LITERATURE

LITERATURE

LITERATURE

An Introduction to

Fiction, Poetry, and Drama

Fifth Edition

X. J. Kennedy

■■ HarperCollins*Publishers*

An Instructor's Manual for *Literature: An Introduction to Fiction, Poetry, and Drama, Fifth Edition*, is available through your local HarperCollins representative or by writing to Literature Acquisitions Editor, HarperCollins College Division, 10 East 53rd Street, New York, NY 10022.

Sponsoring Editor: Lisa Moore
Development Editor: Marisa L'Heureux
Project Coordination: PC & F, Inc.
Cover Illustration: C. Michael Dudash
Production: Michael Weinstein
Compositor: PC & F, Inc.
Printer and Binder: R. R. Donnelley & Sons, Inc.
Cover Printer: New England Book Components

Literature: An Introduction to Fiction, Poetry, and Drama, Fifth Edition

Copyright © 1991 by X. J. Kennedy.
All Rights Reserved. Printed in the United States of America. No part of this book may be used or reproduced in any manner whatsoever without written permission, except in the case of brief quotations embodied in critical articles and reviews. For information address HarperCollins Publishers Inc., 10 East 53rd Street, New York, NY 10022.

Library of Congress Cataloguing-in-Publication Data

Literature: an introduction to fiction, poetry, and drama / [compiled
by] X. J. Kennedy.—5th ed.
    p.   cm.
Includes bibliographical references and index.
ISBN 0-673-52046-3
    1. Literature—Collections.   I. Kennedy, X. J.
PN6014.L58   1991
808—dc20   90-44489
                                                   CIP

(Student Edition) ISBN 0-673-52046-3

(Teacher Edition) ISBN 0-673-52159-1

    91 92 93 9 8 7 6 5 4 3 2

ACKNOWLEDGMENTS

FICTION

Margaret Atwood. "The Sin Eater" from *Dancing Girls* and Other Stories by Margaret Atwood. Copyright © 1977, 1982 by O. W. Toad, Ltd. Reprinted by permission of Simon & Schuster, Inc.

Toni Cade Bambara. "Blues Ain't No Mockin' Bird." Copyright © 1971 by Toni Cade Bambara. Reprinted from *Gorilla, My Love* by Toni Cade Bambara, by permission of Random House, Inc.

Jorge Luis Borges. "The Secret Miracle" from *A Personal Anthology* by Jorge Luis Borges. Reprinted by permission of Grove Weidenfeld, a division of Wheatland Corporation. Copyright © 1967 by Grove Press, Inc.

T. Coraghessan Boyle. "Greasy Lake." From *Greasy Lake and Other Stories* by T. Coraghessan Boyle. Copyright © 1982 by T. Coraghessan Boyle. Reprinted by permission of Viking Penguin, a division of Penguin Books USA Inc.

Raymond Carver. "Cathedral," "A Small, Good Thing," and "Where I'm Calling From." From *Cathedral* by Raymond Carver. Copyright © 1983 by

Raymond Carver. Reprinted by permission of Alfred A. Knopf, Inc. Excerpt from "A Storyteller's Shoptalk," *The New York Times* (Book Review), February 15, 1981. Copyright © 1981 by The New York Times Company. Reprinted by permission.

Anton Chekhov. "The Darling" from *Anton Chekhov: Selected Stories* translated by Ann Dunnigan. Copyright © 1960 by Ann Dunnigan. Reprinted by permission of New American Library, a division of Penguin Books USA Inc. "The Man in a Case" from *Stories of Russian Life* by Anton Chekhov, translated by Marian Fell, published by Charles Scribner's Sons. "Vanka" from *The Image of Chekhov: Forty Stories by Anton Chekhov*, translated by Robert Payne. Copyright © 1963 by Alfred A. Knopf, Inc. Reprinted by permission of the publisher.

Continued on page 1537.

Topical Contents

AUSTIN COMMUNITY COLLEGE
LEARNING RESOURCE SERVICE

POETRY 495

DRAMA 951

Contents

14 *Listening to a Voice*   509

16 *Saying and Suggesting* 560

17 *Imagery* 569

18   *Figures of Speech*   584

19 *Song*   604

20 *Sound*

21 *Rhythm* 641

22 *Closed Form, Open Form* 660

24 *Symbol* 701

25 *Myth* 713

26 *Alternatives* 727

27 *Evaluating a Poem* 740

28 What Is Poetry?   769

29 Poems for Further Reading   773

30 Lives of the Poets 903

31 Criticism: On Poetry 934

DRAMA

Supplement: Writing 1453

Preface

Literature, in the widest sense, is just about anything written. It is even what you receive in the mail if you send for free information about a weight-reducing plan or a motorcycle. In the sense that matters to us in this book, literature is a kind of art, usually written, which offers pleasure and illumination. We say it is *usually* written, for we have an oral literature, too. Few would deny the name of literature to "Bonny Barbara Allan" and other immortal folk ballads, though they were not set down in writing until centuries after they were originated.

Literature—the book in your hands—is really three books between one cover. Its opening third contains the whole of the text-anthology *An Introduction to Fiction, Fifth Edition;* its middle third, the whole of *An Introduction to Poetry, Seventh Edition;* and its closing third is a text-anthology of drama that includes fourteen plays. All together, the book is an attempt to provide the college student with a reasonably compact introduction to the study and appreciation of stories, poems, and plays.

I assume that appreciation begins in loving attention to words on a page. Speed reading has its uses; but at times, as Robert Frost said, the reader who reads for speed "misses the best part of what a good writer puts into it." Close reading, then, is essential. Still, I do not believe that close reading tells us everything, that it is wrong to read a literary work by any light except that of the work itself. At times I suggest different approaches: referring to facts of an author's life; comparing an early draft with a finished version, looking for myth; seeing the conventions (or usual elements) of a kind of writing—seeing, for instance, that an old mansion, cobwebbed and creaking, is the setting for a Gothic horror story.

Although I cannot help having a few convictions about the meanings of stories, poems, and plays, I have tried to step back and give you room to make up your own mind. Here and there, in the wording of a question, a conviction may stick out. If you should notice any, please ignore it. Be assured that no one interpretation, laid down by authority, is the only right one, for any work of literature. Trust your own interpretation—provided that, in making it, you have looked clearly and carefully at the evidence.

Reading literature often will provide you with reason to write. At the back of the book, the large supplement has for the student writer some practical advice. It will guide you, step by step, in finding a topic, planning an essay, writing, revising, and putting your paper into finished form. Further, you will find there specific help in writing about fiction, poetry, and drama, and even sections with pointers for writing stories, poems, and plays of your own. (Even if you don't venture into creative writing, you will find these sections full of glimpses into the processes of literary composition.)

To help you express yourself easily and accurately, both in writing papers and in class discussion, this book supplies critical terms that may be of use to you. These words and phrases appear in **boldface** when they are first defined. If anywhere in this book you meet a critical term you don't know or don't recall—what is a *carpe diem* poem? a *dramatic question?*—just look it up in the Index of Terms on the inside back cover.

A WORD ABOUT CAREERS

Most students agree that to read celebrated writers such as Faulkner and Tolstoi is probably good for the spirit, and most even take some pleasure in the experience. But many, not planning to teach English and impatient to begin some other career, wonder if the study of literature, however enjoyable, isn't a waste of time—or at least, an annoying obstacle.

This objection, reasonable though it may seem, rests on a shaky assumption. On the contrary, it can be argued, success in a career is not merely a matter of learning the information and skills required to join a profession. In most careers, according to one senior business executive, people often fail not because they don't understand their jobs, but because they don't understand the people they work with, or their clients or customers. They don't ever see the world from another person's point of view. Their problem is a failure of imagination.

To leap over the wall of self, to look through another's eyes—this is valuable experience, which literature offers. If you are lucky, you may never meet (or have to do business with) anyone *exactly* like Mrs. Turpin in the story "Revelation," and yet you will learn much about the kind of person she is from Flannery O'Connor's fictional portrait of her. In reading Tolstoi's "The Death of Ivan Ilych," you will enter the mind and heart of another human being. He is someone unlike you: a Russian petty bureaucrat of the nineteenth century. Still, you may find him amazingly similar to many people now living in America.

What is it like to be black, a white may wonder? Gwendolyn Brooks, Langston Hughes, James C. Kilgore, Jamaica Kincaid, Dudley Randall, Toni Cade Bambara, August Wilson, and others have knowledge to impart. What is it like to be a woman? If a man would learn, let him read (for a start) Kate Chopin, Susan Glaspell, Sylvia Plath, Katherine Anne Porter, Flannery O'Connor, Tillie Olsen, Adrienne Rich, Edith Wharton—perhaps, too, John Steinbeck's "The Chrysanthemums" and Anton Chekhov's "The Darling."

Plodding singlemindedly toward careers, some people are like horses wearing blinders. For many, the goals look fixed and predictable. Competent nurses, accountants, and dental technicians seem always in demand. Others may find that in our society some careers, like waves in the sea, will rise or fall unexpectedly. Think how many professions we now take for granted, which only a few years ago didn't even exist: computer programming, energy conservation, tofu manufacture, videotape rental. Others that once looked like lifetime meal tickets have been cut back and nearly ruined: shoe repairing, commercial fishing, railroading.

In a society perpetually in change, it may be risky to lock yourself on one track to a career, refusing to consider any other. "We are moving," writes John Naisbitt in *Megatrends*, a study of our changing society, "from the specialist, soon obsolete, to the generalist who can adapt." Perhaps the greatest opportunity in your whole life lies in a career that has yet to be invented. If you do change your career as you go along, you will be like most people. According to U.S. Department of Labor statistics, the average person in a working life changes occupations three times. When for some unforeseen reason you have to make such a change, basic skills may be your most valuable credentials—and a knowledge of humanity.

Literature has much practical knowledge to offer you. An art of words, it can help you become more sensitive to language, both your own and other people's. It can make you aware of the difference between the word that is exactly right and the word that is merely good enough—Mark Twain calls it "the difference between the lightning and the lightning-bug." Read a fine work of literature alertly, and some of its writer's sensitivity to words may grow on you. A Supreme Court justice, John Paul Stevens, gave his opinion (informally) that the best preparation for law school is to study poetry. Why? George D. Gopen, an English professor with a law degree, says it may be because "no other discipline so closely replicates the central question asked in the study of legal thinking: Here is a text; in how many ways can it have meaning?" (By the way, if a career you plan has anything to do with advertising, whether writing it or buying it or resisting it, be sure to read Chapter 16, "Saying and Suggesting," on the hints inherent in words.)

Many careers today, besides law, call for close reading and for clear thinking expressed on paper. Lately, college placement directors have reported more demand for graduates who are good readers and writers. The reason is evident: employers need people who can handle words. In a recent survey conducted by Cornell University, business executives were asked to rank in importance the traits they look for when hiring. Leadership was first, but skill in writing and speaking came in fourth, ahead of managerial skill, ahead of skill in analysis. Times change, but to think cogently and to express yourself well are abilities the world still needs.

That is why most colleges, however thorough the career training they may provide, still insist on general training as well, including basic courses in the humanities. No one can promise that your study of literature will result in cash profit, but at least the kind of wealth that literature provides is immune to fluctuations of the Dow Jones average. A highly paid tool and die maker, asked by his community college English instructor why he had enrolled in an evening literature course, said, "Oh, I just decided there has to be more to life than work, a few beers, and the bowling alley." If you should discover in yourself a fondness for great reading, then in no season of your life are you likely to become incurably bored or feel totally alone— even after you make good in your career, even when there is nothing on television.

To the Instructor: Changes in This Edition

Once again, scores of instructors made valuable suggestions for change. Stories, poems, and plays that scored high with users of the book have been retained, while those less well favored have been retired.

The chief innovation in the FICTION section is Chapter Ten: Three Fiction Writers in Depth, featuring three stories each by Raymond Carver, Anton Chekhov, and Flannery O'Connor. Although the book has long had two stories by William Faulkner (and still has them), it has never before offered several representative stories by a writer, for those who wish to teach that writer's work in greater detail. "Suggestions for Writing" are provided for Carver, Chekhov, and O'Connor. In fact, the whole FICTION section has been enlarged, to give you a wider choice. This edition increases the count from 41 stories to 53, of which 27 stories—about half—are new. Now there is a second selection by James Thurber and a second by Kate Chopin besides.

POETRY has a new look in its opening chapter. Following the wishes of many, this opening chapter now contains sections on Lyric Poetry and Narrative Poetry, to try to make these rough but serviceable disctinctions clear from the start. A different array of poems has been called for, but if you are looking for Housman's "Loveliest of Trees," Robert Hayden's "Those Winter Sundays," Linda Pastan's "Ethics," Robert Francis's "Catch," or Marvell's "To His Coy Mistress," please be assured that all are still aboard. Some 76 of the book's 439 complete poems are new, 44 of these in the Poems for Further Reading.

In DRAMA, the opening chapter now offers a choice of four one-act plays, which may be used (if you like) to introduce both tragedy and comedy immediately. In all, there are seven plays not present last time, with new selections by W. C. Fields, Maria Irene Fornes, Lady Gregory (whose *Workhouse Ward* is restored in answer to several demands), Tom Stoppard, John Millington Synge, August Wilson, and Wendy Wasserstein (whose short play is a dramatic version of Chekhov's story "The Man in a Case," which, for ready comparison, is given in Chapter Ten).

Again, the book's representation of woman writers and minority writers has become stronger. The capsule biographies now come with portraits; no old question has gone unquestioned; and a few editorial discussions were put on a reducing diet. Further details about changes in the book and the thinking behind them will be found in the preface to the newly revised and updated *Instructor's Manual to Accompany Literature, Fifth Edition,* written together with Dorothy M. Kennedy.

HarperCollins has also assembled an impressive array of high-quality videos and audiotapes of a variety of literary works in each genre, including a Harper-Collins video designed specifically to accompany *Literature.* These can be used to broaden students' experience of literature. Instructors are invited to learn more about the HarperCollins video and audiotape library and request a complimentary copy of the Instructor's Manual from their HarperCollins representative or the publisher.

USING THIS BOOK TO TEACH WRITING

The "Supplement: Writing," especially in "Writing about Literature," continues to derive from recent research. Until the last edition, this book's advice on writing had been traditional, quite uninformed by recent research in composition.

In earlier editions, I used to see the writing of a paper as a lockstep trip through stages, with an always-foreseeable product at the end. This advice has since been recast, more accurately to describe real life. Strategies for discovering material are given priority. Students are still told they may find it helpful to state a thesis, but this advice is offered as only one possible way to write. Editing and mechanics, while given careful attention, take a back seat to more vital matters, such as the tendency of fresh ideas to arrive when it's time to revise. The directions for documenting sources now follow the latest MLA *Handbook for Writers of Research Papers, Third Edition* (1988).

Many instructors use this book in teaching a combined literature-and-writing course. To serve their needs, I have tried again to improve the guidance offered to student writers—improve, but not too greatly lengthen it. This book keeps its essential focus on literature; it tries not to let apparatus intrude or dominate. The editor's prose, I believe, matters less to the study of fiction than William Faulkner's or Tillie Olsen's.

Several of the suggestions for writing, at the end of each main chapter, have been rethought. Some instructors prefer to let students discover their own topics, and in that case, these suggestions may be helpful to start them thinking on their own. The well-received sections "Criticism: On Fiction", "Criticism: On Poetry", and "Criticism: On Drama" remain, and while an instructor need not do anything about them, they can provide not only ideas for class discussion but also further writing possibilities.

Besides lending support to the student creative writer, the section "Writing a Story" may interest others: it contains remarks by celebrated fiction writers, telling how they write.

TEXTS, DATES, AND A POSSIBLY PUZZLING ASTERISK

Every effort has been made to supply each selection in its most accurate text and (where necessary) in a lively, faithful translation. For the reader who wishes to know when a work was written, at the right of each title appears the date of its first publication in book form. Brackets around a date indicate the work's date of composition, given when it was composed much earlier than when it was first published. In the case of plays, a date in brackets indicates a first production.

In the poetry section, "Lives of the Poets" (Chapter 30) offers 71 brief biographies: one for each poet represented by two selections or more. For easy reference, they are tucked in one place (pages 903–933). Throughout the poetry pages, an asterisk (*) after a poet's by-line indicates the subject of a biography.

FICTION AND POETRY AVAILABLE SEPARATELY

Instructors who wish to use only the fiction section or the poetry section of this book are assured that An *Introduction to Fiction, Fifth Edition,* and An *Introduction to Poetry, Seventh Edition,* contain the full and complete contents of these sections. Each book has a "Supplement: Writing" applicable to its subject, including "Writing about Literature."

For examination copies of either book, please contact your HarperCollins representative, or write to Humanities Marketing Manager, College Division, HarperCollins Publishers Inc., 10 East 53rd Street, New York, NY 10022.

THANKS

Once again, in revising this book and its manual, I have depended on the reactions and generous suggestions of many instructors. I remain grateful to hundreds of people named in prefaces past, much of whose thinking and experience is still here. For new contributions, I owe deep thanks to Ila Abernathy, University of Arizona; Stephen Adams, University of Minnesota at Duluth; Jonathan Aldrich, Portland School of Art; Karen Alkalay-Gut, Tel Aviv University; Robert F. Baron, Mesa Community College; R. M. Bedell, Virginia Military Institute; William W. Betts, Jr., Indiana University of Pennsylvania; Ellen Sternberg Bevan, St. John Fisher College; Peggy L. Brayfield, Eastern Illinois University; Laurel Brodsley, UCLA; Joyce Moss Brown, Catonsville Community College; Mary M. Burns, South Central Community College; Ellen Miller Casey, University of Scranton; Steven R. Centola, Millersville University; Joe R. Christopher, Tarleton State University; Saul Cohen, County College of Morris; Robert F. Coleman, Palomar College; Ruth Corson, Norwalk Community College; LuDene Dallimore, Weber State College; Emanuel di Pasquale, Middlesex County Community College; Dan Doll, University of New Orleans; Judi Doumas, Old Dominion University; Charles Clay Doyle, University of Georgia; William D. Eisenberg, Bloomsburg University of Pennsylvania; Ed Eleazer, Albany (Georgia) Junior College; Toni Empringham, El Camino Community College; SallyAnn H. Ferguson, North Carolina A & T State University; Matthew A. Fike, University of Michigan, Eastern Michigan University; Robert Foster, SUNY College, Potsdam; Norman Fruman, University of Minnesota, Twin Cities; G. Dale Gleason, Hutchinson Community College; Len Gougeon, University of Scranton; R. S. Gwynn, Lamar University; Sally M. Hanson, University of South Dakota; Diane Harris, Kent State University; Charles O. Hartman, Connecticut College; Norleen M. Healy, Sheridan College; James Heldman, Western Kentucky University; Randel Helms, Arizona State University; Leonard J. Leff, Oklahoma State University; Richard Lessa, University of Hawaii at Manoa; Roselle Lewis, Los Angeles Valley College; Stephen Shu-ning Liu, Clark County Community College; Joe Lostracco, Austin Community College; Kathy L. May, Virginia Polytechnic Institute and State University; Robert McGovern, Ashland College; Mary Nardo, Brevard Community College; Bruce Naschak, Mesa College; Janet C. Nosek, University of Alaska, Anchorage; L. Anderson Orr, Virginia Wesleyan College; Linda Pannill, Transylvania University; David Peck, California State University, Long Beach; Barb Powell, University of Regina; Judith K. Powers, University of Wyoming; Helon H. Raines, Casper College; Linda C. Rollins, Motlow State Community College; Julie Ryden, University of Connecticut; Arthrell D. Sanders, North Carolina Central University; B. Sandlin, Scottsdale Community College; Ellery Sedgwick, Longwood College; Debra J. Sheffer, Central Missouri State University; Carol Sklenicka, Milwaukee

Institute of Art and Design; Michael J. Smith, Highline Community College; Paul H. Stacy, University of Hartford; Al Starr, Essex Community College; Dabney Stuart, Washington and Lee University; Joseph L. Swonk, Rappahannock Community College; Ray S. Williams, Brigham Young University; and Stephen Caldwell Wright, Seminole Community College. Patricia Winters, a student at Southern Illinois University at Edwardsville, sent valuable corrections. Many other students, some of them using the questionnaire at the back of the book, wrote reactions and suggestions. I wish there were space to name them all, and to thank properly all the students at Tufts, Michigan, North Carolina (Greensboro), and Leeds who have let me read literature in their company.

On the publisher's staff, I am indebted to many people, especially Lisa Moore, Ted Simpson, Marisa L. L'Heureux (who saw the book into shape), Garret White, Francis Byrne, Ann Stypuloski, Debbie Costello, Kelly Mountain, and Rosemary Hunter. Guy Huff obtained poetry permissions, and once again, Carolyn Woznick valiantly sought permissions for the stories and plays. Mary Maguire, Margaret Saunders, and Dorothy Lindon of PC & F, Inc., proved invaluable. Other friends assisted: Peter and Jo Cone helped annotate Tom Stoppard's slang. Sylvan Barnet, who showed me how to write textbooks to begin with, once again criticized and corrected the poetry pages. Alan Nordstrom and Henry Taylor supplied profound corrections. Dorothy M. Kennedy contributed questions, writing topics, intelligence, and much besides.

X. J. Kennedy

FICTION

Here is a story, one of the shortest ever written and one of the most difficult to forget:

> A woman is sitting in her old, shuttered house. She knows that she is alone in the whole world; every other thing is dead.
>
> The doorbell rings.

In a brief space this small tale of terror, credited to Thomas Bailey Aldrich, makes itself memorable. It sets a promising scene—is this a haunted house?—introduces a character, and places her in a strange and intriguing situation. Although in reading a story that is over so quickly we don't come to know the character well, for a moment we enter her thoughts and begin to share her feelings. Then something amazing happens. The story leaves us to wonder: who or what rang that bell?

Like many richer, longer, more complicated stories, this one, in its few words, engages the imagination. Evidently, how much a story contains and suggests doesn't depend on its size. In the opening chapter of this book, we will look first at other brief stories—examples of two ancient kinds of fiction, a fable and a tale—then at a contemporary short story. We will consider the elements of fiction one after another. By seeing a few short stories broken into their parts, you will come to a keener sense of how a story is put together. Not all stories are short, of course; later in the book, you will meet a chapter on reading novels and long stories.

All in all, here are fifty-three stories. Among them, may you find at least a few you'll enjoy and care to remember.

1   Reading a Story

After the shipwreck that marooned him on his desert island, Robinson Crusoe, in the story by Daniel Defoe, stood gazing over the water where pieces of cargo from his ship were floating by. Along came "two shoes, not mates." It is the qualification *not mates* that makes the detail memorable. We could well believe that a thing so striking and odd must have been seen, and not invented. But in truth Defoe, like other masters of the art of fiction, had the power to make us believe his imaginings. Borne along by the art of the storyteller, we trust what we are told, even though the story may be sheer fantasy.

Fiction (from the latin *fictio*, "a shaping, a counterfeiting") is a name for stories not entirely factual, but at least partially shaped, made up, imagined. It is true that in some fiction, such as a historical novel, a writer draws upon factual information in presenting scenes, events, and characters. But the factual information in a historical novel, unlike that in a history book, is of secondary importance. Many firsthand accounts of the American Civil War were written by men who had fought in it, but few eyewitnesses give us so keen a sense of actual life on the battlefront as the author of *The Red Badge of Courage*, Stephen Crane, born after the war was over. In fiction, the "facts" may or may not be true, and a story is none the worse for their being entirely imaginary. We expect from fiction a sense of how people act, not an authentic chronicle of how, at some past time, a few people acted.

As children, we used to read (if we were lucky and formed the habit) to steep ourselves in romance, mystery, and adventure. As adults, we still do: at an airport, while waiting for a flight, we pass the time with some newsstand paperback full of fast action and brisk dialogue. Certain fiction, of course, calls for closer attention. To read a novel by the Russian master Dostoevsky instead of a thriller about secret agent James Bond is somewhat like playing chess instead of a game of tic-tac-toe. Not that a great novel does not provide entertainment. In fact, it may offer more deeply satisfying entertainment than a novel of violence and soft-core pornography, in which stick figures connive, go to bed, and kill one another in accord with some market-tested formula. Reading literary fiction (as distinguished from fiction as a commercial product—the formula kind of spy, detective, Western, love, jungle, or other adventure story), we are not necessarily led on by the promise of thrills; we do not keep reading mainly to find out what happens next. Indeed, a literary story might even disclose in its opening lines everything that happened, then spend the rest of its length revealing what that happening meant. Reading literary fiction is no merely passive activity, but one that demands both attention and insight-lending participation. In return, it offers rewards. In some works of literary fiction, in Stephen Crane's "The Open Boat" and Leo Tolstoi's "The Death of Ivan Ilych," we see more deeply into the minds and hearts of the characters than we ever see into those of our family, our close friends, our lovers—or even ourselves.

FABLE AND TALE

Modern literary fiction in English has been dominated by two forms: the novel and the short story. The two have many elements in common (and in this book a further discussion of the novel as a special form will be given in Chapter Nine). Perhaps we will be able to define the short story more meaningfully—for it has traits more essential than just a particular length—if first, for comparison, we consider some related varieties of fiction: the fable and the tale. Ancient forms whose origins date back to the time of word-of-mouth storytelling, the fable and the tale are relatively simply in structure; in them we can plainly see elements also found in the short story (and in the novel). To begin, here is a **fable:** a brief story that sets forth some pointed statement of truth. The writer, W. Somerset Maugham, an English novelist and playwright (1874–1965), is retelling an Arabian folk story. (Samarra, by the way, is a city sixty miles from Bagdad.)

W. *Somerset Maugham*

THE APPOINTMENT IN SAMARRA   1933

Death speaks: There was a merchant in Bagdad who sent his servant to market to buy provisions and in a little while the servant came back, white and trembling, and said, Master, just now when I was in the market-place I was jostled by a woman in the crowd and when I turned I saw it was Death that jostled me. She looked at me and made a threatening gesture; now, lend me your horse, and I will ride away from this city and avoid my fate. I will go to Samarra and there Death will not find me. The merchant lent him his horse, and the servant mounted it, and he dug his spurs in its flanks and as fast as the horse could gallop he went. Then the merchant went down to the marketplace and he saw me standing in the crowd and he came to me and said, Why did you make a threatening gesture to my servant when you saw him this morning? That was not a threatening gesture, I said, it was only a start of surprise. I was astonished to see him in Bagdad, for I had an appointment with him tonight in Samarra.

This brief story seems practically all skin and bones; that is, it contains little decoration. For in a fable everything leads directly to the **moral,** or message, sometimes stated at the end ("Moral: Haste makes waste"). In "The Appointment in Samarra" the moral isn't stated outright, it is merely implied. How would you state it in your own words?

You are probably acquainted with some of the fables credited to the Greek slave Aesop (about 620–560 B.C.), whose stories seem designed to teach lessons about human life. Such is the fable of "The Fox and the Grapes," in which a fox, unable to reach a bunch of grapes that hangs too high, decides that they were sour anyway. (Implied moral: It is easy to spurn what we cannot attain.) Another is the fable of "The Tortoise and the Hare" (implied moral: "Slow, steady plodding wins the race"). The characters in a fable may be talking animals (as in many of Aesop's fables), inanimate objects, or people and supernatural beings (as in "The Appointment in Samarra"). Whoever they may be, these characters are merely sketched, not greatly developed. Evidently, it would not have helped Maugham's fable to put across its point if he had portrayed the merchant, the servant, and Death in fuller detail. A more elaborate description of the market-place would not have improved the story. Probably, such a description would strike us as unnecessary and distracting. By its very bareness and simplicity, a fable fixes itself—and its message—in memory.

The name *tale* (from the Old English *talu,* "speech") is sometimes applied to any story, whether short or long, true or fictitious. *Tale* being a more evocative name than *story,* writers sometimes call their stories "tales" as if to imply something handed down from the past. But defined in a more limited sense, a **tale** is a story, usually short, that sets forth strange and wonderful events in more or less bare summary, without detailed character-drawing. "Tale" is pretty much synonymous with "yarn," for it implies a story in which the goal is revelation of the marvelous rather than revelation of character. In the English folk tale "Jack and the Beanstalk," we take away a more vivid impression of the miraculous beanstalk and the giant who dwells at its top than of Jack's mind or personality. Because such venerable stories were told aloud before someone set them down in writing, the storytellers had to limit themselves to brief descriptions. Probably spoken around a fire or hearth, such a tale tends to be less complicated and less closely detailed than a story written for the printed page, whose reader can linger over it. Still, such tales *can* be complicated. It is not merely greater length that makes a short story different from a tale or a fable: a mark of a short story is a fully delineated character.

Even modern tales favor supernatural or fantastic events: for instance, the **tall tale,** that variety of folk story which recounts the deeds of a superhero (Paul Bunyan, John Henry, Mike Fink) or of the storyteller. If the storyteller is telling about his own imaginary experience, his bragging yarn is usually told with a straight face to listeners who take pleasure in scoffing at it. Although the **fairy tale,** set in a world of magic and enchantment, is sometimes the work of a modern author (notably Hans Christian Andersen), well-known examples are those German folk-tales probably originated in the Middle Ages, collected by the brothers Grimm. The label *fairy tale* is something of an English misnomer, for in the Grimm stories, though witches and goblins abound, fairies are a minority.

Jakob and Wilhelm Grimm

GODFATHER DEATH   1812 (from oral tradition)

Translated by Lore Segal

Jakob Grimm (1785–1863) and Wilhelm Grimm (1786–1859), brothers and scholars, were born near Frankfurt-am-Main, Germany. For most of their lives they worked together—lived together, too, even when in 1825 Wilhelm married. In 1838, as librarians, they began toiling on their Deutsch Wörterbuch, *or German dictionary, a vast project that was to outlive them by a century. (It was completed only in 1960.) In 1840 King Friedrich Wilhelm IV appointed both brothers to the Royal Academy of Sciences, and both taught at the University of Berlin for the rest of their days. Although Jakob had a side-career as a diplomat, wrote a great* Deutsche Grammatik, *or German grammar (1819–37), and*

Jakob and Wilhelm Grimm

propounded Grimm's Law (an explanation of shifts in consonant sounds, of interest to students of linguistics), the name Grimm is best known to us for that splendid collection of ancient German folk stories we call Grimm's Fairy Tales—*in German, Kinder- und Hausmärchen ("Childhood and Household Tales," 1812–15). This classic work spread German children's stories around the world. Many tales we hear early in life were collected by the Grimms: "Hansel and Gretel," "Snow White and the Seven Dwarfs," "Rapunzel," "Puss-in-Boots," "Little Red Riding Hood," "Rumpelstiltskin." Versions of some of these tales had been written down as early as the sixteenth century, but mainly the brothers relied on the memories of Hessian peasants who recited the stories aloud for them.*

A poor man had twelve children and worked night and day just to get enough bread for them to eat. Now when the thirteenth came into the world, he did not know what to do and in his misery ran out onto the great highway to ask the first person he met to be godfather. The first to come along was God, and he already knew what it was that weighed on the man's mind and said, "Poor man, I pity you. I will hold your child at the font and I will look after it and make it happy upon earth." "Who are you?" asked the man. "I am God." "Then I don't want you for a godfather," the man said. "You give to the rich and let the poor go hungry." That was how the man talked because he did not understand how wisely God shares out wealth and poverty, and thus he turned from the Lord and walked on. Next came the Devil and said, "What is it you want? If you let me be godfather to your child, I will give him gold as much as he can use, and all the pleasures of the world besides." "Who are you?" asked the man. "I am the Devil." "Then I don't want you for a godfather," said the man. "You deceive and mislead mankind." He walked on and along came spindle-legged Death striding toward him and said, "Take me as godfather." The man asked, "Who are you?" "I am Death who makes all men equal." Said the man, "Then you're the one for me; you take rich and poor without distinction. You shall be godfather." Answered Death: "I will make your child rich and famous, because the one who has me for a friend shall want for nothing." The man said, "Next Sunday is the baptism. Be there in good time." Death appeared as he had promised and made a perfectly fine godfather.

When the boy was of age, the godfather walked in one day, told him to come along, and led him out into the woods. He showed him an herb which grew there and said, "This is your christening gift. I shall make you into a famous doctor. When you are called to a patient's bedside I will appear and if I stand at the sick man's head you can boldly say that you will cure him and if you give him some of this herb he will recover. But if I stand at the sick man's feet, then he is mine, and you must say there is no help for him and no doctor on this earth could save him. But take care not to use the herb against my will or it could be the worse for you."

It wasn't long before the young man had become the most famous doctor in the whole world. "He looks at a patient and right away he knows how things stand, whether he will get better or if he's going to die." That is what they said about him, and from near and far the people came, took him to see the sick, and gave him so much money he became a rich man. Now it happened that the king fell ill. The doctor was summoned to say if he was going to get well. When he came to the bed, there stood Death at the feet of the sick man, so that no herb on earth could have done him any good. If I could only just this once outwit Death! thought the doctor. He'll be annoyed, I know, but I am his godchild and he's sure to turn a blind eye. I'll take my chance. And so he lifted the sick man and laid him the other way around so that Death was standing at his head. Then he gave him some of the herb and the king began to feel better and was soon in perfect health. But Death came toward the doctor, his face dark and angry, threatened him with raised forefinger, and said, "You have tricked me. This time I will let it pass because you are my godchild, but if you ever dare do such a thing again, you put your own head in the noose and it is you I shall carry away with me."

Soon after that, the king's daughter lapsed into a deep illness. She was his only child, he wept day and night until his eyes failed him and he let it be known that whoever saved the princess from death should become her husband and inherit the crown. When the doctor came to the sick girl's bed, he saw Death at her feet. He ought to have remembered his godfather's warning, but the great beauty of the princess and the happiness of becoming her husband so bedazzled him that he threw caution to the winds, nor did he see Death's angry glances and how he lifted his hand in the air and threatened him with his bony fist. He picked the sick girl up and laid her head where her feet had lain, then he gave her some of the herb and at once her cheeks reddened and life stirred anew.

When Death saw himself cheated of his property the second time, he strode 5
toward the doctor on his long legs and said, "It is all up with you, and now it
is your turn," grasped him harshly with his ice-cold hand so that the doctor could
not resist, and led him to an underground cave, and here he saw thousands upon
thousands of lights burning in rows without end, some big, some middle-sized,
others small. Every moment some went out and others lit up so that the little
flames seemed to be jumping here and there in perpetual exchange. "Look," said
Death, "these are the life lights of mankind. The big ones belong to children,
the middle-sized ones to married couples in their best years, the little ones belong
to very old people. Yet children and the young often have only little lights." "Show
me my life light," said the doctor, imagining that it must be one of the big ones.
Death pointed to a little stub threatening to go out and said, "Here it is." "Ah,
dear godfather," said the terrified doctor, "light me a new one, do it, for my sake,
so that I may enjoy my life and become king and marry the beautiful princess."
"I cannot," answered Death. "A light must go out before a new one lights up."
"Then set the old on top of a new one so it can go on burning when the first
is finished," begged the doctor. Death made as if to grant his wish, reached for
a tall new taper, but because he wanted revenge he purposely fumbled and the
little stub fell over and went out. Thereupon the doctor sank to the ground and
had himself fallen into the hands of death.

PLOT

Like a fable, the Grimm brothers' tale seems stark in its lack of detail and in the
swiftness of its telling. Compared with the fully portrayed characters of many
modern stories, the characters of father, son, king, princess, and even Death himself seem hardly more than stick figures. It may have been that to draw ample
characters would not have contributed to the storytellers' design; that, indeed,
to have done so would have been inartistic. Yet "Godfather Death" is a compelling story. By what methods does it arouse and sustain our interest?

From the opening sentence of the tale, we watch the unfolding of a **dramatic
situation:** a person is involved in some conflict. First, this character is a poor
man with children to feed, in conflict with the world; very soon, we find him
in conflict with God and with the Devil besides. Drama in fiction occurs in any
clash of wills, desires, or powers—whether it be a conflict of character against
character, character against society, character against some natural force, or, as
in "Godfather Death," character against some supernatural entity.

Like any shapely tale, "Godfather Death" has a beginning, a middle, and an
end. In fact, it is unusual to find a story so clearly displaying the elements of structure that critics have found in many classic works of fiction and drama. The tale
begins with an **exposition:** the opening portion that sets the scene (if any), introduces the main characters, tells us what happened before the story opened,
and provides any other background information that we need in order to understand and care about the events to follow. In "Godfather Death," the exposition
is brief—all in the opening paragraph. The middle section of the story begins with

Death's giving the herb to the boy, and his warning not to defy him. This moment introduces a new conflict (a **complication**), and by this time it is clear that the son and not the father is to be the central human character of the story. Death's godson is the principal person who strives: the **protagonist** (a better term than **hero,** for it may apply equally well to a central character who is not especially brave or virtuous).

The **suspense,** the pleasurable anxiety we feel that heightens our attention to the story, inheres in our wondering how it will all turn out. Will the doctor triumph over Death? Even though we suspect, early in the story, that the doctor stands no chance against such a superhuman **antagonist,** we want to see for ourselves the outcome of his defiance. A storyteller can try to incite our anticipation by giving us some **foreshadowing** or indication of events to come. In "Godfather Death" the foreshadowings are apparent in Death's warnings ("but if you ever dare do such a thing again, you put your own head in the noose"). When the doctor defies his godfather for the first time—when he saves the king—we have a **crisis,** a moment of high tension. The tension is momentarily resolved when Death lets him off. Then an even greater crisis—the turning point in the action—occurs with the doctor's second defiance in restoring the princess to life. In the last section of the story, with the doctor in the underworld, events come to a **climax,** the moment of greatest tension at which the outcome is to be decided, when the terrified doctor begs for a new candle. Will Death grant him one? Will he live, become king, and marry the princess? The outcome or **conclusion**—also called the **resolution** or **dénouement** ("the untying of the knot")—quickly follows as Death allows the little candle to go out.

Such a structure of events arising out of a conflict may be called the plot of the story. Like many terms used in literary discussion, *plot* is blessed with several meanings. Sometimes it refers simply to the events in a story. In this book, **plot** will mean the artistic arrangement of those events. Different arrangements of the same material are possible. A writer might decide to tell of the events in chronological order, beginning with the earliest; or he might open his story with the last event, then tell what led up to it. Sometimes a writer chooses to skip rapidly over the exposition and begin **in medias res** (Latin, "in the midst of things"), first presenting some exciting or significant moment, then filling in what happened earlier. This method is by no means a modern invention: Homer begins the *Odyssey* with his hero mysteriously late in returning from war and his son searching for him; John Milton's *Paradise Lost* opens with Satan already defeated in his revolt against the Lord. A device useful to writers for filling in what happened earlier is the **flashback** (or **retrospect**), a scene relived in a character's memory.

To have a plot, a story does not need an intense, sustained conflict such as we find in "Godfather Death," a tale especially economical in its structure of crisis, climax, and conclusion. Although a highly dramatic story may tend to assume such a clearly recognizable structure, many contemporary writers avoid it, considering it too contrived and arbitrary. In commercial fiction, in which exciting conflict is everything and in which the writer has to manufacture all possible suspense, such a structure is often obvious. In popular detective, Western, and adventure novels; in juvenile fiction (the perennial Hardy Boys and Nancy Drew books); and in popular series on television (soap operas, police and hospital thrillers, mysteries, and cowboy stories), it is often easy to recognize crisis, climax, and conclusion. The presence of these elements does not necessarily indicate inferior literature (as "Godfather Death" shows); yet when reduced to parts of a formula, the result may seem stale and contrived.[1] Such plots may be (as contemporary French novelist Alain Robbe-Grillet describes them) mere anecdotes, providing trumped-up surprises for "the panting reader."

THE SHORT STORY

The teller of a tale relies heavily upon the method of **summary:** terse, general narration as in "Godfather Death" ("It wasn't long before the young man had become the most famous doctor in the whole world"). But in a **short story,** a form more realistic than the tale and of modern origin, the writer usually presents the main events in greater fullness. Fine writers of short stories, although they may use summary at times (often to give some portion of a story less emphasis), are skilled in rendering a **scene:** a vivid or dramatic moment described in enough detail to create the illusion that the reader is practically there. Avoiding long summary, they try to *show* rather than simply to *tell;* as if following Mark Twain's advice to authors: "Don't say, 'The old lady screamed.' Bring her on and let her scream."

A short story is more than just a sequence of happenings. A finely wrought short story has the richness and conciseness of an excellent lyric poem. Spontaneous and natural as the finished story may seem, the writer has written it so artfully that there is meaning in even seemingly casual speeches and apparently trivial details. If we skim it hastily, skipping the descriptive passages, we miss significant parts. Some literary short stories, unlike commercial fiction in which the main interest is in physical action or conflict, tell of an **epiphany:** some moment of insight, discovery, or revelation by which a character's life, or view of life, is greatly altered.[2] (For such moments in fiction, see the stories in this book by James Joyce, Leo Tolstoi, John Steinbeck, Edith Wharton, and Joyce Carol Oates.) Other short stories tell of a character initiated into experience or maturity: one such **story of initiation** is William Faulkner's "Barn Burning" (Chapter Five), in which a boy finds it necessary to defy his father and suddenly to grow into manhood. Less obviously dramatic, perhaps, than "Godfather Death," such a story may be no less powerful.

---

[1]In the heyday of the **pulp magazines** (so called for their cheap paper), some professional writers even relied on a mechanical device called Plotto: a tin arrow-spinner pointed to numbers and the writer looked them up in a book that listed necessary ingredients—type of hero, type of villain, sort of conflict, crisis, climax, conclusion.

[2]From the Greek *epiphainein*, "to show forth." In Christian tradition, the Feast of the Epiphany commemorates the revelation to the Magi of the birth of Christ. For James Joyce's description of epiphanies in everyday life, see page 489.

The fable and the tale are ancient forms; the short story is of more recent origin. In the nineteenth century, writers of fiction were encouraged by a large, literate audience of middle-class readers who wanted to see their lives reflected in faithful mirrors. Skillfully representing ordinary life, many writers perfected the art of the short story: in Russia, Anton Chekhov; in France, Honoré de Balzac, Gustave Flaubert, and Guy de Maupassant; and in America, Nathaniel Hawthorne and Edgar Allan Poe (although the Americans seem less fond of everyday life than of dream and fantasy). It would be false to claim that, in passing from the fable and the tale to the short story, fiction has made a triumphant progress; or to claim that, because short stories are modern, they are superior to fables and tales. Fable, tale, and short story are distinct forms, each achieving its own effects. (Incidentally, fable and tale are far from being extinct today: you can find many recent examples.) Lately, in the hands of Donald Barthelme, Joyce Carol Oates, John Barth, and other innovative writers, the conventions of the short story have been changing; and at the moment, stories of epiphany and initiation have become scarcer.

But let us begin with a contemporary short story whose protagonist *does* undergo an initiation into maturity. To notice the difference between a short story and a tale, you may find it helpful to compare John Updike's "A & P" with "Godfather Death." Although Updike's short story is centuries distant from the Grimm tale in its method of telling and in its setting, you may be reminded of "Godfather Death" in the main character's dramatic situation. To defend a young woman, a young man has to defy his mentor—here, the boss of a supermarket! So doing, he places himself in jeopardy. Updike has the protagonist tell his own story, amply and with humor. How does it differ from a tale?

John Updike

A & P   1961

John Updike, born in Shillington, Pennsylvania, in 1932, received his B.A. from Harvard, then went to Oxford to study drawing and fine art. In the mid-1950s he worked on the staff of The New Yorker, *at times doing errands for the aged James Thurber. But although he left the magazine to become a full-time writer, Updike has continued to supply it with memorable stories and searching reviews. His more than thirty books include essays, art criticism, light verse, and serious poetry. Updike is best known, however, as a hardworking, versatile, highly productive writer of fiction. For his novel* The Centaur *(1963) he received a National Book Award and for* Rabbit Is Rich

John Updike

(1982), a Pulitzer prize and an American Book Award. Recently, The Witches of East-wick (1984) was successfully adapted for a film starring Jack Nicholson. S. (1988), an interesting later novel, was partly inspired by Nathaniel Hawthorne's The Scarlet Letter.

In walks three girls in nothing but bathing suits. I'm in the third check-out slot, with my back to the door, so I don't see them until they're over by the bread. The one that caught my eye first was the one in the plaid green two-piece. She was a chunky kid, with a good tan and a sweet broad soft-looking can with those two crescents of white just under it, where the sun never seems to hit, at the top of the backs of her legs. I stood there with my hand on a box of HiHo crackers trying to remember if I rang it up or not. I ring it up again and the customer starts giving me hell. She's one of these cash-register-watchers, a witch about fifty with rouge on her cheekbones and no eyebrows, and I know it made her day to trip me up. She'd been watching cash registers for fifty years and probably never seen a mistake before.

By the time I got her feathers smoothed and her goodies into a bag—she gives me a little snort in passing, if she'd been born at the right time they would have burned her over in Salem—by the time I get her on her way the girls had circled around the bread and were coming back, without a pushcart, back my way along the counters, in the aisle between the check-outs and the Special bins. They didn't even have shoes on. There was this chunky one, with the two-piece—it was bright green and the seams on the bra were still sharp and her belly was still pretty pale so I guessed she just got it (the suit)—there was this one, with one of those chubby berry-faces, the lips all bunched together under her nose, this one, and a tall one, with black hair that hadn't quite frizzed right, and one of these sunburns right across under the eyes, and a chin that was too long—you know, the kind of girl other girls think is very "striking" and "attractive" but never quite makes it, as they very well know, which is why they like her so much—and then the third one, that wasn't quite so tall. She was the queen. She kind of led them, the other two peeking around and making their shoulders round. She didn't look around, not this queen, she just walked straight on slowly, on these long white primadonna legs. She came down a little hard on her heels, as if she didn't walk in her bare feet that much, putting down her heels and then letting the weight move along to her toes as if she was testing the floor with every step, putting a little deliberate extra action into it. You never know for sure how girls' minds work (do you really think it's a mind in there or just a little buzz like a bee in a glass jar?) but you got the idea she had talked the other two into coming in here with her, and now she was showing them how to do it, walk slow and hold yourself straight.

She had on a kind of dirty-pink—beige maybe, I don't know—bathing suit with a little nubble all over it and, what got me, the straps were down. They were off her shoulders looped loose around the cool tops of her arms, and I guess as a result the suit had slipped a little on her, so all around the top of the cloth there was this shining rim. If it hadn't been there you wouldn't have known there could have been anything whiter than those shoulders. With the straps pushed off, there was nothing between the top of the suit and the top of her head except just *her*, this clean bare plane of the top of her chest down from the shoulder bones like a dented sheet of metal tilted in the light. I mean, it was more than pretty.

She had sort of oaky hair that the sun and salt had bleached, done up in a bun that was unraveling, and a kind of prim face. Walking into the A & P with your straps down, I suppose it's the only kind of face you *can* have. She held her head so high her neck, coming up out of those white shoulders, looked kind of stretched, but I didn't mind. The longer her neck was, the more of her there was.

She must have felt in the corner of her eye me and over my shoulder Stokesie   5 in the second slot watching, but she didn't tip. Not this queen. She kept her eyes moving across the racks, and stopped, and turned so slow it made my stomach rub the inside of my apron, and buzzed to the other two, who kind of huddled against her for relief, and they all three of them went up the cat-and-dog-food-breakfast-cereal-macaroni-rice-raisins-seasonings-spreads-spaghetti-soft-drinks-crackers-and-cookies aisle. From the third slot I look straight up this aisle to the meat counter, and I watched them all the way. The fat one with the tan sort of fumbled with the cookies, but on second thought she put the packages back. The sheep pushing their carts down the aisle—the girls were walking against the usual traffic (not that we have one-way signs or anything)—were pretty hilarious. You could see them, when Queenie's white shoulders dawned on them, kind of jerk, or hop, or hiccup, but their eyes snapped back to their own baskets and on they pushed. I bet you could set off dynamite in an A & P and the people would by and large keep reaching and checking oatmeal off their lists and muttering "Let me see, there was a third thing, began with A, asparagus, no, ah, yes, applesauce!" or whatever it is they do mutter. But there was no doubt, this jiggled them. A few houseslaves in pin curlers even looked around after pushing their carts past to make sure what they had seen was correct.

You know, it's one thing to have a girl in a bathing suit down on the beach, where what with the glare nobody can look at each other much anyway, and another thing in the cool of the A & P, under the fluorescent lights, against all those stacked packages, with her feet padding along naked over our checkerboard green-and-cream rubber-tile floor.

"Oh Daddy," Stokesie said beside me. "I feel so faint."

"Darling," I said. "Hold me tight." Stokesie's married, with two babies chalked up on his fuselage already, but as far as I can tell that's the only difference. He's twenty-two, and I was nineteen this April.

"Is it done?" he asks, the responsible married man finding his voice. I forgot to say he thinks he's going to be manager some sunny day, maybe in 1990 when it's called the Great Alexandrov and Petrooshki Tea Company or something.

What he meant was, our town is five miles from a beach, with a big summer   10 colony out on the Point, but we're right in the middle of town, and the women generally put on a shirt or shorts or something before they get out of the car into the street. And anyway these are usually women with six children and varicose veins mapping their legs and nobody, including them, could care less. As I say, we're right in the middle of town, and if you stand at our front doors you can see two banks and the Congregational church and the newspaper store and three real-estate offices and about twenty-seven old freeloaders tearing up Central Street because the sewer broke again. It's not as if we're on the Cape; we're north of Boston and there's people in this town haven't seen the ocean for twenty years.

The girls had reached the meat counter and were asking McMahon something. He pointed, they pointed, and they shuffled out of sight behind a pyramid of Diet Delight peaches. All that was left for us to see was old McMahon patting his mouth and looking after them sizing up their joints. Poor kids, I began to feel sorry for them, they couldn't help it.

Now here comes the sad part of the story, at least my family says it's sad but I don't think it's sad myself. The store's pretty empty, it being Thursday afternoon, so there was nothing much to do except lean on the register and wait for the girls to show up again. The whole store was like a pinball machine and I didn't know which tunnel they'd come out of. After a while they come around out of the far aisle, around the light bulbs, records at discount of the Caribbean Six or Tony Martin Sings or some such gunk you wonder they waste the wax on, six-packs of candy bars, and plastic toys done up in cellophane that fall apart when a kid looks at them anyway. Around they come, Queenie still leading the way, and holding a little gray jar in her hand. Slots Three through Seven are unmanned and I could see her wondering between Stokes and me, but Stokesie with his usual luck draws an old party in baggy gray pants who stumbles up with four giant cans of pineapple juice (what do these bums *do* with all that pineapple juice? I've often asked myself) so the girls come to me. Queenie puts down the jar and I take it into my fingers icy cold. Kingfish Fancy Herring Snacks in Pure Sour Cream: 49¢. Now her hands are empty, not a ring or a bracelet, bare as God made them, and I wonder where the money's coming from. Still with that prim look she lifts a folded dollar bill out of the hollow at the center of her nubbled pink top. The jar went heavy in my hand. Really, I thought that was so cute.

Then everybody's luck begins to run out. Lengel comes in from haggling with a truck full of cabbages on the lot and is about to scuttle into that door marked MANAGER behind which he hides all day when the girls touch his eye. Lengel's pretty dreary, teaches Sunday school and the rest, but he doesn't miss that much. He comes over and says, "Girls, this isn't the beach."

Queenie blushes, though maybe it's just a brush of sunburn I was noticing for the first time, now that she was so close. "My mother asked me to pick up a jar of herring snacks." Her voice kind of startled me, the way voices do when you see the people first, coming out so flat and dumb yet kind of tony, too, the way it ticked over "pick up" and "snacks." All of a sudden I slid right down her voice into her living room. Her father and the other men were standing around in ice-cream coats and bow ties and the women were in sandals picking up herring snacks on toothpicks off a big plate and they were all holding drinks the color of water with olives and sprigs of mint in them. When my parents have somebody over they get lemonade and if it's a real racy affair Schlitz in tall glasses with "They'll Do It Every Time" cartoons stencilled on.

"That's all right," Lengel said. "But this isn't the beach." His repeating this struck me as funny, as if it had just occurred to him, and he had been thinking all these years the A & P was a great big dune and he was the head lifeguard. He didn't like my smiling—as I say he doesn't miss much—but he concentrates on giving the girls that sad Sunday-school-superintendent stare.

15

Queenie's blush is no sunburn now, and the plump one in plaid, that I liked better from the back—a really sweet can—pipes up, "We weren't doing any shopping. We just came in for the one thing."

"That makes no difference," Lengel tells her, and I could see from the way his eyes went that he hadn't noticed she was wearing a two-piece before. "We want you decently dressed when you come in here."

"We *are* decent," Queenie says suddenly, her lower lip pushing, getting sore now that she remembers her place, a place from which the crowd that runs the A & P must look pretty crummy. Fancy Herring Snacks flashed in her very blue eyes.

"Girls, I don't want to argue with you. After this come in here with your shoulders covered. It's our policy." He turns his back. That's policy for you. Policy is what the kingpins want. What the others want is juvenile delinquency.

All this while, the customers had been showing up with their carts but, you know, sheep, seeing a scene, they had all bunched up on Stokesie, who shook open a paper bag as gently as peeling a peach, not wanting to miss a word. I could feel in the silence everybody getting nervous, most of all Lengel, who asks me, "Sammy, have you rung up this purchase?"

I thought and said "No" but it wasn't about that I was thinking. I go through the punches, 4, 9, GROC, TOT—it's more complicated than you think, and after you do it often enough, it begins to make a little song, that you hear words to, in my case "Hello (*bing*) there, you (*gung*) hap-py *pee*-pul (*splat*)!"—the *splat* being the drawer flying out. I uncrease the bill, tenderly as you may imagine, it just having come from between the two smoothest scoops of vanilla I had ever known were there, and pass a half and a penny into her narrow pink palm, and nestle the herrings in a bag and twist its neck and hand it over, all the time thinking.

The girls, and who'd blame them, are in a hurry to get out, so I say "I quit" to Lengel quick enough for them to hear, hoping they'll stop and watch me, their unsuspected hero. They keep right on going, into the electric eye; the door flies open and they flicker across the lot to their car, Queenie and Plaid and Big Tall Goony-Goony (not that as raw material she was so bad), leaving me with Lengel and a kink in his eyebrow.

"Did you say something, Sammy?"

"I said I quit."

"I thought you did."

"You didn't have to embarrass them."

"It was they who were embarrassing us."

I started to say something that came out "Fiddle-de-doo." It's a saying of my grandmother's, and I know she would have been pleased.

"I don't think you know what you're saying," Lengel said.

"I know you don't," I said. "But I do." I pull the bow at the back of my apron and start shrugging it off my shoulders. A couple customers that had been heading for my slot begin to knock against each other, like scared pigs in a chute.

Lengel sighs and begins to look very patient and old and gray. He's been a friend of my parents for years. "Sammy, you don't want to do this to your Mom and Dad," he tells me. It's true, I don't. But it seems to me that once you begin a gesture it's fatal not to go through with it. I fold the apron, "Sammy" stitched in red on the pocket, and put it on the counter, and drop the bow tie on top of it. The bow tie is theirs, if you've ever wondered. "You'll feel this for the rest of your life," Lengel says, and I know that's true, too, but remembering how he made that pretty girl blush makes me so scrunchy inside I punch the No Sale tab and the machine whirs "pee-pul" and the drawer splats out. One advantage to this scene taking place in summer, I can follow this up with a clean exit, there's no fumbling around getting your coat and galoshes, I just saunter into the electric eye in my white shirt that my mother ironed the night before, and the door heaves itself open, and outside the sunshine is skating around on the asphalt.

I look around for my girls, but they're gone, of course. There wasn't anybody but some young married screaming with her children about some candy they didn't get by the door of a powder-blue Falcon station wagon. Looking back in the big windows, over the bags of peat moss and aluminum lawn furniture stacked on the pavement, I could see Lengel in my place in the slot, checking the sheep through. His face was dark gray and his back stiff, as if he'd just had an injection of iron, and my stomach kind of fell as I felt how hard the world was going to be to me hereafter.

QUESTIONS

1. Notice how artfully Updike arranges details to set the story in a perfectly ordinary supermarket. What details stand out for you as particularly true to life? What does this close attention to detail contribute to the story?
2. How fully does Updike draw the character of Sammy? What traits (admirable or otherwise) does Sammy show? Is he any less a hero for wanting the girls to notice his heroism? To what extent is he more thoroughly and fully portrayed than the doctor in "Godfather Death"?
3. What part of the story seems exposition? (See the definition of *exposition* on page 6.) Of what value to the story is the carefully detailed portrait of Queenie, the leader of the three girls?
4. As the story develops, do you detect any change in Sammy's feelings toward the girls?
5. Where in "A & P" does the dramatic conflict become apparent? What moment in the story brings the crisis? What is the climax of the story?
6. Why, exactly, does Sammy quit his job?
7. Does anything lead you to *expect* Sammy to make some gesture of sympathy for the three girls? What incident earlier in the story (before Sammy quits) seems a foreshadowing?
8. What do you understand from the conclusion of the story? What does Sammy mean when he acknowledges "how hard the world was going to be . . . hereafter"?
9. What comment does Updike—through Sammy—make on supermarket society?

James Thurber

THE UNICORN IN THE GARDEN   1940

James Thurber (1894–1961), a humorist
sometimes mentioned in the same breath with
Mark Twain, was born in Columbus, Ohio,
and took a degree from Ohio State University.
As a young man he gravitated to New York,
where he became a prolific contributor to The
New Yorker *along with E. B. White, his col-*
laborator on a book-length spoof of popular psy-
chology, Is Sex Necessary? *(1929). Despite*
weak eyesight, Thurber gained fame as a car-
toonist known for his childlike drawings of timid
little men and hound dogs with floppy ears. As
blindness descended in his last years, Thurber
drew less and less, wrote more and more. Be-
sides essays and stories, his works include a
fable for children, The Thirteen Clocks
(1950); a memoir of working on The New
Yorker *staff,* The Years with Ross *(1959);*
and with Elliott Nugent, a comedy, The Male
Animal, *produced on Broadway in 1940.*

James Thurber

Once upon a sunny morning a man who sat in a breakfast nook looked up
from his scrambled eggs to see a white unicorn with a gold horn quietly cropping
the roses in the garden. The man went up to the bedroom where his wife was
still asleep and woke her. "There's a unicorn in the garden," he said. "Eating roses."
She opened one unfriendly eye and looked at him. "The unicorn is a mythical
beast," she said, and turned her back on him. The man walked slowly downstairs
and out into the garden. The unicorn was still there; he was now browsing among
the tulips. "Here, unicorn," said the man, and he pulled up a lily and gave it to
him. The unicorn ate it gravely. With a high heart, because there was a unicorn
in his garden, the man went upstairs and roused his wife again. "The unicorn,"
he said, "ate a lily." His wife sat up in bed and looked at him, coldly. "You are
a booby," she said, "and I am going to have you put in the booby-hatch." The
man, who had never liked the words "booby" and "booby-hatch," and who liked
them even less on a shining morning when there was a unicorn in the garden,
thought for a moment. "We'll see about that," he said. He walked over to the
door. "He has a golden horn in the middle of his forehead," he told her. Then
he went back to the garden to watch the unicorn; but the unicorn had gone away.
The man sat down among the roses and went to sleep.

As soon as the husband had gone out of the house, the wife got up and dressed
as fast as she could. She was very excited and there was a gloat in her eye. She

telephoned the police and she telephoned a psychiatrist; she told them to hurry to her house and bring a strait-jacket. When the police and the psychiatrist arrived they sat down in chairs and looked at her, with great interest. "My husband," she said, "saw a unicorn this morning." The police looked at the psychiatrist and the psychiatrist looked at the police. "He told me it ate a lily," she said. The psychiatrist looked at the police and the police looked at the psychiatrist. "He told me it had a golden horn in the middle of its forehead," she said. At a solemn signal from the psychiatrist, the police leaped from their chairs and seized the wife. They had a hard time subduing her, for she put up a terrific struggle, but they finally subdued her. Just as they got her into the strait-jacket, the husband came back into the house.

"Did you tell your wife you saw a unicorn?" asked the police. "Of course not," said the husband. "The unicorn is a mythical beast." "That's all I wanted to know," said the psychiatrist. "Take her away. I'm sorry, sir, but your wife is as crazy as a jay bird." So they took her away, cursing and screaming, and shut her up in an institution. The husband lived happily ever after.

Moral: Don't count your boobies until they are hatched.

QUESTIONS

1. How does Thurber's fable (one of his "Fables for Our Time") differ from the kind of fable Maugham retells in "An Appointment in Samarra"?
2. What do you understand to be the writer's attitudes toward the unicorn, the husband, and the wife? Does this fable seem to exist only to lead up to a pun, or do you find any point in it?
3. Take a lingering look at the drawing that accompanies "The Unicorn in the Garden." Then attack or defend Thurber as an illustrator.

SUGGESTIONS FOR WRITING

1. In a paragraph or two, referring to John Updike's "A & P," consider this remark: "Sammy is a sexist pig who suddenly sees the light." What evidence supporting (or refuting) this comment do you find in the story?
2. Imagining you are Sammy, write a brief letter to a friend explaining why you quit your job.
3. Look up Anne Sexton's retelling of the Grimm tale "Godfather Death" in her book of poems *Transformations* (1971); also included in *The Complete Poems of Anne Sexton* (1981). In a short essay of three to five paragraphs, discuss the differences you find between the Grimm and Sexton versions. What is the effect of Sexton's retelling? What does she retain from the original? Which version of the story do you prefer? Why?
4. If you have had an experience in telling stories aloud (to children or to others), write a brief but detailed account of your experience, giving tips to adults who wish to become storytellers.
5. Write a brief fable of your own invention, perhaps illustrating some familiar proverb ("Too many cooks spoil the broth," "A rolling stone gathers no moss"). Your fable might be inspired by "The Appointment in Samarra" or "The Unicorn in the Garden," or by a fable by Aesop. You can state a moral at the end, or, if you prefer, let the moral be unstated but obvious.
6. After you have written such a fable, write a short account of your writing process. Tell of the problems you encountered in thinking up your fable and in writing it, and how you surmounted them.
7. Compare "The Unicorn in the Garden" with Thurber's short story "The Catbird Seat" (page 465) and explain, in a paragraph or two, how the two works differ and what they have in common.

2 Point of View

In the opening lines of *The Adventures of Huckleberry Finn*, Mark Twain takes care to separate himself from the leading character, who is to tell his own story:

> You don't know about me, without you have read a book by the name of
> *The Adventures of Tom Sawyer*, but that ain't no matter. That book was made
> by Mr. Mark Twain, and he told the truth, mainly.

Twain wrote the novel, but the **narrator** or speaker is Huck Finn, the one from whose perspective the story is told. Obviously, in *Huckleberry Finn*, the narrator of a story is not the same person as the "real-life" author, the one given the by-line. In employing Huck as his narrator, Twain selects a special angle of vision: not his own, exactly, but that of a resourceful boy moving through the thick of events, with a mind at times shrewd, at other times innocent. Through Huck's eyes, Twain takes in certain scenes, actions, and characters and—as only Huck's angle of vision could have enabled Twain to do so well—records them memorably.

Not every narrator in fiction is, like Huck Finn, a main character, one in the thick of events. Some narrators play only minor parts in the stories they tell; others take no active part at all. In the tale of "Godfather Death," we have a narrator who does not participate in the events he recounts. He is not a character in the story but is someone not even named, who stands at some distance from the action recording what the main characters say and do; recording also, at times, what they think, feel, or desire. He seems to have unlimited knowledge: he even knows the mind of Death, who "because he wanted revenge" let the doctor's candle go out. More humanly restricted in their knowledge, other narrators can see into the mind of only one character. They may be less willing to express opinions than the narrator of "Godfather Death" ("He ought to have remembered his godfather's warning"). A story may even be told by a narrator who seems so impartial and aloof that he limits himself to reporting only overheard conversation and to describing, without comment or opinion, the appearances of things. Evidently, narrators greatly differ in kind; however, because stories usually are told by some-one, almost every story has some kind of narrator.[1] It is rare in modern fiction for the "real-life" author to try to step out from behind the typewriter and tell the story. Real persons can tell stories, but when such a story is *written*, the result is usually *nonfiction*: a memoir, an account of travels, an autobiography.[2]

To identify the narrator of a story, describing any part he or she plays in the events and any limits placed upon his knowledge, is to identify the story's **point of view.** In a short story, it is usual for the writer to maintain one point of view from beginning to end, but there is nothing to stop him from introducing other points of view as well. In his long, panoramic novel *War and Peace*, Leo Tolstoi, encompassing the vast drama of Napoleon's invasion of Russia, freely shifts the point of view in and out of the minds of many characters, among them Napoleon himself.

Theoretically, a great many points of view are possible. A narrator who says "I" might conceivably be involved in events to a much greater or a much lesser degree: as the protagonist, as some other major character, as some minor charac-ter, as a mere passive spectator, or even as a character who arrives late upon the scene and then tries to piece together what happened. Evidently, too, a narrator's knowledge might vary in gradations from total omniscience to almost total ignor-ance. But in reading fiction, again and again we encounter familiar and recogniz-able points of view. Here is a list of them—admittedly just a rough abstraction—that may provide a few terms with which to discuss the stories that you read and to describe their points of view:

Narrator a participant (writing in the first person):

1. a major character
2. a minor character

Narrator a nonparticipant (writing in the third person):

3. all-knowing (seeing into any of the characters)
4. seeing into one major character
5. seeing into one minor character
6. objective (not seeing into any characters)

When the narrator is cast as a **participant** in the events of the story, he or she is a dramatized character who says "I." Such a narrator may be the protagonist (Huck Finn) or may be an **observer,** a minor character standing a little to one side, watching a story unfold that mainly involves someone else.

[1]Some theorists reserve the term *narrator* for a character who tells a story in the first person. We use it in a wider sense: to mean a recording consciousness that an author creates, who may or may not be a participant in the events of the story. In the view of Wayne C. Booth, the term *narrator* can be dispensed with in dealing with a rigorously impersonal "fly-on-the-wall" story, containing no editorializing and confined to the presentation of surfaces: "In Hemingway's 'The Killers,' for exam-ple, there is no narrator other than the implicit second self that Hemingway creates as he writes (*The Rhetoric of Fiction* [Chicago: U of Chicago P, 1961] 151).

[2]Another relationship between the author and the story will be discussed in Chapter Five, "Tone and Style."

A narrator who remains a **nonparticipant** does not appear in the story as a character. Viewing the characters, perhaps seeing into the minds of one or more of them, such a narrator refers to them as "he," "she," or "they." When **all-knowing** (or **omniscient**), the narrator sees into the minds of all (or some) characters, moving when necessary from one to another. This is the point of view in "Godfather Death," whose narrator knows the feelings and motives of the father, of the doctor, and even of Death himself. In that he adds an occasional comment or opinion, this narrator may be said also to show **editorial omniscience** (as we can tell from his disapproving remark that the doctor "ought to have remembered" and his observation that the father did not understand "how wisely God shares out wealth and poverty"). A narrator who shows **impartial omniscience** presents the thoughts and actions of the characters, but does not judge them or comment on them.

When a nonparticipating narrator sees events throught the eyes of a single character, whether a major character or a minor one, the resulting point of view is sometimes called **limited omniscience** or **selective omniscience.** The author, of course, selects which character to see through; the omniscience is his and not the narrator's. In William Faulkner's "Barn Burning" (Chapter Five), the narrator is almost entirely confined to knowing the thoughts and perceptions of a boy, the central character. Here is another example. Early in his novel *Madame Bovary*, Gustave Flaubert tells of the first time a young country doctor, Charles Bovary, meets Emma, the woman later to become his wife. The doctor has been summoned late at night to set the broken leg of a farmer, Emma's father.

A young woman wearing a blue merino dress with three flounces came to the door of the house to greet Monsieur Bovary, and she ushered him into the kitchen, where a big open fire was blazing. Around its edges the farm hands' breakfast was bubbling in small pots of assorted sizes. Damp clothes were drying inside the vast chimney-opening. The fire shovel, the tongs, and the nose of the bellows, all of colossal proportions, shone like polished steel; and along the walls hung a lavish array of kitchen utensils, glimmering in the bright light of the fire and in the first rays of the sun that were now beginning to come in through the window-panes.

Charles went upstairs to see the patient. He found him in bed, sweating under blankets, his nightcap lying where he had flung it. He was a stocky little man of fifty, fair-skinned, blue-eyed, bald in front and wearing earrings. On a chair beside him was a big decanter of brandy: he had been pouring himself drinks to keep up his courage. But as soon as he saw the doctor he dropped his bluster, and instead of cursing as he had been doing for the past twelve hours he began to groan weakly.

The fracture was a simple one, without complications of any kind. Charles couldn't have wished for anything easier. Then he recalled his teachers' bedside manner in accident cases, and proceeded to cheer up his patient with all kinds of facetious remarks—a truly surgical attention, like the oiling of a scalpel. For splints, they sent someone to bring a bundle of laths from the carriage shed. Charles selected one, cut it into lengths and smoothed it down with a piece of broken window glass, while the maidservant tore sheets for bandages and Mademoiselle Emma tried to sew some pads. She was a long time finding her workbox, and her father showed his impatience. She made no reply; but as she sewed she kept pricking her fingers and raising them to her mouth to suck.

Charles was surprised by the whiteness of her fingernails. They were almond-shaped, tapering, as polished and shining as Dieppe ivories. Her hands, however, were not pretty—not pale enough, perhaps, a little rough at the knuckles; and they were too long, without softness of line. The finest thing about her was her eyes. They were brown, but seemed black under the long eyelashes; and she had an open gaze that met yours with fearless candor.[3]

In this famous scene, Charles Bovary is beholding people and objects in a natural sequence. On first meeting Emma, he notices only her dress, as though less interested in the woman who opens the door than in passing through to the warm fire. Needing pads for his patient's splint, the doctor observes just the hands of the woman sewing them. Obliged to wait for the splints, he then has the leisure to notice her face, her remarkable eyes. (By the way, notice the effect of the word *yours* in the last sentence of the passage. It is as if the reader, seeing through the doctor's eyes, suddenly became one with him.) Who is the narrator? Not Charles Bovary, nor Gustave Flaubert, but someone able to enter the minds of others— here limited to knowing the thoughts and perceptions of one character.

In the **objective** point of view, the narrator does not enter the mind of any character but describes events from the outside. Telling us what people say and how their faces look, he leaves us to infer their thoughts and feelings. So inconspicuous is the narrator that this point of view has been called "the fly on the wall." This metaphor assumes the existence of a fly with a highly discriminating gaze, who knows which details to look for to communicate the deepest meaning. Some critics would say that in the objective point of view, the narrator disappears altogether. Consider this passage by a writer famous for remaining objective, Dashiell Hammett, in his mystery novel *The Maltese Falcon*, describing his private detective Sam Spade:

Spade's thick fingers made a cigarette with deliberate care, sifting a measured quantity of tan flakes down into curved paper, spreading the flakes so that they lay equal at the ends with a slight depression in the middle, thumbs rolling the paper's inner edge down and up under the outer edge as forefingers pressed it over, thumb and fingers sliding to the paper cylinder's ends to hold it even while tongue licked the flap, left forefinger and thumb pinching their ends while right forefinger and thumb smoothed the damp seam, right forefinger and thumb twisting their end and lifting the other to Spade's mouth.[4]

[3]*Madame Bovary*, translated by Francis Steegmuller (New York: Random, 1957) 16–17.
[4]Chapter Two, "Death in the Fog," *The Maltese Falcon* (New York: Knopf, 1929).

In Hammett's novel, this sentence comes at a moment of crisis: just after Spade has been roused from bed in the middle of the night by a phone call telling him that his partner has been murdered. Even in time of stress (we infer) Spade is deliberate, cool, efficient, and painstaking. Hammett refrains from applying all those adjectives to Spade; to do so would be to exercise editorial omniscience and to destroy the objective point of view.

Besides the common points of view just listed, uncommon points of view are possible. In *Flush*, a fictional biography of Elizabeth Barrett Browning, Virginia Woolf employs an unusual observer as narrator: the poet's pet cocker spaniel. In "The Circular Valley," a short story by Paul Bowles, a man and a woman are watched by a sinister spirit trying to take possession of them, and we see the human characters through the spirit's vague consciousness. Possible also, but unusual, is a story written in the second person, *you*. This point of view results in an attention-getting directness, as in Jay McInerney's novel *Bright Lights, Big City* (1985), which begins:

> You are not the kind of guy who would be at a place like this at this time of the morning. But here you are, and you cannot say that the terrain is entirely unfamiliar, although the details are fuzzy. You are at a nightclub talking to a girl with a shaved head.

This arresting way to tell a story is effective, too, in a novel by Carlos Fuentes, *Aura* (1962), in some startling stories by Lorrie Moore in *Self-Help* (1985), and in a currently popular line of juvenile paperbound books, "The Adventures of You Series."[5]

The attitudes and opinions of a narrator aren't necessarily those of the author; in fact, we may notice a lively conflict between what we are told and what, apparently, we are meant to believe. A story may be told by an **innocent narrator** or a **naive narrator,** a character who fails to understand all the implications of the story. One such innocent narrator (despite his sometimes shrewd perceptions) is Huckleberry Finn. Because Huck accepts without question the morality and lawfulness of slavery, he feels guilty about helping Jim, a runaway slave. But, far from condemning Huck for his defiance of the law—"All right, then, I'll *go* to hell," Huck tells himself, deciding against returning Jim to captivity—the author, and the reader along with him, silently applaud. Naive in the extreme is the narrator of one part of William Faulkner's novel *The Sound and the Fury*, the idiot Benjy, a grown man with the intellect of a child. In a story told by an **unreliable narrator,** the point of view is that of a person who, we perceive, is deceptive, self-deceptive, deluded, or deranged. As though seeking ways to be faithful to uncertainty, contemporary writers have been particularly fond of unreliable narrators.

---

[5]Each book starts out with you, the main character, facing some challenge or danger. Then you are offered a choice: "Will you leap forward and struggle with the vampire? Turn to page 20. Will you flee? Turn to page 22." If you choose badly, you may be told, "Suddenly you feel the searing pain of a spear in your back. You sink to the ground—finished for good" (from Edward Packard, *Sugarcane Island* [New York: Pocket, 1978] 60).

Virginia Woolf compared life to "a luminous halo, a semi-transparent envelope surrounding us from the beginning of consciousness to the end."[6] To capture such a reality, modern writers of fiction have employed many strategies. One is the method of writing called **stream of consciousness,** from a phrase coined by psychologist William James to describe the procession of thoughts passing through the mind. In fiction, the stream of consciousness is a kind of selective omniscience: the presentation of thoughts and sense impressions in a lifelike fashion—not in a sequence arranged by logic, but mingled randomly. When in his novel *Ulysses* James Joyce takes us into the mind of Leopold Bloom, an ordinary Dublin mind well-stocked with trivia and fragments of odd learning, the reader may have an impression not of a smoothly flowing stream but of an ocean of miscellaneous things, all crowded and jostling.

As he set foot on O'Connell bridge a puffball of smoke plumed up from the parapet. Brewery barge with export stout. England. Sea air sours it, I heard. Be interesting some day to get a pass through Hancock to see the brewery. Regular world in itself. Vats of porter, wonderful. Rats get in too. Drink themselves bloated as big as a collie floating.[7]

Perceptions—such as the smoke from the brewery barge—trigger Bloom's reflections. A moment later, as he casts a crumpled paper ball off the bridge, he recalls a bit of science he learned in school, the rate of speed of a falling body: "thirty-two feet per sec."

Stream-of-consciousness writing usually occurs in relatively short passages, but in *Ulysses* Joyce employs it extensively. Similar in method, an **interior monologue** is an extended presentation of a character's thoughts, not in the seemingly helter-skelter order of a stream of consciousness, but in an arrangement as if the character were speaking out loud to himself, for us to overhear. A famous interior monologue comes at the end of *Ulysses* when Joyce gives us the rambling memories and reflections of earth-mother Molly Bloom.

Every point of view has limitations. Even **total omniscience,** a knowledge of the minds of all the characters, has its disadvantages. Such a point of view requires high skill to manage, without the storyteller's losing his way in a multitude of perspectives. In fact, there are evident advantages in having a narrator not know everything. We are accustomed to seeing the world through one pair of eyes, to having truths gradually occur to us. Henry James, whose theory and practice of fiction have been influential, held that an excellent way to tell a story was through the fine but bewildered mind of an observer. "It seems probable," James wrote, "that if we were never bewildered there would never be a story to tell about us; we should partake of the superior nature of the all-knowing immortals whose annals are dreadfully dull so long as flurried humans are not, for the positive relief of bored Olympians, mixed up with them."[8]

[6]"Modern Fiction," in *Collected Essays* (New York: Harcourt, 1967).
[7]*Ulysses* (New York: Random, 1934) 150.
[8]Preface to *The Princess Casamassima*, reprinted in *The Art of the Novel*, ed. R. P. Blackmur (New York: Scribner's, 1934).

By using a particular point of view, an author may artfully withhold information, if need be, rather than immediately present it to us. If, for instance, the suspense in a story depends upon our not knowing until the end that the protagonist is a secret agent, the author would be ill advised to tell the story from the protagonist's point of view. If a character acts as the narrator, the author must make sure that the character possesses (or can obtain) enough information to tell the story adequately. Clearly, the author makes a fundamental decision in selecting, from many possibilities, a story's point of view. What we readers admire, if the story is effective, is not only skill in execution, but also judicious choice.

Here is a short story memorable for many reasons, among them for its point of view.

William Faulkner

A ROSE FOR EMILY   1931

William Faulkner (1897–1962) spent most of his days in Oxford, Mississippi, where he attended the University of Mississippi and where he served as postmaster until angry townspeople ejected him after they had long failed to receive mail. During World War I he served with the Royal Canadian Air Force and afterward worked as a feature writer for the New Orleans Times-Picayune. *Faulkner's private life was a long struggle to stay solvent: even after fame came to him, he had to write Hollywood scripts and teach at the University of Virginia. The violent comic novel* Sanctuary *(1931) caused a stir and turned a profit, but critics tend most to admire* The Sound and the Fury *(1929), a tale partially told through the eyes of an idiot;* As I Lay Dying *(1930);*

William Faulkner

Light in August *(1932);* Absalom, Absalom *(1936); and* The Hamlet *(1940). Beginning with* Sartoris *(1929), Faulkner in his fiction imagines a Mississippi county named Yoknapatawpha and traces the fortunes of several of its families, including the aristocratic Compsons and Sartorises and the white-trash, dollar-grabbing Snopeses, from the Civil War to modern times. His influence on his fellow Southern writers (and others) has been profound. In 1950 he received the Nobel Prize for Literature with a stirring speech (quoted on pages 490–491). Although we think of Faulkner primarily as a novelist, he wrote nearly a hundred short stories. Forty-two of the best are available in his* Collected Stories *(1950).*

I

When Miss Emily Grierson died, our whole town went to her funeral: the men through a sort of respectful affection for a fallen monument, the women mostly out of curiosity to see the inside of her house, which no one save an old manservant—a combined gardener and cook—had seen in at least ten years.

It was a big, squarish frame house that had once been white, decorated with cupolas and spires and scrolled balconies in the heavily lightsome style of the seventies, set on what had once been our most select street. But garages and cotton gins had encroached and obliterated even the august names of that neighborhood; only Miss Emily's house was left, lifting its stubborn and coquettish decay above the cotton wagons and the gasoline pumps—an eyesore among eyesores. And now Miss Emily had gone to join the representatives of those august names where they lay in the cedar-bemused cemetery among the ranked and anonymous graves of Union and Confederate soldiers who fell at the battle of Jefferson.

Alive, Miss Emily had been a tradition, a duty, and a care; a sort of hereditary obligation upon the town, dating from that day in 1894 when Colonel Sartoris, the mayor—he who fathered the edict that no Negro woman should appear on the streets without an apron—remitted her taxes, the dispensation dating from the death of her father on into perpetuity. Not that Miss Emily would have accepted charity. Colonel Sartoris invented an involved tale to the effect that Miss Emily's father had loaned money to the town, which the town, as a matter of business, preferred this way of repaying. Only a man of Colonel Sartoris' generation and thought could have invented it, and only a woman could have believed it.

When the next generation, with its more modern ideas, became mayors and aldermen, this arrangement created some little dissatisfaction. On the first of the year they mailed her a tax notice. February came, and there was no reply. They wrote her a formal letter, asking her to call at the sheriff's office at her convenience. A week later the mayor wrote her himself, offering to call or to send his car for her, and received in reply a note on paper of an archaic shape, in a thin, flowing calligraphy in faded ink, to the effect that she no longer went out at all. The tax notice was also enclosed, without comment.

They called a special meeting of the Board of Aldermen. A deputation waited upon her, knocked at the door through which no visitor had passed since she ceased giving china-painting lessons eight or ten years earlier. They were admitted by the old Negro into a dim hall from which a stairway mounted into still more shadow. It smelled of dust and disuse—a close, dank smell. The Negro led them into the parlor. It was furnished in heavy, leather-covered furniture. When the Negro opened the blinds of one window, they could see that the leather was cracked; and when they sat down, a faint dust rose sluggishly about their thighs, spinning with slow motes in the single sun-ray. On a tarnished gilt easel before the fireplace stood a crayon portrait of Miss Emily's father.

They rose when she entered—a small, fat woman in black, with a thin gold chain descending to her waist and vanishing into her belt, leaning on an ebony cane with a tarnished gold head. Her skeleton was small and spare; perhaps that was why what would have been merely plumpness in another was obesity in her. She looked bloated, like a body long submerged in motionless water, and of that pallid hue. Her eyes, lost in the fatty ridges of her face, looked like two small pieces of coal pressed into a lump of dough as they moved from one face to another while the visitors stated their errand.

She did not ask them to sit. She just stood in the door and listened quietly until the spokesman came to a stumbling halt. Then they could hear the invisible watch ticking at the end of the gold chain.

Her voice was dry and cold. "I have no taxes in Jefferson. Colonel Sartoris explained it to me. Perhaps one of you can gain access to the city records and satisfy yourselves."

"But we have. We are the city authorities, Miss Emily. Didn't you get a notice from the sheriff, signed by him?"

"I received a paper, yes," Miss Emily said. "Perhaps he considers himself the   10
sheriff . . . I have no taxes in Jefferson."

"But there is nothing on the books to show that, you see. We must go by the—"

"See Colonel Sartoris. I have no taxes in Jefferson."

"But, Miss Emily—"

"See Colonel Sartoris." (Colonel Sartoris had been dead almost ten years.) "I have no taxes in Jefferson. Tobe!" The Negro appeared. "Show these gentlemen out."

II

So she vanquished them, horse and foot, just as she had vanquished their   15
fathers thirty years before about the smell. That was two years after her father's death and a short time after her sweetheart—the one we believed would marry her—had deserted her. After her father's death she went out very little; after her sweetheart went away, people hardly saw her at all. A few of the ladies had the temerity to call, but were not received, and the only sign of life about the place was the Negro man—a young man then—going in and out with a market basket.

"Just as if a man—any man—could keep a kitchen properly," the ladies said; so they were not surprised when the smell developed. It was another link between the gross, teeming world and the high and mighty Griersons.

A neighbor, a woman, complained to the mayor, Judge Stevens, eighty years old.

"But what will you have me do about it, madam?" he said.

"Why, send her word to stop it," the woman said. "Isn't there a law?"

"I'm sure that won't be necessary," Judge Stevens said. "It's probably just a   20
snake or a rat that nigger of hers killed in the yard. I'll speak to him about it."

The next day he received two more complaints, one from a man who came in diffident deprecation. "We really must do something about it, Judge. I'd be the last one in the world to bother Miss Emily, but we've got to do something." That night the Board of Aldermen met—three graybeards and one younger man, a member of the rising generation.

"It's simple enough," he said. "Send her word to have her place cleaned up. Give her a certain time to do it in, and if she don't . . . "

"Dammit, sir," Judge Stevens said, "will you accuse a lady to her face of smelling bad?"

So the next night, after midnight, four men crossed Miss Emily's lawn and slunk about the house like burglars, sniffing along the base of the brickwork and at the cellar openings while one of them performed a regular sowing motion with his hand out of a sack slung from his shoulder. They broke open the cellar door and sprinkled lime there, and in all the outbuildings. As they recrossed the lawn, a window that had been dark was lighted and Miss Emily sat in it, the light behind her, and her upright torso motionless as that of an idol. They crept quietly across the lawn and into the shadow of the locusts that lined the street. After a week or two the smell went away.

That was when people had begun to feel really sorry for her. People in our town, remembering how old lady Wyatt, her great-aunt, had gone completely crazy at last, believed that the Griersons held themselves a little too high for what they really were. None of the young men were quite good enough for Miss Emily and such. We had long thought of them as a tableau, Miss Emily a slender figure in white in the background, her father a spraddled silhouette in the foreground, his back to her and clutching a horsewhip, the two of them framed by the back-flung front door. So when she got to be thirty and was still single, we were not pleased exactly, but vindicated; even with insanity in the family she wouldn't have turned down all of her chances if they had really materialized.

When her father died, it got about that the house was all that was left to her; and in a way, people were glad. At last they could pity Miss Emily. Being left alone, and a pauper, she had become humanized. Now she too would know the old thrill and the old despair of a penny more or less.

The day after his death all the ladies prepared to call at the house and offer condolence and aid, as is our custom. Miss Emily met them at the door, dressed as usual and with no trace of grief on her face. She told them that her father was not dead. She did that for three days, with the ministers calling on her, and the doctors, trying to persuade her to let them dispose of the body. Just as they were about to resort to law and force, she broke down, and they buried her father quickly.

We did not say she was crazy then. We believed she had to do that. We remembered all the young men her father had driven away, and we knew that with nothing left, she would have to cling to that which had robbed her, as people will.

III

She was sick for a long time. When we saw her again, her hair was cut short, making her look like a girl, with a vague resemblance to those angels in colored church windows—sort of tragic and serene.

The town had just let the contracts for paving the sidewalks, and in the summer after her father's death they began the work. The construction company came with niggers and mules and machinery, and a foreman named Homer Barron, a Yankee—a big, dark, ready man, with a big voice and eyes lighter than his face. The little boys would follow in groups to hear him cuss the niggers, and the niggers singing in time to the rise and fall of picks. Pretty soon he knew everybody in town. Whenever you heard a lot of laughing anywhere about the square, Homer Barron would be in the center of the group. Presently we began to see him and

Miss Emily on Sunday afternoons driving in the yellow-wheeled buggy and the matched team of bays from the livery stable.

At first we were glad that Miss Emily would have an interest, because the ladies all said, "Of course a Grierson would not think seriously of a Northerner, a day laborer." But there were still others, older people, who said that even grief could not cause a real lady to forget *noblesse oblige*°—without calling it *noblesse oblige*. They just said, "Poor Emily. Her kinsfolk should come to her." She had some kin in Alabama; but years ago her father had fallen out with them over the estate of old lady Wyatt, the crazy woman, and there was no communication between the two families. They had not even been represented at the funeral.

And as soon as the old people said, "Poor Emily," the whispering began. "Do you suppose it's really so?" they said to one another. "Of course it is. What else could . . ." This behind their hands; rustling of craned silk and satin behind jalousies closed upon the sun of Sunday afternoon as the thin, swift clop-clop-clop of the matched team passed: "Poor Emily."

She carried her head high enough—even when we believed that she was fallen. It was as if she demanded more than ever the recognition of her dignity as the last Grierson; as if it had wanted that touch of earthiness to reaffirm her imperviousness. Like when she bought the rat poison, the arsenic. That was over a year after they had begun to say "Poor Emily," and while the two female cousins were visiting her.

"I want some poison," she said to the druggist. She was over thirty then, still a slight woman, though thinner than usual, with cold, haughty black eyes in a face the flesh of which was strained across the temples and about the eye-sockets as you imagine a lighthouse-keeper's face ought to look. "I want some poison," she said.

"Yes, Miss Emily. What kind? For rats and such? I'd recom—"   35

"I want the best you have. I don't care what kind."

The druggist named several. "They'll kill anything up to an elephant. But what you want is—"

"Arsenic," Miss Emily said. "Is that a good one?"

"Is . . . arsenic? Yes, ma'am. But what you want—"

"I want arsenic."   40

The druggist looked down at her. She looked back at him, erect, her face like a strained flag. "Why, of course," the druggist said. "If that's what you want. But the law requires you to tell what you are going to use it for."

Miss Emily just stared at him, her head tilted back in order to look him eye for eye, until he looked away and went and got the arsenic and wrapped it up. The Negro delivery boy brought her the package; the druggist didn't come back. When she opened the package at home there was written on the box, under the skull and bones: "For rats."

IV

So the next day we all said, "She will kill herself"; and we said it would be the best thing. When she had first begun to be seen with Homer Barron, we had said, "She will marry him." Then we said, "She will persuade him yet," because Homer

noblesse oblige: the obligation of a member of the nobility to behave with honor and dignity.

himself had remarked—he liked men, and it was known that he drank with the younger men in the Elks' Club—that he was not a marrying man. Later we said, "Poor Emily" behind the jalousies as they passed on Sunday afternoon in the glittering buggy, Miss Emily with her head high and Homer Barron with his hat cocked and a cigar in his teeth, reins and whip in a yellow glove.

Then some of the ladies began to say that it was a disgrace to the town and a bad example to the young people. The men did not want to interfere, but at last the ladies forced the Baptist minister—Miss Emily's people were Episcopal— to call upon her. He would never divulge what happened during that interview, but he refused to go back again. The next Sunday they again drove about the streets, and the following day the minister's wife wrote to Miss Emily's relations in Alabama.

So she had blood-kin under her roof again and we sat back to watch developments. At first nothing happened. Then we were sure that they were to be married. We learned that Miss Emily had been to the jeweler's and ordered a man's toilet set in silver, with the letters H. B. on each piece. Two days later we learned that she had bought a complete outfit of men's clothing, including a nightshirt, and we said, "They are married." We were really glad. We were glad because the two female cousins were even more Grierson than Miss Emily had ever been. 45

So we were not surprised when Homer Barron—the streets had been finished some time since—was gone. We were a little disappointed that there was not a public blowing-off, but we believed that he had gone on to prepare for Miss Emily's coming, or to give her a chance to get rid of the cousins. (By that time it was a cabal, and we were all Miss Emily's allies to help circumvent the cousins.) Sure enough, after another week they departed. And, as we had expected all along, within three days Homer Barron was back in town. A neighbor saw the Negro man admit him at the kitchen door at dusk one evening.

And that was the last we saw of Homer Barron. And of Miss Emily for some time. The Negro man went in and out with the market basket, but the front door remained closed. Now and then we would see her at a window for a moment, as the men did that night when they sprinkled the lime, but for almost six months she did not appear on the streets. Then we knew that this was to be expected too; as if that quality of her father which had thwarted her women's life so many times had been too virulent and too furious to die.

When we next saw Miss Emily, she had grown fat and her hair was turning gray. During the next few years it grew grayer and grayer until it attained an even pepper-and-salt iron-gray, when it ceased turning. Up to the day of her death at seventy-four it was still that vigorous iron-gray, like the hair of an active man.

From that time on her front door remained closed, save for a period of six or seven years, when she was about forty, during which she gave lessons in china-painting. She fitted up a studio in one of the downstairs rooms, where the daughters and granddaughters of Colonel Sartoris' contemporaries were sent to her with the same regularity and in the same spirit that they were sent to church on Sundays with a twenty-five-cent piece for the collection plate. Meanwhile her taxes had been remitted.

Then the newer generation became the backbone and the spirit of the town, and the painting pupils grew up and fell away and did not send their children to her with boxes of color and tedious brushes and pictures cut from the ladies' 50 magazines. The front door closed upon the last one and remained closed for good. When the town got free postal delivery, Miss Emily alone refused to let them fasten the metal numbers above her door and attach a mailbox to it. She would not listen to them.

Daily, monthly, yearly we watched the Negro grow grayer and more stooped, going in and out with the market basket. Each December we sent her a tax notice, which would be returned by the post office a week later, unclaimed. Now and then we would see her in one of the downstairs windows—she had evidently shut up the top floor of the house—like the carven torso of an idol in a niche, looking or not looking at us, we could never tell which. Thus she passed from generation to generation—dear, inescapable, impervious, tranquil, and perverse.

And so she died. Fell ill in the house filled with dust and shadows, with only a doddering Negro man to wait on her. We did not even know she was sick; we had long since given up trying to get any information from the Negro. He talked to no one, probably not even to her, for his voice had grown harsh and rusty, as if from disuse.

She died in one of the downstairs rooms, in a heavy walnut bed with a curtain, her gray head propped on a pillow yellow and moldy with age and lack of sunlight.

V

The Negro met the first of the ladies at the front door and let them in, with their hushed, sibilant voices and their quick, curious glances, and then he disappeared. He walked right through the house and out the back and was not seen again.

The two female cousins came at once. They held the funeral on the second day, with the town coming to look at Miss Emily beneath a mass of bought flowers, with the crayon face of her father musing profoundly above the bier and the ladies sibilant and macabre; and the very old men—some in their brushed Confederate uniforms—on the porch and the lawn, talking of Miss Emily as if she had been a contemporary of theirs, believing that they had danced with her and courted her perhaps, confusing time with its mathematical progression, as the old do, to whom all the past is not a diminishing road but, instead, a huge meadow which no winter ever quite touches, divided from them now by the narrow bottleneck of the most recent decade of years.

Already we knew that there was one room in that region above stairs which no one had seen in forty years, and which would have to be forced. They waited until Miss Emily was decently in the ground before they opened it.

The violence of breaking down the door seemed to fill this room with pervading dust. A thin, acrid pall as of the tomb seemed to lie everywhere upon this room decked and furnished as for a bridal: upon the valance curtains of faded rose color, upon the rose-shaded lights, upon the dressing table, upon the delicate array of crystal and the man's toilet things backed with tarnished silver, silver so tarnished that the monogram was obscured. Among them lay collar and tie, as if they had just been removed, which, lifted, left upon the surface a pale crescent in the dust. Upon a chair hung the suit, carefully folded; beneath it the two mute shoes and the discarded socks.

The man himself lay in the bed.

For a long while we just stood there, looking down at the profound and flesh-less grin. The body had apparently once lain in the attitude of an embrace, but now the long sleep that outlasts love, that conquers even the grimace of love, had cuckolded him. What was left of him, rotted beneath what was left of the nightshirt, had become inextricable from the bed in which he lay; and upon him and upon the pillow beside him lay that even coating of the patient and biding dust.

Then we noticed that in the second pillow was the indentation of a head. 60 One of us lifted something from it, and leaning forward, that faint and invisible dust dry and acrid in the nostrils, we saw a long strand of iron-gray hair.

QUESTIONS

1. What is meaningful in the final detail that the strand of hair on the second pillow is *iron-gray*?
2. Who is the unnamed narrator? For whom does he profess to be speaking?
3. Why does "A Rose for Emily" seem better told from his point of view than if it were told (like John Updike's "A & P") from the point of view of the main character?
4. What foreshadowings of the discovery of the body of Homer Barron are we given earlier in the story? Share your experience in reading "A Rose for Emily": did the foreshadowings give away the ending for you? Did they heighten your interest?
5. What contrasts does the narrator draw between changing reality and Emily's refusal or inability to recognize change?
6. How do the character and background of Emily Grierson differ from those of Homer Barron? What general observations about the society that Faulkner depicts can be made from his portraits of these two characters and from his account of life in this one Mississippi town?
7. Does the story seem to you totally grim, or do you find any humor in it?
8. What do you infer to be the author's attitude toward Emily Grierson? Is she simply a murderous madwoman? Why do you suppose Faulkner calls his story "A Rose . . . "?

Katherine Mansfield

MISS BRILL   1922

Katherine Mansfield Beauchamp (1888–1923), who shortened her byline, was born into a sedate Victorian family in New Zealand, daughter of a successful businessman. At fifteen she emigrated to England to attend school and did not ever permanently return Down Under. In 1918, after a time of wild-oat sowing in bohemian London, she married the journalist and critic John Middleton Murray. All at once, Mansfield found herself struggling to define her sexual identity, to earn a living by her pen, to endure World War I (in which her brother was killed in action), and to survive the ravages of tuberculosis. She died

Katherine Mansfield

at thirty-four, in France, at a spiritualist commune where she had sought to regain her health. Mansfield wrote no novels, but during her brief career concentrated on the short story, in which form of art she has few peers. Bliss (1920) and The Garden-Party and Other Stories (1922) were greeted with an acclaim that has continued; her Short Stories were collected in 1937. Some celebrate life, others wryly poke fun at it. Many reveal, in ordinary lives, small incidents that open like doorways into significances.

Although it was so brilliantly fine—the blue sky powdered with gold and great spots of light like white wine splashed over the Jardins Publiques—Miss Brill was glad that she had decided on her fur. The air was motionless, but when you opened your mouth there was just a faint chill, like a chill from a glass of iced water before you sip, and now and again a leaf came drifting—from nowhere, from the sky. Miss Brill put up her hand and touched her fur. Dear little thing! It was nice to feel it again. She had taken it out of its box that afternoon, shaken out the moth-powder, given it a good brush, and rubbed the life back into the dim little eyes. "What has been happening to me?" said the sad little eyes. Oh, how sweet it was to see them snap at her again from the red eiderdown! . . . But the nose, which was of some black composition, wasn't at all firm. It must have had a knock, somehow. Never mind—a little dab of black sealing-wax when the time came— when it was absolutely necessary. . . . Little rogue! Yes, she really felt like that about it. Little rogue biting its tail just by her left ear. She could have taken it off and laid it on her lap and stroked it. She felt a tingling in her hands and arms, but that came from walking, she supposed. And when she breathed, something light and sad—no, not sad, exactly—something gentle seemed to move in her bosom.

There were a number of people out this afternoon, far more than last Sunday. And the band sounded louder and gayer. That was because the Season had begun. For although the band played all year round on Sundays, out of season it was never the same. It was like some one playing with only the family to listen; it didn't care how it played if there weren't any strangers present. Wasn't the conductor wearing a new coat, too? She was sure it was new. He scraped with his foot and flapped his arms like a rooster about to crow, and the bandsmen sitting in the green rotunda blew out their cheeks and glared at the music. Now there came a little "flutey" bit—very pretty!—a little chain of bright drops. She was sure it would be repeated. It was; she lifted her head and smiled.

Only two people shared her "special" seat: a fine old man in a velvet coat, his hands clasped over a huge carved walking-stick, and a big old woman, sitting upright, with a roll of knitting on her embroidered apron. They did not speak. This was disappointing, for Miss Brill always looked forward to the conversation. She had become really quite expert, she thought, at listening as though she didn't listen, at sitting in other people's lives just for a minute while they talked round her.

She glanced, sideways, at the old couple. Perhaps they would go soon. Last Sunday, too, hadn't been as interesting as usual. An Englishman and his wife, he wearing a dreadful Panama hat and she button boots. And she'd gone on the whole time about how she ought to wear spectacles; she knew she needed them; but that it was no good getting any; they'd be sure to break and they'd never keep on. And he'd been so patient. He'd suggested everything—gold rims, the kind that curved round your ears, little pads inside the bridge. No, nothing would please her. "They'll always be sliding down my nose!" Miss Brill wanted to shake her.

The old people sat on the bench, still as statues. Never mind, there was always the crowd to watch. To and fro, in front of the flower-beds and the band rotunda, the couples and groups paraded, stopped to talk, to greet, to buy a handful of flowers from the old beggar who had his tray fixed to the railings. Little children ran among them, swooping and laughing; little boys with big white silk bows under their chins, little girls, little French dolls, dressed up in velvet and lace. And sometimes a tiny staggerer came suddenly rocking into the open from under the trees, stopped, stared, as suddenly sat down "flop," until its small high-stepping mother, like a young hen, rushed scolding to its rescue. Other people sat on the benches and green chairs, but they were nearly always the same, Sunday after Sunday, and—Miss Brill had often noticed—there was something funny about nearly all of them. They were odd, silent, nearly all old, and from the way they stared they looked as though they'd just come from dark little rooms or even—even cupboards!

Behind the rotunda the slender trees with yellow leaves down drooping, and through them just a line of sea, and beyond the blue sky with gold-veined clouds.

Tum-tum-tum tiddle-um! tiddle-um! tum tiddley-um tum ta! blew the band.

Two young girls in red came by and two young soldiers in blue met them, and they laughed and paired and went off arm-in-arm. Two peasant women with funny straw hats passed, gravely, leading beautiful smoke-colored donkeys. A cold, pale nun hurried by. A beautiful woman came along and dropped her bunch of violets, and a little boy ran after to hand them to her, and she took them and threw them away as if they'd been poisoned. Dear me! Miss Brill didn't know whether to admire that or not! And now an ermine toque and a gentleman in grey met just in front of her. He was tall, stiff, dignified, and she was wearing the ermine toque she'd bought when her hair was yellow. Now everything, her hair, her face, even her eyes, was the same color as the shabby ermine, and her hand, in its cleaned glove, lifted to dab her lips, was a tiny yellowish paw. Oh, she was so pleased to see him—delighted! She rather thought they were going to meet that afternoon. She described where she'd been—everywhere, here, there, along by the sea. The day was so charming—didn't he agree? And wouldn't he, perhaps? . . . But he shook his head, lighted a cigarette, slowly breathed a great deep puff into her face, and, even while she was still talking and laughing, flicked the match away and walked on. The ermine toque was alone; she smiled more brightly than ever. But even the band seemed to know what she was feeling and played more softly, played tenderly, and the drum beat, "The Brute! The Brute!" over and over. What would she do? What was going to happen now? But as Miss Brill wondered, the ermine toque turned, raised her hand as though she'd seen some one else, much nicer, just over there, and pattered away. And the band changed again and played more quickly, more gaily than ever, and the old couple on Miss Brill's seat got up and marched away, and such a funny old man with long whiskers hobbled along in time to the music and was nearly knocked over by four girls walking abreast.

Oh, how fascinating it was! How she enjoyed it! How she loved sitting here, watching it all! It was like a play. It was exactly like a play. Who could believe the sky at the back wasn't painted? But it wasn't till a little brown dog trotted on solemn and then slowly trotted off, like a little "theatre" dog, a little dog that had been drugged, that Miss Brill discovered what it was that made it so exciting. They were all on the stage. They weren't only the audience, not only looking on; they were acting. Even she had a part and came every Sunday. No doubt somebody would have noticed if she hadn't been there; she was part of the performance after all. How strange she'd never thought of it like that before! And yet it explained why she made such a point of starting from home at just the same time each week—so as not to be late for the performance—and it also explained why she had quite a queer, shy feeling at telling her English pupils how she spent her Sunday afternoons. No wonder! Miss Brill nearly laughed out loud. She was on the stage. She thought of the old invalid gentleman to whom she read the newspaper four afternoons a week while he slept in the garden. She had got quite used to the frail head on the cotton pillow, the hollowed eyes, the open mouth and the high pinched nose. If he'd been dead she mightn't have noticed for weeks; she wouldn't have minded. But suddenly he knew he was having the paper read to him by an actress! "An actress!" The old head lifted; two points of light quivered in the old eyes. "An actress—are ye?" And Miss Brill smoothed the newspaper as though it were the manuscript of her part and said gently: "Yes, I have been an actress for a long time."

The band had been having a rest. Now they started again. And what they 10 played was warm, sunny, yet there was just a faint chill—a something, what was it?—not sadness—no, not sadness—a something that made you want to sing. The tune lifted, lifted, the light shone; and it seemed to Miss Brill that in another moment all of them, all the whole company, would begin singing. The young ones, the laughing ones who were moving together, they would begin, and the men's voices, very resolute and brave, would join them. And then she too, she too, and the others on the benches—they would come in with a kind of accompaniment—something low, that scarcely rose or fell, something so beautiful—moving . . . . And Miss Brill's eyes filled with tears and she looked smiling at all the other members of the company. Yes, we understand, we understand, she thought—though what they understood she didn't know.

Just at that moment a boy and a girl came and sat down where the old couple had been. They were beautifully dressed; they were in love. The hero and heroine, of course, just arrived from his father's yacht. And still soundlessly singing, still with that trembling smile, Miss Brill prepared to listen.

"No, not now," said the girl. "Not here, I can't."

"But why? Because of that stupid old thing at the end there?" asked the boy. "Why does she come here at all—who wants her? Why doesn't she keep her silly old mug at home?"

"It's her fu-fur which is so funny," giggled the girl. "It's exactly like a fried whiting."

"Ah, be off with you!" said the boy in an angry whisper. Then: "Tell me, my 15 petite chérie—"

"No, not here," said the girl. "Not yet."

On her way home she usually bought a slice of honeycake at the baker's. It was her Sunday treat. Sometimes there was an almond in her slice, sometimes not. It made a great difference. If there was an almond it was like carrying home a tiny present—a surprise—something that might very well not have been there. She hurried on the almond Sundays and struck the match for the kettle in quite a dashing way.

But to-day she passed the baker's boy, climbed the stairs, went into the little dark room—her room like a cupboard—and sat down on the red eiderdown. She sat there for a long time. The box that the fur came out of was on the bed. She unclasped the necklet quickly; quickly, without looking, laid it inside. But when she put the lid on she thought she heard something crying.

QUESTIONS

1. What is the point of view in "Miss Brill"? Why is the story the better for this method of telling?
2. Where and in what season does Mansfield's story take place? How do we know? Would the effect be the same if the story were set, say, in a remote Alaskan village in the summertime?
3. What details provide revealing insights into Miss Brill's character and lifestyle?
4. What draws Miss Brill to the park every Sunday? What is the nature of the startling revelation that delights her on the day this story takes place?
5. Comment on the last line. What possible explanations might there be for Miss Brill's thinking that she "heard something crying"?
6. See Katherine Mansfield's comment on the writing of "Miss Brill" (page 490). Then indicate—and read aloud—any passage or passages in the story that, you believe, illustrate what she was striving for.

Toni Cade Bambara

BLUES AIN'T NO MOCKIN BIRD   1971

Toni Cade Bambara, author, teacher, and civil rights activist, was born Toni Cade in New York in 1939, legally adding her last name in 1970. She grew up in Harlem and in the city's troubled Bedford-Stuyvesant district. After taking her master's degree at City College, she worked for the New York State Welfare Department as a case investigator. Later, she set out to learn dance and film-making; she studied commedia dell'arte in Florence, mime in Paris. After her fiction began to spread her fame, she accepted invitations to teach at Duke, Stephens, Emory, and Spelman College, and in 1969–74 was an assistant professor at Rutgers University. Bambara's works of fiction

Toni Cade Bambara

include Gorilla, My Love *(1972),* The Sea Birds Are Still Alive *(1977),* The Salt Eaters *(1980), and the recent novel* If Blessing Comes *(1987). She has conducted workshops on writing and community organization at museums, prisons, libraries, colleges,* community centers, and independent schools, and has directed a recreation program for psychiatric patients at New York City's Metropolitan Hospital. As a storyteller Bambara has devoted herself to correcting stereotyped images of African-Americans. She has written screenplays and has edited two anthologies of African-American literature.

The puddle had frozen over, and me and Cathy went stompin in it. The twins from next door, Tyrone and Terry, were swingin so high out of sight we forgot we were waitin our turn on the tire. Cathy jumped up and came down hard on her heels and started tap-dancin. And the frozen patch splinterin every which way underneath kinda spooky. "Looks like a plastic spider web," she said. "A sort of weird spider, I guess, with many mental problems." But really it looked like the crystal paperweight Granny kept in the parlor. She was on the back porch, Granny was, making the cakes drunk. The old ladle dripping rum into the Christmas tins, like it used to drip maple syrup into the pails when we lived in the Judsons' woods, like it poured cider into the vats when we were on the Cooper place, like it used to scoop buttermilk and soft cheese when we lived at the dairy.

"Go tell that man we ain't a bunch of trees."

"Ma'am?"

"I said to tell that man to get away from here with that camera." Me and Cathy look over toward the meadow where the men with the station wagon'd been roamin around all mornin. The tall man with a huge camera lassoed to his shoulder was buzzin our way.

"They're makin movie pictures," yelled Tyrone, stiffenin his legs and twistin so the tire'd come down slow so they could see.   5

"They're makin movie pictures," sang out Terry.

"That boy don't never have anything original to say," say Cathy grown-up.

By the time the man with the camera had cut across our neighbor's yard, the twins were out of the trees swingin low and Granny was onto the steps, the screen door bammin soft and scratchy against her palms. "We thought we'd get a shot or two of the house and everything and then—"

"Good mornin," Granny cut him off. And smiled that smile.

"Good mornin," he said, head all down the way Bingo does when you yell   10
at him about the bones on the kitchen floor. "Nice place you got here, Aunty. We thought we'd take a—"

"Did you?" said Granny with her eyebrows. Cathy pulled up her socks and giggled.

"Nice things here," said the man, buzzin his camera over the yard. The pecan barrels, the sled, me and Cathy, the flowers, the printed stones along the driveway, the trees, the twins, the toolshed.

"I don't know about the thing, the it, and the stuff," said Granny, still talkin with her eyebrows. "Just people here is what I tend to consider."

Camera man stopped buzzin. Cathy giggled into her collar.

"Mornin, ladies," a new man said. He had come up behind us when we weren't   15
lookin. "And gents," discoverin the twins givin him a nasty look. "We're filmin for the county," he said with a smile. "Mind if we shoot a bit around here?"

"I do indeed," said Granny with no smile. Smilin man was smiling up a storm. So was Cathy. But he didn't seem to have another word to say, so he and the camera man backed on out of the yard, but you could hear the camera buzzin still. "Suppose you just shut that machine off," said Granny real low through her teeth, and took a step down off the porch and then another.

"Now, Aunty," Camera said, pointin the thing straight at her.

"Your mama and I are not related."

Smilin man got his notebook out and a chewed-up pencil. "Listen," he said movin back into our yard, "we'd like to have a statement from you . . . for the film. We're filmin for the county, see. Part of the food-stamp campaign. You know about the food stamps?"

Granny said nuthin.   20

"Maybe there's somethin you want to say for the film. I see you grow your own vegetables," he smiled real nice. "If more folks did that, see, there'd be no need—"

Granny wasn't sayin nuthin. So they backed on out, buzzin at our clothesline and the twins' bicycles, then back on down to the meadow. The twins were danglin in the tire, lookin at Granny. Me and Cathy were waitin, too, cause Granny always got somethin to say. She teaches steady with no letup. "I was on this bridge one time," she started off. "Was a crowd cause this man was goin to jump, you understand. And a minister was there and the police and some other folks. His woman was there, too."

"What was they doin?" asked Tyrone.

"Tryin to talk him out of it was what they was doin. The minister talkin about how it was a mortal sin, suicide. His woman takin bites out of her own hand and not even knowin it, so nervous and cryin and talkin fast."

"So what happened?" asked Tyrone.   25

"So here comes . . . this person . . . with a camera, takin pictures of the man and the minister and the woman. Takin pictures of the man in his misery about to jump, cause life so bad and people been messin with him so bad. This person takin up the whole roll of film practically. But savin a few, of course."

"Of course," said Cathy, hatin the person. Me standin there wonderin how Cathy knew it was "of course" when I didn't and it was *my* grandmother.

After a while Tyrone say, "Did he jump?"

"Yeh, did he jump?" say Terry all eager.

And Granny just stared at the twins till their faces swallow up the eager and   30
they don't even care any more about the man jumpin. Then she goes back onto the porch and lets the screen door go for itself. I'm lookin to Cathy to finish the story cause she knows Granny's whole story before me even. Like she knew how come we move so much and Cathy ain't but a third cousin we picked up on the way last Thanksgivin visitin. But she knew it was on account of people drivin Granny crazy till she'd get up in the night and start packin. Mumblin and packin and wakin everybody up sayin, "Let's get away from here before I kill me somebody." Like people wouldn't pay her for things like they said they would. Or Mr. Judson bringin us boxes of old clothes and raggedy magazines. Or Mrs. Cooper comin in our kitchen and touchin everything and sayin how clean it all was. Granny goin crazy, and Granddaddy Cain pullin her off the people, sayin, "Now, now, Cora." But next day loadin up the truck, with rocks all in his jaw, madder than Granny in the first place.

"I read a story once," said Cathy soundin like Granny teacher. "About this lady Goldilocks who barged into a house that wasn't even hers. And not invited, you understand. Messed over the people's groceries and broke up the people's furniture. Had the nerve to sleep in the folks' bed."

"Then what happened?" asked Tyrone. "What they do, the folks, when they come in to all this mess?"

"Did they make her pay for it?" asked Terry, makin a fist. "I'd've made her pay me."

I didn't even ask. I could see Cathy actress was very likely to just walk away and leave us in mystery about this story which I heard was about some bears.

"Did they throw her out?" asked Tyrone, like his father sounds when he's bein 35
extra nasty-plus to the washin-machine man.

"Woulda," said Terry. "I woulda gone upside her head with my fist and—"

"You woulda done whatcha always do—go cry to Mama, you big baby," said Tyrone. So naturally Terry starts hittin on Tyrone, and next thing you know they tumblin out the tire and rollin on the ground. But Granny didn't say a thing or send the twins home or step out on the steps to tell us about how we can't afford to be fightin amongst ourselves. She didn't say nuthin. So I get into the tire to take my turn. And I could see her leanin up against the pantry table, starin at the cakes she was puttin up for the Christmas sale, mumblin real low and grumpy and holdin her forehead like it wanted to fall off and mess up the rum cakes.

Behind me I hear before I can see Granddaddy Cain comin through the woods in his field boots. Then I twist around to see the shiny black oilskin cuttin through what little left there was of yellows, red, and oranges. His great white head not quite round cause of this bloody thing high on his shoulder, like he was wearin a cap on sideways. He takes the shortcut through the pecan grove, and the sound of twigs snapping overhead and underfoot travels clear and cold all the way up to us. And here comes Smilin and Camera up behind him like they was going to do somethin. Folks like to go for him sometimes. Cathy say it's because he's so tall and quiet and like a king. And people just can't stand it. But Smilin and Camera don't hit him on the head or nuthin. They just buzz on him as he stalks by with the chicken hawk slung over his shoulder, squawkin, drippin red down the back of the oilskin. He passes the porch and stops a second for Granny to see he's caught the hawk at last, but she's just starin and mumblin, and not at the hawk. So he nails the bird to the toolshed door, the hammerin crackin through the eardrums. And the bird flappin himself to death and droolin down the door to paint the gravel on the driveway red, then brown, then black. And the two men movin up on tiptoe like they was invisible or we were blind, one.

"Get them persons out of my flower bed, Mister Cain," say Granny moanin real low like at a funeral.

"How come your grandmother calls her husband 'Mister Cain' all the time?" 40
Tyrone whispers all loud and noisy and from the city and don't know no better. Like his mama, Miss Myrtle, tell us never mind the formality as if we had no better breeding than to call her Myrtle, plain. And then this awful thing—a giant hawk—come wailin up over the meadow, flyin low and tilted and screamin, zigzaggin through the pecan grove, breakin branches and hollerin, snappin past the clothesline, flyin every which way, flyin into things reckless with crazy.

"He's come to claim his mate," say Cathy fast, and ducks down. We all fall quick and flat into the gravel driveway, stones scrapin my face. I squinch my eyes open again at the hawk on the door, tryin to fly up out of her death like it was just a sack flown into by mistake. Her body holdin her there on that nail, though. The mate beatin the air overhead and clutchin for hair, for heads, for landin space.

The camera man duckin and bendin and runnin and fallin, jigglin the camera and scared. And Smilin jumpin up and down swipin at the huge bird, tryin to bring the hawk down with just his raggedy ole cap. Granddaddy Cain straight up and silent, watchin the circles of the hawk, then aimin the hammer off his wrist. The giant bird fallin, silent and slow. Then here comes Camera and Smilin all big and bad now that the awful screechin thing is on its back and broken, here they come. And Granddaddy Cain looks up at them like it was the first time noticin, but not payin them too much mind cause he's listenin, we all listenin, to that low groanin music comin from the porch. And we figure any minute, somethin in my back tells me any minute now, Granny gonna bust through that screen with somethin in her hand and murder on her mind. So Granddaddy say above the buzzin, but quiet, "Good day, gentlemen." Just like that. Like he'd invited them in to play cards and they'd stayed too long and all the sandwiches were gone and Reverend Webb was droppin by and it was time to go.

They didn't know what to do. But like Cathy say, folks can't stand Granddaddy tall and silent and like a king. They can't neither. The smile the men smilin is pullin the mouth back and showin the teeth. Lookin like the wolf man, both of them. Then Grandaddy holds his hand out—this huge hand I used to sit in when I was a baby and he'd carry me through the house to my mother like I was a gift on a tray. Like he used to on the trains. They called the other men just waiters. But they spoke of Granddaddy separate and said, The Waiter. And said he had engines in his feet and motors in his hands and couldn't no train throw him off and couldn't nobody turn him round. They were big enough for motors, his hands were. He held that one hand out all still and it gettin to be not at all a hand but a person in itself.

"He wants you to hand him the camera," Smilin whispers to Camera, tiltin his head to talk secret like they was in the jungle or somethin and come upon a native that don't speak the language. The men start untyin the straps, and they put the camera into that great hand speckled with the hawk's blood all black and crackly now. And the hand don't even drop with the weight, just the fingers move, curl up around the machine. But Granddaddy lookin straight at the men. They lookin at each other and everywhere but at Granddaddy's face.

"We filmin for the county, see," say Smilin. "We puttin together a movie for the foodstamp program . . . filmin all around these parts. Uhh, filmin for the county."

"Can I have my camera back?" say the tall man with no machine on his shoulder, but still keepin it high like the camera was still there or needed to be. "Please, sir."

Then Granddaddy's other hand flies up like a sudden and gentle bird, slaps down fast on top of the camera and lifts off half like it was a calabash cut for sharing.

"Hey," Camera jumps forward. He gathers up the parts into his chest and everything unrollin and fallin all over. "Whatcha tryin to do? You'll ruin the film."

He looks down into his chest of metal reels and things like he's protectin a kitten from the cold.

"You standin in the misses' flower beds," say Granddaddy. "This is our own place."

The two men look at him, then at each other, then back at the mess in the cameraman's chest, and they just back off. One sayin over and over all the way down to the meadow, "Watch it, Bruno. Keep ya fingers off the film." Then Granddaddy picks up the hammer and jams it into the oilskin pocket, scrapes his boots, and goes into the house. And you can hear the squish of his boots headin through the house. And you can see the funny shadow he throws from the parlor window onto the ground by the string-bean patch. The hammer draggin the pocket of the oilskin out so Granddaddy looked even wider. Granny was hummin now—high, not low and grumbly. And she was doin the cakes again, you could smell the molasses from the rum.

"There's this story I'm goin to write one day," say Cathy dreamer. "About the proper use of the hammer."

"Can I be in it?" Tyrone say with his hand up like it was a matter of first come, first served.

"Perhaps," say Cathy, climbin onto the tire to pump us up. "If you there and ready."

QUESTIONS

1. From whose point of view is "Blues Ain't No Mockin Bird" told? Suppose the story were told in the third person, from the point of view of a nonparticipant narrator. What do you think the story would lose, or gain?
2. What is Cathy's function in the story?
3. What motivates the family in this story to move from place to place so often?
4. What makes the grandmother resist the cameramen who want to photograph her and her surroundings?
5. What details give a clear picture of the grandfather? Is he cruel? How do you explain his nailing the bloody, still living, female hawk to the toolshed door? How does he kill her mate?
6. How do you explain the interesting fact that the birds in "Blues Ain't No Mockin Bird" are not mockingbirds but hawks? What rich suggestions do the hawks add to the story's meaning?

Edgar Allan Poe

THE TELL-TALE HEART

1850

Edgar Allan Poe (1809–1849), orphaned child of traveling actors, was raised by well-off foster parents, John and Frances Allan, in Richmond, Virginia. At eighteen he published his first book of poems. When Poe ran up heavy gambling debts as as student at the University of Virginia, Allan called him home and eventually disowned him. After two years in the army and a brief stay at West Point, Poe became a successful editor in Richmond, Philadelphia, and New York and an industrious contributor to newspapers and magazines. Marriage in 1836 to his thirteen-year-old cousin Virginia Clemm increased his happiness but also his burdens; mercilessly, he drove his pen to support wife, self, and mother-in-law. Virginia, five years an invalid, died of tuberculosis in 1847. Poe, whose tolerance for alcohol was low, increased his drinking. He was found dead in a street in

Edgar Allan Poe

Baltimore. As a writer, Poe was a true innovator. His bizarre, macabre tales have held generations spellbound, as have some of his highly musical poems ("The Raven," "Annabel Lee"). His tales of private sleuth C. Auguste Dupin ("The Murders in the Rue Morgue," "The Purloined Letter") have earned him the title of father of the modern detective story. Other tales and his one novel, The Narrative of Arthur Gordon Pym, figure in the history of science fiction. A trail-blazing critic, Poe laid down laws for the short story (see page 485). His work has profoundly influenced not only American literature but European literature through French translations by Charles Baudelaire.

True!—nervous—very, very dreadfully nervous I had been and am; but why will you say that I am mad? The disease had sharpened my senses—not destroyed—not dulled them. Above all was the sense of hearing acute. I heard all things in the heaven and in the earth. I heard many things in hell. How, then, am I mad? Hearken! and observe how healthily—how calmly I can tell you the whole story.

It is impossible to say how first the idea entered my brain; but once conceived, it haunted me day and night. Object there was none. Passion there was none. I loved the old man. He had never wronged me. He had never given me insult. For his gold I had no desire. I think it was his eye! yes, it was this! One of his eyes resembled that of a vulture—a pale blue eye, with a film over it. Whenever it fell upon me, my blood ran cold; and so by degrees—very gradually—I made up my mind to take the life of the old man, and thus rid myself of the eye for ever.

Now this is the point. You fancy me mad. Madmen know nothing. But you should have seen *me*. You should have seen how wisely I proceeded—with what caution—with what foresight—with what dissimulation I went to work! I was never kinder to the old man than during the whole week before I killed him. And every night, about midnight, I turned the latch of his door and opened it—oh, so gently! And then, when I had made an opening sufficient for my head, I put in a dark lantern, all closed, closed, so that no light shone out, and then I thrust in my head. Oh, you would have laughed to see how cunningly I thrust it in! I moved it slowly—very, very slowly, so that I might not disturb the old man's sleep. It took me an hour to place my whole head within the opening so far that I could see him as he lay upon his bed. Ha!—would a madman have been so wise as this? And then, when my head was well in the room, I undid the lantern cautiously— oh, so cautiously—cautiously (for the hinges creaked)—I undid it just so much that a single thin ray fell upon the vulture eye. And this I did for seven long nights— every night just at midnight—but I found the eye always closed; and so it was impossible to do the work; for it was not the old man who vexed me, but his Evil Eye. And every morning, when the day broke, I went boldly into the chamber, and spoke courageously to him, calling him by name in a hearty tone, and inquir- ing how he had passed the night. So you see he would have been a very profound old man, indeed, to suspect that every night, just at twelve, I looked in upon him while he slept.

Upon the eighth night I was more than usually cautious in opening the door. A watch's minute hand moves more quickly than did mine. Never before that night had I *felt* the extent of my own powers—of my sagacity. I could scarcely contain my feelings of triumph. To think that there I was, opening the door, lit- tle by little, and he not even to dream of my secret deeds or thoughts. I fairly chuckled at the idea; and perhaps he heard me; for he moved on the bed sud- denly, as if startled. Now you may think that I drew back—but no. His room was as black as pitch with the thick darkness (for the shutters were close fastened, through fear of robbers), and so I knew that he could not see the opening of the door, and I kept pushing it on steadily, steadily.

I had my head in, and was about to open the lantern, when my thumb slipped upon the tin fastening, and the old man sprang up in the bed, crying out—"Who's there?"

I kept quite still and said nothing. For a whole hour I did not move a muscle, and in the meantime I did not hear him lie down. He was still sitting up in the bed listening;—just as I have done, night after night, hearkening to the death watches° in the wall.

Presently I heard a slight groan, and I knew it was the groan of mortal terror. It was not a groan of pain or of grief—oh, no!—it was the low stifled sound that arises from the bottom of the soul when overcharged with awe. I knew the sound very well. Many a night, just at midnight, when all the world slept, it has welled up from my own bosom, deepening, with its dreadful echo, the terrors that dis-

5

---

death watches: beetles that infest timbers. Their clicking sound was thought to be an omen of death.

tracted me. I say I knew it well. I knew what the old man felt, and pitied him, although I chuckled at heart. I knew that he had been lying awake ever since the first slight noise, when he had turned in the bed. His fears had been ever since growing upon him. He had been trying to fancy them causeless, but could not. He had been saying to himself—"It is nothing but the wind in the chimney—it is only a mouse crossing the floor," or "it is merely a cricket which has made a single chirp." Yes, he had been trying to comfort himself with these suppositions; but he had found all in vain. *All in vain*; because Death, in approaching him, had stalked with his black shadow before him, and enveloped the victim. And it was the mournful influence of the unperceived shadow that caused him to feel— although he neither saw nor heard—to *feel* the presence of my head within the room.

When I had waited a long time, very patiently, without hearing him lie down, I resolved to open a little—a very, very little crevice in the lantern. So I opened it—you cannot imagine how stealthily, stealthily—until, at length, a single dim ray, like the thread of the spider, shot from out the crevice and full upon the vulture eye.

It was open—wide, wide open—and I grew furious as I gazed upon it. I saw it with perfect distinctness—all a dull blue, with a hideous veil over it that chilled the very marrow in my bones; but I could see nothing else of the old man's face or person: for I had directed the ray as if by instinct, precisely upon the damned spot.

And now have I not told you that what you mistake for madness is but over- acuteness of the senses?—now, I say, there came to my ears a low, dull, quick sound, such as a watch makes when enveloped in cotton. I knew *that* sound well too. It was the beating of the old man's heart. It increased my fury, as the beating of a drum stimulates the soldier into courage.

But even yet I refrained and kept still. I scarcely breathed. I held the lantern motionless. I tried how steadily I could maintain the ray upon the eye. Meantime the hellish tattoo of the heart increased. It grew quicker and quicker, and louder and louder every instant. The old man's terror *must* have been extreme! It grew louder, I say, louder every moment!—do you mark me well? I have told you that I am nervous: so I am. And now at the dead hour of the night, amid the dreadful silence of that old house, so strange a noise as this excited me to uncontrollable terror. Yet, for some minutes longer I refrained and stood still. But the beating grew louder, louder! I thought the heart must burst. And now a new anxiety seized me—the sound would be heard by a neighbor! The old man's hour had come! With a loud yell, I threw open the lantern and leaped into the room. He shrieked once— once only. In an instant I dragged him to the floor, and pulled the heavy bed over him. I then smiled gaily, to find the deed so far done. But, for many minutes, the heart beat on with a muffled sound. This, however, did not vex me; it would not be heard through the wall. At length it ceased. The old man was dead. I re- moved the bed and examined the corpse. Yes, he was stone, stone dead. I placed my hand upon the heart and held it there many minutes. There was no pulsation. He was stone dead. His eye would trouble me no more.

If still you think me mad, you will think so no longer when I describe the wise precautions I took for the concealment of the body. The night waned, and

10

I worked hastily, but in silence. First of all I dismembered the corpse. I cut off the head and the arms and the legs.

I then took up three planks from the flooring of the chamber, and deposited all between the scantlings. I then replaced the boards so cleverly, so cunningly, that no human eye—not even *his*—could have detected anything wrong. There was nothing to wash out—no stain of any kind—no bloodspot whatever. I had been too wary for that. A tub had caught all—ha! ha!

When I had made an end of these labors, it was four o'clock—still dark as midnight. As the bell sounded the hour, there came a knocking at the street door. I went down to open it with a light heart,—for what had I *now* to fear? There entered three men, who introduced themselves, with perfect suavity, as officers of the police. A shriek had been heard by a neighbor during the night; suspicion of foul play had been aroused; information had been lodged at the police office, and they (the officers) had been deputed to search the premises.

I smiled,—for *what* had I to fear? I bade the gentlemen welcome. The shriek, I said, was my own in a dream. The old man, I mentioned, was absent in the country. I took my visitors all over the house. I bade them search—search *well*. I led them, at length, to *his* chamber. I showed them his treasures, secure, undisturbed. In the enthusiasm of my confidence, I brought chairs into the room, and desired them *here* to rest from their fatigues, while I myself, in the wild audacity of my perfect triumph, placed my own seat upon the very spot beneath which reposed the corpse of the victim.

The officers were satisfied. My *manner* had convinced them. I was singularly at ease. They sat, and while I answered cheerily, they chatted familiar things. But, ere long, I felt myself getting pale and wished them gone. My head ached, and I fancied a ringing in my ears: but still they sat and still chatted. The ringing became more distinct:—it continued and became more distinct: I talked more freely to get rid of the feeling: but it continued and gained definitiveness—until, at length, I found that the noise was *not* within my ears.

No doubt I now grew *very* pale:—but I talked more fluently, and with a heightened voice. Yet the sound increased—and what could I do? It was *a low, dull, quick sound—much such a sound as a watch makes when enveloped in cotton.* I gasped for breath—and yet the officers heard it not. I talked more quickly—more vehemently; but the noise steadily increased. I arose and argued about trifles, in a high key and with violent gesticulations, but the noise steadily increased. Why *would* they not be gone? I paced the floor to and fro with heavy strides, as if excited to fury by the observation of the men—but the noise steadily increased. Oh God! what *could* I do? I foamed—I raved—I swore! I swung the chair upon which I had been sitting, and grated it upon the boards, but the noise arose over all and continually increased. It grew louder—louder—*louder*! And still the men chatted pleasantly, and smiled. Was it possible they heard not? Almighty God!—no, no! They heard!—they suspected!—they *knew*!—they were making a mockery of my horror!—this I thought, and this I think. But any thing was better than this agony! Any thing was more tolerable than this derision! I could bear those hypocritical smiles no longer! I felt that I must scream or die!—and now—again!—hark! louder! louder! louder! *louder*!—

"Villians!" I shrieked, "dissemble no more! I admit the deed!—tear up the planks!—here, here!—it is the beating of his hideous heart!"

QUESTIONS

1. From what point of view is Poe's story told? Why is this point of view particularly effective for "The Tell-Tale Heart"?
2. Point to details in the story that identify its speaker as an unreliable narrator.
3. What do we know about the old man in the story? What motivates the narrator to kill him?
4. In spite of all his precautions, the narrator does not commit the perfect crime. What trips him up?
5. How do you account for the police officers' chatting calmly with the murderer instead of reacting to the sound that stirs the murderer into a frenzy?
6. See the students' comments on this story in "Writing about a Story" in the Supplement: Writing. What do they point out that enlarges your own appreciation of Poe's art?

SUGGESTIONS FOR WRITING

1. Here is a writing exercise to help you sense what a difference a point of view makes. Write a short statement from the point of view of one of these characters:
   William Faulkner's Homer Barron (on "My Affair with Miss Emily").
   Toni Cade Bambara's camera man (on the difficulties of documentary film-making).
   Edgar Allan Poe's old man (on "My Live-in Servant and His Little Peculiarities").
2. Write a brief narrative account of a decisive moment in your life—one that changed your outlook or your future—from two quite different, contrasting points of view. One instance: a memory of buying a first car, told in two ways: from the first-person point of view of the buyer and from the third-person point of view of a worried parent or a gloating car dealer. Another example: An account of meeting a person who profoundly affected your life, from (1) your point of view and then (2) from the point of view of that other person.
3. Topic for an essay of two or three paragraphs: How William Faulkner Sees North and South in "A Rose for Emily."
4. Taking examples from short stories in other chapters, point out some differences between male and female ways of looking at things. Some stories especially to consider: "A & P," "The Jilting of Granny Weatherall," "The Found Boat," "The Darling," "Big Bertha Stories," "First Confession," and "I Stand Here Ironing." (Note: Because a character holds a certain attitude in a specific situation doesn't oblige you to argue that such an attitude is universally held by women and men.)
5. Adopt the point of view of a naive, innocent commentator—either a younger, less-knowing version of yourself, or some imagined character. From this point of view, discuss the proposed ban on nuclear weapons, the case for legislation against the sale of pornography, or another issue in the news. Sound off like a true ignoramus. An effective paper will make clear to your reader that your speaker is full of malarkey. (This task means that you, the knowing writer, and not the uninformed speaker who is your mask, will need to know something about your subject.)
6. Choosing one of the "Stories for Further Reading" (in Chapter Eleven), briefly describe whatever point of view you find in it. Then, in a paragraph or two, explain why this

angle of vision seems right and fitting to the telling of this story. If you like, you may argue that the story might be told more effectively from some other point of view.

7. Write a one-paragraph story in the first person. Some recent small event in your life is a possible subject. Then rewrite your story from the *objective*, or "fly-on-the-wall," point of view. (See the passage by Dashiell Hammett on page 21 for an illustration.) Following your two terse stories, make a comment summing up what this exercise told you about point of view.

3 Character

From popular fiction and drama, both classic and contemporary, we are acquainted with many stereotyped characters. Called **stock characters,** they are often known by some outstanding trait or traits: the *bragging* soldier of Greek and Roman comedy, the prince *charming* of fairy tales, the *mad* scientist of horror movies, the *loyal* sidekick of Westerns, the *greedy* explorer of Tarzan films, the *brilliant but alcoholic* brain surgeon of medical thrillers on television. Stock characters are especially convenient for writers of commercial fiction: they require little detailed portraiture, for we already know them well. Most writers of the literary story, however, attempt to create characters who strike us not as stereotypes but as unique individuals. Although stock characters tend to have single dominant virtues and vices, characters in the finest contemporary short stories tend to have many facets, like people we meet.

A **character,** then, is presumably an imagined person who inhabits a story—although that simple definition may admit to a few exceptions. In George Stewart's novel *Storm,* the protagonist is the wind; in Richard Adams's *Watership Down,* the main characters are rabbits. But usually we recognize, in the main characters of a story, human personalities that become familiar to us. If the story seems "true to life," we generally find that its characters act in a reasonably consistent manner, and that the author has provided them with **motivation:** sufficient reason to behave as they do. Should a character behave in a sudden and unexpected way, seeming to deny what we have been told about his nature or personality, we trust that he had a reason and that sooner or later we will discover it. This is not to claim that *all* authors insist that their characters behave with absolute consistency, for (as we shall see later in this chapter) some contemporary stories feature characters who sometimes act without apparent reason. Nor can we say that, in good fiction, characters never change or develop. In "A Christmas Carol," Charles Dickens tells how Ebeneezer Scrooge, a tightfisted miser, reforms overnight, suddenly gives to the poor, and endeavors to assist his clerk's struggling family. But Dickens amply demonstrates why Scrooge had such a change of heart: four ghostly visitors, stirring kind memories the old miser had forgotten and also warning him of the probable consequences of his habits, provide the character (and hence the story) with adequate motivation.

To borrow the useful terms of the English novelist E. M. Forster, characters may seem **flat** or **round,** depending on whether a writer sketches or sculptures them. A flat character has only one outstanding trait or feature, or at most a few distinguishing marks: for example, the familiar stock character of the mad scientist, with his lust for absolute power and his crazily gleaming eyes. Flat characters, however, need not be stock characters: in all of literature there is probably only one Tiny Tim, though his functions in "A Christmas Carol" are mainly to invoke blessings and to remind others of their Christian duties. Some writers, notably Balzac, who peopled his many novels with hosts of characters, try to distinguish the flat ones by giving each a single odd physical feature or mannerism—a nervous twitch, a piercing gaze, an obsessive fondness for oysters. Round characters, however, present us with more facets—that is, their authors portray them in greater depth and in more generous detail. Such a round character may appear to us only as he appears to the other characters in the story. If their views of him differ, we will see him from more than one side. In other stories, we enter a character's mind and come to know him through his own thoughts, feelings, and perceptions. By the time we finish reading Katherine Mansfield's "Miss Brill" (in Chapter Two), we are well acquainted with the central character and find her amply three-dimensional.

Flat characters tend to stay the same throughout a story, but round characters often change—learn or become enlightened, grow or deteriorate. In William Faulkner's "Barn Burning" (Chapter Five), the boy Sarty Snopes, driven to defy his proud and violent father, becomes at the story's end more knowing and more mature. (Some critics call a fixed character **static;** a changing one, **dynamic.**) This is not to damn a flat character as an inferior work of art. In most fiction—even the greatest—minor characters tend to be flat instead of round. Why? Rounding them would cost time and space; and so enlarged, they might only distract us from the main characters.

"A character, first of all, is the noise of his name," according to novelist William Gass.[1] Names, chosen artfully, can indicate natures. A simple illustration is the completely virtuous Squire Allworthy, the foster father in *Tom Jones* by Henry Fielding. Subtler, perhaps, is the custom of giving a character a name that makes an **allusion:** a reference to some famous person, place, or thing in history, in other fiction, or in actuality. For his central characters in *Moby-Dick*, Herman Melville chose names from the Old Testament, calling his tragic and domineering Ahab after a Biblical tyrant who came to a bad end, and his wandering narrator Ishmael after a Biblical outcast. Whether or not it includes an allusion, a good name often reveals the character of the character. Charles Dickens, a vigorous and richly suggestive christener, named a charming confidence man Mr. Jingle

---

[1]"The Concept of Character in Fiction," in *Fiction and the Figures of Life* (New York: Knopf, 1970).

(suggesting something jingly, light, and superficially pleasant), named a couple of shyster lawyers Dodgson and Fogg (suggesting dodging evasiveness and foglike obfuscation), and named two heartless educators, who grimly drill their schoolchildren in "hard facts," Gradgind and M'Choakumchild. Henry James, who so loved names that he kept lists of them for characters he might someday conceive, chose for a sensitive, cultured gentleman the name of Lambert Strether; for a down-to-earth benevolent individual, the name of Mrs. Bread. (But James may have wished to indicate that names cannot be identified with people absolutely, in giving the fragile, considerate heroine of *The Spoils of Poynton* the harshsounding name of Fleda Vetch.)

Instead of a hero, many a recent novel has featured an **antihero:** an ordinary, unglorious twentieth-century citizen, usually drawn (according to Sean O'Faolain) as someone "groping, puzzled, cross, mocking, frustrated, and isolated."[2] (Obviously, there are antiheroines, too.) If epic poets once drew their heroes as decisive leaders of their people, embodying their people's highest ideals, antiheroes tend to be loners, without perfections, just barely able to survive. Antiheroes lack "character," as defined by psychologist Anthony Quinton to mean a person's conduct or "persistence and consistency in seeking to realize his longterm aims."[3] A gulf separates Leopold Bloom, antihero of James Joyce's novel *Ulysses*, from the hero of the Greek *Odyssey*. In Homer's epic, Ulysses wanders the Mediterranean, battling monsters and overcoming enchantments. In Joyce's novel, Bloom wanders the littered streets of Dublin, peddling advertising space. In contemporary fiction, by the way, female antiheroes abound: Ellen, for instance, the aimlessly drifting central character of Edna O'Brien's novel *August Is a Wicked Month.*

Evidently, not only fashions in heroes but also attitudes toward human nature have undergone change. In the eighteenth century, Scottish philosopher David Hume argued that the nature of an individual is relatively fixed and unalterable. Hume mentioned, however, a few exceptions: "A person of an obliging disposition gives a peevish answer; but he has the toothache or has not dined. A stupid fellow discovers an obvious alacrity in his carriage; but he has met with a sudden piece of good fortune." For a long time after Hume, novelists and short-story writers seem to have assumed that characters behave nearly always in a predictable fashion and that their actions ought to be consistent with their personalities. Now and again, a writer differed: Jane Austen in *Pride and Prejudice* has her protagonist Elizabeth Bennet remark to the citified Mr. Darcy, who fears that life in the country cannot be amusing, "But people themselves alter so much, that there is something to be observed in them forever."

Many contemporary writers of fiction would deny even that people have definite selves to alter. Following Sigmund Freud and other modern psychologists, they assume that a large part of human behavior is shaped in the unconscious—that, for instance, a person might fear horses, not because of a basi-

---

[2] *The Vanishing Hero* (Boston: Little, 1957).
[3] "The Continuity of Persons," *Times Literary Supplement* issue on "The Nature of Character," 27 July 1973.

cally timid nature, but because of unconscious memories of having been nearly trampled by a horse when a child. To some writers it now appears that what Hume called a "disposition" (now called a "personality") is more vulnerable to change from such causes as age, disease, neurosis, psychic shock, or brainwashing than was once believed. Hence, some characters in twentieth-century fiction appear to be shifting bundles of impulses. "You mustn't look in my novel for the old stable ego of character," wrote D. H. Lawrence to a friend about *The Rainbow;* and in that novel and other novels Lawrence demonstrated his view of individuals as bits of one vast Life Force, spurred to act by incomprehensible passions and urges—the "dark gods" in them. The idea of the **gratuitous act,** a deed without cause or motive, is explored in André Gide's novel *Lafcadio's Adventures,* in which an ordinary young man without homicidal tendencies abruptly and for no reason pushes a stranger from a speeding train. The usual limits of character are playfully violated by Virginia Woolf in *Orlando,* a novel whose protagonist, defying time, lives right on from Elizabethan days into the present, changing in midstory from a man into a woman. Characterization, as practiced by nineteenth-century novelists, almost entirely disappears in Franz Kafka's *The Castle,* whose protagonist has no home, no family, no definite appearance—not even a name, just the initial K. Characters are things of the past, insists the contemporary French novelist Alain Robbe-Grillet. Still, many writers of fiction go on portraying them.

Katherine Anne Porter

THE JILTING OF GRANNY WEATHERALL   1930

Katherine Anne Porter (1890–1980) was born in Indian Creek, Texas. Her mother died when she was two, and Porter was raised by a grandmother who surrounded the growing girl with books. At sixteen, apparently bored with her studies at an Ursuline convent, Porter ran away from home. Three years later, she began supporting herself as a news reporter in Chicago, Denver, and Fort Worth, and sometimes as an actress and ballad singer traveling through the South. Sojourns in Europe and in Mexico supplied her with matter for some of her finest stories. Her brilliant, sensitive short fiction, first collected in Flowering Judas *(1930), won her a high reputation. Her one novel,* Ship of Fools *(1962), with which she had struggled for twenty years, received harsh critical notices, but proved a commercial success. Made into a movie, it ended Porter's*

Katherine Anne Porter

lifelong struggle to earn a living. In 1965 her Collected Stories *received a Pulitzer prize and a National Book Award.*

She flicked her wrist neatly out of Doctor Harry's pudgy careful fingers and pulled the sheet up to her chin. The brat ought to be in knee breeches. Doctoring around the country with spectacles on his nose! "Get along now, take your school-books and go. There's nothing wrong with me."

Doctor Harry spread a warm paw like a cushion on her forehead where the forked green vein danced and made her eyelids twitch. "Now, now, be a good girl, and we'll have you up in no time."

"That's no way to speak to a woman nearly eighty years old just because she's down. I'd have you respect your elders, young man."

"Well, Missy, excuse me." Doctor Harry patted her cheek. "But I've got to warn you, haven't I? You're a marvel, but you must be careful or you're going to be good and sorry."

"Don't tell me what I'm going to be. I'm on my feet now, morally speaking. It's Cornelia. I had to go to bed to get rid of her." 5

Her bones felt loose, and floated around in her skin, and Doctor Harry floated like a balloon around the foot of the bed. He floated and pulled down his waist-coat and swung his glasses on a cord. "Well, stay where you are, it certainly can't hurt you."

"Get along and doctor your sick," said Granny Weatherall. "Leave a well woman alone. I'll call for you when I want you. . . . Where were you forty years ago when I pulled through milk leg and double pneumonia? You weren't even born. Don't let Cornelia lead you on," she shouted, because Doctor Harry appeared to float up to the ceiling and out. "I pay my own bills, and I don't throw my money away on nonsense!"

She meant to wave good-by, but it was too much trouble. Her eyes closed of themselves, it was like a dark curtain drawn around the bed. The pillow rose and floated under her, pleasant as a hammock in a light wind. She listened to the leaves rustling outside the window. No, somebody was swishing newspapers: no, Cornelia and Doctor Harry were whispering together. She leaped broad awake, thinking they whispered in her ear.

"She was never like this, *never* like this!" "Well, what can we expect?" "Yes, eighty years old. . . . "

Well, and what if she was? She still had ears. It was like Cornelia to whisper 10 around doors. She always kept things secret in such a public way. She was always being tactful and kind. Cornelia was dutiful; that was the trouble with her. Duti-ful and good: "So good and dutiful," said Granny, "that I'd like to spank her." She saw herself spanking Cornelia and making a fine job of it.

"What'd you say, Mother?"

Granny felt her face tying up in hard knots.

"Can't a body think, I'd like to know?"

"I thought you might want something."

"I do. I want a lot of things. First off, go away and don't whisper." 15

She lay and drowsed, hoping in her sleep that the children would keep out and let her rest a minute. It had been a long day. Not that she was tired. It was always pleasant to snatch a minute now and then. There was always so much to be done, let me see: tomorrow.

Tomorrow was far away and there was nothing to trouble about. Things were finished somehow when the time came; thank God there was always a little margin over for peace: then a person could spread out the plan of life and tuck in the edges orderly. It was good to have everything clean and folded away, with the hair brushes and tonic bottles sitting straight on the white embroidered linen: the day started without fuss and the pantry shelves laid out with rows of jelly glasses and brown jugs and white stone-china jars with blue whirligigs and words painted on them: coffee, tea, sugar, ginger, cinnamon, allspice: and the bronze clock with the lion on top nicely dusted off. The dust that lion could collect in twenty-four hours! The box in the attic with all those letters tied up, well, she'd have to go through that tomorrow. All those letters—George's letters and John's letters and her letters to them both—lying around for the children to find afterwards made her uneasy. Yes, that would be tomorrow's business. No use to let them know how silly she had been once.

While she was rummaging around she found death in her mind and it felt clammy and unfamiliar. She had spent so much time preparing for death there was no need for bringing it up again. Let it take care of itself now. When she was sixty she had felt very old, finished, and went around making farewell trips to see her children and grandchildren, with a secret in her mind: This is the very last of your mother, children! Then she made her will and came down with a long fever. That was all just a notion like a lot of other things, but it was lucky too, for she had once for all got over the idea of dying for a long time. Now she couldn't be worried. She hoped she had better sense now. Her father had lived to be one hundred and two years old and had drunk a noggin of strong hot toddy on his last birthday. He told the reporters it was his daily habit, and he owed his long life to it. He had made quite a scandal and was very pleased about it. She believed she'd just plague Cornelia a little.

"Cornelia! Cornelia!" No footsteps, but a sudden hand on her cheek. "Bless you, where have you been?"

"Here, Mother." 20

"Well, Cornelia, I want a noggin of hot toddy."

"Are you cold, darling?"

"I'm chilly, Cornelia. Lying in bed stops the circulation. I must have told you that a thousand times."

Well, she could just hear Cornelia telling her husband that Mother was getting a little childish and they'd have to humor her. The thing that most annoyed her was that Cornelia thought she was deaf, dumb, and blind. Little hasty glances and tiny gestures tossed around her and over her head saying, "Don't cross her, let her have her way, she's eighty years old," and she sitting there as if she lived in a thin glass cage. Sometimes Granny almost made up her mind to pack up and move back to her own house where nobody could remind her every minute that she was old. Wait, wait, Cornelia, till your own children whisper behind your back!

In her day she had kept a better house and had got more work done. She 25 wasn't too old yet for Lydia to be driving eighty miles for advice when one of the children jumped the track, and Jimmy still dropped in and talked things over:

"Now, Mammy, you've a good business head, I want to know what you think of this? . . ." Old. Cornelia couldn't change the furniture around without asking. Little things, little things! They had been so sweet when they were little. Granny wished the old days were back again with the children young and everything to be done over. It had been a hard pull, but not too much for her. When she thought of all the food she had cooked, and all the clothes she had cut and sewed, and all the gardens she had made—well, the children showed it. There they were, made out of her, and they couldn't get away from that. Sometimes she wanted to see John again and point to them and say, Well, I didn't do so badly, did I? But that would have to wait. That was for tomorrow. She used to think of him as a man, but now all the children were older than their father, and he would be a child beside her if she saw him now. It seemed strange and there was something wrong in the idea. Why, he couldn't possibly recognize her. She had fenced in a hundred acres once, digging the post holes herself and clamping the wires with just a negro boy to help. That changed a woman. John would be looking for a young woman with the peaked Spanish comb in her hair and the painted fan. Digging post holes changed a woman. Riding country roads in the winter when women had their babies was another thing: sitting up nights with sick horses and sick negroes and sick children and hardly every losing one. John, I hardly ever lost one of them! John would see that in a minute, that would be something he could understand, she wouldn't have to explain anything!

It made her feel like rolling up her sleeves and putting the whole place to rights again. No matter if Cornelia was determined to be everywhere at once, there were a great many things left undone on this place. She would start tomorrow and do them. It was good to be strong enough for everything, even if all you made melted and changed and slipped under your hands, so that by the time you finished you almost forgot what you were working for. What was it I set out to do? she asked herself intently, but she could not remember. A fog rose over the valley, she saw it marching across the creek swallowing the trees and moving up the hill like an army of ghosts. Soon it would be at the near edge of the orchard, and then it was time to go in and light the lamps. Come in, children, don't stay out in the night air.

Lighting the lamps had been beautiful. The children huddled up to her and breathed like little calves waiting at the bars in the twilight. Their eyes followed the match and watched the flame rise and settle in a blue curve, then they moved away from her. The lamp was lit, they didn't have to be scared and hang on to mother any more. Never, never, never more. God, for all my life I thank Thee. Without Thee, my God, I could never have done it. Hail, Mary, full of grace.

I want you to pick all the fruit this year and see that nothing is wasted. There's always someone who can use it. Don't let good things rot for want of using. You waste life when you waste good food. Don't let things get lost. It's bitter to lose things. Now, don't let me get to thinking, not when I am tired and taking a little nap before supper. . . .

The pillow rose about her shoulders and pressed against her heart and the memory was being squeezed out of it: oh, push down the pillow, somebody: it would smother her if she tried to hold it. Such a fresh breeze blowing and such a green day with no threats in it. But he had not come, just the same. What does a woman do when she has put on the white veil and set out the white cake for a man and he doesn't come? She tried to remember. No, I swear he never harmed me but in that. He never harmed me but in that . . . and what if he did? There was the day, the day, but a whirl of dark smoke rose and covered it, crept up and over into the bright field where everything was planted so carefully in orderly rows. That was hell, she knew hell when she saw it. For sixty years she had prayed against remembering him and against losing her soul in the deep pit of hell, and now the two things were mingled in one and the thought of him was a smoky cloud from hell that moved and crept in her head when she had just got rid of Doctor Harry and was trying to rest a minute. Wounded vanity, Ellen, said a sharp voice in the top of her mind. Don't let your wounded vanity get the upper hand of you. Plenty of girls get jilted. You were jilted, weren't you? Then stand up to it. Her eyelids wavered and let in streamers of blue-gray light like tissue paper over her eyes. She must get up and pull the shades down or she'd never sleep. She was in bed again and the shades were not down. How could that happen? Better turn over, hide from the light, sleeping in the light gave you nightmares. "Mother, how do you feel now?" and a stinging wetness on her forehead. But I don't like having my face washed in cold water!

Hapsy? George? Lydia? Jimmy? No, Cornelia, and her features were swollen 30 and full of little puddles. "They're coming, darling, they'll all be here soon." Go wash your face, child, you look funny.

Instead of obeying, Cornelia knelt down and put her head on the pillow. She seemed to be talking but there was no sound. "Well, are you tongue-tied? Whose birthday is it? Are you going to give a party?"

Cornelia's mouth moved urgently in strange shapes. "Don't do that, you bother me, daughter."

"O, no, Mother. Oh, no. . . . "

Nonsense. It was strange about children. They disputed your every word. "No what, Cornelia?"

"Here's Doctor Harry." 35

"I won't see that boy again. He just left three minutes ago."

"That was this morning, Mother. It's night now. Here's the nurse."

"This is Doctor Harry, Mrs. Weatherall. I never saw you look so young and happy!"

"Ah, I'll never be young again—but I'd be happy if they'd let me lie in peace and get rested."

She thought she spoke up loudly, but no one answered. A warm weight on 40 her forehead, a warm bracelet on her wrist, and a breeze went on whispering, trying to tell her something. A shuffle of leaves in the everlasting hand of God. He blew on them and they danced and rattled. "Mother, don't mind, we're going to give you a little hypodermic." "Look here, daughter, how do ants get in this bed? I saw sugar ants yesterday." Did you send for Hapsy too?

It was Hapsy she really wanted. She had to go a long way back through a great many rooms to find Hapsy standing with a baby on her arm. She seemed to herself to be Hapsy also, and the baby on Hapsy's arm was Hapsy and himself and herself, all at once, and there was no surprise in the meeting. Then Hapsy melted from within and turned flimsy as gray gauze and the baby was a gauzy shadow, and Hapsy came up close and said, "I thought you'd never come," and looked at her very searchingly and said, "You haven't changed a bit!" They leaned forward to kiss, when Cornelia began whispering from a long way off, "Oh, is there anything you want to tell me? Is there anything I can do for you?"

Yes, she had changed her mind after sixty years and she would like to see George. I want you to find George. Find him and be sure to tell him I forgot him. I want him to know I had my husband just the same and my children and my house like any other woman. A good house too and a good husband that I loved and fine children out of him. Better than I hoped for even. Tell him I was given back everything he took away and more. Oh, no, oh, God, no, there was something else besides the house and the man and the children. Oh, surely they were not all? What was it? Something not given back . . . Her breath crowded down under her ribs and grew into a monstrous frightening shape with cutting edges; it bored up into her head, and the agony was unbelievable: Yes, John, get the Doctor now, no more talk, my time has come.

When this one was born it should be the last. The last. It should have been born first, for it was the one she had truly wanted. Everything came in good time. Nothing left out, left over. She was strong, in three days she would be as well as ever. Better. A woman needed milk in her to have her full health.

"Mother, do you hear me?"

"I've been telling you—"   45

"Mother, Father Connolly's here."

"I went to Holy Communion only last week. Tell him I'm not so sinful as all that."

"Father just wants to speak to you."

He could speak as much as he pleased. It was like him to drop in and inquire about her soul as if it were a teething baby, and then stay for a cup of tea and a round of cards and gossip. He always had a funny story of some sort, usually about an Irishman who made his little mistakes and confessed them, and the point lay in some absurd thing he would blurt out in the confessional showing his struggles between native piety and original sin. Granny felt easy about her soul. Cornelia, where are your manners? Give Father Connolly a chair. She had her secret comfortable understanding with a few favorite saints who cleared a straight road to God for her. All as surely signed and sealed as the papers for the new Forty Acres. Forever . . . heirs and assigns forever. Since the day the wedding cake was not cut, but thrown out and wasted. The whole bottom dropped out of the world, and there she was blind and sweating with nothing under her feet and walls falling away. His hand had caught her under the breast, she had not fallen, there was the freshly polished floor with the green rug on it, just as before. He had cursed like a sailor's parrot and said, "I'll kill him for you." Don't lay a hand on him, for my sake leave something to God. "Now, Ellen, you must believe what I tell you . . . ."

So there was nothing, nothing to worry about any more, except sometimes   50
in the night one of the children screamed in a nightmare, and they both hustled out shaking and hunting for the matches and calling, "There, wait a minute, here we are!" John, get the doctor now, Hapsy's time has come. But there was Hapsy standing by the bed in a white cap. "Cornelia, tell Hapsy to take off her cap. I can't see her plain."

Her eyes opened very wide and the room stood out like a picture she had seen somewhere. Dark colors with the shadows rising towards the ceiling in long angles. The tall black dresser gleamed with nothing on it but John's picture, enlarged from a little one, with John's eyes very black when they should have been blue. You never saw him, so how do you know how he looked? But the man insisted the copy was perfect, it was very rich and handsome. For a picture, yes, but it's not my husband. The table by the bed had a linen cover and a candle and a crucifix. The light was blue from Cornelia's silk lampshades. No sort of light at all, just frippery. You had to live forty years with kerosene lamps to appreciate honest electricity. She felt very strong and she saw Doctor Harry with a rosy nimbus around him.

"You look like a saint, Doctor Harry, and I vow that's as near as you'll ever come to it."

"She's saying something."

"I heard you, Cornelia. What's all this carrying-on?"

"Father Connolly's saying—"

Cornelia's voice staggered and bumped like a cart in a bad road. It rounded corners and turned back again and arrived nowhere. Granny stepped up in the cart very lightly and reached for the reins, but a man sat beside her and she knew him by his hands, driving the cart. She did not look in his face, for she knew without seeing, but looked instead down the road where the trees leaned over and bowed to each other and a thousand birds were singing a Mass. She felt like singing too, but she put her hand in the bosom of her dress and pulled out a rosary, and Father Connolly murmured Latin in a very solemn voice and tickled her feet. My God, will you stop that nonsense? I'm a married woman. What if he did run away and leave me to face the priest by myself? I found another a whole world better. I wouldn't have exchanged my husband for anybody except St. Michael himself, and you may tell him that for me with a thank you in the bargain.

Light flashed on her closed eyelids, and a deep roaring shook her. Cornelia, is that lightning? I hear thunder. There's going to be a storm. Close all the windows. Call the children in. . . . "Mother, here we are, all of us." "Is that you, Hapsy?" "Oh, no, I'm Lydia. We drove as fast as we could." Their faces drifted above her, drifted away. The rosary fell out of her hands and Lydia put it back. Jimmy tried to help, their hands fumbled together, and Granny closed two fingers around Jimmy's thumb. Beads wouldn't do, it must be something alive. She was so amazed her thoughts ran round and round. So, my dear Lord, this is my death and I wasn't even thinking about it. My children have come to see me die. But I can't, it's not time. Oh, I always hated surprises. I wanted to give Cornelia the amethyst set—Cornelia, you're to have the amethyst set, but Hapsy's to wear it when she wants, and, Doctor Harry, do shut up. Nobody sent for you. Oh, my dear Lord, do wait a minute. I meant to do something about the Forty Acres, Jimmy doesn't need it and Lydia will later on, with that worthless husband of hers. I meant to finish the altar cloth and send six bottles of wine to Sister Borgia for her dyspepsia. I want to send six bottles of wine to Sister Borgia, Father Connolly, now don't let me forget.

Cornelia's voice made short turns and tilted over and crashed, "Oh, Mother, oh, Mother, oh, Mother. . . . "

"I'm not going, Cornelia. I'm taken by surprise. I can't go."

You'll see Hapsy again. What about her? "I thought you'd never come." Granny ⁶⁰ made a long journey outward, looking for Hapsy. What if I don't find her? What then? Her heart sank down and down, there was no bottom to death, she couldn't come to the end of it. The blue light from Cornelia's lampshade drew into a tiny point in the center of her brain, it flickered and winked like an eye, quietly it fluttered and dwindled. Granny lay curled down within herself, amazed and watchful, staring at the point of light that was herself; her body was now only a deeper mass of shadow in an endless darkness and this darkness would curl around the light and swallow it up. God, give a sign!

For the second time there was no sign. Again no bridegroom and the priest in the house. She could not remember any other sorrow because this grief wiped them all away. Oh, no, there's nothing more cruel than this—I'll never forgive it. She stretched herself with a deep breath and blew out the light.

QUESTIONS

1. In the very first paragraph, what does the writer tell us about Ellen (Granny) Weatherall?
2. What does the name of Weatherall have to do with Granny's nature (or her life story)? What other traits or qualities do you find in her?
3. "Her bones felt loose, and floated around in her skin, and Doctor Harry floated like a balloon" (paragraph 6). What do you understand from this statement? By what other remarks does the writer indicate Granny's condition? In paragraph 56, why does Father Connolly tickle Granny's feet? At what other moments in the story does she fail to understand what is happening, or confuse the present with the past?
4. Exactly what happened to Ellen Weatherall sixty years earlier? What effects did this event have on her?
5. In paragraph 49, who do you guess to be the man who "cursed like a sailor's parrot"? In paragraph 56, who do you assume to be the man driving the cart? Is the fact that these persons are not clearly labeled and identified a failure on the author's part?
6. What is stream of consciousness? (The term is discussed on page 23.) Would you call "The Jilting of Granny Weatherall" a stream of consciousness story? Refer to the story in your reply.
7. Sum up the character of the daughter Cornelia.
8. Why doesn't Granny's last child Hapsy come to her mother's deathbed?
9. Would you call the character of Doctory Harry "flat" or "round"? Why is his flatness (or roundness) appropriate to the story?
10. How is this the story of another "jilting"? What is similar between that fateful day of sixty years ago (described in paragraphs 29, 49, and 61) and the moment when Granny is dying? This time, who is the "bridegroom" not in the house?
11. "This is the story of an eighty-year-old woman lying in bed, getting groggy, and dying; I can't see why it should interest anybody." How would you answer this critic?

GIRL 1978

Jamaica Kincaid, born in 1941 in St. John's, capital of the West Indian island nation of Antigua and Barbuda, now lives in New York, where she has worked for The New Yorker *magazine as a staff writer. She has won wide attention for* At the Bottom of the River, *the collection of stories that includes "Girl" (1983); as well as for* Annie John, *a coherent cycle of short stories about growing up in Antigua (1985); and* A Small Place, *a memoir, (1988), and* Lucy, *a recent novel (1990). A naturalized U.S. citizen, Kincaid once remarked of her adopted country: "It's given me a place to be myself—but myself as I was formed somewhere else."*

Jamaica Kincaid

Wash the white clothes on Monday and put them on the stone heap; wash the color clothes on Tuesday and put them on the clothes-line to dry; don't walk barehead in the hot sun; cook pumpkin fritters in very hot sweet oil; soak your little cloths right after you take them off; when buying cotton to make yourself a nice blouse, be sure that it doesn't have gum on it, because that way it won't hold up well after a wash; soak salt fish overnight before you cook it; is it true that you sing benna° in Sunday school?; always eat your food in such a way that it won't turn someone else's stomach; on Sundays try to walk like a lady and not like the slut you are so bent on becoming; don't sing benna in Sunday school; you mustn't speak to wharf-rat boys, not even to give directions; don't eat fruits on the street—flies will follow you; *but I don't sing benna on Sundays at all and never in Sunday school;* this is how to sew on a button; this is how to make a buttonhole for the button you have just sewed on; this is how to hem a dress when you see the hem coming down and so to prevent yourself from looking like the slut I know you are so bent on becoming; this is how you iron your father's khaki shirt so that it doesn't have a crease; this is how you iron your father's khaki pants so that they don't have a crease; this is how you grow okra—far from the house, because okra tree harbors red ants; when you are growing dasheen, make sure it gets plenty of water or else it makes your throat itch when you are eating it; this is how you sweep a corner; this is how you sweep a whole house; this is how you sweep a yard; this is how you smile to someone you don't like too much; this is how you smile to someone you don't like at all; this is how you smile to someone you like completely; this is how you set a table for tea; this is how you set a table for dinner; this is how you set a table for dinner with an important guest; this

---

benna: Kincaid defined this word, for two editors who inquired, as meaning "songs of the sort your parents didn't want you to sing, at first calypso and later rock and roll" (quoted by Sylvan Barnet and Marcia Stubbs, *The Little Brown Reader, Second Edition* [Boston: Little, Brown, 1980], 74).

is how you set a table for lunch; this is how you set a table for breakfast; this is how to behave in the presence of men who don't know you very well, and this way they won't recognize immediately the slut I have warned you against becoming; be sure to wash every day, even if it is with your own spit; don't squat down to play marbles—you are not a boy, you know; don't pick people's flowers—you might catch something; don't throw stones at blackbirds, because it might not be a blackbird at all; this is how to make a bread pudding; this is how to make doukona; this is how to make pepper pot; this is how to make a good medicine for a cold; this is how to make a good medicine to throw away a child before it even becomes a child; this is how to catch a fish; this is how to throw back a fish you don't like, and that way something bad won't fall on you; this is how to bully a man; this is how a man bullies you; this is how to love a man, and if this doesn't work there are other ways, and if they don't work don't feel too bad about giving up; this is how to spit up in the air if you feel like it, and this is how to move quick so that it doesn't fall on you; this is how to make ends meet; always squeeze bread to make sure it's fresh; *but what if the baker won't let me feel the bread?*; you mean to say that after all you are really going to be the kind of woman who the baker won't let near the bread?

QUESTIONS

1. How would you characterize the main speaker in "Girl"? To whom are her words addressed? How does the listener react to them?
2. What is this story about? Does it have a theme?
3. What, if anything, identifies "Girl" as a work of fiction and not merely a kind of tape recording taken from life?

Margaret Atwood

THE SIN EATER   1977

Margaret Atwood, born in Ottawa, Ontario, in 1939, is a distinguished Canadian writer of fiction and poetry whose fame has extended far beyond her native land. In 1962, the year she was graduated from the University of Toronto, she published her first book, the poetry collection Double Persephone. *Her fiction and poetry, at once grim and wryly humorous, often concern alienation and destructive human relationships, as does her recent novel,* Cat's Eye (1989), *about a woman whose childhood friend is also her lifelong tormenter. Her* Selected Poems (1976) *and* Selected Poems II (1987) *include much of her best work in poetry;* Second Words (1982) *gathers some of her critical essays.* Bluebeard's Egg (1986)

Margaret Atwood

includes several of her best stories. Atwood has also written Survival, *a ground-breaking study of Canadian writers (1972), and has edited* The Oxford Book of Canadian Verse *(1982) and* The Oxford Book of Canadian Short Stories in English *(with Robert Weaver, 1987).*

This is Joseph, in maroon leather bedroom slippers, flattened at the heels, scuffed at the toes, wearing also a seedy cardigan of muddy off-yellow that reeks of bargain basements, sucking at his pipe, his hair greying and stringy, his articulation as beautiful and precise and English as ever:

"In Wales," he says, "mostly in the rural areas, there was a personage known as the Sin Eater. When someone was dying the Sin Eater would be sent for. The people of the house would prepare a meal and place it on the coffin. They would have the coffin all ready, of course: once they'd decided you were going off, you had scarcely any choice in the matter. According to other versions, the meal would be placed on the dead person's body, which must have made for some sloppy eating one would have thought. In any case the Sin Eater would devour this meal and would also be given a sum of money. It was believed that all the sins the dying person had accumulated during his lifetime would be removed from him and transmitted to the Sin Eater. The Sin Eater thus became absolutely bloated with other people's sins. She'd accumulate such a heavy load of them that nobody wanted to have anything to do with her; a kind of syphilitic of the soul, you might say. They'd even avoid speaking to her, except of course when it was time to summon her to another meal."

"Her?" I say.

Joseph smiles, that lopsided grin that shows the teeth in one side of his mouth, the side not engaged with the stem of his pipe. An ironic grin, wolvish, picking up on what? What have I given away this time?

"I think of them as old women," he says, "though there's no reason why they shouldn't have been men, I suppose. They could be anything as long as they were willing to eat the sins. Destitute old creatures who had no other way of keeping body and soul together, wouldn't you think? A sort of geriatric spiritual whoring." 5

He gazes at me, grinning away, and I remember certain stories I've heard about him, him and women. He's had three wives, to begin with. Nothing with me though, ever, though he does try to help me on with my coat a bit too lingeringly. Why should I worry? It's not as though I'm susceptible. Besides which he's at least sixty, and the cardigan is truly gross, as my sons would say.

"It was bad luck to kill one of them, though," he says, "and there must have been other perks. In point of fact I think Sin Eating has a lot to be said for it."

Joseph's not one of the kind who'll wait in sensitive, indulgent silence when you've frozen on him or run out of things to say. If you won't talk to him, he'll bloody well talk to you, about the most boring things he can think of, usually. I've heard all about his flower beds and his three wives and how to raise calla lilies in your cellar; I've heard all about the cellar too, I could give guided tours. He says he thinks it's healthy for his patients—he won't call them "clients," no pussyfooting around, with Joseph—to know he's a human being too, and God do we know it. He'll drone on and on until you figure out that you aren't paying him so you can listen to him talk about his house plants, you're paying him so he can listen to you talk about yours.

Sometimes, though, he's really telling you something. I pick up my coffee cup, wondering whether this is one of those occasions.

"Okay," I say, "I'll bite. Why?"

"It's obvious," he says, lighting his pipe again, spewing out fumes. "First, the patients have to wait until they're dying. A true life crisis, no fakery and invention. They aren't permitted to bother you until then, until they can demonstrate that they're serious, you might say. Second, somebody gets a good square meal out of it." He laughs ruefully. We both know that half his patients don't bother to pay him, not even the money the government pays them. Joseph has a habit of taking on people nobody else will touch with a barge pole, not because they're too sick but because they're too poor. Mothers on welfare and so on; bad credit risks, like Joseph himself. He once got fired from a loony bin for trying to institute worker control.

"And think of the time saving," he goes on. "A couple of hours per patient, sum total, as opposed to twice a week for years and years, with the same result in the end."

"That's pretty cynical," I say disapprovingly. I'm supposed to be the cynical one, but maybe he's outflanking me, to force me to give up this corner. Cynicism is a defense, according to Joseph.

"You wouldn't even have to listen to them," he says. "Not a blessed word. The sins are transmitted in the food."

Suddenly he looks sad and tired. "You're telling me I'm wasting your time?" I say.

"Not mine, my dear," he says. "I've got all the time in the world."

I interpret this as condescension, the one thing above all that I can't stand. I don't throw my coffee cup at him, however. I'm not as angry as I would have been once.

We've spent a lot of time on it, this anger of mine. It was only because I found reality so unsatisfactory; that was my story. So unfinished, so sloppy, so pointless, so endless. I wanted things to make sense.

I thought Joseph would try to convince me that reality was actually fine and dandy and then try to adjust me to it, but he didn't do that. Instead he agreed with me, cheerfully and at once. Life in most ways was a big pile of shit, he said. That was axiomatic. "Think of it as a desert island," he said. "You're stuck on it, now you have to decide how best to cope."

"Until rescued?" I said.

"Forget about the rescue," he said.

"I can't," I said.

This conversation is taking place in Joseph's office, which is just as tatty as he is and smells of unemptied ashtrays, feet, misery and twice-breathed air. But it's also taking place in my bedroom, on the day of the funeral. Joseph's, who didn't have all the time in the world.

"He fell out of a tree," said Karen, notifying me. She'd come to do this in person, rather than using the phone. Joseph didn't trust phones. Most of the message in any act of communication, he said, was non-verbal.

Karen stood in my doorway, oozing tears. She was one of his too, one of us; it was through her I'd got him. By now there's a network of us, it's like recommending a hairdresser, we've passed him from hand to hand like the proverbial eye or tooth. Smart women with detachable husbands or genius-afflicted children with nervous tics, smart women with deranged lives, overjoyed to find someone who wouldn't tell us we were too smart for our own good and should all have frontal lobotomies. Smartness was an asset, Joseph maintained. We should only see what happened to the dumb ones.

"Out of a *tree?*" I said, almost screaming.

"Sixty feet, onto his head," said Karen. She began weeping again. I wanted to shake her.

"What the bloody hell was he doing up at the top of a sixty-foot *tree?*" I said.

"Pruning it," said Karen. "It was in his garden. It was cutting off the light to his flower beds."

"The old fart," I said. I was furious with him. It was an act of desertion. What made him think he had the right to go climbing up to the top of a sixty-foot tree, risking all our lives? Did his flower beds mean more to him than we did?

"What are we going to do?" said Karen.

What am I going to do? is one question. It can always be replaced by *What am I going to wear?* For some people it's the same thing. I go through the cupboard, looking for the blackest things I can find. What I wear will be the non-verbal part of the communication. Joseph will notice. I have a horrible feeling I'll turn up at the funeral home and find they've laid him out in his awful yellow cardigan and those tacky maroon leather bedroom slippers.

I needn't have bothered with black. It's no longer demanded. The three wives are in pastels, the first in blue, the second in mauve, the third, the current one, in beige. I know a lot about the three wives, from those off-days of mine when I didn't feel like talking.

Karen is here too, in an Indian-print dress, snivelling softly to herself. I envy her. I want to feel grief, but I can't quite believe Joseph is dead. It seems like some joke he's playing, some anecdote that's supposed to make us learn something. Fakery and invention. *All right, Joseph,* I want to call, *we have the answer, you can come out now.* But nothing happens, the closed coffin remains closed, no wisps of smoke issue from it to show there's life.

The closed coffin is the third wife's idea. She thinks it's more dignified, says the grapevine, and it probably is. The coffin is of dark wood, in good taste, no showy trim. No one has made a meal and placed it on this coffin, no one has eaten from it. No destitute old creature, gobbling down the turnips and mash and the heavy secrecies of Joseph's life along with them. I have no idea what Joseph might have had on his conscience. Nevertheless I feel this as an omission: what then have become of Joseph's sins? They hover around us, in the air, over the bowed heads, while a male relative of Joseph's, unknown to me, tells us all what a fine man he was.

30

35

After the funeral we go back to Joseph's house, to the third wife's house, for what used to be called the wake. Not any more: now it's coffee and refreshments.

The flower beds are tidy, gladioli at this time of year, already fading and a little ragged. The tree branch, the one that broke, is still on the lawn.

"I kept having the feeling he wasn't really there," says Karen as we go up the walk.

"Really where?" I say.

"There," says Karen. "In the coffin." 40

"For Christ's sake," I say, "don't start that." I can tolerate that kind of sentimental fiction in myself, just barely, as long as I don't do it out loud. "Dead is dead, that's what he'd say. Deal with here and now, remember?"

Karen, who'd once tried suicide, nodded and started to cry again. Joseph is an expert on people who try suicide. He's never lost one yet.

"How does he do it?" I asked Karen once. Suicide wasn't one of my addictions, so I didn't know.

"He makes it sound so *boring*," she said.

"That can't be all," I said. 45

"He makes you imagine," she said, "what it's like to be dead."

There are people moving around quietly, in the living room and in the dining room, where the table stands, arranged by the third wife with a silver tea urn and a vase of chrysanthemums, pink and yellow. Nothing too funereal, you can hear her thinking. On the white tablecloth there are cups, plates, cookies, coffee, cakes. I don't know why funerals are supposed to make people hungry, but they do. If you can still chew you know you're alive.

Karen is beside me, stuffing down a piece of chocolate cake. On the other side is the first wife.

"I hope you aren't one of the loonies," she says to me abruptly. I've never really met her before, she's just been pointed out to me, by Karen, at the funeral. She's wiping her fingers on a paper napkin. On her powder-blue lapel is a gold brooch in the shape of a bird's nest, complete with the eggs. It reminds me of high school: felt skirts with appliqués of cats and telephones, a world of replicas.

I ponder my reply. Does she mean *client*, or is she asking whether I am by 50 chance genuinely out of my mind?

"No," I say.

"Didn't think so," says the first wife. "You don't look like it. A lot of them were, the place was crawling with them. I was afraid there might be an *incident*. When I lived with Joseph there were always these *incidents*, phone calls at two in the morning, always killing themselves, throwing themselves all over him, you couldn't believe what went on. Some of them were *devoted* to him. If he'd told them to shoot the Pope or something, they'd have done it just like that."

"He was very highly thought of," I say carefully.

"You're telling *me*," says the first wife. "Had the idea he was God himself, some of them. Not that he minded all that much."

The paper napkin isn't adequate, she's licking her fingers. "Too rich," she says. 55 "*Hers.*" She jerks her head in the direction of the second wife, who is wispier than the first wife and is walking past us, somewhat aimlessly, in the direction of the living room. "You can have it, I told him finally. I just want some peace and quiet before I start pushing up the daisies." Despite the richness, she helps herself to another piece of chocolate cake. "*She* had this nutty idea that we should have some of them stand up and give little testimonies about him, right at the ceremony. Are you totally out of your tree? I told her. It's your funeral, but if I was you I'd try to keep it in mind that some of the people there are going to be a whole lot saner than others. Luckily she listened to me."

"Yes," I say. There's chocolate icing on her cheek: I wonder if I should tell her.

"I did what I could," she says, "which wasn't that much, but still. I was fond of him in a way. You can't just wipe out ten years of your life. I brought the cookies," she adds, rather smugly. "Least I could do."

I look down at the cookies. They're white, cut into the shapes of stars and moons and decorated with colored sugar and little sugar balls. They remind me of Christmas, of festivals and celebrations. They're the kind of cookies you make to please someone; to please a child.

I've been here long enough. I look around for the third wife, the one in charge, to say goodbye. I finally locate her, standing in an open doorway. She's crying, something she didn't do at the funeral. The first wife is beside her, holding her hand.

"I'm keeping it just like this," says the third wife, to no one in particular. 60 Past her shoulder I can see into the room, Joseph's study evidently. It would take a lot of strength to leave that rummage sale untouched, untidied. Not to mention the begonias withering on the sill. But for her it will take no strength at all, because Joseph is in this room, unfinished, a huge boxful of loose ends. He refuses to be packed up and put away.

"Who do you hate the most?" says Joseph. This, in the middle of a lecture he's been giving me about the proper kind of birdbath for one's garden. He knows of course that I don't have a garden.

"I have absolutely no idea," I say.

"Then you should find out," says Joseph. "I myself cherish an abiding hatred for the boy who lived next door to me when I was eight."

"Why is that?" I ask, pleased to be let off the hook.

"He picked my sunflower," he says. "I grew up in a slum, you know. We had 65 an area of sorts at the front, but it was solid cinders. However I did manage to grow this one stunted little sunflower, God knows how. I used to get up early every morning just to look at it. And the little bugger picked it. Pure bloody malice. I've forgiven a lot of later transgressions but if I ran into the little sod tomorrow I'd stick a knife into him."

I'm shocked, as Joseph intends me to be. "He was only a child," I say.

"So was I," he says. "The early ones are the hardest to forgive. Children have no charity; it has to be learned."

Is this Joseph proving yet once more that he's a human being, or am I intended to understand something about myself? Maybe, maybe not. Sometimes Joseph's stories are parables, but sometimes they're just running off at the mouth.

In the front hall the second wife, she of the mauve wisps, ambushes me. "He didn't fall," she whispers.

"Pardon?" I say.

The three wives have a family resemblance—they're all blondish and vague around the edges—but there's something else about this one, a glittering of the eyes. Maybe it's grief; or maybe Joseph didn't always draw a totally firm line between his personal and his professional lives. The second wife has a faint aroma of client.

"He wasn't happy," she says. "I could tell. We were still very close, you know."

What she wants me to infer is that he jumped. "He seemed all right to me," I say.

"He was good at keeping up a front," she says. She takes a breath, she's about to confide in me, but whatever these revelations are I don't want to hear them. I want Joseph to remain as he appeared: solid, capable, wise and sane. I do not need his darkness.

I go back to the apartment. My sons are away for the weekend. I wonder whether I should bother making dinner just for myself. It's hardly worth it. I wander around the too-small living room, picking things up. No longer my husband's: as befits the half-divorced, he lives elsewhere.

One of my sons has just reached the shower-and-shave phase, the other hasn't, but both of them leave a deposit every time they pass through a room. A sort of bathtub ring of objects—socks, paperback books left face-down and open in the middle, sandwiches with bites taken out of them, and, lately, cigarette butts.

Under a dirty T-shirt I discover the Hare Krishna magazine my younger son brought home a week ago. I was worried that it was a spate of adolescent religious mania, but no, he'd given them a quarter because he felt sorry for them. He was a dead-robin-burier as a child. I take the magazine into the kitchen to put it in the trash. On the front there's a picture of Krishna playing the flute, surrounded by adoring maidens. His face is bright blue, which makes me think of corpses: some things are not cross-cultural. If I read on I could find out why meat and sex are bad for you. Not such a poor idea when you think about it: no more terrified cows, no more divorces. A life of abstinence and prayer. I think of myself, standing on a street corner, ringing a bell, swathed in flowing garments. Selfless and removed, free from sin. Sin in this world, says Krishna. This world is all we have, says Joseph. It's all you have to work with. It is not too much for you. You will not be rescued.

I could walk to the corner for a hamburger or I could phone out for pizza. I decide on the pizza.

"Do you like me?" Joseph says from his armchair.

"What do you mean, do I *like* you?" I say. It's early on; I haven't given any thought to whether or not I like Joseph.

"Well, do you?" he says.

"Look," I say. I'm speaking calmly but in fact I'm outraged. This is a demand, and Joseph is not supposed to make demands of me. There are too many demands being made of me already. That's why I'm here, isn't it? Because the demands exceed the supply. "You're like my dentist," I say. "I don't think about whether or not I like my dentist. I don't *have* to like him. I'm paying him to fix my teeth. You and my dentist are the only people in the whole world that I don't *have* to *like*."

"But if you met me under other circumstances," Joseph persists, "would you like me?"

"I have no idea," I say. "I can't imagine any other circumstances."

This is a room at night, a night empty except for me. I'm looking at the ceiling, across which the light from a car passing outside is slowly moving. My apartment is on the first floor: I don't like heights. Before this I always lived in a house.

I've been having a dream about Joseph. Joseph was never much interested in dreams. At the beginning I used to save them up for him and tell them to him, the ones I thought were of interest, but he would always refuse to say what they meant. He'd make me tell him, instead. Being awake, according to Joseph, was more important than being asleep. He wanted me to prefer it.

Nevertheless, there was Joseph in my dream. It's the first time he's made an appearance. I think that it will please him to have made it, finally, after all those other dreams about preparations for dinner parties, always one plate short. But then I remember that he's no longer around to be told. Here it is, finally, the shape of my bereavement: Joseph is no longer around to be told. There is no one left in my life who is there only to be told.

I'm in an airport terminal. The plane's been delayed, all the planes have been delayed, perhaps there's a strike, and people are crammed in and milling around. Some of them are upset, there are children crying, some of the women are crying too, they've lost people, they push through the crowd calling out names, but elsewhere there are clumps of men and women laughing and singing, they've had the foresight to bring cases of beer with them to the airport and they're passing the bottles around. I try to get some information but there's no one at any of the ticket counters. Then I realize I've forgotten my passport. I decide to take a taxi home to get it, and by the time I make it back maybe they'll have everything straightened out.

I push towards the exit doors, but someone is waving to me across the heads of the crowd. It's Joseph. I'm not at all surprised to see him, though I do wonder about the winter overcoat he's wearing, since it's still summer. He also has a yellow muffler wound around his neck, and a hat. I've never seen him in any of these clothes before. Of course, I think, he's cold, but now he's pushed through the people, he's beside me. He's wearing a pair of heavy leather gloves and he takes the right one off to shake my hand. His own hand is bright blue, a flat tempera-paint blue, a picture-book blue. I hesitate, then I shake the hand, but he doesn't let go, he holds my hand, confidingly, like a child, smiling at me as if we haven't met for a long time.

"I'm glad you got the invitation," he says.

Now he's leading me towards a doorway. There are fewer people now. To one side there's a stand selling orange juice. Joseph's three wives are behind the counter, all in identical costumes, white hats and frilly aprons, like waitresses of the forties. We go through the doorway; inside, people are sitting at small round tables, though there's nothing on the tables in front of them, they appear to be waiting.

I sit down at one of the tables and Joseph sits opposite me. He doesn't take off his hat or his coat, but his hands are on the table, no gloves, they're the normal color again. There's a man standing beside us, trying to attract our attention. He's holding out a small white card covered with symbols, hands and fingers. A deaf-mute, I decide, and sure enough when I look his mouth is sewn shut. Now he's tugging at Joseph's arm, he's holding out something else, it's a large yellow flower. Joseph doesn't see him.

"Look," I say to Joseph, but the man is already gone and one of the waitresses has come instead. I resent the interruption, I have so much to tell Joseph and there's so little time, the plane will go in a minute, in the other room I can already hear the crackle of announcements, but the woman pushes in between us, smiling officiously. It's the first wife; behind her, the other two wives stand in attendance. She sets a large plate in front of us on the table.

"Will that be all?" she says, before she retreats.

The plate is filled with cookies, children's-party cookies, white ones, cut into 95
the shapes of moons and stars, decorated with silver balls and colored sugar. They look too rich.

"My sins," Joseph says. His voice sounds wistful but when I glance up he's smiling at me. Is he making a joke?

I look down at the plate again. I have a moment of panic: this is not what I ordered, it's too much for me, I might get sick. Maybe I could send it back; but I know this isn't possible.

I remember now that Joseph is dead. The plate floats up towards me, there is no table, around us is dark space. There are thousands of stars, thousands of moons, and as I reach out for one they begin to shine.

QUESTIONS

1. Which characters in "The Sin Eater" are round characters and which are flat?
2. Characterize the relationship between Joseph and the narrator.
3. What contradictions exist within the character of Joseph?
4. Who in the story most resembles the Welsh Sin Eater of Joseph's anecdote? Find evidence for your answer.
5. What explanation does Atwood give for the narrator's refusal to listen to the second wife's revelations about Joseph (paragraph 74)? What further explanation for this refusal can you find in the story as a whole?
6. Explain the significance of the dream that ends the story.

Isaac Bashevis Singer

GIMPEL THE FOOL 1953

Translated by Saul Bellow

Isaac Bashevis Singer

Isaac Bashevis Singer, born in Poland in 1904, the son of a rabbi, grew up in the Jewish ghetto in Warsaw in a family where money was scarce, but intellectual stimuli plentiful. "My father's house," he recalls, "was a study house, a court of justice, a house of prayer, of storytelling." For a time he pursued rabbinical studies. In 1935, when the Nazi invasion of Poland was imminent, he came to New York and became a journalist for the Jewish Daily Forward, a Yiddish-language newspaper for which, ever since, he has continued to write. For years he contributed a daily serial story to the Forward and for a time wrote scripts for a Yiddish soap opera on radio station WEVD. He became a naturalized United States citizen in 1943. Only in 1950 when The Family Moskat, a novel of three generations of Warsaw Jews, appeared in English translation, did a larger audience become aware of him. (Singer, whose command of English is excellent, has always worked closely with his translators.) In 1978 he was awarded the Nobel prize for literature. Singer's work often (as in "Gimpel the Fool") recreates the vanished world of the shtetl, or Jewish village of Eastern Europe. Traditional Jewish legends inform many of his novels, including Satan in Goray (1955), The Magician of Lublin (1960), and The Golem (1982). Singer has also written many volumes of short fiction (see Collected Stories, 1982), children's books, the play Yentl (1975), and three volumes of autobiography.

I

I am Gimpel the fool. I don't think myself a fool. On the contrary. But that's what folks call me. They gave me the name while I was still in school. I had seven names in all: imbecile, donkey, flax-head, dope, glump, ninny, and fool. The last name stuck. What did my foolishness consist of? I was easy to take in. They said, "Gimpel, you know the rabbi's wife has been brought to childbed?" So I skipped school. Well, it turned out to be a lie. How was I supposed to know? She hadn't had a big belly. But I never looked at her belly. Was that really so foolish? The gang laughed and hee-hawed, stomped and danced and chanted a good-night prayer. And instead of the raisins they give when a woman's lying in, they stuffed my hand full of goat turds. I was no weakling. If I slapped someone he'd see all the way to Cracow. But I'm really not a slugger by nature. I think to myself, Let it pass. So they take advantage of me.

I was coming home from school and heard a dog barking. I'm not afraid of dogs, but of course I never want to start up with them. One of them may be mad, and if he bites there's not a Tartar in the world who can help you. So I made tracks. Then I looked around and saw the whole market place wild with laughter. It was no dog at all but Wolf-Leib the thief. How was I supposed to know it was he? It sounded like a howling bitch.

When the pranksters and leg-pullers found that I was easy to fool, every one of them tried his luck with me. "Gimpel, the Czar is coming to Frampol; Gimpel, the moon fell down in Turbeen; Gimpel, little Hodel Furpiece found a treasure behind the bathhouse." And I like a *golem*° believed everyone. In the first place, everything is possible, as it is written in the Wisdom of the Fathers, I've forgotten just how. Second, I had to believe when the whole town came down on me! If I ever dared to say, "Ah, you're kidding!" there was trouble. People got angry. "What do you mean! You want to call everyone a liar?" What was I to do? I believed them, and I hope at least that did them some good.

I was an orphan. My grandfather who brought me up was already bent toward the grave. So they turned me over to a baker, and what a time they gave me there! Every woman or girl who came to bake a pan of cookies or dry a batch of noodles had to fool me at least once. "Gimpel, there's a fair in heaven; Gimpel, the rabbi gave birth to a calf in the seventh month; Gimpel, a cow flew over the roof and laid brass eggs." A student from the *yeshiva*° came once to buy a roll, and he said, "You, Gimpel, while you stand here scraping with your baker's shovel the Messiah has come. The dead have arisen." "What do you mean?" I said. "I heard no one blowing the ram's horn!" He said, "Are you deaf?" And all began to cry, "We heard it, we heard!" Then in came Reitze the candle-dipper and called out in her hoarse voice, "Gimpel, your father and mother have stood up from the grave. They're looking for you."

To tell the truth, I knew very well that nothing of the sort had happened, but all the same, as folks were talking, I threw on my wool vest and went out. Maybe something had happened. What did I stand to lose by looking? Well, what a cat music went up! And then I took a vow to believe nothing more. But that was no go either. They confused me so that I didn't know the big end from the small.

I went to the rabbi to get some advice. He said, "It is written, better to be a fool all your days than for one hour to be evil. You are not a fool. They are the fools. For he who causes his neighbor to feel shame loses Paradise himself." Nevertheless the rabbi's daughter took me in. As I left the rabbinical court she said, "Have you kissed the wall yet?" I said, "No; what for?" She answered, "It's a law; you've got to do it after every visit." Well, there didn't seem to be any harm in it. And she burst out laughing. It was a fine trick. She put one over on me, all right.

golem: simpleton. From the Hebrew: "a yet-unformed thing" (*Psalms* 139:16); a mere robot, a shapeless mass.   *yeshiva*: school of theology.

I wanted to go off to another town, but then everyone got busy matchmaking, and they were after me so they nearly tore my coat tails off. They talked at me and talked until I got water on the ear. She was no chaste maiden, but they told me she was virgin pure. She had a limp, and they said it was deliberate, from coyness. She had a bastard, and they told me the child was her little brother. I cried, "You're wasting your time. I'll never marry that whore." But they said indignantly, "What a way to talk! Aren't you ashamed of yourself? We can take you to the rabbi and have you fined for giving her a bad name." I saw then that I wouldn't escape them so easily and I thought, They're set on making me their butt. But when you're married the husband's the master, and if that's all right with her it's agreeable to me too. Besides, you can't pass through life unscathed, nor expect to.

I went to her clay house, which was built on the sand, and the whole gang, hollering and chorusing, came after me. They acted like bearbaiters. When we came to the well they stopped all the same. They were afraid to start anything with Elka. Her mouth would open as if it were on a hinge, and she had a fierce tongue. I entered the house. Lines were strung from wall to wall and clothes were drying. Barefoot she stood by the tub, doing the wash. She was dressed in a worn hand-me-down gown of plush. She had her hair put up in braids and pinned across her head. It took my breath away, almost, the reek of it all.

Evidently she knew who I was. She took a look at me and said, "Look who's here! He's come, the drip. Grab a seat."

I told her all; I denied nothing. "Tell me the truth," I said, "are you really   10
a virgin, and is that mischievous Yechiel actually your little brother? Don't be deceitful with me, for I'm an orphan."

"I'm an orphan myself," she answered, "and whoever tries to twist you up, may the end of his nose take a twist. But don't let them think they can take advantage of me. I want a dowry of fifty guilders, and let them take up a collection besides. Otherwise they can kiss my you-know-what." She was very plain-spoken. I said, "Don't bargain with me. Either a flat 'yes' or a flat 'no'—go back where you came from."

I thought, No bread will ever be baked from *this* dough. But ours is not a poor town. They consented to everything and proceeded with the wedding. It so happened that there was a dysentery epidemic at the time. The ceremony was held at the cemetery gates, near the little corpse-washing hut. The fellows got drunk. While the marriage contract was being drawn up I heard the most pious high rabbi ask, "Is the bride a widow or a divorced woman?" And the sexton's wife answered for her, "Both a widow and divorced." It was a black moment for me. But what was I to do, run away from under the marriage canopy?

There was singing and dancing. An old granny danced opposite me, hugging a braided white *chalah*°. The master of revels made a "God 'a mercy" in memory of the bride's parents. The schoolboys threw burrs, as on *Tishe b' Av* fast day°. There were a lot of gifts after the sermon: a noodle board, a kneading trough,

---

chalah: loaf of bread glazed with egg white, a Sabbath and holiday delicacy.   *Tishe b' Av:* day of mourning that commemorates disasters and persecutions.

a bucket, brooms, ladles, household articles galore. Then I took a look and saw two strapping young men carrying a crib. "What do we need this for?" I asked. So they said, "Don't rack your brains about it. It's all right, it'll come in handy." I realized I was going to be rooked. Take it another way though, what did I stand to lose? I reflected, I'll see what comes of it. A whole town can't go altogether crazy.

II

At night I came where my wife lay, but she wouldn't let me in. "Say, look here, is this what they married us for?" I said. And she said, "My monthly has come." "But yesterday they took you to the ritual bath, and that's afterward, isn't it supposed to be?" "Today isn't yesterday," said she, "and yesterday's not today. You can beat it if you don't like it." In short, I waited.

Not four months later she was in childbed. The townsfolk hid their laughter with their knuckles. But what could I do? She suffered intolerable pains and clawed at the walls. "Gimpel," she cried, "I'm going. Forgive me!" The house filled with women. They were boiling pans of water. The screams rose to the welkin.

The thing to do was to go to the House of Prayer to repeat Psalms, and that was what I did.

The townsfolk liked that, all right. I stood in a corner saying Psalms and prayers, and they shook their heads at me. "Pray, pray!" they told me. "Prayer never made any woman pregnant." One of the congregation put a straw to my mouth and said, "Hay for the cows." There was something to that too, by God!

She gave birth to a boy. Friday at the synagogue the sexton stood up before the Ark, pounded on the reading table, and announced, "The wealthy Reb Gimpel invites the congregation to a feast in honor of the birth of a son." The whole House of Prayer rang with laughter. My face was flaming. But there was nothing I could do. After all, I *was* the one responsible for the circumcision honors and rituals.

Half the town came running. You couldn't wedge another soul in. Women brought peppered chick-peas, and there was a keg of beer from the tavern. I ate and drank as much as anyone, and they all congratulated me. Then there was a circumcision, and I named the boy after my father, may he rest in peace. When all were gone and I was left with my wife alone, she thrust her head through the bed-curtain and called me to her.

"Gimpel," said she, "why are you silent? Has your ship gone and sunk?"

"What shall I say?" I answered. "A fine thing you've done to me! If my mother had known of it she'd have died a second time."

She said, "Are you crazy, or what?"

"How can you make such a fool," I said, "of one who should be the lord and master?"

"What's the matter with you?" she said. "What have you taken it into your head to imagine?"

I saw that I must speak bluntly and openly. "Do you think this is the way to use an orphan?" I said. "You have borne a bastard."

She answered, "Drive this foolishness out of your head. The child is yours."

"How can he be mine?" I argued. "He was born seventeen weeks after the wedding."

She told me then that he was premature. I said, "Isn't he a little too premature?" She said she had had a grandmother who carried just as short a time and she resembled this grandmother of hers as one drop of water does another. She swore to it with such oaths that you would have believed a peasant at the fair if he had used them. To tell the plain truth, I didn't believe her; but when I talked it over the next day with the schoolmaster he told me that the very same thing had happened to Adam and Eve. Two they went up to bed, and four they descended.

"There isn't a woman in the world who is not the granddaughter of Eve," he said.

That was how it was—they argued me dumb. But then, who really knows how such things happen? 30

I began to forget my sorrow. I loved the child madly, and he loved me too. As soon as he saw me he'd wave his little hands and want me to pick him up, and when he was colicky I was the only one who could pacify him. I bought him a little bone teething ring and a little gilded cap. He was forever catching the evil eye from someone, and then I had to run to get one of those abracadabras for him that would get him out of it. I worked like an ox. You know how expenses go up when there's an infant in the house. I don't want to lie about it; I didn't dislike Elka either, for that matter. She swore at me and cursed, and I couldn't get enough of her. What strength she had! One of her looks could rob you of the power of speech. And her orations! Pitch and sulphur, that's what they were full of, and yet somehow also full of charm. I adored her every word. She gave me bloody wounds though.

In the evening I brought her a white loaf as well as a dark one, and also poppy-seed rolls I baked myself. I thieved because of her and swiped everything I could lay hands on, macaroons, raisins, almonds, cakes. I hope I may be forgiven for stealing from the Saturday pots the women left to warm in the baker's oven. I would take out scraps of meat, a chunk of pudding, a chicken leg or head, a piece of tripe, whatever I could nip quickly. She ate and became fat and handsome.

I had to sleep away from home all during the week, at the bakery. On Friday nights when I got home she always made an excuse of some sort. Either she had heartburn, or a stitch in the side, or hiccups, or headaches. You know what women's excuses are. I had a bitter time of it. It was rough. To add to it, this little brother of hers, the bastard, was growing bigger. He'd put lumps on me, and when I wanted to hit back she'd open her mouth and curse so powerfully I saw a green haze floating before my eyes. Ten times a day she threatened to divorce me. Another man in my place would have taken French leave and disappeared. But I'm the type that bears it and says nothing. What's one to do? Shoulders are from God, and burdens too.

One night there was a calamity in the bakery; the oven burst, and we almost had a fire. There was nothing to do but go home, so I went home. Let me, I thought, also taste the joy of sleeping in bed in midweek. I didn't want to wake the sleeping mite and tiptoed into the house. Coming in, it seemed to me that I heard not the snoring of one but, as it were, a double snore, one a thin enough snore and the other like the snoring of a slaughtered ox. Oh, I didn't like that! I didn't like it at all. I went up to the bed, and things suddenly turned black. Next to Elka lay a man's form. Another in my place would have made an uproar, and enough noise to rouse the whole town, but the thought occurred to me that I might wake the child. A little thing like that—why frighten a little swallow like that, I thought. All right then, I went back to the bakery and stretched out on a sack of flour, and till morning I never shut an eye. I shivered as if I had had malaria. "Enough of being a donkey," I said to myself. "Gimpel isn't going to be a sucker all his life. There's a limit even to the foolishness of a fool like Gimpel."

In the morning I went to the rabbi to get advice, and it made a great commotion in the town. They sent the beadle for Elka right away. She came, carrying the child. And what do you think she did? She denied it, denied everything, bone and stone! "He's out of his head," she said. "I know nothing of dreams or divinations." They yelled at her, warned her, hammered on the table, but she stuck to her guns: it was a false accusation, she said. 35

The butchers and the horse-traders took her part. One of the lads from the slaughterhouse came by and said to me, "We've got our eye on you, you're a marked man." Meanwhile the child started to bear down and soiled itself. In the rabbinical court there was an Ark of the Covenant, and they couldn't allow that, so they sent Elka away.

I said to the rabbi, "What shall I do?"
"You must divorce her at once," said he.
"And what if she refuses?" I asked.
He said, "You must serve the divorce, that's all you'll have to do." 40
I said, "Well, all right, Rabbi. Let me think about it."
"There's nothing to think about," said he. "You mustn't remain under the same roof with her."
"And if I want to see the child?" I asked.
"Let her go, the harlot," said he, "and her brood of bastards with her."
The verdict he gave was that I mustn't even cross her threshold—never again, as long as I should live. 45

During the day it didn't bother me so much. I thought, It was bound to happen, the abscess had to burst. But at night when I stretched out upon the sacks I felt it all very bitterly. A longing took me, for her and for the child. I wanted to be angry, but that's my misfortune exactly, I don't have it in me to be really angry. In the first place—this was how my thoughts went—there's bound to be a slip sometimes. You can't live without errors. Probably that lad who was with her led her on and gave her presents and what not, and women are often long on hair and short on sense, and so he got around her. And then since she denies it so, maybe I was only seeing things? Hallucinations do happen. You see a figure or a mannikin or something, but when you come up closer it's nothing, there's not a thing there. And if that's so, I'm doing her an injustice. And when I got so far in my thoughts I started to weep. I sobbed so that I wet the flour where I lay. In the morning I went to the rabbi and told him that I had made a mistake. The rabbi wrote on with his quill, and he said that if that were so he would have to reconsider the whole case. Until he had finished I wasn't to go near my wife, but I might send her bread and money by messenger.

III

Nine months passed before all the rabbis could come to an agreement. Letters went back and forth. I hadn't realized that there could be so much erudition about a matter like this.

Meantime Elka gave birth to still another child, a girl this time. On the Sabbath I went to the synagogue and invoked a blessing on her. They called me up to the Torah, and I named the child for my mother-in-law, may she rest in peace. The louts and loudmouths of the town who came into the bakery gave me a going over. All Frampol refreshed its spirits because of my trouble and grief. However, I resolved that I would always believe what I was told. What's the good of *not* believing? Today it's your wife you don't believe; tomorrow it's God Himself you won't take stock in.

By an apprentice who was her neighbor I sent her daily a corn or a wheat loaf, or a piece of pastry, rolls or bagels, or, when I got the chance, a slab of pudding, a slice of honeycake, or wedding strudel—whatever came my way. The apprentice was a goodhearted lad, and more than once he added something on his own. He had formerly annoyed me a lot, plucking my nose and digging me in the ribs, but when he started to be a visitor to my house he became kind and friendly. "Hey, you, Gimpel," he said to me, "you have a very decent little wife and two fine kids. You don't deserve them."

"But the things people say about her," I said.   50

"Well, they have long tongues," he said, "and nothing to do with them but babble. Ignore it as you ignore the cold of last winter."

One day the rabbi sent for me and said, "Are you certain, Gimpel, that you were wrong about your wife?"

I said, "I'm certain."

"Why, but look here! You yourself saw it."

"It must have been a shadow," I said.   55

"The shadow of what?"

"Just of one of the beams, I think."

"You can go home then. You owe thanks to the Yanover rabbi. He found an obscure reference in Maimonides° that favored you.

I seized the rabbi's hand and kissed it.

I wanted to run home immediately. It's no small thing to be separated for   60
so long a time from wife and child. Then I reflected, I'd better go back to work now, and go home in the evening. I said nothing to anyone, although as far as my heart was concerned it was like one of the Holy Days. The women teased and twitted me as they did every day, but my thought was, Go on, with your loose talk. The truth is out, like the oil upon the water. Maimonides says it's right, and therefore it is right!

At night, when I had covered the dough to let it rise, I took my share of bread and a little sack of flour and started homeward. The moon was full and the stars were glistening, something to terrify the soul. I hurried onward, and be-

---

Maimonides: Jewish philosopher (1135–1204) whose *Guide for the Perplexed* (1190) attempted to reconcile Judaism and the teachings of Aristotle.

fore me darted a long shadow. It was winter, and a fresh snow had fallen. I had a mind to sing, but it was growing late and I didn't want to wake the householders. Then I felt like whistling, but remembered that you don't whistle at night because it brings the demons out. So I was silent and walked as fast as I could.

Dogs in the Christian yards barked at me when I passed, but I thought, Bark your teeth out! What are you but mere dogs? Whereas I am a man, the husband of a fine wife, the father of promising children.

As I approached the house my heart started to pound as though it were the heart of a criminal. I felt no fear, but my heart went thump! thump! Well, no drawing back. I quietly lifted the latch and went in. Elka was asleep. I looked at the infant's cradle. The shutter was closed, but the moon forced its way through the cracks. I saw the newborn child's face and loved it as soon as I saw it— immediately—each tiny bone.

Then I came nearer to the bed. And what did I see but the apprentice lying there beside Elka. The moon went out all at once. It was utterly black, and I trembled. My teeth chattered. The bread fell from my hands and my wife waked and said, "Who is that, ah?"

I muttered, "It's me." 65

"Gimpel?" she asked. "How come you're here? I thought it was forbidden."

"The rabbi said," I answered and shook as with a fever.

"Listen to me, Gimpel," she said, "go out to the shed and see if the goat's all right. It seems she's been sick." I have forgotten to say that we had a goat. When I heard she was unwell I went into the yard. The nannygoat was a good little creature. I had a nearly human feeling for her.

With hesitant steps I went up to the shed and opened the door. The goat stood there on her four feet. I felt her everywhere, drew her by the arms, examined her udders, and found nothing wrong. She had probably eaten too much bark. "Good night, little goat," I said. "Keep well." And the little beast answered with a "Maa" as though to thank me for the good will.

I went back. The apprentice had vanished. 70

"Where," I asked, "is the lad?"

"What lad?" my wife answered.

"What do you mean?" I said. "The apprentice. You were sleeping with him."

"The things I have dreamed this night and the night before," she said, "may they come true and lay you low, body and soul! An evil spirit has taken root in you and dazzles your sight." She screamed out, "You hateful creature! You moon calf! You spook! You uncouth man! Get out, or I'll scream all Frampol out of bed!"

Before I could move, her brother sprang out from behind the oven and struck 75 me a blow on the back of the head. I thought he had broken my neck. I felt that something about me was deeply wrong, and I said, "Don't make a scandal. All that's needed now is that people should accuse me of raising spooks and *dybbuks°*." For that was what she had meant. "No one will touch bread of my baking."

In short, I somehow calmed her.

"Well," she said, "that's enough. Lie down, and be shattered by wheels."

dybbuks: demons, or souls of the dead, who take possession of people.

Next morning I called the apprentice aside. "Listen here, brother!" I said. And so on and so forth. "What do you say?" He stared at me as though I had dropped from the roof or something.

"I swear," he said, "you'd better go to an herb doctor or some healer. I'm afraid you have a screw loose, but I'll hush it up for you." And that's how the thing stood.

To make a long story short, I lived twenty years with my wife. She bore me six children, four daughters and two sons. All kinds of things happened, but I neither saw nor heard. I believed, and that's all. The rabbi recently said to me, "Belief in itself is beneficial. It is written that a good man lives by his faith."

Suddenly my wife took sick. It began with a trifle, a little growth upon the breast. But she evidently was not destined to live long; she had no years. I spent a fortune on her. I have forgotten to say that by this time I had a bakery of my own and in Frampol was considered to be something of a rich man. Daily the healer came, and every witch doctor in the neighborhood was brought. They decided to use leeches, and after that to try cupping. They even called a doctor from Lublin, but it was too late. Before she died she called me to her bed and said, "Forgive me, Gimpel."

I said, "What is there to forgive? You have been a good and faithful wife."

"Woe, Gimpel!" she said. "It was ugly how I deceived you all these years. I want to go clean to my Maker, and so I have to tell you that the children are not yours."

If I had been clouted on the head with a piece of wood it couldn't have bewildered me more.

"Whose are they?" I asked.

"I don't know," she said, "there were a lot. . . . But they're not yours." And as she spoke she tossed her head to the side, her eyes turned glassy, and it was all up with Elka. On her whitened lips there remained a smile.

I imagined that, dead as she was, she was saying, "I deceived Gimpel. That was the meaning of my brief life."

IV

One night, when the period of mourning was done, as I lay dreaming on the flour sacks, there came the Spirit of Evil himself and said to me, "Gimpel, why do you sleep?"

I said, "What should I be doing? Eating kreplach°?"

"The whole world deceives you," he said, "and you ought to deceive the world in your turn."

"How can I deceive all the world?" I asked him.

He answered, "You might accumulate a bucket of urine every day and at night pour it into the dough. Let the sages of Frampol eat filth."

"What about judgment in the world to come?" I said.

"There is no world to come," he said. "They've sold you a bill of goods and talked you into believing you carried a cat in your belly. What nonsense!"

kreplach: a kind of dumpling containing meat, cheese, or other filling.

"Well then," I said, "and is there a God?"

He answered, "There is no God either."

"What," I said, "is there, then?"

"A thick mire."

He stood before my eyes with a goatish beard and horns, longtoothed, and with a tail. Hearing such words, I wanted to snatch him by the tail, but I tumbled from the flour sacks and nearly broke a rib. Then it happened that I had to answer the call of nature, and, passing, I saw the risen bread, which seemed to say to me, "Do it!" In brief, I let myself be persuaded.

At dawn the apprentice came. We kneaded the dough, scattered caraway seeds on it, and set it to bake. Then the apprentice went away, and I was left sitting in the little trench by the oven, on a pile of rags. Well, Gimpel, I thought, you've revenged yourself on them for all the shame they've put on you. Outside the frost glittered, but it was warm beside the oven. The flames heated my face. I bent my head and fell into a doze.

I saw in a dream, at once, Elka in her shroud. She called to me, "What have you done, Gimpel?"

I said to her, "It's all your fault," and started to cry.

"You fool!" she said. "You fool! Because I was false is everything false too? I never deceived anyone but myself. I'm paying for it all, Gimpel. They spare you nothing here."

I looked at her face. It was black. I was startled and waked, and remained sitting dumb. I sensed that everything hung in the balance. A false step now and I'd lose Eternal Life. But God gave me His help. I seized the long shovel and took out the loaves, carried them into the yard, and started to dig a hole in the frozen earth.

My apprentice came back as I was doing it. "What are you doing, boss?" he said, and grew pale as a corpse.

"I know what I'm doing," I said, and I buried it all before his very eyes.

Then I went home, took my hoard from its hiding place, and divided it among the children. "I saw your mother tonight," I said. "She's turning black, poor thing."

They were so astounded they couldn't speak a word.

"Be well," I said, "and forget that such a one as Gimpel ever existed." I put on my short coat, a pair of boots, took the bag that held my prayer shawl in one hand, my stick in the other, and kissed the mezzuzah°. When people saw me in the street they were greatly surprised.

"Where are you going?" they said.

I answered, "Into the world." And so I departed from Frampol.

I wandered over the land, and good people did not neglect me. After many years I became old and white; I heard a great deal, many lies and falsehoods, but the longer I lived the more I understood that there were really no lies. Whatever doesn't really happen is dreamed at night. It happens to one if it doesn't happen to another, tomorrow if not today, or a century hence if not next year. What

---

mezzuzah: a small oblong container, affixed near the front door of the house, which holds copies of Biblical verses (including a reminder to obey God's laws when traveling away from home).

difference can it make? Often I heard tales of which I said, "Now this is a thing that cannot happen." But before a year had elapsed I heard that it actually had come to pass somewhere.

Going from place to place, eating at strange tables, it often happens that I spin yarns—improbable things that could never have happened—about devils, magicians, windmills, and the like. The children run after me, calling, "Grandfather, tell us a story." Sometimes they ask for particular stories, and I try to please them. A fat young boy once said to me, "Grandfather, it's the same story you told us before." The little rogue, he was right.

So it is with dreams too. It is many years since I left Frampol, but as soon as I shut my eyes I am there again. And whom do you think I see? Elka. She is standing by the washtub, as at our first encounter, but her face is shining and her eyes as radiant as the eyes of a saint, and she speaks outlandish words to me, strange things. When I wake I have forgotten it all. But while the dream lasts I am comforted. She answers all my queries, and what comes out is that all is right. I weep and implore, "Let me be with you." And she consoles me and tells me to be patient. The time is nearer than it is far. Sometimes she strokes and kisses me and weeps upon my face. When I awaken I feel her lips and taste the salt of her tears.

No doubt the world is entirely an imaginary world, but it is only once removed from the true world. At the door of the hovel where I lie, there stands the plank on which the dead are taken away. The gravedigger Jew has his spade ready. The grave waits and the worms are hungry; the shrouds are prepared—I carry them in my beggar's sack. Another *shnorrer*° is waiting to inherit my bed of straw. When the time comes I will go joyfully. Whatever may be there, it will be real, without complication, without ridicule, without deception. God be praised: there even Gimpel cannot be deceived. 115

Questions

1. In what ways does Gimpel appear to deserve his nickname *the fool?* In what other ways is Gimpel not foolish at all?
2. What does Gimpel find to love in the character of Elka? Consider in particular the scene of her deathbed confession and her later appearance in Gimpel's dreams.
3. Why does Gimpel momentarily listen to the Devil? How is he delivered from temptation? For what reasons does he finally divide his wealth and become a poor wanderer? Would you call him a dynamic character, or a static character—one who grows and develops in the course of the story, or one who remains unchanged?
4. "No doubt the world is entirely an imaginary world, but it is only once removed from the true world." Comment on this statement in the closing paragraph. What do you think it means?
5. What elements of the supernatural do you find in "Gimpel the Fool"? What details of down-to-earth realism?
6. In what respects does the story resemble a fable? Is it possible to draw any moral from it?

shnorrer: a beggar, a traveling panhandler.

SUGGESTIONS FOR WRITING

1. Here is a topic for a lively essay if you are familiar with some variety of popular fiction—detective stories, science fiction, Gothic novels, romances, "adolescent agony" novels written for teenagers, or other kinds of paperback storytelling. Portray some of the stock characters you find prevalent in it. Suggestion: It might be simplistic to condemn stock characters as bad. They have long been valuable ingredients in much excellent literature. (For a discussion of stock characters, see page 47.)

2. Alternate topic: Portray a few stock characters we meet in current television programs. It might focus your essay to confine it to just one variety of stock character (for instance, the little man who peddles information to the police, the glamorous spy), or to just one kind of program (situation comedies, say, or soap operas, or police thrillers).

3. In a brief essay, study a dynamic character in a story, showing exactly how that character changed, or grew and developed. Possible subjects: Granny Weatherall, Gimpel, Sammy in John Updike's "A & P," the narrator in T. Coraghessan Boyle's "Greasy Lake," the boy Sarty Snopes in William Faulkner's "Barn Burning," Eva and Carol in Alice Munro's "The Found Boat," the central character in Leo Tolstoi's "The Death of Ivan Ilych," Mrs. Turpin in Flannery O'Connor's "Revelation," the narrators in Raymond Carver's "Where I'm Calling From" and in Tess Gallagher's "The Lover of Horses." (For a discussion of dynamic characters, see page 48.)

4. Alternate topic: Have you ever in your life known anyone whose character, over months or years, has altered deeply? If so, try to explain what may have caused that person to be a "dynamic character."

5. Topics for brief papers:
   The motivation of Gimpel in leaving Frampol to wander the world.
   The motivation of Sammy in quitting his job (in "A & P").
   The motivation of someone (whether in your reading or in your experience) who made a similar gesture of throwing over everything.

4 Setting

By the **setting** of a story, we mean its time and place. The word might remind you of the metal that holds a diamond in a ring, or of a *set* used in a play—perhaps a bare chair in front of a slab of painted canvas. But often, in an effective short story, setting may figure as more than mere background or underpinning. It can make things happen. It can prompt characters to act, bring them to realizations, or cause them to reveal their inmost natures.

To be sure, the idea of setting includes the physical environment of a story: a house, a street, a city, a landscape, a region. (*Where* a story takes place is sometimes called its **locale**.) Physical places mattered so greatly to French novelist Honoré de Balzac that sometimes, before writing a story set in a town, he would visit that town, select a few houses, and describe them in detail, down to their very smells. "The place in which an event occurred," Henry James admiringly said of him, "was in his view of equal moment with the event itself . . . it had a part to play; it needed to be made as definite as anything else."

But besides place, setting may crucially involve the *time* of the story—hour, year, or century. It might matter greatly that a story takes place at dawn, or on the day of the first moon landing. When we begin to read a historical novel, we are soon made aware that we aren't reading about life in the 1990s. In *The Scarlet Letter*, nineteenth-century author Nathaniel Hawthorne, by a long introduction and a vivid opening scene at a prison door, prepares us to witness events in the Puritan community of Boston in the earlier seventeenth century. This setting, together with scenes of Puritan times we recall from high school history, helps us understand what happens in the novel. We can appreciate the shocked agitation in town when a woman is accused of adultery: she has given illegitimate birth. Such an event might seem more nearly common today, but in the stern, God-fearing New England Puritan community, it was a flagrant defiance of church and state, which are all-powerful (and are all one). That reader will make no sense of *The Scarlet Letter* who ignores its setting—if to ignore the setting is possible, so much attention does Hawthorne pay to it.

That Hawthorne's novel takes place in a time remote from our own leads us to expect different customs, different attitudes. Some critics and teachers regard the setting of a story as its whole society, including the beliefs and assumptions of its characters. Still, we suggest that for now you keep your working definition of *setting* simple. Call it time and place. If later you should feel that your definition needs widening and deepening, you can always widen and deepen it.

Besides time and place, setting may also include the weather—which indeed, in some stories, may be crucial. Climate seems as substantial as any character in William Faulkner's "Dry September." After sixty-two rainless days, a long-unbroken spell of late-summer heat has frayed every nerve in a small town and caused the main character, a hotheaded white supremacist, to feel more and more irritation. The weather, someone remarks, is "enough to make a man do anything." When a false report circulates that a woman has been raped by a black man, the rumor, like a match flung into a dry field, ignites rage and provokes a lynching. Evidently, to understand the story we have to recognize its locale, a small town in Mississippi. The time (the 1930s) and that infernal heat wave matter, too. Fully to take in the meaning of Faulkner's story, we have to take in the setting in its entirety.

Physical place, by the way, is especially vital to a **regional writer,** who usually sets stories (or other work) in one geographic area. Such a writer, often a native of the place, tries to bring it alive to readers who live no matter where. William Faulkner, a distinguished regional writer, almost always sets his novels and stories in his native Mississippi. Though born in St. Louis, Kate Chopin became known as a regional writer for writing about Louisiana in many of her short stories and in her novel *The Awakening.* Willa Cather, for her novels of frontier Nebraska, often is regarded as another outstanding regionalist (though she also set fiction in Quebec, the Southwest, and in "Paul's Case," in Pittsburgh and New York). The expression is generally heard only in discussions of American and Canadian writing. (In a sense, we might think of James Joyce as a regional writer, in that all his fiction takes place in the city of Dublin, but instead we usually call him an Irish one.)

As such writers show, a place can profoundly affect the character who grew up in it. Willa Cather is fond of portraying strong-minded, independent women, such as the heroine of her novel *My Antonia.* strengthened in part by years of coping with the hardships of life on the wind-lashed prairie. Not that every writer of stories in which a place matters greatly will draw the characters as helpless puppets of their environment. Few writers do so, although that may be what you find in novels of **naturalism**—fiction of grim realism, in which the writer observes human characters like a scientist observing ants, seeing them as the products and victims of environment and heredity.[1] Theodore Dreiser carries on the tradition of naturalism in such novels such as *The Financier* (1912). It begins in a city setting. A young lad (who will grow up to be a ruthless industrialist) is watching

---

[1]The founder of naturalism in fiction was French novelist Émile Zola (1840–1902), who in a vast series of twenty novels about the family Rougon-Macquart traced a case of syphilis through several generations. In America, Stephen Crane wrote an early naturalist novel, *Maggie: A Girl of the Streets* (1893), and showed the way for later novelists such as Dreiser, Frank Norris, Upton Sinclair, and James T. Farrell.

a battle to death between a lobster and a squid in a fish-market tank. Dented for the rest of his life by this grim scene, he decides that's exactly the way to live in human society.

Setting may operate more subtly than that fish tank. Often, setting and character will reveal each other. Recall how Faulkner, at the start of "A Rose for Emily," depicts Emily Grierson's house, once handsome but now "an eyesore among eyesores" surrounded by gas stations. Still standing, refusing to yield its old-time horse-and-buggy splendor to the age of the automobile, the house in "its stubborn and coquettish decay" embodies the character of its owner. In some fiction, setting is closely bound with theme (what the story is saying)—as you will find in John Steinbeck's "The Chrysanthemums" (Chapter 7), a story beginning with a fog that has sealed off a valley from the rest of the world—a fog like the lid on a pot. In *The Scarlet Letter*, even small details contain powerful hints. At the beginning of his story, Hawthorne remarks of a colonial jailhouse:

> Before this ugly edifice, and between it and the wheel-track of the street, was a grass-plot, much overgrown with burdock, pigweed, apple-peru, and such unsightly vegetation, which evidently found something congenial in the soil that had so early borne the black flower of civilized society, a prison. But, on one side of the portal, and rooted almost at the threshold, was a wild rose-bush, covered, in this month of June, with its delicate gems, which might be imagined to offer their fragrance and fragile beauty to the prisoner as he went in, and to the condemned criminal as he came forth to his doom, in token that the deep heart of Nature could pity and be kind to him.

Apparently, Hawthorne wishes to show us that Puritan Boston, a town of rutted streets and an ugly jail with a tangled grass-plot, may be rough but has beauty in it. As the story unfolds, he will further suggest (among other things) that secret sin and a beautiful child may go together like pigweed and wild roses. In his artfully crafted novel, setting is one with—not separate from—characters, theme, and symbols.

In some stories, a writer will seem to draw a setting mainly to evoke atmosphere. In such a story, setting starts us feeling whatever the storyteller would have us feel. In "The Tell-Tale Heart," Poe's setting the action in an old, dark, lantern-lit house greatly contributes to our sense of unease—and so helps the story's effectiveness. (Old, dark mansions are favorite settings for the Gothic story, a long-popular kind of fiction mentioned again on page 210.)

But be warned: you'll meet stories in which setting appears hardly to matter. In W. Somerset Maugham's fable, "The Appointment in Samarra," all we need be told about the setting is that it is a marketplace in Bagdad. In that brief fable, the inevitability of death is the point, not an exotic setting. In this chapter, though, you will meet three fine stories in which setting, for one reason or another, counts greatly. Without it, none of these stories could happen.

THE STORM   1898

Kate Chopin (1851–1904) was born Katherine O'Flaherty in St. Louis, daughter of an Irish immigrant grown wealthy in retailing. On his death, young Kate was raised by her mother's family: aristocratic Creoles, descendants of the French and Spaniards who had colonized Louisiana. Young Kate received a convent schooling, and at nineteen married Oscar Chopin, a Creole cotton broker from New Orleans. Later, the Chopins lived on a plantation near Cloutierville, Louisiana, a region whose varied people—Creoles, Cajuns, blacks—Kate Chopin was later to write about with loving care in Bayou Folk *(1894) and* A Night in Arcadia *(1897). The shock of her husband's sudden death in 1883, which left her with the raising of six children, seems to have plunged*

Kate Chopin

Kate Chopin into writing. She read and admired fine woman writers of her day, such as the Maine realist Sarah Orne Jewett. She also read Maupassant, Zola, and other new (and scandalous) French naturalist writers. She began to bring into American fiction some of their hard-eyed observation and their passion for telling unpleasant truths. Determined, in defiance of her times, frankly to show the sexual feelings of her characters, Chopin suffered from neglect and censorship. When her major novel, The Awakening, *appeared in 1899, critics were outraged by her candid portrait of a woman who seeks sexual and professional independence. After causing such a literary scandal, Chopin was unable to get her later work published, and wrote little more before she died. The Awakening and many of her stories had to wait seven decades for a sympathetic audience.*

I

The leaves were so still that even Bibi thought it was going to rain. Bobinôt, who was accustomed to converse on terms of perfect equality with his little son, called the child's attention to certain somber clouds that were rolling with sinister intention from the west, accompanied by a sullen, threatening roar. They were at Friedheimer's store and decided to remain there till the storm had passed. They sat within the door on two empty kegs. Bibi was four years old and looked very wise.

"Mama'll be 'fraid, yes," he suggested with blinking eyes.

"She'll shut the house. Maybe she got Sylvie helpin' her this evenin'," Bobinôt responded reassuringly.

"No; she ent got Sylvie. Sylvie was helpin' her yistiday," piped Bibi.

Bobinôt arose and going across to the counter purchased a can of shrimps, of which Calixta was very fond. Then he returned to his perch on the keg and   5 sat stolidly holding the can of shrimps while the storm burst. It shook the wooden store and seemed to be ripping great furrows in the distant field. Bibi laid his little hand on his father's knee and was not afraid.

II

Calixta, at home, felt no uneasiness for their safety. She sat at a side window sewing furiously on a sewing machine. She was greatly occupied and did not notice the approaching storm. But she felt very warm and often stopped to mop her face on which the perspiration gathered in beads. She unfastened her white sacque at the throat. It began to grow dark, and suddenly realizing the situation she got up hurriedly and went about closing windows and doors.

Out on the small front gallery she had hung Bobinôt's Sunday clothes to air and she hastened out to gather them before the rain fell. As she stepped outside, Alcée Laballière rode in at the gate. She had not seen him very often since her marriage, and never alone. She stood there with Bobinôt's coat in her hands, and the big rain drops began to fall. Alcée rode his horse under the shelter of a side projection where the chickens had huddled and there were plows and a harrow piled up in the corner.

"May I come and wait on your gallery till the storm is over, Calixta?" he asked.

"Come 'long in, M'sieur Alcée."

His voice and her own startled her as if from a trance, and she seized Bobinôt's vest. Alcée, mounting to the porch, grabbed the trousers and snatched Bibi's braided jacket that was about to be carried away by a sudden gust of wind. He expressed an intention to remain outside, but it was soon apparent that he might as well have been out in the open: the water beat in upon the boards in driving sheets, and he went inside, closing the door after him. It was even necessary to put something beneath the door to keep the water out.

"My! what a rain! It's good two years sence it rain like that," exclaimed Calixta as she rolled up a piece of bagging and Alcée helped her to thrust it beneath the crack.

She was a little fuller of figure than five years before when she married; but she had lost nothing of her vivacity. Her blue eyes still retained their melting quality; and her yellow hair, dishevelled by the wind and rain, kinked more stubbornly than ever about her ears and temples.

The rain beat upon the low, shingled roof with a force and clatter that threatened to break an entrance and deluge them there. They were in the dining room— the sitting room—the general utility room. Adjoining was her bed room, with Bibi's couch along side her own. The door stood open, and the room with its white, monumental bed, its closed shutters, looked dim and mysterious.

Alcée flung himself into a rocker and Calixta nervously began to gather up from the floor the lengths of a cotton sheet which she had been sewing.

"If this keeps up, *Dieu sait*° if the levees goin' to stan' it!" she exclaimed.

"What have you got to do with the levees?"

"I got enough to do! An' there's Bobinôt with Bibi out in that storm—if he only didn' left Friedheimer's!"

Dieu sait: God only knows.

"Let us hope, Calixta, that Bobinôt's got sense enough to come in out of a cyclone."

She went and stood at the window with a greatly disturbed look on her face. She wiped the frame that was clouded with moisture. It was stiflingly hot. Alcée got up and joined her at the window, looking over her shoulder. The rain was coming down in sheets obscuring the view of far-off cabins and enveloping the distant wood in a gray mist. The playing of the lightning was incessant. A bolt struck a tall chinaberry tree at the edge of the field. It filled all visible space with a blinding glare and the crash seemed to invade the very boards they stood upon.

Calixta put her hands to her eyes, and with a cry, staggered backward. Alcée's arm encircled her, and for an instant he drew her close and spasmodically to him.

"Bonte!°" she cried, releasing herself from his encircling arm and retreating from the window, "the house'll go next! If I only knew w'ere Bibi was!" She would not compose herself; she would not be seated. Alcée clasped her shoulders and looked into her face. The contact of her warm, palpitating body when he had unthinkingly drawn her into his arms, had aroused all the old-time infatuation and desire for her flesh.

"Calixta," he said, "don't be frightened. Nothing can happen. The house is too low to be struck, with so many tall trees standing about. There! aren't you going to be quiet? say, aren't you?" He pushed her hair back from her face that was warm and steaming. Her lips were as red and moist as pomegranate seed. Her white neck and a glimpse of her full, firm bosom disturbed him powerfully. As she glanced up at him the fear in her liquid blue eyes had given place to a drowsy gleam that unconsciously betrayed a sensuous desire. He looked down into her eyes and there was nothing for him to do but gather her lips in a kiss. It reminded him of Assumption°.

"Do you remember—in Assumption, Calixta?" he asked in a low voice broken by passion. Oh! she remembered; for in Assumption he had kissed her and kissed and kissed her; until his senses would well nigh fail, and to save her he would resort to a desperate flight. If she was not an immaculate dove in those days, she was still inviolate; a passionate creature whose very defenselessness had made her defense, against which his honor forbade him to prevail. Now—well, now—her lips seemed in a manner free to be tasted, as well as her round, white throat and her whiter breasts.

They did not heed the crashing torrents, and the roar of the elements made her laugh as she lay in his arms. She was a revelation in that dim, mysterious chamber; as white as the couch she lay upon. Her firm, elastic flesh that was knowing for the first time its birthright, was like a creamy lily that the sun invites to contribute its breath and perfume to the undying life of the world.

The generous abundance of her passion, without guile or trickery, was like   25
a white flame which penetrated and found response in depths of his own sensuous nature that had never yet been reached.

Bonte!: Heavens!
Assumption: a parish west of New Orleans.

When he touched her breasts they gave themselves up in quivering ecstasy, inviting his lips. Her mouth was a fountain of delight. And when he possessed her, they seemed to swoon together at the very borderland of life's mystery.

He stayed cushioned upon her, breathless, dazed, enervated, with his heart beating like a hammer upon her. With one hand she clasped his head, her lips lightly touching his forehead. The other hand stroked with a soothing rhythm his muscular shoulders.

The growl of the thunder was distant and passing away. The rain beat softly upon the shingles, inviting them to drowsiness and sleep. But they dared not yield.

The rain was over; and the sun was turning the glistening green world into a palace of gems. Calixta, on the gallery, watched Alcée ride away. He turned and smiled at her with a beaming face; and she lifted her pretty chin in the air and laughed aloud.

III

Bobinôt and Bibi, trudging home, stopped without at the cistern to make   30
themselves presentable.

"My! Bibi, w'at will yo' mama say! You ought to be ashame'. You oughtn' put on those good pants. Look at 'em! An' that mud on yo' collar! How you got that mud on yo' collar, Bibi? I never saw such a boy!" Bibi was the picture of pathetic resignation. Bobinôt was the embodiment of serious solicitude as he strove to remove from his own person and his son's the signs of their tramp over heavy roads and through wet fields. He scraped the mud off Bibi's bare legs and feet with a stick and carefully removed all traces from his heavy brogans. Then, prepared for the worst—the meeting with an over-scrupulous housewife, they entered cautiously at the back door.

Calixta was preparing supper. She had set the table and was dripping coffee at the hearth. She sprang up as they came in.

"Oh, Bobinôt! You back! My! but I was uneasy. W'ere you been during the rain? An' Bibi? he ain't wet? he ain't hurt?" She had clasped Bibi and was kissing him effusively. Bobinôt's explanations and apologies which he had been composing all along the way, died on his lips as Calixta felt him to see if he were dry, and seemed to express nothing but satisfaction at their safe return.

"I brought you some shrimps, Calixta," offered Bobinôt, hauling the can from his ample side pocket and laying it on the table.

"Shrimps! Oh, Bobinôt! you too good fo' anything!" and she gave him a smack-   35
ing kiss on the cheek that resounded. *"J'vous reponds°*, we'll have feas' to night! umph-umph!"

Bobinôt and Bibi began to relax and enjoy themselves, and when the three seated themselves at table they laughed much and so loud that anyone might have heard them as far away as Laballière's.

IV

Alcée Laballière wrote to his wife, Clarisse, that night. It was a loving letter, full of tender solicitude. He told her not to hurry back, but if she and the babies

J'vous reponds: Let me tell you.

liked it at Biloxi, to stay a month longer. He was getting on nicely; and though he missed them, he was willing to bear the separation a while longer—realizing that their health and pleasure were the first things to be considered.

V

As for Clarisse, she was charmed upon receiving her husband's letter. She and the babies were doing well. The society was agreeable; many of her old friends and acquaintances were at the bay. And the first free breath since her marriage seemed to restore the pleasant liberty of her maiden days. Devoted as she was to her husband, their intimate conjugal life was something which she was more than willing to forego for a while.

So the storm passed and everyone was happy.

QUESTIONS

1. Exactly where does Chopin's story take place? How can you tell?
2. What circumstances introduced in Part I turn out to have a profound effect on events in the story?
3. What details in "The Storm" emphasize the fact that Bobinôt loves his wife? What details reveal how imperfectly he comprehends her nature?
4. What general attitudes toward sex, love, and marriage does Chopin imply? Cite evidence to support your answer.
5. What meanings do you find in the title "The Storm"?
6. In the story as a whole, how do setting and plot reinforce each other?

Jack London

TO BUILD A FIRE   1910

Jack London (1876–1916), born in San Francisco, won a large popular audience for his
novels of the sea and the Yukon: The Call of
the Wild (1903), The Sea-Wolf (1904), and
White Fang (1906). Like Ernest Hemingway,
he was a writer who lived a strenuous life. In
1893, he marched cross-country in Coxey's
Army, an organized protest of the unemployed;
in 1897, he took part in the Klondike gold rush;
and later as a reporter he covered the Russo-
Japanese war and the Mexican Revolution.
Son of an unmarried mother and a father who
denied his paternity, London grew up in
poverty. At fourteen, he began holding hard
jobs: working in a canning factory and a jute-
mill, serving as a deck hand, pirating oysters
in San Francisco Bay. These experiences persuaded him to join the Socialist Labor Party
and crusade for workers' rights. In his political

Jack London

novel The Iron Heel *(1908), London envisions a grim totalitarian America. Like himself, the hero of his novel* Martin Eden *(1909) is a man of brief schooling who gains fame as a writer, works for a cause, loses faith in it, and finds life without meaning. Though endowed with immense physical energy—he wrote 50 volumes—London drank hard, spent fast, and played out early. While his reputation as a novelist may have declined since his own day, some of his short stories have lasted triumphantly.*

Day had broken cold and gray, exceedingly cold and gray, when the man turned aside from the main Yukon trail and climbed the high earth-bank, where a dim and little-travelled trail led eastward through the fat spruce timberland. It was a steep bank, and he paused for breath at the top, excusing the act to himself by looking at his watch. It was nine o'clock. There was no sun nor hint of sun, though there was not a cloud in the sky. It was a clear day, and yet there seemed an intangible pall over the face of things, a subtle gloom that made the day dark, and that was due to the absence of sun. This fact did not worry the man. He was used to the lack of sun. It had been days since he had seen the sun, and he knew that a few more days must pass before that cheerful orb, due south, would just peep above the sky line and dip immediately from view.

The man flung a look back along the way he had come. The Yukon lay a mile wide and hidden under three feet of ice. On top of this ice were as many feet of snow. It was all pure white, rolling in gentle undulations where the ice jams of the freeze-up had formed. North and south, as far as the eye could see, it was unbroken white, save for a dark hairline that curved and twisted from around the spruce-covered island to the south, and that curved and twisted away into the north, where it disappeared behind another spruce-covered island. This dark hairline was the trail—the main trail—that led south five hundred miles to the Chilcoot Pass, Dyea, and salt water; and that led north seventy miles to Dawson, and still on to the north a thousand miles to Nulato, and finally to St. Michael, on Bering Sea, a thousand miles and half a thousand more.

But all this—the mysterious, far-reaching hairline trail, the absence of sun from the sky, the tremendous cold, and the strangeness and weirdness of it all— made no impression on the man. It was not because he was long used to it. He was a newcomer in the land, a *chechaquo*, and this was his first winter. The trouble with him was that he was without imagination. He was quick and alert in the things of life, but only in the things, and not in the significances. Fifty degrees below zero meant eighty-odd degrees of frost. Such fact impressed him as being cold and uncomfortable, and that was all. It did not lead him to meditate upon his frailty as a creature of temperature, and upon man's frailty in general, able only to live within certain narrow limits of heat and cold; and from there on it did not lead him to the conjectural field of immortality and man's place in the universe. Fifty degrees below zero stood for a bite of frost that hurt and that must be guarded against by the use of mittens, ear flaps, warm moccasins, and thick socks. Fifty degrees below zero was to him just precisely fifty degrees below zero. That there should be anything more to it than that was a thought that never entered his head.

As he turned to go on, he spat speculatively. There was a sharp, explosive crackle that startled him. He spat again. And again, in the air, before it could fall to the snow, the spittle crackled. He knew that at fifty below spittle crackled on the snow, but this spittle had crackled in the air. Undoubtedly it was colder than fifty below—how much colder he did not know. But the temperature did not matter. He was bound for the old claim on the left fork of Henderson Creek, where the boys were already. They had come over across the divide from the Indian Creek country, while he had come the roundabout way to take a look at the possibilities of getting out logs in the spring from the islands in the Yukon. He would be in to camp by six o'clock; a bit after dark, it was true, but the boys would be there, a fire would be going, and a hot supper would be ready. As for lunch, he pressed his hand against the protruding bundle under his jacket. It was also under his shirt, wrapped up in a handkerchief and lying against the naked skin. It was the only way to keep the biscuits from freezing. He smiled agreeably to himself as he thought of those biscuits, each cut open and sopped in bacon grease, and each enclosing a generous slice of fried bacon.

He plunged in among the big spruce trees. The trail was faint. A foot of snow   5
had fallen since the last sled had passed over, and he was glad he was without a sled, travelling light. In fact, he carried nothing but the lunch wrapped in the handkerchief. He was surprised, however, at the cold. It certainly was cold, he concluded, as he rubbed his numb nose and cheekbones with his mittened hand. He was a warm-whiskered man, but the hair on his face did not protect the high cheekbones and the eager nose that thrust itself aggressively into the frosty air.

At the man's heels trotted a dog, a big native husky, the proper wolf dog, gray-coated and without any visible or temperamental difference from its brother, the wild wolf. The animal was depressed by the tremendous cold. It knew that it was no time for travelling. Its instinct told it a truer tale than was told to the man by the man's judgment. In reality, it was not merely colder than fifty below zero; it was colder than sixty below, than seventy below. It was seventy-five below zero. Since the freezing point is thirty-two above zero, it meant that one hundred and seven degrees of frost obtained. The dog did not know anything about thermometers. Possibly in its brain there was no sharp consciousness of a condition of very cold such as was in the man's brain. But the brute had its instinct. It experienced a vague but menacing apprehension that subdued it and made it slink along at the man's heels, and that made it question eagerly every unwonted movement of the man as if expecting him to go into camp or to seek shelter somewhere and build a fire. The dog had learned fire, and it wanted fire, or else to burrow under the snow and cuddle its warmth away from the air.

The frozen moisture of its breathing had settled on its fur in a fine powder of frost, and especially were its jowls, muzzle, and eyelashes whitened by its crystalled breath. The man's red beard and mustache were likewise frosted, but more solidly, the deposit taking the form of ice and increasing with every warm, moist breath he exhaled. Also, the man was chewing tobacco, and the muzzle of ice held his lips so rigidly that he was unable to clear his chin when he expelled the juice. The result was that a crystal beard of the color and solidity of amber was increasing its length on his chin. If he fell down it would shatter itself, like glass, into brittle fragments. But he did not mind the appendage. It was the penalty all tobacco chewers paid in that country, and he had been out before in two cold snaps. They had not been so cold as this, he knew, but by the spirit thermometer at Sixty Mile he knew they had been registered at fifty below and at fifty-five.

He held on through the level stretch of woods for several miles, crossed a wide flat, and dropped down a bank to the frozen bed of a small stream. This was Henderson Creek, and he knew he was ten miles from the forks. He looked at his watch. It was ten o'clock. He was making four miles an hour, and he calculated that he would arrive at the forks at half-past twelve. He decided to celebrate that event by eating his lunch there.

The dog dropped in again at his heels, with a tail drooping discouragement, as the man swung along the creek bed. The furrow of the old sled trail was plainly visible, but a dozen inches of snow covered the marks of the last runners. In a month no man had come up or down that silent creek. The man held steadily on. He was not much given to thinking, and just then particularly he had nothing to think about save that he would eat lunch at the forks and that at six o'clock he would be in camp with the boys. There was nobody to talk to; and, had there been, speech would have been impossible because of the ice muzzle on his mouth. So he continued monotonously to chew tobacco and to increase the length of his amber beard.

Once in a while the thought reiterated itself that it was very cold and that   10
he had never experienced such cold. As he walked along he rubbed his cheekbones and nose with the back of his mittened hand. He did this automatically, now and again changing hands. But, rub as he would, the instant he stopped his cheekbones were numb, and the following instant the end of his nose went numb. He was sure to frost his cheeks; he knew that, and experienced a pang of regret that he had not devised a nose strap of the sort Bud wore in cold snaps. Such a strap passed across the cheeks, as well, and saved them. But it didn't matter much, after all. What were frosted cheeks? A bit painful, that was all; they were never serious.

Empty as the man's mind was of thoughts, he was keenly observant, and he noticed the changes in the creek, the curves and bends and timber jams, and always he sharply noted where he placed his feet. Once, coming around a bend, he shied abruptly, like a startled horse, curved away from the place where he had been walking, and retreated several paces back along the trail. The creek he knew was frozen clear to the bottom—no creek could contain water in that arctic winter—but he knew also that there were springs that bubbled out from the hillsides and ran along under the snow and on top the ice of the creek. He knew that the coldest snaps never froze these springs, and he knew likewise their danger. They were traps. They hid pools of water under the snow that might be three inches deep, or three feet. Sometimes a skin of ice half an inch thick covered them, and in turn was covered by the snow. Sometimes there were alternate layers of water and ice skin, so that when one broke through he kept on breaking through for a while, sometimes wetting himself to the waist.

That was why he had shied in such panic. He had felt the give under his feet and heard the crackle of a snow-hidden ice skin. And to get his feet wet in such a temperature meant trouble and danger. At the very least it meant delay, for he would be forced to stop and build a fire, and under its protection to bare his feet while he dried his socks and moccasins. He stood and studied the creek bed and its banks, and decided that the flow of water came from the right. Here reflected awhile, rubbing his nose and cheeks, then skirted to the left, stepping gingerly and testing the footing for each step. Once clear of the danger, he took a fresh chew of tobacco and swung along at his four-mile gait.

In the course of the next two hours he came upon several similar traps. Usually the snow above the hidden pools had a sunken, candied appearance that advertised the danger. Once again, however, he had a close call; and once, suspecting danger, he compelled the dog to go on in front. The dog did not want to go. It hung back until the man shoved it forward, and then it went quickly across the white, unbroken surface. Suddenly it broke through, floundered to one side, and got away to firmer footing. It had wet its forefeet and legs, and almost immediately the water that clung to it turned to ice. It made quick efforts to lick the ice off its legs, then dropped down in the snow and began to bite out the ice that had formed between the toes. This was a matter of instinct. To permit the ice to remain would mean sore feet. It did not know this. It merely obeyed the mysterious prompting that arose from the deep crypts of its being. But the man knew, having achieved a judgment on the subject, and he removed the mitten from his right hand and helped tear out the ice particles. He did not expose his fingers more than a minute, and was astonished at the swift numbness that smote them. It certainly was cold. He pulled on the mitten hastily, and beat the hand savagely across his chest.

At twelve o'clock the day was at its brightest. Yet the sun was too far south on its winter journey to clear the horizon. The bulge of the earth intervened between it and Henderson Creek, where the men walked under a clear sky at noon and cast no shadow. At half-past twelve, to the minute, he arrived at the forks of the creek. He was pleased at the speed he had made. If he kept it up, he would certainly be with the boys by six. He unbuttoned his jacket and shirt and drew forth his lunch. The action consumed no more than a quarter of a minute, yet in that brief moment the numbness laid hold of the exposed fingers. He did not put the mitten on, but, instead, struck the fingers a dozen sharp smashes against his leg. Then he sat down on a snow-covered log to eat. The sting that followed upon the striking of his fingers against his leg ceased so quickly that he was startled. He had had no chance to take a bite of biscuit. He struck the fingers repeatedly and returned them to the mitten, baring the other hand for the purpose of eating. He tried to take a mouthful, but the ice muzzle prevented. He had forgotten to build a fire and thaw out. He chuckled at his foolishness, and as he chuckled he noted the numbness creeping into the exposed fingers. Also, he noted that the stinging which had first come to his toes when he sat down was already passing away. He wondered whether the toes were warm or numb. He moved them inside the moccasins and decided that they were numb.

He pulled the mitten on hurriedly and stood up. He was a bit frightened. 15 He stamped up and down until the stinging returned into the feet. It certainly was cold, was his thought. That man from Sulphur Creek had spoken the truth when telling how cold it sometimes got in the country. And he had laughed at him at the time! That showed one must not be too sure of things. There was no mistake about it, it *was* cold. He strode up and down, stamping his feet and threshing his arms, until reassured by the returning warmth. Then he got out matches and proceeded to make a fire. From the undergrowth, where high water of the previous spring had lodged a supply of seasoned twigs, he got his firewood. Working carefully from a small beginning, he soon had a roaring fire, over which he thawed the ice from his face and in the protection of which he ate his biscuits. For the moment the cold of space was outwitted. The dog took satisfaction in the fire, stretching out close enough for warmth and far enough away to escape being singed.

When the man had finished, he filled his pipe and took his comfortable time over a smoke. Then he pulled on his mittens, settled the ear flaps of his cap firmly about his ears, and took the creek trail up the left fork. The dog was disappointed and yearned back toward the fire. This man did not know cold. Possibly all the generations of his ancestry had been ignorant of cold, of real cold, of cold one hundred and seven degrees below freezing point. But the dog knew; all its ancestry knew, and it had inherited the knowledge. And it knew that it was not good to walk abroad in such fearful cold. It was the time to lie snug in a hole in the snow and wait for a curtain of cloud to be drawn across the face of outer space whence this cold came. On the other hand, there was no keen intimacy between the dog and the man. The one was the toil slave of the other, and the only caresses it had ever received were the caresses of the whip lash and of harsh and menacing throat sounds that threatened the whip lash. So the dog made no effort to communicate its apprehension to the man. It was not concerned in the welfare of the man; it was for its own sake that it yearned back toward the fire. But the man whistled, and spoke to it with the sound of whip lashes, and the dog swung in at the man's heels and followed after.

The man took a chew of tobacco and proceeded to start a new amber beard. Also, his moist breath quickly powdered with white his mustache, eyebrows, and lashes. There did not seem to be so many springs on the left fork of the Henderson, and for half an hour the man saw no signs of any. And then it happened. At a place where there were no signs, where the soft, unbroken snow seemed to advertise solidity beneath, the man broke through. It was not deep. He wet himself halfway to the knees before he floundered out to the firm crust.

He was angry, and cursed his luck aloud. He had hoped to get into camp with the boys at six o'clock, and this would delay him an hour, for he would have to build a fire and dry out his footgear. This was imperative at that low temperature—he knew that much; and he turned aside to the bank, which he climbed. On top, tangled in the underbrush about the trunks of several small spruce trees, was a high-water deposit of dry firewood—sticks and twigs, principally, but also larger portions of seasoned branches and fine, dry, last year's grasses. He threw down several large pieces on top of the snow. This served for a foundation and prevented the young flame from drowning itself in the snow it otherwise would melt. The flame he got by touching a match to a small shred of birch bark that he took from his pocket. This burned even more readily than paper. Placing it on the foundation, he fed the young flame with wisps of dry grass and with the tiniest dry twigs.

He worked slowly and carefully, keenly aware of his danger. Gradually, as the flame grew stronger, he increased the size of the twigs with which he fed it. He squatted in the snow, pulling the twigs out from their entanglement in the brush and feeding directly to the flame. He knew there must be no failure. When it is seventy-five below zero, a man must not fail in his first attempt to build a fire—that is, if his feet are wet. If his feet are dry, and he fails, he can run along the trail for half a mile and restore his circulation. But the circulation of wet and freezing feet cannot be restored by running when it is seventy five below. No matter how fast he runs, the wet feet will freeze the harder.

All this the man knew. The old-timer on Sulphur Creek had told him about it the previous fall, and now he was appreciating the advice. Already all sensation had gone out of his feet. To build the fire he had been forced to remove his mittens, and the fingers had quickly gone numb. His pace of four miles an hour had kept his heart pumping blood to the surface of his body and to all the extremities. But the instant he stopped, the action of the pump eased down. The cold of space smote the unprotected tip of the planet, and he, being on that unprotected tip, received the full force of the blow. The blood of his body recoiled before it. The blood was alive, like the dog, and like the dog it wanted to hide away and cover itself up from the fearful cold. So long as he walked four miles an hour, he pumped that blood, willy-nilly, to the surface; but now it ebbed away and sank down into the recesses of his body. The extremities were the first to feel its absence. His wet feet froze the faster, and his exposed fingers numbed the faster, though they had not yet begun to freeze. Nose and cheeks were already freezing, while the skin of all his body chilled as it lost its blood.

But he was safe. Toes and nose and cheeks would be only touched by the frost, for the fire was beginning to burn with strength. He was feeding it with twigs the size of his finger. In another minute he would be able to feed it with branches the size of his wrist, and then he could remove his wet footgear, and, while it dried, he could keep his naked feet warm by the fire, rubbing them at first, of course, with snow. The fire was a success. He was safe. He remembered the advice of the old-timer on Sulphur Creek, and smiled. The old-timer had been very serious in laying down the law that no man must travel alone in the Klondike after fifty below. Well, here he was; he had had the accident; he was alone; and he had saved himself. Those old-timers were rather womanish, some of them, he thought. All a man had to do was to keep his head, and he was all right. Any man who was a man could travel alone. But it was surprising, the rapidity with which his cheeks and nose were freezing. And he had not thought his fingers could go lifeless in so short a time. Lifeless they were, for he could scarcely make them move together to grip a twig, and they seemed remote from his body and from him. When he touched a twig, he had to look and see whether or not he had hold of it. The wires were pretty well down between him and his finger ends.

All of which counted for little. There was the fire, snapping and crackling and promising life with every dancing flame. He started to untie his moccasins. They were coated with ice; the thick German socks were like sheaths of iron halfway to the knees; and the moccasin strings were like rods of steel all twisted and knotted as by some conflagration. For a moment he tugged with his numb fingers, then, realizing the folly of it, he drew his sheath knife.

But before he could cut the strings, it happened. It was his own fault or, rather, his mistake. He should not have built the fire under the spruce tree. He should have built it in the open. But it had been easier to pull the twigs from the brush and drop them directly on the fire. Now the tree under which he had done this carried a weight of snow on its boughs. No wind had blown for weeks, and each bough was fully freighted. Each time he had pulled a twig he had communicated a slight agitation to the tree—an imperceptible agitation, so far as he was concerned, but an agitation sufficient to bring about the disaster. High up in the tree one bough capsized its load of snow. This fell on the boughs beneath, capsizing them. This process continued, spreading out and involving the whole tree. It grew like an avalanche, and it descended without warning upon the man and the fire, and the fire was blotted out! Where it had burned was a mantle of fresh and disordered snow.

The man was shocked. It was as though he had just heard his own sentence of death. For a moment he sat and stared at the spot where the fire had been. Then he grew very calm. Perhaps the old-timer on Sulphur Creek was right. If he had only had a trail mate he would have been in no danger now. The trail mate could have built the fire. Well, it was up to him to build the fire over again, and this second time there must be no failure. Even if he succeeded, he would most likely lose some toes. His feet must be badly frozen by now, and there would be some time before the second fire was ready.

Such were his thoughts, but he did not sit and think them. He was busy all the time they were passing through his mind. He made a new foundation for a fire, this time in the open, where no treacherous tree could blot it out. Next he gathered dry grasses and tiny twigs from the high-water flotsam. He could not bring his fingers together to pull them out, but he was able to gather them by the handful. In this way he got many rotten twigs and bits of green moss that were undesirable, but it was the best he could do. He worked methodically, even collecting an armful of the larger branches to be used later when the fire gathered strength. And all the while the dog sat and watched him, a certain yearning wistfulness in its eye, for it looked upon him as the fire provider, and the fire was slow in coming.

When all was ready, the man reached in his pocket for a second piece of birch bark. He knew the bark was there, and, though he could not feel it with his fingers, he could hear its crisp rustling as he fumbled for it. Try as he would, he could not clutch hold of it. And all the time, in his consciousness, was the knowledge that each instant his feet were freezing. This thought tended to put him in a panic, but he fought against it and kept calm. He pulled on his mittens with his teeth, and threshed his arms back and forth, beating his hands with all his might against his sides. He did this sitting down, and he stood up to do it; and all the while the dog sat in the snow, its wolf brush of a tail curled around warmly over its forefeet, its sharp wolf ears pricked forward intently as it watched the man. And the man, as he beat and threshed with his arms and hands, felt a great surge of envy as he regarded the creature that was warm and secure in its natural covering.

After a time he was aware of the first faraway signals of sensation in his beaten fingers. The faint tingling grew stronger till it evolved into a stinging ache that was excruciating, but which the man hailed with satisfaction. He stripped the mitten from his right hand and fetched forth the birch bark. The exposed fingers were quickly going numb again. Next he brought out his bunch of sulphur matches. But the tremendous cold had already driven the life out of his fingers. In his effort to separate one match from the others, the whole bunch fell in the snow. He tried to pick it out of the snow, but failed. The dead fingers could neither touch nor clutch. He was very careful. He drove the thought of his freezing feet, and nose, and cheeks, out of his mind, devoting his whole soul to the matches. He watched, using the sense of vision in place of that of touch, and when he saw his fingers on each side the bunch, he closed them—that is, he willed to close them, for the wires were down, and the fingers did not obey. He pulled the mitten on the right hand, and beat it fiercely against his knee. Then, with both mittened hands, he scooped the bunch of matches, along with much snow, into his lap. Yet he was no better off.

After some manipulation he managed to get the bunch between the heels of his mittened hands. In this fashion he carried it to his mouth. The ice crackled and snapped when by a violent effort he opened his mouth. He drew the lower jaw in, curled the upper lip out of the way, and scraped the bunch with his upper teeth in order to separate a match. He succeeded in getting one, which he dropped on his lap. He was no better off. He could not pick it up. Then he devised a way. He picked it up in his teeth and scratched it on his leg. Twenty times he scratched before he succeeded in lighting it. As it flamed he held it with his teeth to the birch bark. But the burning brimstone went up his nostrils and into his lungs, causing him to cough spasmodically. The match fell into the snow and went out.

The old-timer on Sulphur Creek was right, he thought in the moment of controlled despair that ensued: after fifty below, a man should travel with a partner. He beat his hands, but failed in exciting any sensation. Suddenly he bared both hands, removing the mittens with his teeth. He caught the whole bunch between the heels of his hands. His arm muscles not being frozen enabled him to press the hand heels tightly against the matches. Then he scratched the bunch along his leg. It flared into flame, seventy sulphur matches at once! There was no wind to blow them out. He kept his head to one side to escape the strangling fumes, and held the blazing bunch to the birch bark. As he so held it, he became aware of sensation in his hand. His flesh was burning. He could smell it. Deep down below the surface he could feel it. The sensation developed into pain that grew acute. And still he endured it, holding the flame of the matches clumsily to the bark that would not light readily because his own burning hands were in the way, absorbing most of the flame.

At last, when he could endure no more, he jerked his hands apart. The blazing matches fell sizzling into the snow, but the birch bark was alight. He began laying dry grasses and the tiniest twigs on the flame. He could not pick and choose, for he had to lift the fuel between the heels of his hands. Small pieces of rotten wood and green moss clung to the twigs, and he bit them off as well as he could with his teeth. He cherished the flame carefully and awkwardly. It meant life, and it must not perish. The withdrawal of blood from the surface of his body now made him begin to shiver, and he grew more awkward. A large piece of green moss fell squarely on the little fire. He tried to poke it out with his fingers, but his shivering frame made him poke too far, and he disrupted the nucleus of the little fire, the burning grasses and tiny twigs separating and scattering. He tried to poke them together again, but in spite of the tenseness of the effort, his shivering got away from him, and the twigs were hopelessly scattered. Each twig gushed a puff of smoke and went out. The fire provider had failed. As he looked

30

apathetically about him, his eyes chanced on the dog, sitting across the ruins of the fire from him, in the snow, making restless, hunching movements, slightly lifting one forefoot and then the other, shifting its weight back and forth on them with wistful eagerness.

The sight of the dog put a wild idea into his head. He remembered the tale of the man, caught in the blizzard, who killed a steer and crawled inside the carcass, and so was saved. He would kill the dog and bury his hands in the warm body until the numbness went out of them. Then he could build another fire. He spoke to the dog, calling it to him; but in his voice was a strange note of fear that frightened the animal, who had never known the man to speak in such a way before. Something was the matter, and its suspicious nature sensed danger — it knew not what danger, but somewhere, somehow, in its brain arose an apprehension of the man. It flattened its ears down at the sound of the man's voice, and its restless, hunching movements and the liftings and shiftings of its forefeet became more pronounced; but it would not come to the man. He got on his hands and knees and crawled toward the dog. This unusual posture again excited suspicion, and the animal sidled mincingly away.

The man sat up in the snow for a moment and struggled for calmness. Then he pulled on his mittens, by means of his teeth, and got upon his feet. He glanced down at first in order to assure himself that he was really standing up, for the absence of sensation in his feet left him unrelated to the earth. His erect position in itself started to drive the webs of suspicion from the dog's mind; and when he spoke peremptorily, with the sound of whip lashes in his voice, the dog rendered its customary allegiance and came to him. As it came within reaching distance, the man lost his control. His arms flashed out to the dog, and he experienced genuine surprise when he discovered that his hands could not clutch, that there was neither bend nor feeling in the fingers. He had forgotten for the moment that they were frozen and that they were freezing more and more. All this happened quickly, and before the animal could get away, he encircled its body with his arms. He sat down in the snow, and in this fashion held the dog, while it snarled and whined and struggled.

But it was all he could do, hold its body encircled in his arms and sit there. He realized that he could not kill the dog. There was no way to do it. With his helpless hands he could neither draw nor hold his sheath knife nor throttle the animal. He released it, and it plunged wildly away, with tail between its legs, and still snarling. It halted forty feet away and surveyed him curiously, with ears sharply pricked forward.

The man looked down at his hands in order to locate them, and found them hanging on the ends of his arms. It struck him as curious that one should have to use his eyes in order to find out where his hands were. He began threshing his arms back and forth, beating the mittened hands against his sides. He did this for five minutes, violently, and his heart pumped enough blood up to the surface to put a stop to his shivering. But no sensation was aroused in the hands. He had an impression that they hung like weights on the ends of his arms, but when he tried to run the impression down, he could not find it.

A certain fear of death, dull and oppressive, came to him. This fear quickly became poignant as he realized that it was no longer a mere matter of freezing

35

his fingers and toes, or of losing his hands and feet, but that it was a matter of life and death with the chances against him. This threw him into a panic, and he turned and ran up the creek bed along the old, dim trail. The dog joined in behind and kept up with him. He ran blindly, without intention, in fear such as he had never known in his life. Slowly, as he plowed and floundered through the snow, he began to see things again—the banks of the creek, the old timber jams, the leafless aspens, and the sky. The running made him feel better. He did not shiver. Maybe, if he ran on, his feet would thaw out; and anyway, if he ran far enough, he would reach camp and the boys. Without doubt he would lose some fingers and toes and some of his face; but the boys would take care of him, and save the rest of him when he got there. And at the same time there was another thought in his mind that said he would never get to the camp and the boys; that it was too many miles away, that the freezing had too great a start on him, and that he would soon be stiff and dead. This thought he kept in the background and refused to consider. Sometimes it pushed itself forward and demanded to be heard, but he thrust it back and strove to think of other things.

It struck him as curious that he could run at all on feet so frozen that he could not feel them when they struck the earth and took the weight of his body. He seemed to himself to skim along above the surface, and to have no connection with the earth. Somewhere he had once seen a winged Mercury, and he wondered if Mercury felt as he felt when skimming over the earth.

His theory of running until he reached the camp and the boys had one flaw in it: he lacked the endurance. Several times he stumbled, and finally he tottered, crumpled up, and fell. When he tried to rise, he failed. He must sit and rest, he decided, and next time he would merely walk and keep on going. As he sat and regained his breath, he noted that he was feeling quite warm and comfortable. He was not shivering, and it even seemed that a warm glow had come to his chest and trunk. And yet, when he touched his nose and cheeks, there was no sensation. Running would not thaw them out. Nor would it thaw out his hands and feet. Then the thought came to him that the frozen portions of his body must be extending. He tried to keep this thought down, to forget it, to think of something else; he was aware of the panicky feeling that it caused, and he was afraid of the panic. But the thought asserted itself, and persisted, until it produced a vision of his body totally frozen. This was too much, and he made another wild run along the trail. Once he slowed down to a walk, but the thought of the freezing extending itself made him run again.

And all the time the dog ran with him, at his heels. When he fell down a second time, it curled its tail over its forefeet and sat in front of him, facing him, curiously eager and intent. The warmth and security of the animal angered him, and he cursed it till it flattened down its ears appeasingly. This time the shivering came more quickly upon the man. He was losing in his battle with the frost. It was creeping into his body from all sides. The thought of it drove him on, but he ran no more than a hundred feet, when he staggered and pitched headlong. It was his last panic. When he had recovered his breath and control, he sat up and entertained in his mind the conception of meeting death with dignity. However, the conception did not come to him in such terms. His idea of it was that he had been making a fool of himself, running around like a chicken with its head cut off—such was the simile that occurred to him. Well, he was bound to freeze anyway, and he might as well take it decently. With this new-found peace of mind came the first glimmerings of drowsiness. A good idea, he thought, to sleep off to death. It was like taking an anesthetic. Freezing was not so bad as people thought. There were lots worse ways to die.

He pictured the boys finding his body next day. Suddenly he found himself with them, coming along the trail and looking for himself. And, still with them, he came around a turn in the trail and found himself lying in the snow. He did not belong with himself any more, for even then he was out of himself, standing with the boys and looking at himself in the snow. It certainly was cold, was his thought. When he got back to the States he could tell the folks what real cold was. He drifted on from this to a vision of the old-timer on Sulphur Creek. He could see him quite clearly, warm and comfortable, and smoking a pipe.

"You were right, old hoss; you were right," the man mumbled to the old-timer 40 of Sulphur Creek.

Then the man drowsed off into what seemed to him the most comfortable and satisfying sleep he had ever known. The dog sat facing him and waiting. The brief day drew to a close in a long, slow twilight. There were no signs of a fire to be made, and, besides, never in the dog's experience had it known a man to sit like that in the snow and make no fire. As the twilight drew on, its eager yearning for the fire mastered it, and with a great lifting and shifting of forefeet, it whined softly, then flattened its ears down in anticipation of being chidden by the man. But the man remained silent. Later the dog whined loudly. And still later it crept close to the man and caught the scent of death. This made the animal bristle and back away. A little longer it delayed, howling under the stars that leaped and danced and shone brightly in the cold sky. Then it turned and trotted up the trail in the direction of the camp it knew, where were the other food providers and fire providers.

QUESTIONS

1. Roughly how much of London's story is devoted to describing the setting? What particular details make it memorable?
2. To what extent does setting determine what happens in this story?
3. From what point of view is London's story told?
4. In "To Build a Fire" the man is never given a name. What is the effect of his being called simply "the man" throughout the story?
5. From the evidence London gives us, what stages are involved in the process of freezing to death? What does the story gain from London's detailed account of the man's experience with each successive stage?
6. What are the most serious mistakes the man makes? To what factors do you attribute these errors?

T. Coraghessan Boyle

T. Coraghessan Boyle (the T. stands for Tom) was born in 1948 in Peekskill, New York, the son of Irish immigrants. He grew up, he recalls, "as a sort of pampered punk" who did not read a book until he was eighteen. After a brief period as a high school teacher, he studied in the University of Iowa Writers' Workshop, submitting a collection of stories for his Ph.D. He now teaches writing at the University of Southern California and sometimes plays saxophone in a rockabilly band. His stories in Esquire, Paris Review, The Atlantic, and other magazines quickly won him notice for their outrageous and macabre humor, verve, and inventiveness. Besides three story collections, The Descent of Man (1979), Greasy Lake (1985), and If the River Was Whiskey (1989), Boyle has written four novels: Water Music (1982), about an eighteenth-century expedition to Africa; Budding Prospects (1984),

T. Coraghessan Boyle

a picaresque (or scoundrel-adventure) story of life among marijuana growers; World's End (1987), an account of three families in his native Hudson River Valley which spans three centuries; and East is East (1990), the half serious, half comic story of a Japanese fugitive in an American writers' colony.

It's about a mile down on the dark side of Route 8.
          —Bruce Springsteen

There was a time when courtesy and winning ways went out of style, when it was good to be bad, when you cultivated decadence like a taste. We were all dangerous characters then. We wore torn-up leather jackets, slouched around with toothpicks in our mouths, sniffed glue and ether and what somebody claimed was cocaine. When we wheeled our parents' whining station wagons out onto the street we left a patch of rubber half a block long. We drank gin and grape juice, Tango, Thunderbird, and Bali Hai. We were nineteen. We were bad. We read André Gide° and struck elaborate poses to show that we didn't give a shit about anything. At night, we went up to Greasy Lake.

Through the center of town, up the strip, past the housing developments and shopping malls, street lights giving way to the thin streaming illumination of the

André Gide: controversial French writer (1869–1951) whose novels, including The Counterfeiters and Lafcadio's Adventures, often show individuals in conflict with accepted morality.

headlights, trees crowding the asphalt in a black unbroken wall: that was the way out to Greasy Lake. The Indians had called it Wakan, a reference to the clarity of its waters. Now it was fetid and murky, the mud banks glittering with broken glass and strewn with beer cans and the charred remains of bonfires. There was a single ravaged island a hundred yards from shore, so stripped of vegetation it looked as if the air force had strafed it. We went up to the lake because everyone went there, because we wanted to snuff the rich scent of possibility on the breeze, watch a girl take off her clothes and plunge into the festering murk, drink beer, smoke pot, howl at the stars, savor the incongruous full-throated roar of rock and roll against the primeval susurrus of frogs and crickets. This was nature.

I was there one night, late, in the company of two dangerous characters. Digby wore a gold star in his right ear and allowed his father to pay his tuition at Cornell; Jeff was thinking of quitting school to become a painter/musician/head-shop proprietor. They were both expert in the social graces, quick with a sneer, able to manage a Ford with lousy shocks over a rutted and gutted blacktop road at eighty-five while rolling a joint as compact as a Tootsie Roll Pop stick. They could lounge against a bank of booming speakers and trade "man"s with the best of them or roll out across the dance floor as if their joints worked on bearings. They were slick and quick and they wore their mirror shades at breakfast and dinner, in the shower, in closets and caves. In short, they were bad.

I drove. Digby pounded the dashboard and shouted along with Toots & the Maytals while Jeff hung his head out the window and streaked the side of my mother's Bel Air with vomit. It was early June, the air soft as a hand on your cheek, the third night of summer vacation. The first two nights we'd been out till dawn, looking for something we never found. On this, the third night, we'd cruised the strip sixty-seven times, been in and out of every bar and club we could think of in a twenty-mile radius, stopped twice for bucket chicken and forty-cent hamburgers, debated going to a party at the house of a girl Jeff's sister knew, and chucked two dozen raw eggs at mailboxes and hitchhikers. It was 2:00 A.M.; the bars were closing. There was nothing to do but take a bottle of lemon-flavored gin up to Greasy Lake.

The taillights of a single car winked at us as we swung into the dirt lot with its tufts of weed and washboard corrugations; '57 Chevy, mint, metallic blue. On the far side of the lot, like the exoskeleton of some gaunt chrome insect, a chopper leaned against its kickstand. And that was it for excitement: some junkie half-wit biker and a car freak pumping his girlfriend. Whatever it was we were looking for, we weren't about to find it at Greasy Lake. Not that night.

But then all of a sudden Digby was fighting for the wheel. "Hey, that's Tony Lovett's car! Hey!" he shouted, while I stabbed at the brake pedal and the Bel Air nosed up to the gleaming bumper of the parked Chevy. Digby leaned on the horn, laughing, and instructed me to put my brights on. I flicked on the brights. This was hilarious. A joke. Tony would experience premature withdrawal and expect to be confronted by grim-looking state troopers with flashlights. We hit the horn, strobed the lights, and then jumped out of the car to press our witty faces to Tony's windows; for all we knew we might even catch a glimpse of some little fox's tit, and then we could slap backs with red-faced Tony, roughhouse a little, and go on to new heights of adventure and daring.

The first mistake, the one that opened the whole floodgate, was losing my
grip on the keys. In the excitement, leaping from the car with the gin in one
hand and a roach clip in the other, I spilled them in the grass—in the dark, rank,
mysterious nighttime grass of Greasy Lake. This was a tactical error, as damaging
and irreversible in its way as Westmoreland's decision to dig in at Khe Sanh°.
I felt it like a jab of intuition, and I stopped there by the open door, peering vaguely
into the night that puddled up round my feet.

The second mistake—and this was inextricably bound up with the first—was
identifying the car as Tony Lovett's. Even before the very bad character in greasy
jeans and engineer boots ripped out of the driver's door, I began to realize that
this chrome blue was much lighter than the robin's-egg of Tony's car, and that
Tony's car didn't have rear-mounted speakers. Judging from their expressions, Digby
and Jeff were privately groping toward the same inevitable and unsettling conclusion as I was.

In any case, there was no reasoning with this bad greasy character—clearly
he was a man of action. The first lusty Rockette° kick of his steel-toed boot caught
me under the chin, chipped my favorite tooth, and left me sprawled in the dirt.
Like a fool, I'd gone down on one knee to comb the stiff hacked grass for the
keys, my mind making connections in the most dragged-out, testudineous way,
knowing that things had gone wrong, that I was in a lot of trouble, and that the
lost ignition key was my grail and my salvation. The three or four succeeding blows
were mainly absorbed by my right buttock and the tough piece of bone at the
base of my spine.

Meanwhile, Digby vaulted the kissing bumpers and delivered a savage kung-   10
fu blow to the greasy character's collarbone. Digby had just finished a course in
martial arts for phys-ed credit and had spent the better part of the past two nights
telling us apocryphal tales of Bruce Lee types and of the raw power invested in
lightning blows shot from coiled wrists, ankles, and elbows. The greasy character
was unimpressed. He merely backed off a step, his face like a Toltec mask, and
laid Digby out with a single whistling roundhouse blow . . . but by now Jeff had
got into the act, and I was beginning to extricate myself from the dirt, a tinny
compound of shock, rage, and impotence wadded in my throat.

Jeff was on the guy's back, biting at his ear. Digby was on the ground, cursing.
I went for the tire iron I kept under the driver's seat. I kept it there because bad
characters always keep tire irons under the driver's seat, for just such an occasion
as this. Never mind that I hadn't been involved in a fight since sixth grade, when
a kid with a sleepy eye and two streams of mucus depending from his nostrils hit
me in the knee with a Louisville slugger°, never mind that I'd touched the tire
iron exactly twice before, to change tires: it was there. And I went for it.

I was terrified. Blood was beating in my ears, my hands were shaking, my

Westmoreland's decision . . . Khe Sanh: General William C. Westmoreland commanded United States
troops in Vietnam (1964–68). In late 1967 the North Vietnamese and Viet Cong forces attacked
Khe Sanh (or Khesanh) with a show of strength, causing Westmoreland to expend great effort to
defend a plateau of relatively little tactical importance.   *Rockette:* member of a dancing troupe in
the stage show at Radio City Music Hall, New York, famous for ability to kick fast and high with
wonderful coordination.   *Louisville slugger:* a brand of baseball bat.

heart turning over like a dirtbike in the wrong gear. My antagonist was shirtless, and a single cord of muscle flashed across his chest as he bent forward to peel Jeff from his back like a wet overcoat. "Motherfucker," he spat, over and over, and I was aware in that instant that all four of us—Digby, Jeff, and myself included—were chanting "motherfucker, motherfucker," as if it were a battle cry. (What happened next? the detective asks the murderer from beneath the turned-down brim of his porkpie hat. I don't know, the murderer says, something came over me. Exactly.)

Digby poked the flat of his hand in the bad character's face and I came at him like a kamikaze, mindless, raging, stung with humiliation—the whole thing, from the initial boot in the chin to this murderous primal instant involving no more than sixty hyperventilating, gland-flooding seconds—I came at him and brought the tire iron down across his ear. The effect was instantaneous, astonishing. He was a stunt man and this was Hollywood, he was a big grimacing toothy balloon and I was a man with a straight pin. He collapsed. Wet his pants. Went loose in his boots.

A single second, big as a zeppelin, floated by. We were standing over him in a circle, gritting our teeth, jerking our necks, our limbs and hands and feet twitching with glandular discharges. No one said anything. We just stared down at the guy, the car freak, the lover, the bad greasy character laid low. Digby looked at me; so did Jeff. I was still holding the tire iron, a tuft of hair clinging to the crook like dandelion fluff, like down. Rattled, I dropped it in the dirt, already envisioning the headlines, the pitted faces of the police inquisitors, the gleam of handcuffs, clank of bars, the big black shadows rising from the back of the cell . . . when suddenly a raw torn shriek cut through me like all the juice in all the electric chairs in the country.

It was the fox. She was short, barefoot, dressed in panties and a man's shirt. 15 "Animals!" she screamed, running at us with her fists clenched and wisps of blow-dried hair in her face. There was a silver chain round her ankle, and her toenails flashed in the glare of the headlights. I think it was the toenails that did it. Sure, the gin and the cannabis and even the Kentucky Fried may have had a hand in it, but it was the sight of those flaming toes that set us off—the toad emerging from the loaf in Virgin Spring°, lipstick smeared on a child; she was already tainted. We were on her like Bergman's deranged brothers—see no evil, hear none, speak none—panting, wheezing, tearing at her clothes, grabbing for flesh. We were bad characters, and we were scared and hot and three steps over the line—anything could have happened.

It didn't.

Before we could pin her to the hood of the car, our eyes masked with lust and greed and the purest primal badness, a pair of headlights swung into the lot. There we were, dirty, bloody, guilty, dissociated from humanity and civilization, the first of the Ur-crimes behind us, the second in progress, shreds of nylon panty and spandex brassiere dangling from our fingers, our flies open, lips licked—there we were, caught in the spotlight. Nailed.

Virgin Spring: film by Swedish director Ingmar Bergman.

We bolted. First for the car, and then, realizing we had no way of starting it, for the woods. I thought nothing. I thought escape. The headlights came at me like accusing fingers. I was gone.

Ram-bam-bam, across the parking lot, past the chopper and into the feculent undergrowth at the lake's edge, insects flying up in my face, weeds whipping, frogs and snakes and red-eyed turtles splashing off into the night: I was already ankle-deep in muck and tepid water and still going strong. Behind me, the girl's screams rose in intensity, disconsolate, incriminating, the screams of the Sabine women°, the Christian martyrs, Anne Frank° dragged from the garret. I kept going, pursued by those cries, imagining cops and bloodhounds. The water was up to my knees when I realized what I was doing: I was going to swim for it. Swim the breadth of Greasy Lake and hide myself in the thick clot of woods on the far side. They'd never find me there.

I was breathing in sobs, in gasps. The water lapped at my waist as I looked out over the moon-burnished ripples, the mats of algae that clung to the surface like scabs. Digby and Jeff had vanished. I paused. Listened. The girl was quieter now, screams tapering to sobs, but there were male voices, angry, excited, and the high-pitched ticking of the second car's engine. I waded deeper, stealthy, hunted, the ooze sucking at my sneakers. As I was about to take the plunge—at the very instant I dropped my shoulder for the first slashing stroke—I blundered into something. Something unspeakable, obscene, something soft, wet, moss-grown. A patch of weed? A log? When I reached out to touch it, it gave like a rubber duck, it gave like flesh. 20

In one of those nasty little epiphanies for which we are prepared by films and TV and childhood visits to the funeral home to ponder the shrunken painted forms of dead grandparents, I understood what it was that bobbed there so inadmissibly in the dark. Understood, and stumbled back in horror and revulsion, my mind yanked in six different directions (I was nineteen, a mere child, an infant, and here in the space of five minutes I'd struck down one greasy character and blundered into the waterlogged carcass of a second), thinking, The keys, the keys, why did I have to go and lose the keys? I stumbled back, but the muck took hold of my feet—a sneaker snagged, balance lost—and suddenly I was pitching face forward into the buoyant black mass, throwing out my hands in desperation while simultaneously conjuring the image of reeking frogs and muskrats revolving in slicks of their own deliquescing juices. AAAAArrrgh! I shot from the water like a torpedo, the dead man rotating to expose a mossy beard and eyes cold as the moon. I must have shouted out, thrashing around in the weeds, because the voices behind me suddenly became animated.

"What was that?"

"It's them, it's them: they tried to, tried to . . . *rape* me!" Sobs.

A man's voice, flat Midwestern accent. "You sons a bitches, we'll kill you!"

Sabine women: members of an ancient tribe in Italy, according to legend, forcibly carried off by the early Romans under Romulus to be their wives. The incident is depicted in a famous painting, "The Rape of the Sabine Women," by seventeenth-century French artist Nicolas Poussin.   *Anne Frank:* German Jewish girl (1929–1945) whose diary written during the Nazi occupation of the Netherlands later became world famous. She hid with her family in a secret attic in Amsterdam, but was caught by storm troopers and sent to the concentration camp at Belsen, where she died.

Frogs, crickets.

Then another voice, harsh, *r*-less, Lower East Side: "Motherfucker!" I recognized the verbal virtuosity of the bad greasy character in the engineer boots. Tooth chipped, sneakers gone, coated in mud and slime and worse, crouching breathless in the weeds waiting to have my ass thoroughly and definitively kicked and fresh from the hideous stinking embrace of a three-days-dead-corpse, I suddenly felt a rush of joy and vindication: the son of a bitch was alive! Just as quickly, my bowels turned to ice. "Come on out of there, you pansy mothers!" the bad greasy character was screaming. He shouted curses till he was out of breath.

The crickets started up again, then the frogs. I held my breath. All at once was a sound in the reeds, a swishing, a splash: thunk-a-thunk. They were throwing rocks. The frogs fell silent. I cradled my head. Swish, swish, thunk-a-thunk. A wedge of feldspar the size of a cue ball glanced off my knee. I bit my finger.

It was then that they turned to the car. I heard a door slam, a curse, and then the sound of the headlights shattering—almost a good-natured sound, celebratory, like corks popping from the necks of bottles. This was succeeded by the dull booming of the fenders, metal on metal, and then the icy crash of the windshield. I inched forward, elbows and knees, my belly pressed to the muck, thinking of guerrillas and commandos and *The Naked and the Dead*°. I parted the weeds and squinted the length of the parking lot.

The second car—it was a Trans-Am—was still running, its high beams washing the scene in a lurid stagy light. Tire iron flailing, the greasy bad character was laying into the side of my mother's Bel Air like an avenging demon, his shadow riding up the trunks of the trees. Whomp. Whomp. Whomp-whomp. The other two guys—blond types, in fraternity jackets—were helping out with tree branches and skull-sized boulders. One of them was gathering up bottles, rocks, muck, candy wrappers, used condoms, poptops, and other refuse and pitching it through the window on the driver's side. I could see the fox, a white bulb behind the windshield of the '57 Chevy. "Bobbie," she whined over the thumping, "come *on*." The greasy character paused a moment, took one good swipe at the left taillight, and then heaved the tire iron halfway across the lake. Then he fired up the '57 and was gone.

Blond head nodded at blond head. One said something to the other, too low 30 for me to catch. They were no doubt thinking that in helping to annihilate my mother's car they'd committed a fairly rash act, and thinking too that there were three bad characters connected with that very car watching them from the woods. Perhaps other possibilities occurred to them as well—police, jail cells, justices of the peace, reparations, lawyers, irate parents, fraternal censure. Whatever they were thinking, they suddenly dropped branches, bottles, and rocks and sprang for their car in unison, as if they'd choreographed it. Five seconds. That's all it took. The engine shrieked, the tires squealed, a cloud of dust rose from the rutted lot and then settled back on darkness.

I don't know how long I lay there, the bad breath of decay all around me, my jacket heavy as a bear, the primordial ooze subtly reconstituting itself to accommodate my upper thighs and testicles. My jaws ached, my knee throbbed, my coccyx was on fire. I contemplated suicide, wondered if I'd need bridgework,

The Naked and the Dead: novel (1948) by Norman Mailer, of U.S. Army life in World War II.

scraped the recesses of my brain for some sort of excuse to give my parents—a tree had fallen on the car, I was blinded by a bread truck, hit and run, vandals had got to it while we were playing chess at Digby's. Then I thought of the dead man. He was probably the only person on the planet worse off than I was. I thought about him, fog on the lake, insects chirring eerily, and felt the tug of fear, felt the darkness opening up inside me like a set of jaws. Who was he, I wondered, this victim of time and circumstance bobbing sorrowfully in the lake at my back. The owner of the chopper, no doubt, a bad older character come to this. Shot during a murky drug deal, drowned while drunkenly frolicking in the lake. Another headline. My car was wrecked; he was dead.

When the eastern half of the sky went from black to cobalt and the trees began to separate themselves from the shadows, I pushed myself up from the mud and stepped out into the open. By now the birds had begun to take over for the crickets, and dew lay slick on the leaves. There was a smell in the air, raw and sweet at the same time, the smell of the sun firing buds and opening blossoms. I contemplated the car. It lay there like a wreck along the highway, like a steel sculpture left over from a vanished civilization. Everything was still. This was nature.

I was circling the car, as dazed and bedraggled as the sole survivor of an air blitz, when Digby and Jeff emerged from the trees behind me. Digby's face was crosshatched with smears of dirt; Jeff's jacket was gone and his shirt was torn across the shoulder. They slouched across the lot, looking sheepish, and silently came up beside me to gape at the ravaged automobile. No one said a word. After a while Jeff swung open the driver's door and began to scoop the broken glass and garbage off the seat. I looked at Digby. He shrugged. "At least they didn't slash the tires," he said.

It was true: the tires were intact. There was no windshield, the headlights were staved in, and the body looked as if it had been sledge-hammered for a quarter a shot at the county fair, but the tires were inflated to regulation pressure. The car was drivable. In silence, all three of us bent to scrape the mud and shattered glass from the interior. I said nothing about the biker. When we were finished, I reached in my pocket for the keys, experienced a nasty stab of recollection, cursed myself, and turned to search the grass. I spotted them almost immediately, no more than five feet from the open door, glinting like jewels in the first tapering shaft of sunlight. There was no reason to get philosophical about it: I eased into the seat and turned the engine over.

It was at that precise moment that the silver Mustang with the flame decals rumbled into the lot. All three of us froze; then Digby and Jeff slid into the car and slammed the door. We watched as the Mustang rocked and bobbed across the ruts and finally jerked to a halt beside the forlorn chopper at the far end of the lot. "Let's go," Digby said. I hesitated, the Bel Air wheezing beneath me.

Two girls emerged from the Mustang. Tight jeans, stiletto heels, hair like frozen fur. They bent over the motorcycle, paced back and forth aimlessly, glanced once or twice at us, and then ambled over to where the reeds sprang up in a green fence round the perimeter of the lake. One of them cupped her hands to her mouth. "Al," she called. "Hey, Al!"

"Come on," Digby hissed. "Let's get out of here."

But it was too late. The second girl was picking her way across the lot, unsteady on her heels, looking up at us and then away. She was older—twenty-five or -six—and as she came closer we could see there was something wrong with her: she was stoned or drunk, lurching now and waving her arms for balance. I gripped the steering wheel as if it were the ejection lever of a flaming jet, and Digby spat out my name, twice, terse and impatient.

"Hi," the girl said.

We looked at her like zombies, like war veterans, like deaf-and-dumb pencil peddlers.

40

She smiled, her lips cracked and dry. "Listen," she said, bending from the waist to look in the window, "you guys seen Al?" Her pupils were pinpoints, her eyes glass. She jerked her neck. "That's his bike over there—Al's. You seen him?"

Al. I didn't know what to say. I wanted to get out of the car and retch, I wanted to go home to my parents' house and crawl into bed. Digby poked me in the ribs. "We haven't seen anybody," I said.

The girl seemed to consider this, reaching out a slim veiny arm to brace herself against the car. "No matter," she said, slurring the *t*'s, "he'll turn up." And then, as if she'd just taken stock of the whole scene—the ravaged car and our battered faces, the desolation of the place—she said: "Hey, you guys look like some pretty bad characters—been fightin', huh?" We stared straight ahead, rigid as catatonics. She was fumbling in her pocket and muttering something. Finally she held out a handful of tablets in glassine wrappers: "Hey, you want to party, you want to do some of these with me and Sarah?"

I just looked at her. I thought I was going to cry. Digby broke the silence. "No, thanks," he said, leaning over me. "Some other time."

I put the car in gear and it inched forward with a groan, shaking off pellets of glass like an old dog shedding water after a bath, heaving over the ruts on its worn springs, creeping toward the highway. There was a sheen of sun on the lake. I looked back. The girl was still standing there, watching us, her shoulders slumped, hand outstretched.

45

QUESTIONS

1. Around what year, would you say, was it that "courtesy and winning ways went out of style, when it was good to be bad, when you cultivated decadence like a taste"?
2. What is it about Digby and Jeff that inspires the narrator to call them "bad"?
3. Twice in "Greasy Lake"—in paragraphs 2 and 32—appear the words, "This was nature." What contrasts do you find between the "nature" of the narrator's earlier and later views?
4. What makes the narrator and his friends run off into the woods?
5. How does the heroes' encounter with the two girls at the end of the story differ from their earlier encounter with the girl from the blue Chevy? How do you account for the difference? When at the end of the story the girl offers to party with the three friends, what makes the narrator say, "I thought I was going to cry"?
6. How important to what happens in this story is Greasy Lake itself? What details about the lake and its shores strike you as particularly memorable (whether funny, disgusting, or both)?
7. The setting of Boyle's story is very different from that of James Joyce's "Araby." But in what ways do the two stories resemble each other?

SUGGESTIONS FOR WRITING

1. In a few paragraphs, not necessarily a complete essay or story, recreate a time and place you know intimately. Write about it like a fiction writer, giving reality to a setting in which a story is about to unfold. Imagine this setting in detail—or, if you can, go take a fresh look at it. Ensure that your reader can virtually see, hear, smell, and taste your chosen time and place.

   You might find it revealing to choose for your subject some nearby, present-day place that your audience will recognize, then read your paper aloud in class. If, without your dropping place names or giving them other obvious clues, your listeners can identify your subject, then you will have written well.

2. From a different chapter of this book, or from the Stories for Further Reading, choose a story that particularly interests you. Start out by defining for your reader its exact time and place. Then, in two or three more paragraphs, go on to show how this setting functions in the story. Does the setting supply atmosphere? Make things happen? Reveal the natures of certain people? Prompt a character to a realization? Suggested stories to work on (but your instructor may be saving some stories for other purposes and may wish to narrow or add to this list): "Gimpel the Fool," "A Clean, Well-Lighted Place," "Barn Burning," "Araby," "The Open Boat," "Young Goodman Brown," "The Chrysanthemums," "The Death of Ivan Ilych," "Where I'm Calling From," and "Roman Fever" (Stories for Further Reading).

3. Rewrite the first page or two of a story you have read, picking up the characters and putting them down in an entirely different setting. This new time and place might be the setting of another story, or it might be some actual place your readers will recognize. As you write, you might find yourself deciding to seek laughs, or you might decide to make the rewrite serious. You might try, for instance, a satire in the vein of *Monty Python*, shifting Hawthorne's "Young Goodman Brown" to the setting of Updike's "A & P." Or, without trying to be funny, you might rewrite the opening of Joyce's "Araby," setting the story in the neighborhood where you grew up.

   End with a short comment in answer to the question: "What did this exercise prove to you?" If your attempt should seem to you a failure, try to explain why the original story proved so reluctant to give up its time and place. (The purpose of this exercise is not to produce a new masterpiece, but to experience at first hand how the setting of a story works.)

5 Tone and Style

In many Victorian novels it was customary for some commentator, presumably the author, to interrupt the story from time to time, remarking upon the action, offering philosophic asides, or explaining the procedures to be followed in telling the story.

> Two hours later, Dorothea was seated in an inner room or boudoir of a handsome apartment in the Via Sistina. I am sorry to add that she was sobbing bitterly . . .
> —George Eliot in *Middlemarch* (1873)

> But let the gentle-hearted reader be under no apprehension whatsoever. It is not destined that Eleanor shall marry Mr. Slope or Bertie Stanhope.
> —Anthony Trollope in *Barchester Towers* (1857)

> And, as we bring our characters forward, I will ask leave, as a man and a brother, not only to introduce, but occasionally step down from the platform, and talk about them: if they are good and kindly, to love them and shake them by the hand; if they are silly, to laugh at them confidentially in the reader's sleeve; if they are wicked and heartless, to abuse them in the strongest terms which politeness admits of.
> —William Makepeace Thackeray in *Vanity Fair* (1847–1848)

Of course, the voice of this commentator was not identical with that of the "real life" author—the one toiling over an inkpot, worrying about publication deadlines and whether the rent would be paid. At times the living author might have been far different in personality from that usually wise and cheerful intruder who kept addressing the reader of the book. Much of the time, to be sure, the author probably agreed with whatever attitudes his alter ego expressed. But, in effect, the author created the character of a commentator to speak for him and through out the novel artfully sustained that character's voice.

Such intrusions, although sometimes useful to the "real" author and enjoyable to the reader, are today rare. Modern storytellers, carefully keeping out of sight, seldom comment on their plots and characters. Apparently they agree with Anton Chekhov that a writer should not judge the characters but should serve as their "impartial witness." And yet, no less definitely than Victorian novelists who introduced commentators, writers of effective stories no doubt have feelings toward their characters and events. The authors presumably care about these imaginary people and, in order for the story to grasp and sustain our interest, have to make us see these people in such a way that we, too, will care about them. When at the beginning of the short story "In Exile" Chekhov introduces us to a character, he does so with a description that arouses sympathy:

> The Tartar was worn out and ill, and wrapping himself in his rags, he talked about how good it was in the province of Simbirsk, and what a beautiful and clever wife he had left at home. He was not more than twenty-five, and in the firelight his pale, sickly face and woebegone expression made him seem like a boy.

Other than the comparison of the Tartar to a child, the details in this passage seem mostly factual: the young man's illness, ragged clothes, facial expression, and topics of conversation. But these details form a portrait that stirs pity. By his selection of these imaginary details out of countless others that he might have included, Chekhov firmly directs our feelings about the Tartar, so miserable and pathetic in his sickness and his homesickness. We cannot know, of course, exactly what the living Chekhov felt; but at least we can be sure that we are supposed to share the compassion and tenderness of the narrator—Chekhov's impartial (but human) witness.

Not only the author's choice of details may lead us to infer his or her attitude, but also choice of characters, events, and situations, and choice of words. When the narrator of Joseph Conrad's *Heart of Darkness* comes upon an African outpost littered with abandoned machines and notices "a boiler wallowing in the grass," the exact word *wallowing* conveys an attitude: that there is something swinish about this scene of careless waste. Whatever leads us to infer the author's attitude is commonly called **tone.** Like a tone of voice, the tone of a story may communicate amusement, anger, affection, sorrow, contempt. It implies the feelings of the author, so far as we can sense them. Those feelings may be similar to feelings expressed by the narrator of the story (or by any character), but sometimes they may be dissimilar, even sharply opposed. The characters in a story may regard an event as sad, but we sense that the author regards it as funny. To understand the tone of a story, then, is to understand some attitude more fundamental to the story than whatever attitude the characters explicitly declare.

The tone of a story, like a tone of voice, may convey not simply one attitude, but a medley. Reading "Gimpel the Fool" (Chapter Three), we have mingled feelings toward Gimpel and his "foolishness": amusement that Gimpel is so easily deceived; sympathy, perhaps, for his excessive innocence; admiration for his unwavering faith in God and fellow man. Often the tone of a literary story will be too rich and complicated to sum up in one or two words. But to try to describe the tone of such a story may be a useful way to penetrate to its center and to grasp the whole of it.

One of the clearest indications of the tone of a story is the **style** in which it is written. In general, style refers to the individual traits or characteristics of a piece of writing: to a writer's particular ways of managing words that we come to recognize as habitual or customary. A distinctive style marks the work of a fine writer: we can tell his or her work from that of anyone else. From one story to another, however, the writer may fittingly change style; and in some stories, style may be altered meaningfully as the story goes along. In his novel *As I Lay Dying*, William Faulkner changes narrators with every chapter, and he distinguishes the narrators one from another by giving each an individual style or manner of speaking. Though each narrator has his own style, the book as a whole demonstrates Faulkner's style as well. For instance, one chapter is written from the point of view of a small boy, Vardaman Bundren, member of a family of poor Mississippi tenant farmers, whose view of a horse in a barn reads like this:

> It is as though the dark were resolving him out of his integrity, into an unrelated scattering of components—snuffings and stampings; smells of cooling flesh and ammoniac hair; an illusion of a coordinated whole of splotched hide and strong bones within which, detached and secret and familiar, an *is* different from my *is*.[1]

How can a small boy unaccustomed to libraries use words like *integrity, components, illusion,* and *coordinated*? Elsewhere in the story, Vardaman says aloud, with no trace of literacy, "Hit was a-laying right there on the ground." Apparently, in the passage it is not the voice of the boy that we are hearing, but something resembling the voice of William Faulkner, elevated and passionate, expressing the boy's thoughts in a style that admits Faulknerian words.

Usually, *style* indicates a mode of expression: the language a writer uses. In this sense, the notion of style includes such traits as the length and complexity of sentences, and **diction,** or choice of words: abstract or concrete, bookish ("unrelated scattering of components") or close to speech ("Hit was a-laying right there on the ground"). Involved in the idea of style, too, is any habitual use of imagery, patterns of sound, figures of speech, or other devices.

Lately, several writers of realistic fiction, called **minimalists**—Ann Beattie, Raymond Carver, Mary Robison—have written with a flat, laid-back, unemotional tone, in an appropriately bare, unadorned style. Minimalists seem to give nothing but facts drawn from ordinary life, sometimes in picayune detail. Here is a sample passage, from Raymond Carver's story "A Small, Good Thing":

> She pulled into the driveway and cut the engine. She closed her eyes and leaned her head against the wheel for a minute. She listened to the ticking sounds the engine made as it began to cool. Then she got out of the car. She could hear the dog barking inside the house. She went to the front

[1]Modern Library edition (New York: Random, 1930) 379.

door, which was unlocked. She went inside and turned on lights and put on a kettle of water for tea. She opened some dog food and fed Slug on the back porch. The dog ate in hungry little smacks. It kept running into the kitchen to see that she was going to stay.

Explicit feeling and showy language are kept at a minimum here. Taken out of context, this description may strike you as banal, as if the writer himself was bored; but see how effectively it works as a part of Carver's entire story (page 278). As in all good writing, the style here seems a faithful mirror of what is said in it. At its best, such writing achieves "a hard-won reduction, a painful stripping away of richness, a baring of bone."[2]

To see what style means, compare the stories in this chapter by William Faulkner ("Barn Burning") and by Ernest Hemingway ("A Clean, Well-Lighted Place"). Faulkner frequently falls into a style in which a statement, as soon as uttered, is followed by another statement expressing the idea in a more emphatic way. Sentences are interrupted with parenthetical elements (asides, like this) thrust into them unexpectedly. At times, Faulkner writes of seemingly ordinary matters as if giving a speech in a towering passion. Here, from "Barn Burning," is a description of how a boy's father delivers a rug:

> "Don't you want me to help?" he whispered. His father did not answer and now he heard again that stiff foot striking the hollow portico with that wooden and clocklike deliberation, that outrageous overstatement of the weight it carried. The rug, hunched, not flung (the boy could tell that even in the darkness) from his father's shoulder struck the angle of wall and floor with a sound unbelievably loud, thunderous, then the foot again, unhurried and enormous; a light came on in the house and the boy sat, tense, breathing steadily and quietly and just a little fast, though the foot itself did not increase its beat at all, descending the steps now; now the boy could see him.

Faulkner is not merely indulging in language for its own sake. As you will find when you read the whole story, this rug delivery is vital to the story, and so too is the father's profound defiance—indicated by his walk. By devices of style—by *metaphor* and *simile* ("wooden and clocklike"), by exact qualification ("not flung"), by emphatic adjectives ("loud, thunderous")—Faulkner is carefully placing his emphases. By the words he selects to describe the father's stride, Faulkner directs how we feel toward the man and perhaps also indicates his own wondering but skeptical attitude toward a character whose very footfall is "outrageous" and "enormous." (Fond of long sentences like the last one in the quoted passage, Faulkner remarked that there are sentences that need to be written in the way a circus acrobat pedals a bicycle on a high wire: rapidly, so as not to fall off.)

Hemingway's famous style includes both short sentences and long, but when the sentences are long they tend to be relatively simple in construction. Hemingway likes long compound sentences (clause plus clause plus clause), sometimes joined with "and's." He interrupts such a sentence with a dependent clause or

[2]Letter in *The New York Times Book Review*, June 5, 1988.

a parenthetical element much less frequently than Faulkner does. The effect is like listening to speech:

> In the day time the street was dusty, but at night the dew settled the dust and the old man liked to sit late because he was deaf and now at night it was quiet and he felt the difference.

Hemingway is a master of swift, terse dialogue, and often casts whole scenes in the form of conversation. As if he were a closemouthed speaker unwilling to let his feelings loose, the narrator of a Hemingway story often addresses us in understatement, implying greater depths of feeling than he puts into words. Read the following story and you will see that its style and tone cannot be separated.

Ernest Hemingway

A CLEAN, WELL-LIGHTED PLACE   1933

Ernest Hemingway (1898–1961), born in Oak Park, Illinois, bypassed college to be a cub reporter. In World War I, as an eighteen-year-old volunteer ambulance driver in Italy, he was wounded in action. In 1922 he settled in Paris, then aswarm with writers; he later recalled that time in A Moveable Feast *(1964). Hemingway won swift acclaim for his early stories,* In Our Time *(1925), and for his first, perhaps finest, novel,* The Sun Also Rises *(1926), portraying a "lost generation" of postwar American drifters in France and Spain. For* Whom the Bell Tolls *(1940) depicts life during the Spanish Civil War. Hemingway became a celebrity, often photographed as a marlin fisherman or a lion hunter. A fan of bullfighting, he wrote two nonfiction books on the subject:* Death in the Afternoon *(1932) and* The Dangerous Summer *(1985). After World War II, with his fourth wife, journalist Mary Welsh, he made his home in Cuba,*

Ernest Hemingway

where he wrote The Old Man and the Sea *(1952). The Nobel prize for literature came to him in 1954. In 1961, mentally distressed and physically ailing, he shot himself. Hemingway brought a hard-bitten realism into American fiction. His heroes live dangerously, by personal codes of honor, courage, and endurance. Hemingway's distinctively crisp, unadorned style left American literature permanently changed.*

It was late and every one had left the café except an old man who sat in the shadow the leaves of the tree made against the electric light. In the day time the street was dusty, but at night the dew settled the dust and the old man liked to sit late because he was deaf and now at night it was quiet and he felt the difference. The two waiters inside the café knew that the old man was a little drunk, and while he was a good client they knew that if he became too drunk he would leave without paying, so they kept watch on him.

"Last week he tried to commit suicide," one waiter said.

"Why?"

"He was in despair."

"What about?"

"Nothing."   5

"How do you know it was nothing?"

"He has plenty of money."

They sat together at a table that was close against the wall near the door of the café and looked at the terrace where the tables were all empty except where the old man sat in the shadow of the leaves of the tree that moved slightly in the wind. A girl and a soldier went by in the street. The street light shone on the brass number on his collar. The girl wore no head covering and hurried beside him.

"The guard will pick him up," one waiter said.   10

"What does it matter if he gets what he's after?"

"He had better get off the street now. The guard will get him. They went by five minutes ago."

The old man sitting in the shadow rapped on his saucer with his glass. The younger waiter went over to him.

"What do you want?"

The old man looked at him. "Another brandy," he said.   15

"You'll be drunk," the waiter said. The old man looked at him. The waiter went away.

"He'll stay all night," he said to his colleague. "I'm sleepy now. I never get into bed before three o'clock. He should have killed himself last week."

The waiter took the brandy bottle and another saucer from the counter inside the café and marched out to the old man's table. He put down the saucer and poured the glass full of brandy.

"You should have killed yourself last week," he said to the deaf man. The old man motioned with his finger. "A little more," he said. The waiter poured on into the glass so that the brandy slopped over and ran down the stem into the top saucer of the pile. "Thank you," the old man said. The waiter took the bottle back inside the café. He sat down at the table with his colleague again.

"He's drunk now," he said.   20

"He's drunk every night."°

"He's drunk now," he said. "He's drunk every night": The younger waiter says both these lines. A device of Hemingway's style is sometimes to have a character pause, then speak again—as often happens in actual speech.

"What did he want to kill himself for?"

"How should I know?"

"How did he do it?"

"He hung himself with a rope." 25

"Who cut him down?"

"His niece."

"Why did they do it?"

"Fear for his soul."

"How much money has he got?" 30

"He's got plenty."

"He must be eighty years old."

"Anyway I should say he was eighty."°

"I wish he would go home. I never get to bed before three o'clock. What kind of hour is that to go to bed?"

"He stays up because he likes it." 35

"He's lonely. I'm not lonely. I have a wife waiting in bed for me."

"He had a wife once too."

"A wife would be no good to him now."

"You can't tell. He might be better with a wife."

"His niece looks after him." 40

"I know. You said she cut him down."

"I wouldn't want to be that old. An old man is a nasty thing."

"Not always. This old man is clean. He drinks without spilling. Even now, drunk. Look at him."

"I don't want to look at him. I wish he would go home. He has no regard for those who must work."

The old man looked from his glass across the square, then over at the waiters. 45

"Another brandy," he said, pointing to his glass. The waiter who was in a hurry came over.

"Finished," he said, speaking with that omission of syntax stupid people employ when talking to drunken people or foreigners. "No more tonight. Close now."

"Another," said the old man.

"No. Finished." The waiter wiped the edge of the table with a towel and shook his head.

The old man stood up, slowly counted the saucers, took a leather coin purse 50 from his pocket and paid for the drinks, leaving half a peseta tip.

The waiter watched him go down the street, a very old man walking unsteadily but with dignity.

"Why didn't you let him stay and drink?" the unhurried waiter asked. They were putting up the shutters. "It is not half-past two."

"I want to go home to bed."

"What is an hour?"

"He must be eighty years old." "Anyway I should say he was eighty": Is this another instance of the same character's speaking twice? Clearly, it is the younger waiter who says the next line, "I wish he would go home."

"More to me than to him." 55

"An hour is the same."

"You talk like an old man yourself. He can buy a bottle and drink at home."

"It's not the same."

"No, it is not," agreed the waiter with a wife. He did not wish to be unjust. He was only in a hurry.

"And you? You have no fear of going home before the usual hour?" 60

"Are you trying to insult me?"

"No, hombre, only to make a joke."

"No," the waiter who was in a hurry said, rising from pulling down the metal shutters. "I have confidence. I am all confidence."

"You have youth, confidence, and a job," the older waiter said. "You have everything."

"And what do you lack?" 65

"Everything but work."

"You have everything I have."

"No. I have never had confidence and I am not young."

"Come on. Stop talking nonsense and lock up."

"I am of those who like to stay late at the café," the older waiter said. "With 70 all those who do not want to go to bed. With all those who need a light for the night."

"I want to go home and into bed."

"We are of two different kinds," the older waiter said. He was not dressed to go home. "It is not only a question of youth and confidence although those things are very beautiful. Each night I am reluctant to close up because there may be some one who needs the café."

"Hombre, there are bodegas° open all night long."

"You do not understand. This is a clean and pleasant café. It is well lighted. The light is very good and also, now, there are shadows of the leaves."

"Good night," said the younger waiter. 75

"Good night," the other said. Turning off the electric light he continued the conversation with himself. It is the light of course but it is necessary that the place be clean and pleasant. You do not want music. Certainly you do not want music. Nor can you stand before a bar with dignity although that is all that is provided for these hours. What did he fear? It was not fear or dread. It was a nothing that he knew too well. It was all a nothing and a man was nothing too. It was only that and light was all it needed and a certain cleanness and order. Some lived in it and never felt it but he knew it all was nada y pues nada y nada y pues nada°. Our nada who are in nada, nada be thy name thy kingdom nada thy will be nada in nada as it is in nada. Give us this nada our daily nada and nada us our nada as we nada our nadas and nada us not into nada but deliver us from nada; pues nada. Hail nothing full of nothing, nothing is with thee. He smiled and stood before a bar with a shining steam pressure coffee machine.

---

bodegas: wineshops.   nada y pues . . . nada: nothing and then nothing and nothing and then nothing.

"What's yours?" asked the barman.

"Nada."

"Otro loco más°," said the barman and turned away.

"A little cup," said the waiter.   80

The barman poured it for him.

"The light is very bright and pleasant but the bar is unpolished," the waiter said.

The barman looked at him but did not answer. It was too late at night for conversation.

"You want another copita?°" the barman asked.

"No, thank you," said the waiter and went out. He disliked bars and bodegas.   85
A clean, well-lighted café was a very different thing. Now, without thinking further, he would go home to his room. He would lie in the bed and finally, with daylight, he would go to sleep. After all, he said to himself, it is probably only insomnia. Many must have it.

QUESTIONS

1. What besides insomnia makes the older waiter reluctant to go to bed? Comment especially on his meditation with its *nada* refrain. Why does he so well understand the old man's need for a café? What does the café represent for the two of them?
2. Compare the younger waiter and the older waiter in their attitudes toward the old man. Whose attitude do you take to be closer to that of the author? Even though Hemingway does not editorially state his own feelings, how does he make them clear to us?
3. Point to sentences that establish the style of the story. What is distinctive in them? What repetitions of words or phrases seem particularly effective? Does Hemingway seem to favor a simple or an erudite vocabulary?
4. What is the story's point of view? Discuss its appropriateness.

William Faulkner

BARN BURNING   1939

William Faulkner (1897–1962) receives a capsule biography on page 24, along with his story "A Rose for Emily." His "Barn Burning" is among his many contributions to the history of Yoknapatawpha, an imaginary Mississippi county in which the Sartorises and the de Spains are landed aristocrats living by a code of honor and the Snopeses— most of them—shiftless ne'er-do-wells.

The store in which the Justice of the Peace's court was sitting smelled of cheese. The boy, crouched on his nail keg at the back of the crowded room, knew he smelled cheese, and more: from where he sat he could see the ranked shelves close-packed with the solid, squat, dynamic shapes of tin cans whose labels his stomach read, not from the lettering which meant nothing to his mind but from the scarlet devils and the silver curve of fish—this, the cheese which he knew he smelled and the hermetic meat which his intestines believed he smelled coming in inter-

Otro loco más: another lunatic.   *copita:* little cup.

mittent gusts momentary and brief between the other constant one, the smell and sense just a little of fear because mostly of despair and grief, the old fierce pull of blood. He could not see the table where the Justice sat and before which his father and his father's enemy (*our enemy* he thought in that despair: *ourn! mine and hisn both! He's my father!*) stood, but he could hear them, the two of them that is, because his father had said no word yet:

"But what proof have you, Mr. Harris?"

"I told you. The hog got into my corn. I caught it up and sent it back to him. He had no fence that would hold it. I told him so, warned him. The next time I put the hog in my pen. When he came to get it I gave him enough wire to patch up his pen. The next time I put the hog up and kept it. I rode down to his house and saw the wire I gave him still rolled on to the spool in his yard. I told him he could have the hog when he paid me a dollar pound fee. That evening a nigger came with the dollar and got the hog. He was a strange nigger. He said, 'He say to tell you wood and hay kin burn.' I said, 'What?' 'That whut he say to tell you,' the nigger said. 'Wood and hay kin burn.' That night my barn burned. I got the stock out but I lost the barn."

"Where's the nigger? Have you got him?"

"He was a strange nigger, I tell you. I don't know what became of him."   5

"But that's not proof. Don't you see that's not proof?"

"Get that boy up here. He knows." For a moment the boy thought too that the man meant his older brother until Harris said, "Not him. The little one. The boy," and, crouching, small for his age, small and wiry like his father, in patched and faded jeans even too small for him, with straight, uncombed, brown hair and eyes gray and wild as storm scud, he saw the men between himself and the table part and become a lane of grim faces, at the end of which he saw the Justice, a shabby, collarless, graying man in spectacles, beckoning him. He felt no floor under his bare feet; he seemed to walk beneath the palpable weight of the grim turning faces. His father, still in his black Sunday coat donned not for the trial but for the moving, did not even look at him. *He aims for me to lie,* he thought, again with that frantic grief and despair. *And I will have to do hit.*

"What's your name, boy?" the Justice said.

"Colonel Sartoris Snopes," the boy whispered.

"Hey?" the Justice said. "Talk louder. Colonel Sartoris? I reckon anybody named   10 for Colonel Sartoris in this country can't help but tell the truth, can they?" The boy said nothing. *Enemy! Enemy!* he thought; for a moment he could not even see, could not see that the Justice's face was kindly nor discern that his voice was troubled when he spoke to the man named Harris: "Do you want me to question this boy?" But he could hear, and during those subsequent long seconds while there was absolutely no sound in the crowded little room save that of quiet and intent breathing it was as if he had swung outward at the end of a grape vine, over a ravine, and at the top of the swing had been caught in a prolonged instant of mesmerized gravity, weightless in time.

"No!" Harris said violently, explosively. "Damnation! Send him out of here!" Now time, the fluid world, rushed beneath him again, the voices coming to him again through the smell of cheese and sealed meat, the fear and despair and the old grief of blood:

"This case is closed. I can't find against you, Snopes, but I can give you advice. Leave this country and don't come back to it."

His father spoke for the first time, his voice cold and harsh, level, without emphasis: "I aim to. I don't figure to stay in a country among people who . . ." he said something unprintable and vile, addressed to no one.

"That'll do," the Justice said. "Take your wagon and get out of this country before dark. Case dismissed."

His father turned, and he followed the stiff black coat, the wiry figure walk- 15 ing a little stiffly from where a Confederate provost's man's musket ball had taken him in the heel on a stolen horse thirty years ago, followed the two backs now, since his older brother had appeared from somewhere in the crowd, no taller than the father but thicker, chewing tobacco steadily, between the two lines of grim-faced men and out of the store and across the worn gallery and down the sagging steps and among the dogs and half-grown boys in the mild May dust, where as he passed a voice hissed:

"Barn burner!"

Again he could not see, whirling; there was a face in a red haze, moonlike, bigger than the full moon, the owner of it half again his size, he leaping in the red haze toward the face, feeling no blow, feeling no shock when his head struck the earth, scrabbling up and leaping again, feeling no blow this time either and tasting no blood, scrabbling up to see the other boy in full flight and himself already leaping into pursuit as his father's hand jerked him back, the harsh, cold voice speaking above him: "Go get in the wagon."

It stood in a grove of locusts and mulberries across the road. His two hulking sisters in their Sunday dresses and his mother and her sister in calico and sunbonnets were already in it, sitting on and among the sorry residue of the dozen and more movings which even the boy could remember—the battered stove, the broken beds and chairs, the clock inlaid with mother-of-pearl, which would not run, stopped at some fourteen minutes past two o'clock of a dead and forgotten day and time, which had been his mother's dowry. She was crying, though when she saw him she drew her sleeve across her face and began to descend from the wagon. "Get back," the father said.

"He's hurt. I got to get some water and wash his . . . "

"Get back in the wagon," his father said. He got in too, over the tail-gate. 20 His father mounted to the seat where the older brother already sat and struck the gaunt mules two savage blows with the peeled willow, but without heat. It was not even sadistic; it was exactly that same quality which in later years would cause his descendants to over-run the engine before putting a motor car into motion, striking and reining back in the same movement. The wagon went on, the store with its quiet crowd of grimly watching men dropped behind; a curve in the road hid it. *Forever* he thought. *Maybe he's done satisfied now, now that he has* . . . stopping himself, not to say it aloud even to himself. His mother's hand touched his shoulder.

"Does hit hurt?" she said.

"Naw," he said. "Hit don't hurt. Lemme be."

"Can't you wipe some of the blood off before hit dries?"

"I'll wash to-night," he said. "Lemme be, I tell you."

The wagon went on. He did not know where they were going. None of them
ever did or ever asked, because it was always somewhere, always a house of sorts
waiting for them a day or two days or even three days away. Likely his father had
already arranged to make a crop on another farm before he . . . Again he had
to stop himself. He (the father) always did. There was something about his wolflike
independence and even courage when the advantage was at least neutral which
impressed strangers, as if they got from his latent ravening ferocity not so much
a sense of dependability as a feeling that his ferocious conviction in the rightness
of his own actions would be of advantage to all whose interest lay with his.

That night they camped, in a grove of oaks and beeches where a spring ran.
The nights were still cool and they had a fire against it, of a rail lifted from a
nearby fence and cut into lengths—a small fire, neat, niggard almost, a shrewd
fire; such fires were his father's habit and custom always, even in freezing weather.
Older, the boy might have remarked this and wondered why not a big one; why
should not a man who had not only seen the waste and extravagance of war, but
who had in his blood an inherent voracious prodigality with material not his own,
have burned everything in sight? Then he might have gone a step farther and
thought that that was the reason: that niggard blaze was the living fruit of nights
passed during those four years in the woods hiding from all men, blue and gray,
with his strings of horses (captured horses, he called them). And older still, he
might have divined the true reason: that the element of fire spoke to some deep
mainspring of his father's being, as the element of steel or of powder spoke to
other men, as the one weapon for the preservation of integrity, else breath were
not worth the breathing, and hence to be regarded with respect and used with
discretion.

But he did not think this now and he had seen those same niggard blazes
all his life. He merely ate his supper beside it and was already half asleep over
his iron plate when his father called him, and once more he followed the stiff
back, the stiff and ruthless limp, up the slope and on to the starlit road where,
turning, he could see his father against the stars but without face or depth—a shape
black, flat, and bloodless as though cut from tin in the iron folds of the frock-
coat which had not been made for him, the voice harsh like tin and without heat
like tin:

"You were fixing to tell them. You would have told him."

He didn't answer. His father struck him with the flat of his hand on the side
of the head, hard but without heat, exactly as he had struck the two mules at
the store, exactly as he would strike either of them with any stick in order to
kill a horse fly, his voice without heat or anger: "You're getting to be a man. You
got to learn. You got to learn to stick to your own blood or you ain't going to
have any blood to stick to you. Do you think either of them, any man there this
morning, would? Don't you know all they wanted was a chance to get at me because they knew I had them beat? Eh?" Later, twenty years later, he was to tell
himself, "If I had said they wanted only truth, justice, he would have hit me again."
But now he said nothing. He was not crying. He just stood there. "Answer me,"
his father said.

"Yes," he whispered. His father turned.

"Get on to bed. We'll be there tomorrow."

Tomorrow they were there. In the early afternoon the wagon stopped before a paintless two-room house identical almost with the dozen others it had stopped before even in the boy's ten years, and again, as on the other dozen occasions, his mother and aunt got down and began to unload the wagon, although his two sisters and his father and brother had not moved.

"Likely hit ain't fitten for hawgs," one of the sisters said.

"Nevertheless, fit it will and you'll hog it and like it," his father said. "Get out of them chairs and help your Ma unload."

The two sisters got down, big, bovine, in a flutter of cheap ribbons; one of them drew from the jumbled wagon bed a battered lantern, the other a worn broom. His father handed the reins to the older son and began to climb stiffly over the wheel. "When they get unloaded, take the team to the barn and feed them." Then he said, and at first the boy thought he was still speaking to his brother: "Come with me." 35

"Me?" he said.

"Yes," his father said. "You."

"Abner," his mother said. His father paused and looked back—the harsh level stare beneath the shaggy, graying, irascible brows.

"I reckon I'll have a word with the man that aims to begin tomorrow owning me body and soul for the next eight months."

They went back up the road. A week ago—or before last night, that is—he would have asked where they were going, but not now. His father had struck him before last night but never before had he paused afterward to explain why; it was as if the blow and the following calm, outrageous voice still rang, repercussed, divulging nothing to him save the terrible handicap of being young, the light weight of his few years, just heavy enough to prevent his soaring free of the world as it seemed to be ordered but not heavy enough to keep him footed solid in it, to resist it and try to change the course of its events. 40

Presently he could see the grove of oaks and cedars and the other flowering trees and shrubs where the house would be, though not the house yet. They walked beside a fence massed with honeysuckle and Cherokee roses and came to a gate swinging open between two brick pillars, and now, beyond a sweep of drive, he saw the house for the first time and at that instant he forgot his father and the terror and despair both, and even when he remembered his father again (who had not stopped) the terror and despair did not return. Because, for all the twelve movings, they had sojourned until now in a poor country, a land of small farms and fields and houses, and he had never seen a house like this before. *Hit's big as a courthouse* he thought quietly, with a surge of peace and joy whose reason he could not have thought into words, being too young for that: *They are safe from him. People whose lives are a part of this peace and dignity are beyond his touch, he no more to them than a buzzing wasp: capable of stinging for a little moment but that's all; the spell of this peace and dignity rendering even the barns and stable and cribs which belong to it impervious to the puny flames he might contrive* . . . this, the peace and joy, ebbing for an instant as he looked again at the stiff black back, the stiff and implacable limp of the figure which was not dwarfed by the house, for the reason that it had never looked big anywhere and which now, against the serene columned backdrop, had more than ever that impervious quality of something cut ruthlessly from tin, depthless, as though, sidewise to the sun, it would cast no shadow. Watching him, the boy remarked the absolutely undeviating course which his father held and saw the stiff foot come squarely down in a pile of fresh droppings where a horse had stood in the drive and which his father could have avoided by a simple change of stride. But it ebbed only a moment, though he could not have thought this into words either, walking on in the spell of the house, which he could even want but without envy, without sorrow, certainly never with that ravening and jealous rage which unknown to him walked in the ironlike black coat before him: *Maybe he will feel it too. Maybe it will even change him now from what maybe he couldn't help but be.*

They crossed the portico. Now he could hear his father's stiff foot as it came down on the boards with clocklike finality, a sound out of all proportion to the displacement of the body it bore and which was not dwarfed either by the white door before it, as though it had attained to a sort of vicious and ravening minimum not to be dwarfed by anything—the flat, wide, black hat, the formal coat of broadcloth which had once been black but which had now that friction-glazed greenish cast of the bodies of old house flies, the lifted sleeve which was too large, the lifted hand like a curled claw. The door opened so promptly that the boy knew the Negro must have been watching them all the time, an old man with neat grizzled hair, in a linen jacket, who stood barring the door with his body, saying, "Wipe yo foots, white man, fo you come in here. Major ain't home nohow."

"Get out of my way, nigger," his father said, without heat too, flinging the door back and the Negro also and entering, his hat still on his head. And now the boy saw the prints of the stiff foot on the doorjamb and saw them appear on the pale rug behind the machinelike deliberation of the foot which seemed to bear (or transmit) twice the weight which the body compassed. The Negro was shouting "Miss Lula! Miss Lula!" somewhere behind them, then the boy, deluged as though by a warm wave by a suave turn of the carpeted stair and a pendant glitter of chandeliers and a mute gleam of gold frames, heard the swift feet and saw her too, a lady—perhaps he had never seen her like before either—in a gray, smooth gown with lace at the throat and an apron tied at the waist and the sleeves turned back, wiping cake or biscuit dough from her hands with a towel as she came up the hall, looking not at his father at all but at the tracks on the blond rug with an expression of incredulous amazement.

"I tried," the Negro cried. "I tole him to . . . "

"Will you please go away?" she said in a shaking voice. "Major de Spain is not at home. Will you please go away?"

His father had not spoken again. He did not speak again. He did not even look at her. He just stood stiff in the center of the rug, in his hat, the shaggy iron-gray brows twitching slightly above the pebble-colored eyes as he appeared to examine the house with brief deliberation. Then with the same deliberation he turned; the boy watched him pivot on the good leg and saw the stiff foot drag around the arc of the turning, leaving a final long and fading smear. His father never looked at it, he never once looked down at the rug. The Negro held the door. It closed behind them, upon the hysteric and indistinguishable woman-wail. His father stopped at the top of the steps and scraped his boot clean on the edge of it. At the gate he stopped again. He stood for a moment, planted stiffly on the stiff foot, looking back at the house. "Pretty and white, ain't it?" he said. "That's sweat. Nigger sweat. Maybe it ain't white enough yet to suit him. Maybe he wants to mix some white sweat with it."

Two hours later the boy was chopping wood behind the house within which his mother and aunt and the two sisters (the mother and aunt, not the two girls, he knew that; even at this distance and muffled by walls the flat loud voices of the two girls emanated an incorrigible idle inertia) were setting up the stove to prepare a meal, when he heard the hooves and saw the linen-clad man on a fine sorrel mare, whom he recognized even before he saw the rolled rug in front of the Negro youth following on a fat bay carriage horse—a suffused, angry face vanishing, still at full gallop, beyond the corner of the house where his father and brother were sitting in the two tilted chairs; and a moment later, almost before he could have put the axe down, he heard the hooves again and watched the sorrel mare go back out of the yard, already galloping again. Then his father began to shout one of the sisters' names, who presently emerged backward from the kitchen door dragging the rolled rug along the ground by one end while the other sister walked behind it.

"If you ain't going to tote, go on and set up the wash pot," the first said.

"You, Sarty!" the second shouted. "Set up the wash pot!" His father appeared at the door, framed against that shabbiness, as he had been against that other bland perfection, impervious to either, the mother's anxious face at his shoulder.

"Go on," the father said. "Pick it up." The two sisters stooped, broad, lethar- 50 gic; stooping, they presented an incredible expanse of pale cloth and a flutter of tawdry ribbons.

"If I thought enough of a rug to have to git hit all the way from France I wouldn't keep hit where folks coming in would have to tromp on hit," the first said. They raised the rug.

"Abner," the mother said. "Let me do it."

"You go back and git dinner," his father said. "I'll tend to this."

From the woodpile through the rest of the afternoon the boy watched them, the rug spread flat in the dust beside the bubbling wash pot, the two sisters stooping over it with that profound and lethargic reluctance, while the father stood over them in turn, implacable and grim, driving them though never raising his voice again. He could smell the harsh homemade lye they were using; he saw his mother come to the door once and look toward them with an expression not anxious now but very like despair; he saw his father turn, and he fell to with the axe and saw from the corner of his eye his father raise from the ground a flattish fragment of field stone and examine it and return to the pot, and this time his mother actually spoke: "Abner. Abner. Please don't. Please, Abner."

Then he was done too. It was dusk; the whippoorwills had already begun. 55 He could smell coffee from the room where they would presently eat the cold food remaining from the mid-afternoon meal, though when he entered the house he realized they were having coffee again probably because there was a fire on the hearth, before which the rug now lay spread over the backs of the two chairs. The tracks of his father's foot were gone. Where they had been were now long, water-cloudy scoriations resembling the sporadic course of a lilliputian mowing machine.

It still hung there while they ate the cold food and then went to bed, scattered without order or claim up and down the two rooms, his mother in one bed, where his father would later lie, the older brother in the other, himself, the aunt, and the two sisters on pallets on the floor. But his father was not in bed yet. The last thing the boy remembered was the depthless, harsh silhouette of the hat and coat bending over the rug and it seemed to him that he had not even closed his eyes when the silhouette was standing over him, the fire almost dead behind it, the stiff foot prodding him awake. "Catch up the mule," his father said.

When he returned with the mule his father was standing in the black door, the rolled rug over his shoulder. "Ain't you going to ride?" he said.

"No. Give me your foot."

He bent his knee into his father's hand, the wiry, surprising power flowed smoothly, rising, he rising with it, on to the mule's bare back (they had owned a saddle once; the boy could remember it though not when or where) and with the same effortlessness his father swung the rug up in front of him. Now in the starlight they retraced the afternoon's path, up the dusty road rife with honeysuckle, through the gate and up the black tunnel of the drive to the lightless house, where he sat on the mule and felt the rough warp of the rug drag across his thighs and vanish.

"Don't you want me to help?" he whispered. His father did not answer and now he heard again that stiff foot striking the hollow portico with that wooden and clocklike deliberation, that outrageous overstatement of the weight it carried. The rug, hunched, not flung (the boy could tell that even in the darkness) from his father's shoulder struck the angle of wall and floor with a sound unbelievably loud, thunderous, then the foot again, unhurried and enormous; a light came on in the house and the boy sat, tense, breathing steadily and quietly and just a little fast, though the foot itself did not increase its beat at all, descending the steps now; now the boy could see him.

"Don't you want to ride now?" he whispered. "We kin both ride now," the light within the house altering now, flaring up and sinking. *He's coming down the stairs now,* he thought. He had already ridden the mule up beside the horse block; presently his father was up behind him and he doubled the reins over and slashed the mule across the neck, but before the animal could begin to trot the hard, thin arm came around him, the hard, knotted hand jerking the mule back to a walk.

In the first red rays of the sun they were in the lot, putting plow gear on the mules. This time the sorrel mare was in the lot before he heard it at all, the rider collarless and even bareheaded, trembling, speaking in a shaking voice as the woman in the house had done, his father merely looking up once before stooping again to the hame he was buckling, so that the man on the mare spoke to his stooping back:

"You must realize you have ruined that rug. Wasn't there anybody here, any of your women . . . " he ceased, shaking, the boy watching him, the older brother leaning now in the stable door, chewing, blinking slowly and steadily at nothing apparently. "It cost a hundred dollars. But you never had a hundred dollars. You never will. So I'm going to charge you twenty bushels of corn against your crop. I'll add it in your contract and when you come to the commissary you can sign it. That won't keep Mrs. de Spain quiet but maybe it will teach you to wipe your feet off before you enter her house again."

Then he was gone. The boy looked at his father, who still had not spoken or even looked up again, who was now adjusting the logger-head in the hame.

"Pap," he said. His father looked at him—the inscrutable face, the shaggy brows beneath where the gray eyes glinted coldly. Suddenly the boy went toward him, fast, stopping as suddenly. "You done the best you could!" he cried. "If he wanted hit done different why didn't he wait and tell you how? He won't git no twenty bushels! He won't git none! We'll gather hit and hide hit! I kin watch . . . "

"Did you put the cutter back in that straight stock like I told you?"

"No, sir," he said.

"Then go do it."

That was Wednesday. During the rest of that week he worked steadily, at what was within his scope and some which was beyond it, with an industry that did not need to be driven nor even commanded twice; he had this from his mother, with the difference that some at least of what he did he liked to do, such as splitting wood with the half-size axe which his mother and aunt had earned, or saved money somehow, to present him with at Christmas. In company with the two older women (and on one afternoon, even one of the sisters), he built pens for the shoat and the cow which were a part of his father's contract with the landlord, and one afternoon, his father being absent, gone somewhere on one of the mules, he went to the field.

They were running a middle buster now, his brother holding the plow straight while he handled the reins, and walking beside the straining mule, the rich black soil shearing cool and damp against his bare ankles, he thought *Maybe this is the end of it. Maybe even that twenty bushels that seems hard to have to pay for just a rug will be a cheap price for him to stop forever and always from being what he used to be;* thinking, dreaming now, so that his brother had to speak sharply to him to mind the mule: *Maybe he even won't collect the twenty bushels. Maybe it will all add up and balance and vanish—corn, rug, fire; the terror and grief; the being pulled two ways like between two teams of horses—gone, done with for ever and ever.*

Then it was Saturday; he looked up from beneath the mule he was harnessing and saw his father in the black coat and hat. "Not that," his father said. "The wagon gear." And then, two hours later, sitting in the wagon bed behind his father and brother on the seat, the wagon accomplished a final curve, and he saw the weathered paintless store with its tattered tobacco- and patent-medicine posters and the tethered wagons and saddle animals below the gallery. He mounted the gnawed steps behind his father and brother, and there again was the lane of quiet, watching faces for the three of them to walk through. He saw the man in spectacles sitting at the plank table and he did not need to be told this was a Justice of the Peace; he sent one glare of fierce, exultant, partisan defiance at the man in collar and cravat now, whom he had seen but twice before in his life, and that on a galloping horse, who now wore on his face an expression not of rage but of amazed unbelief which the boy could not have known was at the incredible circumstance of being sued by one of his own tenants, and came and stood against his father and cried at the Justice: "He ain't done it! He ain't burnt . . . "

"Go back to the wagon," his father said.

"Burnt?" the Justice said. "Do I understand this rug was burned too?"

"Does anybody here claim it was?" his father said. "Go back to the wagon." But he did not, he merely retreated to the rear of the room, crowded as that other had been, but not to sit down this time, instead, to stand pressing among the motionless bodies, listening to the voices:

"And you claim twenty bushels of corn is too high for the damage you did to the rug?"   75

"He brought the rug to me and said he wanted the tracks washed out of it. I washed the tracks out and took the rug back to him."

"But you didn't carry the rug back to him in the same condition it was in before you made the tracks on it."

His father did not answer, and now for perhaps half a minute there was no sound at all save that of breathing, the faint, steady suspiration of complete and intent listening.

"You decline to answer that, Mr. Snopes?" Again his father did not answer. "I'm going to find against you, Mr. Snopes. I'm going to find that you were responsible for the injury to Major de Spain's rug and hold you liable for it. But twenty bushels of corn seems a little high for a man in your circumstances to have to pay. Major de Spain claims it cost a hundred dollars. October corn will be worth about fifty cents. I figure that if Major De Spain can stand a ninety-five dollar loss on something he paid cash for, you can stand a five-dollar loss you haven't earned yet. I hold you in damages to Major de Spain to the amount of ten bushels of corn over and above your contract with him, to be paid to him out of your crop at gathering time. Court adjourned."

It had taken no time hardly, the morning was but half begun. He thought   80
they would return home and perhaps back to the field, since they were late, far behind all other farmers. But instead his father passed on behind the wagon, merely indicating with his hand for the older brother to follow with it, and crossed the road toward the blacksmith shop opposite, pressing on after his father, overtaking him, speaking, whispering up at the harsh, calm face beneath the weathered hat: "He won't git no ten bushels either. He won't git one. We'll . . . " until his father glanced for an instant down at him, the face absolutely calm, the grizzled eyebrows tangled above the cold eyes, the voice almost pleasant, almost gentle:

"You think so? Well, we'll wait till October anyway."

The matter of the wagon—the setting of a spoke or two and the tightening of the tires—did not take long either, the business of the tires accomplished by driving the wagon into the spring branch behind the shop and letting it stand there, the mules nuzzling into the water from time to time, and the boy on the seat with the idle reins, looking up the slope and through the sooty tunnel of the shed where the slow hammer rang and where his father sat on an upended cypress bolt, easily, either talking or listening, still sitting there when the boy brought the dripping wagon up out of the branch and halted it before the door.

"Take them on to the shade and hitch," his father said. He did so and returned. His father and the smith and a third man squatting on his heels inside the door were talking, about crops and animals; the boy, squatting too in the ammoniac dust and hoof-parings and scales of rust, heard his father tell a long and unhurried story out of the time before the birth of the older brother even when he had been a professional horsetrader. And then his father came up beside him where he stood before a tattered last year's circus poster on the other side of the store, gazing rapt and quiet at the scarlet horses, the incredible poisings and convulsions of tulle and tights and the painted leers of comedians, and said, "It's time to eat."

But not at home. Squatting beside his brother against the front wall, he watched his father emerge from the store and produce from a paper sack a segment of cheese and divide it carefully and deliberately into three with his pocket knife and produce crackers from the same sack. They all three squatted on the gallery and ate, slowly, without talking; then in the store again, they drank from a tin dipper tepid water smelling of the cedar bucket and of living beech trees. And still they did not go home. It was a horse lot this time, a tall rail fence upon and along which men stood and sat and out of which one by one horses were led, to be walked and trotted and then cantered back and forth along the road while the slow swapping and buying went on and the sun began to slant westward, they—the three of them—watching and listening, the older brother with his muddy eyes and his steady, inevitable tobacco, the father commenting now and then on certain of the animals, to no one in particular.

It was after sundown when they reached home. They ate supper by lamplight, 85 then, sitting on the doorstep, the boy watched the night fully accomplish, listening to the whippoorwills and the frogs, when he heard his mother's voice: "Abner! No! No! Oh, God. Oh, God. Abner!" and he rose, whirled, and saw the altered light through the door where a candle stub now burned in a bottle neck on the table and his father, still in the hat and coat, at once formal and burlesque as though dressed carefully for some shabby and ceremonial violence, emptying the reservoir of the lamp back into the five-gallon kerosene can from which it had been filled, while the mother tugged at his arm until he shifted the lamp to the other hand and flung her back, not savagely or viciously, just hard, into the wall, her hands flung out against the wall for balance, her mouth open and in her face the same quality of hopeless despair as had been in her voice. Then his father saw him standing in the door.

"Go to the barn and get that can of oil we were oiling the wagon with," he said. The boy did not move. Then he could speak.

"What . . . " he cried. "What are you . . . "

"Go get that oil," his father said. "Go."

Then he was moving, running, outside the house, toward the stable: this the old habit, the old blood which he had not been permitted to choose for himself, which had been bequeathed him willy nilly and which had run for so long (and who knew where, battening on what of outrage and savagery and lust) before it came to him. *I could keep on*, he thought. *I could run on and on and never look back, never need to see his face again. Only I can't. I can't*, the rusted can in his hand now, the liquid sploshing in it as he ran back to the house and into it, into the sound of his mother's weeping in the next room, and handed the can to his father.

"Ain't you going to even send a nigger?" he cried. "At least you sent a nigger 90 before!"

This time his father didn't strike him. The hand came even faster than the blow had, the same hand which had set the can on the table with almost excruciating care flashing from the can toward him too quick for him to follow it, gripping him by the back of his shirt and on to tiptoe before he had seen it quit the can, the face stooping at him in breathless and frozen ferocity, the cold, dead voice speaking over him to the older brother who leaned against the table, chewing with that steady, curious, sidewise motion of cows:

"Empty the can into the big one and go on. I'll catch up with you."

"Better tie him up to the bedpost," the brother said.

"Do like I told you," the father said. Then the boy was moving, his bunched shirt and the hard, bony hand between his shoulder-blades, his toes just touching the floor, across the room and into the other one, past the sisters sitting with spread heavy thighs in the two chairs over the cold hearth, and to where his mother and aunt sat side by side on the bed, the aunt's arm about his mother's shoulders.

"Hold him," the father said. The aunt made a startled movement. "Not you," the father said. "Lennie. Take hold of him. I want to see you do it." His mother took him by the wrist. "You'll hold him better than that. If he gets loose don't you know what he is going to do? He will go up yonder." He jerked his head toward the road. "Maybe I'd better tie him."

"I'll hold him," his mother whispered.

"See you do then." Then his father was gone, the stiff foot heavy and measured upon the boards, ceasing at last.

Then he began to struggle. His mother caught him in both arms, he jerking and wrenching at them. He would be stronger in the end, he knew that. But he had no time to wait for it. "Lemme go!" he cried. "I don't want to have to hit you!"

"Let him go!" the aunt said. "If he don't go, before God, I am going up there myself!"

"Don't you see I can't?" his mother cried. "Sarty! Sarty! No! No! Help me, Lizzie!"

Then he was free. His aunt grasped at him but it was too late. He whirled, running, his mother stumbled forward on to her knees behind him, crying to the nearer sister: "Catch him, Net! Catch him!" But that was too late too, the sister (the sisters were twins, born at the same time, yet either of them now gave the impression of being, encompassing as much living meat and volume and weight as any other two of the family) not yet having begun to rise from the chair, her head, face, alone merely turned, presenting to him in the flying instant an astonishing expanse of young female features untroubled by any surprise even, wearing only an expression of bovine interest. Then he was out of the room, out of the house, in the mild dust of the starlit road and the heavy rifeness of honeysuckle, the pale ribbon unspooling with terrific slowness under his running feet, reaching the gate at last and turning in, running, his heart and lungs drumming, on up the drive toward the lighted house, the lighted door. He did not knock, he burst in, sobbing for breath, incapable for the moment of speech; he saw the astonished face of the Negro in the linen jacket without knowing when the Negro had appeared.

"De Spain!" he cried, panted. "Where's . . ." then he saw the white man too emerging from a white door down the hall. "Barn!" he cried. "Barn!"

"What?" the white man said. "Barn?"

"Yes!" the boy cried. "Barn!"

"Catch him!" the white man shouted.

But it was too late this time too. The Negro grasped his shirt, but the entire sleeve, rotten with washing, carried away, and he was out that door too and in the drive again, and had actually never ceased to run even while he was screaming into the white man's face.

Behind him the white man was shouting. "My horse! Fetch my horse!" and he thought for an instant of cutting across the park and climbing the fence into the road, but he did not know the park nor how the vine-massed fence might be and he dared not risk it. So he ran on down the drive, blood and breath roaring; presently he was in the road again though he could not see it. He could not hear either: the galloping mare was almost upon him before he heard her, and even then he held his course, as if the very urgency of his wild grief and need must in a moment more find him wings, waiting until the ultimate instant to hurl himself aside and into the weed-choked roadside ditch as the horse thundered past and on, for an instant in furious silhouette against the stars, the tranquil early summer night sky which, even before the shape of the horse and rider vanished, stained abruptly and violently upward: a long, swirling roar incredible and soundless, blotting the stars, and he springing up and into the road again, running again, knowing it was too late yet still running even after he heard the shot and an instant later, two shots, pausing now without knowing he had ceased to run, crying, "Pap! Pap!", running again before he knew he had begun to run, stumbling, tripping over something and scrabbling up again without ceasing to run, looking backward over his shoulder at the glare as he got up, running on among the invisible trees, panting, sobbing, "Father! Father!"

At midnight he was sitting on the crest of a hill. He did not know it was midnight and he did not know how far he had come. But there was no glare behind him now and he sat now, his back toward what he had called home for four days anyhow, his face toward the dark woods which he would enter when breath was strong again, small, shaking steadily in the chill darkness, hugging himself into the remainder of his thin, rotten shirt, the grief and despair now no longer terror and fear but just grief and despair. *Father. My father*, he thought. "He was brave!" he cried suddenly, aloud but not loud, no more than a whisper. "He was! He was in the war! He was in Colonel Sartoris' cav'ry!" not knowing that his father had gone to that war a private in the fine old European sense, wearing no uniform, admitting the authority of and giving fidelity to no man or army or flag, going to war as Malbrouck° himself did: for booty—it meant nothing and less than nothing to him if it were enemy booty or his own.

The slow constellations wheeled on. It would be dawn and then sun-up after a while and he would be hungry. But that would be tomorrow and now he was only cold, and walking would cure that. His breathing was easier now and he decided to get up and go on, and then he found that he had been asleep because he knew it was almost dawn, the night almost over. He could tell that from the whippoorwills. They were everywhere now among the dark trees below him, constant and inflectioned and ceaseless, so that, as the instant for giving over to the

---

Malbrouck: John Churchill, Duke of Marlborough (1650–1722), English general victorious in the Battle of Blenheim (1704), which triumph drove the French army out of Germany. The French called him Malbrouck, a name they found easier to pronounce.

day birds drew nearer and nearer, there was no interval at all between them. He got up. He was a little stiff, but walking would cure that too as it would the cold, and soon there would be the sun. He went on down the hill, toward the dark woods within which the liquid silver voices of the birds called unceasing—the rapid and urgent beating of the urgent and quiring heart of the late spring night. He did not look back.

Questions

1. After delivering his warning to Major de Spain, the boy Snopes does not actually witness what happens to his father and brother, nor what happens to the Major's barn. But what do you assume does happen? What evidence is given in the story?
2. What do you understand to be Faulkner's opinion of Abner Snopes? Make a guess, indicating details in the story that convey attitudes.
3. Which adjectives best describe the general tone of the story: calm, amused, disinterested, scornful, marveling, excited, impassioned? Point out passages that may be so described. What do you notice about the style in which these passages are written?
4. In tone and style, how does "Barn Burning" compare with Faulkner's story "A Rose for Emily" (Chapter Two)? To what do you attribute any differences?
5. Suppose that, instead of "Barn Burning," Faulkner had written another story told by Abner Snopes in the first person. Why would such a story need a style different from that of "Barn Burning"? (Suggestion: Notice Faulkner's descriptions of Abner Swopes's voice.)
6. Although "Barn Burning" takes place some thirty years after the Civil War, how does the war figure in it?

Irony

If a friend declares, "Oh, sure, I just *love* to have four papers fall due on the same day," you detect that the statement contains **irony.** This is **verbal irony,** the most familiar kind, in which we understand the speaker's meaning to be far from the usual meaning of the words—in this case, quite the opposite. (When the irony is found, as here, in a somewhat sour statement tinged with mockery, it is called **sarcasm.)**

Irony, of course, occurs in writing as well as in conversation. When in a comic moment in Isaac Bashevis Singer's "Gimpel the Fool" (Chapter Three) the sexton announces, "The wealthy Reb Gimpel invites the congregation to a feast in honor of the birth of a son," the people at the synagogue burst into laughter. They know that Gimpel, in contrast to the sexton's words, is not a wealthy man but a humble baker; that the son is not his own but his wife's lover's; and that the birth brings no honor to anybody. Verbal irony, then, implies a contrast or discrepancy between what is *said* and what is *meant.* But stories often contain other kinds of irony besides such verbal irony. A situation, for example, can be ironic if it contains some wry contrast or incongruity. In Jack London's "To Build a Fire" (Chapter Four), it is ironic that a freezing man, desperately trying to strike a match to light a fire and save himself, accidentally ignites all his remaining matches.

An entire story may be told from an **ironic point of view.** Whenever we sense a sharp distinction between the narrator of a story and the author, irony is likely to occur—especially when the narrator is telling us something that we are clearly expected to doubt or to interpret very differently. In "Gimpel the Fool," Gimpel (who tells his own story) keeps insisting on trusting people; but the author, a shrewder observer, makes it clear to us that the people Gimpel trusts are only tricking him. (This irony, by the way, does not prevent Gimpel from expressing a few things that Isaac Bashevis Singer believes, and perhaps expects us to believe.) And when we read Hemingway's "A Clean, Well-Lighted Place," surely we feel that most of the time the older waiter speaks for the author. Though the waiter gives us a respectful, compassionate view of a lonely old man, and we don't doubt that the view is Hemingway's, still, in the closing lines of the story we are reminded that author and waiter are not identical. Musing on the sleepless night ahead of him, the waiter tries to shrug off his problem—"After all, it is probably only insomnia"—but the reader, who recalls the waiter's bleak view of *nada*, nothingness, knows that it certainly isn't mere insomnia that keeps him awake but a dread of solitude and death. At that crucial moment, Hemingway and the older waiter part company, and we perceive an ironic point of view, and also a verbal irony, "After all, it is probably only insomnia."

Storytellers are sometimes fond of ironic twists of fate—developments that reveal a terrible distance between what people deserve and what they get, between what is and what ought to be. In the novels of Thomas Hardy, some hostile fate keeps playing tricks to thwart the main characters. In *Tess of the D'Urbervilles*, an all-important letter, thrust under a door, by chance slides beneath a carpet and is not received. An obvious prank of fate occurs in O. Henry's short story "The Gift of the Magi," in which a young wife sells her beautiful hair to buy her poor young husband a watch chain for Christmas, not knowing that, to buy combs for her hair, he has sold his watch. Such an irony is sometimes called an **irony of fate** or a **cosmic irony,** for it suggests that some malicious fate (or other spirit in the universe) is deliberately frustrating human efforts. (In O. Henry's story, however, the twist of fate leads to a happy ending; for the author suggests that, by their futile sacrifices, the lovers are drawn closer together.) Evidently, there is an irony of fate in the servant's futile attempt to escape Death in the fable "The Appointment in Samarra," and perhaps in the flaring up of the all precious matches in "To Build a Fire" as well.

To notice an irony gives pleasure. It may move us to laughter, make us feel wonder, or arouse our sympathy. By so involving us, irony—whether in a statement, a situation, an unexpected event, or a point of view—can render a story more likely to strike us, to affect us, and to be remembered.

James Joyce

James Joyce (1884–1941) quit Ireland at twenty to spend his mature life in voluntary exile on the continent, writing of nothing but Dublin, where he was born. In Trieste, Zurich, and Paris, he supported his family with difficulty, sometimes teaching in Berlitz language schools, until his writing won him fame and wealthy patrons. At first Joyce met difficulty in getting his work printed and circulated. Publication of Dubliners (1914), the collection of stories that includes "Araby," was delayed seven years because its prospective Irish publisher feared libel suits. (The book depicts local citizens, some of them recognizable, and views Dubliners mostly as a thwarted, self-deceived lot.) Portrait of the Artist as a Young Man (1916), a novel of thinly veiled autobiography, recounts a young intellectual's breaking away from country, church, and

James Joyce

home. Joyce's immense comic novel, Ulysses (1922), a parody of the Odyssey, spans eighteen hours in the life of a wandering Jew, a Dublin seller of advertising. Frank about sex but untitillating, the book was banned at one time by the U.S. Post Office. Joyce's later work stepped up its demands on readers. The challenging Finnegan's Wake (1939), if read aloud, sounds as though a learned comic poet were sleep-talking, jumbling several languages. Joyce was an innovator whose bold experiments showed many other writers possibilities in fiction that had not earlier been imagined.

North Richmond Street, being blind°, was a quiet street except at the hour when the Christian Brothers' School set the boys free. An uninhabited house of two stories stood at the blind end, detached from its neighbors in a square ground. The other houses of the street, conscious of decent lives within them, gazed at one another with brown imperturbable faces.

The former tenant of our house, a priest, had died in the back drawing-room. Air, musty from having long been enclosed, hung in all the rooms, and the waste room behind the kitchen was littered with old useless papers. Among these I found a few paper-covered books, the pages of which were curled and damp: *The Abbot*, by Walter Scott, *The Devout Communicant* and *The Memoirs of Vidocq°*. I liked the last best because its leaves were yellow. The wild garden behind the house

---

being blind: being a dead-end street.   *The Abbot . . . Vidocq*: a popular historical romance (1820); a book of pious meditations by an eighteenth-century English Franciscan, Pacificus Baker; and the autobiography of François-Jules Vidocq (1775–1857), a criminal who later turned detective.

contained a central apple-tree and a few straggling bushes under one of which I found the late tenant's rusty bicycle-pump. He had been a very charitable priest: in his will he had left all his money to institutions and the furniture of his house to his sister.

When the short days of winter came dusk fell before we had well eaten our dinners. When we met in the street the houses had grown somber. The space of sky above us was the color of ever-changing violet and towards it the lamps of the street lifted their feeble lanterns. The cold air stung us and we played till our bodies glowed. Our shouts echoed in the silent street. The career of our play brought us through the dark muddy lanes behind the houses where we ran the gantlet of the rough tribes from the cottages, to the back doors of the dark dripping gardens where odors arose from the ashpits, to the dark odorous stables where a coachman smoothed and combed the horse or shook music from the buckled harness. When we returned to the street light from the kitchen windows had filled the areas. If my uncle was seen turning the corner we hid in the shadow until we had seen him safely housed. Or if Mangan's sister° came out on the doorstep to call her brother in to his tea we watched her from our shadow peer up and down the street. We waited to see whether she would remain or go in and, if she remained, we left our shadow and walked up to Mangan's steps resignedly. She was waiting for us, her figure defined by the light from the half-opened door. Her brother always teased her before he obeyed and I stood by the railings looking at her. Her dress swung as she moved her body and the soft rope of her hair tossed from side to side.

Every morning I lay on the floor in the front parlor watching her door. The blind was pulled down within an inch of the sash so that I could not be seen. When she came out on the doorstep my heart leaped. I ran to the hall, seized my books and followed her. I kept her brown figure always in my eye and, when we came near the point at which our ways diverged, I quickened my pace and passed her. This happened morning after morning. I had never spoken to her, except for a few casual words, and yet her name was like a summons to all my foolish blood.

Her image accompanied me even in places the most hostile to romance. On   5
Saturday evenings when my aunt went marketing I had to go to carry some of the parcels. We walked through the flaring streets, jostled by drunken men and bargaining women, amid the curses of laborers, the shrill litanies of shopboys who stood on guard by the barrels of pigs' cheeks, the nasal chanting of street singers, who sang a *come-all-you* about O'Donovan Rossa°, or a ballad about the troubles in our native land. These noises converged in a single sensation of life for me: I imagined that I bore my chalice safely through the throng of foes. Her name sprang to my lips at moments in strange prayers and praises which I myself did

---

Mangan's sister: an actual young woman in this story, but the phrase recalls Irish poet James Clarence Mangan (1803–1849) and his best-known poem, "Dark Rosaleen," which personifies Ireland as a beautiful woman for whom the poet yearns.   *come-all-you about O'Donovan Rossa:* the street singers earned their living by singing timely songs that usually began, "Come all you gallant Irishmen / And listen to my song." Their subject, also called Dynamite Rossa, was a popular hero jailed by the British for advocating violent rebellion.

not understand. My eyes were often full of tears (I could not tell why) and at times a flood from my heart seemed to pour itself out into my bosom. I thought little of the future. I did not know whether I would ever speak to her or not or, if I spoke to her, how I could tell her of my confused adoration. But my body was like a harp and her words and gestures were like fingers running upon the wires.

One evening I went into the back drawing-room in which the priest had died. It was a dark rainy evening and there was no sound in the house. Through one of the broken panes I heard the rain impinge upon the earth, the fine incessant needles of water playing in the sodden beds. Some distant lamp or lighted window gleamed below me. I was thankful that I could see so little. All my senses seemed to desire to veil themselves and, feeling that I was about to slip from them, I pressed the palms of my hands together until they trembled, murmuring: *O love! O love!* many times.

At last she spoke to me. When she addressed the first words to me I was so confused that I did not know what to answer. She asked me was I going to *Araby*. I forget whether I answered yes or no. It would be a splendid bazaar, she said; she would love to go.

—And why can't you? I asked.

While she spoke she turned a silver bracelet round and round her wrist. She could not go, she said, because there would be a retreat that week in her convent°. Her brother and two other boys were fighting for their caps and I was alone at the railings. She held one of the spikes, bowing her head towards me. The light from the lamp opposite our door caught the white curve of her neck, lit up her hair that rested there and, falling, lit up the hand upon the railing. It fell over one side of her dress and caught the white border of a petticoat, just visible as she stood at ease.

—It's well for you, she said.

—If I go, I said, I will bring you something.

What innumerable follies laid waste my waking and sleeping thoughts after that evening! I wished to annihilate the tedious intervening days. I chafed against the work of school. At night in my bedroom and by day in the classroom her image came between me and the page I strove to read. The syllables of the word *Araby* were called to me through the silence in which my soul luxuriated and cast an Eastern enchantment over me. I asked for leave to go to the bazaar on Saturday night. My aunt was surprised and hoped it was not some Freemason° affair. I answered few questions in class. I watched my master's face pass from amiability to sternness; he hoped I was not beginning to idle. I could not call my wandering thoughts together. I had hardly any patience with the serious work of life which, now that it stood between me and my desire, seemed to me child's play, ugly monotonous child's play.

On Saturday morning I reminded my uncle that I wished to go to the bazaar in the evening. He was fussing at the hall-stand, looking for the hatbrush, and answered me curtly:

—Yes, boy, I know.

10

a retreat . . . in her convent: a week devoted to religious observances more intense than usual, at the convent school Miss Mangan attends; probably she will have to listen to a number of hellfire sermons.
Freemason: Catholics in Ireland viewed the Masonic order as a Protestant conspiracy against them.

As he was in the hall I could not go into the front parlor and lie at the window. I left the house in bad humor and walked slowly towards the school. The
air was pitilessly raw and already my heart misgave me.

When I came home to dinner my uncle had not yet been home. Still it was
early. I sat staring at the clock for some time and, when its ticking began to irri-
tate me, I left the room. I mounted the staircase and gained the upper part of
the house. The high cold empty gloomy rooms liberated me and I went from room
to room singing. From the front window I saw my companions playing below in
the street. Their cries reached me weakened and indistinct and, leaning my forehead against the cool glass, I looked over at the dark house where she lived. I
may have stood there for an hour, seeing nothing but the brown-clad figure cast
by my imagination, touched discreetly by the lamplight at the curved neck, at
the hand upon the railings and at the border below the dress.

When I came downstairs again I found Mrs. Mercer sitting at the fire. She
was an old garrulous woman, a pawnbroker's widow, who collected used stamps
for some pious purpose. I had to endure the gossip of the tea-table. The meal was
prolonged beyond an hour and still my uncle did not come. Mrs. Mercer stood
up to go: she was sorry she couldn't wait any longer, but it was after eight o'clock
and she did not like to be out late, as the night air was bad for her. When she
had gone I began to walk up and down the room, clenching my fists. My aunt said:

—I'm afraid you may put off your bazaar for this night of Our Lord.

At nine o'clock I heard my uncle's latchkey in the halldoor. I heard him talking to himself and heard the hall-stand rocking when it had received the weight
of his overcoat. I could interpret these signs. When he was midway through his
dinner I asked him to give me the money to go to the bazaar. He had forgotten.

—The people are in bed and after their first sleep now, he said.

I did not smile. My aunt said to him energetically:

—Can't you give him the money and let him go? You've kept him late enough
as it is.

My uncle said he was very sorry he had forgotten. He said he believed in
the old saying: *All work and no play makes Jack a dull boy*. He asked me where
I was going and, when I had told him a second time he asked me did I know *The
Arab's Farewell to His Steed*°. When I left the kitchen he was about to recite the
opening lines of the piece to my aunt.

I held a florin tightly in my hand as I strode down Buckingham Street towards
the station. The sight of the streets thronged with buyers and glaring with gas
recalled to me the purpose of my journey. I took my seat in a third-class carriage
of a deserted train. After an intolerable delay the train moved out of the station
slowly. It crept onward among ruinous houses and over the twinkling river. At
Westland Row Station a crowd of people pressed to the carriage doors; but the
porters moved them back, saying that it was a special train for the bazaar. I remained alone in the bare carriage. In a few minutes the train drew up beside an

---

The Arab's Farewell to His Steed: This sentimental ballad by a popular poet, Caroline Norton (1808–1877),
tells the story of a nomad of the desert who, in a fit of greed, sells his beloved horse, then regrets
the loss, flings away the gold he has received, and takes back his horse. Notice the echo of "Araby"
in the song title.

improvised wooden platform. I passed out on to the road and saw by the lighted dial of a clock that it was ten minutes to ten. In front of me was a large building which displayed the magical name.

I could not find any sixpenny entrance and, fearing that the bazaar would be closed, I passed in quickly through a turnstile, handing a shilling to a weary-looking man. I found myself in a big hall girdled at half its height by a gallery. Nearly all the stalls were closed and the greater part of the hall was in darkness. I recognized a silence like that which pervades a church after a service. I walked into the center of the bazaar timidly. A few people were gathered about the stalls which were still open. Before a curtain, over which the words *Café Chantant°* were written in colored lamps, two men were counting money on a salver°. I listened to the fall of the coins.

Remembering with difficulty why I had come I went over to one of the stalls and examined porcelain vases and flowered tea-sets. At the door of the stall a young lady was talking and laughing with two young gentlemen. I remarked their English accents and listened vaguely to their conversation.

—O, I never said such a thing!

—O, but you did!

—O, but I didn't!

—Didn't she say that?

—Yes. I heard her.

—O, there's a . . . fib!

Observing me the young lady came over and asked me did I wish to buy anything. The tone of her voice was not encouraging; she seemed to have spoken to me out of a sense of duty. I looked humbly at the great jars that stood like eastern guards at either side of the dark entrance to the stall and murmured:

—No, thank you.

The young lady changed the position of one of the vases and went back to the two young men. They began to talk of the same subject. Once or twice the young lady glanced at me over her shoulder.

I lingered before her stall, though I knew my stay was useless, to make my interest in her wares seem the more real. Then I turned away slowly and walked down the middle of the bazaar. I allowed the two pennies to fall against the sixpence in my pocket. I heard a voice call from one end of the gallery that the light was out. The upper part of the hall was now completely dark.

Gazing up into the darkness I saw myself as a creature driven and derided by vanity; and my eyes burned with anguish and anger.

QUESTIONS

1. What images does the name of the bazaar conjure up for the boy? What ironic discrepancies appear between his dream of Araby and the reality?
2. How can it be claimed that "Araby" is told from an ironic point of view? Does the narrator of the story seem a boy—a naive or innocent narrator—or a mature man looking back through a boy's eyes?

Café Chantant: name for a Paris nightspot featuring topical songs.   *salver:* a tray like that used in serving Holy Communion.

3. Who besides the boy is the other central character in the story? How do we know that the boy's view of this character is not exactly the author's view? (It may help to look closely at the narrator's descriptions of the other major character, and of his own feelings.)
4. At what other moments in the story does the boy romanticize, or project an air of enchantment upon things?
5. In general, how would you describe the physical setting of "Araby" as Joyce details it in the first five paragraphs? Does he make Dublin seem a beautiful metropolis, a merry town, an ugly backwater, or what? And what do you make of the detail, in the opening sentence, that the boy's street has a dead end?
6. How does the time of day matter to this story? What is meaningful or suggestive, in the end, about the fall of night?

Anne Tyler

AVERAGE WAVES IN UNPROTECTED WATERS   1977

Anne Tyler, born in 1941 in Minneapolis, grew up in North Carolina and at nineteen received her bachelor's degree from Duke University. After graduate study at Columbia, she returned to Duke as a bibliographer. Tyler, who has lived in Montreal and, since 1965, in Baltimore, is a writer who values privacy and discourages visits from reporters and interviewers. She has gained a legion of readers for her eleven novels, including Celestial Navigation *(1974),* Dinner in the Homesick Restaurant *(1982),* The Accidental Tourist *(1985), the basis for a popular film, and* Breathing Lessons *(1988). Tyler's people, whom she views with compassion and wry humor, are often slightly eccentric citizens of Baltimore, able to relate only with difficulty to one another and to society. "Average Waves in Unprotected Waters" was originally published in* The New Yorker.

Anne Tyler

As soon as it got light, Bet woke him and dressed him, and then she walked him over to the table and tried to make him eat a little cereal. He wouldn't, though. He could tell something was up. She pressed the edge of the spoon against his lips till she heard it click on his teeth, but he just looked off at a corner of the ceiling—a knobby child with great glassy eyes and her own fair hair. Like any other nine-year-old, he wore a striped shirt and jeans, but the shirt was too neat and the jeans too blue, unpatched and unfaded, and would stay that way till he outgrew them. And his face was elderly—pinched, strained, tired—though it should have looked as unused as his jeans. He hardly ever changed his expression.

She left him in his chair and went to make the beds. Then she raised the yellowed shade, rinsed a few spoons in the bathroom sink, picked up some bits of magazines he'd torn the night before. This was a rented room in an ancient, crumbling house, and nothing you could do to it would lighten its cluttered look. There was always that feeling of too many lives layered over other lives, like the layers of brownish wallpaper her child had peeled away in the corner by his bed.

She slipped her feet into flat-heeled loafers and absently patted the front of her dress, a worn beige knit she usually saved for Sundays. Maybe she should take it in a little; it hung from her shoulders like a sack. She felt too slight and frail, too wispy for all she had to do today. But she reached for her coat anyhow, and put it on and tied a blue kerchief under her chin. Then she went over to the table and slowly spun, modelling the coat. "See, Arnold?" she said. "We're going out."

Arnold went on looking at the ceiling, but his gaze turned wild and she knew he'd heard.

She fetched his jacket from the closet—brown corduroy, with a hood. It had set her back half a week's salary. But Arnold didn't like it; he always wanted his old one, a little red duffel coat he'd long ago outgrown. When she came toward him, he started moaning and rocking and shaking his head. She had to struggle to stuff his arms in the sleeves. Small though he was, he was strong, wiry; he was getting to be too much for her. He shook free of her hands and ran over to his bed. The jacket was on, though. It wasn't buttoned, the collar was askew, but never mind; that just made him look more real. She always felt bad at how he stood inside his clothes, separate from them, passive, unaware of all the buttons and snaps she'd fastened as carefully as she would a doll's. 5

She gave a last look around the room, checked to make sure the hot plate was off, and then picked up her purse and Arnold's suitcase. "Come along, Arnold," she said.

He came, dragging out every step. He looked at the suitcase suspiciously, but only because it was new. It didn't have any meaning for him. "See?" she said. "It's yours. It's Arnold's. It's going on the train with us."

But her voice was all wrong. He would pick it up, for sure. She paused in the middle of locking the door and glanced over at him fearfully. Anything could set him off nowadays. He hadn't noticed, though. He was too busy staring around the hallway, goggling at a freckled, walnut-framed mirror as if he'd never seen it before. She touched his shoulder. "Come, Arnold," she said.

They went down the stairs slowly, both of them clinging to the sticky mahogany railing. The suitcase banged against her shins. In the entrance hall, old Mrs. Puckett stood waiting outside her door—a huge, soft lady in a black crêpe dress and orthopedic shoes. She was holding a plastic bag of peanut-butter cookies, Arnold's favorites. There were tears in her eyes. "Here, Arnold," she said, quavering. Maybe she felt to blame that he was going. But she'd done the best she could: babysat him all these years and only given up when he'd grown too strong and wild to manage. Bet wished Arnold would give the old lady some sign— hug her, make his little crowing noise, just take the cookies, even. But he was too excited. He raced on out the front door, and it was Bet who had to take them. "Well, thank you, Mrs. Puckett," she said. "I know he'll enjoy them later."

"Oh, no . . . " said Mrs. Puckett, and she flapped her large hands and gave
up, sobbing.

They were lucky and caught a bus first thing. Arnold sat by the window. He must have thought he was going to work with her; when they passed the red-and-gold Kresge's sign, he jabbered and tried to stand up. "No, honey," she said, and took hold of his arm. He settled down then and let his hand stay curled in hers awhile. He had very small, cool fingers, and nails as smooth as thumbtack heads.

At the train station, she bought the tickets and then a pack of Wrigley's spearmint gum. Arnold stood gaping at the vaulted ceiling, with his head flopped back and his arms hanging limp at his sides. People stared at him. She would have liked to push their faces in. "Over here, honey," she said, and she nudged him toward the gate, straightening his collar as they walked.

He hadn't been on a train before and acted a little nervous, bouncing up and down in his seat and flipping the lid of his ashtray and craning forward to see the man ahead of them. When the train started moving, he crowed and pulled at her sleeve. "That's right, Arnold. Train. We're taking a trip," Bet said. She unwrapped a stick of chewing gum and gave it to him. He loved gum. If she didn't watch him closely, he sometimes swallowed it—which worried her a little because she'd heard it clogged your kidneys; but at least it would keep him busy. She looked down at the top of his head. Through the blond prickles of his hair, cut short for practical reasons, she could see his skull bones moving as he chewed. He was so thin-skinned, almost transparent; sometimes she imagined she could see the blood travelling in his veins.

When the train reached a steady speed, he grew calmer, and after a while he nodded over against her and let his hands sag on his knees. She watched his eyelashes slowly drooping—two colorless, fringed crescents, heavier and heavier, every now and then flying up as he tried to fight off sleep. He had never slept well, not ever, not even as a baby. Even before they'd noticed anything wrong, they'd wondered at his jittery, jerky catnaps, his tiny hands clutching tight and springing open, his strange single wail sailing out while he went right on sleeping. Avery said it gave him the chills. And after the doctor talked to them Avery wouldn't have anything to do with Arnold anymore—just walked in wide circles around the crib, looking stunned and sick. A few weeks later, he left. She wasn't surprised. She even knew how he felt, more or less. Halfway, he blamed her; halfway, he blamed himself. You can't believe a thing like this will just fall on you out of nowhere.

She'd had moments herself of picturing some kind of evil gene in her husband's ordinary, stocky body—a dark little egg like a black jelly bean, she imagined
it. All his fault. But other times she was sure the gene was hers. It seemed so natural; she never could do anything as well as most people. And then other times she blamed their marriage. They'd married too young, against her parents' wishes. All she'd wanted was to get away from home. Now she couldn't remember why. What was wrong with home? She thought of her parents' humped green trailer, perched

on cinder blocks near a forest of masts in Salt Spray, Maryland. At this distance (parents dead, trailer rusted to bits, even Salt Spray changed past recognition), it seemed to her that her old life had been beautifully free and spacious. She closed her eyes and saw wide gray skies. Everything had been ruled by the sea. Her father (who'd run a fishing boat for tourists) couldn't arrange his day till he'd heard the marine forecast—the wind, the tides, the small-craft warnings, the height of average waves in unprotected waters. He loved to fish, offshore and on, and he swam every chance he could get. He'd tried to teach her to bodysurf, but it hadn't worked out. There was something about the breakers: she just gritted her teeth and stood staunch and let them slam into her. As if standing staunch were a virtue, really. She couldn't explain it. Her father thought she was scared, but it wasn't that at all.

She'd married Avery against their wishes and been sorry ever since—sorry to move so far from home, sorrier when her parents died within a year of each other, sorriest of all when the marriage turned grim and cranky. But she never would have thought of leaving him. It was Avery who left; she would have stayed forever. In fact, she did stay on in their apartment for months after he'd gone, though the rent was far too high. It wasn't that she expected him back. She just took some comfort from enduring.

Arnold's head snapped up. He looked around him and made a gurgling sound. His chewing gum fell onto the front of his jacket. "Here, honey," she told him. She put the gum in her ashtray. "Look out the window. See the cows?"

He wouldn't look. He began bouncing in his seat, rubbing his hands together rapidly.

"Arnold? Want a cookie?"

If only she'd brought a picture book. She'd meant to and then forgot. She wondered if the train people sold magazines. If she let him get too bored, he'd go into one of his tantrums, and then she wouldn't be able to handle him. The doctor had given her pills just in case, but she was always afraid that while he was screaming he would choke on them. She looked around the car. "Arnold," she said, "see the . . . see the hat with feathers on? Isn't it pretty? See the red suitcase? See the, um . . . "

The car door opened with a rush of clattering wheels and the conductor burst in, singing "Girl of my dreams, I love you." He lurched down the aisle, plucking pink tickets from the back of each seat. Just across from Bet and Arnold, he stopped. He was looking down at a tiny black lady in a purple coat, with a fox fur piece biting its own tail around her neck. "You!" he said.

The lady stared straight ahead.

"You, I saw you. You're the one in the washroom."

A little muscle twitched in her cheek.

"You got on this train in Beulah, didn't you. Snuck in the washroom. Darted back like you thought you could put something over on me. I saw that bit of purple! Where's your ticket gone to?"

She started fumbling in a blue cloth purse. The fumbling went on and on. The conductor shifted his weight.

"Why!" she said finally. "I must've left it back in my other seat."

"What other seat?"

"Oh, the one back . . . " She waved a spidery hand.

The conductor sighed. "Lady," he said, "you owe me money."30

"I do no such thing!" she said. "Viper! Monger! Hitler!" Her voice screeched up all at once; she sounded like a parrot. Bet winced and felt herself flushing, as if *she* were the one. But then at her shoulder she heard a sudden, rusty clang, and she turned and saw that Arnold was laughing. He had his mouth wide open and his tongue curled, the way he did when he watched "Sesame Street." Even after the scene had worn itself out, and the lady had paid and the conductor had moved on, Arnold went on chortling and la-la-ing, and Bet looked gratefully at the little black lady, who was settling her fur piece fussily and muttering under her breath.

From the Parkinsville Railroad Station, which they seemed to be tearing down or else remodeling—she couldn't tell which—they took a taxicab to Parkins State Hospital. "Oh, I been out there many and many a time," said the driver. "Went out there just the other—"

But she couldn't stop herself; she had to tell him before she forgot. "Listen," she said, "I want you to wait for me right in the driveway. I don't want you to go on away."

"Well, fine," he said.

"Can you do that? I want you to be sitting right by the porch or the steps35 or whatever, right where I come out of, ready to take me back to the station. Don't just go off and—"

"I *got* you, I got you," he said.

She sank back. She hoped he understood.

Arnold wanted a peanut-butter cookie. He was reaching and whimpering. She didn't know what to do. She wanted to give him anything he asked for, anything; but he'd get it all over his face and arrive not looking his best. She couldn't stand it if they thought he was just ordinary and unattractive. She wanted them to see how small and neat he was, how somebody cherished him. But it would be awful if he went into one of his rages. She broke off a little piece of cookie from the bag. "Here," she told him. "Don't mess, now."

He flung himself back in the corner and ate it, keeping one hand flattened across his mouth while he chewed.

The hospital looked like someone's great, pillared mansion, with square brick40 buildings all around it. "Here we are," the driver said.

"Thank you," she said. "Now you wait here, please. Just wait till I get—"

"*Lady*," he said, "I'll wait."

She opened the door and nudged Arnold out ahead of her. Lugging the suitcase, she started toward the steps. "Come on, Arnold," she said.

He hung back.

"Arnold?"45

Maybe he wouldn't allow it, and they would go on home and never think of this again.

But he came, finally, climbing the steps in his little hobbled way. His face was clean, but there were a few cookie crumbs on his jacket. She set down the suitcase to brush them off. Then she buttoned all his buttons and smoothed his shirt collar over his jacket collar before she pushed open the door.

140   TONE AND STYLE

In the admitting office, a lady behind a wooden counter showed her what papers to sign. Secretaries were clacketing typewriters all around. Bet thought Arnold might like that, but instead he got lost in the lights—chilly, hanging ice-cube-tray lights with a little flicker to them. He gazed upward, looking astonished. Finally a flat-fronted nurse came in and touched his elbow. "Come along, Arnold. Come, Mommy. We'll show you where Arnold is staying," she said.

They walked back across the entrance hall, then up wide marble steps with hollows worn in them. Arnold clung to the bannister. There was a smell Bet hated, pine-oil disinfectant, but Arnold didn't seem to notice. You never knew; sometimes smells could just put him in a state.

The nurse unlocked a double door that had chicken-wired windows. They   50
walked through a corridor, passing several fat, ugly women in shapeless gray dresses and ankle socks. "Ha!" one of the women said, and fell giggling into the arms of a friend. The nurse said, "*Here* we are." She led them into an enormous hallway lined with little white cots. Nobody else was in it; there wasn't a sign that children lived here except for a tiny cardboard clown picture hanging on one vacant wall. "This one is your bed, Arnold," said the nurse. Bet laid the suitcase on it. It was made up so neatly, the sheets might have been painted on. A steely-gray blanket was folded across the foot. She looked over at Arnold, but he was pivoting back and forth to hear how his new sneakers squeaked on the linoleum.

"Usually," said the nurse, "we like to give new residents six months before the family visits. That way they settle in quicker, don't you see." She turned away and adjusted the clown picture, though as far as Bet could tell it was fine the way it was. Over her shoulder, the nurse said, "You can tell him goodbye now, if you like."

"Oh," Bet said. "All right." She set her hands on Arnold's shoulders. Then she laid her face against his hair, which felt warm and fuzzy. "Honey," she said. But he went on pivoting. She straightened and told the nurse, "I brought his special blanket."

"Oh, fine," said the nurse, turning toward her again. "We'll see that he gets it."

"He always likes to sleep with it; he has ever since he was little."

"All right."   55

"Don't wash it. He hates if you wash it."

"Yes. Say goodbye to Mommy now, Arnold."

"A lot of times he'll surprise you. I mean there's a whole lot to him. He's not just—"

"We'll take very good care of him, Mrs. Blevins, don't worry."

"Well," she said. "Bye, Arnold."   60

She left the ward with the nurse and went down the corridor. As the nurse was unlocking the doors for her, she heard a single, terrible scream, but the nurse only patted her shoulder and pushed her gently on through.

In the taxi, Bet said, "Now, I've just got fifteen minutes to get to the station. I wonder if you could hurry?"

"Sure thing," the driver said.

She folded her hands and looked straight ahead. Tears seemed to be coming down her face in sheets.

Once she'd reached the station, she went to the ticket window. "Am I in time for the twelve-thirty-two?" she asked. 65

"Easily," said the man. "It's twenty minutes late."

"What?"

"Got held up in Norton somehow."

"But you can't!" she said. The man looked startled. She must be a sight, all swollen-eyed and wet-cheeked. "Look," she said, in a lower voice. "I figured this on purpose. I chose the one train from Beulah that would let me catch another one back without waiting. I do not want to sit and wait in this station."

"Twenty *minutes*, lady. That's all it is." 70

"What am I going to do?" she asked him.

He turned back to his ledgers.

She went over to a bench and sat down. Ladders and scaffolding towered above her, and only ten or twelve passengers were dotted through the rest of the station. The place looked bombed out—nothing but a shell. "Twenty minutes?" she said aloud. "What am I going to do?"

Through the double glass doors at the far end of the station, a procession of gray-suited men arrived with briefcases. More men came behind them, dressed in work clothes, carrying folding chairs, black trunklike boxes with silver hinges, microphones, a wooden lectern, and an armload of bunting. They set the lectern down in the center of the floor, not six feet from Bet. They draped the bunting across it—an arc of red, white, and blue. Wires were connected, floodlights were lit. A microphone screeched. One of the workmen said, "Try her, Mayor." He held the microphone out to a fat man in a suit, who cleared his throat and said, "Ladies and gentlemen, on the occasion of the expansion of this fine old railroad station—"

"Sure do get an echo here," the workmen said. "Keep on going." 75

The Mayor cleared his throat again. "If I may," he said, "I'd like to take about twenty minutes of your time, friends."

He straightened his tie. Bet blew her nose, and then she wiped her eyes and smiled. They had come just for her sake, you might think. They were putting on a sort of private play. From now on, all the world was going to be like that—just something on a stage, for her to sit back and watch.

QUESTIONS

1. How early in the story do we perceive that Bet's child is not an ordinary nine-year-old? What has made his mother decide to put him in Parkins State Hospital?
2. Is Tyler's story told from an ironic point of view? Cite evidence for your answer.
3. What ironies do you detect in the scene at the hospital?
4. The title "Average Waves in Unprotected Waters" echoes a phrase used in paragraph 15. To what does it refer? How does the phrase (and therefore the title) apply to the story as a whole?
5. How would you characterize Bet? Why is she so upset when she learns that the twelve-thirty-two is to be twenty minutes late, and so pleased when the Mayor says "I'd like to take about twenty minutes of your time, friends"?
6. How do you account for Bet's view of her early life as "beautifully free and spacious"?

Suggestions for Writing

1. Choose a subject you admire greatly: some person, place, film, sports team, work of fiction, or whatever. In a paragraph, describe it so that you make clear your admiration. Then rewrite the paragraph from the point of view of someone who detests the same subject. Try not to declare "I love this" or "I hate this," but select details and characteristics of your subject that will make the tone of each paragraph unmistakable.

2. Consider a short story in which the narrator is the central character: perhaps "A & P," "Greasy Lake," "Araby," "Where I'm Calling From," "I Stand Here Ironing," or "The Use of Force." In a brief essay, show how the character of the narrator determines the style of the story. Examine language in particular—words or phrases, slang expressions, figures of speech, local or regional speech.

3. Take a short story or novel not included in this book—one by a writer of high reputation and distinctive style, such as William Faulkner, Ernest Hemingway, Raymond Carver, Flannery O'Connor, or another writer suggested by your instructor. Then write a passage of your own, in which you imitate the writer's style as closely as possible. Pay attention to tone, vocabulary, length and variety of sentences, amount of description. Find some place in the story to insert your original passage. Then type out two or three pages of the story, including your forgery, and make copies for the other members of the class. See if anyone can tell where the writer's prose stops and yours begins.

4. Freewrite for fifteen or twenty minutes, rapidly jotting down any thoughts you may have in answer to this question: From your daily contacts with people, what ironies do you at times become aware of? Consider ironies of language (in deliberately misleading or sarcastic remarks), ironies of situation (here you are, a trained computer programmer unable to convince a counterperson in a fast-food joint that you can correctly add up a check). Then, using any good perceptions you have generated, write and polish a short answer to the question, illustrating your remarks by reference to your own recalled experience and recent observations. Of course you might also find it useful to cite some ironies in any stories about everyday life.

5. Here are some other topics: "Irony in 'A Rose for Emily.'" "Irony in 'Greasy Lake.'" "Irony in 'The Jilting of Granny Weatherall.'" (Or what other story have you read that more keenly interests you?) What sorts of irony make the story more effective? In dealing with any of them, you may find the method of analysis a help to you. Before you write, read about this useful method in "Writing about a Story" in Supplement: Writing.

6 Theme

The **theme** of a story is whatever general idea or insight the entire story reveals. In some stories the theme is unmistakable. At the end of Aesop's fable about the council of the mice that can't decide who will bell the cat, the theme is stated in the moral: *It is easier to propose a thing than to carry it out.* In a work of commercial fiction, too, the theme (if any) is usually obvious. Consider a typical detective thriller in which, say, a rookie policeman trained in scientific methods of crime detection sets out to solve a mystery sooner than his rival, a veteran sleuth whose only laboratory is carried under this hat. Perhaps the veteran solves the case, leading to the conclusion (and the theme), "The old ways are the best ways after all." Another story by the same writer might dramatize the same rivalry but reverse the outcome, having the rookie win, thereby reversing the theme: "The times are changing! Let's shake loose from old-fashioned ways." In such commercial entertainments, a theme is like a length of rope with which the writer, patently and mechanically, trusses the story neatly (usually too neatly) into meaningful shape.

In literary fiction, a theme is seldom so obvious. That is, a theme need not be a moral or a message; it may be what the happenings add up to, what the story is about. When we come to the end of a finely wrought short story such as Ernest Hemingway's "A Clean, Well-Lighted Place" (Chapter Five), it may be easy to sum up the plot—to say what happens—but it is more difficult to sum up the story's main idea. Evidently, Hemingway relates events—how a younger waiter gets rid of an old man and how an older waiter then goes to a coffee bar—but in themselves these events seem relatively slight, though the story as a whole seems large (for its size) and full of meaning. For the meaning, we must look to other elements in the story besides what happens in it. And it is clear that Hemingway is most deeply interested in the thoughts and feelings of the older waiter, the character who has more and more to say as the story progresses, until at the end the story is entirely confined to his thoughts and perceptions. What is meaningful in these thoughts and perceptions? The older waiter understands the old man and sympathizes with his need for a clean, well-lighted place. If we say that, we are still talking about what happens in the story, though we have gone beyond merely recording its external events. But a theme is usually stated in *general* words. Another try: "Solitary people who cannot sleep need a cheerful, orderly place where they can drink with dignity." That's a little better. We have indicated, at least, that Hemingway's story is about more than just an old man and a couple of waiters. But what about the older waiter's meditation on *nada*, nothingness? Coming near the end of the story, it takes great emphasis; and probably no good statement of Hemingway's theme can leave it out. Still another try at a statement: "Solitary people need a place of refuge from their terrible awareness that their lives (or perhaps, human lives) are essentially meaningless." Neither this nor any other statement of the story's theme is unarguably right, but at least the sentence helps the reader to bring into focus one primary idea that Hemingway seems to be driving at. When we finish reading "A Clean, Well-Lighted Place," we feel that there *is* such a theme, a unifying vision, even though we cannot reduce it absolutely to a tag. Like some freshwater lake alive with creatures, Hemingway's story is a broad expanse, reflecting in many directions. No wonder that many readers will view it differently.

Moral inferences may be drawn from the story, no doubt—for Hemingway is indirectly giving us advice for properly regarding and sympathizing with the lonely, the uncertain, and the old. But the story doesn't set forth a lesson that we are supposed to put into practice. One could argue that "A Clean, Well-Lighted Place" contains *several* themes—and other statements could be made to take in Hemingway's views of love, of communication between people, of dignity. Great short stories, like great symphonies, frequently have more than one theme.

In many a fine short story, theme is the center, the moving force, the principle of unity. Clearly, such a theme is something other than the characters and events of its story. To say of James Joyce's "Araby" (page 131) that it is about a boy who goes to a bazaar to buy a gift for a young woman, only to arrive too late, is to summarize plot, not theme. (The theme *might* be put, "The illusions of a romantic child are vulnerable," or it might be put in any of a few hundred other ways.) Although the title of Isaac Bashevis Singer's "Gimpel the Fool" (Chapter Three) indicates the main character and suggests the subject (his "foolishness"), the theme—the larger realization that the story leaves us with—has to do not with foolishness, but with how to be wise.

Sometimes you will hear it said that the theme of a story (say, Faulkner's "Barn Burning") is "loss of innocence" or "initiation into maturity"; or that the theme of some other story (Thurber's "The Catbird Seat," for instance) is "the revolt of the downtrodden." This is to use *theme* in a larger and more abstract sense than we use it here. Although such general descriptions of theme can be useful—as in sorting a large number of stories into rough categories—we suggest that, in the beginning, you look for whatever truth or insight you think the writer of a story reveals. Try to sum it up *in a sentence*. By doing so, you will find yourself looking closely at the story, trying to define its principal meaning. You may find it helpful, in making your sentence-statement of theme, to consider these points:

1. Look back once more at the title of the story. From what you have read, what does it indicate?
2. Does the main character in any way change in the story? Does this character arrive at any eventual realization or understanding? Are you left with any realization or understanding you did not have before?
3. Does the author make any general observations about life or human nature? Do the characters make any? (Caution: Characters now and again will utter opinions with which the reader is not necessarily supposed to agree.)
4. Does the story contain any especially curious objects, mysterious flat characters, significant animals, repeated names, song titles, or whatever, that hint toward meanings larger than such things ordinarily have? In literary stories, such symbols may point to central themes. (For a short discussion of symbolism and a few illustrations, see Chapter Seven.)
5. When you have worded your statement of theme, have you cast your statement into general language, not just given a plot summary?
6. Does your statement hold true for the story as a whole, not for just part of it?

In distilling a statement of theme from a rich and complicated story, we have, of course, no more encompassed the whole story than a paleontologist taking a plaster mold of a petrified footprint has captured a living brontosaurus. A writer (other than a fabulist) does not usually set out with theme in hand, determined to make every detail in the story work to demonstrate it. Well then, the skeptical reader may ask, if only *some* stories have themes, if those themes may be hard to sum up, and if readers will probably disagree in their summations, why bother to state themes? Isn't it too much trouble? Surely it is, unless the effort to state a theme ends in pleasure and profit. Trying to sum up the point of a story in our own words is merely one way to make ourselves better aware of whatever we may have understood vaguely and tentatively. Attempted with loving care, such statements may bring into focus our scattered impressions of a rewarding story, may help to clarify and hold fast whatever wisdom the storyteller has offered us.

Stephen Crane

Stephen Crane (1871–1900) was born in Newark, New Jersey, a Methodist minister's last and fourteenth child. After flunking out of both Lafayette College and Syracuse University, he became a journalist in New York, specializing in grim life among the down-and-out who people his early self-published novel Maggie: A Girl of the Streets (1893). Restlessly generating material for stories, Crane trekked to the Southwest, New Orleans, and Mexico. "The Open Boat" is based on experience. En route to Havana to report the Cuban revolution for the New York Press, Crane was shipwrecked when the SS. Commodore sank in heavy seas east of New Smyrna, Florida, on January 2, 1897. He escaped in a ten-foot lifeboat with the captain and

Stephen Crane

two members of the crew. Later that year, Crane moved into a stately home in England with Cora Taylor, former madam of a Florida brothel, hobnobbed with literary greats, and lived beyond his means. Hounded by creditors, afflicted by tuberculosis, he died in Germany at twenty-eight. Crane has been called the first writer of American realism. His famed novel The Red Badge of Courage (1895) gives an imagined but convincing account of a young Union soldier's initiation into battle. A handful of his short stories appear immortal. He was an original poet, too, writing terse, sardonic poems in open forms, at the time considered radical. In his short life, Crane greatly helped American literature to come of age.

A Tale Intended to be after the Fact:
Being the Experience of Four Men from the Sunk Steamer Commodore

I

None of them knew the color of the sky. Their eyes glanced level, and were fastened upon the waves that swept toward them. These waves were of the hue of slate, save for the tops, which were of foaming white, and all of the men knew the colors of the sea. The horizon narrowed and widened, and dipped and rose, and at all times its edge was jagged with waves that seemed thrust up in points like rocks.

Many a man ought to have a bathtub larger than the boat which here rode upon the sea. These waves were most wrongfully and barbarously abrupt and tall, and each frothtop was a problem in small-boat navigation.

The cook squatted in the bottom, and looked with both eyes at the six inches of gunwale which separated him from the ocean. His sleeves were rolled over his fat forearms, and the two flaps of his unbuttoned vest dangled as he bent to bail out the boat. Often he said, "Gawd! that was a narrow clip." As he remarked it he invariably gazed eastward over the broken sea.

The oiler, steering with one of the two oars in the boat, sometimes raised himself suddenly to keep clear of water that swirled in over the stern. It was a thin little oar, and it seemed often ready to snap.

The correspondent°, pulling at the other oar, watched the waves and won- 5
dered why he was there.

The injured captain, lying in the bow, was at this time buried in that profound dejection and indifference which comes, temporarily at least, to even the bravest and most enduring when, willy-nilly, the firm fails, the army loses, the ship goes down. The mind of the master of a vessel is rooted deep in the timbers of her, though he command for a day or a decade; and this captain had on him the stern impression of a scene in the grays of dawn of seven turned faces, and later a stump of a topmast with a white ball on it, that slashed to and fro at the waves, went low and lower, and down. Thereafter there was something strange in his voice. Although steady, it was deep with mourning, and of a quality beyond oration or tears.

"Keep 'er a little more south, Billie," said he.

"A little more south, sir," said the oiler in the stern.

A seat in this boat was not unlike a seat upon a bucking broncho, and by the same token a broncho is not much smaller. The craft pranced and reared and plunged like an animal. As each wave came, and she rose for it, she seemed like a horse making at a fence outrageously high. The manner of her scramble over these walls of water is a mystic thing, and, moreover, at the top of them were ordinarily these problems in white water, the foam racing down from the summit of each wave requiring a new leap, and a leap from the air. Then, after scornfully bumping a crest, she would slide and race and splash down a long incline, and arrive bobbing and nodding in front of the next menace.

A singular disadvantage of the sea lies in the fact that after successfully sur- 10
mounting one wave you discover that there is another behind it just as important and just as nervously anxious to do something effective in the way of swamping boats. In a ten-foot dinghy one can get an idea of the resources of the sea in the line of waves that is not probable to the average experience which is never at sea in a dinghy. As each slaty wall of water approached, it shut all else from the view of the men in the boat, and it was not difficult to imagine that this particular wave was the final outburst of the ocean, the last effort of the grim water. There was a terrible grace in the move of the waves, and they came in silence, save for the snarling of the crests.

In the wan light the faces of the men must have been gray. Their eyes must have glinted in strange ways as they gazed steadily astern. Viewed from a balcony, the whole thing would doubtless have been weirdly picturesque. But the men in the boat had no time to see it, and if they had had leisure, there were other things to occupy their minds. The sun swung steadily up the sky, and they knew it was broad day because the color of the sea changed from slate to emerald green streaked

correspondent: foreign correspndent, newspaper reporter.

with amber lights, and the foam was like tumbling snow. The process of the breaking day was unknown to them. They were aware only of this effect upon the color of the waves that rolled toward them.

In disjointed sentences the cook and the correspondent argued as to the difference between a life-saving station and a house of refuge. The cook had said: "There's a house of refuge just north of the Mosquito Inlet Light, and as soon as they see us they'll come off in their boat and pick us up."

"As soon as who see us?" said the correspondent.

"The crew," said the cook.

"Houses of refuge don't have crews," said the correspondent. "As I understand them, they are only places where clothes and grub are stored for the benefit of shipwrecked people. They don't carry crews." 15

"Oh, yes, they do," said the cook.

"No, they don't," said the correspondent.

"Well, we're not there yet, anyhow," said the oiler, in the stern.

"Well," said the cook, "perhaps it's not a house of refuge that I'm thinking of as being near Mosquito Inlet Light; perhaps it's a life-saving station."

"We're not there yet," said the oiler in the stern. 20

II

As the boat bounced from the top of each wave the wind tore through the hair of the hatless men, and as the craft plopped her stern down again the spray slashed past them. The crest of each of these waves was a hill, from the top of which the men surveyed for a moment a broad tumultuous expanse, shining and wind-riven. It was probably splendid, it was probably glorious, this play of the free sea, wild with lights of emerald and white and amber.

"Bully good thing it's an on-shore wind," said the cook. "If not, where would we be? Wouldn't have a show."

"That's right," said the correspondent.

The busy oiler nodded his assent.

Then the captain, in the bow, chuckled in a way that expressed humor, contempt, tragedy, all in one. "Do you think we've got much of a show now, boys?" said he. 25

Whereupon the three were silent, save for a trifle of hemming and hawing. To express any particular optimism at this time they felt to be childish and stupid, but they all doubtless possessed this sense of the situation in their minds. A young man thinks doggedly at such times. On the other hand, the ethics of their condition was decidely against any open suggestion of hopelessness. So they were silent.

"Oh, well," said the captain, soothing his children, "we'll get ashore all right."

But there was that in his tone which made them think; so the oiler quoth, "Yes! if this wind holds."

The cook was bailing. "Yes! if we don't catch hell in the surf."

Canton-flannel gulls flew near and far. Sometimes they sat down on the sea, near patches of brown seaweed that rolled over the waves with a movement like carpets on a line in a gale. The birds sat comfortably in groups, and they were envied by some in the dinghy, for the wrath of the sea was no more to them than 30 it was to a covey of prairie chickens a thousand miles inland. Often they came very close and stared at the men with black bead-like eyes. At these times they were uncanny and sinister in their unblinking scrutiny, and the men hooted angrily at them, telling them to be gone. One came, and evidently decided to alight on the top of the captain's head. The bird flew parallel to the boat and did not circle, but made short sidelong jumps in the air in chicken-fashion. His black eyes were wistfully fixed upon the captain's head. "Ugly brute," said the oiler to the bird. "You look as if you were made with a jacknife." The cook and the correspondent swore darkly at the creature. The captain naturally wished to knock it away with the end of the heavy painter, but he did not dare do it, because anything resembling an emphatic gesture would have capsized this freighted boat; and so, with his open hand, the captain gently and carefully waved the gull away. After it had been discouraged from the pursuit the captain breathed easier on account of his hair, and others breathed easier because the bird struck their minds at this time as being somehow gruesome and ominous.

In the meantime the oiler and the correspondent rowed. And also they rowed. They sat together in the same seat, and each rowed an oar. Then the oiler took both oars; then the correspondent took both oars; then the oiler; then the correspondent. They rowed and they rowed. The very ticklish part of the business was when the time came for the reclining one in the stern to take his turn at the oars. By the very last star of truth, it is easier to steal eggs from under a hen than it was to change seats in the dinghy. First the man in the stern slid his hand along the thwart and moved with care, as if he were of Sèvres.° Then the man in the rowing-seat slid his hand along the other thwart. It was all done with the most extraordinary care. As the two sidled past each other, the whole party kept watchful eyes on the coming wave, and the captain cried: "Look out, now! Steady, there!"

The brown mats of seaweed that appeared from time to time were like islands, bits of earth. They were travelling, apparently, neither one way nor the other. They were, to all intents, stationary. They informed the men in the boat that it was making progress slowly toward the land.

The captain, rearing cautiously in the bow after the dinghy soared on a great swell, said that he had seen the lighthouse at Mosquito Inlet. Presently the cook remarked that he had seen it. The correspondent was at the oars then, and for some reason he too wished to look at the lighthouse; but his back was toward the far shore, and the waves were important, and for some time he could not seize an opportunity to turn his head. But at last there came a wave more gentle than the others, and when at the crest of it he swiftly scoured the western horizon.

"See it?" said the captain.

"No," said the correspondent, slowly; "I didn't see anything."   35

"Look again," said the captain. He pointed. "It's exactly in that direction."

At the top of another wave the correspondent did as he was bid, and this time his eyes chanced on a small, still thing on the edge of the swaying horizon. It was precisely like the point of a pin. It took an anxious eye to find a lighthouse so tiny.

Sèvres: chinaware made in this French town.

"Think we'll make it, Captain?"

"If this wind holds and the boat don't swamp, we can't do much else," said the captain.

The little boat, lifted by each towering sea and splashed viciously by the crests, 40 made progress that in the absence of seaweed was not apparent to those in her. She seemed just a wee thing wallowing, miraculously top up, at the mercy of five oceans. Occasionally a great spread of water, like white flames, swarmed into her.

"Bail her, cook," said the captain, serenely.

"All right, Captain," said the cheerful cook.

III

It would be difficult to describe the subtle brotherhood of men that was here established on the seas. No one said that it was so. No one mentioned it. But it dwelt in the boat, and each man felt it warm him. They were a captain, an oiler, a cook, and a correspondent, and they were friends—friends in a more curiously iron-bound degree than may be common. The hurt captain, lying against the water-jar in the bow, spoke always in a low voice and calmly; but he could never command a more ready and swiftly obedient crew than the motley three of the dinghy. It was more than a mere recognition of what was best for the common safety. There was surely in it a quality that was personal and heart-felt. And after this devotion to the commander of the boat, there was this comradeship, that the correspondent, for instance, who had been taught to be cynical of men, knew even at the time was the best experience of his life. But no one said that it was so. No one mentioned it.

"I wish we had a sail," remarked the captain. "We might try my overcoat on the end of an oar, and give you two boys a chance to rest." So the cook and the correspondent held the mast and spread wide the overcoat; the oiler steered; and the little boat made good way with her new rig. Sometimes the oiler had to scull sharply to keep a sea from breaking into the boat, but otherwise sailing was a success.

Meanwhile the lighthouse had been growing slowly larger. It had now almost 45 assumed color, and appeared like a little gray shadow on the sky. The man at the oars could not be prevented from turning his head rather often to try for a glimpse of this little gray shadow.

At last, from the top of each wave, the men in the tossing boat could see land. Even as the lighthouse was an upright shadow on the sky, this land seemed but a long black shadow on the sea. It certainly was thinner than paper. "We must be about opposite New Smyrna," said the cook, who had coasted this shore often in schooners. "Captain, by the way, I believe they abandoned that life-saving station there about a year ago."

"Did they?" said the captain.

The wind slowly died away. The cook and the correspondent were not now obliged to slave in order to hold high the oar. But the waves continued their old impetuous swooping at the dinghy, and the little craft, no longer under way, struggled woundily over them. The oiler or the correspondent took the oars again.

Shipwrecks are apropos of nothing. If men could only train for them and have them occur when the men had reached pink condition, there would be less drowning at sea. Of the four in the dinghy none had slept any time worth mentioning for two days and two nights previous to embarking in the dinghy, and in the excitement of clambering about the deck of a foundering ship they had also forgotten to eat heartily.

For these reasons, and for others, neither the oiler nor the correspondent   50
was fond of rowing at this time. The correspondent wondered ingenuously how in the name of all that was sane could there be people who thought it amusing to row a boat. It was not an amusement; it was a diabolical punishment, and even a genius of mental aberrations could never conclude that it was anything but a horror to the muscles and crime against the back. He mentioned to the boat in general how the amusement of rowing struck him, and the weary-faced oiler smiled in full sympathy. Previously to the foundering, by the way, the oiler had worked double watch in the engine-room of the ship.

"Take her easy now, boys," said the captain. "Don't spend yourselves. If we have to run a surf you'll need all your strength, because we'll sure have to swim for it. Take your time."

Slowly the land arose from the sea. From a black line it became a line of black and a line of white—trees and sand. Finally the captain said that he could make out a house on the shore. "That's the house of refuge, sure," said the cook. "They'll see us before long, and come out after us."

The distant lighthouse reared high. "The keeper ought to be able to make us out now, if he's looking through a glass," said the captain. "He'll notify the life-saving people."

"None of those other boats could have got ashore to give word of the wreck," said the oiler, in a low voice, "else the life-boat would be out hunting us."

Slowly and beautifully the land loomed out of the sea. The wind came again.   55
It had veered from the north-east to the south-east. Finally a new sound struck the ears of the men in the boat. It was the low thunder of the surf on the shore. "We'll never be able to make the lighthouse now," said the captain. "Swing her head a little more north, Billie."

"A little more north, sir," said the oiler.

Whereupon the little boat turned her nose once more down the wind, and all but the oarsman watched the shore grow. Under the influence of this expansion doubt and direful apprehension were leaving the minds of the men. The management of the boat was still most absorbing, but it could not prevent a quiet cheerfulness. In an hour, perhaps, they would be ashore.

Their backbones had become thoroughly used to balancing in the boat, and they now rode this wild colt of a dinghy like circus men. The correspondent thought that he had been drenched to the skin, but happening to feel in the top pocket of his coat, he found therein eight cigars. Four of them were soaked with sea-water; four were perfectly scatheless. After a search, somebody produced three dry matches; and thereupon the four waifs rode impudently in their little boat and, with an assurance of an impending rescue shining in their eyes, puffed at the big cigars, and judged well and ill of all men. Everybody took a drink of water.

IV

"Cook," remarked the captain, "there don't seem to be any signs of life about your house of refuge."

"No," replied the cook. "Funny they don't see us!" 60

A broad stretch of lowly coast lay before the eyes of the men. It was of low dunes topped with dark vegetation. The roar of the surf was plain, and sometimes they could see the white lip of a wave as it spun up the beach. A tiny house was blocked out black upon the sky. Southward, the slim lighthouse lifted its little gray length.

Tide, wind, and waves were swinging the dinghy northward. "Funny they don't see us," said the men.

The surf's roar was here dulled, but its tone was nevertheless thunderous and mighty. As the boat swam over the great rollers the men sat listening to this roar. "We'll swamp sure," said everybody.

It is fair to say here that there was not a life-saving station within twenty miles in either direction; but the men did not know this fact, and in consequence they made dark and opprobrious remarks concerning the eyesight of the nation's life-savers. Four scowling men sat in the dinghy and surpassed records in the invention of epithets.

"Funny they don't see us." 65

The light-heartedness of a former time had completely faded. To their sharpened minds it was easy to conjure pictures of all kinds of incompetency and blindness and, indeed, cowardice. There was the shore of the populous land, and it was bitter and bitter to them that from it came no sign.

"Well," said the captain, ultimately, "I suppose we'll have to make a try for ourselves. If we stay out here too long, we'll none of us have strength left to swim after the boat swamps."

And so the oiler, who was at the oars, turned the boat straight for the shore. There was a sudden tightening of muscles. There was some thinking.

"If we don't all get ashore," said the captain—"if we don't all get ashore, I suppose you fellows know where to send news of my finish?"

They then briefly exchanged some addresses and admonitions. As for the reflec- 70 tions of the men, there was a great deal of rage in them. Perchance they might be formulated thus: "If I am going to be drowned—if I am going to be drowned—if I am going to be drowned, why, in the name of the seven mad gods who rule the sea, was I allowed to come thus far and contemplate sand and trees? Was I brought here merely to have my nose dragged away as I was about to nibble the sacred cheese of life? It is preposterous. If this old ninny-woman, Fate, cannot do better than this, she should be deprived of the management of men's fortunes. She is an old hen who knows not her intention. If she has decided to drown me, why did she not do it in the beginning and save me all this trouble? The whole affair is absurd.—But no; she cannot mean to drown me. She dare not drown me. She cannot drown me. Not after all this work." Afterward the man might have had an impulse to shake his fist at the clouds. "Just you drown me, now, and then hear what I call you!"

The billows that came at this time were more formidable. They seemed always just about to break and roll over the little boat in a turmoil of foam. There was a preparatory and long growl in the speech of them. No mind unused to the sea would have concluded that the dinghy could ascend these sheer heights in time. The shore was still afar. The oiler was a wily surfman. "Boys," he said swiftly, "she won't live three minutes more, and we're too far out to swim. Shall I take her to sea again, Captain?"

"Yes; go ahead!" said the captain.

This oiler, by a series of quick miracles and fast and steady oarsmanship, turned the boat in the middle of the surf and took her safely to sea again.

There was a considerable silence as the boat bumped over the furrowed sea to deeper water. Then somebody in gloom spoke: "Well, anyhow, they must have seen us from the shore by now."

The gulls went in slanting flight up the wind toward the gray, desolate east. 75
A squall, marked by dinghy clouds and clouds brick-red like smoke from a burning building, appeared from the south-east.

"What do you think of those life-saving people? Ain't they peaches?"

"Funny they haven't seen us."

"Maybe they think we're out here for sport! Maybe they think we're fishin'. Maybe they think we're damned fools."

It was a long afternoon. A changed tide tried to force them southward, but wind and wave said northward. Far ahead, where coast-line, sea, and sky formed their mighty angle, there were little dots which seemed to indicate a city on the shore.

"St. Augustine?" 80

The captain shook his head. "Too near Mosquito Inlet."

And the oiler rowed, and then the correspondent rowed; then the oiler rowed. It was a weary business. The human back can become the seat of more aches and pains than are registered in books for the composite anatomy of a regiment. It is a limited area, but it can become the theatre of innumerable muscular conflicts, tangles, wrenches, knots, and other comforts.

"Did you ever like to row, Billie?" asked the correspondent.

"No," said the oiler; "hang it!"

When one exchanged the rowing-seat for a place in the bottom of the boat, 85
he suffered a bodily depression that caused him to be careless of everything save an obligation to wiggle one finger. There was cold sea-water swashing to and fro in the boat, and he lay in it. His head, pillowed on a thwart, was within an inch of the swirl of a wave-crest, and sometimes a particularly obstreperous sea came inboard and drenched him once more. But these matters did not annoy him. It is almost certain that if the boat had capsized he would have tumbled comfortably upon the ocean as if he felt sure that it was a great soft mattress.

"Look! There's a man on the shore!"

"Where?"

"There! See 'im?"

"Yes, sure! He's walking along."

"Now he's stopped. Look! He's facing us!" 90

"He's waving at us!"

"So he is! By thunder!"

"Ah, now we're all right! Now we're all right! There'll be a boat out here for us in half an hour."

"He's going on. He's running. He's going up to that house there."

The remote beach seemed lower than the sea, and it required a searching glance to discern the little black figure. The captain saw a floating stick, and they rowed to it. A bath towel was by some weird chance in the boat, and, trying this on the stick, the captain waved it. The oarsman did not dare turn his head, so he was obliged to ask questions.

"What's he doing now?"

"He's standing still again. He's looking, I think.—There he goes again—toward the house.—Now he's stopped again."

"Is he waving at us?"

"No, not now; he was, though."

"Look! There comes another man!"

"He's running."

"Look at him go, would you!"

"Why, he's on a bicycle. Now he's met the other man. They're both waving at us. Look!"

"There comes something up the beach."

"What the devil is that thing?"

"Why, it looks like a boat."

"Why, certainly, it's a boat."

"No; it's on wheels."

"Yes, so it is. Well, that must be the life-boat. They drag them along shore on a wagon."

"That's the life-boat, sure."

"No, by God, it's—it's an omnibus."

"I tell you it's a life-boat."

"It is not! It's an omnibus. I can see it plain. See? One of the these big hotel omnibuses."

"By thunder, you're right. It's an omnibus, sure as fate. What do you suppose they are doing with an omnibus? Maybe they are going around collecting the life-crew, hey?"

"That's it, likely. Look! There's a fellow waving a little black flag. He's standing on the steps of the omnibus. There come those other two fellows. Now they're all talking together. Look at the fellow with the flag. Maybe he ain't waving it!"

"That ain't a flag, is it? That's his coat. Why, certainly, that's his coat."

"So it is; it's his coat. He's taken it off and is waving it around his head. But would you look at him swing it!"

"Oh, say, there isn't any life-saving station there. That's just a winter-resort hotel omnibus that has brought over some of the boarders to see us drown."

"What's that idiot with the coat mean? What's he signalling, anyhow?"

"It looks as if he were trying to tell us to go north. There must be a life-saving station up there."

"No; he thinks we're fishing. Just giving us a merry hand. See? Ah, there, Willie!"

"Well, I wish I could make something out of those signals. What do you suppose he means?"

"He don't mean anything; he's just playing."

"Well, if he'd just signal us to try the surf again, or to go to sea and wait, or go north, or go south, or go to hell, there would be some reason in it. But look at him! He just stands there and keeps his coat revolving like a wheel. The ass!"

"There come more people."

"Now there's quite a mob. Look! Isn't that a boat?"

"Where? Oh, I see where you mean. No, that's no boat."

"That fellow is still waving his coat."

"He must think we like to see him do that. Why don't he quit it? It don't mean anything."

"I don't know. I think he is trying to make us go north. It must be that there's a life-saving station there somewhere."

"Say, he ain't tired yet. Look at 'im wave!"

"Wonder how long he can keep that up. He's been revolving his coat ever since he caught sight of us. He's an idiot. Why aren't they getting men to bring a boat out? A fishingboat—one of those big yawls—could come out here all right. Why don't he do something?"

"Oh, it's all right now."

"They'll have a boat out here for us in less than no time, now that they've seen us."

A faint yellow tone came into the sky over the low land. The shadows on the sea slowly deepened. The wind bore coldness with it, and the men began to shiver.

"Holy smoke!" said one, allowing his voice to express his impious mood, "If we keep on monkeying out here! If we've got to flounder out here all night!"

"Oh, we'll never have to stay here all night! Don't you worry. They've seen us now, and it won't be long before they'll come chasing out after us."

The shore grew dusky. The man waving a coat blended gradually into this gloom, and it swallowed in the same manner the omnibus and the group of people. The spray, when it dashed uproariously over the side, made the voyagers shrink and swear like men who were being branded.

"I'd like to catch the chump who waved the coat. I feel like socking him one, just for luck."

"Why? What did he do?"

"Oh, nothing, but then he seemed so damned cheerful."

In the meantime the oiler rowed, and then the correspondent rowed, and then the oiler rowed. Gray-faced and bowed forward, they mechanically, turn by turn, plied the leaden oars. The form of the lighthouse had vanished from the southern horizon, but finally a pale star appeared, just lifting from the sea. The streaked saffron in the west passed before the all-merging darkness, and the sea to the east was black. The land had vanished, and was expressed only by the low and drear thunder of the surf.

"If I am going to be drowned—if I am going to be drowned—if I am going to be drowned, why, in the name of the seven gods who rule the sea, was I allowed to come thus far and contemplate sand and trees? Was I brought here merely to have my nose dragged away as I was about to nibble the sacred cheese of life?"

The patient captain, drooped over the water-jar, was sometimes obliged to speak to the oarsman.

"Keep her head up! Keep her head up!"

"Keep her head, up, sir." The voices were weary and low.

This was surely a quiet evening. All save the oarsman lay heavily and listlessly in the boat's bottom. As for him, his eyes were just capable of noting the tall black waves that swept forward in a most sinister silence, save for an occasional subdued growl of a crest.

The cook's head was on a thwart, and he looked without interest at the water under this nose. He was deep in other scenes. Finally he spoke. "Billie," he murmured, dreamfully, "what kind of pie do you like best?"

V

"Pie!" said the oiler and the correspondent, agitatedly. "Don't talk about those things, blast you!"

"Well," said the cook, "I was just thinking about ham sandwiches, and—"

A night on the sea in an open boat is a long night. As darkness settled finally, the shine of the light, lifting from the sea in the south, changed to full gold. On the northern horizon a new light appeared, a small bluish gleam on the edge of the waters. These two lights were the furniture of the world. Otherwise there was nothing but waves.

Two men huddled in the stern, and distances were so magnificent in the dinghy that the rower was enabled to keep his feet partly warm by thrusting them under his companions. Their legs indeed extended far under the rowingseat until they touched the feet of the captain forward. Sometimes, despite the efforts of the tired oarsman, a wave came piling into the boat, an icy wave of the night, and the chilling water soaked them anew. They would twist their bodies for a moment and groan, and sleep the dead sleep once more, while the water in the boat gurgled about them as the craft rocked.

The plan of the oiler and the correspondent was for one to row until he lost the ability, and then arouse the other from his sea-water couch in the bottom of the boat.

The oiler plied the oars until his head drooped forward and the overpowering sleep blinded him; and he rowed yet afterward. Then he touched a man in the bottom of the boat, and called his name. "Will you spell me for a little while?" he said meekly.

"Sure, Billie," said the correspondent, awaking and dragging himself to a sitting position. They exchanged places carefully, and the oiler, cuddling down in the sea-water at the cook's side, seemed to go to sleep instantly.

The particular violence of the sea had ceased. The waves cames without snarling. The obligation of the man at the oars was to keep the boat headed so that the tilt of the roller would not capsize her, and to preserve her from filling when the crests rushed past. The black waves were silent and hard to be seen in the darkness. Often one was almost upon the boat before the oarsman was aware.

In a low voice the correspondent addressed the captain. He was not sure that the captain was awake, although this iron man seemed to be always awake. "Captain, shall I keep her making for that light north, sir?"

The same steady voice answered him. "Yes. Keep it about two points off the port bow."

The cook had tied a life-belt around himself in order to get even the warmth which this clumsy cork contrivance could donate, and he seemed almost stove-like when a rower, whose teeth invariably chattered wildly as soon as he ceased his labor, dropped down to sleep.

The correspondent, as he rowed, looked down at the two men sleeping underfoot. The cook's arm was around the oiler's shoulders, and, with their fragmentary clothing and haggard faces, they were the babes of the sea – a grotesque rendering of the old babes in the wood.

Later he must have grown stupid at his work, for suddenly there was a growling of water, and a crest came with a roar and a swash into the boat, and it was a wonder that it did not set the cook afloat in his life-belt. The cook continued to sleep, but the oiler sat up, blinking his eyes and shaking with the new cold.

"Oh, I'm awful sorry, Billie," said the correspondent, contritely.

"That's all right, old boy," said the oiler, and lay down again and was asleep.

Presently it seemed that even the captain dozed, and the correspondent thought that he was the one man afloat on all the oceans. The wind had a voice as it came over the waves, and it was sadder than the end.

There was a long, loud swishing astern of the boat, and a gleaming trail of phosphorescence, like blue flame, was furrowed on the black waters. It might have been made by a monstrous knife.

Then there came a stillness, while the correspondent breathed with open mouth and looked at the sea.

Suddenly there was another swish and another long flash of bluish light, and this time it was alongside the boat, and might almost have been reached with an oar. The correspondent saw an enormous fin speed like a shadow through the water, hurling the crystalline spray and leaving the long glowing trail.

The correspondent looked over his shoulder at the captain. His face was hidden, and he seemed to be asleep. He looked at the babes of the sea. They certainly were asleep. So, being bereft of sympathy, he leaned a little way to one side and swore softly into the sea.

But the thing did not then leave the vicinity of the boat. Ahead or astern, on one side or the other, at intervals long or short, fled the long sparkling streak, and there was to be heard the *whirroo* of the dark fin. The speed and power of the thing was greatly to be admired. It cut the water like a gigantic and keen projectile.

The presence of this biding thing did not affect the man with the same horror that it would if he had been a picnicker. He simply looked at the sea dully and swore in an undertone.

Nevertheless, it is true that he did not wish to be alone with the thing. He wished one of his companions to awake by chance and keep him company with it. But the company hung motionless over the water-jar, and the oiler and the cook in the bottom of the boat were plunged in slumber.

160

165

170

VI

"If I am going to be drowned—if I am going to be drowned – if I am going to be drowned, why, in the name of the seven mad gods who rule the sea, was I allowed to come thus far and contemplate sand and trees?"

During this dismal night, it may be remarked that a man would conclude that it was really the intention of the seven mad gods to drown him, despite the abominable injustice of it. For it was certainly an abominable injustice to drown a man who had worked so hard, so hard. The man felt it would be a crime most unnatural. Other people had drowned at sea since galleys swarmed with painted sails, but still—

When it occurs to a man that nature does not regard him as important, and that she feels she would not maim the universe by disposing of him, he at first wishes to throw bricks at the temple, and he hates deeply the fact that there are no bricks and no temples. Any visible expression of nature would surely be pelleted with his jeers.

Then, if there be no tangible thing to hoot, he feels, perhaps, the desire to 175 confront a personification and indulge in pleas, bowed to one knee, and with hands supplicant, saying, "Yes, but I love myself."

A high cold star on a winter's night is the word he feels that she says to him. Thereafter he knows the pathos of his situation.

The men in the dinghy had not discussed these matters, but each had, no doubt, reflected upon them in silence and according to his mind. There was seldom any expression upon their faces save the general one of complete weariness. Speech was devoted to the business of the boat.

To chime the notes of his emotion, a verse mysteriously entered the correspondent's head. He had even forgotten that he had forgotten this verse, but it suddenly was in his mind.

> A soldier of the Legion lay dying in Algiers;
> There was lack of woman's nursing, there was dearth of woman's tears;
> But a comrade stood beside him, and he took that comrade's hand,
> And he said, "I never more shall see my own, my native land.'"

In his childhood the correspondent had been made acquainted with the fact 180 that a soldier of the Legion lay dying in Algiers, but he had never regarded the fact as important. Myriads of his school-fellows had informed him of the soldier's plight, but the dinning had naturally ended by making him perfectly indifferent. He had never considered it his affair that a soldier of the Legion lay dying in Algiers, nor had it appeared to him as a matter for sorrow. It was less to him than the breaking of a pencil's point.

Now, however, it quaintly came to him as a human, living thing. It was no longer merely a picture of a few throes in the breast of a poet, meanwhile drinking tea and warming his feet at the grate; it was an actuality—stern, mournful, and fine.

A soldier of the Legion . . . native land: The correspondent remembers a Victorian ballad about a German dying in the French Foreign Legion, "Bingen on the Rhine" by Caroline Norton.

The correspondent plainly saw the soldier. He lay on the sand with his feet out straight and still. While his pale left hand was upon his chest in an attempt to thwart the going of his life, the blood came between his fingers. In the far Algerian distance, a city of low square forms was set against a sky that was faint with the last sunset hues. The correspondent, plying the oars and dreaming of the slow and slower movements of the lips of the soldier, was moved by a profound and perfectly impersonal comprehension. He was sorry for the soldier of the Legion who lay dying in Algiers.

The thing which had followed the boat and waited had evidently grown bored at the delay. There was no longer to be heard the slash of the cutwater, and there was no longer the flame of the long trail. The light in the north still glimmered, but it was apparently no nearer to the boat. Sometimes the boom of the surf rang in the correspondent's ears, and he turned the craft seaward then and rowed harder. Southward, some one had evidently built a watch-fire on the beach. It was too low and too far to be seen, but it made a shimmering, roseate reflection upon the bluff in back of it, and this could be discerned from the boat. The wind came stronger, and sometimes a wave suddenly raged out like a mountain cat, and there was to be seen the sheen and sparkle of a broken crest.

The captain, in the bow, moved on his water-jar and sat erect. "Pretty long night," he observed to the correspondent. He looked at the shore. "Those life-saving people take their time."

"Did you see that shark playing around?"   185

"Yes, I saw him. He was a big fellow, all right."

"Wish I had known you were awake."

Later the correspondent spoke into the bottom of the boat.

"Billie!" There was a slow and gradual disentanglement.

"Billie, will you spell me?"   190

"Sure," said the oiler.

As soon as the correspondent touched the cold, comfortable sea-water in the bottom of the boat and had huddled close to the cook's life-belt he was deep in sleep, despite the fact that his teeth played all the popular airs. This sleep was so good to him that it was but a moment before he heard a voice call his name in a tone that demonstrated the last stages of exhaustion. "Will you spell me?"

"Sure, Billie."

The light in the north had mysteriously vanished, but the correspondent took his course from the wide-awake captain.

Later in the night they took the boat farther out to sea, and the captain   195
directed the cook to take one oar at the stern and keep the boat facing the seas. He was to call out if he should hear the thunder of the surf. This plan enabled the oiler and the correspondent to get respite together. "We'll give those boys a chance to get into shape again," said the captain. They curled down and, after a few preliminary chatterings and trembles, slept once more the dead sleep. Neither knew they had bequeathed to the cook the company of another shark, or perhaps the same shark.

As the boat caroused on the waves, spray occasionally bumped over the side and gave them a fresh soaking, but this had no power to break their repose. The ominous slash of the wind and the water affected them as it would have affected mummies.

"Boys," said the cook, with the notes of every reluctance in his voice, "she's drifted in pretty close. I guess one of you had better take her to sea again." The correspondent, aroused, heard the crash of the toppled crests.

As he was rowing, the captain gave him some whisky-and-water, and this steadied the chills out of him. "If I ever get ashore and anybody shows me even a photograph of an oar—"

At last there was a short conversation.

"Billie!—Billie, will you spell me?"

"Sure," said the oiler.

VII

When the correspondent again opened his eyes, the sea and sky were each of the gray hue of the dawning. Later, carmine and gold was painted upon the waters. The morning appeared finally, in its splendor, with a sky of pure blue, and the sunlight flamed on the tips of the waves.

On the distant dunes were set many little black cottages, and a tall white windmill reared above them. No man, nor dog, nor bicycle appeared on the beach. The cottages might have formed a deserted village.

The voyagers scanned the shore. A conference was held in the boat. "Well," said the captain, "if no help is coming, we might better try a run through the surf right away. If we stay out here much longer we will be too weak to do anything for ourselves at all." The others silently acquiesced in this reasoning. The boat was headed for the beach. The correspondent wondered if none ever ascended the tall wind-tower, and if they never looked seaward. This tower was a giant, standing with its back to the plight of the ants. It represented in a degree, to the correspondent, the serenity of nature amid the struggles of the individual—nature in the wind, and nature in the vision of men. She did not seem cruel to him then, nor beneficent, nor treacherous, nor wise. But she was indifferent, flatly indifferent. It is, perhaps, plausible that a man in this situation, impressed with the unconcern of the universe, should see the innumerable flaws of life, and have them taste wickedly in his mind, and wish for another chance. A distinction between right and wrong seems absurdly clear to him, then, in this new ignorance of the grave-edge, and he understands that if he were given another opportunity he would mend his conduct and his words, and be better and brighter during an introduction or at a tea.

"Now, boys," said the captain, "she is going to swamp sure. All we can do is to work her in as far as possible, and then when she swamps, pile out and scramble for the beach. Keep cool now, and don't jump until she swamps sure."

The oiler took the oars. Over his shoulders he scanned the surf. "Captain," he said, "I think I'd better bring her about and keep her head-on to the seas and back her in."

"All right, Billie," said the captain. "Back her in." The oiler swung the boat then, and, seated in the stern, the cook and the correspondent were obliged to look over their shoulders to contemplate the lonely and indifferent shore.

The monstrous inshore rollers heaved the boat high until the men were again enabled to see the white sheets of water scudding up the slanted beach. "We won't get in very close," said the captain. Each time a man could wrest his attention from the rollers, he turned his glance toward the shore, and in the expression of the eyes during this contemplation there was a singular quality. The correspondent, observing the others, knew that they were not afraid, but the full meaning of their glances was shrouded.

As for himself, he was too tired to grapple fundamentally with the fact. He tried to coerce his mind into thinking of it, but the mind was dominated at this time by the muscles, and the muscles said they did not care. It merely occurred to him that if he should drown it would be a shame.

There were no hurried words, no pallor, no plain agitation. The men simply looked at the shore. "Now, remember to get well clear of the boat when you jump," said the captain. 210

Seaward the crest of a roller suddenly fell with a thunderous crash, and the long white comber came roaring down upon the boat.

"Steady now," said the captain. The men were silent. They turned their eyes from the shore to the comber and waited. The boat slid up the incline, leaped at the furious top, bounced over it, and swung down the long back of the wave. Some water had been shipped, and the cook bailed it out.

But the next crest crashed also. The tumbling, boiling flood of white water caught the boat and whirled it almost perpendicular. Water swarmed in from all sides. The correspondent had his hands on the gunwale at this time, and when the water entered at that place he swiftly withdrew his fingers, as if he objected to wetting them.

The little boat, drunken with this weight of water, reeled and snuggled deeper into the sea.

"Bail her out, cook! Bail her out!" said the captain. 215

"All right, Captain," said the cook.

"Now, boys, the next one will do for us sure," said the oiler. "Mind to jump clear of the boat."

The third wave moved forward, huge, furious, implacable. It fairly swallowed the dinghy, and almost simultaneously the men tumbled into the sea. A piece of life-belt had lain in the bottom of the boat, and as the correspondent went overboard he held this to his chest with his left hand.

The January water was icy, and he reflected immediately that it was colder than he had expected to find it off the coast of Florida. This appeared to his dazed mind as a fact important enough to be noted at the time. The coldness of the water was sad; it was tragic. This fact was somehow mixed and confused with his opinion of his own situation, so that it seemed almost a proper reason for tears. The water was cold.

When he came to the surface he was conscious of little but the noisy water. 220 Afterward he saw his companions in the sea. The oiler was ahead in the race. He was swimming strongly and rapidly. Off to the correspondent's left, the cook's great white and corked back bulged out of the water; and in the rear the captain was hanging with his one good hand to the keel of the overturned dinghy.

There is a certain immovable quality to a shore, and the correspondent wondered at it amid the confusion of the sea.

It seemed also very attractive; but the correspondent knew that it was a long journey, and he paddled leisurely. The piece of life-preserver lay under him, and sometimes he whirled down the incline of a wave as if he were on a handsled.

But finally he arrived at a place in the sea where travel was beset with difficulty. He did not pause swimming to inquire what manner of current had caught him, but there his progress ceased. The shore was set before him like a bit of scenery on a stage, and he looked at it and understood with his eyes each detail of it.

As the cook passed, much farther to the left, the captain was calling to him, "Turn over on your back, cook! Turn over on your back and use the oar."

"All right, sir." The cook turned on his back, and, paddling with an oar, went ahead as if he were a canoe. 225

Presently the boat also passed to the left of the correspondent, with the captain clinging with one hand to the kneel. He would have appeared like a man raising himself to look over a board fence if it were not for the extraordinary gymnastics of the boat. The correspondent marvelled that the captain could still hold to it.

They passed on nearer to shore—the oiler, the cook, the captain—and following them went the water-jar, bouncing gaily over the seas.

The correspondent remained in the grip of this strange new enemy—a current. The shore, with its white slope of sand and its green bluff topped with little silent cottages, was spread like a picture before him. It was very near to him then, but he was impressed as one who, in a gallery, looks at a scene from Brittany or Algiers.

He thought: "I am going to drown? Can it be possible? Can it be possible? Can it be possible?" Perhaps an individual must consider his own death to be the final phenomenon of nature.

But later a wave perhaps whirled him out of this small deadly current, for he found suddenly that he could again make progress toward the shore. Later still he was aware that the captain, clinging with one hand to the keel of the dinghy, had his face turned away from the shore and toward him, and was calling his name. "Come to the boat! Come to the boat!" 230

In his struggle to reach the captain and the boat, he reflected that when one gets properly wearied drowning must really be a comfortable arrangement—a cessation of hostilities accompanied by a large degree of relief; and he was glad of it, for the main thing in his mind for some moments had been horror of the temporary agony. He did not wish to be hurt.

Presently he saw a man running along the shore. He was undressing with most remarkable speed. Coat, trousers, shirt, everything flew magically off him.

"Come to the boat!" called the captain.

"All right, Captain." As the correspondent paddled, he saw the captain let himself down to bottom and leave the boat. Then the correspondent performed his one little marvel of the voyage. A large wave caught him and flung him with ease and supreme speed completely over the boat and far beyond it. It struck him even then as an event in gymnastics and a true miracle of the sea. An overturned boat in the surf is not a plaything to a swimming man.

The correspondent arrived in water that reached only to his waist, but his condition did not enable him to stand for more than a moment. Each wave knocked him into a heap, and the undertow pulled at him. 235

Then he saw the man who had been running and undressing, and undressing and running, come bounding into the water. He dragged ashore the cook, and then waded toward the captain; but the captain waved him away and sent him to the correspondent. He was naked—naked as a tree in winter; but a halo was about his head, and he shone like a saint. He gave a strong pull, and a long drag, and a bully heave at the correspondent's hand. The correspondent, schooled in the minor formulae, said, "Thanks, old man." But suddenly the man cried, "What's that?" He pointed a swift finger. The correspondent said, "Go."

In the shallows, face downward, lay the oiler. His forehead touched sand that was periodically, between each wave, clear of the sea.

The correspondent did not know all that transpired afterward. When he achieved safe ground he fell, striking the sand with each particular part of his body. It was as if he had dropped from a roof, but the thud was grateful to him.

It seems that instantly the beach was populated with men with blankets, clothes, and flasks, and women with coffee-pots and all the remedies sacred to their minds. The welcome of the land to the men from the sea was warm and generous; but a still and dripping shape was carried slowly up the beach, and the land's welcome for it could only be the different and sinister hospitality of the grave.

When it came night, the white waves paced to and fro in the moonlight, 240 and the wind brought the sound of the great sea's voice to the men on the shore, and they felt that they could then be interpreters.

QUESTIONS

1. In actuality, Crane, the captain of the *Commodore*, and the two crew members spent nearly thirty hours in the open boat. William Higgins, the oiler, was drowned as Crane describes. Does a knowledge of these facts in any way affect your response to the story? Would you admire the story less if you believed it to be pure fiction?
2. Sum up the personalities of each of the four men in the boat: captain, cook, oiler, and correspondent.
3. What is the point of view of the story?
4. In paragraph 9, we are told that as each wave came, the boat "seemed like a horse making for a fence outrageously high." Point to the other vivid similes or figures of speech. What do they contribute to the story's effectiveness?
5. Notice some of the ways in which Crane, as a storyteller conscious of plot, builds suspense. What enemies or obstacles do the men in the boat confront? What is the effect of the scene of the men who wave from the beach (paragraphs 86–141)? What is the climax of the story? (If you need to be refreshed on the meaning of *climax*, see page 7.)
6. In paragraph 70 (and again in paragraph 143), the men wonder, "Was I brought here merely to have my nose dragged away as I was about to nibble the sacred cheese of life?" What variety of irony do you find in this quotation?
7. Why does the scrap of verse about the soldier dying in Algiers (paragraph 179) suddenly come to mean so much to the correspondent?
8. What theme in "The Open Boat" seems most important to you? Where is it stated?
9. What secondary themes also enrich the story? See for instance paragraph 43 (the thoughts on comradeship).
10. How do you define *heroism*? Who is a hero in "The Open Boat"?

Nathaniel Hawthorne

Nathaniel Hawthorne (1804–1864) was born in the clipper-ship seaport of Salem, Massachusetts, son of a merchant captain and grandson of a judge at the notorious Salem witchcraft trials. Hawthorne takes a keen interest in New England's sin-and-brimstone Puritan past in this and many other of his stories and in The Scarlet Letter *(1848), that enduring novel of a woman taken in adultery. After college, Hawthorne lived at home and trained to be a writer. Only when his first collection,* Twice-Told Tales *(1837), made money did he feel secure enough to marry Sophia Peabody and settle in the Old Manse in Concord, Massachusetts. Three more novels followed* The Scarlet Letter: The House of the Seven Gables *(1851, a story tinged with nightmarish humor),* The Blithedale Romance *(1852, drawn from his short, disgrun-*

Nathaniel Hawthorne

tled stay at a Utopian commune, Brook Farm), and The Marble Faun *(1860, inspired by a stay in Italy). Hawthorne wrote for children, too, retelling classic legends in* The Wonder Book *(1852) and* Tanglewood Tales *(1853). At Bowdoin College, he had been a classmate of Franklin Pierce; later, when Pierce ran for President of the United States, Hawthorne wrote him a campaign biography. The victorious Pierce appointed his old friend American consul at Liverpool, England. With his contemporary, Edgar Allan Poe, Hawthorne sped the transformation of the American short story from popular magazine filler into a form of art.*

Young Goodman° Brown came forth, at sunset, into the street of Salem village°, but put his head back, after crossing the threshold, to exchange a parting kiss with his young wife. And Faith, as the wife was aptly named, thrust her own pretty head into the street, letting the wind play with the pink ribbons of her cap, while she called to Goodman Brown.

"Dearest heart," whispered she, softly and rather sadly, when her lips were close to his ear, "pray thee, put off your journey until sunrise, and sleep in your own bed to-night. A lone woman is troubled with such dreams and such thoughts, that she's afraid of herself, sometimes. Pray, tarry with me this night, dear husband, of all nights in the year!"

Goodman: title given by Puritans to a male head of a household: a farmer or other ordinary citizen.
Salem village: in England's Massachusetts Bay Colony.

"My love and my Faith," replied young Goodman Brown, "of all nights in the year, this one night must I tarry away from thee. My journey, as thou callest it, forth and back again, must needs be done 'twixt now and sunrise. What, my sweet, pretty wife, dost thou doubt me already, and we but three months married!"

"Then, God bless you!" said Faith, with the pink ribbons, "and may you find all well, when you come back."

"Amen!" cried Goodman Brown. "Say thy prayers, dear Faith, and go to bed at dusk, and no harm will come to thee." 5

So they parted; and the young man pursued his way, until, being about to turn the corner by the meeting-house, he looked back, and saw the head of Faith still peeping after him, with a melancholy air, in spite of her pink ribbons.

"Poor little Faith!" thought he, for his heart smote him. "What a wretch am I, to leave her on such an errand! She talks of dreams, too. Methought, as she spoke, there was trouble in her face, as if a dream had warned her what work is to be done to-night. But, no, no! 'twould kill her to think it. Well; she's a blessed angel on earth; and after this one night, I'll cling to her skirts and follow her to Heaven."

With this excellent resolve for the future, Goodman Brown felt himself justified in making more haste on his present evil purpose. He had taken a dreary road, darkened by all the gloomiest trees of the forest, which barely stood aside to let the narrow path creep through, and closed immediately behind. It was all as lonely as could be; and there is this peculiarity in such a solitude, that the traveller knows not who may be concealed by the innumerable trunks and the thick boughs overhead; so that, with lonely footsteps, he may yet be passing through an unseen multitude.

"There may be a devilish Indian behind every tree," said Goodman Brown, to himself; and he glanced fearfully behind him, as he added, "What if the devil himself should be at my very elbow!"

His head being turned back, he passed a crook of the road, and looking forward again, beheld the figure of a man, in grave and decent attire, seated at the foot of an old tree. He arose, at Goodman Brown's approach, and walked onward, side by side with him. 10

"You are late, Goodman Brown," said he. "The clock of the Old South was striking as I came through Boston; and that is full fifteen minutes agone°."

"Faith kept me back awhile," replied the young man, with a tremor in his voice, caused by the sudden appearance of his companion, though not wholly unexpected.

It was now deep dusk in the forest, and deepest in that part of it where these two were journeying. As nearly as could be discerned, the second traveller was about fifty years old, apparently in the same rank of life as Goodman Brown, and bearing a considerable resemblance to him, though perhaps more in expression than features. Still, they might have been taken for father and son. And yet, though the elder person was as simply clad as the younger, and as simple in manner too, he had an indescribable air of one who knew the world, and would not have felt

full fifteen minutes agone: Apparently this mystery-man has traveled in a flash from Boston's Old South Church all the way to the woods beyond Salem—as the crow flies, a good sixteen miles.

abashed at the governor's dinner-table, or in King William's court,° were it possible that his affairs should call him thither. But the only thing about him, that could be fixed upon as remarkable, was his staff, which bore the likeness of a great black snake, so curiously wrought, that it might almost be seen to twist and wriggle itself, like a living serpent. This, of course, must have been an ocular deception, assisted by the uncertain light.

"Come, Goodman Brown!" cried his fellow-traveller, "this is dull pace for the beginning of a journey. Take my staff, if you are so soon weary."

"Friend," said the other, exchanging his slow pace for a full stop, "having kept covenant by meeting thee here, it is my purpose now to return whence I came. I have scruples, touching the matter thou wot'st° of." 15

"Sayest thou so?" replied he of the serpent, smiling apart. "Let us walk on, nevertheless, reasoning as we go, and if I convince thee not, thou shalt turn back. We are but a little way in the forest, yet."

"Too far, too far!" exclaimed the goodman, unconsciously resuming his walk. "My father never went into the woods on such an errand, nor his father before him. We have been a race of honest men and good Christians, since the days of the martyrs°. And shall I be the first of the name of Brown, that ever took this path, and kept—"

"Such company, thou wouldst say," observed the elder person, interpreting his pause. "Well said, Goodman Brown! I have been as well acquainted with your family as with ever a one among the Puritans; and that's no trifle to say. I helped your grandfather, the constable, when he lashed the Quaker woman so smartly through the streets of Salem. And it was I that brought your father a pitch-pine knot, kindled at my own hearth, to set fire to an Indian village, in King Philip's war°. They were my good friends, both; and many a pleasant walk have we had along this path, and returned merrily after midnight. I would fain be friends with you, for their sake."

"If it be as thou sayest," replied Goodman Brown, "I marvel they never spoke of these matters. Or, verily, I marvel not, seeing that the least rumor of the sort would have driven them from New-England. We are a people of prayer, and good works, to boot, and abide no such wickedness."

"Wickedness or not," said the traveller with the twisted staff, "I have a very general acquaintance here in New-England. The deacons of many a church have drunk the communion wine with me; the selectmen, of divers towns, make me their chairman; and a majority of the Great and general Court are firm supporters of my interest. The governor and I, too—but these are state-secrets." 20

"Can this be so!" cried Goodman Brown, with a stare of amazement at his undisturbed companion. "Howbeit, I have nothing to do with the governor and

---

King William's court: back in England, where William III reigned in 1689–1702.   wot'st: know. days of the martyrs: a time when many forebears of the New England Puritans had given their lives for their religious convictions—when Mary I (Mary Tudor, nicknamed "Bloody Mary"), queen of England from 1553 to 1558, briefly re-established the Roman Catholic Church in England and launched a campaign of persecution against Protestants.   King Philip's war: Metacomet, or King Philip (as the English called him), chief of the Wampanoag Indians, had led a bitter, widespread uprising of several New England tribes (1675–78). Metacomet died in the war, as did one out of every ten white male colonists.

council; they have their own ways, and are no rule for a simple husbandman, like me. But, were I to go on with thee, how should I meet the eye of that good old man, our minister, at Salem village? Oh, his voice would make me tremble, both Sabbath-day and lecture-day°!"

Thus far, the elder traveller had listened with due gravity, but now burst into a fit of irrepressible mirth, shaking himself so violently, that his snake-life staff actually seemed to wriggle in sympathy.

"Ha! ha! ha!" shouted he, again and again; then composing himself, "Well, go on, Goodman Brown, go on; but pray thee, don't kill me with laughing!"

"Well, then, to end the matter at once," said Goodman Brown, considerably nettled, "there is my wife, Faith. It would break her dear little heart; and I'd rather break my own!"

"Nay, if that be the case," answered the other, "e'en go thy ways, Goodman   25
Brown. I would not, for twenty old women like the one hobbling before us, that Faith should come to any harm."

As he spoke, he pointed his staff at a female figure on the path, in whom Goodman Brown recognized a very pious and exemplary dame, who had taught him his catechism, in youth, and was still his moral and spiritual adviser, jointly with the minister and Deacon Gookin.

"A marvel, truly, that Goody° Cloyse should be so far in the wilderness, at night-fall!" said he. "But, with your leave, friend, I shall take a cut through the woods, until we have left this Christian woman behind. Being a stranger to you, she might ask whom I was consorting with, and whither I was going."

"Be it so," said his fellow-traveller. "Betake you to the woods, and let me keep the path."

Accordingly, the young man turned aside, but took care to watch his companion, who advanced softly along the road, until he had come within a staff's length of the old dame. She, meanwhile, was making the best of her way, with singular speed for so aged a woman, and mumbling some indistinct words, a prayer, doubtless, as she went. The traveller put forth his staff, and touched her withered neck with what seemed the serpent's tail.

"The devil!" screamed the pious old lady.   30

"Then Goody Cloyse knows her old friend?" observed the traveller, confronting her, and leaning on his writhing stick.

"Ah, forsooth, and is it your worship, indeed?" cried the good dame. "Yea, truly is it, and in the very image of my old gossip°, Goodman Brown, the grandfather of the silly fellow that now is. But—would your worship believe it?—my broomstick hath strangely disappeared, stolen, as I suspect, by that unhanged witch, Goody Cory, and that, too, when I was all anointed with the juice of smallage and cinque-foil and wolf's bane—°"

---

lecture-day: a weekday when everyone had to go to church to hear a sermon or Bible-reading.   *Goody:* short for Goodwife, title for a married woman of ordinary station. In his story, Hawthorne borrows from history the names of two "Goodys"—Goody Cloyse and Goody Cory—and one unmarried woman, Martha Carrier. In 1692 Hawthorne's great-grandfather, John Hawthorne, a judge in the Salem witch-craft trials, had condemned all three to be hanged.   *gossip:* friend or kinsman.   *smallage and cin-quefoil and wolf's bane:* wild plants—here, ingredients for a witch's brew.

"Mingled with fine wheat and the fat of a new-born babe," said the shape of old Goodman Brown.

"Ah, your worship knows the receipt," cried the old lady, cackling aloud. "So, as I was saying, being all ready for the meeting, and no horse to ride on, I made up my mind to foot it; for they tell me, there is a nice young man to be taken into communion to-night. But now your good worship will lend me your arm, and we shall be there in a twinkling."

"That can hardly be," answered her friend. "I may not spare you my arm, Goody 35 Cloyse, but here is my staff, if you will."

So saying, he threw it down at her feet, where, perhaps, it assumed life, being one of the rods which its owner had formerly lent to the Egyptian Magi°. Of this fact, however, Goodman Brown could not take cognizance. He had cast up his eyes in astonishment, and looking down again, beheld neither Goody Cloyse nor the serpentine staff, but his fellow-traveller alone, who waited for him as calmly as if nothing had happened.

"That old woman taught me my catechism!" said the young man; and there was a world of meaning in this simple comment.

They continued to walk onward, while the elder traveller exhorted his companion to make good speed and persevere in the path, discoursing so aptly, that his arguments seemed rather to spring up in the bosom of his auditor, than to be suggested by himself. As they went, he plucked a branch of maple, to serve for a walking-stick, and began to strip it of the twigs and little boughs, which were wet with evening dew. The moment his fingers touched them, they became strangely withered and dried up, as with a week's sunshine. Thus the pair proceeded, at a good free pace, until suddenly, in a gloomy hollow of the road, Goodman Brown sat himself down on the stump of a tree, and refused to go any farther.

"Friend," said he, stubbornly, "my mind is made up. Not another step will I budge on this errand. What if a wretched old woman do choose to go to the devil, when I thought she was going to Heaven! Is that any reason why I should quit my dear Faith, and go after her?"

"You will think better of this, by-and-by," said his acquaintance, composedly. 40 "Sit here and rest yourself awhile; and when you feel like moving again, there is my staff to help you along."

Without more words, he threw his companion the maple stick, and was as speedily out of sight, as if he had vanished into the deepening gloom. The young man sat a few moments, by the road-side, applauding himself greatly, and thinking with how clear a conscience he should meet the minister, in his morning-walk, nor shrink from the eye of good old Deacon Gookin. And what calm sleep would be his, that very night, which was to have been spent so wickedly, but purely and sweetly now, in the arms of Faith! Amidst these pleasant and praiseworthy meditations, Goodman Brown heard the tramp of horses along the road, and deemed it advisable to conceal himself within the verge of the forest, conscious of the guilty purpose that had brought him thither, though now so happily turned from it.

Egyptian Magi: In the Bible, Pharaoh's wise men and sorcerers who by their magical powers changed their rods into live serpents. (This incident, part of the story of Moses and Aaron, is related in Exodus 7:8–12.)

On came the hoof-tramps and the voices of the riders, two grave old voices, conversing soberly as they drew near. These mingled sounds appeared to pass along the road, within a few yards of the young man's hiding-place; but owing, doubt-less, to the depth of the gloom, at that particular spot, neither the travellers nor their steeds were visible. Though their figures brushed the small boughs by the way-side, it could not be seen that they intercepted, even for a moment, the faint gleam from the strip of bright sky, athwart which they must have passed. Good-man Brown alternately crouched and stood on tip-toe, pulling aside the branches, and thrusting forth his head as far as he durst, without discerning so much as a shadow. It vexed him the more, because he could have sworn, were such a thing possible, that he recognized the voices of the minister and Deacon Gookin, jog-ging along quietly, as they were wont to do, when bound to some ordination or ecclesiastical council. While yet within hearing, one of the riders stopped to pluck a switch.

"Of the two, reverend Sir," said the voice like the deacon's, "I had rather miss an ordination-dinner than to-night's meeting. They tell me that some of our community are to be here from Falmouth and beyond, and others from Connec-ticut and Rhode-Island; besides several of the Indian powows°, who, after their fashion, know almost as much deviltry as the best of us. Moreover, there is a goodly young woman to be taken into communion."

"Mighty well, Deacon Gookin!" replied the solemn old tones of the minister. "Spur up, or we shall be late. Nothing can be done, you know, until I get on the ground."

The hoofs clattered again, and the voices, talking so strangely in the empty air, passed on through the forest, where no church had ever been gathered, nor solitary Christian prayed. Whither, then, could these holy men by journeying, so deep into the heathen wilderness? Young Goodman Brown caught hold of a tree, for support, being ready to sink down on the ground, faint and overburdened with the heavy sickness of his heart. He looked up to the sky, doubting whether there really was a Heaven above him. Yet, there was the blue arch, and the stars brightening in it.

"With Heaven above, and Faith below, I will yet stand firm against the devil!" cried Goodman Brown.

While he still gazed upward, into the deep arch of the firmament, and had lifted his hands to pray, a cloud, though no wind was stirring, hurried across the zenith, and hid the brightening stars. The blue sky was still visible, except directly overhead, where this black mass of cloud was sweeping swiftly northward. Aloft in the air, as if from the depths of the cloud, came a confused and doubtful sound of voices. Once, the listener fancied that he could distinguish the accents of town's-people of his own, men and women, both pious and ungodly, many of whom he had met at the communion-table, and had seen others rioting at the tavern. The next moment, so indistinct were the sounds, he doubted whether he had heard aught but the murmur of the old forest, whispering without a wind. Then came a stronger swell of those familiar tones, heard daily in the sunshine, at Salem vil-lage, but never, until now, from a cloud of night. There was one voice, of a young

powows: Indian priests or medicine men.

woman, uttering lamentations, yet with an uncertain sorrow, and entreating for some favor, which, perhaps, it would grieve her to obtain. And all the unseen multitude, both saints and sinners, seemed to encourage her onward.

"Faith!" shouted Goodman Brown, in a voice of agony and desperation; and the echoes of the forest mocked him, crying—"Faith! Faith!" as if bewildered wretches were seeking her, all through the wilderness.

The cry of grief, rage, and terror, was yet piercing the night, when the unhappy husband held his breath for a response. There was a scream, drowned immediately in a louder murmur of voices, fading into far-off laughter, as the dark cloud swept away, leaving the clear and silent sky above Goodman Brown. But something fluttered lightly down through the air, and caught on the branch of a tree. The young man seized it, and beheld a pink ribbon.

"My Faith is gone!" cried he, after one stupefied moment. "There is no good on earth; and sin is but a name. Come, devil! for to thee is this world given." 50

And maddened with despair, so that he laughed loud and long, did Goodman Brown grasp his staff and set forth again, at such a rate, that he seemed to fly along the forest-path, rather than to walk or run. The road grew wilder and drearier, and more faintly traced, and vanished at length, leaving him in the heart of the dark wilderness, still rushing onward, with the instinct that guides mortal man to evil. The whole forest was peopled with frightful sounds; the creaking of the trees, the howling of wild beasts, and the yell of Indians; while, sometimes, the wind tolled like a distant church-bell, and sometimes gave a broad roar around the traveller, as if all Nature were laughing him to scorn. But he was himself the chief horror of the scene, and shrank not from its other horrors.

"Ha! ha! ha!" roared Goodman Brown, when the wind laughed at him. "Let us hear which will laugh loudest! Think not to frighten me with your deviltry! Come witch, come wizard, come Indian powow, come devil himself! and here comes Goodman Brown. You may as well fear him as he fear you!"

In truth, all through the haunted forest, there could be nothing more frightful than the figure of Goodman Brown. On he flew, among the black pines, brandishing his staff with frenzied gestures, now giving vent to an inspiration of horrid blasphemy, and now shouting forth such laughter, as set all the echoes of the forest laughing like demons around him. The fiend in his own shape is less hideous, than when he rages in the breast of man. Thus sped the demoniac on his course, until, quivering among the trees, he saw a red light before him, as when the felled trunks and branches of a clearing have been set on fire, and throw up their lurid blaze against the sky, at the hour of midnight. He paused, in a lull of the tempest that had driven him onward, and heard the swell of what seemed a hymn, rolling solemnly from a distance, with the weight of many voices. He knew the tune; it was a familiar one in the choir of the village meeting-house. The verse died heavily away, and was lengthened by a chorus, not of human voices, but of all the sounds of the benighted wilderness, pealing in awful harmony together. Goodman Brown cried out; and his cry was lost to his own ear, by its unison with the cry of the desert.

In the interval of silence, he stole forward, until the light glared full upon his eyes. At one extremity of an open space, hemmed in by the dark wall of the forest, arose a rock, bearing some rude, natural resemblance either to an altar or a pulpit, and surrounded by four blazing pines, their tops aflame, their stems untouched, like candles at an evening meeting. The mass of foliage, that had overgrown the summit of the rock, was all on fire, blazing high into the night, and fitfully illuminating the whole field. Each pendent twig and leafy festoon was in a blaze. As the red light arose and fell, a numerous congregation alternately shone forth, then disappeared in shadow, and again grew, as it were, out of the darkness, peopling the heart of the solitary woods at once.

"A grave and dark-clad company!" quoth Goodman Brown.   55

In truth, they were such. Among them, quivering to-and-fro, between gloom and splendor, appeared faces that would be seen, next day, at the council-board of the province, and others which, Sabbath after Sabbath, looked devoutly heavenward, and benignantly over the crowded pews, from the holiest pulpits in the land. Some affirm that the lady of the governor was there. At least, there were high dames well known to her, and wives of honored husbands, and widows, a great multitude, and ancient maidens, all of excellent repute, and fair young girls, who trembled, lest their mothers should espy them. Either the sudden gleams of light, flashing over the obscure field, bedazzled Goodman Brown, or he recognized a score of the church-members of Salem village, famous for their especial sanctity. Good old Deacon Gookin had arrived, and waited at the skirts of that venerable saint, his revered pastor. But, irreverently consorting with these grave, reputable, and pious people, these elders of the church, these chaste dames and dewy virgins, there were men of dissolute lives and women of spotted fame, wretches given over to all mean and filthy vice, and suspected even of horrid crimes. It was strange to see, that the good shrank not from the wicked, nor were the sinners abashed by the saints. Scattered, also, among their pale-faced enemies, were the Indian priests, or powows, who had often scared their native forest with more hideous incantations than any known to English witchcraft.

"But, where is Faith?" thought Goodman Brown; and, as hope came into his heart, he trembled.

Another verse of the hymn arose, a slow and mournful strain, such as the pious love, but joined to words which expressed all that our nature can conceive of sin, and darkly hinted at far more. Unfathomable to mere mortals is the lore of fiends. Verse after verse was sung, and still the chorus of the desert swelled between, like the deepest tone of a mighty organ. And, with the final peal of that dreadful anthem, there came a sound, as if the roaring wind, the rushing streams, the howling beasts, and every other voice of the unconverted wilderness, were mingling and according with the voice of guilty man, in homage to the prince of all. The four blazing pines threw up a loftier flame, and obscurely discovered shapes and visages of horror on the smoke-wreaths, above the impious assembly. At the same moment, the fire on the rock shot redly forth, and formed a glowing arch above its base, where now appeared a figure. With reverence be it spoken, the figure bore no slight similitude, both in garb and manner, to some grave divine of the New-England churches.

"Bring forth the converts!" cried a voice, that echoed through the field and rolled into the forest.

At the word, Goodman Brown stepped forth from the shadow of the trees,   60
and approached the congregation, with whom he felt a loathful brotherhood, by

the sympathy of all that was wicked in his heart. He could have well nigh sworn, that the shape of his own dead father beckoned him to advance, looking downward from a smoke-wreath, while a woman, with dim features of despair, threw out her hand to warn him back. Was it his mother? But he had no power to retreat one step, nor to resist, even in thought, when the minister and good old Deacon Gookin seized his arms, and led him to the blazing rock. Thither came also the slender form of a veiled female, led between Goody Cloyse, that pious teacher of the catechism, and Martha Carrier, who had received the devil's promise to be queen of hell. A rampant hag was she! And there stood the proselytes°, beneath the canopy of fire.

"Welcome, my children," said the dark figure, "to the communion of your race! Ye have found, thus young, your nature and your destiny. My children, look behind you!"

They turned; and flashing forth, as it were, in a sheet of flame, the fiend-worshippers were seen; the smile of welcome gleamed darkly on every visage.

"There," resumed the sable form, "are all whom ye have reverenced from youth. Ye deemed them holier than yourselves, and shrank from your own sin, contrasting it with their lives of righteousness, and prayerful aspirations heavenward. Yet, here are they all, in my worshipping assembly! This night it shall be granted you to know their secret deeds; how hoary-bearded elders of the church have whispered wanton words to the young maids of their households; how many a woman, eager for widow's weeds, has given her husband a drink at bed-time, and let him sleep his last sleep in her bosom; how beardless youths have made haste to inherit their fathers' wealth; and how fair damsels—blush not, sweet ones!—have dug little graves in the garden, and bidden me, the sole guest, to an infant's funeral. By the sympathy of your human hearts for sin, ye shall scent out all the places—whether in church, bed-chamber, street, field, or forest—where crime has been committed, and shall exult to behold the whole earth one stain of guilt, one mighty blood-spot. Far more than this! It shall be yours to penetrate, in every bosom, the deep mystery of sin, the fountain of all wicked arts, and which inexhaustibly supplies more evil impulses than human power—than my power, at its utmost!—can make manifest in deeds. And now, my children, look upon each other."

They did so; and, by the blaze of the hell-kindled torches, the wretched man beheld his Faith, and the wife her husband, trembling before that unhallowed altar.

"Lo! there ye stand, my children," said the figure, in a deep and solemn tone, almost sad, with its despairing awfulness, as if his once angelic nature could yet mourn for our miserable race. "Depending upon one another's hearts, ye had still hoped, that virtue were not all a dream. Now are ye undeceived! Evil is the nature of mankind. Evil must be your only happiness. Welcome, again, my children, to the communion of your race!"

"Welcome!" repeated the fiend-worshippers, in one cry of despair and triumph.

And there they stood, the only pair, as it seemed, who were yet hesitating on the verge of wickedness, in this dark world. A basin was hollowed, naturally, in the rock. Did it contain water, reddened by the lurid light? or was it blood? or, perchance, a liquid flame? Herein did the Shape of Evil dip his hand, and prepare to lay the

proselytes: new converts.

mark of baptism upon their foreheads, that they might be partakers of the mystery of sin, more conscious of the secret guilt of others, both in deed and thought, than they could now be of their own. The husband cast one look at his pale wife, and Faith at him. What polluted wretches would the next glance show them to each other, shuddering alike at what they disclosed and what they saw!

"Faith! Faith!" cried the husband. "Look up to Heaven, and resist the Wicked one!"

Whether Faith obeyed, he knew not. Hardly had he spoken, when he found himself amid calm night and solitude, listening to a roar of the wind, which died heavily away through the forest. He staggered against the rock and felt it chill and damp, while a hanging twig, that had been all on fire, besprinkled his cheek with the coldest dew.

The next morning, young Goodman Brown came slowly into the street of Salem village, staring around him like a bewildered man. The good old minister was taking a walk along the grave-yard, to get an appetite for breakfast and meditate his sermon, and bestowed a blessing, as he passed, on Goodman Brown. He shrank from the venerable saint, as if to avoid an anathema°. Old Deacon Goodkin was at domestic worship, and the holy words of his prayer were heard through the open window. "What God doth the wizard pray to?" quoth Goodman Brown. Goody Cloyse, that excellent old Christian, stood in the early sunshine, at her own lattice, catechizing a little girl, who had brought her a pint of morning's milk. Goodman Brown snatched away the child, as from the grasp of the fiend himself. Turning the corner by the meeting-house, he spied the head of Faith, with the pink ribbons, gazing anxiously forth, and bursting into such joy at sight of him, that she skipt along the street, and almost kissed her husband before the whole village. But, Goodman Brown looked sternly and sadly into her face, and passed on without a greeting.

Had Goodman Brown fallen asleep in the forest, and only dreamed a wild dream of a witch-meeting?

Be it so, if you will. But, alas! it was a dream of evil omen for young Goodman Brown. A stern, a sad, a darkly meditative, a distrustful, if not a desperate man, did he become, from the night of that fearful dream. On the Sabbath-day, when the congregation were singing a holy psalm, he could not listen, because an anthem of sin rushed loudly upon his ear, and drowned all the blessed strain. When the minister spoke from the pulpit, with power and fervid eloquence, and, with his hand on the open Bible, of the sacred truths of our religion, and of saint-like lives and triumphant deaths, and of future bliss or misery unutterable, then did Goodman Brown turn pale, dreading, lest the roof should thunder down upon the gray blasphemer and his hearers. Often, awakening suddenly at midnight, he shrank from the bosom of Faith, and at morning or eventide, when the family knelt down at prayer, he scowled, and muttered to himself, and gazed sternly at his wife, and turned away. And when he had lived long, and was borne to his grave, a hoary corpse, followed by Faith, an aged woman, and children and grand-children, a goodly procession, besides neighbors, not a few, they carved no hopeful verse upon his tombstone; for his dying hour was gloom.

°*anathema*: an official curse, a decree that casts one out of a church and bans him from receiving the sacraments.

1. When we learn (in the opening sentence) that this story begins in Salem village, what suggestions come to mind from our knowledge of American history? How does Salem make a more appropriate setting than some other colonial American village?
2. Why is Brown's wife Faith "aptly named" (as we are told in the opening paragraph)? Point to any passages in which the author seems to be punning on her name. What do you understand from them?
3. What do you make of the fact that the strange man in the woods closely resembles Brown himself (paragraphs 13, 32)?
4. As Brown and the stranger proceed deeper into the woods, what does Brown find out that troubles him? When the pink ribbon flutters to the ground, as though fallen from something airborne (paragraph 49), what does Brown assume? What effect does this event have upon his determination to resist the devil?
5. What is the purpose of the ceremony in the woods? Bring to your understanding of it anything you have heard or read about witchcraft, the witches' Sabbath, and the notion of making a pact with the devil.
6. What power does the devil promise to give his communicants (63)?
7. "Evil is the nature of mankind," declares the devil (65). Does Hawthorne agree with him? (Exactly what do we find in this story to suggest the author's view?)
8. Was Brown's experience in the woods all a dream, or wasn't it? Does Hawthorne favor one explanation, or the other?
9. Discuss this comment: "Even though Brown, at the last possible moment, refuses the "mark of baptism" and rejects the devil's gift, it turns out that he really did receive the gift after all. For the rest of his days, he definitely possesses the very same ability that the devil offered him."
10. How would you state the main theme of the story?

Kurt Vonnegut, Jr.

HARRISON BERGERON   1961

Kurt Vonnegut, Jr., was born in Indianapolis in 1922. After graduation from the University of Chicago, he worked as a reporter and a public relations man and later took a graduate degree in anthropology. Although Vonnegut first won popularity with science fiction fans for his stories and novels such as Piano Player *(1952), his work eventually found its way to a wider audience:* Cat's Cradle *(1963) became a best-seller. Despite his early intention to make a career in biochemistry, Vonnegut seems often hostile in his views of science and technology. Among his later popular novels are* Bluebeard *(1987) and* Hocus Pocus *(1990). Vonnegut has also written many essays, collected in* Wampeters, Foma and Granfalloons *(1982), a play,* Happy Birthday, Wanda June *(1970), and several scripts for television.*

Kurt Vonnegut, Jr.

The year was 2081, and everybody was finally equal. They weren't only equal before God and the law. They were equal every which way. Nobody was smarter than anybody else. Nobody was better looking than anybody else. Nobody was stronger or quicker than anybody else. All this equality was due to the 211th, 212th, and 213th Amendments to the Constitution, and to the unceasing vigilance of agents of the United States Handicapper General.

Some things about living still weren't quite right, though. April, for instance, still drove people crazy by not being springtime. And it was in that clammy month that the H-G men took George and Hazel Bergeron's fourteen-year-old son, Harrison, away.

It was tragic, all right, but George and Hazel couldn't think about it very hard. Hazel had a perfectly average intelligence, which meant she couldn't think about anything except in short bursts. And George, while his intelligence was way above normal, had a little mental handicap radio in his ear. He was required by law to wear it at all times. It was tuned to a government transmitter. Every twenty seconds or so, the transmitter would send out some sharp noise to keep people like George from taking unfair advantage of their brains.

George and Hazel were watching television. There were tears on Hazel's cheeks, but she'd forgotten for the moment what they were about.

On the television screen were ballerinas.   5

A buzzer sounded in George's head. His thoughts fled in panic, like bandits from a burglar alarm.

"That was a real pretty dance, that dance they just did," said Hazel.

"Huh?" said George.

"That dance—it was nice," said Hazel.

"Yup," said George. He tried to think a little about the ballerinas. They weren't   10 really very good—no better than anybody else would have been, anyway. They were burdened with sashweights and bags of birdshot, and their faces were masked, so that no one, seeing a free and graceful gesture or a pretty face, would feel like something the cat drug in. George was toying with the vague notion that maybe dancers shouldn't be handicapped. But he didn't get very far with it before another noise in his ear radio scattered his thoughts.

George winced. So did two out of the eight ballerinas.

Hazel saw him wince. Having no mental handicap herself, she had to ask George what the latest sound had been.

"Sounded like somebody hitting a milk bottle with a ball peen hammer," said George.

"I'd think it would be real interesting, hearing all the different sounds," said Hazel, a little envious. "All the things they think up."

"Um," said George.   15

"Only, if I was Handicapper General, you know what I would do?" said Hazel. Hazel, as a matter of fact, bore a strong resemblance to the Handicapper General, a woman named Diana Moon Glampers. "If I was Diana Moon Glampers," said Hazel, "I'd have chimes on Sunday—just chimes. Kind of in honor of religion."

"I could think, if it was just chimes," said George.

"Well—maybe make 'em real loud," said Hazel. "I think I'd make a good Handicapper General."

"Good as anybody else," said George.

"Who knows better'n I do what normal is?" said Hazel.

"Right," said George. He began to think glimmeringly about his abnormal son who was now in jail, about Harrison, but a twenty-one-gun salute in his head stopped that.

"Boy!" said Hazel, "that was a doozy, wasn't it?"

It was such a doozy that George was white and trembling, and tears stood on the rims of his red eyes. Two of the eight ballerinas had collapsed to the studio floor, were holding their temples.

"All of a sudden you look so tired," said Hazel. "Why don't you stretch out on the sofa, so's you can rest your handicap bag on the pillows, honeybunch." She was referring to the forty-seven pounds of birdshot in a canvas bag, which was padlocked around George's neck. "Go on and rest the bag for a little while," she said. "I don't care if you're not equal to me for a while."

George weighed the bag with his hands. "I don't mind it," he said. "I don't notice it any more. It's just a part of me."

"You been so tired lately—kind of wore out," said Hazel. "If there was just some way we could make a little hole in the bottom of the bag, and just take out a few of them lead balls. Just a few."

"Two years in prison and two thousand dollars fine for every ball I took out," said George. "I don't call that a bargain."

"If you could just take a few out when you came home from work," said Hazel. "I mean—you don't compete with anybody around here. You just set around."

"If I tried to get away with it," said George, "then other people'd get away with it—and pretty soon we'd be right back to the dark ages again, with everybody competing against everybody else. You wouldn't like that, would you?"

"I'd hate it," said Hazel.

"There you are," said George. "The minute people start cheating on laws, what do you think happens to society?"

If Hazel hadn't been able to come up with an answer to this question, George couldn't have supplied one. A siren was going off in his head.

"Reckon it'd fall all apart," said Hazel.

"What would?" said George blankly.

"Society," said Hazel uncertainly. "Wasn't that what you just said?"

"Who knows?" said George.

The television program was suddenly interrupted for a news bulletin. It wasn't clear at first as to what the bulletin was about, since the announcer, like all announcers, had a serious speech impediment. For about half a minute, and in a state of high excitement, the announcer tried to say, "Ladies and gentlemen—"

He finally gave up, handed the bulletin to a ballerina to read.

"That's all right—" Hazel said of the announcer, "he tried. That's the big thing. He tried to do the best he could with what God gave him. He should get a nice raise for trying so hard."

"Ladies and gentlemen—" said the ballerina, reading the bulletin. She must have been extraordinarily beautiful, because the mask she wore was hideous. And it was easy to see that she was the strongest and most graceful of all the dancers, for her handicap bags were as big as those worn by two-hundred-pound men.

KURT VONNEGUT, JR.   177

And she had to apologize at once for her voice, which was a very unfair voice for a woman to use. Her voice was a warm, luminous, timeless melody. "Excuse me—" she said, and she began again, making her voice absolutely uncompetitive.

"Harrison Bergeron, age fourteen," she said in a grackle squawk, "has just escaped from jail, where he was held on suspicion of plotting to overthrow the government. He is a genius and an athlete, is under-handicapped, and should be regarded as extremely dangerous."

A police photograph of Harrison Bergeron was flashed on the screen upside down, then sideways, upside down again, then right side up. The picture showed the full length of Harrison against a background calibrated in feet and inches. He was exactly seven feet tall.

The rest of Harrison's appearance was Halloween and hardware. Nobody had ever borne heavier handicaps. He had outgrown hindrances faster than the H-G men could think them up. Instead of a little ear radio for a mental handicap, he wore a tremendous pair of earphones, and spectacles with thick wavy lenses. The spectacles were intended to make him not only half blind, but to give him whanging headaches besides.

Scrap metal was hung all over him. Ordinarily, there was a certain symmetry, a military neatness to the handicaps issued to strong people, but Harrison looked like a walking junkyard. In the race of life, Harrison carried three hundred pounds. 45

And to offset his good looks, the H-G men required that he wear at all times a red rubber ball for a nose, keep his eyebrows shaved off, and cover his even white teeth with black caps at snaggle-tooth random.

"If you see this boy," said the ballerina, "do not—I repeat, do not—try to reason with him."

There was the shriek of a door being torn from its hinges.

Screams and barking cries of consternation came from the television set. The photograph of Harrison Bergeron on the screen jumped again and again, as though dancing to the tune of an earthquake.

George Bergeron correctly identified the earthquake, and well he might have—for many was the time his own home had danced to the same crashing tune. "My God—" said George, "that must be Harrison!" 50

The realization was blasted from his mind instantly by the sound of an automobile collision in his head.

When George could open his eyes again, the photograph of Harrison was gone. A living, breathing Harrison filled the screen.

Clanking, clownish, and huge, Harrison stood in the center of the studio. The knob of the uprooted studio door was still in his hand. Ballerinas, technicians, musicians, and announcers cowered on their knees before him, expecting to die.

"I am the Emperor!" cried Harrison. "Do you hear? I am the Emperor! Everybody must do what I say at once!" He stamped his foot and the studio shook.

"Even as I stand here—" he bellowed, "crippled, hobbled, sickened—I am a greater ruler than any man who ever lived! Now watch me become what I *can* become!" 55

Harrison tore the straps of his handicap harness like wet tissue paper, tore straps guaranteed to support five thousand pounds.

Harrison's scrap-iron handicaps crashed to the floor.

Harrison thrust his thumbs under the bar of the padlock that secured his head harness. The bar snapped like celery. Harrison smashed his headphones and spectacles against the wall.

He flung away his rubber-ball nose, revealed a man that would have awed Thor, the god of thunder.

"I shall now select my Empress!" he said, looking down on the cowering people. "Let the first woman who dares rise to her feet claim her mate and her throne!"

A moment passed, and then a ballerina arose, swaying like a willow.

Harrison plucked the mental handicap from her ear, snapped off her physical handicaps with marvelous delicacy. Last of all, he removed her mask.

She was blindingly beautiful.

"Now—" said Harrison, taking her hand, "shall we show the people the meaning of the word dance? Music!" he commanded.

The musicians scrambled back into their chairs, and Harrison stripped them of their handicaps, too. "Play your best," he told them, "and I'll make you barons and dukes and earls."

The music began. It was normal at first—cheap, silly, false. But Harrison snatched two musicians from their chairs, waved them like batons as he sang the music as he wanted it played. He slammed them back into their chairs.

The music began again and was much improved.

Harrison and his Empress merely listened to the music for a while—listened gravely, as though synchronizing their heartbeats with it.

They shifted their weights to their toes.

Harrison placed his big hands on the girl's tiny waist, letting her sense the weightlessness that would soon be hers.

And then, in an explosion of joy and grace, into the air they sprang!

Not only were the laws of the land abandoned, but the law of gravity and the laws of motion as well.

They reeled, whirled, swiveled, flounced, capered, gamboled, and spun.

They leaped like deer on the moon.

The studio ceiling was thirty feet high, but each leap brought the dancers nearer to it.

It became their obvious intention to kiss the ceiling.

They kissed it.

And then, neutralizing gravity with love and pure will, they remained suspended in air inches below the ceiling, and they kissed each other for a long, long time.

It was then that Diana Moon Glampers, the Handicapper General, came into the studio with a double-barreled ten-gauge shotgun. She fired twice, and the Emperor and the Empress were dead before they hit the floor.

Diana Moon Glampers loaded the gun again. She aimed it at the musicians and told them they had ten seconds to get their handicaps back on.

It was then that the Bergerons' television tube burned out.

Hazel turned to comment about the blackout to George. But George had gone out into the kitchen for a can of beer.

George came back in with the beer, paused while a handicap signal shook him up. And then he sat down again. "You been crying?" he said to Hazel.

"Yup," she said.

"What about?" he said.

"I forget," she said. "Something real sad on television."

"What was it?" he said.

"It's all kind of mixed up in my mind," said Hazel.

"Forget sad things," said George.

"I always do," said Hazel.

"That's my girl," said George. He winced. There was the sound of a rivetting gun in his head.

"Gee—I could tell that one was a doozy," said Hazel.

"You can say that again," said George.

"Gee—" said Hazel, "I could tell that one was a doozy."

QUESTIONS

1. What tendencies in present-day American society is Vonnegut satirizing? Does the story argue *for* anything? How would you sum up its theme?

2. Is Diana Moon Glampers a "flat" or a "round" character? (If you need to review these terms, see page 48.) Would you call Vonnegut's characterization of her "realistic"? If not, why doesn't it need to be?

3. From what point of view is the story told? Why is it more effective than if Harrison Bergeron had told his own story in the first person?

4. Two sympathetic critics of Vonnegut's work, Karen and Charles Wood, have said of his stories: "Vonnegut proves repeatedly . . . that men and women remain fundamentally the same, no matter what technology surrounds them." Try applying this comment to "Harrison Bergeron." Do you agree?

5. Stanislaw Lem, Polish author of *Solaris* and other novels, once made this thoughtful criticism of many of his contemporary science fiction writers:

> The revolt against the machine and against civilization, the praise of the "aesthetic" nature of catastrophe, the dead-end course of human civilization— these are their foremost problems, the intellectual content of their works. Such SF is as it were *a priori* vitiated by pessimism, in the sense that anything that may happen will be for the worse. ("The Time-Travel Story and Related Matters of SF Structuring," *Science Fiction Studies 1* [1974], 143–154.)

How might Lem's objection be raised against "Harrison Bergeron"? In your opinion, does it negate the value of Vonnegut's story?

SUGGESTIONS FOR WRITING

1. Have you, like the narrator of "The Open Boat," ever been in physical danger? Not that your life needs to be a television thriller, but think and see what you can recall. What have you learned from your experience? Tell of it, comparing your memory with what Crane observes of people in danger, with what Crane's reporter notices within himself.

   Note: In a sense, you are often in real danger from forces sometimes beyond your control (storms, rapists and other criminals, crazed souls who tamper with capsules in drugstores, disease carriers). In a way, passively to face such ordinary perils may seem less heroic than rowing an open boat in a heaving sea. In another way—well, if you're looking for a danger to recall, you might think about this comparison. Reading Crane's story, do you feel that, in any sense, you and the news correspondent are in the same boat?

2. In "The Open Boat," recall the poem that comes to matter greatly to the correspondent (paragraphs 179 – 182). Have you ever been in a situation when a story, an Aesop fable, a saying, a line of poetry, or a song lyric took on fresh and immediate meaning for you? If so, relate your experience. (If no such experience has befallen you, don't make one up.)

3. In 500 words or more, explain what you believe to be Hawthorne's opinion of the Puritans, as shown in "Young Goodman Brown."

4. Pick a story not included in this chapter and, in your own words, sum up its main theme. Then indicate what you find in the story that makes this theme clear. Among stories whose themes stand out are "Gimpel the Fool," "Barn Burning," "The Chrysanthemums," "The Death of Ivan Ilych," "A Small, Good Thing," "The Man in a Case," "I Stand Here Ironing," and "The Use of Force." Is the author making any statement you can agree or disagree with? Why do you feel the way you do?

6. Compare two stories similar in theme. Both Joyce in "Araby" and Singer in "Gimpel the Fool" set forth a conflict between illusion and reality. Flannery O'Connor's "A Good Man Is Hard To Find" and "Revelation" show how, by the grace of God, an ordinary individual can receive enlightenment. Browse in other chapters and in "Stories for Further Reading" and see what other pairs of stories go together in theme. Then set them side by side and point out their similarities and differences. This topic will lead you to compare and contrast, as discussed in "Writing about a Story" in Supplement: Writing.

7. Here is a topic for science fiction fans: Trace a general theme in two or more science fiction novels or stories you know. Choose works that express similar views. Suggestion: If you know two science fiction writers who distrust the benefits of technology, or who take a keen interest in the future of women, look closely at their work and you will probably find an intriguing theme.

7 Symbol

In F. Scott Fitzgerald's novel *The Great Gatsby*, a huge pair of bespectacled eyes stares across a wilderness of ash heaps, from a billboard advertising the services of an oculist. Repeatedly entering into the story, the advertisement comes to mean more than simply the availability of eye examinations. Fitzgerald has a character liken it to the eyes of God; he hints that some sad, compassionate spirit is brooding as it watches the passing procession of humanity. Such an object is a **symbol:** in literature, a thing that suggests more than its literal meaning. Symbols generally do not "stand for" any one meaning, nor for anything absolutely definite; they point, they hint, or, as Henry James put it, they cast long shadows. To take a large example: in Herman Melville's *Moby-Dick,* the great white whale of the book's title apparently means more than the literal dictionary-definition meaning of an aquatic mammal. He also suggests more than the devil, to whom some of the characters liken him. The great whale, as the story unfolds, comes to imply an amplitude of meanings: among them the forces of nature and the whole created universe.

This indefinite multiplicity of meanings is characteristic of a symbolic story and distinguishes it from an **allegory,** a story in which persons, places, and things form a system of clearly labeled equivalents. In a simple allegory, characters and other ingredients often stand for other definite meanings, which are often abstractions. You met such a character in the last chapter: Faith in Hawthorne's "Young Goodman Brown." Supreme allegories are found in some biblical parables ("The kingdom of Heaven is like a man who sowed good seed in his field . . . ," Matthew 13:24–30).[1] A classic allegory is the medieval play *Everyman*, whose hero represents us all, and who, deserted by false friends called Kindred and Goods, faces the judgment of God accompanied only by a faithful friend called Good Deeds. In John Bunyan's seventeenth-century *Pilgrim's Progress*, the protagonist, Chris-

---

[1]A **parable** is a brief story that teaches a lesson. Some (but not all) parables are allegories.

tian, struggles along the difficult road toward salvation, meeting along the way persons such as Mr. Worldly Wiseman, who directs him into a more comfortable path (a wrong turn), and the residents of a town called Fair Speech, among them a hypocrite named Mr. Facing-both-ways. Not all allegories are simple: Dante's *Divine Comedy*, written in the Middle Ages, continues to reveal new meanings to careful readers. Allegory was much beloved in the Middle Ages, but in contemporary fiction it is rare. One modern instance is George Orwell's long fable *Animal Farm*, in which (among its double meanings) barnyard animals stand for human victims and totalitarian oppressors.

Symbols in fiction are not generally abstract terms like *love* or *truth*, but are likely to be perceptible objects (or worded descriptions that cause us to imagine them). In William Faulker's "A Rose for Emily" (Chapter Two), Miss Emily's invisible watch ticking at the end of a golden chain not only indicates the passage of time, but suggests that time passes without even being noticed by the watch's owner, and the golden chain carries suggestions of wealth and authority. Often the symbols we meet in fiction are inanimate objects, but other things also may function symbolically. In James Joyce's "Araby" (Chapter Five), the very name of the bazaar, Araby—the poetic name for Arabia—suggests magic, romance, and *The Arabian Nights*; its syllables (the narrator tells us) "cast an Eastern enchantment over me." Even a locale, or a feature of physical topography, can provide rich suggestions. Recall Ernest Hemingway's "A Clean, Well-Lighted Place" (Chapter Five), in which the café is not merely a café, but an island of refuge from night, chaos, loneliness, old age, and impending death.

In some novels and stories, symbolic characters make brief cameo appearances. Such characters often are not well-rounded and fully known, but are seen fleetingly and remain slightly mysterious. In *Heart of Darkness*, a short novel by Joseph Conrad, a steamship company that hires men to work in the Congo maintains in its waiting room two women who knit black wool—like the classical Fates. Usually such a symbolic character is more a portrait than a person—or somewhat portraitlike, as Faulkner's Miss Emily, who twice appears at a window of her house "like the carven torso of an idol in a niche." Though Faulkner invests Miss Emily with life and vigor, he also clothes her in symbolic hints: she seems almost to personify the vanishing aristocracy of the antebellum South, still maintaining a black servant and being ruthlessly betrayed by a moneymaking Yankee. Sometimes a part of a character's body or an attribute may convey symbolic meaning: a baleful eye, as in Edgar Allan Poe's "The Tell-Tale Heart" (page 41).

Much as a symbolic whale holds more meaning than an ordinary whale, a **symbolic act** is a gesture with larger significance than usual. For the boy's father in Faulkner's "Barn Burning" (Chapter Five), the act of destroying a barn is no mere act of spite, but an expression of his profound hatred for anything not belonging to him. Faulkner adds that burning a barn reflects the father's memories of the "waste and extravagance of war"; and further adds that "the element of fire spoke to some deep mainspring" in his being. A symbolic act, however, doesn't have to be a gesture as large as starting a conflagration. Before setting out in pursuit of the great white whale, Melville's Captain Ahab in *Moby-Dick* deliberately snaps his tobacco pipe and throws it away, as if to suggest (among other things) that he will let no pleasure or pastime distract him from his vengeance.

Why do writers have to symbolize—why don't they tell us outright? One advantage of a symbol is that it is so compact, and yet so fully laden. Both starkly concrete and slightly mysterious, like Miss Emily's invisibly ticking watch, it may impress us with all the force of something beheld in a dream or in a nightmare. The watch suggests, among other things, the slow and invisible passage of time. What this symbol says, it says more fully and more memorably than could be said, perhaps, in a long essay on the subject.

To some extent (it may be claimed), all stories are symbolic. Merely by holding up for our inspection these characters and their actions, the writer lends them *some* special significance. But this is to think of *symbol* in an extremely broad and inclusive way. For the usual purposes of reading a story and understanding it, there is probably little point in looking for symbolism in every word, in every stick or stone, in every striking of a match, in every minor character. Still, to be on the alert for symbols when reading fiction is perhaps wiser than to ignore them. Not to admit that symbolic meanings may be present, or to refuse to think about them, would be another way to misread a story—or to read no further than its outer edges.

How, then, do you recognize a symbol in fiction when you meet it? Fortunately, the storyteller often gives the symbol particular emphasis. It may be mentioned repeatedly throughout the story; it may even supply the story with a title ("Araby," "Barn Burning," "A Clean, Well-Lighted Place"). At times, a crucial symbol will open a story or end it. Unless an object, act, or character is given some such special emphasis and importance, we may generally feel safe in taking it at face value. Probably it isn't a symbol if it points clearly and unmistakably toward some one meaning, like a whistle in a factory, whose blast at noon means lunch. But an object, an act, or a character is surely symbolic (and almost as surely displays high literary art) if, when we finish the story, we realize that it was that item—those gigantic eyes; that clean, well-lighted café; that burning of a barn—which led us to the author's theme, the essential meaning.

John Steinbeck

John Steinbeck

John Steinbeck (1902–1968), was born in Salinas, California, in the fertile valley he remembers in "The Chrysanthemums." Off and on, he attended Stanford University, then sojourned in New York as a reporter and a bricklayer. After years of struggle to earn his living by fiction, Steinbeck reached a large audience with Tortilla Flat *(1935), a loosely woven novel portraying Mexican-Americans in Monterey with fondness and sympathy. Great acclaim greeted* The Grapes of Wrath *(1939), the story of a family of Oklahoma farmers who, ruined by dust storms in the 1930s, join a mass migration to California. Like Ernest Hemingway and Stephen Crane, Steinbeck prided himself on his journalism: in World War II, he filed dispatches from battlefronts in Italy and Africa, and in 1966 he wrote a column from South Vietnam. Known widely behind the Iron Curtain, Steinbeck accepted an invitation to visit the Soviet Union, and reported his trip in* A Russian Journal *(1948). In 1962 he became the seventh American to win the Nobel prize for literature, but critics have never placed Steinbeck on the same high shelf with Faulkner and Hemingway. He wrote much, not all good, and yet his best work adds to an impressive total. Besides* The Grapes of Wrath, *it includes* In Dubious Battle *(1936), a novel of an apple-pickers' strike;* Of Mice and Men, *a powerful short novel (also a play) of comradeship between a hobo and a moron;* The Log from the Sea of Cortez, *a nonfiction account of a marine biological expedition; and the short stories in* The Long Valley *(1938). Throughout the fiction he wrote in his prime, Steinbeck maintains an appealing sympathy for the poor and downtrodden, the lonely and dispossessed.*

The high grey-flannel fog of winter closed off the Salinas Valley° from the sky and from all the rest of the world. On every side it sat like a lid on the mountains and made of the great valley a closed pot. On the broad, level land floor the gang plows bit deep and left the black earth shining like metal where the shares had cut. On the foothill ranches across the Salinas River, the yellow stubble fields seemed to be bathed in pale cold sunshine, but there was no sunshine in the valley now in December. The thick willow scrub along the river flamed with sharp and positive yellow leaves.

Salinas Valley: south of San Francisco in the Coast Ranges region of California.

It was a time of quiet and of waiting. The air was cold and tender. A light wind blew up from the southwest so that the farmers were mildly hopeful of a good rain before long; but fog and rain do not go together.

Across the river, on Henry Allen's foothill ranch there was little work to be done, for the hay was cut and stored and the orchards were plowed up to receive the rain deeply when it should come. The cattle on the higher slopes were becoming shaggy and rough-coated.

Elisa Allen, working in her flower garden, looked down across the yard and saw Henry, her husband, talking to two men in business suits. The three of them stood by the tractor shed, each man with one foot on the side of the little Fordson. They smoked cigarettes and studied the machine as they talked.

Elisa watched them for a moment and then went back to her work. She was thirty-five. Her face was lean and strong and her eyes were as clear as water. Her figure looked blocked and heavy in her gardening costume, a man's black hat pulled low down over her eyes, clod-hopper shoes, a figured print dress almost completely covered by a big corduroy apron with four big pockets to hold the snips, the trowel and scratcher, the seeds and the knife she worked with. She wore heavy leather gloves to protect her hands while she worked.

She was cutting down the old year's chrysanthemum stalks with a pair of short and powerful scissors. She looked down toward the men by the tractor shed now and then. Her face was eager and mature and handsome; even her work with the scissors was over-eager, over-powerful. The chrysanthemum stems seemed too small and easy for her energy.

She brushed a cloud of hair out of her eyes with the back of her glove, and left a smudge of earth on her cheek in doing it. Behind her stood the neat white farm house with red geraniums close-banked around it as high as the windows. It was a hard-swept looking little house with hard-polished windows, and a clean mud-mat on the front steps.

Elisa cast another glance toward the tractor shed. The strangers were getting into their Ford coupe. She took off a glove and put her strong fingers down into the forest of new green chrysanthemum sprouts that were growing around the old roots. She spread the leaves and looked down among the close-growing stems. No aphids were there, no sowbugs or snails or cutworms. Her terrier fingers destroyed such pests before they could get started.

Elisa started at the sound of her husband's voice. He had come near quietly, and he leaned over the wire fence that protected her flower garden from cattle and dogs and chickens.

"At it again," he said. "You've got a strong new crop coming." 10

Elisa straightened her back and pulled on the gardening glove again. "Yes. They'll be strong this coming year." In her tone and on her face there was a little smugness.

"You've got a gift with things," Henry observed. "Some of those yellow chrysanthemums you had this year were ten inches across. I wish you'd work out in the orchard and raise some apples that big."

Her eyes sharpened. "Maybe I could do it, too. I've a gift with things, all right. My mother had it. She could stick anything in the ground and make it grow. She said it was having planters' hands that knew how to do it."

"Well, it sure works with flowers," he said.

"Henry, who were those men you were talking to?"

"Why, sure, that's what I came to tell you. They were from the Western Meat Company. I sold those thirty head of three-year-old steers. Got nearly my own price, too."

"Good," she said. "Good for you."

"And I thought," he continued, "I thought how it's Saturday afternoon, and we might go into Salinas for dinner at a restaurant, and then to a picture show— to celebrate, you see."

"Good," she repeated. "Oh, yes. That will be good."

Henry put on his joking tone. "There's fights tonight. How'd you like to go to the fights?"

"Oh, no," she said breathlessly. "No, I wouldn't like fights."

"Just fooling, Elisa. We'll go to a movie. Let's see. It's two now. I'm going to take Scotty and bring down those steers from the hill. It'll take us maybe two hours. We'll go in town about five and have dinner at the Cominos Hotel. Like that?"

"Of course I'll like it. It's good to eat away from home."

"All right, then. I'll go get up a couple of horses."

She said, "I'll have plenty of time to transplant some of these sets, I guess."

She heard her husband calling Scotty down by the barn. And a little later she saw the two men ride up the pale yellow hillside in search of the steers.

There was a little square sandy bed kept for rooting the chrysanthemums. With her trowel she turned the soil over and over, and smoothed it and patted it firm. Then she dug ten parallel trenches to receive the sets. Back at the chrysanthemum bed she pulled out the little crisp shoots, trimmed off the leaves of each one with her scissors and laid it on a small orderly pile.

A squeak of wheels and plod of hoofs came from the road. Elisa looked up. The country road ran along the dense bank of willows and cottonwoods that bordered the river, and up this road came a curious vehicle, curiously drawn. It was an old spring-wagon, with a round canvas top on it like the cover of a prairie schooner. It was drawn by an old bay horse and a little grey-and-white burro. A big stubble-bearded man sat between the cover flaps and drove the crawling team. Underneath the wagon, between the hind wheels, a lean and rangy mongrel dog walked sedately. Words were painted on the canvas, in clumsy, crooked letters. "Pots, pans, knives, sisors, lawn mores, Fixed." Two rows of articles, and the triumphantly definitive "Fixed" below. The black paint had run down in little sharp points beneath each letter.

Elisa, squatting on the ground, watched to see the crazy, loose-jointed wagon pass by. But it didn't pass. It turned into the farm road in front of her house, crooked old wheels skirling and squeaking. The rangy dog darted from between the wheels and ran ahead. Instantly the two ranch shepherds flew out at him. Then all three stopped, and with stiff and quivering tails, with taut straight legs, with ambassadorial dignity, they slowly circled, sniffing daintily. The caravan pulled up to Elisa's wire fence and stopped. Now the newcomer dog, feeling out-numbered, lowered his tail and retired under the wagon with raised hackles and bared teeth.

The man on the wagon seat called out, "That's a bad dog in a fight when he gets started."

Elisa laughed. "I see he is. How soon does he generally get started?"

The man caught up her laughter and echoed it heartily. "Sometimes not for weeks and weeks," he said. He climbed stiffly down, over the wheel. The horse and the donkey drooped like unwatered flowers.

Elisa saw that he was a very big man. Although his hair and beard were greying, he did not look old. His worn black suit was wrinkled and spotted with grease. The laughter had disappeared from his face and eyes the moment his laughing voice ceased. His eyes were dark, and they were full of the brooding that gets in the eyes of teamsters and of sailors. The calloused hands he rested on the wire fence were cracked, and every crack was a black line. He took off his battered hat.

"I'm off my general road, ma'am," he said. "Does this dirt road cut over across the river to the Los Angeles highway?"

Elisa stood up and shoved the thick scissors in her apron pocket. "Well, yes, it does, but it winds around and then fords the river. I don't think your team could pull through the sand."

He replied with some asperity. "It might surprise you what them beasts can pull through."

"When they get started?" she asked.

He smiled for a second. "Yes. When they get started."

"Well," said Elisa, "I think you'll save time if you go back to the Salinas road and pick up the highway there."

He drew a big finger down the chicken wire and made it sing. "I ain't in any hurry, ma'am. I go from Seattle to San Diego and back every year. Takes all my time. About six months each way. I aim to follow nice weather."

Elisa took off her gloves and stuffed them in the apron pocket with the scissors. She touched the under edge of her man's hat, searching for fugitive hairs. "That sounds like a nice kind of a way to live," she said.

He leaned confidentially over the fence. "Maybe you noticed the writing on my wagon. I mend pots and sharpen knives and scissors. You got any of them things to do?"

"Oh, no," she said quickly. "Nothing like that." Her eyes hardened with resistance.

"Scissors is the worst thing," he explained. "Most people just ruin scissors trying to sharpen 'em, but I know how. I got a special tool. It's a little bobbit kind of thing, and patented. But it sure does the trick."

"No. My scissors are all sharp."

"All right, then. Take a pot," he continued earnestly, "a bent pot, or a pot with a hole. I can make it like new so you don't have to buy no new ones. That's a saving for you."

"No," she said shortly. "I tell you I have nothing like that for you to do."

His face fell to an exaggerated sadness. His voice took on a whining undertone. "I ain't had a thing to do today. Maybe I won't have no supper tonight. You see I'm off my regular road. I know folks on the highway clear from Seattle to San Diego. They save their things for me to sharpen up because they know I do it so good and save them money."

"I'm sorry," Elisa said irritably. "I haven't anything for you to do."

His eyes left her face and fell to searching the ground. They roamed about until they came to the chrysanthemum bed where she had been working. "What's them plants, ma'am?"

The irritation and resistance melted from Elisa's face. "Oh, those are chrysanthemums, giant whites and yellows. I raise them every year, bigger than anybody around here."

"Kind of a long-stemmed flower? Looks like a quick puff of colored smoke?" he asked.

"That's it. What a nice way to describe them."

"They smell kind of nasty till you get used to them," he said.

"It's a good bitter smell," she retorted, "not nasty at all."

He changed his tone quickly. "I like the smell myself."

"I had ten-inch blooms this year," she said.

The man leaned farther over the fence. "Look. I know a lady down the road a piece, has got the nicest garden you ever seen. Got nearly every kind of flower but no chrysanthemums. Last time I was mending a copper-bottom washtub for her (that's a hard job but I do it good), she said to me, 'If you ever run acrost some nice chrysanthemums I wish you'd try to get me a few seeds.' That's what she told me."

Elisa's eyes grew alert and eager. "She couldn't have known much about chrysanthemums. You *can* raise them from seed, but it's much easier to root the little sprouts you see there."

"Oh," he said. "I s'pose I can't take none to her, then."

"Why yes you can," Elisa cried. "I can put some in damp sand, and you can carry them right along with you. They'll take root in the pot if you keep them damp. And then she can transplant them."

"She'd sure like to have some, ma'am. You say they're nice ones?"

"Beautiful," she said. "Oh, beautiful." Her eyes shone. She tore off the battered hat and shook out her dark pretty hair. "I'll put them in a flower pot, and you can take them right with you. Come into the yard."

While the man came through the picket gate Elisa ran excitedly along the geranium-bordered path to the back of the house. And she returned carrying a big red flower pot. The gloves were forgotten now. She kneeled on the ground by the starting bed and dug up the sandy soil with her fingers and scooped it into the bright new flower pot. Then she picked up the little pile of shoots she had prepared. With her strong fingers she pressed them in the sand and tamped around them with her knuckles. The man stood over her. "I'll tell you what to do," she said. "You remember so you can tell the lady."

"Yes, I'll try to remember."

"Well, look. These will take root in about a month. Then she must set them out, about a foot apart in good rich earth like this, see?" She lifted a handful of dark soil for him to look at. "They'll grow fast and tall. Now remember this: In July tell her to cut them down, about eight inches from the ground."

"Before they bloom?" he asked.

"Yes, before they bloom." Her face was tight with eagerness. "They'll grow right up again. About the last of September the buds will start."

She stopped and seemed perplexed. "It's the budding that takes the most care," she said hesitantly. "I don't know how to tell you." She looked deep into his eyes, searchingly. Her mouth opened a little, and she seemed to be listening. "I'll try to tell you," she said. "Did you ever hear of planting hands?"

"Can't say I have, ma'am." 70

"Well, I can only tell you what it feels like. It's when you're picking off the buds you don't want. Everything goes right down into your fingertips. You watch your fingers work. They do it themselves. You can feel how it is. They pick and pick the buds. They never make a mistake. They're with the plant. Do you see? Your fingers and the plant. You can feel that, right up your arm. They know. They never make a mistake. You can feel it. When you're like that you can't do anything wrong. Do you see that? Can you understand that?"

She was kneeling on the ground looking up at him. Her breast swelled passionately.

The man's eyes narrowed. He looked away self-consciously. "Maybe I know," he said. "Sometimes in the night in the wagon there—"

Elisa's voice grew husky. She broke in on him, "I've never lived as you do, but I know what you mean. When the night is dark—why, the stars are sharp-pointed, and there's quiet. Why, you rise up and up! Every pointed star gets driven into your body. It's like that. Hot and sharp and—lovely."

Kneeling there, her hand went out toward his legs in the greasy black trousers. 75 Her hesitant fingers almost touched the cloth. Then her hand dropped to the ground. She crouched low like a fawning dog.

He said, "It's nice, just like you say. Only when you don't have no dinner, it ain't."

She stood up then, very straight, and her face was ashamed. She held the flower pot out to him and placed it gently in his arms. "Here. Put it in your wagon, on the seat, where you can watch it. Maybe I can find something for you to do."

At the back of the house she dug in the can pile and found two old and battered aluminum saucepans. She carried them back and gave them to him. "Here, maybe you can fix these."

His manner changed. He became professional. "Good as new I can fix them." At the back of his wagon he set a little anvil, and out of an oily tool box dug a small machine hammer. Elisa came through the gate to watch him while he pounded out the dents in the kettles. His mouth grew sure and knowing. At a difficult part of the work he sucked his under-lip.

"You sleep right in the wagon?" Elisa asked. 80

"Right in the wagon, ma'am. Rain or shine I'm dry as a cow in there."

"It must be nice," she said. "It must be very nice. I wish women could do such things."

"It ain't the right kind of a life for a woman."

Her upper lip raised a little, showing her teeth. "How do you know? How can you tell?" she said.

"I don't know, ma'am," he protested. "Of course I don't know. Now here's 85 your kettles, done. You don't have to buy no new ones."

"How much?"

"Oh, fifty cents'll do. I keep my prices down and my work good. That's why I have all them satisfied customers up and down the highway."

Elisa brought him a fifty-cent piece from the house and dropped it in his hand. "You might be surprised to have a rival some time. I can sharpen scissors, too. And I can beat the dents out of little pots. I could show you what a woman might do."

He put his hammer back in the oily box and shoved the little anvil out of sight. "It would be a lonely life for a woman, ma'am, and a scarey life, too, with animals creeping under the wagon all night." He climbed over the single-tree, steadying himself with a hand on the burro's white rump. He settled himself in the seat, picked up the lines. "Thank you kindly, ma'am," he said. "I'll do like you told me; I'll go back and catch the Salinas road."

"Mind," she called, "if you're long in getting there, keep the sand damp." 90

"Sand, ma'am? . . . Sand? Oh, sure. You mean around the chrysanthemums. Sure I will." He clucked his tongue. The beasts leaned luxuriously into their collars. The mongrel dog took his place between the back wheels. The wagon turned and crawled out the entrance road and back the way it had come, along the river.

Elisa stood in front of her wire fence watching the slow progress of the caravan. Her shoulders were straight, her head thrown back, her eyes half-closed, so that the scene came vaguely into them. Her lips moved silently, forming the words "Good-bye—good-bye." Then she whispered, "That's a bright direction. There's a glowing there." The sound of her whisper startled her. She shook herself free and looked about to see whether anyone had been listening. Only the dogs had heard. They lifted their heads toward her from their sleeping in the dust, and then stretched out their chins and settled asleep again. Elisa turned and ran hurriedly into the house.

In the kitchen she reached behind the stove and felt the water tank. It was full of hot water from the noonday cooking. In the bathroom she tore off her soiled clothes and flung them into the corner. And then she scrubbed herself with a little block of pumice, legs and thighs, loins and chest and arms, until her skin was scratched and red. When she had dried herself she stood in front of a mirror in her bedroom and looked at her body. She tightened her stomach and threw out her chest. She turned and looked over her shoulder at her back.

After a while she began to dress, slowly. She put on her newest under-clothing and her nicest stockings and the dress which was the symbol of her prettiness. She worked carefully on her hair, penciled her eyebrows and rouged her lips.

Before she was finished she heard the little thunder of hoofs and the shouts 95 of Henry and his helper as they drove the red steers into the corral. She heard the gate bang shut and set herself for Henry's arrival.

His step sounded on the porch. He entered the house calling, "Elisa, where are you?"

"In my room, dressing. I'm not ready. There's hot water for your bath. Hurry up. It's getting late."

When she heard him splashing in the tub, Elisa laid his dark suit on the bed, and shirt and socks and tie beside it. She stood his polished shoes on the floor beside the bed. Then she went to the proch and sat primly and stiffly down. She looked toward the river road where the willow-line was still yellow with frosted leaves so that under the high grey fog they seemed a thin band of sunshine. This was the only color in the grey afternoon. She sat unmoving for a long time. Her eyes blinked rarely.

Henry came banging out of the door, shoving his tie inside his vest as he came. Elisa stiffened and her face grew tight. Henry stopped short and looked at her. "Why—why, Elisa. You look so nice!"

"Nice? You think I look nice? What do you mean by 'nice'?" 100

Henry blundered on. "I don't know. I mean you look different, strong and happy."

"I am strong? Yes, strong. What do you mean 'strong'?"

He looked bewildered. "You're playing some kind of a game," he said helplessly. "It's a kind of a play. You look strong enough to break a calf over your knee, happy enough to eat it like a watermelon."

For a second she lost her rigidity. "Henry! Don't talk like that. You didn't know what you said." She grew complete again. "I'm strong," she boasted. "I never knew before how strong."

Henry looked down toward the tractor shed, and when he brought his eyes 105 back to her, they were his own again. "I'll get out the car. You can put on your coat while I'm starting."

Elisa went into the house. She heard him drive to the gate and idle down his motor, and then she took a long time to put on her hat. She pulled it here and pressed it there. When Henry turned the motor off she slipped into her coat and went out.

The little roadster bounced along on the dirt road by the river, raising the birds and driving the rabbits into the brush. Two cranes flapped heavily over the willow-line and dropped into the river-bed.

Far ahead on the road Elisa saw a dark speck. She knew.

She tried not to look as they passed it, but her eyes would not obey. She whispered to herself sadly, "He might have thrown them off the road. That wouldn't have been much trouble, not very much. But he kept the pot," she explained. "He had to keep the pot. That's why he couldn't get them off the road."

The roadster turned a bend and she saw the caravan ahead. She swung full 110 around toward her husband so she could not see the little covered wagon and the mismatched team as the car passed them.

In a moment it was over. The thing was done. She did not look back.

She said loudly, to be heard above the motor, "It will be good, tonight, a good dinner."

"Now you're changed again," Henry complained. He took one hand from the wheel and patted her knee. "I ought to take you in to dinner oftener. It would be good for both of us. We get so heavy out on the ranch."

"Henry," she asked, "could we have wine at dinner?"

"Sure we could. Say! That will be fine." 115

She was silent for a while; then she said, "Henry, at those prize fights, do the men hurt each other very much?"

"Sometimes a little, not often. Why?"

"Well, I've read how they break noses, and blood runs down their chests. I've read how the fighting gloves get heavy and soggy with blood."

He looked around at her. "What's the matter, Elisa? I didn't know you read things like that." He brought the car to a stop, then turned to the right over the Salinas River bridge.

"Do any women ever go to the fights?" she asked.

"Oh, sure, some. What's the matter, Elisa? Do you want to go? I don't think you'd like it, but I'll take you if you really want to go."

She relaxed limply in the seat. "Oh, no. No. I don't want to go. I'm sure I don't." Her face was turned away from him. "It will be enough if we can have wine. It will be plenty." She turned up her coat collar so he could not see that she was crying weakly—like an old woman.

QUESTIONS

1. When we first meet Elisa in her garden, with what details does Steinbeck delineate her character for us?
2. Elisa works inside a "wire fence that protected her flower garden from cattle and dogs and chickens" (paragraph 9). What does this wire fence suggest?
3. How would you describe Henry and Elisa's marriage? Cite details from the story to support your description.
4. For what motive does the traveling salesman take an interest in Elisa's chrysanthemums? What immediate effect does his interest have on Elisa?
5. For what possible purpose does Steinbeck give us such a detailed account of Elisa's preparations for her evening out? Notice her tearing off her soiled clothes, her scrubbing her body with pumice (paragraphs 93–94).
6. Of what significance to Elisa is the sight of the contents of the flower pot discarded in the road? Notice that, as her husband's car overtakes the covered wagon, Elisa averts her eyes; and then Steinbeck adds, "In a moment it was over. The thing was done. She did not look back" (paragraph 111). Explain this passage.
7. How do you interpret Elisa's asking for wine with dinner? How do you account for her new interest in prize fights?
8. In a sentence, try to state this short story's theme.
9. Why are Elisa Allen's chrysanthemums so important to this story? Sum up what you understand them to mean.

THE LOTTERY 1948

Shirley Jackson (1919–1965), a native of San Francisco, moved in her teens to Rochester, New York. She started college at the University of Rochester, but had to drop out, stricken by severe depression, a problem that was to recur at intervals throughout her life. Later she was graduated from Syracuse University. With her husband Stanley Edgar Hyman, a literary critic, she settled in Bennington, Vermont, in a sprawling house built in the nineteenth century. There Jackson conscientiously set herself to produce a fixed number of words each day. She wrote novels: The Road Through the Wall *(1948), and three psychological thrillers—* Hangsaman *(1951),* The Haunting of Hill House *(1959), and* We Have Always Lived in the Castle *(1962). She wrote light, witty articles for* Good Housekeeping *and other popular magazines about the horrors*

Shirley Jackson

of housekeeping and rearing four children, collected in Life among the Savages *(1953) and* Raising Demons *(1957); but she claimed to have written these only for money. When in 1948 "The Lottery" appeared in* The New Yorker, *that issue of the magazine quickly sold out. Her purpose in writing the story, Jackson declared, had been "to shock the story's readers with a graphic demonstration of the pointless violence and general inhumanity in their own lives."*

The morning of June 27th was clear and sunny, with the fresh warmth of a full-summer day; the flowers were blossoming profusely and the grass was richly green. The people of the village began to gather in the square, between the post office and the bank, around ten o'clock; in some towns there were so many people that the lottery took two days and had to be started on June 26th, but in this village, where there were only about three hundred people, the whole lottery took less than two hours, so it could begin at ten o'clock in the morning and still be through in time to allow the villagers to get home for noon dinner.

The children assembled first, of course. School was recently over for the summer, and the feeling of liberty sat uneasily on most of them; they tended to gather together quietly for a while before they broke into boisterous play, and their talk was still of the classroom and the teacher, of books and reprimands. Bobby Martin had already stuffed his pockets full of stones, and the other boys soon followed his example, selecting the smoothest and roundest stones; Bobby and Harry Jones and Dickie Delacroix—the villagers pronounced this name "Dellacroy"—eventually made a great pile of stones in one corner of the square and guarded it against the raids of the other boys. The girls stood aside, talking among themselves, looking over their shoulders at the boys, and the very small children rolled in the dust or clung to the hands of their older brothers or sisters.

Soon the men began to gather, surveying their own children, speaking of planting and rain, tractors and taxes. They stood together, away from the pile of stones in the corner, and their jokes were quiet and they smiled rather than laughed. The women, wearing faded house dresses and sweaters, came shortly after their menfolk. They greeted one another and exchanged bits of gossip as they went to join their husbands. Soon the women, standing by their husbands, began to call to their children, and the children came reluctantly, having to be called four or five times. Bobby Martin ducked under his mother's grasping hand and ran, laughing, back to the pile of stones. His father spoke up sharply, and Bobby came quickly and took his place between his father and his oldest brother.

The lottery was conducted—as were the square dances, the teenage club, the Halloween program—by Mr. Summers, who had time and energy to devote to civic activities. He was a roundfaced, jovial man and he ran the coal business, and people were sorry for him, because he had no children and his wife was a scold. When he arrived in the square, carrying the black wooden box, there was a murmur of conversation among the villagers and he waved and called, "Little late today, folks." The postmaster, Mr. Graves, followed him, carrying a three-legged stool, and the stool was put in the center of the square and Mr. Summers set the black box down on it. The villagers kept their distance, leaving a space between themselves and the stool, and when Mr. Summers said, "Some of you fellows want to give me a hand?" there was a hesitation before two men, Mr. Martin and his oldest son, Baxter, came forward to hold the box steady on the stool while Mr. Summers stirred up the papers inside it.

The original paraphernalia for the lottery had been lost long ago, and the   5
black box now resting on the stool had been put into use even before Old Man Warner, the oldest man in town, was born. Mr. Summers spoke frequently to the villagers about making a new box, but no one liked to upset even as much tradition as was represented by the black box. There was a story that the present box had been made with some pieces of the box that had preceded it, the one that had been constructed when the first people settled down to make a village here. Every year, after the lottery, Mr. Summers began talking again about a new box, but every year the subject was allowed to fade off without anything's being done. The black box grew shabbier each year; by now it was no longer completely black but splintered badly along one side to show the original wood color, and in some places faded or stained.

Mr. Martin and his oldest son, Baxter, held the black box securely on the stool until Mr. Summers had stirred the papers thoroughly with his hand. Because so much of the ritual had been forgotten or discarded, Mr. Summers had been successful in having slips of paper substituted for the chips of wood that had been used for generations. Chips of wood, Mr. Summers had argued, had been all very well when the village was tiny, but now that the population was more than three hundred and likely to keep on growing, it was necessary to use something that would fit more easily into the black box. The night before the lottery, Mr. Summers and Mr. Graves made up the slips of paper and put them in the box, and it was then taken to the safe of Mr. Summers's coal company and locked up until Mr. Summers was ready to take it to the square next morning. The rest of the year, the box was put away, sometimes one place, sometimes another; it had spent one year in Mr. Graves's barn and another year underfoot in the post office, and sometimes it was set on a shelf in the Martin grocery and left there.

There was a great deal of fussing to be done before Mr. Summers declared the lottery open. There were lists to make up—of heads of families, heads of households in each family, members of each household in each family. There was the proper swearing-in of Mr. Summers by the postmaster, as the official of the lottery; at one time, some people remembered, there had been a recital of some sort, performed by the official of the lottery, a perfunctory, tuneless chant that had been rattled off duly each year; some people believed that the official of the lottery used to stand just so when he said or sang it, others believed that he was supposed to walk among the people, but years and years ago this part of the ritual had been allowed to lapse. There had been, also, a ritual salute, which the official of the lottery had had to use in addressing each person who came up to draw from the box, but this also had changed with time, until now it was felt necessary only for the official to speak to each person approaching. Mr. Summers was very good at all this; in his clean white shirt and blue jeans, with one hand resting carelessly on the black box, he seemed very proper and important as he talked interminably to Mr. Graves and the Martins.

Just as Mr. Summers finally left off talking and turned to the assembled villagers, Mrs. Hutchinson came hurriedly along the path to the square, her sweater thrown over her shoulders, and slid into place in the back of the crowd. "Clean forgot what day it was," she said to Mrs. Delacroix, who stood next to her, and they both laughed softly. "Thought my old man was out back stacking wood," Mrs. Hutchinson went on, "and then I looked out the window and the kids were gone, and then I remembered it was the twenty-seventh and came a-running." She dried her hands on her apron, and Mrs. Delacroix said, "You're in time, though. They're still talking away up there."

Mrs. Hutchinson craned her neck to see through the crowd and found her husband and children standing near the front. She tapped Mrs. Delacroix on the arm as a farewell and began to make her way through the crowd. The people separated good-humoredly to let her through; two or three people said, in voices just loud enough to be heard across the crowd, "Here comes your Missus, Hutchinson," and "Bill, she made it after all." Mrs. Hutchinson reached her husband, and Mr. Summers, who had been waiting, said cheerfully, "Thought we were going to have to get on without you, Tessie." Mrs. Hutchinson said, grinning, "Wouldn't have me leave m'dishes in the sink, now would you, Joe?" and soft laughter ran through the crowd as the people stirred back into position after Mrs. Hutchinson's arrival.

"Well, now," Mr. Summers said soberly, "guess we better get started, get this over with, so's we can go back to work. Anybody ain't here?" 10

"Dunbar," several people said. "Dunbar, Dunbar."

Mr. Summers consulted his list. "Clyde Dunbar," he said. "That's right. He's broke his leg, hasn't he? Who's drawing for him?"

"Me, I guess," a woman said, and Mr. Summers turned to look at her. "Wife draws for her husband," Mr. Summers said. "Don't you have a grown boy to do it for you, Janey?" Although Mr. Summers and everyone else in the village knew the answer perfectly well, it was the business of the official of the lottery to ask such questions formally. Mr. Summers waited with an expression of polite interest while Mrs. Dunbar answered.

"Horace's not but sixteen yet," Mrs. Dunbar said regretfully. "Guess I gotta fill in for the old man this year."

"Right," Mr. Summers said. He made a note on the list he was holding. Then he asked, "Watson boy drawing this year?"

15

A tall boy in the crowd raised his hand. "Here," he said. "I'm drawing for m'mother and me." He blinked his eyes nervously and ducked his head as several voices in the crowd said things like "Good fellow, Jack," and "Glad to see your mother's got a man to do it."

"Well," Mr. Summers said, "guess that's everyone. Old Man Warner make it?"

"Here," a voice said, and Mr. Summers nodded.

A sudden hush fell on the crowd as Mr. Summers cleared his throat and looked at the list. "All ready?" he called. "Now, I'll read the names—heads of families first—and the men come up and take a paper out of the box. Keep the paper folded in your hand without looking at it until everyone has had a turn. Everything clear?"

The people had done it so many times that they only half listened to the directions; most of them were quiet, wetting their lips, not looking around. Then Mr. Summers raised one hand high and said, "Adams." A man disengaged himself from the crowd and came forward. "Hi, Steve," Mr. Summers said, and Mr. Adams said, "Hi, Joe." They grinned at one another humorlessly and nervously. Then Mr. Adams reached into the black box and took out a folded paper. He held it firmly by one corner as he turned and went hastily back to his place in the crowd, where he stood a little apart from his family, not looking down at his hand.

20

"Allen," Mr. Summers said. "Anderson. . . . Bentham."

"Seems like there's no time at all between lotteries any more," Mrs. Delacroix said to Mrs. Graves in the back row. "Seems like we got through with the last one only last week."

"Time sure goes fast," Mrs. Graves said.

"Clark. . . . Delacroix."

"There goes my old man," Mrs. Delacroix said. She held her breath while her husband went forward.

25

"Dunbar," Mr. Summers said, and Mrs. Dunbar went steadily to the box while one of the women said, "Go on, Janey," and another said, "There she goes."

"We're next," Mrs. Graves said. She watched while Mr. Graves came around from the side of the box, greeted Mr. Summers gravely, and selected a slip of paper from the box. By now, all through the crowd there were men holding the small folded papers in their large hands, turning them over and over nervously. Mrs. Dunbar and her two sons stood together, Mrs. Dunbar holding the slip of paper.

"Harburt. . . . Hutchinson."

"Get up there, Bill," Mrs. Hutchinson said, and the people near her laughed.

"Jones."

30

"They do say," Mr. Adams said to Old Man Warner, who stood next to him, "that over in the north village they're talking of giving up the lottery."

Old Man Warner snorted. "Pack of crazy fools," he said. "Listening to the young folks, nothing's good enough for *them*. Next thing you know, they'll be wanting to go back to living in caves, nobody work any more, live *that* way for a while. Used to be a saying about 'Lottery in June, corn be heavy soon.' First thing you know, we'd all be eating stewed chickweed and acorns. There's *always* been a lottery," he added petulantly. "Bad enough to see young Joe Summers up there joking with everybody."

"Some places have already quit lotteries," Mrs. Adams said.

"Nothing but trouble in *that*," Old Man Warner said stoutly. "Pack of young fools."

"Martin." And Bobby Martin watched his father go forward. "Over-   35
dyke. . . . Percy."

"I wish they'd hurry," Mrs. Dunbar said to her older son. "I wish they'd hurry."

"They're almost through," her son said.

"You get ready to run tell Dad," Mrs. Dunbar said.

Mr. Summers called his own name and then stepped forward precisely and selected a slip from the box. Then he called, "Warner."

"Seventy-seventh year I been in the lottery," Old Man Warner said as he   40
went through the crowd. "Seventy-seventh time."

"Watson." The tall boy came awkwardly through the crowd. Someone said, "Don't be nervous, Jack," and Mr. Summers said, "Take your time, son."

"Zanini."

After that, there was a long pause, a breathless pause, until Mr. Summers, holding his slip of paper in the air, said, "All right, fellows." For a minute, no one moved, and then all the slips of paper were opened. Suddenly, all women began to speak at once, saying, "Who is it?" "Who's got it?" "Is it the Dunbars?" "Is it the Watsons?" Then the voices began to say, "It's Hutchinson. It's Bill." "Bill Hutchinson's got it."

"Go tell your father," Mrs. Dunbar said to her older son.

People began to look around to see the Hutchinsons. Bill Hutchinson was   45
standing quiet, staring down at the paper in his hand. Suddenly, Tessie Hutchinson shouted to Mr. Summers, "You didn't give him time enough to take any paper he wanted. I saw you. It wasn't fair!"

"Be a good sport, Tessie," Mrs. Delacroix called, and Mrs. Graves said, "All of us took the same chance."

"Shut up, Tessie," Bill Hutchinson said.

"Well, everyone," Mr. Summers said, "that was done pretty fast, and now we've got to be hurrying a little more to get done in time." He consulted his next list. "Bill," he said, "you draw for the Hutchinson family. You got any other households in the Hutchinsons?"

"There's Don and Eva," Mrs. Hutchinson yelled. "Make *them* take their chance!"

"Daughters draw with their husbands' families, Tessie," Mr. Summers said   50
gently. "You know that as well as anyone else."

"It wasn't fair," Tessie said.

"I guess not, Joe," Bill Hutchinson said regretfully. "My daughter draws with her husband's family, that's only fair. And I've got no other family except the kids."

"Then, as far as drawing for families is concerned, it's you," Mr. Summers said in explanation, "and as far as drawing for households is concerned, that's you, too. Right?"

"Right," Bill Hutchinson said.

"How many kids, Bill?" Mr. Summers asked formally. 55

"Three," Bill Hutchinson said. "There's Bill, Jr., and Nancy, and little Dave. And Tessie and me."

"All right, then," Mr. Summers said. "Harry, you got their tickets back?"

Mr. Graves nodded and held up the slips of paper. "Put them in the box, then," Mr. Summers directed. "Take Bill's and put it in."

"I think we ought to start over," Mrs. Hutchinson said, as quietly as she could. "I tell you it wasn't *fair*. You didn't give him time enough to choose. *Everybody* saw that."

Mr. Graves had selected the five slips and put them in the box, and he dropped 60 all the papers but those onto the ground, where the breeze caught them and lifted them off.

"Listen, everybody," Mrs. Hutchinson was saying to the people around her.

"Ready, Bill?" Mr. Summers asked, and Bill Hutchinson, with one quick glance around at his wife and children, nodded.

"Remember," Mr. Summers said, "take the slips and keep them folded until each person has taken one. Harry, you help little Dave." Mr. Graves took the hand of the little boy, who came willingly with him up to the box. "Take a paper out of the box, Davy," Mr. Summers said. Davy put his hand into the box and laughed. "Take just *one* paper," Mr. Summers said. "Harry, you hold it for him." Mr. Graves took the child's hand and removed the folded paper form the tight fist and held it while little Dave stood next to him and looked up at him wonderingly.

"Nancy next," Mr. Summers said. Nancy was twelve, and her school friends breathed heavily as she went forward, switching her skirt, and took a slip daintily from the box. "Bill, Jr.," Mr. Summers said, and Billy, his face red and his feet over-large, nearly knocked the box over as he got a paper out. "Tessie," Mr. Summers said. She hesitated for a minute, looking around defiantly, and then set her lips and went up to the box. She snatched a paper out and held it behind her.

"Bill," Mr. Summers said, and Bill Hutchinson reached into the box and felt 65 around, bringing his hand out at last with the slip of paper in it.

The crowd was quiet. A girl whispered, "I hope it's not Nancy," and the sound of the whisper reached the edges of the crowd.

"It's not the way it used to be," Old Man Warner said clearly. "People ain't the way they used to be."

"All right," Mr. Summers said. "Open the papers. Harry, you open little Dave's."

Mr. Graves opened the slip of paper and there was a general sigh through the crowd as he held it up and everyone could see that it was blank. Nancy and Bill, Jr., opened theirs at the same time, and both beamed and laughed, turning around to the crowd and holding their slips of paper above their heads.

"Tessie," Mr. Summers said. There was a pause, and then Mr. Summers looked 70 at Bill Hutchinson, and Bill unfolded his paper and showed it. It was blank.

"It's Tessie," Mr. Summers said, and his voice was hushed. "Show us her paper, Bill."

Bill Hutchinson went over to his wife and forced the slip of paper out of her hand. It had a black spot on it, the black spot Mr. Summers had made the night before with the heavy pencil in the coal-company office. Bill Hutchinson held it up, and there was a stir in the crowd.

"All right, folks," Mr. Summers said, "let's finish quickly."

Although the villagers had forgotten the ritual and lost the original black box, they still remembered to use stones. The pile of stones the boys had made earlier was ready; there were stones on the ground with the blowing scraps of paper that had come out of the box. Mrs. Delacroix selected a stone so large she had to pick it up with both hands and turned to Mrs. Dunbar. "Come on," she said. "Hurry up."

Mrs. Dunbar had small stones in both hands, and she said, gasping for breath, 75 "I can't run at all. You'll have to go ahead and I'll catch up with you."

The children had stones already, and someone gave little Davy Hutchinson a few pebbles.

Tessie Hutchinson was in the center of a cleared space by now, and she held her hands out desperately as the villagers moved in on her. "It isn't fair," she said. A stone hit her on the side of the head.

Old Man Warner was saying, "Come on, come on, everyone." Steve Adams was in the front of the crowd of villagers, with Mrs. Graves beside him.

"It isn't fair, it isn't right," Mrs. Hutchinson screamed, and then they were upon her.

QUESTIONS

1. Where do you think "The Lottery" takes place? What purpose do you suppose the writer has in making this setting appear so familiar and ordinary?
2. In paragraphs 2 and 3, what details foreshadow the ending of the story?
3. Take a close look at Jackson's description of the black wooden box (paragraph 5) and of the black spot on the fatal slip of paper (paragraph 72). What do these objects suggest to you? Are there any other symbols in the story?
4. What do you understand to be the writer's own attitude toward the lottery and the stoning? Exactly what in the story makes her attitude clear to us?
5. What do you make of Old Man Warner's saying, "Lottery in June, corn be heavy soon"?
6. What do you think Shirley Jackson is driving at? Consider each of the following interpretations and, looking at the story, see if you can find any evidence for it.

Jackson takes a primitive fertility rite and playfully transfers it to a small town in North America.

Jackson, writing her story soon after World War II, indirectly expresses her horror at the Holocaust. She assumes that the massacre of the Jews was carried out by unwitting, obedient people, like these villagers. (This suggestion has been advanced by critic Richard Moore.)

Jackson is satirizing our own society, in which men are selected for the army by lottery.

Jackson is just writing a memorable, entertaining story that signifies nothing at all.

Alice Munro

THE FOUND BOAT   1974

*Alice Munro, one of the most widely admired
contemporary writers in Canada, was born of
farm parents in 1931 in Wingham, in south-
western Ontario, an area in which she has
spent most of her life. Its small-town people
figure in many of her stories. For two years,
she attended the University of Western Ontario, but dropped out at twenty, after her first
marriage. The mother of three daughters,
Munro is a particularly sensitive explorer of
the relations between parents and children, yet
she ranges widely in choosing her themes. She
has written seven remarkable collections of
short fiction:* Dance of the Happy Shades
(1968), Lives of Girls and Women *(1971),*
Something I've Been Meaning to Tell You
(1974), The Beggar Maid *(1982),* The
Moons of Jupiter *(1983),* The Progress of
Love *(1986), and* Friend of My Youth
(1990). Three of her books have won Canada's

Alice Munro

prestigious Governor General's Literary Award. Although Lives of Girls and Women
*has been called a novel, Atwood regards it as a book of "interrelated stories." Clearly
the short story is her medium, and she has declared her preference for "the story that
will zero in and give you intense, but not connected, moments of experience."*

At the end of Bell Street, McKay Street, Mayo Street, there was the Flood.
It was the Wawanash River, which every spring overflowed its banks. Some springs,
say one in every five, it covered the roads on that side of town and washed over
the fields, creating a shallow choppy lake. Light reflected off the water made everything bright and cold, as it is in a lakeside town, and woke or revived in people
certain vague hopes of disaster. Mostly during the late afternoon and early evening, there were people straggling out to look at it, and discuss whether it was
still rising, and whether this time it might invade the town. In general, those
under fifteen and over sixty-five were most certain that it would.

Eva and Carol rode out on their bicycles. They left the road—it was the end of
Mayo Street, past any houses—and rode right into a field, over a wire fence entirely
flattened by the weight of the winter's snow. They coasted a little way before the
long grass stopped them, then left their bicycles lying down and went to the water.

"We have to find a log and ride on it," Eva said.

"Jesus, we'll freeze our legs off."

"Jesus, we'll freeze our legs off!" said one of the boys who were there too at   5
the water's edge. He spoke in a sour whine, the way boys imitated girls although

it was nothing like the way girls talked. These boys—there were three of them—were all in the same class as Eva and Carol at school and were known to them by name (their names being Frank, Bud and Clayton), but Eva and Carol, who had seen and recognized them from the road, had not spoken to them or looked at them or, even yet, given any sign of knowing they were there. The boys seemed to be trying to make a raft, from lumber they had salvaged from the water.

Eva and Carol took off their shoes and socks and waded in. The water was so cold it sent pain up their legs, like blue electric sparks shooting through their veins, but they went on, pulling their skirts high, tight behind and bunched so they could hold them in front.

"Look at the fat-assed ducks in wading."

"Fat-assed fucks."

Eva and Carol, of course, gave no sign of hearing this. They laid hold of a log and climbed on, taking a couple of boards floating in the water for paddles. There were always things floating around in the Flood—branches, fence-rails, logs, road signs, old lumber; sometimes boilers, washtubs, pots and pans, or even a car seat or stuffed chair, as if somewhere the Flood had got into a dump.

They paddled away from shore, heading out into the cold lake. The water   10
was perfectly clear, they could see the brown grass swimming along the bottom. Suppose it was the sea, thought Eva. She thought of drowned cities and countries. Atlantis. Suppose they were riding in a Viking boat—Viking boats on the Atlantic were more frail and narrow than this log on the Flood—and they had miles of clear sea beneath them, then a spired city, intact as a jewel irretrievable on the ocean floor.

"This is a Viking boat," she said. "I am the carving on the front." She stuck her chest out and stretched her neck, trying to make a curve, and she made a face, putting out her tongue. Then she turned and for the first time took notice of the boys.

"Hey, you sucks!" she yelled at them. "You'd be scared to come out here, this water is ten feet deep!"

"Liar," they answered without interest, and she was.

They steered the log around a row of trees, avoiding floating barbed wire, and got into a little bay created by a natural hollow of the land. Where the bay was now, there would be a pond full of frogs later in the spring, and by the middle of summer there would be no water visible at all, just a low tangle of reeds and bushes, green, to show that mud was still wet around their roots. Larger bushes, willows, grew around the steep bank of this pond and were still partly out of the water. Eva and Carol let the log ride in. They saw a place where something was caught.

It was a boat, or part of one. An old rowboat with most of one side ripped   15
out, the board that had been the seat just dangling. It was pushed up among the branches, lying on what would have been its side, if it had a side, the prow caught high.

Their idea came to them without consultation, at the same time:

"You guys! Hey, you guys!"

"We found you a boat!"

"Stop building your stupid raft and come and look at the boat!"

What surprised them in the first place was that the boys really did come, scram- 20
bling overland, half running, half sliding down the bank, wanting to see.

"Hey, where?"

"Where is it, I don't see no boat."

What surprised them in the second place was that when the boys did actually
see what boat was meant, this old flood-smashed wreck held up in the branches,
they did not understand that they had been fooled, that a joke had been played
on them. They did not show a moment's disappointment, but seemed as pleased
at the discovery as if the boat had been whole and new. They were already barefoot,
because they had been wading in the water to get lumber, and they waded in here
without a stop, surrounding the boat and appraising it and paying no attention
even of an insulting kind to Eva and Carol who bobbed up and down on their
log. Eva and Carol had to call to them.

"How do you think you're going to get it off?"

"It won't float anyway."   25

"What makes you think it will float?"

"It'll sink. Glub-blub-blub, you'll all be drownded."

The boys did not answer, because they were too busy walking around the
boat, pulling at it in a testing way to see how it could be got off with the least
possible damage. Frank, who was the most literate, talkative and inept of the three,
began referring to the boat as *she*, an affectation which Eva and Carol acknowledged
with fish-mouths of contempt.

"She's caught two places. You got to be careful not to tear a hole in her bottom. She's heavier than you'd think."

It was Clayton who climbed up and freed the boat, and Bud, a tall fat boy,   30
who got the weight of it on his back to turn it into the water so that they could
half float, half carry it to shore. All this took some time. Eva and Carol abandoned their log and waded out of the water. They walked overland to get their
shoes and socks and bicycles. They did not need to come back this way but they
came. They stood at the top of the hill, leaning on their bicycles. They did not
go on home, but they did not sit down and frankly watch, either. They stood
more or less facing each other, but glancing down at the water and at the boys
struggling with the boat, as if they had just halted for a moment out of curiosity,
and staying longer than they intended, to see what came of this unpromising
project.

About nine o'clock, or when it was nearly dark—dark to people inside the
houses, but not quite dark outside—they all returned to town, going along Mayo
Street in a sort of procession. Frank and Bud and Clayton came carrying the boat,
upside-down, and Eva and Carol walked behind, wheeling their bicycles. The boys'
heads were almost hidden in the darkness of the overturned boat, with its smell
of soaked wood, cold swampy water. The girls could look ahead and see the street
lights in their tin reflectors, a necklace of lights climbing Mayo Street, reaching
all the way up to the standpipe. They turned onto Burns Street heading for Clayton's house, the nearest house belonging to any of them. This was not the way
home for Eva or for Carol either, but they followed along. The boys were perhaps
too busy carrying the boat to tell them to go away. Some younger children were
still out playing, playing hopscotch on the sidewalk though they could hardly see.
At this time of year the bare sidewalk was still such a novelty and delight. These

children cleared out of the way and watched the boat go by with unwilling respect; they shouted questions after it, wanting to know where it came from and what was going to be done with it. No one answered them. Eva and Carol as well as the boys refused to answer or even look at them.

The five of them entered Clayton's yard. The boys shifted weight, as if they were going to put the boat down.

"You better take it round to the back where nobody can see it," Carol said. That was the first thing any of them had said since they came into town.

The boys said nothing but went on, following a mud path between Clayton's house and a leaning board fence. They let the boat down in the back yard.

"It's a stolen boat, you know," said Eva, mainly for the effect. "It must've belonged to somebody. You stole it."   35

"You was the ones who stole it then," Bud said, short of breath. "It was you seen it first."

"It was you took it."

"It was all of us then. If one of us gets in trouble then all of us does."

"Are you going to tell anybody on them?" said Carol as she and Eva rode home, along the streets which were dark between the lights now and potholed from winter.

"It's up to you. I won't if you won't."   40

"I won't if you won't."

They rode in silence, relinquishing something, but not discontented.

The board fence in Clayton's back yard had every so often a post which supported it, or tried to, and it was on these posts that Eva and Carol spent several evenings sitting, jauntily but not very comfortably. Or else they just leaned against the fence while the boys worked on the boat. During the first couple of evenings neighborhood children attracted by the sound of hammering tried to get into the yard to see what was going on, but Eva and Carol blocked their way.

"Who said you could come in here?"

"Just us can come in this yard."   45

These evenings were getting longer, the air milder. Skipping was starting on the sidewalks. Further along the street there was a row of hard maples that had been tapped. Children drank the sap as fast as it could drip into the buckets. The old man and woman who owned the trees, and who hoped to make syrup, came running out of the house making noises as if they were trying to scare away crows. Finally, every spring, the old man would come out on his porch and fire his shotgun into the air, and then the thieving would stop.

None of those working on the boat bothered about stealing sap, though all had done so last year.

The lumber to repair the boat was picked up here and there, along back lanes. At this time of year things were lying around—old boards and branches, sodden mitts, spoons flung out with the dishwater, lids of pudding pots that had been set in the snow to cool, all the debris that can sift through and survive winter. The tools came from Clayton's cellar—left over, presumably, from the time when his father was alive—and though they had nobody to advise them the boys seemed to figure out more or less the manner in which boats are built, or rebuilt. Frank was the one who showed up with diagrams from books and *Popular Mechanics* magazines. Clayton looked at these diagrams and listened to Frank read the instructions and then went ahead and decided in his own way what was to be done. Bud was best at sawing. Eva and Carol watched everything from the fence and offered criticism and thought up names. The names for the boat that they thought of were: Water Lily, Sea Horse, Flood Queen, and Caro-Eve, after them because they had found it. The boys did not say which, if any, of these names they found satisfactory.

The boat had to be tarred. Clayton heated up a pot of tar on the kitchen stove and brought it out and painted slowly, his thorough way, sitting astride the overturned boat. The other boys were sawing a board to make a new seat. As Clayton worked, the tar cooled and thickened so that finally he could not move the brush any more. He turned to Eva and held out the pot and said, "You can go in and heat this on the stove."

Eva took the pot and went up the back steps. The kitchen seemed black after   50 outside, but it must be light enough to see in, because there was Clayton's mother standing at the ironing board, ironing. She did that for a living, took in wash and ironing.

"Please may I put the tar pot on the stove?" said Eva, who had been brought up to talk politely to parents, even wash-and-iron ladies, and who for some reason especially wanted to make a good impression on Clayton's mother.

"You'll have to poke up the fire then," said Clayton's mother, as if she doubted whether Eva would know how to do that. But Eva could see now, and she picked up the lid with the stove-lifter, and took the poker and poked up a flame. She stirred the tar as it softened. She felt privileged. Then and later. Before she went to sleep a picture of Clayton came to her mind; she saw him sitting astride the boat, tarpainting, with such concentration, delicacy, absorption. She thought of him speaking to her, out of his isolation, in such an ordinary peaceful taking-for-granted voice.

On the twenty-fourth of May, a school holiday in the middle of the week, the boat was carried out of town, a long way now, off the road over fields and fences that had been repaired, to where the river flowed between its normal banks. Eva and Carol, as well as the boys, took turns carrying it. It was launched in the water from a cow-trampled spot between willow bushes that were fresh out in leaf. The boys went first. They yelled with triumph when the boat did float, when it rode amazingly down the river current. The boat was painted black, and green inside, with yellow seats, and a strip of yellow all the way around the outside. There was no name on it, after all. The boys could not imagine that it needed any name to keep it separate from the other boats in the world.

Eva and Carol ran along the bank, carrying bags full of peanut butter-and-jam sandwiches, pickles, bananas, chocolate cake, potato chips, graham crackers stuck together with corn syrup and five bottles of pop to be cooled in the river water. The bottles bumped against their legs. They yelled for a turn.

"If they don't let us they're bastards," Carol said, and they yelled together,   55 "We found it! We found it!"

The boys did not answer, but after a while they brought the boat in, and Carol and Eva came crashing, panting down the bank.

"Does it leak?"

"It don't leak yet."

"We forgot a bailing can," wailed Carol, but nevertheless she got in, with Eva, and Frank pushed them off, crying, "Here's to a Watery Grave!"

And the thing about being in a boat was that it was not solidly bobbing, like a log, but was cupped in the water, so that riding in it was not like being on something in the water, but like being in the water itself. Soon they were all going out in the boat in mixed-up turns, two boys and a girl, two girls and a boy, a girl and a boy, until things were so confused it was impossible to tell whose turn came next, and nobody cared anyway. They went down the river—those who weren't riding, running along the bank to keep up. They passed under two bridges, one iron, one cement. Once they saw a big carp just resting, it seemed to smile at them, in the bridge-shaded water. They did not know how far they had gone on the river, but things had changed—the water had got shallower, and the land flatter. Across an open field they saw a building that looked like a house, abandoned. They dragged the boat up on the bank and tied it and set out across the field.

"That's the old station," Frank said. "That's Pedder Station." The others had heard this name but he was the one who knew, because his father was the station agent in town. He said that this was a station on a branch line that had been torn up, and that there had been a sawmill here, but a long time ago.

Inside the station it was dark, cool. All the windows were broken. Glass lay in shards and in fairly big pieces on the floor. They walked around finding the larger pieces of glass and tramping on them, smashing them, it was like cracking ice on puddles. Some partitions were still in place, you could see where the ticket window had been. There was a bench lying on its side. People had been here, it looked as if people came here all the time, though it was so far from anywhere. Beer bottles and pop bottles were lying around, also cigarette packages, gum and candy wrappers, the paper from a loaf of bread. The walls were covered with dim and fresh pencil and chalk writings and carved with knives.

I LOVE RONNIE COLES
I WANT TO FUCK
KILROY WAS HERE
RONNIE COLES IS AN ASS-HOLE
WHAT ARE YOU DOING HERE?
WAITING FOR A TRAIN
DAWNA MARY-LOU BARBARA JOANNE

It was exciting to be inside this large, dark, empty place, with the loud noise of breaking glass and their voices ringing back from the underside of the roof. They tipped the old beer bottles against their mouths. That reminded them that they were hungry and thirsty and they cleared a place in the middle of the floor and sat down and ate the lunch. They drank the pop just as it was, lukewarm. They ate everything there was and licked the smears of peanut butter and jam off the bread-paper in which the sandwiches had been wrapped.

They played Truth or Dare.

"I dare you to write on the wall, I am a Stupid Ass, and sign your name." 65

"Tell the truth—what is the worst lie you ever told?"

"Did you ever wet the bed?"

"Did you ever dream you were walking down the street without any clothes on?"

"I dare you to go outside and pee on the railway sign."

It was Frank who had to do that. They could not see him, even his back, but they knew he did it, they heard the hissing sound of his pee. They all sat still, amazed, unable to think of what the next dare would be.

"I dare everybody," said Frank from the doorway, "I dare—Everybody."

"What?"

"Take off all our clothes."

Eva and Carol screamed.

"Anybody who won't do it has to walk—has to *crawl*—around this floor on their hands and knees."

They were all quiet, till Eva said, almost complacently, "What first?"

"Shoes and socks."

"Then we have to go outside, there's too much glass here."

They pulled off their shoes and socks in the doorway, in the sudden blinding sun. The field before them was bright as water. They ran across where the tracks used to go.

"That's enough, that's enough," said Carol. "Watch out for thistles!"

"Tops! Everybody take off their tops!"

"I won't! We won't, will we, Eva?"

But Eva was whirling round and round in the sun where the track used to be. "I don't care, I don't care! Truth or Dare! Truth or Dare!"

She unbuttoned her blouse as she whirled, as if she didn't know what her hand was doing, she flung it off.

Carol took off hers. "I wouldn't have done it, if you hadn't!"

"Bottoms!"

Nobody said a word this time, they all bent and stripped themselves. Eva, naked first, started running across the field, and then all the others ran, all five of them running bare through the knee-high hot grass, running towards the river. Not caring now about being caught but in fact leaping and yelling to call attention to themselves, if there was anybody to hear or see. They felt as if they were going to jump off a cliff and fly. They felt that something was happening to them different from anything that had happened before, and it had to do with the boat, the water, the sunlight, the dark ruined station, and each other. They thought of each other now hardly as names or people, but as echoing shrieks, reflections, all bold and white and loud and scandalous, and as fast as arrows. They went running without a break into the cold water and when it came almost to the tops of their legs they fell on it and swam. It stopped their noise. Silence, amazement, came over them in a rush. They dipped and floated and separated, sleek as mink.

Eva stood up in the water her hair dripping, water running down her face. She was waist deep. She stood on smooth stones, her feet fairly wide apart, water flowing between her legs. About a yard away from her Clayton also stood up, and they were blinking the water out of their eyes, looking at each other. Eva did not turn or try to hide; she was quivering from the cold of the water, but also with pride, shame, boldness, and exhilaration.

Clayton shook his head violently, as if he wanted to bang something out of it, then bent over and took a mouthful of river water. He stood up with his cheeks full and made a tight hole of his mouth and shot the water at her as if it was coming out of a hose, hitting her exactly, first one breast and then the other. Water from his mouth ran down her body. He hooted to see it, a loud self-conscious sound that nobody would have expected, from him. The others looked up from wherever they were in the water and closed in to see.

Eva crouched down and slid into the water, letting her head go right under. She swam, and when she let her head out downstream, Carol was coming after her and the boys were already on the bank, already running into the grass, showing their skinny backs, their white, flat buttocks. They were laughing and saying things to each other but she couldn't hear, for the water in her ears.

"What did he do?" said Carol.

"Nothing."

They crept in to shore. "Let's stay in the bushes till they go," said Eva. "I hate them anyway. I really do. Don't you hate them?"

"Sure," said Carol, and they waited, not very long, until they heard the boys still noisy and excited coming down to the place a bit upriver where they had left the boat. They heard them jump in and start rowing.

"They've got all the hard part, going back," said Eva, hugging herself and shivering violently. "Who cares? Anyway. It never was our boat."

"What if they tell?" said Carol.

"We'll say it's all a lie."

Eva hadn't thought of this solution until she said it, but as soon as she did she felt almost light-hearted again. The ease and scornfulness of it did make them both giggle, and slapping themselves and splashing out of the water they set about developing one of those fits of laughter in which, as soon as one showed signs of exhaustion, the other would snort and start up again, and they would make helpless—soon genuinely helpless—faces at each other and bend over and grab themselves as if they had the worst pain.

Questions

1. By what hints does Alice Munro indicate the age of the characters in her story and their level of maturity?
2. Of what importance is it that "The Found Boat" is set in the springtime? In other words, how does the setting matter to what happens in the story?
3. Munro carefully describes the water of the Wawanash River. What role does it play in the story? What changes take place in the water during the course of the story? What changes take place in the characters?
4. What is the "something" that the girls relinquish in paragraph 42?
5. What is the point of view in "The Found Boat"? At what places in the story do you find the point of view shifting?
6. What does the boat suggest to you? What other details in the story are suggestive enough to be called symbolic?
7. Where do you find evidence of Eva's growing attraction to Clayton? How would you describe his character?
8. What do you make of the change of heart that Eva suddenly displays in paragraph 93?

Suggestions for Writing

1. Reexamine one of these stories you have already read: "A Rose for Emily," "The Tell-Tale Heart," "Greasy Lake," "Barn Burning," "A Clean, Well-Lighted Place," "The Storm," "Araby," "The Open Boat," "Young Goodman Brown." Reread carefully, looking for rich hints. In writing, indicate what actions and objects now seem to you symbolic in their suggestions. Do these actions or objects point toward any central theme in the story? (Note: Watch out for Poe. He eschews messages, and his stories keep away from central themes.)

2. For an alternate topic, look for symbols in a story you have not read before. In the Stories for Further Reading, you might take a look at "The Lover of Horses," "The Man Who Did Not Smile," and "Where Are You Going, Where Have You Been?"

3. Write a short comment inspired by the title "Absolutely Nothing Is Symbolic" or "There Isn't a Thing You Can't Make a Symbol of." Draw upon your experiences in reading the stories in this chapter, or any other literature. Give concrete examples.

4. Pick a tangible *thing* that intrigues you—an animal, a plant, or another part of nature; a house or another man-made object. Recall it, observe it, meditate on it. Then write an opening paragraph for a story that will make a symbol of that object, doing your best to fill the passage with hints. For inspiration, look back over John Steinbeck's "The Chrysanthemums" and Alice Munro's "The Found Boat."

8 Evaluating a Story

When we **evaluate** a story, we consider it and place a value on it. Perhaps we decide that it is a masterpiece, or a bit of trash, or (like most fiction we read) a work of some value in between. No cut-and-dried method of judgment will work on every story, and so in this chapter I have none to propose. Still, there are things we can look for in a story—usually clear indications of its author's competence.

In judging the quality of a baseball glove, we first have to be aware that a catcher's mitt differs—for good reasons—from a first baseman's glove. It is no less true that, before evaluating a story, we need to recognize its nature. To see, for instance, that a story is a fable (or perhaps a tale) may save us from condemning it as a failed short story.

Good critics of literature have at least a working knowledge of some of its conventions. By **conventions** we mean usual devices and features of a literary work, by which we can recognize its kind. When in movies or on television we watch a yarn about a sinister old mansion full of horrors, we recognize the conventions of that long-lived species of fiction, the **Gothic story.** The Castle of Otranto, A Gothic Story (1764), by English author Horace Walpole, started the genre, supplied its name, and established its favorite trappings. In Walpole's short novel, Otranto is a cobwebbed ruin full of underground passages and massive doors that slam unexpectedly. There are awful objects: a statue that bleeds, a portrait that steps from its frame, a giant helmet that falls and leaves its victim "dashed to pieces." Atmosphere is essential to a Gothic story: dusty halls, shadowy landscapes, whispering servants "seen at a distance imperfectly through the dusk" (I quote from Anne Radcliffe's novel The Mysteries of Udolpho, 1794). In Charlotte Brontë's Jane Eyre (1847), we find the model for a legion of heroines in the Gothic fiction of our own day. In the best-selling Gothic romances of Victoria Holt, Phyllis A. Whitney, and others, young women similarly find love while working as governesses in ominous mansions. Lacking for English castles, American authors of Gothic fiction have had to make do with dark old houses—like those in Nathaniel

Hawthorne's novel *The House of the Seven Gables* and in the short stories of Edgar Allan Poe, such as "The Tell-Tale Heart." William Faulkner, who brought the tradition to Mississippi, gives "A Rose for Emily" some familiar conventions: a rundown mansion, a mysterious servant, a madwoman, a hideous secret. But Faulkner's story, in its portrait of an aristocrat who refuses to admit that her world has vanished, goes far beyond Gothic conventions. Evidently, when you set up court as a judge of stories, to recognize such conventions will be an advantage. Knowing a Gothic story for what it is, you won't condemn it for lacking "realism." And to be aware of the Gothic elements in "A Rose for Emily" may help you see how original Faulkner manages to be, though employing some handed-down conventions.

Is the story a piece of commercial fiction tailored to a formula, or is it unique in its design? You can't demand the subtlety of a Katherine Anne Porter of a writer of hard-boiled detective stories. Neither can you put down "The Jilting of Granny Weatherall" for lacking slam-bang action. Some stories are no more than light, entertaining bits of fluff—no point in damning them, unless you dislike fluff or find them written badly. Of course, you are within your rights to prefer solidity to fluff, or to prefer a Porter story to a typical paperback romance by a hack writer. James Thurber's "The Catbird Seat," though a simpler and briefer story than Leo Tolstoi's "The Death of Ivan Ilych," is no less finished, complete, and satisfactory a work of art. Yet, considered in another light, Tolstoi's short novel may well seem a greater work than Thurber's. It reveals greater meaning and enfolds more life.

Masterpieces often have flaws; and so, whenever we can, we need to consider a story in its entirety. Some novels by Thomas Hardy and by Theodore Dreiser impress (on the whole), despite passages of stilted dialogue and other clumsy writing. If a story totally fails to enlist our sympathies, probably it suffers from some basic ineptitude: choice of an inappropriate point of view, a style ill suited to its theme, or possibly insufficient knowledge of human beings. In some ineffectual stories, things important to the writer (and to the story) remain private and unmentioned. In other stories, the writer's interests may be perfectly clear but they may not interest the reader, for they are not presented with sufficient art.

Some stories fail from **sentimentality**, a defect in a work whose writer seems to feel tremendous emotion and implies that we too should feel it, but does not provide us enough reason to share such feelings. Sentimentality is rampant in televised weekday afternoon soap operas, whose characters usually palpitate with passion for reasons not quite known, and who speak in melodramatic tones as if heralding the end of the world. In some fiction, conventional objects (locks of baby hair, posthumously awarded medals, pressed roses) frequently signal, "Let's have a good cry!" Revisiting home after her marriage, the character Amelia in William Makepeace Thackeray's *Vanity Fair* effuses about the bed she slept in when a virgin: "Dear little bed! how many a long night had she wept on its pillow."[1]

---

[1]Sentimentality in fiction is older than the Victorians. Popular in eighteenth-century England, the **sentimental novel** (or **novel of sensibility**) specialized in characters whose ability to shed quick and copious tears signified their virtuous hearts. Oliver Goldsmith's *The Vicar of Wakefield* (1766) and Henry Mackenzie's *The Man of Feeling* (1771) are classics of the genre. An abundance of tears does not prevent such novels from having merit.

Teary sentimentality is more common in nineteenth-century fiction than in ours. We have gone to the other extreme, some critics think, into a sentimentality of the violent and the hard-boiled. But in a grossly sentimental work of any kind, failure inheres in our refusal to go along with the author's implied attitudes. We laugh when we are expected to cry, feel delight when we are supposed to be horrified.

In evaluating a story, we may usefully ask a few questions:

1. What is the tone of the story? By what means and how effectively is it communicated?
2. What is the point of view? Does it seem appropriate and effective in this story? Imagine the story told from a different point of view; would such a change be for the worse or for the better?
3. Does the story show us unique and individual scenes, events, and characters—or weary stereotypes?
4. Are any symbols evident? If so, do they direct us to the story's central theme, or do they distract us from it?
5. How appropriate to the theme of the story, and to its subject matter, are its tone and style? Is it ever difficult or impossible to sympathize with the attitudes of the author (insofar as we can tell what they are)?
6. Does our interest in the story mainly depend on following its plot, on finding out what will happen next? Or does the author go beyond the events to show us what they mean? Are the events (however fantastic) credible, or are they incredibly melodramatic? Does the plot greatly depend upon farfetched coincidence?
7. Has the writer caused characters, events, and settings to come alive? Are they full of breath and motion, or simply told about in the abstract ("She was a lovable girl whose life had been highly exciting")? Unless the story is a fable or a tale, which need no detailed description or deep portrayal of character, then we may well expect the story to contain enough vividly imagined detail to make us believe in it.

SUGGESTIONS FOR WRITING

1. In a short essay, take two stories that you find differing markedly in quality and evaluate them, giving evidence to support your judgments. Stories similar enough to compare might include two character studies of women, as in "The Jilting of Granny Weatherall" and "The Chrysanthemums."
2. Write a blast against a story in this book that you dislike intensely. Stick to the text of the story in making your criticisms and support your charges with plenty of evidence.
3. By comparing two stories that strike you as similar ("'Greasy Lake' and 'Barn Burning': Two Stories of Hard-won Maturity"), evaluate them.

9 Reading Long Stories and Novels

Among the forms of imaginative literature in our language, the novel has been the favorite of both writers and readers for more than two hundred years. Broadly defined, a **novel** is a book-length story in prose, whose author tries to create the sense that while we read, we experience actual life.

This sense of actuality, also found in artful short stories, may be the quality that sets the novel apart from other long prose narratives. Why do we not apply the name *novel* to, for instance, *Gulliver's Travels?* In his marvel-filled account of Lemuel Gulliver's voyages among pygmies, giants, civilized horses, and noxious humanoid swine, Jonathan Swift does not seem primarily to care if we find his story credible. Though he arrays the adventures of Gulliver in painstaking detail (and, ironically, has Gulliver swear to the truth of them), Swift neither attempts nor achieves a convincing illusion of life. For his book is a fantastic satire that finds resemblances between noble horses and man's reasoning faculties, between debased apes and man's kinship with the beasts.

Unlike other major literary forms—drama, lyric, ballad, and epic—the novel is a relative newcomer. Originally, the drama in ancient Greece came alive only when actors performed it; the epic or heroic poem (from the classic *Iliad* through the Old English *Beowulf*), only when a bard sang or chanted it. But the English novel came to maturity in literate times, in the eighteenth century, and by its nature was something different: a story to be communicated silently, at whatever moment and at whatever pace (whether quickly or slowly and meditatively) the reader desired.

Some definitions of the novel would more strictly limit its province. "The Novel is a picture of real life and manners, and of the time in which it was written," declared Clara Reeve in 1785, thus distinguishing the novel from the romance, which "describes what never happened nor is likely to happen." By so specifying that the novel depicts life in the present day, the critic was probably observing the derivation of the word *novel.* Akin to the French word for "news" (*nouvelles*), it comes from the Italian *novella* ("something new and small"), a term applied to a newly made story taking place in recent times, and not a traditional story taking place long ago.

Also drawing a line between novel and romance, Nathaniel Hawthorne, in his preface to *The House of the Seven Gables* (1851), restricted the novel "not merely to the possible, but to the probable and ordinary course of man's experience." A **romance** had no such limitations. Such a definition would deny the name of *novel* to any fantastic or speculative story—to, say, the Gothic novel and the science fiction novel. Carefully bestowed, the labels *novel* and *romance* may be useful to distinguish between the true-to-life story of usual people in ordinary places (such as George Eliot's *Silas Marner* or John Updike's *Couples*) and the larger-than-life story of daring deeds and high adventure, set in the past or future or in some timeless land (such as Walter Scott's *Ivanhoe* or J.R.R. Tolkien's *Lord of the Rings*). But the labels are difficult to apply to much modern fiction, in which ordinary life is sometimes mingled with outlandishness. Who can say that James Joyce's *Ulysses* is not a novel, though it contains moments of dream and drunken hallucination? And yet the total effect, as in any successful novel, is a sense of the actual.

This sense of the actual is, perhaps, the hallmark of a novel, whether or not the events it relates are literally possible. To achieve this sense, novelists have employed many devices, and frequently have tried to pass off their storytelling as reporting. Nathaniel Hawthorne, in his introduction to *The Scarlet Letter*, gives a minute account of his finding documents on which he claims to base his novel, tied with a faded red ribbon and gathering dust in a customshouse. More recently, Vladimir Nabokov's *Pale Fire* (1962) tells its story in the form of a scholarly edition of a 999-line poem, complete with a biographical commentary by a friend of the late poet. Samuel Richardson's casting *Pamela* (1740) into the form of personal letters helped lend the story an appearance of being not invented, but discovered. Alice Walker's *The Color Purple* (1982) is also an **epistolary novel,** though some of the letters that tell the story are addressed to God. Another method favored by novelists is to write as though setting down a memoir or an autobiography. Daniel Defoe, whose skill in feigning such memoirs was phenomenal, even succeeded in writing the supposedly true confessions of a woman retired from a life of crime, *Moll Flanders* (1722), and in maintaining a vivid truthfulness:

> Going through Aldersgate Street, there was a pretty little child who had been at a dancing-school, and was going home all alone: and my prompter, like a true devil, set me upon this innocent creature. I talked to it, and it prattled to me again, and I took it by the hand and led it along till I came to a paved alley that goes into Bartholomew Close, and I led it in there. The child said that was not its way home. I said, "Yes, my dear, it is; I'll show you the way home." The child had a little necklace on of gold beads, and I had my eye upon that, and in the dark of the alley I stooped, pretending to mend the child's clog that was loose, and took off her necklace, and the child never felt it, and so led the child on again. Here, I say, the devil put me upon killing the child in the dark alley, that it might not cry, but the very thought frighted me so that I was ready to drop down; but I turned the child about and bade it go back again. . . . The last affair left no great

concern upon me, for as I did the poor child no harm, I only said to myself, I had given the parents a just reproof for their negligence in leaving the poor little lamb to come home by itself, and it would teach them to take more care of it another time.

What could sound more like the voice of an experienced child-robber than this manner of excusing her crime, and even justifying it?

Informed that a student had given up the study of mathematics to become a novelist, the logician David Hilbert drily remarked, "It was just as well: he did not have enough imagination to become a first-rate mathematician."[1] It is true that some novelists place great emphasis on research and notetaking. Arthur Halley, author of bestsellers such as *Wheels* (about the Detroit car industry) and *Airport,* reportedly starts work on a novel by interviewing people in whatever glamorous profession he plans to expose, gathering stacks of note cards to make sure that his slightest detail is accurate. Clearly, however, any novel can grow to completion only through a procedure of creation, selection, and arrangement. Raw facts cannot leap into a novel by themselves—whether the novel is a paperback shocker about a famous crime, or Theodore Dreiser's impressive study of a murder case, inspired by newspaper accounts, *An American Tragedy.*

In "The Open Boat," Stephen Crane brings high literary art to bear upon his own experience. The result is a short story based on fact. More recently, we have heard much about the **nonfiction novel,** in which the author presents actual people and events in story form. Norman Mailer, in *The Executioner's Song* (1979), chronicles the life and death of Gary Gilmore, the Utah murderer who demanded his own execution. Truman Capote's *In Cold Blood* (1966) sets forth an account of crime and punishment in Kansas, based on interviews with the accused and other principals. Perhaps the name "nonfiction novel" (Capote's name for it) or "true life novel" (as Mailer calls his Gilmore story) is newer than the form. In the past, writers of autobiography have cast their memoirs into what looks like novel form: Richard Wright in *Black Boy* (1945), William Burroughs in *Junkie* (1953). Derived not from the author's memory but from his reporting, John Hersey's *Hiroshima* (1946) reconstructs the lives of six survivors of the atom bomb as if they were fictional. In reading such works we may nearly forget we are reading literal truth, so well do the techniques of the novel lend remembered facts an air of immediacy.

A familiar kind of fiction that claims a basis in fact is the **historical novel,** a detailed reconstruction of life in another time, perhaps in another place. In some historical novels the author attempts a faithful picture of daily life in another era, as does Robert Graves in *I, Claudius* (1934), a novel of patrician Rome. More often, history is a backdrop for an exciting story of love and heroic adventure. Nathaniel Hawthorne's *The Scarlet Letter* (set in Puritan Boston), Herman Melville's *Moby-Dick* (set in the heyday of Yankee whalers), and Stephen Crane's *The Red Badge of Courage* (set in the battlefields of the Civil War) are historical novels in that their authors lived considerably later than the scenes and events that they depicted—and strove for truthfulness, by imaginative means.

[1]Quoted by William H. Gass, *Fiction and the Figures of Life* (New York: Knopf, 1970).

Other varieties of novel will be familiar to anyone who scans the racks of paperback books in any drugstore: the mystery or detective novel, the Western novel, the science fiction novel, and other enduring types. Classified according to less well-known species, novels are sometimes said to belong to a category if they contain some recognizable kind of structure or theme. Such a category is the **bildungsroman** (German for a "novel of growth or development"), sometimes call the **apprenticeship novel** after its classic example, *Wilhelm Meister's Apprenticeship* (1796) by Johann Wolfgang von Goethe. This is the kind of novel in which a youth struggles toward maturity, seeking, perhaps, some consistent world view or philosophy of life. Sometimes the apprenticeship novel is evidently the author's recollection of his own early life: James Joyce's *Portrait of the Artist as a Young Man* and Mark Twain's *Tom Sawyer*.

In a **picaresque novel** (another famous category), a likable scoundrel wanders through adventures, living by his wits, duping the straight citizenry. The name comes from Spanish: *Picaro*, "rascal" or "rogue." The classic picaresque novel is the anonymous Spanish *Life of Lazarillo de Tormes* (1554), imitated by many English writers, among them Henry Fielding in his story of a London thief and racketeer, *Jonathan Wild* (1743). Mark Twain's *Huckleberry Finn* owes something to the tradition; like early picaresque novels, it is told in episodes rather than in one all-unifying plot and is narrated in the first person by a hero at odds with respectable society ("dismal regular and decent," Huck Finn calls it). In Twain's novel, however, the traveling swindlers who claim to be a duke and a dauphin are much more typical rogues of picaresque fiction than Huck himself, an honest innocent. Modern novels worthy of the name include J.P. Donleavy's *The Ginger Man* (1965), Saul Bellow's *The Adventures of Augie March* (1953), and Erica Jong's *Fanny* (1981).

Mainly (but not merely) a description of size, the term **short novel** refers to a narrative midway in length between a short story and a novel (the latter, according to E.M. Forster, has to have at least 50,000 words). Generally a short novel, like a short story, is focused on just one or two characters but, unlike a short story, has room to reveal them in greater fullness and depth, sometimes taking in a longer span of time. A short novel is included in this book: Leo Tolstoi's *The Death of Ivan Ilych*. Sometimes a short novel is also called a **novelette** (a name formerly much used by magazines that featured long fiction), or a **nouvelle,** or a **novella;** but these names are out of fashion.

Trying to perceive a novel as a whole, we may find it helpful to look for the same elements that we have noticed in reading short stories. By asking ourselves leading questions, we may be drawn more deeply into the novel's world, and may come to recognize and appreciate the techniques of the novelist. Does the novel have themes, or an overall theme? Who is its main character? What is the author's kind of narrative voice? What do we know about the tone, style, and use of irony? Why is this novel written from one point of view rather than from another? If the novel in question is large and thickly populated, it may help to read it with a pencil, taking brief notes. Forced to put the novel aside and later return to it, the reader may find that the notes refresh the memory. Notetaking habits differ, but perhaps these might be no more than, say, "Theme introduced, p. 27," or,

"Old clothes dealer, p. 109—walking symbol?" Some readers find it useful to list briefly whatever each chapter accomplishes. Others make lists of a novel's characters, especially when reading classic Russian novels in which the reader has to recall that Alexey Karamazov is also identified by his pet name Aloysha, or that, in Leo Tolstoi's *Anna Karenina*, Princess Catherine Alexándrovna Shcherbátskaya and "Kitty" are one and the same.

Once our reading of a novel is finished and we prepare to discuss it or write about it, it may be a good idea to browse through it again, rereading brief portions. This method of overall browsing may also help when first approaching a bulky and difficult novel. Just as an explorer mapping unfamiliar territory may find it best to begin by taking an aerial view of it, so too the reader approaching an exceptionally thick and demanding novel may wish, at the start, to look for its general shape. This is the method of some professional book reviewers, who size up a novel (even an easy-to-read spy story, because they are not reading for pleasure) by skimming the first chapter, a middle chapter or two, and the last chapter; then going back and browsing at top speed through the rest. Reading a novel in this grim fashion, of course, the reviewer does not really know it thoroughly, any more than a tourist knows the mind and heart of foreign people after just strolling in a capital city and riding a tour bus to a few monuments. The reviewer's method will, however, provide a general notion of what the author is doing, and at the very least will tell something of her tone, style, point of view, and competence. We suggest this method only as a way to *approach* a book that, otherwise, the reader might not want to approach at all. It may be a comfort in studying some obdurate-looking or highly experimental novel, such as James Joyce's *Ulysses* or Henry James's *The Sacred Fount*. But the reader will find it necessary to return to the book, in order to know it, and to read it honestly, in detail. There is, of course, no short cut to novel reading, and probably the best method is to settle in comfort and read the book through: with your own eyes, not with the borrowed glasses of literary criticism.

The death of the novel is continually being predicted. The competition of television drama is too much for it, some believe; indeed, some evidence says that such competition is taking hold. In Brittany, France, when antigovernment protesters blew up the only television transmitter in the province, booksellers the very next day reported their business increased by as much as twenty percent. But in England and North America, television dramas have been sending people in vast numbers back to the books dramatized: Evelyn Waugh's *Brideshead Revisited*, Charles Dickens's *A Tale of Two Cities*. Meanwhile, each year new novels by the hundreds continue to appear, their authors wistfully looking for a public. A chosen few reach tens of thousands of readers through book clubs, and, through paperback reprint editions, occasionally millions more. To forecast the end of the novel seems risky. For the novel exercises the imagination of the beholder. At any hour, at a touch of the hand, it opens and (with no warm-up) begins to speak. Once printed, it consumes no further energy. Often so small it may be carried in a pocket, it may yet survive by its ability to contain multitudes (a "capacious vessel," Henry James called it): a thing both a work of art and an amazingly compact system for the storage and retrieval of imagined life.

Leo Tolstoi

THE DEATH OF IVAN ILYCH   1886

Translated by Louise and Aylmer Maude

Leo Tolstoi

Leo Tolstoi (1828–1910), who inherited the title of Count, was born into a family who owned vast lands in Tula province, Russia. As a young man disgruntled with self and schooling, he left Kazan University without taking a degree. After a period of fast living in Moscow and St. Petersburg, he became an army officer and took part in the siege of Sevastopol in the Crimean War. Returning to his estate, Tolstoi opened a school for the children of serfs, based on the ideas (then radical) that learning should be a joy and that individuals should be taught according to their needs. In 1862 he married young, well-educated Sophia Bers. Thirteen children followed, and Tolstoi's years of tremendous achievement as a novelist. About 1876, after a religious illumination, Tolstoi became convinced that one should do good, eschew alcohol, tobacco, meat, and violence, and stop owning things. These tenets brought him into conflict with his wife and family, the Russian Orthodox Church, and the Czarist government. Tolstoi renounced his lands and his book royalties. He dressed like a peasant, made his own boots, and dug potatoes. From his driven pen poured books, tracts, and articles expounding his radically Christian moral and social ideas. In What Is Art? (1898) he held that artists have a God-given duty to produce only what most people can understand and appreciate. In his seventh decade Tolstoi returned to the novel, seeing in fiction a means to preach. Yet, impressive though they are, The Kreutzer Sonata (1891) and Resurrection (1899) have never won readers' love as have his earlier masterpieces War and Peace (1863–69), that immense saga of Russian society before, during, and after Napoleon's invasion, and Anna Karenina (1875–77), a compassionate history of the decline and fall of a woman who defies convention.

I

During an interval in the Melvinski trial in the large building of the Law Courts, the members and public prosecutor met in Ivan Egorovich Shebek's private room, where the conversation turned on the celebrated Krasovski case. Fëdor Vasilievich warmly maintained that it was not subject to their jurisdiction, Ivan Egorovich maintained the contrary, while Peter Ivanovich, not having entered into the discussion at the start, took no part in it but looked through the *Gazette* which had just been handed in.

"Gentlemen," he said, "Ivan Ilych has died!"

"You don't say so!"

"Here, read it yourself," replied Peter Ivanovich, handing Fëdor Vasilievich the paper still damp from the press. Surrounded by a black border were the words: "Praskovya Fëdorovna Goloviná, with profound sorrow, informs relatives and friends of the demise of her beloved husband Ivan Ilych Golovin, Member of the Court of Justice, which occurred on February the 4th of this year 1882. The funeral will take place on Friday at one o'clock in the afternoon."

Ivan Ilych had been a colleague of the gentlemen present and was liked by 5 them all. He had been ill for some weeks with an illness said to be incurable. His post had been kept open for him, but there had been conjectures that in case of his death Alexeev might receive his appointment, and that either Vinnikov or Shtabel would succeed Alexeev. So on receiving the news of Ivan Ilych's death the first thought of each of the gentlemen in that private room was of the changes and promotions it might occasion among themselves or their acquaintances.

"I shall be sure to get Shtabel's place or Vinnikov's," thought Fëdor Vasilievich. "I was promised that long ago, and the promotion means an extra eight hundred rubles a year for me besides the allowance."

"Now I must apply for my brother-in-law's transfer from Kaluga," thought Peter Ivanovich. "My wife will be very glad, and then she won't be able to say that I never do anything for her relations."

"I thought he would never leave his bed again," said Peter Ivanovich aloud. "It's very sad."

"But what really was the matter with him?"

"The doctors couldn't say—at least they could, but each of them said some- 10 thing different. When last I saw him I thought he was getting better."

"And I haven't been to see him since the holidays. I always meant to go."

"Had he any property?"

"I think his wife had a little—but something quite trifling."

"We shall have to go to see her, but they live so terribly far away."

"Far away from you, you mean. Everything's far away from your place." 15

"You see, he never can forgive my living on the other side of the river," said Peter Ivanovich, smiling at Shebek. Then, still talking of the distances between different parts of the city, they returned to the Court.

Besides considerations as to the possible transfers and promotions likely to result from Ivan Ilych's death, the mere fact of the death of a near acquaintance aroused, as usual, in all who heard of it the complacent feeling that "it is he who is dead and not I."

Each one thought or felt, "Well, he's dead but I'm alive!" But the more intimate of Ivan Ilych's acquaintances, his so-called friends, could not help thinking also that they would now have to fulfil the very tiresome demands of propriety by attending the funeral service and paying a visit of condolence to the widow.

Fëdor Vasilievich and Peter Ivanovich had been his nearest acquaintances. Peter Ivanovich had studied law with Ivan Ilych and had considered himself to be under obligations to him.

Having told his wife at dinner-time of Ivan Ilych's death and of his conjec- 20 ture that it might be possible to get her brother transferred to their circuit, Peter

Ivanovich sacrificed his usual nap, put on his evening clothes, and drove to Ivan Ilych's house.

At the entrance stood a carriage and two cabs. Leaning against the wall in the hall downstairs near the cloak-stand was a coffin-lid covered with cloth of gold, ornamented with gold cord and tassels, that had been polished up with metal powder. Two ladies in black were taking off their fur cloaks. Peter Ivanovich recognized one of them as Ivan Ilych's sister, but the other was a stranger to him. His colleague Schwartz was just coming downstairs, but on seeing Peter Ivanovich enter he stopped and winked at him, as if to say: "Ivan Ilych has made a mess of things—not like you and me."

Schwartz's face with his Piccadilly whiskers and his slim figure in evening dress had as usual an air of elegant solemnity which contrasted with the playfulness of his character and had a special piquancy here, or so it seemed to Peter Ivanovich.

Peter Ivanovich allowed the ladies to precede him and slowly followed them upstairs. Schwartz did not come down but remained where he was, and Peter Ivanovich understood that he wanted to arrange where they should play bridge that evening. The ladies went upstairs to the widow's room, and Schwartz with seriously compressed lips but a playful look in his eyes, indicated by a twist of his eyebrows the room to the right where the body lay.

Peter Ivanovich, like everyone else on such occasions, entered feeling uncertain what he would have to do. All he knew was that at such times it is always safe to cross oneself. But he was not quite sure whether one should make obeisances while doing so. He therefore adopted a middle course. On entering the room he began crossing himself and made a slight movement resembling a bow. At the same time, as far as the motion of his head and arm allowed, he surveyed the room. Two young men—apparently nephews, one of whom was a high-school pupil—were leaving the room, crossing themselves as they did so. An old woman was standing motionless, and a lady with strangely arched eyebrows was saying something to her in a whisper. A vigorous, resolute Church Reader, in a frock-coat, was reading something in a loud voice with an expression that precluded any contradiction. The butler's assistant, Gerasim, stepping lightly in front of Peter Ivanovich, was strewing something on the floor. Noticing this, Peter Ivanovich was immediately aware of a faint odor of a decomposing body.

The last time he had called on Ivan Ilych, Peter Ivanovich had seen Gerasim in the study. Ivan Ilych had been particularly fond of him and he was performing the duty of a sick nurse.

Peter Ivanovich continued to make the sign of the cross, slightly inclining his head in an intermediate direction between the coffin, the Reader, and the icons on the table in a corner of the room. Afterwards, when it seemed to him that this movement of his arm in crossing himself had gone on too long, he stopped and began to look at the corpse.

The dead man lay, as dead men always lie, in a specially heavy way, his rigid limbs sunk in the soft cushions of the coffin, with the head forever bowed on the pillow. His yellow waxen brow with bald patches over his sunken temples was thrust up in the way peculiar to the dead, the protruding nose seeming to press on the upper lip. He was much changed and had grown even thinner since Peter

25

Ivanovich had last seen him, but, as is always the case with the dead, his face was handsomer and above all more dignified than when he was alive. The expression on the face said that what was necessary had been accomplished, and accomplished rightly. Besides this there was in that exprerssion a reproach and a warning to the living. This warning seemed to Peter Ivanovich out of place, or at least not applicable to him. He felt a certain discomfort and so he hurriedly crossed himself once more and turned and went out of the door—too hurriedly and too regardless of propriety, as he himself was aware.

Schwartz was waiting for him in the adjoining room with legs spread wide apart and both hands toying with his top-hat behind his back. The mere sight of that playful, well-groomed, and elegant figure refreshed Peter Ivanovich. He felt that Schwartz was above all these happenings and would not surrender to any depressing influences. His very look said that this incident of a church service for Ivan Ilych could not be a sufficient reason for infringing the order of the session—in other words, that it would certainly not prevent his unwrapping a new pack of cards and shuffling them that evening while a footman placed four fresh candles on the table: in fact, that there was no reason for supposing that this incident would hinder their spending the evening agreeably. Indeed he said this in a whisper as Peter Ivanovich passed him, proposing that they should meet for a game at Fëdor Vasilievich's. But apparently Peter Ivanovich was not destined to play bridge that evening. Praskovya Fëdorovna (a short, fat woman who despite all efforts to the contrary had continued to broaden steadily from her shoulders downwards and who had the same extraordinarily arched eyebrows as the lady who had been standing by the coffin), dressed all in black, her head covered with lace, came out of her own room with some other ladies, conducted them to the room where the dead body lay, and said: "The service will begin immediately. Please go in."

Schwartz, making an indefinite bow, stood still, evidently neither accepting nor declining this invitation. Praskovya Fëdorovna, recognizing Peter Ivanovich, sighed, went close up to him, took his hand, and said: "I know you were a true friend of Ivan Ilych . . . " and looked at him awaiting some suitable response. And Peter Ivanovich knew that, just as it had been the right thing to cross himself in that room, so what he had to do here was to press her hand, sigh, and say, "Believe me . . . ." So he did all this and as he did it felt that the desired result had been achieved: that both he and she were touched.

"Come with me. I want to speak to you before it begins," said the widow. 30 "Give me your arm."

Peter Ivanovich gave her his arm and they went to the inner rooms, passing Schwartz, who winked at Peter Ivanovich compassionately.

"That does for our bridge! Don't object if we find another player. Perhaps you can cut in when you do escape," said his playful look.

Peter Ivanovich sighed still more deeply and despondently, and Praskovya Fëdorovna pressed his arm gratefully. When they reached the drawing-room, upholstered in pink cretonne and lighted by a dim lamp, they sat down at the table—she on a sofa and Peter Ivanovich on a low pouffe, the springs of which yielded spasmodically under his weight. Praskovya Fëdorovna had been on the point of warning him to take another seat, but felt that such a warning was out of keeping with her present condition and so changed her mind. As he sat down on the pouffe Peter Ivanovich recalled how Ivan Ilych had arranged this room and had consulted him regarding this pink cretonne with green leaves. The whole room was full of furniture and knick-knacks, and on her way to the sofa the lace of the widow's black shawl caught on the carved edge of the table. Peter Ivanovich rose to detach it, and the springs of the pouffe, relieved of his weight, rose also and gave him a push. The widow began detaching her shawl herself, and Peter Ivanovich again sat down, suppressing the rebellious springs of the pouffe under him. But the widow had not quite freed herself and Peter Ivanovich got up again, and again the pouffe rebelled and even creaked. When this was all over she took out a clean cambric handkerchief and began to weep. The episode with the shawl and the struggle with the pouffe had cooled Peter Ivanovich's emotions and he sat there with a sullen look on his face. This awkward situation was interrupted by Sokolov, Ivan Ilych's butler, who came to report that the plot in the cemetery that Praskovya Fëdorovna had chosen would cost two hundred rubles. She stopped weeping and, looking at Peter Ivanovich with the air of a victim, remarked in French that it was very hard for her. Peter Ivanovich made a silent gesture signifying his full conviction that it must indeed be so.

"Please smoke," she said in a magnanimous yet crushed voice, and turned to discuss with Sokolov the price of the plot for the grave.

Peter Ivanovich while lighting his cigarette heard her inquiring very circum- 35 stantially into the prices of different plots in the cemetery and finally decide which she would take. When that was done she gave instructions about engaging the choir. Sokolov then left the room.

"I look after everything myself," she told Peter Ivanovich, shifting the albums that lay on the table; and noticing that the table was endangered by his cigarette-ash, she immediately passed him an ashtray, saying as she did so: "I consider it an affectation to say that my grief prevents my attending to practical affairs. On the contrary, if anything can—I won't say console me, but—distract me, it is seeing to everything concerning him." She again took out her handkerchief as if preparing to cry, but suddenly, as if mastering her feeling, she shook herself and began to speak calmly. "But there is something I want to talk to you about."

Peter Ivanovich bowed, keeping control of the springs of the pouffe, which immediately began quivering under him.

"He suffered terribly the last few days."

"Did he?" said Peter Ivanovich.

"Oh, terribly! He screamed unceasingly, not for minutes but for hours. For 40 the last three days he screamed incessantly. It was unendurable. I cannot understand how I bore it; you could hear him three rooms off. Oh, what I have suffered!"

"Is it possible that he was conscious all that time?" asked Peter Ivanovich.

"Yes," she whispered. "To the last moment. He took leave of us a quarter of an hour before he died, and asked us to take Volodya away."

The thought of the sufferings of this man he had known so intimately, first as a merry little boy, then as a school-mate, and later as a grown-up colleague, suddenly struck Peter Ivanovich with horror, despite an unpleasant consciousness of his own and this woman's dissimulation. He again saw that brow, and that nose pressing down on the lip, and felt afraid for himself.

"Three days of frightful suffering and then death! Why, that might suddenly, at any time, happen to me," he thought, and for a moment felt terrified. But—he did not himself know how—the customary reflection at once occurred to him that this had happened to Ivan Ilych and not to him, and that it should not and could not happen to him, and that to think that it could would be yielding to depression which he ought not to do, as Schwartz's expression plainly showed. After which reflection Peter Ivanovich felt reassured, and began to ask with interest about the details of Ivan Ilych's death, as though death was an accident natural to Ivan Ilych but certainly not to himself.

After many details of the really dreadful physical sufferings Ivan Ilych had endured (which details he learnt only from the effect those sufferings had produced on Praskovya Fëdorovna's nerves) the widow apparently found it necessary to get to business. 45

"Oh, Peter Ivanovich, how hard it is! How terribly, terribly hard!" and she again began to weep.

Peter Ivanovich sighed and waited for her to finish blowing her nose. When she had done so he said, "Believe me . . . " and she again began talking and brought out what was evidently her chief concern with him—namely, to question him as to how she could obtain a grant of money from the government on the occasion of her husband's death. She made it appear that she was asking Peter Ivanovich's advice about her pension, but he soon saw that she already knew about that to the minutest detail, more even than he did himself. She knew how much could be got out of the government in consequence of her husband's death, but wanted to find out whether she could not possibly extract something more. Peter Ivanovich tried to think of some means of doing so, but after reflecting for a while and, out of propriety, condemning the government for its niggardliness, he said he thought that nothing more could be got. Then she sighed and evidently began to devise means of getting rid of her visitor. Noticing this, he put out his cigarette, rose, pressed her hand, and went out into the anteroom.

In the dining-room where the clock stood that Ivan Ilych had liked so much and had bought at an antique shop, Peter Ivanovich met a priest and a few acquaintances who had come to attend the service, and he recognized Ivan Ilych's daughter, a handsome young woman. She was in black and her slim figure appeared slimmer than ever. She had a gloomy, determined, almost angry expression, and bowed to Peter Ivanovich as though he were in some way to blame. Behind her, with the same offended look, stood a wealthy young man, an examining magistrate, whom Peter Ivanovich also knew and who was her fiancé, as he had heard. He bowed mournfully to them and was about to pass into the death-chamber, when from under the stairs appeared the figure of Ivan Ilych's schoolboy son, who was extremely like his father. He seemed a little Ivan Ilych, such as Peter Ivanovich remembered when they studied law together. His tear-stained eyes had in them the look that is seen in the eyes of boys of thirteen or fourteen who are not pureminded. When he saw Peter Ivanovich he scowled morosely and shamefacedly. Peter Ivanovich nodded to him and entered the death-chamber. The service began: candles, groans, incense, tears, and sobs. Peter Ivanovich stood looking gloomily down at his feet. He did not look once at the dead man, did not yield to any depressing influence, and was one of the first to leave the room. There was no one in the anteroom, but Gerasim darted out of the dead man's room, rummaged with his strong hands among the fur coats to find Peter Ivanovich's, and helped him on with it.

"Well, friend Gerasim," said Peter Ivanovich, so as to say something. "It's a sad affair, isn't it?"

"It's God's will. We shall all come to it some day," said Gerasim, displaying   50
his teeth—the even, white teeth of a healthy peasant—and, like a man in the thick of urgent work, he briskly opened the front door, called the coachman, helped Peter Ivanovich into the sledge, and sprang back to the porch as if in readiness for what he had to do next.

Peter Ivanovich found the fresh air particularly pleasant after the smell of incense, the dead body, and carbolic acid.

"Where to, sir?" asked the coachman.

"It's not too late even now . . . I'll call round on Fëdor Vasilievich."

He accordingly drove there and found them just finishing the first rubber, so that it was quite convenient for him to cut in.

II

Ivan Ilych's life had been most simple and most ordinary and therefore most   55
terrible.

He had been a member of the Court of Justice, and died at the age of forty-five. His father had been an official who after serving in various ministries and departments in Petersburg had made the sort of career which brings men to positions from which by reason of their long service they cannot be dismissed, though they are obviously unfit to hold any responsible position, and for whom therefore posts are specially created, which though fictitious carry salaries of from six to ten thousand rubles that are not fictitious, and in receipt of which they live on to a great age.

Such was the Privy Councillor and superfluous member of various superfluous institutions, Ilya Epimovich Golovin.

He had three sons, of whom Ivan Ilych was the second. The eldest son was following in his father's footsteps only in another department, and was already approaching that stage in the service at which a similar sinecure would be reached. The third son was a failure. He had ruined his prospects in a number of positions and was now serving in the railway department. His father and brothers, and still more their wives, not merely disliked meeting him, but avoided remembering his existence unless compelled to do so. His sister had married Baron Greff, a Petersburg official of her father's type. Ivan Ilych was le phénix de la famille° as people said. He was neither as cold and formal as his elder brother nor as wild as the younger, but was a happy mean between them—an intelligent, polished, lively, and agreeable man. He had studied with his younger brother at the School of Law, but the latter had failed to complete the course and was expelled when he was in the fifth class. Ivan Ilych finished the course well. Even when he was at the School of Law he was just what he remained for the rest of his life: a capable,

le phénix de la famille: "the prize of the family."

cheerful, good-natured, and sociable man, though strict in the fulfillment of what he considered to be his duty: and he considered his duty to be what was so considered by those in authority. Neither as a boy nor as a man was he a toady, but from early youth was by nature attracted to people of high station as a fly is drawn to the light, assimilating their ways and views of life and establishing friendly relations with them. All the enthusiasms of childhood and youth passed without leaving much trace on him; he succumbed to sensuality, to vanity, and latterly among the highest classes to liberalism, but always within limits which his instinct unfailingly indicated to him as correct.

At school he had done things which had formerly seemed to him very horrid and made him feel disgusted with himself when he did them; but when later on he saw that such actions were done by people of good position and that they did not regard them as wrong, he was able not exactly to regard them as right, but to forget about them entirely or not be at all troubled at remembering them.

Having graduated from the School of Law and qualified for the tenth rank of the civil service, and having received money from his father for his equipment, Ivan Ilych ordered himself clothes at Scharmer's, the fashionable tailor, hung a medallion inscribed *respice finem°* on his watch-chain, took leave of his professor and the prince who was patron of the school, had a farewell dinner with his comrades at Donon's first-class restaurant, and with his new and fashionable portmanteau, linen, clothes, shaving and other toilet appliances, and a travelling rug all purchased at the best shops, he set off for one of the provinces where through his father's influence, he had been attached to the Governor as an official for special service. 60

In the province Ivan Ilych soon arranged as easy and agreeable a position for himself as he had had at the School of Law. He performed his official tasks, made his career, and at the same time amused himself pleasantly and decorously. Occasionally he paid official visits to country districts, where he behaved with dignity both to his superiors and inferiors, and performed the duties entrusted to him, which related chiefly to the sectarians°, with an exactness and incorruptible honesty of which he could not but feel proud.

In official matters, despite his youth and taste for frivolous gaiety, he was exceedingly reserved, punctilious, and even severe; but in society he was often amusing and witty, and always good-natured, correct in his manner, and *bon enfant°*, as the Governor and his wife—with whom he was like one of the family—used to say of him.

In the province he had an affair with a lady who made advances to the elegant young lawyer, and there was also a milliner; and there were carousals with aides-de-camp who visited the district, and after-supper visits to a certain outlying street of doubtful reputation; and there was too some obsequiousness to his chief and even to his chief's wife, but all this was done with such a tone of good breeding that no hard names could be applied to it. It all came under the heading

---

respice finem: "Think of the end (of your life)." *sectarians:* dissenters from the Orthodox Church. *bon enfant:* like a well-behaved child.

of the French saying: *"Il faut que jeunesse se passe."* ° It was all done with clean hands, in clean linen, with French phrases, and above all among people of the best society and consequently with the approval of people of rank.

So Ivan Ilych served for five years and then came a change in his official life. The new and reformed judicial institutions were introduced, and new men were needed. Ivan Ilych became such a new man. He was offered the post of examining magistrate, and he accepted it though the post was in another province and obliged him to give up the connections he had formed and to make new ones. His friends met to give him a send-off; they had a group-photograph taken and presented him with a silver cigarette-case, and he set off to his new post.

As examining magistrate Ivan Ilych was just as *comme il faut* ° and decorous 65 a man, inspiring general respect and capable of separating his official duties from his private life, as he had been when acting as an official on special service. His duties now as examining magistrate were far more interesting and attractive than before. In his former position it had been pleasant to wear an undress uniform made by Scharmer, and to pass through the crowd of petitioners and officials who were timorously awaiting an audience with the Governor, and who envied him as with free and easy gait he went straight into his chief's private room to have a cup of tea and a cigarette with him. But not many people had been directly dependent on him—only police officials and the sectarians when he went on special missions—and he liked to treat them politely, almost as comrades, as if he were letting them feel that he who had the power to crush them was treating them in this simple, friendly way. There were then but few such people. But now, as an examining magistrate, Ivan Ilych felt that everyone without exception, even the most important and self-satisfied, was in his power, and that he need only write a few words on a sheet of paper with a certain heading, and this or that important, self-satisfied person would be brought before him in the role of an accused person or a witness, and if he did not choose to allow him to sit down, would have to stand before him and answer his questions. Ivan Ilych never abused his power; he tried on the contrary to soften its expression, but the consciousness of it and of the possibility of softening its effect, supplied the chief interest and attraction of his office. In his work itself, especially in his examinations, he very soon acquired a method of eliminating all considerations irrelevant to the legal aspect of the case, and reducing even the most complicated case to a form in which it would be presented on paper only in its externals, completely excluding his personal opinion of the matter, while above all observing every prescribed formality. The work was new and Ivan Ilych was one of the first men to apply the new Code of 1864°.

On taking up the post of examining magistrate in a new town, he made new acquaintances and connections, placed himself on a new footing, and assumed a somewhat different tone. He took up an attitude of rather dignified aloofness towards the provincial authorities, but picked out the best circle of legal gentle-

---

"Il faut que jeunesse se passe": "Youth doesn't last."   *comme il faut*: "as required," rule-abiding.   *Code of 1864*: The emancipation of the serfs in 1861 was followed by a thorough all-round reform of judicial proceedings. [Translators' note.]

men and wealthy gentry living in the town and assumed a tone of slight dissatisfaction with the government, of moderate liberalism, and of enlightened citizen-
ship. At the same time, without at all altering the elegance of his toilet, he ceased
shaving his chin and allowed his beard to grow as it pleased.

Ivan Ilych settled down very pleasantly in this new town. The society there,
which inclined towards opposition to the Governor, was friendly, his salary was
larger, and he began to play *vint*°, which he found added not a little to the pleasure of life, for he had a capacity for cards, played good-humoredly, and calculated rapidly and astutely, so that he usually won.

After living there for two years he met his future wife, Praskovya Fëdorovna
Mikhel, who was the most attractive, clever, and brilliant girl of the set in which
he moved, and among other amusements and relaxations from his labors as examining magistrate, Ivan Ilych established light and playful relations with her.

While he had been an official on special service he had been accustomed
to dance, but now as an examining magistrate it was exceptional for him to do
so. If he danced now, he did it as if to show that though he served under the
reformed order of things, and had reached the fifth official rank, yet when it came
to dancing he could do it better than most people. So at the end of an evening
he sometimes danced with Praskovya Fëdorovna, and it was chiefly during these
dances that he captivated her. She fell in love with him. Ivan Ilych had at first
no definite intention of marrying, but when the girl fell in love with him he said
to himself: "Really, why shouldn't I marry?"

Praskovya Fëdorovna came of a good family, was not bad-looking, and had   70
some little property. Ivan Ilych might have aspired to a more brilliant match,
but even this was good. He had his salary, and she, he hoped, would have an
equal income. She was well connected, and was a sweet, pretty, and thoroughly
correct young woman. To say that Ivan Ilych married because he fell in love with
Praskovya Fëdorovna and found that she sympathized with his views of life would
be as incorrect as to say that he married because his social circle approved of the
match. He was swayed by both these considerations: the marriage gave him personal satisfaction, and at the same time it was considered the right thing by the
most highly placed of his associates.

So Ivan Ilych got married.

The preparations for marriage and the beginning of married life, with its conjugal caresses, the new furniture, new crockery, and new linen, were very pleasant
until his wife became pregnant—so that Ivan Ilych had begun to think that marriage would not impair the easy, agreeable, gay, and always decorous character
of his life, approved of by society and regarded by himself as natural, but would
even improve it. But from the first months of his wife's pregnancy, something
new, unpleasant, depressing, and unseemly, and from which there was no way
of escape, unexpectedly showed itself.

His wife, without any reason—*de gaieté de coeur*° as Ivan Ilych expressed it
to himself—began to disturb the pleasure and propriety of their life. She began

---

vint: a form of bridge. [Translators' note.]   *de gaieté de coeur*: "from pure whim."

to be jealous without any cause, expected him to devote his whole attention to her, found fault with everything, and made coarse and ill-mannered scenes.

At first Ivan Ilych hoped to escape from the unpleasantness of this state of affairs by the same easy and decorous relation to life that had served him heretofore: he tried to ignore his wife's disagreeable moods, continued to live in his usual easy and pleasant way, invited friends to his house for a game of cards, and also tried going out to his club or spending his evenings with friends. But one day his wife began upbraiding him so vigorously, using such coarse words, and continued to abuse him every time he did not fulfil her demands, so resolutely and with such evident determination not to give way till he submitted—that is, till he stayed at home and was bored just as she was —that he became alarmed. He now realized that matrimony—at any rate with Praskovya Fëdorovna—was not always conducive to the pleasures and amenities of life, but on the contrary often infringed both comfort and propriety, and that he must therefore entrench himself against such infringement. And Ivan Ilych began to seek for means of doing so. His official duties were the one thing that imposed upon Praskovya Fëdorovna, and by means of his official work and the duties attached to it he began struggling with his wife to secure his own independence.

With the birth of their child, the attempts to feed it and the various failures   75
in doing so, and with the real and imaginary illnesses of mother and child, in which Ivan Ilych's sympathy was demanded but about which he understood nothing, the need of securing for himself an existence outside his family life became still more imperative.

As his wife grew more irritable and exacting and Ivan Ilych transferred the center of gravity of his life more and more to his official work, so did he grow to like his work better and become more ambitious than before.

Very soon, within a year of his wedding, Ivan Ilych had realized that marriage, though it may add some comforts to life, is in fact a very intricate and difficult affair towards which in order to perform one's duty, that is, to lead a decorous life approved of by society, one must adopt a definite attitude just as towards one's official duties.

And Ivan Ilych evolved such an attitude towards married life. He only required of it those coveniences—dinner at home, housewife, and bed—which it could give him, and above all that propriety of external forms required by public opinion. For the rest he looked for light-hearted pleasure and propriety, and was very thankful when he found them, but if he met with antagonism and querulousness he at once retired into his separate fenced-off world of official duties, where he found satisfaction.

Ivan Ilych was esteemed a good official, and after three years was made Assistant Public Prosecutor. His new duties, their importance, the possibility of indicting and imprisoning anyone he chose, the publicity his speeches received, and the success he had in all these things, made his work still more attractive.

More children came. His wife became more and more querulous and ill-   80
tempered, but the attitude Ivan Ilych had adopted towards his home life rendered him almost impervious to her grumbling.

After seven years' service in that town he was transferred to another province as Public Prosecutor. They moved, but were short of money and his wife did not like the place they moved to. Though the salary was higher the cost of living was greater, besides which two of their children died and family life became still more unpleasant for him.

Praskovya Fëdorovna blamed her husband for every inconvenience they encountered in their new home. Most of the conversations between husband and wife, especially as to the children's education, led to topics which recalled former disputes, and those disputes were apt to flare up again at any moment. There remained only those rare periods of amorousness which still came to them at times but did not last long. These were islets at which they anchored for a while and then again set out upon that ocean of veiled hostility which showed itself in their aloofness from one another. This aloofness might have grieved Ivan Ilych had he considered that it ought not to exist, but he now regarded the position as normal, and even made it the goal at which he aimed in family life. His aim was to free himself more and more from those unpleasantnesses and to give them a semblance of harmlessness and propriety. He attained this by spending less and less time with his family, and when obliged to be at home he tried to safeguard his position by the presence of outsiders. The chief thing, however, was that he had his official duties. The whole interest of his life now centered in the official world and that interest absorbed him. The consciousness of his power, being able to ruin anybody he wished to ruin, the importance, even the external dignity of his entry into court, or meetings with his subordinates, his success with superiors and inferiors, and above all his masterly handling of cases, of which he was conscious—all this gave him pleasure and filled his life, together with chats with his colleagues, dinners, and bridge. So that on the whole Ivan Ilych's life continued to flow as he considered it should do—pleasantly and properly.

So things continued for another seven years. His eldest daughter was already sixteen, another child had died, and only one son was left, a schoolboy and a subject of dissension. Ivan Ilych wanted to put him in the School of Law, but to spite him Praskovya Fëdorovna entered him at the High School. The daughter had been educated at home and had turned out well; the boy did not learn badly either.

III

So Ivan Ilych lived for seventeen years after his marriage. He was already a Public Prosecutor of long standing, and had declined several proposed transfers while awaiting a more desirable post, when an unanticipated and unpleasant occurrence quite upset the peaceful course of his life. He was expecting to be offered the post of presiding judge in a University town, but Happe somehow came to the front and obtained the appointment instead. Ivan Ilych became irritable, reproached Happe, and quarrelled both with him and with his immediate superiors—who became colder to him and again passed him over when other appointments were made.

This was in 1880, the hardest year of Ivan Ilych's life. It was then that it 85 became evident on the one hand that his salary was insufficient for them to live on, and on the other that he had been forgotten, and not only this, but that what was for him the greatest and most cruel injustice appeared to others a quite ordinary occurrence. Even his father did not consider it his duty to help him. Ivan Ilych felt himself abandoned by everyone, and that they regarded his position with a salary of 3,500 rubles as quite normal and even fortunate. He alone knew that with the consciousness of the injustices done him, with his wife's incessant nagging, and with the debts he had contracted by living beyond his means, his position was far from normal.

In order to save money that summer he obtained leave of absence and went with his wife to live in the country at her brother's place.

In the country, without his work, he experienced *ennui* for the first time in his life, and not only *ennui* but intolerable depression, and he decided that it was impossible to go on living like that, and that it was necessary to take energetic measures.

Having passed a sleepless night pacing up and down the veranda, he decided to go to Petersburg and bestir himself, in order to punish those who had failed to appreciate him and to get transferred to another ministry.

Next day, despite many protests from his wife and her brother, he started for Petersburg with the sole object of obtaining a post with a salary of five thousand rubles a year. He was no longer bent on any particular department, or tendency, or kind of activity. All he now wanted was an appointment to another post with a salary of five thousand rubles, either in the administration, in the banks, with the railways, in one of the Empress Marya's Institutions°, or even in the customs—but it had to carry with it a salary of five thousand rubles and be in a ministry other than that in which they had failed to appreciate him.

And this quest of Ivan Ilych's was crowned with remarkable and unexpected success. At Kursk an acquaintance of his, F. I. Ilyin, got into the first-class carriage, sat down beside Ivan Ilych, and told him of a telegram just received by the Governor of Kursk announcing that a change was about to take place in the ministry: Peter Ivanovich was to be superseded by Ivan Semënovich.

The proposed change, apart from its significance for Russia, had a special significance for Ivan Ilych, because by bringing forward a new man, Peter Petrovich, and consequently his friend Zachar Ivanovich, it was highly favorable for Ivan Ilych, since Zachar Ivanovich was a friend and colleague of his.

In Moscow this news was confirmed, and on reaching Petersburg Ivan Ilych found Zachar Ivanovich and received a definite promise of an appointment in his former department of Justice.

A week later he telegraphed to his wife: "Zachar in Miller's place. I shall receive appointment on presentation of report."

Thanks to this change of personnel, Ivan Ilych had unexpectedly obtained an appointment in his former ministry which placed him two stages above his former colleagues besides giving him five thousand rubles salary and three thousand five hundred rubles for expenses connected with his removal. All his ill humor towards his former enemies and the whole department vanished, and Ivan Ilych was completely happy.

He returned to the country more cheerful and contented than he had been for a long time. Praskovya Fëdorovna also cheered up and a truce was arranged

Empress Marya's Institutions: orphanages.

between them. Ivan Ilych told of how he had been fêted by everybody in Petersburg, how all those who had been his enemies were put to shame and now fawned on him, how envious they were of his appointment, and how much everybody in Petersburg had liked him.

Praskovya Fëdorovna listened to all this and appeared to believe it. She did not contradict anything, but only made plans for their life in the town to which they were going. Ivan Ilych saw with delight that these plans were his plans, that he and his wife agreed, and that, after a stumble, his life was regaining its due and natural character of pleasant lightheartedness and decorum.

Ivan Ilych had come back for a short time only, for he had to take up his new duties on the 10th of September. Moreover, he needed time to settle into the new place, to move all his belongings from the province, and to buy and order many additional things: in a word, to make such arrangements as he had resolved on, which were almost exactly what Praskovya Fëdorovna too had decided on.

Now that everything had happened so fortunately, and that he and his wife were at one in their aims and moreover saw so little of one another, they got on together better than they had done since the first years of marriage. Ivan Ilych had thought of taking his family away with him at once, but the insistence of his wife's brother and her sister-in-law, who had suddenly become particularly amiable and friendly to him and his family, induced him to depart alone.

So he departed, and the cheerful state of mind induced by his success and by the harmony between his wife and himself, the one intensifying the other, did not leave him. He found a delightful house, just the thing both he and his wife had dreamt of. Spacious, lofty reception rooms in the old style, a convenient and dignified study, rooms for his wife and daughter, a study for his son—it might have been specially built for them. Ivan Ilych himself superintended the arrangements, chose the wallpapers, supplemented the furniture (preferably with antiques which he considered particularly *comme il faut*), and supervised the upholstering. Everything progressed and progressed and approached the ideal he had set himself: even when things were only half completed they exceeded his expectations. He saw what a refined and elegant character, free from vulgarity, it would all have when it was ready. On falling asleep he pictured to himself how the reception-room would look. Looking at the yet unfinished drawing-room he could see the fireplace, the screen, the what-not, the little chairs dotted here and there, the dishes and plates on the walls, and the bronzes, as they would be when everything was in place. He was pleased by the thought of how his wife and daughter, who shared his taste in this matter, would be impressed by it. They were certainly not expecting as much. He had been particularly successful in finding, and buying cheaply, antiques which gave a particularly aristocratic character to the whole place. But in his letters he intentionally understated everything in order to be able to surprise them. All this so absorbed him that his new duties—though he liked his official work—interested him less than he had expected. Sometimes he even had moments of absentmindedness during the Court Sessions, and would consider whether he should have straight or curved cornices for his curtains. He was so interested in it all that he often did things himself, rearranging the furniture, or rehanging the curtains. Once when mounting a stepladder to show the upholsterer, who did not understand, how he wanted the hangings draped, he made a false step and slipped, but being a strong and agile man he clung on and only knocked his side against the knob of the window frame. The bruised place was painful but the pain soon passed, and he felt particularly bright and well just then. He wrote: "I feel fifteen years younger." He thought he would have everything ready by September, but it dragged on till mid-October. But the result was charming not only in his eyes but to everyone who saw it.

In reality it was just what is usually seen in the houses of people of moderate 100 means who want to appear rich, and therefore succeed only in resembling others like themselves: there were damasks, dark wood, plants, rugs, and dull and polished bronzes—all the things people of a certain class have in order to resemble other people of that class. His house was so like the others that it would never have been noticed, but to him it all seemed to be quite exceptional. He was very happy when he met his family at the station and brought them to the newly furnished house all lit up, where a footman in a white tie opened the door into the hall decorated with plants, and when they went on into the drawing-room and the study uttering exclamations of delight. He conducted them everywhere, drank in their praises eagerly, and beamed with pleasure. At tea that evening, when Praskovya Fëdorovna among other things asked him about his fall, he laughed and showed them how he had gone flying and had frightened the upholsterer.

"It's a good thing I'm a bit of an athlete. Another man might have been killed, but I merely knocked myself, just there; it hurts when it's touched, but it's passing off already—it's only a bruise."

So they began living in their new home—in which, as always happens, when they got thoroughly settled in they found they were just one room short—and with the increased income, which as always was just a little (some five hundred rubles) too little, but it was all very nice.

Things went particularly well at first, before everything was finally arranged and while something had still to be done: this thing bought, that thing ordered, another thing moved, and something else adjusted. Though there were some disputes between husband and wife, they were both so well satisfied and had so much to do that it all passed off without any serious quarrels. When nothing was left to arrange it became rather dull and something seemed to be lacking, but they were then making acquaintances, forming habits, and life was growing fuller.

Ivan Ilych spent his mornings at the law courts and came home to dinner, and at first he was generally in good humor, though he occasionally became irritable just on account of his house. (Every spot on the tablecloth or the upholstery, and every broken window-blind string, irritated him. He had devoted so much trouble to arranging it all that every disturbance of it distressed him.) But on the whole his life ran its course as he believed life should do: easily, pleasantly, and decorously.

He got up at nine, drank his coffee, read the paper, and then put on his un- 105 dress uniform and went to the law courts. There the harness in which he worked had already been stretched to fit him and he donned it without a hitch: petitioners, inquiries at the chancery, the chancery itself, and the sittings public and administrative. In all this the thing was to exclude everything fresh and vital, which always disturbs the regular course of official business, and to admit only official relations with people, and then only on official grounds. A man would come, for instance, wanting some information. Ivan Ilych, as one in whose sphere the matter did not lie, would have nothing to do with him: but if the man had some business with him in his official capacity, something that could be expressed on officially stamped paper, he would do everything, positively everything he could within the limits of such relations, and in doing so would maintain the semblance of friendly human relations, that is, would observe the courtesies of life. As soon as the official relations ended, so did everything else. Ivan Ilych possessed this capacity to separate his real life from the official side of affairs and not mix the two, in the highest degree, and by long practice and natural aptitude had brought it to such a pitch that sometimes, in the manner of a virtuoso, he would even allow himself to let the human and official relations mingle. He let himself do this just because he felt that he could at any time he chose resume the strictly official attitude again and drop the human relation. And he did it all easily, pleasantly, correctly, and even artistically. In the intervals between the sessions he smoked, drank tea, chatted a little about politics, a little about general topics, a little about cards, but most of all about official appointments. Tired, but with the feelings of a virtuoso—one of the first violins who has played his part in an orchestra with precision—he would return home to find that his wife and daughter had been out paying calls, or had a visitor, and that his son had been to school, had done his homework with his tutor, and was duly learning what is taught at High Schools. Everything was as it should be. After dinner, if they had no visitors, Ivan Ilych sometimes read a book that was being much discussed at the time, and in the evening settled down to work, that is, read official papers, compared the depositions of witnesses, and noted paragraphs of the Code applying to them. This was neither dull nor amusing. It was dull when he might have been playing bridge, but if no bridge was available it was at any rate better than doing nothing or sitting with his wife. Ivan Ilych's chief pleasure was giving little dinners to which he invited men and women of good social position, and just as his drawing-room resembled all other drawing-rooms so did his enjoyable little parties resemble all other such parties.

Once they even gave a dance. Ivan Ilych enjoyed it and everything went off well, except that it led to a violent quarrel with his wife about the cakes and sweets. Praskovya Fëdorovna had made her own plans, but Ivan Ilych insisted on getting everything from an expensive confectioner and ordered too many cakes, and the quarrel occurred because some of those cakes were left over and the confectioner's bill came to forty-five rubles. It was a great and disagreeable quarrel. Praskovya Fëdorovna called him "a fool and an imbecile," and he clutched at his head and made angry allusions to divorce.

But the dance itself had been enjoyable. The best people were there, and Ivan Ilych had danced with Princess Trufonova, a sister of the distinguished founder of the Society "Bear My Burden."

The pleasures connected with his work were pleasures of ambition; his social pleasures were those of vanity; but Ivan Ilych's greatest pleasure was playing bridge. He acknowledged that whatever disagreeable incident happened in his life, the pleasure that beamed like a ray of light above everything else was to sit down to bridge with good players, not noisy partners, and of course to four-handed bridge (with five players it was annoying to have to stand out, though one pretended not to mind), to play a clever and serious game (when the cards allowed it), and then to have supper and drink a glass of wine. After a game of bridge, especially if he had won a little (to win a large sum was unpleasant), Ivan Ilych went to bed in specially good humor.

So they lived. They formed a circle of acquaintances among the best people and were visited by people of importance and by young folk. In their views as to their acquaintances, husband, wife, and daughter were entirely agreed, and tacitly and unanimously kept at arm's length and shook off the various shabby friends and relations who, with much show of affection, gushed into the drawing-room with its Japanese plates on the walls. Soon these shabby friends ceased to obtrude themselves and only the best people remained in the Golovins' set.

Young men made up to Lisa, and Petrishchev, an examining magistrate and 110 Dmitri Ivanovich Petrischev's son and sole heir, began to be so attentive to her that Ivan Ilych had already spoken to Praskovya Fëdorovna about it, and considered whether they should not arrange a party for them, or get up some private theatricals.

So they lived, and all went well, without change, and life followed pleasantly.

IV

They were all in good health. It could not be called ill health if Ivan Ilych sometimes said that he had a queer taste in his mouth and felt some discomfort in his left side.

But this discomfort increased and, though not exactly painful, grew into a sense of pressure in his side accompanied by ill humor. And his irritability became worse and worse and began to mar the agreeable, easy, and correct life that had established itself in the Golovin family. Quarrels between husband and wife became more and more frequent, and soon the ease and amenity disappeared and even the decorum was barely maintained. Scenes again became frequent, and very few of those islets remained on which husband and wife could meet without an explosion. Praskovya Fëdorovna now had good reason to say that her husband's temper was trying. With characteristic exaggeration she said he had always had a dreadful temper, and that it had needed all her good nature to put up with it for twenty years. It was true that now the quarrels were started by him. His bursts of temper always came just before dinner, often just as he began to eat his soup. Sometimes he noticed that a plate or dish was chipped, or the food was not right, or his son put his elbow on the table, or his daughter's hair was not done as he liked it, and for all this he blamed Praskovya Fëdorovna. At first she retorted and said disagreeable things to him, but once or twice he fell into such a rage at the beginning of dinner that she realized it was due to some physical derangement brought on by taking food, and so she restrained herself and did not answer, but only hurried to get the dinner over. She regarded this self-restraint as highly praiseworthy. Having come to the conclusion that her husband had a dreadful temper and made her life miserable, she began to feel sorry for herself, and the more she pitied herself the more she hated her husband. She began to wish he would die; yet she did not want him to die because then his salary would cease. And this irritated her against him still more. She considered herself dreadfully unhappy just because not even his death could save her, and though she concealed her exasperation, that hidden exasperation of hers increased his irritation also.

After one scene in which Ivan Ilych had been particularly unfair and after which he had said in explanation that he certainly was irritable but that it was due to his not being well, she said that if he was ill it should be attended to, and insisted on his going to see a celebrated doctor.

He went. Everything took place as he had expected and as it always does. 115 There was the usual waiting and the important air assumed by the doctor, with which he was so familiar (resembling that which he himself assumed in court), and the sounding and listening, and the questions which called for answers that were foregone conclusions and were evidently unnecessary, and the look of importance which implied that "if only you put yourself in our hands we will arrange everything—we know indubitably how it has to be done, always in the same way for everybody alike." It was all just as it was in the law courts. The doctor put on just the same air towards him as he himself put on towards an accused person.

The doctor said that so-and-so indicated that there was so-and-so inside the patient, but if the investigation of so-and-so did not confirm this, then he must assume that and that. If he assumed that and that, then . . . and so on. To Ivan Ilych only one question was important: was his case serious or not? But the doctor ignored that inappropriate question. From his point of view it was not the one under consideration, the real question was to decide between a floating kidney, chronic catarrh, or appendicitis. It was not a question of Ivan Ilych's life or death, but one between a floating kidney and appendicitis. And that question the doctor solved brilliantly, as it seemed to Ivan Ilych, in favor of the appendix, with the reservation that should an examination of the urine give fresh indications the matter would be reconsidered. All this was just what Ivan Ilych had himself brilliantly accomplished a thousand times in dealing with men on trial. The doctor summed up just as brilliantly, looking over his spectacles triumphantly and even gaily at the accused. From the doctor's summing up Ivan Ilych concluded that things were bad, but that for the doctor, and perhaps for everybody else, it was a matter of indifference, though for him it was bad. And this conclusion struck him painfully, arousing in him a great feeling of pity for himself and of bitterness towards the doctor's indifference to a matter of such importance.

He said nothing of this, but rose, placed the doctor's fee on the table, and remarked with a sigh: "We sick people probably often put inappropriate questions. But tell me, in general, is this complaint dangerous, or not? . . . "

The doctor looked at him sternly over his spectacles with one eye, as if to say: "Prisoner, if you will not keep to the questions put to you, I shall be obliged to have you removed from the court."

"I have already told you what I consider necessary and proper. The analysis may show something more." And the doctor bowed.

Ivan Ilych went out slowly, seated himself disconsolately in his sledge, and 120 drove home. All the way home he was going over what the doctor had said, trying to translate those complicated, obscure, scientific phrases into plain language and find in them an answer to the question: "Is my condition bad? Is it very bad? Or is there as yet nothing much wrong?" And it seemed to him that the meaning of what the doctor had said was that it was very bad. Everything in the streets seemed depressing. The cabmen, the houses, the passers-by, and the shops, were dismal. His ache, this dull gnawing ache that never ceased for a moment, seemed to have acquired a new and more serious significance from the doctor's dubious remarks. Ivan Ilych now watched it with a new and oppressive feeling.

He reached home and began to tell his wife about it. She listened, but in the middle of his account his daughter came in with her hat on, ready to go out with her mother. She sat down reluctantly to listen to this tedious story, but could not stand it long, and her mother too did not hear him to the end.

"Well, I am very glad," she said. "Mind now to take your medicine regularly. Give me the prescription and I'll send Gerasim to the chemist's." And she went to get ready to go out.

While she was in the room Ivan Ilych had hardly taken time to breathe, but he sighed deeply when she left it.

"Well," he thought, "perhaps it isn't so bad after all."

He began taking his medicine and following the doctor's directions, which had been altered after the examination of the urine. But then it happened that there was a contradiction between the indications drawn from the examination of the urine and the symptoms that showed themselves. It turned out that what was happening differed from what the doctor had told him, and that he had either forgotten, or blundered, or hidden something from him. He could not, however, be blamed for that, and Ivan Ilych still obeyed his orders implicitly and at first derived some comfort from doing so.

From the time of his visit to the doctor, Ivan Ilych's chief occupation was the exact fulfilment of the doctor's instructions regarding hygiene and the taking of medicine, and the observation of his pain and his excretions. His chief interests came to be people's ailments and people's health. When sickness, deaths, or recoveries were mentioned in his presence, especially when the illness resembled his own, he listened with agitation which he tried to hide, asked questions, and applied what he heard to his own case.

The pain did not grow less, but Ivan Ilych made efforts to force himself to think that he was better. And he could do this so long as nothing agitated him. But as soon as he had any unpleasantness with his wife, any lack of success in his official work, or held bad cards at bridge, he was at once acutely sensible of his disease. He had formerly borne such mischances, hoping soon to adjust what was wrong, to master it and attain success, or make a grand slam. But now every mischance upset him and plunged him into despair. He would say to himself: "There now, just as I was beginning to get better and the medicine had begun to take effect, comes this accursed misfortune, or unpleasantness . . . ." And he was furious with the mishap, or with the people who were causing the unpleasantness and killing him, for he felt that this fury was killing him but could not restrain it. One would have thought that it should have been clear to him that this exasperation with circumstances and people aggravated his illness, and that he ought therefore to ignore unpleasant occurrences. But he drew the very opposite conclusion: he said that he needed peace, and he watched for everything that might disturb it and became irritable at the slightest infringement of it. His condition was rendered worse by the fact that he read medical books and consulted doctors.

The progress of his disease was so gradual that he could deceive himself when comparing one day with another—the difference was so slight. But when he consulted the doctors it seemed to him that he was getting worse, and even very rapidly. Yet despite this he was continually consulting them.

That month he went to see another celebrity, who told him almost the same as the first had done but put his questions rather differently, and the interview with this celebrity only increased Ivan Ilych's doubts and fears. A friend of a friend of his, a very good doctor, diagnosed his illness again quite differently from the others, and though he predicted recovery, his questions and suppositions bewildered Ivan Ilych still more and increased his doubts. A homeopathist diagnosed the disease in yet another way, and prescribed medicine which Ivan Ilych took secretly for a week. But after a week, not feeling any improvement and having lost confidence both in the former doctor's treatment and in this one's, he became still more despondent. One day a lady acquaintance mentioned a cure effected by a wonder-working icon. Ivan Ilych caught himself listening attentively and beginning to believe that it had occurred. This incident alarmed him. "Has my mind really weakened to such an extent?" he asked himself. "Nonsense! It's all rubbish. I mustn't give way to nervous fears but having chosen a doctor must keep strictly to his treatment. That is what I will do. Now it's all settled. I won't think about it, but will follow the treatment seriously till summer, and then we shall see. From now there must be no more of this wavering!" This was easy to say but impossible to carry out. The pain in his side oppressed him and seemed to grow worse and more incessant, while the taste in his mouth grew stranger and stranger. It seemed to him that his breath had a disgusting smell, and he was conscious of a loss of appetite and strength. There was no deceiving himself: something terrible, new, and more important than anything before in his life, was taking place within him of which he alone was aware. Those about him did not understand or would not understand it, but thought everything in the world was going on as usual. That tormented Ivan Ilych more than anything. He saw that his household, especially his wife and daughter who were in a perfect whirl of visiting, did not understand anything of it and were annoyed that he was so depressed and so exacting, as if he were to blame for it. Though they tried to disguise it he saw that he was an obstacle in their path, and that his wife had adopted a definite line in regard to his illness and kept to it regardless of anything he said or did. Her attitude was this: "You know," she would say to her friends, "Ivan Ilych can't do as other people do, and keep to the treatment prescribed for him. One day he'll take his drops and keep strictly to his diet and go to bed in good time, but the next day unless I watch him he'll suddenly forget his medicine, eat sturgeon—which is forbidden—and sit up playing cards till one o'clock in the morning."

"Oh, come, when was that?" Ivan Ilych would ask in vexation. "Only once at Peter Ivanovich's."

"And yesterday with Shebek."

"Well, even if I hadn't stayed up, this pain would have kept me awake."

"Be that as it may you'll never get well like that, but will always make us wretched."

Praskovya Fëdorovna's attitude to Ivan Ilych's illness, as she expressed it both to others and to him, was that it was his own fault and was another of the

130

annoyances he caused her. Ivan Ilych felt that this opinion escaped her involuntarily—but that did not make it easier for him.

At the law courts too, Ivan Ilych noticed, or thought he noticed, a strange attitude towards himself. It sometimes seemed to him that people were watching him inquisitively as a man whose place might soon be vacant. Then again, his friends would suddenly begin to chaff him in a friendly way about his low spirits, as if the awful, horrible, and unheard-of thing that was going on within him, incessantly gnawing at him and irresistibly drawing him away, was a very agreeable subject for jests. Schwartz in particular irritated him by his jocularity, vivacity, and *savoir-faire*, which reminded him of what he himself had been ten years ago.

Friends came to make up a set and they sat down to cards. They dealt, bending the new cards to soften them, and he sorted the diamonds in his hand and found he had seven. His partner said "No trumps" and supported him with two diamonds. What more could be wished for? It ought to be jolly and lively. They would make a grand slam. But suddenly Ivan Ilych was conscious of that gnawing pain, that taste in his mouth, and it seemed ridiculous that in such circumstances he should be pleased to make a grand slam.

He looked at his partner Mikhail Mikhaylovich, who rapped the table with his strong hand and instead of snatching up the tricks pushed the cards courteously and indulgently towards Ivan Ilych that he might have the pleasure of gathering them up without the trouble of stretching out his hand for them. "Does he think I am too weak to stretch out my arm?" thought Ivan Ilych, and forgetting what he was doing he over-trumped his partner, missing the grand slam by three tricks. And what was most awful of all was that he saw how upset Mikhail Mikhaylovich was about it but did not himself care. And it was dreadful to realize why he did not care.

They all saw that he was suffering, and said: "We can stop if you are tired. Take a rest." Lie down? No, he was not at all tired, and he finished the rubber. All were gloomy and silent. Ivan Ilych felt that he had diffused this gloom over them and could not dispel it. They had supper and went away, and Ivan Ilych was left alone with the consciousness that his life was poisoned and was poisoning the lives of others, and that this poison did not weaken but penetrated more and more deeply into his whole being.

With this consciousness, and with physical pain besides the terror, he must go to bed, often to lie awake the greater part of the night. Next morning he had to get up again, dress, go to the law courts, speak, and write; or if he did not go out, spend at home those twenty-four hours a day each of which was a torture. And he had to live thus all alone on the brink of an abyss, with no one who understood or pitied him.

V

So one month passed and then another. Just before the New Year his brother-in-law came to town and stayed at their house. Ivan Ilych was at the law courts and Praskovya Fëdorovna had gone shopping. When Ivan Ilych came home and entered his study he found his brother-in-law there—a healthy, florid man—unpacking his portmanteau himself. He raised his head on hearing Ivan Ilych's footsteps and looked up at him for a moment without a word. That stare told Ivan Ilych everything. His brother-in-law opened his mouth to utter an exclamation of surprise but checked himself, and that action confirmed it all.

"I have changed, eh?"

"Yes, there is a change."

And after that, try as he would to get his brother-in-law to return to the subject of his looks, the latter would say nothing about it. Praskovya Fëdorovna came home and her brother went out to her. Ivan Ilych locked the door and began to examine himself in the glass, first full face, then in profile. He took up a portrait of himself taken with his wife, and compared it with what he saw in the glass. The change in him was immense. Then he bared his arms to the elbow, looked at them, drew the sleeves down again, sat down on an ottoman, and grew blacker than night.

"No, no, this won't do!" he said to himself, and jumped up, went to the table, took up some law papers, and began to read them, but could not continue. He unlocked the door and went into the reception-room. The door leading to the drawing-room was shut. He approached it on tiptoe and listened.

"No, you are exaggerating!" Praskovya Fëdorovna was saying.

"Exaggerating! Don't you see it? Why, he's a dead man! Look at his eyes— there's no light in them. But what is it that is wrong with him?"

"No one knows. Nikolaevich said something, but I don't know what. And Leshchetitsky° said quite the contrary . . . "

Ivan Ilych walked away, went to his own room, lay down, and began musing: "The kidney, a floating kidney." He recalled all the doctors had told him of how it detached itself and swayed about. And by an effort of imagination he tried to catch that kidney and arrest it and support it. So little was needed for this, it seemed to him. "No, I'll go to see Peter Ivanovich° again." He rang, ordered the carriage, and got ready to go.

"Where are you going, Jean?" asked his wife, with a specially sad and exceptionally kind look.

This exceptionally kind look irritated him. He looked morosely at her.

"I must go to see Peter Ivanovich."

He went to see Peter Ivanovich, and together they went to see his friend, the doctor. He was in, and Ivan Ilych had a long talk with him.

Reviewing the anatomical and physiological details of what in the doctor's opinion was going on inside him, he understood it all.

There was something, a small thing, in the vermiform appendix. It might all come right. Only stimulate the energy of one organ and check the activity of another, then absorption would take place and everything would come right. He got home rather late for dinner, ate his dinner, and conversed cheerfully, but could not for a long time bring himself to go back to work in his room. At last, however, he went to his study and did what was necessary, but the consciousness that he had put something aside—an important, intimate matter which he would revert to when his work was done—never left him. When he finished his work

Nikolaevich, Leshchetitsky: two doctors, the latter a celebrated specialist. [Translators' note.]   *Peter Ivanovich:* That was the friend whose friend was a doctor. [Translators' note.]

he remembered that this intimate matter was the thought of his vermiform appendix. But he did not give himself up to it, and went to the drawing-room for tea. There were callers there, including the examining magistrate who was a desirable match for his daughter, and they were conversing, playing the piano, and singing. Ivan Ilych, as Praskovya Fëdorovna remarked, spent that evening more cheerfully than usual, but he never for a moment forgot that he had postponed the important matter of the appendix. At eleven o'clock he said good-night and went to his bedroom. Since his illness he had slept alone in a small room next to his study. He undressed and took up a novel by Zola, but instead of reading it he fell into thought, and in his imagination that desired improvement in the vermiform appendix occurred. There was the absorption and evacuation and the re-establishment of normal activity. "Yes, that's it!" he said to himself. "One need only assist nature, that's all." He remembered his medicine, rose, took it, and lay down on his back watching for the beneficent action of the medicine and for it to lessen the pain. "I need only take it regularly and avoid all injurious influences. I am already feeling better, much better." He began touching his side: it was not painful to the touch. "There, I really don't feel it. It's much better already." He put out the light and turned on his side . . . "The appendix is getting better, absorption is occurring." Suddenly he felt the old, familiar, dull, gnawing pain, stubborn and serious. There was the same familiar loathsome taste in this mouth. His heart sank and he felt dazed. "My God! My God!" he muttered. "Again, again! and it will never cease." And suddenly the matter presented itself in a quite different aspect. "Vermiform appendix! Kidney!" he said to himself. "It's not a question of appendix or kidney, but of life and . . . death. Yes, life was there and now it is going, going and I cannot stop it. Yes. Why deceive myself? Isn't it obvious to everyone but me that I'm dying, and that it's only a question of weeks, days . . . it may happen this moment. There was light and now there is darkness. I was here and now I'm going there! Where?" A chill came over him, his breathing ceased, and he felt only the throbbing of his heart.

"When I am not, what will there be? There will be nothing. Then where shall I be when I am no more? Can this be dying? No, I don't want to!" He jumped up and tried to light the candle, felt for it with trembling hands, dropped candle and candlestick on the floor, and fell back on his pillow.

"What's the use? It makes no difference," he said to himself, staring with wide-open eyes into the darkness. "Death. Yes, death. And none of them know or wish to know it, and they have no pity for me. Now they are playing." (He heard through the door the distant sound of a song and its accompaniment.) "It's all the same to them, but they will die too! Fools! I first, and they later, but it will be the same for them. And now they are merry . . . the beasts!"

Anger choked him and he was agonizingly, unbearably miserable. "It is impossible that all men have been doomed to suffer this awful horror!" He raised himself.

"Something must be wrong. I must calm myself—must think it all over from the beginning." And he again began thinking. "Yes, the beginning of my illness: I knocked my side, but I was still quite well that day and the next. It hurt a little, then rather more. I saw the doctors, then followed despondency and anguish, more doctors, and I drew nearer to the abyss. My strength grew less and I kept coming nearer and nearer, and now I have wasted away and there is no light in my eyes. I think of the appendix—but this is death! I think of mending the appendix, and all the while here is death! Can it really be death?" Again terror seized him and he gasped for breath. He leant down and began feeling for the matches, pressing with his elbow on the stand beside the bed. It was in his way and hurt him, he grew furious with it, pressed on it still harder, and upset it. Breathless and in despair he fell on his back, expecting death to come immediately.

Meanwhile the visitors were leaving. Praskovya Fëdorovna was seeing them off. She heard something fall and came in.

"What has happened?"

"Nothing. I knocked it over accidentally."   160

She went out and returned with a candle. He lay there panting heavily, like a man who has run a thousand yards, and stared upwards at her with a fixed look.

"What is it, Jean?"

"No . . . o . . . thing. I upset it." ("Why speak of it? She won't understand," he thought.

And in truth she did not understand. She picked up the stand, lit his candle, and hurried away to see another visitor off. When she came back he still lay on his back, looking upwards.

"What is it? Do you feel worse?"   165

"Yes."

She shook her head and sat down.

"Do you know, Jean, I think we must ask Leshchetitsky to come and see you here."

This meant calling in the famous specialist, regardless of expense. He smiled malignantly and said "No." She remained a little longer and then went up to him and kissed his forehead.

While she was kissing him he hated her from the bottom of his soul and with   170
difficulty refrained from pushing her away.

"Good-night. Please God you'll sleep."

"Yes."

VI

Ivan Ilych saw that he was dying, and he was in continual despair.

In the depth of his heart he knew he was dying, but not only was he not accustomed to the thought, he simply did not and could not grasp it.

The syllogism he had learnt from Kiezewetter's Logic: "Caius is a man, men   175
are mortal, therefore Caius is mortal," had always seemed to him correct as ap-
plied to Caius, but certainly not as applied to himself. That Caius—man in the abstract—was mortal, was perfectly correct, but he was not Caius, not an abstract man, but a creature quite, quite separate from all others. He had been little Vanya, with a mamma and a papa, with Mitya and Volodya, with the toys, a coachman and a nurse, afterwards with Katenka and with all the joys, griefs, and delights of childhood, boyhood, and youth. What did Caius know of the smell of that striped leather ball Vanya had been so fond of? Had Caius kissed his mother's hand like that, and did the silk of her dress rustle so for Caius? Had he rioted like that at

school when the pastry was bad? Had Caius been in love like that? Could Caius preside at a session as he did? "Caius really was mortal, and it was right for him to die; but for me, little Vanya, Ivan Ilych, with all my thoughts and emotions, it's altogether a different matter. It cannot be thought I ought to die. That would be too terrible."

Such was his feeling.

"If I had to die like Caius I should have known it was so. An inner voice would have told me so, but there was nothing of the sort in me and I and all my friends felt that our case was quite different from that of Caius. And now here it is!" he said to himself. "It can't be. It's impossible! But here it is. How is this? How is one to understand it?"

He could not understand it, and tried to drive this false, incorrect, morbid thought away and to replace it by other proper and healthy thoughts. But that thought, and not the thought only but the reality itself, seemed to come and confront him.

And to replace that thought he called up a succession of others, hoping to find in them some support. He tried to get back into the former current of thoughts that had once screened the thought of death from him. But strange to say, all that had formerly shut off, hidden, and destroyed his consciousness of death, no longer had that effect. Ivan Ilych now spent most of his time in attempting to re-establish that old current. He would say to himself: "I will take up my duties again—after all I used to live by them." And banishing all doubts he would go to the law courts, enter into conversation with his colleagues, and sit carelessly as was his wont, scanning the crowd with a thoughtful look and leaning both his emaciated arms on the arms of his oak chair; bending over as usual to a colleague and drawing his papers nearer he would interchange whispers with him, and then suddenly raising his eyes and sitting erect would pronounce certain words and open the proceedings. But suddenly in the midst of those proceedings the pain in his side, regardless of the stage the proceedings had reached, would begin its own gnawing work. Ivan Ilych would turn his attention to it and try to drive the thought of it away, but without success. It would come and stand before him and look at him, and he would be petrified and the light would die out of his eyes, and he would again begin asking himself whether It alone was true. And his colleagues and subordinates would see with surprise and distress that he, the brilliant and subtle judge, was becoming confused and making mistakes. He would shake himself, try to pull himself together, manage somehow to bring the sitting to a close, and return home with the sorrowful consciousness that his judicial labors could not as formerly hide from him what he wanted them to hide, and could not deliver him from It. And what was worst of all was that It drew his attention to itself not in order to make him take some action but only that he should look at It, look it straight in the face: look at it and, without doing anything, suffer inexpressibly.

And to save himself from this condition Ivan Ilych looked for consolation— new screens—and new screens were found and for a while seemed to save him, but then they immediately fell to pieces or rather became transparent, as if It penetrated them and nothing could veil It.

180

In these latter days he would go into the drawing-room he had arranged—that drawing-room where he had fallen and for the sake of which (how bitterly ridiculous it seemed) he had sacrificed his life—for he knew that his illness originated with that knock. He would enter and see that something had scratched the polished table. He would look for the cause of this and find that it was the bronze ornamentation of an album, that had got bent. He would take up the expensive album which he had lovingly arranged, and feel vexed with his daughter and her friends for their untidiness—for the album was torn here and there and some of the photographs turned upside down. He would put it carefully in order and bend the ornamentation back into position. Then it would occur to him to place all those things in another corner of the room, near the plants. He could call the footman, but his daughter or wife would come to help him. They would not agree, and his wife would contradict him, and he would dispute and grow angry. But that was all right, for then he did not think about It. It was invisible.

But then, when he was moving something himself, his wife would say: "Let the servants do it. You will hurt yourself again." And suddenly It would flash through the screen and he would see it. It was just a flash, and he hoped it would disappear, but he would involuntarily pay attention to his side. "It sits there as before, gnawing just the same!" And he could no longer forget It, but could distinctly see it looking at him from behind the flowers. "What is it all for?"

"It really is so! I lost my life over that curtain as I might have done when storming a fort. Is that possible? How terrible and how stupid. It can't be true! It can't, but it is."

He would go to his study, lie down, and again be alone with It: face to face with It. And nothing could be done with It except to look at it and shudder.

VII

How it happened it is impossible to say because it came about step by step, unnoticed, but in the third month of Ivan Ilych's illness, his wife, his daughter, his son, his acquaintances, the doctors, the servants, and above all he himself, were aware that the whole interest he had for the other people was whether he would soon vacate his place, and at last release the living from the discomfort caused by his presence and be himself released from his sufferings.

He slept less and less. He was given opium and hypodermic injections of morphine, but this did not relieve him. The dull depression he experienced in a somnolent condition at first gave him a little relief, but only as something new, afterwards it became as distressing as the pain itself or even more so.

Special foods were prepared for him by the doctor's orders, but all those foods became increasingly distasteful and disgusting to him.

For his excretions also special arrangements had to be made, and this was a torment to him every time—a torment from the uncleanliness, the unseemliness, and the smell, and from knowing that another person had to take part in it.

But just through this most unpleasant matter, Ivan Ilych obtained comfort. Gerasim, the butler's young assistant, always came in to carry the things out. Gerasim was a clean, fresh peasant lad, grown stout on town food and always cheerful and bright. At first the sight of him, in his clean Russian peasant costume, engaged on that disgusting task embarrassed Ivan Ilych.

Once when he got up from the commode too weak to draw up his trousers, 190
he dropped into a soft armchair and looked with horror at his bare, enfeebled
thighs with the muscles so sharply marked on them.

Gerasim with a firm light tread, his heavy boots emitting a pleasant smell
of tar and fresh winter air, came in wearing a clean Hessian apron, the sleeves
of his print shirt tucked up over his strong, bare young arms; and refraining from
looking at his sick master out of consideration for his feelings, and restraining
the joy of life that beamed from his face, he went up to the commode.

"Gerasim!" said Ivan Ilych in a weak voice.

Gerasim started, evidently afraid he might have committed some blunder,
and with a rapid movement turned his fresh, kind, simple young face which just
showed the first downy signs of a beard.

"Yes, sir?"

"That must be very unpleasant for you. You must forgive me. I am helpless." 195

"Oh, why, sir," and Gerasim's eyes beamed and he showed his glistening white
teeth, "what's a little trouble? It's a case of illness with you, sir."

And his deft strong hands did their accustomed task, and he went out of the
room stepping lightly. Five minutes later he as lightly returned.

Ivan Ilych was still sitting in the same position in the armchair.

"Gerasim," he said when the latter had replaced the freshly-washed utensil.
"Please come here and help me." Gerasim went up to him. "Lift me up. It is hard
for me to get up, and I have sent Dmitri away."

Gerasim went up to him, grasped his master with his strong arms deftly but 200
gently, in the same way that he stepped—lifted him, supported him with one hand,
and with the other drew up his trousers and would have set him down again, but
Ivan Ilych asked to be led to the sofa. Gerasim, without an effort and without
apparent pressure, led him, almost lifting him, to the sofa and placed him on it.

"Thank you. How easily and well you do it all!"

Gerasim smiled again and turned to leave the room. But Ivan Ilych felt his
presence such a comfort that he did not want to let him go.

"One thing more, please move up that chair. No, the other one—under my
feet. It is easier for me when my feet are raised."

Gerasim brought the chair, set it down gently in place, and raised Ivan Ilych's legs on to it. It seemed to Ivan Ilych that he felt better while Gerasim was
holding up his legs.

"It's better when my legs are higher," he said. "Place that cushion under them." 205

Gerasim did so. He again lifted the legs and placed them, and again Ivan
Ilych felt better while Gerasim held his legs. When he set them down Ivan Ilych
fancied he felt worse.

"Gerasim," he said. "Are you busy now?"

"Not at all, sir," said Gerasim, who had learnt from the townsfolk how to
speak to gentlefolk.

"What have you still to do?"

"What have I to do? I've done everything except chopping the logs for 210
tomorrow."

"Then hold my legs up a bit higher, can you?"

"Of course I can. Why not?" And Gerasim raised his master's legs higher and Ivan Ilych thought that in that position he did not feel any pain at all.

"And how about the logs?"

"Don't trouble about that, sir. There's plenty of time."

Ivan Ilych told Gerasim to sit down and hold his legs, and began to talk to him. And strange to say it seemed to him that he felt better while Gerasim held his legs up.

After that Ivan Ilych would sometimes call Gerasim and get him to hold his legs on his shoulders, and he liked talking to him. Gerasim did it all easily, willingly, simply, and with a good nature that touched Ivan Ilych. Health, strength, and vitality in other people were offensive to him, but Gerasim's strength and vitality did not mortify but soothed him.

What tormented Ivan Ilych most was the deception, the lie, which for some reason they all accepted, that he was not dying but was simply ill, and that he only need keep quiet and undergo a treatment and then something very good would result. He, however, knew that do what they would nothing would come of it, only still more agonizing suffering and death. This deception tortured him — their not wishing to admit what they all knew and what he knew, but wanting to lie to him concerning his terrible condition, and wishing and forcing him to participate in that lie. Those lies — lies enacted over him on the eve of his death and destined to degrade this awful, solemn act to the level of their visitings, their curtains, their sturgeon for dinner — were a terrible agony for Ivan Ilych. And strangely enough, many times when they were going through their antics over him he had been within a hairbreadth of calling out to them: "Stop lying! You know and I know that I am dying. Then at least stop lying about it!" But he had never had the spirit to do it. The awful, terrible act of his dying was, he could see, reduced by those about him to the level of a casual, unpleasant, and almost indecorous incident (as if someone entered a drawing-room diffusing an unpleasant odor) and this was done by that very decorum which he had served all his life long. He saw that no one felt for him, because no one even wished to grasp his position. Only Gerasim recognized it and pitied him. And so Ivan Ilych felt at ease only with him. He felt comforted when Gerasim supported his legs (sometimes all night long) and refused to go to bed, saying: "Don't you worry, Ivan Ilych. I'll get sleep enough later on," or when he suddenly became familiar and exclaimed: "If you weren't sick it would be another matter, but as it is, why should I grudge a little trouble?" Gerasim alone did not lie; eveything showed that he alone understood the facts of the case and did not consider it necessary to disguise them, but simply felt sorry for his emaciated and enfeebled master. Once when Ivan Ilych was sending him away he even said straight out: "We shall all of us die, so why should I grudge a little trouble?" — expressing the fact that he did not think his work burdensome, because he was doing it for a dying man and hoped someone would do the same for him when his time came.

Apart from this lying, or because of it, what most tormented Ivan Ilych was that no one pitied him as he wished to be pitied. At certain moments after prolonged suffering he wished most of all (though he would have been ashamed to confess it) for someone to pity him as a sick child is pitied. He longed to be petted and comforted. He knew he was an important functionary, that he had a beard turning grey, and that therefore what he longed for was impossible, but still he longed for it. And in Gerasim's attitude towards him there was something akin to what he wished for, and so that attitude comforted him. Ivan Ilych wanted to weep, wanted to be petted and cried over, and then his colleague Shebek would come, and instead of weeping and being petted, Ivan Ilych would assume a serious, severe, and profound air, and by force of habit would express his opinion on a decision of the Court of Cassation and would stubbornly insist on that view. This falsity around him and within him did more than anything else to poison his last days.

VIII

It was morning. He knew it was morning because Gerasim had gone, and Peter the footman had come and put out the candles, drawn back one of the curtains, and begun quietly to tidy up. Whether it was morning or evening, Friday or Sunday, made no difference, it was all just the same: the gnawing, unmitigated, agonizing pain, never ceasing for an instant, the consciousness of life inexorably waning but not yet extinguished, the approach of that ever dreaded and hateful Death which was the only reality, and always the same falsity. What were days, weeks, hours, in such a case?

"Will you have some tea, sir?"   220

"He wants things to be regular, and wishes the gentlefolk to drink tea in the morning," thought Ivan Ilych, and only said "No."

"Wouldn't you like to move onto the sofa, sir?"

"He wants to tidy up the room, and I'm in the way. I am uncleanliness and disorder," he thought, and said only:

"No, leave me alone."

The man went on bustling about. Ivan Ilych stretched out his hand. Peter   225
came up, ready to help.

"What is it, sir?"

"My watch."

Peter took the watch which was close at hand and gave it to his master.

"Half-past eight. Are they up?"

"No, sir, except Vladimir Ivanovich" (the son) "who has gone to school.   230
Praskovya Fëdorovna ordered me to wake her if you asked for her. Shall I do so?"

"No, there's no need to." "Perhaps I'd better have some tea," he thought, and added aloud: "Yes, bring me some tea."

Peter went to the door, but Ivan Ilych dreaded being left alone. "How can I keep him here? Oh yes, my medicine." "Peter, give me my medicine." "Why not? Perhaps it may still do me some good." He took a spoonful and swallowed it. "No, it won't help. It's all tomfoolery, all deception," he decided as soon as he became aware of the familiar, sickly, hopeless taste. "No, I can't believe in it any longer. But the pain, why this pain? If it would only cease just for a moment!" And he moaned. Peter turned towards him. "It's all right. Go and fetch me some tea."

Peter went out. Left alone Ivan Ilych groaned not so much with pain, terrible though that was, as from mental anguish. Always and forever the same, always these endless days and nights. If only it would come quicker! If only *what* would come quicker? Death, darkness? . . . No, no! Anything rather than death!

When Peter returned with the tea on a tray, Ivan Ilych stared at him for a time in perplexity, not realizing who and what he was. Peter was disconcerted by that look and his embarrassment brought Ivan Ilych to himself.

"Oh, tea! All right, put it down. Only help me to wash and put on a clean shirt." 235

And Ivan Ilych began to wash. With pauses for rest, he washed his hands and then his face, cleaned his teeth, brushed his hair, and looked in the glass. He was terrified by what he saw, especially by the limp way in which his hair clung to his pallid forehead.

While his shirt was being changed he knew that he would be still more frightened at the sight of his body, so he avoided looking at it. Finally he was ready. He drew on a dressing-gown, wrapped himself in a plaid, and sat down in the armchair to take his tea. For a moment he felt refreshed, but soon as he began to drink the tea he was again aware of the same taste, and the pain also returned. He finished it with an effort, and then lay down stretching out his legs, and dismissed Peter.

Always the same. Now a spark of hope flashes up, then a sea of despair rages, and always pain; always pain, always despair, and always the same. When alone he had a dreadful and distressing desire to call someone, but he knew beforehand that with others present it would be still worse. "Another dose of morphine—to lose consciousness. I will tell him, the doctor, that he must think of something else. It's impossible, impossible, to go on like this."

An hour and another pass like that. But now there is a ring at the door bell. Perhaps it's the doctor? It is. He comes in fresh, hearty, plump, and cheerful, with that look on his face that seems to say: "There now, you're in a panic about something, but we'll arrange it all for you directly!" The doctor knows this expression is out of place here, but he has put it on once for all and can't take it off—like a man who has put on a frock-coat in the morning to pay a round of calls.

The doctor rubs his hands vigorously and reassuringly. 240

"Brr! How cold it is! There's such a sharp frost; just let me warm myself!" he says, as if it were only a matter of waiting till he was warm, and then he would put everything right.

"Well now, how are you?"

Ivan Ilych feels that the doctor would like to say: "Well, how are our affairs?" but that even he feels that this would not do, and says instead: "What sort of a night have you had?"

Ivan Ilych looks at him as much as to say: "Are you really never ashamed of lying?" But the doctor does not wish to understand this question, and Ivan Ilych says: "Just as terrible as ever. The pain never leaves me and never subsides. If only something . . . "

"Yes, you sick people are always like that. . . . There, now I think I am warm 245 enough. Even Praskovya Fëdorovna, who is so particular, could find no fault with my temperature. Well, now I can say good-morning," and the doctor presses his patient's hand.

Then, dropping his former playfulness, he begins with a most serious face to examine the patient, feeling his pulse and taking his temperature, and then begins the sounding and auscultation.

Ivan Ilych knows quite well and definitely that all this is nonsense and pure deception, but when the doctor, getting down on his knee, leans over him, putting his ear first higher then lower, and performs various gymnastic movements over him with a significant expression on his face, Ivan Ilych submits to it all as he used to submit to the speeches of the lawyers, though he knew very well that they were all lying and why they were lying.

The doctor, kneeling on the sofa, is still sounding him when Praskovya Fëdorovna's silk dress rustles at the door and she is heard scolding Peter for not having let her know of the doctor's arrival.

She comes in, kisses her husband, and at once proceeds to prove that she has been up a long time already, and only owing to a misunderstanding failed to be there when the doctor arrived.

Ivan Ilych looks at her, scans her all over, sets against her the whiteness and 250 plumpness and cleanness of her hands and neck, the gloss of her hair, and the sparkle of her vivacious eyes. He hates her with his whole soul. And the thrill of hatred he feels for her makes him suffer from her touch.

Her attitude towards him and his disease is still the same. Just as the doctor had adopted a certain relation to his patient which he could not abandon, so had she formed one towards him—that he was not doing something he ought to do and was himself to blame, and that she reproached him lovingly for this—and she could not now change that attitude.

"You see he doesn't listen to me and doesn't take his medicine at the proper time. And above all he lies in a position that is no doubt bad for him—with his legs up."

She described how he made Gerasim hold his legs up.

The doctor smiled with a contemptuous affability that said: "What's to be done? These sick people do have foolish fancies of that kind, but we must forgive them."

When the examination was over the doctor looked at his watch, and then 255 Praskovya Fëdorovna announced to Ivan Ilych that it was of course as he pleased, but she had sent today for a celebrated specialist who would examine him and have a consultation with Michael Danilovich (their regular doctor).

"Please don't raise any objections. I am doing this for my own sake," she said ironically, letting it be felt that she was doing it all for his sake and only said this to leave him no right to refuse. He remained silent, knitting his brows. He felt that he was so surrounded and involved in a mesh of falsity that it was hard to unravel anything.

Everything she did for him was entirely for her own sake, and she told him she was doing for herself what she actually was doing for herself, as if that was so incredible that he must understand the opposite.

At half-past eleven the celebrated specialist arrived. Again the sounding began and the significant conversations in his presence and in another room, about the kidneys and the appendix, and the questions and answers, with such an air of importance that again, instead of the real question of life and death which now alone confronted him, the question arose of the kidney and appendix which were not behaving as they ought to and would now be attacked by Michael Danilovich and the specialist and forced to amend their ways.

The celebrated specialist took leave of him with a serious though not hopeless look, and in reply to the timid question Ivan Ilych, with eyes glistening with fear and hope, put to him as to whether there was a chance of recovery, said that he could not vouch for it but there was a possibility. The look of hope with which Ivan Ilych watched the doctor out was so pathetic that Praskovya Fëdorovna, seeing it, even wept as she left the room to hand the doctor his fee.

The gleam of hope kindled by the doctor's encouragement did not last long. The same room, the same pictures, curtains, wallpaper, medicine bottles, were all there, and the same aching suffering body, and Ivan Ilych began to moan. They gave him a subcutaneous injection and he sank into oblivion.

It was twilight when he came to. They brought him his dinner and he swallowed some beef tea with difficulty, and then everything was the same again and night was coming on.

After dinner, at seven o'clock, Praskovya Fëdorovna came into the room in evening dress, her full bosom pushed up by her corset, and with traces of powder on her face. She had reminded him in the morning that they were going to the theatre. Sarah Bernhardt was visiting the town and they had a box, which he had insisted on their taking. Now he had forgotten about it and her toilet offended him, but he concealed his vexation when he remembered that he had himself insisted on their securing a box and going because it would be an instructive and aesthetic pleasure for the children.

Praskovya Fëdorovna came in, self-satisfied but yet with a rather guilty air. She sat down and asked how he was, but, as he saw, only for the sake of asking and not in order to learn about it, knowing that there was nothing to learn—and then went on to what she really wanted to say: that she would not on any account have gone but that the box had been taken and Helen and their daughter were going, as well as Petrishchev (the examining magistrate, their daughter's fiancé), and that it was out of the question to let them go alone; but that she would have much preferred to sit with him for a while; and he must be sure to follow the doctor's orders while she was away.

"Oh, and Fëdor Petrovich" (the fiancé) "would like to come in. May he? And Lisa?"

"All right."

Their daughter came in in full evening dress, her fresh young flesh exposed (making a show of that very flesh which in his own case caused so much suffering), strong, healthy, evidently in love, and impatient with illness, suffering, and death, because they interfered with her happiness.

Fëdor Petrovich came in too, in evening dress, his hair curled à la Capoul°, a tight stiff collar round his long sinewy neck, an enormous white shirtfront, and

à la Capoul: imitating the hair-do of Victor Capoul, a contemporary French singer.

narrow black trousers tightly stretched over his strong thighs. He had one white glove tightly drawn on, and was holding his opera hat in his hand.

Following him the schoolboy crept in unnoticed, in a uniform, poor little fellow, and wearing gloves. Terribly dark shadows showed under his eyes, the meaning of which Ivan Ilych knew well.

His son had always seemed pathetic to him, and now it was dreadful to see the boy's frightened look of pity. It seemed to Ivan Ilych that Vasya was the only one besides Gerasim who understood and pitied him.

They all sat down and again asked how he was. A silence followed. Lisa asked 270 her mother about the opera-glasses, and there was an altercation between mother and daughter as to who had taken them and where they had been put. This occasioned some unpleasantness.

Fëdor Petrovich inquired of Ivan Ilych whether he had ever seen Sarah Bernhardt. Ivan Ilych did not at first catch the question, but then replied: "No, have you seen her before?"

"Yes, in *Adrienne Lecouvreur*."

Praskovya Fëdorovna mentioned some rôles in which Sarah Bernhardt was particularly good. Her daughter disagreed. Conversation sprang up as to the elegance and realism of her acting—the sort of conversation that is always repeated and is always the same.

In the midst of the conversation Fëdor Petrovich glanced at Ivan Ilych and became silent. The others also looked at him and grew silent. Ivan Ilych was staring with glittering eyes straight before him, evidently indignant with them. This had to be rectified, but it was impossible to do so. The silence had to be broken, but for a time no one dared to break it and they all became afraid that the conventional deception would suddenly become obvious and the truth become plain to all. Lisa was the first to pluck up courage and break that silence, but by trying to hide what everybody was feeling, she betrayed it.

"Well, if we are going it's time to start," she said, looking at her watch, a 275 present from her father, and with a faint and significant smile at Fëdor Petrovich relating to something known only to them. She got up with a rustle of her dress.

They all rose, said good-night, and went away.

When they had gone it seemed to Ivan Ilych that he felt better: the falsity had gone with them. But the pain remained—that same pain and that same fear that made everything monotonously alike, nothing harder and nothing easier. Everything was worse.

Again minute followed minute and hour followed hour. Everything remained the same and there was no cessation. And the inevitable end of it all became more and more terrible.

"Yes, send Gerasim here," he replied to a question Peter asked.

IX

His wife returned late at night. She came in on tiptoe, but he heard her, 280 opened his eyes, and made haste to close them again. She wished to send Gerasim away and to sit with him herself, but he opened his eyes and said: "No, go away."

"Are you in great pain?"

"Always the same."

"Take some opium."

He agreed and took some. She went away.

Till about three in the morning he was in a state of stupefied misery. It seemed to him that he and his pain were being thrust into a narrow, deep black sack, but though they were pushed further and further in they could not be pushed to the bottom. And this, terrible enough in itself, was accompanied by suffering. He was frightened yet wanted to fall through the sack, he struggled but yet cooperated. And suddenly he broke through, fell, and regained consciousness. Gerasim was sitting at the foot of the bed dozing quietly and patiently, while he himself lay with his emaciated stockinged legs resting on Gerasim's shoulders; the same shaded candle was there and the same unceasing pain.

"Go away, Gerasim," he whispered.

"It's all right, sir. I'll stay a while."

"No. Go away."

He removed his legs from Gerasim's shoulders, turned sideways onto his arm, and felt sorry for himself. He only waited till Gerasim had gone into the next room and then restrained himself no longer but wept like a child. He wept on account of his helplessness, his terrible loneliness, the cruelty of man, the cruelty of God, and the absence of God.

"Why hast Thou done all this? Why hast Thou brought me here? Why, why dost Thou torment me so terribly?"

He did not expect an answer and yet wept because there was no answer and could be none. The pain grew more acute, but he did not stir and did not call. He said to himself: "Go on! Strike me! But what is it for? What have I done to Thee? What is it for?"

Then he grew quiet and not only ceased weeping but even held his breath and became all attention. It was as though he was listening not to an audible voice but to the voice of his soul, to the current of thoughts arising within him.

"What is it you want?" was the first clear conception capable of expression in words, that he heard.

"What do you want? What do you want?" he repeated to himself.

"What do I want? To live and not to suffer," he answered.

And again he listened with such concentrated attention that even his pain did not distract him.

"To live? How?" asked his inner voice.

"Why, to live as I used to—well and pleasantly."

"As you lived before, well and pleasantly?" the voice repeated.

And in imagination he began to recall the best moments of his pleasant life. But strange to say none of those best moments of his pleasant life now seemed at all what they had then seemed—none of them except the first recollections of childhood. There, in childhood, there had been something really pleasant with which it would be possible to live if it could return. But the child who had experienced that happiness existed no longer, it was like a reminiscence of somebody else.

As soon as the period began which had produced the present Ivan Ilych, all that had then seemed joys now melted before his sight and turned into something trival and often nasty.

And the further he departed from childhood and the nearer he came to the present the more worthless and doubtful were the joys. This began with the School of Law. A little that was really good was still found there—there was lightheartedness, friendship, and hope. But in the upper classes there had already been fewer of such good moments. Then during the first years of his official career, when he was in the service of the Governor, some pleasant moments again occurred; they were the memories of love for a woman. Then all became confused and there was still less of what was good; later on again there was still less that was good, and the further he went the less there was. His marriage, a mere accident, then the disenchantment that followed it, his wife's bad breath and the sensuality and hypocrisy; then that deadly official life and those preoccupations about money, a year of it, and two, and ten, and twenty, and always the same thing. And the longer it lasted the more deadly it became. "It is as if I had been going downhill while I imagined I was going up. And that is really what it was. I was going up in public opinion, but to the same extent life was ebbing away from me. And now it is all done and there is only death."

"Then what does it mean? Why? It can't be that life is so senseless and horrible. But if it really has been so horrible and senseless, why must I die and die in agony? There is something wrong!"

"Maybe I did not live as I ought to have done," it suddenly occurred to him. "But how could that be, when I did everything properly?" he replied, and immediately dismissed from his mind this, the sole solution of all the riddles of life and death, as something quite impossible.

"Then what do you want now? To live? Live how? Live as you lived in the law courts when the usher proclaimed 'The judge is coming!' The judge is coming, the judge!" he repeated to himself. "Here he is, the judge. But I am not guilty!" he exclaimed angrily. "What is it for?" And he ceased crying, but turning his face to the wall continued to ponder on the same question: Why, and for what purpose, is there all this horror? But however much he pondered he found no answer. And whenever the thought occurred to him, as it often did, that it all resulted from his not having lived as he ought to have done, he at once recalled the correctness of his whole life and dismissed so strange an idea. 305

X

Another fortnight passed. Ivan Ilych now no longer left his sofa. He would not lie in bed but lay on the sofa, facing the wall nearly all the time. He suffered ever the same unceasing agonies and in his loneliness pondered always on the same insoluble question: "What is this? Can it be that it is Death?" And the inner voice answered: "Yes, it is Death."

"Why these sufferings?" And the voice answered, "For no reason—they just are so." Beyond and besides this there was nothing.

From the very beginning of his illness, ever since he had first been to see the doctor, Ivan Ilych's life had been divided between two contrary and alternating moods: now it was despair and the expectation of this uncomprehended and terrible death, and now hope and an intently interested observation of the functioning of his organs. Now before his eyes there was only a kidney or an intestine that temporarily evaded its duty, and now only that incomprehensible and dreadful death from which it was impossible to escape.

These two states of mind had alternated from the very beginning of his illness, but the further it progressed the more doubtful and fantastic became the conception of the kidney, and the more real the sense of impending death.

He had but to call to mind what he had been three months before and what ³¹⁰ he was now, to call to mind with what regularity he had been going downhill, for every possibility of hope to be shattered.

Latterly during that loneliness in which he found himself as he lay facing the back of the sofa, a loneliness in the midst of a populous town and surrounded by numerous acquaintances and relations but that yet could not have been more complete anywhere—either at the bottom of the sea or under the earth—during that terrible loneliness Ivan Ilych had lived only in memories of the past. Pictures of his past rose before him one after another. They always began with what was nearest in time and then went back to what was most remote—to his childhood—and rested there. If he thought of the stewed prunes that had been offered him that day, his mind went back to the raw shrivelled French plums of his childhood, their peculiar flavor and the flow of saliva when he sucked their stones, and along with the memory of that taste came a whole series of memories of those days: his nurse, his brother, and their toys. "No, I mustn't think of that. . . . It is too painful," Ivan Ilych said to himself, and brought himself back to the present—to the button on the back of the sofa and the creases in its morocco. "Morocco is expensive, but it does not wear well: there had been a quarrel about it. It was a different kind of quarrel and a different kind of morocco that time when we tore father's portfolio and were punished, and mamma brought us some tarts. . . . " And again his thoughts dwelt on his chiildhood, and again it was painful and he tried to banish them and fix his mind on something else.

Then again together with that chain of memories another series passed through his mind—of how his illness had progressed and grown worse. There also the further back he looked the more life there had been. There had been more of what was good in life and more of life itself. The two merged together. "Just as the pain went on getting worse and worse, so my life grew worse and worse," he thought. "There is one bright spot there at the back, at the beginning of life, and afterwards all becomes blacker and blacker and proceeds more and more rapidly—in inverse ratio to the square of the distance from death," thought Ivan Ilych. And the example of a stone falling downwards with increasing velocity entered his mind. Life, a series of increasing sufferings, flies further and further towards its end—the most terrible suffering. "I am flying. . . . " He shuddered, shifted himself, and tried to resist, but was already aware that resistance was impossible, and again, with eyes weary of gazing but unable to cease seeing what was before them, he stared at the back of the sofa and waited—awaiting that dreadful fall and shock and destruction.

"Resistance is impossible!" he said to himself. "If I could only understand what it is all for! But that too is impossible. An explanation would be possible if it could be said that I have not lived as I ought to. But it is impossible to say that," and he remembered all the legality, correctitude, and propriety of his life. "That at any rate can certainly not be admitted," he thought, and his lips smiled ironically as if someone could see that smile and be taken in by it. "There is no explanation! Agony, death. . . . What for?"

XI

Another two weeks went by in this way and during that fortnight an event occurred that Ivan Ilych and his wife had desired. Petrishchev formally proposed. It happened in the evening. The next day Praskovya Fëdorovna came into her husband's room considering how best to inform him of it, but that very night there had been a fresh change for the worse in his condition. She found him still lying on the sofa but in a different position. He lay on his back, groaning and staring fixedly straight in front of him.

She began to remind him of his medicines, but he turned his eyes towards her with such a look that she did not finish what she was saying; so great an animosity, to her in particular, did that look express.

"For Christ's sake let me die in peace!" he said.

She would have gone away, but just then their daughter came in and went up to say good morning. He looked at her as he had done at his wife, and in reply to her inquiry about his health said dryly that he would soon free them all of himself. They were both silent and after sitting with him for a while went away.

"Is it our fault?" Lisa said to her mother. "It's as if we were to blame! I am sorry for papa, but why should we be tortured?"

The doctor came at his usual time. Ivan Ilych answered "Yes" and "No," never taking his angry eyes from him, and at last said: "You know you can do nothing for me, so leave me alone."

"We can ease your sufferings."

"You can't even do that. Let me be."

The doctor went into the drawing-room and told Praskovya Fëdorovna that the case was very serious and that the only resource left was opium to allay her husband's sufferings, which must be terrible.

It was true, as the doctor said, that Ivan Ilych's physical sufferings were terrible, but worse than the physical sufferings were his mental sufferings, which were his chief torture.

His mental sufferings were due to the fact that one night, as he looked at Gerasim's sleepy, good-natured face with its prominent cheekbones, the question suddenly occurred to him: "What if my whole life has really been wrong?"

It occurred to him that what had appeared perfectly impossible before, namely that he had not spent his life as he should have done, might after all be true. It occurred to him that his scarcely perceptible attempts to struggle against what was considered good by the most highly placed people, those scarcely noticeable impulses which he had immediately suppressed, might have been the real thing, and all the rest false. And his professional duties and the whole arrangement of his life and of his family, and all his social and official interests, might all have been false. He tried to defend all those things to himself and suddenly felt the weakness of what he was defending. There was nothing to defend.

"But if that is so," he said to himself, "and I am leaving this life with the consciousness that I have lost all that was given me and it is impossible to rectify it—what then?"

He lay on his back and began to pass his life in review in quite a new way. In the morning when he saw first his footman, then his wife, then his daughter, and then the doctor, their every word and movement confirmed to him the awful truth that had been revealed to him during the night. In them he saw himself— all that for which he had lived—and saw clearly that it was not real at all, but a terrible and huge deception which had hidden both life and death. This consciousness intensified his physical suffering tenfold. He groaned and tossed about, and pulled at his clothing which choked and stifled him. And he hated them on that account.

He was given a large dose of opium and became unconscious, but at noon his sufferings began again. He drove everybody away and tossed from side to side.

His wife came to him and said:

"Jean, my dear, do this for me. It can't do any harm and often helps. Healthy people often do it." 330

He opened his eyes wide.

"What? Take communion? Why? It's unnecessary! However . . . "

She began to cry.

"Yes, do, my dear. I'll send for our priest. He is such a nice man."

"All right. Very well," he muttered. 335

When the priest came and heard his confession, Ivan Ilych was softened and seemed to feel a relief from his doubts and consequently from his sufferings, and for a moment there came a ray of hope. He again began to think of the vermiform appendix and the possibility of correcting it. He received the sacrament with tears in his eyes.

When they laid him down again afterwards he felt a moment's ease, and the hope that he might live awoke in him again. He began to think of the operation that had been suggested to him. "To live! I want to live!" he said to himself.

His wife came in to congratulate him after his communion, and when uttering the usual conventional words she added:

"You feel better, don't you?"

Without looking at her he said "Yes." 340

Her dress, her figure, the expression of her face, the tone of her voice, all revealed the same thing. "This is wrong, it is not as it should be. All you have lived for and still live for is falsehood and deception, hiding life and death from you." And as soon as he admitted that thought, his hatred and his agonizing physical suffering again sprang up, and with that suffering a consciousness of the unavoidable, approaching end. And to this was added a new sensation of grinding shooting pain and a feeling of suffocation.

The expression of his face when he uttered that "yes" was dreadful. Having uttered it, he looked her straight in the eyes, turned on his face with a rapidity extraordinary in his weak state and shouted:

"Go away! Go away and leave me alone!"

XII

From that moment the screaming began that continued for three days, and was so terrible that one could not hear it through two closed doors without horror. At the moment he answered his wife he realized that he was lost, that there was no return, that the end had come, the very end, and his doubts were still unsolved and remained doubts.

"Oh! Oh! Oh!" he cried in various intonations. He had begun by screaming 345 "I won't!" and continued screaming on the letter O.

For three whole days, during which time did not exist for him, he struggled in that black sack into which he was being thrust by an invisible, resistless force. He struggled as a man condemned to death struggles in the hands of the executioner, knowing that he cannot save himself. And every moment he felt that despite all his efforts he was drawing nearer and nearer to what terrified him. He felt that his agony was due to his being thrust into that black hole and still more to his not being able to get right into it. He was hindered from getting into it by his conviction that his life had been a good one. That very justification of his life held him fast and prevented his moving forward, and it caused him most torment of all.

Suddenly some force struck him in the chest and side, making it still harder to breathe, and he fell through the hole and there at the bottom was a light. What had happened to him was like the sensation one sometimes experiences in a railway carriage when one thinks one is going backwards while one is really going forwards and suddenly becomes aware of the real direction.

"Yes, it was all not the right thing," he said to himself, "but that's no matter. It can be done. But what is the right thing?" he asked himself, and suddenly grew quiet.

This occurred at the end of the third day, two hours before his death. Just then his schoolboy son had crept softly in and gone up to the bedside. The dying man was still screaming desperately and waving his arms. His hand fell on the boy's head, and the boy caught it, pressed it to his lips, and began to cry.

At that very moment Ivan Ilych fell through and caught sight of the light, 350 and it was revealed to him that though his life had not been what it should have been, this could still be rectified. He asked himself, "What is the right thing?" and grew still, listening. Then he felt that someone was kissing his hand. He opened his eyes, looked at his son, and felt sorry for him. His wife came up to him and he glanced at her. She was gazing at him open-mouthed, with undried tears on her nose and cheek and a despairing look on her face. He felt sorry for her too.

"Yes, I am making them wretched," he thought. "They are sorry, but it will be better for them when I die." He wished to say this but had not the strength to utter it. "Besides, why speak? I must act," he thought. With a look at his wife he indicated his son and said: "Take him away . . . sorry for him . . . sorry for you too . . . ." He tried to add, "Forgive me," but said "forgo" and waved his hand, knowing that He whose understanding mattered would understand.

And suddenly it grew clear to him that what had been oppressing him and would not leave him was all dropping away at once from two sides, from ten sides, and from all sides. He was sorry for them, he must act so as not to hurt them: release them and free himself from these sufferings. "How good and how simple!" he thought. "And the pain?" he asked himself. "What has become of it? Where are you, pain?"

He turned his attention to it.

"Yes, here it is. Well, what of it? Let the pain be."

"And death . . . where is it?"

He sought his former accustomed fear of death and did not find it. "Where is it? What death?" There was no fear because there was no death.

In place of death there was light.

"So that's what it is!" he suddenly exclaimed aloud. "What joy!"

To him all this happened in a single instant, and the meaning of that instant did not change. For those present his agony continued for another two hours. Something rattled in his throat, his emaciated body twitched, then the gasping and rattle became less and less frequent.

"It is finished!" said someone near him.

He heard these words and repeated them in his soul.

"Death is finished," he said to himself. "It is no more!"

He drew in a breath, stopped in the midst of a sigh, stretched out, and died.

355

360

QUESTIONS

1. Sum up the reactions of Ivan's colleagues to the news of his death. What is implied in Tolstoi's calling them not friends but "nearest acquaintances"?
2. What comic elements do you find in the account of the wake that Peter Ivanovich attends?
3. In Tolstoi's description of the corpse and its expression (paragraph 27), what details seem especially revealing and meaningful?
4. Do you think Tolstoi would have improved the story had he placed the events in chronological order? What if the opening scene of Ivan's colleagues at the Law Courts and the wake scene were to be given last? What would be lost?
5. Would you call Ivan, when we first meet him, a religious man? Sum up his goals in life, his values, his attitudes.
6. By what "virtues" and abilities does Ivan rise through the ranks? While he continues to succeed in his career, what happens to his marriage?
7. "Every spot on the tablecloth or the upholstery, and every broken window-blind string, irritated him. He had devoted so much trouble to arranging it all that every disturbance of it distressed him" (paragraph 104). What do you make of this passage? What is its tone? Does the narrator sympathize with Ivan's attachment to his possessions?
8. Consider the account of Ivan's routine ("He got up at nine . . . .," paragraph 105). What elements of a full life, what higher satisfactions, does this routine omit?
9. What caused Ivan's illness? How would it probably be diagnosed today? What is the narrator's attitude toward Ivan's doctors?
10. In what successive stages does Tolstoi depict Ivan's growing isolation as his progressive illness sets him more and more apart?
11. What are we apparently supposed to admire in the character and conduct of the servant Gerasim?
12. What do you understand from the statement that Ivan's justification of his life "prevented his moving forward, and it caused him most torment of all" (paragraph 346)?
13. What is memorable in the character of Ivan's schoolboy son? Why is he crucial to the story? (Suggestion: Look closely at paragraphs 349–350.)
14. What realization allows Ivan to triumph over pain? Why does he die gladly?
15. Henri Troyat has said that through the story of Ivan Ilych we imagine what our own deaths will be. Is it possible to identify with an aging, selfish, wordly, nineteenth-century Russian judge?

READING LONG STORIES AND NOVELS   **257**

SUGGESTIONS FOR WRITING

1. In a single, carefully thought-out paragraph, try to sum up what you believe Tolstoi is saying in *The Death of Ivan Ilych*.
2. Compares Tolstoi's short novel with another story of spiritual awakening: Flannery O'Connor's "Revelation" or "A Good Man Is Hard To Find," or perhaps Isaac Bashevis Singer's "Gimpel the Fool." In each, what brings about the enlightenment of the central character?
3. Compare the last thoughts of Ivan Ilych with the last thoughts of Katherine Anne Porter's Granny Weatherall.
4. Topic for a long term paper: Read either *War and Peace* or *Anna Karenina* and show how some theme present in *Ivan Ilych* is essential to it as well.
5. Read a novel chosen from a list provided by your instructor, or chosen with your instructor's approval. Selecting some element in it that interests you, write an essay in which you demonstrate the importance to the book of that one element. You might write, for instance, on "The Character of the Monster in Mary Shelley's *Frankenstein*"; for an essay on theme, "A Plea for Paganism in D. H. Lawrence's *The Plumed Serpent*"; "Setting as a Force in Thomas Pyncheon's *Vineland*"; "Symbolism in *The Scarlet Letter*" (or in *The Great Gatsby*). (Suggestion: You might find it helpful to read the discussion of analysis in "Writing about a Story" in Supplement: Writing.)

10   *Three Fiction Writers in Depth*

Raymond Carver

CATHEDRAL   1983

Raymond Carver, whose stories are mainly set in his native Pacific Northwest, was born in Clatskanie, Oregon, in 1938, the son of a laborer. At nineteen, he found himself married and the father of two children. After a series of low-paying jobs — picking tulips, pumping gas, working as hospital janitor — he took a degree in 1963 from Humboldt State University (now California State University, Humboldt), and in 1966 received an M.F.A. from the University of Iowa. His first book, Near Klamath (1968) was poetry; so is his recent, posthumous book, A New Path to the Waterfall (1989). Among his widely praised story collections are Will You Please Be Quiet, Please? *(1977),* What We Talk About When We Talk About Love *(1981),* Raymond Carver

Cathedral (1984), and a volume of new and selected stories, Where I'm Calling From *(1988). Carver taught creative writing at several schools: the University of California in Berkeley and Santa Cruz, the University of Texas in El Paso, Goddard College, and Syracuse University. In his last years, he lived in Port Angeles, Washington, with his second wife, the poet and short story writer Tess Gallagher. He died in 1988, a victim of lung cancer. Recently, Carver has received acclaim as a contemporary master of the short story, and his work has been translated into more than twenty languages. His stories have been much admired for, among other things, their knowledge of poor working people; but Carver once said that, until he read critics' reviews, he had not realized that his characters could be pitied: "I never felt the people I was writing about were so bad off."*

This blind man, an old friend of my wife's, he was on his way to spend the night. His wife had died. So he was visiting the dead wife's relatives in Connecticut. He called my wife from his in-laws'. Arrangements were made. He would come by train, a five-hour trip, and my wife would meet him at the station. She hadn't seen him since she worked for him one summer in Seattle ten years ago. But she and the blind man had kept in touch. They made tapes and mailed them back and forth. I wasn't enthusiastic about his visit. He was no one I knew. And his being blind bothered me. My idea of blindness came from the movies. In the movies, the blind moved slowly and never laughed. Sometimes they were led by seeing-eye dogs. A blind man in my house was not something I looked forward to.

That summer in Seattle she had needed a job. She didn't have any money. The man she was going to marry at the end of the summer was in officers' training school. He didn't have any money, either. But she was in love with the guy, and he was in love with her, etc. She'd seen something in the paper: HELP WANTED— Reading to Blind Man, and a telephone number. She phoned and went over, was hired on the spot. She'd worked with this blind man all summer. She read stuff to him, case studies, reports, that sort of thing. She helped him organize his little office in the county social-service department. They'd become good friends, my wife and the blind man. How do I know these things? She told me. And she told me something else. On her last day in the office, the blind man asked if he could touch her face. She agreed to this. She told me he touched his fingers to every part of her face, her nose—even her neck! She never forgot it. She even tried to write a poem about it. She was always trying to write a poem. She wrote a poem or two every year, usually after something really important had happened to her.

When we first started going out together, she showed me the poem. In the poem, she recalled his fingers and the way they had moved around over her face. In the poem, she talked about what she had felt at the time, about what went through her mind when the blind man touched her nose and lips. I can remember I didn't think much of the poem. Of course, I didn't tell her that. Maybe I just don't understand poetry. I admit it's not the first thing I reach for when I pick up something to read.

Anyway, this man who'd first enjoyed her favors, the officer-to-be, he'd been her childhood sweetheart. So okay. I'm saying that at the end of the summer she let the blind man run his hands over her face, said good-bye to him, married her childhood etc., who was now a commissioned officer, and she moved away from Seattle. But they'd kept in touch, she and the blind man. She made the first contact after a year or so. She called him up one night from an Air Force base in Alabama. She wanted to talk. They talked. He asked her to send a tape and tell him about her life. She did this. She sent the tape. On the tape, she told the blind man about her husband and about their life together in the military. She told the blind man she loved her husband but she didn't like it where they lived and she didn't like it that he was part of the military-industrial thing. She told the blind man she'd written a poem and he was in it. She told him that she was writing a poem about what it was like to be an Air Force officer's wife. The poem wasn't finished yet. She was still writing it. The blind man made a tape. He sent her the tape. She made a tape. This went on for years. My wife's officer was posted to one base and then another. She sent tapes from Moody AFB, McGuire, McConnell, and finally Travis, near Sacramento, where one night she got to feeling lonely and cut off from people she kept losing in that moving-around life. She got to feeling she couldn't go it another step. She went in and swallowed all the pills and capsules in the medicine chest and washed them down with a bottle of gin. Then she got into a hot bath and passed out.

But instead of dying, she got sick. She threw up. Her officer—why should 5
he have a name? he was the childhood sweetheart, and what more does he want?—
came home from somewhere, found her, and called the ambulance. In time, she
put it all on a tape and sent the tape to the blind man. Over the years, she put
all kinds of stuff on tapes and sent the tapes off lickety-split. Next to writing a
poem every year, I think it was her chief means of recreation. On one tape, she
told the blind man she'd decided to live away from her officer for a time. On another
tape, she told him about her divorce. She and I began going out, and of course
she told her blind man about it. She told him everything, or so it seemed to me.
Once she asked me if I'd like to hear the latest tape from the blind man. This
was a year ago. I was on the tape, she said. So I said okay, I'd listen to it. I got
us drinks and we settled down in the living room. We made ready to listen. First
she inserted the tape into the player and adjusted a couple of dials. Then she pushed
a lever. The tape squeaked and someone began to talk in this loud voice. She
lowered the volume. After a few minutes of harmless chitchat, I heard my own
name in the mouth of this stranger, this blind man I didn't even know! And then
this: "From all you've said about him, I can only conclude—" But we were interrupted, a knock at the door, something, and we didn't ever get back to the tape.
Maybe it was just as well. I'd heard all I wanted to.

Now this same blind man was coming to sleep in my house.

"Maybe I could take him bowling," I said to my wife. She was at the draining
board doing scalloped potatoes. She put down the knife she was using and turned
around.

"If you love me," she said, "you can do this for me. If you don't love me, okay.
But if you had a friend, any friend, and the friend came to visit, I'd make him
feel comfortable." She wiped her hands with the dish towel.

"I don't have any blind friends," I said.

"You don't have *any* friends," she said. "Period. Besides," she said, "goddamn 10
it, his wife's just died! Don't you understand that? The man's lost his wife!"

I didn't answer. She'd told me a little about the blind man's wife. Her name
was Beulah. Beulah! That's a name for a colored woman.

"Was his wife a Negro?" I asked.

"Are you crazy?" my wife said. "Have you just flipped or something?" She picked
up a potato. I saw it hit the floor, then roll under the stove. "What's wrong with
you?" she said. "Are you drunk?"

"I'm just asking," I said.

Right then my wife filled me in with more detail than I cared to know. I 15 made a drink and sat at the kitchen table to listen. Pieces of the story began to fall into place.

Beulah had gone to work for the blind man the summer after my wife had stopped working for him. Pretty soon Beulah and the blind man had themselves a church wedding. It was a little wedding—who'd want to go to such a wedding in the first place?—just the two of them, plus the minister and the minister's wife. But it was a church wedding just the same. It was what Beulah had wanted, he'd said. But even then Beulah must have been carrying the cancer in her glands. After they had been inseparable for eight years—my wife's word, *inseparable*—Beulah's health went into a rapid decline. She died in a Seattle hospital room, the blind man sitting beside the bed and holding on to her hand. They'd married, lived and worked together, slept together—had sex, sure—and then the blind man had to bury her. All this without his having ever seen what the goddamned woman looked like. It was beyond my understanding. Hearing this, I felt sorry for the blind man for a little bit. And then I found myself thinking what a pitiful life this woman must have led. Imagine a woman who could never see herself as she was seen in the eyes of her loved one. A woman who could go on day after day and never receive the smallest compliment from her beloved. A woman whose husband could never read the expression on her face, be it misery or something better. Someone who could wear makeup or not—what difference to him? She could, if she wanted, wear green eye-shadow around one eye, a straight pin in her nostril, yellow slacks, and purple shoes, no matter. And then to slip off into death, the blind man's hand on her hand, his blind eyes streaming tears—I'm imagining now—her last thought maybe this: that he never even knew what she looked like, and she on an express to the grave. Robert was left with a small insurance policy and a half of a twenty-peso Mexican coin. The other half of the coin went into the box with her. Pathetic.

So when the time rolled around, my wife went to the depot to pick him up. With nothing to do but wait—sure, I blamed him for that—I was having a drink and watching the TV when I heard the car pull into the drive. I got up from the sofa with my drink and went to the window to have a look.

I saw my wife laughing as she parked the car. I saw her get out of the car and shut the door. She was still wearing a smile. Just amazing. She went around to the other side of the car to where the blind man was already starting to get out. This blind man, feature this, he was wearing a full beard! A beard on a blind man! Too much, I say. The blind man reached into the backseat and dragged out a suitcase. My wife took his arm, shut the car door, and, talking all the way, moved him down the drive and then up the steps to the front porch. I turned off the TV. I finished my drink, rinsed the glass, dried my hands. Then I went to the door.

My wife said, "I want you to meet Robert. Robert, this is my husband. I've told you all about him." She was beaming. She had this blind man by his coat sleeve.

The blind man let go of his suitcase and up came his hand. 20

I took it. He squeezed hard, held my hand, and then he let it go.

"I feel like we've already met," he boomed.

"Likewise," I said. I didn't know what else to say. Then I said, "Welcome. I've heard a lot about you." We began to move then, a little group, from the porch into the living room, my wife guiding him by the arm. The blind man was carrying his suitcase in his other hand. My wife said things like, "To your left here, Robert. That's right. Now watch it, there's a chair. That's it. Sit down right here. This is the sofa. We just bought this sofa two weeks ago."

I started to say something about the old sofa. I'd liked that old sofa. But I didn't say anything. Then I wanted to say something else, small-talk, about the scenic ride along the Hudson. How going *to* New York, you should sit on the right-hand side of the train, and coming *from* New York, the left-hand side.

"Did you have a good train ride?" I said. "Which side of the train did you sit on, by the way?"

"What a question, which side!" my wife said. "What's it matter which side?" she said.

"I just asked," I said.

"Right side," the blind man said. "I hadn't been on a train in nearly forty years. Not since I was a kid. With my folks. That's been a long time. I'd nearly forgotten the sensation. I have winter in my beard now," he said. "So I've been told, anyway. Do I look distinguished, my dear?" the blind man said to my wife.

"You look distinguished, Robert," she said. "Robert," she said. "Robert, it's just so good to see you."

My wife finally took her eyes off the blind man and looked at me. I had the feeling she didn't like what she saw. I shrugged.

I've never met, or personally known, anyone who was blind. This blind man was late forties, a heavy-set, balding man with stooped shoulders, as if he carried a great weight there. He wore brown slacks, brown shoes, a light-brown shirt, a tie, a sports coat. Spiffy. He also had this full beard. But he didn't use a cane and he didn't wear dark glasses. I'd always thought dark glasses were a must for the blind. Fact was, I wished he had a pair. At first glance, his eyes looked like anyone else's eyes. But if you looked close, there was something different about them. Too much white in the iris, for one thing, and the pupils seemed to move around in the sockets without his knowing it or being able to stop it. Creepy. As I stared at his face, I saw the left pupil turn in toward his nose while the other made an effort to keep in one place. But it was only an effort, for that eye was on the roam without his knowing it or wanting it to be.

I said, "Let me get you a drink. What's your pleasure? We have a little of everything. It's one of our pastimes."

"Bub, I'm a Scotch man myself," he said fast enough in this big voice.

"Right," I said. Bub! "Sure you are. I knew it."

He let his fingers touch his suitcase, which was sitting alongside the sofa. He was taking his bearings. I didn't blame him for that.

"I'll move that up to your room," my wife said.

"No, that's fine," the blind man said loudly. "It can go up when I go up."

"A little water with the Scotch?" I said.

"Very little," he said.

"I knew it," I said.

He said, "Just a tad. The Irish actor, Barry Fitzgerald? I'm like that fellow. When I drink water, Fitzgerald said, I drink water. When I drink whiskey, I drink whiskey." My wife laughed. The blind man brought his hand up under his beard.

He lifted his beard slowly and let it drop.

I did the drinks, three big glasses of Scotch with a splash of water in each. Then we made ourselves comfortable and talked about Robert's travels. First the long flight from the West Coast to Connecticut, we covered that. Then from Connecticut up here by train. We had another drink concerning that leg of the trip.

I remembered having read somewhere that the blind didn't smoke because, as speculation had it, they couldn't see the smoke they exhaled. I thought I knew that much and that much only about blind people. But this blind man smoked his cigarette down to the nubbin and then lit another one. This blind man filled his ashtray and my wife emptied it.

When we sat down at the table for dinner, we had another drink. My wife heaped Robert's plate with cube steak, scalloped potatoes, green beans. I buttered him up two slices of bread. I said, "Here's bread and butter for you." I swallowed some of my drink. "Now let us pray," I said, and the blind man lowered his head. My wife looked at me, her mouth agape. "Pray the phone won't ring and the food doesn't get cold," I said.

We dug in. We ate everything there was to eat on the table. We ate like there was no tomorrow. We didn't talk. We ate. We scarfed. We grazed that table. We were into serious eating. The blind man had right away located his foods, he knew just where everything was on his plate. I watched with admiration as he used his knife and fork on the meat. He'd cut two pieces of meat, fork the meat into his mouth, and then go all out for the scalloped potatoes, the beans next, and then he'd tear off a hunk of buttered bread and eat that. He'd follow this up with a big drink of milk. It didn't seem to bother him to use his fingers once in a while, either.

We finished everything, including half a strawberry pie. For a few moments, we sat as if stunned. Sweat beaded on our faces. Finally, we got up from the table and left the dirty plates. We didn't look back. We took ourselves into the living room and sank into our places again. Robert and my wife sat on the sofa. I took the big chair. We had us two or three more drinks while they talked about the major things that had come to pass for them in the past ten years. For the most part, I just listened. Now and then I joined in. I didn't want him to think I'd left the room, and I didn't want her to think I was feeling left out. They talked of things that had happened to them—to them!—these past ten years. I waited in vain to hear my name on my wife's sweet lips: "And then my dear husband came into my life"—something like that. But I heard nothing of the sort. More talk of Robert. Robert had done a little of everything, it seemed, a regular blind jack-of-all-trades. But most recently he and his wife had had an Amway distributorship, from which, I gathered, they'd earned their living, such as it was. The blind man was also a ham radio operator. He talked in his loud voice about conversations he'd had with fellow operators in Guam, in the Philippines, in Alaska, and even in Tahiti. He said he'd have a lot of friends there if he ever wanted to go visit those places. From time to time, he'd turn his blind face toward me, put his hand under his beard, ask me something. How long had I been in my present position? (Three years.) Did I like my work? (I didn't.) Was I going to stay with it? (What were the options?) Finally, when I thought he was beginning to run down, I got up and turned on the TV.

My wife looked at me with irritation. She was heading toward a boil. Then she looked at the blind man and said, "Robert, do you have a TV?"

The blind man said, "My dear, I have two TVs. I have a color set and a black-and-white thing, an old relic. It's funny, but if I turn the TV on, and I'm always turning it on, I turn on the color set. It's funny, don't you think?"

I didn't know what to say to that. I had absolutely nothing to say to that. No opinion. So I watched the news program and tried to listen to what the announcer was saying.

"This is a color TV," the blind man said. "Don't ask me how, but I can tell." 50

"We traded up a while ago," I said.

The blind man had another taste of his drink. He lifted his beard, sniffed it, and let it fall. He leaned forward on the sofa. He positioned his ashtray on the coffee table, then put the lighter to his cigarette. He leaned back on the sofa and crossed his legs at the ankles.

My wife covered her mouth, and then she yawned. She stretched. She said, "I think I'll go upstairs and put on my robe. I think I'll change into something else. Robert, you make yourself comfortable," she said.

"I'm comfortable," the blind man said.

"I want you to feel comfortable in this house," she said. 55

"I am comfortable," the blind man said.

After she'd left the room, he and I listened to the weather report and then to the sports roundup. By that time, she'd been gone so long I didn't know if she was going to come back. I thought she might have gone to bed. I wished she'd come back downstairs. I didn't want to be left alone with a blind man. I asked him if he wanted another drink, and he said sure. Then I asked if he wanted to smoke some dope with me. I said I'd just rolled a number. I hadn't, but I planned to do so in about two shakes.

"I'll try some with you," he said.

"Damn right," I said. "That's the stuff."

I got our drinks and sat down on the sofa with him. Then I rolled us two 60 fat numbers. I lit one and passed it. I brought it to his fingers. He took it and inhaled.

"Hold it as long as you can," I said. I could tell he didn't know the first thing.

My wife came back downstairs wearing her pink robe and her pink slippers.

"What do I smell?" she said.

"We thought we'd have us some cannabis," I said.

My wife gave me a savage look. Then she looked at the blind man and said, 65 "Robert, I didn't know you smoked."

He said, "I do now, my dear. There's a first time for everything. But I don't feel anything yet."

"This stuff is pretty mellow," I said. "This stuff is mild. It's dope you can reason with," I said. "It doesn't mess you up."

"Not much it doesn't, bub," he said, and laughed.

My wife sat on the sofa between the blind man and me. I passed her the number. She took it and toked and then passed it back to me. "Which way is this going?" she said. Then she said, "I shouldn't be smoking this. I can hardly keep my eyes open as it is. That dinner did me in. I shouldn't have eaten so much."

"It was the strawberry pie," the blind man said. "That's what did it," he said, and he laughed his big laugh. Then he shook his head.

"There's more strawberry pie," I said.

"Do you want some more, Robert?" my wife said.

"Maybe in a little while," he said.

We gave our attention to the TV. My wife yawned again. She said, "Your bed is made up when you feel like going to bed, Robert. I know you must have had a long day. When you're ready to go to bed, say so." She pulled his arm. "Robert?"

He came to and said, "I've had a real nice time. This beats tapes, doesn't it?"

I said, "Coming at you," and I put the number between his fingers. He inhaled, held the smoke, and then let it go. It was like he'd been doing it since he was nine years old.

"Thanks, bub," he said. "But I think this is all for me. I think I'm beginning to feel it," he said. He held the burning roach out for my wife.

"Same here," she said. "Ditto. Me, too." She took the roach and passed it to me. "I may just sit here for a while between you two guys with my eyes closed. But don't let me bother you, okay? Either one of you. If it bothers you, say so. Otherwise, I may just sit here with my eyes closed until you're ready to go to bed," she said. "Your bed's made up, Robert, when you're ready. It's right next to our room at the top of the stairs. We'll show you up when you're ready. You wake me up now, you guys, if I fall asleep." She said that and then she closed her eyes and went to sleep.

The news program ended. I got up and changed the channel. I sat back down on the sofa. I wished my wife hadn't pooped out. Her head lay across the back of the sofa, her mouth open. She'd turned so that her robe slipped away from her legs, exposing a juicy thigh. I reached to draw her robe back over her, and it was then that I glanced at the blind man. What the hell! I flipped the robe open again.

"You say when you want some strawberry pie," I said.

"I will," he said.

I said, "Are you tired? Do you want me to take you up to your bed? Are you ready to hit the hay?"

"Not yet," he said. "No, I'll stay up with you, bub. If that's all right. I'll stay up until you're ready to turn in. We haven't had a chance to talk. Know what I mean? I feel like me and her monopolized the evening." He lifted his beard and he let it fall. He picked up his cigarettes and his lighter.

"That's all right," I said. Then I said, "I'm glad for the company."

And I guess I was. Every night I smoked dope and stayed up as long as I could before I fell asleep. My wife and I hardly ever went to bed at the same time. When I did go to sleep, I had these dreams. Sometimes I'd wake up from one of them, my heart going crazy.

Something about the church and the Middle Ages was on the TV. Not your run-of-the-mill TV fare. I wanted to watch something else. I turned to the other channels. But there was nothing on them, either. So I turned back to the first channel and apologized.

"Bub, it's all right," the blind man said. "It's fine with me. Whatever you want to watch is okay. I'm always learning something. Learning never ends. It won't hurt me to learn something tonight. I got ears," he said.

We didn't say anything for a time. He was leaning forward with his head turned at me, his right ear aimed in the direction of the set. Very disconcerting. Now and then his eyelids drooped and then they snapped open again. Now and then he put his fingers into his beard and tugged, like he was thinking about something he was hearing on the television.

On the screen, a group of men wearing cowls was being set upon and tormented by men dressed in skeleton costumes and men dressed as devils. The men dressed as devils wore devil masks, horns, and long tails. This pageant was part of a procession. The Englishman who was narrating the thing said it took place in Spain once a year. I tried to explain to the blind man what was happening.

"Skeletons," he said. "I know about skeletons," he said, and he nodded.   90

The TV showed this one cathedral. Then there was a long, slow look at another one. Finally, the picture switched to the famous one in Paris, with its flying buttresses and its spires reaching up to the clouds. The camera pulled away to show the whole of the cathedral rising above the skyline.

There were times when the Englishman who was telling the thing would shut up, would simply let the camera move around the cathedrals. Or else the camera would tour the countryside, men in fields walking behind oxen. I waited as long as I could. Then I felt I had to say something. I said, "They're showing the outside of this cathedral now. Gargoyles. Little statues carved to look like monsters. Now I guess they're in Italy. Yeah, they're in Italy. There's paintings on the walls of this one church."

"Are those fresco paintings, bub?" he asked, and he sipped from his drink.

I reached for my glass. But it was empty. I tried to remember what I could remember. "You're asking me are those frescoes?" I said. "That's a good question. I don't know."

The camera moved to a cathedral outside Lisbon. The differences in the Por-   95 tuguese cathedral compared with the French and Italian were not that great. But they were there. Mostly the interior stuff. Then something occurred to me, and I said, "Something has occurred to me. Do you have any idea what a cathedral is? What they look like, that is? Do you follow me? If somebody says cathedral to you, do you have any notion what they're talking about? Do you know the difference between that and a Baptist church, say?"

He let the smoke dribble from his mouth. "I know they took hundreds of workers fifty or a hundred years to build," he said. "I just heard the man say that, of course. I know generations of the same families worked on a cathedral. I heard him say that, too. The men who began their life's work on them, they never lived to see the completion of their work. In that wise, bub, they're no different from the rest of us, right?" He laughed. Then his eyelids drooped again. His head nodded. He seemed to be snoozing. Maybe he was imagining himself in Portugal. The

TV was showing another cathedral now. This one was in Germany. The English-man's voice droned on. "Cathedrals," the blind man said. He sat up and rolled his head back and forth. "If you want the truth, bub, that's about all I know. What I just said. What I heard him say. But maybe you could describe one to me? I wish you'd do it. I'd like that. If you want to know, I really don't have a good idea."

I stared hard at the shot of the cathedral on the TV. How could I even begin to describe it? But say my life depended on it. Say my life was being threatened by an insane guy who said I had to do it or else.

I stared some more at the cathedral before the picture flipped off into the countryside. There was no use. I turned to the blind man and said, "To begin with, they're very tall." I was looking around the room for clues. "They reach way up. Up and up. Toward the sky. They're so big, some of them, they have to have these supports. To help hold them up, so to speak. These supports are called but-tresses. They remind me of viaducts, for some reasons. But maybe you don't know viaducts, either? Sometimes the cathedrals have devils and such carved into the front. Sometimes lords and ladies. Don't ask me why this is," I said.

He was nodding. The whole upper part of his body seemed to be moving back and forth.

"I'm not doing so good, am I?" I said.   100

He stopped nodding and leaned forward on the edge of the sofa. As he listened to me, he was running his fingers through his beard. I wasn't getting through to him, I could see that. But he waited for me to go on just the same. He nodded, like he was trying to encourage me. I tried to think what else to say. "They're really big," I said. "They're massive. They're built of stone. Marble, too, some-times. In those olden days, when they built cathedrals, men wanted to be close to God. In those olden days, God was an important part of everyone's life. You could tell this from their cathedral-building. I'm sorry," I said, "but it looks like that's the best I can do for you. I'm just no good at it."

"That's all right, bub," the blind man said. "Hey, listen. I hope you don't mind my asking you. Can I ask you something? Let me ask you a simple question, yes or no. I'm just curious and there's no offense. You're my host. But let me ask if you are in any way religious? You don't mind my asking?"

I shook my head. He couldn't see that, though. A wink is the same as a nod to a blind man. "I guess I don't believe in it. In anything. Sometimes it's hard. You know what I'm saying?"

"Sure, I do," he said.

"Right," I said.   105

The Englishman was still holding forth. My wife sighed in her sleep. She drew a long breath and went on with her sleeping.

"You'll have to forgive me," I said. "But I can't tell you what a cathedral looks like. It just isn't in me to do it. I can't do any more than I've done."

The blind man sat very still, his head down, as he listened to me.

I said, "The truth is, cathedrals don't mean anything special to me. Nothing. Cathedrals. They're something to look at on late-night TV. That's all they are."

It was then that the blind man cleared his throat. He brought something up.   110
He took a handkerchief from his back pocket. Then he said, "I get it, bub. It's okay. It happens. Don't worry about it," he said. "Hey, listen to me. Will you do

me a favor? I got an idea. Why don't you find us some heavy paper? And a pen. We'll do something. We'll draw one together. Get us a pen and some heavy paper. Go on, bub, get the stuff," he said.

So I went upstairs. My legs felt like they didn't have any strength in them. They felt like they did after I'd done some running. In my wife's room, I looked around. I found some ballpoints in a little basket on her table. And then I tried to think where to look for the kind of paper he was talking about.

Downstairs, in the kitchen, I found a shopping bag with onion skins in the bottom of the bag. I emptied the bag and shook it. I brought it into the living room and sat down with it near his legs. I moved some things, smoothed the wrinkles from the bag, spread it out on the coffee table.

The blind man got down from the sofa and sat next to me on the carpet.

He ran his fingers over the paper. He went up and down the sides of the paper. The edges, even the edges. He fingered the corners.

"All right," he said. "All right, let's do her." 115

He found my hand, the hand with the pen. He closed his hand over my hand. "Go ahead, bub, draw," he said. "Draw. You'll see. I'll follow along with you. It'll be okay. Just begin now like I'm telling you. You'll see. Draw," the blind man said.

So I began. First I drew a box that looked like a house. It could have been the house I lived in. Then I put a roof on it. At either end of the roof, I drew spires. Crazy.

"Swell," he said. "Terrific. You're doing fine," he said. "Never thought anything like this could happen in your lifetime, did you, bub? Well, it's a strange life, we all know that. Go on now. Keep it up."

I put in windows with arches. I drew flying buttresses. I hung great doors. I couldn't stop. The TV station went off the air. I put down the pen and closed and opened my fingers. The blind man felt around over the paper. He moved the tips of his fingers over the paper, all over what I had drawn, and he nodded.

"Doing fine," the blind man said. 120

I took up the pen again, and he found my hand. I kept at it. I'm no artist. But I kept drawing just the same.

My wife opened up her eyes and gazed as us. She sat up on the sofa, her robe hanging open. She said, "What are you doing? Tell me, I want to know."

I didn't answer her.

The blind man said, "We're drawing a cathedral. Me and him are working on it. Press hard," he said to me. "That's right. That's good," he said. "Sure. You got it, bub, I can tell. You didn't think you could. But you can, can't you? You're cooking with gas now. You know what I'm saying? We're going to really have us something here in a minute. How's the old arm?" he said. "Put some people in there now. What's a cathedral without people?"

My wife said, "What's going on? Robert, what are you doing? What's going 125 on?"

"It's all right," he said to her. "Close your eyes now," the blind man said to me.

I did it. I closed them just like he said.

"Are they closed?" he said. "Don't fudge."

"They're closed," I said.

"Keep them that way," he said. He said, "Don't stop now. Draw." 130

So we kept on with it. His fingers rode my fingers as my hand went over the paper. It was like nothing else in my life up to now.

Then he said, "I think that's it. I think you got it," he said. "Take a look. What do you think?"

But I had my eyes closed. I thought I'd keep them that way for a little longer. I thought it was something I ought to do.

"Well?" he said. "Are you looking?"

My eyes were still closed. I was in my house. I knew that. But I didn't feel 135
like I was inside anything.

"It's really something," I said.

QUESTIONS

1. What details in "Cathedral" make clear the narrator's initial attitude toward blind people? What hints does the author give about the reasons for this attitude? At what point in the story do the narrator's preconceptions about blind people start to change?
2. For what reason does the wife keep asking Robert if he'd like to go to bed (paragraphs 74–78)? What motivates the narrator to make the same suggestion in paragraph 82? What effect does Robert's reply have on the narrator?
3. What makes the narrator start explaining what he's seeing on television?
4. How does the point of view contribute to the effectiveness of the story?
5. At the end, the narrator has an epiphany. How would you describe it?
6. How would you state the theme of "Cathedral" in your own words?

Raymond Carver

A SMALL, GOOD THING   1983

Saturday afternoon she drove to the bakery in the shopping center. After looking through a loose-leaf binder with photographs of cakes taped onto the pages, she ordered chocolate, the child's favorite. The cake she chose was decorated with a spaceship and launching pad under a sprinkling of white stars, and a planet made of red frosting at the other end. His name, SCOTTY, would be in green letters beneath the planet. The baker, who was an older man with a thick neck, listened without saying anything when she told him the child would be eight years old next Monday. The baker wore a white apron that looked like a smock. Straps cut under his arms, went around in back and then to the front again, where they were secured under his heavy waist. He wiped his hands on his apron as he listened to her. He kept his eyes down on the photographs and let her talk. He let her take her time. He'd just come to work and he'd be there all night, baking, and he was in no real hurry.

She gave the baker her name, Ann Weiss, and her telephone number. The cake would be ready on Monday morning, just out of the oven, in plenty of time for the child's party that afternoon. The baker was not jolly. There were no pleasantries between them, just the minimum exchange of words, the necessary information. He made her feel uncomfortable, and she didn't like that. While he was bent over the counter with the pencil in his hand, she studied his coarse features and wondered if he'd ever done anything else with his life besides be a baker. She was a mother and thirty-three years old, and it seemed to her that everyone, especially someone the baker's age—a man old enough to be her father—must have children who'd gone through this special time of cakes and birthday parties. There must be that between them, she thought. But he was abrupt with her—not rude, just abrupt. She gave up trying to make friends with him. She looked into the back of the bakery and could see a long, heavy wooden table with aluminum pie pans stacked at one end; and beside the table a metal container filled with empty racks. There was an enormous oven. A radio was playing country-Western music.

The baker finished printing the information on the special order card and closed up the binder. He looked at her and said, "Monday morning." She thanked him and drove home.

On Monday morning, the birthday boy was walking to school with another boy. They were passing a bag of potato chips back and forth and the birthday boy was trying to find out what his friend intended to give him for his birthday that afternoon. Without looking, the birthday boy stepped off the curb at an intersection and was immediately knocked down by a car. He fell on his side with his head in the gutter and his legs out in the road. His eyes were closed, but his legs moved back and forth as if he were trying to climb over something. His friend dropped the potato chips and started to cry. The car had gone a hundred feet or so and stopped in the middle of the road. The man in the driver's seat looked back over his shoulder. He waited until the boy got unsteadily to his feet. The boy wobbled a little. He looked dazed, but okay. The driver put the car into gear and drove away.

The birthday boy didn't cry, but he didn't have anything to say about anything either. He wouldn't answer when his friend asked him what it felt like to be hit by a car. He walked home, and his friend went on to school. But after the birthday boy was inside his house and was telling his mother about it—she sitting beside him on the sofa, holding his hands in her lap, saying, "Scotty, honey, are you sure you feel all right, baby?" thinking she would call the doctor anyway—he suddenly lay back on the sofa, closed his eyes, and went limp. When she couldn't wake him up, she hurried to the telephone and called her husband at work. Howard told her to remain calm, remain calm, and then he called an ambulance for the child and left for the hospital himself.

Of course, the birthday party was canceled. The child was in the hospital with a mild concussion and suffering from shock. There'd been vomiting, and his lungs had taken in fluid which needed pumping out that afternoon. Now he simply seemed to be in a very deep sleep—but no coma, Dr. Francis had emphasized, no coma, when he saw the alarm in the parents' eyes. At eleven o'clock that night, when the boy seemed to be resting comfortably enough after the many X-rays and the lab work, and it was just a matter of his waking up and coming around, Howard left the hospital. He and Ann had been at the hospital with the child since that afternoon, and he was going home for a short while to bathe and change clothes. "I'll be back in an hour," he said. She nodded. "It's fine," she said. "I'll

5

be right here." He kissed her on the forehead, and they touched hands. She sat in the chair beside the bed and looked at the child. She was waiting for him to wake up and be all right. Then she could begin to relax.

Howard drove home from the hospital. He took the wet, dark streets very fast, then caught himself and slowed down. Until now, his life had gone smoothly and to his satisfaction—college, marriage, another year of college for the advanced degree in business, a junior partnership in an investment firm. Fatherhood. He was happy and, so far, lucky—he knew that. His parents were still living, his brothers and his sister were established, his friends from college had gone out to take their places in the world. So far, he had kept away from any real harm, from those forces he knew existed and that could cripple or bring down a man if the luck went bad, if things suddenly turned. He pulled into the driveway and parked. His left leg began to tremble. He sat in the car for a minute and tried to deal with the present situation in a rational manner. Scotty had been hit by a car and was in the hospital, but he was going to be all right. Howard closed his eyes and ran his hand over his face. He got out of the car and went up to the front door. The dog was barking inside the house. The telephone rang and rang while he unlocked the door and fumbled for the light switch. He shouldn't have left the hospital, he shouldn't have. "Goddamn it!" he said. He picked up the receiver and said, "I just walked in the door!"

"There's a cake here that wasn't picked up," the voice on the other end of the line said.

"What are you saying?" Howard asked.

"A cake," the voice said. "A sixteen-dollar cake."　　　　　　　　　　　　　　10

Howard held the receiver against his ear, trying to understand. "I don't know anything about a cake," he said. "Jesus, what are you talking about?"

"Don't hand me that," the voice said.

Howard hung up the telephone. He went into the kitchen and poured himself some whiskey. He called the hospital. But the child's condition remained the same; he was still sleeping and nothing had changed there. While water poured into the tub, Howard lathered his face and shaved. He'd just stretched out in the tub and closed his eyes when the telephone rang again. He hauled himself out, grabbed a towel, and hurried through the house, saying, "Stupid, stupid," for having left the hospital. But when he picked up the receiver and shouted, "Hello!" there was no sound at the other end of the line. Then the caller hung up.

He arrived back at the hospital a little after midnight. Ann still sat in the chair beside the bed. She looked up at Howard, and then she looked back at the child. The child's eyes stayed closed, the head was still wrapped in bandages. His breathing was quiet and regular. From an apparatus over the bed hung a bottle of glucose with a tube running from the bottle to the boy's arm.

"How is he?" Howard said. "What's all this?" waving at the glucose and the tube.　　15

"Dr. Francis's orders," she said. "He needs nourishment. He needs to keep up his strength. Why doesn't he wake up, Howard? I don't understand, if he's all right."

Howard put his hand against the back of her head. He ran his fingers through her hair. "He's going to be all right. He'll wake up in a little while. Dr. Francis knows what's what."

After a time, he said, "Maybe you should go home and get some rest. I'll stay here. Just don't put up with this creep who keeps calling. Hang up right away."

"Who's calling?" she asked.

"I don't know who, just somebody with nothing better to do than call up people. You go on now." 20

She shook her head. "No," she said, "I'm fine."

"Really," he said. "Go home for a while, and then come back and spell me in the morning. It'll be all right. What did Dr. Francis say? He said Scotty's going to be all right. We don't have to worry. He's just sleeping now, that's all."

A nurse pushed the door open. She nodded at them as she went to the bedside. She took the left arm out from under the covers and put her fingers on the wrist, found the pulse, then consulted her watch. In a little while, she put the arm back under the covers and moved to the foot of the bed, where she wrote something on a clipboard attached to the bed.

"How is he?" Ann said. Howard's hand was a weight on her shoulder. She was aware of the pressure from his fingers.

"He's stable," the nurse said. Then she said, "Doctor will be in again shortly. 25 Doctor's back in the hospital. He's making rounds right now."

"I was saying maybe she'd want to go home and get a little rest," Howard said. "After the doctor comes," he said.

"She could do that," the nurse said. "I think you should both feel free to do that, if you wish." The nurse was a big Scandinavian woman with blond hair. There was the trace of an accent in her speech.

"We'll see what the doctor says," Ann said. "I want to talk to the doctor. I don't think he should keep sleeping like this. I don't think that's a good sign." She brought her hand up to her eyes and let her head come forward a little. Howard's grip tightened on her shoulder, and then his hand moved up to her neck, where his fingers began to knead the muscles there.

"Dr. Francis will be here in a few minutes," the nurse said. Then she left the room.

Howard gazed at his son for a time, the small chest quietly rising and falling 30 under the covers. For the first time since the terrible minutes after Ann's telephone call to him at his office, he felt a genuine fear starting in his limbs. He began shaking his head. Scotty was fine, but instead of sleeping at home in his own bed, he was in a hospital bed with bandages around his head and a tube in his arm. But this help was what he needed right now.

Dr. Francis came in and shook hands with Howard, though they'd just seen each other a few hours before. Ann got up from the chair. "Doctor?"

"Ann," he said and nodded. "Let's just first see how he's doing," the doctor said. He moved to the side of the bed and took the boy's pulse. He peeled back one eyelid and then the other. Howard and Ann stood beside the doctor and watched. Then the doctor turned back the covers and listened to the boy's heart and lungs with his stethoscope. He pressed his fingers here and there on the abdomen. When he was finished, he went to the end of the bed and studied the chart. He noted the time, scribbled something on the chart, and then looked at Howard and Ann.

"Doctor, how is he?" Howard said. "What's the matter with him exactly?"

"Why doesn't he wake up?" Ann said.

The doctor was a handsome, big-shouldered man with a tanned face. He wore 35
a three-piece blue suit, a striped tie, and ivory cuff links. His gray hair was combed
along the sides of his head, and he looked as if he had just come from a concert.
"He's all right," the doctor said. "Nothing to shout about, he could be better, I
think. But he's all right. Still, I wish he'd wake up. He should wake up pretty
soon." The doctor looked at the boy again. "We'll know some more in a couple
of hours, after the results of a few more tests are in. But he's all right, believe
me, except for the hairline fracture of the skull. He does have that."

"Oh, no," Ann said.

"And a bit of a concussion, as I said before. Of course, you know he's in shock,"
the doctor said. "Sometimes you see this in shock cases. This sleeping."

"But he's out of any real danger?" Howard said. "You said before he's not in
a coma. You wouldn't call this a coma, then—would you, doctor?" Howard waited.
He looked at the doctor.

"No, I don't want to call it a coma," the doctor said and glanced over at the
boy once more. "He's just in a very deep sleep. It's a restorative measure the body
is taking on its own. He's out of any real danger, I'd say that for certain, yes. But
we'll know more when he wakes up and the other tests are in," the doctor said.

"It's a coma," Ann said. "Of sorts." 40

"It's not a coma yet, not exactly," the doctor said. "I wouldn't want to call
it coma. Not yet, anyway. He's suffered shock. In shock cases, this kind of reaction is common enough; it's a temporary reaction to bodily trauma. Coma. Well,
coma is a deep, prolonged unconsciousness, something that could go on for days,
or weeks even. Scotty's not in that area, not as far as we can tell. I'm certain his
condition will show improvement by morning. I'm betting that it will. We'll know
more when he wakes up, which shouldn't be long now. Of course, you may do
as you like, stay here or go home for a time. But by all means feel free to leave
the hospital for a while if you want. This is not easy, I know." The doctor gazed
at the boy again, watching him, and then he turned to Ann and said, "You try
not to worry, little mother. Believe me, we're doing all that can be done. It's just
a question of a little more time now." He nodded at her, shook hands with Howard
again, and then he left the room.

Ann put her hand over the child's forehead. "At least he doesn't have a fever,"
she said. Then she said, "My God, he feels so cold, though. Howard? Is he supposed to feel like this? Feel his head."

Howard touched the child's temples. His own breathing had slowed. "I think
he's supposed to feel this way right now," he said. "He's in shock, remember? That's
what the doctor said. The doctor was just in here. He would have said something
if Scotty wasn't okay."

Ann stood there a while longer, working her lip with her teeth. Then she
moved over to her chair and sat down.

Howard sat in the chair next to her chair. They looked at each other. He 45
wanted to say something else and reassure her, but he was afraid, too. He took
her hand and put it in his lap, and this made him feel better, her hand being
there. He picked up her hand and squeezed it. Then he just held her hand. They
sat like that for a while, watching the boy and not talking. From time to time,
he squeezed her hand. Finally, she took her hand away.

"I've been praying," she said.

He nodded.

She said, "I almost thought I'd forgotten how, but it came back to me. All I had to do was close my eyes and say, 'Please God, help us—help Scotty,' and then the rest was easy. The words were right there. Maybe if you prayed, too," she said to him.

"I've already prayed," he said. "I prayed this afternoon—yesterday afternoon, I mean—after you called, while I was driving to the hospital. I've been praying," he said.

"That's good," she said. For the first time, she felt they were together in it, 50 this trouble. She realized with a start that, until now, it had only been happening to her and to Scotty. She hadn't let Howard into it, though he was there and needed all along. She felt glad to be his wife.

The same nurse came in and took the boy's pulse again and checked the flow from the bottle hanging above the bed.

In an hour, another doctor came in. He said his name was Parsons, from Radiology. He had a bushy moustache. He was wearing loafers, a Western shirt, and a pair of jeans.

"We're going to take him downstairs for more pictures," he told them. "We need to do some more pictures, and we want to do a scan."

"What's that?" Ann said. "A scan?" She stood between this new doctor and the bed. "I thought you'd already taken all your X-rays."

"I'm afraid we need some more," he said. "Nothing to be alarmed about. We 55 just need some more pictures, and we want to do a brain scan on him."

"My God," Ann said.

"It's perfectly normal procedure in cases like this," this new doctor said. "We just need to find out for sure why he isn't back awake yet. It's normal medical procedure, and nothing to be alarmed about. We'll be taking him down in a few minutes," this doctor said.

In a little while, two orderlies came into the room with a gurney. They were black-haired, dark-complexioned men in white uniforms, and they said a few words to each other in a foreign tongue as they unhooked the boy from the tube and moved him from his bed to the gurney. Then they wheeled him from the room. Howard and Ann got on the same elevator. Ann gazed at the child. She closed her eyes as the elevator began its descent. The orderlies stood at either end of the gurney without saying anything, though once one of the men made a comment to the other in their own language, and the other man nodded slowly in response.

Later that morning, just as the sun was beginning to lighten the windows in the waiting room outside the X-ray department, they brought the boy out and moved him back up to his room. Howard and Ann rode up on the elevator with him once more, and once more they took up their places beside the bed.

They waited all day, but still the boy did not wake up. Occasionally, one 60 of them would leave the room to go downstairs to the cafeteria to drink coffee and then, as if suddenly remembering and feeling guilty, get up from the table and hurry back to the room. Dr. Francis came again that afternoon and examined the boy once more and then left after telling them he was coming along and could wake up at any minute now. Nurses, different nurses from the night before, came in from time to time. Then a young woman from the lab knocked and entered the room. She wore white slacks and a white blouse and carried a little tray of things which she put on the stand beside the bed. Without a word to them, she took blood from the boy's arm. Howard closed his eyes as the woman found the right place on the boy's arm and pushed the needle in.

"I don't understand this," Ann said to the woman.

"Doctor's orders," the young woman said. "I do what I'm told. They say draw that one, I draw. What's wrong with him, anyway?" she said. "He's a sweetie."

"He was hit by a car," Howard said. "A hit-and-run."

The young woman shook her head and looked again at the boy. Then she took her tray and left the room.

"Why won't he wake up?" Ann said. "Howard? I want some answers from these people." 65

Howard didn't say anything. He sat down again in the chair and crossed one leg over the other. He rubbed his face. He looked at his son and then he settled back in the chair, closed his eyes, and went to sleep.

Ann walked to the window and looked out at the parking lot. It was night, and cars were driving into and out of the parking lot with their lights on. She stood at the window with her hands gripping the sill, and knew in her heart that they were into something now, something hard. She was afraid, and her teeth began to chatter until she tightened her jaws. She saw a big car stop in front of the hospital and someone, a woman in a long coat, get into the car. She wished she were that woman and somebody, anybody, was driving her away from here to somewhere else, a place where she would find Scotty waiting for her when she stepped out of the car, ready to say Mom and let her gather him in her arms.

In a little while, Howard woke up. He looked at the boy again. Then he got up from the chair, stretched, and went over to stand beside her at the window. They both stared out at the parking lot. They didn't say anything. But they seemed to feel each other's insides now, as though the worry had made them transparent in a perfectly natural way.

The door opened and Dr. Francis came in. He was wearing a different suit and tie this time. His gray hair was combed along the sides of his head, and he looked as if he had just shaved. He went straight to the bed and examined the boy. "He ought to have come around by now. There's just no good reason for this," he said. "But I can tell you we're all convinced he's out of any danger. We'll just feel better when he wakes up. There's no reason, absolutely none, why he shouldn't come around. Very soon. Oh, he'll have himself a dilly of a headache when he does, you can count on that. But all of his signs are fine. They're as normal as can be."

"It is a coma, then?" Ann said. 70

The doctor rubbed his smooth cheek. "We'll call it that for the time being, until he wakes up. But you must be worn out. This is hard. I know this is hard. Feel free to go out for a bite," he said. "It would do you good. I'll put a nurse in here while you're gone if you'll feel better about going. Go and have yourselves something to eat."

"I couldn't eat anything," Ann said.

"Do what you need to do, of course," the doctor said. "Anyway, I wanted to tell you that all the signs are good, the tests are negative, nothing showed up at all, and just as soon as he wakes up he'll be over the hill."

"Thank you, doctor," Howard said. He shook hands with the doctor again. The doctor patted Howard's shoulder and went out.

"I suppose one of us should go home and check on things," Howard said. "Slug needs to be fed, for one thing." 75

"Call one of the neighbors," Ann said. "Call the Morgans. Anyone will feed a dog if you ask them to."

"All right," Howard said. After a while, he said, "Honey, why don't *you* do it? Why don't you go home and check on things, and then come back? It'll do you good. I'll be right here with him. Seriously," he said. "We need to keep up our strength on this. We'll want to be here for a while even after he wakes up."

"Why don't *you* go?" she said. "Feed Slug. Feed yourself."

"I already went," he said. "I was gone for exactly an hour and fifteen minutes. You go home for an hour and freshen up. Then come back."

She tried to think about it, but she was too tired. She closed her eyes and 80 tried to think about it again. After a time, she said, "Maybe I *will* go home for a few minutes. Maybe if I'm not just sitting right here watching him every second, he'll wake up and be all right. You know? Maybe he'll wake up if I'm not here. I'll go home and take a bath and put on clean clothes. I'll feed Slug. Then I'll come back."

"I'll be right here," he said. "You go on home, honey. I'll keep an eye on things here." His eyes were bloodshot and small, as if he'd been drinking for a long time. His clothes were rumpled. His beard had come out again. She touched his face, and then she took her hand back. She understood he wanted to be by himself for a while, not have to talk or share his worry for a time. She picked her purse up from the nightstand, and he helped her into her coat.

"I won't be gone long," she said.

"Just sit and rest for a little while when you get home," he said. "Eat something. Take a bath. After you get out of the bath, just sit for a while and rest. It'll do you a world of good, you'll see. Then come back," he said. "Let's try not to worry. You heard what Dr. Francis said."

She stood in her coat for a minute trying to recall the doctor's exact words, looking for any nuances, any hint of something behind his words other than what he had said. She tried to remember if his expression had changed any when he bent over to examine the child. She remembered the way his features had composed themselves as he rolled back the child's eyelids and then listened to his breathing.

She went to the door, where she turned and looked back. She looked at the 85 child, and then she looked at the father. Howard nodded. She stepped out of the room and pulled the door closed behind her.

She went past the nurses' station and down to the end of the corridor, looking for the elevator. At the end of the corridor, she turned to her right and entered a little waiting room where a Negro family sat in wicker chairs. There was a middle-aged man in a khaki shirt and pants, a baseball cap pushed back on his head. A large woman wearing a housedress and slippers was slumped in one of the chairs. A teenaged girl in jeans, hair done in dozens of little braids, lay stretched out in one of the chairs smoking a cigarette, her legs crossed at the ankles. The family swung their eyes to Ann as she entered the room. The little table was littered with hamburger wrappers and Styrofoam cups.

"Franklin," the large woman said as she roused herself. "Is it about Franklin?" Her eyes widened. "Tell me now, lady," the woman said. "Is it about Franklin?" She was trying to rise from her chair, but the man had closed his hand over her arm.

"Here, here," he said. "Evelyn."

"I'm sorry," Ann said. "I'm looking for the elevator. My son is in the hospital, and now I can't find the elevator."

"Elevator is down that way, turn left," the man said as he aimed a finger.   90

The girl drew on her cigarette and stared at Ann. Her eyes were narrowed to slits, and her broad lips parted slowly as she let the smoke escape. The Negro woman let her head fall on her shoulder and looked away from Ann, no longer interested.

"My son was hit by a car," Ann said to the man. She seemed to need to explain herself. "He has a concussion and a little skull fracture, but he's going to be all right. He's in shock now, but it might be some kind of coma, too. That's what really worries us, the coma part. I'm going out for a little while, but my husband is with him. Maybe he'll wake up while I'm gone."

"That's too bad," the man said and shifted in the chair. He shook his head. He looked down at the table, and then he looked back at Ann. She was still standing there. He said, "Our Franklin, he's on the operating table. Somebody cut him. Tried to kill him. There was a fight where he was at. At this party. They say he was just standing and watching. Not bothering nobody. But that don't mean nothing these days. Now he's on the operating table. We're just hoping and praying, that's all we can do now." He gazed at her steadily.

Ann looked at the girl again, who was still watching her, and at the older woman, who kept her head down, but whose eyes were now closed. Ann saw the lips moving silently, making words. She had an urge to ask what those words were. She wanted to talk more with these people who were in the same kind of waiting she was in. She was afraid, and they were afraid. They had that in common. She would have liked to have said something else about the accident, told them more about Scotty, that it had happened on the day of his birthday, Monday, and that he was still unconscious. Yet she didn't know how to begin. She stood looking at them without saying anything more.

She went down the corridor the man had indicated and found the elevator.   95 She waited a minute in front of the closed doors, still wondering if she was doing the right thing. Then she put out her finger and touched the button.

She pulled into the driveway and cut the engine. She closed her eyes and leaned her head against the wheel for a minute. She listened to the ticking sounds the engine made as it began to cool. Then she got out of the car. She could hear the dog barking inside the house. She went to the front door, which was unlocked. She went inside and turned on lights and put on a kettle of water for tea. She opened some dog food and fed Slug on the back porch. The dog ate in hungry little smacks. It kept running into the kitchen to see that she was going to stay. As she sat down on the sofa with her tea, the telephone rang.

"Yes!" she said as she answered. "Hello!"

"Mrs. Weiss," a man's voice said. It was five o'clock in the morning, and she thought she could hear machinery or equipment of some kind in the background.

"Yes, yes! What is it?" she said. "This is Mrs. Weiss. This is she. What is it, please?" She listened to whatever it was in the background. "Is it Scotty, for Christ's sake?"

"Scotty," the man's voice said. "It's about Scotty, yes. It has to do with Scotty, 100 that problem. Have you forgotten about Scotty?" the man said. Then he hung up.

She dialed the hospital's number and asked for the third floor. She demanded information about her son from the nurse who answered the telephone. Then she asked to speak to her husband. It was, she said, an emergency.

She waited, turning the telephone cord in her fingers. She closed her eyes and felt sick at her stomach. She would have to make herself eat. Slug came in from the back porch and lay down near her feet. He wagged his tail. She pulled at his ear while he licked her fingers. Howard was on the line.

"Somebody just called here," she said. She twisted the telephone cord. "He said it was about Scotty," she cried.

"Scotty's fine," Howard told her. "I mean, he's still sleeping. There's been no change. The nurse has been in twice since you've been gone. A nurse or else a doctor. He's all right."

"This man called. He said it was about Scotty," she told him. 105

"Honey, you rest for a little while, you need the rest. It must be that same caller I had. Just forget it. Come back down here after you've rested. Then we'll have breakfast or something."

"Breakfast," she said. "I don't want any breakfast."

"You know what I mean," he said. "Juice, something. I don't know. I don't know anything, Ann. Jesus, I'm not hungry, either. Ann, it's hard to talk now. I'm standing here at the desk. Dr. Francis is coming again at eight o'clock this morning. He's going to have something to tell us then, something more definite. That's what one of the nurses said. She didn't know any more than that. Ann? Honey, maybe we'll know something more then. At eight o'clock. Come back here before eight. Meanwhile, I'm right here and Scotty's all right. He's still the same," he added.

"I was drinking a cup of tea," she said, "when the telephone rang. They said it was about Scotty. There was a noise in the background. Was there a noise in the background on that call you had, Howard?"

"I don't remember," he said. "Maybe the driver of the car, maybe he's a psy- 110 chopath and found out about Scotty somehow. But I'm here with him. Just rest like you were going to do. Take a bath and come back by seven or so, and we'll talk to the doctor together when he gets here. It's going to be all right, honey. I'm here, and there are doctors and nurses around. They say his condition is stable."

"I'm scared to death," she said.

She ran water, undressed, and got into the tub. She washed and dried quickly, not taking the time to wash her hair. She put on clean underwear, wool slacks, and a sweater. She went into the living room, where the dog looked up at her and let its tail thump once against the floor. It was just starting to get light outside when she went out to the car.

She drove into the parking lot of the hospital and found a space close to the front door. She felt she was in some obscure way responsible for what had happened to the child. She let her thoughts move to the Negro family. She remembered the name Franklin and the table that was covered with hamburger papers, and the teenaged girl staring at her as she drew on her cigarette. "Don't have children," she told the girl's image as she entered the front door of the hospital. "For God's sake, don't."

She took the elevator up to the third floor with two nurses who were just going on duty. It was Wednesday morning, a few minutes before seven. There was a page for a Dr. Madison as the elevator doors slid open on the third floor. She got off behind the nurses, who turned in the other direction and continued the conversation she had interrupted when she'd gotten into the elevator. She walked down the corridor to the little alcove where the Negro family had been waiting. They were gone now, but the chairs were scattered in such a way that it looked as if people had just jumped up from them the minute before. The tabletop was cluttered with the same cups and papers, the ashtray was filled with cigarette butts.

She stopped at the nurses' station. A nurse was standing behind the counter, brushing her hair and yawning. 115

"There was a Negro boy in surgery last night," Ann said. "Franklin was his name. His family was in the waiting room. I'd like to inquire about his condition."

A nurse who was sitting at a desk behind the counter looked up from a chart in front of her. The telephone buzzed and she picked up the receiver, but she kept her eyes on Ann.

"He passed away," said the nurse at the counter. The nurse held the hairbrush and kept looking at her. "Are you a friend of the family or what?"

"I met the family last night," Ann said. "My own son is in the hospital. I guess he's in shock. We don't know for sure what's wrong. I just wondered about Franklin, that's all. Thank you." She moved down the corridor. Elevator doors the same color as the walls slid open and a gaunt, bald man in white pants and white canvas shoes pulled a heavy cart off the elevator. She hadn't noticed these doors last night. The man wheeled the cart out into the corridor and stopped in front of the room nearest the elevator and consulted a clipboard. Then he reached down and slid a tray out of the cart. He rapped lightly on the door and entered the room. She could smell the unpleasant odors of warm food as she passed the cart. She hurried on without looking at any of the nurses and pushed open the door to the child's room.

Howard was standing at the window with his hands behind his back. He turned 120 around as she came in.

"How is he?" she said. She went over to the bed. She dropped her purse on the floor beside the nightstand. It seemed to her she had been gone a long time. She touched the child's face. "Howard?"

"Dr. Francis was here a little while ago," Howard said. She looked at him closely and thought his shoulders were bunched a little.

"I thought he wasn't coming until eight o'clock this morning," she said quickly.

"There was another doctor with him. A neurologist."

"A neurologist," she said. 125

Howard nodded. His shoulders were bunching, she could see that. "What'd they say, Howard? For Christ's sake, what'd they say? What is it?"

"They said they're going to take him down and run more tests on him, Ann. They think they're going to operate, honey. Honey, they *are* going to operate. They can't figure out why he won't wake up. It's more than just shock or concussion, they know that much now. It's in his skull, the fracture, it has something, something to do with that, they think. So they're going to operate. I tried to call you, but I guess you'd already left the house."

"Oh, God," she said. "Oh, please, Howard, please," she said, taking his arms.

"Look!" Howard said. "Scotty! Look, Ann!" He turned her toward the bed.

The boy had opened his eyes, then closed them. He opened them again now. 130 The eyes stared straight ahead for a minute, then moved slowly in his head until they rested on Howard and Ann, then traveled away again.

"Scotty," his mother said, moving to the bed.

"Hey, Scott," his father said. "Hey, son."

They leaned over the bed. Howard took the child's hand in his hands and began to pat and squeeze the hand. Ann bent over the boy and kissed his forehead again and again. She put her hands on either side of his face. "Scotty, honey, it's Mommy and Daddy," she said. "Scotty?"

The boy looked at them, but without any sign of recognition. Then his mouth opened, his eyes scrunched closed, and he howled until he had no more air in his lungs. His face seemed to relax and soften then. His lips parted as his last breath was puffed through his throat and exhaled gently through the clenched teeth.

The doctors called it a hidden occlusion and said it was a one-in-a-million 135 circumstance. Maybe if it could have been detected somehow and surgery undertaken immediately, they could have saved him. But more than likely not. In any case, what would they have been looking for? Nothing had shown up in the tests or in the X-rays.

Dr. Francis was shaken. "I can't tell you how badly I feel. I'm so very sorry, I can't tell you," he said as he led them into the doctors' lounge. There was a doctor sitting in a chair with his legs hooked over the back of another chair, watching an early-morning TV show. He was wearing a green delivery-room outfit, loose green pants and green blouse, and a green cap that covered his hair. He looked at Howard and Ann and then looked at Dr. Francis. He got to his feet and turned off the set and went out of the room. Dr. Francis guided Ann to the sofa, sat down beside her, and began to talk in a low, consoling voice. At one point, he leaned over and embraced her. She could feel his chest rising and falling evenly against her shoulder. She kept her eyes open and let him hold her. Howard went into the bathroom, but he left the door open. After a violent fit of weeping, he ran water and washed his face. Then he came out and sat down at the little table that held a telephone. He looked at the telephone as though deciding what to do first. He made some calls. After a time, Dr. Francis used the telephone.

"Is there anything else I can do for the moment?" he asked them.

Howard shook his head. Ann stared at Dr. Francis as if unable to comprehend his words.

The doctor walked them to the hospital's front door. People were entering and leaving the hospital. It was eleven o'clock in the morning. Ann was aware of how slowly, almost reluctantly, she moved her feet. It seemed to her that Dr. Francis was making them leave when she felt they should stay, when it would be more the right thing to do to stay. She gazed out into the parking lot and then turned around and looked back at the front of the hospital. She began shaking her head. "No, no," she said. "I can't leave him here, no." She heard herself say that and thought how unfair it was that the only words that came out were the sort of words used on TV shows where people were stunned by violent or sudden deaths. She wanted her words to be her own. "No," she said, and for some reason the memory of the Negro woman's head lolling on the woman's shoulder came to her. "No," she said again.

"I'll be talking to you later in the day," the doctor was saying to Howard.   140 "There are still some things that have to be done, things that have to be cleared up to our satisfaction. Some things that need explaining."

"An autopsy," Howard said.

Dr. Francis nodded.

"I understand," Howard said. Then he said, "Oh, Jesus. No, I don't understand, doctor. I can't, I can't. I just can't."

Dr. Francis put his arm around Howard's shoulders. "I'm sorry. God, how I'm sorry." He let go of Howard's shoulders and held out his hand. Howard looked at the hand, and then he took it. Dr. Francis put his arms around Ann once more. He seemed full of some goodness she didn't understand. She let her head rest on his shoulder, but her eyes stayed open. She kept looking at the hospital. As they drove out of the parking lot, she looked back at the hospital.

At home, she sat on the sofa with her hands in her coat pockets. Howard   145 closed the door to the child's room. He got the coffee-maker going and then he found an empty box. He had thought to pick up some of the child's things that were scattered around the living room. But instead he sat down beside her on the sofa, pushed the box to one side, and leaned forward, arms between his knees. He began to weep. She pulled his head over into her lap and patted his shoulder. "He's gone," she said. She kept patting his shoulder. Over his sobs, she could hear the coffee-maker hissing in the kitchen. "There, there," she said tenderly. "Howard, he's gone. He's gone and now we'll have to get used to that. To being alone."

In a little while, Howard got up and began moving aimlessly around the room with the box, not putting anything into it, but collecting some things together on the floor at one end of the sofa. She continued to sit with her hands in her coat pockets. Howard put the box down and brought coffee into the living room. Later, Ann made calls to relatives. After each call had been placed and the party had answered, Ann would blurt out a few words and cry for a minute. Then she would quietly explain, in a measured voice, what had happened and tell them about arrangements. Howard took the box out to the garage, where he saw the child's bicycle. He dropped the box and sat down on the pavement beside the bicycle. He took hold of the bicycle awkwardly so that it leaned against his chest. He held it, the rubber pedal sticking into his chest. He gave the wheel a turn.

Ann hung up the telephone after talking to her sister. She was looking up another number when the telephone rang. She picked it up on the first ring.

"Hello," she said, and she heard something in the background, a humming noise. "Hello!" she said. "For God's sake," she said. "Who is this? What is it you want?"

"Your Scotty, I got him ready for you," the man's voice said. "Did you forget him?"

"You evil bastard!" she shouted into the receiver. "How can you do this, you evil son of a bitch!"

"Scotty," the man said. "Have you forgotten about Scotty?" Then the man hung up on her.

Howard heard the shouting and came in to find her with her head on her arms over the table, weeping. He picked up the receiver and listened to the dial tone.

Much later, just before midnight, after they had dealt with many things, the telephone rang again.

"You answer it," she said. "Howard, it's him, I know." They were sitting at the kitchen table with coffee in front of them. Howard had a small glass of whiskey beside his cup. He answered on the third ring.

"Hello," he said. "Who is this? Hello! Hello!" The line went dead. "He hung up," Howard said. "Whoever it was."

"It was him," she said. "That bastard, I'd like to kill him," she said. "I'd like to shoot him and watch him kick," she said.

"Ann, my God," he said.

"Could you hear anything?" she said. "In the background? A noise, machinery, something humming?"

"Nothing, really. Nothing like that," he said. "There wasn't much time. I think there was some radio music. Yes, there was a radio going, that's all I could tell. I don't know what in God's name is going on," he said.

She shook her head. "If I could, could get my hands on him." It came to her then. She knew who it was. Scotty, the cake, the telephone number. She pushed the chair away from the table and got up. "Drive me down to the shopping center," she said. "Howard."

"What are you saying?"

"The shopping center. I know who it is who's calling. I know who it is. It's the baker, the son-of-a-bitching baker, Howard. I had him bake a cake for Scotty's birthday. That's who's calling. That's who has the number and keeps calling us. To harass us about that cake. The baker, that bastard."

They drove down to the shopping center. The sky was clear and stars were out. It was cold, and they ran the heater in the car. They parked in front of the bakery. All of the shops and stores were closed, but there were cars at the far end of the lot in front of the movie theater. The bakery windows were dark, but when they looked through the glass they could see a light in the back room and, now and then, a big man in an apron moving in and out of the white, even light. Through the glass, she could see the display cases and some little tables with chairs. She tried the door. She rapped on the glass. But if the baker heard them, he gave no sign. He didn't look in their direction.

They drove around behind the bakery and parked. They got out of the car. There was a lighted window too high up for them to see inside. A sign near the back door said THE PANTRY BAKERY, SPECIAL ORDERS. She could hear faintly a radio playing inside and something creak—an oven door as it was pulled down? She knocked on the door and waited. Then she knocked again, louder. The radio was turned down and there was a scraping sound now, the distinct sound of something, a drawer, being pulled open and then closed.

Someone unlocked the door and opened it. The baker stood in the light and 165 peered out at them. "I'm closed for business," he said. "What do you want at this hour? It's midnight. Are you drunk or something?"

She stepped into the light that fell through the open door. He blinked his heavy eyelids as he recognized her. "It's you," he said.

"It's me," she said. "Scotty's mother. This is Scotty's father. We'd like to come in."

The baker said, "I'm busy now. I have work to do."

She had stepped inside the doorway anyway. Howard came in behind her. The baker moved back. "It smells like a bakery in here. Doesn't it smell like a bakery in here, Howard?"

"What do you want?" the baker said. "Maybe you want your cake? That's it, 170 you decided you want your cake. You ordered a cake, didn't you?"

"You're pretty smart for a baker," she said. "Howard, this is the man who's been calling us." She clenched her fists. She stared at him fiercely. There was a deep burning inside her, an anger that made her feel larger than herself, larger than either of these men.

"Just a minute here," the baker said. "You want to pick up your three-day-old cake? That it? I don't want to argue with you, lady. There it sits over there, getting stale. I'll give it to you for half of what I quoted you. No. You want it? You can have it. It's no good to me, no good to anyone now. It cost me time and money to make that cake. If you want it, okay, if you don't, that's okay, too. I have to get back to work." He looked at them and rolled his tongue behind his teeth.

"More cakes," she said. She knew she was in control of it, of what was increasing in her. She was calm.

"Lady, I work sixteen hours a day in this place to earn a living," the baker said. He wiped his hands on his apron. "I work night and day in here, trying to make ends meet." A look crossed Ann's face that made the baker move back and say, "No trouble, now." He reached to the counter and picked up a rolling pin with his right hand and began to tap it against the palm of his other hand. "You want the cake or not? I have to get back to work. Bakers work at night," he said again. His eyes were small, mean-looking, she thought, nearly lost in the bristly flesh around his cheeks. His neck was thick with fat.

"I know bakers work at night," Ann said. "They make phone calls at night, too. You bastard," she said.

The baker continued to tap the rolling pin against his hand. He glanced at Howard. "Careful, careful," he said to Howard.

"My son's dead," she said with a cold, even finality. "He was hit by a car Monday morning. We've been waiting with him until he died. But, of course, you couldn't be expected to know that, could you? Bakers can't know everything—can they, Mr. Baker? But he's dead. He's dead, you bastard!" Just as suddenly as it had welled in her, the anger dwindled, gave way to something else, a dizzy feeling of nausea. She leaned against the wooden table that was sprinkled with flour, put her hands over her face, and began to cry, her shoulders rocking back and forth. "It isn't fair," she said. "It isn't, isn't fair."

Howard put his hand at the small of her back and looked at the baker. "Shame on you," Howard said to him. "Shame."

The baker put the rolling pin back on the counter. He undid his apron and threw it on the counter. He looked at them, and then he shook his head slowly. He pulled a chair out from under the card table that held papers and receipts, an adding machine, and a telephone directory. "Please sit down," he said. "Let me get you a chair," he said to Howard. "Sit down now, please." The baker went into the front of the shop and returned with two little wrought-iron chairs. "Please sit down, you people."

Ann wiped her eyes and looked at the baker. "I wanted to kill you," she said. "I wanted you dead."

The baker had cleared a space for them at the table. He shoved the adding machine to one side, along with the stacks of notepaper and receipts. He pushed the telephone directory onto the floor, where it landed with a thud. Howard and Ann sat down and pulled their chairs up to the table. The baker sat down, too.

"Let me say how sorry I am," the baker said, putting his elbows on the table. "God alone knows how sorry. Listen to me. I'm just a baker. I don't claim to be anything else. Maybe once, maybe years ago, I was a different kind of human being. I've forgotten, I don't know for sure. But I'm not any longer, if I ever was. Now I'm just a baker. That don't excuse my doing what I did, I know. But I'm deeply sorry. I'm sorry for your son, and sorry for my part in this," the baker said. He spread his hands out on the table and turned them over to reveal his palms. "I don't have any children myself, so I can only imagine what you must be feeling. All I can say to you now is that I'm sorry. Forgive me, if you can," the baker said. "I'm not an evil man, I don't think. Not evil, like you said on the phone. You got to understand what it comes down to is I don't know how to act anymore, it would seem. Please," the man said, "let me ask you if you can find it in your hearts to forgive me?"

It was warm inside the bakery. Howard stood up from the table and took off his coat. He helped Ann from her coat. The baker looked at them for a minute and then nodded and got up from the table. He went to the oven and turned off some switches. He found cups and poured coffee from an electric coffee-maker. He put a carton of cream on the table, and a bowl of sugar.

"You probably need to eat something," the baker said. "I hope you'll eat some of my hot rolls. You have to eat and keep going. Eating is a small, good thing in a time like this," he said.

He served them warm cinnamon rolls just out of the oven, the icing still runny. 185 He put butter on the table and knives to spread the butter. Then the baker sat down at the table with them. He waited. He waited until they each took a roll from the platter and began to eat. "It's good to eat something," he said, watching them. "There's more. Eat up. Eat all you want. There's all the rolls in the world in here."

They ate rolls and drank coffee. Ann was suddenly hungry, and the rolls were warm and sweet. She ate three of them, which pleased the baker. Then he began to talk. They listened carefully. Although they were tired and in anguish, they listened to what the baker had to say. They nodded when the baker began to speak of loneliness, and of the sense of doubt and limitation that had come to him in his middle years. He told them what it was like to be childless all these years. To repeat the days with the ovens endlessly full and endlessly empty. The party food, the celebrations he'd worked over. Icing knuckle-deep. The tiny wedding couples stuck into cakes. Hundreds of them, no, thousands by now. Birthdays. Just imagine all those candles burning. He had a necessary trade. He was a baker. He was glad he wasn't a florist. It was better to be feeding people. This was a better smell anytime than flowers.

"Smell this," the baker said, breaking open a dark loaf. "It's a heavy bread, but rich." They smelled it, then he had them taste it. It had the taste of molasses and coarse grains. They listened to him. They ate what they could. They swallowed the dark bread. It was like daylight under the fluorescent trays of light. They talked on into the early morning, the high, pale cast of light in the windows, and they did not think of leaving.

QUESTIONS

1. What is the point of view of "A Small, Good Thing"?
2. Describe the tone of Carver's story. To what extent do point of view and tone work together to produce an effect? How would you characterize that effect?
3. What does the story's setting contribute to its impact?
4. At what point in the story did you begin to feel that the doctor's reassurances no longer presaged a happy ending?
5. What motivates the Weisses in paragraph 163 to set out for the bakery?
6. What is ironic about the story's final scene? Where else in "A Small, Good Thing" do you find irony?
7. Does it seem to you that, besides telling a story, Carver is making some comment about contemporary life? If so, what is he saying?
8. What similarities do you find between this story and "Cathedral" (pages 259–270)?

Raymond Carver

WHERE I'M CALLING FROM   1983

J.P. and I are on the front porch at Frank Martin's drying-out facility. Like the rest of us at Frank Martin's, J.P. is first and foremost a drunk. But he's also a chimney sweep. It's his first time here, and he's scared. I've been here once before. What's to say? I'm back. J.P.'s real name is Joe Penny, but he says I should call him J.P. He's about thirty years old. Younger than I am. Not much younger, but a little. He's telling me how he decided to go into his line of work, and he wants to use his hands when he talks. But his hands tremble. I mean, they won't keep still. "This has never happened to me before," he says. He means the trembling. I tell him I sympathize. I tell him the shakes will idle down. And they will. But it takes time.

We've only been in here a couple of days. We're not out of the woods yet. J.P. has these shakes, and every so often a nerve—maybe it isn't a nerve, but it's something—begins to jerk in my shoulder. Sometimes it's at the side of my neck. When this happens, my mouth dries up. It's an effort just to swallow then. I know something's about to happen and I want to head it off. I want to hide from it, that's what I want to do. Just close my eyes and let it pass by, let it take the next man. J.P. can wait a minute.

I saw a seizure yesterday morning. A guy they call Tiny. A big fat guy, an electrician from Santa Rosa. They said he'd been in here for nearly two weeks and that he was over the hump. He was going home in a day or two and would spend New Year's Eve with his wife in front of the TV. On New Year's Eve, Tiny planned to drink hot chocolate and eat cookies. Yesterday morning he seemed just fine when he came down for breakfast. He was letting out with quacking noises, showing some guy how he called ducks right down onto his head. "Blam. Blam," said Tiny, picking off a couple. Tiny's hair was damp and was slicked back along the sides of his head. He'd just come out of the shower. He'd also nicked himself on the chin with his razor. But so what? Just about everybody at Frank Martin's has nicks on his face. It's something that happens. Tiny edged in at the head of the table and began telling about something that had happened on one of his drinking bouts. People at the table laughed and shook their heads as they shoveled up their eggs. Tiny would say something, grin, then look around the table for a sign of recognition. We'd all done things just as bad and crazy, so, sure, that's why we laughed. Tiny had scrambled eggs on his plate, and some biscuits and honey. I was at the table, but I wasn't hungry. I had some coffee in front of me. Suddenly, Tiny wasn't there anymore. He'd gone over in his chair with a big clatter. He was on his back on the floor with his eyes closed, his heels drumming the linoleum. People hollered for Frank Martin. But he was right there. A couple of guys got down on the floor beside Tiny. One of the guys put his fingers inside Tiny's mouth and tried to hold his tongue. Frank Martin yelled, "Everybody stand back!" Then I noticed that the bunch of us were leaning over Tiny, just looking at him, not able to take our eyes off him. "Give him air!" Frank Martin said. Then he ran into the office and called the ambulance.

Tiny is on board again today. Talk about bouncing back. This morning Frank Martin drove the station wagon to the hospital to get him. Tiny got back too late for his eggs, but he took some coffee into the dining room and sat down at the table anyway. Somebody in the kitchen made toast for him, but Tiny didn't eat it. He just sat with his coffee and looked into his cup. Every now and then he moved his cup back and forth in front of him.

I'd like to ask him if he had any signal just before it happened. I'd like to know if he felt his ticker skip a beat, or else begin to race. Did his eyelid twitch? But I'm not about to say anything. He doesn't look like he's hot to talk about it anyway. But what happened to Tiny is something I won't ever forget. Old Tiny flat on the floor, kicking his heels. So every time this little flitter starts up anywhere, I draw some breath and wait to find myself on my back, looking up, somebody's fingers in my mouth.

In his chair on the front porch, J.P. keeps his hands in his lap. I smoke cigarettes and use an old coal bucket for an ashtray. I listen to J.P. ramble on. It's eleven o'clock in the morning—an hour and a half until lunch. Neither one of us is hungry. But just the same we look forward to going inside and sitting down at the table. Maybe we'll get hungry.

What's J.P. talking about, anyway? He's saying how when he was twelve years old he fell into a well in the vicinity of the farm he grew up on. It was a dry well, lucky for him. "Or unlucky," he says, looking around him and shaking his head. He says how late that afternoon, after he'd been located, his dad hauled him out with a rope. J.P. had wet his pants down there. He'd suffered all kinds of terror in that well, hollering for help, waiting, and then hollering some more. He hollered himself hoarse before it was over. But he told me that being at the bottom of that well had made a lasting impression. He'd sat there and looked up at the well mouth. Way up at the top, he could see a circle of blue sky. Every once in a while a white cloud passed over. A flock of birds flew across, and it seemed to J.P. their wingbeats set up this odd commotion. He heard other things. He heard tiny rustlings above him in the well, which made him wonder if things might fall down into his hair. He was thinking of insects. He heard wind blow over the well mouth, and that sound made an impression on him, too. In short, everything about his life was different for him at the bottom of that well. But nothing fell on him and nothing closed off that little circle of blue. Then his dad came along with the rope, and it wasn't long before J.P. was back in the world he'd always lived in.

"Keep talking, J.P. Then what?" I say.

When he was eighteen or nineteen years old and out of high school and had nothing whatsoever he wanted to do with his life, he went across town one afternoon to visit a friend. This friend lived in a house with a fireplace. J.P. and his friend sat around drinking beer and batting the breeze. They played some records. Then the doorbell rings. The friend goes to the door. This young woman chimney sweep is there with her cleaning things. She's wearing a top hat, the sight of which knocked J.P. for a loop. She tells J.P.'s friend that she has an appointment to clean the fireplace. The friend lets her in and bows. The young woman doesn't pay him any mind. She spreads a blanket on the hearth and lays out her gear. She's wearing these black pants, black shirt, black shoes and socks. Of course, by now she's taken her hat off. J.P. says it nearly drove him nuts to look at her. She does the work, she cleans the chimney, while J.P. and his friend play records and drink beer. But they watch her and they watch what she does. Now and then J.P. and his friend look at each other and grin, or else they wink. They raise their eyebrows when the upper half of the young woman disappears into the chimney. She was all-right looking, too, J.P. said.

When she'd finished her work, she rolled her things up in the blanket. From J.P.'s friend, she took a check that had been made out to her by his parents. And

10

then she asks the friend if he wants to kiss her. "It's supposed to bring good luck," she says. That does it for J.P. The friend rolls his eyes. He clowns some more. Then, probably blushing, he kisses her on the cheek. At this minute, J.P. made his mind up about something. He put his beer down. He got up from the sofa. He went over to the young woman as she was starting to go out the door.

"Me, too?" J.P. said to her.

She swept her eyes over him. J.P. says he could feel his heart knocking. The young woman's name, it turns out, is Roxy.

"Sure," Roxy says. "Why not? I've got some extra kisses." And she kissed him a good one right on the lips and then turned to go.

Like that, quick as a wink, J.P. followed her onto the porch. He held the porch screen door for her. He went down the steps with her and out to the drive, where she'd parked her panel truck. It was something that was out of his hands. Nothing else in the world counted for anything. He knew he'd met somebody who could set his legs atremble. He could feel her kiss still burning on his lips, etc. J.P. couldn't begin to sort anything out. He was filled with sensations that were carrying him every which way.

He opened the rear door of the panel truck for her. He helped her store her things inside. "Thanks," she told him. Then he blurted it out—that he'd like to see her again. Would she go to a movie with him sometime? He'd realized, too, what he wanted to do with his life. He wanted to do what she did. He wanted to be a chimney sweep. But he didn't tell her that then.

J.P. says she put her hands on her hips and looked him over. Then she found a business card in the front seat of her truck. She gave it to him. She said, "Call this number after ten tonight. We can talk. I have to go now." She put the top hat on and then took it off. She looked at J.P. once more. She must have liked what she saw, because this time she grinned. He told her there was a smudge near her mouth. Then she got into her truck, tooted the horn, and drove away.

"Then what?" I say. "Don't stop now, J.P."

I was interested. But I would have listened if he'd been going on about how one day he'd decided to start pitching horseshoes.

It rained last night. The clouds are banked up against the hills across the valley. J.P. clears his throat and looks at the hills and the clouds. He pulls his chin. Then he goes on with what he was saying.

Roxy starts going out with him on dates. And little by little he talks her into letting him go along on jobs with her. But Roxy's in business with her father and brother and they've got just the right amount of work. They don't need anybody else. Besides, who was this guy J.P.? J.P. what? Watch out, they warned her.

So she and J.P. saw some movies together. They went to a few dances. But mainly the courtship revolved around their cleaning chimneys together. Before you know it, J.P. says, they're talking about tying the knot. And after a while they do it, they get married. J.P.'s new father-in-law takes him in as a full partner. In a year or so, Roxy has a kid. She's quit being a chimney sweep. At any rate, she's quit doing the work. Pretty soon she has another kid. J.P.'s in his mid-twenties

15

20

by now. He's buying a house. He says he was happy with his life. "I was happy with the way things were going," he says. "I had everything I wanted. I had a wife and kids I loved, and I was doing what I wanted to do with my life." But for some reason—who knows why we do what we do?—his drinking picks up. For a long time he drinks beer and beer only. Any kind of beer—it didn't matter. He says he could drink beer twenty-four hours a day. He'd drink beer at night while he watched TV. Sure, once in a while he drank hard stuff. But that was only if they went out on the town, which was not often, or else when they had company over. Then a time comes, he doesn't know why, when he makes the switch from beer to gin-and-tonic. And he'd have more gin-and-tonic after dinner, sitting in front of the TV. There was always a glass of gin-and-tonic in his hand. He says he actually liked the taste of it. He began stopping off after work for drinks before he went home to have more drinks. Then he began missing some dinners. He just wouldn't show up. Or else he'd show up, but he wouldn't want anything to eat. He'd filled up on snacks at the bar. Sometimes he'd walk in the door and for no good reason throw his lunch pail across the living room. When Roxy yelled at him, he'd turn around and go out again. He moved his drinking time up to early afternoon, while he was still supposed to be working. He tells me that he was starting off the morning with a couple of drinks. He'd have a belt of the stuff before he brushed his teeth. Then he'd have his coffee. He'd go to work with a thermos bottle of vodka in his lunch pail.

J.P. quits talking. He just clams up. What's going on? I'm listening. It's helping me relax, for one thing. It's taking me away from my own situation. After a minute, I say, "What the hell? Go on, J.P." He's pulling his chin. But pretty soon he starts talking again.

J.P. and Roxy are having some real fights now. I mean *fights*. J.P. says that one time she hit him in the face with her fist and broke his nose. "Look at this," he says. "Right here." He shows me a line across the bridge of his nose. "That's a broken nose." He returned the favor. He dislocated her shoulder for her. Another time he split her lip. They beat on each other in front of the kids. Things got out of hand. But he kept on drinking. He couldn't stop. And nothing could make him stop. Not even with Roxy's dad and her brother threatening to beat the hell out of him. They told Roxy she should take the kids and clear out. But Roxy said it was her problem. She got herself into it, and she'd solve it.

Now J.P. gets real quiet again. He hunches his shoulders and pulls down in his chair. He watches a car driving down the road between this place and the hills.

I say, "I want to hear the rest of this, J.P. You better keep talking." 25

"I just don't know," he says. He shrugs.

"It's all right," I say. And I mean it's okay for him to tell it. "Go on, J.P."

One way she tried to fix things, J.P. says, was by finding a boyfriend. J.P. would like to know how she found the time with the house and kids.

I look at him and I'm surprised. He's a grown man. "If you want to do that," I say, "you find the time. You make the time."

J.P. shakes his head. "I guess so," he says. 30

Anyway, he found out about it—about Roxy's boyfriend—and he went wild. He manages to get Roxy's wedding ring off her finger. And when he does, he cuts it into several pieces with a pair of wire-cutters. Good, solid fun. They'd already gone a couple of rounds on this occasion. On his way to work the next morning, he gets arrested on a drunk charge. He loses his driver's license. He can't drive the truck to work anymore. Just as well, he says. He'd already fallen off a roof the week before and broken his thumb. It was just a matter of time until he broke his neck, he says.

He was here at Frank Martin's to dry out and to figure how to get his life back on track. But he wasn't here against his will, any more than I was. We weren't locked up. We could leave any time we wanted. But a minimum stay of a week was recommended, and two weeks or a month was, as they put it, "strongly advised."

As I said, this is my second time at Frank Martin's. When I was trying to sign a check to pay in advance for a week's stay, Frank Martin said, "The holidays are always bad. Maybe you should think of sticking around a little longer this time? Think in terms of a couple of weeks. Can you do a couple of weeks? Think about it, anyway. You don't have to decide anything right now," he said. He held his thumb on the check and I signed my name. Then I walked my girlfriend to the front door and said goodbye. "Goodbye," she said, and she lurched into the door-jamb and then onto the porch. It's late afternoon. It's raining. I go from the door to the window. I move the curtain and watch her drive away. She's in my car. She's drunk. But I'm drunk, too, and there's nothing I can do. I make it to a big chair that's close to the radiator, and I sit down. Some guys look up from their TV. Then they shift back to what they were watching. I just sit there. Now and then I look up at something that's happening on the screen.

Later that afternoon the front door banged open and J.P. was brought in between these two big guys—his father-in-law and brother-in-law, I find out afterward. They steered J.P. across the room. The old guy signed him in and gave Frank Martin a check. Then these two guys helped J.P. upstairs. I guess they put him to bed. Pretty soon the old guy and the other guy came downstairs and headed for the front door. They couldn't seem to get out of this place fast enough. It was like they couldn't wait to wash their hands of all this. I didn't blame them. Hell, no. I don't know how I'd act if I was in their shoes.

A day and a half later J.P. and I meet up on the front porch. We shake hands and comment on the weather. J.P. has a case of the shakes. We sit down and prop our feet up on the railing. We lean back in our chairs like we're just out there taking our ease, like we might be getting ready to talk about our bird dogs. That's when J.P. gets going with his story.

It's cold out, but not too cold. It's a little overcast. Frank Martin comes outside to finish his cigar. He has on a sweater buttoned all the way up. Frank Martin is short and heavy. He has curly gray hair and a small head. His head is too small for the rest of his body. Frank Martin puts the cigar in his mouth and stands with his arms crossed over his chest. He works that cigar in his mouth and looks across the valley. He stands there like a prizefighter, like somebody who knows the score.

J.P. gets quiet again. I mean, he's hardly breathing. I toss my cigarette into the coal bucket and look hard at J.P., who scoots farther down in his chair. J.P. pulls up his collar. What the hell's going on? I wonder. Frank Martin uncrosses his arms and takes a puff on the cigar. He lets the smoke carry out of his mouth. Then he raises his chin toward the hills and says, "Jack London used to have a big place on the other side of this valley. Right over there behind that green hill you're looking at. But alcohol killed him. Let that be a lesson to you. He was a better man than any of us. But he couldn't handle the stuff, either." Frank Martin looks at what's left of his cigar. It's gone out. He tosses it into the bucket. "You guys want to read something while you're here, read that book of his, *The Call of the Wild*. You know the one I'm talking about? We have it inside if you want to read something. It's about this animal that's half dog and half wolf. End of sermon," he says, and then hitches his pants up and tugs his sweater down. "I'm going inside," he says. "See you at lunch."

"I feel like a bug when he's around," J.P. says. "He makes me feel like a bug." J.P. shakes his head. Then he says, "Jack London. What a name! I wish I had me a name like that. Instead of the name I got."

My wife brought me up here the first time. That's when we were still together, trying to make things work out. She brought me here and she stayed around for an hour or two, talking to Frank Martin in private. Then she left. The next morning Frank Martin got me aside and said, "We can help you. If you want help and want to listen to what we say." But I didn't know if they could help me or not. Part of me wanted help. But there was another part.

This time around, it was my girlfriend who drove me here. She was driving 40 my car. She drove us through a rainstorm. We drank champagne all the way. We were both drunk when she pulled up in the drive. She intended to drop me off, turn around, and drive home again. She had things to do. One thing she had to do was to go to work the next day. She was a secretary. She had an okay job with this electronic-parts firm. She also had this mouthy teenaged son. I wanted her to get a room in town, spend the night, and then drive home. I don't know if she got the room or not. I haven't heard from her since she led me up the front steps the other day and walked me into Frank Martin's office and said, "Guess who's here."

But I wasn't mad at her. In the first place, she didn't have any idea what she was letting herself in for when she said I could stay with her after my wife asked me to leave. I felt sorry for her. The reason I felt sorry for her was that on the day before Christmas her Pap smear came back, and the news was not cheery. She'd have to go back to the doctor, and real soon. That kind of news was reason enough for both of us to start drinking. So what we did was get ourselves good and drunk. And on Christmas Day we were still drunk. We had to go out to a restaurant to eat, because she didn't feel like cooking. The two of us and her mouthy teenaged son opened some presents, and then we went to this steakhouse near her apartment. I wasn't hungry. I had some soup and a hot roll. I drank a bottle of wine with the soup. She drank some wine, too. Then we started in on Bloody Marys. For the next couple of days, I didn't eat anything except salted nuts. But I drank a lot of bourbon. Then I said to her, "Sugar, I think I'd better pack up. I better go back to Frank Martin's."

She tried to explain to her son that she was going to be gone for a while and he'd have to get his own food. But right as we were going out the door, this mouthy kid screamed at us. He screamed, "The hell with you! I hope you never come back. I hope you kill yourselves!" Imagine this kid!

Before we left town, I had her stop at the package store, where I bought us the champagne. We stopped someplace else for plastic glasses. Then we picked up a bucket of fried chicken. We set out for Frank Martin's in this rainstorm, drinking and listening to music. She drove. I looked after the radio and poured. We tried to make a little party of it. But we were sad, too. There was that fried chicken, but we didn't eat any.

I guess she got home okay. I think I would have heard something if she didn't. But she hasn't called me, and I haven't called her. Maybe she's had some news about herself by now. Then again, maybe she hasn't heard anything. Maybe it was all a mistake. Maybe it was somebody else's smear. But she has my car, and I have things at her house. I know we'll be seeing each other again.

They clang an old farm bell here to call you for mealtime. J.P. and I get out 45 of our chairs and we go inside. It's starting to get too cold on the porch, anyway. We can see our breath drifting out from us as we talk.

New Year's Eve morning I try to call my wife. There's no answer. It's okay. But even if it wasn't okay, what am I supposed to do? The last time we talked on the phone, a couple of weeks ago, we screamed at each other. I hung a few names on her. "Wet brain!" she said, and put the phone back where it belonged.

But I wanted to talk to her now. Something had to be done about my stuff. I still had things at her house, too.

One of the guys here is a guy who travels. He goes to Europe and places. That's what he says, anyway. Business, he says. He also says he has his drinking under control and he doesn't have any idea why he's here at Frank Martin's. But he doesn't remember getting here. He laughs about it, about his not remembering. "Anyone can have a blackout," he says. "That doesn't prove a thing." He's not a drunk—he tells us this and we listen. "That's a serious charge to make," he says. "That kind of talk can ruin a good man's prospects." He says that if he'd only stick to whiskey and water, no ice, he'd never have these blackouts. It's the ice they put into your drink that does it. "Who do you know in Egypt?" he asks me. "I can use a few names over there."

For New Year's Eve dinner Frank Martin serves steak and baked potato. My appetite's coming back. I clean up everything on my plate and I could eat more. I look over at Tiny's plate. Hell, he's hardly touched a thing. His steak is just sitting there. Tiny is not the same old Tiny. The poor bastard had planned to be at home tonight. He'd planned to be in his robe and slippers in front of the TV, holding hands with his wife. Now he's afraid to leave. I can understand. One seizure means you're ready for another. Tiny hasn't told any more nutty stories on himself since it happened. He's stayed quiet and kept to himself. I ask him if I can have his steak, and he pushes his plate over to me.

Some of us are still up, sitting around the TV, watching Times Square, when 50 Frank Martin comes in to show us his cake. He brings it around and shows it to each of us. I know he didn't make it. It's just a bakery cake. But it's still a cake. It's a big white cake. Across the top there's writing in pink letters. The writing says, HAPPY NEW YEAR—ONE DAY AT A TIME.

"I don't want any fucking cake," says the guy who goes to Europe and places. "Where's the champagne?" he says, and laughs.

We all go into the dining room. Frank Martin cuts the cake. I sit next to J.P. He eats two pieces and drinks a Coke. I eat a piece and wrap another piece in a napkin, thinking of later.

J.P. lights a cigarette—his hands are steady now—and he tells me his wife is coming in the morning, the first day of the new year.

"That's great," I say. I nod. I lick the frosting off my finger. "That's good news, J.P."

"I'll introduce you," he says.   55

"I look forward to it," I say.

We say goodnight. We say Happy New Year. I use a napkin on my fingers. We shake hands.

I go to the phone, put in a dime, and call my wife collect. But nobody answers this time, either. I think about calling my girlfriend, and I'm dialing her number when I realize I really don't want to talk to her. She's probably at home watching the same thing on TV that I've been watching. Anyway, I don't want to talk to her. I hope she's okay. But if she has something wrong with her, I don't want to know about it.

After breakfast, J.P. and I take coffee out to the porch. The sky is clear, but it's cold enough for sweaters and jackets.

"She asked me if she should bring the kids," J.P. says. "I told her she should   60 keep the kids at home. Can you imagine? My God, I don't want my kids up here."

We use the coal bucket for an ashtray. We look across the valley to where Jack London used to live. We're drinking more coffee when this car turns off the road and comes down the drive.

"That's her!" J.P. says. He puts his cup next to his chair. He gets up and goes down the steps.

I see this woman stop the car and set the brake. I see J.P. open the door. I watch her get out, and I see them hug each other. I look away. Then I look back. J.P. takes her by the arm and they come up the stairs. This woman broke a man's nose once. She has had two kids, and much trouble, but she loves this man who has her by the arm. I get up from the chair.

"This is my friend," J.P. says to his wife. "Hey, this is Roxy."

Roxy takes my hand. She's a tall, good-looking woman in a knit cap. She   65 has on a coat, a heavy sweater, and slacks. I recall what J.P. told me about the boyfriend and the wire-cutters. I don't see any wedding ring. That's in pieces somewhere, I guess. Her hands are broad and the fingers have these big knuckles. This is a woman who can make fists if she has to.

"I've heard about you," I say. "J.P. told me how you got acquainted. Something about a chimney, J.P. said."

"Yes, a chimney," she says. "There's probably a lot else he didn't tell you," she says. "I bet he didn't tell you everything," she says, and laughs. Then—she can't wait any longer—she slips her arm around J.P. and kisses him on the cheek. They start to move to the door. "Nice meeting you," she says. "Hey, did he tell you he's the best sweep in the business?"

"Come on now, Roxy," J.P. says. He has his hand on the doorknob.

"He told me he learned everything he knew from you," I say.

"Well, that much is sure true," she says. She laughs again. But it's like she's thinking about something else. J.P. turns the doorknob. Roxy lays her hand over his. "Joe, can't we go into town for lunch? Can't I take you someplace?" 70

J.P. clears his throat. He says, "It hasn't been a week yet." He takes his hand off the doorknob and brings his fingers to his chin. "I think they'd like it if I didn't leave the place for a little while yet. We can have some coffee here," he says.

"That's fine," she says. Her eyes work over to me again. "I'm glad Joe's made a friend. Nice to meet you," she says.

They start to go inside. I know it's a dumb thing to do, but I do it anyway. "Roxy," I say. And they stop in the doorway and look at me. "I need some luck," I say. "No kidding. I could do with a kiss myself."

J.P. looks down. He's still holding the knob, even though the door is open. He turns the knob back and forth. But I keep looking at her. Roxy grins. "I'm not a sweep anymore," she says. "Not for years. Didn't Joe tell you that? But, sure, I'll kiss you, sure."

She moves over. She takes me by the shoulders—I'm a big man—and she plants this kiss on my lips. "How's that?" she says. 75

"That's fine," I say.

"Nothing to it," she says. She's still holding me by the shoulders. She's looking me right in the eyes. "Good luck," she says, and then she lets go of me.

"See you later, pal," J.P. says. He opens the door all the way, and they go in.

I sit down on the front steps and light a cigarette. I watch what my hand does, then I blow out the match. I've got the shakes. I started out with them this morning. This morning I wanted something to drink. It's depressing, but I didn't say anything about it to J.P. I try to put my mind on something else.

I'm thinking about chimney sweeps—all that stuff I heard from J.P.—when for some reason I start to think about a house my wife and I once lived in. That 80 house didn't have a chimney, so I don't know what makes me remember it now. But I remember the house and how we'd only been in there a few weeks when I heard a noise outside one morning. It was Sunday morning and it was still dark in the bedroom. But there was this pale light coming in from the bedroom window. I listened. I could hear something scrape against the side of the house. I jumped out of bed and went to look.

"My God!" my wife says, sitting up in bed and shaking the hair away from her face. Then she starts to laugh. "It's Mr. Venturini," she says. "I forgot to tell you. He said he was coming to paint the house today. Early. Before it gets too hot. I forgot all about it," she says, and laughs. "Come on back to bed, honey. It's just him."

"In a minute," I say.

I push the curtain away from the window. Outside, this old guy in white coveralls is standing next to his ladder. The sun is just starting to break above the mountains. The old guy and I look each other over. It's the landlord, all right—this old guy in coveralls. But his coveralls are too big for him. He needs a shave, too. And he's wearing this baseball cap to cover his bald head. Goddamn it, I think, if he isn't a weird old fellow. And a wave of happiness comes over me that I'm not him—that I'm me and that I'm inside this bedroom with my wife.

He jerks his thumb toward the sun. He pretends to wipe his forehead. He's letting me know he doesn't have all that much time. He breaks into a grin. It's then I realize I'm naked. I look down at myself. I look at him again and shrug. What did he expect?

My wife laughs. "Come *on*," she says. "Get back in this bed. Right now. This minute. Come on back to bed." 85

I let go of the curtain. But I keep standing there at the window. I can see the old fellow nod to himself like he's saying, "Go on, sonny, go back to bed. I understand." He tugs on the bill of his cap. Then he sets about his business. He picks up his bucket. He starts climbing the ladder.

I lean back into the step behind me now and cross one leg over the other. Maybe later this afternoon I'll try calling my wife again. And then I'll call to see what's happening with my girlfriend. But I don't want to get her mouthy kid on the line. If I do call, I hope he'll be out somewhere doing whatever he does when he's not around the house. I try to remember if I ever read any Jack London books. I can't remember. But there was a story of his I read in high school. "To Build a Fire," it was called. This guy in the Yukon is freezing. Imagine it—he's actually going to freeze to death if he can't get a fire going. With a fire, he can dry his socks and things and warm himself.

He gets his fire going, but then something happens to it. A branchful of snow drops on it. It goes out. Meanwhile, it's getting colder. Night is coming on.

I bring some change out of my pocket. I'll try my wife first. If she answers, I'll wish her a Happy New Year. But that's it. I won't bring up business. I won't raise my voice. Not even if she starts something. She'll ask me where I'm calling from, and I'll have to tell her. I won't say anything about New Year's resolutions. There's no way to make a joke out of this. After I talk to her, I'll call my girlfriend. Maybe I'll call her first. I'll just have to hope I don't get her kid on the line. "Hello, sugar," I'll say when she answers. "It's me."

Questions

1. In paragraph 2 the narrator expresses a wish to hide from what is "about to happen." Do you think the reader is meant to regard this as a healthy or an unhealthy reaction? Explain.
2. What effect does Tiny's seizure have on the other patients at Frank Martin's drying-out facility? How does the narrator, in particular, react? To what other event in the story does he react in similar fashion?
3. Reread J.P.'s tale about falling down a well when he was twelve. What parallels can you find between that experience and his stay at Frank Martin's?
4. How do you explain Roxy's impact first on J.P. and then on the narrator?

5. Explain the references to Jack London in Carver's story. What "sermon" are J.P. and the narrator supposed to find in Frank Martin's reference to *The Call of the Wild?* How would you explain the narrator's response to his memory of "To Build a Fire" (in this book, pp. 87–98)?
6. Most readers consider Carver's story a life-affirming one. How does the ending appear to signal hope for both J.P. and the narrator?

SUGGESTIONS FOR WRITING: *On Raymond Carver*

1. After reading the three Carver stories in this book, write a response to the critic who said, "Carver doesn't write stories at all, just rambling, simpleminded anecdotes about not much of anything. They lack plot, style, theme, irony, and symbolism—in short, everything that makes fiction worthy of notice. So drab, obtuse, and lacking in moral sensibility are the characters he creates that it's impossible to care about any of them. With Carver, fiction is going to the dogs."
2. Imagining that Raymond Carver is still alive and that you are he, write a plot outline, a statement of theme, and an opening paragraph for your next story. Who will the characters be? What will happen to them? From what sources will the story's main conflict stem? How will the conflict be resolved? As you work, keep in mind that the object of this exercise is not to embark on a deathless work of literature but rather to demonstrate your awareness of the elements that make up a typical Carver story.
3. Compare and contrast Carver's "A Small, Good Thing" with either Anne Tyler's "Average Waves in Unprotected Waters" or Tillie Olsen's "I Stand Here Ironing." Focusing especially on matters of tone and style, point of view, and character development, ask yourself: What are the similarities between the two stories? What important differences throw light on each writer's aims and methods?
4. After consulting "Writing about a Story" in the Supplement: Writing, where you will find directions for writing a card report, make an analysis of any one of the Carver stories in this book, terse enough to fit on an index card no larger than 5 x 8 inches.

Anton Chekhov

THE DARLING   1898

Translated by Ann Dunnigan

Anton Chekhov (1860–1904), one of the Russian writers who helped shape modern fiction, is remembered especially for his plays and short stories. Born in the provincial town of Taganrog, the grandson of a serf who had bought his own freedom, Chekhov as a boy worked in his father's general store, a hangout for vodka-drinking storytellers. As a young man, he studied at Moscow University and became a doctor of medicine. To earn money while a medical student, he wrote his first stories for magazines. By 1886, his work had become so celebrated that he gave up medicine for writing, though continuing to treat

Anton Chekhov

sick peasants at his home without fee and to work in clinics during times of famine and epidemic. From 1896 to 1904, Chekhov wrote his great plays for the Moscow Art Theater, where they were directed by the influential director Konstantin Stanislavsky: The Seagull, The Cherry Orchard, Uncle Vanya, *and* The Three Sisters. *Chekhov's last years were brightened by his marriage to Olga Knipper, a star of the theater company. He died at 44, after a long struggle against tuberculosis.*

Olenka, the daughter of the retired collegiate assessor Plemyannikov, was sitting on the little porch that faced the courtyard, lost in thought. It was hot, the flies were annoyingly persistent, and it was pleasant to think that it would soon be evening. Dark rain clouds were gathering from the east, bringing with them an occasional breath of moisture.

Kukin, a theater manager who ran an amusement garden known as the Tivoli, and who lodged in the wing of the house, was standing in the middle of the courtyard staring up at the sky.

"Again!" he said in despair. "It's going to rain again! Every day it rains; every day, as if to spite me! I might just as well put a noose around my neck! It's ruin! Every day terrible losses!"

He clasped his hands, turned to Olenka and went on, "That's our life for you, Olga Semyonovna. It's enough to make you weep! You work, you do your very best, you worry and lose sleep, always thinking how to make it better—and what happens? On the one hand, the public is ignorant, barbarous. I give them the very best operetta, a pantomime, magnificent vaudeville artists—but do you think that's what they want? Do you think they understand it? What they want is slapstick! Give them trash! And then, look at the weather! Rain almost every evening. It started the tenth of May and it's been raining incessantly ever since—all May and June. Simply dreadful! The public doesn't come, but I still have to pay the rent, don't I—and the artists?"

The next day toward evening the clouds again appeared, and, laughing hysterically, Kukin said, "Well, go on, rain! Flood the whole park, drown me! Bad luck to me in this world and the next! Let the artists sue me! Let them send me to prison—to Siberia—to the scaffold! Ha! Ha! Ha!"

And the third day it was the same. . . .

Olenka listened to Kukin gravely, silently, and sometimes tears would come into her eyes. She was so moved by his misfortunes that she ended by falling in love with him. He was an emaciated little man with a yellow face and hair combed down over his temples; he spoke in a thin tenor voice, twisting his mouth to one side, and despair was permanently engraved on his face; nevertheless, he aroused a deep and genuine feeling in her. She was always in love with someone and could not live otherwise. First it had been her papa, who was now ill and sat in an armchair in a darkened room, breathing with difficulty; then it had been her aunt, who used to come from Bryansk every other year; and before that, when she was at school, she had been in love with her French teacher. She was a quiet, good-natured, compassionate girl with meek, gentle eyes and very good health. At the sight of her full, rosy cheeks, her soft, white neck with a dark little mole on it, and the kind, ingenuous smile that came over her face when she listened to anything pleasant, men thought, "Yes, not bad!" and smiled too, while the ladies present could not refrain from suddenly seizing her hand in the middle of a conversation and exclaiming in an outburst of delight, "You darling!"

The house she had lived in since birth, and which, according to her father's will, was to be hers, was located on the outskirts of the city on Gypsy Road, not far from the Tivoli. In the evenings and at night when she heard the band playing and skyrockets exploding, it seemed to her that it was Kukin at war with his fate, assaulting his chief enemy, the apathetic public; then her heart melted, she had no desire to sleep, and when he returned home at daybreak she would tap softly at her bedroom window and, letting him see only her face and one shoulder through the curtain, would smile tenderly at him. . . .

He proposed to her and they were married. And when he had a good look at her neck and her plump, fine shoulders, he clapped his hands together and exclaimed, "Darling!"

He was happy, but as it rained both the day and the night of the wedding, 10 his expression of despair remained unchanged.

They got on well together. She presided over the box office, looked after things in the garden, kept the accounts and paid the salaries; and her rosy cheeks, her sweet, artless smile, shone now in the box-office window, now in the wings of the theater, now at the buffet. She began telling her friends that the most remarkable, the most important and essential thing in the whole world was the theater— that only through the theater could one derive true pleasure and become a cultivated and humane person.

"But do you suppose the public understands that?" she would ask. "What it wants is slapstick! Yesterday we gave *Faust Inside Out,* and almost every box was empty, but if Vanichka and I had put on some kind of trash, then, believe me, the theater would have been packed. Tomorrow Vanichka and I are putting on *Orpheus in Hell.* Do come."

Whatever Kukin said about the theater and the actors she repeated. Like him she despised the public for its ignorance and indifference to art; she took a hand in the rehearsals, correcting the actors, kept an eye on the conduct of the musicians, and when there was an unfavorable notice in the local newspaper, shed tears, and then went to the editor for an explanation.

The actors loved her and called her "Vanichka and I" and "the darling." She was sorry for them and used to lend them small sums of money, and if they deceived her she wept in secret but did not complain to her husband.

They got on well in the winter too. They leased the municipal theater for 15 the season and sublet it for short periods to a Ukrainian troupe, a magician, or a local dramatic club. Olenka grew plumper and was always beaming with satisfaction, while Kukin grew thinner and yellower and complained of terrible losses, although business was not bad during the winter. He coughed at night and she would give him an infusion of raspberries and linden blossoms, rub him with eau de Cologne, and wrap him in her soft shawls.

"What a sweet precious you are!" she would say with perfect sincerity, as she stroked his hair. "My handsome pet!"

At Lent he went to Moscow to gather a new troupe, and without him she could not sleep, but sat all night at the window looking at the stars. She likened herself to the hens, which also stay awake all night and are uneasy when the cock is not in the henhouse. Kukin was detained in Moscow, wrote that he would return by Easter, and in his letters sent instructions regarding the Tivoli. But on the Monday of Passion Week°, late in the evening, there was a sudden, ominous knocking at the gate; someone was hammering at the wicket as if it were a barrel— boom! boom! boom! The sleepy cook, splashing through the puddles in her bare feet, ran to open the gate.

"Open, please!" said someone on the other side of the gate in a deep bass voice. "There is a telegram for you!"

Olenka had received telegrams from her husband before, but this time for some reason she felt numb with fright. She opened the telegram with trembling hands and read:

> IVAN PETROVICH DIED SUDDENLY TODAY AWAIT-
> ING THISD INSTRUCTIONS FUFUNERAL TUESDAY.

That was exactly the way the telegram had it: "fufuneral" and the incom- 20 prehensible word "thisd"; it was signed by the director of the operetta company.

"My precious!" Olenka sobbed. "Vanichka, my precious, my dearest! Why did we ever meet? Why did I know you and love you? Whom can your poor forsaken Olenka turn to now?"

Kukin was buried on Tuesday in the Vagankovo cemetery in Moscow. Olenka returned home on Wednesday, and as soon as she reached her room sank onto the bed and sobbed so loudly that she could be heard in the street and in the neighboring courtyards.

"The darling!" said the neighbors, crossing themselves. "Darling Olga Semyonovna! Poor soul, how she grieves!"

Three months later Olenka was returning from mass one day, in deep mourning and very sad. It happened that one of her neighbors, Vasily Andreich Pustovalov, the manager of Babakayev's lumberyard, was also returning from church and walked with her. He wore a straw hat, a white waistcoat with a gold watch chain, and looked more like a landowner than a merchant.

"Everything happens as it is ordained, Olga Semyonovna," he said gravely, 25 with a note of sympathy in his voice, "and if one of our dear ones passes on, we must take ourselves in hand and bear it submissively."

Having seen Olenka to her gate, he said good-bye and went on. All day long she seemed to hear his grave voice, and as soon as she closed her eyes she dreamed of his dark beard. She liked him very much. And apparently she had made an

Passion Week: week preceding Easter.

impression on him too, because not long afterwards an elderly lady whom she scarcely knew came to have coffee with her, and as soon as she was seated at the table began to talk of Pustovalov, saying that he was a fine steady man and that any marriageable woman would be happy to marry him. Three days later Pustovalov himself paid her a visit. He did not stay long, not more than ten minutes, and said little, but Olenka fell in love with him—she was so much in love that she lay awake all night, inflamed as with a fever, and in the morning she sent for the elderly lady. The betrothal was arranged, and the wedding followed soon afterwards.

After they were married Pustovalov and Olenka got on very well together. As a rule he was in the lumberyard till dinnertime, then he went out on business and Olenka took his place and sat in the office till evening, making out bills and dispatching orders.

"Every year the price of lumber rises twenty per cent," she would say to customers and acquaintances. "Why, we used to deal in local timber, but now Vasichka has to travel to the province of Mogilev every year for wood. And the freight!" she would add, covering her cheeks with her hands in horror. "The freight!"

It seemed to her that she had been in the lumber business for ages and ages, that lumber was the most important and essential thing in life, and she found something touching, dear to her, in such words as girder, beam, plank, batten, boxboard, lath, scantling, slab. . . . At night she would dream of whole mountains of boards and planks, long endless caravans of wagons carrying lumber to some distant place; she dreamed of a whole regiment of 8-inch beams 28 feet long standing on end, marching on the lumberyard, beams, girders, slabs, striking against one another with the hollow sound of dry wood, all falling, then rising, piling themselves one upon another. . . . When she cried out in her sleep Pustovalov would speak to her tenderly, saying, "Olenka, what's the matter, darling? Cross yourself!"

Whatever ideas her husband had became her own. If he thought the room was hot or business was slow, she thought so too. Her husband did not care for entertainment of any kind, and on holidays stayed at home, and so did she.

"You are always at home or in the office," her friends said to her. "You ought to go to the theater, darling, or to the circus."

"Vasichka and I have no time for the theater," she would reply sedately. "We are working people, we're not interested in such foolishness. What's the good of those theaters?"

On Saturday evenings they would go to vespers, on holidays to early mass, and as they walked home side by side their faces reflected the emotion of the service. There was an agreeable aroma about them both, and her silk dress rustled pleasantly. At home they had tea and buns with various kinds of jam, and afterwards a pie. Every day at noon, in the yard and beyond the gate in the street, there was a delicious smell of borsch and roast lamb or duck and, on fast days, fish; no one could pass their gate without feeling hungry. In the office the samovar was always boiling and the customers were treated to tea and cracknels°. Once a week they went to the baths and returned side by side, both very red.

cracknels: hard, crusty biscuits.

"Yes, everything goes well with us, thank God," Olenka would say to her friends. "I wish everyone were as happy as Vasichka and I."

When Pustovalov went to the province of Mogilev to buy timber, she missed 35 him dreadfully, and lay awake nights crying. Sometimes in the evening Smirnin, a young army veterinarian to whom they rented the wing of the house, came to see her. They chatted or played cards, and this diverted her. She was especially interested in what he told her of his domestic life. He was married and had a son, but was separated from his wife because she had been unfaithful to him, and now he hated her; he sent her forty rubles a month for the support of the child. Listening to all this, Olenka sighed, shook her head, and was sorry for him.

"Well, God keep you," she would say, accompanying him to the stairs with a candle. "Thank you for passing the time with me, and may the Queen of Heaven give you health."

She always expressed herself in this grave, circumspect manner in imitation of her husband. Just as the veterinarian was about to disappear behind the door below, she would call to him and say, "You know, Vladimir Platonych, you ought to make it up with your wife. For your son's sake, you should forgive her! The little fellow probably understands everything."

When Pustovalov returned she would tell him in a low voice all about the veterinarian and his unhappy life, and they both would sigh, shake their heads, and talk about the little boy, who very likely missed his father. Then, by some strange association of ideas, they both stood before the icons°, bowed to the ground, and prayed that God would send them children.

Thus the Pustovalovs lived quietly and peaceably, in love and complete harmony for six years. Then one winter day, after drinking hot tea in the office, Vasily Andreich went out without his cap to dispatch some lumber, caught cold, and was taken ill. He was treated by the best doctors, but the illness had its way with him, and after four months he died. And again Olenka was a widow.

"Whom can I turn to, my darling?" she sobbed, after burying her husband. 40 "How can I live without you, miserable and unhappy as I am? Good people, pity me!"

She went about in a black dress with weepers°, gave up wearing a hat and gloves for good, seldom went out of the house except to go to church or to visit her husband's grave, and at home she lived like a nun. Only after six months did she take off her widow's weeds and open the shutters of her windows. Occasionally she was seen in the mornings, going with her cook to the market, but how she lived and what went on in her house could only be surmised. People based their conjectures on the fact that she was seen drinking tea in her garden with the veterinarian, that he read the newspaper aloud to her, and that, on meeting an acquaintance in the post office, she said, "There is no proper veterinary inspection in our city, and that's why there is so much sickness around. You often hear of people getting ill from milk or catching infections from horses and cows.

---

icons: religious pictures, painted on small wooden panels, often seen in Russian Orthodox and other Christian churches in Eastern Europe.   *weepers*: badges or emblems of mourning.

The health of domestic animals ought to be just as well looked after as the health of human beings."

She repeated the ideas of the veterinarian, and now was of the same opinion as he about everything. It was clear that she could not live even a year without some attachment, and had found new happiness in the wing of her own house. Another woman would have been censured for this, but no one could think ill of Olenka; everything about her was so natural. Neither she nor the veterinarian spoke to anyone of the change in their relations, and tried, indeed, to conceal it, but they did not succeed because Olenka could not keep a secret. When his regimental colleagues visited him, while she poured tea for them or served supper she would talk of the cattle plague, the pearl disease, the municipal slaughterhouses. He would be dreadfully embarrassed, and when the guests had gone, would seize her by the arm and hiss angrily, "I've asked you before not to talk about things you don't understand! When we veterinarians are talking among ourselves, please don't interfere! It's really annoying!"

She would look at him in amazement and anxiously inquire, "But, Volodochka, what am I to talk about?" Then, with tears in her eyes, she would embrace him, begging him not to be angry, and they were both happy.

This happiness did not last long. The veterinarian went away with his regiment, went away forever, as the regiment was transferred to some distant place—it may even have been Siberia. And Olenka was left alone.

Now she was quite alone. Her father had died long ago; his armchair lay in the attic, covered with dust and with one leg missing. She grew thin and plain, and when people met her in the street they did not glance at her and smile as they used to; clearly, her best years were over and behind her, and now a new, uncertain life was beginning, one that did not bear thinking of. In the evening, as she sat on her porch, Olenka could hear the band playing and skyrockets going off at the Tivoli, but this no longer called up anything to her mind. She gazed indifferently into her empty courtyard, thought of nothing, wished for nothing, and later, when darkness fell, she went to bed and dreamed of the empty courtyard. She ate and drank as though involuntarily.

Above all—and worst of all—she no longer had any opinions whatever. She saw objects about her, understood what was going on, but could not form an opinion about anything and did not know what to talk about. And how awful it is to have no opinions! You see a bottle, for instance, or rain, or a peasant driving a cart, but what the bottle, the rain, or the peasant may be for, what the significance of them is, you cannot say, and could not even for a thousand rubles. When Kukin was with her, or Pustovalov, or later, the veterinarian, Olenka could explain everything, could express an opinion on anything you like, but now there was the same emptiness in her mind and heart as in her courtyard. It was painful, and bitter as wormwood in the mouth.

Little by little the town was spreading in all directions; Gypsy Road was now a street, and where the gardens of the Tivoli and the lumberyards had been, houses sprang up and lanes formed. How swiftly time passes! Olenka's house grew shabby, the roof was rusty, the shed sloped, and the whole yard was overgrown with tall grass and prickly nettles. Olenka herself had aged and grown plain; in the summer she sat on the porch, and her soul was empty, bleak, and bitter; in the winter

45

she sat at the window and stared at the snow. There were times when a breath of spring or the sound of church bells brought to her on the wind would suddenly provoke a rush of memories; then her heart melted, her eyes brimmed with tears, but this lasted only a moment, and there was again emptiness and uncertainty as to the purpose of life. Bryska, the black kitten, rubbed against her, purring softly, but Olenka was not affected by these feline caresses. Was that what she needed? She wanted a love that would take possession of her whole soul, her mind, that would give her ideas, a direction in life, that would warm her old blood. She shook the black kitten off her lap and said irritably, "Get away! Go on! There's nothing for you here!"

And so it was, day after day, year after year, no joy whatsoever, no opinions of any sort. Whatever Mavra the cook said, she accepted.

One hot July day, toward evening, when the cattle were being driven home and the whole yard was filled with clouds of dust, someone unexpectedly knocked at the gate. Olenka went to open it herself and was astounded at what she saw: there stood Smirnin, the veterinarian, his hair gray, and in civilian dress. All at once she remembered everything and, unable to control herself, burst into tears, dropping her head onto his breast without a word. She was so moved that she scarcely was aware of going into the house and sitting down to tea with him.

"My dear!" she murmured, trembling with joy. "Vladimir Platonych! What   50
brings you here?"

"I have come here for good," he said. "I've retired from the army and I want to settle down and try my luck on my own. And besides, it's time for my son to go to high school. He's growing up. I am reconciled with my wife, you know."

"Where is she?" asked Olenka.

"She's at the hotel with the boy, and I'm out looking for lodgings."

"Good heavens, my dear, take my house! Lodgings! Goodness, I wouldn't take any rent for it," cried Olenka, growing excited and weeping again. "You live here, and the wing will do for me. Heavens, how glad I am!"

The next day they began painting the roof and whitewashing the walls, and   55
Olenka, with her arms akimbo, walked about the yard giving orders. Her face beamed with her old smile, and she was animated and fresh, as though she had waked from a long sleep. The veterinarian's wife arrived, thin and homely, with short hair and a capricious expression. With her came the little boy, Sasha, small for his age (he was going on ten), chubby, with bright blue eyes and dimples in his cheeks. No sooner had he entered the courtyard than he began chasing the cat, and immediately his gay and joyous laughter could be heard.

"Auntie, is that your cat?" he asked Olenka. "When she has little ones, please give us one of her kittens. Mama is terribly afraid of mice."

Olenka talked to him, gave him tea, and her heart grew suddenly warm and there was a sweet ache in her bosom, as if this little boy were her own son. In the evening when he sat in the dining room doing his homework, she gazed at him with tenderness and pity as she whispered, "My darling, my pretty one. . . . How clever you are, my little one, and so fair!"

"An island," he read aloud from the book, "is a body of land entirely surrounded by water."

"An island is a body of land . . ." she repeated, and this was the first opinion she had uttered with conviction after years of silence and emptiness of mind.

She now had opinions of her own, and at supper she talked to Sasha's parents about how difficult the lessons were for children in the high school, but that, nevertheless, a classical education was better than a technical course, because it opened all avenues—you could be a doctor . . . an engineer. . . .

Sasha started going to high school. His mother went to Kharkov to visit her sister and did not come back; his father used to go away every day to inspect herds, and he sometimes was away for three days together. It seemed to Olenka that Sasha was quite forsaken, that he was unwanted, that he was being starved to death, and she moved him into the wing with her and settled him in a little room there.

For six months now Sasha has been living in her wing. Every morning Olenka goes into his room where he lies fast asleep, his hand under his cheek, breathing quietly. She is always sorry to wake him.

"Sashenka," she says sadly, "get up, darling. It's time for school."

He gets up, dresses, says his prayers, and sits down to breakfast; he drinks three glasses of tea, eats two large cracknels and half a buttered roll. He is still not quite awake and consequently ill-humored.

"Now, Sashenka, you have not learned your fable very well," Olenka says, gazing at him as if she were seeing him off on a long journey. "You are such a worry to me! You must do your best, darling; you must study. . . . Pay attention to your teachers."

"Oh, leave me alone, please!" he says.

Then he walks down the street to school, a little figure in a big cap, with a knapsack on his back. Olenka silently follows him.

"Sashenka-a!" she calls. And when he looks round she thrusts a date or a caramel into his hand. When they turn in to the school lane he feels ashamed of being followed by a tall, stout lady; he looks back and says, "You'd better go home, Auntie. I can go alone now."

She stops, but does not take her eyes off him until he has disappeared into the school entrance. Ah, how she loves him! Not one of her former attachments had been so deep; never before had her soul surrendered itself so devotedly and with such joy as now, when her maternal feelings have been quickened. For this little boy who is not her own, for the dimples in his cheeks, for his cap, she would give her whole life, would give it with joy and tears of tenderness. Why? But who knows why?

Having seen Sasha off to school she goes quietly home, contented, serene, full of love; her face, grown younger in the last six months, beams with joy; people meeting her look at her with pleasure and say, "Good morning, Olga Semyonovna, darling. How are you, darling?"

"The lessons in school are so difficult nowadays," she says, as she goes about her marketing. "It's no joke. Yesterday in the first class they gave him a fable to learn by heart, a Latin translation, and a problem. . . . You know, it's too much for the little fellow."

And she begins talking about the teachers, the lessons, the textbooks—saying just what Sasha says about them.

At three o'clock they have dinner together; in the evening they do the home-work together, and cry. When she puts him to bed she takes a long time making the sign of the cross over him and whispering a prayer. Then she goes to bed and dreams of that faraway, misty future when Sasha, having finished his studies, will become a doctor or an engineer, will have a large house of his own, horses, a carriage, when he will marry and have children of his own. . . . She falls asleep, still thinking of the same thing, and the tears run down her cheeks from under closed eyelids, while the black cat lies beside her purring: mrr . . . mrr . . . mrr. . . .

Suddenly there is a loud knock at the gate and Olenka wakes up, breathless with fear, her heart pounding. Half a minute later there is another knock.

"It's a telegram from Kharkov," she thinks, her whole body trembling. "Sasha's mother is sending for him. . . . Oh, Lord!" 75

She is in despair, her head, hands, and feet are cold, and it seems to her that she is the most unfortunate woman in the whole world. But another moment passes, she hears voices: it is the veterinarian coming home from the club.

"Well, thank God!" she thinks. Gradually the weight on her heart lifts, and she feels relieved; she goes back to bed and thinks of Sasha, who is fast asleep in the next room, sometimes crying out in his sleep, "I'll give it to you! Go on! No fighting!"

QUESTIONS

1. What is Chekhov's attitude toward Olenka? How can you tell?
2. What essential traits in the character of Olenka does Chekhov reveal? How does she form her opinions? What becomes consistent and predictable in her relationships with Kukin, the theatrical impresario; Pustovalov, the manager of the lumberyard; Smirnin, the veterinarian; and in her behavior toward Sasha, the more or less abandoned child?
3. What contrast does Chekhov draw between the character and appearance of Kukin and Olenka's view of him? Between the little boy Sasha and Olenka's view of him? What do you suppose these contrasts indicate about Olenka herself?
4. Would you call Olenka's life "a decline and fall" (as one critic has put it); a kind of moral progress and final triumph; an ordinary, meandering life without pattern to it; or what?
5. Try stating in your own words the theme of the story.

Anton Chekhov

THE MAN IN A CASE   1898

Translated by Marian Fell

On the outskirts of the village of Mironitski, in a shed belonging to the bailiff Prokofi, some belated huntsmen were encamped for the night. There were two of them: the veterinary surgeon Ivan Ivanitch and the schoolteacher Burkin. Ivan Ivanitch had a rather strange, hyphenated surname, Tchimsha-Himalaiski, which did not suit him at all, and so he was known all over the province simply by his two Christian names. He lived on a stud farm near the town and had now come out hunting to get a breath of fresh air. Burkin, the schoolteacher, had long been at home in this neighborhood, for he came every year as the guest of Count P——.

They were not asleep. Ivan Ivanitch, a tall, spare old man with a long mustache, sat at the door of the shed, with the moon shining on him, smoking his pipe. Burkin lay inside on the hay and was invisible in the shadows.

They were telling stories. Among other things, they spoke of Mavra, the bailiff's wife, a healthy, intelligent woman who had never in her life been outside of her native village and who had never seen the town nor the railway; they remembered that she had sat beside the stove now for the last ten years, never going out into the street except after nightfall.

"There is nothing so very surprising in that," said Burkin. "There are not a few people in this world who, like hermit crabs and snails, are always trying to retire into their shells. Perhaps this is a manifestation of atavism, a harking back to the time when man's forebears were not yet gregarious animals but lived alone in their dens, or perhaps it is simply one of the many phases of human character— who can say? I am not an anthropologist and it is not my business to meddle with such questions; I only mean to say that people like Mavra are not an uncommon phenomenon. Here! We don't have to go far to seek an illustration. Two months ago a certain Byelinkoff died in our town, a colleague of mine, a teacher of Greek. You must have heard of him. He was remarkable for one thing: no matter how fine the weather was, he always went out in galoshes, carrying an umbrella and wearing a warm, wadded overcoat. And his umbrella he always kept in a case and his watch in a case of gray chamois, and when he took out his penknife to sharpen a pencil that, too, was in a little case. Even his face seemed to be in a case, for he always kept it concealed behind the turned-up collar of his coat. He wore dark spectacles and a warm waistcoat, and he kept cotton wool in his ears and he had the hood raised whenever he got into a cab. In a word, one saw in this man a perpetual and irresistible longing to wrap some covering around himself—one might call it a case—which would isolate him from external impressions. Reality chafed and alarmed him and kept him in a state of perpetual apprehension, and it was, perhaps, to justify his timidity and his aversion to the present that he always exalted the past and things which had never existed. The ancient languages which he taught were at bottom the galoshes and umbrella behind which he hid himself from the realities of existence.

" 'Oh, how musical, how beautiful is the Greek tongue!' he would cry with a beaming look, and, as if in proof of what he had said, he would half shut his eyes, hold up one finger, and pronounce the word 'anthropos'!

"And his opinions, too, Byelinkoff tried to confine in a case. Only bulletins and newspaper articles in which something was prohibited were clear to him. If he saw a bulletin forbidding the scholars to go out on the street after nine o'clock, or if he read an article enjoining him from carnal love, that was fixed and clear to him—and basta!° For to him there was always an element of doubt, something unspoken and confused, concealed in license and liberty of action. When it was permitted to start a dramatic or reading club in the town he would shake his head and say softly:

" 'That is all very well and very fine, but I shouldn't wonder if something unpleasant would come of it.'

basta!: "Enough!" (Spanish), exclamation of triumph, made when playing the trump in a game of cards.

"Every transgression and deviation from the right plunged him into dejection, although one wondered what business it was of his. If one of his colleagues came late to prayers, or if he heard rumors of some prank of the schoolboys, or if one of the lady superintendents was seen late at night with an officer, he would grow tremendously excited and always insist that something unpleasant would come of it. At the teachers' meetings he used to drive us absolutely mad by his prudence and his scruples and his absolutely caselike reflections. 'Oh,' he would cry, 'the boys and girls in the school behave so very badly and make such a noise in the classrooms! Oh, what if this should reach the governor's ears, and what if something unpleasant should come of it? If only Petroff could be expelled from the second class and Yegorieff from the fourth, how good it would be!' And what was the result? We would grow so oppressed with his sighing and his moaning and his dark spectacles on his white face that we would give in—give Petroff and Yegorieff bad-conduct marks, put them under arrest, and finally expel them.

"He had a strange habit—he used to make the tour of our rooms. He would come into a master's room and just sit and say nothing, as if he were looking for something. He would sit like that for an hour or so and then would go out. This he called 'keeping on good terms with his comrades,' but it was plainly a heavy burden for him to come and sit with us, and he only did it because he considered it his duty as our comrade. All of us teachers were afraid of him. Even the director feared him. Our teachers are all a thoughtful and thoroughly steady lot, brought up on Turgenieff and Shedrin°, and yet this man, with his galoshes and his umbrella, held the whole school in the hollow of his hand for fifteen years. The whole school, did I say? The whole town! The ladies did not dare to get up little plays on Saturday evenings for fear he should hear of it, and the clergy were ashamed to eat meat and play cards in his presence. Under the influence of men like Byelinkoff the people of our town in the last ten or fifteen years have begun to fear everything. They are afraid of sending letters, of making acquaintances, of speaking aloud, of reading books, of helping or teaching the poor—"

Ivan Ivanitch coughed as a sign that he wanted to make a remark, but he first finished his pipe, then gazed at the moon, and then at last, pausing at intervals, said:

"Yes, they are thoughtful and steady; they read Shedrin and Turgenieff and others, and therefore they have submitted patiently—that is just it."

"Byelinkoff lived in the same house that I did," Burkin went on, "on the same floor. His door was opposite mine. We often met, and I was familiar with his domestic life. It was the same old story when he was at home. He wore a dressing gown and a nightcap and had shutters to his windows and bolts to his doors—a perfect array of restraints and restrictions and of 'oh-something-unpleasant-might-come-of-its.' Lenten fare was bad for the health, but to eat flesh was impossible because

10

Turgenieff and Shedrin: two widely read novelists of the previous generation, both of whom Chekhov himself admired but whose influence the liberal, reform-minded Ivan Ivanovich appears to resent (in his remark in paragraph 11). Ivan Turgenieff, or Turgenev (1818–1883), often wrote of thwarted liberals like Bazarov, a character in his best-known novel, Fathers and Sons (1862). Shedrin, or Schedrin, was the pen name of Mikhail Saltykov (1826–1889), author of a social satire, The Golovlyov Family (1876). When Saltykov died, Chekhov called him a great enemy of "the mean spirit that inhabits the petty, average, spiritually distorted Russian intellectual."

somebody might say that Byelinkoff did not keep the fasts; therefore he ate perch fried in butter, which was not Lenten fare, but neither could it be called meat. He would not keep a woman servant for fear that people might think ill of him, so he employed as a cook an old man named Afanasi, a besotted semi-idiot of sixty who had once been an officer's servant and could cook after a fashion. This Afanasi would stand at the door with folded arms, sigh deeply, and always mutter one and the same thing:

" 'There's a whole lot of *them* out today!'

"Byelinkoff's bedroom was like a little box and curtains hung around his bed. When he went to sleep he would pull the blankets over his head. The room would be stuffy and hot, the wind rattle the closed doors and rumble in the stove, and sighs, ominous sighs, would be heard from the kitchen; and he would shake under his bedclothes. He was afraid that something unpleasant might come of it—that Afanasi might murder him, that burglars might break in. All night he would be a prey to alarming dreams, and in the morning, as we walked to the school together, he would be melancholy and pale, and one could see that the crowded school toward which he was going dismayed him and was repugnant to his whole being, and that it was burdensome for a man of his solitary disposition to be walking beside me.

" 'There is so much noise in the classrooms,' he would say as if seeking an   15 explanation of his depression.

"And think of it, this teacher of Greek, this man in a case, once very nearly got married!"

Ivan Ivanitch looked quickly around into the shed and said: "You're joking!"

"Yes, he nearly got married, strange as it may appear. A new teacher of history and geography was appointed to our school, a certain Little Russian named Kovalenko. He did not come alone but brought his sister Varenka with him. He was young and tall and dark, with huge hands and a face from which it could be guessed that he possessed a bass voice. As a matter of fact, when he spoke his voice did sound as if it were coming out of a barrel—boo—boo—boo—. As for her, she was no longer young, thirty perhaps, but she was tall, too, and graceful, dark-eyed and red-cheeked—a sugar-plum of a girl, and so boisterous and jolly! She was always singing Little Russian songs and ha-ha-ing. At the slightest provocation she would break into loud peals of laughter—ha! ha! ha! I remember the first time we met the Kovalenkos; it was at a birthday party at the director's. Among the stern, tiresome teachers who go to birthday parties out of a sense of duty, we suddenly beheld a new Aphrodite risen from the waves, strolling about with her arms akimbo, laughing, singing, and dancing. She sang 'The Wind Blows' with feeling, and then another song, and then another, and fascinated us all, even Byelinkoff. He sat down beside her and said with a sweet smile: 'The Little Russian tongue with its tenderness and pleasant sonorousness reminds me of ancient Greek.'

"This flattered her, and she began earnestly and with feeling to tell him that she had a farm in the province of Gadiatch, that her mamma lived there and that there were such pears and such melons there and such inns! Little Russians call gourds 'inns,' and make a soup out of the little red ones and the little blue ones that is 'so good, so good it is simply—awful!'

"We listened and listened, and the same thought suddenly crossed the minds 20 of all of us.

" 'How nice it would be to make a match between them!' said the director's wife to me quietly.

"For some reason we all remembered that our Byelinkoff was unmarried, and it now seemed strange to us that until this moment we had not noticed, had somehow quite overlooked this important detail in his life. By the way, how does he regard women? we asked ourselves. How does he solve this daily problem? This had not interested us before at all; perhaps we had not even entertained the idea that a man who wore galoshes in all weathers and slept behind bed curtains could possibly fall in love.

" 'He is already long past forty, but she is thirty herself,' the director's wife expressed her opinion. 'I think she would marry him.'

"How many wrong and foolish deeds are committed in our country towns because we are bored! What need was there to have tried to marry off Byelinkoff, whom one could not even conceive of as being married? The director's wife and the inspector's wife and all the ladies of our school brightened and bloomed as if they had suddenly discovered the object of their existence. The director's wife takes a box at the theater, and, behold! in it sits Varenka waving a fan, radiant and happy, and beside her is Byelinkoff, small and depressed, as if they had pulled him out of his room with a pair of pincers. I give an evening party, and the ladies insist that I shall invite both Byelinkoff and Varenka. In a word, the mills were grinding. It appeared that Varenka was not averse to marriage. It was not particularly cheerful for her living at her brother's, for they scolded and squabbled the day long. Here's a picture for you: Kovalenko is stalking down the street, a tall, lusty fellow in an embroidered shirt with his forelock hanging down over his forehead from under the brim of his cap. In one hand he carries a bundle of books, in the other a thick, knotted stick. Behind him walks his sister, also carrying books.

" 'But you haven't read it, Mihailik!' she argues loudly. 'I tell you, I swear to 25 you, you haven't read it at all!'

" 'But I tell you I have read it!' shouts Kovalenko, rattling his stick on the sidewalk.

" 'Oh, Lord have mercy, Mintchik! What are you getting so angry about; does it matter?'

" 'But I tell you that I have read it!' shouts Kovalenko still louder.

"And at home, as soon as an outsider came in they would open fire at each other. A life like that was probably growing wearisome for her; she wanted a nook of her own; and then her age should be taken into account; at her years there's little time for picking and choosing—a woman takes what she can get, even if the man be a teacher of Greek. And, as a matter of fact, the majority of our young ladies will marry whom they can, only to get married. Well, be it as it may, Varenka began to show our Byelinkoff marked favor.

"And what about Byelinkoff? He called on the Kovalenkos as he did on the 30 rest of us. He would go to their rooms and sit and say nothing. He would say nothing, but Varenka would sing 'The Wind Blows' for him, or gaze at him pensively out of her dark eyes, or suddenly break into peals of merry laughter—ha! ha! ha!

"In affairs of the heart, and especially in marriage, a large part is played by suggestion. Everyone—both the ladies and Byelinkoff's colleagues—all began to assure him that he ought to get married, that there was nothing for him to do but to marry. We all congratulated him and said all sorts of silly things with grave faces—that marriage was a serious step, and so forth. Besides that, Varenka was pretty and attractive; she was the daughter of a state councilor and owned a farm of her own; and, above all, she was the first woman who had treated him kindly and affectionately. His head was turned and he fancied that he really must marry."

"Now would have been the time to get rid of his galoshes and his umbrella," said Ivan Ivanitch.

"Will you believe it? That proved to be impossible. He put a photograph of Varenka on his table, and kept coming to me and talking to me about Varenka and family life, and about what a serious step marriage was; he was much at the Kovalenkos, but he did not change his way of living one atom. On the contrary, his resolve to get married affected him painfully; he grew thin and pale and seemed to shrink still further into his case.

" 'I like Miss Varenka,' he said to me once with a wry smile, 'and I know every man ought to marry, but—all this has happened so suddenly; I must think it over a bit.'

" 'What is there to think over?' I answered. 'Marry her! That's all there is to it.'   35

" 'No, marriage is a serious step; one must first weigh the consequences and duties and responsibilities—so that nothing unpleasant shall come of it. All this worries me so that I can't sleep any more at night. And, to tell you the truth, I am alarmed: she and her brother have such a queer way of thinking; they reason somehow so strangely, and she has a very bold character. One might marry her and, before one knew it, get mixed up in some scandal.'

"And so he did not propose, but still kept putting it off, to the deep chagrin of the director's wife and of all of our ladies; he still kept weighing those duties and responsibilities, though he went walking every day with Varenka, thinking, no doubt, that this was due to a man placed as he was. He still kept coming to me to discuss family life.

"But in all probability he would have proposed at last, and one of those bad and foolish matches would have been consummated, as so many thousands are, simply because people have nothing better to do with themselves, had we not been suddenly overwhelmed by a colossal scandal.

"I must tell you that Varenka's brother could not abide Byelinkoff.

" 'I can't understand,' he would say to us with a shrug of his shoulders, 'I can't   40
imagine how you can stomach that sneak with his horrid face. Oh, friends, how can you live here? Your whole atmosphere here is stifling and nauseating. Are you instructors and teachers? No, you are sycophants, and this isn't a temple of learning; it's a detective office, stinking as sour as a police court. No, brothers, I'm going to stay here a little while longer, and then I'm going back to my farm to catch crawfish and teach young Little Russians. I am going, and you can stay here with your Judas.'

"Or else he would laugh and laugh till the tears rolled down his cheeks, now in a deep voice, now in a high squeaky one, and demand of me, spreading out his hands:

"'What does he sit in my room for? What is he after? He just sits and stares.'

"He even called Byelinkoff 'the spider,' and, of course, we avoided mentioning to him that his sister was thinking of marrying this 'spider.' When the director's wife once hinted to him that it would be a good idea to settle his sister with such a steady, universally respected man as Byelinkoff he frowned and growled: 'That's none of my business. Let her marry a reptile if she likes. I can't endure interfering in other people's affairs.'

"And now listen to what followed. Some wag made a caricature of Byelinkoff in galoshes and cotton trousers, holding up an umbrella, with Varenka on his arm. Underneath was written: 'The Amorous Anthropos.' His expression was caught to perfection. The artist must have worked more nights than one, for every teacher in our school, every teacher in the seminary, and every official received a copy. Byelinkoff got one, too. The caricature made the most painful impression on him.

"We were coming out of our house together. It was on a Sunday, the first 45 of May, and all of us, teachers and pupils, had agreed to meet at the school and from there walk out beyond the town into the woods. So we came out together, and his face was absolutely green; he looked like a thundercloud.

"'What bad, what unkind people there are!' he burst out, and his lips quivered.

"I really felt sorry for him. As we walked along, we suddenly saw Kovalenko riding toward us on a bicycle, followed by Varenka, also on a bicycle. She was scarlet and dusty, but merry and gay nevertheless.

"'We are going on ahead!' she cried. 'This weather is so glorious, so glorious, it's simply awful!'

"And they disappeared from view.

"Our Byelinkoff's face turned from green to white, and he seemed paralyzed. 50 He stopped and looked at me.

"'Allow me, what do I see?' he asked. 'Or does my eyesight deceive me? Is it proper for schoolteachers and women to ride bicycles?'

"'What is there improper about it?' said I. 'Let them ride to their hearts' content.'

"'But how is it possible?' he shrieked, stupefied by my calmness. 'What are you saying?'

"And he was so shocked that he did not want to go on any farther, but turned and went home.

"Next day he rubbed his hands nervously all the time and trembled, and we 55 could see from his face that he was not well. He left his work—the first time in his life that this had happened to him—and did not come to dinner. Toward evening he dressed himself warmly, although the weather was now quite summer-like, and crawled over to the Kovalenkos. Varenka was not at home; he found her brother alone.

"'Sit down,' said Kovalenko coldly and frowned. He looked sleepy; he had just had a nap after his dinner and was in a very bad humor.

"Byelinkoff sat for ten minutes in silence and then said: 'I have come to you to relieve my mind. I am very, very much grieved. Some lampooner has made a picture of myself and a person who is near to us both in a ridiculous position. I consider it my duty to assure you that I have had nothing to do with this; I have never given any occasion for such a jest; I have always behaved with perfect propriety all the time.'

"Kovalenko sat moodily without saying a word. Byelinkoff waited a few minutes and then went on in a sad, low voice: 'And I have something else to say to you. I have been a teacher for many years, and your career is just beginning: I consider it my duty as an older man to give you a word of warning. You ride the bicycle—now, this amusement is quite improper for a teacher of the young.'

"'Why?' asked Kovalenko in a deep voice.

"'Need I really explain that to you, Kovalenko? Isn't it obvious? If the master goes about on a bicycle, what is there left for the pupils to go about on? Only their heads! And if permission to do it has not been given in a bulletin, it must not be done. I was horrified yesterday. My head swam when I saw your sister—a woman or a girl on a bicycle—how terrible!' 60

"'What do you want, anyhow?'

"'I only want one thing: I want to caution you. You are a young man, the future lies before you, you must be very, very careful, or you will make a mistake. Oh, what a mistake you will make! You go about wearing embroidered shirts, you are always on the street with some book or other, and now you ride a bicycle! The director will hear of it; it will reach the ears of the trustees that you and your sister ride the bicycle—what is the use?'

"'It is nobody's business whether my sister and I ride the bicycle or not,' said Kovalenko, flushing deeply. 'And whoever interferes in my domestic and family affairs I will kick to the devil.'

"Byelinkoff paled and rose.

"'If you talk to me in that way I cannot continue,' he said. 'I must ask you never to refer to the heads of the school in that tone in my presence. You should have more respect for the authorities.' 65

"'Did I say anything against the authorities?' asked Kovalenko, glaring angrily at him. 'Please leave me alone, I am an honorable man, and I decline to talk to a person like you. I don't like sneaks!'

"Byelinkoff began nervously to bustle about and put on his things. You see, this was the first time in his life that he had heard such rudeness.

"'You can say what you like,' he cried as he stepped out of the hall onto the landing of the stairs. 'I must only warn you of one thing. Someone may have overheard our conversation and I shall have to report it to the director in its principal features, as it might be misinterpreted and something unpleasant might come of it. I shall be obliged to do this.'

"'To report it? Go ahead, report it!'

"Kovalenko seized him by the nape of the neck and pushed, and Byelinkoff tumbled downstairs with his galoshes rattling after him. The staircase was long and steep, but he rolled safely to the bottom, picked himself up, and touched his nose to make sure that his spectacles were all right. At the very moment of his descent Varenka had come in with two ladies; they stood at the foot of the stairs and watched him, and for Byelinkoff this was the most terrible thing of all. He would rather have broken his neck and both legs than to have appeared ridiculous; the whole town would now know it, the director, the trustees would hear of it—oh, something unpleasant would come of it! There would be another caricature, and the end of it would be that he would have to resign. 70

"As he picked himself up Varenka recognized him. When she caught sight of his absurd face, his wrinkled overcoat, and his galoshes, not knowing what had happened but supposing that he had fallen downstairs of his own accord, she could not control herself and laughed till the whole house rang: 'Ha! ha! ha!'

"This pealing and rippling 'ha! ha! ha!' settled everything—it put an end to the wedding and to the earthly career of Byelinkoff.

"He did not hear what Varenka said to him; he saw nothing before his eyes. When he reached home he first took Varenka's picture off the table, then he went to bed and never got up again.

"Three days later Afanasi came to me and asked me whether he ought not to send for a doctor, as something was happening to his master. I went to see Byelinkoff. He was lying speechless behind his bed curtains, covered with a blanket, and when a question was asked him he only answered yes or no, and not another sound did he utter. There he lay, and about the bed roamed Afanasi, gloomy, scowling, sighing profoundly, and reeking of vodka like a taproom.

"A month later Byelinkoff died. We all went to his funeral, that is, the boys' and girls' schools and the seminary. As he lay in his coffin the expression on his face was timid and sweet, even gay, as if he were glad to be put in a case at last out of which he need never rise. Yes, he had attained his ideal! As if in his honor, the day of his funeral was overcast and rainy, and all of us wore galoshes and carried umbrellas. Varenka, too, was at the funeral and burst into tears when the coffin was lowered into the grave. I have noticed that Little Russian women always either laugh or cry, they know no middle state. 75

"I must confess that it is a great pleasure to bury such people as Byelinkoff. On our way back from the cemetery we all wore sober, Lenten expressions; no one wished to betray this feeling of pleasure, the same feeling that we used to have long, long ago in childhood when our elders went away from home and we could run about the garden for a few hours in perfect liberty. Oh, liberty, liberty! Even a hint, even a faint hope of its possibility lends the soul wings, does it not?

"We returned from the cemetery in a good humor, but before a week had elapsed our life was trickling on as sternly, as wearily, as senselessly as before; a life not prohibited in a bulletin and yet not quite permitted—no better than it had been!

"And, as a matter of fact, though we had buried Byelinkoff, how many more people in cases there were left! How many more there will be!"

"Yes, so, so, quite right," said Ivan Ivanitch, smoking his pipe.

"How many more there will be!" Burkin repeated. 80

The schoolmaster stepped out of the shed. He was a small man, fat, quite bald, with a black beard that reached almost to his waist; two dogs followed him out.

"What a moon! What a moon!" he exclaimed, looking up.

It was already midnight. To the right the whole village lay visible, its long street stretching away for three or four miles. Everything was wrapped in deep, peaceful slumber; not a movement, not a sound; it did not seem possible that nature could lie so silent. Peace fills the soul when one sees the broad street of a village on a moonlit night with its huts and its haystacks and its dreaming willows. It looks so gentle and beautiful and sad in its rest, screened by the shades of night from care and grief and toil. The stars, too, seem to be gazing at it with tenderness and emotion, and one feels that there is no evil in the world and that all is well. To the left the fields began at the edge of the village and were visible for miles down to the horizon; in all this broad expanse there was also neither movement nor sound.

"Yes, so, so, quite right," Ivan Ivanitch repeated. "But think how we live in town, so hot and cramped, writing unnecessary papers and playing vint°—isn't that also a case? And isn't our whole life, which we spend among rogues and back-biters and stupid, idle women, talking and listening to nothing but folly—isn't that a case? Here! If you like I'll tell you a very instructive story."

"No, it's time to go to sleep," Burkin said. "Tomorrow!"   85

Both men went into the shed and lay down on the hay. They had already covered themselves up and were half asleep when they suddenly heard light foot-steps approaching—tip—tip. Somebody was walking by the shed. The footsteps went on and stopped, and in a minute came back again—tip—tip. The dogs growled.

"That was Mavra," said Burkin as the sound died away.

"One hears and sees all this lying," said Ivan Ivanitch, turning over on the other side. "Nobody calls one a fool for standing it all, for enduring insults and humilia-tions without daring to declare oneself openly on the side of free and honest peo-ple. One has to lie oneself and smile, all for a crust of bread, a corner to live in, and a little rank, which is not worth a penny—no, a man can't go on living like this."

"Oh, come, that's out of another opera, Ivan Ivanitch," said the schoolmaster. "Let's go to sleep!"

And ten minutes later Burkin was already asleep. But Ivan Ivanitch, sighing,   90 still tossed from side to side, and at last got up and went out again and sat in the doorway smoking his pipe.

QUESTIONS

1. What is the matter with Byelinkoff? Have you ever known anyone at all like him? Do you find him a round or a flat character? A credible character or an incredible one?
2. Why do you suppose Chekhov chooses to tell Byelinkoff's history as remembered by another person, as a story inside another story? What additional insights do we get from the story's frame? Suggestion: Consider Burkin's comments on his fellow townspeople (paragraph 9) and Ivan Ivanitch's remarks (85 and 89).
3. Why do people conspire to make a match between Byelinkoff and Varenka?
4. How does the character of Mavra, the bailiff's wife, relate to the rest of the story?
5. Sum up what you understand to be the story's central theme.

Anton Chekhov

VANKA   1886

Translated by Robert Payne

Nine-year-old Vanka Zhukov, who was apprenticed three months ago to the shoe-maker Alyakhin, did not go to bed on Christmas Eve. He waited till the master and mistress and the more senior apprentices had gone to the early service, and

---

vint: a card game similar to bridge.

then he took a bottle of ink and a pen with a rusty nib from his master's cupboard, and began to write on a crumpled sheet of paper spread out in front of him. Before tracing the shape of the first letter, he looked several times fearfully in the direction of the doors and windows, and then he gazed up at the dark icon, flanked on either side by shelves filled with cobbler's lasts, and then he heaved a broken sigh. With the paper spread over the bench, Vanka knelt on the floor beside it.

"Dear Grandfather Konstantin Makarich," he wrote. "I am writing a letter to you. I wish you a Merry Christmas and all good things from the Lord God. I have no father and mother, and you are all I have left."

Vanka raised his eyes to the dark windowpane, on which there gleamed the reflection of a candle flame, and in his vivid imagination he saw his grandfather Konstantin Makarich standing there. His grandfather was a night watchman on the estate of some gentlefolk called Zhivaryov, a small, thin, unusually lively and nimble old man of about sixty-five, his face always crinkling with laughter, and his eyes bleary from drink. In the daytime the old man slept in the servants' kitchen or cracked jokes with the cooks. At night, wrapped in an ample sheepskin coat, he made the rounds of the estate, shaking his clapper. Two dogs followed him with drooping heads—one was the old bitch Brownie, the other was called Eel from his black coat and long weaselly body. Eel always seemed to be extraordinarily respectful and endearing, gazing with the same fond eyes on friends and strangers alike; yet no one trusted him. His deference and humility concealed a most jesuitical malice. No one knew better how to creep stealthily behind someone and take a nip at his leg, or how to crawl into the icehouse, or how to scamper off with a peasant's chicken. More than once they just about broke his hind legs, twice a noose was put round his neck, and every week he was beaten until he was only half alive, yet he always managed to survive.

At this very moment Grandfather was probably standing by the gates, screwing up his eyes at the bright red windows of the village church, stamping about in his felt boots and cracking jokes with the servants. His clapper hung from his belt. He would be throwing out his arms and then hugging himself against the cold, and, hiccoughing as old men do, he would be pinching one of the servant girls or one of the cooks.

"What about a pinch of snuff, eh?" he would say, holding out his snuffbox 5 to the women.

Then the women would take a pinch and sneeze, and the old man would be overcome with indescribable ecstasies, laughing joyously and exclaiming: "Fine for frozen noses, eh!"

The dogs, too, were given snuff. Brownie would sneeze, shake her head, and walk away looking offended, while Eel, too polite to sneeze, only wagged his tail. The weather was glorious. The air was still, transparently clear, and fresh. The night was very dark, but the whole white-roofed village with its snowdrifts and trees silvered with hoarfrost and smoke steaming from the chimneys could be seen clearly. The heavens were sprinkled with gay, glinting stars, and the Milky Way stood out as clearly as if it had been washed and scrubbed with snow for the holidays.

Vanka sighed, dipped his pen in the ink, and went on writing:

"Yesterday I was given a thrashing. The master dragged me by the hair into the yard and gave me a beating with a stirrup strap because when I was rocking the baby in the cradle, I misfortunately fell asleep. And then last week the mistress ordered me to gut a herring, and because I began with the tail, she took the head of the herring and rubbed it all over my face. The other apprentices made fun of me, sent me to the tavern for vodka, and made me steal the master's cucumbers for them, and then the master beat me with the first thing that came to hand. And there's nothing to eat. In the morning they give me bread, there is porridge for dinner, and in the evening only bread again. They never give me tea or cabbage soup—they gobble it all up themselves. They make me sleep in the passageway, and when their baby cries, I don't get any sleep at all because I have to rock the cradle. Dear Grandfather, please for God's sake take me away from here, take me to the village, it's more than I can bear. . . . I kneel down before you. I'll pray to God to keep you forever, but take me away from here, or I shall die."

Vanka grimaced, rubbed his eyes with his black fists, and sobbed.

10

"I'll grind your snuff for you," he went on. "I will pray to God to keep you, and if I ever do anything wrong, you can flog me all you like. If you think there's no place for me, then I'll ask the manager for Christ's sake to let me clean boots or take Fedya's place as a shepherd boy. Dear Grandfather, it's more than I can bear, it will be the death of me. I thought of running away to the village, but I haven't any boots, and I am afraid of the ice. If you'll do this for me, I'll feed you when I grow up, and won't let anyone harm you, and when you die I'll pray for the repose of your soul, just like I do for my mother, Pelageya.

"Moscow is such a big city. There are so many houses belonging to the gentry, so many horses, but no sheep anywhere, and the dogs aren't vicious. The boys don't go about with the Star of Christmas, and they don't let you sing in the choir, and once I saw fishhooks in the shopwindow with the fishing lines for every kind of fish, very fine ones, even one hook which would hold a skate fish weighing forty pounds. I've seen shops selling guns which are just like the master's at home, and each one must cost a hundred rubles. In the butcher shops they have woodcocks and partridges and hares, but the people in the shop won't tell you where they were shot.

"Dear Grandfather, when they put up the Christmas tree at the big house, please take down a golden walnut for me and hide it in the green chest. Ask the young mistress, Olga Ignatyevna, and say it is for Vanka."

Vanka heaved a convulsive sigh, and once more he gazed in the direction of the window. He remembered it was Grandfather who always went to the forest to cut down a Christmas tree for the gentry, taking his grandson with him. They had a wonderful time together. Grandfather chuckled, the frost crackled, and Vanka, not to be outdone, clucked away cheerfully. Before chopping down the fir tree Grandfather would smoke a pipe, take a long pinch of snuff, and make fun of Vanka, who was shivering in the cold. The young fir trees, garlanded with hoarfrost, stood perfectly still, waiting to see which of them would die. . . . Suddenly out of nowhere a hare came springing across the snowdrifts, quick as an arrow, and Grandfather would be unable to prevent himself from shouting: "Hold him! Hold him! Hold that bobtailed devil, eh!"

When the tree had been chopped down, Grandfather would drag it to the big house and they would start decorating it. The young mistress, Olga Ignatyevna, Vanka's favorite, was the busiest of all. While Vanka's mother, Pelageya, was alive, serving as a chambermaid, Olga Ignatyevna used to stuff him with sugar candy, and it amused her to teach him to read and write, to count up to a hundred, and even to dance the quadrille. But when Pelageya died, they relegated the orphan Vanka to the servants' kitchen to be with his Grandfather, and from there he went to Moscow to the shoemaker Alyakhin. . . .

"Come to me, dear Grandfather," Vanka went on. "I beseech you for Christ's sake, take me away from here! Have pity on me, a poor orphan, they are always beating me, and I am terribly hungry, and so miserable I can't tell you, and I'm always crying. The other day the master hit me on the head with a last, and I fell down and thought I would never get up again. It's worse than a dog's life, and so miserable. I send greetings to Alyona, to one-eyed Yegor, and to the coachman, and don't give my harmonica away. I remain your grandson Ivan Zhukov, dear Grandfather, and come soon!"

Vanka twice folded the sheet of paper and then he put it in an envelope bought the previous day for a kopeck. He reflected for a while, dipped the pen in ink, and wrote the address:

To Grandfather in the Village

Then he scratched his head and thought for a while, and added the words: *Konstantin Makarich.* Pleased because no one interrupted him when he was writing, he threw on his cap, and without troubling to put on a coat, he ran out into the street in his shirt sleeves.

When he talked to the clerks in the butcher shop the previous day, they told him that letters were dropped in boxes, and from these boxes they were carried all over the world on mail coaches drawn by three horses and driven by drunken drivers, while the bells jingled. Vanka ran to the nearest mailbox and thrust his precious letter into the slot.

An hour later, lulled by sweetest hopes, he was fast asleep. He dreamed of a stove. His grandfather was sitting on the stove, bare feet dangling down, while he read the letter aloud to the cooks. Eel was walking round the stove, wagging his tail.

QUESTIONS

1. How would you describe the tone and atmosphere of "Vanka"? What picture does the author draw of Russian society in the 1880s?
2. What sort of person is Vanka? How would you characterize his grandfather?
3. Of what importance to Chekhov's story are the dogs Brownie and Eel?
4. Where in "Vanka" do you find irony?

SUGGESTIONS FOR WRITING: *On Anton Chekhov*

1. In an essay of at least 1,000 words, consider one of these topics, modifying the suggested title if necessary:

   "Isolation and Loneliness in Chekhov's Stories"
   "Chekhov as Portrait Artist of Children"
   "Chekhov's Eccentrics" (a study of those of his characters whose behavior seems whimsical, odd, or irrational)
   "Anton Chekhov and Raymond Carver: Two Realists with Different Techniques"

2. Think about Chekhov's insistence on the importance of a writer's noticing small details and minute particulars in "Natural description and 'the center of gravity' " (page 488). How do you find him living up to this principle in these three stories?
3. What if Olenka of "The Darling" were to marry Byelinkoff of "The Man in a Case"? In about 500 words, imagine the consequences for both of them.

Flannery O'Connor

EVERYTHING THAT RISES MUST CONVERGE   1965

Mary Flannery O'Connor (she dropped the first name from her byline) spent most of her life (1925–1964) in Milledgeville, Georgia. While she was a student at Georgia State College for Women, in her home town, her fledgling stories won her local fame. She went on to study at the Writers Workshop of the University of Iowa, from which in 1946 she obtained her M.F.A. degree. On discovering that she was afflicted with lupus erythematosus, the progressive and incurable blood disease that had killed her father, O'Connor returned to Milledgeville to live with her mother, undergo treatment, raise peacocks, and write. The bulk of her work consists of two novels, Wise Blood *(1952) and* The Violent Bear It Away *(1960);* Complete Stories of Flannery O'Connor *(1971); a book of essays and talks,* Mystery and Manners *(1961); her*

Flannery O'Connor

brilliant, modest, cheerful letters, collected in The Habit of Being *(1979); and terse book reviews written for Catholic newspapers in Georgia, collected in* The Presence of Grace *(1983). Since O'Connor's early death, her fiction, once blamed as gratuitously violent and jarringly grotesque, has enjoyed a steady and triumphant rise in critical favor. Its themes derive from her devoutly Christian faith, but its dark and often hilarious humor derives from her own view—perhaps also from a native Georgian tradition of tall-tale telling.*

Her doctor had told Julian's mother that she must lose twenty pounds on account of her blood pressure, so on Wednesday nights Julian had to take her downtown on the bus for a reducing class at the Y. The reducing class was designed for working girls over fifty, who weighed from 165 to 200 pounds. His mother was one of the slimmer ones, but she said ladies did not tell their age or weight. She would not ride the buses by herself at night since they had been integrated, and because the reducing class was one of her few pleasures, necessary for her health, and *free*, she said Julian could at least put himself out to take her, considering all she did for him. Julian did not like to consider all she did for him, but every Wednesday night he braced himself and took her.

She was almost ready to go, standing before the hall mirror, putting on her hat, while he, his hands behind him, appeared pinned to the door frame, waiting like Saint Sebastian for the arrows to begin piercing him°. The hat was new and had cost her seven dollars and a half. She kept saying, "Maybe I shouldn't have paid that for it. No, I shouldn't have. I'll take it off and return it tomorrow. I shouldn't have bought it."

Julian raised his eyes to heaven. "Yes, you should have bought it," he said. "Put it on and let's go." It was a hideous hat. A purple velvet flap came down on one side of it and stood up on the other; the rest of it was green and looked like a cushion with the stuffing out. He decided it was less comical than jaunty and pathetic. Everything that gave her pleasure was small and depressed him.

She lifted the hat one more time and set it down slowly on top of her head. Two wings of gray hair protruded on either side of her florid face, but her eyes, sky-blue, were as innocent and untouched by experience as they must have been when she was ten. Were it not that she was a widow who had struggled fiercely to feed and clothe and put him through school and who was supporting him still, "until he got on his feet," she might have been a little girl that he had to take to town.

"It's all right, it's all right," he said. "Let's go." He opened the door himself 5 and started down the walk to get her going. The sky was a dying violet and the houses stood out darkly against it, bulbous liver-colored monstrosities of a uniform ugliness though no two were alike. Since this had been a fashionable neighborhood forty years ago, his mother persisted in thinking they did well to have an apartment in it. Each house had a narrow collar of dirt around it in which sat, usually, a grubby child. Julian walked with his hands in his pockets, his head down and thrust forward and his eyes glazed with the determination to make himself completely numb during the time he would be sacrificed to her pleasure.

The door closed and he turned to find the dumpy figure, surmounted by the atrocious hat, coming toward him. "Well," she said, "you only live once and paying a little more for it, I at least won't meet myself coming and going."

"Some day I'll start making money," Julian said gloomily—he knew he never would—"and you can have one of those jokes whenever you take the fit." But first they would move. He visualized a place where the nearest neighbors would be three miles away on either side.

"I think you're doing fine," she said, drawing on her gloves. "You've only been out of school a year. Rome wasn't built in a day."

She was one of the few members of the Y reducing class who arrived in hat and gloves and who had a son who had been to college: "It takes time," she said, "and the world is in such a mess. This hat looked better on me than any of the others, though when she brought it out I said, 'Take that thing back. I wouldn't have it on my head,' and she said, 'Now wait till you see it on,' and when she put it on me, I said, 'We-ull,' and she said, 'If you ask me, that hat does something for you and you do something for the hat, and besides,' she said, 'with that hat, you won't meet yourself coming and going.'"

Saint Sebastian . . . piercing him: During the reign of the Roman emperor Diocletian (284–305 A.D.), Sebastian was sentenced to be shot to death by archers. Painters of the Italian Renaissance portrayed him riddled with arrows.

Julian thought he could have stood his lot better if she had been selfish, if she had been an old hag who drank and screamed at him. He walked along, saturated in depression, as if in the midst of his martyrdom he had lost his faith. Catching sight of his long, hopeless, irritated face, she stopped suddenly with a grief-stricken look, and pulled back on his arm. "Wait on me," she said. "I'm going back to the house and take this thing off and tomorrow I'm going to return it. I was out of my head. I can pay the gas bill with that seven-fifty."

He caught her arm in a vicious grip. "You are not going to take it back," he said. "I like it."

"Well," she said, "I don't think I ought . . . "

"Shut up and enjoy it," he muttered, more depressed than ever.

"With the world in the mess it's in," she said, "it's a wonder we can enjoy anything. I tell you, the bottom rail is on the top."

Julian sighed.

"Of course," she said, "if you know who you are, you can go anywhere." She said this every time he took her to the reducing class. "Most of them in it are not our kind of people," she said, "but I can be gracious to anybody. I know who I am."

"They don't give a damn for your graciousness," Julian said savagely. "Knowing who you are is good for one generation only. You haven't the foggiest idea where you stand now or who you are."

She stopped and allowed her eyes to flash at him. "I most certainly do know who I am," she said, "and if you don't know who you are, I'm ashamed of you."

"Oh hell," Julian said.

"Your great-grandfather was a former governor of this state," she said. "Your grandfather was a prosperous landowner. Your grandmother was a Godhigh."

"Will you look around you," he said tensely, "and see where you are now?" and he swept his arm jerkily out to indicate the neighborhood, which the growing darkness at least made less dingy.

"You remain what you are," she said. "Your great-grandfather had a plantation and two hundred slaves."

"There are no more slaves," he said irritably.

"They were better off when they were," she said. He groaned to see that she was off on that topic. She rolled onto it every few days like a train on an open track. He knew every stop, every junction, every swamp along the way, and knew the exact point at which her conclusion would roll majestically into the station: "It's ridiculous. It's simply not realistic. They should rise, yes, but on their own side of the fence."

"Let's skip it," Julian said.

"The ones I feel sorry for," she said, "are the ones that are half white. They're tragic."

"Will you skip it?"

"Suppose we were half white. We would certainly have mixed feelings."

"I have mixed feelings now," he groaned.

"Well let's talk about something pleasant," she said. "I remember going to Grandpa's when I was a little girl. Then the house had double stairways that went up to what was really the second floor—all the cooking was done on the first. I used to like to stay down in the kitchen on account of the way the walls smelled.

I would sit with my nose pressed against the plaster and take deep breaths. Actually the place belonged to the Godhighs but your grandfather Chestny paid the mortgage and saved it for them. They were in reduced circumstances," she said, "but reduced or not, they never forgot who they were."

"Doubtless that decayed mansion reminded them," Julian muttered. He never spoke of it without contempt or thought of it without longing. He had seen it once when he was a child before it had been sold. The double stairways had rotted and been torn down. Negroes were living in it. But it remained in his mind as his mother had known it. It appeared in his dreams regularly. He would stand on the wide porch, listening to the rustle of oak leaves, then wander through the high-ceilinged hall into the parlor that opened onto it and gaze at the worn rugs and faded draperies. It occurred to him that it was he, not she, who could have appreciated it. He preferred its threadbare elegance to anything he could name and it was because of it that all the neighborhoods they had lived in had been a torment to him—whereas she had hardly known the difference. She called her insensitivity "being adjustable."

"And I remember the old darky who was my nurse, Caroline. There was no better person in the world. I've always had a great respect for my colored friends," she said. "I'd do anything in the world for them and they'd . . . "

"Will you for God's sake get off that subject?" Julian said. When he got on a bus by himself, he made it a point to sit down beside a Negro, in reparation as it were for his mother's sins.

"You're mighty touchy tonight," she said. "Do you feel all right?"

"Yes I feel all right," he said. "Now lay off." 35

She pursed her lips. "Well, you certainly are in a vile humor," she observed. "I just won't speak to you at all."

They had reached the bus stop. There was no bus in sight and Julian, his hands still jammed in his pockets and his head thrust forward, scowled down the empty street. The frustration of having to wait on the bus as well as ride on it began to creep up his neck like a hot hand. The presence of his mother was borne in upon him as she gave a pained sigh. He looked at her bleakly. She was holding herself very erect under the preposterous hat, wearing it like a banner of her imaginary dignity. There was in him an evil urge to break her spirit. He suddenly unloosened his tie and pulled it off and put it in his pocket.

She stiffened. "Why must you look like *that* when you take me to town?" she said. "Why must you deliberately embarrass me?"

"If you'll never learn where you are," he said, "you can at least learn where I am."

"You look like a—thug," she said. 40

"Then I must be one," he murmured.

"I'll just go home," she said. "I will not bother you. If you can't do a little thing like that for me . . . "

Rolling his eyes upward, he put his tie back on. "Restored to my class," he muttered. He thrust his face toward her and hissed, "True culture is in the mind, the *mind*," he said, and tapped his head, "the mind."

"It's in the heart," she said, "and in how you do things and how you do things is because of who you *are*."

"Nobody in the damn bus cares who you are." 45

"I care who I am," she said icily.

The lighted bus appeared on top of the next hill and as it approached, they moved out into the street to meet it. He put his hand under her elbow and hoisted her up on the creaking step. She entered with a little smile, as if she were going into a drawing room where everyone had been waiting for her. While he put in the tokens, she sat down on one of the broad front seats for three which faced the aisle. A thin woman with protruding teeth and long yellow hair was sitting on the end of it. His mother moved up beside her and left room for Julian beside herself. He sat down and looked at the floor across the aisle where a pair of thin feet in red and white canvas sandals were planted.

His mother immediately began a general conversation meant to attract anyone who felt like talking. "Can it get any hotter?" she said and removed from her purse a folding fan, black with a Japanese scene on it, which she began to flutter before her.

"I reckon it might could," the woman with the protruding teeth said, "but I know for a fact my apartment couldn't get no hotter."

"It must get the afternoon sun," his mother said. She sat forward and looked up and down the bus. It was half filled. Everybody was white. "I see we have the bus to ourselves," she said. Julian cringed. 50

"For a change," said the woman across the aisle, the owner of the red and white canvas sandals. "I come on one the other day and they were thick as fleas— up front and all through."

"The world is in a mess everywhere," his mother said. "I don't know how we've let it get in this fix."

"What gets my goat is all those boys from good families stealing automobile tires," the woman with the protruding teeth said. "I told my boy, I said you may not be rich but you been raised right and if I ever catch you in any such mess, they can send you on to the reformatory. Be exactly where you belong."

"Training tells," his mother said. "Is your boy in high school?"

"Ninth grade," the woman said. 55

"My son just finished college last year. He wants to write but he's selling typewriters until he gets started," his mother said.

The woman leaned forward and peered at Julian. He threw her such a malevolent look that she subsided against the seat. On the floor across the aisle there was an abandoned newspaper. He got up and got it and opened it out in front of him. His mother discreetly continued the conversation in a lower tone but the woman across the aisle said in a loud voice, "Well that's nice. Selling typewriters is close to writing. He can go right from one to the other."

"I tell him," his mother said, "that Rome wasn't built in a day."

Behind the newspaper Julian was withdrawing into the inner compartment of his mind where he spent most of his time. This was a kind of mental bubble in which he established himself when he could not bear to be a part of what was going on around him. From it he could see out and judge but in it he was safe from any kind of penetration from without. It was the only place where he felt free of the general idiocy of his fellows. His mother had never entered it but from it he could see her with absolute clarity.

The old lady was clever enough and he thought that if she had started from 60
any of the right premises, more might have been expected of her. She lived according to the laws of her own fantasy world, outside of which he had never seen

her set foot. The law of it was to sacrifice herself for him after she had first created the necessity to do so by making a mess of things. If he had permitted her sacrifices, it was only because her lack of foresight had made them necessary. All of her life had been a struggle to act like a Chestny without the Chestny goods, and to give him everything she thought a Chestny ought to have; but since, said she, it was fun to struggle, why complain? And when you had won, as she had won, what fun to look back on the hard times! He could not forgive her that she had enjoyed the struggle and that she thought *she* had won.

What she meant when she said she had won was that she had brought him up successfully and had sent him to college and that he had turned out so well—good looking (her teeth had gone unfilled so that his could be straightened), intelligent (he realized he was too intelligent to be a success), and with a future ahead of him (there was of course no future ahead of him). She excused his gloominess on the grounds that he was still growing up and his radical ideas on his lack of practical experience. She said he didn't yet know a thing about "life," that he hadn't even entered the real world—when already he was as disenchanted with it as a man of fifty.

The further irony of all this was that in spite of her, he had turned out so well. In spite of going to only a third-rate college, he had, on his own initiative, come out with a first-rate education; in spite of growing up dominated by a small mind, he had ended up with a large one; in spite of all her foolish views, he was free of prejudice and unafraid to face facts. Most miraculous of all, instead of being blinded by love for her as she was for him, he had cut himself emotionally free of her and could see her with complete objectivity. He was not dominated by his mother.

The bus stopped with a sudden jerk and shook him from his meditation. A woman from the back lurched forward with little steps and barely escaped falling in his newspaper as she righted herself. She got off and a large Negro got on. Julian kept his paper lowered to watch. It gave him a certain satisfaction to see injustice in daily operation. It confirmed his view that with a few exceptions there was no one worth knowing within a radius of three hundred miles. The Negro was well dressed and carried a briefcase. He looked around and then sat down on the other end of the seat where the woman with the red and white canvas sandals was sitting. He immediately unfolded a newspaper and obscured himself behind it. Julian's mother's elbow at once prodded insistently into his ribs. "Now you see why I won't ride on these buses by myself," she whispered.

The woman with the red and white canvas sandals had risen at the same time the Negro sat down and had gone further back in the bus and taken the seat of the woman who had got off. His mother leaned forward and cast her an approving look.

Julian rose, crossed the aisle, and sat down in the place of the woman with the canvas sandals. From this position, he looked serenely across at his mother. Her face had turned an angry red. He stared at her, making his eyes the eyes of a stranger. He felt his tension suddenly lift as if he had openly declared war on her.

He would have liked to get in conversation with the Negro and to talk with him about art or politics or any subject that would be above the comprehension of those around them, but the man remained entrenched behind his paper. He

65

was either ignoring the change of seating or had never noticed it. There was no way for Julian to convey his sympathy.

His mother kept her eyes fixed reproachfully on his face. The woman with the protruding teeth was looking at him avidly as if he were a type of monster new to her.

"Do you have a light?" he asked the Negro.

Without looking away from his paper, the man reached in his pocket and handed him a packet of matches.

"Thanks," Julian said. For a moment he held the matches foolishly. A NO SMOKING sign looked down upon him from over the door. This alone would not have deterred him; he had no cigarettes. He had quit smoking some months before because he could not afford it. "Sorry," he muttered and handed back the matches. The Negro lowered the paper and gave him an annoyed look. He took the matches and raised the paper again.

His mother continued to gaze at him but she did not take advantage of his momentary discomfort. Her eyes retained their battered look. Her face seemed to be unnaturally red, as if her blood pressure had risen. Julian allowed no glimmer of sympathy to show on his face. Having got the advantage, he wanted desperately to keep it and carry it through. He would have liked to teach her a lesson that would last her a while, but there seemed no way to continue the point. The Negro refused to come out from behind his paper.

Julian folded his arms and looked stolidly before him, facing her but as if he did not see her, as if he had ceased to recognize her existence. He visualized a scene in which, the bus having reached their stop, he would remain in his seat and when she said, "Aren't you going to get off?" he would look at her as at a stranger who had rashly addressed him. The corner they got off on was usually deserted, but it was well lighted and it would not hurt her to walk by herself the four blocks to the Y. He decided to wait until the time came and then decide whether or not he would let her get off by herself. He would have to be at the Y at ten to bring her back, but he could leave her wondering if he was going to show up. There was no reason for her to think she could always depend on him.

He retired again into the high-ceilinged room sparsely settled with large pieces of antique furniture. His soul expanded momentarily but then he became aware of his mother across from him and the vision shriveled. He studied her coldly. Her feet in little pumps dangled like a child's and did not quite reach the floor. She was training on him an exaggerated look of reproach. He felt completely detached from her. At that moment he could with pleasure have slapped her as he would have slapped a particularly obnoxious child in his charge.

He began to imagine various unlikely ways by which he could teach her a lesson. He might make friends with some distinguished Negro professor or lawyer and bring him home to spend the evening. He would be entirely justified but her blood pressure would rise to 300. He could not push her to the extent of making her have a stroke, and moreover, he had never been successful at making any Negro friends. He had tried to strike up an acquaintance on the bus with some of the better types, with ones that looked like professors or ministers or lawyers. One morning he had sat down next to a distinguished-looking dark brown man who had answered his questions with a sonorous solemnity but who had turned out to be an undertaker. Another day he had sat down beside a cigar-smoking Negro with a diamond ring on his finger, but after a few stilted pleasantries, the Negro had rung the buzzer and risen, slipping two lottery tickets into Julian's hand as he climbed over him to leave.

He imagined his mother lying desperately ill and his being able to secure only a Negro doctor for her. He toyed with that idea for a few minutes and then dropped it for a momentary vision of himself participating as a sympathizer in a sit-in demonstration. This was possible but he did not linger with it. Instead, he approached the ultimate horror. He brought home a beautiful suspiciously Negroid woman. Prepare yourself, he said. There is nothing you can do about it. This is the woman I've chosen. She's intelligent, dignified, even good, and she's suffered and she hasn't thought it *fun*. Now persecute us, go ahead and persecute us. Drive her out of here, but remember, you're driving me too. His eyes were narrowed and through the indignation he had generated, he saw his mother across the aisle, purple-faced, shrunken to the dwarf-like proportions of her moral nature, sitting like a mummy beneath the ridiculous banner of her hat.

He was tilted out of his fantasy again as the bus stopped. The door opened with a sucking hiss and out of the dark a large, gaily dressed, sullen-looking colored woman got on with a little boy. The child, who might have been four, had on a short plaid suit and a Tyrolean hat with a blue feather in it. Julian hoped that he would sit down beside him and that the woman would push in beside his mother. He could think of no better arrangement.

As she waited for her tokens, the woman was surveying the seating possibilities—he hoped with the idea of sitting where she was least wanted. There was something familiar-looking about her but Julian could not place what it was. She was a giant of a woman. Her face was set not only to meet opposition but to seek it out. The downward tilt of her large lower lip was like a warning sign: DON'T TAMPER WITH ME. Her bulging figure was encased in a green crepe dress and her feet overflowed in red shoes. She had on a hideous hat. A purple velvet flap came down on one side of it and stood up on the other; the rest of it was green and looked like a cushion with the stuffing out. She carried a mammoth red pocketbook that bulged throughout as if it were stuffed with rocks.

To Julian's disappointment, the little boy climbed up on the empty seat beside his mother. His mother lumped all children, black and white, into the common category, "cute," and she thought little Negroes were on the whole cuter than little white children. She smiled at the little boy as he climbed on the seat.

Meanwhile the woman was bearing down upon the empty seat beside Julian. To his annoyance, she squeezed herself into it. He saw his mother's face change as the woman settled herself next to him and he realized with satisfaction that this was more objectionable to her than it was to him. Her face seemed almost gray and there was a look of dull recognition in her eyes, as if suddenly she had sickened at some awful confrontation. Julian saw that it was because she and the woman had, in a sense, swapped sons. Though his mother would not realize the symbolic significance of this, she would feel it. His amusement showed plainly on his face.

THREE FICTION WRITERS IN DEPTH

The woman next to him muttered something unintelligible to herself. He was conscious of a kind of bristling next to him, a muted growling like that of an angry cat. He could not see anything but the red pocketbook upright on the bulging green thighs. He visualized the woman as she had stood waiting for her tokens—the ponderous figure, rising from the red shoes upward over the solid hips, the mammoth bosom, the haughty face, to the green and purple hat.

His eyes widened.

The vision of the two hats, identical, broke upon him with the radiance of a brilliant sunrise. His face was suddenly lit with joy. He could not believe that Fate had thrust upon his mother such a lesson. He gave a loud chuckle so that she would look at him and see that he saw. She turned her eyes on him slowly. The blue in them seemed to have turned a bruised purple. For a moment he had an uncomfortable sense of her innocence, but it lasted only a second before principle rescued him. Justice entitled him to laugh. His grin hardened until it said to her as plainly as if he were saying aloud: Your punishment exactly fits your pettiness. This should teach you a permanent lesson.

Her eyes shifted to the woman. She seemed unable to bear looking at him and to find the woman preferable. He became conscious again of the bristling presence at his side. The woman was rumbling like a volcano about to become active. His mother's mouth began to twitch slightly at one corner. With a sinking heart, he saw incipient signs of recovery on her face and realized that this was going to strike her suddenly as funny and was going to be no lesson at all. She kept her eyes on the woman and an amused smile came over her face as if the woman were a monkey that had stolen her hat. The little Negro was looking up at her with large fascinated eyes. He had been trying to attract her attention for some time.

"Carver!" the woman said suddenly. "Come heah!"

When he saw that the spotlight was on him at last, Carver drew his feet up and turned himself toward Julian's mother and giggled.

"Carver!" the woman. "You heah me? Come heah!"

Carver slid down from the seat but remained squatting with his back against the base of it, his head turned slyly around toward Julian's mother, who was smiling at him. The woman reached a hand across the aisle and snatched him to her. He righted himself and hung backwards on her knees, grinning at Julian's mother. "Isn't he cute?" Julian's mother said to the woman with the protruding teeth.

"I reckon he is," the woman said without conviction.

The Negress yanked him upright but he eased out of her grip and shot across the aisle and scrambled, giggling wildly, onto the seat beside his love.

"I think he likes me," Julian's mother said, and smiled at the woman. It was the smile she used when she was being particularly gracious to an inferior. Julian saw everything lost. The lesson had rolled off her like rain on a roof.

The woman stood up and yanked the little boy off the seat as if she were snatching him from contagion. Julian could feel the rage in her at having no weapon like his mother's smile. She gave the child a sharp slap across his leg. He howled once and then thrust his head into her stomach and kicked his feet against her shins. "Be-have," she said vehemently.

The bus stopped and the Negro who had been reading the newspaper got off. The woman moved over and set the little boy down with a thump between herself and Julian. She held him firmly by the knee. In a moment he put his hands in front of his face and peeped at Julian's mother through his fingers.

"I see yoooooooo!" she said and put her hand in front of her face and peeped at him.

The woman slapped his hand down. "Quit yo' foolishness," she said, "before I knock the living Jesus out of you!"

Julian was thankful that the next stop was theirs. He reached up and pulled   95
the cord. The woman reached up and pulled it at the same time. Oh my God, he thought. He had the terrible intuition that when they got off the bus together, his mother would open her purse and give the little boy a nickel. The gesture would be as natural to her as breathing. The bus stopped and the woman got up and lunged to the front, dragging the child, who wished to stay on, after her. Julian and his mother got up and followed. As they neared the door, Julian tried to relieve her of her pocketbook.

"No," she murmured. "I want to give the little boy a nickel."

"No!" Julian hissed. "No!"

She smiled down at the child and opened her bag. The bus door opened and the woman picked him up by the arm and descended with him, hanging at her hip. Once in the street she set him down and shook him.

Julian's mother had to close her purse while she got down the bus step but as soon as her feet were on the ground, she opened it again and began to rummage inside. "I can't find but a penny," she whispered, "but it looks like a new one."

"Don't do it!" Julian said fiercely between his teeth. There was a streetlight   100
on the corner and she hurried to get under it so that she could better see into her pocketbook. The woman was heading off rapidly down the street with the child still hanging backward on her hand.

"Oh little boy!" Julian's mother called and took a few quick steps and caught up with them just beyond the lamppost. "Here's a bright new penny for you," and she held out the coin, which shone bronze in the dim light.

The huge woman turned and for a moment stood, her shoulders lifted and her face frozen with frustrated rage, and stared at Julian's mother. Then all at once she seemed to explode like a piece of machinery that had been given one ounce of pressure too much. Julian saw the black fist swing out with the red pocketbook. He shut his eyes and cringed as he heard the woman shout, "He don't take nobody's pennies!" When he opened his eyes, the woman was disappearing down the street with the little boy staring wide-eyed over her shoulder. Julian's mother was sitting on the sidewalk.

"I told you not to do that," Julian said angrily. "I told you not to do that!"

He stood over her for a minute, gritting his teeth. Her legs were stretched out in front of her and her hat was on her lap. He squatted down and looked her in the face. It was totally expressionless. "You got exactly what you deserved," he said. "Now get up."

He picked up her pocketbook and put what had fallen out back in it. He   105
picked the hat up off her lap. The penny caught his eye on the sidewalk and he picked that up and let it drop before her eyes into the purse. Then he stood up

and leaned over and held his hands out to pull her up. She remained immobile. He sighed. Rising above them on either side were black apartment buildings, marked with irregular rectangles of light. At the end of the block a man came out of a door and walked off in the opposite direction. "All right," he said, "suppose somebody happens by and wants to know why you're sitting on the sidewalk?"

She took the hand and, breathing hard, pulled heavily up on it and then stood for a moment, swaying slightly as if the spots of light in the darkness were circling around her. Her eyes, shadowed and confused, finally settled on his face. He did not try to conceal his irritation. "I hope this teaches you a lesson," he said. She leaned forward and her eyes raked his face. She seemed trying to determine his identity. Then, as if she found nothing familiar about him, she started off with a headlong movement in the wrong direction.

"Aren't you going on to the Y?" he asked.

"Home," she muttered.

"Well, are we walking?"

For answer she kept going. Julian followed along, his hands behind him. He 110 saw no reason to let the lesson she had had go without backing it up with an explanation of its meaning. She might as well be made to understand what had happened to her. "Don't think that was just an uppity Negro woman," he said. "That was the whole colored race which will no longer take your condescending pennies. That was your black double. She can wear the same hat as you, and to be sure," he added gratuitously (because he thought it was funny), "it looked better on her than it did on you. What all this means," he said, "is that the old world is gone. The old manners are obsolete and your graciousness is not worth a damn." He thought bitterly of the house that had been lost for him. "You aren't who you think you are," he said.

She continued to plow ahead, paying no attention to him. Her hair had come undone on one side. She dropped her pocketbook and took no notice. He stooped and picked it up and handed it to her but she did not take it.

"You needn't act as if the world had come to an end," he said. "because it hasn't. From now on you've got to live in a new world and face a few realities for a change. Buck up," he said, "it won't kill you."

She was breathing fast.

"Let's wait on the bus," he said.

"Home," she said thickly. 115

"I hate to see you behave like this," he said. "Just like a child. I should be able to expect more of you." He decided to stop where he was and make her stop and wait for a bus. "I'm not going any farther," he said, stopping. "We're going on the bus."

She continued to go on as if she had not heard him. He took a few steps and caught her arm and stopped her. He looked into her face and caught his breath. He was looking into a face he had never seen before. "Tell Grandpa to come get me," she said.

He stared, stricken.

"Tell Caroline to come get me," she said.

Stunned, he let her go and she lurched forward again, walking as if one leg 120 were shorter than the other. A tide of darkness seemed to be sweeping her from him. "Mother!" he cried. "Darling, sweetheart, wait!" Crumpling, she fell to the pavement. He dashed forward and fell at her side, crying, "Mamma, Mamma!" He turned her over. Her face was fiercely distorted. One eye, large and staring, moved slightly to the left as if it had become unmoored. The other remained fixed on him, raked his face again, found nothing and closed.

"Wait here, wait here!" he cried and jumped up and began to run for help toward a cluster of lights he saw in the distance ahead of him. "Help, help!" he shouted, but his voice was thin, scarcely a thread of sound. The lights drifted farther away the faster he ran and his feet moved numbly as if they carried him nowhere. The tide of darkness seemed to sweep him back to her, postponing from moment to moment his entry into the world of guilt and sorrow.

QUESTIONS

1. In what ways is Julian's mother, in her attitudes and assumptions, typical of an earlier generation of privileged people? What is her family history?
2. How would you describe Julian's attitude toward his mother? His attitude toward himself? The author's view of him? (How can you tell? Look for evidence.)
3. Julian thinks his mother lives in "her own fantasy world" (paragraph 60). How might it be charged that, ironically, he lives in a fantasy world of his own?
4. Think about the mother's offering Carver a penny—and the consequences of this small act. What are we to think of it? Do you take it, as perhaps Carver's mother does, to be a gesture of contempt and bigotry?
5. What does O'Connor make of the fact that Julian's and Carver's mother happen to wear identical hats? How does Julian interpret this fact, and what does it tell us about him?
6. What do you make of the title, "Everything That Rises Must Converge"?
7. Try stating the theme of the story.
8. If you have read Chekhov's story "The Man in a Case," how does Julian remind you of Byelinkoff? (See especially O'Connor's paragraph 59.)

Flannery O'Connor

A GOOD MAN IS HARD TO FIND   1955

The grandmother didn't want to go to Florida. She wanted to visit some of her connections in east Tennessee and she was seizing at every chance to change Bailey's mind. Bailey was the son she lived with, her only boy. He was sitting on the edge of his chair at the table, bent over the orange sports section of the *Journal*. "Now look here, Bailey," she said, "see here, read this," and she stood with one hand on her thin hip and the other rattling the newspaper at his bald head. "Here this fellow that calls himself The Misfit is aloose from the Federal Pen and headed toward Florida and you read here what it says he did to these people. Just you read it. I wouldn't take my children in any direction with a criminal like that aloose in it. I couldn't answer to my conscience if I did."

Bailey didn't look up from his reading so she wheeled around then and faced the children's mother, a young woman in slacks, whose face was as broad and innocent as a cabbage and was tied around with a green head-kerchief that had two points on the top like rabbit's ears. She was sitting on the sofa, feeding the baby his apricots out of a jar. "The children have been to Florida before," the old lady said. "You all ought to take them somewhere else for a change so they would see different parts of the world and be broad. They never have been to east Tennessee."

The children's mother didn't seem to hear her but the eight-year-old boy, John Wesley, a stocky child with glasses, said, "If you don't want to go to Florida, why dontcha stay at home?" He and the little girl, June Star, were reading the funny papers on the floor.

"She wouldn't stay at home to be queen for a day," June Star said without raising her yellow head.

"Yes and what would you do if this fellow, The Misfit, caught you?" the grand- 5 mother said.

"I'd smack his face," John Wesley said.

"She wouldn't stay at home for a million bucks," June Star said. "Afraid she'd miss something. She has to go everywhere we go."

"All right, Miss," the grandmother said. "Just remember that the next time you want me to curl your hair."

June Star said her hair was naturally curly.

The next morning the grandmother was the first one in the car, ready to go. 10 She had her big black valise that looked like the head of a hippopotamus in one corner, and underneath it she was hiding a basket with Pitty Sing, the cat, in it. She didn't intend for the cat to be left alone in the house for three days be- cause he would miss her too much and she was afraid he might brush against one of the gas burners and accidentally asphyxiate himself. Her son, Bailey, didn't like to arrive at a motel with a cat.

She sat in the middle of the back seat with John Wesley and June Star on either side of her. Bailey and the children's mother and the baby sat in front and they left Atlanta at eight forty-five with the mileage on the car at 55890. The grandmother wrote this down because she thought it would be interesting to say how many miles they had been when they got back. It took them twenty minutes to reach the outskirts of the city.

The old lady settled herself comfortably, removing her white cotton gloves and putting them up with her purse on the shelf in front of the back window. The children's mother still had on slacks and still had her hair tied up in a green kerchief, but the grandmother had on a navy blue straw sailor hat with a bunch of white violets on the brim and a navy blue dress with a small white dot in the print. Her collars and cuffs were white organdy trimmed with lace and at her neck- line she had pinned a purple spray of cloth violets containing a sachet. In case of an accident, anyone seeing her dead on the highway would know at once that she was a lady.

She said she thought it was going to be a good day for driving, neither too hot nor too cold, and she cautioned Bailey that the speed limit was fifty-five miles an hour and that the patrolmen hid themselves behind billboards and small clumps of trees and sped out after you before you had a chance to slow down. She pointed out interesting details of the scenery: Stone Mountain; the blue granite that in some places came up to both sides of the highway; the brilliant red clay banks slightly streaked with purple; and the various crops that made rows of green lacework on the ground. The trees were full of silver-white sunlight and the meanest of them sparkled. The children were reading comic magazines and their mother had gone back to sleep.

"Let's go through Georgia fast so we won't have to look at it much," John Wesley said.

"If I were a little boy," said the grandmother, "I wouldn't talk about my native state that way. Tennessee has the mountains and Georgia has the hills." 15

"Tennessee is just a hillbilly dumping ground," John Wesley said, "and Georgia is a lousy state too."

"You said it," June Star said.

"In my time," said the grandmother, folding her thin veined fingers, "children were more respectful of their native states and their parents and everything else. People did right then. Oh look at the cute little pickaninny!" she said and pointed to a Negro child standing in the door of a shack. "Wouldn't that make a picture, now?" she asked and they all turned and looked at the little Negro out of the back window. He waved.

"He didn't have any britches on," June Star said.

"He probably didn't have any," the grandmother explained. "Little niggers in the country don't have things like we do. If I could paint, I'd paint that picture," she said. 20

The children exchanged comic books.

The grandmother offered to hold the baby and the children's mother passed him over the front seat to her. She set him on her knee and bounced him and told him about the things they were passing. She rolled her eyes and screwed up her mouth and stuck her leathery thin face into his smooth bland one. Occasionally he gave her a faraway smile. They passed a large cotton field with five or six graves fenced in the middle of it, like a small island. "Look at the graveyard!" the grandmother said, pointing it out. "That was the old family burying ground. That belonged to the plantation."

"Where's the plantation?" John Wesley asked.

"Gone With the Wind," said the grandmother. "Ha. Ha."

When the children finished all the comic books they had brought, they opened the lunch and ate it. The grandmother ate a peanut butter sandwich and an olive and would not let the children throw the box and the paper napkins out the window. When there was nothing else to do they played a game by choosing a cloud and making the other two guess what shape it suggested. John Wesley took one the shape of a cow and June Star guessed a cow and John Wesley said, no, an automobile, and June Star said he didn't play fair, and they began to slap each other over the grandmother. 25

The grandmother said she would tell them a story if they would keep quiet. When she told a story, she rolled her eyes and waved her head and was very dramatic. She said once when she was a maiden lady she had been courted by a Mr. Edgar Atkins Teagarden from Jasper, Georgia. She said he was a very good-looking man and a gentleman and that he brought her a watermelon every Saturday afternoon with his initials cut in it, E. A. T. Well, one Saturday, she said, Mr. Teagarden brought the watermelon and there was nobody at home and he left it on the front porch and returned in his buggy to Jasper, but she never got the watermelon, she said, because a nigger boy ate it when he saw the initials, E. A. T.! This story tickled John Wesley's funny bone and he giggled and giggled but June Star didn't think it was any good. She said she wouldn't marry a man that just brought her a watermelon on Saturday. The grandmother said she would have done well to marry Mr. Teagarden because he was a gentlemen and had bought Coca-Cola stock when it first came out and that he had died only a few years ago, a very wealthy man.

They stopped at The Tower for barbecued sandwiches. The Tower was a part stucco and part wood filling station and dance hall set in a clearing outside of Timothy. A fat man named Red Sammy Butts ran it and there were signs stuck here and there on the building and for miles up and down the highway saying, TRY RED SAMMY'S FAMOUS BARBECUE. NONE LIKE FAMOUS RED SAMMY'S! RED SAM! THE FAT BOY WITH THE HAPPY LAUGH. A VETERAN! RED SAMMY'S YOUR MAN!

Red Sammy was lying on the bare ground outside The Tower with his head under a truck while a gray monkey about a foot high, chained to a small chinaberry tree, chattered nearby. The monkey sprang back into the tree and got on the highest limb as soon as he saw the children jump out of the car and run toward him.

Inside, The Tower was a long dark room with a counter at one end and tables at the other and dancing space in the middle. They all sat down at a board table next to the nickelodeon and Red Sam's wife, a tall burnt-brown woman with hair and eyes lighter than her skin, came and took their order. The children's mother put a dime in the machine and played "The Tennessee Waltz," and the grandmother said that tune always made her want to dance. She asked Bailey if he would like to dance but he only glared at her. He didn't have a naturally sunny disposition like she did and trips made him nervous. The grandmother's brown eyes were very bright. She swayed her head from side to side and pretended she was dancing in her chair. June Star said play something she could tap to so the children's mother put in another dime and played a fast number and June Star stepped out onto the dance floor and did her tap routine.

"Ain't she cute?" Red Sam's wife said, leaning over the counter. "Would you like to come be my little girl?" 30

"No I certainly wouldn't," June Star said. "I wouldn't live in a broken-down place like this for a million bucks!" and she ran back to the table.

"Ain't she cute?" the woman repeated, stretching her mouth politely.

"Arn't you ashamed?" hissed the grandmother.

Red Sam came in and told his wife to quit lounging on the counter and hurry up with these people's order. His khaki trousers reached just to his hip bones and his stomach hung over them like a sack of meal swaying under his shirt. He came over and sat down at a table nearby and let out a combination sigh and yodel. "You can't win," he said. "You can't win," and he wiped his sweating red face off with a gray handkerchief. "These days you don't know who to trust," he said. "Ain't that the truth?"

"People are certainly not nice like they used to be," said the grandmother. 35

"Two fellers come in here last week," Red Sammy said, "driving a Chrysler. It was a old beat-up car but it was a good one and these boys looked all right to me. Said they worked at the mill and you know I let them fellers charge the gas they bought? Now why did I do that?"

"Because you're a good man!" the grandmother said at once.

"Yes'm, I suppose so," Red Sam said as if he were struck with this answer.

His wife brought the orders, carrying the five plates all at once without a tray, two in each hand and one balanced on her arm. "It isn't a soul in this green world of God's that you can trust," she said. "And I don't count nobody out of that, not nobody," she repeated, looking at Red Sammy.

"Did you read about that criminal, The Misfit, that's escaped?" asked the grand- 40 mother.

"I wouldn't be a bit surprised if he didn't attact this place right here," said the woman. "If he hears about it being here, I wouldn't be none surprised to see him. If he hears it's two cent in the cash register, I wouldn't be a tall surprised if he . . . "

"That'll do," Red Sam said. "Go bring these people their Co'-Colas," and the woman went off to get the rest of the order.

"A good man is hard to find," Red Sammy said. "Everything is getting terrible. I remember the day you could go off and leave your screen door unlatched. Not no more."

He and the grandmother discussed better times. The old lady said that in her opinion Europe was entirely to blame for the way things were now. She said the way Europe acted you would think we were made of money and Red Sam said it was no use talking about it, she was exactly right. The children ran outside into the white sunlight and looked at the monkey in the lacy chinaberry tree. He was busy catching fleas on himself and biting each one carefully between his teeth as if it were a delicacy.

They drove off again into the hot afternoon. The grandmother took cat naps 45 and woke up every five minutes with her own snoring. Outside of Toombsboro she woke up and recalled an old plantation that she had visited in this neighborhood once when she was a young lady. She said the house had six white columns across the front and that there was an avenue of oaks leading up to it and two little wooden trellis arbors on either side in front where you sat down with your suitor after a stroll in the garden. She recalled exactly which road to turn off to get to it. She knew that Bailey would not be willing to lose any time looking at an old house, but the more she talked about it, the more she wanted to see it once again and find out if the little twin arbors were still standing. "There was a secret panel in this house," she said craftily, not telling the truth but wishing that she were, "and the story went that all the family silver was hidden in it when Sherman° came through but it was never found . . . "

"Hey!" John Wesley said. "Let's go see it! We'll find it! We'll poke all the woodwork and find it! Who lives there? Where do you turn off at? Hey, Pop, can't we turn off there?"

"We never have seen a house with a secret panel!" June Star shrieked. "Let's go to the house with the secret panel! Hey Pop, can't we go see the house with the secret panel!"

Sherman: General William Tecumseh Sherman, Union commander, whose troops burned Atlanta in 1864, then made a devastating march to the sea.

"It's not far from here, I know," the grandmother said. "It wouldn't take over twenty minutes."

Bailey was looking straight ahead. His jaw was as rigid as a horseshoe. "No," he said.

The children began to yell and scream that they wanted to see the house   50
with the secret panel. John Wesley kicked the back of the front seat and June Star hung over her mother's shoulder and whined desperately into her ear that they never had any fun even on their vacation, that they could never do what THEY wanted to do. The baby began to scream and John Wesley kicked the back of the seat so hard that his father could feel the blows in his kidney.

"All right!" he shouted and drew the car to a stop at the side of the road. "Will you all shut up? Will you all just shut up for one second? If you don't shut up, we won't go anywhere."

"It would be very educational for them," the grandmother murmured.

"All right," Bailey said, "but get this: this is the only time we're going to stop for anything like this. This is the one and only time."

"The dirt road that you have to turn down is about a mile back," the grandmother directed. "I marked it when we passed."

"A dirt road," Bailey groaned.   55

After they had turned around and were headed toward the dirt road, the grandmother recalled other points about the house, the beautiful glass over the front doorway and the candle-lamp in the hall. John Wesley said that the secret panel was probably in the fireplace.

"You can't go inside this house," Bailey said. "You don't know who lives there."

"While you all talk to the people in front, I'll run around behind and get in a window," John Wesley suggested.

"We'll all stay in the car," his mother said.

They turned onto the dirt road and the car raced roughly along in a swirl   60
of pink dust. The grandmother recalled the times when there were no paved roads and thirty miles was a day's journey. The dirt road was hilly and there were sudden washes in it and sharp curves on dangerous embankments. All at once they would be on a hill, looking down over the blue tops of trees for miles around, then the next minute, they would be in a red depression with the dust-coated trees looking down on them.

"This place had better turn up in a minute," Bailey said, "or I'm going to turn around."

The road looked as if no one had traveled on it for months.

"It's not much farther," the grandmother said and just as she said it, a horrible thought came to her. The thought was so embarrassing that she turned red in the face and her eyes dilated and her feet jumped up, upsetting her valise in the corner. The instant the valise moved, the newspaper top she had over the basket under it rose with a snarl and Pitty Sing, the cat, sprang onto Bailey's shoulder.

The children were thrown to the floor and their mother, clutching the baby, was thrown out the door onto the ground; the old lady was thrown into the front seat. The car turned over once and landed right-side-up in a gulch off the side of the road. Bailey remained in the driver's seat with the cat—gray-striped with a broad white face and an orange nose—clinging to his neck like a caterpillar.

As soon as the children saw they could move their arms and legs, they scrambled out of the car, shouting, "We've had an ACCIDENT!" The grandmother
was curled up under the dashboard, hoping she was injured so that Bailey's wrath
would not come down on her all at once. The horrible thought she had had before the accident was that the house she had remembered so vividly was not in
Georgia but in Tennessee.

Bailey removed the cat from his neck with both hands and flung it out the
window against the side of a pine tree. Then he got out of the car and started
looking for the children's mother. She was sitting against the side of the red gutted ditch, holding the screaming baby, but she only had a cut down her face and
a broken shoulder. "We've had an ACCIDENT!" the children screamed in a frenzy
of delight.

"But nobody's killed," June Star said with disappointment as the grandmother
limped out of the car, her hat still pinned to her head but the broken front brim
standing up at a jaunty angle and the violet spray hanging off the side. They all
sat down in the ditch, except the children, to recover from the shock. They were
all shaking.

"Maybe a car will come along," said the children's mother hoarsely.

"I believe I have injured an organ," said the grandmother, pressing her side,
but no one answered her. Bailey's teeth were clattering. He had on a yellow sport
shirt with bright blue parrots designed in it and his face was as yellow as the shirt.
The grandmother decided that she would not mention that the house was in Tennessee.

The road was about ten feet above and they could see only the tops of the
trees on the other side of it. Behind the ditch they were sitting in there were
more woods, tall and dark and deep. In a few minutes they saw a car some
distance away on top of a hill, coming slowly as if the occupants were watching
them. The grandmother stood up and waved both her arms dramatically to
attract their attention. The car continued to come on slowly, disappeared around
a bend and appeared again, moving even slower, on top of the hill they had gone
over. It was a big black battered hearse-like automobile. There were three men in it.

It came to a stop just over them and for some minutes, the driver looked
down with a steady expressionless gaze to where they were sitting, and didn't
speak. Then he turned his head and muttered something to the other two
and they got out. One was a fat boy in black trousers and a red sweat shirt with
a silver stallion embossed on the front of it. He moved around on the right side
of them and stood staring, his mouth partly open in a kind of loose grin. The
other had on khaki pants and a blue striped coat and a gray hat pulled down very
low, hiding most of his face. He came around slowly on the left side. Neither
spoke.

The driver got out of the car and stood by the side of it, looking down at
them. He was an older man than the other two. His hair was just beginning to
gray and he wore silver-rimmed spectacles that gave him a scholarly look. He had
a long creased face and didn't have on any shirt or undershirt. He had on blue
jeans that were too tight for him and was holding a black hat and a gun. The
two boys also had guns.

"We've had an ACCIDENT!" the children screamed.

The grandmother had the peculiar feeling that the bespectacled man was someone she knew. His face was as familiar to her as if she had known him all her
life but she could not recall who he was. He moved away from the car and began
to come down the embankment, placing his feet carefully so that he wouldn't
slip. He had on tan and white shoes and no socks, and his ankles were red and
thin. "Good afternoon," he said. "I see you all had you a little spill."

"We turned over twice!" said the grandmother.   75

"Oncet," he corrected. "We seen it happen. Try their car and see will it run,
Hiram," he said quietly to the boy with the gray hat.

"What you got that gun for?" John Wesley asked. "Whatcha gonna do with
that gun?"

"Lady," the man said to the children's mother, "would you mind calling them
children to sit down by you? Children make me nervous. I want all you all to
sit down right together there where you're at."

"What are you telling US what to do for?" June Star asked.

Behind them the line of woods gaped like a dark open mouth. "Come here,"   80
said their mother.

"Look here now," Bailey began suddenly, "we're in a predicament! We're
in . . ."

The grandmother shrieked. She scrambled to her feet and stood staring. "You're
The Misfit!" she said. "I recognized you at once!"

"Yes'm," the man said, smiling slightly as if he were pleased in spite of himself
to be known, "but it would have been better for all of you, lady, if you hadn't
of reckernized me."

Bailey turned his head sharply and said something to his mother that shocked
even the children. The old lady began to cry and The Misfit reddened.

"Lady," he said, "don't you get upset. Sometimes a man says things he don't   85
mean. I don't reckon he meant to talk to you thataway."

"You wouldn't shoot a lady, would you?" the grandmother said and removed
a clean handkerchief from her cuff and began to slap at her eyes with it.

The Misfit pointed the toe of his shoe into the ground and made a little hole
and then covered it up again. "I would hate to have to," he said.

"Listen," the grandmother almost screamed, "I know you're a good man. You
don't look a bit like you have common blood. I know you must come from nice
people!"

"Yes ma'am," he said, "finest people in the world." When he smiled he showed
a row of strong white teeth. "God never made a finer woman than my mother
and my daddy's heart was pure gold," he said. The boy with the red sweat shirt
had come around behind them and was standing with his gun at his hip. The
Misfit squatted down on the ground. "Watch them children, Bobby Lee," he said.
"You know they make me nervous." He looked at the six of them huddled together
in front of him and he seemed to be embarrassed as if he couldn't think of anything to say. "Ain't a cloud in the sky," he remarked, looking up at it. "Don't see
no sun but don't see no cloud neither."

"Yes, it's a beautiful day," said the grandmother. "Listen," she said, "you   90
shouldn't call yourself The Misfit because I know you're a good man at heart. I
can just look at you and tell."

"Hush!" Bailey yelled. "Hush! Everybody shut up and let me handle this!" He was squatting in the position of a runner about to sprint forward but he didn't move.

"I pre-chate that, lady," the Misfit said and drew a little circle in the ground with the butt of his gun.

"It'll take a half a hour to fix this here car," Hiram called, looking over the raised hood of it.

"Well, first you and Bobby Lee get him and that little boy to step over yonder with you," The Misfit said, pointing to Bailey and John Wesley. "The boys want to ast you something," he said to Bailey. "Would you mind stepping back in them woods there with them?"

"Listen," Bailey began, "we're in a terrible predicament! Nobody realizes what   95 this is," and his voice cracked. His eyes were as blue and intense as the parrots in his shirt and he remained perfectly still.

The grandmother reached up to adjust her hat brim as if she were going to the woods with him but it came off in her hand. She stood staring at it and after a second she let it fall on the ground. Hiram pulled Bailey up by the arm as if he were assisting an old man. John Wesley caught hold of his father's hand and Bobby Lee followed. They went off toward the woods and just as they reached the dark edge, Bailey turned and supporting himself against a gray naked pine trunk, he shouted, "I'll be back in a minute, Mamma, wait on me!"

"Come back this instant!" his mother shrilled but they all disappeared into the woods.

"Bailey Boy!" the grandmother called in a tragic voice but she found she was looking at The Misfit squatting on the ground in front of her. "I just know you're a good man," she said desperately. "You're not a bit common!"

"Nome, I ain't a good man," The Misfit said after a second as if he had considered her statement carefully, "but I ain't the worst in the world neither. My daddy said I was a different breed of dog from my brothers and sisters. 'You know,' Daddy said, 'it's some that can live their whole life out without asking about it and it's others has to know why it is, and this boy is one of the latters. He's going to be into everything!" He put on his black hat and looked up suddenly and then away deep into the woods as if he were embarrassed again. "I'm sorry I don't have on a shirt before you ladies," he said, hunching his shoulders slightly. "We buried our clothes that we had on when we escaped and we're just making do until we can get better. We borrowed these from some folks we met," he explained.

"That's perfectly all right," the grandmother said. "Maybe Bailey has an extra   100 shirt in his suitcase."

"I'll look and see terrectly," The Misfit said.

"Where are they taking him?" the children's mother screamed.

"Daddy was a card himself," The Misfit said. "You couldn't put anything over on him. He never got in trouble with the Authorities though. Just had the knack of handling them."

"You could be honest too if you'd only try," said the grandmother. "Think how wonderful it would be to settle down and live a comfortable life and not have to think about somebody chasing you all the time."

The Misfit kept scratching in the ground with the butt of his gun as if he   105 were thinking about it. "Yes'm, somebody is always after you," he murmured.

The grandmother noticed how thin his shoulder blades were just behind his hat because she was standing up looking down on him. "Do you ever pray?" she asked.

He shook his head. All she saw was the black hat wiggle between his shoulder blades. "Nome," he said.

There was a pistol shot from the woods, followed closely by another. Then silence. The old lady's head jerked around. She could hear the wind move through the tree tops like a long satisfied insuck of breath. "Bailey Boy!" she called.

"I was a gospel singer for a while," The Misfit said. "I been most everything. Been in the arm service, both land and sea, at home and abroad, been twict married, been an undertaker, been with the railroads, plowed Mother Earth, been in a tornado, seen a man burnt alive oncet," and he looked up at the children's mother and the little girl who were sitting close together, their faces white and their eyes glassy; "I even seen a woman flogged," he said.

"Pray, pray," the grandmother began, "pray, pray . . ."   110

"I never was a bad boy that I remember of," The Misfit said in an almost dreamy voice, "but somewheres along the line I done something wrong and got sent to the penitentiary. I was buried alive," and he looked up and held her attention to him by a steady stare.

"That's when you should have started to pray," she said. "What did you do to get sent up to the penitentiary that first time?"

"Turn to the right, it was a wall," The Misfit said, looking up again at the cloudless sky. "Turn to the left, it was a wall. Look up it was a ceiling, look down it was a floor. I forget what I done, lady. I set there and set there, trying to remember what it was I done and I ain't recalled it to this day. Oncet in a while, I would think it was coming to me, but it never come."

"Maybe they put you in by mistake," the old lady said vaguely.

"Nome," he said. "It wasn't no mistake. They had the papers on me."   115

"You must have stolen something," she said.

The Misfit sneered slightly. "Nobody had nothing I wanted," he said. "It was a head-doctor at the penitentiary said what I had done was kill my daddy but I known that for a lie. My daddy died in nineteen ought nineteen of the epidemic flu and I never had a thing to do with it. He was buried in the Mount Hopewell Baptist churchyard and you can go there and see for yourself."

"If you would pray," the old lady said, "Jesus would help you."

"That's right," The Misfit said.

"Well then, why don't you pray?" she asked trembling with delight suddenly.   120

"I don't want no hep," he said. "I'm doing all right by myself."

Bobby Lee and Hiram came ambling back from the woods. Bobby Lee was dragging a yellow shirt with bright blue parrots in it.

"Thow me that shirt, Bobby Lee," The Misfit said. The shirt came flying at him and landed on his shoulder and he put it on. The grandmother couldn't name what the shirt reminded her of. "No, lady," The Misfit said while he was buttoning it up, "I found out the crime don't matter. You can do one thing or you can do another, kill a man or take a tire off his car, because sooner or later you're going to forget what it was you done and just be punished for it."

The children's mother had begun to make heaving noises as if she couldn't get her breath. "Lady," he asked, "would you and that little girl like to step off yonder with Bobby Lee and Hiram and join your husband?"

"Yes, thank you," the mother said faintly. Her left arm dangled helplessly and she was holding the baby, who had gone to sleep, in the other. "Hep that lady up, Hiram," The Misfit said as she struggled to climb out of the ditch, "and Bobby Lee, you hold onto that little girl's hand."

"I don't want to hold hands with him," June Star said. "He reminds me of a pig."

The fat boy blushed and laughed and caught her by the arm and pulled her off into the woods after Hiram and her mother.

Alone with The Misfit, the grandmother found that she had lost her voice. There was not a cloud in the sky nor any sun. There was nothing around her but woods. She wanted to tell him that he must pray. She opened and closed her mouth several times before anything came out. Finally she found herself saying, "Jesus. Jesus," meaning, Jesus will help you, but the way she was saying it, it sounded as if she might be cursing.

"Yes'm," The Misfit said as if he agreed. "Jesus thown everything off balance. It was the same case with Him as with me except He hadn't committed any crime and they could prove I had committed one because they had the papers on me. Of course," he said, "they never shown me my papers. That's why I sign myself now. I said long ago, you get you a signature and sign everything you do and keep a copy of it. Then you'll know what you done and you can hold up the crime to the punishment and see do they match and in the end you'll have something to prove you ain't been treated right. I call myself The Misfit," he said, "because I can't make what all I done wrong fit what all I gone through in punishment."

There was a piercing scream from the woods, followed closely by a pistol report. 130 "Does it seem right to you, lady, that one is punished a heap and another ain't punished at all?"

"Jesus!" the old lady cried. "You've got good blood! I know you wouldn't shoot a lady! I know you come from nice people! Pray! Jesus, you ought not to shoot a lady. I'll give you all the money I've got!"

"Lady," The Misfit said, looking beyond her far into the woods, "there never was a body that give the undertaker a tip."

There were two more pistol reports and the grandmother raised her head like a parched old turkey hen crying for water and called, "Bailey Boy, Bailey Boy!" as if her heart would break.

"Jesus was the only One that ever raised the dead," The Misfit continued, "and He shouldn't have done it. He thown everything off balance. If He did what He said, then it's nothing for you to do but thow away everything and follow Him, and if He didn't, then it's nothing for you to do but enjoy the few minutes you got left the best way you can—by killing somebody or burning down his house or doing some other meanness to him. No pleasure but meanness," he said and his voice had become almost a snarl.

"Maybe He didn't raise the dead," the old lady mumbled, not knowing what 135 she was saying and feeling so dizzy that she sank down in the ditch with her legs twisted under her.

"I wasn't there so I can't say He didn't," The Misfit said. "I wisht I had of been there," he said, hitting the ground with his fist. "It ain't right I wasn't there because if I had of been there I would of known. Listen lady," he said in a high voice, "if I had of been there I would of known and I wouldn't be like I am now." His voice seemed about to crack and the grandmother's head cleared for an instant. She saw the man's face twisted close to her own as if he were going to cry and she murmured, "Why you're one of my babies. You're one of my own children!" She reached out and touched him on the shoulder. The Misfit sprang back as if a snake had bitten him and shot her three times through the chest. Then he put his gun down on the ground and took off his glasses and began to clean them.

Hiram and Bobby Lee returned from the woods and stood over the ditch, looking down at the grandmother who half sat and half lay in a puddle of blood with her legs crossed under her like a child's and her face smiling up at the cloudless sky.

Without his glasses, The Misfit's eyes were red-rimmed and pale and defenseless-looking. "Take her off and thow her where you thown the others," he said, picking up the cat that was rubbing itself against his leg.

"She was a talker, wasn't she?" Bobby Lee said, sliding down the ditch with a yodel.

"She would of been a good woman," The Misfit said, "if it had been somebody   140 there to shoot her every minute of her life."

"Some fun!" Bobby Lee said.

"Shut up, Bobby Lee," The Misfit said. "It's no real pleasure in life."

QUESTIONS

1. How early in the story does O'Connor foreshadow what will happen in the end? What further hints does she give us along the way? How does the scene at Red Sammy's Barbecue advance the story toward its conclusion?
2. When we first meet the grandmother, what kind of person is she? What do her various remarks reveal about her? Does she remain a static character, or does she in any way change as the story goes on?
3. When the grandmother's head clears for an instant (paragraph 136), what does she suddenly understand? Reread this passage carefully and prepare to discuss what it means.
4. What do we learn from the conversation between The Misfit and the grandmother while the others go out to the woods? How would you describe The Misfit's outlook on the world? Compare it with the author's, from whatever you know about Flannery O'Connor and from the story itself.
5. How would you respond to a reader who complained, "The title of this story is just an obvious platitude"?

Flannery O'Connor

REVELATION   1965

The doctor's waiting room, which was very small, was almost full when the Turpins entered and Mrs. Turpin, who was very large, made it look even smaller by her presence. She stood looming at the head of the magazine table set in the center of it, a living demonstration that the room was inadequate and ridiculous. Her little bright black eyes took in all the patients as she sized up the seating situation. There was one vacant chair and a place on a sofa occupied by a blond child in a dirty blue romper who should have been told to move over and make room for the lady. He was five or six, but Mrs. Turpin saw at once that no one was going to tell him to move over. He was slumped down in the seat, his arms idle at his sides and his eyes idle in his head; his nose ran unchecked.

Mrs. Turpin put a firm hand on Claud's shoulder and said in a voice that included anyone who wanted to listen, "Claud, you sit in that chair there," and gave him a push down into the vacant one. Claud was florid and bald and sturdy, somewhat shorter than Mrs. Turpin, but he sat down as if he were accustomed to doing what she told him to.

Mrs. Turpin remained standing. The only man in the room besides Claud was a lean stringy old fellow with a rusty hand spread out on each knee, whose eyes were closed as if he were asleep or dead or pretending to be so as not to get up and offer her his seat. Her gaze settled agreeably on a well-dressed grey-haired lady whose eyes met hers and whose expression said: if that child belonged to me, he would have some manners and move over—there's plenty of room there for you and him too.

Claud looked up with a sigh and made as if to rise.

"Sit down," Mrs. Turpin said. "You know you're not supposed to stand on   5
that leg. He has an ulcer on his leg," she explained.

Claud lifted his foot onto the magazine table and rolled his trouser leg up to reveal a purple swelling on a plump marble-white calf.

"My!" the pleasant lady said. "How did you do that?"

"A cow kicked him," Mrs. Turpin said.

"Goodness!" said the lady.

Claud rolled his trouser leg down.   10

"Maybe the little boy would move over," the lady suggested, but the child did not stir.

"Somebody will be leaving in a minute," Mrs. Turpin said. She could not understand why a doctor—with as much money as they made charging five dollars a day to just stick their head in the hospital door and look at you—couldn't afford a decent-sized waiting room. This one was hardly bigger than a garage. The table was cluttered with limp-looking magazines and at one end of it there was a big green glass ash tray full of cigaret butts and cotton wads with little blood spots on them. If she had had anything to do with the running of the place, that would have been emptied every so often. There were no chairs against the wall at the head of the room. It had a rectangular-shaped panel in it that permitted a view of the office where the nurse came and went and the secretary listened to the radio. A plastic fern in a gold pot sat in the opening and trailed its fronds down almost to the floor. The radio was softly playing gospel music.

Just then the inner door opened and a nurse with the highest stack of yellow hair Mrs. Turpin had ever seen put her face in the crack and called for the next patient. The woman sitting beside Claud grasped the two arms of her chair and hoisted herself up; she pulled her dress free from her legs and lumbered through the door where the nurse had disappeared.

Mrs. Turpin eased into the vacant chair, which held her tight as a corset. "I wish I could reduce," she said, and rolled her eyes and gave a comic sigh.

"Oh, *you* aren't fat," the stylish lady said.

"Ooooo I am too," Mrs. Turpin said. "Claud he eats all he wants to and never weighs over one hundred and seventy-five pounds, but me I just look at something good to eat and I gain some weight," and her stomach and shoulders shook with laughter. "You can eat all you want to, can't you, Claud?" she asked, turning to him.

Claud only grinned.

"Well, as long as you have such a good disposition," the stylish lady said, "I don't think it makes a bit of difference what size you are. You just can't beat a good disposition."

Next to her was a fat girl of eighteen or nineteen, scowling into a thick blue book which Mrs. Turpin saw was entitled *Human Development.* The girl raised her head and directed her scowl at Mrs. Turpin as if she did not like her looks. She appeared annoyed that anyone should speak while she tried to read. The poor girl's face was blue with acne and Mrs. Turpin thought how pitiful it was to have a face like that at that age. She gave the girl a friendly smile but the girl only scowled the harder. Mrs. Turpin herself was fat but she had always had good skin, and, though she was forty-seven years old, there was not a wrinkle in her face except around her eyes from laughing too much.

Next to the ugly girl was the child, still in exactly the same position, and next to him was a thin leathery old woman in a cotton print dress. She and Claud had three sacks of chicken feed in their pump house that was in the same print. She had seen from the first that the child belonged with the old woman. She could tell by the way they sat—kind of vacant and white-trashy, as if they would sit there until Doomsday if nobody called and told them to get up. And at right angles but next to the well-dressed pleasant lady was a lank-faced woman who was certainly the child's mother. She had on a yellow sweat shirt and wine-colored slacks, both gritty-looking, and the rims of her lips were stained with snuff. Her dirty yellow hair was tied behind with a little piece of red paper ribbon. Worse than niggers any day, Mrs. Turpin thought.

The gospel hymn playing was, "When I looked up and He looked down," and Mrs. Turpin, who knew it, supplied the last line mentally, "And wona these days I know I'll we-eara crown."

Without appearing to, Mrs. Turpin always noticed people's feet. The well-dressed lady had on red and grey suede shoes to match her dress. Mrs. Turpin had on her good black patent leather pumps. The ugly girl had on Girl Scout shoes and heavy socks. The old woman had on tennis shoes and the white-trashy mother had on what appeared to be bedroom slippers, black straw with gold braid threaded through them—exactly what you would have expected her to have on.

Sometimes at night when she couldn't go to sleep, Mrs. Turpin would occupy herself with the question of who she would have chosen to be if she couldn't have been herself. If Jesus had said to her before he made her, "There's only two places available for you. You can either be a nigger or white-trash," what would she have said? "Please, Jesus, please," she would have said, "just let me wait until there's another place available," and he would have said, "No, you have to go right now and I have only those two places so make up your mind." She would have wiggled and squirmed and begged and pleaded but it would have been no use and finally she would have said, "All right, make me a nigger then—but that don't mean a trashy one." And he would have made her a neat clean respectable Negro-woman, herself but black.

Next to the child's mother was a red-headed youngish woman, reading one of the magazines and working a piece of chewing gum, hell for leather, as Claud would say. Mrs. Turpin could not see the woman's feet. She was not white-trash, just common. Sometimes Mrs. Turpin occupied herself at night naming the classes of people. On the bottom of the heap were most colored people, not the kind she would have been if she had been one, but most of them; then next to them— not above, just away from—were the white-trash; then above them were the home-owners, and above them the home-and-land owners, to which she and Claud belonged. Above she and Claud° were people with a lot of money and much bigger houses and much more land. But here the complexity of it would begin to bear in on her, for some of the people with a lot of money were common and ought to be below she and Claud and some of the people who had good blood had lost their money and had to rent and then there were colored people who owned their homes and land as well. There was a colored dentist in town who had two red Lincolns and a swimming pool and a farm with registered white-face cattle on it. Usually by the time she had fallen asleep all the classes of people were moiling and roiling around in her head, and she would dream they were all crammed in together in a box car, being ridden off to be put in a gas oven.

"That's a beautiful clock," she said and nodded to her right. It was a big wall clock, the face encased in a brass sunburst.   25

"Yes, it's very pretty," the stylish lady said agreeably. "And right on the dot too," she added, glancing at her watch.

The ugly girl beside her cast an eye upward at the clock, smirked, then looked directly at Mrs. Turpin and smirked again. Then she returned her eyes to her book. She was obviously the lady's daughter because, although they didn't look anything alike as to disposition, they both had the same shape of face and the same blue eyes. On the lady they sparkled pleasantly but in the girl's seared face they appeared alternately to smolder and to blaze.

What if Jesus had said, "All right, you can be white-trash or a nigger or ugly"!

Mrs. Turpin felt an awful pity for the girl, though she thought it was one thing to be ugly and another to act ugly.

The woman with the snuff-stained lips turned around in her chair and looked   30 up at the clock. Then she turned back and appeared to look a little to the side of Mrs. Turpin. There was a cast in one of her eyes. "You want to know wher you can get one of themther clocks?" she asked in a loud voice.

"No, I already have a nice clock," Mrs. Turpin said. Once somebody like her got a leg in the conversation, she would be all over it.

"You can get you one with green stamps," the woman said. "That's most likely wher he got hisn. Save you up enough, you can get you most anythang. I got me some joo'ry."

Above she and Claud: ungrammatical construction. Putting herself first, Mrs. Turpin presumably would say (if she were speaking aloud), "Above I and Claud . . . "

Ought to have got you a wash rag and some soap, Mrs. Turpin thought.

"I get contour sheets with mine," the pleasant lady said.

The daughter slammed her book shut. She looked straight in front of her, 35 directly through Mrs. Turpin and on through the yellow curtain and the plate glass window which made the wall behind her. The girl's eyes seemed lit all of a sudden with a peculiar light, an unnatural light like night road signs give. Mrs. Turpin turned her head to see if there was anything going on outside that she should see, but she could not see anything. Figures passing cast only a pale shadow through the curtain. There was no reason the girl should single her out for her ugly looks.

"Miss Finley," the nurse said, cracking the door. The gum chewing woman got up and passed in front of her and Claud and went into the office. She had on red high-heeled shoes.

Directly across the table, the ugly girl's eyes were fixed on Mrs. Turpin as if she had some very special reason for disliking her.

"This is wonderful weather, isn't it?" the girl's mother said.

"It's good weather for cotton if you can get the niggers to pick it," Mrs. Turpin said, "but niggers don't want to pick cotton any more. You can't get the white folks to pick it and now you can't get the niggers—because they got to be right up there with the white folks."

"They gonna *try* anyways," the white-trash woman said, leaning forward. 40

"Do you have one of those cotton-picking machines?" the pleasant lady asked.

"No," Mrs. Turpin said, "they leave half the cotton in the field. We don't have much cotton anyway. If you want to make it farming now, you have to have a little of everything. We got a couple of acres of cotton and a few hogs and chickens and just enough white-face that Claud can look after them himself."

"One thang I don't want," the white-trash woman said, wiping her mouth with the back of her hands. "Hogs. Nasty stinking things, a-gruntin and a-rootin all over the place."

Mrs. Turpin gave her the merest edge of her attention. "Our hogs are not dirty and they don't stink," she said. "They're cleaner than some children I've seen. Their feet never touch the ground. We have a pig-parlor—that's where you raise them on concrete," she explained to the pleasant lady, "and Claud scoots them down with the hose every afternoon and washes off the floor." Cleaner by far than that child right there, she thought. Poor nasty little thing. He had not moved except to put the thumb of his dirty hand into his mouth.

The woman turned her face away from Mrs. Turpin. "I know I wouldn't scoot 45 down no hog with no hose," she said to the wall.

You wouldn't have no hog to scoot down, Mrs. Turpin said to herself.

"A-gruntin and a-rootin and a-groanin," the woman muttered.

"We got a little of everything," Mrs. Turpin said to the pleasant lady. "It's no use in having more than you can handle yourself with help like it is. We found enough niggers to pick our cotton this year but Claud he has to go after them and take them home again in the evening. They can't walk that half a mile. No they can't. I tell you," she said and laughed merrily, "I sure am tired of buttering up niggers, but you got to love em if you want em to work for you. When they come in the morning, I run out and I say, 'Hi yawl this morning?' and when Claud

drives them off to the field I just wave to beat the band and they just wave back."
And she waved her hand rapidly to illustrate.

"Like you read out of the same book," the lady said, showing she understood
perfectly.

"Child, yes," Mrs. Turpin said. "And when they come in from the field, I   50
run out with a bucket of icewater. That's the way it's going to be from now on,"
she said. "You may as well face it."

"One thang I know," the white-trash woman said. "Two thangs I ain't going
to do: love no niggers or scoot down no hog with no hose." And she let out a
bark of contempt.

The look that Mrs. Turpin and the pleasant lady exchanged indicated they
both understood that you had to *have* certain things before you could *know* certain things. But every time Mrs. Turpin exchanged a look with the lady, she was
aware that the ugly girl's peculiar eyes were still on her, and she had trouble bringing
her attention back to the conversation.

"When you got something," she said, "you got to look after it." And when
you ain't got a thing but breath and britches, she added to herself, you can afford
to come to town every morning and just sit on the Court House coping and spit.

A grotesque revolving shadow passed across the curtain behind her and was
thrown palely on the opposite wall. Then a bicycle clattered down against the
outside of the building. The door opened and a colored boy glided in with a tray
from the drug store. It had two large red and white paper cups on it with tops
on them. He was a tall, very black boy in discolored white pants and a green nylon
shirt. He was chewing gum slowly, as if to music. He set the tray down in the
office opening next to the fern and stuck his head through to look for the secretary. She was not in there. He rested his arms on the ledge and waited, his narrow
bottom stuck out, swaying slowly to the left and right. He raised a hand over his
head and scratched the base of his skull.

"You see that button there, boy?" Mrs. Turpin said. "You can punch that and   55
she'll come. She's probably in the back somewhere."

"Is thas right?" the boy said agreeably, as if he had never seen the button before. He leaned to the right and put his finger on it. "She sometime out," he said
and twisted around to face his audience, his elbows behind him on the counter.
The nurse appeared and he twisted back again. She handed him a dollar and he
rooted in his pocket and made the change and counted it out to her. She gave
him fifteen cents for a tip and he went out with the empty tray. The heavy door
swung to slowly and closed at length with the sound of suction. For a moment
no one spoke.

"They ought to send all them niggers back to Africa," the white-trash woman
said. "That's wher they come from in the first place."

"Oh, I couldn't do without my good colored friends," the pleasant lady said.

"There's a heap of things worse than a nigger," Mrs. Turpin agreed. "It's all
kinds of them just like it's all kinds of us."

"Yes, and it takes all kinds to make the world go round," the lady said in her   60
musical voice.

As she said it, the raw-complexioned girl snapped her teeth together. Her
lower lip turned downwards and inside out, revealing the pale pink inside of her

mouth. After a second it rolled back up. It was the ugliest face Mrs. Turpin had ever seen anyone make and for a moment she was certain that the girl had made it at her. She was looking at her as if she had known and disliked her all her life—all of Mrs. Turpin's life, it seemed too, not just all the girl's life. Why, girl, I don't even know you, Mrs. Turpin said silently.

She forced her attention back to the discussion. "It wouldn't be practical to send them back to Africa," she said. "They wouldn't want to go. They got it too good here."

"Wouldn't be what they wanted—if I had anythang to do with it," the woman said.

"It wouldn't be a way in the world you could get all the niggers back over there," Mrs. Turpin said. "They'd be hiding out and lying down and turning sick on you and wailing and hollering and raring and pitching. It wouldn't be a way in the world to get them over there."

"They got over here," the trashy woman said. "Get back like they got over."   65

"It wasn't so many of them then," Mrs. Turpin explained.

The woman looked at Mrs. Turpin as if here was an idiot indeed but Mrs. Turpin was not bothered by the look, considering where it came from.

"Nooo," she said, "they're going to stay here where they can go to New York and marry white folks and improve their color. That's what they all want to do, every one of them, improve their color."

"You know what comes of that, don't you?" Claud asked.

"No, Claud, what?" Mrs. Turpin said.   70

Claud's eyes twinkled. "White-faced niggers," he said with never a smile.

Everybody in the office laughed except the white-trash and the ugly girl. The girl gripped the book in her lap with white fingers. The trashy woman looked around her from face to face as if she thought they were all idiots. The old woman in the feed sack dress continued to gaze expressionless across the floor at the high-top shoes of the man opposite her, the one who had been pretending to be asleep when the Turpins came in. He was laughing heartily, his hands still spread out on his knees. The child had fallen to the side and was lying now almost face down in the old woman's lap.

While they recovered from their laughter, the nasal chorus on the radio kept the room from silence.

> "You go to blank blank
> And I'll go to mine
> But we'll all blank along
> To-geth-ther,
> And all along the blank
> We'll hep each other out
> Smile-ling in any kind of
> Weath-ther!"

Mrs. Turpin didn't catch every word but she caught enough to agree with   75
the spirit of the song and it turned her thoughts sober. To help anybody out that needed it was her philosophy of life. She never spared herself when she found somebody in need, whether they were white or black, trash or decent. And of

all she had to be thankful for, she was most thankful that this was so. If Jesus had said, "You can be high society and have all the money you want and be thin and svelte-like, but you can't be a good woman with it," she would have had to say, "Well don't make me that then. Make me a good woman and it don't matter what else, how fat or how ugly or how poor!" Her heart rose. He had not made her a nigger or white-trash or ugly! He had made her herself and given her a little of everything. Jesus, thank you! she said. Thank you thank you thank you! Whenever she counted her blessings she felt as buoyant as if she weighed one hundred and twenty-five pounds instead of one hundred and eighty.

"What's wrong with your little boy?" the pleasant lady asked the white-trashy woman.

"He has a ulcer," the woman said proudly. "He ain't give me a minute's peace since he was born. Him and her are just alike," she said, nodding at the old woman, who was running her leathery fingers through the child's pale hair. "Look like I can't get nothing down them two but Co' Cola and candy."

That's all you try to get down em, Mrs. Turpin said to herself. Too lazy to light the fire. There was nothing you could tell her about people like them that she didn't know already. And it was not just that they didn't have anything. Because if you gave them everything, in two weeks it would all be broken or filthy or they would have chopped it up for lightwood. She knew all this from her own experience. Help them you must, but help them you couldn't.

All at once the ugly girl turned her lips inside out again. Her eyes were fixed like two drills on Mrs. Turpin. This time there was no mistaking that there was something urgent behind them.

Girl, Mrs. Turpin exclaimed silently, I haven't done a thing to you! The girl   80
might be confusing her with somebody else. There was no need to sit by and let herself be intimidated. "You must be in college," she said boldly, looking directly at the girl. "I see you reading a book there."

The girl continued to stare and pointedly did not answer.

Her mother blushed at this rudeness. "The lady asked you a question, Mary Grace," she said under her breath.

"I have ears," Mary Grace said.

The poor mother blushed again. "Mary Grace goes to Wellesley College," she explained. She twisted one of the buttons on her dress. "In Massachusetts," she added with a grimace. "And in the summer she just keeps right on studying. Just reads all the time, a real book worm. She's done real well at Wellesley; she's taking English and Math and History and Psychology and Social Studies," she rattled on, "and I think it's too much. I think she ought to get out and have fun."

The girl looked as if she would like to hurl them all through the plate glass   85
window.

"Way up north," Mrs. Turpin murmured and thought, well, it hasn't done much for her manners.

"I'd almost rather to have him sick," the white-trash woman said, wrenching the attention back to herself. "He's so mean when he ain't. Look like some children just take natural to meanness. It's some gets bad when they get sick but he was the opposite. Took sick and turned good. He don't give me no trouble now. It's me waitin to see the doctor," she said.

If I was going to send anybody back to Africa, Mrs. Turpin thought, it would be your kind, woman. "Yes, indeed," she said aloud, but looking up at the ceiling, "it's a heap of things worse than a nigger." And dirtier than a hog, she added to herself.

"I think people with bad dispositions are more to be pitied than anyone on earth," the pleasant lady said in a voice that was decidedly thin.

"I thank the Lord he has blessed me with a good one," Mrs. Turpin said. "The day has never dawned that I couldn't find something to laugh at."   90

"Not since she married me anyways," Claud said with a comical straight face.

Everybody laughed except the girl and the white-trash.

Mrs. Turpin's stomach shook. "He's such a caution," she said, "that I can't help but laugh at him."

The girl made a loud ugly noise through her teeth.

Her mother's mouth grew thin and straight. "I think the worst thing in the   95 world," she said, "is an ungrateful person. To have everything and not appreciate it. I know a girl," she said, "who has parents who would give her anything, a little brother who loves her dearly, who is getting a good education, who wears the best clothes, but who can never say a kind word to anyone, who never smiles, who just criticizes and complains all day long."

"Is she too old to paddle?" Claud asked.

The girl's face was almost purple.

"Yes," the lady said, "I'm afraid there's nothing to do but leave her to her folly. Some day she'll wake up and it'll be too late."

"It never hurt anyone to smile," Mrs. Turpin said. "It just makes you feel better all over."

"Of course," the lady said sadly, "but there are just some people you can't tell   100 anything to. They can't take criticism."

"If it's one thing I am," Mrs. Turpin said with feeling, "it's grateful. When I think who all I could have been besides myself and what all I got, a little of everything, and a good disposition besides, I just feel like shouting, 'Thank you, Jesus, for making everything the way it is!' It could have been different!" For one thing, somebody else could have got Claud. At the thought of this, she was flooded with gratitude and a terrible pang of joy ran through her. "Oh thank you, Jesus, Jesus, thank you!" she cried aloud.

The book struck her directly over her left eye. It struck almost at the same instant that she realized the girl was about to hurl it. Before she could utter a sound, the raw face came crashing across the table toward her, howling. The girl's fingers sank like clamps into the soft flesh of her neck. She heard the mother cry out and Claud shout, "Whoa!" There was an instant when she was certain that she was about to be in an earthquake.

All at once her vision narrowed and she saw everything as if it were happening in a small room far away, or as if she were looking at it through the wrong end of a telescope. Claud's face crumpled and fell out of sight. The nurse ran in, then out, then in again. Then the gangling figure of the doctor rushed out of the inner door. Magazines flew this way and that as the table turned over. The girl fell with a thud and Mrs. Turpin's vision suddenly reversed itself and she saw everything large instead of small. The eyes of the white-trashy woman were staring hugely at the floor. There the girl, held down on one side by the nurse and on the other by her mother, was wrenching and turning in their grasp. The doctor was kneeling astride her, trying to hold her arm down. He managed after a second to sink a long needle into it.

Mrs. Turpin felt entirely hollow except for her heart which swung from side to side as if it were agitated in a great empty drum of flesh.

"Somebody that's not busy call for the ambulance," the doctor said in the off-hand voice young doctors adopt for terrible occasions. 105

Mrs. Turpin could not have moved a finger. The old man who had been sitting next to her skipped nimbly into the office and made the call, for the secretary still seemed to be gone.

"Claud!" Mrs. Turpin called.

He was not in his chair. She knew she must jump up and find him but she felt like some one trying to catch a train in a dream, when everything moves in slow motion and the faster you try to run the slower you go.

"Here I am," a suffocated voice, very unlike Claud's, said.

He was doubled up in the corner on the floor, pale as paper, holding his leg. 110 She wanted to get up and go to him but she could not move. Instead, her gaze was drawn slowly downward to the churning face on the floor, which she could see over the doctor's shoulder.

The girl's eyes stopped rolling and focused on her. They seemed a much lighter blue than before, as if a door that had been tightly closed behind them was now open to admit light and air.

Mrs. Turpin's head cleared and her power of motion returned. She leaned forward until she was looking directly into the fierce brilliant eyes. There was no doubt in her mind that the girl did know her, knew her in some intense and personal way, beyond time and place and condition. "What you got to say to me?" she asked hoarsely and held her breath, waiting, as for a revelation.

The girl raised her head. Her gaze locked with Mrs. Turpin's. "Go back to hell where you came from, you old wart hog," she whispered. Her voice was low but clear. Her eyes burned for a moment as if she saw with pleasure that her message had struck its target.

Mrs. Turpin sank back in her chair.

After a moment the girl's eyes closed and she turned her head wearily to the side. 115

The doctor rose and handed the nurse the empty syringe. He leaned over and put both hands for a moment on the mother's shoulders, which were shaking. She was sitting on the floor, her lips pressed together, holding Mary Grace's hand in her lap. The girl's fingers were gripped like a baby's around her thumb. "Go on to the hospital," he said. "I'll call and make the arrangements."

"Now let's see that neck," he said in a jovial voice to Mrs. Turpin. He began to inspect her neck with his first two fingers. Two little moon-shaped lines like pink fish bones were indented over her windpipe. There was the beginning of an angry red swelling above her eye. His fingers passed over this also.

"Lea' me be," she said thickly and shook him off. "See about Claud. She kicked him."

"I'll see about him in a minute," he said and felt her pulse. He was a thin grey-haired man, given to pleasantries. "Go home and have yourself a vacation the rest of the day," he said and patted her on the shoulder.

Quit your pattin me, Mrs. Turpin growled to herself.

"And put an ice pack over that eye," he said. Then he went and squatted down beside Claud and looked at his leg. After a moment he pulled him up and Claud limped after him into the office.

Until the ambulance came, the only sounds in the room were the tremulous moans of the girl's mother, who continued to sit on the floor. The white-trash woman did not take her eyes off the girl. Mrs. Turpin looked straight ahead at nothing. Presently the ambulance drew up, a long dark shadow, behind the curtain. The attendants came in and set the stretcher down beside the girl and lifted her expertly onto it and carried her out. The nurse helped the mother gather up her things. The shadow of the ambulance moved silently away and the nurse came back in the office.

"That ther girl is going to be a lunatic, ain't she?" the white-trash woman asked the nurse, but the nurse kept on to the back and never answered her.

"Yes, she's going to be a lunatic," the white-trash woman said to the rest of them.

"Po' critter," the old woman murmured. The child's face was still in her lap. His eyes looked idly out over her knees. He had not moved during the disturbance except to draw one leg up under him.

"I thank Gawd," the white-trash woman said fervently, "I ain't a lunatic."

Claud came limping out and the Turpins went home.

As their pick-up truck turned into their own dirt road and made the crest of the hill, Mrs. Turpin gripped the window ledge and looked out suspiciously. The land sloped gracefully down through a field dotted with lavender weeds and at the start of the rise their small yellow frame house, with its little flower beds spread out around it like a fancy apron, sat primly in its accustomed place between two giant hickory trees. She would not have been startled to see a burnt wound between two blackened chimneys.

Neither of them felt like eating so they put on their house clothes and lowered the shade in the bedroom and lay down, Claud with his leg on a pillow and herself with a damp washcloth over her eye. The instant she was flat on her back, the image of a razor-backed hog with warts on its face and horns coming out behind its ears snorted into her head. She moaned, a low quiet moan.

"I am not," she said tearfully, "a wart hog. From hell." But the denial had no force. The girl's eyes and her words, even the tone of her voice, low but clear, directed only to her, brooked no repudiation. She had been singled out for the message, though there was trash in the room to whom it might justly have been applied. The full force of this fact struck her only now. There was a woman there who was neglecting her own child but she had been overlooked. The message had been given to Ruby Turpin, a respectable, hard-working, church-going woman. The tears dried. Her eyes began to burn instead with wrath.

She rose on her elbow and the washcloth fell into her hand. Claud was lying on his back, snoring. She wanted to tell him what the girl had said. At the same time, she did not wish to put the image of herself as a wart hog from hell into his mind.

"Hey, Claud," she muttered and pushed his shoulder.

Claud opened one pale baby blue eye.

She looked into it warily. He did not think about anything. He just went his way.

"Wha, whasit?" he said and closed the eye again.

"Nothing," she said. "Does your leg pain you?"

"Hurts like hell," Claud said.

"It'll quit terreckly," she said and lay back down. In a moment Claud was snoring again. For the rest of the afternoon they lay there. Claud slept. She scowled at the ceiling. Occasionally she raised her fist and made a small stabbing motion over her chest as if she was defending her innocence to invisible guests who were like the comforters of Job, reasonable-seeming but wrong.

About five-thirty Claud stirred. "Got to go after those niggers," he sighed, not moving.

She was looking straight up as if there were unintelligible handwriting on the ceiling. The protuberance over her eye had turned a greenish-blue. "Listen here," she said.

"What?"

"Kiss me."

Claud leaned over and kissed her loudly on the mouth. He pinched her side and their hands interlocked. Her expression of ferocious concentration did not change. Claud got up, groaning and growling, and limped off. She continued to study the ceiling.

She did not get up until she heard the pick-up truck coming back with the Negroes. Then she rose and thrust her feet in her brown oxfords, which she did not bother to lace, and stumped out onto the back porch and got her red plastic bucket. She emptied a tray of ice cubes into it and filled it half full of water and went out into the back yard. Every afternoon after Claud brought the hands in, one of the boys helped him put out hay and the rest waited in the back of the truck until he was ready to take them home. The truck was parked in the shade under one of the hickory trees.

"Hi yawl this evening?" Mrs. Turpin asked grimly, appearing with the bucket and the dipper. There were three women and a boy in the truck.

"Us doin nicely," the oldest woman said. "Hi you doin?" and her gaze stuck immediately on the dark lump on Mrs. Turpin's forehead. "You done fell down, ain't you?" she asked in a solicitous voice. The old woman was dark and almost toothless. She had on an old felt hat of Claud's set back on her head. The other two women were younger and lighter and they both had new bright green sun hats. One of them had hers on her head; the other had taken hers off and the boy was grinning beneath it.

Mrs. Turpin set the bucket down on the floor of the truck. "Yawl hep yourselves," she said. She looked around to make sure Claud had gone. "No. I didn't fall down," she said, folding her arms. "It was something worse than that."

"Ain't nothing bad happen to you!" the old woman said. She said it as if they all knew Mrs. Turpin was protected in some special way by Divine Providence. "You just had you a little fall."

"We were in town at the doctor's office for where the cow kicked Mr. Turpin," Mrs. Turpin said in a flat tone that indicated they could leave off their foolishness. "And there was this girl there. A big fat girl with her face all broke out. I could look at that girl and tell she was peculiar but I couldn't tell how. And me and her mama were just talking and going along and all of a sudden WHAM! She throws this big book she reading at me and . . . "

"Naw!" the old woman cried out. 150

"And then she jumps over the table and commences to choke me."

"Naw!" they all exclaimed, "naw!"

"Hi come she do that?" the old woman asked. "What ail her?"

Mrs. Turpin only glared in front of her.

"Something ail her," the old woman said. 155

"They carried her off in an ambulance," Mrs. Turpin continued, "but before she went she was rolling on the floor and they were trying to hold her down to give her a shot and she said something to me." She paused. "You know what she said to me?"

"What she say?" they asked.

"She said," Mrs. Turpin began, and stopped, her face very dark and heavy. The sun was getting whiter and whiter, blanching the sky overhead so that the leaves of the hickory tree were black in the face of it. She could not bring forth the words. "Something real ugly," she muttered.

"She sho shouldn't said nothin ugly to you," the old woman said. "You so sweet. You the sweetest lady I know."

"She pretty too," the one with the hat on said. 160

"And stout," the other one said. "I never knowed no sweeter white lady."

"That's the truth befo' Jesus," the old woman said. "Amen! You des as sweet and pretty as you can be."

Mrs. Turpin knew just exactly how much Negro flattery was worth and it added to her rage. "She said," she began again and finished this time with a fierce rush of breath, "that I was an old wart hog from hell."

There was an astounded silence.

"Where she at?" the youngest woman cried in a piercing voice. 165

"Lemme see her. I'll kill her!"

"I'll kill her with you!" the other one cried.

"She b'long in the sylum," the old woman said emphatically. "You the sweetest white lady I know."

"She pretty too," the other two said. "Stout as she can be and sweet. Jesus satisfied with her!"

"Deed he is," the old woman declared. 170

Idiots! Mrs. Turpin growled to herself. You could never say anything intelligent to a nigger. You could talk at them but not with them. "Yawl ain't drunk your water," she said shortly. "Leave the bucket in the truck when you're finished with it. I got more to do than just stand around and pass the time of day," and she moved off and into the house.

She stood for a moment in the middle of the kitchen. The dark protuberance over her eye looked like a miniature tornado cloud which might any moment sweep across the horizon of her brow. Her lower lip protruded dangerously. She squared her massive shoulders. Then she marched into the front of the house and out the side door and started down the road to the pig parlor. She had the look of a woman going single-handed, weaponless, into battle.

The sun was a deep yellow now like a harvest moon and was riding westward very fast over the far tree line as if it meant to reach the hogs before she did. The road was rutted and she kicked several good-sized stones out of her path as she strode along. The pig parlor was on a little knoll at the end of a lane that ran off from the side of the barn. It was a square of concrete as large as a small room, with a board fence about four feet high around it. The concrete floor sloped slightly so that the hog wash could drain off into a trench where it was carried to the field for fertilizer. Claud was standing on the outside, on the edge of the concrete, hanging onto the top board, hosing down the floor inside. The hose was connected to the faucet of a water trough nearby.

Mrs. Turpin climbed up beside him and glowered down at the hogs inside. There were seven long-snouted bristly shoats in it—tan with liver-colored spots— and an old sow a few weeks off from farrowing. She was lying on her side grunting. The shoats were running about shaking themselves like idiot children, their little slit pig eyes searching the floor for anything left. She had read that pigs were the most intelligent animal. She doubted it. They were supposed to be smarter than dogs. There had even been a pig astronaut. He had performed his assignment perfectly but died of a heart attack afterwards because they left him in his electric suit, sitting upright throughout his examination when naturally a hog should be on all fours.

A-gruntin and a-rootin and a-groanin.   175

"Gimme that hose," she said, yanking it away from Claud. "Go on and carry them niggers home and then get off that leg."

"You look like you might have swallowed a mad dog," Claud observed, but he got down and limped off. He paid no attention to her humors.

Until he was out of earshot, Mrs. Turpin stood on the side of the pen, holding the hose and pointing the stream of water at the hind quarters of any shoat that looked as if it might try to lie down. When he had had time to get over the hill, she turned her head slightly and her wrathful eyes scanned the path. He was nowhere in sight. She turned back again and seemed to gather herself up. Her shoulders rose and she drew in her breath.

"What do you send me a message like that for?" she said in a low fierce voice, barely above a whisper but with the force of a shout in its concentrated fury. "How am I a hog and me both? How am I saved and from hell too?" Her free fist was knotted and with the other she gripped the hose, blindly pointing the stream of water in and out of the eye of the old sow whose outraged squeal she did not hear.

The pig parlor commanded a view of the back pasture where their twenty   180 beef cows were gathered around the hay-bales Claud and the boy had put out. The freshly cut pasture sloped down to the highway. Across it was their cotton field and beyond that a dark green dusty wood which they owned as well. The sun was behind the wood, very red, looking over the paling of trees like a farmer inspecting his own hogs.

"Why me?" she rumbled. "It's no trash around here, black or white, that I haven't given to. And break my back to the bone every day working. And do for the church."

She appeared to be the right size woman to command the arena before her. "How am I a hog?" she demanded. "Exactly how am I like them?" and she jabbed the stream of water at the shoats. "There was plenty of trash there. It didn't have to be me."

"If you like trash better, go get yourself some trash then," she railed. "You could have made me trash. Or a nigger. If trash is what you wanted why didn't you make me trash?" She shook her fist with the hose in it and a watery snake appeared momentarily in the air. "I could quit working and take it easy and be filthy," she growled. "Lounge about the sidewalks all day drinking root beer. Dip snuff and spit in every puddle and have it all over my face. I could be nasty.

"Or you could have made me a nigger. It's too late for me to be a nigger," she said with deep sarcasm, "but I could act like one. Lay down in the middle of the road and stop traffic. Roll on the ground."

In the deepening light everything was taking on a mysterious hue. The pasture 185 was growing a peculiar glassy green and the streak of highway had turned lavender. She braced herself for a final assault and this time her voice rolled out over the pasture. "Go on," she yelled, "call me a hog! Call me a hog again. From hell. Call me a wart hog from hell. Put that bottom rail on top. There'll still be a top and bottom!"

A garbled echo returned to her.

A final surge of fury shook her and she roared, "Who do you think you are?"

The color of everything, field and crimson sky, burned for a moment with a transparent intensity. The question carried over the pasture and across the highway and the cotton field and returned to her clearly like an answer from beyond the wood.

She opened her mouth but no sound came out of it.

A tiny truck, Claud's, appeared on the highway, heading rapidly out of sight. 190 Its gears scraped thinly. It looked like a child's toy. At any moment a bigger truck might smash into it and scatter Claud's and the niggers' brains all over the road.

Mrs. Turpin stood there, her gaze fixed on the highway, all her muscles rigid, until in five or six minutes the truck reappeared, returning. She waited until it had had time to turn into their own road. Then like a monumental statue coming to life, she bent her head slowly and gazed, as if through the very heart of mystery, down into the pig parlor at the hogs. They had settled all in one corner around the old sow who was grunting softly. A red glow suffused them. They appeared to pant with a secret life.

Until the sun slipped finally behind the tree line, Mrs. Turpin remained there with her gaze bent to them as if she were absorbing some abysmal life-giving knowledge. At last she lifted her head. There was only a purple streak in the sky, cutting through a field of crimson and leading, like an extension of the highway, into the descending dusk. She raised her hands from the side of the pen in a gesture hieratic and profound. A visionary light settled in her eyes. She saw the streak as a vast swinging bridge extending upward from the earth through a field of living fire. Upon it a vast horde of souls were rumbling toward heaven. There were whole companies of white-trash, clean for the first time in their lives, and bands of black niggers in white robes, and battalions of freaks and lunatics shouting and clapping and leaping like frogs. And bringing up the end of the procession was a tribe of people whom she recognized at once as those who, like herself and Claud, had always had a little of everything and the God-given wit to use it right. She leaned forward to observe them closer. They were marching behind the others with great dignity, accountable as they had always been for good order and common sense and respectable behavior. They alone were on key. Yet she could see by their shocked and altered faces that even their virtues were being burned away. She lowered her hands and gripped the rail of the hog pen, her eyes small but fixed unblinkingly on what lay ahead. In a moment the vision faded but she remained where she was, immobile.

At length she got down and turned off the faucet and made her slow way on the darkening path to the house. In the woods around her the invisible cricket choruses had struck up, but what she heard were the voices of the souls climbing upward into the starry field and shouting hallelujah.

QUESTIONS

1. How does Mrs. Turpin see herself before Mary Grace calls her a wart hog?
2. What is the narrator's attitude toward Mrs. Turpin in the beginning of the story? How can you tell? Does this attitude change, or stay the same, at the end?
3. Describe the relationship between Mary Grace and her mother. What annoying platitudes does the mother mouth? Which of Mrs. Turpin's opinions seem especially to anger Mary Grace?
4. Sketch the plot of the story. What moment or event do you take to be the crisis, or turning point? What is the climax? What is the conclusion?
5. What do you infer from Mrs. Turpin's conversation with the black farm workers? Is she their friend? Why does she now find their flattery unacceptable ("Jesus satisfied with her")?
6. When, near the end of the story, Mrs. Turpin roars, "Who do you think you are?" an echo "returned to her clearly like an answer from beyond the wood" (paragraph 188). Explain.
7. What is the final revelation given to Mrs. Turpin? (To state it is to state the theme of the story.) What new attitude does the revelation impart? (How is Mrs. Turpin left with a new vision of humanity?)
8. Other stories in this book contain revelations: "Gimpel the Fool," "The Death of Ivan Ilych," "Young Goodman Brown," "The Secret Miracle," "On the Road." If you have read them, try to sum up the supernatural revelation made to the central character in each story. In each, is the revelation the same as a statement of the story's main theme?

SUGGESTIONS FOR WRITING: On Flannery O'Connor

1. How do the stories of Flannery O'Connor make manifest the principles she states in her remarks entitled "The serious writer and the tired reader" on page 491–92?
2. Compare Mrs. Turpin's defiance of God in "Revelation" ("Who do you think you are?," paragraph 187) with the urge of a shipwrecked man in "The Open Boat" to shake his fist at the clouds ("Just you drown me, now, and then hear what I call you!," 70). Do Flannery O'Connor and Stephen Crane express similar or different concepts of Whoever runs the universe?
3. "In most good stories it is the character's personality that creates the action of the story," O'Connor declares in her essay "Writing Short Stories." "If you start with a real personality, a real character, then something is bound to happen." Discuss this statement as it applies to one or more of the O'Connor stories you have read. Do O'Connor's characters seem to you to be real people, or do you see them as mere vessels for the author's religious views?
4. Compare the woman protagonists in these three stories of Flannery O'Connor: Julian's mother, the grandmother who confronts The Misfit, and Mrs. Turpin.
5. In 750–1,000 words, comment on O'Connor's use of humor. How does comedy help her say what she has to say?

11 Stories for Further Reading

For human intercourse, as soon as we look at it for its own sake and not as a social adjunct, is seen to be haunted by a specter. We cannot understand each other, except in a rough-and-ready way; we cannot reveal ourselves, even when we want to; what we call intimacy is only a makeshift; perfect knowledge is an illusion. But in the novel we can know people perfectly, and, apart from the general pleasure of reading, we can find here a compensation for their dimness in life. In this direction fiction is truer than history, because it goes beyond the evidence, and each of us knows from his own experience that there is something beyond the evidence, and even if the novelist has not got it correctly, well—he has tried.

—E. M. Forster, *Aspects of the Novel*

Ambrose Bierce

An Occurrence at Owl Creek Bridge   1891

Ambrose Bierce (1842–1914?) was born in Horse Cave Creek, Ohio, the youngest child of nine in an impoverished farm family. A year at Kentucky Military Academy was his only formal schooling. Enlisting as a drummer boy in the Union Army, Bierce saw action at Shiloh and Chickamauga, took part in Sherman's march to the sea, and came out of the army a brevet major. Then he became a writer, later an editor, for San Francisco newspapers. For a while Bierce thrived. He and his wife, on her ample dowry, lived five years in London, where Bierce wrote for London papers, honed his style, and cultivated his wit. But his wife left

Ambrose Bierce

him, his two sons died (one of gunfire and the other of alcoholism), and in late life Bierce came to deserve his nickname "Bitter Bierce." In 1913, at seventy-one, he trekked off to Mexico and vanished without a trace, although one report had him riding with the forces of revolutionist Pancho Villa. (A recent movie, Old Gringo, imagines Bierce's last days.) Bierce, who regarded the novel as "a short story padded," favored shorter lengths: short story, fable, newspaper column, aphorism. Sardonically, in The Devil's Dictionary (1911), he defines diplomacy as "the patriotic art of lying for one's country," and saint as "a dead sinner revised and edited." Master of both realism and of the ghost story, he collected his best Civil War fiction, including "An Occurrence at Owl Creek Bridge," in Tales of Soldiers and Civilians (1891), later retitled In the Midst of Life.

I

A man stood upon a railroad bridge in northern Alabama, looking down into the swift water twenty feet below. The man's hands were behind his back, the wrists bound with a cord. A rope closely encircled his neck. It was attached to a stout cross-timber above his head and the slack fell to the level of his knees. Some loose boards laid upon the sleepers supporting the metals of the railway supplied a footing for him and his executioners—two private soldiers of the Federal army, directed by a sergeant who in civil life may have been a deputy sheriff. At a short remove upon the same temporary platform was an officer in the uniform of his rank, armed. He was a captain. A sentinel at each end of the bridge stood with his rifle in the position known as "support," that is to say, vertical in front of the left shoulder, the hammer resting on the forearm thrown straight across the chest—a formal and unnatural position, enforcing an erect carriage of the body. It did not appear to be the duty of these two men to know what was occurring at the center of the bridge; they merely blockaded the two ends of the foot planking that traversed it.

Beyond one of the sentinels nobody was in sight; the railroad ran straight away into a forest for a hundred yards, then, curving, was lost to view. Doubtless there was an outpost farther along. The other bank of the stream was open ground—a gentle acclivity topped with a stockade of vertical tree trunks, loop-holed for rifles, with a single embrasure through which protruded the muzzle of a brass cannon commanding the bridge. Midway of the slope between bridge and fort were the spectators—a single company of infantry in line, at "parade rest," the butts of the rifles on the ground, the barrels inclining slightly backward against the right shoulder, the hands crossed upon the stock. A lieutenant stood at the right of the line, the point of his sword upon the ground, his left hand resting upon his right. Excepting the group of four at the center of the bridge, not a man moved. The company faced the bridge, staring stonily, motionless. The sentinels, facing the banks of the stream, might have been statues to adorn the bridge. The captain stood with folded arms, silent, observing the work of his subordinates, but making no sign. Death is a dignitary who when he comes announced is to be received with formal manifestations of respect, even by those most familiar with him. In the code of military etiquette silence and fixity are forms of deference.

The man who was engaged in being hanged was apparently about thirty-five years of age. He was a civilian, if one might judge from his habit, which was that of a planter. His features were good—a straight nose, firm mouth, broad forehead, from which his long, dark hair was combed straight back, falling behind his ears to the collar of his well-fitting frock-coat. He wore a mustache and pointed beard, but no whiskers; his eyes were large and dark gray, and had a kindly expression which one would hardly have expected in one whose neck was in the hemp. Evidently this was no vulgar assassin. The liberal military code makes provision for hanging many kinds of persons, and gentlemen are not excluded.

The preparations being complete, the two private soldiers stepped aside and each drew away the plank upon which he had been standing. The sergeant turned to the captain, saluted and placed himself immediately behind that officer, who in turn moved apart one pace. These movements left the condemned man and the sergeant standing on the two ends of the same plank, which spanned three of the cross-ties of the bridge. The end upon which the civilian stood almost, but not quite, reached a fourth. This plank had been held in place by the weight of the captain; it was now held by that of the sergeant. At a signal from the former the latter would step aside, the plank would tilt and the condemned man go down between two ties. The arrangement commended itself to his judgment as simple and effective. His face had not been covered nor his eyes bandaged. He looked a moment at his "unsteadfast footing," then let his gaze wander to the swirling water of the stream racing madly beneath his feet. A piece of dancing driftwood caught his attention and his eyes followed it down the current. How slowly it appeared to move! What a sluggish stream!

He closed his eyes in order to fix his last thoughts upon his wife and children. 5 The water, touched to gold by the early sun, the brooding mists under the banks at some distance down the stream, the fort, the soldiers, the piece of drift—all had distracted him. And now he became conscious of a new disturbance. Striking through the thought of his dear ones was a sound which he could neither ignore nor understand, a sharp, distinct, metallic percussion like the stroke of a blacksmith's hammer upon the anvil; it had the same ringing quality. He wondered what it was, and whether immeasurably distant or near by—it seemed both. Its recurrence was regular, but as slow as the tolling of a death knell. He awaited each stroke with impatience and—he knew not why—apprehension. The intervals of silence grew progressively longer; the delays became maddening. With their greater infrequency the sounds increased in strength and sharpness. They hurt his ear like the thrust of a knife; he feared he would shriek. What he heard was the ticking of his watch.

He unclosed his eyes and saw again the water below him. "If I could free my hands," he thought, "I might throw off the noose and spring into the stream. By diving I could evade the bullets and, swimming vigorously, reach the bank, take to the woods and get away home. My home, thank God, is as yet outside their lines; my wife and little ones are still beyond the invader's farthest advance."

As these thoughts, which have here to be set down in words, were flashed into the doomed man's brain rather than evolved from it the captain nodded to the sergeant. The sergeant stepped aside.

II

Peyton Farquhar was a well-to-do planter, of an old and highly respected Alabama family. Being a slave owner and like other slave owners a politician he was naturally an original secessionist and ardently devoted to the Southern cause. Circumstances of an imperious nature, which it is unnecessary to relate here, had prevented him from taking service with the gallant army that had fought the disastrous campaigns ending with the fall of Corinth, and he chafed under the inglorious restraint, longing for the release of his energies, the larger life of the soldier, the opportunity for distinction. That opportunity, he felt, would come, as it comes to all in war time. Meanwhile he did what he could. No service was too humble to him to perform in aid of the South, no adventure too perilous for him to undertake if consistent with the character of a civilian who was at heart a soldier, and who in good faith and without too much qualification assented to at least a part of the frankly villainous dictum that all is fair in love and war.

One evening while Farquhar and his wife were sitting on a rustic bench near the entrance to his grounds, a gray-clad soldier rode up to the gate and asked for a drink of water. Mrs. Farquhar was only too happy to serve him with her own white hands. While she was fetching the water her husband approached the dusty horseman and inquired eagerly for news from the front.

"The Yanks are repairing the railroads," said the man, "and are getting ready 10 for another advance. They have reached the Owl Creek bridge, put it in order and built a stockade on the north bank. The commandant has issued an order, which is posted everywhere, declaring that any civilian caught interfering with the railroad, its bridges, tunnels or trains will be summarily hanged. I saw the order."

"How far is it to the Owl Creek bridge?" Farquhar asked.

"About thirty miles."

"Is there no force on this side the creek?"

"Only a picket post half a mile out, on the railroad, and a single sentinel at this end of the bridge."

"Suppose a man—a civilian and student of hanging—should elude the picket 15 post and perhaps get the better of the sentinel," said Farquhar, smiling, "what could he accomplish?"

The soldier reflected. "I was there a month ago," he replied. "I observed that the flood of last winter had lodged a great quantity of driftwood against the wooden pier at this end of the bridge. It is now dry and would burn like tow."

The lady had now brought the water, which the soldier drank. He thanked her ceremoniously, bowed to her husband and rode away. An hour later, after nightfall, he repassed the plantation, going northward in the direction from which he had come. He was a Federal scout.

III

As Peyton Farquhar fell straight downward through the bridge he lost consciousness and was as one already dead. From this state he was awakened—ages later, it seemed to him—by the pain of a sharp pressure upon his throat, followed by a sense of suffocation. Keen, poignant agonies seemed to shoot from his neck downward through every fiber of his body and limbs. These pains appeared to flash along well-defined lines of ramification and to beat with an inconceivably rapid periodicity. They seemed like streams of pulsating fire heating him to an intolerable temperature. As to his head, he was conscious of nothing but a feeling of fulness—of congestion. These sensations were unaccompanied by thought. The intellectual part of his nature was already effaced; he had power only to feel, and feeling was torment. He was conscious of motion. Encompassed in a luminous cloud, of which he was now merely the fiery heart, without material substance, he swung through unthinkable arcs of oscillation, like a vast pendulum. Then all at once, with terrible suddenness, the light about him shot upward with the noise of a loud plash; a frightful roaring was in his ears, and all was cold and dark. The power of thought was restored; he knew that the rope had broken and he had fallen into the stream. There was no additional strangulation; the noose about his neck was already suffocating him and kept the water from his lungs. To die of hanging at the bottom of a river!—the idea seemed to him ludicrous. He opened his eyes in the darkness and saw above him a gleam of light, but how distant, how inaccessible! He was still sinking, for the light became fainter and fainter until it was a mere glimmer. Then it began to grow and brighten, and he knew that he was rising toward the surface—knew it with reluctance, for he was now very comfortable. "To be hanged and drowned," he thought, "that is not so bad; but I do not wish to be shot. No; I will not be shot; that is not fair."

He was not conscious of an effort, but a sharp pain in his wrist apprised him that he was trying to free his hands. He gave the struggle his attention, as an idler might observe the feat of a juggler, without interest in the outcome. What splendid effort!—what magnificent, what superhuman strength! Ah, that was a fine endeavor! Bravo! The cord fell away; his arms parted and floated upward, the hands dimly seen on each side in the growing light. He watched them with a new interest as first one and then the other pounced upon the noose at his neck. They tore it away and thrust it fiercely aside, its undulations resembling those of a water-snake. "Put it back, put it back!" He thought he shouted these words to his hands, for the undoing of the noose had been succeeded by the direst pang that he had yet experienced. His neck ached horribly; his brain was on fire; his heart, which had been fluttering faintly, gave a great leap, trying to force itself out at his mouth. His whole body was racked and wrenched with an insupportable anguish! But his disobedient hands gave no heed to the command. They beat the water vigorously with quick, downward strokes, forcing him to the surface. He felt his head emerge; his eyes were blinded by the sunlight; his chest expanded convulsively, and with a supreme and crowning agony his lungs engulfed a great draught of air, which instantly he expelled in a shriek!

He was now in full possession of his physical senses. They were, indeed, preter- naturally keen and alert. Something in the awful disturbance of his organic sys- tem had so exalted and refined them that they made record of things never before perceived. He felt the ripples upon his face and heard their separate sounds as they struck. He looked at the forest on the bank of the stream, saw the individual trees, the leaves and the veining of each leaf—saw the very insects upon them: the locusts, the brilliant-bodied flies, the gray spiders stretching their webs from twig to twig. He noted the prismatic colors in all the dewdrops upon a million blades of grass. The humming of the gnats that danced above the eddies of the

20

stream, the beating of the dragon-flies' wings, the strokes of the water-spiders' legs, like oars which had lifted their boat—all these made audible music. A fish slid along beneath his eyes and he heard the rush of its body parting the water.

He had come to the surface facing down the stream; in a moment the visible world seemed to wheel slowly round, himself the pivotal point, and he saw the bridge, the fort, the soldiers upon the bridge, the captain, the sergeant, the two privates, his executioners. They were in silhouette against the blue sky. They shouted and gesticulated, pointing at him. The captain had drawn his pistol, but did not fire; the others were unarmed. Their movements were grotesque and horrible, their forms gigantic.

Suddenly he heard a sharp report and something struck the water smartly within a few inches of his head, spattering his face with spray. He heard a second report, and saw one of the sentinels with his rifle at his shoulder, a light cloud of blue smoke rising from the muzzle. The man in the water saw the eye of the man on the bridge gazing into his own through the sights of the rifle. He observed that it was a gray eye and remembered having read that gray eyes were keenest, and that all famous markmen had them. Nevertheless, this one had missed.

A counter-swirl had caught Farquhar and turned him half round; he was again looking into the forest on the bank opposite the fort. The sound of a clear, high voice in a monotonous singsong now rang out behind him and came across the water with a distinctness that pierced and subdued all other sounds, even the beating of the ripples in his ears. Although no soldier, he had frequented camps enough to know the dread significance of that deliberate, drawling, aspirated chant; the lieutenant on shore was taking a part in the morning's work. How coldly and pitilessly—with what an even, calm intonation, presaging, and enforcing tranquility in the men—with what accurately measured intervals fell those cruel words:

"Attention, company! . . . Shoulder arms! . . . Ready! . . . Aim! . . . Fire!"

Farquhar dived—dived as deeply as he could. The water roared in his ears 25 like the voice of Niagara, yet he heard the dulled thunder of the volley and, rising again toward the surface, met shining bits of metal, singularly flattened, oscillating slowly downward. Some of them touched him on the face and hands, then fell away, continuing their descent. One lodged between his collar and neck; it was uncomfortably warm and he snatched it out.

As he rose to the surface, gasping for breath, he saw that he had been a long time under water; he was perceptibly farther down stream—nearer to safety. The soldiers had almost finished reloading; the metal ramrods flashed all at once in the sunshine as they were drawn from the barrels, turned in the air, and thrust into their sockets. The two sentinels fired again, independently and ineffectually.

The hunted man saw all this over his shoulder; he was now swimming vigorously with the current. His brain was as energetic as his arms and legs; he thought with the rapidity of lightning.

"The officer," he reasoned, "will not make that martinet's error a second time. It is as easy to dodge a volley as a single shot. He has probably already given the command to fire at will. God help me, I cannot dodge them all!"

An appalling plash within two yards of him was followed by a loud, rushing sound, *diminuendo*°, which seemed to travel back through the air to the fort and

---

diminuendo: diminishing (Italian); a term from music indicating a gradual decrease in loudness or force.

died in an explosion which stirred the very river to its deeps! A rising sheet of water curved over him, fell down upon him, blinded him, strangled him! The cannon had taken a hand in the game. As he shook his head free from the commotion of the smitten water he heard the deflected shot humming through the air ahead, and in an instant it was cracking and smashing the branches in the forest beyond.

"They will not do that again," he thought; "the next time they will use a charge 30 of grape. I must keep my eye upon the gun; the smoke will apprise me—the report arrives too late; it lags behind the missile. That is a good gun."

Suddenly he felt himself whirled round and round—spinning like a top. The water, the banks, the forests, the now distant bridge, fort and men—all were commingled and blurred. Objects were represented by their colors only; circular horizontal streaks of color—that was all he saw. He had been caught in a vortex and was being whirled on with a velocity of advance and gyration that made him giddy and sick. In a few moments he was flung upon the gravel at the foot of the left bank of the stream—the southern bank—and behind a projecting point which concealed him from his enemies. The sudden arrest of his motion, the abrasion of one of his hands on the gravel, restored him, and he wept with delight. He dug his fingers into the sand, threw it over himself in handfuls and audibly blessed it. It looked like diamonds, rubies, emeralds; he could think of nothing beautiful which it did not resemble. The trees upon the bank were giant garden plants; he noted a definite order in their arrangement, inhaled the fragrance of their blooms. A strange, roseate light shone through the spaces among their trunks and the wind made in their branches the music of æolian harps. He had no wish to perfect his escape—was content to remain in that enchanting spot until retaken.

A whiz and rattle of grapeshot among the branches high above his head roused him from his dream. The baffled cannoneer had fired him a random farewell. He sprang to his feet, rushed up the sloping bank, and plunged into the forest.

All that day he traveled, laying his course by the rounding sun. The forest seemed interminable; nowhere did he discover a break in it, not even a woodman's road. He had not known that he lived in so wild a region. There was something uncanny in the revelation.

By nightfall he was fatigued, footsore, famishing. The thought of his wife and children urged him on. At last he found a road which led him in what he knew to be the right direction. It was as wide and straight as a city street, yet it seemed untraveled. No fields bordered it, no dwelling anywhere. Not so much as the barking of a dog suggested human habitation. The black bodies of the trees formed a straight wall on both sides, terminating on the horizon in a point, like a diagram in a lesson in perspective. Overhead, as he looked up through this rift in the wood, shone great golden stars looking unfamiliar and grouped in strange constellations. He was sure they were arranged in some order which had a secret and malign significance. The wood on either side was full of singular noises, among which—once, twice, and again—he distinctly heard whispers in an unknown tongue.

His neck was in pain and lifting his hand to it he found it horribly swollen. 35 He knew that it had a circle of black where the rope had bruised it. His eyes felt congested; he could no longer close them. His tongue was swollen with thirst;

he relieved its fever by thrusting it forward from between his teeth into the cold air. How softly the turf had carpeted the untraveled avenue—he could no longer feel the roadway beneath his feet!

Doubtless, despite his suffering, he had fallen asleep while walking, for now he sees another scene—perhaps he has merely recovered from a delirium. He stands at the gate of his own home. All is as he left it, and all bright and beautiful in the morning sunshine. He must have traveled the entire night. As he pushes open the gate and passes up the wide white walk, he sees a flutter of female garments; his wife, looking fresh and cool and sweet, steps down from the veranda to meet him. At the bottom of the steps she stands waiting, with a smile of ineffable joy, an attitude of matchless grace and dignity. Ah, how beautiful she is! He springs forward with extended arms. As he is about to clasp her he feels a stunning blow upon the back of the neck; a blinding white light blazes all about him with a sound like the shock of a cannon—then all is darkness and silence!

Peyton Farquhar was dead; his body, with a broken neck, swung gently from side to side beneath the timbers of the Owl Creek bridge.

Jorge Luis Borges

THE SECRET MIRACLE   1961

Translated by Anthony Kerrigan

Jorge Luis Borges

Jorge Luis Borges (1899–1986), an outstanding modern writer of Latin America, was born in Buenos Aires into a family prominent in Argentine history. Borges grew up bilingual, learning English from his English grandmother and receiving his early education from an English tutor. Caught in Europe by the outbreak of World War II, Borges lived in Switzerland and later Spain, where he joined the Ultraists, a group of experimental poets who renounced realism. On returning to Argentina, he edited a poetry magazine printed in the form of a poster and affixed to city walls. For his opposition to the regime of Colonel Juan Perón, Borges was forced to resign his post as a librarian and was mockingly offered a job as a chicken inspector. In 1955, after Perón was deposed, Borges became director of the national library and Professor of English Literature at the University of Buenos Aires. Since childhood a sufferer from poor eyesight, Borges eventually went blind. His eye problems may have encouraged him to work mainly in short, highly crafted forms: stories, essays, fables, and lyric poems full of elaborate music. His short stories, in Ficciones (1944), El hacedor (1960; translated as Dreamtigers, 1964), and Labyrinths (1962), have been admired worldwide.

And God made him die during the course of a hundred years and then He revived him and said:
"How long have you been here?"
"A day, or part of a day," he replied.

—*The Koran*, II 261

On the night of March 14, 1939, in an apartment on the Zelternergasse in Prague, Jaromir Hladík, author of the unfinished tragedy *The Enemies*, of a *Vindication of Eternity*, and of an inquiry into the indirect Jewish sources of Jakob Boehme°, dreamt a long-drawn-out chess game. The antagonists were not two individuals, but two illustrious families. The contest had begun many centuries before. No one could any longer describe the forgotten prize, but it was rumored that it was enormous and perhaps infinite. The pieces and the chessboard were set up in a secret tower. Jaromir (in his dream) was the first-born of one of the contending families. The hour for the next move, which could not be postponed, struck on all the clocks. The dreamer ran across the sands of a rainy desert—and he could not remember the chessmen or the rules of chess. At this point he awoke. The din of the rain and the clangor of the terrible clocks ceased. A measured unison, sundered by voices of command, arose from the Zelternergasse. Day had dawned, and the armored vanguards of the Third Reich were entering Prague.

On the nineteenth, the authorities received an accusation against Jaromir Hladík; on the same day, at dusk, he was arrested. He was taken to a barracks, aseptic and white, on the opposite bank of the Moldau. He was unable to refute a single one of the charges made by the Gestapo: his maternal surname was Jaroslavski, his blood was Jewish, his study of Boehme was Judaizing, his signature had helped to swell the final census of those protesting the *Anschluss*°. In 1928, he had translated the *Sepher Yezirah* for the publishing house of Hermann Barsdorf; the effusive catalogue issued by this firm had exaggerated, for commercial reasons, the translator's renown; this catalogue was leafed through by Julius Rothe, one of the officials in whose hands lay Hladík's fate. The man does not exist who, outside his own specialty, is not credulous: two or three adjectives in Gothic script sufficed to convince Julius Rothe of Hladík's preeminence, and of the need for the death penalty, *pour encourager les autres*°. The execution was set for the twenty-ninth of March, at nine in the morning. This delay (whose importance the reader will appreciate later) was due to a desire on the part of the authorities to act slowly and impersonally, in the manner of planets or vegetables.

Hladík's first reaction was simply one of horror. He was sure he would not have been terrified by the gallows, the block, or the knife; but to die before a firing squad was unbearable. In vain he repeated to himself that the pure and general act of dying, not the concrete circumstances, was the dreadful fact. He did not grow weary of imagining these circumstances: he absurdly tried to exhaust all the variations. He infinitely anticipated the process, from the sleepless dawn to the mysterious discharge of the rifles. Before the day set by Julius Rothe, he died

---

Jakob Boehme: German philosopher and mystic (1575–1624).   *Anschluss:* the annexation of Austria by Nazi Germany in 1938.   *pour encourager les autres:* "to encourage others (to obey)."

hundreds of deaths, in courtyards whose shapes and angles defied geometry, shot down by changeable soldiers whose number varied and who sometimes put an end to him from close up and sometimes from far away. He faced these imaginary executions with true terror (perhaps with true courage). Each simulacrum lasted a few seconds. Once the circle was closed, Jaromir returned interminably to the tremulous eve of his death. Then he would reflect that reality does not tend to coincide with forecasts about it. With perverse logic he inferred that to foresee a circumstantial detail is to prevent its happening. Faithful to this feeble magic, he would invent, *so that they might not happen,* the most atrocious particulars. Naturally, he finished by fearing that these particulars were prophetic. During his wretched nights he strove to hold fast somehow to the fugitive substance of time. He knew that time was precipitating itself toward the dawn of the twenty-ninth. He reasoned aloud: *I am now in the night of the twenty-second. While this night lasts (and for six more nights to come) I am invulnerable, immortal.* His nights of sleep seemed to him deep, dark pools into which he might submerge. Sometimes he yearned impatiently for the firing squad's definitive volley, which would redeem him, for better or worse, from the vain compulsion of his imagination. On the twenty-eighth, as the final sunset reverberated across the high barred windows, he was distracted from all these abject considerations by thought of his drama, *The Enemies.*

Hladík was past forty. Apart from a few friendships and many habits, the problematic practice of literature constituted his life. Like every writer, he measured the virtues of other writers by their performance, and asked that they measure him by what he conjectured or planned. All of the books he had published merely moved him to a complex repentance. His investigation of the work of Boehme, of Ibn Ezra°, and of Fludd° was essentially a product of mere application; his translation of the *Sepher Yezirah* was characterized by negligence, fatigue, and conjecture. He judged his *Vindication of Eternity* to be perhaps less deficient: the first volume is a history of the diverse eternities devised by man, from the immutable Being of Parmenides° to the alterable past of Hinton°; the second volume denies (with Francis Bradley°) that all the events in the universe make up a temporal series. He argues that the number of experiences possible to man is not infinite, and that a single "repetition" suffices to demonstrate that time is a fallacy. . . . Unfortunately, the arguments that demonstrate this fallacy are not any less fallacious. Hladík was in the habit of running through these arguments with certain disdainful perplexity. He had also written a series of expressionist poems; these, to the discomfiture of the author, were included in an anthology in 1924, and there was no anthology of later date which did not inherit them. Hladík was anxious to redeem himself from his equivocal and languid past with his verse drama, *The Enemies.* (He favored the verse form in the theater because it prevents the spectators from forgetting unreality, which is the necessary condition of art.)

Ibn Ezra: Hebrew poet of Muslim Spain (c. 1060–c. 1139).   *Fludd:* Robert Fludd, English physician and mystic (1574–1637).   *Parmenides:* Greek philosopher of the fifth century B.C.   *Hinton:* James Hinton, English physiologist and philosopher (1822–1875).   *Francis Bradley:* English philosopher (1846–1924).

This opus preserved the dramatic unities (time, place, and action). It trans- 5
pires in Hradcany, in the library of the Baron Roemerstadt, on one of the last
evenings of the nineteenth century. In the first scene of the first act, a stranger
pays a visit to Roemerstadt. (A clock strikes seven, the vehemence of a setting
sun glorifies the window panes, the air transmits familiar and impassioned Hungarian music.) This visit is followed by others; Roemerstadt does not know the
people who come to importune him, but he has the uncomfortable impression
that he has seem them before: perhaps in a dream. All the visitors fawn upon
him, but it is obvious—first to the spectators of the drama, and then to the Baron
himself—that they are secret enemies, sworn to ruin him. Roemerstadt manages
to outwit, or evade, their complex intrigues. In the course of the dialogue, mention is made of his betrothed, Julia de Weidenau, and of a certain Jaroslav Kubin,
who at one time had been her suitor. Kubin has now lost his mind and thinks
he is Roemerstadt. . . . The dangers multiply. Roemerstadt, at the end of the second act, is forced to kill one of the conspirators. The third and final act begins.
The incongruities gradually mount up: actors who seemed to have been discarded
from the play reappear; the man who had been killed by Romerstadt returns, for
an instant. Someone notes that the time of day has not advanced: the clock strikes
seven, the western sun reverberates in the high windowpanes, impassioned Hungarian music is carried on the air. The first speaker in the play reappears and repeats
the words he had spoken in the first scene of the first act. Roemerstadt addresses
him without the least surprise. The spectator understands that Roemerstadt is
the wretched Jaroslav Kubin. The drama has never taken place: it is the circular
delirium which Kubin unendingly lives and relives.

Hladík had never asked himself whether this tragicomedy of errors was
preposterous or admirable, deliberate or casual. Such a plot, he intuited, was the
most appropriate invention to conceal his defects and to manifest his strong points,
and it embodied the possibility of redeeming (symbolically) the fundamental meaning of his life. He had already completed the first act and a scene or two of the
third. The metrical nature of the work allowed him to go over it continually,
rectifying the hexameters, without recourse to the manuscript. He thought of the
two acts still to do, and of his coming death. In the darkness, he addressed himself to God. *If I exist at all, if I am not one of Your repetitions and errata, I exist as
the author of the* The Enemies. *In order to bring this drama, which may serve to justify
me, to justify You, I need one more year. Grant me that year, You to whom belong
the centuries and all time.* It was the last, the most atrocious night, but ten minutes
later sleep swept over him like a dark ocean and drowned him.

Toward dawn, he dreamt he had hidden himself in one of the naves of the
Clementine Library. A librarian wearing dark glasses asked him: *What are you
looking for?* Hladík answered: *God.* The Librarian told him: *God is in one of the
letters on one of the pages of one of the 400,000 volumes of the Clementine. My fathers
and the fathers of my fathers have sought after that letter. I've gone blind looking for
it.* He removed his glasses, and Hladík saw that his eyes were dead. A reader came
in to return an atlas. *This atlas is useless,* he said, and handed it to Hladík, who
opened it at random. As if through a haze, he saw a map of India. With a sudden
rush of assurance, he touched one of the tiniest letters. An ubiquitous voice said:
The time for your work has been granted. Hladík awoke.

He remembered that the dreams of men belong to God, and that Maimonides wrote that the words of a dream are divine, when they are all separate and clear and are spoken by someone invisible. He dressed. Two soldiers entered his cell and ordered him to follow them.

From behind the door, Hladík had visualized a labyrinth of passageways, stairs, and connecting blocks. Reality was less rewarding: the party descended to an inner courtyard by a single iron stairway. Some soldiers—uniforms unbuttoned—were testing a motorcycle and disputing their conclusions. The sergeant looked at his watch: it was 8:44. They must wait until nine. Hladík, more insignificant than pitiful, sat down on a pile of firewood. He noticed that the soldiers' eyes avoided his. To make his wait easier, the sergeant offered him a cigarette. Hladík did not smoke. He accepted the cigarette out of politeness or humility. As he lit it, he saw that his hands shook. The day was clouding over. The soldiers spoke in low tones, as though he were already dead. Vainly, he strove to recall the woman of whom Julia de Weidenau was the symbol . . . .

The firing squad fell in and was brought to attention. Hladík, standing against 10 the barracks wall, waited for the volley. Someone expressed fear the wall would be splashed with blood. The condemned man was ordered to step forward a few paces. Hladík recalled, absurdly, the preliminary maneuvers of a photographer. A heavy drop of rain grazed one of Hladík's temples and slowly rolled down his cheek. The sergeant barked the final command.

The physical universe stood still.

The rifles converged upon Hladík, but the men assigned to pull the triggers were immobile. The sergeant's arm eternalized an inconclusive gesture. Upon a courtyard flagstone a bee cast a stationary shadow. The wind had halted, as in a painted picture. Hladík began a shriek, a syllable, a twist of the hand. He realized he was paralyzed. Not a sound reached him from the stricken world.

He thought: *I'm in hell, I'm dead.*

He thought: *I've gone mad.*

He thought: *Time has come to a halt.* 15

Then he reflected that in that case, his thought, too, would have come to a halt. He was anxious to test this possibility: he repeated (without moving his lips) the mysterious Fourth Eclogue of Virgil. He imagined that the already remote soldiers shared his anxiety; he longed to communicate with them. He was astonished that he felt no fatigue, no vertigo from his protracted immobility. After an indeterminate length of time he fell asleep. On awakening he found the world still motionless and numb. The drop of water still clung to his cheek; the shadow of the bee still did not shift in the courtyard; the smoke from the cigarette he had thrown down did not blow away. Another "day" passed before Hladík understood.

He had asked God for an entire year in which to finish his work: His omnipotence had granted him the time. For his sake, God projected a secret miracle: German lead would kill him, at the determined hour, but in his mind a year would elapse between the command to fire and its execution. From perplexity he passed to stupor, from stupor to resignation, from resignation to sudden gratitude.

He disposed of no document but his own memory; the mastering of each hexameter as he added it, had imposed upon him a kind of fortunate discipline not imagined by those amateurs who forget their vague, ephemeral paragraphs. He did not work for posterity, nor even for God, of whose literary preferences he possessed scant knowledge. Meticulous, unmoving, secretive, he wove his lofty invisible labyrinth in time. He worked the third act over twice. He eliminated some rather too-obvious symbols: the repeated striking of the hour, the music. There were no circumstances to constrain him. He omitted, condensed, amplified; occasionally, he chose the primitive version. He grew to love the courtyard, the barracks; one of the faces endlessly confronting him made him modify his conception of Roemerstadt's character. He discovered that the hard cacophonies which so distressed Flaubert are mere visual superstitions: debilities and annoyances of the written word, not of the sonorous, the sounding one . . . . He brought his drama to a conclusion: he lacked only a single phrase. He found it: the drop of water slid down his cheek. He began a wild cry, moved his face aside. A quadruple blast brought him down.

Jaromir Hladík died on March 29, at 9:02 in the morning.

Willa Cather

PAUL'S CASE   1905

Willa Cather (1876–1947) was born in Gore, Virginia, but at nine moved to Webster County, Nebraska, where pioneer sod houses still clung to the windswept plains. There, mainly in the town of Red Cloud, she grew up among Scandinavians, Czechs, Bohemians, and other immigrant settlers, for whom she felt a quick kinship: they too had been displaced from their childhood homes. After graduation from the University of Nebraska, Cather went east to spend ten years in Pittsburgh, where the story "Paul's Case" opens. (When she wrote the story, she was a high school teacher of Latin and English and music critic for a newspaper.) Then, because her early stories had attracted notice, New York beckoned. A job on the staff of McClure's led to her becoming managing editor of the popular magazine. Her early novels of Nebraska won immense popularity: Willa Cather

Willa Cather

O Pioneers! *(1913),* My Ántonia *(1918), and* A Lost Lady *(1923). In her later novels Cather explores other regions of the North American past: in* Death Comes to the Archbishop *(1927), frontier New Mexico; in* Shadows on the Rock *(1931), seventeenth-century Quebec. She does not romanticize the rugged lives of farm people on the plains, or glamorize village life. Often, as in* The Song of the Lark *(1915), the story of a Colorado girl who becomes an opera singer, she depicts a small town as stifling. With remarkable skill, she may tell a story from a man's point of view, but her favorite characters are likely to be women of strong will who triumph over obstacles.*

It was Paul's afternoon to appear before the faculty of the Pittsburgh High School to account for his varous misdemeanors. He had been suspended a week ago, and his father had called at the Principal's office and confessed his perplexity about his son. Paul entered the faculty room suave and smiling. His clothes were a trifle outgrown and the tan velvet on the collar of his open overcoat was frayed and worn; but for all that there was something of the dandy about him, and he wore an opal pin in his neatly knotted black four-in-hand, and a red carnation in his buttonhole. This latter adornment the faculty somehow felt was not properly significant of the contrite spirit befitting a boy under the ban of suspension.

Paul was tall for his age and very thin, with high, cramped shoulders and a narrow chest. His eyes were remarkable for a certain hysterical brilliancy and he continually used them in a conscious, theatrical sort of way, peculiarly offensive in a boy. The pupils were abnormally large, as though he were addicted to belladonna, but there was a glassy glitter about them which that drug does not produce.

When questioned by the Principal as to why he was there, Paul stated, politely enough, that he wanted to come back to school. This was a lie, but Paul was quite accustomed to lying; found it, indeed, indispensable for overcoming friction. His teachers were asked to state their respective charges against him, which they did with such a rancor and aggrievedness as evinced that this was not a usual case. Disorder and impertinence were among the offenses named, yet each of his instructors felt that it was scarcely possible to put into words the real cause of the trouble, which lay in a sort of hysterically defiant manner of the boy's; in the contempt which they all knew he felt for them, and which he seemingly made not the least effort to conceal. Once, when he had been making a synopsis of a paragraph at the blackboard, his English teacher had stepped to his side and attempted to guide his hand. Paul had started back with a shudder and thrust his hands violently behind him. The astonished woman could scarcely have been more hurt and embarrassed had he struck at her. The insult was so involuntary and definitely personal as to be unforgettable. In one way and another, he had made all his teachers, men and women alike, conscious of the same feeling of physical aversion. In one class he habitually sat with his hand shading his eyes; in another he always looked out of the window during the recitation; in another he made a running commentary on the lecture, with humorous intention.

His teachers felt this afternoon that his whole attitude was symbolized by his shrug and his flippantly red carnation flower, and they fell upon him without mercy, his English teacher leading the pack. He stood through it smiling, his pale lips parted over his white teeth. (His lips were continually twitching, and he had a habit of raising his eyebrows that was contemptuous and irritating to the last degree.) Older boys than Paul had broken down and shed tears under that baptism of fire, but his set smile did not once desert him, and his only sign of discomfort was the nervous trembling of the fingers that toyed with the buttons of his overcoat, and an occasional jerking of the other hand that held his hat. Paul was always smiling, always glancing about him, seeming to feel that people might be watching him and trying to detect something. This conscious expression, since it was as far as possible from boyish mirthfulness, was usually attributed to insolence or "smartness."

As the inquisition proceeded, one of his instructors repeated an impertinent remark of the boy's, and the Principal asked him whether he thought that a courteous speech to have made a woman. Paul shrugged his shoulders slightly and his eyebrows twitched. 5

"I don't know," he replied. "I didn't mean to be polite or impolite, either. I guess it's a sort of way I have of saying things regardless."

The Principal, who was a sympathetic man, asked him whether he didn't think that a way it would be well to get rid of. Paul grinned and said he guessed so. When he was told that he could go, he bowed gracefully and went out. His bow was but a repetition of the scandalous red carnation.

His teachers were in despair, and his drawing master voiced the feeling of them all when he declared there was something about the boy which none of them understood. He added: "I don't really believe that smile of his comes altogether from insolence; there's something sort of haunted about it. The boy is not strong, for one thing. I happen to know that he was born in Colorado, only a few months before his mother died out there of a long illness. There is something wrong about the fellow."

The drawing master had come to realize that, in looking at Paul, one saw only his white teeth and the forced animation of his eyes. One warm afternoon the boy had gone to sleep at his drawing-board, and his master had noted with amazement what a white, blue-veined face it was; drawn and wrinkled like an old man's about the eyes, the lips twitching even in his sleep, and stiff with a nervous tension that drew them back from his teeth.

His teachers left the building dissatisfied and unhappy; humiliated to have felt so vindictive toward a mere boy, to have uttered this feeling in cutting terms, and to have set each other on, as it were, in the gruesome game of intemperate reproach. Some of them remembered having seen a miserable street cat set at bay by a ring of tormentors. 10

As for Paul, he ran down the hill whistling the Soldiers' Chorus from *Faust*°, looking wildly behind him now and then to see whether some of his teachers were not there to writhe under his light-heartedness. As it was now late in the afternoon and Paul was on duty that evening as usher at Carnegie Hall°, he decided that he would not go home to supper. When he reached the concert hall the doors were not yet open and, as it was chilly outside, he decided to go up into the picture gallery—always deserted at this hour—where there were some of Raffaelli's° gay studies of Paris streets and an airy blue Venetian scene or two that always exhilarated him. He was delighted to find no one in the gallery but the old guard, who sat in one corner, a newspaper on his knee, a black patch over one eye and

---

Faust: tragic grand opera (1859) by French composer Charles Gounod.   *Carnegie Hall*: concert hall endowed by Pittsburgh steel manufacturer Andrew Carnegie, not to be confused with the better-known Carnegie Hall in New York City.   *Raffaelli*: Jean-Francois Raffaelli (1850–1921), painter and graphic artist, native and lifelong resident of Paris, attained great popularity for his paintings and drawings of that city.

the other closed. Paul possessed himself of the place and walked confidently up and down, whistling under his breath. After a while he sat down before a blue Rico° and lost himself. When he bethought him to look at his watch, it was after seven o'clock, and he rose with a start and ran downstairs, making a face at Augustus, peering out from the cast-room°, and an evil gesture at the Venus of Milo as he passed her on the stairway.

When Paul reached the ushers' dressing-room half-a-dozen boys were there already, and he began excitedly to tumble into his uniform. It was one of the few that at all approached fitting, and Paul thought it very becoming—though he knew that the tight, straight coat accentuated his narrow chest, about which he was exceedingly sensitive. He was always considerably excited while he dressed, twanging all over to the tuning of the strings and the preliminary flourishes of the horns in the music-room; but tonight he seemed quite beside himself, and he teased and plagued the boys until, telling him that he was crazy, they put him down on the floor and sat on him.

Somewhat calmed by his suppression, Paul dashed out to the front of the house to seat the early comers. He was a model usher; gracious and smiling he ran up and down the aisles; nothing was too much trouble for him; he carried messages and brought programmes as though it were his greatest pleasure in life, and all the people in his section thought him a charming boy, feeling that he remembered and admired them. As the house filled, he grew more and more vivacious and animated, and the color came to his cheeks and lips. It was very much as though this were a great reception and Paul were the host. Just as the musicians came out to take their places, his English teacher arrived with checks for the seats which a prominent manufacturer had taken for the season. She betrayed some embarrassment when she handed Paul the tickets, and a *hauteur*° which subsequently made her feel very foolish. Paul was startled for a moment, and had the feeling of wanting to put her out; what business had she here among all these fine people and gay colors? He looked her over and decided that she was not appropriately dressed and must be a fool to sit downstairs in such togs. The tickets had probably been sent her out of kindness, he reflected as he put down a seat for her, and she had about as much right to sit there as he had.

When the symphony began Paul sank into one of the rear seats with a long sigh of relief, and lost himself as he had done before the Rico. It was not that symphonies, as such, meant anything in particular to Paul, but the first sigh of the instruments seemed to free some hilarious and potent spirit within him; something that struggled there like the Genius° in the bottle found by the Arab fisherman. He felt a sudden zest of life; the lights danced before his eyes and the concert hall blazed into unimaginable splendor. When the soprano soloist came on, Paul forgot even the nastiness of his teacher's being there and gave himself up to the peculiar stimulus such personages always had for him. The soloist chanced to be

---

Rico: (flourished 1500–1550), painter of the Byzantine school, a native of Crete.   Augustus . . . cast-room: Paul mocks a plaster cast of the Vatican Museum's famous statue of the first Roman emperor (63 B.C.-A.D. 14), whom an unknown sculptor posed sternly pointing an index finger at his beholders.   hauteur: haughtiness.   Genius: genie in a tale from *The Arabian Nights*.

a German woman, by no means in her first youth, and the mother of many children; but she wore an elaborate gown and a tiara, and above all she had that indefinable air of achievement, that world-shine upon her, which, in Paul's eyes, made her a veritable queen of Romance.

After a concert was over Paul was always irritable and wretched until he got 15 to sleep, and tonight he was even more than usually restless. He had the feeling of not being able to let down, of its being impossible to give up this delicious excitement which was the only thing that could be called living at all. During the last number he withdrew and, after hastily changing his clothes in the dressing-room, slipped out to the side door where the soprano's carriage stood. Here he began pacing rapidly up and down the walk, waiting to see her come out.

Over yonder the Schenley, in its vacant stretch, loomed big and square through the fine rain, the windows of its twelve stories glowing like those of a lighted cardboard house under a Christmas tree. All the actors and singers of the better class stayed there when they were in the city, and a number of the big manufacturers of the place lived there in the winter. Paul had often hung about the hotel, watching the people go in and out, longing to enter and leave school-masters and dull care behind him forever.

At last the singer came out, accompanied by the conductor, who helped her into her carriage and closed the door with a cordial *auf wiedersehen*° which set Paul to wondering whether she were not an old sweetheart of his. Paul followed the carriage over to the hotel, walking so rapidly as not to be far from the entrance when the singer alighted and disappeared behind the swinging glass doors that were opened by a negro in a tall hat and a long coat. In the moment that the door was ajar it seemed to Paul that he, too, entered. He seemed to feel himself go after her up the steps, into the warm, lighted building, into an exotic, a tropical world of shiny, glistening surfaces and basking ease. He reflected upon the mysterious dishes that were brought into the dining-room, the green bottles in buckets of ice, as he had seen them in the supper party pictures of the *Sunday World* supplement. A quick gust of wind brought the rain down with sudden vehemence, and Paul was startled to find that he was still outside in the slush of the gravel driveway; that his boots were letting in the water and his scanty over-coat was clinging wet about him; that the lights in front of the concert hall were out, and that the rain was driving in sheets between him and the orange glow of the windows above him. There it was, what he wanted—tangibly before him, like the fairy world of a Christmas pantomime, but mocking spirits stood guard at the doors, and, as the rain beat in his face, Paul wondered whether he were destined always to shiver in the black night outside, looking up at it.

He turned and walked reluctantly toward the car tracks. The end had to come sometime; his father in his night-clothes at the top of the stairs, explanations that did not explain, hastily improvised fictions that were forever tripping him up, his upstairs room and its horrible yellow wall-paper, the creaking bureau with the

auf wiedersehen: German equivalent of *au revoir*, or "here's to seeing you again."

greasy plush collar-box, and over his painted wooden bed the pictures of George Washington and John Calvin°, and the framed motto, "Feed my Lambs," which had been worked in red worsted by his mother.

Half an hour later, Paul alighted from his car and went slowly down one of the side streets off the main thoroughfare. It was a highly respectable street, where all the houses were exactly alike, and where businessmen of moderate means begot and reared large families of children, all of whom went to Sabbath-school and learned the shorter catechism, and were interested in arithmetic; all of whom were as exactly alike as their homes, and of a piece with the monotony in which they lived. Paul never went up Cordelia Street without a shudder of loathing. His home was next to the house of the Cumberland° minister. He approached it tonight with the nerveless sense of defeat, the hopeless feeling of sinking back forever into ugliness and commonness that he had always had when he came home. The moment he turned into Cordelia Street he felt the waters close above his head. After each of these orgies of living, he experienced all the physical depression which follows a debauch; the loathing of respectable beds, of common food, of a house penetrated by kitchen odors; a shuddering repulsion for the flavorless, colorless mass of every-day existence; a morbid desire for cool things and soft lights and fresh flowers.

The nearer he approached the house, the more absolutely unequal Paul felt to the sight of it all; his ugly sleeping chamber; the cold bathroom with the grimy zinc tub, the cracked mirror, the dripping spigots; his father, at the top of the stairs, his hairy legs sticking out from his night-shirt, his feet thrust into carpet slippers. He was so much later than usual that there would certainly be inquiries and reproaches. Paul stopped short before the door. He felt that he could not be accosted by his father tonight; that he could not toss again on that miserable bed. He would not go in. He would tell his father that he had no car fare, and it was raining so hard he had gone home with one of the boys and stayed all night.

Meanwhile, he was wet and cold. He went around to the back of the house-and tried one of the basement windows, found it open, raised it cautiously, and scrambled down the cellar wall to the floor. There he stood, holding his breath, terrified by the noise he had made, but the floor above him was silent, and there was no creak on the stairs. He found a soap-box, and carried it over to the soft ring of light that streamed from the furnace door, and sat down. He was horribly afraid of rats, so he did not try to sleep, but sat looking distrustfully at the dark, still terrified lest he might have awakened his father. In such reactions, after one of the experiences which made days and nights out of the dreary blanks of the calendar, when his senses were deadened, Paul's head was always singularly clear. Suppose his father had heard him getting in at the window and had come down and shot him for a burglar? Then, again, suppose his father had come down, pistol in hand, and he had cried out in time to save himself, and his father had been horrified to think how nearly he had killed him? Then, again, suppose a day should

°John Calvin: French Protestant theologian of the Reformation (1509–1564) whose teachings are the basis of Presbyterianism. °Cumberland: The minister, a Cumberland Presbyterian, belongs to a frontier denomination that had splintered away from the Presbyterian Church and whose ministers were ordained after a briefer training.

come when his father would remember that night, and wish there had been no warning cry to stay his hand? With this last supposition Paul entertained himself until daybreak.

The following Sunday was fine; the sodden November chill was broken by the last flash of autumnal summer. In the morning Paul had to go to church and Sabbath-school, as always. On seasonable Sunday afternoons the burghers of Cordelia Street always sat out on their front "stoops," and talked to their neighbors on the next stoop, or called to those across the street in neighborly fashion. The men usually sat on gay cushions placed upon the steps that led down to the sidewalk, while the women, in their Sunday "waists," sat in rockers on the cramped porches, pretending to be greatly at their ease. The children played in the streets; there was so many of them that the place resembled the recreation grounds of a kindergarten. The men on the steps—all in their shirt sleeves, their vests unbuttoned—sat with their legs well apart, their stomachs comfortably protruding, and talked of the prices of things, or told anecdotes of the sagacity of their various chiefs and overlords. They occasionally looked over the multitude of squabbling children, listened affectionately to their high-pitched, nasal voices, smiling to see their own proclivities reproduced in their offspring, and interspersed their legends of the iron kings with remarks about their sons' progress at school, their grades in arithmetic, and the amounts they had saved in their toy banks.

On this last Sunday of November, Paul sat all the afternoon on the lowest step of his "stoop," staring into the street, while his sisters, in their rockers, were talking to the minister's daughters next door about how many shirt-waists they had made in the last week, and how many waffles some one had eaten at the last church supper. When the weather was warm, and his father was in a particularly jovial frame of mind, the girls made lemonade, which was always brought out in a red-glass pitcher, ornamented with forget-me-nots in blue enamel. This the girls thought very fine, and the neighbors always joked about the suspicious color of the pitcher.

Today Paul's father sat on the top step, talking to a young man who shifted a restless baby from knee to knee. He happened to be the young man who was daily held up to Paul as a model, and after whom it was his father's dearest hope that he would pattern. This young man was of a ruddy complexion, with a compressed, red mouth, and faded, near-sighted eyes, over which he wore thick spectacles, with gold bows that curved about his ears. He was clerk to one of the magnates of a great steel corporation, and was looked upon in Cordelia Street as a young man with a future. There was a story that, some five years ago—he was now barely twenty-six—he had been a trifle dissipated but in order to curb his appetites and save the loss of time and strength that a sowing of wild oats might have entailed, he had taken his chief's advice oft reiterated to his employees, and at twenty-one had married the first woman whom he could persuade to share his fortunes. She happened to be an angular school-mistress, much older than he, who also wore thick glasses, and who had now borne him four children, all near-sighted, like herself.

The young man was relating how his chief, now cruising in the Mediterra- 25 nean, kept in touch with all the details of the business, arranging his office hours on his yacht just as though he were at home, and "knocking off work enough to keep two stenographers busy." His father told, in turn, the plan his corporation was considering, of putting in an electric railway plant at Cairo. Paul snapped his teeth; he had an awful apprehension that they might spoil it all before he got there. Yet he rather liked to hear these legends of the iron kings, that were told and retold on Sundays and holidays; these stories of palaces in Venice, yachts on the Mediterranean, and high play at Monte Carlo appealed to his fancy, and he was interested in the triumphs of these cash boys who had become famous, though he had no mind for the cash-boy stage.

After supper was over, and he had helped to dry the dishes, Paul nervously asked his father whether he could go to George's to get some help in his geometry, and still more nervously asked for car fare. This latter request he had to repeat, as his father, on principle, did not like to hear requests for money, whether much or little. He asked Paul whether he could not go to some boy who lived nearer, and told him that he ought not to leave his school work until Sunday; but he gave him the dime. He was not a poor man, but he had a worthy ambition to come up in the world. His only reason for allowing Paul to usher was, that he thought a boy ought to be earning a little.

Paul bounded upstairs, scrubbed the greasy odor of the dish-water from his hands with the ill-smelling soap he hated, and then shook over his fingers a few drops of violet water from the bottle he kept hidden in his drawer. He left the house with his geometry conspicuously under his arm, and the moment he got out of Cordelia Street and boarded a downtown car, he shook off the lethargy of two deadening days, and began to live again.

The leading juvenile of the permanent stock company which played at one of the downtown theatres was an acquaintance of Paul's, and the boy had been invited to drop in at the Sunday-night rehearsals whenever he could. For more than a year Paul had spent every available moment loitering about Charley Edwards's dressing-room. He had won a place among Edwards's following not only because the young actor, who could not afford to employ a dresser, often found him useful, but because he recognized in Paul something akin to what churchmen term "vocation."

It was at the theatre and at Carnegie Hall that Paul really lived; the rest was but a sleep and a forgetting. This was Paul's fairy tale, and it had for him all the allurement of a secret love. The moment he inhaled the gassy, painty, dusty odor behind the scenes, he breathed like a prisoner set free, and felt within him the possibility of doing or saying splendid, brilliant, poetic things. The moment the cracked orchestra beat out the overture from *Martha*°, or jerked at the serenade from *Rigoletto*°, all stupid and ugly things slid from him, and his senses were deliciously, yet delicately fired.

Perhaps it was because, in Paul's world, the natural nearly always wore the guise of ugliness, that a certain element of artificiality seemed to him necessary in beauty. Perhaps it was because his experience of life elsewhere was so full of Sabbath-school picnics, petty economies, wholesome advice as to how to succeed

30

Martha: grand opera about romance among English aristocrats (1847) by German composer Friedrich von Flotow.   *Rigoletto:* tragic grand opera (1851) by Italian composer Giuseppe Verdi.

in life, and the unescapable odors of cooking, that he found this existence so alluring, these smartly-clad men and women so attractive, that he was so moved by these starry apple orchards that bloomed perennially under the lime-light.

It would be difficult to put it strongly enough how convincingly the stage entrance of that theatre was for Paul the actual portal of Romance. Certainly none of the company ever suspected it, least of all Charley Edwards. It was very like the old stories that used to float about London of fabulously rich Jews, who had subterranean halls there, with palms, and fountains, and soft lamps and richly apparelled women who never saw the disenchanting light of Londay day. So, in the midst of that smoke-palled city, enamored of figures and grimy toil, Paul had his secret temple, his wishing carpet, his bit of blue-and-white Mediterranean shore bathed in perpetual sunshine.

Several of Paul's teachers had a theory that his imagination had been perverted by garish fiction, but the truth was that he scarcely ever read at all. The books at home were not such as would either tempt or corrupt a youthful mind, and as for reading the novels that some of his friends urged upon him—well, he got what he wanted much more quickly from music; any sort of music, from an orchestra to a barrel organ. He needed only the spark, the indescribable thrill that made his imagination master of his senses, and he could make plots and pictures enough of his own. It was equally true that he was not stage struck—not, at any rate, in the usual acceptation of that expression. He had no desire to become an actor, any more than he had to become a musician. He felt no necessity to do any of these things; what he wanted was to see, to be in the atmosphere, float on the wave of it, to be carried out, blue league after blue league, away from everything.

After a night behind the scenes, Paul found the school-room more than ever repulsive; the bare floors and naked walls; the prosy men who never wore frock coats, or violets in their buttonholes; the women with their dull gowns, shrill voices, and pitiful seriousness about prepositions that govern the dative. He could not bear to have the other pupils think, for a moment, that he took these people seriously; he must convey to them that he considered it all trivial, and was there only by way of a jest, anyway. He had autographed pictures of all the members of the stock company which he showed his classmates, telling them the most incredible stories of his familiarity with these people, of his acquaintance with the soloists who came to Carnegie Hall, his suppers with them and the flowers he sent them. When these stories lost their effect, and his audience grew listless, he became desperate and would bid all the boys good-bye, announcing that he was going to travel for a while; going to Naples, to Venice, to Egypt. Then, next Monday, he would slip back, conscious and nervously smiling; his sister was ill, and he should have to defer his voyage until spring.

Matters went steadily worse with Paul at school. In the itch to let his instructors know how heartily he despised them and their homilies, and how thoroughly he was appreciated elsewhere, he mentioned once or twice that he had no time to fool with theorems; adding—with a twitch of the eyebrows and a touch of that nervous bravado which so perplexed them—that he was helping the people down at the stock company; they were old friends of his.

The upshot of the matter was that the Principal went to Paul's father, and 35
Paul was taken out of school and put to work. The manager at Carnegie Hall
was told to get another usher in his stead; the door-keeper at the theatre was warned
not to admit him to the house; and Charley Edwards remorsefully promised the
boy's father not to see him again.

The members of the stock company were vastly amused when some of Paul's
stories reached them—especially the women. They were hardworking women, most
of them supporting indigent husbands or brothers, and they laughed rather bitterly at having stirred the boy to such fervid and florid inventions. They agreed
with the faculty and with his father that Paul's was a bad case.

The east-bound train was ploughing through a January snow-storm; the dull
dawn was beginning to show grey when the engine whistled a mile out of Newark. Paul started up from the seat where he had lain curled in uneasy slumber,
rubbed the breath-misted window glass with his hand, and peered out. The snow
was whirling in curling eddies above the white bottom lands, and the drifts lay
already deep in the fields and along the fences, while here and there the long
dead grass and dried weed stalks protruded black above it. Lights shone from the
scattered houses, and a gang of laborers who stood beside the track waved their
lanterns.

Paul had slept very little, and he felt grimy and uncomfortable. He had made
the all-night journey in a day coach, partly because he was ashamed, dressed as
he was, to go into a Pullman, and partly because he was afraid of being seen there
by some Pittsburgh businessmen, who might have noticed him in Denny & Carson's office. When the whistle awoke him, he clutched quickly at his breast pocket,
glancing about him with an uncertain smile. But the little, clay-bespattered Italians
were still sleeping, the slatternly women across the aisle were in open-mouthed
oblivion, and even the crumby, crying babies were for the nonce stilled. Paul settled back to struggle with his impatience as best as he could.

When he arrived at the Jersey City station, he hurried through his breakfast,
manifestly ill at ease and keeping a sharp eye about him. After he reached the
Twenty-third Street station°, he consulted a cabman, and had himself driven to
a men's furnishing establishment that was just opening for the day. He spent upward of two hours there, buying with endless reconsidering and great care. His
new street suit he put on in the fitting-room; the frock coat and dress clothes
he had bundled into the cab with his linen. Then he drove to a hatter's and a
shoe house. His next errand was at Tiffany's, where he selected his silver and a
new scarf-pin. He would not wait to have his silver marked, he said. Lastly, he
stopped at a trunk shop on Broadway, and had his purchases packed into various
travelling bags.

It was a little after one-o'clock when he drove up to the Waldorf, and after 40
settling with the cabman, went into the office. He registered from Washington;
said his mother and father had been abroad, and that he had come down to await

Twenty-third Street station: The scene is now New York City.

the arrival of their steamer. He told his story plausibly and had no trouble, since he volunteered to pay for them in advance, in engaging his rooms; a sleeping-room, sitting-room and bath.

Not once, but a hundred times Paul had planned this entry into New York. He had gone over every detail of it with Charley Edwards, and in his scrap book at home there were pages of description about New York hotels, cut from the Sunday papers. When he was shown to his sitting-room on the eighth floor, he saw at a glance that everything was as it should be; there was but one detail in his mental picture that the place did not realize, so he rang for the bell boy and sent him down for flowers. He moved about nervously until the boy returned, putting away his new linen and fingering it delightedly as he did so. When the flowers came, he put them hastily into water, and then tumbled into a hot bath. Presently he came out of his white bath-room, resplendent in his new silk under-wear, and playing with the tassels of his red robe. The snow was whirling so fiercely outside his windows that he could scarcely see across the street, but within the air was deliciously soft and fragrant. He put the violets and jonquils on the taboret beside the couch, and threw himself down, with a long sigh, covering himself with a Roman blanket. He was thoroughly tired; he had been in such haste, he had stood up to such a strain, covered so much ground in the last twenty-four hours, that he wanted to think how it had all come about. Lulled by the sound of the wind, the warm air, and the cool fragrance of the flowers, he sank into deep, drowsy retrospection.

It had been wonderfully simple; when they had shut him out of the theatre and concert hall, when they had taken away his bone, the whole thing was virtu-ally determined. The rest was a mere matter of opportunity. The only thing that at all surprised him was his own courage—for he realized well enough that he had always been tormented by fear, a sort of apprehensive dread that, of late years, as the meshes of the lies he had told closed about him, had been pulling the mus-cles of his body tighter and tighter. Until now, he could not remember the time when he had not been dreading something. Even when he was a little boy, it was always there—behind him, or before, or on either side. There had always been the shadowed corner, the dark place into which he dared not look, but from which something seemed always to be watching him—and Paul had done things that were not pretty to watch, he knew.

But now he had a curious sense of relief, as though he had at last thrown down the gauntlet to the thing in the corner.

Yet it was but a day since he had been sulking in the traces; but yesterday afternoon that he had been sent to the bank with Denny & Carson's deposit, as usual—but this time he was instructed to leave the book to be balanced. There was above two thousand dollars in checks, and nearly a thousand in the bank notes which he had taken from the book and quietly transferred to his pocket. At the bank he had made out a new deposit slip. His nerves had been steady enough to permit of his returning to the office, where he had finished his work and asked for a full day's holiday tomorrow, Saturday, giving a perfectly reasonable pretext. The bank book, he knew, would not be returned before Monday or Tuesday, and his father would be out of town for the next week. From the time he slipped the bank notes into his pocket until he boarded the night train for New York, he had not known a moment's hesitation. It was not the first time Paul had steered through treacherous waters.

How astonishingly easy it had all been; here he was, the thing done; and 45 this time there would be no awakening, no figure at the top of the stairs. He watched the snow flakes whirling by his window until he fell asleep.

When he awoke, it was three o'clock in the afternoon. He bounded up with a start; half of one of his precious days gone already! He spent more than an hour in dressing, watching every stage of his toilet carefully in the mirror. Everything was quite perfect; he was exactly the kind of boy he had always wanted to be.

When he went downstairs, Paul took a carriage and drove up Fifth Avenue toward the Park. The snow had somewhat abated; carriages and tradesmen's wagons were hurrying soundlessly to and fro in the winter twilight; boys in woollen mufflers were shovelling off the doorsteps; the avenue stages made fine spots of color against the white street. Here and there on the corners were stands, with whole flower gardens blooming under glass cases, against the sides of which the snow flakes stuck and melted; violets, roses, carnations, lilies of the valley—somewhat vastly more lovely and alluring that they blossomed thus unnaturally in the snow. The Park itself was a wonderful stage winterpiece.

When he returned, the pause of the twilight had ceased, and the tune of the streets had changed. The snow was falling faster, lights streamed from the hotels that reared their dozen stories fearlessly up into the storm, defying the raging Atlantic winds. A long, black stream of carriages poured down the avenue, intersected here and there by other streams, tending horizontally. There were a score of cabs about the entrance of his hotel, and his driver had to wait. Boys in livery were running in and out of the awning stretched across the sidewalk, up and down the red velvet carpet laid from the door to the street. Above, about, within it all was the rumble and roar, the hurry and toss of thousands of human beings as hot for pleasure as himself, and on every side of him towered the glaring affirmation of the omnipotence of wealth.

The boy set his teeth and drew his shoulders together in a spasm of realization: the plot of all dramas, the text of all romances, the nerve-stuff of all sensations was whirling about him like the snow flakes. He burnt like a faggot in a tempest.

When Paul went down to dinner, the music of the orchestra came floating 50 up the elevator shaft to greet him. His head whirled as he stepped into the thronged corridor, and he sank back into one of the chairs against the wall to get his breath. The lights, the chatter, the perfumes, the bewildering medley of color—he had, for a moment, the feeling of not being able to stand it. But only for a moment; these were his own people, he told himself. He went slowly about the corridors, through the writing-rooms, smoking-rooms, reception-rooms, as though he were exploring the chambers of an enchanted palace, built and peopled for him alone.

When he reached the dining-room he sat down at a table near a window. The flowers, the white linen, the many-colored wine glasses, the gay toilettes of the women, the low popping of corks, the undulating repetitions of the *Blue Danube* from the orchestra, all flooded Paul's dream with bewildering radiance. When the roseate tinge of his champagne was added—that cold, precious, bubbling stuff that creamed and foamed in his glass—Paul wondered that there were honest men in the world at all. This was what all the world was fighting for, he reflected; this was what all the struggle was about. He doubted the reality of his past. Had he ever known a place called Cordelia Street, a place where fagged-looking business-men got on the early car; mere rivets in a machine they seemed to Paul—sickening men, with combings of children's hair always hanging to their coats, and the smell of cooking in their clothes. Cordelia Street—Ah! that belonged to another time and country; had he not always been thus, had he not sat here night after night, from as far back as he could remember, looking pensively over just such shimmer-ing textures, and slowly twirling the stem of a glass like this one between his thumb and middle finger? He rather thought he had.

He was not in the least abashed or lonely. He had no especial desire to meet or to know any of these people; all he demanded was the right to look on and conjecture, to watch the pageant. The mere stage properties were all he contended for. Nor was he lonely later in the evening, in his loge at the Metropolitan. He was now entirely rid of his nervous misgivings, of his forced aggressiveness, of the imperative desire to show himself different from his surroundings. He felt now that his surroundings explained him. Nobody questioned the purple; he had only to wear it passively. He had only to glance down at his attire to reassure himself that here it would be impossible for anyone to humiliate him.

He found it hard to leave his beautiful sitting-room to go to bed that night, and sat long watching the raging storm from his turret window. When he went to sleep it was with the lights turned on in his bedroom; partly because of his old timidity, and partly so that, if he should wake in the night, there would be no wretched moment of doubt, no horrible suspicion of yellow wall-paper, or of Washington and Calvin above his bed.

Sunday morning the city was practically snow-bound. Paul breakfasted late, and in the afternoon he fell in with a wild San Francisco boy, a freshman at Yale, who said he had run down for a "little flyer" over Sunday. The young man offered to show Paul the night side of the town, and the two boys went out together after dinner, not returning to the hotel until seven o'clock the next morning. They had started out in the confiding warmth of a champagne friendship, but their part-ing in the elevator was singularly cool. The freshman pulled himself together to make his train, and Paul went to bed. He awoke at two o'clock in the afternoon, very thirsty and dizzy, and rang for ice-water, coffee, and the Pittsburgh papers.

On the part of the hotel management, Paul excited no suspicion. There was this to be said for him, that he wore his spoils with dignity and in no way made himself conspicuous. Even under the glow of his wine he was never boisterous, though he found the stuff like a magician's wand for wonder-building. His chief greediness lay in his ears and eyes, and his excesses were not offensive ones. His dearest pleasures were the grey winter twilights in his sitting-room; his quiet en-joyment of his flowers, his clothes, his wide divan, his cigarette, and his sense of power. He could not remember a time when he had felt so at peace with him-self. The mere release from the necessity of petty lying, lying every day and every day, restored his self-respect. He had never lied for pleasure, even at school; but to be noticed and admired, to assert his difference from other Cordelia Street boys; and he felt a good deal more manly, more honest, even, now that he had no need for boastful pretensions, now that he could, as his actor friends used to say, "dress the part." It was characteristic that remorse did not occur to him. His golden days went by without a shadow, and he made each as perfect as he could.

On the the eighth day after his arrival in New York, he found the whole affair exploited in the Pittsburgh papers, exploited with a wealth of detail which indicated that local news of a sensational nature was at a low ebb. The firm of Denny & Carson announced that the boy's father had refunded the full amount of the theft, and that they had no intention of prosecuting. The Cumberland minister had been interviewed, and expressed his hope of yet reclaiming the motherless lad, and his Sabbath-school teacher declared that she would spare no effort to that end. The rumor had reached Pittsburgh that the boy had been seen in a New York hotel, and his father had gone East to find him and bring him home.

Paul had just come in to dress for dinner; he sank into a chair, weak to the knees, and clasped his head in his hands. It was to be worse than jail, even; the tepid waters of Cordelia Street were to close over him finally and forever. The grey monotony stretched before him in hopeless, unrelieved years; Sabbath-school, Young People's Meeting, the yellow-papered room, the damp dish-towels; it all rushed back upon him with a sickening vividness. He had the old feeling that the orchestra had suddenly stopped, the sinking sensation that the play was over. The sweat broke out on his face, and he sprang to his feet, looked about him with his white, conscious smile, and winked at himself in the mirror. With something of the old childish belief in miracles with which he had so often gone to class, all his lessons unlearned, Paul dressed and dashed whistling down the corridor to the elevator.

He had no sooner entered the dining-room and caught the measure of the music than his remembrance was lightened by his old elastic power of claiming the moment, mounting with it, and finding it all sufficient. The glare and glitter about him, the mere scenic accessories had again, and for the last time, their old potency. He would show himself that he was game, he would finish the thing splendidly. He doubted, more than ever, the existence of Cordelia Street, and for the first time he drank his wine recklessly. Was he not, after all, one of those fortunate beings born to the purple, was he not still himself and in his own place? He drummed a nervous accompaniment to the Pagliacci music and looked about him, telling himself over and over that it had paid.

He reflected drowsily, to the swell of the music and the chill sweetness of his wine, that he might have done it more wisely. He might have caught an outbound steamer and been well out of their clutches before now. But the other side of the world had seemed too far away and too uncertain then; he could not have waited for it; his need had been too sharp. If he had to choose over again, he would do the same thing tomorrow. He looked affectionately about the dining-room, now gilded with a soft mist. Ah, it had paid indeed!

Paul was awakened next morning by a painful throbbing in his head and feet. 60 He had thrown himself across the bed without undressing, and had slept with his shoes on. His limbs and hands were lead heavy, and his tongue and throat were parched and burnt. There came upon him one of those fateful attacks of clear-headedness that never occurred except when he was physically exhausted and his nerves hung loose. He lay still and closed his eyes and let the tide of things wash over him.

His father was in New York; "stopping at some joint or other," he told himself. The memory of successive summers on the front stoop fell upon him like a weight of black water. He had not a hundred dollars left; and he knew now, more than ever, that money was everything, the wall that stood between all he loathed and all he wanted. The thing was winding itself up; he had thought of that on his first glorious day in New York, and had even provided a way to snap the thread. It lay on his dressing-table now; he had got it out last night when he came blindly up from dinner, but the shiny metal hurt his eyes, and he disliked the looks of it.

He rose and moved about with a painful effort, succumbing now and again to attacks of nausea. It was the old depression exaggerated; all the world had become Cordelia Street. Yet somehow he was not afraid of anything, was absolutely calm; perhaps because he had looked into the dark corner at last and knew. It was bad enough, what he saw there, but somehow not so bad as his long fear of it had been. He saw everything clearly now. He had a feeling that he had made the best of it, that he had lived the sort of life he was meant to live, and for half an hour he sat staring at the revolver. But he told himself that was not the way, so he went downstairs and took a cab to the ferry.

When Paul arrived at Newark, he got off the train and took another cab, directing the driver to follow the Pennsylvania tracks out of the town. The snow lay heavy on the roadways and had drifted deep in the open fields. Only here and there the dead grass or dried weed stalks projected, singularly black, above it. Once well into the country, Paul dismissed the carriage and walked, floundering along the tracks, his mind a medley of irrelevant things. He seemed to hold in his brain an actual picture of everything he had seen that morning. He remembered every feature of both his drivers, of the toothless old woman from whom he had bought the red flowers in his coat, the agent from whom he had got his ticket, and all of his fellow-passengers on the ferry. His mind, unable to cope with vital matters near at hand, worked feverishly and deftly at sorting and grouping these images. They made for him a part of the ugliness of the world, of the ache in his head, and the bitter burning on his tongue. He stooped and put a handful of snow into his mouth as he walked, but that, too, seemed hot. When he reached a little hillside, where the tracks ran through a cut some twenty feet below him, he stopped and sat down.

The carnations in his coat were drooping with the cold, he noticed; their red glory all over. It occurred to him that all the flowers he had seen in the glass cases that first night must have gone the same way, long before this. It was only one splendid breath they had, in spite of their brave mockery at the winter outside the glass; and it was a losing game in the end, it seemed, this revolt against the homilies by which the world is run. Paul took one of the blossoms carefully from his coat and scooped a little hole in the snow, where he covered it up. Then he dozed a while, from his weak condition, seemingly insensible to the cold.

The sound of an approaching train awoke him, and he started to his feet, remembering only his resolution, and afraid lest he should be too late. He stood watching the approaching locomotive, his teeth chattering, his lips drawn away from them in a frightened smile; once or twice he glanced nervously sidewise, as though he were being watched. When the right moment came, he jumped. 65

As he fell, the folly of his haste occurred to him with merciless clearness, the vastness of what he had left undone. There flashed through his brain, clearer than ever before, the blue of Adriatic water, the yellow of Algerian sands.

He felt something strike his chest, and that his body was being thrown swiftly through the air, on and on, immeasurably far and fast, while his limbs were gently relaxed. Then, because the picture making mechanism was crushed, the disturbing visions flashed into black, and Paul dropped back into the immense design of things.

Maxine Chernoff

THE SPIRIT OF GIVING   1986

Maxine Chernoff, born in 1952 in Chicago, still lives in her native city. Her stories and poems have appeared in Iowa Review, Story, Mississippi Review, Paris Review, Playgirl, Triquarterly, Partisan Review, *and other magazines, and she has published collections of poetry including* New Faces of 1952, *which won the 1985 Carl Sandburg Award. In 1987, Vintage Contemporaries reprinted* Bop, *a collection of stories published by Coffee House Press a year earlier, from which "The Spirit of Giving" is taken.* Bop *won the 1988 LSU/Southern Review Short Fiction Award. With her husband, the writer Paul Hoover, she edits and publishes* New American Writing, *a literary journal. She teaches creative writing at the Art Institute and is an assistant professor of English in the Chicago City Colleges.*

Maxine Chernoff

My sister collects primitive art, so on her birthday I sent her an Eskimo calendar. Each month shows a different block print of Eskimos hunting, sitting around a fire, or stretching seal skins on frames. The prints are done in rich primary colors. They are striking in their simplicity. After the year is over, the prints are suitable for framing.

My sister and I are close. Although she lives in San Francisco, we talk several times a month. When I didn't hear from her for three weeks after I'd sent the gift, I decided to call her.

"I hate it," she said on the phone in a nervous voice. "I know it's unkind of me to tell you, but I'm used to speaking the truth. The prints are finely executed, but I hate what's omitted. All the blood spilled, all the flesh rendered."

"I should have sent you photos of bok choy°," I suggested. "Or of a tribe that only eats dead bumblebees they find in the grass. It's life, Martha."

"I know," she answered. "Who's the anthropologist?" 5

She is. We talked about other things—Andy, the kids, nuclear war. Then she told me she had to go to her stained-glass workshop. Seemed she was in hot pursuit of a hummingbird.

After the call I went back to my desk to write her a letter. I asked her how it felt to be such a sentimentalist. I questioned her own studies of primitive art, if much of it isn't sacrifice and blood, even human blood spilled to assure favor. I never sent the letter.

Two months later I was looking through those shopping catalogues I get in the mail, the ones from famous Texas gift stores. Last year I could have bought a ticket to ride on the first space shuttle to carry passengers or an oil painting by Richard Nixon called "Boats Escaping, Retirement Years." I opted for a new bathrobe of green velour. I bought Ted some sheepskin earmuffs he never wore. In fact, when I gave them to him, he said, "You have to be kidding, Jane. I'm a translator!"

"Maybe you wanted a plastic replica of the Rosetta stone?" I asked. Our relationship has gone downhill since. Sometimes we meet for pasta and Chianti, but our conversations are strained.

This Christmas I'm determined to choose gifts with more care. Martha still 10 hasn't forgiven me, though her hummingbird was a success. She sold it at a small art fair for a hundred twenty-six dollars and fifty cents. The fifty cents might have discouraged customers, but she's uncompromising.

First I consider gift certificates, but they're safe as white bread. Then I call a friend and ask her what she buys for her sister. "House slippers. My sister loves house slippers. This year I bought her a pair monogrammed MM. I found them in an art-deco shop."

"Are those her initials?"

"Marilyn Monroe. They're her initials. I thought my sister would get a kick out of wearing Marilyn Monroe's slippers."

My friend is no help. My sister would call me uncaring. "That poor woman died in her bed. Some people even say she was murdered. How sad to own the slippers in which she thought her last thoughts."

A few nights later I'm reading a journal of aging. As we all know, the Es- 15 kimos used to leave their elderly to die on ice floes. The old took it in good spirits, but even so. Now it's more popular to have the elderly move in with unmarried daughters, who not only care for them in their illness but if they have no teeth, chew the tough and gristly seal meat for them.

That night I dream I'm a young Eskimo woman with very strong teeth. My job is to chew seal meat not only for my parents but for my in-laws, my great-aunt Ida, who has red hair in my dream, and her pet retriever, Yuk-Yuk. When I wake up, my jaws ache, and I remember it's December seventeenth. If I don't send Martha a present soon, I'll have to send her an apology.

---

bok choy: Chinese vegetable similar to cabbage.

When I get home that night from dinner with Ted, this time moo-shoo pork in a crowded basement in Chinatown, I call Martha.

"Did you ever eat moo-shoo pork?" I ask.

"It looks like chewed food. I don't like it," she says.

How is it that my sister always knows my thoughts and critiques them before 20
they're announced?

"Did you know that Eskimos no longer let their parents die on ice floes? Rather, they chew the food for their toothless elders and care for them the rest of their lives."

"The job usually falls to the unmarried daughter," she adds, meaning me.

"That's right! I'd be the one chewing the food."

Martha chortles. I can hear Andy in the background telling the kids not to paint on the white rug.

"How are you and Ted?" she asks. 25

"He didn't like the earmuffs I gave him."

"Speaking of presents," she says, "I sent you a purse I got at an ethnic fair. It's from China. It shows a duck hiding in some rushes while a feast is taking place in the palace to the left. I thought it wonderfully humorous."

"Did you ever think," I ask her, "how nothing is funny except predation? Think of cartoons, the roadrunner eluding the coyote, Bugs Bunny hiding from Elmer Fudd. The punch line is 'You can't eat me.'"

"You're deep, Jane." We say goodbye soon after.

The next day I'm in a little gourmet shop that specializes in French cheeses 30
and dessert items. Still thinking of those Eskimo women chewing for their parents, I'm having trouble doing any worthwhile shopping. Finally, I buy Ted two pounds of brandied cherries. As long as he can't wear them on his ears, I feel certain he'll like them. Now for Martha. I look up at a shining mountain of white food processors, able to grind, purée, stir, aerate, among other verbs. I ask the clerk to wrap one and enclose this card: "When Mother needs an ice floe, remember who owns the food processor. Love, Jane."

Kate Chopin

THE STORY OF AN HOUR   1894

Kate Chopin (1851–1904) demonstrates again, as in "The Storm" in Chapter Four, her ability to write short stories of compressed intensity. For a brief biography and a portrait see page 83.

Knowing that Mrs. Mallard was afflicted with a heart trouble, great care was taken to break to her as gently as possible the news of her husband's death.

It was her sister Josephine who told her, in broken sentences, veiled hints that revealed in half concealing. Her husband's friend Richards was there, too, near her. It was he who had been in the newspaper office when intelligence of the railroad disaster was received, with Brently Mallard's name leading the list of "killed." He had only taken the time to assure himself of its truth by a second telegram, and had hastened to forestall any less careful, less tender friend in bearing the sad message.

She did not hear the story as many women have heard the same, with a paralyzed inability to accept its significance. She wept at once, with sudden, wild abandonment, in her sister's arms. When the storm of grief had spent itself she went away to her room alone. She would have no one follow her.

There stood, facing the open window, a comfortable, roomy armchair. Into this she sank, pressed down by a physical exhaustion that haunted her body and seemed to reach into her soul.

She could see in the open square before her house the tops of trees that were 5 all aquiver with the new spring life. The delicious breath of rain was in the air. In the street below a peddler was crying his wares. The notes of a distant song which some one was singing reached her faintly, and countless sparrows were twittering in the eaves.

There were patches of blue sky showing here and there through the clouds that had met and piled one above the other in the west facing her window.

She sat with her head thrown back upon the cushion of the chair, quite motionless, except when a sob came up into her throat and shook her, as a child who has cried itself to sleep continues to sob in its dreams.

She was young, with a fair, calm face, whose lines bespoke repression and even a certain strength. But now there was a dull stare in her eyes, whose gaze was fixed away off yonder on one of those patches of blue sky. It was not a glance of reflection, but rather indicated a suspension of intelligent thought.

There was something coming to her and she was waiting for it, fearfully. What was it? She did not know; it was too subtle and elusive to name. But she felt it, creeping out of the sky, reaching toward her through the sounds, the scents, the color that filled the air.

Now her bosom rose and fell tumultuously. She was beginning to recognize 10 this thing that was approaching to possess her, and she was striving to beat it back with her will—as powerless as her two white slender hands would have been.

When she abandoned herself a little whispered word escaped her slightly parted lips. She said it over and over under her breath: "Free, free, free!" The vacant stare and the look of terror that had followed it went from her eyes. They stayed keen and bright. Her pulses beat fast, and the coursing blood warmed and relaxed every inch of her body.

She did not stop to ask if it were not a monstrous joy that held her. A clear and exalted perception enabled her to dismiss the suggestion as trivial.

She knew that she would weep again when she saw the kind, tender hands folded in death; the face that had never looked save with love upon her, fixed and gray and dead. But she saw beyond that bitter moment a long procession of years to come that would belong to her absolutely. And she opened and spread her arms out to them in welcome.

There would be no one to live for during those coming years; she would live for herself. There would be no powerful will bending her in that blind persistence with which men and women believe they have a right to impose a private will upon a fellow creature. A kind intention or a cruel intention made the act seem no less a crime as she looked upon it in that brief moment of illumination.

And yet she had loved him—sometimes. Often she had not. What did it mat- 15
ter! What could love, the unsolved mystery, count for in face of this possession
of self-assertion which she suddenly recognized as the strongest impulse of her being.

"Free! Body and soul free!" she kept whispering.

Josephine was kneeling before the closed door with her lips to the keyhole,
imploring for admission. "Louise, open the door! I beg; open the door—you will
make yourself ill. What are you doing, Louise? For heaven's sake open the door."

"Go away. I am not making myself ill." No; she was drinking in a very elixir
of life through that open window.

Her fancy was running riot along those days ahead of her. Spring days, and
summer days, and all sorts of days that would be her own. She breathed a quick
prayer that life might be long. It was only yesterday she had thought with a shudder that life might be long.

She arose at length and opened the door to her sister's importunities. There 20
was a feverish triumph in her eyes, and she carried herself unwittingly like a goddess of Victory. She clasped her sister's waist, and together they descended the
stairs. Richards stood waiting for them at the bottom.

Some one was opening the front door with a latchkey. It was Brently Mallard who entered, a little travel-stained, composedly carrying his gripsack and umbrella. He had been far from the scene of the accident, and did not even know
there had been one. He stood amazed at Josephine's piercing cry; at Richards'
quick motion to screen him from the view of his wife.

But Richards was too late.

When the doctors came they said she had died of heart disease—of joy that
kills.

Tess Gallagher

THE LOVER OF HORSES   1986

*Tess Gallagher, poet and fiction writer of the
Pacific Northwest, was born in Port Angeles,
Washington, in 1932, eldest of five children
of parents who worked in the logging industry. She entered the University of Washington in time to enroll in the last course offered
by the poet Theodore Roethke, and later
received master's degrees from both Washington and the University of Iowa. She has
traveled and lived in both Northern Ireland and
the Irish Republic and has taught at colleges
and universities including St. Lawrence, Kirk-
land, Montana, Arizona, and Syracuse. With
her husband, the story writer and poet Raymond Carver, she returned to make her home
again in her native Port Angeles. Her volumes
of poetry include* Instructions to the Double

Tess Gallagher

(1976), Under Stars (1978), Willingly (1984), and Amplitude: New and Selected Poems (1987). Gallagher has also written critical prose, gathered in A Concert of Tenses (1986), and two screenplays, The Night Belongs to the Police (1982) and (with Carver) Dostoevsky (1988). So far, The Lover of Horses (1986) is her one volume of stories.

They say my great-grandfather was a gypsy, but the most popular explanation for his behavior was that he was a drunk. How else could the women have kept up the scourge of his memory all these years, had they not had the usual malady of our family to blame? Probably he was both a gypsy and a drunk.

Still, I have reason to believe the gypsy in him had more to do with the turn his life took than his drinking. I used to argue with my mother about this, even though most of the information I have about my great-grandfather came from my mother, who got it from her mother. A drunk, I kept telling her, would have had no initiative. He would simply have gone down with his failures and had nothing to show for it. But my great-grandfather had eleven children, surely a sign of industry, and he was a lover of horses. He had so many horses he was what people called "horse poor."

I did not learn, until I traveled to where my family originated at Collenamore in the west of Ireland, that my great-grandfather had most likely been a "whisperer," a breed of men among the gypsies who were said to possess the power of talking sense into horses. These men had no fear of even the most malicious and dangerous horses. In fact, they would often take the wild animal into a closed stall in order to perform their skills.

Whether a certain intimacy was needed or whether the whisperers simply wanted to protect their secret conversations with horses is not known. One thing was certain—that such men gained power over horses by whispering. What they whispered no one knew. But the effectiveness of their methods was renowned, and anyone for counties around who had an unruly horse could send for a whisperer and be sure that the horse would take to heart whatever was said and reform his behavior from that day forth.

By all accounts, my great-grandfather was like a huge stallion himself, and 5 when he went into a field where a herd of horses was grazing, the horses would suddenly lift their heads and call to him. Then his bearded mouth would move, and though he was making sounds that could have been words, which no horse would have had reason to understand, the horses would want to hear; and one by one they would move toward him across the open space of the field. He could turn his back and walk down the road, and they would follow him. He was probably drunk my mother said, because he was swaying and mumbling all the while. Sometimes he would stop deadstill in the road and the horses would press up against him and raise and lower their heads as he moved his lips. But because these things were only seen from a distance, and because they have eroded in the telling, it is now impossible to know whether my great-grandfather said anything of importance to the horses. Or even if it was his whispering that had brought about their good behavior. Nor was it clear, when he left them in some barnyard as suddenly as he'd come to them, whether they had arrived at some new understanding of the difficult and complex relationship between men and horses.

Only the aberrations of my great-grandfather's relationship with horses have survived—as when he would bathe in the river with his favorite horse or when, as my grandmother told my mother, he insisted on conceiving his ninth child in the stall of a bay mare named Redwing. Not until I was grown and going through the family Bible did I discover that my grandmother had been this ninth child, and so must have known something about the matter.

These oddities in behavior lead me to believe that when my great-grandfather, at the age of fifty-two, abandoned his wife and family to join a circus that was passing through the area, it was not simply drunken bravado, nor even the understandable wish to escape family obligations. I believe the gypsy in him finally got the upper hand, and it led to such a remarkable happening that no one in the family has so far been willing to admit it: not the obvious transgression—that he had run away to join the circus—but that he was in all likelihood a man who had been stolen by a horse.

This is not an easy view to sustain in the society we live in. But I have not come to it frivolously, and have some basis for my belief. For although I have heard the story of my great-grandfather's defection time and again since childhood, the one image which prevails in all versions is that of a dappled gray stallion that had been trained to dance a variation of the mazurka. So impressive was this animal that he mesmerized crowds with his sliding step-and-hop to the side through the complicated figures of the dance, which he performed, not in the way of Lippizaners°—with other horses and their riders—but riderless and with the men of the circus company as his partners.

It is known that my great-grandfather became one of these dancers. After that he was reputed, in my mother's words, to have gone "completely to ruin." The fact that he walked from the house with only the clothes on his back, leaving behind his own beloved horses (twenty-nine of them to be exact), further supports my idea that a powerful force must have held sway over him, something more profound than the miseries of drink or the harsh imaginings of his abandoned wife.

Not even the fact that seven years later he returned and knocked on his wife's door, asking to be taken back, could exonerate him from what he had done, even though his wife did take him in and looked after him until he died some years later. But the detail that no one takes note of in the account is that when my great-grandfather returned, he was carrying a saddle blanket and the black plumes from the headgear of one of the circus horses. This passes by even my mother as simply a sign of the ridiculousness of my great-grandfather's plight—for after all, he was homeless and heading for old age as a "good for nothing drunk" and a "fool for horses." 10

No one has bothered to conjecture what these curious emblems—saddle blanket and plumes—must have meant to my great-grandfather. But he hung them over the foot of his bed—"like a fool," my mother said. And sometimes when he got very drunk he would take up the blanket and, wrapping it like a shawl over his shoulders, he would grasp the plumes. Then he would dance the mazurka. He did not dance in the living room but took himself out into the field, where the horses stood at attention and watched as if suddenly experiencing the smell of the sea or a change of wind in the valley. "Drunks don't care what they do," my mother would say as she finished her story about my great-grandfather. "Talking to a drunk is like talking to a stump."

Lippizaners: world-famous Austrian show horses trained at the Spanish Riding School of Vienna.

Ever since my great-grandfather's outbreaks of gypsy necessity, members of my family have been stolen by things—by mad ambitions, by musical instruments, by otherwise harmless pursuits from mushroom hunting to childbearing or, as was my father's case, by the more easily recognized and popular obsession with card playing. To some extent, I still think it was failure of imagination in this respect that brought about his diminished prospects in the life of our family.

But even my mother had been powerless against the attraction of a man so convincingly driven. When she met him at a birthday dance held at the country house of one of her young friends, she asked him what he did for a living. My father pointed to a deck of cards in his shirt pocket and said, "I play cards." But love is such as it is, and although my mother was otherwise a deadly practical woman, it seemed she could fall in love with no man but my father.

So it is possible that the propensity to be stolen is somewhat contagious when ordinary people come into contact with people such as my father. Though my mother loved him at the time of the marriage, she soon began to behave as if she had been stolen from a more fruitful and upright life which she was always imagining might have been hers.

My father's card playing was accompanied, to no one's surprise, by bouts of drinking. The only thing that may have saved our family from a life of poverty was the fact that my father seldom gambled with money. Such were his charm and powers of persuasion that he was able to convince other players to accept his notes on everything from the fish he intended to catch next season to the sale of his daughter's hair.

I know about this last wager because I remember the day he came to me with a pair of scissors and said it was time to cut my hair. Two snips and it was done. I cannot forget the way he wept onto the backs of his hands and held the braids together like a broken noose from which a life had suddenly slipped. I was thirteen at the time and my hair had never been cut. It was his pride and joy that I had such hair. But for me it was only a burdensome difference between me and my classmates, so I was glad to be rid of it. What anyone else could have wanted with my long shiny braids is still a mystery to me.

When my father was seventy-three he fell ill and the doctors gave him only a few weeks to live. My father was convinced that his illness had come on him because he'd hit a particularly bad losing streak at cards. He had lost heavily the previous month, and items of value, mostly belonging to my mother, had disappeared from the house. He developed the strange idea that if he could win at cards he could cheat the prediction of the doctors and live at least into his eighties.

By this time I had moved away from home and made a life for myself in an attempt to follow the reasonable dictates of my mother, who had counseled her children severely against all manner of rash ambition and foolhardiness. Her entreaties were leveled especially in my direction since I had shown a suspect enthusiasm for a certain pony at around the age of five. And it is true I felt I had lost a dear friend when my mother saw to it that the neighbors who owned this pony moved it to pasture elsewhere.

But there were other signs that I might wander off into unpredictable pursuits. The most telling of these was that I refused to speak aloud to anyone until the age of eleven. I whispered everything, as if my mind were a repository of secrets which could only be divulged in this intimate manner. If anyone asked me a question, I was always polite about answering, but I had to do it by putting my mouth near the head of my inquisitor and using only my breath and lips to make my reply.

My teachers put my whispering down to shyness and made special accommodations for me. When it came time for recitations I would accompany the teacher into the cloakroom and there whisper to her the memorized verses or the speech I was to have prepared. God knows, I might have continued on like this into the present if my mother hadn't plotted with some neighborhood boys to put burrs into my long hair. She knew by other signs that I had a terrible temper, and she was counting on that to deliver me into the world where people shouted and railed at one another and talked in an audible fashion about things both common and sacred.

When the boys shut me into a shed, according to plan, there was nothing for me to do but to cry out for help and to curse them in a torrent of words I had only heard used by adults. When my mother heard this she rejoiced, thinking that at last she had broken the treacherous hold of the past over me, of my great-grandfather's gypsy blood and the fear that against all her efforts I might be stolen away, as she had been, and as my father had, by some as yet unforeseen predilection. Had I not already experienced the consequences of such a life in our household, I doubt she would have been successful, but the advantages of an ordinary existence among people of a less volatile nature had begun to appeal to me.

It was strange, then, that after all the care my mother had taken for me in this regard, when my father's illness came on him, my mother brought her appeal to me. "Can you do something?" she wrote, in her cramped, left-handed scrawl. "He's been drinking and playing cards for three days and nights. I am at my wit's end. Come home at once."

Somehow I knew this was a message addressed to the very part of me that most baffled and frightened my mother—the part that belonged exclusively to my father and his family's inexplicable manias.

When I arrived home my father was not there.

"He's at the tavern. In the back room," my mother said. "He hasn't eaten for days. And if he's slept, he hasn't done it here."

I made up a strong broth, and as I poured the steaming liquid into a Thermos I heard myself utter syllables and other vestiges of language which I could not reproduce if I wanted to. "What do you mean by that?" my mother demanded, as if a demon had leapt out of me. "What did you say?" I didn't—I couldn't—answer her. But suddenly I felt that an unsuspected network of sympathies and distant connections had begun to reveal itself to me in my father's behalf.

There is a saying that when lovers have need of moonlight, it is there. So it seemed, as I made my way through the deserted town toward the tavern and card room, that all nature had been given notice of my father's predicament, and that the response I was waiting for would not be far off.

But when I arrived at the tavern and had talked my way past the barman and into the card room itself, I saw that my father had an enormous pile of blue chips at his elbow. Several players had fallen out to watch, heavy-lidded and smoking their cigarettes like weary gangsters. Others were slumped on folding chairs near the coffee urn with its empty "Pay Here" styrofoam cup.

My father's cap was pushed to the back of his head so that his forehead shone in the dim light, and he grinned over his cigarette at me with the serious preoccupation of a child who has no intention of obeying anyone. And why should he, I thought as I sat down just behind him and loosened the stopper on the Thermos. The five or six players still at the table casually appraised my presence to see if it had tipped the scales of their luck in an even more unfavorable direction. Then they tossed their cards aside, drew fresh cards, or folded.

In the center of the table were more blue chips, and poking out from my father's coat pocket I recognized the promissory slips he must have redeemed, for he leaned to me and in a low voice, without taking his eyes from his cards, said, "I'm having a hell of a good time. The time of my life."

He was winning. His face seemed ravaged by the effort, but he was clearly playing on a level that had carried the game far beyond the realm of mere card playing and everyone seemed to know it. The dealer cocked an eyebrow as I poured broth into the plastic Thermos cup and handed it to my father, who slurped from it noisily, then set it down.

"Tell the old kettle she's got to put up with me a few more years," he said, and lit up a fresh cigarette. His eyes as he looked at me, however, seemed over-brilliant, as if doubt, despite all his efforts, had gained a permanent seat at his table. I squeezed his shoulder and kissed him hurriedly on his forehead. The men kept their eyes down, and as I paused at the door, there was a shifting of chairs and a clearing of throats. Just outside the room I nearly collided with the barman, who was carrying in a fresh round of beer. His heavy jowls waggled as he recovered himself and looked hard at me over the icy bottles. Then he disappeared into the card room with his provisions.

I took the long way home, finding pleasure in the fact that at this hour all the stoplights had switched onto a flashing-yellow caution cycle. Even the teenagers who usually cruised the town had gone home or to more secluded spots. *Doubt,* I kept thinking as I drove with my father's face before me, that's the real thief. And I knew my mother had brought me home because of it, because she knew that once again a member of our family was about to be stolen.

Two more days and nights I ministered to my father at the card room. I would never stay long because I had the fear myself that I might spoil his luck. But many unspoken tendernesses passed between us in those brief appearances as he accepted the nourishment I offered, or when he looked up and handed me his beer bottle to take a swig from—a ritual we'd shared since my childhood.

My father continued to win—to the amazement of the local barflies who poked their faces in and out of the card room and gave the dwindling three or four stalwarts who remained at the table a commiserating shake of their heads. There had never been a winning streak like it in the history of the tavern, and indeed, we heard later that the man who owned the card room and tavern had to sell out and open a fruit stand on the edge of town as a result of my father's extraordinary good luck.

Twice during this period my mother urged the doctor to order my father home. She was sure my father would, at some fateful moment, risk the entire winnings in some mad rush toward oblivion. But his doctor spoke of a new "gaming therapy" for the terminally ill, based on my father's surge of energies in the pursuit of his gambling. Little did he know that my father was, by that stage, oblivious to even his winning, he had gone so far into exhaustion.

Luckily for my father, the hour came when, for lack of players, the game folded. Two old friends drove him home and helped him down from the pickup. They paused in the driveway, one on either side of him, letting him steady himself. When the card playing had ended there had been nothing for my father to do but to get drunk.

My mother and I watched from the window as the men steered my father toward the hydrangea bush at the side of the house, where he relieved himself with perfect precision on one mammoth blossom. Then they hoisted him up the stairs and into the entryway. My mother and I took over from there.

"Give 'em hell, boys," my father shouted after the men, concluding some conversation he was having with himself.

"You betcha," the driver called back, laughing. Then he climbed with his companion into the cab of his truck and roared away. 40

Tied around my father's waist was a cloth sack full of bills and coins which flapped and jingled against his knees as we bore his weight between us up the next flight of stairs and into the living room. There we deposited him on the couch, where he took up residence, refusing to sleep in his bed—for fear, my mother claimed, that death would know where to find him. But I preferred to think he enjoyed the rhythms of the household; from where he lay at the center of the house, he could overhear all conversations that took place and add his opinions when he felt like it.

My mother was so stricken by the signs of his further decline that she did everything he asked, instead of arguing with him or simply refusing. Instead of taking his winnings straight to the bank so as not to miss a day's interest, she washed an old goldfish bowl and dumped all the money into it, most of it in twenty-dollar bills. Then she placed it on the coffee table near his head so he could run his hand through it at will, or let his visitors do the same.

"Money feels good on your elbow," he would say to them. "I played them under the table for that. Yes sir, take a feel of that!" Then he would lean back on his pillows and tell my mother to bring his guests a shot of whiskey. "Make sure she fills my glass up," he'd say to me so that my mother was certain to overhear. And my mother, who'd never allowed a bottle of whiskey to be brought into her house before now, would look at me as if the two of us were more than any woman should have to bear.

"If you'd only brought him home from that card room," she said again and again. "Maybe it wouldn't have come to this."

This included the fact that my father had radically altered his diet. He lived 45 only on greens. If it was green he would eat it. By my mother's reckoning, the reason for his change of diet was that if he stopped eating what he usually ate, death would think it wasn't him and go look for somebody else.

Another request my father made was asking my mother to sweep the doorway after anyone came in or went out.

"To make sure death wasn't on their heels; to make sure death didn't slip in as they left." This was my mother's reasoning. But my father didn't give any reasons. Nor did he tell us finally why he wanted all the furniture moved out of the room except for the couch where he lay. And the money, they could take that away too.

But soon his strength began to ebb, and more and more family and friends crowded into the vacant room to pass the time with him, to laugh about stories remembered from his childhood or from his nights as a young man at the country dances when he and his older brother would work all day in the cotton fields, hop a freight train to town and dance all night. Then they would have to walk home, getting there just at daybreak in time to go straight to work again in the cotton fields.

"We were like bulls then," my father would say in a burst of the old vigor, then close his eyes suddenly as if he hadn't said anything at all.

As long as he spoke to us, the inevitability of his condition seemed easier   50
to bear. But when, at the last, he simply opened his mouth for food or stared silently toward the far wall, no one knew what to do with themselves.

My own part in that uncertain time came to me accidentally. I found myself in the yard sitting on a stone bench under a little cedar tree my father loved because he liked to sit there and stare at the ocean. The tree whispered, he said. He said it had a way of knowing what your troubles were. Suddenly a craving came over me. I wanted a cigarette, even though I don't smoke, hate smoking, in fact. I was sitting where my father had sat, and to smoke seemed a part of some rightness that had begun to work its way within me. I went into the house and bummed a pack of cigarettes from my brother. For the rest of the morning I sat under the cedar tree and smoked. My thoughts drifted with its shifting and murmurings, and it struck me what a wonderful thing nature is because it knows the value of silence, the innuendos of silence and what they could mean for a word-bound creature such as I was.

I passed the rest of the day in a trance of silences, moving from place to place, revisiting the sites I knew my father loved—the "dragon tree," a hemlock which stood at the far end of the orchard, so named for how the wind tossed its triangular head; the rose arbor where he and my mother had courted; the little marina where I sat in his fishing boat and dutifully smoked the hated cigarettes, flinging them one by one into the brackish water.

I was waiting to know what to do for him, he who would soon be a piece of useless matter of no more consequence than the cigarette butts that floated and washed against the side of his boat. I could feel some action accumulating in me through the steadiness of water raising and lowering the boat, through the sad petal-fall of roses in the arbor and the tossing of the dragon tree.

That night when I walked from the house I was full of purpose. I headed toward the little cedar tree. Without stopping to question the necessity of what I was doing, I began to break off the boughs I could reach and to pile them on the ground.

"What are you doing?" my brother's children wanted to know, crowding around   55
me as if I might be inventing some new game for them.

"What does it look like?" I said.

"Pulling limbs off the tree," the oldest said. Then they dashed away in a pack under the orchard trees, giggling and shrieking.

As I pulled the boughs from the trunk I felt a painful permission, as when two silences, tired of holding back, give over to each other some shared regret. I made my bed on the boughs and resolved to spend the night there in the yard, under the stars, with the hiss of the ocean in my ear, and the maimed cedar tree standing over me like a gift torn out of its wrappings.

My brothers, their wives and my sister had now begun their nightly vigil near my father, taking turns at staying awake. The windows were open for the breeze and I heard my mother trying to answer the question of why I was sleeping outside on the ground—"like a damned fool" I knew they wanted to add.

"She doesn't want to be here when death comes for him" my mother said, with an air of clairvoyance she had developed from a lifetime with my father. "They're too much alike," she said. 60

The ritual of night games played by the children went on and on past their bedtimes. Inside the house, the kerosene lantern, saved from my father's childhood home, had been lit—another of his strange requests during the time before his silence. He liked the shadows it made and the sweet smell of the kerosene. I watched the darkness as the shapes of my brothers and sister passed near it, gigantic and misshapen where they bent or raised themselves or crossed the room.

Out on the water the wind had come up. In the orchard the children were spinning around in a circle, faster and faster until they were giddy and reeling with speed and darkness. Then they would stop, rest a moment, taking quick ecstatic breaths before plunging again into the opposite direction, swirling round and round in the circle until the excitement could rise no higher, their laughter and cries brimming over, then scattering as they flung one another by the arms or chased each other toward the house as if their lives depended on it.

I lay awake for a long while after their footsteps had died away and the car doors had slammed over the goodbyes of the children being taken home to bed and the last of the others had been bedded down in the house while the adults went on waiting.

It was important to be out there alone and close to the ground. The pungent smell of the cedar boughs was around me, rising up in the crisp night air toward the tree, whose turnings and swayings had altered, as they had to, in order to accompany the changes about to overtake my father and me. I thought of my great-grandfather bathing with his horse in the river, and of my father who had just passed through the longest period in his life without the clean feel of cards falling through his hands as he shuffled or dealt them.He was too weak now even to hold a cigarette; there was a burn mark on the hardwood floor where his last cigarette had fallen. His winnings were safely in the bank and the luck that was to have saved him had gone back to that place luck goes to when it is finished with us.

So this is what it comes to, I thought, and listened to the wind as it mixed 65 gradually with the memory of children's voices which still seemed to rise and fall in the orchard. There was a soft crooning of syllables that was satisfying to my ears, but ultimately useless and absurd. Then it came to me that I was the author of those unwieldy sounds, and that my lips had begun to work of themselves.

In a raw pulsing of language I could not account for, I lay awake through the long night and spoke to my father as one might speak to an ocean or the wind, letting him know by that threadbare accompaniment that the vastness he was about to enter had its rhythms in me also. And that he was not forsaken. And that I was letting him go. That so far I had denied the disreputable world of dancers and drunkards, gamblers and lovers of horses to which I most surely belonged. But from that night forward I vowed to be filled with the first unsavory desire that would have me. To plunge myself into the heart of my life and be ruthlessly lost forever

Langston Hughes

ON THE ROAD   1952

Langston Hughes (1902–1967), who dropped his first name, James, was born in Joplin, Missouri. As a high school senior in Cleveland, he wrote a poem still often reprinted, "The Negro Speaks of Rivers." When a young man, he worked as a merchant seaman, visited Africa, and lived for a time in Paris and Rome. The Weary Blues (1926) earned him an immediate reputation as a poet; his interest in fiction developed later. In his autobiography I Wonder As I Wander (1956), he credits D. H. Lawrence's stories, particularly "The Rocking-Horse Winner," with inspiring him to write short fiction himself. Hughes's writing won him a scholarship to Lincoln University, from which he was graduated in 1929. He became a major figure in the Harlem Renaissance of the 1920s and early 1930s, a period when that section of New York City proved a lively center for African-American writers, artists,

Langston Hughes

and musicians. Tireless in his efforts to win new respect for African-American culture, Hughes compiled twenty-eight anthologies of African-American folklore and poetry. He was a prolific and protean writer: among his original works are plays, song lyrics, children's books, memoirs, newspaper columns, translations, and essays reporting his imaginary conversations with a Harlem citizen called Simple, a streetwise philosopher. A Langston Hughes Reader (1958) gives some idea of the scope of his writing, its richness and variety.

He was not interested in snow. When he got off the freight, one early evening during the depression, Sargeant never even noticed the snow. But he must have felt it seeping down his neck, cold, wet, sopping in his shoes. But if you had asked him, he wouldn't have known it was snowing. Sargeant didn't see the snow, not even under the bright lights of the main street, falling white and flaky against the night. He was too hungry, too sleepy, too tired.

The Reverend Mr. Dorset, however, saw the snow when he switched on his porch light, opened the front door of his parsonage, and found standing there before him a big black man with snow on his face, a human piece of night with snow on his face—obviously unemployed.

Said the Reverend Mr. Dorset before Sargeant even realized he'd opened his mouth: "I'm sorry. No! Go right on down this street four blocks and turn to your left, walk up seven and you'll see the Relief Shelter. I'm sorry. No!" He shut the doorSargeant wanted to tell the holy man that he had already been to the Relief Shelter, been to hundreds of relief shelters during the depression years, the beds were always gone and supper was over, the place was full, and they drew the color line anyhow. But the minister said, "No," and shut the door. Evidently he didn't want to hear about it. And he *had* a door to shut.

The big black man turned away. And even yet he didn't see the snow, walk-ing right into it. Maybe he sensed it, cold, wet, sticking to his jaws, wet on his black hands, sopping in his shoes. He stopped and stood on the sidewalk hunched over—hungry, sleepy, cold—looking up and down. Then he looked right where he was—in front of a church! Of course! A church! Sure, right next to a parsonage, certainly a church.

It had *two* doors.

Broad white steps in the night all snowy white. Two high arched doors with slender stone pillars on either side. And way up, a round lacy window with a stone crucifix in the middle and Christ on the crucifix in stone. All this was pale in the street lights, solid and stony pale in the snow.

Sargeant blinked. When he looked up, the snow fell into his eyes. For the first time that night he *saw* the snow. He shook his head. He shook the snow from his coat sleeves, felt hungry, felt lost, felt not lost, felt cold. He walked up the steps of the church. He knocked at the door. No answer. He tried the handle. Locked. He put his shoulder against the door and his long black body slanted like a ramrod. He pushed. With loud rhythmic grunts, like the grunts in a chain-gang song, he pushed against the door.

"I'm tired . . . Huh! . . . Hongry . . . Uh! . . . I'm sleepy . . . Huh! I'm cold . . . I got to sleep somewheres," Sargeant said. "This here is a church, ain't it? Well, uh!"

He pushed against the door.

Suddenly, with an undue cracking and screaking, the door began to give way to the tall black Negro who pushed ferociously against it.

By now two or three white people had stopped in the street, and Sargeant was vaguely aware of some of them yelling at him concerning the door. Three or four more came running, yelling at him.

"Hey!" they said. "Hey!"

"Uh-huh," answered the big tall Negro, "I know it's a white folks' church, but I got to sleep somewhere." He gave another lunge at the door. "Huh!"

And the door broke open.

But just when the door gave way, two white cops arrived in a car, ran up the steps with their clubs, and grabbed Sargeant. But Sargeant for once had no intention of being pulled or pushed away from the door.

Sargeant grabbed, but not for anything so weak as a broken door. He grabbed for one of the tall stone pillars beside the door, grabbed at it and caught it. And

5

10

15

held it. The cops pulled Sargeant pulled. Most of the people in the street got behind the cops and helped them pull.

"A big black unemployed Negro holding onto our church!" thought the people. "The idea!"

The cops began to beat Sargeant over the head, and nobody protested. But he held on.

And then the church fell down.

Gradually, the big stone front of the church fell down, the walls and the rafters, the crucifix and the Christ. Then the whole thing fell down, covering the cops and the people with bricks and stones and debris. The whole church fell down in the snow.

Sargeant got out from under the church and went walking on up the street with the stone pillar on his shoulder. He was under the impression that he had buried the parsonage and the Reverend Mr. Dorset who said, "No!" So he laughed, and threw the pillar six blocks up the street and went on.

Sargeant thought he was alone, but listening to the *crunch, crunch, crunch* on the snow of his own footsteps, he heard other footsteps, too, doubling his own. He looked around, and there was Christ walking along beside him, the same Christ that had been on the cross on the church—still stone with a rough stone surface, walking along beside him just like he was broken off the cross when the church fell down.

"Well, I'll be dogged," said Sargeant. "This here's the first time I ever seed you off the cross."

"Yes," said Christ, crunching his feet in the snow. "You had to pull the church down to get me off the cross."

"You glad?" said Sargeant.

"I sure am," said Christ.

They both laughed.

"I'm a hell of a fellow, ain't I?" said Sargeant. "Done pulled the church down!"

"You did a good job," said Christ. "They have kept me nailed on a cross for nearly two thousand years."

"Whee-ee-e!" said Sargeant. "I know you are glad to get off."

"I sure am," said Christ.

They walked on in the snow. Sargeant looked at the man of stone.

"And you have been up there two thousand years?"

"I sure have," Christ said.

"Well, if I had a little cash," said Sargeant, "I'd show you around a bit."

"I been around," said Christ

"Yeah, but that was a long time ago."

"All the same," said Christ, "I've been around."

They walked on in the snow until they came to the railroad yards. Sargeant was tired, sweating and tired.

"Where you goin'?" Sargeant said, stopping by the tracks. He looked at Christ. Sargeant said, "I'm just a bum on the road. How about you? Where you goin'?"

"God knows," Christ said, "but I'm leavin' here."

They saw the red and green lights of the railroad yard half veiled by the snow that fell out of the night. Away down the track they saw a fire in a hobo jungle.

"I can go there and sleep," Sargeant said.

"You can?"   45

"Sure," said Sargeant. "That place ain't got no doors."

Outside the town, along the tracks, there were barren trees and bushes below the embankment, snow-gray in the dark. And down among the trees and bushes there were makeshift houses made out of boxes and tin and old pieces of wood and canvas. You couldn't see them in the dark, but you knew they were there if you'd ever been on the road, if you had ever lived with the homeless and hungry in a depression.

"I'm side-tracking," Sargeant said. "I'm tired."

"I'm gonna make it on to Kansas City," said Christ.

"O.K.," Sargeant said. "So long!"   50

He went down into the hobo jungle and found himself a place to sleep. He never did see Christ no more. About 6:00 A.M. a freight came by. Sargeant scrambled out of the jungle with a dozen or so more hobos and ran along the track, grabbing at the freight. It was dawn, early dawn, cold and gray.

"Wonder where Christ is by now?" Sargeant thought. "He musta gone on way on down the road. He didn't sleep in this jungle."

Sargeant grabbed the train and started to pull himself up into a moving coal car, over the edge of a wheeling coal car. But strangely enough, the car was full of cops. The nearest cop rapped Sargeant soundly across the knuckles with his night stick. Wham! Rapped his big black hands for clinging to the top of the car. Wham! But Sargeant did not turn loose. He clung on and tried to pull himself into the car. He hollered at the top of his voice, "Damn it, lemme in this car!"

"Shut up," barked the cop. "You crazy coon!" He rapped Sargeant across the knuckles and punched him in the stomach. "You ain't out in no jungle now. This ain't no train. You in jail."

Wham! across his bare black fingers clinging to the bars of his cell. Wham!   55
between the steel bars low down against his shins.

Suddenly Sargeant realized that he really was in jail. He wasn't on no train. The blood of the night before had dried on his face, his head hurt terribly, and a cop outside in the corridor was hitting him across the knuckles for holding onto the door, yelling and shaking the cell door.

"They musta took me to jail for breaking down the door last night," Sargeant thought, "that church door."

Sargeant went over and sat on a wooden bench against the cold stone wall. He was emptier than ever. His clothes were wet, clammy cold wet, and shoes sloppy with snow water. It was just about dawn. There he was, locked up behind a cell door, nursing his bruised fingers.

The bruised fingers were his, but not the *door*.

Not the *club* but the fingers.   60

"You wait," mumbled Sargeant, black against the jail wall. "I'm gonna break down this door, too."

"Shut up—or I'll paste you one," said the cop.

"I'm gonna break down this door," yelled Sargeant as he stood up in his cell.

Then he must have been talking to himself because he said, "I wonder where Christ's gone? I wonder if he's gone to Kansas City?"

Franz Kafka

THE BUCKET RIDER 1918

Translated by Willa and Edwin Muir

Franz Kafka

Franz Kafka (1883–1924) was born into a German-speaking Jewish family in Prague, Czechoslovakia (then part of Austria). After taking a doctor's degree in law, he settled into the routine of a government claims investigator. By night when he couldn't sleep he toiled on stories. Kafka's work is rich in macabre humor and unforgettable nightmares: the long story The Metamorphosis *(1915), for instance, begins with the great line, "As Gregor Samsa awoke one morning from uneasy dreams he found himself transformed in his bed into a gigantic insect." Kafka was a writer of such impeccably high standards that he could bring himself to publish little in his lifetime; he never finished his major novels* The Trial *and* The Castle. *Both depict huge, remote, bumbling, irresponsible bureaucracies in whose power an individual feels helplessly isolated. Before he died, Kafka left his friend Max Brod orders to burn his incomplete manuscripts; Brod pondered, but didn't obey. Kafka, who succumbed to tuberculosis, did not live to see his stories appear startlingly prophetic to readers looking back on them by the later light of the Holocaust. Only after World War II did his work achieve international fame.*

Coal all spent; the bucket empty; the shovel useless; the stove breathing out cold; the room freezing; the leaves outside the window rigid, covered with rime; the sky a silver shield against any one who looks for help from it. I must have coal; I cannot freeze to death; behind me is the pitiless stove, before me the pitiless sky, so I must ride out between them and on my journey seek aid from the coaldealer. But he has already grown deaf to ordinary appeals; I must prove irrefutably to him that I have not a single grain of coal left, and that he means to me the very sun in the firmament. I must approach like a beggar, who, with the death rattle already in his throat, insists on dying on the doorstep, and to whom the grand people's cook accordingly decides to give the dregs of the coffeepot; just so must the coaldealer, filled with rage, but acknowledging the command, "Thou shalt not kill," fling a shovelful of coal into my bucket.

My mode of arrival must decide the matter; so I ride off on the bucket. Seated on the bucket, my hands on the handle, the simplest kind of bridle, I propel myself with difficulty down the stairs; but once down below my bucket ascends, superbly, superbly; camels humbly squatting on the ground do not rise with more dignity, shaking themselves under the sticks of their drivers. Through the hard frozen streets we go at a regular canter; often I am upraised as high as the first story of a house; never do I sink as low as the house doors. And at last I float at an extraordinary height above the vaulted cellar of the dealer, whom I see far below crouching over his table, where he is writing; he has opened the door to let out the excessive heat.

"Coaldealer!" I cry in a voice burned hollow by the frost and muffled in the cloud made by my breath, "please, coaldealer, give me a little coal. My bucket is so light that I can ride on it. Be kind. When I can I'll pay you."

The dealer puts his hand to his ear. "Do I hear rightly?" he throws the question over his shoulder to his wife. "Do I hear rightly? A customer."

"I hear nothing," says his wife, breathing in and out peacefully while she knits   5
on, her back pleasantly warmed by the heat.

"Oh, yes, you must hear," I cry. "It's me; an old customer; faithful and true; only without means at the moment."

"Wife," says the dealer, "it's someone, it must be; my ears can't have deceived me so much as that; it must be an old, a very old customer, that can move me so deeply."

"What ails you, man?" says his wife, ceasing from her work for a moment and pressing her knitting to her bosom. "It's nobody, the street is empty, all our customers are provided for; we could close down the shop for several days and take a rest."

"But I'm sitting up here on the bucket," I cry, and unfeeling frozen tears dim my eyes, "please look up here, just once; you'll see me directly; I beg you, just a shovelful; and if you give me more it'll make me so happy that I won't know what to do. All the other customers are provided for. Oh, if I could only hear the coal clattering into the bucket!"

"I'm coming," says the coaldealer, and on his short legs he makes to climb   10
the steps of the cellar, but his wife is already beside him, holds him back by the arm and says: "You stay here; seeing you persist in your fancies I'll go myself. Think of the bad fit of coughing you had during the night. But for a piece of business, even if it's one you've only fancied in your head, you're prepared to forget your wife and child and sacrifice your lungs. I'll go."

"Then be sure to tell him all the kinds of coal we have in stock; I'll shout out the prices after you."

"Right," says his wife, climbing up to the street. Naturally she sees me at once. "Frau Coaldealer," I cry, "my humblest greetings; just one shovelful of coal; here in my bucket; I'll carry it home myself. One shovelful of the worst you have. I'll pay you in full for it, of course, but not just now, not just now." What a knell-like sound the words "not just now" have, and how bewilderingly they mingle with the evening chimes that fall from the church steeple near by!

"Well, what does he want?" shouts the dealer. "Nothing," his wife shouts back, "there's nothing here; I see nothing, I hear nothing; only six striking, and now we must shut up the shop. The cold is terrible; tomorrow we'll likely have lots to do again."

She sees nothing and hears nothing; but all the same she loosens her apron strings and waves her apron to waft me away. She succeeds, unluckily. My bucket has all the virtues of a good steed except powers of resistance, which it has not; it is too light; a woman's apron can make it fly through the air.

"You bad woman!" I shout back, while she, turning into the shop, half con- 15
temptuous, half reassured, flourishes her fist in the air. "You bad woman! I begged you for a shovelful of the worst coal and you would not give it me." And with that I ascend into the regions of the ice mountains and am lost for ever.

Yasunari Kawabata

THE MAN WHO DID NOT SMILE   1929

Translated by J. Martin Holman

Yasunari Kawabata, who in 1968 became Japan's first recipient of the Nobel Prize for Literature, was born in Osaka in 1899. As an infant he lost his parents, and soon after, his only sister; and at fourteen he had to live in a school dormitory. These facts may help account for the sense of isolation and loss that pervades much of his fiction. Kawabata had hoped to be a painter, but his first stories appeared in print while he was still in high school, and he was encouraged to become a writer instead. He became known in the West for his poetic novels, including The Izu Dancer *(1927),* Snow Country *(1947),* Thousand Cranes *(1959),* The Old Capital *(1962),*

Yasunari Kawabata

House of the Sleeping Beauties *(1969),* The Sound of the Mountain *(1970), and* The Master of Go *(1972), all available in English. Kawabata writes a prose deeply steeped in Japanese tradition, yet often sets his stories against landscapes of modern industry. Some of his novels seem compilations of stories; undoubtedly the short-short story was the form he most loved. "Many writers in their youth write poetry," Kawabata once said; "I, instead of poetry, wrote tiny stories."* Palm-of-the-Hand Stories, *translated by Lane Dunlop and J. Martin Holman (San Francisco, 1988), collects 70 of his 146 short-short stories, written both early and late. In April 1972 he died by his own hand, for reasons known only to himself.*

The sky had turned a deep shade; it looked like the surface of a beautiful celadon° porcelain piece. From my bed I gazed out on the Kamo River where the water was tinged with the color of morning.

For a week now, filming for the movie had continued through the middle of the night because the actor playing the lead role was scheduled to appear on

celadon: ceramic glaze ranging in color from grayish to bluish green.

stage in ten days. I was merely the author, so all I had to do was casually witness the filming. But my lips had grown chapped, and I was so tired that I could not keep my eyes open, even as I stood next to the burning white carbide lamps. I had returned to my hotel room that morning about the time the stars were beginning to disappear.

However, the celadon-colored sky refreshed me. I felt that some beautiful daydream was about to take shape.

First, the scenery of Shijō Street came to mind. The previous day I had eaten lunch at Kikusui, a Western-style restaurant near Ōhashi. The mountains appeared before my eyes. I could see the new green of the trees of Higashiyama outside the third-story window. That was to be expected, but for me, having just come from Tokyo, it was startlingly fresh. Next, I recalled a mask I had seen in the display window of a curio shop. It was an old smiling mask.

"I have it. I've found a beautiful daydream," I whispered, overjoyed, as I drew   5 some blank manuscript paper toward me and gathered the daydream into words. I rewrote the last scene of the movie script. When I had finished, I added a letter to the director.

"I shall make the last scene a daydream. Gentle smiling masks will appear all over the screen. Since I could not hope to show a bright smile at the end of this dark story, at least I could wrap reality in a beautiful, smiling mask."

I took the manuscript to the studio. The only thing at the office was the morning paper. The cafeteria woman was cleaning up sawdust in front of the prop room.

"Would you please leave this at the director's bedside?"

This movie took place at a mental hospital. It pained me to see the wretched lives of the insane people we filmed every day. I had begun to think that I would feel hopeless unless I could somehow add a bright ending. I was afraid that I could not find a happy ending because my own personality was too gloomy.

So I was elated that I had thought of the masks. I had a pleasant sensation   10 when I imagined having every last person in the mental hospital wear a laughing mask.

The glass roof of the studio shone green. The color of the sky had lightened with the daylight. Relieved, I went back to my lodging and slept soundly.

The man who had gone to buy the masks returned to the studio about eleven o'clock that night.

"I've been running around to all the toy stores in Kyoto since morning, but there aren't any good masks anywhere."

"Let me see what you've got."

I was disappointed when I unwrapped the package. "This? Well . . . ."   15

"I know. They won't do. I thought I'd be able to find masks just anywhere. I'm sure I've seen them at all kinds of shops, but this is the only thing I could come up with the whole day."

"What I envisioned was something like a Noh° mask. If the mask itself isn't artistic, it will simply look ridiculous on film." I felt as though I might cry as I took the child's paper clown-mask in my hand. "For one thing, this color would look like faded black when photographed. And if it doesn't have a gentler smile with a whitish luster on the skin, then . . . "

The red tongue stuck out from the brown face.

"They're trying white paint on it now in the office."

Filming had stopped temporarily, so the director, too, came out of the hospital-room set, stared at everyone, and laughed. There was no way to collect enough masks; they had to shoot the last scene the next day. If they could not get old masks, he wanted at least to have celluloid ones.   20

"If there aren't any artistic masks, then we'd better give up," a man from the script department said, perhaps sympathizing with my disappointment. "Shall we go out looking one last time? It's only eleven o'clock, so they'll probably still be awake in Kyōgoku."

"Would you?"

We hurried by car straight along the dikes of the Kamo River. The bright lights in the windows of the university hospital on the opposite bank reflected in the water. I could not imagine that there were many patients suffering in a hospital with all those beautifully illuminated windows. I wondered if we might show the lights in the hospital windows instead, if we could not find suitable masks.

We walked around to each of the toy shops in Shinkyōgoku as they were beginning to close. We knew it was hopeless. We bought twenty paper turtle-masks. They were cute, but they could hardly be called artistic. Shijō Street was already asleep.

"Wait a moment." The script man turned down an alley. "There are a lot   25 of shops here that sell old Buddhist altar fittings. I think they have Noh theater equipment, too."

But no one was awake on the street. I peeped inside at the shops through the doors.

"I'll come again tomorrow morning about seven. I'll be up all night tonight anyway."

"I'll come along, too. Please wake me up," I said. But the next day he went alone. When I woke up, they had already started filming the masks. They had found five masks used in ancient music performances. My idea was to use twenty or thirty of the same kind of mask, but, touched by what it would be like to be floating in the gentle smiles of those five masks, I relaxed. I felt I had fulfilled my responsibility to the insane.

"I rented them because they were too expensive to buy. If you get them dirty, they can't be returned, so be careful."

After the script man spoke, the actors all washed their hands and picked up   30 the masks with their fingertips, gazing at them as if viewing a treasure.

"If they were washed, the paint would peel, wouldn't it?"

Noh: Classical Japanese drama, featuring music and dance, performed by actors in stylized masks designed to indicate love, grief, anger, and other emotions.

"Well, then, I'll buy them." I did actually want them. I daydreamed as if awaiting the future when the world would be in harmony and people would all wear the same gentle face as these masks.

As soon as I got back home to Tokyo, I went straight to my wife's hospital room.

The children laughed with joy, putting on one mask after another. I felt a vague sense of satisfaction.

"Daddy, put one on." 35

"No."

"Please put one on."

"No."

"Put one on."

My second son stood up and tried to push the mask onto my face. 40

"Stop it!" I shouted.

My wife saved me from this awkward moment. "Here, I'll put one on."

In the midst of the children's laughter, I turned pale. "What are you doing? You're ill."

How horrifying it was to see this laughing mask lying in her sickbed!

When my wife took off the mask, her breathing became labored. But that 45 was not what horrified me. The moment she removed the mask, my wife's face somehow appeared ugly. My skin grew clammy as I gazed at her haggard face. I was shocked at having discovered my wife's face for the first time. She had been enclosed for three minutes in the beautiful, gentle, smiling expression of the mask, so now I was able to perceive the ugliness of her own countenance for the first time. But no, rather than ugliness, it was the pained expression of one crushed by misfortune. After it had been hidden by the beautiful mask, her face had revealed this shadow of a wretched life.

"Daddy, put it on."

"It's Daddy's turn now." The children pressed me again.

"No." I stood up. If I were to put on the mask, then take it off again, I would look like an ugly demon to my wife. I was afraid of the beautiful mask. And that fear aroused in me suspicions that the ever-smiling gentle face of my wife might itself be a mask or that my wife's smile might be artifice, just like the mask.

The mask is no good. Art is no good.

I wrote a telegram to send to the studio in Kyoto. 50

"Cut the mask scene."

Then I tore the telegram to shreds.

D. H. Lawrence

David Herbert Lawrence (1885–1930) was born in Nottinghamshire, England, child of a coalminer and a schoolteacher who hated her husband's toil and vowed that her son should escape it. He took up fiction writing, attaining early success. During World War I, Lawrence and his wife were unjustly suspected of treason (he because of his pacifism, she because of her aristocratic German birth). After the armistice they left England and, seeking a climate healthier for Lawrence, who suffered from tuberculosis, wandered in Italy, France, Australia, Mexico, and the American Southwest. Lawrence is an impassioned spokesman for our unconscious, instinctive natures, which we moderns (he argues) have neglected in favor of our overweening intellects. In Lady Chatterley's Lover (1928), he strove to restore explicit sexuality to English fiction. The book,

D.H. Lawrence

which today seems tame and repetitious, was long banned in Britain and the United States. Deeper Lawrence novels include Sons and Lovers (1913), a veiled account of his breaking away from his fiercely possessive mother; The Rainbow (1915); Women in Love (1921); and The Plumed Serpent (1926), about a revival of pagan religion in Mexico. Besides fiction, Lawrence left a rich legacy of poetry, essays, criticism (Studies in Classic American Literature, 1923, is especially shrewd and funny), and travel writing. Lawrence exerted deep influence on others, both by the message in his work and by his personal magnetism.

There was a woman who was beautiful, who started with all the advantages, yet she had no luck. She married for love, and the love turned to dust. She had bonny children, yet she felt they had been thrust upon her, and she could not love them. They looked at her coldly, as if they were finding fault with her. And hurriedly she felt she must cover up some fault in herself. Yet what it was that she must cover up she never knew. Nevertheless, when her children were present, she always felt the center of her heart go hard. This troubled her, and in her manner she was all the more gentle and anxious for her children, as if she loved them very much. Only she herself knew that at the center of her heart was a hard little place that could not feel love, no, not for anybody. Everybody else said of her: "She is such a good mother. She adores her children." Only she herself, and her children themselves, knew it was not so. They read it in each other's eyes.

There were a boy and two little girls. They lived in a pleasant house, with a garden, and they had discreet servants, and felt themselves superior to anyone in the neighborhood.

Although they lived in style, they felt always an anxiety in the house. There was never enough money. The mother had a small income, and the father had a small income, but not nearly enough for the social position which they had to keep up. The father went in to town to some office. But though he had good prospects, these prospects never materialized. There was always the grinding sense of the shortage of money, though the style was always kept up.

At last the mother said: "I will see if I can't make something." But she did not know where to begin. She racked her brains, and tried this thing and the other, but could not find anything successful. The failure made deep lines come into her face. Her children were growing up, they would have to go to school. There must be more money, there must be more money. The father, who was always very handsome and expensive in his tastes, seemed as if he never *would* be able to do anything worth doing. And the mother, who had a great belief in herself, did not succeed any better, and her tastes were just as expensive.

And so the house came to be haunted by the unspoken phrase: *There must* 5 *be more money! There must be more money!* The children could hear it all the time, though nobody said it aloud. They heard it at Christmas, when the expensive and splendid toys filled the nursery. Behind the shining modern rocking-horse, behind the smart doll's house, a voice would start whispering: "There *must* be more money! There *must* be more money!" And the children would stop playing, to listen for a moment. They would look into each other's eyes, to see if they had all heard. And each one saw in the eyes of the other two that they too had heard. "There *must* be more money! There *must* be more money!"

It came whispering from the springs of the still-swaying rocking-horse, and even the horse, bending his wooden, champing head, heard it. The big doll, sitting so pink and smirking in her new pram, could hear it quite plainly, and seemed to be smirking all the more self-consciously because of it. The foolish puppy, too, that took the place of the teddy-bear, he was looking so extraordinarily foolish for no other reason but that he heard the secret whisper all over the house: "There *must* be more money!"

Yet nobody ever said it aloud. The whisper was everywhere, and therefore no one spoke it. Just as no one ever says: "We are breathing!" in spite of the fact that breath is coming and going all the time.

"Mother," said the boy Paul one day, "why don't we keep a car of our own? Why do we always use uncle's, or else a taxi?"

"Because we're the poor members of the family," said the mother.

"But why *are* we, mother?" 10

"Well—I suppose," she said slowly and bitterly, "it's because your father has no luck."

The boy was silent for some time.

"Is luck money, mother?" he asked rather timidly.

"No, Paul. Not quite. It's what causes you to have money."

"Oh!" said Paul vaguely. "I thought when Uncle Oscar said *filthy lucker*, it 15 meant money."

"*Filthy lucre* does mean money," said the mother. "But it's lucre, not luck."

"Oh!" said the boy. "Then what *is* luck, mother?"

"It's what causes you to have money. If you're lucky you have money. That's why it's better to be born lucky than rich. If you're rich, you may lose your money. But if you're lucky, you will always get more money."

"Oh! Will you? And is father not lucky?"

"Very unlucky, I should say," she said bitterly.

The boy watched her with unsure eyes.

"Why?" he asked.

"I don't know. Nobody ever knows why one person is lucky and another unlucky."

"Don't they? Nobody at all? Does *nobody* know?"

"Perhaps God. But He never tells."

"He ought to, then. And aren't you lucky either, mother?"

"I can't be, if I married an unlucky husband."

"But by yourself, aren't you?"

"I used to think I was, before I married. Now I think I am very unlucky indeed."

"Why?"

"Well—never mind! Perhaps I'm not really," she said.

The child looked at her, to see if she meant it. But he saw, by the lines of her mouth, that she was only trying to hide something from him.

"Well, anyhow," he said stoutly, "I'm a lucky person."

"Why?" said his mother, with a sudden laugh.

He stared at her. He didn't even know why he had said it.

"God told me," he asserted, brazening it out.

"I hope He did, dear!" she said, again with a laugh, but rather bitter.

"He did, mother!"

"Excellent!" said the mother, using one of her husband's exclamations.

The boy saw she did not believe him; or, rather, that she paid no attention to his assertion. This angered him somewhat, and made him want to compel her attention.

He went off by himself, vaguely, in a childish way, seeking for the clue to "luck." Absorbed, taking no heed of other people, he went about with a sort of stealth, seeking inwardly for luck. He wanted luck, he wanted it, he wanted it. When the two girls were playing dolls in the nursery, he would sit on his big rocking-horse, charging madly into space, with a frenzy that made the little girls peer at him uneasily. Wildly the horse careered, the waving dark hair of the boy tossed, his eyes had a strange glare in them. The little girls dared not speak to him.

When he had ridden to the end of his mad little journey, he climbed down and stood in front of his rocking-horse, staring fixedly into its lowered face. Its red mouth was slightly open, its big eye was wide and glassy-bright.

"Now!" he would silently command the snorting steed. "Now, take me to where there is luck! Now take me!"

And he would slash the horse on the neck with the little whip he had asked Uncle Oscar for. He *knew* the horse could take him to where there was luck, if only he forced it. So he would mount again, and start on his furious ride, hoping at last to get there. He knew he could get there.

"You'll break your horse, Paul!" said the nurse.

"He's always riding like that! I wish he'd leave off!" said his elder sister Joan.

But he only glared down on them in silence. Nurse gave him up. She could make nothing of him. Anyhow he was growing beyond her.

One day his mother and his Uncle Oscar came in when he was on one of his furious rides. He did not speak to them.

"Hallo, you young jockey! Riding a winner?" said his uncle.

"Aren't you growing too big for a rocking-horse? You're not a very little boy any longer, you know," said his mother.

But Paul only gave a blue glare from his big, rather close-set eyes. He would speak to nobody when he was in full tilt. His mother watched him with an anxious expression on her face.

At last he suddenly stopped forcing his horse into the mechanical gallop, and slid down.

"Well, I got there!" he announced fiercely, his blue eyes still flaring, and his sturdy long legs straddling apart.

"Where did you get to?" asked his mother.

"Where I wanted to go," he flared back at her.

"That's right, son!" said Uncle Oscar. "Don't you stop till you get there. What's the horse's name?"

"He doesn't have a name," said the boy.

"Gets on without all right?" asked the uncle.

"Well, he has different names. He was called Sansovino last week."

"Sansovino, eh? Won the Ascot. How did you know his name?"

"He always talks about horse-races with Bassett," said Joan.

The uncle was delighted to find that his small nephew was posted with all the racing news. Bassett, the young gardener, who had been wounded in the left foot in the war and had got his present job through Oscar Cresswell, whose batman° he had been, was a perfect blade of the "turf." He lived in the racing events, and the small boy lived with him.

Oscar Cresswell got it all from Bassett.

"Master Paul comes and asks me, so I can't do more than tell him, sir," said Bassett, his face terribly serious, as if he were speaking of religious matters.

"And does he ever put anything on a horse he fancies?"

"Well—I don't want to give him away—he's a young sport, a fine sport, sir. Would you mind asking him himself? He sort of takes a pleasure in it, and perhaps he'd feel I was giving him away, sir, if you don't mind."

Bassett was serious as a church.

The uncle went back to his nephew and took him off for a ride in the car.

"Say, Paul, old man, do you ever put anything on a horse?" the uncle asked.

The boy watched the handsome man closely.

"Why, do you think I oughtn't to?" he parried.

"Not a bit of it. I thought perhaps you might give me a tip for the Lincoln."

The car sped on into the country, going down to Uncle Oscar's place in Hampshire.

batman: In the game of cricket, one who carries a player's equipment (like a caddy in golf).

"Honor bright?" said the nephew.

"Honor bright, son!" said the uncle.

"Well, then, Daffodil."

"Daffodil! I doubt it, sonny. What about Mirza?"

"I only know the winner," said the boy. "That's Daffodil."

"Daffodil, eh?"

There was a pause. Daffodil was an obscure horse comparatively. 80

"Uncle!"

"Yes, son?"

"You won't let it go any further, will you? I promised Bassett."

"Bassett be damned, old man! What's he got to do with it?"

"We're partners. We've been partners from the first. Uncle, he lent me my 85
first five shillings, which I lost. I promised him, honor bright, it was only between
me and him; only you gave me that ten-shilling note I started winning with, so
I thought you were lucky. You won't let it go any further, will you?"

The boy gazed at his uncle from those big, hot, blue eyes, set rather close
together. The uncle stirred and laughed uneasily.

"Right you are, son! I'll keep your tip private. Daffodil, eh? How much are
you putting on him?"

"All except twenty pounds," said the boy. "I keep that in reserve."

The uncle thought it a good joke.

"You keep twenty pounds in reserve, do you, you young romancer? What are 90
you betting, then?"

"I'm betting three hundred," said the boy gravely. "But it's between you and
me, Uncle Oscar! Honor bright?"

The uncle burst into a roar of laughter.

"It's between you and me all right, you young Nat Gould°," he said, laughing. "But where's your three hundred?"

"Bassett keeps it for me. We're partners."

"You are, are you! And what is Bassett putting on Daffodil?" 95

"He won't go quite as high as I do, I expect. Perhaps he'll go a hundred and
fifty."

"What, pennies?" laughed the uncle.

"Pounds," said the child, with a surprised look at his uncle. "Bassett keeps
a bigger reserve than I do."

Between wonder and amusement Uncle Oscar was silent. He pursued the
matter no further, but he determined to take his nephew with him to the Lincoln
races.

"Now, son," he said, "I'm putting twenty on Mirza, and I'll put five for you 100
on any horse you fancy. What's your pick?"

"Daffodil, uncle,"

"No, not the fiver on Daffodil!"

"I should if it was my own fiver," said the child.

"Good! Good! Right you are! A fiver for me and a fiver for you on Daffodil."

Nat Gould: celebrated English gambler of the 1920s.

The child had never been to a race-meeting before, and his eyes were blue 105
fire. He pursed his mouth tight, and watched. A Frenchman just in front had put
his money on Lancelot. Wild with excitement, he flayed his arms up and down,
yelling, "*Lancelot! Lancelot!*" in his French accent.

Daffodil came in first, Lancelot second, Mirza third. The child, flushed and
with eyes blazing, was curiously serene. His uncle brought him four five-pound
notes, four to one.

"What am I to do with these?" he cried, waving them before the boy's eyes.

"I suppose we'll talk to Bassett," said the boy. "I expect I have fifteen hundred
now; and twenty in reserve; and this twenty."

His uncle studied him for some moments.

"Look here, son!" he said. "You're not serious about Bassett and that fifteen 110
hundred, are you?"

"Yes, I am. But it's between you and me, uncle. Honor bright!"

"Honor bright all right, son! But I must talk to Bassett."

"If you'd like to be a partner, uncle, with Bassett and me, we could all be
partners. Only, you'd have to promise, honor bright, uncle, not to let it go beyond us three. Bassett and I are lucky, and you must be lucky, because it was your
ten shillings I started winning with. . . ."

Uncle Oscar took both Bassett and Paul into Richmond Park for an afternoon, and there they talked.

"It's like this, you see, sir," Bassett said. "Master Paul would get me talking 115
about racing events, spinning yarns, you know, sir. And he was always keen on
knowing if I'd made or if I'd lost. It's about a year since, now, that I put five shillings on Blush of Dawn for him—and we lost. Then the luck turned, and with
that ten shillings he had from you, that we put on Singhalese. And since that
time, it's been pretty steady, all things considering. What do you say, Master Paul?"

"We're all right when we're sure," said Paul. "It's when we're not quite sure
that we go down."

"Oh, but we're careful then," said Bassett.

"But when are you *sure?*" smiled Uncle Oscar.

"It's Master Paul, sir," said Bassett, in a secret, religious voice. "It's as if he
had it from heaven. Like Daffodil, now, for the Lincoln. That was as sure as eggs."

"Did you put anything on Daffodil?" asked Oscar Cresswell. 120

"Yes, sir. I made my bit."

"And my nephew?"

Bassett was obstinately silent, looking at Paul.

"I made twelve hundred, didn't I, Bassett? I told uncle I was putting three
hundred on Daffodil."

"That's right," said Bassett, nodding. 125

"But where's the money?" asked the uncle.

"I keep it safe locked up, sir. Master Paul he can have it any minute he likes
to ask for it."

"What, fifteen hundred pounds?"

"And twenty! And *forty*, that is, with the twenty he made on the course."

"It's amazing!" said the uncle. 130

"If Master Paul offers you to be partners, sir, I would, if I were you; if you'll
excuse me," said Bassett.

Oscar Cresswell thought about it.

"I'll see the money," he said.

They drove home again, and sure enough, Bassett came round to the garden-house with fifteen hundred pounds in notes. The twenty pounds reserve was left with Joe Glee, in the Turf Commission deposit.

"You see, it's all right, uncle, when I'm *sure!* Then we go strong, for all we're 135 worth. Don't we, Bassett!"

"We do that, Master Paul."

"And when are you sure?" said the uncle, laughing.

"Oh, well, sometimes I'm *absolutely* sure, like about Daffodil," said the boy; "and sometimes I have an idea; and sometimes I haven't even an idea, have I, Bassett? Then we're careful, because we mostly go down."

"You do, do you! And when you're sure, like about Daffodil, what makes you sure, sonny?"

"Oh, well, I don't know," said the boy uneasily. "I'm sure, you know, uncle; 140 that's all."

"It's as if he had it from heaven, sir," Bassett reiterated.

"I should say so!" said the uncle.

But he became a partner. And when the Leger was coming on, Paul was "sure" about Lively Spark, which was a quite inconsiderable horse. The boy insisted on putting a thousand on the horse, Bassett went for five hundred, and Oscar Cresswell two hundred. Lively Spark came in first, and the betting had been ten to one against him. Paul had made ten thousand.

"You see," he said, "I was absolutely sure of him."

Even Oscar Cresswell had cleared two thousand. 145

"Look here, son," he said, "this sort of thing makes me nervous."

"It needn't, uncle! Perhaps I shan't be sure again for a long time."

"But what are you going to do with your money?" asked the uncle.

"Of course," said the boy, "I started it for mother. She said she had no luck, because father is unlucky, so I thought if I was lucky, it might stop whispering."

"What might stop whispering?" 150

"Our house. I *hate* our house for whispering."

"What does it whisper?"

"Why—why"—the boy fidgeted—"why, I don't know. But it's always short of money, you know, uncle."

"I know it, son, I know it."

"You know people send mother writs, don't you, uncle?" 155

"I'm afraid I do," said the uncle.

"And then the house whispers, like people laughing at you behind your back. It's awful, that is! I thought if I was lucky . . ."

"You might stop it," added the uncle.

The boy watched him with big blue eyes, that had an uncanny cold fire in them, and he said never a word.

"Well, then!" said the uncle. "What are we doing?" 160

"I shouldn't like mother to know I was lucky," said the boy.

"Why not, son?"

"She'd stop me."

"I don't think she would."

"Oh!"—and the boy writhed in an odd way—"I *don't* want her to know, uncle." 165

"All right, son! We'll manage it without her knowing."

They managed it very easily. Paul, at the other's suggestion, handed over five thousand pounds to his uncle, who deposited it with the family lawyer, who was then to inform Paul's mother that a relative had put five thousand pounds into his hands, which sum was to be paid out a thousand pounds at a time, on the mother's birthday, for the next five years.

"So she'll have a birthday present of a thousand pounds for five successive years," said Uncle Oscar. "I hope it won't make it all the harder for her later."

Paul's mother had her birthday in November. The house had been "whispering" worse than ever lately, and, even in spite of his luck, Paul could not bear up against it. He was very anxious to see the effect of the birthday letter, telling his mother about the thousand pounds.

When there were no visitors, Paul now took his meals with his parents, as 170 he was beyond the nursery control. His mother went into town nearly every day. She had discovered that she had an odd knack of sketching furs and dress materials, so she worked secretly in the studio of a friend who was the chief "artist" for the leading drapers. She drew the figures of ladies in furs and ladies in silk and sequins for the newspaper advertisements. This young woman artist earned several thousand pounds a year, but Paul's mother only made several hundreds, and she was again dissatisfied. She so wanted to be first in something, and she did not succeed, even in making sketches for drapery advertisements.

She was down to breakfast on the morning of her birthday. Paul watched her face as she read the letters. He knew the lawyer's letter. As his mother read it, her face hardened and became more expressionless. Then a cold, determined look came on her mouth. She hid the letter under the pile of others, and said not a word about it.

"Didn't you have anything nice in the post for your birthday, mother?" said Paul.

"Quite moderately nice," she said, her voice cold and absent.

She went away to town without saying more.

But in the afternoon Uncle Oscar appeared. He said Paul's mother had had 175 a long interview with the lawyer, asking if the whole five thousand could not be advanced at once, as she was in debt.

"What do you think, uncle?" said the boy.

"I leave it to you, son."

"Oh, let her have it, then! We can get some more with the other," said the boy.

"A bird in the hand is worth two in the bush, laddie!" said Uncle Oscar.

"But I'm sure to *know* for the Grand National; or the Lincolnshire; or else 180 the Derby. I'm sure to know for *one* of them," said Paul.

So Uncle Oscar signed the agreement, and Paul's mother touched the whole five thousand. Then something very curious happened. The voices in the house suddenly went mad, like a chorus of frogs on a spring evening. There were certain new furnishings, and Paul had a tutor. He was *really* going to Eton, his father's school, in the following autumn. There were flowers in the winter, and a blossoming of the luxury Paul's mother had been used to. And yet the voices in the house, behind the sprays of mimosa and almond blossom, and from under the piles of iridescent cushions, simply trilled and screamed in a sort of ecstasy: "There *must* be more money! Oh-h-h; there *must* be more money. Oh, now, now-w! Now-w-w—there *must* be more money—more than ever! More than ever!"

It frightened Paul terribly. He studied away at his Latin and Greek with his tutors. But his intense hours were spent with Bassett. The Grand National had gone by: he had not "known," and had lost a hundred pounds. Summer was at hand. He was in agony for the Lincoln. But even for the Lincoln he didn't "know," and he lost fifty pounds. He became wild-eyed and strange, as if something were going to explode in him.

"Let it alone, son! Don't you bother about it!" urged Uncle Oscar. But it was as if the boy couldn't really hear what his uncle was saying.

"I've got to know for the Derby! I've got to know for the Derby!" the child reiterated, his big blue eyes blazing with a sort of madness.

His mother noticed how overwrought he was.   185

"You'd better go to the seaside. Wouldn't you like to go now to the seaside, instead of waiting? I think you'd better," she said, looking down at him anxiously, her heart curiously heavy because of him.

But the child lifted his uncanny blue eyes.

"I couldn't possibly go before the Derby, mother!" he said. "I couldn't possibly!"

"Why not?" she said, her voice becoming heavy when she was opposed. "Why not? You can still go from the seaside to see the Derby with your Uncle Oscar, if that's what you wish. No need for you to wait here. Besides, I think you care too much about these races. It's a bad sign. My family has been a gambling family, and you won't know till you grow up how much damage it has done. But it has done damage. I shall have to send Bassett away, and ask Uncle Oscar not to talk racing to you, unless you promise to be reasonable about it; go away to the seaside and forget it. You're all nerves!"

"I'll do what you like, mother, so long as you don't send me away till after   190
the Derby," the boy said.

"Send you away from where? Just from this house?"

"Yes," he said, gazing at her.

"Why, you curious child, what makes you care about this house so much, suddenly? I never knew you loved it."

He gazed at her without speaking. He had a secret within a secret, something he had not divulged, even to Bassett or to his Uncle Oscar.

But his mother, after standing undecided and a little bit sullen for some mo-   195
ments, said:

"Very well, then! Don't go to the seaside till after the Derby, if you don't wish it. But promise me you won't let your nerves go to pieces. Promise you won't think so much about horse-racing and *events*, as you call them!"

"Oh, no," said the boy casually. "I won't think much about them, mother. You needn't worry. I wouldn't worry, mother, if I were you."

"If you were me and I were you," said his mother, "I wonder what we *should* do!"

"But you know you needn't worry, mother, don't you?" the boy repeated.

"I should be awfully glad to know it," she said wearily.   200

"Oh, well, you *can*, you know. I mean, you *ought* to know you needn't worry," he insisted.

"Ought I? Then I'll see about it," she said.

Paul's secret of secrets was his wooden horse, that which had no name. Since he was emancipated from a nurse and a nursery-governess, he had had his rocking-horse removed to his own bedroom at the top of the house.

"Surely, you're too big for a rocking-horse!" his mother had remonstrated.

"Well, you see, mother, till I can have a *real* horse, I like to have *some* sort 205 of animal about," had been his quaint answer.

"Do you feel he keeps you company? she laughed.

"Oh, yes! He's very good, he always keeps me company, when I'm there," said Paul.

So the horse, rather shabby, stood in an arrested prance in the boy's bedroom.

The Derby was drawing near, and the boy grew more and more tense. He hardly heard what was spoken to him, he was very frail, and his eyes were really uncanny. His mother had sudden strange seizures of uneasiness about him. Sometimes, for half-an-hour, she would feel a sudden anxiety about him that was almost anguish. She wanted to rush to him at once, and know he was safe.

Two nights before the Derby, she was at a big party in town, when one of 210 her rushes of anxiety about her boy, her first-born, gripped her heart till she could hardly speak. She fought with the feeling, might and main, for she believed in common-sense. But it was too strong. She had to leave the dance and go downstairs to telephone to the country. The children's nursery-governess was terribly surprised and startled at being rung up in the night.

"Are the children all right, Miss Wilmot?"

"Oh, yes, they are quite all right."

"Master Paul? Is he all right?"

"He went to bed as right as a trivet. Shall I run up and look at him?"

"No," said Paul's mother reluctantly. "No! Don't trouble. It's all right. Don't 215 sit up. We shall be home fairly soon." She did not want her son's privacy intruded upon.

"Very good," said the governess.

It was about one-o'clock when Paul's mother and father drove up to their house. All was still. Paul's mother went to her room and slipped off her white fur cloak. She had told her maid not to wait up for her. She heard her husband downstairs, mixing a whisky-and-soda.

And then, because of the strange anxiety at her heart, she stole upstairs to her son's room. Noiselessly she went along the upper corridor. Was there a faint noise? What was it?

She stood, with arrested muscles, outside his door, listening. There was a strange, heavy, and yet not loud noise. Her heart stood still. It was a soundless noise, yet rushing and powerful. Something huge, in violent, hushed motion. What was it? What in God's name was it? She ought to know. She felt that she knew the noise. She knew what it was.

Yet she could not place it. She couldn't say what it was. And on and on it 220 went, like a madness.

Softly, frozen with anxiety and fear, she turned the door-handle.

The room was dark. Yet in the space near the window, she heard and saw something plunging to and fro. She gazed in fear and amazement.

Then suddenly she switched on the light, and saw her son, in his green pajamas, madly surging on the rocking-horse. The blaze of light suddenly lit him up, as he urged the wooden horse, and lit her up, as she stood, blonde, in her dress of pale green and crystal, in the doorway.

"Paul!" she cried. "Whatever are you doing?"

"It's Malabar!" he screamed, in a powerful, strange voice. "It's Malabar!" 225

His eyes blazed at her for one strange and senseless second, as he ceased urging his wooden horse. Then he fell with a crash to the ground, and she, all her tormented motherhood flooding upon her, rushed to gather him up.

But he was unconscious, and unconscious he remained, with some brainfever. He talked and tossed, and his mother sat stonily by his side.

"Malabar! It's Malabar! Bassett, Bassett I *know*! It's Malabar!"

So the child cried, trying to get up and urge the rocking-horse that gave him his inspiration.

"What does he mean by Malabar?" asked the heart-frozen mother. 230

"I don't know," said the father stonily.

"What does he mean by Malabar?" she asked her brother Oscar.

"It's one of the horses running for the Derby," was the answer.

And, in spite of himself, Oscar Cresswell spoke to Bassett, and himself put a thousand on Malabar: at fourteen to one.

The third day of the illness was critical: they were waiting for a change. The 235 boy, with his rather long, curly hair, was tossing ceaselessly on the pillow. He neither slept nor regained consciousness, and his eyes were like blue stones. His mother sat, feeling her heart had gone, turned actually into a stone.

In the evening, Oscar Cresswell did not come, but Bassett sent a message, saying could he come up for one moment, just one moment? Paul's mother was very angry at the intrusion, but on second thought she agreed. The boy was the same. Perhaps Bassett might bring him to consciousness.

The gardener, a shortish fellow with a little brown moustache, and sharp little brown eyes, tiptoed into the room, touched his imaginary cap to Paul's mother, and stole to the bedside, staring with glittering, smallish eyes, at the tossing, dying child.

"Master Paul!" he whispered. "Master Paul! Malabar came in first all right, a clean win. I did as you told me. You've made over seventy thousand pounds, you have; you've got over eighty thousand. Malabar came in all right, Master Paul."

"Malabar! Malabar! Did I say Malabar, mother? Did I say Malabar? Do you think I'm lucky, mother? I knew Malabar, didn't I? Over eighty thousand pounds! I call that lucky, don't you, mother? Over eighty thousand pounds! I knew, didn't I know I knew? Malabar came in all right. If I ride my horse till I'm sure, then I tell you, Bassett, you can go as high as you like. Did you go for all you were worth, Bassett?"

"I went a thousand on it, Master Paul." 240

"I never told you, mother, that if I can ride my horse, and *get there*, then I'm absolutely sure—oh, absolutely! Mother, did I ever tell you? I *am* lucky!"

"No, you never did," said the mother.

But the boy died in the night.

And even as he lay dead, his mother heard her brother's voice saying to her: "My God, Hester, you're eighty-odd thousand to the good, and a poor devil of a son to the bad. But, poor devil, poor devil, he's best gone out of a life where he rides his rocking-horse to find a winner."

Bobbie Ann Mason

BIG BERTHA STORIES   1989

Bobbie Ann Mason, one of the leading voices in the new Southern fiction, was born in 1940 in Mayfield, Kentucky, growing up on a dairy farm in a region of western Kentucky whose people often appear in her stories. After her graduation from the University of Kentucky, she wrote for popular magazines including Movie Life *and* TV Star Parade, *then began a now-suspended career in college teaching, taking her Ph.D. at the University of Connecticut and writing the critical studies* Nabokov's Garden *(1974) and* The Girl Sleuth: A Feminist Guide to the Bobbsey Twins, Nancy Drew, and Their Sisters *(1975). Her first collection,* Shiloh and Other Stories *(1982), received wide attention, and with the novels* In Country *(1985) and* Spence & Lila *(1988), her audience has continued to grow. Anonymously, Mason has also written many contributions to the feature "Talk of the Town" in* The New Yorker. *"Big Bertha Stories" first*

Bobbie Ann Mason

appeared in Mother Jones *magazine, later in a second collection of stories,* Love Life *(1989).*

Donald is home again, laughing and singing. He comes home from Central City, near the strip mines, only when he feels like it, like an absentee landlord checking on his property. He is always in such a good humor when he returns that Jeannette forgives him. She cooks for him—ugly, pasty things she gets with food stamps. Sometimes he brings steaks and ice cream, occasionally money. Rodney, their child, hides in the closet when he arrives, and Donald goes around the house talking loudly about the little boy named Rodney who used to live there—the one who fell into a septic tank, or the one stolen by gypsies. The stories change. Rodney usually stays in the closet until he has to pee, and then he hugs his father's knees, forgiving him, just as Jeannette does. The way Donald saunters through the door, swinging a six-pack of beer, with a big grin on his face, takes her breath away. He leans against the door facing, looking sexy in his baseball cap and his shaggy red beard and his sunglasses. He wears sunglasses to be like the Blues Brothers, but he in no way resembles either of the Blues Brothers. I should have my head examined, Jeannette thinks.

The last time Donald was home, they went to the shopping center to buy Rodney some shoes advertised on sale. They stayed at the shopping center half the afternoon, just looking around. Donald and Rodney played video games. Jeannette felt they were a normal family. Then, in the parking lot, they stopped to watch a man on a platform demonstrating snakes. Children were petting a twelve-foot python coiled around the man's shoulders. Jeannette felt faint.

"Snakes won't hurt you unless you hurt them," said Donald as Rodney stroked the snake.

"It feels like chocolate," he said.

The snake man took a tarantula from a plastic box and held it lovingly in   5
his palm. He said, "If you drop a tarantula, it will shatter like a Christmas ornament."

"I hate this," said Jeannette.

"Let's get out of here," said Donald.

Jeannette felt her family disintegrating like a spider shattering as Donald hurried them away from the shopping center. Rodney squalled and Donald dragged him along. Jeannette wanted to stop for ice cream. She wanted them all to sit quietly together in a booth, but Donald rushed them to the car, and he drove them home in silence, his face growing grim.

"Did you have bad dreams about the snakes?" Jeannette asked Rodney the next morning at breakfast. They were eating pancakes made with generic pancake mix. Rodney slapped his fork in the pond of syrup on his pancakes. "The black racer is the farmer's friend," he said soberly, repeating a fact learned from the snake man.

"Big Bertha kept black racers," said Donald. "She trained them for the 500."   10
Donald doesn't tell Rodney ordinary children's stories. He tells him a series of strange stories he makes up about Big Bertha. Big Bertha is what he calls the huge strip-mining machine in Muhlenberg County, but he has Rodney believing that Big Bertha is a female version of Paul Bunyan.

"Snakes don't run in the 500," said Rodney.

"This wasn't the Indy 500 or the Daytona 500—none of your well-known 500s," said Donald. "This was the Possum Trot 500, and it was a long time ago. Big Bertha started the original 500, with snakes. Black racers and blue racers mainly. Also some red-and-white-striped racers, but those are rare."

"We always ran for the hoe if we saw a black racer," Jeannette said, remembering her childhood in the country.

In a way, Donald's absences are a fine arrangement, even considerate. He is sparing them his darkest moods, when he can't cope with his memories of Vietnam. Vietnam had never seemed such a meaningful fact until a couple of years ago, when he grew depressed and moody, and then he started going away to Central City. He frightened Jeannette, and she always said the wrong thing in her efforts to soothe him. If the welfare people find out he is spending occasional weekends at home, and even bringing some money, they will cut off her assistance. She applied for welfare because she can't depend on him to send money, but she knows he blames her for losing faith in him. He isn't really working regularly at the strip mines. He is mostly just hanging around there, watching the land being scraped away, trees coming down, bushes flung in the air. Sometimes he operates a steam shovel, and when he comes home his clothes are filled with the clay and it is caked on his shoes. The clay is the color of butterscotch pudding.

At first, he tried to explain to Jeannette. He said, "If we could have had tanks 15 over there as big as Big Bertha, we wouldn't have lost the war. Strip mining is just like what we were doing over there. We were stripping off the top. The top-soil is like the culture and the people, the best part of the land and the country. America was just stripping off the top, the best. We ruined it. Here, at least the coal companies have to plant vetch and loblolly pines and all kinds of trees and bushes. If we'd done that in Vietnam, maybe we'd have left that country in better shape."

"Wasn't Vietnam a long time ago?" Jeannette asked.

She didn't want to hear about Vietnam. She thought it was unhealthy to dwell on it so much. He should live in the present. Her mother is afraid Donald will do something violent, because she once read in the newspaper that a veteran in Louisville held his little girl hostage in their apartment until he had a shootout with the police and was killed. But Jeannette can't imagine Donald doing anything so extreme. When she first met him, several years ago, at her parents' pit-barbecue luncheonette, where she was working then, he had a good job at a lumberyard and he dressed nicely. He took her out to eat at a fancy restaurant. They got plastered and ended up in a motel in Tupelo, Mississippi, on Elvis Presley Boulevard. Back then, he talked nostalgically about his year in Vietnam, about how beautiful it was, how different the people were. He could never seem to explain what he meant. "They're just different," he said.

They went riding around in a yellow 1957 Chevy convertible. He drives too fast now, but he didn't then, maybe because he was so protective of the car. It was a classic. He sold it three years ago and made a good profit. About the time he sold the Chevy, his moods began changing, his even-tempered nature shifting, like driving on a smooth interstate and then switching to a secondary road. He had headaches and bad dreams. But his nightmares seemed trivial. He dreamed of riding a train through the Rocky Mountains, of hijacking a plane to Cuba, of stringing up barbed wire around the house. He dreamed he lost a doll. He got drunk and rammed the car, the Chevy's successor, into a Civil War statue in front of the courthouse. When he got depressed over the meaninglessness of his job, Jeannette felt guilty about spending money on something nice for the house, and she tried to make him feel his job had meaning by reminding him that, after all, they had a child to think of. "I don't like his name," Donald said once. "What a stupid name. Rodney. I never did like it."

Rodney has dreams about Big Bertha, echoes of his father's nightmare, like TV cartoon versions of Donald's memories of the war. But Rodney loves the stories, even though they are confusing, with lots of loose ends. The latest in the

Big Bertha series is "Big Bertha and the Neutron Bomb." Last week it was "Big Bertha and the MX Missile." In the new story, Big Bertha takes a trip to California to go surfing with Big Mo, her male counterpart. On the beach, corn dogs and snow cones are free and the surfboards turn into dolphins. Everyone is having fun until the neutron bomb comes. Rodney loves the part where everyone keels over dead. Donald acts it out, collapsing on the rug. All the dolphins and the surfers keel over, everyone except Big Bertha. Big Bertha is so big she is immune to the neutron bomb.

"Those stories aren't true," Jeannette tells Rodney.

Rodney staggers and falls down on the rug, his arms and legs akimbo. He gets the giggles and can't stop. When his spasms finally subside, he says, "I told Scottie Bidwell about Big Bertha and he didn't believe me."

Donald picks Rodney up under the armpits and sets him upright. "You tell Scottie Bidwell if he saw Big Bertha he would pee in his pants on the spot, he would be so impressed."

"Are you scared of Big Bertha?"

"No, I'm not. Big Bertha is just like a wonderful woman, a big fat woman who can sing the blues. Have you ever heard Big Mama Thornton?"

"No."

"Well, Big Bertha's like her, only she's the size of a tall building. She's slow as a turtle and when she crosses the road they have to reroute traffic. She's big enough to straddle a four-lane highway. She's so tall she can see all the way to Tennessee, and when she belches, there's a tornado. She's really something. She can even fly."

"She's too big to fly," Rodney says doubtfully. He makes a face like a wadded-up washrag and Donald wrestles him to the floor again.

Donald has been drinking all evening, but he isn't drunk. The ice cubes melt and he pours the drink out and refills it. He keeps on talking. Jeannette cannot remember him talking so much about the war. He is telling her about an ammunitions dump. Jeannette had the vague idea that an ammo dump is a mound of shotgun shells, heaps of cartridge casings and bomb shells, or whatever is left over, a vast waste pile from the war, but Donald says that is wrong. He has spent an hour describing it in detail, so that she will understand.

He refills the glass with ice, some 7-Up, and a shot of Jim Beam. He slams doors and drawers, looking for a compass. Jeannette can't keep track of the conversation. It doesn't matter that her hair is uncombed and her lipstick eaten away. He isn't seeing her.

"I want to draw the compound for you," he says, sitting down at the table with a sheet of Rodney's tablet paper.

Donald draws the map in red and blue ballpoint, with asterisks and technical labels that mean nothing to her. He draws some circles with the compass and measures some angles. He makes a red dot on an oblique line, a patch that leads to the ammo dump.

"That's where I was. Right there," he says. "There was a water buffalo that tripped a land mine and its horn just flew off and stuck in the wall of the barracks like a machete thrown backhanded." He puts a dot where the land mine was, and he doodles awhile with the red ballpoint pen, scribbling something on the edge of the map that looks like feathers. "The dump was here and I was there and over there was where we piled the sandbags. And here were the tanks." He draws tanks, a row of squares with handles—guns sticking out.

"Why are you going to so much trouble to tell me about a buffalo horn that got stuck in a wall?" she wants to know.

But Donald just looks at her as though she has asked something obvious.

"Maybe I *could* understand if you'd let me," she says cautiously.   35

"You could never understand." He draws another tank.

In bed, it is the same as it has been since he started going away to Central City—the way he claims his side of the bed, turning away from her. Tonight, she reaches for him and he lets her be close to him. She cries for a while and he lies there, waiting for her to finish, as though she were merely putting on makeup.

"Do you want me to tell you a Big Bertha story?" he asks playfully.

"You act like you're in love with Big Bertha."

He laughs, breathing on her. But he won't come closer.   40

"You don't care what I look like anymore," she says. "What am I supposed to think?"

"There's nobody else. There's not anybody but you."

Loving a giant machine is incomprehensible to Jeannette. There must be another woman, someone that large in his mind. Jeannette has seen the strip-mining machine. The top of the crane is visible beyond a rise along the parkway. The strip mining is kept just out of sight of travelers because it would give them a poor image of Kentucky.

For three weeks, Jeannette has been seeing a psychologist at the free mental health clinic. He's a small man from out of state. His name is Dr. Robinson, but she calls him The Rapist, because the word *therapist* can be divided into two words, *the rapist*. He doesn't think her joke is clever, and he acts as though he has heard it a thousand times before. He has a habit of saying, "Go with that feeling," the same way Bob Newhart did on his old TV show. It's probably the first lesson in the textbook, Jeannette thinks.

She told him about Donald's last days on his job at the lumberyard—how   45
he let the stack of lumber fall deliberately and didn't know why, and about how he went away soon after that, and how the Big Bertha stories started. Dr. Robinson seems to be waiting for her to make something out of it all, but it's maddening that he won't tell her what to do. After three visits, Jeannette has grown angry with him, and now she's holding back things. She won't tell him whether Donald slept with her or not when he came home last. Let him guess, she thinks.

"Talk about yourself," he says.

"What about me?"

"You speak so vaguely about Donald that I get the feeling that you see him as somebody larger than life. I can't quite picture him. That makes me wonder what that says about you." He touches the end of his tie to his nose and sniffs it.

When Jeannette suggests that she bring Donald in, the therapist looks bored and says nothing.

"He had another nightmare when he was home last," Jeannette says. "He 50 dreamed he was crawling through tall grass and people were after him."

"How do *you* feel about that?" The Rapist asks eagerly.

"I didn't have the nightmare," she says coldly. "Donald did. I came to you to get advice about Donald, and you're acting like I'm the one who's crazy. I'm not crazy. But I'm lonely."

Jeannette's mother, behind the counter of the luncheonette, looks lovingly at Rodney pushing buttons on the jukebox in the corner. "It's a shame about that youngun," she says tearfully. "That boy needs a daddy."

"What are you trying to tell me? That I should file for divorce and get Rodney a new daddy?"

Her mother looks hurt. "No, honey," she says. "You need to get Donald to 55 seek the Lord. And you need to pray more. You haven't been going to church lately."

"Have some barbecue," Jeannette's father booms, as he comes in from the back kitchen. "And I want you to take a pound home with you. You've got a growing boy to feed."

"I want to take Rodney to church," Mama says. "I want to show him off, and it might do some good."

"People will think he's an orphan," Dad says.

"I don't care," Mama says. "I just love him to pieces and I want to take him to church. Do you care if I take him to church, Jeannette?"

"No. I don't care if you take him to church." She takes the pound of barbecue 60 from her father. Grease splotches the brown wrapping paper. Dad has given them so much barbecue that Rodney is burned out on it and won't eat it anymore.

Jeannette wonders if she would file for divorce if she could get a job. It is a thought—for the child's sake, she thinks. But there aren't many jobs around. With the cost of a baby-sitter, it doesn't pay her to work. When Donald first went away, her mother kept Rodney and she had a good job, waitressing at a steak house, but the steak house burned down one night—a grease fire in the kitchen. After that, she couldn't find a steady job, and she was reluctant to ask her mother to keep Rodney again because of her bad hip. At the steak house, men gave her tips and left their telephone numbers on the bill when they paid. They tucked dollar bills and notes in the pockets of her apron. One note said, "I want to hold your muffins." They were real-estate developers and businessmen on important missions for the Tennessee Valley Authority. They were boisterous and they drank too much. They said they'd take her for a cruise on the *Delta Queen*, but she didn't believe them. She knew how expensive that was. They talked about their speed-boats and invited her for rides on Lake Barkley, or for spins in their private planes. They always used the word *spin*. The idea made her dizzy. Once, Jeannette let an electronics salesman take her for a ride in his Cadillac, and they breezed down the wilderness road through the Land Between the Lakes. His car had automatic windows and a stereo system and lighted computer-screen numbers on the dash that told him how many miles to the gallon he was getting and other statistics. He said the numbers distracted him and he had almost had several wrecks. At the restaurant, he had been flamboyant, admired by his companions. Alone with Jeannette in the Cadillac, on The Trace, he was shy and awkward, and really not very interesting. The most interesting thing about him, Jeannette thought, was all the lighted numbers on his dashboard. The Cadillac had everything but video games. But she'd rather be riding around with Donald, no matter where they ended up.

While the social worker is there, filling out her report, Jeannette listens for Donald's car. When the social worker drove up, the flutter and wheeze of her car sounded like Donald's old Chevy, and for a moment Jeannette's mind lapsed back in time. Now she listens, hoping he won't drive up. The social worker is younger than Jeannette and has been to college. Her name is Miss Bailey, and she's excessively cheerful, as though in her line of work she has seen hardships that make Jeannette's troubles seem like a trip to Hawaii.

"Is your little boy still having those bad dreams?" Miss Bailey asks, looking up from her clipboard.

Jeannette nods and looks at Rodney, who has his finger in his mouth and won't speak.

"Has the cat got your tongue?" Miss Bailey asks.   65

"Show her your pictures, Rodney." Jeannette explains, "He won't talk about the dreams, but he draws pictures of them."

Rodney brings his tablet of pictures and flips through them silently. Miss Bailey says, "Hmm." They are stark line drawings, remarkably steady lines for his age. "What is this one?" she asks. "Let me guess. Two scoops of ice cream?"

The picture is two huge circles, filling the page, with three tiny stick people in the corner.

"These are Big Bertha's titties," says Rodney.

Miss Bailey chuckles and winks at Jeannette. "What do you like to read, hon?"   70 she asks Rodney.

"Nothing."

"He can read," says Jeannette. "He's smart."

"Do you like to read?" Miss Bailey asks Jeannette. She glances at the pile of paperbacks on the coffee table. She is probably going to ask where Jeannette got the money for them.

"I don't read," says Jeannette. "If I read, I just go crazy."

When she told The Rapist she couldn't concentrate on anything serious, he   75 said she read romance novels in order to escape from reality. "Reality, hell!" she had said. "Reality's my whole problem."

"It's too bad Rodney's not here," Donald is saying. Rodney is in the closet again. "Santa Claus has to take back all these toys. Rodney would love this bicycle! And this Pac-Man game. Santa has to take back so many things he'll have to have a pickup truck!"

"You didn't bring him anything. You never bring him anything," says Jeannette.

He has brought doughnuts and dirty laundry. The clothes he is wearing are caked with clay. His beard is lighter from working out in the sun, and he looks his usual joyful self, the way he always is before his moods take over, like migraine headaches, which some people describe as storms.

Donald coaxes Rodney out of the closet with the doughnuts.

"Were you a good boy this week?"   80

"I don't know."

"I hear you went to the shopping center and showed out." It is not true that Rodney made a big scene. Jeannette has already explained that Rodney was upset because she wouldn't buy him an Atari. But she didn't blame him for crying. She was tired of being unable to buy him anything.

Rodney eats two doughnuts and Donald tells him a long, confusing story about Big Bertha and a rock-and-roll band. Rodney interrupts him with dozens of questions. In the story, the rock-and-roll band gives a concert in a place that turns out to be a toxic-waste dump and the contamination is spread all over the country. Big Bertha's solution to this problem is not at all clear. Jeannette stays in the kitchen, trying to think of something original to do with instant potatoes and leftover barbecue.

"We can't go on like this," she says that evening in bed. "We're just hurting each other. Something has to change."

He grins like a kid. "Coming home from Muhlenberg County is like R and   85
R—rest and recreation. I explain that in case you think R and R means rock and roll. Or maybe rumps and rears. Or rust and rot." He laughs and draws a circle in the air with his cigarette.

"I'm not that dumb."

"When I leave, I go back to the mines." He sighs, as though the mines were some eternal burden.

Her mind skips ahead to the future: Donald locked away somewhere, coloring in a coloring book and making clay pots, her and Rodney in some other town, with another man—someone dull and not at all sexy. Summoning up her courage, she says, "I haven't been through what you've been through and maybe I don't have a right to say this, but sometimes I think you act superior because you went to Vietnam, like nobody can ever know what you know. Well, maybe not. But you've still got your legs, even if you don't know what to do with what's between them anymore." Bursting into tears of apology, she can't help adding, "You can't go on telling Rodney those awful stories. He has nightmares when you're gone."

Donald rises from bed and grabs Rodney's picture from the dresser, holding it as he might have held a hand grenade. "Kids betray you," he says, turning the picture in his hand.

"If you cared about him, you'd stay here." As he sets the picture down, she   90
asks, "What can I do? How can I understand what's going on in your mind? Why do you go there? Strip mining's bad for the ecology and you don't have any business strip mining."

"My job is serious, Jeannette. I run that steam shovel and put the topsoil back on. I'm reclaiming the land." He keeps talking, in a gentler voice, about strip mining, the same old things she has heard before, comparing Big Bertha to a supertank. If only they had had Big Bertha in Vietnam. He says, "When they strip off the top, I keep looking for those tunnels where the Viet Cong hid. They had so many tunnels it was unbelievable. Imagine Mammoth Cave going all the way across Kentucky."

"Mammoth Cave's one of the natural wonders of the world," says Jeannette brightly. She is saying the wrong thing again.

At the kitchen table at 2 A.M., he's telling about C-5A's. A C-5A is so big it can carry trooops and tanks and helicopters, but it's not big enough to hold Big Bertha. Nothing could hold Big Bertha. He rambles on, and when Jeannette shows him Rodney's drawing of the circles, Donald smiles. Dreamily, he begins talking about women's breasts and thighs—the large, round thighs and big round breasts of American women, contrasted with the frail, delicate beauty of the Orientals. It is like comparing oven broilers and banties, he says. Jeannette relaxes. A confession about another lover from long ago is not so hard to take. He seems stuck on the breasts and thighs of American women—insisting that she understand how small and delicate the Orientals are, but then he abruptly returns to tanks and helicopters.

"A Bell Huey Cobra—my God, what a beautiful machine. So efficient!" Donald takes the food processor blade from the drawer where Jeannette keeps it. He says, "A rotor blade from a chopper could just slice anything to bits."

"Don't do that," Jeannette says.   95

He is trying to spin the blade on the counter, like a top. "Here's what would happen when a chopper blade hits a power line—not many of those over there!—or a tree. Not many trees, either, come to think of it, after all the Agent Orange." He drops the blade and it glances off the open drawer and falls to the floor, spiking the vinyl.

At first, Jeannette thinks the screams are hers, but they are his. She watches him cry. She has never seen anyone cry so hard, like an intense summer thundershower. All she knows to do is shove Kleenex at him. Finally, he is able to say, "You thought I was going to hurt you. That's why I'm crying."

"Go ahead and cry," Jeannette says, holding him close.

"Don't go away."

"I'm right here. I'm not going anywhere."   100

In the night, she still listens, knowing his monologue is being burned like a tattoo into her brain. She will never forget it. His voice grows soft and he plays with a ballpoint pen, jabbing holes in a paper towel. Bullet holes, she thinks. His beard is like a bird's nest, woven with dark corn silks.

"This is just a story," he says. "Don't mean nothing. Just relax." She is sitting on the hard edge of the kitchen chair, her toes cold on the floor, waiting. His tears have dried up and left a slight catch in his voice.

"We were in a big camp near a village. It was pretty routine and kind of soft there for a while. Now and then we'd go into Da Nang and whoop it up. We had been in the jungle for several months, so the two months at this village was

A sort of rest—an R and R almost. Don't shiver. This is just a little story. Don't mean nothing! This is nothing, compared to what I could tell you. Just listen. We lost our fear. At night there would be some incoming and we'd see these tracers in the sky, like shooting stars up close, but it was all pretty minor and we didn't take it seriously, after what we'd been through. In the village I knew this Vietnamese family—a woman and her two daughters. They sold Cokes and beer to GIs. The oldest daughter was named Phan. She could speak a little English. She was really smart. I used to go see them in their hooch in the afternoons—in the siesta time of day. It was so hot there. Phan was beautiful, like the country. The village was ratty, but the country was pretty. And she was beautiful, just like she had grown up out of the jungle, like one of those flowers that bloomed high up in the trees and freaked us out sometimes, thinking it was a sniper. She was so gentle, with these eyes shaped like peach pits, and she was no bigger than a child of maybe thirteen or fourteen. I felt funny about her size at first, but later it didn't matter. It was just some wonderful feature about her, like a woman's hair, or her breasts."

He stops and listens, the way they used to listen for crying sounds when Rodney was a baby. He says, "She'd take those big banana leaves and fan me while I lay there in the heat."

"I didn't know they had bananas over there." 105

"There's a lot you don't know! Listen! Phan was twenty-three, and her brothers were off fighting. I never even asked which side they were fighting on." He laughs. "She got a kick out of the word *fan*. I told her that *fan* was the same word as her name. She thought I meant her name was banana. In Vietnamese the same word can have a dozen different meanings, depending on your tone of voice. I bet you didn't know that, did you?"

"No. What happened to her?"

"I don't know."

"Is that the end of the story?"

"I don't know." Donald pauses, then goes on talking about the village, the 110 girl, the banana leaves, talking in a monotone that is making Jeannette's flesh crawl. He could be the news radio from the next room.

"You must have really liked that place. Do you wish you could go back there to find out what happened to her?"

"It's not there anymore," he says. "It blew up."

Donald abruptly goes to the bathroom. She hears the water running, the pipes in the basement shaking.

"It was so pretty," he says when he returns. He rubs his elbow absentmindedly. "That jungle was the most beautiful place in the world. You'd have thought you were in paradise. But we blew it sky-high."

In her arms, he is shaking, like the pipes in the basement, which are still 115 vibrating. Then the pipes let go, after a long shudder, but he continues to tremble.

They are driving to the Veterans Hospital. It was Donald's idea. She didn't have to persuade him. When she made up the bed that morning—with a finality that shocked her, as though she knew they wouldn't be in it again together—he told her it would be like R and R. Rest was what he needed. Neither of them had slept at all during the night. Jeannette felt she had to stay awake, to listen for more.

"Talk about strip mining," she says now. "That's what they'll do to your head. They'll dig out all those ugly memories, I hope. We don't need them around here." She pats his knee.

It is a cloudless day, not the setting for this sober journey. She drives and Donald goes along obediently, with the resignation of an old man being taken to a rest home. They are driving through southern Illinois, known as Little Egypt, for some obscure reason Jeannette has never understood. Donald still talks, but very quietly, without urgency. When he points out the scenery, Jeannette thinks of the early days of their marriage, when they would take a drive like this and laugh hysterically. Now Jeannette points out funny things they see. The Little Egypt Hot Dog World, Pharaoh Cleaners, Pyramid Body Shop. She is scarcely aware that she is driving, and when she sees a sign, LITTLE EGYPT STARLITE CLUB, she is confused for a moment, wondering where she has been transported.

As they part, he asks, "What will you tell Rodney if I don't come back? What if they keep me here indefinitely?"

"You're coming back. I'm telling him you're coming back soon."   120

"Tell him I went off with Big Bertha. Tell him she's taking me on a sea cruise, to the South Seas."

"No. You can tell him that yourself."

He starts singing "Sea Cruise." He grins at her and pokes her in the ribs.

"You're coming back," she says.

Donald writes from the VA Hospital, saying that he is making progress. They   125 are running tests, and he meets in a therapy group in which all the veterans trade memories. Jeannette is no longer on welfare because she now has a job waitressing at Fred's Family Restaurant. She waits on families, waits for Donald to come home so they can come here and eat together like a family. The fathers look at her with downcast eyes, and the children throw food. While Donald is gone, she rearranges the furniture. She reads some books from the library. She does a lot of thinking. It occurs to her that even though she loved him, she has thought of Donald primarily as a husband, a provider, someone whose name she shared, the father of her child, someone like the fathers who come to the Wednesday night all-you-can-eat fish fry. She hasn't thought of him as himself. She wasn't brought up that way, to examine someone's soul. When it comes to something deep inside, nobody will take it out and examine it, the way they will look at clothing in a store for flaws in the manufacturing. She tries to explain all this to The Rapist, and he says she's looking better, got sparkle in her eyes. "Big deal," says Jeannette. "Is that all you can say?"

She takes Rodney to the shopping center, their favorite thing to do together, even though Rodney always begs to buy something. They go to Penney's perfume counter. There, she usually hits a sample bottle of cologne—Chantilly or Charlie or something strong. Today she hits two or three and comes out of Penney's smelling like a flower garden.

"You stink!" Rodney cries, wrinkling his nose like a rabbit.

"Big Bertha smells like this, only a thousand times worse, she's so big," says Jeannette impulsively. "Didn't Daddy tell you that?"

"Daddy's a messenger from the devil."

This is an idea he must have gotten from church. Her parents have been 130 taking him every Sunday. When Jeannette tries to reassure him about his father, Rodney is skeptical. "He gets that funny look on his face like he can see through me," the child says.

"Something's missing," Jeannette says, with a rush of optimism, a feeling of recognition. "Something happened to him once and took out the part that shows how much he cares about us."

"The way we had the cat fixed?"

"I guess. Something like that." The appropriateness of his remark stuns her, as though, in a way, her child has understood Donald all along. Rodney's pictures have been more peaceful lately, pictures of skinny trees and airplanes flying low. This morning he drew pictures of tall grass, with creatures hiding in it. The grass is tilted at an angle, as though a light breeze is blowing through it.

With her paycheck, Jeannette buys Rodney a present, a miniature trampo- 135 line they have seen advertised on television. It is called Mr. Bouncer. Rodney is thrilled about the trampoline, and he jumps on it until his face is red. Jeannette discovers that she enjoys it, too. She puts it out on the grass, and they take turns jumping. She has an image of herself on the trampoline, her sailor collar flapping, at the moment when Donald returns and sees her flying. One day a neighbor driving by slows down and calls out to Jeannette as she is bouncing on the trampoline, "You'll tear your insides loose!" Jeannette starts thinking about that, and the idea is so horrifying she stops jumping so much. That night, she has a nightmare about the trampoline. In her dream, she is jumping on soft moss, and then it turns into a springy pile of dead bodies.

Joyce Carol Oates

WHERE ARE YOU GOING, WHERE HAVE YOU BEEN?   1970

Joyce Carol Oates was born in 1938 into a blue-collar family in Lockport, New York. As an undergraduate at Syracuse University, she won a Mademoiselle *magazine award for fiction. After graduation with top honors, she took a master's degree in English at the University of Wisconsin and went on to teach at universities: Detroit, Windsor, and Princeton. She now lives in Princeton, New Jersey, where together with her husband, Raymond Smith, she directs the Ontario Review Press, literary publishers. A remarkably prolific writer, Oates so far has produced nearly half a hundred collections of stories; more than twenty novels including* Them, *winner of a National Book Award in 1970, and* Because It Is Bitter, and

Joyce Carol Oates

Because It Is My Heart (1990); poetry, plays and literary criticism. Woman Writer: *Occasions & Opportunities (1988) is a book of varied essays;* On Boxing *(1987) is a nonfiction memoir and study of fighters and fighting. Violence and the macabre may inhabit her best stories, but Oates has insisted that these elements in her work are never gratuitous.* Smooth Talk, *a recent film directed by Joyce Chopra, was based on "Where Are You Going, Where Have You Been?"*

For Bob Dylan

Her name was Connie. She was fifteen and she had a quick nervous giggling habit of craning her neck to glance into mirrors, or checking other people's faces to make sure her own was all right. Her mother, who noticed everything and knew everything and who hadn't much reason any longer to look at her own face, always scolded Connie about it. "Stop gawking at yourself, who are you? You think you're so pretty?" she would say. Connie would raise her eyebrows at these familiar complaints and look right through her mother, into a shadowy vision of herself as she was right at that moment: she knew she was pretty and that was everything. Her mother had been pretty once too, if you could believe those old snapshots in the album, but now her looks were gone and that was why she was always after Connie.

"Why don't you keep your room clean like your sister? How've you got your hair fixed—what the hell stinks? Hair spray? You don't see your sister using that junk."

Her sister June was twenty-four and still lived at home. She was a secretary in the high school Connie attended, and if that wasn't bad enough—with her in the same building—she was so plain and chunky and steady that Connie had to hear her praised all the time by her mother and her mother's sisters. June did this, June did that, she saved money and helped clean the house and cooked and Connie couldn't do a thing, her mind was all filled with trashy daydreams. Their father was away at work most of the time and when he came home he wanted supper and he read the newspaper at supper and after supper he went to bed. He didn't bother talking much to them, but around his bent head Connie's mother kept picking at her until Connie wished her mother was dead and she herself was dead and it was all over. "She makes me want to throw up sometimes," she complained to her friends. She had a high, breathless, amused voice which made everything she said sound a little forced, whether it was sincere or not.

There was one good thing: June went places with girl friends of hers, girls who were just as plain and steady as she, and so when Connie wanted to do that her mother had no objections. The father of Connie's best girl friend drove the girls the three miles to town and left them off at a shopping plaza, so that they could walk through the stores or go to a movie, and when he came to pick them up again at eleven he never bothered to ask what they had done.

They must have been familiar sights, walking around that shopping plaza in   5
their shorts and flat ballerina slippers that always scuffed the sidewalk, with charm bracelets jingling on their thin wrists; they would lean together to whisper and laugh secretly if someone passed by who amused or interested them. Connie had long dark blond hair that drew anyone's eye to it, and she wore part of it pulled

up on her head and puffed out and the rest of it she let fall down her back. She wore a pull-over jersey blouse that looked one way when she was at home and another way when she was away from home. Everything about her had two sides to it, one for home and one for anywhere that was not home: her walk that could be childlike and bobbing, or languid enough to make anyone think she was hearing music in her head, her mouth which was pale and smirking most of the time, but bright and pink on these evenings out, her laugh which was cynical and drawling at home—"Ha, ha, very funny"—but high-pitched and nervous anywhere else, like the jingling of the charms on her bracelet.

Sometimes they did go shopping or to a movie, but sometimes they went across the highway, ducking fast across the busy road, to a drive-in restaurant where older kids hung out. The restaurant was shaped like a big bottle, though squatter than a real bottle, and on its cap was a revolving figure of a grinning boy who held a hamburger aloft. One night in mid-summer they ran across, breathless with daring, and right away someone leaned out a car window and invited them over, but it was just a boy from high school they didn't like. It made them feel good to be able to ignore him. They went up through the maze of parked and cruising cars to the bright-lit, fly-infested restaurant, their faces pleased and expectant as if they were entering a sacred building that loomed out of the night to give them what haven and what blessing they yearned for. They sat at the counter and crossed their legs at the ankles, their thin shoulders rigid with excitement, and listened to the music that made everything so good: the music was always in the background like music at a church service, it was something to depend upon.

A boy named Eddie came in to talk with them. He sat backwards on his stool, turning himself jerkily around in semi-circles and then stopping and turning again, and after a while he asked Connie if she would like something to eat. She said she did and so she tapped her friend's arm on her way out—her friend pulled her face up into a brave droll look—and Connie said she would meet her at eleven, across the way. "I just hate to leave her like that," Connie said earnestly, but the boy said that she wouldn't be alone for long. So they went out to his car and on the way Connie couldn't help but let her eyes wander over the windshields and faces all around her, her face gleaming with a joy that had nothing to do with Eddie or even this place; it might have been the music. She drew her shoulders up and sucked in her breath with the pure pleasure of being alive, and just at that moment she happened to glance at a face just a few feet from hers. It was a boy with shaggy black hair, in a convertible jalopy painted gold. He stared at her and then his lips widened into a grin. Connie slit her eyes at him and turned away, but she couldn't help glancing back and there he was still watching her. He wagged a finger and laughed and said, "Gonna get you, baby," and Connie turned away again without Eddie noticing anything.

She spent three hours with him, at the restaurant where they ate hamburgers and drank Cokes in wax cups that were always sweating, and then down an alley a mile or so away, and when he left her off at five to eleven only the movie house was still open at the plaza. Her girl friend was there, talking with a boy. When Connie came up the two girls smiled at each other and Connie said, "How was the movie?" and the girl said, "You should know." They rode off with the girl's father, sleepy and pleased, and Connie couldn't help but look at the darkened shopping plaza with its big empty parking lot and its signs that were faded and ghostly now, and over at the drive-in restaurant where cars were still circling tirelessly. She couldn't hear the music at this distance.

Next morning June asked her how the movie was and Connie said, "So-so."

She and that girl and occasionally another girl went out several times a week that way, and the rest of the time Connie spent around the house—it was summer vacation—getting in her mother's way and thinking, dreaming, about the boys she met. But all the boys fell back and dissolved into a single face that was not even a face, but an idea, a feeling, mixed up with the urgent insistent pounding of the music and the humid night air of July. Connie's mother kept dragging her back to the daylight by finding things for her to do or saying, suddenly, "What's this about the Pettinger girl?" 10

And Connie would say nervously, "Oh, her. That dope." She always drew thick clear lines between herself and such girls, and her mother was simple and kindly enough to believe her. Her mother was so simple, Connie thought, that it was maybe cruel to fool her so much. Her mother went scuffling around the house in old bedroom slippers and complained over the telephone to one sister about the other, then the other called up and the two of them complained about the third one. If June's name was mentioned her mother's tone was approving, and if Connie's name was mentioned it was disapproving. This did not really mean she disliked Connie and actually Connie thought that her mother preferred her to June because she was prettier, but the two of them kept up a pretense of exasperation, a sense that they were tugging and struggling over something of little value to either of them. Sometimes, over coffee, they were almost friends, but something would come up—some vexation that was like a fly buzzing suddenly around their heads—and their faces went hard with contempt.

One Sunday Connie got up at eleven—none of them bothered with church—and washed her hair so that it could dry all day long, in the sun. Her parents and sister were going to a barbecue at an aunt's house and Connie said no, she wasn't interested, rolling her eyes to let her mother know just what she thought of it. "Stay home alone then," her mother said sharply. Connie sat out back in a lawn chair and watched them drive away, her father quiet and bald, hunched around so that he could back the car out, her mother with a look that was still angry and not at all softened through the windshield, and in the back seat poor old June all dressed up as if she didn't know what a barbecue was, with all the running yelling kids and the flies. Connie sat with her eyes closed in the sun, dreaming and dazed with the warmth about her as if this were a kind of love, the caresses of love, and her mind slipped over onto thoughts of the boy she had been with the night before and how nice he had been, how sweet it always was, not the way someone like June would suppose but sweet, gentle, the way it was in movies and promised in songs; and when she opened her eyes she hardly knew where she was, the back yard ran off into weeds and a fence-line of trees and behind it the sky was perfectly blue and still. The asbestos "ranch house" that was now three years old startled her—it looked small. She shook her head as if to get awake.

It was too hot. She went inside the house and turned on the radio to drown out the quiet. She sat on the edge of her bed, barefoot, and listened for an hour and a half to a program called XYZ Sunday Jamboree, record after record of hard, fast, shrieking songs she sang along with, interspersed by exclamations from "Bobby King": "An' look here you girls at Napoleon's—Son and Charley want you to pay real close attention to this song coming up!"

And Connie paid close attention herself, bathed in a glow of slow-pulsed joy that seemed to rise mysteriously out of the music itself and lay languidly about the airless little room, breathed in and breathed out with each gentle rise and fall of her chest.

After a while she heard a car coming up the drive. She sat up at once, star- 15 tled, because it couldn't be her father so soon. The gravel kept crunching all the way in from the road—the driveway was long—and Connie ran to the window. It was a car she didn't know. It was an open jalopy, painted a bright gold that caught the sunlight opaquely. Her heart began to pound and her fingers snatched at her hair, checking it, and she whispered "Christ. Christ," wondering how bad she looked. The car came to a stop at the side door and the horn sounded four short taps as if this were a signal Connie knew.

She went into the kitchen and approached the door slowly, then hung out the screen door, her bare toes curling down off the step. There were two boys in the car and now she recognized the driver: he had shaggy, shabby black hair that looked crazy as a wig and he was grinning at her.

"I ain't late, am I?" he said.

"Who the hell do you think you are?" Connie said.

"Toldja I'd be out, didn't I?"

"I don't even know who you are." 20

She spoke sullenly, careful to show no interest or pleasure, and he spoke in a fast bright monotone. Connie looked past him to the other boy, taking her time. He had fair brown hair, with a lock that fell onto his forehead. His sideburns gave him a fierce, embarrassed look, but so far he hadn't even bothered to glance at her. Both boys wore sunglasses. The driver's glasses were metallic and mirrored everything in miniature.

"You wanta come for a ride?" he said.

Connie smirked and let her hair fall loose over one shoulder.

"Don'tcha like my car? New paint job," he said. "Hey."

"What?" 25

"You're cute."

She pretended to fidget, chasing flies away from the door.

"Don'tcha believe me, or what?" he said.

"Look, I don't even know who you are," Connie said in disgust.

"Hey, Ellie's got a radio, see. Mine's broke down." He lifted his friend's arm 30 and showed her the little transistor the boy was holding, and now Connie began to hear the music. It was the same program that was playing inside the house.

"Bobby King?" she said.

"I listen to him all the time. I think he's great."

"He's kind of great," Connie said reluctantly.

"Listen, that guy's *great*. He knows where the action is."

Connie blushed a little, because the glasses made it impossible for her to see 35 just what this boy was looking at. She couldn't decide if she liked him or if he was just a jerk, and so she dawdled in the doorway and wouldn't come down or go back inside. She said, "What's all that stuff painted on your car?"

"Can'tcha read it?" He opened the door very carefully, as if he was afraid it might fall off. He slid out just as carefully, planting his feet firmly on the ground, the tiny metallic world in his glasses slowing down like gelatine hardening and in the midst of it Connie's bright green blouse. "This here is my name, to begin with," he said. ARNOLD FRIEND was written in tarlike black letters on the side, with a drawing of a round grinning face that reminded Connie of a pumpkin, except it wore sunglasses. "I wanta introduce myself, I'm Arnold Friend and that's my real name and I'm gonna be your friend, honey, and inside the car's Ellie Oscar, he's kinda shy." Ellie brought his transistor radio up to his shoulder and balanced it there. "Now these numbers are a secret code, honey," Arnold Friend explained. He read off the numbers 33, 19, 17 and raised his eyebrows at her to see what she thought of that, but she didn't think much of it. The left rear fender had been smashed and around it was written, on the gleaming gold background: DONE BY CRAZY WOMAN DRIVER. Connie had to laugh at that. Arnold Friend was pleased at her laughter and looked up at her. "Around the other side's a lot more—you wanta come and see them?"

"No."

"Why not?"

"Why should I?"

"Don'tcha wanta see what's on the car? Don'tcha wanta go for a ride?"   40

"I don't know."

"Why not?"

"I got things to do."

"Like what?"

"Things."   45

He laughed as if she had said something funny. He slapped his thighs. He was standing in a strange way, leaning back against the car as if he were balancing himself. He wasn't tall, only an inch or so taller than she would be if she came down to him. Connie liked the way he was dressed, which was the way all of them dressed: tight faded jeans stuffed into black, scuffed boots, a belt that pulled his waist in and showed how lean he was, and a white pull-over shirt that was a little soiled and showed the hard small muscles of his arms and shoulders. He looked as if he probably did hard work, lifting and carrying things. Even his neck looked muscular. And his face was a familiar face, somehow: the jaw and chin and cheeks slightly darkened, because he hadn't shaved for a day or two, and the nose long and hawk-like, sniffing as if she were a treat he was going to gobble up and it was all a joke.

"Connie, you ain't telling the truth. This is your day set aside for a ride with me and you know it," he said, still laughing. The way he straightened and recovered from his fit of laughing showed that it had been all fake.

"How do you know what my name is?" she said suspiciously.

"It's Connie."

"Maybe and maybe not."   50

"I know my Connie," he said, wagging his finger. Now she remembered him even better, back at the restaurant, and her cheeks warmed at the thought of how she sucked in her breath just at the moment she passed him—how she must have looked to him. And he had remembered her. "Ellie and I come out here especially for you," he said. "Ellie can sit in back. How about it?"

"Where?"

"Where what?"

"Where're we going?"

He looked at her. He took off the sunglasses and she saw how pale the skin 55
around his eyes was, like holes that were not in shadow but instead in light. His eyes were chips of broken glass that catch the light in an amiable way. He smiled. It was as if the idea of going for a ride somewhere, to some place, was a new idea to him.

"Just for a ride, Connie sweetheart."

"I never said my name was Connie," she said.

"But I know what it is. I know your name and all about you, lots of things," Arnold Friend said. He had not moved yet but stood still leaning back against the side of his jalopy. "I took a special interest in you, such a pretty girl, and found out all about you like I know your parents and sister are gone somewheres and I know where and how long they're going to be gone, and I know who you were with last night, and your best girl friend's name is Betty. Right?"

He spoke in a simple lilting voice, exactly as if he were reciting the words to a song. His smile assured her that everything was fine. In the car Ellie turned up the volume on his radio and did not bother to look around at them.

"Ellie can sit in the back seat," Arnold Friend said. He indicated his friend 60
with a casual jerk of his chin, as if Ellie did not count and she should not bother with him.

"How'd you find out all that stuff?" Connie said.

"Listen: Betty Schultz and Tony Fitch and Jimmy Pettinger and Nancy Pettinger," he said, in a chant. "Raymond Stanley and Bob Hutter—"

"Do you know all those kids?"

"I know everybody."

"Look, you're kidding. You're not from around here." 65

"Sure."

"But—how come we never saw you before?"

"Sure you saw me before," he said. He looked down at his boots, as if he were a little offended. "You just don't remember."

"I guess I'd remember you," Connie said.

"Yeah?" He looked up at this, beaming. He was pleased. He began to mark 70
time with the music from Ellie's radio, tapping his fists lightly together. Connie looked away from his smile to the car, which was painted so bright it almost hurt her eyes to look at it. She looked at that name, ARNOLD FRIEND. And up at the front fender was an expression that was familiar—MAN THE FLYING SAUCERS. It was an expression kids had used the year before, but didn't use this year. She looked at if for a while as if the words meant something to her that she did not yet know.

"What're you thinking about? Huh?" Arnold Friend demanded. "Not worried about your hair blowing around in the car, are you?"

"No."

"Think I maybe can't drive good?"

"How do I know?"

"You're a hard girl to handle. How come?" he said. "Don't you know I'm your 75 friend? Didn't you see me put my sign in the air when you walked by?"

"What sign?"

"My sign." And he drew an X in the air, leaning out toward her. They were maybe ten feet apart. After his hand fell back to his side the X was still in the air, almost visible. Connie let the screen door close and stood perfectly still inside it, listening to the music from her radio and the boy's blend together. She stared at Arnold Friend. He stood there so stiffly relaxed, pretending to be relaxed, with one hand idly on the door handle as if he were keeping himself up that way and had no intention of ever moving again. She recognized most things about him, the tight jeans that showed his thighs and buttocks and the greasy leather boots and the tight shirt, and even that slippery friendly smile of his, that sleepy dreamy smile that all the boys used to get across ideas they didn't want to put into words. She recognized all this and also the singsong way he talked, slightly mocking, kidding, but serious and a little melancholy, and she recognized the way he tapped one fist against the other in homage to the perpetual music behind him. But all these things did not come together.

She said suddenly, "Hey, how old are you?"

His smile faded. She could see then that he wasn't a kid, he was much older— thirty, maybe more. At this knowledge her heart began to pound faster.

"That's a crazy thing to ask. Can'tcha see I'm your own age?" 80

"Like hell you are."

"Or maybe a coupla years older, I'm eighteen."

"Eighteen?" she said doubtfully.

He grinned to reassure her and lines appeared at the corners of his mouth. His teeth were big and white. He grinned so broadly his eyes became slits and she saw how thick the lashes were, thick and black as if painted with a black tarlike material. Then he seemed to become embarrassed, abruptly, and looked over his shoulder at Ellie. "*Him,* he's crazy," he said. "Ain't he a riot, he's a nut, a real character." Ellie was still listening to the music. His sunglasses told nothing about what he was thinking. He wore a bright orange shirt unbuttoned halfway to show his chest, which was a pale, bluish chest and not muscular like Arnold Friend's. His shirt collar was turned up all around and the very tips of the collar pointed out past his chin as if they were protecting him. He was pressing the transistor radio up against his ear and sat there in a kind of daze, right in the sun.

"He's kinda strange," Connie said. 85

"Hey, she says you're kinda strange! Kinda strange!" Arnold Friend cried. He pounded on the car to get Ellie's attention. Ellie turned for the first time and Connie saw with shock that he wasn't a kid either—he had a fair, hairless face, cheeks reddened slightly as if the veins grew too close to the surface of his skin, the face of a forty-year-old baby. Connie felt a wave of dizziness rise in her at this sight and she stared at him as if waiting for something to change the shock of the moment, make it all right again. Ellie's lips kept shaping words, mumbling along, with the words blasting in his ear.

"Maybe you two better go away," Connie said faintly.

"What? How come?" Arnold Friend cried. "We come out here to take you for a ride. It's Sunday." He had the voice of the man on the radio now. It was the same voice, Connie thought. "Don'tcha know it's Sunday all day and honey, no matter who you were with last night today you're with Arnold Friend and don't you forget it!—Maybe you better step out here," he said, and this last was in a different voice. It was a little flatter, as if the heat was finally getting to him.

"No. I got things to do."

"Hey." 90

"You two better leave."

"We ain't leaving until you come with us."

"Like hell I am—"

"Connie, don't fool around with me. I mean, I mean, don't fool *around*," he said, shaking his head. He laughed incredulously. He placed his sunglasses on top of his head, carefully, as if he were indeed wearing a wig, and brought the stems down behind his ears. Connie stared at him, another wave of dizziness and fear rising in her so that for a moment he wasn't even in focus but was just a blur, standing there against his gold car, and she had the idea that he had driven up the driveway all right but had come from nowhere before that and belonged nowhere and that everything about him and even about the music that was so familiar to her was only half real.

"If my father comes and sees you—" 95

"He ain't coming. He's at the barbecue."

"How do you know that?"

"Aunt Tillie's. Right now they're—uh—they're drinking. Sitting around," he said vaguely, squinting as if he were staring all the way to town and over to Aunt Tillie's backyard. Then the vision seemed to get clear and he nodded energetically. "Yeah. Sitting around. There's your sister in a blue dress, huh? And high heels, the poor sad bitch—nothing like you, sweetheart! And your mother's helping some fat woman with the corn, they're cleaning the corn—husking the corn—"

"What fat woman?" Connie cried.

"How do I know what fat woman. I don't know every goddam fat woman 100 in the world!" Arnold Friend laughed.

"Oh, that's Mrs. Hornby . . . . Who invited her?" Connie said. She felt a little light-headed. Her breath was coming quickly.

"She's too fat. I don't like them fat. I like them the way you are, honey," he said, smiling sleepily at her. They stared at each other for a while, through the screen door. He said softly, "Now what you're going to do is this: you're going to come out that door. You're going to sit up front with me and Ellie's going to sit in the back, the hell with Ellie, right? This isn't Ellie's date. You're my date. I'm your lover, honey."

"What? You're crazy—"

"Yes, I'm your lover. You don't know what that is but you will," he said. "I know that too. I know all about you. But look: it's real nice and you couldn't ask for nobody better than me, or more polite. I always keep my word. I'll tell you how it is, I'm always nice at first, the first time. I'll hold you so tight you won't think you have to try to get away or pretend anything because you'll know you can't. And I'll come inside you where it's all secret and you'll give in to me and you'll love me—"

"Shut up! You're crazy!" Connie said. She backed away from the door. She put her hands against her ears as if she'd heard something terrible, something not meant for her. "People don't talk like that, you're crazy," she muttered. Her heart was almost too big now for her chest and its pumping made sweat break out all over her. She looked out to see Arnold Friend pause and then take a step toward the porch lurching. He almost fell. But, like a clever drunken man, he managed to catch his balance. He wobbled in his high boots and grabbed hold of one of the porch posts.

"Honey?" he said. "You still listening?"

"Get the hell out of here!"

"Be nice, honey. Listen."

"I'm going to call the police—"

He wobbled again and out of the side of his mouth came a fast spat curse, an aside not meant for her to hear. But even this "Christ!" sounded forced. Then he began to smile again. She watched this smile come, awkward as if he were smiling from inside a mask. His whole face was a mask, she thought wildly, tanned down onto his throat but then running out as if he had plastered make-up on his face but had forgotten about his throat.

"Honey—? Listen, here's how it is. I always tell the truth and I promise you this: I ain't coming in that house after you."

"You better not! I'm going to call the police if you—if you don't—"

"Honey," he said, talking right through her voice, "honey, I'm not coming in there but you are coming out here. You know why?"

She was panting. The kitchen looked like a place she had never seen before, some room she had run inside but which wasn't good enough, wasn't going to help her. The kitchen window had never had a curtain, after three years, and there were dishes in the sink for her to do—probably—and if you ran your hand across the table you'd probably feel something sticky there.

"You listening, honey? Hey?"

"—going to call the police—"

"Soon as you touch the phone I don't need to keep my promise and can come inside. You won't want that."

She rushed forward and tried to lock the door. Her fingers were shaking. "But why lock it," Arnold Friend said gently, talking right into her face. "It's just a screen door. It's just nothing." One of his boots was at a strange angle, as if his foot wasn't in it. It pointed out to the left, bent at the ankle. "I mean, anybody can break through a screen door and glass and wood and iron or anything else if he needs to, anybody at all and specially Arnold Friend. If the place got lit up with a fire honey you'd come running out into my arms, right into my arms and safe at home—like you knew I was your lover and'd stopped fooling around. I don't mind a nice shy girl but I don't like no fooling around." Part of those words were spoken with a slight rhythmic lilt, and Connie somehow recognized them—the echo of a song from last year, about a girl rushing into her boy friend's arms and coming home again—

Connie stood barefoot on the linoleum floor, staring at him. "What do you want?" she whispered.

"I want you," he said. 120

"What?"

"Seen you that night and thought, that's the one, yes sir. I never needed to look any more."

"But my father's coming back. He's coming to get me. I had to wash my hair first—" She spoke in a dry, rapid voice, hardly raising it for him to hear.

"No, your daddy is not coming and yes, you had to wash your hair and you washed it for me. It's nice and shining and all for me, I thank you, sweetheart," he said, with a mock bow, but again he almost lost his balance. He had to bend and adjust his boots. Evidently his feet did not go all the way down; the boots must have been stuffed with something so that he would seem taller. Connie stared out at him and behind him Ellie in the car, who seemed to be looking off toward Connie's right, into nothing. This Ellie said, pulling the words out of the air one after another as if he were just discovering them, "You want me to pull out the phone?"

"Shut your mouth and keep it shut," Arnold Friend said, his face red from 125 bending over or maybe from embarrassment because Connie had seen his boots. "This ain't none of your business."

"What—what are you doing? What do you want?" Connie said. "If I call the police they'll get you, they'll arrest you—"

"Promise was not to come in unless you touch that phone, and I'll keep that promise," he said. He resumed his erect position and tried to force his shoulders back. He sounded like a hero in a movie, declaring something important. He spoke too loudly and it was as if he were speaking to someone behind Connie. "I ain't made plans for coming in that house where I don't belong but just for you to come out to me, the way you should. Don't you know who I am?"

"You're crazy," she whispered. She backed away from the door but did not want to go into another part of the house, as if this would give him permission to come through the door. "What do you . . . You're crazy, you . . . "

"Huh? What're you saying, honey?"

Her eyes darted everywhere in the kitchen. She could not remember what 130 it was, this room.

"This is how it is, honey: you come out and we'll drive away, have a nice ride. But if you don't come out we're gonna wait till your people come home and then they're all going to get it."

"You want that telephone pulled out?" Ellie said. He held the radio away from his ear and grimaced, as if without the radio the air was too much for him.

"I toldja shut up, Ellie," Arnold Friend said, "you're deaf, get a hearing aid, right? Fix yourself up. This little girl's no trouble and's gonna be nice to me, so Ellie keep to yourself, this ain't your date—right? Don't hem in on me. Don't hog. Don't crush. Don't bird dog. Don't trail me," he said in a rapid meaningless voice, as if he were running through all the expressions he'd learned but was no longer sure which one of them was in style, then rushing on to new ones, making them up with his eyes closed, "Don't crawl under my fence, don't squeeze in my chipmunk hole, don't sniff my glue, suck my popsicle, keep your own greasy fingers on yourself!" He shaded his eyes and peered in at Connie, who was backed against the kitchen table. "Don't mind him honey he's just a creep. He's a dope. Right? I'm the boy for you and like I said you come out here nice like a lady and give me your hand, and nobody else gets hurt, I mean, your nice old bald-headed daddy and your mummy and your sister in her high heels. Because listen: why bring them in this?"

"Leave me alone," Connie whispered.

"Hey, you know that old woman down the road, the one with the chickens 135
and stuff—you know her?"

"She's dead!"

"Dead? What? You know her?" Arnold Friend said.

"She's dead—"

"Don't you like her?"

"She's dead—she's—she isn't here any more—" 140

"But don't you like her, I mean, you got something against her? Some grudge or something?" Then his voice dipped as if he were conscious of a rudeness. He touched the sunglasses perched on top of his head as if to make sure they were still there. "Now you be a good girl."

"What are you going to do?"

"Just two things, or maybe three," Arnold Friend said. "But I promise it won't last long and you'll like me that way you get to like people you're close to. You will. It's all over for you here, so come on out. You don't want your people in any trouble, do you?"

She turned and bumped against a chair or something, hurting her leg, but she ran into the back room and picked up the telephone. Something roared in her ear, a tiny roaring, and she was so sick with fear that she could do nothing but listen to it—the telephone was clammy and very heavy and her fingers groped down to the dial but were too weak to touch it. She began to scream into the phone, into the roaring. She cried out, she cried for her mother, she felt her breath start jerking back and forth in her lungs as if it were something Arnold Friend were stabbing her with again and again with no tenderness. A noisy sorrowful wailing rose all about her and she was locked inside it the way she was locked inside the house.

After a while she could hear again. She was sitting on the floor with her wet 145
back against the wall.

Arnold Friend was saying from the door, "That's a good girl. Put the phone back."

She kicked the phone away from her.

"No, honey. Pick it up. Put it back right."

She picked it up and put it back. The dial tone stopped.

"That's a good girl. Now come outside." 150

She was hollow with what had been fear, but what was now just an emptiness. All that screaming had blasted it out of her. She sat, one leg cramped under her, and deep inside her brain was something like a pinpoint of light that kept going and would not let her relax. She thought, I'm not going to see my mother again. She thought, I'm not going to sleep in my bed again. Her bright green blouse was all wet.

Arnold Friend said, in a gentle-loud voice that was like a stage voice, "The place where you came from ain't there any more, and where you had in mind to go is cancelled out. This place you are now—inside your daddy's house—is nothing but a cardboard box I can knock down any time. You know that and always did know it. You hear me?"

She thought, I have got to think. I have to know what to do.

"We'll go out to a nice field, out in the country here where it smells so nice and it's sunny," Arnold Friend said. "I'll have my arms around you so you won't need to try to get away and I'll show you what love is like, what it does. The hell with this house! It looks solid all right," he said. He ran a fingernail down the screen and the noise did not make Connie shiver, as it would have the day before. "Now put your hand on your heart, honey. Feel that? That feels solid too but we know better, be nice to me, be sweet like you can because what else is there for a girl like you but to be sweet and pretty and give in?—and get away before her people come back?"

She felt her pounding heart. Her hand seemed to enclose it. She thought   155
for the first time in her life that it was nothing that was hers, that belonged to her, but just a pounding, living thing inside this body that wasn't really hers either.

"You don't want them to get hurt," Arnold Friend went on. "Now get up, honey. Get up all by yourself."

She stood up.

"Now turn this way. That's right. Come over here to me—Ellie, put that away, didn't I tell you? You dope. You miserable creepy dope," Arnold Friend said. His words were not angry but only part of an incantation. The incantation was kindly. "Now come out through the kitchen to me honey and let's see a smile, try it, you're a brave sweet little girl and now they're eating corn and hotdogs cooked to bursting over an outdoor fire, and they don't know one thing about you and never did and honey you're better than them because not a one of them would have done this for you."

Connie felt the linoleum under her feet; it was cool. She brushed her hair back out of her eyes. Arnold Friend let go of the post tentatively and opened his arms for her, his elbows pointing in toward each other and his wrists limp, to show that this was an embarrassed embrace and a little mocking, he didn't want to make her self-conscious.

She put out her hand against the screen. She watched herself push the door   160
slowly open as if she were safe back somewhere in the other doorway, watching this body and this head of long hair moving out into the sunlight where Arnold Friend waited.

"My sweet little blue-eyed girl," he said, in a half-sung sigh that had nothing to do with her brown eyes but was taken up just the same by the vast sunlit reaches of the land behind him and on all sides of him, so much land that Connie had never seen before and did not recognize except to know that she was going to it.

Frank O'Connor

Frank O'Connor

Frank O'Connor was the pen name that Michael O'Donovan (1903–1966) adopted when he feared that to be known as a writer would hurt his career in civil service. He was born in Cork, Ireland's second city. Desperate poverty forced his parents to take him out of school after he had completed only fourth grade. During the troubles of 1918–21 that led to the new Irish Free State, he served in the Republican Army. After peace came, he worked as a librarian and for several years served as a director of Dublin's influential Abbey Theatre. America offered O'Connor-O'Donovan early hospitality: in 1931 The Atlantic printed his first story. In the 1950s he lived in America, teaching at Northwestern and Harvard. For a time he regularly appeared on CBS television on Sunday mornings, just sitting and telling stories. A fine literary critic, besides, he wrote The Mirror in the Roadway *(1956), a study of the novel, and* The Lonely Voice *(1963), a study of the short story. In* Kings, Lords & Commons *(1959), he proved himself a master translator of Gaelic poetry. O'Connor toiled hard over his stories, trying to polish each to the perfection of a good lyric. "First Confession" appeared in print in three versions because he kept rewriting it. The story is based upon his boyhood memories.*

All the trouble began when my grandfather died and my grandmother—my father's mother—came to live with us. Relations in the one house are a strain at the best of times, but, to make matters worse, my grandmother was a real old countrywoman and quite unsuited to the life in town. She had a fat, wrinkled old face, and, to Mother's great indignation, went round the house in bare feet—the boots had her crippled, she said. For dinner she had a jug of porter and a pot of potatoes with—sometimes—a bit of salt fish, and she poured out the potatoes on the table and ate them slowly, with great relish, using her fingers by way of a fork.

Now, girls are supposed to be fastidious, but I was the one who suffered most from this. Nora, my sister, just sucked up to the old woman for the penny she got every Friday out of the old-age pension, a thing I could not do. I was too honest, that was my trouble; and when I was playing with Bill Connell, the sergeant-major's son, and saw my grandmother steering up the path with the jug of porter sticking out from beneath her shawl I was mortified. I made excuses not to let him come into the house, because I could never be sure what she would be up to when we went in.

When Mother was at work and my grandmother made the dinner I wouldn't touch it. Nora once tried to make me, but I hid under the table from her and took the bread-knife with me for protection. Nora let on to be very indignant (she wasn't, of course, but she knew Mother saw through her, so she sided with Gran) and came after me. I lashed out at her with the bread-knife, and after that she left me alone. I stayed there till Mother came in from work and made my dinner, but when Father came in later Nora said in a shocked voice: "Oh, Dadda, do you know what Jackie did at dinnertime?" Then, of course, it all came out; Father gave me a flaking; Mother interfered, and for days after that he didn't speak to me and Mother barely spoke to Nora. And all because of that old woman! God knows, I was heart-scalded.

Then, to crown my misfortunes, I had to make my first confession and communion. It was an old woman called Ryan who prepared us for these. She was about the one age with Gran; she was well-to-do, lived in a big house on Montenotte, wore a black cloak and bonnet, and came every day to school at three o'clock when we should have been going home, and talked to us of hell. She may have mentioned the other place as well, but that could only have been by accident, for hell had the first place in her heart.

She lit a candle, took out a new half-crown, and offered it to the first boy who would hold one finger—only one finger!—in the flame for five minutes by the school clock. Being always very ambitious I was tempted to volunteer, but I thought it might look greedy. Then she asked were we afraid of holding one finger—only one finger!—in a little candle flame for five minutes and not afraid of burning all over in roasting hot furnaces for all eternity. "All eternity! Just think of that! A whole lifetime goes by and it's nothing, not even a drop in the ocean of your sufferings." The woman was really interesting about hell, but my attention was all fixed on the half-crown. At the end of the lesson she put it back in her purse. It was a great disappointment; a religious woman like that, you wouldn't think she'd bother about a thing like a half-crown.

Another day she said she knew a priest who woke one night to find a fellow he didn't recognize leaning over the end of his bed. The priest was a bit frightened—naturally enough—but he asked the fellow what he wanted, and the fellow said in a deep, husky voice that he wanted to go to confession. The priest said it was an awkward time and wouldn't it do in the morning, but the fellow said that last time he went to confession, there was one sin he kept back, being ashamed to mention it, and now it was always on his mind. Then the priest knew it was a bad case, because the fellow was after making a bad confession and committing a mortal sin. He got up to dress, and just then the cock crew in the yard outside, and—lo and behold!—when the priest looked round there was no sign of the fellow, only a smell of burning timber, and when the priest looked at his bed didn't he see the print of two hands burned in it? That was because the fellow had made a bad confession. This story made a shocking impression on me.

But the worst of all was when she showed us how to examine our conscience. Did we take the name of the Lord, our God, in vain? Did we honor our father and our mother? (I asked her did this include grandmothers and she said it did.)

5

Did we love our neighbors as ourselves? Did we covet our neighbor's goods? (I thought of the way I felt about the penny that Nora got every Friday.) I decided that, between one thing and another, I must have broken the whole ten commandments, all on account of that old woman, and so far as I could see, so long as she remained in the house I had no hope of ever doing anything else.

I was scared to death of confession. The day the whole class went I let on to have a toothache, hoping my absence wouldn't be noticed; but at three o'clock, just as I was feeling safe, along comes a chap with a message from Mrs. Ryan that I was to go to confession myself on Saturday and be at the chapel for communion with the rest. To make it worse, Mother couldn't come with me and sent Nora instead.

Now, that girl had ways of tormenting me that Mother never knew of. She held my hand as we went down the hill, smiling sadly and saying how sorry she was for me, as if she were bringing me to the hospital for an operation.

"Oh, God help us!" she moaned. "Isn't it a terrible pity you weren't a good   10
boy? Oh, Jackie, my heart bleeds for you! How will you ever think of all your sins? Don't forget you have to tell him about the time you kicked Gran on the shin."

"Lemme go!" I said, trying to drag myself free of her. "I don't want to go to confession at all."

"But sure, you'll have to go to confession, Jackie," she replied in the same regretful tone. "Sure, if you didn't, the parish priest would be up to the house, looking for you. 'Tisn't, God knows, that I'm not sorry for you. Do you remember the time you tried to kill me with the bread-knife under the table? And the language you used to me? I don't know what he'll do with you at all, Jackie. He might have to send you up to the bishop."

I remember thinking bitterly that she didn't know the half of what I had to tell—if I told it. I knew I couldn't tell it, and understood perfectly why the fellow in Mrs. Ryan's story made a bad confession; it seemed to me a great shame that people wouldn't stop criticizing him. I remember that steep hill down to the church, and the sunlit hillsides beyond the valley of the river, which I saw in the gaps between the houses like Adam's last glimpse of Paradise.

Then, when she had maneuvered me down the long flight of steps to the chapel yard, Nora suddenly changed her tone. She became the raging malicious devil she really was.

"There you are!" she said with a yelp of triumph, hurling me through the church   15
door. "And I hope he'll give you the penitential psalms, you dirty little caffler.°"

I knew then I was lost, given up to eternal justice. The door with the colored-glass panels swung shut behind me, the sunlight went out and gave place to deep shadow, and the wind whistled outside so that the silence within seemed to crackle like ice under my feet. Nora sat in front of me by the confession box. There were a couple of old women ahead of her, and then a miserable-looking poor devil came and wedged me in at the other side, so that I couldn't escape even if I had the courage. He joined his hands and rolled his eyes in the direction of the roof, muttering aspirations in an anguished tone, and I wondered had he a grandmother too. Only a grandmother could account for a fellow behaving in that heartbroken

caffler: scamp, rascal.

way, but he was better off than I, for he at least could go and confess his sins; while I would make a bad confession and then die in the night and be continually coming back and burning people's furniture.

Nora's turn came, and I heard the sound of something slamming, and then her voice as if butter wouldn't melt in her mouth, and then another slam, and out she came. God, the hypocrisy of women! Her eyes were lowered, her head was bowed, and her hands were joined very low down on her stomach, and she walked up the aisle to the side altar looking like a saint. You never saw such an exhibition of devotion; and I remembered the devilish malice with which she had tormented me all the way from our door, and wondered were all religious people like that, really. It was my turn now. With the fear of damnation in my soul I went in, and the confessional door closed of itself behind me.

It was pitch-dark and I couldn't see priest or anything else. Then I really began to be frightened. In the darkness it was a matter between God and me, and He had all the odds. He knew what my intentions were before I even started; I had no chance. All I had ever been told about confession got mixed up in my mind, and I knelt to one wall and said: "Bless me, father, for I have sinned; this is my first confession." I waited for a few minutes, but nothing happened, so I tried it on the other wall. Nothing happened there either. He had me spotted all right.

It must have been then that I noticed the shelf at about one height with my head. It was really a place for grown-up people to rest their elbows, but in my distracted state I thought it was probably the place you were supposed to kneel. Of course, it was on the high side and not very deep, but I was always good at climbing and managed to get up all right. Staying up was the trouble. There was room only for my knees, and nothing you could get a grip on but a sort of wooden moulding a bit above it. I held on to the moulding and repeated the words a little louder, and this time something happened all right. A slide was slammed back; a little light entered the box, and a man's voice said: "Who's there?"

"'Tis me, father," I said for fear he mightn't see me and go away again. I couldn't   20
see him at all. The place the voice came from was under the moulding, about level with my knees, so I took a good grip of the moulding and swung myself down till I saw the astonished face of a young priest looking up at me. He had to put his head on one side to see me, and I had to put mine on one side to see him, so we were more or less talking to one another upside-down. It struck me as a queer way of hearing confessions, but I didn't feel it my place to criticize.

"Bless me, father, for I have sinned; this is my first confession," I rattled off all in one breath, and swung myself down the least shade more to make it easier for him.

"What are you doing up there?" he shouted in an angry voice, and the strain the politeness was putting on my hold of the moulding, and the shock of being addressed in such an uncivil tone, were too much for me. I lost my grip, tumbled, and hit the door an unmerciful wallop before I found myself flat on my back in the middle of the aisle. The people who had been waiting stood up with their mouths open. The priest opened the door of the middle box and came out, pushing his biretta back from his forehead; he looked something terrible. Then Nora came scampering down the aisle.

"Oh, you dirty little caffler!" she said. "I might have known you'd do it. I might have known you'd disgrace me. I can't leave you out of my sight for one minute."

Before I could even get to my feet to defend myself she bent down and gave me a clip across the ear. This reminded me that I was so stunned I had even forgotten to cry, so that people might think I wasn't hurt at all, when in fact I was probably maimed for life. I gave a roar out of me.

"What's all this about?" the priest hissed, getting angrier than ever and pushing Nora off me. "How dare you hit the child like that, you little vixen?"   25

"But I can't do my penance with him, father," Nora cried, cocking an outraged eye up at him.

"Well, go and do it, or I'll give you some more to do," he said, giving me a hand up. "Was it coming to confession you were, my poor man?" he asked me.

" 'Twas, father," said I with a sob.

"Oh," he said respectfully, "a big hefty fellow like you must have terrible sins. Is this your first?"

" 'Tis, father," said I.   30

"Worse and worse," he said gloomily. "The crimes of a life-time. I don't know will I get rid of you at all today. You'd better wait now till I'm finished with these old ones. You can see by the looks of them they haven't much to tell."

"I will, father," I said with something approaching joy.

The relief of it was really enormous. Nora stuck out her tongue at me from behind his back, but I couldn't even be bothered retorting. I knew from the very moment that man opened his mouth that he was intelligent above the ordinary. When I had time to think, I saw how right I was. It only stood to reason that a fellow confessing after seven years would have more to tell then people that went every week. The crimes of a lifetime, exactly as he said. It was only what he expected, and the rest was the cackle of old women and girls with their talk of hell, the bishop, and the penitential psalms. That was all they knew. I started to make my examination of conscience, and barring the one bad business of my grandmother it didn't seem so bad.

The next time, the priest steered me into the confession box himself and left the shutter back the way I could see him get in and sit down at the further side of the grille from me.

"Well, now," he said, "what do they call you?"   35

"Jackie, father," said I.

"And what's a-trouble to you, Jackie?"

"Father," I said, feeling I might as well get it over while I had him in good humor, "I had it all arranged to kill my grandmother."

He seemed a bit shaken by that, all right, because he said nothing for quite a while.

"My goodness," he said at last, "that'd be a shocking thing to do. What put   40
that into your head?"

"Father," I said, feeling very sorry for myself, "she's an awful woman."

"Is she?" he asked. "What way is she awful?"

"She takes porter, father," I said, knowing well from the way Mother talked of it that this was a mortal sin, and hoping it would make the priest take a more favorable view of my case.

"Oh my!" he said, and I could see he was impressed.

"And snuff, father," said I.   45

"That's a bad case, sure enough, Jackie," he said.

"And she goes round in her bare feet, father," I went on in a rush of self-pity, "and she knows I don't like her, and she gives pennies to Nora and none to me, and my da sides with her and flakes me, and one night I was so heart-scalded I made up my mind I'd have to kill her."

"And what would you do with the body?" he asked with great interest.

"I was thinking I could chop that up and carry it away in a barrow I have," I said.

"Begor, Jackie," he said, "do you know you're a terrible child?"   50

"I know, father," I said, for I was just thinking the same thing myself. "I tried to kill Nora too with a bread-knife under the table, only I missed her."

"Is that the little girl that was beating you just now?" he asked.

" 'Tis, father."

"Someone will go for her with a bread-knife one day, and he won't miss her," he said rather cryptically. "You must have great courage. Between ourselves, there's a lot of people I'd like to do the same to but I'd never have the nerve. Hanging is an awful death."

"Is it, father?" I asked with the deepest interest—I was always very keen on   55
hanging. "Did you ever see a fellow hanged?"

"Dozens of them," he said solemnly. "And they all died roaring."

"Jay!" I said.

"Oh, a horrible death!" he said with great satisfaction. "Lots of the fellows I saw killed their grandmothers too, but they all said 'twas never worth it."

He had me there for a full ten minutes talking, and then walked out the chapel yard with me. I was genuinely sorry to part with him, because he was the most entertaining character I'd ever met in the religious line. Outside, after the shadow of the church, the sunlight was like the roaring of waves on a beach; it dazzled me; and when the frozen silence melted and I heard the screech of trams on the road my heart soared. I knew now I wouldn't die in the night and come back, leaving marks on my mother's furniture. It would be a great worry to her, and the poor soul had enough.

Nora was sitting on the railing, waiting for me, and she put on a very sour   60
puss when she saw the priest with me. She was mad jealous because a priest had never come out of the church with her.

"Well," she asked coldly, after he left me, "what did he give you?"

"Three Hail Marys," I said.

"Three Hail Marys," she repeatedly incredulously. "You mustn't have told him anything."

"I told him everything," I said confidently.

"About Gran and all?"   65

"About Gran and all."

(All she wanted was to be able to go home and say I'd made a bad confession.)

"Did you tell him you went for me with the bread-knife?" she asked with a frown.

"I did to be sure."

"And he only gave you three Hail Marys?"   70

"That's all."

She slowly got down from the railing with a baffled air. Clearly, this was beyond her. As we mounted the steps back to the main road she looked at me suspiciously.

"What are you sucking?" she asked.

"Bullseyes."

"Was it the priest gave them to you"

75

" 'Twas."

"Lord God," she wailed bitterly, "some people have all the luck! 'Tis no advantage to anybody trying to be good. I might just as well be a sinner like you."

Tillie Olsen

I Stand Here Ironing   1961

Tillie Olsen was born in Omaha in 1912, into a family of blue-collar workers who had fled Czarist Russia to escape persecution. Olsen grew up in poverty and quit school in eleventh grade to work. She later declared, "Public libraries were my college." As a member of the Young Communist League, she strove to organize Kansas City meat-packers, and was once thrown into jail. After her first husband deserted her, leaving her with one child, she married a printer and labor activist, Jack Olsen, by whom she had three more children. Although in the 1930s she published fiction in a distinguished little magazine, Partisan Review, *the demands of motherhood, political activity, and factory and office jobs left her scant time to write until 1955. Then her* Tillie Olsen
youngest daughter began school and Olsen was awarded a creative-writing fellowship at Stanford University. Long a crusader for causes, she has been active in the recent feminist movement. "I Stand Here Ironing," from her first book, Tell Me a Riddle *(1961), reads like autobiography. Olsen has since published* Yonnondio *(1974), an unfinished novel begun at age nineteen, and* Silences *(1978), a study of why writers—especially women writers—dry up. She holds several honorary degrees. In 1981 the city of San Francisco, where she has long resided, designated a Tillie Olsen day.*

I stand here ironing, and what you asked me moves tormented back and forth with the iron.

"I wish you would manage the time to come in and talk with me about your daughter. I'm sure you can help me understand her. She's a youngster who needs help and whom I'm deeply interested in helping."

"Who needs help." . . . Even if I came, what good would it do? You think because I am her mother I have a key, or that in some way you could use me as a key? She has lived for nineteen years. There is all that life that has happened outside of me, beyond me.

And when is there time to remember, to sift, to weigh, to estimate, to total? I will start and there will be an interruption and I will have to gather it all together again. Or I will become engulfed with all I did or did not do, with what should have been and what cannot be helped.

She was a beautiful baby. The first and only one of our five that was beautiful   5
at birth. You do not guess how new and uneasy her tenancy in her now-loveliness. You did not know her all those years she was thought homely, or see her poring over her baby pictures, making me tell her over and over how beautiful she had been—and would be, I would tell her—and was now, to the seeing eye. But the seeing eyes were few or nonexistent. Including mine.

I nursed her. They feel that's important nowadays. I nursed all the children, but with her, with all the fierce rigidity of first motherhood, I did like the books then said. Though her cries battered me to trembling and my breasts ached with swollenness, I waited till the clock decreed.

Why do I put that first? I do not even know if it matters, or if it explains anything.

She was a beautiful baby. She blew shining bubbles of sound. She loved motion, loved light, loved color and music and textures. She would lie on the floor in her blue overalls patting the surface so hard in ecstasy her hands and feet would blur. She was a miracle to me, but when she was eight months old I had to leave her daytimes with the woman downstairs to whom she was no miracle at all, for I worked or looked for work and for Emily's father, who "could no longer endure" (he wrote in his good-bye note) "sharing want with us."

I was nineteen. It was the pre-relief, pre-WPA world of the depression. I would start running as soon as I got off the streetcar, running up the stairs, the place smelling sour, and awake or asleep to startle awake, when she saw me she would break into a clogged weeping that could not be comforted, a weeping I can hear yet.

After a while I found a job hashing at night so I could be with her days,   10
and it was better. But it came to where I had to bring her to his family and leave her.

It took a long time to raise the money for her fare back. Then she got chicken pox and I had to wait longer. When she finally came, I hardly knew her, walking quick and nervous like her father, looking like her father, thin, and dressed in a shoddy red that yellowed her skin and glared at the pockmarks. All the baby loveliness gone.

She was two. Old enough for nursery school they said, and I did not know then what I know now—the fatigue of the long day, and the lacerations of group life in the kinds of nurseries that are only parking places for children.

Except that it would have made no difference if I had known. It was the only place there was. It was the only way we could be together, the only way I could hold a job.

And even without knowing, I knew. I knew the teacher that was evil because all these years it has curdled into my memory, the little boy hunched in the corner, her rasp, "why aren't you outside, because Alvin hits you? that's no reason, go out, scaredy." I knew Emily hated it even if she did not clutch and implore "don't go Mommy" like the other children, mornings.

She always had a reason why we should stay home. Momma, you look sick. 15 Momma, I feel sick. Momma, the teachers aren't there today, they're sick. Momma, we can't go, there was a fire there last night. Momma, it's a holiday today, no school, they told me.

But never a direct protest, never rebellion. I think of our others in their three-, four-year-oldness—the explosions, the tempers, the denunciations, the demands—and I feel suddenly ill. I put the iron down. What in me demanded that goodness in her? And what was the cost, the cost to her of such goodness?

The old man living in the back once said in his gentle way: "You should smile at Emily more when you look at her." What *was* in my face when I looked at her? I loved her. There were all the acts of love.

It was only with the others I remembered what he said, and it was the face of joy, and not of care or tightness or worry I turned to them—too late for Emily. She does not smile easily, let alone almost always as her brothers and sisters do. Her face is closed and somber, but when she wants, how fluid. You must have seen it in her pantomimes, you spoke of her rare gift for comedy on the stage that rouses laughter out of the audience so dear they applaud and applaud and do not want to let her go.

Where does it come from, that comedy? There was none of it in her when she came back to me that second time, after I had had to send her away again. She had a new daddy now to learn to love, and I think perhaps it was a better time.

Except when we left her alone nights, telling ourselves she was old enough. 20

"Can't you go some other time, Mommy, like tomorrow?" she would ask. "Will it be just a little while you'll be gone? Do you promise?"

The time we came back, the front door open, the clock on the floor in the hall. She rigid awake. "It wasn't just a little while. I didn't cry. Three times I called you, just three times, and then I ran downstairs to open the door so you could come faster. The clock talked loud. I threw it away, it scared me what it talked."

She said the clock talked loud again that night I went to the hospital to have Susan. She was delirious with the fever that comes from red measles, but she was fully conscious all the week I was gone and the week after we were home when she could not come near the new baby or me.

She did not get well. She stayed skeleton thin, not wanting to eat, and night after night she had nightmares. She would call for me, and I would rouse from exhaustion to sleepily call back: "You're all right, darling, go to sleep, it's just a dream," and if she still called, in a sterner voice, "now go to sleep, Emily, there's nothing to hurt you." Twice, only twice, when I had to get up for Susan anyhow, I went in to sit with her.

Now when it is too late (as if she would let me hold and comfort her like 25 I do the others) I get up and go to her at once at her moan or restless stirring. "Are you awake, Emily? Can I get you something?" And the answer is always the same: "No, I'm all right, go back to sleep, Mother."

They persuaded me at the clinic to send her away to a convalescent home in the country where "she can have the kind of food and care you can't manage for her, and you'll be free to concentrate on the new baby." They still send children to that place. I see pictures on the society page of sleek young women planning affairs to raise money for it, or dancing at the affairs, or decorating Easter eggs or filling Christmas stockings for the children.

They never have a picture of the children so I do not know if the girls still wear those gigantic red bows and the ravaged looks on the every other Sunday when parents can come to visit "unless otherwise notified"—as we were notified the first six weeks.

Oh it is a handsome place, green lawns and tall trees and fluted flower beds. High up on the balconies of each cottage the children stand, the girls in their red bows and white dresses, the boys in white suits and giant red ties. The parents stand below shrieking up to be heard and the children shriek down to be heard, and between them the invisible wall: "Not to Be Contaminated by Parental Germs or Physical Affection."

There was a tiny girl who always stood hand in hand with Emily. Her parents never came. One visit she was gone. "They moved her to Rose Cottage," Emily shouted in explanation. "They don't like you to love anybody here."

She wrote once a week, the labored writing of a seven-year-old. "I am fine. 30 How is the baby. If I write my leter nicly I will have a star. Love." There never was a star. We wrote every other day, letters she could never hold or keep but only hear read—once. "We simply do not have room for children to keep any personal possessions," they patiently explained when we pieced one Sunday's shrieking together to plead how much it would mean to Emily, who loved so to keep things, to be allowed to keep her letters and cards.

Each visit she looked frailer. "She isn't eating," they told us.

(They had runny eggs for breakfast or mush with lumps, Emily said later, I'd hold it in my mouth and not swallow. Nothing ever tasted good, just when they had chicken.)

It took us eight months to get her released home, and only the fact that she gained back so little of her seven lost pounds convinced the social worker.

I used to try to hold and love her after she came back, but her body would stay stiff, and after a while she'd push away. She ate little. Food sickened her, and I think much of life too. Oh she had physical lightness and brightness, twinkling by on skates, bouncing like a ball up and down up and down over the jump rope, skimming over the hill: but these were momentary.

She fretted about her appearance, thin and dark and foreign-looking at a time 35 when every little girl was supposed to look or thought she should look a chubby blonde replica of Shirley Temple. The doorbell sometimes rang for her, but no one seemed to come and play in the house or be a best friend. Maybe because we moved so much.

There was a boy she loved painfully through two school semesters. Months later she told me how she had taken pennies from my purse to buy him candy. "Licorice was his favorite and I brought him some every day, but he still liked Jennifer better'n me. Why, Mommy?" The kind of question for which there is no answer.

School was a worry to her. She was not glib or quick in a world where glibness and quickness were easily confused with ability to learn. To her overworked and exasperated teachers she was an overconscientious "slow learner" who kept trying to catch up and was absent entirely too often.

I let her be absent, though sometimes the illness was imaginary. How different from my now-strictness about attendance with the others. I wasn't working. We had a new baby, I was home anyhow. Sometimes, after Susan grew old enough, I would keep her home from school, too, to have them all together.

Mostly Emily had asthma, and her breathing, harsh and labored, would fill the house with a curiously tranquil sound. I would bring the two old dresser mirrors and her boxes of collections to her bed. She would select beads and single earrings, bottle tops and shells, dried flowers and pebbles, old postcards and scraps, all sorts of oddments; then she and Susan would play Kingdom, setting up landscapes and furniture, peopling them with action.

Those were the only times of peaceful companionship between her and Susan. 40 I have edged away from it, that poisonous feeling between them, that terrible balancing of hurts and needs I had to do between the two, and did so badly, those earlier years.

Oh there are conflicts between the others too, each one human, needing, demanding, hurting, taking—but only between Emily and Susan, no, Emily toward Susan that corroding resentment. It seems so obvious on the surface, yet it is not obvious. Susan, the second child, Susan, golden- and curly-haired and chubby, quick and articulate and assured, everything in appearance and manner Emily was not; Susan, not able to resist Emily's precious things, losing or sometimes clumsily breaking them; Susan telling jokes and riddles to company for applause while Emily sat silent (to say to me later: that was *my* riddle, Mother, I told it to Susan); Susan, who for all the five years' difference in age was just a year behind Emily in developing physically.

I am glad for that slow physical development that widened the difference between her and her contemporaries, though she suffered over it. She was too vulnerable for that terrible world of youthful competition, of preening and parading, of constant measuring of yourself against every other, of envy, "If I had the copper hair," "If I had that skin . . . ." She tormented herself enough about not looking like the others, there was enough of the unsureness, the having to be conscious of words before you speak, the constant caring—what are they thinking of me? without having it all magnified by the merciless physical drives.

Ronnie is calling. He is wet and I change him. It is rare there is such a cry now. That time of motherhood is almost behind me when the ear is not one's own but must always be racked and listening for the child cry, the child call. We sit for a while and I hold him, looking out over the city spread in charcoal with its soft aisles of light. "Shoogily," he breathes and curls closer. I carry him back to bed, asleep. *Shoogily*. A funny word, a family word, inherited from Emily, invented by her to say: *comfort*.

In this and other ways she leaves her seal, I say aloud. And startle at my saying it. What do I mean? What did I start to gather together, to try and make coherent? I was at the terrible, growing years. War years. I do not remember them well. I was working, there were four smaller ones now, there was not time for her. She had to help be a mother, and housekeeper, and shopper. She had to set her seal. Mornings of crisis and near hysteria trying to get lunches packed, hair combed, coats and shoes found, everyone to school or Child Care on time, the baby ready for transportation. And always the paper scribbled on by a smaller one, the book looked at by Susan then mislaid, the homework not done. Running out to that huge school where she was one, she was lost, she was a drop; suffering over the unpreparedness, stammering and unsure in her classes.

There was so little time left at night after the kids were bedded down. She 45 would struggle over books, always eating (it was in those years she developed her enormous appetite that is legendary in our family) and I would be ironing, or preparing food for the next day, or writing V-mail to Bill, or tending the baby. Sometimes, to make me laugh, or out of her despair, she would imitate happenings or types at school.

I think I said once: "Why don't you do something like this in the school amateur show?" One morning she phoned me at work, hardly understandable through the weeping: "Mother, I did it. I won, I won; they gave me first prize; they clapped and clapped and wouldn't let me go."

Now suddenly she was Somebody, and as imprisoned in her difference as she had been in anonymity.

She began to be asked to perform at other high schools, even in colleges, then at city and statewide affairs. The first one we went to, I only recognized her that first moment when thin, shy, she almost drowned herself into the curtains. Then: Was this Emily? The control, the command, the convulsing and deadly clowning, the spell, then the roaring, stamping audience, unwilling to let this rare and precious laughter out of their lives.

Afterwards: You ought to do something about her with a gift like that—but without money or knowing how, what does one do? We have left it all to her, and the gift has as often eddied inside, clogged and clotted, as been used and growing.

She is coming. She runs up the stairs two at a time with her light graceful 50 step, and I know she is happy tonight. Whatever it was that occasioned your call did not happen today.

"Aren't you ever going to finish the ironing, Mother? Whistler painted his mother in a rocker. I'd have to paint mine standing over an ironing board." This is one of her communicative nights and she tells me everything and nothing as she fixes herself a plate of food out of the icebox.

She is so lovely. Why did you want me to come in at all? Why were you concerned? She will find her way.

She starts up the stairs to bed. "Don't get me up with the rest in the morning." "But I thought you were having midterms." "Oh, those," she comes back in, kisses me, and says quite lightly, "in a couple of years when we'll all be atomdead they won't matter a bit."

She has said it before. She *believes* it. But because I have been dredging the past, and all that compounds a human being is so heavy and meaningful in me, I cannot endure it tonight.

I will never total it all. I will never come in to say: She was a child seldom 55 smiled at. Her father left me before she was a year old. I had to work her first six years when there was work, or I sent her home and to his relatives. There were years she had care she hated. She was dark and thin and foreign-looking in a world where the prestige went to blondeness and curly hair and dimples, she was slow where glibness was prized. She was a child of anxious, not proud, love. We were poor and could not afford for her the soil of easy growth. I was a young mother, I was a distracted mother. There were other children pushing up, demanding. Her younger sister seemed all that she was not. There were years she did not want me to touch her. She kept too much in herself, her life was such she had to keep too much in herself. My wisdom came too late. She has much to her and probably little will come of it. She is a child of her age, of depression, of war, of fear.

Let her be. So all that is in her will not bloom—but in how many does it? There is still enough left to live by. Only help her to know—help make it so there is cause for her to know—that she is more than this dress on the ironing board, helpless before the iron.

Philip Roth

THE CONVERSION OF THE JEWS   1959

Philip Roth, called "the inventor of the Jewish novel of manners," was born in 1933 in Newark, New Jersey. He first attended college on the local campus of Rutgers University, later transferred to Bucknell, completed his M.A. degree at the University of Chicago, and served a year in the Army. He has taught fiction writing at three universities: Iowa, Pennsylvania, and Princeton. Roth's first book, the collection of stories Goodbye, Columbus *(1955), from which we take "The Conversion of the Jews," won him immediate fame.* Portnoy's Complaint, *a sardonically comic novel of a man's sexual obsession, topped the bestseller list in 1969. Three novels about a writer named Zuckerman have been collected as* Zuckerman Bound *(1985); Zuckerman's saga is amplified in* The Counterlife *(1988) and* Deception *(1990). Roth has also written plays and literary criticism, notably* Reading Myself and Others *(1975), and* The Facts: A Novelist's Autobiography *(1988).*

Philip Roth

"You're a real one for opening your mouth in the first place," Itzie said. "What do you open your mouth all the time for?"

"I didn't bring it up, Itz, I didn't," Ozzie said.

"What do you care about Jesus Christ for anyway?"

"I didn't bring up Jesus Christ. He did. I didn't even know what he was talking about. Jesus is historical, he kept saying. Jesus is historical." Ozzie mimicked the monumental voice of Rabbi Binder.

"Jesus was a person that lived like you and me," Ozzie continued. "That's what   5
Binder said—"

"Yeah? . . . So what! What do I give two cents whether he lived or not. And what do you gotta open your mouth!" Itzie Lieberman favored closed-mouthedness, especially when it came to Ozzie Freedman's questions. Mrs. Freedman had to see Rabbi Binder twice before about Ozzie's questions and this Wednesday at four-thirty would be the third time. Itzie preferred to keep *his* mother in the kitchen; he settled for behind-the-back subtleties such as gestures, faces, snarls and other less delicate barnyard noises.

"He was a real person, Jesus, but he wasn't like God, and we don't believe he is God." Slowly, Ozzie was explaining Rabbi Binder's position to Itzie, who had been absent from Hebrew School the previous afternoon.

"The Catholics," Itzie said helpfully, "they believe in Jesus Christ, that he's God." Itzie Lieberman used "the Catholics" in its broadest sense—to include the Protestants.

Ozzie received Itzie's remark with a tiny head bob, as though it were a foot-note, and went on. "His mother was Mary, and his father probably was Joseph," Ozzie said. "But the New Testament says his real father was God."

"His *real* father?"   10

"Yeah," Ozzie said, "that's the big thing, his father's supposed to be God."

"Bull."

"That's what Rabbi Binder says, that it's impossible—"

"Sure it's impossible. That stuff's all bull. To have a baby you gotta get laid," Itzie theologized. "Mary hadda get laid."

"That's what Binder says: 'The only way a woman can have a baby is to have   15
intercourse with a man.' "

"He said *that*, Ozz?" For a moment it appeared that Itzie had put the theologi-cal question aside. "He said that, intercourse?" A little curled smile shaped itself in the lower half of Itzie's face like a pink mustache. "What you guys do, Ozz, you laugh or something?"

"I raised my hand."

"Yeah? Whatja say?"

"That's when I asked the question."

Itzie's face lit up. "Whatja ask about—intercourse?"   20

"No, I asked the question about God, how if He could create the heaven and earth in six days, and make all the animals and the fish and the light in six days— the light especially, that's what always gets me, that He could make the light. Making fish and animals, that's pretty good—"

"That's damn good." Itzie's appreciation was honest but unimaginative: it was as though God had just pitched a one-hitter.

"But making light . . . I mean when you think about it, it's really some-thing," Ozzie said. "Anyway, I asked Binder if He could make all that in six days, and He could *pick* the six days He wanted right out of nowhere, why couldn't He let a woman have a baby without having intercourse?"

"You said intercourse, Ozz, to Binder?"

"Yeah."

"Right in class?"

"Yeah."

Itzie smacked the side of his head.

"I mean, no kidding around," Ozzie said, "that'd really be nothing. After all that other stuff, that'd practically be nothing."

Itzie considered a moment. "What'd Binder say?"

"He started all over again explaining how Jesus was historical and how he lived like you and me but he wasn't God. So I said I understood that. What I wanted to know was different."

What Ozzie wanted to know was always different. The first time he had wanted to know how Rabbi Binder could call the Jews "The Chosen People" if the Declaration of Independence claimed all men to be created equal. Rabbi Binder tried to distinguish for him between political equality and spiritual legitimacy, but what Ozzie wanted to know, he insisted vehemently, was different. That was the first time his mother had to come.

Then there was the plane crash. Fifty-eight people had been killed in a plane crash at La Guardia°. In studying a casualty list in the newspaper his mother had discovered among the list of those dead eight Jewish names (his grandmother had nine but she counted Miller as a Jewish name); because of the eight she said the plane crash was "a tragedy." During free-discussion time on Wednesday Ozzie had brought to Rabbi Binder's attention this matter of "some of his relations" always picking out the Jewish names. Rabbi Binder had begun to explain cultural unity and some other things when Ozzie stood up at his seat and said that what he wanted to know was different. Rabbi Binder insisted that he sit down and it was then that Ozzie shouted that he wished all fifty-eight were Jews. That was the second time his mother came.

"And he kept explaining about Jesus being historical, and so I kept asking him. No kidding, Itz, he was trying to make me look stupid."

"So what he finally do?"

"Finally he starts screaming that I was deliberately simple-minded and a wise guy, and that my mother had to come, and this was the last time. And that I'd never get bar-mitzvahed if he could help it. Then, Itz, then he starts talking in that voice like a statue, real slow and deep, and he says that I better think over what I said about the Lord. He told me to go to his office and think it over." Ozzie leaned his body towards Itzie. "Itz, I thought it over for a solid hour, and now I'm convinced God could do it."

Ozzie had planned to confess his latest transgression to his mother as soon as she came home from work. But it was a Friday night in November and already dark, and when Mrs. Freedman came through the door she tossed off her coat, kissed Ozzie quickly on the face, and went to the kitchen table to light the three yellow candles, two for the Sabbath and one for Ozzie's father.

La Guardia: a New York City airport.

When his mother lit the candles she would move her two arms slowly towards her, dragging them through the air, as though persuading people whose minds were half made up. And her eyes would get glassy with tears. Even when his father was alive Ozzie remembered that her eyes had gotten glassy, so it didn't have anything to do with his dying. It had something to do with lighting the candles.

As she touched the flaming match to the unlit wick of a Sabbath candle, the phone rang, and Ozzie, standing only a foot from it, plucked it off the receiver and held it muffled to his chest. When his mother lit candles Ozzie felt there should be no noise; even breathing, if you could manage it, should be softened. Ozzie pressed the phone to his breast and watched his mother dragging whatever she was dragging, and he felt his own eyes get glassy. His mother was a round, tired, gray-haired penguin of a woman whose gray skin had begun to feel the tug of gravity and the weight of her own history. Even when she was dressed up she didn't look like a chosen person. But when she lit candles she looked like something better; like a woman who knew momentarily that God could do anything.

After a few mysterious minutes she was finished. Ozzie hung up the phone   40
and walked to the kitchen table where she was beginning to lay the two places for the four-course Sabbath meal. He told her that she would have to see Rabbi Binder next Wednesday at four-thirty, and then he told her why. For the first time in their life together she hit Ozzie across the face with her hand.

All through the chopped liver and chicken soup part of the dinner Ozzie cried; he didn't have any appetite for the rest.

On Wednesday, in the largest of the three basement classrooms of the synagogue, Rabbi Marvin Binder, a tall, handsome, broad-shouldered man of thirty with thick strong-fibered black hair, removed his watch from his pocket and saw that it was four o'clock. At the rear of the room Yakov Blotnik, the seventy-one-year-old custodian, slowly polished the large window, mumbling to himself, unaware that it was four o'clock or six o'clock, Monday or Wednesday. To most of the students Yakov Blotnik's mumbling, along with his brown curly beard, scythe nose, and two heel-trailing black cats, made of him an object of wonder, a foreigner, a relic, towards whom they were alternately fearful and disrespectful. To Ozzie the mumbling had always seemed a monotonous, curious prayer; what made it curious was that old Blotnik had been mumbling so steadily for so many years, Ozzie suspected he had memorized the prayers and forgotten all about God.

"It is now free-discussion time," Rabbi Binder said. "Feel free to talk about any Jewish matter at all—religion, family, politics, sports—"

There was silence. It was a gusty, clouded November afternoon and it did not seem as though there ever was or could be a thing called baseball. So nobody this week said a word about that hero from the past, Hank Greenberg—which limited free discussion considerably.

And the soul-battering Ozzie Freedman had just received from Rabbi Binder   45
had imposed its limitation. When it was Ozzie's turn to read aloud from the Hebrew book the rabbi had asked him petulantly why he didn't read more rapidly. He was showing no progress. Ozzie said he could read faster but that if he did he was sure not to understand what he was reading. Nevertheless, at the rabbi's repeated suggestion Ozzie tried, and showed a great talent, but in the midst of a long

passage he stopped short and said he didn't understand a word he was reading, and started in again at a drag-footed pace. Then came the soul-battering.

Consequently when free-discussion time rolled around none of the students felt too free. The rabbi's invitation was answered only by the mumbling of feeble old Blotnik.

"Isn't there anything at all you would like to discuss?" Rabbi Binder asked again, looking at his watch. "No questions or comments?"

There was a small grumble from the third row. The rabbi requested that Ozzie rise and give the rest of the class the advantage of his thought.

Ozzie rose. "I forget it now," he said, and sat down in his place.

Rabbi Binder advanced a seat towards Ozzie and poised himself on the edge 50 of the desk. It was Itzie's desk and the rabbi's frame only a dagger's-length away from his face snapped him to sitting attention.

"Stand up again, Oscar," Rabbi Binder said calmly, "and try to assemble your thoughts."

Ozzie stood up. All his classmates turned in their seats and watched as he gave an unconvincing scratch to his forehead.

"I can't assemble any," he announced, and plunked himself down.

"Stand up!" Rabbi Binder advanced from Itzie's desk to the one directly in front of Ozzie; when the rabbinical back was turned Ozzie gave it five-fingers off the tip of his nose, causing a small titter in the room. Rabbi Binder was too absorbed in squelching Ozzie's nonsense once and for all to bother with titters. "Stand up, Oscar. What's your question about?"

Ozzie pulled a word out of the air. It was the handiest word. "Reli- 55 gion."

"Oh, now you remember?"

"Yes."

"What is it?"

Trapped, Ozzie blurted the first thing that came to him. "Why can't He make anything He wants to make!"

As Rabbi Binder prepared an answer, a final answer, Itzie, ten feet behind 60 him, raised one finger on his left hand, gestured it meaningfully towards the rabbi's back, and brought the house down.

Binder twisted quickly to see what had happened and in the midst of the commotion Ozzie shouted into the rabbi's back what he couldn't have shouted to his face. It was a loud, toneless sound that had the timbre of something stored inside for about six days.

"You don't know! You don't know anything about God!"

The rabbi spun back towards Ozzie. "What?"

"You don't know—you don't—"

"Apologize, Oscar, apologize!" It was a threat. 65

"You don't—"

Rabbi Binder's hand flicked out at Ozzie's cheek. Perhaps it had only been meant to clamp the boy's mouth shut, but Ozzie ducked and the palm caught him squarely on the nose.

The blood came in a short, red spurt on to Ozzie's shirt front.

The next moment was all confusion. Ozzie screamed, "You bastard, you bastard!" and broke for the classroom door. Rabbi Binder lurched a step backwards, as though his own blood had started flowing violently in the opposite direction, then gave a clumsy lurch forward and bolted out the door after Ozzie. The class followed after the rabbi's huge blue-suited back, and before old Blotnik could turn from his window, the room was empty and everyone was headed full speed up the three flights leading to the roof.

If one should compare the light of the day to the life of man: sunrise to birth;   70
sunset—the dropping down over the edge—to death; then as Ozzie Freedman wiggled through the trapdoor of the synagogue roof, his feet kicking backwards bronco-style at Rabbi Binder's outstretched arms—at that moment the day was fifty years old. As a rule, fifty or fifty-five reflects accurately the age of late afternoons in November, for it is in that month, during those hours, that one's awareness of light seems no longer a matter of seeing, but of hearing: light begins clicking away. In fact, as Ozzie locked shut the trapdoor in the rabbi's face, the sharp click of the bolt into the lock might momentarily have been mistaken for the sound of the heavier gray that had just throbbed through the sky.

With all his weight Ozzie kneeled on the locked door; any instant he was certain that Rabbi Binder's shoulder would fling it open, splintering the wood into shrapnel and catapulting his body into the sky. But the door did not move and below him he heard only the rumble of feet, first loud and then dim, like thunder rolling away.

A question shot through his brain. "Can this be *me*?" For a thirteen-year-old who had just labeled his religious leader a bastard, twice, it was not an improper question. Louder and louder the question came to him—"Is it me? Is it me?"—until he discovered himself no longer kneeling, but racing crazily towards the edge of the roof, his eyes crying, his throat screaming, and his arms flying everywhich-way as though not his own.

"Is it me? Is it me ME ME ME ME! It has to be me—but is it!"

It is the question a thief must ask himself the night he jimmies open his first window, and it is said to be the question with which bridegrooms quiz themselves before the altar.

In the few wild seconds it took Ozzie's body to propel him to the edge of the   75
roof, his self-examination began to grow fuzzy. Gazing down at the street, he became confused as to the problem beneath the question: was it, is-it-me-who-called-Binder-a-bastard? or, is-it-me-prancing-around-on-the-roof? However, the scene below settled all, for there is an instant in any action when whether it is you or somebody else is academic. The thief crams the money in his pockets and scoots out the window. The bridegroom signs the hotel register for two. And the boy on the roof finds a streetful of people gaping at him, necks stretched backwards, faces up, as though he were the ceiling of the Hayden Planetarium. Suddenly you know it's you.

"Oscar! Oscar Freedman!" A voice rose from the center of the crowd, a voice that, could it have been seen, would have looked like the writing on a scroll. "Oscar Freedman, get down from there. Immediately!" Rabbi Binder was pointing one arm stiffly up at him; and at the end of that arm, one finger aimed menacingly. It was the attitude of a dictator, but one—the eyes confessed all—whose personal valet had spit neatly in his face.

Ozzie didn't answer. Only for a blink's length did he look towards Rabbi Binder. Instead his eyes began to fit together the world beneath him, to sort out people from places, friends from enemies, participants from spectators. In little jagged starlike clusters his friends stood around Rabbi Binder, who was still pointing. The topmost point on a star compounded not of angels but of five adolescent boys was Itzie. What a world it was, with those stars below, Rabbi Binder below . . . Ozzie, who a moment earlier hadn't been able to control his own body, started to feel the meaning of the word control: he felt Peace and he felt Power.

"Oscar Freedman, I'll give you three to come down."

Few dictators give their subjects three to do anything; but, as always, Rabbi Binder only looked dictatorial.

"Are you ready, Oscar?"   80

Ozzie nodded his head yes, although he had no intention in the world—the lower one or the celestial one he'd just entered—of coming down even if Rabbi Bender should give him a million.

"All right then," said Rabbi Binder. He ran a hand through his black Samson hair as though it were the gesture prescribed for uttering the first digit. Then, with his other hand cutting a circle out of the small piece of sky around him, he spoke. "One!"

There was no thunder. One the contrary, at that moment, as though "one" was the cue for which he had been waiting, the world's least thunderous person appeared on the synagogue steps. He did not so much come out the synagogue door as lean out, onto the darkening air. He clutched at the doorknob with one hand and looked up at the roof.

"Oy!"

Yakov Blotnik's old mind hobbled slowly, as if on crutches, and though he   85
couldn't decide precisely what the boy was doing on the roof, he knew it wasn't good—that is, it wasn't-good-for-the-Jews. For Yakov Blotnik life had fractionated itself simply: things were either good-for-the-Jews or no-good-for-the-Jews.

He smacked his free hand to his in-sucked cheek, gently. "Oy, Gut!" And then quickly as he was able, he jacked down his head and surveyed the street. There was Rabbi Binder (like a man at an auction with only three dollars in his pocket, he had just delivered a shaky "Two!"); there were the students, and that was all. So far it-wasn't-so-bad-for-the-Jews. But the boy had to come down immediately, before anybody saw. The problem: how to get the boy off the roof?

Anybody who has ever had a cat on the roof knows how to get him down. You call the fire department. Or first you call the operator and you ask her for the fire department. And the next thing there is great jamming of brakes and clanging of bells and shouting of instructions. And then the cat is off the roof. You do the same thing to get a boy off the roof.

That is, you do the same thing if you are Yakov Blotnik and you once had a cat on the roof.

When the engines, all four of them, arrived, Rabbi Binder had four times given Ozzie the count of three. The big hook-and-ladder swung around the corner and one of the firemen leaped from it, plunging headlong towards the yellow fire hydrant in front of the synagogue. With a huge wrench he began to unscrew the top nozzle. Rabbi Binder raced over him and pulled at his shoulder.

"There's no fire . . . " 90

The fireman mumbled back over his shoulder and, heatedly, continued working at the nozzle.

"But there's no fire, there's no fire . . . " Binder shouted. When the fireman mumbled again, the rabbi grasped his face with both his hands and pointed it up at the roof.

To Ozzie it looked as though Rabbi Binder was trying to tug the fireman's head out of his body, like a cork from a bottle. He had to giggle at the picture they made: it was a family portrait—rabbi in black skullcap, fireman in red hat, and the little yellow hydrant squatting beside like a kid brother, bareheaded. From the edge of the roof Ozzie waved at the portrait, a one-handed, flapping, mocking wave; in doing it his right foot slipped from under him. Rabbi Binder covered his eyes with his hands.

Firemen work fast. Before Ozzie had even regained his balance, a big, round, yellowed net was being held on the synagogue lawn. The firemen who held it looked up at Ozzie with stern, feelingless faces.

One of the firemen turned his head towards Rabbi Binder. "What, is the kid 95 nuts or something?"

Rabbi Binder unpeeled his hands from his eyes, slowly, painfully, as if they were tape. Then he checked: nothing on the sidewalk, no dents in the net.

"Is he gonna jump, or what?" the fireman shouted.

In a voice not at all like a statue, Rabbi Binder finally answered. "Yes, yes, I think so . . . He's been threatening to . . . "

Threatening to? Why, the reason he was on the roof, Ozzie remembered, was to get away; he hadn't even thought about jumping. He had just run to get away, and the truth was that he hadn't really headed for the roof as much as he'd been chased there.

"What's his name, the kid?" 100

"Freedman," Rabbi Binder answered. "Oscar Freedman."

The fireman looked up at Ozzie. "What is it with you, Oscar? You gonna jump, or what?"

Ozzie did not answer. Frankly, the question had just arisen.

"Look, Oscar, if you're gonna jump, jump—and if you're not gonna jump, don't jump. But don't waste our time, willya?"

Ozzie looked at the fireman and then at Rabbi Binder. He wanted to see Rabbi 105 Binder cover his eyes one more time.

"I'm going to jump."

And then he scampered around the edge of the roof to the corner, where there was no net below, and he flapped his arms at his sides, swishing the air and smacking his palms to his trousers on the downbeat. He began screaming like some kind of engine, "Wheeeee . . . wheeeeee," and leaning way out over the edge with the upper half of his body. The firemen whipped around to cover the ground with the net. Rabbi Binder mumbled a few words to Somebody and covered his eyes. Everything happened quickly, jerkily, as in a silent movie. The crowd, which had arrived with the fire engines, gave out a long, Fourth-of-July fireworks oooh-aahhh. In the excitement no one had paid the crowd much heed, except, of course, Yakov Blotnik, who swung from the doorknob counting heads. "Fier und tsvan-sik . . . finf und tsvantsik . . . Oy, Gut!"° It wasn't like this with the cat.

Rabbi Binder peeked through his fingers, checked the sidewalk and net. Empty. But there was Ozzie racing to the other corner. The firemen raced with him but were unable to keep up. Whenever Ozzie wanted to he might jump and splatter himself upon the sidewalk, and by the time the firemen scooted to the spot all they could do with their net would be to cover the mess.

"Wheeeee . . . wheeeee . . . "

"Hey, Oscar," the winded fireman yelled, "What the hell is this, a game or something?" 110

"Wheeeee . . . wheeeee . . . "

"Hey, Oscar—"

But he was off now to the other corner, flapping his wings fiercely. Rabbi Binder couldn't take it any longer—the fire engines from nowhere, the screaming suicidal boy, the net. He fell to his knees, exhausted, and with his hands curled together in front of his chest like a little dome, he pleaded, "Oscar, stop it, Oscar. Don't jump, Oscar. Please come down . . . Please don't jump."

And further back in the crowd a single voice, a single young voice, shouted a lone word to the boy on the roof.

"Jump!" 115

It was Itzie. Ozzie momentarily stopped flapping.

"Go ahead, Ozz—jump!" Itzie broke off his point of the star and courageously, with the inspiration not of a wise-guy but of a disciple, stood alone. "Jump, Ozz, jump!"

Still on his knees, his hands still curled, Rabbi Binder twisted his body back. He looked at Itzie, then, agonizingly, back to Ozzie.

"OSCAR, DON'T JUMP! PLEASE, DON'T JUMP . . . please please . . . "

"Jump!" This time it wasn't Itzie but another point of the star. By the time 120 Mrs. Freedman arrived to keep her four-thirty appointment with Rabbi Binder, the whole little upside down heaven was shouting and pleading for Ozzie to jump, and Rabbi Binder no longer was pleading with him not to jump, but was crying into the dome of his hands.

Understandably Mrs. Freedman couldn't figure out what her son was doing on the roof. So she asked.

"Ozzie, my Ozzie, what are you doing? My Ozzie, what is it?"

Ozzie stopped wheeeeeing and slowed his arms down to a cruising flap, the kind birds use in soft winds, but he did not answer. He stood against the low, clouded, darkening sky—light clicked down swiftly now, as on a small gear—flapping softly and gazing down at the small bundle of a woman who was his mother.

"What are you doing, Ozzie?" She turned towards the kneeling Rabbi Binder and rushed so close that only a paper-thickness of dusk lay between her stomach and his shoulders.

Fier . . . Gut! "Twenty-four . . . twenty-five . . . Oh, God!"

"What is my baby doing?"

Rabbi Binder gaped up at her but he too was mute. All that moved was the dome of his hands; it shook back and forth like a weak pulse.

"Rabbi, get him down! He'll kill himself. Get him down, my only baby . . . "

"I can't," Rabbi Binder said, "I can't . . . " and he turned his handsome head towards the crowd of boys behind him. "It's them. Listen to them."

And for the first time Mrs. Freedman saw the crowd of boys, and she heard what they were yelling.

"He's doing it for them. He won't listen to me. It's them." Rabbi Binder spoke like one in a trance.

"For them?"

"Yes."

"Why for them?"

"They want him to . . . "

Mrs. Freedman raised her two arms upward as though she were conducting the sky. "For them he's doing it!" And then in a gesture older than pyramids, older than prophets and floods, her arms came slapping down to her sides. "A martyr I have. Look!" She tilted her head to the roof. Ozzie was still flapping softly. "My martyr."

"Oscar, come down, *please*," Rabbi Binder groaned.

In a startlingly even voice Mrs. Freedman called to the boy on the roof. "Ozzie, come down, Ozzie. Don't be a martyr, my baby."

As though it were a litany, Rabbi Binder repeated her words. "Don't be a martyr, my baby. Don't be a martyr."

"Gawhead, Ozz—be a Martin!" It was Itzie. "Be a Martin, be a Martin," and all the voices joined in singing for Martindom, whatever *it* was. "Be a Martin, be a Martin . . . "

Somehow when you're on a roof the darker it gets the less you can hear. All Ozzie knew was that two groups wanted two new things; his friends were spirited and musical about what they wanted; his mother and the rabbi were even-toned, chanting, about what they didn't want. The rabbi's voice was without tears now and so was his mother's.

The big net stared up at Ozzie like a sightless eye. The big, clouded sky pushed down. From beneath it looked like a gray corrugated board. Suddenly, looking up into that unsympathetic sky, Ozzie realized all the strangeness of what these people, his friends, were asking: they wanted him to jump, to kill himself; they were singing about it now—it made them that happy. And there was an even greater strangeness: Rabbi Binder was on his knees, trembling. If there was a question to be asked now it was not "Is it me?" but rather "Is it us? . . . Is it us?"

Being on the roof, it turned out, was a serious thing. If he jumped would the singing become dancing? Would it? What would jumping stop? Yearningly, Ozzie wished he could rip open the sky, plunge his hands through, and pull out the sun; and on the sun, like a coin, would be stamped JUMP or DON'T JUMP.

Ozzie's knees rocked and sagged a little under him as though they were setting him for a dive. His arms tightened, stiffened, froze, from shoulders to fingernails. He felt as if each part of his body were going to vote as to whether he should kill himself or not—and each part as though it were independent of *him*.

The light took an unexpected click down and the new darkness, like a gag, hushed the friends singing for this and the mother and rabbi chanting for that.

Ozzie stopped counting votes, and in a curiously high voice, like one who 145 wasn't prepared for speech, he spoke.

"Mamma?"

"Yes, Oscar."

"Mamma, get down on your knees, like Rabbi Binder."

"Oscar—"

"Get down on your knees," he said, "or I'll jump." 150

Ozzie heard a whimper, then a quick rustling, and when he looked down where his mother had stood he saw the top of a head and beneath that a circle of dress. She was kneeling beside Rabbi Binder.

He spoke again. "Everybody kneel." There was the sound of everybody kneeling.

Ozzie looked around. With one hand he pointed towards the synagogue entrance. "Make *him* kneel."

There was a noise, not of kneeling, but of body-and-cloth stretching. Ozzie could hear Rabbi Binder saying in a gruff whisper, " . . . or he'll *kill* himself," and when next he looked there was Yakov Blotnik off the doorknob and for the first time in his life upon his knees in the Gentile posture of prayer.

As for the firemen—it is not as difficult as one might imagine to hold a net 155 taut while you are kneeling.

Ozzie looked around again; and then he called to Rabbi Binder.

"Rabbi?"

"Yes, Oscar."

"Rabbi Binder, do you believe in God?"

"Yes." 160

"Do you believe God can do Anything?" Ozzie leaned his head out into the darkness. "Anything?"

"Oscar, I think—"

"Tell me you believe God can do Anything."

There was a second's hesitation. Then: "God can do Anything."

"Tell me you believe God can make a child without intercourse." 165

"He can."

"Tell me!"

"God," Rabbi Binder admitted, "can make a child without intercourse."

"Mamma, you tell me."

"God can make a child without intercourse," his mother said. 170

"Make *him* tell me." There was no doubt who *him* was.

In a few moments Ozzie heard an old comical voice say something to the increasing darkness about God.

Next, Ozzie made everybody say it. And then he made them all say they believed in Jesus Christ—first one at a time, then all together.

When the catechizing was through it was the beginning of evening. From the street it sounded as if the boy on the roof might have sighed.

"Ozzie?" A woman's voice dared to speak. "You'll come down now?"

There was no answer, but the woman waited, and when a voice finally did speak it was thin and crying, and exhausted as that of an old man who has just finished pulling the bells.

"Mamma, don't you see—you shouldn't hit me. He shouldn't hit me. You shouldn't hit me about God, Mamma. You should never hit anybody about God—"

"Ozzie, please come down now."

"Promise me, promise me you'll never hit anybody about God."

He had asked only his mother, but for some reason everyone kneeling in the
street promised he would never hit anybody about God.

Once again there was silence.

"I can come down now, Mamma," the boy on the roof finally said. He turned his head both ways as though checking the traffic lights. "Now I can come down . . ."

And he did, right into the center of the yellow net that glowed in the evening's edge like an overgrown halo.

James Thurber

The Catbird Seat   1945

James Thurber (1894–1961), besides achieving success as a fabulist, a playwright, a cartoonist, and a writer of humorous sketches, was noted for his short stories. For a capsule biography and portrait see "The Unicorn in the Garden," page 51.

Mr. Martin bought the pack of Camels on Monday night in the most crowded cigar store on Broadway. It was theater time and seven or eight men were buying cigarettes. The clerk didn't even glance at Mr. Martin, who put the pack in his overcoat pocket and went out. If any of the staff at F & S had seen him buy the cigarettes, they would have been astonished, for it was generally known that Mr. Martin did not smoke, and never had. No one saw him.

It was just a week to the day since Mr. Martin had decided to rub out Mrs. Ulgine Barrows. The term "rub out" pleased him because it suggested nothing more than the correction of an error—in this case an error of Mr. Fitweiler. Mr. Martin had spent each night of the past week working out his plan and examining it. As he walked home now he went over it again. For the hundredth time he resented the element of imprecision, the margin of guesswork that entered into the business. The project as he had worked it out was casual and bold, the risks were considerable. Something might go wrong anywhere along the line. And therein lay the cunning of his scheme. No one would ever see in it the cautious, painstaking hand of Erwin Martin, head of the filing department at F & S, of whom Mr. Fitweiler had once said, "Man is fallible but Martin isn't." No one would see his hand, that is, unless it were caught in the act.

Sitting in his apartment, drinking a glass of milk, Mr. Martin reviewed his case against Mrs. Ulgine Barrows, as he had every night for seven nights. He began at the beginning. Her quacking voice and braying laugh had first profaned the halls of F & S on March 7, 1941 (Mr. Martin had a head for dates). Old Roberts, the personnel chief, had introduced her as the newly appointed special adviser to the president of the firm, Mr. Fitweiler. The woman had appalled Mr. Martin instantly, but he hadn't shown it. He had given her his dry hand, a look of studious concentration, and a faint smile. "Well," she had said, looking at the papers on his desk, "are you lifting the oxcart out of the ditch?" As Mr. Martin recalled that moment, over his milk, he squirmed slightly. He must keep his mind on her crimes as a special adviser, not on her peccadillos as a personality. This he found difficult to do, in spite of entering an objection and sustaining it. The faults of the woman as a woman kept chattering on in his mind like an unruly witness. She had, for almost two years now, baited him. In the halls, in the elevator, even in his own office, into which she romped now and then like a circus horse, she was constantly shouting out these silly questions at him. "Are you lifting the ox-cart out of the ditch? Are you tearing up the pea patch? Are you hollering down the rain barrel? Are you scraping around the bottom of the pickle barrel? Are you sitting in the catbird seat?"

It was Joey Hart, one of Mr. Martin's two assistants, who had explained what the gibberish meant. "She must be a Dodger fan°," he had said. "Red Barber announces the Dodger games over the radio and he uses those expressions—picked 'em up down South." Joey had gone on to explain one or two. "Tearing up the pea patch" meant going on a rampage; "sitting in the catbird seat" meant sitting pretty, like a batter with three balls and no strikes on him. Mr. Martin dismissed all this with an effort. It had been annoying, it had driven him near to distraction, but he was too solid a man to be moved to murder by anything so childish. It was fortunate, he reflected as he passed on to the important charges against Mrs. Barrows, that he had stood up under it so well. He had maintained always an outward appearance of polite tolerance. "Why, I even believe you like the woman," Miss Paird, his other assistant, had once said to him. He had simply smiled.

A gavel rapped in Mr. Martin's mind and the case proper was resumed. Mrs. 5 Ulgine Barrows stood charged with willful, blatant, and persistent attempts to destroy the efficiency and system of F & S. It was competent, material, and relevant to review her advent and rise to power. Mr. Martin had got the story from Miss Paird, who seemed always able to find things out. According to her, Mrs. Barrows had met Mr. Fitweiler at a party, where she had rescued him from the embraces of a powerfully built drunken man who had mistaken the president of F & S for a famous retired Middle Western football coach. She had led him to a sofa and somehow worked upon him a monstrous magic. The aging gentleman had jumped to the conclusion there and then that this was a woman of singular attainments, equipped to bring out the best in him and in the firm. A week later he had introduced her into F & S as his special adviser. On that day confusion got its foot in the door. After Miss Tyson, Mr. Brundage, and Mr. Bartlett had been fired and Mr. Munson had taken his hat and stalked out, mailing in his resignation later, old Roberts had been emboldened to speak to Mr. Fitweiler. He mentioned that Mr. Munson's department had been "a little disrupted" and hadn't they perhaps better resume the old system there? Mr. Fitweiler had said certainly

Dodger fan: At the time of this story, the Dodgers were the Brooklyn Dodgers.

not. He had the greatest faith in Mrs. Barrow's ideas. "They require a little seasoning, a little seasoning is all," he had added. Mr. Roberts had given it up. Mr. Martin reviewed in detail all the changes wrought by Mrs. Barrows. She had begun chipping at the cornices of the firm's edifice and now she was swinging at the foundation stones with a pickaxe.

Mr. Martin came now, in his summing up, to the afternoon of Monday, November 2, 1942—just one week ago. On that day, at 3 P.M., Mrs. Barrows had bounced into his office. "Boo!" she had yelled. "Are you scraping around the bottom of the pickle barrel?" Mr. Martin had looked at her from under his green eyeshade, saying nothing. She had begun to wander about the office, taking it in with her great, popping eyes. "Do you really need *all* these filing cabinets?" she had demanded suddenly. Mr. Martin's heart had jumped. "Each of these files," he had said, keeping his voice even, "plays an indispensable part in the system of F & S." She had brayed at him, "Well, don't tear up the pea patch!" and gone to the door. From there she had bawled, "But you sure have got a lot of fine scrap in here!" Mr. Martin could no longer doubt that the finger was on his beloved department. Her pickaxe was on the upswing, poised for the first blow. It had not come yet; he had received no blue memo from the enchanted Mr. Fitweiler bearing nonsensical instructions deriving from the obscene woman. But there was no doubt in Mr. Martin's mind that one would be forthcoming.He must act quickly. Already a precious week had gone by. Mr. Martin stood up in his living room, still holding his milk glass. "Gentlemen of the jury," he said to himself, "I demand the death penalty for this horrible person."

The next day Mr. Martin followed his routine, as usual. He polished his glasses more often and once sharpened an already sharp pencil, but not even Miss Paird noticed. Only once did he catch sight of his victim; she swept past him in the hall with a patronizing "Hi!" At five-thirty he walked home, as usual, and had a glass of milk, as usual. He had never drunk anything stronger in his life—unless you could count ginger ale. The late Sam Schlosser, the S of F & S, had praised Mr. Martin at a staff meeting several years before for his temperate habits. "Our most efficient worker neither drinks nor smokes," he had said. "The results speak for themselves." Mr. Fitweiler had sat by, nodding approval.

Mr. Martin was still thinking about that red-letter day as he walked over to the Schrafft's on Fifth Avenue near Forty-sixth Street. He got there, as he always did, at eight o'clock. He finished his dinner and the financial page of the *Sun* at a quarter to nine, as he always did. It was his custom after dinner to take a walk. This time he walked down Fifth Avenue at a casual pace. His gloved hands felt moist and warm, his forehead cold. He transferred the Camels from his overcoat to a jacket pocket. He wondered, as he did so, if they did not represent an unnecessary note of strain. Mrs. Barrows smoked only Luckies. It was his idea to puff a few puffs on a Camel (after the rubbing-out), stub it out in the ashtray holding her lipstick-stained Luckies, and thus drag a small red herring across the trail. Perhaps it was not a good idea. It would take time. He might even choke, too loudly.

Mr. Martin had never seen the house on West Twelfth Street where Mrs. Barrows lived, but he had a clear enough picture of it. Fortunately, she had bragged to everybody about her ducky first-floor apartment in the perfectly darling three-story redbrick. There would be no doorman or other attendants; just the tenants of the second and third floors. As he walked along, Mr. Martin realized that he would get there before nine-thirty. He had considered walking north on Fifth Avenue from Schrafft's to a point from which it would take him until ten o'clock to reach the house. At that hour people were less likely to be coming in or going out. But the procedure would have made an awkward loop in the straight thread of his casualness, and he had abandoned it. It was impossible to figure when people would be entering or leaving the house, anyway. There was a great risk at any hour. If he ran into anybody, he would simply have to place the rubbing-out of Ulgine Barrows in the inactive file forever. The same thing would hold true if there were someone in her apartment. In that case he would just say that he had been passing by, recognized her charming house and thought to drop in.

It was eighteen minutes after nine when Mr. Martin turned into Twelfth Street. A man passed him, and a man and a woman talking. There was no one within fifty paces when he came to the house, halfway down the block. He was up the steps and in the small vestibule in no time, pressing the bell under the card that said "Mrs. Ulgine Barrows." When the clicking in the lock started, he jumped forward against the door. He got inside fast, closing the door behind him. A bulb in a lantern hung from the hall ceiling on a chain seemed to give a monstrously bright light. There was nobody on the stair, which went up ahead of him along the left wall. A door opened down the hall in the wall on the right. He went toward it swiftly, on tiptoe.

"Well, for God's sake, look who's here!" bawled Mrs. Barrows, and her braying laugh rang out like the report of a shotgun. He rushed past her like a football tackle, bumping her. "Hey, quit shoving!" she said, closing the door behind them. They were in her living room, which seemed to Mr. Martin to be lighted by a hundred lamps. "What's after you?" she said. "You're as jumpy as a goat." He found he was unable to speak. His heart was wheezing in his throat. "I—yes," he finally brought out. She was jabbering and laughing as she started to help him off with his coat. "No, no," he said. "I'll put it there." He took it off and put it on a chair near the door. "Your hat and gloves, too," she said. "You're in a lady's house." He put his hat on top of the coat. Mrs. Barrows seemed larger than he had thought. He kept his gloves on. "I was passing by," he said. "I recognized—is there anyone here?" She laughed louder than ever. "No," she said, "we're all alone. You're as white as a sheet, you funny man. Whatever *has* come over you? I'll mix you a toddy." She started toward a door across the room. "Scotch-and-soda be all right? But say, you don't drink, do you?" She turned and gave him her amused look. Mr. Martin pulled himself together. "Scotch-and-soda will be all right," he heard himself say. He could hear her laughing in the kitchen.

Mr. Martin looked quickly around the living room for the weapon. He had counted on finding one there. There were andirons and a poker and something in a corner that looked like an Indian club. None of them would do. It couldn't be that way. He began to pace around. He came to a desk. On it lay a metal knife with an ornate handle. Would it be sharp enough? He reached for it and knocked over a small brass jar. Stamps spilled out of it and it fell to the floor with a clatter. "Hey," Mrs. Barrows yelled from the kitchen, "are you tearing up the pea patch?" Mr. Martin gave a strange laugh. Picking up the knife, he tried its point against his left wrist. It was blunt. It wouldn't do.

When Mrs. Barrows reappeared, carrying two highballs, Mr. Martin, standing there with his gloves on, became acutely conscious of the fantasy he had wrought. Cigarettes in his pocket, a drink prepared for him—it was all too grossly improbable. It was more than that; it was impossible. Somewhere in the back of his mind a vague idea stirred, sprouted. "For heaven's sake, take off those gloves," said Mrs. Barrows. "I always wear them in the house," said Mr. Martin. The idea began to bloom, strange and wonderful. She put the glasses on a coffee table in front of a sofa and sat on the sofa. "Come over here, you odd little man," she said. Mr. Martin went over and sat beside her. It was difficult getting a cigarette out of the pack of Camels, but he managed it. She held a match for him, laughing. "Well," she said, handing him his drink, "this is perfectly marvelous. You with a drink and cigarette."

Mr. Martin puffed, not too awkwardly, and took a gulp of the highball. "I drink and smoke all the time," he said. He clinked his glass against hers. "Here's nuts to that old windbag, Fitweiler," he said, and gulped again. The stuff tasted awful, but he made no grimace. "Really, Mr. Martin," she said, her voice and posture changing, "you are insulting our employer." Mrs. Barrows was now all special adviser to the president. "I am preparing a bomb," said Mr. Martin, "which will blow the old goat higher than hell." He had only had a little of the drink, which was not strong. It couldn't be that. "Do you take dope or something?" Mrs. Barrows asked coldly. "Heroin," said Mr. Martin. "I'll be coked to the gills when I bump that old buzzard off." "Mr. Martin!" she shouted, getting to her feet. "That will be all of that. You must go at once." Mr. Martin took another swallow of his drink. He tapped his cigarette out in the ashtray and put the pack of Camels on the coffee table. Then he got up. She stood glaring at him. He walked over and put on his hat and coat. "Not a word about this," he said, and laid an index finger against his lips. All Mrs. Barrows could bring out was "Really!" Mr. Martin put his hand on the doorknob. "I'm sitting in the catbird seat," he said. He stuck his tongue out at her and left. Nobody saw him go.

Mr. Martin got to his apartment, walking, well before eleven. No one saw him go in. He had two glasses of milk after brushing his teeth, and he felt elated. It wasn't tipsiness, because he hadn't been tipsy. Anyway, the walk had worn off all effects of the whiskey. He got in bed and read a magazine for a while. He was asleep before midnight.

Mr. Martin got to the office at eight-thirty the next morning, as usual. At a quarter to nine, Ulgine Barrows, who had never before arrived at work before ten, swept into his office. "I'm reporting to Mr. Fitweiler now!" she shouted. "If he turns you over to the police, it's no more than you deserve!" Mr. Martin gave her a look of shocked surprise. "I beg your pardon?" he said. Mrs. Barrows snorted

15

and bounced out of the room, leaving Miss Paird and Joey Hart staring after her. "What's the matter with that old devil now?" asked Miss Paird. "I have no idea," said Mr. Martin, resuming his work. The other two looked at him and then at each other. Miss Paird got up and went out. She walked slowly past the closed door of Mr. Fitweiler's office. Mrs. Barrows was yelling inside, but she was not braying. Miss Paird could not hear what the woman was saying. She went back to her desk.

Forty-five minutes later, Mrs. Barrows left the president's office and went into her own, shutting the door. It wasn't until half an hour later that Mr. Fitweiler sent for Mr. Martin. The head of the filing department, neat, quiet, attentive, stood in front of the old man's desk. Mr. Fitweiler was pale and nervous. He took his glasses off and twiddled them. He made a small, bruffing sound in his throat. "Martin," he said, "you have been with us more than twenty years." "Twenty-two, sir," said Mr. Martin. "In that time," pursued the president, "your work and your—uh—manner have been exemplary." "I trust so, sir," said Mr. Martin. "I have understood, Martin," said Mr. Fitweiler, "that you have never taken a drink or smoked." "That is correct, sir," said Mr. Martin. "Ah, yes." Mr. Fitweiler polished his glasses. "You may describe what you did after leaving the office yesterday, Martin," he said. Mr. Martin allowed less than a second for his bewildered pause. "Certainly, sir," he said. "I walked home. Then I went to Schrafft's for dinner. Afterward I walked home again. I went to bed early, sir, and read a magazine for a while. I was asleep before eleven." "Ah, yes," said Mr. Fitweiler again. He was silent for a moment, searching for the proper words to say to the head of the filing department. "Mrs. Barrows," he said finally, "Mrs. Barrows has worked hard, Martin, very hard. It grieves me to report that she has suffered a severe breakdown. It has taken the form of a persecution complex accompanied by distressing hallucinations." "I am very sorry, sir," said Mr. Martin. "Mrs. Barrows is under the delusion," continued Mr. Fitweiler, "that you visited her last evening and behaved yourself in an—uh—unseemly manner." He raised his hand to silence Mr. Martin's little pained outcry. "It is the nature of these psychological diseases," Mr. Fitweiler said, "to fix upon the least likely and most innocent party as the—uh—source of persecution. These matters are not for the lay mind to grasp, Martin. I've just had my psychiatrist, Dr. Fitch, on the phone. He would not, of course, commit himself, but he made enough generalizations to substantiate my suspicions. I suggested to Mrs. Barrows when she had completed her—uh—story to me this morning, that she visit Dr. Fitch, for I suspected a condition at once. She flew, I regret to say, into a rage, and demanded—uh—requested that I call you on the carpet. You may not know, Martin, but Mrs. Barrows had planned a reorganization of your department—subject to my approval, of course, subject to my approval. This brought you, rather than anyone else, to her mind—but again that is a phenomenon for Dr. Fitch and not for us. So, Martin, I am afraid Mrs. Barrows' usefulness here is at an end." "I am dreadfully sorry, sir," said Mr. Martin.

It was at this point that the door to the office blew open with the suddenness of a gas-main explosion and Mrs. Barrows catapulted through it. "Is the little rat denying it?" she screamed. "He can't get away with that!" Mr. Martin got up and moved discreetly to a point beside Mr. Fitweiler's chair. "You drank and smoked at my apartment," she bawled at Mr. Martin, "and you know it! You called Mr. Fitweiler an old windbag and said you were going to blow him up when you got coked to the gills on your heroin!" She stopped yelling to catch her breath and a new glint came into her popping eyes. "If you weren't such a drab, ordinary little man," she said, "I'd think you'd planned it all. Sticking your tongue out, saying you were sitting in the catbird seat, because you thought no one would believe me when I told it! My God, it's really too perfect!" She brayed loudly and hysterically, and the fury was on her again. She glared at Mr. Fitweiler. "Can't you see how he has tricked us, you old fool? Can't you see his little game?" But Mr. Fitweiler had been surreptitiously pressing all the buttons under the top of his desk and employees of F & S began pouring into the room. "Stockton," said Mr. Fitweiler, "you and Fishbein will take Mrs. Barrows to her home. Mrs. Powell, you will go with them." Stockton, who had played a little football in high school, blocked Mrs. Barrows as she made for Mr. Martin. It took him and Fishbein together to force her out of the door into the hall, crowded with stenographers and office boys. She was still screaming imprecations at Mr. Martin, tangled and contradictory imprecations. The hubbub finally died out down the corridor.

"I regret that this has happened," said Mr. Fitweiler. "I shall ask you to dismiss it from your mind, Martin." "Yes, sir," said Mr. Martin, anticipating his chief's "That will be all," by moving to the door. "I will dismiss it." He went out and shut the door, and his step was light and quick in the hall. When he entered his department he had slowed down to his customary gait, and he walked quietly across the room to the W20 file, wearing a look of studious concentration.

Edith Wharton

ROMAN FEVER   1936

Edith Wharton (1862–1937), born Edith Newbold Jones, grew up in a world she later dissected in her fiction: that of wealthy New York socialites. Although her parents frowned on her ambition to write—after all, why would she need money?—young Edith set out to perfect her own elegant, forceful prose style. In her early twenties she began placing stories in popular magazines and kept on to become America's most celebrated woman author. A long, unhappy marriage to Edward Wharton, a rich nonreader thirteen years her senior, was cheered by the building of The Manse, a stately home in the Berkshires outside Lenox, Massachusetts. Divorced in 1913, she settled permanently in France. During World War I, she worked tirelessly to aid refugees. Friendship with American novelist Henry James inspired Wharton to study her craft still more thoroughly. Among her twenty-seven books of

Edith Wharton

fiction are the novels The House of Mirth *(1905)*, The Custom of the Country *(1913)*, Summer *(1917)*, and The Age of Innocence *(1920)*. *Today her best-known novel may be that short, powerful tale of thwarted lovers in a New England village,* Ethan Frome *(1911). Besides, Wharton wrote fine ghost stories, memoirs, and a critical study,* The Writing of Fiction *(1925). As her biographer R. W. B. Lewis has shown in* Edith Wharton *(1975), she was a generous, wise, and impassioned woman whose best stories refuse to go away.*

I

From the table at which they had been lunching two American ladies of ripe but well-cared-for middle age moved across the lofty terrace of the Roman restaurant and, leaning on its parapet, looked first at each other, and then down on the outspread glories of the Palatine and the Forum, with the same expression of vague but benevolent approval.

As they leaned there a girlish voice echoed up gaily from the stairs leading to the court below. "Well, come along, then," it cried, not to them but to an invisible companion, "and let's leave the young things to their knitting"; and a voice as fresh laughed back: "Oh, look here, Babs, not actually *knitting—*" "Well, I mean figuratively," rejoined the first. "After all, we haven't left our poor parents much else to do . . . ." and at that point the turn of the stairs engulfed the dialogue.

The two ladies looked at each other again, this time with a tinge of smiling embarrassment, and the smaller and paler one shook her head and colored slightly.

"Barbara!" she murmured, sending an unheard rebuke after the mocking voice in the stairway.

The other lady, who was fuller, and higher in color, with a small determined 5 nose supported by vigorous black eyebrows, gave a good-humored laugh. "That's what our daughters think of us!"

Her companion replied by a deprecating gesture. "Not of us individually. We must remember that. It's just the collective modern idea of Mothers. And you see—" Half-guiltily she drew from her handsomely mounted black handbag a twist of crimson silk run through by two fine knitting needles. "One never knows," she murmured. "The new system has certainly given us a good deal of time to kill; and sometimes I get tired just looking—even at this." Her gesture was now addressed to the stupendous scene at their feet.

The dark lady laughed again, and they both relapsed upon the view, contemplating it in silence, with a sort of diffused serenity which might have been borrowed from the spring effulgence of the Roman skies. The luncheon hour was long past, and the two had their end of the vast terrace to themselves. At its opposite extremity a few groups, detained by a lingering look at the outspread city, were gathering up guidebooks and fumbling for tips. The last of them scattered, and the two ladies were alone on the air-washed height.

"Well, I don't see why we shouldn't just stay here," said Mrs. Slade, the lady of the high color and energetic brows. Two derelict basket chairs stood near, and she pushed them into the angle of the parapet, and settled herself in one, her gaze upon the Palatine. "After all, it's still the most beautiful view in the world."

"It always will be, to me," assented her friend Mrs. Ansley, with so slight a stress on the "me" that Mrs. Slade, though she noticed it, wondered if it were not merely accidental, like the random underlinings of old-fashioned letter writers.

"Grace Ansley was always old-fashioned," she thought; and added aloud, with a retrospective smile: "It's a view we've both been familiar with for a good many years. When we first met here we were younger than our girls are now. You remember?" 10

"Oh, yes, I remember," murmured Mrs. Ansley, with the same undefinable stress. "There's that headwaiter wondering," she interpolated. She was evidently far less sure than her companion of herself and of her rights in the world.

"I'll cure him of wondering," said Mrs. Slade, stretching her hand toward a bag as discreetly opulent-looking as Mrs. Ansley's. Signing to the headwaiter, she explained that she and her friend were old lovers of Rome, and would like to spend the end of the afternoon looking down on the view—that is, if it did not disturb the service? The headwaiter, bowing over her gratuity, assured her that the ladies were most welcome, and would be still more so if they would condescend to remain for dinner. A full-moon night, they would remember . . . .

Mrs. Slade's black brows drew together, as though references to the moon were out of place and even unwelcome. But she smiled away her frown as the headwaiter retreated. "Well, why not? We might do worse. There's no knowing, I suppose, when the girls will be back. Do you even know back from *where*? I don't!"

Mrs. Ansley again colored slightly. "I think those young Italian aviators we met at the Embassy invited them to fly to Tarquinia for tea. I suppose they'll want to wait and fly back by moonlight."

"Moonlight—moonlight! What a part it still plays. Do you suppose they're as sentimental as we were?" 15

"I've come to the conclusion that I don't in the least know what they are," said Mrs. Ansley. "And perhaps we didn't know much more about each other."

"No; perhaps we didn't."

Her friend gave her a shy glance. "I never should have supposed you were sentimental, Alida."

"Well, perhaps I wasn't." Mrs. Slade drew her lids together in retrospect; and for a few moments the two ladies, who had been intimate since childhood, reflected how little they knew each other. Each one, of course, had a label ready to attach to the other's name; Mrs. Delphin Slade, for instance, would have told herself, or anyone who asked her, that Mrs. Horace Ansley, twenty-five years ago, had been exquisitely lovely—no, you wouldn't believe it, would you? . . . though, of course, still charming, distinguished . . . .Well, as a girl she had been exquisite; far more beautiful than her daughter Barbara, though certainly Babs, according to the new standards at any rate, was more effective—had more *edge*, as they say. Funny where she got it, with those two nullities as parents. Yes; Horace Ansley was—well, just the duplicate of his wife. Museum specimens of old New York. Good-looking, irreproachable, exemplary. Mrs. Slade and Mrs. Ansley had lived opposite each other—actually as well as figuratively—for years. When the drawing-room curtains in No. 20 East 73rd Street were renewed, No. 23, across the way, was always aware of it. And of all the movings, buyings, travels, anniversaries, illnesses—the tame chronicle of an estimable pair. Little of it escaped Mrs. Slade.

But she had grown bored with it by the time her husband made his big *coup* in Wall Street, and when they bought in upper Park Avenue had already begun to think: "I'd rather live opposite a speakeasy for a change; at least one might see it raided." The idea of seeing Grace raided was so amusing that (before the move) she launched it at a woman's lunch. It made a hit, and went the rounds—she sometimes wondered if it had crossed the street, and reached Mrs. Ansley. She hoped not, but didn't much mind. Those were the days when respectability was at a discount, and it did the irreproachable no harm to laugh at them a little.

A few years later, and not many months apart, both ladies lost their husbands. There was an appropriate exchange of wreaths and condolences, and a brief renewal of intimacy in the half-shadow of their mourning; and now, after another interval, they had run across each other in Rome, at the same hotel, each of them the modest appendage of a salient daughter. The similarity of their lot had again drawn them together, lending itself to mild jokes, and the mutual confession that, if in old days it must have been tiring to "keep up" with daughters, it was now, at times, a little dull not to.

No doubt, Mrs. Slade reflected, she felt her unemployment more than poor Grace ever would. It was a big drop from being the wife of Delphin Slade to being his widow. She had always regarded herself (with a certain conjugal pride) as his equal in social gifts, as contributing her full share to the making of the exceptional couple they were: but the difference after his death was irremediable. As the wife of the famous corporation lawyer, always with an international case or two on hand, every day brought its exciting and unexpected obligation: the impromptu entertaining of eminent colleagues from abroad, the hurried dashes on legal business to London, Paris or Rome, where the entertaining was so handsomely reciprocated; the amusement of hearing in her wake: "What, that handsome woman with the good clothes and the eyes is Mrs. Slade—*the* Slade's wife? Really? Generally the wives of celebrities are such frumps."

Yes; being *the* Slade's widow was a dullish business after that. In living up to such a husband all her faculties had been engaged; now she had only her daughter to live up to, for the son who seemed to have inherited his father's gifts had died suddenly in boyhood. She had fought through that agony because her husband was there, to be helped and to help; now, after the father's death, the thought of the boy had become unbearable. There was nothing left but to mother her daughter; and dear Jenny was such a perfect daughter that she needed no excessive mothering. "Now with Babs Ansley I don't know that I *should* be so quiet," Mrs. Slade sometimes half-enviously reflected; but Jenny, who was younger than her brilliant friend, was that rare accident, an extremely pretty girl who somehow made youth and prettiness seem as safe as their absence. It was all perplexing— and to Mrs. Slade a little boring. She wished that Jenny would fall in love—with the wrong man, even; that she might have to be watched, out-maneuvered, rescued. And instead, it was Jenny who watched her mother, kept her out of drafts, made sure that she had taken her tonic . . . .

Mrs. Ansley was much less articulate than her friend, and her mental portrait of Mrs. Slade was slighter, and drawn with fainter touches. "Alida Slade's awfully brilliant; but not as brilliant as she thinks," would have summed it up; though she would have added, for the enlightenment of strangers, that Mrs. Slade had been an extremely dashing girl; much more so than her daughter, who was pretty, of course, and clever in a way, but had none of her mother's—well, "vividness," someone had once called it. Mrs. Ansley would take up current words like this, and cite them in quotation marks, as unheard-of audacities. No; Jenny was not like her mother. Sometimes Mrs. Ansley thought Alida Slade was disappointed; on the whole she had had a sad life. Full of failures and mistakes; Mrs. Ansley had always been rather sorry for her . . . .

So these two ladies visualized each other, each through the wrong end of her little telescope.

II

For a long time they continued to sit side by side without speaking. It seemed as though, to both, there was a relief in laying down their somewhat futile activities in the presence of the vast Memento Mori which faced them. Mrs. Slade sat quite still, her eyes fixed on the golden slope of the Palace of the Caesars, and after a while Mrs. Ansley ceased to fidget with her bag, and she too sank into meditation. Like many intimate friends, the two ladies had never before had occasion to be silent together, and Mrs. Ansley was slightly embarrassed by what seemed, after so many years, a new stage in their intimacy, and one with which she did not yet know how to deal.

Suddenly the air was full of that deep clangor of bells which periodically covers Rome with a roof of silver. Mrs. Slade glanced at her wristwatch. "Five o'clock already," she said, as though surprised.

Mrs. Ansley suggested interrogatively: "There's bridge at the Embassy at five." For a long time Mrs. Slade did not answer. She appeared to be lost in contemplation, and Mrs. Ansley thought the remark had escaped her. But after a while she said, as if speaking out of a dream: "Bridge, did you say? Not unless you want to. . . . But I don't think I will, you know."

"Oh, no," Mrs. Ansley hastened to assure her. "I don't care to at all. It's so lovely here; and so full of old memories, as you say." She settled herself in her chair, and almost furtively drew forth her knitting. Mrs. Slade took sideway note of this activity, but her own beautifully cared-for hands remained motionless on her knee.

"I was just thinking," she said slowly, "what different things Rome stands for to each generation of travelers. To our grandmothers, Roman fever; to our mothers, sentimental dangers—how we used to be guarded!—to our daughters, no more dangers than the middle of Main Street. They don't know it—but how much they're missing!"

The long golden light was beginning to pale, and Mrs. Ansley lifted her knitting a little closer to her eyes. "Yes; how we were guarded!"

"I always used to think," Mrs. Slade continued, "that our mothers had a much more difficult job than our grandmothers. When Roman fever stalked the streets it must have been comparatively easy to gather in the girls at the danger hour; but when you and I were young, with such beauty calling us, and the spice of disobedience thrown in, and no worse risk than catching cold during the cool hour after sunset, the mothers used to be put to it to keep us in—didn't they?"

She turned again toward Mrs. Ansley, but the latter had reached a delicate point in her knitting. "One, two, three—slip two; yes, they must have been," she assented, without looking up.

Mrs. Slade's eyes rested on her with a deepened attention. "She can knit—in the face of *this!* How like her . . . ."

Mrs. Slade leaned back, brooding, her eyes ranging from the ruins which faced her to the long green hollow of the Forum, the fading glow of the church fronts beyond it, and the outlying immensity of the Colosseum. Suddenly she thought: "It's all very well to say that our girls have done away with sentiment and moonlight. But if Babs Ansley isn't out to catch that young aviator—the one who's a Marchese—then I don't know anything. And Jenny has no chance beside her. I know that too. I wonder if that's why Grace Ansley likes the two girls to go everywhere together? My poor Jenny as a foil—!" Mrs. Slade gave a hardly audible laugh, and at the sound Mrs. Ansley dropped her knitting.

"Yes—?"   35

"I—oh, nothing. I was only thinking how your Babs carries everything before her. That Campolieri boy is one of the best matches in Rome. Don't look so innocent, my dear—you know he is. And I was wondering, ever so respectfully, you understand . . . wondering how two such exemplary characters as you and Horace had managed to produce anything quite so dynamic." Mrs. Slade laughed again, with a touch of asperity.

Mrs. Ansley's hands lay inert across her needles. She looked straight out at the great accumulated wreckage of passion and splendor at her feet. But her small profile was almost expressionless. At length she said: "I think you overrate Babs, my dear."

Mrs. Slade's tone grew easier. "No; I don't. I appreciate her. And perhaps envy you. Oh, my girl's perfect; if I were a chronic invalid I'd—well, I think I'd rather be in Jenny's hands. There must be times . . . but there! I always wanted a brilliant daughter . . . and never quite understood why I got an angel instead."

Mrs. Ansley echoed her laugh in a faint murmur. "Babs is an angel too."

"Of course—of course! But she's got rainbow wings. Well, they're wandering   40
by the sea with their young men; and here we sit . . . and it all brings back the past a little too acutely."

Mrs. Ansley had resumed her knitting. One might almost have imagined (if one had known her less well, Mrs. Slade reflected) that, for her also, too many memories rose from the lengthening shadows of those august ruins. But no; she was simply absorbed in her work. What was there for her to worry about? She knew that Babs would almost certainly come back engaged to the extremely eligible Campolieri. "And she'll sell the New York house, and settle down near them in Rome, and never be in their way . . . she's much too tactful. But she'll have an excellent cook, and just the right people in for bridge and cocktails . . . and a perfectly peaceful old age among her grandchildren."

Mrs. Slade broke off this prophetic flight with a recoil of self-disgust. There was no one of whom she had less right to think unkindly than of Grace Ansley. Would she never cure herself of envying her? Perhaps she had begun too long ago.

She stood up and leaned against the parapet, filling her troubled eyes with the tranquilizing magic of the hour. But instead of tranquilizing her the sight seemed to increase her exasperation. Her gaze turned toward the Colosseum. Already its golden flank was drowned in purple shadow, and above it the sky curved crystal clear, without light or color. It was the moment when afternoon and evening hang balanced in midheaven.

Mrs. Slade turned back and laid her hand on her friend's arm. The gesture was so abrupt that Mrs. Ansley looked up, startled.

"The sun's set. You're not afraid, my dear?"   45

"Afraid—?"

"Of Roman fever or pneumonia? I remember how ill you were that winter. As a girl you had a very delicate throat, hadn't you?"

"Oh, we're all right up here. Down below, in the Forum, it does get deathly cold, all of a sudden . . . but not here."

"Ah, of course you know because you had to be so careful." Mrs. Slade turned back to the parapet. She thought: "I must make one more effort not to hate her." Aloud she said: "Whenever I look at the Forum from up here, I remember that story about a great-aunt of yours, wasn't she? A dreadfully wicked great-aunt?"

"Oh, yes: great-aunt Harriet. The one who was supposed to have sent her   50 young sister out to the Forum after sunset to gather a night-blooming flower for her album. All our great-aunts and grandmothers used to have albums of dried flowers."

Mrs. Slade nodded. "But she really sent her because they were in love with the same man—"

"Well, that was the family tradition. They said Aunt Harriet confessed it years afterward. At any rate, the poor little sister caught the fever and died. Mother used to frighten us with the story when we were children."

"And you frightened me with it, that winter when you and I were here as girls. The winter I was engaged to Delphin."

Mrs. Ansley gave a faint laugh. "Oh, did I? Really frightened you? I don't believe you're easily frightened."

"Not often; but I was then. I was easily frightened because I was too happy.   55 I wonder if you know what that means?"

"I—yes . . . " Mrs. Ansley faltered.

"Well, I suppose that was why the story of your wicked aunt made such an impression on me. And I thought: There's no more Roman fever, but the Forum is deathly cold after sunset—especially after a hot day. And the Colosseum's even colder and damper."

"The Colosseum—?"

"Yes. It wasn't easy to get in, after the gates were locked for the night. Far from easy. Still, in those days it could be managed; it *was* managed, often. Lovers met there who couldn't meet elsewhere. You knew that?"

"I—I dare say. I don't remember."   60

"You don't remember? You don't remember going to visit some ruins or other one evening, just after dark, and catching a bad chill? You were supposed to have gone to see the moon rise. People always said that expedition was what caused your illness."

There was a moment's silence; then Mrs. Ansley rejoined: "Did they? It was all so long ago."

"Yes. And you got well again—so it didn't matter. But I suppose it struck your friends—the reason given for your illness, I mean—because everybody knew you were so prudent on account of your throat, and your mother took such care of you . . . . You *had* been out late sight-seeing, hadn't you, that night?"

"Perhaps I had. The most prudent girls aren't always prudent. What made you think of it now?"

Mrs. Slade seemed to have no answer ready. But after a moment she broke out: "Because I simply can't bear it any longer—!"

Mrs. Ansley lifted her head quickly. Her eyes were wide and very pale. "Can't bear what?"

"Why—your not knowing that I've always known why you went."

"Why I went—?"

"Yes. You think I'm bluffing, don't you? Well, you went to meet the man I was engaged to—and I can repeat every word of the letter that took you there."

While Mrs. Slade spoke Mrs. Ansley had risen unsteadily to her feet. Her bag, her knitting and gloves, slid in a panic-stricken heap to the ground. She looked at Mrs. Slade as though she were looking at a ghost.

"No, no—don't," she faltered out.

"Why not? Listen, if you don't believe me. 'My one darling, things can't go on like this. I must see you alone. Come to the Colosseum immediately after dark tomorrow. There will be somebody to let you in. No one whom you need fear will suspect'—but perhaps you've forgotten what the letter said?"

Mrs. Ansley met the challenge with an unexpected composure. Steadying herself against the chair she looked at her friend, and replied: "No; I know it by heart too."

"And the signature? 'Only *your* D.S.' Was that it? I'm right, am I? That was the letter that took you out that evening after dark?"

Mrs. Ansley was still looking at her. It seemed to Mrs. Slade that a slow struggle was going on behind the voluntarily controlled mask of her small quiet face. "I shouldn't have thought she had herself so well in hand," Mrs. Slade reflected, almost resentfully. But at this moment Mrs. Ansley spoke. "I don't know how you knew. I burnt that letter at once."

"Yes; you would, naturally—you're so prudent!" The sneer was open now. "And if you burnt the letter you're wondering how on earth I know what was in it. That's it, isn't it?"

Mrs. Slade waited, but Mrs. Ansley did not speak.

"Well, my dear, I know what was in the letter because I wrote it!"

"You wrote it?"

"Yes."

The two women stood for a minute staring at each other in the last golden light. Then Mrs. Ansley dropped back into her chair. "Oh," she murmured, and covered her face with her hands.

Mrs. Slade waited nervously for another word or movement. None came, and at length she broke out: "I horrify you."

Mrs. Ansley's hands dropped to her knee. The face they uncovered was streaked with tears. "I wasn't thinking of you. I was thinking—it was the only letter I ever had from him!"

"And I wrote it. Yes; I wrote it! But I was the girl he was engaged to. Did you happen to remember that?"

Mrs. Ansley's head drooped again. "I'm not trying to excuse myself . . . I remembered . . . ." 85

"And still you went?"

"Still I went."

Mrs. Slade stood looking down on the small bowed figure at her side. The flame of her wrath had already sunk, and she wondered why she had ever thought there would be any satisfaction in inflicting so purposeless a wound on her friend. But she had to justify herself.

"You do understand? I'd found out—and I hated you, hated you. I knew you were in love with Delphin—and I was afraid; afraid of you, of your quiet ways, your sweetness . . . your . . . well, I wanted you out of the way, that's all. Just for a few weeks; just till I was sure of him. So in a blind fury I wrote that letter. . . . I don't know why I'm telling you now."

"I suppose," said Mrs. Ansley slowly, "it's because you've always gone on hating me." 90

"Perhaps. Or because I wanted to get the whole thing off my mind." She paused. "I'm glad you destroyed the letter. Of course I never thought you'd die."

Mrs. Ansley relapsed into silence, and Mrs. Slade, leaning above her, was conscious of a strange sense of isolation, of being cut off from the warm current of human communion. "You think me a monster!"

"I don't know. . . . It was the only letter I had, and you say he didn't write it?"

"Ah, how you care for him still!"

"I cared for that memory," said Mrs. Ansley. 95

Mrs. Slade continued to look down on her. She seemed physically reduced by the blow—as if, when she got up, the wind might scatter her like a puff of dust. Mrs. Slade's jealousy suddenly leapt up again at the sight. All these years the woman had been living on that letter. How she must have loved him, to treasure the mere memory of its ashes! The letter of the man her friend was engaged to. Wasn't it she who was the monster?

"You tried your best to get him away from me, didn't you? But you failed; and I kept him. That's all."

"Yes. That's all."

"I wish now I hadn't told you. I'd no idea you'd feel about it as you do; I thought you'd be amused. It all happened so long ago, as you say; and you must do me the justice to remember that I had no reason to think you'd ever taken it seriously. How could I, when you were married to Horace Ansley two months afterward? As soon as you could get out of bed your mother rushed you off to Florence and married you. People were rather surprised—they wondered at its being done so quickly; but I thought I knew. I had an idea you did it out of *pique*—to be able to say you'd got ahead of Delphin and me. Girls have such silly reasons for doing the most serious things. And your marrying so soon convinced me that you'd never really cared."

"Yes. I suppose it would," Mrs. Ansley assented. 100

The clear heaven overhead was emptied of all its gold. Dusk spread over it, abruptly darkening the Seven Hills. Here and there lights began to twinkle through the foliage at their feet. Steps were coming and going on the deserted terrace—waiters looking out of the doorway at the head of the stairs, then reappearing with trays and napkins and flasks of wine. Tables were moved, chairs straightened. A feeble string of electric lights flickered out. Some vases of faded flowers were carried away, and brought back replenished. A stout lady in a dust coat suddenly appeared, asking in broken Italian if anyone had seen the elastic band which held together her tattered Baedeker. She poked with her stick under the table at which she had lunched, the waiters assisting.

The corner where Mrs. Slade and Mrs. Ansley sat was still shadowy and deserted. For a long time neither of them spoke. At length Mrs. Slade began again: "I suppose I did it as a sort of joke—"

"A joke?"

"Well, girls are ferocious sometimes, you know. Girls in love especially. And I remember laughing to myself all that evening at the idea that you were waiting around there in the dark, dodging out of sight, listening for every sound, trying to get in—Of course I was upset when I heard you were so ill afterward."

Mrs. Ansley had not moved for a long time. But now she turned slowly toward her companion. "But I didn't wait. He'd arranged everything. He was there. We were let in at once," she said.

Mrs. Slade sprang up from her leaning position. "Delphin there? They let you in?—Ah, now you're lying!" she burst out with violence.

Mrs. Ansley's voice grew clearer, and full of surprise. "But of course he was there. Naturally he came—"

"Came? How did he know he'd find you there? You must be raving!"

Mrs. Ansley hesitated, as though reflecting. "But I answered the letter. I told him I'd be there. So he came."

Mrs. Slade flung her hands up to her face. "Oh, God—you answered! I never thought of your answering . . . ."

"It's odd you never thought of it, if you wrote the letter."

"Yes. I was blind with rage."

Mrs. Ansley rose, and drew her fur scarf about her. "It is cold here. We'd better go. . . . I'm sorry for you," she said, as she clasped the fur about her throat.

The unexpected words sent a pang through Mrs. Slade. "Yes; we'd better go." She gathered up her bag and cloak. "I don't know why you should be sorry for me," she muttered.

Mrs. Ansley stood looking away from her toward the dusky secret mass of the Colosseum. "Well—because I didn't have to wait that night."

Mrs. Slade gave an unquiet laugh. "Yes; I was beaten there. But I oughtn't to begrudge it to you, I suppose. At the end of all these years. After all, I had everything; I had him for twenty-five years. And you had nothing but that one letter that he didn't write."

Mrs. Ansley was again silent. At length she turned toward the door of the terrace. She took a step, and turned back, facing her companion.

"I had Barbara," she said, and began to move ahead of Mrs. Slade toward the stairway.

William Carlos Williams

THE USE OF FORCE   1938

William Carlos Williams (1883–1963) was
born in Rutherford, New Jersey, studied at the
universities of Pennsylvania and Leipzig, then
practiced medicine as a pediatrician in his home
town for forty-one years. His mother, who was
Puerto Rican, gave him his Spanish middle
name. Amazingly prolific for a busy doctor,
Williams even wrote during office hours: between patients, he would haul out his typewriter and devote every spare minute to literary
work. His encouragement of younger writers,
among them Allen Ginsberg (whose baby-
doctor he was), and the influential example of
his formally open poetry made him a father
figure to a generation of poets that included
Gary Snyder, Denise Levertov, Robert Creeley, and Robert Lowell. Williams believed in

William Carlos Williams

truthtelling and in the worth of ordinary life. Some of his stories, like "The Use of Force,"
read like tales drawn from his working experience. In all his writing, Williams championed plain speech "out of the mouths of Polish mothers." His fiction included four novels,
among them White Mule (1937) and its sequel In the Money (1940), and stories collected in The Farmer's Daughter (1961). Combining poetry with prose (including documents and statistics), his five-part poem Paterson (1946–58) explores the past, present,
and future of the New Jersey industrial city near which he lived. For the shorter poems
see Collected Poems in two volumes (1986 and 1988). Williams also wrote plays, criticism, history (In the American Grain, 1925), and an Autobiography (1951).

They were new patients to me, all I had was the name, Olson. Please come
down as soon as you can, my daughter is very sick.

When I arrived I was met by the mother, a big startled looking woman, very
clean and apologetic who merely said, Is this the doctor? and let me in. In the
back, she added. You must excuse us, doctor, we have her in the kitchen where
it is warm. It is very damp here sometimes.

The child was fully dressed and sitting on her father's lap near the kitchen
table. He tried to get up, but I motioned for him not to bother, took off my overcoat and started to look things over. I could see that they were all very nervous,
eyeing me up and down distrustfully. As often, in such cases, they weren't telling
me more than they had to, it was up to me to tell them; that's why they were
spending three dollars on me.

The child was fairly eating me up with her cold, steady eyes, and no expression to her face whatever. She did not move and seemed, inwardly, quiet; an

unusually attractive little thing, and as strong as a heifer in appearance. But her face was flushed, she was breathing rapidly, and I realized that she had a high fever. She had magnificent blonde hair, in profusion. One of those picture children often reproduced in advertising leaflets and the photogravure sections of the Sunday papers.

She's had a fever for three days, began the father and we don't know what it comes from. My wife has given her things, you know, like people do, but it don't do no good. And there's been a lot of sickness around. So we tho't you'd better look her over and tell us what is the matter.

As doctors often do I took a trial shot at it as a point of departure. Has she had a sore throat?

Both parents answered me together, No . . . No, she says her throat don't hurt her.

Does your throat hurt you? added the mother to the child. But the little girl's expression didn't change nor did she move her eyes from my face.

Have you looked?

I tried to, said the mother, but I couldn't see.

As it happens we had been having a number of cases of diphtheria in the school to which this child went during that month and we were all, quite apparently, thinking of that, though no one had as yet spoken of the thing.

Well, I said, suppose we take a look at the throat first. I smiled in my best professional manner and asking for the child's first name I said, come on, Mathilda, open your mouth and let's take a look at your throat.

Nothing doing.

Aw, come on, I coaxed, just open your mouth wide and let me take a look. Look, I said opening both hands wide, I haven't anything in my hands. Just open up and let me see.

Such a nice man, put in the mother. Look how kind he is to you. Come on, do what he tells you to. He won't hurt you.

At that I ground my teeth in disgust. If only they wouldn't use the word "hurt" I might be able to get somewhere. But I did not allow myself to be hurried or disturbed but speaking quietly and slowly I approached the child again.

As I moved my chair a little nearer suddenly with one cat-like movement both her hands clawed instinctively for my eyes and she almost reached them too. In fact she knocked my glasses flying and they fell, though unbroken, several feet away from me on the kitchen floor.

Both the mother and father almost turned themselves inside out in embarrassment and apology. You bad girl, said the mother, taking her and shaking her by one arm. Look what you've done. The nice man . . .

For heaven's sake, I broke in. Don't call me a nice man to her. I'm here to look at her throat on the chance that she might have diphtheria and possibly die of it. But that's nothing to her. Look here, I said to the child, we're going to look at your throat. You're old enough to understand what I'm saying. Will you open it now by yourself or shall we have to open it for you?

Not a move. Even her expression hadn't changed. Her breaths however were coming faster and faster. Then the battle began. I had to do it. I had to have a throat culture for her own protection. But first I told the parents that it was entirely up to them. I explained the danger but said that I would not insist on a throat examination so long as they would take the responsibility.

If you don't do what the doctor says you'll have to go to the hospital, the mother admonished her severely.

Oh yeah? I had to smile to myself. After all, I had already fallen in love with the savage brat, the parents were contemptible to me. In the ensuing struggle they grew more and more abject, crushed, exhausted while she surely rose to magnificent heights of insane fury of effort bred of her terror of me.

The father tried his best, and he was a big man but the fact that she was his daughter, his shame at her behavior and his dread of hurting her made him release her just at the critical moment several times when I had almost achieved success, till I wanted to kill him. But his dread also that she might have diphtheria made him tell me to go on, go on though he himself was almost fainting, while the mother moved back and forth behind us raising and lowering her hands in an agony of apprehension.

Put her in front of you on your lap, I ordered, and hold both her wrists.

But as soon as he did the child let out a scream. Don't, you're hurting me. 25 Let go of my hands. Let them go I tell you. Then she shrieked terrifyingly, hysterically. Stop it! Stop it! You're killing me!

Do you think she can stand it, doctor! said the mother.

You get out, said the husband to his wife. Do you want her to die of diphtheria? Come on now, hold her, I said.

Then I grasped the child's head with my left hand and tried to get the wooden tongue depressor between her teeth. She fought, with clenched teeth, desperately! But now I also had grown furious—at a child. I tried to hold myself down but I couldn't. I know how to expose a throat for inspection. And I did my best. When finally I got the wooden spatula behind the last teeth and just the point of it into the mouth cavity, she opened up for an instant but before I could see anything she came down again and gripping the wooden blade between her molars she reduced it to splinters before I could get it out again.

Aren't you ashamed, the mother yelled at her. Aren't you ashamed to act 30 like that in front of the doctor?

Get me a smooth-handled spoon of some sort, I told the mother. We're going through with this. The child's mouth was already bleeding. Her tongue was cut and she was screaming in wild hysterical shrieks. Perhaps I should have desisted and come back in an hour or more. No doubt it would have been better. But I have seen at least two children lying dead in bed of neglect in such cases, and feeling that I must get a diagnosis now or never I went at it again. But the worst of it was that I too had got beyond reason. I could have torn the child apart in my own fury and enjoyed it. It was a pleasure to attack her. My face was burning with it.

The damned little brat must be protected against her own idiocy, one says to one's self at such times. Others must be protected against her. It is social necessity. And all these things are true. But a blind fury, a feeling of adult shame, bred of a longing for muscular release are the operatives. One goes on to the end.

In a final unreasoning assault I overpowered the child's neck and jaws. I forced the heavy silver spoon back of her teeth and down her throat till she gagged. And there it was—both tonsils covered with membrane. She had fought valiantly to keep me from knowing her secret. She had been hiding that sore throat for three days at least and lying to her parents in order to escape just such an outcome as this.

Now truly she *was* furious. She had been on the defensive before but now she attacked. Tried to get off her father's lap and fly at me while tears of defeat blinded her eyes.

12 Criticism: On Fiction

The critical power is of lower rank than the creative. True, but in assenting to this proposition, one or two things are to be kept in mind. It is undeniable that the exercise of a creative power, that of a free creative activity, is the true function of man; it is proved to be so by man's finding in it his true happiness. But it is undeniable, also, that men may have the sense of exercising this free creative activity in other ways than in producing great works of literature or art; if it were not so, all but a very few men would be shut out from the true happiness of all men; they may have it in well-doing, they may have it in learning, they may have it even in criticizing.

—Matthew Arnold, "The Function of Criticism"

Edgar Allan Poe (1809–1849)

THE TALE AND ITS EFFECT   1842

Were we called upon, however, to designate that class of composition which, next to [a short lyric poem], should best fulfill the demands of high genius—should offer it the most advantageous field of exertion—we should unhesitatingly speak of the prose tale, as Mr. Hawthorne has here exemplified it. We allude to the short prose narrative, requiring from a half-hour to one or two hours in its perusal. The ordinary novel is objectionable, from its length, for reasons already stated in substance. As it cannot be read at one sitting, it deprives itself, of course, of the immense force derivable from *totality*. Worldly interests intervening during the pauses of perusal, modify, annul, or counteract, in a greater or less degree, the impressions of the book. But simple cessation in reading would, of itself, be sufficient to destroy the true unity. In the brief tale, however, the author is enabled to carry out the fullness of his intention, be it what it may. During the hour of perusal the soul of the reader is at the writer's control. There are no external or extrinsic influences—resulting from weariness or interruption.

A skillful literary artist has constructed a tale. If wise, he has not fashioned his thoughts to accommodate his incidents; but having conceived, with deliberate care, a certain unique or single *effect* to be wrought out, he then invents such incidents—he then combines such events as may best aid him in establishing this preconceived effect. If his very initial sentence tend not to the outbringing of this effect, then he has failed in his first step. In the whole composition there should be no word written, of which the tendency, direct or indirect, is not to the one pre-established design. And by such means, with such care and skill, a picture is at length painted which leaves in the mind of him who contemplates it with a kindred art, a sense of the fullest satisfaction. The idea of the tale has been presented unblemished, because undisturbed; and this is an end unattainable by the novel. Undue brevity is just as exceptionable here as in the poem; but undue length is yet more to be avoided.

—*Twice-Told Tales*, by Nathaniel Hawthorne: A Review

Charlotte Brontë (1816–1855)

THE WRITER'S PASSIVE WORK   1850

Whether it is right or advisable to create beings like Heathcliff°, I do not know: I scarcely think it is. But this I know: the writer who possesses the creative gift owns something of which he is not always master—something that, at times, strangely wills and works for itself. He may lay down rules and devise principles, and to rules and principles it will perhaps for years lie in subjection; and then, haply without any warning of revolt, there comes a time when it will no longer consent to "harrow the valleys, or be bound with a band in the furrow"—when it "laughs at the multitude of the city, and regards not the crying of the driver"—when, refusing absolutely to make ropes out of sea-sand any longer, it sets to work on statue-hewing, and you have a Pluto or Jove, a Tisiphone or a Psyche, a Mermaid or a Madonna, as Fate or Inspiration direct. Be the work grim or glorious, dread or divine, you have little choice left but quiescent adoption. As for you—the nominal artist—your share in it has been to work passively under dictates you neither delivered nor could question—that would not be uttered at your prayer, nor suppressed nor changed at your caprice. If the result be attractive, the World will praise you, who little deserve praise; if it be repulsive, the same World will blame you, who almost as little deserve blame.

—Preface to the Second Edition of *Wuthering Heights* (by Emily Brontë)

Heathcliff: Central character of the novel *Wuthering Heights:* "a man's shape animated by demon life" (in Charlotte Brontë's view).

Gustave Flaubert (1821–1880)

THE LABOR OF STYLE   1854

Translated by Francis Steegmuller

I have just made a fresh copy of what I have written since New Year, or rather since the middle of February, for on my return from Paris I burned all my January work. It amounts to thirteen pages, no more, no less, thirteen pages in seven weeks. However, they are in shape, I think, and as perfect as I can make them. There are only two or three repetitions of the same word which must be removed, and two turns of phrase that are still too much alike. At last something is completed. It was a difficult transition: the reader had to be led gradually and imperceptibly from psychology to action. Now I am about to begin the dramatic, eventful part. Two or three more big pushes and the end will be in sight. By July or August I hope to tackle the denouement. What a struggle it has been! My God, what a struggle! Such drudgery! Such discouragement! I spent all last evening frantically poring over surgical texts. I am studying the theory of clubfeet. In three hours I devoured an entire volume on this interesting subject and took notes. I came upon some really fine sentences. "The maternal breast is an impenetrable and mysterious sanctuary, where . . . etc." An excellent treatise, incidentally. Why am I not young? How I should work! One ought to know everything, to write. All of us scribblers are monstrously ignorant. If only we weren't so lacking in stamina, what a rich field of ideas and similes we could tap! Books that have been the source of entire literatures, like Homer and Rabelais, contain the sum of all the knowledge of their times. They knew everything, those fellows, and we know nothing. Ronsard's poetics contain a curious precept: he advises the poet to become well versed in the arts and crafts—to frequent blacksmiths, goldsmiths, locksmiths, etc.—in order to enrich his stock of metaphors. And indeed that is the sort of thing that makes for rich and varied language. The sentences in a book must quiver like the leaves in a forest, all dissimilar in their similarity.
—Letter to Louise Colet, April 7, 1854, during the writing of *Madame Bovary*

Henry James (1843–1916)

THE MIRROR OF A CONSCIOUSNESS   1908

This in fact I have ever found rather terribly the point—that the figures in any picture, the agents in any drama, are interesting only in proportion as they feel their respective situations; since the consciousness, on their part, of the complication exhibited forms for us their link of connection with it. But there are degrees of feeling—the muffled, the faint, the just sufficient, the barely intelligent, as we may say; and the acute, the intense, the complete, in a word—the power to be finely aware and richly responsible. It is those moved in this latter fashion who "get most" out of all that happens to them and who in so doing enable us, as readers of their record, as participators by a fond attention, also to get most. Their being finely aware—as Hamlet and Lear, say, are finely aware—*makes* absolutely the intensity of their adventure, gives the maximum of sense to what befalls them. We care, our curiosity and our sympathy care, comparatively little for what happens to the stupid, the coarse and the blind; care for it, and for the effects of it, at the most as helping to precipitate what happens to the more deeply wondering, to the really sentient. Hamlet and Lear are surrounded, amid their complications, by the stupid and the blind, who minister in all sorts of ways to their recorded fate . . . .

Verily even, I think, no "story" is possible without its fools—as most of the fine painters of life, Shakespeare, Cervantes and Balzac, Fielding, Scott, Thackeray, Dickens, George Meredith, George Eliot, Jane Austen, have abundantly felt. At the same time I confess I never see the *leading* interest of any human hazard but in a consciousness (on the part of the moved and moving creature) subject to fine intensification and wide enlargement. It is as mirrored in that consciousness that the gross fools, the headlong fools, the fatal fools play their part for us—they have much less to show us in themselves. The troubled life mostly at the center of our subject—whatever our subject, for the artistic hour, happens to be—embraces them and deals with them for its amusement and its anguish: they are apt largely indeed, on a near view, to be all the cause of its trouble. This means, exactly, that the person capable of feeling in the given case more than another of what is to be felt for it, and so serving in the highest degree to *record* it dramatically and objectively, is the only sort of person on whom we can count not to betray, to cheapen or, as we say, give away, the value and beauty of the thing. By so much as the affair matters *for* some such individual, by so much do we get the best there is of it, and by so much as it falls within the scope of a denser and duller, a more vulgar and more shallow capacity, do we get a picture dim and meager.

The great chroniclers have clearly always been aware of this; they have at least always either placed a mind of some sort—in the sense of a reflecting and coloring medium—in possession of the general adventure . . . or else paid signally, as to the interest created for their failure to do so.

—Preface to *The Princess Casamassima*

Anton Chekhov (1860–1904)

NATURAL DESCRIPTION AND "THE CENTER OF GRAVITY"   1886

Translated by Irina Prishvin

A fine description of nature, I think, has to be brief and to the point. Banalities— "the setting sun, drowning in the darkening waves of the sea," and all that, or, "the swallows, skimming over the crest of the ocean, tweeted happily"—such banalities have to be left out. When describing nature, a writer should seize upon small details, arranging them so that the reader will see an image in his mind after he closes his eyes. For instance: you will capture the truth of a moonlit night if you'll write that a gleam like starlight shone from the pieces of a broken bottle, and then the dark, plump shadow of a dog or wolf appeared. You will bring life to nature only if you don't shrink from similes that liken its activities to those of humankind.

In displaying the psychology of your characters, minute particulars are essential. God save us from vague generalizations! Be sure *not* to discuss your hero's state of mind. Make it clear from his actions. Nor is it necessary to portray many main characters. Let two people be the center of gravity in your story: he and she.

—Letter to his brother Alexander Chekhov, May 10, 1886.

James Joyce (1882–1941)

EPIPHANIES   1904–1906

He° was passing through Eccles Street one evening, one misty evening, with all these thoughts dancing the dance of unrest in his brain when a trivial incident set him composing some ardent verses which he entitled a 'Villanelle of the Temptress.' A young lady was standing on the steps of one of those brown brick houses which seem the very incarnation of Irish paralysis. A young gentleman was leaning on the rusty railings of the area. Stephen as he passed on his quest heard the following fragment of colloquy out of which he received an impression keen enough to afflict his sensitiveness very severely.

THE YOUNG LADY—(drawling discreetly) . . . O, yes . . . I was . . . at the . . . cha . . . pel . . . .

THE YOUNG GENTLEMAN—(inaudibly) . . . I . . . (again inaudibly) . . . I . . .

THE YOUNG LADY—(softly) . . . O . . . but you're . . . ve . . . ry . . . wick . . . ed . . . .

This triviality made him think of collecting many such moments together in a book of epiphanies. By an epiphany he meant a sudden spiritual manifestation, whether in the vulgarity of speech or of gesture or in a memorable phase of the mind itself. He believed that it was for the man of letters to record these epiphanies with extreme care, seeing that they themselves are the most delicate and evanescent of moments. He told Cranly° that the clock of the Ballast Office was capable of an epiphany. Cranly questioned the inscrutable dial of the Ballast Office with his no less inscrutable countenance.

—Yes, said Stephen. I will pass it time after time, allude to it, refer to it, catch a glimpse of it. It is only an item in the catalogue of Dublin's street furniture. Then all at once I see it and I know at once what it is: epiphany . . . .

—Stephen Hero

He: Stephen Dedalus, protagonist of Joyce's novel (an early version of *Portrait of the Artist as a Young Man*), a young Dublin intellectual resembling Joyce himself.   Cranly: a fellow student.

Katherine Mansfield (1888–1923)

WRITING "MISS BRILL"   1921

In "Miss Brill," I choose not only the length of every sentence, but even the sound of every sentence. I choose the rise and fall of every paragraph to fit her, and to fit her on that day at that very moment. After I'd written it I read it aloud— numbers of times—just as one would *play over* a musical composition—trying to get it nearer and nearer to the expression of Miss Brill—until it fitted her.

Don't think I'm vain about the little sketch. It's only the method I wanted to explain. I often wonder whether other writers do the same—if a thing has really come off it seems to me there mustn't be one single word out of place, or one word that could be taken out. That's how I *aim* at writing. It will take some time to get anywhere near there.

                                        —Letter to Richard Murry

William Faulkner (1897–1962)

"THE HUMAN HEART IN CONFLICT WITH ITSELF"   1950

Our tragedy today is a general and universal physical fear so long sustained by now that we can even bear it. There are no longer problems of the spirit. There is only the question: When will I be blown up? Because of this, the young man or woman writing today has forgotten the problems of the human heart in conflict with itself which alone can make good writing because only that is worth writing about, worth the agony and the sweat.

He must learn them again. He must teach himself that the basest of all things is to be afraid; and, teaching himself that, forget it forever, leaving no room in his workshop for anything but the verities and truths of the heart, the old universal truths lacking which any story is ephemeral and doomed—love and honor and pity and pride and compassion and sacrifice. Until he does so, he labors under a curse. He writes not of love but of lust, of defeats in which nobody loses anything of value, of victories without hope and, worst of all, without pity or compassion. His griefs grieve on no universal bones, leaving no scars. He writes not of the heart but of the glands.

Until he relearns these things, he will write as though he stood among and watched the end of man. I decline to accept the end of man. It is easy enough to say that man is immortal simply because he will endure; that when the last ding-dong of doom has clanged and faded from the last worthless rock hanging tideless in the last red and dying evening, that even then there will still be one more sound: that of his puny inexhaustible voice, still talking. I refuse to accept this. I believe that man will not merely endure: he will prevail. He is immortal, not because he alone among creatures has an inexhaustible voice, but because he has a soul, a spirit capable of compassion and sacrifice and endurance. The poet's, the writer's, duty is to write about these things. It is his privilege to help man endure by lifting his heart, by reminding him of the courage and honor and hope and pride and compassion and pity and sacrifice which have been the glory of his past. The poet's voice need not merely be the record of man, it can be one of the props, the pillars to help him endure and prevail.

—Speech of Acceptance for the award of the Nobel Prize for Literature

Flannery O'Connor (1925–1964)

THE SERIOUS WRITER AND THE TIRED READER   1960

Those writers who speak for and with their age are able to do so with a great deal more ease and grace than those who speak counter to prevailing attitudes. I once received a letter from an old lady in California who informed me that when the tired reader comes home at night, he wishes to read something that will lift up his heart. And it seems her heart had not been lifted up by anything of mine she had read. I think that if her heart had been in the right place, it would have been lifted up.

You may say that the serious writer doesn't have to bother about the tired reader, but he does, because they are all tired. One old lady who wants her heart lifted up wouldn't be so bad, but you multiply her two hundred and fifty thousand times and what you get is a book club. I used to think it should be possible to write for some supposed elite, for the people who attend the universities and sometimes know how to read, but I have since found that though you may publish your stories in Botteghe Oscure°, if they are any good at all, you are eventually going to get a letter from some old lady in California, or some inmate of the Federal Penitentiary or the state insane asylum or the local poorhouse, telling you where you have failed to meet his needs.

And his need, of course, is to be lifted up. There is something in us, as storytellers and as listeners to stories, that demands the redemptive act, that demands that what falls at least be offered the chance to be restored. The reader of today looks for this motion, and rightly so, but what he has fogotten is the cost of it. His sense of evil is diluted or lacking altogether and so he has forgotten the price of restoration. When he reads a novel, he wants either his senses tormented or his spirits raised. He wants to be transported, instantly, either to a mock damnation or a mock innocence.

I am often told that the model of balance for the novelist should be Dante, who divided his territory up pretty evenly between hell, purgatory and paradise. There can be no objection to this, but also there can be no reason to assume that the result of doing it in these times will give us the balanced picture that it gave in Dante's. Dante lived in the 13th century when that balance was achieved in the faith of his age. We live now in an age which doubts both fact and value, which is swept this way and that by momentary convictions. Instead of reflecting a balance from the world around him, the novelist now has to achieve one from

Botteghe Oscure: distinguished (and high-priced) literary magazine of the time, published in Rome for a small international audience.

a felt balance inside himself. There are ages when it is possible to woo the reader; there are others when something more drastic is necessary.

There is no literary orthodoxy that can be prescribed as settled for the fiction writer, not even that of Henry James who balanced the elements of traditional realism and romance so admirably within each of his novels. But this much can be said. The great novels we get in the future are not going to be those that the public thinks it wants, or those that critics demand. They are going to be the kind of novels that interest the novelist. And the novels that interest the novelist are those that have not already been written. They are those that put the greatest demands on him, that require him to operate at the maximum of his intelligence and his talents, and to be true to the particularities of his own vocation. The direction of many of us will be toward concentration and the distortion that is necessary to get our vision across; it will be more toward poetry than toward the traditional novel.

The problem for such a novelist will be to know how far he can distort without destroying, and in order not to destroy, he will have to descend far enough into himself to reach those underground springs that give life to his work. This descent into himself will, at the same time, be a descent into his region. It will be a descent through the darkness of the familiar into a world where, like the blind man cured in the gospels, he sees men as if they were trees, but walking. This is the beginning of vision, and I feel it is a vision which we in the South must at least try to understand if we want to participate in the continuance of a vital Southern literature. I hate to think that in twenty years Southern writers too may be writing about men in grey flannel suits and may have lost their ability to see that these gentlemen are even greater freaks than what we are writing about now. I hate to think of the day when the Southern writer will satisfy the tired reader.

—"The Grotesque in Southern Fiction."

Stanley Fish (b. 1938)

AN ESKIMO "A ROSE FOR EMILY"   1980

The fact that it remains easy to think of a reading that most of us would dismiss out of hand does not mean that the text excludes it but that there is as yet no elaborated interpretive procedure for producing that text. . . . Norman Holland's analysis of Faulkner's "A Rose for Emily" is a case in point. Holland is arguing for a knd of psychoanalytic pluralism. The text, he declares, is "at most a matrix of psychological possibilities for its readers," but, he insists, "only some possibilities . . . truly fit the matrix": "One would not say, for example, that a reader of . . . 'A Rose for Emily' who thought the 'tableau' [of Emily and her father in the doorway] described an Eskimo was really responding to the story at all—only pursuing some mysterious inner exploration."

Holland is making two arguments: first, that anyone who proposes an Eskimo reading of "A Rose for Emily" will not find a hearing in the literary community. And that, I think, is right. ("We are right to rule out at least some readings.")

His second argument is that the unacceptability of the Eskimo reading is a function of the text, of what he calls its "sharable promptuary", the public "store of structured language" that sets limits to the interpretations the words can accommodate. And that, I think, is wrong. The Eskimo reading is unacceptable because there is at present no interpretive strategy for producing it, no way of "looking" or reading (and remember, all acts of looking or reading are "ways") that would result in the emergence of obviously Eskimo meanings. This does not mean, however, that no such strategy could ever come into play, and it is not difficult to imagine the circumstances under which it would establish itself. One such circumstance would be the discovery of a letter in which Faulkner confides that he has always believed himself to be an Eskimo changeling. (The example is absurd only if one forgets Yeats's *Vision* or Blake's Swedenborgianism° or James Miller's recent elaboration of a homosexual reading of *The Waste Land*°.) Immediately the workers in the Faulkner industry would begin to reinterpret the canon in the light of this newly revealed "belief" and the work of reinterpretation would involve the elaboration of a symbolic or allusive system (not unlike mythological or typological criticism) whose application would immediately transform the text into one informed everywhere by Eskimo meanings. It might seem that I am admitting that there is a text to be transformed, but the object of transformation would be the text (or texts) given by whatever interpretive strategies the Eskimo strategy was in the process of dislodging or expanding. The result would be that whereas we now have a Freudian "A Rose for Emily," a mythological "A Rose for Emily," a Christological "A Rose for Emily," a regional "A Rose for Emily," a sociological "A Rose for Emily," a linguistic "A Rose for Emily," we would in addition have an Eskimo "A Rose for Emily," existing in some relation of compatibility or incompatibility with the others.

Again the point is that while there are always mechanisms for ruling out readings, their source is not the text but the presently recognized interpretive strategies for producing the text. It follows, then, that no reading, however outlandish is might appear, is inherently an impossible one.

—*Is There a Text in This Class?*

Raymond Carver (1938–1988)

"COMMONPLACE BUT PRECISE LANGUAGE"   1983

It's possible, in a poem or a short story, to write about commonplace things and objects using commonplace but precise language, and to endow those things—a chair, a window curtain, a fork, a stone, a woman's earring—with immense, even startling power. It is possible to write a line of seemingly innocuous dialogue and have it send a chill along the reader's spine—the source of artistic delight, as

Yeats's Vision *or* Blake's Swedenborgianism: Irish poet William Butler Yeats and Swedish mystical writer Emanuel Swedenborg both claimed to have received revelations from the spirit world; some of Swedenborg's ideas are embodied in the long poems of William Blake.   The Waste Land: influential poem by T. S. Eliot.

Nabokov would have it. That's the kind of writing that most interests me. I hate sloppy or haphazard writing whether it flies under the banner of experimentation or else is just clumsily rendered realism. In Isaac Babel's wonderful short story, "Guy de Maupassant," the narrator has this to say about the writing of fiction: "No iron can pierce the heart with such force as a period put just at the right place." This too ought to go on a three-by-five.

Evan Connell said once that he knew he was finished with a short story when he found himself going through it and taking out commas and then going through the story again and putting commas back in the same places. I like that way of working on something. I respect that kind of care for what is being done. That's all we have, finally, the words, and they had better be the right ones, with the punctuation in the right places so that they can best say what they are meant to say. If the words are heavy with the writer's own unbridled emotions, of if they are imprecise and inaccurate for some other reason—if the words are in any way blurred—the reader's eyes will slide right over them and nothing will be achieved. The reader's own artistic sense will simply not be engaged. Henry James called this sort of hapless writing "weak specification."

I have friends who've told me they had to hurry a book because they needed the money, their editor or their wife was leaning on them or leaving them—something, some apology for the writing not being very good. "It would have been better if I'd taken the time." I was dumbfounded when I heard a novelist friend say this. I still am, if I think about it, which I don't. It's none of my business. But if the writing can't be made as good as it is within us to make it, then why do it? In the end, the satisfaction of having done our best, and the proof of that labor, is the one thing we can take into the grave.

—"On Writing," Fires

POETRY

TO THE MUSE

Give me leave, Muse, in plain view to array
Your shift and bodice by the light of day.
I would have brought an epic. Be not vexed
Instead to grace a niggling schoolroom text;
Let down your sanction, help me to oblige
Him who would lead fresh devots to your liege,
And at your altar, grant that in a flash
They, he and I know incense from dead ash.
                                              —X.J.K.

What is poetry? Pressed for an answer, Robert Frost made a classic reply: "Poetry is the kind of thing poets write." In all likelihood, Frost was not trying merely to evade the question but to chide his questioner into thinking for himself. A trouble with definitions is that they may stop thought. If Frost had said, "Poetry is a rhythmical composition of words expressing an attitude, designed to surprise and delight, and to arouse an emotional response," the questioner might have settled back in his chair, content to have learned the truth about poetry. He would have learned nothing, or not so much as he might learn by continuing to wonder.

The nature of poetry eludes simple definitions. (In this respect it is rather like jazz. Asked after one of his concerts, "What is jazz?" Louis Armstrong replied, "Man, if you gotta ask, you'll never know.") Definitions will be of little help at first, if we are to know poetry and respond to it. We have to go to it willing to see and hear. For this reason, you are asked in reading this book not to be in any hurry to decide what poetry is, but instead to study poems and to let them grow in your mind. At the end of our discussions of poetry, the problem of definition will be taken up again (for those who may wish to pursue it).

Confronted with a formal introduction to poetry, you may be wondering, "Who needs it?" and you may well be right. It's unlikely that you have avoided meeting poetry before; and perhaps you already have a friendship, or at least a fair acquaintance, with some of the great English-speaking poets of all time. What this book provides is an introduction to the *study* of poetry. It tries to help you look at a poem closely, to offer you a wider and more accurate vocabulary with which to express what poems say to you. It will suggest ways to judge for yourself the poems you read. It may set forth some poems new to you.

A frequent objection is that poetry ought not to be studied at all. In this view, a poem is either a series of gorgeous noises to be funneled through one ear and out the other without being allowed to trouble the mind, or an experience so holy that to analyze it in a classroom is as cruel and mechanical as dissecting a hummingbird. To the first view, it might be countered that a good poem has something to say that is well worth listening to. To the second view, it might be argued that poems are much less perishable than hummingbirds, and luckily, we can study them in flight. The risk of a poem's dying from observation is not nearly so great as the risk of not really seeing it at all. It is doubtful that any excellent poem has ever vanished from human memory because people have read it too closely. More likely, poems that vanish are poems that no one reads closely, for no one cares.

That poetry matters to the people who write it has been shown unmistakably by the ordeal of Soviet poet Irina Ratushinskaya, now living in the West. Sentenced to prison for three and a half years, she was given paper and pencil only twice a month to write letters to her husband and her parents and was not allowed to write anything else. Nevertheless, Ratushinskaya composed more than two hundred poems in her cell, engraving them with a burnt match in a bar of soap, then memorizing the lines. "I would read the poem and read it," she said, "until it was committed to memory—then with one washing of my hands, it would be gone."[1]

Good poetry is something that readers and listeners, too, can care about. In fact, an ancient persuasion of humankind is that the hearing of a poem, as well as the making of a poem, can be a religious act. Poetry, in speech and song, was part of classic Greek drama, which for playwright, actor, and spectator alike was a holy-day ceremony. The Greeks' belief that a poet writes a poem only by supernatural assistance is clear from the invocations to the Muse that begin the *Iliad* and the *Odyssey* and from the opinion of Socrates (in Plato's *Ion*) that a poet has no powers of invention until divinely inspired. Among the ancient Celts, poets were regarded as magicians and priests, and whoever insulted one of them might expect to receive a curse in rime potent enough to afflict him with boils and to curdle the milk of his cows. Such identification between the poet and the magician are less common these days, although we know that poetry is involved in the primitive white-magic of children, who bring themselves good luck in a game with the charm "Roll, roll, Tootsie-roll! / Roll the marble in the hole!" and who warn against a hex while jumping along a sidewalk: "Step on a crack, / Break your mother's back." But in this age when we pride outselves that a computer may solve the riddle of all creation as soon as it is programmed, magic seems to some people of small importance and so too does poetry. It is dangerous, however, to dismiss what we do not logically understand. To read a poem at all, we have to be willing to offer it responses *besides* a logical understanding. Whether we attribute the effect of a poem to a divine spirit or to the reactions of our glands and cortexes, we have to take the reading of poetry seriously (not solemnly), if only because—as some of the poems in this book may demonstrate—few other efforts can repay us so generously, both in wisdom and in joy.

If, as I hope you will do, you sometimes browse in the book for fun, you may be annoyed to see so many questions following the poems. Should you feel this way, try reading with a slip of paper to cover up the questions. You will then—if the Muse should inspire you—have paper in hand to write a poem.

---

[1]Reported in the *New York Times*, December 19, 1986.

496

13 Reading a Poem

How do you read a poem? The literal-minded might say, "Just let your eye light on it"; but there is more to poetry than meets the eye. What Shakespeare called "the mind's eye" also plays a part. Many a reader who has no trouble understanding and enjoying prose finds poetry difficult. This is to be expected. At first glance, a poem usually will make some sense and give some pleasure, but it may not yield everything at once. Sometimes it only hints at meaning still to come if we will keep after it. Poetry is not to be galloped over like the daily news: a poem differs from most prose in that it is to be read slowly, carefully, and attentively. Not all poems are difficult, of course, and some can be understood and enjoyed on first seeing. But good poems yield more if read twice; and the best poems—after ten, twenty, or a hundred readings—still go on yielding.

Approaching a thing written in lines and surrounded with white space, we need not expect it to be a poem just because it is **verse.** (Any composition in lines of more or less regular rhythm, usually ending in rimes, is verse.) Here, for instance, is a specimen of verse that few will call poetry:

> Thirty days hath September,
> April, June, and November;
> All the rest have thirty-one
> Excepting February alone,
> To which we twenty-eight assign
> Till leap year makes it twenty-nine.

To a higher degree than that classic memory-tickler, poetry appeals to the mind and arouses feelings. Poetry may state facts, but, more important, it makes imaginative statements that we may value even if its facts are incorrect. Coleridge's error in placing a star within the horns of the crescent moon in "The Rime of the Ancient Mariner" does not stop the passage from being good poetry, though it is faulty astronomy. According to one poet, Gerard Manley Hopkins, poetry is "to be heard for its own sake and interest even over and above its interest of meaning." There are other elements in a poem besides plain prose sense: sounds, images, rhythms, figures of speech. These may strike us and please us even before we ask, "But what does it all mean?"

This is a truth not readily grasped by anyone who regards a poem as a kind of puzzle written in secret code with a message slyly concealed. The effect of a poem (one's whole mental and emotional response to it) consists in much more than simply a message. By its musical qualities, by its suggestions, it can work on the reader's unconscious. T. S. Eliot put it well when he said in *The Use of Poetry and the Use of Criticism* that the prose sense of a poem is chiefly useful in keeping the reader's mind "diverted and quiet, while the poem does its work upon him." Eliot went on to liken the meaning of a poem to the bit of meat a burglar brings along to throw to the family dog. What is the work of a poem? To touch us, to stir us, to make us glad, and possibly even to tell us something.

How to set about reading a poem? Here are a few suggestions.

To begin with, read the poem once straight through, with no particular expectations; read open-mindedly. Let yourself experience whatever you find, without worrying just yet about the large general and important ideas the poem contains (if indeed it contains any). Don't dwell on a troublesome word or difficult passage—just push on. Some of the difficulties may seem smaller when you read the poem for a second time; at least, they will have become parts of a whole for you.

On second reading, read for the exact sense of all the words; if there are words you don't understand, look them up in a dictionary. Dwell on any difficult parts as long as you need to.

If you read the poem silently to yourself, sound its words in your mind. (This is a technique that will get you nowhere in a speed-reading course, but it may help the poem to do its work on you.) Better still, read the poem aloud, or hear someone else read it. You may discover meanings you didn't perceive in it before. Even if you are no actor, to decide how to speak a poem can be an excellent method of getting to understand it. Some poems, like bells, seem heavy till heard. Listen while reading the following lines from Alexander Pope's *Dunciad.* Attacking the minor poet James Ralph, who had sung the praises of a mistress named Cynthia, Pope makes the goddess of Dullness exclaim:

"Silence, ye wolves! while Ralph to Cynthia howls,
And makes night hideous—answer him, ye owls!"

When *ye owls* slide together and become *yowls,* poor Ralph's serenade is turned into the nightly outcry of a cat.

Try to **paraphrase** the poem as a whole, or perhaps just the more difficult lines. In paraphrasing, we put into our own words what we understand the poem to say, restating ideas that seem essential, coming out and stating what the poem may only suggest. This may sound like a heartless thing to do to a poem, but good poems can stand it. In fact, to compare a poem to its paraphrase is a good way to see the distance between poetry and prose. In making a paraphrase, we generally work through a poem or a passage line by line. The statement that results may take as many words as the original, if not more. A paraphrase, then, is ampler than a **summary,** a brief condensation of gist, main idea, or story. (Summary of a horror film in *TV Guide:* "Demented biologist, coveting power over New York, swells sewer rats to hippopotamus-size.") Here is a poem worth considering line by line. The poet writes of an island in a lake in the west of Ireland where he spent many summers as a boy. (The asterisk on Yeats's name means that his biography appears in "Lives of the Poets," pages 903–933.)

William Butler Yeats (1865–1939)*

THE LAKE ISLE OF INNISFREE   1892

I will arise and go now, and go to Innisfree,
And a small cabin build there, of clay and wattles made:
Nine bean-rows will I have there, a hive for the honey-bee,
And live alone in the bee-loud glade.

And I shall have some peace there, for peace comes dropping slow,   5
Dropping from the veils of the morning to where the cricket sings;
There midnight's all a glimmer, and noon a purple glow,
And evening full of the linnet's wings.

I will arise and go now, for always night and day
I hear lake water lapping with low sounds by the shore;   10
While I stand on the roadway, or on the pavements gray,
I hear it in the deep heart's core.

Though relatively simple, this poem is far from simple-minded. We need to absorb it slowly and thoughtfully. At the start, for most of us, it raises problems: what are *wattles,* from which the speaker's dream-cabin is to be made? We might guess, but in this case it will help to consult a dictionary: they are "poles interwoven with sticks or branches, formerly used in building as frameworks to support walls or roofs." Evidently, this getaway house will be built in an old-fashioned way: it won't be a prefabricated log cabin or A-frame house, nothing modern or citified. The phrase *bee-loud glade* certainly isn't commonplace language of the sort we find on a cornflake package, but right away, we can understand it, at least partially: it's a place loud with bees. What is a *glade?* Experience might tell us that it is an open space in woods, but if that word stops us, we can look it up. Although the *linnet* doesn't live in North America, it is a creature with wings—a songbird of the finch family, adds the dictionary. But even if we don't make a special trip to the dictionary to find *linnet,* we recognize that the word means "bird," and the line makes sense to us.

A paraphrase of the whole poem might go something like this (in language easier to forget than that of the original): "I'm going to get up now, go to Innisfree, build a cabin, plant beans, keep bees, and live peacefully by myself amid nature and beautiful light. I want to, because I can't forget the sound of that lake water. When I'm in the city, a gray and dingy place, I seem to hear it deep inside me."

These dull remarks, roughly faithful to what Yeats is saying, seem a long way from poetry. Nevertheless, they make certain things clear. For one, they spell out what the poet merely hints at in his choice of the word *gray*: that he finds the city dull and depressing. He stresses the word; instead of saying *gray pavements,* in the usual word-order, he turns the phrase around and makes *gray* stand at the end of the line, where it rimes with *day* and so takes extra emphasis. The grayness of the city therefore seems important to the poem, and the paraphrase tries to make its meaning obvious.

Whenever you paraphrase, you stick your neck out. You affirm what the poem gives you to understand. And making a paraphrase can help you see the central thought of the poem, its **theme.** Theme isn't the same as **subject,** the main topic, whatever the poem is "about." In Yeats's poem, the subject is the lake isle of Innisfree, or a wish to retreat to it. But the theme is, "I yearn for an ideal place where I will find perfect peace and happiness." Themes can be stated variously, depending on what you believe most matters in the poem. Taking a different view of the poem, placing more weight on the speaker's wish to escape the city, you might instead state the theme: "This city is getting me down—I want to get back to nature." But after taking a second look at that statement, you might want to sharpen it. After all, this Innisfree seems a special, particular place, where the natural world means more to the poet than just any old trees and birds he might see in a park. Perhaps a stronger statement of theme, one closer to what matters most in the poem, might be: "I want to quit the city for my heaven on earth." That, of course, is saying in an obvious way what Yeats says more subtly, more memorably.

Not all poems clearly assert a proposition, but many do; some even declare their themes in their opening lines: "Gather ye rose-buds while ye may!"—that is, enjoy love before it's too late. This theme, stated in that famous first line of Robert Herrick's "To the Virgins, to Make Much of Time" (page 825), is so familiar that we give it a name: **carpe diem,** Latin for "seize the day." It is a favorite argument of poets since Roman times. You will meet it in more than one poem in this book.

A paraphrase, of course, never tells *all* that a poem contains; nor will every reader agree that a particular paraphrase is accurate. We all make our own interpretations; and sometimes the total meaning of a poem evades even the poet who wrote it. Asked to explain his difficult *Sordello,* Robert Browning replied that when he had written the poem only God and he knew what it meant; but "Now, only God knows." Still, to analyze a poem *as if* we could be certain of its meaning is, in general, more fruitful than to proceed as if no certainty could ever be had. The latter approach is likely to end in complete subjectivity: the attitude of the reader who says, "Yeats's 'Lake Isle of Innisfree' is really about the lost island of Atlantis. It is, because I think it is. How can you prove me wrong?" Interpretations can't be proven "wrong." A more fruitful question might be, "What can we understand from the poem's very words?"

All of us bring personal associations to the poems we read. "The Lake Isle of Innisfree" might give you special pleasure if you have ever vacationed on a small island or on the shore of a lake. Such associations are inevitable, even to be welcomed, as long as they don't interfere with our reading the words on the page. We need to distinguish irrelevant responses from those the poem calls for. The reader who can't stand "The Lake Isle of Innisfree" because she is afraid of bees isn't reading a poem by Yeats, but one of her own invention.

Now and again we meet a poem—perhaps startling and memorable—into which the method of paraphrase won't take us far. Some portion of any deep poem resists explanation, but certain poems resist it almost entirely. Many poems of religious mystics seem closer to dream than waking. So do poems that purport to record drug experiences, such as Coleridge's "Kubla Khan" (page 795), as well as poems that embody some private system of beliefs, such as Blake's "The Sick Rose" (page 787), or the same poet's lines from *Jerusalem*,

> For a Tear is an Intellectual thing,
> And a Sigh is the Sword of an Angel King.

So do nonsense poems, translations of primitive folk songs, and surreal poems.[1] Such poetry may move us and give pleasure (although not, perhaps, the pleasure of mental understanding). We do it no harm by trying to paraphrase it, though we may fail. Whether logically clear or strangely opaque, good poems appeal to the intelligence and do not shrink from it.

So far, we have taken for granted that poetry differs from prose; yet all our strategies for reading poetry—plowing straight on through and then going back, isolating difficulties, trying to paraphrase, reading aloud, using a dictionary—are no different from those we might employ in unraveling a complicated piece of prose. Poetry, after all, is similar to prose in most respects. At the very least, it is written in the same language. Like prose, poetry shares knowledge with us. It tells us, for instance, of a beautiful island in Lake Gill, County Sligo, Ireland, of how one man feels toward it. Maybe the poet knows no more about Innisfree than a writer of a travel guidebook knows. And yet Yeats's poem indicates a kind of knowledge that tourist guidebooks do not ordinarily reveal: that the human heart can yearn for peace and happiness, that the lake isle of Innisfree with its "low sounds by the shore" can echo and reecho in memory forever.

LYRIC POETRY

Originally, as its Greek name suggests, a *lyric* was a poem sung to the music of a lyre. This earlier meaning—a poem made for singing—is still current today, when we use *lyrics* to mean the words of a popular song. But the kind of printed poem we now call a *lyric* is usually something else, for over the past five hundred

---

[1]The French poet André Breton, founder of **surrealism,** a movement in art and writing, declared that a higher reality exists, which to mortal eyes looks absurd. To mirror that reality, surrealist poets are fond of bizarre and dreamlike objects such as soluble fish and white-haired revolvers.

years, the nature of lyric poetry has changed greatly. Ever since the rise of the printing press in the fifteenth century, poets have written less often for singers, more often for readers. In general, this tendency has made lyric poems contain less word-music and (since they can be pondered on a page) more thought—and perhaps more complicated feelings.

Here is a rough definition of a **lyric** as it is written today: a short poem expressing the thoughts and feelings of a single speaker. Probably, it won't report conversations between two or more speakers, as does a poem given later in this chapter, "Sir Patrick Spence." Often a poet will write a lyric in the first person ("I will arise and go now, and go to Innisfree"), but not always. Instead, a lyric might describe an object or recall an experience without the speaker's ever bringing himself or herself into it. (For an example of such a lyric, one in which the poet refrains from saying "I," see William Carlos Williams's "The Red Wheelbarrow" on page 521, Theodore Roethke's "Root Cellar" on page 571, or Gerard Manley Hopkin's "Pied Beauty" on page 576.)

Perhaps because, rightly or wrongly, some people still think of lyrics as lyre-strummings, they expect a lyric to be an outburst of feeling, somewhat resembling a song, at least containing musical elements such as rime, rhythm, or sound effects. Such expectations are fulfilled in "The Lake Isle of Innisfree," that impassioned lyric full of language rich in sound (as you will hear if you'll read it aloud). In practice, though, many contemporary poets write short poems in which they voice opinions or complicated feelings—poems that no reader would dream of trying to sing. Most people would call such poems lyrics, too; one recent commentator has argued that a lyric may contain an argument.[2]

But in the sense in which we use it, *lyric* will usually apply to a kind of poem you can easily recognize. Here, for instance, are two lyrics. They differ sharply in subject and theme, but they have traits in common: both are short, and (as you will find) both set forth one speaker's definite, unmistakable feelings.

D. H. Lawrence (1885 – 1930)*

PIANO   1918

Softly, in the dusk, a woman is singing to me;
Taking me back down the vista of years, till I see
A child sitting under the piano, in the boom of the tingling strings
And pressing the small, poised feet of a mother who smiles as she
    sings.

In spite of myself, the insidious mastery of song   5
Betrays me back, till the heart of me weeps to belong
To the old Sunday evenings at home, with winter outside
And hymns in the cozy parlor, the tinkling piano our guide.

[2]Jeffrey Walker, "Aristotle's Lyric," *College English* 51 (January, 1989) 5–26.

So now it is vain for the singer to burst into clamor
With the great black piano appassionato. The glamor   10
Of childish days is upon me, my manhood is cast
Down in the flood of remembrance, I weep like a child for the past.

QUESTIONS

1. Jot down a brief paraphrase of this poem. In your paraphrase, clearly show what the
   speaker says is happening at present and also what he finds himself remembering.
   Make clear which seems the more powerful in its effect on him.
2. What are the speaker's various feelings? What do you understand from the words
   insidious and *betrays?*
3. With what specific details does the poem make the past seem real?
4. What is the subject of Lawrence's poem? How would you state its theme?

Marianne Moore (1887 – 1972)*

THE WOOD-WEASEL   1944

emerges daintily, the skunk—
don't laugh—in sylvan black and white chipmunk
regalia. The inky thing
adaptively whited with glistening
goat-fur, is wood-warden. In his   5
ermined well-cuttlefish-inked wool, he is
determination's totem. Out-
lawed? His sweet face and powerful feet go about
in chieftain's coat of Chilkat cloth.
He is his own protection from the moth,   10

noble little warrior. That
otter-skin on it, the living pole-cat,
smothers anything that stings. Well,—
this same weasel's playful and his weasel
associates are too. Only   15
Wood-weasels shall associate with me.

THE WOOD-WEASEL. 9 *Chilkat cloth:* Fine cloth made by the Chilkats, a Native American people
of southeastern Alaska.

QUESTIONS

1. What traits and features does Marianne Moore find in her subject to admire?
2. In what ways does the language of "The Wood-Weasel" differ from most prose you've
   read lately? (Suggestion: read the poem aloud.)
3. The poet uses three different names for the same animal: *wood-weasel, skunk,* and
   pole-cat. What possible reasons might she have for preferring the first?
4. "To hell with people—I'll take skunks." How accurate would that be as a statement
   of the poem's theme?

Narrative Poetry

Although a lyric sometimes relates an incident, or like "Piano" draws a scene, it does not usually relate a series of events. That happens in a **narrative poem,** one whose main purpose is to tell a story.

In Western literature, narrative poetry dates back to the Babylonian epic of Gilgamesh (composed before 2000 B.C.) and Homer's epic *Iliad* and *Odyssey* (composed before 700 B.C.). It may well have originated much earlier. In England and Scotland, storytelling poems have long been popular; in the late Middle Ages, ballads—or storytelling songs—circulated widely. Some, like "Sir Patrick Spence" and "Bonny Barbara Allan," survive in our day, and folksingers sometimes perform them.

Evidently the art of narrative poetry invites the skills of a writer of fiction: the ability to draw characters and settings briefly, to engage attention, to shape a plot. Needless to say, it calls for all the skills of a poet besides. Here are two narrative poems: one medieval, one modern. How would you paraphrase the stories they tell? How do they hold your attention to their stories?

Anonymous (traditional Scottish ballad)

Sir Patrick Spence

The king sits in Dumferling toune,
    Drinking the blude-reid wine:
"O whar will I get guid sailor
    To sail this schip of mine?"

Up and spak an eldern knicht,   5
    Sat at the kings richt kne:
"Sir Patrick Spence is the best sailor
    That sails upon the se."

The king has written a braid letter,
    And signed it wi' his hand,   10
And sent it to Sir Patrick Spence,
    Was walking on the sand.

The first line that Sir Patrick red,
    A loud lauch lauchèd he;
The next line that Sir Patrick red,   15
    The teir blinded his ee.

"O wha° is this has don this deid,   *who*
    This ill deid don to me,
To send me out this time o' the yeir,
    To sail upon the se!   20

"Mak haste, mak haste, my mirry men all,
    Our guid schip sails the morne."
"O say na sae°, my master deir,   so
    For I feir a deadlie storme.

"Late late yestreen I saw the new moone,   25
    Wi' the auld moone in hir arme,
And I feir, I feir, my deir master,
    That we will cum to harme."

O our Scots nobles wer richt laith°   loath
    To weet° their cork-heild schoone°,   wet; shoes   30
Bot lang owre° a' the play wer playd,   before
    Their hats they swam aboone°.   above (their heads)

O lang, lang may their ladies sit,
    Wi' their fans into their hand,
Or ere° they se Sir Patrick Spence   long before   35
    Cum sailing to the land.

O lang, lang may the ladies stand,
    Wi' their gold kems° in their hair,   combs
Waiting for their ain° deir lords,   own
    For they'll se thame na mair.   40

Haf owre°, haf owre to Aberdour,   halfway over
    It's fiftie fadom deip,
And thair lies guid Sir Patrick Spence,
    Wi' the Scots lords at his feit.

SIR PATRICK SPENCE. 9 *braid*: Broad, but broad in what sense? Among guesses are *plain-spoken*,
official, and *on wide paper*.

QUESTIONS

1. That the king drinks "blood-red wine" (line 2)—what meaning do you find in that
   detail? What does it hint, or foreshadow?
2. What do you make of this king and his motives for sending Spence and the Scots
   lords out into an impending storm? Is he a fool, is he cruel and inconsiderate, is he
   deliberately trying to drown Sir Patrick and his crew, or can't we possibly know? Let
   your answer depend on the poem alone, not on anything you read into it.
3. Comment on this ballad's methods of storytelling. Is the story told too briefly for us
   to care what happens to Spence and his men, or does the poet by any means make
   us feel compassion for them? Do you resent the lack of a detailed account of the
   shipwreck?
4. Lines 25–28—the new moon with the old moon in her arm—has been much admired
   as poetry. What does this stanza contribute to the story as well?

Robert Frost (1874 – 1963)*

"Out, Out—" 1916

The buzz-saw snarled and rattled in the yard
And made dust and dropped stove-length sticks of wood,
Sweet-scented stuff when the breeze drew across it.
And from there those that lifted eyes could count
Five mountain ranges one behind the other   5
Under the sunset far into Vermont.
And the saw snarled and rattled, snarled and rattled,
As it ran light, or had to bear a load.
And nothing happened: day was all but done.
Call it a day, I wish they might have said   10
To please the boy by giving him the half hour
That a boy counts so much when saved from work.
His sister stood beside them in her apron
To tell them "Supper." At the word, the saw,
As if to prove saws knew what supper meant,   15
Leaped out at the boy's hand, or seemed to leap—
He must have given the hand. However it was,
Neither refused the meeting. But the hand!
The boy's first outcry was a rueful laugh,
As he swung toward them holding up the hand   20
Half in appeal, but half as if to keep
The life from spilling. Then the boy saw all—
Since he was old enough to know, big boy
Doing a man's work, though a child at heart—
He saw all spoiled. "Don't let him cut my hand off—   25
The doctor, when he comes. Don't let him, sister!"
So. But the hand was gone already.
The doctor put him in the dark of ether.
He lay and puffed his lips out with his breath.
And then—the watcher at his pulse took fright.   30
No one believed. They listened at his heart.
Little—less—nothing!—and that ended it.
No more to build on there. And they, since they
Were not the one dead, turned to their affairs.

"Out, Out—" The title of this poem echoes the words of Shakespeare's Macbeth on receiving news that his queen is dead: "Out, out, brief candle! / Life's but a walking shadow, a poor player / That struts and frets his hour upon the stage / And then is heard no more. It is a tale / Told by an idiot, full of sound and fury, / Signifying nothing" (*Macbeth* V, v, 23–28).

Questions

1. How does Frost make the buzz-saw appear sinister? How does he make it seem, in another way, like a friend?

2. What do you make of the people who surround the boy—the "they" of the poem? Who might they be? Do they seem to you concerned and compassionate, cruel, indifferent, or what?
3. What does Frost's reference to *Macbeth* contribute to your understanding of "Out, Out—"? How would you state the theme of Frost's poem?
4. Set this poem side by side with "Sir Patrick Spence." How does "Out, Out—" resemble that medieval folk ballad in subject, or differ from it? How is Frost's poem similar or different in its way of telling a story?

Today, lyrics in the English language seem more plentiful than other kinds of poetry. Long narrative poems still appear, but have a far smaller audience than Henry Wadsworth Longfellow's *Evangeline* and Alfred, Lord Tennyson's *Idylls of the King* enjoyed in the nineteenth century.

Also more fashionable in former times was a third variety of poetry, **didactic poetry:** that apparently written to state a message or teach a body of knowledge. In a lyric, a speaker may express sadness; in a didactic poem, he or she may explain that sadness is inherent in life. Poems that impart a body of knowledge, like Ovid's *Art of Love* and Lucretius's *On the Nature of Things,* are didactic. Such instructive poetry was favored especially by classical Latin poets and by English poets of the eighteenth century. In *The Fleece* (1757), John Dyer celebrated the British woolen industry and included practical advice on raising sheep:

> In cold stiff soils the bleaters oft complain
> Of gouty ails, by shepherds termed the halt:
> Those let the neighboring fold or ready crook
> Detain, and pour into their cloven feet
> Corrosive drugs, deep-searching arsenic,
> Dry alum, verdegris, or vitriol keen.

One might agree with Dr. Johnson's comment on Dyer's effort: "The subject, Sir, cannot be made poetical." But it may be argued that the subject of didactic poetry does not make it any less poetical. Good poems, it seems, can be written about anything under the sun. In a splendid poem, Robert Lowell tells of an encounter with a garbage-eating skunk, while in another fine poem, James Merrill shows us a woman dissecting live turtles in a laboratory. Like Dyer, John Milton also described sick sheep in "Lycidas," a poem few readers have thought unpoetic:

> The hungry sheep look up, and are not fed,
> But, swoll'n with wind and the rank mist they draw,
> Rot inwardly, and foul contagion spread . . .

What makes Milton's lines better poetry than Dyer's is, among other things, a difference in attitude. Sick sheep to Dyer mean the loss of a few shillings and pence; to Milton, whose sheep stand for English Christendom, they mean a moral catastrophe.

Suggestion for Writing

Write a concise, accurate paraphrase of a poem from the Poems for Further Reading (pages 773–902). Your instructor may wish to suggest a poem or poems. Although your paraphrase should take in the entire poem, it need not mention everything. Just try to include the points that seem most vital and try to state the poem's main thought, or *theme*. Be ready to share your paraphrase with the rest of the class and to compare it with other paraphrases of the same poem. You may then be able to test yourself as a reader of poetry. What in the poem whizzed by you that other students noticed? What did you discover that others ignored?

14   *Listening to a Voice*

TONE

In late-show Westerns, when one hombre taunts another, it is customary for the second to drawl, "Smile when you say that, pardner" or "Mister, I don't like your tone of voice." Sometimes in reading a poem, although we can neither see a face nor hear a voice, we can infer the poet's attitude from other evidence.

Like tone of voice, **tone** in literature often conveys an attitude toward the person addressed. Like the manner of a person, the manner of a poem may be friendly or belligerent toward its reader, condescending or respectful. Again like tone of voice, the tone of a poem may tell us how the speaker feels about himself or herself: cocksure or humble, sad or glad. But usually when we ask, "What is the tone of a poem?" we mean, "What attitude does the poet take toward a theme or a subject?" Is the poet being affectionate, hostile, earnest, playful, sarcastic, or what? We may never be able to know, of course, the poet's personal feelings. All we need know is how to feel when we read the poem.

Strictly speaking, tone isn't an attitude; it is whatever in the poem makes an attitude clear to us: the choice of certain words instead of others, the picking out of certain details. In Housman's "Loveliest of trees," for example, the poet communicates his admiration for a cherry tree's beauty by singling out for attention its white blossoms; had he wanted to show his dislike for the tree, he might have concentrated on its broken branches, birdlime, or snails. Rightly to perceive the tone of a poem, we need to read the poem carefully, paying attention to whatever suggestions we find in it.

Theodore Roethke (1908 – 1963)*

MY PAPA'S WALTZ   1948

The whiskey on your breath
Could make a small boy dizzy;
But I hung on like death:
Such waltzing was not easy.

We romped until the pans   5
Slid from the kitchen shelf;
My mother's countenance
Could not unfrown itself.

The hand that held my wrist
Was battered on one knuckle;   10
At every step you missed
My right ear scraped a buckle.

You beat time on my head
With a palm caked hard by dirt,
Then waltzed me off to bed   15
Still clinging to your shirt.

What is the tone of this poem? Most readers find the speaker's attitude toward his father affectionate and take this recollection of childhood to be a happy one. But at least one reader, concentrating on certain details, once wrote: "Roethke expresses his resentment for his father, a drunken brute with dirty hands and a whiskey breath who carelessly hurt the child's ear and manhandled him." Although this reader accurately noticed some of the events in the poem and perceived that in the son's hanging on to the father "like death" there is something desperate, he missed the tone of the poem and so misunderstood it altogether. Among other things, this reader didn't notice the rollicking rhythms of the poem; the playfulness of a rime like *dizzy* and *easy*; the joyful suggestions of the words *waltz, waltzing,* and *romped.* Probably the reader didn't stop to visualize this scene in all its comedy, with kitchen pans falling and the father happily using his son's head for a drum. Nor did he stop to feel the suggestions in the last line, with the boy *still clinging* with persistent love.

Such a poem, though it includes lifelike details that aren't pretty, has a tone relatively easy to recognize. So does **satiric poetry,** a kind of comic poetry that generally conveys a message. Usually its tone is one of detached amusement, withering contempt, and implied superiority. In a satiric poem, the poet ridicules some person or persons (or perhaps some kind of human behavior), examining the victim by the light of certain principles and implying that the reader, too, ought to feel contempt for the victim.

Countee Cullen (1903 – 1946)

FOR A LADY I KNOW   1925

She even thinks that up in heaven
    Her class lies late and snores,
While poor black cherubs rise at seven
    To do celestial chores.

QUESTIONS

1. What is Cullen's message?
2. How would you characterize the tone of this poem? Wrathful? Amused?

    In some poems the poet's attitude may be plain enough; while in other poems attitudes may be so mingled that it is hard to describe them tersely without doing injustice to the poem. Does Andrew Marvell in "To His Coy Mistress" (page 846) take a serious or playful attitude toward the fact that he and his lady are destined to be food for worms? No one-word answer will suffice. And what of T. S. Eliot's "Love Song of J. Alfred Prufrock" (page 806)? In his attitude toward his redemption-seeking hero who wades with trousers rolled, Eliot is seriously funny. Such a mingled tone may be seen in the following poem by the wife of a governor of the Massachusetts Bay Colony and the earliest American poet of note. Anne Bradstreet's first book, *The Tenth Muse Lately Sprung Up in America* (1650), had been published in England without her consent. She wrote these lines to preface a second edition:

Anne Bradstreet (1612? – 1672)

THE AUTHOR TO HER BOOK   1678

Thou ill-formed offspring of my feeble brain,
Who after birth did'st by my side remain,
Till snatched from thence by friends, less wise than true,
Who thee abroad exposed to public view;
Made thee in rags, halting, to the press to trudge,   5
Where errors were not lessened, all may judge.
At thy return my blushing was not small,
My rambling brat (in print) should mother call;
I cast thee by as one unfit for light,
Thy visage was so irksome in my sight;   10
Yet being mine own, at length affection would
Thy blemishes amend, if so I could:
I washed thy face, but more defects I saw,
And rubbing off a spot, still made a flaw.
I stretched thy joints to make thee even feet,   15
Yet still thou run'st more hobbling than is meet;

In better dress to trim thee was my mind,
But nought save homespun cloth in the house I find.
In this array, 'mongst vulgars may'st thou roam;
In critics' hands beware thou dost not come;   20
And take thy way where yet thou are not known.
If for thy Father asked, say thou had'st none;
And for thy Mother, she alas is poor,
Which caused her thus to send thee out of door.

In the author's comparison of her book to an illegitimate ragamuffin, we may
be struck by the details of scrubbing and dressing a child: details that might
well occur to a mother who had scrubbed and dressed many. As she might feel
toward such a child, so she feels toward her book. She starts by deploring it
but, as the poem goes on, cannot deny it her affection. Humor enters (as in the
pun in line 15). She must dress the creature in *homespun cloth*, something both
crude and serviceable. By the end of her poem, Bradstreet seems to regard her
book-child with tenderness, amusement, and a certain indulgent awareness of
its faults. To read this poem is to sense its mingling of several attitudes.
Simultaneously, a poet can be merry and in earnest.

Walt Whitman (1819 – 1892)*

TO A LOCOMOTIVE IN WINTER   1881

Thee for my recitative,
Thee in the driving storm even as now, the snow, the winter-day
    declining,
Thee in thy panoply°, thy measur'd dual throbbing and thy   *suit of*
    beat convulsive,   *armor*
Thy black cylindric body, golden brass and silvery steel,
Thy ponderous side-bars, parallel and connecting rods, gyrating,
    shuttling at thy sides,   5
Thy metrical, now swelling pant and roar, now tapering in the
    distance,
Thy great protruding head-light fix'd in front,
Thy long, pale, floating vapor-pennants, tinged with delicate purple,
The dense and murky clouds out-belching from thy smoke-stack,
Thy knitted frame, thy springs and valves, the tremulous twinkle of
    thy wheels,   10
Thy train of cars behind, obedient, merrily following,
Through gale or calm, now swift, now slack, yet steadily careering;
Type of the modern — emblem of motion and power — pulse of the
    continent,
For once come serve the Muse and merge in verse, even as here I see
    thee,

With storm and buffeting gusts of wind and falling snow, 15
By day thy warning ringing bell to sound its notes,
By night thy silent signal lamps to swing.
Fierce-throated beauty!
Roll through my chant with all thy lawless music, thy swinging lamps
    at night,
Thy madly-whistled laughter, echoing, rumbling like an earthquake,
  ⟶ rousing all, 20
Law of thyself complete, thine own track firmly holding,
(No sweetness debonair of tearful harp or glib piano thine,)
Thy trills of shrieks by rocks and hills return'd,
Launch'd o'er the prairies wide, across the lakes,
To the free skies unpent and glad and strong. 25

Emily Dickinson (1830 – 1886)*

I LIKE TO SEE IT LAP THE MILES   (about 1862)

I like to see it lap the Miles –
And lick the Valleys up –
And stop to feed itself at Tanks –
And then – prodigious step

Around a Pile of Mountains – 5
And supercilious peer
In Shanties – by the sides of Roads –
And then a Quarry pare

To fit its Ribs
And crawl between
Complaining all the while 10
In horrid – hooting stanza –
Then chase itself down Hill –

And neigh like Boanerges –
Then – punctual as a Star 15
Stop – docile and omnipotent
At its own stable door –

QUESTIONS

1. What differences in tone do you find between Whitman's and Dickinson's poems?
   Point out in each poem whatever contributes to these differences.
2. *Boanerges* in Dickinson's last stanza means "sons of thunder," a name given by Jesus
   to the disciples John and James (see Mark 3:17). How far should the reader work out
   the particulars of this comparison? Does it make the tone of the poem serious?
3. In Whitman's opening line, what is a *recitative*? What other specialized terms from
   the vocabulary of music and poetry does each poem contain? How do they help
   underscore Whitman's theme?

4. Poets and song-writers probably have regarded the locomotive with more affection than they have shown most other machines. Why do you suppose this to be? Can you think of any other poems or songs for example?
5. What do these two poems tell you about locomotives that you would not be likely to find in a technical book on railroading?
6. Are the subjects of the two poems identical? Discuss.

Langston Hughes (1902 – 1967)*

HOMECOMING   1959

I went back in the alley
And I opened up my door.
All her clothes was gone:
She wasn't home no more.

I pulled back the covers,   5
I made down the bed.
A *whole* lot of room
Was the only thing I had.

QUESTIONS

1. How does the speaker feel about this sudden disappearance? Exactly what in the poem makes his feelings clear?
2. Suppose the speaker had ranted, cried, felt sorry for himself, and discussed his anger, frustration, and grief at great length. Do you suppose a better poem might have resulted? What do you find to admire in the poem as it is?

John Milton (1608 – 1674)*

ON THE LATE MASSACRE IN PIEMONT   (1655)

Avenge, O Lord, thy slaughtered saints, whose bones
   Lie scattered on the Alpine mountains cold;
   Even them who kept thy truth so pure of old,
When all our fathers worshiped stocks and stones,
Forget not: in thy book record their groans   5
   Who were thy sheep, and in their ancient fold
   Slain by the bloody Piemontese, that rolled
Mother with infant down the rocks. Their moans
The vales redoubled to the hills, and they
   To heaven. Their martyred blood and ashes sow   10
O'er all the Italian fields, where still doth sway
   The triple Tyrant; that from these may grow
   A hundredfold, who, having learnt thy way,
Early may fly the Babylonian woe.

On the Late Massacre in Piemont. Despite hostility between Catholics and Protestants, the Waldenses, members of a Puritan sect, had been living in the Piemont, that region in northwest Italy bounded by the crests of the Alps. In 1655, ignoring a promise to observe religious liberty, troops of the Roman Catholic ruler of the Piemont put to death several members of the sect. 4 *When . . . stones:* Englishmen had been Catholics, worshiping stone and wooden statues (so Milton charges) when the Waldensian sect was founded in the twelfth century. 12 *The triple Tyrant:* The Pope, to whom is attributed authority over earth, heaven, and hell. 14 *Babylonian woe:* Destruction expected to befall the city of Babylon at the world's end as punishment for its luxury and other wickedness (see Revelation 18:1 – 24). Protestants took Babylon to mean the Church of Rome.

Question

What is Milton's attitude toward the massacre? Does he express a single feeling, or a mingling of feelings?

The Person in the Poem

The tone of a poem, we said, is like tone of voice in that both communicate feelings. Still, this comparison raises a question: When we read a poem, whose "voice" speaks to us?

"The poet's" is one possible answer; and in the case of many a poem, that answer may be right. Reading Anne Bradstreet's "The Author to Her Book," we can be reasonably sure that the poet speaks of her very own book, and of her own experiences. In order to read a poem, we seldom need to read a poet's biography; but in truth there are certain poems whose full effect depends upon our knowing at least a fact or two of the poet's life. In this poem, surely the poet refers to himself:

Trumbull Stickney (1874 – 1904)

Sir, say no more   1905

Sir, say no more,
Within me 'tis as if
The green and climbing eyesight of a cat
Crawled near my mind's poor birds.

The subject of Stickney's poem is not some nightmare or hallucination. The poem may mean more to you if you know that Stickney, who wrote it shortly before his death, had been afflicted by cancer of the brain. But the poem is not a prosaic entry in the diary of a dying man, nor is it a good poem because a dying man wrote it. Not only does it tell truth from experience, it speaks in memorable words.

Most of us can tell the difference between a person we meet in life and a person we meet in a work of art — unlike the moviegoer in the Philippines who, watching a villain in an exciting film, pulled out a revolver and peppered the screen. And yet, in reading poems, we are liable to temptation. When the poet says "I," we may want to assume that he or she, like Trumbull Stickney, is making a personal statement. But reflect: do all poems have to be personal? Here is a brief poem inscribed on the tombstone of an infant in Burial Hill cemetery, Plymouth, Massachusetts:

> Since I have been so quickly done for,
> I wonder what I was begun for.

We do not know who wrote those lines, but it is clear that the poet was not a short-lived infant writing from personal experience. In other poems, the speaker is obviously a **persona** or fictitious character: not the poet, but the poet's creation. As a grown man, William Blake, a skilled professional engraver, wrote a poem in the voice of a boy, an illiterate chimney sweeper. (The poem appears on page 532.) No law decrees that the speaker in a poem even has to be human: good poems have been uttered by clouds, pebbles, and cats. A **dramatic monologue** is a poem written as a speech made at some decisive or revealing moment. It is usually addressed by the speaker to some other character (who remains silent). Robert Browning, who developed the form, liked to put words into the mouths of characters stupider, weaker, or nastier than he: for instance, see "Soliloquy of the Spanish Cloister" (page 792), in which the speaker is an insanely proud and jealous monk.

Let's consider a poem spoken not by a poet but by a persona — in this case, a woman. The poem is a monologue, but not a dramatic monologue. (It gives us the spoken thoughts of one person, but the moment isn't particularly dramatic.)

Philip Larkin (1922 – 1985)*

WEDDING-WIND   1951

The wind blew all my wedding-day,
And my wedding-night was the night of the high wind;
And a stable door was banging, again and again,
That he must go and shut it, leaving me
Stupid in candlelight, hearing rain,   5
Seeing my face in the twisted candlestick,
Yet seeing nothing. When he came back
He said the horses were restless, and I was sad
That any man or beast that night should lack
The happiness I had.

               Now in the day   10
All's ravelled under the sun by the wind's blowing.
He has gone to look at the floods, and I
Carry a chipped pail to the chicken-run,
Set it down, and stare. All is the wind
Hunting through clouds and forests, thrashing   15
My apron and the hanging cloths on the line.

Can it be borne, this bodying-forth by wind
Of joy my actions turn on, like a thread
Carrying beads? Shall I be let to sleep
Now this perpetual morning shares my bed?   20
Can even death dry up
These new delighted lakes, conclude
Our kneeling as cattle by all-generous waters?

QUESTIONS

1. Who is the speaker and what are her circumstances? Where does the poem take place?
2. Does the poet, in your view, exaggerate the joy of feeding chickens? What accounts for the intensity of the speaker's happiness?
3. How successful do you find this male poet in imagining a woman's feelings?

In a famous definition, William Wordsworth calls poetry "the spontaneous overflow of powerful feelings . . . recollected in tranquillity."[1] But in the case of the following poem, Wordsworth's feelings weren't all his; they didn't just overflow spontaneously; and the process of tranquil recollection had to go on for years.

William Wordsworth (1770 – 1850)*

I WANDERED LONELY AS A CLOUD   1807

I wandered lonely as a cloud
   That floats on high o'er vales and hills,
When all at once I saw a crowd,
   A host, of golden daffodils,
Beside the lake, beneath the trees,   5
Fluttering and dancing in the breeze.

Continuous as the stars that shine
   And twinkle on the milky way,
They stretched in never-ending line
   Along the margin of a bay: 10
Ten thousand saw I at a glance,
Tossing their heads in sprightly dance.

The waves beside them danced; but they
   Out-did the sparkling waves in glee;
A poet could not but be gay,   15
   In such a jocund company;
I gazed — and gazed — but little thought
What wealth the show to me had brought:

[1]For a fuller text of Wordsworth's statement, see page 939.

For oft, when on my couch I lie
   In vacant or in pensive mood,
They flash upon that inward eye
   Which is the bliss of solitude;
And then my heart with pleasure fills,
And dances with the daffodils.

20

Between the first printing of the poem in 1807 and the version of 1815 given here, Wordsworth made several deliberate improvements. He changed *dancing* to *golden* in line 4, *Along* to *Beside* in line 5, *Ten thousand* to *Fluttering and* in line 6, *laughing* to *jocund* in line 16, and he added a whole stanza (the second). In fact, the writing of the poem was unspontaneous enough for Wordsworth, at a loss for lines 21 - 22, to take them from his wife Mary. It is likely that the experience of daffodil-watching was not entirely his to begin with but was derived in part from the recollections his sister Dorothy Wordsworth had set down in her journal of April 15, 1802, two years before he first drafted his poem:

> When we were in the woods beyond Gowbarrow Park we saw a few daffodils close to the water-side. We fancied that the lake had floated the seeds ashore, and that the little colony had so sprung up. But as we went along there were more and yet more; and at last, under the boughs of the trees, we saw that there was a long belt of them along the shore, about the breadth of a country turnpike road. I never saw daffodils so beautiful. They grew among the mossy stones about and about them; some rested their heads upon these stones as on a pillow for weariness; and the rest tossed and reeled and danced, and seemed as if they verily laughed with the wind, that flew upon them over the Lake; they looked so gay, ever glancing, ever changing. This wind blew directly over the Lake to them. There was here and there a little knot, and a few stragglers a few yards higher up; but they were so few as not to disturb the simplicity, unity, and life of that one busy highway.

Notice that Wordsworth's poem echoes a few of his sister's observations. Weaving poetry out of their mutual memories, Wordsworth has offered the experience as if altogether his own, made himself lonely, and left Dorothy out. The point is not that Wordsworth is a liar or a plagiarist but that, like any other good poet, he has transformed ordinary life into art. A process of interpreting, shaping, and ordering had to intervene between the experience of looking at daffodils and the finished poem.

We need not deny that a poet's experience can contribute to a poem nor that the emotion in the poem can indeed be the poet's. Still, to write a good poem one has to do more than live and feel. It seems a pity that, as Randall Jarrell has said, a cardinal may write verses worse than his youngest choirboy's. But writing poetry takes skill and imagination — qualities that extensive travel and wide experience do not necessarily give. For much of her life, Emily Dickinson seldom strayed from her family's house and grounds in Amherst,

Massachusetts; yet her rimed lifestudies of a snake, a bee, and a hummingbird contain more poetry than we find in any firsthand description (so far) of the surface of the moon.

James Stephens (1882 – 1950)*

A GLASS OF BEER   1918

The lanky hank of a she in the inn over there
Nearly killed me for asking the loan of a glass of beer;
May the devil grip the whey-faced slut by the hair,
And beat bad manners out of her skin for a year.

That parboiled ape, with the toughest jaw you will see   5
On virtue's path, and a voice that would rasp the dead,
Came roaring and raging the minute she looked at me,
And threw me out of the house on the back of my head!

If I asked her master he'd give me a cask a day;
But she, with the beer at hand, not a gill° would arrange!   *quarter-pint* 10
May she marry a ghost and bear him a kitten, and may
The High King of Glory permit her to get the mange.

QUESTIONS

1. Who do you take to be the speaker? Is it the poet? The speaker may be angry, but what is the tone of this poem?
2. Would you agree with a commentator who said, "To berate anyone in truly memorable language is practically a lost art in America"? How well does the speaker (an Irishman) succeed? Which of his epithets and curses strike you as particularly imaginative?

Mary Elizabeth Coleridge (1861 – 1907)

WE NEVER SAID FAREWELL   1897

We never said farewell, nor even looked
    Our last upon each other, for no sign
Was made when we the linkèd chain unhooked
    And broke the level line.

And here we dwell together, side by side,   5
    Our places fixed for life upon the chart.
Two islands that the roaring seas divide
    Are not more far apart.

1. In "We never said farewell," who do you suppose to be the *we?* How do you know?
   Are both persons speaking, or just one of them?
2. How would you state this poem's theme?

Paul Zimmer (b. 1934)

THE DAY ZIMMER LOST RELIGION   1976

The first Sunday I missed Mass on purpose
I waited all day for Christ to climb down
Like a wiry flyweight from the cross and
Club me on my irreverent teeth, to wade into
My blasphemous gut and drop me like a   5
Red hot thurible°, the devil roaring in   *vessel for incense*
Reserved seats until he got the hiccups.

It was a long cold way from the old days
When cassocked and surpliced I mumbled Latin
At the old priest and rang his obscure bell.   10
A long way from the dirty wind that blew
The soot like venial sins across the school yard
Where God reigned as a threatening,
One-eyed triangle high in the fleecy sky.

The first Sunday I missed Mass on purpose   15
I waited all day for Christ to climb down
Like the playground bully, the cuts and mice
Upon his face agleam, and pound me
Till my irreligious tongue hung out.
But of course He never came, knowing that   20
I was grown up and ready for Him now.

QUESTIONS

1. Who is the person in this poem? The mature poet? The poet as a child? Some fictitious
   character?
2. What do you understand to be the speaker's attitude toward religion at the present
   moment?

EXPERIMENT: *Reading with and without Biography*

Read the following poem and state what you understand from it. Then consider the
circumstances in which it probably came to be written. (Some information is offered in
a note on page 532.) Does the meaning of the poem change? To what extent does an appreciation of the poem need the support of biography?

William Carlos Williams (1883 – 1963)*

THE RED WHEELBARROW   1923

so much depends
upon

a red wheel
barrow

glazed with rain   5
water

beside the white
chickens.

IRONY

To see a distinction between the poet and the words of a fictitious character — between Philip Larkin and "Wedding-Wind" — is to be aware of **irony:**
a manner of speaking that implies a discrepancy. If the mask says one thing and
we sense that the writer is in fact saying something else, the writer has adopted
an **ironic point of view.** No finer illustration exists in English than Jonathan
Swift's "A Modest Proposal," an essay in which Swift speaks as an earnest,
humorless citizen who sets forth his reasonable plan to aid the Irish poor. The
plan is so monstrous no sane reader can assent to it: the poor are to sell their
children as meat for the tables of their landlords. From behind his falseface,
Swift is actually recommending not cannibalism but love and Christian charity.

A poem is often made complicated and more interesting by another kind
of irony. **Verbal irony** occurs whenever words say one thing but mean something else, usually the opposite. The word *love* means *hate* here: "I just *love* to
stay home and do my hair on a Saturday night!" If the verbal irony is conspicuously bitter, heavy-handed, and mocking, it is **sarcasm:** "Oh, he's the biggest
spender in the world, all right!" (The sarcasm, if that statement were spoken,
would be underscored by the speaker's tone of voice.) A famous instance of
sarcasm is Mark Antony's line in his oration over the body of slain Julius
Caesar: "Brutus is an honorable man." Antony repeats this line until the
enraged populace begins shouting exactly what he means to call Brutus and the
other conspirators: traitors, villains, murderers. We had best be alert for irony
on the printed page, for if we miss it, our interpretations of a poem may go wild.

Robert Creeley (b. 1926)

OH NO   1959

If you wander far enough
you will come to it
and when you get there
they will give you a place to sit

for yourself only, in a nice chair,   5
and all your friends will be there
with smiles on their faces
and they will likewise all have places.

This poem is rich in verbal irony. The title helps point out that between the speaker's words and attitude lie deep differences. In line 2, what is *it*? Old age? The wandering suggests a conventional metaphor: the journey of life. Is *it* literally a rest home for "senior citizens," or perhaps some naïve popular concept of heaven (such as we meet in comic strips: harps, angels with hoops for halos) in which the saved all sit around in a ring, smugly congratulating one another? We can't be sure, but the speaker's attitude toward this final sitting-place is definite. It is a place for the selfish, as we infer from the phrase *for yourself only*. And *smiles on their faces* may hint that the smiles are unchanging and forced. There is a difference between saying "They had smiles on their faces" and "They smiled": the latter suggests that the smiles came from within. The word *nice* is to be regarded with distrust. If we see through this speaker, as Creeley implies we can do, we realize that, while pretending to be sweet-talking us into a seat, actually he is revealing the horror of a little hell. And the title is the poet's reaction to it (or the speaker's unironic, straightforward one): "Oh no! Not *that!*"

Dramatic irony, like verbal irony, contains an element of contrast, but it usually refers to a situation in a play wherein a character, whose knowledge is limited, says, does, or encounters something of greater significance than he or she knows. We, the spectators, realize the meaning of this speech or action, for the playwright has afforded us superior knowledge. In Sophocles' *King Oedipus*, when Oedipus vows to punish whoever has brought down a plague upon the city of Thebes, we know — as he does not — that the man he would punish is himself. (Referring to such a situation that precedes the downfall of a hero in a tragedy, some critics speak of **tragic irony** instead of dramatic irony.) Superior knowledge can be enjoyed not only by spectators in a theater but by readers of poetry as well. In *Paradise Lost*, we know in advance that Adam will fall into temptation, and we recognize his overconfidence when he neglects a warning. The situation of Oedipus contains also **cosmic irony,** or **irony of fate:** some Fate with a grim sense of humor seems cruelly to trick a human being. Cosmic irony clearly exists in poems in which fate or the Fates are personified and seen as hostile, as in Thomas Hardy's "The Convergence of the Twain" (page 816); and it may be said to occur too in Robinson's "Richard Cory" (page 610). Evidently it is a twist of fate for the most envied man in town to kill himself.

To sum up: the effect of irony depends upon the reader's noticing some incongruity or discrepancy between two things. In *verbal irony*, there is a contrast between the speaker's words and meaning; in an *ironic point of view*, between the writer's attitude and what is spoken by a fictitious character; in *dramatic irony*, between the limited knowledge of a character and the fuller knowledge of the reader or spectator; in *cosmic irony*, between a character's aspiration and the treatment he or she receives at the hands of Fate. Although in the work of an inept poet irony can be crude and obvious sarcasm, it is invaluable to a poet of more complicated mind, who imagines more than one perspective.

W. H. Auden (1907 – 1973)*

THE UNKNOWN CITIZEN   1940

(To JS/07/M/378
This Marble Monument
Is Erected by the State)

He was found by the Bureau of Statistics to be
One against whom there was no official complaint,
And all the reports on his conduct agree
That, in the modern sense of an old-fashioned word, he was a saint,
For in everything he did he served the Greater Community.   5
Except for the War till the day he retired
He worked in a factory and never got fired,
But satisfied his employers, Fudge Motors Inc.
Yet he wasn't a scab or odd in his views,
For his Union reports that he paid his dues,   10
(Our report on his Union shows it was sound)
And our Social Psychology workers found
That he was popular with his mates and liked a drink.
The Press are convinced that he bought a paper every day
And that his reactions to advertisements were normal in every way.   15
Policies taken out in his name prove that he was fully insured,
And his Health-card shows he was once in hospital but left it cured.
Both Producers Research and High-Grade Living declare
He was fully sensible to the advantages of the Installment Plan
And had everything necessary to the Modern Man,   20
A phonograph, a radio, a car and a frigidaire.
Our researchers into Public Opinion are content
That he held the proper opinions for the time of year;
When there was peace, he was for peace; when there was war, he
    went.
He was married and added five children to the population,   25
Which our Eugenist says was the right number for a parent of his
    generation,
And our teachers report that he never interfered with their
    education.
Was he free? Was he happy? The question is absurd:
Had anything been wrong, we should certainly have heard.

1. Read the three-line epitaph at the beginning of the poem as carefully as you read what follows. How does the epitaph help establish the voice by which the rest of the poem is spoken?
2. Who is speaking?
3. What ironic discrepancies do you find between the speaker's attitude toward the subject and that of the poet himself? By what is the poet's attitude made clear?
4. In the phrase "The Unknown Soldier" (of which "The Unknown Citizen" reminds us), what does the word *unknown* mean? What does it mean in the title of Auden's poem?
5. What tendencies in our civilization does Auden satirize?
6. How would you expect the speaker to define a Modern Man, if a phonograph, a radio, a car, and a refrigerator are "everything" a Modern Man needs?

Herbert Scott (b. 1931)

THE GROCER'S CHILDREN   1976

The grocer's children
eat day-old bread,
moldy cakes and cheese,
soft black bananas
on stale shredded wheat,   5
weeviled rice, their plates
heaped high with wilted
greens, bruised fruit,
surprise treats
from unlabeled cans,   10
tainted meat.
The grocer's children
never go hungry.

QUESTIONS

1. At what point, in reading "The Grocer's Children," do you realize that the poem is ironic?
2. Does the speaker reveal his own attitude toward what he reports? If so, how does he make it clear to us?

John Betjeman (1906 – 1984)

IN WESTMINSTER ABBEY   1940

Let me take this other glove off
    As the *vox humana* swells,
And the beauteous fields of Eden
    Bask beneath the Abbey bells.
Here, where England's statesmen lie,   5
Listen to a lady's cry.

Gracious Lord, oh bomb the Germans.
   Spare their women for Thy Sake,
And if that is not too easy
   We will pardon Thy Mistake.   10
But, gracious Lord, whate'er shall be,
Don't let anyone bomb me.

Keep our Empire undismembered,
   Guide our Forces by Thy Hand,
Gallant blacks from far Jamaica,   15
   Honduras and Togoland;
Protect them Lord in all their fights,
And, even more, protect the whites.

Think of what our Nation stands for:
   Books from Boots' and country lanes,   20
Free speech, free passes, class distinction,
   Democracy and proper drains.
Lord, put beneath Thy special care
One-eighty-nine Cadogan Square.

Although dear Lord I am a sinner,   25
   I have done no major crime;
Now I'll come to Evening Service
   Whensoever I have the time.
So, Lord, reserve for me a crown,
And do not let my shares° go down.   *stocks* 30

I will labor for Thy Kingdom,
   Help our lads to win the war,
Send white feathers to the cowards,
   Join the Women's Army Corps,
Then wash the Steps around Thy Throne   35
In the Eternal Safety Zone.

Now I feel a little better,
   What a treat to hear Thy Word,
Where the bones of leading statesmen
   Have so often been interred.   40
And now, dear Lord, I cannot wait
Because I have a luncheon date.

IN WESTMINSTER ABBEY. First printed during World War II. 2 *vox humana:* an organ stop that makes tones similar to those of the human voice. 20 *Boots':* a chain of pharmacies whose branches had lending libraries.

QUESTIONS

1. Who is the speaker? What do we know about her life style? About her prejudices?
2. Point out some of the places in which she contradicts herself.
3. How would you describe the speaker's attitude toward religion?
4. Through the medium of irony, what positive points do you believe Betjeman makes?

Sarah N. Cleghorn (1876 – 1959)

THE GOLF LINKS   1917

The golf links lie so near the mill
    That almost every day
The laboring children can look out
    And see the men at play.

QUESTIONS

1. Is this brief poem satiric? Does it contain any verbal irony? Is the poet making a matter-of-fact statement in words that mean just what they say?
2. What other kind of irony is present in the poem?
3. Sarah N. Cleghorn's poem dates from before the enactment of legislation against child labor. Is it still a good poem, or is it hopelessly dated?
4. How would you state its theme?
5. Would you call this poem lyric, narrative, or didactic?

EXERCISE: *Detecting Irony*

Point out the kinds of irony that occur in the following poem.

Thomas Hardy (1840 – 1928)*

THE WORKBOX   1914

"See, here's the workbox, little wife,
    That I made of polished oak."
He was a joiner°, of village life;   *carpenter*
    She came of borough folk.

He holds the present up to her   5
    As with a smile she nears
And answers to the profferer,
    " 'Twill last all my sewing years!"

"I warrant it will. And longer too.
    'Tis a scantling that I got   10
Off poor John Wayward's coffin, who
    Died of they knew not what.

"The shingled pattern that seems to cease
    Against your box's rim
Continues right on in the piece   15
    That's underground with him.

"And while I worked it made me think
    Of timber's varied doom:
One inch where people eat and drink,
    The next inch in a tomb.   20

"But why do you look so white, my dear,
     And turn aside your face?
You knew not that good lad, I fear,
     Though he came from your native place?"

"How could I know that good young man,   25
     Though he came from my native town,
When he must have left far earlier than
     I was a woman grown?"

"Ah, no. I should have understood!
     It shocked you that I gave   30
To you one end of a piece of wood
     Whose other is in a grave?"

"Don't, dear, despise my intellect,
     Mere accidental things
Of that sort never have effect   35
     On my imaginings."

Yet still her lips were limp and wan,
     Her face still held aside,
As if she had known not only John,
     But known of what he died.   40

Robert Burns (1759 – 1796)*

THE TOAD-EATER   (1783?)

What of earls with whom you have supped,
     And of dukes that you dined with yestreen°?   *last night*
Lord! an insect's an insect at most,
     Though it crawl on the curls of a Queen.

QUESTIONS

1. A toad-eater was originally (according to the Oxford English Dictionary) "the attendant of a charlatan, employed to eat or pretend to eat toads (held to be poisonous)
   to enable his master to exhibit his skill in expelling poison." Later, *toad-eater* was
   shortened to *toady*. What does that word mean today? (If you don't know, infer what
   it means from Burns's poem. The meaning hasn't changed.)
2. What ironic contrast does Burns draw in the last two lines?
3. How would you describe this speaker's tone of voice?

FOR REVIEW AND FURTHER STUDY

EXERCISE: *Telling Tone*

Here are two radically different poems on a similar subject. Try stating the theme of each
poem in your own words. How is tone (the speaker's attitude) different in the two poems?

Richard Lovelace (1618 – 1658)

TO LUCASTA   1649

On Going to the Wars

Tell me not, Sweet, I am unkind
    That from the nunnery
Of thy chaste breast and quiet mind,
    To war and arms I fly.

True, a new mistress now I chase,   5
    The first foe in the field;
And with a stronger faith embrace
    A sword, a horse, a shield.

Yet this inconstancy is such
    As you too shall adore;   10
I could not love thee, Dear, so much,
    Loved I not Honor more.

Wilfred Owen (1893 – 1918)*

DULCE ET DECORUM EST   1920

Bent double, like old beggars under sacks,
Knock-kneed, coughing like hags, we cursed through sludge,
Till on the haunting flares we turned our backs
And towards our distant rest began to trudge.
Men marched asleep. Many had lost their boots   5
But limped on, blood-shod. All went lame; all blind;
Drunk with fatigue; deaf even to the hoots
Of tired, outstripped Five-Nines° that dropped behind.   *gas-shells*

Gas! Gas! Quick, boys! — An ecstasy of fumbling,
Fitting the clumsy helmets just in time;   10
But someone still was yelling out and stumbling
And flound'ring like a man in fire or lime . . .
Dim, through the misty panes and thick green light,
As under a green sea, I saw him drowning.
In all my dreams, before my helpless sight,   15
He plunges at me, guttering, choking, drowning.

If in some smothering dreams you too could pace
Behind the wagon that we flung him in,
And watch the white eyes writhing in his face,
His hanging face, like a devil's sick of sin;   20

If you could hear, at every jolt, the blood
Come gargling from the froth-corrupted lungs,
Obscene as cancer, bitter as the cud
Of vile, incurable sores on innocent tongues, —
My friend, you would not tell with such high zest   25
To children ardent for some desperate glory,
The old Lie: Dulce et decorum est
Pro patria mori.

DULCE ET DECORUM EST. Owen was a British infantry officer in World War I. 17 *you too*: Some
manuscript versions of this poem carry the dedication "To Jessie Pope" (a writer of patriotic verse)
or "To a certain Poetess." 27 – 28 *Dulce et . . . mori*: a quotation from the Latin poet Horace, "It
is sweet and fitting to die for one's country."

Bettie Sellers (b. 1926)

IN THE COUNSELOR'S WAITING ROOM   1981

The terra cotta girl
with the big flat farm feet
traces furrows in the rug
with her toes,
reads an existentialist paperback   5
from psychology class,
finds no ease there
from the guilt of loving
the quiet girl down the hall.
Their home soil has seen to this visit,   10
their Baptist mothers,
who weep for the waste of sturdy hips
ripe for grandchildren.

IN THE COUNSELOR'S WAITING ROOM. The poet is a teacher and administrator at a small college in
Georgia. 1 *terra cotta*: fired clay, light brownish orange in hue. 5 *existentialist*: of the twentieth-
century school of philosophy that holds (among other tenets) that an individual is alone and
isolated, free and yet responsible, and ordinarily subject to guilt, anxiety, and dread.

QUESTIONS

1. For what sort of counseling is this girl waiting?
2. Point out all the words that refer to plowing, to clay and earth. Why are the mothers
   called "home soil"? How do these references to earth relate to the idea in the last
   line?
3. What irony inheres in this situation?
4. Does the poet appear to sympathize with the girls? With their weeping mothers? In
   what details does this poem hint at any of the poet's own attitude or attitudes?

Jonathan Swift (1667 – 1745)*

ON STELLA'S BIRTHDAY   (1718 – 1719)

Stella this day is thirty-four
(We shan't dispute a year or more) —
However, Stella, be not troubled,
Although thy size and years are doubled,
Since first I saw thee at sixteen,   5
The brightest virgin on the green,
So little is thy form declined,
Made up so largely in thy mind.
Oh, would it please the gods, to split
Thy beauty, size, and years, and wit,   10
No age could furnish out a pair
Of nymphs so graceful, wise, and fair,
With half the luster of your eyes,
With half your wit, your years, and size.
And then, before it grew too late,   15
How should I beg of gentle Fate
(That either nymph might have her swain)
To split my worship too in twain.

ON STELLA'S BIRTHDAY. For many years Swift made an annual birthday gift of a poem to his close friend Mrs. Esther Johnson, the degree of whose nearness to the proud and lonely Swift remains an enigma to biographers. 18 *my worship:* as Dean of St. Patrick's in Dublin, Swift was addressed as "Your Worship."

QUESTIONS

1. If you were Stella, would you be amused or insulted by the poet's references to your *size?*
2. According to Swift in lines 7 – 8, what has compensated Stella for what the years have taken away?
3. Comment on the last four lines. Does Swift exempt himself from growing old?
4. How would you describe the tone of this poem? Offensive (like the speaker's complaints in "A Glass of Beer")? Playfully tender? Sad over Stella's growing fat and old?

Robert Flanagan (b. 1941)

REPLY TO AN EVICTION NOTICE   1978

My mother and father camped in such apartments
in their time, landlord, promoter
of cramped endurances,
your rightful inheritance. Your father
purchased shrewdly and practiced ungiving   5
well. Mine did not.

So my sweaty bursts of living
are managed in rooms
gauged like parking meters, narrow as coin slots,
while from the landscaped, architect-designed   10
vantage of your home,
the town lies before you like a Monopoly board.
Ownership is your reward
and punishment; movement mine.

QUESTIONS

1. What does the poem tell us about this anonymous landlord? What is the speaker's
   attitude toward him or her?
2. Paraphrase, in your own words, the last two lines.

John Ciardi (1916 – 1986)

IN PLACE OF A CURSE   1959

At the next vacancy for God, if I am elected,
I shall forgive last the delicately wounded
who, having been slugged no harder than anyone else,
never got up again, neither to fight back,
nor to finger their jaws in painful admiration.   5

They who are wholly broken, and they in whom
mercy is understanding, I shall embrace at once
and lead to pillows in heaven. But they who are
the meek by trade, baiting the best of their betters
with the extortions of a mock-helplessness   10

I shall take last to love, and never wholly.
Let them all into Heaven—I abolish Hell—
but let it be read over them as they enter:
"Beware the calculations of the meek, who gambled nothing,
gave nothing, and could never receive enough."   15

QUESTIONS

1. What kinds of people does the speaker dislike? Whom does he feel compassion for?
2. How would you describe the tone of this poem? How can you tell it isn't entirely
   serious?

William Blake (1757 – 1827)*

THE CHIMNEY SWEEPER   1789

When my mother died I was very young,
And my father sold me while yet my tongue
Could scarcely cry " 'weep! 'weep! 'weep! 'weep!"
So your chimneys I sweep, and in soot I sleep.

There's little Tom Dacre, who cried when his head,   5
That curled like a lamb's back, was shaved: so I said
"Hush, Tom! never mind it, for when your head's bare
You know that the soot cannot spoil your white hair."

And so he was quiet, and that very night,
As Tom was a-sleeping, he had such a sight!   10
That thousands of sweepers, Dick, Joe, Ned, and Jack,
Were all of them locked up in coffins of black.

And by came an Angel who had a bright key,
And he opened the coffins and set them all free;
Then down a green plain leaping, laughing, they run,   15
And wash in a river, and shine in the sun.

Then naked and white, all their bags left behind,
They rise upon clouds and sport in the wind;
And the Angel told Tom, if he'd be a good boy,
He'd have God for his father, and never want joy.   20

And so Tom awoke; and we rose in the dark,
And got with our bags and our brushes to work.
Though the morning was cold, Tom was happy and warm;
So if all do their duty they need not fear harm.

QUESTIONS

1. What does Blake's poem reveal about conditions of life in the London of his day?
2. What does this poem have in common with "The Golf Links" (page 526)?
3. Sum up your impressions of the speaker's character. What does he say and do that displays it to us?
4. What pun do you find in line 3? Is its effect comic or serious?
5. In Tom Dacre's dream (lines 11 – 20), what wishes come true? Do you understand them to be the wishes of the chimney sweepers, of the poet, or of both?
6. In the last line, what is ironic in the speaker's assurance that the dutiful *need not fear harm*? What irony is there in his urging all to *do their duty*? (Who have failed in their duty to *him*?)
7. What is the tone of Blake's poem? Angry? Hopeful? Sorrowful? Compassionate? (Don't feel obliged to sum it up in a single word.)

INFORMATION FOR EXPERIMENT: *Reading with and without Biography*

THE RED WHEELBARROW (page 521). Dr. William's poem reportedly contains a personal experience: he was gazing from the window of the house where one of his patients, a small girl, lay suspended between life and death. (This account, from the director of the public library in Williams's native Rutherford, N.J., is given by Geri M. Rhodes in "The Paterson Metaphor in William Carlos Williams' *Paterson*," master's essay, Tufts University, June 1965.)

SUGGESTIONS FOR WRITING

1. In a paragraph, sum up your initial reactions to "The Red Wheelbarrow." Then, taking another look at the poem in light of information noted above, write a second paragraph summing up your further reactions.
2. Write a short essay titled "What Thomas Hardy Leaves Unsaid in 'The Workbox'."
3. Write a verbal profile or short character sketch of the speaker of John Betjeman's "In Westminster Abbey."
4. In a brief essay, consider the tone of two poems on a similar subject. Compare and contrast Walt Whitman and Emily Dickinson as locomotive-fanciers; or, in the poems by Richard Lovelace and Wilfred Owen, compare and contrast attitudes toward war. (For advice on writing about poetry by the method of comparison and contrast, see page 1499.)

15 Words

LITERAL MEANING: WHAT A POEM SAYS FIRST

Although successful as a painter, Edgar Degas struggled to produce sonnets, and found poetry discouragingly hard to write. To his friend, the poet Stéphane Mallarmé, he complained, "What a business! My whole day gone on a blasted sonnet, without getting an inch further . . . and it isn't ideas I'm short of . . . I'm full of them, I've got too many . . ."

"But Degas," said Mallarmé, "you can't make a poem with ideas — you make it with *words!*"[1]

Like the celebrated painter, some people assume that all it takes to make a poem is a bright idea. Poems state ideas, to be sure, and sometimes the ideas are invaluable; and yet the most impressive idea in the world will not make a poem unless its words are selected and arranged with loving art. Some poets take great pains to find the right word. Unable to fill a two-syllable gap in an unfinished line that went, "The seal's wide – – gaze toward Paradise," Hart Crane paged through an unabridged dictionary. When he reached S, he found the object of his quest in *spindrift:* "spray skimmed from the sea by a strong wind." The word is exact and memorable. Any word can be the right word, however, if artfully chosen and placed. It may be a word as ordinary as *from.* Consider the difference between "The sedge is withered *on* the lake" (a misquotation of a line by Keats) and "The sedge is withered *from* the lake" (what Keats in fact wrote). Keats's original line suggests, as the altered line doesn't, that because the sedge (a growth of grasslike plants) has withered *from* the lake, it has withdrawn mysteriously.

---

[1]Paul Valéry, *Degas . . . Manet . . . Morisot,* translated by David Paul (New York: Pantheon, 1960) 62.

In reading a poem, some people assume that its words can be skipped over rapidly, and they try to leap at once to the poem's general theme. It is as if they fear being thought clods unless they can find huge ideas in the poem (whether or not there are any). Such readers often ignore the literal meanings of words: the ordinary, matter-of-fact sense to be found in a dictionary. (As you will see in Chapter Four, "Saying and Suggesting," words possess not only dictionary meanings — **denotations** — but also many associations and suggestions — **connotations**.) Consider the following poem and see what you make of it.

William Carlos Williams (1883 – 1963)*

THIS IS JUST TO SAY   1934

I have eaten
the plums
that were in
the icebox
and which   5
you were probably
saving
for breakfast

Forgive me
they were delicious   10
so sweet
and so cold

Some readers distrust a poem so simple and candid. They think, "What's wrong with me? There has to be more to it than this!" But poems seldom are puzzles in need of solutions. We can begin by accepting the poet's statements, without suspecting the poet of trying to hoodwink us. On later reflection, of course, we might possibly decide that the poet is playfully teasing or being ironic; but Williams gives us no reason to think that. There seems no need to look beyond the literal sense of his words, no profit in speculating that the plums symbolize worldly joys and that the icebox stands for the universe. Clearly, a reader who held such a grand theory would have overlooked (in eagerness to find a significant idea) the plain truth that the poet makes clear to us: that ice-cold plums are a joy to taste, especially if one knows they'll be missed the next morning.

To be sure, Williams's small poem is simpler than most poems are; and yet in reading any poem, no matter how complicated, you will do well to reach slowly and reluctantly for a theory to explain it by. To find the general theme of a poem, you first need to pay attention to its words. Recall Yeats's "The Lake Isle of Innisfree" (page 499), a poem that makes a statement—crudely summed up, "I yearn to leave the city and retreat to a place of ideal peace and happiness." And yet before we can realize this theme, we have to notice details: nine bean rows, a glade loud with bees, "lake water lapping with low sounds by the shore," the gray of a pavement. These details and not some abstract remark make clear what the poem is saying: that the city is drab, while the island hideaway is sublimely beautiful.

Poets often strive for words that point to physical details and solid objects. They may do so even when speaking of an abstract idea:

> Beauty is but a flower
> Which wrinkles will devour;
> Brightness falls from the air,
> Queens have died young and fair,
> Dust hath closed Helen's eye.
> I am sick, I must die:
>   Lord, have mercy on us!

In these lines by Thomas Nashe, the abstraction *beauty* has grown petals that shrivel. Brightness may be a general name for light, but Nashe succeeds in giving it the weight of a falling body.

If a poem reads *daffodils* instead of *plant life*, *diaper years* instead of *infancy*, we call its **diction,** or choice of words, **concrete** rather than **abstract.** Concrete words refer to what we can immediately perceive with our senses: *dog, actor, chemical,* or particular individuals who belong to those general classes: *Bonzo the fox terrier, Clint Eastwood, hydrogen sulfate.* Abstract words express ideas or concepts: *love, time, truth.* In abstracting, we leave out some characteristics found in each individual, and instead observe a quality common to many. The word *beauty,* for instance, denotes what may be observed in numerous persons, places, and things. Most poets tend to favor concrete diction, at least part of the time. In an apt criticism, William Butler Yeats once took to task the poems of W. E. Henley for being "abstract, as even an actor's movement can be when the thought of doing is plainer to his mind than the doing itself: the straight line from cup to lip, let us say, more plain than the hand's own sensation weighed down by that heavy spillable cup."[2] To convey the sense of that heavy spillable cup was to Yeats a goal, one that surely he attained in "Among School Children" by describing a woman's stark face: "Hollow of cheek as though it drank the wind / And took a mess of shadows for its meat." A more abstract-minded poet might have written "Her hollow cheek and wasted, hungry look."

Ezra Pound gave a famous piece of advice to his fellow poets: "Go in fear of abstractions." This is not to say that a poet cannot employ abstract words, nor that all poems have to be about physical things. Much of T. S. Eliot's *Four Quartets* is concerned with time, eternity, history, language, reality, and other things that cannot be handled. But Eliot, however high he may soar for a larger view, keeps returning to earth. He makes us aware of *things*, as Thomas Carlyle said a good writer has to do: "Wonderful it is with what cutting words, now

---

[2]*The Trembling of the Veil* (1922), reprinted in *The Autobiography of William Butler Yeats* (New York: Macmillan, 1953) 177.

and then, he severs asunder the confusion; shears it down, were it furlongs deep, into the true center of the matter; and there not only hits the nail on the head, but with crushing force smites it home, and buries it." Like other good writers, good poets remind us of that smitten nail and that spillable cup.

Knute Skinner (b. 1929)

THE COLD IRISH EARTH   1968

I shudder thinking
of the cold Irish earth.
The firelighter flares
in the kitchen range,
but a cold rain falls   5
all around Liscannor.
It scours the Hag's face
on the Cliffs of Moher.
It runs through the bog
and seeps up into mounds   10
of abandoned turf.
My neighbor's fields are chopped
by the feet of cattle
sinking down to the roots
of winter grass.   15
That coat hangs drying now
by the kitchen range,
but down at Healy's cross
the Killaspuglonane graveyard
is wet to the bone.   20

QUESTIONS

1. To what familiar phrase does Skinner's poem lend fresh meaning? What is its usual meaning?
2. What details in the poem show us that, in using the old phrase, Skinner literally means what he says?

Henry Taylor (b. 1942)

RIDING A ONE-EYED HORSE   1975

One side of his world is always missing.
You may give it a casual wave of the hand
or rub it with your shoulder as you pass,
but nothing on his blind side ever happens.

Hundreds of trees slip past him into darkness, 5
drifting into a hollow hemisphere
whose sounds you will have to try to explain.
Your legs will tell him not to be afraid

if you learn never to lie. Do not forget
to turn his head and let what comes come seen: 10
he will jump the fences he has to if you swing
toward them from the side that he can see

and hold his good eye straight. The heavy dark
will stay beside you always; let him learn
to lean against it. It will steady him 15
and see you safely through diminished fields.

Question

Do you read this poem as a fable in which the horse stands for something, or as a set
of instructions for riding a one-eyed horse?

Robert Graves (1895 – 1985)

Down, Wanton, Down! 1933

Down, wanton, down! Have you no shame
That at the whisper of Love's name,
Or Beauty's, presto! up you raise
Your angry head and stand at gaze?

Poor bombard-captain, sworn to reach 5
The ravelin and effect a breach —
Indifferent what you storm or why,
So be that in the breach you die!

Love may be blind, but Love at least
Knows what is man and what mere beast; 10
Or Beauty wayward, but requires
More delicacy from her squires.

Tell me, my witless, whose one boast
Could be your staunchness at the post,
When were you made a man of parts 15
To think fine and profess the arts?

Will many-gifted Beauty come
Bowing to your bald rule of thumb,
Or Love swear loyalty to your crown?
Be gone, have done! Down, wanton, down! 20

Down, Wanton, Down! 5 bombard-captain: officer in charge of a bombard, an early type of cannon
that hurled stones. 6 ravelin: fortification with two faces that meet in a protruding angle. effect a
breach: break an opening through (a fortification). 15 man of parts: man of talent or ability.

1. How do you define a wanton?
2. What wanton does the poet address?
3. Explain the comparison drawn in the second stanza.
4. In line 14, how many meanings do you find in *staunchness at the post*?
5. Explain any other puns you find in lines 15 – 19.
6. Do you take this to be a cynical poem making fun of Love and Beauty, or is Graves making fun of stupid, animal lust?

Peter Davison (b. 1928)

THE LAST WORD   1970

When I saw your head bow, I knew I had beaten you.
You shed no tears — not near me — but held your neck
Bare for the blow I had been too frightened
Ever to deliver, even in words. And now,
In spite of me, plummeting it came.   5
Frozen we both waited for its fall.

Most of what you gave me I have forgotten
With my mind but taken into my body,
But this I remember well: the bones of your neck
And the strain in my shoulders as I heaved up that huge   10
Double blade and snapped my wrists to swing
The handle down and hear the axe's edge
Nick through your flesh and creak into the block.

QUESTIONS

1. "The Last Word" stands fourth in a series titled "Four Love Poems." Sum up what happens in this poem. Do you take this to be *merely* a literal account of an execution? Explain the comparison.
2. Which words embody concrete things and show us physical actions? Which words have sounds that especially contribute to the poem's effectiveness?

Bruce Guernsey (b. 1944)

GLOVE   1987

If in this word
is love itself
then love is bone
and blood inside
the form that warms   5
your lovely hand—

your hand is love
and mine that takes
your love in mine
without your hand   10
is nothing but
an empty word.

QUESTIONS

1. What double meaning do you find in "the form that warms your lovely hand"?
2. What does this poem say about love? (Suggestion: How would you paraphrase lines 7–12?)

John Donne (1572 – 1631)*

BATTER MY HEART, THREE-PERSONED GOD, FOR YOU   (about 1610)

Batter my heart, three-personed God, for You
As yet but knock, breathe, shine, and seek to mend.
That I may rise and stand, o'erthrow me, and bend
Your force to break, blow, burn, and make me new.
I, like an usurped town to another due,   5
Labor to admit You, but Oh! to no end.
Reason, Your viceroy in me, me should defend,
But is captived, and proves weak or untrue.
Yet dearly I love You, and would be lovèd fain,
But am betrothed unto Your enemy;   10
Divorce me, untie or break that knot again;
Take me to You, imprison me, for I,
Except You enthrall me, never shall be free,
Nor ever chaste, except You ravish me.

QUESTIONS

1. In the last line of this sonnet, to what does Donne compare the onslaught of God's love? Do you think the poem weakened by the poet's comparing a spiritual experience to something so grossly carnal? Discuss.
2. Explain the seeming contradiction in the last line: in what sense can a ravished person be *chaste?* Explain the seeming contradictions in lines 3 – 4 and 12 – 13: how can a person thrown down and destroyed be enabled to *rise and stand;* an imprisoned person be *free?*
3. In lines 5 – 6 the speaker compares himself to a *usurped town* trying to throw off its conqueror by admitting an army of liberation. Who is the "usurper" in this comparison?
4. Explain the comparison of *Reason* to a *viceroy* (lines 7 – 8).
5. Sum up in your own words the message of Donne's poem. In stating its theme, did you have to read the poem for literal meanings, figurative comparisons, or both?

THE VALUE OF A DICTIONARY

If a poet troubles to seek out the best words available, the least we can do is to find out what the words mean. The dictionary is a firm ally in reading poems; if the poems are more than a century old, it is indispensable. Meanings change. When the Elizabethan poet George Gascoigne wrote, "O Abraham's brats, O brood of blessed seed," the word *brats* implied neither irritation nor contempt. When in the seventeenth century Andrew Marvell imagined two lovers' "vegetable love," he referred to a vegetative or growing love, not one resembling a lettuce. And when King George III called a building an "awful artificial spectacle," he was not condemning it but praising it as an awe-inspiring work of art.

In reading poetry, there is nothing to be done about this inevitable tendency of language except to watch out for it. If you suspect that a word has shifted in meaning over the years, most standard desk dictionaries will be helpful, an unabridged dictionary more helpful yet, and most helpful of all the *Oxford English Dictionary (OED)*, which gives, for each definition, successive examples of the word's written use through the past thousand years. You need not feel a grim obligation to keep interrupting a poem in order to rummage the dictionary; but if the poem is worth reading very closely, you may wish any aid you can find.

One of the valuable services of poetry is to recall for us the concrete, physical sense that certain words once had, but since have lost. As the English critic H. Coombes has remarked in *Literature and Criticism*,

> We use a word like *powerful* without feeling that it is really "power-full."
> We do not seem today to taste the full flavor of words as we feel that
> Falstaff (and Shakespeare, and probably his audience) tasted them when
> he was applauding the virtues of "good sherris-sack," which makes the
> brain "apprehensive, quick, forgetive, full of nimble, fiery, and delectable
> shapes." And being less aware of the life and substantiality of words, we
> are probably less aware of the things . . . that these words stand for.

"Every word which is used to express a moral or intellectual fact," said Emerson in his study *Nature*, "if traced to its root, is found to be borrowed from some material appearance. *Right* means straight; *wrong* means twisted. *Spirit* primarily means wind; *transgression*, the crossing of a line; *supercilious*, the raising of an eyebrow." Browse in a dictionary and you will discover such original concretenesses. These are revealed in your dictionary's etymologies, or brief notes on the derivation of words, given in most dictionaries near the beginning of an entry on a word; in some dictionaries, at the end of the entry. Look up *squirrel*, for instance, and you will find it comes from two Greek words meaning "shadow-tail." For another example of a common word that originally contained a poetic metaphor, look up the origin of *daisy*.

Much of the effect of the following poem depends upon our awareness of the precision with which the poet has selected his words. We can better see this by knowing their derivations. For instance, *potpourri* comes from French: *pot* plus *pourri.* What do these words mean? (If you do not know French, look up the etymology of the word in a dictionary.) Look up the definitions and etymologies of *revenance, circumstance, inspiration, conceptual, commotion, cordial,* and *azure;* and try to state the meanings these words have in Wilbur's poem.

Richard Wilbur (b. 1921)*

IN THE ELEGY SEASON   1950

Haze, char, and the weather of All Souls':
A giant absence mopes upon the trees:
Leaves cast in casual potpourris
Whisper their scents from pits and cellar-holes.

Or brewed in gulleys, steeped in wells, they spend   5
In chilly steam their last aromas, yield
From shallow hells a revenance of field
And orchard air. And now the envious mind

Which could not hold the summer in my head
While bounded by that blazing circumstance   10
Parades these barrens in a golden trance,
Remembering the wealthy season dead,

And by an autumn inspiration makes
A summer all its own. Green boughs arise
Through all the boundless backward of the eyes,   15
And the soul bathes in warm conceptual lakes.

Less proud than this, my body leans an ear
Past cold and colder weather after wings'
Soft commotion, the sudden race of springs,
The goddess' tread heard on the dayward stair,   20

Longs for the brush of the freighted air, for smells
Of grass and cordial lilac, for the sight
Of green leaves building into the light
And azure water hoisting out of wells.

An **allusion** is an indirect reference to any person, place, or thing — fictitious, historical, or actual. Sometimes, to understand an allusion in a poem, we have to find out something we didn't know before. But usually the poet asks of us only common knowledge. When Edgar Allan Poe refers to "the glory that was Greece / And the grandeur that was Rome," he assumes that we have heard of those places, and that we will understand his allusion to the cultural achievement of those nations (implicit in *glory* and *grandeur*).

Allusions not only enrich the meaning of a poem, they also save space. In "The Love Song of J. Alfred Prufrock" (page 806), T. S. Eliot, by giving a brief introductory quotation from the speech of a damned soul in Dante's *Inferno*, is able to suggest that his poem will be the confession of a soul in torment, who sees no chance of escape.

Often in reading a poem you will meet a name you don't recognize, on which the meaning of a line (or perhaps a whole poem) seems to depend. In this book, most such unfamiliar references and allusions are glossed or footnoted, but when you venture out on your own in reading poems, you may find yourself needlessly perplexed unless you look up such names, the way you look up any other words. Unless the name is one that the poet made up, you will probably find it in one of the larger desk dictionaries, such as *Webster's New Collegiate Dictionary, The American Heritage Dictionary*, or *Webster's II.* If you don't solve your problem there, try an encyclopedia, a world atlas, or *The New Century Cyclopedia of Names.*

Some allusions are quotations from other poems. In L. E. Sissman's "In and Out: A Home Away from Home," the narrator, a male college student, describes his sleeping love,

> This Sally now does like a garment wear
> The beauty of the evening; silent, bare,
> Hips, shoulders, arms, tresses, and temples lie.

(For the source of these lines, see Wordsworth's "Composed upon Westminster Bridge," page 896.)

EXERCISE: *Catching Allusions*

From your knowledge, supplemented by a dictionary or other reference work if need be, explain the allusions in the following four poems.

J. V. Cunningham (1911 – 1985)*

FRIEND, ON THIS SCAFFOLD THOMAS MORE LIES DEAD   1960

Friend, on this scaffold Thomas More lies dead
Who would not cut the Body from the Head.

Herman Melville (1819 – 1891)

THE PORTENT   1859

Hanging from the beam,
    Slowly swaying (such the law),
Gaunt the shadow on your green,
    Shenandoah!

The cut is on the crown
   (Lo, John Brown),
And the stabs shall heal no more.

Hidden in the cap
   Is the anguish none can draw;
So your future veils its face,
   Shenandoah!

But the streaming beard is shown
   (Weird John Brown),
The meteor of the war.

Lucille Clifton (b. 1936)

WINNIE SONG   1987

a dark wind is blowing
the townships into town.
they have burned your house
winnie mandela
but your house has been on fire
a hundred years.
they have locked your husband
in a cage
and it has made him free.
Mandela. Mandala. Mandala
is the universe. the universe
is burning. a dark wind is blowing
the homelands into home.

Laurence Perrine (b. 1915)

JANUS   1984

Janus writes books for women's liberation;
His wife types up the scripts from his dictation.

John Clare (1793 – 1864)

MOUSE'S NEST   (about 1835)

I found a ball of grass among the hay
And progged it as I passed and went away;
And when I looked I fancied something stirred,
And turned again and hoped to catch the bird —

When out an old mouse bolted in the wheats   5
With all her young ones hanging at her teats;
She looked so odd and so grotesque to me,
I ran and wondered what the thing could be,
And pushed the knapweed bunches where I stood;
Then the mouse hurried from the craking° brood.   *crying* 10
The young ones squeaked, and as I went away
She found her nest again among the hay.
The water o'er the pebbles scarce could run
And broad old cesspools glittered in the sun.

Questions

1. "To prog" (line 2) means "to poke about for food, to forage." In what ways does this
   word fit more exactly here than *prodded, touched,* or *searched?*
2. Is *craking* (line 10) better than *crying?* Which word better fits the poem? Why?
3. What connections do you find between the last two lines and the rest of the poem?
   To what are water that *scarce could run* and *broad old cesspools* (lines 13 and 14)
   likened?

Word Choice and Word Order

Even if Samuel Johnson's famous *Dictionary* of 1755 had been as thick as
Webster's unabridged, an eighteenth-century poet searching through it for
words to use would have had a narrower choice. For in English literature of the
neoclassical period or **Augustan age** — that period from about 1660 into the
late eighteenth century — many poets subscribed to a belief in **poetic diction**:
"A system of words," said Dr. Johnson, "refined from the grossness of domestic
use." The system admitted into a serious poem only certain words and subjects,
excluding others as violations of **decorum** (propriety). Accordingly such common words as *rat, cheese, big, sneeze,* and *elbow,* although admissible to satire,
were thought inconsistent with the loftiness of tragedy, epic, ode, and elegy. Dr.
Johnson's biographer, James Boswell, tells how a poet writing an epic reconsidered the word "rats" and instead wrote "the whiskered vermin race." Johnson
himself objected to Lady Macbeth's allusion to her "keen knife," saying that
"we do not immediately conceive that any crime of importance is to be committed with a knife; or who does not, at last, from the long habit of connecting
a knife with sordid offices, feel aversion rather than terror?" Probably Johnson
was here the victim of his age, and Shakespeare was right, but Johnson in one
of his assumptions was right too: there are inappropriate words as well as
appropriate ones.

Neoclassical poets chose their classical models more often from Roman
writers than from Greek, as their diction suggests by the frequency of Latin
derivatives. For example, a *net,* according to Dr. Johnson's dictionary, is "any
thing reticulated or decussated, at equal distances, with interstices between the
intersections." In company with Latinate words often appeared fixed combinations of adjective and noun ("finny prey" for "fish"), poetic names (a song to
a lady named Molly might rechristen her Parthenia), and allusions to classical
mythology. Neoclassical poetic diction was evidently being abused when, instead of saying "uncork the bottle," a poet could write,

Apply thine engine to the spongy door,
Set *Bacchus* from his glassy prison free,

in some bad lines ridiculed by Alexander Pope in *Peri Bathous, or, Of the Art of Sinking in Poetry.*

Not all poetic diction is excess baggage. To a reader who knew at first hand both living sheep and the pastoral poems of Virgil — as most readers nowadays do not — such a fixed phrase as "the fleecy care," which seems stilted to us, conveyed pleasurable associations. But "fleecy care" was more than a highfalutin way of saying "sheep"; as one scholar has pointed out, "when they wished, our poets could say 'sheep' as clearly and as often as anybody else. In the first place, 'fleecy' drew attention to wool, and demanded the appropriate visual image of sheep; for aural imagery the poets would refer to 'the bleating kind'; it all depended upon what was happening in the poem."[3]

Other poets have found some special kind of poetic language valuable: Old English poets, with their standard figures of speech ("whale-road" for the sea, "ring-giver" for a ruler); makers of folk ballads who, no less than neoclassicists, love fixed epithet-noun combinations ("milk-white steed," "blood-red wine," "steel-driving man"); and Edmund Spenser, whose example made popular the adjective ending in -y (*fleecy, grassy, milky*).

When Wordsworth, in his Preface to *Lyrical Ballads*, asserted that "the language really spoken by men," especially by humble rustics, is plainer, more emphatic, and conveys "elementary feelings . . . in a state of greater simplicity," he was, in effect, advocating a new poetic diction. Wordsworth's ideas invited freshness into English poetry and, by admitting words that neoclassical poets would have called "low" ("His poor old *ankles* swell"), helped rid poets of the fear of being thought foolish for mentioning a commonplace.

This theory of the superiority of rural diction was, as Coleridge pointed out, hard to adhere to, and, in practice, Wordsworth was occasionally to write a language as Latinate and citified as these lines on yew trees:

Huge trunks! — and each particular trunk a growth
Of intertwisted fibers serpentine
Up-coiling, and inveterately convolved . . .

Language so Latinate sounds pedantic to us, especially the phrase *inveterately convolved.* In fact, some poets, notably Gerard Manley Hopkins, have subscribed to the view that English words derived from Anglo-Saxon (Old English) have more force and flavor than their Latin equivalents. *Kingly*, one may feel, has more power than *regal.* One argument for this view is that so many words of Old English origin — *man, wife, child, house, eat, drink, sleep* — are basic to our living speech. It may be true that a language closer to Old English is particularly fit for rendering abstract notions concretely — as does the memorable title of a medieval work of piety, the *Ayenbite of Inwit* ("again-bite of inner

[3]Bonamy Dobrée, *English Literature in the Early Eighteenth Century, 1700 – 1740* (New York: Oxford UP, 1959) 161.

wisdom" or "remorse of conscience"). And yet this view, if accepted at all, must be accepted with reservations. Some words of Latin origin carry meanings both precise and physical. In the King James Bible is the admonition, "See then that ye walk circumspectly, not as fools, but as wise" (Ephesians 5:15). To be *circumspect* (a word from two Latin roots meaning "to look" and "around") is to be watchful on all sides — a meaning altogether lost in a modernized wording of the passage once printed on a subway poster for a Bible society: "Be careful how you live, not thoughtlessly but thoughtfully."

When E. E. Cummings begins a poem, "mr youse needn't be so spry / concernin questions arty," we recognize another kind of diction available to poetry: **vulgate** (speech not much affected by schooling). Handbooks of grammar sometimes distinguish various **levels of usage**. A sort of ladder is imagined, on whose rungs words, phrases, and sentences may be ranked in an ascending order of formality, from the curses of an illiterate thug to the commencement-day address of a doctor of divinity. These levels range from vulgate through **colloquial** (the casual conversation or informal writing of literate people) and **general English** (most literate speech and writing, more studied than colloquial but not pretentious), up to **formal English** (the impersonal language of educated persons, usually only written, possibly spoken on dignified occasions). Recently, however, lexicographers have been shunning such labels. The designation *colloquial* has been expelled (*bounced* would be colloquial; *trun out*, vulgate) from *Webster's Third New International Dictionary* on the grounds that "it is impossible to know whether a word out of context is colloquial or not" and that the diction of Americans nowadays is more fluid than the labels suggest. Aware that we are being unscientific, we may find the labels useful. They may help roughly to describe what happens when, as in the following poem, a poet shifts from one level of usage to another. This poem employs, incidentally, a colloquial device throughout: omitting the subjects of sentences. In keeping the characters straight, it may be helpful to fill in the speaker for each *said* and for the verbs *saw* and *ducked* (lines 9 and 10).

Josephine Miles (1911 – 1985)

REASON   1955

Said, Pull her up a bit will you, Mac, I want to unload there.
Said, Pull her up my rear end, first come first serve.
Said, Give her the gun, Bud, he needs a taste of his own bumper.
Then the usher came out and got into the act:
Said, Pull her up, pull her up a bit, we need this space, sir.   5
Said, For God's sake, is this still a free country or what?
You go back and take care of Gary Cooper's horse
And leave me handle my own car.

Saw them unloading the lame old lady,
Ducked out under the wheel and gave her an elbow,   10
Said, All you needed to do was just explain;
Reason, Reason is my middle name.

Language on more than one level enlivens this miniature comedy; the vulgate
of the resentful driver ("Pull her up my rear end," "leave me handle my own
car") and the colloquial of the bystander ("Give her the gun"). There is also
a contrast in formality between the old lady's driver, who says "Mac," and the
usher, who says "sir." These varied levels of language distinguish the speakers
in the poem from one another.

The diction of "Reason" is that of speech; that of Coleridge's "Kubla
Khan" (page 795) is more bookish. Coleridge is not at fault, however: the
language of Josephine Miles's reasonable driver might not have contained
Kubla Khan's stately pleasure dome. At present, most poetry in English appears
to be shunning expressions such as "fleecy care" in favor of general English and
the colloquial. In Scotland, there has been an interesting development: the
formation of an active group of poets who write in Scots, a **dialect** (variety of
language spoken by a social group or spoken in a certain locality). Perhaps,
whether poets write in language close to speech or in language of greater
formality, their poems will ring true if they choose appropriate words.

EXPERIMENT: *Wheeshts into Hushes*

Reword the following poem from Scots dialect into general English, using the closest
possible equivalents. Then try to assess what the poem has gained or lost. (In line 4, a
"ploy," as defined by *Webster's Third New International Dictionary,* is a pursuit or activity,
"especially one that requires eagerness or finesse.")

Hugh MacDiarmid
[Christopher Murray Grieve] (1892 – 1978)

WHEESHT, WHEESHT   1926

Wheesht°, wheesht, my foolish hert,	*hush*
For weel ye ken°	*know*
I widna ha'e ye stert	
Auld ploys again.	
It's guid to see her lie	
Sae snod° an' cool,	*smooth*
A' lust o' lovin' by –	
Wheesht, wheesht, ye fule!	

Not only the poet's choice of words makes a poem seem more formal, or less,
but also the way the words are arranged into sentences. Compare these lines,

Jack and Jill went up the hill
To fetch a pail of water.
Jack fell down and broke his crown
And Jill came tumbling after.

with Milton's account of a more significant downfall:

Earth trembled from her entrails, as again
In pangs, and Nature gave a second groan;
Sky loured, and, muttering thunder, some sad drops
Wept at completing of the mortal sin
Original; while Adam took no thought
Eating his fill, nor Eve to iterate
Her former trespass feared, the more to soothe
Him with her loved society, that now
As with new wine intoxicated both
They swim in mirth, and fancy that they feel
Divinity within them breeding wings
Wherewith to scorn the Earth.

Not all the words in Milton's lines are bookish: indeed, many of them can be found in nursery rimes. What helps, besides diction, to distinguish this account of the Biblical fall from "Jack and Jill" is that Milton's nonstop sentence seems further removed from usual speech in its length (83 words), in its complexity (subordinate clauses), and in its word order ("with new wine intoxicated both" rather than "both intoxicated with new wine"). Should we think less (or more highly) of Milton for choosing a style so elaborate and formal? No judgment need be passed: both Mother Goose and the author of *Paradise Lost* use language appropriate to their purposes.

Among languages, English is by no means the most flexible. English words must be used in fairly definite and inviolable patterns, and whoever departs too far from them will not be understood. In the sentence "Cain slew Abel," if you change the word order, you change the meaning: "Abel slew Cain." Such inflexibility was not true of Latin, in which a poet could lay down words in almost any sequence and, because their endings (inflections) showed what parts of speech they were, could trust that no reader would mistake a subject for an object or a noun for an adjective. (E. E. Cummings has striven, in certain of his poems, for the freedom of Latin. One such poem, "anyone lived in a pretty how town," appears on page 556.)

The rigidity of English word order invites the poet to defy it and to achieve unusual effects by inverting it. It is customary in English to place adjective in front of noun (*a blue mantle, new pastures*). But an unusual emphasis is achieved when Milton ends "Lycidas" by reversing the pattern:

At last he rose, and twitched his mantle blue:
Tomorrow to fresh woods, and pastures new.

Perhaps the inversion in *mantle blue* gives more prominence to the color associated with heaven (and in "Lycidas," heaven is of prime importance). Perhaps the inversion in *pastures new*, stressing the *new*, heightens the sense of a rebirth.

Coleridge offered two "homely definitions of prose and poetry; that is, *prose:* words in their best order; *poetry:* the best words in the best order." If all goes well, a poet may fasten the right word into the right place, and the result may be — as T. S. Eliot said in "Little Gidding" — a "complete consort dancing together."

Emma Lee Warrior (b. 1941)

How I Came to Have a Man's Name   1988

It's a good thing Dad deserted Mom
and all us kids for a cousin's wiles,
cause then we learned from Grampa
how to pray to the Sun, the Moon and Stars.

Before a January dawn, under a moondog sky,   5
Yellow Dust hitched up a team to a strawfilled sleigh.
Snow squeaked against the runners
in reply to the crisp crackling cottonwoods.
They bundled up bravely in buffalo robes,
their figures pronounced by the white of night;   10
the still distance of the Wolf Trail° greeted them,   *Milky Way*
and Ipisowahs,° the boy child of Natosi,°   *morning star/the sun*
and Kokomiikiisom° watched their hurry.   *the moon*
My momma's body was bent with pain.
Otohkostskaksin° sensed the Morning Star's   *Yellow Dust* 15
presence and so he beseeched him:

"Aayo, Ipisowahs, you see us now,
pitiful creatures.
We are thankful there is no wind.
We are thankful for your light.   20
Guide us safely to our destination.
May my daughter give birth in a warm place.
May her baby be a boy; may he have your name.
May he be fortunate because of your name.
May he live long and be happy.   25
Bestow your name upon him, Ipisowahs.
His name will be Ipisowahs.
Aayo, help us, we are pitiful."

And Ipisowahs led them that icy night
through the Old Man River Valley   30

and out onto the frozen prairie.
They rushed to the hospital
where my mother pushed me into this world
and nobody bothered to change my name.

How I Came to Have a Man's Name. The words glossed in the margin of the poem are the poet's translations from the Blackfoot language.

QUESTIONS

1. What do the words from the Blackfoot language contribute to this poem? (Suggestion: Try reading them aloud as best you can.)
2. If the unborn child was to be named Ipisowahs, "morning star," then why do you suppose the poet signs herself Emma Lee Warrior?

Thomas Hardy (1840 – 1928)*

THE RUINED MAID   1901

"O 'Melia, my dear, this does everything crown!
Who could have supposed I should meet you in Town?
And whence such fair garments, such prosperi-ty?" —
"O didn't you know I'd been ruined?" said she.

— "You left us in tatters, without shoes or socks,   5
Tired of digging potatoes, and spudding up docks°;   *spading up dockweed*
And now you've gay bracelets and bright feathers three!" —
"Yes: that's how we dress when we're ruined," said she.

— "At home in the barton° you said 'thee' and 'thou,'   *farmyard*
And 'thik oon,' and 'theäs oon,' and 't'other'; but now   10
Your talking quite fits 'ee for high compa-ny!" —
"Some polish is gained with one's ruin," said she.

— "Your hands were like paws then, your face blue and bleak
But now I'm bewitched by your delicate cheek,
And your little gloves fit as on any la-dy!" —   15
"We never do work when we're ruined," said she.

— "You used to call home-life a hag-ridden dream,
And you'd sigh, and you'd sock°; but at present you seem   *groan*
To know not of megrims° or melancho-ly!" —   *blues*
"True. One's pretty lively when ruined," said she.   20

— "I wish I had feathers, a fine sweeping gown,
And a delicate face, and could strut about Town!" —
"My dear — a raw country girl, such as you be,
Cannot quite expect that. You ain't ruined," said she.

1. Where does this dialogue take place? Who are the two speakers?
2. Comment on Hardy's use of the word *ruined*. What is the conventional meaning of the word when applied to a woman? As 'Melia applies it to herself what is its meaning?
3. Sum up the attitude of each speaker toward the other. What details of the new 'Melia does the first speaker most dwell upon? Would you expect Hardy to be so impressed by all these details, or is there, between his view of the characters and their view of themselves, any hint of an ironic discrepancy?
4. In losing her country dialect (*thik oon* and *theäs oon* for *this one* and *that one*), 'Melia is presumed to have gained in sophistication. What does Hardy suggest by her *ain't* in the last line?

Richard Eberhart (b. 1904)

THE FURY OF AERIAL BOMBARDMENT   1947

You would think the fury of aerial bombardment
Would rouse God to relent; the infinite spaces
Are still silent. He looks on shock-pried faces.
History, even, does not know what is meant.

You would feel that after so many centuries   5
God would give man to repent; yet he can kill
As Cain could, but with multitudinous will,
No farther advanced than in his ancient furies.

Was man made stupid to see his own stupidity?
Is God by definition indifferent, beyond us all?   10
Is the eternal truth man's fighting soul
Wherein the Beast ravens in its own avidity?

Of Van Wettering I speak, and Averill,
Names on a list, whose faces I do not recall
But they are gone to early death, who late in school   15
Distinguished the belt feed lever from the belt holding pawl.

QUESTIONS

1. As a naval officer during World War II, Richard Eberhart was assigned for a time as an instructor in a gunnery school. How has this experience apparently contributed to the diction of his poem?
2. In his *Life of John Dryden*, complaining about a description of a sea fight Dryden had filled with nautical language, Samuel Johnson argued that technical terms should be excluded from poetry. Is this criticism applicable to Eberhart's last line? Can a word succeed for us in a poem, even though we may not be able to define it? (For more evidence, see also the technical terms in Henry Reed's "Naming of Parts," page 863.)
3. Some readers have found a contrast in tone between the first three stanzas of this poem and the last stanza. How would you describe this contrast? What does diction contribute to it?

Wole Soyinka (b. 1934)

LOST TRIBE   1988

Ants disturbed by every passing tread,
The wandering tribe still scurries round
In search of lost community. Love by rote,
Care by inscription. Incantations without magic.
Straws outstretched to suck at every passing broth,   5
Incessant tongues pretend to a way of thought—
Where language mints are private franchise,
The coins prove counterfeit on open markets.

Hard-sell pharmacies dispense all social pills:
"Have a nice day now." "Touch someone."   10
There's premium on the verb imperative—some
Instant fame psychologist pronounced it on TV—
He's now forgotten like tomorrow's guru,
Instant cult, disposable as paper diaper—
Firm commands denote sincerity;   15
The wish is wishy-washy, lacks "contact
Positive." The waiter barks: "Enjoy your meal,"
Or crisper still: *"Enjoy!"* You feel you'd better!
Buses, subway, park seats push the gospel,
Slogans like tickertapes emblazon foreheads—   20
"Talk it over with someone—now, not later!"
"Take down fences, not mend them."
"Give a nice smile to someone." But, a tear-duct
Variant: "Have you hugged your child today?"

QUESTIONS

1. What criticisms of our use of the English language is this Nigerian poet making?
2. What do you understand from lines 7–8, with their reference to "language mints" and counterfeit coins?
3. Explain the allusion in the title of this poem. How might it apply to Americans?

FOR REVIEW AND FURTHER STUDY

David B. Axelrod (b. 1943)

ONCE IN A WHILE A PROTEST POEM   1976

Over and over again the papers print
the dried-out tit of an African woman
holding her starving child. Over

and over, cropping it each time to one
prominent, withered tit, the feeble   5
infant face. Over and over to toughen
us, teach us to ignore the foam turned
dusty powder on the infant's lips,
the mother's sunken face (is cropped)
and filthy dress. The tit remains;   10
the tit held out for everyone to see,
reminding us only that we are not so hungry
ogling the tit, admiring it and in our
living rooms, making it a symbol of starving
millions; our sympathy as real as silicone.   15

QUESTIONS

1. Why is the last word in this poem especially meaningful?
2. What does the poet protest?

Lewis Carroll
[Charles Lutwidge Dodgson] (1832 – 1898)

JABBERWOCKY   1871

'Twas brillig, and the slithy toves
    Did gyre and gimble in the wabe:
All mimsy were the borogoves,
    And the mome raths outgrabe.

"Beware the Jabberwock, my son!   5
    The jaws that bite, the claws that catch!
Beware the Jubjub bird, and shun
    The frumious Bandersnatch!"

He took his vorpal sword in hand;
    Long time the manxome foe he sought —   10
So rested he by the Tumtum tree
    And stood awhile in thought.

And, as in uffish thought he stood,
    The Jabberwock, with eyes of flame,
Came whiffling through the tulgey wood,   15
    And burbled as it came!

One, two! One, two! And through and through
    The vorpal blade went snicker-snack!
He left it dead, and with its head
    He went galumphing back.   20

"And hast thou slain the Jabberwock?
    Come to my arms, my beamish boy!
O frabjous day! Callooh, Callay!"
    He chortled in his joy.

'Twas brillig, and the slithy toves   25
    Did gyre and gimble in the wabe:
All mimsy were the borogoves,
    And the mome raths outgrabe.

JABBERWOCKY. Fussy about pronunciation, Carroll in his preface to *The Hunting of the Snark* declares: "The first 'o' in 'borogoves' is pronounced like the 'o' in 'borrow.' I have heard people try to give it the sound of the 'o' in 'worry.' Such is Human Perversity." *Toves*, he adds, rimes with *groves*.

QUESTIONS

1. Look up *chortled* (line 24) in your dictionary and find out its definition and origin.
2. In *Through the Looking-Glass*, Alice seeks the aid of Humpty Dumpty to decipher the meaning of this nonsense poem. *"Brillig,"* he explains, "means four o'clock in the afternoon — the time when you begin *broiling* things for dinner." Does *brillig* sound like any other familiar word?
3. *"Slithy,"* the explanation goes on, "means 'lithe and slimy.' 'Lithe' is the same as 'active.' You see it's like a portmanteau — there are two meanings packed up into one word." *Mimsy* is supposed to pack together both "flimsy" and "miserable." In the rest of the poem, what other portmanteau — or packed suitcase — words can you find?

Wallace Stevens (1879 – 1955)*

METAMORPHOSIS   1942

Yillow, yillow, yillow,
Old worm, my pretty quirk,
How the wind spells out
Sep - tem - ber. . . .

Summer is in bones.   5
Cock-robin's at Caracas.
Make o, make o, make o,
Oto - otu - bre.

And the rude leaves fall.
The rain falls. The sky   10
Falls and lies with the worms.
The street lamps

Are those that have been hanged.
Dangling in an illogical
To and to and fro   15
Fro Niz - nil - imbo.

1. Explain the title. Of the several meanings of *metamorphosis* given in a dictionary, which best applies to the process that Stevens sees in the natural world?
2. What metamorphosis is also taking place in the *language* of the poem? How does it continue from line 4 to line 8 to line 16?
3. In the last line, which may recall the thickening drone of a speaker lapsing into sleep, *Niz - nil - imbo* seems not only a pun on the name of a month, but also a portmanteau word into which at least two familiar words are packed. Say it aloud. What are they?
4. What dictionary definitions of the word *quirk* seem relevant to line 2? How can a worm be a quirk? What else in this poem seems quirky?

E. E. Cummings (1894 – 1962)*

ANYONE LIVED IN A PRETTY HOW TOWN   1940

anyone lived in a pretty how town
(with up so floating many bells down)
spring summer autumn winter
he sang his didn't he danced his did.

Women and men (both little and small)   5
cared for anyone not at all
they sowed their isn't they reaped their same
sun moon stars rain

children guessed (but only a few
and down they forgot as up they grew   10
autumn winter spring summer)
that noone loved him more by more

when by now and tree by leaf
she laughed his joy she cried his grief
bird by snow and stir by still   15
anyone's any was all to her

someones married their everyones
laughed their cryings and did their dance
(sleep wake hope and then) they
said their nevers they slept their dream   20

stars rain sun moon
(and only the snow can begin to explain
how children are apt to forget to remember
with up so floating many bells down)

one day anyone died i guess   25
(and noone stooped to kiss his face)
busy folk buried them side by side
little by little and was by was

all by all and deep by deep
and more by more they dream their sleep   30
noone and anyone earth by april
wish by spirit and if by yes.

Women and men (both dong and ding)
summer autumn winter spring
reaped their sowing and went their came   35
sun moon stars rain

QUESTIONS

1. Summarize the story told in this poem. Who are the characters?
2. Rearrange the words in the two opening lines into the order you would expect them usually to follow. What effect does Cummings obtain by his unconventional word order?
3. Another of Cummings's strategies is to use one part of speech as if it were another; for instance, in line 4, *didn't* and *did* ordinarily are verbs, but here they are used as nouns. What other words in the poem perform functions other than their expected ones?

EXERCISE: *Different Kinds of English*

Read the following poems and see what kinds of diction and word order you find in them. Which poems are least formal in their language and which most formal? Is there any use of vulgate English? Any dialect? What does each poem achieve that its own kind of English makes possible?

Anonymous (American oral verse)

CARNATION MILK   (about 1900?)

Carnation Milk is the best in the land;
Here I sit with a can in my hand —
No tits to pull, no hay to pitch,
You just punch a hole in the son of a bitch.

CARNATION MILK. "This quatrain is imagined as the caption under a picture of a rugged-looking cowboy seated upon a bale of hay," notes William Harmon in his *Oxford Book of American Light Verse* (New York: Oxford UP, 1979). Possibly the first to print this work was David Ogilvy (b. 1911), who quotes it in his *Confessions of an Advertising Man* (New York: Atheneum, 1963).

A. R. Ammons (b. 1926)

SPRING COMING   1970

The caryophyllaceae
like a scroungy
frost are

rising through the lawn:
many-fingered as leggy
    copepods:
a suggestive delicacy,
lacework, like
the scent of wild plum
    thickets: 10
also the grackles
with their incredible
vertical, horizontal,
reversible
tails have arrived: 15
such nice machines.

William Wordsworth (1770 – 1850)*

MY HEART LEAPS UP WHEN I BEHOLD   1807

My heart leaps up when I behold
    A rainbow in the sky:
So was it when my life began;
So is it now I am a man;
So be it when I shall grow old,   5
    Or let me die!
The Child is father of the Man;
And I could wish my days to be
Bound each to each by natural piety.

William Wordsworth (1770 – 1850)*

MUTABILITY   1822

From low to high doth dissolution climb,
And sink from high to low, along a scale
Of awful notes, whose concord shall not fail;
A musical but melancholy chime,
Which they can hear who meddle not with crime,   5
Nor avarice, nor over-anxious care.
Truth fails not; but her outward forms that bear
The longest date do melt like frosty rime°,   *frozen dew*
That in the morning whitened hill and plain
And is no more; drop like the tower sublime   10
Of yesterday, which royally did wear
His crown of weeds, but could not even sustain
Some casual shout that broke the silent air,
Or the unimaginable touch of Time.

Anonymous

SCOTTSBORO   1936

Paper come out — done strewed de news
Seven po' chillun moan deat' house blues,
Seven po' chillun moanin' deat' house blues.
Seven nappy° heads wit' big shiny eye   *frizzy*
All boun' in jail and framed to die,   5
All boun' in jail and framed to die.

Messin' white woman — snake lyin' tale
Hang and burn and jail wit' no bail.
Dat hang and burn and jail wit' no bail.
Worse ol' crime in white folks' lan'   10
Black skin coverin' po' workin' man,
Black skin coverin' po' workin' man.

Judge and jury — all in de stan'
Lawd, biggety name for same lynchin' ban',
Lawd, biggety name for same lynchin' ban'.   15
White folks and nigger in great co't house
Like cat down cellar wit' nohole mouse.
Like cat down cellar wit' nohole mouse.

SCOTTSBORO. This folk blues, collected by Lawrence Gellert in *Negro Songs of Protest* (New York: Carl Fischer, Inc., 1936), is a comment on the Scottsboro case. In 1931 nine black youths of Scottsboro, Alabama, were arrested and charged with the rape of two white women. Though eventually, after several trials, they were found not guilty, some of them at the time this song was composed had been convicted and sentenced to death.

SUGGESTIONS FOR WRITING

1. Choosing a poem that strikes you as particularly inventive or unusual in its language, such as Wallace Steven's "Metamorphosis" (page 555), E. E. Cummings's "anyone lived in a pretty how town" (page 556), or Gerard Manley Hopkins's "The Windhover" (page 830), write a brief analysis of it. Concentrate on the diction of the poem and its word order. For what possible purposes does the poet depart from standard English? (To find some pointers on writing about poetry by the method of analysis, see page 1497.)
2. In a short essay, set forth the pleasures of browsing in a dictionary. As you browse, see if you can discover any "found poems".
3. "Printing poetry in dialect, such as 'Scottsboro,' insults the literacy of a people." Think about this critical charge and comment on it.
4. Write a short defense of a poet's right to employ the language of science and technology. Alternatively, point out some of the dangers and drawbacks of using such language in poetry. For evidence, see the poems in this chapter by Richard Eberhart and A. R. Ammons and those in the Poems for Further Reading by James Merrill (page 848) and Henry Reed (page 863).

16 Saying and Suggesting

To write so clearly that they might bring "all things as near the mathematical plainness" as possible — that was the goal of scientists according to Bishop Thomas Sprat, who lived in the seventeenth century. Such an effort would seem bound to fail, because words, unlike numbers, are ambiguous indicators. Although it may have troubled Bishop Sprat, the tendency of a word to have multiplicity of meaning rather than mathematical plainness opens broad avenues to poetry.

Every word has at least one **denotation:** a meaning as defined in a dictionary. But the English language has many a common word with so many denotations that a reader may need to think twice to see what it means in a specific context. The noun *field,* for instance, can denote a piece of ground, a sports arena, the scene of a battle, part of a flag, a profession, and a number system in mathematics. Further, the word can be used as a verb ("he fielded a grounder") or an adjective ("field trip," "field glasses").

A word also has **connotations:** overtones or suggestions of additional meaning that it gains from all the contexts in which we have met it in the past. The word *skeleton,* according to a dictionary, denotes "the bony framework of a human being or other vertebrate animal, which supports the flesh and protects the organs." But by its associations, the word can rouse thoughts of war, of disease and death, or (possibly) of one's plans to go to medical school. Think, too, of the difference between "Old Doc Jones" and "Abner P. Jones, M.D." In the mind's eye, the former appears in his shirtsleeves; the latter has a gold nameplate on his door. That some words denote the same thing but have sharply different connotations is pointed out in this anonymous Victorian jingle:

Here's a little ditty that you really ought to know:
Horses "sweat" and men "perspire," but ladies only "glow."

The terms *druggist, pharmacist,* and *apothecary* all denote the same occupation, but apothecaries lay claim to special distinction.

Poets aren't the only people who care about the connotations of language. Advertisers know that connotations make money. Nowadays many automobile dealers advertise their secondhand cars not as "used" but as "pre-owned," as if fearing that "used car" would connote an old heap with soiled upholstery and mysterious engine troubles that somebody couldn't put up with. "Pre-owned," however, suggests that the previous owner has taken the trouble of breaking in the car for you. Not long ago prune-packers, alarmed by a slump in sales, sponsored a survey to determine the connotations of prunes in the public consciousness. Asked, "What do you think of when you hear the word *prunes?*" most people replied, "dried up," "wrinkled," or "constipated." Dismayed, the packers hired an advertising agency to create a new image for prunes, in hopes of inducing new connotations. Soon, advertisements began to show prunes in brightly colored settings, in the company of bikinied bathing beauties.

In imaginative writing, connotations are as crucial as they are in advertising. Consider this sentence: "A new brand of journalism is being born, or spawned" (Dwight Macdonald writing in *The New York Review of Books*). The last word, by its associations with fish and crustaceans, suggests that this new journalism is scarcely the product of human beings. And what do we make of Romeo's assertion that Juliet "is the sun"? Surely even a lovesick boy cannot mean that his sweetheart is "the incandescent body of gases about which the earth and other planets revolve" (a dictionary definition). He means, of course, that he thrives in her sight, that he feels warm in her presence or even at the thought of her, that she illumines his world and is the center of his universe. Because in the mind of the hearer these and other suggestions are brought into play, Romeo's statement, literally absurd, makes excellent sense.

Here is a famous poem that groups together things with similar connotations: certain ships and their cargoes. (A *quinquireme,* by the way, was an ancient Assyrian vessel propelled by sails and oars.)

John Masefield (1878 – 1967)

CARGOES   1902

Quinquireme of Nineveh from distant Ophir,
Rowing home to haven in sunny Palestine,
With a cargo of ivory,
And apes and peacocks,
Sandalwood, cedarwood, and sweet white wine.   5

Stately Spanish galleon coming from the Isthmus,
Dipping through the Tropics by the palm-green shores,
With a cargo of diamonds,
Emeralds, amethysts,
Topazes, and cinnamon, and gold moidores°.   *Portuguese coins*   10

Dirty British coaster with a salt-caked smoke stack,
Butting through the Channel in the mad March days,
With a cargo of Tyne coal,
Road-rails, pig-lead,
Firewood, iron-ware, and cheap tin trays.   15

To us, as well as to the poet's original readers, the place-names in the first two
stanzas suggest the exotic and faraway. Ophir, a vanished place, may have been
in Arabia; according to the Bible, King Solomon sent there for its celebrated
pure gold, also for ivory, apes, peacocks, and other luxury items. (See I Kings
9 – 10.) In his final stanza, Masefield groups commonplace things (mostly heavy
and metallic), whose suggestions of crudeness, cheapness, and ugliness he deliberately contrasts with those of the precious stuffs he has listed earlier. For
British readers, the Tyne is a stodgy and familiar river; the English Channel in
March, choppy and likely to upset a stomach. The quinquireme is *rowing*, the
galleon is *dipping*, but the dirty British freighter is *butting*, aggressively pushing.
Conceivably, the poet could have described firewood and even coal as beautiful,
but evidently he wants them to convey sharply different suggestions here, to go
along with the rest of the coaster's cargo. In drawing such a sharp contrast
between past and present, Masefield does more than merely draw up bills-of-
lading. Perhaps he even implies a wry and unfavorable comment upon life in
the present day. His meaning lies not so much in the dictionary definitions of
his words ("*moidores*: Portuguese gold coins formerly worth approximately five
pounds sterling") as in their rich and vivid connotations.

William Blake (1757 – 1827)*

LONDON   1794

I wander through each chartered street,
Near where the chartered Thames does flow,
And mark in every face I meet
Marks of weakness, marks of woe.

In every cry of every man,   5
In every infant's cry of fear,
In every voice, in every ban,
The mind-forged manacles I hear.

How the chimney-sweeper's cry
Every black'ning church appalls   10

And the hapless soldier's sigh
Runs in blood down palace walls.

But most through midnight streets I hear
How the youthful harlot's curse
Blasts the new born infant's tear   15
And blights with plagues the marriage hearse.

Here are only a few of the possible meanings of three of Blake's words:

chartered (lines 1, 2)

> DENOTATIONS: Established by a charter (a written grant or a certificate of
> incorporation); leased or hired.
>
> CONNOTATIONS: Defined, limited, restricted, channeled, mapped, bound by
> law; bought and sold (like a slave or an inanimate object); Magna Carta;
> charters given crown colonies by the King.
>
> OTHER WORDS IN THE POEM WITH SIMILAR CONNOTATIONS: *Ban,* which can
> denote (1) a legal prohibition; (2) a churchman's curse or malediction;
> (3) in medieval times, an order summoning a king's vassals to fight for
> him. *Manacles,* or shackles, restrain movement. *Chimney-sweeper, soldier,*
> and *harlot* are all hirelings.
>
> INTERPRETATION OF THE LINES: The street has had mapped out for it the
> direction in which it must go; the Thames has had laid down to it the
> course it must follow. Street and river are channeled, imprisoned, en-
> slaved (like every inhabitant of London).

black'ning (line 10)

> DENOTATION: Becoming black.
>
> CONNOTATIONS: The darkening of something once light, the defilement of
> something once clean, the deepening of guilt, the gathering of darkness
> at the approach of night.
>
> OTHER WORDS IN THE POEM WITH SIMILAR CONNOTATIONS: Objects becoming
> marked or smudged (*marks of weakness, marks of woe* in the faces of
> passers-by; bloodied walls of a palace; marriage blighted with plagues);
> the word *appalls* (denoting not only "to overcome with horror" but "to
> make pale" and also "to cast a pall or shroud over"); *midnight streets.*
>
> INTERPRETATION OF THE LINE: Literally, every London church grows black
> from soot and hires a chimney-sweeper (a small boy) to help clean it. But
> Blake suggests too that by profiting from the suffering of the child
> laborer, the church is soiling its original purity.

Blasts, blights (lines 15 – 16) ·

> DENOTATIONS: Both *blast* and *blight* mean "to cause to wither" or "to ruin
> and destroy." Both are terms from horticulture. Frost *blasts* a bud and
> kills it; disease *blights* a growing plant.
>
> CONNOTATIONS: Sickness and death; gardens shriveled and dying; gusts of
> wind and the ravages of insects; things blown to pieces or rotted and
> warped.

OTHER WORDS IN THE POEM WITH SIMILAR CONNOTATIONS: Faces marked with weakness and woe; the child become a chimney-sweep; the soldier killed by war; blackening church and bloodied palace; young girl turned harlot; wedding carriage transformed into a hearse.

INTERPRETATION OF THE LINES: Literally, the harlot spreads the plague of syphilis, which, carried into marriage, can cause a baby to be born blind. In a larger and more meaningful sense, Blake sees the prostitution of even one young girl corrupting the entire institution of matrimony and endangering every child.

Some of these connotations are more to the point than others; the reader of a poem nearly always has the problem of distinguishing relevant associations from irrelevant ones. We need to read a poem in its entirety and, when a word leaves us in doubt, look for other things in the poem to corroborate or refute what we think it means. Relatively simple and direct in its statement, Blake's account of his stroll through the city at night becomes an indictment of a whole social and religious order. The indictment could hardly be this effective if it were "mathematically plain," its every word restricted to one denotation clearly spelled out.

Wallace Stevens (1879 – 1955)*

DISILLUSIONMENT OF TEN O'CLOCK   1923

The houses are haunted
By white night-gowns.
None are green,
Or purple with green rings,
Or green with yellow rings,   5
Or yellow with blue rings.
None of them are strange,
With socks of lace
And beaded ceintures.
People are not going   10
To dream of baboons and periwinkles.
Only, here and there, an old sailor,
Drunk and asleep in his boots,
Catches tigers
In red weather.   15

QUESTIONS

1. What are *beaded ceintures*? What does the phrase suggest?
2. What contrast does Stevens draw between the people who live in these houses and the old sailor? What do the connotations of *white night-gowns* and *sailor* add to this contrast?
3. What is lacking in these people who wear white night-gowns? Why should the poet's view of them be a "disillusionment"?

Gwendolyn Brooks (b. 1917)*

THE BEAN EATERS   1960

They eat beans mostly, this old yellow pair.
Dinner is a casual affair.
Plain chipware on a plain and creaking wood,
Tin flatware.

Two who are Mostly Good.   5
Two who have lived their day,
But keep on putting on their clothes
And putting things away.

And remembering . . .
Remembering, with tinklings and twinges,   10
As they lean over the beans in their rented back room that is full of
    beads and receipts and dolls and cloths, tobacco crumbs, vases
    and fringes.

QUESTIONS

1. What do we infer about this old couple and their life style from the details in lines
   1–4 about their diet, dishes, dinnertable, and cutlery?
2. In that long last line, what is suggested by the things they have saved and stored?

Timothy Steele (b. 1948)*

EPITAPH   1979

Here lies Sir Tact, a diplomatic fellow
Whose silence was not golden, but just yellow.

QUESTIONS

1. To what famous saying does the poet allude?
2. What are the connotations of *golden?* Of *yellow?*

Geoffrey Hill (b. 1932)

MERLIN   1959

I will consider the outnumbering dead:
For they are the husks of what was rich seed.
Now, should they come together to be fed,
They would outstrip the locusts' covering tide.

Arthur, Elaine, Mordred; they are all gone   5
Among the raftered galleries of bone.

By the long barrows of Logres they are made one,
And over their city stands the pinnacled corn.

MERLIN. In medieval legend, Merlin was a powerful magician and a seer, an aide of King Arthur.
5 *Elaine:* in Arthurian romance, the beloved of Sir Launcelot. *Mordred:* Arthur's treacherous
nephew by whose hand the king died. 7 *barrows:* earthworks for burial of the dead. *Logres:* name
of an ancient British kingdom, according to the twelfth-century historian Geoffrey of Monmouth,
who gathered legends of King Arthur.

QUESTIONS

1. What does the title "Merlin" contribute to this poem? Do you prefer to read the
   poem as though it is Merlin who speaks to us — or the poet?
2. Line 4 alludes to the plague of locusts that God sent upon Egypt (Exodus 10): "For
   they covered the face of the whole earth, so that the land was darkened . . ." With
   this allusion in mind, explain the comparison of the dead to locusts.
3. Why are the suggestions inherent in the names of *Arthur, Elaine,* and *Mordred* more
   valuable to this poem than those we might find in the names of other dead persons
   called, say, Gus, Tessie, and Butch?
4. Explain the phrase in line 6: *the raftered galleries of bone.*
5. In the last line, what *city* does the poet refer to? Does he mean some particular city,
   or is he making a comparison?
6. What is interesting in the adjective *pinnacled?* How can it be applied to corn?

Wallace Stevens (1879 – 1955)*

THE EMPEROR OF ICE-CREAM   1923

Call the roller of big cigars,
The muscular one, and bid him whip
In kitchen cups concupiscent curds.
Let the wenches dawdle in such dress
As they are used to wear, and let the boys   5
Bring flowers in last month's newspapers.
Let be be finale of seem.
The only emperor is the emperor of ice-cream.

Take from the dresser of deal,
Lacking the three glass knobs, that sheet   10
On which she embroidered fantails once
And spread it so as to cover her face.
If her horny feet protrude, they come
To show how cold she is, and dumb.
Let the lamp affix its beam.   15
The only emperor is the emperor of ice-cream.

THE EMPEROR OF ICE-CREAM. 9 *deal:* fir or pine wood used to make cheap furniture.

QUESTIONS

1. What scene is taking place in the first stanza? Describe it in your own words. What
   are your feelings about it?

2. Who do you suppose to be the dead person in the second stanza? What can you infer about her? What do you know about her for sure?
3. Make a guess about this mysterious emperor. Who do you take him to be?
4. What does ice cream mean to you? In this poem, what do you think it means to Stevens?

Walter de la Mare (1873 – 1956)

THE LISTENERS   1912

"Is there anybody there?" said the Traveller,
    Knocking on the moonlit door;
And his horse in the silence champed the grasses
    Of the forest's ferny floor:
And a bird flew up out of the turret,   5
    Above the Traveller's head:
And he smote upon the door again a second time;
    "Is there anybody there?" he said.
But no one descended to the Traveller;
    No head from the leaf-fringed sill   10
Leaned over and looked into his gray eyes,
    Where he stood perplexed and still.
But only a host of phantom listeners
    That dwelt in the lone house then
Stood listening in the quiet of the moonlight   15
    To that voice from the world of men:
Stood thronging the faint moonbeams on the dark stair
    That goes down to the empty hall,
Hearkening in an air stirred and shaken
    By the lonely Traveller's call.   20
And he felt in his heart their strangeness,
    Their stillness answering his cry,
While his horse moved, cropping the dark turf,
    'Neath the starred and leafy sky;
For he suddenly smote on the door, even   25
    Louder, and lifted his head: —
"Tell them I came, and no one answered,
    That I kept my word," he said.
Never the least stir made the listeners,
    Though every word he spake   30
Fell echoing through the shadowiness of the still house
    From the one man left awake:
Ay, they heard his foot upon the stirrup,
    And the sound of iron on stone,
And how the silence surged softly backward,   35
    When the plunging hoofs were gone.

QUESTIONS

1. Before you had read this poem, what suggestions did its title bring to mind?
2. Now that you have read the poem, what do you make of these "listeners"? Who or what do you imagine them to be?
3. Why is *the moonlit door* (in line 2) a phrase more valuable to this poem than if the poet had written simply "the door"?
4. What does *turret* (in line 5) suggest?
5. Reconstruct some earlier events that might have preceded the Traveller's visit. Who might this Traveller be? Who are the unnamed persons — "them" (line 27) — for whom the Traveller leaves a message? What promise has he kept? (The poet doesn't tell us; we can only guess.)
6. Do you think this poem any the worse for the fact that its setting, characters, and action are so mysterious? What does "The Listeners" gain from not telling us all?

Robert Frost (1874 – 1963)*

FIRE AND ICE   1923

Some say the world will end in fire, A
Some say in ice. B
From what I've tasted of desire A
I hold with those who favor fire. A
But if it had to perish twice, B   5
I think I know enough of hate C
To say that for destruction ice B
Is also great C
And would suffice. B

QUESTIONS

1. To whom does Frost refer in line 1? In line 2?
2. What connotations of *fire* and *ice* contribute to the richness of Frost's comparison?

SUGGESTIONS FOR WRITING

1. In a short essay, analyze a poem full of words that radiate suggestions. Looking into the Poems for Further Reading that begin on page 773, you might consider T. S. Eliot's "The Love Song of J. Alfred Prufrock," John Keats's "To Autumn," Sylvia Plath's "Daddy," or many others. Focus on particular words: explain their connotations and show how these suggestions are part of the poem's meaning. (For guidelines on writing about poetry by the method of analysis, see page 1497.)
2. In a current newspaper or magazine, select an advertisement that tries to surround a product with an aura. A new car, for instance, might be described in terms of some powerful jungle cat ("purring power, ready to spring"). Likely hunting-grounds for such ads are magazines that cater to the affluent (*New Yorker*, *Vogue*, and others). Clip or photocopy the ad and circle words in it that seem especially suggestive. Then, in an accompanying paper, unfold the suggestions in these words and try to explain the ad's appeal. How is the purpose of connotative language used in advertising copy different from that of such language when used in poetry?

17 Imagery

Ezra Pound (1885 – 1972)*

In a Station of the Metro   1916

The apparition of these faces in the crowd;
Petals on a wet, black bough.

  Pound said he wrote this poem to convey an experience: emerging one day from a train in the Paris subway *(Métro)*, he beheld "suddenly a beautiful face, and then another and another." Originally he had described his impression in a poem thirty lines long. In this final version, each line contains an **image,** which, like a picture, may take the place of a thousand words.

  Though the term *image* suggests a thing seen, when speaking of images in poetry we generally mean *a word or sequence of words that refers to any sensory experience.* Often this experience is a sight (**visual imagery,** as in Pound's poem), but it may be a sound (**auditory imagery**) or a touch (**tactile imagery,** as a perception of roughness or smoothness). It may be an odor or a taste or perhaps a bodily sensation such as pain, the prickling of gooseflesh, the quenching of thirst, or — as in the following brief poem — the perception of something cold.

Taniguchi Buson (1715 – 1783)

The piercing chill I feel   (about 1760)

The piercing chill I feel:
    my dead wife's comb, in our bedroom,
        under my heel . . .
                    — Translated by Harold G. Henderson

As in this **haiku** (in Japanese, a poem of about seventeen syllables) an image can convey a flash of understanding. Had he wished, the poet might have spoken of the dead woman, of the contrast between her death and his memory of her, of his feelings toward death in general. But such a discussion would be quite different from the poem he actually wrote. Striking his bare foot against the comb, now cold and motionless but associated with the living wife (perhaps worn in her hair), the widower feels a shock as if he had touched the woman's corpse. A literal, physical sense of death is conveyed; the abstraction "death" is understood through the senses. To render the abstract in concrete terms is what poets often try to do; in this attempt, an image can be valuable.

An image may occur in a single word, a phrase, a sentence, or, as in this case, an entire short poem. To speak of the **imagery** of a poem — all its images taken together — is often more useful than to speak of separate images. To divide Buson's haiku into five images — *chill, wife, comb, bedroom, heel* — is possible, for any noun that refers to a visible object or a sensation is an image, but this is to draw distinctions that in themselves mean little and to disassemble a single experience.

Does an image cause a reader to experience a sense impression? Not quite. Reading the word *petals,* no one literally sees petals; but the occasion is given for imagining them. The image asks to be seen with the mind's eye. And although "In a Station of the Metro" records what Ezra Pound saw, it is of course not necessary for a poet actually to have lived through a sensory experience in order to write of it. Keats may never have seen a newly discovered planet through a telescope, despite the image in his sonnet on Chapman's Homer (p. 837).

It is tempting to think of imagery as mere decoration, particularly when we read Keats, who fills his poems with an abundance of sights, sounds, odors, and tastes. But a successful image is not just a dab of paint or a flashy bauble. When Keats opens "The Eve of St. Agnes" with what have been called the coldest lines in literature, he evokes by a series of images a setting and a mood:

> St. Agnes' eve — Ah, bitter chill it was!
> The owl, for all his feathers, was a-cold;
> The hare limped trembling through the frozen grass,
> And silent was the flock in woolly fold:
> Numb were the Beadsman's fingers, while he told
> His rosary, and while his frosted breath,
> Like pious incense from a censer old,
> Seemed taking flight for heaven, without a death, . . .

Indeed, some literary critics look for much of the meaning of a poem in its imagery, wherein they expect to see the mind of the poet more truly revealed than in whatever the poet explicitly claims to believe. In his investigation of Wordsworth's "Ode: Intimations of Immortality," the critic Cleanth Brooks devotes his attention to the imagery of light and darkness, which he finds carries on and develops Wordsworth's thought.[1]

[1]"Wordsworth and the Paradox of the Imagination," in *The Well Wrought Urn* (New York: Harcourt, 1956).

Though Shakespeare's Theseus (in A *Midsummer Night's Dream*) accuses poets of being concerned with "airy nothings," poets are usually very much concerned with what is in front of them. This concern is of use to us. Perhaps, as Alan Watts has remarked, Americans are not the materialists they are sometimes accused of being. How could anyone taking a look at an American city think that its inhabitants deeply cherish material things? Involved in our personal hopes and apprehensions, anticipating the future so hard that much of the time we see the present through a film of thought across our eyes, perhaps we need a poet occasionally to remind us that even the coffee we absentmindedly sip comes in (as Yeats put it) a "heavy spillable cup."

T. S. Eliot (1888 – 1965)*

THE WINTER EVENING SETTLES DOWN   1917

The winter evening settles down
With smell of steaks in passageways.
Six o'clock.
The burnt-out ends of smoky days.
And now a gusty shower wraps   5
The grimy scraps
Of withered leaves about your feet
And newspapers from vacant lots;
The showers beat
On broken blinds and chimney-pots,   10
And at the corner of the street
A lonely cab-horse steams and stamps.

And then the lighting of the lamps.

QUESTIONS

1. What mood is evoked by the images in Eliot's poem?
2. What kind of city neighborhood has the poet chosen to describe? How can you tell?

Theodore Roethke (1908 – 1963)*

ROOT CELLAR   1948

Nothing would sleep in that cellar, dank as a ditch,
Bulbs broke out of boxes hunting for chinks in the dark,
Shoots dangled and drooped,
Lolling obscenely from mildewed crates,
Hung down long yellow evil necks, like tropical snakes.   5
And what a congress of stinks! —

Roots ripe as old bait,
Pulpy stems, rank, silo-rich,
Leaf-mold, manure, lime, piled against slippery planks.
Nothing would give up life: 10
Even the dirt kept breathing a small breath.

QUESTIONS

1. As a boy growing up in Saginaw, Michigan, Theodore Roethke spent much of his
   time in a large commercial greenhouse run by his family. What details in his poem
   show more than a passing acquaintance with growing things?
2. What varieties of image does "Root Cellar" contain? Point out examples.
3. What do you understand to be Roethke's attitude toward the root cellar? Does he
   view it as a disgusting chamber of horrors? Pay special attention to the last two lines.

Elizabeth Bishop (1911 – 1979)*

THE FISH   1946

I caught a tremendous fish
and held him beside the boat
half out of water, with my hook
fast in a corner of his mouth.
He didn't fight.   5
He hadn't fought at all.
He hung a grunting weight,
battered and venerable
and homely. Here and there
his brown skin hung in strips   10
like ancient wall-paper,
and its pattern of darker brown
was like wall-paper:
shapes like full-blown roses
stained and lost through age.   15
He was speckled with barnacles,
fine rosettes of lime,
and infested
with tiny white sea-lice,
and underneath two or three   20
rags of green weed hung down.
While his gills were breathing in
the terrible oxygen
— the frightening gills,
fresh and crisp with blood,   25

that can cut so badly—
I thought of the coarse white flesh
packed in like feathers,
the big bones and the little bones,
the dramatic reds and blacks   30
of his shiny entrails,
and the pink swim-bladder
like a big peony.
I looked into his eyes
which were far larger than mine   35
but shallower, and yellowed,
the irises backed and packed
with tarnished tinfoil
seen through the lenses
of old scratched isinglass.   40
They shifted a little, but not
to return my stare.
— It was more like the tipping
of an object toward the light.
I admired his sullen face,   45
the mechanism of his jaw,
and then I saw
that from his lower lip
— if you could call it a lip —
grim, wet, and weapon-like,   50
hung five old pieces of fish-line,
or four and a wire leader
with the swivel still attached,
with all their five big hooks
grown firmly in his mouth.   55
A green line, frayed at the end
where he broke it, two heavier lines,
and a fine black thread
still crimped from the strain and snap
when it broke and he got away.   60
Like medals with their ribbons
frayed and wavering,
a five-haired beard of wisdom
trailing from his aching jaw.
I stared and stared   65
and victory filled up
the little rented boat,
from the pool of bilge
where oil had spread a rainbow
around the rusted engine   70
to the bailer rusted orange,

the sun-cracked thwarts,
the oarlocks on their strings,
the gunnels — until everything
was rainbow, rainbow, rainbow!   75
And I let the fish go.

QUESTIONS

1. How many abstract words does this poem contain? What proportion of the poem is
   imagery?
2. What is the speaker's attitude toward the fish? Comment in particular on lines
   61 – 64.
3. What attitude do the images of the rainbow of oil (line 69), the orange bailer (bailing
   bucket, line 71), the *sun-cracked thwarts* (line 72) convey? Does the poet expect us to
   feel mournful because the boat is in such sorry condition?
4. What is meant by *rainbow, rainbow, rainbow*?
5. How do these images prepare us for the conclusion? Why does the speaker let the
   fish go?

Oscar Wilde (1854 – 1900)

SYMPHONY IN YELLOW   1889

An omnibus across the bridge
   Crawls like a yellow butterfly,
   And, here and there, a passer-by
Shows like a little restless midge°.   *a tiny fly*

Big barges full of yellow hay   5
   Are moored against the shadowy wharf,
   And, like a yellow silken scarf,
The thick fog hangs along the quay.

The yellow leaves begin to fade
   And flutter from the Temple elms,   10
   And at my feet the pale green Thames
Lies like a rod of rippled jade.

QUESTIONS

1. What season is it?
2. What is fresh and surprising in this view of an ordinary city scene?
3. To which of your senses does this poem most appeal?

John Haines (b. 1924)

WINTER NEWS   1966

They say the wells
are freezing
at Northway where
the cold begins.

Oil tins bang   5
as evening comes on,
and clouds of
steaming breath drift
in the street.

Men go out to feed   10
the stiffening dogs,

the voice of the snowman
calls the white-
haired children home.

QUESTIONS

1. Which of the images in this poem strike you as the most vivid? To which senses do
   Haines's images appeal?
2. Why are the children described as "white-haired"?

Emily Dickinson (1830 – 1886)*

A ROUTE OF EVANESCENCE   (1879)

A Route of Evanescence
With a revolving Wheel –
A Resonance of Emerald –
A Rush of Cochineal° –   *red dye*
And every Blossom on the Bush   5
Adjusts its tumbled Head –
The mail from Tunis, probably,
An easy Morning's Ride –

A ROUTE OF EVANESCENCE. 1 *Evanescence*; ornithologist's term for the luminous sheen of certain
birds' feathers. 7 *Tunis*: capital city of Tunisia, North Africa.

QUESTION

What is the subject of this poem? How can you tell?

Jean Toomer (1894 – 1967)

REAPERS   1923

Black reapers with the sound of steel on stones
Are sharpening scythes. I see them place the hones
In their hip-pockets as a thing that's done,
And start their silent swinging, one by one.
Black horses drive a mower through the weeds,   5
And there, a field rat, startled, squealing bleeds,
His belly close to ground. I see the blade,
Blood-stained, continue cutting weeds and shade.

QUESTIONS

1. Imagine the scene Jean Toomer describes. Which particulars most vividly strike the mind's eye?
2. What kind of image is *silent swinging*?
3. Read the poem aloud. Notice especially the effect of the words *sound of steel on stones* and *field rat, startled, squealing bleeds*. What interesting sounds are present in the very words that contain these images?
4. What feelings do you get from this poem as a whole? Would you agree with someone who said, "This poem gives us a sense of happy, carefree life down on the farm, close to nature"? Exactly what in "Reapers" makes you feel the way you do? Besides appealing to our auditory and visual imagination, what do the images contribute?

Gerard Manley Hopkins (1844 – 1889)*

PIED BEAUTY   (1877)

Glory be to God for dappled things —
    For skies of couple-color as a brinded° cow;   *streaked*
       For rose-moles all in stipple upon trout that swim;
Fresh-firecoal chestnut-falls; finches' wings;
    Landscape plotted and pieced — fold, fallow, and plow;   5
       And áll trádes, their gear and tackle and trim°.   *equipment*

All things counter, original, spare, strange;
    Whatever is fickle, freckled (who knows how?)
       With swift, slow; sweet, sour; adazzle, dim;
He fathers-forth whose beauty is past change: 10
       Praise him.

QUESTIONS

1. What does the word *pied* mean? (Hint: what does a Pied Piper look like?)
2. According to Hopkins, what do *skies, cow, trout, ripe chestnuts, finches' wings,* and *landscapes* all have in common? What landscapes can the poet have in mind? (Have you ever seen any *dappled* landscape while looking down from an airplane, or from a mountain or high hill?)

3. What do you make of line 6: what can carpenters' saws and ditch-diggers' spades possibly have in common with the dappled things in lines 2 – 4?
4. Does Hopkins refer only to contrasts that meet the eye? What other kinds of variation interest him?
5. Try to state in your own words the theme of this poem. How essential to our understanding of this theme are Hopkins's images?

About Haiku

On the one-ton temple bell
a moonmoth, folded into sleep,
sits still.
— Taniguchi Buson

The name *haiku* means "beginning-verse" — perhaps because the form may have originated in a game. Players, given a haiku, were supposed to extend its three lines into a longer poem. Haiku (the word can also be plural) tend to consist mainly of imagery, but as we saw in Buson's lines on the cold comb, their imagery is not always only pictorial.

Heat-lightning streak —
through darkness pierces
the heron's shriek.
— Matsuo Basho

In the poet's account of his experience, are sight and sound neatly distinguished from each other?

Note that a haiku has little room for abstract thoughts or general observations. The following attempt, though in seventeen syllables, is far from haiku in spirit:

Now that our love is gone
I feel within my soul
a nagging distress.

Unlike the author of those lines, haiku poets look out upon a literal world, seldom looking inward to *discuss* their feelings. Japanese haiku tend to be seasonal in subject, but because they are so highly compressed, they usually just *imply* a season: a blossom indicates spring; a crow on a branch, autumn; snow, winter. Not just pretty little sketches of nature (as some Westerners think), haiku assume a view of the universe in which observer and nature are not separated.

A haiku in Japanese is rimeless, its seventeen syllables usually arranged in three lines, often following a pattern of five, seven, and five syllables. Haiku written in English frequently ignore such a pattern; they may be rimed (like the English versions of Buson and Basho), or unrimed, as the poet prefers.

John Ridland (b. 1933)

THE LAZY MAN'S HAIKU   1975

out in the night
a wheelbarrowful
of moonlight

If you care to try your hand at haiku-writing, here are a few suggestions. Make every word matter. Include few adjectives, shun needless conjunctions. Set your poem in the present — "Haiku," said Basho, "is simply what is happening in this place at this moment." Confine your poem to what can be seen, heard, smelled, tasted, or touched. Mere sensory reports, however, will be meaningless unless they make the reader feel something — as a contemporary American writer points out in this spoof.

Richard Brautigan (1935 – 1985)

HAIKU AMBULANCE   1968

A piece of green pepper fell
off the wooden salad bowl:
so what?

Here, freely translated, are two more Japanese haiku to inspire you. The first is by master poet Basho (1644 – 1694), sometimes called the Shakespeare of the haiku.

In the old stone pool
a frogjump:
splishhhhh.

The second (in a translation by Cid Corman) is by Issa (1763 – 1827), a poet noted for wit.

only one guy and
only one fly trying to
make the guest room do

Finally, here are eight more recent haiku written in English. (Don't expect them all to observe a strict arrangement of seventeen syllables.) Haiku, in any language, is an art of few words, many suggestions. A haiku starts us thinking and feeling. "So the reader," Raymond Roseliep wrote, "keeps getting on where the poet got off."

Sprayed with strong poison
my roses are crisp this year
in the crystal vase
    — Paul Goodman

After weeks of watching the roof leak
I fixed it tonight
by moving a single board
    — Gary Snyder

Dusk over the lake;
   a turtle's head emerges
      then silently sinks
          — Virgil Hutton

broken bowl
the pieces
still rocking
      — Penny Harter

campfire extinguished,
the woman washing dishes
in a pan of stars
      — Raymond Roseliep

on the cardboard box
holding the frozen wino:
Fragile: Do not crush.
      — Nicholas A. Virgilio

The green cockleburs
Caught in the thick woolly hair
Of the black boy's head.
      — Richard Wright

A dawn in a tree of birds.
Another.
And then another.
      — Kenneth Rexroth

FOR REVIEW AND FURTHER STUDY

John Keats (1795 – 1821)*

BRIGHT STAR! WOULD I WERE
STEADFAST AS THOU ART   (1819)

Bright star! would I were steadfast as thou art —
   Not in lone splendor hung aloft the night,
And watching, with eternal lids apart,
   Like nature's patient, sleepless Eremite°   *hermit*
The moving waters at their priest-like task   5
   Of pure ablution round earth's human shores,
Or gazing on the new soft-fallen mask
   Of snow upon the mountains and the moors —
No — yet still steadfast, still unchangeable,
   Pillowed upon my fair love's ripening breast,   10
To feel for ever its soft fall and swell,
   Awake for ever in a sweet unrest,
Still, still to hear her tender-taken breath,
And so live ever — or else swoon to death.

QUESTIONS

1. Stars are conventional symbols for love and a loved one. (Love, Shakespeare tells us in a sonnet, "is the star to every wandering bark.") In this sonnet, why is it not possible for the star to have this meaning? How does Keats use it?
2. What seems concrete and particular in the speaker's observations?
3. Suppose Keats had said *slow and easy* instead of *tender-taken* in line 13? What would have been lost?

Timothy Steele (b. 1948)

WAITING FOR THE STORM   1986

Breeze sent a wrinkling darkness
Across the bay. I knelt
Beneath an upturned boat,
And, moment by moment, felt

The sand at my feet grow colder,   5
The damp air chill and spread.
Then the first raindrops sounded
On the hull above my head.

QUESTIONS

1. How many sensory experiences does this poem evoke?
2. By what means does the poem build an atmosphere of suspenseful expectation?
3. Read the poem aloud. What do you notice that differentiates "Waiting for the Storm" from prose?

EXPERIMENT: *Writing with Images*

Taking the following poems as examples from which to start rather than as models to be slavishly copied, try to compose a brief poem that consists largely of imagery.

Walt Whitman (1819 – 1892)*

THE RUNNER   1867

On a flat road runs the well-train'd runner;
He is lean and sinewy, with muscular legs;
He is thinly clothed — he leans forward as he runs,
With lightly closed fists, and arms partially rais'd.

T. E. Hulme (1883 – 1917)

IMAGE   (about 1910)

Old houses were scaffolding once
                 and workmen whistling.

William Carlos Williams (1883 – 1963)*

THE GREAT FIGURE   1921

Among the rain
and lights
I saw the figure 5
in gold
on a red   5
firetruck
moving
tense
unheeded
to gong clangs   10
siren howls
and wheels rumbling
through the dark city.

Robert Bly (b. 1926)*

DRIVING TO TOWN LATE TO MAIL A LETTER   1962

It is a cold and snowy night. The main street is deserted.
The only things moving are swirls of snow.
As I lift the mailbox door, I feel its cold iron.
There is a privacy I love in this snowy night.
Driving around, I will waste more time.

Gary Snyder (b. 1930)

MID-AUGUST AT SOURDOUGH MOUNTAIN LOOKOUT   1959

Down valley a smoke haze
Three days heat, after five days rain
Pitch glows on the fir-cones
Across rocks and meadows
Swarms of new flies.   5

I cannot remember things I once read
A few friends, but they are in cities.
Drinking cold snow-water from a tin cup
Looking down for miles
Through high still air.   10

MID-AUGUST AT SOURDOUGH MOUNTAIN LOOKOUT. *Sourdough Mountain:* in the state of Washington,
where the poet's job at the time was to watch for forest fires.

H. D. [Hilda Doolittle] (1886–1961)

HEAT   1916

O wind, rend open the heat,
cut apart the heat,
rend it to tatters.

Fruit cannot drop
through this thick air —   5
fruit cannot fall into heat
that presses up and blunts
the points of pears
and rounds the grapes.

Cut the heat —   10
plough through it,
turning it on either side
of your path.

Emanuel di Pasquale (b. 1943)

A SENSUAL, FOR EZRA POUND   1989

A girl is feeding
grapes to three leopards.
The leopards are black.
The grapes are also black.
Blue black.   5
And the girl is naked.
Like ripening grapes,
her breasts, her small breasts,
lean lightly into the air.

Linda Gregg (b. 1942)

THE GRUB   1981

The almost transparent white grub moves
slowly along the edge of the frying pan.
The grease makes the only sound, loud
in the empty room. Even the rim is cooking him.
The worm stops. Raises his head slightly.   5
Lowers it, moving tentatively down the side.
He seems to be moving on his own time,
but he is falling by definition. He moves forward
touching the frying grease with his whole face.

Mary Oliver (b. 1935)

RAIN IN OHIO   1983

The robin cries: *rain!*
The crow calls: *plunder!*

The blacksnake climbing
in the vines halts
his long ladder of muscle   5

while the thunderheads whirl up
out of the white west,

their dark hooves nicking
the tall trees as they come.

Rain, rain, rain! sings the robin   10
frantically, then flies for cover.

The crow hunches.
The blacksnake

pours himself swift and heavy
into the ground.   15

SUGGESTIONS FOR WRITING

1. Choose, from the Poems for Further Reading that begins on page 773, a poem that appeals to you. Then write a brief account of your experience in reading it, paying special notice to its imagery. What images strike you, and why? What do they contribute to the poem as a whole? Poems rich in imagery include Samuel Taylor Coleridge's "Kubla Khan," Robert Frost's "Birches," John Keats's "Ode on Melancholy," Charlotte Mew's "The Farmer's Bride," William Carlos Williams's "Spring and All (By the road to the contagious hospital)" and many more.
2. After you have read the haiku and the discussion of haiku-writing in this chapter, write three or four haiku of your own. Then write a brief prose account of your experience in writing them. What, if anything, did you find out?
3. Reflect on Samuel Johnson's famous remarks on "the business of the poet" (page 938). Try applying Johnson's view to some recent poem—say, Elizabeth Bishop's "The Fish" (in this chapter). Would Johnson find Bishop a seer of "general and transcendental truths" or a counter of tulip-streaks? Then, in a short critical statement of your own, support or attack Johnson's view.

18   Figures of Speech

WHY SPEAK FIGURATIVELY?

"I will speak daggers to her, but use none," says Hamlet, preparing to confront his mother. His statement makes sense only because we realize that *daggers* is to be taken two ways: literally (denoting sharp, pointed weapons) and nonliterally (referring to something that can be used *like* weapons — namely, words). Reading poetry, we often meet comparisons between two things whose similarity we have never noticed before. When Marianne Moore observes that a fir tree has "an emerald turkey-foot at the top," the result is a pleasure that poetry richly affords: the sudden recognition of likenesses.

A treetop like a turkey-foot, words like daggers — such comparisons are called **figures of speech.** In its broadest definition, a figure of speech may be said to occur whenever a speaker or writer, for the sake of freshness or emphasis, departs from the usual denotations of words. Certainly, when Hamlet says he will speak daggers, no one expects him to release pointed weapons from his lips, for *daggers* is not to be read solely for its denotation. Its connotations — sharp, stabbing, piercing, wounding — also come to mind, and we see ways in which words and daggers work alike. (Words too can hurt: by striking through pretenses, possibly, or by wounding their hearer's self-esteem.) In the statement "A razor is sharper than an ax," there is no departure from the usual denotations of *razor* and *ax,* and no figure of speech results. Both objects are of the same class; the comparison is not offensive to logic. But in "How sharper than a serpent's tooth it is to have a thankless child," the objects — snake's tooth (fang) and ungrateful offspring — are so unlike that no reasonable comparison may be made between them. To find similarity, we attend to the connotations of *serpent's tooth* — biting, piercing, venom, pain — rather than to its denotations. If we are aware of the connotations of *red rose* (beauty, softness, freshness, and so forth), then the line "My love is like a red, red rose" need not call to mind a woman with a scarlet face and a thorny neck.

Figures of speech are not devices to state what is demonstrably untrue. Indeed they often state truths that more literal language cannot communicate; they call attention to such truths; they lend them emphasis.

Alfred, Lord Tennyson (1809 – 1892)*

THE EAGLE   1851

He clasps the crag with crooked hands;
Close to the sun in lonely lands,
Ringed with the azure world, he stands.

The wrinkled sea beneath him crawls;
He watches from his mountain walls,
And like a thunderbolt he falls.

This brief poem is rich in figurative language. In the first line, the phrase *crooked hands* may surprise us. An eagle does not have hands, we might protest; but the objection would be a quibble, for evidently Tennyson is indicating exactly how an eagle clasps a crag, in the way that human fingers clasp a thing. By implication, too, the eagle is a person. *Close to the sun,* if taken literally, is an absurd exaggeration, the sun being a mean distance of 93,000,000 miles from the earth. For the eagle to be closer to it by the altitude of a mountain is an approach so small as to be insignificant. But figuratively, Tennyson conveys that the eagle stands above the clouds, perhaps silhouetted against the sun, and for the moment belongs to the heavens rather than to the land and sea. The word *ringed* makes a circle of the whole world's horizons and suggests that we see the world from the eagle's height; the sea becomes an aged, sluggish animal; *mountain walls,* possibly literal, also suggests a fort or castle; and finally the eagle itself is likened to a thunderbolt in speed and in power, perhaps also in that its beak is — like our abstract conception of a lightning bolt — pointed. How much of the poem can be taken literally? Only *he clasps the crag, he stands, he watches, he falls.* The rest is made of figures of speech. The result is that, reading Tennyson's poem, we gain a bird's-eye view of sun, sea, and land — and even of bird. Like imagery, figurative language refers us to the physical world.

William Shakespeare (1564 – 1616)*

SHALL I COMPARE THEE TO A SUMMER'S DAY?   1609

Shall I compare thee to a summer's day?
Thou art more lovely and more temperate.
Rough winds do shake the darling buds of May,
And summer's lease hath all too short a date.

Sometime too hot the eye of heaven shines,   5
And often is his gold complexion dimmed;
And every fair° from fair sometimes declines,   *fair one*
By chance, or nature's changing course, untrimmed.
But thy eternal summer shall not fade,
Nor lose possession of that fair thou ow'st°;   *ownest, have* 10
Nor shall death brag thou wand'rest in his shade,
When in eternal lines to time thou grow'st.
    So long as men can breathe or eyes can see,
    So long lives this, and this gives life to thee.

Howard Moss (1922 – 1987)

Shall I Compare Thee to a Summer's Day?   1976

Who says you're like one of the dog days?
You're nicer. And better.
Even in May, the weather can be gray,
And a summer sub-let doesn't last forever.
Sometimes the sun's too hot;   5
Sometimes it is not.
Who can stay young forever?
People break their necks or just drop dead!
But you? Never!
If there's just one condensed reader left   10
Who can figure out the abridged alphabet,
    After you're dead and gone,
    In this poem you'll live on!

Questions

1. In Howard Moss's streamlined version of Shakespeare, from a series called "Modified Sonnets (Dedicated to adapters, abridgers, digesters, and condensers everywhere)," to what extent does the poet use figurative language? In Shakespeare's original sonnet, how high a proportion of Shakespeare's language is figurative?

2. Compare some of Moss's lines to the corresponding lines in Shakespeare's sonnet. Why is *Even in May, the weather can be gray* less interesting than the original? In the lines on the sun (5 – 6 in both versions), what has Moss's modification deliberately left out? Why is Shakespeare's seeing death as a braggart memorable? Why aren't you greatly impressed by Moss's last two lines?

3. Can you explain Shakespeare's play on the word *untrimmed* (line 8)? Evidently the word can mean "divested of trimmings," but what other suggestions do you find in it?

4. How would you answer someone who argued, "Maybe Moss's language isn't as good as Shakespeare's, but the meaning is still there. What's wrong with putting Shakespeare into up-to-date words that can be understood by everybody?"

Jon Stallworthy (b. 1935)

Sindhi Woman   1963

Barefoot through the bazaar,
and with the same undulant grace
as the cloth blown back from her face,
she glides with a stone jar
high on her head   5
and not a ripple in her tread.

Watching her cross erect
stones, garbage, excrement, and crumbs
of glass in the Karachi slums,
I, with my stoop, reflect   10
they stand most straight
who learn to walk beneath a weight.

Sindhi Woman. The Sindhi are the predominantly Moslem people of Sind, a former province of India now in Pakistan. 9 *Karachi:* located on the Arabian Sea, from 1948 to 1959 the capital of Pakistan.

Question

Where in the poem does the most striking figurative language occur? What other figurative language does the poet use?

Metaphor and Simile

> Life, like a dome of many-colored glass,
> Stains the white radiance of Eternity.

The first of these lines (from Shelley's "Adonais") is a **simile:** a comparison of two things, indicated by some connective, usually *like, as, than,* or a verb such as *resembles.* A simile expresses a similarity. Still, for a simile to exist, the things compared have to be dissimilar in kind. It is no simile to say, "Your fingers are like mine," it is a literal observation. But to say, "Your fingers are like sausages" is to use a simile. Omit the connective — say, "Your fingers are sausages" — and the result is a **metaphor,** a statement that one thing *is* something else, which, in a literal sense, it is not. In the second of Shelley's lines, it is *assumed* that Eternity is light or radiance, and we have an **implied metaphor,** one that uses neither a connective nor the verb *to be.* Here are examples:

Oh, my love is like a red, red rose.	*Simile*
Oh, my love resembles a red, red rose.	*Simile*
Oh, my love is redder than a rose.	*Simile*
Oh, my love is a red, red rose.	*Metaphor*
Oh, my love has red petals and sharp thorns.	*Implied metaphor*
Oh, I placed my love into a long-stem vase	
And I bandaged my bleeding thumb.	*Implied metaphor*

Often you can tell a metaphor from a simile by much more than just the presence or absence of a connective. In general, a simile refers to only one characteristic that two things have in common, while a metaphor is not plainly limited in the number of resemblances it may indicate. To use the simile "He eats like a pig" is to compare man and animal in one respect: eating habits. But to say "He's a pig" is to use a metaphor that might involve comparisons of appearance and morality as well.

For scientists as well as poets, the making of metaphors is customary. In 1933 George Lemaitre, the Belgian priest and physicist credited with the Big Bang theory of the origin of the universe, conceived of a primal atom that existed before anything else, which expanded and produced everything. And so, he remarked, making a wonderful metaphor, the evolution of the cosmos as it is today "can be compared to a display of fireworks that has just ended." As astrophysicist and poet Alan Lightman has noted, we can't help envisioning scientific discoveries in terms of things we know from daily life—spinning balls, waves in water, pendulums, weights on springs. "We have no other choice," Lightman reasons. "We cannot avoid forming mental pictures when we try to grasp the meaning of our equations, and how can we picture what we have not seen?"[1] In science as well as in poetry, it would seem, metaphors are necessary instruments of understanding.

In everyday speech, simile and metaphor occur frequently. We use metaphors ("She's a doll") and similes ("The tickets are selling like hotcakes") without being fully conscious of them. If, however, we are aware that words possess literal meanings as well as figurative ones, we do not write *died in the wool* for *dyed in the wool* or *tow the line* for *toe the line*, nor do we use **mixed metaphors** as did the writer who advised, "Water the spark of knowledge and it will bear fruit," or the speaker who urged, "To get ahead, keep your nose to the grindstone, your shoulder to the wheel, your ear to the ground, and your eye on the ball." Perhaps the unintended humor of these statements comes from our seeing that the writer, busy stringing together stale metaphors, was not aware that they had any physical reference.

Unlike a writer who thoughtlessly mixes metaphors, a good poet can join together incongruous things and still keep the reader's respect. In his ballad "Thirty Bob a Week," John Davidson has a British workingman tell how it feels to try to support a large family on small wages:

> It's a naked child against a hungry wolf;
>   It's playing bowls upon a splitting wreck;
> It's walking on a string across a gulf
>   With millstones fore-and-aft about your neck;
> But the thing is daily done by many and many a one;
>   And we fall, face forward, fighting, on the deck.

Like the man with his nose to the grindstone, Davidson's wage-earner is in an absurd fix; but his balancing act seems far from merely nonsensical. For every

[1]"Physicists' Use of Metaphor," *The American Scholar* (Winter 1989) 99.

one of the poet's comparisons — of workingman to child, to bowler, to tight-rope walker, and to seaman — offer suggestions of a similar kind. All help us see (and imagine) the workingman's hard life: a brave and unyielding struggle against impossible odds.

A poem may make a series of comparisons, like Davidson's, or the whole poem may be one extended comparison:

Richard Wilbur (b. 1917)*

A SIMILE FOR HER SMILE   1950

Your smiling, or the hope, the thought of it,
Makes in my mind such pause and abrupt ease
As when the highway bridgegates fall,
Balking the hasty traffic, which must sit
On each side massed and staring, while   5
Deliberately the drawbridge starts to rise:

Then horns are hushed, the oilsmoke rarifies,
Above the idling motors one can tell
The packet's smooth approach, the slip,
Slip of the silken river past the sides,   10
The ringing of clear bells, the dip
And slow cascading of the paddle wheel.

How much life metaphors bring to poetry may be seen by comparing two poems by Tennyson and Blake.

Alfred, Lord Tennyson (1809 – 1892)*

FLOWER IN THE CRANNIED WALL   1869

Flower in the crannied wall,
I pluck you out of the crannies,
I hold you here, root and all, in my hand,
Little flower — but *if* I could understand
What you are, root and all, and all in all,
I should know what God and man is.

How many metaphors does this poem contain? None. Compare it with a briefer poem on a similar theme: the quatrain that begins Blake's "Auguries of Inno-cence." (We follow here the opinion of W. B. Yeats, who, in editing Blake's poems, thought the lines ought to be printed separately.)

William Blake (1757 – 1827)*

TO SEE A WORLD IN A GRAIN OF SAND   (about 1803)

To see a world in a grain of sand
And a heaven in a wild flower,
Hold infinity in the palm of your hand
And eternity in an hour.

Set beside Blake's poem, Tennyson's — short though it is — seems lengthy.
What contributes to the richness of "To see a world in a grain of sand" is
Blake's use of a metaphor in every line. And every metaphor is loaded with
suggestion. Our world does indeed resemble a grain of sand: in being round,
in being stony, in being one of a myriad (the suggestions go on and on). Like
Blake's grain of sand, a metaphor holds much, within a small circumference.

Sylvia Plath (1932 – 1963)*

METAPHORS   1960

I'm a riddle in nine syllables,
An elephant, a ponderous house,
A melon strolling on two tendrils.
O red fruit, ivory, fine timbers!
This loaf's big with its yeasty rising.   5
Money's new-minted in this fat purse.
I'm a means, a stage, a cow in calf.
I've eaten a bag of green apples,
Boarded the train there's no getting off.

QUESTIONS

1. To what central fact do all the metaphors in this poem refer?
2. In the first line, what has the speaker in common with a riddle? Why does she say
   she has *nine* syllables?
3. How would you describe the tone of this poem? (Perhaps the poet expresses more
   than one attitude.) What attitude is conveyed in the metaphors of an elephant, "a
   ponderous house," "a melon strolling on two tendrils"? By the metaphors of red fruit,
   ivory, fine timbers, new-minted money? By the metaphor in the last line?

Emily Dickinson (1830 – 1886)*

IT DROPPED SO LOW – IN MY REGARD   (about 1863)

It dropped so low – in my Regard –
I heard it hit the Ground –
And go to pieces on the Stones
At bottom of my Mind –

Yet blamed the Fate that flung it–*less*
Than I denounced Myself,
For entertaining Plated Wares
Upon My Silver Shelf –

QUESTIONS

1. What is *it*? What two things are compared?
2. How much of the poem develops and amplifies this comparison?

James C. Kilgore (1928–1988)

THE WHITE MAN PRESSED THE LOCKS   1970

Driving down the concrete artery,
Away from the smoky heart,
Through the darkening, blighted body,
Pausing at varicose veins,
The white man pressed the locks   5
   on all the sedan's doors,
Sped toward the white corpuscles
   in the white arms
     hugging the black city.

QUESTIONS

1. Explain the two implied metaphors in this poem: what are the two bodies?
2. How do you take the word *hugging*? Is this a loving embrace or a stranglehold?
3. What, in your own words, is the poet's theme?

Peter Williams (b. 1937)

WHEN SHE WAS HERE, LI BO, SHE WAS
LIKE COLD SUMMER LAGER   1978

Her presence was a roomful of flowers,
Her absence is an empty bed.
           — Li Bo (701 – 762)

When she was here, Li Bo, she was like cold
   summer lager,
Like hot pastrami at Katz's on Houston Street,
Like a bright nickname on my downtown express,
Like every custardy honey from the old art books:
She was quadraphonic° Mahler   *four-channeled*   5
And the perfect little gymnast.

Now she's gone, it's like flat Coke on Sunday morning,
Like a melted Velveeta on white, eaten
Listening to Bobby Vinton —
Like the Philadelphia Eagles.   10

QUESTIONS

1. What do the lines from the Chinese poet Li Bo (in the **epigraph** or introductory
   quotation) have to do with the poem that ensues?
2. In the first six lines of the poem, what quality or qualities does the poet find in the
   things he likens to the presence of his lover? In the last lines, how are the four things
   that resemble her absence all alike?
3. This poem is full of allusions: in the first part, to a famous New York delicatessen
   and to a much-admired Austrian composer. Explain the allusions in part two.
4. What is the tone of the poem? (Sorrowful? Bitter? Or what?) How do the similes help
   communicate the poet's attitude?

EXPERIMENT: *Likening*

Write a two-part poem that follows the method of Peter Williams, finding your own
similes to express a joyful experience in terms of things you admire, and a glum experience in terms of things you dislike. Possible subjects: Before meeting a loved one and
after. Having a dull, badly paid job and then quitting it. Losing weight and putting it
back on.

Ruth Whitman (b. 1922)

CASTOFF SKIN   1973

She lay in her girlish sleep at ninety-six,
small as a twig.
Pretty good figure

for an old lady, she said to me once.
Then she crawled away, leaving   5
a tiny stretched transparence

behind her. When I kissed her paper cheek
I thought of the snake,
of his quick motion.

QUESTIONS

1. Explain the central metaphor in "Castoff Skin."
2. What other figures of speech does the poem contain?

EXERCISE: *What Is Similar?*

Each of these quotations contains a simile or a metaphor. In each of these figures of
speech, what two things is the poet comparing? Try to state exactly what you understand
the two things to have in common: the most striking similarity or similarities that the
poet sees.

1. Think of the storm roaming the sky uneasily
   like a dog looking for a place to sleep in,
   listen to it growling.
                    — Elizabeth Bishop, "Little Exercise"
2. When the hounds of spring are on winter's traces . . .
                    — Algernon Charles Swinburne, "Atalanta in Calydon"
3. . . . the sun gnaws the night's bone
   down through the meat and gristle.
                    —John Ridland, "Elegy for My Aunt"
4. The scarlet of the maples can shake me like a cry
   Of bugles going by.
                    — Bliss Carman, "A Vagabond Song"
5. "Hope" is the thing with feathers –
   That perches in the soul –
   And sings the tune without the words –
   And never stops – at all –
                    — Emily Dickinson, an untitled poem
6. Work without Hope draws nectar in a sieve . . .
                    —Samuel Taylor Coleridge, "Work Without Hope"
7. A new electric fence,
   Its five barbed wires tight
   As a steel-stringed banjo.
                    — Van K. Brock, "Driving at Dawn"
8. Spring stirs Gossamer Beynon schoolmistress like a spoon.
                    — Dylan Thomas, *Under Milk Wood*

OTHER FIGURES

When Shakespeare asks, in a sonnet,

> O! how shall summer's honey breath hold out
> Against the wrackful siege of batt'ring days,

it might seem at first that he mixes metaphors. How can a *breath* confront the battering ram of an invading army? But it is summer's breath and, by giving it to summer, Shakespeare makes the season a man or woman. It is as if the fragrance of summer were the breath within a person's body, and winter were the onslaught of old age.

Such is one instance of **personification**: a figure of speech in which a thing, an animal, or an abstract term (*truth, nature*) is made human. A personification extends throughout this whole short poem:

James Stephens (1882 – 1950)*

THE WIND   1915

The wind stood up and gave a shout.
He whistled on his fingers and

Kicked the withered leaves about
And thumped the branches with his hand

And said he'd kill and kill and kill,
And so he will and so he will.

The wind is a wild man, and evidently it is not just any autumn breeze but a hurricane or at least a stiff gale. In poems that do not work as well as this one, personification may be employed mechanically. Hollow-eyed personifications walk the works of lesser English poets of the eighteenth century: Coleridge has quoted the beginning of one such neoclassical ode, "Inoculation! heavenly Maid, descend!" It is hard for the contemporary reader to be excited by William Collins's "The Passions, An Ode for Music" (1747), which personifies, stanza by stanza, Fear, Anger, Despair, Hope, Revenge, Pity, Jealousy, Love, Hate, Melancholy, and Cheerfulness, and has them listen to Music, until even "Brown Exercise rejoiced to hear, / And Sport leapt up, and seized his beechen spear." Still, the portraits of the Seven Deadly Sins in the fourteenth-century *Vision of Piers Plowman* remain memorable: "Thanne come Slothe al bislabered, with two slimy eiyen. . . ." In "Two Sonnets on Fame" John Keats makes an abstraction come alive in seeing Fame as "a wayward girl."

Hand in hand with personification often goes **apostrophe:** a way of addressing someone or something invisible or not ordinarily spoken to. In an apostrophe, a poet (in these examples Wordsworth) may address an inanimate object ("Spade! with which Wilkinson hath tilled his lands"), some dead or absent person ("Milton! thou shouldst be living at this hour"), an abstract thing ("Return, Delights!"), or a spirit ("Thou Soul that art the eternity of thought"). More often than not, the poet uses apostrophe to announce a lofty and serious tone. An "O" may even be put in front of it ("O moon!") since, according to W. D. Snodgrass, every poet has a right to do so at least once in a lifetime. But apostrophe doesn't have to be highfalutin. It is a means of giving life to the inanimate. It is a way of giving body to the intangible, a way of speaking to it person to person, as in the words of a moving American spiritual: "Death, ain't you got no shame?"

Most of us, from time to time, emphasize a point with a statement containing exaggeration: "Faster than greased lightning," "I've told him a thousand times." We speak, then, not literal truth but use a figure of speech called **overstatement** (or **hyperbole**). Poets too, being fond of emphasis, often exaggerate for effect. Instances are Marvell's profession of a love that should grow "Vaster than empires, and more slow" and John Burgon's praise for Petra: "A rose-red city, half as old as Time." Overstatement can be used also for humorous purposes, as in a fat woman's boast (from a blues song): "Every time I shake, some skinny gal loses her home."[2] The opposite is **understatement,** implying more than is said. Mark Twain in *Life on the Mississippi* recalls how, as an apprentice steamboat-pilot asleep when supposed to be on watch, he was roused by the pilot and sent clambering to the pilot house: "Mr. Bixby was close behind, commenting." Another example is Robert Frost's line "One could do worse than be a swinger of birches" — the conclusion of a poem that has

[2]Quoted by Amiri Baraka [LeRoi Jones] in *Blues People* (New York: Morrow, 1963).

suggested that to swing on a birch tree is one of the most deeply satisfying activities in the world.

In **metonymy,** the name of a thing is substituted for that of another closely associated with it. For instance, we say "The White House decided," and mean the president did. When John Dyer writes in "Grongar Hill,"

> A little rule, a little sway,
> A sun beam on a winter's day,
> Is all the proud and mighty have
> Between the cradle and the grave,

we recognize that *cradle* and *grave* signify birth and death. A kind of metonymy, **synecdoche** is the use of a part of a thing to stand for the whole of it or vice versa. We say "She lent a hand," and mean that she lent her entire presence. Similarly, Milton in "Lycidas" refers to greedy clergymen as "blind mouths." Another kind of metonymy is the **transferred epithet**: a device of emphasis in which the poet attributes some characteristic of a thing to another thing closely associated with it. When Thomas Gray observes that, in the evening pastures, "drowsy tinklings lull the distant folds," he well knows that sheep's bells do not drowse, but sheep do. When Hart Crane, describing the earth as seen from an airplane, speaks of "nimble blue plateaus," he attributes the airplane's motion to the earth.

Paradox occurs in a statement that at first strikes us as self-contradictory but that on reflection makes some sense. "The peasant," said G. K. Chesterton, "lives in a larger world than the globe-trotter." Here, two different meanings of *larger* are contrasted: "greater in spiritual values" versus "greater in miles." Some paradoxical statements, however, are much more than plays on words. In a moving sonnet, the blind John Milton tells how one night he dreamed he could see his dead wife. The poem ends in a paradox:

> But oh, as to embrace me she inclined,
> I waked, she fled, and day brought back my night.

EXERCISE: *Paradox*

What paradoxes do you find in the following poem? For each, explain the sense that underlies the statement.

Chidiock Tichborne (1568? – 1586)

ELEGY, WRITTEN WITH HIS OWN HAND
IN THE TOWER BEFORE HIS EXECUTION   1586

> My prime of youth is but a frost of cares,
>   My feast of joy is but a dish of pain,
> My crop of corn is but a field of tares°,   *weeds*

And all my good is but vain hope of gain:
The day is past, and yet I saw no sun,   5
And now I live, and now my life is done.

My tale was heard, and yet it was not told,
    My fruit is fall'n, and yet my leaves are green,
My youth is spent, and yet I am not old,
    I saw the world, and yet I was not seen: 10
My thread is cut, and yet it is not spun,
And now I live, and now my life is done.

I sought my death, and found it in my womb,
    I looked for life, and saw it was a shade,
I trod the earth, and knew it was my tomb,   15
    And now I die, and now I was but made:
My glass is full, and now my glass is run,
And now I live, and now my life is done.

ELEGY, WRITTEN WITH HIS OWN HAND. Accused of taking part in the Babington Conspiracy, a plot
by Roman Catholics against the life of Queen Elizabeth I, eighteen-year-old Chidiock Tichborne
was hanged, drawn, and quartered at the Tower of London. That is virtually all we know about
him.

　　Asked to tell the difference between men and women, Samuel Johnson
replied, "I can't conceive, madam, can you?" The great dictionary-maker was
using a figure of speech known to classical rhetoricians as *paronomasia*, better
known to us as a **pun** or play on words. How does a pun operate? It reminds
us of another word (or other words) of similar or identical sound but of very
different denotation. Although puns at their worst can be mere piddling quib-
bles, at best they can sharply point to surprising but genuine resemblances. The
name of a dentist's country estate, Tooth Acres, is accurate: aching teeth paid
for the property. In his novel *Moby-Dick*, Herman Melville takes up questions
about whales that had puzzled scientists: for instance, are the whale's spoutings
water or gaseous vapor? And when Melville speaks pointedly of the great whale
"sprinkling and mistifying the gardens of the deep," we catch his pun, and
conclude that the creature both mistifies and mystifies at once.
　　In poetry, a pun may be facetious, as in Thomas Hood's ballad of "Faithless
Nelly Gray":

Ben Battle was a soldier bold,
    And used to war's alarms;
But a cannon-ball took off his legs,
    So he laid down his arms!

Or it may be serious, as in these lines on war by E. E. Cummings:

the bigness of cannon
is skillful,

(*is skillful* becoming *is kill-ful* when read aloud), or perhaps, as in Shakespeare's
song in *Cymbeline*, "Fear no more the heat o' th' sun," both facetious and
serious at once:

Golden lads and girls all must,
As chimney-sweepers, come to dust.

George Herbert (1593 – 1633)*

THE PULLEY   1633

When God at first made man,
Having a glass of blessings standing by —
Let us (said he) pour on him all we can;
Let the world's riches, which dispersèd lie,
    Contract into a span.   5

So strength first made a way,
Then beauty flowed, then wisdom, honor, pleasure:
When almost all was out, God made a stay,
Perceiving that, alone of all His treasure,
    Rest in the bottom lay.   10

For if I should (said he)
Bestow this jewel also on My creature,
He would adore My gifts instead of Me,
And rest in Nature, not the God of Nature:
    So both should losers be.   15

Yet let him keep the rest,
But keep them with repining restlessness;
Let him be rich and weary, that at least,
If goodness lead him not, yet weariness
    May toss him to My breast.   20

QUESTIONS

1. What different senses of the word *rest* does Herbert bring into this poem?
2. How do God's words in line 16, *Yet let him keep the rest*, seem paradoxical?
3. What do you feel to be the tone of Herbert's poem? Does the punning make the poem seem comic?
4. Why is the poem called "The Pulley"? What is its implied metaphor?

To sum up: even though figures of speech are not to be taken *only* literally, they refer us to a tangible world. By *personifying* an eagle, Tennyson reminds us that the bird and humankind have certain characteristics in common. Through *metonymy*, a poet can focus our attention on a particular detail in a larger object; through *hyperbole* and *understatement*, make us see the physical actuality in back of words. *Pun* and *paradox* cause us to realize this actuality, too, and probably surprise us enjoyably at the same time. Through *apostrophe*, the poet animates the inanimate and asks it to listen — speaks directly to an immediate god or to the revivified dead. Put to such uses, figures of speech have power. They are more than just ways of playing with words.

Edmund Waller (1606 – 1687)

ON A GIRDLE   1645

That which her slender waist confined,
Shall now my joyful temples bind;
No monarch but would give his crown,
His arms might do what this has done.

It was my heaven's extremest sphere,   5
The pale° which held that lovely deer;   *enclosure*
My joy, my grief, my hope, my love,
Did all within this circle move!

A narrow compass! and yet there
Dwelt all that's good, and all that's fair!   10
Give me but what this riband bound,
Take all the rest the sun goes round!

ON A GIRDLE. This girdle is a waistband or sash — not, of course, a modern "foundation garment."
1 – 2 *That which . . . temples bind:* A courtly lover might bind his brow with a lady's ribbon, to
signify he was hers. 5 *extremest sphere:* In Ptolemaic astronomy, the outermost of the concentric
spheres that surround the earth. In its wall the farthest stars are set.

QUESTIONS

1. To what things is the girdle compared?
2. Explain the pun in line 4. What effect does it have upon the tone of the poem?
3. Why is the effect of this pun different from that of Thomas Hood's play on the same
   word in "Faithless Nelly Gray" (quoted on p. 596)?
4. What does *compass* denote in line 9?
5. What paradox occurs in lines 9 – 10?
6. How many of the poem's statements are hyperbolic? Is the compliment the speaker
   pays his lady too grandiose to be believed? Explain.

Theodore Roethke (1908 – 1963)*

I KNEW A WOMAN   1958

I knew a woman, lovely in her bones,
When small birds sighed, she would sigh back at them;
Ah, when she moved, she moved more ways than one:
The shapes a bright container can contain!
Of her choice virtues only gods should speak,   5
Or English poets who grew up on Greek
(I'd have them sing in chorus, cheek to cheek).

How well her wishes went! She stroked my chin,
She taught me Turn, and Counter-turn, and Stand;
She taught me Touch, that undulant white skin;   10

I nibbled meekly from her proffered hand;
She was the sickle; I, poor I, the rake,
Coming behind her for her pretty sake
(But what prodigious mowing we did make).

Love likes a gander, and adores a goose: 15
Her full lips pursed, the errant note to seize;
She played it quick, she played it light and loose;
My eyes, they dazzled at her flowing knees;
Her several parts could keep a pure repose,
Or one hip quiver with a mobile nose   20
(She moved in circles, and those circles moved).

Let seed be grass, and grass turn into hay:
I'm martyr to a motion not my own;
What's freedom for? To know eternity.
I swear she cast a shadow white as stone.   25
But who would count eternity in days?
These old bones live to learn her wanton ways:
(I measure time by how a body sways).

QUESTIONS

1. What outrageous puns do you find in Roethke's poem? Describe the effect of them.
2. What kind of figure of speech occurs in all three lines: *Of her choice virtues only gods should speak*; *My eyes, they dazzled at her flowing knees*; and *I swear she cast a shadow white as stone*?
3. What sort of figure is the poet's reference to himself as *old bones*?
4. Do you take *Let seed be grass, and grass turn into hay* as figurative language, or literal statement?
5. If you agree that the tone of this poem is witty and playful, do you think the poet is making fun of the woman? What is his attitude toward her? What part do figures of speech play in communicating it?

FOR REVIEW AND FURTHER STUDY

Robert Frost (1874 – 1963)*

THE SILKEN TENT   1942

She is as in a field a silken tent
At midday when a sunny summer breeze
Has dried the dew and all its ropes relent,
So that in guys° it gently sways at ease,   *attachments that steady it*
And its supporting central cedar pole,   5
That is its pinnacle to heavenward
And signifies the sureness of the soul,

Seems to owe naught to any single cord,
But strictly held by none, is loosely bound
By countless silken ties of love and thought   10
To everything on earth the compass round,
And only by one's going slightly taut
In the capriciousness of summer air
Is of the slightest bondage made aware.

QUESTIONS

1. Is Frost's comparison of woman and tent a simile or a metaphor?
2. What are the ropes or cords?
3. Does the poet convey any sense of this woman's character? What sort of person do
   you believe her to be?
4. Paraphrase the poem, trying to state its implied meaning. (If you need to be refreshed
   about paraphrase, turn back to pages 498–499.) Be sure to include the implications of
   the last three lines.

Denise Levertov (b. 1923)*

LEAVING FOREVER   1964

He says the waves in the ship's wake
are like stones rolling away.
I don't see it that way.
But I see the mountain turning,
turning away its face as the ship
takes us away.

QUESTIONS

1. What do you understand to be the man's feelings about leaving forever? How does
   the speaker feel? With what two figures of speech does the poet express these
   conflicting views?
2. Suppose that this poem had ended in another simile (instead of its three last lines):

   I see the mountain as a suitcase
   left behind on the shore
   as the ship takes us away.

   How is Denise Levertov's choice of a figure of speech a much stronger one?

Jane Kenyon (b. 1947)

THE SUITOR   1978

We lie back to back. Curtains
lift and fall,
like the chest of someone sleeping.
Wind moves the leaves of the box elder;
they show their light undersides,   5

turning all at once
like a school of fish.
Suddenly I understand that I am happy.
For months this feeling
has been coming closer, stopping   10
for short visits, like a timid suitor.

QUESTION

In each simile you find in this poem, exactly what is the similarity?

Richard Wilbur (b. 1921)*

SLEEPLESS AT CROWN POINT   1976

All night, this headland
Lunges into the rumpling
Capework of the wind.

Robert Frost (1874 – 1963)*

THE SECRET SITS   1936

We dance round in a ring and suppose,
But the Secret sits in the middle and knows.

Margaret Atwood (b. 1939)

YOU FIT INTO ME   1971

you fit into me
like a hook into an eye

a fish hook
an open eye

Grace Schulman

HEMISPHERES   1984

Our bodies, luminary under bedclothes,
fit tightly like the pieces of a broken
terra cotta vase that is newly mended,
smooth surfaces, no jagged edges visible.

I've read that countries were so interlocked   5
before the oceans fractured them and splayed
Mexico enfolding Mauritania;
Brazil's round shoulder hoisted to Nigeria;
Italy pressing Libya; Alaska
so linked with Russia in the Bering Straits   10
that fingers touched, like dead hands on a harp.
Our tremulous hands held fast in sleep at dawn;
legs, arms entwined, one continent, one mass.

John Tagliabue (b. 1923)

MAINE VASTLY COVERED WITH MUCH SNOW   1984

4 squirrels
are as busy as monks
looking for seeds; inside the seeds is a
          scripture;
nourishing themselves they trace their pre-history   5
          and future;
is theology something like the flourish of their tails?
          alert, aware of changing seasons,
          aware of other blokes about
          they persist in their   10
          scrutiny of syllables.

John Ashbery (b. 1927)*

THE CATHEDRAL IS   1979

Slated for demolition.

W. S. Merwin (b. 1927)

SONG OF MAN CHIPPING AN ARROWHEAD   1973

Little children you will all go
but the one you are hiding
will fly

Robert Burns (1759 – 1796)*

OH, MY LOVE IS LIKE A RED, RED ROSE   (about 1788)

Oh, my love is like a red, red rose
   That's newly sprung in June;
My love is like the melody
   That's sweetly played in tune.

So fair art thou, my bonny lass,   5
   So deep in love am I;
And I will love thee still, my dear,
   Till a' the seas gang° dry.   go

Till a' the seas gang dry, my dear,
   And the rocks melt wi' the sun;   10
And I will love thee still, my dear,
   While the sands o' life shall run.

And fare thee weel, my only love!
   And fare thee weel awhile!
And I will come again, my love   15
   Though it were ten thousand mile.

SUGGESTIONS FOR WRITING

1. Freely using your imagination, write a paragraph in which you make as many hyperbolic statements as possible. Then write another version, changing all your exaggeration to understatement. Then, in a concluding paragraph, sum up what this experiment shows you about figurative language. Some possible topics are "The Most Gratifying (or Terrifying) Moment of My Life," "The Job I Almost Landed," "The Person I Most Admire."
2. Choose a short poem rich in figurative language: Sylvia Plath's "Metaphors," say, or Burns's "Oh, my love is like a red, red rose." Rewrite the poem, taking for your model Howard Moss's deliberately bepiddling version of "Shall I compare thee to a summer's day?" Eliminate every figure of speech. Turn the poem into language as flat and unsuggestive as possible. (Just ignore any rime or rhythm in the original.) Then, in a paragraph, indicate lines in your revised version that seem glaringly worsened. In conclusion, sum up what your barbaric rewrite tells you about the nature of poetry.

19 Song

SINGING AND SAYING

Most poems are more memorable than most ordinary speech, and when music is combined with poetry the result can be more memorable still. The differences between speech, poetry, and song may appear if we consider, first of all, this fragment of an imaginary conversation between two lovers:

> Let's not drink; let's just sit here and look at each other. Or put a kiss inside my goblet and I won't want anything to drink.

Forgettable language, we might think; but let's try to make it a little more interesting:

> Drink to me only with your eyes, and I'll pledge my love to you with my
> eyes;
> Or leave a kiss within the goblet, that's all I'll want to drink.

The passage is closer to poetry, but still has a distance to go. At least we now have a figure of speech — the metaphor that love is wine, implied in the statement that one lover may salute another by lifting an eye as well as by lifting a goblet. But the sound of the words is not yet especially interesting. Here is another try, by Ben Jonson:

> Drink to me only with thine eyes,
>   And I will pledge with mine;
> Or leave a kiss but in the cup,
>   And I'll not ask for wine.

In these opening lines from Jonson's poem "To Celia," the improvement is noticeable. These lines are poetry; their language has become special. For one thing, the lines rime (with an additional rime sound on *thine*). There is interest, too, in the proximity of the words *kiss* and *cup:* the repetition (or alliteration) of the *k* sound. The rhythm of the lines has become regular; generally every other word (or syllable) is stressed:

DRINK to me ON-ly WITH thine EYES,
And I will PLEDGE with MINE;
OR LEAVE a KISS but IN the CUP,
And I'LL not ASK for WINE.

All these devices of sound and rhythm, together with metaphor, produce a pleasing effect — more pleasing than the effect of "Let's not drink; let's look at each other." But the words became more pleasing still when later set to music:

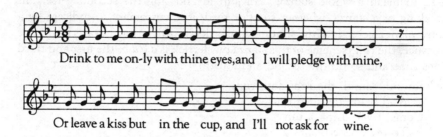

Drink to me on-ly with thine eyes, and I will pledge with mine,

Or leave a kiss but in the cup, and I'll not ask for wine.

In this memorable form, the poem is still alive today.

Ben Jonson (1573? – 1637)*

To Celia   1616

Drink to me only with thine eyes,
    And I will pledge with mine;
Or leave a kiss but in the cup,
    And I'll not ask for wine.
The thirst that from the soul doth rise   5
    Doth ask a drink divine;
But might I of Jove's nectar sup,
    I would not change for thine.

I sent thee late a rosy wreath,
    Not so much honoring thee   10
As giving it a hope that there
    It could not withered be.
But thou thereon didst only breathe,
    And sent'st it back to me;
Since when it grows, and smells, I swear,   15
    Not of itself but thee.

A compliment to a lady has rarely been put in language more graceful, more wealthy with interesting sounds. Other figures of speech besides metaphor make them unforgettable: for example, the hyperbolic tributes to the power of the lady's sweet breath, which can start picked roses growing again, and her kisses, which even surpass the nectar of the gods.

This song falls into stanzas — as many poems that resemble songs also do. A **stanza** (Italian for "station," "stopping-place," or "room") is a group of lines whose pattern is repeated throughout the poem. Most songs have more than one stanza. When printed, the stanzas of songs and poems usually are set off from one another by space. When sung, stanzas of songs are indicated by a pause or by the introduction of a refrain, or chorus (a line or lines repeated). The word **verse,** which strictly refers to one line of a poem, is sometimes loosely used to mean a whole stanza: "All join in and sing the second verse!" In speaking of a stanza, whether sung or read, it is customary to indicate by a convenient algebra its **rime scheme,** the order in which rimed words recur. For instance, the rime scheme of this stanza by Herrick is *a b a b*; the first and third lines rime and so do the second and fourth:

> Round, round, the roof doth run;
> And being ravished thus,
> Come, I will drink a tun
> To my Propertius.

Refrains are words, phrases, or lines repeated at intervals in a song or songlike poem. A refrain usually follows immediately after a stanza, and when it does, it is called **terminal refrain.** A refrain whose words change slightly with each recurrence is called an **incremental refrain.** Sometimes we also hear an **internal refrain:** one that appears within a stanza, generally in a position that stays fixed throughout a poem. Both internal refrains and terminal refrains are used to great effect in the traditional song "The Cruel Mother":

Anonymous (traditional Scottish ballad)

THE CRUEL MOTHER

> She sat down below a thorn,
>   *Fine flowers in the valley,*
> And there she has her sweet babe born
>   *And the green leaves they grow rarely.*
>
> "Smile na sae° sweet, my bonny babe,"   *so*   5
>   *Fine flowers in the valley,*
> "And° ye smile sae sweet, ye'll smile me dead."   *if*
>   *And the green leaves they grow rarely.*
>
> She's taen out her little pen-knife,
>   *Fine flowers in the valley,*   10
> And twinned° the sweet babe o' its life,   *severed*
>   *And the green leaves they grow rarely.*

She's howket° a grave by the light of the moon,   *dug*
    Fine flowers in the valley,
And there she's buried her sweet babe in   15
    And the green leaves they grow rarely.

As she was going to the church,
    Fine flowers in the valley,
She saw a sweet babe in the porch
    And the green leaves they grow rarely.   20

"O sweet babe, and thou were mine,"
    Fine flowers in the valley,
"I wad cleed° thee in the silk so fine."   *dress*
    And the green leaves they grow rarely.

"O mother dear, when I was thine,"   25
    Fine flowers in the valley,
"You did na prove to me sae kind."
    And the green leaves they grow rarely.

Taken by themselves, the refrain lines might seem mere pretty nonsense. But interwoven with the story of the murdered child, they form a terrible counterpoint. What do they come to mean? Possibly that Nature keeps going about her chores, unmindful of sin and suffering. The effect is an ironic contrast. Besides, by hearing the refrain over and over and over, we find it hard to forget.

Unlike many poems we read on the printed page, songs tend to be written in language simple enough to understand on first hearing. This immediate clarity is essential to **rap**, a form of popular music in which words are recited to a driving rhythmic beat. In Black English, *rap* means "to talk" ("Let's rap about it"), and in most current rap songs, the singer talks or recites at top speed, dazzling us with long, rhythmic, four-stress lines that end in rimes. Although today many rap singers and groups use electronic backgrounds, rap began on city streets in the game of "signifying," in which two poets aim rimed insults at each other, sometimes accompanying their tirades with a beat made by clapping or finger-snapping. Anyone interested in the form will enjoy listening to Run DMC, Grandmaster Flash, L. L. Cool J, the Fat Boys, and other performers currently popular. Here, for instance, is the opening of a rap lyric, "Parents Just Don't Understand," by W. Smith, J. Townes, and Pete Q. Harris, and performed by D. J. Jazzy Jeff and The Fresh Prince on a recent recording.[1] We listen in on a high school lad's lament:

> You know, parents are the same, no matter time nor place.
> They don't understand that us kids are gonna make *some* mistakes.
> So, to you other kids, all across the land—
> There's no need to argue, parents just don't understand.

[1] *He's the DJ, I'm the Rapper* (Jive LP album 1091-1-J, 1988. Copyright © 1988 by Zomba Enterprises, Inc., ASCAP).

I remember one year, my mom took me school shopping—
It was me, my brother, my mom—oh, my pop and
My little sister all hopped in the car.
We headed downtown to the gallery mall.
My mom started buggin' with the clothes she chose.
I didn't say nothing at first, I just turned up my nose.
She said, "What's wrong? This shirt cost twenty dollars!"
I said, "Mom, the shirt is plaid, with a butterfly collar."
The next half-hour was the same old thing,
My mother buying me clothes from nineteen sixty-three,
And then she lost her mind and did the ultimate:
I asked her for Adidas and she bought me Zips!
I said, "Mom, what are you doing? You'll ruin my rep!"
She said, "You're only sixteen, you don't *have* a rep yet."
I said, "Mom, let's put these clothes back, please?"
She said, "No! You go to school to learn, not for a fashion show."
I said, "Decision time, and now—come on, Mom, I'm not Bowser.
Mom, please put back the bell-bottom Brady Bunch trousers.
But if you don't want to, I can live with that,
But you gotta put back the double-knit reversible slacks."
She wasn't givin' in, everything stayed the same.
Inevitably the first day of school came.
I thought I could get over. I tried to play sick,
But my mom said, "No, no way—uh uh—forget it!"
There was nothing I could do. I tried to relax.
I got dressed up in those ancient artifacts
And when I walked in the school, it was just as I thought:
The kids were cracking up laughing at the clothes Mom bought.
And those who weren't laughing still had a ball
'Cause they were pointing and whispering as I walked down the hall.
I got home and told my mom how my day went—
She said, "If they were laughing you don't need them 'cause they're not
    good friends."
For the next six hours, I tried to explain to my mom
That I was gonna have to go through this about two hundred more times.
So to you other kids, all across the land—
There's no need to argue, parents just don't understand.

As the story continues, the speaker takes a joyride in his parents' Porsche with
a twelve-year-old runaway until a police car catches him. Although some of
these rimes are clever and unexpected (*Bowser / trousers, relax / artifacts*), most
of this language sounds ordinary, written to be talked fast and understood at
once.

Not all popular songs are so plainspoken: Bob Dylan, Sting, Bono, Elvis
Costello, Michelle Shocked, and others have written complicated lyrics full of
strange, dreamlike imagery. To unravel them, a listener may have to play a
recording many times, with the treble turned up all the way.

Many familiar poems began life as songs, but today, their tunes forgotten, they survive only in poetry anthologies. Shakespeare studded his plays with songs, and many of his contemporaries wrote verse to fit existing tunes. Some poets, themselves musicians (like Thomas Campion), composed both words and music. In Shakespeare's day, **madrigals,** short secular songs for three or more voice-parts arranged in counterpoint, enjoyed great favor. A madrigal by Chidiock Tichborne is given on page 595 and another by an anonymous poet, "The Silver Swan," on page 618.

Some poets who were not composers printed their work in madrigal books for others to set to music. In the seventeenth century, however, poetry and song seem to have fallen away from each other. By the end of the century, much new poetry, other than songs for plays, was written to be printed and to be silently read. Poets who wrote popular songs — like Thomas D'Urfey, compiler of the collection *Pills to Purge Melancholy* — were considered somewhat disreputable. With the notable exceptions of John Gay, who took existing popular tunes for *The Beggar's Opera,* and Robert Burns, who rewrote folk songs or made completely new words for them, few important English poets since Campion have been first-rate song-writers.

Occasionally, a poet has learned a thing or two from music. "But for the opera I could never have written *Leaves of Grass,*" said Walt Whitman, who loved the Italian art form for its expansiveness. Coleridge, Hardy, Auden, and many others have learned from folk ballads, and T. S. Eliot patterned his thematically repetitive *Four Quartets* after the structure of a quartet in classical music. "Poetry," said Ezra Pound, "begins to atrophy when it gets too far from music." Still, even in the twentieth century, the poet has been more often a corrector of printer's proofs than a tunesmith or performer.

Some people think that to make a poem and to travel about singing it, as many rock singer-composers now do, is a return to the venerable tradition of the **troubadours,** minstrels of the late Middle Ages. But there are differences. No doubt the troubadours had to please their patrons, but for better or worse their songs were not affected by a stopwatch in a producer's hand or by the technical resources of a sound studio. Bob Dylan has denied that he is a poet, and Paul Simon once told an interviewer, "If you want poetry read Wallace Stevens." Nevertheless, much has been made lately of current song lyrics as poetry. Are rock songs poems? Clearly some, but not all, are. That the lyrics of a song cannot stand the scrutiny of a reader does not necessarily invalidate them, though; song-writers do not usually write in order to be read. Pete Seeger has quoted a saying of his father: "A printed folk song is like a photograph of a bird in flight." Still there is no reason not to photograph birds, or to read song lyrics. If the words seem rich and interesting, we may possibly increase our enjoyment of them and perhaps be able to sing them more accurately. Like most poems and songs of the past, most current songs may end in the trash can of time. And yet, certain memorable rimed and rhythmic lines may live on, especially if music has served them for a base and if singers have given them wide exposure.

EXERCISE: *Comparing Poem and Song*

Compare the following poem by Edwin Arlington Robinson and a popular song lyric based on it. Notice what Paul Simon had to do to Robinson's original in order to make it into a song, and how Simon altered Robinson's conception.

Edwin Arlington Robinson (1869 – 1935)

RICHARD CORY   1897

Whenever Richard Cory went down town,
We people on the pavement looked at him:
He was a gentleman from sole to crown,
Clean favored, and imperially slim.

And he was always quietly arrayed,   5
And he was always human when he talked;
But still he fluttered pulses when he said,
"Good-morning," and he glittered when he walked.

And he was rich — yes, richer than a king —
And admirably schooled in every grace: 10
In fine°, we thought that he was everything   *in short*
To make us wish that we were in his place.

So on we worked, and waited for the light,
And went without the meat, and cursed the bread;
And Richard Cory, one calm summer night,   15
Went home and put a bullet through his head.

Paul Simon (b. 1942)

RICHARD CORY   1966

With Apologies to E. A. Robinson

They say that Richard Cory owns
One half of this old town,
With elliptical connections
To spread his wealth around.
Born into Society,   5
A banker's only child,
He had everything a man could want:
Power, grace and style.

Refrain:

But I, I work in his factory
And I curse the life I'm livin'
And I curse my poverty   10
And I wish that I could be
Oh I wish that I could be
Oh I wish that I could be
Richard Cory.   15

The papers print his picture
Almost everywhere he goes:
Richard Cory at the opera,
Richard Cory at a show
And the rumor of his party   20
And the orgies on his yacht —
Oh he surely must be happy
With everything he's got.   (Refrain.)

He freely gave to charity,
He had the common touch,   25
And they were grateful for his patronage
And they thanked him very much,
So my mind was filled with wonder
When the evening headlines read:
    "Richard Cory went home last night   30
    And put a bullet through his head."   (Refrain.)

RICHARD CORY by Paul Simon. If possible, listen to the ballad sung by Simon and Garfunkel on
Sounds of Silence (Columbia recording CL 2469, stereo CS 9269), © 1966 by Paul Simon. Used
by permission.

BALLADS

Any narrative song, like Paul Simon's "Richard Cory," may be called a **ballad.**
In English, some of the most famous ballads are **folk ballads,** loosely defined
as anonymous story-songs transmitted orally before they were ever written
down. Sir Walter Scott, a pioneer collector of Scottish folk ballads, drew the
ire of an old woman whose songs he had transcribed: "They were made for
singing and no' for reading, but ye ha'e broken the charm now and they'll never
be sung mair." The old singer had a point. Print freezes songs and tends to hold
them fast to a single version. If Scott and others had not written them down,
however, many would have been lost.

In his monumental work *The English and Scottish Popular Ballads*
(1882 – 1898), the American scholar Francis J. Child winnowed out 305 folk
ballads he considered authentic — that is, creations of illiterate or semiliterate
people who had preserved them orally. Child, who worked by insight as well
as by learning, did such a good job of telling the difference between folk ballads
and other kinds that later scholars have added only about a dozen ballads to

his count. Often called **Child ballads,** his texts include "The Three Ravens," "Sir Patrick Spence," "The Twa Corbies," "Edward," "The Cruel Mother," and many others still on the lips of singers. Here is one of the best-known Child ballads.

Anonymous (traditional Scottish ballad)

Bonny Barbara Allan

It was in and about the Martinmas time,
    When the green leaves were afalling,
That Sir John Graeme, in the West Country,
    Fell in love with Barbara Allan.

He sent his men down through the town,   5
    To the place where she was dwelling;
"O haste and come to my master dear,
    Gin° ye be Barbara Allan."   *if*

O hooly°, hooly rose she up,   *slowly*
    To the place where he was lying,   10
And when she drew the curtain by:
    "Young man, I think you're dying."

"O it's I'm sick, and very, very sick,
    And 'tis a' for Barbara Allan." —
"O the better for me ye's never be,   15
    Tho your heart's blood were aspilling.

"O dinna ye mind°, young man," said she,   *don't you remember*
    "When ye was in the tavern adrinking,
That ye made the health° gae round and round,   *toasts*
    And slighted Barbara Allan?"   20

He turned his face unto the wall,
    And death was with him dealing:
"Adieu, adieu, my dear friends all,
    And be kind to Barbara Allan."

And slowly, slowly raise she up,   25
    And slowly, slowly left him,
And sighing said she could not stay,
    Since death of life had reft him.

She had not gane a mile but twa,
    When she heard the dead-bell ringing,   30
And every jow° that the dead-bell geid,   *stroke*
    It cried, "Woe to Barbara Allan!"

"O mother, mother, make my bed!
    O make it saft and narrow!
Since my love died for me today,   35
    I'll die for him tomorrow."

BONNY BARBARA ALLAN. 1 *Martinmas:* Saint Martin's day, November 11.

QUESTIONS

1. In any line does the Scottish dialect cause difficulty? If so, try reading the line aloud.
2. Without ever coming out and explicitly calling Barbara hard-hearted, this ballad reveals that she is. In which stanza and by what means is her cruelty demonstrated?
3. At what point does Barbara evidently have a change of heart? Again, how does the poem dramatize this change without explicitly talking about it?
4. In many American versions of this ballad, noble knight John Graeme becomes an ordinary citizen. The gist of the story is the same, but at the end are these further stanzas, incorporated from a different ballad:

    They buried Willie in the old churchyard
        And Barbara in the choir;
    And out of his grave grew a red, red rose,
        And out of hers a briar.

    They grew and grew to the steeple top
        Till they could grow no higher;
    And there they locked in a true love's knot,
        The red rose round the briar.

    Do you think this appendage heightens or weakens the final impact of the story? Can the American ending be defended as an integral part of a new song? Explain.
5. Paraphrase lines 9, 15 – 16, 22, 25 – 28. By putting these lines into prose, what has been lost?

As you can see from "Bonny Barbara Allan," in a traditional English or Scottish folk ballad the storyteller speaks of the lives and feelings of others. Even if the pronoun "I" occurs, it rarely has much personality. Characters often exchange dialogue, but no one character speaks all the way through. Events move rapidly, perhaps because some of the dull transitional stanzas have been forgotten. The events themselves, as ballad scholar Albert B. Friedman has said, are frequently "the stuff of tabloid journalism — sensational tales of lust, revenge and domestic crime. Unwed mothers slay their newborn babes; lovers unwilling to marry their pregnant mistresses brutally murder the poor women, for which, without fail, they are justly punished."[2] There are also many ballads of the supernatural ("The Twa Corbies") and of gallant knights ("Sir Patrick Spence"), and there are a few humorous ballads, usually about unhappy marriages.

The ballad-spinner has at hand a fund of ready-made epithets: steeds are usually "milk-white" or "berry-brown," lips "rosy" or "ruby-red," corpses and graves "clay-cold," beds (like Barbara Allan's) "soft and narrow." At the least,

[2]Introduction to *The Viking Book of Folk Ballads of the English-Speaking World,* edited by Albert B. Friedman (New York: Viking, 1956).

these conventional phrases are terse and understandable. Sometimes they add meaning: the king who sends Sir Patrick Spence to his doom drinks "blood-red wine." The clothing, steeds, and palaces of ladies and lords are always luxurious: a queen may wear "grass-green silk" or "Spanish leather" and ride a horse with "fifty silver bells and nine." Such descriptions are naive, for as Friedman points out, ballad-singers were probably peasants imagining what they had seen only from afar: the life of the nobility. This may be why the skin of ladies in folk ballads is ordinarily "milk-white," "lily-white," or "snow-white." In an agrarian society, where most people worked in the fields, not to be suntanned was a sign of gentility.

A favorite pattern of ballad-makers is the so-called **ballad stanza**, four lines rimed *a b c b*, tending to fall into 8, 6, 8, and 6 syllables:

> Clerk Saunders and Maid Margaret
>> Walked owre yon garden green,
> And deep and heavy was the love
>> That fell thir twa between°. *between those two*

Though not the only possible stanza for a ballad, this easily singable quatrain has continued to attract poets since the Middle Ages. Close kin to the ballad stanza is **common meter**, a stanza found in hymns such as "Amazing Grace," by the eighteenth-century English hymnist John Newton:

> Amazing grace! how sweet the sound
>> That saved a wretch like me!
> I once was lost, but now am found,
>> Was blind, but now I see.

Notice that its pattern is that of the ballad stanza except for its *two* pairs of rimes. That all its lines rime is probably a sign of more literate artistry than we usually hear in folk ballads. Another sign of schoolteachers' influence is that Newton's rimes are exact. (Rimes in folk ballads are often rough-and-ready, as if made by ear, rather than polished and exact, as if the riming words had been matched for their similar spellings. In "Barbara Allan," for instance, the hard-hearted lover's name rimes with *afalling, dwelling, aspilling, dealing,* and even with *ringing* and *adrinking*.) That so many hymns were written in common meter may have been due to convenience. If a congregation didn't know the tune to a hymn in common meter, they readily could sing its words to the tune of another such hymn they knew. Besides hymnists, many poets have favored common meter, among them A. E. Housman and Emily Dickinson.

Related to traditional folk ballads but displaying characteristics of their own, **broadside ballads** (so called because they were printed on one sheet of paper) often were set to traditional tunes. Most broadside ballads were an early form of journalism made possible by the development of cheap printing and by the growth of audiences who could read, just barely. Sometimes merely humorous or tear-jerking, often they were rimed accounts of sensational news events. That they were widespread and often scorned in Shakespeare's day is attested by the character of Autolycus in *A Winter's Tale*, an itinerant hawker of ballads about sea monsters and strange pregnancies ("a usurer's wife was brought to bed of twenty money-bags"). Although many broadsides tend to be **doggerel** (verse full of irregularities due not to skill but to incompetence), many excellent poets had their work taken up and peddled in the streets — among them Marvell, Swift, and Byron.[3]

Literary ballads, not meant for singing, are written by sophisticated poets for book-educated readers who enjoy being reminded of folk ballads. Literary ballads imitate certain features of folk ballads: they may tell of dramatic conflicts or of mortals who encounter the supernatural; they may use conventional figures of speech or ballad stanzas. Well-known poems of this kind include Keats's "La Belle Dame Sans Merci," Coleridge's "Rime of the Ancient Mariner," and (in our time) Dudley Randall's "Ballad of Birmingham."

Dudley Randall (b. 1914)

BALLAD OF BIRMINGHAM   1966

(On the Bombing of a Church in Birmingham, Alabama, 1963)

"Mother dear, may I go downtown
Instead of out to play,
And march the streets of Birmingham
In a Freedom March today?"

"No, baby, no, you may not go,   5
For the dogs are fierce and wild,
And clubs and hoses, guns and jail
Aren't good for a little child."

"But, mother, I won't be alone.
Other children will go with me,
And march the streets of Birmingham   10
To make our country free."

"No, baby, no, you may not go,
For I fear those guns will fire.
But you may go to church instead   15
And sing in the children's choir."

She has combed and brushed her night-dark hair,
And bathed rose petal sweet,

---

[3]A generous collection of broadsides has been assembled by Vivian de Sola Pinto and A. E. Rodway in *The Common Muse: An Anthology of Popular British Ballad Poetry, XVth – XXth Century* (St. Clair Shores, Mich.: Scholarly Press, 1957). See also *Irish Street Ballads,* edited by Colm O. Lochlainn (New York: Corinth Books, 1960), and Olive Woolley Burt, *American Murder Ballads and Their Stories* (New York: Oxford UP, 1958).

And drawn white gloves on her small brown hands,
And white shoes on her feet.   20

The mother smiled to know her child
Was in the sacred place,
But that smile was the last smile
To come upon her face.

For when she heard the explosion,   25
Her eyes grew wet and wild.
She raced through the streets of Birmingham
Calling for her child.

She clawed through bits of glass and brick,
Then lifted out a shoe.   30
"O here's the shoe my baby wore,
But, baby, where are you?"

QUESTIONS

1. This poem, about a dynamite blast set off in a black people's church by a racial terrorist (later convicted), delivers a message without preaching. How would you sum up this message, its implied theme?
2. What is ironic in the mother's denying her child permission to take part in a protest march?
3. How does this modern poem resemble a traditional ballad?

EXPERIMENT: *Seeing the Traits of Ballads*

In the Anthology at the back of this book, read the Child ballads "Edward," "The Three Ravens," and "The Twa Corbies" (pages 774–776). With these ballads in mind, consider one or more of these modern poems:

  W. H. Auden, "As I Walked Out One Evening" (page 781)
  William Jay Smith, "American Primitive" (page 879)
  William Butler Yeats, "Crazy Jane Talks with the Bishop" (page 901)

What characteristics of folk ballads do you find in them? In what ways do these modern poets depart from the traditions of folk ballads of the Middle Ages?

FOR REVIEW AND FURTHER STUDY

John Lennon (1940 – 1980)
Paul McCartney (b. 1942)

ELEANOR RIGBY   1966

Ah, look at all the lonely people!
Ah, look at all the lonely people!

Eleanor Rigby
Picks up the rice in the church where a wedding has been,
Lives in a dream,   5

Waits at the window
Wearing the face that she keeps in a jar by the door.
Who is it for?

All the lonely people,
Where do they all come from?   10
All the lonely people,
Where do they all belong?

Father McKenzie,
Writing the words of a sermon that no one will hear,
No one comes near   15
Look at him working,
Darning his socks in the night when there's nobody there.
What does he care?

All the lonely people
Where do they all come from?   20
All the lonely people
Where do they all belong?

Eleanor Rigby
Died in the church and was buried along with her name.
Nobody came.   25
Father McKenzie,
Wiping the dirt from his hands as he walks from the grave,
No one was saved.

All the lonely people,
Where do they all come from?   30
All the lonely people,
Where do they all belong?

Ah, look at all the lonely people!
Ah, look at all the lonely people!

ELEANOR RIGBY by John Lennon and Paul McCartney. This song first appeared in 1966 on the Beatles' album *Revolver* (Capital ST 2576).

Copyright © 1966 Northern Songs Ltd. All rights for the United States, Canada, and Mexico controlled and administered by Blackwood Music, Inc. under license from ATV Music (Maclen). All rights reserved. International copyright secured. Used by permission.

QUESTION

Is there any reason to call this famous song lyric a ballad? Compare it with a traditional ballad, such as "Bonny Barbara Allan." Do you notice any similarity? What are the differences?

EXERCISE: *Songs or Poems or Both?*

Consider each of the following song lyrics. Which do you think can stand not only to be sung but to be read as poetry? Which probably should not be seen but only heard?

Anonymous (English madrigal)

FA, MI, FA, RE, LA, MI   1609

Fa, mi, fa, re, la, mi,
Begin, my son, and follow me;
   Sing flat, fa mi,
  So shall we well agree.
    Hey tro loly lo.   5
    Hold fast, good son,
  With hey tro lily lo.
O sing this once again, lustily.

Anonymous (English madrigal)

THE SILVER SWAN, WHO LIVING HAD NO NOTE   1612

The silver swan, who living had no note,
When death approached unlocked her silent throat;
Leaning her breast against the reedy shore,
Thus sung her first and last, and sung no more.
Farewell, all joys; O death, come close mine eyes;
More geese than swans now live, more fools than wise.

Bruce Springsteen (b. 1949)

BORN TO RUN   1975

In the day we sweat it out in the streets
    of a runaway American dream
At night we ride through mansions of
    glory in suicide machines
Sprung from cages out on Highway 9
Chrome wheeled, fuel injected
And steppin' out over the line   5
Baby this town rips the bones from your back
It's a death trap, it's a suicide rap
We gotta get out while we're young
'Cause tramps like us, baby we were born to run.

Wendy, let me in, I wanna be your friend   10
I want to guard your dreams and visions
Just wrap your legs round these velvet rims
And strap your hands across my engines
Together we could break this trap
We'll run till we drop, baby we'll never go back   15

Will you walk with me out on the wire
'Cause baby I'm just a scared and lonely rider
But I gotta know how it feels
I want to know if your love is wild
Girl I want to know if love is real   20

Beyond the Palace hemi-powered drones
        scream down the boulevard
The girls comb their hair in rear-view mirrors
And the boys try to look so hard
The amusement park rises bold and stark
Kids are huddled on the beach in a mist   25
I wanna die with you out on the streets tonight
In an everlasting kiss

The highways jammed with broken heroes
On a last chance power drive
Everybody's out on the run tonight   30
But there's no place left to hide
Together, Wendy, we can live with the sadness
I'll love you with all the madness in my soul
Someday girl, I don't know when,
        we're gonna get to that place
Where we really want to go   35
And we'll walk in the sun
But till then tramps like us
Baby we were born to run

Suggestions for Writing

1. Write a short study of a lyric (or lyrics) by a recent popular song-writer. Show why you believe the song-writer's work deserves the name of poetry.
2. Compare and contrast the English folk ballad "The Three Ravens" with the Scottish folk ballad "The Twa Corbies" (both in the Anthology).
3. Compare the versions of "Richard Cory" by Edwin Arlington Robinson and by Paul Simon. Point out changes Simon apparently made in the poem to render it singable. What other changes did he make? How did he alter Robinson's story and its characters?
4. After listening to some recent examples of rap (see page 607), compose a short rap lyric of your own, one that tells a story.

20 Sound

SOUND AS MEANING

Isak Dinesen, in a memoir of her life on a plantation in East Africa, tells how some Kikuyu tribesmen reacted to their first hearing of rimed verse:

> The Natives, who have a strong sense of rhythm, know nothing of verse, or at least did not know anything before the times of the schools, where they were taught hymns. One evening out in the maize-field, where we had been harvesting maize, breaking off the cobs and throwing them on to the ox-carts, to amuse myself, I spoke to the field laborers, who were mostly quite young, in Swahili verse. There was no sense in the verses, they were made for the sake of rime — "Ngumbe na-penda chumbe, Malaya mbaya. Wakamba na-kula mamba." The oxen like salt — whores are bad — The Wakamba eat snakes. It caught the interest of the boys, they formed a ring round me. They were quick to understand that meaning in poetry is of no consequence, and they did not question the thesis of the verse, but waited eagerly for the rime, and laughed at it when it came. I tried to make them themselves find the rime and finish the poem when I had begun it, but they could not, or would not, do that, and turned away their heads. As they had become used to the idea of poetry, they begged: "Speak again. Speak like rain." Why they should feel verse to be like rain I do not know. It must have been, however, an expression of applause, since in Africa rain is always longed for and welcomed.[1]

What the tribesmen had discovered is that poetry, like music, appeals to the ear. However limited it may be in comparison with the sound of an orchestra — or a tribal drummer — the sound of words in itself gives pleasure. However,

---

[1]Isak Dinesen, *Out of Africa* (New York: Random, 1972).

we might doubt Isak Dinesen's assumption that "meaning in poetry is of no consequence." "Hey nonny-nonny" and such nonsense has a place in song lyrics and other poems, and we might take pleasure in hearing rimes in Swahili; but most good poetry has meaningful sound as well as musical sound. Certainly the words of a song have an effect different from that of wordless music: they go along with their music and, by making statements, add more meaning. The French poet Isidore Isou, founder of a literary movement called *lettrisme*, maintained that poems can be written not only in words but in letters (sample lines: *xyl, xyl, / prprali dryl / znglo trpylo pwi*). But the sound of letters alone, without denotation and connotation, has not been enough to make Letterist poems memorable. In the response of the Kikuyu tribesmen, there may have been not only the pleasure of hearing sounds but also the agreeable surprise of finding that things not usually associated had been brought together.

More powerful when in the company of meaning, not apart from it, the sounds of consonants and vowels can contribute greatly to a poem's effect. The sound of *s*, which can suggest the swishing of water, has rarely been used more accurately than in Surrey's line "Calm is the sea, the waves work less and less." When, in a poem, the sound of words working together with meaning pleases mind and ear, the effect is **euphony,** as in the following lines from Tennyson's "Come down, O maid":

> Myriads of rivulets hurrying through the lawn,
> The moan of doves in immemorial elms,
> And murmuring of innumerable bees.

Its opposite is **cacophony:** a harsh, discordant effect. It too is chosen for the sake of meaning. We hear it in Milton's scornful reference in "Lycidas" to corrupt clergymen whose songs "Grate on their scrannel pipes of wretched straw." (Read that line and one of Tennyson's aloud and see which requires lips, teeth, and tongue to do more work.) But note that although Milton's line is harsh in sound, the line (when we meet it in his poem) is pleasing because it is artful. In a famous passage from his *Essay on Criticism,* Pope has illustrated both euphony and cacophony. (Given here as Pope printed it, the passage relies heavily on italics and capital letters, for particular emphasis. If you will read these lines aloud, dwelling a little longer or harder on the words italicized, you will find that Pope has given you very good directions for a meaningful reading.)

Alexander Pope (1688 – 1744)*

TRUE EASE IN WRITING COMES FROM ART, NOT CHANCE   1711

True Ease in Writing comes from Art, not Chance,
As those move easiest who have learned to dance.
'Tis not enough no Harshness gives Offence,
The *Sound* must seem an *Echo* to the *Sense.*
Soft is the strain when *Zephyr°* gently blows,   *the west wind*   5

And the *smooth Stream* in *smoother Numbers*° flows;   *metrical rhythm*
But when loud Surges lash the sounding Shore,
The *hoarse, rough Verse* should like the *Torrent* roar.
When *Ajax* strives, some Rock's vast Weight to throw,
The Line too *labors*, and the Words move *slow*;   10
Not so, when swift *Camilla* scours the Plain,
Flies o'er th' unbending Corn, and skims along the Main°.   *expanse (of sea)*
Hear how *Timotheus'* varied Lays surprise,
And bid Alternate Passions fall and rise!
While, at each Change, the Son of *Lybian Jove*   15
Now *burns* with Glory, and then *melts* with Love;
Now his *fierce Eyes* with *sparkling Fury* glow;
Now *Sighs* steal out, and *Tears begin to flow:*
Persians and Greeks like *Turns of Nature* found,
And the *World's Victor* stood subdued by *Sound!*   20
The *Pow'rs of Music* all our Hearts allow;
And what *Timotheus* was, is *Dryden* now.

TRUE EASE IN WRITING COMES FROM ART, NOT CHANCE (*An Essay on Criticism*, lines 362–383). 9
Ajax: Greek hero, almost a superman, who in Homer's account of the siege of Troy hurls an
enormous rock that momentarily flattens Hector, the Trojan prince (*Iliad* VII, 268–272). 11
Camilla: a kind of Amazon or warrior woman of the Volcians, whose speed and lightness of step
are praised by the Roman poet Virgil: "She could have skimmed across an unmown grainfield /
Without so much as bruising one tender blade; / She could have sped across an ocean's surge /
Without so much as wetting her quicksilver soles" (*Aeneid* VII, 808–811). 13 *Timotheus*: favorite
musician of Alexander the Great. In "Alexander's Feast, or The Power of Music," John Dryden
imagines him: "Timotheus, placed on high / Amid the tuneful choir, / With flying fingers touched
the lyre: / The trembling notes ascend the sky, / And heavenly joys inspire." 15 *Lybian Jove*: name
for Alexander. A Libyan oracle had declared the king to be the son of the god Zeus Ammon.

Notice the pleasing effect of all the *s* sounds in the lines about the west wind
and the stream, and in another meaningful place, the effect of the consonants
in *Ajax strives*, a phrase that makes our lips work almost as hard as Ajax
throwing the rock.

Is sound identical with meaning in lines such as these? Not quite. In the
passage from Tennyson, for instance, the cooing of doves is not *exactly* a moan.
As John Crowe Ransom pointed out, the sound would be almost the same but
the meaning entirely different in "The murdering of innumerable beeves."
While it is true that the consonant sound *sl-* will often begin a word that
conveys ideas of wetness and smoothness — *slick, slimy, slippery, slush* — we are
so used to hearing it in words that convey nothing of the kind — *slave, slow,
sledgehammer* — that it is doubtful whether, all by itself, the sound communicates anything definite. The most beautiful phrase in the English language,
according to Dorothy Parker, is *cellar door*. Another wit once nominated, as our
most euphonious word, not *sunrise* or *silvery* but *syphilis*.

Relating sound more closely to meaning, the device called **onomatopoeia**
is an attempt to represent a thing or action by a word that imitates the sound
associated with it: *zoom, whiz, crash, bang, ding-dong, pitter-patter, yakety-yak*.
Onomatopoeia is often effective in poetry, as in Emily Dickinson's line about
the fly with its "uncertain stumbling Buzz," in which the nasal sounds *n, m, ng*

and the sibilants *c, s* help make a droning buzz, and in Robert Lowell's transcription of a bird call, "yuck-a, yuck-a, yuck-a" (in "Falling Asleep over the Aeneid").

Like the Kikuyu tribesmen, others who care for poetry have discovered in the sound of words something of the refreshment of cool rain. Dylan Thomas, telling how he began to write poetry, said that from early childhood words were to him "as the notes of bells, the sounds of musical instruments, the noises of wind, sea, and rain, the rattle of milkcarts, the clopping of hooves on cobbles, the fingering of branches on the window pane, might be to someone, deaf from birth, who has miraculously found his hearing."[2] For readers, too, the sound of words can have a magical spell, most powerful when it points to meaning. James Weldon Johnson in *God's Trombones* has told of an old-time preacher who began his sermon, "Brothers and sisters, this morning I intend to explain the unexplainable — find out the indefinable — ponder over the imponderable — and unscrew the inscrutable!" The repetition of sound in *unscrew* and *inscrutable* has appeal, but the magic of the words is all the greater if they lead us to imagine the mystery of all Creation as an enormous screw that the preacher's mind, like a screw-driver, will loosen. Though the sound of a word or the meaning of a word may have value all by itself, both become more memorable when taken together.

William Butler Yeats (1865 – 1939)*

WHO GOES WITH FERGUS?   1892

Who will go drive with Fergus now,
And pierce the deep wood's woven shade,
And dance upon the level shore?
Young man, lift up your russet brow,
And lift your tender eyelids, maid,   5
And brood on hopes and fear no more.

And no more turn aside and brood
Upon love's bitter mystery;
For Fergus rules the brazen cars°,   *chariots*
And rules the shadows of the wood,   10
And the white breast of the dim sea
And all dishevelled wandering stars.

WHO GOES WITH FERGUS? *Fergus:* Irish king who gave up his throne to be a wandering poet.

QUESTIONS

1. In what lines do you find euphony?
2. In what line do you find cacophony?
3. How do the sounds of these lines stress what is said in them?

[2]"Notes on the Art of Poetry," *Modern Poetics,* ed. James Scully (New York: McGraw-Hill, 1965).

EXERCISE: *Listening to Meaning*

Read aloud the following brief poems. In the sounds of which particular words are meanings well captured? In which of the poems below do you find onomatopoeia?

John Updike (b. 1932)*

WINTER OCEAN   1960

Many-maned scud-thumper, tub
of male whales, maker of worn wood, shrub-
ruster, sky-mocker, rave!
portly pusher of waves, wind-slave.

Frances Cornford (1886 – 1960)

THE WATCH   1923

I wakened on my hot, hard bed,
Upon the pillow lay my head;
Beneath the pillow I could hear
My little watch was ticking clear.
I thought the throbbing of it went   5
Like my continual discontent.
I thought it said in every tick:
I am so sick, so sick, so sick.
O death, come quick, come quick, come quick,
Come quick, come quick, come quick, come quick!   10

William Wordsworth (1770 – 1850)*

A SLUMBER DID MY SPIRIT SEAL   1800

A slumber did my spirit seal;
    I had no human fears —
She seemed a thing that could not feel
    The touch of earthly years.

No motion has she now, no force;   5
    She neither hears nor sees;
Rolled round in earth's diurnal course,
    With rocks, and stones, and trees.

Emanuel di Pasquale (b. 1943)*

RAIN   1971

Like a drummer's brush,
the rain hushes the surface of tin porches.

Aphra Behn (1640?–1689)

WHEN MAIDENS ARE YOUNG   1687

When maidens are young, and in their spring,
Of pleasure, of pleasure let 'em take their full swing,
   Full swing, full swing,
And love, and dance, and play, and sing,
For Silvia, believe it, when youth is done,   5
There's nought but hum-drum, hum-drum, hum-drum,
There's nought but hum-drum, hum-drum, hum-drum.

ALLITERATION AND ASSONANCE

Listening to a symphony in which themes are repeated throughout each
movement, we enjoy both their recurrence and their variation. We take similar
pleasure in the repetition of a phrase or a single chord. Something like this
pleasure is afforded us frequently in poetry.

Analogies between poetry and wordless music, it is true, tend to break
down when carried far, since poetry — to mention a single difference — has
denotation. But like musical compositions, poems have patterns of sounds.
Among such patterns long popular in English poetry is **alliteration**, which has
been defined as a succession of similar sounds. Alliteration occurs in the
repetition of the same consonant sound at the beginning of successive
words — "round and round the rugged rocks the ragged rascal ran" — or
inside the words, as in Milton's description of the gates of Hell:

> On a sudden open fly
> With impetuous recoil and jarring sound
> The infernal doors, and on their hinges grate
> Harsh thunder, that the lowest bottom shook
> Of Erebus.

The former kind is called **initial alliteration**, the latter **internal alliteration**
or **hidden alliteration**. We recognize alliteration by sound, not by spelling:
know and *nail* alliterate, *know* and *key* do not. In a line by E. E. Cummings,

"colossal hoax of clocks and calendars," the sound of *x* within *hoax* alliterates with the *cks* in *clocks*. Incidentally, the letter *r* does not *always* lend itself to cacophony: elsewhere in *Paradise Lost* Milton said that

> Heaven opened wide
> Her ever-during gates, harmonious sound
> On golden hinges moving . . .

By itself, a letter-sound has no particular meaning. This is a truth forgotten by people who would attribute the effectiveness of Milton's lines on the Heavenly Gates to, say, "the mellow *o*'s and liquid *l* of *harmonious* and *golden.*" Mellow *o*'s and liquid *l*'s occur also in the phrase *moldy cold oatmeal*, which may have a quite different effect. Meaning depends on larger units of language than letters of the alphabet.

Today good prose writers usually avoid alliteration; in the past, some cultivated it. "There is nothing more swifter than time, nothing more sweeter," wrote John Lyly in *Euphues* (1579), and he went on — playing especially with the sounds of *v, n, t, s, l,* and *b* — "we have not, as Seneca saith, little time to live, but we lose much; neither have we a short life by nature, but we make it shorter by naughtiness." Poetry, too, formerly contained more alliteration than it usually contains today. In Old English verse, each line was held together by alliteration, a basic pattern still evident in the fourteenth century, as in the following description of the world as a "fair field" in *Piers Plowman*:

> A *f*eir *f*eld *f*ul of *f*olk *f*ond I ther bi-twene,
> Of alle *m*aner of *m*en, the *m*ene and the riche . . .

Most poets nowadays save alliteration for special occasions. They may use it to give emphasis, as Edward Lear does: "*F*ar and *f*ew, *f*ar and *f*ew, / Are the *l*ands where the Jumblies *l*ive." With its aid they can point out the relationship between two things placed side by side, as in Pope's line on things of little worth: "The courtier's *p*romises, and sick man's *p*rayers." Alliteration, too, can be a powerful aid to memory. It is hard to forget such tongue twisters as "Peter Piper picked a peck of pickled peppers," or common expressions like "green as grass," "tried and true," and "from stem to stern." In fact, because alliteration directs our attention to something, it had best be used neither thoughtlessly nor merely for decoration, lest it call attention to emptiness. A case in point may be a line by Philip James Bailey, a reaction to a lady's weeping: "I saw, but *s*pared to *s*peak." If the poet chose the word *spared* for any meaningful reason other than that it alliterates with *speak*, the reason is not clear.

As we have seen, to repeat the sound of a consonant is to produce alliteration, but to repeat the sound of a *vowel* is to produce **assonance**. Like alliteration, assonance may occur either initially — "*a*ll the *aw*ful *au*guries"[3] — or internally — Edmund Spenser's "Her goodly *ey*es *l*ike sapphires shining

---

[3]Some prefer to call the repetition of an initial vowel-sound by the name of alliteration: "apt alliteration's artful aid."

bright, / Her forehead ivory white . . ." and it can help make common phrases unforgettable: "eager beaver," "holy smoke." Like alliteration, it slows the reader down and focuses attention.

A. E. Housman (1859 – 1936)*

EIGHT O'CLOCK   1922

He stood, and heard the steeple
    Sprinkle the quarters on the morning town.
One, two, three, four, to market-place and people
    It tossed them down.

Strapped, noosed, nighing his hour,   5
    He stood and counted them and cursed his luck;
And then the clock collected in the tower
    Its strength, and struck.

QUESTIONS

1. Why does the protagonist in this brief drama curse his luck? What is his situation?
2. For so short a poem, "Eight O'Clock" carries a great weight of alliteration. What patterns of initial alliteration do you find? What patterns of internal alliteration? What effect is created by all this heavy emphasis?

Robert Herrick (1591 – 1674)*

UPON JULIA'S VOICE   1648

So smooth, so sweet, so silv'ry is thy voice,
As, could they hear, the damned would make no noise,
But listen to thee (walking in thy chamber)
Melting melodious words, to lutes of amber.

UPON JULIA'S VOICE. 4 *amber:* either the fossilized resin from which pipestems are sometimes made today, and which might have inlaid the body of a lute; or an alloy of four parts silver and one part gold.

QUESTIONS

1. Is Julia speaking or singing? How do we know for sure?
2. In what moments in this brief poem does the sound of words especially help convey meaning?
3. Does Herrick's reference to *the damned* (presumably howling from Hell's torments) seem out of place?

Janet Lewis (b. 1899)

GIRL HELP   1927

Mild and slow and young,
She moves about the room,
And stirs the summer dust
With her wide broom.

In the warm, lofted air,   5
Soft lips together pressed,
Soft wispy hair,
She stops to rest,

And stops to breathe,
Amid the summer hum,   10
The great white lilac bloom
Scented with days to come.

QUESTIONS

1. What assonance and alliteration do you find in this poem? (Suggestion: It may help
   to read the poem aloud.)
2. In this particular poem, how are these repetitions (or echoes) of sound valuable?

EXERCISE: *Hearing How Sound Helps*

Which of these translations of the same passage from Petrarch do you think is better
poetry? Why? What do assonance and alliteration have to do with your preference?

1. Love that liveth and reigneth in my thought,
   That built his seat within my captive breast,
   Clad in the arms wherein with me he fought,
   Oft in my face he doth his banner rest.
                      —Henry Howard, Earl of Surrey (1517? – 1547)

2. The long love that in my thought doth harbor,
   And in mine heart doth keep his residence,
   Into my face presseth with bold pretense
   And therein campeth, spreading his banner.
                      —Sir Thomas Wyatt (1503? – 1542)

EXPERIMENT: *Reading for Assonance*

Try reading aloud as rapidly as possible the following poem by Tennyson. From the
difficulties you encounter, you may be able to sense the slowing effect of assonance. Then
read the poem aloud a second time, with consideration.

Alfred, Lord Tennyson (1809 – 1892)*

THE SPLENDOR FALLS ON CASTLE WALLS   1850

The splendor falls on castle walls
    And snowy summits old in story;
The long light shakes across the lakes,
    And the wild cataract leaps in glory.
Blow, bugle, blow, set the wild echoes flying,   5
Blow, bugle; answer, echoes, dying, dying, dying.

    O hark, O hear! how thin and clear,
        And thinner, clearer, farther going!
    O sweet and far from cliff and scar°   *jutting rock*
        The horns of Elfland faintly blowing!   10
Blow, let us hear the purple glens replying:
Blow, bugle; answer, echoes, dying, dying, dying.

    O love, they die in yon rich sky,
        They faint on hill or field or river;
    Our echoes roll from soul to soul,   15
        And grow for ever and for ever.
Blow, bugle, blow, set the wild echoes flying,
And answer, echoes, answer, dying, dying, dying.

RIME

Isak Dinesen's tribesmen, to whom rime was a new phenomenon, recognized at once that rimed language is special language. So do we, for, although much English poetry is unrimed, rime is one means to set poetry apart from ordinary conversation and bring it closer to music. A **rime** (or rhyme), defined most narrowly, occurs when two or more words or phrases contain an identical or similar vowel-sound, usually accented, and the consonant-sounds (if any) that follow the vowel-sound are identical: *hay* and *sleigh, prairie schooner* and *piano tuner.* [4] From these examples it will be seen that rime depends not on spelling but on sound.

    Excellent rimes surprise. It is all very well that a reader may anticipate which vowel-sound is coming next, for patterns of rime give pleasure by satisfying expectations; but riming becomes dull clunking if, at the end of each line, the reader can predict the word that will end the next. Hearing many a jukebox song for the first time, a listener can do so: *charms* lead to *arms, skies above* to *love.* As Alexander Pope observes of the habits of dull rimesters,

[4]Some definitions of *rime* would apply the term to the repetition of any identical or similar sound, not only a vowel-sound. In this sense, assonance is a kind of rime; so is alliteration (called **initial rime**).

Where'er you find "the cooling western breeze,"
In the next line it "whispers through the trees";
If crystal streams "with pleasing murmurs creep,"
The reader's threatened (not in vain) with "sleep" . . .

But who — given the opening line of this comic poem — could predict the lines
that follow?

William Cole (b. 1919)

ON MY BOAT ON LAKE CAYUGA   1985

On my boat on Lake Cayuga
I have a horn that goes "Ay-oogah!"
I'm not the modern kind of creep
Who has a horn that goes "beep beep."

Robert Herrick, in a more subtle poem, made good use of rime to indicate a
startling contrast:

Then while time serves, and we are but decaying,
Come, my Corinna, come, let's go a-Maying.

Though good rimes seem fresh, not all will startle, and probably few will call
to mind things so unlike as *May* and *decay, Cayuga* and *Ay-oogah.* Some masters
of rime often link words that, taken out of text, might seem common and
unevocative. Here, for instance, is Alexander Pope's comment on a trifling
courtier:

Yet let me flap this bug with gilded wings,
This painted child of dirt, that stinks and stings;
Whose buzz the witty and the fair annoys,
Yet wit ne'er tastes, and beauty ne'er enjoys:
So well-bred spaniels civilly delight
In mumbling of the game they dare not bite.
Eternal smiles his emptiness betray,
As shallow streams run dimpling all the way.

Pope's rime-words are not especially memorable — and yet these lines are,
because (among other reasons) they rime. Wit may be driven home without
rime, but it is rime that rings the doorbell. Admittedly, some rimes wear thin
from too much use. More difficult to use freshly than before the establishment
of Tin Pan Alley, rimes such as *moon, June, croon* seem leaden and to ring true
would need an extremely powerful context. *Death* and *breath* are a rime that
poets have used with wearisome frequency; another is *birth, earth, mirth.* And
yet we cannot exclude these from the diction of poetry, for they might be the
very words a poet would need in order to say something new and original. The
following brief poem seems fresher than its rimes (if taken out of context) would
lead us to expect.

William Blake (1757 – 1827)*

THE ANGEL THAT PRESIDED O'ER MY BIRTH   (1808 – 1811)

The Angel that presided o'er my birth
Said, "Little creature, formed of Joy and Mirth,
Go love without the help of any thing on earth."

What matters to rime is freshness — not of a word but of the poet's way of seeing.

Good poets, said John Dryden, learn to make their rime "so properly a part of the verse, that it should never mislead the sense, but itself be led and governed by it." The comment may remind us that skillful rime — unlike poor rime — is never a distracting ornament. "Rime the rudder is of verses, / With which, like ships, they steer their courses," wrote the seventeenth-century poet Samuel Butler. Like other patterns of sound, rime can help a poet to group ideas, emphasize particular words, and weave a poem together. It can start reverberations between words and can point to connections of meaning.

To have an **exact rime,** sounds following the vowel sound have to be the same: *red* and *bread, wealthily* and *stealthily, walk to her* and *talk to her.* If final consonant sounds are the same but the vowel sounds are different, the result is **slant rime,** also called **near rime, off rime,** or **imperfect rime:** *sun* riming with *bone, moon, rain, green, gone, thin.* By not satisfying the reader's expectation of an exact chime, but instead giving a clunk, a slant rime can help a poet say some things in a particular way. It works especially well for disappointed let-downs, negations, and denials, as in Blake's couplet:

He who the ox to wrath has moved
Shall never be by woman loved.

Many poets have admired the unexpected and arresting effect of a slant rime. As a student in high school, Kenneth Burke (later to become known as a critic, poet, and fiction writer) decided that "the most nearly perfect possible imperfect rime" was the combination of *widow-shadow-meadow.* "Ever since then," he wrote, "I have been trying to fit them just right into a poem—and maybe some day I'll succeed." Here is one attempt.

Kenneth Burke (b. 1897)

THE HABIT OF IMPERFECT RHYMING   1968

Lips now rhyme with slops
Hips with blobs
Passion with nuclear fission
And beauty with shoddy.
The word for lovely leisure, *school,*   5

Is now in line with urban sprawl.
Are we blunted or haunted?
Is last year's auto a dodo?
Let widow be bedded
With shadow and meadow.   10

All this is necessary
Says the secretary—
Else moan, groan, bone must go with alone,
As breath must go with death.

Consonance, a kind of slant rime, occurs when the rimed words or phrases
have the same consonant sounds but a different vowel, as in *chitter* and *chatter.*
It is used in a traditional nonsense poem, "The Cutty Wren": " 'O where are
you going?' says *Milder* to *Malder.*" (W. H. Auden wrote a variation on it that
begins, " 'O where are you going?' said *reader* to *rider,*" thus keeping the
consonance.)

End rime, as its name indicates, comes at the ends of lines, **internal rime**
within them. Most rime tends to be end rime. Few recent poets have used
internal rime so heavily as Wallace Stevens in the beginning of "Bantams in
Pine-Woods": "Chieftain Iffucan of Azcan in caftan / Of tan with henna
hackles, halt!" (lines also heavy on alliteration). A poet may employ both end
rime and internal rime in the same poem, as in Robert Burns's satiric ballad
"The Kirk's Alarm":

> Orthodox, Orthodox, wha believe in John Knox,
>   Let me sound an alarm to your conscience:
> There's a heretic blast has been blawn i' the wast°,   *west*
>   "That what is not sense must be nonsense."

Masculine rime is a rime of one-syllable words (*jail, bail*) or (in words of
more than one syllable) stressed final syllables: *di-VORCE, re-MORSE,* or *horse,
re-MORSE.* **Feminine rime** is a rime of two or more syllables, with stress on
a syllable other than the last: *TUR-tle, FER-tile,* or (to take an example from
Byron) *in-tel-LECT-u-al, hen-PECKED you all.* Often it lends itself to comic
verse, but can occasionally be valuable to serious poems, as in Wordsworth's
"Resolution and Independence":

> We poets in our youth begin in gladness,
> But thereof come in the end despondency and madness.

or as in Anne Sexton's seriously witty "Eighteen Days Without You":

> and of course we're not married, we are a pair of scissors
> who come together to cut, without towels saying His. Hers.

Serious poems containing feminine rimes of three syllables have been attempted, notably by Thomas Hood in "The Bridge of Sighs":

Take her up tenderly,
Lift her with care;
Fashioned so slenderly,
Young, and so fair!

But the pattern is hard to sustain without lapsing into unintended comedy, as
in the same poem:

Still, for all slips of hers,
One of Eve's family —
Wipe those poor lips of hers,
Oozing so clammily.

It works better when comedy is wanted:

Hilaire Belloc (1870 – 1953)

THE HIPPOPOTAMUS   1896

I shoot the Hippopotamus
  with bullets made of platinum,
Because if I use leaden ones
  his hide is sure to flatten 'em.

In **eye rime,** spellings look alike but pronunciations differ — *rough* and
dough, idea and *flea, Venus* and *menus.* Strictly speaking, eye rime is not rime
at all.

In the early 1960s in American poetry, rime suffered a tremendous fall from
favor. A new generation of poets took for models the open forms of Whitman
and William Carlos Williams. Only lately has skilled rime prominently reappeared, in the work of new poets such as R. L. Barth, Amy Clampitt, Dana
Gioia, R. S. Gwynn, Marilyn Hacker, Gjertrud Schnackenberg, and Timothy
Steele. Here is a recent sample:

Brad Leithauser (b. 1953)

TRAUMA   1982

You will carry this suture
  Into the future.
The past never passes.
  It simply amasses.

Still, most American poets don't write in rime; some even consider it exhausted. Such a view may be a reaction against the wearing-thin of rimes by overuse or the mechanical and meaningless application of a rime scheme. Yet anyone who listens to children skipping rope in the street, making up rimes to delight themselves as they go along, may doubt that the pleasures of rime are ended; and certainly the practice of Yeats and Emily Dickinson, to name only two, suggests that the possibilities of slant rime may be nearly infinite. If successfully employed, as it has been at times by a majority of English-speaking poets whose work we care to save, rime runs through its poem like a spine: the creature moves by means of it.

William Butler Yeats (1865 – 1939)*

LEDA AND THE SWAN   1924

A sudden blow: the great wings beating still
Above the staggering girl, her thighs caressed
By the dark webs, her nape caught in his bill,
He holds her helpless breast upon his breast.

How can those terrified vague fingers push   5
The feathered glory from her loosening thighs?
And how can body, laid in that white rush,
But feel the strange heart beating where it lies?

A shudder in the loins engenders there
The broken wall, the burning roof and tower   10
And Agamemnon dead.
                         Being so caught up,
So mastered by the brute blood of the air,
Did she put on his knowledge with his power
Before the indifferent beak could let her drop?

QUESTIONS

1. According to Greek mythology, the god Zeus in the form of a swan descended upon Leda, a Spartan queen. Among the offspring of this union were Clytemnestra, Agamemnon's unfaithful wife who conspired in his murder, and Helen, on whose account the Trojan war was fought. What does a knowledge of these allusions contribute to our understanding of the poem's last two lines?
2. The slant rime up / drop (lines 11, 14) may seem accidental or inept. Is it? Would this poem have ended nearly so well if Yeats had made an exact rime like up / cup or like stop / drop?

Gerard Manley Hopkins (1844 – 1889)*

GOD'S GRANDEUR (1877)

The world is charged with the grandeur of God.
    It will flame out, like shining from shook foil;
    It gathers to a greatness, like the ooze of oil
Crushed. Why do men then now not reck his rod?
Generations have trod, have trod, have trod;   5
    And all is seared with trade; bleared, smeared with toil;
    And wears man's smudge and shares man's smell: the soil
Is bare now, nor can foot feel, being shod.

And for all this, nature is never spent;
    There lives the dearest freshness deep down things;   10
And though the last lights off the black West went
    Oh, morning, at the brown brink eastward, springs —
Because the Holy Ghost over the bent
    World broods with warm breast and with ah! bright wings.

GOD'S GRANDEUR. 1 *charged:* as though with electricity. 3–4 *It gathers . . . Crushed:* The grandeur of God will rise and be manifest, as oil rises and collects from crushed olives or grain. 4 *reck his rod:* heed His law. 10 *deep down things:* Tightly packing the poem, Hopkins omits the preposition *in* or *within* before *things.* 11 *last lights . . . went:* When in 1534 Henry VIII broke ties with the Roman Catholic Church and created the Church of England?

QUESTIONS

1. In a letter Hopkins explained *shook foil* (line 2): "I mean foil in its sense of leaf or tinsel. . . . Shaken goldfoil gives off broad glares like sheet lightning and also, and this is true of nothing else, owing to its zigzag dints and creasings and network of small many cornered facets, a sort of fork lightning too." What do you think he meant by the phrase *ooze of oil* (line 3)? Would you call this phrase an example of alliteration?
2. What instances of internal rime does the poem contain? How would you describe their effects?
3. Point out some of the poet's uses of alliteration and assonance. Do you believe that Hopkins perhaps goes too far in his heavy use of devices of sound, or would you defend his practice?
4. Why do you suppose Hopkins, in the last two lines, says *over the bent / World* instead of (as we might expect) *bent over the world?* How can the world be bent? Can you make any sense out of this wording, or is Hopkins just trying to get his rime scheme to work out?

James Whitehead (b. 1936)

THE COUNTRY MUSIC STAR BEGINS HIS POLITICS   1979

There are no deadlier Americas
Than those I see from stages where I work,
And over coffee in the bad cafes,
Which is how everyone is going broke
Investing in good times and sentiment   5
Which pays my wages.
                 Squandering their love
The size of death and a revival tent
A troubled pride is what I have to give.

Whatever else they want they hardly say,
And I don't either. I am paid to strum   10
And make up songs that help grown children play.
The thing I do has prospered and gone wrong.
Lord, we are multiplied and we mean well.
There's murder in the darkness I can't kill.

QUESTIONS

1. What ironies trouble the speaker in this sonnet?
2. What suggestions emanate from Whitehead's title?
3. Notice the off-rimes, especially *work / broke, strum / wrong,* and *well / kill.* To what extent do they help to illuminate the poem's theme?

Robert Frost (1874 – 1963)*

DESERT PLACES   1936

Snow falling and night falling fast, oh, fast
In a field I looked into going past,
And the ground almost covered smooth in snow,
But a few weeds and stubble showing last.

The woods around it have it — it is theirs.   5
All animals are smothered in their lairs,
I am too absent-spirited to count;
The loneliness includes me unawares.

And lonely as it is, that loneliness
Will be more lonely ere it will be less —   10
A blanker whiteness of benighted snow
With no expression, nothing to express.

They cannot scare me with their empty spaces
Between stars — on stars where no human race is.
I have it in me so much nearer home   15
To scare myself with my own desert places.

1. What are these desert places that the speaker finds in himself? (More than one theory is possible. What is yours?)
2. Notice how many times, within the short space of lines 8 – 10, Frost says *lonely* (or *loneliness*). What other words in the poem contain similar sounds that reinforce these words?
3. In the closing stanza, the feminine rimes *spaces, race is,* and *places* might well occur in light or comic verse. Does "Desert Places" leave you laughing? If not, what does it make you feel?

READING AND HEARING POEMS ALOUD

Thomas Moore's "The light that lies in women's eyes" — a line rich in internal rime, alliteration, and assonance — is harder to forget than "The light burning in the gaze of a woman." Because of sound, it is possible to remember the obscure line Christopher Smart wrote while in an insane asylum: "Let Ross, house of Ross rejoice with the Great Flabber Dabber Flat Clapping Fish with hands." Such lines, striking as they are even when read silently, become still more effective when said out loud. Reading poems aloud is a way to understand them. For this reason, practice the art of lending poetry your voice.

Before trying to read a poem aloud to other people, understand its meaning as thoroughly as possible. If you know what the poet is saying and the poet's attitude toward it, you will be able to find an appropriate tone of voice and to give each part of the poem a proper emphasis.

Except in the most informal situations and in some class exercises, read a poem to yourself before trying it on an audience. No actor goes before the footlights without first having studied the script, and the language of poems usually demands even more consideration than the language of most contemporary plays. Prepare your reading in advance. Check pronunciations you are not sure of. Underline things to be emphasized.

Read deliberately, more slowly than you would read aloud from a newspaper. Keep in mind that you are saying something to somebody. Don't race through the poem as if you are eager to get it over with.

Don't lapse into singsong. A poem may have a definite swing, but swing should never be exaggerated at the cost of sense. If you understand what the poem is saying and utter the poem as if you do, the temptation to fall into such a mechanical intonation should not occur. Observe the punctuation, making slight pauses for commas, longer pauses for full stops (periods, question marks, exclamation points).

If the poem is rimed, don't raise your voice and make the rimes stand out unnaturally. They should receive no more volume than other words in the poem, though a faint pause at the end of each line will call the listener's attention to them. This advice is contrary to a school that holds that, if a line does not end in any punctuation, one should not pause but run it together with the line following. The trouble is that, from such a reading, a listener may not be able to identify the rimes; besides, the line, that valuable unit of rhythm, is destroyed.

In some older poems rimes that look like slant rimes may have been exact rimes in their day:

> Still so perverse and opposite,
> As if they worshiped God for spite.
> — Samuel Butler, *Hudibras* (1663)

> Soft yielding minds to water glide away,
> And sip, with nymphs, their elemental tea.
> — Alexander Pope, "The Rape of the Lock" (1714)

You may wish to establish a consistent policy toward such shifting usage: is it worthwhile to distort current pronunciation for the sake of the rime?

Listening to a poem, especially if it is unfamiliar, calls for concentration. Merciful people seldom read poetry uninterruptedly to anyone for more than a few minutes at a time. Robert Frost, always kind to his audiences, used to intersperse poems with many silences and seemingly casual remarks — shrewdly giving his hearers a chance to rest from their labors and giving his poems a chance to settle in.

If, in first listening to a poem, you don't take in all its meaning, don't be discouraged. With more practice in listening, your attention span and your ability to understand poems read aloud will increase. Incidentally, following the text of poems in a book while hearing them read aloud may increase your comprehension, but it may not necessarily help you to *listen*. At least some of the time, close your book and let your ears make the poems welcome. That way, their sounds may better work for you.

Hearing recordings of poets reading their work can help both your ability to read aloud and your ability to listen. Not all poets read their poems well, but there is much to be relished in both the highly dramatic reading style of a Dylan Thomas and the quiet underplay of a Robert Frost. You need feel no obligation, of course, to imitate the poet's reading of a poem. You have to feel about the poem in your own way, in order to read it with conviction and naturalness.

Even if you don't have an audience, the act of speaking poetry can have its own rewards. Perhaps that is what James Wright is driving at in the following brief prose poem.

James Wright (1927 – 1980)*

SAYING DANTE ALOUD   1976

You can feel the muscles and veins rippling in widening and rising
  circles, like a bird in flight under your tongue.

EXERCISE: *Reading for Sound and Meaning*

Read these brief poems aloud. What devices of sound do you find in each of them? Try to explain what sound contributes to the total effect of the poem and how it reinforces what the poet is saying.

Michael Stillman (b. 1940)

In Memoriam John Coltrane   1972

Listen to the coal
rolling, rolling through the cold
    steady rain, wheel on

  wheel, listen to the
turning of the wheels this night   5
    black as coal dust, steel

  on steel, listen to
these cars carry coal, listen
    to the coal train roll.

In Memoriam John Coltrane. John Coltrane (1926 – 1967) was a saxophonist whose originality, passion, and technical wizardry have had a deep influence on the history of modern jazz.

William Shakespeare (1564 – 1616)*

Full fathom five thy father lies   (about 1611)

Full fathom five thy father lies;
  Of his bones are coral made;
Those are pearls that were his eyes:
  Nothing of him that doth fade,
But doth suffer a sea change   5
Into something rich and strange.
Sea nymphs hourly ring his knell:
  Ding-dong.
Hark! now I hear them — Ding-dong, bell.

Full fathom five thy father lies. The spirit Ariel sings this song in The Tempest to Ferdinand, prince of Naples, who mistakenly thinks his father is drowned.

A. E. Housman (1859 – 1936)*

With rue my heart is laden   1896

With rue my heart is laden
  For golden friends I had,
For many a rose-lipt maiden
  And many a lightfoot lad.

By brooks too broad for leaping   5
  The lightfoot boys are laid;
The rose-lipt girls are sleeping
  In fields where roses fade.

T. S. Eliot (1888 – 1965)*

VIRGINIA   1934

Red river, red river,
Slow flow heat is silence
No will is still as a river
Still. Will heat move
Only through the mocking-bird   5
Heard once? Still hills
Wait. Gates wait. Purple trees,
White trees, wait, wait,
Delay, decay. Living, living,
Never moving. Ever moving   10
Iron thoughts came with me
And go with me:
Red river, river, river.

VIRGINIA. This poem is one of a series entitled "Landscapes."

SUGGESTIONS FOR WRITING

1. Write about a personal experience with reading poems aloud.
2. Explain why contemporary poets are right (or wrong) to junk rime.
3. Consider the verbal music in W. H. Auden's "As I Walked Out One Evening" (or
   another selection from the Poems for Further Reading). Analyze the poem for language
   with ear-appeal and show how the poem's sound is of a piece with its meaning.

21 Rhythm

STRESSES AND PAUSES

Rhythms affect us powerfully. We are lulled by a hammock's sway, awakened by an alarm clock's repeated yammer. Long after we come home from a beach, the rising and falling of waves and tides continue in memory. How powerfully the rhythms of poetry also move us may be felt in folk songs of railroad workers and chain gangs whose words were chanted in time to the lifting and dropping of a sledgehammer, and in verse that marching soldiers shout, putting a stress on every word that coincides with a footfall:

Your LEFT! TWO! THREE! FOUR!
Your LEFT! TWO! THREE! FOUR!
You LEFT your WIFE and TWEN-ty-one KIDS
And you LEFT! TWO! THREE! FOUR!
You'll NEV-er get HOME to-NIGHT!

A rhythm is produced by a series of recurrences: the returns and departures of the seasons, the repetitions of an engine's stroke, the beats of the heart. A rhythm may be produced by the recurrence of a sound (the throb of a drum, a telephone's busy-signal), but rhythm and sound are not identical. A totally deaf person at a parade can sense rhythm from the motions of the marchers' arms and feet, from the shaking of the pavement as they tramp. Rhythms inhere in the motions of the moon and stars, even though when they move we hear no sound.

In poetry, several kinds of recurrent *sound* are possible, including (as we saw in the last chapter) rime, alliteration, and assonance. But most often when we speak of the **rhythm** of a poem we mean the recurrence of stresses and pauses in it. When we hear a poem read aloud, stresses and pauses are, of course, part of its sound. It is possible to be aware of rhythms in poems read silently, too.

A **stress** (or **accent**) is a greater amount of force given to one syllable in speaking than is given to another. We favor a stressed syllable with a little more breath and emphasis, with the result that it comes out slightly louder, higher in pitch, or longer in duration than other syllables. In this manner we place a stress on the first syllable of words such as *eagle, impact, open,* and *statue,* and on the second syllable in *cigar, mystique, precise,* and *until.* Each word in English carries at least one stress, except (usually) for the articles *a, an,* and *the,* and one-syllable prepositions: *at, by, for, from, of, to, with.* Even these, however, take a stress once in a while: "Get WITH it!" "You're not THE Dolly Parton?" One word by itself is seldom long enough for us to notice a rhythm in it. Usually a sequence of at least a few words is needed for stresses to establish their pattern: a line, a passage, a whole poem. Strong rhythms may be seen in most Mother Goose rimes, to which children have been responding for hundreds of years. This rime is for an adult to chant while jogging a child up and down on a knee:

Here goes my lord
A trot, a trot, a trot, a trot!
Here goes my lady
A canter, a canter, a canter, a canter!
Here goes my young master
Jockey-hitch, jockey-hitch, jockey-hitch, jockey-hitch!
Here goes my young miss
An amble, an amble, an amble, an amble!
The footman lags behind to tipple ale and wine
And goes gallop, a gallop, a gallop, to make up his time.

More than one rhythm occurs in these lines, as the make-believe horse changes pace. How do these rhythms differ? From one line to the next, the interval between stresses lengthens or grows shorter. In "a TROT a TROT a TROT a TROT," the stress falls on every other syllable. But in the middle of the line "A CAN-ter a CAN-ter a CAN-ter a CAN-ter," the stress falls on every third syllable. When stresses recur at fixed intervals as in these lines, the result is called a **meter.** The line "A trot a trot a trot a trot" is in **iambic** meter, a succession of alternate unstressed and stressed syllables.[1] Of all rhythms in the English language, this one is most familiar; most of our traditional poetry is written in it and ordinary speech tends to resemble it. Most poems, less obvious in rhythm than nursery rimes are, rarely stick to their meters with such jog-trot regularity. The following lines also contain a horseback-riding rhythm. (The poet, Gerard Manley Hopkins, is comparing the pell-mell plunging of a burn — Scottish word for a brook — to the motion of a wild horse.)

This darksome burn, horseback brown,
His rollrock highroad roaring down,
In coop and in comb the fleece of his foam
Flutes and low to the lake falls home.

[1]Another kind of meter is possible, in which the intervals between stresses vary. This is **accentual** meter, not often found in contemporary poetry. It is discussed in the second part of this chapter.

In the third line, when the brook courses through coop and comb ("hollow" and "ravine"), the passage breaks into a gallop; then, with the two-beat *falls home,* almost seems reined to a sudden halt.

Stresses embody meanings. Whenever two or more fall side by side, words gain in emphasis. Consider these hard-hitting lines from John Donne, in which accent marks have been placed, dictionary-fashion, to indicate the stressed syllables:

> Bat'ter my heart', three'-per'soned God', for You'
> As yet' but knock', breathe', shine', and seek' to mend';
> That I may rise' and stand', o'er'throw' me, and bend'
> Your force' to break', blow', burn', and make' me new'.

Unstressed (or **slack**) syllables also can direct our attention to what the poet means. In a line containing few stresses and a great many unstressed syllables, there can be an effect not of power and force but of hesitation and uncertainty. Yeats asks in "Among School Children" what young mother, if she could see her baby grown to be an old man, would think him

> A com'pen·sa'tion for the pang' of his birth'
> Or the un·cer'tain·ty of his set'ting forth'?

When unstressed syllables recur in pairs, the result is a rhythm that trips and bounces, as in Robert Service's rollicking line:

> A bunch' of the boys' were whoop'ing it up' in the Mal'a·mute sa·loon'
> . . .

or in Poe's lines — also light but probably supposed to be serious:

> For the moon' nev·er beams' with·out bring'ing me dreams'
> Of the beau'ti·ful An'na·bel Lee'.

Apart from the words that convey it, the rhythm of a poem has no meaning. There are no essentially sad rhythms, nor any essentially happy ones. But some rhythms enforce certain meanings better than others do. The bouncing rhythm of Service's line seems fitting for an account of a merry night in a Klondike saloon; but it may be distracting when encountered in Poe's wistful elegy.

EXERCISE: *Appropriate and Inappropriate Rhythms*

In each of the following passages decide whether rhythm enforces meaning and tone or works against these elements and consequently against the poem's effectiveness.

1. Alfred, Lord Tennyson, "Break, break, break":

> Break, break, break,
> On thy cold gray stones, O Sea!

2. Edgar Allan Poe, "Ulalume":

> Then my heart it grew ashen and sober
>   As the leaves that were crispèd and sere —
>   As the leaves that were withering and sere,

And I cried: "It was surely October
    On *this* very night of last year
    That I journey — I journeyed down here —
    That I brought a dread burden down here —
    On this night of all nights in the year,
    Ah, what demon has tempted me here?"

3. Greg Keeler, "There Ain't No Such Thing as a Montana Cowboy" (a song lyric):

I couldn't be cooler, I come from Missoula,
And I rope and I chew and I ride.
But I'm a heroin dealer, and I drive a four-wheeler
With stereo speakers inside.
My ol' lady Phoebe's out rippin' off C.B.'s
From the rigs at the Wagon Wheel Bar,
Near a Montana truck stop and a shit-outta-luck stop
For a trucker who's driven too far.

4. Eliza Cook, "Song of the Sea-Weed":

Many a lip is gaping for drink,
    And madly calling for rain;
And some hot brains are beginning to think
    Of a messmate's opened vein.

5. William Shakespeare, song from *The Tempest*:

The master, the swabber, the boatswain, and I,
The gunner and his mate
Loved Moll, Meg, and Marian, and Margery,
But none of us cared for Kate;
For she had a tongue with a tang
Would cry to a sailor "Go hang!" —
She loved not the savor of tar nor of pitch
Yet a tailor might scratch her where'er she did itch;
Then to sea, boys, and let her go hang!

Rhythms in poetry are due not only to stresses but also to pauses. "Every nice ear," observed Alexander Pope (*nice* meaning "finely tuned"), "must, I believe, have observed that in any smooth English verse of ten syllables, there is naturally a pause either at the fourth, fifth, or sixth syllable." Such a light but definite pause within a line is called a **cesura** (or caesura), "a cutting." More liberally than Pope, we apply the name to any pause in a line of any length, after any word in the line. In studying a poem, we often indicate a cesura by double lines(‖). Usually, a cesura will occur at a mark of punctuation, but there can be a cesura even if no punctuation is present. Sometimes you will find it at the end of a phrase or clause or, as in these lines by William Blake, after an internal rime:

And priests in black gowns‖were walking their rounds
And binding with briars‖my joys and desires.

Lines of ten or twelve syllables (as Pope knew) tend to have just one cesura, though sometimes there are more:

Cover her face:‖mine eyes dazzle:‖she died young.

Pauses also tend to recur at more prominent places — namely, after each line. At the end of a verse (from *versus,* "a turning"), the reader's eye, before turning to go on to the next line, makes a pause, however brief. If a line ends in a full pause — usually indicated by some mark of punctuation — we call it **end-stopped.** All the lines in this stanza by Theodore Roethke are end-stopped:

> Let seed be grass and grass turn into hay:
> I'm martyr to a motion not my own;
> What's freedom for? To know eternity.
> I swear she cast a shadow white as stone.
> But who would count eternity in days?
> These old bones live to learn her wanton ways:
> (I measure time by how a body sways).[2]

A line that does not end in punctuation and that therefore is read with only a slight pause after it is called a **run-on line.** Because a run-on line gives us only part of a phrase, clause, or sentence, we have to read on to the line or lines following, in order to complete a thought. All these lines from Robert Browning's "My Last Duchess" are run-on lines:

> . . . Sir, 'twas not
> Her husband's presence only, called that spot
> Of joy into the Duchess' cheek: perhaps
> Frà Pandolf chanced to say "Her mantle laps
> Over my lady's wrist too much," or "Paint
> Must never hope to reproduce the faint
> Half-flush that dies along her throat." Such stuff
> Was courtesy, she thought . . .

A passage in run-on lines has a rhythm different from that of a passage like Roethke's in end-stopped lines. When emphatic pauses occur in the quotation from Browning, they fall within a line rather than at the end of one. The passage by Roethke and that by Browning are in lines of the same meter (iambic) and the same length (ten syllables). What makes the big difference in their rhythms is the running on, or lack of it.

To sum up: rhythm is recurrence. In poems, it is made of stresses and pauses. The poet can produce it by doing any of several things: making the intervals between stresses fixed or varied, long or short; indicating pauses (cesuras) within lines; end-stopping lines or running them over; writing in short or long lines. Rhythm in itself cannot convey meaning. And yet if a poet's words have meaning, their rhythm must be one with it.

[2]The complete poem, "I Knew a Woman," appears on page 598.

Gwendolyn Brooks (b. 1917)*

WE REAL COOL   1960

The Pool Players.
Seven at the Golden Shovel.

We real cool. We
Left school. We

Lurk late. We
Strike straight. We

Sing sin. We   5
Thin gin. We

Jazz June. We
Die soon.

QUESTION

Describe the rhythms of this poem. By what techniques are they produced?

Robert Frost (1874 – 1963)*

NEVER AGAIN WOULD BIRDS' SONG BE THE SAME   1942

He would declare and could himself believe
That the birds there in all the garden round
From having heard the daylong voice of Eve
Had added to their own an oversound,
Her tone of meaning but without the words.   5
Admittedly an eloquence so soft
Could only have had an influence on birds
When call or laughter carried it aloft.
Be that as may be, she was in their song.
Moreover her voice upon their voices crossed   10
Had now persisted in the woods so long
That probably it never would be lost.
Never again would birds' song be the same.
And to do that to birds was why she came.

QUESTIONS

1. Who is *he*?
2. In reading aloud line 9, do you stress *may*? (Do you say "as MAY be" or "as may BE"?) What guide do we have to the poet's wishes here?
3. Which lines does Frost cast mostly or entirely into monosyllables? How would you describe the impact of these lines?
4. In his *Essay on Criticism*, Alexander Pope made fun of poets who wrote mechanically, without wit: "And ten low words oft creep in one dull line." Do you think this criticism applicable to Frost's lines of monosyllables? Explain.

Ben Jonson (1573? – 1637)*

SLOW, SLOW, FRESH FOUNT, KEEP TIME
WITH MY SALT TEARS   1600

Slow, slow, fresh fount, keep time with my salt tears;
    Yet slower yet, oh faintly, gentle springs;
List to the heavy part the music bears,
    Woe weeps out her division° when she sings.   *a part in a song*
        Droop herbs and flowers,   5
        Fall grief in showers;
        Our beauties are not ours;
           Oh, I could still,
Like melting snow upon some craggy hill,
    Drop, drop, drop, drop,   10
Since nature's pride is now a withered daffodil.

SLOW, SLOW, FRESH FOUNT. The nymph Echo sings this lament over the youth Narcissus in Jonson's play *Cynthia's Revels*. In mythology, Nemesis, goddess of vengeance, to punish Narcissus for loving his own beauty, caused him to pine away and then transformed him into a narcissus (another name for a *daffodil*, line 11).

QUESTIONS

1. Read the first line aloud rapidly. Why is it difficult to do so?
2. Which lines rely most heavily on stressed syllables?
3. In general, how would you describe the rhythm of this poem? How is it appropriate to what is said?

Alexander Pope (1688 – 1744)*

ATTICUS   1735

How did they fume, and stamp, and roar, and chafe!
And swear, not Addison himself was safe.
    Peace to all such! but were there one whose fires
True genius kindles, and fair fame inspires;
Blest with each talent, and each art to please,   5
And born to write, converse, and live with ease,
Should such a man, too fond to rule alone,
Bear, like the Turk, no brother near the throne,
View him with scornful, yet with jealous eyes,
And hate for arts that caused himself to rise;   10
Damn with faint praise, assent with civil leer,
And, without sneering, teach the rest to sneer;
Willing to wound, and yet afraid to strike,
Just hint a fault, and hesitate dislike;
Alike reserved to blame, or to commend,   15
A timorous foe, and a suspicious friend;

Dreading e'en fools, by flatterers besieged,
And so obliging, that he ne'er obliged;
Like Cato, give his little Senate laws,
And sit attentive to his own applause: 20
While wits and Templars every sentence raise,
And wonder with a foolish face of praise —
Who but must laugh, if such a man there be?
Who would not weep, if Atticus were he?

ATTICUS. In this selection from "An Epistle to Dr. Arbuthnot," Pope has been referring to dull
versifiers and their angry reception of his satiric thrusts at them. With *Peace to all such!* (line 3)
he turns to his celebrated portrait of a rival man of letters, Joseph Addison. 19 *Cato:* Roman
senator about whom Addison had written a tragedy. 21 *Templars:* London lawyers who dabbled
in literature.

QUESTIONS

1. In these lines — one of the most famous damnations in English poetry — what
   positive virtues, in Pope's view, does Addison lack?
2. Which lines are end-stopped? What is the effect of these lines upon the rhythm of
   this passage? (Suggestion: Read "Atticus" aloud.)

EXERCISE: *Two Kinds of Rhythm*

The following compositions in verse have lines of similar length, yet they differ greatly
in rhythm. Explain how they differ and why.

Sir Thomas Wyatt (1503? – 1542)*

WITH SERVING STILL   (1528 – 1536)

With serving still°   *continually*
   This have I won,
For my goodwill
   To be undone;

And for redress   5
   Of all my pain,
Disdainfulness
   I have again°;   *in return*

And for reward
   Of all my smart   10
Lo, thus unheard,
   I must depart!

Wherefore all ye
   That after shall
By fortune be,   15
   As I am, thrall,

Example take
    What I have won,
Thus for her sake
    To be undone!   20

Dorothy Parker (1893 – 1967)

RÉSUMÉ   1926

Razors pain you;
Rivers are damp;
Acids stain you;
And drugs cause cramp.
Guns aren't lawful;   5
Nooses give;
Gas smells awful;
You might as well live.

METER

To enjoy the rhythms of a poem, no special knowledge of meter is necessary.
All you need do is pay attention to stresses and where they fall, and you will
perceive the basic pattern, if there is any. However, there is nothing occult
about the study of meter. Most people find they can master its essentials in no
more time than it takes to learn a complicated game such as chess. If you take
the time, you will then have the pleasure of knowing what is happening in the
rhythms of many a fine poem, and pleasurable knowledge may even deepen
your insight into poetry. The following discussion, then, will be of interest only
to those who care to go deeper into **prosody**, the study of metrical structures
in poetry.

Far from being artificial constructions found only in the minds of poets,
meters occur in everyday speech and prose. As the following example will show,
they may need only a poet to recognize them. The English satirist Max Beerbohm, after contemplating the title page of his first book, took his pen and
added two more lines.

Max Beerbohm (1872 – 1956)

ON THE IMPRINT OF THE FIRST ENGLISH EDITION OF
THE WORKS OF MAX BEERBOHM   (1896)

"London: JOHN LANE, *The Bodley Head*
    New York: Charles Scribner's Sons."
This plain announcement, nicely read,
    Iambically runs.

In everyday life, nobody speaks or writes in perfect iambic rhythm, except at moments: "a HAM on RYE and HIT the MUStard HARD!" (As we have seen, iambic rhythm consists of a series of syllables alternately unstressed and stressed.) Poets rarely speak in it for long, either — at least, not with absolute consistency. If you read aloud Max Beerbohm's lines, you'll hear an iambic rhythm, but not an unvarying one. And yet all of us speak with a rising and falling of stress *somewhat like* iambic meter. Perhaps, as the poet and scholar John Thompson has maintained, "The iambic metrical pattern has dominated English verse because it provides the best symbolic model of our language."[3]

To make ourselves aware of a meter, we need only listen to a poem, or sound its words to ourselves. If we care to work out exactly what a poet is doing, we *scan* a line or a poem by indicating the stresses in it. **Scansion**, the art of so doing, is not just a matter of pointing to syllables; it is also a matter of listening to a poem and making sense of it. To scan a poem is one way to indicate how to read it aloud; in order to see where stresses fall, you have to see the places where the poet wishes to put emphasis. That is why, when scanning a poem, you may find yourself suddenly understanding it.

An objection might be raised against scanning: isn't it too simple to pretend that all language (and poetry) can be divided neatly into stressed syllables and unstressed syllables? Indeed it is. As the linguist Otto Jespersen has said, "In reality there are infinite gradations of stress, from the most penetrating scream to the faintest whisper."[4] However, the idea in scanning a poem is not to reproduce the sound of a human voice. For that we would do better to buy a tape recorder. To scan a poem, rather, is to make a diagram of the stresses (and absences of stress) we find in it. Various marks are used in scansion; in this book we use ´ for a stressed syllable and ˘ for an unstressed syllable. Some scanners, wishing a little more precision, also use the **half-stress** (`); this device can be helpful in many instances when a syllable usually not stressed comes at a place where it takes some emphasis, as in the last syllable in a line:

Bound each to each with natˑuˑral piˑeˑty.

Here, with examples, are some of the principal meters we find in English poetry. Each is named for its basic **foot,** or molecule (usually one stressed and one or two unstressed syllables).

1. **Iambic** (foot: the **iamb,** ˘´):
   Thĕ fállˑĭng oút ŏf fáithˑfŭl friénds, rĕˑnéwˑĭng ĭs ŏf lóve

2. **Anapestic** (foot: the **anapest,** ˘˘´):
   Ĭ ăm mónˑărch ŏf áll Ĭ sŭrˑvéy

3. **Trochaic** (foot: the **trochee,** ´˘):
   Doúˑblĕ, doúˑblĕ, tóil ănd troúˑblĕ

[3]*The Founding of English Metre* (New York: Columbia UP, 1966) 12.
[4]"Notes on Metre," (1933), reprinted in *The Structure of Verse: Modern Essays on Prosody,* ed. Harvey Gross, 2nd ed. (New York: Echo Press, 1978).

4. **Dactylic** (foot: the **dactyl**, ´˘˘):

Táke hĕr ŭp tén·dĕr·lў

Iambic and anapestic meters are called **rising** meters because their movement rises from unstressed syllable (or syllables) to stress; trochaic and dactylic meters are called **falling**. In the twentieth century, the bouncing meters — anapestic and dactylic — have been used more often for comic verse than for serious poetry. Called feet, though they contain no unaccented syllables, are the **monosyllabic foot** (´) and the **spondee** (´´). Meters are not ordinarily made up of them; if one were, it would be like the steady impact of nails being hammered into a board — no pleasure to hear or to dance to. But inserted now and then, they can lend emphasis and variety to a meter, as Yeats well knew when he broke up the predominantly iambic rhythm of "Who Goes with Fergus?" (page 623) with the line,

Ănd thĕ whíte breást ŏf thĕ dím seá,

in which occur two spondees. Meters are classified also by line lengths: *trochaic monometer*, for instance, is a line one trochee long, as in this anonymous brief comment on microbes:

Adam
Had 'em.

A frequently heard metrical description is **iambic pentameter:** a line of five iambs, a meter especially familiar because it occurs in all blank verse (such as Shakespeare's plays and Milton's *Paradise Lost*), heroic couplets, and sonnets. The commonly used names for line lengths follow:

monometer	one foot	**pentameter**	five feet
dimeter	two feet	**hexameter**	six feet
trimeter	three feet	**heptameter**	seven feet
tetrameter	four feet	**octameter**	eight feet

Lines of more than eight feet are possible but are rare. They tend to break up into shorter lengths in the listening ear.

When Yeats chose the spondees *white breast* and *dim sea,* he was doing what poets who write in meter do frequently for variety — using a foot other than the expected one. Often such a substitution will be made at the very beginning of a line, as in the third line of this passage from Christopher Marlowe's *Tragical History of Doctor Faustus:*

Wăs thĭs thĕ fáce thăt láunched ă thoú·sănd shíps

Ănd búrnt thĕ tóp·lĕss tów'rs ŏf Íl·ĭ·um?

Sweét Hél·en, máke mĕ im·mór·tăl wíth ă kíss.

How, we might wonder, can that last line be called iambic at all? But it is, just as a waltz that includes an extra step or two, or leaves a few steps out, remains a waltz. In the preceding lines the basic iambic pentameter is established, and though in the third line the regularity is varied from, it does not altogether disappear. It continues for a while to run on in the reader's mind, where (if the poet does not stay away from it for too long) the meter will be when the poem comes back to it.

Like a basic dance step, a meter is not to be slavishly adhered to. The fun in reading a metrical poem often comes from watching the poet continually departing from perfect regularity, giving a few heel-kicks to display a bit of joy or ingenuity, then easing back into the basic step again. Because meter is orderly and the rhythms of living speech are unruly, poets can play one against the other, in a sort of counterpoint. Robert Frost, a master at pitting a line of iambs against a very natural-sounding and irregular sentence, declared, "I am never more pleased than when I can get these into strained relation. I like to drag and break the intonation across the meter as waves first comb and then break stumbling on a shingle."[5]

Evidently Frost's skilled effects would be lost to a reader who, scanning a Frost poem or reading it aloud, distorted its rhythms to fit the words exactly to the meter. With rare exceptions, a good poem can be read and scanned the way we would speak its sentences if they were ours. This, for example, is an unreal scansion:

That's mý lăst Dúch·ĕss páint·ĕd ón thĕ wáll.

— because no speaker of English would say that sentence in that way. We are likely to stress *That's* and *last*.

Variety in rhythm is not merely desirable in poetry, it is a necessity, and the poem that fails to depart often enough from absolute regularity is in trouble. If the beat of its words slips into a mechanical pattern, the poem marches robot-like right into its grave. Luckily, few poets, except writers of greeting cards, favor rhythms that go "a TROT a TROT a TROT a TROT" for very long. Robert Frost told an audience one time that if when writing a poem he found its rhythm becoming monotonous, he knew that the poem was going wrong and that he himself didn't believe what it was saying.

Although in good poetry we seldom meet a very long passage of absolute metrical regularity, we sometimes find (in a line or so) a monotonous rhythm that is effective. Words fall meaningfully in Macbeth's famous statement of world-weariness: "Tomorrow and tomorrow and tomorrow . . ." and in the opening lines of Thomas Gray's "Elegy":

The cŭr·fĕw tólls thĕ knéll ŏf párt·ĭng dáy,
The lów·ĭng hérd wĭnd slów·lў o'ér thĕ léa,
The plów·măn hóme·wărd plóds hĭs wéar·ў way,
Ănd léaves thĕ wórld tŏ dárk·nĕss ănd tŏ mé.[6]

Although certain unstressed syllables in these lines seem to call for more emphasis than others — you might, for instance, care to throw a little more

[5]Letter to John Cournos in 1914, in *Selected Letters of Robert Frost*, ed. Lawrance Thompson (New York: Holt, 1964) 128.
[6]The complete poem, "Elegy Written in a Country Churchyard," appears on page 264.

weight on the second syllable of *curfew* in the opening line — we can still say the lines are notably iambic. Their almost unvarying rhythm seems just right to convey the tolling of a bell and the weary setting down of one foot after the other.

Besides the two rising meters (iambic, anapestic) and the two falling meters (trochaic, dactylic), English poets have another valuable meter. It is **accentual meter,** in which the poet does not write in feet (as in the other meters) but instead counts accents (stresses). The idea is to have the same number of stresses in every line. The poet may place them anywhere in the line and may include practically any number of unstressed syllables, which do not count. In "Christabel," for instance, Coleridge keeps four stresses to a line, though the first line has only eight syllables and the last line has eleven:

> There is not wind e·nough to twirl
> The one red leaf, the last of its clan,
> That dan·ces as of·ten as dance it can,
> Hang·ing so light, and hang·ing so high,
> On the top-most twig that looks up at the sky.

The history of accentual meter is long and honorable. Old English poetry was written in a kind of accentual meter, but its line was more rule-bound than Coleridge's: four stresses arranged two on either side of a cesura, plus alliteration of three of the stressed syllables. In "Junk," Richard Wilbur revives the pattern:

> An axe an·gles ‖ from my neigh·bor's ash·can . . .

Many poets, from the authors of Mother Goose rimes to Gerard Manley Hopkins, have sometimes found accentual meters congenial.

It has been charged that the importation of Greek names for meters and of the classical notion of feet was an unsuccessful attempt to make a Parthenon out of English wattles. The charge is open to debate, but at least it is certain that Greek names for feet cannot mean to us what they meant to Aristotle. Greek and Latin poetry is measured not by stressed and unstressed syllables but by long and short vowel sounds. An iamb in classical verse is one short syllable followed by a long syllable. Such a meter constructed on the principle of vowel length is called a **quantitative meter.** Campion's "Rose-cheeked Laura" was an attempt to demonstrate it in English, but probably we enjoy the rhythm of the poem's well-placed stresses whether or not we notice its vowel sounds.

Thomas Campion (1567 – 1620)*

ROSE-CHEEKED LAURA, COME   1602

Rose-cheeked Laura, come,
Sing thou smoothly with thy beauty's
Silent music, either other
      Sweetly gracing.

Lovely forms do flow   5
From concent° divinely framèd;   *harmony*
Heav'n is music, and thy beauty's
    Birth is heavenly.

These dull notes we sing
Discords need for helps to grace them;   10
Only beauty purely loving
    Knows no discord,

But still moves delight,
Like clear springs renewed by flowing,
Ever perfect, ever in them-   15
    Selves eternal.

Although less popular among poets today than formerly, meter endures. Major poets from Shakespeare through Yeats have fashioned their work by it, and if we are to read their poems with full enjoyment, we need to be aware of it. To enjoy metrical poetry — even to write it — you do not have to slice lines into feet; you do need to recognize when a meter is present in a line, and when the line departs from it. An argument in favor of meter is that it reminds us of body rhythms such as breathing, walking, the beating of the heart. In an effective metrical poem, these rhythms cannot be separated from what the poet is saying — or, in the words of an old jazz song, "It don't mean a thing if you ain't got that swing." As critic Paul Fussell has put it: "No element of a poem is more basic — and I mean physical — in its effect upon the reader than the metrical element, and perhaps no technical triumphs reveal more readily than the metrical the poet's sympathy with that universal human nature . . . which exists outside his own."[7]

Walter Savage Landor (1775 – 1864)

ON SEEING A HAIR OF LUCRETIA BORGIA   (1825)

Borgia, thou once wert almost too august
And high for adoration; now thou'rt dust.
All that remains of thee these plaits unfold,
Calm hair, meandering in pellucid gold.

QUESTIONS

1. Who was Lucretia Borgia and when did she live? Because of her reputation, what connotations does her name add to Landor's poem?
2. What does *meander* mean? How can a hair meander?

[7]*Poetic Meter and Poetic Form* (New York: Random, 1965) 110.

3. Scan the poem, indicating stressed syllables. What is the basic meter of most of the poem? What happens to this meter in the last line? Note especially *meandering in pel-*. How many light, unstressed syllables are there in a row? Does rhythm in any way reinforce what Landor is saying?

EXERCISE: *Meaningful Variation*

At what place or places in each of these passages does the poet depart from basic iambic meter? How does each departure help underscore the meaning?

1. John Dryden, "Mac Flecknoe" (speech of Flecknoe, prince of Nonsense, referring to Thomas Shadwell, poet and playwright):

    Shadwell alone of all my sons is he
    Who stands confirmed in full stupidity.
    The rest to some faint meaning make pretense,
    But Shadwell never deviates into sense.

2. Alexander Pope, *An Essay on Criticism:*

    A needless Alexandrine ends the song
    That, like a wounded snake, drags its slow length along.

3. Henry King, "The Exequy" (an apostrophe to his wife):

    'Tis true, with shame and grief I yield,
    Thou like the van° first tookst the field,   vanguard
    And gotten hath the victory
    In thus adventuring to die
    Before me, whose more years might crave
    A just precedence in the grave.
    But hark! my pulse like a soft drum
    Beats my approach, tells thee I come;
    And slow howe'er my marches be,
    I shall at last sit down by thee.

4. Henry Wadsworth Longfellow, "Mezzo Cammin":

    Half-way up the hill, I see the Past
        Lying beneath me with its sounds and sights, —
    A city in the twilight dim and vast,
        With smoking roofs, soft bells, and gleaming lights, —
    And hear above me on the autumnal blast
        The cataract of Death far thundering from the heights.

5. Wallace Stevens, "Sunday Morning":

    Deer walk upon our mountains, and the quail
    Whistle about us their spontaneous cries;
    Sweet berries ripen in the wilderness;
    And, in the isolation of the sky,
    At evening, casual flocks of pigeons make
    Ambiguous undulations as they sink,
    Downward to darkness, on extended wings.

EXERCISE: *Recognizing Rhythms*

Which of the following poems contain predominant meters? Which poems are not wholly metrical, but are metrical in certain lines? Point out any such lines. What reasons do you see, in such places, for the poet's seeking a metrical effect?

Edna St. Vincent Millay (1892 – 1950)*

COUNTING-OUT RHYME   1928

Silver bark of beech, and sallow
Bark of yellow birch and yellow
    Twig of willow.

Stripe of green in moosewood maple,
Color seen in leaf of apple,   5
    Bark of popple.

Wood of popple pale as moonbeam,
Wood of oak for yoke and barn-beam,
    Wood of hornbeam.

Silver bark of beech, and hollow   10
Stem of elder, tall and yellow
    Twig of willow.

A. E. Housman (1859 – 1936)*

WHEN I WAS ONE-AND-TWENTY   1896

When I was one-and-twenty
    I heard a wise man say,
"Give crowns and pounds and guineas
    But not your heart away;
Give pearls away and rubies   5
    But keep your fancy free."
But I was one-and-twenty,
    No use to talk to me.

When I was one-and-twenty
    I heard him say again,   10
"The heart out of the bosom
    Was never given in vain;
'Tis paid with sighs a plenty
    And sold for endless rue."
And I am two-and-twenty,   15
    And oh, 'tis true, 'tis true.

William Carlos Williams (1883 – 1963)*

THE DESCENT OF WINTER (SECTION 10/30)   1934

To freight cars in the air

all the slow
   clank, clank
   clank, clank
moving about the treetops   5

the
   wha, wha
of the hoarse whistle

   pah, pah, pah
   pah, pah, pah, pah, pah   10
   piece and piece
   piece and piece
moving still trippingly
through the morningmist

long after the engine   15
has fought by
        and disappeared
in silence
       to the left

Walt Whitman (1819 – 1892)*

BEAT! BEAT! DRUMS!   (1861)

Beat! beat! drums! — blow! bugles! blow!
Through the windows — through doors — burst like a ruthless force,
Into the solemn church, and scatter the congregation,
Into the school where the scholar is studying;
Leave not the bridegroom quiet — no happiness must he have now
   with his bride,   5
Nor the peaceful farmer any peace, ploughing his field or gathering
   his grain,
So fierce you whirr and pound you drums — so shrill you bugles
   blow.

Beat! beat! drums! — blow! bugles! blow!
Over the traffic of cities — over the rumble of wheels in the streets;
Are beds prepared for sleepers at night in the houses? no sleepers
   must sleep in those beds,   10

No bargainer's bargains by day — no brokers or speculators — would
    they continue?
Would the talkers be talking? would the singer attempt to sing?
Would the lawyer rise in the court to state his case before the judge?
Then rattle quicker, heavier drums — you bugles wilder blow.

Beat! beat! drums! — blow! bugles! blow!   15
Make no parley — stop for no expostulation,
Mind not the timid — mind not the weeper or prayer,
Mind not the old man beseeching the young man,
Let not the child's voice be heard, nor the mother's entreaties,
Make even the trestles to shake the dead where they lie awaiting the
    hearses.   20
So strong you thump O terrible drums — so loud you bugles blow.

Langston Hughes (1902–1967)*

DREAM BOOGIE   1951

Good morning, daddy!
Ain't you heard
The boogie-woogie rumble
Of a dream deferred?

Listen closely: 5
You'll hear their feet
Beating out and beating out a—

    You think
    It's a happy beat?

Listen to it closely: 10
Ain't you heard
something underneath
like a—

    What did I say?

Sure,   15
I'm happy!
Take it away!

    Hey, pop!
    Re-bop!
    Mop!   20

     Y-e-a-h!

Suggestions for Writing

1. When has a rhythm of any kind (whether or not in poetry) stirred you, picked you up, and carried you along with it? Write an account of your experience.
2. The fact that most contemporary poets have given up meter, in the view of Stanley Kunitz, has made poetry "easier to write, but harder to remember." Why so? Comment on Kunitz's remark, or quarrel with it, in two or three paragraphs.
3. Ponder Robert Frost's idea of "the sound of sense" (page 942). Then, in a paragraph or two, try to show what light this idea sheds upon Frost's "Never Again Would Birds' Song Be the Same" (or any other Frost poem in this book).

22   Closed Form, Open Form

Form, as a general idea, is the design of a thing as a whole, the configuration of all its parts. No poem can escape having some kind of form, whether its lines are as various in length as broomstraws, or all in hexameter. To put this point in another way: if you were to listen to a poem read aloud in a language unknown to you, or if you saw the poem printed in that foreign language, whatever in the poem you could see or hear would be the form of it.[1]

Writing in closed form, a poet follows (or finds) some sort of pattern, such as that of a sonnet with its rime scheme and its fourteen lines of iambic pentameter. On a page, poems in closed form tend to look regular and symmetrical, often falling into stanzas that indicate groups of rimes. Along with William Butler Yeats, who held that a successful poem will "come shut with a click, like a closing box," the poet who writes in closed form apparently strives for a kind of perfection — seeking, perhaps, to lodge words so securely in place that no word can be budged without a worsening. For the sake of meaning, though, a competent poet often will depart from a symmetrical pattern. As Robert Frost observed, there is satisfaction to be found in things not mechanically regular: "We enjoy the straight crookedness of a good walking stick."

The poet who writes in open form usually seeks no final click. Often, such a poet views the writing of a poem as a process, rather than a quest for an absolute. Free to use white space for emphasis, able to shorten or lengthen lines as the sense seems to require, the poet lets the poem discover its shape as it goes along, moving as water flows downhill, adjusting to its terrain, engulfing obstacles.

Most poetry of the past is in closed form, exhibiting at least a pattern of rime or meter, but since the early 1960s most American poets have preferred forms that stay open. Lately, the situation has been changing yet again, with

[1]For a good summary of the uses of the term form in criticism of poetry, see the article "Form" by G. N. G. Orsini in *Princeton Encyclopedia of Poetry and Poetics,* 2nd ed., eds. Preminger, Warnke, and Hardison (Princeton: Princeton UP, 1975).

closed form reappearing in much recent poetry. Whatever the fashion of the moment, the reader who seeks a wide understanding of poetry of both the present and the past will need to know both the closed and open varieties.

CLOSED FORM: BLANK VERSE, STANZA, SONNET

Closed form gives some poems a valuable advantage: it makes them more easily memorable. The **epic** poems of nations — long narratives tracing the adventures of popular heroes: the Greek *Iliad* and *Odyssey,* the French *Song of Roland,* the Spanish *Cid* — tend to occur in patterns of fairly consistent line length or number of stresses because these works were sometimes transmitted orally. Sung to the music of a lyre or chanted to a drumbeat, they may have been easier to memorize because of their patterns. If a singer forgot something, the song would have a noticeable hole in it, so rime or fixed meter probably helped prevent an epic from deteriorating when passed along from one singer to another. It is no coincidence that so many English playwrights of Shakespeare's day favored iambic pentameter. Companies of actors, often called upon to perform a different play daily, could count on a fixed line length to aid their burdened memories.

Some poets complain that closed form is a straitjacket, a limit to free expression. Other poets, however, feel that, like fires held fast in a narrow space, thoughts stated in a tightly binding form may take on a heightened intensity. "Limitation makes for power," according to one contemporary practitioner of closed form, Richard Wilbur; "the strength of the genie comes of his being confined in a bottle." Compelled by some strict pattern to arrange and rearrange words, delete, and exchange them, poets must focus on them the keenest attention. Often they stand a chance of discovering words more meaningful than the ones they started out with. And at times, in obedience to a rime scheme, the poet may be surprised by saying something quite unexpected. Composing a poem is like walking blindfolded down a dark road, with one's hand in the hand of an inexorable guide. With the conscious portion of the mind, the poet may wish to express what seems to be a good idea. But a line ending in *year* must be followed by another ending in *atmosphere, beer, bier, bombardier, cashier, deer, friction-gear, frontier,* or some other rime word that otherwise might not have entered the poem. That is why rime schemes and stanza patterns can be mighty allies and valuable disturbers of the unconscious. As Rolfe Humphries has said about strict form: "It makes you think of better things than you would all by yourself."

The best-known one-line pattern for a poem in English is **blank verse:** unrimed iambic pentameter. (This pattern is not a stanza: stanzas have more than one line.) Most portions of Shakespeare's plays are in blank verse, and so are Milton's *Paradise Lost,* Tennyson's "Ulysses," certain dramatic monologues of Browning and Frost, and thousands of other poems. Here is a poem in blank verse that startles us by dropping out of its pattern in the final line. Keats appears to have written it late in his life to his fiancée Fanny Brawne.

John Keats (1795 – 1821)*

THIS LIVING HAND, NOW WARM AND CAPABLE (1819?)

This living hand, now warm and capable
Of earnest grasping, would, if it were cold
And in the icy silence of the tomb,
So haunt thy days and chill thy dreaming nights
That thou wouldst wish thine own heart dry of blood   5
So in my veins red life might stream again,
And thou be conscience-calmed — see here it is —
I hold it towards you.

The **couplet** is a two-line stanza, usually rimed. Its lines often tend to be equal in length, whether short or long. Here are two examples:

Blow,
Snow!

As I in hoary winter's night stood shivering in the snow,
Surprised I was with sudden heat which made my heart to glow.

Actually, any pair of rimed lines that contains a complete thought is called a couplet, even if it is not a stanza, such as the couplet that ends a sonnet by Shakespeare. Unlike other stanzas, couplets are often printed solid, one couplet not separated from the next by white space. This practice is usual in printing the **heroic couplet** — or **closed couplet** — two rimed lines of iambic pentameter, the first ending in a light pause, the second more heavily end-stopped. George Crabbe, in *The Parish Register*, described a shotgun wedding:

Next at our altar stood a luckless pair,
Brought by strong passions and a warrant there:
By long rent cloak, hung loosely, strove the bride,
From every eye, what all perceived, to hide;
While the boy bridegroom, shuffling in his place,
Now hid awhile and then exposed his face.
As shame alternately with anger strove
The brain confused with muddy ale to move,
In haste and stammering he performed his part,
And looked the rage that rankled in his heart.

Though employed by Chaucer, the heroic couplet was named from its later use by Dryden and others in poems, translations of classical epics, and verse plays of epic heroes. It continued in favor through most of the eighteenth century. Much of our pleasure in reading good heroic couplets comes from the seemingly easy precision with which a skilled poet unites statements and strict pattern. In doing so, the poet may place a pair of words, phrases, clauses, or sentences side by side in agreement or similarity, forming a **parallel,** or in contrast and opposition, forming an **antithesis.** The effect is neat. For such skill in manipulating parallels and antitheses, John Denham's lines on the river Thames were much admired:

O could I flow like thee, and make thy stream
My great example, as it is my theme!
Though deep, yet clear; though gentle, yet not dull;
Strong without rage, without o'erflowing full.

These lines were echoed by Pope, ridiculing a poetaster, in two heroic couplets in *The Dunciad*:

Flow, Welsted, flow! like thine inspirer, Beer:
Though stale, not ripe; though thin, yet never clear;
So sweetly mawkish, and so smoothly dull;
Heady, not strong; o'erflowing, though not full.

Reading long poems in so exact a form, one may feel like a spectator at a ping-pong match unless the poet skillfully keeps varying rhythms. One way of escaping such metronome-like monotony is to keep the cesura (see page 644) shifting about from place to place—now happening early in a line, now happening late—and at times unexpectedly to hurl in a second or third cesura. This skill, among other things, distinguishes the work of Dryden and Pope. If you care to see it in action, try working through Dryden's elegy for Oldham (page 803) or Pope's acid portrait of Atticus (page 651), noticing where the cesuras fall. You'll find that the pauses skip around with lively variety.

A **tercet** is a group of three lines. If rimed, they usually keep to one rime sound, as in this anonymous English children's jingle:

Julius Caesar,
The Roman geezer,
Squashed his wife with a lemon-squeezer.

(That, by the way, is a great demonstration of surprising and unpredictable rimes.) **Terza rima,** the form Dante employs in *The Divine Comedy,* is made of tercets linked together by the rime scheme *a b a, b c b, c d c, d e d, e f e,* and so on. Harder to do in English than in Italian — with its greater resources of riming words — the form nevertheless has been managed by Shelley in "Ode to the West Wind" (with the aid of some slant rimes):

Make me thy lyre, even as the forest is:
What if my leaves are falling like its own!
The tumult of thy mighty harmonies

Will take from both a deep, autumnal tone,
Sweet though in sadness. Be thou, spirit fierce,
My spirit! Be thou me, impetuous one!

The workhorse of English stanzas is the **quatrain,** used for more rimed poems than any other form. It comes in many line lengths, and sometimes contains lines of varying length, as in the ballad stanza (see page 614).

Longer and more complicated stanzas are, of course, possible, but couplet, tercet, and quatrain have been called the building blocks of our poetry because most longer stanzas are made up of them. What short stanzas does John Donne mortar together to make the longer stanza of his "Song"?

John Donne (1572 – 1631)*

SONG   1633

Go and catch a falling star,
   Get with child a mandrake root,
Tell me where all past years are,
   Or who cleft the Devil's foot,
Teach me to hear mermaids singing,   5
   Or to keep off envy's stinging,
      And find
      What wind
Serves to advance an honest mind.

If thou be'st borne to strange sights,   10
   Things invisible to see,
Ride ten thousand days and nights,
   Till age snow white hairs on thee,
Thou, when thou return'st, wilt tell me
   All strange wonders that befell thee,   15
      And swear
      Nowhere
Lives a woman true, and fair.

If thou findst one, let me know,
   Such a pilgrimage were sweet —   20
Yet do not, I would not go,
   Though at next door we might meet;
Though she were true, when you met her,
   And last, till you write your letter,
      Yet she   25
      Will be
False, ere I come, to two, or three.

Recently in vogue is a form known as **syllabic verse**, in which the poet establishes a pattern of a certain number of syllables to a line. Either rimed or rimeless but usually stanzaic, syllabic verse has been hailed as a way for poets to escape "the tyranny of the iamb" and discover less conventional rhythms, since, if they take as their line length an *odd* number of syllables, then iambs, being feet of *two* syllables, cannot fit perfectly into it. Offbeat victories have been scored in syllabics by such poets as W. H. Auden, W. D. Snodgrass, Donald Hall, Thom Gunn, and Marianne Moore. A well-known syllabic poem is Dylan Thomas's "Fern Hill" (page 886). Notice its shape on the page, count the syllables in its lines, and you'll perceive its perfect symmetry. Although like playing a game, the writing of such a poem is apparently more than finger exercise: the discipline can help a poet to sing well, though (with Thomas) singing "in . . . chains like the sea."

Poets who write in demanding forms seem to enjoy taking on an arbitrary task for the fun of it, as ballet dancers do, or weightlifters. Much of our pleasure in reading such poems comes from watching words fall into a shape. It is the pleasure of seeing any hard thing done skillfully — a leap executed in a dance, a basketball swished through a basket. Still, to be excellent, a poem needs more than skill; and to enjoy a poem it isn't always necessary for the reader to be aware of the skill that went into it. Unknowingly, the editors of *The New Yorker* once printed an **acrostic** — a poem in which the initial letter of each line, read downward, spells out a word or words — that named (and insulted) a well-known anthologist. Evidently, besides being ingenious, the acrostic was a printable poem. In the Old Testament book of Lamentations, profoundly moving songs tell of the sufferings of the Jews after the destruction of Jerusalem. Four of the songs are written as an alphabetical acrostic, every stanza beginning with a letter of the Hebrew alphabet. However ingenious, such sublime poetry cannot be dismissed as merely witty; nor can it be charged that a poet who writes in such a form does not express deep feeling.

Patterns of sound and rhythm can, however, be striven after in a dull mechanical way, for which reason many poets today think them dangerous. Swinburne, who loved alliterations and tripping meters, had enough detachment to poke fun at his own excessive patterning:

> From the depth of the dreamy decline of the dawn through a notable
>   nimbus of nebulous noonshine,
>   Pallid and pink as the palm of the flag-flower that flickers with fear of
>   the flies as they float,
> Are the looks of our lovers that lustrously lean from a marvel of mystic
>   miraculous moonshine,
>   These that we feel in the blood of our blushes that thicken and
>   threaten with throbs through the throat?

This is bad, but bad deliberately. Viewed mechanically, as so many empty boxes somehow to be filled up, stanzas can impose the most hollow sort of discipline, and a poem written in these stanzas becomes no more than finger-exercise. If any good at all, a poem in a fixed pattern, such as a sonnet, is created not only by the craftsman's chipping away at it but by the explosion of a sonnet-shaped *idea*.

Ronald Gross (b. 1935)

Yield   1967

Yield.
No Parking.
Unlawful to Pass.
Wait for Green Light.
Yield.   5

Stop.
Narrow Bridge.
Merging Traffic Ahead
Yield.

Yield.   10

QUESTIONS

1. This poem by Ronald Gross is a "found poem." After reading it, how would you
   define **found poetry**?
2. Does "Yield" have a theme? If so, how would you state it?
3. What makes "Yield" mean more than traffic signs ordinarily mean to us?

Ronald Gross, who produces his "found poetry" by arranging prose from such
unlikely places as traffic signs and news stories into poem-like lines, has told of
making a discovery:

> As I worked with labels, tax forms, commercials, contracts, pin-up cap-
> tions, obituaries, and the like, I soon found myself rediscovering all the
> traditional verse forms in found materials: ode, sonnet, epigram, haiku,
> free verse. Such finds made me realize that these forms are not mere
> artifices, but shapes that language naturally takes when carrying powerful
> thoughts or feelings.[2]

Though Gross is a playful experimenter, his remark is true of serious
poetry. Traditional verse forms like sonnets and haiku aren't a lot of hollow
pillowcases for a poet to stuff with verbiage. At best, in the hands of a skilled
poet, they can be shapes into which living language seems to fall naturally.

It is fun to see words tumble gracefully into such a shape. Consider, for
instance, one famous "found poem," a sentence discovered in a physics textbook: "And so no force, however great, can stretch a cord, however fine, into
a horizontal line which shall be absolutely straight."[3] What a good clear sentence containing effective parallels ("however great . . . however fine"), you
might say, taking pleasure in it. Yet this plain statement gives extra pleasure
if arranged like this:

> And so no force, however great,
>   Can stretch a cord, however fine,
>   Into a horizontal line
> Which shall be absolutely straight.

So spaced, in lines that reveal its built-in rimes and rhythms, the sentence
would seem one of those "shapes that language naturally takes" that Ronald
Gross finds everywhere. (It is possible, of course, that the textbook writer was

[2]"Speaking of Books: Found Poetry," *The New York Times Book Review*, June 11, 1967. See also
Gross's *Pop Poems* (New York: Simon, 1967).
[3]William Whewell, *Elementary Treatise on Mechanics* (Cambridge, England, 1819).

gleefully planting a quatrain for someone to find; but perhaps it is more likely that he knew much rimed, metrical poetry by heart and couldn't help writing it unconsciously.) Inspired by pop artists who reveal fresh vistas in Brillo boxes and comic strips, found poetry has had a recent flurry of activity. Earlier practitioners include William Carlos Williams, whose long poem *Paterson* quotes historical documents and statistics. Prose, wrote Williams, can be a "laboratory" for poetry: "It throws up jewels which may be cleaned and grouped." Such a jewel may be the sentence Rosmarie Waldrop found in *The Joy of Cooking* and arranged as verse.

Rosmarie Waldrop (b. 1935)

THE RELAXED ABALONE   1970

Abalone, like inkfish,
needs prodigious pounding
if it has died in a state
of tension.

EXPERIMENT: *Finding a Poem*

In a newspaper, magazine, catalogue, textbook, or advertising throwaway, find a sentence or passage that (with a little artistic manipulation on your part) shows promise of becoming a poem. Copy it into lines like poetry, being careful to place what seem to be the most interesting words at the ends of lines to give them greatest emphasis. According to the rules of found poetry, you may excerpt, delete, repeat, and rearrange elements but not add anything. What does this experiment tell you about poetic form? About ordinary prose?

When we speak, with Ronald Gross, of "traditional verse forms," we usually mean **fixed forms.** If written in a fixed form a poem inherits from other poems certain familiar elements of structure: an unvarying number of lines, say, or a stanza pattern. In addition, it may display certain **conventions:** expected features such as themes, subjects, attitudes, or figures of speech. In medieval folk ballads a "milk-white steed" is a conventional figure of speech; and if its rider be a cruel and beautiful witch who kidnaps mortals, she is a conventional character. (*Conventional* doesn't necessarily mean uninteresting.)

In the poetry of western Europe and America, the **sonnet** is the fixed form that has attracted for the longest time the largest number of noteworthy practitioners. Originally an Italian form (*sonnetto:* "little song"), the sonnet owes much of its prestige to Petrarch (1304 – 1374), who wrote in it of his love for the unattainable Laura. So great was the vogue for sonnets in England at the end of the sixteenth century that a gentleman might have been thought a boor if he couldn't turn out a decent one. Not content to adopt merely the sonnet's fourteen-line pattern, English poets also tried on its conventional mask of the tormented lover. They borrowed some of Petrarch's similes (a lover's heart, for instance, is like a storm-tossed boat) and invented others. (If you would like more illustrations of Petrarchan conventions, see Shakespeare's sonnet on page 756.)

Soon after English poets imported the sonnet in the middle of the sixteenth century, they worked out their own rime scheme — one easier for them to follow than Petrarch's, which calls for a greater number of riming words than English can readily provide. (In Italian, according to an exaggerated report, practically everything rimes.) In the following **English sonnet,** sometimes called a **Shakespearean sonnet,** the rimes cohere in four clusters: *a b a b, c d c d, e f e f, g g.* Because a rime scheme tends to shape the poet's statements to it, the English sonnet has three places where the procession of thought is likely to turn in another direction. Within its form, a poet may pursue one idea throughout the three quatrains and then in the couplet end with a surprise.

Michael Drayton (1563 – 1631)

SINCE THERE'S NO HELP, COME LET US KISS AND PART   1619

Since there's no help, come let us kiss and part;
Nay, I have done, you get no more of me,
And I am glad, yea, glad with all my heart
That thus so cleanly I myself can free;
Shake hands for ever, cancel all our vows,   5
And when we meet at any time again,
Be it not seen in either of our brows
That we one jot of former love retain.
Now at the last gasp of Love's latest breath,
When, his pulse failing, Passion speechless lies,   10
When Faith is kneeling by his bed of death,
And Innocence is closing up his eyes,
   Now if thou wouldst, when all have given him over,
   From death to life thou mightst him yet recover.

Less frequently met in English poetry, the **Italian sonnet,** or **Petrarchan sonnet,** follows the rime scheme *a b b a, a b b a* in its first eight lines, the **octave,** and then adds new rime sounds in the last six lines, the **sestet.** The sestet may rime *c d c d c d, c d e c d e, c d c c d c,* or in almost any other variation that doesn't end in a couplet. This organization into two parts sometimes helps arrange the poet's thoughts. In the octave, the poet may state a problem, and then, in the sestet, may offer a resolution. A lover, for example, may lament all octave long that a loved one is neglectful, then in line 9 begin to foresee some outcome: the speaker will die, or accept unhappiness, or trust that the beloved will have a change of heart.

Elizabeth Barrett Browning (1806 – 1861)

GRIEF   1844

I tell you, hopeless grief is passionless;
    That only men incredulous of despair,
    Half-taught in anguish, through the midnight air
Beat upward to God's throne in loud access
Of shrieking and reproach. Full desertness   5
    In souls, as countries, lieth silent-bare
    Under the blanching, vertical eye-glare
Of the absolute Heavens. Deep-hearted man, express
Grief for the Dead in silence like to death:
    Most like a monumental statue set   10
In everlasting watch and moveless woe
Till itself crumble to the dust beneath.
    Touch it: the marble eyelids are not wet —
If it could weep, it could arise and go.

In this Italian sonnet, the division in thought comes a bit early — in the middle of line 8. Few English-speaking poets who have used the form seem to feel strictly bound by it.

"The sonnet," in the view of Robert Bly, a modern critic, "is where old professors go to die." And yet the use of the form by such twentieth-century poets as Yeats, Frost, Auden, Thomas, Pound, Cummings, Berryman, and Lowell suggests that it may be far from exhausted. Like the hero of the popular ballad "Finnegan's Wake," literary forms (though not professors) declared dead have a habit of springing up again. No law compels sonnets to adopt an exalted tone, or confines them to an Elizabethan vocabulary, as this sonnet by a contemporary poet makes clear.

R. S. Gwynn (b. 1948)

SCENES FROM THE PLAYROOM   1986

Now Lucy with her family of dolls
Disfigures Mother with an emery board,
While Charles, with match and rubbing alcohol,
Readies the struggling cat, for Chuck is bored.

The young ones pour more ink into the water   5
Through which the latest goldfish gamely swims,
Laughing, pointing at naked, neutered Father.
The toy chest is a Buchenwald of limbs.

Mother is so lovely; Father, so late.
The cook is off, yet dinner must go on.   10
With onions as her only cause for tears
She hacks the red meat from the slippery bone,
Setting the table, where the children wait,
Her grinning babies, clean behind the ears.

QUESTIONS

1. Explain the allusion to Buchenwald in line 8.
2. What do we know about this family and their life-style? What is revealed by the word *latest* (line 6)?
3. What do you think of these children and their parents? What does the poet think of them? By what details is his attitude made clear?

EXERCISE: *Knowing Two Kinds of Sonnet*

Find other sonnets in this book. Which are English in form? Which are Italian? Which are variations on either form or combinations of the two? You may wish to try your hand at writing both kinds of sonnet and experience the difference for yourself.

Oscar Wilde said that a cynic is "a man who knows the price of everything and the value of nothing." Such a terse, pointed statement is called an epigram. In poetry, however, an **epigram** is a form: "A short poem ending in a witty or ingenious turn of thought, to which the rest of the composition is intended to lead up" (according to the *Oxford English Dictionary*). Often it is a malicious gibe with an unexpected stinger in the final line — perhaps in the very last word:

Alexander Pope (1688 – 1744)*

EPIGRAM ENGRAVED ON THE COLLAR OF A DOG
WHICH I GAVE TO HIS ROYAL HIGHNESS   1738

I am his Highness' dog at Kew;
Pray tell me, sir, whose dog are you?

Cultivated by the Roman poet Martial — for whom the epigram was a short poem, sometimes satiric but not always — this form has been especially favored by English poets who love Latin. Few characteristics of the English epigram seem fixed. Its pattern tends to be brief and rimed, its tone playfully merciless.

Martial (A.D. 40?–102?)

READERS AND LISTENERS PRAISE MY BOOKS   A.D. 90

Readers and listeners praise my books;
You swear they're worse than a beginner's.
Who cares? I always plan my dinners
To please the diners, not the cooks.
— Translated by R. L. Barth

Sir John Harrington (1561?–1612)

OF TREASON   1618

Treason doth never prosper; what's the reason?
For if it prosper, none dare call it treason.

William Blake (1757–1827)*

HER WHOLE LIFE IS AN EPIGRAM   (1793)

Her whole life is an epigram: smack smooth°, and   *perfectly smooth*
    neatly penned,
Platted° quite neat to catch applause, with a sliding   *plaited, woven*
    noose at the end.

E. E. Cummings (1894–1962)*

A POLITICIAN   1944

a politician is an arse upon
which everyone has sat except a man

Langston Hughes (1902–1967)*

GREEN MEMORY   1951

A wonderful time—the War:
when money rolled in
and blood rolled out.

But blood
was far away
from here—

Money was near.

5

J. V. Cunningham (1911–1985)*

THIS *Humanist* WHOM NO BELIEFS CONSTRAINED   1947

This *Humanist* whom no beliefs constrained
Grew so broad-minded he was scatter-brained.

John Frederick Nims (b. 1914)*

CONTEMPLATION   1967

"I'm Mark's alone!" you swore. Given cause to doubt you,
I think less of you, dear. But more about you.

Stevie Smith (1902–1971)*

THIS ENGLISHWOMAN   1937

This Englishwoman is so refined
She has no bosom and no behind.

Robert Crawford (b. 1959)

MY IAMBIC PENTAMETER LINES   1986

Three drunks, a leg on one quite gone, bereft
Of sense, and traveling on five feet, all left.

Paul Ramsey (b. 1924)

A POET DEFENDED 1984

You claim his poems are garbage. Balderdash!
Garbage includes some meat. His poems are trash.

R. L. Barth (b. 1947)*

DEFINITION 1984

The epigram is not artillery,
Blockbusters, automatic weaponry,
Napalm or rockets; but, hunkered in mire,
The sniper-scoped guerilla's small-arms fire.

Bruce Bennett (b. 1940)

LEADER 1984

                A man shot himself
in the foot.

                "OW!" he howled,
hopping this way and
that. "Do something!
Do something!"   5

                "We are! We are!"
shouted those around
him. "We're hopping!
We're hopping!"   10

EXPERIMENT: *Expanding an Epigram*

Rewrite any of the preceding epigrams, taking them out of rime (if they are in rime) and adding a few more words to them. See if your revisions have nearly the same effect as the originals.

EXERCISE: *Reading for Couplets*

Read all the sonnets by Shakespeare in this book. How do the final couplets of some of them resemble epigrams? Does this similarity diminish their effect of "seriousness"?

In English the only other fixed form to rival the sonnet and the epigram in favor is the **limerick:** five anapestic lines usually riming *a a b b a.* Here is a sample, attributed to W. R. Inge (1860 – 1954):

> There was an old man of Khartoum
> Who kept a tame sheep in his room,
>> "To remind me," he said,
>> "Of someone who's dead,
> But I never can recollect whom."

The limerick was made popular by Edward Lear (1812 – 1888), English painter and author of nonsense, whose own custom was to make the last line hark back to the first: "That oppressive old man of Khartoum."

EXPERIMENT: *Contriving a Clerihew*

The **clerihew,** a fixed form named for its inventor, Edmund Clerihew Bentley (1875 – 1956), has straggled behind the limerick in popularity. Here are four examples: how would you define the form and what are its rules? Who or what is its conventional subject matter? Try writing your own example.

> James Watt
> Was the hard-boiled kind of Scot:
> He thought any dream
> Sheer waste of steam.
>> — W. H. Auden

> Sir Christopher Wren
> Said, "I am going to dine with some men.
> If anybody calls
> Say I am designing St. Paul's."
>> — Edmund Clerihew Bentley

> Etienne de Silhouette
> (It's a good bet)
> Has the shadiest claim
> To fame.
>> — Cornelius J. Ter Maat

Dylan Thomas (1914 – 1953)*

DO NOT GO GENTLE INTO THAT GOOD NIGHT   1952

Do not go gentle into that good night,
Old age should burn and rave at close of day;
Rage, rage against the dying of the light.

Though wise men at their end know dark is right,
Because their words had forked no lightning they   5
Do not go gentle into that good night.

Good men, the last wave by, crying how bright
Their frail deeds might have danced in a green bay,
Rage, rage against the dying of the light.

Wild men who caught and sang the sun in flight,   10
And learn, too late, they grieved it on its way,
Do not go gentle into that good night.

Grave men, near death, who see with blinding sight
Blind eyes could blaze like meteors and be gay,
Rage, rage against the dying of the light.   15

And you, my father, there on the sad height,
Curse, bless, me now with your fierce tears, I pray,
Do not go gentle into that good night.
Rage, rage against the dying of the light.

QUESTIONS

1. "Do not go gentle into that good night" is a **villanelle:** a fixed form originated by French courtly poets of the Middle Ages. What are its rules?
2. Is Thomas's poem, like many another villanelle, just an elaborate and trivial exercise? Whom does the poet address? What is he saying?

OPEN FORM

Writing in **open form**, a poet seeks to discover a fresh and individual arrangement for words in every poem. Such a poem, generally speaking, has neither a rime scheme nor a basic meter informing the whole of it. Doing without those powerful (some would say hypnotic) elements, the poet who writes in open form relies on other means to engage and to sustain the reader's attention. Novice poets often think that open form looks easy, not nearly so hard as riming everything; but in truth, formally open poems are easy to write only if written carelessly. To compose lines with keen awareness of open form's demands, and of its infinite possibilities, calls for skill: at least as much as that needed to write in meter and rime, if not more. Should the poet succeed, then the discovered arrangement will seem exactly right for what the poem is saying. Words will seem at home in their positions, as naturally as the words of a decent sonnet.

Denise Levertov (b. 1923)*

SIX VARIATIONS (PART III)   1961

Shlup, shlup, the dog
as it laps up
water
makes intelligent
music, resting   5
now and then to take breath in irregular
measure.

Open form, in this brief poem, affords Denise Levertov certain advantages. Able to break off a line at whatever point she likes (a privilege not available to the poet writing, say, a conventional sonnet, who has to break off each line after its tenth syllable), she selects her pauses artfully. Line-breaks lend emphasis: a word or phrase at the end of a line takes a little more stress (and receives a little more attention), because the ending of the line compels the reader to make a slight pause, if only for the brief moment it takes to sling back one's eyes (like a typewriter carriage) and fix them on the line following. Slight pauses, then, follow the words and phrases *the dog / laps up / water / intelligent / resting / irregular / measure* — all of these being elements that apparently the poet wishes to call our attention to. (The pause after a line-break also casts a little more weight upon the *first* word or phrase of each succeeding line.) Levertov makes the most of white space — another means of calling attention to things, as any good picture-framer knows. By setting a word all alone on a line (*water / measure*), she makes it stand out more than it would do in a line of pentameter. She feels free to include a bit of rime (*Shlup, shlup / up*). She creates rhythms: if you will read aloud the phrases *intelligent / music* and *irregular / measure,* you will sense that in each phrase the arrangement of pauses and stresses is identical. Like the dog's halts to take breath, the lengths of the lines seem naturally irregular. The result is a fusion of meaning and form: indeed, an "intelligent music."

Poetry in open form used to be called **free verse** (from the French **vers libre**), suggesting a kind of verse liberated from the shackles of rime and meter. "Writing free verse," said Robert Frost, who wasn't interested in it, "is like playing tennis with the net down." And yet, as Denise Levertov and many other poets demonstrate, high scores can be made in such an unconventional game, provided it doesn't straggle all over the court. For a successful poem in open form, the term *free verse* seems inaccurate. "Being an art form," said William Carlos Williams, "verse cannot be 'free' in the sense of having *no* limitations or guiding principles."[4] Various substitute names have been suggested: organic poetry, composition by field, raw (as against cooked) poetry, open form poetry. "But what does it matter what you call it?" remark the editors of an anthology called *Naked Poetry.* The best poems of the last twenty years "don't rhyme (usually) and don't move on feet of more or less equal duration (usually). That nondescription moves toward the only technical principle they all have in common."[5]

And yet many poems in open form have much more in common than absences and lacks. One positive principle has been Ezra Pound's famous suggestion that poets "compose in the sequence of the musical phrase, not in the sequence of the metronome" — good advice, perhaps, even for poets who write inside fixed forms. In Charles Olson's influential theory of **projective verse**, poets compose by listening to their own breathing. On paper, they indicate the rhythms of a poem by using a little white space or a lot, a slight

[4]"Free Verse," article in *Princeton Encyclopedia of Poetry and Poetics.*
[5]Stephen Berg and Robert Mezey, eds., foreword to *Naked Poetry: Recent American Poetry in Open Forms* (Indianapolis: Bobbs, 1969).

indentation or a deep one, depending on whether a short pause or a long one is intended. Words can be grouped in clusters on the page (usually no more words than a lungful of air can accommodate). Heavy cesuras are sometimes shown by breaking a line in two and lowering the second part of it.[6] (An Olson poem appears on page 692.)

To the poet working in open form, no less than to the poet writing a sonnet, line length can be valuable. Walt Whitman, who loved to expand vast sentences for line after line, knew well that an impressive rhythm can accumulate if the poet will keep long lines approximately the same length, causing a pause to recur at about the same interval after every line. Sometimes, too, Whitman repeats the same words at each line's opening. An instance is the masterly sixth section of "When Lilacs Last in the Dooryard Bloom'd," an elegy for Abraham Lincoln:

> Coffin that passes through lanes and streets,
> Through day and night with the great cloud darkening the land,
> With the pomp of the inloop'd flags with the cities draped in black,
> With the show of the States themselves as of crape-veil'd women standing,
> With processions long and winding and the flambeaus of the night,
> With the countless torches lit, with the silent sea of faces and the unbared
>   heads,
> With the waiting depot, the arriving coffin, and the somber faces,
> With dirges through the night, with the thousand voices rising strong and
>   solemn,
> With all the mournful voices of the dirges pour'd around the coffin,
> The dim-lit churches and the shuddering organs — where amid these you
>   journey,
> With the tolling tolling bells' perpetual clang,
> Here, coffin that slowly passes,
> I give you my sprig of lilac.

There is music in such solemn, operatic arias. Whitman's lines echo another model: the Hebrew **psalms**, or sacred songs, as translated in the King James Version of the Bible. In Psalm 150, repetition also occurs inside of lines:

> Praise ye the Lord. Praise God in his sanctuary: praise him in the firmament of his power.
> Praise him for his mighty acts: praise him according to his excellent greatness.
> Praise him with the sound of the trumpet: praise him with the psaltery and harp.
> Praise him with the timbrel and dance: praise him with stringed instruments and organs.
> Praise him upon the loud cymbals: praise him upon the high sounding cymbals.
> Let every thing that hath breath praise the Lord. Praise ye the Lord.

[6]See Olson's essays "Projective Verse" and "Letter to Elaine Feinstein" in *Selected Writings*, edited by Robert Creeley (New York: New Directions, 1966). Olson's letters to Cid Corman are fascinating: *Letters for Origin, 1950 – 1955*, edited by Albert Glover (New York: Grossman, 1970).

In Biblical Psalms, we are in the presence of (as Robert Lowell has said) "supreme poems, written when their translators merely intended prose and were forced by the structure of their originals to write poetry."[7]

Whitman was a more deliberate craftsman than he let his readers think, and to anyone interested in writing in open form, his work will repay close study. He knew that repetitions of any kind often make memorable rhythms, as in this passage from "Song of Myself," with every line ending on an *-ing* word (a stressed syllable followed by an unstressed syllable):

> Here and there with dimes on the eyes walking,
> To feed the greed of the belly the brains liberally spooning,
> Tickets buying, taking, selling, but in to the feast never once going,
> Many sweating, ploughing, thrashing, and then the chaff for payment
> receiving,
> A few idly owning, and they the wheat continually claiming.

Much more than simply repetition, of course, went into the music of those lines — the internal rime *feed, greed,* the use of assonance, the trochees that begin the third and fourth lines, whether or not they were calculated.

In such classics of open form poetry, sound and rhythm are positive forces. When speaking a poem in open form, you often may find that it makes a difference for the better if you pause at the end of each line. Try pausing there, however briefly; but don't allow your voice to drop. Read just as you would normally read a sentence in prose (except for the pauses, of course). Why do the pauses matter? Open form poetry usually has no meter to lend it rhythm. *Some* lines in an open form poem, as we have seen in Whitman's "dimes on the eyes" passage, do fall into metrical feet; sometimes the whole poem does. Usually lacking meter's aid, however, open form, in order to have more and more noticeable rhythms, has need of all the recurring pauses it can get. When reading their own work aloud, open form poets like Robert Creeley and Allen Ginsberg often pause very definitely at each line break. Such a habit makes sense only in reading artful poems.

Some poems, to be sure, seem more widely open in form than others. A poet, for instance, may employ rime, but have the rimes recur at various intervals; or perhaps rime lines of various lengths. (See T. S. Eliot's famous "Love Song of J. Alfred Prufrock" on page 806. Is it a closed poem left ajar or an open poem trying to slam itself?) No law requires a poet to split thoughts into verse lines at all. Charles Baudelaire, Rainer Maria Rilke, Jorge Luis Borges, Alexander Solzhenitsyn, T. S. Eliot, and many others have written **prose poems**, in which, without caring that eye appeal and some of the rhythm of a line structure may be lost, the poet prints words in a block like a prose paragraph. For an example see Karl Shapiro's "The Dirty Word" (page 873).[8]

"Farewell, stale pale skunky pentameters (the only honest English meter, gloop! gloop!)," Kenneth Koch has gleefully exclaimed, suggesting that it was high time

---

[7]"On Freedom in Poetry," in Berg and Mezey, *Naked Poetry.*
[8]For more examples see *The Prose Poem, An International Anthology,* edited by Michael Benedikt (New York: Dell, 1976).

to junk such stale conventions. Many poets who agree with him believe that it is wrong to fit words into any pattern that already exists, and instead believe in letting a poem seek its own shape as it goes along. (Traditionalists might say that that is what all good poems do anyway: sonnets rarely know they are going to be sonnets until the third line has been written. However, there is no doubt that the sonnet form already exists, at least in the back of the head of any poet who has ever read sonnets.) Some open form poets offer a historical motive: they want to reflect the nervous, staccato, disconnected pace of our bumper-to-bumper society. Others see open form as an attempt to suit thoughts and words to a more spontaneous order than the traditional verse forms allow. "Better," says Gary Snyder, quoting from Zen, "the perfect, easy discipline of the swallow's dip and swoop, 'without east or west.' "[9]

At the moment, much exciting new poetry is being written in both open form and closed. Today, many younger poets (labeled New Formalists) have taken up rime and meter and have been writing sonnets, epigrams, and poems in rimed stanzas, giving "pale skunky pentameters" a fresh lease on life.[10]

E. E. Cummings (1894 – 1962)*

BUFFALO BILL 'S   1923

Buffalo Bill 's
defunct
        who used to
        ride a watersmooth-silver
                                    stallion   5
and break onetwothreefourfive pigeonsjustlikethat
                                            Jesus
he was a handsome man
                        and what i want to know is
how do you like your blueeyed boy   10
Mister Death

QUESTION

Cummings's poem would look like this if given conventional punctuation and set in a solid block like prose:

Buffalo Bill's defunct, who used to ride a water-smooth silver stallion and break one, two, three, four, five pigeons just like that. Jesus, he was a handsome man. And what I want to know is: "How do you like your blue-eyed boy, Mister Death?"

If this were done, by what characteristics would it still be recognizable as poetry? But what would be lost?

[9]"Some Yips & Barks in the Dark," in Berg and Mezey, *Naked Poetry*.
[10]For more samples of recent formal poetry than this book provides, see *The Direction of Poetry* ed. Robert Richman (Boston: Houghton, 1988), *Ecstatic Occasions, Expedient Forms* ed. David Lehman (New York: Collier, 1987), and *Strong Measures: Contemporary American Poetry in Traditional Forms* ed. Philip Dacey and David Jauss (New York: Harper, 1986).

Emily Dickinson (1830 – 1886)*

VICTORY COMES LATE   (1861)

Victory comes late –
And is held low to freezing lips –
Too rapt with frost
To take it –
How sweet it would have tasted –   5
Just a Drop –
Was God so economical?
His Table's spread too high for Us –
Unless We dine on tiptoe –
Crumbs – fit such little mouths –   10
Cherries – suit Robins –
The Eagle's Golden Breakfast strangles – Them –
God keep His Oath to Sparrows –
Who of little Love – know how to starve –

QUESTIONS

1. In this specimen of poetry in open form, can you see any other places at which the poet might have broken off any of her lines? To place a word last in a line gives it a greater emphasis; she might, for instance, have ended line 12 with *Breakfast* and begun a new line with the word *strangles*. Do you think she knows what she is doing here or does the pattern of this poem seem decided by whim? Discuss.
2. Read the poem aloud. Try pausing for a fraction of a second at every dash. Is there any justification for the poet's unorthodox punctuation?

"THE KERMESS" by Pieter Brueghel (1520?–1569)

William Carlos Williams (1883 – 1963)*

THE DANCE   1944

In Brueghel's great picture, The Kermess,
the dancers go round, they go round and
around, the squeal and the blare and the
tweedle of bagpipes, a bugle and fiddles
tipping their bellies (round as the thick-   5
sided glasses whose wash they impound)
their hips and their bellies off balance
to turn them. Kicking and rolling about
the Fair Grounds, swinging their butts, those
shanks must be sound to bear up under such   10
rollicking measures, prance as they dance
in Brueghel's great picture, The Kermess.

THE DANCE. Brueghel, a Flemish painter known for his scenes of peasant activities, represented in "The Kermess" a celebration on the feast day of a local patron saint.

QUESTIONS

1. Scan this poem and try to describe the effect of its rhythms.
2. Williams, widely admired for his free verse, insisted for many years that what he sought was a form not in the least bit free. What effect does he achieve by ending lines on such weak words as the articles *and* and *the*? By splitting *thick- / sided*? By splitting a prepositional phrase with the break at the end of line 8? By using line breaks to split *those* and *such* from what they modify? What do you think he is trying to convey?
3. Is there any point in his making line 12 a repetition of the opening line?
4. Look at the reproduction of Brueghel's painting "The Kermess" (also called "Peasants Dancing"). Aware that the rhythms of dancers, the rhythms of a painting, and the rhythms of a poem are not all the same, can you put in your own words what Breughel's dancing figures have in common with Williams's descriptions of them?
5. Compare with "The Dance" another poem that refers to a Brueghel painting: W. H. Auden's "Musée des Beaux Arts" on page 783. What seems to be each poet's main concern: to convey in words a sense of the painting, or to visualize the painting in order to state some theme?

Stephen Crane (1871 – 1900)

THE HEART   1895

In the desert
I saw a creature, naked, bestial,
Who, squatting upon the ground,
Held his heart in his hands,
And ate of it.   5

I said, "Is it good, friend?"
"It is bitter — bitter," he answered;
"But I like it
Because it is bitter,
And because it is my heart."   10

Walt Whitman (1819 – 1892)*

CAVALRY CROSSING A FORD   (1865)

A line in long array where they wind betwixt green islands,
They take a serpentine course, their arms flash in the sun — hark to
      the musical clank,
Behold the silvery river, in it the splashing horses loitering stop to
      drink,
Behold the brown-faced men, each group, each person a picture, the
      negligent rest on the saddles,
Some emerge on the opposite bank, others are just entering the
      ford — while,   5
Scarlet and blue and snowy white,
The guidon flags flutter gayly in the wind.

QUESTIONS
The following nit-picking questions are intended to help you see exactly what makes
these two open form poems by Crane and Whitman so different in their music.
1. What devices of sound occur in Whitman's phrase *silvery river* (line 3)? Where else
   in his poem do you find these devices?
2. Does Crane use any such devices?
3. In number of syllables, Whitman's poem is almost twice as long as Crane's. Which
   poem has more pauses in it? (Count pauses at the ends of lines, at marks of punctuation.)
4. Read the two poems aloud. In general, how would you describe the effect of their
   sounds and rhythms? Is Crane's poem necessarily an inferior poem for having less
   music?

Wallace Stevens (1879 – 1955)*

THIRTEEN WAYS OF LOOKING AT A BLACKBIRD   1923

I

Among twenty snowy mountains,
The only moving thing
Was the eye of the blackbird.

II

I was of three minds,
Like a tree
In which there are three blackbirds.

III

The blackbird whirled in the autumn winds.
It was a small part of the pantomime.

IV

A man and a woman
Are one.
A man and a woman and a blackbird
Are one.

V

I do not know which to prefer,
The beauty of inflections
Or the beauty of innuendoes,
The blackbird whistling
Or just after.

VI

Icicles filled the long window
With barbaric glass.
The shadow of the blackbird
Crossed it, to and fro.
The mood
Traced in the shadow
An indecipherable cause.

VII

O thin men of Haddam,
Why do you imagine golden birds?
Do you not see how the blackbird
Walks around the feet
Of the women about you?

VIII

I know noble accents
And lucid, inescapable rhythms;
But I know, too,
That the blackbird is involved
In what I know.

IX

When the blackbird flew out of sight,
It marked the edge
Of one of many circles.

X

At the sight of blackbirds
Flying in a green light,
Even the bawds of euphony
Would cry out sharply.

XI

He rode over Connecticut
In a glass coach.
Once, a fear pierced him,
In that he mistook
The shadow of his equipage
For blackbirds.

XII

The river is moving.
The blackbird must be flying.

XIII

It was evening all afternoon.
It was snowing
And it was going to snow.
The blackbird sat
In the cedar-limbs.

THIRTEEN WAYS OF LOOKING AT A BLACKBIRD. 25 *Haddam:* This Biblical-sounding name is that of a town in Connecticut.

QUESTIONS

1. What is the speaker's attitude toward the men of Haddam? What attitude toward this world does he suggest they lack? What is implied by calling them *thin* (line 25)?

2. What do the landscapes of winter contribute to the poem's effectiveness? If Stevens had chosen images of summer lawns, what would have been lost?

3. In which sections of the poem does Stevens suggest that a unity exists between human being and blackbird, between blackbird and the entire natural world? Can we say that Stevens "philosophizes"? What role does imagery play in Stevens's statement of his ideas?

4. What sense can you make of Part X? Make an enlightened guess.

5. Consider any one of the thirteen parts. What patterns of sound and rhythm do you find in it? What kind of structure does it have?

6. If the thirteen parts were arranged in some different order, would the poem be just as good? Or can we find a justification for its beginning with Part I and ending with Part XIII?

7. Does the poem seem an arbitrary combination of thirteen separate poems? Or is there any reason to call it a whole?

Gary Gildner (b. 1938)

First Practice   1969

After the doctor checked to see
we weren't ruptured,
the man with the short cigar took us
under the grade school,
where we went in case of attack   5
or storm, and said
he was Clifford Hill, he was
a man who believed dogs
ate dogs, he had once killed
for his country, and if   10
there were any girls present
for them to leave now.
           No one
left. OK, he said, he said I take
that to mean you are hungry
men who hate to lose as much   15
as I do. OK. Then
he made two lines of us
facing each other,
and across the way, he said,
is the man you hate most   20
in the world,
and if we are to win
that title I want to see how.
But I don't want to see
any marks when you're dressed,   25
he said. He said, *Now.*

1. What do you make of Hill and his world-view?
2. How does the speaker reveal his own view? Why, instead of quoting Hill directly ("This is a dog-eat-dog world"), does he call him *a man who believed dogs ate dogs* (lines 8 – 9)?
3. What effect is made by breaking off and lowering *No one* at the end of line 12?
4. What is gained by having a rime on the poem's last word?
5. For the sake of understanding how right the form of Gildner's poem is for it, imagine the poem in meter and a rime scheme, and condensed into two stanzas:

> Then he made two facing lines of us
> And he said, Across the way,
> Of all the men there are in the world
> Is the man you most want to slay,
>
> And if we are to win that title, he said,
> I want you to show me how.
> But I don't want to see any marks when you're dressed,
> He said. Go get him. *Now.*

Why would that rewrite be so unfaithful to what Gildner is saying?
6. How would you answer someone who argued, "This can't be a poem — its subject is ugly and its language isn't beautiful"?

Michael Heffernan (b. 1942)

LIVING ROOM   1988

Christmas Eve at Beitzinger's Hardware
John & Phil had bourbon in the backroom for the customers
along with a cooker full of braised raccoon.

I would have eaten some, only Bill Allen,
who was in there replumbing his toilet,   5
said This coon is a little blue,

and John had referred to cooking it long enough
to get the strangeness out.
So I drank my bourbon and stepped into the light

on Broadway and went next door to buy   10
Kathy a wristwatch from Bud Benelli,
who was delighted to see me buy something for a change.

The great thing is, I thought,
that down here in the real world nobody's gods win
and nobody's demons either.   15

Which is why Phil had placed that poor beast's forepaw
on a piece of hardcrust bread
and laid it in the scalepan where they weigh the nails

and Uncle Bud had seen fit that she should come
into the living room with that watch on   20
dancing to something on the radio.

QUESTIONS

1. What do you take to be the setting of this poem? Is this Broadway, New York? Point to evidence.
2. What contrasts do you find between the feast in the backroom and what followed after the speaker "stepped into the light"?
3. In your own words, what is the theme of the poem? Where is this theme summed up? How do the last two stanzas illustrate it?
4. Comment on the form of this poem. How does it differ from prose?

FOR REVIEW AND FURTHER STUDY

Leigh Hunt (1784 – 1859)

RONDEAU   1838

Jenny kissed me when we met,
    Jumping from the chair she sat in;
Time, you thief, who love to get
    Sweets into your list, put that in:
Say I'm weary, say I'm sad,   5
    Say that health and wealth have missed me,
Say I'm growing old, but add,
    Jenny kissed me.

QUESTION

Here is a fresh contemporary version of Hunt's "Rondeau" that yanks open the form of the rimed original:

Jenny kissed me when we met,
jumping from her chair;
Time, you thief, who love to add
sweets into your list, put that in:
say I'm weary, say I'm sad,
say I'm poor and in ill health,
say I'm growing old — but note, too,
Jenny kissed me.

That revised version says approximately the same thing as Hunt's original, doesn't it? Why is it less effective?

Keith Waldrop (b. 1932)*

PROPOSITION II   1975

Each grain of sand has an architecture, but
a desert displays the structure of the wind.

QUESTIONS

1. How is this poem like an epigram?
2. How is it dissimilar?

Elizabeth Bishop (1911 – 1979)*

SESTINA   1965

September rain falls on the house.
In the failing light, the old grandmother
sits in the kitchen with the child
beside the Little Marvel Stove,
reading the jokes from the almanac,   5
laughing and talking to hide her tears.

She thinks that her equinoctial tears
and the rain that beats on the roof of the house
were both foretold by the almanac,
but only known to a grandmother.   10
The iron kettle sings on the stove.
She cuts some bread and says to the child,

It's time for tea now; but the child
is watching the teakettle's small hard tears
dance like mad on the hot black stove,   15
the way the rain must dance on the house.
Tidying up, the old grandmother
hangs up the clever almanac

on its string. Birdlike, the almanac
hovers half open above the child,   20
hovers above the old grandmother
and her teacup full of dark brown tears.
She shivers and says she thinks the house
feels chilly, and puts more wood in the stove.

It was to be, says the Marvel Stove.   25
I know what I know, says the almanac.
With crayons the child draws a rigid house
and a winding pathway. Then the child
puts in a man with buttons like tears
and shows it proudly to the grandmother.   30

But secretly, while the grandmother
busies herself about the stove,
the little moons fall down like tears

from between the pages of the almanac
into the flower bed the child   35
has carefully placed in the front of the house.

Time to plant tears, says the almanac.
The grandmother sings to the marvellous stove
and the child draws another inscrutable house.

SESTINA. As its title indicates, this poem is written in the trickiest of medieval fixed forms, that of
the **sestina** (or "song of sixes"), said to have been invented in Provence in the thirteenth century
by the troubadour poet Arnaut Daniel. In six six-line stanzas, the poet repeats six end-words (in
a prescribed order), then reintroduces the six repeated words (in any order) in a closing **envoy**
of three lines. Elizabeth Bishop strictly follows the troubadour rules for the order in which the
end-words recur. (If you care, you can figure out the formula: in the first stanza, the six words are
arranged A B C D E F; in the second, F A E B D C; and so on.) Notable sestinas in English have
been written also by Sir Philip Sidney, Algernon Charles Swinburne, and Rudyard Kipling, more
recently by Ezra Pound ("Sestina: Altaforte"), by W. H. Auden ("Hearing of Harvests Rotting in
the Valleys" and others), and by contemporary poets, among them John Ashbery, Dana Gioia,
Marilyn Hacker, Michael Heffernan, Donald Justice, Peter Klappert, William Meredith, Howard
Nemerov, John Frederick Nims, Robert Pack, Henry Taylor, and Mona Van Duyn.

QUESTIONS

1. A perceptive comment from a student: "Something seems to be going on here that
   the child doesn't understand. Maybe some terrible loss has happened." Test this
   guess by reading the poem closely.
2. Then consider this possibility. We don't know that "Sestina" is autobiographical;
   still, does any information about the poet's early life contribute to your reading of
   the poem? (See "Lives of the Poets," page 905).
3. In the "little moons" that fall from the almanac (line 33), does the poem introduce
   dream or fantasy, or do you take these to be small round pieces of paper?
4. What is the tone of this poem — the speaker's apparent attitude toward the scene
   described?
5. In an essay, "The Sestina," in *A Local Habitation* (U of Michigan P, 1985), John
   Frederick Nims defends the form against an obvious complaint against it:

   A shallow view of the sestina might suggest that the poet writes a stanza, and then
   is stuck with six words which he has to juggle into the required positions through
   five more stanzas and an envoy — to the great detriment of what passion and
   sincerity would have him say. But in a good sestina the poet has six words, six images,
   six ideas so urgently in his mind that he cannot get away from them; he wants to
   test them in all possible combinations and come to a conclusion about their relationship.

   How well does this description of a good sestina fit "Sestina"?

EXPERIMENT: *Urgent Repetition*

Write a sestina and see what you find out by doing so. (Even if you fail in the attempt,
you just might learn something interesting.) To start, pick six words you think worth
repeating six times. This elaborate pattern gives you much help: as John Ashbery has
pointed out, writing a sestina is "like riding downhill on a bicycle and having the pedals
push your feet." Here is some encouragement from a poet and critic, John Heath-Stubbs:
"I have never read a sestina that seemed to me a total failure."

YOUR ẎEN TWO WOL SLEE ME SODENLY (late fourteenth century)

Your ÿen° two wol slee° me sodenly;   *eyes; slay*
I may the beautee of hem° not sustene°,   *them; resist*
So woundeth hit thourghout my herte kene.

And but° your word wol helen° hastily   *unless, heal*
My hertes wounde, while that hit is grene°,   *new*   5
    Your ÿen two wol slee me sodenly;
    I may the beautee of hem not sustene.

Upon my trouthe° I sey you feithfully   *word*
That ye ben of my lyf and deeth the quene;
For with my deeth the trouthe° shal be sene.   *truth*   10
    Your ÿen two wol slee me sodenly;
    I may the beautee of hem not sustene,
    So woundeth it thourghout my herte kene.

YOUR ẎEN TWO WOL SLEE ME SODENLY. This poem is one of a group of three in the same fixed form, entitled "Merciles Beaute." 3 *so woundeth . . . kene:* "So deeply does it wound me through the heart."

QUESTIONS

1. This is a **roundel** (or **rondel**), an English form. What are its rules? How does it remind you of French courtly forms such as the villanelle, employed by Dylan Thomas (page 674)?
2. Try writing a roundel of your own in modern English. Although tricky, the form isn't extremely difficult: write only three lines and your poem is already eight-thirteenths finished. Here are some possible opening lines:

Baby, your eyes will slay me. Shut them tight.
Against their glow, I can't hold out for long. . . .

Your eyes present a pin to my balloon:
One pointed look and I start growing small. . . .

Since I escaped from love, I've grown so fat,
I barely can remember being thin. . . .

EXERCISE: *Seeing the Logic of Open Form Verse*

Read the following poems in open form silently to yourself, noticing what each poet does with white space, repetitions, line breaks, and indentations. Then read the poems aloud, trying to indicate by slight pauses where lines end and also pausing slightly at any space inside a line. Can you see any reasons for the poet's placing his words in this arrangement rather than in a prose paragraph? Do any of these poets seem to care also about visual effect? (As with other kinds of poetry, there may not be any obvious logical reason for everything that happens in these poems.)

E. E. Cummings (1894 – 1962)*

IN JUST-   1923

in Just-
spring   when the world is mud-
luscious the little
lame balloonman

whistles   far   and wee   5

and eddieandbill come
running from marbles and
piracies and it's
spring

when the world is puddle-wonderful   10

the queer
old balloonman whistles
far   and   wee
and bettyandisbel come dancing

from hop-scotch and jump-rope and   15

it's
spring
and
    the

        goat-footed   20

balloonMan   whistles
far
and
wee

Linda Pastan (b. 1932)*

JUMP CABLING   1984

When our cars   touched
When you lifted the hood   of mine
To see the intimate workings   underneath,
When we were bound   together
By a pulse of pure   energy,   5
When my car like the   princess
In the tale woke with a   start,
I thought why not ride the rest of the way together?

Donald Finkel (b. 1929)

GESTURE   1970

My arm sweeps down
    a pliant arc
        whatever I am
            streams through my
                negligent wrist: 5

the poem
        uncoils
            like a
                whip, and

snaps   10
softly   an inch from your enchanted face.

Charles Olson (1910 – 1970)

LA CHUTE   1967

my drum, hollowed out thru the thin slit,
carved from the cedar wood, the base I took
when the tree was felled

o my lute, wrought from the tree's crown

my drum, whose lustiness   5
was not to be resisted
                my lute,

from whose pulsations
not one could turn away

                    They   10
are where the dead are, my drum fell
where the dead are, who
will bring it up, my lute
who will bring it up where it fell in the face of them
where they are, where my lute and drum have fallen?   15

LA CHUTE. The French title means "The Fall."

SUGGESTIONS FOR WRITING

1. William Carlos Williams, in an interview, delivered this blast:

   Forcing twentieth-century America into a sonnet—gosh, how I hate sonnets—is like
   putting a crab into a square box. You've got to cut his legs off to make him fit. When
   you get through, you don't have a crab any more.

In a two-page essay, defend the modern American sonnet against Williams's charge. Or instead, open fire on it, using Williams's view for ammunition. Some sonnets to consider: R. S. Gwynn's "Scenes from the Playroom" (page 669), Gwendolyn Brooks's "The Rites for Cousin Vit" (page 791), and Archibald MacLeish's "The End of the World" (page 845).

2. Write an unserious argument for or against the abolition of limericks. Give illustrations of limericks you think worthy of abolition (or preservation).

3. Is "free verse" totally free? Argue this question in a short essay, drawing evidence from open-form poems that interest you.

23 Poems for the Eye

Let's look at a famous poem with a distinctive visible shape. In the seventeenth century, ingenious poets trimmed their lines into the silhouettes of altars and crosses, pillars and pyramids. Here is one. Is it anything more than a demonstration of ingenuity?

George Herbert (1593 – 1633)*

EASTER WINGS   1633

Lord, who createdst man in wealth and store,
Though foolishly he lost the same,
Decaying more and more
Till he became
Most poor;
With thee
Oh, let me rise
As larks, harmoniously,
And sing this day thy victories;
Then shall the fall further the flight in me.

My tender age in sorrow did begin;
And still with sicknesses and shame
Thou didst so punish sin,
That I became
Most thin.
With thee
Let me combine,
And feel this day thy victory;
For if I imp my wing on thine,
Affliction shall advance the flight in me.

In the next-to-last line, *imp* is a term from falconry meaning to repair the wing of an injured bird by grafting feathers into it.

If we see it merely as a picture, we will have to admit that Herbert's word design does not go far. It renders with difficulty shapes that a sketcher's pencil could set down in a flash, in more detail, more accurately. Was Herbert's effort wasted? It might have been, were there not more to his poem than meets the eye. The mind, too, is engaged by the visual pattern, by the realization that the words *most thin* are given emphasis by their narrow form. Here, visual pattern points out meaning. Heard aloud, too, "Easter Wings" gives further pleasure. Its rimes, its rhythm are perceptible.

Ever since George Herbert's day, poets have continued to experiment with the looks of printed poetry. Notable efforts to entertain the eye are Lewis Carroll's rimed mouse's tail in *Alice in Wonderland;* and the *Calligrammes* of Guillaume Apollinaire, who arranged words in the shapes of a necktie, of the Eiffel Tower, of spears of falling rain. Here is a bird-shaped poem of more recent inspiration than Herbert's. What does its visual form have to do with what the poet is saying?

John Hollander (b. 1929)

SWAN AND SHADOW   1969

```
                    Dusk
                  Above the
              water hang the
                        loud
                        flies
                        Here
                        O so
                        gray
                        then
              What                    A pale signal will appear
              When                    Soon before its shadow fades
              Where                   Here in this pool of opened eye
              In us          No Upon us As at the very edges
                 of where we take shape in the dark air
                   this object bares its image awakening
                     ripples of recognition that will
                       brush darkness up into light
    even after this bird this hour both drift by atop the perfect sad instant now
                       already passing out of sight
                     toward yet-untroubled reflection
                   this image bears its object darkening
                 into memorial shades Scattered bits of
              light          No of water Or something across
              water                   Breaking up No Being regathered
              soon                    Yet by then a swan will have
              gone                    Yet out of mind into what
                        vast
                        pale
                        hush
                        of a
                        place
                        past
              sudden dark as
                if a swan
                    sang
```

A whole poem doesn't need to be such a verbal silhouette, of course, for its appearance on the page to seem meaningful. In some lines of a longer poem, William Carlos Williams has conveyed the way an energetic bellhop (or hotel porter) runs downstairs:

> ta tuck a
>   ta tuck a
>   ta tuck a
>   ta tuck a
>   ta tuck a

This is not only good onomatopoeia and an accurate description of a rhythm; the steplike appearance of the lines goes together with their meaning.

At least some of our pleasure in silently reading a poem derives from the way it looks upon its page. A poem in an open form can engage the eye with snowfields of white space and thickets of close-set words. A poem in stanzas can please us by its visual symmetry. And, far from being merely decorative, the visual devices of a poem can be meaningful, too. White space — as poets demonstrate who work in open forms — can indicate pauses. If white space entirely surrounds a word or phrase or line, then that portion of the poem obviously takes special emphasis. Typographical devices such as capital letters and italics also can lay stress upon words. In most traditional poems, a capital letter at the beginning of each new line helps indicate the importance the poet places upon line-divisions, whose regular intervals make a rhythm out of pauses. And the poet may be trying to show us that certain lines rime by indenting them.

Though too much importance can be given to the visual element of poetry and though many poets seem hardly to care about it, it can be another dimension that sets apart poetry from prose. It is at least arguable that some of Walt Whitman's long-line, page-filling descriptions of the wide ocean, open landscapes, and broad streets of his America, which meet the eye as wide expanses of words, would lose something — besides rhythm — if couched in lines only three or four syllables long. Another poet who deeply cared about visual appearance was William Blake (1757 – 1827), graphic artist and engraver as well as a master artist in words. By publishing his *Songs of Innocence* and *Songs of Experience* (among other works) with illustrations and accompanying hand-lettered poems, often interwoven with the lines of the poems, Blake apparently strove to make poem and appearance of poem a unity, striking mind and eye at the same time.

A POISON TREE.

I was angry with my friend:
I told my wrath, my wrath did end.
I was angry with my foe:
I told it not, my wrath did grow.

And I water'd it in fears,
Night & morning with my tears:
And I sunned it with smiles,
And with soft deceitful wiles.

And it grew both day and night.
Till it bore an apple bright.
And my foe beheld it shine,
And he knew that it was mine.

And into my garden stole,
When the night had veild the pole:
In the morning glad I see;
My foe outstretchd beneath the tree:

Some poets who write in English have envied poets who write in Chinese, a language in which certain words look like the things they represent. Consider this Chinese poem:

Wang Wei (701 – 761)

BIRD-SINGING STREAM (about 750)

人靜月時　閒夜出鳴　桂春驚春　花山山澗　落空鳥中

Substituting English words for ideograms, the poem becomes:

man	leisure	cassia	flower	fall
quiet	night	spring	mountain	empty
moon	rise	startle	mountain	bird
at times	sing	spring	stream	middle

Even without the aid of English crib-notes, all of us can read some Chinese if we can recognize a picture of a man. What resemblances can you see between any of the other ideograms and the things they stand for?[1]

Wai-lim Yip, the poet and critic who provided the Chinese text and translation, has also translated the poem into more usual English word order, still keeping close to the original sequence of ideas:

Man at leisure. Cassia flowers fall.
Quiet night. Spring mountain is empty.
Moon rises. Startles — a mountain bird.
It sings at times in the spring stream.

One envious Western poet was Ezra Pound, who included a few Chinese ideograms in his *Cantos* as illustrations. From the scholar Ernest Fenollosa, Pound said he had come to understand why a language written in ideograms "simply *had to stay poetic*; simply couldn't help being and staying poetic in a way that a column of English type might very well not stay poetic."[2] Having an imperfect command of Chinese, Pound greatly overestimated the tendency of the language to depict things. (Only a small number of characters in modern Chinese are pictures; Chinese characters, like Western alphabets, also indicate the sounds of words.) Still, Pound's misunderstanding was fruitful. Thanks to his influence, many other recent poets were encouraged to consider the appearance of words.[3] E. E. Cummings, in a poem that begins "mOOn Over tOwns mOOn," has reveled in the fact that O's are moonshaped. Aram Saroyan, in a poem entitled "crickets," makes capital of the fact that the word *cricket* somewhat resembles the snub-nosed insect of approximately the same length. The poem begins,

crickets
crickets
crickets
crickets

[1]To help you compare English and Chinese, the Chinese original has been arranged in Western word-order. (Ordinarily, in Chinese, the word for "man" would appear at the upper right.)
[2]*The ABC of Reading* (Norfolk, Conn., 1960) 22.
[3]For a brief discussion of Pound's misunderstanding and its influence, see Milton Klonsky's introduction to his anthology *Speaking Pictures: A Gallery of Pictorial Poetry from the Sixteenth Century to the Present* (New York: Harmony, 1975).

and goes on down its page like that, for thirty-seven lines. (Read aloud, by the way, the poem sounds somewhat like crickets chirping!)

In recent years, a movement called **concrete poetry** has traveled far and wide. Though practitioners of the art disagree over its definition, what most concretists seem to do is make designs out of letters and words. Other concrete poets wield typography like a brush dipped in paint, using such techniques as blow-up, montage, and superimposed elements (the same words printed many times on top of the same impression, so that the result is blurriness). They may even keep words in a usual order, perhaps employing white space as freely as any writer of open form verse. (More freely sometimes — Aram Saroyan has a concrete poem that consists of a page blank except for the word *oxygen.*) Poet Richard Kostelanetz has suggested that a more accurate name for concrete poetry might be "word-imagery." He sees it occupying an area somewhere between conventional poetry and visual art.[4]

Admittedly, some concrete poems mean less than meets the eye. That many pretentious doodlers have taken up concretism may have caused a *Time* writer to sneer: did Joyce Kilmer miss all that much by never having seen a poem lovely as a

```
    t
   ttt
  rrrrr
 rrrrrrr
eeeeeeeee
   ???
```

Like other structures of language, however, concrete poems evidently can have the effect of poetry, if written by poets. Whether or not it ought to be dubbed "poetry," this art can do what poems traditionally have done: use language in delightful ways that reveal meanings to us.

Edwin Morgan (b. 1920)

Siesta of a Hungarian Snake   1968

s   sz   sz   SZ   sz   SZ   sz   ZS   zs   ZS   zs   zs   z

Questions

1. What do you suppose Morgan is trying to indicate by reversing the order of the two letters in mid line?
2. What, if anything, about this snake seems Hungarian?
3. Does the sound of its consonants matter?

---

[4]Introduction to his anthology *Imaged Words and Worded Images* (New York: Outerbridge and Dienstfrey, 1970).

Dorthi Charles (b. 1963)

Concrete Cat   1971

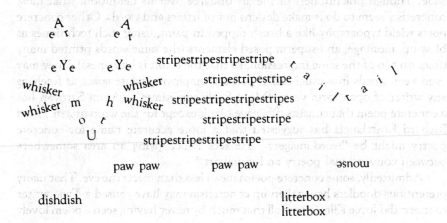

Questions

1. What does this writer indicate by capitalizing the *a* in *ear*? The *y* in *eye*? The *u* in *mouth*? By using spaces between the letters in the word *tail*?
2. Why is the word *mouse* upside down?
3. What possible pun might be seen in the cat's middle stripe?
4. What is the tone of "Concrete Cat"? How is it made evident?
5. Do these words seem chosen for their connotations or only for their denotations? Would you call this work of art a poem?

Experiment: *Do It Yourself*

Make a concrete poem of your own. If you need inspiration, pick some familiar object or animal and try to find words that look like it. For more ideas, study the typography of a magazine or newspaper; cut out interesting letters and numerals and try pasting them into arrangements. What (if anything) do your experiments tell you about familiar letters and words?

Suggestions for Writing

1. Consider whether concrete poetry is a vital new art form or merely visual trivia.
2. Should a poem be illustrated, or is it better left to the mind's eye? Discuss this question in a brief essay. You might care to consider William Blake's illustration for "A Poison Tree" or the illustrations in a collection of poems for children.

24 Symbol

The national flag is supposed to bestir our patriotic feelings. When a black cat crosses his path, a superstitious man shivers, foreseeing bad luck. To each of these, by custom, our society expects a standard response. A flag, a black cat's crossing one's path — each is a **symbol:** a visible object or action that suggests some further meaning in addition to itself. In literature, a symbol might be the word *flag* or the words *a black cat crossed his path* or every description of flag or cat in an entire novel, story, play, or poem.

A flag and the crossing of a black cat may be called **conventional symbols,** since they can have a conventional or customary effect on us. Conventional symbols are also part of the language of poetry, as we know when we meet the red rose, emblem of love, in a lyric, or the Christian cross in the devotional poems of George Herbert. More often, however, symbols in literature have no conventional, long-established meaning, but particular meanings of their own. In Melville's novel *Moby-Dick,* to take a rich example, whatever we associate with the great white whale is *not* attached unmistakably to white whales by custom. Though Melville tells us that men have long regarded whales with awe and relates Moby Dick to the celebrated fish that swallowed Jonah, the reader's response is to one particular whale, the creature of Herman Melville. Only the experience of reading the novel in its entirety can give Moby Dick his particular meaning.

We should say *meanings,* for as Eudora Welty has observed, it is a good thing Melville made Moby Dick a whale, a creature large enough to contain all that critics have found in him. A symbol in literature, if not conventional, has more than just one meaning. In "The Raven," by Edgar Allan Poe, the appearance of a strange black bird in the narrator's study is sinister; and indeed, if we take the poem seriously, we may even respond with a sympathetic shiver of dread. Does the bird mean death, fate, melancholy, the loss of a loved one, knowledge in the service of evil? All these, perhaps. Like any well-chosen symbol, Poe's raven sets going within the reader an unending train of feelings and associations.

We miss the value of a symbol, however, if we think it can mean absolutely anything we wish. If a poet has any control over our reactions, the poem will guide our responses in a certain direction.

T. S. Eliot (1888 – 1965)*

THE *BOSTON EVENING TRANSCRIPT*   1917

The readers of the *Boston Evening Transcript*
Sway in the wind like a field of ripe corn.

When evening quickens faintly in the street,
Wakening the appetites of life in some
And to others bringing the *Boston Evening Transcript,*   5
I mount the steps and ring the bell, turning
Wearily, as one would turn to nod good-bye to La Rochefoucauld,
If the street were time and he at the end of the street,
And I say, "Cousin Harriet, here is the *Boston Evening Transcript.*"

The newspaper, whose name Eliot purposely repeats so monotonously, indicates what this poem is about. Now defunct, the *Transcript* covered in detail the slightest activity of Boston's leading families and was noted for the great length of its obituaries. Eliot, then, uses the newspaper as a symbol for an existence of boredom, fatigue *(Wearily),* petty and unvarying routine (since an evening newspaper, like night, arrives on schedule). The *Transcript* evokes a way of life without zest or passion, for, opposed to people who read it, Eliot sets people who do not: those whose desires revive, not expire, when the working day is through. Suggestions abound in the ironic comparison of the *Transcript*'s readers to a cornfield late in summer. To mention only a few: the readers sway because they are sleepy; they vegetate; they are drying up; each makes a rattling sound when turning a page. It is not necessary that we know the remote and similarly disillusioned friend to whom the speaker might nod: La Rochefoucauld, whose cynical *Maxims* entertained Parisian society under Louis XIV (sample: "All of us have enough strength to endure the misfortunes of others"). We understand that the nod is symbolic of an immense weariness of spirit. We know nothing about Cousin Harriet, whom the speaker addresses, but imagine from the greeting she inspires that she is probably a bore.

If Eliot wishes to say that certain Bostonians lead lives of sterile boredom, why does he couch his meaning in symbols? Why doesn't he tell us directly what he means? These questions imply two assumptions not necessarily true: first, that Eliot has a message to impart; second, that he is concealing it. We have reason to think that Eliot did not usually have a message in mind when beginning a poem, for as he once told a critic: "The conscious problems with which one is concerned in the actual writing are more those of a quasi musical nature . . . than of a conscious exposition of ideas." Poets sometimes discover what they have to say while in the act of saying it. And it may be that in his *Transcript* poem, Eliot is saying exactly what he means. By communicating his meaning through symbols instead of statements, he may be choosing the only kind of language appropriate to an idea of great subtlety and complexity. (The paraphrase "Certain Bostonians are bored" hardly begins to describe the poem in all its possible meaning.) And by his use of symbolism, Eliot affords us the pleasure of finding our own entrances to his poem. Another great strength of a symbol is that, like some figures of speech, it renders the abstract in concrete terms, and, like any other image, refers to what we can perceive — an object like a newspaper, a gesture like a nod. Eliot might, like Robert Frost, have called himself a "synecdochist." Frost explained: "Always a larger significance. A little thing touches a larger thing."

This power of suggestion that a symbol contains is, perhaps, its greatest advantage. Sometimes, as in the following poem by Emily Dickinson, a symbol will lead us from a visible object to something too vast to be perceived.

Emily Dickinson (1830 – 1886)*

THE LIGHTNING IS A YELLOW FORK   (about 1870)

The Lightning is a yellow Fork
From Tables in the sky
By inadvertent fingers dropt
The awful Cutlery

Of mansions never quite disclosed   5
And never quite concealed
The Apparatus of the Dark
To ignorance revealed.

If the lightning is a fork, then whose are the fingers that drop it, the table from which it slips, the household to which it belongs? The poem implies this question without giving an answer. An obvious answer is "God," but can we be sure? We wonder, too, about these partially lighted mansions: if our vision were clearer, what would we behold?[1]

"But how am I supposed to know a symbol when I see one?" The best approach is to read poems closely, taking comfort in the likelihood that it is better not to notice symbols at all than to find significance in every literal stone

[1]In its suggestion of an infinite realm that mortal eyes cannot quite see, but whose nature can be perceived fleetingly through things visible, Emily Dickinson's poem, by coincidence, resembles the work of late-nineteenth-century French poets called **symbolists.** To a symbolist the shirt-tail of Truth is continually seen disappearing around a corner. With their Neoplatonic view of ideal realities existing in a great beyond, whose corresponding symbols are the perceptible cats that bite us and tangible stones we stumble over, French poets such as Charles Baudelaire, Jules Laforgue, and Stéphane Mallarmé were profoundly to affect poets writing in English, notably Yeats (who said a poem "entangles . . . a part of the Divine essence") and Eliot. But we consider in this chapter symbolism as an element in certain poems, not Symbolism, the literary movement.

and huge meanings in every thing. In looking for the symbols in a poem, pick out all the references to concrete objects — newspapers, black cats, twisted pins. Consider these with special care. Notice any that the poet emphasizes by detailed description, by repetition, or by placing at the very beginning or end of the poem. Ask: What is the poem about, what does it add up to? If, when the poem is paraphrased, the paraphrase depends primarily upon the meaning of certain concrete objects, these richly suggestive objects may be the symbols.

There are some things a literary symbol usually is *not*. A symbol is not an abstraction. Such terms as *truth, death, love,* and *justice* cannot work as symbols (unless personified, as in the traditional figure of Justice holding a scale). Most often, a symbol is something we can see in the mind's eye: a newspaper, a lightning bolt, a gesture of nodding good-bye.

In narratives, a well-developed character who speaks much dialogue and is not the least bit mysterious is usually not a symbol. But watch out for an executioner in a black hood; a character, named for a Biblical prophet, who does little but utter a prophecy; a trio of old women who resemble the Three Fates. (It has been argued, with good reason, that Milton's fully rounded character of Satan in *Paradise Lost* is a symbol embodying evil and human pride, but a narrower definition of symbol is more frequently useful.) A symbol *may* be a part of a person's body (the baleful eye of the murder victim in Poe's story "The Tell-Tale Heart") or a look, a voice, a mannerism.

A symbol usually is not the second term of a metaphor. In the line "The lightning is a yellow fork," the symbol is the lightning, not the fork.

Sometimes a symbol addresses a sense other than sight: the sound of a mysterious harp at the end of Chekhov's play *The Cherry Orchard*; or, in William Faulkner's tale "A Rose for Emily," the odor of decay that surrounds the house of the last survivor of a town's leading family — suggesting not only physical dissolution but also the decay of a social order. A symbol is a special kind of image, for it exceeds the usual image in the richness of its connotations. The dead wife's cold comb in the haiku of Buson (discussed on page 569) works symbolically, suggesting among other things the chill of the grave, the contrast between the living and the dead.

Holding a narrower definition than that used in this book, some readers of poetry prefer to say that a symbol is always a concrete object, never an act. They would deny the label "symbol" to Ahab's breaking his tobacco pipe before setting out to pursue Moby Dick (suggesting, perhaps, his determination to allow no pleasure to distract him from the chase) or to any large motion (as Ahab's whole quest). This distinction, while confining, does have the merit of sparing one from seeing all motion to be possibly symbolic. Some would call Ahab's gesture not a symbol but a **symbolic act.**

To sum up: a symbol radiates hints or casts long shadows (to use Henry James's metaphor). We are unable to say it "stands for" or "represents" a meaning. It evokes, it suggests, it manifests. It demands no single necessary interpretation, such as the interpretation a driver gives to a red traffic light.

Rather, like Emily Dickinson's lightning bolt, it points toward an indefinite meaning, which may lie in part beyond the reach of words. In a symbol, as Thomas Carlyle said in *Sartor Resartus,* "the Infinite is made to blend with the Finite, to stand visible, and as it were, attainable there."

Thomas Hardy (1840 – 1928)*

NEUTRAL TONES   1898

We stood by a pond that winter day,
And the sun was white, as though chidden of God,
And a few leaves lay on the starving sod;
   — They had fallen from an ash, and were gray.

Your eyes on me were as eyes that rove   5
Over tedious riddles of years ago;
And some words played between us to and fro
   On which lost the more by our love.

The smile on your mouth was the deadest thing
Alive enough to have strength to die;   10
And a grin of bitterness swept thereby
   Like an ominous bird a-wing. . . .

Since then, keen lessons that love deceives,
And wrings with wrong, have shaped to me
Your face, and the God-curst sun, and a tree,   15
   And a pond edged with grayish leaves.

QUESTIONS

1. Sum up the story told in this poem. In lines 1 – 12, what is the dramatic situation? What has happened in the interval between the experience related in these lines and the reflection in the last stanza?
2. What meanings do you find in the title?
3. Explain in your own words the metaphor in line 2.
4. What connotations appropriate to this poem does the *ash* (line 4) have, that *oak* or *maple* would lack?
5. What visible objects in the poem function symbolically? What actions or gestures?

If we read of a ship, its captain, its sailors, and the rough seas, and we realize we are reading about a commonwealth and how its rulers and workers keep it going even in difficult times, then we are reading an **allegory.** Closely akin to symbolism, allegory is a description — usually narrative — in which persons, places, and things are employed in a continuous system of equivalents.

Although more strictly limited in its suggestions than symbolism, allegory need not be thought inferior. Few poems continue to interest readers more than Dante's allegorical *Divine Comedy*. Sublime evidence of the appeal of allegory may be found in Christ's use of the **parable:** a brief narrative — usually allegorical but sometimes not — that teaches a moral.

Matthew 13:24–30 (Authorized or King James Version, 1611)

THE PARABLE OF THE GOOD SEED

The kingdom of heaven is likened unto a man which sowed good seed in his field:

But while men slept, his enemy came and sowed tares among the wheat, and went his way.

But when the blade was sprung up, and brought forth fruit, then appeared the tares also.

So the servants of the householder came and said unto him, Sir, didst not thou sow good seed in thy field? From whence then hath it tares?

He said unto them, An enemy hath done this. The servants said unto him, Wilt thou then that we go and gather them up?   5

But he said, Nay; lest while ye gather up the tares, ye root up also the wheat with them.

Let both grow together until the harvest: and in the time of harvest I will say to the reapers, Gather ye together first the tares, and bind them in bundles to burn them: but gather the wheat into my barn.

The sower is the Son of man, the field is the world, the good seed are the children of the Kingdom, the tares are the children of the wicked one, the enemy is the devil, the harvest is the end of the world, the reapers are angels. "As therefore the tares are gathered and burned in the fire; so shall it be in the end of this world" (Matthew 13:36 – 42).

Usually, as in this parable, the meanings of an allegory are plainly labeled or thinly disguised. In John Bunyan's allegorical narrative *The Pilgrim's Progress*, it is clear that the hero Christian, on his journey through places with such pointed names as Vanity Fair, the Valley of the Shadow of Death, and Doubting Castle, is the soul, traveling the road of life on the way toward Heaven. An allegory, when carefully built, is systematic. It makes one principal comparison, the working out of whose details may lead to further comparisons, then still further comparisons: Christian, thrown by Giant Despair into the dungeon of Doubting Castle, escapes by means of a key called Promise. Such a complicated design may take great length to unfold, as in Spenser's *Faerie Queene*; but the method may be seen in a short poem:

George Herbert (1593 – 1633)*

REDEMPTION   1633

Having been tenant long to a rich Lord,
   Not thriving, I resolvèd to be bold,
And make a suit unto him to afford
   A new small-rented lease and cancel th' old.
In Heaven at his manor I him sought.   5
   They told me there that he was lately gone
About some land which he had dearly bought
   Long since on earth, to take possessiòn.
I straight returned, and knowing his great birth,
   Sought him accordingly in great resorts,   10
   In cities, theaters, gardens, parks, and courts.
At length I heard a ragged noise and mirth
   Of thieves and murderers; there I him espied,
Who straight "Your suit is granted," said, and died.

QUESTIONS

1. In this allegory, what equivalents does Herbert give each of these terms: *tenant, Lord, not thriving, suit, new lease, old lease, manor, land, dearly bought, take possession, his great birth?*
2. What scene is depicted in the last three lines?

An object in allegory is like a bird whose cage is clearly lettered with its identity — "RAVEN, *Corvus corax*; habitat of specimen, Maine." A symbol, by contrast, is a bird with piercing eyes that mysteriously appears one evening in your library. It is there; you can touch it. But what does it mean? You look at it. It continues to look at you.

Whether an object in literature is a symbol, part of an allegory, or no such thing at all, it has at least one sure meaning. Moby Dick is first a whale, the *Boston Evening Transcript* a newspaper. Besides deriving a multitude of intangible suggestions from the title symbol in Eliot's long poem *The Waste Land*, its readers cannot fail to carry away a sense of the land's physical appearance: a river choked with sandwich papers and cigarette ends, London Bridge "under the brown fog of a winter dawn." A virtue of *The Pilgrim's Progress* is that its walking abstractions are no mere abstractions but are also human: Giant Despair is a henpecked husband. The most vital element of a literary work may pass us by, unless before seeking further depths in a thing, we look to the thing itself.

Emily Dickinson (1830 – 1886)*

I HEARD A FLY BUZZ – WHEN I DIED   (about 1862)

I heard a Fly buzz – when I died –
The Stillness in the Room
Was like the Stillness in the Air –
Between the Heaves of Storm –

The Eyes around – had wrung them dry –   5
And Breaths were gathering firm
For that last Onset – when the King
Be witnessed – in the Room –

I willed my Keepsakes – Signed away
What portion of me be   10
Assignable – and then it was
There interposed a Fly –

With Blue – uncertain stumbling Buzz –
Between the light – and me –
And then the Windows failed – and then   15
I could not see to see –

QUESTIONS

1. Why is the poem written in the past tense? Where is the speaker at present?
2. What do you understand from the repetition of the word *see* in the last line?
3. What does the poet mean by *Eyes around* (line 5), *that last Onset* (line 7), *the King* (line 7), and *What portion of me be / Assignable* (lines 10 – 11)?
4. In line 13, how can a sound be called *Blue* and *stumbling*?
5. What further meaning might *the Windows* (line 15) suggest, in addition to denoting the windows of the room?
6. What connotations of the word *fly* seem relevant to an account of a death?
7. Summarize your interpretation of the poem. What does the fly mean?

Robert Frost (1874–1963)*

THE ROAD NOT TAKEN   1916

Two roads diverged in a yellow wood,
And sorry I could not travel both
And be one traveler, long I stood
And looked down one as far as I could
To where it bent in the undergrowth;   5

Then took the other, as just as fair,
And having perhaps the better claim,
Because it was grassy and wanted wear;
Though as for that the passing there
Had worn them really about the same,   10

And both that morning equally lay
In leaves no step had trodden black.
Oh, I kept the first for another day!
Yet knowing how way leads on to way,
I doubted if I should ever come back.   15

I shall be telling this with a sigh
Somewhere ages and ages hence:
Two roads diverged in a wood, and I—
I took the one less traveled by,
And that has made all the difference.   20

QUESTION

What symbolism do you find in this poem, if any? Back up your claim with evidence.

Christina Rossetti (1830 – 1894)

UPHILL   1862

Does the road wind uphill all the way?
    Yes, to the very end.
Will the day's journey take the whole long day?
    From morn to night, my friend.

But is there for the night a resting-place?   5
    A roof for when the slow dark hours begin.
May not the darkness hide it from my face?
    You cannot miss that inn.

Shall I meet other wayfarers at night?
    Those who have gone before.   10
Then must I knock, or call when just in sight?
    They will not keep you standing at that door.

Shall I find comfort, travel-sore and weak?
    Of labor you shall find the sum.
Will there be beds for me and all who seek?   15
    Yea, beds for all who come.

QUESTIONS

1. At what line in reading this poem did you tumble to the fact that the poet is building
   an allegory?
2. For what does each thing stand?
3. What does the title of the poem suggest to you?
4. Recast the meaning of line 14, a knotty line, in your own words.
5. Discuss the possible identities of the two speakers — the apprehensive traveler and
   the character with all the answers. Are they specific individuals? Allegorical figures?
6. Compare "Uphill" with Robert Creeley's "Oh No" (page 521). What striking similarities do you find in these two dissimilar poems?

Gjertrud Schnackenberg (b. 1953)

SIGNS   1974

Threading the palm, a web of little lines
Spells out the lost money, the heart, the head,
The wagging tongues, the sudden deaths, in signs
We would smooth out, like imprints on a bed,

In signs that can't be helped, geese heading south,   5
In signs read anxiously, like breath that clouds
A mirror held to a barely open mouth,
Like telegrams, the gathering of crowds —

The plane's X in the sky, spelling disaster:
Before the whistle and hit, a tracer flare;   10
Before rubble, a hairline crack in plaster
And a housefly's panicked scribbling on the air.

QUESTIONS

1. What are "signs" in this poet's sense of the word?
2. The poem gives a list of signs. What unmistakable meaning does each indicate?
3. Compare Schnackenberg's fly and Emily Dickinson's (page 708). Which insect seems loaded with more suggestions?
4. Can you think of any familiar signs that *aren't* ominous?
5. This poem was written when the poet was a student at Mount Holyoke College. Knowing this fact, do you like it any less, or any more?

EXERCISE: *Symbol Hunting*

After you have read each of these poems, decide which description best suits it:

1. The poem has a central symbol.
2. The poem contains no symbolism, but is to be taken literally.

Sir Philip Sidney (1554 – 1586)

YOU THAT WITH ALLEGORY'S CURIOUS FRAME   1591

You that with allegory's curious frame
    Of others' children changelings use to make,
    With me those pains, for God's sake, do not take;
I list not° dig so deep for brazen fame.   *I do not choose to*
When I say Stella, I do mean the same   5
    Princess of beauty for whose only sake
    The reins of love I love, though never slake,
And joy therein, though nations count it shame.
I beg no subject to use eloquence,
    Nor in hid ways do guide philosophy;   10

Look at my hands for no such quintessence,
    But know that I in pure simplicity
    Breathe out the flames which burn within my heart,
    Love only reading unto me this art.

William Carlos Williams (1883 – 1963)*

POEM   1934

As the cat
climbed over
the top of

the jamcloset
first the right   5
forefoot

carefully
then the hind
stepped down
into the pit of   10
the empty
flowerpot

Theodore Roethke (1908 – 1963)*

NIGHT CROW   1948

When I saw that clumsy crow
Flap from a wasted tree,
A shape in the mind rose up:
Over the gulfs of dream
Flew a tremendous bird   5
Further and further away
Into a moonless black,
Deep in the brain, far back.

John Donne (1572 – 1631)*

A BURNT SHIP   1633

Out of a fired ship which by no way
But drowning could be rescued from the flame
Some men leaped forth, and ever as they came
Near the foe's ships, did by their shot decay;
So all were lost, which in the ship were found,
    They in the sea being burnt, they in the burnt ship drowned.

Wallace Stevens (1879 – 1955)*

ANECDOTE OF THE JAR   1923

I placed a jar in Tennessee,
And round it was, upon a hill.
It made the slovenly wilderness
Surround that hill.

The wilderness rose up to it,   5
And sprawled around, no longer wild.
The jar was round upon the ground
And tall and of a port in air.

It took dominion everywhere.
The jar was gray and bare.   10
It did not give of bird or bush,
Like nothing else in Tennessee.

SUGGESTIONS FOR WRITING

1. Write a paraphrase of Emily Dickinson's "I heard a Fly buzz — when I died." Make
   clear whatever meanings you find in the fly (and other concrete objects).
2. Discuss the symbolism in a poem in the Poems for Further Reading beginning on page
   773. Likely poems to study (among many) are Louise Bogan's "The Dream," T. S. Eliot's
   "The Love Song of J. Alfred Prufrock," Robert Lowell's "Skunk Hour," Howard Nemerov's
   "The Snow Globe" and Adrienne Rich's "Aunt Jennifer's Tigers."
3. Take some relatively simple, straightforward poem, such as William Carlos Williams's
   "This Is Just to Say" (page 535), and write a burlesque critical interpretation of it.
   Claim to discover symbols in the poem that it doesn't contain. While letting your
   ability to "read into" a poem run wild, don't invent anything that you can't somehow
   support from the text of the poem itself. At the end of your burlesque, add a
   paragraph summing up what this exercise indicates about how to read poems, or how
   not to.

25 Myth

Poets have long been fond of retelling **myths,** narrowly defined as traditional stories of immortal beings. Such stories taken collectively may also be called **myth** or **mythology.** In one of the most celebrated collections of myth ever assembled, the *Metamorphoses,* the poet Ovid has told — to take one example from many — how Phaeton, child of the sun god, rashly tried to drive his father's fiery chariot on its daily round, lost control of the horses, and caused disaster both to himself and to the world. Our use of the term *myth* in discussing poetry, then, differs from its use in expressions such as "the myth of communism" and "the myth of democracy." In these examples, myth, in its broadest sense, is any idea people believe in, whether true or false. Nor do we mean — to take another familiar use of the word — a cock-and-bull story: "Judge Rapp doesn't roast speeders alive; that's just a *myth.*" In the following discussion, *myth* will mean — as critic Northrop Frye has put it — "the imitation of actions near or at the conceivable limits of desire." Myths tell us of the exploits of the gods — their battles, the ways in which they live, love, and perhaps suffer — all on a scale of magnificence larger than our life. We envy their freedom and power; they enact our wishes and dreams. Whether we believe in them or not, their adventures are myths: Ovid, it seems, placed no credence in the stories he related, for he declared, "I prate of ancient poets' monstrous lies."

And yet it is characteristic of a myth that it *can* be believed. Throughout history, myths have accompanied religious doctrines and rituals. They have helped sanction or recall the reasons for religious observances. A sublime instance is the New Testament account of the Last Supper. Because of it and its record of the words of Jesus, "This do in remembrance of Me," Christians have continued to re-enact the offering and partaking of the body and blood of their Lord, under the appearances of bread and wine. It is essential to recall that, just because a myth narrates the acts of a god, we do not necessarily mean by the term a false or fictitious narrative. When we speak of the "myth of Islam" or "the Christian myth," we do so without implying either belief or disbelief.

Myths can also help sanction customs and institutions other than religious ones. At the same time as the baking of bread was introduced to ancient Greece — one theory goes — there was introduced the myth of Demeter, goddess of grain, who had kindly sent her emissary Triptolemus to teach humankind this valuable art — thus helping to persuade the distrustful that bread was a good thing. Some myths seem made to divert and regale, not to sanction anything. Such may be the story of the sculptor Pygmalion, who fell in love with his statue of a woman; so exquisite was his work, so deep was his feeling, that Aphrodite brought the statue to life. And yet perhaps the story goes deeper than mere diversion: perhaps it is a way of saying that works of art achieve a reality of their own, that love can transform or animate its object.

How does a myth begin? Several theories have been proposed, none universally accepted. One is that a myth is a way to explain some natural phenomenon. Winter comes and the vegetation perishes because Persephone, child of Demeter, must return to the underworld for four months every year. This theory, as classical scholar Edith Hamilton has pointed out, may lead us to think incorrectly that Greek mythology was the creation of a primitive people. Tales of the gods of Mount Olympus may reflect an earlier inheritance, but Greek myths known to us were transcribed in an era of high civilization. Anthropologists have questioned whether primitive people generally find beauty in the mysteries of nature. "From my own study of living myths among savages," wrote Bronislaw Malinowski, "I should say that primitive man has to a very limited extent the purely artistic or scientific interest in nature; there is but little room for symbolism in his ideas and tales; and myth, in fact, is not an idle rhapsody . . . but a hard-working, extremely important cultural force."[1] Such a practical function was seen by Sir James Frazer in *The Golden Bough:* myths were originally expressions of human hope that nature would be fertile. Still another theory is that, once upon a time, heroes of myth were human prototypes. The Greek philosopher Euhemerus declared myths to be tales of real persons, which poets had exaggerated. Most present-day historians of myth would seek no general explanation but would say that different myths probably have different origins.

Poets have many coherent mythologies on which to draw; perhaps those most frequently consulted by British and American poets are the classical, the Christian, the Norse, and folk myth of the American frontier (embodying the deeds of superhuman characters such as Paul Bunyan). Some poets have taken inspiration from other myths as well: T. S. Eliot's *The Waste Land,* for example, is enriched by allusions to Buddhism and to pagan vegetation-cults.

As a tour through any good art museum will demonstrate, myth pervades much of the graphic art of Western civilization. In literature, one evidence of its continuing value to recent poets and storytellers is the frequency with which myths — both primitive and civilized — are retold. William Faulkner's story

[1]Bronislaw Malinowski, *Myth in Primitive Psychology* (1926); reprinted in *Magic, Science and Religion* (New York: Doubleday, 1954) 97.

"The Bear" recalls tales of Indian totem animals; John Updike's novel *The Centaur* presents the horse-man Chiron as a modern high school teacher; Hart Crane's poem "For the Marriage of Faustus and Helen" unites two figures of different myths, who dance to jazz; T. S. Eliot's plays bring into the drawing room the myths of Alcestis (*The Cocktail Party*) and the Eumenides (*The Family Reunion*); Jean Cocteau's film *Orphée* shows us Eurydice riding to the underworld with an escort of motorcycles. Popular interest in such works may testify to the profound appeal myths continue to hold for us. Like any other large body of knowledge that can be alluded to, myth offers the poet an instant means of communication — if the reader also knows the particular myth cited. Writing "Lycidas," John Milton could depend upon his readers — mostly persons of similar classical learning — to understand him without footnotes. Today, a poet referring to a traditional myth must be sure to choose a reasonably well-known one, or else write as well as T. S. Eliot, whose work has compelled his readers to single out his allusions and look them up. Like other varieties of poetry, myth is a kind of knowledge, not at odds with scientific knowledge but existing in addition to it.

D. H. Lawrence (1885 – 1930)*

BAVARIAN GENTIANS   1932

Not every man has gentians in his house
in soft September, at slow, sad Michaelmas.

Bavarian gentians, big and dark, only dark
darkening the daytime, torch-like with the smoking blueness of
    Pluto's gloom,
ribbed and torch-like, with their blaze of darkness spread blue   5
down flattening into points, flattened under the sweep of white day
torch-flower of the blue-smoking darkness, Pluto's dark-blue daze,
black lamps from the halls of Dis, burning dark blue,
giving off darkness, blue darkness, as Demeter's pale lamps give off
    light,
lead me then, lead the way.   10

Reach me a gentian, give me a torch!
let me guide myself with the blue, forked torch of this flower
down the darker and darker stairs, where blue is darkened on
    blueness
even where Persephone goes, just now, from the frosted September
to the sightless realm where darkness is awake upon the dark   15
and Persephone herself is but a voice

or a darkness invisible enfolded in the deeper dark
of the arms Plutonic, and pierced with the passion of dense gloom,
among the splendor of torches of darkness, shedding darkness on the
    lost bride and her groom.

BAVARIAN GENTIANS. 4 *Pluto:* Roman name for Hades, in Greek mythology the ruler of the underworld, who abducted Persephone to be his bride. Each spring Persephone returns to earth and is
welcomed by her mother Demeter, goddess of fruitfulness; each winter she departs again, to dwell
with her husband below. 8 *Dis:* Pluto's realm.

QUESTIONS

1. Read this poem aloud. What devices of sound do you hear in it?
2. What characteristics of gentians appear to remind Lawrence of the story of Persephone? What significance do you attach to the poem's being set in September? How
   does the fact of autumn matter to the gentians and to Persephone?

Thomas Hardy (1840 – 1928)*

THE OXEN

1915

Christmas Eve, and twelve of the clock.
    "Now they are all on their knees,"
An elder said as we sat in a flock
    By the embers in hearthside ease.

We pictured the meek mild creatures where   5
    They dwelt in their strawy pen,
Nor did it occur to one of us there
    To doubt they were kneeling then.

So fair a fancy few would weave
    In these years! Yet, I feel,   10
If someone said on Christmas Eve,
    "Come; see the oxen kneel

"In the lonely barton° by yonder coomb°   *farmyard; a hollow*
    Our childhood used to know,"
I should go with him in the gloom,   15
    Hoping it might be so.

THE OXEN. This ancient belief has had wide currency among peasants and farmers of Western
Europe. Some also say that on Christmas Eve the beasts can speak.

QUESTIONS

1. What body of myth is Hardy's subject and what are his speaker's attitudes toward
   it? Perhaps, in Hardy's view, the pious report about oxen is only part of it.
2. Read this poem aloud and notice its sound and imagery. What contrast do you find
   between the sounds of the first stanza and the sounds of the last stanza? Which words

make the difference? What images enforce a contrast in tone between the beginning of the poem and its ending?
3. G. K. Chesterton, writing as a defender of Christian faith, called Hardy's writings "the mutterings of the village atheist." See other poems by Hardy (particularly "Four Satires of Circumstance," page 819). What do you think Chesterton might have meant? Can "The Oxen" be called a hostile mutter?

William Wordsworth (1770 – 1850)*

THE WORLD IS TOO MUCH WITH US   1807

The world is too much with us; late and soon,
Getting and spending, we lay waste our powers;
Little we see in Nature that is ours;
We have given our hearts away, a sordid boon!
This Sea that bares her bosom to the moon;   5
The winds that will be howling at all hours,
And are up-gathered now like sleeping flowers;
For this, for everything, we are out of tune;
It moves us not. Great God! I'd rather be
A Pagan suckled in a creed outworn;   10
So might I, standing on this pleasant lea,
Have glimpses that would make me less forlorn;
Have sight of Proteus rising from the sea;
Or hear old Triton blow his wreathèd horn.

QUESTIONS
1. In this sonnet by Wordsworth what condition does the poet complain about? To what does he attribute this condition?
2. How does it affect him as an individual?

When Plato in *The Republic* relates the Myth of Er, he introduces supernatural characters he himself originated. Poets, too, have been inspired to make up myths of their own, for their own purposes. "I must create a system or be enslaved by another man's," said William Blake, who in his "prophetic books" peopled the cosmos with supernatural beings having names like Los, Urizen, and Vala (side by side with recognizable figures from the Old Testament and New Testament). This kind of system-making probably has advantages and drawbacks. T. S. Eliot, in his essay on Blake, wishes that the author of *The Four Zoas* had accepted traditional myths, and he compares Blake's thinking to a piece of homemade furniture whose construction diverted valuable energy from the writing of poems. Others have found Blake's untraditional cosmos an achievement — notably William Butler Yeats, himself the author of an elaborate personal mythology. Although we need not know all of Yeats's mythology to enjoy his poems, to know of its existence can make a few great poems deeper for us and less difficult.

William Butler Yeats (1865 – 1939)*

THE SECOND COMING   1921

Turning and turning in the widening gyre°   *spiral*
The falcon cannot hear the falconer;
Things fall apart; the center cannot hold;
Mere anarchy is loosed upon the world,
The blood-dimmed tide is loosed, and everywhere   5
The ceremony of innocence is drowned;
The best lack all conviction, while the worst
Are full of passionate intensity.

Surely some revelation is at hand;
Surely the Second Coming is at hand;   10
The Second Coming! Hardly are those words out
When a vast image out of *Spiritus Mundi*
Troubles my sight: somewhere in sands of the desert
A shape with lion body and the head of a man,
A gaze blank and pitiless as the sun,   15
Is moving its slow thighs, while all about it
Reel shadows of the indignant desert birds.
The darkness drops again; but now I know
That twenty centuries of stony sleep
Were vexed to nightmare by a rocking cradle,   20
And what rough beast, its hour come round at last,
Slouches towards Bethlehem to be born?

What kind of Second Coming does Yeats expect? Evidently it is not to be
a Christian one. Yeats saw human history as governed by the turning of a Great
Wheel, whose phases influence events and determine human personalities —
rather like the signs of the Zodiac in astrology. Every two thousand years comes
a horrendous moment: the Wheel completes a turn; one civilization ends and
another begins. Strangely, a new age is always announced by birds and by acts
of violence. Thus the Greek-Roman world arrives with the descent of Zeus in
swan's form and the burning of Troy, the Christian era with the descent of the
Holy Spirit — traditionally depicted as a dove — and the Crucifixion. In 1919
when Yeats wrote "The Second Coming," his Ireland was in the midst of
turmoil and bloodshed; the Western Hemisphere had been severely shaken by
World War I. A new millennium seemed imminent. What sphinxlike, savage
deity would next appear on earth, with birds proclaiming it angrily? Yeats
imagines it emerging from *Spiritus Mundi,* Soul of the World, a collective
unconscious from which a human being (since the individual soul touches it)
receives dreams, nightmares, and racial memories.[2]

---

[2]Yeats fully explains his system in *A Vision* (1938; reprinted New York: Macmillan, 1956).

It is hard to say whether a poet who discovers a personal myth does so to have something to live by or to have something to write about. Robert Graves, who professed his belief in a White Goddess ("Mother of All Living, the ancient power of love and terror"), declared that he wrote his poetry in a trance, inspired by his Goddess-Muse.[3] Luckily, we do not have to know a poet's religious affiliation before we can read the poems. Perhaps most personal myths that enter poems are not acts of faith but works of art: stories that resemble traditional mythology.

Dick Allen (b. 1939)

NIGHT DRIVING   1987

Cold hands on the cold wheel of his car,
Driving from Bridgeport, he watches
The long line of red taillights
Curving before him, remembers
How his father used to say they were cats' eyes   5
Staring back at them, a long line of cats
Watching from the distance—never Fords,
Buicks, Chevrolets, filled with the heads
Of children, lovers, lonely businessmen,
But cats in the darkness. Half asleep,   10
He can believe, or make himself believe
The truth of his father—all the lies
Not really lies: images which make
The world come closer, cats' eyes up ahead.

QUESTIONS

1. How does personal myth function in this poem?
2. What suggestions can you find in the poem's title?

Harvey Shapiro (b. 1924)

NATIONAL COLD STORAGE COMPANY   1966

The National Cold Storage Company contains
More things than you can dream of.
Hard by the Brooklyn Bridge it stands
In a litter of freight cars,
Tugs to one side; the other, the traffic   5
Of the Long Island Expressway.

[3]See Graves's *The White Goddess*, rev. ed. (New York: Farrar, 1966), or for a terser statement of his position, see his lecture "The Personal Muse" in *On Poetry: Collected Talks and Essays* (New York: Doubleday, 1969).

I myself have dropped into it in seven years
Midnight tossings, plans for escape, the shakes.
Add this to the national total—
Grant's tomb, the Civil War, Arlington,   10
The young President dead.
Above the warehouse and beneath the stars
The poets creep on the harp of the Bridge.
But see,
They fall into the National Cold Storage Company   15
One by one. The wind off the river is too cold,
Or the times too rough, or the Bridge
Is not a harp at all. Or maybe
A monstrous birth inside the warehouse
Must be fed by everything—ships, poems,   20
Stars, all the years of our lives.

QUESTIONS

1. Do you take the National Cold Storage Company to be a real company, some
   imagined afterworld, or both? What different things is it said to keep?
2. In line 13, Brooklyn Bridge is a harp; in lines 17–18 it is not a harp. Does the poet
   contradict himself?
3. What do you make of this monster—the "monstrous birth"—about whose existence
   the poet speculates in his closing lines?

John Milton (1608 – 1674)*

LYCIDAS   1637

*In this monody the author bewails a learned friend, unfortunately drowned
in his passage from Chester on the Irish Seas, 1637. And by occasion
foretells the ruin of our corrupted clergy then in their height.*

Yet once more, O ye laurels, and once more,
Ye myrtles brown°, with ivy never sere,   *dark*
I come to pluck your berries harsh and crude°,   *immature*
And with forced fingers rude
Shatter your leaves before the mellowing year.   5
Bitter constraint and sad occasion dear
Compels me to disturb your season due;
For Lycidas is dead, dead ere his prime,
Young Lycidas, and hath not left his peer.

Lycidas. A *monody* is a song for a single voice, generally a lament. Milton's *learned friend* was Edward
King, scholar and poet, a fellow student at Cambridge University, where King had been preparing
for the ministry. In calling him Lycidas, Milton employs a conventional name for a young shepherd
in **pastoral poetry** (which either portrays the world of shepherds with some realism, as in Virgil's
Eclogues, or makes it a prettified Eden, as in Marlowe's "The Passionate Shepherd to His Love").
1 – 2 *laurels, myrtles:* Evergreens in the crowns traditionally bestowed upon poets.

Who would not sing for Lycidas? he knew   10
Himself to sing, and build the lofty rhyme.
He must not float upon his wat'ry bier
Unwept, and welter° to the parching wind,   *toss about*
Without the meed° of some melodious tear.   *tribute*
     Begin, then, Sisters of the Sacred Well   15
That from beneath the seat of Jove doth spring,
Begin, and somewhat loudly sweep the string.
Hence with denial vain and coy excuse:
So may some gentle Muse°   *poet*
With lucky words favor my destined urn,   20
And, as he passes, turn,
And bid fair peace be to my sable shroud!
For we were nursed upon the self-same hill,
Fed the same flocks, by fountain, shade, and rill;
     Together both, ere the high lawns appeared   25
Under the opening eyelids of the Morn,
We drove a-field, and both together heard
What time the gray-fly winds° her sultry horn,   *sounds*
Batt'ning° our flocks with the fresh dews of night,   *feeding*
Oft till the star that rose at evening bright   30
Toward Heav'n's descent had sloped his westering wheel.
Meanwhile the rural ditties were not mute,
Tempered to the oaten° flute,   *made of an oat stalk*
Rough satyrs danced, and fauns with cloven heel
From the glad sound would not be absent long;   35
And old Damoetas loved to hear our song.
     But, O the heavy change, now thou art gone,
Now thou art gone, and never must return!
Thee, Shepherd, thee the woods and desert caves,
With wild thyme and the gadding° vine o'ergrown,   *wandering* 40
And all their echoes mourn.
The willows, and the hazel copses green,
Shall now no more be seen
Fanning their joyous leaves to thy soft lays.
As killing as the canker to the rose,   45
Or taint-worm to the weanling herds that graze,
Or frost to flowers, that their gay wardrobe wear
When first the white thorn blows°;   *blossoms*
Such, Lycidas, thy loss to shepherd's ear.
     Where were ye, Nymphs, when the remorseless deep   50
Closed o'er the head of your loved Lycidas?
For neither were ye playing on the steep
Where your old bards, the famous Druids, lie,
Nor on the shaggy top of Mona high,

36 *Damoetas:* Perhaps some Cambridge tutor. 53 *Druids:* priests and poets of the Celts in pre-Christian Britain. 54 *Mona:* Roman name for the Isle of Man, near which King was drowned.

Nor yet where Deva spreads her wizard stream.   55
Ay me! I fondly° dream!   *foolishly*
"Had ye been there" — for what could that have done?
What could the Muse herself that Orpheus bore,
The Muse herself, for her enchanting son,
Whom universal Nature did lament,   60
When, by the rout° that made the hideous roar,   *mob*
His gory visage down the stream was sent,
Down the swift Hebrus to the Lesbian shore?
    Alas! What boots it° with uncessant care   *what good does it do*
To tend the homely, slighted shepherd's trade,   65
And strictly meditate the thankless Muse?
Were it not better done, as others use°,   *do*
To sport with Amaryllis in the shade,
Or with the tangles of Neaera's hair?
Fame is the spur that the clear spirit doth raise   70
(That last infirmity of noble mind)
To scorn delights and live laborious days;
But the fair guerdon when we hope to find,
And think to burst out into sudden blaze
Comes the blind Fury with th' abhorrèd shears,   75
And slits the thin-spun life. "But not the praise,"
Phoebus replied, and touched my trembling ears:
"Fame is no plant that grows on mortal soil,
Nor in the glistering° foil,   *glittering*
Set off to the world, nor in broad rumor° lies,   *reputation*   80
But lives and spreads aloft by those pure eyes
And perfect witness of all-judging Jove;
As he pronounces lastly on each deed,
Of so much fame in Heav'n expect thy meed."
    O fountain Arethuse, and thou honored flood,   85
Smooth-sliding Mincius, crowned with vocal reeds,
That strain I heard was of a higher mood:
But now my oat proceeds,
And listens to the Herald of the Sea,
That came in Neptune's plea.   90
He asked the waves, and asked the felon winds,
What hard mishap hath doomed this gentle swain?
And questioned every gust of rugged wings
That blows from off each beakèd promontory:
They knew not of his story;   95

55 *Deva:* the River Dee, flowing between England and Wales. Its shifts in course were said to augur good luck for one country or the other. 68 – 69 *Amaryllis, Neaera:* conventional names for shepherdesses. 70 *the clear spirit doth raise:* doth raise the clear spirit. 77 *touched . . . ears:* gesture signifying "Remember!" 79 *foil:* a setting of gold or silver leaf, used to make a gem appear more brilliant. 85 – 86 *Arethuse, Minicius:* a fountain and river near the birthplaces of Theocritus and Virgil, respectively, hence recalling the most celebrated writer of pastorals in Greek and the most celebrated in Latin. 90 *in Neptune's plea:* bringing the sea-god's plea, "not guilty."

And sage Hippotades their answer brings,
That not a blast was from his dungeon strayed:
The air was calm, and on the level brine
Sleek Panope with all her sisters played.
It was that fatal and perfidious bark,   100
Built in th' eclipse, and rigged with curses dark,
That sunk so low that sacred head of thine.
    Next, Camus, reverend sire, went footing slow,
His mantle hairy, and his bonnet sedge,
Inwrought with figures dim, and on the edge   105
Like to that sanguine flower inscribed with woe.
"Ah! who hath reft," quoth he, "my dearest pledge?"
Last came, and last did go,
The pilot of the Galilean lake;
Two massy keys he bore of metals twain   110
(The golden opes, the iron shuts amain°).   *with force*
He shook his mitered locks, and stern bespake: —
"How well could I have spared for thee, young swain,
Enow° of such as for their bellies' sake,   *enough*
Creep, and intrude, and climb into the fold!   115
Of other care they little reck'ning make
Than how to scramble at the shearers' feast,
And shove away the worthy bidden guest.
Blind mouths! that scarce themselves know how to hold
A sheep-hook, or have learned aught else the least   120
That to the faithful herdsman's art belongs!
What recks it them? What need they? they are sped°;   *prosperous*
And, when they list°, their lean and flashy songs   *so incline*
Grate on their scrannel° pipes of wretched straw;   *feeble, harsh*
The hungry sheep look up, and are not fed,   125
But, swoll'n with wind and the rank mist they draw,
Rot inwardly, and foul contagion spread;
Besides what the grim wolf with privy° paw   *stealthy*
Daily devours apace, and nothing said;
But that two-handed engine at the door   130
Stands ready to smite once, and smite no more."

---

99 *Panope:* a sea nymph. Her name means "one who sees all." 101 *eclipse:* thought to be an omen
of evil fortune. 103 *Camus:* spirit of the river Cam and personification of Cambridge University.
109–112 *pilot:* Saint Peter, once a fisherman in Galilee, to whom Jesus gave the keys of Heaven
(Matthew 16:19). As first Bishop of Rome, he wears the miter, a bishop's emblematic head-covering.
115 *fold:* the Church of England. 120 *sheep-hook:* a bishop's staff or crozier, which resembles a
shepherd's crook. 128 *wolf:* probably the Church of Rome. Jesuits in England at the time were
winning converts. 130 *two-handed engine:* This disputed phrase may refer (among other possibilities)
to the punishing sword of The Word of God (Revelation 19:13–15 and Hebrews 4:12). Perhaps
Milton sees it as a lightning bolt, as does Spenser, to whom Jove's wrath is a "three-forked engine"
(*Faerie Queene,* VIII, 9). 131 *smite once . . . no more:* Because, in the proverb, lightning never strikes
twice in the same place?

Return, Alpheus; the dread voice is past
That shrunk thy streams; return, Sicilian Muse,
And call the vales, and bid them hither cast
Their bells and flow'rets of a thousand hues.   135
Ye valleys low, where the mild whispers use°   resort
Of shades, and wanton winds, and gushing brooks,
On whose fresh lap the swart star sparely looks,
Throw hither all your quaint enameled eyes,
That on the green turf suck the honied showers,   140
And purple all the ground with vernal flowers.
Bring the rathe° primrose that forsaken dies,   early
The tufted crow-toe, and pale jessamine,
The white pink, and the pansy freaked° with jet,   streaked
The glowing violet,   145
The musk-rose, and the well-attired woodbine,
With cowslips wan that hang the pensive head,
And every flower that sad embroidery wears;
Bid amaranthus all his beauty shed,
And daffadillies fill their cups with tears,   150
To strew the laureate hearse where Lycid lies.
For so, to interpose a little ease,
Let our frail thoughts dally with false surmise,
Ay me! whilst thee the shores and sounding seas
Wash far away, where'er thy bones are hurled;   155
Whether beyond the stormy Hebrides,
Where thou, perhaps, under the whelming tide
Visit'st the bottom of the monstrous° world;   full of sea monsters
Or whether thou, to our moist vows° denied,   prayers
Sleep'st by the fable of Bellerus old,   160
Where the great Vision of the guarded mount
Looks toward Namancos and Bayona's hold°:   stronghold
Look homeward, angel, now, and melt with ruth°;   pity
And, O ye dolphins, waft the hapless youth.
Weep no more, woeful shepherds, weep no more,   165
For Lycidas, your sorrow, is not dead,
Sunk though he be beneath the wat'ry floor:
So sinks the day-star in the ocean bed
And yet anon repairs his drooping head,
And tricks° his beams, and with new-spangled ore°   arrays; gold 170
Flames in the forehead of the morning sky:
So Lycidas sunk low, but mounted high,

---

133 *Sicilian Muse:* who inspired Theocritus, a native of Sicily. 138 *swart star:* Sirius, at its zenith
in summer, was thought to turn vegetation black. 153 *false surmise:* futile hope that the body of
Lycidas could be recovered. 160 *Bellerus:* legendary giant of Land's End, the far tip of Cornwall.
161 *guarded mount:* Saint Michael's Mount, off Land's End, said to be under the protection of the
archangel. 162 *Namancos, Bayona:* on the coast of Spain. 164 *dolphins:* In Greek legend, these kindly
mammals carried the spirits of the dead to the Blessed Isles.

Through the dear might of Him that walked the waves,
Where, other groves and other streams along,
With nectar pure his oozy locks he laves, 175
And hears the unexpressive nuptial song,
In the blest kingdoms meek of Joy and Love.
There entertain him all the Saints above,
In solemn troops, and sweet societies,
That sing, and singing in their glory move, 180
And wipe the tears forever from his eyes.
Now, Lycidas, the shepherds weep no more;
Henceforth thou art the Genius° of the shore, *guardian spirit*
In thy large recompense, and shalt be good
To all that wander in that perilous flood. 185

    Thus sang the uncouth° swain to th' oaks and rills, *rustic (or little-known)*
While the still Morn went out with sandals gray;
He touched the tender stops of various quills°, *reeds of a shepherd's pipe*
With eager thought warbling his Doric lay:
And now the sun had stretched out all the hills, 190
And now was dropped into the western bay.
At last he rose, and twitched° his mantle blue: *donned*
Tomorrow to fresh woods and pastures new.

---

176 *unexpressive nuptial song:* inexpressibly beautiful song for the marriage feast of the Lamb
(Revelation 19:9). 189 *Doric lay:* pastoral poem. Doric is the dialect of Greek employed by Theocritus.

QUESTIONS AND EXERCISES

1. With the aid of an encyclopedia or a handbook of classical mythology (such as
   Bulfinch's *Mythology*, Edith Hamilton's *Mythology*, or H. J. Rose's *Handbook of Greek
   Mythology*) learn more about the following myths or mythical figures and places to
   which Milton alludes:

   Line 15   Sisters of the Sacred Well (Muses)
        16   seat of Jove (Mount Olympus)
        58   the Muse . . . that Orpheus bore (Calliope)
    61 – 63   (the death of Orpheus)
        75   Fury with the . . . shears (Atropos, one of the three Fates)
        77   Phoebus
        89   Herald of the Sea (Triton)
        90   Neptune
        96   Hippotades
      106   (Hyacinthus)
      132   Alpheus

   Then reread Milton's poem. As a result of your familiarity with these myths,
   what details become clear?
2. Read the parable of the Good Shepherd (John 10:1 – 18). What relationships does
   Milton draw between the Christian idea of the shepherd and pastoral poetry?

3. "With these trifling fictions [allusions to classical mythology]," wrote Samuel Johnson about "Lycidas," "are mingled the most awful and sacred truths, such as ought never to be polluted with such irreverend combinations." Does this mingling of paganism and Christianity detract from Milton's poem? Discuss.
4. In "Lycidas" does Milton devise any new myth or myths?

SUGGESTIONS FOR WRITING

1. Write an explication of D. H. Lawrence's "Bavarian Gentians" or Thomas Hardy's "The Oxen." (For hints on writing about poetry by the method of explication, see page 1492.)
2. In a brief essay, either serious or otherwise, invent a brand new personal myth.

26 Alternatives

THE POET'S REVISIONS

"He / Who casts to write a living line must sweat, / . . . and strike the second heat / Upon the Muse's anvil," wrote Ben Jonson. Indeed, few if any immortal poems can have been perfected with the first blow. As a result, a poet may leave us two or more versions of a poem — perhaps (as Robert Graves has said of his work drafts) "hatched and cross-hatched by puzzling layers of ink."

We need not, of course, rummage the poet's wastebasket in order to evaluate a poem. If we wish, we can follow a suggestion of the critic Austin Warren: take any fine poem and make changes in it. Then compare the changes with the original. We may then realize why the poem is as it is instead of something else. However, there is a certain undeniable pleasure in watching a poem go through its growth stages. Some readers have claimed that the study of successive versions gives them insight into the process by which poems come to be. More important to a reader whose concern is to read poems with appreciation, we stand to learn something about the rightness of a finished poem from seeing what alternatives occurred to the poet. To a critic who protested two lines in Wordsworth's "The Thorn," a painfully flat description of an infant's grave,

> I've measured it from side to side;
> 'Tis three feet long and two feet wide,

Wordsworth retorted, "They ought to be liked." However, he thought better of them and later made this change:

> Though but of compass small, and bare
> To thirsty suns and parching air.

William Butler Yeats, who enjoyed revision, kept trying to improve the poems of his youth. A merciless self-critic, Yeats discarded lines that a lesser poet would have been grateful for. In some cases his final version was practically a new poem.

William Butler Yeats (1865 – 1939)*

THE OLD PENSIONER   1890

I had a chair at every hearth,
When no one turned to see
With "Look at that old fellow there;
And who may he be?"
And therefore do I wander on,   5
And the fret is on me.

The road-side trees keep murmuring —
Ah, wherefore murmur ye
As in the old days long gone by,
Green oak and poplar tree!   10
The well-known faces are all gone,
And the fret is on me.

William Butler Yeats (1865 – 1939)

THE LAMENTATION OF THE OLD PENSIONER   1939

Although I shelter from the rain
Under a broken tree
My chair was nearest to the fire
In every company
That talked of love or politics,   5
Ere Time transfigured me.

Though lads are making pikes again
For some conspiracy,
And crazy rascals rage their fill
At human tyranny,   10
My contemplations are of Time
That has transfigured me.

There's not a woman turns her face
Upon a broken tree,
And yet the beauties that I loved   15
Are in my memory;
I spit into the face of Time
That has transfigured me.

QUESTIONS

1. "The Old Pensioner" is this poem's first printed version; "Lamentation," its last.
   From the original, what elements has Yeats in the end retained?
2. What does the final version add to our knowledge of the old man (his character,
   attitudes, circumstances)?

3. Compare in sound and rhythm the refrain in the "Lamentation" with the original refrain.
4. Why do the statements in the final version seem to follow one another more naturally, and the poem as a whole seem more tightly woven together?

Yeats's practice seems to document the assertion of critic A. F. Scott that "the work of correction is often quite as inspired as the first onrush of words and ideas." Yeats made a revealing comment on his methods of revision:

> In dream poetry, in "Kubla Khan," . . . every line, every word can carry its unanalyzable, rich associations; but if we dramatize some possible singer or speaker we remember that he is moved by one thing at a time, certain words must be dull and numb. Here and there in correcting my early poems I have introduced such numbness and dullness, turned, for instance, the "curd-pale moon" into the "brilliant moon," that all might seem, as it were, remembered with indifference, except some one vivid image. When I began to rehearse a play I had the defects of my early poetry; I insisted upon obvious all-pervading rhythm. Later on I found myself saying that only in those lines or words where the beauty of the passage came to its climax, must rhythm be obvious.[1]

In changing colorful words for "dull and numb" ones, in breaking up and varying rhythms, Yeats evidently is trying for improvement not in a particular line, but in an entire poem.

Not all revisions are successful. An instance might be the alterations Keats made in "La Belle Dame sans Merci," in which a stanza with "wild wild eyes" and exactly counted kisses,

> She took me to her elfin grot,
>   And there she wept and sighed full sore,
> And there I shut her wild wild eyes
>   With kisses four.

was scrapped in favor of:

> She took me to her elfin grot,
>   And there she gazed and sighèd deep,
> And there I shut her wild sad eyes —
>   So kissed to sleep.

When Mark Antony begins his funeral oration, "Friends, Romans, countrymen: lend me your ears," Shakespeare makes him ask something quite different from the modernized version in one high school English textbook: "Friends, Romans, countrymen: listen to me." Strictly speaking, any revised version of a poem is a different poem, even if its only change is a single word.

---

[1]"Dramatis Personae, 1896–1902," in *The Autobiography of William Butler Yeats* (New York: Macmillan, 1953).

EXERCISE: *Early and Late Versions*

In each of the following pairs, which details of the revised version show an improvement of the earlier one? Exactly what makes the poet's second thoughts seem better (if you agree that they are)? Italics indicate words of one text not found in the other. Notice that in some cases, the poet has also changed word order.

1. Samuel Taylor Coleridge, "The Rime of the Ancient Mariner," from Part III:

    a. One after one, by the hornèd Moon
        (Listen, O Stranger! to me)
       Each turn'd his face with a ghastly pang
       And curs'd me with his *ee.*

    　　　　　　　　(1799 version)

    b. One after one, by the *star-dogged* Moon,
       Too quick for groan or sigh,
       Each turned his face with a ghastly pang
       And cursed me with his *eye.*

    　　　　　　　　(1817 version)

2. William Blake, last stanza of "London" (complete poem given on 562):

    a. But most the midnight harlot's curse
       From every *dismal* street I hear,
       Weaves around the marriage hearse
       And blasts the new born infant's tear.

    　　　　　　　　(first draft, 1793)

    b. But most *through* midnight streets I hear
       How the *youthful* harlot's curse
       Blasts the new born infant's tear
       And *blights with plagues* the marriage hearse.

    　　　　　　　　(1794 version)

3. Edward FitzGerald, *The Rubáiyát of Omar Khayyám*, a quatrain:

    a. For *in and out, above, about, below,*
       'Tis nothing but a Magic Shadow-show,
        Play'd in a Box whose Candle is the Sun,
       Round *which* we *Phantom Figures* come and go.

    　　　　　　　　(first version, 1859 edition)

    b. We *are no other than a moving row*
       Of Magic Shadow-*shapes that* come and go
       Round *with* the Sun-*illumined Lantern held*
       In Midnight by the Master of the Show; . . .

    　　　　　　　　(fifth version, 1889 edition)

Walt Whitman (1819 – 1892)*

A NOISELESS PATIENT SPIDER

A noiseless patient spider,
I mark'd where on a little promontory it stood isolated,
Mark'd how to explore the vacant vast surrounding,
It launch'd forth filament, filament, filament, out of itself,

Ever unreeling them, ever tirelessly speeding them.   5
And you O my soul where you stand,
Surrounded, detached, in measureless oceans of space,
Ceaselessly musing, venturing, throwing, seeking the spheres to
    connect them,
Till the bridge you will need be form'd, till the ductile anchor hold,
Till the gossamer thread you fling catch somewhere, O my soul.   10

Walt Whitman (1819 – 1892)

THE SOUL, REACHING, THROWING OUT FOR LOVE

The Soul, reaching, throwing out for love,
As the spider, from some little promontory, throwing out filament
    after filament, tirelessly out of itself, that one at least may catch
    and form a link, a bridge, a connection
O I saw one passing along, saying hardly a word — yet full of love I
    detected him, by certain signs
O eyes wishfully turning! O silent eyes!
For then I thought of you o'er the world,   5
O latent oceans, fathomless oceans of love!
O waiting oceans of love! yearning and fervid! and of you sweet souls
    perhaps in the future, delicious and long:
But Death, unknown on the earth — ungiven, dark here, unspoken,
    never born:
You fathomless latent souls of love — you pent and unknown oceans
    of love!

QUESTIONS

1. One of these two versions of a poem by Whitman is an early draft from the poet's
   notebook. The other is the final version completed in 1871, about ten years later.
   Which is the final version?
2. In the final version, what has Whitman done to render his central metaphor (the
   comparison of soul and spider) more vivid and exact? What proportion of the final
   version is devoted to this metaphor?
3. In the early draft, what lines seem distracting or nonessential?

TRANSLATIONS

Poetry, said Robert Frost, is what gets lost in translation. If absolutely true, the
comment is bad news for most of us, who have to depend on translations for
our only knowledge of great poems in many other languages. However, some
translators seem able to save a part of their originals and bring it across the
language gap. At times they may even add more poetry of their own, as if to
try to compensate for what is lost.

Unlike the writer of an original poem, the translator begins with a meaning that already exists. To convey it, the translator may decide to stick closely to the denotations of the original words or else to depart from them, more or less freely, after something he or she values more. The latter aim is evident in the *Imitations* of Robert Lowell, who said he had been "reckless with literal meaning" and instead had "labored hard to get the tone." Particularly defiant of translation are poems in dialect, uneducated speech, and slang: what can be used for English equivalents? Ezra Pound, in a bold move, translates the song of a Chinese peasant in *The Classic Anthology Defined by Confucius:*

> Yaller bird, let my corn alone,
> Yaller bird, let my crawps alone,
> These folks here won't let me eat,
> I wanna go back whaar I can meet
> the folks I used to know at home,
>   I got a home an' I wanna' git goin'.

Here, it is our purpose to judge a translation not by its fidelity to its original, but by the same standards we apply to any other poem written in English. To do so may be another way to see the difference between appropriate and inappropriate words.

Federico García Lorca (1899 – 1936)

LA GUITARRA	1921	GUITAR	1967

Empieza el llanto	Begins the crying
de la guitarra.	of the guitar.
Se rompen las copas	From earliest dawn
de la madrugada.	the strokes are breaking.
Empieza el llanto	Begins the crying
de la guitarra.	of the guitar.
Es inútil	It is futile
callarla.	to stop its sound.
Es imposible	It is impossible
callarla.	to stop its sound.
Llora monótona	It is crying a monotone
como llora el agua,	like the crying of water,
como llora el viento	like the crying of wind
sobre la nevada.	over fallen snow.
Es imposible	It is impossible
callarla.	to stop its sound.
Llora por cosas	It is crying over things
lejanas.	far off.

Arena del Sur caliente	Burning sand of the South	
que pide camelias blancas.	which covets white camelias.	20
Llora flecha sin blanco,	It is crying the arrow without aim,	
la tarde sin mañana,	the evening without tomorrow,	
y el primer pájaro muerto	and the first dead bird on the branch.	
sobre la rama.	O guitar!	
¡Oh, guitarra!	Heart heavily wounded	25
Corazón malherido	by five sharp swords.	
por cinco espadas.		

— Translated by Keith Waldrop

QUESTIONS

1. Someone who knows Spanish should read aloud the original and the translation. Although it is impossible for any translation fully to capture the resonance of García Lorca's poem, in what places is the English version most nearly able to approximate it?
2. Another translation renders line 21: "It mourns for the targetless arrow." What is the difference between mourning for something and being the cry of it?
3. Throughout his translation, Waldrop closely follows the line divisions of the original, but in line 23 he combines García Lorca's lines 23 and 24. Can you see any point in his doing so? Would "on the branch" by itself be a strong line of English poetry?

EXERCISE: *Comparing Translations*

Which English translation of each of the following poems is the best poetry? The originals may be of interest to some. For those who do not know the foreign language, the editor's line-by-line prose paraphrases may help indicate what the translator had to work with and how much of the translation is the translator's own idea. In which do you find the diction most felicitous? In which do pattern and structure best move as one? What differences in tone are apparent? It is doubtful that any one translation will surpass the others in every detail.

Horace (65 – 8 B.C.)

ODES I (38)   (about 20 B.C.)

Persicos odi, puer, apparatus,
Displicent nexae philyra coronae;
Mitte sectari, rosa quo locorum
      Sera moretur.
Simplici myrto nihil allabores   5
Sedulus curo: neque te ministrum
Dedecet myrtus neque me sub arta
      Vite bibentem.

ODES I (38). Prose translation: (1) Persian pomp, boy, I detest, (2) garlands woven of linden bark displease me; (3 – 4) give up searching for the place where the late-blooming rose is. (5 – 6) Put no laborious trimmings on simple myrtle: (6 – 7) for myrtle is unbecoming neither to you, a servant, nor to me, under the shade of this (8) vine, drinking.

1. SIMPLICITY   (about 1782)

Boy, I hate their empty shows,
    Persian garlands I detest,
Bring me not the late-blown rose
    Lingering after all the rest:
Plainer myrtle pleases me   5
    Thus outstretched beneath my vine,
Myrtle more becoming thee,
    Waiting with thy master's wine.
                        — William Cowper

2. FIE ON EASTERN LUXURY!   (about 1830)

Nay, nay, my boy — 'tis not for me,
    This studious pomp of Eastern luxury;
Give me no various garlands — fine
    With linden twine,
Nor seek, where latest lingering blows,   5
    The solitary rose.

Earnest I beg — add not with toilsome pain,
One far-sought blossom to the myrtle plain,
For sure, the fragrant myrtle bough
    Looks seemliest on thy brow;   10
Nor me mis-seems, while, underneath the vine,
Close interweaved, I quaff the rosy wine.
                        — Hartley Coleridge

3. THE PREFERENCE DECLARED   1892

Boy, I detest the Persian pomp;
    I hate those linden-bark devices;
And as for roses, holy Moses!
    They can't be got at living prices!
Myrtle is good enough for us, —   5
    For *you*, as bearer of my flagon;
For *me*, supine beneath this vine,
    Doing my best to get a jag on!
                        — Eugene Field

Charles Baudelaire (1821 – 1867)

RECUEILLEMENT   1866

Sois sage, ô ma Douleur, et tiens-toi plus tranquille.
Tu réclamais le Soir; il descend; le voici:
Une atmosphère obscure enveloppe la ville,
Aux uns portant la paix, aux autres le souci.

"MEDITATION." Prose translation: (1) Behave yourself [as a mother would say to her child], O my
Sorrow, and keep calmer. (2) You called for Evening; it descends; here it is: (3) a dim atmosphere
envelops the city, (4) Bringing peace to some; to others anxiety.

Pendant que des mortels la multitude vile,   5
Sous le fouet du Plaisir, ce bourreau sans merci,
Va cueillir des remords dans la fête servile,
Ma Douleur, donne-moi la main; viens par ici,

Loin d'eux. Vois se pencher les défuntes Années,
Sur les balcons du ciel, en robes surannées;   10
Surgir du fond des eaux le Regret souriant;

Le Soleil moribond s'endormir sous une arche,
Et, comme un long linceul traînant à l'Orient,
Entends, ma chère, entends la douce Nuit qui marche.

(5) While the vile multitude of mortals (6) under the whip of Pleasure, that merciless executioner,
(7) go to gather remorse in the servile festival, (8) my Sorrow, give me your hand; come this way,
(9) far from them. See the dead years lean (10) on the balconies of the sky, in old-fashioned dresses;
(11) [see] Regret, smiling, emerge from the depths of the waters; (12) [see] the dying Sun go to sleep
under an arch; (13) and like a long shroud trailing in the East, (14) hear, my darling, hear the soft
Night who is walking.

1. Peace, be at peace, O thou my heaviness   1919

Peace, be at peace, O thou my heaviness,
Thou callèdst for the evening, lo! 'tis here,
The City wears a somber atmosphere
That brings repose to some, to some distress.
Now while the heedless throng make haste to press   5
Where pleasure drives them, ruthless charioteer,
To pluck the fruits of sick remorse and fear,
Come thou with me, and leave their fretfulness.
See how they hang from heaven's high balconies,
The old lost years in faded garments dressed,   10
And see Regret with faintly smiling mouth;
And while the dying sun sinks in the west,
Hear how, far off, Night walks with velvet tread,
And her long robe trails all about the south.
    — Lord Alfred Douglas

2. Inward Conversation   1961

Be reasonable, my pain, and think with more detachment.
You asked to see the dusk; it descends; it is here:
A sheath of dark light robes the city,
To some bringing peace, to some the end of peace.
Now while the rotten herds of mankind,   5
Flogged by pleasure, that lyncher without touch,
Go picking remorse in their filthy holidays,
Let us join hands, my pain; come this way,

Far from them. Look at the dead years that lean on
The balconies of the sky, in their clothes long out of date;   10
The sense of loss that climbs from the deep waters with a smile;

The sun, nearly dead, that drops asleep beneath an arch;
And listen to the night, like a long shroud being dragged
Toward the east, my love, listen, the soft night is moving.
    — Robert Bly

3. MEDITATION   1961

   Calm down, my Sorrow, we must move with care.
   You called for evening; it descends; it's here.
   The town is coffined in its atmosphere,
   bringing relief to some, to others care.

   Now while the common multitude strips bare,   5
   feels pleasure's cat o' nine tails on its back,
   and fights off anguish at the great bazaar,
   give me your hand, my Sorrow. Let's stand back;

   back from these people! Look, the dead years dressed
   in old clothes crowd the balconies of the sky.   10
   Regret emerges smiling from the sea,

   the sick sun slumbers underneath an arch,
   and like a shroud strung out from east to west,
   listen, my Dearest, hear the sweet night march!
                    — Robert Lowell

4. MEDITATION   1982

   Behave, my Sorrow! let's have no more scenes.
   Evening's what you wanted — Evening's here:
   a gradual darkness overtakes the town,
   bringing peace to some, to others pain.

   Now, while humanity racks up remorse   5
   in low distractions under Pleasure's lash,
   grovelling for a ruthless master — come
   away, my Sorrow, leave them! Give me your hand . . .

   See how the dear departed dowdy years
   crowd the balconies of heaven, leaning down,   10
   while smiling out of the sea appears Regret;

   the Sun will die in its sleep beneath a bridge,
   and trailing westward like a winding-sheet —
   listen, my dear — how softly Night arrives.
                    — Richard Howard

PARODY

In a **parody**, one writer imitates another writer or another work, for the
purpose of poking fun. Parody is a favorite medium for child poets, as shown
in this jingle made up by children on the streets of Edinburgh.

Anonymous

WE FOUR LADS FROM LIVERPOOL ARE   (about 1963)

We four lads from Liverpool are—
Paul in a taxi, John in a car,
George on a scooter, tootin' his hooter,
Following Ringo Starr.

Skillfully written, parody can be a devastating form of literary criticism. Rather than merely flinging abuse, the wise parodist imitates with understanding, even with sympathy. The many crude parodies of T. S. Eliot's difficult poem *The Waste Land* show parodists mocking what they cannot fathom, with the result that, instead of illuminating the original, they belittle it (and themselves). Good parodists have an ear for the sounds and rhythms of their originals, as does James Camp, who echoes Walt Whitman's stately "Out of the Cradle Endlessly Rocking" in his line "Out of the crock endlessly ladling" (what a weary teacher feels he is doing). Parody can be aimed at poems good or bad; yet there are poems of such splendor and dignity that no parodist seems able to touch them without looking like a small dog defiling a cathedral, and others so illiterate that good parody would be squandered on them. In the following original by T. E. Brown, what failings does the parodist, J. A. Lindon, jump upon? (*God wot*, by the way, is an archaism for "God knows.")

T. E. Brown (1830 – 1897)

MY GARDEN   1887

A garden is a lovesome thing,
  God wot!
Rose plot,
Fringed pool,
Ferned grot —
The veriest school
Of peace; and yet the fool
Contends that God is not —
Not God! in gardens! when the eve
  is cool?
Nay, but I have a sign;
'Tis very sure God walks in mine.

J. A. Lindon (b. 1914)

My GARDEN   1959

A garden is a *lovesome* thing?
  What rot!
Weed plot,
Scum pool,
Old pot,   5
Snail-shiny stool
In pieces; yet the fool
Contends that snails are not —
Not snails! in gardens! when
  the eve is cool?
Nay, but I see their trails!   10
'Tis very sure *my* garden's full
  of snails!

Hugh Kingsmill
[Hugh Kingsmill Lunn] (1889 – 1949)

WHAT, STILL ALIVE AT TWENTY-TWO?   (about 1920)

What, still alive at twenty-two,
A clean, upstanding chap like you?
Sure, if your throat 'tis hard to slit,
Slit your girl's, and swing for it.

Like enough, you won't be glad   5
When they come to hang you, lad:

But bacon's not the only thing
That's cured by hanging from a string.

So, when the spilt ink of the night
Spreads o'er the blotting-pad of light,   10
Lads whose job is still to do
Shall whet their knives, and think of you.

QUESTIONS

1. A. E. Housman considered this the best of many parodies of his poetry. Read his poems
   in this book, particularly "Eight O'Clock" (page 627), "When I was one-and-twenty" (page
   656), and "To an Athlete Dying Young" (page 832). What characteristics of theme, form,
   and language does Hugh Kingsmill's parody convey?
2. What does Kingsmill exaggerate?

Kenneth Koch (b. 1925)

MENDING SUMP   1960

"Hiram, I think the sump is backing up.
The bathroom floor boards for above two weeks
Have seemed soaked through. A little bird, I think,
Has wandered in the pipes, and all's gone wrong."
"Something there is that doesn't hump a sump,"   5
He said; and through his head she saw a cloud
That seemed to twinkle. "Hiram, well," she said,
"Smith is come home! I saw his face just now
While looking through your head. He's come to die
Or else to laugh, for hay is dried-up grass   10
When you're alone." He rose, and sniffed the air.
"We'd better leave him in the sump," he said.

QUESTIONS

1. What poet is the object of this parody? Which of his poems are echoed in it?
2. Koch gains humor by making outrageous statements in the tone and language of his
   original. Looking at other poems in this book by the poet being parodied, how would
   you describe their tone? Their language?
3. Suppose, instead of casting his parody into blank verse, Koch had written:

   "Hiram, the sump is backing up.
   The bathroom floor boards
   For above two weeks
   Have been soaking through. A little bird,
   I think, has wandered in
   The pipes, and all's gone wrong."

   Why would the biting edge of his parody have been blunted?
4. What, by the way, is a sump?

EXERCISE: *Spotting the Originals*

In the following parody, what poem or poet is being kidded? Does the parodist seem only to be having fun, or is he making any critical point?

George Starbuck (b. 1931)

MARGARET ARE YOU DRUG   1966

Cool it Mag.
Sure it's a drag
With all that green flaked out.
Next thing you know they'll be changing the color of bread.

But look, Chick,   5
Why panic?
Sevennyeighty years, we'll *all* be dead.

Roll with it, Kid.
I did.
Give it the old benefit of the doubt.   10

I mean leaves
Schmeaves.
You sure you aint just feeling sorry for yourself?

MARGARET ARE YOU DRUG. This is one of a series of "Translations from the English."

SUGGESTIONS FOR WRITING

1. Write a poem in the manner of Emily Dickinson, William Carlos Williams, E. E. Cummings, or any other modern poet whose work interests you and which you feel able to imitate. Decide, before you start, whether to write a serious imitation (that could be slipped into the poet's *Collected Poems* without anyone being the wiser), or a humorous parody. Read all the poet's poems included in this book; perhaps you will find it helpful also to consult a larger selection or collection of the poet's work. It might be simplest to choose a particular poem as your model; but, if you like, you may echo any number of poems. Choose a model within the range of your own skill: to imitate a sonnet, for instance, you need to be able to rime and to write in meter. Probably, if your imitation is serious, and not a parody, it is a good idea to pick a subject or theme characteristic of the poet. This is a difficult project, but if you can do it even fairly well, you will know a great deal more about poetry and your poet.
2. Compare and contrast the earlier version of Robert Frost's poem originally titled "In White" with the finished version "Design" (page 1493). What specific improvements did the poet make? Why do you think he made them? What was the matter with his first thoughts?
3. Word-processing systems, it is claimed, now enable writers to revise swiftly and efficiently. If you are familiar with word processors or computers, point out any possible advantages and disadvantages to poetry that may result from this recent development in technology.

27 Evaluating a Poem

TELLING GOOD FROM BAD

Why do we call some poems "bad"? We are talking not about their moral implications. Rather, we mean that, for one or more of many possible reasons, the poem has failed to move us or to engage our sympathies. Instead, it has made us doubt that the poet is in control of language and vision; perhaps it has aroused our antipathies or unwittingly appealed to our sense of the comic, though the poet is serious. Some poems can be said to succeed despite burdensome faults. But in general such faults are symptoms of deeper malady: some weakness in a poem's basic conception or in the poet's competence.

Nearly always, a bad poem reveals only a dim and distorted awareness of its probable effect on its audience. Perhaps the sound of words may clash with what a poem is saying, as in the jarring last word of this opening line of a tender lyric (author unknown, quoted by Richard Wilbur): "Come into the tent, my love, and close the flap." Perhaps a metaphor may fail by calling to mind more differences than similarities, as in Emily Dickinson's lines "Our lives are Swiss — / So still — so cool." A bad poem usually overshoots or falls short of its mark by the poet's thinking too little or too much. Thinking too much, a poet contrives an excess of ingenuity like that quoted by Alexander Pope in *Peri Bathous, or Of the Art of Sinking in Poetry*: a hounded stag who "Hears his own feet, and thinks they sound like more; / And fears the hind feet will o'ertake the fore." Thinking too little, a poet writes redundantly, as Wordsworth in "The Thorn": "And they had fixed the wedding-day, / The morning that must wed them both."

In a poem that has a rime scheme or a set line length, when all is well, pattern and structure move inseparably with the rest of their poem, the way a tiger's skin and bones move with their tiger. But sometimes, in a poem that fails, the poet evidently has had difficulty in fitting the statements into a formal pattern. English poets have long felt free to invert word order for a special effect (Milton: "ye myrtles brown"), but the poet having trouble keeping to a rime scheme may invert words for no apparent reason but convenience. Needing a rime for *barge* may lead to ending a line with a *policedog large* instead of *a large policedog.* Another sign of trouble is a profusion of adjectives. If a line of iambic pentameter reads, "Her lovely skin, like dear sweet white old silk," we suspect the poet of stuffing the line to make it long enough. (But no one suspects Matthew Arnold of padding the last line of "To Marguerite": "The unplumbed, salt, estranging sea.")

Because, over his or her dead body, even a poet's slightest and feeblest efforts may be collected, some lines in the canon of celebrated bards make us wonder, "How could they have written this?" Wordsworth, Shelley, Whitman, and Browning are among the great whose failures can be painful, and sometimes an excellent poem will have a bad spot in it. To be unwilling to read them, though, would be as ill advised as to refuse to see Venice just because the Grand Canal is said to contain impurities. The seasoned reader of poetry thinks no less of Tennyson for having written, "Form, Form, Riflemen Form! . . . Look to your butts, and take good aims!" The collected works of a duller poet may contain no such lines of unconscious double meaning, but neither do they contain any poem as good as "Ulysses." If the duller poet never had a spectacular failure, it may be because of failure to take risks. "In poetry," said Ronsard, "the greatest vice is mediocrity."

Often, inept poems fall into familiar categories. At one extreme is the poem written entirely in conventional diction, dimly echoing Shakespeare, Wordsworth, and the Bible, but garbling them. Couched in a rhythm that ticks along like a metronome, this kind of poem shows no sign that its author has ever taken a hard look at anything that can be tasted, handled, and felt. It employs loosely and thoughtlessly the most abstract of words: *love, beauty, life, death, time, eternity.* Littered with old-fashioned contractions (*'tis, o'er, where'er*), it may end in a simple preachment or platitude. George Orwell's complaint against much contemporary writing (not only poetry) is applicable: "As soon as certain topics are raised" — and one thinks of such standard topics for poetry as spring, a first kiss, and stars — "the concrete melts into the abstract and no one seems able to think of turns of speech that are not hackneyed." Writers, Orwell charged, too often make their sentences out of tacked-together phrases "like the sections of a prefabricated hen-house."[1] Versifiers often do likewise.

At the opposite extreme is the poem that displays no acquaintance with poetry of the past but manages, instead, to fabricate its own clichés. Slightly paraphrased, a manuscript once submitted to *The Paris Review* began:

Vile

    rottenflush

        o   — *screaming* —

        f CORPSEBLOOD!!   ooze

STRANGLE my

    eyes . . .

                  HELL's

         O, ghastly   stench***!!!

[1] George Orwell, "Politics and the English Language," from *Shooting an Elephant and Other Essays* (New York: Harcourt, 1945).

At most, such a work has only a private value. The writer has vented personal frustrations upon words, instead of kicking stray dogs. In its way, "Vile Rotten-flush" is as self-indulgent as the oldfangled "first kiss in spring" kind of poem. "I dislike," said John Livingston Lowes, "poems that black your eyes, or put up their mouths to be kissed."

As jewelers tell which of two diamonds is fine by seeing which scratches the other, two poems may be tested by comparing them. This method works only on poems similar in length and kind: an epigram cannot be held up to test an epic. Most poems we meet are neither sheer trash nor obvious master-pieces. Because good diamonds to be proven need softer ones to scratch, in this chapter you will find a few clear-cut gems and a few clinkers.

Anonymous (English)

O MOON, WHEN I GAZE ON THY BEAUTIFUL FACE   (about 1900)

O Moon, when I gaze on thy beautiful face,
Careering along through the boundaries of space,
The thought has often come into my mind
If I ever shall see thy glorious behind.

O MOON. Sir Edmund Gosse, the English critic (1849 – 1928), offered this quatrain as the work of his maidservant, but there is reason to suspect him of having written it.

QUESTIONS

1. To what fact of astronomy does the last line refer?
2. Which words seem chosen with too little awareness of their denotations and connotations?
3. Even if you did not know that these lines probably were deliberately bad, how would you argue with someone who maintained that the opening O in the poem was admirable as a bit of concrete poetry? (See the quotation from E. E. Cummings on page 698.)

Grace Treasone

LIFE   (about 1963)

Life is like a jagged tooth
that cuts into your heart;
fix the tooth and save the root,
and laughs, not tears, will start.

QUESTIONS

1. Try to paraphrase this poem. What is the poet saying?
2. How consistent is the working out of the comparison of life to a tooth?

Stephen Tropp (b. 1930)

MY WIFE IS MY SHIRT   1960

My wife is my shirt
I put my hands through her armpits
slide my head through her mouth
& finally button her blood around my hands

QUESTIONS

1. How consistently is the metaphor elaborated?
2. Why can this metaphor be said to work in exactly the opposite way from a personification?
3. A paraphrase might discover this simile: "My wife is as intimate, familiar, and close to me as the shirt on my back." If this is the idea and the poem is supposed to be a love poem, how precisely is its attitude expressed?

William McGonagall (1830? – 1902)

THE ALBION BATTLESHIP CALAMITY   (1898)

'Twas in the year of 1898, and on the 21st of June,
The launching of the Battleship Albion caused a great gloom,
Amongst the relatives of many persons who were drowned in the
    River Thames,
Which their relatives will remember while life remains.

The vessel was christened by the Duchess of York,   5
And the spectators' hearts felt as light as cork
As the Duchess cut the cord that was holding the fine ship,
Then the spectators loudly cheered as the vessel slid down the slip.

The launching of the vessel was very well carried out,
While the guests on the stands cheered without any doubt,   10
Under the impression that everything would go well;
But, alas! instantaneously a bridge and staging fell.

Oh! little did the Duchess of York think that day
That so many lives would be taken away
At the launching of the good ship Albion,   15
But when she heard of the catastrophe she felt woebegone.

But accidents will happen without any doubt,
And often the cause thereof is hard to find out;
And according to report, I've heard people say,
'Twas the great crowd on the bridge caused it to give way.   20

Just as the vessel entered the water the bridge and staging gave way,
Immersing some three hundred people which caused great dismay

Amongst thousands of spectators that were standing there,
And in the faces of the bystanders were depicted despair.

Then the police boats instantly made for the fatal spot,   25
And with the aid of dockyard hands several people were got,
While some scrambled out themselves, the best way they could—
And the most of them were the inhabitants of the neighborhood.

Part of them were the wives and daughters of the dockyard hands,
And as they gazed upon them they in amazement stands;   30
And several bodies were hauled up quite dead,
Which filled the onlookers' hearts with pity and dread.

One of the first rescued was a little baby,
Which was conveyed away to a mortuary;
And several were taken to the fitter's shed, and attended to there   35
By the firemen and several nurses with the greatest care.

Meanwhile heartrending scenes were taking place,
Whilst the tears ran down many a Mother and Father's face,
That had lost their children in the River Thames,
Which they will remember while life remains.   40

Oh, Heaven! it was horrible to see the bodies laid out in rows,
And as Fathers and Mothers passed along, adown their cheeks the
        tears flows,
While their poor, sickly hearts were throbbing with fear.

A great crowd had gathered to search for the missing dead,
And many strong men broke down because their heart with pity bled,   45
As they looked upon the distorted faces of their relatives dear,
While adown their cheeks flowed many a silent tear.

The tenderest sympathy, no doubt, was shown to them,
By the kind hearted Police and Firemen;
The scene in fact was most sickening to behold,   50
And enough to make one's blood run cold,
To see tear-stained men and women there
Searching for their relatives, and in their eyes a pitiful stare.

There's one brave man in particular I must mention,
And I'm sure he's worthy of the people's attention: 55
His name is Thomas Cooke, of No. 6 Percy Road, Canning Town,
Who's name ought to be to posterity handed down,
Because he leapt into the River Thames, and heroically did behave,
And rescued five persons from a watery grave.

Mr. Wilson, a young Electrician, got a terrible fright,   60
When he saw his mother and sister dead—he was shocked at the
        sight,
Because his sister had not many days returned from her honeymoon,
And in his countenance, alas! there was a sad gloom.

Her Majesty has sent a message of sympathy to the bereaved ones in
    distress,
And the Duke and Duchess of York have sent 25 guineas I must
    confess,   65
And £1000 from the Directors of the Thames Ironworks and
    Shipbuilding Company,
Which I hope will help to fill the bereaved one's hearts with glee.

And in conclusion I will venture to say,
That accidents will happen by night and by day;
And I will say without any fear,   70
Because to me it appears quite clear,
That the stronger we our houses do build,
The less chance we have of being killed.

THE ALBION BATTLESHIP CALAMITY. The poetry of McGonagall, handloom weaver and amateur
Shakespearean actor of Dundee, Scotland, has become popular not for its merits but for its
flamboyant faults. Like a writer of broadside ballads, McGonagall revels in fires, accidents, bridge
disasters, shipwrecks, mine cave-ins, and other catastrophes. In England and Scotland, his *Poetic
Gems* (1890, reprinted 1934) and *More Poetic Gems* (1966) are classics.

QUESTIONS

1. With a pencil, delete anything in this poem that seems to you repetitious. What would
   you remove? (Don't say "The whole poem"; look for glaring redundancies.)
2. In what places does the poet appear to make a remark for no reason other than to
   round out his rime?
3. How vivid and exact is McGonagall's description of the sudden collapse of the bridge
   and staging? How clear and detailed are his portraits of victims and relatives? What
   words or phrases seem particularly vague and woolly?
4. Inspect the lines about Mr. Wilson (60–63). Why is the word *shocked* such an unlucky
   choice? Even granting that this might be a deliberate pun, why is it bad?
5. In the next-to-last stanza, what is the poet's attitude toward money?
6. Comment on the wisdom of the last two lines.
7. As best you can tell from this poem, how sharp is the poet's awareness of his readers
   and their possible reactions?

Emily Dickinson (1830 – 1886)*

A DYING TIGER – MOANED FOR DRINK   (ABOUT 1862)

A Dying Tiger – moaned for Drink –
I hunted all the Sand –
I caught the Dripping of a Rock
And bore it in my Hand –

His Mighty Balls – in death were thick –   5
But searching – I could see
A Vision on the Retina
Of Water – and of me –

'Twas not my blame – who sped too slow –
'Twas not his blame – who died   10
While I was reaching him –
But 'twas – the fact that He was dead –

QUESTION

How does this poem compare in success with other poems of Emily Dickinson that you know? Justify your opinion by pointing to some of this poem's particulars.

EXERCISE: *Seeing What Went Wrong*

Here is a small anthology of bad moments in poetry. For what reasons does each selection fail? In which passages do you attribute the failure to inappropriate sound or diction? To awkward word order? To inaccurate metaphor? To excessive overstatement? To forced rime? To monotonous rhythm? To redundancy? To simple-mindedness or excessive ingenuity?

1. Last lines of *Enoch Arden* by Alfred, Lord Tennyson:

   So passed the strong heroic soul away.
   And when they buried him, the little port
   Had seldom seen a costlier funeral.

2. From *Purely Original Verse* (1891) by J. Gordon Coogler (1865–1901), of Columbia, South Carolina:

   Alas for the South, her books have grown fewer—
   She never was much given to literature.

3. From "Lines Written to a Friend on the Death of His Brother, Caused by a Railway Train Running Over Him Whilst He Was in a State of Inebriation" by James Henry Powell:

   Thy mangled corpse upon the rails in frightful shape was found.
   The ponderous train had killed thee as its heavy wheels went round,
   And thus in dreadful form thou met'st a drunkard's awful death
   And I, thy brother, mourn thy fate, and breathe a purer breath.

4. From *Dolce Far Niente* by the American poet Francis Saltus Saltus, who flourished in the 1890s:

   Her laugh is like sunshine, full of glee,
   And her sweet breath smells like fresh-made tea.

5. From another gem by Francis Saltus Saltus, "The Spider":

   Then all thy feculent majesty recalls
      The nauseous mustiness of forsaken bowers,
   The leprous nudity of deserted halls—
      The positive nastiness of sullied flowers.

   And I mark the colours yellow and black
      That fresco thy lithe, dictatorial thighs,
   I dream and wonder on my drunken back
      How God could possibly have created flies!

6. From "Song to the Suliotes" by George Gordon, Lord Byron:

   Up to battle! Sons of Suli
   Up, and do your duty duly!
   There the wall—and there the moat is:

Bouwah! Bouwah! Suliotes,
There is booty—there is beauty!
Up my boys and do your duty!

7. From a juvenile poem of John Dryden, "Upon the Death of the Lord Hastings" (a
victim of smallpox):

Each little pimple had a tear in it,
To wail the fault its rising did commit . . .

8. From "I Kissed Pa Twice After His Death" by Mattie J. Peterson (1866–1947), the
self-styled "Poetissima Laureatissima of Bladen County":

I saw him coming stepping high,
Which was of his walk the way . . .

9. From "The Abbey Mason" by Thomas Hardy:

When longer yet dank death had wormed
The brain wherein the style had germed

From Gloucester church it flew afar—
The style called Perpendicular.—

To Winton and to Westminster
It ranged, and grew still beautifuller . . .

10. A metaphor from "The Crucible of Life" by the once-popular American newspaper
poet Edgar A. Guest:

Sacred and sweet is the joy that must come
From the furnace of life when you've poured off the scum.

11. From an elegy for Queen Victoria by one of her subjects:

Dust to dust, and ashes to ashes,
Into the tomb the Great Queen dashes.

Sentimentality is a failure of writers who seem to feel a great emotion but
who fail to give us sufficient grounds for sharing it. The emotion may be an
anger greater than its object seems to call for, as in these lines to a girl who
caused scandal (the exact nature of her act never being specified): "The gossip
in each hall / Will curse your name . . . / Go! better cast yourself right down
the falls!"[2] Or it may be an enthusiasm quite unwarranted by its subject: in
The Fleece John Dyer temptingly describes the pleasures of life in a workhouse
for the poor. The sentimental poet is especially prone to tenderness. Great tears
fill his eyes at a glimpse of an aged grandmother sitting by a hearth. For all the
poet knows, she may be the manager of a casino in Las Vegas who would be
startled to find herself an object of pity, but the sentimentalist doesn't care to
know about the woman herself. She is a general excuse for feeling maudlin. Any
other conventional object will serve as well: a faded valentine, the strains of an
old song, a baby's cast-off pacifier. An instance of such emotional self-indul-
gence is "The Old Oaken Bucket," by Samuel Woodworth, a stanza of which
goes:

[2]Ali. S. Hilmi, "The Preacher's Sermon," in *Verse at Random* (Larnaca, Cyprus: Ohanian Press,
1953).

How sweet from the green, mossy brim to receive it,
   As, poised on the curb, it inclined to my lips!
Not a full-flushing goblet could tempt me to leave it,
   Tho' filled with the nectar that Jupiter sips.
And now, far removed from the loved habitation,
   The tear of regret will intrusively swell,
As fancy reverts to my father's plantation,
   And sighs for the bucket that hung in the well.

The staleness of the phrasing and imagery (Jove's nectar, *tear of regret*) suggests that the speaker is not even seeing the actual physical bucket, and the tripping meter of the lines is inappropriate to an expression of tearful regret. Perhaps the poet's nostalgia is genuine. Indeed, as Keith Waldrop has put it, "a bad poem is always sincere." However sincere in their feelings, sentimental poets are insincere in their art — otherwise, wouldn't they trouble to write better poems? Wet-eyed and sighing for a bucket, Woodworth achieves not pathos but **bathos:** a description that can move us to laughter instead of tears.[3] Tears, of course, can be shed for good reason. A piece of sentimentality is not to be confused with a well-wrought poem whose tone is tenderness.

Rod McKuen (b. 1933)

THOUGHTS ON CAPITAL PUNISHMENT   1954

There ought to be capital punishment for cars
that run over rabbits and drive into dogs
and commit the unspeakable, unpardonable crime
of killing a kitty cat still in his prime.

Purgatory, at the very least   5
                       should await the driver
   driving over a beast.

Those hurrying headlights coming out of the dark
that scatter the scampering squirrels in the park
should await the best jury that one might compose   10
of fatherless chipmunks and husbandless does.

And then found guilty, after too fair a trial
should be caged in a cage with a hyena's smile
or maybe an elephant with an elephant gun
should shoot out his eyes when the verdict is done.   15

---

[3]*Bathos* in poetry can also mean an abrupt fall from the sublime to the trivial or incongruous. A sample, from Nicholas Rowe's play *The Fair Penitent:* "Is it the voice of thunder, or my father?" Another, from John Close, a minor Victorian: "Around their heads a dazzling halo shone, / No need of mortal robes, or any hat." When, however, such a letdown is used for a *desirable* effect of humor or contrast, it is usually called an **anticlimax:** as in Alexander Pope's lines on the queen's palace, "Here thou, great Anna! whom three realms obey, / Dost sometimes counsel take — and sometimes tea."

There ought to be something, something that's fair
to avenge Mrs. Badger as she waits in her lair
for her husband who lies with his guts spilling out
cause he didn't know what automobiles are about.

Hell on the highway, at the very least   20
                    should await the driver
        driving over a beast.

Who kills a man kills a bit of himself
But a cat too is an extension of God.

William Stafford (b. 1914)*

TRAVELING THROUGH THE DARK   1962

Traveling through the dark I found a deer
dead on the edge of the Wilson River road.
It is usually best to roll them into the canyon:
that road is narrow; to swerve might make more dead.

By glow of the tail-light I stumbled back of the car   5
and stood by the heap, a doe, a recent killing;
she had stiffened already, almost cold.
I dragged her off; she was large in the belly.

My fingers touching her side brought me the reason —
her side was warm; her fawn lay there waiting,   10
alive, still, never to be born.
Beside that mountain road I hesitated.

The car aimed ahead its lowered parking lights;
under the hood purred the steady engine.
I stood in the glare of the warm exhaust turning red;   15
around our group I could hear the wilderness listen.

I thought hard for us all — my only swerving —
then pushed her over the edge into the river.

QUESTIONS

1. Compare these poems by Rod McKuen and William Stafford. How are they similar?
2. Explain Stafford's title. Who are all those traveling through the dark?
3. Comment on McKuen's use of language. Consider especially: *unspeakable, unpardonable crime* (line 3), *kitty cat* (4), *scatter the scampering squirrels* (9), and *cause he didn't know* (19).
4. Compare the meaning of Stafford's last two lines and McKuen's last two. Does either poem have a moral? Can either poem be said to moralize?
5. Which poem might be open to the charge of sentimentality? Why?

Which of the following five poems do you find sentimental? Which would you defend? At least one kind of evidence to look for is minute, detailed observation of physical objects. In a successful poem, the poet is likely at least occasionally to notice the world beyond his or her own skin; in a sentimental poem, this world is likely to be ignored.

Julia A. Moore (1847 – 1920)

LITTLE LIBBY   1876

One more little spirit to Heaven has flown,
    To dwell in that mansion above,
Where dear little angels, together roam,
    In God's everlasting love.

One little flower has withered and died,   5
    A bud nearly ready to bloom,
Its life on earth is marked with pride;
    Oh, sad it should die so soon.

Sweet little Libbie, that precious flower
    Was a pride in her parents' home,   10
They miss their little girl *every* hour,
    Those friends that are left to mourn.

Her sweet silvery voice no more is heard
    In the home where she once roamed;
Her place is *vacant* around the hearth,   15
    Where her friends are mourning lone.

They are mourning the loss of a little girl,
    With black eyes and auburn hair,
She was a treasure to them in this world,
    This beautiful child so fair.   20

One morning in April, a short time ago,
    Libbie was active and gay;
Her Saviour called her, she had to go,
    E're the close of that pleasant day.

While eating dinner, this dear little child   25
    Was choked on a piece of beef.
Doctors came, tried their skill awhile,
    But none could give relief.

She was ten years of age, I am told,
    And in school stood very high.   30
Her little form now the earth enfolds,
    In her embrace it must ever lie.

Her friends and schoolmates will not forget
    Little Libbie that is no more;
She is waiting on the shining step,   35
    To welcome home friends once more.

Bill Knott (b. 1940)

POEM   1968

The only response
to a child's grave is
to lie down before it and play dead

Dabney Stuart (b. 1937)

CRIB DEATH   1987

Kisses are for the living.
Even if the terrible breath of the dead
Never rose from the earth's mouth,
Dread of it would turn our heads aside
As relatives at a funeral meet and kiss.   5
Living in such air is what the living have,
Less choice than a stone what's cut into its face.

Leo Connellan (b. 1928)

SCOTT HUFF   1978

Think tonight of sixteen
year old Scott Huff of
Maine driving home fell asleep at
the wheel, his car sprang awake
from the weight of his foot head on   5
into a tree. God, if you need him
take him asking me to believe in
you because there are yellow buttercups,
salmon for my heart in the rivers,
fresh springs of ice cold water running away.   10
You can have all these back for Scott Huff.

Ted Kooser (b. 1939)

A Child's Grave Marker   1985

A small block of granite
engraved with her name and the dates
just wasn't quite pretty enough
for this lost little girl
or her parents, who added a lamb   5
cast in plaster of paris,
using the same kind of cake mold
my grandmother had—iron,
heavy and black as a skillet.
The lamb came out coconut-white,   10
and seventy years have proven it
soft in the rain. On this hill,
overlooking a river in Iowa,
it melts in its own sweet time.

KNOWING EXCELLENCE

How can we tell an excellent poem from any other? To give reasons for excellence in poetry is harder than to give reasons for failure in poetry (so often due to familiar kinds of imprecision and sentimentality). A bad poem tends to be stereotyped, an excellent poem unique. In judging either, we can have no absolute specifications. A poem is not like an electric toaster that an inspector can test by a check-off list. It has to be judged on the basis of what it is trying to be and how well it succeeds in the effort.

To judge a poem, we first have to understand it. At least, we need to understand it *almost* all the way; there is, to be sure, a poem such as Hopkins's "The Windhover" (page 830), which most readers probably would call excellent even though its meaning is still being debated. Although it is a good idea to give a poem at least a couple of considerate readings before judging it, sometimes our first encounter starts turning into an act of evaluation. Moving along into the poem, becoming more deeply involved in it, we may begin forming an opinion. In general, the more a poem contains for us to understand, the more rewarding we are likely to find it. Of course, an obscure and highly demanding poem is not always to be preferred to a relatively simple one. Difficult poems can be pretentious and incoherent; still, there is something to be said for the poem complicated enough to leave us something to discover on our fifteenth reading (unlike most limericks, which yield their all at a look). Here is such a poem, one not readily fathomed and exhausted.

William Butler Yeats (1865 – 1939)*

SAILING TO BYZANTIUM   1927

That is no country for old men. The young
In one another's arms, birds in the trees
— Those dying generations — at their song,
The salmon-falls, the mackerel-crowded seas,
Fish, flesh, or fowl, commend all summer long   5
Whatever is begotten, born, and dies.
Caught in that sensual music all neglect
Monuments of unaging intellect.

An aged man is but a paltry thing,
A tattered coat upon a stick, unless   10
Soul clap its hands and sing, and louder sing
For every tatter in its mortal dress,
Nor is there singing school but studying
Monuments of its own magnificence;
And therefore I have sailed the seas and come   15
To the holy city of Byzantium.

O sages standing in God's holy fire
As in the gold mosaic of a wall,
Come from the holy fire, perne in a gyre°,   *spin down a spiral*
And be the singing-masters of my soul.   20
Consume my heart away; sick with desire
And fastened to a dying animal
It knows not what it is; and gather me
Into the artifice of eternity.

Once out of nature I shall never take   25
My bodily form from any natural thing,
But such a form as Grecian goldsmiths make
Of hammered gold and gold enameling
To keep a drowsy Emperor awake;
Or set upon a golden bough to sing   30
To lords and ladies of Byzantium
Of what is past, or passing, or to come.

SAILING TO BYZANTIUM. Byzantium was the capital of the Byzantine Empire, the city now called Istanbul. Yeats means, though, not merely the physical city. Byzantium is also a name for his conception of paradise.

Though *salmon-falls* (line 4) suggests Yeats's native Ireland, the poem, as we find out in line 25, is about escaping from the entire natural world. If the poet desires this escape, then probably the *country* mentioned in the opening line is no political nation but the cycle of birth and death in which human beings are trapped; and, indeed, the poet says his heart is "fastened to a dying animal." Imaginary landscapes, it would seem, are merging with the historical Byzantium. Lines 17 – 18 refer to mosaic images, adornments of the Byzantine cathedral of St. Sophia, in which the figures of saints are inlaid against backgrounds of gold. The clockwork bird of the last stanza is also a reference to something actual. Yeats noted: "I have read somewhere that in the Emperor's palace at Byzantium was a tree made of gold and silver, and artificial birds that sang." This description of the role the poet would seek — that of a changeless, immortal singer — directs us back to the earlier references to music and singing. Taken all together, they point toward the central metaphor of the poem: the craft of poetry can be a kind of singing. One kind of everlasting monument is a great poem. To study masterpieces of poetry is the only "singing school" — the only way to learn to write a poem.

We have no more than skimmed through a few of this poem's suggestions, enough to show that, out of allusion and imagery, Yeats has woven at least one elaborate metaphor. Surely one thing the poem achieves is that, far from merely puzzling us, it makes us aware of relationships between what a person can imagine and the physical world. There is the statement that a human heart is bound to the body that perishes, and yet it is possible to see consciousness for a moment independent of flesh, to sing with joy at the very fact that the body is crumbling away. Expressing a similar view of mortality, the Japanese artist Hokusai has shown a withered tree letting go of its few remaining leaves, while under it two graybeards shake with laughter. Like Hokusai's view, that of Yeats is by no means simple. Much of the power of Yeats's poem comes from the physical terms with which he states the ancient quarrel between body and spirit, body being a "tattered coat upon a stick." There is all the difference in the world between the work of the poet like Yeats whose eye is on the living thing and whose mind is awake and passionate, and that of the slovenly poet whose dull eye and sleepy mind focus on nothing more than some book read hastily long ago. The former writes a poem out of compelling need, the latter as if it seems a nice idea to write something.

Yeats's poem has the three qualities essential to beauty, according to the definition of Thomas Aquinas: wholeness, harmony, and radiance. The poem is all one; its parts move in peace with one another; it shines with emotional intensity. There is an orderly progression going on in it: from the speaker's statement of his discontent with the world of "sensual music," to his statement that he is quitting this world, to his prayer that the sages will take him in, and his vision of future immortality. And the images of the poem relate to one another — *dying generations* (line 3), *dying animal* (line 22), and the undying golden bird (lines 27 – 32) — to mention just one series of related things. "Sailing to Byzantium" is not the kind of poem that has, in Pope's words, "One simile, that solitary shines / In the dry desert of a thousand lines." Rich in figurative language, Yeats's whole poem develops a metaphor, with further metaphors as its tributaries.

"Sailing to Byzantium" has a theme that matters to us. What human being does not long, at times, to shed timid, imperfect flesh, to live in a state of absolute joy, unperishing? Being human, perhaps we too are stirred by Yeats's prayer: "Consume my heart away, sick with desire / And fastened to a dying animal. . . ." If it is true that in poetry (as Ezra Pound declared) "only emotion endures," then Yeats's poem ought to endure. (No reasons to be moved by a poem, however, can be of much use. If you happen not to feel moved by this poem, try another — but come back to "Sailing to Byzantium" after a while.)

Most excellent poems, it might be argued, contain significant themes, as does "Sailing to Byzantium." But the presence of such a theme is not enough to render a poem excellent. Not theme alone makes an excellent poem, but how well a theme is stated.

Yeats's poem, some would say, is the match for any lyric in our language. Some might call it inferior to an epic (to Milton's *Paradise Lost,* say, or to the *Iliad*), but this claim is to lead us into a different argument: whether certain genres are innately better than others. Such an argument usually leads to a dead end. Evidently, *Paradise Lost* has greater range, variety, matter, length, and ambitiousness. But any poem — whether an epic or an epigram — may be judged by how well it fulfills the design it undertakes. God, who created both fleas and whales, pronounced all good. Fleas, like epigrams, have no reason to feel inferior.

EXERCISE: *Two Poems to Compare*

Here are two poems with a similar theme. Which contains more qualities of excellent poetry? Decide whether the other is bad or whether it may be praised for achieving something different.

Arthur Guiterman (1871 – 1943)

ON THE VANITY OF EARTHLY GREATNESS   1936

The tusks that clashed in mighty brawls
Of mastodons, are billiard balls.

The sword of Charlemagne the Just
Is ferric oxide, known as rust.

The grizzly bear whose potent hug   5
Was feared by all, is now a rug.

Great Caesar's bust is on the shelf,
And I don't feel so well myself.

Percy Bysshe Shelley (1792 – 1822)

OZYMANDIAS   1818

I met a traveler from an antique land
Who said: Two vast and trunkless legs of stone
Stand in the desert. Near them, on the sand,
Half sunk, a shattered visage lies, whose frown,
And wrinkled lip, and sneer of cold command,   5
Tell that its sculptor well those passions read
Which yet survive, stamped on these lifeless things,
The hand that mocked° them and the heart that fed;   *imitated*
And on the pedestal these words appear:
"My name is Ozymandias, king of kings: 10
Look on my works, ye Mighty, and despair!"
Nothing beside remains. Round the decay
Of that colossal wreck, boundless and bare
The lone and level sands stretch far away.

Some excellent poems of the past will remain sealed to us unless we are willing to sympathize with their conventions. Pastoral poetry, for instance — Marlowe's "Passionate Shepherd" and Milton's "Lycidas" — asks us to accept certain conventions and situations that may seem old-fashioned: idle swains, oaten flutes. We are under no grim duty, of course, to admire poems whose conventions do not appeal to us. But there is no point in blaming a poet for playing a particular game or for observing its rules.

Bad poems, of course, can be woven together out of conventions, like patchwork quilts made of old unwanted words. In Shakespeare's England, poets were busily imitating the sonnets of Petrarch, the Italian poet whose praise of his beloved Laura had become well known. The result of their industry was a surplus of Petrarchan **conceits,** or elaborate comparisons (from the Italian *concetto*: concept, bright idea). In the following sonnet, Shakespeare, who at times helped himself generously from the Petrarchan stockpile, pokes fun at poets who thoughtlessly use such handed-down figures of speech.

William Shakespeare (1564 – 1616)*

MY MISTRESS' EYES ARE NOTHING LIKE THE SUN   1609

My mistress' eyes are nothing like the sun;
Coral is far more red than her lips' red;
If snow be white, why then her breasts are dun;
If hairs be wires, black wires grow on her head.
I have seen roses damasked red and white,   5
But no such roses see I in her cheeks;

And in some perfumes is there more delight
Than in the breath that from my mistress reeks.
I love to hear her speak, yet well I know
That music hath a far more pleasing sound;   10
I grant I never saw a goddess go:
My mistress, when she walks, treads on the ground.
    And yet, by heaven, I think my love as rare
    As any she°, belied with false compare.   *woman*

Contrary to what you might expect, for years after Shakespeare's time, poets
continued to write fine poems with Petrarchan conventions.

Thomas Campion (1567 – 1620)*

THERE IS A GARDEN IN HER FACE   1617

    There is a garden in her face
Where roses and white lilies grow;
    A heav'nly paradise is that place
Wherein all pleasant fruits do flow.
    There cherries grow which none may buy   5
    Till "Cherry-ripe" themselves do cry.

    Those cherries fairly do enclose
Of orient pearl a double row,
    Which when her lovely laughter shows,
They look like rose-buds filled with snow;   10
    Yet them nor° peer nor prince can buy,   *neither*
    Till "Cherry-ripe" themselves do cry.

    Her eyes like angels watch them still;
Her brows like bended bows do stand,
    Threat'ning with piercing frowns to kill   15
All that attempt, with eye or hand
    Those sacred cherries to come nigh
    Till "Cherry-ripe" themselves do cry.

THERE IS A GARDEN IN HER FACE. 6 *"Cherry-ripe"*: cry of fruit-peddlers in London streets.

QUESTIONS

1. What does Campion's song owe to Petrarchan tradition?
2. What in it strikes you as fresh observation of actual life?
3. Comment in particular on the last stanza. Does the comparison of eyebrows to
   threatening bowmen seem too silly or far-fetched? What sense do you find in it?
4. Try to describe the tone of this poem. What do you understand, from this portrait
   of a young girl, to be the poet's feelings?

Excellent poetry might be easier to recognize if each poet had a fixed position on the slopes of Mount Parnassus, but from one century to the next, the reputations of some poets have taken humiliating slides, or made impressive clambers. We decide for ourselves which poems to call excellent, but readers of the future may reverse our opinions. Most of us no longer would share this popular view of Walt Whitman by one of his contemporaries:

> Walt Whitman (1819 – 1892), by some regarded as a great poet; by others, as no poet at all. Most of his so-called poems are mere catalogues of things, without meter or rime, but in a few more regular poems and in lines here and there he is grandly poetical, as in "O Captain! My Captain!"[1]

Walt Whitman (1819 – 1892)*

O CAPTAIN! MY CAPTAIN!   1865

O Captain! my Captain! our fearful trip is done,
The ship has weather'd every rack, the prize we sought is won,
The port is near, the bells I hear, the people all exulting,
While follow eyes the steady keel, the vessel grim and daring;
    But O heart! heart! heart!   5
      O the bleeding drops of red,
        Where on the deck my Captain lies,
        Fallen cold and dead.

O Captain! my Captain! rise up and hear the bells;
Rise up — for you the flag is flung — for you the bugle trills,   10
For you bouquets and ribbon'd wreaths — for you the shores
    a-crowding,
For you they call, the swaying mass, their eager faces turning;
    Here Captain! dear father!
      This arm beneath your head!
        It is some dream that on the deck,   15
        You've fallen cold and dead.

My Captain does not answer, his lips are pale and still,
My father does not feel my arm, he has no pulse nor will,
The ship is anchor'd safe and sound, its voyage closed and done,
From fearful trip the victor ship comes in with object won;   20
    Exult O shores, and ring O bells!
      But I with mournful tread,
        Walk the deck my Captain lies,
        Fallen cold and dead.

O CAPTAIN! MY CAPTAIN! Written soon after the death of Abraham Lincoln, this was, in Whitman's lifetime, by far the most popular of his poems.

[1] J. Willis Westlake, A.M., in *Common-school Literature, English and American, with Several Hundred Extracts to be Memorized* (Philadelphia, 1898).

1. Compare this with other Whitman poems. (See another elegy for Lincoln, "When Lilacs Last in the Dooryard Bloom'd.") In what ways is "O Captain! My Captain!" uncharacteristic of his works? Do you agree with J. Willis Westlake that this is one of the few occasions on which Whitman is "grandly poetical?"
2. Comment on the appropriateness to its subject of the poem's rhythms.
3. Do you find any evidence in this poem that an excellent poet wrote it?

There is nothing to do but commit ourselves and praise or blame and, if need be, let time erase our error. In a sense, all readers of poetry are constantly reexamining the judgments of the past by choosing those poems they care to go on reading. In the end, we have to admit that the critical principles set forth in this chapter are all very well for admiring excellent poetry we already know, but they cannot be carried like a yardstick in the hand, to go out looking for it. As Ezra Pound said in his *ABC of Reading*, "A classic is classic not because it conforms to certain structural rules, or fits certain definitions (of which its author had quite probably never heard). It is classic because of a certain eternal and irrepressible freshness."

The best poems, like "Sailing to Byzantium," may offer a kind of religious experience. In the last decade of the twentieth century, some of us rarely set foot outside an artificial environment. Whizzing down four-lane superhighways, we observe lakes and trees in the distance. In a way our cities are to us as anthills are to ants: no less than anthills, they are "natural" structures. But the "unnatural" world of school or business is, as Wordsworth says, too much with us. Locked in the shells of our ambitions, our self-esteem, we forget our kinship to earth and sea. We fabricate self-justifications. But a great poem shocks us into another order of perception. It points beyond language to something still more essential. It ushers us into an experience so moving and true that we feel (to quote King Lear) "cut to the brain." In bad or indifferent poetry, words are all there is.

Carl Sandburg (1878 – 1967)

FOG   1916

The fog comes
on little cat feet.
It sits looking
over harbor and city
on silent haunches
and then moves on.

QUESTION

In lines 15–22 of "The Love Song of J. Alfred Prufrock" (page 806), T. S. Eliot also likens fog to a cat. Compare Sandburg's lines and Eliot's. Which passage tells us more about fogs and cats?

Thomas Gray (1716 – 1771)*

ELEGY WRITTEN IN A COUNTRY CHURCHYARD   1753

The curfew tolls the knell of parting day,
   The lowing herd wind slowly o'er the lea,
The plowman homeward plods his weary way,
   And leaves the world to darkness and to me.

Now fades the glimmering landscape on the sight,   5
   And all the air a solemn stillness holds,
Save where the beetle wheels his droning flight,
   And drowsy tinklings lull the distant folds;

Save that from yonder ivy-mantled tower
   The moping owl does to the moon complain   10
Of such, as wand'ring near her secret bower,
   Molest her ancient solitary reign.

Beneath those rugged elms, that yew tree's shade,
   Where heaves the turf in many a mold'ring heap,
Each in his narrow cell forever laid,   15
   The rude° forefathers of the hamlet sleep.   *simple, ignorant*

The breezy call of incense-breathing morn,
   The swallow twitt'ring from the straw-built shed,
The cock's shrill clarion, or the echoing horn°,   *fox-hunters' horn*
   No more shall rouse them from their lowly bed.   20

For them no more the blazing hearth shall burn,
   Or busy housewife ply her evening care;
No children run to lisp their sire's return,
   Or climb his knees the envied kiss to share.

Oft did the harvest to their sickle yield,   25
   Their furrow oft the stubborn glebe° has broke;   *turf*
How jocund did they drive their team afield!
   How bowed the woods beneath their sturdy stroke!

Let not Ambition mock their useful toil,
   Their homely joys, and destiny obscure;   30
Nor Grandeur hear with a disdainful smile
   The short and simple annals of the poor.

The boast of heraldry°, the pomp of pow'r,   *noble birth*
   And all that beauty, all that wealth e'er gave,
Awaits alike th' inevitable hour.   35
   The paths of glory lead but to the grave.

ELEGY WRITTEN IN A COUNTRY CHURCHYARD. In English poetry, an **elegy** has come to mean a lament or a sadly meditative poem, sometimes written on the occasion of a death. Other elegies in this book include Chidiock Tichborne's "Elegy," Milton's "Lycidas," A. E. Housman's "To an Athlete Dying Young," and in more recent poetry, "The Rites for Cousin Vit" by Gwendolyn Brooks and "Elegy for Jane" by Theodore Roethke.

Nor you, ye proud, impute to these the fault,
   If Mem'ry o'er their tomb no trophies raise,
Where through the long-drawn aisle and fretted° vault   *inlaid with designs*
   The pealing anthem swells the note of praise.   40

Can storied urn or animated bust
   Back to its mansion call the fleeting breath?
Can Honor's voice provoke the silent dust,
   Or Flatt'ry soothe the dull cold ear of Death?

Perhaps in this neglected spot is laid   45
   Some heart once pregnant with celestial fire;
Hands that the rod of empire might have swayed,
   Or waked to ecstasy the living lyre.

But knowledge to their eyes her ample page
   Rich with the spoils of time did ne'er unroll;   50
Chill Penury° repressed their noble rage,   *Poverty*
   And froze the genial current of the soul.

Full many a gem of purest ray serene,
   The dark unfathomed caves of ocean bear:
Full many a flower is born to blush unseen,   55
   And waste its sweetness on the desert air.

Some village Hampden, that with dauntless breast
   The little tyrant of his field withstood;
Some mute inglorious Milton here may rest,
   Some Cromwell, guiltless of his country's blood.   60

Th' applause of list'ning senates to command,
   The threats of pain and ruin to despise,
To scatter plenty o'er a smiling land,
   And read their hist'ry in a nation's eyes,

Their lot forbade; nor circumscribed alone   65
   Their growing virtues, but their crimes confined;
Forbade to wade through slaughter to a throne,
   And shut the gates of mercy on mankind,

The struggling pangs of conscious truth to hide,
   To quench the blushes of ingenuous° shame,   *innocent* 70
Or heap the shrine of Luxury and Pride
   With incense kindled at the Muse's flame.

41 *storied urn:* vessel holding the ashes of the dead after cremation. *Storied* can mean (1) decorated
with scenes; (2) inscribed with a life's story; or (3) celebrated in story or history. The *animated bust*
is a lifelike sculpture of the dead, placed on a tomb. 57 *Hampden:* John Hampden (1594 – 1643),
member of Parliament, had resisted illegal taxes on his lands imposed by Charles I. 60 *Cromwell
. . . his country's blood:* Gray blames Oliver Cromwell (1599 – 1658) for strife and tyranny. As general
of the armies of Parliament, Cromwell had won the Civil War against Charles I and had signed
the king's death warrant. As Lord Protector of England (1653 – 1658), he had ruled with an iron
hand. 71 – 72 *heap the shrine . . . Muse's flame:* Gray chides mercenary poets who write poems to
please their rich, high-living patrons.

Far from the madding° crowd's ignoble strife,   *frenzied*
   Their sober wishes never learned to stray;
Along the cool sequestered vale of life   75
   They kept the noiseless tenor° of their way.   *ongoing motion*

Yet ev'n these bones from insult to protect
   Some frail memorial still erected nigh,
With uncouth rhymes and shapeless sculpture decked,
   Implores the passing tribute of a sigh.   80

Their name, their years, spelt by th' unlettered Muse,
   The place of fame and elegy supply:
And many a holy text around she strews,
   That teach the rustic moralist to die.

For who to dumb Forgetfulness a prey,   85
   This pleasing anxious being e'er resigned,
Left the warm precincts of the cheerful day,
   Nor cast one longing ling'ring look behind?

On some fond breast the parting soul relies,
   Some pious drops the closing eye requires;   90
Ev'n from the tomb the voice of Nature cries,
   Ev'n in our ashes live their wonted° fires.   *customary*

For thee, who mindful of th' unhonored dead
   Dost in these lines their artless tale relate;
If chance°, by lonely contemplation led,   *if by chance*   95
   Some kindred spirit shall inquire thy fate,

Haply° some hoary-headed swain° may say,   *perhaps; gray-haired shepherd*
   "Oft have we seen him at the peep of dawn
Brushing with hasty steps the dews away
   To meet the sun upon the upland lawn.   100

"There at the foot of yonder nodding beech
   That wreathes its old fantastic roots so high,
His listless length at noontide would he stretch,
   And pore upon the brook that babbles by.

"Hard by yon wood, now smiling as in scorn,   105
   Mutt'ring his wayward fancies he would rove,
Now drooping, woeful wan, like one forlorn,
   Or crazed with care, or crossed in hopeless love.

"One morn I missed him, on the customed hill,
   Along the heath and near his fav'rite tree;   110
Another came; nor yet beside the rill°,   *brook*
   Nor up the lawn, nor at the wood was he;

"The next with dirges due in sad array
   Slow through the churchway path we saw him borne.
Approach and read (for thou canst read) the lay°,   song or poem 115
   Graved on the stone beneath yon aged thorn."

The Epitaph

Here rests his head upon the lap of Earth
   A youth to Fortune and to Fame unknown.
Fair Science° frowned not on his humble birth,   Knowledge
   And Melancholy marked him for her own.   120

Large was his bounty, and his soul sincere,
   Heav'n did a recompense as largely send:
He gave to Mis'ry all he had, a tear,
   He gained from Heav'n ('twas all he wished) a friend.

No farther seek his merits to disclose,   125
   Or draw his frailties from their dread abode,
(There they alike in trembling hope repose),
   The bosom of His Father and his God.

QUESTIONS

1. In contrasting the unknown poor buried in this village churchyard and famous men buried in cathedrals (in *fretted vault*, line 39), what is Gray's theme? What do you understand from the line, *The paths of glory lead but to the grave?*
2. Carl J. Weber thinks that Gray's compassion for the village poor anticipates the democratic sympathies of the American Revolution: "Thomas Gray is the pioneer literary spokesman for the Ordinary Man." But another critic, Lyle Glazier, argues that the "Elegy" isn't political at all: that we misread if we think the poet meant "to persuade the poor and obscure that their barren lives are meaningful"; and also misread if we think he meant to assure the privileged classes "in whose ranks Gray was proud to consider himself" that they need not worry about the poor, "who have already all essential riches." How much truth do you find in either of these views?
3. Cite lines and phrases that show Gray's concern for the musical qualities of words.
4. Who is the *youth* of the closing Epitaph? By *thee* (line 93) does Gray mean himself? Does he mean some fictitious poet supposedly writing the "Elegy" — the first-person speaker (line 4)? Does he mean some village stonecutter, a crude poet whose illiterate Muse (line 81) inspired him to compose tombstone epitaphs? Or could the Epitaph possibly refer to Gray's close friend of school and undergraduate days, the promising poet Richard West, who had died in 1742? Which interpretation seems to you the most reasonable? (Does our lack of absolute certainty negate the value of the poem?)
5. Walter Savage Landor called the Epitaph a tin kettle tied to the tail of a noble dog. Do you agree that the Epitaph is inferior to what has gone before it? What is its function in Gray's poem?
6. Many sources for Gray's phrases and motifs have been found in earlier poets: Virgil, Horace, Dante, Milton, and many more. Even if it could be demonstrated that

Gray's poem has not one original line in it, would it be possible to dismiss the "Elegy" as a mere rag-bag of borrowings?

7. Gray's poem, a pastoral elegy, is in the same genre as another famous English poem: John Milton's "Lycidas." What conventions are common to both?

8. In the earliest surviving manuscript of Gray's poem, lines 73 – 76 read:

No more with Reason and thyself at strife;
Give anxious cares and endless wishes room
But through the cool sequester'd vale of Life
Pursue the silent tenor of thy doom.

In what ways does the final version of those lines seem superior?

9. Perhaps the best-known poem in English, Gray's "Elegy" has inspired hundreds of imitations, countless parodies, and translations into eighteen or more languages. (Some of these languages contain dozens of attempts to translate it.) To what do you attribute the poem's fame? What do you suppose has proved so universally appealing in it?

10. Compare Gray's "Elegy" with Shelley's "Ozymandias" and Arthur Guiterman's "On the Vanity of Earthly Greatness." What do the three poems have in common? How would you rank them in order of excellence?

EXERCISE: *Evaluating the Unfamiliar*

In this exercise you will read work by two American poets who differ in many ways. At present, they are seldom included in literature textbooks and anthologies. For each, you will find not one but three short poems, to give you a deeper sense of their work than a lone poem might supply. (Brief biographies for these poets appear in the Lives of the Poets section, but before you look at their facts, read the poems.)

Read the poems carefully and make your own personal, tentative evaluation of the poet's work—what you now know of it. Here are some questions you might ask yourself (taking the poets one at a time):

Do these poems at all engage your sympathies? Do they stir you and touch your feelings?

What, if anything, might make them memorable? Do they have any vivid images? Any metaphors, understatement, overstatement, or other figures of speech? Do these poems appeal to the ear?

What are the poets saying? Do they tell you anything?

Do the poems exhibit any wild incompetence such as you found in William McGonagall's "Albion Battleship Calamity"? Do you find any forced rimes, inappropriate words, or other unintentionally comic features? Can the poems be accused of bathos or sentimentality, or do you trust the poet to report honest feelings?

How well does the poet seem in control of language? Does the poet's language reflect in any detail the physical world we know?

Do these poems seem entirely drawn from other poetry of the past, or do you have a sense that the poet is thinking and feeling on her (or his) own? Does the poet show any evidence of having read other poets' poetry?

Try setting these poems side by side with any similar poems you know and admire. (You might try, for instance, comparing Lorine Niedecker's work with that of William Carlos Williams, or James Hayford's with that of Robert Frost.) Are they fit to be seen in the same company?

Are these poems sufficiently rich and interesting to repay more than one reading?

What do you suppose the poet is trying to do? How successful is the attempt, in your opinion?

Do you or don't you think this poet's work deserving of a larger audience?

Lorine Niedecker

Lorine Niedecker (1903 – 1970)*

POPCORN-CAN COVER   (c. 1959)

Popcorn-can cover
screwed to the wall
over a hole
    so the cold
can't mouse in   5

Lorine Niedecker (1903–1970)*

I TAKE IT SLOW   (c. 1950)

I take it slow
   alone the river
wild sunflowers
   over my head
the dead
   who gave me life   5
give me this
   our relative the air
floods
   our rich friend   10
silt

Lorine Niedecker (1903 – 1970)*

SORROW MOVES IN WIDE WAVES   (c. 1950)

Sorrow moves in wide waves,
    it passes, lets us be.
It uses us, we use it,
    it's blind while we see.

Consciousness is illimitable,   5
    too good to forsake
tho what we feel be misery
    and we know will break.

Old Mother turns blue and from us,
    "Don't let my head drop to the earth.   10
I'm blind and deaf." Death from the heart,
    a thimble in her purse.

"It's a long day since last night.
    Give me space. I need
floors. Wash the floors, Lorine!   15
    Wash clothes! Weed!"

James Hayford (b. 1913)

BEHIND THE WALL   1983

What shall we find behind this wall,
Only the room next door?
I never went in from here before.
Better stand by in case I call—

In case when I pry off this lath   5
We find a sealed staircase
Or someone's secret burial place,
Or even a charmed garden path—

A pocket of old night is all.
Wait; what's this down in the dark?   10
A carpenter's hammer old as the ark—
The hand long dead that let you fall.

James Hayford

James Hayford (b. 1913)

UNDER THE HOLY EYE   1983

The world and I when young
And backward and content
Were visible among
The several bodies hung
About the firmament   5

Under the holy eye.
Though we all strove alone,
Some cloistered behind stone,
Some under the wide sky,
Our struggles yet were known,   10

Our Bibles still were true.
Then everything proved vast,
And numerous, and fast,
And, Father, either you
Or we flew out of view.   15

James Hayford (b. 1913)

DRY NOON   1983

Their low house nooning in the maple shade,
The pair inside remember having hayed.

The day today is dry and very fine—
Good haying weather, he has said, yes sir—
He who will hay no more, come rain or shine.   5

In all the valley, not a breeze to stir
The old man's breeches drying on the line.

SUGGESTIONS FOR WRITING

1. Write your brief evaluation of the poems of Lorine Niedecker, or those of James Hayford.
2. Concoct the worst poem you can write and, in a brief accompanying essay, recount the difficulties you met and overcame in writing it. Quote, for instance, any lines you thought of but had to discard for not being bad enough.
3. In the Poems for Further Reading that begin on page 773, find a poem you especially admire, or dislike. In a brief essay (300–500 words), evaluate it. Refer to particulars in the poem to support your opinion of it.

28 What Is Poetry?

Robert Francis (1901 – 1987)

CATCH   1950

Two boys uncoached are tossing a poem together,
Overhand, underhand, backhand, sleight of hand, every hand,
Teasing with attitudes, latitudes, interludes, altitudes,
High, make him fly off the ground for it, low, make him stoop,
Make him scoop it up, make him as-almost-as-possible miss it,   5
Fast, let him sting from it, now, now fool him slowly,
Anything, everything tricky, risky, nonchalant,
Anything under the sun to outwit the prosy,
Over the tree and the long sweet cadence down,
Over his head, make him scramble to pick up the meaning,   10
And now, like a posy, a pretty one plump in his hands.

As Robert Francis hints in this playful poem, the pitching poet keeps the catching reader alert by creating little difficulties. Reading some of the poems in this book, you have probably felt like the boy or girl on the receiving end: sometimes having to work to make the catch, once in a while encountering a poem that lands with an easy *plump* right in the middle of your understanding.

What, then, is poetry? By now, perhaps, you have formed your own idea, whether or not you can define it. Robert Frost made a try at a definition: "A poem is an idea caught in the act of dawning." Just in case further efforts at definition can be useful, here are a few memorable ones (including, for a second look, some given earlier):

the art of uniting pleasure with truth by calling imagination to the help of reason.
— Samuel Johnson

the best words in the best order.
                        — Samuel Taylor Coleridge

the record of the best and happiest moments of the happiest and best minds.
                        — Percy Bysshe Shelley

musical Thought.
                        — Thomas Carlyle

at bottom a criticism of life.
                        — Matthew Arnold

If I read a book and it makes my whole body so cold no fire can ever warm me, I know that it is poetry. If I feel physically as if the top of my head were taken off, I know that it is poetry. These are the only ways I know it. Is there any other way?
                        — Emily Dickinson

speech framed . . . to be heard for its own sake and interest even over and above its interest of meaning.
                        — Gerard Manley Hopkins

a revelation in words by means of the words.
                        — Wallace Stevens

not the assertion that something is true, but the making of that truth more fully real to us.
                        — T. S. Eliot

the body of linguistic constructions that men usually refer to as poems.
                        — J. V. Cunningham

anything said in such a way, or put on the page in such a way, as to invite from the hearer or the reader a certain kind of attention.
                        — William Stafford

the clear expression of mixed feelings.
                        — W. H. Auden

A poem differs from most prose in several ways. For one, both writer and reader tend to regard it differently. The poet's attitude is something like this: I offer this piece of writing to be read not as prose but as a poem — that is, more perceptively, thoughtfully, and considerately, with more attention to sounds and connotations. This is a great deal to expect, but in return, the reader, too, has a right to certain expectations. Approaching the poem in the anticipation of out-of-the-ordinary knowledge and pleasure, the reader assumes that the poem may use certain enjoyable devices not available to prose: rime, alliteration, meter, and rhythms — definite, various, or emphatic. (The poet may not *always* decide to use these things.) The reader expects the poet to make greater use, perhaps, of resources of meaning such as figurative language, allusion, symbol, and imagery. As readers of prose we might seek no more than meaning: no more than what could be paraphrased without serious loss. Meeting any figurative language or graceful turns of word order, we think them pleasant extras. But in poetry all these "extras" matter as much as the paraphraseable content, if not more. For, when we finish reading a good poem, we cannot explain precisely to ourselves what we have experienced — without repeating, word for word, the language of the poem itself. Archibald MacLeish makes this point memorably in his "Ars Poetica":

A poem should not mean
But be.

"Poetry is to prose as dancing is to walking," remarked Paul Valéry. It is doubtful, however, that anyone can draw an immovable boundary between poetry and prose. Certain prose needs only to be arranged in lines to be seen as poetry — especially prose that conveys strong emotion in vivid, physical imagery and in terse, figurative, rhythmical language. Even in translation the words of Chief Joseph of the Nez Percé tribe, at the moment of his surrender to the U.S. Army in 1877, still move us and are memorable:

Hear me, my warriors, my heart is sick and sad:
Our chiefs are killed,
The old men all are dead,
It is cold and we have no blankets.

The little children freeze to death.

Hear me, my warriors, my heart is sick and sad:
From where the sun now stands I will fight no more forever.

It may be that a poem can point beyond words to something still more essential. Language has its limits, and probably Edgar Allan Poe was the only poet ever to claim he could always find words for whatever he wished to express. For, of all a human being can experience and imagine, words say only part. "Human speech," said Flaubert, who strove after the best of it, "is like a cracked kettle on which we hammer out tunes to make bears dance, when what we long for is the compassion of the stars."

Like Yeats's chestnut-tree in "Among School Children" (which when asked whether it is leaf, blossom, or bole, has no answer), a poem is to be seen not as a confederation of form, rime, image, metaphor, tone, and theme, but as a whole. We study a poem one element at a time because the intellect best comprehends what it can separate. But only our total attention, involving the participation of our blood and marrow, can see all elements in a poem fused, all dancing together. Yeats knew how to make poems and how to read them:

God guard me from those thoughts men think
In the mind alone;
He that sings a lasting song
Thinks in a marrow-bone.

Throughout this book, we have been working on the assumption that the patient and conscious explication of poems will sharpen unconscious perceptions. We can only hope that it will; the final test lies in whether you care to go on by yourself, reading other poems, finding in them pleasure and enlightenment. Pedagogy must have a stop; so too must the viewing of poems as if their elements fell into chapters. For the total experience of reading a poem surpasses the mind's categories. The wind in the grass, says a proverb, cannot be taken into the house.

29 Poems for Further Reading

Sit a while dear son,
Here are biscuits to eat and here is milk to drink,
But as soon as you sleep and renew yourself in sweet clothes,
I kiss you with a good-by kiss and open the gates for your egress
    hence.

Long enough have you dream'd contemptible dreams,
Now I wash the gum from your eyes,
You must habit yourself to the dazzle of the light and of every
    moment of your life.

Long have you timidly waded holding a plank by the shore,
Now I will you to be a bold swimmer,
To jump off in the midst of the sea, rise again, nod to me, shout, and
    laughingly dash with your hair.
        — Walt Whitman, "Song of Myself"

EDWARD

"Why dois your brand° sae° drap wi' bluid,   *sword; so*
        Edward, Edward?
Why dois your brand sae drap wi' bluid?
    And why sae sad gang° yee, O?"   *go*
"O, I hae killed my hauke sae guid,   5
        Mither, mither,
O, I hae killed my hauke sae guid,
    And I had nae mair bot° hee, O."   *but*

"Your haukis bluid was nevir sae reid,
        Edward, Edward,   10
Your haukis bluid was nevir sae reid,
    My deir son I tell thee, O."
"O, I hae killed my reid-roan steid,
        Mither, mither,
O, I hae killed my reid-roan steid,   15
    That erst° was sa fair and frie°, O."   *once; free*

"Your steid was auld, and ye hae gat mair,
        Edward, Edward,
Your steid was auld, and ye hae gat mair,
    Sum other dule° ye drie°, O."   *sorrow; suffer*   20
"O, I hae killed my fadir deir,
        Mither, mither,
O, I hae killed my fadir deir,
    Alas, and wae° is mee, O!"   *woe*

"And whatten penance wul ye drie for that,   25
        Edward, Edward?
And whatten penance will ye drie for that?
    My deir son, now tell me, O."
"Ile set my feit in yonder boat,
        Mither, mither,   30
Ile set my feit in yonder boat,
    And Ile fare ovir the sea, O."

"And what wul ye doe wi' your towirs and your ha°,   *hall*
        Edward, Edward,
And what wul ye doe wi' your towirs and your ha',   35
    That were sae fair to see, O?"
"Ile let thame stand tul they doun fa',
        Mither, mither,
Ile let thame stand tul they doun fa',
    For here nevir mair maun° I bee, O."   *must*   40

"And what wul ye leive to your bairns° and your wife,   *children*
    Edward, Edward?
And what wul ye leive to your bairns and your wife,
    When ye gang ovir the sea, O?"
"The warldis° room, late° them beg thrae° life,   *world's; let; through*   45
    Mither, mither
The warldis room, late them beg thrae life,
    For thame nevir mair wul I see, O."

"And what wul ye leive to your ain° mither deir,   *own*
    Edward, Edward?   50
And what wul ye leive to your ain mither deir?
    My deir son, now tell me, O."
"The curse of hell frae me sall ye beir,
    Mither, mither,
The curse of hell frae me sall ye beir,   55
    Sic° counseils° ye gave to me, O."   *such; counsel*

COMPARE:

"Edward" with a modern ballad such as "Ballad of Birmingham" by Dudley Randall
(page 615).

Anonymous (traditional English ballad)

THE THREE RAVENS

There were three ravens sat on a tree,
    Down a down, hay down, hay down,
There were three ravens sat on a tree,
    With a down,
There were three ravens sat on a tree,   5
They were as black as they might be.
    With a down derry, derry, derry, down, down.

The one of them said to his mate,
"Where shall we our breakfast take?"

"Down in yonder greene field,   10
There lies a knight slain under his shield.

"His hounds they lie down at his feet,
So well they can their master keep.

"His hawks they fly so eagerly,
There's no fowl dare him come nigh."   15

Down there comes a fallow doe,
As great with young as she might go.

She lift up his bloody head,
And kist his wounds that were so red.

She got him up upon her back,
And carried him to earthen lake°.   20   the grave

She buried him before the prime,
She was dead herself ere evensong time.

God send every gentleman
Such hawks, such hounds, and such a leman°.   lover   25

THE THREE RAVENS. The lines of refrain are repeated in each stanza. "Perhaps in the folk mind the doe is the form the soul of a human mistress, now dead, has taken," Albert B. Friedman has suggested (in *The Viking Book of Folk Ballads*). "Most probably the knight's beloved was understood to be an enchanted woman who was metamorphosed at certain times into an animal." 22–23 *prime, evensong*: two of the canonical hours set aside for prayer and worship. Prime is at dawn, evensong at dusk.

Anonymous (traditional Scottish ballad)

THE TWA CORBIES

As I was walking all alane,
I heard twa corbies° making a mane°;   ravens; moan
The tane° unto the t'other say,   one
"Where sall we gang° and dine today?"   go

"In behint yon auld fail dyke°,   turf wall   5
I wot° there lies a new slain knight;   know
And naebody kens° that he lies there,   knows
But his hawk, his hound, and lady fair.

"His hound is to the hunting gane,
His hawk to fetch the wild-fowl hame,   10
His lady's ta'en another mate,
So we may mak our dinner sweet.

"Ye'll sit on his white hause-bane°,   neck bone
And I'll pike out his bonny blue een;
Wi' ae° lock o' his gowden hair   one   15
We'll theek° our nest when it grows bare.   thatch

"Mony a one for him makes mane,
But nane sall ken where he is gane;
O'er his white banes, when they are bare,
The wind sall blaw for evermair."   20

THE TWA CORBIES. Sir Walter Scott, the first to print this ballad in his *Minstrelsy of the Scottish Border* (1802 – 1803), calls it "rather a counterpart than a copy" of "The Three Ravens." M. J. C. Hodgart and other scholars think he may have written most of it himself.

Anonymous (English lyric)

SUMER IS ICUMEN IN   (thirteenth century)

Sumer is icumen in	Summer is acoming in —
Lhude sing cuccu	Loudly sing, cuckoo!
Groweþ sed and bloweþ med	Groweth seed and bloweth mead
and springþ þe wde nu	And springeth the wood new.
Sing cuccu	Sing, cuckoo! 5
Awe bleteþ after lomb	Ewe bleateth after lamb,
Ihouþ after calue cu	Loweth after calf cow,
Bulluc sterteþ bucke uerteþ	Bullock starteth, buck farteth —
Murie sing cuccu	Merrily sing, cuckoo!
Cuccu cuccu	Cuckoo, cuckoo, 10
Wel singes þu cuccu	Well singest thou, cuckoo!
ne swik þu nauer nu	Cease thou never now.
Sing cuccu nu Sing cuccu	Sing, cuckoo now! Sing, cuckoo!
Sing cuccu Sing cuccu nu	Sing, cuckoo! Sing, cuckoo, now!

SUMER IS ICUMEN IN. On the left, this famous song is printed as it appears in a thirteenth-century manuscript: a commonplace book, or book of songs and obituaries set down by various monks at Reading Abbey (Harley manuscript 978, now in the British Museum). On the right, words and spellings have been modernized and punctuation added, but word-order kept unaltered. In the opening line, *acoming* is not quite a faithful translation: *is icumen* means "has come." Summer is already here. The character þ is called a *thorn*, and is pronounced like the spelling *th*. 8 *starteth*: starts, jumps up and runs.

Anonymous (English lyric)

I SING OF A MAIDEN   (fifteenth century)

I sing of a maiden	that is makeless°,	*matchless (or mateless)*
King of alle kinges	to° her son che ches°.	*to be; she chose*
He cam all so stille	there° his moder was	*where*
As dew in Aprille	that falleth on the grass.	

| He cam all so stille | to his moderes bower | 5 |
| As dew in Aprille | that falleth on the flower. | |

| He cam all so stille | there his moder lay | |
| As dew in Aprille | that falleth on the spray. | |

| Moder and maiden | was never none but she — | |
| Well may swich° a lady | Godes moder be. | *such* 10 |

I SING OF A MAIDEN. To keep the rhythm, pronounce the final *e* in *alle, stille,* and *Aprille* like *e* in *the.* 5 *bower:* dwelling place, room, or bedchamber.

Anonymous (English lyric)

WESTERN WIND   (about 1500)

Western wind, when wilt thou blow,
The° small rain down can rain?   *(so that) the*
Christ, if my love were in my arms,
And I in my bed again!

COMPARE:

"Western Wind" with "Wedding-Wind" by Philip Larkin (page 516).

Matthew Arnold (1822 – 1888)

DOVER BEACH   1867

The sea is calm tonight.
The tide is full, the moon lies fair
Upon the straits; — on the French coast the light
Gleams and is gone; the cliffs of England stand,
Glimmering and vast, out in the tranquil bay.   5
Come to the window, sweet is the night-air!
Only, from the long line of spray
Where the sea meets the moon-blanched land,
Listen! you hear the grating roar
Of pebbles which the waves draw back, and fling,   10
At their return, up the high strand,
Begin, and cease, and then again begin,
With tremulous cadence slow, and bring
The eternal note of sadness in.

Sophocles long ago   15
Heard it on the Aegean, and it brought
Into his mind the turbid ebb and flow
Of human misery; we
Find also in the sound a thought,
Hearing it by this distant northern sea.   20

The Sea of Faith
Was once, too, at the full, and round earth's shore
Lay like the folds of a bright girdle furled.
But now I only hear
Its melancholy, long, withdrawing roar,   25
Retreating, to the breath
Of the night-wind, down the vast edges drear
And naked shingles° of the world.   *gravel beaches*

Ah, love, let us be true
To one another! for the world, which seems   30
To lie before us like a land of dreams,
So various, so beautiful, so new,
Hath really neither joy, nor love, nor light,
Nor certitude, nor peace, nor help for pain;
And we are here as on a darkling° plain   *darkened or darkening* 35
Swept with confused alarms of struggle and flight,
Where ignorant armies clash by night.

John Ashbery (b. 1927)*

At North Farm   1984

Somewhere someone is traveling furiously toward you,
At incredible speed, traveling day and night,
Through blizzards and desert heat, across torrents, through narrow
        passes.
But will he know where to find you,
Recognize you when he sees you,   5
Give you the thing he has for you?

Hardly anything grows here,
Yet the granaries are bursting with meal,
The sacks of meal piled to the rafters.
The streams run with sweetness, fattening fish;   10
Birds darken the sky. Is it enough
That the dish of milk is set out at night,
That we think of him sometimes,
Sometimes and always, with mixed feelings?

Margaret Atwood

Margaret Atwood (b. 1939)*

ALL BREAD   1978

All bread is made of wood,
cow dung, packed brown moss,
the bodies of dead animals, the teeth
and backbones, what is left
after the ravens. This dirt   5
flows through the stems into the grain,
into the arm, nine strokes
of the axe, skin from a tree,
good water which is the first
gift, four hours.   10

Live burial under a moist cloth,
a silver dish, the row
of white famine bellies
swollen and taut in the oven,
lungfuls of warm breath stopped   15
in the heat from an old sun.

Good bread has the salt taste
of your hands after nine
strokes of the axe, the salt
taste of your mouth, it smells   20
of its own small death, of the deaths
before and after.

Lift these ashes
into your mouth, your blood;
to know what you devour   25
is to consecrate it,
almost. All bread must be broken
so it can be shared. Together
we eat this earth.

W. H. Auden

W. H. Auden (1907 – 1973)*

As I Walked Out One Evening   1940

As I walked out one evening,
 Walking down Bristol Street,
The crowds upon the pavement
 Were fields of harvest wheat.

And down by the brimming river   5
 I heard a lover sing
Under an arch of the railway:
 "Love has no ending.

"I'll love you, dear, I'll love you
 Till China and Africa meet,   10
And the river jumps over the mountain
 And the salmon sing in the street,

"I'll love you till the ocean
 Is folded and hung up to dry
And the seven stars go squawking   15
 Like geese about the sky.

"The years shall run like rabbits,
 For in my arms I hold
The Flower of the Ages,
 And the first love of the world."   20

But all the clocks in the city
   Began to whirr and chime:
"O let not Time deceive you,
   You cannot conquer Time.

"In the burrows of the Nightmare   25
   Where Justice naked is,
Time watches from the shadow
   And coughs when you would kiss.

"In headaches and in worry
   Vaguely life leaks away,   30
And Time will have his fancy
   Tomorrow or today.

"Into many a green valley
   Drifts the appalling snow;
Time breaks the threaded dances   35
   And the diver's brilliant bow.

"O plunge your hands in water,
   Plunge them in up to the wrist;
Stare, stare in the basin
   And wonder what you've missed.   40

"The glacier knocks in the cupboard,
   The desert sighs in the bed,
And the crack in the teacup opens
   A lane to the land of the dead.

"Where the beggars raffle the banknotes   45
   And the Giant is enchanting to Jack,
And the Lily-white Boy is a Roarer,
   And Jill goes down on her back.

"O look, look in the mirror,
   O look in your distress;
Life remains a blessing   50
   Although you cannot bless.

"O stand, stand at the window
   As the tears scald and start;
You shall love your crooked neighbor   55
   With your crooked heart."

It was late, late in the evening,
   The lovers they were gone;
The clocks had ceased their chiming,
   And the deep river ran on.   60

"THE FALL OF ICARUS" by Pieter Brueghel (1520?–1569)

W. H. Auden (1907 – 1973)*

MUSÉE DES BEAUX ARTS   1940

About suffering they were never wrong,
The Old Masters: how well they understood
Its human position; how it takes place
While someone else is eating or opening a window or just walking
    dully along;
How, when the aged are reverently, passionately waiting   5
For the miraculous birth, there always must be
Children who did not specially want it to happen, skating
On a pond at the edge of the wood:
They never forgot
That even the dreadful martyrdom must run its course   10
Anyhow in a corner, some untidy spot
Where the dogs go on with their doggy life and the torturer's horse
Scratches its innocent behind on a tree.

In Brueghel's *Icarus*, for instance: how everything turns away
Quite leisurely from the disaster; the ploughman may   15
Have heard the splash, the forsaken cry,
But for him it was not an important failure; the sun shone
As it had to on the white legs disappearing into the green
Water; and the expensive delicate ship that must have seen
Something amazing, a boy falling out of the sky,   20
Had somewhere to get to and sailed calmly on.

COMPARE:

"Musée des Beaux Arts" with "The Dance" by William Carlos Williams (page 681) and
the painting by Pieter Brueghel to which each poem refers.

Jimmy Santiago Baca (b. 1952)

SPLICED WIRE   1982

I filled your house with light.
There was warmth in all corners
of the house. My words I gave you
like soft warm toast in early morning.
I brewed your tongue   5
to a rich dark coffee, and drank
my fill. I turned on the music for you,
playing notes along the crest
of your heart, like birds,
eagles, ravens, owls on rim of red canyon,   10

I brought reception clear to you,
and made the phone ring at your request,
from Paris or South America,
you could talk to any of the people,
as my words gave them life,   15
from a child in a boat with his father,
to a prisoner in a concentration camp,
all at your bedside.

And then you turned away, wanted
a larger mansion. I said no. I left you.   20
The plug pulled out, the house blinked out,
Into a quiet darkness, swallowing wind,
collecting autumn leaves like stamps
between its old boards where they stick.

You say, or carry the thought with you   25
to comfort you, that faraway somewhere,
lightning knocked down all the power lines.
But no my love, it was I,

pulling the plug. Others will come, plug in,
but often the lights will dim weakly   30
in storms, the music stop to a drawl,
the warmth shredded by cold drafts.

R. L. Barth (b. 1947)*

THE INSERT   1981

Our view of sky, jungle, and fields constricts
Into a sink hole covered with sawgrass

Undulating, soon whipped slant as the chopper
Hovers at four feet. Rapt, boot-deep in slime,

We deploy ourselves in a loose perimeter,   5
Listening for incoming rockets above

The thump of rotor blades; edgy for contact,
Junkies of terror impatient to shoot up.

Nothing moves, nothing sounds: then, single file,
We move across a streambed toward high ground.   10

The terror of the insert's quickly over.
Too quickly . . . and more quickly every time . . .

THE INSERT. R. L. Barth, a U.S. Marine in 1966 – 69, served as a long-range reconnaissance leader
in Vietnam. An *insert* is the dropping of troops into an area by helicopter.

COMPARE:

"The Insert" with the poems of Wilfred Owen: "Dulce et Decorum Est" (page 528) and
"Anthem for Doomed Youth" (page 854).

Elizabeth Bishop (1911 – 1979)*

FILLING STATION   1965

Oh, but it is dirty!
— this little filling station,
oil-soaked, oil-permeated
to a disturbing, over-all
black translucency.   5
Be careful with that match!

Father wears a dirty,
oil-soaked monkey suit
that cuts him under the arms,
and several quick and saucy   10
and greasy sons assist him
(it's a family filling station),
all quite thoroughly dirty.

Do they live in the station?
It has a cement porch
behind the pumps, and on it
a set of crushed and grease-
impregnated wickerwork;
on the wicker sofa
a dirty dog, quite comfy.

Some comic books provide
the only note of color —
of certain color. They lie
upon a big dim doily
draping a taboret
(part of the set), beside
a big hirsute begonia.

Why the extraneous plant?
Why the taboret?
Why, oh why, the doily?
(Embroidered in daisy stitch
with marguerites, I think,
and heavy with gray crochet.)

Somebody embroidered the doily.
Somebody waters the plant,
or oils it, maybe. Somebody
arranges the rows of cans
so that they softly say:
ESSO — SO — SO — SO
to high-strung automobiles.
Somebody loves us all.

15

20

25

30

35

40

COMPARE:

"Filling Station" with "MECANIC ON DUTY AT ALL TIMES" by Miller Williams (page 893).

Elizabeth Bishop

Elizabeth Bishop (1911–1979)*

ONE ART   1976

The art of losing isn't hard to master;
so many things seem filled with the intent
to be lost that their loss is no disaster.

Lose something every day. Accept the fluster
of lost door keys, the hour badly spent.   5
The art of losing isn't hard to master.

Then practice losing farther, losing faster:
places, and names, and where it was you meant
to travel. None of these will bring disaster.

I lost my mother's watch. And look! my last, or   10
next-to-last, of three loved houses went.
The art of losing isn't hard to master.

I lost two cities, lovely ones. And, vaster,
some realms I owned, two rivers, a continent.
I miss them, but it wasn't a disaster.   15

—Even losing you (the joking voice, a gesture
I love) I shan't have lied. It's evident
the art of losing's not too hard to master
though it may look like (*Write* it!) like disaster.

COMPARE:

"One Art" with "Do not go gentle into that good night" by Dylan Thomas (page 674) and
"Sestina" by Elizabeth Bishop (page 688).

William Blake (1757 – 1827)*

THE SICK ROSE   1794

O Rose, thou art sick!
The invisible worm
That flies in the night,
In the howling storm,

Has found out thy bed   5
Of crimson joy,
And his dark secret love
Does thy life destroy.

William Blake

William Blake (1757 – 1827)*

THE TYGER   1794

Tyger! Tyger! burning bright
In the forests of the night,
What immortal hand or eye
Could frame thy fearful symmetry?

In what distant deeps or skies   5
Burnt the fire of thine eyes?
On what wings dare he aspire?
What the hand dare seize the fire?

And what shoulder, and what art,
Could twist the sinews of thy heart?   10
And when thy heart began to beat,
What dread hand? and what dread feet?

What the hammer? what the chain?
In what furnace was thy brain?
What the anvil? what dread grasp   15
Dare its deadly terrors clasp?

When the stars threw down their spears,
And watered heaven with their tears,
Did he smile his work to see?
Did he who made the Lamb make thee?   20

Tyger! Tyger! burning bright
In the forests of the night,
What immortal hand or eye
Dare frame thy fearful symmetry?

Louise Bogan (1897 – 1970)

THE DREAM   1941

O God, in the dream the terrible horse began
To paw at the air, and make for me with his blows.
Fear kept for thirty-five years poured through his mane,
And retribution equally old, or nearly, breathed through his nose.

Coward complete, I lay and wept on the ground   5
When some strong creature appeared, and leapt for the rein.
Another woman, as I lay half in a swound,
Leapt in the air, and clutched at the leather and chain.

Give him, she said, something of yours as a charm.
Throw him, she said, some poor thing you alone claim.   10
No, no, I cried, he hates me; he's out for harm,
And whether I yield or not, it is all the same.

But, like a lion in a legend, when I flung the glove
Pulled from my sweating, my cold right hand,
The terrible beast, that no one may understand,   15
Came to my side, and put down his head in love.

Mark Alexander Boyd (1563 – 1601)

CUPID AND VENUS   (late sixteenth century)

Fra bank to bank, fra wood to wood I rin°,   *run*
   Ourhailit° with my feeble fantasie,   *overcome*
   Like til° a leaf that fallis from a tree   *to*
Or til a reed ourblawin with the win.
Twa gods guides me: the ane of them is blin,   5
   Yea, and a bairn° brocht up in vanitie,   *child*
   The next a wife ingenrit° of the sea,   *engendered, born*
And lichter nor° a dauphin° with her fin.   *than; dolphin*

Unhappy is the man for evermair
That tills the sand and sawis° in the air;   *sows* 10
   But twice unhappier is he, I lairn,
That feidis° in his hairt a mad desire   *feeds*
And follows on a woman thro the fire,
   Led by a blind and teachit by a bairn.

Joseph Brodsky (b. 1940)*

BELFAST TUNE   1988

Here's a girl from a dangerous town.
    She crops her dark hair short
so that less of her has to frown
    when someone gets hurt.

She folds her memories like a parachute.   5
    Dropped, she collects the peat
and cooks her veggies at home: they shoot
    here where they eat.

Ah, there's more sky in these parts than, say,
    ground. Hence her voice's pitch,   10
and her stare stains your retina like a gray
    bulb when you switch

hemispheres, and her knee-length quilt
    skirt's cut to catch the squall.
I dream of her either loved or killed   15
    because the town's too small.

Gwendolyn Brooks (b. 1917)*

A BLACK WEDDING SONG   1981

This love is a rich cry over
the deviltries and the death.
A weapon-song. Keep it strong.

Keep it strong.
Keep it logic and magic and lightning and muscle.   5

Strong hand in strong hand, stride to
the Assault that is promised you (knowing
no armor assaults a pudding or a mush.)

Here is your Wedding Day.
Here is your launch.   10

Come to your Wedding Song.

For you
I wish the kindness that romps or sorrows along.
Or kneels.

I wish you the daily forgiveness of each other.   15
For war comes in from the World
and puzzles a darling duet—
tangles tongues,
tears hearts, mashes minds;
there will be the need to forgive.   20

I wish you jewels of Black love.
Come to your Wedding Song.

Gwendolyn Brooks (b. 1917)*

THE RITES FOR COUSIN VIT   1949

Carried her unprotesting out the door.
Kicked back the casket-stand. But it can't hold her,
That stuff and satin aiming to enfold her,
The lid's contrition nor the bolts before.
Oh oh. Too much. Too much. Even now, surmise,   5
She rises in the sunshine. There she goes,
Back to the bars she knew and the repose
In love-rooms and the things in people's eyes.
Too vital and too squeaking. Must emerge.
Even now she does the snake-hips with a hiss,   10
Slops the bad wine across her shantung, talks
Of pregnancy, guitars and bridgework, walks
In parks or alleys, comes haply on the verge
Of happiness, haply hysterics. Is.

Gwendolyn Brooks

Robert Browning (1812 – 1889)*

SOLILOQUY OF THE SPANISH CLOISTER   1842

Gr-r-r — there go, my heart's abhorrence!
    Water your damned flower-pots, do!
If hate killed men, Brother Lawrence,
    God's blood, would not mine kill you!
What? your myrtle-bush wants trimming?   5
    Oh, that rose has prior claims —
Needs its leaden vase filled brimming?
    Hell dry you up with its flames!

At the meal we sit together;
    Salve tibi!° I must hear   Hail to thee!   10
Wise talk of the kind of weather,
    Sort of season, time of year:
Not a plenteous cork-crop: scarcely
    Dare we hope oak-galls, I doubt;
What's the Latin name for "parsley"?   15
What's the Greek name for "swine's snout"?

Whew! We'll have our platter burnished,
    Laid with care on our own shelf!
With a fire-new spoon we're furnished,
    And a goblet for ourself,   20
Rinsed like something sacrificial
    Ere 'tis fit to touch our chaps —
Marked with L. for our initial!
    (He-he! There his lily snaps!)

Saint, forsooth! While Brown Dolores   25
    Squats outside the Convent bank
With Sanchicha, telling stories,
    Steeping tresses in the tank,
Blue-black, lustrous, thick like horsehairs,
    — Can't I see his dead eye glow,   30
Bright as 'twere a Barbary corsair's?
    (That is, if he'd let it show!)

When he finishes refection,
    Knife and fork he never lays
Cross-wise, to my recollection,   35
    As I do, in Jesu's praise.
I the Trinity illustrate,
    Drinking watered orange-pulp —
In three sips the Arian frustrate;
    While he drains his at one gulp!   40

SOLILOQUY OF THE SPANISH CLOISTER. 3 *Brother Lawrence*: one of the speaker's fellow monks. 31
Barbary corsair: a pirate operating off the Barbary coast of Africa. 39 *Arian*: a follower of Arius,
heretic who denied the doctrine of the Trinity.

Oh, those melons! if he's able
    We're to have a feast; so nice!
One goes to the Abbot's table,
    All of us get each a slice.
How go on your flowers? None double?   45
    Not one fruit-sort can you spy?
Strange! — And I, too, at such trouble,
    Keep them close-nipped on the sly!

There's a great text in Galatians,
    Once you trip on it, entails   50
Twenty-nine distinct damnations,
    One sure, if another fails;
If I trip him just a-dying,
    Sure of heaven as sure can be,
Spin him round and send him flying   55
    Off to hell, a Manichee?

Or, my scrofulous French novel
    On grey paper with blunt type!
Simply glance at it, you grovel
    Hand and foot in Belial's gripe;   60
If I double down its pages
    At the woeful sixteenth print,
When he gathers his greengages,
    Ope a sieve and slip it in't?

Or, there's Satan! — one might venture   65
    Pledge one's soul to him, yet leave
Such a flaw in the indenture
    As he'd miss till, past retrieve,
Blasted lay that rose-acacia
    We're so proud of! Hy, Zy, Hine. . . .   70
'St, there's Vespers! *Plena gratia*
    Ave, Virgo!° Gr-r-r — you swine!   *Hail, Virgin, full of grace!*

49 *a great text in Galatians:* a difficult verse in this book of the Bible. Brother Lawrence will be
damned as a heretic if he wrongly interprets it. 56 *Manichee:* another kind of heretic, one who (after
the Persian philosopher Mani) sees in the world a constant struggle between good and evil, neither
able to win. 60 *Belial:* Here, not specifically Satan but (as used in the Old Testament) a name for
wickedness. 70 *Hy, Zy, Hine:* Possibly the sound of a bell to announce evening devotions.

Thomas Carew (1594? – 1640)

ASK ME NO MORE WHERE JOVE BESTOWS   1640

Ask me no more where Jove bestows,
When June is past, the fading rose;
For in your beauty's orient deep
These flowers, as in their causes, sleep.

Ask me no more whither do stray   5
The golden atoms of the day;
For in pure love heaven did prepare
Those powders to enrich your hair.

Ask me no more whither doth haste
The nightingale when May is past,   10
For in your sweet dividing throat
She winters, and keeps warm her note.

Ask me no more where those stars light
That downwards fall in dead of night,
For in your eyes they sit, and there   15
Fixèd become, as in their sphere.

Ask me no more if east or west
The phoenix builds her spicy nest,
For unto you at last she flies
And in your fragrant bosom dies.   20

ASK ME NO MORE WHERE JOVE BESTOWS. 3 *orient:* radiant, glowing. (In our time, this sense of the
word is obsolete.) 4 *These flowers . . . sleep:* as they slept before they came into existence. (A *cause,*
that which gives being, is a term from Aristotle and the Scholastic philosophers.) 11 *dividing:*
singing, uttering a "division" or melodic phrase added to a basic tune. 18 *phoenix:* In legend, an
Arabian bird believed to subsist on incense and perfumes. It was supposed to reproduce by going
up in flames, to rise again out of its ashes.

Fred Chappell (b. 1936)

SKIN FLICK   1971

The selfsame surface that billowed once with
The shapes of Trigger and Gene. New faces now
Are in the saddle. Tits and buttocks
Slide rattling down the beam as down
A coal chute; in the splotched light   5
The burning bush strikes dumb.
Different sort of cattle drive:
No water for miles and miles.

In the aisles, new bugs and rats
Though it's the same Old Paint.   10
Audience of lepers, hopeless and homeless,
Or like the buffalo, at home
In the wind only. No
Mushy love stuff for them.

They eye the violent innocence they always knew.   15
Is that the rancher's palomino daughter?
Is this her eastern finishing school?
Same old predicament:
No water for miles and miles,
The horizon breeds no cavalry.   20

Men, draw your wagons in a circle. Be ready.

G. K. Chesterton (1874 – 1936)

THE DONKEY   1900

When fishes flew and forests walked
  And figs grew upon thorn,
Some moment when the moon was blood
  Then surely I was born;

With monstrous head and sickening cry   5
  And ears like errant wings,
The devil's walking parody
  On all four-footed things.

The tattered outlaw of the earth,
  Of ancient crooked will;   10
Starve, scourge, deride me: I am dumb,
  I keep my secret still.

Fools! For I also had my hour;
  One far fierce hour and sweet:
There was a shout about my ears,   15
  And palms before my feet.

THE DONKEY. For more details of the donkey's hour of triumph see Matthew 21:1 – 8.

Samuel Taylor Coleridge (1772 – 1834)*

KUBLA KHAN   (1797 – 1798)

Or, a Vision in a Dream. A Fragment.

In Xanadu did Kubla Khan
A stately pleasure-dome decree:
Where Alph, the sacred river, ran
Through caverns measureless to man
  Down to a sunless sea.   5
So twice five miles of fertile ground
With walls and towers were girdled round;
And there were gardens bright with sinuous rills,
Where blossomed many an incense-bearing tree;
And here were forests ancient as the hills,   10
Enfolding sunny spots of greenery.

But oh! that deep romantic chasm which slanted
Down the green hill athwart a cedarn cover!
A savage place! as holy and enchanted
As e'er beneath a waning moon was haunted   15
By woman wailing for her demon-lover!

And from this chasm, with ceaseless turmoil seething,
As if this earth in fast thick pants were breathing,
A mighty fountain momently was forced:
Amid whose swift half-intermitted burst   20
Huge fragments vaulted like rebounding hail,
Or chaffy grain beneath the thresher's flail:
And 'mid these dancing rocks at once and ever
It flung up momently the sacred river.
Five miles meandering with a mazy motion   25
Through wood and dale the sacred river ran,
Then reached the caverns measureless to man,
And sank in tumult to a lifeless ocean:
And 'mid this tumult Kubla heard from far
Ancestral voices prophesying war!   30

    The shadow of the dome of pleasure
    Floated midway on the waves;
    Where was heard the mingled measure
    From the fountain and the caves.
It was a miracle of rare device,   35
A sunny pleasure-dome with caves of ice!

    A damsel with a dulcimer
    In a vision once I saw:
    It was an Abyssinian maid,
    And on her dulcimer she played,   40
    Singing of Mount Abora.
    Could I revive within me
    Her symphony and song,
    To such a deep delight 'twould win me,
That with music loud and long,   45
I would build that dome in air,
That sunny dome! those caves of ice!
And all who heard should see them there,
And all should cry, Beware! Beware!
His flashing eyes, his floating hair!   50
Weave a circle round him thrice,
And close your eyes with holy dread,
For he on honey-dew hath fed,
And drunk the milk of Paradise.

KUBLA KHAN. There was an actual Kublai Khan, a thirteenth-century Mongol emperor, and a
Chinese city of Xamdu; but Coleridge's dream vision also borrows from travelers' descriptions of
such other exotic places as Abyssinia and America. 51 *circle*: a magic circle drawn to keep away
evil spirits.

Emily Dickinson

Emily Dickinson (1830 – 1886)*

BECAUSE I COULD NOT STOP FOR DEATH   (1863)

Because I could not stop for Death –
He kindly stopped for me –
The Carriage held but just Ourselves –
And Immortality.

We slowly drove – He knew no haste   5
And I had put away
My labor and my leisure too,
For His Civility –

We passed the School, where Children strove
At Recess – in the Ring –   10
We passed the Fields of Gazing Grain –
We passed the Setting Sun –

Or rather – He passed Us –
The Dews drew quivering and chill –
For only Gossamer, my Gown –   15
My Tippet° – only Tulle –   *cape*

We paused before a House that seemed
A Swelling of the Ground –

BECAUSE I COULD NOT STOP FOR DEATH. In the version of this poem printed by Emily Dickinson's first editors in 1890, stanza four was left out. In line 9 *strove* was replaced by *played*; line 10 was made to read "Their lessons scarcely done".

The Roof was scarcely visible –
The Cornice – in the Ground –

Since then – 'tis Centuries – and yet
Feels shorter than the Day
I first surmised the Horses' Heads
Were toward Eternity –

20, "The cornice but a mound"; 21, "Since then 'tis centuries, but each"; and capitalization and
punctuation were made conventional.

Emily Dickinson (1830 – 1886)*

I STARTED EARLY – TOOK MY DOG   (1862)

I started Early – Took my Dog –
And visited the Sea –
The Mermaids in the Basement
Came out to look at me –

And Frigates – in the Upper Floor   5
Extended Hempen Hands –
Presuming Me to be a Mouse –
Aground – upon the Sands –

But no Man moved Me – till the Tide
Went past my simple Shoe –   10
And past my Apron – and my Belt
And past my Bodice – too –

And made as He would eat me up –
As wholly as a Dew
Upon a Dandelion's Sleeve –   15
And then – I started – too –

And He – He followed – close behind –
I felt His Silver Heel
Upon my Ankle – Then my Shoes
Would overflow with Pearl –   20

Until We met the Solid Town –
No One He seemed to know –
And bowing – with a Mighty look –
At me – The Sea withdrew –

Emily Dickinson (1830 – 1886)*

MY LIFE HAD STOOD – A LOADED GUN   (about 1863)

My Life had stood – a Loaded Gun –
In Corners – till a Day
The Owner passed – identified –
And carried Me away –

And now We roam in Sovereign Woods –   5
And now We hunt the Doe –
And every time I speak for Him –
The Mountains straight reply –

And do I smile, such cordial light
Upon the Valley glow –   10
It is as a Vesuvian face
Had let its pleasure through –

And when at Night – Our good Day done –
I guard My Master's Head –
'Tis better than the Eider-Duck's   15
Deep Pillow – to have shared –

To foe of His – I'm deadly foe –
None stir the second time –
On whom I lay a Yellow Eye –
Or an emphatic Thumb –   20

Though I than He – may longer live
He longer must – than I –
For I have but the power to kill,
Without – the power to die –

Deborah Digges (b. 1950)

FOR *The Daughters of Hannah Bible Class* OF TIPTON, MISSOURI'S WOMEN'S PRISON: MOTHER'S DAY, 1959   1986

I remember the gifts we brought that Sunday.
We were no one to them.
We were another woman's children.
The number of blossoms they chose from the red
carnations we'd bound with wire at the stems   5
told how many children they had.

But today, driving through Tipton,
I couldn't remember their faces.
I must have been afraid if I looked too long
I might take on the expression of the thief   10
or the murderess—I had my own sins to contend with
that bloomed in dreams like bruises,
like corsages pinned to faded identical dresses
or strapped like watches to their wrists.
We'd fan ourselves with hymnals, out of rhythm,   15
while my mother's piano played out songs of forgiveness.
The afternoon went sunblind as an old grief,
the way my small son coming from sleep now
sees the last dream above him erased.
Still, they must have felt something break   20
open inside they didn't know had sealed
each spring when the roads cleared.
For the first time in months they could hold
their children, they could lift them up
onto the prison's ageless yard toys   25
and feel their own full weight all visiting hour—
so that the evening that followed would be blessed
somehow as each one waited for sleep,
when the voices along the corridors were only echoes,
the static on guardhouse radios, their weather.   30
Once they were every young girl escaping,
driving fast past these small towns.
Here, on the sun-side the last ice lining the eaves
catches the light cleanly, and hits ground,
the sound unmistakable, or hangs on,   35
shining, through the first thaw.

John Donne (1572 – 1631)*

THE FLEA   1633

Mark but this flea, and mark in this
How little that which thou deny'st me is;
It sucked me first, and now sucks thee,
And in this flea our two bloods mingled be;
Thou know'st that this cannot be said   5
A sin, nor shame, nor loss of maidenhead,
    Yet this enjoys before it woo,
    And pampered swells with one blood made of two,
    And this, alas, is more than we would do.

Oh stay, three lives in one flea spare, 10
Where we almost, yea more than married are.
This flea is you and I, and this
Our marriage bed, and marriage temple is;
Though parents grudge, and you, we're met
And cloistered in these living walls of jet. 15
   Though use° make you apt to kill me, *custom*
   Let not to that, self-murder added be,
   And sacrilege, three sins in killing three.

Cruel and sudden, hast thou since
Purpled thy nail in blood of innocence? 20
Wherein could this flea guilty be,
Except in that drop it sucked from thee?
Yet thou triumph'st, and say'st that thou
Find'st not thyself, nor me, the weaker now;
   'Tis true; then learn how false, fears be; 25
   Just so much honor, when thou yield'st to me,
   Will waste, as this flea's death took life from thee.

John Donne

John Donne (1572 – 1631)*

A VALEDICTION: FORBIDDING MOURNING   (1611)

As virtuous men pass mildly away,
   And whisper to their souls to go,
Whilst some of their sad friends do say
   The breath goes now, and some say no:

So let us melt, and make no noise, 5
   No tear-floods, nor sigh-tempests move;
'Twere profanation of our joys
   To tell the laity° our love. *common people*

Moving of th' earth° brings harms and fears;   *earthquake*
    Men reckon what it did and meant;   10
But trepidation of the spheres,
    Though greater far, is innocent°.   *harmless*

Dull sublunary lovers' love
    (Whose soul is sense) cannot admit
Absence, because it doth remove   15
    Those things which elemented° it.   *constituted*

But we, by a love so much refined
    That ourselves know not what it is,
Inter-assurèd of the mind,
    Care less, eyes, lips, and hands to miss.   20

Our two souls, therefore, which are one,
    Though I must go, endure not yet
A breach, but an expansìon,
    Like gold to airy thinness beat.

If they be two, they are two so   25
    As stiff twin compasses are two:
Thy soul, the fixed foot, makes no show
    To move, but doth, if th' other do.

And though it in the center sit,
    Yet when the other far doth roam,   30
It leans and harkens after it,
    And grows erect as that comes home.

Such wilt thou be to me, who must,
    Like th' other foot, obliquely run;
Thy firmness makes my circle just°,   *perfect*   35
    And makes me end where I begun.

A VALEDICTION: FORBIDDING MOURNING. According to Donne's biographer Izaak Walton, Donne's
wife received this poem as a gift before the poet departed on a journey to France. 11 *spheres:* In
Ptolemaic astronomy, the concentric spheres surrounding the earth. The trepidation or motion of
the ninth sphere was thought to change the date of the equinox. 19 *Inter-assurèd of the mind:* each
sure in mind that the other is faithful. 24 *gold to airy thinness:* Gold is so malleable that, if beaten
to the thickness of gold leaf (1/250,000 of one inch), one ounce of gold would cover 250 square
feet.

Rita Dove (b. 1952)

DAYSTAR   1986

She wanted a little room for thinking:
but she saw diapers steaming on the line,
a doll slumped behind the door.

So she lugged a chair behind the garage
to sit out the children's naps.   5

Sometimes there were things to watch—
the pinched armor of a vanished cricket,
a floating maple leaf. Other days
she stared until she was assured
when she closed her eyes   10
she'd see only her own vivid blood.

She had an hour, at best, before Liza appeared
pouting from the top of the stairs.
And just *what* was mother doing
out back with the field mice? Why,   15

building a palace. Later
that night when Thomas rolled over and
lurched into her, she would open her eyes
and think of the place that was hers
for an hour—where   20
she was nothing,
pure nothing, in the middle of the day.

John Dryden (1631 – 1700)*

To the Memory of Mr. Oldham   1684

Farewell, too little and too lately known,
Whom I began to think and call my own;
For sure our souls were near allied, and thine
Cast in the same poetic mold with mine.
One common note on either lyre did strike,   5
And knaves and fools we both abhorred alike.
To the same goal did both our studies drive:
The last set out the soonest did arrive.
Thus Nissus fell upon the slippery place,
While his young friend performed and won the race.   10
O early ripe! to thy abundant store
What could advancing age have added more?
It might (what Nature never gives the young)
Have taught the numbers° of thy native tongue.   *meters*
But satire needs not those, and wit will shine   15
Through the harsh cadence of a rugged line.
A noble error, and but seldom made,

To the Memory of Mr. Oldham. John Oldham, poet best remembered for his *Satires upon the
Jesuits*, had died at thirty. 9 – 10 *Nissus; his young friend:* These two close friends, as Virgil tells us
in the *Aeneid*, ran a race for the prize of an olive crown.

When poets are by too much force betrayed.
Thy gen'rous fruits, though gathered ere their
    prime,
Still showed a quickness; and maturing time   20
But mellows what we write to the dull sweets of
    rhyme.
Once more, hail, and farewell! farewell, thou young
But ah! too short, Marcellus of our tongue!
Thy brows with ivy and with laurels bound;
But fate and gloomy night encompass thee around.   25

23 *Marcellus:* Had he not died in his twentieth year, he would have succeeded the Roman emperor
Augustus. 25 This line echoes the *Aeneid* (VI, 886), in which Marcellus is seen walking under the
black cloud of his impending doom.

COMPARE:

"To the Memory of Mr. Oldham" with "Lycidas" by John Milton (page 720).

T. S. Eliot (1888 – 1965)*

JOURNEY OF THE MAGI   1927

"A cold coming we had of it,
Just the worst time of the year
For a journey, and such a long journey:
The ways deep and the weather sharp,
The very dead of winter."   5
And the camels galled, sore-footed, refractory,
Lying down in the melting snow.
There were times we regretted
The summer palaces on slopes, the terraces,
And the silken girls bringing sherbet.   10
Then the camel men cursing and grumbling
And running away, and wanting their liquor and women,
And the night-fires going out, and the lack of shelters,
And the cities hostile and the towns unfriendly
And the villages dirty and charging high prices: 15
A hard time we had of it.
At the end we preferred to travel all night,
Sleeping in snatches,
With the voices singing in our ears, saying
That this was all folly.   20

Then at dawn we came down to a temperate valley,
Wet, below the snow line, smelling of vegetation;
With a running stream and a water-mill beating the darkness,
And three trees on the low sky,
And an old white horse galloped away in the meadow.   25

Then we came to a tavern with vine-leaves over the lintel,
Six hands at an open door dicing for pieces of silver,
And feet kicking the empty wine-skins.
But there was no information, and so we continued
And arrived at evening, not a moment too soon   30
Finding the place; it was (you may say) satisfactory.
All this was a long time ago, I remember,
And I would do it again, but set down
This set down
This: were we led all that way for   35
Birth or Death? There was a Birth, certainly,
We had evidence and no doubt. I had seen birth and death,
But had thought they were different; this Birth was
Hard and bitter agony for us, like Death, our death.
We returned to our places, these Kingdoms,   40
But no longer at ease here, in the old dispensation,
With an alien people clutching their gods.
I should be glad of another death.

JOURNEY OF THE MAGI. The story of the Magi, the three wise men who traveled to Bethlehem to behold the baby Jesus, is told in Matthew 2:1 – 12. That the three were kings is a later tradition. 1 – 5 A *cold coming . . . winter:* Eliot quotes with slight changes from a sermon preached on Christmas day, 1622, by Bishop Lancelot Andrewes. 24 *three trees:* foreshadowing the three crosses on Calvary (see Luke 23:32 – 33). 25 *white horse:* perhaps the steed that carried the conquering Christ in the vision of St. John the Divine (Revelation 19:11 – 16). 41 *old dispensation:* older, pagan religion about to be displaced by Christianity.

COMPARE:

"Journey of the Magi" with "The Magi" by William Butler Yeats (page 902).

T. S. Eliot

T. S. Eliot (1888 – 1965)*

THE LOVE SONG OF J. ALFRED PRUFROCK   1917

S'io credessi che mia risposta fosse
A persona che mai tornasse al mondo,
Questa fiamma staria senza piu scosse.
Ma perciocche giammai di questo fondo
Non torno vivo alcun, s'i'odo il vero,
Senza tema d'infamia ti rispondo.

Let us go then, you and I,
When the evening is spread out against the sky
Like a patient etherized upon a table;
Let us go, through certain half-deserted streets,
The muttering retreats   5
Of restless nights in one-night cheap hotels
And sawdust restaurants with oyster-shells:
Streets that follow like a tedious argument
Of insidious intent
To lead you to an overwhelming question . . .   10
Oh, do not ask, "What is it?"
Let us go and make our visit.

In the room the women come and go
Talking of Michelangelo.

The yellow fog that rubs its back upon the window-panes,   15
The yellow smoke that rubs its muzzle on the window-panes
Licked its tongue into the corners of the evening,
Lingered upon the pools that stand in drains,
Let fall upon its back the soot that falls from chimneys,
Slipped by the terrace, made a sudden leap,   20
And seeing that it was a soft October night,
Curled once about the house, and fell asleep.

And indeed there will be time
For the yellow smoke that slides along the street,
Rubbing its back upon the window-panes;   25
There will be time, there will be time
To prepare a face to meet the faces that you meet;
There will be time to murder and create,
And time for all the works and days of hands
That lift and drop a question on your plate;   30
Time for you and time for me,
And time yet for a hundred indecisions,
And for a hundred visions and revisions,
Before the taking of a toast and tea.

In the room the women come and go   35
Talking of Michelangelo.

And indeed there will be time
To wonder, "Do I dare?" and, "Do I dare?"
Time to turn back and descend the stair,
With a bald spot in the middle of my hair —   40
(They will say: "How his hair is growing thin!")
My morning coat, my collar mounting firmly to the chin,
My necktie rich and modest, but asserted by a simple pin —
(They will say: "But how his arms and legs are thin!")
Do I dare   45
Disturb the universe?
In a minute there is time
For decisions and revisions which a minute will reverse.

For I have known them all already, known them all: —
Have known the evenings, mornings, afternoons,   50
I have measured out my life with coffee spoons;
I know the voices dying with a dying fall
Beneath the music from a farther room.
    So how should I presume?

And I have known the eyes already, known them all —   55
The eyes that fix you in a formulated phrase,
And when I am formulated, sprawling on a pin,
When I am pinned and wriggling on the wall,
Then how should I begin
To spit out all the butt-ends of my days and ways?   60
    And how should I presume?

And I have known the arms already, known them all —
Arms that are braceleted and white and bare
(But in the lamplight, downed with light brown hair!)
Is it perfume from a dress   65
That makes me so digress?
Arms that lie along a table, or wrap about a shawl.
    And should I then presume?
    And how should I begin?

                         .   .   .   .   .

Shall I say, I have gone at dusk through narrow streets   70
And watched the smoke that rises from the pipes
Of lonely men in shirt-sleeves, leaning out of windows? . . .

I should have been a pair of ragged claws
Scuttling across the floors of silent seas.

And the afternoon, the evening, sleeps so peacefully!   75
Smoothed by long fingers,
Asleep . . . tired . . . or it malingers,
Stretched on the floor, here beside you and me.
Should I, after tea and cakes and ices,
Have the strength to force the moment to its crisis?   80

But though I have wept and fasted, wept and prayed,
Though I have seen my head (grown slightly bald) brought in upon a
    platter,
I am no prophet — and here's no great matter;
I have seen the moment of my greatness flicker,
And I have seen the eternal Footman hold my coat, and snicker,   85
And in short, I was afraid.

And would it have been worth it, after all,
After the cups, the marmalade, the tea,
Among the porcelain, among some talk of you and me,
Would it have been worth while,   90
To have bitten off the matter with a smile,
To have squeezed the universe into a ball
To roll it toward some overwhelming question,
To say: "I am Lazarus, come from the dead,
Come back to tell you all, I shall tell you all" —   95
If one, settling a pillow by her head,
    Should say: "That is not what I meant at all.
    That is not it, at all."

And would it have been worth it, after all,
Would it have been worth while,   100
After the sunsets and the dooryards and the sprinkled streets,
After the novels, after the teacups, after the skirts that trail along the
    floor —
And this, and so much more? —
It is impossible to say just what I mean!
But as if a magic lantern threw the nerves in patterns on a screen: 105
Would it have been worth while
If one, settling a pillow or throwing off a shawl,
And turning toward the window, should say:
    "That is not it at all,
    That is not what I meant, at all."   110

. . . . .

No! I am not Prince Hamlet, nor was meant to be;
Am an attendant lord, one that will do
To swell a progress, start a scene or two,
Advise the prince; no doubt, an easy tool,
Deferential, glad to be of use,   115
Politic, cautious, and meticulous;
Full of high sentence, but a bit obtuse;
At times, indeed, almost ridiculous —
Almost, at times, the Fool.

I grow old . . . I grow old . . .   120
I shall wear the bottoms of my trousers rolled.

Shall I part my hair behind? Do I dare to eat a peach?
I shall wear white flannel trousers, and walk upon the beach.
I have heard the mermaids singing, each to each.

I do not think that they will sing to me. 125

I have seen them riding seaward on the waves
Combing the white hair of the waves blown back
When the wind blows the water white and black.

We have lingered in the chambers of the sea
By sea-girls wreathed with seaweed red and brown 130
Till human voices wake us, and we drown.

THE LOVE SONG OF J. ALFRED PRUFROCK. The epigraph, from Dante's *Inferno*, is the speech of one dead and damned, who thinks that his hearer also is going to remain in Hell. Count Guido da Montefeltro, whose sin has been to give false counsel after a corrupt prelate had offered him prior absolution and whose punishment is to be wrapped in a constantly burning flame, offers to tell Dante his story: "If I thought my reply were to someone who could ever return to the world, this flame would waver no more. But since, I'm told, nobody ever escapes from this pit, I'll tell you without fear of ill fame." 29 *works and days*: title of a poem by Hesiod (eighth century B.C.), depicting his life as a hard-working Greek farmer and exhorting his brother to be like him. 82 *head . . . platter*: like that of John the Baptist, prophet and praiser of chastity, whom King Herod beheaded at the demand of Herodias, his unlawfully wedded wife (see Mark 6:17 – 28). 92 – 93 *squeezed . . . To roll it*: an echo from Marvell's "To His Coy Mistress," lines 41 – 42 (see page 847). 94 *Lazarus*: Probably the Lazarus whom Jesus called forth from the tomb (John 11:1 – 44), but possibly the beggar seen in Heaven by the rich man in Hell (Luke 16:19 – 25).

Louise Erdrich (b. 1954)

INDIAN BOARDING SCHOOL: THE RUNAWAYS 1984

Home's the place we head for in our sleep.
Boxcars stumbling north in dreams
don't wait for us. We catch them on the run.
The rails, old lacerations that we love,
shoot parallel across the face and break 5
just under Turtle Mountains. Riding scars
you can't get lost. Home is the place they cross.

The lame guard strikes a match and makes the dark
less tolerant. We watch through cracks in boards
as the land starts rolling, rolling till it hurts 10
to be here, cold in regulation clothes.
We know the sheriff's waiting at midrun
to take us back. His car is dumb and warm.
The highway doesn't rock, it only hums
like a wing of long insults. The worn-down welts 15
of ancient punishments lead back and forth.

All runaways wear dresses, long green ones,
the color you would think shame was. We scrub
the sidewalks down because it's shameful work.
Our brushes cut the stone in watered arcs   20
and in the soak frail outlines shiver clear
a moment, things us kids pressed on the dark
face before it hardened, pale, remembering
delicate old injuries, the spines of names and leaves.

INDIAN BOARDING SCHOOL: THE RUNAWAYS. 6. *Turtle Mountains:* in North Dakota and Manitoba.
The poet, of German and Native American descent, belongs to the Turtle Mountain Band of the
Chippewa.

Robert Frost (1874–1963)*

AWAY!   1962

Now I out walking
The world desert,
And my shoe and my stocking
Do me no hurt.

I leave behind   5
Good friends in town.
Let them get well-wined
And go lie down.

Don't think I leave
For the outer dark   10
Like Adam and Eve
Put out of the Park.

Forget the myth.
There is no one I
Am put out with   15
Or put out by.

Unless I'm wrong
I but obey
The urge of a song:
I'm—bound—away!   20

And I may return
If dissatisfied
With what I learn
From having died.

Robert Frost (1874–1963)*

BIRCHES   1916

When I see birches bend to left and right
Across the lines of straighter darker trees,
I like to think some boy's been swinging them.
But swinging doesn't bend them down to stay
As ice storms do. Often you must have seen them   5
Loaded with ice a sunny winter morning
After a rain. They click upon themselves
As the breeze rises, and turn many-colored
As the stir cracks and crazes their enamel.
Soon the sun's warmth makes them shed crystal shells   10
Shattering and avalanching on the snow crust—
Such heaps of broken glass to sweep away
You'd think the inner dome of heaven had fallen.
They are dragged to the withered bracken by the load,
And they seem not to break; though once they are bowed   15
So low for long, they never right themselves:
You may see their trunks arching in the woods
Years afterwards, trailing their leaves on the ground
Like girls on hands and knees that throw their hair
Before them over their heads to dry in the sun.   20
But I was going to say when Truth broke in
With all her matter of fact about the ice storm,
I should prefer to have some boy bend them
As he went out and in to fetch the cows—
Some boy too far from town to learn baseball,   25
Whose only play was what he found himself,
Summer or winter, and could play alone.
One by one he subdued his father's trees
By riding them down over and over again
Until he took the stiffness out of them,   30
And not one but hung limp, not one was left
For him to conquer. He learned all there was
To learn about not launching out too soon
And so not carrying the tree away
Clear to the ground. He always kept his poise   35
To the top branches, climbing carefully
With the same pains you use to fill a cup
Up to the brim, and even above the brim.
Then he flung outward, feet first, with a swish,
Kicking his way down through the air to the ground.   40

So was I once myself a swinger of birches.
And so I dream of going back to be.
It's when I'm weary of considerations,
And life is too much like a pathless wood
Where your face burns and tickles with the cobwebs   45
Broken across it, and one eye is weeping
From a twig's having lashed across it open.
I'd like to get away from earth awhile
And then come back to it and begin over.
May no fate willfully misunderstand me   50
And half grant what I wish and snatch me away
Not to return. Earth's the right place for love:
I don't know where it's likely to go better.
I'd like to go by climbing a birch tree,
And climb black branches up a snow-white trunk   55
Toward heaven, till the tree could bear no more,
But dipped its top and set me down again.
That would be good both going and coming back.
One could do worse than be a swinger of birches.

Robert Frost (1874 – 1963)*

STOPPING BY WOODS ON A SNOWY EVENING   1923

Whose woods these are I think I know.
His house is in the village though;
He will not see me stopping here
To watch his woods fill up with snow.

My little horse must think it queer   5
To stop without a farmhouse near
Between the woods and frozen lake
The darkest evening of the year.

He gives his harness bells a shake
To ask if there is some mistake.   10
The only other sound's the sweep
Of easy wind and downy flake.

The woods are lovely, dark and deep,
But I have promises to keep,
And miles to go before I sleep,   15
And miles to go before I sleep.

COMPARE:

"Stopping by Woods on a Snowy Evening" with "Desert Places" by Robert Frost (page 636).

Allen Ginsberg (b. 1926)

A SUPERMARKET IN CALIFORNIA   1956

What thoughts I have of you tonight, Walt Whitman, for I walked down the sidestreets under the trees with a headache self-conscious looking at the full moon.

In my hungry fatigue, and shopping for images, I went into the neon fruit supermarket, dreaming of your enumerations!

What peaches and what penumbras! Whole families shopping at night! Aisles full of husbands! Wives in the avocados, babies in the tomatoes! — and you, Garcia Lorca, what were you doing down by the watermelons?

I saw you, Walt Whitman, childless, lonely old grubber, poking among the meats in the refrigerator and eyeing the grocery boys.

I heard you asking questions of each: Who killed the pork chops? What price bananas? Are you my Angel?   5

I wandered in and out of the brilliant stacks of cans following you, and followed in my imagination by the store detective.

We strode down the open corridors together in our solitary fancy tasting artichokes, possessing every frozen delicacy, and never passing the cashier.

Where are we going, Walt Whitman? The doors close in an hour. Which way does your beard point tonight?

(I touch your book and dream of our odyssey in the supermarket and feel absurd.)

Will we walk all night through solitary streets? The trees add shade to shade, lights out in the houses, we'll both be lonely.   10

Will we stroll dreaming of the lost America of love past blue automobiles in driveways, home to our silent cottage?

Ah, dear father, graybeard, lonely old courage-teacher, what America did you have when Charon quit poling his ferry and you got out on a smoking bank and stood watching the boat disappear on the black waters of Lethe?

A SUPERMARKET IN CALIFORNIA. 2 *enumerations:* Many of Whitman's poems contain lists of observed details. 3 *Garcia Lorca:* modern Spanish poet who wrote an "Ode to Walt Whitman" in his booklength sequence *Poet in New York.* (A poem by Lorca appears on page 732.) 12 *Charon . . . Lethe:* Is the poet confusing two underworld rivers? Charon, in Greek and Roman mythology, is the boatman who ferries the souls of the dead across the River Styx. The River Lethe also flows through Hades, and a drink of its waters makes the dead lose their painful memories of loved ones thay have left behind.

COMPARE:

"A Supermarket in California" with Walt Whitman's "To a Locomotive in Winter" (page 512) and "I Saw in Louisiana a Live-Oak Growing" (page 890).

Dana Gioia (b. 1950)

CALIFORNIA HILLS IN AUGUST   1982

I can imagine someone who found
these fields unbearable, who climbed
the hillside in the heat, cursing the dust,
cracking the brittle weeds underfoot,
wishing a few more trees for shade.   5

An Easterner especially, who would scorn
the meagreness of summer, the dry
twisted shapes of black elm,
scrub oak, and chaparral — a landscape
August has already drained of green.   10

One who would hurry over the clinging
thistle, foxtail, golden poppy,
knowing everything was just a weed,
unable to conceive that these trees
and sparse brown bushes were alive.   15

And hate the bright stillness of the noon,
without wind, without motion,
the only other living thing
a hawk, hungry for prey, suspended
in the blinding, sunlit blue.   20

And yet how gentle it seems to someone
raised in a landscape short of rain —
the skyline of a hill broken by no more
trees than one can count, the grass,
the empty sky, the wish for water.   25

H. D. [Hilda Doolittle] (1886–1961)*

HELEN   1924

All Greece hates
the still eyes in the white face,
the lustre as of olives
where she stands,
and the white hands.   5

All Greece reviles
the wan face when she smiles,
hating it deeper still
when it grows wan and white,
remembering past enchantments   10
and past ills.

Greece sees unmoved,
God's daughter, born of love,
the beauty of cool feet
and slenderest knees,   15
could love indeed the maid,
only if she were laid,
white ash amid funereal cypresses.

HELEN. In Greek mythology, Helen, most beautiful of all women, was the daughter of a mortal, Leda, by the god Zeus. Her kidnapping set off the long and devastating Trojan War. While married to Menelaus, king of the Greek city-state of Sparta, Helen was carried off by Paris, prince of Troy. Menelaus and his brother Agammemnon raised an army, besieged Troy for ten years, and eventually recaptured her. One episode of the Trojan War is related in the *Iliad*, Homer's epic poem, composed before 700 B.C.

COMPARE:

"Helen" with "Long-legged Fly" by William Butler Yeats (page 900).

H. D.

Donald Hall (b. 1928)

NAMES OF HORSES   1978

All winter your brute shoulders strained against collars, padding
and steerhide over the ash hames, to haul
sledges of cordwood for drying through spring and summer,
for the Glenwood stove next winter, and for the simmering range.

In April you pulled cartloads of manure to spread on the fields,   5
dark manure of Holsteins, and knobs of your own clustered with oats.
All summer you mowed the grass in meadow and hayfield, the
    mowing machine
clacketing beside you, while the sun walked high in the morning;

and after noon's heat, you pulled a clawed rake through the same
    acres,
gathering stacks, and dragged the wagon from stack to stack,   10
and the built hayrack back, uphill to the chaffy barn,
three loads of hay a day from standing grass in the morning.

Sundays you trotted the two miles to church with the light load
of a leather quartertop buggy, and grazed in the sound of hymns.
Generation on generation, your neck rubbed the windowsill   15
of the stall, smoothing the wood as the sea smooths glass.

When you were old and lame, when your shoulders hurt bending to
    graze,
one October the man, who fed you and kept you, and harnessed you
    every morning,
led you through corn stubble to sandy ground above Eagle Pond,
and dug a hole beside you where you stood shuddering in your skin,   20

and lay the shotgun's muzzle in the boneless hollow behind your ear,
and fired the slug into your brain, and felled you into your grave,
shoveling sand to cover you, setting goldenrod upright above you,
where by next summer a dent in the ground made your monument.

For a hundred and fifty years, in the pasture of dead horses,   25
roots of pine trees pushed through the pale curves of your ribs,
yellow blossoms flourished above you in autumn, and in winter
frost heaved your bones in the ground — old toilers, soil makers:

O Roger, Mackerel, Riley, Ned, Nellie, Chester, Lady Ghost.

COMPARE:

"Names of Horses" with "The Bull Calf" by Irving Layton (page 840).

Thomas Hardy (1840 – 1928)*

THE CONVERGENCE OF THE TWAIN   1912

Lines on the Loss of the "Titanic"

I

    In a solitude of the sea
    Deep from human vanity,
And the Pride of Life that planned her, stilly couches she.

II

    Steel chambers, late the pyres
    Of her salamandrine fires,
Cold currents thrid°, and turn to rhythmic tidal lyres.   5   *thread*

III

        Over the mirrors meant
        To glass the opulent
The sea-worm crawls — grotesque, slimed, dumb, indifferent.

IV

        Jewels in joy designed   10
        To ravish the sensuous mind
Lie lightless, all their sparkles bleared and black and blind.

V

        Dim moon-eyed fishes near
        Gaze at the gilded gear
And query: "What does this vaingloriousness down here?"   15

VI

        Well: while was fashioning
        This creature of cleaving wing,
The Immanent Will that stirs and urges everything

VII

        Prepared a sinister mate
        For her — so gaily great —   20
A Shape of Ice, for the time far and dissociate.

VIII

        And as the smart ship grew
        In stature, grace, and hue,
In shadowy silent distance grew the Iceberg too.

IX

        Alien they seemed to be: 25
        No mortal eye could see
The intimate welding of their later history,

X

        Or sign that they were bent
        By paths coincident
On being anon twin halves of one august event.   30

XI

        Till the Spinner of the Years
        Said "Now!" And each one hears,
And consummation comes, and jars two hemispheres.

THE CONVERGENCE OF THE TWAIN. The luxury liner *Titanic*, supposedly unsinkable, went down in 1912 after striking an iceberg, on its first Atlantic voyage. 5 *salamandrine:* like the salamander, a lizard that supposedly thrives in fires, or like a spirit of the same name that inhabits fire (according to alchemists).

COMPARE:

"The Covergence of the Twain" with "Titanic" by David R. Slavitt (page 875).

Thomas Hardy

Thomas Hardy (1840–1928)*

During Wind and Rain   1917

They sing their dearest songs—
He, she, all of them—yea,
Treble and tenor and bass,
   And one to play;
With the candles mooning each face. . . .   5
   Ah, no; the years O!
How the sick leaves reel down in throngs!

They clear the creeping moss—
Elders and juniors—aye,
Making the pathways neat   10
   And the garden gay;
And they build a shady seat. . . .
   Ah, no; the years, the years;
See, the white storm-birds wing across!

They are blithely breakfasting all—   15
Men and maidens—yea,
Under the summer tree,
   With a glimpse of the bay,
While pet fowl come to the knee. . . .
   Ah, no! the years O!   20
And the rotten rose is ripped from the wall.

They change to a high new house,
He, she, all of them—aye,
Clocks and carpets and chairs
    On the lawn all day,   25
And brightest things that are theirs. . . .
    Ah, no; the years, the years;
Down their carved names the rain-drop plows.

COMPARE:

"During Wind and Rain" with "anyone lived in a pretty how town" by E. E. Cummings
(page 556).

Thomas Hardy (1840 – 1928)*

FOUR SATIRES OF CIRCUMSTANCE   1914

In Church

"And now to God the Father," he ends,
And his voice thrills up to the topmost tiles:
Each listener chokes as he bows and bends,
And emotion pervades the crowded aisles.
Then the preacher glides to the vestry-door,   5
And shuts it, and thinks he is seen no more.

The door swings softly ajar meanwhile,
And a pupil of his in the Bible class,
Who adores him as one without gloss or guile
Sees her idol stand with a satisfied smile   10
And re-enact at the vestry-glass
Each pulpit gesture in deft dumb-show
That had moved the congregation so.

In the Room of the Bride-elect

"Would it had been the man of our wish!"
Sighs her mother. To whom with vehemence she   15
In the wedding-dress — the wife to be —
"Then why were you so mollyish
As not to insist on him for me!"
The mother, amazed: "Why, dearest one,
Because you pleaded for this or none!"   20

"But Father and you should have stood out strong!
Since then, to my cost, I have lived to find
That you were right and that I was wrong;

This man is a dolt to the one declined. . . .
Ah! — here he comes with his button-hole rose.   25
Good God — I must marry him I suppose!"

In the Cemetery

"You see those mothers squabbling there?"
Remarks the man of the cemetery.
"One says in tears, ' 'Tis mine lies here!'
Another, 'Nay, mine, you Pharisee°!'   hypocrite   30
Another, 'How dare you move my flowers
And put your own on this grave of ours!'
But all their children were laid therein
At different times, like sprats in a tin°.   sardines in a can

"And then the main drain had to cross,   35
And we moved the lot some nights ago,
And packed them away in the general foss°   ditch
With hundreds more. But their folks don't know,
And as well cry over a new-laid drain
As anything else, to ease your pain!"   40

In the Nuptial Chamber

"O that mastering tune!" And up in the bed
Like a lace-robed phantom springs the bride;
"And why?" asks the man she had that day wed,
With a start, as the band plays on outside.
"It's the townsfolk's cheery compliment   45
Because of our marriage, my Innocent."

"O but you don't know! 'Tis the passionate air
To which my old Love waltzed with me,
And I swore as we spun that none should share
My home, my kisses, till death, save he!   50
And he dominates me and thrills me through,
And it's he I embrace while embracing you!"

FOUR SATIRES OF CIRCUMSTANCE. The series "Satires of Circumstance" consists of fifteen short
poems; this is a sampling of them.

COMPARE:
"Four Satires of Circumstance" with Thomas Hardy's "The Workbox" (page 526) and "The
Ruined Maid" (page 551).

Robert Hayden (1913–1980)

THOSE WINTER SUNDAYS   1962

Sundays too my father got up early
and put his clothes on in the blueblack cold,
then with cracked hands that ached
from labor in the weekday weather made
banked fires blaze. No one ever thanked him.   5

I'd wake and hear the cold splintering, breaking.
When the rooms were warm, he'd call,
and slowly I would rise and dress,
fearing the chronic angers of that house,

Speaking indifferently to him,   10
who had driven out the cold
and polished my good shoes as well.
What did I know, what did I know
of love's austere and lonely offices?

COMPARE:

"Those Winter Sundays" with "My Father's Martial Art" by Stephen Shu-ning Liu
(page 843) and "Daddy" by Sylvia Plath (page 857).

Seamus Heaney (b. 1939)*

DIGGING   1966

Between my finger and my thumb
The squat pen rests; snug as a gun.

Under my window, a clean rasping sound
When the spade sinks into gravelly ground.
My father, digging. I look down   5

Till his straining rump among the flowerbeds
Bends low, comes up twenty years away
Stooping in rhythm through potato drills
Where he was digging.

The coarse boot nestled on the lug, the shaft   10
Against the inside knee was levered firmly.
He rooted out tall tops, buried the bright edge deep
To scatter new potatoes that we picked
Loving their cool hardness in our hands.

By God, the old man could handle a spade.   15
Just like his old man.

My grandfather cut more turf in a day
Than any other man on Toner's bog.
Once I carried him milk in a bottle
Corked sloppily with paper. He straightened up   20
To drink it, then fell to right away

Nicking and slicing neatly, heaving sods
Over his shoulder, going down and down
For the good turf. Digging.

The cold smell of potato mould, the squelch and slap   25
Of soggy peat, the curt cuts of an edge
Through living roots awaken in my head.
But I've no spade to follow men like them.

Between my finger and my thumb
The squat pen rests.   30
I'll dig with it.

Seamus Heaney (b. 1939)*

MOTHER OF THE GROOM   1972

What she remembers
Is his glistening back
In the bath, his small boots
In the ring of boots at her feet.

Hands in her voided lap,   5
She hears a daughter welcomed.
It's as if he kicked when lifted
And slipped her soapy hold.

Once soap would ease off
The wedding ring   10
That's bedded forever now
In her clapping hand.

Anthony Hecht (b. 1923)

THE VOW   1967

In the third month, a sudden flow of blood.
The mirth of tabrets ceaseth, and the joy
Also of the harp. The frail image of God
Lay spilled and formless. Neither girl nor boy,

But yet blood of my blood, nearly my child. 5
        All that long day
Her pale face turned to the window's mild
        Featureless grey.

And for some nights she whimpered as she dreamed
The dead thing spoke, saying: "Do not recall 10
Pleasure at my conception. I am redeemed
From pain and sorrow. Mourn rather for all
Who breathlessly issue from the bone gates,
        The gates of horn,
For truly it is best of all the fates 15
        Not to be born.

"Mother, a child lay gasping for bare breath
On Christmas Eve when Santa Claus had set
Death in the stocking, and the lights of death
Flamed in the tree. O, if you can, forget 20
You were the child, turn to my father's lips
        Against the time
When his cold hand puts forth its fingertips
        Of jointed lime."

Doctors of Science, what is man that he 25
Should hope to come to a good end? *The best*
Is not to have been born. And could it be
That Jewish diligence and Irish jest
The consent of flesh and a midwinter storm
        Had reconciled, 30
Was yet too bold a mixture to inform
        A simple child?

Even as gold is tried, Gentile and Jew.
If that ghost was a girl's, I swear to it:
Your mother shall be far more blessed than you. 35
And if a boy's, I swear: The flames are lit
That shall refine us; they shall not destroy
        A living hair.
Your younger brothers shall confirm in joy
        This that I swear. 40

THE VOW. 2 *tabrets:* small drums used to accompany traditional Jewish dances. 14 *gates of horn:* According to Homer and Virgil pleasant, lying dreams emerge from the underworld through gates of ivory; ominous, truth-telling dreams, through gates of horn.

George Herbert

George Herbert (1593 – 1633)*

LOVE   1633

Love bade me welcome; yet my soul drew back,
        Guilty of dust and sin.
But quick-eyed Love, observing me grow slack
        From my first entrance in,
Drew nearer to me, sweetly questioning   5
        If I lacked anything.

"A guest," I answered, "worthy to be here";
        Love said, "You shall be he."
"I, the unkind, ungrateful? Ah, my dear,
        I cannot look on Thee."   10
Love took my hand, and smiling did reply,
        "Who made the eyes but I?"

"Truth, Lord, but I have marred them; let my shame
        Go where it doth deserve."
"And know you not," says Love, "who bore the blame?"   15
        "My dear, then I will serve."
"You must sit down," says Love, "and taste My meat."
        So I did sit and eat.

COMPARE

"Love" with "Batter my heart, three-personed God" by John Donne (page 540).

Robert Herrick (1591–1674)*

THE BAD SEASON MAKES THE POET SAD   1648

Dull to myself and almost dead to these
My many fresh and fragrant mistresses,
Lost to all music now, since everything
Puts on the semblance here of sorrowing.
Sick is the land to th' heart, and doth endure   5
More dangerous faintings by her desp'rate cure.
But if that golden age would come again
And Charles here rule, as he before did reign,
If smooth and unperplexed the seasons were
As when the sweet Maria lived here,   10
I should delight to have my curls half drowned
In Tyrian dews, and head with roses crowned,
And once more yet, ere I am laid out dead,
Knock at a star with my exalted head.

THE BAD SEASON MAKES THE POET SAD. 1–2 *these . . . mistresses:* This line may appear to suggest
that Herrick was a Don Juan, but see his brief biography in *Lives of the Poets* (page 914). To what
"mistresses" might he refer? 5 *Sick is the land:* Civil War had erupted in England in 1642. 6 *desp'rate
cure:* Herrick probably means rule by Parliament, which had brought an uneasy peace. In 1645 the
forces of Parliament, led by Oliver Cromwell, had defeated the armies of Charles I, and the king
had fled the country. 10 *Maria:* Henrietta Maria, wife of Charles. 12 *Tyrian dews:* perfumes from
Tyre, in ancient Phoenicia.

Robert Herrick (1591 – 1674)*

TO THE VIRGINS, TO MAKE MUCH OF TIME   1648

Gather ye rose-buds while ye may,
    Old Time is still a-flying;
And this same flower that smiles today,
    Tomorrow will be dying.

The glorious lamp of heaven, the sun,   5
    The higher he's a-getting,
The sooner will his race be run,
    And nearer he's to setting.

That age is best which is the first,
    When youth and blood are warmer;   10
But being spent, the worse, and worst
    Times still succeed the former.

Then be not coy, but use your time,
   And while ye may, go marry;
For having lost but once your prime,   15
   You may for ever tarry.

COMPARE:

"To the Virgins, to Make Much of Time" with "To His Coy Mistress" by Andrew
Marvell (page 846) and "Go, Lovely Rose" by Edmund Waller (page 889).

Garrett Hongo (b. 1951)*

THE CADENCE OF SILK   1988

When I lived in Seattle, I loved watching
the Sonics play basketball; something
about that array of trained and energetic
bodies set in motion to attack a more
sluggish, less physically intelligent opponent   5
appealed to me, taught me about cadence
and play, the offguard breaking free
before the rebound, "releasing," as is said
in the parlance of the game, getting to
the center's downcourt pass and streaking   10
to the basket for a scoopshot layup
off the glass, all in rhythm, all in
perfect declensions of action, smooth
and strenuous as Gorgiasian rhetoric.
I was hooked on the undulant ballet   15
of the pattern offense, on the set play
back-door under the basket, and, at times,
even on the auctioneer's pace and elocution
of the play-by-play man. Now I watch
the Lakers, having returned to Los Angeles   20
some years ago, love them even more than
the Seattle team, long since broken up and aging.
The Lakers are incomparable, numerous
options for any situation, their players
the league's quickest, most intelligent,   25
and, it is my opinion, frankly, the most *cool.*

Few bruisers, they are sleek as arctic seals,
especially the small forward
as he dodges through the key, away from
the ball, rubbing off his man on the screen,   30
setting for his shot. Then, slick as spit,
comes the ball from the point guard,
and my man goes up, cradling the ball
in his right hand like a waiter balancing
a tray piled with champagne in stemmed glasses,   35
cocking his arm and bringing the ball
back behind his ear, pumping, letting fly then
as he jumps, popcorn-like, in the corner,
while the ball, launched, slung dextrously
with a slight backspin, slashes through   40
the basket's silk net with a small,
sonorous splash of completion.

THE CADENCE OF SILK. 14 *Gorgiasian rhetoric:* art of persuasive speaking as practiced by Gorgias (485?–380? B.C.), Greek Sophist philosopher, who argued that nothing exists.

COMPARE:

"The Cadence of Silk" with "Ex-Basketball Player" by John Updike (page 888).

Garrett Hongo

Garrett Hongo (b. 1951)*

THE HONGO STORE
29 MILES VOLCANO
HILO, HAWAII   1982

From a photograph

My parents felt those rumblings
Coming deep from the earth's belly,
Thudding like the bell of the Buddhist Church.
Tremors in the ground swayed the bathinette
Where I lay squalling in soapy water.   5

My mother carried me around the house,
Back through the orchids, ferns, and plumeria
Of that greenhouse world behind the store,
And jumped between gas pumps into the car.

My father gave it the gun   10
And said, "Be quiet," as he searched
The frequencies, flipping for the right station
(The radio squealing more loudly than I could cry).

And then even the echoes stopped —
The only sound the Edsel's grinding   15
And the bark and crackle of radio news
Saying stay home or go to church.

"Dees time she no blow!"
My father said, driving back
Over the red ash covering the road.   20
"I worried she went go for broke already!"

So in this print the size of a matchbook,
The dark skinny man, shirtless and grinning,
A toothpick in the corner of his smile,
Lifts a naked baby above his head —   25
Behind him the plate glass of the store only
    cracked.

Gerard Manley Hopkins

Gerard Manley Hopkins (1844 – 1889)*

SPRING AND FALL (1880)

To a Young Child

Márgarét, are you grieving
Over Goldengrove unleaving°?   shedding its leaves
Leáves, like the things of man, you
With your fresh thoughts care for, can you?
Ah! ás the heart grows older   5
It will come to such sights colder
By and by, nor spare a sigh
Though worlds of wanwood leafmeal lie;
And yet you will weep and know why.
Now no matter, child, the name: 10
Sórrow's springs áre the same.
Nor mouth had, no nor mind, expressed
What heart heard of, ghost° guessed: spirit
It is the blight man was born for,
It is Margaret you mourn for.   15

COMPARE:

"Spring and Fall" with "Margaret Are You Drug" by George Starbuck (page 739).

THOU ART INDEED JUST, LORD, IF I CONTEND   (1889)

Justus quidem tu es, Domine, si disputem tecum: verumtamen justa
    loquar ad te: Quare via impiorum prosperatur? &c.

Thou art indeed just, Lord, if I contend
With thee; but, sir, so what I plead is just.
Why do sinners' ways prosper? and why must
Disappointment all I endeavor end?
Wert thou my enemy, O thou my friend,   5
How wouldst thou worse, I wonder than thou dost
Defeat, thwart me? Oh, the sots and thralls of lust
Do in spare hours more thrive than I that spend,

Sir, life upon thy cause. See, banks and brakes°   *ferny marshes*
Now, leavèd how thick! lacèd they are again   10
With fretty chervil°, look, and fresh wind shakes   *wild herb*

Them; birds build — but not I build; no, but strain,
Time's eunuch, and not breed one work that wakes.
Mine, O thou lord of life, send my roots rain.

THOU ART INDEED JUST, LORD, IF I CONTEND. In the first two sentences of this poem, Hopkins
translates the Latin quotation from the Vulgate Bible (Jeremiah 12:1).

COMPARE:

"Thou art indeed just, Lord . . ." with "When I consider how my light is spent" by John
Milton (page 850).

THE WINDHOVER   (1877)

To Christ Our Lord

I caught this morning morning's minion, king-
    dom of daylight's dauphin, dapple-dawn-drawn Falcon, in his riding
    Of the rolling level underneath him steady air, and striding
High there, how he rung upon the rein of a wimpling wing
In his ecstasy! then off, off forth on swing,   5

As a skate's heel sweeps smooth on a bow-bend: the hurl and
   gliding
Rebuffed the big wind. My heart in hiding
Stirred for a bird, — the achieve of, the mastery of the thing!

Brute beauty and valor and act, oh, air, pride, plume, here
   Buckle! AND the fire that breaks from thee then, a billion   10
Times told lovelier, more dangerous, O my chevalier!

   No wonder of it: shéer plód makes plow down sillion°   *furrow*
Shine, and blue-bleak embers, ah my dear,
   Fall, gall themselves, and gash gold-vermilion.

THE WINDHOVER. A windhover is a kestrel, or small falcon, so called because it can hover upon
the wind. 4 *rung . . . wing:* A horse is "rung upon the rein" when its trainer holds the end of a
long rein and has the horse circle him. The possible meanings of *wimpling* include (1) curving; (2)
pleated, arranged in many little folds one on top of another; (3) rippling or undulating like the
surface of a flowing stream.

A. E. Housman (1859 – 1936)*

LOVELIEST OF TREES, THE CHERRY NOW   1896

Loveliest of trees, the cherry now
Is hung with bloom along the bough,
And stands about the woodland ride°   *path*
Wearing white for Eastertide.

Now, of my threescore years and ten,   5
Twenty will not come again,
And take from seventy springs a score,
It only leaves me fifty more.

And since to look at things in bloom
Fifty springs are little room,
About the woodlands I will go   10
To see the cherry hung with snow.

COMPARE:

"Loveliest of trees, the cherry now" with "To the Virgins, to Make Much of Time" by
Robert Herrick (page 825) and "Spring and Fall" by Gerard Manley Hopkins (page 829).

A. E. Housman

A. E. Housman (1859 – 1936)*

To an Athlete Dying Young   1896

The time you won your town the race
We chaired you through the market-place;
Man and boy stood cheering by,
And home we brought you shoulder-high.

Today, the road all runners come,   5
Shoulder-high we bring you home,
And set you at your threshold down,
Townsman of a stiller town.

Smart lad, to slip betimes away
From fields where glory does not stay,   10
And early though the laurel grows
It withers quicker than the rose.

Eyes the shady night has shut
Cannot see the record cut,
And silence sounds no worse than cheers   15
After earth has stopped the ears.

Now you will not swell the rout
Of lads that wore their honors out,
Runners whom renown outran
And the name died before the man.   20

So set, before its echoes fade,
The fleet foot on the sill of shade,
And hold to the low lintel up
The still-defended challenge-cup.

And round that early-laureled head
Will flock to gaze the strengthless dead,
And find unwithered on its curls
The garland briefer than a girl's.

COMPARE:

"To an Athlete Dying Young" with "Ex-Basketball Player" by John Updike (page 888).

Langston Hughes (1902 – 1967)*

DREAM DEFERRED   1951

What happens to a dream deferred?

    Does it dry up
    like a raisin in the sun?
    Or fester like a sore —
    And then run?   5
    Does it stink like rotten meat?
    Or crust and sugar over —
    like a syrupy sweet?

    Maybe it just sags
    like a heavy load.   10

    Or does it explode?

COMPARE:

"Dream Deferred" with Langston Hughes's "Dream Boogie" (page 658) and "Ballad of Birmingham" by Dudley Randall (page 615).

Langston Hughes

Langston Hughes (1902–1967)*

ISLAND   1959

Wave of sorrow,
Do not drown me now:

I see the island
Still ahead somehow.

I see the island   5
And its sands are fair:

Wave of sorrow,
Take me there.

COMPARE:

"Island" with "The Lake Isle of Innisfree" by William Butler Yeats (page 499).

Randall Jarrell (1914 – 1965)

THE DEATH OF THE BALL TURRET GUNNER   1945

From my mother's sleep I fell into the State
And I hunched in its belly till my wet fur froze.
Six miles from earth, loosed from its dream of life,
I woke to black flak and the nightmare fighters.
When I died they washed me out of the turret with a hose.

Randall Jarrell

THE DEATH OF THE BALL TURRET GUNNER. Jarrell has written: "A ball turret was a plexiglass sphere set into the belly of a B-17 or B-24, and inhabited by two .50 caliber machine-guns and one man, a short small man. When this gunner tracked with his machine-guns a fighter attacking his bomber from below, he revolved with the turret; hunched in his little sphere, he looked like the fetus in the womb. The fighters which attacked him were armed with cannon firing explosive shells. The hose was a steam hose."

COMPARE:

"The Death of the Ball Turret Gunner" with "Dulce et Decorum Est" by Wilfred Owen (page 834) and "The Insert" by R. L. Barth (page 785).

Robinson Jeffers (1887–1962)

TO THE STONE-CUTTERS   1925

Stone-cutters fighting time with marble, you foredefeated
Challengers of oblivion
Eat cynical earnings, knowing rock splits, records fall down,
The square-limbed Roman letters
Scale in the thaws, wear in the rain. The poet as well   5
Builds his monument mockingly;
For man will be blotted out, the blithe earth die, the brave
   sun
Die blind, his heart blackening:
Yet stones have stood for a thousand years, and pained
   thoughts found
The honey peace in old poems.   10

COMPARE:

"To the Stone-cutters" with "Not marble nor the gilded monuments" by William Shakespeare (page 870).

Elizabeth Jennings (b. 1926)

DELAY   1953

The radiance of that star that leans on me
Was shining years ago. The light that now
Glitters up there my eye may never see,
And so the time lag teases me with how

Love that loves now may not reach me until   5
Its first desire is spent. The star's impulse
Must wait for eyes to claim it beautiful
And love arrived may find us somewhere else.

COMPARE:

"Delay" with "Bright star! would I were steadfast as thou art" by John Keats (page 579).

Ben Jonson (1573? – 1637)*

ON MY FIRST SON   (1603)

Farewell, thou child of my right hand, and joy.
My sin was too much hope of thee, loved boy;
Seven years thou wert lent to me, and I thee pay,
Exacted by thy fate, on the just day.
Oh, could I lose all father° now. For why   fatherhood   5
Will man lament the state he should envy? —
To have so soon 'scaped world's and flesh's rage,
And, if no other misery, yet age.
Rest in soft peace, and asked, say, "Here doth lie
Ben Jonson his best piece of poetry,"   10
For whose sake henceforth all his vows be such
As what he loves may never like° too much.   thrive

ON MY FIRST SON. 1 *child of my right hand:* Jonson's son was named Benjamin; this phrase translates
the Hebrew name. 4 *the just day:* the very day. The boy had died on his seventh birthday.

COMPARE:

"On My First Son" with "To Her Son, H. P." by Katherine Philips (page 856).

Donald Justice (b. 1925)

ON THE DEATH OF FRIENDS IN CHILDHOOD   1960

We shall not ever meet them bearded in heaven,
Nor sunning themselves among the bald of hell;
If anywhere, in the deserted schoolyard at twilight,
Forming a ring, perhaps, or joining hands
In games whose very names we have forgotten.   5
Come, memory, let us seek them there in the shadows.

COMPARE:

"On the Death of Friends in Childhood" and "With rue my heart is laden" by A. E. Housman (page 639).

John Keats (1795 – 1821)*

ON FIRST LOOKING INTO CHAPMAN'S HOMER   1816

Much have I traveled in the realms of gold,
   And many goodly states and kingdoms seen;
   Round many western islands have I been
Which bards in fealty to Apollo hold.
Oft of one wide expanse had I been told   5
   That deep-browed Homer ruled as his demesne°,   *domain*
   Yet did I never breathe its pure serene
Till I heard Chapman speak out loud and bold.
Then felt I like some watcher of the skies
   When a new planet swims into his ken;   10
Or like stout Cortez when with eagle eyes
   He stared at the Pacific — and all his men
Looked at each other with a wild surmise —
   Silent, upon a peak in Darien.

ON FIRST LOOKING INTO CHAPMAN'S HOMER. When one evening in October 1816 Keats's friend and former teacher Cowden Clarke introduced the young poet to George Chapman's vigorous Elizabethan translations of the *Iliad* and the *Odyssey*, Keats stayed up all night reading and discussing them in high excitement; then went home at dawn to compose this sonnet, which Clarke received at his breakfast table. 4 *fealty*: in feudalism, the loyalty of a vassal to his lord; *Apollo*: classical god of poetic inspiration. 11 *stout Cortez*: the best-known boner in English poetry. (What Spanish explorer *was* the first European to view the Pacific?) 14 *Darien*: old name for the Isthmus of Panama.

John Keats

John Keats (1795–1821)*

WHEN I HAVE FEARS THAT I MAY CEASE TO BE   (1818)

When I have fears that I may cease to be
  Before my pen has gleaned my teeming brain,
Before high-pilèd books, in charact'ry°,   *written language*
  Hold like rich garners° the full-ripened grain;   *storehouses*
When I behold, upon the night's starred face,   5
  Huge cloudy symbols of a high romance,
And think that I may never live to trace
  Their shadows with the magic hand of chance;
And when I feel, fair creature of an hour,
  That I shall never look upon thee more,   10
Never have relish in the fairy° power   *supernatural*
  Of unreflecting love—then on the shore
Of the wide world I stand alone, and think
  Till love and fame to nothingness do sink.

WHEN I HAVE FEARS THAT I MAY CEASE TO BE. 12 *unreflecting:* thoughtless and spontaneous, rather than deliberate.

John Keats (1795 – 1821)*

TO AUTUMN   1820

I

Season of mists and mellow fruitfulness,
  Close bosom-friend of the maturing sun;
Conspiring with him how to load and bless
  With fruit the vines that round the thatch-eaves run;
To bend with apples the mossed cottage-trees,   5
  And fill all fruit with ripeness to the core;
    To swell the gourd, and plump the hazel shells
With a sweet kernel; to set budding more,
And still more, later flowers for the bees,
Until they think warm days will never cease,   10
    For Summer has o'er-brimmed their clammy cells.

II

Who hath not seen thee oft amid thy store?
  Sometimes whoever seeks abroad may find
Thee sitting careless on a granary floor,
  Thy hair soft-lifted by the winnowing wind;   15

Or on a half-reaped furrow sound asleep,
   Drowsed with the fume of poppies, while thy hook°   *sickle*
      Spares the next swath and all its twinèd flowers:
And sometimes like a gleaner thou dost keep
   Steady thy laden head across a brook;   20
   Or by a cider-press, with patient look,
      Thou watchest the last oozings hours by hours.

III

Where are the songs of Spring? Ay, where are they?
   Think not of them, thou hast thy music too, —
While barrèd clouds bloom the soft-dying day,   25
   And touch the stubble-plains with rosy hue;
Then in a wailful choir the small gnats mourn
   Among the river sallows°, borne aloft   *willows*
      Or sinking as the light wind lives or dies;
And full-grown lambs loud bleat from hilly bourn;   30
   Hedge-crickets sing; and now with treble soft
   The red-breast whistles from a garden-croft°   *garden plot*
      And gathering swallows twitter in the skies.

ODE TO AUTUMN. 12 *thee:* Autumn personified. 14 *Thy hair . . . winnowing wind:* Autumn's hair is a billowing cloud of straw. In winnowing, whole blades of grain were laid on a granary floor and beaten with wooden flails, then the beaten mass was tossed in a blanket until the yellow straw (or *chaff*) drifted away on the air, leaving kernels of grain. 30 *bourn:* perhaps meaning a brook. In current English, the word is a cousin of *burn,* as in the first line of Gerard Manley Hopkins's "Inversnaid"; but in archaic English, which Keats sometimes liked, a *bourn* can also be a boundary, or a destination. What possible meaning makes most sense to you?

COMPARE:

"To Autumn" with "In the Elegy Season" by Richard Wilbur (page 542).

Philip Larkin (1922 – 1985)*

HOME IS SO SAD   1964

Home is so sad. It stays as it was left,
Shaped to the comfort of the last to go
As if to win them back. Instead, bereft
Of anyone to please, it withers so,
Having no heart to put aside the theft   5

And turn again to what it started as,
A joyous shot at how things ought to be,
Long fallen wide. You can see how it was:
Look at the pictures and the cutlery.
The music in the piano stool. That vase.   10

Philip Larkin (1922–1985)*

POETRY OF DEPARTURES   1955

Sometimes you hear, fifth-hand,
As epitaph:
He chucked up everything
And just cleared off,
And always the voice will sound   5
Certain you approve
This audacious, purifying,
Elemental move.

And they are right, I think.
We all hate home   10
And having to be there:
I detest my room,
Its specially-chosen junk,
The good books, the good bed,
And my life, in perfect order: 15
So to hear it said

He walked out on the whole crowd
Leaves me flushed and stirred,
Like *Then she undid her dress*
Or *Take that you bastard;*   20
Surely I can, if he did?
And that helps me stay
Sober and industrious.
But I'd go today,

Yes, swagger the nut-strewn roads,   25
Crouch in the fo'c'sle
Stubbly with goodness, if
It weren't so artificial,
Such a deliberate step backwards
To create an object: 30
Books; china; a life
Reprehensibly perfect.

Irving Layton (b. 1912)

THE BULL CALF   1959

The thing could barely stand. Yet taken
from his mother and the barn smells
he still impressed with his pride,

with the promise of sovereignty in the way
his head moved to take us in.   5
The fierce sunlight tugging the maize from the ground
licked at his shapely flanks.
He was too young for all that pride.
I thought of the deposed Richard II.

"No money in bull calves," Freeman had said.   10
The visiting clergyman rubbed the nostrils
now snuffing pathetically at the windless day.
"A pity," he sighed.
My gaze slipped off his hat toward the empty sky
that circled over the black knot of men,   15
over us and the calf waiting for the first blow.

Struck,
the bull calf drew in his thin forelegs
as if gathering strength for a mad rush . . .
tottered . . . raised his darkening eyes to us,   20
and I saw we were at the far end
of his frightened look, growing smaller and smaller
till we were only the ponderous mallet
that flicked his bleeding ear
and pushed him over on his side, stiffly,   25
like a block of wood.

Below the hill's crest
the river snuffled on the improvised beach.
We dug a deep pit and threw the dead calf into it.
It made a wet sound, a sepulchral gurgle,   30
as the warm sides bulged and flattened.
Settled, the bull calf lay as if asleep,
one foreleg over the other,
bereft of pride and so beautiful now,
without movement, perfectly still in the cool pit,   35
I turned away and wept.

COMPARE:

"The Bull Calf" with "Names of Horses" by Donald Hall (page 815).

Denise Levertov

Denise Levertov (b. 1923)*

DIVORCING   1975

> One garland
> of flowers, leaves, thorns
> was twined round our two necks.
> Drawn tight, it could choke us,
> yet we loved its scratchy grace,   5
> our fragrant yoke.
>
> We were Siamese twins.
> Our blood's not sure
> if it can circulate,
> now we are cut apart.   10
> Something in each of us is waiting
> to see if we can survive,
> severed.

COMPARE:

"Divorcing" with "You fit into me" by Margaret Atwood and "Hemispheres" by Grace
Schulman (both on page 601).

Philip Levine (b. 1928)

ANIMALS ARE PASSING FROM OUR LIVES   1968

It's wonderful how I jog
on four honed-down ivory toes
my massive buttocks slipping
like oiled parts with each light step.

I'm to market. I can smell   5
the sour, grooved block, I can smell
the blade that opens the hole
and the pudgy white fingers

that shake out the intestines
like a hankie. In my dreams   10
the snouts drool on the marble,
suffering children, suffering flies,

suffering the consumers
who won't meet their steady eyes
for fear they could see. The boy   15
who drives me along believes

that any moment I'll fall
on my side and drum my toes
like a typewriter or squeal
and shit like a new housewife   20

discovering television,
or that I'll turn like a beast
cleverly to hook his teeth
with my teeth. No. Not this pig.

COMPARE:

"Animals Are Passing from Our Lives" with "Butcher Shop" by Charles Simic (page
875).

Stephen Shu-ning Liu (b. 1930)

MY FATHER'S MARTIAL ART   1982

When he came home Mother said he looked
like a monk and stank of green fungus.
At the fireside he told us about life
at the monastery: his rock pillow,
his cold bath, his steel-bar lifting   5
and his wood-chopping. He didn't see
a woman for three winters, on Mountain O Mei.

"My Master was both light and heavy.
He skipped over treetops like a squirrel.
Once he stood on a chair, one foot tied   10
to a rope. We four pulled; we couldn't
move him a bit. His kicks could split
a cedar's trunk."

I saw Father break into a pumpkin
with his fingers. I saw him drop a hawk   15
with bamboo arrows. He rose before dawn, filled
our backyard with a harsh sound *hah, hah, hah:*
there was his Black Dragon Sweep, his Crane Stand,
his Mantis Walk, his Tiger Leap, his Cobra Coil . . .
Infrequently he taught me tricks and made me   20
fight the best of all the village boys.

From a busy street I brood over high cliffs
on O Mei, where my father and his Master sit:
shadows spread across their faces as the smog
between us deepens into a funeral pyre.   25

But don't retreat into night, my father.
Come down from the cliffs. Come
with a single Black Dragon Sweep and hush
this oncoming traffic with your *hah, hah, hah.*

Robert Lowell (1917 – 1977)*

SKUNK HOUR   1959

For Elizabeth Bishop

Nautilus Island's hermit
heiress still lives through winters in her Spartan cottage;
her sheep still graze above the sea.
Her son's a bishop. Her farmer
is first selectman in our village;   5
she's in her dotage.

Thirsting for
the hierarchic privacy
of Queen Victoria's century,
she buys up all   10
the eyesores facing her shore,
and lets them fall.

The season's ill —
we've lost our summer millionaire,
who seemed to leap from an L. L. Bean   15
catalogue. His nine-knot yawl
was auctioned off to lobstermen.
A red fox stain covers Blue Hill.

And now our fairy
decorator brightens his shop for fall;   20
his fishnet's filled with orange cork,

orange, his cobbler's bench and awl;
there is no money in his work,
he'd rather marry.

One dark night,   25
my Tudor Ford climbed the hill's skull;
I watched for love-cars. Lights turned down,
they lay together, hull to hull,
where the graveyard shelves on the town. . . .
My mind's not right.   30

A car radio bleats,
"Love, O careless Love. . . ." I hear
my ill-spirit sob in each blood cell,
as if my hand were at its throat. . . .
I myself am hell;   35
nobody's here —

only skunks, that search
in the moonlight for a bite to eat.
They march on their soles up Main Street:
white stripes, moonstruck eyes' red fire   40
under the chalk-dry and spar spire
of the Trinitarian Church.

I stand on top
of our back steps and breathe the rich air —
a mother skunk with her column of kittens swills the garbage pail.   45
She jabs her wedge-head in a cup
of sour cream, drops her ostrich tail,
and will not scare.

COMPARE:
"Skunk Hour" with "The Wood-Weasel" by Marianne Moore (page 503).

Archibald MacLeish (1892 – 1982)

THE END OF THE WORLD   1926

Quite unexpectedly as Vasserot
The armless ambidextrian was lighting
A match between his great and second toe,
And Ralph the lion was engaged in biting
The neck of Madame Sossman while the drum   5
Pointed, and Teeny was about to cough
In waltz-time swinging Jocko by the thumb —
Quite unexpectedly the top blew off:

And there, there overhead, there, there hung over
Those thousands of white faces, those dazed eyes,   10
There in the starless dark the poise, the hover,
There with vast wings across the canceled skies,
There in the sudden blackness the black pall
Of nothing, nothing, nothing — nothing at all.

Charles Martin (b. 1942)

ROUGH DRAFT   1987

Popping gum, cracking wise,
   At poolside she defies
Gravity: lifted in her not quite skin-
   tight pink maillol, she shrieks uproar-
iously as the boyfriend starts to spin   5
   Her across one brawny shoulder:

No Rogers, no Astaire:
   Her legs scissor the air
With an unglamorously panicked glee,
   And he's too stocky and too short   10
For idoldom: set down, she lurches free:
   Her taunting cry, his low retort:

Ignoring the cold print
   Forbidding it, they sprint
Outrageously around the pool: arrive   15
   In a final burst of laughter
At the deep end: turn without pause and dive
   Into enveloping water:

Explode at the other
   End, breathless, together.   20
Dripping, subdued, they recompose themselves
   And then go walking off. Traces
Of a distant light lie broken on the waves
   Their passage scribbles and erases.

Andrew Marvell (1621 – 1678)

TO HIS COY MISTRESS   1681

Had we but world enough and time,
This coyness°, lady, were no crime.   *modesty, reluctance*
We would sit down and think which way
To walk, and pass our long love's day.
Thou by the Indian Ganges' side   5
Should'st rubies find; I by the tide
Of Humber would complain°. I would   *sing sad songs*

Love you ten years before the Flood,
And you should, if you please, refuse
Till the conversion of the Jews.   10
My vegetable° love should grow   *vegetative, flourishing*
Vaster than empires, and more slow.
An hundred years should go to praise
Thine eyes, and on thy forehead gaze,
Two hundred to adore each breast,   15
But thirty thousand to the rest.
An age at least to every part,
And the last age should show your heart.
For, lady, you deserve this state°,   *pomp, ceremony*
Nor would I love at lower rate.   20
    But at my back I always hear
Time's wingèd chariot hurrying near,
And yonder all before us lie
Deserts of vast eternity.
Thy beauty shall no more be found,   25
Nor in thy marble vault shall sound
My echoing song; then worms shall try
That long preserved virginity,
And your quaint honor turn to dust,
And into ashes all my lust.   30
The grave's a fine and private place,
But none, I think, do there embrace.
    Now therefore, while the youthful hue
Sits on thy skin like morning glew°   *glow*
And while thy willing soul transpires   35
At every pore with instant° fires,   *eager*
Now let us sport us while we may;
And now, like amorous birds of prey,
Rather at once our time devour
Than languish in his slow-chapped° power.   *slow-jawed* 40
Let us roll all our strength and all
Our sweetness up into one ball
And tear our pleasures with rough strife
Thorough° the iron gates of life.   *through*
Thus, though we cannot make our sun   45
Stand still, yet we will make him run.

To His Coy Mistress. 7 *Humber:* a river that flows by Marvell's town of Hull (on the side of the world opposite from the Ganges). 10 *conversion of the Jews:* an event that, according to St. John the Divine, is to take place just before the end of the world. 35 *transpires:* exudes, as a membrane lets fluid or vapor pass through it.

Compare:

"To His Coy Mistress" with "To the Virgins, to Make Much of Time" by Robert Herrick (page 825).

George Meredith (1828 – 1909)

LUCIFER IN STARLIGHT   1883

On a starred night Prince Lucifer uprose,
   Tired of his dark dominion, swung the fiend
   Above the rolling ball in cloud part screened,
Where sinners hugged their specter of repose.
Poor prey to his hot fit of pride were those.   5
   And now upon his western wing he leaned,
   Now his huge bulk o'er Afric's sands careened,
Now the black planet shadowed Arctic snows.
Soaring through wider zones that pricked his scars
   With memory of the old revolt from Awe,   10
He reached a middle height, and at the stars,
Which are the brain of heaven, he looked, and sank.
Around the ancient track marched, rank on rank,
   The army of unalterable law.

James Merrill (b. 1926)

LABORATORY POEM   1958

Charles used to watch Naomi, taking heart
And a steel saw, open up turtles, live.
While she swore they felt nothing, he would gag
At blood, at the blind twitching, even after
The murky dawn of entrails cleared, revealing   5
Contours he knew, egg-yellows like lamps paling.

Well then. She carried off the beating heart
To the kymograph and rigged it there, a rag
In fitful wind, now made to strain, now stopped
By her solutions tonic or malign   10
Alternately in which it would be steeped.
What the heart bore, she noted on a chart,

For work did not stop only with the heart.
He thought of certain human hearts, their climb
Through violence into exquisite disciplines   15
Of which, as it now appeared, they all expired.
Soon she would fetch another and start over,
Easy in the presence of her lover.

LABORATORY POEM. 8 *kymograph:* device to record wavelike motions or pulsations on a piece of
paper fastened to a revolving drum.

Charlotte Mew (1869–1928)

The Farmer's Bride   1916

Three Summers since I chose a maid,
Too young maybe—but more's to do
At harvest-time than bide and woo.
    When us was wed she turned afraid
Of love and me and all things human;   5
Like the shut of a winter's day.
Her smile went out, and 'twasn't a woman—
    More like a little frightened fay.°   *elf*
        One night, in the Fall, she runned away.

"Out 'mong the sheep, her be," they said,   10
'Should properly have been abed;
But sure enough she wasn't there
Lying awake with her wide brown stare.
So over seven-acre field and up-along across the down
We chased her, flying like a hare   15
Before our lanterns. To Church-Town
    All in a shiver and a scare
We caught her, fetched her home at last
    And turned the key upon her, fast.

She does the work about the house   20
As well as most, but like a mouse:
    Happy enough to chat and play
    With birds and rabbits and such as they,
    So long as men-folk keep away.
"Not near, not near!" her eyes beseech   25
When one of us comes within reach.
    The women say that beasts in stall
    Look round like children at her call.
    I've hardly heard her speak at all.
Shy as a leveret, swift as he,   30
Straight and slight as a young larch tree,
Sweet as the first wild violets, she,
To her wild self. But what to me?

The short days shorten and the oaks are brown,
    The blue smoke rises to the low gray sky,   35
One leaf in the still air falls slowly down,
    A magpie's spotted feathers lie
On the black earth spread white with rime,°   *frost*
The berries redden up to Christmas-time.

What's Christmas-time without there be   40
Some other in the house than we!

She sleeps up in the attic there
Alone, poor maid. 'Tis but a stair
Betwixt us. Oh! my God! the down,
The soft young down of her, the brown,   45
The brown of her—her eyes, her hair, her hair!

Edna St. Vincent Millay (1892–1950)*

RECUERDO   1920

We were very tired, we were very merry—
We had gone back and forth all night on the ferry.
It was bare and bright, and smelled like a stable—
But we looked into a fire, we leaned across a table,
We lay on a hill-top underneath the moon;   5
And the whistles kept blowing, and the dawn came soon.

We were very tired, we were very merry—
We had gone back and forth all night on the ferry;
And you ate an apple, and I ate a pear,
From a dozen of each we had bought somewhere;   10
And the sky went wan, and the wind came cold,
And the sun rose dripping, a bucketful of gold.

We were very tired, we were very merry,
We had gone back and forth all night on the ferry.
We hailed, "Good morrow, mother!" to a shawl-covered head,   15
And bought a morning paper, which neither of us read;
And she wept, "God bless you!" for the apples and pears,
And we gave her all our money but our subway fares.

RECUERDO. The Spanish title means "a recollection" or "a memory."

John Milton (1608 – 1674)*

WHEN I CONSIDER HOW MY LIGHT IS SPENT   (1655?)

When I consider how my light is spent,
   Ere half my days in this dark world and wide,
   And that one talent which is death to hide
Lodged with me useless, though my soul more bent
To serve therewith my Maker, and present   5
   My true account, lest He returning chide;
   "Doth God exact day-labor, light denied?"

I fondly° ask. But Patience, to prevent   *foolishly*
That murmur, soon replies, "God doth not need
     Either man's work or His own gifts. Who best   10
     Bear His mild yoke, they serve Him best. His state
Is kingly: thousands at His bidding speed,
     And post o'er land and ocean without rest;
     They also serve who only stand and wait."

WHEN I CONSIDER HOW MY LIGHT IS SPENT. 1 *my light is spent:* Milton had become blind. 3 *that one talent:* For Jesus's parable of the talents (measures of money), see Matthew 25:14 – 30.

COMPARE:

"When I consider how my light is spent" with "Thou art indeed just, Lord, if I contend" by Gerard Manley Hopkins (page 830).

Marianne Moore

Marianne Moore (1887 – 1972)*

THE MIND IS AN ENCHANTING THING   1944

is an enchanted thing
     like the glaze on a
katydid-wing
          subdivided by sun
          till the nettings are legion.   5
Like Gieseking playing Scarlatti;

like the apteryx-awl
     as a beak, or the
kiwi's rain-shawl
          of haired feathers, the mind   10
          feeling its way as though blind,
walks along with its eyes on the ground.

It has memory's ear
       that can hear without
having to hear.   15
              Like the gyroscope's fall,
              truly unequivocal
because trued by regnant certainty,

it is a power of
       strong enchantment. It   20
is like the dove-
              neck animated by
              sun; it is memory's eye;
it's conscientious inconsistency.

It tears off the veil; tears   25
       the temptation, the
mist the heart wears,
              from its eyes, — if the heart
              has a face; it takes apart
dejection. It's fire in the dove-neck's   30

iridescence; in the
       inconsistencies
of Scarlatti.
              Unconfusion submits
              its confusion to proof; it's   35
not a Herod's oath that cannot change.

THE MIND IS AN ENCHANTING THING. 6 *Gieseking . . . Scarlatti:* Walter Gieseking (1895 – 1956),
German pianist, was a celebrated performer of the difficult sonatas of Italian composer Domenico
Scarlatti (1685 – 1757). 7 *apteryx-awl:* awl-shaped beak of the apteryx, one of the kiwi family. (An
awl is a pointed tool for piercing wood or leather.) 36 *Herod's oath:* King Herod's order condemning
to death all infants in Bethlehem (Matthew 2:1 – 16). In one medieval English version of the Herod
story, a pageant play, the king causes the death of his own child by refusing to withdraw his
command.

Howard Nemerov (b. 1920)

THE SNOW GLOBE   1955

A long time ago, when I was a child,
They left my light on while I went to sleep,
As though they would have wanted me beguiled
By brightness if at all; dark was too deep.

And they left me one toy, a village white   5
With the fresh snow and silently in glass
Frozen forever. But if you shook it,
The snow would rise up in the rounded space

And from the limits of the universe
Snow itself down again. O world of white,   10
First home of dreams! Now that I have my dead,
I want so cold an emblem to rehearse
How many of them have gone from the world's light,
As I have gone, too, from my snowy bed.

John Frederick Nims (b. 1914)*

LOVE POEM   1947

My clumsiest dear, whose hands shipwreck vases,
At whose quick touch all glasses chip and ring,
Whose palms are bulls in china, burs in linen,
And have no cunning with any soft thing

Except all ill-at-ease fidgeting people: 5
The refugee uncertain at the door
You make at home; deftly you steady
The drunk clambering on his undulant floor.

Unpredictable dear, the taxi drivers' terror,
Shrinking from far headlights pale as a dime   10
Yet leaping before red apoplectic streetcars —
Misfit in any space. And never on time.

A wrench in clocks and the solar system. Only
With words and people and love you move at ease.
In traffic of wit expertly manoeuvre   15
And keep us, all devotion, at your knees.

Forgetting your coffee spreading on our flannel,
Your lipstick grinning on our coat,
So gayly in love's unbreakable heaven
Our souls on glory of spilt bourbon float.   20

Be with me, darling, early and late. Smash glasses —
I will study wry music for your sake.
For should your hands drop white and empty
All the toys of the world would break.

Sharon Olds (b. 1942)

THE ONE GIRL AT THE BOYS PARTY   1983

When I take my girl to the swimming party
I set her down among the boys. They tower and
bristle, she stands there smooth and sleek,
her math scores unfolding in the air around her.
They will strip to their suits, her body hard and   5
indivisible as a prime number,
they'll plunge in the deep end, she'll subtract
her height from ten feet, divide it into
hundreds of gallons of water, the numbers
bouncing in her mind like molecules of chlorine   10
in the bright blue pool. When they climb out,
her ponytail will hang its pencil lead
down her back, her narrow silk suit
with hamburgers and french fries printed on it
will glisten in the brilliant air, and they will   15
see her sweet face, solemn and
sealed, a factor of one, and she will
see their eyes, two each,
their legs, two each, and the curves of their sexes,
one each, and in her head she'll be doing her   20
wild multiplying, as the drops
sparkle and fall to the power of a thousand from her body.

Wilfred Owen (1893 – 1918)*

ANTHEM FOR DOOMED YOUTH   (1917?)

What passing-bells for these who die as cattle?
        Only the monstrous anger of the guns.
Only the stuttering rifles' rapid rattle
Can patter out their hasty orisons.
No mockeries now for them; no prayers nor bells,   5
        Nor any voice of mourning save the choirs, —
The shrill, demented choirs of wailing shells;
        And bugles calling for them from sad shires°.   *counties*

What candles may be held to speed them all?
        Not in the hands of boys, but in their eyes   10
        Shall shine the holy glimmers of good-byes.
The pallor of girls' brows shall be their pall;
Their flowers the tenderness of patient minds,
And each slow dusk a drawing-down of blinds.

Linda Pastan

Linda Pastan (b. 1932)*

ETHICS   1980

In ethics class so many years ago
our teacher asked this question every fall:
if there were a fire in a museum
which would you save, a Rembrandt painting
or an old woman who hadn't many   5
years left anyhow? Restless on hard chairs
caring little for pictures or old age
we'd opt one year for life, the next for art
and always half-heartedly. Sometimes
the woman borrowed my grandmother's face   10
leaving her usual kitchen to wander
some drafty, half imagined museum.
One year, feeling clever, I replied
why not let the woman decide herself?
Linda, the teacher would report, eschews   15
the burdens of responsibility.
This fall in a real museum I stand
before a real Rembrandt, old woman,
or nearly so, myself. The colors
within this frame are darker than autumn,   20
darker even than winter — the browns of earth,
though earth's most radiant elements burn
through the canvas. I know now that woman
and painting and season are almost one
and all beyond saving by children.   25

Katherine Philips (1632–1664)

On Her Son, H.P.   (1655?)

What on earth deserves our trust?
Youth and beauty both are dust.
Long we gathering are with pain
What one moment calls again.
Seven years' childless marriage past,   5
A son, a son is born at last:
So exactly limned and fair,
Full of good spirits, mien, and air,
As a long life promisèd,
Yet, in less than six weeks, dead.   10
Too promising, too great a mind
In so small room to be confined;
Therefore, fit in Heaven to dwell,
He quickly broke the prison shell.
So the subtle° alchemist   *ingenious*   15
Can't with Hermes' seal resist
The powerful spirit's subtler flight,
But 'twill bid him long good night.
So the sun, if it arise
Half so glorious as his eyes,   20
Like this infant takes a shroud,
Buried in a morning cloud.

On Her Son, H. P. In 1655, after seven years of marriage, the poet gave birth to her first child, Hector Philips, who lived only a few days. When this poem was first published (posthumously, in 1667), Philips's friend and editor Sir Charles Cotterell called it "EPITAPH. On Her Son H.P. at St. Syth's Church where her body also lies Interred." 7 *limned:* drawn or outlined in sharp detail (also a pun on *limbed*). 16 *Hermes' seal:* hermetic seal, such as might render an alchemist's bottle or beaker airtight (but still, in Philips's simile, fail to prevent its contents from leaking or evaporating). 22 *morning:* another pun.

COMPARE:

"On Her Son, H.P." with "On My First Son" by Ben Jonson (page 340).

Robert Phillips (b. 1938)

Running on Empty   1981

As a teenager I would drive Father's
Chevrolet cross-county, given me

reluctantly: "Always keep the tank
half full, boy, half full, ya hear?"

The fuel gauge dipping, dipping   5
toward Empty, hitting Empty, then

— thrilling! — 'way below Empty,
myself driving cross-county

mile after mile, faster and faster,
all night long, this crazy kid driving   10

the earth's rolling surface,
against all laws, defying chemistry,

rules, and time, riding on nothing
but fumes, pushing luck harder

than anyone pushed before, the wind   15
screaming past like the Furies . . .

I stranded myself only once, a white
night with no gas station open, ninety miles

from nowhere. Panicked for a while,
at standstill, myself stalled.   20

At dawn the car and I both refilled. But,
Father, I am running on empty still.

RUNNING ON EMPTY. 16 *Furies:* In Greek mythology, deities who pursue and torment evildoers.

Sylvia Plath (1932 – 1963)*

DADDY   1965

You do not do, you do not do
Any more, black shoe
In which I have lived like a foot
For thirty years, poor and white,
Barely daring to breathe or Achoo.   5

Daddy, I have had to kill you.
You died before I had time —
Marble-heavy, a bag full of God,
Ghastly statue with one grey toe
Big as a Frisco seal   10

And a head in the freakish Atlantic
Where it pours bean green over blue
In the waters off beautiful Nauset.
I used to pray to recover you.
Ach, du.   15

In the German tongue, in the Polish town
Scraped flat by the roller
Of wars, wars, wars.
But the name of the town is common.
My Polack friend   20

Says there are a dozen or two.
So I never could tell where you
Put your foot, your root,
I never could talk to you.
The tongue stuck in my jaw.   25

It stuck in a barb wire snare.
Ich, ich, ich, ich,
I could hardly speak.
I thought every German was you.
And the language obscene   30

An engine, an engine
Chuffing me off like a Jew.
A Jew to Dachau, Auschwitz, Belsen.
I began to talk like a Jew.
I think I may well be a Jew.   35

The snows of the Tyrol, the clear beer of Vienna
Are not very pure or true.
With my gypsy ancestress and my weird luck
And my Taroc pack and my Taroc pack
I may be a bit of a Jew.   40

I have always been scared of *you*,
With your Luftwaffe, your gobbledygoo.
And your neat moustache
And your Aryan eye, bright blue.
Panzer-man, panzer-man, O You—   45

Not God but a swastika
So black no sky could squeak through.
Every woman adores a Fascist,
The boot in the face, the brute
Brute heart of a brute like you.   50

You stand at the blackboard, daddy,
In the picture I have of you,
A cleft in your chin instead of your foot
But no less a devil for that, no not
Any less the black man who   55

15 *Ach, du:* Oh, you. 27 *Ich, ich, ich, ich:* I, I, I, I. 51 *blackboard:* Otto Plath had been a professor
of biology at Boston University.

Bit my pretty red heart in two.
I was ten when they buried you.
At twenty I tried to die
And get back, back, back to you.
I thought even the bones will do.   60

But they pulled me out of the sack,
And they stuck me together with glue.
And then I knew what to do.
I made a model of you,
A man in black with a Meinkampf look   65

And a love of the rack and the screw.
And I said I do, I do.
So daddy, I'm finally through.
The black telephone's off at the root,
The voices just can't worm through.   70

If I've killed one man, I've killed two —
The vampire who said he was you
And drank my blood for a year,
Seven years, if you want to know.
Daddy, you can lie back now.   75

There's a stake in your fat black heart
And the villagers never liked you.
They are dancing and stamping on you.
They always *knew* it was you.
Daddy, daddy, you bastard, I'm through.   80

DADDY. Introducing this poem in a reading, Sylvia Plath remarked:

The poem is spoken by a girl with an Electra complex. Her father died while she thought he was God. Her case is complicated by the fact that her father was also a Nazi and her mother very possibly part Jewish. In the daughter the two strains marry and paralyze each other — she has to act out the awful little allegory before she is free of it.

(Quoted by A. Alvarez, *Beyond All This Fiddle*, New York, 1971.) In some details "Daddy" is autobiography: the poet's father, Otto Plath, a German, had come to the United States from Grabow, Poland. He had died following amputation of a gangrened foot and leg, when Sylvia was eight years old. Politically, Otto Plath was a Republican, not a Nazi; but was apparently a somewhat domineering head of the household. (See the recollections of the poet's mother, Aurelia Schober Plath, in her edition of *Letters Home* by Sylvia Plath, New York, 1975.)

65 *Meinkampf*: Adolf Hitler entitled his autobiography *Mein Kampf* ("My Struggle").

COMPARE:

"Daddy" with "American Primitive" by William Jay Smith (page 879).

Sylvia Plath

Sylvia Plath (1932 – 1963)*

MORNING SONG   1965

Love set you going like a fat gold watch.
The midwife slapped your footsoles, and your bald cry
Took its place among the elements.

Our voices echo, magnifying your arrival. New statue.   5
In a drafty museum, your nakedness
Shadows our safety. We stand round blankly as walls.

I'm no more your mother
Than the cloud that distills a mirror to reflect its own slow
Effacement at the wind's hand.

All night your moth-breath   10
Flickers among the flat pink roses. I wake to listen:
A far sea moves in my ear.

One cry, and I stumble from bed, cow-heavy and floral
In my Victorian nightgown.
Your mouth opens clean as a cat's. The window square   15

Whitens and swallows its dull stars. And now you try
Your handful of notes;
The clear vowels rise like balloons.

Ezra Pound

Ezra Pound (1885 – 1972)*

THE RIVER-MERCHANT'S WIFE: A LETTER   1915

While my hair was still cut straight across my forehead
I played about the front gate, pulling flowers.
You came by on bamboo stilts, playing horse,
You walked about my seat, playing with blue plums.
And we went on living in the village of Chokan: 5
Two small people, without dislike or suspicion.
At fourteen I married My Lord you.
I never laughed, being bashful.
Lowering my head, I looked at the wall.
Called to, a thousand times, I never looked back.   10

At fifteen I stopped scowling,
I desired my dust to be mingled with yours
Forever and forever and forever.
Why should I climb the lookout?

At sixteen you departed,   15
You went into far Ku-to-yen, by the river of swirling eddies,
And you have been gone five months.
The monkeys make sorrowful noise overhead.

You dragged your feet when you went out.
By the gate now, the moss is grown, the different mosses,   20
Too deep to clear them away!
The leaves fall early this autumn, in wind.
The paired butterflies are already yellow with August
Over the grass in the West garden;
They hurt me. I grow older.   25

If you are coming down through the narrows of the river Kiang,
Please let me know before hand,
And I will come out to meet you
     As far as Cho-fu-sa.

THE RIVER-MERCHANT'S WIFE: A LETTER. A free translation from the Chinese poet Li Po (eighth century).

Dudley Randall (b. 1914)*

OLD WITHERINGTON   1966

Old Witherington had drunk too much again.
The children changed their play and packed around him
To jeer his latest brawl. Their parents followed.

Prune-black, with bloodshot eyes and one white tooth,
He tottered in the night with legs spread wide   5
Waving a hatchet. "Come on, come on," he piped,
"And I'll baptize these bricks with bloody kindling.
I may be old and drunk, but not afraid
To die. I've died before. A million times
I've died and gone to hell. I live in hell.   10
If I die now I die, and put an end
To all this loneliness. Nobody cares
Enough to even fight me now, except
This crazy bastard here."

                  And with these words
He cursed the little children, cursed his neighbors,   15
Cursed his father, mother, and his wife,
Himself, and God, and all the rest of the world,
All but his grinning adversary, who, crouched,
Danced tenderly around him with a jag-toothed bottle,
As if the world compressed to one old man   20
Who was the sun, and he sole faithful planet.

Dudley Randall

John Crowe Ransom (1888–1974)

BELLS FOR JOHN WHITESIDE'S DAUGHTER   1924

There was such speed in her little body,
And such lightness in her footfall,
It is no wonder her brown study
Astonishes us all.

Her wars were bruited in our high window.   5
We looked among orchard trees and beyond,
Where she took arms against her shadow,
Or harried unto the pond

The lazy geese, like a snow cloud
Dripping their snow on the green grass,   10
Tricking and stopping, sleepy and proud,
Who cried in goose, Alas,

For the tireless heart within the little
Lady with rod that made them rise
From their noon apple-dreams, and scuttle   15
Goose-fashion under the skies!

But now go the bells, and we are ready;
In one house we are sternly stopped
To say we are vexed at her brown study,
Lying so primly propped.   20

COMPARE:

"Bells for John Whiteside's Daughter" with "Elegy for Jane" by Theodore Roethke (page 867).

Henry Reed (1914–1986)

NAMING OF PARTS   1946

Today we have naming of parts. Yesterday,
We had daily cleaning. And tomorrow morning,
We shall have what to do after firing. But today,
Today we have naming of parts. Japonica
Glistens like coral in all of the neighboring gardens,   5
      And today we have naming of parts.

This is the lower sling swivel. And this
Is the upper sling swivel, whose use you will see,
When you are given your slings. And this is the piling swivel,
Which in your case you have not got. The branches   10
Hold in the gardens their silent, eloquent gestures,
      Which in our case we have not got.

This is the safety-catch, which is always released
With an easy flick of the thumb. And please do not let me
See anyone using his finger. You can do it quite easy   15
If you have any strength in your thumb. The blossoms
Are fragile and motionless, never letting anyone see
        Any of them using their finger.

And this you can see is the bolt. The purpose of this
Is to open the breech, as you see. We can slide it   20
Rapidly backwards and forwards: we call this
Easing the spring. And rapidly backwards and forwards
The early bees are assaulting and fumbling the flowers:
        They call it easing the Spring.

They call it easing the Spring: it is perfectly easy   25
If you have any strength in your thumb: like the bolt,
And the breech, and the cocking-piece, and the point of balance,
Which in our case we have not got; and the almond-blossom
Silent in all of the gardens and the bees going backwards and
    forwards,
        For today we have naming of parts.   30

COMPARE:

"Naming of Parts" with "The Fury of Aerial Bombardment" by Richard Eberhart (page
552).

Adrienne Rich (b. 1929)*

AUNT JENNIFER'S TIGERS   1951

Aunt Jennifer's tigers prance across a screen,
Bright topaz denizens of a world of green.
They do not fear the men beneath the tree;
They pace in sleek chivalric certainty.

Aunt Jennifer's fingers fluttering through her wool   5
Find even the ivory needle hard to pull.
The massive weight of Uncle's wedding band
Sits heavily upon Aunt Jennifer's hand.

When Aunt is dead, her terrified hands will lie
Still ringed with ordeals she was mastered by.   10
The tigers in the panel that she made
Will go on prancing, proud and unafraid.

Adrienne Rich

Adrienne Rich (b. 1929)*

THE NINTH SYMPHONY OF BEETHOVEN UNDERSTOOD AT LAST AS A SEXUAL MESSAGE   1973

A man in terror of impotence
or infertility, not knowing the difference
a man trying to tell something
howling from the climacteric
music of the entirely   5
isolated soul
yelling at Joy from the tunnel of the ego
music without the ghost
of another person in it, music
trying to tell something the man   10
does not want out, would keep if he could
gagged and bound and flogged with chords of Joy
where everything is silence and the
beating of a bloody fist upon
a splintered table   15

THE NINTH SYMPHONY OF BEETHOVEN UNDERSTOOD AT LAST AS A SEXUAL MESSAGE. In 1824, three years before his death, Ludwig van Beethoven (1770–1827), increasingly isolated by severe deafness, wrote his final (and, some say, greatest) symphony. 4 *climacteric music:* music written at a turning point or critical stage in life. In women, the *climacteric* is menopause; in men, it is that corresponding time when sexual activity and potency decline. 7 *yelling at Joy:* In the symphony's closing movement, four leading singers and a full chorus sing poet Friedrich von Schiller's ode "An die freude" ("To Joy"). This triumphant, rousing finale (in the words of critic Stefan Kunze) makes "an ecstatic, enthusiastic appeal to all humanity to unite in honor of a joy that shall flood every soul alive."

Adrienne Rich (b. 1929)*

TRYING TO TALK WITH A MAN   1973

Out in this desert we are testing bombs,
that's why we came here.

Sometimes I feel an underground river
forcing its way between deformed cliffs
an acute angle of understanding   5
moving itself like a locus of the sun
into this condemned scenery.

What we've had to give up to get here—
whole LP collections, films we starred in
playing in the neighborhoods, bakery windows   10
full of dry, chocolate-filled Jewish cookies,
the language of love-letters, of suicide notes,
afternoons on the riverbank
pretending to be children

Coming out to this desert   15
we meant to change the face of
driving among dull green succulents
walking at noon in the ghost town
surrounded by a silence

that sounds like the silence of the place   20
except that it came with us
and is familiar
and everything we were saying until now
was an effort to blot it out—
coming out here we are up against it   25

Out here I feel more helpless
with you than without you

You mention the danger
and list the equipment
we talk of people caring for each other   30
in emergencies—laceration, thirst—
but you look at me like an emergency

Your dry heat feels like power
your eyes are stars of a different magnitude
they reflect lights that spell out: EXIT   35
when you get up and pace the floor

talking of the danger
as if it were not ourselves
as if we were testing anything else.

COMPARE:

"Trying to Talk with a Man" with "Once in a While a Protest Poem" by David B.
Axelrod (page 553).

Theodore Roethke

Theodore Roethke (1908 – 1963)*

ELEGY FOR JANE   1953

My Student, Thrown by a Horse

I remember the neckcurls, limp and damp as tendrils;
And her quick look, a sidelong pickerel smile;
And how, once startled into talk, the light syllables leaped for her,
And she balanced in the delight of her thought,
A wren, happy, tail into the wind,   5
Her song trembling the twigs and small branches.
The shade sang with her;
The leaves, their whispers turned to kissing;
And the mold sang in the bleached valleys under the rose.

Oh, when she was sad, she cast herself down into such a pure depth,   10
Even a father could not find her:
Scraping her cheek against straw;
Stirring the clearest water.

My sparrow, you are not here,
Waiting like a fern, making a spiny shadow.   15
The sides of wet stones cannot console me,
Nor the moss, wound with the last light.

If only I could nudge you from this sleep,
My maimed darling, my skittery pigeon.
Over this damp grave I speak the words of my love: 20
I, with no rights in this matter,
Neither father nor lover.

COMPARE:

"Elegy for Jane" with "Bells for John Whiteside's Daughter" by John Crowe Ransom (page 863).

Gibbons Ruark (b. 1941)

Waiting for You with the Swallows 1983

I was waiting for you
Where the four lanes wander
Into a city street,
Listening to the freight
Train's whistle and thunder 5
Come racketing through,

And I saw beyond black
Empty branches the light
Turn swiftly to a flurry
Of wingbeats in a hurry 10
For nowhere but the flight
From steeple-top and back

To steeple-top again.
I thought of how the quick
Hair shadows your lit face 15
Till laughter in your voice
Awoke and brought me back
And you stepped from the train.

I was waiting for you
Not a little too long 20
To learn what swallows said
Darkening overhead:
When we had time, we sang.
After we sang, we flew.

Paul Ruffin (b. 1941)

HOTEL FIRE: NEW ORLEANS   1980

From first light we fear falling:
after the fever of birth, impetus
toward that natural window, we
reach, cling, our fingers and toes
curled to grip, after the fire   5
that tempers us for the sun.

There I saw them — I see them still —
thrust from windows,
flailing like children
who know the earth has failed them: 10
they snatch at chinks, to ledges,
tumble to the wet street below,
the fire an old and certain death,
the leap the only faith that's left.

Anne Sexton

Anne Sexton (1928–1974)

THE KISS   1969

My mouth blooms like a cut.
I've been wronged all year, tedious
nights, nothing but rough elbows in them
and delicate boxes of Kleenex calling *crybaby*
crybaby, you fool!   5

Before today my body was useless.
Now it's tearing at its square corners.
It's tearing old Mary's garments off, knot by knot
and see—Now it's shot full of these electric bolts.
Zing! A resurrection!   10

Once it was a boat, quite wooden
and with no business, no salt water under it
and in need of some paint. It was no more
than a group of boards. But you hoisted her, rigged her.
She's been elected.   15

My nerves are turned on. I hear them like
musical instruments. Where there was silence
the drums, the strings are incurably playing. You did this.
Pure genius at work. Darling, the composer has stepped
into fire.   20

COMPARE:

"The Kiss" with "The Ninth Symphony of Beethoven Understood at Last as a Sexual
Message" by Adrienne Rich (page 865).

William Shakespeare (1564–1616)*

NOT MARBLE NOR THE GILDED MONUMENTS   1609

Not marble, nor the gilded monuments
Of princes, shall outlive this powerful rhyme;
But you shall shine more bright in these contents
Than unswept stone, besmeared with sluttish time.
When wasteful war shall statues overturn,   5
And broils root out the work of masonry,
Nor Mars his sword nor war's quick fire shall burn
The living record of your memory.
'Gainst death and all-oblivious enmity
Shall you pace forth; your praise shall still find room   10
Even in the eyes of all posterity
That wear this world out to the ending doom.
    So, till the judgment that yourself arise.
    You live in this, and dwell in lovers' eyes.

COMPARE:

"Not marble nor the gilded monuments" with "To the Stone-cutters" by Robinson Jeffers
(page 835).

William Shakespeare

William Shakespeare (1564 – 1616)*

THAT TIME OF YEAR THOU MAYST IN ME BEHOLD   1609

That time of year thou mayst in me behold
When yellow leaves, or none, or few, do hang
Upon those boughs which shake against the cold,
Bare ruined choirs where late the sweet birds sang.
In me thou see'st the twilight of such day   5
As after sunset fadeth in the west,
Which by-and-by black night doth take away,
Death's second self that seals up all in rest.
In me thou see'st the glowing of such fire
That on the ashes of his youth doth lie,   10
As the deathbed whereon it must expire,
Consumed with that which it was nourished by.
   This thou perceiv'st, which makes thy love more strong,
   To love that well which thou must leave ere long.

William Shakespeare (1564 – 1616)*

WHEN, IN DISGRACE WITH FORTUNE AND MEN'S EYES   1609

When, in disgrace with Fortune and men's eyes,
I all alone beweep my outcast state,
And trouble deaf heaven with my bootless° cries,   *futile*
And look upon myself and curse my fate,
Wishing me like to one more rich in hope,   5
Featured like him, like him with friends possessed,
Desiring this man's art, and that man's scope,
With what I most enjoy contented least,
Yet in these thoughts myself almost despising,
Haply° I think on thee, and then my state,   *luckily*   10
Like to the lark at break of day arising
From sullen earth, sings hymns at heaven's gate;
     For thy sweet love rememb'red such wealth brings
     That then I scorn to change my state with kings.

William Shakespeare (1564 – 1616)*

WHEN DAISIES PIED AND VIOLETS BLUE   1598

When daisies pied and violets blue
     And lady-smocks all silver-white
And cuckoo-buds° of yellow hue   *buttercups*
     Do paint the meadows with delight,
The cuckoo then, on every tree,   5
Mocks married men; for thus sings he,
           "Cuckoo,
Cuckoo, cuckoo!" — O word of fear,
Unpleasing to a married ear!

When shepherds pipe on oaten straws,   10
     And merry larks are ploughmen's clocks,
When turtles tread°, and rooks, and daws,   *turtledoves mate*
     And maidens bleach their summer smocks,
The cuckoo then, on every tree,
Mocks married men; for thus sings he,   15
           "Cuckoo,
Cuckoo, cuckoo!" — O word of fear,
Unpleasing to a married ear!

WHEN DAISIES PIED. This song and "When icicles hang by the wall" conclude the play *Love's Labor's Lost.* 2 *lady-smocks:* also named cuckoo-flowers. 8 *O word of fear:* because it sounds like *cuckold,* a man whose wife has deceived him.

William Shakespeare (1564 – 1616)*

WHEN ICICLES HANG BY THE WALL   1598

When icicles hang by the wall,
  And Dick the shepherd blows his nail,
And Tom bears logs into the hall,
  And milk comes frozen home in pail,
When blood is nipped and ways° be foul,   *roads*   5
  Then nightly sings the staring owl:
      "Tu-whit, to-who!"
    A merry note,
While greasy Joan doth keel° the pot.   *cool (as by skimming or stirring)*

When all aloud the wind doth blow,   10
  And coughing drowns the parson's saw°,   *old saw, platitude*
And birds sit brooding in the snow,
  And Marian's nose looks red and raw,
When roasted crabs° hiss in the bowl,   *crab apples*
  Then nightly sings the staring owl: 15
      "Tu-whit, to-who!"
    A merry note,
While greasy Joan doth keel the pot.

Karl Shapiro (b. 1913)

THE DIRTY WORD   1947

The dirty word hops in the cage of the mind like the Pondicherry
vulture, stomping with its heavy left claw on the sweet meat of the brain
and tearing it with its vicious beak, ripping and chopping the flesh.
Terrified, the small boy bears the big bird of the dirty word into the
house, and grunting, puffing, carries it up the stairs to his own room in   5
the skull. Bits of black feather cling to his clothes and his hair as he locks
the staring creature in the dark closet.

All day the small boy returns to the closet to examine and feed the
bird, to caress and kick the bird, that now snaps and flaps its wings
savagely whenever the door is opened. How the boy trembles and delights   10
at the sight of the white excrement of the bird! How the bird leaps and
rushes against the walls of the skull, trying to escape from the zoo of the
vocabulary! How wildly snaps the sweet meat of the brain in its rage.

And the bird outlives the man, being freed at the man's death-funeral
by a word from the rabbi.   15

(But I one morning went upstairs and opened the door and entered
the closet and found in the cage of my mind the great bird dead. Softly
I wept it and softly removed it and softly buried the body of the bird in

the hollyhock garden of the house I lived in twenty years before. And out
of the worn black feathers of the wing have I made these pens to write   20
these elegies, for I have outlived the bird, and I have murdered it in my
early manhood.)

Richard Shelton (b. 1933)

MEXICO   1978

once each year
after a warm day in April
when darkness comes to the desert
uninvited but planning to spend the night
something hits me like a shovel   5
and I am stunned into believing
anything is possible

there is no overture to frenzy
I simply look up and see Scorpio
most dangerous of friends   10
with the last two stars in his tail
blinking like lights at a railroad crossing
while in one claw he holds the top
of a mountain in Mexico

and suddenly I know   15
everything I need is waiting for me
south of here in another country
and I have been walking through empty
rooms and talking to furniture

then I say to myself   20
why should I stay home and listen to Bach
such precision could have happened
to anyone to an infinite number
of monkeys with harpsichords

and next morning I start south   25
with my last chances flapping their wings
while birds of passage stream over me
in the opposite direction

I never find what I am looking for
and each time I return older   30
with my ugliness intact
but with the knowledge that if it isn't there
in the darkness under Scorpio
it isn't anywhere

Charles Simic (b. 1938)

Butcher Shop   1971

Sometimes walking late at night
I stop before a closed butcher shop.
There is a single light in the store
Like the light in which the convict digs his tunnel.

An apron hangs on the hook: 5
The blood on it smeared into a map
Of the great continents of blood,
The great rivers and oceans of blood.

There are knives that glitter like altars
In a dark church   10
Where they bring the cripple and the imbecile
To be healed.

There's a wooden block where bones are broken,
Scraped clean—a river dried to its bed
Where I am fed,   15
Where deep in the night I hear a voice.

COMPARE:

"Butcher Shop" with "Animals Are Passing from Our Lives" by Philip Levine (page 842).

David R. Slavitt (b. 1935)

Titanic   1983

Who does not love the *Titanic?*
If they sold passage tomorrow for that same crossing,
who would not buy?

To go down . . . We all go down, mostly
alone. But with crowds of people, friends, servants,   5
well fed, with music, with lights! Ah!

And the world, shocked, mourns, as it ought to do
and almost never does. There will be the books and movies
to remind our grandchildren who we were
and how we died, and give them a good cry.   10

Not so bad, after all. The cold
water is anaesthetic and very quick.
The cries on all sides must be a comfort.

We all go: only a few, first-class.

COMPARE:

"Titanic" with "The Convergence of the Twain" by Thomas Hardy (page 816).

Christopher Smart (1722 – 1771)*

FOR I WILL CONSIDER MY CAT JEOFFRY   (1759 – 1763)

For I will consider my Cat Jeoffry.
For he is the servant of the Living God, duly and daily serving him.
For at the first glance of the glory of God in the East he worships in
    his way.
For is this done by wreathing his body seven times round with
    elegant quickness.
For then he leaps up to catch the musk°, which is the   *catnip*
    blessing of God upon his prayer.   5
For he rolls upon prank to work it in.
For having done duty and received blessing he begins to consider
    himself.
For this he performs in ten degrees.
For first he looks upon his fore-paws to see if they are clean.
For secondly he kicks up behind to clear away there.   10
For thirdly he works it upon stretch° with the fore-paws   *he works his*
    extended.   *muscles, stretching*
For fourthly he sharpens his paws by wood.
For fifthly he washes himself.
For sixthly he rolls upon wash.
For seventhly he fleas himself, that he may not be interrupted upon
    the beat°.   *his patrol*   15
For eighthly he rubs himself against a post.
For ninthly he looks up for his instructions.
For tenthly he goes in quest of food.
For having considered God and himself he will consider his neighbor.
For if he meets another cat he will kiss her in kindness.   20
For when he takes his prey he plays with it to give it a chance.
For one mouse in seven escapes by his dallying.
For when his day's work is done his business more properly begins.
For he keeps the Lord's watch in the night against the Adversary.
For he counteracts the powers of darkness by his electrical skin and
    glaring eyes.   25
For he counteracts the Devil, who is death, by brisking about the life.
For in his morning orisons he loves the sun and the sun loves him.
For he is of the tribe of Tiger.
For the Cherub Cat is a term of the Angel Tiger.
For he has the subtlety and hissing of a serpent, which in goodness
    he suppresses.   30
For he will not do destruction if he is well-fed, neither will he spit
    without provocation.
For he purrs in thankfulness when God tells him he's a good Cat.

For he is an instrument for the children to learn benevolence upon.
For every house is incomplete without him, and a blessing is lacking
    in the spirit.
For the Lord commanded Moses concerning the cats at the departure
    of the Children of Israel from Egypt.   35
For every family had one cat at least in the bag.
For the English cats are the best in Europe.
For he is the cleanest in the use of his fore-paws of any quadruped.
For the dexterity of his defense is an instance of the love of God to
    him exceedingly.
For he is the quickest to his mark of any creature.   40
For he is tenacious of his point.
For he is a mixture of gravity and waggery.
For he knows that God is his Savior.
For there is nothing sweeter than his peace when at rest.
For there is nothing brisker than his life when in motion.   45
For he is of the Lord's poor, and so indeed is he called by
    benevolence perpetually — Poor Jeoffry! poor Jeoffry! the rat has
    bit thy throat.
For I bless the name of the Lord Jesus that Jeoffry is better.
For the divine spirit comes about his body to sustain it in complete
    cat.
For his tongue is exceeding pure so that it has in purity what it wants
    in music.
For he is docile and can learn certain things.   50
For he can sit up with gravity which is patience upon approbation.
For he can fetch and carry, which is patience in employment.
For he can jump over a stick which is patience upon proof positive.
For he can spraggle upon waggle at the word of command.
For he can jump from an eminence into his master's bosom.   55
For he can catch the cork and toss it again.
For he is hated by the hypocrite and miser.
For the former is afraid of detection.
For the latter refuses the charge.
For he camels his back to bear the first notion of business.   60
For he is good to think on, if a man would express himself neatly.
For he made a great figure in Egypt for his signal services.
For he killed the Icneumon-rat, very pernicious by land.
For his ears are so acute that they sting again.

FOR I WILL CONSIDER MY CAT JEOFFRY. This is a self-contained extract from Smart's long poem
Jubilate Agno ("Rejoice in the Lamb"), written during his confinement for insanity. 35 *For the Lord
commanded Moses concerning the cats:* No such command is mentioned in Scripture. 54 *spraggle upon
waggle:* W. F. Stead, in his edition of Smart's poem, suggests that this means Jeoffry will sprawl when
his master waggles a finger or a stick. 59 *the charge:* perhaps the cost of feeding a cat.

For from this proceeds the passing quickness of his attention. 65
For by stroking of him I have found out electricity.
For I perceived God's light about him both wax and fire.
For the electrical fire is the spiritual substance which God sends from
    heaven to sustain the bodies both of man and beast.
For God has blessed him in the variety of his movements.
For, though he cannot fly, he is an excellent clamberer. 70
For his motions upon the face of the earth are more than any other
    quadruped.
For he can tread to all the measures upon the music.
For he can swim for life.
For he can creep.

Stevie Smith (1902 – 1971)*

I REMEMBER 1957

It was my bridal night I remember,
An old man of seventy-three
I lay with my young bride in my arms,
A girl with t.b.
It was wartime, and overhead 5
The Germans were making a particularly heavy raid on Hampstead.
What rendered the confusion worse, perversely
Our bombers had chosen that moment to set out for Germany.
Harry, do they ever collide?
I do not think it has ever happened, 10
Oh my bride, my bride.

Stevie Smith

William Jay Smith (b. 1918)

AMERICAN PRIMITIVE   1953

Look at him there in his stovepipe hat,
His high-top shoes, and his handsome collar;
Only my Daddy could look like that,
And I love my Daddy like he loves his Dollar.

The screen door bangs, and it sounds so funny —   5
There he is in a shower of gold;
His pockets are stuffed with folding money,
His lips are blue, and his hands feel cold.

He hangs in the hall by his black cravat,
The ladies faint, and the children holler: 10
Only my Daddy could look like that,
And I love my Daddy like he loves his Dollar.

COMPARE:

"American Primitive" with "Daddy" by Sylvia Plath (page 857).

W. D. Snodgrass (b. 1926)

SEEING YOU HAVE . . .   1959

Seeing you have a woman
Whose loves grow thick as the weeds
That keep songsparrows through the year,
Why are you envious of boys
Who prowl the streets all night in packs   5
So they are equal to the proud
Slender girls they fear?

She's like the tall grass, common,
That sends roots, where it needs,
Six feet into the prairies.   10
Why do you teach yourself the loud
Hankering voices of blue jays
That quarrel branch by branch to peck
And spoil the bitter cherries?

William Stafford (b. 1914)*

AT THE KLAMATH BERRY FESTIVAL   1966

The war chief danced the old way —
the eagle wing he held before his mouth —
and when he turned the boom-boom
stopped. He took two steps. A sociologist
was there; the Scout troop danced.   5
I envied him the places where he had not been.

The boom began again. Outside he heard
the stick game, and the Blackfoot gamblers
arguing at poker under lanterns.
Still-moccasined and bashful, holding   10
the eagle wing before his mouth,
listening and listening, he danced after others stopped.

He took two steps, the boom caught up,
the mountains rose, the still deep river
slid but never broke its quiet.   15
I looked back when I left:
he took two steps, he took two steps,
past the sociologist.

AT THE KLAMATH BERRY FESTIVAL. The Klamath Indians have a reservation at the base of the
Cascade Range in southern Oregon.

Wallace Stevens (1879 – 1955)*

PETER QUINCE AT THE CLAVIER   1923

I

Just as my fingers on these keys
Make music, so the selfsame sounds
On my spirit make a music, too.

Music is feeling, then, not sound;
And thus it is that what I feel,   5
Here in this room, desiring you,

Thinking of your blue-shadowed silk,
Is music. It is like the strain
Waked in the elders by Susanna.

Of a green evening, clear and warm,   10
She bathed in her still garden, while
The red-eyed elders watching, felt

The basses of their beings throb
In witching chords, and their thin blood
Pulse pizzicati of Hosanna.   15

II

In the green water, clear and warm,
Susanna lay.
She searched
The touch of springs,

And found   20
Concealed imaginings.
She sighed,
For so much melody.

Upon the bank, she stood
In the cool   25
Of spent emotions.
She felt, among the leaves,
The dew
Of old devotions.

She walked upon the grass,   30
Still quavering.
The winds were like her maids,
On timid feet,
Fetching her woven scarves,
Yet wavering.   35

A breath upon her hand
Muted the night.
She turned —
A cymbal crashed,
And roaring horns.   40

III

Soon, with a noise like tambourines,
Came her attendant Byzantines.

They wondered why Susanna cried
Against the elders by her side;

And as they whispered, the refrain   45
Was like a willow swept by rain.

Anon, their lamps' uplifted flame
Revealed Susanna and her shame.

And then, the simpering Byzantines
Fled, with a noise like tambourines.   50

IV

Beauty is momentary in the mind —
The fitful tracing of a portal;
But in the flesh it is immortal.

The body dies; the body's beauty lives.
So evenings die, in their green going,   55
A wave, interminably flowing.
So gardens die, their meek breath scenting
The cowl of winter, done repenting.
So maidens die, to the auroral
Celebration of a maiden's choral.   60

Susanna's music touched the bawdy strings
Of those white elders; but, escaping,
Left only Death's ironic scraping.
Now, in its immortality, it plays
On the clear viol of her memory,   65
And makes a constant sacrament of praise.

PETER QUINCE AT THE CLAVIER. In Shakespeare's *Midsummer Night's Dream*, Peter Quince is a
clownish carpenter who stages a mock-tragic play. In The Book of Susanna in the Apocrypha, two
lustful elders who covet Susanna, a virtuous married woman, hide in her garden, spy on her as
she bathes, then threaten to make false accusations against her unless she submits to them. When
she refuses, they cry out, and her servants come running. All ends well when the prophet Daniel
cross-examines the elders and proves them liars. 15 *pizzicati:* thin notes made by plucking a stringed
instrument. 42 *Byzantines:* Susanna's maidservants.

Wallace Stevens

Ruth Stone (b. 1915)

SECOND HAND COAT   1982

I feel
in her pockets; she wore nice cotton gloves,
kept a handkerchief box, washed her undies,
ate at the Holiday Inn, had a basement freezer,
belonged to a bridge club.   5
I think when I wake in the morning
that I have turned into her.
She hangs in the hall downstairs,
a shadow with pulled threads.
I slip her over my arms, skin of a matron.   10
Where are you? I say to myself, to the orphaned body,
and her coat says,
Get your purse, have you got your keys?

Jonathan Swift (1667 – 1745)*

A DESCRIPTION OF THE MORNING   1711

Now hardly here and there an hackney-coach°,   *horse-drawn cab*
Appearing, showed the ruddy morn's approach.
Now Betty from her master's bed had flown
And softly stole to discompose her own.
The slipshod 'prentice from his master's door   5
Had pared the dirt, and sprinkled round the floor.
Now Moll had whirled her mop with dextrous airs,
Prepared to scrub the entry and the stairs.
The youth with broomy stumps began to trace
The kennel°-edge, where wheels had worn the place.   *gutter*   10
The small-coal man was heard with cadence deep
Till drowned in shriller notes of chimneysweep,
Duns° at his lordship's gate began to meet,   *bill-collectors*
And Brickdust Moll had screamed through half the street.
The turnkey° now his flock returning sees,   *jailkeeper* 15
Duly let out a-nights to steal for fees;
The watchful bailiffs° take their silent stands;   *constables*
And schoolboys lag with satchels in their hands.

A DESCRIPTION OF THE MORNING. 9 *youth with broomy stumps:* a young man sweeping the gutter's edge with worn-out brooms, looking for old nails fallen from wagonwheels, which were valuable. 14 *Brickdust Moll:* woman selling brickdust to be used for scouring.

Alfred, Lord Tennyson

Alfred, Lord Tennyson (1809 – 1892)*

DARK HOUSE, BY WHICH ONCE MORE I STAND   1850

Dark house, by which once more I stand
   Here in the long unlovely street,
   Doors, where my heart was used to beat
So quickly, waiting for a hand,

A hand that can be clasped no more —   5
   Behold me, for I cannot sleep,
   And like a guilty thing I creep
At earliest morning to the door.

He is not here; but far away
   The noise of life begins again,
   And ghastly through the drizzling rain   10
On the bald street breaks the blank day.

DARK HOUSE. This poem is one part of the series *In Memoriam,* an elegy for Tennyson's friend
Arthur Henry Hallam.

Alfred, Lord Tennyson (1809 – 1892)*

ULYSSES   (1833)

It little profits that an idle king,
By this still hearth, among these barren crags,
Matched with an agèd wife, I mete and dole
Unequal laws unto a savage race
That hoard, and sleep, and feed, and know not me.   5
I cannot rest from travel; I will drink
Life to the lees. All times I have enjoyed
Greatly, have suffered greatly, both with those
That loved me, and alone; on shore, and when
Through scudding drifts the rainy Hyades   10
Vexed the dim sea. I am become a name;
For always roaming with a hungry heart
Much have I seen and known — cities of men
And manners, climates, councils, governments,
Myself not least, but honored of them all —   15
And drunk delight of battle with my peers,
Far on the ringing plains of windy Troy.
I am a part of all that I have met;
Yet all experience is an arch wherethrough
Gleams that untraveled world whose margin fades   20
Forever and forever when I move.
How dull it is to pause, to make an end,
To rust unburnished, not to shine in use!
As though to breathe were life! Life piled on life
Were all too little, and of one to me   25
Little remains; but every hour is saved
From that eternal silence, something more,
A bringer of new things; and vile it were
For some three suns to store and hoard myself,
And this grey spirit yearning in desire   30
To follow knowledge like a sinking star,
Beyond the utmost bound of human thought.
    This is my son, mine own Telemachus,
To whom I leave the scepter and the isle —
Well-loved of me, discerning to fulfill   35
This labor, by slow prudence to make mild
A rugged people, and through soft degrees
Subdue them to the useful and the good.
Most blameless is he, centered in the sphere
Of common duties, decent not to fail   40
In offices of tenderness, and pay
Meet adoration to my household gods,
When I am gone. He works his work, I mine.

There lies the port; the vessel puffs her sail;
There gloom the dark, broad seas. My mariners,   45
Souls that have toiled, and wrought, and thought with me —
That ever with a frolic welcome took
The thunder and the sunshine, and opposed
Free hearts, free foreheads — you and I are old;
Old age hath yet his honor and his toil.   50
Death closes all; but something ere the end,
Some work of noble note, may yet be done,
Not unbecoming men that strove with Gods.
The lights begin to twinkle from the rocks;
The long day wanes; the low moon climbs; the deep   55
Moans round with many voices. Come, my friends,
'Tis not too late to seek a newer world.
Push off, and sitting well in order smite
The sounding furrows; for my purpose holds
To sail beyond the sunset, and the baths   60
Of all the western stars, until I die.
It may be that the gulfs will wash us down;
It may be we shall touch the Happy Isles,
And see the great Achilles, whom we knew.
Though much is taken, much abides; and though   65
We are not now that strength which in old days
Moved earth and heaven, that which we are, we are —
One equal temper of heroic hearts,
Made weak by time and fate, but strong in will
To strive, to seek, to find, and not to yield.   70

ULYSSES. 10 *Hyades*: daughters of Atlas, who were transformed into a group of stars. Their rising
with the sun was thought to be a sign of rain. 63 *Happy Isles*: Elysium, a paradise believed to be
attainable by sailing west.

COMPARE:

"Ulysses" with "Sir Patrick Spence" (page 504).

Dylan Thomas (1914 – 1953)*

FERN HILL   1946

Now as I was young and easy under the apple boughs
About the lilting house and happy as the grass was green,
             The night above the dingle° starry,   *wooded valley*
                     Time let me hail and climb
                 Golden in the heydays of his eyes,   5

And honored among wagons I was prince of the apple towns
And once below a time I lordly had the trees and leaves
        Trail with daisies and barley
     Down the rivers of the windfall light.

And as I was green and carefree, famous among the barns   10
About the happy yard and singing as the farm was home,
       In the sun that is young once only,
         Time let me play and be
     Golden in the mercy of his means,
And green and golden I was huntsman and herdsman, the calves   15
Sang to my horn, the foxes on the hills barked clear and cold,
        And the sabbath rang slowly
     In the pebbles of the holy streams.

All the sun long it was running, it was lovely, the hay
Fields high as the house, the tunes from the chimneys, it was air   20
      And playing, lovely and watery
        And fire green as grass.
      And nightly under the simple stars
As I rode to sleep the owls were bearing the farm away,
All the moon long I heard, blessed among stables, the nightjars   25
      Flying with the ricks, and the horses
       Flashing into the dark.

And then to awake, and the farm, like a wanderer white
With the dew, come back, the cock on his shoulder: it was all
      Shining, it was Adam and maiden,   30
       The sky gathered again
      And the sun grew round that very day.
So it must have been after the birth of the simple light
In the first, spinning place, the spellbound horses walking warm
      Out of the whinnying green stable   35
       On to the fields of praise.

And honored among foxes and pheasants by the gay house
Under the new made clouds and happy as the heart was long,
      In the sun born over and over,
        I ran my heedless ways,   40
      My wishes raced through the house high hay
And nothing I cared, at my sky blue trades, that time allows
In all his tuneful turning so few and such morning songs
      Before the children green and golden
       Follow him out of grace,   45

Nothing I cared, in the lamb white days, that time would take me
Up to the swallow thronged loft by the shadow of my hand,
    In the moon that is always rising,
        Nor that riding to sleep
    I should hear him fly with the high fields   50
And wake to the farm forever fled from the childless land.
Oh as I was young and easy in the mercy of his means,
        Time held me green and dying
    Though I sang in my chains like the sea.

John Updike (b. 1932)*

EX-BASKETBALL PLAYER   1958

Pearl Avenue runs past the high-school lot,
Bends with the trolley tracks, and stops, cut off
Before it has a chance to go two blocks,
At Colonel McComsky Plaza. Berth's Garage
Is on the corner facing west, and there,   5
Most days, you'll find Flick Webb, who helps Berth out.

Flick stands tall among the idiot pumps —
Five on a side, the old bubble-head style,
Their rubber elbows hanging loose and low.
One's nostrils are two S's, and his eyes   10
An E and O. And one is squat, without
A head at all — more of a football type.

Once Flick played for the high-school team, the Wizards.
He was good: in fact, the best. In '46
He bucketed three hundred ninety points,   15
A county record still. The ball loved Flick.
I saw him rack up thirty-eight or forty
In one home game. His hands were like wild birds.

He never learned a trade, he just sells gas,
Checks oil, and changes flats. Once in a while,   20
As a gag, he dribbles an inner tube,
But most of us remember anyway.
His hands are fine and nervous on the lug wrench.
It makes no difference to the lug wrench, though.

Off work, he hangs around Mae's luncheonette.   25
Grease-gray and kind of coiled, he plays pinball,
Smokes those thin cigars, nurses lemon phosphates.
Flick seldom says a word to Mae, just nods
Beyond her face toward bright applauding tiers
Of Necco Wafers, Nibs, and Juju Beads.   30

COMPARE:

"Ex-Basketball Player" with "The Cadence of Silk" by Garrett Hongo (page 826) and "To
An Athlete Dying Young" by A. E. Housman (page 832).

Edmund Waller (1606 – 1687)*

GO, LOVELY ROSE   1645

    Go, lovely rose,
Tell her that wastes her time and me
    That now she knows,
When I resemble° her to thee,   *compare*
How sweet and fair she seems to be.   5

    Tell her that's young
And shuns to have her graces spied,
    That hadst thou sprung
In deserts where no men abide,
Thou must have uncommended died.   10

    Small is the worth
Of beauty from the light retired:
    Bid her come forth,
Suffer herself to be desired,
And not blush so to be admired.   15

    Then die, that she
The common fate of all things rare
    May read in thee,
How small a part of time they share
That are so wondrous sweet and fair.   20

COMPARE:

"Go, Lovely Rose" with "To the Virgins, to Make Much of Time" by Robert Herrick
(page 825) and "To His Coy Mistress" by Andrew Marvell (page 846).

Walt Whitman

Walt Whitman (1819 – 1892)*

I SAW IN LOUISIANA A LIVE-OAK GROWING   1867

I saw in Louisiana a live-oak growing,
All alone stood it and the moss hung down from the branches,
Without any companion it grew there uttering joyous leaves of dark
    green,
And its look, rude, unbending, lusty, made me think of myself,
But I wonder'd how it could utter joyous leaves standing alone there
    without its friend near, for I knew I could not,   5
And I broke off a twig with a certain number of leaves upon it, and
    twined around it a little moss,
And brought it away, and I have placed it in sight in my room,
It is not needed to remind me as of my own dear friends,
(For I believe lately I think of little else than of them,)
Yet it remains to me a curious token, it makes me think of manly
    love;   10
For all that, and though the live-oak glistens there in Louisiana
    solitary in a wide flat space,
Uttering joyous leaves all its life without a friend a lover near,
I know very well I could not.

COMPARE:

"I Saw in Louisiana a Live-Oak Growing" with "A Supermarket in California" by Allen
Ginsberg (page 813).

Richard Wilbur

Richard Wilbur (b. 1921)*

TRANSIT

1988

A woman I have never seen before
Steps from the darkness of her town-house door
At just that crux of time when she is made
So beautiful that she or time must fade.

What use to claim that as she tugs her gloves   5
A phantom heraldry of all the loves
Blares from the lintel? That the staggered sun
Forgets, in his confusion, how to run?

Still, nothing changes as her perfect feet
Click down the walk that issues in the street.   10
Leaving the stations of her body there
As a whip maps the countries of the air.

Richard Wilbur (b. 1921)*

THE WRITER

1976

In her room at the prow of the house
Where light breaks, and the windows are tossed with linden,
My daughter is writing a story.

I pause in the stairwell, hearing
From her shut door a commotion of typewriter-keys   5
Like a chain hauled over a gunwale.

Young as she is, the stuff
Of her life is a great cargo, and some of it heavy:
I wish her a lucky passage.

But now it is she who pauses,   10
As if to reject my thought and its easy figure.
A stillness greatens, in which

The whole house seems to be thinking,
And then she is at it again with a bunched clamor
Of strokes, and again is silent.   15

I remember the dazed starling
Which was trapped in that very room, two years ago;
How we stole in, lifted a sash

And retreated, not to affright it;
And how for a helpless hour, through the crack of the door,   20
We watched the sleek, wild, dark

And iridescent creature
Batter against the brilliance, drop like a glove
To the hard floor, or the desk-top.

And wait then, humped and bloody,   25
For the wits to try it again; and how our spirits
Rose when, suddenly sure,

It lifted off from a chair-back,
Beating a smooth course for the right window
And clearing the sill of the world.   30

It is always a matter, my darling,
Of life or death, as I had forgotten. I wish
What I wished you before, but harder.

Nancy Willard (b. 1936)

MARRIAGE AMULET   1974

You are polishing me like old wood.
At night we curl together like two rings
on a dark hand. After many nights,
the rough edges wear down.

If this is aging, it is warm as fleece.   5
I will gleam like ancient wood.
I will wax smooth, my crags and cowlicks
well-rubbed to show my grain.

Some sage will keep us in his hand for peace.

Miller Williams (b. 1930)

MECANIC ON DUTY AT ALL TIMES   1986

The license plate was another state and year.
The man's slow hands, as if they had no part
in whatever happened here, followed the hollows
and hills of his broad belt. Inside the car
four children, his face again, with eyes like washers,   5
were as still as the woman, two fingers touching her cheek.
"How much?" he said. "Well maybe fifty dollars
if I can find a used one. I guess I can."
The hands paid no attention. Out in the sun
light wires dipped and rose and dipped again   10
until they disappeared. *Flats fixed* and *Gas*
and *Quaker State* squeaked in the wind. Just that.
And the speeding trucks, wailing through their tires.

COMPARE:

"MECANIC ON DUTY AT ALL TIMES" with "Filling Station" by Elizabeth Bishop (page 785).

William Carlos Williams (1883 – 1963)*

SPRING AND ALL   1923

By the road to the contagious hospital
under the surge of the blue
mottled clouds driven from the
northeast — a cold wind. Beyond, the
waste of broad, muddy fields   5
brown with dried weeds, standing and fallen

patches of standing water
the scattering of tall trees

All along the road the reddish
purplish, forked, upstanding, twiggy   10

stuff of bushes and small trees
with dead, brown leaves under them
leafless vines —

Lifeless in appearance, sluggish
dazed spring approaches —   15

They enter the new world naked,
cold, uncertain of all
save that they enter. All about them
the cold, familiar wind —

Now the grass, tomorrow   20
the stiff curl of wildcarrot leaf
One by one objects are defined —
It quickens: clarity, outline of leaf

But now the stark dignity of
entrance — Still, the profound change   25
has come upon them: rooted, they
grip down and begin to awaken

Compare:

"Spring and All" with "in Just-" by E. E. Cummings (page 691) and "Root Cellar" by Theodore Roethke (page 571).

William Carlos Williams

William Carlos Williams (1883 – 1963)*

To Waken an Old Lady   1921

Old age is
a flight of small
cheeping birds
skimming
bare trees   5
above a snow glaze.
Gaining and failing
they are buffeted
by a dark wind —
But what?   10
On harsh weedstalks
the flock has rested,
the snow
is covered with broken
seedhusks   15
and the wind tempered
by a shrill
piping of plenty.

COMPARE:

"To Waken an Old Lady" with "Castoff Skin" by Ruth Whitman (page 592).

Yvor Winters (1900 – 1968)

At the San Francisco Airport   1960

To My Daughter, 1954

This is the terminal: the light
Gives perfect vision, false and hard;
The metal glitters, deep and bright.
Great planes are waiting in the yard —
They are already in the night.   5

And you are here beside me, small,
Contained and fragile, and intent
On things that I but half recall —
Yet going whither you are bent.
I am the past, and that is all.   10

But you and I in part are one:
The frightened brain, the nervous will,
The knowledge of what must be done,
The passion to acquire the skill
To face that which you dare not shun.   15

The rain of matter upon sense
Destroys me momently. The score:
There comes what will come. The expense
Is what one thought, and something more —
One's being and intelligence. 20

This is the terminal, the break.
Beyond this point, on lines of air,
You take the way that you must take;
And I remain in light and stare —
In light, and nothing else, awake. 25

William Wordsworth (1770 – 1850)*

COMPOSED UPON WESTMINSTER BRIDGE 1807

Earth has not anything to show more fair:
Dull would he be of soul who could pass by
A sight so touching in its majesty:
This City now doth, like a garment, wear
The beauty of the morning; silent, bare, 5
Ships, towers, domes, theatres, and temples lie
Open unto the fields, and to the sky;
All bright and glittering in the smokeless air.
Never did sun more beautifully steep
In his first splendor, valley, rock, or hill; 10
Ne'er saw I, never felt, a calm so deep!
The river glideth at his own sweet will:
Dear God! the very houses seem asleep;
And all that mighty heart is lying still!

William Wordsworth

James Wright

James Wright (1927 – 1980)*

A BLESSING   1961

Just off the highway to Rochester, Minnesota,
Twilight bounds softly forth on the grass.
And the eyes of those two Indian ponies
Darken with kindness.
They have come gladly out of the willows   5
To welcome my friend and me.
We step over the barbed wire into the pasture
Where they have been grazing all day, alone.
They ripple tensely, they can hardly contain their happiness
That we have come.   10
They bow shyly as wet swans. They love each other.
There is no loneliness like theirs.
At home once more,
They begin munching the young tufts of spring in the darkness.
I would like to hold the slenderer one in my arms,   15
For she has walked over to me
And nuzzled my left hand.
She is black and white,
Her mane falls wild on her forehead,
And the light breeze moves me to caress her long ear   20
That is delicate as the skin over a girl's wrist.
Suddenly I realize
That if I stepped out of my body I would break
Into blossom.

James Wright (1927 – 1980)*

Autumn Begins in Martins Ferry, Ohio   1963

In the Shreve High football stadium,
I think of Polacks nursing long beers in Tiltonsville,
And gray faces of Negroes in the blast furnace at Benwood,
And the ruptured night watchman of Wheeling Steel,
Dreaming of heroes.   5

All the proud fathers are ashamed to go home.
Their women cluck like starved pullets,
Dying for love.

Therefore,
Their sons grow suicidally beautiful   10
At the beginning of October,
And gallop terribly against each other's bodies.

Sir Thomas Wyatt (1503? – 1542)*

They Flee From Me That Sometime Did Me Sekë   (about 1535)

They flee from me that sometime did me sekë
   With naked fotë° stalking in my chamber.   *foot*
I have seen them gentle, tame and mekë
   That now are wild, and do not remember
   That sometime they put themself in danger   5
To take bread at my hand; and now they range
Busily seeking with a continual change.

Thankèd be fortune, it hath been otherwise
   Twenty times better; but once in speciàll,
In thin array, after a pleasant guise,   10
   When her loose gown from her shoulders did fall,
   And she me caught in her armës long and small,
Therëwith all sweetly did me kiss,
And softly said, *Dear heart, how like you this?*

It was no dremë: I lay broadë waking.   15
   But all is turned thorough° my gentleness   *through*

Into a strangë fashion of forsaking;
   And I have leave to go of her goodness,
   And she also to use newfangleness°.   *to seek novelty*
But since that I so kindëly am served   20
I would fain knowë what she hath deserved.

THEY FLEE FROM ME THAT SOMETIME DID ME SEKë. Some latter-day critics have called Sir Thomas Wyatt a careless poet because some of his lines appear faltering and metrically inconsistent; others have thought he knew what he was doing. It is uncertain whether the final *e*'s in English spelling were still pronounced in Wyatt's day as they were in Chaucer's, but if they were, perhaps Wyatt has been unjustly blamed. In this text, spellings have been modernized except in words where the final *e* would make a difference in rhythm. To sense how it matters, try reading the poem aloud leaving out the *e*'s and then putting them in wherever indicated. Sound them like the *a* in *sofa.* 20 *kindëly:* according to my kind (or hers); that is, as befits the nature of man (or woman). Perhaps there is also irony here, and the word means "unkindly."

Elinor Wylie (1885–1928)

THE EAGLE AND THE MOLE   1921

Avoid the reeking herd,
Shun the polluted flock,
Live like that stoic bird,
The eagle of the rock.

The huddled warmth of crowds   5
Begets and fosters hate;
He keeps, above the clouds,
His cliff inviolate.

When flocks are folded warm,
And herds to shelter run,   10
He sails above the storm,
He stares into the sun.

If in the eagle's track
Your sinews cannot leap,
Avoid the lathered pack,   15
Turn from the steaming sheep.

If you would keep your soul
From spotted sight or sound,
Live like the velvet mole;
Go burrow underground.   20

And there hold intercourse
With roots of trees and stones,
With rivers at their source,
And disembodied bones.

William Butler Yeats

William Butler Yeats (1865–1939)

LONG-LEGGED FLY   1940

That civilization may not sink,
Its great battle lost,
Quiet the dog, tether the pony
To a distant post;
Our master Caesar is in the tent   5
Where the maps are spread,
His eyes fixed upon nothing,
A hand under his head.

Like a long-legged fly upon the stream
His mind moves upon silence.   10

That the topless towers be burnt
And men recall that face,
Move most gently if move you must
In this lonely place.
She thinks, part woman, three parts a child,   15
That nobody looks; her feet
Practice a tinker shuffle
Picked up on the street.

Like a long-legged fly upon the stream
Her mind moves upon silence.   20

That girls at puberty may find
The first Adam in their thought,
Shut the door of the Pope's chapel,
Keep those children out.
There on that scaffolding reclines   25
Michael Angelo.
With no more sound than the mice make
His hand moves to and fro.

Like a long-legged fly upon the stream
His mind moves upon silence.   30

LONG-LEGGED FLY. This "fly" is the fresh-water insect also known as the water strider. 11 *topless towers*: of Troy, burned by the Greeks. Yeats echoes the description of Helen of Troy (whose abduction started the war) given in Christopher Marlowe's play *The Tragical History of Doctor Faustus*: "Was this the face that launched a thousand ships, / And burnt the topless towers of Ilium?" 23 *the Pope's Chapel*: Michelangelo had to lie on his back to paint upon the ceiling of the Sistine Chapel his celebrated frescoes depicting the creation, fall, and final judgment of humankind.

COMPARE:

"Long-legged Fly" with "Helen" by H.D. (page 815).

William Butler Yeats (1865–1939)

CRAZY JANE TALKS WITH THE BISHOP   1933

I met the Bishop on the road
And much said he and I.
"Those breasts are flat and fallen now,
Those veins must soon be dry;
Live in a heavenly mansion,   5
Not in some foul sty."

"Fair and foul are near of kin,
And fair needs foul," I cried.
"My friends are gone, but that's a truth
Nor° grave nor bed denied,   *neither*   10
Learned in bodily lowliness
And in the heart's pride.

"A woman can be proud and stiff
When on love intent;
But Love has pitched his mansion in   15
The place of excrement;
For nothing can be sole or whole
That has not been rent."

William Butler Yeats (1865 – 1939)*

THE MAGI   1914

Now as at all times I can see in the mind's eye,
In their stiff, painted clothes, the pale unsatisfied ones
Appear and disappear in the blue depth of the sky
With all their ancient faces like rain-beaten stones,
And all their helms of silver hovering side by side,   5
And all their eyes still fixed, hoping to find once more,
Being by Calvary's turbulence unsatisfied,
The uncontrollable mystery on the bestial floor.

COMPARE:

"The Magi" with "Journey of the Magi" by T. S. Eliot (page 804).

30   *Lives of the Poets*

Here you will find a brief biographical note for each poet represented in the book by more than one selection. There is also a note for Thomas Gray, author of the long poem "Elegy in a Country Churchyard."

John Ashbery

John Ashbery, born in Rochester, New York, in 1927, was educated at Deerfield Academy, Harvard, and Columbia. In 1960 he became an art critic in Paris for the *New York Herald Tribune*, and from 1966 to 1972 served as executive editor of the magazine *Art News* in New York. His first full collection of poetry, *Some Trees* (1956), was chosen by W. H. Auden for publication in the Yale Series of Younger Poets; his *Self-Portrait in a Convex Mirror* (1976) garnered praise and three leading literary prizes, and sold well for a book of serious poetry. Ashbery has written plays and a novel (with James Schuyler), *A Nest of Ninnies* (1969). He now lives in New York and teaches part time in the writing program at Brooklyn College. Some critics have speculated that Ashbery's experience as an art critic has tinged his poetry: that he performs in words what an abstract expressionist performs on canvas in oils. His work can annoy readers who expect poems to make clear statements to be taken in only one way; others think him the foremost living American poet and major heir to the tradition of Wallace Stevens — that is, to the art of suggesting rather than depicting, of arranging words primarily for their own sake.

Margaret Atwood

Margaret Atwood, born in Ottawa in 1939, is a staunchly Canadian poet, short story writer, and novelist whose literary reputation has extended well beyond the borders of her native country. She published her first book of poems,

Double Persephone, in 1962, the same year she was graduated from the University of Toronto. She went on to earn a master's degree at Radcliffe and to study Victorian fantasy at Harvard. She has advanced her country's cultural identity by publishing *Survival* (1972), a book about Canadian literature, and has edited *The Oxford Book of Canadian Verse* (1982). Her fiction and poetry, at once comic and grim, often deal with alienation and the destructive nature of human relationships. Her most recent novel, *Cat's Eye* (1989), has won attention on both sides of the Canadian border. The cream of her poetry has been skimmed in *Selected Poems* (1976) and *Selected Poems II* (1987).

W. H. Auden

W. H. Auden (1907 – 1973), born in York, England, in 1907, as a young man in the 1930s became the acknowledged spokesman for a generation of English poets that included Stephen Spender, C. Day Lewis, Christopher Isherwood, and Louis MacNeice. His early work was characterized by blithe wit, a Marxist outlook, and a knowledge of Freudian psychology; in later life, he professed Christianity and (in his views of poetry) increasing conservatism. In 1939 Auden emigrated to America, and in 1946 became a United States citizen. A prolific editor, anthologist, and translator of poetry, he collaborated on verse plays, travel memoirs, and (with his longtime friend Chester Kallman) librettos for operas, including Igor Stravinsky's *The Rake's Progress* (1951). He wrote influential criticism, notably that collected in *The Dyer's Hand* (1962). Auden divided his last years among England, Italy, Austria, and New York.

R. L. Barth

R. L. Barth was born in 1947 in Covington, Kentucky. From 1966 until 1969 he served as a patrol leader with the First Reconnaissance Battalion of the U.S. Marines in Vietnam. Later he held a Wallace Stegner fellowship in creative writing at Stanford. He now teaches English at Xavier University in Cincinnati, and has twice been a visiting lecturer at the University of California, Santa Barbara. As Robert L. Barth, he operates a small publishing house in Florence, Kentucky, issuing books and chapbooks of poetry by contemporary formalists Edgar Bowers, Turner Cassity, Dick Davis, Timothy Dekin, Thom Gunn, Charles Gullans, Warren Hope, Janet Lewis, Raymond Oliver, John Ridland, Don Stanford, Timothy Steele, Wesley Trimpi, William Wilborn, and others. His own classically taut poems of the Vietnam war have been gathered in *A Soldier's Time* (1987), and his work as a translator includes *Earthenware: XLVI Epigrams from Martial* (1988).

Elizabeth Bishop

Elizabeth Bishop (1911 – 1979) was born in Worcester, Massachusetts. After her father died (in her first year) and her mother was stricken with mental illness, she lived until age six with her grandmother in a coastal village in Nova Scotia. A sufferer from asthma, she received scant elementary schooling, but she read widely and deeply at home. At sixteen she entered Walnut Hill, a boarding school, and later graduated from Vassar. Her undergraduate poems won her the friendship of the poet Marianne Moore, who persuaded her not to go on to medical school, but instead to write. Fond of travel and flower-filled climates, Bishop lived for nine years in Key West, Florida, then for fifteen years in Brazil, dividing her time between the mountains and Rio de Janeiro. In 1966 she returned to the United States to teach: first at the University of Washington, then at Harvard from 1969 until 1977, when she retired. Most of her sparely disciplined work is contained in two volumes: *Complete Poems 1927 – 1979* (1983) and *Collected Prose* (1984). Her sharp-eyed poems, full of vivid images and apt metaphors, have affected the work of other poets, among them her friends Randall Jarrell and Robert Lowell.

William Blake

William Blake (1757 – 1827), poet, painter, and visionary, was born in the Soho district of London and early in life was apprenticed to an engraver. Becoming a skilled craftsman, he earned his living illustrating books, among them Dante's *Divine Comedy*, Milton's poems, and the Book of Job. A remarkable and original graphic artist whose only formal training came from a few months at the Royal Academy, Blake published his own poems, engraving them in a careful script embellished with hand-colored illustrations and decorations. His wife Catherine Boucher, whom he taught to read and write, shared his visions and helped him do the coloring. *Songs of Innocence* (1789) and *Songs of Experience* (1794), brief lyrics written from a child's point of view, are easy to enjoy; but anyone deeply interested in Blake copes also with the longer, more demanding "Prophetic Books," among them *The Book of Thel* (1789), *The Marriage of Heaven and Hell* (1790), and *Jerusalem* (1804 – 20). In these later works, out of his readings in alchemy, the Bible, and the works of Plato and Swedenborg, Blake derived support for his lifelong hatred of scientific rationalism and created his own mythology, complete with devils and deities. A sympathizer with both American and French revolutions, Blake was once accused of sedition, but the charges were dismissed. In his lifetime, Wordsworth and Coleridge were among the few admirers of his short lyrics; his "Prophetic Books" have had to wait until our century for compassionate readers.

Robert Bly

Robert Bly was born on a farm in Madison, Minnesota, in 1926, and continued to live there for most of his life. He was graduated from Harvard, where he began studies in mathematics before deciding to devote his life to poetry. Rather than teaching, Bly has preferred to support himself and his family by giving poetry readings and by translating books and poems from Scandinavian and other languages. In 1958 he launched a poetry magazine, The Fifties (later renamed, as decades went by, The Sixties and The Seventies). In it he spoofed academic critics, urged American poets to open their work to dream and surrealism, and introduced in translation the work of important poets of Europe and Latin America. Bly has vitally influenced the work of James Wright, Donald Hall, and many younger poets. His readings, in which he sometimes chants and dons primitive masks, have drawn throngs. In the 1960s he organized (with David Ray) American Writers Against the Vietnam War, and over the years has championed many causes, usually pacifist and antinuclear. Lately he has been leading retreats for men, trying to help them understand their male natures.

Gwendolyn Brooks

Gwendolyn Brooks, born in 1917 in Topeka, Kansas, moved early in life to Chicago's South Side, whose people she has commemorated in her poetry and in a novel, Maud Martha (1953). Recipient of the Pulitzer prize for poetry in 1950, for Annie Allen, Brooks has long been recognized as a leading voice in modern American letters. She has combined several teaching positions with raising two children. Since 1967, when she took part in a conference for black writers at Fisk University and was impressed with young black poets' views, she has increasingly been an activist, teaching teen-age black writers in Chicago and addressing her work especially to black audiences. Instead of continuing to publish with a mainstream New York publishing house, she switched her work to Broadside, a small literary press in Detroit founded by black poet Dudley Randall. Her memoir Report from Part One (1972) discusses her altered outlook. In 1985 she was named Consultant in Poetry to the Library of Congress. Her goals in life, she has declared, are "to be clean of heart, clear of mind, and claiming of what is right and just."

Robert Browning

Robert Browning (1812 – 1889), born in a suburb of London, was educated mainly in his father's six-thousand-volume library. With Pauline (1833), he began to print his poetry. After the death of his wife Elizabeth Barrett Browning, with whom he had lived in Italy, he returned to England to become (Henry James wrote) an "accomplished, saturated, sane, sound man of the London world." There, as he neared sixty, he enjoyed late but loud applause and the adulation of the Browning Society: faithful readers whose local groups met over their teacups to explicate him. Readers have most greatly favored Browning's story-poems in a form he perfected, the dramatic monologue — such as "My Last Duchess" and "Soliloquy of the Spanish Cloister" — in which he brings to life persons from the past (some of them famous), has them speak their inmost thoughts and reveal their characters. His masterpiece, *The Ring and the Book* (1868 – 69), is a long narrative poem in twelve monologues, based on a seventeenth-century Roman murder trial. Browning also wrote several plays, among them *A Blot in the 'Scutcheon* (1842). Through the praise and emulation of his later admirers Ezra Pound and T. S. Eliot, Browning has profoundly affected modern poetry. A formal experimenter, he speaks to us in energetic, punchy words — and like many later poets he introduces learning into his poems without apology. More important, Browning is among the great yea-sayers in English poetry: an affirmer and celebrant of life.

Robert Burns

Robert Burns (1759 – 1796), the preeminent poet of Scotland, was born in a two-room farm cottage in Alloway, a hamlet on the River Doon, the son of a farmer who worked himself to death. For most of his days Burns too struggled to farm poor soil. Though his schooling lasted only three years, he eagerly read Shakespeare and Pope as a boy and let poetry pour from his own pen. Only in 1786, when he felt he needed money to emigrate to Jamaica, did he publish his *Poems, Chiefly in the Scottish Dialect,* depicting Scottish rural life with warm humor, tender compassion, and rugged exuberance. The book scored an immediate hit and Burns remained in Scotland for the rest of his days. After Edinburgh's stylish society, which had lionized him for a time, let him drop, he returned to his plough, married Jean Armour (who earlier had borne him two sets of twins), and continued to farm until 1791, when he retired to the easier life of a tax official. But worn from toil, hardship, and poverty, Burns died at thirty-seven. Among his legacies are songs, such as "Flow Gently, Sweet Afton," "Comin' Through the Rye," and a song still heard in this country each New Year's eve, "Auld Lang Syne." Like Hugh MacDiarmid, Burns wrote poetry in both standard English and Scots dialect — in the latter whenever, as in "The Jolly Beggars" and "Address to the Unco Guid," he expressed defiantly unconventional views.

Thomas Campion

Thomas Campion (1567 – 1620), Elizabethan courtier, physician, musician, and poet, was the author of several books of solo songs with lute accompaniment, much admired for their masterly unity of words and music. In 1602

Campion wrote a tract, *Observations in the Art of English Poesy*, in which he argued in favor of writing quantitative verse in English, after the example of the ancient Greek and Latin poets. "Rose-cheeked Laura" was apparently written to illustrate his theories. In the same tract, he opposed the writing of any more poetry in rime and traditional English meters — in which, however, he excelled.

Samuel Taylor Coleridge

Samuel Taylor Coleridge (1772–1834) was born in Devonshire, England, a clergyman's thirteenth child. With poet Robert Southey, a fellow student at Cambridge University, he once planned to go to the United States and found a utopian community, but the scheme was never fulfilled. A brilliant talker and sometime professional lecturer, Coleridge wrote ably on philosophy and religion as well as on literature. As a young man, he collaborated with William Wordsworth on the influential *Lyrical Ballads* (1798), a milestone of English Romantic poetry. Among Coleridge's best-known poems are "The Rime of the Ancient Mariner," "Cristabel," and "Kubla Khan"—ornate poems of the exotic and supernatural. His *Biographia Literaria* (1817) combines literary criticism with autobiography, and sets forth views of poetry and the imagination (see page 940) heavily indebted to German idealist philosophy. Long troubled by an addiction to opium, Coleridge went to London in 1816 to live in the household of Dr. James Gilman, under whose care he passed the rest of his days.

E. E. Cummings

E[dward] E[stlin] Cummings (1894 – 1962) was born in Cambridge, Massachusetts, the son of a minister. As a young man at Harvard, he studied Greek and Latin. In World War I, while serving as an ambulance driver, he was mistakenly arrested and confined to a French prison — an experience that gave rise to a novel filled with vivid portraits of his fellow prisoners, *The Enormous Room* (1922). Off and on throughout the 1920s, Cummings lived in Paris. In *Eimi* (1933) he scathingly and satirically reported on a trip to the Soviet Union. Although many of his lyric poems revel in typographical experiment, in theme and sentiment they are often more conventional than they appear. Besides poetry Cummings wrote essays, plays including *Him* (1927) and *Santa Claus* (1946), and the ballet *Tom* (1935), and produced substantial work as a painter and a graphic artist. Throughout his career, he upheld simple themes: love is good, pomp is silly, one individual is worth a thousand faceless societies.

J. V. Cunningham

J[ames] V[incent] Cunningham (1911 – 1985) was born in Maryland, but spent his early life in Montana. A Shakespeare scholar with a Stanford Ph.D., Cunningham taught English at Brandeis for many years (1953 – 80) and for eight years served as chairman of the department. A reader of Latin and Greek, he became the modern master of the terse, pithy English verse epigram in the classical manner. All his poems have a similar brevity, firm control, and a cold, hardboiled manner. "Poetry is what looks like poetry, what sounds like poetry," he stated. "It is metrical composition." His relatively slim *Collected Poems and Epigrams* (1971) gathers most of his work in verse; his *Collected Essays* (1976), most of his work in prose, including an earlier study, *Woe or Wonder: The Emotional Effect of Shakespearean Tragedy*. In a late critical work, *Dickinson: Lyric and Legend* (1980), Cunningham took a withering look at the bard of Amherst.

Emily Dickinson

Emily Dickinson (1830 – 1886) passed nearly all her life in her family home in Amherst, Massachusetts. Her father was a prominent lawyer and for a time a United States congressman. One trip to Washington, D.C. and a short, unhappy period as a college student at New England Female Seminary (later Mount Holyoke) were the extent of her distant travels, and as the years passed Dickinson withdrew from town activities and retired into deeper seclusion. Though she wrote more than a thousand poems, she published only seven. The extent of her work was known only after her death, when her manuscripts were discovered in a trunk in the homestead attic, stitched into little booklets and peppered with an idiosyncratic system of punctuation. From 1890 until midcentury, nine posthumous collections of her poems were assembled by friends and relatives, some of whom rewrote her work to make it more conventional. Thomas H. Johnson's three-volume edition of the *Poems* (1955) established a better text. In relatively few and simple forms clearly indebted to the hymns she heard in church, Dickinson succeeded in being a true visionary and a poet of colossal originality.

Emanuel di Pasquale

Emanuel di Pasquale, born in Sicily in 1943, emigrated to America with his mother after his father died. Although he did not learn English until he was sixteen, he began to write poetry at an early age and is now an English professor at Middlesex Community College in New Jersey. For years, di Pasquale has published poetry in *The Nation, New York Times, Sewanee Review,* and other places, but has only recently brought out a first collection, *Genesis* (1989). Lately, he has become known for his poems for children, which appear in several anthologies.

John Donne

John Donne (1572 – 1631), English poet and divine, wrote his subtle, worldly love lyrics as a young man in the court of Queen Elizabeth I. At the time, he came to be known in London as (wrote his contemporary, Richard Baker) "a great visitor of ladies, a great frequenter of plays, a great writer of conceited verses." The poems of his *Songs and Sonnets* were first circulated in manuscript, for in his lifetime Donne printed little. When in 1601 he married without the consent of his bride's father, he was dismissed from his secretarial post at court. For several years he endured poverty. His longer poems, *The First Anniversary* and *The Second Anniversary* (1611, 1612), suffused with gloom, see the order of the universe shaken by science and doubt. In 1615 Donne — apparently with some reluctance, for he had been raised a Catholic — became a priest of the Anglican church. From 1621 until he died he was dean of St. Paul's Cathedral in London, where he preached sermons known for their eloquence. His "Holy Sonnets" date from later life. Almost forgotten for two centuries, Donne's work has had much influence in our time. H. J. C. Grierson brought out a great scholarly edition of it in 1912; shortly thereafter it was championed by T. S. Eliot.

T. S. Eliot

T[homas] S[tearns] Eliot (1888 – 1965) was born of a New England family who had moved to St. Louis. After study at Harvard, Eliot emigrated to London, became a bank clerk and later an influential editor for the publishing house of Faber. In 1927 he became a British citizen and joined the Church of England. During the fire bombings of London in World War II, he served as an air raid warden. Although Eliot strove to keep his private life private, a recent biographer, Peter Ackroyd in *T. S. Eliot* (1984), throws light upon his troubled early marriage. Early poems such as "The Love Song of J. Alfred Prufrock" (1917) and *The Waste Land* (1922), an allusive and seemingly disconnected complaint about the sterility of contemporary city life, enormously influenced young poets. Eliot was mainly responsible for bringing French Symbolism into English poetry, and as a critic he helped revive interest in John Donne and other Metaphysical poets. In an early essay, "Tradition and the Individual Talent" (1919), he finds a necessary continuity in Western civilization. *Four Quartets*, completed in 1943, was Eliot's last major work of poetry: an attempt to structure a long thematic poem like a work of music. In later years he devoted himself to writing verse plays for the London stage; the best received was *The Cocktail Party* (1950), in which Alec Guinness played a psychiatrist. In 1948 Eliot received the Nobel Prize for Literature.

Robert Frost

Robert Frost (1874 – 1963), though born in San Francisco, came to be popularly known as a spokesman of rural New England. In periods of farming, teaching school, and raising chickens and writing for poultry journals, Frost struggled until his late thirties to support his family and to publish his poems, with little success. Moving to England to write and farm in 1912 – 15, he had his first book published in London: *A Boy's Will* (1913). Returning to America, he settled in New Hampshire, later teaching for many years (in a casual way) at Amherst College in Massachusetts. Audiences responded warmly to the poet's public readings; he was awarded four Pulitzer prizes. In late years the white-haired Frost became a sort of elder statesman and poet laureate of the John F. Kennedy administration: invited to read a poem at President Kennedy's inauguration, dispatched to Russia as a cultural emissary. Frost is sometimes admired for putting colloquial Yankee speech into poetry — and he did, but more essentially he mastered the art of laying conversational American speech along a metrical line. In a three-volume biography (1966 – 76), Lawrance Thompson made Frost out to be an overweening egotist who tormented his family, and we are only now coming around again to seeing him as more than that.

Thomas Gray

Thomas Gray (1716 – 1771), author of the most often quoted poem in English, was born in London into a middle-class home (his father was a scrivener, his mother kept a hat shop). He was the only one of twelve children to survive infancy. He attended Eton and later Cambridge University, where he studied for four years but did not take a degree. After a tour of Europe with his schoolmate Horace Walpole (the first Gothic novelist) and a short sojourn with his mother in the village of Stoke Poges, Gray returned to Cambridge to spend the rest of his life in seclusion as a sort of perpetual graduate student. He stayed around the university so long and became so widely learned in architecture, heraldry, botany, Greek, Old Norse, and other matters that in 1768, at fifty-two, he was appointed Regius Professor of History. So retiring was Gray that he first published his "Elegy in a Country Churchyard" anonymously — and only when friends browbeat him into printing it. He seems to have suffered from a constitutional lack of energy. He dreaded being known, and when the post of poet laureate was offered him, he rejected it. A dilettante, Gray considered himself an amateur in whatever he did. Poetry was only one of his interests, but in his "Elegy" and his Pindaric odes "The Bard" and "The Progress of Poesy," he spurred English poetry to break away from neoclassicism and move toward plainer speech, more various forms, infatuation with the colorful, primitive Old English past, and love of nature and countryside. Gray is buried in Stoke Poges, in the churchyard for which we remember him.

H. D. (Hilda Doolittle)

Hilda Doolittle (1886 – 1961), daughter of a Moravian mother and a professor of mathematics and astronomy, spent her first eight years in Bethlehem, Pennsylvania. At Bryn Mawr, she failed English and suffered a nervous collapse. By 1911, she had become a confirmed expatriate, living in London. At one time she was engaged to Ezra Pound, who submitted her early poems to Harriet Monroe's magazine *Poetry* and signed them "H. D. Imagiste." In 1913, she married poet and translator Richard Aldington, and in 1916 published *Sea Change*, her first book of poems. During World War I, H. D. went through a marital breakup and a number of misfortunes recalled in her novel *Palimpsest* (1926). Alone and in poor health, she was rescued by Winifred Ellerman, a writer signing herself Bryher, who adopted the poet's daughter by Cecil Gray and befriended H. D. for life. During 1933 and 1934, H. D. was a patient of Sigmund Freud, an experience she recalls in *Tribute to Freud* (1956). After World War II, the poet moved to Switzerland. Her last works of poetry were epic-long: *Trilogy* (1944 – 46) and the dramatic monologue *Helen in Egypt* (1961). Her earlier poems are available in *Collected Poems 1912 – 1944* (1983), edited by Louis L. Martz. In 1960, back in the United States for the last time, H. D. was given the American Academy of Arts and Letters Award of Merit for Poetry.

Thomas Hardy

Thomas Hardy (1840 – 1928) was both a major Victorian novelist and a great poet of the twentieth century. After his novel *Jude the Obscure* (1896) was trounced by critics who objected to its dismal morbidity, Hardy, who by then had made a modest fortune from his fiction, switched exclusively to his first love, poetry. Hardy was born in the English county of Dorsetshire ("Wessex" in his fiction and poetry), and as a young man worked as an architect. Determined to be a novelist, he first won success with *Far from the Madding Crowd* (1874), followed by *The Return of the Native* (1878), *The Mayor of Casterbridge* (1886), and his masterpiece *Tess of the D'Urbervilles* (1891). After the death of his first wife Emma, with whom he appears to have had had a rather cold and troubled relationship, Hardy was inspired to write a great spate of love poems in her memory. In old age he wrote a two-volume autobiography and charged his second wife, Florence, to publish it after his death under her own name. In both fiction and poetry, Hardy's view of the universe is somber: God appears to have forgotten us, and happiness usually arrives too late. *The Dynasts* (1903 – 08), a long epic poem, makes amused gods sneer down on the Napoleonic wars. Many modern poets have credited Hardy with teaching them a good deal, probably about irony and the use of spoken language, among them W. H. Auden, Philip Larkin, Dylan Thomas, and W. D. Snodgrass.

James Hayford

James Hayford has lived most of his life in Vermont: born in Montpelier in 1913, he now makes his home in Orleans, near the Canadian border. On his graduation from Amherst, he received a Robert Frost Fellowship, given him by the elder poet himself. Hayford has earned a living mainly as a teacher of English, history, and music; he has also worked as a carpenter, raised goats, and edited textbooks. As choirmaster for the Orleans Federated Church, Hayford has composed music for poems by Frost, Herbert, and himself. His work has appeared in *Harper's, The New Yorker,* and other magazines. The poet Robert Francis, an admirer of his work, published his collection *Processional with Wheelbarrow* in 1970; later, Hayford self-published his own collections. Recently the New England Press of Shelburne, Vermont, has brought out his children's novel *Gridley Firing* (1987) with woodcuts by Mary Azarian, and his *Star in the Shed Window: Collected Poems* (1989).

Seamus Heaney

Seamus Heaney, the best-known living Irish poet, was born on a farm in County Derry, Northern Ireland, in 1939. He taught at Queens University, Belfast, before leaving Northern Ireland in 1972 to make his home in Dublin. A guest lecturer at the University of California in Berkeley during the 1971 – 1972 academic year, he now divides his time between Dublin and America, where he teaches at Harvard. Among his recent books of verse are *Station Island* (1985) and *The Haw Lantern* (1987). Rich with images of love and loss, Heaney's poetry draws inventively on the history of Ireland and the Irish from ancient times to the violent present.

George Herbert

George Herbert (1593 – 1633), English devotional poet, the son of an aristocratic family, began writing poems as an undergraduate at Cambridge University. After dabbling for a time in worldly affairs, he entered the priesthood of the Church of England, to live out his days in a country parish. Herbert's poems have many references to music; according to his contemporary John Aubrey, he "had a very good hand on the lute, and set [to music] his own lyrics and sacred poems." Herbert did not publish his poems in his lifetime, but after his death friends collected them in *The Temple* (1633). The book is said to have stimulated Henry Vaughan to follow in Herbert's footsteps as a poet. Herbert makes the religious experience personal, definite, and familiar. For his use of startling "metaphysical" figures of speech, he has been compared with John Donne; but a rare sweetness and plain-spokenness make him unique among poets in English.

Robert Herrick

Robert Herrick (1591 – 1674), after serving as a goldsmith's apprentice, entered Cambridge University at twenty-two, then a late age. For nine years he seems to have lived in London, consorting with a group of poets and wits whose chief was Ben Jonson. In 1629 he became parish priest in Dean Prior, in rural Devonshire, where he lived out his days, sometimes chafing about the boorishness of his parishioners. When in 1647 the Puritans temporarily ousted him from his pulpit, Herrick returned to London. There at fifty-six he brought out his first book, *Noble Numbers* (1647), pious poems; then reprinted them together with five times as many sportive, secular poems in *Hesperides* (1648). Unluckily, the books came too late to cause a stir, Herrick's early fame as a poet having withered and the vogue for chiseled classical lyrics having gone by. Like his master Jonson, Herrick writes songlike poems inspired by Greek and Latin pastoral (or shepherd-and-shepherdess) poetry. We go to him not for profound ideas, but for fresh, tough speech and resonant music. Herrick, who remained a bachelor clergyman, probably imagined the mistresses he praised. He declared in *Hesperides,* "To his book's end this last line he'd have placed: / Jocund his Muse was, but his life was chaste."

Garrett Hongo

Garrett Hongo was born of Japanese ancestry in Volcano, Hawaii, in 1951, and grew up in Oahu and Los Angeles. He earned a B.A. degree at Pomona College and, after doing graduate work in Japanese at the University of Michigan, received an M.F.A. degree from the University of California, Irvine. Hongo has taught at the University of Southern California, the University of California, Irvine, and, most recently, at the University of Missouri, Columbia. His books of poetry include *Yellow Light* (1982) and *The River of Heaven* (1988), which won the Lamont Poetry Prize of the Academy of American Poets.

Gerard Manley Hopkins

Gerard Manley Hopkins (1844 – 1889), born in Essex, England, was, like Emily Dickinson, a major poet not known until our century. At twenty, a student at Oxford, he was converted to Roman Catholicism and received into that church by Cardinal Newman. Ordained a Jesuit, Hopkins at first served as parish priest and teacher in working-class sections of large cities (London, Glasgow, Liverpool, Manchester), where poverty and suffering distressed him. But his sermons were reportedly so strange (in one, he likened the church to a cow we milk and whose moo we follow) that his superiors removed him from public view, making him Professor of Greek at University College, Dublin. He died of typhoid fever at forty-four. Nearly thirty years after Hopkins's death, his friend Robert Bridges published his *Poems* (1918), having thought them too demanding for earlier readers. That much of Hopkins's work sounds odd to us may be due to the poet's admiration for Old English, with its gutsy monosyllables, and for Welsh poetry, rich in patterns of sound. Hopkins developed his own theory of versification: "sprung rhythm" — in brief, a kind of accentual verse. Though on entering the priesthood he had renounced poetry, he welcomed the suggestion of a superior that he contribute to a Jesuit magazine a poem on the drowning of five Franciscan nuns. The result, "The Wreck of the *Deutschland*," received a rejection slip. This challenging poem has been called "the dragon guarding the door to Hopkins's poetry," but most readers have gone in by the back door of his more quickly accessible nature poems. In these, the sensuous world bursts forth in irrepressible testimony to its Maker's glory.

A. E. Housman

A. E. Housman (1859 – 1936), English poet and professor of Latin, was born in a village in rural Shropshire, England. Although as a student at Oxford he distinguished himself as a promising scholar of the classics, he failed his exams, apparently because of some inner crisis precipitated by his love for a fellow male student. Determined to overcome this setback, Housman, while working as a clerk in the British Patent Office, at night wrote scholarly articles. Within ten years these academic writings, bristling with cold sarcasms and scathing putdowns of rival scholars, had won him such high repute that he was invited to be Professor of Latin at the University of London. Later he stepped up to Cambridge University, to spend the rest of his days living a retiring academic life befitting his shy temperament. Though Housman published only two slim collections of poems — the instantly and enormously popular *A Shropshire Lad* (1898) and the conclusively titled *Last Poems* (1922) — his place as a minor master of the English lyric seems unshakable. Like many Latin poets he admired, he insists in well-turned lines that life is short and comes to a bad end.

Langston Hughes

Langston Hughes (1902 – 1967), who dropped his first name, James, was born in Joplin, Missouri. As a high school senior in Cleveland, he wrote a poem still often reprinted, "The Negro Speaks of Rivers." When a young man, Hughes worked as a merchant seaman, visited Africa, and lived for a time in Rome and Paris. While working as a busboy at a Washington, D.C., hotel, he showed his poems to hotel guest Vachel Lindsay, a poet then celebrated, and Lindsay urged them on a publisher. *The Weary Blues* (1926) earned him a considerable reputation. Hughes's work in poetry won him a scholarship to Lincoln University, from which he was graduated in 1929. He became a major figure in the Harlem Renaissance of the 1920s and early 1930s — a period when that district of New York City became a lively center for black writers, artists, and musicians. A versatile writer and teacher, Hughes, one of the first practicing poets to teach poetry writing in elementary schools, was also among the few poets to earn a living by giving readings and lecturing. Among his other works are novels, stories, plays, song lyrics, children's books, memoirs, translations, and essays reporting conversations with a Harlem dweller called Simple, a streetwise philosopher. *A Langston Hughes Reader* (1958) gives some idea of his richness and variety.

Randall Jarrell

Randall Jarrell (1914 – 1965) was born in Nashville, Tennessee, and served as a private in the army air force in World War II, an experience that gave rise to several of his best early poems. Much of his life was spent in academe. At Vanderbilt, a psychology major, he studied literature with poet-critic John Crowe Ransom, who changed the direction of Jarrell's career. When Ransom moved to Kenyon College, Jarrell followed as an English instructor. At Kenyon, he formed another lifelong friendship: with a student who was to become a distinguished poet, Robert Lowell. Later Jarrell taught at the University of Texas, Sarah Lawrence, Princeton, Illinois, and for many years (1947 – 65) at the Woman's College of the University of North Carolina (now the U.N.C., Greensboro). His one novel, *Pictures from an Institution* (1954), is a satire set on a campus. As poetry editor for *The Nation* in the mid-1940s, Jarrell drew attention for his witty, astute, outspoken reviews of poetry. *Poetry and the Age* (1953) includes especially brilliant essays on Robert Frost and Wallace Stevens. Jarrell, who loved the German language, translated Goethe's *Faust* (Part I) and some of the Grimm fairy tales. In late years he wrote four books for children (with beautiful drawings by Maurice Sendak) including *The Bat Poet* (1964) and the posthumous *Fly by Night* (1976).

Ben Jonson

Ben Jonson (1573? – 1637), posthumous son of a Scottish minister, was a native Londoner. As a boy he received a firm grounding in Latin and Greek at

Westminster School, but instead of enrolling in a university, took up bricklaying, then served as a soldier in Flanders. Home from the wars, he married and became an actor and playwright in London. Although a coolly rational classicist by persuasion, Jonson seems to have been an outspoken hothead, given to quarrels and brawls. In 1598 he killed a fellow actor in a duel and escaped the gallows only by claiming an ancient law that forbade hanging anyone who could read. From about 1606, Jonson frequented the Mermaid Tavern in London's Fleet Street, a favorite hangout of writers and actors. There, on the first Friday of each month, he presided over famed literary discussions; according to one report, his friend Shakespeare would take part at times and match wits with him. Later changing pubs (to the Devil and St. Dunstan), Jonson and his circle became known as the "Tribe of Ben"; Thomas Carew and Robert Herrick were younger members. Later Jonson became the leading writer of masks, elaborate plays with music and dancing produced at court. As a poet Jonson, in his precise Latinate lyrics, odes, and epigrams, helped get rid of worn-out Petrarchan conventions (those Shakespeare mocks in "My mistress' eyes are nothing like the sun"). As a playwright, he excelled; his comedies, especially *Volpone, or The Fox* (1606) and *The Alchemist* (1610), are among the crown jewels of the English stage.

John Keats

John Keats (1795 – 1821), son of a London stable keeper, studied to become a physician and served as a surgeon's apprentice before deciding on poetry as a career. In 1817 he published his first book, *Poems,* including "On First Looking into Chapman's Homer." Despite critics' hostility to his narrative poem *Endymion* (1818), Keats persisted. In 1818 he fell in love with sixteen-year-old Fanny Brawne, but, stricken with tuberculosis, postponed plans for marriage. In 1820, shortly after publication of his third and last book, Keats went to Italy in hopes of regaining his health, but his poetry soon slowed to a stop. In the following year, at twenty-five, he died in Rome and was buried there beneath the epitaph he wrote for himself: "Here lies one whose name was writ in water." His name, however, has continued to endure. No English poet wrote poems richer in sensuous imagery (as in his great odes, among them "Ode on Melancholy" and "To Autumn"), nor quite so beautifully reimagined the Middle Ages (in poems such as "La Belle Dame sans Merci" and "The Eve of St. Agnes"). He wrote several of the finest sonnets in the language, an unfinished epic of great interest, *Hyperion,* hilarious light verse, and scores of superb letters.

Philip Larkin

Philip Larkin (1922 – 1985), born in Coventry, England, has been called the most influential British poet since World War II. After studies at Oxford, he drifted into being a librarian, and for many years was head librarian for the University of Hull. Early in his career Larkin wrote two novels, *Jill* (1946) and *A Girl in Winter* (1947). He also reviewed jazz recordings for a London newspaper. A self-declared foe of modernism in music, art, and literature, he published only four slim volumes of poems, traditional in form. The earliest collection was heavily indebted to Yeats: *The North Ship* (1945, reissued in 1966 with a preface making fun of it). With *The Less Deceived* (1955), Larkin hit his characteristic stride, writing most of the poems in the voice of a tough-minded, disillusioned, self-deprecating man facing a dreary urban landscape of quiet frustration. This voice drew an immediate response from readers in postwar England.

D. H. Lawrence

David Herbert Lawrence (1885 – 1930) was born in Nottinghamshire, England, child of a coalminer and a schoolteacher who hated her husband's toil and vowed that her son should escape it. He took up fiction writing, attaining early success. During World War I, Lawrence and his wife were unjustly suspected of treason (he because of his pacifism, she because of her aristocratic German birth). After the armistice they left England and, seeking a climate healthier for Lawrence, who suffered from tuberculosis, wandered in Italy, France, Australia, Mexico, and the American Southwest. Lawrence is an impassioned spokesman for our unconscious, instinctive natures, which we moderns (he argues) have neglected in favor of our overweening intellects. In *Lady Chatterley's Lover* (1928), he strove to restore explicit sexuality to English fiction. The book, which today seems tame and repetitious, was long banned in Britain and the United States. Deeper Lawrence novels include *Sons and Lovers* (1913), a veiled account of his breaking away from his fiercely possessive mother; *The Rainbow* (1915); *Women in Love* (1921); and *The Plumed Serpent* (1926), about a revival of pagan religion in Mexico. Besides fiction, Lawrence left a rich legacy of poetry, essays, criticism (*Studies in Classic American Literature*, 1923, is especially shrewd and funny), and travel writing. Lawrence exerted deep influence on others, both by the message in his work and by his personal magnetism.

Denise Levertov

Denise Levertov was born in 1923 in Essex, England, daughter of a Welsh mother and a Russian Jewish-born priest of the Anglican church. She was educated at home, reading in her father's library. She served as a nurse in World War II. In 1947 she married an American novelist, Mitchell Goodman, and in the following year came to the United States. Her first book, published in England, had observed traditional poetic conventions (including rime and meter), but in America she discovered the work of William Carlos Williams and other open-form poets, and began to write in a different, freer mode. With

Robert Creeley and others of the Black Mountain group, she has exerted much influence among younger poets. Her critical essays have been collected in *The Poet in the World* (1973) and *Light up the Cave* (1981). Levertov has been a tireless political activist, prominent in peace movements of the 1960s, 1970s, and 1980s. She now makes her home in Somerville, Massachusetts, and recently has been teaching poetry writing at Stanford on one coast and at Brandeis on the other.

Robert Lowell

Robert Lowell (1917 – 1977), born in Boston, came from a famous New England family that included three distinguished poets: James Russell, Maria, and Amy. He attended Harvard, then on the advice of his psychiatrist transferred to Kenyon, where he studied with poet-critics John Crowe Ransom and Randall Jarrell. During World War II he served time in a federal prison for resisting the draft. Lowell's early poems in *Lord Weary's Castle* (1946) were violent in imagery and tightly traditional in form. With the deliberately looser *Life Studies* (1959), he showed that he had learned from William Carlos Williams and the Beat poets, and his work became more open in form, more colloquial in speech, and more direct in its use of his own experience. Some of these poems were labeled "confessional poetry." As "Skunk Hour" tells us, Lowell's mind was sometimes "not right"; he suffered from recurrent manic depression that required him to spend periods in a hospital. Besides poetry, he wrote plays based on stories by Hawthorne and Melville: *The Old Glory* (1964, enlarged edition 1968) — as well as English versions of the *Phaedra* of Racine (1961) and the *Prometheus Bound* of Aeschylus (1969). Lowell was also a remarkable critic of poetry.

Edna St. Vincent Millay

Edna St. Vincent Millay (1892 – 1950), born in Rockland, Maine, was the eldest of three daughters. When she was twelve, her father deserted the family. At twenty, she had already published "Renascence," one of her most celebrated poems. In 1917, she was graduated from Vassar College and settled in Greenwich Village, where she became as famous for her vivacious personality, her bohemian life-style, her acting and playwriting, and her femininism, as for her verse. Even as she wrote *The Harp Weaver*, a serious volume of verse that won her a Pulitzer Prize in 1923, Millay did hack writing to pay her bills. Among other work for which she is known are verse dramas such as *Aria da Capo* (1920) and the sonnet cycle *Fatal Interview* (1931). In 1923, she married Eugen Jan Boissevain, Dutch businessman and widower of feminist Inez Milholland. In 1927, Millay's political activism expressed itself in poems about Sacco and Vanzetti, two anarchists accused of murder, and involved her in an unsuccessful campaign to prevent their execution. Though she kept writing poetry well into the 1940s and received several honorary degrees, her reputation waned. Darkened by a nervous breakdown in 1944 and the poet's growing sense that the public had deserted her, Millay's life ended with a heart attack.

John Milton

John Milton (1608 – 1674), author of *Paradise Lost*, the greatest English epic, was born in London, the son of a scrivener who composed music. His mother early began schooling him to be a minister. He studied zealously. As he later recalled: "From my twelfth year I scarcely ever went to bed before midnight, which was the first cause of injury to my eyes." After he received his B.A. from Cambridge University in 1629, his father supported him through eight years of further study. "Lycidas" (1638), a poem of this period, shows his deepening seriousness about religion and his growing resentment of corruptions in the church, which were to lead him to the Puritan cause. Milton wrote much prose in the service of causes. In *Areopagitica* (1644), he argues for freedom of the press and opposes the strict censorship that had been imposed by Parliament. His unhappy marriage to Mary Powell led him to write tracts in favor of divorce. When Oliver Cromwell and the Puritans ousted King Charles and declared England a commonwealth, Milton's writings were remembered, and earned him a post as Cromwell's foreign secretary. His eyesight strained by years of hard study, Milton went blind and had to dictate his correspondence (in Latin) to clerks, one of whom was fellow poet Andrew Marvell. With the Restoration of Charles II in 1660, Milton's world came crashing down. In retirement, at last he turned to a project he had planned as a young man: his major heroic poem, *Paradise Lost* (1667), about Satan's rebellion and the Fall of Adam and Eve. This epic was followed by *Paradise Regained* (1671) and a verse drama modeled on a Greek tragedy, *Samson Agonistes* (1671).

Marianne Moore

Marianne Moore (1887 – 1972), whose poems earned praise from fellow poets as dissimilar as William Carlos Williams and T.S. Eliot, was born in Kirkwood, Missouri, a suburb of St. Louis. Her father abandoned the family in 1894, and Moore moved to Pennsylvania. In 1909, she was graduated from Bryn Mawr, where a classmate was the poet H.D. For a time, Moore taught business courses at the U.S. Indian School in Carlisle, Pennsylvania, where the athlete Jim Thorpe was among her students. By 1915, her poems — witty, satirical, intellectual, disruptive, and innovative — had begun to appear in *Poetry* magazine. Until her mother died in 1947, Moore, a dutiful daughter, lived with her in Brooklyn, supporting herself by a series of conventional jobs. From 1925 to 1929 she edited *The Dial*, a literary magazine in whose pages she published many of the best poets of her day. Besides poems, Moore wrote essays, reviews, and translations including *The Fables of La Fontaine* (1945). For her *Collected Poems* (1951), she won a Pulitzer Prize, the Bollingen Prize, and a National Book Award; her *Complete Poems* appeared in 1967. Late in life, Moore became a media figure for her fondness for the Brooklyn Dodgers and her penchant for three-cornered hats. She stayed in Brooklyn, writing and rewriting, through an active and vigorous old age.

Lorine Niedecker

Lorine Niedecker (1903 – 1970) spent nearly all her life on Blackhawk Island near Fort Atkinson, Wisconsin, where her father worked as a carp fisherman. After two years at Beloit College, she returned home to care for her ailing mother. Following a brief marriage in 1928, Niedecker held jobs as proofreader, librarian's helper, and cleaning worker in a hospital. After her marriage in 1963 she lived in Milwaukee, but on her husband's retirement the couple moved into a house they had built by the Rock River, and the poet returned to her native grounds. Although she lived an outwardly quiet life remote from publishing centers, Niedecker read widely and maintained a vigorous life of the mind. In the early 1930s she struck up a correspondence with poet and teacher Louis Zukofsky, who encouraged her poetry. In the 1950s poet Cid Corman printed her work in his avant garde little magazine *Origin*. During her lifetime she published sparingly, but *From This Condensery: The Complete Writing of Lorine Niedecker* (1985) contains a large body of poems, as well as critical essays, experimental prose, and five radio plays. Her life and work are the subject of Kristine Thatcher's play *Niedecker*, given an off-Broadway production in 1989.

John Frederick Nims

John Frederick Nims, born in 1913 in Muskegon, Michigan, has had a distinguished career as poet and translator, teacher and editor. He has taught at Florida, Illinois (Urbana and Chicago), Missouri, Notre Dame, Toronto, and other universities, and has held visiting professorships at Harvard and in Florence, Milan, and Madrid. The poems in his first book *The Iron Pastoral* (1947) deal wittily with jukeboxes, penny arcades, poolrooms, and other features of the contemporary scene. In *Of Flesh and Bone* (1967) Nims shows his mastery of the epigram. His *Selected Poems* appeared in 1982. A translator of poetry from languages as varied as classical Greek, Catalan, and Galacian, Nims has splendidly rendered into English *The Poems of St. John of the Cross* (1959, revised edition 1968). For several years (1978 – 85) he was editor of *Poetry* magazine. He is the author of an introduction to poetry, *Western Wind*, and editor of *The Harper Anthology of Poetry* (1981).

Wilfred Owen

Wilfred Owen (1893 – 1918) was, like A. E. Housman, a native of Shropshire, England. He attended London University and for a time served as lay assistant to a minister, helping the sick and poor. In 1916, during World War I, he enlisted in the British army, became a company commander, and in less than two years wrote all his famous antiwar poems of life in the trenches. The army seems suddenly to have changed Owen from a competent minor poet with little to say into a powerful voice of pacifism. At age twenty-five, while trying to get his men across a canal under enemy fire on the French front, he was killed in action only a week before the war ended. Though Owen published only four poems, after his death a collection of his work was edited by another front-line war poet, Siegfried Sassoon (1920). Owen is preeminent among English poets who wrote of that conflict, and the reputation of his work has continued to grow.

Linda Pastan

Linda Pastan was born Linda Olenik in New York in 1932. After her graduation from Radcliffe, she took two master's degrees at Simmons (M.L.S.) and Brandeis (M.A.). She married in 1953 and has a daughter and two sons. Her first book, A Perfect Circle of Sun (1971), established her as an up-and-comer; Selected Poems appeared in 1979, confirming her accomplishment. Her subtle, often powerful poems are exceptionally clear and accessible.

Sylvia Plath

Sylvia Plath (1932 – 1963), one of the most remarkable poets in English of the past half-century, was born in Boston, the daughter of German immigrants who both taught at Boston University. The death of her father when the poet was eight came as a trauma from which she seems never quite to have recovered. As a scholarship-winning student at Smith College, Plath revealed early promise, and her work received early publication. Like Esther Greenwood, protagonist of her one novel The Bell Jar (1963), Plath won a student contest that sent her to work in New York for a national magazine, and struggled with a year-long siege of mental illness for which she underwent shock treatments. Returning to Smith, she was graduated with top honors. Later she studied at Cambridge University in England, where she met and in 1956 married the poet Ted Hughes. Estranged from her husband, she died a suicide in London, leaving two children and, in manuscript, the intense, powerful poems that went into her posthumous, highly acclaimed collection, Ariel (1965).

Alexander Pope

Alexander Pope (1688 – 1744), the leading English poet of the early eighteenth century, was born in London, son of a Roman Catholic linen merchant. A sickly, stunted, pockmarked child, he suffered from weak health and continual exhaustion throughout his life, and was said to have worn padded clothes to disguise his misshapen frame. Pope early excelled as a poet, composing his *Pastorals* (1709) at age sixteen. His rimed translations of the *Iliad* (1720) and the *Odyssey* (1725 – 26) and his edition of Shakespeare (1725), bestsellers in their day, made him independently wealthy, and he was able to buy an estate at Twickenham and live in style. Pope did not write an epic, but instead translated epics and wrote great mock epics: *The Rape of the Lock* (1714), in which he voices compassion for women transformed into wives, and *The Dunciad* (1728 – 43), in which he mocks his many literary enemies. He was a master satirist and splendid craftsman of the heroic couplet. Romantic critics generally think him no poet at all, but G. K. Chesterton remarked, "If Pope be not a poet, then who is?"

Ezra Pound

Ezra Pound (1885 – 1972), among the most influential (and still controversial) poets of our century, was born in Hailey, Idaho. He readied himself for a teaching career, but when in 1907 he lost his job at Wabash College for sheltering a penniless prostitute, he left America. Settling in England and later in Paris, he wielded influence on the work of T. S. Eliot, whose long poem *The Waste Land* he edited; W. B. Yeats, whom he served as secretary and critic; and James Joyce. Pound was perpetually championing writers then unknown, like Robert Frost. In 1924 Pound settled permanently in Italy, where he came to admire Mussolini's economic policies. During World War II he made broadcasts to America by Italian radio, deemed treasonous. When American armed forces arrested him in 1944, Pound spent three weeks in a cage in an army camp in Pisa. Flown to the United States to stand trial, he was declared incompetent and for twelve years was confined in St. Elizabeth's in Washington, a hospital for the criminally insane. In 1958, at the intervention of Robert Frost, Archibald MacLeish, and other old friends, he was pronounced incurable and allowed to return to Italy to spend his last, increasingly silent years. In his prime, Pound is a swaggeringly confident critic, a berater of smugness and mediocrity, a delectable humorist. Among his lasting books are *Personae* (enlarged edition, 1949), short poems; his *ABC of Reading* (1934), an introduction to poetry; and *Literary Essays* (1954). His *Cantos*, a vast poem woven of historical themes published in instalments over forty years, Pound never finished. He is a great translator of poetry from Italian, Provençal, Chinese, and other languages. Pare away his delusions, and a remarkable human being and splendid poet remains.

Dudley Randall

Dudley Randall was born in 1914 in Washington, D.C. He was graduated from Wayne State University and the University of Michigan, and has worked as librarian and poet-in-residence at the University of Detroit. A pioneer in the modern movement to publish the work of black writers, Randall founded what has been called the most influential small publishing house in America, Broadside Press. He also edited an important anthology, *The Black Poets* (1971). Randall's *A Litany of Friends: New and Selected Poems* was published in 1981.

Adrienne Rich

Adrienne Rich was born in Baltimore in 1929, into a father-dominated Jewish family of comfortable means. While still an undergraduate at Radcliffe, she published her first book of poems, *A Change of World* (1951), with an introduction by W. H. Auden. Later she studied at Oxford. In 1953 she married an economist and soon bore three sons — an experience she said had been "radicalizing." During the Vietnam War, she took an active part in the peace movement. In 1970 after the suicide of her estranged husband, perhaps obliquely referred to in the poem "Diving into the Wreck," Rich turned increasingly to feminist matters, expressed not only in poetry but in prose: in *Of Woman Born* (1976), a study of the institution of motherhood. With Michelle Cliff, she has coedited *Sinister Wisdom*, a lesbian little magazine. Rich has taught at City College of New York, Columbia, Brandeis, Smith, Douglass, and elsewhere. Few woman poets in recent years have commanded a more devoted audience.

Theodore Roethke

Theodore Roethke (1908 – 1963) was born in Saginaw, Michigan, where his family ran a large greenhouse. (No poet seems wealthier in his knowledge of vegetation.) He went to the University of Michigan and (for a year) to Harvard. As a young poet teaching college at a time when creative writing teachers without Ph.D.s were suspect, Roethke held impermanent jobs before coming to rest at the University of Washington in Seattle. There, from 1947 until his death, he was an influential teacher of poetry and poetry writing; among his students were Carolyn Kizer, David Wagoner, and James Wright. Roethke was a large, heavyset man light on his feet (he once coached varsity tennis at Lafayette), and would sometimes prepare for a poetry reading by pacing the stage like an athlete warming up. His poetry developed from rather conventional and imitative lyrics through a phase of disconnected stream of consciousness into (at the end) a meditative poetry reminiscent in its open lines of Walt Whitman's.

William Shakespeare

William Shakespeare (1564 – 1616), the supreme writer of English, was born, baptized, and buried in the market town of Stratford-on-Avon, eighty miles from London. Son of a glovemaker and merchant who was high bailiff (or mayor) of the town, he probably attended grammar school and learned to read Latin authors in the original. At eighteen he married Anne Hathaway, twenty-six, by whom he had three children, including twins. By 1592 he had become well known and envied as an actor and playwright in London. From 1594 until he retired, he belonged to the same theatrical company, the Lord Chamberlain's Men (later renamed the King's Men in honor of their patron, James I), for whom he wrote thirty-six plays — some of them, such as *Hamlet* and *King Lear*, profound reworkings of old plays. As an actor, Shakespeare is believed to have played supporting roles, such as Hamlet's father's ghost. The company prospered, moved into the Globe in 1599, and in 1608 bought the fashionable Blackfriars as well; Shakespeare owned an interest in both theaters. When plagues shut down the theaters from 1592 to 1594, Shakespeare turned to poetry; his great Sonnets (published only in 1609) probably date from the 1590s. Plays were regarded as entertainments of little literary merit, like comic books today, and Shakespeare did not bother to supervise their publication. He did, however, carefully see through press his sonnets and the narrative poems *Venus and Adonis* (1593) and *The Rape of Lucrece* (1594).

Percy Bysshe Shelley

Percy Bysshe Shelley (1792 – 1822) married his first wife, sixteen-year-old Harriet Westbrook, in 1811, the same year he was expelled from Oxford for coauthoring a pamphlet defending atheism. His first major poem, *Queen Mab*, which advocated the abolishment of a number of established institutions, was privately printed in 1813. In 1814 Shelley went to France with Mary Wollstonecraft, later famous as the author of *Frankenstein* (1818). They were married after Harriet's suicide in 1816. In 1818 they settled in Italy, where Shelley wrote some of his best lyrics, including "Ode to the West Wind," "To a Skylark," and "Ozymandias"; poetic dramas; and *Adonais*, an elegy to his friend John Keats. "A Defense of Poetry," the poet's most important prose work, was written in 1821. While sailing during a storm, Shelley was drowned. He is remembered as a staunch believer in the eighteenth-century ideals of reason and the perfectibility of the human race.

Stevie Smith

Stevie Smith (1902 – 1971), was born in Hull, Yorkshire, christened Florence Margaret Smith. Being wiry and short, she acquired her nickname from a popular jockey, Stevie Donahue. For more than sixty years, beginning at age three, Smith lived with her aunt in Palmers Green, a suburb of London, and worked for thirty years as a publisher's secretary. Of her three novels, *Novel on Yellow Paper* (1936) is the best known. Her poetry readings, in public and on BBC radio, widened her audience. *Collected Poems* (1976) is illustrated with her own witty, slapdash, and rakishly charming drawings. *Me Again: Uncollected Writings* (1982) contains poems, stories, essays, and a play for radio. In a film, *Stevie* (1978), based on a stage play by Hugh Whitemore, Glenda Jackson plays the poet with keen empathy.

William Stafford

William Stafford, born in 1914 in Hutchinson, Kansas, was graduated from the University of Kansas and later took a doctorate at the University of Iowa. During World War II he was interned as a conscientious objector, an experience he recalls in his prose memoir *Down in My Heart* (1947). For many years he taught at Lewis and Clark College in Portland, Oregon, and in 1970–71 he served as Consultant in Poetry for the Library of Congress. *Traveling Through the Dark* (1962) won the National Book Award, and in 1977 Stafford published a large volume of his collected poems, *Stories That Could Be True*. In much of his work he traces the landscapes of the Midwest and of the Pacific Northwest, where he has long lived. He describes his poetry as "much like talk, with some enhancement."

Timothy Steele

Timothy Steele, born in Burlington, Vermont, in 1948, took his doctorate in English at Brandeis, where he studied literature with J. V. Cunningham. A Californian by adoption, he has taught and held a Wallace Stegner fellowship in creative writing at Stanford, and currently teaches at California State University, Los Angeles. His first collection, *Uncertainties and Rest*, appeared in 1979, and his most recent, *Sapphics Against Anger and Other Poems*, in 1986. *Missing Measures: Modern Poetry and the Revolt against Meter* (1990) is a critical study in literary history. His poems wear a Yankee reticence and a tendency toward precise understatement, holding much power within their strict limits. Steele writes exclusively in traditional forms, in which he demonstrates mastery.

James Stephens

James Stephens (1882–1950), born in Dublin, Ireland, was a famous member of the Irish Literary Renaissance, a movement early in the century that included William Butler Yeats and the playwrights Lady Gregory, J. M. Synge, and Sean O'Casey. As a young man Stephens took a job as a typist in a lawyer's office, where access to a typewriter started him writing fantastic fiction, some of it based on Irish folklore, such as his most popular novel, *The Crock of Gold* (1912). Other imaginative novels followed, including *The Demi-Gods* (1914) and *Deirdre* (1923). *Irish Fairy Tales* (1920) retells classic legends for young readers. Although best remembered for such books, Stephens was a considerable poet as well. His first collection appeared in 1909, and in 1926 he published his *Collected Poems.* Some of his poems are actually free translations from the Irish: "A Glass of Beer," for instance, is a version of a poem by Dáibhí Ó Bruadair (about 1625 – 98).

Wallace Stevens

Wallace Stevens (1879 – 1955) was born in Reading, Pennsylvania; his father was a successful lawyer; his mother, a former schoolteacher. As a special student at Harvard, he became president of the student literary magazine, the *Harvard Advocate,* but he did not want a liberal arts degree. Instead, he became a lawyer in New York City, and in 1916 joined the legal staff of the Hartford Accident and Indemnity Company. In 1936 he was elected a vice-president. Stevens, who would write poems in his head while walking to work and then dictate them to his secretary, was a leading expert on surety claims. Once asked how he was able to combine poetry and insurance, he replied that the two occupations had an element in common: "calculated risk." As a young man in New York, Stevens made lasting friendships with poets Marianne Moore and William Carlos Williams, but he did not seek literary society. Though his poems are full of references to Europe and remote places, his only travels were annual vacation trips to Key West. He printed his early poems in *Poetry* magazine, but did not publish a book until *Harmonium* appeared in 1923, when he was forty-four. Living quietly in Hartford, Connecticut, Stevens sought to discover order in a chaotic world with his subtle and exotic imagination. His critical essays, collected in *The Necessary Angel* (1951), and his *Letters* (1966), edited by his daughter Holly Stevens, reveal a penetrating, philosophic mind. His *Collected Poems* (1954), published on his seventy-fifth birthday, garnered major prizes and belated recognition for Stevens as a major American poet.

Jonathan Swift

Jonathan Swift (1667 – 1745), Anglo-Irish poet, satirist, journalist, and clergyman, was born in Dublin, said to have been sired by an English steward. Uncles helped him attend Trinity College, Dublin, from which he was graduated "by special grace," having shone only in his studies of the classics. In 1694 Swift entered the Church of England and held parish appointments in Ireland, finally becoming Dean of St. Patrick's Cathedral, Dublin — to his disappointment, for he loved London and had hoped for a position there. His cousin John

Dryden is reported to have told him, "Cousin Swift, you will never be a poet," a prophecy that time has proved inaccurate. In a life crowded with church duties, political agitation, literary society, and long and perhaps sexless love affairs, especially with his former pupil Esther Johnson (whom he called Stella), Swift found occasion to write much excellent verse. Still, he is best remembered for *Gulliver's Travels* (1726), an affectionate tribute to the reasoning part of "that animal called man," a scathing and scatological rebuke to the rest of him.

Alfred, Lord Tennyson

Alfred, Lord Tennyson (1809 – 1892), was born Alfred Tennyson in Lincolnshire, England, the son of an alcoholic rural minister. When Queen Victoria made him a baron in 1883 (at seventy-five), he added the "Lord" to his byline. A precocious poet, Tennyson began writing verse at five, and when still in his teens collaborated with his brother Charles on *Poems by Two Brothers* (1827). As a student at Cambridge, he was unusual: he kept a snake for a pet, won a medal for poetry, and went home without taking a degree. But in college he made influential friendships, especially that of Arthur Hallam, whose death in 1833 inspired Tennyson's *In Memoriam* (1850), the elegiac sequence that contains "Dark house by which once more I stand." The year 1850 was a banner one for Tennyson in other ways: he at last felt prosperous enough to marry Emily Sellwood, who had remained engaged to him for fourteen years, and Queen Victoria named him poet laureate, in which capacity he served for four decades, writing poems for state occasions. Between 1859 and 1888 Tennyson completed *Idylls of the King*, a twelve-part narrative poem of Arthur and his Round Table. In his mid-sixties he wrote several plays. A spokesman for the Victorian age and its militant colonialism, Tennyson is still respected as a poet of varied assets, including an excellent ear.

Dylan Thomas

Dylan Thomas (1914 – 1953) was born in the coastal town of Swansea, Wales, the son of a teacher of English. Much of Thomas's life was a bitter struggle to support his wife and children, a struggle intensified by fondness for spending freely. Lacking a university education, Thomas found most paying literary work barred to him in Britain, although late in life he received many assignments to write film and radio scripts. A resonant reader-aloud of poetry, he made broadcasts for BBC radio and undertook several immensely popular reading tours of America, preceded by a reputation for heavy drinking and gustatorial lovemaking. He died in a hospital in New York City after drinking a procession of straight whiskeys, apparently courting the end. Thomas wrote not only poems (in the early ones he brought surrealism into English poetry), he also wrote remarkable stories and a "play for voices," *Under Milk Wood* (1954), based on memories of his home town in Wales.

John Updike

John Updike, born in Shillington, Pennsylvania, in 1932, is primarily regarded as a novelist. But his first book was verse, *The Carpentered Hen* (1954), from which we take "Ex-Basketball Player"; and ever since, he has continued to produce verse both light and serious. He received his B.A. from Harvard, then went to Oxford to study drawing and fine art. From 1955 to 1957 he worked on the staff of *The New Yorker*. Though he left the magazine to write full-time, he has continued to supply it with bright stories and searching book reviews. Hardly a fall goes by without a new Updike novel. *The Witches of Eastwick* (1984) was recently a made into a successful motion picture.

Keith Waldrop

Keith Waldrop, born in 1932 in Emporia, Kansas, grew up in a family divided by his father's militant atheism and his mother's pious Christian fundamentalism. He took his doctorate at the University of Michigan with a thesis on obscenity in literature, and has since taught at Wesleyan University and at Brown. Waldrop has directed and acted in films and plays. His first book of poems, *A Windmill near Calvary* (1968), was nominated for the National Book Award. He lives in Providence, Rhode Island, with his wife, the poet and translator Rosmarie Waldrop, thousands of books and recordings, and a basement printing press that produces more books under the imprint Burning Deck.

Edmund Waller

Edmund Waller (1606 – 1687), born into a rich country family, is remembered in England not only as a poet but also as a member of Parliament. In 1643 he hatched "Waller's Plot," an attempt to turn London over to the exiled Charles I; it failed, but Parliament later pardoned him. His smooth, elegant poems included tributes to important public figures as well as courtly love lyrics. Written chiefly in iambic pentameter couplets, these later helped establish the heroic couplet as a favorite poetic form among English poets of the eighteenth century.

Walt Whitman

Walt Whitman (1819 – 1892) was born on Long Island, son of an impoverished farmer. He spent his early years as a school teacher, a temperance propagandist, a carpenter, a printer, and a newspaper editor on the Brooklyn *Eagle*. He began writing poetry in youth, sometimes declaiming his lines above the crash of waves on New York beaches. Apparently he was also inspired to write wide, spacious, confident lines by attending performances of Italian opera. His self-published *Leaves of Grass* (1855) won praise from Ralph Waldo Emerson and gained Whitman readers in England. For the rest of his life, he kept revising and enlarging it, ceasing with a ninth or "deathbed edition" in 1891 – 92. Americans at first were slow to accept Whitman's unconventionally open verse forms, his sexual frankness, and his gregarious egoism. The poet of boundless faith in American democracy, Whitman tempered his vision by his experiences as a volunteer hospital nurse during the Civil War (described in his poems *Drum-Taps* and his wartime letters). After the war, he held secretarial jobs to support himself, and lost one such job when his employer's scandalized eye fell upon the *Leaves*. In old age, a semi-invalid after a stroke, Whitman made his home in Camden, New Jersey. Before he died he saw his work finally winning respect and worldwide acceptance. Whitman's influence on later American poetry has been profound, both by the example of his open forms and by his bold encompassing of subject matter that had formerly been considered unpoetic. (In "Song of the Exposition," read aloud at an industrial show in New York, the poet exclaims of his Muse: "She's here, install'd amid the kitchen ware!")

Richard Wilbur

Richard Wilbur, born in 1917 in New York City, was graduated from Amherst College, then served in the army in World War II. He has taught English at Harvard, Wellesley, Wesleyan, and Smith. With his first two collections, *The Beautiful Changes* (1947) and *Ceremony* (1950), Wilbur acquired a high reputation for a poetry of sensitivity, wit, grace, and command of traditional forms. Besides writing poetry, for which he has received many prizes, including two Pulitzer Prizes and a National Book Award, Wilbur has edited the poetry of Shakespeare and Poe. He has written song lyrics for *Candide*, a Broadway musical by Lillian Hellman and Leonard Bernstein (1956); *Loudmouse*, a story for children (1963); and *Responses*, literary criticism (1976); and he has translated plays of Moliere and Racine into wonderfully skillful English verse. He divides his time between Cummington, Massachusetts, where he has a home adjacent to an apple orchard, and Key West, Florida. In 1987 he was named United States Poet Laureate by the Library of Congress. His *New and Collected Poems* (1988) gathers most of his original work in poetry.

William Carlos Williams

William Carlos Williams (1883 – 1963) was born in Rutherford, New Jersey, where he remained in later life as a practicing pediatrician. While taking his M.D. degree at the University of Pennsylvania, he made friends with the poets Ezra Pound and H.D. (Hilda Doolittle). Surprisingly prolific for a busy doctor, Williams wrote (besides poetry) novels and short stories, plays, criticism, and essays in history (*In the American Grain*, 1939). He kept a fliptop desk in his office and between patients would haul out his typewriter and dash off poems. His encouragement of younger poets, among them Allen Ginsberg (whose doctor he was when Ginsberg was a baby), and the long-sustained example of his formally open poetry made him an appealing father figure to the generation of the Beat poets and the Black Mountain poets — Ginsberg, Gary Snyder, and Robert Creeley. But he also had great influence on Robert Lowell, and on a whole younger generation of American poets in our day. Williams believed in truthtelling about ordinary life, championed plain speech "out of the mouths of Polish mothers," and insisted that there can be "no ideas but in things." Combining poetry with prose (including documents and statistics), his long poem in five parts, *Paterson* (1946 – 58) explores the past, present, and future of the New Jersey industrial city near which Williams lived for most of his days.

Yvor Winters

Arthur Yvor Winters (1900 – 1968) is as well remembered for his controversial books of criticism as for his poetry. (As a critic, Winters championed tradition, morality, reason, and certain little-read poets such as Elizabeth Daryush and Frederick Goddard Tuckerman.) Born in Chicago, he returned to that city for high school and college after spending his childhood in California and Oregon. During his first year at the University of Chicago, he contracted tuberculosis and moved to Santa Fe, New Mexico, where he remained for his health until 1925. From 1928 until his retirement in 1966, he taught at Stanford University. He was married to poet and novelist Janet Lewis. Described as an Imagist for his first book of verse, *The Immobile Wind* (1921), Winters later abandoned free verse for strict traditional forms. Though the audience for his poems was never large, he exerted a powerful formative influence on the work of many poets he taught. For his poetry, see *Collected Poems* (1978); for his criticism, *In Defense of Reason* (1947), *The Function of Criticism* (1957), and *Forms of Discovery* (1968).

William Wordsworth

William Wordsworth (1770 – 1850) was born in England's Lake District, whose landscapes and people were to inform many of his poems. As a young man he visited France, sympathized with the Revolution, and met a young French-woman who bore him a child. The Reign of Terror prevented him from returning to France, and he and Annette Vallon never married. With his sister Dorothy (1771 – 1855), his lifelong intellectual companion and the author of remarkable journals, he settled in Dorsetshire. Later they moved to Grasmere, in the Lake District, where Wordsworth lived the rest of his life. In 1798 his friendship with Samuel Taylor Coleridge resulted in their joint publication of *Lyrical Ballads*, a book credited with introducing Romanticism to English poetry. (Wordsworth contributed "Tintern Abbey" and other poems.) To the second edition of 1800, Wordsworth supplied a preface calling for a poetry written "in the real language of men." Time brought him a small official job, a marriage, a swing from left to right in his political sentiments, and appointment as poet laureate. Although he kept on writing, readers have generally preferred his earlier poems. *The Prelude*, a long poem-memoir completed in 1805, did not appear till after the poet's death. One of the most original of writers, Wordsworth—especially for his poems of nature and simple rustics—occupies a popular place in English poetry, much like that of Robert Frost in America.

James Wright

James Wright (1927 – 1980) was born in Martins Ferry, Ohio. After taking his doctorate at the University of Washington, where he studied with Theodore Roethke, he taught at the University of Minnesota, Macalester College, and Hunter College in New York. His first book, *A Green Wall* (1957), in the Yale Series of Younger Poets, established him as a traditional formalist of great skill. With Robert Bly, by whom he was persuaded to branch out of traditional forms, he translated the poems of Cesar Valejo, Pablo Neruda, and George Trakl. In 1972 he received the Pulitzer Prize for his *Collected Poems*. Wright was a memorable teacher, a great quoter of poetry from memory, and a fine critic. "I try and say how I love my country and how I despise the way it is treated," he declared. "I try and speak of the beauty and again of the ugliness in the lives of the poor and neglected."

Sir Thomas Wyatt

Sir Thomas Wyatt (1503? – 1542) was both poet and man of action: diplomat, soldier, and courtier. He was born in his father's castle in Kent, England, and as a boy he was sent to court. In 1516 he entered St. John's College, Cambridge. Wyatt twice saw the inside of prison when he slipped from the favor of King Henry VIII. He is thought to have been a lover of Anne Boleyn, later the King's wife, a fact that perhaps affects some of his remarkable love lyrics. A prominent man in Tudor England, Wyatt carried out diplomatic missions, served as ambassador to Spain, was a member of Parliament and the king's privy council, and was Commander of the Fleet. Wyatt's mission to Italy in 1527 had great consequence for English poetry, for he brought back knowledge of the works of Petrarch and other Italian love poets. In imitation of them, Wyatt wrote some of the first sonnets in our language — also lyrics, rondels, satires, and psalms.

William Butler Yeats

William Butler Yeats (1865 – 1939), poet and playwright, an Irishman of English ancestry, was born in Dublin, the son of painter John Butler Yeats. For a time he studied art himself and was irregularly schooled in Dublin and in London. Early in life Yeats sought to transform Irish folklore and legend into mellifluous poems. He overcame shyness to take an active part in cataclysmic events: he became involved in the movement for an Irish nation (partly drawn into it by his unrequited love for Maud Gonne, a crusading nationalist) and in founding the Irish Literary Theatre (1898) and the Irish National Theatre, which in 1904 moved to the renowned Abbey Theatre in Dublin. Dublin audiences were difficult: in 1899 they jeered Yeats's first play, *The Countess Cathleen,* for portraying a woman who, defying the church, sells her soul to the devil to buy bread for starving peasants. Eventually Yeats retired from the fray, to write plays given in drawing rooms, like *Purgatory.* After the establishment of the Irish Free State, Yeats served as a senator (1922 – 28). His lifelong interest in the occult culminated in his writing of *A Vision* (1937), a view of history as governed by the phases of the moon; Yeats believed the book inspired by spirit masters who dictated communications to his wife, Georgie Hyde-Lees. Had Yeats stopped writing in 1900, he would be remembered as an outstanding minor Victorian. Instead, he went on to become one of the most influential poets of the twentieth century.

31 Criticism: On Poetry

What is a modern Poet's fate?
To write his thoughts upon a slate —
The Critic spits on what is done,
Gives it a wipe — and all is gone.
                    — Thomas Hood, "To the Reviewers"

The critical power is of lower rank than the creative. True, but in assenting
to this proposition, one or two things are to be kept in mind. It is undeniable
that the exercise of a creative power, that a free creative activity, is the true
function of man; it is proved to be so by man's finding in it his true happiness.
But it is undeniable, also, that men may have the sense of exercising this free
creative activity in other ways than in producing great works of literature or
art; if it were not so, all but a very few men would be shut out from the true
happiness of all men; they may have it in well-doing, they may have it in
learning, they may have it even in criticizing.
                    — Matthew Arnold, "The Function of Criticism"

Plato (427? – 347? B.C.)

INSPIRATION[1]   (ABOUT 390 B.C.)

Ion: The world agrees with me in thinking that I do speak better and have more
    to say about Homer than any other man. But I do not speak equally well
    about others — tell me the reason for this.

[1]Translated by Benjamin Jowett.

Socrates: I perceive, Ion; and I will proceed to explain to you what I imagine to be the reason for this. The gift which you possess of speaking excellently about Homer is not an art, but, as I was just saying, an inspiration; there is a divinity moving you, like that contained in the stone which Euripides calls a magnet, but which is commonly known as the stone of Heraclea. This stone not only attracts iron rings, but also imparts to them a similar power of attracting other rings; and sometimes you may see a number of pieces of iron and rings suspended from one another so as to form quite a long chain: and all of them derive their power of suspension from the original stone. In like manner the Muse first of all inspires men herself; and from these inspired persons a chain of other persons is suspended, who take the inspiration. For all good poets, epic as well as lyric, compose their beautiful poems not by art, but because they are inspired and possessed. And as the Corybantian revelers when they dance are not in their right mind, so the lyric poets are not in their right mind when they are composing their beautiful strains: but when falling under the power of music and meter they are inspired and possessed; like Bacchic maidens who draw milk and honey from the rivers when they are under the influence of Dionysus but not when they are in their right mind. And the soul of the lyric poet does the same, as they themselves say; for they tell us that they bring songs from honeyed fountains, culling them out of the gardens and dells of the Muses; they, like the bees, winging their way from flower to flower. And this is true. For the poet is a light and winged and holy thing, and there is no invention in him until he has been inspired and is out of his senses, and the mind is no longer in him: when he has not attained to this state, he is powerless and is unable to utter his oracles. Many are the noble words in which poets speak concerning the actions of men; but like yourself when speaking about Homer, they do not speak of them by any rules of art: they are simply inspired to utter that to which the Muse impels them, and that only; and when inspired, one of them will make dithyrambs, another hymns of praise, another choral strains, another epic or iambic verses — and he who is good at one is not good at any other kind of verse: for not by art does the poet sing, but by power divine. Had he learned by rules of art, he would have known how to speak not of one theme only, but of all; and therefore God takes away the minds of poets, and uses them as his ministers, as he also uses diviners and holy prophets, in order that we who hear them may know them to be speaking not of themselves who utter these priceless words in a state of unconsciousness, but that God himself is the speaker, and that through them he is conversing with us. And Tynnichus the Chalcidian affords a striking instance of what I am saying: he wrote nothing that any one would care to remember but the famous paean which is in every one's mouth, one of the finest poems ever written, simply an invention of the Muses, as he himself says. For in this way the God would seem to indicate to us and not allow us to doubt that these beautiful poems are not human, or the work of man, but divine and the work of God; and that the poets are only the interpreters of the Gods by whom they are severally possessed. Was not this the lesson which the God intended to teach when by the mouth of the worst of poets he sang the best of songs? Am I not right, Ion?

Ion

INSPIRATION. Plato records a dialogue between his master, the philosopher Socrates (469 B.C. – 399 B.C.) and Ion, a young man of Athens. *Corybantian revellers:* The Corybants, priests or attendants of the nature goddess Cybele, deity of the ancient peoples of Asia Minor, were given to orgiastic rites and frenzied dances. *Bacchic maidens:* attendants of the god of wine and fertility, called Dionysus by the Greeks, Bacchus by the Romans. *Muses:* In Greek mythology, nine sister goddesses who presided over poetry and song, the arts and sciences.

Plato (427? – 347? B.C.)

SOCRATES BANISHES POETS FROM HIS IDEAL STATE[2]

(ABOUT 373 B.C.)

Socrates: Hear and judge: The best of us, I conceive, when we listen to a passage of Homer, or one of the tragedians, in which he represents some pitiful hero who is drawling out his sorrows in a long oration, or weeping, and smiting his breast — the best of us, you know, delight in giving way to sympathy, and are in raptures at the excellence of the poet who stirs our feelings most.

Glaucon: Yes, of course I know.

Socrates: But when any sorrow of our own happens to us, then you may observe that we pride ourselves on the opposite quality — we would fain be quiet and patient; this is the manly part, and the other which delighted us in the recitation is now deemed to be the part of a woman.

Glaucon: Very true.

Socrates: Now can we be right in praising and admiring another who is doing that which any one of us would abominate and be ashamed of in his own person?

Glaucon: No, that is certainly not reasonable.

Socrates: Nay, quite reasonable from one point of view.

Glaucon: What point of view?

Socrates: If you consider that when in misfortune we feel a natural hunger and desire to relieve our sorrow by weeping and lamentation, and that this feeling which is kept under control in our own calamities is satisfied and delighted by the poets; — the better nature in each of us, not having been sufficiently trained by reason or habit, allows the sympathetic element to break loose because the sorrow is another's; and the spectator fancies that there can be no disgrace to himself in praising and pitying any one who comes telling him what a good man he is, and making a fuss about his troubles; he thinks that

[2]Translated by Benjamin Jowett.

the pleasure is a gain, and why should he be supercilious and lose this and the poem too? Few persons ever reflect, as I should imagine, that from the evil of other men something of evil is communicated to themselves. And so the feeling of sorrow which has gathered strength at the sight of the misfortunes of others is with difficulty repressed in our own.

Glaucon: How very true!

Socrates: And does not the same hold also of the ridiculous? There are jests which you would be ashamed to make yourself, and yet on the comic stage, or indeed in private, when you hear them, you are greatly amused by them, and are not at all disgusted at their unseemliness; — the case of pity is repeated; — there is a principle in human nature which is disposed to raise a laugh, and this which you once restrained by reason, because you were afraid of being thought a buffoon, is now let out again; and having stimulated the risible faculty at the theater, you are betrayed unconsciously to yourself into playing the comic poet at home.

Glaucon: Quite true.

Socrates: And the same may be said of lust and anger and all the other affections, of desire and pain and pleasure, which are held to be inseparable from every action — in all of them poetry feeds and waters the passions instead of drying them up; she lets them rule, although they ought to be controlled, if mankind are ever to increase in happiness and virtue.

Glaucon: I cannot deny it.

Socrates: Therefore, Glaucon, whenever you meet with any of the eulogists of Homer declaring that he has been the educator of Hellas, and that he is profitable for education and for the ordering of human things, and that you should take him up again and again and get to know him and regulate your whole life according to him, we may love and honor those who say these things — they are excellent people, as far as their lights extend; and we are ready to acknowledge that Homer is the greatest of poets and first of tragedy writers; but we must remain firm in our conviction that hymns to the gods and praises of famous men are the only poetry which ought to be admitted into our State. For if you go beyond this and allow the honeyed muse to enter, either in epic or lyric verse, not law and the reason of mankind, which by common consent have ever been deemed best, but pleasure and pain will be the rulers in our State.

Glaucon: That is most true.

Socrates: And now since we have reverted to the subject of poetry, let this our defense serve to show the reasonableness of our former judgment in sending away out of our State an art having the tendencies which we have described; for reason constrained us. But that she may not impute to us any harshness or want of politeness, let us tell her that there is an ancient quarrel between philosophy and poetry; of which there are many proofs, such as the saying of 'the yelping hound howling at her lord,' or of one 'mighty in the vain talk of fools,' and 'the mob of sages circumventing Zeus,' and the 'subtle thinkers who are beggars after all'; and there are innumerable other signs of ancient enmity between them. Notwithstanding this, let us assure our sweet friend and the sister arts of imitation, that if she will only prove her title to exist in a well-ordered State we shall be delighted to receive her — we are very conscious of her charms; but we may not on that account betray the truth.

The Republic, X

Aristotle (384 – 322 B.C.)

TWO CAUSES OF POETRY[3]   (ABOUT 330 B.C.)

Poetry in general seems to have sprung from two causes, each of them lying deep in our nature. First, the instinct of imitation is implanted in man from childhood, one difference between him and other animals being that he is the most imitative of living creatures; and through imitation he learns his earliest lessons; and no less universal is the pleasure felt in things imitated. We have evidence of this in the facts of experience. Objects which in themselves we view with pain, we delight to contemplate when reproduced with minute fidelity: such as the forms of the most ignoble animals and of dead bodies. The cause of this again is, that to learn gives the liveliest pleasure, not only to philosophers but to men in general; whose capacity, however, of learning is more limited. Thus the reason why men enjoy seeing a likeness is, that in contemplating it they find themselves learning or inferring, and saying perhaps, "Ah, that is he." For if you happen not to have seen the original, the pleasure will be due not to the imitation as such, but to the execution, the coloring, or some such other cause.

Imitation, then, is one instinct of our nature. Next, there is the instinct for "harmony" and rhythm, meters being manifestly sections of rhythm. Persons, therefore, starting with this natural gift developed by degrees their special aptitudes, till their rude improvisations gave birth to Poetry.

Poetics, IV

Samuel Johnson (1709 – 1784)

THE BUSINESS OF A POET   1759

The business of a poet is to examine, not the individual, but the species; to remark general properties and large appearances; he does not number the streaks of the tulip, or describe the different shades in the verdure of the forest. He is to exhibit in his portraits of nature such prominent and striking features as recall the original to every mind, and must neglect the minuter discriminations, which one may have remarked and another have neglected, for those characteristics which are alike obvious to vigilance and carelessness.

[3]Translated by S. H. Butcher.

But the knowledge of nature is only half the task of a poet; he must be acquainted likewise with all the modes of life. His character requires that he estimate the happiness and misery of every condition, observe the power of all the passions in all their combinations, and trace the changes of the human mind as they are modified by various institutions and accidental influences of climate or custom, from the sprightliness of infancy to the despondency of decrepitude. He must divest himself of the prejudices of his age or country; he must consider right and wrong in their abstracted and variable state; he must disregard present laws and opinions, and rise to general and transcendental truths, which will always be the same.

The History of Rasselas,
Prince of Abyssinia

William Wordsworth (1770 – 1850)

EMOTION RECOLLECTED IN TRANQUILLITY   1800

I have said that poetry is the spontaneous overflow of powerful feelings: it takes its origin from emotion recollected in tranquillity: the emotion is contemplated till, by a species of reaction, the tranquillity gradually disappears, and an emotion, kindred to that which was before the subject of contemplation, is gradually produced, and does itself actually exist in the mind. In this mood successful composition generally begins, and in a mood similar to this it is carried on; but the emotion, of whatever kind, and in whatever degree, from various causes, is qualified by various pleasures, so that in describing any passions whatsoever, which are voluntarily described, the mind will, upon the whole, be in a state of enjoyment. If Nature be thus cautious to preserve in a state of enjoyment a being so employed, the Poet ought to profit by the lesson held forth to him, and ought especially to take care, that, whatever passions he communicates to his Reader, those passions, if his Reader's mind be sound and vigorous, should always be accompanied with an overbalance of pleasure. Now the music of harmonious metrical language, the sense of difficulty overcome, and the blind association of pleasure which has been previously received from works of rhyme or meter of the same or similar construction, an indistinct perception perpetually renewed of language closely resembling that of real life, and yet, in the circumstance of meter, differing from it so widely — all these imperceptibly make up a complex feeling of delight, which is of the most important use in tempering the painful feeling always found intermingled with powerful descriptions of the deeper passions. This effect is always produced in pathetic and impassioned poetry; while, in lighter compositions, the ease and gracefulness with which the Poet manages his numbers are themselves confessedly a principal source of the gratification of the Reader. All that it is *necessary* to say, however, upon this subject, may be effected by affirming, what few persons will deny, that, of two descriptions, either of passions, manners, or characters, each of them equally well executed, the one in prose and the other in verse, the verse will be read a hundred times where the prose is read once.

Preface to Lyrical Ballads,
second edition

EMOTION RECOLLECTED IN TRANQUILLITY. For information on Wordsworth's methods of composition in his poem "I Wandered Lonely as a Cloud," see page 517.

Samuel Taylor Coleridge (1772 – 1834)

IMAGINATION   1817

What is poetry? — is so nearly the same question with, what is a poet? — that the answer to the one is involved in the solution of the other. For it is a distinction resulting from the poetic genius itself, which sustains and modifies the images, thoughts, and emotions of the poet's own mind.

The poet, described in ideal perfection, brings the whole soul of man into activity, with the subordination of its faculties to each other according to their relative worth and dignity. He diffuses a tone and spirit of unity, that blends, and (as it were) *fuses*, each into each, by that synthetic and magical power, to which I would exclusively appropriate the name of Imagination. This power, first put in action by the will and understanding, and retained under their irremissive, though gentle and unnoticed, control, *laxis effertur habenis*°, reveals itself in the balance or reconcilement of opposite or discordant qualities; of sameness, with difference; of the general with the concrete; the idea with the image; the individual with the representative; the sense of novelty and freshness with old and familiar objects; a more than usual state of emotion with more than usual order; judgment ever awake and steady self-possession, with enthusiasm and feeling profound and vehement; and while it blends and harmonizes the natural and the artificial, still subordinates art to nature; the manner to the matter; and our admiration of the poet to our sympathy with the poetry.

Biographia Literaria: or, Biographical Sketches
of My Literary Life and Opinions, Chapter XIV

IMAGINATION. The Latin phrase *laxis effertur habenis* means "is driven with reins relaxed."

Percy Bysshe Shelley (1792 – 1822)

UNACKNOWLEDGED LEGISLATORS   (1821)

The most unfailing herald, companion, and follower of the awakening of a great people to work a beneficial change in opinion or institution, is poetry. At such periods there is an accumulation of the power of communicating and receiving intense and impassioned conceptions respecting man and nature. The persons in whom this power resides, may often, as far as regards many portions of their nature, have little apparent correspondence with that spirit of good of which they are the ministers. But even whilst they deny and abjure, they are yet compelled to serve, the power which is seated on the throne of their own soul. It is impossible to read the compositions of the most celebrated writers of the present day without being startled with the electric life which burns within their words. They measure the circumference and sound the depths of human nature with a comprehensive and all-penetrating spirit, and they are themselves perhaps the most sincerely astonished at its manifestations; for it is less their spirit than the spirit of the age. Poets are the hierophants of an unapprehended inspiration; the mirrors of the gigantic shadows which futurity casts upon the present; the words which express what they understand not; the trumpets which sing to battle, and feel not what they inspire; the influence which is moved not, but moves. Poets are the unacknowledged legislators of the world.

A Defense of Poetry

Ralph Waldo Emerson (1803 – 1882)

METER-MAKING ARGUMENT   1844

I took part in a conversation the other day concerning a recent writer of lyrics, a man of subtle mind, whose head appeared to be a music-box of delicate tunes and rhythms, and whose skill and command of language we could not sufficiently praise. But when the question arose whether he was not only a lyrist but a poet, we were obliged to confess that he is plainly a contemporary, not an eternal man. He does not stand out of our low limitations, like a Chimborazo under the line°, running up from a torrid base through all the climates of the globe, with belts of the herbage of every latitude on its high and mottled sides; but this genius is the landscape-garden of a modern house adorned with fountains and statues, with well-bred men and women standing and sitting in the walks and terraces. We hear, through all the varied music, the ground-tone of conventional life. Our poets are men of talents who sing, and not the children of music. The argument is secondary, the finish of the verses is primary.

For it is not meters, but a meter-making argument that makes a poem, — a thought so passionate and alive that like the spirit of a plant or an animal it has an architecture of its own, and adorns nature with a new thing. The thought and the form are equal in the order of time, but in the order of genesis the thought is prior to the form. The poet has a new thought; he has a whole new experience to unfold; he will tell us how it was with him, and all men will be the richer in his fortune. For the experience of each new age requires a new confession, and the world seems always waiting for its poet.

The Poet

METER-MAKING ARGUMENT. *Chimborazo under the line:* mountain in Ecuador, south of the Equator.

Edgar Allan Poe (1809 – 1849)

A LONG POEM DOES NOT EXIST   1848

I hold that a long poem does not exist. I maintain that the phrase, "a long poem," is simply a flat contradiction in terms.

I need scarcely observe that a poem deserves its title only inasmuch as it excites, by elevating the soul. The value of the poem is in the ratio of its elevative excitement. But all excitements are, through a psychal necessity, transient. That degree of excitement which would entitle a poem to be so called at all cannot be sustained throughout a composition of any great length. After the lapse of half an hour, at the very utmost, its flags — fails — a revulsion ensues — and then the poem is in effect, and in fact, no longer such.

The Poetic Principle

Robert Frost (1874 – 1963)

THE SOUND OF SENSE   (1913)

I alone of English writers have consciously set myself to make music out of what I may call the sound of sense. Now it is possible to have sense without the sound of sense (as in much prose that is supposed to pass muster but makes very dull reading) and the sound of sense without sense (as in Alice in Wonderland which makes anything but dull reading). The best place to get the abstract sound of sense is from voices behind a door that cuts off the words. Ask yourself how these sentences would sound without the words in which they are embodied:

> You mean to tell me you can't read?
> I said no such thing.
> Well read then.
> You're not my teacher.
>
> .   .   .
>
> He says it's too late.
> Oh, say!
> Damn an Ingersoll watch anyway.
>
> .   .   .
>
> One-two-three — go!
> No good! Come back — come back.
> Haslam go down there and make those kids get out of the track.
>
> .   .   .

Those sounds are summoned by the [audial] imagination and they must be positive, strong, and definitely and unmistakably indicated by the context. The reader must be at no loss to give his voice the posture proper to the sentence. The simple declarative sentence used in making a plain statement is one sound.

But Lord love ye it mustn't be worked to death. It is against the law of nature that whole poems should be written in it. If they are written they won't be read. The sound of sense, then. You get that. It is the abstract vitality of our speech. It is pure sound — pure form. One who concerns himself with it more than the subject is an artist. But remember we are still talking merely of the raw material of poetry. An ear and an appetite for these sounds of sense is the first qualification of a writer, be it of prose or verse. But if one is to be a poet he must learn to get cadences by skillfully breaking the sounds of sense with all their irregularity of accent across the regular beat of the meter. Verse in which there is nothing but the beat of the meter furnished by the accents of the polysyllabic words we call doggerel. Verse is not that. Neither is it the sound of sense alone. It is a resultant from those two. There are only two or three meters that are worth anything. We depend for variety on the infinite play of accents in the sound of sense. The high possibility of emotional expression all lets in this mingling of sense-sound and word-accent. A curious thing. And all this has its bearing on your prose, me boy. Never if you can help it write down a sentence in which the voice will not know how to posture *specially*.

Letter to John T. Bartlett, from *Selected Letters*
of Robert Frost, ed. Lawrance Thompson
(New York: Holt, 1964)

Wallace Stevens (1879 – 1955)

PROVERBS   1957

The poet makes silk dresses out of worms.

After one has abandoned a belief in God, poetry is that essence which takes its place as life's redemption.

All poetry is experimental poetry.

One reads poetry with one's nerves.

A poet looks at the world as a man looks at a woman.

Aristotle is a skeleton.

Thought tends to collect in pools.

Poetry must resist the intelligence almost successfully.

One cannot spend one's time in being modern when there are so many more important things to be.

Adagia, Opus Posthumous

William Carlos Williams (1883 – 1963)

THE RHYTHM PERSISTS (1913?)

No action, no creative action is complete but a period from a greater action going in rhythmic course. . . . Imagination creates an image, point by point, piece by piece, segment by segment — into a whole, living. But each part as it plays into its neighbor, each segment into its neighbor segment and every part into every other, causing the whole — exists naturally in rhythm, and as there are waves there are tides and as there are ridges in the sand there are bars after bars. . . .

I do not believe in *vers libre,* this contradiction in terms. Either the motion continues or it does not continue, either there is rhythm or no rhythm. *Vers libre* is prose. In the hands of Whitman it was a good tool, a kind of synthetic chisel — the best he had. In his bag of chunks even lie some of the pieces of rhythmic life of which we must build. This is honor enough. *Vers libre* is finished — Whitman did all that was necessary with it. Verse has nothing to gain here and all to lose. . . .

Each piece of work, rhythmic in whole, is then in essence an assembly of tides, waves, ripples — in short, of greater and lesser rhythmic particles regularly repeated or destroyed.

Essay "Speech Rhythm" quoted by Mike Weaver,
William Carlos Williams, The American Background
(New York: Cambridge University Press, 1971)

Ezra Pound (1885 – 1972)

POETRY AND MUSIC 1934

The great lyric age lasted while Campion made his own music, while Lawes set Waller's verses, while verses, if not actually sung or set to music, were at least made with the intention of going to music.

Music rots when it gets *too far* from the dance. Poetry atrophies when it gets too far from music.

ABC of Reading

T. S. Eliot (1888 – 1965)

EMOTION AND PERSONALITY

1920

It is not in his personal emotions, the emotions provoked by particular events in his life, that the poet is in any way remarkable or interesting. His particular emotions may be simple, or crude, or flat. The emotion in his poetry will be a very complex thing, but not with the complexity of the emotions of people who have very complex or unusual emotions in life. One error, in fact, of eccentricity in poetry is to seek for new human emotions to express; and in this search for novelty in the wrong place it discovers the perverse. The business of the poet is not to find new emotions, but to use the ordinary ones and, in working them up into poetry, to express feelings which are not in actual emotions at all. And emotions which he has never experienced will serve his turn as well as those familiar to him. Consequently, we must believe that "emotion recollected in tranquillity" is an inexact formula. For it is neither emotion, nor recollection, nor, without distortion of meaning, tranquillity. It is a concentration, and a new thing resulting from the concentration, of a very great number of experiences which to the practical and active person would not seem to be experiences at all; it is a concentration which does not happen consciously or of deliberation. These experiences are not "recollected," and they finally unite in an atmosphere which is "tranquil" only in that it is a passive attending upon the event. Of course this is not quite the whole story. There is a great deal, in the writing of poetry, which must be conscious and deliberate. In fact, the bad poet is usually unconscious where he ought to be conscious, and conscious where he ought to be unconscious. Both errors tend to make him "personal." Poetry is not a turning loose of emotion, but an escape from emotion; it is not the expression of personality, but an escape from personality. But, of course, only those who have personality and emotions know what it means to want to escape from these things.

Tradition and the Individual Talent

Yvor Winters (1900 – 1968)

THE FALLACY OF EXPRESSIVE FORM

1939

I cannot grasp the contemporary notion that the traditional virtues of style are incompatible with a poetry of modern subject matter; it appears to rest on the fallacy of expressive form, the notion that the form of the poem should express the matter. This fallacy results in the writing of chaotic poetry about the traffic; of loose poetry about our sprawling nation; of semi-conscious poetry about our semi-conscious states. But the matter of poetry is and always has been chaotic; it is raw nature. To let the form of the poem succumb to its matter is and always will be the destruction of poetry and may be the destruction of intelligence.

Before Disaster

Randall Jarrell (1914 – 1965)

ON THE CHARGE THAT MODERN POETRY IS OBSCURE 1953

That the poet, the modern poet, is, understandably enough, for all sorts of good reasons, more obscure than even he has any imaginable right to be — this is one of those great elementary (or, as people say nowadays, *elemental*) attitudes about which it is hard to write anything that is not sensible and gloomily commonplace; one might as well talk on faith and works, on heredity and environment, or on that old question: why give the poor bath-tubs when they only use them to put coal in? Anyone knows enough to reply to this question: "They don't; and, even if they did, *that's* not the reason you don't want to help pay for the tubs." Similarly, when someone says, "I don't read modern poetry because it's all stuff that nobody on earth can understand," I know enough to be able to answer, though not aloud: "It isn't; and, even if it were, *that's* not the reason you don't read it." . . . And people who have inherited the custom of not reading poets justify it by referring to the obscurity of the poems they have never read — since most people decide that poets are obscure very much as legislators decide that books are pornographic: by glancing at a few fragments someone has strung together to disgust them. When a person says accusingly that he can't understand Eliot, his tone implies that most of his happiest hours are spent at the fireside among worn copies of the *Agamemnon, Phèdre,* and the Symbolic Books of William Blake; and it is melancholy to find, as one commonly will, that for months at a time he can be found pushing eagerly through the pages of *Gone with the Wind* or *Forever Amber.*°

The Obscurity of the Poet,
Poetry and the Age

ON THE CHARGE THAT MODERN POETRY IS OBSCURE. *Forever Amber:* novel by Kathleen Winsor, a best-seller in its day (1945). Much of its action takes place in bed.

Sylvia Plath (1932 – 1963)

THE MAGIC MOUNTAINS 1957

The artist's life nourishes itself on the particular, the concrete: that came to me last night as I despaired about writing poems on the concept of the seven deadly sins and told myself to get rid of the killing idea: this must be a great work of philosophy. Start with the mat-green fungus in the pine woods yesterday: words about it, describing it — and a poem will come. Daily, simply, and then it won't lower in the distance, an untouchable object. Write about the cow, Mrs. Spaulding's heavy eyelids, the smell of vanilla flavoring in a brown bottle. That's where the magic mountains begin.

Journals

Robert Scholes (b. 1929)

'HOW DO WE MAKE A POEM?'   1982

Let us begin with one of the shortest poetic texts in the English language,
"Elegy" by W. S. Merwin:

Who would I show it to

One line, one sentence, unpunctuated, but proclaimed an interrogative by its
grammar and syntax — what makes it a poem? Certainly without its title it
would not be a poem; but neither would the title alone constitute a poetic text.
Nor do the two together simply make a poem by themselves. Given the title
and the text, the *reader* is encouraged to make a poem. He is not forced to do
so, but there is not much else he can do with this material, and certainly
nothing else so rewarding. (I will use the masculine pronoun here to refer to
the reader, not because all readers are male but because I am, and my hypotheti-
cal reader is not a pure construct but an idealized version of myself.)

How do we make a poem out of this text? There are only two things to work
on, the title and the question posed by the single, colloquial line. The line is
not simply colloquial, it is prosaic; with no words of more than one syllable,
concluded by a preposition, it is within the utterance range of every speaker
of English. It is, in a sense, completely intelligible. But in another sense it is
opaque, mysterious. Its three pronouns — who, I, it — pose problems of reference. Its conditional verb phrase — would . . . show to — poses a problem of
situation. The context that would supply the information required to make that
simple sentence meaningful as well as intelligible is not there. It must be
supplied by the reader.

To make a poem of this text the reader must not only know English, he
must know a poetic code as well: the code of the funeral elegy, as practiced in
English from the Renaissance to the present time. The "words on the page"
do not constitute a poetic "work," complete and self-sufficient, but a "text,"
a sketch or outline that must be completed by the active participation of a
reader equipped with the right sort of information. In this case part of that
information consists of an acquaintance with the elegiac tradition: its procedures, assumptions, devices, and values. One needs to know works like Milton's
"Lycidas," Shelley's "Adonais," Tennyson's "In Memoriam," Whitman's
"When Lilacs Last in the Dooryard Bloomed," Thomas's "Refusal to Mourn
the Death by Fire of a Child in London," and so on, in order to "read" this
simple poem properly. In fact, it could be argued that the more elegies one can
bring to bear on a reading of this one, the better, richer poem this one becomes.
I would go even further, suggesting that a knowledge of the critical tradition
— of Dr. Johnson's objections to "Lycidas," for instance, or Wordsworth's
critique of poetic diction — will also enhance one's reading of this poem. For

the poem is, of course, an anti-elegy, a refusal not simply to mourn, but to write a sonorous, eloquent, mournful, but finally acquiescent, accepting — in a word, "elegiac" — poem at all.

Reading the poem involves, then, a special knowledge of its tradition. It also involves a special interpretive skill. The forms of the short, written poem as they have developed in English over the past few centuries can be usefully seen as compressed, truncated, or fragmented imitations of other verbal forms, especially the play, story, public oration, and personal essay. The reasons for this are too complicated for consideration here, but the fact will be apparent to all who reflect upon the matter. Our short poems are almost always elliptical version of what can easily be conceived of as dramatic, narrative, oratorical, or meditative texts. Often, they are combinations of these and other modes of address. To take an obvious example, the dramatic monologue in the hands of Robert Browning is like a speech from a play (though usually more elongated than most such speeches). But to "read" such a monologue we must imagine the setting, the situation, the context, and so on. The dramatic monologue is "like" a play but gives us less information of certain sorts than a play would, requiring us to provide that information by decoding the clues in the mono-logue itself in the light of our understanding of the generic model. Most short poems work this way. They require both special knowledge and special skills to be "read."

To understand "Elegy" we must construct a situation out of the clues provided. The "it" in "Who would I show it to" is of course the elegy itself. The "I" is the potential writer of the elegy. The "Who" is the audience for the poem. But the verb phrase "would . . . show to" indicates a condition contrary to fact. Who would I show it to *if* I were to write it? This implies in turn that for the potential elegiac poet there is one person whose appreciation means more than that of all the rest of the potential audience for the poem he might write, and it further implies that the death of this particular person is the one imagined in the poem. If this person were dead, the poet suggests, so would his inspiration be dead. With no one to write for, no poem would be forthcoming. This poem is not only a "refusal to mourn," like that of Dylan Thomas, it is a refusal to elegize. The whole elegiac tradition, like its cousin the funeral oration, turns finally away from mourning toward acceptance, revival, renewal, a return to the concerns of life, symbolized by the very writing of the poem. Life goes on; there *is* an audience; and the mourned person will live through accomplishments, influence, descendants, and also (not least) in the elegiac poem itself. Merwin rejects all that. *If* I wrote an elegy for X, the person for whom I have always written, X would not be alive to read it; therefore, there is no reason to write an elegy for the one person in my life who most deserves one; therefore, there is no reason to write any elegy, anymore, ever. Finally, and of course, this poem called "Elegy" is not an elegy.

Semiotics and Interpretation

Sandra M. Gilbert (b. 1936) and **Susan Gubar** (b. 1944)

The Freedom of Emily Dickinson   1985

[Emily Dickinson] defined herself as a *woman* writer, reading the works of female precursors with special care, attending to the implications of novels like Charlotte Brontë's *Jane Eyre*, Emily Brontë's *Wuthering Heights*, and George Eliot's *Middlemarch* with the same absorbed delight that characterized her devotion to Elizabeth Barrett Browning's *Aurora Leigh*. Finally, then, the key to her enigmatic identity as a "supposed person" who was called the "Myth of Amherst" may rest, not in investigations of her questionable romance, but in studies of her unquestionably serious reading as well as in analyses of her disquietingly powerful writing. Elliptically phrased, intensely compressed, her poems are more linguistically innovative than any other nineteenth-century verses, with the possible exception of some works by Walt Whitman and Gerard Manley Hopkins, her two most radical male contemporaries. Throughout her largely secret but always brilliant career, moreover, she confronted precisely the questions about the individual and society, time and death, flesh and spirit, that major precursors from Milton to Keats had faced. Dreaming of "Amplitude and Awe," she recorded sometimes vengeful, sometimes mystical visions of social and personal transformation in poems as inventively phrased and imaginatively constructed as any in the English language.

Clearly such accomplishments required not only extraordinary talent but also some measure of freedom. Yet because she was the unmarried daughter of conservative New Englanders, Dickinson was obliged to take on many household tasks; as a nineteenth-century New England wife, she would have had the same number of obligations, if not more. Some of these she performed with pleasure; in 1856, for instance, she was judge of a bread-baking contest, and in 1857 she won a prize in that contest. But as Higginson's "scholar," as a voracious reader and an ambitious writer, Dickinson had to win herself time for "Amplitude and Awe," and it is increasingly clear that she did so through a strategic withdrawal from her ordinary world. A story related by her niece Martha Dickinson Bianchi reveals that the poet herself knew from the first what both the price and the prize might be: on one occasion, said Mrs. Bianchi, Dickinson took her up to the room in which she regularly sequestered herself, and, mimicking locking herself in, "thumb and forefinger closed on an imaginary key," said "with a quick turn of her wrist, 'It's just a turn — and freedom, Matty!'"

In the freedom of her solitary, but not lonely, room, Dickinson may have become what her Amherst neighbors saw as a bewildering "myth." Yet there, too, she created myths of her own. Reading the Brontës and Barrett Browning, studying Transcendentalism and the Bible, she contrived a theology which is powerfully expressed in many of her poems. That it was at its most hopeful a female-centered theology is revealed in verses like those she wrote about the women artists she admired, as well as in more general works like her gravely pantheistic address to the "Sweet Mountains" who "tell me no lie," with its definition of the hills around Amherst as "strong Madonnas" and its description of the writer herself as "The Wayward Nun — beneath the Hill — / Whose service is to You — ." As Dickinson's admirer and descendant Adrienne Rich has accurately observed, this passionate poet consistently chose to confront her society — to "have it out" — "on her own premises."

Introduction to Emily Dickinson,
The Norton Anthology of Literature by Women

DRAMA

Unlike a short story or a novel, a **play** is a work of storytelling in which actors represent the characters. In another essential, a play differs from a work of fiction: it is addressed not to readers but to spectators.

To be part of an audience in a theater is an experience far different from reading a story in solitude. Expectant as the house lights dim and the curtain rises, we become members of a community. The responses of people around us affect our own responses. We, too, contribute to the community's response whenever we laugh, sigh, applaud, murmur in surprise, or catch our breath in excitement. In contrast, when all alone we watch a movie by means of a videocassette recorder—say, a slapstick comedy—we probably laugh less often than if we were watching the same film in a theater, surrounded by a roaring crowd. Of course, no one is spilling popcorn down the back of our necks. Each kind of theatrical experience, to be sure, has its advantages.

A theater of live actors has another advantage: a sensitive give-and-take between actors and audience. Such rapport, of course, depends on the actors being skilled and the audience perceptive. Although professional actors may try to give a top-class performance on all occasions, it is natural for them to feel more keenly inspired by a lively, appreciative audience than by a dull, lethargic one. No doubt a large turnout of spectators also helps draw the best from performers on stage: the *Othello* you get may be somewhat less inspired if you are part of an audience that may be counted on the fingers of one hand. But at any rate, as veteran playgoers well know, something unique and wonderful can happen when good actors and a good audience respond to each other.

In another sense, a play is more than actors and audience: Like a short story or a poem, a play is a work of art made of words. The playwright devoted thought and care and skill to the selection and arrangement of language. Watching a play, of course, we do not notice the playwright standing between us and the characters.[1] If the play is absorbing, it flows before our eyes. In a silent reading, the usual play consists mainly of **dialogue,** exchanges of speech, punctuated by stage directions.[2] In performance, though, stage directions vanish. And although the thoughtful efforts of perhaps a hundred people—actors, director, producer, stage designer, costumer, makeup artist, technicians—may have gone into a production, a successful play makes us forget its artifice. We may even forget that the play is literature, for its gestures, facial expressions, bodily stances, lighting, and special effects are as much a part of it as the playwright's written words. Even though words are not all there is to a living play, they are its bones. And the whole play, the finished production, is the total of whatever transpires on stage.

The sense of immediacy we derive from **drama** is suggested by the root of the word. *Drama* means "action" or "deed" (from the Greek *dran*, "to do"). We use *drama* as a synonym for *plays*, but the word has several meanings. Sometimes it refers to one play ("a stirring drama"); or to the work of a playwright, or **dramatist** ("Ibsen's drama"); or perhaps to a body of plays written in a particular time or place ("Elizabethan drama," "French drama of the seventeenth century"). In yet another familiar sense, *drama* often means events that elicit high excitement: "A real-life drama," a news story might begin, "was enacted today before lunchtime crowds in downtown Manhattan as firemen battled to free two children trapped on the sixteenth floor of a burning building." In this sense, whatever is "dramatic" implies suspense, tension, or conflict. Plays, as we shall see, frequently contain such "dramatic" chains of events; and yet, if we expect all plays to be crackling with suspense or conflict, we may be disappointed. Some, such as Maria Irene Fornes' *A Vietnamese Wedding*, create little suspense, but they do compel our attention. "Good drama," said critic George Jean Nathan, "is anything that interests an intelligently emotional group of persons assembled together in an illuminated hall."

In partaking of the nature of ritual—something to be repeated in front of an audience on a special occasion—drama is akin to a festival (whether a religious festival or a rock festival) or a church service. Twice in the history of Europe, drama has sprung forth as a part of worship: when in ancient Greece, plays were performed on feast days; and when in the Christian church of the Middle Ages, a play was introduced as an adjunct to the Easter mass with the enactment of the meeting between the three Marys and the angel at Jesus' empty tomb. Evidently something in drama remains constant over the years—something as old, perhaps, as the deepest desires and highest aspirations of humanity.

---

[1] The word *playwright*, by the way, invites misspelling. Notice that it is not *playwrite*. The suffix *-wright* (from Old English) means "one who makes"—like a *boatwright*, a worker in a trade.

[2] Not all plays employ dialogue. There is also **pantomime**—generally, a play without words (sometimes also called a **dumb show**). Originally, in ancient Rome, a pantomime meant an actor who singlehandedly played all the parts. An eminent modern pantomime (or **mime**) is French stage and screen actor Marcel Marceau.

32   Reading a Play

Most plays are written not to be read in books but to be performed. Finding plays in a literature anthology, the student may well ask, Isn't there something wrong with the idea of reading plays on the printed page? To do so—to treat them as literature—isn't that a perversion of their nature?

True, plays are meant to be seen on stage, but equally true, reading a play may afford advantages. One is that it is better to know some masterpieces by reading them than never to know them at all. Even if you live in a large city with many theaters, even if you attend a college with many theatrical productions, to succeed in your lifetime in witnessing, say, all the plays of Shakespeare might well be impossible. In print, they are as near-to-hand as a book on a shelf, ready to be enacted (if you like) on the stage of the mind.

After all, a play is literature before it comes alive in a theater; and it might be argued that when we read an unfamiliar play, we meet it in the same form in which it first appears to its actors and its director. If a play is rich and complex, or if it dates from the remote past and contains difficulties of language and allusion, to read it on the page enables us to study it at our leisure, to return to the parts that demand greater scrutiny.

Let us admit, by the way, that some plays, whatever the intentions of their authors, are destined to be read more often than they are acted. Such a play is sometimes called a **closet drama**—"closet" meaning a small, private room. Percy Bysshe Shelley's neo-Shakespearean tragedy The Cenci (1819) has seldom escaped from its closet, even though Shelley tried without luck to have it performed on the London stage. Perhaps too rich in talk to please an audience or too sparse in opportunities for actors to use their bodies, such works nevertheless may lead long, respectable lives on their own, solely as literature.

But even if a play may be seen in a theater, sometimes to read it in print may be our way of knowing it as the author wrote it in its entirety. Far from regarding Shakespeare's words as holy writ, producers of Hamlet, King Lear, Othello, and other masterpieces often leave out whole speeches and scenes, or shorten them. Besides, the nature of the play, as far as you can tell from a stage production, may depend upon decisions of the director. Shall *Othello* dress as a Renaissance Moor, or as a jet-set contemporary? Every actor who plays Iago in *Othello* makes his own interpretation of this knotty character. Some see Iago as a figure of pure evil; others, as a madman; still others, as a suffering human being consumed by hatred, jealousy, and pride. What do you think Shakespeare meant? You can always read the play and decide for yourself. If every stage production of a play is a fresh interpretation, so too is every reader's reading of it.

Some readers, when silently reading a play to themselves, try to visualize a stage, imagining the characters in costume and under lights. If such a reader is an actor or a director and is reading the play with an eye to staging it, then that reader may try to imagine every detail of a possible production, even shades of makeup and loudness of sound effects. But the nonprofessional reader, who regards the play as literature, need not attempt such exhaustive imagining. Although some readers find it enjoyable to imagine the play taking place upon a stage, others prefer to imagine the people and events that the play brings vividly to mind. Sympathetically following the tangled life of Nora in *A Doll House* by Henrik Ibsen, we forget that we are reading printed stage directions and instead find ourselves in the presence of human conflict. Thus regarded, a play becomes a form of storytelling, and the playwright's instructions to the actors and the director become a conventional mode of narrative that we accept much as we accept the methods of a novel or short story. If we read *A Doll House* caring more about Nora's fate than the imagined appearance of an actress portraying her, we speed through an ordinary passage such as this (from a scene in which Nora's husband hears the approach of an unwanted caller, Dr. Rank):

> Helmer (*with quiet irritation*): Oh, what does he want now? (*Aloud.*) Hold on. (*Goes and opens the door.*) Oh, how nice that you didn't just pass us by!

We read the passage, if the story absorbs us, as though we were reading a novel whose author, employing the conventional devices for recording speech in fiction, might have written:

> "Oh, what does he want now?" said Helmer under his breath, in annoyance. Aloud, he called, "Hold on," then walked to the door and opened it and greeted Rank with all the cheer he could muster—"Oh, how nice that you didn't pass us by!"

Such is the power of an excellent play to make us ignore the playwright's artistry that it becomes a window through which the reader's gaze, given focus, encompasses more than language and typography and beholds a scene of imagined life.

Most plays, whether seen in a theater or in print, employ *some* **conventions**: customary methods of presenting an action, usual and recognizable devices that an audience is willing to accept. In reading a great play from the past, such as *Oedipus the King* or *Othello*, it will help if we know some of the conventions of the classical Greek theater or the Elizabethan theater. When in *Oedipus the King* we encounter a character called the Chorus, it may be useful to be aware that this is a group of citizens who stand to one side of the action, conversing with the principal character and commenting. In *Othello*, when the sinister Iago, left on stage alone, begins to speak (at the end of Act II, Scene 1), we recognize the conventional device of a **soliloquy,** a dramatic monologue in which we seem to overhear the character's inmost thoughts uttered aloud. Like conventions in poetry, such familiar methods of staging a story afford us a happy shock of recognition. Often, as in these examples, they are ways of making clear to us exactly what the playwright would have us know.

A Play in Its Elements

When we read a play on the printed page and find ourselves swept forward by the motion of its story, we need not wonder how—and of what ingredients—the playwright put it together. Still, to analyze the structure of a play is one way to understand and appreciate a playwright's art. Analysis is complicated, however, because in an excellent play the elements (including plot, theme, and characters) do not stand in isolation. Often, deeds clearly follow from the kinds of people the characters are, and from those deeds it is left to the reader to infer the **theme** of the play—the general point or truth about human beings that may be drawn from it. Perhaps the most meaningful way to study the elements of a play (and certainly the most enjoyable) is to consider a play in its entirety.

Here is a short, famous one-act play worth reading for the boldness of its elements—and for its own sake. *Trifles* tells the story of a murder. As you will discover, the "trifles" mentioned in its title are not of trifling stature. In reading the play, you will probably find yourself imagining what you might see on stage if you were in a theater. You may also care to imagine what took place in the lives of the characters before the curtain rose. All this imagining may sound like a tall order, but don't worry. Just read the play for enjoyment the first time through, and then we will consider whatever makes it effective.

TRIFLES   1916

*Susan Glaspell (1882–1948), grew up in her
native Davenport, Iowa, daughter of a grain
dealer. After four years at Drake University
and a reporting job in Des Moines, she settled
in New York's Greenwich Village. In 1915,
with her husband George Cram Cook, a
theatrical director, she founded the Provincetown Players, the first influential noncommercial theater troupe in America. Summers,
in a makeshift playhouse on a Cape Cod pier,
the Players staged the earliest plays of Eugene
O'Neill and work by John Reed, Edna St. Vincent Millay, and Glaspell herself. (Later trans-
planting the company to New York, Glaspell
and Cook renamed it the Playwrights' Theater.)
Glaspell wrote several still-remembered plays,
among them a pioneering work of feminist
drama, The Verge (1921), and the Pulitzer
prize-winning Alison's House (1930), about
the family of a reclusive poet like Emily Dick-*

Susan Glaspell

*inson who, after her death, squabble over the right to publish her poems. First widely
known for her fiction with an Iowa background, Glaspell wrote ten novels, including
Fidelity (1915) and The Morning Is Near Us (1939). Shortly after writing the play*
Trifles, she rewrote it as a short story, "A Jury of Her Peers."

Characters

George Henderson, county attorney
Henry Peters, sheriff
Lewis Hale, a neighboring farmer
Mrs. Peters
Mrs. Hale

Scene. *The kitchen in the now abandoned farmhouse of John Wright, a gloomy kitchen,
and left without having been put in order—unwashed pans under the sink, a loaf of bread
outside the breadbox, a dish towel on the table—other signs of incompleted work. At
the rear the outer door opens and the Sheriff comes in followed by the County Attorney
and Hale. The Sheriff and Hale are men in middle life, the County Attorney is a young
man; all are much bundled up and go at once to the stove. They are followed by two
women—the Sheriff's wife first; she is a slight wiry woman, a thin nervous face. Mrs.
Hale is larger and would ordinarily be called more comfortable looking, but she is disturbed now and looks fearfully about as she enters. The women have come in slowly,
and stand close together near the door.*

County Attorney: [Rubbing his hands.] This feels good. Come up to the fire, ladies.

Mrs. Peters: [After taking a step forward.] I'm not—cold.

Sheriff: [Unbuttoning his overcoat and stepping away from the stove as if to mark the beginning of official business.] Now, Mr. Hale, before we move things about, you explain to Mr. Henderson just what you saw when you came here yesterday morning.

County Attorney: By the way, has anything been moved? Are things just as you left them yesterday?

Sheriff: [Looking about.] It's just the same. When it dropped below zero last night I thought I'd better send Frank out this morning to make a fire for us—no use getting pneumonia with a big case on, but I told him not to touch anything except the stove—and you know Frank.

County Attorney: Somebody should have been left here yesterday.

Sheriff: Oh—yesterday. When I had to send Frank to Morris Center for that man who went crazy—I want you to know I had my hands full yesterday, I knew you could get back from Omaha by today and as long as I went over everything here myself—

County Attorney: Well, Mr. Hale, tell just what happened when you came here yesterday morning.

Hale: Harry and I had started to town with a load of potatoes. We came along the road from my place and as I got here I said, "I'm going to see if I can't get John Wright to go in with me on a party telephone." I spoke to Wright about it once before and he put me off, saying folks talked too much anyway, and all he asked was peace and quiet—I guess you know about how much he talked himself; but I thought maybe if I went to the house and talked about it before his wife, though I said to Harry that I didn't know as what his wife wanted made much difference to John—

County Attorney: Let's talk about that later, Mr. Hale. I do want to talk about that, but tell now just what happened when you got to the house.

Hale: I didn't hear or see anything; I knocked at the door, and still it was all quiet inside. I knew they must be up, it was past eight o'clock. So I knocked again, and I thought I heard somebody say, "Come in." I wasn't sure, I'm not sure yet, but I opened the door—this door [Indicating the door by which the two women are still standing] and there in that rocker—[Pointing to it] sat Mrs. Wright.

[They all look at the rocker.]

County Attorney: What—was she doing?

Hale: She was rockin' back and forth. She had her apron in her hand and was kind of—pleating it.

County Attorney: And how did she—look?

Hale: Well, she looked queer.

County Attorney: How do you mean—queer?

Hale: Well, as if she didn't know what she was going to do next. And kind of done up.

County Attorney: How did she seem to feel about your coming?

Hale: Why, I don't think she minded—one way or other. She didn't pay much attention. I said, "How do, Mrs. Wright, it's cold, ain't it?" And she said, "Is it?"—and went on kind of pleating at her apron. Well, I was surprised; she didn't ask me to come up to the stove, or to set down, but just sat there, not even looking at me, so I said, "I want to see John." And then she—laughed. I guess you would call it a laugh. I thought of Harry and the team outside, so I said a little sharp: "Can't I see John?" "No," she says, kind o' dull like. "Ain't he home?" says I. "Yes," says she, "he's home." "Then why can't I see him?" I asked her, out of patience. " 'Cause he's dead," says she. "*Dead?*" says I. She just nodded her head, not getting a bit excited, but rockin' back and forth. "Why—where is he?" says I, not knowing what to say. She just pointed upstairs—like that [*Himself pointing to the room above.*] I got up, with the idea of going up there. I walked from there to here—then I says, "Why, what did he die of?" "He died of a rope round his neck," says she, and just went on pleatin' at her apron. Well, I went out and called Harry. I thought I might— need help. We went upstairs and there he was lyin'—

County Attorney: I think I'd rather have you go into that upstairs, where you can point it all out. Just go on now with the rest of the story.

Hale: Well, my first thought was to get that rope off. It looked . . . [*Stops, his face twitches*] . . . but Harry, he went up to him, and he said, "No, he's dead all right, and we'd better not touch anything." So we went back down stairs. She was still sitting that same way. "Has anybody been notified?" I asked. "No," says she, unconcerned. "Who did this, Mrs. Wright?" said Harry. He said it businesslike—and she stopped pleatin' of her apron. "I don't know," she says. "You don't *know?*" says Harry. "No," says she. "Weren't you sleepin' in the bed with him?" says Harry. "Yes," says she, "but I was on the inside." "Somebody slipped a rope round his neck and strangled him and you didn't wake up?" says Harry. "I didn't wake up," she said after him. We must 'a looked as if we didn't see how that could be, for after a minute she said, "I sleep sound." Harry was going to ask her more questions but I said maybe we ought to let her tell her story first to the coroner, or the sheriff, so Harry went fast as he could to Rivers' place, where there's a telephone.

County Attorney: And what did Mrs. Wright do when she knew that you had gone for the coroner?

Hale: She moved from that chair to this one over here [*Pointing to a small chair in the corner*] and just sat there with her hands held together and looking down. I got a feeling that I ought to make some conversation, so I said I had come in to see if John wanted to put in a telephone, and at that she started to laugh, and then she stopped and looked at me—scared. [*The County Attorney, who has had his notebook out, makes a note.*] I dunno, maybe it wasn't scared. I wouldn't like to say it was. Soon Harry got back, and then Dr. Lloyd came, and you, Mr. Peters, and so I guess that's all I know that you don't.

County Attorney: [*Looking around.*] I guess we'll go upstairs first—and then out to the barn and around there. [*To the Sheriff*] You're convinced that there was nothing important here—nothing that would point to any motive.

Sheriff: Nothing here but kitchen things.

[*The County Attorney, after again looking around the kitchen, opens the door of a cupboard closet. He gets up on a chair and looks on a shelf. Pulls his hand away, sticky.*]

County Attorney: Here's a nice mess.

[The women draw nearer.]

Mrs. Peters: [To the other woman.] Oh, her fruit; it did freeze. [To the County Attorney] She worried about that when it turned so cold. She said the fire'd go out and her jars would break.
Sheriff: Well, can you beat the women! Held for murder and worryin' about her preserves.
County Attorney: I guess before we're through she may have something more serious than preserves to worry about.
Hale: Well, women are used to worrying over trifles.

[The two women move a little closer together.]

County Attorney: [With the gallantry of a young politician.] And yet, for all their worries, what would we do without the ladies? [The women do not unbend. He goes to the sink, takes a dipperful of water from the pail and pouring it into a basin, washes his hands. Starts to wipe them on the roller towel, turns it for a cleaner place.] Dirty towels! [Kicks his foot against the pans under the sink.] Not much of a housekeeper, would you say, ladies?
Mrs. Hale: [Stiffly.] There's a great deal of work to be done on a farm.
County Attorney: To be sure. And yet [With a little bow to her] I know there are some Dickson county farmhouses which do not have such roller towels.

[He gives it a pull to expose its full length again.]

Mrs. Hale: Those towels get dirty awful quick. Men's hands aren't always as clean as they might be.
County Attorney: Ah, loyal to your sex, I see. But you and Mrs. Wright were neighbors. I suppose you were friends, too.
Mrs. Hale: [Shaking her head.] I've not seen much of her of late years. I've not been in this house—it's more than a year.
County Attorney: And why was that? You didn't like her?
Mrs. Hale: I liked her all well enough. Farmers' wives have their hands full, Mr. Henderson. And then—
County Attorney: Yes—?
Mrs. Hale: [Looking about.] It never seemed a very cheerful place.
County Attorney: No—it's not cheerful. I shouldn't say she had the homemaking instinct.
Mrs. Hale: Well, I don't know as Wright had, either.
County Attorney: You mean that they didn't get on very well?
Mrs. Hale: No, I don't mean anything. But I don't think a place'd be any cheerfuller for John Wright's being in it.
County Attorney: I'd like to talk more of that a little later. I want to get the lay of things upstairs now.

[He goes to the left, where three steps lead to a stair door.]

Sheriff: I suppose anything Mrs. Peters does'll be all right. She was to take in some clothes for her, you know, and a few little things. We left in such a hurry yesterday.

County Attorney: Yes, but I would like to see what you take, Mrs. Peters, and keep an eye out for anything that might be of use to us.

Mrs. Peters: Yes, Mr. Henderson.

[The women listen to the men's steps on the stairs, then look about the kitchen.]

Mrs. Hale: I'd hate to have men coming into my kitchen, snooping around and criticizing.

[She arranges the pans under sink which the County Attorney had shoved out of place.]

Mrs. Peters: Of course it's no more than their duty.

Mrs. Hale: Duty's all right, but I guess that deputy sheriff that came out to make the fire might have got a little of this on. *[Gives the roller towel a pull.]* Wish I'd thought of that sooner. Seems mean to talk about her for not having things slicked up when she had to come away in such a hurry.

Mrs. Peters: *[Who has gone to a small table in the left rear corner of the room, and lifted one end of a towel that covers a pan.]* She had bread set.

[Stands still.]

Mrs. Hale: *[Eyes fixed on a loaf of bread beside the breadbox, which is on a low shelf at the other side of the room. Moves slowly toward it.]* She was going to put this in there. *[Picks up loaf, then abruptly drops it. In a manner of returning to familiar things.]* It's a shame about her fruit. I wonder if it's all gone. *[Gets up on the chair and looks.]* I think there's some here that's all right, Mrs. Peters. Yes— here; *[Holding it toward the window]* this is cherries, too. *[Looking again.]* I declare I believe that's the only one. *[Gets down, bottle in her hand. Goes to the sink and wipes it off on the outside.]* She'll feel awful bad after all her hard work in the hot weather. I remember the afternoon I put up my cherries last summer.

[She puts the bottle on the big kitchen table, center of the room. With a sigh, is about to sit down in the rocking-chair. Before she is seated realizes what chair it is; with a slow look at it, steps back. The chair which she has touched rocks back and forth.]

Mrs. Peters: Well, I must get those things from the front room closet. *[She goes to the door at the right, but after looking into the other room, steps back.]* You coming with me, Mrs. Hale? You could help me carry them.

[They go in the other room; reappear, Mrs. Peters carrying a dress and skirt, Mrs. Hale following with a pair of shoes.]

Mrs. Peters: My, it's cold in there.

[She puts the clothes on the big table, and hurries to the stove.]

Mrs. Hale: *[Examining her skirt.]* Wright was close. I think maybe that's why she kept so much to herself. She didn't even belong to the Ladies Aid. I suppose she felt she couldn't do her part, and then you don't enjoy things when you feel shabby. She used to wear pretty clothes and be lively, when she was Minnie Foster, one of the town girls singing in the choir. But that—oh, that was thirty years ago. This all you was to take in?

Mrs. Peters: She said she wanted an apron. Funny thing to want, for there isn't much to get you dirty in jail, goodness knows. But I suppose just to make her feel more natural. She said they was in the top drawer in this cupboard. Yes, here. And then her little shawl that always hung behind the door. [Opens stair door and looks.] Yes, here it is.

[Quickly shuts door leading upstairs.]

Mrs. Hale: [Abruptly moving toward her.] Mrs. Peters?

Mrs. Peters: Yes, Mrs. Hale?

Mrs. Hale: Do you think she did it?

Mrs. Peters: [In a frightened voice.] Oh, I don't know.

Mrs. Hale: Well, I don't think she did. Asking for an apron and her little shawl. Worrying about her fruit.

Mrs. Peters: [Starts to speak, glances up, where footsteps are heard in the room above. In a low voice.] Mr. Peters says it looks bad for her. Mr. Henderson is awful sarcastic in a speech and he'll make fun of her sayin' she didn't wake up.

Mrs. Hale: Well, I guess John Wright didn't wake when they was slipping that rope under his neck.

Mrs. Peters: No, it's strange. It must have been done awful crafty and still. They say it was such a—funny way to kill a man, rigging it all up like that.

Mrs. Hale: That's just what Mr. Hale said. There was a gun in the house. He says that's what he can't understand.

Mrs. Peters: Mr. Henderson said coming out that what was needed for the case was a motive; something to show anger, or—sudden feeling.

Mrs. Hale: [Who is standing by the table.] Well, I don't see any signs of anger around here. [She puts her hand on the dish towel which lies on the table, stands looking down at table, one half of which is clean, the other half messy.] It's wiped to here. [Makes a move as if to finish work, then turns and looks at loaf of bread outside the breadbox. Drops towel. In that voice of coming back to familiar things.] Wonder how they are finding things upstairs. I hope she had it a little more red-up° up there. You know, it seems kind of sneaking. Locking her up in town and then coming out here and trying to get her own house to turn against her!

Mrs. Peters: But Mrs. Hale, the law is the law.

Mrs. Hale: I s'pose 'tis. [Unbuttoning her coat.] Better loosen up your things, Mrs. Peters. You won't feel them when you go out.

[Mrs. Peters takes off her fur tippet, goes to hang it on hook at back of room, stands looking at the under part of the small corner table.]

Mrs. Peters: She was piecing a quilt.

[She brings the large sewing basket and they look at the bright pieces.]

Mrs. Hale: It's log cabin pattern. Pretty, isn't it? I wonder if she was goin' to quilt it or just knot it?

red-up: (slang) readied up, ready to be seen.

[Footsteps have been heard coming down the stairs. The Sheriff enters followed by Hale and the County Attorney.]

Sheriff: They wonder if she was going to quilt it or just knot it!

[The men laugh; the women look abashed.]

County Attorney: [Rubbing his hands over the stove.] Frank's fire didn't do much up there, did it? Well, let's go out to the barn and get that cleared up.

[The men go outside.]

Mrs. Hale: [Resentfully.] I don't know as there's anything so strange, our takin' up our time with little things while we're waiting for them to get the evidence. *[She sits down at the big table smoothing out a block with decision.]* I don't see as it's anything to laugh about.

Mrs. Peters: [Apologetically.] Of course they've got awful important things on their minds.

[Pulls up a chair and joins Mrs. Hale at the table.]

Mrs. Hale: [Examining another block.] Mrs. Peters, look at this one. Here, this is the one she was working on, and look at the sewing! All the rest of it has been so nice and even. And look at this! It's all over the place! Why, it looks as if she didn't know what she was about!

[After she has said this they look at each, then start to glance back at the door. After an instant Mrs. Hale has pulled at a knot and ripped the sewing.]

Mrs. Peters: Oh, what are you doing, Mrs. Hale?

Mrs. Hale: [Mildly.] Just pulling out a stitch or two that's not sewed very good. *[Threading a needle.]* Bad sewing always made me fidgety.

Mrs. Peters: [Nervously.] I don't think we ought to touch things.

Mrs. Hale: I'll just finish up this end. *[Suddenly stopping and leaning forward.]* Mrs. Peters?

Mrs. Peters: Yes, Mrs. Hale?

Mrs. Hale: What do you suppose she was so nervous about?

Mrs. Peters: Oh—I don't know. I don't know as she was nervous. I sometimes sew awful queer when I'm just tired. *[Mrs. Hale starts to say something, looks at Mrs. Peters, then goes on sewing.]* Well, I must get these things wrapped up. They may be through sooner than we think. *[Putting apron and other things together.]* I wonder where I can find a piece of paper, and string.

Mrs. Hale: In that cupboard, maybe.

Mrs. Peters: [Looking in cupboard.] Why, here's a birdcage. *[Holds it up.]* Did she have a bird, Mrs. Hale?

Mrs. Hale: Why, I don't know whether she did or not—I've not been here for so long. There was a man around last year selling canaries cheap, but I don't know as she took one; maybe she did. She used to sing real pretty herself.

Mrs. Peters: [Glancing around.] Seems funny to think of a bird here. But she must have had one, or why would she have a cage? I wonder what happened to it.

Mrs. Hale: I s'pose maybe the cat got it.

Mrs. Peters: No, she didn't have a cat. She's got that feeling some people have about cats—being afraid of them. My cat got in her room and she was real upset and asked me to take it out.

Mrs. Hale: My sister Bessie was like that. Queer, ain't it?

Mrs. Peters: [Examining the cage.] Why, look at this door. It's broke. One hinge is pulled apart.

Mrs. Hale: [Looking too.] Looks as if someone must have been rough with it.

Mrs. Peters: Why, yes.

[She brings the cage forward and puts it on the table.]

Mrs. Hale: I wish if they're going to find any evidence they'd be about it. I don't like this place.

Mrs. Peters: But I'm awful glad you came with me, Mrs. Hale. It would be lonesome for me sitting here alone.

Mrs. Hale: It would, wouldn't it? [Dropping her sewing.] But I tell you what I do wish, Mrs. Peters. I wish I had come over sometimes when she was here. I— [Looking around the room.]—wish I had.

Mrs. Peters: But of course you were awful busy, Mrs. Hale—your house and your children.

Mrs. Hale: I could've come. I stayed away because it weren't cheerful—and that's why I ought to have come. I—I've never liked this place. Maybe because it's down in a hollow and you don't see the road. I dunno what it is but it's a lonesome place and always was. I wish I had come over to see Minnie Foster sometimes. I can see now—

[Shakes her head.]

Mrs. Peters: Well, you mustn't reproach yourself, Mrs. Hale. Somehow we just don't see how it is with other folks until—something comes up.

Mrs. Hale: Not having children makes less work—but it makes a quiet house, and Wright out to work all day, and no company when he did come in. Did you know John Wright, Mrs. Peters?

Mrs. Peters: Not to know him; I've seen him in town. They say he was a good man.

Mrs. Hale: Yes—good; he didn't drink, and kept his word as well as most, I guess, and paid his debts. But he was a hard man, Mrs. Peters. Just to pass the time of day with him—[Shivers.] Like a raw wind that gets to the bone. [Pauses, her eye falling on the cage.] I should think she would 'a wanted a bird. But what do you suppose went with it?

Mrs. Peters: I don't know, unless it got sick and died.

[She reaches over and swings the broken door, swings it again. Both women watch it.]

Mrs. Hale: You weren't raised round here, were you? [Mrs. Peters shakes her head.] You didn't know—her?

Mrs. Peters: Not till they brought her yesterday.

Mrs. Hale: She—come to think of it, she was kind of a like a bird herself—real sweet and pretty, but kind of timid and—fluttery. How—she—did—change. [Silence; then as if struck by a happy thought and relieved to get back to everyday *things.]* Tell you what, Mrs. Peters, why don't you take the quilt in with you? It might take up her mind.

Mrs. Peters: Why, I think that's a real nice idea, Mrs. Hale. There couldn't possibly be any objection to it, could there? Now, just what would I take? I wonder if her patches are in here—and her things.

[They look in the sewing basket.]

Mrs. Hale: Here's some red. I expect this has got sewing things in it. *[Brings out a fancy box.]* What a pretty box. Looks like something somebody would give you. Maybe her scissors are in here. *[Opens box. Suddenly puts her hand to her nose.]* Why—*[Mrs. Peters bends nearer, then turns her face away.]* There's something wrapped up in this piece of silk.

Mrs. Peters: Why, this isn't her scissors.

Mrs. Hale: *[Lifting the silk.]* Oh, Mrs. Peters—it's—

[Mrs. Peters bends closer.]

Mrs. Peters: It's the bird.

Mrs. Hale: *[Jumping up.]* But, Mrs. Peters—look at it! Its neck! Look at its neck! It's all—other side *to*.

Mrs. Peters: Somebody—wrung—its—neck.

[Their eyes meet. A look of growing comprehension, of horror. Steps are heard outside. Mrs. Hale slips box under quilt pieces, and sinks into her chair. Enter Sheriff and County Attorney. Mrs. Peters rises.]

County Attorney: *[As one turning from serious things to little pleasantries.]* Well, ladies, have you decided whether she was going to quilt it or knot it?

Mrs. Peters: We think she was going to—knot it.

County Attorney: Well, that's interesting, I'm sure. *[Seeing the birdcage.]* Has the bird flown?

Mrs. Hale: *[Putting more quilt pieces over the box.]* We think the—cat got it.

County Attorney: *[Preoccupied.]* Is there a cat?

[Mrs. Hale glances in a quick covert way at Mrs. Peters.]

Mrs. Peters: Well, not *now*. They're superstitious, you know. They leave.

County Attorney: *[To Sheriff Peters, continuing an interrupted conversation.]* No sign at all of anyone having come from the outside. Their own rope. Now let's go up again and go over it piece by piece. *[They start upstairs.]* It would have to have been someone who knew just the—

[Mrs. Peters sits down. The two women sit there not looking at one another, but as if peering into something and at the same time holding back. When they talk now it is in the manner of feeling their way over strange ground, as if afraid of what they are saying, but as if they can not help saying it.]

Mrs. Hale: She liked the bird. She was going to bury it in that pretty box.

Mrs. Peters: *[In a whisper.]* When I was a girl—my kitten—there was a boy took a hatchet, and before my eyes—and before I could get there—*[Covers her face an instant]* If they hadn't held me back I would have—*[Catches herself, looks upstairs where steps are heard, falters weakly]*—hurt him.

Mrs. Hale: *[With a slow look around her.]* I wonder how it would seem never to have had any children around. *[Pause.]* No, Wright wouldn't like the bird—a thing that sang. She used to sing. He killed that, too.

Mrs. Peters: *[Moving uneasily.]* We don't know who killed the bird.

Mrs. Hale: I knew John Wright.

Mrs. Peters: It was an awful thing was done in this house that night, Mrs. Hale. Killing a man while he slept, slipping a rope around his neck that choked the life out of him.

Mrs. Hale: His neck. Choked the life out of him.

[Her hand goes out and rests on the birdcage.]

Mrs. Peters: *[With rising voice.]* We don't know who killed him. We don't know.

Mrs. Hale: *[Her own feeling not interrupted.]* If there'd been years and years of nothing, then a bird to sing to you, it would be awful—still, after the bird was still.

Mrs. Peters: *[Something within her speaking.]* I know what stillness is. When we homesteaded in Dakota, and my first baby died—after he was two years old, and me with no other then—

Mrs. Hale: *[Moving.]* How soon do you suppose they'll be through, looking for the evidence?

Mrs. Peters: I know what stillness is. *[Pulling herself back.]* The law has got to punish crime, Mrs. Hale.

Mrs. Hale: *[Not as if answering that.]* I wish you'd seen Minnie Foster when she wore a white dress with blue ribbons and stood up there in the choir and sang. *[A look around the room.]* Oh, I *wish* I'd come over here once in a while! That was a crime! That was a crime! Who's going to punish that?

Mrs. Peters: *[Looking upstairs.]* We mustn't—take on.

Mrs. Hale: I might have known she needed help! I know how things can be—for women. I tell you, it's queer, Mrs. Peters. We live close together and we live far apart. We all go through the same things—it's all just a different kind of the same thing. *[Brushes her eyes; noticing the bottle of fruit, reaches out for it.]* If I was you I wouldn't tell her her fruit was gone. Tell her it *ain't.* Tell her it's all right. Take this in to prove it to her. She—she may never know whether it was broke or not.

Mrs. Peters: *[Takes the bottle, looks about for something to wrap it in; takes petticoat from the clothes brought from the other room, very nervously begins winding this around the bottle. In a false voice.]* My, it's a good thing the men couldn't hear us. Wouldn't they just laugh! Getting all stirred up over a little thing like a—dead canary. As if that could have anything to do with—with—wouldn't they *laugh!*

[The men are heard coming down stairs.]

Mrs. Hale: *[Under her breath.]* Maybe they would—maybe they wouldn't.

County Attorney: No, Peters, it's all perfectly clear except a reason for doing it. But you know juries when it comes to women. If there was some definite thing. Something to show—something to make a story about—a thing that would connect up with this strange way of doing it—

[*The women's eyes meet for an instant. Enter Hale from outer door.*]

Hale: Well, I've got the team around. Pretty cold out there.

County Attorney: I'm going to stay here a while myself. [*To the Sheriff.*] You can send Frank out for me, can't you? I want to go over everything. I'm not satisfied that we can't do better.

Sheriff: Do you want to see what Mrs. Peters is going to take in?

[*The County Attorney goes to the table, picks up the apron, laughs.*]

County Attorney: Oh, I guess they're not very dangerous things the ladies have picked out. [*Moves a few things about, disturbing the quilt pieces which cover the box. Steps back.*] No, Mrs. Peters doesn't need supervising. For that matter, a sheriff's wife is married to the law. Ever think of it that way, Mrs. Peters?

Mrs. Peters: Not—just that way.

Sheriff: [*Chuckling.*] Married to the law. [*Moves toward the other room.*] I just want you to come in here a minute, George. We ought to take a look at these windows.

County Attorney: [*Scoffingly.*] Oh, windows!

Sheriff: We'll be right out, Mr. Hale.

[*Hale goes outside. The Sheriff follows the County Attorney into the other room. Then Mrs. Hale rises, hands tight together, looking intensely at Mrs. Peters, whose eyes make a slow turn, finally meeting Mrs. Hale's. A moment Mrs. Hale holds her, then her own eyes point the way to where the box is concealed. Suddenly Mrs. Peters throws back quilt pieces and tries to put the box in the bag she is wearing. It is too big. She opens box, starts to take bird out, cannot touch it, goes to pieces, stands there helpless. Sound of a knob turning in the other room. Mrs. Hale snatches the box and puts it in the pocket of her big coat. Enter County Attorney and Sheriff.*]

County Attorney: [*Facetiously.*] Well, Henry, at least we found out that she was not going to quilt it. She was going to—what is it you call it, ladies?

Mrs. Hale: [*Her hand against her pocket.*] We call it—knot it, Mr. Henderson.

CURTAIN

QUESTIONS

1. What attitudes toward women do the Sheriff and the County Attorney express? How do Mrs. Hale and Mrs. Peters react to these sentiments?
2. Why does the County Attorney care so much about discovering a motive for the killing?
3. What does Glaspell show us about the position of women in this early twentieth-century community?
4. What do we learn about the married life of the Wrights? By what means is this knowledge revealed to us?
5. What is the setting of this play and how does it help us to understand Mrs. Wright's deed?
6. What do you infer from the wildly stitched block in Minnie's quilt? Why does Mrs. Hale rip out the crazy stitches?
7. What is so suggestive in the ruined birdcage and the dead canary wrapped in silk? What do these objects have to do with Minnie Foster Wright? What similarity do you notice between the way the canary died and John Wright's own death?

8. What thoughts and memories confirm Mrs. Peters and Mrs. Hale in their decision to help Minnie beat the murder rap?
9. In what places does Mrs. Peters show that she is trying to be a loyal, law-abiding sheriff's wife? How do she and Mrs. Hale differ in background and temperament?
10. What ironies does the play contain? Comment on Mrs. Hale's closing speech: "We call it—knot it, Mr. Henderson." Why is that little hesitation before "knot it" such a meaningful pause?
11. Point out some moments in the play when the playwright gives us to understand much without needing a spoken word.
12. How would you sum up the play's major theme?
13. How does this play, first produced in 1916, show its age? In what ways does it seem still remarkably new?
14. "Trifles is a lousy mystery. All the action took place before the curtain went up. Almost in the beginning, on the third page, we find out 'who done it.' So there isn't really much reason for us to sit through the rest of the play." Discuss this view.

Some plays endure, perhaps because (among other reasons) actors take pleasure in performing them. Trifles is such a play: a showcase for the skills of its two principals. While the men importantly bumble about, trying to discover a motive, Mrs. Peters and Mrs. Hale solve the case right under their dull noses. The two players in these leading roles face a challenging task: to show both characters growing onstage before us. Discovering a secret that binds them, the two must realize painful truths in their own lives, become aware of all they have in common with Minnie Wright, and gradually resolve to side with the accused against the men. That Trifles has lately enjoyed a revival of attention may reflect its evident feminist views, its convincing portrait of two women forced reluctantly to make a moral judgment and to make a defiant move.

Some critics say that the essence of drama is conflict. Evidently, Glaspell's play is rich in this essential, even though its most violent conflict—the war between John and Minnie Wright—takes place earlier, off scene. Right away, when the menfolk barge through the door into the warm room, letting the women trail in after them; right away, when the sheriff makes fun of Minnie for worrying about "trifles" and the county attorney (that slick politician) starts crudely trying to flatter the "ladies," we sense a conflict between officious, self-important men and the women they expect to wait on them. What is the play's *theme*? Surely the title points to it: Women, who men say worry over trifles, can find in those little things large meanings.

Like a carefully constructed traditional short story, Trifles has a **plot,** a term sometimes taken to mean whatever happens in a story, but more exactly referring to the unique arrangement of events that the author has made. (For more about plot in a story, see Chapter One.) If Glaspell had elected to tell the story of John and Minnie Wright in chronological order, the sequence in which events took place in time, she might have written a much longer play, opening perhaps with a scene of Minnie's buying her canary and John's cold complaint, "That damned bird keeps twittering all day long!" She might have included scenes showing John strangling the canary and swearing when it beaks him; the Wrights in their loveless bed while Minnie knots her noose; and farmer Hale's entrance after the murder, with Minnie rocking. Only at the end would she have shown us what happened after the crime. That arrangement of events would have made for a quite different play than the short, tight one Glaspell wrote. By telling of events in retrospect, by having the women detectives piece together what happened, Glaspell leads us to focus not only on the murder but, more important, on the developing bond between the two women and their growing compassion for the accused.

If *Trifles* may be said to have a **protagonist,** a leading character—a word we usually save for the primary figure of a larger and more eventful play such as *Othello* or *Death of a Salesman*—then you would call the two women dual protagonists. Both act in unison to make the plot unfold. Or you could argue that Mrs. Hale, because she destroys the wild stitching in the quilt; because she finds the dead canary; because she invents a cat to catch the bird (thus deceiving the county attorney); and because in the end when Mrs. Peters helplessly "goes to pieces" it is she who takes the initiative and seizes the evidence, deserves to be called the protagonist. More than anyone else in the play, you could claim, the more decisive Mrs. Hale makes things happen.

A vital part in most plays is an **exposition,** the part in which we first meet the characters, learn what happened before the curtain rose, and find out what is happening now. For a one-act play, *Trifles* has a fairly long exposition, extending from the opening of the kitchen door through the end of farmer Hale's story. Clearly, this substantial exposition is necessary to set the situation and to fill in the facts of the crime. By comparison, Shakespeare's far longer *Tragedy of Richard III* begins almost abruptly, with its protagonist, a duke who yearns to be king, summing up history in an opening speech and revealing his evil character: "And therefore, since I cannot prove a lover . . . I am determined to prove a villain." But Glaspell, too, knows her craft. In the exposition, we are given a **foreshadowing** (or hint of what is to come) in Hale's dry remark, "I didn't know as what his wife wanted made much difference to John." The remark announces the play's theme that men often ignore women's feelings, and it hints at Minnie Wright's motive, later to be revealed. The county attorney, failing to pick up a valuable clue, tables the discussion. (Still another foreshadowing occurs in Mrs. Hale's ripping out the wild, panicky stitches in Minnie's quilt. In the end, Mrs. Hale will make a similar final move to conceal the evidence.)

With the county attorney's speech to the sheriff, "You're convinced that there was nothing important here—nothing that would point to any motive," we begin to understand what he seeks. As he will make even clearer later, the attorney needs a motive in order to convict the accused wife of murder in the first degree. Will Minnie's motive in killing her husband be discovered? Through the first two-thirds of *Trifles*, this is the play's **dramatic question.** Whether or not we state such a question in our minds, and it is doubtful that we do, our interest quickens as we sense that here is a problem to be solved, an uncertainty to be dissipated. When Mrs. Hale and Mrs. Peters find the dead canary with the twisted neck, the question is answered. We know that Minnie killed John to repay him for his act of gross cruelty. But the playwright now raises a *new* dramatic question. Having discovered Minnie's motive, will the women reveal it to the lawmen? Or (if you care to phrase the new question differently), what will they do with the incriminating evidence? We keep reading, or stay clamped to our theater seats, because we want that question answered. We share the women's secret now, and we want to see what they will do with it.

Tightly packed, the one-act *Trifles* contains but one plot: the story of how two women discover evidence that might hang another woman and then hide it. But some plays, usually longer ones, may be more complicated. They may contain a **double plot** (or **subplot**), a secondary arrangement of incidents, involving not the protagonist but someone less important. In Henrik Ibsen's *A Doll House*, the main plot involves a woman and her husband. But they are joined by a second couple, whose fortunes we also follow with interest and whose futures pose another dramatic question.

Step by step, *Trifles* builds to a **climax:** a moment, usually coming late in a play, when tension reaches its greatest height. At such a moment, we sense that the play's dramatic question (or its final dramatic question, if the writer has posed two or more) is about to be answered. In *Trifles*, this climax occurs when Mrs. Peters finds herself torn between her desire to save Minnie and her duty to the law. "It was an awful thing that was done in this house that night," she reminds herself in one speech, suggesting that Minnie deserves to be punished; then in the next speech she insists, "We don't know who killed him. We don't *know*." Shortly after that, in one speech she voices two warring attitudes. Remembering the loss of her first child, she sympathizes with Minnie: "I know what stillness is." But in her next breath she recalls once more her duty to be a loyal sheriff's wife: "The law has got to punish crime, Mrs. Hale." For a moment, she is placed in conflict with Mrs. Hale, who knew Minnie personally. The two now stand on the edge of a fateful brink. Which way will they decide?[1]

From this moment of climax, the play, like its protagonist (or if you like, protagonists), will make a final move. Mrs. Peters takes her stand. Mrs. Hale, too, decides. She owes Minnie something to make up for her own "crime"—her failure to visit the desperate woman. The plot now charges ahead to its outcome or **resolution,** also called the **conclusion** or **dénouement** (French: untying of a knot). The two women act: they scoop up the damaging evidence. Seconds before the very end, Glaspell heightens the **suspense,** our enjoyable anxiety, by making Mrs. Peters fumble with the incriminating box as the sheriff and the county attorney draw near. Mrs. Hale's swift grab for the evidence saves the day and presumably saves Minnie's life. The sound of the doorknob turning in the next room, as the lawmen return, is a small but effective bit of **stage business**—any nonverbal action that engages the attention of an audience. When Mrs. Hale almost sits down in Minnie's place, the empty chair that ominously starts rocking is another brilliant piece of stage business. Not only does it give us something interesting to watch, it gives us something to think about.

---

[1]You will sometimes hear *climax* used in a different sense: to mean any **crisis**—that is, a moment of tension when one or another outcome is possible. What *crisis* means will be easy to remember if you think of a crisis in medicine: the turning point in a disease when it becomes clear that a patient will either die or recover. In talking about plays, you will probably find both *crisis* and *climax* useful. You can say that a play has more than one crisis, perhaps several. In such a play, the last and most decisive crisis is the climax. A play has only one climax.

Some critics maintain that events in a plot can be arranged in the outline of a pyramid.[2] In this view, a play begins with a **rising action,** that part of the story (including the exposition) in which events start moving toward a climax. After the climax, the story tapers off in a **falling action:** the subsequent events, including a resolution. In a tragedy, this falling action usually is recognizable: the protagonist's fortunes proceed downhill to an inexorable end.

Some plays indeed have demonstrable pyramids. In *Trifles*, we might claim that in the first two thirds of the play a rising action builds up in intensity. It proceeds through each main incident: the finding of the crazily stitched quilt, Mrs. Hale's ripping out the evidence, the discovery of the birdcage, then the bird itself, and Mrs. Hale's concealing it. At the climax, the peak of the pyramid, the two women seem about to clash as Mrs. Peters wavers uncertainly. The action then falls to a swift resolution. But if you outlined that pyramid on paper, it would look lopsided—a long rise and a short, steep fall. The pyramid metaphor seems more meaningfully to fit longer plays, among them some classic tragedies. Try it on *Oedipus the King*, or for an even neater fit, on Shakespeare's *Julius Caesar*—an unusual play in that its climax, the assassination of Caesar, occurs exactly in the middle (III, 1), right where a good pyramid's point ought to be. But in most other plays, it is hard to find a symmetrical pyramid. (For a demonstration of another, quite different way to outline *Trifles*, see "Writing a Card Report" on pages 1524–1527.)

Because its action occurs all at one time, in one place, *Trifles* happens to observe the **unities,** certain principles laid down by Italian literary critics in the sixteenth century. Interpreting the theories of Aristotle as binding laws, these critics decreed that the action of a play must take place within twenty-four hours and in one single location. Further, they insisted, it has to be entirely serious or entirely funny, and not a mingling. That Glaspell consciously strove to obey those critics is doubtful, and certainly many great plays, like Shakespeare's *Othello*, defy such arbitrary rules. Still, it is at least arguable that some of the power of *Trifles*, and of Sophocles' *Oedipus the King*, come from the intensity of its playwright's concentration on what happens in one place, in one short expanse of time.

Brief though it is, *Trifles* has main elements you will find in much longer, more complicated plays. It even has **symbols,** things that hint at large meanings: the broken birdcage and the dead canary, both suggesting the music and the joy that John Wright stifled in Minnie and the terrible stillness that followed his killing the one thing she loves. Perhaps the lone remaining jar of cherries, too, radiates suggestions: it is the one bright, cheerful thing poor Minnie has to show for a whole summer of toil. Symbols in drama may be as big as a house—the home in Ibsen's *A Doll House*, for instance—or they may appear to be trifles. In Glaspell's rich art, such trifles aren't trifling at all.[3]

---

[2]The metaphor of a play as a pyramid was invented by German critic Gustav Freytag in his *Techniques of the Drama*, 1904; reprint ed., New York: Arno (1968).
[3]Plays can also contain symbolic characters (generally flat ones like a prophet who croaks, "Beware the ides of March"), symbolic settings, and symbolic gestures. For more about symbolism, see Chapters Seven and Twenty-four.

TRAGEDY AND COMEDY

By **tragedy,** generally speaking, we mean a play that portrays a conflict between human beings and some superior, overwhelming force. It ends sorrowfully and disastrously, and this outcome seems inevitable. Few spectators of *Oedipus the King* wonder how the play will turn out or wish for a happy ending. "In a tragedy," French playwright Jean Anouilh has remarked, "nothing is in doubt and everyone's destiny is known. . . . Tragedy is restful, and the reason is that hope, that foul, deceitful thing, has no part in it. There isn't any hope. You're trapped. The whole sky has fallen on you, and all you can do about it is shout."[4]

Many of our ideas of tragedy go back to ancient Athens; the plays of the Greek dramatists Sophocles, Aeschylus, and Euripides exemplify the art of tragedy. In the fourth century B.C., the philosopher Aristotle described Sophocles' *Oedipus the King* and other tragedies he had seen, analyzing their elements and trying to account for their power over our emotions. Aristotle's observations will make more sense after you read *Oedipus the King,* so let us save discussion of them for the next chapter. For now, to understand something of the nature of tragedy, we suggest you begin by reading not a classic Greek tragedy but a gripping modern tragedy by the Irish poet and playwright John Millington Synge.

The people of Synge's play are simple fisherfolk who live in the Aran Islands, outposts of barren rock washed by the stormy North Atlantic. They are speakers of Gaelic, the old Irish language. Living in their midst, Synge studied their plain, colorful speech and tried to convey a sense of it in the English of this play. Notice how slowly and quietly the tragedy begins. Gradually, disturbing facts fit into place until we know the whole story of a family that has long struggled with the sea, a dangerous and demanding friend, a relentless enemy.

[4]Preface to *Antigone,* translated by Louis Galantière (New York: Random, 1946).

John Millington Synge

RIDERS TO THE SEA°   1904

John Millington Synge (pronounced "Sing," 1871–1909), a leading figure in the Irish literary revival at the turn of this century, was born near Dublin, where he died. After graduation from Dublin's Trinity College, he studied music in Germany, Italy, and France. In 1899 he struck up a friendship with poet and playwright William Butler Yeats, who advised him to go to the Aran Islands off Ireland's west coast, listen to the spoken language, and observe the life of the islanders. For Synge, this advice bore fruit: in his plays The Shadow of the Glen (1903) and Riders to the Sea (1904), and in a book of impressions, The Aran Islands (1907). When first performed at the Abbey Theater in Dublin in 1907, Synge's dark comedy The Playboy of the Western World caused a riot, some in the audience objecting to its unflattering, satiric view of rural Irishmen. Later, its Irish-American audiences

John Millington Synge

rioted in Boston, Philadelphia, and New York. A considerable poet as well as a playwright, Synge struggled for years against lymphatic sarcoma, which disease curtailed his life. His unfinished tragedy, Deirdre of the Sorrows, was produced after his death.

Characters

Maurya, an old woman
Bartley, her son
Cathleen, her daughter
Nora, a younger daughter
Men and women

Scene. An Island off the West of Ireland.
Cottage kitchen, with nets, oil-skins, spinning-wheel, some new boards standing by the wall, etc. Cathleen, a girl of about twenty, finishes kneading cake, and puts it down in the pot-oven by the fire; then wipes her hands, and begins to spin at the wheel. Nora, a young girl, puts her head in at the door.

Riders to the Sea: The title alludes to a well-known Bible story. After Moses opens a corridor in the sea for the children of Israel to pass through, he obeys the Lord and lets the waters "come again upon the Egyptians, upon their chariots, and upon their horsemen." Then he and the Israelites "sing unto the Lord, for he has triumphed gloriously: the horse and his rider hath he thrown into the sea" (Exodus 14:21–31, 15:1–5).

Nora (in a low voice): Where is she?

Cathleen: She's lying down, God help her, and may be sleeping, if she's able.

Nora comes in softly, and takes a bundle from under her shawl.

Cathleen (spinning the wheel rapidly): What is it you have?

Nora: The young priest is after bringing them°. It's a shirt and a plain stocking were got off a drowned man in Donegal.

Cathleen stops her wheel with a sudden movement, and leans out to listen.

Nora: We're to find out if it's Michael's they are, some time herself will be down looking by the sea.

Cathleen: How would they be Michael's, Nora? How would he go the length of that way to the far north?

Nora: The young priest says he's known the like of it. "If it's Michael's they are," says he, "you can tell yourself he's got a clean burial by the grace of God, and if they're not his, let no one say a word about them, for she'll be getting her death," says he, "with crying and lamenting."

The door which Nora half-closed is blown open by a gust of wind.

Cathleen (looking out anxiously): Did you ask him would he stop Bartley going this day with the horses to the Galway fair?

Nora: "I won't stop him," says he, "but let you not be afraid. Herself does be saying prayers half through the night, and the Almighty God won't leave her destitute," says he, "with no son living."

Cathleen: Is the sea bad by the white rocks, Nora?

Nora: Middling bad, God help us. There's a great roaring in the west, and it's worse it'll be getting when the tide's turned to the wind.

She goes over to the table with the bundle.

Shall I open it now?

Cathleen: Maybe she'd wake up on us, and come in before we'd done. (*Coming to the table.*) It's a long time we'll be, and the two of us crying.

Nora (goes to the inner door and listens): She's moving about on the bed. She'll be coming in a minute.

Cathleen: Give me the ladder, and I'll put them up in the turf-loft, the way she won't know of them at all, and maybe when the tide turns she'll be going down to see would he be floating from the east.

They put the ladder against the gable of the chimney; Cathleen goes up a few steps and hides the bundle in the turf-loft. Maurya comes from the inner room.

Maurya (looking up at Cathleen and speaking querulously): Isn't it turf enough you have for this day and evening?

Cathleen: There's a cake baking at the fire for a short space (*throwing down the turf*) and Bartley will want it when the tide turns if he goes to Connemara.

---

is after bringing them: has just brought them.

Nora picks up the turf and puts it round the pot-oven.

Maurya (sitting down on a stool at the fire): He won't go this day with the wind rising from the south and west. He won't go this day, for the young priest will stop him surely.

Nora: He'll not stop him, mother, and I heard Eamon Simon and Stephen Pheety and Colum Shawn saying he would go.

Maurya: Where is he itself?

Nora: He went down to see would there be another boat sailing in the week, and I'm thinking it won't be long till he's here now, for the tide's turning at the green head, and the hooker's° tacking from the east.

Cathleen: I hear some one passing the big stones.

Nora (looking out): He's coming now, and he in a hurry.

Bartley (comes in and looks round the room. Speaking sadly and quietly): Where is the bit of new rope, Cathleen, was bought in Connemara?

Cathleen (coming down): Give it to him, Nora; it's on a nail by the white boards. I hung it up this morning, for the pig with the black feet was eating it.

Nora (giving him a rope): Is that it, Bartley?

Maurya: You'd do right to leave that rope, Bartley, hanging by the boards. *(Bartley takes the rope.)* It will be wanting in this place. I'm telling you, if Michael is washed up to-morrow morning, or the next morning, or any morning in the week, for it's a deep grave we'll make him by the grace of God.

Bartley (beginning to work with the rope): I've no halter the way I can ride down on the mare, and I must go now quickly. This is the one boat going for two weeks or beyond it, and the fair will be a good fair for horses I heard them saying below.

Maurya: It's a hard thing they'll be saying below if the body is washed up and there's no man in it to make the coffin, and I after giving a big price for the finest white boards you'd find in Connemara.

She looks round at the boards.

Bartley: How would it be washed up, and we after looking each day for nine days, and a strong wind blowing a while back from the west and south?

Maurya: If it wasn't found itself, that wind is raising the sea, and there was a star up against the moon, and it rising in the night. If it was a hundred horses, or a thousand horses you had itself, what is the price of a thousand horses against a son where there is one son only?

Bartley (working at the halter, to Cathleen): Let you go down each day, and see the sheep aren't jumping in on the rye, and if the jobber comes you can sell the pig with the black feet if there is a good price going.

Maurya: How would the like of her get a good price for a pig?

Bartley (to Cathleen): If the west wind holds with the last bit of the moon let you and Nora get up weed enough for another cock for the kelp.° It's hard set we'll be from this day with no one in it but one man to work.

---

hooker: a one-masted fishing boat.   *another cock for the kelp:* another pile of seaweed. The islanders harvest the weed to fertilize their sparse, rocky soil.

Maurya: It's hard set we'll be surely the day you're drownd'd with the rest. What way will I live and the girls with me, and I an old woman looking for the grave?

Bartley lays down the halter, takes off his old coat, and puts on a newer one of the same flannel.

Bartley (to Nora): Is she coming to the pier?

Nora (looking out): She's passing the green head and letting fall her sails.

Bartley (getting his purse and tobacco): I'll have half an hour to go down, and you'll see me coming again in two days, or in three days, or maybe in four days if the wind is bad.

Maurya (turning round to the fire, and putting her shawl over her head): Isn't it a hard and cruel man won't hear a word from an old woman, and she holding him from the sea?

Cathleen: It's the life of a young man to be going on the sea, and who would listen to an old woman with one thing and she saying it over?

Bartley (taking the halter): I must go now quickly. I'll ride down on the red mare, and the gray pony'll run behind me. . . . The blessing of God on you.

He goes out.

Maurya (crying out as he is in the door): He's gone now, God spare us, and we'll not see him again. He's gone now, and when the black night is falling I'll have no son left me in the world.

Cathleen: Why wouldn't you give him your blessing and he looking round in the door? Isn't it sorrow enough is on every one in this house without your sending him out with an unlucky word behind him, and a hard word in his ear?

Maurya takes up the tongs and begins raking the fire aimlessly without looking round.

Nora (turning towards her): You're taking away the turf from the cake.

Cathleen (crying out): The Son of God forgive us, Nora, we're after forgetting his bit of bread.

She comes over to the fire.

Nora: And it's destroyed he'll be going till dark night, and he after eating nothing since the sun went up.

Cathleen (turning the cake out of the oven): It's destroyed he'll be, surely. There's no sense left on any person in a house where an old woman will be talking for ever.

Maurya sways herself on her stool.

Cathleen (cutting off some of the bread and rolling it in a cloth; to Maurya): Let you go down now to the spring well and give him this and he passing. You'll see him then and the dark word will be broken, and you can say "God speed you," the way he'll be easy in his mind.

Maurya (taking the bread): Will I be in it as soon as himself?

Cathleen: If you go now quickly.

Maurya (standing up unsteadily): It's hard set I am to walk.

Cathleen (looking at her anxiously): Give her the stick, Nora, or maybe she'll slip
    on the big stones.
Nora: What stick?
Cathleen: The stick Michael brought from Connemara.
Maurya (taking a stick Nora gives her): In the big world the old people do be leaving
    things after them for their sons and children, but in this place it is the young
    men do be leaving things behind for them that do be old.

    She goes out slowly. Nora goes over to the ladder.

Cathleen: Wait, Nora, maybe she'd turn back quickly. She's that sorry, God help
    her, you wouldn't know the thing she'd do.
Nora: Is she gone around by the bush?
Cathleen (looking out): She's gone now. Throw it down quickly, for the Lord knows
    when she'll be out of it again.
Nora (getting the bundle from the loft): The young priest said he'd be passing to-
    morrow, and we might go down and speak to him below if it's Michael's they
    are surely.
Cathleen (taking the bundle): Did he say what way they were found?
Nora (coming down): "There were two men," says he, "and they rowing round with
    poteen before the cocks crowed°, and the oar of one of them caught the
    body, and they passing the black cliffs of the north."
Cathleen (trying to open the bundle): Give me a knife, Nora, the strings perished
    with the salt water, and there's a black knot on it you wouldn't loosen in
    a week.
Nora (giving her a knife): I've heard tell it was a long way to Donegal.
Cathleen (cutting the string): It is surely. There was a man in here a while ago—the
    man sold us that knife—and he said if you set off walking from the rock be-
    yond, it would be seven days you'd be in Donegal.
Nora: And what time would a man take, and he floating?

    Cathleen opens the bundle and takes out a bit of a stocking. They look at them eagerly.

Cathleen (in a low voice): The Lord spare us, Nora! isn't it a queer hard thing to
    say if it's his they are surely?
Nora: I'll get his shirt off the hook the way we can put the one flannel on the
    other. (She looks through some clothes hanging in the corner.) It's not with them,
    Cathleen, and where will it be?
Cathleen: I'm thinking Bartley put it on him in the morning, for his own shirt
    was heavy with the salt in it. (Pointing to the corner.) There's a bit of a sleeve
    was of the same stuff. Give me that and it will do.

    Nora brings it to her and they compare the flannel.

Cathleen: It's the same stuff, Nora; but if it is itself aren't there great rolls of it
    in the shops of Galway, and isn't it many another man may have a shirt of
    it as well as Michael himself?

rowing round with poteen . . . crowed: transporting moonshine whiskey under cover of darkness.

Nora (who has taken up the stocking and counted the stitches, crying out): It's Michael, Cathleen, it's Michael; God spare his soul, and what will herself say when she hears this story, and Bartley on the sea?

Cathleen (taking the stocking): It's a plain stocking.

Nora: It's the second one of the third pair I knitted, and I put up three score stitches, and I dropped four of them.

Cathleen (counts the stitches): It's that number is in it. (*Crying out.*) Ah, Nora, isn't it a bitter thing to think of him floating that way to the far north, and no one to keen° him but the black hags that do be flying on the sea?

Nora (swinging herself round, and throwing out her arms on the clothes.) And isn't it a pitiful thing when there is nothing left of a man who was a great rower and fisher, but a bit of an old shirt and a plain stocking?

Cathleen (after an instant): Tell me is herself coming, Nora? I hear a little sound on the path.

Nora (looking out): She is, Cathleen. She's coming up to the door.

Cathleen: Put these things away before she'll come in. Maybe it's easier she'll be after giving her blessing to Bartley, and we won't let on we've heard anything the time he's on the sea.

Nora (helping Cathleen to close the bundle): We'll put them here in the corner.

They put them into a hole in the chimney corner. Cathleen goes back to the spinning-wheel.

Nora: Will she see it was crying I was?

Cathleen: Keep your back to the door the way the light'll not be on you.

Nora sits down at the chimney corner, with her back to the door. Maurya comes in very slowly, without looking at the girls, and goes over to her stool at the other side of the fire. The cloth with the bread is still in her hand. The girls look at each other, and Nora points to the bundle of bread.

Cathleen (after spinning for a moment): You didn't give him his bit of bread?

Maurya begins to keen softly, without turning round.

Cathleen: Did you see him riding down?

Maurya goes on keening.

Cathleen (a little impatiently): God forgive you; isn't it a better thing to raise your voice and tell what you seen, than to be making lamentation for a thing that's done? Did you see Bartley, I'm saying to you.

Maurya (with a weak voice): My heart's broken from this day.

Cathleen (as before): Did you see Bartley?

Maurya: I seen the fearfulest thing.

Cathleen (leaves her wheel and looks out): God forgive you; he's riding the mare now over the green head, and the gray pony behind him.

Maurya (starts, so that her shawl falls back from her head and shows her white tossed hair. With a frightened voice): The gray pony behind him.

---

keen: weep and wail.

Cathleen (coming to the fire): What is it ails you, at all?

Maurya (speaking very slowly): I've seen the fearfulest thing any person has seen, since the day Bride Dara seen the dead man with the child in his arms.

Cathleen and Nora: Uah.°

They crouch down in front of the old woman at the fire.

Nora: Tell us what it is you seen.

Maurya: I went down to the spring well, and I stood there saying a prayer to my-self. Then Bartley came along, and he riding on the red mare with the gray pony behind him. *(She puts up her hands, as if to hide something from her eyes.)* The Son of God spare us, Nora!

Cathleen: What is it you seen?

Maurya: I seen Michael himself.

Cathleen (speaking softly): You did not mother; it wasn't Michael you seen, for his body is after being found in the far north, and he's got a clean burial by the grace of God.

Maurya (a little defiantly): I'm after seeing him this day, and he riding and gallop-ing. Bartley came first on the red mare; and I tried to say "God speed you," but something choked the words in my throat. He went by quickly; and "the blessing of God on you," says he, and I could say nothing. I looked up then, and I crying, at the gray pony, and there was Michael upon it—with fine clothes on him, and new shoes on his feet.

Cathleen (begins to keen): It's destroyed we are from this day. It's destroyed, surely.

Nora: Didn't the young priest say the Almighty God wouldn't leave her destitute with no son living?

Maurya (in a low voice, but clearly): It's little the like of him knows of the sea. . . . Bartley will be lost now, and let you call in Eamon and make me a good coffin out of the white boards, for I won't live after them. I've had a husband, and a husband's father, and six sons in this house—six fine men, though it was a hard birth I had with every one of them and they coming to the world—and some of them were found and some of them were not found, but they're gone now the lot of them. . . . There were Stephen, and Shawn, were lost in the great wind, and found after in the Bay of Gregory of the Golden Mouth, and carried up the two of them on the one plank, and in by that door.

She pauses for a moment, the girls start as if they heard something through the door that is half open behind them.

Nora (in a whisper): Did you hear that, Cathleen? Did you hear a noise in the north-east?

Cathleen (in a whisper): There's some one after crying out by the seashore.

Maurya (continues without hearing anything): There was Sheamus and his father, and his own father again, were lost in a dark night, and not a stick or sign was seen of them when the sun went up. There was Patch after was drowned

---

Uah: exclamation of horror and surprise.

out of a curagh° that turned over. I was sitting here with Bartley, and he a baby, lying on my two knees, and I seen two women, and three women, and four women coming in, and they crossing themselves, and not saying a word. I looked out then, and there were men coming after them, and they holding a thing in the half of a red sail, and water dripping out of it—it was a dry day, Nora—and leaving a track to the door.

She pauses again with her hand stretched out towards the door. It opens softly and old women begin to come in, crossing themselves on the threshold, and kneeling down in front of the stage with red petticoats over their heads.

Maurya (half in a dream, to Cathleen): Is it Patch, or Michael, or what is it at all?

Cathleen: Michael is after being found in the far north, and when he is found there how could he be here in this place?

Maurya: There does be a power of young men floating round in the sea, and what way would they know if it was Michael they had, or another man like him, for when a man is nine days in the sea, and the wind blowing, it's hard set his own mother would be to say what man was it.

Cathleen: It's Michael, God spare him, for they're after sending us a bit of his clothes from the far north.

She reaches out and hands Maurya the clothes that belonged to Michael. Maurya stands up slowly and takes them in her hand. Nora looks out.

Nora: They're carrying a thing among them and there's water dripping out of it and leaving a track by the big stones.

Cathleen (in a whisper to the women who have come in): Is it Bartley it is?

One of the Women: It is surely, God rest his soul.

Two younger women come in and pull out the table. Then men carry in the body of Bartley, laid on a plank, with a bit of sail over it, and lay it on the table.

Cathleen (to the women, as they are doing so): What way was he drowned?

One of the Women: The gray pony knocked him into the sea, and he was washed out where there is a great surf on the white rocks.

Maurya has gone over and knelt down at the head of the table. The women are keening softly and swaying themselves with a slow movement. Cathleen and Nora kneel at the other end of the table. The men kneel near the door.

Maurya (raising her head and speaking as if she did not see the people around her): They're all gone now, and there isn't anything more the sea can do to me. . . . I'll have no call now to be up crying and praying when the wind breaks from the south and you can hear the surf is in the east, and the surf is in the west, making a great stir with the two noises, and they hitting one on the other. I'll have no call now to be going down and getting Holy Water in the dark nights after Samhain,° and I won't care what way the sea is when the other

---

curagh: a canvas-bottomed boat.   *Samhain:* All Saints' Day.

women will be keening. (*To Nora.*) Give me the Holy Water, Nora, there's a small sup still on the dresser.

Nora gives it to her.

Maurya (drops Michael's clothes across Bartley's feet, and sprinkles the Holy Water over him.): It isn't that I haven't prayed for you, Bartley, to the Almighty God. It isn't that I haven't said prayers in the dark night till you wouldn't know what I'ld be saying; but it's a great rest I'll have now, and it's time surely. It's a great rest I'll have now, and great sleeping in the long nights after Samhain, if it's only a bit of wet flour we do have to eat, and maybe a fish that would be stinking.

She kneels down again, crossing herself, and saying prayers under her breath.

Cathleen (to an old man): Maybe yourself and Eamon would make a coffin when the sun rises. We have fine white boards herself bought, God help her, thinking Michael would be found, and I have a new cake you can eat while you'll be working.
The Old Man (looking at the boards): Are there nails with them?
Cathleen: There are not, Colum; we didn't think of the nails.
Another Man: It's a great wonder she wouldn't think of the nails, and all the coffins she's been made already.
Cathleen: It's getting old she is, and broken.

Maurya stands up again very slowly and spreads out the pieces of Michael's clothes beside the body, sprinkling them with the last of the Holy Water.

Nora (in a whisper to Cathleen): She's quiet now and easy; but the day Michael was drowned you could hear her crying out from this to the spring well. It's fonder she was of Michael, and would any one have thought that?
Cathleen (slowly and clearly): An old woman will be soon tired with anything she will do, and isn't it nine days herself is after crying and keening, and making great sorrow in the house?
Maurya (puts the empty cup mouth downwards on the table, and lays her hands together on Bartley's feet): They're all together this time, and the end is come. May the Almighty God have mercy on Bartley's soul, and on Michael's soul, and on the souls of Sheamus and Patch, and Stephen and Shawn (*bending her head*); and may He have mercy on my soul, Nora, and on the soul of every one is left living in the world.

She pauses, and the keen rises a little more loudly from the women, then sinks away.

Maurya (continuing): Michael has a clean burial in the far north, by the grace of the Almighty God. Bartley will have a fine coffin out of the white boards, and a deep grave surely. What more can we want than that? No man at all can be living for ever, and we must be satisfied.

She kneels down again and the curtain falls slowly.

QUESTIONS

1. What is the situation at the start of *Riders to the Sea?* What motivates Cathleen and Nora to hide Michael's clothes from their mother?
2. What suggestions of deeper meaning do you find in the abruptness with which Cathleen stops her spinning wheel at Nora's mention of the clothes that have been found? In the gust of wind that opens the half-closed door?
3. What motivates the priest not to interfere with Bartley's plan to take the horses to the Galway fair? Why does his mother want him to stay home? How do Cathleen, Nora, and Bartley react to their mother's request?
4. What does Maurya see when she goes to the spring well to give Bartley his bread? What is there about her account of it that makes Cathleen say, "It's destroyed we are from this day. It's destroyed, surely"?
5. How does Bartley die? At what moment is his death foreshadowed?
6. Do you agree with Cathleen's observation at the end of the play that Maurya is "broken"? Explain.
7. Does *Riders to the Sea* have any protagonist? If so, what character has this central role?

Comedy, from the Greek *komos,* "a revel," is thought to have originated in festivities to celebrate spring: ritual performances in praise of Dionysus, god of fertility and wine. In drama, comedy may be broadly defined as whatever makes us laugh. A comedy may be a name for one entire play, or we may say that there is comedy in only part of a play—as in a comic character or a comic situation.

The best-known traditional emblem of drama—a pair of masks, one sorrowful (representing tragedy) and one smiling (representing comedy)—suggests that tragedy and comedy, although opposites, are close relatives. Often, comedy shows people getting into trouble through error or weakness; in this respect it is akin to tragedy. But an important difference between comedy and tragedy lies in the attitude toward human failing that is expected of us. When a main character in a comedy suffers from over-weening pride, as does Oedipus, or if he fails to recognize that his bride-to-be is actually his mother, we laugh—something we would never do in watching a competent performance of *Oedipus the King.*

Many theories have been propounded to explain why we laugh; most of these are likely to be of a few familiar types. One school, maintained by French philosopher Henri Bergson, sees laughter as a form of ridicule, implying a feeling of disinterested superiority: all jokes are *on* somebody. Bergson suggests that laughter springs from situations in which we sense a conflict between some mechanical or rigid pattern of behavior and our sense of a more natural or "organic" kind of behavior that is possible.[1] An example occurs in Buster Keaton's comic film *The Boat:* having launched a little boat that springs a leak, Keaton rigidly goes down with it, with frozen face. (The more natural and organic thing to do would be to swim for shore.) Other thinkers view laughter as our response to expectations fulfilled, or to expectations set up but then suddenly frustrated. Some hold it to be the expression of our delight in seeing our suppressed urges acted out (as when a comedian hurls an egg at a pompous stuffed shirt); some, to be our defensive reaction to a painful and disturbing truth.

1 See Bergson's essay *Le Rire* (1900), translated as "Laughter" in *Comedy,* ed. Wylie Sypher (New York: Anchor, 1956).

Derisive humor is basic to **satiric comedy,** in which human weakness or folly is ridiculed from a vantage point of supposedly enlightened superiority. Satiric comedy may be coolly malicious and gently biting, but it tends to be critical of people, their manners, and their morals. It is at least as old as the comedies of Aristophanes, who thrived in the fifth century B.C. In *Lysistrata,* the satirist shows how the women of two warring cities speedily halt a war: by agreeing to deny themselves to their husbands. (The satirist's target is men so proud that they go to war rather than make the slightest concession.)

Comedy is sometimes divided into "high" and "low" categories. **High comedy** relies on wit and verbal humor rather than physical action. It appeals to a sophisticated audience fond of epigrams ("A fellow that lives in a windmill has not a more whimsical dwelling than the heart of a man that is lodged in a woman"—an **epigram,** or short, sententious statement, from William Congreve's *The Way of the World,* 1700). A species of high comedy, the **comedy of manners,** or witty satire set in high society, was written by Congreve and other English playwrights of the **Restoration period** (the period following the year 1660, when Charles II, restored to the throne, reopened the London theaters, which had been closed by the Puritans). In more recent times, splendid comedies of manners have been written by Oscar Wilde—notably *The Importance of Being Earnest* (1895)—and by Bernard Shaw, whose play *Pygmalion* (1913) contrasts life in the streets with life in aristocratic drawing rooms.

Low comedy (the opposite extreme) places greater emphasis on physical action, and its verbal jokes do not require much intellect to appreciate. ("I've got a goat with no nose."—"No nose, eh? How does the poor thing smell?"—"Just terrible.") Low comedy includes several distinct types. One is the **burlesque,** a broadly humorous parody or travesty of another play or kind of play. (In America, *burlesque* is something else: a form of show business once popular featuring stripteases interspersed with bits of ribald low comedy.)

Another valuable type of low comedy is the **farce,** a broadly humorous play whose action is usually fast-moving and improbable. The farce is a descendant of the Italian **commedia dell' arte** ("artistic comedy") of the late Renaissance, a kind of theater developed by comedians who traveled from town to town, regaling crowds at country fairs and in marketplaces. This popular art featured familiar stock characters in masks or whiteface: Harlequin, a clown; Columbine, his peppery sweetheart; and Pantaloon, a doddering duffer. Lately making a comeback, the more modern farces of French playwright Georges Feydeau (1862–1891) are practically all plot, with only the flattest of characters: mindless ninnies who play frantic games of hide-and-seek in order to deceive their spouses. **Slapstick comedy** (such as that of the Three Stooges) is a kind of farce. Featuring pratfalls, fisticuffs, pie-throwing, and other violent action, it takes its name from a circus clown's device: a bat with two boards that loudly clap together when one clown swats another.

Still another traditional sort of comedy, **romantic comedy,** is subtler. Its main characters are generally lovers, and its plot unfolds their ultimately successful strivings to be united. Unlike satiric comedy, romantic comedy portrays its characters not with withering contempt but with kindly indulgence. It may take place in the everyday world, or perhaps in some never-never land, such as the forest of Arden in Shakespeare's *As You Like It*.

In *Riders to the Sea*, you encountered a tragedy by a playwright of the Irish literary revival, a movement of writers at the beginning of the twentieth century. Here, to enable you to make a close comparison, is a comedy by another playwright of that same time and place. *The Workhouse Ward* makes comedy out of a situation that might sound grim and sorrowful. As the curtain rises, two old men, decrepit and bedridden, are lying in the hospital ward of a public workhouse for the destitute. Will this play seem a tragedy? How can there be any laughter in it?

Lady Gregory

THE WORKHOUSE WARD   1908

Lady Gregory (1852–1932) was born Isabella Augusta Persse in County Galway, Ireland, into a family of Anglo-Irish landowners. Her title came by marriage in 1880 to Sir William Gregory, a neighbor and a member of Parliament; but only after his death in 1892 did she embark on a literary career. In 1898 she met the poet William Butler Yeats and became his lifelong friend and patron. With Yeats and George Moore, she founded the Irish Literary Theater in 1899. For years she served as a director of the struggling Abbey in Dublin, a historic little theater that first staged plays by Yeats, John Millington Synge, Sean O'Casey, and others. Aware that the Abbey needed a few realistic plays in actual speech, Lady Gregory became a playwright herself. Her many successful plays include Spreading the News *(1904),* The Gaol Gate *(1906),* The Rising of the Moon *(1907), and fantasies*

Lady Gregory

such as The Golden Apple *(1916) and* The Dragon *(1920). She brilliantly translated four plays of Molière into Kiltartan, a lilting dialect spoken in her native Galway. Lady Gregory worked tirelessly to preserve and perpetuate Irish folklore and legends and wove together some ancient Irish epics in appealing new versions:* Cuchulain of Muirthemne *(1902) and* Gods and Fighting Men *(1904).* The Workhouse Ward, *according to theater historian John Gassner, "has had few rivals for the title of the best one-act comedy in the English language."*

Persons

Mike McInerney ⎫
Michael Miskell ⎬ paupers
Mrs. Donohoe, a countrywoman

Scene. *A ward in Cloon Workhouse. The two old men in their beds.*

Michael Miskell: Isn't it a hard case, Mike McInerney, myself and yourself to be left here in the bed, and it the feast day of Saint Colman, and the rest of the ward attending on the Mass.

Mike McInerney: Is it sitting up by the hearth you are wishful to be, Michael Miskell, with cold in the shoulders and with speckled shins? Let you rise up so, and you well able to do it, not like myself that has pains the same as tin-tacks within in my inside.

Michael Miskell: If you have pains within in your inside there is no one can see it or know of it the way they can see my own knees that are swelled up with the rheumatism, and my hands that are twisted in ridges the same as an old cabbage stalk. It is easy to be talking about soreness and about pains, and they maybe not to be in it at all.

Mike McInerney: To open me and to analyze me you would know what sort of a pain and a soreness I have in my heart and in my chest. But I'm not one like yourself to be cursing and praying and tormenting the time the nuns are at hand, thinking to get a bigger share than myself of the nourishment and of the milk.

Michael Miskell: That's the way you do be picking at me and faulting me. I had a share and a good share in my early time, and it's well you know that, and the both of us reared in Skehanagh.

Mike McInerney: You may say that, indeed, we are both of us reared in Skehanagh. Little wonder you to have good nourishment the time we were both rising, and you bringing away my rabbits out of the snare.

Michael Miskell: And you didn't bring away my own eels, I suppose, I was after spearing in the Turlough? Selling them to the nuns in the convent you did, and letting on they to be your own. For you were always a cheater and a schemer, grabbing every earthly thing for your own profit.

Mike McInerney: And you were no grabber yourself, I suppose, till your land and all you had grabbed wore away from you!

Michael Miskell: If I lost it itself, it was through the crosses I met with and I going through the world. I never was a rambler and a card-player like yourself, Mike McInerney, that ran through all and lavished it unknown to your mother!

Mike McInerney: Lavished it, is it? And if I did was it you yourself led me to lavish it or some other one? It is on my own floor I would be today and in the face of my family, but for the misfortune I had to be put with a bad next door neighbor that was yourself. What way did my means go from me is it? Spending on fencing, spending on walls, making up gates, putting up doors, that would keep your hens and your ducks from coming in through starvation on my floor, and every four-footed beast you had from preying and trespassing on my oats and my mangolds° and my little lock of hay!

Michael Miskell: O to listen to you! And I striving to please you and to be kind to you and to close my ears to the abuse you would be calling and letting out of your mouth. To trespass on your crops is it? It's little temptation there was for my poor beasts to ask to cross the mering°. My God Almighty! What had you but a little corner of a field!

Mike McInerney: And what do you say to my garden that your two pigs had destroyed on me the year of the big tree being knocked, and they making gaps in the wall.

Michael Miskell: Ah, there does be a great deal of gaps knocked in a twelve-month. Why wouldn't they be knocked by thunder, the same as the tree, or some storm that came up from the west?

Mike McInerney: It was the west wind, I suppose, that devoured my green cabbage? And that rooted up my Champion potatoes? And that ate the gooseberries themselves from off the bush?

Michael Miskell: What are you saying? The two quietest pigs ever I had, no way wicked and well ringed. They were not ten minutes in it. It would be hard for them eat strawberries in that time, let alone gooseberries that's full of thorns.

Mike McInerney: They were not quiet, but very ravenous pigs you had that time, as active as a fox they were, killing my young ducks. Once they had blood tasted you couldn't stop them.

Michael Miskell: And what happened myself the fair day of Esserkelly, the time I was passing your door? Two brazened dogs that rushed out and took a piece of me. I never was the better of it or of the start I got, but wasting from then till now!

Mike McInerney: Thinking you were a wild beast they did, that had made his escape out of the traveling show, with the red eyes of you and the ugly face of you, and the two crooked legs of you that wouldn't hardly stop a pig in a gap. Sure any dog that had any life in it at all would be roused and stirred seeing the like of you going the road!

Michael Miskell: I did well taking out a summons against you that time. It is a great wonder you not to have been bound over° through your lifetime, but the laws of England is queer.

Mike McInerney: What ailed me that I did not summons yourself after you stealing away the clutch of eggs I had in the barrel, and I away in Ardrahan searching out a clocking° hen.

Michael Miskell: To steal your eggs is it? Is that what you are saying now? *(Holds up his hands.)* The Lord is in heaven, and Peter and the saints, and yourself that was in Ardrahan that day put a hand on them as soon as myself! Isn't it a bad story for me to wearing out my days beside you the same as a

---

mangolds: beets.   mering: property line.   bound over: required by law to pay an indemnity.   clocking: setting.

spancelled° goat. Chained I am and tethered I am to a man that is ransacking his mind for lies!

Mike McInerney: If it is a bad story for you, Michael Miskell, it is a worse story again for myself. A Miskell to be next and near me through the whole of the four quarters of the year. I never heard there to be any great name on the Miskells as there was on my own race and name.

Michael Miskell: You didn't, is it? Well, you could hear it if you had but ears to hear it. Go across to Lisheen Crannagh and down to the sea and to Newtown Lynch and the mills of Duras and you'll find a Miskell, and as far as Dublin!

Mike McInerney: What signifies Crannagh and the mills of Duras? Look at all my own generations that are buried at the Seven Churches. And how many generations of the Miskells are buried in it? Answer me that!

Michael Miskell: I tell you but for the wheat that was to be sowed there would be more side cars and more common cars° at my father's funeral (God rest his soul!) than at any funeral ever left your own door. And as to my mother, she was a Cuffe from Claregalway, and it's she had the purer blood!

Mike McInerney: And what do you say to the banshee°? Isn't she apt to have knowledge of the ancient race? Was ever she heard to screech or to cry for the Miskells? Or the Cuffes from Claregalway? She was not, but for the six families, the Hyneses, the Foxes, the Faheys, the Dooleys, the McInerneys. It is of the nature of the McInerneys she is I am thinking, crying them the same as a king's children.

Michael Miskell: It is a pity the banshee not to be crying for yourself at this minute, and giving you a warning to quit your lies and your chat and your arguing and your contrary ways; for there is no one under the rising sun could stand you. I tell you you are not behaving as in the presence of the Lord!

Mike McInerney: Is it wishful for my death you are? Let it come and meet me now and welcome so long as it will part me from yourself! And I say, and I would kiss the book on it, I to have one request only to be granted, and I leaving it in my will, it is what I would request, nine furrows of the field, nine ridges of the hills, nine waves of the ocean to be put between your grave and my own grave the time we will be laid in the ground!

Michael Miskell: Amen to that! Nine ridges, is it? No, but let the whole ridge of the world separate us till the Day of Judgment! I would not be laid anear you at the Seven Churches, I to get Ireland without a divide!

Mike McInerney: And after that again! I'd sooner than ten pound in my hand, I to know that my shadow and my ghost will not be knocking about with your shadow and your ghost, and the both of us waiting our time. I'd sooner be delayed in Purgatory! Now, have you anything to say?

Michael Miskell: I have everything to say, if I had but the time to say it!

Mike McInerney (sitting up): Let me up out of this till I'll choke you!

---

spancelled: tied fast by a span of rope or chain.   side cars . . . common cars: horse-drawn carts. The fancier side cars (also called *jaunting cars*) seat the passengers facing either side of the road. Miskell means that important persons would have come to the funeral.   *banshee:* spirit whose strange wail foretells death.

Michael Miskell: You scolding pauper you!

Mike McInerney (shaking his fist at him): Wait a while!

Michael Miskell (shaking at fist): Wait a while yourself!

> *Mrs. Donohoe comes in with a parcel. She is a countrywoman with a frilled cap and a shawl. She stands still a minute. The two old men lie down and compose themselves.*

Mrs. Donohoe: They bade me come up here by the stair. I never was in this place at all. I don't know am I right. Which now of the two of ye is Mike McInerney?

Mike McInerney: Who is it is calling me by my name?

Mrs. Donohoe: Sure amn't I your sister, Honor McInerney that was, that is now Honor Donohoe.

Mike McInerney: So you are, I believe. I didn't know you till you pushed anear me. It is time indeed for you to come see me, and I in this place five year or more. Thinking me to be no credit to you, I suppose, among that tribe of the Donohoes. I wonder they to give you leave to come ask am I living yet or dead?

Mrs. Donohoe: Ah, sure, I buried the whole string of them. Himself was the last to go. *(Wipes her eyes.)* The Lord be praised he got a fine natural death. Sure we must go through our crosses. And he got a lovely funeral; it would delight you to hear the priest reading the Mass. My poor John Donohoe! A nice clean man, you couldn't but be fond of him. Very severe on the tobacco he was, but he wouldn't touch the drink.

Mike McInerney: And is it in Curranroe you are living yet?

Mrs. Donohoe: It is so. He left all to myself. But it is a lonesome thing the head of a house to have died!

Mike McInerney: I hope that he has left you a nice way of living?

Mrs. Donohoe: Fair enough, fair enough. A wide lovely house I have; a few acres of grass land . . . the grass does be very sweet that grows among the stones. And as to the sea, there is something from it every day of the year, a handful of periwinkles to make kitchen, or cockles maybe. There is many a thing in the sea is not decent, but cockles is fit to put before the Lord!

Mike McInerney: You have all that! And you without ere a man in the house?

Mrs. Donohoe: It is what I am thinking, yourself might come and keep me company. It is no credit to me a brother of my own to be in this place at all.

Mike McInerney: I'll go with you! Let me out of this! It is the name of the McInerneys will be rising on every side!

Mrs. Donohoe: I don't know. I was ignorant of you being kept to the bed.

Mike McInerney: I am not kept to it, but maybe an odd time when there is a colic rises up within me. My stomach always gets better the time there is a change in the moon. I'd like well to draw anear you. My heavy blessing on you, Honor Donohoe, for the hand you have held out to me this day.

Mrs. Donohoe: Sure you could be keeping the fire in, and stirring the pot with the bit of Indian meal for the hens, and milking the goat and taking the tacklings off the donkey at the door; and maybe putting out the cabbage plants in their time. For when the old man died the garden died.

Mike McInerney: I could to be sure, and be cutting the potatoes for seed. What luck could there be in a place and a man not to be in it? Is that now a suit of clothes you have brought with you?

Mrs. Donohoe: It is so, the way you will be tasty coming in among the neighbors at Curranroe.

Mike McInerney: My joy you are! It is well you earned me! Let me up out of this! *(He sits up and spreads out the clothes and tries on the coat.)* That now is a good frieze coat° . . . and a hat in the fashion. . . . *(He puts on hat.)*

Michael Miskell (alarmed): And is it going out of this you are, Mike McInerney?

Mike McInerney: Don't you hear I am going? To Curranroe I am going. Going I am to a place where I will get every good thing!

Michael Miskell: And is it to leave me here after you, you will?

Mike McInerney (in a rising chant): Every good thing! The goat and the kid are there, the sheep and the lamb are there, the cow does be running and she coming to be milked! Ploughing and seed sowing, blossom at Christmas time, the cuckoo speaking through the dark days of the year! Ah, what are you talking about? Wheat high in the hedges, no talk about the rent! Salmon in the rivers as plenty as turf! Spending and getting and nothing scarce! Sport and pleasure, and music on the strings! Age will go from me and I will be young again. Geese and turkeys for the hundreds and drinks for the whole world!

Michael Miskell: Ah, Mike, is it truth you are saying, you to go from me and to leave me with rude people and with townspeople, and with people of every parish in the union, and they having no respect for me or no wish for me at all!

Mike McInerney: Whist now and I'll leave you . . . my pipe *(hands it over)*; and I'll engage it is Honor Donohoe won't refuse to be sending you a few ounces of tobacco an odd time, and neighbors coming to the fair in November or in the month of May.

Michael Miskell: Ah, what signifies tobacco? All that I am craving is the talk. There to be no one at all to say out to whatever thought might be rising in my innate mind! To be lying here and no conversible person in it would be the abomination of misery!

Mike McInerney: Look now, Honor. . . . It is what I often heard said, two to be better than one. . . . Sure if you had an old trouser was full of holes . . . or a skirt . . . wouldn't you put another in under it that might be as tattered as itself, and the two of them together would make some sort of a decent show?

Mrs. Donohoe: Ah, what are you saying? There is no holes in that suit I brought you now, but as sound it is as the day I spun it for himself.

Mike McInerney: It is what I am thinking, Honor . . . I do be weak an odd time . . . any load I would carry, it preys upon my side . . . and this man does be weak an odd time with the swelling in his knees . . . but the two of us together it's not likely it is at the one time we would fail. Bring the both of us with you, Honor, and the height of the castle of luck on you, and the both of us together will make one good hardy man!

---

frieze coat: coat made of Frisian cloth, a coarse woolen material.

Mrs. Donohoe: I'd like my job! Is it queer in the head you are grown asking me to bring in a stranger off the road?

Michael Miskell: I am not, ma'am, but an old neighbor I am. If I had forecasted this asking I would have asked it myself. Michael Miskell I am, that was in the next house to you in Skehanagh!

Mrs. Donohoe: For pity's sake! Michael Miskell is it? That's worse again. Yourself and Mike that never left fighting and scolding and attacking one another like two young pups you were, and threatening one another after like two grown dogs!

Mike McInerney: All the quarrelling was ever in the place it was myself did it. Sure his anger rises fast and goes away like the wind. Bring him out with myself now, Honor Donohoe, and God bless you.

Mrs. Donohoe: Well, then, I will not bring him out, and I will not bring yourself out, and you not to learn better sense. Are you making yourself ready to come?

Mike McInerney: I am thinking, maybe . . . it is a mean thing for a man that is shivering into seventy years to go changing from place to place.

Mrs. Donohoe: Well, take your luck or leave it. All I asked was to save you from the hurt and the harm of the year.

Mike McInerney: Bring the both of us with you or I will not stir out of this.

Mrs. Donohoe: Give me back my fine suit so *(begins gathering up the clothes)*, till I'll go look for a man of my own!

Mike McInerney: Let you go so, as you are so unnatural and so disobliging, and look for some man of your own, God help him! For I will not go with you at all!

Mrs. Donohoe: It is too much time I lost with you, and dark night waiting to overtake me on the road. Let the two of you stop together, and the back of my hand to you. It is I will leave you there the same as God left the Jews!

She goes out. The old men lie down and are silent for a moment.

Michael Miskell: Maybe the house is not so wide as what she says.

Mike McInerney: Why wouldn't it be wide?

Michael Miskell: Ah, there does be a good deal of middling poor houses down by the sea.

Mike McInerney: What would you know about wide houses? Whatever sort of a house you had yourself it was too wide for the provision you had into it.

Michael Miskell: Whatever provision I had in my house it was wholesome provision and natural provision. Herself and her periwinkles! Periwinkles is a hungry sort of food.

Mike McInerney: Stop your impudence and your chat or it will be the worse for you. I'd bear with my own father and mother as long as any man would, but if they'd vex me I would give them the length of a rope as soon as another!

Michael Miskell: I would never ask at all to go eating periwinkles.

Mike McInerney (sitting up): Have you anyone to fight me?

Michael Miskell (whimpering): I have not, only the Lord!

Mike McInerney: Let you leave putting insults on me so, and death picking at you!

Michael Miskell: Sure I am saying nothing at all to displease you. It is why I wouldn't go eating periwinkles, I'm in dread I might swallow the pin.

Mike McInerney: Who in the world wide is asking you to eat them? You're as tricky as a fish in the full tide!

Michael Miskell: Tricky is it! Oh, my curse and the curse of the four and twenty men upon you!

Mike McInerney: That the worm may chew you from skin to marrow bone! *(Seizes his pillow.)*

Michael Miskell (seizing his own pillow): I'll leave my death on you, you scheming vagabone!

Mike McInerney: By cripes! I'll pull out your pin feathers! *(Throwing pillow.)*

Michael Miskell (throwing pillow): You tyrant! You big bully you!

Mike McInerney (throwing pillow and seizing mug): Take this so, you stobbing ruffian you!

They throw all within their reach at one another, mugs, prayer books, pipes, etc.

CURTAIN

QUESTIONS

1. Try dividing this play into its elements. How much of the play seems *exposition*? Does it have any *protagonist*? If so, who is it? When Mrs. Donohoe arrives to take Mike home with her, what *dramatic question* does the playwright introduce? What is the *climax* of the play, the moment when tension is at its height and the question about to be answered? What is the *resolution* or conclusion?
2. What is suggestive about Honor Donohoe's bringing Mike new clothes, then gathering them up again?
3. How would you state the theme of this comedy? Does the playwright seem to be making any general reflection or observation about people?
4. Do any labels apply to *The Workhouse Ward*, or any parts of it—high comedy, low comedy, satiric comedy, romantic comedy, farce, slapstick? Or does it escape labeling? Discuss.
5. In what respects does its characters' language recall that of *Riders to the Sea*? Point to a few similar examples.

W. C. Fields

STOLEN BONDS   1923

W. C. Fields (1879–1946), christened William Claude Dukinfield in Philadelphia, was raised over a saloon, the son of a London-born bartender. At fourteen, he began a career in vaudeville and musical comedy, soon perfecting his act as a comic juggler. In 1915, while a star of Broadway's leading variety show, the Ziegfield Follies, he began making movies. The screen extended his fame as a dextrous comedian with expert timing and a look of bibulous rascality. With the advent of sound, millions heard his deadpan, singsong voice deliver outrageous lines (out of the side of his mouth), and he was soon among Hollywood's top come-

W.C. Fields

dians. His film hits include Million Dollar Legs *(1932),* You Can't Cheat an Honest Man *(1939),* The Bank Dick *(1940),* My Little Chickadee *(also 1940, with sultry comic Mae West), and* Never Give a Sucker an Even Break *(1941). In 1934, Fields memorably played two supporting roles: as the dictatorial Humpty Dumpty in* Alice in Wonderland *and as the affable ne'er-do-well Micawber in* David Copperfield. *He wrote many of his own screenplays under names such as Charles Bogle, Otis Cribblecoblis, and Mahatma Kane Jeeves. Off screen, Fields worked hard at maintaining his image of a raffish, hard-drinking cynic (whom in life he resembled). "Anybody who hates children and dogs," he once quipped, "can't be all bad."* Stolen Bonds *was first staged on Broadway in a musical comedy review,* Earl Carroll's Vanities, *with Fields playing Snavely. When in 1933 producer Mack Sennett made it into a short film starring Fields, it was expanded and retitled* The Fatal Glass of Beer.[1]

Characters

Chief Big Spear
Little Small Blanket
Snavely
Mrs. Snavely
Chester

Scene. The interior of an old country farmhouse made of logs in the Canadian Northwest. There is a living room on the left—a small bedroom right. There is a window in the center of the living room and electric lights with chain attachment at each side of the window. An old lantern hangs on the wall. Several skins are thrown about the floor. A small table with two chairs is off center of the living room. Door stage right. Old fashioned telephone hung on wall near this door. In the bedroom there is a bed and a curtain hangs over doorway. A few sticks of firewood lie near the fireplace. On the table in living room are two plates, knives, forks, spoons, one trick spoon (for Snavely), and a long loaf of French bread. At rise, two Indians in blankets are seated by the fire. The wind howls outside. Snow is falling. Door at back opens and Snavely enters. As he opens the door, velocity of wind can be heard more plainly and a quantity of snow is blown into the living room. Dogs can be heard howling outside. The room is dimly lighted. Snavely is carrying one gold nugget about the size of a human skull, which he carefully deposits on the table with a thud.

Snavely: It ain't a fit night for man or beast and it's been a-stormin' for a fortnit. Hello thar, hello thar, hello, hello—

[*Crosses to phone and takes it off the hook and speaks into it.*]

---

[1]Available on videotape with two other short Fields comedies of the early 1930s: in *The Best of W. C. Fields* (Spotlite Video, VHS V7058).

Hello!

[Replaces the phone on the hook.]

Indian Chief: How, Mr. Snavely.
Snavely: How, Chief.
Second Indian: How!
Snavely: And how! Vamoose! Ewscray!

[Indians move to door, Indian Chief exits. Wind blows and finally Second Indian is yanked off by the Chief. Snavely crosses to the door and closes it.]

It ain't a fit night out for man or beast.

[He looks about the room furtively, then pulls the chain on one of the electric lights. The light on the other side of the window lights up. He goes to the lighted lamp, pulls the cord and the opposite light flashes on.]

Mrs. Snavely: [Offstage] Who's thar?
Snavely: 'S'me, Ma.
Mrs. Snavely: [Entering] Did you find any gold down in the gulch?
Snavely: I found a nugget. Thar it be on the table.
Mrs. Snavely: [Seeing the nugget, she effusively exclaims] A nugget, a golden nugget. [Picks it up with great care and deliberation] A golden nugget—just what you have combed them thar hills for, for nigh onto thirty years. It must be worth almost a hundred dollars.
Snavely: That will help to pay off the mortgage on the old shack. [Picks up a paper from the table.] Has that pill from Medicine Hat been here again?
Mrs. Snavely: Yes, and he wants more money.
Snavely: Drat his hide.
Mrs. Snavely: He says if he don't get it, he'll take our malamutes.
Snavely: He won't take old Balto, my lead dog!
Mrs. Snavely: Why not, Pa?
Snavely: Because I et him. He was mighty good with mustard. We was a-mushin' all last night over Blind Nag Rim and I got pretty hungry.
Mrs. Snavely: You'd better take off your mucklucks, Pa. Captain Pipitone of the Canadian Mounted smuggled a police dog across the border for you.

[During this she has been taking off his mucklucks.]

Snavely: He's got a police dog for me?
Mrs. Snavely: Yes, he says for you to keep it under your hat.
Snavely: How big is it?
Mrs. Snavely: [Indicating about two feet high] About that high.
Snavely: He's crazy.
Mrs. Snavely: Come on, Pa, have your vittles. [They start supper.] Pa, do you know it's three years ago today since they put our dear son in jail for stealing them thar bonds and I know he never stole them.
Snavely: Certainly he didn't, Ma. Our Chester never stole nothing from nobody never.

[He gets up and puts his arm on Mrs. Snavely's shoulder.]

Mrs. Snavely: Do you think he'll come a-headin' for home, Pa, when they turn him loose from that plagued jail?

Snavely: I reckon, guess and calculate he will, Ma.

[There is a knock at the door. Snavely turns and looks at the door, as does Mrs. Snavely.]

Who's thar?

[Door opens—wind is howling—more snow is thrown into the room. Chester enters.]

Mrs. Snavely: *[Going to Chester]* Chester, my dear, my darling boy!

[She takes Chester in her arms and weeps aloud.]

Snavely: *[Closing door]* T'ain't a fit night out for man or beast. There, Ma, don't cry, we got our son back agin now. Welcome home, Chester. *[He goes to table and stands with his hand on the back of the chair.]* But I don't suppose we'll have him with us long. Once the big city gits into a boy's system, he loses his hankerin' for the country.

Chester: *[Coming down to back of table]* No, Dad, I ain't ever a-goin' to leave the old farm agin. I've come back here to stay with you and Mother. I ain't ever goin' to leave agin.

[Mrs. Snavely has brought another chair to the table and placed it for Chester. She hands him a plate of soup from the table. Snavely reaches for it.]

Snavely: 'S'my soup, Ma.

[Mrs. Snavely gets Chester another plate.]

Chester: Dad, it's so good to see you both. I'm so glad to be home agin to see you and Mother—I can't talk. I'd like to go to my little room and lay on the bed and cry like I was a baby agin.

[Puts his head on his arms and cries. Snavely breaks down, rises and crosses to left.]

Snavely: It ain't a fit night out for man or beast.

Mrs. Snavely: *[Leading Chester to bedroom]* Go in your room, dear, and have a good cry. I know how you feel.

Chester: *[Still crying]* Good night, Dad, dear.

Snavely: Good night, Chester.

Chester: Good night, Ma, dear.

Mrs. Snavely: Good night, Chester.

[Chester exits into the bedroom and slowly begins disrobing. Mrs. Snavely gazes after him admiringly. Snavely removes lantern from the wall and proceeds to light it. Then he puts on his hat.]

Snavely: Ain't it good to have him back agin? I think I'll go out and lock up the cow. *[He opens the door—more wind and snow.]* It ain't a fit night out for man or beast.

[He exits and passes window. Mrs. Snavely goes to Chester's door.]

Mrs. Snavely: Chester?

Chester: *[Offstage]* Yes, Mother, dear?

Mrs. Snavely: Can I see you for just a moment before you go to sleep?

Chester: *[Coming into room]* Yes, Ma.

Mrs. Snavely: *[Leading him to a chair, pathetically asks]* Chester, did you steal them bonds?

Chester: Yes, Ma! *[She sinks into the chair. He kneels beside her.]* I stole the bonds. I was a bank messenger at the time. They caught me fair and square. I wasn't framed.

Mrs. Snavely: I thought you stole 'em, Cheater, but I never would admit it to your father. If he thought you stole 'em it would break his old heart. He thinks you're innocent. Never tell him any different. Good night, Chester.

[She kisses him and rises from the chair.]

Chester: *[Rises]* Good night, Ma, and God bless you.

[He exits into bedroom. Snavely is seen crossing window. He enters. More wind and snow, as before.]

Snavely: It ain't a fit night out for man or beast. *[Takes his hat and scarf off.]* Has Chester gone to bed yet, Ma?

Mrs. Snavely: *[Moving chair away from table]* I don't think so, Pa.

[She exits left.]

Snavely: *[Crosses to Chester's room. Whispers]* Chester!

[Crosses to door through which Mrs. Snavely has just exited and starts to close it. It squeaks. He crosses back to Chester's room and again calls.]

Chester!

Chester: *[Offstage]* Yes, Dad?

Snavely: Come and sit down, Son. *[Chester enters. Snavely crosses to back of table.]* Sit down.

[Indicates chair—Chester sits.]

Son, did you steal them bonds?

[Chester hangs his head. Mrs. Snavely appears in doorway.]

I knowed you was guilty, Son, but I never admitted it to your mother. If she thought you stole them bonds, it would break her old heart. She thinks you are innocent. Never tell her any different.

Chester: *[Raises head]* Oh, it's good to be home, Dad. I'm going to stay now with you and Mother for all time.

Snavely: Have you any of the bonds with you, Son, or any of that money?

Chester: No, Dad, I haven't a cent of the tainted money and I took those bonds and I threw them away.

Snavely: And you came back here to Ma and me?

Chester: [*Turns head to Snavely*] Yes, Dad!
Snavely: [*Quickly picking up long loaf of bread*] To sponge on us for the rest of your life!

[*Smashes Chester with loaf. Chester falls. Mrs. Snavely screams and comes to table.*]

Mrs. Snavely: My God! Do you want to kill him?
Snavely: Yes, I do!
Mrs. Snavely: [*Handing him the nugget*] Then hit him with this!

BLACKOUT

QUESTIONS

1. Would you call *Stolen Bonds* high comedy or low comedy? What techniques does Fields use to get laughs? Are there any instances of verbal humor? Sight gags? Slapstick? Expectations set up and deliberately thwarted?
2. "Every character in *Stolen Bonds* is a stock character." Test this observation, character by character, and decide whether or not you agree with it. (A stock character, remember, is one who exhibits some outstanding trait or traits, which we immediately recognize.)

SUGGESTIONS FOR WRITING

1. Write an account of the *Trifles* case—the discovery of the murder and the arrest of Mrs. Wright—as a newspaper might have reported it. Then, in a separate paragraph or two, sum up the important facts that a reporter couldn't know, but that Susan Glaspell makes clear to us.
2. Write an essay in praise of the language spoken by the characters in *Riders to the Sea* and *The Workhouse Ward*. Arrive at some generalizations about it. (One suggestion: Turn back to Chapter 18 and refresh your acquaintance with metaphors and other figures of speech.)
3. "Comedy on Campus," or "Comedy in Everyday Life." This essay might depend on what you have lately observed, heard reported in conversation, or noticed in current news media. Give an array of examples.
4. Watch *The Fatal Glass of Beer* on videotape (in *The Best of W. C. Fields*—try the "classics" section of a video rental shop) and compare it with its original, *Stolen Bonds*. What did Fields add, subtract, or alter in transferring his vaudeville sketch to the screen? For what possible reasons?

33 The Theater of Sophocles

For a citizen of Athens in the fifth century B.C. when the surviving classical Greek tragedies originated, a play was a religious occasion. Plays were given at the Lenaea, or feast of the winepress, in January; or during the Great Dionysia, the feast of Dionysus, god of wine and crops, in the spring. So well did the Athenians love contests that at the spring festival each playwright was to present—in competition—three tragedies on successive days, the last tragedy to be followed by a short comedy of a special sort. The comedy was a **satyr play,** a parody of a mythic story, with a chorus of actors playing *satyrs*, creatures half goat or horse, half man.

Seated in the open air, in a hillside amphitheater, as many as fourteen thousand spectators could watch a performance that must have somewhat resembled an opera or a modern musical. The audience, arranged in rows, looked out across a rounded **orchestra** or dancing-place, where the chorus of fifteen (the number was fixed by Sophocles) sang passages of lyric poetry and executed dance movements. (It is also possible that actors and chorus sometimes shared the orchestra.) In these song and dance interludes may have originated the modern custom of dividing a play into acts and scenes. Besides providing stage business, the chorus had a function in telling the story: in the plays of Sophocles, they converse with the main character and sometimes comment on the action, offering words of warning and other unwanted advice. As they *physically* stand between audience and principal actors, the members of the chorus serve as middlemen who seem to voice the spectators' reactions.

Behind the orchestra stood the actors, in front of a stage house or **skene** (the source of our word *scene*). Originally, the *skene* was a dressing room; later it is believed to have borne a painted backdrop. Directly behind the *skene*, a **colonnade** or row of pillars provided (according to one scholarly guess) a ready-made set for a palace. (This is a rough description of the Athenian theater of Dionysus; several other Greek cities had theaters, each unique in details.)

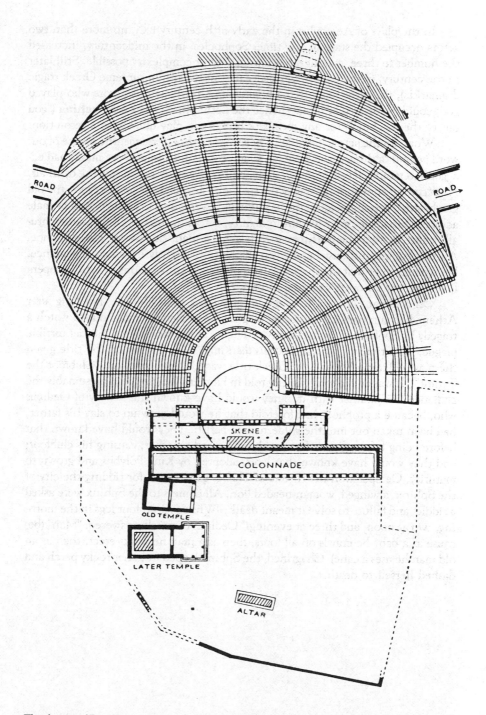

ROAD

ROAD

SKENE

COLONNADE

OLD TEMPLE

LATER TEMPLE

ALTAR

The theater of Dionysus at Athens in the time of Sophocles; a modern drawing based on scholarly guesswork. From R. C. Flickinger, *The Greek Theater and Its Drama* (1918).

In the plays of Aeschylus in the early fifth century B.C., no more than two actors occupied the stage at any time. Sophocles, in the midcentury, increased the number to three, making situations of greater complexity possible. Still later in the century, in the time of Euripedes (last of the trio of supreme Greek tragic dramatists), the *skene* supported a hook-and-pulley by which actors who played gods could be lowered or lifted—hence the Latin phrase **deus ex machina** ("god out of the machine") for any means of bringing a play quickly to a resolution.

What did the actors look like? They wore **masks** (*personae*, the source of our word *person*: "a thing through which sound comes"); some of these masks had exaggerated mouthpieces, probably designed to project speech across the open air. From certain conventional masks the spectators recognized familiar types: the old graybeard, the young soldier, the beautiful girl (women's parts were played by male actors). Perhaps in order to gain in dignity, actors in the Greek theater eventually came to wear the **cothurnus** or buskin, a high, thick-soled elevator shoe. All this equipment must have given the actors a slightly inhuman appearance, but we may infer that the spectators accepted such conventions as easily as opera lovers accept an opera's natural artifice.

On a Great Dionysia feast day in about the year 430 B.C., not long after Athens had survived a devastating plague, the audience turned out to watch a tragedy by Sophocles, set in the city of Thebes at the moment of another terrible plague. This timely play was *Oedipus the King* ("King Clubfoot," the title given the play by later scholars—the Greek title was *Oedipus Tyrannos*, "Clubfoot the Tyrant"). It was an old story, briefly told in Homer's *Odyssey*, and presumably the audience was familiar with it. They would have known the history of Oedipus who, because a prophecy had foretold that he would grow up to slay his father, had been taken out into the wilderness to perish. They would have known that before being left to die his feet had been pinned together, causing his clubfoot; and they would have known that later, adopted by King Polybus and grown to maturity, Oedipus won the throne of Thebes as a reward for ridding the city of the Sphinx, a winged, woman-headed lion. All comers to the Sphinx were asked a riddle, and failure to solve it meant death: "What goes on four legs in the morning, two at noon, and three at evening?" Oedipus correctly answered, "Man" (because as a baby he crawls on all fours, then as a man he walks erect, then as an old man he uses a cane). Chagrined, the Sphinx leaped from her rocky perch and dashed herself to death.

Sophocles

OEDIPUS THE KING

Translated by David Grene

Sophocles (496?–406 B.C.), tragic dramatist, priest, for a time one of ten Athenian generals, was among three great ancient Greek writers of tragedy. (The other two were his contemporaries: Aeschylus, his senior, and Euripides, his junior.) Sophocles won his first victory in the Athenian spring drama competition in 468 B.C., when a tragedy he had written defeated a tragedy by Aeschylus. He went on to win many prizes, writing more than 120 plays, of which only seven have survived entire—Ajax, Antigone, Oedipus the King, Electra, Philoctetes, The Trachinian Women, and Oedipus at Colonus. (Of the lost plays, about a thousand fragments remain.) In his long life, Sophocles saw Greece rise to supremacy over the Persian Empire. He enjoyed the favor of the statesman Pericles, who, making peace with enemy Sparta, ruled Athens during a Golden Age (461–429 B.C.) during which the Parthe-

Sophocles

non was built and music, art, drama, and philosophy flourished. The playwright lived on to see his native city-state in decline, its strength drained by the disastrous Peloponnesian War. His last play, Oedipus at Colonus, set twenty years after the events of Oedipus the King, shows the former king in old age, ragged and blind, cast into exile by his sons, but still accompanied by his faithful daughter Antigone. It was written when Sophocles was nearly ninety. Oedipus the King is believed to have been first produced in 425 B.C., five years after plague had broken out in Athens.

Characters

Oedipus, king of Thebes
Jocasta, his wife
Creon, his brother-in-law
Teiresias, an old blind prophet
A Priest
First Messenger
Second Messenger
A Herdsman
A Chorus of Old Men of Thebes

Scene: *In front of the palace of Oedipus at Thebes. To the right of the stage near the altar stands the Priest with a crowd of children. Oedipus emerges from the central door.*

Oedipus: Children, young sons and daughters of old Cadmus°,
    why do you sit here with your suppliant crowns°?
    The town is heavy with a mingled burden
    of sounds and smells, of groans and hymns and incense;
    I did not think it fit that I should hear   5
    of this from messengers but came myself,—
    I Oedipus whom all men call the Great.

    (He turns to the Priest.)

    You're old and they are young; come, speak for them.
    What do you fear or want, that you sit here
    suppliant? Indeed I'm willing to give all   10
    that you may need; I would be very hard
    should I not pity suppliants like these.
Priest: O ruler of my country, Oedipus,
    you see our company around the altar;
    you see our ages; some of us, like these,   15
    who cannot yet fly far, and some of us
    heavy with age; these children are the chosen
    among the young, and I the priest of Zeus.
    Within the market place sit others crowned
    with suppliant garlands, at the double shrine   20
    of Pallas and the temple where Ismenus°
    gives oracles by fire. King, you yourself
    have seen our city reeling like a wreck
    already; it can scarcely lift its prow
    out of the depths, out of the bloody surf.   25
    A blight is on the fruitful plants of the earth,
    A blight is on the cattle in the fields,
    a blight is on our women that no children
    are born to them; a God that carries fire,
    a deadly pestilence, is on our town,   30
    strikes us and spares not, and the house of Cadmus
    is emptied of its people while black Death
    grows rich in groaning and in lamentation.

---

1 *Cadmus:* hero who, according to legend, had founded the city of Thebes, where the play takes place.   2 *suppliant crowns:* Suppliants, persons come to beg a favor of the king, traditionally wore headbands of flowers.   21 *shrine of Pallas and . . . Ismensus:* temples to Athena, goddess of wisdom, and Apollo, god of music, poetry, medicine, and prophecy. At Ismensus, the ashes of fires were used to foretell the future. An *oracle* is a message from a god, also the name for a priestess who, while in a trance, would speak the message.

We have not come as suppliants to this altar
because we thought of you as of a God,   35
but rather judging you the first of men
in all the chances of this life and when
we mortals have to do with more than man.
You came and by your coming saved our city,
freed us from tribute which we paid of old   40
to the Sphinx, cruel singer. This you did
in virtue of no knowledge we could give you,
in virtue of no teaching; it was God
that aided you, men say, and you are held
with God's assistance to have saved our lives.   45
Now Oedipus, Greatest in all men's eyes,
here falling at your feet we all entreat you,
find us some strength for rescue.
Perhaps you'll hear a wise word from some God,
perhaps you will learn something from a man   50
(for I have seen that for the skilled of practice
the outcome of their counsels live the most).
Noblest of men, go, and raise up our city,
go—and give heed. For now this land of ours
calls you its savior since you saved it once.   55
So, let us never speak about your reign
as of a time when first our feet were set
secure on high, but later fell to ruin.
Raise up our city, save it and raise it up.
Once you have brought us luck with happy omen;   60
be no less now in fortune.
If you will rule this land, as now you rule it,
better to rule it full of men than empty.
For neither tower nor ship is anything
when empty, and none live in it together.   65
Oedipus: I pity you, children. You have come full of longing,
but I have known the story before you told it
only too well. I know you are all sick,
yet there is not one of you, sick though you are,
that is as sick as I myself.   70
Your several sorrows each have single scope
and touch but one of you. My spirit groans
for city and myself and you at once.
You have not roused me like a man from sleep;
know that I have given many tears to this,   75
gone many ways wandering in thought,
but as I thought I found only one remedy
and that I took. I sent Menoeceus' son
Creon, Jocasta's brother, to Apollo,

to his Pythian temple°,   80
that he might learn there by what act or word
I could save this city. As I count the days,
it vexes me what ails him; he is gone
far longer than he needed for the journey.
But when he comes, then, may I prove a villain,   85
if I shall not do all the God commands.

Priest: Thanks for your gracious words. Your servants here
   signal that Creon is this moment coming.

Oedipus: His face is bright. O holy Lord Apollo,
   grant that his news too may be bright for us   90
   and bring us safety.

Priest: It is happy news
   I think, for else his head would not be crowned
   with sprigs of fruitful laurel.

Oedipus: We will know soon,
   he's within hail. Lord Creon, my good brother,
   what is the word you bring us from the God?   95

   (Creon enters.)

Creon: A good word—for things hard to bear themselves
   if in the final issue all is well
   I count complete good fortune.

Oedipus: What do you mean?
   What you have said so far
   leaves me uncertain whether to trust or fear.   100

Creon: If you will hear my news before these others
   I am ready to speak, or else to go within.

Oedipus: Speak it to all;
   the grief I bear, I bear it more for these
   than for my own heart.

Creon: I will tell you, then,   105
   what I heard from the God.
   King Phoebus° in plain words commanded us
   to drive out a pollution from our land,
   pollution grown ingrained within the land;
   drive it out, said the God, not cherish it,   110
   till it's past cure.

Oedipus: What is the rite
   of purification? How shall it be done?

Creon: By banishing a man, or expiation
   of blood by blood, since it is murder guilt
   which holds our city in this destroying storm.   115

Oedipus: Who is this man whose fate the God pronounces?

---

80 *Pythian temple:* Oedipus has sent his brother-in-law Creon to the oracle at Delphi (or Pytho) to
seek divine advice.   107 *King Phoebus:* the sun god, Phoebus Apollo. In the fifth century B.C., when
Sophocles writes, the sun god and Apollo were coming to be regarded as one.

Creon: My Lord, before you piloted the state
    we had a king called Laius.
Oedipus: I know of him by hearsay. I have not seen him.
Creon: The God commanded clearly: let some one   120
    punish with force this dead man's murderers.
Oedipus: Where are they in the world? Where would a trace
    of this old crime be found? It would be hard
    to guess where.
Creon: The clue is in this land;
    that which is sought is found: 125
    the unheeded thing escapes:
    so said the God.
Oedipus: Was it at home,
    or in the country that death came upon him,
    or in another country travelling?
Creon: He went, he said himself, upon an embassy,   130
    but never returned when he set out from home.
Oedipus: Was there no messenger, no fellow traveller
    who knew what happened? Such a one might tell
    something of use.
Creon: They were all killed save one. He fled in terror   135
    and he could tell us nothing in clear terms
    of what he knew, nothing, but one thing only.
Oedipus: What was it?
    If we could even find a slim beginning
    in which to hope, we might discover much.   140
Creon: This man said that the robbers they encountered
    were many and the hands that did the murder
    were many; it was no man's single power.
Oedipus: How could a robber dare a deed like this
    were he not helped with money from the city,   145
    money and treachery?
Creon: That indeed was thought.
    But Laius was dead and in our trouble
    there was none to help.
Oedipus: What trouble was so great to hinder you
    inquiring out the murder of your king?   150
Creon: The riddling Sphinx induced us to neglect
    mysterious crimes and rather seek solution
    of troubles at our feet.
Oedipus: I will bring this to light again. King Phoebus
    fittingly took this care about the dead,   155
    and you too fittingly.
    And justly you will see in me an ally,
    a champion of my country and the God.
    For when I drive pollution from the land
    I will not serve a distant friend's advantage,   160

but act in my own interest. Whoever
he was that killed the king may readily
wish to dispatch me with his murderous hand;
so helping the dead king I help myself.
Come, children, take your suppliant boughs and go;   165
up from the altars now. Call the assembly
and let it meet upon the understanding
that I'll do everything. God will decide
whether we prosper or remain in sorrow.
Priest: Rise, children—it was this we came to seek,   170
which of himself the king now offers us.
May Phoebus who gave us the oracle
come to our rescue and stay the plague.

(Exeunt all but the Chorus.)

Chorus°:
[Strophe:] What is the sweet spoken word of God from the shrine of Pytho
    rich in gold
    that has come to glorious Thebes?   175
I am stretched on the rack of doubt, and terror and trembling hold
my heart, O Delian Healer°, and I worship full of fears
for what doom you will bring to pass, new or renewed in the revolving
    years.
Speak to me, immortal voice,
child of golden Hope.   180
[Antistrophe:] First I call on you, Athene, deathless daughter of Zeus,
    and Artemis°, Earth Upholder,
    who sits in the midst of the market place in the throne which men call
        Fame,
    and Phoebus, the Far Shooter, three averters of Fate,
    come to us now, if ever before, when ruin rushed upon the state,   185
    you drove destruction's flame away
    out of our land.
[Strophe:] Our sorrows defy number;
    all the ship's timbers are rotten;
    taking of thought is no spear for the driving away of the plague.   190
    There are no growing children in this famous land;
    there are no women bearing the pangs of childbirth.
    You may see them one with another, like birds swift on the wing,
    quicker than fire unmastered,
    speeding away to the coast of the Western God.   195
[Antistrophe:] In the unnumbered deaths
    of its people the city dies;

Chorus: A *strophe*, according to theory, was a passage sung while the chorus danced from stage right
to stage left; an *antistrophe*, while they danced back again.   177 *Delian Healer*: Apollo, in his capacity as god of medicine.   182 *Artemis*: twin sister of Apollo, goddess of the moon and of the hunt.

those children that are born lie dead on the naked earth
unpitied, spreading contagion of death; and grey haired mothers and
    wives
everywhere stand at the altar's edge, suppliant, moaning;   200
the hymn to the healing God rings out but with the wailing voices are
    blended.
From these our sufferings grant us, O golden Daughter of Zeus, glad-
    faced deliverance.

[Strophe:] There is no clash of brazen shields but our fight is with the War
    God,
a War God ringed with the cries of men, a savage God who burns us;   205
grant that he turn in racing course backwards out of our country's bounds
to the great palace of Amphitrite or where the waves of the Thracian sea
deny the stranger safe anchorage.
Whatsoever escapes the night
at last the light of day revisits;   210
so smite the War God, Father Zeus,
beneath your thunderbolt,
for you are the Lord of the lightning, the lightning that carries fire.
[Antistrophe:] And your unconquered arrow shafts, winged by the golden
    corded   bow,
Lycean King, I beg to be at our side for help;   215
and the gleaming torches of Artemis with which she scours the Lycean
    hills,
and I call on the God with the turban of gold, who gave his name
    to this country of ours,
the Bacchic God with the wine flushed face,
Evian One, who travel
with the Maenad company°,   220
combat the God that burns us
with your torch of pine;
for the God that is our enemy is a God unhonored among the Gods.

(Oedipus returns.)

Oedipus: For what you ask me—if you will hear my words,
and hearing welcome them and fight the plague,   225
you will find strength and lightening of your load.

Hark to me; what I say to you, I say
as one that is a stranger to the story
as stranger to the deed. For I would not
be far upon the track if I alone   230
were tracing it without a clue. But now,
since after all was finished, I became

---

220 *God with the turban of gold . . . Maenad company:* Bacchus, or Dionysus, god of wine, said to travel
with a company of Maenads, girl revelers.

a citizen among you, citizens—
now I proclaim to all the men of Thebes:
who so among you knows the murderer   235
by whose hand Laius, son of Labdacus,
died—I command him to tell everything
to me—yes, though he fears himself to take the blame
on his own head; for bitter punishment
he shall have none, but leave this land unharmed.   240
Or if he knows the murderer, another,
a foreigner, still let him speak the truth.
For I will pay him and be grateful, too.
But if you shall keep silence, if perhaps
some one of you, to shield a guilty friend,   245
or for his own sake shall reject my words—
hear what I shall do then:
I forbid that man, whoever he be, my land,
my land where I hold sovereignty and throne;
and I forbid any to welcome him   250
or cry him greeting or make him a sharer
in sacrifice or offering to the Gods,
or give him water for his hands to wash.
I command all to drive him from their homes,
since he is our pollution, as the oracle   255
of Pytho's God proclaimed him now to me.
So I stand forth a champion of the God
and of the man who died.
Upon the murderer I invoke this curse—
whether he is one man and all unknown,   260
or one of many—may he wear out his life
in misery to miserable doom!
If with my knowledge he lives at my hearth
I pray that I myself may feel my curse.
On you I lay my charge to fulfill all this   265
for me, for the God, and for this land of ours
destroyed and blighted, by the God forsaken.

Even were this no matter of God's ordinance
it would not fit you so to leave it lie,
unpurified, since a good man is dead   270
and one that was a king. Search it out.
Since I am now the holder of his office,
and have his bed and wife that once was his,
and had his line not been unfortunate
we would have common children—(fortune leaped   275
upon his head)—because of all these things,
I fight in his defence as for my father,
and I shall try all means to take the murderer

of Laius the son of Labdacus
the son of Polydorus and before him   280
of Cadmus and before him of Agenor.
Those who do not obey me, may the Gods
grant no crops springing from the ground they plough
nor children to their women! May a fate
like this, or one still worse than this consume them!   285
For you whom these words please. the other Thebans,
may Justice as your ally and all the Gods
live with you, blessing you now and for ever!

Chorus: As you have held me to my oath, I speak:
I neither killed the king nor can declare   290
the killer; but since Phoebus set the quest
it is his part to tell who the man is.

Oedipus: Right; but to put compulsion on the Gods
against their will—no man can do that.

Chorus: May I then say what I think second best?   295

Oedipus: If there's a third best, too, spare not to tell it.

Chorus: I know that what the Lord Teiresias
sees, is most often what the Lord Apollo
sees. If you should inquire of this from him
you might find out most clearly.   300

Oedipus: Even in this my actions have not been sluggard.
On Creon's word I have sent two messengers
and why the prophet is not here already
I have been wondering.

Chorus: His skill apart
there is besides only an old faint story.   305

Oedipus: What is it?
I look at every story.

Chorus: It was said
that he was killed by certain wayfarers.

Oedipus: I heard that, too, but no one saw the killer.

Chorus: Yet if he has a share of fear at all,   310
his courage will not stand firm, hearing your curse.

Oedipus: The man who in the doing did not shrink
will fear no word.

Chorus: Here comes his prosecutor:
led by your men the godly prophet comes
in whom alone of mankind truth is native.   315

(*Enter Teiresias, led by a little boy.*)

Oedipus: Teiresias, you are versed in everything,
things teachable and things not to be spoken,
things of the heaven and earth-creeping things.
You have no eyes but in your mind you know
with what a plague our city is afflicted.   320

My lord, in you alone we find a champion,
in you alone one that can rescue us.
Perhaps you have not heard the messengers,
but Phoebus sent in answer to our sending
an oracle declaring that our freedom   325
from this disease would only come when we
should learn the names of those who killed King Laius,
and kill them or expel from our country.
Do not begrudge us oracles from birds,
or any other way of prophecy   330
within your skill; save yourself and the city,
save me; redeem the debt of our pollution
that lies on us because of this dead man.
We are in your hands; pains are most nobly taken
to help another when you have means and power.   335

Teiresias: Alas, how terrible is wisdom when
it brings no profit to the man that's wise!
This I knew well, but had forgotten it,
else I would not have come here.

Oedipus: What is this?
How sad you are now you have come!

Teiresias: Let me   340
go home. It will be easiest for us both
to bear our several destinies to the end
if you will follow my advice.

Oedipus: You'd rob us
of this your gift of prophecy? You talk
as one who had no care for law nor love   345
for Thebes who reared you.

Teiresias: Yes, but I see that even your own words
miss the mark; therefore I must fear for mine.

Oedipus: For God's sake if you know of anything,
do not turn from us; all of us kneel to you,   350
all of us here, your suppliants.

Teiresias: All of you here know nothing. I will not
bring to the light of day my troubles, mine—
rather than call them yours.

Oedipus: What do you mean?
You know of something but refuse to speak.   355
Would you betray us and destroy the city?

Teiresias: I will not bring this pain upon us both,
neither on you nor on myself. Why is it
you question me and waste your labor? I
will tell you nothing.   360

Oedipus: You would provoke a stone! Tell us, you villain,
tell us, and do not stand there quietly
unmoved and balking at the issue.

Teiresias: You blame my temper but you do not see
    your own that lives within you; it is me   365
    you chide.
Oedipus: Who would not feel his temper rise
    at words like these with which you shame our city?
Teiresias: Of themselves things will come, although I hide them
    and breathe no word of them.
Oedipus: Since they will come
    tell them to me.
Teiresias: I will say nothing further.   370
    Against this answer let your temper rage
    as wildly as you will.
Oedipus: Indeed I am
    so angry I shall not hold back a jot
    of what I think. For I would have you know
    I think you were complotter of the deed   375
    and the doer of the deed save in so far
    as for the actual killing. Had you had eyes
    I would have said alone you murdered him.
Teiresias: Yes? Then I warn you faithfully to keep
    the letter of your proclamation and   380
    from this day forth to speak no work of greeting
    to these nor me; you are the land's pollution.
Oedipus: How shamelessly you started up this taunt!
    How do you think you will escape?
Teiresias: I have.
    I have escaped; the truth is what I cherish   385
    and that's my strength.
Oedipus: And who has taught you truth?
    Not your profession surely!
Teiresias: You have taught me,
    for you have made me speak against my will.
Oedipus: Speak what? Tell me again that I may learn it better.
Teiresias: Did you not understand before or would you   390
    provoke me into speaking?
Oedipus: I did not grasp it,
    not so to call it known. Say it again.
Teiresias: I say you are the murderer of the king
    whose murderer you seek.
Oedipus: Not twice you shall
    say calumnies like this and stay unpunished.   395
Teiresias: Shall I say more to tempt your anger more?
Oedipus: As much as you desire; it will be said
    in vain.
Teiresias: I say that with those you love best
    you live in foulest shame unconsciously
    and do not see where you are in calamity.   400

Oedipus: Do you imagine you can always talk
   like this, and live to laugh at it hereafter?
Teiresias: Yes, if the truth has anything of strength.
Oedipus: It has, but not for you; it has no strength
   for you because you are blind in mind and ears   405
   as well as in your eyes.
Teiresias: You are a poor wretch
   to taunt me with the very insults which
   every one soon will heap upon yourself.
Oedipus: Your life is one long night so that you cannot
   hurt me or any other who sees the light.   410
Teiresias: It is not fate that I should be your ruin,
   Apollo is enough; it is his care
   to work this out.
Oedipus: Was this your own design
   or Creon's?
Teiresias: Creon is no hurt to you,
   but you are to yourself.   415
Oedipus: Wealth, sovereignty and skill outmatching skill
   for the contrivance of an envied life!
   Great store of jealousy fill your treasury chests,
   if my friend Creon, friend from the first and loyal,
   thus secretly attacks me, secretly   420
   desires to drive me out and secretly
   suborns this juggling, trick devising quack,
   this wily beggar who has only eyes
   for his own gains, but blindness in his skill.
   For, tell me, where have you seen clear, Teiresias,   425
   with your prophetic eyes? When the dark singer,
   the sphinx, was in your country, did you speak
   word of deliverance to its citizens?
   And yet the riddle's answer was not the province
   of a chance comer. It was a prophet's task   430
   and plainly you had no such gift of prophecy
   from birds nor otherwise from any God
   to glean a word of knowledge. But I came,
   Oedipus, who knew nothing, and I stopped her.
   I solved the riddle by my wit alone.   435
   Mine was no knowledge got from birds. And now
   you would expel me,
   because you think that you will find a place
   by Creon's throne. I think you will be sorry,
   both you and your accomplice, for your plot   440
   to drive me out. And did I not regard you
   as an old man, some suffering would have taught you
   that what was in your heart was treason.

Chorus: We look at this man's words and yours, my king,
　　　and we find both have spoken them in anger.　　　　　　　445
　　　We need no angry words but only thought
　　　how we may best hit the God's meaning for us.
Teiresias: If you are king, at least I have the right
　　　no less to speak in my defense against you.
　　　Of that much I am master. I am no slave　　　　　　　　450
　　　of yours, but Loxias', and so I shall not
　　　enroll myself with Creon for my patron.
　　　Since you have taunted me with being blind,
　　　here is my word for you.
　　　You have your eyes but see not where you are　　　　　　455
　　　in sin, nor where you live, nor whom you live with.
　　　Do you know who your parents are? Unknowing
　　　you are an enemy to kith and kin
　　　in death, beneath the earth, and in this life.
　　　A deadly footed, double striking curse,　　　　　　　　460
　　　from father and mother both, shall drive you forth
　　　out of this land, with darkness on your eyes,
　　　that now have such straight vision. Shall there be
　　　a place will not be harbor to your cries,
　　　a corner of Cithaeron° will not ring　　　　　　　　　　465
　　　in echo to your cries, soon, soon—
　　　when you shall learn the secret of your marriage,
　　　which steered you to a haven in this house—
　　　haven no haven, after lucky voyage?
　　　And of the multitude of other evils　　　　　　　　　　470
　　　establishing a grim equality
　　　between you and your children, you know nothing.
　　　So, muddy with contempt my words and Creon's!
　　　Misery shall grind no man as it will you.
Oedipus: Is it endurable that I should hear　　　　　　　　475
　　　such words from him? Go and a curse go with you!
　　　Quick, home with you! Out of my house at once!
Teiresias: I would not have come either had you not called me.
Oedipus: I did not know then you would talk like a fool—
　　　or it would have been long before I called you.　　　　480
Teiresias: I am a fool then, as it seems to you—
　　　but to the parents who have bred you, wise.
Oedipus: What parents? Stop! Who are they of all the world?
Teiresias: This day will show your birth and will destroy you.
Oedipus: How needlessly your riddles darken everything.　　485
Teiresias: But it's in riddle answering you are strongest.
Oedipus: Yes. Taunt me where you will find me great.

465 Cithaeron: mountain outside Thebes where the child Oedipus had been abandoned to die.

Teiresias: It is this very luck that has destroyed you.

Oedipus: I do not care, if it has saved this city.

Teiresias: Well, I will go. Come, boy, lead me away.   490

Oedipus: Yes, lead him off. So long as you are here,
    you'll be a stumbling block and a vexation;
    once gone, you will not trouble me again.

Teiresias: I have said
    what I came here to say not fearing your
    countenance: there is no way you can hurt me.   495
    I tell you, king, this man, this murderer
    (whom you have long declared you are in search of,
    indicting him in threatening proclamation
    as murderer of Laius)—he is here.
    In name he is a stranger among citizens   500
    but soon he will be shown to be a citizen
    true native Theban, and he'll have no joy
    of the discovery: blindness for sight
    and beggary for riches his exchange,
    he shall go journeying to a foreign country   505
    tapping his way before him with a stick.
    He shall be proved father and brother both
    to his own children in his house; to her
    that gave him birth, a son and husband both;
    a fellow sower in his father's bed   510
    with that same father that he murdered.
    Go within, reckon that out, and if you find me
    mistaken, say I have no skill in prophecy.

    (*Exeunt separately Teiresias and Oedipus.*)

Chorus:

[*Strophe:*] Who is the man proclaimed
    by Delphi's prophetic rock°   515
    as the bloody handed murderer,
    the doer of deeds that none dare name?
    Now is the time for him to run
    with a stronger foot
    than Pegasus°   520
    for the child of Zeus° leaps in arms upon him
    with fire and the lightning bolt,
    and terribly close on his heels
    are the Fates that never miss.

[*Antistrophe:*] Lately from snowy Parnassus   525

---

515 *Delphi's prophetic rock:* The shrine at Delphi, thought to stand at the geographical center of the world, featured a holy stone known as the Navel of the Earth.   520 *Pegasus:* in Greek mythology, the winged horse born from the neck of the dying gorgon Medusa. A blow of his hoof caused the stream Hippocrene to spring forth from Mount Helicon; its waters were thought to inspire poets to write.   521 *child of Zeus:* Apollo, armed with the thunderbolts of his father.

clearly the voice flashed forth,
bidding each Theban track him down,
the unknown murderer.
In the savage forests he lurks and in
the caverns like   530
the mountain bull.
He is sad and lonely, and lonely his feet
that carry him far from the navel of earth;
but its prophecies, ever living,
flutter around his head.   535

[Strophe:] The augur has spread confusion,
terrible confusion;
I do not approve what was said
nor can I deny it.
I do not know what to say;   540
I am in a flutter of foreboding;
I never heard in the present
nor past of a quarrel between
the sons of Labdacus and Polybus°,
that I might bring as proof   545
in attacking the popular fame
of Oedipus, seeking
to take vengeance for undiscovered
death in the line of Labdacus.

[Antistrophe:] Truly Zeus and Apollo are wise   550
and in human things all knowing;
but amongst men there is no
distinct judgment, between the prophet
and me—which of us is right.
One man may pass another in wisdom   555
but I would never agree
with those that find fault with the king
till I should see the word
proved right beyond doubt. For once
in visible form the Sphinx   560
came on him and all of us
saw his wisdom and in that test
he saved the city. So he will not be condemned by my mind.

(Enter Creon.)

Creon: Citizens, I have come because I heard
deadly words spread about me, that the king   565
accuses me. I cannot take that from him.
If he believes that in these present troubles
he has been wronged by me in word or deed

544 *sons of Labdacus and Polybus:* the son of Labdacus, remember, was Laius, previous king of Thebes.
At this moment in the play Oedipus is assumed to be the son of Polybus, king of Corinth.

I do not want to live on with the burden
of such a scandal on me. The report   570
injures me doubly and most vitally—
for I'll be called a traitor to my city
and traitor also to my friends and you.
Chorus: Perhaps it was a sudden gust of anger
that forced that insult from him, and no judgment.   575
Creon: But did he say that it was in compliance
with schemes of mine that the seer told him lies?
Chorus: Yes, he said that, but why, I do not know.
Creon: Were his eyes straight in his head? Was his mind right
when he accused me in this fashion?   580
Chorus: I do not know; I have no eyes to see
what princes do. Here comes the king himself.

(Enter Oedipus.)

Oedipus: You, sir, how is it you come here? Have you so much
brazen-faced daring that you venture in
my house although you are proved manifestly   585
the murderer of that man, and though you tried,
openly, highway robbery of my crown?
For God's sake, tell me what you saw in me,
what cowardice or what stupidity,
that made you lay a plot like this against me?   590
Did you imagine I should not observe
the crafty scheme that stole upon me or
seeing it, take no means to counter it?
Was it not stupid of you to make the attempt,
to try to hunt down royal power without   595
the people at your back or friends? For only
with the people at your back or money can
the hunt end in the capture of a crown.
Creon: Do you know what you're doing? Will you listen
to words to answer yours, and then pass judgment?   600
Oedipus: You're quick to speak, but I am slow to grasp you,
for I have found you dangerous—and my foe.
Creon: First of all hear what I shall say to that.
Oedipus: At least don't tell me that you are not guilty.
Creon: If you think obstinacy without wisdom   605
a valuable possession, you are wrong.
Oedipus: And you are wrong if you believe that one,
a criminal, will not be punished only
because he is my kinsman.
Creon: This is but just—
but tell me, then, of what offense I'm guilty?   610
Oedipus: Did you or did you not urge me to send
to this prophetic mumbler?

Creon: I did indeed,
   and I shall stand by what I told you.
Oedipus: How long ago is it since Laius. . . .
Creon: What about Laius? I don't understand.   615
Oedipus: Vanished—died—was murdered?
Creon: It is long,
   a long, long time to reckon.
Oedipus: Was this prophet
   in the profession then?
Creon: He was, and honored
   as highly as he is today.
Oedipus: At that time did he say a word about me?   620
Creon: Never, at least when I was near him.
Oedipus: You never made a search for the dead man?
Creon: We searched, indeed, but never learned of anything.
Oedipus: Why did our wise old friend not say this then?
Creon: I don't know; and when I know nothing, I   625
   usually hold my tongue.
Oedipus: You know this much,
   and can declare this much if you are loyal.
Creon: What is it? If I know, I'll not deny it.
Oedipus: That he would not have said that I killed Laius
   had he not met you first.
Creon: You know yourself   630
   whether he said this, but I demand that I
   should hear as much from you as you from me.
Oedipus: Then hear—I'll not be proved a murderer.
Creon: Well, then. You're married to my sister.
Oedipus: Yes,
   that I am not disposed to deny.
Creon: You rule   635
   this country giving her an equal share
   in the government?
Oedipus: Yes, everything she wants
   she has from me.
Creon: And I, as thirdsman to you,
   am rated as the equal of you two?
Oedipus: Yes, and it's there you've proved yourself false friend. 640
Creon: Not if you will reflect on it as I do.
   Consider, first, if you think any one
   would choose to rule and fear rather than rule
   and sleep untroubled by a fear if power
   were equal in both cases. I, at least,   645
   I was not born with such a frantic yearning
   to be a king—but to do what kings do.
   And so it is with every one who has learned
   wisdom and self-control. As it stands now,

the prizes are all mine—and without fear. 650
But if I were the king myself, I must
do much that went against the grain.
How should despotic rule seem sweeter to me
than painless power and an assured authority?
I am not so besotted yet that I 655
want other honors than those that come with profit.
Now every man's my pleasure; every man greets me;
now those who are your suitors fawn on me—
success for them depends upon my favor.
Why should I let all this go to win that? 660
My mind would not be traitor if it's wise;
I am no treason lover, of my nature,
nor would I ever dare to join a plot.
Prove what I say. Go to the oracle
at Pytho and inquire about the answers, 665
if they are as I told you. For the rest,
if you discover I laid any plot
together with the seer, kill me, I say,
not only by your vote but by my own.
But do not charge me on obscure opinion 670
without some proof to back it. It's not just
lightly to count your knaves as honest men,
nor honest men as knaves. To throw away
an honest friend is, as it were, to throw
your life away, which a man loves the best. 675
In time you will know all with certainty;
time is the only test of honest men,
one day is space enough to know a rogue.
Chorus: His words are wise, king, if one fears to fall.
Those who are quick of temper are not safe. 680
Oedipus: When he that plots against me secretly
moves quickly, I must quickly counterplot.
If I wait taking no decisive measure
his business will be done, and mine be spoiled.
Creon: What do you want to do then? Banish me? 685
Oedipus: No, certainly; kill you, not banish you.
Creon: I do not think that you've your wits about you.
Oedipus: For my own interests, yes.
Creon: But for mine, too,
you should think equally.
Oedipus: You are a rogue.
Creon: Suppose you do not understand?
Oedipus: But yet 690
I must be ruler.
Creon: Not if you rule badly.

Oedipus: O, city, city!
Creon: I too have some share
   in the city; it is not yours alone.
Chorus: Stop, my lords! Here—and in the nick of time
   I see Jocasta coming from the house;   695
   with her help lay the quarrel that now stirs you.

   (Enter Jocasta.)

Jocasta: For shame! Why have you raised this foolish squabbling
   brawl? Are you not ashamed to air your private
   griefs when the country's sick? Go in, you, Oedipus,
   and you, too, Creon, into the house. Don't magnify   700
   your nothing troubles.
Creon: Sister, Oedipus,
   your husband, thinks he has the right to do
   terrible wrongs—he has but to choose between
   two terrors: banishing or killing me.
Oedipus: He's right, Jocasta; for I find him plotting   705
   with knavish tricks against my person.
Creon: That God may never bless me! May I die
   accursed, if I have been guilty of
   one tittle of the charge you bring against me!
Jocasta: I beg you, Oedipus, trust him in this,   710
   spare him for the sake of this his oath to God,
   for my sake, and the sake of those who stand here.
Chorus: Be gracious, be merciful,
   we beg of you.
Oedipus: In what would you have me yield?   715
Chorus: He has been no silly child in the past.
   He is strong in his oath now.
   Spare him.
Oedipus: Do you know what you ask?
Chorus: Yes.   720
Oedipus: Tell me then.
Chorus: He has been your friend before all men's eyes; do not cast him
   away dishonored on an obscure conjecture.
Oedipus: I would have you know that this request of yours
   really requests my death or banishment.   725
Chorus: May the Sun God, king of Gods, forbid! May I die without God's
   blessing, without friends' help, if I had any such thought. But my spirit
   is broken by my unhappiness for my wasting country; and this would
   but add troubles amongst ourselves to the other troubles.
Oedipus: Well, let him go then—if I must die ten times for it,
   or be sent out dishonored into exile.
   It is your lips that prayed for him I pitied,
   not his; wherever he is, I shall hate him.

Creon: I see you sulk in yielding and you're dangerous
   when you are out of temper; natures like yours
   are justly heaviest for themselves to bear.
Oedipus: Leave me alone! Take yourself off, I tell you.
Creon: I'll go, you have not known me, but they have,   735
   and they have known my innocence.

   (Exit.)

Chorus: Won't you take him inside, lady?
Jocasta: Yes, when I've found out what was the matter.
Chorus: There was some misconceived suspicion of a story, and on the other
   side the sting of injustice.
Jocasta: So, on both sides?   740
Chorus: Yes.
Jocasta: What was the story?
Chorus: I think it best, in the interests of the country, to leave it where
   it ended.
Oedipus: You see where you have ended, straight of judgment
   although you are, by softening my anger.   745
Chorus: Sir, I have said before and I say again—be sure that I would have
   been proved a madman, bankrupt in sane council, if I should put you
   away, you who steered the country I love safely when she was crazed
   with troubles. God grant that now, too, you may prove a fortunate guide
   for us.
Jocasta: Tell me, my lord, I beg of you, what was it
   that roused your anger so?
Oedipus: Yes, I will tell you.
   I honor you more than I honor them.
   It was Creon and the plots he laid against me.   750
Jocasta: Tell me—if you can clearly tell the quarrel—
Oedipus: Creon says
   that I'm the murderer of Laius.
Jocasta: Of his own knowledge or on information?
Oedipus: He sent this rascal prophet to me, since
   he keeps his own mouth clean of any guilt.   755
Jocasta: Do not concern yourself about this matter;
   listen to me and learn that human beings
   have no part in the craft of prophecy.
   Of that I'll show you a short proof.
   There was an oracle once that came to Laius—   760
   I will not say that it was Phoebus' own,
   but it was from his servants—and it told him
   that it was fate that he should die a victim
   at the hands of his own son, a son to be born
   of Laius and me. But, see now, he,   765
   the king, was killed by foreign highway robbers
   at a place where three roads meet—so goes the story;

and for the son—before three days were out
after his birth King Laius pierced his ankles
and by the hands of others cast him forth   770
upon a pathless hillside. So Apollo
failed to fulfill his oracle to the son,
that he should kill his father, and to Laius
also proved false in that the thing he feared,
death at his son's hands, never came to pass.   775
So clear in this case were the oracles,
so clear and false. Give them no heed, I say;
what God discovers need of, easily
he shows to us himself.

Oedipus: O dear Jocasta,
as I hear this from you, there comes upon me   780
a wandering of the soul—I could run mad.

Jocasta: What trouble is it, that you turn again
and speak like this?

Oedipus: I thought I heard you say
that Laius was killed at a crossroads.

Jocasta: Yes, that was how the story went and still   785
that word goes round.

Oedipus: Where is this place, Jocasta,
where he was murdered?

Jocasta: Phocis is the country
and the road splits there, one of two roads from Delphi,
another comes from Daulia.

Oedipus: How long ago is this?

Jocasta: The news came to the city just before   790
you became king and all men's eyes looked to you.
What is it, Oedipus, that's in your mind?

Oedipus: What have you designed, O Zeus, to do with me?

Jocasta: What is the thought that troubles your heart?

Oedipus: Don't ask me yet—tell me of Laius—   795
How did he look? How old or young was he?

Jocasta: He was a tall man and his hair was grizzled
already—nearly white—and in his form
not unlike you.

Oedipus: O God, I think I have
called curses on myself in ignorance.   800

Jocasta: What do you mean? I am terrified
when I look at you.

Oedipus: I have a deadly fear
that the old seer had eyes. You'll show me more
if you can tell me one more thing.

Jocasta: I will.
I'm frightened—but if I can understand,   805
I'll tell you all you ask.

Oedipus: How was his company?
    Had he few with him when he went this journey,
    or many servants, as would suit a prince?
Jocasta: In all there were but five, and among them
    a herald; and carriage for the king.   810
Oedipus: It's plain—its plain—who was it told you?
Jocasta: The only servant that escaped safe home.
Oedipus: Is he at home now?
Jocasta: No, when he came home again
    and saw you king and Laius was dead,
    he came to me and touched my hand and begged   815
    that I should send him to the fields to be
    my shepherd and so he might see the city
    as far off as he might. So I
    sent him away. He was an honest man,
    as slaves go, and was worthy of far more   820
    that what he asked of me.
Oedipus: O, how I wish that he could come back quickly!
Jocasta: He can. Why is your heart so set on this?
Oedipus: O dear Jocasta, I am full of fears
    that I have spoken far too much; and therefore   825
    I wish to see this shepherd.
Jocasta: He will come;
    but, Oedipus, I think I'm worthy too
    to know what it is that disquiets you.
Oedipus: It shall not be kept from you, since my mind
    has gone so far with its forebodings. Whom   830
    should I confide in rather than you, who is there
    of more importance to me who have passed
    through such a fortune?
    Polybus was my father, king of Corinth,
    and Merope, the Dorian, my mother.   835
    I was held greatest of the citizens
    in Corinth till a curious chance befell me
    as I shall tell you—curious, indeed,
    but hardly worth the store I set upon it.
    There was a dinner and at it a man,   840
    a drunken man, accused me in his drink
    of being bastard. I was furious
    but held my temper under for that day.
    Next day I went and taxed my parents with it;
    they took the insult very ill from him,   845
    the drunken fellow who had uttered it.
    So I was comforted for their part, but
    still this thing rankled always, for the story
    crept about widely. And I went at last
    to Pytho, though my parents did not know.   850

But Phoebus sent me home again unhonored
in what I came to learn, but he foretold
other and desperate horrors to befall me,
that I was fated to lie with my mother,
and show to daylight an accursed breed   855
which men would not endure, and I was doomed
to be murderer of the father that begot me.
When I heard this I fled, and in the days
that followed I would measure from the stars
the whereabouts of Corinth—yes, I fled   860
to somewhere where I should not see fulfilled
the infamies told in that dreadful oracle.
And as I journeyed I came to the place
where, as you say, this king met with his death.
Jocasta, I will tell you the whole truth.   865
When I was near the branching of the crossroads,
going on foot, I was encountered by
a herald and a carriage with a man in it,
just as you tell me. He that led the way
and the old man himself wanted to thrust me   870
out of the road by force. I became angry
and struck the coachman who was pushing me.
When the old man saw this he watched his moment,
and as I passed he struck me from his carriage,
full on the head with his two pointed goad.   875
But he was paid in full and presently
my stick had struck him backwards from the car
and he rolled out of it. And then I killed them
all. If it happened there was any tie
of kinship twixt this man and Laius,   880
who is then now more miserable than I,
what man on earth so hated by the Gods,
since neither citizen nor foreigner
may welcome me at home or even greet me,
but drive me out of doors? And it is I,   885
I and no other have so cursed myself.
And I pollute the bed of him I killed
by the hands that killed him. Was I not born evil?
Am I not utterly unclean? I had to fly
and in my banishment not even see   890
my kindred nor set foot in my own country,
or otherwise my fate was to be yoked
in marriage with my mother and kill my father,
Polybus who begot me and had reared me.
Would not one rightly judge and say that on me   895
these things were sent by some malignant God?
O no, no, no—O holy majesty

of God on high, may I not see that day!
May I be gone out of men's sight before
I see the deadly taint of this disaster   900
come upon me.

Chorus: Sir, we too fear these things. But until you see this man face to
face and hear his story, hope.

Oedipus: Yes, I have just this much of hope—to wait until the herdsman
comes.

Jocasta: And when he comes, what do you want with him?

Oedipus: I'll tell you; if I find that his story is the same as yours, I at least
will be clear of this guilt.   905

Jocasta: Why what so particularly did you learn from my story?

Oedipus: You said that he spoke of highway *robbers* who killed Laius. Now
if he uses the same number, it was not I who killed him. One man cannot be the same as many. But if he speaks of a man travelling alone,
then clearly the burden of the guilt inclines towards me.

Jocasta: Be sure, at least, that this was how he told the story. He cannot
unsay it now, for every one in the city heard it—not I alone. But, Oedipus, even if he diverges from what he said then, he shall never prove
that the murder of Laius squares rightly with the prophecy—for Loxias
declared that the king should be killed by his own son. And that poor
creature did not kill him surely—for he died himself first. So as far as
prophecy goes, henceforward I shall not look to the right hand or the
left.

Oedipus: Right. But yet, send some one for the peasant to bring him here;
do not neglect it.

Jocasta: I will send quickly. Now let me go indoors. I will do nothing except
what pleases you.   910

(*Exeunt.*)

Chorus:
[*Strophe:*] May destiny ever find me
    pious in word and deed
    prescribed by the laws that live on high:
    laws begotten in the clear air of heaven,
    whose only father is Olympus;   915
    no mortal nature brought them to birth,
    no forgetfulness shall lull them to sleep;
    for God is great in them and grows not old.

[*Antistrophe:*] Insolence breeds the tyrant, insolence
    if it is glutted with a surfeit, unseasonable, unprofitable,   920
    climbs to the roof-top and plunges
    sheer down to the ruin that must be,
    and there its feet are no service.
    But I pray that the God may never
    abolish the eager ambition that profits the state.   925
    For I shall never cease to hold the God as our protector.

[Strophe:] If a man walks with haughtiness
of hand or word and gives no heed
to Justice and the shrines of Gods
despises—may an evil doom   930
smite him for his ill-starred pride of heart!—
if he reaps gains without justice
and will not hold from impiety
and his fingers itch for untouchable things.
When such things are done, what man shall contrive   935
to shield his soul from the shafts of the God?
When such deeds are held in honor,
why should I honor the Gods in the dance?
[Antistrophe:] No longer to the holy place,
to the navel of earth I'll go,   940
to worship nor to Abae
nor to Olympia,
unless the oracles are proved to fit,
for all men's hands to point at.
O Zeus, if you are rightly called   945
the sovereign lord, all-mastering,
let this not escape you nor your ever-living power!
The oracles concerning Laius
are old and dim and men regard them not.
Apollo is nowhere clear in honor; God's service perishes. 950

(Enter Jocasta, carrying garlands.)

Jocasta: Princes of the land, I have had the thought to go
to the Gods' temples, bringing in my hand
garlands and gifts of incense, as you see.
For Oedipus excites himself too much
at every sort of trouble, not conjecturing,   955
like a man of sense, what will be from what was,
but he is always at the speaker's mercy,
when he speaks terrors. I can do no good
by my advice, and so I came as suppliant
to you, Lycaean Apollo, who are nearest.   960
These are the symbols of my prayer and this
my prayer: grant us escape free of the curse.
Now when we look to him we are all afraid;
he's pilot of our ship and he is frightened.

(Enter Messenger.)

Messenger: Might I learn from you, sirs, where is the house of Oedipus? Or
best of all, if you know, where is the king himself?   965
Chorus: This is his house and he is within doors. This lady is his wife and
mother of his children.

Messenger: God bless you, lady, and God bless your household! God bless
   Oedipus' noble wife!
Jocasta: God bless you, sir, for your kind greeting! What do you want of
   us that you have come here? What have you to tell us?
Messenger: Good news, lady. Good for your home and for your husband.
Jocasta: What is your news? Who sent you to us?   970
Messenger: I come from Corinth and the news I bring will give you pleasure.
   Perhaps a little pain too.
Jocasta: What is this news of double meaning?
Messenger: The people of the Isthmus will choose Oedipus to be their king.
   That is the rumor there.
Jocasta: But isn't their king still old Polybus?
Messenger: No. He is in his grave. Death has got him.   975
Jocasta: Is that the truth? Is Oedipus' father dead?
Messenger: May I die myself if it be otherwise!
Jocasta (to a servant): Be quick and run to the King with the news! O oracles
   of the Gods, where are you now? It was from this man Oedipus fled,
   lest he should be his murderer! And now he is dead, in the course of
   nature, and not killed by Oedipus.

   (Enter Oedipus.)

Oedipus: Dearest Jocasta, why have you sent for me?
Jocasta: Listen to this man and when you hear reflect what is the outcome
   of the holy oracles of the Gods.   980
Oedipus: Who is he? What is his message for me?
Jocasta: He is from Corinth and he tells us that your father Polybus is dead
   and gone.
Oedipus: What's this you say, sir? Tell me yourself.
Messenger: Since this is the first matter you want clearly told: Polybus has
   gone down to death. You may be sure of it.
Oedipus: By treachery or sickness?   985
Messenger: A small thing will put old bodies asleep.
Oedipus: So he died of sickness, it seems—poor old man!
Messenger: Yes, and of age—the long years he had measured.
Oedipus: Ha! Ha! O dear Jocasta, why should one
   look to the Pythian hearth°? Why should one look   990
   to the birds screaming overhead? They prophesied
   that I should kill my father! But he's dead,
   and hidden deep in earth, and I stand here
   who never laid a hand on spear against him—
   unless perhaps he died of longing for me.   995
   and thus I am his murderer. But they,
   the oracles, as they stand—he's taken them
   away with him, they're dead as he himself is,
   and worthless.

990 *Pythian hearth:* the oracle at Delphi.

Jocasta: That I told you before now.
Oedipus: You did, but I was misled by my fear.   1000
Jocasta: They lay no more of them to heart, not one.
Oedipus: But surely I must fear my mother's bed?
Jocasta: Why should man fear since chance is all in all
    for him, and he can clearly foreknow nothing?
    Best to live lightly, as one can, unthinkingly.   1005
    As to your mother's marriage bed—don't fear it.
    Before this, in dreams too, as well as oracles,
    many a man has lain with his own mother.
    But he to whom such things are nothing bears
    his life most easily.   1010
Oedipus: All that you say would be said perfectly
    if she were dead; but since she lives I must
    still fear, although you talk so well, Jocasta.
Jocasta: Still in your father's death there's light of comfort?
Oedipus: Great light of comfort; but I fear the living.   1015
Messenger: Who is the woman that makes you afraid?
Oedipus: Merope, old man, Polybus' wife.
Messenger: What about her frightens the queen and you?
Oedipus: A terrible oracle, stranger, from the Gods.
Messenger: Can it be told? Or does the sacred law   1020
    forbid another to have knowledge of it?
Oedipus: O no! Once on a time Loxias said
    that I should lie with my own mother and
    take on my hands the blood of my own father.
    And so for these long years I've lived away   1025
    from Corinth; it has been to my great happiness;
    but yet it's sweet to see the face of parents.
Messenger: This was the fear which drove you out of Corinth?
Oedipus: Old man, I did not wish to kill my father.
Messenger: Why should I not free you from this fear, sir,   1030
    since I have come to you in all goodwill?
Oedipus: You would not find me thankless if you did.
Messenger: Why, it was just for this I brought the news—
    to earn your thanks when you had come safe home.
Oedipus: No, I will never come near my parents.
Messenger: Son,   1035
    it's very plain you don't know what you're doing.
Oedipus: What do you mean, old man? For God's sake, tell me.
Messenger: If your homecoming is checked by fears like these.
Oedipus: Yes, I'm afraid that Phoebus may prove right.
Messenger: The murder and the incest?
Oedipus: Yes, old man;   1040
    that is my constant terror.
Messenger: Do you know
    that all your fears are empty?

Oedipus: How is that,
   if they are father and mother and I their son?
Messenger: Because Polybus was no kin to you in blood.
Oedipus: What, was not Polybus my father?   1045
Messenger: No more than I but just so much.
Oedipus: How can
   my father be my father as much as one
   that's nothing to me?
Messenger: Neither he nor I
   begat you.
Oedipus: Why then did he call me son?
Messenger: A gift he took you from these hands of mine.   1050
Oedipus: Did he love so much what he took from another's
   hand?
Messenger: His childlessness before persuaded him.
Oedipus: Was I a child you bought or found when I
   was given to him?
Messenger: On Cithaeron's slopes
   in the twisting thickets you were found.
Oedipus: And why   1055
   were you a traveller in those parts?
Messenger: I was
   in charge of mountain flocks.
Oedipus: You were a shepherd?
   A hireling vagrant?
Messenger: Yes, but at least at that time
   the man that saved your life, son.
Oedipus: What ailed me when you took me in your arms?   1060
Messenger: In that your ankles should be witnesses.
Oedipus: Why do you speak of that old pain?
Messenger: I loosed you;
   the tendons of your feet were pierced and fettered—
Oedipus: My swaddling clothes brought me a rare disgrace.
Messenger: So that from this you're called your present name°.   1065
Oedipus: Was this my father's doing or my mother's?
   For God's sake, tell me.
Messenger: I don't know, but he
   who gave you to me has more knowledge than I.
Oedipus: You yourself did not find me then? You took me
   from someone else?
Messenger: Yes, from another shepherd.   1070
Oedipus: Who was he? Do you know him well
   enough to tell?
Messenger: He was called Laius' man.

1065 your present name: Oedipus's name means "swollen foot" or "clubfoot."

Oedipus: You mean the king who reigned here in the old days?
Messenger: Yes, he was that man's shepherd.
Oedipus: Is he alive
   still, so that I could see him?
Messenger: You who live here   1075
   would know that best.
Oedipus: Do any of you here
   know of this shepherd whom he speaks about
   in town or in the fields? Tell me. It's time
   that this was found out once for all.
Chorus: I think he is none other than the peasant   1080
   whom you have sought to see already; but
   Jocasta here can tell us best of that.
Oedipus: Jocasta, do you know about this man
   whom we have sent for? Is he the man he mentions?
Jocasta: Why ask of whom he spoke? Don't give it heed;   1085
   nor try to keep in mind what has been said.
   It will be wasted labor.
Oedipus: With such clues
   I could not fail to bring my birth to light.
Jocasta: I beg you—do not hunt this out—I beg you,
   if you have any care for your own life.   1090
   What I am suffering is enough.
Oedipus: Keep up
   your heart, Jocasta. Though I'm proved a slave,
   thrice slave, and though my mother is thrice slave,
   you'll not be shown to be of lowly lineage.
Jocasta: O be persuaded by me, I entreat you;
   do not do this.   1095
Oedipus: I will not be persuaded to let be
   the chance of finding out the whole thing clearly.
Jocasta: It is because I wish you well that I
   give you this counsel—and it's the best counsel.
Oedipus: Then the best counsel vexes me, and has   1100
   for some while since.
Jocasta: O Oedipus, God help you!
   God keep you from the knowledge of who you are!
Oedipus: Here, some one, go and fetch the shepherd for me;
   and let her find her joy in her rich family!
Jocasta: O Oedipus, unhappy Oedipus!   1105
   that is all I can call you, and the last thing
   that I shall ever call you.

   (*Exit.*)

Chorus: Why has the queen gone, Oedipus, in wild
   grief rushing from us? I am afraid that trouble
   will break out of this silence.   1110

Oedipus: Break out what will! I at least shall be
   willing to see my ancestry, though humble.
   Perhaps she is ashamed of my low birth,
   for she has all a woman's high-flown pride.
   But I account myself a child of Fortune,   1115
   beneficent Fortune, and I shall not be
   dishonored. She's the mother from whom I spring;
   the months, the brothers, marked me, now as small,
   and now again as mighty. Such is my breeding,
   and I shall never prove so false to it,   1120
   as not to find the secret of my birth.

Chorus:
[*Strophe:*] If I am a prophet and wise of heart
   you shall not fail, Cithaeron,
   by the limitless sky, you shall not!—
   to know at tomorrow's full moon   1125
   that Oedipus honors you,
   as native to him and mother and nurse at once;
   and that you are honored in dancing by us, as finding favor in sight
      of our king.
   Apollo, to whom we cry, find these things pleasing!
[*Antistrophe:*] Who was it bore you, child? One of   1130
   the long-lived nymphs who lay with Pan°—
   the father who treads the hills?
   Or was she a bride of Loxias, your mother? The grassy slopes
   are all of them dear to him. Or perhaps Cyllene's king°
   or the Bacchantes' God° that lives on the tops   1135
   of the hills received you a gift from some
   one of the Helicon Nymphs, with whom he mostly plays?

   (*Enter an old man, led by Oedipus' servants.*)

Oedipus: If some one like myself who never met him
   may make a guess—I think this is the herdsman,
   whom we are seeking. His old age is consonant   1140
   with the other. And besides, the men who bring him
   I recognize as my own servants. You
   perhaps may better me in knowledge since
   you've seen the man before.
Chorus: You can be sure
   I recognize him. For if Laius   1145
   had ever an honest shepherd, this was he.

1131 *nymphs who lay with Pan:* In Greek mythology, nymphs are beautiful young immortals associated
with features of nature or specific places. Pan is the goat-footed god of wildlife and the flocks. In this
passage the chorus speculates that Oedipus is the child of a nymph by some god.   1134 *Cyllene's
king:* Hermes, messenger of the gods.   1135 *Bacchantes' God:* Dionysus. Bacchantes are the same
as Maenads, the wine god's groupies or priestesses.

Oedipus: You, sir, from Corinth, I must ask you first,
    is this the man you spoke of?
Messenger: This is he
    before your eyes.
Oedipus: Old man, look here at me
    and tell me what I ask you. Were you ever   1150
    a servant of King Laius?
Herdsman: I was—
    no slave he bought but reared in his own house.
Oedipus: What did you do as work? How did you live?
Herdsman: Most of my life was spent among the flocks.
Oedipus: In what part of the country did you live?   1155
Herdsman: Cithaeron and the places near to it.
Oedipus: And somewhere there perhaps you knew this man?
Herdsman: What was his occupation? Who?
Oedipus: This man here,
    have you had any dealings with him?
Herdsman: No—
    not such that I can quickly call to mind.   1160
Messenger: That is no wonder, master. But I'll make him remember what
    he does not know. For I know, that he well knows the country of Cithae-
    ron, how he with two flocks, I with one kept company for three years—
    each year half a year—from spring till autumn time and then when
    winter came I drove my flocks to our fold home again and he to Laius'
    steadings. Well—am I right or not in what I said we did?
Herdsman: You're right—although it's a long time ago.
Messenger: Do you remember giving me a child
    to bring up as my foster child?
Herdsman: What's this?
    Why do you ask this question?
Messenger: Look, old man,   1165
    here he is—here's the man who was that child!
Herdsman: Death take you! Won't you hold your tongue?
Oedipus: No, no,
    do not find fault with him, old man. Your words
    are more at fault than his.
Herdsman: O best of masters,
    how do I give offense?
Oedipus: When you refuse   1170
    to speak about the child of whom he asks you.
Herdsman: He speaks out of his ignorance, without meaning.
Oedipus: If you'll not talk to gratify me, you
    will talk with pain to urge you.
Herdsman: O please, sir,
    don't hurt an old man, sir.
Oedipus: (to the servants):   Here, one of you,   1175
    twist his hands behind him.

Herdsman: Why, God help me, why?
  What do you want to know?
Oedipus: You gave a child
  to him—the child he asked you of?
Herdsman: I did.
  I wish I'd died the day I did.
Oedipus: You will
  unless you tell me truly.
Herdsman: And I'll die   1180
  far worse if I should tell you.
Oedipus: This fellow
  is bent on more delays, as it would seem.
Herdsman: O no, no! I have told you that I gave it.
Oedipus: Where did you get this child from? Was it your own or did you
  get it from another?
Herdsman: Not   1185
  my own at all; I had it from some one.
Oedipus: One of these citizens? or from what house?
Herdsman: O master, please—I beg you, master, please
  don't ask me more.
Oedipus: You're a dead man if I
  ask you again.
Herdsman: It was one of the children   1190
  of Laius.
Oedipus: A slave? Or born in wedlock?
Herdsman: O God, I am on the brink of frightful speech.
Oedipus: And I of frightful hearing. But I must hear.
Herdsman: The child was called his child; but she within,
  your wife would tell you best how all this was.   1195
Oedipus: She gave it to you?
Herdsman: Yes, she did, my lord.
Oedipus: To do what with it?
Herdsman: Make away with it.
Oedipus: She was so hard—its mother?
Herdsman: Aye, through fear
  of evil oracles.
Oedipus: Which?
Herdsman: They said that he
  should kill his parents.
Oedipus: How was it that you   1200
  gave it away to this old man?
Herdsman: O master,
  I pitied it, and thought that I could send it
  off to another country and this man
  was from another country. But he saved it
  for the most terrible troubles. If you are   1205
  the man he says you are, you're bred to misery.

Oedipus: O, O, O, they will all come,
all come out clearly! Light of the sun, let me
look upon you no ...ore after today!
I who first saw the light bred of a match   1210
accursed, and accursed in my living
with them I lived with, cursed in my killing.

(Exeunt all but the Chorus.)

Chorus:
[*Strophe:*] O generations of men, how I
count you as equal with those who live
not at all!   1215
What man, what man on earth wins more
of happiness than a seeming
and after that turning away?
Oedipus, you are my pattern of this,
Oedipus, you and your fate!   1220
Luckless Oedipus, whom of all men
I envy not at all.
[*Antistrophe:*] In as much as he shot his bolt
beyond the others and won the prize
of happiness complete—   1225
O Zeus—and killed and reduced to nought
the hooked taloned maid of the riddling speech,
standing a tower against death for my land:
hence he was called my king and hence
was honored the highest of all   1230
honors; and hence he ruled
in the great city of Thebes.
[*Strophe:*] But now whose tale is more miserable?
Who is there lives with a savager fate?
Whose troubles so reverse his life as his?   1235

O Oedipus, the famous prince
for whom a great haven°
the same both as father and son
sufficed for generation,
how, O how, have the furrows ploughed   1240
by your father endured to bear you, poor wretch,
and hold their peace so long?
Antistrophe: Time who sees all has found you out
against your will; judges your marriage accursed,
begetter and begot at one in it.   1245

1237 *a great haven:* the womb of Jocasta.

O child of Laius,
would I had never seen you.
I weep for you and cry
a dirge of lamentation.

To speak directly, I drew my breath   1250
from you at the first and so now I lull
my mouth to sleep with your name.

(*Enter a second messenger.*)

Second Messenger: O Princes always honored by our country,
what deeds you'll hear of and what horrors see,
what grief you'll feel, if you as true born Thebans   1255
care for the house of Labdacus's sons.
Phasis nor Ister cannot purge this house,
I think, with all their streams, such things
it hides, such evils shortly will bring forth
into the light, whether they will or not;   1260
and troubles hurt the most
when they prove self-inflicted.
Chorus: What we had known before did not fall short
of bitter groaning's worth; what's more to tell?
Second Messenger: Shortest to hear and tell—our glorious queen   1265
Jocasta's dead.
Chorus: Unhappy woman! How?
Second Messenger: By her own hand. The worst of what was done
you cannot know. You did not see the sight.
Yet in so far as I remember it
you'll hear the end of our unlucky queen.   1270
When she came raging into the house she went
straight to her marriage bed, tearing her hair
with both her hands, and crying upon Laius
long dead—Do you remember, Laius,
that night long past which bred a child for us   1275
to send you to your death and leave
a mother making children with her son?
And then she groaned and cursed the bed in which
she brought forth husband by her husband, children
by her own child, an infamous double bond.   1280
How after that she died I do not know—
for Oedipus distracted us from seeing.
He burst upon us shouting and we looked
to him as he paced frantically around,
begging us always: Give me a sword, I say,   1285
to find this wife no wife, this mother's womb,
this field of double sowing whence I sprang
and where I sowed my children! As he raved
some god showed him the way—none of us there.

Bellowing terribly and led by some   1290
invisible guide he rushed on the two doors—
wrenching the hollow bolts out of their sockets,
he charged inside. There, there, we saw his wife
hanging, the twisted rope around her neck.
When he saw her, he cried out fearfully   1295
and cut the dangling noose. Then, as she lay,
poor woman, on the ground, what happened after,
was terrible to see. He tore the brooches—
the gold chased brooches fastening her robe—
away from her and lifting them up high   1300
dashed them on his own eyeballs, shrieking out
such things as: they will never see the crime
I have committed or had done upon me!
Dark eyes, now in the days to come look on
forbidden faces, do not recognize   1305
those whom you long for—with such imprecations
he struck his eyes again and yet again
with the brooches. And the bleeding eyeballs gushed
and stained his beard—no sluggish oozing drops
but a black rain and bloody hail poured down.   1310

So it has broken—and not on one head
but troubles mixed for husband and for wife.
The fortune of the days gone by was true
good fortune—but today groans and destruction
and death and shame—of all ills can be named   1315
not one is missing.
Chorus: Is he now in any ease from pain?
Second Messenger: He shouts
for some one to unbar the doors and show him
to all the men of Thebes, his father's killer,
his mother's—no I cannot say the word,   1320
it is unholy—for he'll cast himself,
out of the land, he says, and not remain
to bring a curse upon his house, the curse
he called upon it in his proclamation. But
he wants for strength, aye, and some one to guide him;   1325
his sickness is too great to bear. You, too,
will be shown that. The bolts are opening.
Soon you will see a sight to waken pity
even in the horror of it.

(*Enter the blinded Oedipus.*)

Chorus: This is a terrible sight for men to see!   1330
I never found a worse!
Poor wretch, what madness came upon you!
What evil spirit leaped upon your life

to your ill-luck—a leap beyond man's strength!
Indeed I pity you, but I cannot   1335
look at you, though there's much I want to ask
and much to learn and much to see.
I shudder at the sight of you.
Oedipus: O, O,
where am I going? Where is my voice   1340
borne on the wind to and fro?
Spirit, how far have you sprung?
Chorus: To a terrible place whereof men's ears
may not hear, nor their eyes behold it.
Oedipus: Darkness!   1345
Horror of darkness enfolding, resistless, unspeakable visitant sped
by an ill wind in haste!
madness and stabbing pain and memory
of evil deeds I have done!
Chorus: In such misfortunes it's no wonder
if double weighs the burden of your grief.   1350
Oedipus: My friend,
you are the only one steadfast, the only one that attends on me;
you still stay nursing the blind man.
Your care is not unnoticed. I can know
your voice, although this darkness is my world.   1355
Chorus: Doer of dreadful deeds, how did you dare
so far to do despite to your own eyes?
What spirit urged you to it?
Oedipus: It was Apollo, friends, Apollo,
that brought this bitter bitterness, my sorrows to completion.   1360
But the hand that struck me
was none but my own.
Why should I see
whose vision showed me nothing sweet to see?
Chorus: These things are as you say.   1365
Oedipus: What can I see to love?
What greeting can touch my ears with joy?
Take me away, and haste—to a place out of the way!
Take me away, my friends, the greatly miserable,
the most accursed, whom God too hates   1370
above all men on earth!
Chorus: Unhappy in your mind and your misfortune,
would I had never known you!
Oedipus: Curse on the man who took
the cruel bonds from off my legs, as I lay in the field.   1375
He stole me from death and saved me,
no kindly service.
Had I died then
I would not be so burdensome to friends.
Chorus: I, too, could have wished it had been so.   1380

Oedipus: Then I would not have come
    to kill my father and marry my mother infamously.
    Now I am godless and child of impurity,
    begetter in the same seed that created my wretched self.
    If there is any ill worse than ill,   1385
    that is the lot of Oedipus.
Chorus: I cannot say your remedy was good;
    you would be better dead than blind and living.
Oedipus: What I have done here was best done—don't tell me
    otherwise, do not give me further counsel.   1390
    I do not know with what eyes I could look
    upon my father when I die and go
    under the earth, nor yet my wretched mother—
    those two to whom I have done things deserving
    worse punishment than hanging. Would the sight   1395
    of children, bred as mine are, gladden me?
    No, not these eyes, never. And my city,
    its towers and sacred places of the Gods,
    of these I robbed my miserable self
    when I commanded all to drive *him* out,   1400
    the criminal since proved by God impure
    and of the race of Laius.
    To this guilt I bore witness against myself—
    with what eyes shall I look upon my people?
    No. If there were a means to choke the fountain   1405
    of hearing I would not have stayed my hand
    from locking up my miserable carcass,
    seeing and hearing nothing; it is sweet
    to keep our thoughts out of the range of hurt.

    Cithaeron, why did you receive me? why   1410
    having received me did you not kill me straight?
    And so I had not shown to men my birth.

    O Polybus and Corinth and the house,
    the old house that I used to call my father's—
    what fairness you were nurse to, and what foulness   1415
    festered beneath! Now I am found to be
    a sinner and a son of sinners. Crossroads,
    and hidden glade, oak and the narrow way
    at the crossroads, that drank my father's blood
    offered you by my hands, do you remember   1420
    still what I did as you looked on, and what
    I did when I came here? O marriage, marriage!
    you bred me and again when you had bred
    bred children of your child and showed to men
    brides, wives and mothers and the foulest deeds   1425
    that can be in this world of ours.

Come—it's unfit to say what is unfit
to do.—I beg of you in God's name hide me
somewhere outside your country, yes, or kill me,
or throw me into the sea, to be forever   1430
out of your sight. Approach and deign to touch me
for all my wretchedness, and do not fear.
No man but I can bear my evil doom.

Chorus: Here Creon comes in fit time to perform
   or give advice in what you ask of us.   1435
   Creon is left sole ruler in your stead.

Oedipus: Creon! Creon! What shall I say to him?
   How can I justly hope that he will trust me?
   In what is past I have been proved towards him
   an utter liar.

(Enter Creon.)

Creon: Oedipus, I've come   1440
   not so that I might laugh at you nor taunt you
   with evil of the past. But if you still
   are without shame before the face of men
   reverence at least the flame that gives all life,
   our Lord the Sun, and do not show unveiled   1445
   to him pollution such that neither land
   nor holy rain nor light of day can welcome.

(To a servant.)

   Be quick and take him in. It is most decent
   that only kin should see and hear the troubles
   of kin.

Oedipus: I beg you, since you've torn me from   1450
   my dreadful expectations and have come
   in a most noble spirit to a man
   that has used you vilely—do a thing for me.
   I shall speak for your own good, not for my own.

Creon: What do you need that you would ask of me?   1455

Oedipus: Drive me from here with all the speed you can
   to where I may not hear a human voice.

Creon: Be sure, I would have done this had not I
   wished first of all to learn from the God the course
   of action I should follow.

Oedipus: But his word   1460
   has been quite clear to let the parricide,
   the sinner, die.

Creon: Yes, that indeed was said.
   But in the present need we had best discover
   what we should do.

Oedipus: And will you ask about
a man so wretched?
Creon: Now even you will trust   1465
the God.
Oedipus: So. I command you—and will beseech you—
to her that lies inside that house give burial
as you would have it; she is yours and rightly
you will perform the rites for her. For me—
never let this my father's city have me   1470
living a dweller in it. Leave me live
in the mountains where Cithaeron is, that's called
my mountain, which my mother and my father
while they were living would have made my tomb.
So I may die by their decree who sought   1475
indeed to kill me. Yet I know this much:
no sickness and no other thing will kill me.
I would not have been saved from death if not
for some strange evil fate. Well, let my fate
go where it will.
                          Creon, you need not care   1480
about my sons; they're men and so wherever
they are, they will not lack a livelihood.
But my two girls—so sad and pitiful—
whose table never stood apart from mine,
and everything I touched they always shared—   1485
O Creon, have a thought for them! And most
I wish that you might suffer me to touch them
and sorrow with them.

(Enter Antigone and Ismene, Oedipus' two daughters.)

O my Lord! O true noble Creon! Can I
really be touching them, as when I saw?   1490
What shall I say?
Yes, I can hear them sobbing—my two darlings!
and Creon has had pity and has sent me
what I loved most?
Am I right?   1495
Creon: You're right: it was I gave you this
because I knew from old days how you loved them
as I see now.
Oedipus: God bless you for it, Creon,
and may God guard you better on your road
than he did me!
                          O children,   1500
where are you? Come here, come to my hands,
a brother's hands which turned your father's eyes,

those bright eyes you knew once, to what you see,
a father seeing nothing, knowing nothing,
begetting you from his own source of life,   1505
I weep for you—I cannot see your faces—
I weep when I think of the bitterness
there will be in your lives, how you must live
before the world. At what assemblages
of citizens will you make one? to what   1510
gay company will you go and not come home
in tears instead of sharing in the holiday?
And when you're ripe for marriage, who will he be,
the man who'll risk to take such infamy
as shall cling to my children, to bring hurt   1515
on them and those that marry with them? What
curse is not there? "Your father killed his father
and sowed the seed where he had sprung himself
and begot you out of the womb that held him."
These insults you will hear. Then who will marry you?   1520
No one, my children; clearly you are doomed
to waste away in barrenness unmarried.
Son of Menoeceus, since you are all the father
left these two girls, and we, their parents, both
are dead to them—do not allow them wander   1525
like beggars, poor and husbandless.
They are of your own blood.
And do not make them equal with myself
in wretchedness; for you can see them now
so young, so utterly alone, save for you only.   1530
Touch my hand, noble Creon, and say yes.
If you were older, children, and were wiser,
there's much advice I'd give you. But as it is,
let this be what you pray: give me a life
wherever there is opportunity   1535
to live, and better life than was my father's.

Creon: Your tears have had enough of scope; now go within the house.
Oedipus: I must obey, though bitter of heart.
Creon: In season, all is good.
Oedipus: Do you know on what conditions I obey?
Creon: You tell me them,   1540
    and I shall know them when I hear.
Oedipus: That you shall send me out
    to live away from Thebes.
Creon: That gift you must ask of the God.
Oedipus: But I'm now hated by the Gods.
Creon: So quickly you'll obtain your prayer.
Oedipus: You consent then?
Creon: What I do not mean, I do not use to say. 1545

Oedipus: Now lead me away from here.
Creon: Let go the children, then, and come.
Oedipus: Do not take them from me.
Creon: Do not seek to be master in everything,
for the things you mastered did not follow you throughout your life.   1550

(As Creon and Oedipus go out.)

Chorus: You that live in my ancestral Thebes, behold this Oedipus, —
him who knew the famous riddles and was a man most masterful;
not a citizen who did not look with envy on his lot—
see him now and see the breakers of misfortune swallow him!
Look upon that last day always. Count no mortal happy till   1555
he has passed the final limit of his life secure from pain.

QUESTIONS

1. How explicitly does the prophet Teiresias reveal the guilt of Oedipus? Does it seem to you stupidity on the part of Oedipus, or a defect in Sophocles' play, that the king takes so long to recognize his guilt and to admit to it?
2. How does Oedipus exhibit weakness of character? Point to lines that reveal him as imperfectly noble in his words, deeds, or treatment of others.
3. "Oedipus is punished not for any fault in himself, but for his ignorance. Not knowing his family history, unable to recognize his parents on sight, he is blameless; and in slaying his father and marrying his mother, he behaves as any sensible person might behave in the same circumstances." Do you agree with this interpretation?
4. Besides the predictions of Teiresias, what other foreshadowings of the shepherd's revelation does the play contain?
5. Consider the character of Jocasta. Is she a "flat" character—a generalized queen figure—or an individual with distinctive traits of personality? Point to speeches or details in the play to back up your opinion.
6. Do the choral interludes merely interrupt the play with wordy poetry? Other than providing song, dance, and variety, do they have any value to the telling of the story?
7. What is dramatic irony? Besides the example given on page 522, what other instances of dramatic irony do you find in *Oedipus the King*? What do they contribute to the effectiveness of the play?
8. In the drama of Sophocles, violence and bloodshed take place offstage; thus, the suicide of Jocasta is only reported to us. Nor do we witness Oedipus' removal of his eyes; this horror is only given in the report by the second messenger. Of what advantage or disadvantage to the play is this limitation?
9. For what reason does Oedipus blind himself? What meaning, if any, do you find in his choice of a surgical instrument?
10. What are your feelings toward him as the play ends?
11. Read the famous interpretation of this play offered by Sigmund Freud (page 1437). How well does Freud explain why the play moves you?
12. With what attitude toward the gods does the play leave you? By inflicting a plague upon Thebes, by causing barrenness, by cursing both the people and their king, do the gods seem cruel, unjust, or tyrannical? Does the play show any reverence toward them?
13. Does this play end in total gloom?
14. How readily adaptable to the contemporary stage does *Oedipus the King* seem? Suppose you were to stage a production of the play with the aim of making it come alive for the playgoer today. What problems would you encounter? How would you deal with them?

Aristotle's Concept of Tragedy

> A tragedy, then, is an imitation of an action that is serious, complete in itself, and of a certain magnitude; in a language embellished with each kind of artistry . . . cast in the form of drama, not narrative; accomplishing through incidents that arouse pity and fear the purgation of these emotions.
>
> —Aristotle, *Poetics*, Chapter VI

Aristotle's famous definition of tragedy, constructed in the fourth century B.C., is the testimony of one who probably saw many classical tragedies performed. In making his observations, Aristotle does not seem to be laying down laws for what a tragedy ought to be. More likely, he is drawing—from tragedies he has seen or read—a general description of them.

Aristotle observes that the protagonist, the hero or chief character of a tragedy, is a person of "high estate," apparently a king or queen or other member of a royal family. In thus being as keenly interested as contemporary dramatists in the private lives of the powerful, Greek dramatists need not be accused of snobbery. It is the nature of tragedy that the protagonist must fall from power and from happiness; his high estate gives him a place of dignity to fall from and perhaps makes his fall seem all the more a calamity in that it involves an entire nation or people. Nor is the protagonist extraordinary merely in his position in society. Oedipus is not only a king but a noble soul who suffers profoundly and who employs splendid speech to express his suffering.

But the tragic hero is not a superman; he is fallible. The hero's downfall is the result, as Aristotle said, of his **hamartia**: his error or transgression or (as some translators would have it) his flaw or weakness of character. The notion that a tragic hero has such a **tragic flaw** has often been attributed to Aristotle, but it is by no means clear that Aristotle meant just that. According to this interpretation, every tragic hero has some fatal weakness, some moral Achilles' heel, that brings him to a bad end. In some classical tragedies, his transgression is a weakness the Greeks called **hubris**: extreme pride, leading to overconfidence.

Whatever Aristotle had in mind, however, many later critics find value in the idea of the tragic flaw. In this view, the downfall of a hero follows from his very nature. But whatever view we take—whether we find the hero's sufferings due to a flaw of character or to an error of judgment—we will probably find that his downfall results from acts for which he himself is responsible. In a Greek tragedy, the hero is a character amply capable of making choices—capable, too, of accepting the consequences.

It may be useful to take another look at Aristotle's definition of tragedy, with which we began. By **purgation** (or **katharsis**), did the ancient theorist mean that after witnessing a tragedy we feel relief, having released our pent-up emotions? Or did he mean that our feelings are purified, refined into something more ennobling? Scholars continue to argue. Whatever his exact meaning, clearly Aristotle implies that after witnessing a tragedy we feel better, not worse—not depressed but somehow elated. We take a kind of pleasure in the spectacle of a noble man being abased, but surely this pleasure is a legitimate one. For tragedy, Edith Hamilton wrote, affects us as "pain transmuted into exaltation by the alchemy of poetry."[1]

Aristotle, in describing the workings of this inexorable force in *Oedipus the King*, uses terms that later critics have found valuable. One is **recognition** or discovery *(anagnorisis)*: the revelation of some fact not known before, or some person's true identity. Oedipus makes such a discovery: he recognizes that he himself was the child whom his mother had given over to be destroyed. Such a recognition also occurs in Shakespeare's *Macbeth* when Macduff reveals himself to have been "from his mother's womb / Untimely ripped," thus disclosing a double meaning in the witches' prophecy that Macbeth could be harmed by "none of woman born," and sweeping aside Macbeth's last shred of belief that he is infallible. Modern critics have taken the term to mean also the terrible enlightenment that accompanies such a recognition. "To see things plain—that is *anagnorisis*," Clifford Leech observes, "and it is the ultimate experience we shall have if we have leisure at the point of death. . . . It is what tragedy ultimately is about: the realization of the unthinkable."[2]

Having made his discovery, Oedipus suffers a reversal in his fortunes: he goes off into exile, blinded and dethroned. Such a fall from happiness seems intrinsic to tragedy, but we should know that Aristotle has a more particular meaning for his term **reversal** *(peripeteia*, anglicized as **peripety)**. He means an action that turns out to have the opposite effect from the one its doer had intended. One of his illustrations of such an ironic reversal is from *Oedipus the King*: the first messenger intends to cheer Oedipus with the partially good news that, contrary to the prophecy that Oedipus would kill his father, his father has died of old age. The reversal is in the fact that, when the messenger further reveals that old Polybus was Oedipus' father only by adoption, the king, instead of having his fears allayed, is stirred to new dread.

We are not altogether sorry, perhaps, to see an arrogant man such as Oedipus humbled, and yet it is difficult not to feel that the punishment of Oedipus is greater than he deserves. Possibly this feeling is what Aristotle meant in his observation that a tragedy arouses our pity and our fear: our compassion for Oedipus, and our terror as we sense the remorselessness of a universe in which a man is doomed. Notice, however, that at the end of the play Oedipus does not curse God and die. Although such a complex play is open to many interpretations, it is probably safe to say that the play is not a bitter complaint against the universe. At last, Oedipus accepts the divine will, prays for blessings upon his children, and prepares to endure his exile—fallen from high estate, but uplifted in moral dignity.

[1]"The Idea of Tragedy" in *The Greek Way to Western Civilization* (New York: Norton, 1942).
[2]*Tragedy* (London: Methuen, 1969) 65.

SUGGESTIONS FOR WRITING

1. Suppose you face the task of directing and producing a new stage production of *Oedipus the King*. Decide how you would go about it. Would you use masks? How would you render the chorus? Would you set the play in contemporary North America? Justify your decisions by referring to the play itself.
2. Write a brief comment on the play, under the title: "Does Sophocles' Oedipus have an Oedipus complex?" Consider psychiatrist Sigmund Freud's famous observations (quoted on page 1437). Your comment can be either serious or light.
3. Compare the version of *Oedipus the King* given in this book with a different English translation of the play. You might see, for instance, any of the versions by Gilbert Murray, J.T. Sheppard, and H.D.F. Kitto; by Paul Roche (in a Signet paperback); by William Butler Yeats (in his *Collected Plays*); by Dudley Fitts and Robert Fitzgerald; or by Stephen Berg and Diskin Clay (Oxford UP, 1978). Point to significant differences between the two texts. What decisions did the translators have to make? Which version do you prefer? Why?
4. Read the *Antigone* (in "Plays for Further Reading"), and in a brief essay demonstrate its relationship to *Oedipus the King*.
5. John Millington Synge's *Riders to the Sea* (in Chapter One) has been called the closest approximation to a Greek tragedy in English. Does Synge's play resemble a tragedy of Sophocles in any ways? How does it noticeably differ?

34 The Theater of Shakespeare

Compared with the technical resources of a theater of today, those of a London public theater in the time of Queen Elizabeth I seem hopelessly limited. Plays had to be performed by daylight and scenery had to be kept simple: a table, a chair, a throne, perhaps an artificial tree or two to suggest a forest. But these limitations were in a sense advantages. What the theater of today can spell out for us realistically, with massive scenery and electric lighting, Elizabethan playgoers had to imagine and the playwright had to make vivid for them by means of language. Not having a lighting technician to work a panel, Shakespeare had to indicate the dawn by having Horatio, in *Hamlet,* say in a speech rich in metaphor and descriptive detail:

> But look, the morn in russet mantle clad
> Walks o'er the dew of yon high eastward hill.

And yet the theater of Shakespeare was not bare, for the playwright did have *some* valuable technical resources. Costumes could be elaborate, and apparently some costumes conveyed recognized meanings: one theater manager's inventory included "a robe for to go invisible in." There could be musical accompaniment and sound effects such as gunpowder explosions and the beating of a pan to simulate thunder.

The stage itself was remarkably versatile. At its back were doors for exits and entrances and a curtained booth or alcove useful for hiding inside. Above the stage was a higher acting area—perhaps a porch or balcony—useful for a Juliet to stand upon and for a Romeo to raise his eyes to. And in the stage floor was a trapdoor leading to a "hell" or cellar, especially useful for ghosts or devils who had to appear or disappear. The stage itself was a rectangular platform that projected into a yard enclosed by three-storied galleries.

The building was round or octagonal: in *Henry V,* Shakespeare calls it a "wooden O." The audience sat in these galleries or else stood in the yard in front of the stage and at its sides. A roof or awning protected the stage and the high-priced gallery seats, but in a sudden rain, the *groundlings*, who paid a penny to stand in the yard, must have been dampened.

Built by the theatrical company to which Shakespeare belonged, the Globe, most celebrated of Elizabethan theaters, was not in the city of London itself but

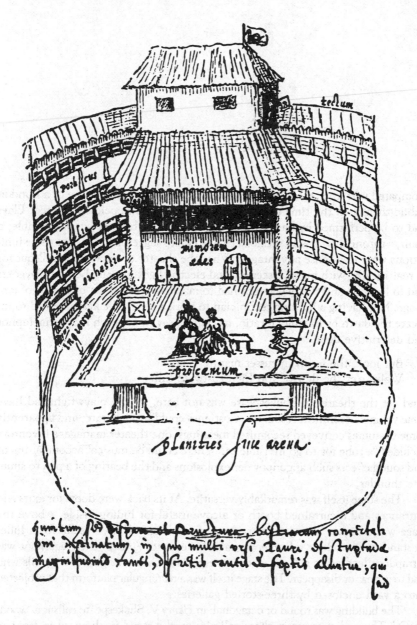

Johannes de Witt, a Continental visitor to London, made a drawing of the Swan Theater about 1596. The original drawing is lost; this is Arend van Buchel's copy of it.

on the south bank of the Thames River. This location had been chosen because earlier, in 1574, public plays had been banished from the city by an ordinance that blamed them for "corruptions of youth and other enormities" (such as providing opportunities for prostitutes and purse-cutters).

A playwright had to please all members of the audience, not only the mannered and educated. This obligation may help to explain the wide range of matter and tone in an Elizabethan play: passages of subtle poetry, of deep philosophy, of coarse bawdry; scenes of sensational violence and of quiet psychological conflict (not that most members of the audience did not enjoy all these elements). Because he was an actor as well as a playwright, Shakespeare well knew what his company could do, and what his audience wanted. In devising a play, he could write a part to take advantage of some actor's specific skills; or he could avoid straining the company's resources (some of his plays have few female parts, perhaps because of a shortage of competent boy actors). The company might offer as many as thirty plays in a season, customarily changing the program daily. The actors thus had to hold many parts in their heads, which may account for Elizabethan playwrights' fondness for blank verse. Lines of fixed length were easier for actors to commit to memory.

The Tragedy of Othello, here offered for study, may be (if you are fortunate) new to you. It is seldom taught in high school, for it is ablaze with passion and violence. But if you already know the play, we trust that you (like your instructor and your editor) still have much more to learn from it. Following his usual practice, Shakespeare based the play on a story he had appropriated—from a tale, "Of the Unfaithfulness of Husbands and Wives," by a sixteenth-century Italian writer, Giraldi Cinthio. And as he could not help but do, Shakespeare freely transformed his source material. In the original tale, the heroine Disdemona (whose name Shakespeare so hugely improved) is beaten to death with a stocking full of sand—a shoddier death than the Bard imagined for her.

Surely no character in literature can touch us more than Desdemona, no character can shock and disgust us more than Iago. Between these two extremes stands Othello, a black man of courage and dignity—and yet human, capable of being fooled, a pushover for bad advice. Besides breathing life into these characters and a host of others, Shakespeare—as brilliant a writer as any the world has known—enables them to speak poetry. Sometimes, this poetry seems splendid and rich in imagery; at other times, quiet and understated. Always, it seems to grow naturally from the nature of Shakespeare's characters and from their situations. *The Tragedy of Othello* has never ceased to grip readers and beholders alike. It is a safe bet that it will triumphantly live as long as fathers dislike whomever their daughters marry, as long as husbands suspect their wives of cheating, as long as blacks remember slavery, and as long as the ambitious court favor and the jealous work deceit. The play may well make sense as long as public officials connive behind smiling faces, and it may even endure as long as the world makes room for the kind, the true, the beautiful—the blessed pure in heart.

THE TRAGEDY OF OTHELLO   1604?

The Moor of Venice

Edited by Alvin Kernan°

*William Shakespeare (1564–1616), the su-
preme writer of English, was born, baptized,
and buried in the market town of Stratford-
on-Avon, eighty miles from London. Son of
a glovemaker and merchant who was high
bailiff (or mayor) of the town, he probably attended grammar school and learned to read
Latin authors in the original. At eighteen he
married Anne Hathaway, twenty-six, by
whom he had three children, including twins.
By 1592 he had become well known and envied as an actor and playwright in London.
From 1594 until he retired, he belonged to the*   William Shakespeare
*same theatrical company, the Lord Cham-
berlain's Men (later renamed the King's Men in honor of their patron, James I), for whom
he wrote thirty-six plays—some of them, such as Hamlet and King Lear, profound reworkings of old plays. As an actor, Shakespeare is believed to have played supporting
roles, such as Hamlet's father's ghost. The company prospered, moved into the Globe
in 1599, and in 1608 bought the fashionable Blackfriars as well; Shakespeare owned
an interest in both theaters. When plagues shut down the theaters from 1592 to 1594,
Shakespeare turned to story poems; his great Sonnets (published only in 1609) probably
also date from the 1590s. Plays were regarded as entertainments of little literary merit,
like comic books today, and Shakespeare did not bother to supervise their publication.
After The Tempest (1611), the last play entirely from his hand, he retired to Stratford,
where since 1597 he had owned the second largest house in town. Most critics agree
that when he wrote Othello, about 1604, Shakespeare was at the height of his powers.*

Characters

Othello, the Moor
Brabantio, father to Desdemona

Edited by Alvin Kernan: This text of *Othello* is based on that of the First Folio, or large collection,
of Shakespeare's plays (1623). But there are many differences between the Folio text and that of the
play's first printing in the Quarto, or small volume, of 1621 (eighteen or nineteen years after the play's
first performance). Some readings from the Quarto are included. For the reader's convenience, some
material has been added by the editor (some indications of scene, some stage directions). Such additions are enclosed in brackets. Mr. Kernan's text and notes were prepared for the edition of *Othello*
in the Signet Classic Shakespeare series (New York: NAL, 1963), under the general editorship of
Sylvan Barnet.

Cassio, an honorable lieutenant
Iago, a villain
Roderigo, a Venetian gentleman
Duke of Venice
Senators
Montano, Governor of Cyprus
Gentlemen of Cyprus
Lodovico and Gratiano, two noble Venetians
Sailors
Clown
Desdemona, wife to Othello
Emilia, wife to Iago
Bianca, a courtesan
[Messenger, Herald, Officers, Gentlemen, Musicians, Attendants]

Scene. Venice and Cyprus.

ACT I

Scene I [Venice. A street.]

Roderigo: Tush! Never tell me? I take it much unkindly
    That thou, Iago, who hast had my purse
    As if the strings were thine, shouldst know of this.
Iago: 'Sblood°, but you'll not hear me! If ever I did dream
    Of such a matter, abhor me.
Roderigo: Thou told'st me   5
    Thou didst hold him in thy hate.
Iago: Despise me
    If I do not. Three great ones of the city,
    In personal suit to make me his lieutenant,
    Off-capped° to him; and, by the faith of man,
    I know my price; I am worth no worse a place.   10
    But he, as loving his own pride and purposes,
    Evades them with a bombast circumstance°,
    Horribly stuffed with epithets of war,
    Nonsuits° my mediators. For, "Certes," says he,
    "I have already chose my officer." And what was he?   15
    Forsooth, a great arithmetician°,

I.i. 4 'Sblood: by God's blood.   9 Off-capped: doffed their caps—as a mark of respect.   12 bombast circumstance: stuffed, roundabout speech.   14 Nonsuits: rejects.   16 arithmetician: theorist (rather than practical).

One Michael Cassio, a Florentine,
(A fellow almost damned in a fair wife)°
That never set a squadron in the field,
Nor the division of a battle knows   20
More than a spinster; unless the bookish theoric,
Wherein the tonguèd° consuls can propose
As masterly as he. Mere prattle without practice
Is all his soldiership. But he, sir, had th' election;
And I, of whom his eyes had seen the proof   25
At Rhodes, at Cyprus, and on other grounds
Christian and heathen, must be belee'd and calmed
By debitor and creditor. This counter-caster°,
He, in good time, must his lieutenant be,
And I—God bless the mark!—his Moorship's ancient°.   30
Roderigo: By heaven, I rather would have been his hangman.
Iago: Why, there's no remedy. 'Tis the curse of service:
Preferment goes by letter and affection°,
And not by old gradation°, where each second
Stood heir to th' first. Now, sir, be judge yourself,   35
Whether I in any just term am affined°
To love the Moor.
Roderigo: I would not follow him then.
Iago: Oh, sir, content you.
I follow him to serve my turn upon him.
We cannot all be masters, nor all masters   40
Cannot be truly followed. You shall mark
Many a duteous and knee-crooking° knave
That, doting on his own obsequious bondage,
Wears out his time, much like his master's ass,
For naught but provender; and when he's old, cashiered.   45
Whip me such honest knaves! Others there are
Who, trimmed in forms and visages of duty,
Keep yet their hearts attending on themselves,
And, throwing but shows of service on their lords,
Do well thrive by them, and when they have lined their coats,   50
Do themselves homage. These fellows have some soul;
And such a one do I profess myself. For, sir,

---

18 *A . . . wife:* (a much-disputed passage, probably best taken as a general sneer at Cassio as a dandy
and a ladies' man. But in the story from which Shakespeare took his plot the counterpart of Cassio
is married, and it may be that at the beginning of the play Shakespeare had decided to keep him
married but later changed his mind).   22 *tonguèd:* eloquent.   28 *counter-caster:* i.e., a bookkeeper
who *casts* (reckons up) figures on a *counter* (abacus).   30 *ancient:* standard-bearer; an under-
officer.   33 *letter and affection:* recommendations (from men of power) and personal preference.
34 *old gradation:* seniority.   36 *affined:* bound.   42 *knee-crooking:* bowing.

It is as sure as you are Roderigo,
Were I the Moor, I would not be Iago.
In following him, I follow but myself. 55
Heaven is my judge, not I for love and duty,
But seeming so, for my peculiar° end;
For when my outward action doth demonstrate
The native° act and figure of my heart
In complement extern°, 'tis not long after 60
But I will wear my heart upon my sleeve
For daws to peck at; I am not what I am.
Roderigo: What a full fortune does the thick-lips owe°
If he can carry't thus!
Iago: Call up her father,
Rouse him. Make after him, poison his delight, 65
Proclaim him in the streets, incense her kinsmen,
And though he in a fertile climate dwell,
Plague him with flies; though that his joy be joy,
Yet throw such chances of vexation on't
As it may lose some color. 70
Roderigo: Here is her father's house. I'll call aloud.
Iago: Do, with like timorous° accent and dire yell
As when, by night and negligence, the fire
Is spied in populous cities.
Roderigo: What, ho, Brabantio! Signior Brabantio, ho! 75
Iago: Awake! What, ho, Brabantio! Thieves! Thieves!
Look to your house, your daughter, and your bags!
Thieves! Thieves!

Brabantio above° [at a window].

Brabantio: What is the reason of this terrible summons?
What is the matter there? 80
Roderigo: Signior, is all your family within?
Iago: Are your doors locked?
Brabantio: Why, wherefore ask you this?
Iago: Zounds, sir, y'are robbed! For shame. Put on your gown!
Your heart is burst, you have lost half your soul.
Even now, now, very now, an old black ram 85
Is tupping your white ewe. Arise, arise!
Awake the snorting citizens with the bell,
Or else the devil will make a grandsire of you.
Arise, I say!

---

57 *peculiar:* personal   59 *native:* natural, innate.   60 *complement extern:* outward appearance.
63 *owe:* own.   72 *timorous:* frightening.   78 *above:* (i.e., on the small upper stage above and to
the rear of the main platform stage, which resembled the projecting upper story of an Elizabethan house).

Brabantio:	What, have you lost your wits?	
Roderigo:	Most reverend signior, do you know my voice?	90
Brabantio:	Not I. What are you?	
Roderigo:	My name is Roderigo.	
Brabantio:	The worser welcome!	

I have charged thee not to haunt about my doors.
In honest plainness thou has heard me say
My daughter is not for thee; and now, in madness,   95
Being full of supper and distemp'ring draughts°,
Upon malicious knavery dost thou come
To start° my quiet.

Roderigo: Sir, sir, sir—

Brabantio: But thou must needs be sure
My spirits and my place° have in their power   100
To make this bitter to thee.

Roderigo: Patience, good sir.

Brabantio: What tell'st thou me of robbing? This is Venice,
My house is not a grange°.

Roderigo: Most grave Brabantio,
In simple and pure soul I come to you.

Iago: Zounds sir, you are one of those that will not serve   105
God if the devil bid you. Because we come to do you service and you
think we are ruffians, you'll have your daughter covered with a
Barbary° horse, you'll have your nephews° neigh to you, you'll have
coursers for cousins°, and gennets for germans°.

Brabantio: What profane wretch art thou?   110

Iago: I am one, sir, that comes to tell you your daughter and the Moor are
making the beast with two backs.

Brabantio: Thou art a villain.

Iago: You are—a senator.

Brabantio: This thou shalt answer. I know thee, Roderigo.

Roderigo: Sir, I will answer anything. But I beseech you,   115
If't be your pleasure and most wise consent,
As partly I find it is, that your fair daughter,
At this odd-even° and dull watch o' th' night,
Transported, with no worse nor better guard
But with a knave of common hire, a gondolier,   120
To the gross clasps of a lascivious Moor—
If this be known to you, and your allowance,

---

96 *distemp'ring draughts:* unsettling drinks.   98 *start:* disrupt.   100 *place:* rank, i.e., of senator.
103 *grange:* isolated house.   107 *Barbary:* Arabian, i.e., Moorish.   105 *nephews:* i.e., grandsons.
109 *cousins:* relations.   109 *gennets for germans:* Spanish horses for blood relatives.   118 *odd-even:*
between night and morning.

We then have done you bold and saucy wrongs;
But if you know not this, my manners tell me
We have your wrong rebuke. Do not believe   125
That from the sense of all civility°
I thus would play and trifle with your reverence.
Your daughter, if you have not given her leave,
I say again, hath made a gross revolt,
Tying her duty, beauty, wit, and fortunes   130
In an extravagant° and wheeling stranger
Of here and everywhere. Straight satisfy yourself.
If she be in her chamber, or your house,
Let loose on me the justice of the state
For thus deluding you.

Brabantio: Strike on the tinder, ho!   135
Give me a taper! Call up all my people!
This accident° is not unlike my dream.
Belief of it oppresses me already.
Light, I say! Light!   *Exit [above].*

Iago: Farewell, for I must leave you.
It seems not meet, nor wholesome to my place,   140
To be produced—as, if I stay, I shall—
Against the Moor. For I do know the State,
However this may gall him with some check°,
Cannot with safety cast° him; for he's embarked
With such loud reason to the Cyprus wars,   145
Which even now stands in act°, that for their souls
Another of his fathom° they have none
To lead their business; in which regard,
Though I do hate him as I do hell-pains,
Yet, for necessity of present life,   150
I must show out a flag and sign of love,
Which is indeed but sign. That you shall surely find him,
Lead to the Sagittary° that raisèd search:
And there will I be with him. So farewell.   *[Exit.]*

Enter Brabantio [in his nightgown], with Servants and torches.

Brabantio: It is too true an evil. Gone she is;   155
And what's to come of my despisèd time

126 *sense of all civility:* feeling of what is proper.   131 *extravagant:* vagrant, wandering (Othello is
not Venetian and thus may be considered a wandering soldier of fortune).   137 *accident:* happening.   143 *check:* restraint.   144 *cast:* dismiss.   146 *stands in act:* takes place.   147 *fathom:* ability.   153 *Sagittary:* (probably the name of an inn).

Is naught but bitterness. Now, Roderigo,
Where didst though see her?—O unhappy girl!—
With the Moor, say'st thou?—Who would be a father?—
How didst thou know 'twas she?—O, she deceives me   160
Past thought!—What said she to you? Get moe° tapers!
Raise all my kindred!—Are they married, think you?
Roderigo: Truly I think they are.
Brabantio: O heaven! How got she out? O treason of the blood!
Fathers, from hence trust not your daughters' minds   165
By what you see them act°. Is there not charms
By which the property° of youth and maidhood
May be abused? Have you not read, Roderigo,
Of some such thing?
Roderigo: Yes, sir, I have indeed.
Brabantio: Call up my brother.—O, would you had had her!—   170
Some one way, some another.—Do you know
Where we may apprehend her and the Moor?
Roderigo: I think I can discover him, if you please
To get good guard and go along with me.
Brabantio: Pray you lead on. At every house I'll call;   175
I may command at most.—Get weapons, ho!
And raise some special officers of night.—
On, good Roderigo; I will deserve your pains°.   [*Exeunt°.*]

Scene II [*A street.*]

Enter Othello, Iago, Attendants with torches.

Iago: Though in the trade of war I have slain men,
Yet do I hold it very stuff° o' th' conscience
To do no contrived murder. I lack iniquity
Sometime to do me service. Nine or ten times
I had thought t' have yerked° him here, under the ribs.   5
Othello: 'Tis better as it is.
Iago: Nay, but he prated,
And spoke such scurvy and provoking terms
Against your honor, that with the little godliness I have
I did full hard forbear him. But I pray you, sir,
Are you fast married? Be assured of this,   10
That the magnifico° is much beloved,
And hath in his effect a voice potential
As double as the Duke's°. He will divorce you,

---

161 *moe:* more.   166 *act:* do.   167 *property:* true nature.   178 *deserve your pains:* be worthy
of (and reward) your efforts.   178 *Exeunt:* Latin, "They go out," a direction indicating that all characters
leave the stage. I.ii. 2 *stuff:* essence.   5 *yerked:* stabbed.   11 *magnifico:* nobleman.
12–13 *hath . . . Duke's:* i.e., can be as effective as the Duke.

Or put upon you what restraint or grievance
The law, with all his might to enforce it on,   15
Will give him cable°.
Othello: Let him do his spite.
My services which I have done the Signiory°
Shall out-tongue his complaints. 'Tis yet to know°—
Which when I know that boasting is an honor
I shall promulgate—I fetch my life and being   20
From men of royal siege°, and my demerits°
May speak unbonneted to as proud a fortune
As this that I have reached°. For know, Iago,
But that I love the gentle Desdemona,
I would not my unhousèd free condition   25
Put into circumscription and confine
For the seas' worth. But look, what lights come yond?

Enter Cassio, with [Officers and] torches.

Iago: Those are the raisèd father and his friends.
You were best go in.
Othello: Not I. I must be found.
My parts, my title, and my perfect soul°   30
Shall manifest me rightly. Is it they?
Iago: By Janus, I think no.
Othello: The servants of the Duke? And my lieutenant?
The goodness of the night upon you, friends.
What is the news?
Cassio: The Duke does greet you, general;   35
And he requires your haste-posthaste appearance
Even on the instant.
Othello: What is the matter, think you?
Cassio: Something from Cyprus, as I may divine.
It is a business of some heat. The galleys
Have sent a dozen sequent° messengers   40
This very night at one another's heels,
And many of the consuls, raised and met,
Are at the Duke's already. You have been hotly called for.
When, being not at your lodging to be found,
The Senate hath sent about three several° quests   45
To search you out.

---

16 *cable:* range, scope.   17 *Signiory:* the rulers of Venice.   18 *yet to know:* unknown as yet.
21 *siege:* rank.   21 *demerits:* deserts.   22–23 *May . . . reached:* i.e., are the equal of the family I have married into.   25 *unhousèd:* unconfined.   30 *perfect soul:* clear, unflawed conscience.
40 *sequent:* successive.   45 *several:* separate.

Othello: 'Tis well I am found by you.
    I will but spend a word here in the house,
    And go with you.   [Exit.]
Cassio: Ancient, what makes he here?
Iago: Faith, he tonight hath boarded a land carack°.
    If it prove lawful prize, he's made forever.   50
Cassio: I do not understand.
Iago: He's married.
Cassio: To who?

    [Enter Othello.]

Iago: Marry°, to—Come captain, will you go?
Othello: Have with you.
Cassio: Here comes another troop to seek for you.

    Enter Brabantio, Roderigo, with Officers and torches.

Iago: It is Brabantio. General, be advised.
    He comes to bad intent.
Othello: Holla! Stand there!   55
Roderigo: Signior, it is the Moor.
Brabantio: Down with him, thief! [They draw swords.]
Iago: You, Roderigo? Come, sir, I am for you.
Othello: Keep up your bright swords, for the dew will rust them.
    Good signior, you shall more command with years
    Than with your weapons.   60
Brabantio: O thou foul thief, where hast thou stowed my daughter?
    Damned as thou art, thou hast enchanted her!
    For I'll refer me to all things of sense°,
    If she in chains of magic were not bound,
    Whether a maid so tender, fair, and happy,   65
    So opposite to marriage that she shunned
    The wealthy, curlèd darlings of our nation,
    Would ever have, t'incur a general mock°,
    Run from her guardage to the sooty bosom
    Of such a thing as thou—to fear, not to delight.   70
    Judge me the world if 'tis not gross in sense°
    That thou has practiced° on her with foul charms,
    Abused her delicate youth with drugs or minerals
    That weaken motion°. I'll have't disputed on;
    'Tis probable, and palpable to thinking.   75
    I therefore apprehend and do attach° thee
    For an abuser of the world, a practicer

---

49 carack: treasure ship.   52 Marry: By Mary (an interjection).   63 refer . . . sense: i.e., base (my argument) on all ordinary understanding of nature.   68 general mock: public shame.   71 gross in sense: obvious.   72 practiced: used tricks.   74 motion: thought, i.e., reason.   76 attach: arrest.

Of arts inhibited and out of warrant°.
Lay hold upon him. If he do resist,
Subdue him at his peril.
Othello: Hold your hands,   80
Both you of my inclining and the rest.
Were it my cue to fight, I should have known it
Without a prompter. Whither will you that I go
To answer this your charge?
Brabantio: To prison, till fit time
Of law and course of direct session   85
Call thee to answer.
Othello: What if I do obey?
How may the Duke be therewith satisfied,
Whose messengers are here about my side
Upon some present° business of the state
To bring me to him?
Officer: 'Tis true, most worthy signior.   90
The Duke's in council, and your noble self
I am sure is sent for.
Brabantio: How? The Duke in council?
In this time of the night? Bring him away.
Mine's not an idle cause. The Duke himself,
Or any of my brothers° of the state,   95
Cannot but feel this wrong as 'twere their own;
For if such actions may have passage free,
Bondslaves and pagans shall our statesmen be.   *Exeunt.*

Scene III [*A council chamber.*]

Enter *Duke, Senators,* and *Officers* [*set at a table, with lights and Attendants.*]

Duke: There's no composition° in this news
That gives them credit°.
First Senator: Indeed, they are disproportioned.
My letters say a hundred and seven galleys.
Duke: And mine a hundred forty.
Second Senator: And mine two hundred.
But though they jump° not on a just accompt°—   5
As in these cases where the aim° reports
'Tis oft with difference—yet do they all confirm
A Turkish fleet, and bearing up to Cyprus.
Duke: Nay, it is possible enough to judgment°.

---

78 *inhibited . . . warrant:* prohibited and illegal (black magic).   89 *present:* immediate.   95 *brothers:*
i.e., the other senators.   I.iii. 1 *composition:* agreement.   2 *gives them credit:* makes them believa-
ble.   5 *jump:* agree.   5 *just accompt:* exact counting.   6 *aim:* approximation.   9 *to judgment:*
when carefully considered.

I do not so secure me in the error,   10
But the main article I do approve
In fearful sense°.
Sailor (Within):   What, ho! What, ho! What, ho!

  Enter Sailor.

Officer: A messenger from the galleys.
Duke: Now? What's the business?
Sailor: The Turkish preparation makes for Rhodes.
So was I bid report here to the State   15
By Signior Angelo.
Duke: How say you by this change?
First Senator: This cannot be
By no assay of reason. 'Tis a pageant°
To keep us in false gaze°. When we consider
Th' importancy of Cyprus to the Turk,   20
And let ourselves again but understand
That, as it more concerns the Turk than Rhodes,
So may he with more facile question° bear it,
For that it stands not in such warlike brace°,
But altogether lacks th' abilities   25
That Rhodes is dressed in. If we make thought of this,
We must not think the Turk is so unskillful
To leave that latest which concerns him first,
Neglecting an attempt of ease and gain
To wake and wage a danger profitless.   30
Duke: Nay, in all confidence he's not for Rhodes.
Officer: Here is more news.

  Enter a Messenger.

Messenger: The Ottomites, reverend and gracious,
Steering with due course toward the isle of Rhodes,
Have there injointed them with an after° fleet.   35
First Senator: Ay, so I thought. How many, as you guess?
Messenger: Of thirty sail; and now they do restem
Their backward course, bearing with frank appearance
Their purposes toward Cyprus. Signior Montano,
Your trusty and most valiant servitor,   40
With his free duty° recommends° you thus,
And prays you to believe him.
Duke: 'Tis certain then for Cyprus.

10–12 *I do . . . sense:* i.e., just because the numbers disagree in the reports, I do not doubt that the
principal information (that the Turkish fleet is out) is fearfully true.   18 *pageant:* show, pretense.
19 *in false gaze:* looking the wrong way.   23 *facile question:* easy struggle.   24 *warlike brace:* "military posture."   35 *after:* following.   41 *free duty:* unlimited respect.   41 *recommends:* informs.

Marcus Luccicos, is not he in town?
First Senator: He's now in Florence.   45
Duke: Write from us to him; post-posthaste dispatch.
First Senator: Here comes Brabantio and the valiant Moor.

Enter Brabantio, Othello, Cassio, Iago, Roderigo, and Officers.

Duke: Valiant Othello, we must straight° employ you
    Against the general° enemy Ottoman.
    [*To Brabantio*] I did not see you. Welcome, gentle signior.   50
    We lacked your counsel and your help tonight.
Brabantio: So did I yours. Good your grace, pardon me.
    Neither my place, nor aught I heard of business,
    Hath raised me from my bed; nor doth the general care
    Take hold on me; for my particular grief   55
    Is of so floodgate and o'erbearing nature
    That it engluts and swallows other sorrows,
    And it is still itself.
Duke: Why, what's the matter?
Brabantio: My daughter! O, my daughter!
Senators: Dead?
Brabantio: Ay, to me.
    She is abused, stol'n from me, and corrupted   60
    By spells and medicines bought of mountebanks;
    For nature so prepost'rously to err,
    Being not deficient, blind, or lame of sense,
    Sans° witchcraft could not.
Duke: Whoe'er he be that in this foul proceeding   65
    Hath thus beguiled your daughter of herself,
    And you of her, the bloody book of law
    You shall yourself read in the bitter letter
    After your own sense; yea, though our proper° son
    Stood in your action°.
Brabantio: Humbly I thank your Grace.   70
    Here is the man—this Moor, whom now, it seems,
    Your special mandate for the state affairs
    Hath hither brought.
All: We are very sorry for't.
Duke [To Othello]: What in your own part can you say to this?
Brabantio: Nothing, but this is so.   75
Othello: Most potent, grave, and reverend signiors,
    My very noble and approved° good masters,
    That I have ta'en away this old man's daughter,
    It is most true; true I have married her.

---

48 *straight:* at once.   49 *general:* universal.   64 *Sans:* without.   69 *proper:* own.   70 *Stood in your action:* were the accused in your suit.   77 *approved:* tested, proven by past performance.

The very head and front° of my offending 80
Hath this extent, no more. Rude am I in my speech,
And little blessed with the soft phrase of peace.
For since these arms of mine had seven years' pith°
Till now some nine moons wasted°, they have used
Their dearest° action in the tented field; 85
And little of this great world can I speak
More than pertains to feats of broils and battle;
And therefore little shall I grace my cause
In speaking for myself. Yet, by your gracious patience,
I will a round° unvarnished tale deliver 90
Of my whole course of love—what drugs, what charms,
What conjuration, and what mighty magic,
For such proceeding I am charged withal,
I won his daughter—
Brabantio: A maiden never bold,
Of spirit so still and quiet that her motion 95
Blushed at herself°, and she, in spite of nature,
Of years, of country, credit, everything,
To fall in love with what she feared to look on!
It is a judgment maimed and most imperfect
That will confess perfection so could err 100
Against all rules of nature, and must be driven
To find out practices of cunning hell
Why this should be. I therefore vouch again
That with some mixtures pow'rful o'er the blood,
Or with some dram, conjured to this effect, 105
He wrought upon her.
Duke: To vouch this is no proof,
Without more wider and more overt test
Than these thin habits° and poor likelihoods
Of modern° seeming do prefer against him.
First Senator: But, Othello, speak. 110
Did you by indirect and forcèd courses
Subdue and poison this young maid's affections?
Or came it by request, and such fair question°
As soul to soul affordeth?
Othello: I do beseech you,
Send for the lady to the Sagittary 115
And let her speak of me before her father.
If you do find me foul in her report,
The trust, the office, I do hold of you

80 *head and front*: extreme form (*front* = forehead).   83 *pith*: strength.   84 *wasted*: past.
85 *dearest*: most important.   90 *round*: blunt.   95–96 *her motion/Blushed at herself*: i.e., she was
so modest that she blushed at every thought (and movement).   108 *habits*: clothing.   109 *modern*:
trivial.   113 *question*: discussion.

Not only take away, but let your sentence
Even fall upon my life.
Duke: Fetch Desdemona hither.   120
Othello: Ancient, conduct them; you best know the place.

[Exit Iago, with two or three Attendants.]

And till she come, as truly as to heaven
I do confess the vices of my blood,
So justly to your grave ears I'll present
How I did thrive in this fair lady's love,   125
And she in mine.
Duke: Say it, Othello.
Othello: Her father loved me; oft invited me;
Still° questioned me the story of my life
From year to year, the battle, sieges, fortune
That I have passed.   130
I ran it through, even from my boyish days
To th' very moment that he bade me tell it.
Wherein I spoke of most disastrous chances,
Of moving accidents by flood and field,
Of hairbreadth scapes i' th' imminent° deadly breach,   135
Of being taken by the insolent foe
And sold to slavery, of my redemption thence
And portance° in my travel's history,
Wherein of anters° vast and deserts idle°,
Rough quarries, rocks, and hills whose heads touch heaven,   140
It was my hint to speak. Such was my process.
And of the Cannibals that each other eat,
The Anthropophagi°, and men whose heads
Grew beneath their shoulders. These things to hear
Would Desdemona seriously incline;   145
But still the house affairs would draw her thence;
Which ever as she could with haste dispatch,
She'd come again, and with a greedy ear
Devour up my discourse. Which I observing,
Took once a pliant hour, and found good means   150
To draw from her a prayer of earnest heart
That I would all my pilgrimage dilate°,
Whereof by parcels she had something heard,
But not intentively°. I did consent,
And often did beguile her of her tears   155
When I did speak of some distressful stroke

128 Still: regularly.   135 imminent: threatening.   138 portanc: manner of acting.   139 anters: caves.   139 idle: empty, sterile.   143 Anthropophagi: maneaters.   152 dilate: relate in full.   154 intentively: at length and in sequence.

That my youth suffered. My story being done,
She gave me for my pains a world of kisses.
She swore in faith 'twas strange, 'twas passing° strange;
'Twas pitiful, 'twas wondrous pitiful.   160
She wished she had not heard it; yet she wished
That heaven had made her such a man. She thanked me,
And bade me, if I had a friend that loved her,
I should but teach him how to tell my story,
And that would woo her. Upon this hint I spake.   165
She loved me for the dangers I had passed,
And I loved her that she did pity them.
This only is the witchcraft I have used.
Here comes the lady. Let her witness it.

                              Enter Desdemona, Iago, Attendants.

Duke: I think this tale would win my daughter too.   170
   Good Brabantio, take up this mangled matter at the best°.
   Men do their broken weapons rather use
   Than their bare hands.
Brabantio: I pray you hear her speak.
   If she confess that she was half the wooer,
   Destruction on my head if my bad blame   175
   Light on the man. Come hither, gentle mistress.
   Do you perceive in all this noble company
   Where must you owe obedience?
Desdemona: My noble father,
   I do perceive here a divided duty.
   To you I am bound for life and education;   180
   My life and education both do learn me
   How to respect you. You are the lord of duty,
   I am hitherto your daughter. But here's my husband,
   And so much duty as my mother showed
   To you, preferring you before her father,   185
   So much I challenge° that I may profess
   Due to the Moor my lord.
Brabantio: God be with you. I have done.
   Please it your Grace, on to the state affairs.
   I had rather to adopt a child than get° it.
   Come hither, Moor.   190
   I here do give thee that with all my heart
   Which, but thou hast already, with all my heart
   I would keep from thee. For your sake°, jewel,
   I am glad at soul I have no other child,

159 *passing:* surpassing.   171 *take . . . best:* i.e., make the best of this disaster.   186 *challenge:* claim
as right.   189 *get:* beget.   193 *For your sake:* because of you.

For thy escape would teach me tyranny, 195
To hang clogs on them. I have done, my lord.
Duke: Let me speak like yourself and lay a sentence°
Which, as a grise° or step, may help these lovers.
When remedies are past, the griefs are ended
By seeing the worst, which late on hopes depended°. 200
To mourn a mischief that is past and gone
Is the next° way to draw new mischief on.
What cannot be preserved when fortune takes,
Patience her injury a mock'ry makes.
The robbed that smiles, steals something from the thief; 205
He robs himself that spends a bootless° grief.
Brabantio: So let the Turk of Cyprus us beguile:
We lose it not so long as we can smile.
He bears the sentence well that nothing bears
But the free comfort which from thence he hears; 210
But he bears both the sentence and the sorrow
That to pay grief must of poor patience borrow.
These sentences, to sugar, or to gall,
Being strong on both sides, are equivocal.
But words are words. I never yet did hear 215
That the bruisèd heart was piercèd° through the ear.
I humbly beseech you, proceed to th' affairs of state.
Duke: The Turk with a most mighty preparation makes for Cyprus. Othello,
the fortitude° of the place is best known to you; and though we have
there a substitute° of most allowed sufficiency°, yet opinion, a more 220
sovereign mistress of effects, throws a more safer voice on you°. You
must therefore be content to slubber° the gloss of your new fortunes
with this more stubborn and boisterous° expedition.
Othello: The tyrant Custom, most grave senators,
Hath made the flinty and steel couch of war 225
My thrice-driven° bed of down. I do agnize°
A natural and prompt alacrity
I find in hardness and do undertake
These present wars against the Ottomites.
Most humbly, therefore, bending to your state, 230
I crave fit disposition for my wife,

---

197 *lay a sentence:* provide a maxim.   198 *grise:* step.   200 *late on hopes depended:* was supported
by hope (of a better outcome) until lately.   202 *next:* closest, surest.   206 *bootless:* valueless.
216 *piercèd:* (some editors emend to *pieced* i.e., "healed". But *piercèd* makes good sense: Brabantio is
saying in effect that his heart cannot be further hurt [pierced] by the indignity of the useless, conventional advice the Duke offers him. *Pierced* can also mean, however, "lanced" in the medical sense,
and would then mean "treated").   219 *fortitude:* fortification.   220 *substitute:* viceroy.   220 *most
allowed sufficiency:* generally acknowledged capability.   220–221 *opinion . . . you:* i.e., the general opinion, which finally controls affairs, is that you would be the best man in this situation.
222 *slubber:* besmear.   223 *stubborn and boisterous:* rough and violent.   226 *thrice-driven:* i.e.,
softest.   226 *agnize:* know in myself.

Due reference of place, and exhibition°,
With such accommodation and besort
As levels with° her breeding.
Duke: Why, at her father's.
Brabantio: I will not have it so.
Othello: Nor I.   235
Desdemona: Nor would I there reside,
    To put my father in impatient thoughts
    By being in his eye. Most gracious Duke,
    To my unfolding° lend your prosperous° ear,
    And let me find a charter° in your voice,   240
    T' assist my simpleness.
Duke: What would you, Desdemona?
Desdemona: That I love the Moor to live with him,
    My downright violence, and storm of fortunes,
    May trumpet to the world. My heart's subdued
    Even to the very quality of my lord.°   245
    I saw Othello's visage in his mind,
    And to his honors and his valiant parts
    Did I my soul and fortunes consecrate.
    So that, dear lords, if I be left behind,
    A moth of peace, and he go to the war,   250
    The rites° for why I love him are bereft me,
    And I a heavy interim shall support
    By his dear absence. Let me go with him.
Othello: Let her have your voice°.
    Vouch with me, heaven, I therefore beg it not   255
    To please the palate of my appetite,
    Nor to comply with heat°—the young affects°
    In me defunct—and proper satisfaction°;
    But to be free and bounteous to her mind;
    And heaven defend° your good souls that you think 260
    I will your serious and great business scant
    When she is with me. No, when light-winged toys
    Of feathered Cupid seel° with wanton° dullness
    My speculative and officed instrument°,
    That my disports corrupt and taint my business,   265
    Let housewives make a skillet of my helm,
    And all indign° and base adversities

232 *exhibition:* grant of funds.   234 *levels with:* is suitable to.   239 *unfolding:* explanation.
239 *prosperous:* favoring.   240 *charter:* permission.   244–245 *My . . . lord:* i.e., I have
become one in nature and being with the man I married (therefore, I too would go to the wars
like a soldier).   251 *rites:* (may refer either to the marriage rites or to the rites, formalities,
of war).   254 *voice:* consent.   257 *heat:* lust.   257 *affects:* passions.   258 *proper satisfaction:* i.e., consummation of the marriage.   260 *defend:* forbid.   263 *seel:* sew up.   263 *wanton:*
lascivious.   264 *speculative . . . instrument:* i.e., sight (and, by extension, the mind).   267 *indign:*
unworthy.

Make head° against my estimation°!—

Duke: Be it as you shall privately determine,
    Either for her stay or going. Th' affair cries haste,   270
    And speed must answer it.

First Senator: You must away tonight.

Othello: With all my heart.

Duke: At nine i' th' morning here we'll meet again.
    Othello, leave some officer behind,
    And he shall our commission bring to you,   275
    And such things also of quality and respect
    As doth import you.

Othello: So please your grace, my ancient;
    A man he is of honesty and trust.
    To his conveyance I assign my wife,
    With what else needful your good grace shall think   280
    To be sent after me.

Duke: Let it be so.
    Good night to every one. *[To Brabantio]* And, noble signior,
    If virtue no delighted° beauty lack,
    Your son-in-law is far more fair than black.

First Senator: Adieu, brave Moor. Use Desdemona well.   285

Brabantio: Look to her, Moor, if thou hast eyes to see:
    She has deceived her father, and may thee.

                  [Exeunt Duke, Senators, Officers, & c.]

Othello: My life upon her faith! Honest Iago,
    My Desdemona must I leave to thee.
    I prithee let thy wife attend on her,   290
    And bring them after in the best advantage°.
    Come, Desdemona. I have but an hour
    Of love, of worldly matter, and direction
    To spend with thee. We must obey the time.

                       Exit [Moor with Desdemona].

Roderigo: Iago?   295

Iago: What say'st thou, noble heart?

Roderigo: What will I do, think'st thou?

Iago: Why, go to bed and sleep.

Roderigo: I will incontinently° drown myself.

Iago: If thou dost, I shall never love thee after. Why, thou silly gentle-   300
    man?

Roderigo: It is silliness to live when to live is torment and then have we
    a prescription to die when death is our physician.

---

268 *Make head:* form an army, i.e., attack.   268 *estimation:* reputation.   283 *delighted:* delightful.   291 *advantage:* opportunity.   299 *incontinently:* at once.

Iago: O villainous! I have looked upon the world for four times seven years, and since I could distinguish betwixt a benefit and an injury, I never found man that knew how to love himself. Ere I would say I would drown myself for the love of a guinea hen, I would change my humanity with a baboon. 305

Roderigo: What should I do? I confess it is my shame to be so fond, but it is not in my virtue° to amend it. 310

Iago: Virtue? A fig! 'Tis in ourselves that we are thus, or thus. Our bodies are our gardens, to the which our wills are gardeners; so that if we will plant nettles or sow lettuce, set hyssop and weed up thyme, supply it with one gender of herbs or distract° it with many—either to have it sterile with idleness or manured with industry—why the power and corrigible° authority of this lies in our wills. If the balance of our lives had not one scale of reason to poise another of sensuality, the blood and baseness of our natures would conduct us to most prepost'rous conclusions°. But we have reason to cool our raging motions, our carnal sting or unbitted° lusts, whereof I take this that you call love to be a sect or scion°. 315 320

Roderigo: It cannot be.

Iago: It is merely a lust of the blood and a permission of the will. Come, be a man! Drown thyself? Drown cats and blind puppies! I have professed me thy friend, and I confess me knit to thy deserving with cables of perdurable toughness. I could never better stead° thee than now. Put money in thy purse. Follow thou the wars; defeat thy favor° with an usurped° beard. I say, put money in thy purse. It cannot be long that Desdemona should continue her love to the Moor. Put money in thy purse. Nor he his to her. It was a violent commencement in her and thou shalt see an answerable° sequestration—put but money in thy purse. These Moors are changeable in their wills—fill thy purse with money. The food that to him now is as luscious as locusts° shall be to him shortly as bitter as coloquintida°. She must change for youth; when she is sated with his body, she will find the errors of her choice. Therefore, put money in thy purse. If thou wilt needs damn thyself, do it a more delicate way than drowning. Make all the money thou canst. If sanctimony° and a frail vow betwixt an erring° barbarian and supersubtle Venetian be not too hard for my wits, and all the tribe of hell, thou shalt enjoy her. Therefore, make money. A pox of drowning thyself, it is clean out of the way. Seek thou rather to be hanged in compassing° thy joy than to be drowned and go without her. 325 330 335 340

Roderigo: Wilt thou be fast to my hopes, if I depend on the issue?

---

310 *virtue:* strength (Roderigo is saying that his nature controls him).   314 *distract:* vary.   316 *corrigible:* corrective.   319 *conclusions:* ends.   320 *unbitted:* i.e., uncontrolled.   321 *sect or scion:* off-shoot.   326 *stead:* serve.   327–328 *defeat thy favor:* disguise your face.   328 *usurped:* assumed.   331 *answerable:* similar.   333 *locusts:* (a sweet fruit).   334 *coloquintida:* a purgative derived from a bitter apple.   338 *sanctimony:* sacred bond (of marriage).   338 *erring:* wandering. 342 *compassing:* encompassing, achieving.

Iago: Thou art sure of me. Go, make money. I have told thee often, and
I retell thee again and again, I hate the Moor. My cause is hearted°;   345
thine hath no less reason. Let us be conjunctive° in our revenge against
him. If thou canst cuckold him, thou dost thyself a pleasure, me a sport.
There are many events in the womb of time, which will be delivered.
Traverse, go, provide thy money! We will have more of this tomorrow.
Adieu.   350

Roderigo: Where shall we meet i' th' morning?

Iago: At my lodging.

Roderigo: I'll be with thee betimes.

Iago: Go to, farewell. Do you hear, Roderigo?

Roderigo: I'll sell all my land.   355

Exit.

Iago: Thus do I ever make my fool my purse;
    For I mine own gained knowledge° should profane
    If I would time expend with such a spine
    But for my sport and profit. I hate the Moor,
    And it is thought abroad that 'twixt my sheets   360
    H'as done my office. I know not if't be true,
    But I, for mere suspicion in that kind
    Will do, as if for surety°. He holds me well;
    The better shall my purpose work on him.
    Cassio's a proper° man. Let me see now: 365
    To get his place, and to plume up my will°
    In double knavery. How? How? Let's see.
    After some time, to abuse Othello's ears
    That he is too familiar with his wife.
    He hath a person and a smooth dispose°   370
    To be suspected—framed° to make women false.
    The Moor is of a free and open nature
    That thinks men honest that but seem to be so;
    And will as tenderly be led by th' nose
    As asses are.   375
    I have't! It is engendered! Hell and night
    Must bring this monstrous birth to the world's light.   *[Exit.]*

ACT II

Scene I *[Cyprus.]*

Enter Montano and two Gentlemen [one above]°.

345 *hearted:* deepseated in the heart.   346 *conjunctive:* joined.   357 *gained knowledge:* i.e., practical, worldly wisdom.   363 *surety:* certainty.   365 *proper:* handsome.   366 *plume up my will:* (many
explanations have been offered for this crucial line, which in Q¹ reads "make up my will." The general
sense is something like "to make more proud and gratify my ego").   370 *dispose:* manner.
371 *framed:* designed.   II.i. stage direction (the Folio text requires that the First Gentleman stand
above—on the upper stage—and act as a lookout reporting sights that cannot be seen by Montano
standing below on the main stage).

Montano: What from the cape can you discern at sea?

First Gentleman: Nothing at all, it is a high-wrought flood.
 I cannot 'twixt the heaven and the main
 Descry a sail.

Montano: Methinks the wind hath spoke aloud at land;   5
 A fuller blast ne'er shook our battlements.
 If it hath ruffianed so upon the sea,
 What ribs of oak, when mountains melt on them,
 Can hold the mortise? What shall we hear of this?

Second Gentleman: A segregation° of the Turkish fleet.   10
 For do but stand upon the foaming shore,
 The chidden billow seems to pelt the clouds;
 The wind-shaked surge, with high and monstrous main°,
 Seems to cast water on the burning Bear
 And quench the guards of th' ever-fixèd pole.°   15
 I never did like molestation view
 On the enchafèd flood.

Montano: If that the Turkish fleet
 Be not ensheltered and embayed, they are drowned;
 It is impossitle to bear it out.

 Enter a [third] Gentleman.

Third Gentleman: News, lads! Our wars are done.   20
 The desperate tempest hath so banged the Turks
 That their designment halts. A noble ship of Venice
 Hath seen a grievous wrack and sufferance°
 On most part of their fleet.

Montano: How? Is this true?

Third Gentleman: The ship is here put in,   25
 A Veronesa; Michael Cassio,
 Lieutenant to the warlike Moor Othello,
 Is come on shore; the Moor himself at sea,
 And is in full commission here for Cyprus.

Montano: I am glad on't. 'Tis a worthy governor.   30

Third Gentleman: But this same Cassio, though he speak of comfort
 Touching the Turkish loss, yet he looks sadly
 And prays the Moor be safe, for they were parted
 With foul and violent tempest.

Montano: Pray heavens he be;
 For I have served him, and the man commands   35
 Like a full soldier. Let's to the seaside, ho!
 As well to see the vessel that's come in

---

10 *segregation:* separation.   13 *main:* (both "ocean" and "strength").   14–15 *Seems . . . pole:* (the constellation Ursa Minor contains two stars that are the *guards*, or companions, of the *pole*, or North Star).   23 *sufferance:* damage.

As to throw out our eyes for brave Othello,
Even till we make the main and th' aerial blue
An indistinct regard°.
Third Gentleman: Come, let's do so;   40
For every minute is expectancy
Of more arrivancie°.

Enter Cassio.

Cassio: Thanks, you the valiant of the warlike isle,
That so approve° the Moor. O, let the heavens
Give him defense against the elements,   45
For I have lost him on a dangerous sea.
Montano: Is he well shipped?
Cassio: His bark is stoutly timbered, and his pilot
Of very expert and approved allowance°;
Therefore my hopes, not surfeited to death°,   50
Stand in bold cure°. (*Within:* A sail, a sail, a sail!)
Cassio: What noise?
First Gentleman: The town is empty; on the brow o' th' sea
Stand ranks of people, and they cry, "A sail!"
Cassio: My hopes do shape him for the governor.   [*A shot.*]   55
Second Gentleman: They do discharge their shot of courtesy:
Our friends at least.
Cassio: I pray you, sir, go forth
And give us truth who 'tis that is arrived.
Second Gentleman: I shall.   [*Exit.*]
Montano: But, good lieutenant, is your general wived?   60
Cassio: Most fortunately. He hath achieved a maid
That paragons° description and wild fame°;
One that excels the quirks of blazoning pens°,
And in th' essential vesture of creation°
Does tire the ingener°.

Enter [Second] Gentleman.

                    How now? Who has put in?   65
Second Gentleman: 'Tis one Iago, ancient to the general.
Cassio: H'as had most favorable and happy speed:
Tempests themselves, high seas, and howling winds,
The guttered° rocks and congregated° sands,
Traitors ensteeped° to enclog the guiltless keel,   70

39–40 *the main . . . regard:* i.e., the sea and sky become indistinguishable.   42 *arrivancie:* arrivals.
44 *approve:* ("honor" or, perhaps, "are as warlike and valiant as your governor").   49 *approved allowance:* known and tested.   50 *not surfeited to death:* i.e., not so great as to be in danger.
51 *Stand in bold cure:* i.e., are likely to be restored.   62 *paragons:* exceeds.   62 *wild fame:* extravagant report.   63 *quirks of blazoning pens:* ingenuities of praising pens.   64 *essential vesture of creation:* essential human nature as given by the Creator.   65 *tire the ingener:* a difficult line that probably means something like "outdo the human ability to imagine and picture."   69 *guttered:* jagged.   69 *congregated:* gathered.   70 *ensteeped:* submerged.

As having sense° of beauty, do omit
Their mortal° natures, letting go safely by
The divine Desdemona.
Montano: What is she?
Cassio: She that I spake of, our great captain's captain,
Left in the conduct of the bold Iago,   75
Whose footing° here anticipates our thoughts
A se'nnight's° speed. Great Jove, Othello guard,
And swell his sail with thine own pow'rful breath,
That he may bless this bay with his tall° ship,
Make love's quick pants in Desdemona's arms,   80
Give renewed fire to our extincted spirits.

Enter Desdemona, Iago, Roderigo, and Emilia.

O, behold! The riches of the ship is come on shore!
You men of Cyprus, let her have your knees.   *[Kneeling.]*
Hail to thee, lady! and the grace of heaven,
Before, behind thee, and on every hand,   85
Enwheel thee round.
Desdemona: I thank you, valiant Cassio.
What tidings can you tell me of my lord?
Cassio: He is not yet arrived, nor know I aught
But that he's well and will be shortly here.
Desdemona: O but I fear. How lost you company?   90
Cassio: The great contention of sea and skies
Parted our fellowship. (*Within:* A sail, a sail!)   *[A shot.]*
But hark. A sail!
Second Gentleman: They give this greeting to the citadel;
This likewise is a friend.
Cassio: See for the news.   *[Exit Gentleman.]*   95
Good ancient, you are welcome. *[To Emilia]* Welcome, mistress.
Let it not gall your patience, good Iago,
That I extend° my manners. 'Tis my breeding°
That gives me this bold show of courtesy.   *[Kisses Emilia.]*
Iago: Sir, would she give you so much of her lips   100
As of her tongue she oft bestows on me,
You would have enough.
Desdemona: Alas, she has no speech.
Iago: In faith, too much.
I find it still when I have leave to sleep°.
Marry, before your ladyship°, I grant,   105

---

71 *sense:* awareness.   72 *mortal:* deadly.   76 *footing:* landing.   77 *se'nnight's:* week's.   79 *tall:*
brave.   98 *extend:* stretch.   98 *breeding:* careful training in manners (Cassio is considerably more
the polished gentleman than Iago, and aware of it).   104 *still . . . sleep:* i.e., even when she allows
me to sleep she continues to scold.   105 *before your ladyship:* in your presence.

She puts her tongue a little in her heart
And chides with thinking.
Emilia: You have little cause to say so.
Iago: Come on, come on! You are pictures° out of door,
    Bells in your parlors, wildcats in your kitchens,
    Saints in your injuries°, devils being offended,   110
    Players in your housewifery°, and housewives in your beds.
Desdemona: O, fie upon thee, slanderer!
Iago: Nay, it is true, or else I am a Turk:
    You rise to play, and go to bed to work.
Emilia: You shall not write my praise.
Iago: No, let me not.   115
Desdemona: What wouldst write of me, if thou shouldst praise me?
Iago: O gentle lady, do not put me to't.
    For I am nothing if not critical.
Desdemona: Come on, assay. There's one gone to the harbor?
Iago: Ay, madam.   120
Desdemona [Aside]: I am not merry; but I do beguile
    The thing I am by seeming otherwise.—
    Come, how wouldst thou praise me?
Iago: I am about it; but indeed my invention
    Comes from my pate as birdlime° does from frieze°—   125
    It plucks out brains and all. But my Muse labors,
    And thus she is delivered:
    If she be fair° and wise: fairness and wit,
    The one's for use, the other useth it.
Desdemona: Well praised. How if she be black° and witty?   130
Iago: If she be black, and thereto have a wit,
    She'll find a white that shall her blackness fit.
Desdemona: Worse and worse!
Emilia: How if fair and foolish?
Iago: She never yet was foolish that was fair,   135
    For even her folly helped her to an heir.
Desdemona: Those are old fond° paradoxes to make fools laugh i' th' ale-
    house. What miserable praise hast thou for her that's foul and foolish?
Iago: There's none so foul, and foolish thereunto,
    But does foul pranks which fair and wise ones do.   140
Desdemona: O heavy ignorance. Thou praisest the worst best. But what praise
    couldst thou bestow on a deserving woman indeed—one that in the
    authority of her merit did justly put on the vouch of very malice itself°?

108 *pictures:* models (of virtue).   110 *in your injuries:* when you injure others.   111 *housewifery:*
this word can mean "careful, economical household management," and Iago would then be accusing
women of only pretending to be good housekeepers, while in bed they are either (1) economical of
their favors, or more likely (2) serious and dedicated workers.   125 *birdlime:* a sticky substance put
on branches to catch birds.   125 *frieze:* rough cloth.   128 *fair:* light-complexioned.   130 *black:*
brunette.   137 *fond:* foolish.   142–143 *one . . . itself:* i.e., a woman so honest and deserving that
even malice would be forced to approve of her.

Iago: She that was ever fair, and never proud;
　　Had tongue at will, and yet was never loud;　　　　　　145
　　Never lacked gold, and yet went never gay;
　　Fled from her wish, and yet said "Now I may";
　　She that being angered, her revenge being nigh,
　　Bade her wrong stay, and her displeasure fly;
　　She that in wisdom never was so frail　　　　　　　　150
　　To change the cod's head for the salmon's tail°;
　　She that could think, and nev'r disclose her mind;
　　See suitors following, and not look behind:
　　She was a wight° (if ever such wights were)—
Desdemona: To do what?　　　　　　　　　　　　　　155
Iago: To suckle fools and chronicle small beer.°
Desdemona: O most lame and impotent conclusion. Do not learn of him,
　　Emilia, though he be thy husband. How say you, Cassio? Is he not a
　　most profane and liberal° counselor?
Cassio: He speaks home°, madam. You may relish him more in° the soldier　160
　　than in the scholar. *[Takes Desdemona's hand.]*
Iago [Aside]: He takes her by the palm. Ay, well said, whisper! With as little
　　a web as this will I ensnare as great a fly as Cassio. Ay, smile upon her,
　　do! I will gyve° thee in thine own courtship.—You say true; 'tis so, in
　　deed!—If such tricks as these strip you out of your lieutenantry, it had　165
　　been better you had not kissed your three fingers so oft—which now
　　again you are most apt to play the sir° in. Very good! Well kissed! An
　　excellent curtsy°! 'Tis so, indeed. Yet again your fingers to your lips?
　　Would they were clyster pipes° for your sake! *[Trumpets within.]* The
Moor! I know his trumpet°.　　　　　　　　　　　　　170
Cassio: 'Tis truly so.
Desdemona: Let's meet him and receive him.
Cassio: Lo, where he comes.

　　Enter Othello and Attendants.

Othello: O my fair warrior!
Desdemona:　　　　　　　My dear Othello.
Othello: It gives me wonder great as my content　　　　　　175
　　To see you here before me. O my soul's joy!
　　If after every tempest come such calms,
　　May the winds blow till they have wakened death.
　　And let the laboring bark climb hills of seas
　　Olympus-high, and duck again as low　　　　　　　180
　　As hell's from heaven. If it were now to die,

---

151 *To . . . tail:* i.e., to exchange something valuable for something useless.　154 *wight:* person.
156 *chronicle small beer:* i.e., keep household accounts (the most trivial of occupations in Iago's opinion).　159 *liberal:* licentious.　160 *speaks home:* thrusts deeply with his speech.　160 *relish him
more in:* enjoy him more as.　164 *gyve:* bind.　167 *the sir:* the fashionable gentleman.　168 *curtsy:*
courtesy, i.e., bow.　169 *clyster pipes:* enema tubes.　170 *his trumpet:* (great men had their own
distinctive calls).

'Twere now to be most happy; for I fear
My soul hath her content so absolute
That not another comfort like to this
Succeeds in unknown fate.
Desdemona: The heavens forbid   185
But that our loves and comforts should increase
Even as our days do grow.
Othello: Amen to that, sweet powers!
I cannot speak enough of this content:
It stops me here [touches his heart]; it is too much of joy.
And this, and this, the greatest discords be   [They kiss.]   190
That e'er our hearts shall make!
Iago [Aside]:   O, you are well tuned now!
But I'll set down the pegs° that make this music,
As honest as I am.
Othello: Come, let us to the castle.
News, friends! Our wars are done; the Turks are drowned.
How does my old acquaintance of this isle?   195
Honey, you shall be well desired in Cyprus;
I have found great love amongst them. O my sweet,
I prattle out of fashion, and I dote
In mine own comforts. I prithee, good Iago,
Go to the bay and disembark my coffers.   200
Bring thou the master to the citadel;
He is a good one and his worthiness
Does challenge° much respect. Come, Desdemona,
Once more well met at Cyprus.

Exit Othello and Desdemona [and all but Iago and Roderigo].

Iago [To an Attendant]: Do thou meet me presently at the Harbor. [To   205
Roderigo] Come hither. If thou be'st valiant (as they say base men being
in love have then a nobility in their natures more than is native to
them), list me. The lieutenant tonight watches on the court of guard°.
First, I must tell thee this: Desdemona is directly in love with him.
Roderigo: With him? Why, 'tis not possible.   210
Iago: Lay thy finger thus [puts his finger to his lips], and let thy soul be instructed. Mark me with what violence she first loved the Moor but for
bragging and telling her fantastical lies. To love him still for prating?
Let not thy discreet heart think it. Her eye must be fed. And what delight
shall she have to look on the devil? When the blood is made dull with   215
the act of sport, there should be a game° to inflame it and to give sati-
ety a fresh appetite, loveliness in favor°, sympathy in years°, manners,
and beauties; all which the Moor is defective in. Now for want of these

192 set down the pegs: loosen the strings (to produce discord).   203 challenge: require, exact.
208 court of guard: guardhouse.   216 game: sport (with the added sense of "gamey," "rank").
217 favor: countenance, appearance.   217 sympathy in years: sameness of age.

required conveniences°, her delicate tenderness will find itself abused,
begin to heave the gorge°, disrelish and abhor the Moor. Very nature   220
will instruct her in it and compel her to some second choice. Now sir,
this granted—as it is a most pregnant° and unforced position—who
stands so eminent in the degree of this fortune as Cassio does? A knave
very voluble; no further conscionable° than in putting on the mere
form of civil and humane° seeming for the better compass of his salt°   225
and most hidden loose° affection. Why, none! Why, none! A slipper°
and subtle knave, a finder of occasion, that has an eye can
stamp and counterfeit advantages, though true advantage never present
itself. A devilish knave. Besides, the knave is handsome, young, and
hath all those requisites in him that folly and green minds look after.   230
A pestilent complete knave, and the woman hath found him already.

Roderigo: I cannot believe that in her; she's full of most blessed condition.

Iago: Blessed fig's-end! The wine she drinks is made of grapes. If she had
been blessed, she would never have loved the Moor. Blessed pudding!
Didst thou not see her paddle with the palm of his hand? Didst not   235
mark that?

Roderigo: Yes, that I did; but that was but courtesy.

Iago: Lechery, by this hand! *[Extends his index finger.]* An index° and obscure prologue to the history of lust and foul thoughts. They met so
near with their lips that their breaths embraced together. Villainous   240
thoughts, Roderigo. When these mutualities so marshal the way, hard
at hand comes the master and main exercise, th' incorporate° conclusion: Pish! But, sir, be you ruled by me. I have brought you from Venice.
Watch you tonight; for the command, I'll lay't upon you. Cassio knows
you not. I'll not be far from you. Do you find some occasion to anger   245
Cassio, either by speaking too loud, or tainting° his discipline, or from
what other course you please which the time shall more favorably
minister.

Roderigo: Well.

Iago: Sir, he's rash and very sudden in choler°, and haply may strike at you.   250
Provoke him that he may; for even out of that will I cause these of
Cyprus to mutiny, whose qualification shall come into no true taste°
again but by the displanting of Cassio. So shall you have a shorter journey to your desires by the means I shall then have to prefer them; and
the impediment most profitably removed without the which there were   255
no expectation of our prosperity.

Roderigo: I will do this if you can bring it to any opportunity.

Iago: I warrant thee. Meet me by and by at the citadel. I must fetch his
necessaries ashore. Farewell.

---

219 *conveniences:* advantages.   220 *heave the gorge:* vomit.   222 *pregnant:* likely.   224 *no further conscionable:* having no more conscience.   225 *humane:* polite.   225 *salt:* lecherous.
226 *loose:* immoral.   226 *slipper:* slippery.   238 *index:* pointer.   242 *incorporate:* carnal.
246 *tainting:* discrediting.   250 *choler:* anger.   252 *qualification . . . taste:* i.e., appeasement will
not be brought about (wine was "qualified" by adding water).

Roderigo: Adieu.   *Exit.*   260
Iago: That Cassio loves her, I do well believe't;
     That she loves him, 'tis apt and of great credit.
     The Moor, howbeit that I endure him not,
     Is of a constant, loving, noble nature,
     And I dare think he'll prove to Desdemona   265
     A most dear° husband. Now I do love her too;
     Not out of absolute° lust, though peradventure°
     I stand accountant for as great a sin,
     But partly led to diet° my revenge,
     For that I do suspect the lusty Moor   270
     Hath leaped into my seat; the thought whereof
     Doth, like a poisonous mineral, gnaw my inwards;
     And nothing can or shall content my soul
     Till I am evened with him, wife for wife.
     Or failing so, yet that I put the Moor   275
     At least into a jealousy so strong
     That judgment cannot cure. Which thing to do,
     If this poor trash of Venice, whom I trace°
     For his quick hunting, stand the putting on,
     I'll have our Michael Cassio on the hip,   280
     Abuse him to the Moor in the right garb°
     (For I fear Cassio with my nightcap too),
     Make the Moor thank me, love me, and reward me
     For making him egregiously an ass
     And practicing upon° his peace and quiet,   285
     Even to madness. 'Tis here, but yet confused:
     Knavery's plain face is never seen till used.   *Exit.*

Scene II [A street.]

Enter Othello's Herald, with a proclamation.

Herald: It is Othello's pleasure, our noble and valiant general, that upon
certain tidings now arrived importing the mere perdition° of the Turkish fleet, every man put himself into triumph. Some to dance, some
to make bonfires, each man to what sport and revels his addition° leads
him. For, besides these beneficial news, it is the celebration of his nup-   5
tial. So much was his pleasure should be proclaimed. All offices° are
open, and there is full liberty of feasting from this present hour of five
till the bell have told eleven. Bless the isle of Cyprus and our noble
general Othello!   *Exit.*

266 *dear:* expensive.   267 *out of absolute:* absolutely out of.   267 *peradventure:* perchance.
269 *diet:* feed.   278 *trace:* (most editors emend to "trash," meaning to hang weights on a dog to
slow his hunting: but "trace" clearly means something like "put on the trace" or "set on the track").
281 *right garb:* i.e., "proper fashion."   285 *practicing upon:* scheming to destroy.   II.ii. 2 *mere per-*
dition: absolute destruction.   4 *addition:* rank.   6 *offices:* kitchens and storerooms of food.

Scene III *[The citadel of Cyprus.]*

Enter Othello, Desdemona, Cassio, and Attendants.

Othello: Good Michael, look you to the guard tonight.
　　Let's teach ourselves that honorable stop,
　　Not to outsport direction.
Cassio: Iago hath discretion what to do;
　　But notwithstanding, with my personal eye　　　　　　　　　　5
　　Will I look to't.
Othello:　　　　　　　Iago is most honest.
　　Michael, good night. Tomorrow with your earliest
　　Let me have speech with you. *[To Desdemona]* Come, my dear love,
　　The purchase made, the fruits are to ensue.
　　That profit's yet to come 'tween me and you.　　　　　　　　　10
　　Good night.　　　　　　*Exit [Othello with Desdemona and Attendants.]*

Enter Iago.

Cassio: Welcome, Iago. We must to the watch.
Iago: Not this hour, lieutenant; 'tis not yet ten o' th' clock. Our general
　　cast° us thus early for the love of his Desdemona; who let us not there-
　　fore blame. He hath not yet made wanton the night with her, and she　15
　　is sport for Jove.
Cassio: She's a most exquisite lady.
Iago: And, I'll warrant her, full of game.
Cassio: Indeed, she's a most fresh and delicate creature.
Iago: What an eye she has! Methinks it sounds a parley to provocation.　20
Cassio: An inviting eye; and yet methinks right modest.
Iago: And when she speaks, is it not an alarum° to love?
Cassio: She is indeed perfection.
Iago: Well, happiness to their sheets! Come, lieutenant, I have a stoup° of
　　wine, and here without are a brace of Cyprus gallants that would fain　25
　　have a measure to the health of black Othello.
Cassio: Not tonight, good Iago. I have very poor and unhappy brains for
　　drinking; I could well wish courtesy would invent some other custom
　　of entertainment.
Iago: O, they are our friends. But one cup! I'll drink for you.　　　　30
Cassio: I have drunk but one tonight, and that was craftily qualified° too;
　　and behold what innovation it makes here. I am unfortunate in the
　　infirmity and dare not task my weakness with any more.
Iago: What, man! 'Tis a night of revels, the gallants desire it.
Cassio: Where are they?　　　　　　　　　　　　　　　　　　35
Iago: Here, at the door. I pray you call them in.
Cassio: I'll do't, but it dislikes me.　　　　　　　　　　　*Exit.*
Iago: If I can fasten but one cup upon him
　　With that which he hath drunk tonight already,

II.iii. 14 *cast:* dismissed.　　22 *alarum:* the call to action, "general quarters."　　24 *stoup:* two-quart
tankard.　　31 *qualified:* diluted.

He'll be as full of quarrel and offense 40
As my young mistress' dog. Now, my sick fool Roderigo,
Whom love hath turned almost the wrong side out,
To Desdemona hath tonight caroused
Potations pottle-deep°; and he's to watch.
Three else° of Cyprus, noble swelling spirits, 45
That hold their honors in a wary distance°,
The very elements of this warlike isle,
Have I tonight flustered wtih flowing cups,
And they watch too. Now, 'mongst this flock of drunkards
Am I to put our Cassio in some action 50
That may offend the isle. But here they come.

Enter Cassio, Montano, and Gentlemen.

If consequence do but approve my dream,
My boat sails freely, both with wind and stream.
Cassio: 'Fore God, they have given me a rouse° already.
Montano: Good faith, a little one; not past a pint, as I am a soldier. 55
Iago: Some wine, ho!
    [Sings] And let me the canakin clink, clink;
        And let me the canakin clink.
        A soldier's a man;
        O man's life's but a span. 60
        Why then, let a soldier drink.
    Some wine, boys!
Cassio: 'Fore God, an excellent song!
Iago: I learned it in England, where indeed they are most potent in potting.
    Your Dane, your German, and your swag-bellied° Hollander—Drink, 65
    ho!—are nothing to your English.
Cassio: Is your Englishman so exquisite° in his drinking?
Iago: Why, he drinks you with facility your Dane dead drunk; he sweats
    not to overthrow your Almain; he gives your Hollander a vomit ere
    the next pottle can be filled. 70
Cassio: To the health of our general!
Montano: I am for it, lieutenant, and I'll do you justice.
Iago: O sweet England!
    [Sings] King Stephen was and a worthy peer;
        His breeches cost him but a crown; 75
        He held them sixpence all too dear,
        With that he called the tailor lown°.
        He was a wight of high renown,
        And thou art but of low degree:

44 *pottle-deep*: to the bottom of the cup.   45 *else*: others.   46 *hold . . . distance*: are scrupulous in
maintaining their honor.   54 *rouse*: drink.   65 *swag-bellied*: pendulous-bellied.   67 *exquisite*: superb.   77 *lown*: lout.

'Tis pride that pulls the country down;
And take thine auld cloak about thee. 80
      Some wine, ho!
Cassio: 'Fore God, this is a more exquisite song than the other.
Iago: Will you hear't again?
Cassio: No, for I hold him to be unworthy of his place that does those things. 85
      Well, God's above all; and there be souls must be saved, and there be
      souls must not be saved.
Iago: It's true, good lieutenant.
Cassio: For mine own part—no offense to the general, nor any man of
      quality—I hope to be saved. 90
Iago: And so do I too, lieutenant.
Cassio: Ay, but, by your leave, not before me. The lieutenant is to be saved
      before the ancient. Let's have no more of this; let's to our affairs.—God
      forgive us our sins!—Gentlemen, let's look to our business. Do not think,
      gentlemen, I am drunk. This is my ancient; this is my right hand, and 95
      this is my left. I am not drunk now. I can stand well enough, and I
      speak well enough.
Gentlemen: Excellent well!
Cassio: Why, very well then. You must not think then that I am drunk.
                                                        Exit.

Montano: To th' platform, masters. Come, let's set the watch. 100
Iago: You see this fellow that is gone before.
      He's a soldier fit to stand by Caesar
      And give direction; and do but see his vice.
      'Tis to his virtue a just equinox°,
      The one as long as th' other. 'Tis pity of him. 105
      I fear the trust Othello puts him in,
      On some odd time of his infirmity,
      Will shake this island.
Montano: But is he often thus?
Iago: 'Tis evermore his prologue to his sleep:
      He'll watch the horologe a double set° 110
      If drink rock not his cradle.
Montano: It were well
      The general were put in mind of it.
      Perhaps he sees it not, or his good nature
      Prizes the virtue that appears in Cassio
      And looks not on his evils. Is not this true? 115

      Enter Roderigo.

Iago [Aside]: How now, Roderigo?
      I pray you after the lieutenant, go!

---

104 *just equinox:* exact balance (of dark and light).   110 *watch . . . set:* stay awake twice around the
clock.

Montano: And 'tis great pity that the noble Moor
    Should hazard such a place as his own second
    With one of an ingraft° infirmity.   120
    It were an honest action to say so
    To the Moor.
Iago: Not I, for this fair island!
    I do love Cassio well and would do much
    To cure him of this evil.   (Help! Help! *Within.*)
    But hark! What noise?   125

    Enter Cassio, pursuing Roderigo.

Cassio: Zounds, you rogue! You rascal!
Montano: What's the matter, lieutenant?
Cassio: A knave teach me my duty? I'll beat the knave into a twiggen°
    bottle.
Roderigo: Beat me?   130
Cassio: Dost thou prate, rogue?   *[Strikes him.]*
Montano: Nay, good lieutenant! I pray for you, sir, hold your hand.

                                        [Stays him.]

Cassio: Let me go, sir, or I'll knock you o'er the mazzard°.
Montano: Come, come, you're drunk!
Cassio: Drunk?   *[They fight.]* 135
Iago [Aside to Roderigo]: Away, I say! Go out and cry a mutiny!

                                    [Exit Roderigo.]

    Nay, good lieutenant. God's will, gentlemen!
    Help, ho! Lieutenant. Sir. Montano.
    Help, masters! Here's a goodly watch indeed!   *[A bell rung.]*
    Who's that which rings the bell? Diablo, ho!   140
    The town will rise. God's will, lieutenant,
    You'll be ashamed forever.

    Enter Othello and Attendants.

Othello: What is the matter here?
Montano: Zounds, I bleed still. I am hurt to the death.
    He dies.   *[He and Cassio fight again.]*
Othello: Hold for your lives!   145
Iago: Hold, ho! Lieutenant. Sir. Montano. Gentlemen!
    Have your forgot all place of sense and duty?
    Hold! The general speaks to you. Hold, for shame!
Othello: Why, how now, ho? From whence ariseth this?
    Are we turned Turks, and to ourselves do that   150
    Which heaven hath forbid the Ottomites°?

120 *ingraft:* ingrained.   128 *twiggen:* wicker-covered.   133 *mazzard:* head.   151 *heaven . . . Otto-*
mites: i.e., by sending the storm which dispersed the Turks.

For Christian shame put by this barbarous brawl!
He that stirs next to carve for his own rage
Holds his soul light°; he dies upon his motion.
Silence that dreadful bell! It frights the isle   155
From her propriety°. What is the matter, masters?
Honest Iago, that looks dead with grieving,
Speak. Who began this? On thy love, I charge thee.

Iago: I do not know. Friends all, but now, even now,
In quarter° and in terms like bride and groom   160
Devesting them for bed; and then, but now—
As if some planet had unwitted men—
Swords out, and tilting one at other's breasts
In opposition bloody. I cannot speak
Any beginning to this peevish odds°,   165
And would in action glorious I had lost
Those legs that brought me to a part of it!

Othello: How comes it, Michael, you are thus forgot?

Cassio: I pray you pardon me; I cannot speak.

Othello: Worthy Montano, you were wont to be civil;   170
Thy gravity and stillness of your youth
The world hath noted, and your name is great
In mouths of wisest censure°. What's the matter
That you unlace° your reputation thus
And spend your rich opinion° for the name   175
Of a night-brawler? Give me answer to it.

Montano: Worthy Othello, I am hurt to danger.
Your officer, Iago, can inform you.
While I spare speech, which something now offends° me,
Of all that I do know; nor know I aught   180
By me that's said or done amiss this night,
Unless self-charity be sometimes a vice,
And to defend ourselves it be a sin
When violence assails us.

Othello: Now, by heaven,
My blood begins my safer guides to rule,   185
And passion, having my best judgment collied°,
Assays to lead the way. If I once stir
Or do but lift this arm, the best of you
Shall sink in my rebuke. Give me to know
How this foul rout began, who set it on;   190
And he that is approved in this offense,
Though he had twinned with me, both at a birth,
Shall lose me. What? In a town of war

---

154 *Holds his soul light:* values his soul lightly.   156 *propriety:* proper order.   160 *In quarter:* on
duty.   165 *odds:* quarrel.   173 *censure:* judgment.   174 *unlace:* undo (the term refers specifically
to the dressing of a wild boar killed in the hunt).   175 *opinion:* reputation.   179 *offends:* harms,
hurts.   186 *collied:* darkened.

Yet wild, the people's hearts brimful of fear,
To manage° private and domestic quarrel?   195
In night, and on the court and guard of safety?
'Tis monstrous. Iago, who began't?
Montano: If partially affined, or leagued in office°,
Thou dost deliver more or less than truth,
Thou art no soldier.
Iago: Touch me not so near.   200
I had rather have this tongue cut from my mouth
Than it should do offense to Michael Cassio.
Yet I persuade myself to speak the truth
Shall nothing wrong him. This it is, general.
Montano and myself being in speech,   205
There comes a fellow crying out for help,
And Cassio following him with determined sword
To execute upon him. Sir, this gentleman
Steps in to Cassio and entreats his pause.
Myself the crying fellow did pursue,   210
Lest by his clamor—as it so fell out—
The town might fall in fright. He, swift of foot,
Outran my purpose; and I returned then rather
For that I heard the clink and fall of swords,
And Cassio high in oath; which till tonight   215
I ne'er might say before. When I came back—
For this was brief—I found them close together
At blow and thrust, even as again they were
When you yourself did part them.
More of this matter cannot I report;   220
But men are men; the best sometimes forget.
Though Cassio did some little wrong to him,
As men in rage strike those that wish them best,
Yet surely Cassio I believe received
From him that fled some strange indignity,   225
Which patience could not pass°.
Othello: I know, Iago,
Thy honesty and love doth mince° this matter,
Making it light to Cassio. Cassio, I love thee;
But never more be officer of mine.

Enter Desdemona, attended.

Look if my gentle love be not raised up.   230
I'll make thee an example.
Desdemona: What is the matter, dear?

---

195 *manage:* conduct.   198 *If . . . office:* if you are partial because you are related ("affined") or the
brother officer (of Cassio).   226 *pass:* allow to pass.   227 *mince:* cut up (i.e., tell only part of).

Othello: All's well, sweeting; come away to bed.

[*To Montano*] Sir, for your hurts, myself will be your surgeon.

Lead him off.   [*Montano led off.*]

Iago, look with care about the town   235

And silence those whom this vile brawl distracted.

Come, Desdemona: 'tis the soldiers' life

To have their balmy slumbers waked with strife.

                          Exit [with all but Iago and Cassio].

Iago: What, are you hurt, lieutenant?

Cassio: Ay, past all surgery.   240

Iago: Marry, God forbid!

Cassio: Reputation, reputation, reputation! Oh, I have lost my reputation! I have lost the immortal part of myself, and what remains is bestial. My reputation, Iago, my reputation.

Iago: As I am an honest man, I had thought you had received some bodily   245
wound. There is more sense° in that than in reputation. Reputation is an idle and most false imposition°, oft got without merit and lost without deserving. You have lost no reputation at all unless you repute yourself such a loser. What, man, there are more ways to recover the general again. You are but now cast in his mood°—a punishment more   250
in policy° than in malice—even so as one would beat his offenseless dog to affright an imperious lion. Sue to him again, and he's yours.

Cassio: I will rather sue to be despised than to deceive so good a commander with so slight, so drunken, and so indiscreet an officer. Drunk! And speak parrot°! And squabble! Swagger! Swear! and discourse fustian°   255
with one's own shadow! O thou invisible spirit of wine, if thou hast no name to be known by, let us call thee devil!

Iago: What was he that you followed with your sword? What had he done to you?

Cassio: I know not.   260

Iago: Is't possible?

Cassio: I remember a mass of things, but nothing distinctly: a quarrel, but nothing wherefore. O God, that men should put an enemy in their mouths to steal away their brains! that we should with joy, pleasance, revel, and applause transform ourselves into beasts!   265

Iago: Why, but you are now well enough. How came you thus recovered?

Cassio: It hath pleased the devil drunkenness to give place to the devil wrath. One unperfectness shows me another, to make me frankly despise myself.

Iago: Come, you are too severe a moraler. As the time, the place, and the condition of this country stands, I could heartily wish this had not be-   270
fall'n; but since it is as it is, mend it for your own good.

---

246 *sense:* physical feeling.   247 *imposition:* external thing.   250 *cast in his mood:* dismissed because of his anger.   251 *in policy:* politically necessary.   255 *speak parrot:* gabble without sense.   255 *discourse fustian:* speak nonsense ("fustian" was a coarse cotton cloth used for stuffing).

Cassio: I will ask him for my place again: he shall tell me I am a drunkard. Had I as many mouths as Hydra, such an answer would stop them all. To be now a sensible man, by and by a fool, and presently a beast! O strange! Every inordinate cup is unblest, and the ingredient is a devil.   275

Iago: Come, come, good wine is a good familiar creature if it be well used. Exclaim no more against it. And, good lieutenant, I think you think I love you.

Cassio: I have well approved it, sir. I drunk?

Iago: You or any man living may be drunk at a time, man. I tell you what   280
you shall do. Our general's wife is now the general. I may say so in this respect, for all he hath devoted and given up himself to the contemplation, mark, and devotement of her parts° and graces. Confess yourself freely to her; importune her help to put you in your place again. She is of so free, so kind, so apt, so blessed a disposition she holds it a vice   285
in her goodness not to do more than she is requested. This broken joint between you and her husband entreat her to splinter°; and my fortunes against any lay° worth naming, this crack of your love shall grow stronger than it was before.

Cassio: You advise me well.   290

Iago: I protest, in the sincerity of love and honest kindness.

Cassio: I think it freely; and betimes in the morning I will beseech the virtuous Desdemona to undertake for me. I am desperate of my fortunes if they check° me.

Iago: You are in the right. Good night, lieutenant; I must to the watch.   295

Cassio: Good night, honest Iago.   *Exit Cassio.*

Iago: And what's he then that says I play the villain,
     When this advice is free° I give, and honest,
     Probal to° thinking, and indeed the course
     To win the Moor again? For 'tis most easy   300
     Th' inclining° Desdemona to subdue
     In any honest suit; she's framed as fruitful°
     As the free elements°. And then for her
     To win the Moor—were't to renounce his baptism,
     All seals and symbols of redeemèd sin—   305
     His soul is so enfettered to her love
     That she may make, unmake, do what she list,
     Even as her appetite° shall play the god
     With his weak function°. How am I then a villain
     To counsel Cassio to this parallel course,   310
     Directly to his good? Divinity of hell!
     When devils will the blackest sins put on°,
     They do suggest at first with heavenly shows°,

283 *devotement of her parts:* devotion to her qualities.   287 *splinter:* splint.   288 *lay:* wager.
294 *check:* repulse.   298 *free:* generous and open.   299 *Probal to:* provable by.   301 *inclining:* inclined (to be helpful).   302 *framed as fruitful:* made as generous.   303 *elements:* i.e., basic nature.
308 *appetite:* liking.   309 *function:* thought.   312 *put on:* advance, further.   313 *shows:* appearances.

As I do now. For whiles this honest fool
Plies Desdemona to repair his fortune,   315
And she for him pleads strongly to the Moor,
I'll pour this pestilence into his ear:
That she repeals him° for her body's lust;
And by how much she strives to do him good,
She shall undo her credit with the Moor.   320
So will I turn her virtue into pitch,
And out of her own goodness make the net
That shall enmesh them all. How now, Roderigo?

Enter Roderigo.

Roderigo: I do not follow here in the chase, not like a hound that hunts,
but one that fills up the cry°. My money is almost spent; I have been   325
tonight exceedingly well cudgeled; and I think the issue will be, I shall
have so much experience for my pains; and so, with no money at all,
and a little more wit, return again to Venice.

Iago: How poor are they that have not patience!
What wound did ever heal but by degrees?   330
Thou know'st we work by wit, and not by witchcraft;
And wit depends on dilatory time.
Does't not go well? Cassio hath beaten thee,
And thou by that small hurt hath cashiered Cassio.
Though other things grow fair against the sun,   335
Yet fruits that blossom first will first be ripe.
Content thyself awhile. By the mass, 'tis morning!
Pleasure and action make the hours seem short.
Retire thee, go where thou are billeted.
Away, I say! Thou shalt know more hereafter.   340
Nay, get thee gone!   *Exit Roderigo.*
                    Two things are to be done:
My wife must move° for Cassio to her mistress;
I'll set her on;
Myself awhile° to draw the Moor apart
And bring him jump° when he may Cassio find   345
Soliciting his wife. Ay, that's the way!
Dull not device by coldness and delay.   *Exit.*

Act III

Scene I [A street.]

Enter Cassio [and] Musicians.

Cassio: Masters, play here. I will content your pains°.

---

318 *repeals him:* asks for (Cassio's reinstatement).   325 *fills up the cry:* makes up one of the hunting
pack, adding to the noise but not actually tracking.   342 *move:* petition.   344 *awhile:* at the same
time.   345 *jump:* at the precise moment and place.   III.i. 1 *content your pains:* reward your efforts.

Something that's brief; and bid "Good morrow, general."

[They play.]

[Enter Clown°.]

Clown: Why, masters, have your instruments been in Naples° that they
speak i' th' nose thus?

Musician: How, sir, how?   5

Clown: Are these, I pray you, wind instruments?

Musician: Ay, marry, are they, sir.

Clown: O, thereby hangs a tale.

Musician: Whereby hangs a tale, sir?

Clown: Marry, sir, by many a wind instrument that I know. But, masters,   10
here's money for you; and the general so likes your music that he desires
you, for love's sake, to make no more noise with it.

Musician: Well, sir, we will not.

Clown: If you have any music that may not be heard, to't again. But, as they
say, to hear music the general does not greatly care.   15

Musician: We have none such, sir.

Clown: Then put up your pipes in your bag, for I'll away. Go, vanish into
air, away!   *Exit Musicians.*

Cassio: Dost thou hear me, mine honest friend?

Clown: No. I hear not your honest friend. I hear you.   20

Cassio: Prithee keep up thy quillets°. There's a poor piece of gold for thee.
If the gentlewoman that attends the general's wife be stirring, tell her
there's one Cassio entreats her a little favor of speech. Wilt thou do this?

Clown: She is stirring, sir. If she will stir hither, I shall seem to notify unto
her°.   *Exit Clown.*   25

Enter Iago.

Cassio: In happy time, Iago.

Iago: You have not been abed then?

Cassio: Why no, the day had broke before we parted.
I have made bold, Iago, to send in to your wife;
My suit to her is that she will to virtuous Desdemona
Procure me some access.

Iago: I'll send her to you presently,   30
And I'll devise a mean to draw the Moor
Out of the way, that your converse and business
May be more free.

Cassio: I humbly thank you for't.   *Exit [Iago].*
                            I never knew
A Florentine° more kind and honest.   35

---

s.d. *Clown:* fool.   3 *Naples:* this may refer either to the Neapolitan nasal tone, or to syphilis—rife
in Naples—which breaks down the nose.   21 *quillets:* puns.   24–25 *seem . . . her:* (the Clown is
mocking Cassio's overly elegant manner of speaking).   35 *Florentine:* i.e., Iago is as kind as if he
were from Cassio's home town, Florence.

Enter Emilia.

Emilia: Good morrow, good lieutenant. I am sorry
   For your displeasure°; but all will sure be well.
   The general and his wife are talking of it,
   And she speaks for you stoutly. The Moor replies
   That he you hurt is of great fame in Cyprus   40
   And great affinity°, and that in wholesome wisdom
   He might not but refuse you. But he protests he loves you.
   And needs no other suitor but his likings
   To bring you in again.
Cassio: Yet I beseech you,
   If you think fit, or that it may be done,   45
   Give me advantage of some brief discourse
   With Desdemona alone.
Emilia: Pray you come in.
   I will bestow you where you shall have time
   To speak your bosom° freely.
Cassio: I am much bound to you.   [*Exeunt.*] 50

Scene II [*The citadel.*]

Enter Othello, Iago, and Gentlemen.

Othello: These letters give, Iago, to the pilot
   And by him do my duties to the Senate.
   That done, I will be walking on the works;
   Repair° there to me.
Iago: Well, my good lord, I'll do't.
Othello: This fortification, gentlemen, shall we see't?   5
Gentlemen: We'll wait upon your lordship.   *Exeunt.*

Scene III [*The citadel.*]

Enter Desdemona, Cassio, and Emilia.

Desdemona: Be thou assured, good Cassio, I will do
   All my abilities in thy behalf.
Emilia: Good madam, do. I warrant it grieves my husband
   As if the cause were his.
Desdemona: O, that's an honest fellow. Do not doubt, Cassio,   5
   But I will have my lord and you again
   As friendly as you were.
Cassio: Bounteous madam,
   Whatever shall become of Michael Cassio,
   He's never anything but your true servant.
Desdemona: I know't; I thank you. You do love my lord.   10
   You have known him long, and be you well assured

37 *displeasure:* discomforting.   41 *affinity:* family.   49 *bosom:* inmost thoughts.   III.ii. 4 *Repair:* go.

He shall in strangeness stand no farther off
Than in a politic distance°.
Cassio: Ay, but, lady,
That policy may either last so long,
Or feed upon such nice° and waterish diet,   15
Or breed itself so out of circumstances°,
That, I being absent, and my place supplied°,
My general will forget my love and service.
Desdemona: Do not doubt° that; before Emilia here
I give thee warrant of thy place. Assure thee,   20
If I do vow a friendship, I'll perform it
To the last article. My lord shall never rest;
I'll watch him tame° and talk him out of patience;
His bed shall seem a school, his board a shrift°;
I'll intermingle everything he does   25
With Cassio's suit. Therefore be merry, Cassio,
For thy solicitor shall rather die
Than give thy cause away.

    Enter Othello and Iago [at a distance].

Emilia: Madam, here comes my lord.
Cassio: Madam, I'll take my leave.   30
Desdemona: Why, stay, and hear me speak.
Cassio: Madam, not now. I am very ill at ease,
Unfit for mine own purposes.
Desdemona: Well, do your discretion.   *Exit Cassio.*
Iago: Ha! I like not that.
Othello: What dost thou say?   35
Iago: Nothing, my lord; or if—I know not what.
Othello: Was not that Cassio parted from my wife?
Iago: Cassio, my lord? No, sure, I cannot think it
That he would steal away so guilty-like,
Seeing you coming.
Othello: I do believe 'twas he.   40
Desdemona [Coming to them]: How now, my lord?
I have been talking with a suitor here,
A man that languishes in your displeasure.
Othello: Who is 't you mean?
Desdemona: Why, your lieutenant, Cassio. Good my lord,   45
If I have any grace or power to move you,
His present° reconciliation take.

III.iii. 12–13 *He . . . distance:* i.e., he shall act no more distant to you than is necessary for political reasons.   15 *nice:* trivial.   16 *Or . . . circumstances:* i.e., or grow so on the basis of accidental happenings and political needs.   17 *supplied:* filled.   19 *doubt:* imagine.   23 *watch him tame:* (animals were tamed by being kept awake).   24 *board a shrift:* table (seem) a confessional.   47 *present:* immediate.

For if he be not one that truly loves you,
That errs in ignorance, and not in cunning,
I have no judgment in an honest face.   50
I prithee call him back.
Othello: Went he hence now?
Desdemona: I' sooth so humbled
That he hath left part of his grief with me
To suffer with him. Good love, call him back.
Othello: Not now, sweet Desdemon; some other time.   55
Desdemona: But shall't be shortly?
Othello: The sooner, sweet, for you.
Desdemona: Shall't be tonight at supper?
Othello: No, not tonight.
Desdemona: Tomorrow dinner then?
Othello: I shall not dine at home;
I meet the captains at the citadel.
Desdemona: Why then, tomorrow night, on Tuesday morn,   60
On Tuesday noon, or night, on Wednesday morn.
I prithee name the time, but let it not
Exceed three days. In faith, he's penitent;
And yet his trespass, in our common reason
(Save that, they say, the wars must make example   65
Out of her best), is not almost a fault
T' incur a private check.° When shall he come?
Tell me, Othello. I wonder in my soul
What you would ask me that I should deny
Or stand so mamm'ring° on. What? Michael Cassio,   70
That came awooing with you, and so many a time,
When I have spoke of you dispraisingly,
Hath ta'en your part—to have so much to do
To bring him in? By'r Lady, I could do much—
Othello: Prithee no more. Let him come when he will!   75
I will deny thee nothing.
Desdemona: Why, this is not a boon;
'Tis as I should entreat you wear your gloves,
Or feed on nourishing dishes, or keep you warm,
Or sue to you to do a peculiar profit°
To your own person. Nay, when I have a suit   80
Wherein I mean to touch your love indeed,
It shall be full of poise° and difficult weight,
And fearful to be granted.
Othello: I will deny thee nothing!
Whereon I do beseech thee grant me this,
To leave me but a little to myself.   85

66–67 *is . . . check:* is almost not serious enough for a private rebuke (let alone a public disgrace).
70 *mamm'ring:* hesitating.   79 *peculiar profit:* particularly personal good.   82 *poise:* weight.

Desdemona: Shall I deny you? No. Farewell, my lord.
Othello: Farewell, my Desdemona: I'll come to thee straight°.
Desdemona: Emilia, come. Be as your fancies teach you;
    Whate'er you be, I am obedient.   *Exit [with Emilia].*
Othello: Excellent wretch! Perdition catch my soul   90
    But I do love thee! And when I love thee not,
    Chaos is come again.
Iago: My noble lord—
Othello: What dost thou say, Iago?
Iago: Did Michael Cassio, when you wooed my lady,
    Know of your love?   95
Othello: He did, from first to last. Why dost thou ask?
Iago: But for a satisfaction of my thought,
    No further harm.
Othello: Why of thy thought, Iago?
Iago: I did not think he had been acquainted with her.
Othello: O, yes, and went between us° very oft.   100
Iago: Indeed?
Othello: Indeed? Ay, indeed! Discern'st thou aught in that?
    Is he not honest?
Iago: Honest, my lord?
Othello: Honest? Ay, honest.
Iago: My lord, for aught I know.
Othello: What dost thou think?
Iago: Think, my lord?
Othello: Think, my lord?   105
    By heaven, thou echoest me,
    As if there were some monster in thy thought
    Too hideous to be shown. Thou dost mean something.
    I heard thee say even now, thou lik'st not that,
    When Cassio left my wife. What didst not like?   110
    And when I told thee he was of my counsel°
    Of my whole course of wooing, thou cried'st "Indeed?"
    And didst contract and purse thy brow together,
    As if thou then hadst shut up in thy brain
    Some horrible conceit°. If thou dost love me,   115
    Show me thy thought.
Iago: My lord, you know I love you.
Othello: I think thou dost;
    And, for I know thou'rt full of love and honesty
    And weigh'st thy words before thou giv'st them breath,
    Therefore these stops° of thine fright me the more;   120
    For such things in a false disloyal knave
    Are tricks of custom°; but in a man that's just

---

87 *straight:* at once.   100 *between us:* i.e., as messenger.   111 *of my counsel:* in my confidence.
115 *conceit:* thought.   120 *stops:* interruptions.   122 *of custom:* customary.

They're close dilations°, working from the heart
That passion cannot rule.
Iago: For Michael Cassio,
I dare be sworn, I think that he is honest.   125
Othello: I think so too.
Iago: Men should be what they seem;
Or those that be not, would they might seem none!
Othello: Certain, men should be what they seem.
Iago: Why then, I think Cassio's an honest man.
Othello: Nay, yet there's more in this?   130
I prithee speak to me as to thy thinkings,
As thou dost ruminate, and give thy worst of thoughts
The worst of words.
Iago: Good my lord, pardon me:
Though I am bound to every act of duty,
I am not bound to that all slaves are free to.   135
Utter my thoughts? Why, say they are vile and false,
As where's that palace whereinto foul things
Sometimes intrude not? Who has that breast so pure
But some uncleanly apprehensions
Keep leets and law days°, and in sessions sit   140
With meditations lawful?
Othello: Thou dost conspire against thy friend, Iago,
If thou but think'st him wronged, and mak'st his ear
A stranger to thy thoughts.
Iago: I do beseech you—
Though I perchance am vicious in my guess   145
(As I confess it is my nature's plague
To spy into abuses, and of my jealousy
Shape faults that are not), that your wisdom
From one that so imperfectly conceits
Would take no notice, nor build yourself a trouble   150
Out of his scattering and unsure observance.
It were not for your quiet nor your good,
Nor for my manhood, honesty, and wisdom,
To let you know my thoughts.
Othello: What dost thou mean?
Iago: Good name in man and woman, dear my lord,   155
Is the immediate jewel of their souls.
Who steals my purse steals trash; 'tis something, nothing;
'Twas mine, 'tis his, and has been slave to thousands;
But he that filches from me my good name
Robs me of that which not enriches him   160
And makes me poor indeed.

---

123 *close dilations:* expressions of hidden thoughts.   140 *leets and law days:* meetings of local courts.

Othello: By heaven, I'll know thy thoughts!

Iago: You cannot, if my heart were in your hand;
　　Nor shall not whilst 'tis in my custody.

Othello: Ha!

Iago: 　　　　O, beware, my lord, of jealousy!   165
　　It is the green-eyed monster, which doth mock
　　The meat it feeds on. That cuckold lives in bliss
　　Who, certain of his fate, loves not his wronger;
　　But O, what damnèd minutes tells° he o'er
　　Who dotes, yet doubts—suspects, yet fondly° loves!   170

Othello: O misery.

Iago: Poor and content is rich, and rich enough;
　　But riches fineless° is as poor as winter
　　To him that ever fears he shall be poor.
　　Good God the souls of all my tribe defend   175
　　From jealousy!

Othello: 　　　　Why? Why is this?
　　Think'st thou I'd make a life of jealousy,
　　To follow still° the changes of the moon
　　With fresh suspicions? No! To be once in doubt
　　Is to be resolved. Exchange me for a goat   180
　　When I shall turn the business of my soul
　　To such exsufflicate and blown° surmises,
　　Matching thy inference. 'Tis not to make me jealous
　　To say my wife is fair, feeds well, loves company,
　　Is free of speech, sings, plays, and dances;   185
　　Where virtue is, these are more virtuous.
　　Nor from mine own weak merits will I draw
　　The smallest fear or doubt of her revolt,
　　For she had eyes, and chose me. No, Iago;
　　I'll see before I doubt; when I doubt, prove;   190
　　And on the proof there is no more but this:
　　Away at once with love or jealousy!

Iago: I am glad of this; for now I shall have reason
　　To show the love and duty that I bear you
　　With franker spirit. Therefore, as I am bound,   195
　　Receive it from me. I speak not yet of proof.
　　Look to your wife; observe her well with Cassio;
　　Wear your eyes thus: not jealous nor secure.
　　I would not have your free and noble nature
　　Out of self-bounty° be abused. Look to't.   200
　　I know our country disposition well:
　　In Venice they do let heaven see the pranks

---

169 *tells:* counts.　170 *fondly:* foolishly.　173 *fineless:* infinite.　178 *To follow still:* to change always (as the phases of the moon).　182 *exsufflicate and blown:* inflated and flyblown.　200 *self-bounty:* innate kindness (which attributes his own motives to others).

They dare not show their husbands; their best conscience
Is not to leave't undone, but kept unknown.°
Othello: Dost thou say so?   205
Iago: She did deceive her father, marrying you;
And when she seemed to shake and fear your looks,
She loved them most.
Othello: And so she did.
Iago: Why, go to then!
She that so young could give out such a seeming
To seel° her father's eyes up close as oak°—   210
He thought 'twas witchcraft. But I am much to blame.
I humbly do beseech you of your pardon
For too much loving you.
Othello: I am bound to thee forever.
Iago: I see this hath a little dashed your spirits.
Othello: Not a jot, not a jot.
Iago: Trust me, I fear it has.   215
I hope you will consider what is spoke
Comes from my love. But I do see y' are moved.
I am to pray you not to strain° my speech
To grosser issues nor to larger reach°
Than to suspicion.   220
Othello: I will not.
Iago: Should you do so, my lord,
My speech should fall into such vile success
Which my thoughts aimed not. Cassio's my worthy friend—
My lord, I see y' are moved.
Othello: No, not much moved.
I do not think but Desdemona's honest.   225
Iago: Long live she so. And long live you to think so.
Othello: And yet, how nature erring from itself—
Iago: Ay, there's the point, as (to be bold with you)
Not to affect many proposèd matches
Of her own clime, complexion, and degree°,   230
Whereto we see in all things nature tends°—
Foh! one may smell in such a will most rank,
Foul disproportions, thoughts unnatural.
But, pardon me, I do not in position°
Distinctly° speak of her; though I may fear   235
Her will, recoiling to her better judgment,
May fall to match° you with her country forms°,
And happily° repent.

203–4 *their . . . unknown:* i.e., their morality does not forbid adultery, but it does forbid being found out.   210 *seel:* hoodwink.   210 *oak:* (a close-grained wood).   218 *strain:* enlarge the meaning.   219 *reach:* meaning.   230 *degree:* social station.   231 *in . . . tends:* i.e., all things in nature seek out their own kind.   234 *position:* general argument.   235 *Distinctly:* specifically.   237 *fall to match:* happen to compare.   237 *country forms:* i.e., the familiar appearance of her countrymen.   238 *happily:* by chance.

Othello: Farewell, farewell!
    If more thou dost perceive, let me know more.
    Set on thy wife to observe. Leave me, Iago.   240
Iago: My lord, I take my leave.   [Going.]
Othello: Why did I marry? This honest creature doubtless
    Sees and knows more, much more, than he unfolds.
Iago [Returns]: My lord, I would I might entreat your honor
    To scan this thing no farther. Leave it to time.   245
    Although 'tis fit that Cassio have his place,
    For sure he fills it up with great ability,
    Yet, if you please to hold him off awhile,
    You shall by that perceive him and his means.
    Note if your lady strains his entertainment°   250
    With any strong or vehement importunity;
    Much will be seen in that. In the meantime
    Let me be thought too busy in my fears
    (As worthy cause I have to fear I am)
    And hold her free, I do beseech your honor.   255
Othello: Fear not my government°.
Iago: I once more take my leave.   Exit.
Othello: This fellow's of exceeding honesty,
    And knows all qualities°, with a learnèd spirit
    Of human dealings. If I do prove her haggard°,
    Though that her jesses° were my dear heartstrings,   260
    I'd whistle her off and let her down the wind°
    To prey at fortune. Haply for° I am black
    And have not those soft parts° of conversation
    That chamberers° have, or for I am declined
    Into the vale of years—yet that's not much—   265
    She's gone. I am abused, and my relief
    Must be to loathe her. O curse of marriage,
    That we can call these delicate creatures ours,
    And not their appetites! I had rather be a toad
    And live upon the vapor of a dungeon   270
    Than keep a corner in the thing I love
    For others' uses. Yet 'tis the plague to great ones;
    Prerogatived are they less than the base.
    'Tis destiny unshunnable, like death.
    Even then this forkèd° plague is fated to us   275
    When we do quicken°. Look where she comes.

---

250 *strains his entertainment*: urge strongly that he be reinstated.   256 *government*: self-control.
258 *qualities*: natures, types of people.   259 *haggard*: a partly trained hawk which has gone wild
again.   260 *jesses*: straps which held the hawk's legs to the trainer's wrist.   261 *I'd . . . wind*: I
would release her (like an untamable hawk) and let her fly free.   262 *Haply for*: it may be because.   263 *soft parts*: gentle qualities and manners.   264 *chamberers*: courtiers—or, perhaps, accomplished seducers.   275 *forkèd*: horned (the sign of the cuckold was horns).   276 *do quicken*:
are born.

Enter Desdemona and Emilia.

If she be false, heaven mocked itself!
I'll not believe't.
Desdemona: How now, my dear Othello?
Your dinner, and the generous islanders
By you invited, do attend° your presence.   280
Othello: I am to blame.
Desdemona: Why do you speak so faintly?
Are you not well?
Othello: I have a pain upon my forehead, here°.
Desdemona: Why, that's with watching; 'twill away again,
Let me but bind it hard, within this hour   285
It will be well.
Othello: Your napkin° is too little;

[He pushes the handkerchief away, and it falls.]

Let it° alone. Come, I'll go in with you.
Desdemona: I am very sorry that you are not well.   *Exit [with Othello].*
Emilia: I am glad I have found this napkin;
This was her first remembrance from the Moor.   290
My wayward husband hath a hundred times
Wooed me to steal it; but she so loves the token
(For he conjured her she should ever keep it)
That she reserves it evermore about her
To kiss and talk to. I'll have the work ta'en out°   295
And give't Iago. What he will do with it,
Heaven knows not, not I; I nothing° but to please his fantasy°.

     Enter Iago.

Iago: How now? What do you here alone?
Emilia: Do not you chide; I have a thing for you.
Iago: You have a thing for me? It is a common thing—   300
Emilia: Ha?
Iago: To have a foolish wife.
Emilia: O, is that all? What will you give me now
For that same handkerchief?
Iago: What handkerchief?
Emilia: What handkerchief!   305
Why, that the Moor first gave to Desdemona,
That which so often you did bid me steal.
Iago: Hast stol'n it from her?

---

280 *attend:* wait.   283 *here:* (he points to his imaginary horns).   286 *napkin:* elaborately worked
handkerchief.   287 *it:* (it makes a considerable difference in the interpretation of later events whether
this "it" refers to Othello's forehead or to the handkerchief; nothing in the text makes the reference
clear).   295 *work ta'en out:* needlework copied.   297 *I nothing:* I wish nothing.   297 *fantasy:*
fancy, whim.

Emilia: No, but she let it drop by negligence,
   And to th' advantage°, I, being here, took't up.   310
   Look, here't is.
Iago: A good wench. Give it me.
Emilia: What will you do with't, that you have been so earnest
   To have me filch it?
Iago: Why, what is that to you?   *[Takes it.]*
Emilia: If it be not for some purpose of import°,
   Give't me again. Poor lady, she'll run mad   315
   When she shall lack° it.
Iago: Be not acknown on't°.
   I have use for it. Go, leave me.   *Exit Emilia.*
   I will in Cassio's lodging lose this napkin
   And let him find it. Trifles light as air
   Are to the jealous confirmations strong   320
   As proofs of Holy Writ. This may do something.
   The Moor already changes with my poison:
   Dangerous conceits are in their natures poisons,
   Which at the first are scarce found to distaste°,
   But with a little°, act upon the blood,   325
   Burn like the mines of sulfur. I did say so.

   Enter Othello.

   Look where he comes! Not poppy nor mandragora°,
   Nor all the drowsy syrups of the world,
   Shall ever medicine thee to that sweet sleep
   Which thou owedst° yesterday.
Othello: Ha! ha! False to me?   330
Iago: Why, how now, general? No more of that.
Othello: Avaunt! be gone! Thou hast set me on the rack.
   I swear 'tis better to be much abused
   Than but to know't a little.
Iago: How now, my lord?
Othello: What sense had I of her stol'n hours of lust?   335
   I saw't not, thought it not, it harmed not me;
   I slept the next night well, fed well, was free and merry;
   I found not Cassio's kisses on her lips.
   He that is robbed, not wanting° what is stol'n,
   Let him not know't, and he's not robbed at all.   340
Iago: I am sorry to hear this.
Othello: I had been happy if the general camp,
   Pioners° and all, had tasted her sweet body,

---

310 *to th' advantage:* being lucky.   314 *import:* importance.   316 *lack:* miss.   316 *Be not acknown on't:* forget you ever saw it.   324 *are scarce found to distaste:* scarcely can be tasted.   325 *with a little:* in a short time.   327 *poppy nor mandragora:* soporifics.   330 *owedst:* possessed.   339 *wanting:* missing.   343 *Pioners:* the basest manual laborers in the army, who dug trenches and mines.

So I had nothing known. O now, forever
Farewell the tranquil mind! Farewell content!   345
Farewell the plumèd troops, and the big wars
That make ambition virtue! O, farewell!
Farewell the neighing steed and the shrill trump,
The spirit-stirring drum, th' ear-piercing fife,
The royal banner, and all quality,   350
Pride, pomp, and circumstance° of glorious war!
And O you mortal engines° whose rude throats
Th' immortal Jove's dread clamors° counterfeit,
Farewell! Othello's occupation's gone!
Iago: Is't possible, my lord?   355
Othello: Villain, be sure thou prove my love a whore!
Be sure of it; give me the ocular proof;
Or, by the worth of mine eternal soul,
Thou hadst been better have been born a dog
Than answer my waked wrath!
Iago: Is't come to this?   360
Othello: Make me to see't; or at the least so prove it
That the probation° bear no hinge nor loop
To hang a doubt on—or woe upon thy life!
Iago: My noble lord—
Othello: If thou dost slander her and torture me,   365
Never pray more; abandon all remorse;
On horror's head horrors accumulate;
Do deeds to make heaven weep, all earth amazed;
For nothing canst thou to damnation add
Greater than that.
Iago: O grace! O heaven forgive me!   370
Are you a man? Have you a soul or sense?
God b' wi' you! Take mine office. O wretched fool,
That lov'st to make thine honesty a vice!
O monstrous world! Take note, take note, O world,
To be direct and honest is not safe.   375
I thank you for this profit, and from hence
I'll love no friend, sith° love breeds such offense.
Othello: Nay, stay. Thou shouldst be honest.
Iago: I should be wise; for honesty's a fool
And loses that it works for.
Othello: By the world,   380
I think my wife be honest, and think she is not;
I think that thou art just, and think thou art not.
I'll have some proof. My name, that was as fresh
as Dian's° visage, is now begrimed and black

---

351 *circumstance:* pageantry.   352 *mortal engines:* lethal weapons, i.e., cannon.   353 *clamors:* i.e.,
thunder.   362 *probation:* proof.   377 *sith:* since.   384 *Dian's:* Diana's (goddess of the moon and
of chastity).

As mine own face. If there be cords, or knives,   385
Poison, or fire, or suffocating streams,
I'll not endure it. Would I were satisfied!
Iago: I see you are eaten up with passion.
I do repent me that I put it to you.
You would be satisfied?
Othello: Would? Nay, and I will.   390
Iago: And may; but how? How satisfied, my lord?
Would you, the supervisor°, grossly gape on?
Behold her topped?
Othello: Death and damnation! O!
Iago: It were a tedious° difficulty, I think,
To bring them to that prospect°. Damn them then,   395
If ever mortal eyes to see them bolster°
More than their own! What then? How then?
What shall I say? Where's satisfaction?
It is impossible you should see this,
Were they as prime° as goats, as hot as monkeys,   400
As salt° as wolves in pride°, and fools as gross
As ignorance made drunk. But yet, I say,
If imputation and strong circumstances
Which lead directly to the door of truth
Will give you satisfaction, you might hav't.   405
Othello: Give me a living reason she's disloyal.
Iago: I do not like the office°.
But sith I am entered in this cause so far,
Pricked° to't by foolish honesty and love,
I will go on. I lay with Cassio lately,   410
And being troubled with a raging tooth,
I could not sleep.
There are a kind of men so loose of soul
That in their sleeps will mutter their affairs.
One of this kind is Cassio.   415
In sleep I heard him say, "Sweet Desdemona,
Let us be wary, let us hide our loves!"
And then, sir, would he gripe° and wring my hand,
Cry "O sweet creature!" Then kiss me hard,
As if he plucked up kisses by the roots   420
That grew upon my lips; laid his leg o'er my thigh,
And sigh, and kiss, and then cry, "Cursèd fate
That gave thee to the Moor!"
Othello: O monstrous! monstrous!

---

392 *supervisor:* onlooker.   394 *tedious:* hard to arrange.   395 *prospect:* sight (where they can be seen).   396 *bolster:* go to bed with.   400–1 *prime, salt:* lustful.   401 *pride:* heat.   407 *office:* duty.   409 *Pricked:* spurred.   418 *gripe:* seize.

Iago: Nay, this was but his dream.

Othello: But this denoted a foregone conclusion°,   425
    'Tis a shrewd doubt°, though it be but a dream.

Iago: And this may help to thicken other proofs
    That do demonstrate° thinly.

Othello: I'll tear her all to pieces!

Iago: Nay, yet be wise. Yet we see nothing done;
    She may be honest yet. Tell me but this: 430
    Have you not sometimes seen a handkerchief
    Spotted with strawberries in your wife's hand?

Othello: I gave her such a one; 'twas my first gift.

Iago: I know not that; but such a handkerchief—
    I am sure it was your wife's—did I today   435
    See Cassio wipe his beard with.

Othello: If it be that—

Iago: If it be that or any that was hers,
    It speaks against her with the other proofs.

Othello: O, that the slave had forty thousand lives!
    One is too poor, too weak for my revenge   440
    Now do I see 'tis true. Look here, Iago:
    All my fond love thus do I blow to heaven.
    'Tis gone.
    Arise, black vengeance, from the hollow hell!
    Yield up, O love, thy crown and hearted° throne   445
    To tyrannous hate! Swell, bosom, with thy fraught°,
    For 'tis of aspics'° tongues.

Iago: Yet be content°.

Othello: O, blood, blood, blood!

Iago: Patience, I say. Your mind may change.

Othello: Never, Iago. Like to the Pontic Sea°,   450
    Whose icy current and compulsive course
    Nev'r keeps retiring ebb, but keeps due on
    To the Propontic and the Hellespont,
    Even so my bloody thoughts, with violent pace,
    Shall nev'r look back, nev'r ebb to humble love,   455
    Till that a capable and wide° revenge
    Swallow them up. *[He kneels.]* Now, by yond marble heaven,
    In the due reverence of a sacred vow
    I here engage my words.

Iago: Do not rise yet.   *[Iago kneels.]*
    Witness, you ever-burning lights above,   460
    You elements that clip° us round about,

---

425 *foregone conclusion:* consummated fact.   426 *shrewd doubt:* penetrating guess.   428 *demonstrate:* show, appear.   445 *hearted:* seated in the heart.   446 *fraught:* burden.   447 *aspics':* asps'.   447 *content:* patient, quiet.   450 *Pontic Sea:* the Black Sea (famous for the strong and constant current with which it flows through the Bosporus into the Mediterranean, where the water level is lower).   456 *capable and wide:* sufficient and far-reaching.   461 *clip:* enfold.

Witness that here Iago doth give up
The execution° of his wit, hands, heart
To wronged Othello's service! Let him command,
And to obey shall be in me remorse°,   465
What bloody business ever°.   [They rise.]
Othello: I greet thy love,
Not with vain thanks but with acceptance bounteous°,
And will upon the instant put thee to 't°.
Within these three days let me hear thee say
That Cassio's not alive.   470
Iago: My friend is dead. 'Tis done at your request.
But let her live.
Othello: Damn her, lewd minx! O, damn her! Damn her!
Come, go with me apart. I will withdraw
To furnish me with some swift means of death
For the fair devil. Now art thou my lieutenant.   475
Iago: I am your own forever.   Exeunt.

Scene IV [A street.]

Enter Desdemona, Emilia, and Clown.

Desdemona: Do you know, sirrah, where Lieutenant Cassio lies°?
Clown: I dare not say he lies anywhere.
Desdemona: Why, man?
Clown: He's a soldier, and for me to say a soldier lies, 'tis stabbing.
Desdemona: Go to. Where lodges he?   5
Clown: To tell you where he lies is to tell you where I lie.
Desdemona: Can anything be made of this?
Clown: I know not where he lies, and for me to devise a lodging, and say
    he lies here or he lies there, were to lie in mine own throat°.
Desdemona: Can you enquire him out, and be edified° by report?   10
Clown: I will catechize the world for him; that is, make questions, and by
    them answer.
Desdemona: Seek him, bid him come hither. Tell him I have moved° my
    lord on his behalf and hope all will be well.
Clown: To do this is within the compass° of man's wit, and therefore I will 15
    attempt the doing it.   Exit Clown.
Desdemona: Where should° I lose the handkerchief, Emilia?
Emilia: I know not, madam.
Desdemona: Believe me, I had rather have lost my purse
    Full of crusadoes°. And but my noble Moor   20

___

463 execution: workings, action.   465 remorse: pity.   466 ever: soever.   467 bounteous: absolute.   468 to't: i.e., to the work you have said you are prepared to do.   III.iv. 1 lies: lodges.
9 lie in mine own throat: (to lie in the throat is to lie absolutely and completely).   10 edified: enlightened (Desdemona mocks the Clown's overly elaborate diction).   13 moved: pleaded with.
15 compass: reach.   17 should: might.   20 crusadoes: Portuguese gold coins.

Is true of mind, and made of no such baseness
As jealous creatures are, it were enough
To put him to ill thinking.
Emilia: Is he not jealous?
Desdemona: Who? He? I think the sun where he was born
Drew all such humors° from him.
Emilia: Look where he comes.   25

Enter Othello.

Desdemona: I will not leave him now till Cassio
Be called to him. How is't with you, my lord?
Othello: Well, my good lady. *[Aside]* O, hardness to
dissemble°!—
How do you, Desdemona?
Desdemona: Well, my good lord.   30
Othello: Give me your hand. This hand is moist°, my lady.
Desdemona: It hath felt no age nor known no sorrow.
Othello: This argues° fruitfulness and liberal° heart.
Hot, hot, and moist. This hand of yours requires
A sequester° from liberty; fasting and prayer;   35
Much castigation; exercise devout;
For here's a young and sweating devil here
That commonly rebels. 'Tis a good hand,
A frank one.
Desdemona: You may, indeed, say so;
For 'twas that hand that gave away my heart.   40
Othello: A liberal hand! The hearts of old gave hands,
But our new heraldry° is hands, not hearts.
Desdemona: I cannot speak of this. Come now, your promise!
Othello: What promise, chuck?
Desdemona: I have sent to bid Cassio come speak with you.   45
Othello: I have a salt and sorry rheum° offends me.
Lend me thy handkerchief.
Desdemona: Here, my lord.
Othello: That which I gave you.
Desdemona: I have it not about me.
Othello: Not?
Desdemona: No, indeed, my lord.
Othello: That's a fault.   50
That handkerchief
Did an Egyptian to my mother give.

---

24 *humors*: characteristics.   29 *hardness to dissemble*: (Othello may refer here either to the difficulty
he has in maintaining his appearance of composure, or to what he believes to be Desdemona's hardened
hypocrisy).   31 *moist*: (a moist, hot hand was taken as a sign of a lustful nature).   33 *argues*: suggests.   33 *liberal*: free, open (but also with a suggestion of "licentious"; from here on in this scene
Othello's words bear a double meaning, seeming to be normal but accusing Desdemona of being unfaithful).   35 *sequester*: separation.   42 *heraldry*: heraldic symbolism.   46 *a salt and sorry rheum*:
a heavy, running head cold.

She was a charmer°, and could almost read
The thoughts of people. She told her, while she kept it
'Twould make her amiable° and subdue my father   55
Entirely to her love; but if she lost it
Or made a gift of it, my father's eye
Should hold her loathèd, and his spirits should hunt
After new fancies. She, dying, gave it me,
And bid me, when my fate would have me wived,   60
To give it her. I did so; and take heed on't;
Make it a darling like your precious eye.
To lose't or give't away were such perdition
As nothing else could match.
Desdemona: Is't possible?
Othello: 'Tis true. There's magic in the web° of it.   65
A sibyl that had numbered in the world
The sun to course two hundred compasses,
In her prophetic fury° sewed the work;
The worms were hallowed that did breed the silk,
And it was dyed in mummy° which the skillful   70
Conserved of maidens' heart.
Desdemona: Indeed? Is't true?
Othello: Most veritable. Therefore look to't well.
Desdemona: Then would to God that I had never seen't!
Othello: Ha! Wherefore?
Desdemona: Why do you speak so startingly and rash?   75
Othello: Is't lost? Is't gone? Speak, is it out o' th' way?
Desdemona: Heaven bless us!
Othello: Say you?
Desdemona: It is not lost. But what an if it were?
Othello: How?   80
Desdemona: I say it is not lost.
Othello: Fetch't, let me see't!
Desdemona: Why, so I can; but I will not now.
   This is a trick to put me from my suit:
   Pray you let Cassio be received again.   85
Othello: Fetch me the handkerchief! My mind misgives.
Desdemona: Come, come!
   You'll never meet a more sufficient° man—
Othello: The handkerchief!
Desdemona: A man that all his time
   Hath founded his good fortunes on your love,   90
   Shared dangers with you—
Othello: The handkerchief!

---

53 *charmer:* magician.   55 *amiable:* desirable.   65 *web:* weaving.   68 *prophetic fury:* seized by
the spirit and able to prophesy.   70 *mummy:* liquid drained from embalmed bodies.   88 *sufficient:*
complete, with all proper qualities.

Desdemona: I'faith, you are to blame.

Othello: Away! Exit Othello.

Emilia: Is not this man jealous? 95

Desdemona: I nev'r saw this before.
　　Sure there's some wonder in this handkerchief;
　　I am most unhappy in the loss of it.

Emilia: Tis not a year or two shows us a man.
　　They are all but stomachs, and we all but food; 100
　　They eat us hungerly, and when they are full,
　　They belch us.

　　Enter Iago and Cassio.

　　　　　　Look you, Cassio and my husband.

Iago: There is no other way; 'tis she must do't.
　　And lo the happiness! Go and importune her.

Desdemona: How now, good Cassio? What's the news with you? 105

Cassio: Madam, my former suit. I do beseech you
　　That by your virtuous means I may again
　　Exist, and be a member of his love
　　Whom I with all the office° of my heart
　　Entirely honor. I would not be delayed. 110
　　If my offense be of such mortal kind
　　That nor my service past, nor present sorrows,
　　Nor purposed merit in futurity,
　　Can ransom me into his love again,
　　But to know so must be my benefit°, 115
　　So shall I clothe me in a forced content,
　　And shut myself up in some other course
　　To fortune's alms.

Desdemona:　　　　　Alas, thrice-gentle Cassio,
　　My advocation° is not now in tune.
　　My lord is not my lord; nor should I know him 120
　　Were he in favor° as in humor altered.
　　So help me every spirit sanctified
　　As I have spoken for you all my best
　　And stood within the blank° of his displeasure
　　For my free speech. You must awhile be patient. 125
　　What I can do I will; and more I will
　　Than for myself I dare. Let that suffice you.

Iago: Is my lord angry?

Emilia:　　　　　He went hence but now,
　　And certainly in strange unquietness.

Iago: Can he be angry? I have seen the cannon 130
　　When it hath blown his ranks into the air

---

109 *office*: duty.　115 *benefit*: good.　119 *advocation*: advocacy.　121 *favor*: countenance.
124 *blank*: bull's-eye of a target.

And, like the devil, from his very arm
Puffed his own brother. And is he angry?
Something of moment° then. I will go meet him.
There's matter in't indeed if he be angry.   135
Desdemona: I prithee do so.   *Exit [Iago.]*
                        Something sure of state°,
Either from Venice or some unhatched practice°
Made demonstrable here in Cyprus to him,
Hath puddled° his clear spirit; and in such cases
Men's natures wrangle with inferior things,   140
Though great ones are their object. 'Tis even so.
For let our finger ache, and it endues°
Our other, healthful members even to a sense
Of pain. Nay, we must think men are not gods,
Nor of them look for such observancy   145
As fits the bridal. Beshrew me such, Emilia,
I was, unhandsome warrior as I am,
Arraigning his unkindness with my soul;
But now I find I had suborned the witness,
And he's indicted falsely.
Emilia: Pray heaven it be   150
State matters, as you think, and no conception
Nor no jealous toy° concerning you.
Desdemona: Alas the day! I never gave him cause.
Emilia: But jealous souls will not be answered so;
They are not ever jealous for the cause,   155
But jealous for they're jealous. It is a monster
Begot upon itself, born on itself.
Desdemona: Heaven keep the monster from Othello's mind!
Emilia: Lady, amen.
Desdemona: I will go seek him. Cassio, walk here about.   160
If I do find him fit°, I'll move your suit
And seek to effect it to my uttermost.
Cassio: I humbly thank your ladyship.   *Exit [Desdemona with Emilia].*

    Enter Bianca.

Bianca: Save you, friend Cassio!
Cassio: What make you from home?
How is't with you, my most fair Bianca?   165
I' faith, sweet love, I was coming to your house.
Bianca: And I was going to your lodging, Cassio.
What, keep a week away? Seven days and nights?
Eightscore eight hours? And lovers' absent hours

---

134 *moment:* importance.   136 *of state:* state affairs.   137 *unhatched practice:* undisclosed plot.
139 *puddled:* muddied.   142 *endues:* leads.   152 *toy:* trifle.   161 *fit:* receptive.

More tedious than the dial eightscore times? 170
O weary reck'ning°.

Cassio: Pardon me, Bianca.
I have this while with leaden thoughts been pressed,
But I shall in a more continuate° time
Strike off this score° of absence. Sweet Bianca,

[Gives her Desdemona's handkerchief.]

Take me this work out.

Bianca: O Cassio, whence came this? 175
This is some token from a newer friend.
To the felt absence now I feel a cause.
Is't come to this? Well, well.

Cassio: Go to, woman!
Throw your vile guesses in the devil's teeth,
From whence you have them. You are jealous now 180
That this is from some mistress, some remembrance.
No, by my faith, Bianca.

Bianca: Why, whose is it?

Cassio: I know not neither; I found it in my chamber.
I like the work well; ere it be demanded°,
As like enough it will, I would have it copied. 185
Take it and do't, and leave me for this time.

Bianca: Leave you? Wherefore?

Cassio: I do attend here on the general
And think it no addition, nor my wish,
To have him see me womaned.

Bianca: Why, I pray you? 190

Cassio: Not that I love you not.

Bianca: But that you do not love me!
I pray you bring° me on the way a little,
And say if I shall see you soon at night.

Cassio: 'Tis but a little way that I can bring you,
For I attend here; but I'll see you soon. 195

Bianca: 'Tis very good. I must be circumstanced°.   *Exeunt omnes.*

ACT IV

Scene I [A street.]

Enter Othello and Iago.

Iago: Will you think so?

---

171 *reck'ning:* addition.   173 *continuate:* uninterrupted.   174 *Strike off this score:* i.e., pay this bill
(the *score* being the account of drinks kept in a tavern).   184 *demanded:* asked for (by the person
who lost it).   192 *bring:* accompany.   196 *be circumstanced:* accept things as they are.

Othello: Think so, Iago?

Iago: What,
   To kiss in private?

Othello: An unauthorized° kiss?

Iago: Or to be naked with her friend in bed
   An hour or more, not meaning any harm?

Othello: Naked in bed, Iago, and not mean harm?   5
   It is hypocrisy against the devil.
   They that mean virtuously, and yet do so,
   The devil their virtue tempts, and they tempt heaven.

Iago: If they do nothing, 'tis a venial slip.
   But if I give my wife a handkerchief—   10

Othello: What then?

Iago: Why, then 'tis hers, my lord; and being hers,
   She may, I think, bestow't on any man.

Othello: She is protectress of her honor too.
   May she give that?   15

Iago: Her honor is an essence that's not seen;
   They have it very oft that have it not.
   But for the handkerchief—

Othello: By heaven, I would most gladly have forgot it!
   Thou said'st—O, it comes o'er my memory   20
   As doth the raven° o'er the infected house,
   Boding to all—he had my handkerchief.

Iago: Ay, what of that?

Othello: That's not so good now.

Iago: What if I had said I had seen him do you wrong?
   Or heard him say—as knaves be such abroad°   25
   Who having, by their own importunate suit,
   Or voluntary dotage° of some mistress,
   Convincèd or supplied° them, cannot choose
   But they must blab—

Othello: Hath he said anything?

Iago: He hath, my lord; but be you well assured,   30
   No more than he'll unswear.

Othello: What hath he said?

Iago: Why, that he did—I know not what he did.

Othello: What? what?

Iago: Lie—

Othello: With her?

Iago: With her, on her; what you will.   35

Othello: Lie with her? Lie on her?—We say lie on her when they belie her.—
   Lie with her! Zounds, that's fulsome°.—Handkerchief—confessions—

IV.i. 2 *unauthorized:* illicit.   21 *raven:* (a harbinger of death.)   25 *abroad:* i.e., in the world.
27 *voluntary dotage:* weakness of the will.   28 *Convincèd or supplied:* persuaded or gratified (the mistress).   37 *fulsome:* foul, repulsive.

handkerchief!—To confess, and be hanged for his labor—first to be
hanged, and then to confess! I tremble at it. Nature would not invest
herself in such shadowing passion without some instruction°. It is not   40
words that shakes me thus.—Pish! Nose, ears, and lips? Is't possible?—
Confess?—Handkerchief?—O devil!   *Falls in a trance.*

Iago: Work on.
My med'cine works! Thus credulous fools are caught,
And many worthy and chaste dames even thus,   45
All guiltless, meet reproach°. What, ho! My lord!
My lord, I say! Othello!

Enter Cassio.

                                    How now, Cassio?
Cassio: What's the matter?
Iago: My lord is fall'n into an epilepsy.
This is his second fit; he had one yesterday.   50
Cassio: Rub him about the temples.
Iago: The lethargy° must have his quiet course.
If not, he foams at mouth, and by and by
Breaks out to savage madness. Look, he stirs.
Do you withdraw yourself a little while.   55
He will recover straight. When he is gone,
I would on great occasion° speak with you.   *[Exit Cassio.]*
How is it, general? Have you not hurt your head?
Othello: Dost thou mock° me?
Iago: I mock you not, by heaven.
Would you would bear your fortune like a man.   60
Othello: A hornèd man's a monster and a beast.
Iago: There's many a beast then in a populous city,
And many a civil° monster.
Othello: Did he confess it?
Iago: Good, sir, be a man.
Think every bearded fellow that's but yoked   65
May draw° with you. There's millions now alive
That nightly lie in those unproper° beds
Which they dare swear peculiar.° Your case is better.
O, 'tis the spite of hell, the fiend's arch-mock,
To lip a wanton in a secure couch,   70
And to suppose her chaste. No, let me know;
And knowing what I am, I know what she shall be.
Othello: O, thou are wise! 'Tis certain.

39–40 *Nature . . . instruction:* i.e., my mind would not become so darkened (with anger) unless there
were something to this (accusation); remember that Othello believes in the workings of magic and
supernatural forces.   46 *reproach:* shame.   52 *lethargy:* coma.   57 *great occasion:* very important matter.   59 *mock:* (Othello takes Iago's comment as a reference to his horns—which it is).
63 *civil:* city-dwelling.   66 *draw:* i.e., like the horned ox.   67 *unproper:* i.e., not exclusively the
husband's.   68 *peculiar:* their own alone.

Iago: Stand you awhile apart;
    Confine yourself but in a patient list.°
    Whilst you were here, o'erwhelmèd with your grief—   75
    A passion most unsuiting such a man—
    Cassio came hither. I shifted him away°
    And laid good 'scuses upon your ecstasy°,
    Bade him anon return, and here speak with me;
    The which he promised. Do but encave° yourself   80
    And mark the fleers°, the gibes, and notable° scorns
    That dwell in every region of his face.
    For I will make him tell the tale anew:
    Where, how, how oft, how long ago, and when
    He hath, and is again to cope your wife.   85
    I say, but mark his gesture. Marry patience,
    Or I shall say you're all in all in spleen°,
    And nothing of a man.
Othello: Dost thou hear, Iago?
    I will be found most cunning in my patience;
    But—dost thou hear?—most bloody.
Iago: That's not amiss;   90
    But yet keep time in all. Will you withdraw?

    [*Othello moves to one side, where his remarks are not audible
    to Cassio and Iago.*]

    Now will I question Cassio of Bianca,
    A huswife° that by selling her desires
    Buys herself bread and cloth. It is a creature
    That dotes on Cassio, as 'tis the strumpet's plague   95
    To beguile many and be beguiled by one.
    He, when he hears of her, cannot restrain
    From the excess of laughter. Here he comes.

    Enter Cassio.

    As he shall smile, Othello shall go mad:
    And his unbookish° jealousy must conster°   100
    Poor Cassio's smiles, gestures, and light behaviors
    Quite in the wrong. How do you, lieutenant?
Cassio: The worser that you give me the addition°
    Whose want even kills me.

---

74 *a patient list:* the bounds of patience.   77 *shifted him away:* got rid of him by a stratagem
78 *ecstasy:* trance (the literal meaning, "outside oneself," bears on the meaning of the change Othello
is undergoing).   80 *encave:* hide.   81 *fleers:* mocking looks or speeches.   81 *notable:* obvious.   87 *spleen:* passion, particularly anger.   93 *huswife:* housewife (but with the special meaning
here of "prostitute").   100 *unbookish:* ignorant.   100 *conster:* construe.   103 *addition:* title.

Iago: Ply Desdemona well, and you are sure on't.   105
    Now, if this suit lay in Bianca's power,
    How quickly should you speed!
Cassio: Alas, poor caitiff!°
Othello: Look how he laughs already!
Iago: I never knew woman love man so.
Cassio: Alas, poor rogue! I think, i' faith, she loves me.   110
Othello: Now he denies it faintly, and laughs it out.
Iago: Do you hear, Cassio?
Othello: Now he importunes him
    To tell it o'er. Go to! Well said, well said!
Iago: She gives it out that you shall marry her.
    Do you intend it?   115
Cassio: Ha, ha, ha!
Othello: Do ye triumph, Roman? Do you triumph?
Cassio: I marry? What, a customer°? Prithee bear some charity to my wit;
    do not think it so unwholesome. Ha, ha, ha!
Othello: So, so, so, so. They laugh that win.   120
Iago: Why, the cry goes that you marry her.
Cassio: Prithee, say true.
Iago: I am a very villain else.
Othello: Have you scored° me? Well.
Cassio: This is the monkey's own giving out. She is persuaded I will marry   125
    her out of her own love and flattery, not out of my promise.
Othello: Iago beckons me; now he begins the story.

[Othello moves close enough to hear.]

Cassio: She was here even now; she haunts me in every place. I was the
    other day talking on the sea bank with certain Venetians, and thither
    comes the bauble°, and falls me thus about my neck—   130
Othello: Crying "O dear Cassio!" as it were. His gesture imports it.
Cassio: So hangs, and lolls, and weeps upon me; so shakes and pulls me!
    Ha, ha, ha!
Othello: Now he tells how she plucked him to my chamber. O, I see that
    nose of yours, but not that dog I shall throw it to.   135
Cassio: Well, I must leave her company.
Iago: Before me!° Look where she comes.

    Enter Bianca.

Cassio: 'Tis such another fitchew!° Marry a perfumed one? What do you
    mean by this haunting of me?

---

107 *caitiff:* wretch.   118 *customer:* one who sells, a merchant (here, a prostitute).   124 *scored:*
marked, defaced.   130 *bauble:* plaything.   137 *Before me!:* (an exclamation of surprise).
138 *fitchew:* polecat, i.e., strong-smelling creature.

Bianca: Let the devil and his dam haunt you! What did you mean by that   140
   same handkerchief you gave me even now? I was a fine fool to take
   it. I must take out the work? A likely piece of work that you should
   find it in your chamber and know not who left it there! This is some
   minx's token, and I must take out the work? There! [*She throws down
   the handkerchief.*] Give it your hobbyhorse°. Wheresoever you had it,   145
   I'll take out no work on't.
Cassio: How now, my sweet Bianca? How now? how now?
Othello: By heaven, that should be my handkerchief!
Bianca: If you'll come to supper tonight, you may; if you will not, come when
   you are next prepared for°.   *Exit.*   150
Iago: After her, after her!
Cassio: Faith, I must; she'll rail in the streets else.
Iago: Will you sup there?
Cassio: Yes, I intend so.
Iago: Well, I may chance to see you, for I would very fain speak with
   you.   155
Cassio: Prithee come. Will you?
Iago: Go to, say no more.   [*Exit Cassio.*]
Othello [Comes forward]: How shall I murder him, Iago?
Iago: Did you perceive how he laughed at his vice?
Othello: O Iago!   160
Iago: And did you see the handkerchief?
Othello: Was that mine?
Iago: Yours, by this hand! And to see how he prizes the foolish woman your
   wife! She gave it him, and he hath giv'n it his whore.
Othello: I would have him nine years a-killing!—A fine woman, a fair woman,   165
   a sweet woman!
Iago: Nay, you must forget that.
Othello: Ay, let her rot, and perish, and be damned tonight; for she shall
   not live. No, my heart is turned to stone; I strike it, and it hurts my
   hand. O, the world hath not a sweeter creature! She might lie by an   170
   emperor's side and command him tasks.
Iago: Nay, that's not your way°.
Othello: Hang her! I do but say what she is. So delicate with her needle.
   An admirable musician. O, she will sing the savageness out of a bear!
   Of so high and plenteous wit and invention°—   175
Iago: She's the worse for all this.
Othello: O, a thousand, a thousand times. And then, of so gentle a
   condition°?
Iago: Ay, too gentle.
Othello: Nay, that's certain. But yet the pity of it, Iago. O Iago, the pity   180
   of it, Iago.

---

145 *hobbyhorse:* prostitute.   150 *next prepared for:* next expected—i.e., never.   172 *way:* proper
course.   175 *invention:* imagination.   177–178 *gentle a condition:* (1) well born (2) of a gentle nature.

Iago: If you are so fond over her iniquity, give her patent to offend; for if
   it touch° not you, it comes near nobody.
Othello: I will chop her into messes°. Cuckold me!
Iago: O, 'tis foul in her.   185
Othello: With mine officer!
Iago: That's fouler.
Othello: Get me some poison, Iago, this night. I'll not expostulate with her,
   lest her body and beauty unprovide my mind° again. This night, Iago!
Iago: Do it not with poison. Strangle her in her bed, even the bed she hath   190
   contaminated.
Othello: Good, good! The justice of it pleases. Very good!
Iago: And for Cassio, let me be his undertaker°. You shall hear more by
   midnight.
Othello: Excellent good!   *[A trumpet.]*
                    What trumpet is that same?   195
Iago: I warrant something from Venice.

   Enter Lodovico, Desdemona, and Attendants.

                                                      'Tis Lodovico.
   This comes from the Duke. See, your wife's with him.
Lodovico: God save you, worthy general.
Othello: With° all my heart, sir.
Lodovico: The Duke and the senators of Venice greet you.

                                         [Gives him a letter.]

Othello: I kiss the instrument of their pleasures.   200

                              [Opens the letter and reads.]

Desdemona: And what's the news, good cousin Lodovico?
Iago: I am very glad to see you, signior.
   Welcome to Cyprus.
Lodovico: I thank you. How does Lieutenant Cassio?
Iago: Lives, sir.
Desdemona: Cousin, there's fall'n between him and my lord   205
   An unkind° breach; but you shall make all well.
Othello: Are you sure of that?
Desdemona: My lord?
Othello [Reads]: "This fail you not to do, as you will—"
Lodovico: He did not call; he's busy in the paper.   210
   Is there division 'twixt my lord and Cassio?
Desdemona: A most unhappy one. I would do much
   T' atone° them, for the love I bear to Cassio.

---

183 *touch:* affects.   184 *messes:* bits.   189 *unprovide my mind:* undo my resolution.   193 *under-*
taker: (not "burier" but "one who undertakes to do something").   198 *With:* i.e., I greet you with.
206 *unkind:* unnatural.   213 *atone:* reconcile.

Othello: Fire and brimstone!
Desdemona: My lord?
Othello: Are you wise?
Desdemona: What, is he angry?
Lodovico: May be th' letter moved him;   215
    For, as I think, they do command him home,
    Deputing Cassio in his government°.
Desdemona: Trust me, I am glad on't.
Othello: Indeed?
Desdemona: My lord?
Othello: I am glad to see you mad.
Desdemona: Why, sweet Othello—
Othello: Devil!   *[Strikes her.]*   220
Desdemona: I have not deserved this.
Lodovico: My lord, this would not be believed in Venice,
    Though I should swear I saw't. 'Tis very much.
    Make her amends; she weeps.
Othello: O devil, devil!
    If that the earth could teem° with woman's tears,   225
    Each drop she falls° would prove a crocodile°.
    Out of my sight!
Desdemona: I will not stay to offend you.   *[Going.]*
Lodovico: Truly, an obedient lady.
    I do beseech your lordship call her back.
Othello: Mistress!
Desdemona: My lord?
Othello: What would you with her, sir?   230
Lodovico: Who? I, my lord?
Othello: Ay! You did wish that I make her turn.
    Sir, she can turn, and turn, and yet go on
    And turn again; and she can weep, sir, weep;
    And she's obedient; as you say, obedient.   235
    Very obedient. Proceed you in your tears.
    Concerning this, sir—O well-painted passion!
    I am commanded home.—Get you away;
    I'll send for you anon.—Sir, I obey the mandate
    And will return to Venice.—Hence, avaunt!   *[Exit Desdemona.]*   240
    Cassio shall have my place. And, sir, tonight
    I do entreat that we may sup together.
    You are welcome, sir, to Cyprus.—Goats and monkeys!   Exit.
Lodovico: Is this the noble Moor whom our full Senate
    Call all in all sufficient? Is this the nature   245
    Whom passion could not shake? whose solid virtue

---

217 *government:* office.   225 *teem:* conceive.   226 *falls:* drops.   226 *crocodile:* (the crocodile was supposed to shed false tears to lure its victims).

The shot of accident nor dart of chance
Could neither graze nor pierce?
Iago: He is much changed.
Lodovico: Are his wits safe? Is he not light of brain?
Iago: He's that he is; I may not breathe my censure.   250
What he might be (if, what he might, he is not)
I would to heaven he were!
Lodovico: What, strike his wife?
Iago: Faith, that was not so well; yet would I knew
That stroke would prove the worst.
Lodovico: Is it his use?°
Or did the letters work upon his blood°   255
And new-create his fault?
Iago: Alas, alas!
It is not honesty in me to speak
What I have seen and known. You shall observe him,
And his own courses° will denote him so
That I may save my speech. Do but go after   260
And mark how he continues.
Lodovico: I am sorry that I am deceived in him.   *Exeunt.*

Scene II *[The citadel.]*

Enter Othello and Emilia.

Othello: You have seen nothing then?
Emilia: Nor ever heard, nor ever did suspect.
Othello: Yes, you have seen Cassio and she together.
Emilia: But then I saw no harm, and then I heard
Each syllable that breath made up° between them.   5
Othello: What, did they never whisper?
Emilia: Never, my lord.
Othello: Nor send you out o' th' way?
Emilia: Never.
Othello: To fetch her fan, her gloves, her mask, nor nothing?
Emilia: Never, my lord.   10
Othello: That's strange.
Emilia: I durst, my lord, to wager she is honest,
Lay down my soul at stake°. If you think other,
Remove your thought. It doth abuse your bosom.
If any wretch have put this in your head,   15
Let heaven requite it with the serpent's curse°,
For if she be not honest°, chaste, and true,
There's no man happy. The purest of their wives
Is foul as slander.

---

254 *use:* habit.   255 *blood:* passion.   259 *courses:* actions.   IV.ii. 5 *that breath made up:*
spoken.   13 *at stake:* as the wager.   16 *serpent's curse:* (God's curse on the serpent after the fall
in Eden).   17 *honest:* chaste.

Othello: Bid her come hither. Go.   *Exit Emilia.*   20
She says enough; yet she's a simple bawd°
That cannot say as much. This is a subtle whore,
A closet lock and key of villainous secrets,
And yet she'll kneel and pray; I have seen her do't.

Enter Desdemona and Emilia.

Desdemona: My lord, what is your will?
Othello: Pray you, chuck, come hither.
Desdemona: What is your pleasure?
Othello: Let me see your eyes.   25
Look in my face.
Desdemona: What horrible fancy's this?
Othello [To Emilia]: Some of your function°, mistress:
Leave procreants alone and shut the door;
Cough or cry hem if anybody come.
Your mystery°, your mystery! Nay, dispatch!   *Exit Emilia.*   30
Desdemona: Upon my knee, what doth your speech import?
I understand a fury in your words°.
Othello: Why, what art thou?
Desdemona: Your wife, my lord; your true
And loyal wife.
Othello: Come, swear it, damn thyself;
Lest, being like one of heaven, the devils themselves   35
Should fear to seize thee. Therefore be doubledamned:
Swear thou art honest.
Desdemona: Heaven doth truly know it.
Othello: Heaven truly knows that thou art false as hell.
Desdemona: To whom, my lord? With whom? How am I false?
Othello: Ah, Desdemon! Away! Away! Away!   40
Desdemona: Alas the heavy day! Why do you weep?
Am I the motive° of these tears, my lord?
If haply° you my father do suspect
An instrument of this your calling back,
Lay not your blame on me. If you have lost him,   45
I have lost him too.
Othello: Had it pleased heaven
To try me with affliction, had they rained
All kinds of sores and shames on my bare head,
Steeped° me in poverty to the very lips,
Given to captivity me and my utmost hopes,   50
I should have found in some place of my soul
A drop of patience. But alas, to make me
The fixèd figure for the time of scorn°

20 *bawd:* procuress.   27 *Some of your function:* do your proper work (as the operator of a brothel).
30 *mystery:* trade.   32 *words:* (Q₁ adds to this line, "But not the words").   42 *motive:*
cause.   43 *haply:* by chance.   49 *Steeped:* submerged.   53 *The . . . scorn:* the very image of scorn
in our time.

To point his slow and moving finger at.
Yet could I bear that too, well, very well. 55
But there where I have garnered up my heart,
Where either I must live or bear no life,
The fountain from the which my current runs
Or else dries up—to be discarded thence,
Or keep it as a cistern for foul toads 60
To knot and gender° in—turn thy complexion there,
Patience, thou young and rose-lipped cherubin!
I here look grim as hell!°
Desdemona: I hope my noble lord esteems me honest.
Othello: O, ay, as summer flies are in the shambles°, 65
That quicken even with blowing°. O thou weed,
Who art so lovely fair, and smell'st so sweet,
That the sense aches at thee, would thou hadst never been born!
Desdemona: Alas, what ignorant° sin have I committed?
Othello: Was this fair paper, this most goodly book, 70
Made to write "whore" upon? What committed?
Committed? O thou public commoner°,
I should make very forges of my cheeks
That would to cinders burn up modesty,
Did I but speak thy deeds. What committed? 75
Heaven stops the nose at it, and the moon winks°;
The bawdy wind that kisses all it meets
Is hushed within the hollow mine of earth
And will not hear't. What committed?
Desdemona: By heaven, you do me wrong! 80
Othello: Are not you a strumpet?
Desdemona: No, as I am a Christian!
If to preserve this vessel for my lord
From any other foul unlawful touch
Be not to be a strumpet, I am none.
Othello: What, not a whore?
Desdemona: No, as I shall be saved! 85
Othello: Is't possible?
Desdemona: O, heaven forgive us!
Othello: I cry you mercy° then.
I took you for that cunning whore of Venice
That married with Othello. *[Calling]* You, mistress,

Enter Emilia.

---

61 *knot and gender:* twist in bunches and procreate.   61–63 *turn . . . hell:* (the rough sense would
seem to be "even Patience would grow pale, turn complexion, at Desdemona's perfidy, but that Othello
looks grimly on").   66 *quicken even with blowing:* become impregnated as soon as they lay their
eggs.   69 *ignorant:* unknowing.   72 *commoner:* prostitute.   76 *winks:* closes its eyes (the moon
was the symbol of chastity).   87 *cry you mercy:* ask your pardon.

That have the office opposite to Saint Peter   90
And keep the gate of hell! You, you, ay, you!
We have done our course; there's money for your pains.

                                        [Throws her some coins.]

I pray you turn the key and keep our counsel.   *Exit.*
Emilia: Alas, what does this gentleman conceive?
    How do you, madam? How do you, my good lady?   95
Desdemona: Faith, half asleep.
Emilia: Good madam, what's the matter with my lord?
Desdemona: With who?
Emilia: Why, with my lord, madam.
Desdemona: Who is thy lord?
Emilia: He that is yours, sweet lady.   100
Desdemona: I have none. Do not talk to me, Emilia.
    I cannot weep, nor answers have I none
    But what should go by water°. Prithee tonight
    Lay on my bed my wedding sheets, remember;
    And call thy husband hither.
Emilia: Here's a change indeed!   *[Exit.]*   105
Desdemona: 'Tis meet I should be used so, very meet.
    How have I been behaved, that he might stick
    The small'st opinion on my least misuse°?

    Enter Iago and Emilia.

Iago: What is your pleasure, madam? How is't with you?
Desdemona: I cannot tell. Those that do teach young babes   110
    Do it with gentle means and easy tasks.
    He might have chid me so; for, in good faith,
    I am a child to chiding.
Iago: What is the matter, lady?
Emilia: Alas, Iago, my lord hath so bewhored her,
    Thrown such despite° and heavy terms upon her   115
    That true hearts cannot bear it.
Desdemona: Am I that name, Iago?
Iago: What name, fair lady?
Desdemona: Such as she said my lord did say I was.
Emilia: He called her whore. A beggar in his drink
    Could not have laid such terms upon his callet°.   120
Iago: Why did he so?
Desdemona: I do not know; I am sure I am none such.
Iago: Do not weep, do not weep. Alas the day.
Emilia: Hath she forsook so many noble matches,
    Her father and her country, and her friends,   125
    To be called whore? Would it not make one weep?

103 *water*: tears.   107–08 *stick . . . misuse*: base any doubt on my smallest fault.   115 *despite*:
abuse.   120 *callet*: slut.

Desdemona: It is my wretched fortune.

Iago: Beshrew° him for't!
    How comes this trick upon him?

Desdemona: Nay, heaven doth know.

Emilia: I will be hanged if some eternal villain,
    Some busy and insinuating rogue,   130
    Some cogging°, cozening slave, to get some office,
    Have not devised this slander. I will be hanged else.

Iago: Fie, there is no such man! It is impossible.

Desdemona: If any such there be, heaven pardon him.

Emilia: A halter pardon him! And hell gnaw his bones!   135
    Why should he call her whore? Who keeps her company?
    What place? What time? What form? What likelihood?
    The Moor's abused by some most villainous knave,
    Some base notorious knave, some scurvy fellow.
    O heavens, that such companions° thou'dst unfold°,   140
    And put in every honest hand a whip
    To lash the rascals naked through the world
    Even from the east to th' west!

Iago: Speak within door°.

Emilia: O, fie upon them! Some such squire° he was
    That turned your wit the seamy side without   145
    And made you to suspect me with the Moor.

Iago: You are a fool. Go to.

Desdemona: Alas, Iago,
    What shall I do to win my lord again?
    Good friend, go to him, for, by this light of heaven,
    I know not how I lost him. Here I kneel: 150
    If e'er my will did trespass 'gainst his love
    Either in discourse of thought° or actual deed,
    Or that mine eyes, mine ears, or any sense
    Delighted them in any other form;
    Or that I do not yet, and ever did,   155
    And ever will (though he do shake me off
    To beggarly divorcement) love him dearly,
    Comfort forswear me. Unkindness may do much,
    And his unkindness may defeat° my life,
    But never taint my love. I cannot say "whore."   160
    It does abhor me now I speak the word;
    To do the act that might the addition earn
    Not the world's mass of vanity could make me.

Iago: I pray you be content. 'Tis but his humor°.
    The business of the state does him offense.   165

Desdemona: If 'twere no other.

---

127 *Beshrew:* curse.   131 *cogging:* cheating.   140 *companions:* fellows, rogues.   140 *unfold:* disclose.
143 *within door:* more quietly and moderately.   144 *squire:* (a term of contempt).   152 *discourse of*
thought: thinking.   159 *defeat:* destroy.   164 *humor:* mood.

Iago: It is but so, I warrant.   *[Trumpets within.]*
     Hark how these instruments summon to supper.
     The messengers of Venice stay the meat°.
     Go in, and weep not. All things shall be well.

                       [Exeunt Desdemona and Emilia.]

Enter Roderigo.

How now, Roderigo?   170
Roderigo: I do not find that thou deal'st justly with me.
Iago: What in the contrary?
Roderigo: Every day thou daff'st° me with some device,° Iago, and rather,
     as it seems to me now, keep'st from me all conveniency° than suppli-
     est me with the least advantage of hope. I will indeed no longer endure   175
     it; nor am I yet persuaded to put up° in peace what already I have fool-
     ishly suffered.
Iago: Will you hear me, Roderigo?
Roderigo: I have heard too much, and your words and performances are no
     kin together.   180
Iago: You charge me most unjustly.
Roderigo: With naught but truth. I have wasted myself out of my means.
     The jewels you have had from me to deliver Desdemona would half
     have corrupted a votarist°. You have told me she hath received them,
     and returned me expectations and comforts of sudden respect° and ac-   185
     quaintance; but I find none.
Iago: Well, go to; very well.
Roderigo: Very well? Go to? I cannot go to, man; nor 'tis not very well.
     Nay, I think it is scurvy, and begin to find myself fopped° in it.
Iago: Very well.   190
Roderigo: I tell you 'tis not very well. I will make myself known to Desdemona.
     If she will return me my jewels, I will give over my suit and repent my unlaw-
     ful solicitation. If not, assure yourself I will seek satisfaction of you.
Iago: You have said now?   195
Roderigo: Ay, and said nothing but what I protest° intendment of doing.
Iago: Why, now I see there's mettle° in thee, and even from this instant
     do build on thee a better opinion than ever before. Give me thy hand,
     Roderigo. Thou hast taken against me a most just exception°, but yet
     I protest I have dealt most directly° in thy affair.   200
Roderigo: It hath not appeared.
Iago: I grant indeed it hath not appeared, and your suspicion is not without
     wit and judgment. But, Roderigo, if thou hast that in thee indeed which
     I have greater reason to believe now than ever—I mean purpose, courage,
     and valor—this night show it. If thou the next night following enjoy   205

---

168 *stay the meat:* await the meal.   173 *daff'st:* put off.   173 *device:* scheme.   174 *con-veniency:* what is needful.   176 *put up:* accept.   184 *votarist:* nun.   185 *sudden respect:* immediate consideration.   189 *fopped:* duped.   196 *protest:* aver.   197 *mettle:* spirit.   199–200 *exception:* objection.   200 *directly:* straightforwardly.

not Desdemona, take me from this world with treachery and devise engines for° my life.

Roderigo: Well, what is it? Is it within reason and compass°?

Iago: Sir, there is especial commission come from Venice to depute Cassio
in Othello's place.   210

Roderigo: Is that true? Why, then Othello and Desdemona return again to
Venice.

Iago: O, no; he goes into Mauritania and taketh away with him the fair Desdemona, unless his abode be lingered here by some accident; wherein none
can be so determinate° as the removing of Cassio.   215

Roderigo: How do you mean, removing him?

Iago: Why, by making him incapable of Othello's place—knocking out his
brains.

Roderigo: And that you would have me to do?

Iago: Ay, if you dare do yourself a profit and a right. He sups tonight with   220
a harlotry°, and thither will I go to him. He knows not yet of his
honorable fortune. If you will watch his going thence, which I will
fashion to fall out° between twelve and one, you may take him at your
pleasure. I will be near to second° your attempt, and he shall fall between us. Come, stand not amazed at it, but go along with me. I will   225
show you such a necessity in his death that you shall think yourself
bound to put it on him. It is now high supper time, and the night grows
to waste. About it.

Roderigo: I will hear further reason for this.

Iago: And you shall be satisfied.   *Exeunt.*   230

Scene III [*The citadel.*]

Enter Othello, Lodovico, Desdemona, Emilia, and Attendants.

Lodovico: I do beseech you, sir, trouble yourself no further.

Othello: O, pardon me; 'twill do me good to walk.

Lodovico: Madam, good night. I humbly thank your ladyship.

Desdemona: Your honor is most welcome.

Othello: Will you walk, sir? O, Desdemona.   5

Desdemona: My lord?

Othello: Get you to bed on th' instant; I will be returned forthwith.
Dismiss your attendant there. Look't be done.

Desdemona: I will, my lord.   *Exit [Othello, with Lodovico and Attendants].*

Emilia: How goes it now? He looks gentler than he did.   10

Desdemona: He says he will return incontinent°,
And hath commanded me to go to bed.
And bade me to dismiss you.

Emilia: Dismiss me?

---

207 *engines for*: schemes against.   208 *compass*: possibility.   215 *determinate*: effective.
221 *harlotry*: female.   223 *fall out*: occur.   224 *second*: support.   IV.iii 11 *incontinent*: at once.

Desdemona: It was his bidding; therefore, good Emilia,
    Give me my nightly wearing, and adieu.   15
    We must not now displease him.
Emilia: I would you had never seen him!
Desdemona: So would not I. My love doth so approve him
    That even his stubbornness, his checks°, his frowns—
    Prithee unpin me—have grace and favor.   20
Emilia: I have laid these sheets you bade me on the bed.
Desdemona: All's one°. Good Father, how foolish are our minds!
    If I do die before, prithee shroud me
    In one of these same sheets.
Emilia: Come, come! You talk.
Desdemona: My mother had a maid called Barbary.   25
    She was in love; and he she loved proved mad
    And did forsake her. She had a song of "Willow";
    An old thing 'twas, but it expressed her fortune,
    And she died singing it. That song tonight
    Will not go from my mind; I have much to do   30
    But to go hang my head all at one side
    And sing it like poor Barbary. Prithee dispatch.
Emilia: Shall I go fetch your nightgown?
Desdemona: No, unpin me here.
    This Lodovico is a proper man.   35
Emilia: A very handsome man.
Desdemona: He speaks well.
Emilia: I know a lady in Venice would have walked barefoot to Palestine
    for a touch of his nether lip.
Desdemona [Sings]:
    "The poor soul sat singing by a sycamore tree,   40
        Sing all a green willow;
    Her hand on her bosom, her head on her knee,
        Sing willow, willow, willow;
    The fresh streams ran by her and murmured her moans;
        Sing willow, willow, willow—"   45
    Her salt tears fell from her, and soft'ned the stones—
        Sing willow, willow, willow—"
    Lay by these.   *[Gives Emilia her clothes.]*
    "Willow, Willow"—
    Prithee hie° thee; he'll come anon°.   50
        "Sing all a green willow must be my garland
        Let nobody blame him; his scorn I approve"—
    Nay, that's not next. Hark! Who is't that knocks?
Emilia: It is the wind.

---

19 *checks:* rebukes.   22 *All's one:* no matter.   50 *hie:* hurry.   50 *anon:* at once.

Desdemona [Sings]:
> "I called my love false love; but what said he then?   55
>   Sing willow, willow, willow:
> If I court moe° women, you'll couch with moe men."
So, get thee gone; good night. Mine eyes do itch.
Doth that bode weeping?

Emilia: 'Tis neither here nor there.

Desdemona: I have heard it said so. O, these men, these men.   60
Dost thou in conscience think, tell me, Emilia,
That there be women do abuse their husbands
In such gross kind?

Emilia: There be some such, no question.

Desdemona: Wouldst thou do such a deed for all the world?

Emilia: Why, would not you?

Desdemona: No, by this heavenly light!   65

Emilia: Nor I neither by this heavenly light.
I might do't as well i' th' dark.

Desdemona: Wouldst thou do such a deed for all the world?

Emilia: The world's a huge thing; it is a great price for a small vice.

Desdemona: In troth, I think thou wouldst not.   70

Emilia: In troth, I think I should; and undo't when I had done. Marry, I
would not do such a thing for a joint-ring°, nor for measures of lawn°,
nor for gowns, petticoats, nor caps, nor any petty exhibition°, but for
all the whole world? Why, who would not make her husband a cuckold
to make him a monarch? I should venture purgatory for't.   75

Desdemona: Beshrew me if I would do such a wrong for the whole world.

Emilia: Why, the wrong is but a wrong i' th' world; and having the world
for your labor, 'tis a wrong in your own world, and you might quickly
make it right.

Desdemona: I do not think there is any such woman.   80

Emilia: Yes, a dozen; and as many to th' vantage as would store° the world
    they played for.
But I do think it is their husbands' faults
If wives do fall. Say that they slack their duties
And pour our treasures into foreign° laps;   85
Or else break out in peevish jealousies,
Throwing restraint upon us; or say they strike us,
Or scant our former having in despite°—
Why, we have galls; and though we have some grace,
Yet have we some revenge. Let husbands know   90
Their wives have sense like them. They see, and smell,
And have their palates both for sweet and sour,

---

57 *moe:* more.   72 *joint-ring:* (a ring with interlocking halves).   72 *lawn:* fine linen.   73 *exhibi-*
tion: payment.   81 *to . . . store:* in addition as would fill.   85 *foreign:* alien, i.e., other than the
wife.   88 *scant . . . despite:* reduce, in spite, our household allowance(?).

As husbands have. What is it that they do
When they change° us for others? Is it sport?
I think it is. And doth affection° breed it?   95
I think it doth. Is't frailty that thus errs?
It is so too. And have not we affections?
Desires for sport? and frailty? as men have?
Then let them use us well; else let them know,
The ills we do, their ills instruct us so°.   100
Desdemona: Good night, good night. Heaven me such uses° send,
Not to pick bad from bad, but by bad mend.   *Exeunt.*

ACT V

Scene I *[A street.]*

Enter Iago and Roderigo.

Iago: Here, stand behind this bulk°; straight will he come.
Wear thy good rapier bare, and put it home.
Quick, quick! Fear nothing; I'll be at thy elbow.
It makes us, or it mars us, think on that,
And fix most firm thy resolution.   5
Roderigo: Be near at hand; I may miscarry in't.
Iago: Here, at thy hand. Be bold, and take thy stand.

                                              [Moves to one side.]

Roderigo: I have no great devotion to the deed,
And yet he hath given me satisfying reasons.
'Tis but a man gone. Forth my sword! He dies!   10
Iago: I have rubbed this young quat° almost to the sense°,
And he grows angry. Now, whether he kill Cassio,
Or Cassio him, or each do kill the other,
Every way makes my gain. Live Roderigo,
He calls me to a restitution large   15
Of gold and jewels that I bobbed° from him
As gifts to Desdemona.
It must not be. If Cassio do remain,
He hath a daily beauty in his life
That makes me ugly; and besides, the Moor   20
May unfold me to him; there stand I in much peril.
No, he must die. But so, I hear him coming.

---

94 *change:* exchange.   95 *affection:* strong feeling, desire.   100 *instruct us so:* teach us to do likewise.   101 *uses:* practices.   V.i. 1 *bulk:* projecting stall of a shop.   11 *quat:* pimple.   11 *to
the sense:* raw.   16 *bobbed:* swindled.

Enter Cassio.

Roderigo: I know his gait. 'Tis he. Villain, thou diest!

                                           [Thrusts at Cassio.]

Cassio: That thrust had been mine enemy indeed
    But that my coat° is better than thou know'st.   25
    I will make proof of thine.   *[Fights with Roderigo.]*
Roderigo: O, I am slain!°
Cassio: I am maimed forever. Help, ho! Murder! Murder!

    Enter Othello [to one side].

Othello: The voice of Cassio. Iago keeps his word.
Roderigo: O, villain that I am!
Othello: It is even so.
Cassio: O help, ho! Light! A surgeon!   30
Othello: 'Tis he. O brave Iago, honest and just,
    That hast such noble sense of thy friend's wrong!
    Thou teachest me. Minion°, your dear lies dead,
    And your unblest° fate hies°. Strumpet, I come.
    Forth of my heart those charms, thine eyes, are blotted.   35
    Thy bed, lust-stained, shall with lust's blood be spotted.

                                      Exit Othello.

    Enter Lodovico and Gratiano.

Cassio: What, ho? No watch? No passage°? Murder! Murder!
Gratiano: 'Tis some mischance. The voice is very direful.
Cassio: O, help!
Lodovico: Hark!   40
Roderigo: O wretched villain!
Lodovico: Two or three groan. 'Tis heavy night.
    These may be counterfeits. Let's think't unsafe
    To come into the cry without more help.
Roderigo: Nobody come? Then shall I bleed to death.   45
Lodovico: Hark!

    Enter Iago [with a light].

Gratiano: Here's one comes in his shirt, with light and weapons.
Iago: Who's there? Whose noise is this that cries on murder?
Lodovico: We do not know.
Iago: Do not you hear a cry?

---

25 *coat:* i.e., a mail shirt or bulletproof vest.   26 *slain:* most editors add here a stage direction that has Iago wounding Cassio in the leg from behind, but remaining unseen. However, nothing in the text requires this expedient, and Cassio's wound can be given him in the fight with Roderigo, for presumably when Cassio attacks Roderigo the latter would not simply accept the thrust but would parry. Iago enters again at line 46, so that he must exit after line 2.   33 *Minion:* hussy, i.e., Desdemona.   34 *unblest:* unsanctified.   34 *hies:* approaches swiftly.   37 *passage:* passers-by.

Cassio: Here, here! For heaven's sake, help me!
Iago: What's the matter?   50
Gratiano: This is Othello's ancient, as I take it.
Lodovico: The same indeed, a very valiant fellow.
Iago: What are you here that cry so grievously?
Cassio: Iago? O, I am spoiled, undone by villains.
    Give me some help.   55
Iago: O me, lieutenant! What villains have done this?
Cassio: I think that one of them is hereabout
    And cannot make away.
Iago: O treacherous villains!
    [*To Lodovico and Gratiano*] What are you there?
    Come in, and give some help.
Roderigo: O, help me here!   60
Cassio: That's one of them.
Iago: O murd'rous slave! O villain!

                                                        [*Stabs Roderigo.*]

Roderigo: O damned Iago! O inhuman dog!
Iago: Kill men i' th' dark?—Where be these bloody thieves?—
    How silent is this town!—Ho! Murder! Murder!
    What may you be? Are you of good or evil?   65
Lodovico: As you shall prove us, praise us.
Iago: Signior Lodovico?
Lodovico: He, sir.
Iago: I cry you mercy. Here's Cassio hurt by villains.
Gratiano: Cassio?   70
Iago: How is't, brother?
Cassio: My leg is cut in two.
Iago: Marry, heaven forbid!
    Light, gentlemen. I'll bind it with my shirt.

    Enter Bianca.

Bianca: What is the matter, ho? Who is't that cried?
Iago: Who is't that cried?   75
Bianco: O my dear Cassio! My sweet Cassio!
    O Cassio, Cassio, Cassio!
Iago: O notable strumpet!—Cassio, may you suspect
    Who they should be that have thus mangled you?
Cassio: No.   80
Gratiano: I am sorry to find you thus. I have been to seek you.
Iago: Lend me a garter. So. O for a chair
    To bear him easily hence.
Bianca: Alas, he faints! O Cassio, Cassio, Cassio!
Iago: Gentlemen all, I do suspect this trash   85
    To be a party in this injury.—

Patience awhile, good Cassio.—Come, come.
Lend me a light. Know we this face or no?
Alas, my friend and my dear countryman
Roderigo? No.—Yes, sure.—Yes, 'tis Roderigo!   90

Gratiano: What, of Venice?

Iago: Even he, sir. Did you know him?

Gratiano: Know him? Ay.

Iago: Signior Gratiano? I cry your gentle pardon.
These bloody accidents must excuse my manners
That so neglected you.

Gratiano: I am glad to see you.   95

Iago: How do you, Cassio?—O, a chair, a chair!

Gratiano: Roderigo?

Iago: He, he, 'tis he! *[A chair brought in.]* O, that's well said°; the chair.
Some good man bear him carefully from hence.
I'll fetch the general's surgeon. *[To Bianca]* For you, mistress,   100
Save you your labor. *[To Cassio]* He that lies slain here, Cassio,
Was my dear friend. What malice was between you?

Cassio: None in the world; nor do I know the man.

Iago: What, look you pale?—O, bear him out o' th' air.

                                        [Cassio is carried off.]

Stay you, good gentlemen.—Look you pale, mistress?   105
Do you perceive the gastness° of her eye?
Nay, if you stare, we shall hear more anon.
Behold her well; I pray you look upon her.
Do you see, gentlemen? Nay, guiltiness will speak,
Though tongues were out of use°.   110

[Enter Emilia.]

Emilia: Alas, what is the matter? What is the matter, husband?

Iago: Cassio hath here been set on in the dark
By Roderigo and fellows that are scaped.
He's almost slain, and Roderigo quite dead.

Emilia: Alas, good gentleman! Alas, good Cassio!   115

Iago: This is the fruits of whoring. Prithee, Emilia,
Go know of Cassio where he supped tonight.
[To Bianca] What, do you shake at that?

Bianca: He supped at my house; but I therefore shake not.

Iago: O, did he so? I charge° you go with me.   120

Emilia: O fie upon thee, strumpet!

Bianca: I am no strumpet, but of life as honest
As you that thus abuse me.

Emilia: As I? Fie upon thee!

98 *well said:* well done.   106 *gastness:* terror.   110 *tongues were out of use:* men no longer
spoke.   120 *charge:* command.

Iago: Kind gentlemen, let's go see poor Cassio dressed°.
    [To Bianca] Come, mistress, you must tell's another tale.   125
    Emilia, run you to the citadel
    And tell my lord and lady what hath happed.   *[Exit Emilia.]*
    Will you go afore?   *Exeunt [all but Iago].*
               This is the night
    That either makes me or fordoes me quite°.   *[Exit.]*

Scene II *[Desdemona's chamber.]*

Enter Othello [with a light]; and Desdemona in her bed.

Othello: It is the cause, it is the cause, my soul.
    Let me not name it to you, you chaste stars.
    It is the cause. Yet I'll not shed her blood,
    Nor scar that whiter skin of hers than snow
    And smooth as monumental alabaster.   5
    Yet she must die, else she'll betray more men.
    Put out the light, and then put out the light.
    If I quench thee, thou flaming minister°,
    I can again thy former light restore,
    Should I repent me; but once put out thy light,   10
    Thou cunning'st° pattern of excelling nature,
    I know not where is that Promethean heat°
    That can thy light relume°. When I have plucked the rose,
    I cannot give it vital° growth again:
    It needs must wither. I'll smell thee on the tree.   *[He kisses her.]*   15
    O balmy breath, that dost almost persuade
    Justice to break her sword. One more, one more!
    Be thus when thou art dead, and I will kill thee,
    And love thee after. One more, and that's the last!
    So sweet was ne'er so fatal. I must weep,   20
    But they are cruel tears. This sorrow's heavenly;
    It strikes where it doth love. She wakes.
Desdemona: Who's there? Othello?
Othello: Ay, Desdemona.
Desdemona: Will you come to bed, my lord?
Othello: Have you prayed tonight, Desdemon?
Desdemona: Ay, my Lord.   25
Othello: If you bethink yourself of any crime
    Unreconciled as yet to heaven and grace,
    Solicit for it straight.
Desdemona: Alack, my lord, what may you mean by that?
Othello: Well, do it, and be brief; I will walk by°.   30

---

124 *dressed:* bandaged.   129 *fordoes me quite:* completely ruins me.   V.ii. 8 *minister:* worker, servant.   11 *cunning'st:* most intricate and skillfully wrought (by nature excelling itself).   12 *Promethean heat:* divine fire (Prometheus is the Titan who stole fire from heaven and gave it to man).   13 *relume:* relight.   14 *vital:* living.   30 *by:* nearby.

I would not kill thy unpreparèd spirit.
No, heavens forfend! I would not kill thy soul.
Desdemona: Talk you of killing?
Othello: Ay, I do.
Desdemona: Then heaven
    Have mercy on me!
Othello: Amen, with all my heart.
Desdemona: If you say so, I hope you will not kill me.   35
Othello: Humh.
Desdemona: And yet I fear you; for you're fatal then
    When your eyes roll so. Why I should fear I know not,
    Since guiltiness I know not; but yet I feel I fear.
Othello: Think on thy sins.
Desdemona: They are loves I bear to you.   40
Othello: Ay, and for that thou diest.
Desdemona: That death's unnatural that kills for loving.
    Alas, why gnaw you so your nether lip?
    Some bloody passion shakes your very frame.
    These are portents; but yet I hope, I hope,   45
    They do not point on me.
Othello: Peace and be still.
Desdemona: I will so. What's the matter?
Othello: That handkerchief which I so loved and gave thee,
    Thou gav'st to Cassio.
Desdemona: No, by my life and soul!
    Send for the man and ask him.
Othello: Sweet soul, take heed,   50
    Take heed of perjury; thou art on thy deathbed.
Desdemona: Ay, but not yet to die.
Othello: Presently°.
    Therefore confess thee freely of thy sin,
    For to deny each article° with oath
    Cannot remove nor choke the strong conception   55
    That I do groan withal. Thou art to die.
Desdemona: Then Lord have mercy on me.
Othello: I say, amen.
Desdemona: And have you mercy too. I never did
    Offend you in my life; never loved Cassio
    But with such general warranty° of heaven   60
    As I might love. I never gave him token.
Othello: By heaven, I saw my handerchief in's hand!
    O perjured woman! thou dost stone° my heart,
    And mak'st me call what I intend to do

---

52 *Presently:* immediately.   54 *article:* item (of the charge of adultery. Othello makes heavy use of
legal terms in this scene).   60 *warranty:* allowance.   63 *stone:* turn to stone.

A murder, which I thought a sacrifice.   65
I saw the handkerchief.
Desdemona: He found it then.
I never gave it him. Send for him hither.
Let him confess a truth.
Othello: He hath confessed.
Desdemona: What, my lord?
Othello: That he hath used thee.
Desdemona: How? Unlawfully?
Othello: Ay.   70
Desdemona: He will not say so.
Othello: No, his mouth is stopped.
Honest Iago hath ta'en order for't°.
Desdemona: O, my fear interprets. What, is he dead?
Othello: Had all his hairs been lives, my great revenge
Had stomach° for them all.   75
Desdemona: Alas, he is betrayed, and I undone!
Othello: Out, strumpet! Weep'st thou for him to my face?
Desdemona: O, banish me, my lord, but kill me not!
Othello: Down, strumpet!
Desdemona: Kill me tomorrow; let me live tonight!   80
Othello: Nay, if you strive—
Desdemona: But half an hour!
Othello: Being done, there is no pause.
Desdemona: But while I say one prayer!
Othello: It is too late.   *Smothers her.*

Emilia at the door.

Emilia [Calls within]: My lord, my lord! What, ho, my lord, my lord!
Othello: What noise is this? Not dead? Not yet quite dead?   85
I that am cruel am yet merciful;
I would not have thee linger in thy pain.
Emilia [Within]: What, ho! My lord, my lord!
Othello: So, so. Who's there?
Emilia [Within]: O, good my lord, I would speak a word with you.
Othello: Yes, 'tis Emilia.—By and by.—She's dead.—   90
'Tis like she comes to speak of Cassio's death.
The noise was high.° Ha! No more moving?
Still as the grave.—Shall she come in? Were't good?—
I think she stirs again. No.—What's best to do?
If she come in, she'll sure speak to my wife.   95
My wife! My wife! What wife? I have no wife.
O, insupportable! O heavy hour!

---

72 *ta'en order for't:* made sure of it.   75 *stomach:* appetite.   92 *high:* loud (Q¹ reads "here").

Methinks it should be now a huge eclipse
Of sun and moon, and that th' affrighted globe
Should yawn at alteration.°
Emilia [Within]:   I do beseech you   100
 That I may speak with you, O good my lord!
Othello: I had forgot thee. O, come in, Emilia.
 Soft, by and by.—Let me the curtains draw.—

    [Draws the bed hangings and then opens the door.]

Where art thou?

Enter Emilia.

      What's the matter with thee now?
Emilia: O my good lord, yonder's foul murders done! 105
Othello: What? Now?
Emilia: But now, my lord.
Othello: It is the very error° of the moon.
 She comes more nearer earth than she was wont
 And makes men mad.   110
Emilia: Cassio, my lord, hath killed a young Venetian
 Called Roderigo.
Othello: Roderigo killed?
 And Cassio killed?
Emilia: No, Cassio is not killed.
Othello: Not Cassio killed? Then murder's out of tune,
 And sweet revenge grows harsh.   115
Desdemona: O, falsely, falsely murdered!
Emilia: O Lord! What cry is that?
Othello: That? What?
Emilia: Out and alas! that was my lady's voice.
 Help! Help, ho! Help! O lady, speak again!
 Sweet Desdemona! O sweet mistress, speak! 120
Desdemona: A guiltless death I die.
Emilia: O, who hath done this deed?
Desdemona: Nobody—I myself. Farewell.
 Commend me to my kind lord. O, farewell! *[She dies.]*
Othello: Why, how should she be murd'red?
Emilia: Alas, who knows? 125
Othello: You heard her say herself, it was not I.
Emilia: She said so. I must needs report the truth.
Othello: She's like a liar gone to burning hell!
 'Twas I that killed her.

98–100 *Methinks . . . alteration:* (the Elizabethans believed that great changes in human affairs were reflected by disorders in nature). 100 *yawn:* gape open (as in an earthquake). 108 *error:* wandering out of regular course (disorders in the heavens were believed by some to cause disorders on earth, as well as vice versa).

Emilia: O, the more angel she,
    And you the blacker devil!   130
Othello: She turned to folly, and she was a whore.
Emilia: Thou dost belie her, and thou art a devil.
Othello: She was false as water.
Emilia: Thou art rash as fire to say
    That she was false. O, she was heavenly true!
Othello: Cassio did top her. Ask thy husband else.   135
    O, I were damned beneath all depth in hell
    But that I did proceed upon just grounds
    To this extremity. Thy husband knew it all.
Emilia: My husband?
Othello: Thy husband.
Emilia: That she was false to wedlock?
Othello: Ay, with Cassio. Had she been true,   140
    If heaven would make me such another world
    Of one entire and perfect chrysolite°,
    I'd not have sold her for it.
Emilia: My husband?
Othello: Ay, 'twas he that told me on her first.
    An honest man he is, and hates the slime   145
    That sticks on filthy deeds.
Emilia: My husband?
Othello: What needs this iterance? Woman, I say thy husband.
Emilia: O mistress, villainy hath made mocks with love!
    My husband say she was false?
Othello: He, woman.
    I say, thy husband. Dost understand the word?   150
    My friend, thy husband; honest, honest Iago.
Emilia: If he say so, may his pernicious soul
    Rot half a grain a day! He lies to th' heart.
    She was too fond of her most filthy bargain.
Othello: Hah?   155
Emilia: Do thy worst.
    This deed of thine is no more worthy heaven
    Than thou wast worthy her.
Othello: Peace, you were best°.
Emilia: Thou hast not half that pow'r to do me harm
    As I have to be hurt. O gull! O dolt!   160
    As ignorant as dirt! Thou hast done a deed—

                              [Othello moves to draw his sword.]

    I care not for thy sword; I'll make thee known,
    Though I lost twenty lives. Help! Help! Ho! Help!

---

142 *chrysolite*: topaz.   158 *Peace, you were best*: i.e., you had better be silent.

The Moor hath killed my mistress! Murder! Murder!

Enter Montano, Gratiano, and Iago [and Others].

Montano: What is the matter? How now, general?   165
Emilia: O, are you come, Iago? You have done well,
    That men must lay their murders on your neck.
Gratiano: What is the matter?
Emilia: Disprove this villain, if thou be'st a man.
    He says thou told'st him that his wife was false.   170
    I know thou didst not; thou'rt not such a villain.
    Speak, for my heart is full.
Iago: I told him what I thought, and told no more
    Than what he found himself was apt and true.
Emilia: But did you ever tell him she was false?   175
Iago: I did.
Emilia: You told a lie, an odious damnèd lie!
    Upon my soul, a lie! A wicked lie!
    She false with Cassio? Did you say with Cassio?
Iago: With Cassio, mistress. Go to, charm° your tongue.   180
Emilia: I will not charm my tongue; I am bound to speak:
    My mistress here lies murdered in her bed.
All: O heavens forfend!
Emilia: And your reports have set the murder on.
Othello: Nay, stare not, masters. It is true indeed.   185
Gratiano: 'Tis a strange truth.
Montano: O monstrous act!
Emilia: Villainy, villainy, villainy!
    I think upon't—I think I smell't!—O villainy!
    I thought so then.—I'll kill myself for grief.—
    O villainy, villainy!   190
Iago: What, are you mad? I charge you get you home.
Emilia: Good gentlemen, let me have leave to speak.
    'Tis proper I obey him, but not now.
    Perchance, Iago, I will ne'er go home.
Othello: O! O! O!   *[Falls on the bed.]*
Emilia: Nay, lay thee down and roar,   195
    For thou hast killed the sweetest innocent
    That e'er did lift up eye.
Othello: O, she was foul!   *[Rises.]*
    I scarce did know you, uncle. There lies your niece,
    Whose breath, indeed, these hands have newly stopped.
    I know this act shows horrible and grim.   200
Gratiano: Poor Desdemon! I am glad thy father's dead.
    Thy match was mortal to him, and pure grief
    Shore his old thread in twain. Did he live now,

180 *charm:* control.

This sight would make him do a desperate turn;
Yea, curse his better angel from his side, 205
And fall to reprobation°.
Othello: 'Tis pitiful; but yet Iago knows
That she with Cassio hath the act of shame
A thousand times committed. Cassio confessed it;
And she did gratify his amorous works 210
With that recognizance and pledge of love,
Which I first gave her. I saw it in his hand.
It was a handkerchief, an antique token
My father gave my mother.
Emilia: O God! O heavenly God! 215
Iago: Zounds, hold your peace!
Emilia: 'Twill out, 'twill out! I peace?
No, I will speak as liberal as the north°.
Let heaven and men and devils, let them all,
All, all, cry shame against me, yet I'll speak.
Iago: Be wise, and get you home.
Emilia: I will not. 220

[*Iago draws and threatens Emilia.*]

Gratiano: Fie! Your sword upon a woman?
Emilia: O thou dull Moor, that handkerchief thou speak'st of
I found by fortune, and did give my husband;
For often with a solemn earnestness—
More than indeed belonged to such a trifle— 225
He begged of me to steal't.
Iago: Villainous whore!
Emilia: She give it Cassio? No, alas, I found it,
And I did give't my husband.
Iago: Filth, thou liest!
Emilia: By heaven, I do not, I do not, gentlemen.
O murd'rous coxcomb! What should such a fool 230
Do with so good a wife?
Othello: Are there no stones° in heaven
But what serves for the thunder? Precious villain!

[*The Moor runs at Iago, but is disarmed by Montano. Iago kills his wife.*]

Gratiano: The woman falls. Sure he hath killed his wife.
Emilia: Ay, ay. O, lay me by my mistress' side.   [*Exit Iago.*]
Gratiano: He's gone, but his wife's killed. 235
Montano: 'Tis a notorious° villain. Take you this weapon,
Which I have recovered from the Moor.

---

206 *reprobation:* damnation.   217 *liberal as the north:* freely (and bitingly) as the north wind
blows.   231 *stones:* thunderbolts.   236 *notorious:* out-and-out.

Come, guard the door without. Let him not pass,
But kill him rather. I'll after that same villain,
For 'tis a damnèd slave.   *Exit [with all but Othello and Emilia].*
Othello: I am not valiant neither;   240
But every puny whipster° gets my sword.
But why should honor outlive honesty?
Let it go all.
Emilia: What did thy song bode, lady?
Hark, canst thou hear me? I will play the swan,
And die in music. *[Sings]* "Willow, willow, willow."   245
Moor, she was chaste. She loved thee, cruel Moor,
So come my soul to bliss as I speak true.
So speaking as I think, alas, I die.   *[She dies.]*
Othello: I have another weapon in this chamber;
It was a sword of Spain, the ice-brook's temper.   250
O, here it is.—Uncle, I must come forth.
Gratiano [Within]: If thou attempt it, it will cost thee dear.
Thou hast no weapon, and perforce must suffer.
Othello: Look in upon me then and speak with me,
Or, naked as I am, I will assault thee.   255

[Enter Gratiano.]

Gratiano: What is the matter?
Othello: Behold, I have a weapon;
A better never did itself sustain
Upon a soldier's thigh. I have seen the day
That with this little arm and this good sword
I have made my way through more impediments   260
Than twenty times your stop. But O vain boast!
Who can control his fate? 'Tis not so now.
Be not afraid, though you do see me weaponed.
Here is my journey's end, here is my butt°,
And very seamark of my utmost sail°.   265
Do you go back dismayed? 'Tis a lost fear.
Man but a rush° against Othello's breast.
And he retires. Where should Othello go?
Now, how dost thou look now? O ill-starred wench!
Pale as thy smock! When we shall meet at compt°,   270
This look of thine will hurl my soul from heaven,
And fiends will snatch at it. Cold, cold, my girl?
Even like thy chastity.
O cursèd, cursèd slave! Whip me, ye devils,

241 *puny whipster:* small top-whipping boy (?).   264 *butt:* target, stopping place.   265 *seamark of my utmost sail:* maker of my farthest journey.   267 *Man but a rush:* attack with only a reed. 270 *compt:* Judgment Day.

From the possession of° this heavenly sight!   275
Blow me about in winds! roast me in sulfur!
Wash me in steep-down gulfs of liquid fire!
O Desdemon! Dead Desdemon; dead. O! O!

Enter Lodovico, Cassio, Montano, and Iago [as prisoner], with Officers.

Lodovico: Where is this rash and most unfortunate man?
Othello: That's he that was Othello? Here I am.   280
Lodovico: Where is that viper? Bring the villain forth.
Othello: I look down towards his feet°—but that's a fable.
    If that thou be'st a devil, I cannot kill thee.   *[Wounds Iago.]*
Lodovico: Wrench his sword from him.   *[Othello is disarmed.]*
Iago: I bleed, sir, but not killed.
Othello: I am not sorry neither. I'd have thee live;   285
    For in my sense, 'tis happiness to die.
Lodovico: O thou Othello that was once so good,
    Fall'n in the practice° of a cursèd slave,
    What shall be said to thee?
Othello: Why, anything:
    An honorable murderer, if you will;   290
    For naught I did in hate, but all in honor.
Lodovico: This wretch hath part confessed his villainy.
    Did you and he consent in Cassio's death?
Othello: Ay.
Cassio: Dear general, I never gave you cause.   295
Othello: I do believe it, and I ask your pardon.
    Will you, I pray, demand that demi-devil
    Why he hath thus ensnared my soul and body?
Iago: Demand me nothing. What you know, you know.
    From this time forth I never will speak word.   300
Lodovico: What, not to pray?
Gratiano: Torments will open your lips.
Othello: Well, thou dost best.
Lodovico: Sir, you shall understand what hath befall'n,
    Which, as I think, you know not. Here is a letter
    Found in the pocket of the slain Roderigo;   305
    And here another. The one of them imports
    The death of Cassio to be undertook
    By Roderigo.
Othello: O villain!
Cassio: Most heathenish and most gross!
Lodovico: Now here's another discontented paper   310
    Found in his pocket too; and this, it seems,

275 *the possession of:* being possessed by.   282 *towards his feet:* i.e., for his cloven hoofs.   288 *practice:* plotting.

Roderigo meant t' have sent this damnèd villain;
But that, belike, Iago in the interim
Came in and satisfied him.
Othello: O thou pernicious caitiff!
How came you, Cassio, by that handkerchief   315
That was my wife's?
Cassio: I found it in my chamber;
And he himself confessed it but even now
That there he dropped it for a special purpose
Which wrought to his desire.
Othello: O fool! Fool! Fool!
Cassio: There is besides in Roderigo's letter,   320
How he upbraids Iago that he made him
Brave me upon the watch; whereon it came
That I was cast; and even but now he spake,
After long seeming dead—Iago hurt him,
Iago set him on.   325
Lodovico: You must forsake this room and go with us.
Your power and your command is taken off,
And Cassio rules in Cyprus. For this slave,
If there by any cunning cruelty
That can torment him much and hold him long,   330
It shall be his. You shall close prisoner rest
Till that the nature of your fault be known
To the Venetian state. Come, bring away.
Othello: Soft you, a word or two before you go.
I have done the state some service and they know't.   335
No more of that. I pray you, in your letters,
When you shall these unlucky deeds relate,
Speak of me as I am. Nothing extenuate,
Nor set down aught in malice. Then must you speak
Of one that loved not wisely, but too well;   340
Of one not easily jealous, but, being wrought,
Perplexed in the extreme; of one whose hand,
Like the base Judean°, threw a pearl away
Richer than all his tribe; of one whose subdued eyes,
Albeit unusèd to the melting mood,   345
Drops tears as fast as the Arabian trees
Their med'cinable gum. Set you down this.
And say besides that in Aleppo once,
Where a malignant and a turbaned Turk
Beat a Venetian and traduced the state,   350
I took by th' throat the circumcisèd dog
And smote him—thus.   *[He stabs himself.]*

343 *Judean:* (most editors use the Q¹ reading, "Indian," here, but F is clear: both readings point toward
the infidel, the unbeliever.)

Lodovico: O bloody period!°
Gratiano: All that is spoke is marred.
Othello: I kissed thee ere I killed thee. No way but this,
     Killing myself, to die upon a kiss. *[He falls over Desdemona and dies.]*   355
Cassio: This did I fear, but thought he had no weapon;
     For he was great of heart.
Lodovico [To Iago]:   O Spartan dog,
     More fell° than anguish, hunger, or the sea!
     Look on the tragic loading of this bed.
     This is thy work. The object poisons sight;   360
     Let it be hid.   *[Bed curtains drawn.]*
            Gratiano, keep° the house,
     And seize upon the fortunes of the Moor,
     For they succeed on you. To you, lord governor,
     Remains the censure of this hellish villain,
     The time, the place, the torture. O, enforce it!   365
     Myself will straight aboard, and to the state
     This heavy act with heavy heart relate.   *Exeunt.*

QUESTIONS

ACT I

1. What is Othello's position in society? How is he regarded by those who know him? By his own words, when we first meet him in Scene II, what traits of character does he manifest?
2. How do you account for Brabantio's dismay on learning of his daughter's marriage, despite the fact that Desdemona has married a man so generally honored and admired?
3. What is Iago's view of human nature? In his fondness for likening men to animals (as in I, i, 44–45; I, i, 85–86; and I, iii, 374–375), what does he tell us about himself?
4. What reasons does Iago give for his hatred of Othello?
5. In Othello's defense before the senators (Scene III), how does he explain Desdemona's gradual falling in love with him?
6. Is Brabantio's warning to Othello (I, iii, 286–287) an accurate or an inaccurate prophecy?
7. By what strategy does Iago enlist Roderigo in his plot against the Moor? In what lines do we learn Iago's true feelings toward Roderigo?

ACT II

1. What do the Cypriots think of Othello? Do their words (in Scene I) make him seem to us a lesser man, or a larger one?
2. What cruelty does Iago display toward Emilia? How well founded is his distrust of his wife's fidelity?
3. In II, iii, 227, Othello speaks of Iago's "honesty and love." How do you account for Othello's being so totally deceived?
4. For what major events does the merrymaking (proclaimed in Scene II) give opportunity?

353 *period:* end.   358 *fell:* cruel.   361 *keep:* remain in.

ACT III

1. Trace the steps by which Iago rouses Othello to suspicion. Is there anything in Othello's character or circumstances that renders him particularly susceptible to Iago's wiles?
2. In III, iv, 48–98, Emilia knows of Desdemona's distress over the lost handkerchief. At this moment, how do you explain her failure to relieve Desdemona's mind? Is Emilia aware of her husband's villainy?

ACT IV

1. In this act, what circumstantial evidence is added to Othello's case against Desdemona?
2. How plausible do you find Bianca's flinging the handkerchief at Cassio just when Othello is looking on? How important is the handkerchief in this play? What does it represent? What suggestions or hints do you find in it?
3. What prevents Othello from being moved by Desdemona's appeal (IV, ii, 33–87)?
4. When Roderigo grows impatient with Iago (IV, ii, 171–196), how does Iago make use of his fellow plotter's discontent?
5. What does the conversation between Emilia and Desdemona (Scene III) tell us about the nature of each?
6. In this act, what scenes (or speeches) contain memorable dramatic irony?

ACT V

1. Summarize the events that lead to Iago's unmasking.
2. How does Othello's mistaken belief that Cassio is slain (V, i, 27–33) affect the outcome of the play?
3. What is Iago's motive in stabbing Roderigo?
4. In your interpretation of the play, exactly what impels Othello to kill Desdemona? Jealousy? Desire for revenge? Excess idealism? A wish to be a public avenger who punishes, "else she'll betray more men"?
5. What do you understand by Othello's calling himself "one that loved not wisely but too well" (V, ii, 340)?
6. In your view, does Othello's long speech in V, ii, 334–352 succeed in restoring his original dignity and nobility? Do you agree with Cassio (V, ii, 357) that Othello was "great of heart"?

GENERAL QUESTIONS

1. What motivates Iago to carry out his schemes? Do you find him a devil incarnate, a madman, or a rational human being?
2. Whom besides Othello does Iago deceive? What is Desdemona's opinion of him? Emilia's? Cassio's (before Iago is found out)? To what do you attribute Iago's success as a deceiver?
3. How essential to the play is the fact that Othello is a black man, a Moor, and not a native of Venice?
4. In the introduction to his edition of the play in *The Complete Signet Classic Shakespeare*, Alvin Kernan remarks:

   Othello is probably the most neatly, the most formally constructed of Shakespeare's plays. Every character is, for example, balanced by another similar or contrasting character. Desdemona is balanced by her opposite, Iago; love and concern for others at one end of the scale, hatred and concern for self at the other.

   Besides Desdemona and Iago, what other pairs of characters strike balances?
5. Consider any passage of the play in which there is a shift from verse to prose, or from prose to verse. What is the effect of this shift?

6. Indicate a passage that you consider memorable for its poetry. Does the passage seem introduced for its own sake? Does it in any way advance the action of the play, express theme, or demonstrate character?
7. Does the play contain any tragic *recognition*—as discussed on page 1041, a moment of terrible enlightenment, a "realization of the unthinkable"?
8. Does the downfall of Othello proceed from any flaw in his nature, or is his downfall entirely the work of Iago?

SUGGESTIONS FOR WRITING

1. Write a defense of Iago.
2. "Never was any play fraught, like this of Othello, with improbabilities," wrote Thomas Rymer in a famous attack (*A Short View of Tragedy*, 1692). Consider Rymer's objections to the play (see page 1441), either answering them or finding evidence to back up Rymer.
3. Suppose yourself a casting director assigned to a film version of *Othello*. What well-known stars would you cast in the principal roles? Write a report justifying your choices. Don't merely discuss the stars and their qualifications; discuss (with specific reference to the play) what Shakespeare appears to call for.
4. Emilia's long speech at the end of Act IV (iii, 84–101) has been called a Renaissance plea for women's liberation. Do you agree? Write a brief close analysis of this speech. How timely is it?
5. "The downfall of Oedipus is the work of the gods; the downfall of Othello is self-inflicted." Test this comment with reference to the two plays, and report your findings.

35 The Modern Theater

As the twentieth century began, realism in the theaters of Western Europe, England, and America appeared to have won a resounding victory. (**Realism** in drama, like realism in fiction, may be broadly defined as an attempt to reproduce faithfully the surface appearance of life, especially that of ordinary people in everyday situations.) The theater had been slow to admit controversial or unpleasant themes, and slow to shed its traditional conventions. From Italian playhouses of the sixteenth century, it had inherited the **picture-frame stage:** one that holds the action within a **proscenium arch,** a gateway standing (as the word *proscenium* indicates) "in front of the scenery." This manner of constructing a playhouse in effect divided the actors from their audience; most commercial theaters even today are so constructed. But as the new century began, actors less often declaimed their passions in oratorical style in front of backdrops painted with waterfalls and volcanoes, while stationed exactly at the center of the stage as if to sing "duets meant to bring forth applause" (as Swedish playwright August Strindberg complained). By 1891 even Victorian London had witnessed a production of a play that frankly portrayed a man dying of venereal disease—Henrik Ibsen's *Ghosts.*

In the theater of realism, a room was represented by a **box set**—three walls that joined in two corners and a ceiling that tilted as if seen in perspective—replacing drapery walls that had billowed and doors that had flapped, not slammed. Instead of posing at stage-center to deliver key speeches, actors were instructed to speak from wherever the dramatic situation placed them, and now and then turn their backs upon the audience. They were to behave as if they lived in a room with the fourth wall sliced away, unaware that they had an audience.

This realistic convention is familiar to us today, not only from realistic plays but from the typical television soap opera or situation comedy that takes place in such a three-walled room, with every cup and spoon revealed by the camera. But such realism went against a long tradition. Watching a play by Sophocles, the spectators, we may safely assume, had to exert their imagination. We do not expect an ancient Greek tragedy literally to represent the lives of ordinary people in everyday situations. On the contrary a tragedy, according to Aristotle, its leading ancient theorist, represents an "action of supreme importance," an extraordinary moment in the life of a king or queen or other person of high estate. An open-air stage, though Sophocles adorned it with painted scenery, could hardly change day into night as lighting technicians commonly do today, nor aspire to reproduce in detail a whole palace. Such limitations prevail upon the theater of Shakespeare as well, encouraging the Bard to flesh out his scene with vivid language, making the spectator willing to imagine that the simple stage—the "wooden O"—is a forest, a stormswept landscape, or a battlefield. In the classic No theater of Japan, spectators recognize conventional props: a simple framework is a boat, four posts and a roof are a palace, an actor's fan may be any useful object—a paintbrush, say, or a knife. In such a nonrealistic theater, the playwright, unhampered by stage sets, can shift scenes as rapidly as the audience can imagine.

In the realistic three-walled room, actors could hardly rant (or, Hamlet said, "tear a passion to tatters") without seeming foolish. Another effect of more lifelike direction was to discourage use of such devices as the soliloquy and the **aside** (villain to audience: "Heh! heh! Now she's in me power!"). To encourage actors even further in imitating reality, the influential director Constantin Stanislavsky of the Moscow Art Theater developed his famous system to help actors feel at home inside a playwright's characters. One of Stanislavsky's exercises was to have actors search their memories for personal experiences like those of the characters in the play; another was to have the actors act out things a character did *not* do in the play but might do in life. The system enabled Stanislavsky to bring authenticity to his productions of Chekhov's plays and of Maxim Gorky's *The Lower Depths* (1902), a play that showed the tenants in a sordid lodging house drinking themselves to death (and hanging themselves) in surroundings of realistic squalor.

Gorky's play is a masterpiece of **naturalism,** a kind of realism in fiction and drama dealing with the more brutal or unpleasant aspects of reality. As codified by French novelist and playwright Émile Zola, who influenced Ibsen, naturalism viewed a person as a creature whose acts are determined by heredity and environment; and Zola urged writers to study their characters' behavior with the detachment of zoologists studying animals.

No sooner had realism and naturalism won the day than a reaction arose. One opposing force was the **Symbolist movement** in the French theater, most influentially expressed by Belgian playwright Maurice Maeterlinck. Like French Symbolist poets Charles Baudelaire and Stéphane Mallarmé, Maeterlinck assumes that the visible world reflects a spirit world we cannot directly perceive. Accordingly, his plays are filled with hints and portents: suggestive objects (jeweled rings, veils, distant candles), mysterious locales (crumbling castles, dim grottoes), vague sounds from afar, dialogue rich in silences and unfinished sentences. In *The Intruder,* (1890), a blind man sees the approach of Death. In *Pelléas and Mélisande* (1892) occurs a typical bit of Symbolist stage business: a small boy stands on his grandfather's shoulders to peer through a high window and speak of wonders invisible to an audience. (For more about symbolism and Symbolists, see Chapters Seven and Twenty-four.)

Elsewhere, others were working along similar lines. In Russia, Anton Chekhov, whose plays on the surface appeared realistic, built some of his best around a symbol (*The Seagull, The Cherry Orchard*). In Ireland, poet William Butler Yeats, who in 1899 had helped found the Irish Dramatic Movement, was himself of a different mind from the realistic playwrights whose work he had helped produce in Dublin's Abbey Theater. Drawing on Irish lore and legend, Yeats wrote (among other plays) "plays for dancers" to be performed in drawing rooms, often in friends' homes, with simple costumes and props, a few masked actors, and a very few musicians. In Sweden, August Strindberg, who earlier had won fame as a naturalist, reversed direction and in *The Dream Play* (1902) and *The Ghost Sonata* (1907) introduced characters who change their identities and, ignoring space and time, move across dreamlike landscapes. In these plays Strindberg anticipated the movement called **expressionism** in German theater after World War I. Delighting in bizarre sets and exaggerated makeup and costuming, expressionist playwrights and producers sought to reflect intense states of emotion and, sometimes, to depict the world through lunatic eyes. A classic example (on film) is *The Cabinet of Dr. Caligari*, made in Berlin in 1919–1920, in which a hypnotist sends forth a subject to murder people. Garbed in jet black, the killer sleepwalks through a town of lopsided houses, twisted streets, and railings that tilt at gravity-defying angles. In expressionist movies and plays, madness is objectified and dreams become realities.

In 1893 Strindberg had complained of producers who represented a kitchen by a drapery painted with pictures of kettles; but by 1900, realistic play production had gone to opposite extremes. In the 1920s the curtain rose upon a Broadway play with a detailed replica of a Schrafft's restaurant, complete to the last fork and folded napkin. (Still, critic George Jean Nathan remarked, no matter how elaborate a stage dinner, the table never seemed to have any butter.) Theaters housed increasingly complicated machines, making it all the easier to present scenes full of realistic detail. Elevators lifted heavy sets swiftly and quietly into place; other sets, at the touch of a button, revolved on giant turntables. Theaters became warehouses for huge ready-made scenery.

Some playwrights fought domination by the painstakingly realistic set. Bertolt Brecht in Germany and Luigi Pirandello in Italy conceived plays to be performed on bare stages—gas pipes and plaster in full view—to remind spectators that they beheld events in a theater, not in the world. In reaction against the traditional picture-frame stage new kinds of theater were designed, such as the **arena theater** or **theater in the round,** in which the audience sits on all four sides of the performing area; and the **flexible theater,** in which the seats are movable. Such theaters usually are not commercial (most of which maintain their traditional picture-frame stages, built decades ago). Rather, the alternative theaters are found in college and civic playhouses, in large cities, in storefronts, and in converted lofts. Proponents of arena staging claim that it brings actors and audience into greater intimacy; opponents, that it keeps the actors artificially circulating like goldfish in a bowl. Perhaps it is safe to say only that some plays lend themselves to being seen head-on in a picture frame; others, to being surrounded.

Henrik Ibsen

A DOLL HOUSE   1879

Translated by Rolf Fjelde

Henrik Ibsen

Henrik Ibsen (1828–1906) was born in Skien, a seaport in Norway. When he was six, his father's business losses suddenly reduced his wealthy family to poverty. After a brief attempt to study medicine, young Ibsen worked as a stage manager in provincial Bergen; then, becoming known as a playwright, moved to Oslo as artistic director of the National Theater — practical experiences that gained him firm grounding in his craft. Discouraged when his theater failed and the king turned down his plea for a grant to enable him to write, Ibsen left Norway and for twenty-seven years lived in Italy and Germany. There, in his middle years (1879–91), he wrote most of his famed plays about small-town life, among them A Doll House, Ghosts, An Enemy of the People, The Wild Duck, *and* Hedda Gabler. *Introducing social problems to the stage, these plays aroused storms of controversy. Although best known as a realist, Ibsen early in his career wrote poetic dramas based on Norwegian history and folklore: the tragedy* Brand *(1866) and the powerful, wildly fantastic* Peer Gynt *(1867). He ended as a symbolist in* John Gabriel Borkman *(1896) and* When We Dead Awaken *(1899), both encompassing huge mountains that heaven-assaulting heroes try to climb. Late in life Ibsen returned to Oslo, honored at last both at home and abroad.*

Characters

Torvald Helmer, a lawyer
Nora, his wife
Dr. Rank
Mrs. Linde
Nils Krogstad, a bank clerk
The Helmers' three small children
Anne-Marie, their nurse
Helene, a maid
A Delivery Boy

The action takes place in Helmer's residence.

ACT I

A comfortable room, tastefully but not expensively furnished. A door to the right in the back wall leads to the entryway; another to the left leads to Helmer's study. Between these doors, a piano. Midway in the left-hand wall a door, and farther back a window. Near the window a round table with an armchair and a small sofa. In the right-hand wall, toward the rear, a door, and nearer the foreground a porcelain stove with two armchairs and a rocking chair beside it. Between the stove and the side door, a small table. Engravings on the walls. An étagère with china figures and other small art objects; a small bookcase with richly bound books; the floor carpeted; a fire burning in the stove. It is a winter day.

A bell rings in the entryway; shortly after we hear the door being unlocked. Nora comes into the room, humming happily to herself; she is wearing street clothes and carries an armload of packages, which she puts down on the table to the right. She has left the hall door open and through it a Delivery Boy is seen, holding a Christmas tree and a basket, which he gives to the Maid who let them in.

Nora: Hide the tree well, Helene. The children mustn't get a glimpse of it till this evening, after it's trimmed. (*To the Delivery Boy, taking out her purse.*) How much?

Delivery Boy: Fifty, ma'am.

Nora: There's a crown. No, keep the change. (*The Boy thanks her and leaves. Nora shuts the door. She laughs softly to herself while taking off her street things. Drawing a bag of macaroons from her pocket, she eats a couple, then steals over and listens at her husband's study door.*) Yes, he's home. (*Hums again as she moves to the table right.*)

Helmer (from the study): Is that my little lark twittering out there?

Nora (busy opening some packages): Yes, it is.

Helmer: Is that my squirrel rummaging around?

Nora: Yes!

Helmer: When did my squirrel get in?

Nora: Just now (*Putting the macaroon bag in her pocket and wiping her mouth.*) Do come in, Torvald, and see what I've bought.

Helmer: Can't be disturbed. (*After a moment he opens the door and peers in, pen in hand.*) Bought, you say? All that there? Has the little spendthrift been out throwing money around again?

Nora: Oh, but Torvald, this year we really should let ourselves go a bit. It's the first Christmas we haven't had to economize.

Helmer: But you know we can't go squandering.

Nora: Oh yes, Torvald, we can squander a little now. Can't we? Just a tiny, wee bit. Now that you've got a big salary and are going to make piles and piles of money.

Helmer: Yes—starting New Year's. But then it's a full three months till the raise comes through.

Nora: Pooh! We can borrow that long.

Helmer: Nora! *(Goes over and playfully takes her by the ear.)* Are your scatterbrains off again? What if today I borrowed a thousand crowns, and you squandered them over Christmas week, and then on New Year's Eve a roof tile fell on my head, and I lay there—

Nora (putting her hand on his mouth): Oh! Don't say such things!

Helmer: Yes, but what if it happened—then what?

Nora: If anything so awful happened, then it just wouldn't matter if I had debts or not.

Helmer: Well, but the people I'd borrowed from?

Nora: Them? Who cares about them? They're strangers.

Helmer: Nora, Nora, how like a woman! No, but seriously, Nora, you know what I think about that. No debts! Never borrow! Something of freedom's lost— and something of beauty, too—from a home that's founded on borrowing and debt. We've made a brave stand up to now, the two of us; and we'll go right on like that the little while we have to.

Nora (going toward the stove): Yes, whatever you say, Torvald.

Helmer (following her): Now, now, the little lark's wings mustn't droop. Come on, don't be a sulky squirrel. *(Taking out his wallet.)* Nora, guess what I have here.

Nora (turning quickly): Money!

Helmer: There, see. *(Hands her some notes.)* Good grief, I know how costs go up in a house at Christmastime.

Nora: Ten—twenty—thirty—forty. Oh, thank you, Torvald; I can manage no end on this.

Helmer: You really will have to.

Nora: Oh yes, I promise I will! But come here so I can show you everything I bought. And so cheap! Look, new clothes for Ivar here—and a sword. Here a horse and a trumpet for Bob. And a doll and a doll's bed here for Emmy; they're nothing much, but she'll tear them to bits in no time anyway. And here I have dress material and handkerchiefs for the maids. Old Anne-Marie really deserves something more.

Helmer: And what's in that package there?

Nora (with a cry): Torvald, no! You can't see that till tonight!

Helmer: I see. But tell me now, you little prodigal, what have you thought of for yourself?

Nora: For myself? Oh, I don't want anything at all.

Helmer: Of course you do. Tell me just what—within reason—you'd most like to have.

Nora: I honestly don't know. Oh, listen, Torvald—

Helmer: Well?

Nora (fumbling at his coat buttons, without looking at him): If you want to give me something, then maybe you could—you could—

Helmer: Come on, out with it.

Nora (hurriedly): You could give me money, Torvald. No more than you think you can spare; then one of these days I'll buy something with it.

Helmer: But Nora—

Nora: Oh, please, Torvald darling, do that! I beg you, please. Then I could hang the bills in pretty gilt paper on the Christmas tree. Wouldn't that be fun?

Helmer: What are those little birds called that always fly through their fortunes?

Nora: Oh yes, spendthrifts; I know all that. But let's do as I say, Torvald; then I'll have time to decide what I really need most. That's very sensible, isn't it?

Helmer (smiling): Yes, very—that is, if you actually hung onto the money I give you, and you actually used it to buy yourself something. But it goes for the house and for all sorts of foolish things, and then I only have to lay out some more.

Nora: Oh, but Torvald—

Helmer: Don't deny it, my dear little Nora. *(Putting his arm around her waist.)* Spendthrifts are sweet, but they use up a frightful amount of money. It's incredible what it costs a man to feed such birds.

Nora: Oh, how can you say that! Really, I save everything I can.

Helmer (laughing): Yes, that's the truth. Everything you can. But that's nothing at all.

Nora (humming, with a smile of quiet satisfaction): Hm, if you only knew what expenses we larks and squirrels have, Torvald.

Helmer: You're an odd little one. Exactly the way your father was. You're never at a loss for scaring up money; but the moment you have it, it runs right out through your fingers; you never know what you've done with it. Well, one takes you as you are. It's deep in your blood. Yes, these things are hereditary, Nora.

Nora: Ah, I could wish I'd inherited many of Papa's qualities.

Helmer: And I couldn't wish you anything but just what you are, my sweet little lark. But wait; it seems to me you have a very—what should I call it?—a very suspicious look today—

Nora: I do?

Helmer: You certainly do. Look me straight in the eye.

Nora (looking at him): Well?

Helmer (shaking an admonitory finger): Surely my sweet tooth hasn't been running riot in town today, has she?

Nora: No. Why do you imagine that?

Helmer: My sweet tooth really didn't make a little detour through the confectioner's?

Nora: No, I assure you, Torvald—

Helmer: Hasn't nibbled some pastry?

Nora: No, not at all.

Helmer: Nor even munched a macaroon or two?

Nora: No, Torvald, I assure you, really—

Helmer: There, there now. Of course I'm only joking.

Nora (going to the table, right): You know I could never think of going against you.

Helmer: No, I understand that; and you *have* given me your word. *(Going over to her.)* Well, you keep your little Christmas secrets to yourself, Nora darling. I expect they'll come to light this evening, when the tree is lit.

Nora: Did you remember to ask Dr. Rank?

Helmer: No. But there's no need for that; it's assumed he'll be dining with us. All the same, I'll ask him when he stops by here this morning. I've ordered some fine wine. Nora, you can't imagine how I'm looking forward to this evening.

Nora: So am I. And what fun for the children, Torvald!

Helmer: Ah, it's so gratifying to know that one's gotten a safe, secure job, and with a comfortable salary. It's a great satisfaction, isn't it?

Nora: Oh, it's wonderful!

Helmer: Remember last Christmas? Three whole weeks before, you shut yourself in every evening till long after midnight, making flowers for the Christmas tree, and all the other decorations to surprise us. Ugh, that was the dullest time I've ever lived through.

Nora: It wasn't at all dull for me.

Helmer (smiling): But the outcome *was* pretty sorry, Nora.

Nora: Oh, don't tease me with that again. How could I help it that the cat came in and tore everything to shreds.

Helmer: No, poor thing, you certainly couldn't. You wanted so much to please us all, and that's what counts. But it's just as well that the hard times are past.

Nora: Yes, it's really wonderful.

Helmer: Now I don't have to sit here alone, boring myself, and you don't have to tire your precious eyes and your fair little delicate hands—

Nora (clapping her hands): No, is it really true, Torvald, I don't have to? Oh, how wonderfully lovely to hear! *(Taking his arm.)* Now I'll tell you just how I've thought we should plan things. Right after Christmas—*(The doorbell rings.)* Oh, the bell. *(Straightening the room up a bit.)* Somebody would have to come. What a bore!

Helmer: I'm not at home to visitors, don't forget.

Maid (from the hall doorway): Ma'am, a lady to see you—

Nora: All right, let her come in.

Maid (to Helmer): And the doctor's just come too.

Helmer: Did he go right to my study?

Maid: Yes, he did.

Helmer goes into his room. The Maid shows in Mrs. Linde, dressed in traveling clothes, and shuts the door after her.

Mrs. Linde (in a dispirited and somewhat hesitant voice): Hello, Nora.

Nora (uncertain): Hello—

Mrs. Linde: You don't recognize me.

Nora: No, I don't know—but wait, I think—*(Exclaiming.)* What! Kristine! Is it really you?

Mrs. Linde: Yes, it's me.

Nora: Kristine! To think I didn't recognize you. But then, how could I? *(More quietly.)* How you've changed, Kristine!

Mrs. Linde: Yes, no doubt I have. In nine—ten long years.

Nora: Is it so long since we met! Yes, it's all of that. Oh, these last eight years have been a happy time, believe me. And so now you've come to town, too. Made the long trip in the winter. That took courage.

Mrs. Linde: I just got here by ship this morning.

Nora: To enjoy yourself over Christmas, of course. Oh, how lovely! Yes, enjoy ourselves, we'll do that. But take your coat off. You're not still cold? *(Helping her.)* There now, let's get cozy here by the stove. No, the easy chair there! I'll take the rocker here. *(Seizing her hands.)* Yes, now you have your old look again; it was only in that first moment. You're a bit more pale, Kristine—and maybe a bit thinner.

Mrs. Linde: And much, much older, Nora.

Nora: Yes, perhaps a bit older; a tiny, tiny bit; not much at all. *(Stopping short; suddenly serious.)* Oh, but thoughtless me, to sit here, chattering away. Sweet, good Kristine, can you forgive me?

Mrs. Linde: What do you mean, Nora?

Nora (softly): Poor Kristine, you've become a widow.

Mrs. Linde: Yes, three years ago.

Nora: Oh, I knew it, of course; I read it in the papers. Oh, Kristine, you must believe me; I often thought of writing you then, but I kept postponing it, and something always interfered.

Mrs. Linde: Nora dear, I understand completely.

Nora: No, it was awful of me, Kristine. You poor thing, how much you must have gone through. And he left you nothing?

Mrs. Linde: No.

Nora: And no children?

Mrs. Linde: No.

Nora: Nothing at all, then?

Mrs. Linde: Not even a sense of loss to feed on.

Nora (looking incredulously at her): But Kristine, how could that be?

Mrs. Linde (smiling wearily and smoothing her hair): Oh, sometimes it happens, Nora.

Nora: So completely alone. How terribly hard that must be for you. I have three lovely children. You can't see them now; they're out with the maid. But now you must tell me everything—

Mrs. Linde: No, no, no, tell me about yourself.

Nora: No, you begin. Today I don't want to be selfish. I want to think only of you today. But there *is* something I must tell you. Did you hear of the wonderful luck we had recently?

Mrs. Linde: No, what's that?

Nora: My husband's been made manager in the bank, just think!

Mrs. Linde: Your husband? How marvelous!

Nora: Isn't it? Being a lawyer is such an uncertain living, you know, especially if one won't touch any cases that aren't clean and decent. And of course Torvald would never do that, and I'm with him completely there. Oh, we're simply delighted, believe me! He'll join the bank right after New Year's and start getting a huge salary and lots of commissions. From now on we can live quite differently—just as we want. Oh, Kristine, I feel so light and happy! Won't it be lovely to have stacks of money and not a care in the world?

Mrs. Linde: Well, anyway, it would be lovely to have enough for necessities.

Nora: No, not just for necessities, but stacks and stacks of money!

Mrs. Linde (smiling): Nora, Nora, aren't you sensible yet? Back in school you were such a free spender.

Nora (with a quiet laugh): Yes, that's what Torvald still says. *(Shaking her finger.)* But "Nora, Nora" isn't as silly as you all think. Really, we've been in no position for me to go squandering. We've had to work, both of us.

Mrs. Linde: You too?

Nora: Yes, at odd jobs—needlework, crocheting, embroidery, and such—*(casually)* and other things too. You remember that Torvald left the department when we were married? There was no chance of promotion in his office, and of course he needed to earn more money. But that first year he drove himself terribly. He took on all kinds of extra work that kept him going morning and night. It wore him down, and then he fell deathly ill. The doctors said it was essential for him to travel south.

Mrs. Linde: Yes, didn't you spend a whole year in Italy?

Nora: That's right. It wasn't easy to get away, you know. Ivar had just been born. But of course we had to go. Oh, that was a beautiful trip, and it saved Torvald's life. But it cost a frightful sum, Kristine.

Mrs. Linde: I can well imagine.

Nora: Four thousand, eight hundred crowns it cost. That's really a lot of money.

Mrs. Linde: But it's lucky you had it when you needed it.

Nora: Well, as it was, we got it from Papa.

Mrs. Linde: I see. It was just about the time your father died.

Nora: Yes, just about then. And, you know, I couldn't make that trip out to nurse him. I had to stay here, expecting Ivar any moment, and with my poor sick Torvald to care for. Dearest Papa, I never saw him again, Kristine. Oh, that was the worst time I've known in all my marriage.

Mrs. Linde: I know how you loved him. And then you went off to Italy?

Nora: Yes. We had the means now, and the doctors urged us. So we left a month after.

Mrs. Linde: And your husband came back completely cured?

Nora: Sound as a drum!

Mrs. Linde: But—the doctor?

Nora: Who?

Mrs. Linde: I thought the maid said he was a doctor, the man who came in with me.

Nora: Yes, that was Dr. Rank—but he's not making a sick call. He's our closest friend, and he stops by at least once a day. No, Torvald hasn't had a sick moment since, and the children are fit and strong, and I am, too. *(Jumping up and clapping her hands.)* Oh, dear God, Kristine, what a lovely thing to live and be happy! But how disgusting of me—I'm talking of nothing but my own affairs. *(Sits on a stool close by Kristine, arms resting across her knees.)* Oh, don't be angry with me! Tell me, is it really true that you weren't in love with your husband? Why did you marry him, then?

Mrs. Linde: My mother was still alive, but bedridden and helpless—and I had my two younger brothers to look after. In all conscience, I didn't think I could turn him down.

Nora: No, you were right there. But was he rich at the time?

Mrs. Linde: He was very well off, I'd say. But the business was shaky, Nora. When he died, it all fell apart, and nothing was left.

Nora: And then—?

Mrs. Linde: Yes, so I had to scrape up a living with a little shop and a little teaching and whatever else I could find. The last three years have been like one endless workday without a rest for me. Now it's over, Nora. My poor mother doesn't need me, for she's passed on. Nor the boys, either; they're working now and can take care of themselves.

Nora: How free you must feel—

Mrs. Linde: No—only unspeakably empty. Nothing to live for now. (*Standing up anxiously.*) That's why I couldn't take it any longer out in that desolate hole. Maybe here it'll be easier to find something to do and keep my mind occupied. If I could only be lucky enough to get a steady job, some office work—

Nora: Oh, but Kristine, that's so dreadfully tiring, and you already look so tired. It would be much better for you if you could go off to a bathing resort.

Mrs. Linde (*going toward the window*): I have no father to give me travel money, Nora.

Nora (*rising*): Oh, don't be angry with me.

Mrs. Linde (*going to her*): Nora dear, don't you be angry with me. The worst of my kind of situation is all the bitterness that's stored away. No one to work for, and yet you're always having to snap up your opportunities. You have to live; and so you grow selfish. When you told me the happy change in your lot, do you know I was delighted less for your sakes than for mine?

Nora: How so? Oh, I see. You think Torvald could so something for you.

Mrs. Linde: Yes, that's what I thought.

Nora: And he will, Kristine! Just leave it to me; I'll bring it up so delicately—find something attractive to humor him with. Oh, I'm so eager to help you.

Mrs. Linde: How very kind of you, Nora, to be so concerned over me—doubly kind, considering you really know so little of life's burdens yourself.

Nora: I—? I know so little—?

Mrs. Linde (*smiling*): Well my heavens—a little needlework and such—Nora, you're just a child.

Nora (*tossing her head and pacing the floor*): You don't have to act so superior.

Mrs. Linde: Oh?

Nora: You're just like the others. You all think I'm incapable of anything serious—

Mrs. Linde: Come now—

Nora: That I've never had to face the raw world.

Mrs. Linde: Nora dear, you've just been telling me all your troubles.

Nora: Hm! Trivia! (*Quietly.*) I haven't told you the big thing.

Mrs. Linde: Big thing? What do you mean?

Nora: You look down on me so, Kristine, but you shouldn't. You're proud that you worked so long and hard for your mother.

Mrs. Linde: I don't look down on a soul. But it *is* true: I'm proud—and happy, too—to think it was given to me to make my mother's last days almost free of care.

Nora: And you're also proud thinking of what you've done for your brothers.

Mrs. Linde: I feel I've a right to be.

Nora: I agree. But listen to this, Kristine—I've also got something to be proud and happy for.

Mrs. Linde: I don't doubt it. But whatever do you mean?

Nora: Not so loud. What if Torvald heard! He mustn't, not for anything in the world. Nobody must know, Kristine. No one but you.

Mrs. Linde: But what is it, then?

Nora: Come here. (*Drawing her down beside her on the sofa.*) It's true—I've also got something to be proud and happy for. I'm the one who saved Torvald's life.

Mrs. Linde: Saved—? Saved how?

Nora: I told you about the trip to Italy. Torvald never would have lived if he hadn't gone south—

Mrs. Linde: Of course; your father gave you the means—

Nora (smiling): That's what Torvald and all the rest think, but—

Mrs. Linde: But—?

Nora: Papa didn't give us a pin. I was the one who raised the money.

Mrs. Linde: You? That whole amount?

Nora: Four thousand, eight hundred crowns. What do you say to that?

Mrs. Linde: But Nora, how was it possible? Did you win the lottery?

Nora (disdainfully): The lottery? Pooh! No art to that.

Mrs. Linde: But where did you get it from then?

Nora (humming, with a mysterious smile): Hmm, tra-la-la-la.

Mrs. Linde: Because you couldn't have borrowed it.

Nora: No? Why not?

Mrs. Linde: A wife can't borrow without her husband's consent.

Nora (tossing her head): Oh, but a wife with a little business sense, a wife who knows how to manage—

Mrs. Linde: Nora, I simply don't understand—

Nora: You don't have to. Whoever said I *borrowed* the money? I could have gotten it other ways. (*Throwing herself back on the sofa.*) I could have gotten it from some admirer or other. After all, a girl with my ravishing appeal—

Mrs. Linde: You lunatic.

Nora: I'll bet you're eaten up with curiosity, Kristine.

Mrs. Linde: Now listen here, Nora—you haven't done something indiscreet?

Nora (sitting up again): Is it indiscreet to save your husband's life?

Mrs. Linde: I think it's indiscreet that without his knowledge you—

Nora: But that's the point: he mustn't know! My Lord, can't you understand? He mustn't ever know the close call he had. It was to *me* the doctors came to say his life was in danger—that nothing could save him but a stay in the south. Didn't I try strategy then! I began talking about how lovely it would be for me to travel abroad like other young wives; I begged and I cried; I told him please to remember my condition, to be kind and indulge me; and then I dropped a hint that he could easily take out a loan. But at that, Kristine, he nearly exploded. He said I was frivolous, and it was his duty as man of the house not to indulge me in whims and fancies—as I think he called them. Aha, I thought, now you'll just have to be saved—and that's when I saw my chance.

Mrs. Linde: And your father never told Torvald the money wasn't from him?

Nora: No, never. Papa died right about then. I'd considered bringing him into my secret and begging him never to tell. But he was too sick at the time—and then, sadly, it didn't matter.

Mrs. Linde: And you've never confided in your husband since?

Nora: For heaven's sake, no! Are you serious? He's so strict on that subject. Besides—Torvald, with all his masculine pride—how painfully humiliating for him if he ever found out he was in debt to me. That would just ruin our relationship. Our beautiful, happy home would never be the same.

Mrs. Linde: Won't you ever tell him?

Nora (thoughtfully, half smiling): Yes—maybe sometime, years from now, when I'm no longer so attractive. Don't laugh! I only mean when Torvald loves me less than now, when he stops enjoying my dancing and dressing up and reciting for him. Then it might be wise to have something in reserve—*(Breaking off.)* How ridiculous! That'll never happen—Well, Kristine, what do you think of my big secret? I'm capable of something too, hm? You can imagine, of course, how this thing hangs over me. It really hasn't been easy meeting the payments on time. In the business world there's what they call quarterly interest and what they call amortization, and these are always so terribly hard to manage. I've had to skimp a little here and there, wherever I could, because Torvald has to live well. I couldn't let the children go poorly dressed; whatever I got for them, I felt I had to use up completely—the darlings!

Mrs. Linde: Poor Nora, so it had to come out of your own budget, then?

Nora: Yes, of course. But I was the one most responsible, too. Every time Torvald gave me money for new clothes and such, I never used more than half; always bought the simplest, cheapest outfits. It was a godsend that everything looks so well on me that Torvald never noticed. But it did weigh me down at times, Kristine. It *is* such a joy to wear fine things. You understand.

Mrs. Linde: Oh, of course.

Nora: And then I found other ways of making money. Last winter I was lucky enough to get a lot of copying to do. I locked myself in and sat writing every evening till late in the night. Ah, I was tired so often, dead tired. But still it was wonderful fun, sitting and working like that, earning money. It was almost like being a man.

Mrs. Linde: But how much have you paid off this way so far?

Nora: That's hard to say, exactly. These accounts, you know, aren't easy to figure. I only know that I've paid out all I could scrape together. Time and again I haven't known where to turn. *(Smiling.)* Then I'd sit here dreaming of a rich old gentleman who had fallen in love with me—

Mrs. Linde: What! Who is he?

Nora: Oh, really! And that he'd died, and when his will was opened, there in big letters it said, "All my fortune shall be paid over in cash, immediately, to that enchanting Mrs. Nora Helmer."

Mrs. Linde: But Nora dear—who *was* this gentleman?

Nora: Good grief, can't you understand? The old man never existed; that was only something I'd dream up time and again whenever I was at my wits' end for money. But it makes no difference now; the old fossil can go where he pleases for all I care; I don't need him or his will—because now I'm free. (*Jumping up.*) Oh, how lovely to think of that, Kristine! Carefree! To know you're carefree, utterly carefree; to be able to romp and play with the children, and to keep up a beautiful, charming home—everything just the way Torvald likes it! And think, spring is coming, with big blue skies. Maybe we can travel a little then. Maybe I'll see the ocean again. Oh yes, it *is* so marvelous to live and be happy!

The front doorbell rings.

Mrs. Linde (rising): There's the bell. It's probably best that I go.

Nora: No, stay. No one's expected. It must be for Torvald.

Maid (from the hall doorway): Excuse me, ma'am—there's a gentleman here to see Mr. Helmer, but I didn't know—since the doctor's with him—

Nora: Who is the gentleman?

Krogstad (from the doorway): It's me, Mrs. Helmer.

Mrs. Linde starts and turns away toward the window.

Nora (stepping toward him, tense, her voice a whisper): You? What is it? Why do you want to speak to my husband?

Krogstad: Bank business—after a fashion. I have a small job in the investment bank, and I hear now your husband is going to be our chief—

Nora: In other words, it's—

Krogstad: Just dry business, Mrs. Helmer. Nothing but that.

Nora: Yes, then please be good enough to step into the study. (*She nods indifferently as she sees him out by the hall door, then returns and begins stirring up the stove.*)

Mrs. Linde: Nora—who was that man?

Nora: That was a Mr. Krogstad—a lawyer.

Mrs. Linde: Then it really was him.

Nora: Do you know that person?

Mrs. Linde: I did once—many years ago. For a time he was a law clerk in our town.

Nora: Yes, he's been that.

Mrs. Linde: How he's changed.

Nora: I understand he had a very unhappy marriage.

Mrs. Linde: He's a widower now.

Nora: With a number of children. There now, it's burning. (*She closes the stove door and moves the rocker a bit to one side.*)

Mrs. Linde: They say he has a hand in all kinds of business.

Nora: Oh? That may be true: I wouldn't know. But let's not think about business. It's so dull.

Dr. Rank enters from Helmer's study.

Rank (still in the doorway): No, no, really—I don't want to intrude, I'd just as soon talk a little while with your wife. (*Shuts the door, then notices Mrs. Linde.*) Oh, beg pardon. I'm intruding here, too.

Nora: No, not at all. *(Introducing him.)* Dr. Rank, Mrs. Linde.

Rank: Well now, that's a name much heard in this house. I believe I passed the lady on the stairs as I came.

Mrs. Linde: Yes, I take the stairs very slowly. They're rather hard on me.

Rank: Uh-hm, some touch of internal weakness?

Mrs. Linde: More overexertion, I'd say.

Rank: Nothing else? Then you're probably here in town to rest up in a round of parties?

Mrs. Linde: I'm here to look for work.

Rank: Is that the best cure for overexertion?

Mrs. Linde: One has to live, Doctor.

Rank: Yes, there's a common prejudice to that effect.

Nora: Oh, come on, Dr. Rank—you really do want to live yourself.

Rank: Yes, I really do. Wretched as I am, I'll gladly prolong my torment indefinitely. All my patients feel like that. And it's quite the same, too, with the morally sick. Right at this moment there's one of those moral invalids in there with Helmer—

Mrs. Linde (softly): Ah!

Nora: What do you mean?

Rank: Oh, it's a lawyer, Krogstad, a type you wouldn't know. His character is rotten to the root—but even he began chattering all-importantly about how he had to *live.*

Nora: Oh? What did he want to talk to Torvald about?

Rank: I really don't know. I only heard something about the bank.

Nora: I didn't know that Krog—that this man Krogstad had anything to do with the bank.

Rank: Yes, he's gotten some kind of berth down there. *(To Mrs. Linde.)* I don't know if you also have, in your neck of the woods, a type of person who scuttles about breathlessly, sniffing out hints of moral corruption, and then maneuvers his victim into some sort of key position where he can keep an eye on him. It's the healthy these days that are out in the cold.

Mrs. Linde: All the same, it's the sick who most need to be taken in.

Rank (with a shrug): Yes, there we have it. That's the concept that's turning society into a sanatorium.

Nora, lost in her thoughts, breaks out into quiet laughter and claps her hands.

Rank: Why do you laugh at that? Do you have any real idea of what society is?

Nora: What do I care about dreary old society? I was laughing at something quite different—something terribly funny. Tell me, Doctor—is everyone who works in the bank dependent now on Torvald?

Rank: Is that what you find so terribly funny?

Nora (smiling and humming): Never mind, never mind! *(Pacing the floor.)* Yes, that's really immensely amusing: that we—that Torvald has so much power now over all those people. *(Taking the bag out of her pocket.)* Dr. Rank, a little macaroon on that?

Rank: See here, macaroons! I thought they were contraband here.

Nora: Yes, but these are some that Kristine gave me.

Mrs. Linde: What? I—?

Nora: Now, now, don't be afraid. You couldn't possibly know that Torvald had forbidden them. You see, he's worried they'll ruin my teeth. But hmp! Just this once! Isn't that so, Dr. Rank? Help yourself! *(Puts a macaroon in his mouth.)* And you too, Kristine. And I'll also have one, only a little one—or two, at the most. *(Walking about again.)* Now I'm really tremendously happy. Now there's just one last thing in the world that I have an enormous desire to do.

Rank: Well! And what's that?

Nora: It's something I have such a consuming desire to say so Torvald could hear.

Rank: And why can't you say it?

Nora: I don't dare. It's quite shocking.

Mrs. Linde: Shocking?

Rank: Well, then it isn't advisable. But in front of us you certainly can. What do you have such a desire to say so Torvald could hear?

Nora: I have such a huge desire to say—to hell and be damned!

Rank: Are you crazy?

Mrs. Linde: My goodness, Nora!

Rank: Go on, say it. Here he is.

Nora (hiding the macaroon bag): Shh, shh, shh!

Helmer comes in from his study, hat in hand, overcoat over his arm.

Nora (going toward him): Well, Torvald dear, are you through with him?

Helmer: Yes, he just left.

Nora: Let me introduce you—this is Kristine, who's arrived here in town.

Helmer: Kristine—? I'm sorry, but I don't know—

Nora: Mrs. Linde, Torvald dear. Mrs. Kristine Linde.

Helmer: Of course. A childhood friend of my wife's, no doubt?

Mrs. Linde: Yes, we knew each other in those days.

Nora: And just think, she made the long trip down here in order to talk with you.

Helmer: What's this?

Mrs. Linde: Well, not exactly—

Nora: You see, Kristine is remarkably clever in office work, and so she's terribly eager to come under a capable man's supervision and add more to what she already knows—

Helmer: Very wise, Mrs. Linde.

Nora: And then when she heard that you'd become a bank manager—the story was wired out to the papers—then she came in as fast as she could and— Really, Torvald, for my sake you can do a little something for Kristine, can't you?

Helmer: Yes, it's not at all impossible. Mrs. Linde, I suppose you're a widow?

Mrs. Linde: Yes.

Helmer: Any experience in office work?

Mrs. Linde: Yes, a good deal.

Helmer: Well, it's quite likely that I can make an opening for you—

Nora (clapping her hands): You see, you see!

Helmer: You've come at a lucky moment, Mrs. Linde.

Mrs. Linde: Oh, how can I thank you?

Helmer: Not necessary. (*Putting his overcoat on.*) But today you'll have to excuse me—

Rank: Wait, I'll go with you. (*He fetches his coat from the hall and warms it at the stove.*)

Nora: Don't stay out long, dear.

Helmer: An hour; no more.

Nora: Are you going too, Kristine?

Mrs. Linde (putting on her winter garments): Yes, I have to see about a room now.

Helmer: Then perhaps we can all walk together.

Nora (helping her): What a shame we're so cramped here, but it's quite impossible for us to—

Mrs. Linde: Oh, don't even think of it! Good-bye, Nora dear, and thanks for everything.

Nora: Good-bye for now. Of course you'll be back this evening. And you too, Dr. Rank. What? If you're well enough? Oh, you've got to be! Wrap up tight now.

In a ripple of small talk the company moves out into the hall; children's voices are heard outside on the steps.

Nora: There they are! There they are! (*She runs to open the door. The children come in with their nurse, Anne-Marie.*) Come in, come in! (*Bends down and kisses them.*) Oh, you darlings—! Look at them, Kristine. Aren't they lovely!

Rank: No loitering in the draft here.

Helmer: Come, Mrs. Linde—this place is unbearable now for anyone but mothers.

Dr. Rank, Helmer, and Mrs. Linde go down the stairs. Anne-Marie goes into the living room with the children. Nora follows, after closing the hall door.

Nora: How fresh and strong you look. Oh, such red cheeks you have! Like apples and roses. (*The children interrupt her throughout the following.*) And it was so much fun? That's wonderful. Really? You pulled both Emmy and Bob on the sled? Imagine, all together! Yes, you're a clever boy, Ivar. Oh, let me hold her a bit, Anne-Marie. My sweet little doll baby! (*Takes the smallest from the nurse and dances with her.*) Yes, yes, Mama will dance with Bob as well. What? Did you throw snowballs? Oh, if I'd only been there! No, don't bother, Anne-Marie—I'll undress them myself. Oh yes, let me. It's such fun. Go in and rest; you look half frozen. There's hot coffee waiting for you on the stove. (*The nurse goes into the room to the left. Nora takes the children's winter things off, throwing them about, while the children talk to her all at once.*) Is that so? A big dog chased you? But it didn't bite? No, dogs never bite little, lovely doll babies. Don't peek in the packages, Ivar! What is it? Yes, wouldn't you like to know. No, no, it's an ugly something. Well? Shall we play? What shall we play? Hide-and-seek? Yes, let's play hide-and-seek. Bob must hide first. I must? Yes, let me hide first. (*Laughing and shouting, she and the children play in and out of the living room and the adjoining room to the right. At last Nora hides under the table. The children come storming in, search, but cannot find her, then hear her muffled laughter, dash over to the table, lift the cloth up and find her. Wild shouting. She creeps forward as if to scare them. More shouts. Meanwhile, a knock at the hall door; no one has noticed it. Now the door half opens, and Krogstad appears. He waits a moment; the game goes on.)*

Krogstad: Beg pardon, Mrs. Helmer—

Nora (with a strangled cry, turning and scrambling to her knees): Oh! What do you want?

Krogstad: Excuse me. The outer door was ajar; it must be someone forgot to shut it—

Nora (rising): My husband isn't home, Mr. Krogstad.

Krogstad: I know that.

Nora: Yes—then what do you want here?

Krogstad: A word with you.

Nora: With—? *(To the children, quietly.)* Go in to Anne-Marie. What? No, the strange man won't hurt Mama. When he's gone, we'll play some more. *(She leads the children into the room to the left and shuts the door after them. Then, tense and nervous):* You want to speak to me?

Krogstad: Yes, I want to.

Nora: Today? But it's not yet the first of the month—

Krogstad: No, it's Christmas Eve. It's going to be up to you how merry a Christmas you have.

Nora: What is it you want? Today I absolutely can't—

Krogstad: We won't talk about that till later. This is something else. You do have a moment to spare, I suppose?

Nora: Oh yes, of course—I do, except—

Krogstad: Good. I was sitting over at Olsen's Restaurant when I saw your husband go down the street—

Nora: Yes?

Krogstad: With a lady.

Nora: Yes. So?

Krogstad: If you'll pardon my asking: wasn't that lady a Mrs. Linde?

Nora: Yes.

Krogstad: Just now come into town?

Nora: Yes, today.

Krogstad: She's a good friend of yours?

Nora: Yes, she is. But I don't see—

Krogstad: I also knew her once.

Nora: I'm aware of that.

Krogstad: Oh? You know all about it. I thought so. Well, then let me ask you short and sweet: is Mrs. Linde getting a job in the bank?

Nora: What makes you think you can cross-examine me, Mr. Krogstad—you, one of my husband's employees? But since you ask, you might as well know—yes, Mrs. Linde's going to be taken on at the bank. And I'm the one who spoke for her, Mr. Krogstad. Now you know.

Krogstad: So I guessed right.

Nora (pacing up and down): Oh, one does have a tiny bit of influence, I should hope. Just because I am a woman, don't think it means that—When one has a subordinate position, Mr. Krogstad, one really ought to be careful about pushing somebody who—hm—

Krogstad: Who has influence?

Nora: That's right.

Krogstad (in a different tone): Mrs. Helmer, would you be good enough to use your influence on my behalf?

Nora: What? What do you mean?

Krogstad: Would you please make sure that I keep my subordinate position in the bank?

Nora: What does that mean? Who's thinking of taking away your position?

Krogstad: Oh, don't play the innocent with me. I'm quite aware that your friend would hardly relish the chance of running into me again; and I'm also aware now whom I can thank for being turned out.

Nora: But I promise you—

Krogstad: Yes, yes, yes, to the point: there's still time, and I'm advising you to use your influence to prevent it.

Nora: But Mr. Krogstad, I have absolutely no influence.

Krogstad: You haven't? I thought you were just saying—

Nora: You shouldn't take me so literally. I! How can you believe that I have any such influence over my husband?

Krogstad: Oh, I've known your husband from our student days. I don't think the great bank manager's more steadfast than any other married man.

Nora: You speak insolently about my husband, and I'll show you the door.

Krogstad: The lady has spirit.

Nora: I'm not afraid of you any longer. After New Year's, I'll soon be done with the whole business.

Krogstad (restraining himself): Now listen to me, Mrs. Helmer. If necessary, I'll fight for my little job in the bank as if it were life itself.

Nora: Yes, so it seems.

Krogstad: It's not just a matter of income; that's the least of it. It's something else— All right, out with it! Look, this is the thing. You know, just like all the others, of course, that once, a good many years ago, I did something rather rash.

Nora: I've heard rumors to that effect.

Krogstad: The case never got into court; but all the same, every door was closed in my face from then on. So I took up those various activities you know about. I had to grab hold somewhere; and I dare say I haven't been among the worst. But now I want to drop all that. My boys are growing up. For their sakes, I'll have to win back as much respect as possible here in town. That job in the bank was like the first rung in my ladder. And now your husband wants to kick me right back down in the mud again.

Nora: But for heaven's sake, Mr. Krogstad, it's simply not in my power to help you.

Krogstad: That's because you haven't the will to—but I have the means to make you.

Nora: You certainly won't tell my husband that I owe you money?

Krogstad: Hm—what if I told him that?

Nora: That would be shameful of you. *(Nearly in tears.)* This secret—my joy and my pride—that he should learn it in such a crude and disgusting way—learn it from you. You'd expose me to the most horrible unpleasantness—

Krogstad: Only unpleasantness?

Nora (vehemently): But go on and try. It'll turn out the worse for you, because then my husband will really see what a crook you are, and then you'll *never* be able to hold your job.

Krogstad: I asked if it was just domestic unpleasantness you were afraid of?

Nora: If my husband finds out, then of course he'll pay what I owe at once, and then we'd be through with you for good.

Krogstad (a step closer): Listen, Mrs. Helmer—you've either got a very bad memory, or else no head at all for business. I'd better put you a little more in touch with the facts.

Nora: What do you mean?

Krogstad: When your husband was sick, you came to me for a loan of four thousand, eight hundred crowns.

Nora: Where else could I go?

Krogstad: I promised to get you that sum—

Nora: And you got it.

Krogstad: I promised to get you that sum, on certain conditions. You were so involved in your husband's illness, and so eager to finance your trip, that I guess you didn't think out all the details. It might just be a good idea to remind you. I promised you the money on the strength of a note I drew up.

Nora: Yes, and that I signed.

Krogstad: Right. But at the bottom I added some lines for your father to guarantee the loan. He was supposed to sign down there.

Nora: Supposed to? He did sign.

Krogstad: I left the date blank. In other words, your father would have dated his signature himself. Do you remember that?

Nora: Yes, I think—

Krogstad: Then I gave you the note for you to mail to your father. Isn't that so?

Nora: Yes.

Krogstad: And naturally you sent it at once—because only some five, six days later you brought me the note, properly signed. And with that, the money was yours.

Nora: Well, then; I've made my payments regularly, haven't I?

Krogstad: More or less. But—getting back to the point—those were hard times for you then, Mrs. Helmer.

Nora: Yes, they were.

Krogstad: Your father was very ill, I believe.

Nora: He was near the end.

Krogstad: He died soon after?

Nora: Yes.

Krogstad: Tell me, Mrs. Helmer, do you happen to recall the date of your father's death? The day of the month, I mean.

Nora: Papa died the twenty-ninth of September.

Krogstad: That's quite correct; I've already looked into that. And now we come to a curious thing—*(taking out a paper)* which I simply cannot comprehend.

Nora: Curious thing? I don't know—

Krogstad: This is the curious thing: that your father co-signed the note for your loan three days after his death.

Nora: How—? I don't understand.

Krogstad: Your father died the twenty-ninth of September. But look. Here your father dated his signature October second. Isn't that curious, Mrs. Helmer? *(Nora is silent.)* Can you explain it to me? *(Nora remains silent.)* It's also remarkable that the words "October second" and the year aren't written in your father's hand, but rather in one that I think I know. Well, it's easy to understand. Your father forgot perhaps to date his signature, and then someone or other added it, a bit sloppily, before anyone knew of his death. There's nothing wrong in that. It all comes down to the signature. And there's no question about *that*, Mrs. Helmer. It really *was* your father who signed his own name here, wasn't it?

Nora (after a short silence, throwing her head back and looking squarely at him): No, it wasn't. *I* signed Papa's name.

Krogstad: Wait, now—are you fully aware that this is a dangerous confession?

Nora: Why? You'll soon get your money.

Krogstad: Let me ask you a question—why didn't you send the paper to your father?

Nora: That was impossible. Papa was so sick. If I'd asked him for his signature, I also would have had to tell him what the money was for. But I couldn't tell him, sick as he was, that my husband's life was in danger. That was just impossible.

Krogstad: Then it would have been better if you'd given up the trip abroad.

Nora: I couldn't possibly. The trip was to save my husband's life. I couldn't give that up.

Krogstad: But didn't you ever consider that this was a fraud against me?

Nora: I couldn't let myself be bothered by that. You weren't any concern of mine. I couldn't stand you, with all those cold complications you made, even though you knew how badly off my husband was.

Krogstad: Mrs. Helmer, obviously you haven't the vaguest idea of what you've involved yourself in. But I can tell you this: it was nothing more and nothing worse than I once did—and it wrecked my whole reputation.

Nora: You? Do you expect me to believe that you ever acted bravely to save your wife's life?

Krogstad: Laws don't inquire into motives.

Nora: Then they must be very poor laws.

Krogstad: Poor or not—if I introduce this paper in court, you'll be judged according to law.

Nora: This I refuse to believe. A daughter hasn't a right to protect her dying father from anxiety and care? A wife hasn't a right to save her husband's life? I don't know much about laws, but I'm sure that somewhere in the books these things are allowed. And you don't know anything about it—you who practice the law? You must be an awful lawyer, Mr. Krogstad.

Krogstad: Could be. But business—the kind of business we two are mixed up in—don't you think I know about that? All right. Do what you want now. But I'm telling you *this:* if I get shoved down a second time, you're going to keep me company. (*He bows and goes out through the hall.*)

Nora (*pensive for a moment, then tossing her head*): Oh, really! Trying to frighten me! I'm not so silly as all that. (*Begins gathering up the children's clothes, but soon stops.*) But—? No, but that's impossible! I did it out of love.

The Children (*in the doorway, left*): Mama, that strange man's gone out the door.

Nora: Yes, yes, I know it. But don't tell anyone about the strange man. Do you hear? Not even Papa!

The Children: No, Mama. But now will you play again?

Nora: No, not now.

The Children: Oh, but Mama, you promised.

Nora: Yes, but I can't now. Go inside; I have too much to do. Go in, go in, my sweet darlings. (*She herds them gently back in the room and shuts the door after them. Settling on the sofa, she takes up a piece of embroidery and makes some stitches, but soon stops abruptly.*) No! (*Throws the work aside, rises, goes to the hall door and calls out.*) Helene! Let me have the tree in here. (*Goes to the table, left, opens the table drawer, and stops again.*) No, but that's utterly impossible!

Maid (*with the Christmas tree*): Where should I put it, ma'am?

Nora: There. The middle of the floor.

Maid: Should I bring anything else?

Nora: No, thanks. I have what I need.

The Maid, who has set the tree down, goes out.

Nora (*absorbed in trimming the tree*): Candles here—and flowers here. That terrible creature! Talk, talk, talk! There's nothing to it at all. The tree's going to be lovely. I'll do anything to please you, Torvald. I'll sing for you, dance for you—

Helmer comes in from the hall, with a sheaf of papers under his arm.

Nora: Oh! You're back so soon?

Helmer: Yes. Has anyone been here?

Nora: Here? No.

Helmer: That's odd. I saw Krogstad leaving the front door.

Nora: So? Oh yes, that's true. Krogstad was here a moment.

Helmer: Nora, I can see by your face that he's been here, begging you to put in a good word for him.

Nora: Yes.

Helmer: And it was supposed to seem like your own idea? You were to hide it from me that he'd been here. He asked you that, too, didn't he?

Nora: Yes, Torvald, but—

Helmer: Nora, Nora, and you could fall for that? Talk with that sort of person and promise him anything? And then in the bargain, tell me an untruth.

Nora: An untruth—?

Helmer: Didn't you say that no one had been here? (*Wagging his finger.*) My little songbird must never do that again. A songbird needs a clean beak to warble with. No false notes. (*Putting his arm about her waist.*) That's the way it should be, isn't it? Yes, I'm sure of it. (*Releasing her.*) And so, enough of that. (*Sitting by the stove.*) Ah, how snug and cozy it is here. (*Leafing among his papers.*)

Nora (*busy with the tree, after a short pause*): Torvald!

Helmer: Yes.

Nora: I'm so much looking forward to the Stenborgs' costume party, day after tomorrow.

Helmer: And I can't wait to see what you'll surprise me with.

Nora: Oh, that stupid business!

Helmer: What?

Nora: I can't find anything that's right. Everything seems so ridiculous, so inane.

Helmer: So my little Nora's come to *that* recognition?

Nora (*going behind his chair, her arms resting on its back*): Are you very busy, Torvald?

Helmer: Oh—

Nora: What papers are those?

Helmer: Bank matters.

Nora: Already?

Helmer: I've gotten full authority from the retiring management to make all necessary changes in personnel and procedure. I'll need Christmas week for that. I want to have everything in order by New Year's.

Nora: So that was the reason this poor Krogstad—

Helmer: Hm.

Nora (*still leaning on the chair and slowly stroking the nape of his neck*): If you weren't so very busy, I would have asked you an enormous favor, Torvald.

Helmer: Let's hear. What is it?

Nora: You know, there isn't anyone who has your good taste—and I want so much to look well at the costume party. Torvald, couldn't you take over and decide what I should be and plan my costume?

Helmer: Ah, is my stubborn little creature calling for a lifeguard?

Nora: Yes, Torvald, I can't get anywhere without your help.

Helmer: All right—I'll think it over. We'll hit on something.

Nora: Oh, how sweet of you. (*Goes to the tree again. Pause.*) Aren't the red flowers pretty—? But tell me, was it really such a crime that this Krogstad committed?

Helmer: Forgery. Do you have any idea what that means?

Nora: Couldn't he have done it out of need?

Helmer: Yes, or thoughtlessness, like so many others. I'm not so heartless that I'd condemn a man categorically for just one mistake.

Nora: No, of course not, Torvald!

Helmer: Plenty of men have redeemed themselves by openly confessing their crimes and taking their punishment.

Nora: Punishment—?

Helmer: But now Krogstad didn't go that way. He got himself out by sharp practices, and that's the real cause of his moral breakdown.

Nora: Do you really think that would—?

Helmer: Just imagine how a man with that sort of guilt in him has to lie and cheat and deceive on all sides, has to wear a mask even with the nearest and dearest he has, even with his own wife and children. And with the children, Nora— that's where it's most horrible.

Nora: Why?

Helmer: Because that kind of atmosphere of lies infects the whole life of a home. Every breath the children take in is filled with the germs of something degenerate.

Nora (coming closer behind him): Are you sure of that?

Helmer: Oh, I've seen it often enough as a lawyer. Almost everyone who goes bad early in life has a mother who's a chronic liar.

Nora: Why just—the mother?

Helmer: It's usually the mother's influence that's dominant, but the father's works in the same way, of course. Every lawyer is quite familiar with it. And still this Krogstad's been going home year in, year out, poisoning his own children with lies and pretense; that's why I call him morally lost. *(Reaching his hands out toward her.)* So my sweet little Nora must promise me never to plead his cause. Your hand on it. Come, come, what's this? Give me your hand. There, now. All settled. I can tell you it'd be impossible for me to work alongside of him. I literally feel physically revolted when I'm anywhere near such a person.

Nora (withdraws her hand and goes to the other side of the Christmas tree): How hot it is here! And I've got so much to do.

Helmer (getting up and gathering his papers): Yes, and I have to think about getting some of these read through before dinner. I'll think about your costume, too. And something to hang on the tree in gilt paper, I may even see about that. *(Putting his hand on her head.)* Oh you, my darling little songbird. *(He goes into his study and closes the door after him.)*

Nora (softly, after a silence): Oh, really! It isn't so. It's impossible. It must be impossible.

Anne-Marie (in the doorway, left): The children are begging so hard to come in to Mama.

Nora: No, no, no, don't let them in to me! You stay with them, Anne-Marie.

Anne-Marie: Of course, ma'am. *(Closes the door.)*

Nora (pale with terror): Hurt my children—! Poison my home? *(A moment's pause; then she tosses her head.)* That's not true. Never. Never in all the world.

ACT II

Same room. Beside the piano the Christmas tree now stands stripped of ornaments, burned-down candle stubs on its ragged branches. Nora's street clothes lie on the sofa. Nora, alone in the room, moves restlessly about; at last she stops at the sofa and picks up her coat.

Nora (dropping the coat again): Someone's coming! *(Goes toward the door, listens.)* No—there's no one. Of course—nobody's coming today, Christmas Day—or tomorrow, either. But maybe—*(Opens the door and looks out.)* No, nothing in the mailbox. Quite empty. *(Coming forward.)* What nonsense! He won't do anything serious. Nothing terrible could happen. It's impossible. Why, I have three small children.

Anne-Marie, with a large carton, comes in from the room to the left.

Anne-Marie: Well, at last I found the box with the masquerade clothes.

Nora: Thanks. Put it on the table.

Anne-Marie (does so): But they're all pretty much of a mess.

Nora: Ahh! I'd love to rip them in a million pieces!

Anne-Marie: Oh, mercy, they can be fixed right up. Just a little patience.

Nora: Yes, I'll go get Mrs. Linde to help me.

Anne-Marie: Out again now? In this nasty weather? Miss Nora will catch cold—get sick.

Nora: Oh, worse things could happen—How are the children?

Anne-Marie: The poor mites are playing with their Christmas presents, but—

Nora: Do they ask for me much?

Anne-Marie: They're so used to having Mama around, you know.

Nora: But Anne-Marie, I *can't* be together with them as much as I was.

Anne-Marie: Well, small children get used to anything.

Nora: You think so? Do you think they'd forget their mother if she was gone for good?

Anne-Marie: Oh, mercy—gone for good!

Nora: Wait, tell me, Anne-Marie—I've wondered so often—how could you ever have the heart to give your child over to strangers?

Anne-Marie: But I had to, you know, to become little Nora's nurse.

Nora: Yes, but how could you *do* it?

Anne-Marie: When I could get such a good place? A girl who's poor and who's gotten in trouble is glad enough for that. Because that slippery fish, he didn't do a thing for me, you know.

Nora: But your daughter's surely forgotten you.

Anne-Marie: Oh, she certainly has not. She's written to me, both when she was confirmed and when she was married.

Nora (clasping her about the neck): You old Anne-Marie, you were a good mother for me when I was little.

Anne-Marie: Poor little Nora, with no other mother but me.

Nora: And if the babies didn't have one, then I know that you'd—What silly talk! *(Opening the carton.)* Go in to them. Now I'll have to—Tomorrow you can see how lovely I'll look.

Anne-Marie: Oh, there won't be anyone at the party as lovely as Miss Nora. *(She goes off into the room, left.)*

Nora (begins unpacking the box, but soon throws it aside): Oh, if I dared to go out. If only nobody would come. If only nothing would happen here while I'm out. What craziness—nobody's coming. Just don't think. This muff—needs a brushing. Beautiful gloves, beautiful gloves. Let it go. Let it go! One, two, three, four, five, six—*(With a cry.)* Oh, there they are! *(Poises to move toward the door, but remains irresolutely standing. Mrs. Linde enters from the hall, where she has removed her street clothes.)*

Nora: Oh, it's you, Kristine. There's no one else out there? How good that you've come.

Mrs. Linde: I hear you were up asking for me.

Nora: Yes, I just stopped by. There's something you really can help me with. Let's get settled on the sofa. Look, there's going to be a costume party tomorrow evening at the Stenborgs' right above us, and now Torvald wants me to go as a Neapolitan peasant girl and dance the tarantella that I learned in Capri.

Mrs. Linde: Really, are you giving a whole performance?

Nora: Torvald says yes, I should. See, here's the dress. Torvald had it made for me down there; but now it's all so tattered that I just don't know—

Mrs. Linde: Oh, we'll fix that up in no time. It's nothing more than the trimmings—they're a bit loose here and there. Needle and thread? Good, now we have what we need.

Nora: Oh, how sweet of you!

Mrs. Linde (sewing): So you'll be in disguise tomorrow, Nora. You know what? I'll stop by then for a moment and have a look at you all dressed up. But listen, I've absolutely forgotten to thank you for that pleasant evening yesterday.

Nora (getting up and walking about): I don't think it was as pleasant as usual yesterday. You should have come to town a bit sooner, Kristine—Yes, Torvald really knows how to give a home elegance and charm.

Mrs. Linde: And you do, too, if you ask me. You're not your father's daughter for nothing. But tell me, is Dr. Rank always so down in the mouth as yesterday?

Nora: No, that was quite an exception. But he goes around critically ill all the time—tuberculosis of the spine, poor man. You know, his father was a disgusting thing who kept mistresses and so on—and that's why the son's been sickly from birth.

Mrs. Linde (lets her sewing fall to her lap): But my dearest Nora, how do you know about such things?

Nora (walking more jauntily): Hmp! When you've had three children, then you've had a few visits from—from women who know something of medicine, and they tell you this and that.

Mrs. Linde (resumes sewing; a short pause): Does Dr. Rank come here every day?

Nora: Every blessed day. He's Torvald's best friend from childhood, and *my* good friend, too. Dr. Rank almost belongs to this house.

Mrs. Linde: But tell me—is he quite sincere? I mean, doesn't he rather enjoy flattering people?

Nora: Just the opposite. Why do you think that?

Mrs. Linde: When you introduced us yesterday, he was proclaiming that he'd often heard my name in this house; but later I noticed that your husband hadn't the slightest idea who I really was. So how could Dr. Rank—?

Nora: But it's all true, Kristine. You see, Torvald loves me beyond words, and, as he puts it, he'd like to keep me all to himself. For a long time he'd almost be jealous if I even mentioned any of my old friends back home. So of course I dropped that. But with Dr. Rank I talk a lot about such things, because he likes hearing about them.

Mrs. Linde: Now listen, Nora; in many ways you're still like a child. I'm a good deal older than you, with a little more experience. I'll tell you something: you ought to put an end to all this with Dr. Rank.

Nora: What should I put an end to?

Mrs. Linde: Both parts of it, I think. Yesterday you said something about a rich admirer who'd provide you with money—

Nora: Yes, one who doesn't exist—worse luck. So?

Mrs. Linde: Is Dr. Rank well off?

Nora: Yes, he is.

Mrs. Linde: With no dependents?

Nora: No, no one. But—

Mrs. Linde: And he's over here every day?

Nora: Yes, I told you that.

Mrs. Linde: How can a man of such refinement be so grasping?

Nora: I don't follow you at all.

Mrs. Linde: Now don't try to hide it, Nora. You think I can't guess who loaned you the forty-eight hundred crowns?

Nora: Are you out of your mind? How could you think such a thing! A friend of ours, who comes here every single day. What an intolerable situation that would have been!

Mrs. Linde: Then it really wasn't him.

Nora: No, absolutely not. It never even crossed my mind for a moment—And he had nothing to lend in those days; his inheritance came later.

Mrs. Linde: Well, I think that was a stroke of luck for you, Nora dear.

Nora: No, it never would have occurred to me to ask Dr. Rank—Still, I'm quite sure that if I had asked him—

Mrs. Linde: Which you won't, of course.

Nora: No, of course not. I can't see that I'd ever need to. But I'm quite positive that if I talked to Dr. Rank—

Mrs. Linde: Behind your husband's back?

Nora: I've got to clear up this other thing; *that's* also behind his back. I've *got* to clear it all up.

Mrs. Linde: Yes, I was saying that yesterday, but—

Nora (pacing up and down): A man handles these problems so much better than a woman—

Mrs. Linde: One's husband does, yes.

Nora: Nonsense. *(Stopping.)* When you pay everything you owe, then you get your note back, right?

Mrs. Linde: Yes, naturally.

Nora: And can rip it into a million pieces and burn it up—that filthy scrap of paper!

Mrs. Linde (looking hard at her, laying her sewing aside, and rising slowly): Nora, you're hiding something from me.

Nora: You can see it in my face?

Mrs. Linde: Something's happened to you since yesterday morning. Nora, what is it?

Nora (hurrying toward her): Kristine! *(Listening.)* Shh! Torvald's home. Look, go in with the children a while. Torvald can't bear all this snipping and stitching. Let Anne-Marie help you.

Mrs. Linde (gathering up some of the things): All right, but I'm not leaving here until we've talked this out. *(She disappears into the room, left, as Torvald enters from the hall.)*

Nora: Oh, how I've been waiting for you, Torvald dear.

Helmer: Was that the dressmaker?

Nora: No, that was Kristine. She's helping me fix up my costume. You know, it's going to be quite attractive.

Helmer: Yes, wasn't that a bright idea I had?

Nora: Brilliant! But then wasn't I good as well to give in to you?

Helmer: Good—because you give in to your husband's judgment? All right, you little goose, I know you didn't mean it like that. But I won't disturb you. You'll want to have a fitting, I suppose.

Nora: And you'll be working?

Helmer: Yes. *(Indicating a bundle of papers.)* See. I've been down to the bank. *(Starts toward his study.)*

Nora: Torvald.

Helmer (stops): Yes.

Nora: If your little squirrel begged you, with all her heart and soul, for something—?

Helmer: What's that?

Nora: Then would you do it?

Helmer: First, naturally, I'd have to know what it was.

Nora: Your squirrel would scamper about and do tricks, if you'd only be sweet and give in.

Helmer: Out with it.

Nora: Your lark would be singing high and low in every room—

Helmer: Come on, she does that anyway.

Nora: I'd be a wood nymph and dance for you in the moonlight.

Helmer: Nora—don't tell me it's that same business from this morning!

Nora (coming closer): Yes, Torvald, I beg you, please!

Helmer: And you actually have the nerve to drag that up again?

Nora: Yes, yes, you've got to give in to me; you *have* to let Krogstad keep his job in the bank.

Helmer: My dear Nora, I've slated his job for Mrs. Linde.

Nora: That's awfully kind of you. But you could just fire another clerk instead of Krogstad.

Helmer: This is the most incredible stubbornness! Because you go and give an impulsive promise to speak up for him, I'm expected to—

Nora: That's not the reason, Torvald. It's for your own sake. That man does writing for the worst papers; you said it yourself. He could do you any amount of harm. I'm scared to death of him—

Helmer: Ah, I understand. It's the old memories haunting you.

Nora: What do you mean by that?

Helmer: Of course, you're thinking about your father.

Nora: Yes, all right. Just remember how those nasty gossips wrote in the papers about Papa and slandered him so cruelly. I think they'd have had him dismissed if the department hadn't sent you up to investigate, and if you hadn't been so kind and open-minded toward him.

Helmer: My dear Nora, there's a notable difference between your father and me. Your father's official career was hardly above reproach. But mine is; and I hope it'll stay that way as long as I hold my position.

Nora: Oh, who can ever tell what vicious minds can invent? We could be so snug and happy now in our quiet, carefree home—you and I and the children, Torvald! That's why I'm pleading with you so—

Helmer: And just by pleading for him you make it impossible for me to keep him on. It's already known at the bank that I'm firing Krogstad. What if it's rumored around now that the new bank manager was vetoed by his wife—

Nora: Yes, what then—?

Helmer: Oh yes—as long as our little bundle of stubbornness gets her way—! I should go and make myself ridiculous in front of the whole office—give people the idea I can be swayed by all kinds of outside pressure. Oh, you can bet I'd feel the effects of that soon enough! Besides—there's something that rules Krogstad right out at the bank as long as I'm the manager.

Nora: What's that?

Helmer: His moral failings I could maybe overlook if I had to—

Nora: Yes, Torvald, why not?

Helmer: And I hear he's quite efficient on the job. But he was a crony of mine back in my teens—one of those rash friendships that crop up again and again to embarrass you later in life. Well, I might as well say it straight out: we're on a first-name basis. And that tactless fool makes no effort at all to hide it in front of others. Quite the contrary—he thinks that entitles him to take a familiar air around me, and so every other second he comes booming out with his "Yes, Torvald!" and "Sure thing, Torvald!" I tell you, it's been excruciating for me. He's out to make my place in the bank unbearable.

Nora: Torvald, you can't be serious about all this.

Helmer: Oh no? Why not?

Nora: Because these are such petty considerations.

Helmer: What are you saying? Petty? You think I'm petty!

Nora: No, just the opposite, Torvald dear. That's exactly why—

Helmer: Never mind. You call my motives petty; then I might as well be just that. Petty! All right! We'll put a stop to this for good. (*Goes to the hall door and calls.*) Helene!

Nora: What do you want?

Helmer (*searching among his papers*): A decision. (*The Maid comes in.*) Look here; take this letter; go out with it at once. Get hold of a messenger and have him deliver it. Quick now. It's already addressed. Wait, here's some money.

Maid: Yes, sir. (*She leaves with the letter.*)

Helmer (*straightening his papers*): There, now, little Miss Willful.

Nora (*breathlessly*): Torvald, what was that letter?

Helmer: Krogstad's notice.

Nora: Call it back, Torvald! There's still time. Oh, Torvald, call it back! Do it for my sake—for your sake, for the children's sake! Do you hear, Torvald; do it! You don't know how this can harm us.

Helmer: Too late.

Nora: Yes, too late.

Helmer: Nora dear, I can forgive you this panic, even though basically you're insulting me. Yes, you are! Or isn't it an insult to think that *I* should be afraid of a courtroom hack's revenge? But I forgive you anyway, because this shows so beautifully how much you love me. *(Takes her in his arms.)* This is the way it should be, my darling Nora. Whatever comes, you'll see: when it really counts, I have strength and courage enough as a man to take on the whole weight myself.

Nora (terrified): What do you mean by that?

Helmer: The whole weight, I said.

Nora (resolutely): No, never in all the world.

Helmer: Good. So we'll share it, Nora, as man and wife. That's as it should be. *(Fondling her.)* Are you happy now? There, there, there—not these frightened dove's eyes. It's nothing at all but empty fantasies—Now you should run through your tarantella and practice your tambourine. I'll go to the inner office and shut both doors, so I won't hear a thing; you can make all the noise you like. *(Turning in the doorway.)* And when Rank comes, just tell him where he can find me. *(He nods to her and goes with his papers into the study, closing the door.)*

Nora (standing as though rooted, dazed with fright, in a whisper): He really could do it. He will do it. He'll do it in spite of everything. No, not that, never, never! Anything but that! Escape! A way out—*(The doorbell rings.)* Dr. Rank! Anything but that! *Anything,* whatever it is! *(Her hands pass over her face, smoothing it; she pulls herself together, goes over and opens the hall door. Dr. Rank stands outside, hanging his fur coat up. During the following scene, it begins getting dark.)*

Nora: Hello, Dr. Rank. I recognized your ring. But you mustn't go in to Torvald yet; I believe he's working.

Rank: And you?

Nora: For you, I always have an hour to spare—you know that. *(He has entered, and she shuts the door after him.)*

Rank: Many thanks. I'll make use of these hours while I can.

Nora: What do you mean by that? While you can?

Rank: Does that disturb you?

Nora: Well, it's such an odd phrase. Is anything going to happen?

Rank: What's going to happen is what I've been expecting so long—but I honestly didn't think it would come so soon.

Nora (gripping his arm): What is it you've found out? Dr. Rank, you have to tell me!

Rank (sitting by the stove): It's all over with me. There's nothing to be done about it.

Nora (breathing easier): Is it you—then—?

Rank: Who else? There's no point in lying to one's self. I'm the most miserable of all my patients, Mrs. Helmer. These past few days I've been auditing my internal accounts. Bankrupt! Within a month I'll probably be laid out and rotting in the churchyard.

Nora: Oh, what a horrible thing to say.

Rank: The thing itself is horrible. But the worst of it is all the other horror before it's over. There's only one final examination left; when I'm finished with that, I'll know about when my disintegration will begin. There's something I want to say. Helmer with his sensitivity has a sharp distaste for anything ugly. I don't want him near my sickroom.

Nora: Oh, but Dr. Rank—

Rank: I won't have him in there. Under no condition. I'll lock my door to him— As soon as I'm completely sure of the worst, I'll send you my calling card marked with a black cross, and you'll know then the wreck has started to come apart.

Nora: No, today you're completely unreasonable. And I wanted you so much to be in a really good humor.

Rank: With death up my sleeve? And then to suffer this way for somebody else's sins. Is there any justice in that? And in every single family, in some way or another, this inevitable retribution of nature goes on—

Nora (her hands pressed over her eyes): Oh, stuff! Cheer up! Please—be gay!

Rank: Yes, I'd just as soon laugh at it all. My poor, innocent spine, serving time for my father's gay army days.

Nora (by the table, left): He was so infatuated with asparagus tips and *pâté de foie gras*, wasn't that it?

Rank: Yes—and with truffles.

Nora: Truffles, yes. And then with oysters, I suppose?

Rank: Yes, tons of oysters, naturally.

Nora: And then the port and champagne to go with it. It's so sad that all these delectable things have to strike at our bones.

Rank: Especially when they strike at the unhappy bones that never shared in the fun.

Nora: Ah, that's the saddest of all.

Rank (looks searchingly at her): Hm.

Nora (after a moment): Why did you smile?

Rank: No, it was you who laughed.

Nora: No, it was you who smiled, Dr. Rank!

Rank (getting up): You're even a bigger tease than I'd thought.

Nora: I'm full of wild ideas today.

Rank: That's obvious.

Nora (putting both hands on his shoulders): Dear, dear Dr. Rank, you'll never die for Torvald and me.

Rank: Oh, that loss you'll easily get over. Those who go away are soon forgotten.

Nora (looks fearfully at him): You believe that?

Rank: One makes new connections, and then—

Nora: Who makes new connections?

Rank: Both you and Torvald will when I'm gone. I'd say you're well under way already. What was that Mrs. Linde doing here last evening?

Nora: Oh, come—you can't be jealous of poor Kristine?

Rank: Oh yes, I am. She'll be my successor here in the house. When I'm down under, that woman will probably—

Nora: Shh! Not so loud. She's right in there.

Rank: Today as well. So you see.

Nora: Only to sew on my dress. Good gracious, how unreasonable you are. *(Sitting on the sofa.)* Be nice now, Dr. Rank. Tomorrow you'll see how beautifully I'll dance, and you can imagine then that I'm dancing only for you—yes, and of course for Torvald, too—that's understood. *(Takes various items out of the carton.)* Dr. Rank, sit over here and I'll show you something.

Rank (sitting): What's that?

Nora: Look here. Look.

Rank: Silk stockings.

Nora: Flesh-colored. Aren't they lovely? Now it's so dark here, but tomorrow— No, no, no, just look at the feet. Oh well, you might as well look at the rest.

Rank: Hm—

Nora: Why do you look so critical? Don't you believe they'll fit?

Rank: I've never had any chance to form an opinion on that.

Nora (glancing at him a moment): Shame on you. *(Hits him lightly on the ear with the stockings.)* That's for you. *(Puts them away again.)*

Rank: And what other splendors am I going to see now?

Nora: Not the least bit more, because you've been naughty. *(She hums a little and rummages among her things.)*

Rank (after a short silence): When I sit here together with you like this, completely easy and open, then I don't know—I simply can't imagine—whatever would have become of me if I'd never come into this house.

Nora (smiling): Yes, I really think you feel completely at ease with us.

Rank (more quietly, staring straight ahead): And then to have to go away from it all—

Nora: Nonsense, you're not going away.

Rank (his voice unchanged): —And not even be able to leave some poor show of gratitude behind, scarcely a fleeting regret—no more than a vacant place that anyone can fill.

Nora: And if I asked you now for—? No—

Rank: For what?

Nora: For a great proof of your friendship—

Rank: Yes, yes?

Nora: No, I mean—for an exceptionally big favor—

Rank: Would you really, for once, make me so happy?

Nora: Oh, you haven't the vaguest idea what it is.

Rank: All right, then tell me.

Nora: No, but I can't, Dr. Rank—it's all out of reason. It's advice and help, too— and a favor—

Rank: So much the better. I can't fathom what you're hinting at. Just speak out. Don't you trust me?

Nora: Of course. More than anyone else. You're my best and truest friend, I'm sure. That's why I want to talk to you. All right, then, Dr. Rank: there's something you can help me prevent. You know how deeply, how inexpressibly dearly Torvald loves me; he'd never hesitate a second to give up his life for me.

Rank (leaning close to her): Nora—do you think he's the only one—

Nora (with a slight start): Who—?

Rank: Who'd gladly give up his life for you.

Nora (heavily): I see.

Rank: I swore to myself you should know this before I'm gone. I'll never find a better chance. Yes, Nora, now you know. And also you know now that you can trust me beyond anyone else.

Nora (rising, natural and calm): Let me by.

Rank (making room for her, but still sitting): Nora—

Nora (in the hall doorway): Helene, bring the lamp in. (*Goes over to the stove.*) Ah, dear Dr. Rank, that was really mean of you.

Rank (getting up): That I've loved you just as deeply as somebody else? Was *that* mean?

Nora: No, but that you came out and told me. That was quite unnecessary—

Rank: What do you mean? Have you known—?

The Maid comes in with the lamp, sets it on the table, and goes out again.

Rank: Nora—Mrs. Helmer—I'm asking you: have you known about it?

Nora: Oh, how can I tell what I know or don't know? Really, I don't know what to say—Why did you have to be so clumsy, Dr. Rank! Everything was so good.

Rank: Well, in any case, you now have the knowledge that my body and soul are at your command. So won't you speak out?

Nora (looking at him): After that?

Rank: Please, just let me know what it is.

Nora: You can't know anything now.

Rank: I have to. You mustn't punish me like this. Give me the chance to do whatever is humanly possible for you.

Nora: Now there's nothing you can do for me. Besides, actually, I don't need any help. You'll see—it's only my fantasies. That's what it is. Of course! (*Sits in the rocker, looks at him, and smiles.*) What a nice one you are, Dr. Rank. Aren't you a little bit ashamed, now that the lamp is here?

Rank: No, not exactly. But perhaps I'd better go—for good?

Nora: No, you certainly can't do that. You must come here just as you always have. You know Torvald can't do without you.

Rank: Yes, but *you?*

Nora: You know how much I enjoy it when you're here.

Rank: That's precisely what threw me off. You're a mystery to me. So many times I've felt you'd almost rather be with me than with Helmer.

Nora: Yes—you see, there are some people that one loves most and other people that one would almost prefer being with.

Rank: Yes, there's something to that.

Nora: When I was back home, of course I loved Papa most. But I always thought it was so much fun when I could sneak down to the maids' quarters, because they never tried to improve me, and it was always so amusing, the way they talked to each other.

Rank: Aha, so it's *their* place that I've filled.

Nora (jumping up and going to him): Oh, dear, sweet Dr. Rank, that's not what I mean at all. But you can understand that with Torvald it's just the same as with Papa—

The Maid enters from the hall.

Maid: Ma'am—please! *(She whispers to Nora and hands her a calling card.)*

Nora *(glancing at the card):* Ah! *(Slips it into her pocket.)*

Rank: Anything wrong?

Nora: No, no, not at all. It's only some—it's my new dress—

Rank: Really? But—there's your dress.

Nora: Oh, that. But this is another one—I ordered it—Torvald mustn't know—

Rank: Ah, now we have the big secret.

Nora: That's right. Just go in with him—he's back in the inner study. Keep him there as long as—

Rank: Don't worry. He won't get away. *(Goes into the study.)*

Nora *(to the Maid):* And he's standing waiting in the kitchen?

Maid: Yes, he came up by the back stairs.

Nora: But didn't you tell him somebody was here?

Maid: Yes, but that didn't do any good.

Nora: He won't leave?

Maid: No, he won't go till he's talked with you, ma'am.

Nora: Let him come in, then—but quietly. Helene, don't breathe a word about this. It's a surprise for my husband.

Maid: Yes, yes, I understand—*(Goes out.)*

Nora: This horror—it's going to happen. No, no, no, it can't happen, it mustn't. *(She goes and bolts Helmer's door. The Maid opens the hall door for Krogstad and shuts it behind him. He is dressed for travel in a fur coat, boots, and a fur cap.)*

Nora *(going toward him):* Talk softly. My husband's home.

Krogstad: Well, good for him.

Nora: What do you want?

Krogstad: Some information.

Nora: Hurry up, then. What is it?

Krogstad: You know, of course, that I got my notice.

Nora: I couldn't prevent it, Mr. Krogstad. I fought for you to the bitter end, but nothing worked.

Krogstad: Does your husband's love for you run so thin? He knows everything I can expose you to, and all the same he dares to—

Nora: How can you imagine he knows anything about this?

Krogstad: Ah, no—I can't imagine it either, now. It's not at all like my fine Torvald Helmer to have so much guts—

Nora: Mr. Krogstad, I demand respect for my husband!

Krogstad: Why, of course—all due respect. But since the lady's keeping it so carefully hidden, may I presume to ask if you're also a bit better informed than yesterday about what you've actually done?

Nora: More than you ever could teach me.

Krogstad: Yes, I *am* such an awful lawyer.

Nora: What is it you want from me?

Krogstad: Just a glimpse of how you are, Mrs. Helmer. I've been thinking about you all day long. A cashier, a night-court scribbler, a—well, a type like me also has a little of what they call a heart, you know.

Nora: Then show it. Think of my children.

Krogstad: Did you or your husband ever think of mine? But never mind. I simply wanted to tell you that you don't need to take this thing too seriously. For the present, I'm not proceeding with any action.

Nora: Oh no, really! Well—I knew that.

Krogstad: Everything can be settled in a friendly spirit. It doesn't have to get around town at all; it can stay just among us three.

Nora: My husband must never know anything of this.

Krogstad: How can you manage that? Perhaps you can pay me the balance?

Nora: No, not right now.

Krogstad: Or you know some way of raising the money in a day or two?

Nora: No way that I'm willing to use.

Krogstad: Well, it wouldn't have done you any good, anyway. If you stood in front of me with a fistful of bills, you still couldn't buy your signature back.

Nora: Then tell me what you're going to do with it.

Krogstad: I'll just hold onto it—keep it on file. There's no outsider who'll even get wind of it. So if you've been thinking of taking some desperate step—

Nora: I have.

Krogstad: Been thinking of running away from home—

Nora: I have!

Krogstad: Or even of something worse—

Nora: How could you guess that?

Krogstad: You can drop those thoughts.

Nora: How could you guess I was thinking of *that?*

Krogstad: Most of us think about *that* at first. I thought about it too, but I discovered I hadn't the courage—

Nora (lifelessly): I don't either.

Krogstad (relieved): That's true, you haven't the courage? You too?

Nora: I don't have it—I don't have it.

Krogstad: It would be terribly stupid, anyway. After that first storm at home blows out, why, then—I have here in my pocket a letter for your husband—

Nora: Telling everything?

Krogstad: As charitably as possible.

Nora (quickly): He mustn't ever get that letter. Tear it up. I'll find some way to get money.

Krogstad: Beg pardon, Mrs. Helmer, but I think I just told you—

Nora: Oh, I don't mean the money I owe you. Let me know how much you want from my husband, and I'll manage it.

Krogstad: I don't want any money from your husband.

Nora: What do you want, then?

Krogstad: I'll tell you what. I want to recoup, Mrs. Helmer; I want to get on in the world—and there's where your husband can help me. For a year and a half I've kept myself clean of anything disreputable—all that time struggling with the worst conditions; but I was satisfied, working my way up step by step. Now I've been written right off, and I'm just not in the mood to come crawling back. I tell you, I want to move on. I want to get back in the bank—in a better position. Your husband can set up a job for me—

Nora: He'll never do that!

Krogstad: He'll do it. I know him. He won't dare breathe a word of protest. And once I'm in there together with him, you just wait and see! Inside of a year, I'll be the manager's right-hand man. It'll be Nils Krogstad, not Torvald Helmer, who runs the bank.

Nora: You'll never see the day!

Krogstad: Maybe you think you can—

Nora: I have the courage now—for *that*.

Krogstad: Oh, you don't scare me. A smart, spoiled lady like you—

Nora: You'll see; you'll see!

Krogstad: Under the ice, maybe? Down in the freezing, coal-black water? There, till you float up in the spring, ugly, unrecognizable, with your hair falling out—

Nora: You don't frighten me!

Krogstad: Nor do you frighten me. One doesn't do these things, Mrs. Helmer. Besides, what good would it be? I'd still have him safe in my pocket.

Nora: Afterwards? When I'm no longer—?

Krogstad: Are you forgetting that I'll be in control then over your final reputation? *(Nora stands speechless, staring at him.)* Good; now I've warned you. Don't do anything stupid. When Helmer's read my letter, I'll be waiting for his reply. And bear in mind that it's your husband himself who's forced me back to my old ways. I'll never forgive him for that. Good-bye, Mrs. Helmer. *(He goes out through the hall.)*

Nora (goes to the hall door, opens it a crack, and listens): He's gone. Didn't leave the letter. Oh no, no, that's impossible too! *(Opening the door more and more.)* What's that? He's standing outside—not going downstairs. He's thinking it over? Maybe he'll—?*(A letter falls in the mailbox; then Krogstad's footsteps are heard, dying away down a flight of stairs. Nora gives a muffled cry and runs over toward the sofa table. A short pause.)* In the mailbox. *(Slips warily over to the hall door.)* It's lying there. Torvald, Torvald—now we're lost!

Mrs. Linde (entering with the costume from the room, left): There now. I can't see anything else to mend. Perhaps you'd like to try—

Nora (in a hoarse whisper): Kristine, come here.

Mrs. Linde (tossing the dress on the sofa): What's wrong? You look upset.

Nora: Come here. See that letter? *There!* Look—through the glass in the mailbox.

Mrs. Linde: Yes, yes, I see it.

Nora: That letter's from Krogstad—

Mrs. Linde: Nora—it's Krogstad who loaned you the money!

Nora: Yes, and now Torvald will find out everything.

Mrs. Linde: Believe me, Nora, it's best for both of you.

Nora: There's more you don't know. I forged a name.

Mrs. Linde: But for heaven's sake—?

Nora: I only want to tell you that, Kristine, so that you can be my witness.

Mrs. Linde: Witness? Why should I—?

Nora: If I should go out of my mind—it could easily happen—

Mrs. Linde: Nora!

Nora: Or anything else occurred—so I couldn't be present here—

Mrs. Linde: Nora, Nora, you aren't yourself at all!

Nora: And someone should try to take on the whole weight, all of the guilt, you follow me—

Mrs. Linde: Yes, of course, but why do you think—?

Nora: Then you're the witness that it isn't true, Kristine. I'm very much myself; my mind right now is perfectly clear; and I'm telling you: nobody else has known about this; I alone did everything. Remember that.

Mrs. Linde: I will. But I don't understand all this.

Nora: Oh, how could you ever understand it? It's the miracle now that's going to take place.

Mrs. Linde: The miracle?

Nora: Yes, the miracle. But it's so awful, Kristine. It mustn't take place, not for anything in the world.

Mrs. Linde: I'm going right over and talk with Krogstad.

Nora: Don't go near him; he'll do you some terrible harm!

Mrs. Linde: There was a time once when he'd gladly have done anything for me.

Nora: He?

Mrs. Linde: Where does he live?

Nora: Oh, how do I know? Yes. (*Searches in her pocket.*) Here's his card. But the letter, the letter—!

Helmer (from the study, knocking on the door): Nora!

Nora (with a cry of fear): Oh! What is it? What do you want?

Helmer: Now, now, don't be so frightened. We're not coming in. You locked the door—are you trying on the dress?

Nora: Yes, I'm trying it. I'll look just beautiful, Torvald.

Mrs. Linde (who has read the card): He's living right around the corner.

Nora: Yes, but what's the use? We're lost. The letter's in the box.

Mrs. Linde: And your husband has the key?

Nora: Yes, always.

Mrs. Linde: Krogstad can ask for his letter back unread; he can find some excuse—

Nora: But it's just this time that Torvald usually—

Mrs. Linde: Stall him. Keep him in there. I'll be back as quick as I can. (*She hurries out through the hall entrance.*)

Nora (goes to Helmer's door, opens it, and peers in): Torvald!

Helmer (from the inner study): Well—does one dare set foot in one's own living room at last? Come on, Rank, now we'll get a look—(*In the doorway.*) But what's this?

Nora: What, Torvald dear?

Helmer: Rank had me expecting some grand masquerade.

Rank (in the doorway): That was my impression, but I must have been wrong.

Nora: No one can admire me in my splendor—not till tomorrow.

Helmer: But Nora dear, you look so exhausted. Have you practiced too hard?

Nora: No, I haven't practiced at all yet.

Helmer: You know, it's necessary—

Nora: Oh, it's absolutely necessary, Torvald. But I can't get anywhere without your help. I've forgotten the whole thing completely.

Helmer: Ah, we'll soon take care of that.

Nora: Yes, take care of me, Torvald, please! Promise me that? Oh, I'm so nervous. That big party—You must give up everything this evening for me. No business—don't even touch your pen. Yes? Dear Torvald, promise?

Helmer: It's a promise. Tonight I'm totally at your service—you little helpless thing. Hm—but first there's one thing I want to—(*Goes toward the hall door.*)

Nora: What are you looking for?

Helmer: Just to see if there's any mail.

Nora: No, no, don't do that, Torvald!

Helmer: Now what?

Nora: Torvald, please. There isn't any.

Helmer: Let me look, though. (*Starts out. Nora, at the piano, strikes the first notes of the tarantella. Helmer, at the door, stops.*) Aha!

Nora: I can't dance tomorrow if I don't practice with you.

Helmer (going over to her): Nora dear, are you really so frightened?

Nora: Yes, so terribly frightened. Let me practice right now; there's still time before dinner. Oh, sit down and play for me, Torvald. Direct me. Teach me, the way you always have.

Helmer: Gladly, if it's what you want. (*Sits at the piano.*)

Nora (snatches the tambourine up from the box, then a long, varicolored shawl, which she throws around herself, whereupon she springs forward and cries out): Play for me now! Now I'll dance!

Helmer plays and Nora dances. Rank stands behind Helmer at the piano and looks on.

Helmer (as he plays): Slower. Slow down.

Nora: Can't change it.

Helmer: Not so violent, Nora!

Nora: Has to be just like this.

Helmer (stopping): No, no, that won't do at all.

Nora (laughing and swinging her tambourine): Isn't that what I told you?

Rank: Let me play for her.

Helmer (getting up): Yes, go on. I can teach her more easily then.

Rank sits at the piano and plays; Nora dances more and more wildly. Helmer has stationed himself by the stove and repeatedly gives her directions; she seems not to hear them; her hair loosens and falls over her shoulders; she does not notice, but goes on dancing. Mrs. Linde enters.

Mrs. Linde (standing dumbfounded at the door): Ah—!

Nora (still dancing): See what fun, Kristine!

Helmer: But Nora darling, you dance as if your life were at stake.

Nora: And it is.

Helmer: Rank, stop! This is pure madness. Stop it, I say!

Rank breaks off playing, and Nora halts abruptly.

Helmer (going over to her): I never would have believed it. You've forgotten everything I taught you.

Nora (throwing away the tambourine): You see for yourself.

Helmer: Well, there's certainly room for instruction here.

Nora: Yes, you see how important it is. You've got to teach me to the very last minute. Promise me that, Torvald?

Helmer: You can bet on it.

Nora: You mustn't, either today or tomorrow, think about anything else but me; you mustn't open any letters—or the mailbox—

Helmer: Ah, it's still the fear of that man—

Nora: Oh yes, yes, that too.

Helmer: Nora, it's written all over you—there's already a letter from him out there.

Nora: I don't know. I guess so. But you mustn't read such things now; there mustn't be anything ugly between us before it's all over.

Rank (quietly to Helmer): You shouldn't deny her.

Helmer (putting his arm around her): The child can have her way. But tomorrow night, after you've danced—

Nora: Then you'll be free.

Maid (in the doorway, right): Ma'am, dinner is served.

Nora: We'll be wanting champagne, Helene.

Maid: Very good, ma'am. *(Goes out.)*

Helmer: So—a regular banquet, hm?

Nora: Yes, a banquet—champagne till daybreak! *(Calling out.)* And some macaroons, Helene. Heaps of them—just this once.

Helmer (taking her hands): Now, now, now—no hysterics. Be my own little lark again.

Nora: Oh, I will soon enough. But go on in—and you, Dr. Rank. Kristine, help me put up my hair.

Rank (whispering, as they go): There's nothing wrong—really wrong, is there?

Helmer: Oh, of course not. It's nothing more than this childish anxiety I was telling you about. *(They go out, right.)*

Nora: Well?

Mrs. Linde: Left town.

Nora: I could see by your face.

Mrs. Linde: He'll be home tomorrow evening. I wrote him a note.

Nora: You shouldn't have. Don't try to stop anything now. After all, it's a wonderful joy, this waiting here for the miracle.

Mrs. Linde: What is it you're waiting for?

Nora: Oh, you can't understand that. Go in to them: I'll be along in a moment.

Mrs. Linde *goes into the dining room.* Nora *stands a short while as if composing herself; then she looks at her watch.*

Nora: Five. Seven hours to midnight. Twenty-four hours to the midnight after, and then the tarantella's done. Seven and twenty-four? Thirty-one hours to live.

Helmer (in the doorway, right): What's become of the little lark?

Nora (going toward him with open arms): Here's your lark!

ACT III

Same scene. The table, with chairs around it, has been moved to the center of the room. A lamp on the table is lit. The hall door stands open. Dance music drifts down from the floor above. Mrs. Linde sits at the table, absently paging through a book, trying to read, but apparently unable to focus her thoughts. Once or twice she pauses, tensely listening for a sound at the outer entrance.

Mrs. Linde (glancing at her watch): Not yet—and there's hardly any time left. If only he's not—(Listening again.) Ah, there he is. (She goes out in the hall and cautiously opens the outer door. Quiet footsteps are heard on the stairs. She whispers.) Come in. Nobody's here.

Krogstad (in the doorway): I found a note from you at home. What's back of all this?

Mrs. Linde: I just *had* to talk to you.

Krogstad: Oh? And it just *had* to be here in this house?

Mrs. Linde: At my place it was impossible; my room hasn't a private entrance. Come in; we're all alone. The maid's asleep, and the Helmers are at the dance upstairs.

Krogstad (entering the room): Well, well, the Helmers are dancing tonight? Really?

Mrs. Linde: Yes, why not?

Krogstad: How true—why not?

Mrs. Linde: All right, Krogstad, let's talk.

Krogstad: Do we two have anything more to talk about?

Mrs. Linde: We have a great deal to talk about.

Krogstad: I wouldn't have thought so.

Mrs. Linde: No, because you've never understood me, really.

Krogstad: Was there anything more to understand—except what's all too common in life? A calculating woman throws over a man the moment a better catch comes by.

Mrs. Linde: You think I'm so thoroughly calculating? You think I broke it off lightly?

Krogstad: Didn't you?

Mrs. Linde: Nils—is that what you really thought?

Krogstad: If you cared, then why did you write me the way you did?

Mrs. Linde: What else could I do? If I had to break off with you, then it was my job as well to root out everything you felt for me.

Krogstad (wringing his hands): So that was it. And this—all this, simply for money!

Mrs. Linde: Don't forget I had a helpless mother and two small brothers. We couldn't wait for you, Nils; you had such a long road ahead of you then.

Krogstad: That may be; but you still hadn't the right to abandon me for somebody else's sake.

Mrs. Linde: Yes—I don't know. So many, many times I've asked myself if I did have that right.

Krogstad (more softly): When I lost you, it was as if all the solid ground dissolved from under my feet. Look at me; I'm a half-drowned man now, hanging onto a wreck.

Mrs. Linde: Help may be near.

Krogstad: It was near—but then you came and blocked it off.

Mrs. Linde: Without my knowing it, Nils. Today for the first time I learned that it's you I'm replacing at the bank.

Krogstad: All right—I believe you. But now that you know, will you step aside?

Mrs. Linde: No, because that wouldn't benefit you in the slightest.

Krogstad: Not "benefit" me, hm! I'd step aside anyway.

Mrs. Linde: I've got to be realistic. Life and hard, bitter necessity have taught me that.

Krogstad: And life's taught me never to trust fine phrases.

Mrs. Linde: Then life's taught you a very sound thing. But you do have to trust in actions, don't you?

Krogstad: What does that mean?

Mrs. Linde: You said you were hanging on like a half-drowned man to a wreck.

Krogstad: I've good reason to say that.

Mrs. Linde: I'm also like a half-drowned woman on a wreck. No one to suffer with; no one to care for.

Krogstad: You made your choice.

Mrs. Linde: There wasn't any choice then.

Krogstad: So—what of it?

Mrs. Linde: Nils, if only we two shipwrecked people could reach across to each other.

Krogstad: What are you saying?

Mrs. Linde: Two on one wreck are at least better off than each on his own.

Krogstad: Kristine!

Mrs. Linde: Why do you think I came into town?

Krogstad: Did you really have some thought of me?

Mrs. Linde: I have to work to go on living. All my born days, as long as I can remember, I've worked, and it's been my best and my only joy. But now I'm completely alone in the world; it frightens me to be so empty and lost. To work for yourself—there's no joy in that. Nils, give me something—someone to work for.

Krogstad: I don't believe all this. It's just some hysterical feminine urge to go out and make a noble sacrifice.

Mrs. Linde: Have you ever found me to be hysterical?

Krogstad: Can you honestly mean this? Tell me—do you know everything about my past?

Mrs. Linde: Yes.

Krogstad: And you know what they think I'm worth around here.

Mrs. Linde: From what you were saying before, it would seem that with me you could have been another person.

Krogstad: I'm positive of that.

Mrs. Linde: Couldn't it happen still?

Krogstad: Kristine—you're saying this in all seriousness? Yes, you are! I can see it in you. And do you really have the courage, then—?

Mrs. Linde: I need to have someone to care for; and your children need a mother. We both need each other. Nils, I have faith that you're good at heart—I'll risk everything together with you.

Krogstad (gripping her hands): Kristine, thank you, thank you—Now I know I can win back a place in their eyes. Yes—but I forgot—

Mrs. Linde (listening): Shh! The tarantella. Go now! Go on!

Krogstad: Why? What is it?

Mrs. Linde: Hear the dance up there? When that's over, they'll be coming down.

Krogstad: Oh, then I'll go. But—it's all pointless. Of course, you don't know the move I made against the Helmers.

Mrs. Linde: Yes, Nils, I know.

Krogstad: And all the same, you have the courage to—?

Mrs. Linde: I know how far despair can drive a man like you.

Krogstad: Oh, if I only could take it all back.

Mrs. Linde: You easily could—your letter's still lying in the mailbox.

Krogstad: Are you sure of that?

Mrs. Linde: Positive. But—

Krogstad (looks at her searchingly): Is that the meaning of it, then? You'll save your friend at any price. Tell me straight out. Is that it?

Mrs. Linde: Nils—anyone who's sold herself for somebody else once isn't going to do it again.

Krogstad: I'll demand my letter back.

Mrs. Linde: No, no.

Krogstad: Yes, of course. I'll stay here till Helmer comes down; I'll tell him to give me my letter again—that it only involves my dismissal—that he shouldn't read it—

Mrs. Linde: No, Nils, don't call the letter back.

Krogstad: But wasn't that exactly why you wrote me to come here?

Mrs. Linde: Yes, in that first panic. But it's been a whole day and night since then, and in that time I've seen such incredible things in this house. Helmer's got to learn everything; this dreadful secret has to be aired; those two have to come to a full understanding; all these lies and evasions can't go on.

Krogstad: Well, then, if you want to chance it. But at least there's one thing I can do, and do right away—

Mrs. Linde (listening): Go now, go, quick! The dance is over. We're not safe another second.

Krogstad: I'll wait for you downstairs.

Mrs. Linde: Yes, please do; take me home.

Krogstad: I can't believe it; I've never been so happy. (He leaves by way of the outer door; the door between the room and hall stays open.)

Mrs. Linde (straightening up a bit and getting together her street clothes): How different now! How different! Someone to work for, to live for—a home to build. Well, it is worth the try! Oh, if they'd only come! (Listening.) Ah, there they are. Bundle up. (She picks up her hat and coat. Nora's and Helmer's voices can be heard outside; a key turns in the lock, and Helmer brings Nora into the hall almost by force. She is wearing the Italian costume with a large black shawl about her; he has on evening dress, with a black domino open over it.)

Nora (struggling in the doorway): No, no, no, not inside! I'm going up again. I don't want to leave so soon.

Helmer: But Nora dear—

Nora: Oh, I beg you, please, Torvald. From the bottom of my heart, please—only an hour more!

Helmer: Not a single minute, Nora darling. You know our agreement. Come on, in we go; you'll catch cold out here. (In spite of her resistance, he gently draws her into the room.)

Mrs. Linde: Good evening.

Nora: Kristine!

Helmer: Why, Mrs. Linde—are you here so late?

Mrs. Linde: Yes, I'm sorry, but I did want to see Nora in costume.

Nora: Have you been sitting here, waiting for me?

Mrs. Linde: Yes. I didn't come early enough; you were all upstairs; and then I thought I really couldn't leave without seeing you.

Helmer (removing Nora's shawl): Yes, take a good look. She's worth looking at, I can tell you that, Mrs. Linde. Isn't she lovely?

Mrs. Linde: Yes, I should say—

Helmer: A dream of loveliness, isn't she? That's what everyone thought at the party, too. But she's horribly stubborn—this sweet little thing. What's to be done with her? Can you imagine, I almost had to use force to pry her away.

Nora: Oh, Torvald, you're going to regret you didn't indulge me, even for just a half hour more.

Helmer: There, you see. She danced the tarantella and got a tumultuous hand—which was well earned, although the performance may have been a bit too naturalistic—I mean it rather overstepped the proprieties of art. But never mind—what's important is, she made a success, an overwhelming success. You think I could let her stay on after that and spoil the effect? Oh no; I took my lovely little Capri girl—my capricious little Capri girl, I should say—took her under my arm; one quick tour of the ballroom, a curtsy to every side, and then—as they say in novels—the beautiful vision disappeared. An exit should always be effective, Mrs. Linde, but that's what I can't get Nora to grasp. Phew, it's hot in here. *(Flings the domino on a chair and opens the door to his room.)* Why's it dark in here? Oh yes, of course. Excuse me. *(He goes in and lights a couple of candles.)*

Nora (in a sharp, breathless whisper): So?

Mrs. Linde (quietly): I talked with him.

Nora: And—?

Mrs. Linde: Nora—you must tell your husband everything.

Nora (dully): I knew it.

Mrs. Linde: You've got nothing to fear from Krogstad, but you have to speak out.

Nora: I won't tell.

Mrs. Linde: Then the letter will.

Nora: Thanks, Kristine. I know now what's to be done. Shh!

Helmer (reentering): Well, then, Mrs. Linde—have you admired her?

Mrs. Linde: Yes, and now I'll say good night.

Helmer: Oh, come, so soon? Is this yours, this knitting?

Mrs. Linde: Yes, thanks. I nearly forgot it.

Helmer: Do you knit, then?

Mrs. Linde: Oh yes.

Helmer: You know what? You should embroider instead.

Mrs. Linde: Really? Why?

Helmer: Yes, because it's a lot prettier. See here, one holds the embroidery so, in the left hand, and then one guides the needle with the right—so—in an easy, sweeping curve—right?

Mrs. Linde: Yes, I guess that's—

Helmer: But, on the other hand, knitting—it can never be anything but ugly. Look, see here, the arms tucked in, the knitting needles going up and down—there's something Chinese about it. Ah, that was really a glorious champagne they served.

Mrs. Linde: Yes, good night, Nora, and don't be stubborn any more.

Helmer: Well put, Mrs. Linde!

Mrs. Linde: Good night, Mr. Helmer.

Helmer (accompanying her to the door): Good night, good night. I hope you get home all right. I'd be very happy to—but you don't have far to go. Good night, good night. *(She leaves. He shuts the door after her and returns.)* There, now, at last we got her out the door. She's a deadly bore, that creature.

Nora: Aren't you pretty tired, Torvald?

Helmer: No, not a bit.

Nora: You're not sleepy?

Helmer: Not at all. On the contrary, I'm feeling quite exhilarated. But you? Yes, you really look tired and sleepy.

Nora: Yes, I'm very tired. Soon now I'll sleep.

Helmer: See! You see! I was right all along that we shouldn't stay longer.

Nora: Whatever you do is always right.

Helmer (kissing her brow): Now my little lark talks sense. Say, did you notice what a time Rank was having tonight?

Nora: Oh, was he? I didn't get to speak with him.

Helmer: I scarcely did either, but it's a long time since I've seen him in such high spirits. *(Gazes at her a moment, then comes nearer her.)* Hm—it's marvelous, though, to be back home again—to be completely alone with you. Oh, you bewitchingly lovely young woman!

Nora: Torvald, don't look at me like that!

Helmer: Can't I look at my richest treasure? At all that beauty that's mine, mine alone—completely and utterly.

Nora (moving around to the other side of the table): You mustn't talk to me that way tonight.

Helmer (following her): The tarantella is still in your blood, I can see—and it makes you even more enticing. Listen. The guests are beginning to go. *(Dropping his voice.)* Nora—it'll soon be quiet through this whole house.

Nora: Yes, I hope so.

Helmer: You do, don't you, my love? Do you realize—when I'm out at a party like this with you—do you know why I talk to you so little, and keep such a distance away; just send you a stolen look now and then—you know why I do it? It's because I'm imagining then that you're my secret darling, my secret young bride-to-be, and that no one suspects there's anything between us.

Nora: Yes, yes; oh, yes, I know you're always thinking of me.

Helmer: And then when we leave and I place the shawl over those fine young rounded shoulders—over that wonderful curving neck—then I pretend that you're my young bride, that we're just coming from the wedding, that for the first time I'm bringing you into my house—that for the first time I'm alone with you—completely alone with you, your trembling young beauty! All this evening I've longed for nothing but you. When I saw you turn and sway in the tarantella—my blood was pounding till I couldn't stand it—that's why I brought you down here so early—

Nora: Go away, Torvald! Leave me alone. I don't want all this.

Helmer: What do you mean? Nora, you're teasing me. You will, won't you? Aren't I your husband—?

A knock at the outside door.

Nora (startled): What's that?

Helmer (going toward the hall): Who is it?

Rank (outside): It's me. May I come in a moment?

Helmer (with quiet irritation): Oh, what does he want now? *(Aloud.)* Hold on. *(Goes and opens the door.)* Oh, how nice that you didn't just pass us by!

Rank: I thought I heard your voice, and then I wanted so badly to have a look in. *(Lightly glancing about.)* Ah, me, these old familiar haunts. You have it snug and cozy in here, you two.

Helmer: You seemed to be having it pretty cozy upstairs, too.

Rank: Absolutely. Why shouldn't I? Why not take in everything in life? As much as you can, anyway, and as long as you can. The wine was superb—

Helmer: The champagne especially.

Rank: You noticed that too? It's amazing how much I could guzzle down.

Nora: Torvald also drank a lot of champagne this evening.

Rank: Oh?

Nora: Yes, and that always makes him so entertaining.

Rank: Well, why shouldn't one have a pleasant evening after a well-spent day?

Helmer: Well spent? I'm afraid I can't claim that.

Rank (slapping him on the back): But I can, you see!

Nora: Dr. Rank, you must have done some scientific research today.

Rank: Quite so.

Helmer: Come now—little Nora talking about scientific research!

Nora: And can I congratulate you on the results?

Rank: Indeed you may.

Nora: Then they were good?

Rank: The best possible for both doctor and patient—certainty.

Nora (quickly and searchingly): Certainty?

Rank: Complete certainty. So don't I owe myself a gay evening afterwards?

Nora: Yes, you're right, Dr. Rank.

Helmer: I'm with you—just so long as you don't have to suffer for it in the morning.

Rank: Well, one never gets something for nothing in life.

Nora: Dr. Rank—are you very fond of masquerade parties?

Rank: Yes, if there's a good array of odd disguises—

Nora: Tell me, what should we two go as at the next masquerade?

Helmer: You little featherhead—already thinking of the next!

Rank: We two? I'll tell you what: you must go as Charmed Life—

Helmer: Yes, but find a costume for *that!*

Rank: Your wife can appear just as she looks every day.

Helmer: That was nicely put. But don't you know what you're going to be?

Rank: Yes, Helmer, I've made up my mind.

Helmer: Well?

Rank: At the next masquerade I'm going to be invisible.

Helmer: That's a funny idea.

Rank: They say there's a hat—black, huge—have you never heard of the hat that makes you invisible? You put it on, and then no one on earth can see you.

Helmer (suppressing a smile): Ah, of course.

Rank: But I'm quite forgetting what I came for. Helmer, give me a cigar, one of the dark Havanas.

Helmer: With the greatest pleasure. *(Holds out his case.)*

Rank: Thanks. *(Takes one and cuts off the tip.)*

Nora (striking a match): Let me give you a light.

Rank: Thank you. *(She holds the match for him; he lights the cigar.)* And now good-bye.

Helmer: Good-bye, good-bye, old friend.

Nora: Sleep well, Doctor.

Rank: Thanks for that wish.

Nora: Wish me the same.

Rank: You? All right, if you like—Sleep well. And thanks for the light. *(He nods to them both and leaves.)*

Helmer (his voice subdued): He's been drinking heavily.

Nora (absently): Could be. *(Helmer takes his keys from his pocket and goes out in the hall.)* Torvald—what are you after?

Helmer: Got to empty the mailbox; it's nearly full. There won't be room for the morning papers.

Nora: Are you working tonight?

Helmer: You know I'm not. Why—what's this? Someone's been at the lock.

Nora: At the lock—?

Helmer: Yes, I'm positive. What do you suppose—? I can't imagine one of the maids—? Here's a broken hairpin. Nora, it's yours—

Nora (quickly): Then it must be the children—

Helmer: You'd better break them of that. Hm, hm—well, opened it after all. *(Takes the contents out and calls into the kitchen.)* Helene! Helene, would you put out the lamp in the hall. *(He returns to the room, shutting the hall door, then displays the handful of mail.)* Look how it's piled up. *(Sorting through them.)* Now what's this?

Nora (at the window): The letter! Oh, Torvald, no!

Helmer: Two calling cards—from Rank.

Nora: From Dr. Rank?

Helmer (examining them): "Dr. Rank, Consulting Physician." They were on top. He must have dropped them in as he left.

Nora: Is there anything on them?

Helmer: There's a black cross over the name. See? That's a gruesome notion. He could almost be announcing his own death.

Nora: That's just what he's doing.

Helmer: What! You've heard something? Something he's told you?

Nora: Yes. That when those cards came, he'd be taking his leave of us. He'll shut himself in now and die.

Helmer: Ah, my poor friend! Of course I knew he wouldn't be here much longer. But so soon—And then to hide himself away like a wounded animal.

Nora: If it has to happen, then it's best it happens in silence—don't you think so, Torvald?

Helmer (pacing up and down): He'd grown right into our lives. I simply can't imagine him gone. He with his suffering and loneliness—like a dark cloud setting off our sunlit happiness. Well, maybe it's best this way. For him, at least. *(Standing still.)* And maybe for us too, Nora. Now we're thrown back on each other, completely. *(Embracing her.)* Oh you, my darling wife, how can I hold you close enough? You know what, Nora—time and again I've wished you were in some terrible danger, just so I could stake my life and soul and everything, for your sake.

Nora (tearing herself away, her voice firm and decisive): Now you must read your mail, Torvald.

Helmer: No, no, not tonight. I want to stay with you, dearest.

Nora: With a dying friend on your mind?

Helmer: You're right. We've both had a shock. There's ugliness between us—these thoughts of death and corruption. We'll have to get free of them first. Until then—we'll stay apart.

Nora (clinging about his neck): Torvald—good night! Good night!

Helmer (kissing her on the cheek): Good night, little songbird. Sleep well, Nora. I'll be reading my mail now. *(He takes the letters into his room and shuts the door after him.)*

Nora (with bewildered glances, groping about, seizing Helmer's domino, throwing it around her, and speaking in short, hoarse, broken whispers): Never see him again. Never, never. *(Putting her shawl over her head.)* Never see the children either—them, too. Never, never. Oh, the freezing black water! The depths—down—Oh, I wish it were over—He has it now; he's reading it—now. Oh no, no, not yet. Torvald, good-bye, you and the children—*(She starts for the hall; as she does, Helmer throws open his door and stands with an open letter in his hand.)*

Helmer: Nora!

Nora (screams): Oh—!

Helmer: What is this? You know what's in this letter?

Nora: Yes, I know. Let me go! Let me out!

Helmer (holding her back): Where are you going?

Nora (struggling to break loose): You can't save me, Torvald!

Helmer (slumping back): True! Then it's true what he writes? How horrible! No, no, it's impossible—it can't be true.

Nora: It *is* true. I've loved you more than all this world.

Helmer: Ah, none of your slippery tricks.

Nora (taking one step toward him): Torvald—!

Helmer: What is this you've blundered into?

Nora: Just let me loose. You're not going to suffer for my sake. You're not going to take on my guilt.

Helmer: No more playacting. *(Locks the hall door.)* You stay right here and give me a reckoning. You understand what you've done? Answer! You understand?

Nora (looking squarely at him, her face hardening): Yes. I'm beginning to understand everything now.

Helmer (striding about): Oh, what an awful awakening! In all these eight years— she who was my pride and joy—a hypocrite, a liar—worse, worse—a criminal! How infinitely disgusting it all is! The shame! *(Nora says nothing and goes on looking straight at him. He stops in front of her.)* I should have suspected something of the kind. I should have known. All your father's flimsy values—Be still! All your father's flimsy values have come out in you. No religion, no morals, no sense of duty—Oh, how I'm punished for letting him off! I did it for your sake, and you repay me like this.

Nora: Yes, like this.

Helmer: Now you've wrecked all my happiness—ruined my whole future. Oh, it's awful to think of. I'm in a cheap little grafter's hands; he can do anything he wants with me, ask for anything, play with me like a puppet—and I can't breathe a word. I'll be swept down miserably into the depths on account of a featherbrained woman.

Nora: When I'm gone from this world, you'll be free.

Helmer: Oh, quit posing. Your father had a mess of those speeches too. What good would that ever do me if you were gone from this world, as you say? Not the slightest. He can still make the whole thing known; and if he does, I could be falsely suspected as your accomplice. They might even think that I was behind it—that I put you up to it. And all that I can thank you for—you that I've coddled the whole of our marriage. Can you see now what you've done to me?

Nora (icily calm): Yes.

Helmer: It's so incredible, I just can't grasp it. But we'll have to patch up whatever we can. Take off the shawl. I said, take it off! I've got to appease him somehow or other. The thing has to be hushed up at any cost. And as for you and me, it's got to seem like everything between us is just as it was—to the outside world, that is. You'll go right on living in this house, of course. But you can't be allowed to bring up the children; I don't dare trust you with them—Oh, to have to say this to someone I've loved so much! Well, that's done with. From now on happiness doesn't matter; all that matters is saving the bits and pieces, the appearance—(*The doorbell rings. Helmer starts.*) What's that? And so late. Maybe the worst—? You think he'd—? Hide, Nora! Say you're sick. (*Nora remains standing motionless. Helmer goes and opens the door.*)

Maid (half dressed, in the hall): A letter for Mrs. Helmer.

Helmer: I'll take it. (*Snatches the letter and shuts the door.*) Yes, it's from him. You don't get it; I'm reading it myself.

Nora: Then read it.

Helmer (by the lamp): I hardly dare. We may be ruined, you and I. But—I've got to know. (*Rips open the letter, skims through a few lines, glances at an enclosure, then cries out joyfully.*) Nora! (*Nora looks inquiringly at him.*) Nora! Wait—better check it again—Yes, yes, it's true. I'm saved. Nora, I'm saved!

Nora: And I?

Helmer: You too, of course. We're both saved, both of us. He's sent back your note. He says he's sorry and ashamed—that a happy development in his life— oh, who cares what he says! Nora, we're saved! No one can hurt you. Oh, Nora, Nora—but first, this ugliness all has to go. Let me see—(*Takes a look at the note.*) No, I don't want to see it; I want the whole thing to fade like a dream. (*Tears the note and both the letters to pieces, throws them into the stove and watches them burn.*) There—now there's nothing left—He wrote that since Christmas Eve you—Oh, they must have been three terrible days for you, Nora.

Nora: I fought a hard fight.

Helmer: And suffered pain and saw no escape but—No, we're not going to dwell on anything unpleasant. We'll just be grateful and keep on repeating: it's over now, it's over! You hear me, Nora? You don't seem to realize—it's over. What's it mean—that frozen look? Oh, poor little Nora, I understand. You can't believe I've forgiven you. But I have, Nora; I swear I have. I know that what you did, you did out of love for me.

Nora: That's true.

Helmer: You loved me the way a wife ought to love her husband. It's simply the means that you couldn't judge. But you think I love you any the less for not knowing how to handle your affairs? No, no—just lean on me; I'll guide you and teach you. I wouldn't be a man if this feminine helplessness didn't make you twice as attractive to me. You mustn't mind those sharp words I said— that was all in the first confusion of thinking my world had collapsed. I've forgiven you, Nora; I swear I've forgiven you.

Nora: My thanks for your forgiveness. (She goes out through the door, right.)

Helmer: No, wait—(Peers in.) What are you doing in there?

Nora (inside): Getting out of my costume.

Helmer (by the open door): Yes, do that. Try to calm yourself and collect your thoughts again, my frightened little songbird. You can rest easy now; I've got wide wings to shelter you with. (Walking about close by the door.) How snug and nice our home is, Nora. You're safe here; I'll keep you like a hunted dove I've rescued out of a hawk's claws. I'll bring peace to your poor, shuddering heart. Gradually it'll happen, Nora; you'll see. Tomorrow all this will look different to you; then everything will be as it was. I won't have to go on repeating I forgive you; you'll feel it for yourself. How can you imagine I'd ever conceivably want to disown you—or even blame you in any way? Ah, you don't know a man's heart, Nora. For a man there's something indescribably sweet and satisfying in knowing he's forgiven his wife—and forgiven her out of a full and open heart. It's as if she belongs to him in two ways now: in a sense he's given her fresh into the world again, and she's become his wife and his child as well. From now on that's what you'll be to me—you little, bewildered, helpless thing. Don't be afraid of anything, Nora; just open your heart to me, and I'll be conscience and will to you both—(Nora enters in her regular clothes.) What's this? Not in bed? You've changed your dress?

Nora: Yes, Torvald, I've changed my dress.

Helmer: But why now, so late?

Nora: Tonight I'm not sleeping.

Helmer: But Nora dear—

Nora (looking at her watch): It's still not so very late. Sit down, Torvald; we have a lot to talk over. (She sits at one side of the table.)

Helmer: Nora—what is this? That hard expression—

Nora: Sit down. This'll take some time. I have a lot to say.

Helmer (sitting at the table directly opposite her): You worry me, Nora. And I don't understand you.

Nora: No, that's exactly it. You don't understand me. And I've never understood you either—until tonight. No, don't interrupt. You can just listen to what I say. We're closing out accounts, Torvald.

Helmer: How do you mean that?

Nora (after a short pause): Doesn't anything strike you about our sitting here like this?

Helmer: What's that?

Nora: We've been married now eight years. Doesn't it occur to you that this is the first time we two, you and I, man and wife, have ever talked seriously together?

Helmer: What do you mean—seriously?

Nora: In eight whole years—longer even—right from our first acquaintance, we've never exchanged a serious word on any serious thing.

Helmer: You mean I should constantly go and involve you in problems you couldn't possibly help me with?

Nora: I'm not talking of problems. I'm saying that we've never sat down seriously together and tried to get to the bottom of anything.

Helmer: But dearest, what good would that ever do you?

Nora: That's the point right there: you've never understood me. I've been wronged greatly, Torvald—first by Papa, and then by you.

Helmer: What! By us—the two people who've loved you more than anyone else?

Nora (shaking her head): You never loved me. You've thought it fun to be in love with me, that's all.

Helmer: Nora, what a thing to say!

Nora: Yes, it's true now, Torvald. When I lived at home with Papa, he told me all his opinions, so I had the same ones too; or if they were different I hid them, since he wouldn't have cared for that. He used to call me his doll-child, and he played with me the way I played with my dolls. Then I came into your house—

Helmer: How can you speak of our marriage like that?

Nora (unperturbed): I mean, then I went from Papa's hands into yours. You arranged everything to your own taste, and so I got the same taste as you—or I pretended to; I can't remember. I guess a little of both, first one, then the other. Now when I look back, it seems as if I'd lived here like a beggar—just from hand to mouth. I've lived by doing tricks for you, Torvald. But that's the way you wanted it. It's a great sin what you and Papa did to me. You're to blame that nothing's become of me.

Helmer: Nora, how unfair and ungrateful you are! Haven't you been happy here?

Nora: No, never. I thought so—but I never have.

Helmer: Not—not happy!

Nora: No, only lighthearted. And you've always been so kind to me. But our home's been nothing but a playpen. I've been your doll-wife here, just as at home I was Papa's doll-child. And in turn the children have been my dolls. I thought it was fun when you played with me, just as they thought it fun when I played with them. That's been our marriage, Torvald.

Helmer: There's some truth in what you're saying—under all the raving exaggeration. But it'll all be different after this. Playtime's over; now for the schooling.

Nora: Whose schooling—mine or the children's?

Helmer: Both yours and the children's, dearest.

Nora: Oh, Torvald, you're not the man to teach me to be a good wife to you.

Helmer: And you can say that?

Nora: And I—how am I equipped to bring up children?

Helmer: Nora!

Nora: Didn't you say a moment ago that that was no job to trust me with?

Helmer: In a flare of temper! Why fasten on that?

Nora: Yes, but you were so very right. I'm not up to the job. There's another job I have to do first. I have to try to educate myself. You can't help me with that. I've got to do it alone. And that's why I'm leaving you now.

Helmer (jumping up): What's that?

Nora: I have to stand completely alone, if I'm ever going to discover myself and the world out there. So I can't go on living with you.

Helmer: Nora, Nora!

Nora: I want to leave right away. Kristine should put me up for the night—

Helmer: You're insane! You've no right! I forbid you!

Nora: From here on, there's no use forbidding me anything. I'll take with me whatever is mine. I don't want a thing from you, either now or later.

Helmer: What kind of madness is this!

Nora: Tomorrow I'm going home—I mean, home where I came from. It'll be easier up there to find something to do.

Helmer: Oh, you blind, incompetent child!

Nora: I must learn to be competent, Torvald.

Helmer: Abandon your home, your husband, your children! And you're not even thinking what people will say.

Nora: I can't be concerned about that. I only know how essential this is.

Helmer: Oh, it's outrageous. So you'll run out like this on your most sacred vows.

Nora: What do you think are my most sacred vows?

Helmer: And I have to tell you that! Aren't they your duties to your husband and children?

Nora: I have other duties equally sacred.

Helmer: That isn't true. What duties are they?

Nora: Duties to myself.

Helmer: Before all else, you're a wife and a mother.

Nora: I don't believe in that any more. I believe that, before all else, I'm a human being, no less than you—or anyway, I ought to try to become one. I know the majority thinks you're right, Torvald, and plenty of books agree with you, too. But I can't go on believing what the majority says, or what's written in books. I have to think over these things myself and try to understand them.

Helmer: Why can't you understand your place in your own home? On a point like that, isn't there one everlasting guide you can turn to? Where's your religion?

Nora: Oh, Torvald, I'm really not sure what religion is.

Helmer: What—?

Nora: I only know what the minister said when I was confirmed. He told me religion was this thing and that. When I get clear and away by myself, I'll go into that problem too. I'll see if what the minister said was right, or, in any case, if it's right for me.

Helmer: A young woman your age shouldn't talk like that. If religion can't move you, I can try to rouse your conscience. You do have some moral feeling? Or, tell me—has that gone too?

Nora: It's not easy to answer that, Torvald. I simply don't know. I'm all confused about these things. I just know I see them so differently from you. I find out, for one thing, that the law's not at all what I'd thought—but I can't get it through my head that the law is fair. A woman hasn't a right to protect her dying father or save her husband's life! I can't believe that.

Helmer: You talk like a child. You don't know anything of the world you live in.

Nora: No, I don't. But now I'll begin to learn for myself. I'll try to discover who's right, the world or I.

Helmer: Nora, you're sick; you've got a fever. I almost think you're out of your head.

Nora: I've never felt more clearheaded and sure in my life.

Helmer: And—clearheaded and sure—you're leaving your husband and children?

Nora: Yes.

Helmer: Then there's only one possible reason.

Nora: What?

Helmer: You no longer love me.

Nora: No. That's exactly it.

Helmer: Nora! You can't be serious!

Nora: Oh, this is so hard, Torvald—you've been so kind to me always. But I can't help it. I don't love you any more.

Helmer (struggling for composure): Are you also clearheaded and sure about that?

Nora: Yes, completely. That's why I can't go on staying here.

Helmer: Can you tell me what I did to lose your love?

Nora: Yes, I can tell you. It was this evening when the miraculous thing didn't come—then I knew you weren't the man I'd imagined.

Helmer: Be more explicit; I don't follow you.

Nora: I've waited now so patiently eight long years—for, my Lord, I know miracles don't come every day. Then this crisis broke over me, and such a certainty filled me: *now* the miraculous event would occur. While Krogstad's letter was lying out there, I never for an instant dreamed that you could give in to his terms. I was so utterly sure you'd say to him: go on, tell your tale to the whole wide world. And when he'd done that—

Helmer: Yes, what then? When I'd delivered my own wife into shame and disgrace—!

Nora: When he'd done that, I was so utterly sure that you'd step forward, take the blame on yourself and say: I am the guilty one.

Helmer: Nora—!

Nora: You're thinking I'd never accept such a sacrifice from you? No, of course not. But what good would my protests be against you? That was the miracle I was waiting for, in terror and hope. And to stave that off, I would have taken my life.

Helmer: I'd gladly work for you day and night, Nora—and take on pain and deprivation. But there's no one who gives up honor for love.

Nora: Millions of women have done just that.

Helmer: Oh, you think and talk like a silly child.

Nora: Perhaps. But you neither think nor talk like the man I could join myself to. When your big fright was over—and it wasn't from any threat against me, only for what might damage you—when all the danger was past, for you it was just as if nothing had happened. I was exactly the same, your little lark, your doll, that you'd have to handle with double care now that I'd turned out so brittle and frail. (*Gets up.*) Torvald—in that instant it dawned on me that for eight years I've been living here with a stranger, and that I'd even conceived three children—oh, I can't stand the thought of it! I could tear myself to bits.

Helmer (*heavily*): I see. There's a gulf that's opened between us—that's clear. Oh, but Nora, can't we bridge it somehow?

Nora: The way I am now, I'm no wife for you.

Helmer: I have the strength to make myself over.

Nora: Maybe—if your doll gets taken away.

Helmer: But to part! To part from you! No, Nora, no—I can't imagine it.

Nora (*going out, right*): All the more reason why it has to be. (*She reenters with her coat and a small overnight bag, which she puts on a chair by the table.*)

Helmer: Nora, Nora, not now! Wait till tomorrow.

Nora: I can't spend the night in a strange man's room.

Helmer: But couldn't we live here like brother and sister—

Nora: You know very well how long that would last. (*Throws her shawl about her.*) Good-bye, Torvald. I won't look in on the children. I know they're in better hands than mine. The way I am now, I'm no use to them.

Helmer: But someday, Nora—someday—?

Nora: How can I tell? I haven't the least idea what'll become of me.

Helmer: But you're my wife, now and wherever you go.

Nora: Listen, Torvald—I've heard that when a wife deserts her husband's house just as I'm doing, then the law frees him from all responsibility. In any case, I'm freeing you from being responsible. Don't feel yourself bound, any more than I will. There has to be absolute freedom for us both. Here, take your ring back. Give me mine.

Helmer: That too?

Nora: That too.

Helmer: There it is.

Nora: Good. Well, now it's all over. I'm putting the keys here. The maids know all about keeping up the house—better than I do. Tomorrow, after I've left town, Kristine will stop by to pack up everything that's mine from home. I'd like those things shipped up to me.

Helmer: Over! All over! Nora, won't you ever think about me?

Nora: I'm sure I'll think of you often, and about the children and the house here.

Helmer: May I write you?

Nora: No—never. You're not to do that.

Helmer: Oh, but let me send you—

Nora: Nothing. Nothing.

Helmer: Or help you if you need it.

Nora: No. I accept nothing from strangers.

Helmer: Nora—can I never be more than a stranger to you?

Nora (*picking up the overnight bag*): Ah, Torvald—it would take the greatest miracle of all—

Helmer: Tell me the greatest miracle!

Nora: You and I both would have to transform ourselves to the point that—Oh, Torvald, I've stopped believing in miracles.

Helmer: But I'll believe. Tell me! Transform ourselves to the point that—?

Nora: That our living together could be a true marriage. (*She goes out down the hall.*)

Helmer (sinks down on a chair by the door, face buried in his hands): Nora! Nora! (*Looking about and rising.*) Empty. She's gone. (*A sudden hope leaps in him.*) The greatest miracle—?

From below, the sound of a door slamming shut.

QUESTIONS

ACT I

1. From the opening conversation between Helmer and Nora, what are your impressions of him? Of her? Of their marriage?
2. At what moment in the play do you understand why it is called *A Doll House?*
3. In what ways does Mrs. Linde provide a contrast for Nora?
4. What in Krogstad's first appearance on stage, and in Dr. Rank's remarks about him, indicates that the bank clerk is a menace?
5. Of what illegal deed is Nora guilty? How does she justify it?
6. When the curtain falls on Act I, what problems now confront Nora?

ACT II

1. As Act II opens, what are your feelings on seeing the stripped, ragged Christmas tree? How is it suggestive?
2. What events that soon occur make Nora's situation even more difficult?
3. How does she try to save herself?
4. Why does Nora fling herself into the wild tarantella?

ACT III

1. For what possible reasons does Mrs. Linde pledge herself to Krogstad?
2. How does Dr. Rank's announcement of his impending death affect Nora and Helmer?
3. What is Helmer's reaction to learning the truth about Nora's misdeed? Why does he blame Nora's father? What is revealing (of Helmer's own character) in his remark, "From now on happiness doesn't matter; all that matters is saving the bits and pieces, the appearance . . ."?
4. When Helmer finds that Krogstad has sent back the note, what is his response? How do you feel toward him?
5. How does the character of Nora develop in this act?
6. How do you interpret her final slamming of the door?

GENERAL QUESTIONS

1. In what ways do you find Nora a victim? In what ways at fault?
2. Try to state the theme of the play. Does it involve women's rights? Self-fulfillment?
3. What dramatic question does the play embody? At what moment can this question first be stated?
4. What is the crisis? In what way is this moment or event a "turning point"? (In what new direction does the action turn?)
5. Eric Bentley, in an essay titled "Ibsen, Pro and Con" (*In Search of Theater,* New York: Knopf, 1953), criticizes the character of Krogstad, calling him "a mere pawn of the plot."

"When convenient to Ibsen, he is a blackmailer. When inconvenient, he is converted."
Do you agree or disagree?

6. Why is the play considered a work of realism? Is there anything in it that does not seem realistic?
7. In what respects does A Doll House seem to apply to life today? Is it in any way dated? Could there be a Nora in North America in the 1990s?

EXPERIMENT AND THE ABSURD

In the 1960s, according to one historian of the theater, Arthur Sainer, "Everything came into question." Was the traditional curtained stage necessary? Did a play really need a playhouse, or might it be performed in any public place? Did plays really need written scripts, or might they be improvised as the actors went along?[1]

Some experimental groups took inspiration from Antonin Artaud, French Surrealist poet and playwright, who had argued for a theater without a stage, in which a spectacle takes place all around the spectators, even in their midst.[2] Many young actors and playwrights joined **ensembles,** companies of kindred souls often living in a commune, working together to create new plays. Some ensembles offered plays anywhere they could: in streets, in parks, on rooftops, in parking lots, even in laundromats. Unlike traditional plays, such works obviously sought to shatter the boundary between actors and audience, and to attain such realism that the play can hardly be distinguished from the stream of passing life. At one performance of the Firehouse Theater, the audience was invited to take part:

> "Would you like to see Faust or be Faust?" Those who chose to "see" Faust kept their roles as spectators. Those who chose to "be" Faust were enclosed in a vast communal bedsheet, given a powdered soap with which to perform a ritual hand-washing of one another, and then brought into close physical contact for up to thirty minutes as they swayed back and forth to an om-like chant.[3]

Ensembles, though some have been pretentious, at least have recalled that drama can be a kind of ritual, with living participants. Yet such experiments raise vexing questions. Can a play break down the distinction between art and "real life" without losing any life that, in a conventional play, the playwright's art holds fast? An enduring work of the 1960s, A Vietnamese Wedding by Hispanic-American dramatist Maria Irene Fornes, raises this question in challenging form.

---

[1]Sainer, The Radical Theatre Notebook (New York: Avon, 1975) 15.   [2]See especially "The Theater of Cruelty (First Manifesto)" in The Theater and Its Double, translated by Mary Caroline Richards (New York: Grove, 1958).   [3]Sainer 72.

Maria Irene Fornes

A VIETNAMESE WEDDING

Maria Irene Fornes was born in 1930 in Havana, Cuba. After the death of her father, she came to New York with her mother in 1945, and at first worked in a factory. She studied painting, in night school and later with Hans Hoffman at the Provincetown School. In 1954–57, Fornes lived and painted in Paris, where the original production of Samuel Beckett's Waiting for Godot inspired her to begin writing plays of her own. During the 1960s she took a leading part in the flowering Off-Off Broadway movement, a wave of fresh plays by new playwrights, produced in small, low-rent theaters. Her first major critical success was the musical Promenade (1965, revised in 1969), which enjoyed a long Off-Broadway run. She has also written about

Maria Irene Fornes

two dozen other plays, many highly experimental, in a wide variety of styles, generally set in a pre-industrial society. These include Tango Palace (1963), The Successful Life of Three (1965), Molly's Dream (1968), Fefu and Her Friends (1977), The Danube (1982), Mud (1983), The Conduct of Life (1985), Hunger (1987), and recently And What of the Night? (1990). Over the years Fornes has garnered many grants and prizes, among them seven Obie awards (the Off-Broadway equivalent of Hollywood's Oscar) for her plays, plus another for distinguished direction. For the past several years she has been in charge of Manhattan's INTAR Hispanic Playwrights-in-Residence Laboratory. Fornes has designed and executed costumes and sets for many productions, and she insists on directing her own plays whenever possible. A Vietnamese Wedding was first performed in February 1967 in New York's Washington Square Methodist Church as an event in Angry Arts Week, a series of protests and demonstrations against U.S. involvement in Vietnam.

The following objects are to be set in the manner indicated in the diagram:

10 Chairs
10 5 x 7 cards
3 Flower garlands (about 24″ around)
7 Red sashes (about 5′ long)
8 Red trays or plates
   Areca leaves (or a substitute)
   Betel nuts (or a substitute)
1 Ring
1 Necklace
1 Bracelet

3 Bags of chocolate money
2 3 x 5 cards
1 Colorful floor mat
5 Candles and holders
1 Sheet of red rice paper
1 Match box
1 Pen
4 Whistles
4 Noisemakers
1 Tape of Vietnamese music (*Music of Vietnam*, Ethnic Folkways Library FE 4352, is suggested.)

The ten 5 x 7 cards will indicate the position of the participants and will be placed on the chairs as shown in the diagram.

The flower wreaths are to be placed on the back of chairs 5, 6, 7.

The red sashes are to be placed on the back of chairs 1, 2, 3, 4, 8, 9, 10

Seven trays are to be placed on the floor facing chairs 1, 2, 3, 4, 8, 9, 10. They are to contain areca leaves and betel nuts. Besides these, the Groom's tray will contain the ring, the necklace, and the bracelet; the Father of the Groom's will contain the 3 chocolate money bags and a 3 x 5 card with the following speech:

Friends, neighbors, and
newly acquired family; may we take
your daughter to our house?

The second 3 x 5 card should have the following speech:

Friends, neighbors, and
newly acquired family; we allow you
to take our daughter to your house.

and should be held by Florence.

The eighth red tray should be in a place accessible to Irene, and will contain the pen, the matches and the red rice paper with the following message:

Rose Silk Thread God,
look after our marriage.

Florence, Remy, Aileen and Irene will hold the whistles and noisemakers and use them at the end of the piece.

A *Vietnamese Wedding* is not a play. Rehearsals should serve the sole purpose of getting the readers acquainted with the text and the actions of the piece. The

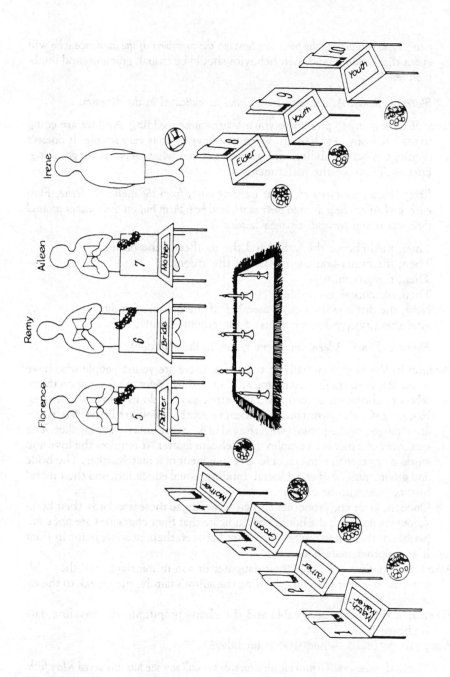

four people conducting the piece are hosts to the members of the audience who will enact the wedding, and their behavior should be casual, gracious, and unobtrusive.

Florence, Remy, Aileen, and Irene stand as indicated in the diagram.

Remy: We are going to present to you a Vietnamese wedding. And we are going to ask a few of you to help us. What you have to do is very simple. It doesn't require any acting ability, and we will tell you what to do as we go along. First, we'll choose the matchmaker.

Remy chooses the members of the wedding party from the audience. Irene, Florence, and Aileen help them to their seats, and help them put on their sashes around their waists and garlands on their heads.

Then, we'll choose the father and the mother of the bride.
Then, the father and the mother of the groom.
Then, the groom.
Then, we choose the bride.
Now, the distinguished elder member of the groom's family.
And then, two young members of the groom's family.

Florence, Remy, Aileen, and Irene return to their positions.

Florence: In Vietnam, especially in the cities, there are young people who have rebelled against traditional customs. That is, they prefer to take it upon themselves to choose their own marital partner as they do in western countries. However, for the most part, Vietnamese youths follow tradition. Marriages are arranged by the parents with the aid of an experienced matchmaker. The matching of a pair is a complex and delicate matter. It requires the love and wisdom of parents, plus the objective judgment of a matchmaker. The bride and groom must be of equal social standing, equal education, and their moral history must also be equal.
Once the bride and groom are chosen according to these standards, their horoscopes are drawn. If the horoscopes indicate that their characters are not compatible or that there might be conflict between them at some point in their lives, another mate is chosen.

Aileen: If a family is asked for their daughter or son in marriage, and they wish to refuse the offer without offending the suitor's family, they speak to the astrologer privately.

Florence: If the offer is acceptable and the charts propitious, the wedding date is chosen.

Remy (To the Bride): When is your birthday?

The Bride answers. To provide an example we will say she has answered May fifth. Remy then passes the information on to Florence.

May fifth.

Florence looks up the date in the accompanying chart and replies.

January 1–20: Capricorn
January 21–31: Aquarius

February 1–19: Aquarius
February 20–28: Pisces
March 1–20: Pisces
March 21–31: Aries
April 1–19: Aries
April 20–30: Taurus
May 1–20: Taurus
May 21–31: Gemini
June 1–21: Gemini
June 22–30: Cancer
July 1–21: Cancer
July 22–31: Leo
August 1–21: Leo
August 22–31: Virgo
September 1–22: Virgo
September 23–30: Libra
October 1–22: Libra
October 23–31: Scorpio
November 1–21: Scorpio
November 22–30: Sagittarius
December 1–21: Sagittarius
December 22–31: Capricorn

Florence: Taurus.
Remy (To the Groom): When is your birthday?

The Groom answers. We will say he was born November fifth.

Remy (To Florence): November fifth.

Florence looks up the date in the chart.

Florence: Scorpio.
Remy: Taurus and Scorpio. Very good!
Aileen: Very, very good!
Florence: Excellent!
Remy: Formerly, girls were wed as young as thirteen and boys at sixteen. The reason for early marriages was usually economic. For some families, to give their daughter away meant one less mouth to feed. For others, to gain a daughter meant one more person to help with the housework. For some, the addition of a male meant another helping hand in the field. There was no general rule as to whether it was convenient to add or to subtract one number in the family. It depended on the particular needs of each household.
These early marriages were usually satisfactory to the family, but as the young people grew, it happened occasionally that they did not find their mate to their liking. A young woman tells us about her unhappy marriage in this popular poem:

Aileen: My mother was greedy.
   She wanted
   A basket of rice,
   A fat pig,
   And a Hang Kung tail.

   I asked her to refuse.
   But she said I was
   Too young to know,
   And brought me to my groom.

   Now, I am fully grown.
   I am tall and my husband is short.

   We are like a pair of unequal chopsticks.

Remy: Child marriages are no longer common in Vietnam.
Aileen: Though many things have changed, the wedding ritual remains the same.
   The betel nut and the areca leaf are symbolic of love and good will, and they
   are always exchanged as a most valuable offering between the bride's and the
   groom's families. The custom derives from an ancient myth.
Florence: During the reign of Hung Wung III, there was a mandarin named Cao,
   who had two beautiful sons, Tan and Sung. One day, the mandarin and his
   wife died, and the two boys were left without a father, a mother, a house,
   or money. The boys had to go from town to town looking for work, and they
   could find none.
   One day them came to the house of Magistrate Luu who happened to be a
   friend of their father Cao. Luu received the boys in his house, and said: "I
   never had a son and now I have two." It was true that Magistrate Luu didn't
   have a son, but he had a daughter who was as fair as a white lotus and as
   fresh as a spring rose. Naturally, both boys loved her the moment they saw
   her. But neither of them spoke to her of his love because each knew his brother
   also loved her.
   Luu realized what was happening. He knew that the boys would become old
   and shriveled before they spoke to the maiden. To prevent that from happening, he decided he would follow the custom and give his daughter to the
   eldest. One day he said to Sung: "Which one of you is the eldest?" And Sung
   said: "Tan is the eldest," but Tan quickly said: "Sung is the eldest." Only one
   of them was telling the truth. But Luu, who was a very clever fellow, decided
   he would not ask any more questions. He knew the boys would keep giving
   him the same answers. Instead, that night for dinner, he placed only one pair
   of chopsticks between the brothers.
   When dinner was served, Sung, without giving it any thought, picked up
   the chopsticks and handed them to Tan. And Tan, without giving it any
   thought, received the chopsticks and bent down to eat, as any older brother
   would. "I found you out," said Luu to Tan. "You are the eldest. You will marry
   my daughter."

Remy: Tan was now the happiest of men in all of Vietnam. He spent all his time taking walks with his new bride, reciting poetry to her, and singing love songs. Sung overcame his love for the fair maiden and accepted his lot, for he wanted only joy and happiness for his beloved brother. But after a while, he realized that he was very lonely. He sat alone in his room waiting for a sign of care, or friendship, from Tan . . . but nothing happened.

In wild sorrow, he ran away from home, for he could stand the sadness no more. He ran and ran, passing leafy forests and flat meadows, until he reached the dark blue sea. Night came and Sung fell exhausted onto the ground, hungry and thirsty. His head was as hot as fire. And he cried and cried until he died and was turned into a white chalky rock.

When Tan realized his brother was gone, he went after him. He passed the leafy forests and the flat meadows and he arrived at the same dark blue sea. He too was exhausted. He sat down by the white chalky rock, and he cried and cried until he died. And he was turned into a tree with a straight stem and green palms. It was the areca tree.

Aileen: The lovely maiden missed her husband so much that she set off one day to look for him. She went along the same way as the brothers and reached the sea and lay down exhausted at the foot of the tall areca tree. Tears of despair rolled down her cheeks and she cried sorrowfully until she died. She was turned into a creeping plant—the betel—which twined around the lofty trunk of the areca tree.

That night, all the people in the village nearby had the same dream. They all dreamt the story of Tan, Sung and the maiden. The strange occurrence came to the ears of King Hung Wung III, who said: "If they were so devoted to each other, let us mix the three things, the rock, the areca leaf, and the betel nut, and see what happens." They burned the rock, which became white and soft, and they wrapped it in an areca leaf. Then they cut a piece of betel nut, and squeezed them all together. The mixture became liquid and red, like blood. The king then said: "This is the true symbol of conjugal and fraternal love. Let the tree and the plant be grown everywhere to remind us of true devotion and love. And let us chew the betel nut so that affection and good will will reign among us."

Florence: The habitual chewing of the betel nut produces a blackening effect on the teeth, until they appear as though they have been lacquered. In the past, such black teeth were an object of admiration. A young man tells us about his loved one's teeth in a popular poem:

Remy: Do you remember me when you go home?
   When I go home I remember your teeth.

   I would pay one hundred taels
   For your beautiful lips.

   But for your black teeth
   I would pay much more.

Aileen: The wedding ceremony.

Florence: The procedure is very formal. The date and hour must be exact, according to horoscopic readings. Everybody wears his best clothing. The boy's family wears red sashes around their waists.

Remy: The boy's family walks from the boy's home to the girl's home in a ceremonial procession.

Irene tells the members of the Groom's party to stand and pick up their trays. She leads them in a procession around the theater aisles, while Aileen reads the following speech. The Vietnamese music is played softly.

Aileen: The matchmaker has previously discussed the amount and kind of gifts. As the gifts are to be distributed among the bride's family and friends, the larger the family the more gifts are required. If the groom's family is rich, the gifts will include sacks of grain, live animals, clothing, candles, incense, tea, cakes, betel nuts and areca leaves, but no matter how poor the family is, there will always be betel nuts and areca leaves.

Florence: The gifts are placed on the ancestral altar by the groom's party.

Irene instructs the party to place the trays on the altar (floor mat). Then she instructs the Groom and his Father to stand to the left of the altar, and the rest to the right.

Remy: The candles are lit.

Irene lights the candles with the help of some of the Groom's family. The music stops.

Aileen: The bridegroom gives the bride jewels—an engagement ring, a necklace and a bracelet.

If the Groom doesn't act of his own accord, Irene will tell him what to do. The same applies to any of the following directions.

Florence: The father of the groom gives the bride, her father, and her mother a certain amount of money.

He does it.

Remy: The groom's father makes a solemn request to take the bride away to their home.

The Groom's Father reads the card on his plate.

Solemnly the father of the bride agrees.

Florence gives the Father of the Bride his card to read. He reads it out loud.

Then they all bow three times.

Everyone bows three times. Irene stands next to the Groom with her tray.

Aileen: A message to the genie of marriage, the Rose Silk Thread God, is written on a red sheet of paper.

Irene gives the red paper to the Groom to sign.

Then, it is burned, so that the message will reach the genie.

The Groom burns the message.

Florence: They all bow three times again, paying their final respect to the genie.

Everyone bows.

Remy: At this point, the couple is considered married.

Irene tells the Groom to take the Bride by the hand and head the procession.

And a party is held with a lot of speechmaking, gift-giving, and merrymaking.

Irene leads the procession, going first around the Readers, then, along the aisles. The music starts softly while Remy reads.

The groom's family traditionally acts as though they are very anxious to take the bride to their home. The groom's entourage then begins the trip home in the form of a procession with the bride and her attendants, friends, and relatives joining in. Little children sometimes set up roadblocks and ask tolls of the wedding party. These are readily paid, as they consider it bad luck to refuse.

Florence: Upon arrival at the groom's house, the party is met by the loud noise of firecrackers.

The music plays loudly. Florence, Remy, and Aileen join the procession, and blow their whistles. Irene also blows her whistle and leads the procession out of the theater.

QUESTIONS

1. Do you agree with the playwright (in her preliminary stage directions) that *A Vietnamese Wedding* "is not a play"? If so, what then would you call it? In what ways does it resemble other plays you have read? In what ways is it different?
2. Fornes's play was first staged in 1967, in a Methodist church in New York City. To what extent might a 1967 audience's reactions have been influenced by U.S. involvement in the Vietnam War? How much would you expect present-day audiences to be affected by that involvement?
3. Does the statement Fornes makes in "Criticism: On Drama" (page 1450) apply in any way to *A Vietnamese Wedding*?

Fresh attitudes toward play production and theater design reflect fresh conceptions of drama. One of the more prominent developments in mid-twentieth-century drama has been the rise of **tragicomedy,** found in plays that not only stir us to pity and fear (echoing Aristotle's description of the effect of tragedy), but to laughter as well. Although tragicomedy is a kind of drama we think modern, it is by no means a new invention. The term was used (although jokingly) by the Roman writer of comedy Plautus in about 185 B.C., and later critics have applied it to plays of the classical Greek dramatist Euripides—notably *Alcestis*, in which apparently tragic events jostle with snappy repartee and end happily.

Since ancient times, playwrights have mingled laughter and tears, defying the neoclassical doctrine requiring adherence to the unities (discussed on page 970). Shakespeare is fond of tragicomic minglings: in *Hamlet*, the prince jokes with a gravedigger; in *Antony and Cleopatra*, the queen commits suicide with a poisonous asp brought to her by a wisecracking clown. In the tragedies of Shakespeare and others, passages of clownish humor are sometimes called **comic relief,** meaning that the comedy introduces a sharp contrast. But such passages can do more than provide relief. In *Othello* (III,iv,1–16), the clown's banter with Desdemona for a moment makes the surrounding tragedy seem, by comparison, more poignant and intense.

No one doubts that *Othello* is a tragedy, but some twentieth-century plays leave us bemused: should we laugh or cry? One of the most talked-about plays since World War II, Samuel Beckett's *Waiting for Godot*, portrays two clownish tramps who mark time in a wasteland, wistfully looking for a savior who never arrives. Contemporary drama has often featured such **antiheroes:** ordinary people, inglorious and inarticulate, who carry on not from bravery but from inertia.[4] We cannot help laughing at the tramps' painful situation; or, turning the idea around, we feel deeply moved by their ridiculous plight. Surely, a modern tragicomedy like *Godot* does not show us great souls suffering greatly—as Edith Hamilton said we are shown in a classical tragedy.

But perhaps the effect of such a play takes time to sink in. Contemporary playwright Edward Albee suggests that sometimes the spectator's sense of relief after experiencing pity and fear (Aristotle calls it *katharsis*) may be a delayed reaction: "I don't feel that catharsis in a play necessarily takes place during the course of a play. Often it should take place afterwards."[5] If Albee is right, we may be amused while watching a tragicomedy, then go home and feel deeply stirred by it.

Straddling the fence between tragedy and comedy, Beckett portrays people whose suffering seems ridiculous. *Godot* belongs to the **theater of the absurd:** a general name for a constellation of plays first staged in Paris in the 1950s. "For the modern critical spirit, nothing can be taken entirely seriously, nor entirely lightly," according to Eugène Ionesco, one of the movement's leading playwrights and chief voices. A human being, such playwrights assume, is a helpless waif alone in a universe that confronts him with ridiculous obstacles. In Ionesco's *Amédée* (1953), a couple share an apartment with a gigantic corpse that keeps swelling relentlessly; in his *Rhinoceros* (1958), the human race starts turning into rhinos, except for one man, who remains human and isolated. A favorite theme in the theater of the absurd is that communication between people is impossible. Language is therefore futile: Ionesco's *The Bald Soprano* (1948) accordingly pokes fun at polite social conversation in a scene with dialogue consisting entirely of illogical strings of catchphrases. In *Endgame* (1957), Samuel Beckett also burlesques small talk, and dramatizes his sense of the present condition of mankind: the main

---

[4]The rise of the antihero in recent fiction is discussed briefly on page 49. These remarks apply to drama as well.   [5]"The Art of the Theater," interview in *The Paris Review*, No. 39, Fall 1966.

character is blind and paralyzed and his legless parents live inside two garbage cans. Oddly, the effect of the play isn't total gloom: we leave the theater both amused and bemused by it.[6]

Fashions in drama change along with playwrights' convictions. In the last two decades, some new plays have been neither absurd nor revolutionary: David Mamet's *American Buffalo* (1975), for one, realistically brings to life three petty thieves in a junk shop as they plot to steal a coin collection. And realistically, for the most part, playwrights of the current **feminist theater** in America have explored the lives, problems, and occasional triumphs of contemporary women. Notable success with both critics and the public has greeted plays such as Marsha Norman's *'Night, Mother* (1983), Beth Henley's *Crimes of the Heart* (1986), and Wendy Wasserstein's *The Heidi Chronicles* (1988).

Some leading critics, among them Richard Gilman, believe that the theater may have entered an era of **new naturalism.**[7] Indeed, many plays of this era analyze the lives of people, especially poor and unhappy people, under a realistic, searching light, showing the forces that shaped them. Sam Shepard in *Buried Child* (1978) explores violence and desperation in a family who dwell on the edge of poverty; while August Wilson, in *Joe Turner's Come and Gone* (1988), convincingly portrays life in a Pittsburgh ghetto lodging house. But if these newly established playwrights sometimes show life as frankly as did the earlier naturalists, both of those particular plays also contain rich and suggestive symbolism, and Wilson's portraits of his characters can be gentle and compassionate.

Yet the influence of the theater of the absurd lives on. In *The Tooth of Crime* (1972), Shepard has characters who transform themselves, even suddenly speak as though they were different people. As in the theater of the absurd, many plays of Shepard, Edward Albee, and Maria Irene Fornes sometimes defy logic, cause and effect, and consistency. Many of our finest contemporary playwrights seem to have learned from the theater of the absurd, among them Tom Stoppard, whose works include both realistic plays and *The Real Inspector Hound*, a bizarre and ingenious comedy. If generalizations are possible, it can only be claimed that playwrights of this moment wear labels unwillingly, and express themselves in profuse variety.

[6]For an excellent study of the theater of the absurd, see Martin Esslin, *The Theatre of the Absurd*, revised edition (New York: Overlook, 1973).   [7]"Out Goes Absurdism—In comes the New Naturalism," *The New York Times Book Review*, 19 March 1978.

THE REAL INSPECTOR HOUND   1968

Tom Stoppard

Tom Stoppard was born Tomas Straussler in 1937 in Zlin, Czechoslovakia, the son of parents who moved to Singapore to escape the Nazis. There he attended a school run by Americans. When Japanese invaders threatened the city, he fled to India with his mother and elder brother; his father remained behind and lost his life. After the war, when his mother remarried, Stoppard took the last name of his English stepfather. As a student in Yorkshire, England, he recalls, his "Czecho-Chinese-American accent" caused his schoolmates to regard him as a curiosity. Leaving school at 17, he went to work as a reporter for a Bristol newspaper, and for a time was a play reviewer (like some of the characters in The Real Inspector Hound). His first major success as a playwright came in 1967 with Rosencrantz and Guildenstern Are Dead, *in which he re-moved two minor characters from Shakespeare's* Hamlet *and built a whole play around them. Since then his witty and often ingenious plays, produced throughout the English-speaking world, have enjoyed success both with the public and with critics. Among these are* Jumpers *(1972),* Travesties *(1974),* Night and Day *(1979),* On the Razzle *(1981), and* The Real Thing *(1982), which won a 1984 Tony Award for best play on Broadway. The prolific Stoppard has also written film scripts, radio and television plays, two novels, and short stories.*

Characters

Moon
Birdboot
Mrs. Drudge
Simon
Felicity
Cynthia
Magnus
Inspector Hound

The first thing is that the audience appear to be confronted by their own reflection in a huge mirror. Impossible. However, back there in the gloom—not at the footlights—a bank of plush seats and pale smudges of faces. The total effect having been established, it can be progressively faded out as the play goes on, until the front row remains to remind us of the rest and then, finally, merely two seats in that row—one of which is now occupied by Moon. Between Moon and the auditorium is an acting area which represents, in as realistic an idiom as possible, the drawing-room of Muldoon Manor. French windows at one side. A telephone fairly well upstage (i.e., towards Moon). The body of a man lies sprawled face down on the floor in front of a large settee. This settee must be of a size and design to allow it to be wheeled over the body, hiding it completely. Silence. The room. The body. Moon.

Moon stares blankly ahead. He turns his head to one side then the other, then up, then down—waiting. He picks up his program and reads the front cover. He turns over the page and reads.

He turns over the page and reads.

He turns over the page and reads.

He turns over the page and reads.

He looks at the back cover and reads.

He puts it down, crosses his legs, and looks about. He stares front. Behind him and to one side, barely visible, a man enters and sits down: Birdboot.

Pause. Moon picks up his program, glances at the front cover and puts it down impatiently. Pause . . . . Behind him there is the crackle of a chocolate-box, absurdly loud. Moon looks round. He and Birdboot see each other. They are clearly known to each other. They acknowledge each other with constrained waves. Moon looks straight ahead. Birdboot comes down to join him.

Note: Almost always, Moon and Birdboot converse in tones suitable for an auditorium, sometimes a whisper. However good the acoustics might be, they will have to have microphones where they are sitting. The effect must be not of sound picked up, amplified and flung out at the audience, but of sound picked up, carried and gently dispersed around the auditorium.

Anyway, Birdboot, with a box of Black Magic chocolates, makes his way down to join Moon and plumps himself down next to him, plumpish, middle-aged Birdboot and younger, taller, less-relaxed Moon.

Birdboot (*sitting down; conspiratorially*): Me and the lads have had a meeting in the bar and decided it's first-class family entertainment but if it goes on beyond half-past ten it's self-indulgent—pass it on . . . (*and laughs jovially.*) I'm on my own tonight, don't mind if I join you?

Moon: Hello, Birdboot.

Birdboot: Where's Higgs?

Moon: I'm standing in.

Moon and Birdboot: Where's Higgs?

Moon: Every time.

Birdboot: What?

Moon: It is as if we only existed one at a time, combining to achieve continuity. I keep space warm for Higgs. My presence defines his absence, his absence confirms my presence, his presence precludes mine . . . . When Higgs and I walk down this aisle together to claim our common seat, the oceans will fall into the sky and the trees will hang with fishes.

Birdboot (*he has not been paying attention, looking around vaguely, now catches up*): Where's Higgs?

Moon: The very sight of me with a complimentary ticket is enough. The streets are impassable tonight, the country is rising and the cry goes up from hill to hill—Where—is—Higgs? (*Small pause.*) Perhaps he's dead at last, or trapped in a lift somewhere, or succumbed to amnesia, wandering the land with his turn-ups° stuffed with ticket-stubs.

Birdboot regards him doubtfully for a moment.

Birdboot: Yes . . . Yes, well I didn't bring Myrtle tonight—not exactly her cup of tea, I thought, tonight.

Moon: Over her head, you mean?

Birdboot: Well, no—I mean it's a sort of a *thriller*, isn't it?

Moon: Is it?

Birdboot: That's what I heard. Who-killed thing?—no-one-will-leave-the-house?

Moon: I suppose so. Underneath.

Birdboot: *Underneath?!?* It's a whodunnit, man!—Look at it!

They look at it. The room. The body. Silence.

Has it started yet?

Moon: Yes.

Pause. They look at it.

Birdboot: Are you sure?

Moon: It's a pause.

Birdboot: You can't start with a *pause!* If you want my opinion there's total panic back there. (*Laughs and subsides.*) Where's Higgs tonight, then?

Moon: It will follow me to the grave and become my epitaph—Here lies Moon the second string: where's Higgs? . . . Sometimes I dream of revolution, a bloody *coup d'état*° by the second rank—troupes of actors slaughtered by their understudies, magicians sawn in half by indefatigably smiling glamor girls, cricket teams wiped out by marauding bands of twelfth men°—I dream of champions chopped down by rabbit-punching sparring partners while eternal bridesmaids turn and rape the bridegrooms over the sausage rolls and parliamentary private secretaries plant bombs in the Minister's Humber°—comedians die on provincial stages, robbed of their feeds by mutely triumphant stooges—And march—an army of assistants and deputies, the seconds-in-command, the runners-up, the right-hand men—storming the palace gates wherein the second son has already mounted the throne having committed regicide with a croquet mallet—stand-ins of the world stand up!—

Beat.

Sometimes I dream of Higgs.

---

turn-ups: trouser cuffs.   *coup d'état:* (French) the sudden overthrow of a government.   *twelfth men:* standby players on a cricket team.   *Humber:* a make of car.

Pause. Birdboot regards him doubtfully. He is at a loss, and grasps reality in the form of his box of chocolates.

Birdboot *(chewing into mike)*: Have a chocolate!
Moon: What kind?
Birdboot *(chewing into mike)*: Black Magic.
Moon: No thanks.

Chewing stops dead. Of such tiny victories and defeats . . .

Birdboot: I'll give you a tip, then. Watch the girl.
Moon: You think she did it?
Birdboot: No, no—the *girl*, watch her.
Moon: What girl?
Birdboot: You won't know her. I'll give you a nudge.
Moon: *You* know her, do you?
Birdboot *(suspiciously, bridling)*: What's *that* supposed to mean?
Moon: I beg your pardon?
Birdboot: I'm trying to tip you a wink—give you a nudge as good as a tip—for God's sake, Moon, what's the matter with you?—you could do yourself some good, spotting her first time out—she's new, from the provinces, going straight to the top. I don't want to put words into your mouth but a word from us and we could make her.
Moon: I suppose you've made dozens of them, like that.
Birdboot *(instantly outraged)*: I'll have you know I'm a family man devoted to my homely but good-natured wife, and if you're suggesting—
Moon: No, no—
Birdboot: —A man of my scrupulous morality—
Moon: I'm sorry.
Birdboot: —falsely besmirched—
Moon: Is that her?

For Mrs. Drudge has entered.

Birdboot: —don't be absurd, wouldn't be seen dead with the old—ah.

Mrs. Drudge is the char, middle-aged, turbanned. She heads straight for the radio, dusting on the trot.

Moon *(reading his program)*: Mrs. Drudge the Help.
Radio *(without preamble, having been switched on by Mrs. Drudge)*: We interrupt our program for a special police message.

Mrs. Drudge stops to listen.

The search still goes on for the escaped madman who is on the run in Essex.
Mrs. Drudge *(fear and dismay)*: Essex!
Radio: County police led by Inspector Hound have received a report that the man has been seen in the desolate marshes around Muldoon Manor.

Fearful gasp from Mrs. Drudge.

The man is wearing a darkish suit with a lightish shirt. He is of medium height and build and youngish. Anyone seeing a man answering to this description and acting suspiciously, is advised to phone the nearest police station.

A man answering this description has appeared behind Mrs. Drudge. He is acting suspiciously. He creeps in. He creeps out. Mrs. Drudge does not see him. He does not see the body.

That is the end of the police message.

Mrs. Drudge turns off the radio and resumes her cleaning. She does not see the body. Quite fortuitously, her view of the body is always blocked, and when it isn't she has her back to it. However, she is dusting and polishing her way towards it.

Birdboot: So that's what they say about me, is it?

Moon: What?

Birdboot: Oh, I know what goes on behind my back—sniggers—slanders—hole-in-corner innuendo—What have you heard?

Moon: Nothing.

Birdboot *(urbanely)*: Tittle tattle. Tittle, my dear fellow, tattle. I take no notice of it—the sly envy of scandal mongers—I can afford to ignore them, I'm a respectable married man—

Moon: Incidentally—

Birdboot: Water off a duck's back, I assure you.

Moon: Who was that lady I saw you with last night?

Birdboot *(unexpectedly stung into fury)*: How dare you! *(More quietly.)* How dare you. Don't you come here with your slimy insinuations! My wife Myrtle understands perfectly well that a man of my critical standing is obliged occasionally to mingle with the world of the footlights, simply by way of keeping *au fait*° with the latest—

Moon: I'm sorry—

Birdboot: That a critic of my scrupulous integrity should be vilified and pilloried in the stocks of common gossip—

Moon: Ssssh—

Birdboot: I have nothing to hide!—why, if this should reach the ears of my beloved Myrtle—

Moon: Can I have a chocolate?

Birdboot: What? Oh—*(Mollified.)* Oh yes—my dear fellow—yes, let's have a chocolate—No point in—yes, good show. *(Pops chocolate into his mouth and chews.)* Which one do you fancy?—Cherry? Strawberry? Coffee cream? Turkish delight?

Moon: I'll have montelimar.

Chewing stops.

Birdboot: Ah. Sorry. *(Just missed that one.)*

Moon: Gooseberry fondue?

---

au fait: (French) acquainted with the facts of something; familiar with.

Birdboot: No.

Moon: Pistacchio fudge? Nectarine cluster? Hickory nut praline? Château Neuf du Pape '55 cracknell°?

Birdboot: I'm afraid not. . . . Caramel?

Moon: Yes, all right.

Birdboot: Thanks very much. (*He gives Moon a chocolate. Pause.*) Incidentally, old chap, I'd be grateful if you didn't mention—I mean, you know how these misunderstandings get about. . . .

Moon: What?

Birdboot: The fact is, Myrtle simply doesn't *like* the theater . . . (*He trails off hopelessly.*)

Mrs. Drudge, whose discovery of the body has been imminent, now—by way of tidying the room—slides the couch over the corpse, hiding it completely. She resumes dusting and humming.

Moon: By the way, congratulations, Birdboot.

Birdboot: What?

Moon: At the Theater Royal. Your entire review reproduced in neon!

Birdboot (pleased): Oh . . . that old thing.

Moon: You've seen it, of course.

Birdboot (vaguely): Well, I was passing. . . .

Moon: I definitely intend to take a second look when it has settled down.

Birdboot: As a matter of fact I have a few color transparencies—I don't know whether you'd care to . . . ?

Moon: Please, please—love to, love to . . .

Birdboot hands over a few color slides and a battery-powered viewer which Moon holds up to his eyes as he speaks.

Yes . . . yes . . . lovely . . . awfully sound. It has scale, it has color, it is, in the best sense of the word, electric. Large as it is, it is a small masterpiece—I would go so far as to say—kinetic without being pop, and having said that, I think it must be said that here we have a review that adds a new dimension to the critical scene. I urge you to make haste to the Theatre Royal, for this is the stuff of life itself. (*Handling back the slides, morosely.*) All I ever got was "Unforgettable" on the posters for . . . What was it?

Birdboot: Oh—yes—I know . . . Was that you? I thought it was Higgs.

The phone rings. Mrs. Drudge seems to have been waiting for it to do so and for the last few seconds has been dusting it with an intense concentration. She snatches it up.

Ms. Drudge (into phone): Hello, the drawing-room of Lady Muldoon's country residence one morning in early spring? . . . Hello!—the draw—Who? Whom did you wish to speak to? I'm afraid there is no one of that name here, this is all very mysterious and I'm sure it's leading up to something, I hope nothing

cracknell: chocolate with crisp texture.

is amiss for we, that is Lady Muldoon and her houseguests, are here cut off from the world, including Magnus, the wheelchair-ridden half-brother of her ladyship's husband Lord Albert Muldoon who ten years ago went out for a walk on the cliffs and was never seen again.

Moon: Derivative, of course.

Birdboot: But quite sound.

Mrs. Drudge: Should a stranger enter our midst, which I very much doubt, I will tell him you called. Good-bye.

She puts down the phone and catches sight of the previously seen suspicious charac-ter who has now entered again, more suspiciously than ever, through the french windows. He senses her stare, freezes, and straightens up.

Simon: Ah!—hello there! I'm Simon Gascoyne, I hope you don't mind, the door was open so I wandered in. I'm a friend of Lady Muldoon, the lady of the house, having made her acquaintance through a mutual friend, Felicity Cun-ningham, shortly after moving into this neighborhood just the other day.

Mrs. Drudge: I'm Mrs. Drudge. I don't live in but I pop in on my bicycle when the weather allows to help in the running of charming though somewhat iso-lated Muldoon Manor. Judging by the time (*she glances at the clock*) you did well to get here before high water cut us off for all practical purposes from the outside world.

Simon: I took the short cut over the cliffs and followed one of the old smugglers' paths through the treacherous swamps that surround this strangely inaccessi-ble house.

Mrs. Drudge: Yes, many visitors have remarked on the topographical quirk in the local strata whereby there are no roads leading from the Manor, though there *are* ways of getting *to* it, weather allowing.

Simon: Yes, well I must say it's a lovely day so far.

Mrs. Drudge: Ah, but now that the cuckoo-beard is in bud there'll be fog before the sun hits Foster's Ridge.

Simon: I say, it's wonderful how you country people really know weather.

Mrs. Drudge (*suspiciously*): Know whether what?

Simon (*glancing out of the window*): Yes, it does seem to be coming on a bit foggy.

Mrs. Drudge: The fog is very treacherous around here—it rolls off the sea without warning, shrouding the cliffs in a deadly mantle of blind man's buff.

Simon: Yes, I've heard it said.

Mrs. Drudge: I've known whole week-ends when Muldoon Manor, as this lovely old Queen Anne house is called, might as well have been floating on the pack ice for all the good it would have done phoning the police. It was on such a week-end as this that Lord Muldoon who had lately brought his beau-tiful bride back to the home of his ancestors, walked out of this house ten years ago, and his body was never found.

Simon: Yes indeed, poor Cynthia.

Mrs. Drudge: His name was Albert.

Simon: Yes indeed, poor Albert. But tell me, is Lady Muldoon about?

Mrs. Drudge: I believe she is playing tennis on the lawn with Felicity Cunningham.

Simon (*startled*): Felicity Cunningham?

Mrs. Drudge: A mutual friend, I believe you said. A happy chance. I will tell them you are here.

Simon: Well, I can't really stay as a matter of fact—please don't disturb them—I really should be off.

Mrs. Drudge: They would be very disappointed. It is some time since we have had a four for pontoon bridge at the Manor, and I don't play cards myself.

Simon: There is another guest, then?

Mrs. Drudge: Major Magnus, the crippled half-brother of Lord Muldoon who turned up out of the blue from Canada just the other day, completes the house-party.

Mrs. Drudge leaves on this. Simon is undecided.

Moon (ruminating quietly): I think I must be waiting for Higgs to die.

Birdboot: What?

Moon: Half-afraid that I will vanish when he does.

The phone rings. Simon picks it up.

Simon: Hello?

Moon: I wonder if it's the same for Puckeridge?

Birdboot and Simon (together): Who?

Moon: Third string.

Birdboot: Your stand-in?

Moon: Does he wait for Higgs and I to write each other's obituary—does he dream—?

Simon: To whom did you wish to speak?

Birdboot: What's he like?

Moon: Bitter.

Simon: There is no one of that name here.

Birdboot: No—as a critic, what's Puckeridge like as a critic?

Moon (laughs poisonously): Nobody knows—

Simon: You must have got the wrong number!

Moon: —There's always been me and Higgs.

Simon replaces the phone and paces nervously. Pause. Birdboot consults his program.

Birdboot: Simon Gascoyne. It's not him, of course.

Moon: What?

Birdboot: I said it's not him.

Moon: Who is it, then?

Birdboot: My guess is Magnus.

Moon: In disguise, you mean?

Birdboot: What?

Moon: You think he's Magnus in disguise?

Birdboot: I don't think you're concentrating, Moon.

Moon: I thought you said—

Birdboot: You keep chattering on about Higgs and Puckeridge—what's the matter with you?

Moon (thoughtfully): I wonder if they talk about me . . . ?

A strange impulse makes Simon turn on the radio.

Radio: Here is another police message. Essex County police are still searching in vain for the madman who is at large in the deadly marshes of the coastal region. Inspector Hound, who is masterminding the operation, is not available for comment but it is widely believed that he has a secret plan . . . . Meanwhile police and volunteers are combing the swamps with loudhailers, shouting, "Don't be a madman, give yourself up." That is the end of the police message.

Simon turns off the radio. He is clearly nervous. Moon and Birdboot are on separate tracks.

Birdboot (knowingly): Oh yes . . .

Moon: Yes, I should think my name is seldom off Puckeridge's lips . . . sad, really. I mean, it's no life at all, a stand-in's stand-in.

Birdboot: Yes . . . yes . . .

Moon: Higgs never gives me a second thought. I can tell by the way he nods.

Birdboot: Revenge, of course.

Moon: What?

Birdboot: Jealousy.

Moon: Nonsense—there's nothing *personal* in it—

Birdboot: The paranoid grudge—

Moon (sharply first, then starting to career . . .): It is merely that it is not enough to wax at another's wane, to be held in reserve, to be on hand, on call, to step in or not at all, the substitute—the near offer—the temporary-acting— for I am Moon, continuous Moon, in my own shoes, Moon in June, April, September and no member of the human race keeps warm my bit of space— yes, I can tell by the way he nods.

Birdboot: Quite mad, of course.

Moon: What?

Birdboot: The answer lies out there in the swamps.

Moon: Oh.

Birdboot: The skeleton in the cupboard is coming home to roost.

Moon: Oh yes. (*He clears his throat . . . for both he and Birdboot have a "public" voice, a critic voice which they turn on for sustained pronouncements of opinion.*) Already in the opening stages we note the classic impact of the catalystic figure— the outsider—plunging through to the center of an ordered world and setting up the disruptions—the shock waves—which unless I am much mistaken will strip these comfortable people—these crustaceans in the rock pool of society— strip them of their shells and leave them exposed as the trembling raw meat which, at heart, is all of us. But there is more to it than that—

Birdboot: I agree—keep your eye on Magnus.

A tennis ball bounces through the french windows, closely followed by Felicity, who is in her twenties. She wears a pretty tennis outfit, and carries a racket.

Felicity (calling behind her): Out!

It takes her a moment to notice Simon who is standing shiftily to one side. Moon is stirred by a memory.

Moon: I say, Birdboot . . .

Birdboot: That's the one.

Felicity (catching sight of Simon): You!

Felicity's manner at the moment is one of great surprise but some pleasure.

Simon (nervously): Er, yes—hello again.

Felicity: What are you doing here?

Simon: Well, I . . .

Moon: She's—

Birdboot: Sssh . . .

Simon: No doubt you're surprised to see me.

Felicity: Honestly, darling, you really are extraordinary.

Simon: Yes, well, here I am.

Felicity: You must have been desperate to see me—I mean, I'm *flattered*, but couldn't it wait till I got back?

Simon (bravely): There is something you don't know.

Felicity: What is it?

Simon: Look, about the things I said—it may be that I got carried away a little— we both did—

Felicity (stiffly): What are you trying to say?

Simon: I love another!

Felicity: I see.

Simon: I didn't make any promises—I merely—

Felicity: You don't have to say any more—

Simon: Oh, I didn't want to hurt you—

Felicity: Of all the nerve!

Simon: Well, I—

Felicity: You philandering coward—

Simon: Let me explain—

Felicity: This is hardly the time and place—you think you can barge in anywhere, whatever I happen to be doing—

Simon: But I want you to know that my admiration for you is sincere—I don't want you to think that I didn't mean those things I said—

Felicity: I'll kill you for this, Simon Gascoyne!

She leaves in tears, passing Mrs. Drudge who has entered in time to overhear her last remark.

Moon: It was her.

Birdboot: I told you—straight to the top—

Moon: No, no—

Birdboot: Sssh. . . .

Simon (to Mrs. Drudge): Yes, what is it?

Mrs. Drudge: I have come to set up the card table, sir.

Simon: I don't think I can stay.

Mrs. Drudge: Oh, Lady Muldoon *will* be disappointed.

Simon: Does she know I'm here?

Mrs. Drudge: Oh yes, sir, I just told her and it put her in quite a tizzy.

Simon: Really? . . . Well, I suppose now that I've cleared the air . . . Quite a tizzy, you say . . . really . . . really . . .

He and Mrs. Drudge start setting up for card game. Mrs. Drudge leaves when this is done.

Moon: Felicity!—she's the one.
Birdboot: Nonsense—red herring.
Moon: I mean, it was *her!*
Birdboot (exasperated): *What* was?
Moon: That lady I saw you with last night!
Birdboot (inhales with fury): Are you suggesting that a man of my scrupulous integrity would trade his pen for a mess of pottage?! Simply because in the course of my profession I happen to have struck up an acquaintance—to have, that is, a warm regard, if you like, for a fellow toiler in the vineyard of greasepaint—I find it simply intolerable to be pillified and viloried—
Moon: I never implied—
Birdboot: —to find myself the object of uninformed malice, the petty slanders of little men—
Moon: I'm sorry—
Birdboot: —to suggest that my good opinion in a journal of unimpeachable integrity is at the disposal of the first coquette who gives me what I want—
Moon: Sssssh—
Birdboot: A ladies' man! . . . Why, Myrtle and I have been together now for—Christ!—who's *that?*

Enter Lady Cynthia Muldoon through french windows. A beautiful woman in her thirties. She wears a cocktail dress, is formally coiffured, and carries a tennis racket. Her effect on Birdboot is also impressive. He half-rises and sinks back agape.

Cynthia (entering): Simon!

A dramatic freeze between her and Simon.

Moon: Lady Muldoon.
Birdboot: No, I mean—who *is* she?
Simon (coming forward): Cynthia!
Cynthia: Don't say anything for a moment—just hold me.

He seizes her and glues his lips to hers, as they say. While their lips are glued—

Birdboot: She's *beautiful*—a vision of eternal grace, a poem . . .
Moon: I think she's got her mouth open.

Cynthia breaks away dramatically.

Cynthia: We can't go on meeting like this!
Simon: We have nothing to be ashamed of!
Cynthia: But darling, this is madness!
Simon: Yes!—I am mad with love for you!
Cynthia: Please—remember where we are!

Simon: Cynthia, I love you!

Cynthia: Don't—I love Albert!

Simon: He's dead! *(Shaking her.)* Do you understand me—Albert's dead!

Cynthia: No—I'll never give up hope! Let me go! We are not free!

Simon: I don't care, we were meant for each other—had we but met in time.

Cynthia: You're a cad, Simon! You will use me and cast me aside as you have cast aside so many others.

Simon: No, Cynthia!—you can make me a better person!

Cynthia: You're ruthless—so strong, so cruel—

> *Ruthlessly he kisses her.*

Moon: The son she never had, now projected in this handsome stranger and transformed into lover—youth, vigor, the animal, the athlete as aesthete—breaking down the barriers at the deepest level of desire.

Birdboot: By jove, I think you're right. Her mouth *is* open.

> *Cynthia breaks away. Mrs. Drudge has entered.*

Cynthia: Stop—can't you see you're making a fool of yourself?

Simon: I'll kill anyone who comes between us!

Cynthia: Yes, what is it, Mrs. Drudge?

Mrs. Drudge: Should I close the windows, my lady? The fog is beginning to roll off the sea like a deadly—

Cynthia: Yes, you'd better. It looks as if we're in for one of those days. Are the cards ready?

Mrs. Drudge: Yes, my lady.

Cynthia: Would you tell Miss Cunningham we are waiting.

Mrs. Drudge: Yes, my lady.

Cynthia: And fetch the Major down.

Mrs. Drudge (as she leaves): I think I hear him coming downstairs now.

> *She does: the sound of a wheelchair approaching down several flights of stairs with landings in between. It arrives bearing Magnus at about 15 m.p.h., knocking Simon over violently.*

Cynthia: Simon!

Magnus (roaring): Never had a chance! Ran under the wheels!

Cynthia: Darling, are you all right?

Magnus: I have witnesses!

Cynthia: Oh, Simon—say something!

Simon (sitting up suddenly): I'm most frightfully sorry.

Magnus (still shouting): How long have you been a pedestrian?

Simon: Ever since I could walk.

Cynthia: Can you walk now . . . ?

> *Simon rises and walks.*

Thank God! Magnus, this is Simon Gascoyne.

Magnus: What's he doing here?

Cynthia: He just turned up.

Magnus: Really? How do you like it here?

Simon (to Cynthia): I could stay forever.

>	*Felicity enters.*

Felicity: So—you're still here.

Cynthia: Of course he's still here. We're going to play cards. There's no need to introduce you two, is there, for I recall now that you, Simon, met me through Felicity, our mutual friend.

Felicity: Yes, Simon is an old friend, though not as old as you, Cynthia dear.

Simon: Yes, I haven't seen Felicity since—

Felicity: Last night.

Cynthia: Indeed? Well, you deal, Felicity. Simon, you help me with the sofa. Will you partner Felicity, Magnus, against Simon and me?

Magnus (aside): Will Simon and you always be partnered against me, Cynthia?

Cynthia: What do you mean, Magnus?

Magnus: You are a damned attractive woman, Cynthia.

Cynthia: Please! Please! Remember Albert!

Magnus: Albert's dead, Cynthia—and you are still young. I'm sure he would have wished that you and I—

Cynthia: No, Magnus, this is not to be!

Magnus: It's Gascoyne, isn't it? I'll kill him if he comes between us.

Cynthia (calling): Simon!

>	*The sofa is shoved towards the card table, once more revealing the corpse, though not to the players.*

Birdboot: Simon's for the chop all right.

Cynthia: Right! Who starts?

Magnus: I do. No bid.

>	*They start playing, putting down and picking up cards.*

Cynthia: Did I hear you say you saw Felicity last night, Simon?

Simon: Did I?—Ah yes, yes quite—your turn, Felicity.

Felicity: I've had my turn, haven't I, Simon?—now, it seems, it's Cynthia's turn.

Cynthia: That's my trick, Felicity dear.

Felicity: Hell hath no fury like a woman scorned, Simon.

Simon: Yes, I've heard it said.

Felicity: So I hope you have not been cheating, Simon.

Simon (standing up and throwing down his cards): No, Felicity, it's just that I hold the cards!

Cynthia: Well done, Simon!

>	*Magnus pays Simon generously in bank notes, while Cynthia deals.*

Felicity: Strange how Simon appeared in the neighborhood from nowhere. We know so little about him.

Simon: It doesn't always pay to show your hand!

Cynthia: Right! Simon, it's your opening on the minor bid.

Simon plays.

Cynthia: Hm, let's see . . . *(Plays.)*
Felicity: I hear there's a dangerous madman on the loose.
Cynthia: Simon?
Simon: Yes—yes—sorry. *(Plays.)*
Cynthia: I meld.
Felicity: Yes—personally, I think he's been hiding out in the deserted cottage on the cliffs *(plays)*.
Simon: Flush!
Cynthia: No! Simon—your luck's in tonight!
Felicity: We shall see—the night is not over yet, Simon Gascoyne! *(She exits.)*

Once more Magnus pays Simon.

Simon (to Magnus): So you're the crippled half-brother of Lord Muldoon who turned up out of the blue from Canada just the other day, are you? It's taken you a long time to get here. What did you do—walk? Oh, I say, I'm most frightfully sorry!
Magnus: Care for a spin round the rose garden, Cynthia?
Cynthia: No Magnus, I must talk to Simon.
Simon: My round, I think, Major.
Magnus: You think so?
Simon: Yes, Major—I do.
Magnus: There's an Old Canadian proverb handed down from the Blackfoot Indians, which says: He who laughs last laughs longest.
Simon: Yes, I've heard it said.
Cynthia (calling): Simon!
Magnus: Well, I think I'll go and oil my gun. *(He exits.)*
Cynthia: I think Magnus suspects something. And Felicity . . . Simon, was there anything between you and Felicity?
Simon: No, no—it's over between her and me, Cynthia—it was a mere passing fleeting thing we had—but now that I have found you—
Cynthia: If I find that you have been untrue to me—if I find that you have falsely seduced me from my dear husband Albert—I will kill you, Simon Gascoyne!

Mrs. Drudge has entered silently to witness this. On this tableau, pregnant with significance, the act ends, the body still undiscovered. Perfunctory applause.
   Moon and Birdboot seem to be completely preoccupied, becoming audible, as it were.

Moon: Camps it around the Old Vic° in his opera cloak and passes me the tat.°
Birdboot: Do you believe in love at first sight?
Moon: It's not that I think I'm a better critic—
Birdboot: I feel my whole life changing—
Moon: I am but it's not that.

Old Vic: London theater occupied by the National Theatre Company.   *passes me the tat*: hands me the dice, that is, gives me the assignment.

Birdboot: Oh, the world will laugh at me, I know . . .

Moon: It is not that they are much in the way of shoes to step into . . .

Birdboot: . . . call me an infatuated old fool . . .

Moon: . . . They are not.

Birdboot: . . . condemn me . . .

Moon: He is standing in my light, that is all.

Birdboot: . . . betrayer of my class . . .

Moon: . . . an almost continuous eclipse, interrupted by the phenomenon of moonlight.

Birdboot: I don't care, I'm a goner.

Moon: And I dream . . .

Birdboot: The Blue Angel° all over again.

Moon: . . . of the day his temperature climbs through the top of his head . . .

Birdboot: Ah, the sweet madness of love . . .

Moon: . . . of the spasm on the stairs . . .

Birdboot: Myrtle, farewell . . .

Moon: . . . dreaming of the stair he'll never reach—

Birdboot: —for I only live but once . . . .

Moon: Sometimes I dream that I've killed him.

Birdboot: What?

Moon: What?

> *They pull themselves together.*

Birdboot: Yes . . . yes. . . . A beautiful performance, a collector's piece. I shall say so.

Moon: A very promising debut. I'll put in a good word.

Birdboot: It would be as hypocritical of me to withhold praise on grounds of personal feelings, as to withhold censure.

Moon: You're right. Courageous.

Birdboot: Oh, I know what people will say—There goes Birdboot buttering up his latest—

Moon: Ignore them—

Birdboot: But I rise above that—The fact is I genuinely believe her performance to be one of the summits in the range of contemporary theater.

Moon: Trim-buttocked, that's the word for her.

Birdboot: —the radiance, the inner sadness—

Moon: Does she actually come across with it?

Birdboot: The part as written is a mere cypher but she manages to make Cynthia a real person—

Moon: Cynthia?

Birdboot: And should she, as a result, care to meet me over a drink, simply by way of er—thanking me, as it were—

Moon: Well, you fickle old bastard!

Birdboot (aggressively): Are you suggesting . . . ? *(He shudders to a halt and clears his throat.)* Well now—shaping up quite nicely, wouldn't you say?

The Blue Angel: classic German film in which Emil Jannings plays an elderly schoolmaster infatuated with a cabaret singer played by Marlene Dietrich.

Moon: Oh yes, yes. A nice trichotomy of forces. One must reserve judgment of course, until the confrontation, but I think it's pretty clear where we're heading.

Birdboot: I agree. It's Magnus a mile off.

Small pause.

Moon: What's Magnus a mile off?

Birdboot: If we knew that we wouldn't be here.

Moon (clears throat): Let me at once say that it has *élan*° while at the same time avoiding *éclat*°. Having said that, and I think it must be said, I am bound to ask—does this play know where it's going?

Birdboot: Well, it seems open and shut to me, Moon—Magnus is not what he pretends to be and he's got his next victim marked down—

Moon: Does it, I repeat, declare its affiliations? There are moments, and I would not begrudge it this, when the play, if we can call it that, and I think on balance we can, aligns itself uncompromisingly on the side of life. *Je suis,* it seems to be saying, *ergo sum*°. But is that enough? I think we are entitled to ask. For what in fact is this play concerned with? It is my belief that here we are concerned with what I have referred to elsewhere as the nature of identity. I think we are entitled to ask—and here one is irresistibly reminded of Voltaire's cry, *"Voilà"*°—I think we are entitled to ask—*Where is God?*

Birdboot (stunned): Who?

Moon: Go-od.

Birdboot (peeping furtively into his program): God?

Moon: I think we are entitled to ask.

The phone rings.
The set re-illumines to reveal Cynthia, Felicity and Magnus about to take coffee, which is being taken round by Mrs. Drudge. Simon is missing. The body lies in position.

Mrs. Drudge (into phone): The same, half an hour later? . . . No, I'm sorry—there's no one of that name here. (*She replaces phone and goes round with coffee. To Cynthia.*) Black or white, my lady?

Cynthia: White please.

Mrs. Drudge pours.

Mrs. Drudge (to Felicity): Black or white, miss?

Felicity: White please.

Mrs. Drudge pours.

Mrs. Drudge (to Magnus): Black or white, Major?

élan: verve, vigor.   *éclat:* brilliance.   *Je suis . . . ergo sum:* Moon mixes French and Latin in misquoting the basic principle of the philosophy of Descartes: "I exist, therefore I am." (Descartes said, "I think. . . .")   *Voilà:* The French philosopher and satirist Voltaire, asked to demonstrate the existence of God, declared, *"Voilà!"* (Look, there He is!).

Magnus: White please.

> *Ditto.*

Mrs. Drudge (to Cynthia): Sugar, my lady?
Cynthia: Yes please.

> *Puts sugar in.*

Mrs. Drudge (to Felicity): Sugar, miss?
Felicity: Yes please.

> *Ditto.*

Mrs. Drudge (to Magnus): Sugar, Major?
Magnus: Yes please.

> *Ditto.*
> *Mrs. Drudge leaves, and reappears with a plate of biscuits.*

Mrs. Drudge (to Cynthia): Biscuit, my lady?
Cynthia: No thank you.
Birdboot (writing elaborately in his notebook): The second act, however, fails to fulfill the promise . . .
Felicity: If you ask me, there's something funny going on.

> *Mrs. Drudge's approach to Felicity makes Felicity jump to her feet in impatience. She goes to the radio while Magnus declines his biscuit, and Mrs. Drudge leaves.*

Radio: We interrupt our program for a special police message. The search for the dangerous madman who is on the loose in Essex has now narrowed to the immediate vicinity of Muldoon Manor. Police are hampered by the deadly swamps and the fog, but believe that the madman spent last night in a deserted cottage on the cliffs. The public is advised to stick together and make sure none of their number is missing. That is the end of the police message.

> *Felicity turns off the radio nervously. Pause.*

Cynthia: Where's Simon?
Felicity: Who?
Cynthia: Simon. Have you seen him?
Felicity: No.
Cynthia: Have you, Magnus?
Magnus: No.
Cynthia: Oh.
Felicity: Yes, there's something foreboding in the air, it is as if one of *us*—
Cynthia: Oh, Felicity, the house is locked up tight—no one can get in—and the police are practically on the doorstep.
Felicity: I don't know—it's just a feeling.
Cynthia: It's only the fog.
Magnus: Hound will never get through on a day like this—
Cynthia (shouting at him): Fog!

Felicity: He means the Inspector.
Cynthia: Is he bringing a dog?
Felicity: Not that I know of.
Magnus: —never get through the swamps. Yes, I'm afraid the madman can show his hand in safety now.

A mournful baying, hooting is heard in the distance, scary.

Cynthia: What's that?!
Felicity (tensely): It sounded like the cry of a gigantic hound!
Birdboot: Rings a bell.
Magnus: Poor devil!
Cynthia: Ssssh!

They listen. The sound is repeated, nearer.

Felicity: There it is again!
Cynthia: It's coming this way—it's right outside the house!

Mrs. Drudge enters.

Mrs. Drudge: Inspector Hound!
Cynthia: A police dog?

Enter Inspector Hound. On his feet are his swamp boots. These are two inflatable— and inflated—pontoons with flat bottoms about two feet across. He carries a foghorn.

Hound: Lady Muldoon?
Cynthia: Yes.
Hound: I came as soon as I could. Where shall I put my foghorn and my swamp boots?
Cynthia: Mrs. Drudge will take them out. Be prepared, as the Force's motto has it, eh, Inspector? How very resourceful!
Hound (divesting himself of boots and foghorn): It takes more than a bit of weather to keep a policeman from his duty.

Mrs. Drudge leaves with chattels. A pause.

Cynthia: Oh—er, Inspector Hound—Felicity Cunningham, Major Magnus Muldoon.
Hound: Good evening.

He and Cynthia continue to look expectantly at each other.

Cynthia and Hound (together): Well?—Sorry—
Cynthia: No, do go on.
Hound: Thank you. Well, tell me about it in your own words—take your time, begin at the beginning and don't leave anything out.
Cynthia: I beg your pardon?
Hound: Fear nothing. You are in safe hands now. I hope you haven't touched anything.

Cynthia: I'm afraid I don't understand.

Hound: I'm Inspector Hound.

Cynthia: Yes.

Hound: Well, what's it all about?

Cynthia: I really have no idea.

Hound: How did it begin?

Cynthia: What?

Hound: The . . . thing.

Cynthia: What thing?

Hound (radpidly losing confidence but exasperated): The trouble!

Cynthia: There hasn't *been* any trouble!

Hound: Didn't you phone the police?

Cynthia: No.

Felicity: I didn't.

Magnus: What for?

Hound: I see. (*Pause.*) This puts me in a very difficult position. (*A steady pause.*) Well, I'll be getting along, then. (*He moves toward the door.*)

Cynthia: I'm terribly sorry.

Hound (stiffly): That's perfectly all right.

Cynthia: Thank you so much for coming.

Hound: Not at all. You never know, there might have been a serious matter.

Cynthia: Drink?

Hound: More serious than that, even.

Cynthia (correcting): Drink before you go?

Hound: No thank you. (*Leaves.*)

Cynthia (through the door): I do hope you find him.

Hound (reappearing at once): Find who, Madam?—out with it!

Cynthia: I thought you were looking for the lunatic.

Hound: And what do you know about that?

Cynthia: It was on the radio.

Hound: Was it, indeed? Well, that's what I'm here about, really. I didn't want to mention it because I didn't know how much you knew. No point in causing unnecessary panic, even with a murderer in our midst.

Felicity: Murderer, did you say?

Hound: Ah—so that was not on the radio?

Cynthia: Whom has he murdered, Inspector?

Hound: Perhaps no one—yet. Let us hope we are in time.

Magnus: You believe he is in our midst, Inspector?

Hound: I do. If anyone of you have recently encountered a youngish good-looking fellow in a smart suit, white shirt, hatless, well-spoken—someone possibly claiming to have just moved into the neighborhood, someone who on the surface seems as sane as you or I, then now is the time to speak!

Felicity: . . . I . . .

Hound: Don't interrupt!

Felicity: Inspector . . .

Hound: Very well.

Cynthia: No. Felicity!

Hound: Please, Lady Cynthia, we are all in this together. I must ask you to put yourself completely in my hands.

Cynthia: Don't, Inspector. I love Albert.

Hound: I don't think you quite grasp my meaning.

Magnus: Is one of us in danger, Inspector?

Hound: Didn't it strike you as odd that on his escape the madman made a beeline for Muldoon Manor? It is my guess that he bears a deep-seated grudge against someone in this very house! Lady Muldoon—where is your husband?

Cynthia: My husband?—you don't mean—?

Hound: I don't know—but I have a reason to believe that one of you is the real McCoy!

Felicity: The real what?

Hound: William Herbert McCoy who as a young man, meeting the madman in the street and being solicited for sixpence for a cup of tea, replied, "Why don't you do a decent day's work, you shifty old bag of horse manure," in Canada all those many years ago and went on to make his fortune. *(He starts to pace intensely.)* The madman was a mere boy at the time but he never forgot that moment, and thenceforth carried in his heart the promise of revenge! *(At which point he finds himself standing on top of the corpse. He looks down carefully.)* Is there anything you have forgotten to tell me?

They all see the corpse for the first time.

Felicity: So the madman has struck!

Cynthia: Oh—it's horrible—horrible—

Hound: Yes, just as I feared. Now you see the sort of man you are protecting.

Cynthia: I can't believe it!

Felicity: I'll have to tell him, Cynthia—Inspector, a stranger of that description has indeed appeared in our midst—Simon Gascoyne. Oh, he had charm, I'll give you that, and he took me in completely. I'm afraid I made a fool of myself over him, and so did Cynthia.

Hound: Where is he now?

Magnus: He must be around the house—he couldn't get away in these conditions.

Hound: You're right. Fear naught, Lady Muldoon—I shall apprehend the man who killed your husband.

Cynthia: My husband? I don't understand.

Hound: Everything points to Gascoyne.

Cynthia: But who's that? *(The corpse.)*

Hound: Your husband.

Cynthia: No, it's not.

Hound: Yes, it is.

Cynthia: I tell you it's not.

Hound: Are you sure?

Cynthia: For goodness sake!

Hound: Then who is it?

Cynthia: I don't know.

Hound: Anybody?

Felicity: I've never seen him before.

Magnus: Quite unlike anybody I've ever met.

Hound: I seem to have made a dreadful mistake. Lady Muldoon, I do apologize.

Cynthia: But what are we going to do?

Hound (snatching the phone): I'll phone the police!

Cynthia: But you are the police!

Hound: Thank God I'm here—the lines have been cut!

Cynthia: You mean—?

Hound: Yes!—we're on our own, cut off from the world and in grave danger!

Felicity: You mean—?

Hound: Yes!—I think the killer will strike again!

Magnus: You mean—?

Hound: Yes! One of us ordinary mortals thrown together by fate and cut off by the elements, is the murderer! He must be found—search the house!

> *All depart speedily in different directions leaving a momentarily empty stage. Simon strolls on.*

Simon (entering, calling): Anyone about?—funny . . . (*He notices the corpse and is surprised. He approaches it and turns it over. He stands up and looks about in alarm.*)

Birdboot: This is where Simon gets the chop.

> *There is a shot. Simon falls dead.*
>
> Inspector Hound runs on and crouches down by Simon's body. Cynthia appears at the french windows. She stops there and stares.

Cynthia: What happened, Inspector?

> *Hound turns to face her.*

Hound: He's dead . . . Simon Gascoyne, I presume. Rough justice even for a killer—unless—unless—We assumed that the body could not have been lying there before Simon Gascoyne entered the house . . . but . . . (*he slides the sofa over the body*) . . . there's your answer. And now—who killed Simon Gascoyne? And why?

> *"Curtain," Freeze, Applause. Exeunt.*

Moon: Why not?

Birdboot: Exactly. Good riddance.

Moon: Yes, getting away with murder must be quite easy provided that one's motive is sufficiently inscrutable.

Birdboot: Fickle young pup! He was deceiving her right, left and center.

Moon (thoughtfully): Of course, I'd still have Puckeridge behind *me* . . .

Birdboot: She needs someone steadier, more mature . . .

Moon: . . . And if I could, so could he . . .

Birdboot: Yes. I know of this rather nice hotel, very discreet, run by a man of the world . . .

Moon: Uneasy lies the head that wears the crown.

Birdboot: Breakfast served in one's room and no questions asked.

Moon: Does Puckeridge dream of me?

Birdboot (pause): Hello—what's happened?

Moon: What? Oh yes—what do you make of it, so far?

Birdboot (clears throat): It is at this point that the play, for me, comes alive. The groundwork has been well and truly laid, and the author has taken the trouble to learn from the masters of the genre. He has created a real situation, and few will doubt his ability to resolve it with a startling dénouement. Certainly that is what it so far lacks, but it has a beginning, a middle and I have no doubt it will prove to have an end. For this let us give thanks, and double thanks for a good clean show without a trace of smut. But perhaps even all this would be for nothing were it not for a performance which I consider to be one of the summits in the range of contemporary theater. In what is possibly the finest Cynthia since the war—

Moon: If we examine this more closely, and I think close examination is the least tribute that this play deserves, I think we will find that within the austere framework of what is seen to be on one level a country-house weekend, and what a useful symbol that is, the author has given us—yes, I will go so far— He has given us the human condition—

Birdboot: More talent in her little finger—

Moon: An uncanny ear that might have belonged to a Van Gogh—

Birdboot: —a public scandal that the Birthday Honors° to date have neglected—

Moon: Faced as we are with such ubiquitous obliquity, it is hard, it is hard indeed, and therefore I will not attempt, to refrain from invoking the names of Kafka, Sartre, Shakespeare, St. Paul, Beckett, Birkett, Pinero, Pirandello, Dante and Dorothy L. Sayers°.

Birdboot: A rattling good evening out. I was held.

The phone starts to ring on the empty stage. Moon tries to ignore it.

Moon: Harder still—Harder still if possible—Harder still if it is possible to be— Neither do I find it easy—Dante and Dorothy L. Sayers. Harder still—

Birdboot: Others taking part included—Moon!

For Moon has lost patience and is bearing down on the ringing phone. He is frankly irritated.

Moon (picking up phone, barks): Hel-lo! (Pause, turns to Birdboot, quietly.) It's for you.

Pause.

Birdboot gets up. He approaches cautiously. Moon gives him the phone and moves back to his seat. Birdboot watches him go. He looks round and smiles weakly, expiating himself.

Birdboot (into phone): Hello. . . . (Explosion.) Oh, for God's sake, Myrtle—I've told you never to phone me at work! (He is naturally embarrassed, looking about with surreptitious fury.) What? Last night? Good God, woman, this is hardly the time to—I assure you, Myrtle, there is absolutely nothing going on between me and—. I took her to dinner simply by way of keeping *au fait* with

---

Birthday Honors: titles and awards annually conferred by the Queen.   Dorothy L. Sayers: British writer of mystery stories and translator of Dante.

the world of the paint and the motley—yes, I promise—Yes, I do—Yes, I *said* yes—I *do*—and you are mine too, Myrtle—darling—I can't—*(whispers)* I'm not alone—*(Up.)* No, she's not!—*(He looks around furtively, licks his lips and mumbles.)* All *right!* I love your little pink ears and you are my own fluffy bunnyboo—Now for God's sake—Good-bye, Myrtle—*(puts down phone)*.

Birdboot mops his brow with his handkerchief. As he turns, a tennis ball bounces in through the french windows, followed by Felicity, as before, in tennis outfit. The lighting is as it was. Everything is as it was. It is, let us say, the same moment of time.

Felicity *(calling)*: Out! *(She catches sight of Birdboot and is amazed.)* You!

Birdboot: Er, yes—hello again.

Felicity: What are you doing here?!

Birdboot: Well, I . . .

Felicity: Honestly, darling, you really are extraordinary—

Birdboot: Yes, well, here I am. *(He looks round sheepishly.)*

Felicity: You must have been desperate to see me—I mean, I'm flattered, but couldn't it wait till I got back?

Birdboot: No, no, you've got it all wrong—

Felicity: What is it?

Birdboot: And about last night—perhaps I gave you the wrong impression—got carried away a bit, perhaps—

Felicity *(stiffly)*: What are you trying to say?

Birdboot: I want to call it off.

Felicity: I see.

Birdboot: I didn't promise anything—and the fact is, I have my reputation—people do talk—

Felicity: You don't have to say any more—

Birdboot: And my wife, too—I don't know how she got to hear of it, but—

Felicity: Of all the nerve!

Birdboot: I'm sorry you had to find out like this—the fact is I didn't mean it this way—

Felicity: You philandering coward!

Birdboot: I'm sorry—but I want you to know that I meant those things I said—oh yes—shows brilliant promise—I shall say so—

Felicity: I'll kill you for this, Simon Gascoyne!

She leaves in tears, passing Mrs. Drudge who has entered in time to overhear her last remark.

Birdboot *(wide-eyed)*: Good God . . .

Mrs. Drudge: I have come to set up the card table, sir.

Birdboot *(wildly)*: I can't stay for a game of *cards!*

Mrs. Drudge: Oh, Lady Muldoon *will* be disappointed.

Birdboot: You mean . . . you mean, she wants to meet me . . . ?

Mrs. Drudge: Oh yes, sir, I just told her and it put her in quite a tizzy.

Birdboot: Really? Yes, well, a man of my influence is not to be sneezed at—I think I have some small name for the making of reputations—mmm, yes, quite a tizzy, you say?

Mrs. Drudge is busied with the card table. Birdboot stands marooned and bemused for a moment.

Moon (*from his seat*): Birdboot!—(*a tense whisper*)—Birdboot!

Birdboot looks round vaguely.

What the hell are you doing?
Birdboot: Nothing.
Moon: Stop making an ass of yourself. Come back.
Birdboot: Oh, I know what you're thinking—but the fact is I genuinely consider her performance to be one of the summits—

Cynthia enters as before. Mrs. Drudge has gone.

Cynthia: Darling!
Birdboot: Ah, good evening—may I say that I genuinely consider—
Cynthia: Don't say anything for a moment—just hold me. (*She falls into his arms.*)
Birdboot: All right!—let us throw off the hollow pretences of the gimcrack codes we live by! Dear lady, from the first moment I saw you, I felt my whole life changing—
Cynthia (*breaking free*): We can't go on meeting like this!
Birdboot: I am not ashamed to proclaim nightly my love for you!—but fortunately that will not be necessary—I know of a very good hotel, discreet—run by a man of the world—
Cynthia: But darling, this is madness!
Birdboot: Yes! I am mad with love.
Cynthia: Please!—remember where we are!
Birdboot: I don't care! Let them think what they like, I love you!
Cynthia: Don't—I love Albert!
Birdboot: He's dead. (*Shaking her.*) Do you understand me—Albert's dead!
Cynthia: No—I'll never give up hope! Let me go! We are not free!
Birdboot: You mean Myrtle? She means nothing to me—nothing!—she's all cocoa and blue nylon fur slippers—not a spark of creative genius in her whole slumping knee-length-knickered body—
Cynthia: You're a cad, Simon! You will use me and cast me aside as you have cast aside so many others!
Birdboot: No, Cynthia—now that I have found you—
Cynthia: You're ruthless—so strong—so cruel—

Birdboot seizes her in an embrace, during which Mrs. Drudge enters, and Moon's fevered voice is heard.

Moon: Have you taken leave of your tiny mind?

Cynthia breaks free.

Cynthia: Stop—can't you see you're making a fool of yourself!
Moon: She's right.
Birdboot (*to Moon*): You keep out of this.

Cynthia: Yes, what is it, Mrs. Drudge?

Mrs. Drudge: Should I close the windows, my lady? The fog—

Cynthia: Yes, you'd better.

Moon: Look, they've got your number—

Birdboot: I'll leave in my own time, thank you very much.

Moon: It's the finish of you, I suppose you know that—

Birdboot: I don't need your twopenny Grub Street° prognostications—I have found something bigger and finer—

Moon (bemused, to himself): If only it were Higgs . . .

Cynthia: . . . And fetch the Major down.

Mrs. Drudge: I think I hear him coming downstairs now.

> *She leaves. The sound of a wheelchair's approach as before. Birdboot prudently keeps out of the chair's former path but it enters from the next wing down and knocks him flying. A babble of anguish and protestation.*

Cynthia: Simon—say something!

Birdboot: That reckless bastard *(as he sits up).*

Cynthia: Thank God!—

Magnus: What's *he* doing here?

Cynthia: He just turned up.

Magnus: Really? How do you like it here?

Birdboot: I couldn't take it night after night.

> *Felicity enters.*

Felicity: So—you're still here.

Cynthia: Of course he's still here. We're going to play cards. There is no need to introduce you two, is there, for I recall now that you, Simon, met me through Felicity, our mutual friend.

Felicity: Yes, Simon is an old friend . . .

Birdboot: Ah—yes—well I like to give young up-and-comers the benefit of my—er—of course, she lacks technique as yet—

Felicity: Last night.

Birdboot: I'm not talking about last night!

Cynthia: Indeed? Well, you deal, Felicity. Simon, you help me with the sofa.

> *Cynthia and Magnus confer as in the earlier scene.*

Birdboot (to Moon): Did you see that? Tried to kill me. I told you it was Magnus—not that it *is* Magnus.

Moon: Who did it, you mean?

Birdboot: What?

Moon: You think it's not Magnus who did it?

Birdboot: Get a grip on yourself, Moon—the facts are staring you in the face. He's after Cynthia for one thing.

Magnus: It's Gascoyne, isn't it?

Grub Street: formerly, a London street where poorly paid hack writers had their lodgings.

Birdboot: Over my dead body!

Magnus: If he comes between us . . .

Moon (angrily): For God's sake sit down!

Cynthia: Simon!

Birdboot: She needs me, Moon. I've got to make up a four.

Cynthia and Birdboot move the sofa as before, and they all sit at the table.

Cynthia: Right! Who starts?

Magnus: I do. I'll dummy for a no-bid ruff and double my holding on South's queen (*while he moves cards*).

Cynthia: Did I hear you say you saw Felicity last night, Simon?

Birdboot: Er—er—

Felicity: Pay twenty-ones or trump my contract. (*Discards.*) Cynthia's turn.

Cynthia: I'll trump your contract with five dummy no-trumps there (*discards*), and I'll move West's rook for the re-bid with a banker ruff on his second trick there. (*Discards.*) Simon?

Birdboot: Would you mind doing that again?

Cynthia: And I'll ruff your dummy with five no-bid trumps there (*discards*), and I support your re-bid with a banker for the solo ruff in the dummy trick there. (*Discards.*)

Birdboot (standing up and throwing down his cards): And I call your bluff!

Cynthia: Well done, Simon!

Magnus pays Birdboot while Cynthia deals.

Felicity: Strange how Simon appeared in the neighborhood from nowhere, we know so little about him.

Cynthia: Right Simon, it's your opening on the minor bid. Hmm. Let's see. I think I'll overbid the spade convention with two no trumps and king's gambit offered there—(*discards*) and West's dummy split double to Queen's Bishop 4 there!

Magnus (as he plays cards): Faites vos jeux. Rien ne va plus. Rouge et noir. Zéro.°

Cynthia: Simon?

Birdboot (triumphantly, leaping to his feet): And I call your bluff!

Cynthia (imperturbably): I meld.

Felicity: I huff.

Magnus: I ruff.

Birdboot: I bluff.

Cynthia: Twist.

Felicity: Bust.

Magnus: Check.

Birdboot: Snap.

Cynthia: How's that?

Felicity: Not out.

Magnus: Double top.

Birdboot: Bingo!

Faites vos jeux . . . Zéro: (French, the chant of a croupier—one in charge of a gaming table): "Place your bets. The betting is closed. Red and black. Zero."

Climax.

Cynthia: No! Simon—your luck's in tonight.

Felicity: We shall see—the night is not over yet, Simon Gascoyne! *(She exits quickly.)*

Birdboot (looking after Felicity): Red herring—smell it a mile off. *(To Magnus.)* Oh yes, she's as clean as a whistle, I've seen it a thousand times. And I've seen you before too, haven't I? Strange—there's something about you . . .

Magnus: Care for a spin round the rose garden, Cynthia?

Cynthia: No Magnus, I must talk to Simon.

Birdboot: There's nothing for you there, you know.

Magnus: You think so?

Birdboot: Oh yes, she knows which side her bread is buttered. I am a man not without a certain influence among those who would reap the limelight—she's not going to throw me over for a heavily disguised cripple.

Magnus: There's an old Canadian proverb—

Birdboot: Don't give me that—I tumbled to you right from the start—oh yes, you chaps are not as clever as you think. . . . Sooner or later you make your mistake. . . . Incidentally, where was it I saw you? . . . I've definitely . . . .

Cynthia (calling): Simon!

Magnus (leaving): Well, I think I'll go and oil my gun. *(Exit.)*

Birdboot (after Magnus): Double bluff!—*(To Cynthia.)* I've seen it a thousand times.

Cynthia: I think Magnus suspects something. And Felicity . . . Simon, was there anything between you and Felicity?

Birdboot: No, no—that's all over now. I merely flattered her a little over a drink, told her she'd go far, that sort of thing. Dear me, the fuss that's been made over a simple flirtation—

Cynthia (as Mrs. Drudge enters behind): If I find you have falsely seduced me from my dear husband Albert, I will kill you, Simon Gascoyne!

The "Curtain" as before. Mrs. Drudge and Cynthia leave. Birdboot starts to follow them.

Moon: Birdboot!

Birdboot stops.

Moon: For God's sake pull yourself together.

Birdboot: I can't help it.

Moon: What do you think you're doing? You're turning it into a complete farce!

Birdboot: I know, I know—but I can't live without her. *(He is making erratic neurotic journeys about the stage.)* I shall resign my position, of course. I don't care I'm a goner, I tell you—*(He has arrived at the body. He looks at it in surprise, hesitates, bends and turns it over.)*

Moon: Birdboot, think of your family, your friends—your high standing in the world of letters—I say, what are you doing?

Birdboot is staring at the body's face.

Birdboot . . . leave it alone. Come and sit down—what's the matter with you?

Birdboot (dead-voiced): It's Higgs.

Moon: What?

Birdboot: It's Higgs.

Pause.

Moon: Don't be silly.
Birdboot: I tell you it's Higgs!

Moon half-rises. Bewildered.

I don't understand . . . He's dead.
Moon: Dead?
Birdboot: Who would want to . . .
Moon: He must have been lying there all the time . . .
Birdboot: . . . kill Higgs?
Moon: But what's he doing here? I was standing in tonight . . .
Birdboot (turning): Moon? . . .
Moon (in wonder, quietly): So it's me and Puckeridge now.
Birdboot: Moon . . . ?
Moon (faltering): But I swear I . . .
Birdboot: I've got it—
Moon: But I didn't—
Birdboot (quietly): My God . . . so that was it . . . (Up.) Moon—now I see—
Moon: —I swear I didn't—
Birdboot: Now—finally—I see it all—

There is a shot and Birdboot falls dead.

Moon: Birdboot! (He runs on, to Birdboot's body.)

Cynthia appears at the french windows. She stops and stares. All as before.

Cynthia: Oh my God—what happened, Inspector?
Moon (almost to himself): He's dead . . . (He rises.) That's a bit rough, isn't it?—a bit extreme!—He may have had his faults—I admit he was a fickle old . . . Who did this, and why?

Moon turns to face her. He stands up and makes swiftly for his seat. Before he gets there he is stopped by the sound of voices. Simon and Hound are occupying the critics' seats. Moon freezes.

Simon: To say that it is without pace, point, focus, interest, drama, wit or originality is to say simply that it does not happen to be my cup of tea. One has only to compare this ragbag with the masters of the genre to see that here we have a trifle that is not my cup of tea at all.
Hound: I'm sorry to be blunt but there is no getting away from it. It lacks pace. A complete ragbag.
Simon: I will go further. Those of you who were fortunate enough to be at the Comédie-Française° on Wednesday last, will not need to be reminded that hysterics are no substitute for éclat.

Comédie-Française: A national theater in Paris, where classical plays are performed with rigorous precision.

Hound: It lacks *élan.*

Simon: Some of the cast seem to have given up acting altogether, apparently aghast, with every reason, at finding themselves involved in an evening that would, and indeed will, make the angels weep.

Hound: I am not a prude but I fail to see any reason for the shower of filth and sexual allusion foisted onto an unsuspected public in the guise of modernity at all costs . . . .

Behind Moon, Felicity, Magnus and Mrs. Drudge have made their entrances, so that he turns to face their semicircle.

Magnus (pointing to Birdboot's body): Well, Inspector, is this your man?

Moon (warily): . . . Yes. . . . Yes. . . .

Cynthia: It's Simon . . .

Moon: Yes . . . yes . . . poor. . . . *(Up.)* Is this some kind of a joke?

Magnus: If it is, Inspector, it's in very poor taste.

Moon pulls himself together and becomes galvanic, a little wild, in grief for Birdboot.

Moon: All right! I'm going to find out who did this! I want everyone to go to the positions they occupied when the shot was fired—

They move; hysterically.

No one will leave the house!

They move back.

Magnus: I think we all had the opportunity to fire the shot, Inspector—

Moon (furious): I am not—

Magnus: —but which of us would want to?

Moon: Perhaps you, Major Magnus!

Magnus: Why should I want to kill him?

Moon: Because he was on to you—yes, he tumbled to you right from the start— and you shot him just when he was about to reveal that you killed—*(Moon points, pauses and then crosses to Higgs' body and falters)*—killed—*(he turns Higgs over)* . . . this . . . chap.

Magnus: But what motive would there be for killing him? *(Pause.)* Who is this chap? *(Pause.)* Inspector?

Moon (rising): I don't know. Quite unlike anyone I've ever met. *(Long pause.)* Well . . . now . . .

Mrs. Drudge: Inspector?

Moon (eagerly): Yes? Yes, what is it, dear lady?

Mrs. Drudge: Happening to enter this room earlier in the day to close the windows, I chanced to overhear a remark made by the deceased Simon Gascoyne to her ladyship, viz., "I will kill anyone who comes between us."

Moon: Ah—yes—well, that's it, then. This . . . chap . . . *(pointing to the body)* was obviously killed by *(pointing to Birdboot's body)* er . . . *(the moment of Moon's betrayal, for which he is to pay with his life)* . . . by *(pause]* Simon.

Cynthia: But he didn't come between us!

Magnus: And who, then, killed Simon?

Mrs. Drudge: Subsequent to that reported remark, I also happened to be in earshot of a remark made by Lady Muldoon to the deceased, to the effect, "I will kill you, Simon Gascoyne!" I hope you don't mind my mentioning it.

Moon: Not at all. I'm glad you did. It is from these chance remarks that we in the Force build up our complete picture before moving in to make the arrest. It will not be long now, I fancy, and I must warn you, Lady Muldoon, that anything you say—

Cynthia: Yes!—I hated Simon Gascoyne, for he had me in his thrall!—But I didn't kill him!

Mrs. Drudge: Prior to that, Inspector, I also chanced to overhear a remark made by Miss Cunningham, no doubt in the heat of the moment, but it stuck in my mind as these things do, viz., "I will kill you for this, Simon Gascoyne!"

Moon: Ah! The final piece of the jigsaw! I think I am now in a position to reveal the mystery. This man *(the corpse)* was, of course, McCoy, the Canadian who, as we heard, meeting Gascoyne in the street and being solicited for sixpence for a toffee apple, smacked him across the ear, with the cry, "How's that for a grudge to harbor, your sniffling little workshy!" all those many years ago. Gascoyne bided his time, but in due course tracked McCoy down to this house, having, on the way, met, in the neighborhood, a simple ambitious girl from the provinces. He was charming, persuasive—told her, I have no doubt, that she would go straight to the top—and she, flattered by his sophistication, taken in by his promises to see her all right on the night, gave in to his simple desires. Perhaps she loved him. We shall never know. But in the very hour of her promised triumph, his eye fell on another—yes, I refer to Lady Cynthia Muldoon. From the moment he caught sight of her there was no other woman for him—he was in her spell, willing to sacrifice anything, even you, Felicity Cunningham. It was only today—unexpectedly finding him here—that you learned the truth. There was a bitter argument which ended with your promise to kill him—a promise that you carried out in this very room at your first opportunity! And I must warn you that anything you say—

Felicity: But it doesn't make sense!

Moon: Not at first glance, *perhaps.*

Magnus: Could not McCoy have been killed by the same person who killed Simon?

Felicity: But why should any of us want to kill a perfect stranger?

Magnus: Perhaps he was not a stranger to *one* of us.

Moon (faltering): But Simon was the madman, wasn't he?

Magnus: We only have your word for that, Inspector. We only have your word for a lot of things. For instance—McCoy. Who is he? Is his name McCoy? Is there any truth in that fantastic and implausible tale of the insult inflicted in the Canadian streets? Or is there something else, something quite unknown to us, behind all this? Suppose for a moment that the madman, having killed this unknown stranger for private and inscrutable reasons of his own, was disturbed before he could dispose of the body, so having cut the telephone wires he decided to return to the scene of the crime, masquerading as—Police Inspector Hound!

Moon: But . . . I'm not mad . . . I'm almost sure I'm not mad . . .

Magnus: . . . only to discover that in the house was a man, Simon Gascoyne, who recognized the corpse as a man against whom you had held a deepseated grudge—!

Moon: But I didn't kill—I'm almost sure I—

Magnus: I put it to you!—are you the real Inspector Hound?!

Moon: You know damn well I'm not! What's it all about?

Magnus: I thought as much.

Moon: I only dreamed . . . sometimes I dreamed—

Cynthia: So it was you!

Mrs. Drudge: The madman!

Felicity: The killer!

Cynthia: Oh, it's horrible, horrible.

Mrs. Drudge: The stranger in our midst!

Magnus: Yes, we had a shrewd suspicion he would turn up here—and he walked into the trap!

Moon: What trap?

Magnus: I am not the real Magnus Muldoon—It was a mere subterfuge!—and (standing up and removing his moustaches) I now reveal myself as—

Cynthia: You mean—?

Magnus: Yes! I am the real Inspector Hound!

Moon (pause): Puckeridge!

Magnus (with pistol): Stand where you are, or I shoot!

Moon (backing): Puckeridge! You killed Higgs—and Birdboot tried to tell me—

Magnus: Stop in the name of the law!

Moon turns to run. Magnus fires. Moon drops to his knees.

I have waited a long time for this moment.

Cynthia: So you are the real Inspector Hound.

Magnus: Not only that!—I have been leading a double life—at least!

Cynthia: You mean—?

Magnus: Yes!—It's been ten long years, but don't you know me?

Cynthia: You mean—?

Magnus: Yes!—it is me, Albert!—who lost his memory and joined the Force, rising by merit to the rank of Inspector, his past blotted out—until fate cast him back into the home he left behind, back to the beautiful woman he had brought here as his girlish bride—in short, my darling, my memory has returned and your long wait is over!

Cynthia: Oh, Albert!

They embrace.

Moon (with a trace of admiration): Puckeridge! . . . you cunning bastard. (He dies.)

THE END

QUESTIONS

1. What do Moon and Birdboot do for a living? What is revealed about each man by the exposition (their opening conversation before the beginning of the play-within-a-play)?
2. At the start of *The Real Inspector Hound*, the big question is "Where's Higgs?" Who is Higgs? Where, in fact, is he?
3. Sum up the two plots in Stoppard's play: first, the plot of the play taking place in Muldoon Manor; and second, the plot based on the personal lives of Moon and Birdboot. In the latter plot, whodunit? Can you establish the killer's motive? Who was first to discover the true identity of the murderer in real life?
4. What connection does Stoppard establish between Birdboot and Simon Gascoyne? Between Moon and the false Inspector Hound (the one who enters wearing inflated pontoons)?
5. What do Magnus, the real Inspector Hound, Cynthia's vanished husband Albert, and Puckeridge all have in common?
6. Explain Stoppard's comment that Moon's speech on page 1230 is "the moment of Moon's betrayal, for which he is to pay with his life."
7. What is Stoppard kidding in *The Real Inspector Hound?*

SUGGESTIONS FOR WRITING

1. Demonstrate, in a paragraph or two, how Nora in *A Doll House* resembles or differs from a feminist of today.
2. Placing yourself in the character of Ibsen's Torvald Helmer, write a defense of him and his attitudes as he himself might write it.
3. Choose the play in this chapter that in your opinion might best lend itself to television. Then tell your reader how you would go about adapting it. What changes or deletions, if any, would you make? What problems would you expect to meet in transferring it to a different medium?
4. This topic calls for a performance of *A Vietnamese Wedding* in your classroom. This will not be difficult and will not even require a rehearsal, provided a few props are obtained in advance. After you have seen the performance or taken part in it, write a paper setting forth whatever it revealed to you.

36 *Evaluating a Play*

To **evaluate** a play is to decide whether the play is any good or not; and if it is good, how good it is in relation to other plays of its kind. In the theater, evaluation is usually thought to be the task of the play reviewer (or, with nobler connotations, "drama critic"), ordinarily a person who sees a new play on its first night and who then tells us, in print or over the air, what the play is about, how well it is done, and whether or not we ought to go to see it. Enthroned in an excellent free seat, the drama critic apparently plies a glamorous trade. What fun it must be to whittle a nasty epigram: to be able to observe, as did a critic of a faltering production of *Uncle Tom's Cabin,* that "the Siberian wolf hound was weakly supported."

Unless you find a job on a large city newspaper or radio station, however, or write for a college paper, or broadcast on a campus FM station, the opportunities to be a drama critic today are probably few and strictly limited. Much more significant, for most of us, is the task of evaluation we undertake for our own satisfaction. We see a play, or a film or a drama on television, and then we make up our minds about it; and we often have to decide whether to recommend it to anyone else.

To evaluate new drama isn't easy. (And in this discussion, let us define *drama* broadly as including not only plays, but anything that actors perform in the movies or on television, for most of us see more movies and television programs than plays.) But at least a part of the process of evaluation has already been accomplished for us. To produce a new play, even in an amateur theater, or to produce a new drama for the movies or for television, is complicated and involves large sums of money and the efforts of many people. Sifted from a mountain of submitted playscripts, already subjected to long scrutiny and evaluation, a new play or film, whether or not it is of deep interest, arrives with a built-in air of professional competence. It is probably seldom that a dull play written by the producer's relative or friend finds enough financial backers to reach the stage; only on the fictitious Broadway of Mel Brooks's film *The Producers* could there be a musical comedy as awful as *Springtime for Hitler.* Nor do most college and civic theaters afford us much opportunity to see thoroughly inept plays; usually they give us new productions of *Oedipus the King* or *Pygmalion;* or else (if they are less adventurous) new versions of whatever succeeded on Broadway in the recent past.

And so new plays—the few that we do see—are usually, like television drama, somebody's safe investment. More often than not, our powers of evaluation confront only slick, pleasant, and efficient mediocrity. We owe it to ourselves to discriminate; and here are a few suggestions designed to help you tell the difference between an ordinary, run-of-the-reel product and a work of drama that may offer high reward.

1. Discard any inexorable rules you may have collected that affirm what a drama ought to be. (One such rule states that a tragedy is innately superior to a comedy, no matter how deep a truth a comedy may strike.) Never mind the misinterpreters of Aristotle who insist that a play must "observe the unities"—that is, must unfold its events in one day and in one place, and must keep tragedy and comedy strictly apart. (Shakespeare ignores such rules.) There is no sense in damning a play for lacking "realism" (what if it's an expressionist play, or a fantasy?), or in belaboring the failure of its plot to fit into a pyramid structure.

2. Instead, watch the play (or read it) alertly, with your mind and your senses open wide. Recall that theaters, such as the classic Greek theater of Sophocles, impose conventions. Do not condemn *Oedipus the King* for the reason one spectator gave: "That damned chorus keeps sticking their noses in!" Do not complain that Hamlet utters soliloquies; nor that, in the same play, some speeches (when the speakers exit) rime unnaturally.

3. Ask yourself if the characters are fully realized. Do their actions follow from the kinds of persons they are, or does the action seem to impose itself upon them, making the play seem falsely contrived? Does the resolution arrive (as in a satisfying play) because of the nature of the characters; or are the characters saved (or destroyed) merely by some *deus ex machina,* or nick-of-time arrival of the Marines?

4. Recognize drama that belongs to a family: a *farce,* say, or a *comedy of manners,* or a **melodrama**—a play in which suspense and physical action are the prime ingredients. Recognizing such a familiar type of drama may help make some things clear to you, and may save you from attacking a play for being what it is, in fact, supposed to be. After all, there can be satisfying melodramas, and excellent plays may have melodramatic elements. What is wrong with thrillers is not that they have suspense, but that suspense is all they have. Awhirl with furious action, they employ stick-figure characters.

5. If there are symbols, ask how well they belong to their surrounding worlds. Do they help to reveal meaning, or merely decorate? In Tennessee Williams's *The Glass Menagerie,* Laura's collection of figurines is much more than simply ornamental.

6. Test the play or film for **sentimentality,** the failure of a dramatist, actor, or director who expects from us a greater emotional response than we

are given reason to feel. (For further discussions of sentimentality, see pages 211 and 747.)

7. Decide what it is that you admire or dislike, and, for a play, whether it is the play that you admire or dislike, or the production. (It is useful to draw this distinction if you are evaluating the play and not the production.)

8. Ask yourself what the theme is. What does the drama reveal? How far and how deeply does its statement go; how readily can we apply it beyond the play to the human world outside? Be slow, of course, to attribute to the playwright the opinions of the characters.

Follow all these steps and you may find that evaluating plays, movies, and television plays is a richly meaningful activity. It may reveal wisdom and pleasure that had previously bypassed you. It may even help you decide what to watch in the future, how to choose those works of drama which help you to fulfill—not merely to spend—your waking life.

SUGGESTIONS FOR WRITING

1. Attend a performance of a play and write a critical review of it. Consider both the play itself and its production. (For advice on reviewing and a sample review, see page 1527.)

2. Read two celebrated, still much performed plays of the same era, *Death of a Salesman* (1949) and *The Glass Menagerie* (1945), both in "Plays for Further Reading." Then, in an essay of 700 words or more, decide which you consider the finer play. Back up your evaluation by referring to both.

3. Read the printed text of a modern or contemporary play not included in this book. (If you can see the play on stage, so much the better.) Then, in an essay of 500 to 750 words, state your considered opinion of it. Among interesting plays to choose from are these:

The Zoo Story by Edward Albee
Waiting for Godot by Samuel Beckett
The Caucasian Chalk Circle or *Mother Courage* by Bertold Brecht
'Master Harold' and the Boys by Athol Fugard
Crimes of the Heart by Beth Henley
Hedda Gabler, The Master Builder, or *Peer Gynt* by Henrik Ibsen
The Bald Soprano or *The Chairs* by Eugene Ionesco
American Buffalo by David Mamet
'Night, Mother by Marsha Norman
Long Day's Journey into Night by Eugene O'Neill
The Birthday Party or *The Caretaker* by Harold Pinter
No Exit by Jean-Paul Sartre
Amadeus or *Equus* by Peter Shaffer
for colored girls who have considered suicide / when the rainbow is enuf by Ntozake Shange
Major Barbara or *Pygmalion* by Bernard Shaw
Buried Child or *True West* by Sam Shepard
Rosencrantz and Guildenstern Are Dead by Tom Stoppard
The Heidi Chronicles by Wendy Wasserstein
Fences or *The Piano Player* by August Wilson

37 *Plays for Further Reading*

All the world's a stage,
And all the men and women merely players:
They have their exits and their entrances,
And one man in his time plays many parts,
His acts being seven ages. At first, the infant
Mewling° and puking in the nurse's arms.   *bawling*
Then the whining schoolboy with his satchel
And shining morning face, creeping like snail
Unwilling to school. And then the lover,
Sighing like furnace, with a woeful ballad
Made to his mistress' eyebrow. Then a soldier
Full of strange oaths and bearded like the pard°,   *leopard*
Jealous in honor, sudden and quick in quarrel,
Seeking the bubble reputation
Even in the cannon's mouth. And then the justice,
In fair round belly with good capon lined,
With eyes severe and beard of formal cut,
Full of wise saws° and modern instances°;   *sayings; examples*
And so he plays his part. The sixth age shifts
Into the lean and slippered pantaloon°,   *old man (from*
With spectacles on nose and pouch on side;   *Pantalone in*
His youthful hose well saved, a world too wide   *the commedia*
For his shrunk shank, and his big manly voice   *dell' arte)*
Turning again toward childish treble, pipes
And whistles in his sound. Last scene of all
That ends this strange eventful history
Is second childishness and mere oblivion,
Sans teeth, sans eyes, sans taste, sans everything.
                    —William Shakespeare, *As You Like It*, II, vii

Arthur Miller

DEATH OF A SALESMAN   1949

Certain Private Conversations in Two Acts and a Requiem

Arthur Miller

Arthur Miller, born in 1915 into a lower-income Jewish family in New York's Harlem, grew up in Brooklyn. He studied playwriting at the University of Michigan (class of '38), later wrote radio scripts, and in World War II worked as a steamfitter. When the New York Drama Critics named his All My Sons best play of 1947, Miller told an interviewer, "I don't see how you can write anything decent without using as your basis the question of right and wrong." (The play is about a guilty manufacturer of defective aircraft parts.) Death of a Salesman (1949) made Miller famous. The Crucible (1953), a dramatic indictment of the Salem witch trials, gained him further attention at a time when Senator Joseph McCarthy was conducting loyalty investigations. For a while (1956–1961) Miller was the husband of actress Marilyn Monroe, whom the main character of his All That Fall (1964) resembles. Among Miller's other plays are A View from the Bridge (1955), The Price (1968), The Creation of the World and Other Businesses (1972), and Playing for Time (1980), written for television. He has written two novels, Focus (1945), a study of antisemitism, and The Misfits (1960), which he made into a screenplay featuring Monroe. Recently, Miller has professed himself disenchanted with Broadway theater. In 1983 he directed an all-Chinese cast in a production of Death of a Salesman in Peking. The play was successfully revived in New York in 1983, and later on television, with Dustin Hoffman playing Willy Loman.

The action takes place in Willy Loman's house and yard and in various places he visits in the New York and Boston of today.

Throughout the play, in the stage directions, left and right mean stage left and stage right.

ACT I

A melody is heard, played upon a flute. It is small and fine, telling of grass and trees and the horizon. The curtain rises.

Before us is the Salesman's house. We are aware of towering, angular shapes behind it, surrounding it on all sides. Only the blue light of the sky falls upon the house and forestage; the surrounding area shows an angry glow of orange. As more light appears, we see a solid vault of apartment houses around the small, fragile-seeming home. An air of the dream clings to the place, a dream rising out of reality. The kitchen at center seems actual enough, for there is a kitchen table with three chairs, and a refrigerator. But no other fixtures are seen. At the back of the kitchen there is a draped entrance, which leads to the livingroom. To the right of the kitchen, on a level raised two feet, is a bedroom furnished only with a brass bedstead and a straight chair. On a shelf over the bed a silver athletic trophy stands. A window opens onto the apartment house at the side.

Behind the kitchen, on a level raised six and a half feet, is the boys' bedroom, at present barely visible. Two beds are dimly seen, and at the back of the room a dormer window. (This bedroom is above the unseen livingroom.) At the left a stairway curves up to it from the kitchen.

The entire setting is wholly or, in some places, partially transparent. The roof-line of the house is one-dimensional; under and over it we see the apartment buildings. Before the house lies an apron, curving beyond the forestage into the orchestra. This forward area serves as the back yard as well as the locale of all Willy's imaginings and of his city scenes. Whenever the action is in the present the actors observe the imaginary wall-lines, entering the house only through the door at the left. But in the scenes of the past these boundaries are broken, and characters enter or leave a room by stepping "through" a wall onto the forestage.

From the right, Willy Loman, the Salesman, enters, carrying two large sample cases. The flute plays on. He hears but is not aware of it. He is past sixty years of age, dressed quietly. Even as he crosses the stage to the doorway of the house, his exhaustion is apparent. He unlocks the door, comes into the kitchen, and thankfully lets his burden down, feeling the soreness of his palms. A word-sigh escapes his lips—it might be, "Oh, boy, oh, boy." He closes the door, then carries his cases out into the livingroom, through the draped kitchen doorway.

Linda, his wife, has stirred in her bed at the right. She gets out and puts on a robe, listening. Most often jovial, she has developed an iron repression of her exceptions to Willy's behavior—she more than loves him, she admires him, as though his mercurial nature, his temper, his massive dreams and little cruelties, served her only as sharp reminders of the turbulent longings within him, longings which she shares but lacks the temperament to utter and follow to their end.

Linda (hearing Willy outside the bedroom, calls with some trepidation): Willy!
Willy: It's all right. I came back.
Linda: Why? What happened? (Slight pause.) Did something happen, Willy?
Willy: No, nothing happened.
Linda: You didn't smash the car, did you?
Willy (with casual irritation): I said nothing happened. Didn't you hear me?
Linda: Don't you feel well?
Willy: I am tired to the death. (The flute has faded away. He sits on the bed beside her, a little numb.) I couldn't make it. I just couldn't make it, Linda.
Linda (very carefully, delicately): Where were you all day? You look terrible.
Willy: I got as far as a little above Yonkers. I stopped for a cup of coffee. Maybe it was the coffee.
Linda: What?
Willy (after a pause): I suddenly couldn't drive any more. The car kept going onto the shoulder, y'know?

Linda (helpfully): Oh. Maybe it was the steering again. I don't think Angelo knows the Studebaker.

Willy: No, it's me, it's me. Suddenly I realize I'm goin' sixty miles an hour and I don't remember the last five minutes. I'm—I can't seem to—keep my mind to it.

Linda: Maybe it's your glasses. You never went for your new glasses.

Willy: No, I see everything. I came back ten miles an hour. It took me nearly four hours from Yonkers.

Linda (resigned): Well, you'll just have to take a rest. Willy, you can't continue this way.

Willy: I just got back from Florida.

Linda: But you didn't rest your mind. Your mind is overactive, and the mind is what counts, dear.

Willy: I'll start out in the morning. Maybe I'll feel better in the morning. (She is taking off his shoes.) These goddam arch supports are killing me.

Linda: Take an aspirin. Should I get you an aspirin? It'll soothe you.

Willy (with wonder): I was driving along, you understand? And I was fine. I was even observing the scenery. You can imagine, me looking at scenery, on the road every week of my life. But it's so beautiful up there, Linda, the trees are so thick, and the sun is warm. I opened the windshield and just let the warm air bathe over me. And then all of a sudden I'm goin' off the road! I'm tellin' ya, I absolutely forgot I was driving. If I'd've gone the other way over the white line I might've killed somebody. So I went on again—and five minutes later I'm dreamin' again, and I nearly—(He presses two fingers against his eyes.) I have such thoughts, I have such strange thoughts.

Linda: Willy, dear. Talk to them again. There's no reason why you can't work in New York.

Willy: They don't need me in New York. I'm the New England man. I'm vital in New England.

Linda: But you're sixty years old. They can't expect you to keep traveling every week.

Willy: I'll have to send a wire to Portland. I'm supposed to see Brown and Morrison tomorrow morning at ten o'clock to show the line. Goddammit, I could sell them! (He starts putting on his jacket.)

Linda (taking the jacket from him): Why don't you go down to the place tomorrow and tell Howard you've simply got to work in New York? You're too accommodating, dear.

Willy: If old man Wagner was alive I'd a been in charge of New York now! That man was a prince, he was a masterful man. But that boy of his, that Howard, he don't appreciate. When I went north the first time, the Wagner Company didn't know where New England was!

Linda: Why don't you tell those things to Howard, dear?

Willy (encouraged): I will, I definitely will. Is there any cheese?

Linda: I'll make you a sandwich.

Willy: No, go to sleep. I'll take some milk. I'll be up right away. The boys in?

Linda: They're sleeping. Happy took Biff on a date tonight.

Willy (interested): That so?

Linda: It was so nice to see them shaving together, one behind the other, in the bathroom. And going out together. You notice? The whole house smells of shaving lotion.

Willy: Figure it out. Work a lifetime to pay off a house. You finally own it, and there's nobody to live in it.

Linda: Well, dear, life is a casting off. It's always that way.

Willy: No, no, some people—some people accomplish something. Did Biff say anything after I went this morning?

Linda: You shouldn't have criticized him, Willy, especially after he just got off the train. You mustn't lose your temper with him.

Willy: When the hell did I lose my temper? I simply asked him if he was making any money. Is that a criticism?

Linda: But, dear, how could he make any money?

Willy (worried and angered): There's such an undercurrent in him. He became a moody man. Did he apologize when I left this morning?

Linda: He was crestfallen, Willy. You know how he admires you. I think if he finds himself, then you'll both be happier and not fight any more.

Willy: How can he find himself on a farm? Is that a life? A farmhand? In the beginning, when he was young, I thought, well, a young man, it's good for him to tramp around, take a lot of different jobs. But it's more than ten years now and he has yet to make thirty-five dollars a week!

Linda: He's finding himself, Willy.

Willy: Not finding yourself at the age of thirty-four is a disgrace!

Linda: Shh!

Willy: The trouble is he's lazy, goddammit!

Linda: Willy, please!

Willy: Biff is a lazy bum.

Linda: They're sleeping. Get something to eat. Go on down.

Willy: Why did he come home? I would like to know what brought him home.

Linda: I don't know. I think he's still lost, Willy. I think he's very lost.

Willy: Biff Loman is lost. In the greatest country in the world a young man with such—personal attractiveness, gets lost. And such a hard worker. There's one thing about Biff—he's not lazy.

Linda: Never.

Willy (with pity and resolve): I'll see him in the morning. I'll have a nice talk with him. I'll get him a job selling. He could be big in no time. My God! Remember how they used to follow him around in high school? When he smiled at one of them their faces lit up. When he walked down the street . . . (*He loses himself in reminiscences.*)

Linda (trying to bring him out of it): Willy, dear, I got a new kind of American-type cheese today. It's whipped.

Willy: Why do you get American when I like Swiss?

Linda: I just thought you'd like a change—

Willy: I don't want a change! I want Swiss cheese. Why am I always being contradicted?

Linda (with a covering laugh): I thought it would be a surprise.

Willy: Why don't you open a window in here, for God's sake?

Linda (with infinite patience): They're all open, dear.

Willy: The way they boxed us in here. Bricks and windows, windows and bricks.

Linda: We should've bought the land next door.

Willy: The street is lined with cars. There's not a breath of fresh air in the neighborhood. The grass don't grow any more, you can't raise a carrot in the back yard. They should've had a law against apartment houses. Remember those two beautiful elm trees out there? When I and Biff hung the swing between them?

Linda: Yeah, like being a million miles from the city.

Willy: They should've arrested the builder for cutting those down. They massacred the neighborhood. *(Lost.)* More and more I think of those days, Linda. This time of year it was lilac and wisteria. And then the peonies would come out, and the daffodils. What fragrance in this room!

Linda: Well, after all, people had to move somewhere.

Willy: No, there's more people now.

Linda: I don't think there's more people. I think—

Willy: There's more people! That's what's ruining this country! Population is getting out of control. The competition is maddening! Smell the stink from that apartment house! And another on the other side . . . How can they whip cheese?

On Willy's last line, Biff and Happy raise themselves up in their beds, listening.

Linda: Go down, try it. And be quiet.

Willy (turning to Linda, guiltily): You're not worried about me, are you, sweetheart?

Biff: What's the matter?

Happy: Listen!

Linda: You've got too much on the ball to worry about.

Willy: You're my foundation and my support, Linda.

Linda: Just try to relax, dear. You make mountains out of molehills.

Willy: I won't fight with him any more. If he wants to go back to Texas, let him go.

Linda: He'll find his way.

Willy: Sure. Certain men just don't get started till later in life. Like Thomas Edison, I think. Or B. F. Goodrich. One of them was deaf. *(He starts for the bedroom doorway.)* I'll put my money on Biff.

Linda: And Willy—if it's warm Sunday we'll drive in the country. And we'll open the windshield, and take lunch.

Willy: No, the windshields don't open on the new cars.

Linda: But you opened it today.

Willy: Me? I didn't. *(He stops.)* Now isn't that peculiar! Isn't that a remarkable— *(He breaks off in amazement and fright as the flute is heard distantly.)*

Linda: What, darling?

Willy: That is the most remarkable thing.

Linda: What, dear?

Willy: I was thinking of the Chevvy. *(Slight pause.)* Nineteen twenty-eight . . . when I had that red Chevvy—*(Breaks off.)* That funny? I coulda sworn I was driving that Chevvy today.

Linda: Well, that's nothing. Something must've reminded you.

Willy: Remarkable. Ts. Remember those days? The way Biff used to simonize that car? The dealer refused to believe there was eighty thousand miles on it. *(He shakes his head. Heh! (To Linda.) Close your eyes, I'll be right up. (He walks out of the bedroom.)*

Happy *(to Biff)*: Jesus, maybe he smashed up the car again!

Linda *(calling after Willy)*: Be careful on the stairs, dear! The cheese is on the middle shelf! *(She turns, goes over to the bed, takes his jacket, and goes out of the bedroom.)*

Light has risen on the boys' room. Unseen, Willy is heard talking to himself, "Eighty thousand miles," and a little laugh. Biff gets out of bed, comes downstage a bit, and stands attentively. Biff is two years older than his brother Happy, well built, but in these days bears a worn air and seems less self-assured. He has succeeded less, and his dreams are stronger and less acceptable than Happy's. Happy is tall, powerfully made. Sexuality is like a visible color on him, or a scent that many women have discovered. He, like his brother, is lost, but in a different way, for he has never allowed himself to turn his face toward defeat and is thus more confused and hard-skinned, although seemingly more content.

Happy *(getting out of bed)*: He's going to get his license taken away if he keeps that up. I'm getting nervous about him, y'know, Biff?

Biff: His eyes are going.

Happy: No, I've driven with him. He sees all right. He just doesn't keep his mind on it. I drove into the city with him last week. He stops at a green light and then it turns red and he goes. *(He laughs.)*

Biff: Maybe he's color-blind.

Happy: Pop? Why he's got the finest eye for color in the business. You know that.

Biff *(sitting down on his bed)*: I'm going to sleep.

Happy: You're not still sour on Dad, are you, Biff?

Biff: He's all right, I guess.

Willy *(underneath them, in the livingroom)*: Yes, sir, eighty thousand miles—eighty-two thousand!

Biff: You smoking?

Happy *(holding out a pack of cigarettes)*: Want one?

Biff *(taking a cigarette)*: I can never sleep when I smell it.

Willy: What a simonizing job, heh!

Happy *(with deep sentiment)*: Funny, Biff, y'know? Us sleeping in here again? The old beds. *(He pats his bed affectionately.)* All the talk that went across those two beds, huh? Our whole lives.

Biff: Yeah. Lotta dreams and plans.

Happy *(with a deep and masculine laugh)*: About five hundred women would like to know what was said in this room.

They share a soft laugh.

Biff: Remember that big Betsy something—what the hell was her name—over on Bushwick Avenue?

Happy *(combing his hair)*: With the collie dog!

Biff: That's the one. I got you in there, remember?

Happy: Yeah, that was my first time—I think. Boy, there was a pig! *(They laugh, almost crudely.)* You taught me everything I know about women. Don't forget that.

Biff: I bet you forgot how bashful you used to be. Especially with girls.

Happy: Oh, I still am, Biff.

Biff: Oh, go on.

Happy: I just control it, that's all. I think I got less bashful and you got more so. What happened, Biff? Where's the old humor, the old confidence? *(He shakes Biff's knee. Biff gets up and moves restlessly about the room.)* What's the matter?

Biff: Why does Dad mock me all the time?

Happy: He's not mocking you, he—

Biff: Everything I say there's a twist of mockery on his face. I can't get near him.

Happy: He just wants you to make good, that's all. I wanted to talk to you about Dad for a long time, Biff. Something's—happening to him. He—talks to himself.

Biff: I noticed that this morning. But he always mumbled.

Happy: But not so noticeable. It got so embarrassing I sent him to Florida. And you know something? Most of the time he's talking to you.

Biff: What's he say about me?

Happy: I can't make it out.

Biff: What's he say about me?

Happy: I think the fact that you're not settled, that you're still kind of up in the air . . .

Biff: There's one or two other things depressing him, Happy.

Happy: What do you mean?

Biff: Never mind. Just don't lay it all on me.

Happy: But I think if you just got started—I mean—is there any future for you out there?

Biff: I tell ya, Hap, I don't know what the future is. I don't know—what I'm supposed to want.

Happy: What do you mean?

Biff: Well, I spent six or seven years after high school trying to work myself up. Shipping clerk, salesman, business of one kind or another. And it's a measly manner of existence. To get on that subway on the hot mornings in summer. To devote your whole life to keeping stock, or making phone calls, or selling or buying. To suffer fifty weeks of the year for the sake of a two-week vacation, when all you really desire is to be outdoors, with your shirt off. And always to have to get ahead of the next fella. And still—that's how you build a future.

Happy: Well, you really enjoy it on a farm? Are you content out there?

Biff (with rising agitation): Hap, I've had twenty or thirty different kinds of jobs since I left home before the war, and it always turns out the same. I just realized it lately. In Nebraska when I herded cattle, and the Dakotas, and Arizona, and now in Texas. It's why I came home now, I guess, because I realized it. This farm I work on, it's spring there now, see? And they've got about fifteen new colts. There's nothing more inspiring or—beautiful than the sight of a mare and a new colt. And it's cool there now, see? Texas is cool now, and it's spring. And whenever spring comes to where I am, I suddenly get the feeling, my God, I'm not gettin' anywhere! What the hell am I doing, playing around with horses, twenty-eight dollars a week! I'm thirty-four years old, I oughta be makin' my future. That's when I come running home. And now, I get here, and I don't know what to do with myself. (*After a pause.*) I've always made a point of not wasting my life, and everytime I come back here I know that all I've done is to waste my life.

Happy: You're a poet, you know that, Biff? You're a—you're an idealist!

Biff: No, I'm mixed up very bad. Maybe I oughta get married. Maybe I oughta get stuck into something. Maybe that's my trouble. I'm like a boy. I'm not married, I'm not in business, I just—I'm like a boy. Are you content, Hap? You're a success, aren't you? Are you content?

Happy: Hell, no!

Biff: Why? You're making money, aren't you?

Happy (moving about with energy, expressiveness): All I can do now is wait for the merchandise manager to die. And suppose I get to be merchandise manager? He's a good friend of mine, and he just built a terrific estate on Long Island. And he lived there about two months and sold it, and now he's building another one. He can't enjoy it once it's finished. And I know that's just what I would do. I don't know what the hell I'm workin' for. Sometimes I sit in my apartment—all alone. And I think of the rent I'm paying. And it's crazy. But then, it's what I always wanted. My own apartment, a car, and plenty of women. And still, goddammit, I'm lonely.

Biff (with enthusiasm): Listen, why don't you come out West with me?

Happy: You and I, heh?

Biff: Sure, maybe we could buy a ranch. Raise cattle, use our muscles. Men built like we are should be working out in the open.

Happy (avidly): The Loman Brothers, heh?

Biff (with vast affection): Sure, we'd be known all over the counties!

Happy (enthralled): That's what I dream about, Biff. Sometimes I want to just rip my clothes off in the middle of the store and outbox that goddam merchandise manager. I mean I can outbox, outrun, and outlift anybody in that store, and I have to take orders from those common, petty sons-of-bitches till I can't stand it any more.

Biff: I'm tellin' you, kid, if you were with me I'd be happy out there.

Happy (enthused): See, Biff, everybody around me is so false that I'm constantly lowering my ideals . . .

Biff: Baby, together we'd stand up for one another, we'd have someone to trust.

Happy: If I were around you—

Biff: Hap, the trouble is we weren't brought up to grub for money. I don't know how to do it.

Happy: Neither can I!

Biff: Then let's go!

Happy: The only thing is—what can you make out there?

Biff: But look at your friend. Builds an estate and then hasn't the peace of mind to live in it.

Happy: Yeah, but when he walks into the store the waves part in front of him. That's fifty-two thousand dollars a year coming through the revolving door, and I got more in my pinky finger than he's got in his head.

Biff: Yeah, but you just said—

Happy: I gotta show some of those pompous, self-important executives over there that Hap Loman can make the grade. I want to walk into the store the way he walks in. Then I'll go with you, Biff. We'll be together yet, I swear. But take those two we had tonight. Now weren't they gorgeous creatures?

Biff: Yeah, yeah, most gorgeous I've had in years.

Happy: I get that any time I want, Biff. Whenever I feel disgusted. The only trouble is, it gets like bowling or something. I just keep knockin' them over and it doesn't mean anything. You still run around a lot?

Biff: Naa. I'd like to find a girl—steady, somebody with substance.

Happy: That's what I long for.

Biff: Go on! You'd never come home.

Happy: I would! Somebody with character, with resistance! Like Mom, y'know? You're gonna call me a bastard when I tell you this. That girl Charlotte I was with tonight is engaged to be married in five weeks. (*He tries on his new hat.*)

Biff: No kiddin'!

Happy: Sure, the guy's in line for the vice-presidency of the store. I don't know what gets into me, maybe I just have an overdeveloped sense of competition or something, but I went and ruined her, and furthermore I can't get rid of her. And he's the third executive I've done that to. Isn't that a crummy characteristic? And to top it all, I go to their weddings! (*Indignantly, but laughing.*) Like I'm not supposed to take bribes. Manufacturers offer me a hundred-dollar bill now and then to throw an order their way. You know how honest I am, but it's like this girl, see. I hate myself for it. Because I don't want the girl, and, still, I take it and—I love it!

Biff: Let's go to sleep.

Happy: I guess we didn't settle anything, heh?

Biff: I just got one idea that I think I'm going to try.

Happy: What's that?

Biff: Remember Bill Oliver?

Happy: Sure, Oliver is very big now. You want to work for him again?

Biff: No, but when I quit he said something to me. He put his arm on my shoulder, and he said, "Biff, if you ever need anything, come to me."

Happy: I remember that. That sounds good.

Biff: I think I'll go to see him. If I could get ten thousand or even seven or eight thousand dollars I could buy a beautiful ranch.

Happy: I bet he'd back you. 'Cause he thought highly of you, Biff, I mean, they all do. You're well liked, Biff. That's why I say to come back here, and we both have the apartment. And I'm tellin' you, Biff, any babe you want . . .

Biff: No, with a ranch I could do the work I like and still be something. I just wonder though. I wonder if Oliver still thinks I stole that carton of basketballs.

Happy: Oh, he probably forgot that long ago. It's almost ten years. You're too sensitive. Anyway, he didn't really fire you.

Biff: Well, I think he was going to. I think that's why I quit. I was never sure whether he knew or not. I know he thought the world of me, though. I was the only one he'd let lock up the place.

Willy (below): You gonna wash the engine, Biff?

Happy: Shh!

Biff looks at Happy, who is gazing down, listening. Willy is mumbling in the parlor.

Happy: You hear that?

They listen. Willy laughs warmly.

Biff (growing angry): Doesn't he know Mom can hear that?

Willy: Don't get your sweater dirty, Biff!

A look of pain crosses Biff's face.

Happy: Isn't that terrible? Don't leave again, will you? You'll find a job here. You gotta stick around. I don't know what to do about him, it's getting embarrassing.

Willy: What a simonizing job!

Biff: Mom's hearing that!

Willy: No kiddin', Biff, you got a date? Wonderful!

Happy: Go on to sleep. But talk to him in the morning, will you?

Biff (reluctantly getting into bed): With her in the house. Brother!

Happy (getting into bed): I wish you'd have a good talk with him.

The light on their room begins to fade.

Biff (to himself in bed): That selfish, stupid . . .

Happy: Sh . . . Sleep, Biff.

Their light is out. Well before they have finished speaking, Willy's form is dimly seen below in the darkened kitchen. He opens the refrigerator, searches in there, and takes out a bottle of milk. The apartment houses are fading out, and the entire house and surroundings become covered with leaves. Music insinuates itself as the leaves appear.

Willy: Just wanna be careful with those girls, Biff, that's all. Don't make any promises. No promises of any kind. Because a girl, y'know, they always believe what you tell 'em, and you're very young, Biff, you're too young to be talking seriously to girls.

Light rises on the kitchen. Willy, talking, shuts the refrigerator door and comes downstage to the kitchen table. He pours milk into a glass. He is totally immersed in himself, smiling faintly.

Willy: Too young entirely, Biff. You want to watch your schooling first. Then when you're all set, there'll be plenty of girls for a boy like you. (*He smiles broadly at a kitchen chair.*) That so? The girls pay for you? (*He laughs.*) Boy, you must really be makin' a hit.

Willy is gradually addressing—physically—a point offstage, speaking through the wall of the kitchen, and his voice has been rising in volume to that of a normal conversation.

Willy: I been wondering why you polish the car so careful. Ha! Don't leave the hubcaps, boys. Get the chamois to the hubcaps. Happy, use newspaper on the windows, it's the easiest thing. Show him how to do it, Biff! You see, Happy? Pad it up, use it like a pad. That's it, that's it, good work. You're doin' all right, Hap. *(He pauses, then nods in approbation for a few seconds, then looks upward.)* Biff, first thing we gotta do when we get time is clip that big branch over the house. Afraid it's gonna fall in a storm and hit the roof. Tell you what. We get a rope and sling her around, and then we climb up there with a couple of saws and take her down. Soon as you finish the car, boys, I wanna see ya. I got a surprise for you, boys.

Biff (offstage): Whatta ya got, Dad?

Willy: No, you finish first. Never leave a job till you're finished—remember that. *(Looking toward the "big trees.")* Biff, up in Albany I saw a beautiful hammock. I think I'll buy it next trip, and we'll hang it right between those two elms. Wouldn't that be something? Just swingin' there under those branches. Boy, that would be . . .

Young Biff and Young Happy appear from the direction Willy was addressing. Happy carries rags and a pail of water. Biff, wearing a sweater with a block "S," carries a football.

Biff (pointing in the direction of the car offstage): How's that, Pop, professional?

Willy: Terrific. Terrific job, boys. Good work, Biff.

Happy: Where's the surprise, Pop?

Willy: In the back seat of the car.

Happy: Boy! *(He runs off.)*

Biff: What is it, Dad? Tell me, what'd you buy?

Willy (laughing, cuffs him): Never mind, something I want you to have.

Biff (turns and starts off): What is it, Hap?

Happy (offstage): It's a punching bag!

Biff: Oh, Pop!

Willy: It's got Gene Tunney's signature on it.

Happy runs onstage with a punching bag.

Biff: Gee, how'd you know we wanted a punching bag?

Willy: Well, it's the finest thing for the timing.

Happy (lies down on his back and pedals with his feet): I'm losing weight, you notice, Pop?

Willy (to Happy): Jumping rope is good too.

Biff: Did you see the new football I got?

Willy (examining the ball): Where'd you get a new ball?

Biff: The coach told me to practice my passing.

Willy: That so? And he gave you the ball, heh?

Biff: Well, I borrowed it from the locker room. *(He laughs confidentially.)*

Willy (laughing with him at the theft): I want you to return that.

Happy: I told you he wouldn't like it!

Biff (angrily): Well, I'm bringing it back!

Willy (stopping the incipient argument, to Happy): Sure, he's gotta practice with a regulation ball, doesn't he? *(To Biff.)* Coach'll probably congratulate you on your initiative.

Biff: Oh, he keeps congratulating my initiative all the time, Pop.

Willy: That's because he likes you. If somebody else took that ball there'd be an uproar. So what's the report, boys, what's the report?

Biff: Where'd you go this time, Dad? Gee we were lonesome for you.

Willy (pleased, puts an arm around each boy and they come down to the apron): Lonesome, heh?

Biff: Missed you every minute.

Willy: Don't say? Tell you a secret, boys. Don't breathe it to a soul. Someday I'll have my own business, and I'll never have to leave home any more.

Happy: Like Uncle Charley, heh?

Willy: Bigger than Uncle Charley! Because Charley is not—liked. He's liked, but he's not—well liked.

Biff: Where'd you go this time, Dad?

Willy: Well, I got on the road, and I went north to Providence. Met the Mayor.

Biff: The Mayor of Providence!

Willy: He was sitting in the hotel lobby.

Biff: What'd he say?

Willy: He said, "Morning!" And I said, "You've got a fine city here, Mayor." And then he had coffee with me. And then I went to Waterbury. Waterbury is a fine city. Big clock city, the famous Waterbury clock. Sold a nice bill there. And then Boston—Boston is the cradle of the Revolution. A fine city. And a couple of other towns in Mass., and on to Portland and Bangor and straight home!

Biff: Gee, I'd love to go with you sometime, Dad.

Willy: Soon as summer comes.

Happy: Promise?

Willy: You and Hap and I, and I'll show you all the towns. America is full of beautiful towns and fine, upstanding people. And they know me, boys, they know me up and down New England. The finest people. And when I bring you fellas up, there'll be open sesame for all of us, 'cause one thing, boys: I have friends. I can park my car in any street in New England, and the cops protect it like their own. This summer, heh?

Biff and Happy (together): Yeah! You bet!

Willy: We'll take our bathing suits.

Happy: We'll carry your bags, Pop!

Willy: Oh, won't that be something! Me comin' into the Boston stores with you boys carryin' my bags. What a sensation!

Biff is prancing around, practicing passing the ball.

Willy: You nervous, Biff, about the game?

Biff: Not if you're gonna be there.

Willy: What do they say about you in school, now that they made you captain?

Happy: There's a crowd of girls behind him everytime the classes change.

Biff (taking Willy's hand): This Saturday, Pop, this Saturday—just for you, I'm going to break through for a touchdown.

Happy: You're supposed to pass.

Biff: I'm takin' one play for Pop. You watch me, Pop, and when I take off my helmet, that means I'm breakin' out. Then you watch me crash through that line!

Willy (kisses Biff): Oh, wait'll I tell this in Boston!

Bernard enters in knickers. He is younger than Biff, earnest and loyal, a worried boy.

Bernard: Biff, where are you? You're supposed to study with me today.

Willy: Hey, looka Bernard. What're you lookin' so anemic about, Bernard?

Bernard: He's gotta study, Uncle Willy. He's got Regents next week.

Happy (tauntingly, spinning Bernard around): Let's box, Bernard!

Bernard: Biff! (He gets away from Happy.) Listen, Biff, I heard Mr. Birnbaum say that if you don't start studyin' math he's gonna flunk you, and you won't graduate. I heard him!

Willy: You better study with him, Biff. Go ahead now.

Bernard: I heard him!

Biff: Oh, Pop, you didn't see my sneakers! (He holds up a foot for Willy to look at.)

Willy: Hey, that's a beautiful job of printing!

Bernard (wiping his glasses): Just because he printed University of Virginia on his sneakers doesn't mean they've got to graduate him, Uncle Willy!

Willy (angrily): What're you talking about? With scholarships to three universities they're gonna flunk him?

Bernard: But I heard Mr. Birnbaum say—

Willy: Don't be a pest, Bernard! (To his boys.) What an anemic!

Bernard: Okay, I'm waiting for you in my house, Biff.

Bernard goes off. The Lomans laugh.

Willy: Bernard is not well liked, is he?

Biff: He's liked, but he's not well liked.

Happy: That's right, Pop.

Willy: That's just what I mean. Bernard can get the best marks in school, y'understand, but when he gets out in the business world, y'understand, you are going to be five times ahead of him. That's why I thank Almighty God you're both built like Adonises. Because the man who makes an appearance in the business world, the man who creates personal interest, is the man who gets ahead. Be liked and you will never want. You take me, for instance. I never have to wait in line to see a buyer. "Willy Loman is here!" That's all they have to know, and I go right through.

Biff: Did you knock them dead, Pop?

Willy: Knocked 'em cold in Providence, slaughtered 'em in Boston.

Happy (on his back, pedaling again): I'm losing weight, you notice, Pop?

Linda enters, as of old, a ribbon in her hair, carrying a basket of washing.

Linda (with youthful energy): Hello, dear!

Willy: Sweetheart!

Linda: How'd the Chevvy run?

Willy: Chevrolet, Linda, is the greatest car every built. (*To the boys.*) Since when do you let your mother carry wash up the stairs?

Biff: Grab hold there, boy!

Happy: Where to, Mom?

Linda: Hang them up on the line. And you better go down to your friends, Biff. The cellar is full of boys. They don't know what to do with themselves.

Biff: Ah, when Pop comes home they can wait!

Willy (*laughs appreciatively*): You better go down and tell them what to do, Biff.

Biff: I think I'll have them sweep out the furnace room.

Willy: Good work, Biff.

Biff (*goes through wall-line of kitchen to doorway at back and calls down*): Fellas! Everybody sweep out the furnace room! I'll be right down!

Voices: All right! Okay, Biff.

Biff: George and Sam and Frank, come out back! We're hangin' up the wash! Come on, Hap, on the double! (*He and Happy carry out the basket.*)

Linda: The way they obey him!

Willy: Well, that's training, the training. I'm tellin' you, I was sellin' thousands and thousands, but I had to come home.

Linda: Oh, the whole block'll be at that game. Did you sell anything?

Willy: I did five hundred gross in Providence and seven hundred gross in Boston.

Linda: No! Wait a minute, I've got a pencil. (*She pulls pencil and paper out of her apron pocket.*) That makes your commission . . . Two hundred—my God! Two hundred and twelve dollars!

Willy: Well, I didn't figure it yet, but . . .

Linda: How much did you do?

Willy: Well, I—I did—about a hundred and eighty gross in Providence. Well, no—it came to—roughly two hundred gross on the whole trip.

Linda (*without hesitation*): Two hundred gross. That's . . . (*She figures.*)

Willy: The trouble was that three of the stores were half closed for inventory in Boston. Otherwise I woulda broke records.

Linda: Well, it makes seventy dollars and some pennies. That's very good.

Willy: What do we owe?

Linda: Well, on the first there's sixteen dollars on the refrigerator—

Willy: Why sixteen?

Linda: Well, the fan belt broke, so it was a dollar eighty.

Willy: But it's brand new.

Linda: Well, the man said that's the way it is. Till they work themselves in, y'know.

They move through the wall-line into the kitchen.

Willy: I hope we didn't get stuck on that machine.

Linda: They got the biggest ads of any of them.

Willy: I know, it's a fine machine. What else?

Linda: Well, there's nine-sixty for the washing machine. And for the vacuum cleaner there's three and a half due on the fifteenth. Then the roof, you got twenty-one dollars remaining.

Willy: It don't leak, does it?

Linda: No, they did a wonderful job. Then you owe Frank for the carburetor.

Willy: I'm not going to pay that man! That goddam Chevrolet, they ought to prohibit the manufacture of that car!

Linda: Well, you owe him three and a half. And odds and ends, comes to around a hundred and twenty dollars by the fifteenth.

Willy: A hundred and twenty dollars! My God, if business don't pick up I don't know what I'm gonna do!

Linda: Well, next week you'll do better.

Willy: Oh, I'll knock them dead next week. I'll go to Hartford. I'm very well liked in Hartford. You know, the trouble is, Linda, people don't seem to take to me.

They move on the forestage.

Linda: Oh, don't be foolish.

Willy: I know it when I walk in. They seem to laugh at me.

Linda: Why? Why would they laugh at you? Don't talk that way, Willy.

Willy moves to the edge of the stage. Linda goes into the kitchen and starts to darn stockings.

Willy: I don't know the reason for it, but they just pass me by. I'm not noticed.

Linda: But you're doing wonderful, dear. You're making seventy to a hundred dollars a week.

Willy: But I gotta be at it ten, twelve hours a day. Other men—I don't know—they do it easier. I don't know why—I can't stop myself—I talk too much. A man oughta come in with a few words. One thing about Charley. He's a man of few words, and they respect him.

Linda: You don't talk too much, you're just lively.

Willy (smiling): Well, I figure, what the hell, life is short, a couple of jokes. (*To himself.*) I joke too much! (*The smile goes.*)

Linda: Why? You're—

Willy: I'm fat. I'm very—foolish to look at, Linda. I didn't tell you, but Christmas time I happened to be calling on F. H. Stewarts, and a salesman I know, as I was going in to see the buyer I heard him say something about—walrus. And I—I cracked him right across the face. I won't take that. I simply will not take that. But they do laugh at me. I know that.

Linda: Darling . . .

Willy: I gotta overcome it. I know I gotta overcome it. I'm not dressing to advantage, maybe.

Linda: Willy, darling, you're the handsomest man in the world—

Willy: Oh, no, Linda.

Linda: To me you are. (*Slight pause.*) The handsomest.

From the darkness is heard the laughter of a woman. Willy doesn't turn to it, but it continues through Linda's lines.

Linda: And the boys, Willy. Few men are idolized by their children the way you are.

Music is heard as behind a scrim, to the left of the house, The Woman, dimly seen, is dressing.

Willy (with great feeling): You're the best there is, Linda, you're a pal, you know that? On the road—on the road I want to grab you sometimes and just kiss the life outa you.

The laughter is loud now, and he moves into a brightening area at the left, where The Woman has come from behind the scrim and is standing, putting on her hat, looking into a "mirror" and laughing.

Willy: 'Cause I get so lonely—especially when business is bad and there's nobody to talk to. I get the feeling that I'll never sell anything again, that I won't make a living for you, or a business, a business for the boys. (*He talks through The Woman's subsiding laughter; The Woman primps at the "mirror."*) There's so much I want to make for—

The Woman: Me? You didn't make me, Willy. I picked you.

Willy (pleased): You picked me?

The Woman (who is quite proper-looking, Willy's age): I did. I've been sitting at that desk watching all the salesmen go by, day in, day out. But you've got such a sense of humor, and we do have such a good time together, don't we?

Willy: Sure, sure. (*He takes her in his arms.*) Why do you have to go now?

The Woman: It's two o'clock . . .

Willy: No, come on in! (*He pulls her.*)

The Woman: . . . my sisters'll be scandalized. When'll you be back?

Willy: Oh, two weeks about. Will you come up again?

The Woman: Sure thing. You do make me laugh. It's good for me. (*She squeezes his arm, kisses him.*) And I think you're a wonderful man.

Willy: You picked me, heh?

The Woman: Sure. Because you're so sweet. And such a kidder.

Willy: Well, I'll see you next time I'm in Boston.

The Woman: I'll put you right through to the buyers.

Willy (slapping her bottom): Right. Well, bottoms up!

The Woman (slaps him gently and laughs): You just kill me, Willy. (*He suddenly grabs her and kisses her roughly.*) You kill me. And thanks for the stockings. I love a lot of stockings. Well, good night.

Willy: Good night. And keep your pores open!

The Woman: Oh, Willy!

The Woman bursts out laughing, and Linda's laughter blends in. The Woman disappears into the dark. Now the area at the kitchen table brightens. Linda is sitting where she was at the kitchen table, but now is mending a pair of silk stockings.

Linda: You are, Willy. The handsomest man. You've got no reason to feel that—

Willy (coming out of The Woman's dimming area and going over to Linda): I'll make it all up to you, Linda, I'll—

Linda: There's nothing to make up, dear. You're doing fine, better than—

Willy (noticing her mending): What's that?

Linda: Just mending my stockings. They're so expensive—

Willy (angrily, taking them from her): I won't have you mending stockings in this house! Now throw them out!

Linda puts the stockings in her pocket.

Bernard (entering on the run): Where is he? If he doesn't study!

Willy (moving to the forestage, with great agitation): You'll give him the answers!

Bernard: I do, but I can't on a Regents! That's a state exam! They're liable to arrest me!

Willy: Where is he? I'll whip him, I'll whip him!

Linda: And he'd better give back that football, Willy, it's not nice.

Willy: Biff! Where is he? Why is he taking everything?

Linda: He's too rough with the girls, Willy. All the mothers are afraid of him!

Willy: I'll whip him!

Bernard: He's driving the car without a license!

The Woman's laugh is heard.

Willy: Shut up!

Linda: All the mothers—

Willy: Shut up!

Bernard (backing quietly away and out): Mr. Birnbaum says he's stuck up.

Willy: Get outa here!

Bernard: If he doesn't buckle down he'll flunk math! *(He goes off.)*

Linda: He's right, Willy, you've gotta—

Willy (exploding at her): There's nothing the matter with him! You want him to be a worm like Bernard? He's got spirit, personality . . .

As he speaks, Linda, almost in tears, exits into the livingroom. Willy is alone in the kitchen, wilting and staring. The leaves are gone. It is night again, and the apartment houses look down from behind.

Willy: Loaded with it. Loaded! What is he stealing? He's giving it back, isn't he? Why is he stealing? What did I tell him? I never in my life told him anything but decent things.

Happy in pajamas has come down the stairs; Willy suddenly becomes aware of Happy's presence.

Happy: Let's go now, come on.

Willy (sitting down at the kitchen table): Huh! Why did she have to wax the floors herself? Everytime she waxes the floors she keels over. She knows that!

Happy: Shh! Take it easy. What brought you back tonight?

Willy: I got an awful scare. Nearly hit a kid in Yonkers. God! Why didn't I go to Alaska with my brother Ben that time! Ben! That man was a genius, that man was success incarnate! What a mistake! He begged me to go.

Happy: Well, there's no use in—

Willy: You guys! There was a man started with the clothes on his back and ended up with diamond mines!

Happy: Boy, someday I'd like to know how he did it.

Willy: What's the mystery? The man knew what he wanted and went out and got it! Walked into a jungle, and comes out, the age of twenty-one, and he's rich! The world is an oyster, but you don't crack it open on a mattress!

Happy: Pop, I told you I'm gonna retire you for life.

Willy: You'll retire me for life on seventy goddam dollars a week? And your women and your car and your apartment, and you'll retire me for life! Christ's sake, I couldn't get past Yonkers today! Where are you guys, where are you? The woods are burning! I can't drive a car!

Charley has appeared in the doorway. He is a large man, slow of speech, laconic, immovable. In all he says, despite what he says, there is pity, and, now, trepidation. He has a robe over his pajamas, slippers on his feet. He enters the kitchen.

Charley: Everything all right?

Happy: Yeah, Charley, everything's . . .

Willy: What's the matter?

Charley: I heard some noise. I thought something happened. Can't we do something about the walls? You sneeze in here, and in my house hats blow off.

Happy: Let's go to bed, Dad. Come on.

Charley signals to Happy to go.

Willy: You go ahead, I'm not tired at the moment.

Happy (to Willy): Take it easy, huh? *(He exits.)*

Willy: What're you doin' up?

Charley (sitting down at the kitchen table opposite Willy): Couldn't sleep good. I had a heartburn.

Willy: Well, you don't know how to eat.

Charley: I eat with my mouth.

Willy: No, you're ignorant. You gotta know about vitamins and things like that.

Charley: Come on, let's shoot. Tire you out a little.

Willy (hesitantly): All right. You got cards?

Charley (taking a deck from his pocket): Yeah, I got them. Someplace. What is it with those vitamins?

Willy (dealing): They build up your bones. Chemistry.

Charley: Yeah, but there's no bones in a heartburn.

Willy: What are you talkin' about? Do you know the first thing about it?

Charley: Don't get insulted.

Willy: Don't talk about something you don't know anything about.

They are playing. Pause.

Charley: What're you doin' home?

Willy: A little trouble with the car.

Charley: Oh. *(Pause.)* I'd like to take a trip to California.

Willy: Don't say.

Charley: You want a job?

Willy: I got a job, I told you that. *(After a slight pause.)* What the hell are you offering me a job for?

Charley: Don't get insulted.

Willy: Don't insult me.

Charley: I don't see no sense in it. You don't have to go on this way.

Willy: I got a good job. *(Slight pause.)* What do you keep comin' in here for?

Charley: You want me to go?

Willy (after a pause, withering): I can't understand it. He's going back to Texas again. What the hell is that?

Charley: Let him go.

Willy: I got nothin' to give him, Charley, I'm clean, I'm clean.

Charley: He won't starve. None a them starve. Forget about him.

Willy: Then what have I got to remember?

Charley: You take it too hard. To hell with it. When a deposit bottle is broken you don't get your nickel back.

Willy: That's easy enough for you to say.

Charley: That ain't easy for me to say.

Willy: Did you see the ceiling I put up in the livingroom?

Charley: Yeah, that's a piece of work. To put up a ceiling is a mystery to me. How do you do it?

Willy: What's the difference?

Charley: Well, talk about it.

Willy: You gonna put up a ceiling?

Charley: How could I put up a ceiling?

Willy: Then what the hell are you bothering me for?

Charley: You're insulted again.

Willy: A man who can't handle tools is not a man. You're disgusting.

Charley: Don't call me disgusting, Willy.

> *Uncle Ben, carrying a valise and an umbrella, enters the forestage from around the right corner of the house. He is a stolid man, in his sixties, with a mustache and an authoritative air. He is utterly certain of his destiny, and there is an aura of far places about him. He enters exactly as Willy speaks.*

Willy: I'm getting awfully tired, Ben.

> *Ben's music is heard. Ben looks around at everything.*

Charley: Good, keep playing; you'll sleep better. Did you call me Ben?

> *Ben looks at his watch.*

Willy: That's funny. For a second there you reminded me of my brother Ben.

Ben: I have only a few minutes. *(He strolls, inspecting the place. Willy and Charley continue playing.)*

Charley: You never heard from him again, heh? Since that time?

Willy: Didn't Linda tell you? Couple of weeks ago we got a letter from his wife in Africa. He died.

Charley: That so.

Ben (chuckling): So this is Brooklyn, eh?

Charley: Maybe you're in for some of his money.

Willy: Naa, he had seven sons. There's just one opportunity I had with that man . . .

Ben: I must make a train, William. There are several properties I'm looking at in Alaska.

Willy: Sure, sure! If I'd gone with him to Alaska that time, everything would've been totally different.

Charley: Go on, you'd froze to death up there.

Willy: What're you talking about?

Ben: Opportunity is tremendous in Alaska, William. Surprised you're not up there.

Willy: Sure, tremendous.

Charley: Heh?

Willy: There was the only man I ever met who knew the answers.

Charley: Who?

Ben: How are you all?

Willy (taking a pot, smiling): Fine, fine.

Charley: Pretty sharp tonight.

Ben: Is Mother living with you?

Willy: No, she died a long time ago.

Charley: Who?

Ben: That's too bad. Fine specimen of a lady, Mother.

Willy (to Charley): Heh?

Ben: I'd hoped to see the old girl.

Charley: Who died?

Ben: Heard anything from Father, have you?

Willy (unnerved): What do you mean, who died?

Charley (taking a pot): What're you talkin' about?

Ben (looking at his watch): William, it's half-past eight!

Willy (as though to dispel his confusion he angrily stops Charley's hand): That's my build!

Charley: I put the ace—

Willy: If you don't know how to play the game I'm not gonna throw my money away on you!

Charley (rising): It was my ace, for God's sake!

Willy: I'm through, I'm through!

Ben: When did Mother die?

Willy: Long ago. Since the beginning you never knew how to play cards.

Charley (picks up the cards and goes to the door): All right! Next time I'll bring a deck with five aces.

Willy: I don't play that kind of game!

Charley (turning to him): You should be ashamed of yourself!

Willy: Yeah?

Charley: Yeah! (He goes out.)

Willy (slamming the door after him): Ignoramus!

Ben (as Willy comes toward him through the wall-line of the kitchen): So you're William.

Willy (shaking Ben's hand): Ben! I've been waiting for you so long! What's the answer? How did you do it?

Ben: Oh, there's a story in that.

Linda enters the forestage, as of old, carrying the wash basket.

Linda: Is this Ben?

Ben (gallantly): How do you do, my dear.

Linda: Where've you been all these years? Willy's always wondered why you—

Willy (*pulling Ben away from her impatiently*): Where is Dad? Didn't you follow him? How did you get started?

Ben: Well, I don't know how much you remember.

Willy: Well, I was just a baby, of course, only three or four years old—

Ben: Three years and eleven months.

Willy: What a memory, Ben!

Ben: I have many enterprises, William, and I have never kept books.

Willy: I remember I was sitting under the wagon in—was it Nebraska?

Ben: It was South Dakota, and I gave you a bunch of wild flowers.

Willy: I remember you walking away down some open road.

Ben (*laughing*): I was going to find Father in Alaska.

Willy: Where is he?

Ben: At that age I had a very faulty view of geography, William. I discovered after a few days that I was heading due south, so instead of Alaska, I ended up in Africa.

Linda: Africa!

Willy: The Gold Coast!

Ben: Principally, diamond mines.

Linda: Diamond mines!

Ben: Yes, my dear. But I've only a few minutes—

Willy: No! Boys! Boys! (*Young Biff and Happy appear.*) Listen to this. This is your Uncle Ben, a great man! Tell my boys, Ben!

Ben: Why, boys, when I was seventeen I walked into the jungle, and when I was twenty-one I walked out. (*He laughs.*) And by God I was rich.

Willy (*to the boys*): You see what I been talking about? The greatest things can happen!

Ben (*glancing at his watch*): I have an appointment in Ketchikan Tuesday week.

Willy: No, Ben! Please tell about Dad. I want my boys to hear. I want them to know the kind of stock they sprang from. All I remember is a man with a big beard, and I was in Mamma's lap, sitting around a fire, and some kind of high music.

Ben: His flute. He played the flute.

Willy: Sure, the flute, that's right!

New music is heard, a high, rollicking tune.

Ben: Father was a very great and a very wild-hearted man. We would start in Boston, and he'd toss the whole family into the wagon, and then he'd drive the team right across the country; through Ohio, and Indiana, Michigan, Illinois, and all the Western states. And we'd stop in the towns and sell the flutes that he'd made on the way. Great inventor, Father. With one gadget he made more in a week than a man like you could make in a lifetime.

Willy: That's just the way I'm bringing them up, Ben—rugged, well liked, all-around.

Ben: Yeah? (*To Biff.*) Hit that, boy—hard as you can. (*He pounds his stomach.*)

Biff: Oh, no, sir!

Ben (*taking boxing stance*): Come on, get to me! (*He laughs.*)

Willy: Go to it, Biff! Go ahead, show him!

Biff: Okay! (*He cocks his fist and starts in.*)

Linda (to Willy): Why must he fight, dear?

Ben (sparring with Biff): Good boy! Good boy!

Willy: How's that, Ben, heh?

Happy: Give him the left, Biff!

Linda: Why are you fighting?

Ben: Good boy! *(Suddenly comes in, trips Biff, and stands over him, the point of his umbrella poised over Biff's eye.)*

Linda: Look out, Biff!

Biff: Gee!

Ben (patting Biff's knee): Never fight fair with a stranger, boy. You'll never get out of the jungle that way. *(Taking Linda's hand and bowing.)* It was an honor and a pleasure to meet you, Linda.

Linda (withdrawing her hand coldly, frightened): Have a nice—trip.

Ben (to Willy): And good luck with your—what do you do?

Willy: Selling.

Ben: Yes. Well . . . *(He raises his hand in farewell to all.)*

Willy: No, Ben, I don't want you to think . . . *(He takes Ben's arm to show him.)* It's Brooklyn, I know, but we hunt too.

Ben: Really, now.

Willy: Oh, sure, there's snakes and rabbits and—that's why I moved out here. Why, Biff can fell any one of these trees in no time! Boys! Go right over to where they're building the apartment house and get some sand. We're gonna rebuild the entire front stoop right now! Watch this, Ben!

Biff: Yes, sir! On the double, Hap!

Happy (as he and Biff run off): I lost weight, Pop, you notice?

Charley enters in knickers, even before the boys are gone.

Charley: Listen, if they steal any more from that building the watchman'll put the cops on them!

Linda (to Willy): Don't let Biff . . .

Ben laughs lustily.

Willy: You shoulda seen the lumber they brought home last week. At least a dozen six-by-tens worth all kinds of money.

Charley: Listen, if that watchman—

Willy: I gave them hell, understand. But I got a couple of fearless characters there.

Charley: Willy, the jails are full of fearless characters.

Ben (clapping Willy on the back, with a laugh at Charley): And the stock exchange, friend!

Willy (joining in Ben's laughter): Where are the rest of your pants?

Charley: My wife bought them.

Willy: Now all you need is a golf club and you can go upstairs and go to sleep. *(To Ben.)* Great athlete! Between him and his son Bernard they can't hammer a nail!

Bernard (rushing in): The watchman's chasing Biff!

Willy (angrily): Shut up! He's not stealing anything!

Linda (alarmed, hurrying off left): Where is he? Biff, dear! *(She exits.)*

Willy (*moving toward the left, away from Ben*): There's nothing wrong. What's the matter with you?

Ben: Nervy boy. Good!

Willy (*laughing*): Oh, nerves of iron, that Biff!

Charley: Don't know what it is. My New England man comes back and he's bleedin', they murdered him up there.

Willy: It's contacts, Charley, I got important contacts!

Charley (*sarcastically*): Glad to hear it, Willy. Come in later, we'll shoot a little casino. I'll take some of your Portland money. (*He laughs at Willy and exits.*)

Willy (*turning to Ben*): Business is bad, it's murderous. But not for me, of course.

Ben: I'll stop by on my way back to Africa.

Willy (*longingly*): Can't you stay a few days? You're just what I need, Ben, because I—I have a fine position, but I—well, Dad left when I was such a baby and I never had a chance to talk to him and I still feel—kind of temporary about myself.

Ben: I'll be late for my train.

They are at opposite ends of the stage.

Willy: Ben, my boys—can't we talk? They'd go into the jaws of hell for me, see, but I—

Ben: William, you're being first-rate with your boys. Outstanding, manly chaps!

Willy (*hanging on to his words*): Oh, Ben, that's good to hear! Because sometimes I'm afraid that I'm not teaching them the right kind of—Ben, how should I teach them?

Ben (*giving great weight to each word, and with a certain vicious audacity*): William, when I walked into the jungle, I was seventeen. When I walked out I was twenty-one. And, by God, I was rich! (*He goes off into darkness around the right corner of the house.*)

Willy: . . . was rich! That's just the spirit I want to imbue them with! To walk into a jungle! I was right! I was right! I was right!

Ben is gone, but Willy is still speaking to him as Linda, in nightgown and robe, enters the kitchen, glances around for Willy, then goes to the door of the house, looks out and sees him. Comes down to his left. He looks at her.

Linda: Willy, dear? Willy?

Willy: I was right!

Linda: Did you have some cheese? (*He can't answer.*) It's very late, darling. Come to bed, heh?

Willy (*looking straight up*): Gotta break your neck to see a star in this yard.

Linda: You coming in?

Willy: What ever happened to that diamond watch fob? Remember? When Ben came from Africa that time? Didn't he give me a watch fob with a diamond in it?

Linda: You pawned it, dear. Twelve, thirteen years ago. For Biff's radio correspondence course.

Willy: Gee, that was a beautiful thing. I'll take a walk.

Linda: But you're in your slippers.

Willy (*starting to go around the house at the left*): I was right! I was! (*Half to Linda, as he goes, shaking his head.*) What a man! There was a man worth talking to. I was right!

Linda (*calling after Willy*): But in your slippers, Willy!

Willy is almost gone when Biff, in his pajamas, comes down the stairs and enters the kitchen.

Biff: What is he doing out there?

Linda: Sh!

Biff: God Almighty, Mom, how long has he been doing this?

Linda: Don't, he'll hear you.

Biff: What the hell is the matter with him?

Linda: It'll pass by morning.

Biff: Shouldn't we do anything?

Linda: Oh, my dear, you should do a lot of things, but there's nothing to do, so go to sleep.

Happy comes down the stairs and sits on the steps.

Happy: I never heard him so loud, Mom.

Linda: Well, come around more often; you'll hear him. (*She sits down at the table and mends the lining of Willy's jacket.*)

Biff: Why didn't you ever write me about this, Mom?

Linda: How would I write to you? For over three months you had no address.

Biff: I was on the move. But you know I thought of you all the time. You know that, don't you, pal?

Linda: I know, dear, I know. But he likes to have a letter. Just to know that there's still a possibility for better things.

Biff: He's not like this all the time, is he?

Linda: It's when you come home he's always the worst.

Biff: When I come home?

Linda: When you write you're coming, he's all smiles, and talks about the future, and—he's just wonderful. And then the closer you seem to come, the more shaky he gets, and then, by the time you get here, he's arguing, and he seems angry at you. I think it's just that maybe he can't bring himself to—to open up to you. Why are you so hateful to each other? Why is that?

Biff (*evasively*): I'm not hateful, Mom.

Linda: But you no sooner come in the door than you're fighting!

Biff: I don't know why. I mean to change. I'm tryin', Mom, you understand?

Linda: Are you home to stay now?

Biff: I don't know. I want to look around, see what's doin'.

Linda: Biff, you can't look around all your life, can you?

Biff: I just can't take hold, Mom. I can't take hold of some kind of a life.

Linda: Biff, a man is not a bird, to come and go with the springtime.

Biff: Your hair . . . (*He touches her hair.*) Your hair got so gray.

Linda: Oh, it's been gray since you were in high school. I just stopped dyeing it, that's all.

Biff: Dye it again, will ya? I don't want my pal looking old. (*He smiles.*)

Linda: You're such a boy! You think you can go away for a year and . . . You've got to get it into your head now that one day you'll knock on this door and there'll be strange people here—

Biff: What are you talking about? You're not even sixty, Mom.

Linda: But what about your father?

Biff (lamely): Well, I meant him too.

Happy: He admires Pop.

Linda: Biff, dear, if you don't have any feeling for him, then you can't have any feeling for me.

Biff: Sure I can, Mom.

Linda: No. You can't just come to see me, because I love him. *(With a threat, but only a threat, of tears.)* He's the dearest man in the world to me, and I won't have anyone making him feel unwanted and low and blue. You've got to make up your mind now, darling, there's no leeway any more. Either he's your father and you pay him that respect, or else you're not to come here. I know he's not easy to get along with—nobody knows that better than me—but . . .

Willy (from the left, with a laugh): Hey, hey, Biffo!

Biff (starting to go out after Willy): What the hell is the matter with him? *(Happy stops him.)*

Linda: Don't—don't go near him!

Biff: Stop making excuses for him! He always, always wiped the floor with you. Never had an ounce of respect for you.

Happy: He's always had respect for—

Biff: What the hell do you know about it?

Happy (surlily): Just don't call him crazy!

Biff: He's got no character—Charley wouldn't do this. Not in his own house—spewing out that vomit from his mind.

Happy: Charley never had to cope with what he's got to.

Biff: People are worse off than Willy Loman. Believe me, I've seen them!

Linda: Then make Charley your father, Biff. You can't do that, can you? I don't say he's a great man. Willy Loman never made a lot of money. His name was never in the paper. He's not the finest character that ever lived. But he's a human being, and a terrible thing is happening to him. So attention must be paid. He's not to be allowed to fall into his grave like an old dog. Attention, attention must be finally paid to such a person. You called him crazy—

Biff: I didn't mean—

Linda: No, a lot of people think he's lost his—balance. But you don't have to be very smart to know what his trouble is. The man is exhausted.

Happy: Sure!

Linda: A small man can be just as exhausted as a great man. He works for a company thirty-six years this March, opens up unheard-of territories to their trademark, and now in his old age they take his salary away.

Happy (indignantly): I didn't know that, Mom!

Linda: You never asked, my dear! Now that you get your spending money someplace else you don't trouble your mind with him.

Happy: But I gave you money last—

Linda: Christmas time, fifty dollars! To fix the hot water it cost ninety-seven fifty! For five weeks he's been on straight commission, like a beginner, an unknown!

Biff: Those ungrateful bastards!

Linda: Are they any worse than his sons? When he brought them business, when he was young, they were glad to see him. But now his old friends, the old buyers that loved him so and always found some order to hand him in a pinch—they're all dead, retired. He used to be able to make six, seven calls a day in Boston. Now he takes his valises out of the car and puts them back and takes them out again and he's exhausted. Instead of walking he talks now. He drives seven hundred miles, and when he gets there no one knows him any more, no one welcomes him. And what goes through a man's mind, driving seven hundred miles home without having earned a cent? Why shouldn't he talk to himself? Why? When he has to go to Charley and borrow fifty dollars a week and pretend to me that it's his pay? How long can that go on? How long? You see what I'm sitting here and waiting for? And you tell me he has no character? The man who never worked a day but for your benefit? When does he get the medal for that? Is this his reward—to turn around at the age of sixty-three and find his sons, who he loved better than his life, one a philandering bum—

Happy: Mom!

Linda: That's all you are, my baby! *(To Biff.)* And you! What happened to the love you had for him? You were such pals! How you used to talk to him on the phone every night! How lonely he was till he could come home to you!

Biff: All right, Mom. I'll live here in my room, and I'll get a job. I'll keep away from him, that's all.

Linda: No, Biff. You can't stay here and fight all the time.

Biff: He threw me out of this house, remember that.

Linda: Why did he do that? I never knew why.

Biff: Because I know he's a fake and he doesn't like anybody around who knows!

Linda: Why a fake? In what way? What do you mean?

Biff: Just don't lay it all at my feet. It's between me and him—that's all I have to say. I'll chip in from now on. He'll settle for half my pay check. He'll be all right. I'm going to bed. *(He starts for the stairs.)*

Linda: He won't be all right.

Biff (turning on the stairs, furiously): I hate this city and I'll stay here. Now what do you want?

Linda: He's dying, Biff.

Happy turns quickly to her, shocked.

Biff (after a pause): Why is he dying?

Linda: He's been trying to kill himself.

Biff (with great horror): How?

Linda: I live from day to day.

Biff: What're you talking about?

Linda: Remember I wrote you that he smashed up the car again? In February?

Biff: Well?

Linda: The insurance inspector came. He said that they have evidence. That all these accidents in the last year—weren't—weren't—accidents.

Happy: How can they tell that? That's a lie.

Linda: It seems there's a woman . . . *(She takes a breath as—)*

Biff (sharply but contained): What woman?

Linda (simultaneously): . . . and this woman . . .

Linda: What?

Biff: Nothing. Go ahead.

Linda: What did you say?

Biff: Nothing. I just said what woman?

Happy: What about her?

Linda: Well, it seems she was walking down the road and saw his car. She says that he wasn't driving fast at all, and that he didn't skid. She says he came to that little bridge, and then deliberately smashed into the railing, and it was only the shallowness of the water that saved him.

Biff: Oh, no, he probably just fell asleep again.

Linda: I don't think he fell asleep.

Biff: Why not?

Linda: Last month . . . *(With great difficulty.)* Oh, boys, it's so hard to say a thing like this! He's just a big stupid man to you, but I tell you there's more good in him than in many other people. *(She chokes, wipes her eyes.)* I was looking for a fuse. The lights blew out, and I went down the cellar. And behind the fuse box—it happened to fall out—was a length of rubber pipe—just short.

Happy: No kidding?

Linda: There's a little attachment on the end of it. I knew right away. And sure enough, on the bottom of the water heater there's a new little nipple on the gas pipe.

Happy (angrily): That—jerk.

Biff: Did you have it taken off?

Linda: I'm—I'm ashamed to. How can I mention it to him? Every day I go down and take away that little rubber pipe. But, when he comes home, I put it back where it was. How can I insult him that way? I don't know what to do. I live from day to day, boys. I tell you, I know every thought in his mind. It sounds so old-fashioned and silly, but I tell you he put his whole life into you and you've turned your backs on him. *(She is bent over in the chair, weeping, her face in her hands.)* Biff, I swear to God! Biff, his life is in your hands!

Happy (to Biff): How do you like that damned fool!

Biff (kissing her): All right, pal, all right. It's all settled now. I've been remiss. I know that, Mom. But now I'll stay, and I swear to you, I'll apply myself. *(Kneeling in front of her, in a fever of self-reproach.)* It's just—you see, Mom, I don't fit in business. Not that I won't try. I'll try, and I'll make good.

Happy: Sure you will. The trouble with you in business was you never tried to please people.

Biff: I know, I—

Happy: Like when you worked for Harrison's. Bob Harrison said you were tops, and then you go and do some damn fool thing like whistling whole songs in the elevator like a comedian.

Biff (against Happy): So what? I like to whistle sometimes.

Happy: You don't raise a guy to a responsible job who whistles in the elevator!

Linda: Well, don't argue about it now.

Happy: Like when you'd go off and swim in the middle of the day instead of taking the line around.

Biff (his resentment rising): Well, don't you run off? You take off sometimes, don't you? On a nice summer day?

Happy: Yeah, but I cover myself!

Linda: Boys!

Happy: If I'm going to take a fade the boss can call any number where I'm supposed to be and they'll swear to him that I just left. I'll tell you something that I hate to say, Biff, but in the business world some of them think you're crazy.

Biff (angered): Screw the business world!

Happy: All right, screw it! Great, but cover yourself!

Linda: Hap! Hap!

Biff: I don't care what they think! They've laughed at Dad for years, and you know why? Because we don't belong in this nut-house of a city! We should be mixing cement on some open plain, or—or carpenters. A carpenter is allowed to whistle!

Willy walks in from the entrance of the house, at left.

Willy: Even your grandfather was better than a carpenter. *(Pause. They watch him.)* You never grew up. Bernard does not whistle in the elevator, I assure you.

Biff (as though to laugh Willy out of it): Yeah, but you do, Pop.

Willy: I never in my life whistled in an elevator! And who in the business world thinks I'm crazy?

Biff: I didn't mean it like that, Pop. Now don't make a whole thing out of it, will ya?

Willy: Go back to the West! Be a carpenter, a cowboy, enjoy yourself!

Linda: Willy, he was just saying—

Willy: I heard what he said!

Happy (trying to quiet Willy): Hey, Pop, come on now . . .

Willy (continuing over Happy's line): They laugh at me, heh? Go to Filene's, go to the Hub, go to Slattery's, Boston. Call out the name Willy Loman and see what happens! Big shot!

Biff: All right, Pop.

Willy: Big!

Biff: All right!

Willy: Why do you always insult me?

Biff: I didn't say a word. *(To Linda.)* Did I say a word?

Linda: He didn't say anything, Willy.

Willy (going to the doorway of the livingroom): All right, good night, good night.

Linda: Willy, dear, he just decided . . .

Willy (to Biff): If you get tired hanging around tomorrow, paint the ceiling I put up in the livingroom.

Biff: I'm leaving early tomorrow.

Happy: He's going to see Bill Oliver, Pop.

Willy (interestedly): Oliver? For what?

Biff (with reserve, but trying, trying): He always said he'd stake me. I'd like to go into business, so maybe I can take him up on it.

Linda: Isn't that wonderful?

Willy: Don't interrupt. What's wonderful about it? There's fifty men in the City of New York who'd stake him. *(To Biff.)* Sporting goods?

Biff: I guess so. I know something about it and—

Willy: He knows something about it! You know sporting goods better than Spalding, for God's sake! How much is he giving you?

Biff: I don't know, I didn't even see him yet, but—

Willy: Then what're you talkin' about?

Biff (getting angry): Well, all I said was I'm gonna see him, that's all!

Willy (turning away): Ah, you're counting your chickens again.

Biff (starting left for the stairs): Oh, Jesus, I'm going to sleep!

Willy (calling after him): Don't curse in this house!

Biff (turning): Since when did you get so clean!

Happy (trying to stop them): Wait a . . .

Willy: Don't use that language to me! I won't have it!

Happy (grabbing Biff, shouts): Wait a minute! I got an idea. I got a feasible idea. Come here, Biff, let's talk this over now, let's talk some sense here. When I was down in Florida last time, I thought of a great idea to sell sporting goods. It just came back to me. You and I, Biff—we have a line, the Loman Line. We train a couple of weeks, and put on a couple of exhibitions, see?

Willy: That's an idea!

Happy: Wait! We form two basketball teams, see? Two water-polo teams. We play each other. It's a million dollars' worth of publicity. Two brothers, see? The Loman Brothers. Displays in the Royal Palms—all the hotels. And banners over the ring and the basketball court: "Loman Brothers." Baby, we could sell sporting goods!

Willy: That is a one-million-dollar idea.

Linda: Marvelous!

Biff: I'm in great shape as far as that's concerned.

Happy: And the beauty of it is, Biff, it wouldn't be like a business. We'd be out playin' ball again . . .

Biff (enthused): Yeah, that's . . .

Willy: Million-dollar . . .

Happy: And you wouldn't get fed up with it, Biff. It'd be the family again. There'd be the old honor, and comradeship, and if you wanted to go off for a swim or somethin'—well, you'd do it! Without some smart cooky gettin' up ahead of you!

Willy: Lick the world! You guys together could absolutely lick the civilized world.

Biff: I'll see Oliver tomorrow. Hap, if we could work that out . . .

Linda: Maybe things are beginning to—

Willy (wildly enthused, to Linda): Stop interrupting! *(To Biff.)* But don't wear sport jacket and slacks when you see Oliver.

Biff: No, I'll—

Willy: A business suit, and talk as little as possible, and don't crack any jokes.

Biff: He did like me. Always liked me.

Linda: He loved you!

Willy (to Linda): Will you stop! *(To Biff.)* Walk in very serious. You are not applying for a boy's job. Money is to pass. Be quiet, fine, and serious. Everybody likes a kidder, but nobody lends him money.

Happy: I'll try to get some myself, Biff. I'm sure I can.

Willy: I can see great things for you, kids, I think your troubles are over. But remember, start big and you'll end big. Ask for fifteen. How much you gonna ask for?

Biff: Gee, I don't know—

Willy: And don't say "Gee." "Gee" is a boy's word. A man walking in for fifteen thousand dollars does not say "Gee!"

Biff: Ten, I think, would be top though.

Willy: Don't be so modest. You always started too low. Walk in with a big laugh. Don't look worried. Start off with a couple of your good stories to lighten things up. It's not what you say, it's how you say it—because personality always wins the day.

Linda: Oliver always thought the highest of him—

Willy: Will you let me talk?

Biff: Don't yell at her, Pop, will ya?

Willy (angrily): I was talking, wasn't I?

Biff: I don't like you yelling at her all the time, and I'm tellin' you, that's all.

Willy: What're you, takin' over the house?

Linda: Willy—

Willy (turning on her): Don't take his side all the time, goddammit!

Biff (furiously): Stop yelling at her!

Willy (suddenly pulling on his cheek, beaten down, guilt ridden): Give my best to Bill Oliver—he may remember me. *(He exits through the livingroom doorway.)*

Linda (her voice subdued): What'd you have to start that for? *(Biff turns away.)* You see how sweet he was as soon as you talked hopefully? *(She goes over to Biff.)* Come up and say good night to him. Don't let him go to bed that way.

Happy: Come on, Biff, let's buck him up.

Linda: Please, dear. Just say good night. It takes so little to make him happy. Come. *(She goes through the livingroom doorway, calling upstairs from within the livingroom.)* Your pajamas are hanging in the bathroom. Willy!

Happy (looking toward where Linda went out): What a woman! They broke the mold when they made her. You know that, Biff?

Biff: He's off salary. My God, working on commission!

Happy: Well, let's face it: he's no hot-shot selling man. Except that sometimes, you have to admit, he's a sweet personality.

Biff (deciding): Lend me ten bucks, will ya? I want to buy some new ties.

Happy: I'll take you to a place I know. Beautiful stuff. Wear one of my striped shirts tomorrow.

Biff: She got gray. Mom got awful old. Gee, I'm gonna go in to Oliver tomorrow and knock him for a—

Happy: Come on up. Tell that to Dad. Let's give him a whirl. Come on.

Biff (steamed up): You know, with ten thousand bucks, boy!

Happy (as they go into the livingroom): That's the talk, Biff, that's the first time I've heard the old confidence out of you! *(From within the livingroom, fading off.)* You're gonna live with me, kid, and any babe you want you just say the word . . . *(The last lines are hardly heard. They are mounting the stairs to their parents' bedroom.)*

Linda (entering her bedroom and addressing Willy, who is in the bathroom. She is straightening the bed for him): Can you do anything about the shower? It drips.

Willy (from the bathroom): All of a sudden everything falls to pieces! Goddam plumbing, oughta be sued, those people. I hardly finished putting it in and the thing . . . *(His words rumble off.)*

Linda: I'm just wondering if Oliver will remember him. You think he might?

Willy (coming out of the bathroom in his pajamas): Remember him? What's the matter with you, you crazy? If he'd've stayed with Oliver he'd be on top by now! Wait'll Oliver gets a look at him. You don't know the average caliber any more. The average young man today—*(he is getting into bed)*—is got a caliber of zero. Greatest thing in the world for him was to bum around.

Biff and Happy enter the bedroom. Slight pause.

Willy (stops short, looking at Biff): Glad to hear it, boy.

Happy: He wanted to say good night to you, sport.

Willy (to Biff): Yeah. Knock him dead, boy. What'd you want to tell me?

Biff: Just take it easy, Pop. Good night. *(He turns to go.)*

Willy (unable to resist): And if anything falls off the desk while you're talking to him—like a package or something—don't you pick it up. They have office boys for that.

Linda: I'll make a big breakfast—

Willy: Will you let me finish? *(To Biff.)* Tell him you were in the business in the West. Not farm work.

Biff: All right, Dad.

Linda: I think everything—

Willy (going right through her speech): And don't undersell yourself. No less than fifteen thousand dollars.

Biff (unable to bear him): Okay. Good night, Mom. *(He starts moving.)*

Willy: Because you got a greatness in you, Biff, remember that. You got all kinds a greatness . . . *(He lies back, exhausted. Biff walks out.)*

Linda (calling after Biff): Sleep well, darling!

Happy: I'm gonna get married, Mom. I wanted to tell you.

Linda: Go to sleep, dear.

Happy (going): I just wanted to tell you.

Willy: Keep up the good work. *(Happy exits.)* God . . . remember that Ebbets Field game? The championship of the city?

Linda: Just rest. Should I sing to you?

Willy: Yeah. Sing to me. *(Linda hums a soft lullaby.)* When that team came out— he was the tallest, remember?

Linda: Oh, yes. And in gold.

Biff enters the darkened kitchen, takes a cigarette, and leaves the house. He comes downstage into a golden pool of light. He smokes, staring at the night.

Willy: Like a young god. Hercules—something like that. And the sun, the sun all around him. Remember how he waved to me? Right up from the field, with the representatives of three colleges standing by? And the buyers I brought, and the cheers when he came out—Loman, Loman, Loman! God Almighty, he'll be great yet. A star like that, magnificent, can never really fade away!

The light on Willy is fading. The gas heater begins to glow through the kitchen wall, near the stairs, a blue flame beneath red coils.

Linda (timidly): Willy, dear, what has he got against you?
Willy: I'm so tired. Don't talk any more.

Biff slowly returns to the kitchen. He stops, stares toward the heater.

Linda: Will you ask Howard to let you work in New York?
Willy: First thing in the morning. Everything'll be all right.

Biff reaches behind the heater and draws out a length of rubber tubing. He is horrified and turns his head toward Willy's room, still dimly lit, from which the strains of Linda's desperate but monotonous humming rise.

Willy (staring through the window into the moonlight): Gee, look at the moon moving between the buildings!

Biff wraps the tubing around his hand and quickly goes up the stairs. Curtain.

ACT II

Music is heard, gay and bright. The curtain rises as the music fades away. Willy, in shirt sleeves, is sitting at the kitchen table, sipping coffee, his hat in his lap. Linda is filling his cup when she can.

Willy: Wonderful coffee. Meal in itself.
Linda: Can I make you some eggs?
Willy: No. Take a breath.
Linda: You look so rested, dear.
Willy: I slept like a dead one. First time in months. Imagine, sleeping till ten on a Tuesday morning. Boys left nice and early, heh?
Linda: They were out of here by eight o'clock.
Willy: Good work!
Linda: It was so thrilling to see them leaving together. I can't get over the shaving lotion in this house.
Willy (smiling): Mmm—
Linda: Biff was very changed this morning. His whole attitude seemed to be hopeful. He couldn't wait to get downtown to see Oliver.
Willy: He's heading for a change. There's no question, there simply are certain men that take longer to get—solidified. How did he dress?

Linda: His blue suit. He's so handsome in that suit. He could be a—anything in that suit!

Willy gets up from the table. Linda holds his jacket for him.

Willy: There's no question, no question at all. Gee, on the way home tonight I'd like to buy some seeds.

Linda (laughing): That'd be wonderful. But not enough sun gets back there. Nothing'll grow any more.

Willy: You wait, kid, before it's all over we're gonna get a little place out in the country, and I'll raise some vegetables, a couple of chickens . . .

Linda: You'll do it yet, dear.

Willy walks out of his jacket. Linda follows him.

Willy: And they'll get married, and come for a weekend. I'd build a little guest house. 'Cause I got so many fine tools, all I'd need would be a little lumber and some peace of mind.

Linda (joyfully): I sewed the lining . . .

Willy: I could build two guest houses, so they'd both come. Did he decide how much he's going to ask Oliver for?

Linda (getting him into the jacket): He didn't mention it, but I imagine ten or fifteen thousand. You going to talk to Howard today?

Willy: Yeah. I'll put it to him straight and simple. He'll just have to take me off the road.

Linda: And Willy, don't forget to ask for a little advance, because we've got the insurance premium. It's the grace period now.

Willy: That's a hundred . . . ?

Linda: A hundred and eight, sixty-eight. Because we're a little short again.

Willy: Why are we short?

Linda: Well, you had the motor job on the car . . .

Willy: That goddam Studebaker!

Linda: And you got one more payment on the refrigerator . . .

Willy: But it just broke again!

Linda: Well, it's old, dear.

Willy: I told you we should've bought a well-advertised machine. Charley bought a General Electric and it's twenty years old and it's still good, that son-of-a-bitch.

Linda: But, Willy—

Willy: Whoever heard of a Hastings refrigerator? Once in my life I would like to own something outright before it's broken! I'm always in a race with the junkyard! I just finished paying for the car and it's on its last legs. The refrigerator consumes belts like a goddam maniac. They time those things. They time them so when you finally paid for them, they're used up.

Linda (buttoning up his jacket as he unbuttons it): All told, about two hundred dollars would carry us, dear. But that includes the last payment on the mortgage. After this payment, Willy, the house belongs to us.

Willy: It's twenty-five years!

Linda: Biff was nine years old when we bought it.

Willy: Well, that's a great thing. To weather a twenty-five year mortgage is—
Linda: It's an accomplishment.
Willy: All the cement, the lumber, the reconstruction I put in this house! There ain't a crack to be found in it any more.
Linda: Well, it served its purpose.
Willy: What purpose? Some stranger'll come along, move in, and that's that. If only Biff would take this house, and raise a family . . . *(He starts to go.)* Good-by, I'm late.
Linda (suddenly remembering): Oh, I forgot! You're supposed to meet them for dinner.
Willy: Me?
Linda: At Frank's Chop House on Forty-eighth near Sixth Avenue.
Willy: Is that so! How about you?
Linda: No, just the three of you. They're gonna blow you to a big meal!
Willy: Don't say! Who thought of that?
Linda: Biff came to me this morning, Willy, and he said, "Tell Dad, we want to blow him to a big meal." Be there six o'clock. You and your two boys are going to have dinner.
Willy: Gee whiz! That's really somethin'. I'm gonna knock Howard for a loop, kid. I'll get an advance, and I'll come home with a New York job. Goddammit, now I'm gonna do it!
Linda: Oh, that's the spirit, Willy!
Willy: I will never get behind a wheel the rest of my life!
Linda: It's changing, Willy, I can feel it changing!
Willy: Beyond a question. G'by, I'm late. *(He starts to go again.)*
Linda (calling after him as she runs to the kitchen table for a handkerchief): You got your glasses?
Willy (feels for them, then comes back in): Yeah, yeah, got my glasses.
Linda (giving him the handkerchief): And a handkerchief.
Willy: Yeah, handkerchief.
Linda: And your saccharine?
Willy: Yeah, my saccharine.
Linda: Be careful on the subway stairs.

She kisses him, and a silk stocking is seen hanging from her hand. Willy notices it.

Willy: Will you stop mending stockings? At least while I'm in the house. It gets me nervous. I can't tell you. Please.

Linda hides the stocking in her hand as she follows Willy across the forestage in front of the house.

Linda: Remember, Frank's Chop House.
Willy (passing the apron): Maybe beets would grow out there
Linda (laughing): But you tried so many times.
Willy: Yeah. Well, don't work hard today. *(He disappears around the right corner of the house.)*
Linda: Be careful!

As Willy vanishes, Linda waves to him. Suddenly the phone rings. She runs across the stage and into the kitchen and lifts it.

Linda: Hello? Oh, Biff! I'm so glad you called, I just . . . Yes, sure, I just told him. Yes, he'll be there for dinner at six o'clock, I didn't forget. Listen, I was just dying to tell you. You know that little rubber pipe I told you about? That he connected to the gas heater? I finally decided to go down the cellar this morning and take it away and destroy it. But it's gone! Imagine? He took it away himself, it isn't there! *(She listens.)* When? Oh, then you took it. Oh— nothing, it's just that I'd hoped he'd taken it away himself. Oh, I'm not worried, darling, because this morning he left in such high spirits, it was like the old days! I'm not afraid any more. Did Mr. Oliver see you? . . . Well, you wait there then. And make a nice impression on him, darling. Just don't perspire too much before you see him. And have a nice time with Dad. He may have big news too! . . . That's right, a New York job. And be sweet to him tonight, dear. Be loving to him. Because he's only a little boat looking for a harbor. *(She is trembling with sorrow and joy.)* Oh, that's wonderful, Biff, you'll save his life. Thanks, darling. Just put your arm around him when he comes into the restaurant. Give him a smile. That's the boy . . . Good-by, dear. . . . You got your comb? . . . That's fine. Good-by, Biff dear.

In the middle of her speech, Howard Wagner, thirty-six, wheels on a small typewriter table on which is a wire-recording machine and proceeds to plug it in. This is on the left forestage. Light slowly fades on Linda as it rises on Howard. Howard is intent on threading the machine and only glances over his shoulder as Willy appears.

Willy: Pst! Pst!
Howard: Hello, Willy, come in.
Willy: Like to have a little talk with you, Howard.
Howard: Sorry to keep you waiting. I'll be with you in a minute.
Willy: What's that, Howard?
Howard: Didn't you ever see one of these? Wire recorder.
Willy: Oh. Can we talk a minute?
Howard: Records things. Just got delivery yesterday. Been driving me crazy, the most terrific machine I ever saw in my life. I was up all night with it.
Willy: What do you do with it?
Howard: I bought it for dictation, but you can do anything with it. Listen to this. I had it home last night. Listen to what I picked up. The first one is my daughter. Get this. *(He flicks the switch and "Roll out the Barrel" is heard being whistled.)* Listen to that kid whistle.
Willy: That is lifelike, isn't it?
Howard: Seven years old. Get that tone.
Willy: Ts, ts. Like to ask a little favor if you . . .

The whistling breaks off, and the voice of Howard's Daughter is heard.

His Daughter: "Now you, Daddy."
Howard: She's crazy for me! *(Again the same song is whistled.)* That's me! Ha! *(He winks.)*
Willy: You're very good!

The whistling breaks off again. The machine runs silent for a moment.

Howard: Sh! Get this now, this is my son.

His Son: "The capital of Alabama is Montgomery; the capital of Arizona is Phoenix; the capital of Arkansas is Little Rock; the capital of California is Sacramento . . ." (*And on, and on.*)

Howard (*holding up five fingers*): Five years old, Willy!

Willy: He'll make an announcer some day!

His Son (*continuing*): "The capital . . ."

Howard: Get that—alphabetical order! (*The machine breaks off suddenly.*) Wait a minute. The maid kicked the plug out.

Willy: It certainly is a—

Howard: Sh, for God's sake!

His Son: "It's nine o'clock, Bulova watch time. So I have to go to sleep."

Willy: That really is—

Howard: Wait a minute! The next is my wife.

They wait.

Howard's Voice: "Go on, say something." (*Pause.*) "Well, you gonna talk?"

His Wife: "I can't think of anything."

Howard's Voice: "Well, talk—it's turning."

His Wife (*shyly, beaten*): "Hello." (*Silence.*) "Oh, Howard, I can't talk into this . . ."

Howard (*snapping the machine off*): That was my wife.

Willy: That is a wonderful machine. Can we—

Howard: I tell you, Willy, I'm gonna take my camera, and my bandsaw, and all my hobbies, and out they go. This is the most fascinating relaxation I ever found.

Willy: I think I'll get one myself.

Howard: Sure, they're only a hundred and a half. You can't do without it. Supposing you wanna hear Jack Benny, see? But you can't be at home at that hour. So you tell the maid to turn the radio on when Jack Benny comes on, and this automatically goes on with the radio . . .

Willy: And when you come home you . . .

Howard: You can come home twelve o'clock, one o'clock, any time you like, and you get yourself a Coke and sit yourself down, throw the switch, and there's Jack Benny's program in the middle of the night!

Willy: I'm definitely going to get one. Because lots of times I'm on the road, and I think to myself, what I must be missing on the radio!

Howard: Don't you have a radio in the car?

Willy: Well, yeah, but who ever thinks of turning it on?

Howard: Say, aren't you supposed to be in Boston?

Willy: That's what I want to talk to you about, Howard. You got a minute?

(*He draws a chair in from the wing.*)

Howard: What happened? What're you doing here?

Willy: Well . . .

Howard: You didn't crack up again, did you?

Willy: Oh, no. No . . .

Howard: Geez, you had me worried there for a minute. What's the trouble?

Willy: Well, to tell you the truth, Howard, I've come to the decision that I'd rather not travel any more.

Howard: Not travel! Well, what'll you do?

Willy: Remember, Christmas time, when you had the party here? You said you'd try to think of some spot for me here in town.

Howard: With us?

Willy: Well, sure.

Howard: Oh, yeah, yeah. I remember. Well, I couldn't think of anything for you, Willy.

Willy: I tell ya, Howard. The kids are all grown up, y'know. I don't need much any more. If I could take home—well, sixty-five dollars a week, I could swing it.

Howard: Yeah, but Willy, see I—

Willy: I tell ya why, Howard. Speaking frankly and between the two of us, y'know—I'm just a little tired.

Howard: Oh, I could understand that, Willy. But you're a road man, Willy, and we do a road business. We've only got a half-dozen salesmen on the floor here.

Willy: God knows, Howard, I never asked a favor of any man. But I was with the firm when your father used to carry you in here in his arms.

Howard: I know that, Willy, but—

Willy: Your father came to me the day you were born and asked me what I thought of the name of Howard, may he rest in peace.

Howard: I appreciate that, Willy, but there just is no spot here for you. If I had a spot I'd slam you right in, but I just don't have a single, solitary spot.

He looks for his lighter. Willy has picked it up and gives it to him. Pause.

Willy (*with increasing anger*): Howard, all I need to set my table is fifty dollars a week.

Howard: But where am I going to put you, kid?

Willy: Look, it isn't a question of whether I can sell merchandise, is it?

Howard: No, but it's a business, kid, and everybody's gotta pull his own weight.

Willy (*desperately*): Just let me tell you a story, Howard—

Howard: 'Cause you gotta admit, business is business.

Willy (*angrily*): Business is definitely business, but just listen for a minute. You don't understand this. When I was a boy—eighteen, nineteen—I was already on the road. And there was a question in my mind as to whether selling had a future for me. Because in those days I had a yearning to go to Alaska. See, there were three gold strikes in one month in Alaska, and I felt like going out. Just for the ride, you might say.

Howard (*barely interested*): Don't say.

Willy: Oh, yeah, my father lived many years in Alaska. He was an adventurous man. We've got quite a little streak of self-reliance in our family. I thought I'd go out with my older brother and try to locate him, and maybe settle in the North with the old man. And I was almost decided to go, when I met a salesman in the Parker House. His name was Dave Singleman. And he was eighty-four years old, and he'd drummed merchandise in thirty-one states. And old Dave, he'd go up to his room, y'understand, put on his green velvet slippers—I'll never forget—and pick up his phone and call the buyers, and without ever leaving his room, at the age of eighty-four, he made his living. And when I saw that, I realized that selling was the greatest career a man could want. 'Cause what could be more satisfying than to be able to go, at the age of eighty-four, into twenty or thirty different cities, and pick up a phone, and be remembered and loved and helped by so many different people? Do you know? When he died—and by the way he died the death of a salesman, in his green velvet slippers in the smoker of the New York, New Haven and Hartford, going into Boston—when he died, hundreds of salesmen and buyers were at his funeral. Things were sad on a lotta trains for months after that. (*He stands up. Howard has not looked at him.*) In those days there was personality in it, Howard. There was respect, and comradeship, and gratitude in it. Today, it's all cut and dried, and there's no chance for bringing friendship to bear—or personality. You see what I mean? They don't know me any more.

Howard (*moving away, to the right*): That's just the thing, Willy.

Willy: If I had forty dollars a week—that's all I'd need. Forty dollars, Howard.

Howard: Kid, I can't take blood from a stone, I—

Willy (*desperation is on him now*): Howard, the year Al Smith was nominated, your father came to me and—

Howard (*starting to go off*): I've got to see some people, kid.

Willy (*stopping him*): I'm talking about your father! There were promises made across this desk! You mustn't tell me you've got people to see—I put thirty-four years into this firm, Howard, and now I can't pay my insurance! You can't eat the orange and throw the peel away—a man is not a piece of fruit! (*After a pause.*) Now pay attention. Your father—in 1928 I had a big year. I averaged a hundred and seventy dollars a week in commissions.

Howard (*impatiently*): Now, Willy, you never averaged—

Willy (*banging his hand on the desk*): I averaged a hundred and seventy dollars a week in the year of 1928! And your father came to me—or rather, I was in the office here—it was right over this desk—and he put his hand on my shoulder—

Howard (*getting up*): You'll have to excuse me, Willy, I gotta see some people. Pull yourself together. (*Going out.*) I'll be back in a little while.

On Howard's exit, the light on his chair grows very bright and strange.

Willy: Pull yourself together! What the hell did I say to him? My God, I was yelling at him! How could I! (*Willy breaks off, staring at the light, which occupies the chair, animating it. He approaches this chair, standing across the desk from it.*) Frank, Frank, don't you remember what you told me that time? How you put your hand on my shoulder, and Frank . . . (*He leans on the desk and as he speaks the dead man's name he accidentally switches on the recorder, and instantly—*)

Howard's Son: " . . . of New York is Albany. The capital of Ohio is Cincinnati, the capital of Rhode Island is . . . " (*The recitation continues.*)

Willy (*leaping away with fright, shouting*): Ha! Howard! Howard! Howard!

Howard (*rushing in*): What happened?

Willy (*pointing at the machine, which continues nasally, childishly, with the capital cities*): Shut it off! Shut it off!

Howard (*pulling the plug out*): Look, Willy . . .

Willy (*pressing his hands to his eyes*): I gotta get myself some coffee. I'll get some coffee . . .

Willy starts to walk out. Howard stops him.

Howard *(rolling up the cord):* Willy, look . . .

Willy: I'll go to Boston.

Howard: Willy, you can't go to Boston for us.

Willy: Why can't I go?

Howard: I don't want you to represent us. I've been meaning to tell you for a long time now.

Willy: Howard, are you firing me?

Howard: I think you need a good long rest, Willy.

Willy: Howard—

Howard: And when you feel better, come back, and we'll see if we can work something out.

Willy: But I gotta earn money, Howard. I'm in no position—

Howard: Where are your sons? Why don't your sons give you a hand?

Willy: They're working on a very big deal.

Howard: This is no time for false pride, Willy. You go to your sons and tell them that you're tired. You've got two great boys, haven't you?

Willy: Oh, no question, no question, but in the meantime . . .

Howard: Then that's that, heh?

Willy: All right, I'll go to Boston tomorrow.

Howard: No, no.

Willy: I can't throw myself on my sons. I'm not a cripple!

Howard: Look, kid, I'm busy this morning.

Willy *(grasping Howard's arm):* Howard, you've got to let me go to Boston!

Howard *(hard, keeping himself under control):* I've got a line of people to see this morning. Sit down, take five minutes, and pull yourself together, and then go home, will ya? I need the office, Willy. *(He starts to go, turns, remembering the recorder, starts to push off the table holding the recorder.)* Oh, yeah. Whenever you can this week, stop by and drop off the samples. You'll feel better, Willy, and then come back and we'll talk. Pull yourself together, kid, there's people outside.

Howard exits, pushing the table off left. Willy stares into space, exhausted. Now the music is heard—Ben's music—first distantly, then closer, closer. As Willy speaks, Ben enters from the right. He carries valise and umbrella.

Willy: Oh, Ben, how did you do it? What is the answer? Did you wind up the Alaska deal already?

Ben: Doesn't take much time if you know what you're doing. Just a short business trip. Boarding ship in an hour. Wanted to say good-by.

Willy: Ben, I've got to talk to you.

Ben *(glancing at his watch):* Haven't the time, William.

Willy *(crossing the apron to Ben):* Ben, nothing's working out. I don't know what to do.

Ben: Now, look here, William. I've bought timberland in Alaska and I need a man to look after things for me.

Willy: God, timberland! Me and my boys in those grand outdoors!

Ben: You've a new continent at your doorstep, William. Get out of these cities, they're full of talk and time payments and courts of law. Screw on your fists and you can fight for a fortune up there.

Willy: Yes, yes! Linda! Linda!

Linda enters as of old, with the wash.

Linda: Oh, you're back?

Ben: I haven't much time.

Willy: No, wait! Linda, he's got a proposition for me in Alaska.

Linda: But you've got—(*To Ben.*) He's got a beautiful job here.

Willy: But in Alaska, kid, I could—

Linda: You're doing well enough, Willy!

Ben (to Linda): Enough for what, my dear?

Linda (frightened of Ben and angry at him): Don't say those things to him! Enough to be happy right here, right now. (*To Willy, while Ben laughs.*) Why must everybody conquer the world? You're well liked, and the boys love you, and someday—(*to Ben*)—why, old man Wagner told him just the other day that if he keeps it up he'll be a member of the firm, didn't he, Willy?

Willy: Sure, sure. I am building something with this firm, Ben, and if a man is building something he must be on the right track, mustn't he?

Ben: What are you building? Lay your hand on it. Where is it?

Willy (hesitantly): That's true, Linda, there's nothing.

Linda: Why? (*To Ben.*) There's a man eighty-four years old—

Willy: That's right, Ben, that's right. When I look at that man I say, what is there to worry about?

Ben: Bah!

Willy: It's true, Ben. All he has to do is go into any city, pick up the phone, and he's making his living and you know why?

Ben (picking up his valise): I've got to go.

Willy (holding Ben back): Look at this boy!

Biff, in his high school sweater, enters carrying suitcase. Happy carries Biff's shoulder guards, gold helmet, and football pants.

Willy: Without a penny to his name, three great universities are begging for him, and from there the sky's the limit, because it's not what you do, Ben. It's who you know and the smile on your face! It's contacts, Ben, contacts! The whole wealth of Alaska passes over the lunch table at the Commodore Hotel, and that's the wonder, the wonder of this country, that a man can end with diamonds here on the basis of being liked! (*He turns to Biff.*) And that's why when you get out on that field today it's important. Because thousands of people will be rooting for you and loving you. (*To Ben, who has again begun to leave.*) And Ben! when he walks into a business office his name will sound out like a bell and all the doors will open to him! I've seen it, Ben, I've seen it a thousand times! You can't feel it with your hand like timber, but it's there!

Ben: Good-by, William.

Willy: Ben, am I right? Don't you think I'm right? I value your advice.

Ben: There's a new continent at your doorstep, William. You could walk out rich. Rich. *(He is gone.)*

Willy: We'll do it here, Ben! You hear me? We're gonna do it here!

Young Bernard rushes in. The gay music of the boys is heard.

Bernard: Oh, gee, I was afraid you left already!

Willy: Why? What time is it?

Bernard: It's half-past one!

Willy: Well, come on, everybody! Ebbets Field next stop! Where's the pennants? *(He rushes through the wall-line of the kitchen and out into the livingroom.)*

Linda (to Biff): Did you pack fresh underwear?

Biff (who has been limbering up): I want to go!

Bernard: Biff, I'm carrying your helmet, ain't I?

Happy: No, I'm carrying the helmet.

Bernard: Oh, Biff, you promised me.

Happy: I'm carrying the helmet.

Bernard: How am I going to get in the locker room?

Linda: Let him carry the shoulder guards. *(She puts her coat and hat on in the kitchen.)*

Bernard: Can I, Biff? 'Cause I told everybody I'm going to be in the locker room.

Happy: In Ebbets Field it's the clubhouse.

Bernard: I meant the clubhouse. Biff!

Happy: Biff!

Biff (grandly, after a slight pause): Let him carry the shoulder guards.

Happy (as he gives Bernard the shoulder guards): Stay close to us now.

Willy rushes in with the pennants.

Willy (handing them out): Everybody wave when Biff comes out on the field. *(Happy and Bernard run off.)* You set now, boy?

The music has died away.

Biff: Ready to go, Pop. Every muscle is ready.

Willy (at the edge of the apron): You realize what this means?

Biff: That's right, Pop.

Willy (feeling Biff's muscles): You're comin' home this afternoon captain of the All-Scholastic Championship Team of the City of New York.

Biff: I got it, Pop. And remember, pal, when I take off my helmet, that touchdown is for you.

Willy: Let's go! *(He is starting out, with his arm around Biff, when Charley enters, as of old, in knickers.)* I got no room for you, Charley.

Charley: Room? For what?

Willy: In the car.

Charley: You goin' for a ride? I wanted to shoot some casino.

Willy (furiously): Casino! *(Incredulously.)* Don't you realize what today is?

Linda: Oh, he knows, Willy. He's just kidding you.

Willy: That's nothing to kid about!

Charley: No, Linda, what's goin' on?

Linda: He's playing in Ebbets Field.

Charley: Baseball in this weather?

Willy: Don't talk to him. Come on, come on! *(He is pushing them out.)*

Charley: Wait a minute, didn't you hear the news?

Willy: What?

Charley: Don't you listen to the radio? Ebbets Field just blew up.

Willy: You go to hell! *(Charley laughs. Pushing them out.)* Come on, come on! We're late.

Charley (as they go): Knock a homer, Biff, knock a homer!

Willy (the last to leave, turning to Charley): I don't think that was funny, Charley. This is the greatest day of his life.

Charley: Willy, when are you going to grow up?

Willy: Yeah, heh? When this game is over, Charley, you'll be laughing out of the other side of your face. They'll be calling him another Red Grange. Twenty-five thousand a year.

Charley (kidding): Is that so?

Willy: Yeah, that's so.

Charley: Well, then, I'm sorry, Willy. But tell me something.

Willy: What?

Charley: Who is Red Grange?

Willy: Put up your hands. Goddam you, put up your hands!

Charley, chuckling, shakes his head and walks away, around the left corner of the stage. Willy follows him. The music rises to a mocking frenzy.

Willy: Who the hell do you think you are, better than everybody else? You don't know everything, you big, ignorant, stupid . . . Put up your hands!

Light rises, on the right side of the forestage, on a small table in the reception room of Charley's office. Traffic sounds are heard. Bernard, now mature, sits whistling to himself. A pair of tennis rackets and an overnight bag are on the floor beside him.

Willy (offstage): What are you walking away for? Don't walk away! If you're going to say something say it to my face! I know you laugh at me behind my back. You'll laugh out of the other side of your goddam face after this game. Touch-down! Touchdown! Eighty thousand people! Touchdown! Right between the goal posts.

Bernard is a quiet, earnest, but self-assured young man. Willy's voice is coming from right upstage now. Bernard lowers his feet off the table and listens. Jenny, his father's secretary, enters.

Jenny (distressed): Say, Bernard, will you go out in the hall?

Bernard: What is that noise? Who is it?

Jenny: Mr. Loman. He just got off the elevator.

Bernard (getting up): Who's he arguing with?

Jenny: Nobody. There's nobody with him. I can't deal with him any more, and your father gets all upset everytime he comes. I've got a lot of typing to do, and your father's waiting to sign it. Will you see him?

Willy (entering): Touchdown! Touch—(He sees Jenny.) Jenny, Jenny, good to see you. How're ya? Workin'? Or still honest?

Jenny: Fine. How've you been feeling?

Willy: Not much any more, Jenny. Ha, ha! *(He is surprised to see the rackets.)*

Bernard: Hello, Uncle Willy.

Willy (almost shocked): Bernard! Well, look who's here! *(He comes quickly, guiltily, to Bernard and warmly shakes his hand.)*

Bernard: How are you? Good to see you.

Willy: What are you doing here?

Bernard: Oh, just stopped by to see Pop. Get off my feet till my train leaves. I'm going to Washington in a few minutes.

Willy: Is he in?

Bernard: Yes, he's in his office with the accountant. Sit down.

Willy (sitting down): What're you going to do in Washington?

Bernard: Oh, just a case I've got there, Willy.

Willy: That so? *(indicating the rackets.)* You going to play tennis there?

Bernard: I'm staying with a friend who's got a court.

Willy: Don't say. His own tennis court. Must be fine people, I bet.

Bernard: They are, very nice. Dad tells me Biff's in town.

Willy (with a big smile): Yeah, Biff's in. Working on a very big deal, Bernard.

Bernard: What's Biff doing?

Willy: Well, he's been doing very big things in the West. But he decided to establish himself here. Very big. We're having dinner. Did I hear your wife had a boy?

Bernard: That's right. Our second.

Willy: Two boys! What do you know!

Bernard: What kind of deal has Biff got?

Willy: Well, Bill Oliver—very big sporting-goods man—he wants Biff very badly. Called him in from the West. Long distance, carte blanche, special deliveries. Your friends have their own private tennis court?

Bernard: You still with the old firm, Willy?

Willy (after a pause): I'm—I'm overjoyed to see how you made the grade, Bernard, overjoyed. It's an encouraging thing to see a young man really—really—Looks very good for Biff—very—*(He breaks off, then.)* Bernard—*(He is so full of emotion, he breaks off again.)*

Bernard: What is it, Willy?

Willy (small and alone): What—what's the secret?

Bernard: What secret?

Willy: How—how did you? Why didn't he ever catch on?

Bernard: I wouldn't know that, Willy.

Willy (confidentially, desperately): You were his friend, his boyhood friend. There's something I don't understand about it. His life ended after that Ebbets Field game. From the age of seventeen nothing good ever happened to him.

Bernard: He never trained himself for anything.

Willy: But he did, he did. After high school he took so many correspondence courses. Radio mechanics; television; God knows what, and never made the slightest mark.

Bernard (taking off his glasses): Willy, do you want to talk candidly?

Willy (rising, faces Bernard): I regard you as a very brilliant man, Bernard. I value your advice.

Bernard: Oh, the hell with the advice, Willy. I couldn't advise you. There's just one thing I've always wanted to ask you. When he was supposed to graduate, and the math teacher flunked him—

Willy: Oh, that son-of-a-bitch ruined his life.

Bernard: Yeah, but, Willy, all he had to do was go to summer school and make up that subject.

Willy: That's right, that's right.

Bernard: Did you tell him not to go to summer school?

Willy: Me? I begged him to go. I ordered him to go!

Bernard: Then why wouldn't he go?

Willy: Why? Why! Bernard, that question has been trailing me like a ghost for the last fifteen years. He flunked the subject, and laid down and died like a hammer hit him!

Bernard: Take it easy, kid.

Willy: Let me talk to you—I got nobody to talk to. Bernard, Bernard, was it my fault? Y'see? It keeps going around in my mind, maybe I did something to him. I got nothing to give him.

Bernard: Don't take it so hard.

Willy: Why did he lay down? What is the story there? You were his friend!

Bernard: Willy, I remember, it was June, and our grades came out. And he'd flunked math.

Willy: That son-of-a-bitch!

Bernard: No, it wasn't right then. Biff just got very angry, I remember, and he was ready to enroll in summer school.

Willy (surprised): He was?

Bernard: He wasn't beaten by it at all. But then, Willy, he disappeared from the block for almost a month. And I got the idea that he'd gone up to New England to see you. Did he have a talk with you then?

Willy stares in silence.

Bernard: Willy?

Willy (with a strong edge of resentment in his voice): Yeah, he came to Boston. What about it?

Bernard: Well, just that when he came back—I'll never forget this, it always mystifies me. Because I'd thought so well of Biff, even though he'd always taken advantage of me. I loved him, Willy, y'know? And he came back after that month and took his sneakers—remember those sneakers with "University of Virginia" printed on them? He was so proud of those, wore them every day. And he took them down in the cellar, and burned them up in the furnace. We had a fist fight. It lasted at least half an hour. Just the two of us, punching each other down the cellar, and crying right through it. I've often thought of how strange it was that I knew he'd given up his life. What happened in Boston, Willy?

Willy looks at him as at an intruder.

Bernard: I just bring it up because you asked me.

Willy (angrily): Nothing. What do you mean, "What happened?" What's that got to do with anything?

Bernard: Well, don't get sore.

Willy: What are you trying to do, blame it on me? If a boy lays down is that my fault?

Bernard: Now, Willy, don't get—

Willy: Well, don't—don't talk to me that way! What does that mean, "What happened?"

Charley enters. He is in his vest, and he carries a bottle of bourbon.

Charley: Hey, you're going to miss that train. *(He waves the bottle.)*

Bernard: Yeah, I'm going. *(He takes the bottle.)* Thanks, Pop. *(He picks up his rackets and bag.)* Good-by, Willy, and don't worry about it. You know, "If at first you don't succeed . . ."

Willy: Yes, I believe in that.

Bernard: But sometimes, Willy, it's better for a man just to walk away.

Willy: Walk away?

Bernard: That's right.

Willy: But if you can't walk away?

Bernard (after a slight pause): I guess that's when it's tough. *(Extending his hand.)* Good-by, Willy.

Willy (shaking Bernard's hand): Good-by, boy.

Charley (an arm on Bernard's shoulder): How do you like this kid? Gonna argue a case in front of the Supreme Court.

Bernard (protesting): Pop!

Willy (genuinely shocked, pained, and happy): No! The Supreme Court!

Bernard: I gotta run. 'By, Dad!

Charley: Knock 'em dead, Bernard!

Bernard goes off.

Willy (as Charley takes out his wallet): The Supreme Court! And he didn't even mention it!

Charley (counting out money on the desk): He don't have to—he's gonna do it.

Willy: And you never told him what to do, did you? You never took any interest in him.

Charley: My salvation is that I never took any interest in anything. There's some money—fifty dollars. I got an accountant inside.

Willy: Charley, look . . . *(With difficulty.)* I got my insurance to pay. If you can manage it—I need a hundred and ten dollars.

Charley doesn't reply for a moment; merely stops moving.

Willy: I'd draw it from my bank but Linda would know, and I . . .

Charley: Sit down, Willy.

Willy (moving toward the chair): I'm keeping an account of everything, remember. I'll pay every penny back. *(He sits.)*

Charley: Now listen to me, Willy.

Willy: I want you to know I appreciate . . .

Charley (sitting down on the table): Willy, what're you doin'? What the hell is goin' on in your head?

Willy: Why? I'm simply . . .

Charley: I offered you a job. You can make fifty dollars a week. And I won't send you on the road.

Willy: I've got a job.

Charley: Without pay? What kind of a job is a job without pay? *(He rises.)* Now, look, kid, enough is enough. I'm no genius but I know when I'm being insulted.

Willy: Insulted!

Charley: Why don't you want to work for me?

Willy: What's the matter with you? I've got a job.

Charley: Then what're you walkin' in here every week for?

Willy (getting up): Well, if you don't want me to walk in here—

Charley: I am offering you a job.

Willy: I don't want your goddam job!

Charley: When the hell are you going to grow up?

Willy (furiously): You big ignoramus, if you say that to me again I'll rap you one! I don't care how big you are! *(He's ready to fight.)*

Pause.

Charley (kindly, going to him): How much do you need, Willy?

Willy: Charley, I'm strapped. I'm strapped. I don't know what to do. I was just fired.

Charley: Howard fired you?

Willy: That snotnose. Imagine that? I named him. I named him Howard.

Charley: Willy, when're you gonna realize that them things don't mean anything? You named him Howard, but you can't sell that. The only thing you got in this world is what you can sell. And the funny thing is that you're a salesman, and you don't know that.

Willy: I've always tried to think otherwise, I guess. I always felt that if a man was impressive, and well liked, that nothing—

Charley: Why must everybody like you? Who liked J. P. Morgan? Was he impressive? In a Turkish bath he'd look like a butcher. But with his pockets on he was very well liked. Now listen, Willy, I know you don't like me, and nobody can say I'm in love with you, but I'll give you a job because—just for the hell of it, put it that way. Now what do you say?

Willy: I—I just can't work for you, Charley.

Charley: What're you, jealous of me?

Willy: I can't work for you, that's all, don't ask me why.

Charley (angered, takes out more bills): You been jealous of me all your life, you damned fool! Here, pay your insurance. *(He puts the money in Willy's hand.)*

Willy: I'm keeping strict accounts.

Charley: I've got some work to do. Take care of yourself. And pay your insurance.

Willy (moving to the right): Funny, y'know? After all the highways, and the trains, and the appointments, and the years, you end up worth more dead than alive.

Charley: Willy, nobody's worth nothin' dead. *(After a slight pause.)* Did you hear what I said?

Willy stands still, dreaming.

Charley: Willy!

Willy: Apologize to Bernard for me when you see him. I didn't mean to argue with him. He's a fine boy. They're all fine boys, and they'll end up big—all of them. Someday they'll all play tennis together. Wish me luck, Charley. He saw Bill Oliver today.

Charley: Good luck.

Willy (*on the verge of tears*): Charley, you're the only friend I got. Isn't that a remarkable thing? (*He goes out.*)

Charley: Jesus!

Charley stares after him a moment and follows. All light blacks out. Suddenly raucous music is heard, and a red glow rises behind the screen at right. Stanley, a young waiter, appears, carrying a table, followed by Happy, who is carrying two chairs.

Stanley (*putting the table down*): That's all right, Mr. Loman, I can handle it myself. (*He turns and takes the chairs from Happy and places them at the table.*)

Happy (*glancing around*): Oh, this is better.

Stanley: Sure, in the front there you're in the middle of all kinds a noise. Whenever you got a party, Mr. Loman, you just tell me and I'll put you back here. Y'know, there's a lotta people they don't like it private, because when they go out they like to see a lotta action around them because they're sick and tired to stay in the house by theirself. But I know you, you ain't from Hackensack. You know what I mean?

Happy (*sitting down*): So how's it coming, Stanley?

Stanley: Ah, it's a dog's life. I only wish during the war they'd a took me in the Army. I coulda been dead by now.

Happy: My brother's back, Stanley.

Stanley: Oh, he come back, heh? From the Far West.

Happy: Yeah, big cattle man, my brother, so treat him right. And my father's coming too.

Stanley: Oh, your father too!

Happy: You got a couple of nice lobsters?

Stanley: Hundred per cent, big.

Happy: I want them with the claws.

Stanley: Don't worry, I don't give you no mice. (*Happy laughs.*) How about some wine? It'll put a head on the meal.

Happy: No. You remember, Stanley, that recipe I brought you from overseas? With the champagne in it?

Stanley: Oh, yeah, sure. I still got it tacked up yet in the kitchen. But that'll have to cost a buck apiece anyways.

Happy: That's all right.

Stanley: What'd you, hit a number or somethin'?

Happy: No, it's a little celebration. My brother is—I think he pulled off a big deal today. I think we're going into business together.

Stanley: Great! That's the best for you. Because a family business, you know what I mean?—that's the best.

Happy: That's what I think.

Stanley: 'Cause what's the difference? Somebody steals? It's in the family. Know what I mean? *(Sotto voce.)* Like this bartender here. The boss is goin' crazy what kinda leak he's got in the cash register. You put it in but it don't come out.

Happy (raising his head): Sh!

Stanley: What?

Happy: You notice I wasn't lookin' right or left, was I?

Stanley: No.

Happy: And my eyes are closed.

Stanley: So what's the—?

Happy: Strudel's comin'.

Stanley (catching on, looks around): Ah, no, there's no—

He breaks off as a furred, lavishly dressed Girl enters and sits at the next table. Both follow her with their eyes.

Stanley: Geez, how'd ya know?

Happy: I got radar or something. *(Staring directly at her profile.)* Oooooooo . . . Stanley.

Stanley: I think that's for you, Mr. Loman.

Happy: Look at that mouth. Oh, God. And the binoculars.

Stanley: Geez, you got a life, Mr. Loman.

Happy: Wait on her.

Stanley (going to The Girl's table): Would you like a menu, ma'am?

Girl: I'm expecting someone, but I'd like a—

Happy: Why don't you bring her—excuse me, miss, do you mind? I sell champagne, and I'd like you to try my brand. Bring her a champagne, Stanley.

Girl: That's awfully nice of you.

Happy: Don't mention it. It's all company money. *(He laughs.)*

Girl: That's a charming product to be selling, isn't it?

Happy: Oh, gets to be like everything else. Selling is selling, y'know.

Girl: I suppose.

Happy: You don't happen to sell, do you?

Girl: No, I don't sell.

Happy: Would you object to a compliment from a stranger? You ought to be on a magazine cover.

Girl (looking at him a little archly): I have been.

Stanley comes in with a glass of champagne.

Happy: What'd I say before, Stanley? You see? She's a cover girl.

Stanley: Oh, I could see, I could see.

Happy (to The Girl): What magazine?

Girl: Oh, a lot of them. *(She takes the drink.)* Thank you.

Happy: You know what they say in France, don't you? "Champagne is the drink of the complexion"—Hya, Biff!

Biff has entered and sits with Happy.

Biff: Hello, kid. Sorry I'm late.

Happy: I just got here. Uh, Miss—?

Girl: Forsythe.

Happy: Miss Forsythe, this is my brother.

Biff: Is Dad here?

Happy: His name is Biff. You might've heard of him. Great football player.

Girl: Really? What team?

Happy: Are you familiar with football?

Girl: No, I'm afraid I'm not.

Happy: Biff is quarterback with the New York Giants.

Girl: Well, that is nice, isn't it? (*She drinks.*)

Happy: Good health.

Girl: I'm happy to meet you.

Happy: That's my name. Hap. It's really Harold, but at West Point they called me Happy.

Girl (now really impressed): Oh, I see. How do you do? (*She turns her profile.*)

Biff: Isn't Dad coming?

Happy: You want her?

Biff: Oh, I could never make that.

Happy: I remember the time that idea would never come into your head. Where's the old confidence, Biff?

Biff: I just saw Oliver—

Happy: Wait a minute. I've got to see that old confidence again. Do you want her? She's on call.

Biff: Oh, no. (*He turns to look at The Girl.*)

Happy: I'm telling you. Watch this. (*Turning to The Girl.*) Honey? (*She turns to him.*) Are you busy?

Girl: Well, I am . . . but I could make a phone call.

Happy: Do that, will you, honey? And see if you can get a friend. We'll be here for a while. Biff is one of the greatest football players in the country.

Girl (standing up): Well, I'm certainly happy to meet you.

Happy: Come back soon.

Girl: I'll try.

Happy: Don't try, honey, try hard.

The Girl exits. Stanley follows, shaking his head in bewildered admiration.

Happy: Isn't that a shame now? A beautiful girl like that? That's why I can't get married. There's not a good woman in a thousand. New York is loaded with them, kid!

Biff: Hap, look—

Happy: I told you she was on call!

Biff (strangely unnerved): Cut it out, will ya? I want to say something to you.

Happy: Did you see Oliver?

Biff: I saw him all right. Now look, I want to tell Dad a couple of things and I want you to help me.

Happy: What? Is he going to back you?

Biff: Are you crazy? You're out of your goddam head, you know that?

Happy: Why? What happened?

Biff (breathlessly): I did a terrible thing today, Hap. It's been the strangest day I ever went through. I'm all numb, I swear.

Happy: You mean he wouldn't see you?

Biff: Well, I waited six hours for him, see? All day. Kept sending my name in. Even tried to date his secretary so she'd get me to him, but no soap.

Happy: Because you're not showin' the old confidence, Biff. He remembered you, didn't he?

Biff (stopping Happy with a gesture): Finally, about five o'clock, he comes out. Didn't remember who I was or anything. I felt like such an idiot, Hap.

Happy: Did you tell him my Florida idea?

Biff: He walked away. I saw him for one minute. I got so mad I could've torn the walls down! How the hell did I ever get the idea I was a salesman there? I even believed myself that I'd been a salesman for him! And then he gave me one look and—I realized what a ridiculous lie my whole life has been! We've been talking in a dream for fifteen years. I was a shipping clerk.

Happy: What'd you do?

Biff (with great tension and wonder): Well, he left, see. And the secretary went out. I was all alone in the waiting-room. I don't know what came over me, Hap. The next thing I know I'm in his office—paneled walls, everything. I can't explain it. I—Hap, I took his fountain pen.

Happy: Geez, did he catch you?

Biff: I ran out. I ran down all eleven flights. I ran and ran and ran.

Happy: That was an awful dumb—what'd you do that for?

Biff (agonized): I don't know, I just—wanted to take something, I don't know. You gotta help me, Hap. I'm gonna tell Pop.

Happy: You crazy? What for?

Biff: Hap, he's got to understand that I'm not the man somebody lends that kind of money to. He thinks I've been spiting him all these years and it's eating him up.

Happy: That's just it. You tell him something nice.

Biff: I can't.

Happy: Say you got a lunch date with Oliver tomorrow.

Biff: So what do I do tomorrow?

Happy: You leave the house tomorrow and come back at night and say Oliver is thinking it over. And he thinks it over for a couple of weeks, and gradually it fades away and nobody's the worse.

Biff: But it'll go on forever!

Happy: Dad is never so happy as when he's looking forward to something!

Willy enters.

Happy: Hello, scout!

Willy: Gee, I haven't been here in years!

Stanley has followed Willy in and sets a chair for him. Stanley starts off but Happy stops him.

Happy: Stanley!

Stanley stands by, waiting for an order.

Biff (*going to Willy with guilt, as to an invalid*): Sit down, Pop. You want a drink?

Willy: Sure, I don't mind.

Biff: Let's get a load on.

Willy: You look worried.

Biff: N-no. (*To Stanley.*) Scotch all around. Make it doubles.

Stanley: Doubles, right. (*He goes.*)

Willy: You had a couple already, didn't you?

Biff: Just a couple, yeah.

Willy: Well, what happened, boy? (*Nodding affirmatively, with a smile.*) Everything go all right?

Biff (*takes a breath, then reaches out and grasps Willy's hand*): Pal . . . (*He is smiling bravely, and Willy is smiling too.*) I had an experience today.

Happy: Terrific, Pop.

Willy: That so? What happened?

Biff (*high, slightly alcoholic, above the earth*): I'm going to tell you everything from first to last. It's been a strange day. (*Silence. He looks around, composes himself as best he can, but his breath keeps breaking the rhythm of his voice.*) I had to wait quite a while for him, and—

Willy: Oliver?

Biff: Yeah, Oliver. All day, as a matter of cold fact. And a lot of—instances—facts, Pop, facts about my life came back to me. Who was it, Pop? Who ever said I was a salesman with Oliver?

Willy: Well, you were.

Biff: No, Dad, I was a shipping clerk.

Willy: But you were practically—

Biff (*with determination*): Dad, I don't know who said it first, but I was never a salesman for Bill Oliver.

Willy: What're you talking about?

Biff: Let's hold on to the facts tonight, Pop. We're not going to get anywhere bullin' around. I was a shipping clerk.

Willy (*angrily*): All right, now listen to me—

Biff: Why don't you let me finish?

Willy: I'm not interested in stories about the past or any crap of that kind because the woods are burning, boys, you understand? There's a big blaze going on all around. I was fired today.

Biff (*shocked*): How could you be?

Willy: I was fired, and I'm looking for a little good news to tell your mother, because the woman has waited and the woman has suffered. The gist of it is that I haven't got a story left in my head, Biff. So don't give me a lecture about facts and aspects. I am not interested. Now what've you got to say to me?

Stanley enters with three drinks. They wait until he leaves.

Willy: Did you see Oliver?

Biff: Jesus, Dad!

Willy: You mean you didn't go up there?

Happy: Sure he went up there.

Biff: I did. I—saw him. How could they fire you?

Willy (on the edge of his chair): What kind of a welcome did he give you?

Biff: He won't even let you work on commission?

Willy: I'm out! *(Driving.)* So tell me, he gave you a warm welcome?

Happy: Sure, Pop, sure!

Biff (driven): Well, it was kind of—

Willy: I was wondering if he'd remember you. *(To Happy.)* Imagine, man doesn't see him for ten, twelve years and gives him that kind of welcome!

Happy: Damn right!

Biff (trying to return to the offensive): Pop, look—

Willy: You know why he remembered you, don't you? Because you impressed him in those days.

Biff: Let's talk quietly and get this down to the facts, huh?

Willy (as though Biff had been interrupting): Well, what happened? It's great news, Biff. Did he take you into his office or'd you talk in the waiting-room?

Biff: Well, he came in, see, and—

Willy (with a big smile): What'd he say? Betcha he threw his arm around you.

Biff: Well, he kinda—

Willy: He's a fine man. *(To Happy.)* Very hard man to see, y'know.

Happy (agreeing): Oh, I know.

Willy (to Biff): Is that where you had the drinks?

Biff: Yeah, he gave me a couple of—no, no!

Happy (cutting in): He told him my Florida idea.

Willy: Don't interrupt. *(To Biff.)* How'd he react to the Florida idea?

Biff: Dad, will you give me a minute to explain?

Willy: I've been waiting for you to explain since I sat down here! What happened? He took you into his office and what?

Biff: Well—I talked. And—and he listened, see.

Willy: Famous for the way he listens, y'know. What was his answer?

Biff: His answer was—*(He breaks off, suddenly angry.)* Dad, you're not letting me tell you what I want to tell you!

Willy (accusing, angered): You didn't see him, did you?

Biff: I did see him!

Willy: What'd you insult him or something? You insulted him, didn't you?

Biff: Listen, will you let me out of it, will you just let me out of it!

Happy: What the hell!

Willy: Tell me what happened!

Biff (to Happy): I can't talk to him!

A single trumpet note jars the ear. The light of green leaves stains the house, which holds the air of night and a dream. Young Bernard enters and knocks on the door of the house.

Young Bernard (frantically): Mrs. Loman, Mrs. Loman!

Happy: Tell him what happened!

Biff (to Happy): Shut up and leave me alone!

Willy: No, no! You had to go and flunk math!

Biff: What math? What're you talking about?

Young Bernard: Mrs. Loman, Mrs. Loman!

Linda appears in the house, as of old.

Willy (wildly): Math, math, math!

Biff: Take it easy, Pop.

Young Bernard: Mrs. Loman!

Willy (furiously): If you hadn't flunked you'd've been set by now!

Biff: Now, look, I'm gonna tell you what happened, and you're going to listen to me.

Young Bernard: Mrs. Loman!

Biff: I waited six hours—

Happy: What the hell are you saying?

Biff: I kept sending in my name but he wouldn't see me. So finally he . . . *(He continues unheard as light fades low on the restaurant.)*

Young Bernard: Biff flunked math!

Linda: No!

Young Bernard: Birnbaum flunked him! They won't graduate him!

Linda: But they have to. He's gotta go to the university. Where is he? Biff! Biff!

Young Bernard: No, he left. He went to Grand Central.

Linda: Grand—You mean he went to Boston?

Young Bernard: Is Uncle Willy in Boston?

Linda: Oh, maybe Willy can talk to the teacher. Oh, the poor, poor boy!

Light on house area snaps out.

Biff (at the table, now audible, holding up a gold fountain pen): . . . so I'm washed up with Oliver, you understand? Are you listening to me?

Willy (at a loss): Yeah, sure. If you hadn't flunked—

Biff: Flunked what? What're you talking about?

Willy: Don't blame everything on me! I didn't flunk math—you did! What pen?

Happy: That was awful dumb, Biff, a pen like that is worth—

Willy (seeing the pen for the first time): You took Oliver's pen?

Biff (weakening): Dad, I just explained it to you.

Willy: You stole Bill Oliver's fountain pen!

Biff: I didn't exactly steal it! That's just what I've been explaining to you!

Happy: He had it in his hand and just then Oliver walked in, so he got nervous and stuck it in his pocket!

Willy: My God, Biff!

Biff: I never intended to do it, Dad!

Operator's voice: Standish Arms, good evening!

Willy (shouting): I'm not in my room!

Biff (frightened): Dad, what's the matter? *(He and Happy stand up.)*

Operator: Ringing Mr. Loman for you!

Willy: I'm not there, stop it!

Biff (horrified, gets down on one knee before Willy): Dad, I'll make good, I'll make good. *(Willy tries to get to his feet. Biff holds him down.)* Sit down now.

Willy: No, you're no good, you're no good for anything.

Biff: I am, Dad, I'll find something else, you understand? Now don't worry about anything. *(He holds up Willy's face.)* Talk to me, Dad.

Operator: Mr. Loman does not answer. Shall I page him?

Willy (attempting to stand, as though to rush and silence the Operator): No, no, no!

Happy: He'll strike something, Pop.

Willy: No, no . . .

Biff (desperately, standing over Willy): Pop, listen! Listen to me! I'm telling you something good. Oliver talked to his partner about the Florida idea. You listening? He—he talked to his partner, and he came to me . . . I'm to be all right, you hear? Dad, listen to me, he said it was just a question of the amount!

Willy: Then you . . . got it?

Happy: He's gonna be terrific, Pop!

Willy (trying to stand): Then you got it, haven't you? You got it! You got it!

Biff (agonized, holds Willy down): No, no. Look, Pop. I'm supposed to have lunch with them tomorrow. I'm just telling you this so you'll know that I can still make an impression, Pop. And I'll make good somewhere, but I can't go tomorrow, see?

Willy: Why not? You simply—

Biff: But the pen, Pop!

Willy: You give it to him and tell him it was an oversight!

Happy: Sure, have lunch tomorrow!

Biff: I can't say that—

Willy: You were doing a crossword puzzle and accidentally used his pen!

Biff: Listen, kid, I took those balls years ago, now I walk in with his fountain pen? That clinches it, don't you see? I can't face him like that! I'll try elsewhere.

Page's voice: Paging Mr. Loman!

Willy: Don't you want to be anything?

Biff: Pop, how can I go back?

Willy: You don't want to be anything, is that what's behind it?

Biff (now angry at Willy for not crediting his sympathy): Don't take it that way! You think it was easy walking into that office after what I'd done to him? A team of horses couldn't have dragged me back to Bill Oliver!

Willy: Then why'd you go?

Biff: Why did I go? Why did I go? Look at you! Look at what's become of you!

Off left, The Woman laughs.

Willy: Biff, you're going to go to that lunch tomorrow, or—

Biff: I can't go. I've got no appointment!

Happy: Biff, for . . . !

Willy: Are you spiting me?

Biff: Don't take it that way! Goddammit!

Willy (strikes Biff and falters away from the table): You rotten little louse! Are you spiting me?

The Woman: Someone's at the door, Willy!

Biff: I'm no good, can't you see what I am?

Happy (separating them): Hey, you're in a restaurant! Now cut it out, both of you! *(The Girls enter.)* Hello, girls, sit down.

The Woman laughs, off left.

Miss Forsythe: I guess we might as well. This is Letta.

The Woman: Willy, are you going to wake up?

Biff (*ignoring Willy*): How're ya, miss, sit down. What do you drink?

Miss Forsythe: Letta might not be able to stay long.

Letta: I gotta get up very early tomorrow. I got jury duty. I'm so excited! Were
    you fellows ever on a jury?

Biff: No, but I been in front of them! (*The Girls laugh.*) This is my father.

Letta: Isn't he cute? Sit down with us, Pop.

Happy: Sit him down, Biff!

Biff (*going to him*): Come on, slugger, drink us under the table. To hell with it!
    Come on, sit down, pal.

On Biff's last insistence, Willy is about to sit.

The Woman (*now urgently*): Willy, are you going to answer the door!

The Woman's call pulls Willy back. He starts right, befuddled.

Biff: Hey, where are you going?

Willy: Open the door.

Biff: The door?

Willy: The washroom . . . the door . . . where's the door?

Biff (*leading Willy to the left*): Just go straight down.

Willy moves left.

The Woman: Willy, Willy, are you going to get up, get up, get up, get up?

Willy exits left.

Letta: I think it's sweet you bring your daddy along.

Miss Forsythe: Oh, he isn't really your father!

Biff (*at left, turning to her resentfully*): Miss Forsythe, you've just seen a prince walk
    by. A fine, troubled prince. A hard-working, unappreciated prince. A pal,
    you understand? A good companion. Always for his boys.

Letta: That's so sweet.

Happy: Well, girls, what's the program? We're wasting time. Come on, Biff. Gather
    round. Where would you like to go?

Biff: Why don't you do something for him?

Happy: Me!

Biff: Don't you give a damn for him, Hap?

Happy: What're you talking about? I'm the one who—

Biff: I sense it, you don't give a good goddam about him. (*He takes the rolled-up
    hose from his pocket and puts it on the table in front of Happy.*) Look what I found
    in the cellar, for Christ's sake. How can you bear to let it go on?

Happy: Me? Who goes away? Who runs off and—

Biff: Yeah, but he doesn't mean anything to you. You could help him—I can't! Don't you understand what I'm talking about? He's going to kill himself, don't you know that?

Happy: Don't I know it! Me!

Biff: Hap, help him! Jesus . . . help him . . . Help me, help me, I can't bear to look at his face! (*Ready to weep, he hurries out, up right.*)

Happy (starting after him): Where are you going?

Miss Forsythe: What's he so mad about?

Happy: Come on, girls, we'll catch up with him.

Miss Forsythe (as Happy pushes her out): Say, I don't like that temper of his!

Happy: He's just a little overstrung, he'll be all right!

Willy (off left, as The Woman laughs): Don't answer! Don't answer!

Letta: Don't you want to tell your father—

Happy: No, that's not my father. He's just a guy. Come on, we'll catch Biff, and, honey, we're going to paint this town! Stanley, where's the check? Hey, Stanley!

They exit. Stanley looks toward left.

Stanley (calling to Happy indignantly): Mr. Loman! Mr. Loman!

Stanley picks up a chair and follows them off. Knocking is heard off left. The Woman enters, laughing. Willy follows her. She is in a black slip; he is buttoning his shirt. Raw, sensuous music accompanies their speech.

Willy: Will you stop laughing? Will you stop?

The Woman: Aren't you going to answer the door? He'll wake the whole hotel.

Willy: I'm not expecting anybody.

The Woman: Whyn't you have another drink, honey, and stop being so damn self-centered?

Willy: I'm so lonely.

The Woman: You know you ruined me, Willy? From now on, whenever you come to the office, I'll see that you go right through to the buyers. No waiting at my desk any more, Willy. You ruined me.

Willy: That's nice of you to say that.

The Woman: Gee, you are self-centered! Why so sad? You are the saddest self-centeredest soul I ever did see-saw. (*She laughs. He kisses her.*) Come on inside, drummer boy. It's silly to be dressing in the middle of the night. (*As knocking is heard.*) Aren't you going to answer the door?

Willy: They're knocking on the wrong door.

The Woman: But I felt the knocking. And he heard us talking in here. Maybe the hotel's on fire!

Willy (his terror rising): It's a mistake.

The Woman: Then tell him to go away!

Willy: There's nobody there.

The Woman: It's getting on my nerves, Willy. There's somebody standing out there and it's getting on my nerves!

Willy (*pushing her away from him*): All right, stay in the bathroom here, and don't come out. I think there's a law in Massachusetts about it, so don't come out. It may be that new room clerk. He looked very mean. So don't come out. It's a mistake, there's no fire.

The knocking is heard again. He takes a few steps away from her, and she vanishes into the wing. The light follows him, and now he is facing Young Biff, who carries a suitcase. Biff steps toward him. The music is gone.

Biff: Why didn't you answer?

Willy: Biff! What are you doing in Boston?

Biff: Why didn't you answer? I've been knocking for five minutes, I called you on the phone—

Willy: I just heard you. I was in the bathroom and had the door shut. Did anything happen at home?

Biff: Dad—I let you down.

Willy: What do you mean?

Biff: Dad . . .

Willy: Biffo, what's this about? (*Putting his arm around Biff.*) Come on, let's go downstairs and get you a malted.

Biff: Dad, I flunked math.

Willy: Not for the term?

Biff: The term. I haven't got enough credits to graduate.

Willy: You mean to say Bernard wouldn't give you the answers?

Biff: He did, he tried, but I only got a sixty-one.

Willy: And they wouldn't give you four points?

Biff: Birnbaum refused absolutely. I begged him, Pop, but he won't give me those points. You gotta talk to him before they close the school. Because if he saw the kind of man you are, and you just talked to him in your way, I'm sure he'd come through for me. The class came right before practice, see, and I didn't go enough. Would you talk to him? He'd like you, Pop. You know the way you could talk.

Willy: You're on. We'll drive right back.

Biff: Oh, Dad, good work! I'm sure he'll change it for you!

Willy: Go downstairs and tell the clerk I'm checkin' out. Go right down.

Biff: Yes, Sir! See, the reason he hates me, Pop—one day he was late for class so I got up at the blackboard and imitated him. I crossed my eyes and talked with a lithp.

Willy (*laughing*): You did? The kids like it?

Biff: They nearly died laughing!

Willy: Yeah? What'd you do?

Biff: The thquare root of thixty twee is . . . (*Willy bursts out laughing; Biff joins him.*) And in the middle of it he walked in!

Willy laughs and The Woman joins in offstage.

Willy (*without hesitating*): Hurry downstairs and—

Biff: Somebody in there?

Willy: No, that was next door.

The Woman laughs offstage.

Biff: Somebody got in your bathroom!

Willy: No, it's the next room, there's a party—

The Woman *(enters, laughing. She lisps this):* Can I come in? There's something in the bathtub, Willy, and it's moving!

Willy looks at Biff, who is staring open-mouthed and horrified at The Woman.

Willy: Ah—you better go back to your room. They must be finished painting by now. They're painting her room so I let her take a shower here. Go back, go back . . . *(He pushes her.)*

The Woman *(resisting):* But I've got to get dressed, Willy, I can't—

Willy: Get out of here! Go back, go back . . . *(Suddenly striving for the ordinary.)* This is Miss Francis, Biff, she's a buyer. They're painting her room. Go back, Miss Francis, go back . . .

The Woman: But my clothes, I can't go out naked in the hall!

Willy *(pushing her offstage):* Get outa here! Go back, go back!

Biff slowly sits down on his suitcase as the argument continues offstage.

The Woman: Where's my stockings? You promised me stockings, Willy!

Willy: I have no stockings here!

The Woman: You had two boxes of size nine sheers for me, and I want them!

Willy: Here, for God's sake, will you get outa here!

The Woman *(enters holding a box of stockings):* I just hope there's nobody in the hall. That's all I hope. *(To Biff.)* Are you football or baseball?

Biff: Football.

The Woman *(angry, humiliated):* That's me too. G'night. *(She snatches her clothes from Willy, and walks out.)*

Willy *(after a pause):* Well, better get going. I want to get to the school first thing in the morning. Get my suits out of the closet. I'll get my valise. *(Biff doesn't move.)* What's the matter? *(Biff remains motionless, tears falling.)* She's a buyer. Buys for J. H. Simmons. She lives down the hall—they're painting. You don't imagine—*(He breaks off. After a pause.)* Now listen, pal, she's just a buyer. She sees merchandise in her room and they have to keep it looking just so . . . *(Pause. Assuming command.)* All right, get my suits. *(Biff doesn't move.)* Now stop crying and do as I say. I gave you an order. Biff, I gave you an order! Is that what you do when I give you an order? How dare you cry! *(Putting his arm around Biff.)* Now look, Biff, when you grow up you'll understand about these things. You mustn't—you mustn't overemphasize a thing like this. I'll see Birnbaum first thing in the morning.

Biff: Never mind.

Willy *(getting down beside Biff):* Never mind! He's going to give you those points. I'll see to it.

Biff: He wouldn't listen to you.

Willy: He certainly will listen to me. You need those points for the U. of Virginia.

Biff: I'm not going there.

Willy: Heh? If I can't get him to change that mark you'll make it up in summer
   school. You've got all summer to—
Biff (his weeping breaking from him): Dad . . .
Willy (infected by it): Oh, my boy . . .
Biff: Dad . . .
Willy: She's nothing to me, Biff. I was lonely, I was terribly lonely.
Biff: You—you gave her Mama's stockings! (His tears break through and he rises to go.)
Willy: (grabbing for Biff): I gave you an order!
Biff: Don't touch me, you—liar!
Willy: Apologize for that!
Biff: You fake! You phony little fake! You fake! (Overcome, he turns quickly and
   weeping fully goes out with his suitcase. Willy is left on the floor on his knees.)
Willy: I gave you an order! Biff, come back here or I'll beat you! Come back here!
   I'll whip you!

   Stanley comes quickly in from the right and stands in front of Willy.

Willy: (shouts at Stanley): I gave you an order . . .
Stanley: Hey, let's pick it up, pick it up, Mr. Loman. (He helps Willy to his feet.)
   Your boys left with the chippies. They said they'll see you at home.

   A second waiter watches some distance away.

Willy: But we were supposed to have dinner together.

   Music is heard, Willy's theme.

Stanley: Can you make it?
Willy: I'll—sure, I can make it. (Suddenly concerned about his clothes.) Do I—I look
   all right?
Stanley: Sure, you look all right. (He flicks a speck off Willy's lapel.)
Willy: Here—here's a dollar.
Stanley: Oh, your son paid me. It's all right.
Willy (putting it in Stanley's hand): No, take it. You're a good boy.
Stanley: Oh, no, you don't have to . . .
Willy: Here—here's some more, I don't need it any more. (After a slight pause.)
   Tell me—is there a seed store in the neighborhood?
Stanley: Seeds? You mean like to plant?

   As Willy turns, Stanley slips the money back into his jacket pocket.

Willy: Yes. Carrots, peas . . .
Stanley: Well, there's hardware stores on Sixth Avenue, but it may be too late now.
Willy (anxiously): Oh, I'd better hurry. I've got to get some seeds. (He starts off
   to the right.) I've got to get some seeds, right away. Nothing's planted. I don't
   have a thing in the ground.

   Willy hurries out as the light goes down. Stanley moves over to the right after him,
   watches him off. The other waiter has been staring at Willy.

Stanley (to the waiter): Well, whatta you looking at?

The waiter picks up the chairs and moves off right. Stanley takes the table and follows him. The light fades on this area. There is a long pause, the sound of the flute coming over. The light gradually rises on the kitchen, which is empty. Happy appears at the door of the house, followed by Biff. Happy is carrying a large bunch of long-stemmed roses. He enters the kitchen, looks around for Linda. Not seeing her, he turns to Biff, who is just outside the house door, and makes a gesture with his hands, indicating "Not here, I guess." He looks into the livingroom and freezes. Inside, Linda, unseen, is seated, Willy's coat on her lap. She rises ominously and quietly and moves toward Happy, who backs up into the kitchen, afraid.

Happy: Hey, what're you doing up? (*Linda says nothing but moves toward him implacably.*) Where's Pop? (*He keeps backing to the right, and now Linda is in full view in the doorway to the livingroom.*) Is he sleeping?

Linda: Where were you?

Happy (*trying to laugh it off*): We met two girls, Mom, very fine types. Here, we brought you some flowers. (*Offering them to her.*) Put them in your room, Ma.

She knocks them to the floor at Biff's feet. He has now come inside and closed the door behind him. She stares at Biff, silent.

Happy: Now what'd you do that for? Mom, I want you to have some flowers—

Linda (*cutting Happy off, violently to Biff*): Don't you care whether he lives or dies?

Happy (*going to the stairs*): Come upstairs, Biff.

Biff (*with a flare of disgust, to Happy*): Go away from me! (*To Linda.*) What do you mean, lives or dies? Nobody's dying around here, pal.

Linda: Get out of my sight! Get out of here!

Biff: I wanna see the boss.

Linda: You're not going near him!

Biff: Where is he? (*He moves into the livingroom and Linda follows.*)

Linda (*shouting after Biff*): You invite him for dinner. He looks forward to it all day—(*Biff appears in his parents' bedroom, looks around, and exits*)—and then you desert him there. There's no stranger you'd do that to!

Happy: Why? He had a swell time with us. Listen, when I—(*Linda comes back into the kitchen*)—desert him I hope I don't outlive the day!

Linda: Get out of here!

Happy: Now look, Mom . . .

Linda: Did you have to go to women tonight? You and your lousy rotten whores!

Biff re-enters the kitchen.

Happy: Mom, all we did was follow Biff around trying to cheer him up! (*To Biff.*) Boy, what a night you gave me!

Linda: Get out of here, both of you, and don't come back! I don't want you tormenting him any more. Go on now, get your things together! (*To Biff.*) You can sleep in his apartment. (*She starts to pick up the flowers and stops herself.*) Pick up this stuff, I'm not your maid any more. Pick it up, you bum, you!

Happy turns his back to her in refusal. Biff slowly moves over and gets down on his knees, picking up the flowers.

Linda: You're a pair of animals! Not one, not another living soul would have had the cruelty to walk out on that man in a restaurant!

Biff (not looking at her): Is that what he said?

Linda: He didn't have to say anything. He was so humiliated he nearly limped when he came in.

Happy: But, Mom he had a great time with us—

Biff (cutting him off violently): Shut up!

Without another word, Happy goes upstairs.

Linda: You! You didn't even go in to see if he was all right!

Biff (still on the floor in front of Linda, the flowers in his hand; with self-loathing): No. Didn't. Didn't do a damned thing. How do you like that, heh? Left him babbling in a toilet.

Linda: You louse. You . . .

Biff: Now you hit it on the nose! *(He gets up, throws the flowers in the wastebasket.)* The scum of the earth, and you're looking at him!

Linda: Get out of here!

Biff: I gotta talk to the boss, Mom. Where is he?

Linda: You're not going near him. Get out of this house!

Biff (with absolute assurance, determination): No. We're gonna have an abrupt conversation, him and me.

Linda: You're not talking to him!

Hammering is heard from outside the house, off right. Biff turns toward the noise.

Linda (suddenly pleading): Will you please leave him alone?

Biff: What's he doing out there?

Linda: He's planting the garden!

Biff (quietly): Now? Oh, my God!

Biff moves outside, Linda following. The light dies down on them and comes up on the center of the apron as Willy walks into it. He is carrying a flashlight, a hoe and a handful of seed packets. He raps the top of the hoe sharply to fix it firmly, and then moves to the left, measuring off the distance with his foot. He holds the flashlight to look at the seed packets, reading off the instructions. He is in the blue of night.

Willy: Carrots . . . quarter-inch apart. Rows . . . one-foot rows. *(He measures it off.)* One foot. *(He puts down a package and measures off.)* Beets. *(He puts down another package and measures again.)* Lettuce. *(He reads the package, puts it down.)* One foot—*(He breaks off as Ben appears at the right and moves slowly down to him.)* What a proposition, ts, ts. Terrific, terrific. 'Cause she's suffered, Ben, the woman has suffered. You understand me? A man can't go out the way he came in, Ben, a man has got to add up to something. You can't, you can't—*(Ben moves toward him as though to interrupt.)* You gotta consider, now. Don't answer so quick. Remember, it's a guaranteed twenty-thousand-dollar proposition. Now look, Ben, I want you to go through the ins and outs of this thing with me. I've got nobody to talk to, Ben, and the woman has suffered, you hear me?

Ben (standing still, considering): What's the proposition?

Willy: It's twenty thousand dollars on the barrelhead. Guaranteed, gilt-edged, you understand?

Ben: You don't want to make a fool of yourself. They might not honor the policy.

Willy: How can they dare refuse? Didn't I work like a coolie to meet every premium on the nose? And now they don't pay off? Impossible!

Ben: It's called a cowardly thing, William.

Willy: Why? Does it take more guts to stand here the rest of my life ringing up a zero?

Ben (yielding): That's a point, William. *(He moves, thinking, turns.)* And twenty thousand—that *is* something one can feel with the hand, it is there.

Willy (now assured, with rising power): Oh, Ben, that's the whole beauty of it! I see it like a diamond, shining in the dark, hard and rough, that I can pick up and touch in my hand. Not like—like an appointment! This would not be another damned-fool appointment, Ben, and it changes all the aspects. Because he thinks I'm nothing, see, and so he spites me. But the funeral— *(Straightening up.)* Ben, that funeral will be massive! They'll come from Maine, Massachusetts, Vermont, New Hampshire! All the old-timers with the strange license plates—that boy will be thunder-struck, Ben, because he never realized—I am known! Rhode Island, New York, New Jersey—I am known, Ben, and he'll see it with his eyes once and for all. He'll see what I am, Ben! He's in for a shock, that boy!

Ben (coming down to the edge of the garden): He'll call you a coward.

Willy (suddenly fearful): No, that would be terrible.

Ben: Yes. And a damned fool.

Willy: No, no, he mustn't, I won't have that! *(He is broken and desperate.)*

Ben: He'll hate you, William.

The gay music of the boys is heard.

Willy: Oh, Ben, how do we get back to all the great times? Used to be so full of light, and comradeship, the sleigh-riding in winter, and the ruddiness on his cheeks. And always some kind of good news coming up, always something nice coming up ahead. And never even let me carry the valises in the house, and simonizing, simonizing that little red car! Why, why can't I give him something and not have him hate me?

Ben: Let me think about it. *(He glances at his watch.)* I still have a little time. Remarkable proposition, but you've got to be sure you're not making a fool of yourself.

Ben drifts off upstage and goes out of sight. Biff comes down from the left.

Willy (suddenly conscious of Biff, turns and looks up at him, then begins picking up the packages of seeds in confusion): Where the hell is that seed? *(Indignantly.)* You can't see nothing out here! They boxed in the whole goddam neighborhood!

Biff: There are people all around here. Don't you realize that?

Willy: I'm busy. Don't bother me.

Biff (taking the hoe from Willy): I'm saying good-by to you, Pop. *(Willy looks at him, silent, unable to move.)* I'm not coming back any more.

Willy: You're not going to see Oliver tomorrow?

Biff: I've got no appointment, Dad.

Willy: He put his arm around you, and you've got no appointment?

Biff: Pop, get this now, will you? Everytime I've left it's been a fight that sent me out of here. Today I realized something about myself and I tried to explain it to you and I—I think I'm just not smart enough to make any sense out of it for you. To hell with whose fault it is or anything like that. *(He takes Willy's arm.)* Let's just wrap it up, heh? Come on in, we'll tell Mom. *(He gently tries to pull Willy to the left.)*

Willy (frozen, immobile, with guilt in his voice): No, I don't want to see her.

Biff: Come on! *(He pulls again, and Willy tries to pull away.)*

Willy (highly nervous): No, no, I don't want to see her.

Biff (tries to look into Willy's face, as if to find the answer there): Why don't you want to see her?

Willy (more harshly now): Don't bother me, will you?

Biff: What do you mean, you don't want to see her? You don't want them calling you yellow, do you? This isn't your fault; it's me, I'm a bum. Now come inside! *(Willy strains to get away.)* Did you hear what I said to you?

Willy pulls away and quickly goes by himself into the house. Biff follows.

Linda (to Willy): Did you plant, dear?

Biff (at the door, to Linda): All right, we had it out. I'm going and I'm not writing any more.

Linda (going to Willy in the kitchen): I think that's the best way, dear. 'Cause there's no use drawing it out, you'll just never get along.

Willy doesn't respond.

Biff: People ask where I am and what I'm doing, you don't know, and you don't care. That way it'll be off your mind and you can start brightening up again. All right? That clears it, doesn't it? *(Willy is silent, and Biff goes to him.)* You gonna wish me luck, scout? *(He extends his hand.)* What do you say?

Linda: Shake his hand, Willy.

Willy (turning to her, seething with hurt): There's no necessity to mention the pen at all, y'know.

Biff (gently): I've got no appointment, Dad.

Willy (erupting fiercely): He put his arm around . . . ?

Biff: Dad, you're never going to see what I am, so what's the use of arguing? If I strike oil I'll send you a check. Meantime forget I'm alive.

Willy (to Linda): Spite, see?

Biff: Shake hands, Dad.

Willy: Not my hand.

Biff: I was hoping not to go this way.

Willy: Well, this is the way you're going. Good-by.

Biff looks at him a moment, then turns sharply and goes to the stairs.

Willy (stops him with): May you rot in hell if you leave this house!

Biff (turning): Exactly what is it that you want from me?

Willy: I want you to know, on the train, in the mountains, in the valleys, wherever you go, that you cut down your life for spite!

Biff: No, no.

Willy: Spite, spite, is the word of your undoing! And when you're down and out, remember what did it. When you're rotting somewhere beside the railroad tracks, remember, and don't you dare blame it on me!

Biff: I'm not blaming it on you!

Willy: I won't take the rap for this, you hear?

Happy comes down the stairs and stands on the bottom step, watching.

Biff: That's just what I'm telling you!

Willy (sinking into a chair at the table, with full accusation): You're trying to put a knife in me—don't think I don't know what you're doing!

Biff: All right, phony! Then let's lay it on the line. (*He whips the rubber tube out of his pocket and puts it on the table.*)

Happy: You crazy—

Linda: Biff! (*She moves to grab the hose, but Biff holds it down with his hand.*)

Biff: Leave it there! Don't move it!

Willy (not looking at it): What is that?

Biff: You know goddam well what that is.

Willy (caged, wanting to escape): I never saw that.

Biff: You saw it. The mice didn't bring it into the cellar! What is this supposed to do, make a hero out of you? This supposed to make me sorry for you?

Willy: Never heard of it.

Biff: There'll be no pity for you, you hear? No pity!

Willy (to Linda): You hear the spite!

Biff: No, you're going to hear the truth—what you are and what I am!

Linda: Stop it!

Willy: Spite!

Happy (coming down toward Biff): You cut it now!

Biff (to Happy): The man don't know who we are! The man is gonna know! (*To Willy.*) We never told the truth for ten minutes in this house!

Happy: We always told the truth!

Biff (turning on him): You big blow, are you the assistant buyer? You're one of the two assistants to the assistant, aren't you?

Happy: Well, I'm practically—

Biff: You're practically full of it! We all are! And I'm through with it. (*To Willy.*) Now hear this, Willy, this is me.

Willy: I know you!

Biff: You know why I had no address for three months? I stole a suit in Kansas City and I was in jail. (*To Linda, who is sobbing.*) Stop crying. I'm through with it.

Linda turns away from them, her hands covering her face.

Willy: I suppose that's my fault!

Biff: I stole myself out of every good job since high school!

Willy: And whose fault is that?

Biff: And I never got anywhere because you blew me so full of hot air I could never stand taking orders from anybody! That's whose fault it is!

Willy: I hear that!

Linda: Don't, Biff!

Biff: It's goddam time you heard that! I had to be boss big shot in two weeks, and I'm through with it!

Willy: Then hang yourself! For spite, hang yourself!

Biff: No! Nobody's hanging himself, Willy! I ran down eleven flights with a pen in my hand today. And suddenly I stopped, you hear me? And in the middle of that office building, do you hear this? I stopped in the middle of that building and I saw—the sky. I saw the things that I love in this world. The work and the food and time to sit and smoke. And I looked at the pen and said to myself, what the hell am I grabbing this for? Why am I trying to become what I don't want to be? What am I doing in an office, making a contemptuous, begging fool of myself, when all I want is out there, waiting for me the minute I say I know who I am! Why can't I say that, Willy? (*He tries to make Willy face him, but Willy pulls away and moves to the left.*)

Willy (with hatred, threateningly): The door of your life is wide open!

Biff: Pop! I'm a dime a dozen, and so are you!

Willy (turning on him now in an uncontrolled outburst): I am not a dime a dozen! I am Willy Loman, and you are Biff Loman!

Biff starts for Willy, but is blocked by Happy. In his fury, Biff seems on the verge of attacking his father.

Biff: I am not a leader of men, Willy, and neither are you. You were never anything but a hard-working drummer who landed in the ash can like all the rest of them! I'm one dollar an hour, Willy! I tried seven states and couldn't raise it. A buck an hour! Do you gather my meaning? I'm not bringing home any prizes any more, and you're going to stop waiting for me to bring them home!

Willy (directly to Biff): You vengeful, spiteful mutt!

Biff breaks from Happy. Willy, in fright, starts up the stairs. Biff grabs him.

Biff (at the peak of his fury): Pop, I'm nothing! I'm nothing, Pop. Can't you understand that? There's no spite in it any more. I'm just what I am, that's all.

Biff's fury has spent itself, and he breaks down, sobbing, holding on to Willy, who dumbly fumbles for Biff's face.

Willy (astonished): What're you doing? What're you doing? (*To Linda.*) Why is he crying?

Biff (crying, broken): Will you let me go, for Christ's sake? Will you take that phony dream and burn it before something happens? (*Struggling to contain himself, he pulls away and moves to the stairs.*) I'll go in the morning. Put him—put him to bed. (*Exhausted, Biff moves up the stairs to his room.*)

Willy (after a long pause, astonished, elevated): Isn't that remarkable? Biff—he likes me!

Linda: He loves you, Willy!

Happy (deeply moved): Always did, Pop.

Willy: Oh, Biff! *(Staring wildly.)* He cried! Cried to me. *(He is choking with his love, and now cries out his promise.)* That boy—that boy is going to be magnificent!

Ben appears in the light just outside the kitchen.

Ben: Yes, outstanding, with twenty thousand behind him.

Linda (sensing the racing of his mind, fearfully, carefully): Now come to bed, Willy. It's all settled now.

Willy (finding it difficult not to rush out of the house): Yes, we'll sleep. Come on. Go to sleep, Hap.

Ben: And it does take a great kind of man to crack the jungle.

In accents of dread, Ben's idyllic music starts up.

Happy (his arm around Linda): I'm getting married, Pop, don't forget it. I'm changing everything. I'm gonna run that department before the year is up. You'll see, Mom. *(He kisses her.)*

Ben: The jungle is dark but full of diamonds, Willy.

Willy turns, moves, listening to Ben.

Linda: Be good. You're both good boys, just act that way, that's all.

Happy: 'Night, Pop. *(He goes upstairs.)*

Linda (to Willy): Come, dear.

Ben (with greater force): One must go in to fetch a diamond out.

Willy (to Linda, as he moves slowly along the edge of the kitchen, toward the door): I just want to get settled down, Linda. Let me sit alone for a little.

Linda (almost uttering her fear): I want you upstairs.

Willy (taking her in his arms): In a few minutes, Linda. I couldn't sleep right now. Go on, you look awful tired. *(He kisses her.)*

Ben: Not like an appointment at all. A diamond is rough and hard to the touch.

Willy: Go on now, I'll be right up.

Linda: I think this is the only way, Willy.

Willy: Sure, it's the best thing.

Ben: Best thing!

Willy: The only way. Everything is gonna be—go on, kid, get to bed. You look so tired.

Linda: Come right up.

Willy: Two minutes.

Linda goes into the livingroom, then reappears in her bedroom. Willy moves just outside the kitchen door.

Willy: Loves me. *(Wonderingly.)* Always loved me. Isn't that a remarkable thing? Ben, he'll worship me for it!

Ben (with promise): It's dark there, but full of diamonds.

Willy: Can you imagine that magnificence with twenty thousand dollars in his pocket?

Linda (calling from her room): Willy! Come up!

Willy (calling from the kitchen): Yes! Yes! Coming! It's very smart, you realize that, don't you, sweetheart? Even Ben sees it. I gotta go, baby. 'By! By! (Going over to Ben, almost dancing.) Imagine? When the mail comes he'll be ahead of Bernard again!

Ben: A perfect proposition all around.

Willy: Did you see how he cried to me? Oh, if I could kiss him, Ben!

Ben: Time, William, time!

Willy: Oh, Ben, I always knew one way or another we were gonna make it, Biff and I!

Ben (looking at his watch): The boat. We'll be late. (He moves slowly off into the darkness.)

Willy (elegiacally, turning to the house): Now when you kick off, boy, I want a seventy-yard boot, and get right down the field under the ball, and when you hit, hit low and hit hard, because it's important, boy. (He swings around and faces the audience.) There's all kinds of important people in the stands, and the first thing you know . . . (Suddenly realizing he is alone.) Ben! Ben, where do I . . . ? (He makes a sudden movement of search.) Ben, how do I . . . ?

Linda (calling): Willy, you coming up?

Willy (uttering a gasp of fear, whirling about as if to quiet her): Sh! (He turns around as if to find his way; sounds, faces, voices, seem to be swarming in upon him and he flicks at them, crying.) Sh! Sh! (Suddenly music, faint and high, stops him. It rises in intensity, almost to an unbearable scream. He goes up and down on his toes, and rushes off around the house.) Shhh!

Linda: Willy?

There is no answer. Linda waits. Biff gets up off his bed. He is still in his clothes. Happy sits up. Biff stands listening.

Linda (with real fear): Willy, answer me! Willy!

There is the sound of a car starting and moving away at full speed.

Linda: No!

Biff (rushing down the stairs): Pop!

As the car speeds off, the music crashes down in a frenzy of sound, which becomes the soft pulsation of a single cello string. Biff slowly returns to his bedroom. He and Happy gravely don their jackets. Linda slowly walks out of her room. The music has developed into a dead march. The leaves of day are appearing over everything. Charley and Bernard, somberly dressed, appear and knock on the kitchen door. Biff and Happy slowly descend the stairs to the kitchen as Charley and Bernard enter. All stop a moment when Linda, in clothes of mourning, bearing a little bunch of roses, comes through the draped doorway into the kitchen. She goes to Charley and takes his arm. Now all move toward the audience, through the wall-line of the kitchen. At the limit of the apron, Linda lays down the flowers, kneels, and sits back on her heels. All stare down at the grave.

Charley: It's getting dark, Linda.

Linda doesn't react. She stares at the grave.

Biff: How about it, Mom? Better get some rest, heh? They'll be closing the gate soon.

Linda makes no move. Pause.

Happy (deeply angered): He had no right to do that! There was no necessity for it. We would've helped him.

Charley (grunting): Hmmm.

Biff: Come along, Mom.

Linda: Why didn't anybody come?

Charley: It was a very nice funeral.

Linda: But where are all the people he knew? Maybe they blame him.

Charley: Naa. It's a rough world, Linda. They wouldn't blame him.

Linda: I can't understand it. At this time especially. First time in thirty-five years we were just about free and clear. He only needed a little salary. He was even finished with the dentist.

Charley: No man only needs a little salary.

Linda: I can't understand it.

Biff: There were a lot of nice days. When he'd come home from a trip; or on Sundays, making the stoop; finishing the cellar; putting on the new porch; when he built the extra bathroom; and put up the garage. You know something, Charley, there's more of him in that front stoop than in all the sales he ever made.

Charley: Yeah. He was a happy man with a batch of cement.

Linda: He was so wonderful with his hands.

Biff: He had the wrong dreams. All, all, wrong.

Happy (almost ready to fight Biff): Don't say that!

Biff: He never knew who he was.

Charley (stopping Happy's movement and reply. To Biff.): Nobody dast blame this man. You don't understand: Willy was a salesman. And for a salesman, there is no rock bottom to the life. He don't put a bolt to a nut, he don't tell you the law or give you medicine. He's a man out there in the blue, riding on a smile and a shoeshine. And when they start not smiling back—that's an earthquake. And then you get yourself a couple of spots on your hat, and you're finished. Nobody dast blame this man. A salesman is got to dream, boy. It comes with the territory.

Biff: Charley, the man didn't know who he was.

Happy (infuriated): Don't say that!

Biff: Why don't you come with me, Happy?

Happy: I'm not licked that easily. I'm staying right in this city, and I'm gonna beat this racket! (*He looks at Biff, his chin set.*) The Loman Brothers!

Biff: I know who I am, kid.

Happy: All right, boy. I'm gonna show you and everybody else that Willy Loman did not die in vain. He had a good dream. It's the only dream you can have—to come out number-one man. He fought it out here, and this is where I'm gonna win it for him.

Biff (with a hopeless glance at Happy, bends toward his mother): Let's go, Mom.

Linda: I'll be with you in a minute. Go on, Charley. *(He hesitates.)* I want to, just for a minute. I never had a chance to say good-by.

Charley moves away, followed by Happy. Biff remains a slight distance up and left of Linda. She sits there, summoning herself. The flute begins, not far away, playing behind her speech.

Linda: Forgive me, dear. I can't cry. I don't know what it is, but I can't cry. I don't understand it. Why did you ever do that? Help me, Willy, I can't cry. It seems to me that you're just on another trip. I keep expecting you. Willy, dear, I can't cry. Why did you do it? I search and search and search, and I can't understand it, Willy. I made the last payment on the house today. Today, dear. And there'll be nobody home. *(A sob rises in her throat.)* We're free and clear. *(Sobbing more fully, released.)* We're free. *(Biff comes slowly toward her.)* We're free . . . We're free . . .

Biff lifts her to her feet and moves out up right with her in his arms. Linda sobs quietly. Bernard and Charley come together and follow them, followed by Happy. Only the music of the flute is left on the darkening stage as over the house the hard towers of the apartment buildings rise into sharp focus, and—

THE CURTAIN FALLS

COMPARE:

Death of a Salesman and Arthur Miller's essay "Tragedy and the Common Man" (page 1448).

Sophocles

ANTIGONE   441 B.C.

Translated by Elizabeth Wyckoff

Sophocles (496?–406 B.C.), Athenian dramatist, is the subject of a biographical note on page 999, preceding his play Oedipus the King. Antigone *was produced in 441 B.C.;* Oedipus the King, *not until fourteen or fifteen years later. Although written earlier than its companion play,* Antigone *relates events supposed to have followed long after.*

Characters

Antigone
Ismene
Chorus of Theban Elders
Creon

A Guard
Haemon
Teiresias
A Messenger
Eurydice

Scene: *Thebes, before the royal palace. Antigone and Ismene emerge from its great central door.*

Antigone: My sister, my Ismene, do you know
    of any suffering from our father sprung°
    that Zeus does not achieve for us survivors?
    There's nothing grievous, nothing free from doom,
    not shameful, not dishonored, I've not seen.   5
    Your sufferings and mine.
    And now, what of this edict which they say
    the commander has proclaimed to the whole people?
    Have you heard anything? Or don't you know
    that the foes' trouble comes upon our friends?   10
Ismene: I've heard no word, Antigone, of our friends.
    Not sweet nor bitter, since that single moment
    when we two lost two brothers
    who died on one day by a double blow.
    And since the Argive army went away   15
    this very night, I have no further news
    of fortune or disaster for myself.
Antigone: I knew it well, and brought you from the house
    for just this reason, that you alone may hear.
Ismene: What is it? Clearly some news has clouded you.   20
Antigone: It has indeed. Creon will give the one
    of our two brothers honor in the tomb;
    the other none.
    Eteocles, with just entreatment treated,
    as law provides he has hidden under earth   25
    to have full honor with the dead below.

2 *Suffering from our father sprung:* As Sophocles tells in *Oedipus the King,* the King of Thebes discovered that he had lived his life under a curse. Unknowingly, he had slain his father and married his mother. On realizing this terrible truth, Oedipus put out his own eyes and departed into exile. Now, years later, as *Antigone* opens, Antigone and Ismene, daughters of Oedipus, are recalling how their two brothers died. After the abdication of their father, the brothers had ruled Thebes together. But they fell to quarreling. When Eteocles expelled Polyneices, the latter returned with an army and attacked the city. The two brothers killed each other in combat, leaving the throne to Creon. The new King of Thebes has buried Eteocles with full honors, but, calling Polyneices a traitor, has decreed that his body shall be left to the crows—an especially terrible decree, for a rotting corpse might offend Zeus, bring down plague, blight, and barrenness upon Thebes, and prevent the soul of a dead hero from entering the Elysian Fields, abode of those favored by the gods.

But Polyneices' corpse who died in pain,
they say he has proclaimed to the whole town
that none may bury him and none bewail,
but leave him unwept, untombed, a rich sweet sight   30
for the hungry birds' beholding.
Such orders they say the worthy Creon gives
to you and me—yes, yes, I say to *me*—
and that he's coming to proclaim it clear
to those who know it not.   35
Further: he has the matter so at heart
that anyone who dares attempt the act
will die by public stoning in the town.
So there you have it and you soon will show
if you are noble, or fallen from your descent.   40
Ismene: If things have reached this stage, what can I do,
    poor sister, that will help to make or amend?
Antigone: Think will you share my labor and my act.
Ismene: What will you risk? And where is your intent?
Antigone: Will you take up that corpse along with me?   45
Ismene: To bury him you mean, when it's forbidden?
Antigone: My brother, and yours, though you may wish he were not.
    I never shall be found to be his traitor.
Ismene: O hard of mind! When Creon spoke against it!
Antigone: It's not for him to keep me from my own.   50
Ismene: Alas. Remember, sister, how our father
    perished abhorred, ill-famed.
    Himself with his own hand, through his own curse
    destroyed both eyes.
    Remember next his mother and his wife   55
    finishing life in the shame of the twisted strings.
    And third two brothers on a single day,
    poor creatures, murdering, a common doom
    each with his arm accomplished on the other.
    And now look at the two of us alone.   60
    We'll perish terribly if we force law
    and try to cross the royal vote and power.
    We must remember that we two are women
    so not to fight with men.
    And that since we are subject to strong power   65
    we must hear these orders, or any that may be worse.
    So I shall ask of them beneath the earth
    forgiveness, for in these things I am forced,
    and shall obey the men in power. I know
    that wild and futile action makes no sense.   70
Antigone: I wouldn't urge it. And if now you wished
    to act, you wouldn't please me as a partner.
    Be what you want to; but that man shall I

bury. For me, the doer, death is best.
Friend shall I lie with him, yes friend and friend,   75
when I have dared the crime of piety.
Longer the time in which to please the dead
than that for those up here.
There shall I lie forever. You may see fit
to keep from honor what the gods have honored.   80

Ismene: I shall do no dishonor. But to act
    against the citizens. I cannot.
Antigone: That's your protection. Now I go, to pile
    the burial-mound for him, my dearest brother.
Ismene: Oh my poor sister. How I fear for you!   85
Antigone: For me, don't borrow trouble. Clear your fate.
Ismene: At least give no one warning of this act;
    you keep it hidden, and I'll do the same.
Antigone: Dear God! Denounce me. I shall hate you more
    if silent, not proclaiming this to all.   90
Ismene: You have a hot mind over chilly things.
Antigone: I know I please those whom I most should please.
Ismene: If but you can. You crave what can't be done.
Antigone: And so, when strength runs out, I shall give over.
Ismene: Wrong from the start, to chase what cannot be.   95
Antigone: If that's your saying, I shall hate you first,
    and next the dead will hate you in all justice.
    But let me and my own ill-counselling
    suffer this terror. I shall suffer nothing
    as great as dying with a lack of grace.   100
Ismene: Go, since you want to. But know this: you go
    senseless indeed, but loved by those who loved you.

*(Ismene returns to the palace; Antigone leaves by one of the side entrances.
The Chorus now enters from the other side.)*

Chorus: Sun's own radiance, fairest light ever shone on the gates of Thebes,
    then did you shine, O golden day's
    eye, coming over Dirce's stream,°   105
    on the Man who had come from Argos° with all his armor
    running now in headlong fear as you shook his bridle free.

    He was stirred by the dubious quarrel of Polyneices.
    So, screaming shrill,
    like an eagle over the land he flew,   110
    covered with white-snow wing,
    with many weapons,
    with horse-hair crested helms.

---

105 *Dirce's stream:* river near Thebes.   106 *Man who had come from Argos:* the enemy, now routed.

He who had stood above our halls, gaping about our seven gates,
with that circle of thirsting spears. 115
Gone, without our blood in his jaws,
before the torch took hold on our tower-crown.
Rattle of war at his back; hard the fight for the dragon's foe.

The boasts of a proud tongue are for Zeus to hate.
So seeing them streaming on 120
in insolent clangor of gold,
he struck with hurling fire him who rushed
for the high wall's top,
to cry conquest abroad.

Swinging, striking the earth he fell 125
fire in hand, who in mad attack,
had raged against us with blasts of hate.
He failed. He failed of his aim.
For the rest great Ares dealt his blows about,
first in the war-team. 130

The captains stationed at seven gates
fought with seven and left behind
their brazen arms as an offering
to Zeus who is turner of battle.
All but those wretches, sons of one man, 135
one mother's sons, who sent their spears
each against each and found the share
of a common death together.

Great-named Victory comes to us
answering Thebe's warrior-joy. 140
Let us forget the wars just done
and visit the shrines of the gods.
All, with night-long dance which Bacchus will lead,
who shakes Thebe's acres.

(*Creon enters from the palace.*)

Now here he comes, the king of the land, 145
Creon, Menoeceus' son,
newly named by the gods' new fate.
What plan that beats about his mind
has made him call this council-session,
sending his summons to all? 150

Creon: My friends, the very gods who shook the state
with mighty surge have set it straight again.

So now I sent for you, chosen from all,
first that I knew you constant in respect
to Laius' royal power; and again 155
when Oedipus had set the state to rights,
and when he perished, you were faithful still
in mind to the descendants of the dead.
When they two perished by a double fate,
on one day struck and striking and defiled 160
each by his own hand, now it comes that I
hold all the power and the royal throne
through close connection with the perished men.
You cannot learn of any man the soul,
the mind, and the intent until he show 165
his practice of the government and law.
For I believe that who controls the state
and does not hold to the best plans of all,
but locks his tongue up through some kind of fear,
that he is worst of all who are or were. 170
And he who counts another greater friend
than his own fatherland, I put him nowhere.
So I—may Zeus all-seeing always know it—
could not keep silent as disaster crept
upon the town, destroying hope of safety. 175
Nor could I count the enemy of the land
friend to myself, not I who know so well
that she it is who saves us, sailing straight,
and only so can we have friends at all.
With such good rules shall I enlarge our state. 180
And now I have proclaimed their brother-edict.
In the matter of the sons of Oedipus,
citizens, know: Eteocles who died,
defending this our town with champion spear,
is to be covered in the grave and granted 185
all holy rites we give the noble dead.
But his brother Polyneices whom I name
the exile who came back and sought to burn
his fatherland, the gods who were his kin,
who tried to gorge on blood he shared, and lead 190
the rest of us as slaves—
it is announced that no one in this town
may give him burial or mourn for him.
Leave him unburied, leave his corpse disgraced,
a dinner for the birds and for the dogs. 195
Such is my mind. Never shall I, myself,
honor the wicked and reject the just.
The man who is well-minded to the state
from me in death and life shall have his honor.

Chorus: This resolution, Creon, is your own,   200
    in the matter of the traitor and the true.
    For you can make such rulings as you will
    about the living and about the dead.
Creon: Now you be sentinels of the decree.
Chorus: Order some younger man to take this on.   205
Creon: Already there are watchers of the corpse.
Chorus: What other order would you give us, then?
Creon: Not to take sides with any who disobey.
Chorus: No fool is fool as far as loving death.
Creon: Death is the price. But often we have known   210
    men to be ruined by the hope of profit.

(Enter, from the side, a guard.)

Guard: Lord, I can't claim that I am out of breath
    from rushing here with light and hasty step,
    for I had many haltings in my thought
    making me double back upon my road.   215
    My mind kept saying many things to me:
    "Why go where you will surely pay the price?"
    "Fool, are you halting? And if Creon learns
    from someone else, how shall you not be hurt?"
    Turning this over, on I dilly-dallied.   220
    And so a short trip turns itself to long.
    Finally, though, my coming here won out.
    If what I say is nothing, still I'll say it.
    For I come clutching to one single hope
    that I can't suffer what is not my fate.   225
Creon: What is it that brings on this gloom of yours?
Guard: I want to tell you first about myself.
    I didn't do it, didn't see who did it.
    It isn't right for me to get in trouble.
Creon: Your aim is good. You fence the fact around.   230
    It's clear you have some shocking news to tell.
Guard: Terrible tidings make for long delays.
Creon: Speak out the story, and then get away.
Guard: I'll tell you. Someone left the corpse just now,
    burial all accomplished, thirsty dust   235
    strewn on the flesh, the ritual complete.
Creon: What are you saying? What man has dared to do it?
Guard: I wouldn't know. There were no marks of picks,
    no grubbed-out earth. The ground was dry and hard,
    no trace of wheels. The doer left no sign.   240
    When the first fellow on the day-shift showed us,
    we all were sick with wonder.
    For he was hidden, not inside a tomb,
    light dust upon him, enough to turn the curse,

no wild beast's track, nor track of any hound   245
having been near, nor was the body torn.
We roared bad words about, guard against guard,
and came to blows. No one was there to stop us.
Each man had done it, nobody had done it
so as to prove it on him—we couldn't tell.   250
We were prepared to hold to red-hot iron,
to walk through fire, to swear before the gods
we hadn't done it, hadn't shared the plan,
when it was plotted or when it was done.
And last, when all our sleuthing came out nowhere,   255
one fellow spoke, who made our heads to droop
low toward the ground. We couldn't disagree.
We couldn't see a chance of getting off.
He said we had to tell you all about it.
We couldn't hide the fact.   260
So he won out. The lot chose poor old me
to win the prize. So here I am unwilling,
quite sure you people hardly want to see me.
Nobody likes the bringer of bad news.
Chorus: Lord, while he spoke, my mind kept on debating.   265
    Isn't this action possibly a god's?
Creon: Stop now, before you fill me up with rage,
    or you'll prove yourself insane as well as old.
    Unbearable, your saying that the gods
    take any kindly forethought for this corpse.   270
    Would it be they had hidden him away,
    honoring his good service, his who came
    to burn their pillared temples and their wealth,
    even their land, and break apart their laws?
    Or have you seen them honor wicked men?   275
    It isn't so.
    No, from the first there were some men in town
    who took the edict hard, and growled against me,
    who hid the fact that they were rearing back,
    not rightly in the yoke, no way my friends.   280
    These are the people—oh it's clear to me—
    who have bribed these men and brought about the deed.
    No current custom among men as bad
    as silver currency. This destroys the state;
    this drives men from their homes; this wicked teacher   285
    drives solid citizens to acts of shame.
    It shows men how to practice infamy
    and know the deeds of all unholiness.
    Every least hireling who helped in this
    brought about then the sentence he shall have.   290
    But further, as I still revere great Zeus,

understand this, I tell you under oath,
if you don't find the very man whose hands
buried the corpse, bring him for me to see,
not death alone shall be enough for you   295
till living, hanging, you make clear the crime.
For any future grabbings you'll have learned
where to get pay, and that it doesn't pay
to squeeze a profit out of every source.
For you'll have felt that more men come to doom   300
through dirty profits than are kept by them.

Guard: May I say something? Or just turn and go?

Creon: Aren't you aware your speech is most unwelcome?

Guard: Does it annoy your hearing or your mind?

Creon: Why are you out to allocate my pain?   305

Guard: The doer hurts your mind. I hurt your ears.

Creon: You are a quibbling rascal through and through.

Guard: But anyhow I never did the deed.

Creon: And you the man who sold your mind for money!

Guard: Oh!   310
    How terrible to guess, and guess at lies!

Creon: Go pretty up your guesswork. If you don't
    show me the doers you will have to say
    that wicked payments work their own revenge.

Guard: Indeed, I pray he's found, but yes or no,   315
    taken or not as luck may settle it,
    you won't see me returning to this place.
    Saved when I neither hoped nor thought to be,
    I owe the gods a mighty debt of thanks.

(Creon enters the palace. The Guard leaves by the way he came.)

Chorus: Many the wonders but nothing walks stranger than man.   320
    This thing crosses the sea in the winter's storm,
    making his path through the roaring waves.
    And she, the greatest of gods, the earth—
    ageless she is, and unwearied—he wears her away
    as the ploughs go up and down from year to year   325
    and his mules turn up the soil.

    Gay nations of birds he snares and leads,
    wild beast tribes and the salty brood of the sea,
    with the twisted mesh of his nets, this clever man.
    He controls with craft the beasts of the open air,   330
    walkers on hills. The horse with his shaggy mane
    he holds and harnesses, yoked about the neck,
    and the strong bull of the mountain.

    Language, and thought like the wind
    and the feelings that make the town,   335

he has taught himself, and shelter against the cold,
refuge from rain. He can always help himself.
He faces no future helpless. There's only death
that he cannot find an escape from. He has contrived
refuge from illnesses once beyond all cure. 340

Clever beyond all dreams
the inventive craft that he has
which may drive him one time or another to well or ill.
When he honors the laws of the land and the gods' sworn right
high indeed is his city; but stateless the man 345
who dares to dwell with dishonor. Not by my fire,
never to share my thoughts, who does these things.

(*The Guard enters with Antigone.*)

My mind is split at this awful sight.
I know her. I cannot deny
Antigone is here. 350
Alas, the unhappy girl,
her unhappy father's child.
Oh what is the meaning of this?
It cannot be you that they bring
for breaking the royal law, 355
caught in open shame.

Guard: This is the woman who has done the deed.
We caught her at the burying. Where's the king?

(*Creon enters.*)

Chorus: Back from the house again just when he's needed.
Creon: What must I measure up to? What has happened? 360
Guard: Lord, one should never swear off anything.
Afterthought makes the first resolve a liar.
I could have vowed I wouldn't come back here
after your threats, after the storm I faced.
But joy that comes beyond the wildest hope 365
is bigger than all other pleasure known.
I'm here, though I swore not to be, and bring
this girl. We caught her burying the dead.
This time we didn't need to shake the lots;
mine was the luck, all mine. 370
So now, lord, take her, you, and question her
and prove her as you will. But I am free.
And I deserve full clearance on this charge.
Creon: Explain the circumstance of the arrest.
Guard: She was burying the man. You have it all. 375
Creon: Is this the truth? And do you grasp its meaning?

Guard: I saw her burying the very corpse
    you had forbidden. Is this adequate?
Creon: How was she caught and taken in the act?
Guard: It was like this: when we got back again   380
    struck with those dreadful threatenings of yours,
    we swept away the dust that hid the corpse.
    We stripped it back to slimy nakedness.
    And then we sat to windward on the hill
    so as to dodge the smell.   385
    We poked each other up with growling threats
    if anyone was careless of his work.
    For some time this went on, till it was noon.
    The sun was high and hot. Then from the earth
    up rose a dusty whirlwind to the sky,   390
    filling the plain, smearing the forest-leaves,
    clogging the upper air. We shut our eyes,
    sat and endured the plague the gods had sent.
    So the storm left us after a long time.
    We saw the girl. She cried the sharp and shrill   395
    cry of a bitter bird which sees the nest
    bare where the young birds lay.
    So this same girl, seeing the body stripped,
    cried with great groanings, cried a dreadful curse
    upon the people who had done the deed.   400
    Soon in her hands she brought the thirsty dust,
    and holding high a pitcher of wrought bronze
    she poured the three libations for the dead.
    We saw this and surged down. We trapped her fast;
    and she was calm. We taxed her with the deeds   405
    both past and present. Nothing was denied.
    And I was glad, and yet I took it hard.
    One's own escape from trouble makes one glad;
    but bringing friends to trouble is hard grief.
    Still, I care less for all these second thoughts   410
    than for the fact that I myself am safe.
Creon: You there, whose head is drooping to the ground,
    do you admit this, or deny you did it?
Antigone: I say I did it and I don't deny it.
Creon (to the guard): Take yourself off wherever you wish to go   415
    free of a heavy charge.
Creon (to Antigone): You—tell me not at length but in a word.
    You knew the order not to do this thing?
Antigone: I knew, of course I knew. The word was plain.
Creon: And still you dared to overstep these laws?   420
Antigone: For me it was not Zeus who made that order.
    Nor did that Justice who lives with the gods below
    mark out such laws to hold among mankind.

Nor did I think your orders were so strong
that you, a mortal man, could over-run   425
the gods' unwritten and unfailing laws.
Not now, nor yesterday's, they always live,
and no one knows their origin in time.
So not through fear of any man's proud spirit
would I be likely to neglect these laws,   430
draw on myself the gods' sure punishment.
I knew that I must die; how could I not?
even without your warning. If I die
before my time, I say it is a gain.
Who lives in sorrows many as are mine   435
how shall he not be glad to gain his death?
And so, for me to meet this fate, no grief.
But if I left that corpse, my mother's son,
dead and unburied I'd have cause to grieve
as now I grieve not.   440
And if you think my acts are foolishness
the foolishness may be in a fool's eye.
Chorus: The girl is bitter. She's her father's child.
She cannot yield to trouble; nor could he.
Creon: These rigid spirits are the first to fall.   445
The strongest iron, hardened in the fire,
most often ends in scraps and shatterings.
Small curbs bring raging horses back to terms.
Slave to his neighbor, who can think of pride?
This girl was expert in her insolence   450
when she broke bounds beyond established law.
Once she had done it, insolence the second,
to boast her doing, and to laugh in it.
I am no man and she the man instead
if she can have this conquest without pain.   455
She is my sister's child, but were she child
of closer kin than any at my hearth,
she and her sister should not so escape
their death and doom. I charge Ismene too.
She shared the planning of this burial.   460
Call her outside. I saw her in the house,
maddened, no longer mistress of herself.
The sly intent betrays itself sometimes
before the secret plotters work their wrong.
I hate it too when someone caught in crime   465
then wants to make it seem a lovely thing.
Antigone: Do you want more than my arrest and death?
Creon: No more than that. For that is all I need.
Antigone: Why are you waiting? Nothing that you say
fits with my thought. I pray it never will.   470

Nor will you ever like to hear my words.
And yet what greater glory could I find
than giving my own brother funeral?
All these would say that they approved my act
did fear not mute them. 475
(A king is fortunate in many ways,
and most, that he can act and speak at will.)

Creon: None of these others see the case this way.

Antigone: They see, and do not say. You have them cowed.

Creon: And you are not ashamed to think alone? 480

Antigone: No, I am not ashamed. When was it shame
   to serve the children of my mother's womb?

Creon: It was not your brother who died against him, then?

Antigone: Full brother, on both sides, my parents' child.

Creon: Your act of grace, in his regard, is crime. 485

Antigone: The corpse below would never say it was.

Creon: When you honor him and the criminal just alike?

Antigone: It was a brother, not a slave, who died.

Creon: Died to destroy this land the other guarded.

Antigone: Death yearns for equal law for all the dead. 490

Creon: Not that the good and bad draw equal shares.

Antigone: Who knows that this is holiness below?

Creon: Never the enemy, even in death, a friend.

Antigone: I cannot share in hatred, but in love.

Creon: Then go down there, if you must love, and love 495
   the dead. No woman rules me while I live.

(Ismene is brought from the palace under guard.)

Chorus: Look there! Ismene is coming out.
   She loves her sister and mourns,
   with clouded brow and bloodied cheeks,
   tears on her lovely face. 500

Creon: You, lurking like a viper in the house,
   who sucked me dry. I looked the other way
   while twin destruction planned against the throne.
   Now tell me, do you say you shared this deed?
   Or will you swear you didn't even know? 505

Ismene: I did the deed, if she agrees I did.
   I am accessory and share the blame.

Antigone: Justice will not allow this. You did not
   wish for a part, nor did I give you one.

Ismene: You are in trouble, and I'm not ashamed 510
   to sail beside you into suffering.

Antigone: Death and the dead, they know whose act it was.
   I cannot love a friend whose love is words.

Ismene: Sister, I pray, don't fence me out from honor,
   from death with you, and honor done the dead. 515

Antigone: Don't die along with me, nor make your own
   that which you did not do. My death's enough.
Ismene: When you are gone what life can be my friend?
Antigone: Love Creon. He's your kinsman and your care.
Ismene: Why hurt me, when it does yourself no good?   520
Antigone: I also suffer, when I laugh at you.
Ismene: What further service can I do you now?
Antigone: To save yourself. I shall not envy you.
Ismene: Alas for me. Am I outside your fate?
Antigone: Yes. For you chose to live when I chose death.   525
Ismene: At least I was not silent. You were warned.
Antigone: Some will have thought you wiser. Some will not.
Ismene: And yet the blame is equal for us both.
Antigone: Take heart. You live. My life died long ago.
   And that has made me fit to help the dead.   530
Creon: One of these girls has shown her lack of sense
   just now. The other had it from her birth.
Ismene: Yes, lord. When people fall in deep distress
   their native sense departs, and will not stay.
Creon: You chose your mind's distraction when you chose   535
   to work out wickedness with this wicked girl.
Ismene: What life is there for me to live without her?
Creon: Don't speak of her. For she is here no more.
Ismene: But will you kill your own son's promised bride?
Creon: Oh, there are other furrows for his plough.   540
Ismene: But where the closeness that has bound these two?
Creon: Not for my sons will I choose wicked wives.
Ismene: Dear Haemon, your father robs you of your rights.
Creon: You and your marriage trouble me too much.
Ismene: You will take away his bride from your own son?   545
Creon: Yes. Death will help me break this marriage off.
Chorus: It seems determined that the girl must die.
Creon: You helped determine it. Now, no delay!
   Slaves, take them in. They must be women now.
   No more free running.   550
   Even the bold will fly when they see Death
   drawing in close enough to end their life.

(Antigone and Ismene are taken inside.)

Chorus: Fortunate they whose lives have no taste of pain.
   For those whose house is shaken by the gods
   escape no kind of doom. It extends to all the kin   555
   like the wave that comes when the winds of Thrace
   run over the dark of the sea.
   The black sand of the bottom is brought from the depth;
   the beaten capes sound back with a hollow cry.

Ancient the sorrow of Labdacus' house° I know.   560
Dead men's grief comes back, and falls on grief.
No generation can free the next.
One of the gods will strike. There is no escape.
So now the light goes out
for the house of Oedipus, while the bloody knife   565
cuts the remaining root. Folly and Fury have done this.

What madness of man, O Zeus, can bind your power?
Not sleep can destroy it who ages all,
nor the weariless months the gods have set. Unaged in time
monarch you rule of Olympus' gleaming light.   570
Near time, far future, and the past,
one law controls them all:
any greatness in human life brings doom.

Wandering hope brings help to many men.
But others she tricks from their giddy loves,   575
and her quarry knows nothing until he has walked into flame.
Word of wisdom it was when someone said,
"The bad becomes the good
to him a god would doom."
Only briefly is that one from under doom.   580

(Haemon enters from the side.)

    Here is your one surviving son.
    Does he come in grief at the fate of his bride,
    in pain that he's tricked of his wedding?

Creon: Soon we shall know more than a seer could tell us.
    Son, have you heard the vote condemned your bride?   585
    And are you here, maddened against your father,
    or are we friends, whatever I may do?
Haemon: My father, I am yours. You keep me straight
    with your good judgment, which I shall ever follow.
    Nor shall a marriage count for more with me   590
    than your kind leading.
Creon: There's my good boy. So should you hold at heart
    and stand behind your father all the way.
    It is for this men pray they may beget
    households of dutiful obedient sons,   595
    who share alike in punishing enemies,
    and give due honor to their father's friends.
    Whoever breeds a child that will not help
    what has he sown but trouble for himself,

560 *Labdacus' house:* the family of Oedipus.

and for his enemies laughter full and free? 600
Son, do not let your lust mislead your mind,
all for a woman's sake, for well you know
how cold the thing he takes into his arms
who has a wicked woman for his wife.
What deeper wounding than a friend no friend? 605
Oh spit her forth forever, as your foe.
Let the girl marry somebody in Hades.
Since I have caught her in the open act,
the only one in town who disobeyed,
I shall not now proclaim myself a liar, 610
but kill her. Let her sing her song of Zeus
who guards the kindred.
If I allow disorder in my house
I'd surely have to license it abroad.
A man who deals in fairness with his own, 615
he can make manifest justice in the state.
But he who crosses law, or forces it,
or hopes to bring the rulers under him,
shall never have a word of praise from me.
The man the state has put in place must have 620
obedient hearing to his least command
when it is right, and even when it's not.
He who accepts this teaching I can trust,
ruler, or ruled, to function in his place,
to stand his ground even in the storm of spears, 625
a mate to trust in battle at one's side.
There is no greater wrong than disobedience.
This ruins cities, this tears down our homes,
this breaks the battle-front in panic-rout.
If men live decently it is because 630
discipline saves their very lives for them.
So I must guard the men who yield to order,
not let myself be beaten by a woman.
Better, if it must happen, that a man
should overset me. 635
I won't be called weaker than womankind.
Chorus: We think—unless our age is cheating us—
that what you say is sensible and right.
Haemon: Father, the gods have given men good sense,
the only sure possession that we have. 640
I couldn't find the words in which to claim
that there was error in your late remarks.
Yet someone else might bring some further light.
Because I am your son I must keep watch
on all men's doing where it touches you, 645
their speech, and most of all, their discontents.

Your presence frightens any common man
from saying things you would not care to hear.
But in dark corners I have heard them say
how the whole town is grieving for this girl,   650
unjustly doomed, if ever woman was,
to die in shame for glorious action done.
She would not leave her fallen, slaughtered brother
there, as he lay, unburied, for the birds
and hungry dogs to make an end of him.   655
Isn't her real desert a golden prize?
This is the undercover speech in town.
Father, your welfare is my greatest good.
What loveliness in life for any child
outweighs a father's fortune and good fame?   660
And so a father feels his children's faring.
Then, do not have one mind, and one alone
that only your opinion can be right.
Who ever thinks that he alone is wise,
his eloquence, his mind, above the rest,   665
come the unfolding, shows his emptiness.
A man, though wise, should never be ashamed
of learning more, and must unbend his mind.
Have you not seen the trees beside the torrent,
the ones that bend them saving every leaf,   670
while the resistant perish root and branch?
And so the ship that will not slacken sail,
the sheet drawn tight, unyielding, overturns.
She ends the voyage with her keel on top.
No, yield your wrath, allow a change of stand.   675
Young as I am, if I may give advice,
I'd say it would be best if men were born
perfect in wisdom, but that failing this
(which often fails) it can be no dishonor
to learn from others when they speak good sense.   680
Chorus: Lord, if your son has spoken to the point
   you should take his lesson. He should do the same.
   Both sides have spoken well.
Creon: At my age I'm to school my mind by his?
   This boy instructor is my master, then?   685
Haemon: I urge no wrong. I'm young, but you should watch
   my actions, not my years, to judge of me.
Creon: A loyal action, to respect disorder?
Haemon: I wouldn't urge respect for wickedness.
Creon: You don't think she is sick with that disease?   690
Haemon: Your fellow-citizens maintain she's not.
Creon: Is the town to tell me how I ought to rule?
Haemon: Now there you speak just like a boy yourself.

Creon: Am I to rule by other mind than mine?
Haemon: No city is property of a single man. 695
Creon: But custom gives possession to the ruler.
Haemon: You'd rule a desert beautifully alone.
Creon (to the Chorus): It seems he's firmly on the woman's side.
Haemon: If you're a woman. It is you I care for.
Creon: Wicked, to try conclusions with your father. 700
Haemon: When you conclude unjustly, so I must.
Creon: Am I unjust, when I respect my office?
Haemon: You tread down the gods' due. Respect is gone.
Creon: Your mind is poisoned. Weaker than a woman!
Haemon: At least you'll never see me yield to shame. 705
Creon: Your whole long argument is but for her.
Haemon: And you, and me, and for the gods below.
Creon: You shall not marry her while she's alive.
Haemon: Then she shall die. Her death will bring another.
Creon: Your boldness has made progress. Threats, indeed! 710
Haemon: No threat, to speak against your empty plan.
Creon: Past due, sharp lessons for your empty brain.
Haemon: If you weren't father, I should call you mad.
Creon: Don't flatter me with "father," you woman's slave.
Haemon: You wish to speak but never wish to hear. 715
Creon: You think so? By Olympus, you shall not
    revile me with these tauntings and go free.
    Bring out the hateful creature; she shall die
    full in his sight, close at her bridegroom's side.
Haemon: Not at my side her death, and you will not 720
    ever lay eyes upon my face again.
    Find other friends to rave with after this.

(Haemon leaves, by one of the side entrances.)

Chorus: Lord, he has gone with all the speed of rage.
    When such a man is grieved his mind is hard.
Creon: Oh, let him go, plan superhuman action. 725
    In any case the girls shall not escape.
Chorus: You plan for both the punishment of death?
Creon: Not her who did not do it. You are right.
Chorus: And what death have you chosen for the other?
Creon: To take her where the foot of man comes not. 730
    There shall I hide her in a hollowed cave
    living, and leave her just so much to eat
    as clears the city from the guilt of death.
    There, if she prays to Death, the only god
    of her respect, she may manage not to die. 735
    Or she may learn at last and even then
    how much too much her labor for the dead.

(Creon returns to the palace.)

Chorus: Love unconquered in fight, love who falls on our havings.
    You rest in the bloom of a girl's unwithered face.
    You cross the sea, you are known in the wildest lairs.   740
    Not the immortal gods can fly,
    nor men of a day. Who has you within him is mad.
    You twist the minds of the just. Wrong they pursue and are ruined.
    You made this quarrel of kindred before us now.
    Desire looks clear from the eyes of a lovely bride: 745
    power as strong as the founded world.
    For there is the goddess at play with whom no man can fight.

(Antigone is brought from the palace under guard.)

    Now I am carried beyond all bounds.
    My tears will not be checked.
    I see Antigone depart   750
    to the chamber where all men sleep.

Antigone: Men of my fathers' land, you see me go
    my last journey. My last sight of the sun,
    then never again. Death who brings all to sleep
    takes me alive to the shore   755
    of the river underground.
    Not for me was the marriage-hymn, nor will anyone start the song
    at a wedding of mine. Acheron° is my mate.
Chorus: With praise as your portion you go
    in fame to the vault of the dead.   760
    Untouched by wasting disease,
    not paying the price of the sword,
    of your own motion you go.
    Alone among mortals will you descend
    in life to the house of Death.   765
Antigone: Pitiful was the death that stranger died,
    our queen once, Tantalus' daughter°. The rock
    it covered her over, like stubborn ivy it grew.
    Still, as she wastes, the rain
    and snow companion her.   770
    Pouring down from her mourning eyes comes the water that soaks the
       stone.
    My own putting to sleep a god has planned like hers.
Chorus: God's child and god she was.
    We are born to death.

---

758 *Acheron:* river in Hades, domain of the dead.   767 *that stranger . . .* Tantalus' daughter: in mythology, Niobe, who when her children were slain wept so copiously that she was transformed to a stone on Mount Sipylus. Her tears became the mountain's streams.

Yet even in death you will have your fame, 775
to have gone like a god to your fate,
in living and dying alike.
Antigone: Laughter against me now. In the name of our fathers' gods,
could you not wait till I went? Must affront be thrown in my face?
O city of wealthy men. 780
I call upon Dirce's spring,
I call upon Thebe's grove in the armored plain,
to be my witnesses, how with no friend's mourning,
by what decree I go to the fresh-made prison-tomb.
Alive to the place of corpses, an alien still, 785
never at home with the living nor with the dead.
Chorus: You went to the furthest verge
of daring, but there you found
the high foundation of justice, and fell.
Perhaps you are paying your father's pain. 790
Antigone: You speak of my darkest thought, my pitiful father's fame,
spread through all the world, and the doom that haunts our house,
the royal house of Thebes.
My mother's marriage-bed.
Destruction where she lay with her husband-son, 795
my father. These are my parents and I their child.
I go to stay with them. My curse is to die unwed.
My brother, you found your fate when you found your bride,
found it for me as well. Dead, you destroy my life.
Chorus: You showed respect for the dead. 800
So we for you: but power
is not to be thwarted so.
Your self-sufficiency has brought you down.
Antigone: Unwept, no wedding-song, unfriended, now I go
the road laid down for me. 805
No longer shall I see this holy light of the sun.
No friend to bewail my fate.

(Creon enters from the palace.)

Creon: When people sing the dirge for their own deaths
ahead of time, nothing will break them off
if they can hope that this will buy delay. 810
Take her away at once, and open up
the tomb I spoke of. Leave her there alone.
There let her choose: death, or a buried life.
No stain of guilt upon us in this case,
but she is exiled from our life on earth. 815
Antigone: O tomb, O marriage-chamber, hollowed out
house that will watch forever, where I go.

To my own people, who are mostly there;
Persephone° has taken them to her.
Last of them all, ill-fated past the rest,   820
shall I descend, before my course is run.
Still when I get there I may hope to find
I come as a dear friend to my dear father,
to you, my mother, and my brother too.
All three of you have known my hand in death.   825
I washed your bodies, dressed them for the grave,
poured out the last libation at the tomb.
Last, Polyneices knows the price I pay
for doing final service to his corpse.
And yet the wise will know my choice was right.   830
Had I had children or their father dead,
I'd let them moulder. I should not have chosen
in such a case to cross the state's decree.
What is the law that lies behind these words?
One husband gone, I might have found another,   835
or a child from a new man in first child's place,
but with my parents hid away in death,
no brother, ever, could spring up for me.
Such was the law by which I honored you.
But Creon thought the doing was a crime,   840
a dreadful daring, brother of my heart.
So now he takes and leads me out by force.
No marriage-bed, no marriage-song for me,
and since no wedding, so no child to rear.
I go, without a friend, struck down by fate,   845
live to the hollow chambers of the dead.
What divine justice have I disobeyed?
Why, in my misery, look to the gods for help?
Can I call any of them my ally?
I stand convicted of impiety,   850
the evidence my pious duty done.
Should the gods think that this is righteousness,
in suffering I'll see my error clear.
But if it is the others who are wrong
I wish them no greater punishment than mine.   855
Chorus: The same tempest of mind
    as ever, controls the girl.
Creon: Therefore her guards shall regret
    the slowness with which they move.
Antigone: That word comes close to death.   860
Creon: You are perfectly right in that.

819 *Persephone:* whom Pluto, god of the underworld, abducted to be his queen. (See D. H. Lawrence's
poem "Bavarian Gentians," page 715.)

Antigone: O town of my fathers in Thebe's land,
   O gods of our house.
   I am led away at last.
   Look, leaders of Thebes,   865
   I am last of your royal line.
   Look what I suffer, at whose command,
   because I respected the right.

(*Antigone is led away. The slow procession should begin during the preceding passage.*)

Chorus: Danaë° suffered too.
   She went from the light to the brass-built room,   870
   chamber and tomb together. Like you, poor child,
   she was of great descent, and more, she held and kept
   the seed of the golden rain which was Zeus.
   Fate has terrible power.
   You cannot escape it by wealth or war.   875
   No fort will keep it out, no ships outrun it.

   Remember the angry king,
   son of Dryas°, who raged at the god and paid,
   pent in a rock-walled prison. His bursting wrath
   slowly went down. As the terror of madness went,   880
   he learned of his frenzied attack on the god.
   Fool, he had tried to stop
   the dancing women possessed of god,
   the fire of Dionysus, the songs and flutes.

   Where the dark rocks divide   885
   sea from sea in Thrace
   is Salmydessus whose savage god°
   beheld the terrible blinding wounds
   dealt to Phineus' sons by their father's wife°.
   Dark the eyes that looked to avenge their mother.   890
   Sharp with her shuttle she struck, and blooded her hands.

   Wasting they wept their fate,
   settled when they were born
   to Cleopatra, unhappy queen.

869 *Danae:* In legend, when an oracle told Acrisius, king of Argos, that his daughter Danae would bear a son who would grow up to slay him, he locked the princess into a chamber made of bronze lest any man impregnate her. But Zeus entered Danae's prison in a shower of gold. The resultant child, Perseus, was accidentally to fulfill the prophecy by killing Acrisius with an ill-aimed discus throw.   877–878 *angry king, son of Dryas:* Lycurgus of Thrace, whom Dionysus caused to go mad.   887 *Salmydessus . . . savage god:* Ares, god of war, said to gloat over bloodshed. 888–889 *wounds dealt to Phineus' sons . . . wife:* King Phineus cast off his first wife Cleopatra (not the later Egyptian queen but the daughter of Boreas, god of the north wind) and imprisoned her in a cave. Out of hatred for Cleopatra, Eidothea, second wife of the king, blinded her stepsons.

She was a princess too, of an ancient house.   895
reared in the cave of the wild north wind, her father.
Half a goddess but, child, she suffered like you.

(*Enter, from the side Teiresias, the blind prophet, led by a boy attendant.*)

Teiresias: Elders of Thebes, we two have come one road,
    two of us looking through one pair of eyes.
    This is the way of walking for the blind.   900
Creon: Teiresias, what news has brought you here?
Teiresias: I'll tell you. You in turn must trust the prophet.
Creon: I've always been attentive to your counsel.
Teiresias: And therefore you have steered this city straight.
Creon: So I can say how helpful you have been.   905
Teiresias: But now you are balanced on a razor's edge.
Creon: What is it? How I shudder at your words!
Teiresias: You'll know, when you hear the signs that I have marked.
    I sat where every bird of heaven comes
    in my old place of augury, and heard   910
    bird-cries I'd never known. They screeched about
    goaded by madness, inarticulate.
    I marked that they were tearing one another
    with claws of murder. I could hear the wing-beats.
    I was afraid, so straight away I tried   915
    burnt sacrifice upon the flaming altar.
    No fire caught my offerings. Slimy ooze
    dripped on the ashes, smoked and sputtered there.
    Gall burst its bladder, vanished into vapor;
    the fat dripped from the bones and would not burn.   920
    These are the omens of the rites that failed,
    as my boy here has told me. He's my guide
    as I am guide to others.
    Why has this sickness struck against the state?
    Through your decision.   925
    All of the altars of the town are choked
    with leavings of the dogs and birds; their feast
    was on that fated, fallen Polyneices.
    So the gods will have no offering from us,
    not prayer, nor flame of sacrifice. The birds   930
    will not cry out a sound I can distinguish,
    gorged with the greasy blood of that dead man.
    Think of these things, my son. All men may err
    but error once committed, he's no fool
    nor yet unfortunate, who gives up his stiffness   935
    and cures the trouble he has fallen in.
    Stubbornness and stupidity are twins.
    Yield to the dead. Why goad him where he lies?
    What use to kill the dead a second time?

I speak for your own good. And I am right. 940
Learning from a wise counsellor is not pain
if what he speaks are profitable words.
Creon: Old man, you all, like bowmen at a mark,
have bent your brows at me. I've had my share
of seers. I've been an item in your accounts. 945
Make profit, trade in Lydian silver-gold,
pure gold of India; that's your chief desire.
But you will never cover up that corpse.
Not if the very eagles tear their food
from him, and leave it at the throne of Zeus. 950
I wouldn't give him up for burial
in fear of that pollution. For I know
no mortal being can pollute the gods.
O old Teiresias, human beings fall;
the clever ones the furthest, when they plead 955
a shameful case so well in hope of profit.
Teiresias: Alas!
What man can tell me, has he thought at all . . .
Creon: What hackneyed saw° is coming from your lips?
Teiresias: How better than all wealth is sound good counsel.
Creon: And so is folly worse than anything. 960
Teiresias: And you're infected with that same disease.
Creon: I'm reluctant to be uncivil to a seer . . .
Teiresias: You're that already. You have said I lie.
Creon: Well, the whole crew of seers are money-mad.
Teiresias: And the whole tribe of tyrants grab at gain. 965
Creon: Do you realize you are talking to a king?
Teiresias: I know. Who helped you save this town you hold?
Creon: You're a wise seer, but you love wickedness.
Teiresias: You'll bring me to speak the unspeakable, very soon.
Creon: Well, speak it out. But do not speak for profit. 970
Teiresias: No, there's no profit in my words for you.
Creon: You'd better realize that you can't deliver
my mind, if you should sell it, to the buyer.
Teiresias: Know well, the sun will not have rolled its course
many more days, before you come to give 975
corpse for these corpses, child of your own loins.
For you've confused the upper and lower worlds.
You sent a life to settle in a tomb;
you keep up here that which belongs below
the corpse unburied, robbed of its release. 980
Not you, nor any god that rules on high
can claim him now.
You rob the nether gods of what is theirs.

958 *hackneyed saw:* stale proverb.

So the pursuing horrors lie in wait
to track you down. The Furies° sent by Hades   985
and by all gods will even you with your victims.
Now say that I am bribed! At no far time
shall men and women wail within your house.
And all the cities that you fought in war
whose sons had burial from wild beasts, or dogs,   990
or birds that brought the stench of your great wrong
back to each hearth, they move against you now.
A bowman, as you said, I send my shafts,
now you have moved me, straight. You'll feel the wound.
Boy, take me home now. Let him spend his rage   995
on younger men, and learn to calm his tongue,
and keep a better mind than now he does.

(Exit.)

Chorus: Lord, he has gone. Terrible prophecies!
    And since the time when I first grew grey hair
    his sayings to the city have been true.   1000
Creon: I also know this. And my mind is torn.
    To yield is dreadful. But to stand against him.
    Dreadful to strike my spirit to destruction.
Chorus: Now you must come to counsel, and take advice.
Creon: What must I do? Speak, and I shall obey.   1005
Chorus: Go free the maiden from that rocky house.
    Bury the dead who lies in readiness.
Creon: This is your counsel? You would have me yield?
Chorus: Quick as you can. The gods move very fast
    when they bring ruin on misguided men.   1010
Creon: How hard, abandonment of my desire.
    But I can fight necessity no more.
Chorus: Do it yourself. Leave it to no one else.
Creon: I'll go at once. Come, followers, to your work.
    You that are here round up the other fellows.   1015
    Take axes with you, hurry to that place
    that overlooks us.
    Now my decision has been overturned
    shall I, who bound her, set her free myself.
    I've come to fear it's best to hold the laws   1020
    of old tradition to the end of life.

(Exit.)

Chorus: God of the many names, Semele's golden child,
    child of Olympian thunder, Italy's lord.

---

985 *Furies:* in Greek mythology, dreaded goddesses of vengeance. They were depicted as hideous hags
with batlike wings, the heads of dogs, and snakes for hair.

Lord of Eleusis, where all men come
to mother Demeter's plain°.   1025
Bacchus, who dwell in Thebes,
by Ismenus' running water,
where wild Bacchic women are at home,
on the soil of the dragon seed.
Seen in the glaring flame, high on the double mount,   1030
with the nymphs of Parnassus at play on the hill,
seen by Kastalia's flowing stream°.

You come from the ivied heights,
from green Euboea's shore.
In immortal words we cry   1035
your name, lord, who watch the ways,
the many ways of Thebes.

This is your city, honored beyond the rest,
the town of your mother's miracle-death°.
Now, as we wrestle our grim disease,   1040
come with healing step from Parnassus' slope
or over the moaning sea.

Leader in dance of the fire-pulsing stars,
overseer of the voices of night,
child of Zeus, be manifest,   1045
with due companionship of Maenad maids°
whose cry is but your name.

(Enter one of those who left with Creon, as messenger.)

Messenger: Neighbors of Cadmus, and Amphion's house°,
there is no kind of state in human life
which I now dare to envy or to blame.   1050
Luck sets it straight, and luck she overturns
the happy or unhappy day by day.
No prophecy can deal with men's affairs.
Creon was envied once, as I believe,
for having saved this city from its foes   1055
and having got full power in this land.

1022–1025 *God of the many names . . . Demeter's plain:* Dionysus, or Bacchus. He was the son of Zeus by Semele, daughter of Cadmus, legendary founder of Thebes. "Lord of Eleusis" is another of his names: he was worshipped at Eleusis, a town northwest of Athens.   1031–1032 *nymphs of Parnassus . . . Kastalia's flowing stream:* In the temple of Delphi, at the foot of Mount Parnassus, priestesses of Dionysus used the waters of a spring, Kastalia, in rites of purification.   1039 *mother's miracle-death:* Semele, mother of Dionysus, burned to death at the sight of Zeus when he appeared before her not in mortal form, but in the form of a god.   1046 *Maenad maids:* women of Thebes said to worship Dionysus with orgiastic rites.   1048 *Amphion's house:* a name for Thebes. Amphion, a son of Zeus, had built a wall around the city by playing so beautifully on his lyre that the charmed stones leaped into their slots.

He steered it well. And he had noble sones.
Now everything is gone.
Yes, when a man has lost all happiness,
he's not alive. Call him a breathing corpse.   1060
Be very rich at home. Live as a king.
But once your joy has gone, though these are left
they are smoke's shadow to lost happiness.
Chorus: What is the grief of princes that you bring?
Messenger: They're dead. The living are responsible.   1065
Chorus: Who died? Who did the murder? Tell us now.
Messenger: Haemon is gone. One of his kin drew blood.
Chorus: But whose arm struck? His father's or his own?
Messenger: He killed himself. His blood is on his father.
Chorus: Seer, all too true the prophecy you told!   1070
Messenger: This is the state of things. Now make your plans.

(Enter, from the palace, Eurydice.)

Chorus: Eurydice is with us now, I see.
   Creon's poor wife. She may have come by chance.
   She may have heard something about her son.
Eurydice: I heard your talk as I was coming out   1075
   to greet the goddess Pallas° with my prayer.
   And as I moved the bolts that held the door
   I heard of my own sorrow.
   I fell back fainting in my women's arms.
   But say again just what the news you bring.   1080
   I, whom you speak to, have known grief before.
Messenger: Dear lady, I was there, and I shall tell,
   leaving out nothing of the true account.
   Why should I make it soft for you with tales
   to prove myself a liar? Truth is right.   1085
   I followed your husband to the plain's far edge,
   where Polyneices' corpse was lying still
   unpitied. The dogs had torn him all apart.
   We prayed the goddess of all journeyings,
   and Pluto, that they turn their wrath to kindness,   1090
   we gave the final purifying bath,
   then burned the poor remains on new-cut boughs,
   and heaped a high mound of his native earth.
   Then turned we to the maiden's rocky bed,
   death's hollow marriage-chamber.   1095
   But, still far off, one of us heard a voice
   in keen lament by that unblest abode.
   He ran and told the master. As Creon came
   he heard confusion crying. He groaned and spoke:

1076 *Pallas:* Pallas Athene, goddess of wisdom.

"Am I a prophet now, and do I tread   1100
the saddest of all roads I ever trod?
My son's voice crying! Servants, run up close,
stand by the tomb and look, push through the crevice
where we built the pile of rock, right to the entry.
Find out if that is Haemon's voice I hear   1105
or if the gods are tricking me indeed."
We obeyed the order of our mournful master.
In the far corner of the tomb we saw
her, hanging by the neck, caught in a noose
of her own linen veiling.   1110
Haemon embraced her as she hung, and mourned
his bride's destruction, dead and gone below,
his father's actions, the unfated marriage.
When Creon saw him, he groaned terribly,
and went toward him, and called him with lament: 1115
"What have you done, what plan have you caught up,
what sort of suffering is killing you?
Come out, my child, I do beseech you, come!"
The boy looked at him with his angry eyes,
spat in his face and spoke no further word.   1120
He drew his sword, but as his father ran,
he missed his aim. Then the unhappy boy,
in anger at himself, leant on the blade.
It entered, half its length, into his side.
While he was conscious he embraced the maiden,   1125
holding her gently. Last, he gasped out blood,
red blood on her white cheek.
Corpse on a corpse he lies. He found his marriage.
Its celebration in the halls of Hades.
So he has made it very clear to men   1130
that to reject good counsel is a crime.

(Eurydice returns to the house.)

Chorus: What do you make of this? The queen has gone
    in silence. We know nothing of her mind.
Messenger: I wonder at her, too. But we can hope
    that she has gone to mourn her son within   1135
    with her own women, not before the town.
    She knows discretion. She will do no wrong.
Chorus: I am not sure. This muteness may portend
    as great disaster as a loud lament.
Messenger: I will go in and see if some deep plan   1140
    hides in her heart's wild pain. You may be right.
    There can be heavy danger in mute grief.

(The messenger goes into the house. Creon enters with his followers. They
are carrying Haemon's body on a bier.)

Chorus: But look, the king draws near.
    His own hand brings
    the witness of his crime,   1145
    the doom he brought on himself.
Creon: O crimes of my wicked heart,
    harshness bringing death.
    You see the killer, you see the kin he killed.
    My planning was all unblest.   1150
    Son, you have died too soon.
    Oh, you have gone away
    through my fault, not your own.
Chorus: You have learned justice, though it comes too late.
Creon: Yes, I have learned in sorrow. It was a god who struck,   1155
    who has weighted my head with disaster; he drove me to wild strange
    ways,
    his heavy heel on my joy.
    Oh sorrows, sorrows of men.

(Re-enter the messenger, from a side door of the palace.)

Messenger: Master, you hold one sorrow in your hands
    but you have more, stored up inside the house.   1160
Creon: What further suffering can come on me?
Messenger: Your wife has died. The dead man's mother in deed,
    poor soul, her wounds are fresh.
Creon: Hades, harbor of all,
    you have destroyed me now.   1165
    Terrible news to hear, horror the tale you tell.
    I was dead, and you kill me again.
    Boy, did I hear you right?
    Did you say the queen was dead,
    slaughter on slaughter heaped?   1170

(The central doors of the palace begin to open.)

Chorus: Now you can see. Concealment is all over.

(The doors are open, and the corpse of Eurydice is revealed.)

Creon: My second sorrow is here. Surely no fate remains
    which can strike me again. Just now, I held my son in my arms.
    And now I see her dead.
    Woe for the mother and son.   1175
Messenger: There, by the altar, dying on the sword,
    her eyes fell shut. She wept her older son
    who died before°, and this one. Last of all
    she cursed you as the killer of her children.

1177–1178 *older son who died before:* Megareus, Haimon's brother, slain in the unsuccessful attack
on Thebes.

Creon: I am mad with fear. Will no one strike   1180
    and kill me with cutting sword?
    Sorrowful, soaked in sorrow to the bone!
Messenger: Yes, for she held you guilty in the death
    of him before you, and the elder dead.
Creon: How did she die?
Messenger: Struck home at her own heart   1185
    when she had heard of Haemon's suffering.
Creon: This is my guilt, all mine. I killed you, I say it clear.
    Servants, take me away, out of the sight of men.
    I who am nothing more than nothing now.
Chorus: Your plan is good—if any good is left.   1190
    Best to cut short our sorrow.
Creon: Let me go, let me go. May death come quick,
    bringing my final day.
    O let me never see tomorrow's dawn.
Chorus: That is the future's. We must look to now.   1195
    What will be is in other hands than ours.
Creon: All my desire was in that prayer of mine.
Chorus: Pray not again. No mortal can escape
    the doom prepared for him.
Creon: Take me away at once, the frantic man who killed   1200
    my son, against my meaning. I cannot rest.
    My life is warped past cure. My fate has struck me down.

(Creon and his attendants enter the house.)

Chorus: Our happiness depends
    on wisdom all the way.
    The gods must have their due.   1205
    Great words by men of pride
    bring greater blows upon them.
    So wisdom comes to the old.

Wendy Wasserstein

THE MAN IN A CASE   1985

*Wendy Wasserstein was born in Brooklyn,
New York, in 1950, youngest of four children
of a textile manufacturer and his theater-loving
wife, both immigrants from central Europe.
She majored in history at Mount Holyoke College, studied creative writing at CCNY with
playwright Israel Horovitz, then went on to
Yale School of Drama. Her satiric plays, serious but crackling with one-liners, have explored
the successes and failures of the feminist move-*
ment. In 1977, Uncommon Woman and
Others, *submitted for her MFA at Yale, was
produced by the National Playwrights Conference at the O'Neill Theatre Center in Water-
ford, Connecticut (a springboard for new
playwrights, among them August Wilson).
Soon it opened Off Broadway, and was fol-*

Wendy Wasserstein

lowed there by Isn't It Romantic *(1980, revised version 1983) and* The Heidi Chronicles *(1988). When in 1989 this last play moved to Broadway, it won a Pulitzer Prize,
a Tony award, and the prize of the New York Critics Circle. Wasserstein has written
several screenplays for television, and the PBS series* Great Performances *has featured
her adaptation of John Cheever's story "The Sorrows of Gin." In 1990 she published
a book of essays,* Bachelor Girls. *She lives in a Greenwich Village flat and claims she
works best in a small space—"the closer it seems to a college dorm, the better." Commissioned by The Acting Company, a national repertory theater,* The Man in a Case *was
first staged as part of* Orchards, *seven plays by seven playwrights inspired by stories
of Anton Chekhov.*

Characters

Byelinkov
Varinka

A small garden in the village of Mironitski. 1898

Byelinkov is pacing. Enter Varinka out of breath.

Byelinkov: You are ten minutes late.
Varinka: The most amazing thing happened on my way over here. You know the
       woman who runs the grocery store down the road. She wears a black wig
       during the week, and a blond wig on Saturday nights. And she has the daughter

who married an engineer in Moscow who is doing very well thank you and is living, God bless them, in a three-room apartment. But he really is the most boring man in the world. All he talks about is his future and his station in life. Well, she heard we were to be married and she gave me this basket of apricots to give to you.

Byelinkov: That is a most amazing thing!

Varinka: She said to me, Varinka, you are marrying the most honorable man in the entire village. In this village he is the only man fit to speak with my son-in-law.

Byelinkov: I don't care for apricots. They give me hives.

Varinka: I can return them. I'm sure if I told her they give you hives she would give me a basket of raisins or a cake.

Byelinkov: I don't know this woman or her pompous son-in-law. Why would she give me her cakes?

Varinka: She adores you!

Byelinkov: She is emotionally loose.

Varinka: She adores you by reputation. Everyone adores you by reputation. I tell everyone I am to marry Byelinkov, the finest teacher in the county.

Byelinkov: You tell them this?

Varinka: If they don't tell me first.

Byelinkov: Pride can be an imperfect value.

Varinka: It isn't pride. It is the truth. You are a great man!

Byelinkov: I am the master of Greek and Latin at a local school at the end of the village of Mironitski.

(Varinka kisses him)

Varinka: And I am to be the master of Greek and Latin's wife!

Byelinkov: Being married requires a great deal of responsibility. I hope I am able to provide you with all that a married man must properly provide a wife.

Varinka: We will be very happy.

Byelinkov: Happiness is for children. We are entering into a social contract, an amicable agreement to provide us with a secure and satisfying future.

Varinka: You are so sweet! You are the sweetest man in the world!

Byelinkov: I'm a man set in his ways who saw a chance to provide himself with a small challenge.

Varinka: Look at you! Look at you! Your sweet round spectacles, your dear collar always starched, always raised, your perfectly pressed pants always creasing at right angles perpendicular to the floor, and my most favorite part, the sweet little galoshes, rain or shine, just in case. My Byelinkov, never taken by surprise. Except by me.

Byelinkov: You speak about me as if I were your pet.

Varinka: You are my pet! My little school mouse.

Byelinkov: A mouse?

Varinka: My sweetest dancing bear with galoshes, my little stale babka°.

Byelinkov: A stale babka?

babka: a cake flavored with rum, almonds, and raisins

Varinka: I am not Pushkin.

Byelinkov (Laughs): That depends what you think of Pushkin.

Varinka: You're smiling. I knew I could make you smile today.

Byelinkov: I am a responsible man. Every day I have for breakfast black bread, fruit, hot tea, and every day I smile three times. I am halfway into my translation of the *Aeneid* from classical Greek hexameter into Russian alexandrines. In twenty years I have never been late to school. I am a responsible man, but no dancing bear.

Varinka: Dance with me.

Byelinkov: Now? It is nearly four weeks before the wedding!

Varinka: It's a beautiful afternoon. We are in your garden. The roses are in full bloom.

Byelinkov: The roses have beetles.

Varinka: Dance with me!

Byelinkov: You are a demanding woman.

Varinka: You chose me. And right. And left. And turn. And right. And left.

Byelinkov: And turn. Give me your hand. You dance like a school mouse. It's a beautiful afternoon! We are in my garden. The roses are in full bloom! And turn. And turn. *(Twirls Varinka around)*

Varinka: I am the luckiest woman!

(Byelinkov stops dancing)

Why are you stopping?

Byelinkov: To place a lilac in your hair. Every year on this day I will place a lilac in your hair.

Varinka: Will you remember?

Byelinkov: I will write it down. *(Takes a notebook from his pocket)* Dear Byelinkov, don't forget the day a young lady, your bride, entered your garden, your peace, and danced on the roses. On that day every year you are to place a lilac in her hair.

Varinka: I love you.

Byelinkov: It is convenient we met.

Varinka: I love you.

Byelinkov: You are a girl.

Varinka: I am thirty.

Byelinkov: But you think like a girl. That is an attractive attribute.

Varinka: Do you love me?

Byelinkov: We've never spoken about housekeeping.

Varinka: I am an excellent housekeeper. I kept house for my family on the farm in Gadyatchsky. I can make a beetroot soup with tomatoes and aubergines which is so nice. Awfully awfully nice.

Byelinkov: You are fond of expletives.

Varinka: My beet soup, sir, is excellent!

Byelinkov: Please don't be cross. I too am an excellent housekeeper. I have a place for everything in the house. A shelf for each pot, a cubby for every spoon, a folder for favorite recipes. I have cooked for myself for twenty years. Though my beet soup is not outstanding, it is sufficient.

Varinka: I'm sure it's very good.

Byelinkov: No. It is awfully, awfully not. What I am outstanding in, however, what gives me greatest pleasure, is preserving those things which are left over. I wrap each tomato slice I haven't used in a wet cloth and place it in the coolest corner of the house. I have had my shoes for seven years because I wrap them in the galoshes you are so fond of. And every night before I go to sleep I wrap my bed in quilts and curtains so I never catch a draft.

Varinka: You sleep with curtains on your bed?

Byelinkov: I like to keep warm.

Varinka: I will make you a new quilt.

Byelinkov: No. No new quilt. That would be hazardous.

Varinka: It is hazardous to sleep under curtains.

Byelinkov: Varinka, I don't like change very much. If one works out the arithmetic the final fraction of improvement is at best less than an eighth of value over the total damage caused by disruption. I never thought of marrying till I saw your eyes dancing among the familiar faces at the headmaster's tea. I assumed I would grow old preserved like those which are left over, wrapped suitably in my case of curtains and quilts.

Varinka: Byelinkov, I want us to have dinners with friends and summer country visits. I want people to say, "Have you spent time with Varinka and Byelinkov? He is so happy now that they are married. She is just what he needed."

Byelinkov: You have already brought me some happiness. But I never was a sad man. Don't ever think I thought I was a sad man.

Varinka: My sweetest darling, you can be whatever you want! If you are sad, they'll say she talks all the time, and he is soft-spoken and kind.

Byelinkov: And if I am difficult?

Varinka: Oh, they'll say he is difficult because he is highly intelligent. All great men are difficult. Look at Lermontov, Tchaikovsky, Peter the Great.

Byelinkov: Ivan the Terrible°.

Varinka: Yes, him too.

Byelinkov: Why are you marrying me? I am none of these things.

Varinka: To me you are.

Byelinkov: You have imagined this. You have constructed an elaborate romance for yourself. Perhaps you are the great one. You are the one with the great imagination.

Varinka: Byelinkov, I am a pretty girl of thirty. You're right, I am not a woman. I have not made myself into a woman because I do not deserve that honor. Until I came to this town to visit my brother I lived on my family's farm. As the years passed I became younger and younger in fear that I would never marry. And it wasn't that I wasn't pretty enough or sweet enough, it was just that no man ever looked at me and saw a wife. I was not the woman who would be there when he came home. Until I met you I thought I would lie all my life and say I never married because I never met a man I loved. I will

Lermontov . . . Ivan the Terrible: Mikhail Lermontov (1814–41), poet and novelist; Peter Ilich Tchaikovsky (1840–93), composer; Peter I (1672–1725) and Ivan IV (1530–84), czars credited with modernizing Russia and raising the country to a world power.

love you, Byelinkov. And I will help you to love me. We deserve the life everyone else has. We deserve not to be different.

Byelinkov: Yes. We are the same as everyone else.

Varinka: Tell me you love me.

Byelinkov: I love you.

Varinka (Takes his hands): We will be very happy. I am very strong. (Pauses) It is time for tea.

Byelinkov: It is too early for tea. Tea is at half past the hour.

Varinka: Do you have heavy cream? It will be awfully nice with apricots.

Byelinkov: Heavy cream is too rich for teatime.

Varinka: But today is special. Today you placed a lilac in my hair. Write in your note pad. Every year we will celebrate with apricots and heavy cream. I will go to my brother's house and get some.

Byelinkov: But your brother's house is a mile from here.

Varinka: Today it is much shorter. Today my brother gave me his bicycle to ride. I will be back very soon.

Byelinkov: You rode to my house by bicycle! Did anyone see you?

Varinka: Of course. I had such fun. I told you I saw the grocery store lady with the son-in-law who is doing very well thank you in Moscow, and the headmaster's wife.

Byelinkov: You saw the headmaster's wife!

Varinka: She smiled at me.

Byelinkov: Did she laugh or smile?

Varinka: She laughed a little. She said, "My dear, you are very progressive to ride a bicycle." She said you and your fiancé Byelinkov must ride together sometime. I wonder if he'll take off his galoshes when he rides a bicycle.

Byelinkov: She said that?

Varinka: She adores you. We had a good giggle.

Byelinkov: A woman can be arrested for riding a bicycle. That is not progressive, it is a premeditated revolutionary act. Your brother must be awfully, awfully careful on behalf of your behavior. He has been careless—oh so careless—in giving you the bicycle.

Varinka: Dearest Byelinkov, you are wrapping yourself under curtains and quilts! I made friends on the bicycle.

Byelinkov: You saw more than the headmaster's wife and the idiot grocery woman.

Varinka: She is not an idiot.

Byelinkov: She is a potato-vending, sausage-armed fool!

Varinka: Shhhh! My school mouse. Shhh!

Byelinkov: What other friends did you make on this bicycle?

Varinka: I saw students from my brother's classes. They waved and shouted, "Anthropos in love! Anthropos in love!!"

Byelinkov: Where is that bicycle?

Varinka: I left it outside the gate. Where are you going?

Byelinkov (Muttering as he exits): Anthropos in love, anthropos in love.

Varinka: They were cheering me on. Careful, you'll trample the roses.

Byelinkov (Returning with the bicycle): Anthropos is the Greek singular for man. Anthropos in love translates as the Greek and Latin master in love. Of course they cheered you. Their instructor, who teaches them the discipline and contained beauty of the classics, is in love with a sprite on a bicycle. It is a good giggle, isn't it? A very good giggle! I am returning this bicycle to your brother.

Varinka: But it is teatime.

Byelinkov: Today we will not have tea.

Varinka: But you will have to walk back a mile.

Byelinkov: I have my galoshes on. (*Gets on the bicycle*) Varinka, we deserve not to be different. (*Begins to pedal. The bicycle doesn't move*)

Varinka: Put the kickstand up.

Byelinkov: I beg your pardon.

Varinka (Giggling): Byelinkov, to make the bicycle move, you must put the kickstand up.

(Byelinkov *puts it up and awkwardly falls off the bicycle as it moves*)

(*Laughing*) Ha ha ha. My little school mouse. You look so funny! You are the sweetest dearest man in the world. Ha ha ha!

(*Pause*)

Byelinkov: Please help me up. I'm afraid my galosh is caught.

Varinka (Trying not to laugh): Your galosh is caught! (*Explodes in laughter again*) Oh, you are so funny! I do love you so. (*Helps Byelinkov up*) You were right, my pet, as always. We don't need heavy cream for tea. The fraction of improvement isn't worth the damage caused by the disruption.

Byelinkov: Varinka, it is still too early for tea. I must complete two stanzas of my translation before late afternoon. That is my regular schedule.

Varinka: Then I will watch while you work.

Byelinkov: No. You had a good giggle. That is enough.

Varinka: Then while you work I will work too. I will make lists of guests for our wedding.

Byelinkov: I can concentrate only when I am alone in my house. Please take your bicycle home to your brother.

Varinka: But I don't want to leave you. You look so sad.

Byelinkov: I never was a sad man. Don't ever think I was a sad man.

Varinka: Byelinkov, it's a beautiful day, we are in your garden. The roses are in bloom.

Byelinkov: Allow me to help you onto your bicycle. (*Takes Varinka's hand as she gets on the bike*)

Varinka: You are such a gentleman. We will be very happy.

Byelinkov: You are a very strong. Good day, Varinka.

(*Varinka pedals off. Byelinkov, alone in the garden, takes out his pad and rips up the note about the lilac, strews it over the garden, then carefully picks up each piece of paper and places them all in a small envelope as lights fade to black*)

COMPARE:

"The Man in a Case" and Anton Chekhov's story "The Man in a Case" (page 306).

THE GLASS MENAGERIE   1945

*Tennessee Williams (1914–1983) was born
Thomas Lanier Williams in Columbus, Mississippi, went to high school in St. Louis, and
was graduated from the University of Iowa.
As an undergraduate, he saw a performance
of Ibsen's Ghosts and determined to be a
playwright himself. His family bore a close
resemblance to the Wingfields in* The Glass
Menagerie: *his mother came from a line of
Southern bluebloods (Tennessee pioneers); his
sister Rose suffered from incapacitating shyness; and as a young man Williams himself,
like Tom, worked at a job he disliked (in a shoe
factory where his father worked), wrote poetry,
sought refuge in moviegoing, and finally left
home to wander and hold odd jobs. He worked
as a bellhop in a New Orleans hotel, a teletype operator in Jacksonville, Florida, an usher
and a waiter in New York. In 1945* The Glass*

Tennessee Williams

Menagerie *scored a success on Broadway, winning a Drama Critics Circle award. Two
years later Williams received a Pulitzer prize for* A Streetcar Named Desire, *a grim,
powerful study of a woman's illusions and frustrations, set in New Orleans. In 1955,
another Pulitzer prize went to* Cat on a Hot Tin Roof. *Besides other plays, including*
Summer and Smoke *(1948),* Sweet Bird of Youth *(1959),* The Night of the Iguana
(1961), Small Craft Warnings *(1973),* Clothes for a Summer Hotel *(1980), and*
A House Not Meant to Stand *(1981), Williams wrote two novels, poetry, essays,
short stories, and* Memoirs *(1975).*

Nobody, not even the rain, has such small hands.
                          E. E. Cummings

Characters

Amanda Wingfield, the mother. A little woman of great but confused vitality clinging frantically to another time and place. Her characterization must be carefully
created, not copied from type. She is not paranoiac, but her life is paranoia. There
is much to admire in Amanda, and as much to love and pity as there is to laugh
at. Certainly she has endurance and a kind of heroism, and though her foolishness makes her unwittingly cruel at times, there is tenderness in her slight person.

Laura Wingfield, her daughter. Amanda, having failed to establish contact with
reality, continues to live vitally in her illusions, but Laura's situation is even graver.

A childhood illness has left her crippled, one leg slightly shorter than the other, and held in a brace. This defect need not be more than suggested on the stage. Stemming from this, Laura's separation increases till she is like a piece of her own glass collection, too exquisitely fragile to move from the shelf.

Tom Wingfield, her son. And the narrator of the play. A poet with a job in a warehouse. His nature is not remorseless, but to escape from a trap he has to act without pity.

Jim O'Connor, the gentleman caller. A nice, ordinary, young man.

Scene. *An alley in St. Louis.*

Part I. *Preparation for a Gentleman Caller.*
Part II. *The Gentleman Calls.*

Time. *Now and the Past.*

Scene I

The Wingfield apartment is in the rear of the building, one of those vast hive-like conglomerations of cellular living-units that flower as warty growths in overcrowded urban centers of lower middle-class population and are symptomatic of the impulse of this largest and fundamentally enslaved section of American society to avoid fluidity and differentiation and to exist and function as one interfused mass of automatism.

The apartment faces an alley and is entered by a fire-escape, a structure whose name is a touch of accidental poetic truth, for all of these huge buildings are always burning with the slow and implacable fires of human desperation. The fire-escape is included in the set—that is, the landing of it and steps descending from it.

The scene is memory and is therefore unrealistic. Memory takes a lot of poetic license. It omits some details; others are exaggerated, according to the emotional value of the articles it touches, for memory is seated predominantly in the heart. The interior is therefore rather dim and poetic.

At the rise of the curtain, the audience is faced with the dark, grim rear wall of the Wingfield tenement. This building, which runs parallel to the footlights, is flanked on both sides by dark, narrow alleys which run into murky canyons of tangled clotheslines, garbage cans and the sinister latticework of neighboring fire-escapes. It is up and down these side alleys that exterior entrances and exits are made, during the play. At the end of Tom's opening commentary, the dark tenement wall slowly reveals (by means of a transparency) the interior of the ground floor Wingfield apartment.

Downstage is the living room, which also serves as a sleeping room for Laura, the sofa unfolding to make her bed. Upstage, center, and divided by a wide arch or second proscenium with transparent faded portieres (or second curtain), is the dining room. In an old-fashioned what-not in the living room are seen scores of transparent glass animals. A blown-up photograph of the father hangs on the wall of the living room, facing the audience, to the left of the archway. It is the face of a very handsome young man in a doughboy's First World War cap. He is gallantly smiling, ineluctably smiling, as if to say, "I will be smiling forever."

The audience hears and sees the opening scene in the dining room through both the transparent fourth wall of the building and the transparent gauze portieres of the dining-room arch. It is during this revealing scene that the fourth wall slowly ascends, out of sight. This transparent exterior wall is not brought down again until the very end of the play, during Tom's final speech.

The narrator is an undisguised convention of the play. He takes whatever license with dramatic convention as is convenient to his purposes.

Tom enters dressed as a merchant sailor from the alley, stage left, and strolls across the front of the stage to the fire-escape. There he stops and lights a cigarette. He addresses the audience.

Tom: Yes, I have tricks in my pocket, I have things up my sleeve. But I am the opposite of a stage magician. He gives you illusion that has the appearance of truth. I give you truth in the pleasant disguise of illusion. To begin with, I turn back time. I reverse it to that quaint period, the thirties, when the huge middle class of America was matriculating in a school for the blind. Their eyes had failed them, or they had failed their eyes, and so they were having their fingers pressed forcibly down on the fiery Braille alphabet of a dissolving economy. In Spain there was revolution. Here there was only shouting and confusion. In Spain there was Guernica. Here there were disturbances of labor, sometimes pretty violent, in otherwise peaceful cities such as Chicago, Cleveland, St. Louis. . . . This is the social background of the play.

(Music.)

The play is memory. Being a memory play, it is dimly lighted, it is sentimental, it is not realistic. In memory everything seems to happen to music. That explains the fiddle in the wings. I am the narrator of the play, and also a character in it. The other characters are my mother, Amanda, my sister, Laura, and a gentleman caller who appears in the final scenes. He is the most realistic character in the play, being an emissary from a world of reality that we were somehow set apart from. But since I have a poet's weakness for symbols, I am using this character also as a symbol; he is the long delayed but always expected something that we live for. There is a fifth character in the play who doesn't appear except in this larger-than-life photograph over the mantel. This is our father who left us a long time ago. He was a telephone man who fell in love with long distances; he gave up his job with the telephone company and skipped the light fantastic out of town. . . . The last we heard of him was a picture post-card from Mazatlan, on the Pacific coast of Mexico, containing a message of two words—"Hello—Good-bye!" and an address. I think the rest of the play will explain itself. . . .

Amanda's voice becomes audible through the portieres.

He divides the portieres and enters the upstage area.

Amanda and Laura are seated at a drop-leaf table. Eating is indicated by gestures without food or utensils. Amanda faces the audience. Tom and Laura are seated in profile.

The interior has lit up softly and through the scrim we see Amanda and Laura seated at the table in the upstage area.

Amanda (calling): Tom?

Tom: Yes, Mother.

Amanda: We can't say grace until you come to the table!

Tom: Coming, Mother. (He bows slightly and withdraws, reappearing a few moments later in his place at the table.)

Amanda (to her son): Honey, don't push with your fingers. If you have to push with something, the thing to push with is a crust of bread. And chew—chew! Animals have sections in their stomachs which enable them to digest food without mastication, but human beings are supposed to chew their food before they swallow it down. Eat food leisurely, son, and really enjoy it. A well-cooked meal has lots of delicate flavors that have to be held in the mouth for appreciation. So chew your food and give your salivary glands a chance to function!

Tom deliberately lays his imaginary fork down and pushes his chair back from the table.

Tom: I haven't enjoyed one bite of this dinner because of your constant directions on how to eat it. It's you that makes me rush through meals with your hawk-like attention to every bite I take. Sickening—spoils my appetite—all this discussion of animals' secretion—salivary glands—mastication!

Amanda (lightly): Temperament like a Metropolitan star! (He rises and crosses downstage.) You're not excused from the table.

Tom: I am getting a cigarette.

Amanda: You smoke too much.

Laura rises.

Laura: I'll bring in the blanc mange.

He remains standing with his cigarette by the portieres during the following.

Amanda (rising): No, sister, no, sister—you be the lady this time and I'll be the darky.

Laura: I'm already up.

Amanda: Resume your seat, little sister—I want you to stay fresh and pretty—for gentlemen callers!

Laura: I'm not expecting any gentlemen callers.

(Legend . . . Neiges."): "Where are the snows (of yesteryear)?" A slide bearing this line by the French poet François Villon is to be projected on a stage wall.

Amanda (crossing out to kitchenette. Airily): Sometimes they come when they are least expected! Why, I remember one Sunday afternoon in Blue Mountain— (Enters kitchenette.)

Tom: I know what's coming!

Laura: Yes. But let her tell it.

Tom: Again?

Laura: She loves to tell it.

Amanda returns with bowl of dessert.

Amanda: One Sunday afternoon in Blue Mountain—your mother received— seventeen!—gentlemen callers! Why, sometimes there weren't chairs enough to accommodate them all. We had to send the nigger over to bring in folding chairs from the parish house.

Tom (remaining at portieres): How did you entertain those gentlemen callers?

Amanda: I understood the art of conversation!

Tom: I bet you could talk.

Amanda: Girls in those days knew how to talk, I can tell you.

Tom: Yes?

(Image: Amanda As A Girl On A Porch Greeting Callers.)

Amanda: They knew how to entertain their gentlemen callers. It wasn't enough for a girl to be possessed of a pretty face and a graceful figure—although I wasn't slighted in either respect. She also needed to have a nimble wit and a tongue to meet all occasions.

Tom: What did you talk about?

Amanda: Things of importance going on in the world! Never anything coarse or common or vulgar. (She addresses Tom as though he were seated in the vacant chair at the table though he remains by portieres. He plays this scene as though he held the book) My callers were gentlemen—all! Among my callers were some of the most prominent young planters of the Mississippi Delta—planters and sons of planters!

Tom motions for music and a spot of light on Amanda. Her eyes lift, her face glows, her voice becomes rich and elegiac.

(Screen Legend: "Où Sont Les Neiges.")

There was young Champ Laughlin who later became vice-president of the Delta Planters Bank. Hadley Stevenson who was drowned in Moon Lake and left his widow one hundred and fifty thousand in Government bonds. There were the Cutrere brothers, Wesley and Bates. Bates was one of my bright particular beaux! He got in a quarrel with that wild Wainright boy. They shot it out on the floor of Moon Lake Casino. Bates was shot through the stomach. Died in the ambulance on his way to Memphis. His widow was also well-provided for, came into eight or ten thousand acres, that's all. She married him on the rebound—never loved her—carried my picture on him the night he died! And there was that boy that every girl in the Delta had set her cap for! That beautiful, brilliant young Fitzhugh boy from Green County!

Tom: What did he leave his widow?

Amanda: He never married! Gracious, you talk as though all of my old admirers had turned up their toes to the daisies!

Tom: Isn't this the first you mentioned that still survives?

Amanda: That Fitzhugh boy went North and made a fortune—came to be known as the Wolf of Wall Street! He had the Midas touch, whatever he touched turned to gold! And I could have been Mrs. Duncan J. Fitzhugh, mind you! But—I picked your *father!*

Laura (rising): Mother, let me clear the table.

Amanda: No dear, you go in front and study your typewriter chart. Or practice your shorthand a little. Stay fresh and pretty!—It's almost time for our gentlemen callers to start arriving. (*She flounces girlishly toward the kitchenette.*) How many do you suppose we're going to entertain this afternoon?

Tom throws down the paper and jumps up with a groan.

Laura (alone in the dining room): I don't believe we're going to receive any, Mother.

Amanda (reappearing, airily): What? No one—not one? You must be joking! (*Laura nervously echoes her laugh. She slips in a fugitive manner through the half-open portieres and draws them gently behind her. A shaft of very clear light is thrown on her face against the jaded tapestry of the curtains.*) **(Music: "The Glass Menagerie" Under Faintly.)** (*Lightly.*) Not one gentleman caller? It can't be true! There must be a flood, there must have been a tornado!

Laura: It isn't a flood, it's not a tornado, Mother. I'm just not popular like you were in Blue Mountain. . . . (*Tom utters another groan. Laura glances at him with a faint, apologetic smile. Her voice catching a little.*) Mother's afraid I'm going to be an old maid.

(The Scene Dims Out With "Glass Menagerie" Music.)

Scene II

"Laura, Haven't You Ever Liked Some Boy?"

On the dark stage the screen is lighted with the image of blue roses.

Gradually Laura's figure becomes apparent and the screen goes out.

The music subsides.

Laura is seated in the delicate ivory chair at the small clawfoot table.

She wears a dress of soft violet material for a kimono—her hair tied back from her forehead with a ribbon.

She is washing and polishing her collection of glass.

Amanda appears on the fire-escape steps. At the sound of her ascent, Laura catches her breath, thrusts the bowl of ornaments away and seats herself stiffly before the diagram of the typewriter keyboard as though it held her spellbound. Something has happened to Amanda. It is written in her face as she climbs to the landing: a look that is grim and hopeless and a little absurd.

She has on one of those cheap or imitation velvety-looking cloth coats with imitation fur collar. Her hat is five or six years old, one of those dreadful cloche hats that were worn in the late twenties, and she is clasping an enormous black patent-leather pocketbook with nickel clasp and initials. This is her fulldress outfit, the one she usually wears to the D.A.R.

Before entering she looks through the door.

She purses her lips, opens her eyes wide, rolls them upward and shakes her head.

Then she slowly lets herself in the door. Seeing her mother's expression Laura touches her lips with a nervous gesture.

Laura: Hello, Mother, I was—(*She makes a nervous gesture toward the chart on the wall. Amanda leans against the shut door and stares at Laura with a martyred look.*)

Amanda: Deception? Deception? (*She slowly removes her hat and gloves, continuing the swift suffering stare. She lets the hat and gloves fall on the floor—a bit of acting.*)

Laura (shakily): How was the D.A.R. meeting? (*Amanda slowly opens her purse and removes a dainty white handkerchief which she shakes out delicately and delicately touches to her lips and nostrils.*) Didn't you go to the D.A.R. meeting, Mother?

Amanda (faintly, almost inaudibly): —No.—No. (*Then more forcibly.*) I did not have the strength—to go to the D.A.R. In fact, I did not have the courage! I wanted to find a hole in the ground and hide myself in it forever! (*She crosses slowly to the wall and removes the diagram of the typewriter keyboard. She holds it in front of her for a second, staring at it sweetly and sorrowfully—then bites her lips and tears it in two pieces.*)

Laura (faintly): Why did you do that, Mother? (*Amanda repeats the same procedure with the chart of the Gregg Alphabet.*) Why are you—

Amanda: Why? Why? How old are you, Laura?

Laura: Mother, you know my age.

Amanda: I thought that you were an adult; it seems that I was mistaken. (*She crosses slowly to the sofa and sinks down and stares at Laura.*)

Laura: Please don't stare at me, Mother.

Amanda closes her eyes and lowers her head. Count ten.

Amanda: What are we going to do, what is going to become of us, what is the future?

Count ten.

Laura: Has something happened, Mother? (*Amanda draws a long breath and takes out the handkerchief again. Dabbing process.*) Mother, has—something happened?

Amanda: I'll be all right in a minute. I'm just bewildered—(*count five*)—by life . . . .

Laura: Mother, I wish that you would tell me what's happened.

Amanda: As you know, I was supposed to be inducted into my office at the D.A.R. this afternoon. **(Image: A Swarm of Typewriters.)** But I stopped off at Rubicam's Business College to speak to your teachers about your having a cold and ask them what progress they thought you were making down there.

Laura: Oh . . .

Amanda: I went to the typing instructor and introduced myself as your mother. She didn't know who you were. Wingfield, she said. We don't have any such student enrolled at the school! I assured her she did, that you had been going to classes since early in January. "I wonder," she said, "if you could be talking about that terribly shy little girl who dropped out of school after only a few days' attendance?" "No," I said, "Laura, my daughter, has been going to school every day for the past six weeks!" "Excuse me," she said. She took the attendance book out and there was your name, unmistakably printed, and all the dates you were absent until they decided that you had dropped out of school.

I still said, "No, there must have been some mistake! There must have been some mix-up in the records!" And she said, "No—I remember her perfectly now. Her hand shook so that she couldn't hit the right keys! The first time we gave a speed-test, she broke down completely—was sick at the stomach and almost had to be carried into the wash-room! After that morning she never showed up any more. We phoned the house but never got any answer"— while I was working at Famous and Barr, I suppose, demonstrating those— Oh! I felt so weak I could barely keep on my feet. I had to sit down while they got me a glass of water! Fifty dollars' tuition, all of our plans—my hopes and ambitions for you—just gone up the spout, just gone up the spout like that. (Laura draws a long breath and gets awkwardly to her feet. She crosses to the victrola and winds it up.) What are you doing?

Laura: Oh! (She releases the handle and returns to her seat.)

Amanda: Laura, where have you been going when you've gone out pretending that you were going to business college?

Laura: I've just been going out walking.

Amanda: That's not true.

Laura: It is. I just went walking.

Amanda: Walking? Walking? In winter? Deliberately courting pneumonia in that light coat? Where did you walk to, Laura?

Laura: It was the lesser of two evils, Mother. (Image: Winter Scene In Park.) I couldn't go back. I—threw up—on the floor!

Amanda: From half past seven till after five every day you mean to tell me you walked around in the park, because you wanted to make me think that you were still going to Rubicam's Business College?

Laura: It wasn't as bad as it sounds. I went inside places to get warmed up.

Amanda: Inside where?

Laura: I went in the art museum and the bird-houses at the Zoo. I visited the penguins every day! Sometimes I did without lunch and went to the movies. Lately I've been spending most of my afternoons in the Jewel-box, that big glass house where they raise the tropical flowers.

Amanda: You did all this to deceive me, just for the deception? (Laura looks down.) Why?

Laura: Mother, when you're disappointed, you get that awful suffering look on your face, like the picture of Jesus' mother in the museum!

Amanda: Hush!

Laura: I couldn't face it.

Pause. A whisper of strings.

(Legend: "The Crust Of Humility.")

Amanda (hopelessly fingering the huge pocketbook): So what are we going to do the rest of our lives? Stay home and watch the parades go by? Amuse ourselves with the glass menagerie, darling? Eternally play those worn-out phonograph records your father left as a painful reminder of him? We won't have a business career—we've given that up because it gave us nervous indigestion! (Laughs wearily.) What is there left but dependence all our lives? I know so well what becomes of unmarried women who aren't prepared to occupy a position. I've seen such pitiful cases in the South—barely tolerated spinsters living upon the grudging patronage of sister's husband or brother's wife!—stuck away in some little mouse-trap of a room—encouraged by one in-law to visit another—little birdlike women without any nest—eating the crust of humility all their life! Is that the future that we've mapped out for ourselves? I swear it's the only alternative I can think of! It isn't a very pleasant alternative, is it? Of course—some girls *do marry*. (*Laura twists her hands nervously*.) Haven't you ever liked some boy?

Laura: Yes I liked one once. (*Rises.*) I came across his picture a while ago.

Amanda (with some interest): He gave you his picture?

Laura: No, it's in the year-book.

Amanda (disappointed): Oh—a high-school boy.

(Screen Image: Jim As A High-School Hero Bearing A Silver Cup.)

Laura: Yes. His name was Jim. (*Laura lifts the heavy annual from the clawfoot table.*) Here he is in *The Pirates of Penzance*.

Amanda (absently): The what?

Laura: The operetta the senior class put on. He had a wonderful voice and we sat across the aisle from each other Mondays, Wednesdays and Fridays in the Aud. Here he is with the silver cup for debating! See his grin?

Amanda (absently): He must have had a jolly disposition.

Laura: He used to call me—Blue Roses.

(Image: Blue Roses.)

Amanda: Why did he call you such a name as that?

Laura: When I had that attack of pleurosis—he asked me what was the matter when I came back. I said pleurosis—he thought that I said Blue Roses! So that's what he always called me after that. Whenever he saw me, he'd holler, "Hello, Blue Roses!" I didn't care for the girl he went out with. Emily Meisenbach. Emily was the best-dressed girl at Soldan. She never struck me, though, as being sincere . . . It says in the Personal Section—they're engaged. That's—six years ago! They must be married by now.

Amanda: Girls that aren't cut out for business careers usually wind up married to some nice man. (*Gets up with a spark of revival.*) Sister, that's what you'll do!

Laura utters a startled, doubtful laugh. She reaches quickly for a piece of glass.

Laura: But, Mother—

Amanda: Yes? (*Crossing to phonograph.*)

Laura (in a tone of frightened apology): I'm—crippled!

(Image: Screen.)

Amanda: Nonsense! Laura, I've told you never, never to use that word. Why, you're not crippled, you just have a little defect—hardly noticeable, even! When people have some slight disadvantage like that, they cultivate other things to make up for it—develop charm—and vivacity—and—*charm!* That's all you have to do! (*She turns again to the phonograph.*) One thing your father had *plenty of*—was *charm!*

Tom motions to the fiddle in the wings.

(The Scene Fades Out With Music.)

Scene III

(Legend On The Screen: "After The Fiasco—")

Tom speaks from the fire-escape landing.

Tom: After the fiasco at Rubicam's Business College, the idea of getting a gentleman caller for Laura began to play a more important part in Mother's calculations. It became an obsession. Like some archetype of the universal
unconscious, the image of the gentleman caller haunted our small apartment. . . . **(Image: Young Man At Door With Flowers.)** An evening at
home rarely passed without some allusion to this image, this spectre, this
hope. . . . Even when he wasn't mentioned, his presence hung in Mother's
preoccupied look and in my sister's frightened, apologetic manner—hung like
a sentence passed upon the Wingfields! Mother was a woman of action as
well as words. She began to take logical steps in the planned direction. Late
that winter and in the early spring—realizing that extra money would be
needed to properly feather the nest and plume the bird—she conducted a
vigorous campaign on the telephone, roping in subscribers to one of those
magazines for matrons called *The Home-maker's Companion,* the type of journal that features the serialized sublimations of ladies of letters who think in
terms of delicate cup-like breasts, slim, tapering waists, rich, creamy thighs,
eyes like wood-smoke in autumn, fingers that soothe and caress like strains
of music, bodies as powerful as Etruscan sculpture.

(Screen Image: Glamor Magazine Cover.)

*Amanda enters with phone on long extension cord. She is spotted in the dim
stage.*

Amanda: Ida Scott? This is Amanda Wingfield! We *missed* you at the D.A.R. last
Monday! I said to myself: She's probably suffering with that sinus condition!
How is that sinus condition? Horrors! Heaven have mercy!—You're a Christian martyr, yes, that's what you are, a Christian martyr! Well, I just now
happened to notice that your subscription to the *Companion's* about to expire! Yes, it expires with the next issue, honey!—just when that wonderful
new serial by Bessie Mae Hopper is getting off to such an exciting start. Oh,
honey, it's something that you can't miss! You remember how *Gone With the
Wind* took everybody by storm? You simply couldn't go out if you hadn't read
it. All everybody *talked* was Scarlett O'Hara. Well, this is a book that critics
already compare to *Gone With the Wind.* It's the *Gone With the Wind* of the
post-World War generation!—What?—Burning?—Oh, honey, don't let them
burn, go take a look in the oven and I'll hold the wire! Heavens—I think
she's hung up!

(Dim Out.)

(Legend On Screen: "You Think I'm In Love With Continental Shoe-makers?")

Before the stage is lighted, the violent voices of Tom and Amanda are heard. They are quarreling behind the portieres. In front of them stands Laura with clenched hands and panicky expression.

A clear pool of light on her figure throughout this scene.

Tom: What in Christ's name am I—
Amanda (shrilly): Don't you use that—
Tom: Supposed to do!
Amanda: Expression! Not in my—
Tom: Ohhh!
Amanda: Presence! Have you gone out of your senses?
Tom: I have, that's true, *driven* out!
Amanda: What is the matter with you, you—big—big—IDIOT!
Tom: Look—I've got *no thing*, no single thing—
Amanda: Lower your voice!
Tom: In my life here that I can call my OWN! Everything is—
Amanda: Stop that shouting!
Tom: Yesterday you confiscated my books! You had the nerve to—
Amanda: I took that horrible novel back to the library—yes! That hideous book by that insane Mr. Lawrence. (*Tom laughs wildly.*) I cannot control the output of diseased minds or people who cater to them—(*Tom laughs still more wildly.*) BUT I WON'T ALLOW SUCH FILTH BROUGHT INTO MY HOUSE! No, no, no, no, no!
Tom: House, house! Who pays rent on it, who makes a slave of himself to—
Amanda (fairly screeching): Don't you DARE to—
Tom: No, no, I mustn't say things! I've got to just—
Amanda: Let me tell you—
Tom: I don't want to hear any more! (*He tears the portieres open. The upstage area is lit with a turgid smoky red glow.*)

Amanda's hair is in metal curlers and she wears a very old bathrobe, much too large for her slight figure, a relic of the faithless Mr. Wingfield.

An upright typewriter and a wild disarray of manuscripts are on the drop-leaf table. The quarrel was probably precipitated by Amanda's interruption of his creative labor. A chair lying overthrown on the floor.

Their gesticulating shadows are cast on the ceiling by the fiery glow.

Amanda: You *will* hear more, you—
Tom: No, I won't hear more, I'm going out!
Amanda: You come right back in—
Tom: Out, out out! Because I'm—
Amanda: Come back here, Tom Wingfield! I'm not through talking to you!
Tom: Oh, go—
Laura (desperately): Tom!
Amanda: You're going to listen, and no more insolence from you! I'm at the end of my patience! (*He comes back toward her.*)

Tom: What do you think I'm at? Aren't I supposed to have any patience to reach the end of, Mother? I know, I know. It seems unimportant to you, what I'm *doing*—what I *want* to do—having a little *difference* between them! You don't think that—

Amanda: I think you've been doing things that you're ashamed of. That's why you act like this. I don't believe that you go every night to the movies. Nobody goes to the movies night after night. Nobody in their right minds goes to the movies as often as you pretend to. People don't go to the movies at nearly midnight, and movies don't let out at two A.M. Come in stumbling. Muttering to yourself like a maniac! You get three hours' sleep and then go to work. Oh, I can picture the way you're doing down there. Moping, doping, because you're in no condition.

Tom (*wildly*): No, I'm in no condition!

Amanda: What right have you got to jeopardize your job? Jeopardize the security of us all? How do you think we'd manage if you were—

Tom: Listen! You think I'm crazy *about* the *warehouse*? (*He bends fiercely toward her slight figure.*) You think I'm in love with the Continental Shoemakers? You think I want to spend fifty-five *years* down there in that—*celotex interior!* with—*fluorescent—tubes!* Look! I'd rather somebody picked up a crowbar and battered out my brains—than go back mornings! I *go!* Every time you come in yelling that God damn "Rise and Shine!" "Rise and Shine!" I say to myself "How *lucky dead* people are!" But I get up. I *go!* For sixty-five dollars a month I give up all that I dream of doing and being *ever!* And you say self—*self's* all I ever think of. Why, listen, if self is what I thought of, Mother, I'd be where he is—GONE! (*Pointing to father's picture.*) As far as the system of transportation reaches! (*He starts past her. She grabs his arm.*) Don't grab at me, Mother!

Amanda: Where are you going?

Tom: I'm going to the *movies!*

Amanda: I don't believe that lie!

Tom (*crouching toward her, overtowering her tiny figure. She backs away, gasping*): I'm going to opium dens! Yes, opium dens, dens of vice and criminals' hangouts, Mother. I've joined the Hogan gang, I'm a hired assassin, I carry a tommygun in a violin case! I run a string of cat-houses in the Valley! They call me Killer, Killer Wingfield, I'm leading a double-life, a simple, honest warehouse worker by day, by night a dynamic *czar* of the *underworld*, Mother. I go to gambling casinos, I spin away fortunes on the roulette table! I wear a patch over one eye and a false mustache, sometimes I put on green whiskers. On those occasions they call me—*El Diablo!* Oh, I could tell you things to make you sleepless! My enemies plan to dynamite this place. They're going to blow us all sky-high some night! I'll be glad, very happy, and so will you! You'll go up, up on a broomstick, over Blue Mountain with seventeen gentlemen callers! You ugly—babbling old—*witch.* . . . (*He goes through a series of violent, clumsy movements, seizing his overcoat, lunging to the door, pulling it fiercely open. The women watch him, aghast. His arm catches in the sleeve of the coat as he struggles to pull it on. For a moment he is pinioned by the bulky garment. With an outraged groan he tears the coat off again, splitting the shoulders of it, and hurls it across the room. It strikes against the shelf of Laura's glass collection, there is a tinkle of shattering glass. Laura cries out as if wounded.)*

(Music Legend: "The Glass Menagerie.")

Laura (shrilly): My glass!—menagerie. . . . *(She covers her face and turns away.)*

But Amanda is still stunned and stupefied by the "ugly witch" so that she barely notices this occurrence. Now she recovers her speech.

Amanda (in an awful voice): I won't speak to you—until you apologize! *(She crosses through portieres and draws them together behind her. Tom is left with Laura. Laura clings weakly to the mantel with her face averted. Tom stares at her stupidly for a moment. Then he crosses to shelf. Drops awkwardly to his knees to collect the fallen glass, glancing at Laura as if he would speak but couldn't.)*

"The Glass Menagerie" steals in as

(The Scene Dims Out.)

Scene IV

The interior is dark. Faint in the alley.

A deep-voiced bell in a church is tolling the hour of five as the scene commences.

Tom appears at the top of the alley. After each solemn boom of the bell in the tower, he shakes a little noise-maker or rattle as if to express the tiny spasm of man in contrast to the sustained power and dignity of the Almighty. This and the unsteadiness of his advance make it evident that he has been drinking.

As he climbs the few steps to the fire-escape landing light steals up inside. Laura appears in night-dress, observing Tom's empty bed in the front room.

Tom fishes in his pockets for the door-key, removing a motley assortment of articles in the search, including a perfect shower of movie-ticket stubs and an empty bottle. At last he finds the key, but just as he is about to insert it, it slips from his fingers. He strikes a match and crouches below the door.

Tom (bitterly): One crack—and it falls through!

Laura opens the door.

Laura: Tom! Tom, what are you doing?
Tom: Looking for a door-key.
Laura: Where have you been all this time?
Tom: I have been to the movies.
Laura: All this time at the movies?
Tom: There was a very long program. There was a Garbo picture and a Mickey Mouse and a travelogue and a newsreel and a preview of coming attractions. And there was an organ solo and a collection for the milk-fund—simultaneously—which ended up in a terrible fight between a fat lady and an usher!
Laura (innocently): Did you have to stay through everything?

Tom: Of course! And, oh, I forgot! There was a big stage show! The headliner on this stage show was Malvolio the Magician. He performed wonderful tricks, many of them, such as pouring water back and forth between pitchers. First it turned to wine and then it turned to beer and then it turned to whiskey. I know it was whiskey it finally turned into because he needed somebody to come up out of the audience to help him, and I came up—both shows! It was Kentucky Straight Bourbon. A very generous fellow, he gave souvenirs. *(He pulls from his back pocket a shimmering rainbow-colored scarf.)* He gave me this. This is his magic scarf. You can have it, Laura. You wave it over a canary cage and you get a bowl of gold-fish. You wave it over the gold-fish bowl and they fly away canaries. . . . But the wonderfullest trick of all was the coffin trick. We nailed him into a coffin and he got out of the coffin without removing one nail. *(He has come inside.)* There is a trick that would come in handy for me—get me out of this 2 by 4 situation! *(Flops onto bed and starts removing shoes.)*

Laura: Tom—Shhh!

Tom: What're you shushing me for?

Laura: You'll wake up Mother.

Tom: Goody, goody! Pay 'er back for all those "Rise an' Shines." *(Lies down, groaning.)* You know it don't take much intelligence to get yourself into a nailed-up coffin, Laura. But who in hell ever got himself out of one without removing one nail?

As if in answer, the father's grinning photograph lights up.

(Scene Dims Out.)

Immediately following: The church bell is heard striking six. At the sixth stroke the alarm clock goes off in Amanda's room, and after a few moments we hear her calling: "Rise and Shine! Rise and Shine! Laura, go tell your brother to rise and shine!"

Tom (sitting up slowly): I'll rise—but I won't shine.

The light increases.

Amanda: Laura, tell your brother his coffee is ready.

Laura slips into front room.

Laura: Tom! it's nearly seven. Don't make Mother nervous. *(He stares at her stupidly. Beseechingly.)* Tom, speak to Mother this morning. Make up with her, apologize, speak to her!

Tom: She won't to me. It's her that started not speaking.

Laura: If you just say you're sorry she'll start speaking.

Tom: Her not speaking—is that such a tragedy?

Laura: Please—please!

Amanda (calling from kitchenette): Laura, are you going to do what I asked you to do, or do I have to get dressed and go out myself?

Laura: Going, going—soon as I get on my coat! *(She pulls on a shapeless felt hat with nervous, jerky movement, pleadingly glancing at Tom. Rushes awkwardly for coat. The coat is one of Amanda's inaccurately made-over, the sleeves too short for Laura.)* Butter and what else?

Amanda (entering upstage): Just butter. Tell them to charge it.

Laura: Mother, they make such faces when I do that.

Amanda: Sticks and stones may break my bones, but the expression on Mr. Garfinkel's face won't harm us! Tell your brother his coffee is getting cold.

Laura (at door): Do what I asked you, will you, will you, Tom?

He looks sullenly away.

Amanda: Laura, go now or just don't go at all!

Laura (rushing out): Going—going! *(A second later she cries out. Tom springs up and crosses to the door. Amanda rushes anxiously in. Tom opens the door.)*

Tom: Laura?

Laura: I'm all right. I slipped, but I'm all right.

Amanda (peering anxiously after her): If anyone breaks a leg on those fire-escape steps, the landlord ought to be sued for every cent he possesses! *(She shuts door. Remembers she isn't speaking and returns to other room.)*

As Tom enters listlessly for his coffee, she turns her back to him and stands rigidly facing the window on the gloomy gray vault of the areaway. Its light on her face with its aged but childish features is cruelly sharp, satirical as a Daumier print.

(Music Under: "Ave Maria.")

Tom glances sheepishly but sullenly at her averted figure and slumps at the table. The coffee is scalding hot; he sips it and gasps and spits it back in the cup. At his gasp, Amanda catches her breath and half turns. Then catches herself and turns back to window.

    Tom blows on his coffee, glancing sidewise at his mother. She clears her throat. Tom clears his. He starts to rise. Sinks back down again, scratches his head, clears his throat again. Amanda coughs. Tom raises his cup in both hands to blow on it, his eyes staring over the rim of it at his mother for several moments. Then he slowly sets the cup down and awkwardly and hesitantly rises from the chair.

Tom (hoarsely): Mother. I—I apologize. Mother. *(Amanda draws a quick, shuddering breath. Her face works grotesquely. She breaks into childlike tears.)* I'm sorry for what I said, for everything that I said, I didn't mean it.

Amanda (sobbingly): My devotion has made me a witch and so I make myself hateful to my children!

Tom: No, you *don't.*

Amanda: I worry so much, don't sleep, it makes me nervous!

Tom (gently): I understand that.

Amanda: I've had to put up a solitary battle all these years. But you're my right-hand bower! Don't fall down, don't fail!

Tom (gently): I try, Mother.

Amanda (with great enthusiasm): Try and you will SUCCEED! *(The notion makes her breathless.)* Why, you—you're just *full* of natural endowments! Both of my children—they're *unusual* children! Don't you think I know it? I'm so—*proud!* Happy and—feel I've—so much to be thankful for but—Promise me one thing, son!

Tom: What, Mother?

Amanda: Promise, son, you'll—never be a drunkard!

Tom (turns to her grinning): I will never be a drunkard, Mother.

Amanda: That's what frightened me so, that you'd be drinking! Eat a bowl of Purina!

Tom: Just coffee, Mother.

Amanda: Shredded wheat biscuit?

Tom: No. No, Mother, just coffee.

Amanda: You can't put in a day's work on an empty stomach. You've got ten minutes—don't gulp! Drinking too-hot liquids makes cancer of the stomach. . . . Put cream in.

Tom: No, thank you.

Amanda: To cool it.

Tom: No! No, thank you, I want it black.

Amanda: I know, but it's not good for you. We have to do all that we can to build ourselves up. In these trying times we live in, all that we have to cling to is—each other. . . . That's why it's so important to—Tom, I—I sent out your sister so I could discuss something with you. If you hadn't spoken I would have spoken to you. *(Sits down.)*

Tom (gently): What is it, Mother, that you want to discuss?

Amanda: Laura!

Tom puts his cup down slowly.

(Legend On Screen: "Laura.")

(Music: "The Glass Menagerie."

Tom: —Oh.—Laura . . .

Amanda (touching his sleeve): You know how Laura is. So quiet but—still water runs deep! She notices things and I think she—broods about them. *(Tom looks up.)* A few days ago I came in and she was crying.

Tom: What about?

Amanda: You.

Tom: Me?

Amanda: She has an idea that you're not happy here.

Tom: What gave her that idea?

Amanda: What gives her any idea? However, you do act strangely. I—I'm not criticizing, understand *that!* I know your ambitions do not lie in the warehouse, that like everybody in the whole wide world—you've had to—make sacrifices, but—Tom—Tom—life's not easy, it calls for—Spartan endurance! There's so many things in my heart that I cannot describe to you! I've never told you but I—*loved* your father. . . .

Tom (gently): I know that, Mother.

Amanda: And you—when I see you taking after his ways! Staying out late—and—well, you *had* been drinking the night you were in that—terrifying condition! Laura says that you hate the apartment and that you go out nights to get away from it! Is that true, Tom?

Tom: No. You say there's so much in your heart that you can't describe to me. That's true of me, too. There's so much in my heart that I can't describe to *you!* So let's respect each other's—

Amanda: But, why—*why,* Tom—are you always so *restless?* Where do you go to, nights?

Tom: I—go to the movies.

Amanda: Why do you go to the movies so much, Tom?

Tom: I go to the movies because—I like adventure. Adventure is something I don't have much of at work, so I go to the movies.

Amanda: But, Tom, you go to the movies *entirely* too *much!*

Tom: I like a lot of adventure.

> *Amanda looks baffled, then hurt. As the familiar inquisition resumes he becomes hard and impatient again. Amanda slips back into her querulous attitude toward him.*

(Image On Screen: Sailing Vessel With Jolly Roger.)

Amanda: Most young men find adventure in their careers.

Tom: Then most young men are not employed in a warehouse.

Amanda: The world is full of young men employed in warehouses and offices and factories.

Tom: Do all of them find adventure in their careers?

Amanda: They do or they do without it! Not everybody has a craze for adventure.

Tom: Man is by instinct a lover, a hunter, a fighter, and none of those instincts are given much play at the warehouse!

Amanda: Man is by instinct! Don't quote instinct to me! Instinct is something that people have got away from! It belongs to animals! Christian adults don't want it!

Tom: What do Christian adults want, then, Mother?

Amanda: Superior things! Things of the mind and the spirit! Only animals have to satisfy instincts! Surely your aims are somewhat higher than theirs! Than monkeys—pigs—

Tom: I reckon they're not.

Amanda: You're joking. However, that isn't what I wanted to discuss.

Tom (rising): I haven't much time.

Amanda (pushing his shoulder): Sit down.

Tom: You want me to punch in red at the warehouse, Mother?

Amanda: You have five minutes. I want to talk about Laura.

(Legend: "Plans And Provisions.")

Tom: All right! What about Laura?

Amanda: We have to be making plans and provisions for her. She's older than you, two years, and nothing has happened. She just drifts along doing nothing. It frightens me terribly how she just drifts along.

Tom: I guess she's the type that people call home girls.

Amanda: There's no such type, and if there is, it's a pity! That is unless the home is hers, with a husband!

Tom: What?

Amanda: Oh, I can see the handwriting on the wall as plain as I see the nose in front of my face! It's terrifying! More and more you remind me of your father! He was out all hours without explanation—Then *left! Goodbye!* And me with the bag to hold. I saw that letter you got from the Merchant Marine. I know what you're dreaming of. I'm not standing here blindfolded. Very well, then. Then *do* it! But not till there's somebody to take your place.

Tom: What do you mean?

Amanda: I mean that as soon as Laura has got somebody to take care of her, married, a home of her own, independent—why, then you'll be free to go wherever you please, on land, on sea, whichever way the wind blows! But until that time you've got to look out for your sister. I don't say me because I'm old and don't matter! I say for your sister because she's young and dependent. I put her in business college—a dismal failure! Frightened her so it made her sick to her stomach. I took her over to the Young People's League at the church. Another fiasco. She spoke to nobody, nobody spoke to her. Now all she does is fool with those pieces of glass and play those worn-out records. What kind of a life is that for a girl to lead!

Tom: What can I do about it?

Amanda: Overcome selfishness! Self, self, self is all that you ever think of! (*Tom springs up and crosses to get his coat. It is ugly and bulky. He pulls on a cap with earmuffs.*) Where is your muffler? Put your wool muffler on! (*He snatches it angrily from the closet and tosses it around his neck and pulls both ends tight.*) Tom! I haven't said what I had in mind to ask you.

Tom: I'm too late to—

Amanda (*catching his arms—very importunately. Then shyly*): Down at the warehouse, aren't there some—nice young men?

Tom: No!

Amanda: There *must* be—*some* . . .

Tom: Mother—

Gesture.

Amanda: Find one that's clean-living—doesn't drink and—ask him out for sister!

Tom: What?

Amanda: For *sister!* To *meet!* Get *acquainted!*

Tom (*stamping to door*): Oh, my go-osh!

Amanda: Will you? (*He opens door. Imploringly.*) Will you? (*He starts down.*) Will you? *Will* you, dear?

Tom (*calling back*): YES!

Amanda closes the door hesitantly and with a troubled but faintly hopeful expression.

(Screen Image: Glamor Magazine Cover.)

Spot Amanda at phone.

Amanda: Ella Cartwright? This is Amanda Wingfield! How are you, honey? How is that kidney condition? (*Count five.*) Horrors! (*Count five.*) You're a Christian martyr, yes, honey, that's what you are, a Christian martyr! Well, I just happened to notice in my little red book that your subscription to the *Companion* has just run out! I knew that you wouldn't want to miss out on the wonderful serial starting in this new issue. It's by Bessie Mae Hopper, the first thing she's written since *Honeymoon for Three*. Wasn't that a strange and interesting story? Well, this one is even lovelier, I believe. It has a sophisticated society background. It's all about the horsey set on Long Island!

(Fade Out.)

Scene V

(Legend On Screen: "Annunciation.") *Fade with music.*

It is early dusk of a spring evening. Supper has just been finished in the Wingfield apartment. Amanda and Laura in light colored dresses are removing dishes from the table, in the upstage area, which is shadowy, their movements formalized almost as a dance or ritual, their moving forms as pale and silent as moths.

Tom, in white shirt and trousers, rises from the table and crosses toward the fire-escape.

Amanda (as he passes her): Son, will you do me a favor?

Tom: What?

Amanda: Comb your hair! You look so pretty when your hair is combed! *(Tom slouches on sofa with evening paper. Enormous caption "Franco Triumphs.")* There is only one respect in which I would like you to emulate your father.

Tom: What respect is that?

Amanda: The care he always took of his appearance. He never allowed himself to look untidy. *(He throws down the paper and crosses to fire-escape.)* Where are you going?

Tom: I'm going out to smoke.

Amanda: You smoke too much. A pack a day at fifteen cents a pack. How much would that amount to in a month? Thirty times fifteen is how much, Tom? Figure it out and you will be astounded at what you could save. Enough to give you a night-school course in accounting at Washington U! Just think what a wonderful thing that would be for you, son!

Tom is unmoved by the thought.

Tom: I'd rather smoke. *(He steps out on landing, letting the screen door slam.)*

Amanda (sharply): I know! That's the tragedy of it. . . . *(Alone, she turns to look at her husband's picture.)*

(Dance Music: "All The World Is Waiting For The Sunrise.")

Tom (to the audience): Across the alley from us was the Paradise Dance Hall. On evenings in spring the windows and doors were open and the music came outdoors. Sometimes the lights were turned out except for a large glass sphere that hung from the ceiling. It would turn slowly about and filter the dusk with delicate rainbow colors. Then the orchestra played a waltz or a tango, something that had a slow and sensuous rhythm. Couples would come outside, to the relative privacy of the alley. You could see them kissing behind ash-pits and telephone poles. This was the compensation for lives that passed like mine, without any change or adventure. Adventure and change were imminent in this year. They were waiting around the corner for all these kids. Suspended in the mist over Berchtesgaden, caught in the folds of Chamberlain's umbrella—In Spain there was Guernica! But here there was only hot swing music and liquor, dance halls, bars, and movies, and sex that hung in the gloom like a chandelier and flooded the world with brief, deceptive rainbows. . . . All the world was waiting for bombardments!

Amanda turns from the picture and comes outside.

Amanda (*sighing*): A fire-escape landing's a poor excuse for a porch. (*She spreads a newspaper on a step and sits down, gracefully and demurely as if she were settling into a swing on a Mississippi veranda.*) What are you looking at?
Tom: The moon.
Amanda: Is there a moon this evening?
Tom: It's rising over Garfinkel's Delicatessen.
Amanda: So it is! A little silver slipper of a moon. Have you made a wish on it yet?
Tom: Um-hum.
Amanda: What did you wish for?
Tom: That's a secret.
Amanda: A secret, huh? Well, I won't tell mine either. I will be just as mysterious as you.
Tom: I bet I can guess what yours is.
Amanda: Is my head so transparent?
Tom: You're not a sphinx.
Amanda: No, I don't have secrets. I'll tell you what I wished for on the moon. Success and happiness for my precious children! I wish for that whenever there's a moon, and when there isn't a moon, I wish for it, too.
Tom: I thought perhaps you wished for a gentleman caller.
Amanda: Why do you say that?
Tom: Don't you remember asking me to fetch one?
Amanda: I remember suggesting that it would be nice for your sister if you brought home some nice young man from the warehouse. I think I've made that suggestion more than once.
Tom: Yes, you have made it repeatedly.
Amanda: Well?
Tom: We are going to have one.
Amanda: What?
Tom: A gentleman caller!

(The Annunciation Is Celebrated With Music.)

Amanda rises.

(Image On Screen: Caller With Bouquet.)

Amanda: You mean you have asked some nice young man to come over?
Tom: Yep. I've asked him to dinner.

Amanda: You really did?

Tom: I did!

Amanda: You did, and did he—*accept?*

Tom: He did!

Amanda: Well, well—well, well! That's—lovely!

Tom: I thought that you would be pleased.

Amanda: It's definite, then?

Tom: Very definite.

Amanda: Soon?

Tom: Very soon.

Amanda: For heaven's sake, stop putting on and tell me some things, will you?

Tom: What things do you want me to tell you?

Amanda: Naturally I would like to know when he's *coming!*

Tom: He's coming tomorrow.

Amanda: *Tomorrow?*

Tom: Yep. Tomorrow.

Amanda: But, Tom!

Tom: Yes, Mother?

Amanda: Tomorrow gives me no time!

Tom: Time for what?

Amanda: Preparations! Why didn't you phone me at once, as soon as you asked him, the minute that he accepted? Then, don't you see, I could have been getting ready!

Tom: You don't have to make any fuss.

Amanda: Oh, Tom, Tom, Tom, of course I have to make a fuss! I want things nice, not sloppy! Not thrown together. I'll certainly have to do some fast thinking, won't I?

Tom: I don't see why you have to think at all.

Amanda: You just don't know. We can't have a gentleman caller in a pig-sty! All my wedding silver has to be polished, the monogrammed table linen ought to be laundered! The windows have to be washed and fresh curtains put up. And how about clothes? We have *wear* something, don't we?

Tom: Mother, this boy is no one to make a fuss over!

Amanda: Do you realize he's the first young man we've introduced to your sister? It's terrible, dreadful, disgraceful that poor little sister has never received a single gentleman caller! Tom, come inside! (*She opens the screen door.*)

Tom: What for?

Amanda: I want to ask you some things.

Tom: If you're going to make such a fuss, I'll call it off, I'll tell him not to come.

Amanda: You certainly won't do anything of the kind. Nothing offends people worse than broken engagements. It simply means I'll have to work like a Turk! We won't be brilliant, but we'll pass inspection. Come on inside. (*Tom follows, groaning.*) Sit down.

Tom: Any particular place you would like me to sit?

Amanda: Thank heavens I've got that new sofa! I'm also making payments on a floor lamp I'll have sent out! And put the chintz covers on, they'll brighten things up! Of course I'd hoped to have these walls re-papered. . . . What is the young man's name?

Tom: His name is O'Connor.

Amanda: That, of course, means fish—tomorrow is Friday! I'll have that salmon loaf—with Durkee's dressing! What does he do? He works at the warehouse?

Tom: Of course! How else would I—

Amanda: Tom, he—doesn't drink?

Tom: Why do you ask me that?

Amanda: Your father *did!*

Tom: Don't get started on that!

Amanda: He *does* drink, then?

Tom: Not that I know of!

Amanda: Make sure, be certain! The last thing I want for my daughter's a boy who drinks!

Tom: Aren't you being a little premature? Mr. O'Connor has not yet appeared on the scene!

Amanda: But will tomorrow. To meet your sister, and what do I know about his character? Nothing! Old maids are better off than wives of drunkards!

Tom: Oh, my God!

Amanda: Be still!

Tom (leaning forward to whisper): Lots of fellows meet girls whom they don't marry!

Amanda: Oh, talk sensibly, Tom—and don't be sarcastic! *(She has gotten a hairbrush.)*

Tom: What are you doing?

Amanda: I'm brushing that cow-lick down! What is this young man's position at the warehouse?

Tom (submitting grimly to the brush and the interrogation): This young man's position is that of a shipping clerk, Mother.

Amanda: Sounds to me like a fairly responsible job, the sort of a job *you* would be in if you just had more *get-up.* What is his salary? Have you got any idea?

Tom: I would judge it to be approximately eighty-five dollars a month.

Amanda: Well—not princely, but—

Tom: Twenty more than I make.

Amanda: Yes, how well I know! But for a family man, eighty-five dollars a month is not much more than you can just get by on. . . .

Tom: Yes, but Mr. O'Connor is not a family man.

Amanda: He might be, mightn't he? Some time in the future?

Tom: I see. Plans and provisions.

Amanda: You are the only young man that I know of who ignores the fact that the future becomes the present, the present the past, and the past turns into everlasting regret if you don't plan for it!

Tom: I will think that over and see what I can make of it.

Amanda: Don't be supercilious with your mother! Tell some more about this—what do you call him?

Tom: James D. O'Connor. The D. is for Delaney.

Amanda: Irish on *both* sides! *Gracious!* And doesn't drink?

Tom: Shall I call him up and ask him right this minute?

Amanda: The only way to find out about those things is to make discreet inquiries at the proper moment. When I was a girl in Blue Mountain and it was suspected that a young man drank, the girl whose attentions he had been receiving, if any girl *was*, would sometimes speak to the minister of his church, *or rather her father would if her father was living, and sort of feel him out on the young man's character. That is the way such things are discreetly handled to keep a young woman from making a tragic mistake!*

Tom: Then how did you happen to make a tragic mistake?

Amanda: That innocent look of your father's had everyone fooled! He *smiled*—the world was *enchanted!* No girl can do worse than put herself at the mercy of a handsome appearance! I hope that Mr. O'Connor is not too good-looking.

Tom: No, he's not too good-looking. He's covered with freckles and hasn't too much of a nose.

Amanda: He's not right-down homely, though?

Tom: Not right-down homely. Just medium homely, I'd say.

Amanda: Character's what to look for in a man.

Tom: That's what I've always said, Mother.

Amanda: You've never said anything of the kind and I suspect you would never give it a thought.

Tom: Don't be suspicious of me.

Amanda: At least I hope he's the type that's up and coming.

Tom: I think he really goes in for self-improvement.

Amanda: What reason have you to think so?

Tom: He goes to night school.

Amanda (beaming): Splendid! What does he do, I mean study?

Tom: Radio engineering and public speaking!

Amanda: Then he has visions of being advanced in the world! Any young man who studies public speaking is aiming to have an executive job some day! And radio engineering? A thing for the future! Both of these facts are very illuminating. Those are the sort of things that a mother should know concerning any young man who comes to call on her daughter. Seriously or—not.

Tom: One little warning. He doesn't know about Laura. I didn't let on that we had dark ulterior motives. I just said, why don't you come have dinner with us? He said okay and that was the whole conversation.

Amanda: I bet it was! You're eloquent as an oyster. However, he'll know about Laura when he gets here. When he sees how lovely and sweet and pretty she is, he'll thank his lucky stars he was asked to dinner.

Tom: Mother, you mustn't expect too much of Laura.

Amanda: What do you mean?

Tom: Laura seems all those things to you and me because she's ours and we love her. We don't even notice she's crippled any more.

Amanda: Don't say crippled! You know that I never allow that word to be used!

Tom: But face facts, Mother. She is and—that not's all—

Amanda: What do you mean "not all"?

Tom: Laura is very different from other girls.

Amanda: I think the difference is all to her advantage.

Tom: Not quite all—in the eyes of others—strangers—she's terribly shy and lives in a world of her own and those things make her seem a little peculiar to people outside the house.

Amanda: Don't say peculiar.

Tom: Face the facts. She is.

(The Dance-hall Music Changes To A Tango That Has A Minor And Somewhat Ominous Tone.)

Amanda: In what way is she peculiar—may I ask?

Tom (gently): She lives in a world of her own—a world of—little glass ornaments, Mother. . . . *(Gets up. Amanda remains holding brush, looking at him, troubled.)* She plays old phonograph records and—that's about all—*(He glances at himself in the mirror and crosses to door.)*

Amanda (sharply): Where are you going?

Tom: I'm going to the movies. *(Out screen door.)*

Amanda: Not to the movies, every night to the movies! *(Follows quickly to screen door.)* I don't believe you always go to the movies! *(He is gone. Amanda looks worriedly after him for a moment. Then vitality and optimism return and she turns from the door. Crossing to portieres.)* Laura! Laura! *(Laura answers from kitchenette.)*

Laura: Yes, Mother.

Amanda: Let those dishes go and come in front! *(Laura appears with dish towel. Gaily.)* Laura, come here and make a wish on the moon!

Laura (entering): Moon—moon?

Amanda: A little silver slipper of a moon. Look over your left shoulder, Laura, and make a wish! *(Laura looks faintly puzzled as if called out of sleep. Amanda seizes her shoulders and turns her at an angle by the door.)* Now! Now, darling, wish!

Laura: What shall I wish for, Mother?

Amanda (her voice trembling and her eyes suddenly filling with tears): Happiness! Good Fortune!

The violin rises and the stage dims out.

Scene VI

(Image: High-School Hero.)

Tom: And so the following evening I brought Jim home to dinner. I had known Jim slightly in high school. In high school Jim was a hero. He had tremendous Irish good nature and vitality with the scrubbed and polished look of white chinaware. He seemed to move in a continual spotlight. He was a star in basketball, captain of the debating club, president of the senior class and the glee club and he sang the male lead in the annual light operas. He was always running or bounding, never just walking. He seemed always at the point of defeating the law of gravity. He was shooting with such velocity through his adolescence that you would logically expect him to arrive at nothing short of the White House by the time he was thirty. But Jim apparently ran into more interference after his graduation from Soldan. His speed had definitely slowed. Six years after he left high school he was holding a job that wasn't much better than mine.

(Image: Clerk.)

He was the only one at the warehouse with whom I was on friendly terms. I was valuable to him as someone who could remember his former glory, who had seen him win basketball games and the silver cup in debating. He knew of my secret practice of retiring to a cabinet of the washroom to work on my poems when business was slack in the warehouse. He called me Shakespeare. And while the other boys in the warehouse regarded me with suspicious hostility, Jim took a humorous attitude toward me. Gradually his attitude affected the others, their hostility wore off and they also began to smile at me as people smile at an oddly fashioned dog who trots across their path at some distance.

I knew that Jim and Laura had known each other at Soldan, and I had heard Laura speak admiringly of his voice. I didn't know if Jim remembered her or not. In high school Laura had been as unobtrusive as Jim had been astonishing. If he did remember Laura, it was not as my sister, for when I asked him to dinner, he grinned and said, "You know, Shakespeare, I never thought of you as having folks!"

He was about to discover that I did. . . .

(Light Up Stage.)

(Legend On Screen: "The Accent Of A Coming Foot.")

Friday evening. It is about five o'clock of a late spring evening which comes "scattering poems in the sky."

A delicate lemony light is in the Wingfield apartment.

Amanda has worked like a Turk in preparation for the gentleman caller. The results are astonishing. The new floor lamp with its rose-silk shade is in place, a colored paper lantern conceals the broken light fixture in the ceiling, new billowing white curtains are at the windows, chintz covers are on chairs and sofa, a pair of new sofa pillows make their initial appearance.

Open boxes and tissue paper are scattered on the floor.

Laura stands in the middle with lifted arms while Amanda crouches before her, adjusting the hem of the new dress, devout and ritualistic. The dress is colored and designed by memory. The arrangement of Laura's hair is changed; it is softer and more becoming. A fragile, unearthly prettiness has come out in Laura: she is like a piece of translucent glass touched by light, given a momentary radiance, not actual, not lasting.

Amanda (impatiently): Why are you trembling?

Laura: Mother, you've made me so nervous!

Amanda: How have I made you nervous?

Laura: By all this fuss! You make it seem so important!

Amanda: I don't understand you, Laura. You couldn't be satisfied with just sitting home, and yet whenever I try to arrange something for you, you seem to resist it. (*She gets up.*) Now take a look at yourself. No, wait! Wait just a moment—I have an idea!

Laura: What is it now?

Amanda produces two power puffs which she wraps in handkerchiefs and stuffs in Laura's bosom.

Laura: Mother, what are you doing?

Amanda: They call them "Gay Deceivers"!

Laura: I won't wear them!

Amanda: You will!

Laura: Why should I?

Amanda: Because, to be painfully honest, your chest is flat.

Laura: You make it seem like we were setting a trap.

Amanda: All pretty girls are a trap, a pretty trap, and men expect them to be. **(Legend: "A Pretty Trap.")** Now look at yourself, young lady. This is the prettiest you will ever be! I've got to fix myself now! You're going to be surprised by your mother's appearance! *(She crosses through portieres, humming gaily.)*

Laura moves slowly to the long mirror and stares solemnly at herself.

A wind blows the white curtains inward in a slow, graceful motion and with a faint, sorrowful sighing.

Amanda (offstage): It isn't dark enough yet. *(She turns slowly before the mirror with a troubled look.)*

(Legend On Screen: "This Is My Sister: Celebrate Her With Strings!" Music.)

Amanda (laughing, off): I'm going to show you something. I'm going to make a spectacular appearance!

Laura: What is it, Mother?

Amanda: Possess your soul in patience—you will see! Something I've resurrected from that old trunk! Styles haven't changed so terribly much after all. . . . *(She parts the portieres.)* Now just look at your mother! *(She wears a girlish frock of yellowed voile with a blue silk sash. She carries a bunch of jonquils—the legend of her youth is nearly revived. Feverishly.)* This is the dress in which I led the cotillion. Won the cakewalk twice at Sunset Hill, wore one spring to the Governor's ball in Jackson! See how I sashayed around the ballroom, Laura? *(She raises her skirt and does a mincing step around the room.)* I wore it on Sundays for my gentlemen callers! I had it on the day I met your father—I had malaria fever all that spring. The change of climate from East Tennessee to the Delta—weakened resistance—I had a little temperature all the time—not enough to be serious—just enough to make me restless and giddy! Invitations poured in—parties all over the Delta!—"Stay in bed," said Mother, "you have fever!"—but I just wouldn't.—I took quinine but kept on going, going!—Evenings, dances!—Afternoons, long, long rides! Picnics—lovely!—So lovely, that country in May.—All lacy with dogwood, literally flooded with jonquils!—That was the spring I had the craze for jonquils. Jonquils became an absolute obsession. Mother said, "Honey, there's no more room for jonquils." And still I kept bringing in more jonquils. Whenever, wherever I saw them, I'd say, "Stop! Stop! I see jonquils!" I made the young men help me gather the jonquils! It was a joke, Amanda and her jonquils! Finally there were no more vases to hold them, every available space was filled with jonquils. No vases to hold them? All right, I'll hold them myself! And then I—*(She stops in front of the picture.)* **(Music.)** met your father! Malaria fever and jonquils and then—this—boy. . . . *(She switches on the rose-colored lamp.)* I hope they get here before it starts to rain. (*She crosses upstage and places the jonquils in bowl on table.*) I gave your brother a little extra change so he and Mr. O'Connor could take the service car home.

Laura (*with altered look*): What did you say his name was?

Amanda: O'Connor.

Laura: What is his first name?

Amanda: I don't remember. Oh, yes, I do. It was—Jim!

Laura sways slightly and catches hold of a chair.

(Legend On Screen: "Not Jim!")

Laura (*faintly*): Not—Jim!

Amanda: Yes, that was it, it was Jim! I've never known a Jim that wasn't nice!

(Music: Ominous.)

Laura: Are you sure his name is Jim O'Connor?

Amanda: Yes. Why?

Laura: Is he the one that Tom used to know in high school?

Amanda: He didn't say so. I think he just got to know him at the warehouse.

Laura: There was a Jim O'Connor we both knew in high school—(*Then, with effort.*) If that is the one that Tom is bringing to dinner—you'll have to excuse me, I won't come to the table.

Amanda: What sort of nonsense is this?

Laura: You asked me once if I'd ever liked a boy. Don't you remember I showed you this boy's picture?

Amanda: You mean the boy you showed me in the year-book?

Laura: Yes, that boy.

Amanda: Laura, Laura, were you in love with that boy?

Laura: I don't know, Mother. All I know is I couldn't sit at the table if it was him!

Amanda: It won't be him! It isn't the least bit likely. But whether it is or not, you will come to the table. You will not be excused.

Laura: I'll have to be, Mother.

Amanda: I don't intend to humor your silliness, Laura. I've had too much from you and your brother, both! So just sit down and compose yourself till they come. Tom has forgotten his key so you'll have to let them in, when they arrive.

Laura (*panicky*): Oh, Mother—*you* answer the door!

Amanda (*lightly*): I'll be in the kitchen—busy!

Laura: Oh, Mother, please answer the door, don't make me do it!

Amanda (*crossing into kitchenette*): I've got to fix the dressing for the salmon. Fuss, fuss—silliness!—over a gentleman caller!

Door swings shut. Laura is left alone.

(Legend: "Terror!")

She utters a low moan and turns off the lamp—sits stiffly on the edge of the sofa, knotting her fingers together.

(Legend On Screen: "The Opening Of A Door!")

Tom and Jim appear on the fire-escape steps and climb to landing. Hearing their approach, Laura rises with a panicky gesture. She retreats to the portieres.

The doorbell. Laura catches her breath and touches her throat. Low drums.

Amanda (*calling*): Laura, sweetheart! The door!

Laura stares at it without moving.

Jim: I think we just beat the rain.

Tom: Uh-huh. (*He rings again, nervously. Jim whistles and fishes for a cigarette.*)

Amanda (*very, very gaily*): Laura, that is your brother and Mr. O'Connor! Will you let them in, darling?

Laura crosses toward kitchenette door.

Laura (*breathlessly*): Mother—you go to the door!

Amanda steps out of kitchenette and stares furiously at Laura. She points imperiously at the door.

Laura: Please, please!

Amanda (*in a fierce whisper*): What is the matter with you, you silly thing?

Laura (*desperately*): Please, you answer it, *please!*

Amanda: I told you I wasn't going to humor you, Laura. Why have you chosen this moment to lose your mind?

Laura: Please, please, please, you go!

Amanda: You'll have to go to the door because I can't!

Laura (*despairingly*): I can't either!

Amanda: Why?

Laura: I'm *sick!*

Amanda: I'm sick, too—of your nonsense! Why can't you and your brother be normal people? Fantastic whims and behavior! (*Tom gives a long ring.*) Preposterous goings on! Can you give me one reason—(*Calls out lyrically.*) COMING! JUST ONE SECOND!—why should you be afraid to open a door? Now you answer it, Laura!

Laura: Oh, oh, oh . . . (*She returns through the portieres. Darts to the victrola and winds it frantically and turns it on.*)

Amanda: Laura Wingfield, you march right to that door!

Laura: Yes—yes, Mother!

A faraway, scratchy rendition of "Dardanella" softens the air and gives her strength to move through it. She slips to the door and draws it cautiously open. Tom enters with the caller, Jim O'Connor.

Tom: Laura, this is Jim. Jim, this is my sister, Laura.

Jim (*stepping inside*): I didn't know that Shakespeare had a sister!

Laura (*retreating stiff and trembling from the door*): How—how do you do?

Jim (heartily extending his hand): Okay!

> *Laura touches it hesitantly with hers.*

Jim: Your hand's cold, Laura!

Laura: Yes, well—I've been playing the victrola. . . .

Jim: Must have been playing classical music on it! You ought to play a little hot swing music to warm you up!

Laura: Excuse me—I haven't finished playing the victrola. . . .

> *She turns awkwardly and hurries into the front room. She pauses a second by the victrola. Then catches her breath and darts through the portieres like a frightened deer.*

Jim (grinning): What was the matter?

Tom: Oh—with Laura? Laura is—terribly shy.

Jim: Shy, huh? It's unusual to meet a shy girl nowadays. I don't believe you ever mentioned you had a sister.

Tom: Well, now you know. I have one. Here is the *Post Dispatch.* You want a piece of it?

Jim: Uh-huh.

Tom: What piece? The comics?

Jim: Sports! (*Glances at it.*) Ole Dizzy Dean is on his bad behavior.

Tom (disinterest): Yeah? (*Lights cigarette and crosses back to fire-escape door.*)

Jim: Where are *you* going?

Tom: I'm going out on the terrace.

Jim (goes after him): You know, Shakespeare—I'm going to sell you a bill of goods!

Tom: What goods?

Jim: A course I'm taking.

Tom: Huh?

Jim: In public speaking! You and me, we're not the warehouse type.

Tom: Thanks—that's good news. But what has public speaking got to do with it?

Jim: It fits you for—executive positions!

Tom: Awww.

Jim: I tell you it's done a helluva lot for me.

(Image: Executive At Desk.)

Tom: In what respect?

Jim: In every! Ask yourself what is the difference between you an' me and men in the office down front? Brains?—No!—Ability?—No! Then what? Just one little thing—

Tom: What is that one little thing?

Jim: Primarily it amounts to—social poise! Being able to square up to people and hold your own on any social level!

Amanda (offstage): Tom?

Tom: Yes, Mother?

Amanda: Is that you and Mr. O'Connor?

Tom: Yes, Mother.

Amanda: Well, you just make yourselves comfortable in there.

Tom: Yes, Mother.

Amanda: Ask Mr. O'Connor if he would like to wash his hands.

Jim: Aw—no—thank you—I took care of that at the warehouse. Tom—

Tom: Yes?

Jim: Mr. Mendoza was speaking to me about you.

Tom: Favorably?

Jim: What do you think?

Tom: Well—

Jim: You're going to be out of a job if you don't wake up.

Tom: I am waking up—

Jim: You show no signs.

Tom: The signs are interior.

(Image On Screen: The Sailing Vessel With Jolly Roger Again.)

Tom: I'm planning to change. (*He leans over the rail speaking with quiet exhilaration. The incandescent marquees and signs of the first-run movie houses light his face from across the alley. He looks like a voyager.*) I'm right at the point of committing myself to a future that doesn't include the warehouse and Mr. Mendoza or even a night-school course in public speaking.

Jim: What are you gassing about?

Tom: I'm tired of the movies.

Jim: Movies!

Tom: Yes, movies! Look at them—(*A wave toward the marvels of Grand Avenue.*) All of those glamorous people—having adventures—hogging it all, gobbling the whole thing up! You know what happens? People go to the *movies* instead of *moving!* Hollywood characters are supposed to have all the adventures for everybody in America, while everybody in America sits in a dark room and watches them have them! Yes, until there's a war. That's when adventure becomes available to the masses! *Everyone's* dish, not only Gable's! Then the people in the dark room come out of the dark room to have some adventures themselves—Goody, goody—It's our turn now, to go to the South Sea Island— to make a safari—to be exotic, far-off—But I'm not patient. I don't want to wait till then. I'm tired of the *movies* and I am *about* to *move!*

Jim (incredulously): Move?

Tom: Yes!

Jim: When?

Tom: Soon!

Jim: Where? Where?

Theme three music seems to answer the question, while Tom thinks it over. He searches among his pockets.

Tom: I'm starting to boil inside. I know I seem dreamy, but inside—well, I'm boiling! Whenever I pick up a shoe, I shudder a little thinking how short life is and what I am doing!—Whatever that means. I know it doesn't mean shoes—except as something to wear on a traveler's feet! (*Finds paper.*) Look—

Jim: What?

Tom: I'm a member.

Jim (reading): The Union of Merchant Seamen.

Tom: I paid my dues this month, instead of the light bill.

Jim: You will regret it when they turn the lights off.

Tom: I won't be here.

Jim: How about your mother?

Tom: I'm like my father. The bastard son of a bastard! See how he grins? And he's been absent going on sixteen years!

Jim: You're just talking, you drip. How does your mother feel about it?

Tom: Shhh—Here comes Mother! Mother is not acquainted with my plans!

Amanda (enters portieres): Where are you all?

Tom: On the terrace, Mother.

> *They start inside. She advances to them. Tom is distinctly shocked at her appearance. Even Jim blinks a little. He is making his first contact with girlish Southern vivacity and in spite of the night-school course in public speaking is somewhat thrown off the beam by the unexpected outlay of social charm.*
>
> *Certain responses are attempted by Jim but are swept aside by Amanda's gay laughter and chatter. Tom is embarrassed but after the first shock Jim reacts very warmly. Grins and chuckles, is altogether won over.*

(Image: Amanda As A Girl.)

Amanda (coyly smiling, shaking her girlish ringlets): Well, well, well, so this is Mr. O'Connor. Introductions entirely unnecessary. I've heard so much about you from my boy. I finally said to him, Tom—good gracious!—why don't you bring this paragon to supper? I'd like to meet this nice young man at the warehouse!—Instead of just hearing him sing your praises so much! I don't know why my son is so stand-offish—that's not Southern behavior! Let's sit down and—I think we could stand a little more air in here! Tom, leave the door open. I felt a nice fresh breeze a moment ago. Where has it gone? Mmm, so warm already! And not quite summer, even. We're going to burn up when summer really gets started. However, we're having—we're having a very light supper. I think light things are better fo' this time of year. The same as light clothes are. Light clothes an' light food are what warm weather calls fo'. You know our blood gets so thick during th' winter—it takes a while fo' us to *adjust* ou'selves!—when the season changes . . . It's come so quick this year. I wasn't prepared. All of a sudden—heavens! Already summer!—I ran to the trunk an' pulled out this light dress—Terribly old! Historical almost! But feels so good—so good an' co-ol, y'know. . . .

Tom: Mother—

Amanda: Yes, honey?

Tom: How about—supper?

Amanda: Honey, you go ask Sister if supper is ready! You know that Sister is in full charge of supper! Tell her you hungry boys are waiting for it. *(To Jim.)* Have you met Laura?

Jim: She—

Amanda: Let you in? Oh, good, you've met already! It's rare for a girl as sweet an' pretty as Laura to be domestic! But Laura is, thank heavens, not only pretty but also very domestic. I'm not at all. I never was a bit. I never could make a thing but angel-food cake. Well, in the South we had so many servants. Gone, gone, gone. All vestiges of gracious living! Gone completely! I wasn't prepared for what the future brought me. All of my gentlemen callers were sons of planters and so of course I assumed that I would be married to one and raise my family on a large piece of land with plenty of servants. But man proposes—and woman accepts the proposal!—To vary that old, old saying a little bit—I married no planter! I married a man who worked for the telephone company!—that gallantly smiling gentleman over there! (*Points to the picture.*) A telephone man who—fell in love with long-distance!—Now he travels and I don't even know where!—But what am I going on for about my—tribulations? Tell me yours—I hope you don't have any! Tom?

Tom (returning): Yes, Mother?

Amanda: Is supper nearly ready?

Tom: It looks to me like supper is on the table.

Amanda: Let me look—(*She rises prettily and looks through portieres.*) Oh, lovely— But where is Sister?

Tom: Laura is not feeling well and she says that she thinks she'd better not come to the table.

Amanda: What?—Nonsense!—Laura? Oh, Laura!

Laura (offstage, faintly): Yes, Mother.

Amanda: You really must come to the table. We won't be seated until you come to the table! Come in, Mr. O'Connor. You sit over there and I'll—Laura? Laura Wingfield! You're keeping us waiting, honey! We can't say grace until you come to the table!

The back door is pushed weakly open and Laura comes in. She is obviously quite faint, her lips trembling, her eyes wide and staring. She moves unsteadily toward the table.

(Legend: "Terror!")

Outside a summer storm is coming abruptly. The white curtains billow inward at the windows and there is a sorrowful murmur and deep blue dusk.

Laura suddenly stumbles—She catches at a chair with a faint moan.

Tom: Laura!

Amanda: Laura! (*There is a clap of thunder.*) **(Legend: "Ah!")** (*Despairingly.*) Why, Laura, you *are* sick, darling! Tom, help your sister into the living room, dear! Sit in the living room, Laura—rest on the sofa. Well! (*To the gentleman caller.*) Standing over the hot stove made her ill!—I told her that it was just too warm this evening, but—(*Tom comes back in. Laura is on the sofa.*) Is Laura all right now?

Tom: Yes.

Amanda: What is that? Rain? A nice cool rain has come up! (*She gives the gentleman caller a frightened look.*) I think we may—have grace—now . . . (*Tom looks at her stupidly.*) Tom, honey—you say grace!

Tom: Oh . . . "For these and all thy mercies—" (*They bow their heads, Amanda stealing a nervous glance at Jim. In the living room Laura, stretched on the sofa, clenches her hand to her lips, to hold back a shuddering sob.*) God's Holy Name be praised—

(The Scene Dims Out.)

Scene VII

(A Souvenir.)

Half an hour later. Dinner is just being finished in the upstage area which is concealed by the drawn portieres.

As the curtain rises Laura is still huddled upon the sofa, her feet drawn under her, her head resting on a pale blue pillow, her eyes wide and mysteriously watchful. The new floor lamp with its shade of rose-colored silk gives a soft, becoming light to her face, bringing out the fragile, unearthly prettiness which usually escapes attention. There is a steady murmur of rain, but it is slackening and stops soon after the scene begins; the air outside becomes pale and luminous as the moon breaks out.

A moment after the curtain rises, the lights in both rooms flicker and go out.

Jim: Hey, there, Mr. Light Bulb!

Amanda laughs nervously.

(Legend: "Suspension Of A Public Service.")

Amanda: Where was Moses when the lights went out? Ha-ha. Do you know the answer to that one, Mr. O'Connor?

Jim: No, Ma'am, what's the answer?

Amanda: In the dark! *(Jim laughs appreciatively.)* Everybody sit still. I'll light the candles. Isn't it lucky we have them on the table? Where's a match? Which of you gentlemen can provide a match?

Jim: Here.

Amanda: Thank you, sir.

Jim: Not at all, Ma'am!

Amanda: I guess the fuse has burnt out. Mr. O'Connor, can you tell a burnt-out fuse? I know I can't and Tom is a total loss when it comes to mechanics. **(Sound: Getting Up: Voices Recede A Little To Kitchenette.)** Oh, be careful you don't bump into something. We don't want our gentleman caller to break his neck. Now wouldn't that be a fine howdy-do?

Jim: Ha-ha! Where is the fuse-box?

Amanda: Right here next to the stove. Can you see anything?

Jim: Just a minute.

Amanda: Isn't electricity a mysterious thing? Wasn't it Benjamin Franklin who tied a key to a kite? We live in such a mysterious universe, don't we? Some people say that science clears up all the mysteries for us. In my opinion it only creates more! Have you found it yet?

Jim: No, Ma'am. All these fuses look okay to me.

Amanda: Tom!

Tom: Yes, Mother?

Amanda: That light bill I gave you several days ago. The one I told you we got the notices about?

Tom: Oh.—Yeah.

Amanda: You didn't neglect to pay it by any chance?

Tom: Why, I—

Amanda: Didn't! I might have known it!

Jim: Shakespeare probably wrote a poem on that light bill, Mrs. Wingfield.

Amanda: I might have known better than to trust him with it! There's such a high price for negligence in this world!

Jim: Maybe the poem will win a ten-dollar prize.

Amanda: We'll just have to spend the remainder of the evening in the nineteenth century, before Mr. Edison made the Mazda lamp!

Jim: Candlelight is my favorite kind of light.

Amanda: That shows you're romantic! But that's no excuse for Tom. Well, we got through dinner. Very considerate of them to let us get through dinner before they plunged us into everlasting darkness, wasn't it, Mr. O'Connor?

Jim: Ha-ha!

Amanda: Tom, as a penalty for your carelessness you can help me with the dishes.

Jim: Let me give you a hand.

Amanda: Indeed you will not!

Jim: I ought to be good for something.

Amanda: Good for something? (*Her tone is rhapsodic.*) You? Why, Mr. O'Connor, nobody, *nobody's* given me this much entertainment in years—as you have!

Jim: Aw, now, Mrs. Wingfield!

Amanda: I'm not exaggerating, not one bit! But Sister is all by her lonesome. You go keep her company in the parlor! I'll give you this lovely old candelabrum that used to be on the altar at the church of the Heavenly Rest. It was melted a little out of shape when the church burnt down. Lightning struck it one spring. Gypsy Jones was holding a revival at the time and he intimated that the church was destroyed because the Episcopalians gave card parties.

Jim: Ha-ha.

Amanda: And how about coaxing Sister to drink a little wine? I think it would be good for her! Can you carry both at once?

Jim: Sure. I'm Superman!

Amanda: Now, Thomas, get into this apron!

The door of kitchenette swings closed on Amanda's gay laughter; the flickering light approaches the portieres.

Laura sits up nervously as he enters. Her speech at first is low and breathless from the almost intolerable strain of being alone with a stranger.

(The Legend: "I Don't Suppose You Remember Me At All!")

In her first speeches in this scene, before Jim's warmth overcomes her paralyzing shyness, Laura's voice is thin and breathless as though she has run up a steep flight of stairs.

Jim's attitude is gently humorous. In playing this scene it should be stressed that while the incident is apparently unimportant, it is to Laura the climax of her secret life.

Jim: Hello, there, Laura.

Laura (faintly): Hello. *(She clears her throat.)*

Jim: How are you feeling now? Better?

Laura: Yes. Yes, thank you.

Jim: This is for you. A little dandelion wine. *(He extends it toward her with extravagant gallantry.)*

Laura: Thank you.

Jim: Drink it—but don't get drunk! *(He laughs heartily. Laura takes the glass uncertainly; laughs shyly.)* Where shall I set the candles?

Laura: Oh—oh, anywhere . . .

Jim: How about here on the floor? Any objections?

Laura: No.

Jim: I'll spread a newspaper under to catch the drippings. I like to sit on the floor. Mind if I do?

Laura: Oh, no.

Jim: Give me a pillow?

Laura: What?

Jim: A pillow!

Laura: Oh . . . *(Hands him one quickly.)*

Jim: How about you? Don't you like to sit on the floor?

Laura: Oh—yes.

Jim: Why don't you, then?

Laura: I—will.

Jim: Take a pillow! *(Laura does. Sits on the other side of the candelabrum. Jim crosses his legs and smiles engagingly at her.)* I can't hardly see you sitting way over there.

Laura: I can—see you.

Jim: I know, but that's not fair, I'm in the limelight. *(Laura moves her pillow closer.)* Good! Now I can see you! Comfortable?

Laura: Yes.

Jim: So am I. Comfortable as a cow. Will you have some gum?

Laura: No, thank you.

Jim: I think that I will indulge, with your permission. *(Musingly unwraps it and holds it up.)* Think of the fortune made by the guy that invented the first piece of chewing gum. Amazing, huh? The Wrigley Building is one of the sights of Chicago.—I saw it summer before last when I went up to the Century of Progress. Did you take in the Century of Progress?

Laura: No, I didn't.

Jim: Well, it was quite a wonderful exposition. What impressed me most was the Hall of Science. Gives you an idea of what the future will be in America, even more wonderful than the present time is! *(Pause. Smiling at her.)* Your brother tells me you're shy. Is that right, Laura?

Laura: I—don't know.

Jim: I judge you to be an old-fashioned type of girl. Well, I think that's a pretty good type to be. Hope you don't think I'm being too personal—do you?

Laura (hastily, out of embarrassment): I believe I *will* take a piece of gum, if you—don't mind. *(Clearing her throat.)* Mr. O'Connor, have you—kept up with your singing?

Jim: Singing? Me?

Laura: Yes. I remember what a beautiful voice you had.

Jim: When did you hear me sing?

(Voice Offstage In The Pause.)

Voice (offstage):

> O blow, ye winds, heigh-ho,
> A-roving I will go!
> I'm off to my love
> With a boxing glove—
> Ten thousand miles away!

Jim: You say you've heard me sing?

Laura: Oh, yes! Yes, very often . . . I—don't suppose you remember me—at all?

Jim (smiling doubtfully): You know I have an idea I've seen you before. I had that idea soon as you opened the door. It seemed almost like I was about to remember your name. But the name that I started to call you—wasn't a name! And so I stopped myself before I said it.

Laura: Wasn't it—Blue Roses?

Jim (springs up, grinning): Blue Roses! My gosh, yes—Blue Roses! That's what I had on my tongue when you opened the door! Isn't it funny what tricks your memory plays? I didn't connect you with the high school somehow or other. But that's where it was; it was high school. I didn't even know you were Shakespeare's sister! Gosh, I'm sorry.

Laura: I didn't expect you to. You—barely knew me!

Jim: But we did have a speaking acquaintance, huh?

Laura: Yes, we—spoke to each other.

Jim: When did you recognize me?

Laura: Oh, right away!

Jim: Soon as I came in the door?

Laura: When I heard your name I thought it was probably you. I knew that Tom used to know you a little in high school. So when you came in the door— Well, then I was—sure.

Jim: Why didn't you *say* something, then?

Laura (breathlessly): I didn't know what to say, I was—too surprised!

Jim: For goodness sakes! You know, this sure is funny!

Laura: Yes! Yes, isn't it, though . . .

Jim: Didn't we have a class in something together?

Laura: Yes, we did.

Jim: What class was that?

Laura: It was—singing—Chorus!

Jim: Aw!

Laura: I sat across the aisle from you in the Aud.

Jim: Aw.

Laura: Mondays, Wednesday and Fridays.

Jim: Now I remember—you always came in late.

Laura: Yes, it was so hard for me, getting upstairs. I had that brace on my leg—it clumped so loud!

Jim: I never heard any clumping.

Laura (wincing at the recollection): To me it sounded like thunder!

Jim: Well, well, well. I never even noticed.

Laura: And everybody was seated before I came in. I had to walk in front of all those people. My seat was in the back row. I had to go clumping all the way up the aisle with everyone watching!

Jim: You shouldn't have been self-conscious.

Laura: I know, but I was. It was always such a relief when the singing started.

Jim: Aw, yes, I've placed you now! I used to call you Blue Roses. How was it that I got started calling you that?

Laura: I was out of school a little while with pleurosis. When I came back you asked me what was the matter. I said I had pleurosis—you thought I said Blue Roses. That's what you always called me after that!

Jim: I hope you didn't mind.

Laura: Oh, no—I liked it. You see, I wasn't acquainted with many—people. . . .

Jim: As I remember you sort of stuck by yourself.

Laura: I—I—never had much luck at—making friends.

Jim: I don't see why you wouldn't.

Laura: Well, I—started out badly.

Jim: You mean being—

Laura: Yes, it sort of—stood between me—

Jim: You shouldn't have let it!

Laura: I know, but it did, and—

Jim: You were shy with people!

Laura: I tried not to be but never could—

Jim: Overcome it?

Laura: No, I—I never could!

Jim: I guess being shy is something you have to work out of kind of gradually.

Laura (sorrowfully): Yes—I guess it—

Jim: Takes time!

Laura: Yes—

Jim: People are not so dreadful when you know them. That's what you have to remember! And everybody has problems, not just you, but practically everybody has got some problems. You think of yourself as having the only problems, as being the only one who is disappointed. But just look around you and you will see lots of people as disappointed as you are. For instance, I hoped when I was going to high school that I would be further along at this time, six years later, than I am now—You remember that wonderful write-up I had in *The Torch?*

Laura: Yes! (*She rises and crosses to table.*)

Jim: It said I was bound to succeed in anything I went into! (*Laura returns with the annual.*) Holy Jeez! *The Torch!* (*He accepts it reverently. They smile across it with mutual wonder. Laura crouches beside him and they begin to turn through it. Laura's shyness is dissolving in his warmth.*)

Laura: Here you are in *Pirates of Penzance!*

Jim (wistfully): I sang the baritone lead in that operetta.

Laura (rapidly): So—beautifully!

Jim (protesting): Aw—

Laura: Yes, yes—beautifully—beautifully!

Jim: You heard me?

Laura: All three times!

Jim: No!

Laura: Yes!

Jim: All three performances?

Laura (looking down): Yes.

Jim: Why?

Laura: I—wanted to ask you to—autograph my program.

Jim: Why didn't you ask me to?

Laura: You were always surrounded by your own friends so much that I never had a chance to.

Jim: You should have just—

Laura: Well, I—thought you might think I was—

Jim: Thought I might think you was—what?

Laura: Oh—

Jim (with reflective relish): I was beleaguered by females in those days.

Laura: You were terribly popular!

Jim: Yeah—

Laura: You had such a—friendly way—

Jim: I was spoiled in high school.

Laura: Everybody—liked you!

Jim: Including you?

Laura: I—yes, I—did, too—*(She gently closes the book in her lap.)*

Jim: Well, well, well!—Give me that program, Laura. *(She hands it to him. He signs it with a flourish.)* There you are—better late than never!

Laura: Oh, I—what a—surprise!

Jim: My signature isn't worth very much right now. But some day—maybe—it will increase in value! Being disappointed is one thing and being discouraged is something else. I am disappointed but I'm not discouraged. I'm twenty-three years old. How old are you?

Laura: I'll be twenty-four in June.

Jim: That's not old age!

Laura: No, but—

Jim: You finished high school?

Laura (with difficulty): I didn't go back.

Jim: You mean you dropped out?

Laura: I made bad grades in my final examinations. *(She rises and replaces the book and the program. Her voice strained.)* How is—Emily Meisenbach getting along?

Jim: Oh, that kraut-head!

Laura: Why do you call her that?

Jim: That's what she was.

Laura: You're not still—going with her?

Jim: I never see her.

Laura: It said in the Personal Section that you were—engaged!

Jim: I know, but I wasn't impressed by that—propaganda!

Laura: It wasn't—the truth?

Jim: Only in Emily's optimistic opinion!
Laura: Oh—

(Legend: "What Have You Done Since High School?")

Jim lights a cigarette and leans indolently back on his elbows smiling at Laura with a warmth and charm which light her inwardly with altar candles. She remains by the table and turns in her hands a piece of glass to cover her tumult.

Jim (after several reflective puffs on a cigarette): What have you done since high school? *(She seems not to hear him.)* Huh? *(Laura looks up.)* I said what have you done since high school, Laura?
Laura: Nothing much.
Jim: You must have been doing something these six long years.
Laura: Yes.
Jim: Well, then, such as what?
Laura: I took a business course at business college—
Jim: How did that work out?
Laura: Well, not very—well—I had to drop out, it gave me—indigestion—

Jim laughs gently.

Jim: What are you doing now?
Laura: I don't do anything—much. Oh, please don't think I sit around doing nothing! My glass collection takes up a good deal of my time. Glass is something you have to take good care of.
Jim: What did you say—about glass?
Laura: Collection I said—I have one—*(She clears her throat and turns away again, acutely shy.)*
Jim (abruptly): You know what I judge to be the trouble with you? Inferiority complex! Know what that is? That's what they call it when someone low-rates himself! I understand it because I had it, too. Although my case was not so aggravated as yours seems to be. I had it until I took up public speaking, developed my voice, and learned that I had an aptitude for science. Before that time I never thought of myself as being outstanding in any way whatsoever! Now I've never made a regular study of it, but I have a friend who says I can analyze people better than doctors that make a profession of it. I don't claim that to be necessarily true, but I can sure guess a person's psychology, Laura! *(Takes out his gum.)* Excuse me, Laura. I always take it out when the flavor is gone. I'll use this scrap of paper to wrap it in. I know how it is to get it stuck on a shoe. Yep—that's what I judge to be your principal trouble. A lack of confidence in yourself as a person. You don't have the proper amount of faith in yourself. I'm basing that fact on a number of your remarks and also on certain observations I've made. For instance that clumping you thought was so awful in high school. You say that you even dreaded to walk into class. You see what you did? You dropped out of school, you gave up an education because of a clump, which as far as I know was practically non-existent! A little physical defect is what you have. Hardly noticeable even! Magnified thousands of times by imagination! You know what my strong advice to you is? Think of yourself as *superior* in some way!

Laura: In what way would I think?

Jim: Why, man alive, Laura! Just look about you a little. What do you see? A world full of common people! All of 'em born and all of 'em going to die! Which of them has one-tenth of your good points! Or mine! Or anyone else's, as far as that goes—Gosh! Everybody excels in some one thing. Some in many! *(Unconsciously glances at himself in the mirror.)* All you've got to do is discover in *what!* Take me, for instance. *(He adjusts his tie at the mirror.)* My interest happens to lie in electro-dynamics. I'm taking a course in radio engineering at night school, Laura, on top of a fairly responsible job at the warehouse. I'm taking that course and studying public speaking.

Laura: Ohhhh.

Jim: Because I believe in the future of television! *(Turning back to her.)* I wish to be ready to go up right along with it. Therefore I'm planning to get in on the ground floor. In fact, I've already made the right connections and all that remains is for the industry itself to get under way! Full steam—*(His eyes are starry.)* Knowledge—Zzzzzp! Money—Zzzzzzp!—Power! That's the cycle democracy is built on! *(His attitude is convincingly dynamic. Laura stares at him, even her shyness eclipsed in her absolute wonder. He suddenly grins.)* I guess you think I think a lot of myself!

Laura: No—o-o-o, I—

Jim: Now how about you? Isn't there something you take more interest in than anything else?

Laura: Well, I do—as I said—have my—glass collection—

A peal of girlish laughter from the kitchen.

Jim: I'm not right sure I know what you're talking about. What kind of glass is it?

Laura: Little articles of it, they're ornaments mostly! Most of them are little animals made out of glass, the tiniest little animals in the world. Mother calls them a glass menagerie! Here's an example of one, if you'd like to see it! This one is one of the oldest. It's nearly thirteen. *(He stretches out his hand.)* **(Music: "The Glass Menagerie.")** Oh, be careful—if you breathe, it breaks!

Jim: I'd better not take it. I'm pretty clumsy with things.

Laura: Go on, I trust you with him! *(Places it in his palm.)* There now—you're holding him gently! Hold him over the light, he loves the light! You see how the light shines through him?

Jim: It sure does shine!

Laura: I shouldn't be partial, but he is my favorite one.

Jim: What kind of a thing is this one supposed to be?

Laura: Haven't you noticed the single horn on his forehead?

Jim: A unicorn, huh?

Laura: Mmm-hmmm!

Jim: Unicorns, aren't they extinct in the modern world?

Laura: I know!

Jim: Poor little fellow, he must feel sort of lonesome.

Laura (smiling): Well, if he does he doesn't complain about it. He stays on a shelf with some horses that don't have horns and all of them seem to get along nicely together.

Jim: How do you know?

Laura (lightly): I haven't heard any arguments among them!

Jim (grinning): No arguments, huh? Well, that's a pretty good sign! Where shall I set him?

Laura: Put him on the table. They all like a change of scenery once in a while!

Jim (stretching): Well, well, well, well—Look how big my shadow is when I stretch!

Laura: Oh, oh, yes—it stretches across the ceiling!

Jim (crossing to door): I think it's stopped raining. (*Opens fire-escape door.*) Where does the music come from?

Laura: From the Paradise Dance Hall across the alley.

Jim: How about cutting the rug a little, Miss Wingfield?

Laura: Oh, I—

Jim: Or is your program filled up? Let me have a look at it. (*Grasps imaginary card.*) Why, every dance is taken! I'll just have to scratch some out. **(Waltz Music: "La Golondrina.")** Ahhh, a waltz! (*He executes some sweeping turns by himself, then holds his arms toward Laura.*)

Laura (breathlessly): I—can't dance!

Jim: There you go, that inferiority stuff!

Laura: I've never danced in my life!

Jim: Come on, try!

Laura: Oh, but I'd step on you!

Jim: I'm not made out of glass.

Laura: How—how—how do we start?

Jim: Just leave it to me. You hold your arms out a little.

Laura: Like this?

Jim: A little bit higher. Right. Now don't tighten up, that's the main thing about it—relax.

Laura (laughing breathlessly): It's hard not to.

Jim: Okay.

Laura: I'm afraid you can't budge me.

Jim: What do you bet I can't? (*He swings her into motion.*)

Laura: Goodness, yes, you can!

Jim: Let yourself go, now, Laura, just let yourself go.

Laura: I'm—

Jim: Come on!

Laura: Trying!

Jim: Not so stiff—Easy does it!

Laura: I know but I'm—

Jim: Loosen th' backbone! There now, that's a lot better.

Laura: Am I?

Jim: Lots, lots better! (*He moves her about the room in a clumsy waltz.*)

Laura: Oh, my!

Jim: Ha-ha!

Laura: Goodness, yes you can!

Jim: Ha-ha-ha! (*They suddenly bump into the table, Jim stops.*) What did we hit on?

Laura: Table.

Jim: Did something fall off it? I think—

Laura: Yes.

Jim: I hope that it wasn't the little glass horse with the horn!

Laura: Yes.

Jim: Aw, aw, aw. Is it broken?

Laura: Now it is just like all the other horses.

Jim: It's lost its—

Laura: Horn! It doesn't matter. Maybe it's a blessing in disguise.

Jim: You'll never forgive me. I bet that that was your favorite piece of glass.

Laura: I don't have favorites much. It's no tragedy, Freckles. Glass breaks so easily. No matter how careful you are. The traffic jars the shelves and things fall off them.

Jim: Still I'm awfully sorry that I was the cause.

Laura (smiling): I'll just imagine he had an operation. The horn was removed to make him feel less—freakish! *(They both laugh.)* Now he will feel more at home with the other horses, the ones that don't have horns . . .

Jim: Ha-ha, that's very funny! *(Suddenly serious.)* I'm glad to see that you have a sense of humor. You know—you're—well—very different! Surprisingly different from anyone else I know! *(His voice becomes soft and hesitant with a genuine feeling.)* Do you mind me telling you that? *(Laura is abashed beyond speech.)* You make me feel sort of—I don't know how to put it! I'm usually pretty good at expressing things, but—This is something that I don't know how to say! *(Laura touches her throat and clears it—turns the broken unicorn in her hands.)* *(Even softer.)* Has anyone ever told you that you were pretty? **(Pause: Music.)** *(Laura looks up slowly, with wonder, and shakes her head.)* Well, you are! In a very different way from anyone else. And all the nicer because of the difference, too. *(His voice becomes low and husky. Laura turns away, nearly faint with the novelty of her emotions.)* I wish you were my sister. I'd teach you to have some confidence in yourself. The different people are not like other people, but being different is nothing to be ashamed of. Because other people are not such wonderful people. They're one hundred times one thousand. You're one times one! They walk all over the earth. You just stay here. They're common as—weeds, but—you—well, you're—*Blue Roses!*

(Image On Screen: Blue Roses.)

(Music Changes.)

Laura: But blue is wrong for—roses . . .

Jim: It's right for you—You're—pretty!

Laura: In what respect am I pretty?

Jim: In all respects—believe me! Your eyes—your hair—are pretty! Your hands are pretty! *(He catches hold of her hand.)* You think I'm making this up because I'm invited to dinner and have to be nice. Oh, I could do that! I could put on an act for you, Laura, and say lots of things without being very sincere. But this time I am. I'm talking to you sincerely. I happened to notice you had this inferiority complex that keeps you from feeling comfortable with people. Somebody needs to build your confidence up and make you proud instead of shy and turning away and—blushing—Somebody ought to—ought to—*kiss* you, Laura! *(His hand slips slowly up her arm to her shoulder.)* **(Music**

Swells Tumultuously.) *(He suddenly turns her about and kisses her on the lips. When he releases her Laura sinks on the sofa with a bright, dazed look. Jim backs away and fishes in his pocket for a cigarette.)* **(Legend On Screen: "Souvenir.")** Stumble-john! *(He lights the cigarette, avoiding her look. There is a peal of girlish laughter from Amanda in the kitchen. Laura slowly raises and opens her hand. It still contains the little broken glass animal. She looks at it with a tender, bewildered expression.)* Stumble-john! I shouldn't have done that—That was way off the beam. You don't smoke, do you? *(She looks up, smiling, not hearing the question. He sits beside her a little gingerly. She looks at him speechlessly—waiting. He coughs decorously and moves a little farther aside as he considers the situation and senses her feelings, dimly, with perturbation. Gently.)* Would you—care for a—mint? *(She doesn't seem to hear him but her look grows brighter even.)* Peppermint—Life Saver? My pocket's a regular drug store—wherever I go . . . *(He pops a mint in his mouth. Then gulps and decides to make a clean breast of it. He speaks slowly and gingerly.)* Laura, you know, if I had a sister like you, I'd do the same thing as Tom, I'd bring out fellows—introduce her to them. The right type of boys of a type to—appreciate her. Only—well—he made a mistake about me. Maybe

I've got no call to be saying this. That may not have been the idea in having me over. But what if it was? There's nothing wrong about that. The only trouble is that in my case—I'm not in a situation to—do the right thing. I can't take down your number and say I'll phone. I can't call up next week and—ask for a date. I thought I had better explain the situation in case you misunderstood it and—hurt your feelings. . . . *(Pause. Slowly, very slowly, Laura's look changes, her eyes returning slowly from his to the ornament in her palm.)*

Amanda utters another gay laugh in the kitchen.

Laura (faintly): You—won't—call again?

Jim: No, Laura, I can't. *(He rises from the sofa.)* As I was just explaining, I've—got strings on me, Laura, I've—been going steady! I go out all the time with a girl named Betty. She's a home-girl like you, and Catholic, and Irish, and in a great many ways we—get along fine. I met her last summer on a moonlight boat trip up the river to Alton, on the *Majestic*. Well—right away from the start it was—love! **(Legend: Love!)** *(Laura sways slightly forward and grips the arm of the sofa. He fails to notice, now enrapt in his own comfortable being.)* Being in love has made a new man of me! *(Leaning stiffly forward, clutching the arm of the sofa, Laura struggles visibly with her storm. But Jim is oblivious, she is a long way off.)* The power of love is really pretty tremendous! Love is something that—changes the whole world, Laura! *(The storm abates a little and Laura leans back. He notices her again.)* It happened that Betty's aunt took sick, she got a wire and had to go to Centralia. So Tom—when he asked me to dinner—I naturally just accepted the invitation, not knowing that you— that he—that I—*(He stops awkwardly.)* Huh—I'm a stumble-john! *(He flops back on the sofa. The holy candles in the altar of Laura's face have been snuffed out! There is a look of almost infinite desolation. Jim glances at her uneasily.)* I wish that you would—say something. *(She bites her lip which was trembling and then bravely smiles. She opens her hand again on the broken glass ornament. Then she gently takes his hand and raises it level with her own. She carefully places the unicorn*

in the palm of his hand, then pushes his fingers closed upon it.) What are you—doing that for? You want me to have him?—Laura? *(She nods.)* What for?
Laura: A—souvenir . . .

She rises unsteadily and crouches beside the victrola to wind it up.

(Legend On Screen: "Things Have A Way Of Turning Out So Badly.")

(Or Image: "Gentleman Caller Waving Good-bye!—Gaily.")

At this moment Amanda rushes brightly back in the front room. She bears a pitcher of fruit punch in an old-fashioned cut-glass pitcher and a plate of macaroons. The plate has a gold border and poppies painted on it.

Amanda: Well, well, well! Isn't the air delightful after the shower? I've made you children a little liquid refreshment. *(Turns gaily to the gentleman caller.)* Jim, do you know that song about lemonade?
　　"Lemonade, lemonade
　　Made in the shade and stirred with a spade—
　　Good enough for any old maid!"
Jim (uneasily): Ha-ha! No—I never heard it.
Amanda: Why, Laura! You look so serious!
Jim: We were having a serious conversation.
Amanda: Good! Now you're better acquainted!
Jim (uncertainly): Ha-ha! Yes.
Amanda: You modern young people are much more serious-minded than my generation. I was so gay as a girl!
Jim: You haven't changed, Mrs. Wingfield.
Amanda: Tonight I'm rejuvenated! The gaiety of the occasion, Mr. O'Connor! *(She tosses her head with a peal of laughter. Spills lemonade.)* Oooo! I'm baptizing myself!
Jim: Here—let me—
Amanda (setting the pitcher down): There now. I discovered we had some maraschino cherries. I dumped them in, juice and all!
Jim: You shouldn't have gone to that trouble, Mrs. Wingfield.
Amanda: Trouble, trouble? Why it was loads of fun! Didn't you hear me cutting up in the kitchen? I bet your ears were burning! I told Tom how outdone with him I was for keeping you to himself so long a time! He should have brought you over much, much sooner! Well, now that you've found your way, I want you to be a very frequent caller! Not just occasional but all the time. Oh, we're going to have a lot of gay times together! I see them coming! Mmm, just breathe that air! So fresh, and the moon's so pretty! I'll skip back out—I know where my place is when young folks are having a—serious conversation!
Jim: Oh, don't go out, Mrs. Wingfield. The fact of the matter is I've got to be going.
Amanda: Going, now? You're joking! Why, it's only the shank of the evening, Mr. O'Connor!
Jim: Well, you know how it is.

Amanda: You mean you're a young workingman and have to keep workingmen's hours. We'll let you off early tonight. But only on the condition that next time you stay later. What's the best night for you? Isn't Saturday night the best night for you workingmen?

Jim: I have a couple of time-clocks to punch, Mrs. Wingfield. One at morning, another one at night!

Amanda: My, but you *are* ambitious! You work at night, too?

Jim: No, Ma'am, not work but—Betty! *(He crosses deliberately to pick up his hat. The band at the Paradise Dance Hall goes into a tender waltz.)*

Amanda: Betty? Betty? Who's—Betty? *(There is an ominous cracking sound in the sky.)*

Jim: Oh, just a girl. The girl I go steady with! *(He smiles charmingly. The sky falls.)*

(Legend: "The Sky Falls.")

Amanda (a long-drawn exhalation): Ohhhh . . . Is it a serious romance, Mr. O'Connor?

Jim: We're going to be married the second Sunday in June.

Amanda: Ohhhh—how nice! Tom didn't mention that you were engaged to be married.

Jim: The cat's not out of the bag at the warehouse yet. You know how they are. They call you Romeo and stuff like that. *(He stops at the oval mirror to put on his hat. He carefully shapes the brim and the crown to give a discreetly dashing effect.)* It's been a wonderful evening, Mrs. Wingfield. I guess this is what they mean by Southern hospitality.

Amanda: It really wasn't anything at all.

Jim: I hope it don't seem like I'm rushing off. But I promised Betty I'd pick her up at the Wabash depot, an' by the time I get my jalopy down there her train'll be in. Some women are pretty upset if you keep 'em waiting.

Amanda: Yes, I know—The tyranny of women! *(Extends her hand.)* Goodbye, Mr. O'Connor. I wish you luck—and happiness—and success! All three of them, and so does Laura!—Don't you, Laura?

Laura: Yes!

Jim (taking her hand): Goodbye, Laura. I'm certainly going to treasure that souvenir. And don't you forget the good advice I gave you. *(Raises his voice to a cheery shout.)* So long, Shakespeare! Thanks again, ladies—Good night!

He grins and ducks jauntily out.

Still bravely grimacing, Amanda closes the door on the gentleman caller. Then she turns back to the room with a puzzled expression. She and Laura don't dare to face each other. Laura crouches beside the victrola to wind it.

Amanda (faintly): Things have a way of turning out so badly. I don't believe that I would play the victrola. Well, well—well—Our gentleman caller was engaged to be married! Tom!

Tom (from back): Yes, Mother?

Amanda: Come in here a minute. I want to tell you something awfully funny.

Tom (enters with macaroon and a glass of the lemonade): Has the gentleman caller gotten away already?

Amanda: The gentleman caller has made an early departure. What a wonderful joke you played on us!

Tom: How do you mean?

Amanda: You didn't mention that he was engaged to be married.

Tom: Jim? Engaged?

Amanda: That's what he just informed us.

Tom: I'll be jiggered! I didn't know about that.

Amanda: That seems very peculiar.

Tom: What's peculiar about it?

Amanda: Didn't you call him your best friend down at the warehouse?

Tom: He is, but how did I know?

Amanda: It seems extremely peculiar that you wouldn't know your best friend was going to be married!

Tom: The warehouse is where I work, not where I know things about people!

Amanda: You don't know things anywhere! You live in a dream; you manufacture illusions! *(He crosses to door.)* Where are you going?

Tom: I'm going to the movies.

Amanda: That's right, now that you've had us make such fools of ourselves. The effort, the preparations, all the expense! The new floor lamp, the rug, the clothes for Laura! All for what? To entertain some other girl's fiancé! Go to the movies, go! Don't think about us, a mother deserted, an unmarried sister who's crippled and has no job! Don't let anything interfere with your selfish pleasure! Just go, go, go—to the movies!

Tom: All right, I will! The more you shout about my selfishness to me the quicker I'll go, and I won't go to the movies!

Amanda: Go, then! Then go to the moon—you selfish dreamer!

> *Tom smashes his glass on the floor. He plunges out on the fire-escape, slamming the door. Laura screams—cut by door.*
>
> *Dance-hall music up. Tom goes to the rail and grips it desperately, lifting his face in the chill white moonlight penetrating the narrow abyss of the alley.*

(Legend On Screen: "And So Good-bye . . .")

> *Tom's closing speech is timed with the interior pantomime. The interior scene is played as though viewed through sound-proof glass. Amanda appears to be making a comforting speech to Laura who is huddled upon the sofa. Now that we cannot hear the mother's speech, her silliness is gone and she has dignity and tragic beauty. Laura's dark hair hides her face until at the end of the speech she lifts it to smile at her mother. Amanda's gestures are slow and graceful, almost dancelike, as she comforts the daughter. At the end of her speech she glances a moment at the father's picture—then withdraws through the portieres. At close of Tom's speech, Laura blows out the candles, ending the play.*

Tom: I didn't go to the movies, I went much further—for time is the longest distance between two places—Not long after that I was fired for writing a poem on the lid of a shoe-box. I left Saint Louis. I descended the steps of this fire-escape for a last time and followed, from then on, in my father's footsteps, attempting to find in motion what was lost in space—I traveled around a great deal. The cities swept about me like dead leaves, leaves that were brightly colored but torn away from the branches. I would have stopped, but was pursued by something. It always came upon me unawares, taking me altogether by surprise. Perhaps it was a familiar bit of music. Perhaps it was only a piece of transparent glass. Perhaps I am walking along a street at night, in some strange city, before I have found companions. I pass the lighted window of a shop where perfume is sold. The window is filled with pieces of colored glass, tiny transparent bottles in delicate colors, like bits of a shattered rainbow. Then all at once my sister touches my shoulder. I turn around and look into her eyes . . . Oh, Laura, Laura, I tried to leave you behind me, but I am more faithful than I intended to be! I reach for a cigarette, I cross the street, I run into the movies or a bar, I buy a drink, I speak to the nearest stranger— anything that can blow your candles out! *(Laura bends over the candles.)*—for nowadays the world is lit by lightning! Blow out your candles, Laura—and so good-bye . . . .

She blows the candles out.

(The Scene Dissolves.)

COMPARE:

The Glass Menagerie and Tennessee Williams's "How to Stage *The Glass Menagerie*" (page 1446).

August Wilson

JOE TURNER'S COME AND GONE   1988

August Wilson was born (in 1945) and raised on The Hill, a Pittsburgh ghetto neighborhood. Although he quit school in the ninth grade when a teacher accused him of submitting a ghost-written paper, which in truth he had written himself, Wilson continued his education in local libraries, supporting himself by cooking and stock-clerking. In 1968 he co-founded a community troupe, the Black Horizons Theater, staging plays by LeRoi Jones and other militants; later he moved from Pittsburgh to Saint Paul, Minnesota, where at last he saw a play of his own performed. Jitney, his first effort, won him entry to a 1982 playwrights' conference at the Eugene O'Neill Theater Center. There, Lloyd Richards, dean of Yale University School of Drama, took an interest in Wilson's work and offered to produce his plays at Yale. Ma Rainey's Black Bottom was the first to reach Broadway (in 1985), where it ran for

August Wilson

ten months and received a prize from the New York Drama Critics Circle. In 1987 Fences, starring Mary Alice and James Paul Jones, won another Critics Circle award, besides a Tony award and the Pulitzer Prize for best American play of its year. It set a box office record for a Broadway nonmusical. Joe Turner's Come and Gone has also received high acclaim, and in 1990 his fourth major work, The Piano Player, won him a second Pulitzer Prize. A published poet, Wilson once told an interviewer, "After writing poetry for twenty-one years, I approach a play the same way. The mental process is poetic: you use metaphor and condense."

Characters

Seth Holly, owner of the boardinghouse
Bertha Holly, his wife
Bynum Walker, a rootworker[1]
Rutherford Selig, a peddler
Jeremy Furlow, a resident
Herald Loomis, a resident
Zonia Loomis, his daughter
Mattie Campbell, a resident
Reuben Scott, boy who lives next door
Molly Cunningham, a resident
Martha Pentecost, Herald Loomis's wife

Setting

August, 1911. A boardinghouse in Pittsburgh. At right is a kitchen. Two doors open off the kitchen. One leads to the outhouse and Seth's workshop. The other to Seth's and Bertha's bedroom. At left is a parlor. The front door opens into the parlor, which gives access to the stairs leading to the upstairs rooms.
    There is a small outside playing area.

The Play

It is August in Pittsburgh, 1911. The sun falls out of heaven like a stone. The fires of the steel mill rage with a combined sense of industry and progress. Barges loaded with coal and iron ore trudge up the river to the mill towns that dot the Monongahela and return with fresh, hard, gleaming steel. The city flexes its muscles. Men throw countless bridges across the river, lay roads and carve tunnels through the hills sprouting with houses.
    From the deep and the near South the sons and daughters of newly freed African slaves wander into the city. Isolated, cut off from memory, having forgotten the names of the gods and only guessing at their faces, they arrive dazed and stunned, their heart kicking in their chest with a song worth singing. They arrive carrying Bibles and guitars, their pockets lined with dust and fresh hope, marked men and women seeking to scrape

rootworker: a conjure man, or voodoo practitioner.

from the narrow, crooked cobbles and the fiery blasts of the coke furnace a way of bludgeoning and shaping the malleable parts of themselves into a new identity as free men of definite and sincere worth.

Foreigners in a strange land, they carry as part and parcel of their baggage a long line of separation and dispersement which informs their sensibilities and marks their conduct as they search for ways to reconnect, to reassemble, to give clear and luminous meaning to the song which is both a wail and a whelp of joy.

ACT I

Scene 1

The lights come up on the kitchen. Bertha busies herself with breakfast preparations. Seth stands looking out the window at Bynum in the yard. Seth is in his early fifties. Born of Northern free parents, a skilled craftsman, and owner of the boardinghouse, he has a stability that none of the other characters have. Bertha is five years his junior. Married for over twenty-five years, she has learned how to negotiate around Seth's apparent orneriness.

Seth (*at the window, laughing*): If that ain't the damndest thing I seen. Look here, Bertha.

Bertha: I done seen Bynum out there with them pigeons before.

Seth: Naw . . . naw . . . look at this. That pigeon flopped out of Bynum's hand and he about to have a fit.

(*Bertha crosses over to the window.*)

He down there on his hands and knees behind that bush looking all over for that pigeon and it on the other side of the yard. See it over there?

Bertha: Come on and get your breakfast and leave that man alone.

Seth: Look at him . . . he still looking. He ain't seen it yet. All that old mumbo jumbo nonsense. I don't know why I put up with it.

Bertha: You don't say nothing when he bless the house.

Seth: I just go along with that 'cause of you. You around here sprinkling salt all over the place . . . got pennies lined up across the threshold . . . all that heebie-jeebie stuff. I just put up with that 'cause of you. I don't pay that kind of stuff no mind. And you going down there to the church and wanna come home and sprinkle salt all over the place.

Bertha: It don't hurt none. I can't say if it help . . . but it don't hurt none.

Seth: Look at him. He done found that pigeon and now he's talking to it.

Bertha: These biscuits be ready in a minute.

Seth: He done drew a big circle with that stick and now he's dancing around. I know he'd better not . . .

(*Seth bolts from the window and rushes to the back door.*)

Hey, Bynum! Don't be hopping around stepping in my vegetables. Hey, Bynum . . . Watch where you stepping!

Bertha: Seth, leave that man alone.

Seth (coming back into the house): I don't care how much he be dancing around . . . just don't be stepping in my vegetables. Man got my garden all messed up now . . . planting them weeds out there . . . burying them pigeons and whatnot.

Bertha: Bynum don't bother nobody. He ain't even thinking about your vegetables.

Seth: I know he ain't! That's why he out there stepping on them.

Bertha: What Mr. Johnson say down there?

Seth: I told him if I had the tools I could go out here and find me four or five fellows and open up my own shop instead of working for Mr. Olowski. Get me four or five fellows and teach them how to make pots and pans. One man making ten pots is five men making fifty. He told me he'd think about it.

Bertha: Well, maybe he'll come to see it your way.

Seth: He wanted me to sign over the house to him. You know what I thought of that idea.

Bertha: He'll come to see you're right.

Seth: I'm going up and talk to Sam Green. There's more than one way to skin a cat. I'm going up and talk to him. See if he got more sense than Mr. Johnson. I can't get nowhere working for Mr. Olowski and selling Selig five or six pots on the side. I'm going up and see Sam Green. See if he loan me the money.

(Seth crosses back to the window.)

Now he got that cup. He done killed that pigeon and now he's putting its blood in that little cup. I believe he drink that blood.

Bertha: Seth Holly, what is wrong with you this morning? Come on and get your breakfast so you can go to bed. You know Bynum don't be drinking no pigeon blood.

Seth: I don't know what he do.

Bertha: Well, watch him, then. He's gonna dig a little hole and bury that pigeon. Then he's gonna pray over that blood . . . pour it on top . . . mark out his circle and come on into the house.

Seth: That's what he doing . . . he pouring that blood on top.

Bertha: When they gonna put you back working daytime? Told me two months ago he was gonna put you back working daytime.

Seth: That's what Mr. Olowski told me. I got to wait till he say when. He tell me what to do. I don't tell him. Drive me crazy to speculate on the man's wishes when he don't know what he want to do himself.

Bertha: Well, I wish he go ahead and put you back working daytime. This working all hours of the night don't make no sense.

Seth: It don't make no sense for that boy to run out of here and get drunk so they lock him up either.

Bertha: Who? Who they got locked up for being drunk?

Seth: That boy that's staying upstairs . . . Jeremy. I stopped down there on Logan Street on my way home from work and one of the fellows told me about it. Say he seen it when they arrested him.

Bertha: I was wondering why I ain't seen him this morning.

Seth: You know I don't put up with that. I told him when he came . . .

(Bynum enters from the yard carrying some plants. He is a short, round man in his early sixties. A conjure man, or rootworker, he gives the impression of always being in control of everything. Nothing ever bothers him. He seems to be lost in a world of his own making and to swallow any adversity or interference with his grand design.)

What you doing bringing them weeds in my house? Out there stepping on my vegetables and now wanna carry them weeds in my house.

Bynum: Morning, Seth. Morning, Sister Bertha.

Seth: Messing up my garden growing them things out there. I ought to go out there and pull up all them weeds.

Bertha: Some gal was by here to see you this morning, Bynum. You was out there in the yard . . . I told her to come back later.

Bynum (To Seth): You look sick. What's the matter, you ain't eating right?

Seth: What if I was sick? You ain't getting near me with none of that stuff.

(Bertha sets a plate of biscuits on the table.)

Bynum: My . . . my . . . Bertha, your biscuits getting fatter and fatter.

(Bynum takes a biscuit and begins to eat.)

Where Jeremy? I don't see him around this morning. He usually be around riffing and raffing on Saturday morning.

Seth: I know where he at. I know just where he at. They got him down there in the jail. Getting drunk and acting a fool. He down there where he belong with all that foolishness.

Bynum: Mr. Piney's boys got him, huh? They ain't gonna do nothing but hold on to him for a little while. He's gonna be back here hungrier than a mule directly.

Seth: I don't go for all that carrying on and such. This is a respectable house. I don't have no drunkards or fools around here.

Bynum: That boy got a lot of country in him. He ain't been up here but two weeks. It's gonna take a while before he can work that country out of him.

Seth: These niggers coming up here with that old backward country style of living. It's hard enough now without all that ignorant kind of acting. Ever since slavery got over with there ain't been nothing but foolish-acting niggers. Word get out they need men to work in the mill and put in these roads . . . and niggers drop everything and head North looking for freedom. They don't know the white fellows looking too. White fellows coming from all over the world. White fellow come over and in six months got more than what I got. But these niggers keep on coming. Walking . . . riding . . . carrying their Bibles. That boy done carried a guitar all the way from North Carolina. What he gonna find out? What he gonna do with that guitar? This the city.

(There is a knock on the door.)

Niggers coming up here from the backwoods . . . coming up here from the country carrying Bibles and guitars looking for freedom. They got a rude awakening.

(Seth goes to answer the door. Rutherford Selig enters. About Seth's age, he is a thin white man with greasy hair. A peddler, he supplies Seth with the raw materials to make pots and pans which he then peddles door to door in the mill towns along the river. He keeps a list of his customers as they move about and is known in the various communities as the People Finder. He carries squares of sheet metal under his arm.)

Ho! Forgot you was coming today. Come on in.

Bynum: If it ain't Rutherford Selig . . . the People Finder himself.

Selig: What say there, Bynum?

Bynum: I say about my shiny man. You got to tell me something. I done give you my dollar . . . I'm looking to get a report.

Selig: I got eight here, Seth.

Seth (Taking the sheet metal): What is this? What you giving me here? What I'm gonna do with this?

Selig: I need some dustpans. Everybody asking me about dustpans.

Seth: Gonna cost you fifteen cents apiece. And ten cents to put a handle on them.

Selig: I'll give you twenty cents apiece with the handles.

Seth: Alright. But I ain't gonna give you but fifteen cents for the sheet metal.

Selig: It's twenty-five cents apiece for the metal. That's what we agreed on.

Seth: This low-grade sheet metal. They ain't worth but a dime. I'm doing you a favor giving you fifteen cents. You know this metal ain't worth no twenty-five cents. Don't come talking that twenty-five cent stuff to me over no low-grade sheet metal.

Selig: Alright, fifteen cents apiece. Just make me some dustpans out of them.

(Seth exits with the sheet metal out the back door.)

Bertha: Sit on down there, Selig. Get you a cup of coffee and a biscuit.

Bynum: Where you coming from this time?

Selig: I been upriver. All along the Monongahela. Past Rankin and all up around Little Washington.

Bynum: Did you find anybody?

Selig: I found Sadie Jackson up in Braddock. Her mother's staying down there in Scotchbottom say she hadn't heard from her and she didn't know where she was at. I found her up in Braddock on Enoch Street. She bought a frying pan from me.

Bynum: You around here finding everybody how come you ain't found my shiny man?

Selig: The only shiny man I saw was the Nigras working on the road gang with the sweat glistening on them.

Bynum: Naw, you'd be able to tell this fellow. He shine like new money.

Selig: Well, I done told you I can't find nobody without a name.

Bertha: Here go one of these hot biscuits, Selig.

Bynum: This fellow don't have no name. I call him John 'cause it was up around Johnstown where I seen him. I ain't even so sure he's one special fellow. That shine could pass on to anybody. He could be anybody shining.

Selig: Well, what's he look like besides being shiny? There's lots of shiny Nigras.

Bynum: He's just a man I seen out on the road. He ain't had no special look. Just a man walking toward me on the road. He come up and asked me which way the road went. I told him everything I knew about the road, where it went and all, and he asked me did I have anything to eat 'cause he was hungry. Say he ain't had nothing to eat in three days. Well, I never be out there on the road without a piece of dried meat. Or an orange or an apple. So I give this fellow an orange. He take and eat that orange and told me to come and go along the road a little ways with him, that he had something he wanted to show me. He had a look about him made me wanna go with him, see what he gonna show me.

We walked on a bit and it's getting kind of far from where I met him when it come up on me all of a sudden, we wasn't going the way he had come from, we was going back my way. Since he said he ain't knew nothing about the road, I asked him about this. He say he had a voice inside him telling him which way to go and if I come and go along with him he was gonna show me the Secret of Life. Quite naturally I followed him. A fellow that's gonna show you the Secret of Life ain't to be taken lightly. We get near this bend in the road . . .

(Seth enters with an assortment of pans.)

Seth: I got six here, Selig.

Selig: Wait a minute, Seth. Bynum's telling me about the secret of life. Go ahead, Bynum. I wanna hear this.

(Seth sets the pots down and exits out the back.)

Bynum: We get near this bend in the road and he told me to hold out my hands. Then he rubbed them together with his and I looked down and see they got blood on them. Told me to take and rub it all over me . . . say that was a way of cleaning myself. Then we went around the bend in that road. Got around that bend and it seem like all of a sudden we ain't in the same place. Turn around that bend and everything look like it was twice as big as it was. The trees and everything bigger than life! Sparrows big as eagles! I turned around to look at this fellow and he had this light coming out of him. I had to cover up my eyes to keep from being blinded. He shining like new money with that light. He shined until all the light seemed like it seeped out of him and then he was gone and I was by myself in this strange place where everything was bigger than life.

I wandered around there looking for that road, trying to find my way back from this big place . . . and I looked over and seen my daddy standing there. He was the same size he always was, except for his hands and his mouth. He had a great big old mouth that look like it took up his whole face and his hands were as big as hams. Look like they was too big to carry around. My daddy called me to him. Said he had been thinking about me and it grieved him to see me in the world carrying other people's songs and not having one of my own. Told me he was gonna show me how to find my song. Then he carried me further into this big place until we come to this ocean. Then he showed me something I ain't got words to tell you. But if you stand to witness it, you done seen something there. I stayed in that place awhile and my daddy taught me the meaning of this thing that I had seen and showed me how to find my song. I asked him about the shiny man and he told me he was the One Who Goes Before and Shows the Way. Said there was lots of shiny men and if I ever saw one again before I died then I would know that my song had been accepted and worked its full power in the world and I could lay down and die a happy man. A man who done left his mark on life. On the way people cling to each other out of the truth they find in themselves. Then he showed me how to get back to the road. I came out where everything was its own size and I had my song. I had the Binding Song. I choose that song because that's what I seen most when I was traveling . . . people walking away and leaving one another. So I takes the power of my song and binds them together.

(Seth enters from the yard carrying cabbages and tomatoes.)

Been binding people ever since. That's why they call me Bynum. Just like glue I sticks people together.

Seth: Maybe they ain't supposed to be stuck sometimes. You ever think of that?

Bynum: Oh, I don't do it lightly. It cost me a piece of myself every time I do. I'm a Binder of What Clings. You got to find out if they cling first. You can't bind what don't cling.

Selig: Well, how is that the Secret of Life? I thought you said he was gonna show you the secret of life. That's what I'm waiting to find out.

Bynum: Oh, he showed me alright. But you still got to figure it out. Can't nobody figure it out for you. You got to come to it on your own. That's why I'm looking for the shiny man.

Selig: Well, I'll keep my eye out for him. What you got there, Seth?

Seth: Here go some cabbage and tomatoes. I got some green beans coming in real nice. I'm gonna take and start me a grapevine out there next year. Butera says he gonna give me a piece of his vine and I'm gonna start that out there.

Selig: How many of them pots you got?

Seth: I got six. That's six dollars minus eight on top of fifteen for the sheet metal come to a dollar twenty out the six dollars leave me four dollars and eighty cents.

Selig (Counting out the money): There's four dollars . . . and . . . eighty cents.

Seth: How many of them dustpans you want?

Selig: As many as you can make out them sheets.

Seth: You can use that many? I get to cutting on them sheets figuring how to make them dustpans . . . ain't no telling how many I'm liable to come up with.

Selig: I can use them and you can make me some more next time.

Seth: Alright, I'm gonna hold you to that, now.

Selig: Thanks for the biscuit, Bertha.

Bertha: You know you welcome anytime, Selig.

Seth: Which way you heading?

Selig: Going down to Wheeling. All through West Virginia there. I'll be back Saturday. They putting in new roads down that way. Makes traveling easier.

Seth: That's what I hear. All up around here too. Got a fellow staying here working on that road by the Brady Street Bridge.

Selig: Yeah, it's gonna make traveling real nice. Thanks for the cabbage, Seth. I'll see you on Saturday.

(*Selig exits.*)

Seth (To Bynum): Why you wanna start all that nonsense talk with that man? All that shiny man nonsense.

Bynum: You know it ain't no nonsense. Bertha know it ain't no nonsense. I don't know if Selig know or not.

Bertha: Seth, when you get to making them dustpans make me a coffeepot.

Seth: What's the matter with your coffee? Ain't nothing wrong with your coffee. Don't she make some good coffee, Bynum?

Bynum: I ain't worried about the coffee. I know she makes some good biscuits.

Seth: I ain't studying no coffeepot, woman. You heard me tell the man I was gonna cut as many dustpans as them sheets will make . . . and all of a sudden you want a coffeepot.

Bertha: Man, hush up and go on and make me that coffeepot.

(*Jeremy enters the front door. About twenty-five, he gives the impression that he has the world in his hand, that he can meet life's challenges head on. He smiles a lot. He is a proficient guitar player, though his spirit has yet to be molded into song.*)

Bynum: I hear Mr. Piney's boys had you.

Jeremy: Fined me two dollars for nothing! Ain't done nothing.

Seth: I told you when you come on here everybody know my house. Know these is respectable quarters. I don't put up with no foolishness. Everybody know Seth Holly keep a good house. Was my daddy's house. This house been a decent house for a long time.

Jeremy: I ain't done nothing, Mr. Seth. I stopped by the Workmen's Club and got me a bottle. Me and Roper Lee from Alabama. Had us a half pint. We was fixing to cut that half in two when they came up on us. Asked us if we was working. We told them we was putting in the road over yonder and that it was our payday. They snatched hold of us to get that two dollars. Me and Roper Lee ain't even had a chance to take a drink when they grabbed us.

Seth: I don't go for all that kind of carrying on.

Bertha: Leave the boy alone, Seth. You know the police do that. Figure there's too many people out on the street they take some of them off. You know that.

Seth: I ain't gonna have folks talking.

Bertha: Ain't nobody talking nothing. That's all in your head. You want some grits and biscuits, Jeremy?

Jeremy: Thank you, Miss Bertha. They didn't give us a thing to eat last night. I'll take one of them big bowls if you don't mind.

(There is a knock at the door. Seth goes to answer it. Enter Herald Loomis and his eleven-year-old daughter, Zonia. Herald Loomis is thirty-two years old. He is at times possessed. A man driven not by the hellhounds that seemingly bay at his heels, but by his search for a world that speaks to something about himself. He is unable to harmonize the forces that swirl around him, and seeks to recreate the world into one that contains his image. He wears a hat and a long wool coat.)

Loomis: Me and my daughter looking for a place to stay, mister. You got a sign say you got rooms.

(Seth stares at Loomis, sizing him up.)

Mister, if you ain't got no rooms we can go somewhere else.
Seth: How long you plan on staying?
Loomis: Don't know. Two weeks or more maybe.
Seth: It's two dollars a week for the room. We serve meals twice a day. It's two dollars for room and board. Pay up in advance.

(Loomis reaches into his pocket.)

It's a dollar extra for the girl.
Loomis: The girl sleep in the same room.
Seth: Well, do she eat off the same plate? We serve meals twice a day. That's a dollar extra for food.
Loomis: Ain't got no extra dollar. I was planning on asking your missus if she could help out with the cooking and cleaning and whatnot.
Seth: Her helping out don't put no food on the table. I need that dollar to buy some food.
Loomis: I'll give you fifty cents extra. She don't eat much.
Seth: Okay . . . but fifty cents don't buy but half a portion.
Bertha: Seth, she can help me out. Let her help me out. I can use some help.
Seth: Well, that's two dollars for the week. Pay up in advance. Saturday to Saturday. You wanna stay on then it's two more come Saturday.

(Loomis pays Seth the money.)

Bertha: My name's Bertha. This my husband, Seth. You got Bynum and Jeremy over there.
Loomis: Ain't nobody else live here?
Bertha: They the only ones live here now. People come and go. They the only ones here now. You want a cup of coffee and a biscuit?
Loomis: We done ate this morning.
Bynum: Where you coming from, Mister . . . I didn't get your name.
Loomis: Name's Herald Loomis. This my daughter, Zonia.
Bynum: Where you coming from?
Loomis: Come from all over. Whicheverway the road take us that's the way we go.
Jeremy: If you looking for a job, I'm working putting in that road down there by the bridge. They can't get enough mens. Always looking to take somebody on.

Loomis: I'm looking for a woman named Martha Loomis. That's my wife. Got married legal with the papers and all.

Seth: I don't know nobody named Loomis. I know some Marthas but I don't know no Loomis.

Bynum: You got to see Rutherford Selig if you wanna find somebody. Selig's the People Finder. Rutherford Selig's a first-class People Finder.

Jeremy: What she look like? Maybe I seen her.

Loomis: She a brownskin woman. Got long pretty hair. About five feet from the ground.

Jeremy: I don't know. I might have seen her.

Bynum: You got to see Rutherford Selig. You give him one dollar to get her name on his list . . . and after she get her name on his list Rutherford Selig will go right on out there and find her. I got him looking for somebody for me.

Loomis: You say he find people. How you find him?

Bynum: You just missed him. He's gone downriver now. You got to wait till Saturday. He's gone downriver with his pots and pans. He come to see Seth on Saturdays. You got to wait till then.

Seth: Come on, I'll show you to your room.

(Seth, Loomis, and Zonia exit up the stairs.)

Jeremy: Miss Bertha, I'll take that biscuit you was gonna give that fellow, if you don't mind. Say, Mr. Bynum, they got somebody like that around here sure enough? Somebody that find people?

Bynum: Rutherford Selig. He go around selling pots and pans and every house he come to he write down the name and address of whoever lives there. So if you looking for somebody, quite naturally you go and see him . . . 'cause he's the only one who know where everybody live at.

Jeremy: I ought to have him look for this old gal I used to know. It be nice to see her again.

Bertha (Giving Jeremy a biscuit): Jeremy, today's the day for you to pull them sheets off the bed and set them outside your door. I'll set you out some clean ones.

Bynum: Mr. Piney's boys done ruined your good time last night, Jeremy . . . what you planning for tonight?

Jeremy: They got me scared to go out, Mr. Bynum. They might grab me again.

Bynum: You ought to take your guitar and go down to Seefus. Seefus got a gambling place down there on Wylie Avenue. You ought to take your guitar and go down there. They got guitar contest down there.

Jeremy: I don't play no contest, Mr. Bynum. Had one of them white fellows cure me of that. I ain't been nowhere near a contest since.

Bynum: White fellow beat you playing guitar?

Jeremy: Naw, he ain't beat me. I was sitting at home just fixing to sit down and eat when somebody come up to my house and got me. Told me there's a white fellow say he was gonna give a prize to the best guitar player he could find. I take up my guitar and go down there and somebody had gone up and got ᴿobo Smith and brought him down there. Him and another fellow called ⁿter. Old Hooter couldn't play no guitar, he do more hollering than play- ᵗ Bobo could go at it awhile.

This fellow standing there say he the one that was gonna give the prize and me and Bobo started playing for him. Bobo play something and then I'd try to play something better than what he played. Old Hooter, he just holler and bang at the guitar. Man was the worst guitar player I ever seen. So me and Bobo played and after a while I seen where he was getting the attention of this white fellow. He'd play something and while he was playing it he be slapping on the side of the guitar, and that made it sound like he was playing more than he was. So I started doing it too. White fellow ain't knew no difference. He ain't knew as much about guitar playing as Hooter did. After we play awhile, the white fellow called us to him and said he couldn't make up his mind, say all three of us was the best guitar player and we'd have to split the prize between us. Then he give us twenty-five cents. That's eight cents apiece and a penny on the side. That cured me of playing contest to this day.

Bynum: Seefus ain't like that. Seefus give a whole dollar and a drink of whiskey.

Jeremy: What night they be down there?

Bynum: Be down there every night. Music don't know no certain night.

Bertha: You go down to Seefus with them people and you liable to end up in a raid and go to jail sure enough. I don't know why Bynum tell you that.

Bynum: That's where the music at. That's where the people at. The people down there making music and enjoying themselves. Some things is worth taking the chance going to jail about.

Bertha: Jeremy ain't got no business going down there.

Jeremy: They got some women down there, Mr. Bynum?

Bynum: Oh, they got women down there, sure. They got women everywhere. Women be where the men is so they can find each other.

Jeremy: Some of them old gals come out there where we be putting in that road. Hanging around there trying to snatch somebody.

Bynum: How come some of them ain't snatched hold of you?

Jeremy: I don't want them kind. Them desperate kind. Ain't nothing worse than a desperate woman. Tell them you gonna leave them and they get to crying and carrying on. That just make you want to get away quicker. They get to cutting up your clothes and things trying to keep you staying. Desperate women ain't nothing but trouble for a man.

(Seth enters from the stairs.)

Seth: Something ain't setting right with that fellow.

Bertha: What's wrong with him? What he say?

Seth: I take him up there and try to talk to him and he ain't for no talking. Say he been traveling . . . coming over from Ohio. Say he a deacon in the church. Say he looking for Martha Pentecost. Talking about that's his wife.

Bertha: How you know it's the same Martha? Could be talking about anybody. Lots of people named Martha.

Seth: You see that little girl? I didn't hook it up till he said it, but that little girl look just like her. Ask Bynum. *(To Bynum.)* Bynum. Don't that little girl look just like Martha Pentecost?

Bertha: I still say he could be talking about anybody.

Seth: The way he described her wasn't no doubt about who he was talking about. Described her right down to her toes.

Bertha: What did you tell him?

Seth: I ain't told him nothing. The way that fellow look I wasn't gonna tell him nothing. I don't know what he looking for her for.

Bertha: What else he have to say?

Seth: I told you he wasn't for no talking. I told him where the outhouse was and to keep that gal off the front porch and out of my garden. He asked if you'd mind setting a hot tub for the gal and that was about the gist of it.

Bertha: Well, I wouldn't let it worry me if I was you. Come on get your sleep.

Bynum: He says he looking for Martha and he a deacon in the church.

Seth: That's what he say. Do he look like a deacon to you?

Bertha: He might be, you don't know. Bynum ain't got no special say on whether he a deacon or not.

Seth: Well, if he the deacon I'd sure like to see the preacher.

Bertha: Come on get your sleep. Jeremy, don't forget to set them sheets outside the door like I told you.

(Bertha exits into the bedroom.)

Seth: Something ain't setting right with that fellow, Bynum. He's one of them mean-looking niggers look like he done killed somebody gambling over a quarter.

Bynum: He ain't no gambler. Gamblers wear nice shoes. This fellow got on clod-hoppers. He been out there walking up and down them roads.

(Zonia enters from the stairs and looks around.)

Bynum: You looking for the back door, sugar? There it is. You can go out there and play. It's alright.

Seth *(Showing her the door)*: You can go out there and play. Just don't get in my garden. And don't go messing around in my workshed.

(Seth exits into the bedroom. There is a knock on the door.)

Jeremy: Somebody at the door.

(Jeremy goes to answer the door. Enter Mattie Campbell. She is a young woman of twenty-six whose attractiveness is hidden under the weight and concerns of a dissatisfied life. She is a woman in an honest search for love and companionship. She has suffered many defeats in her search, and though not always uncompromising, still believes in the possibility of love.)

Mattie: I'm looking for a man named Bynum. Lady told me to come back later.

Jeremy: Sure, he here. Mr. Bynum, somebody here to see you.

Bynum: Come to see me, huh?

Mattie: Are you the man they call Bynum? The man folks say can fix things?

Bynum: Depend on what need fixing. I can't make no promises. But I got a powerful song in some matters.

Mattie: Can you fix it so my man come back to me?

Bynum: Come on in . . . have a sit down.

Mattie: You got to help me. I don't know what else to do.

Bynum: Depend on how all the circumstances of the thing come together. How all the pieces fit.

Mattie: I done everything I knowed how to do. You got to make him come back to me.

Bynum: It ain't nothing to make somebody come back. I can fix it so he can't stand to be away from you. I got my roots and powders, I can fix it so wherever he's at this thing will come up on him and he won't be able to sleep for seeing your face. Won't be able to eat for thinking of you.

Mattie: That's what I want. Make him come back.

Bynum: The roots is a powerful thing. I can fix it so one day he'll walk out his front door . . . won't be thinking of nothing. He won't know what it is. All he knows is that a powerful dissatisfaction done set in his bones and can't nothing he do make him feel satisfied. He'll set his foot down on the road and the wind in the trees be talking to him and everywhere he step on the road, that road'll give back your name and something will pull him right up to your doorstep. Now, I can do that. I can take my roots and fix that easy. But maybe he ain't supposed to come back. And if he ain't supposed to come back . . . then he'll be in your bed one morning and it'll come up on him that he's in the wrong place. That he's lost outside of time from his place that he's supposed to be in. Then both of you be lost and trapped outside of life and ain't no way for you to get back into it. 'Cause you lost from yourselves and where the places come together, where you're supposed to be alive, your heart kicking in your chest with a song worth singing.

Mattie: Make him come back to me. Make his feet say my name on the road. I don't care what happens. Make him come back.

Bynum: What's your man's name?

Mattie: He go by Jack Carper. He was born in Alabama then he come to West Texas and find me and we come here. Been here three years before he left. Say I had a curse prayer on me and he started walking down the road and ain't never come back. Somebody told me, say you can fix things like that.

Bynum: He just got up one day, set his feet on the road, and walked away?

Mattie: You got to make him come back, mister.

Bynum: Did he say goodbye?

Mattie: Ain't said nothing. Just started walking. I could see where he disappeared. Didn't look back. Just keep walking. Can't you fix it so he come back? I ain't got no curse prayer on me. I know I ain't.

Bynum: What made him say you had a curse prayer on you?

Mattie: 'Cause the babies died. Me and Jack had two babies. Two little babies that ain't lived two months before they died. He say it's because somebody cursed me not to have babies.

Bynum: He ain't bound to you if the babies died. Look like somebody trying to keep you from being bound up and he's gone on back to whoever it is 'cause he's already bound up to her. Ain't nothing to be done. Somebody else done got a powerful hand in it and ain't nothing to be done to break it. You got to let him go find where he's supposed to be in the world.

Mattie: Jack done gone off and you telling me to forget about him. All my life I been looking for somebody to stop and stay with me. I done already got too many things to forget about. I take Jack Carper's hand and it feel so rough and strong. Seem like he's the strongest man in the world the way he hold me. Like he's bigger than the whole world and can't nothing bad get to me. Even when he act mean sometimes he still make everything seem okay with the world. Like there's part of it that belongs just to you. Now you telling me to forget about him?

Bynum: Jack Carper gone off to where he belong. There's somebody searching for your doorstep right now. Ain't no need you fretting over Jack Carper. Right now he's a strong thought in your mind. But every time you catch yourself fretting over Jack Carper you push that thought away. You push it out your mind and that thought will get weaker and weaker till you wake up one morning and you won't even be able to call him up on your mind.

(Bynum gives her a small cloth packet.)

Take this and sleep with it under your pillow and it'll bring good luck to you. Draw it to you like a magnet. It won't be long before you forget all about Jack Carper.

Mattie: How much . . . do I owe you?

Bynum: Whatever you got there . . . that'll be alright.

(Mattie hands Bynum two quarters. She crosses to the door.)

You sleep with that under your pillow and you'll be alright.

(Mattie opens the door to exit and Jeremy crosses over to her. Bynum overhears the first part of their conversation, then exits out the back.)

Jeremy: I overheard what you told Mr. Bynum. Had me an old gal did that to me. Woke up one morning and she was gone. Just took off to parts unknown. I woke up that morning and the only thing I could do was look around for my shoes. I woke up and got out of there. Found my shoes and took off. That's the only thing I could think of to do.

Mattie: She ain't said nothing?

Jeremy: I just looked around for my shoes and got out of there.

Mattie: Jack ain't said nothing either. He just walked off.

Jeremy: Some mens do that. Womens too. I ain't gone off looking for her. I just let her go. Figure she had a time to come to herself. Wasn't no use of me standing in the way. Where you from?

Mattie: Texas. I was born in Georgia but I went to Texas with my mama. She dead now. Was picking peaches and fell dead away. I come up here with Jack Carper.

Jeremy: I'm from North Carolina. Down around Raleigh where they got all that tobacco. Been up here about two weeks. I likes it fine except I still got to find me a woman. You got a nice look to you. Look like you have mens standing in your door. Is you got mens standing in your door to get a look at you?

Mattie: I ain't got nobody since Jack left.

Jeremy: A woman like you need a man. Maybe you let me be your man. I got a nice way with the women. That's what they tell me.

Mattie: I don't know. Maybe Jack's coming back.

Jeremy: I'll be your man till he come. A woman can't be by her lonesome. Let me be your man till he come.

Mattie: I just can't go through life piecing myself out to different mens. I need a man who wants to stay with me.

Jeremy: I can't say what's gonna happen. Maybe I'll be the man. I don't know. You wanna go along the road a little ways with me?

Mattie: I don't know. Seem like life say it's gonna be one thing and end up being another. I'm tired of going from man to man.

Jeremy: Life is like you got to take a chance. Everybody got to take a chance. Can't nobody say what's gonna be. Come on . . . take a chance with me and see what the year bring. Maybe you let me come and see you. Where you staying?

Mattie: I got me a room up on Bedford. Me and Jack had a room together.

Jeremy: What's the address? I'll come by and get you tonight and we can go down to Seefus. I'm going down there and play my guitar.

Mattie: You play guitar?

Jeremy: I play guitar like I'm born to it.

Mattie: I live at 1727 Bedford Avenue. I'm gonna find out if you can play guitar like you say.

Jeremy: I plays it sugar, and that ain't all I do. I got a ten-pound hammer and I knows how to drive it down. Good god . . . you ought to hear my hammer ring!

Mattie: Go on with that kind of talk, now. If you gonna come by and get me I got to get home and straighten up for you.

Jeremy: I'll be by at eight o'clock. How's eight o'clock? I'm gonna make you forget all about Jack Carper.

Mattie: Go on, now. I got to get home and fix up for you.

Jeremy: Eight o'clock, sugar.

(*The lights go down in the parlor and come up on the yard outside. Zonia is singing and playing a game.*)

Zonia:
> I went downtown
> To get my grip
> I came back home
> Just a pullin' the skiff
>
> I went upstairs
> To make my bed
> I made a mistake
> And I bumped my head
> Just a pullin' the skiff
>
> I went downstairs
> To milk the cow
> I made a mistake
> And I milked the sow
> Just a pullin' the skiff

Tomorrow, tomorrow
Tomorrow never comes
The marrow the marrow
The marrow in the bone.

(Reuben enters.)

Reuben: Hi.

Zonia: Hi.

Reuben: What's your name?

Zonia: Zonia.

Reuben: What kind of name is that?

Zonia: It's what my daddy named me.

Reuben: My name's Reuben. You staying in Mr. Seth's house?

Zonia: Yeah.

Reuben: That your daddy I seen you with this morning?

Zonia: I don't know. Who you see me with?

Reuben: I saw you with some man had on a great big old coat. And you was walk-
    ing up to Mr. Seth's house. Had on a hat too.

Zonia: Yeah, that's my daddy.

Reuben: You like Mr. Seth?

Zonia: I ain't see him much.

Reuben: My grandpap say he a great big old windbag. How come you living in
    Mr. Seth's house? Don't you have no house?

Zonia: We going to find my mother.

Reuben: Where she at?

Zonia: I don't know. We got to find her. We just go all over.

Reuben: Why you got to find her? What happened to her?

Zonia: She ran away.

Reuben: Why she run away?

Zonia: I don't know. My daddy say some man named Joe Turner did something
    bad to him once and that made her run away.

Reuben: Maybe she coming back and you don't have to go looking for her.

Zonia: We ain't there no more.

Reuben: She could have come back when you wasn't there.

Zonia: My daddy said she ran off and left us so we going looking for her.

Reuben: What he gonna do when he find her?

Zonia: He didn't say. He just say he got to find her.

Reuben: Your daddy say how long you staying in Mr. Seth's house?

Zonia: He don't say much. But we never stay too long nowhere. He say we got
    to keep moving till we find her.

Reuben: Ain't no kids hardly live around here. I had me a friend but he died. He
    was the best friend I ever had. Me and Eugene used to keep secrets. I still
    got his pigeons. He told me to let them go when he died. He say, "Reuben,
    promise me when I die you'll let my pigeons go." But I keep them to remem-
    ber him by. I ain't never gonna let them go. Even when I get to be grown
    up. I'm just always gonna have Eugene's pigeons.

(Pause.)

Mr. Bynum a conjure man. My grandpap scared of him. He don't like me to come over here too much. I'm scared of him too. My grandpap told me not to let him get close enough to where he can reach out his hand and touch me.

Zonia: He don't seem scary to me.

Reuben: He buys pigeons from me . . . and if you get up early in the morning you can see him out in the yard doing something with them pigeons. My grandpap say he kill them. I sold him one yesterday. I don't know what he do with it. I just hope he don't spook me up.

Zonia: Why you sell him pigeons if he's gonna spook you up?

Reuben: I just do like Eugene do. He used to sell Mr. Bynum pigeons. That's how he got to collecting them to sell to Mr. Bynum. Sometime he give me a nickel and sometime he give me a whole dime.

(Loomis enters from the house.)

Loomis: Zonia!

Zonia: Sir?

Loomis: What you doing?

Zonia: Nothing.

Loomis: You stay around this house, you hear? I don't want you wandering off nowhere.

Zonia: I ain't wandering off nowhere.

Loomis: Miss Bertha set that hot tub and you getting a good scrubbing. Get scrubbed up good. You ain't been scrubbing.

Zonia: I been scrubbing.

Loomis: Look at you. You growing too fast. Your bones getting bigger everyday. I don't want you getting grown on me. Don't you get grown on me too soon. We gonna find your mamma. She around here somewhere. I can smell her. You stay on around this house now. Don't you go nowhere.

Zonia: Yes, sir.

(Loomis exits into the house.)

Reuben: Wow, your daddy's scary!

Zonia: He is not! I don't know what you talking about.

Reuben: He got them mean-looking eyes!

Zonia: My daddy ain't got no mean-looking eyes!

Reuben: Aw, girl, I was just messing with you. You wanna go see Eugene's pigeons? Got a great big coop out the back of my house. Come on, I'll show you.

(Reuben and Zonia exit as the lights go down.)

Scene 2

It is Saturday morning, one week later. The lights come up on the kitchen. Bertha is at the stove preparing breakfast while Seth sits at the table.

Seth: Something ain't right about that fellow. I been watching him all week. Something ain't right, I'm telling you.

Bertha: Seth Holly, why don't you hush up about that man this morning?

Seth: I don't like the way he stare at everybody. Don't look at you natural like. He just be staring at you. Like he trying to figure out something about you. Did you see him when he come back in here?

Bertha: That man ain't thinking about you.

Seth: He don't work nowhere. Just go out and come back. Go out and come back.

Bertha: As long as you get your boarding money it ain't your cause about what he do. He don't bother nobody.

Seth: Just go and come back. Going around asking everybody about Martha. Like Henry Allen seen him down at the church last night.

Bertha: The man's allowed to go to church if he want. He say he a deacon. Ain't nothing wrong about him going to church.

Seth: I ain't talking about him going to church. I'm talking about him hanging around *outside* the church.

Bertha: Henry Allen say that?

Seth: Say he be standing around outside the church. Like he be watching it.

Bertha: What on earth he wanna be watching the church for, I wonder?

Seth: That's what I'm trying to figure out. Looks like he fixing to rob it.

Bertha: Seth, now do he look like the kind that would rob the church?

Seth: I ain't saying that. I ain't saying how he look. It's how he do. Anybody liable to do anything as far as I'm concerned. I ain't never thought about how no church robbers look . . . but now that you mention it, I don't see where they look no different than how he look.

Bertha: Herald Loomis ain't the kind of man who would rob no church.

Seth: I ain't even so sure that's his name.

Bertha: Why the man got to lie about his name?

Seth: Anybody can tell anybody anything about what their name is. That's what you call him . . . Herald Loomis. His name is liable to be anything.

Bertha: Well, until he tell me different that's what I'm gonna call him. You just getting yourself all worked up about the man for nothing.

Seth: Talking about Loomis: Martha's name wasn't no Loomis nothing. Martha's name is Pentecost.

Bertha: How you so sure that's her right name? Maybe she changed it.

Seth: Martha's a good Christian woman. This fellow here look like he owe the devil a day's work and he's trying to figure out how he gonna pay him. Martha ain't had a speck of distrust about her the whole time she was living here. They moved the church out there to Rankin and I was sorry to see her go.

Bertha: That's why he be hanging around the church. He looking for her.

Seth: If he looking for her, why don't he go inside and ask? What he doing hanging around outside the church acting sneakly like?

(Bynum enters from the yard.)

Bynum: Morning, Seth. Morning, Sister Bertha.

(Bynum continues through the kitchen and exits up the stairs.)

Bertha: That's who you should be asking the questions. He been out there in that yard all morning. He was out there before the sun come up. He didn't even come in for breakfast. I don't know what he's doing. He had three of them pigeons line up out there. He dance around till he get tired. He sit down awhile then get up and dance some more. He come through here a little while ago looking like he was mad at the world.

Seth: I don't pay Bynum no mind. He don't spook me up with all that stuff.

Bertha: That's how Martha come to be living here. She come to see Bynum. She come to see him when she first left from down South.

Seth: Martha was living here before Bynum. She ain't come on here when she first left from down there. She come on here after she went back to get her little girl. That's when she come on here.

Bertha: Well, where was Bynum? He was here when she came.

Seth: Bynum ain't come till after her. That boy Hiram was staying up there in Bynum's room.

Bertha: Well, how long Bynum been here?

Seth: Bynum ain't been here no longer than three years. That's what I'm trying to tell you. Martha was staying up there and sewing and cleaning for Doc Goldblum when Bynum came. This the longest he ever been in one place.

Bertha: How you know how long the man been in one place?

Seth: I know Bynum. Bynum ain't no mystery to me. I done seen a hundred niggers like him. He's one of them fellows never could stay in one place. He was wandering all around the country till he got old and settled here. The only thing different about Bynum is he bring all this heebie-jeebie stuff with him.

Bertha: I still say he was staying here when she came. That's why she came . . . to see him.

Seth: You can say what you want. I know the facts of it. She come on here four years ago all heartbroken 'cause she couldn't find her little girl. And Bynum wasn't nowhere around. She got mixed up in that old heebie-jeebie nonsense with him after he came.

Bertha: Well, if she came on before Bynum I don't know where she stayed. 'Cause she stayed up there in Hiram's room. Hiram couldn't get along with Bynum and left out of here owing you two dollars. Now, I know you ain't forgot about that!

Seth: Sure did! You know Hiram ain't paid me that two dollars yet. So that's why he be ducking and hiding when he see me down on Logan Street. You right. Martha did come on after Bynum. I forgot that's why Hiram left.

Bertha: Him and Bynum never could see eye to eye. They always rubbed each other the wrong way. Hiram got to thinking that Bynum was trying to put a fix on him and he moved out. Martha came to see Bynum and ended up taking Hiram's room. Now, I know what I'm talking about. She stayed on here three years till they moved the church.

Seth: She out there in Rankin now. I know where she at. I know where they moved the church to. She right out there in Rankin in that place used to be shoe store. Used to be Wolf's shoe store. They moved to a bigger place and they put that church in there. I know where she at. I know just where she at.

Bertha: Why don't you tell the man? You see he looking for her.

Seth: I ain't gonna tell that man where that woman is! What I wanna do that for? I don't know nothing about that man. I don't know why he looking for her. He might wanna do her a harm. I ain't gonna carry that on my hands. He looking for her, he gonna have to find her for himself. I ain't gonna help him. Now, if he had come and presented himself as a gentleman—the way Martha Pentecost's husband would have done—then I would have told him. But I ain't gonna tell this old wild-eyed mean-looking nigger nothing!

Bertha: Well, why don't you get a ride with Selig and go up there and tell her where he is? See if she wanna see him. If that's her little girl . . . you say Martha was looking for her.

Seth: You know me, Bertha. I don't get mixed up in nobody's business.

(Bynum enters from the stairs.)

Bynum: Morning, Seth. Morning, Bertha. Can I still get some breakfast? Mr. Loomis been down here this morning?

Seth: He done gone out and come back. He up there now. Left out of here early this morning wearing that coat. Hot as it is, the man wanna walk around wearing a big old heavy coat. He come back in here paid me for another week, sat down there waiting on Selig. Got tired of waiting and went on back upstairs.

Bynum: Where's the little girl?

Seth: She out there in the front. Had to chase her and that Reuben off the front porch. She out there somewhere.

Bynum: Look like if Martha was around here he would have found her by now. My guess is she ain't in the city.

Seth: She ain't! I know where she at. I know just where she at. But I ain't gonna tell him. Not the way he look.

Bertha: Here go your coffee, Bynum.

Bynum: He says he gonna get Selig to find her for him.

Seth: Selig can't find her. He talk all that . . . but unless he get lucky and knock on her door he can't find her. That's the only way he find anybody. He got to get lucky. But I know just where she at.

Bertha: Here go some biscuits, Bynum.

Bynum: What else you got over there, Sister Bertha? You got some grits and gravy over there? I could go for some of that this morning.

Bertha (Sets a bowl on the table): Seth, come on and help me turn this mattress over. Come on.

Seth: Something ain't right with that fellow, Bynum. I don't like the way he stare at everybody.

Bynum: Mr. Loomis alright, Seth. He just a man got something on his mind. He just got a straightforward mind, that's all.

Seth: What's that fellow that they had around here? Moses, that's Moses Houser. Man went crazy and jumped off the Brady Street Bridge. I told you when I seen him something wasn't right about him. And I'm telling you about this fellow now.

(There is a knock on the door. Seth goes to answer it. Enter Rutherford Selig.)

Ho! Come on in, Selig.

Bynum: If it ain't the People Finder himself.

Selig: Bynum, before you start . . . I ain't seen no shiny man now.

Bynum: Who said anything about that? I ain't said nothing about that. I just called you a first-class People Finder.

Selig: How many dustpans you get out of that sheet metal, Seth?

Seth: You walked by them on your way in. They sitting out there on the porch. Got twenty-eight. Got four out of each sheet and made Bertha a coffeepot out the other one. They a little small but they got nice handles.

Selig: That was twenty cents apiece, right? That's what we agreed on.

Seth: That's five dollars and sixty cents. Twenty on top of twenty-eight. How many sheets you bring me?

Selig: I got eight out there. That's a dollar twenty makes me owe you . . .

Seth: Four dollars and forty cents.

Selig (Paying him): Go on and make me some dustpans. I can use all you can make.

(Loomis enters from the stairs.)

Loomis: I been watching for you. He say you find people.

Bynum: Mr. Loomis here wants you to find his wife.

Loomis: He say you find people. Find her for me.

Selig: Well, let see here . . . find somebody, is it?

(Selig rummages through his pockets. He has several notebooks and he is searching for the right one.)

Alright now . . . what's the name?

Loomis: Martha Loomis. She my wife. Got married legal with the paper and all.

Selig (Writing): Martha . . . Loomis. How tall is she?

Loomis: She five feet from the ground.

Selig: Five feet . . . tall. Young or old?

Loomis: She a young woman. Got long pretty hair.

Selig: Young . . . long . . . pretty . . . hair. Where did you last see her?

Loomis: Tennessee. Nearby Memphis.

Selig: When was that?

Loomis: Nineteen hundred and one.

Selig: Nineteen . . . hundred and one. I'll tell you, mister . . . you better off without them. Now you take me . . . old Rutherford Selig could tell you a thing or two about these women. I ain't met one yet I could understand. Now, you take Sally out there. That's all a man needs is a good horse. I say giddup and she go. Say whoa and she stop. I feed her some oats and she carry me wherever I want to go. Ain't had a speck of trouble out of her since I had her. Now, I been married. A long time ago down in Kentucky. I got up one morning and I saw this look on my wife's face. Like way down deep inside her she was wishing I was dead. I walked around that morning and every time I looked at her she had that look on her face. It seem like she knew I could see it on her. Every time I looked at her I got smaller and smaller. Well, I wasn't gonna stay around there and just shrink away. I walked out on the porch and closed the door behind me. When I closed the door she locked it. I went out and bought me a horse. And I ain't been without one since! Martha Loomis, huh? Well, now I'll do the best I can do. That's one dollar.

Loomis (Holding out dollar suspiciously): How you find her?

Selig: Well now, it ain't no easy job like you think. You can't just go out there and find them like that. There's a lot of little tricks to it. It's not an easy job keeping up with you Nigras the way you move about so. Now you take this woman you looking for . . . this Martha Loomis. She could be anywhere. Time I find her, if you don't keep your eye on her, she'll be gone off someplace else. You'll be thinking she over here and she'll be over there. But like I say there's a lot of little tricks to it.

Loomis: You say you find her.

Selig: I can't promise anything but we been finders in my family for a long time. Bringers and finders. My great-granddaddy used to bring Nigras across the ocean on ships. That's wasn't no easy job either. Sometimes the winds would blow so hard you'd think the hand of God was set against the sails. But it set him well in pay and he settled in this new land and found him a wife of good Christian charity with a mind for kids and the like and well . . . here I am, Rutherford Selig. You're in good hands, mister. Me and my daddy have found plenty Nigras. My daddy, rest his soul, used to find runaway slaves for the plantation bosses. He was the best there was at it. Jonas B. Selig. Had him a reputation stretched clean across the country. After Abraham Lincoln give you all Nigras your freedom papers and with you all looking all over for each other . . . we started finding Nigras for Nigras. Of course, it don't pay as much. But the People Finding business ain't so bad.

Loomis (Hands him the dollar): Find her. Martha Loomis. Find her for me.

Selig: Like I say, I can't promise you anything. I'm going back upriver, and if she's around in them parts I'll find her for you. But I can't promise you anything.

Loomis: When you coming back?

Selig: I'll be back on Saturday. I come and see Seth to pick up my order on Saturday.

Bynum: You going upriver, huh? You going up around my way. I used to go all up through there. Blawknox . . . Clairton. Used to go up to Rankin and take that first righthand road. I wore many a pair of shoes out walking around that way. You'd have thought I was a missionary spreading the gospel the way I wandered all around them parts.

Selig: Okay, Bynum. See you on Saturday.

Seth: Here, let me walk out with you. Help you with them dustpans.

(Seth and Selig exit out the back. Bertha enters from the stairs carrying a bundle of sheets.)

Bynum: Herald Loomis got the People Finder looking for Martha.

Bertha: You can call him a People Finder if you want to. I know Rutherford Selig carries people away too. He done carried a whole bunch of them away from here. Folks plan on leaving plan by Selig's timing. They wait till he get ready to go, then they hitch a ride on his wagon. Then he charge folks a dollar to tell them where he took them. Now, that's the truth of Rutherford Selig. This old People Finding business is for the birds. He ain't never found nobody he ain't took away. Herald Loomis, you just wasted your dollar.

(Bertha exits into the bedroom.)

Loomis: He say he find her. He say he find her by Saturday. I'm gonna wait till Saturday.

(The lights fade to black.)

Scene 3

It is Sunday morning, the next day. The lights come up on the kitchen. Seth sits talking to Bynum. The breakfast dishes have been cleared away.

Seth: They can't see that. Neither one of them can see that. Now, how much sense it take to see that? All you got to do is be able to count. One man making ten pots is five men making fifty pots. But they can't see that. Asked where I'm gonna get my five men. Hell, I can teach anybody how to make a pot. I can teach you. I can take you out there and get you started right now. Inside of two weeks you'd know how to make a pot. All you got to do is want to do it. I can get five men. I ain't worried about getting no five men.

Bertha *(Calls from the bedroom)*: Seth. Come on and get ready now. Reverend Gates ain't gonna be holding up his sermon 'cause you sitting out there talking.

Seth: Now, you take the boy, Jeremy. What he gonna do after he put in that road? He can't do nothing but go put in another one somewhere. Now, if he let me show him how to make some pots and pans . . . then he'd have something can't nobody take away from him. After a while he could get his own tools and go off somewhere and make his own pots and pans. Find him somebody to sell them to. Now, Selig can't make no pots and pans. He can sell them but he can't make them. I get me five men with some tools and we'd make him so many pots and pans he'd have to open up a store somewhere. But they can't see that. Neither Mr. Cohen nor Sam Green.

Bertha *(Calls from the bedroom)*: Seth . . . time be wasting. Best be getting on.

Seth: I'm coming, woman! *(To Bynum.)* Want me to sign over the house to borrow five hundred dollars. I ain't that big a fool. That's all I got. Sign it over to them and then I won't have nothing.

(Jeremy enters waving a dollar and carrying his guitar.)

Jeremy: Look here, Mr. Bynum . . . won me another dollar last night down at Seefus! Me and that Mattie Campbell went down there again and I played contest. Ain't no guitar players down there. Wasn't even no contest. Say, Mr. Seth, I asked Mattie Campbell if she wanna come by and have Sunday dinner with us. Get some fried chicken.

Seth: It's gonna cost you twenty-five cents.

Jeremy: That's alright. I got a whole dollar here. Say Mr. Seth . . . me and Mattie Campbell talked it over last night and she gonna move in with me. If that's alright with you.

Seth: Your business is your business . . . but it's gonna cost her a dollar a week for her board. I can't be feeding nobody for free.

Jeremy: Oh, she know that, Mr. Seth. That's what I told her, say she'd have to pay for her meals.

Seth: You say you got a whole dollar there . . . turn loose that twenty-five cents.

Jeremy: Suppose she move in today, then that make seventy-five cents more, so I'll give you the whole dollar for her now till she gets here.

(Seth pockets the money and exits into the bedroom.)

Bynum: So you and that Mattie Campbell gonna take up together?

Jeremy: I told her she don't need to be by her lonesome, Mr. Bynum. Don't make no sense for both of us to be by our lonesome. So she gonna move in with me.

Bynum: Sometimes you got to be where you supposed to be. Sometimes you can get all mixed up in life and come to the wrong place.

Jeremy: That's just what I told her, Mr. Bynum. It don't make no sense for her to be all mixed up and lonesome. May as well come here and be with me. She a fine woman too. Got them long legs. Knows how to treat a fellow too. Treat you like you wanna be treated.

Bynum: You just can't look at it like that. You got to look at the whole thing. Now, you take a fellow go out there, grab hold to a woman and think he got something 'cause she sweet and soft to the touch. Alright. Touching's part of life. It's in the world like everything else. Touching's nice. It feels good. But you can lay your hand upside a horse or a cat, and that feels good too. What's the difference? When you grab hold to a woman, you got something there. You got a whole world there. You got a way of life kicking up under your hand. That woman can take and make you feel like something. I ain't just talking about in the way of jumping off into bed together and rolling around with each other. Anybody can do that. When you grab hold to that woman and look at the whole thing and see what you got . . . why, she can take and make something out of you. Your mother was a woman. That's enough right there to show you what a woman is. Enough to show you what she can do. She made something out of you. Taught you converse, and all about how to take care of yourself, how to see where you at and where you going tomorrow, how to look out to see what's coming in the way of eating, and what to do with yourself when you get lonesome. That's a mighty thing she did. But you just can't look at a woman to jump off into bed with her. That's a foolish thing to ignore a woman like that.

Jeremy: Oh, I ain't ignoring her, Mr. Bynum. It's hard to ignore a woman got legs like she got.

Bynum: Alright. Let's try it this way. Now, you take a ship. Be out there on the water traveling about. You out there on that ship sailing to and from. And then you see some land. Just like you see a woman walking down the street. You see that land and it don't look like nothing but a line out there on the horizon. That's all it is when you first see it. A line that cross your path out there on the horizon. Now, a smart man know when he see that land, it ain't just a line setting out there. He know that if you get off the water to go take a good look . . . why, there's a whole world right there. A whole world with everything imaginable under the sun. Anything you can think of you can find on that land. Same with a woman. A woman is everything a man need.

To a smart man she water and berries. And that's all a man need. That's all he need to live on. You give me some water and berries and if there ain't nothing else I can live a hundred years. See, you just like a man looking at the horizon from a ship. You just seeing a part of it. But it's a blessing when you learn to look at a woman and see in maybe just a few strands of her hair, the way her cheek curves . . . to see in that everything there is out of life to be gotten. It's a blessing to see that. You know you done right and proud by your mother to see that. But you got to learn it. My telling you ain't gonna mean nothing. You got to learn how to come to your own time and place with a woman.

Jeremy: What about your woman, Mr. Bynum? I know you done had some woman.

Bynum: Oh, I got them in memory time. That lasts longer than any of them ever stayed with me.

Jeremy: I had me an old gal one time . . .

(There is a knock on the door, Jeremy goes to answer it. Enter Molly Cunningham. She is about twenty-six, the kind of woman that "could break in on a dollar anywhere she goes." She carries a small cardboard suitcase, and wears a colorful dress of the fashion of the day. Jeremy's heart jumps out of his chest when he sees her.)

Molly: You got any rooms here? I'm looking for a room.

Jeremy: Yeah . . . Mr. Seth got rooms. Sure . . . wait till I get Mr. Seth. *(Calls.)* Mr. Seth! Somebody here to see you! *(To Molly.)* Yeah, Mr. Seth got some rooms. Got one right next to me. This is a nice place to stay, too. My name's Jeremy. What's yours?

(Seth enters dressed in his Sunday clothes.)

Seth: Ho!

Jeremy: This here woman looking for a place to stay. She say you got any rooms.

Molly: Mister, you got any rooms? I seen your sign say you got rooms.

Seth: How long you plan to staying?

Molly: I ain't gonna be here long. I ain't looking for no home or nothing. I'd be in Cincinnati if I hadn't missed my train.

Seth: Rooms cost two dollars a week.

Molly: Two dollars!

Seth: That includes meals. We serve two meals a day. That's breakfast and dinner.

Molly: I hope it ain't on the third floor.

Seth: That's the only one I got. Third floor to the left. That's pay up in advance week to week.

Molly *(Going into her bosom)*: I'm gonna pay you for one week. My name's Molly. Molly Cunningham.

Seth: I'm Seth Holly. My wife's name is Bertha. She do the cooking and take care of around here. She got sheets on the bed. Towels twenty-five cents a week extra if you ain't got none. You get breakfast and dinner. We got fried chicken on Sundays.

Molly: That sounds good. Here's two dollars and twenty-five cents. Look here, Mister . . . ?

Seth: Holly. Seth Holly.

Molly: Look here, Mr. Holly. I forgot to tell you. I likes me some company from
time to time. I don't like being by myself.

Seth: Your business is your business. I don't meddle in nobody's business. But this
is a respectable house. I don't have no riffraff around here. And I don't have
no women hauling no men up to their rooms to be making their living. As
long as we understand each other then we'll be alright with each other.

Molly: Where's the outhouse?

Seth: Straight through the door over yonder.

Molly: I get my own key to the front door?

Seth: Everybody get their own key. If you come in late just don't be making no
whole lot of noise and carrying on. Don't allow no fussing and fighting around
here.

Molly: You ain't got to worry about that, mister. Which way you say that outhouse was again?

Seth: Straight through that door over yonder.

(Molly exits out the back door. Jeremy crosses to watch her.)

Jeremy: Mr. Bynum, you know what? I think I know what you was talking about
now.

(The lights go down on the scene.)

Scene 4

*The lights come up on the kitchen. It is later the same evening. Mattie and all the resi-
dents of the house, except Loomis, sit around the table. They have finished eating and
most of the dishes have been cleared.*

Molly: That sure was some good chicken.

Jeremy: That's what I'm talking about. Miss Bertha, you sure can fry some chicken.
I thought my mama could fry some chicken. But she can't do half as good
as you.

Seth: I know it. That's why I married her. She don't know that, though. She think
I married her for something else.

Bertha: I ain't studying you, Seth. Did you get your things moved in alright, Mattie?

Mattie: I ain't had that much. Jeremy helped me with what I did have.

Bertha: You'll get to know your way around here. If you have any questions about
anything just ask me. You and Molly both. I get along with everybody. You'll
find I ain't no trouble to get along with.

Mattie: You need some help with the dishes?

Bertha: I got me a helper. Ain't I, Zonia? Got me a good helper.

Zonia: Yes, ma'am.

Seth: Look at Bynum sitting over there with his belly all poked out. Ain't saying
nothing. Sitting over there half asleep. Ho, Bynum!

Bertha: If Bynum ain't saying nothing what you wanna start him up for?

Seth: Ho, Bynum!

Bynum: What you hollering at me for? I ain't doing nothing.

Seth: Come on, we gonna Juba.

Bynum: You know me, I'm always ready to Juba.

Seth: Well, come on, then.

(Seth pulls out a harmonica and blows a few notes.)

Come on there, Jeremy. Where's your guitar? Go get your guitar. Bynum say he's ready to Juba.

Jeremy: Don't need no guitar to Juba. Ain't you never Juba without a guitar?

(Jeremy begins to drum on the table.)

Seth: It ain't that. I ain't never Juba with one! Figured to try it and see how it worked.

Bynum (Drumming on the table): You don't need no guitar. Look at Molly sitting over there. She don't know we Juba on Sunday. We gonna show you something tonight. You and Mattie Campbell both. Ain't that right, Seth?

Seth: You said it! Come on, Bertha, leave them dishes be for a while. We gonna Juba.

Bynum: Alright. Let's Juba down!

(The Juba is reminiscent of the Ring Shouts of the African slaves. It is a call and response dance. Bynum sits at the table and drums. He calls the dance as others clap hands, shuffle and stomp around the table. It should be as African as possible, with the performers working themselves up into a near frenzy. The words can be improvised, but should include some mention of the Holy Ghost. In the middle of the dance Herald Loomis enters.)

Loomis (In a rage): Stop it! Stop!

(They stop and turn to look at him.)

You all sitting up here singing about the Holy Ghost. What's so holy about the Holy Ghost? You singing and singing. You think the Holy Ghost coming? You singing for the Holy Ghost to come? What he gonna do, huh? He gonna come with tongues of fire to burn up your woolly heads? You gonna tie onto the Holy Ghost and get burned up? What you got then? Why God got to be so big? Why he got to be bigger than me? How much big is there? How much big do you want?

(Loomis starts to unzip his pants.)

Seth: Nigger, you crazy!

Loomis: How much big you want?

Seth: You done plumb lost your mind!

(Loomis begins to speak in tongues and dance around the kitchen. Seth starts after him.)

Bertha: Leave him alone, Seth. He ain't in his right mind.

Loomis (*Stops suddenly*): You all don't know nothing about me. You don't know what I done seen. Herald Loomis done seen some things he ain't got words to tell you.

(*Loomis starts to walk out the front door and is thrown back and collapses, terror-stricken by his vision. Bynum crawls to him.*)

Bynum: What you done seen, Herald Loomis?

Loomis: I done seen bones rise up out the water. Rise up and walk across the water. Bones walking on top of the water.

Bynum: Tell me about them bones, Herald Loomis. Tell me what you seen.

Loomis: I come to this place . . . to this water that was bigger than the whole world. And I looked out . . . and I seen these bones rise up out the water. Rise up and begin to walk on top of it.

Bynum: Wasn't nothing but bones and they walking on top of the water.

Loomis: Walking without sinking down. Walking on top of the water.

Bynum: Just marching in a line.

Loomis: A whole heap of them. They come up out the water and started marching.

Bynum: Wasn't nothing but bones and they walking on top of the water.

Loomis: One after the other. They just come up out the water and start to walking.

Bynum: They walking on the water without sinking down. They just walking and walking. And then . . . what happened, Herald Loomis?

Loomis: They just walking across the water.

Bynum: What happened, Herald Loomis? What happened to the bones?

Loomis: They just walking across the water . . . and then . . . they sunk down.

Bynum: The bones sunk into the water. They all sunk down.

Loomis: All at one time! They just all fell in the water at one time.

Bynum: Sunk down like anybody else.

Loomis: When they sink down they made a big splash and this here wave come up . . .

Bynum: A big wave, Herald Loomis. A big wave washed over the land.

Loomis: It washed them out of the water and up on the land. Only . . . only . . .

Bynum: Only they ain't bones no more.

Loomis: They got flesh on them! Just like you and me!

Bynum: Everywhere you look the waves is washing them up on the land right on top of one another.

Loomis: They black. Just like you and me. Ain't no difference.

Bynum: Then what happened, Herald Loomis?

Loomis: They ain't moved or nothing. They just laying there.

Bynum: You just laying there. What you waiting on, Herald Loomis?

Loomis: I'm laying there . . . waiting.

Bynum: What you waiting on, Herald Loomis?

Loomis: I'm waiting on the breath to get into my body.

Bynum: The breath coming into you, Herald Loomis. What you gonna do now?

Loomis: The wind's blowing the breath into my body. I can feel it. I'm starting to breathe again.

Bynum: What you gonna do, Herald Loomis?

Loomis: I'm gonna stand up. I got to stand up. I can't lay here no more. All the breath coming into my body and I got to stand up.

Bynum: Everybody's standing up at the same time.

Loomis: The ground's starting to shake. There's a great shaking. The world's busting half in two. The sky's splitting open. I got to stand up.

(Loomis attempts to stand up.)

My legs . . . my legs won't stand up!

Bynum: Everybody's standing and walking toward the road. What you gonna do, Herald Loomis?

Loomis: My legs won't stand up.

Bynum: They shaking hands and saying goodbye to each other and walking every whichaway down the road.

Loomis: I got to stand up!

Bynum: They walking around here now. Mens. Just like you and me. Come right up out the water.

Loomis: Got to stand up.

Bynum: They walking, Herald Loomis. They walking around here now.

Loomis: I got to stand up. Get up on the road.

Bynum: Come on, Herald Loomis.

(Loomis tries to stand up.)

Loomis: My legs won't stand up! My legs won't stand up!

(Loomis collapses on the floor as the lights go down to black.)

ACT II

Scene 1

The lights come up on the kitchen. Bertha busies herself with breakfast preparations. Seth sits at the table.

Seth: I don't care what his problem is! He's leaving here!

Bertha: You can't put the man out and he got that little girl. Where they gonna go then?

Seth: I don't care where he go. Let him go back where he was before he come here. I ain't asked him to come here. I knew when I first looked at him something wasn't right with him. Dragging that little girl around with him. Looking like he be sleeping in the woods somewhere. I knew all along he wasn't right.

Bertha: A fellow get a little drunk he's liable to say or do anything. He ain't done no big harm.

Seth: I just don't have all that carrying on in my house. When he come down here I'm gonna tell him. He got to leave here. My daddy wouldn't stand for it and I ain't gonna stand for it either.

Bertha: Well, if you put him out you have to put Bynum out too. Bynum right there with him.

Seth: If it wasn't for Bynum ain't no telling what would have happened. Bynum talked to that fellow just as nice and calmed him down. If he wasn't here ain't no telling what would have happened. Bynum ain't done nothing but talk to him and kept him calm. Man acting all crazy with that foolishness. Naw, he's leaving here.

Bertha: What you gonna tell him? How you gonna tell him to leave?

Seth: I'm gonna tell him straight out. Keep it nice and simple. Mister, you got to leave here!

(Molly enters from the stairs.)

Molly: Morning.

Bertha: Did you sleep alright in that bed?

Molly: Tired as I was I could have slept anywhere. It's a real nice room, though. This is a nice place.

Seth: I'm sorry you had to put up with all that carrying on last night.

Molly: It don't bother me none. I done seen that kind of stuff before.

Seth: You won't have to see it around here no more.

(Bynum is heard singing offstage.)

I don't put up with all that stuff. When that fellow come down here I'm gonna tell him.

Bynum (singing):
Soon my work will all be done
Soon my work will all be done
Soon my work will all be done

I'm going to see the king.

Bynum (Enters): Morning, Seth. Morning, Sister Bertha. I see we got Molly Cunningham down here at breakfast.

Seth: Bynum, I wanna thank you for talking to that fellow last night and calming him down. If you hadn't been here ain't no telling what might have happened.

Bynum: Mr. Loomis alright, Seth. He just got a little excited.

Seth: Well, he can get excited somewhere else 'cause he leaving here.

(Mattie enters from the stairs.)

Bynum: Well, there's Mattie Campbell.

Mattie: Good morning.

Bertha: Sit on down there, Mattie. I got some biscuits be ready in a minute. The coffee's hot.

Mattie: Jeremy gone already?

Bynum: Yeah, he leave out of here early. He got to be there when the sun come up. Most working men got to be there when the sun come up. Everybody but Seth. Seth work at night. Mr. Olowski so busy in his shop he got fellows working at night.

(Loomis enters from the stairs.)

Seth: Mr. Loomis, now . . . I don't want no trouble. I keeps me a respectable house here. I don't have no carrying on like what went on last night. This has been a respectable house for a long time. I'm gonna have to ask you to leave.

Loomis: You got my two dollars. That two dollars say we stay till Saturday.

(Loomis and Seth glare at each other.)

Seth: Alright. Fair enough. You stay till Saturday. But come Saturday you got to leave here.

Loomis (Continues to glare at Seth. He goes to the door and calls): Zonia. You stay around this house, you hear? Don't you go anywhere.

(Loomis exits out the front door.)

Seth: I knew it when I first seen him. I knew something wasn't right with him.

Bertha: Seth, leave the people alone to eat their breakfast. They don't want to hear that. Go on out there and make some pots and pans. That's the only time you satisfied is when you out there. Go on out there and make some pots and pans and leave them people alone.

Seth: I ain't bothering anybody. I'm just stating the facts. I told you, Bynum.

(Bertha shoos Seth out the back door and exits into the bedroom.)

Molly (To Bynum): You one of them voo-doo people?

Bynum: I got a power to bind folks if that what you talking about.

Molly: I thought so. The way you talked to that man when he started all that spooky stuff. What you say you had the power to do to people? You ain't the cause of him acting like that, is you?

Bynum: I binds them together. Sometimes I help them find each other.

Molly: How do you do that?

Bynum: With a song. My daddy taught me how to do it.

Molly: That's what they say. Most folks be what they daddy is. I wouldn't want to be like my daddy. Nothing ever set right with him. He tried to make the world over. Carry it around with him everywhere he go. I don't want to be like that. I just take life as it come. I don't be trying to make it over.

(Pause.)

Your daddy used to do that too, huh? Make people stay together?

Bynum: My daddy used to heal people. He had the Healing Song. I got the Binding Song.

Molly: My mama used to believe in all that stuff. If she got sick she would have gone and saw your daddy. As long as he didn't make her drink nothing. She wouldn't drink nothing nobody give her. She was always afraid somebody was gonna poison her. How your daddy heal people?

Bynum: With a song. He healed people by singing over them. I seen him do it. He sung over this little white girl when she was sick. They made a big to-do about it. They carried the girl's bed out in the yard and had all her kinfolk standing around. The little girl laying up there in the bed. Doctors standing around can't do nothing to help her. And they had my daddy come up and sing his song. It didn't sound no different than any other song. It was just somebody singing. But the song was its own thing and it come out and took upon this little girl with its power and it healed her.

Molly: That's sure something else. I don't understand that kind of thing. I guess if the doctor couldn't make me well I'd try it. But otherwise I don't wanna be bothered with that kind of thing. It's too spooky.

Bynum: Well, let me get on out here and get to work.

(Bynum gets up and heads out the back door.)

Molly: I ain't meant to offend you or nothing. What's your name . . . Bynum? I ain't meant to say nothing to make you feel bad now.

(Bynum exits out the back door.)

(to Mattie.) I hope he don't feel bad. He's a nice man. I don't wanna hurt nobody's feelings or nothing.

Mattie: I got to go on up to Doc Goldblum's and finish this ironing.

Molly: Now, that's something I don't never wanna do. Iron no clothes. Especially somebody else's. That's what I believe killed my mama. Always ironing and working, doing somebody else's work. Not Molly Cunningham.

Mattie: It's the only job I got. I got to make it someway to fend for myself.

Molly: I thought Jeremy was your man. Ain't he working?

Mattie: We just be keeping company till maybe Jack come back.

Molly: I don't trust none of these men. Jack or nobody else. These men liable to do anything. They wait just until they get one woman tied and locked up with them . . . then they look around to see if they can get another one. Molly don't pay them no mind. One's just as good as the other if you ask me. I ain't never met one that meant nobody no good. You got any babies?

Mattie: I had two for my man, Jack Carper. But they both died.

Molly: That be the best. These men make all these babies, then run off and leave you to take care of them. Talking about they wanna see what's on the other side of the hill. I make sure I don't get no babies. My mama taught me how to do that.

Mattie: Don't make me no mind. That be nice to be a mother.

Molly: Yeah? Well, you go on, then. Molly Cunningham ain't gonna be tied down with no babies. Had me a man one time who I thought had some love in him. Come home one day and he was packing his trunk. Told me the time come when even the best of friends must part. Say he was gonna send me a Special Delivery some old day. I watched him out the window when he carried that trunk out and down to the train station. Said if he was gonna send me a Special Delivery I wasn't gonna be there to get it. I done found out the harder you try to hold onto them, the easier it is for some gal to pull them away. Molly done learned that. That's why I don't trust nobody but the good Lord above, and I don't love nobody but my mama.

Mattie: I got to get on. Doc Goldblum gonna be waiting.

(Mattie exits out the front door. Seth enters from his workshop with his apron, gloves, goggles, etc. He carries a bucket and crosses to the sink for water.)

Seth: Everybody gone but you, huh?

Molly: That little shack out there by the outhouse . . . that's where you make them pots and pans and stuff?

Seth: Yeah, that's my workshed. I go out there . . . take these hands and make something out of nothing. Take that metal and bend and twist it whatever way I want. My daddy taught me that. He used to make pots and pans. That's how I learned it.

Molly: I never knew nobody made no pots and pans. My uncle used to shoe horses.

(Jeremy enters at the front door.)

Seth: I thought you was working? Ain't you working today?

Jeremy: Naw, they fired me. White fellow come by told me to give him fifty cents if I wanted to keep working. Going around to all the colored making them give him fifty cents to keep hold to their jobs. Them other fellows, they was giving it to him. I kept hold to mine and they fired me.

Seth: Boy, what kind of sense that make? What kind of sense it make to get fired from a job where you making eight dollars a week and all it cost you is fifty cents. That's seven dollars and fifty cents profit! This way you ain't got nothing.

Jeremy: It didn't make no sense to me. I don't make but eight dollars. Why I got to give him fifty cents of it? He go around to all the colored and he got ten dollars extra. That's more than I make for a whole week.

Seth: I see you gonna learn the hard way. You just looking at the facts of it. See, right now, without the job, you ain't got nothing. What you gonna do when you can't keep a roof over your head? Right now, come Saturday, unless you come up with another two dollars, you gonna be out there in the streets. Down up under one of them bridges trying to put some food in your belly and wishing you had given that fellow that fifty cents.

Jeremy: Don't make me no difference. There's a big road out there. I can get my guitar and always find me another place to stay. I ain't planning on staying in one place for too long noway.

Seth: We gonna see if you feel like that come Saturday!

(Seth exits out the back. Jeremy sees Molly.)

Jeremy: Molly Cunningham. How you doing today, sugar?

Molly: You can go on back down there tomorrow and go back to work if you want. They won't even know who you is. Won't even know it's you. I had me a fellow did that one time. They just went ahead and signed him up like they never seen him before.

Jeremy: I'm tired of working anyway. I'm glad they fired me. You sure look pretty today.

Molly: Don't come telling me all that pretty stuff. Beauty wanna come in and sit down at your table asking to be fed. I ain't hardly got enough for me.

Jeremy: You know you pretty. Ain't no sense in you saying nothing about that. Why don't you come on and go away with me?

Molly: You tied up with that Mattie Campbell. Now you talking about running away with me.

Jeremy: I was just keeping her company 'cause she lonely. You ain't the lonely kind. You the kind that know what she want and how to get it. I need a woman like you to travel around with. Don't you wanna travel around and look at some places with Jeremy? With a woman like you beside him, a man can make it nice in the world.

Molly: Moll can make it nice by herself too. Molly don't need nobody leave her cold in hand. The world rough enough as it is.

Jeremy: We can make it better together. I got my guitar and I can play. Won me another dollar last night playing guitar. We can go around and I can play at the dances and we can just enjoy life. You can make it by yourself alright, I agrees with that. A woman like you can make it anywhere she go. But you can make it better if you got a man to protect you.

Molly: What places you wanna go around and look at?

Jeremy: All of them! I don't want to miss nothing. I wanna go everywhere and do everything there is to be got out of life. With a woman like you it's like having water and berries. A man got everything he need.

Molly: You got to be doing more than playing that guitar. A dollar a day ain't hardly what Molly got in mind.

Jeremy: I gambles real good. I got a hand for it.

Molly: Molly don't work. And Molly ain't up for sale.

Jeremy: Sure, baby. You ain't got to work with Jeremy.

Molly: There's one more thing.

Jeremy: What's that, sugar?

Molly: Molly ain't going South.

(*The lights go down on the scene.*)

Scene 2

The lights come up on the parlor. Seth and Bynum sit playing a game of dominoes. Bynum sings to himself.

Bynum (Singing):
> They tell me Joe Turner's come and gone°
> Ohhh Lordy
> They tell me Joe Turner's come and gone
> Ohhh Lordy
> Got my man and gone
>
> Come with forty links of chain
> Ohhh Lordy
> Come with forty links of chain
> Ohhh Lordy
> Got my man and gone

Seth: Come on and play if you gonna play.

Bynum: I'm gonna play. Soon as I figure out what to do.

Joe Turner's come and gone: In Tennessee around the turn of the century, Joe Turner became legendary: a professional bounty hunter, and one who claimed a reward for finding an escaped convict. To increase his profits Turner impressed not only convicts into a chain gang but innocent men as well.

Seth: You can't figure out if you wanna play or you wanna sing.

Bynum: Well sir, I'm gonna do a little bit of both.

(*Playing.*)

There. What you gonna do now?

(*Singing.*)

They tell me Joe Turner's come and gone
Ohhh Lordy
They tell me Joe Turner's come and gone
Ohhh Lordy

Seth: Why don't you hush up that noise.

Bynum: That's a song the women sing down around Memphis. The women down there made up that song. I picked it up down there about fifteen years ago.

(*Loomis enters from the front door.*)

Bynum: Evening, Mr. Loomis.

Seth: Today's Monday, Mr. Loomis. Come Saturday your time is up. We done ate already. My wife roasted up some yams. She got your plate sitting in there on the table. (*To Bynum.*) Whose play is it?

Bynum: Ain't you keeping up with the game? I thought you was a domino player. I just played so it got to be your turn.

(*Loomis goes into the kitchen, where a plate of yams is covered and set on the table. He sits down and begins to eat with his hands.*)

Seth (Plays): Twenty! Give me twenty! You didn't know I had that ace five. You was trying to play around that. You didn't know I had that lying there for you.

Bynum: You ain't done nothing. I let you have that to get mine.

Seth: Come on and play. You ain't doing nothing but talking. I got a hundred and forty points to your eighty. You ain't doing nothing but talking. Come on and play.

Bynum (Singing):
They tell me Joe Turner's come and gone
Ohhh Lordy
They tell me Joe Turner's come and gone
Ohhh Lordy
Got my man and gone

He come with forty links of chain
Ohhh Lordy

Loomis: Why you singing that song? Why you singing about Joe Turner?

Bynum: I'm just singing to entertain myself.

Seth: You trying to distract me. That's what you trying to do.

Bynum (Singing):
Come with forty links of chain
Ohhh Lordy
Come with forty links of chain
Ohhh Lordy

Loomis: I don't like you singing that song, mister!

Seth: Now, I ain't gonna have no more disturbance around here, Herald Loomis. You start any more disturbance and you leavin' here, Saturday or no Saturday.

Bynum: The man ain't causing no disturbance, Seth. He just say he don't like the song.

Seth: Well, we all friendly folk. All neighborly like. Don't have no squabbling around here. Don't have no disturbance. You gonna have to take that some-place else.

Bynum: He just say he don't like the song. I done sung a whole lot of songs people don't like. I respect everybody. He here in the house too. If he don't like the song, I'll sing something else. I know lots of songs. You got "I Belong to the Band," "Don't You Leave Me Here." You got "Praying on the Old Camp-ground," "Keep your Lamp Trimmed and Burning" . . . I know lots of songs. (*Sings.*)

Boys, I'll be so glad when payday come
Captain, Captain, when payday comes
Gonna catch that Illinois Central
Going to Kankakee

Seth: Why don't you hush up that hollering and come on and play dominoes.

Bynum: You ever been to Johnstown, Herald Loomis? You look like a fellow I seen around there.

Loomis: I don't know no place with that name.

Bynum: That's around where I seen my shiny man. See, you looking for this woman. I'm looking for a shiny man. Seem like everybody looking for something.

Seth: I'm looking for you to come and play these dominoes. That's what I'm look-ing for.

Bynum: You a farming man, Herald Loomis? You look like you done some farming.

Loomis: Same as everybody. I done farmed some, yeah.

Bynum: I used to work at farming . . . picking cotton. I reckon everybody done picked some cotton.

Seth: I ain't! I ain't never picked no cotton. I was born up here in the North. My daddy was a freedman. I ain't never even seen no cotton!

Bynum: Mr. Loomis done picked some cotton. Ain't you, Herald Loomis? You done picked a bunch of cotton.

Loomis: How you know so much about me? How you know what I done? How much cotton I picked?

Bynum: I can tell from looking at you. My daddy taught me how to do that. Say when you look at a fellow, if you taught yourself to look for it, you can see his song written on him. Tell you what kind of man he is in the world. Now, I can look at you, Mr. Loomis, and see you a man who done forgot his song. Forgot how to sing it. A fellow forget that and he forget who he is. Forget how he's supposed to mark down life. Now, I used to travel all up and down this road and that . . . looking here and there. Searching. Just like you, Mr. Loomis. I didn't know what I was searching for. The only thing I knew was something was keeping me dissatisfied. Something wasn't making my heart smooth and easy. Then one day my daddy gave me a song. That song had a weight to it that was hard to handle. That song was hard to carry. I fought against it. Didn't want to accept that song. I tried to find my daddy to give him back the song. But I found out it wasn't his song. It was my song. It had come from way deep inside me. I looked long back in memory and gathered up pieces and snatches of things to make that song. I was making it up out of myself. And that song helped me on the road. Made it smooth to where my footsteps didn't bite back at me. All the time that song getting bigger and bigger. That song growing with each step of the road. It got so I used all of myself up in the making of that song. Then I was the song in search of itself. That song rattling in my throat and I'm looking for it. See, Mr. Loomis, when a man forgets his song he goes off in search of it . . . till he find out he's got it with him all the time. That's why I can tell you one of Joe Turner's niggers. 'Cause you forgot how to sing your song.

Loomis: You lie! How you see that? I got a mark on me? Joe Turner done marked me to where you can see it? You telling me I'm a marked man. What kind of mark you got on you?

(Bynum begins singing.)

Bynum:

They tell me Joe Turner's come and gone
Ohhh Lordy
They tell me Joe Turner's come and gone
Ohhh Lordy
Got my man and gone

Loomis: Had a whole mess of men he catched. Just go out hunting regular like you go out hunting possum. He catch you and go home to his wife and family. Ain't thought about you going home to yours. Joe Turner catched me when my little girl was born. Wasn't nothing but a little baby sucking on her mama's titty when he catched me. Joe Turner catched me in nineteen hundred and one. Kept me seven years until nineteen hundred and eight. Kept everybody seven years. He'd go out hunting and bring back forty men at a time. And keep them seven years.

I was walking down this road in this little town outside of Memphis. Come up on these fellows gambling. I was a deacon in the Abundant Life Church. I stopped to preach to these fellows to see if maybe I could turn some of them from their sinning when Joe Turner, brother of the Governor of the great sovereign state of Tennessee, swooped down on us and grabbed everybody there. Kept us all seven years.

My wife Martha gone from me after Joe Turner catched me. Got out from under Joe Turner on his birthday. Me and forty other men put in our seven years and he let us go on his birthday. I made it back to Henry Thompson's place where me and Martha was sharecropping and Martha's gone. She taken my little girl and left her with her mama and took off North. We been looking for her ever since. That's been going on four years now we been looking. That's the only thing I know to do. I just wanna see her face so I can get me a starting place in the world. The world got to start somewhere. That's what I been looking for. I been wandering a long time in somebody else's world. When I find my wife that be the making of my own.

Bynum: Joe Turner tell why he caught you? You ever asked him that?

Loomis: I ain't never seen Joe Turner. Seen him to where I could touch him. I asked one of them fellows one time why he catch niggers. Asked him what I got he want? Why don't he keep on to himself? Why he got to catch me going down the road by my lonesome? He told me I was worthless. Worthless is something you throw away. Something you don't bother with. I ain't seen him throw me away. Wouldn't even let me stay away when I was by my lonesome. I ain't tried to catch him when he going down the road. So I must got something he want. What I got?

Seth: He just want you to do his work for him. That's all.

Loomis: I can look at him and see where he big and strong enough to do his own work. So it can't be that. He must want something he ain't got.

Bynum: That ain't hard to figure out. What he wanted was your song. He wanted to have that song to be his. He thought by catching you he could learn that song. Every nigger he catch he's looking for the one he can learn that song from. Now he's got you bound up to where you can't sing your own song. Couldn't sing it them seven years 'cause you was afraid he would snatch it from under you. But you still got it. You just forgot how to sing it.

Loomis (To Bynum): I know who you are. You one of them bones people.

(The lights go down to black.)

Scene 3

The lights come up on the kitchen. It is the following morning. Mattie, and Bynum, sit at the table. Bertha busies herself at the stove.

Bynum: Good luck don't know no special time to come. You sleep with that up under your pillow and good luck can't help but come to you. Sometimes it come and go and you don't even know it's been there.

Bertha: Bynum, why don't you leave that gal alone? She don't wanna be hearing all that. Why don't you go on and get out the way and leave her alone?

Bynum (Getting up.): Alright, alright. But you mark what I'm saying. It'll draw it to you just like a magnet.

(Bynum exits up the stairs and Loomis enters.)

Bertha: I got some grits here, Mr. Loomis.

(Bertha sets a bowl on the table.)

If I was you, Mattie, I wouldn't go getting all tied up with Bynum in that stuff. That kind of stuff, even if it do work for a while, it don't last. That just get people more mixed up than they is already. And I wouldn't waste my time fretting over Jeremy either. I seen it coming. I seen it when she first come here. She that kind of woman run off with the first man got a dollar to spend on her. Jeremy just young. He don't know what he getting into.

That gal don't mean him no good. She's just using him to keep from being by herself. That's the worst use of a man you can have. You ought to be glad to wash him out of your hair. I done seen all kind of men. I done seen them come and go through here. Jeremy ain't had enough to him for you. You need a man who's got some understanding and who willing to work with that understanding to come to the best he can. You got your time coming. You just tries too hard and can't understand why it don't work for you. Trying to figure it out don't do nothing but give you a troubled mind. Don't no man want a woman with a troubled mind.

You get all that trouble off your mind and just when it look like you ain't never gonna find what you want . . . you look up and it's standing right there. That's how I met my Seth. You gonna look up one day and find everything you want standing right in front of you. Been twenty-seven years now since that happened to me. But life ain't no happy-go-lucky time where everything be just like you want it. You got your time coming. You watch what Bertha's saying.

(Seth enters.)

Seth: Ho!
Bertha: What you doing come in here so late?
Seth: I was standing down there on Logan Street talking with the fellows. Henry Allen tried to sell me that old piece of horse he got.

(He sees Loomis.)

Today's Tuesday, Mr. Loomis.
Bertha *(Pulling him toward the bedroom)*: Come on in here and leave that man alone to eat his breakfast.
Seth: I ain't bothering nobody. I'm just reminding him what day it is.

(Seth and Bertha exit into the bedroom.)

Loomis: That dress got a color to it.
Mattie: Did you really see them things like you said? Them people come up out the ocean?
Loomis: It happened just like that, yeah.
Mattie: I hope you find your wife. It be good for your little girl for you to find her.
Loomis: Got to find her for myself. Find my starting place in the world. Find me a world I can fit in.
Mattie: I ain't never found no place for me to fit. Seem like all I do is start over. It ain't nothing to find no starting place in the world. You just start from where you find yourself.
Loomis: Got to find my wife. That be my starting place.
Mattie: What if you don't find her? What you gonna do then if you don't find her?
Loomis: She out there somewhere. Ain't no such thing as not finding her.
Mattie: How she got lost from you? Jack just walked away from me.
Loomis: Joe Turner split us up. Joe Turner turned the world upside-down. He bound me on to him for seven years.

Mattie: I hope you find her. It be good for you to find her.

Loomis: I been watching you. I been watching you watch me.

Mattie: I was just trying to figure out if you seen things like you said.

Loomis (Getting up): Come here and let me touch you. I been watching you. You a full woman. A man needs a full woman. Come on and be with me.

Mattie: I ain't got enough for you. You'd use me up too fast.

Loomis: Herald Loomis got a mind seem like you a part of it since I first seen you. It's been a long time since I seen a full woman. I can smell you from here. I know you got Herald Loomis on your mind, can't keep him apart from it. Come on and be with Herald Loomis.

(Loomis has crossed to Mattie. He touches her awkwardly, gently, tenderly. Inside he howls like a lost wolf pup whose hunger is deep. He goes to touch her but finds he cannot.)

I done forgot how to touch.

(The lights fade to black.)

Scene 4

It is early the next morning. The lights come up on Zonia and Reuben in the yard.

Reuben: Something spooky going on around here. Last night Mr. Bynum was out in the yard singing and talking to the wind . . . and the wind it just be talking back to him. Did you hear it?

Zonia: I heard it. I was scared to get up and look. I thought it was a storm.

Reuben: That wasn't no storm. That was Mr. Bynum. First he say something . . . and the wind it say back to him.

Zonia: I heard it. Was you scared? I was scared.

Reuben: And then this morning . . . I seen Miss Mabel!

Zonia: Who Miss Mabel?

Reuben: Mr. Seth's mother. He got her picture hanging up in the house. She been dead.

Zonia: How you seen her if she been dead?

Reuben: Zonia . . . if I tell you something you promise you won't tell anybody?

Zonia: I promise.

Reuben: It was early this morning . . . I went out to the coop to feed the pigeons. I was down on the ground like this to open up the door to the coop . . . when all of a sudden I seen some feets in front of me. I looked up . . . and there was Miss Mabel standing there.

Zonia: Reuben, you better stop telling that! You ain't seen nobody!

Reuben: Naw, it's the truth. I swear! I seen her just like I see you. Look . . . you can see where she hit me with her cane.

Zonia: Hit you? What she hit you for?

Reuben: She says, "Didn't you promise Eugene something?" Then she hit me with her cane. She say, "Let them pigeons go." Then she hit me again. That's what made them marks.

Zonia: Jeez man . . . get away from me. You done see a haunt!

Reuben: Shhhh. You promised, Zonia!

Zonia: You sure it wasn't Miss Bertha come over there and hit you with her hoe?

Reuben: It wasn't no Miss Bertha. I told you it was Miss Mabel. She was standing right there by the coop. She had this light coming out of her and then she just melted away.

Zonia: What she had on?

Reuben: A white dress. Ain't even had no shoes or nothing. Just had on that white dress and them big hands . . . and that cane she hit me with.

Zonia: How you reckon she knew about the pigeons? You reckon Eugene told her?

Reuben: I don't know. I sure ain't asked her none. She say Eugene was waiting on them pigeons. Say he couldn't go back home till I let them go. I couldn't get the door to the coop open fast enough.

Zonia: Maybe she an angel? From the way you say she look with that white dress. Maybe she an angel.

Reuben: Mean as she was . . . how she gonna be an angel? She used to chase us out her yard and frown up and look evil all the time.

Zonia: That don't mean she can't be no angel 'cause of how she looked and 'cause she wouldn't let no kids play in her yard. It go by if you got any spots on your heart and if you pray and go to church.

Reuben: What about she hit me with her cane? An angel wouldn't hit me with her cane.

Zonia: I don't know. She might. I still say she was an angel.

Reuben: You reckon Eugene the one who sent old Miss Mabel?

Zonia: Why he send her? Why he don't come himself?

Reuben: Figured if he send her maybe that'll make me listen. 'Cause she old.

Zonia: What you think it feel like?

Reuben: What?

Zonia: Being dead.

Reuben: Like being sleep only you don't know nothing and can't move no more.

Zonia: If Miss Mabel can come back . . . then maybe Eugene can come back too.

Reuben: We can go down to the hideout like we used to! He could come back everyday! It be just like he ain't dead.

Zonia: Maybe that ain't right for him to come back. Feel kinda funny to be playing games with a haunt.

Reuben: Yeah . . . what if everybody came back? What if Miss Mabel came back just like she ain't dead? Where you and your daddy gonna sleep then?

Zonia: Maybe they go back at night and don't need no place to sleep.

Reuben: It still don't seem right. I'm sure gonna miss Eugene. He's the bestest friend anybody ever had.

Zonia: My daddy say if you miss somebody too much it can kill you. Say he missed me till it liked to killed him.

Reuben: What if your mama's already dead and all the time you looking for her?

Zonia: Naw, she ain't dead. My daddy say he can smell her.

Reuben: You can't smell nobody that ain't here. Maybe he smelling old Miss Bertha. Maybe Miss Bertha your mama?

Zonia: Naw, she ain't. My mama got long pretty hair and she five feet from the ground!

Reuben: Your daddy say when you leaving?

(*Zonia doesn't respond.*)

Maybe you gonna stay in Mr. Seth's house and don't go looking for your mama no more.

Zonia: He say we got to leave on Saturday.

Reuben: Dag! You just only been here for a little while. Don't seem like nothing ever stay the same.

Zonia: He say he got to find her. Find him a place in the world.

Reuben: He could find him a place in Mr. Seth's house.

Zonia: It don't look like we never gonna find her.

Reuben: Maybe he find her by Saturday then you don't have to go.

Zonia: I don't know.

Reuben: You look like a spider!

Zonia: I ain't no spider!

Reuben: Got them long skinny arms and legs. You look like one of them Black Widows.

Zonia: I ain't no Black Window nothing! My name is Zonia!

Reuben: That's what I'm gonna call you . . . Spider.

Zonia: You can call me that, but I don't have to answer.

Reuben: You know what? I think maybe I be your husband when I grow up.

Zonia: How you know?

Reuben: I ask my grandpap how you know and he say when the moon falls into a girl's eyes that how you know.

Zonia: Did it fall into my eyes?

Reuben: Not that I can tell. Maybe I ain't old enough. Maybe you ain't old enough.

Zonia: So there! I don't know why you telling me that lie!

Reuben: That don't mean nothing 'cause I can't see it. I know it's there. Just the way you look at me sometimes look like the moon might have been in your eyes.

Zonia: That don't mean nothing if you can't see it. You supposed to see it.

Reuben: Shucks, I see it good enough for me. You ever let anybody kiss you?

Zonia: Just my daddy. He kiss me on the cheek.

Reuben: It's better on the lips. Can I kiss you on the lips?

Zonia: I don't know. You ever kiss anybody before?

Reuben: I had a cousin let me kiss her on the lips one time. Can I kiss you?

Zonia: Okay.

(*Reuben kisses her and lays his head against her chest.*)

What you doing?

Reuben: Listening. Your heart singing?

Zonia: It is not.

Reuben: Just beating like a drum. Let's kiss again.

(*They kiss again.*)

Now you mine, Spider. You my girl, okay?

Zonia: Okay.

Reuben: When I get grown, I come looking for you.
Zonia: Okay.

(*The lights fade to black.*)

Scene 5

The lights come up on the kitchen. It is Saturday. Bynum, Loomis, and Zonia sit at the table. Bertha prepares breakfast. Zonia has on a white dress.

Bynum: With all this rain we been having he might have ran into some washed-out roads. If that wagon got stuck in the mud he's liable to be still upriver somewhere. If he's upriver then he ain't coming until tomorrow.
Loomis: Today's Saturday. He say he be here on Saturday.
Bertha: Zonia, you gonna eat your breakfast this morning.
Zonia: Yes, ma'am.
Bertha: I don't know how you expect to get any bigger if you don't eat. I ain't never seen a child that didn't eat. You about as skinny as a bean pole.

(*Pause.*)

Mr. Loomis, there's a place down on Wylie. Zeke Mayweather got a house down there. You ought to see if he got any rooms.

(*Loomis doesn't respond.*)

Well, you're welcome to some breakfast before you move on.

(*Mattie enters from the stairs.*)

Mattie: Good morning.
Bertha: Morning, Mattie. Sit on down there and get you some breakfast.
Bynum: Well, Mattie Campbell, you been sleeping with that up under your pillow like I told you?
Bertha: Bynum, I done told you to leave that gal alone with all that stuff. You around here meddling in other people's lives. She don't want to hear all that. You ain't doing nothing but confusing her with that stuff.
Mattie (To Loomis): You all fixing to move on?
Loomis: Today's Saturday. I'm paid up till Saturday.
Mattie: Where you going to?
Loomis: Gonna find my wife.
Mattie: You going off to another city?
Loomis: We gonna see where the road take us. Ain't no telling where we wind up.
Mattie: Eleven years is a long time. Your wife . . . she might have taken up with someone else. People do that when they get lost from each other.
Loomis: Zonia. Come on, we gonna find your mama.

(*Loomis and Zonia cross to the door.*)

Mattie (To Zonia): Zonia, Mattie got a ribbon here match your dress. Want Mattie to fix your hair with her ribbon?

(Zonia nods. Mattie ties the ribbon in her hair.)

There . . . it got a color just like your dress. *(To Loomis.)* I hope you find her. I hope you be happy.

Loomis: A man looking for a woman be lucky to find you. You a good woman, Mattie. Keep a good heart.

(Loomis and Zonia exit.)

Bertha: I been watching that man for two weeks . . . and that's the closest I come to seeing him act civilized. I don't know what's between you all, Mattie . . . but the only thing that man needs is somebody to make him laugh. That's all you need in the world is love and laughter. That's all anybody needs. To have love in one hand and laughter in the other.

(Bertha moves about the kitchen as though blessing it and chasing away the huge sadness that seems to envelop it. It is a dance and demonstration of her own magic, her own remedy that is centuries old and to which she is connected by the muscles of her heart and the blood's memory.)

You hear me, Mattie? I'm talking about laughing. The kind of laugh that comes from way deep inside. To just stand and laugh and let life flow right through you. Just laugh to let yourself know you're alive.

(She begins to laugh. It is a near-hysterical laughter that is a celebration of life, both its pain and its blessing. Mattie and Bynum join in the laughter. Seth enters from the front door.)

Seth: Well, I see you all having fun.

(Seth begins to laugh with them.)

That Loomis fellow standing up there on the corner watching the house. He standing right up there on Manila Street.

Bertha: Don't you get started on him. The man done left out of here and that's the last I wanna hear of it. You about to drive me crazy with that man.

Seth: I just say he standing up there on the corner. Acting sneaky like he always do. He can stand up there all he want. As long as he don't come back in here.

(There is a knock on the door. Seth goes to answer it. Enter Martha Loomis [Pentecost]. She is a young woman about twenty-eight. She is dressed as befitting a member of an Evangelist church. Rutherford Selig follows.)

Seth: Look here, Bertha. It's Martha Pentecost. Come on in, Martha. Who that with you? Oh . . . that's Selig. Come on in, Selig.

Bertha: Come on in, Martha. It's sure good to see you.

Bynum: Rutherford Selig, you a sure enough first-class People Finder!

Selig: She was right out there in Rankin. You take that first righthand road . . . right there at that church on Wooster Street. I started to go right past and something told me to stop at the church and see if they needed any dustpans.

Seth: Don't she look good, Bertha.

Bertha: Look all nice and healthy.

Martha: Mr. Bynum . . . Selig told me my little girl was here.

Seth: There's some fellow around here say he your husband. Say his name is Loomis. Say you his wife.

Martha: Is my little girl with him?

Seth: Yeah, he got a little girl with him. I wasn't gonna tell him where you was. Not the way this fellow look. So he got Selig to find you.

Martha: Where they at? They upstairs?

Seth: He was standing right up there on Manila Street. I had to ask him to leave 'cause of how he was carrying on. He come in here one night—

(The door opens and Loomis and Zonia enter. Martha and Loomis stare at each other.)

Loomis: Hello, Martha.

Martha: Herald . . . Zonia?

Loomis: You ain't waited for me, Martha. I got out the place looking to see your face. Seven years I waited to see your face.

Martha: Herald, I been looking for you. I wasn't but two months behind you when you went to my mama's and got Zonia. I been looking for you ever since.

Loomis: Joe Turner let me loose and I felt all turned around inside. I just wanted to see your face to know that the world was still there. Make sure everything still in its place so I could reconnect myself together. I got there and you was gone, Martha.

Martha: Herald . . .

Loomis: Left my little girl motherless in the world.

Martha: I didn't leave her motherless, Herald. Reverend Tolliver wanted to move the church up North 'cause of all the trouble the colored folks was having down there. Nobody knew what was gonna happen traveling them roads. We didn't even know if we was gonna make it up here or not. I left her with my mama so she be safe. That was better than dragging her out on the road having to duck and hide from people. Wasn't no telling what was gonna happen to us. I didn't leave her motherless in the world. I been looking for you.

Loomis: I come up on Henry Thompson's place after seven years of living in hell, and all I'm looking to do is see your face.

Martha: Herald, I didn't know if you was ever coming back. They told me Joe Turner had you and my whole world split half in two. My whole life shattered. It was like I had poured it in a cracked jar and it all leaked out the bottom. When it go like that there ain't nothing you can do to put it back together. You talking about Henry Thompson's place like I'm still gonna be working the land by myself. How I'm gonna do that? You wasn't gone but two months and Henry Thompson kicked me off his land and I ain't had no place to go but to my mama's. I stayed and waited there for five years before I woke up one morning and decided that you was dead. Even if you weren't, you was dead to me. I wasn't gonna carry you with me no more. So I killed you in my heart. I buried you. I mourned you. And then I picked up what was left and went on to make life without you. I was a young woman with life at my beckon. I couldn't drag you behind me like a sack of cotton.

Loomis: I just been waiting to look on your face to say my goodbye. That goodbye got so big at times, seem like it was gonna swallow me up. Like Jonah in the whale's belly I sat up in that goodbye for three years. That goodbye kept me out on the road searching. Not looking on women in their houses. It kept me bound up to the road. All the time that goodbye swelling up in my chest till I'm about to bust. Now that I see your face I can say my goodbye and make my own world.

(*Loomis takes Zonia's hand and presents her to Martha.*)

Martha . . . here go your daughter. I tried to take care of her. See that she had something to eat. See that she was out of the elements. Whatever I know I tried to teach her. Now she need to learn from her mother whatever you got to teach her. That way she won't be no one-sided person.

(*Loomis stoops to Zonia.*)

Zonia, you go live with your mama. She a good woman. You go on with her and listen to her good. You my daughter and I love you like a daughter. I hope to see you again in the world somewhere. I'll never forget you.

Zonia (*Throws her arms around Loomis in a panic*): I won't get no bigger! My bones won't get no bigger! They won't! I promise! Take me with you till we keep searching and never finding. I won't get no bigger! I promise!

Loomis: Go on and do what I told you now.

Martha (*Goes to Zonia and comforts her*): It's alright, baby. Mama's here. Mama's here. Don't worry. Don't cry.

(*Martha turns to Bynum.*)

Mr. Bynum, I don't know how to thank you. God bless you.

Loomis: It was you! All the time it was you that bind me up! You bound me to the road!

Bynum: I ain't bind you, Herald Loomis. You can't bind what don't cling.

Loomis: Everywhere I go people wanna bind me up. Joe Turner wanna bind me up! Reverend Tolliver wanna bind me up. You wanna bind me up. Everybody wanna bind me up. Well, Joe Turner's come and gone and Herald Loomis ain't for no binding. I ain't gonna let nobody bind me up!

(*Loomis pulls out a knife.*)

Bynum: It wasn't you, Herald Loomis. I ain't bound you. I bound the little girl to her mother. That's who I bound. You binding yourself. You bound onto your song. All you got to do is stand up and sing it, Herald Loomis. It's right there kicking at your throat. All you got to do is sing it. Then you be free.

Martha: Herald . . . look at yourself! Standing there with a knife in your hand. You done gone over to the devil. Come on . . . put down the knife. You got to look to Jesus. Even if you done fell away from the church you can be saved again. The Bible say, "The Lord is my shepherd I shall not want. He maketh me to lie down in green pastures. He leads me beside the still water. He restoreth my soul. He leads me in the path of righteousness for His name's sake. Even though I walk through the shadow of death—"

Loomis: That's just where I be walking!

Martha: "I shall fear no evil. For Thou art with me. Thy rod and thy staff, they comfort me."

Loomis: You can't tell me nothing about no valleys. I done been all across the valleys and the hills and the mountains and the oceans.

Martha: "Thou preparest a table for me in the presence of my enemies."

Loomis: And all I seen was a bunch of niggers dazed out of their woolly heads. And Mr. Jesus Christ standing there in the middle of them, grinning.

Martha: "Thou anointest my head with oil, my cup runneth over."

Loomis: He grin that big old grin . . . and niggers wallowing at his feet.

Martha: "Surely goodness and mercy shall follow me all the days of my life, and I shall dwell in the house of the Lord forever."

Loomis: Great big old white man . . . your Mr. Jesus Christ. Standing there with a whip in one hand and tote board in another, and them niggers swimming in a sea of cotton. And he counting. He tallying up the cotton. "Well, Jeremiah . . . what's the matter, you ain't picked but two hundred pounds of cotton today? Got to put you on half rations." And Jeremiah go back and lay up there on his half rations and talk about what a nice man Mr. Jesus Christ is 'cause he give him salvation after he die. Something wrong here. Something don't fit right!

Martha: You got to open up your heart and have faith, Herald. This world is just a trial for the next. Jesus offers you salvation.

Loomis: I been wading in the water. I been walking all over the River Jordan. But what it get me, huh? I done been baptized with blood of the lamb and the fire of the Holy Ghost. But what I got, huh? I got salvation? My enemies all around me picking the flesh from my bones. I'm choking on my own blood and all you got to give me is salvation?

Martha: You got to be clean, Herald. You got to be washed with the blood of the lamb.

Loomis: Blood make you clean? You clean with blood?

Martha: Jesus bled for you. He's the Lamb of God who takest away the sins of the world.

Loomis: I don't need nobody to bleed for me! I can bleed for myself.

Martha: You got to be something, Herald. You just can't be alive. Life don't mean nothing unless it got a meaning.

Loomis: What kind of meaning you got? What kind of clean you got, woman? You want blood? Blood make you clean? You clean with blood?

(Loomis slashes himself across the chest. He rubs the blood over his face and comes to a realization.)

I'm standing! I'm standing. My legs stood up! I'm standing now!

(Having found his song, the song of self-sufficiency, fully resurrected, cleansed and given breath, free from any encumbrance other than the workings of his own heart and the bonds of the flesh, having accepted the responsibility for his own presence in the world, he is free to soar above the environs that weighed and pushed his spirit into terrifying contractions.)

Goodbye, Martha.

(Loomis turns and exits, the knife still in his hands. Mattie looks about the room and rushes out after him.)

Bynum: Herald Loomis, you shining! You shining like new money!

The lights go down to BLACK.

38 Criticism: On Drama

FROM A PROPOSED AGREEMENT BETWEEN THE PLAYWRIGHT AND THE SPECTATOR

It is also agreed that every man here exercise his own judgment and not censure by contagion, or upon trust, from another's voice or face that sits by him . . . that he be fixed and settled in his censure, that what he approves or not approves today he will do the same tomorrow; and, if tomorrow, the next day; and so the next week, if need be; and not be brought about by any that sits on the bench with him, though they indict and arraign plays daily.

—The Scrivener, in Ben Jonson's *Bartholomew Fair* (1614)

Aristotle (384–322 B.C.)

TRAGEDY   (about 330 B.C.)

Translated by L.J. Potts

Tragedy is an imitation of an action of high importance, complete and of some amplitude; in language enhanced by distinct and varying beauties; acted not narrated; by means of pity and fear effecting its purgation of these emotions. By the beauties enhancing the language I mean rhythm and melody; by "distinct and varying" I mean that some are produced by meter alone, and others at another time by melody . . . .

What will produce the tragic effect? Since, then, tragedy, to be at its finest, requires a complex, not a simple, structure, and its structure should also imitate fearful and pitiful events (for that is the peculiarity of this sort of imitation), it is clear: first, that decent people must not be shown passing from good fortune to misfortune (for that is not fearful or pitiful but disgusting); again, vicious people must not be shown passing from misfortune to good fortune (for that is the most untragic situation possible—it has none of the requisites, it is neither humane, not pitiful, nor fearful); nor again should an utterly evil man fall from good fortune into misfortune (for though a plot of that kind would be humane, it would not induce pity or fear—pity is induced by undeserved misfortune, and fear by the misfortunes of normal people, so that this situation will be neither pitiful nor fearful). So we are left with the man between these extremes: that is to say, the kind of man who neither is distinguished for excellence and virtue, nor comes to grief on account of baseness and vice, but on account of some error; a man of great reputation and prosperity, like Oedipus and Thyestes and conspicuous people of such families as theirs. So, to be well formed, a fable must be single rather than (as some say) double—there must be no change from misfortune to good fortune, but only the opposite, from good fortune to misfortune; the cause must not be vice, but a great error; and the man must be either of the type specified or better, rather than worse. This is borne out by the practice of poets; at first they picked a fable at random and made an inventory of its contents, but now the finest tragedies are plotted, and concern a few families—for example, the tragedies about Alcmeon, Oedipus, Orestes, Meleager, Thyestes, Telephus, and any others whose lives were attended by terrible experiences or doings.

This is the plot that will produce the technically finest tragedy. Those critics are therefore wrong who censure Euripides on this very ground—because he does this in his tragedies, and many of them end in misfortune; for it is, as I have said, the right thing to do. This is clearly demonstrated on the stage in the competitions, where such plays, if they succeed, are the most tragic, and Euripides, even if he is inefficient in every other respect, still shows himself the most tragic of our poets. The next best plot, which is said by some people to be the best, is the tragedy with a double plot, like the *Odyssey*, ending in one way for the better people and in the opposite way for the worse. But it is the weakness of theatrical performances that gives priority to this kind; when poets write what the audience would like to happen, they are in leading strings.° This is not the pleasure proper to tragedy, but rather to comedy, where the greatest enemies in the fable, say Orestes and Aegisthus, make friends and go off at the end, and nobody is killed by anybody.

The pity and fear can be brought about by the *Mise en scène*°; but they can also come from the mere plotting of the incidents, which is preferable, and better poetry. For, without seeing anything, the fable ought to have been so plotted that if one heard the bare facts, the chain of circumstances would make one shudder and pity. That would happen to any one who heard the fable of the *Oedipus*. To produce this effect by the *Mise en scène* is less artistic and puts one at the mercy of the technician; and those who use it not to frighten but merely to startle have lost touch with tragedy altogether. We should not try to get all sorts of pleasure from tragedy, but the particular tragic pleasure. And clearly, since this pleasure coming from pity and fear has to be produced by imitation, it is by his handling of the incidents that the poet must create it.

Let us, then, take next the kind of circumstances that seem terrible or lamentable. Now, doings of that kind must be between friends, or enemies, or neither.

TRAGEDY. *in leading strings:* each is led, as by a string, wherever the audience wills.
Mise en scène: arrangement of actors and scenery.

If an enemy injures an enemy, there is no pity either beforehand or at the time, except on account of the bare fact; nor is there if they are neutral; but when sufferings are engendered among the affections—for example, if murder is done or planned, or some similar outrage is committed, by brother on brother, or son on father, or mother on son, or son on mother—that is the thing to aim at. . . .

In Character there are four things to aim at. First and foremost, that it should be good of its kind: a speech or action will be moral if (as I have said) it shows a preference, and the morality will be good if the preference is good of its kind. This is possible in every class. There are good women and good slaves; yet the former class is no doubt inferior, and the latter altogether low.—Secondly, that it should be appropriate: for instance, any one can have a brave character, but there are kinds of courage, as well as kinds of sagacity, that may be inappropriate to a woman.—Thirdly, that it should be lifelike; this is distinct from making the character good and appropriate as defined above.—And fourthly, that it should be consistent; even if the person who is the original of the imitation is inconsistent, and inconsistency is the basis of his character, it is none the less necessary to make him consistently inconsistent. An example of an unnecessarily low character is Menelaus in the *Orestes*; of the unseemly and inappropriate, the lament of Odysseus in the *Scylla*, and the speech of Melanippe; of the inconsistent, Iphigeneia at Aulis—her character as a suppliant is quite unlike her later self.

And in the characterization, as in the plotting of the incidents, the aim should always be either necessity or probability: so that they say or do such things as it is necessary or probable that they would, being what they are; and that for this to follow that is either necessary or probable. (Thus it is clear that the untying of the fable should follow on the circumstances of the fable itself, and not be done *ex machina*, as it is in the *Medea*, or in Book Two of the *Iliad*. But the *deus ex machina*° should be used for matters outside the drama—either things that happened before and that man could not know, or future events that need to be announced prophetically; for we allow the gods to see everything. As for extravagant incidents, there should be none in the story, or if there are they should be kept outside the tragedy, as is the one in the *Oedipus* of Sophocles.)

Since tragedy is an imitation of people above the normal, we must be like good portrait-painters, who follow the original model closely, but refine on it; in the same way the poet, in imitating people whose character is choleric or phlegmatic, and so forth, must keep them as they are and at the same time make them attractive. So Homer made Achilles noble, as well as a pattern of obstinacy.

—*Poetics*, VI, XIII–XV

Sigmund Freud (1856–1939)

THE DESTINY OF OEDIPUS   1900

Translated by James Strachey. The lines from Oedipus the King *are given in the version of David Grene.*

Deus ex machina: "god out of the machine," or an arbitrary way of concluding a play. For a discussion of this term see page 998.

If *Oedipus the King* moves a modern audience no less than it did the contemporary Greek one, the explanation can only be that its effect does not lie in the contrast between destiny and human will, but is to be looked for in the particular nature of the material on which that contrast is exemplified. There must be something which makes a voice within us ready to recognize the compelling force of destiny in the *Oedipus*, while we can dismiss as merely arbitrary such dispositions as are laid down in *Die Ahnfrau*° or other modern tragedies of destiny. And a factor of this kind is in fact involved in the story of King Oedipus. His destiny moves us only because it might have been ours—because the oracle laid the same curse upon us before our birth as upon him. It is the fate of all of us, perhaps, to direct our first sexual impulse towards our mother and our first hatred and our first murderous wish against our father. Our dreams convince us that that is so. King Oedipus, who slew his father Laius and married his mother Jocasta, merely shows us the fulfillment of our own childhood wishes. But, more fortunate than he, we have meanwhile succeeded, insofar as we have not become psychoneurotics, in detaching our sexual impulses from our mothers and in forgetting our jealousy of our fathers. Here is one in whom these primeval wishes of our childhood have been fulfilled, and we shrink back from him with the whole force of the repression by which those wishes have since that time been held down within us. While the poet, as he unravels the past, brings to light the guilt of Oedipus, he is at the same time compelling us to recognize our own inner minds, in which those same impulses, though suppressed, are still to be found. The contrast with which the closing Chorus leaves us confronted—

> . . . behold this Oedipus,—
> him who knew the famous riddles and was a man most masterful;
> not a citizen who did not look with envy on his lot—
> see him now and see the breakers of misfortune swallow him!

—strikes as a warning at ourselves and our pride, at us who since our childhood have grown so wise and so mighty in our own eyes. Like Oedipus, we live in ignorance of these wishes, repugnant to morality, which have been forced upon us by Nature, and after their revelation we may all of us well seek to close our eyes to the scenes of our childhood.

—The Interpretation of Dreams

E. R. Dodds (1893–1979)

SOPHOCLES AND DIVINE JUSTICE   1966

I take it, then, as reasonably certain that while Sophocles did not pretend that the gods are in any human sense just he nevertheless held that they are entitled to our worship. Are those two opinions incompatible? Here once more we cannot hope to understand Greek literature if we persist in looking at it through Christian spectacles. To the Christian it is a necessary part of piety to believe

THE DESTINY OF OEDIPUS. *Die Ahnfrau:* "The Foremother," a verse play by Franz Grillparzer (1791–1872), Austrian dramatist and poet.

that God is just. And so it was to Plato and to the Stoics. But the older world saw no such necessity. If you doubt this, take down the *Iliad* and read Achilles' opinion of what divine justice amounts to (xxiv. 525–33); or take down the Bible and read the Book of Job. Disbelief in divine justice as measured by human yard-sticks can perfectly well be associated with deep religious feelings. "Men," said Heraclitus, "find some things unjust, other things just; but in the eyes of God all things are beautiful and good and just." I think that Sophocles would have agreed.

—On Misunderstanding the *Oedipus Rex*

Charles Paul Segal

ANTIGONE'S WOMANLY NATURE   1964

It is again among the tragic paradoxes of Antigone's position that she who ac-cepts the absolutes of death has a far fuller sense of the complexities of life. Creon, who lacks a true "reverence" for the gods, the powers beyond human life, also lacks a deep awareness of the complexities within the human realm. Hence he tends to see the world in terms of harshly opposed categories, right and wrong, reason and folly, youth and age, male and female. He scornfully joins old age with foolishness in speaking to the chorus (267–268) and refuses to listen to his son's advice because he is younger (684–685). Yet his opposition of old and young is later to be turned against him by Teiresias (921ff.), and he is, in the end, to be "taught" by the young son (685) who dies, Creon laments, "young with a young fate" (1150).

All these categories imply the relation of superior and inferior, stronger and weaker. This highly structured and aggressive view of the world Creon expresses perhaps most strikingly in repeatedly formulating the conflict between Antigone and himself in terms of the woman trying to conquer the man. He sees in An-tigone a challenge to his whole way of living and his basic attitudes toward the world. And of course he is right, for Antigone's full acceptance of her womanly nature, her absolute valuation of the bonds of blood and affection, is a total denial of Creon's obsessively masculine rationality.

Antigone's acceptance of this womanly obligation stands out the more by contrast with Ismene's rejection of it: "We must consider," Ismene says, "that we were born as women with women's nature, and are not such as to fight with men" (63–64). Ismene feels her womanhood as something negative, as a weakness. An-tigone finds in it a source of strength. Ismene capitulates to Creon's view; An-tigone resists and finds in her "nature" a potent heroism which cuts across Creon's dichotomizing of things and has its echoes even after her death in the equally womanly, though less significant, death of Eurydice.

It is Antigone's very "nature," even more than her actions, which stands in such challenging opposition to Creon. Thus she concludes her first, and most im-portant, clash with Creon with the pointed line: "It is my nature not to share in hating (*synechthein*), but to share in loving (*symphilein*)" (494). Her words not only answer Creon's charge that Polyneices is an enemy and hence deserving of hate, not love (493), but also expose more of the fundamental differences be-tween the two protagonists. In the conflict over basic terms like "law," "piety," "profit," lies much of the movement of the play. The words for "love" and "hate" used by Creon and Antigone in 494–495 (and throughout the play) have a certain ambiguity. *Echthros*, "enemy," means also personally "hated"; *philos*, "friend," means also an intimately "loved one." Creon simply identifies the two meanings; that is, he identifies "love" as personal and emotional (*philein*) with political agreement (153ff.) and "hate" with political enmity. But Antigone's being and her action place into dramatic conflict the question of who deserves "love" and who "hate." Hence at the end of their first encounter Creon answers Antigone's "It is my nature not to share in hating but to share in loving" with one of his characteristic dichotomies of man-woman, superior-inferior: "Go below then and love them, if love them you must; but no woman will rule me while I live" (495–496).

Creon's definition of man by his civic or political relations alone extends to areas other than "love." He can conceive of "honor" only for benefactors of the state (198–199) and angrily rejects any idea that the gods could "honor" a traitor (269–276). He again presumes that human and divine—or political and religious—values exactly coincide. Antigone, on the other hand, looks at "honor" in terms of what is due to the gods.

—"Sophocles' Praise of Man and the Conflicts of the *Antigone*"

Thomas Rymer (1643?–1713)

THE FAULTS OF *OTHELLO*   1692

Nothing is more odious in Nature than an improbable lie; and, certainly, never was any play fraught, like this of *Othello*, with improbabilities. . . . Othello is made a Venetian general. We see nothing done by him, nor related concerning him, that comports with the condition of a general, or indeed of a man, unless the killing himself, to avoid a death the law was about to inflict upon him. When his jealousy had wrought him up to a resolution of his taking revenge for the supposed injury, he sets Iago to the fighting part, to kill Cassio, and chooses himself to murder the silly woman his wife, that was like to make no resistance.

His love and his jealousy are no part of a soldier's character, unless for comedy. . . .

So much ado, so much stress, so much passion and repetition about an handkerchief! Why was this not called *The Tragedy of the Handkerchief*? Had it been Desdemona's garter, the sagacious Moor might have smelt a rat, but the handkerchief is so remote a trifle, no booby . . . could make any consequence from it.

We may learn here that a woman never loses her tongue, even though after she is stifled:

Desdemona: O, falsely, falsely murdered!
Emilia: O Lord! What cry is that?
Othello: That? What?
Emilia: Out and alas! that was my lady's voice.
    Help! Help, ho! Help! O lady, speak again!
    Sweet Desdemona! O sweet mistress, speak!
Desdemona: A guiltless death I die.

Emilia: O, who hath done this deed?
Desdemona: Nobody—I myself. Farewell.
      Commend me to my kind lord. O, farewell!   (V, ii, 116–123)

But from this scene to the end of the play we meet with nothing but blood and butchery, described much-what° to the style of the last speeches and confessions of the persons executed at Tyburn,° with this difference: that there we have the fact, and the due course of justice, whereas our poet against all justice and reason, against all law, humanity, and Nature, in a barbarous arbitrary way, executes and makes havoc of his subjects, hab-nab, as they come to hand. Desdemona dropped her handkerchief; therefore, she must be stifled. Othello, by law to be broken on the wheel, by the poet's cunning escapes with cutting his own throat. Cassio, for I know not what, comes off with a broken shin. Iago murders his benefactor Roderigo, as this were poetical gratitude. Iago is not yet killed, because there never yet was such a villain alive.

—A Short View of Tragedy

Samuel Johnson (1709–1784)

"SHAKESPEARE HAS NO HEROES"   1765

Other dramatists can only gain attention by hyperbolical or aggravated characters, by fabulous and unexampled excellence or depravity, as the writers of barbarous romances invigorated the reader by a giant and a dwarf; and he that should form his expectations of human affairs from the play or from the tale would be equally deceived. Shakespeare has no heroes; his scenes are occupied only by men, who act and speak as the reader thinks that he should himself have spoken or acted on the same occasion; even where the agency is supernatural, the dialogue is level with life. Other writers disguise the most natural passions and most frequent incidents so that he who contemplates them in the book will not know them in the world: Shakespeare approximates the remote, and familiarizes the wonderful; the event which he represents will not happen, but, if it were possible, its effects would probably be such as he has assigned; and it may be said that he has not only shown human nature as it acts in real exigencies, but as it would be found in trials to which it cannot be exposed. . . .

Shakespeare's plays are not in the rigorous and critical sense either tragedies or comedies, but compositions of a distinct kind; exhibiting the real state of sublunary nature, which partakes of good and evil, joy and sorrow, mingled with endless variety of proportion and innumerable modes of combination; and expressing the course of the world, in which the loss of one is the gain of another; in which, at the same time, the reveler is hasting to his wine, and the mourner burying his friend; in which the malignity of one is sometimes defeated by the frolic of another; and many mischiefs and many benefits are done and hindered without design.

THE FAULTS OF OTHELLO. *much-what:* nearly or "pretty much."
Tyburn: In London, site of a gallows where criminals were publicly hanged.

Out of this chaos of mingled purposes and casualties the ancient poets, according to the laws which custom had prescribed, selected some of the crimes of men, and some their absurdities; some the momentous vicissitudes of life, and some the lighter occurrences; some the terrors of distress, and some the gaieties of prosperity. Thus rose the two modes of imitation, known by the names of *tragedy* and *comedy*, compositions intended to promote different ends by contrary means, and considered as so little allied that I do not recollect among the Greeks or Romans a single writer who attempted both.

Shakespeare has united the powers of exciting laughter and sorrow not only in one mind, but in one composition. Almost all his plays are divided between serious and ludicrous characters, and, in the successive evolutions of the design, sometimes produce seriousness and sorrow, and sometimes levity and laughter.

That this is a practice contrary to the rules of criticism will be readily allowed; but there is always an appeal open from criticism to nature. The end of writing is to instruct; the end of poetry is to instruct by pleasing. That the mingled drama may convey all the instruction of tragedy or comedy cannot be denied, because it includes both in its alternations of exhibitions, and approaches nearer than either to the appearance of life, by showing how great machinations and slender designs may promote or obviate one another, and the high and the low co-operate in the general system by unavoidable concatenation.

—Preface to Shakespeare

Bernard Shaw (1856–1950)

IBSEN AND THE FAMILIAR SITUATION   1913

Up to a certain point in the last act, *A Doll's House* is a play that might be turned into a very ordinary French drama by the excision of a few lines, and the substitution of a sentimental happy ending for the famous last scene: indeed the very first thing the theatrical wiseacres did with it was to effect exactly this transformation, with the result that the play thus pithed had no success and attracted no notice worth mentioning. But at just that point in the last act, the heroine very unexpectedly (by the wiseacres) stops her emotional acting and says: "We must sit down and discuss all this that has been happening between us." And it was by this new technical feature: this addition of a new movement, as musicians would say, to the dramatic form, that *A Doll's House* conquered Europe and founded a new school of dramatic art. . . .

The drama was born of old from the union of two desires: the desire to have a dance and the desire to hear a story. The dance became a rant: the story became a situation. When Ibsen began to make plays, the art of the dramatist had shrunk into the art of contriving a situation. And it was held that the stranger the situation, the better the play. Ibsen saw that, on the contrary, the more familiar the situation, the more interesting the play. Shakespeare had put ourselves on the stage but not our situations. Our uncles seldom murder our fathers, and cannot legally marry our mothers; we do not meet witches; our kings are not as a rule stabbed and succeeded by their stabbers; and when we raise money by bills we do not promise to pay pounds of our flesh. Ibsen supplies the want left by Shakespeare. He gives us not only ourselves, but ourselves in our own situations. The things that happen to his stage figures are things that happen to us. One consequence is that his plays are much more important to us than Shakespeare's. Another is that they are capable both of hurting us cruelly and of filling us with excited hopes of escape from idealistic tyrannies, and with visions of intenser life in the future.

— The Quintessence of Ibsenism (second edition)

Virginia Woolf (1882–1941)

WHAT IF SHAKESPEARE HAD HAD A SISTER?1929

Let me imagine, since facts are so hard to come by, what would have happened had Shakespeare had a wonderfully gifted sister, called Judith, let us say. Shakespeare himself went, very probably—his mother was an heiress—to the grammar school, where he may have learnt Latin—Ovid, Virgil and Horace—and the elements of grammar and logic. He was, it is well known, a wild boy who poached rabbits, perhaps shot a deer, and had, rather sooner than he should have done, to marry a woman in the neighborhood, who bore him a child rather quicker than was right. That escapade sent him to seek his fortune in London. He had, it seemed, a taste for the theater; he began by holding horses at the stage door. Very soon he got work in the theater, became a successful actor, and lived at the hub of the universe, meeting everybody, knowing everybody, practicing his art on the boards, exercising his wits in the streets, and even getting access to the palace of the queen. Meanwhile his extraordinarily gifted sister, let us suppose, remained at home. She was as adventurous, as imaginative, as agog to see the world as he was. But she was not sent to school. She had no chance of learning grammar and logic, let alone of reading Horace and Virgil. She picked up a book now and then, one of her brother's perhaps, and read a few pages. But then her parents came in and told her to mend the stockings or mind the stew and not moon about with books and papers. They would have spoken sharply but kindly, for they were substantial people who knew the conditions of life for a woman and loved their daughter—indeed, more likely than not she was the apple of her father's eye. Perhaps she scribbled some pages up in an apple loft on the sly, but was careful to hide them or set fire to them. Soon, however, before she was out of her teens, she was to be betrothed to the son of a neighboring wool-stapler. She cried out that marriage was hateful to her, and for that she was severely beaten by her father. Then he ceased to scold her. He begged her instead not to hurt him, not to shame him in this matter of her marriage. He would give her a chain of beads or a fine petticoat, he said; and there were tears in his eyes. How could she disobey him? How could she break his heart? The force of her own gift alone drove her to it. She made up a small parcel of her belongings, let herself down by a rope one summer's night and took the road to London. She was not seventeen. The birds that sang in the hedge were not more musical than she was. She had the quickest fancy, a gift like her brother's, for the tune of words. Like him, she had a taste for the theater. She stood at the stage door; she wanted to act, she said. Men laughed in her face. The manager—a fat, loose-lipped man—guffawed. He bellowed something about poodles dancing and women acting—no woman, he said, could possibly be an actress. He hinted—you can imagine what. She could get no training in her craft. Could she even seek her dinner in a tavern or roam the streets at midnight? Yet her genius was for fiction and lusted to feed abundantly upon the lives of men and women and the study of their ways. At last—for she was very young, oddly like Shakespeare the poet in her face, with the same grey eyes and rounded brows—at last Nick Greene the actor-manager took pity on her; she found herself with child by that gentleman and so—who shall measure the heat and violence of the poet's heart when caught and tangled in a woman's body?—killed herself one winter's night and lies buried at some cross-roads where the omnibuses now stop outside the Elephant and Castle.

That, more or less, is how the story would run, I think, if a woman in Shakespeare's day had had Shakespeare's genius. . . . Any woman born with a great gift in the sixteenth century would certainly have gone crazed, shot herself, or ended her days in some lonely cottage outside the village, half witch, half wizard, feared and mocked at. For it needs little skill in psychology to be sure that a highly gifted girl who had tried to use her gift for poetry would have been so thwarted and hindered by other people, so tortured and pulled asunder by her own contrary instincts, that she must have lost her health and sanity to a certainty. No girl could have walked to London and stood at a stage door and forced her way into the presence of actor-managers without doing herself a violence and suffering an anguish which may have been irrational—for chastity may be a fetish invented by certain societies for unknown reasons—but were none the less inevitable. Chastity had then, it has even now, a religious importance in a woman's life, and has so wrapped itself round with nerves and instincts that to cut it free and bring it to the light of day demands courage of the rarest. To have lived a free life in London in the sixteenth century would have meant for a woman who was poet and playwright a nervous stress and dilemma which might well have killed her. Had she survived, whatever she had written would have been twisted and deformed, issuing from a strained and morbid imagination. And undoubtedly, I thought, looking at the shelf where there are no plays by women, her work would have gone unsigned.

—*A Room of One's Own*

Edward Albee (b. 1928)

THE THEATER OF THE ABSURD   1962

What of this theater in which, for example, a legless old couple live out their lives in twin ashcans, surfacing occasionally for food or conversation (Samuel Beckett's *Endgame*); in which a man is seduced, and rather easily, by a girl with three well-formed and functioning noses (Eugène Ionesco's *Jack, or The Submission*); in which, on the same stage, one group of Negro actors is playing at pretending to be Negro (Jean Genêt's *The Blacks*)?

What of this theater? Is it, as it has been accused of being, obscure, sordid, destructive, anti-theater, perverse, and absurd (in the sense of foolish)? Or is it merely, as I have so often heard it put, that, "This sort of stuff is too depressing, too . . . too mixed up; I go to the theater to relax and have a good time"?

I would submit that it is this latter attitude—that the theater is a place to relax and have a good time—in conflict with the purpose of The Theater of the Absurd—which is to make a man face up to the human condition as it really is— that has produced all the brouhaha and the dissent. I would submit that The Theater of the Absurd, in the sense that it is truly the contemporary theater, facing as it does man's condition as it is, is the Realistic theater of our time; and that the supposed Realistic theater—the term used here to mean most of what is done on Broadway—in the sense that it panders to the public need for self-congratulation and reassurance and presents a false picture of ourselves to ourselves, is, with an occasional very lovely exception, really and truly The Theater of the Absurd.

—"Which Theater Is the Absurd One?"

Tennessee Williams (1914–1983)

HOW TO STAGE THE GLASS MENAGERIE   1945

Being a "memory play," *The Glass Menagerie* can be presented with unusual freedom of convention. Because of its considerably delicate or tenuous material, atmospheric touches and subtleties of direction play a particularly important part. Expressionism and all other unconventional techniques in drama have only one valid aim, and that is a closer approach to truth. When a play employs unconventional techniques, it is not, or certainly shouldn't be, trying to escape its responsibility of dealing with reality, or interpreting experience, but is actually or should be attempting to find a closer approach, a more penetrating and vivid expression of things as they are. The straight realistic play with its genuine Frigidaire and authentic ice-cubes, its characters that speak exactly as its audience speaks, corresponds to the academic landscape and has the same virtue of a photographic likeness. Everyone should know nowadays the unimportance of the photographic in art: that truth, life, or reality is an organic thing which the poetic imagination can represent or suggest, in essence, only through transformation, through changing into other forms than those which were merely present in appearance.

These remarks are not meant as a preface only to this particular play. They have to do with a conception of a new, plastic theater which must take the place of the exhausted theater of realistic conventions if the theater is to resume vitality as a part of our culture.

THE SCREEN DEVICE. There is *only one important difference between the original and acting version of the play* and that is the *omission* in the latter of the device which I tentatively included in my *original* script. This device was the use of a screen on which were projected magic-lantern slides bearing images or titles. I do not regret the omission of this device from the present Broadway production. The extraordinary power of Miss Taylor's performance° made it suitable to have the utmost simplicity in the physical production. But I think it may be interest-

---

HOW TO STAGE THE GLASS MENAGERIE. *Miss Taylor's performance:* In the original Broadway production of the play in 1945, the role of Amanda Wingfield, the mother, was played by veteran actress Laurette Taylor.

ing to some readers to see how this device was conceived. So I am putting it into the published manuscript. These images and legends, projected from behind, were cast on a section of wall between the front-room and dining-room areas, which should be indistinguishable from the rest when not in use.

The purpose of this will probably be apparent. It is to give accent to certain values in each case. Each scene contains a particular point (or several) which is structurally the most important. In an episodic play, such as this, the basic structure or narrative line may be obscured from the audience; the effect may seem fragmentary rather than architectural. This may not be the fault of the play so much as a lack of attention in the audience. The legend or image upon the screen will strengthen the effect of what is merely allusion in the writing and allow the primary point to be made more simply and lightly than if the entire responsibility were on the spoken lines. Aside from this structural value, I think the screen will have a definite emotional appeal, less definable but just as important. An imaginative producer or director may invent many other uses for this device than those indicated in the present script. In fact the possibilities of the device seem much larger to me than the instance of this play can possibly utilize.

THE MUSIC. Another extra-literary accent in this play is provided by the use of music. A single recurring tune, "The Glass Menagerie," is used to give emotional emphasis to suitable passages. This tune is like circus music, not when you are on the grounds or in the immediate vicinity of the parade, but when you are at some distance and very likely thinking of something else. It seems under those circumstances to continue almost interminably and it weaves in and out of your preoccupied consciousness; then it is the lightest, most delicate music in the world and perhaps the saddest. It expresses the surface vivacity of life with the underlying strain of immutable and inexpressible sorrow. When you look at a piece of delicately spun glass you think of two things: how beautiful it is and how easily it can be broken. Both of those ideas should be woven into the recurring tune, which dips in and out of the play as if it were carried on a wind that changes. It serves as a thread of connection and allusion between the narrator with his separate point in time and space and the subject of his story. Between each episode it returns as reference to the emotion, nostalgia, which is the first condition of the play. It is primarily Laura's music and therefore comes out most clearly when the play focuses upon her and the lovely fragility of glass which is her image.

THE LIGHTING. The lighting in the play is not realistic. In keeping with the atmosphere of memory, the stage is dim. Shafts of light are focused on selected areas or actors, sometimes in contradistinction to what is the apparent center. For instance, in the quarrel scene between Tom and Amanda, in which Laura has no active part, the clearest pool of light is on her figure. This is also true of the supper scene, when her silent figure on the sofa should remain the visual center. The light upon Laura should be distinct from the others, having a peculiar pristine clarity such as light used in early religious portraits of female saints or madonnas. A certain correspondence to light in religious paintings, such as El Greco's, where the figures are radiant in atmosphere that is relatively dusky, could be effectively used throughout the play. (It will also permit a more effective use of the screen.) A free, imaginative use of light can be of enormous value in giving a mobile, plastic quality to plays of a more or less static nature.

—The Author's Production Notes to *The Glass Menagerie*

Arthur Miller (b. 1915)

In this age few tragedies are written. It has often been held that the lack is due to a paucity of heroes among us, or else that modern man has had the blood drawn out of his organs of belief by the skepticism of science, and the heroic attack on life cannot feed on an attitude of reserve and circumspection. For one reason or another, we are often held to be below tragedy—or tragedy above us. The inevitable conclusion is, of course, that the tragic mode is archaic, fit only for the very highly placed, the kings or the kingly, and where this admission is not made in so many words it is most often implied.

I believe that the common man is as apt a subject for tragedy in its highest sense as kings were. On the face of it this ought to be obvious in the light of modern psychiatry, which bases its analysis upon classific formulations, such as the Oedipus and Orestes complexes, for instance, which were enacted by royal beings, but which apply to everyone in similar emotional situations.

More simply, when the question of tragedy in art is not at issue, we never hesitate to attribute to the well-placed and the exalted the very same mental processes as the lowly. And finally, if the exaltation of tragic action were truly a property of the high-bred character alone, it is inconceivable that the mass of mankind should cherish tragedy above all other forms, let alone be capable of understanding it.

As a general rule, to which there may be exceptions unknown to me, I think the tragic feeling is evoked in us when we are in the presence of a character who is ready to lay down his life, if need be, to secure one thing—his sense of personal dignity. From Orestes to Hamlet, Medea to Macbeth, the underlying struggle is that of the individual attempting to gain his "rightful" position in his society.

Sometimes he is one who has been displaced from it, sometimes one who seeks to attain it for the first time, but the fateful wound from which the inevitable events spiral is the wound of indignity, and its dominant force is indignation. Tragedy, then, is the consequence of a man's total compulsion to evaluate himself justly.

In the sense of having been initiated by the hero himself, the tale always reveals what has been called his "tragic flaw," a failing that is not peculiar to grand or elevated characters. Nor is it necessarily a weakness. The flaw, or crack in the character, is really nothing—and need be nothing—but his inherent unwillingness to remain passive in the face of what he conceives to be a challenge to his dignity, his image of his rightful status. Only the passive, only those who accept their lot without active retaliation, are "flawless." Most of us are in that category.

But there are among us today, as there always have been, those who act against the scheme of things that degrades them, and in the process of action, everything we have accepted out of fear or insensitivity or ignorance is shaken before us and examined, and from this total onslaught by an individual against the seemingly

---

[1]A complete essay, originally published in *The New York Times*.

stable cosmos surrounding us—from this total examination of the "unchangeable" environment—comes the terror and the fear that is classically associated with tragedy.

More important, from this total questioning of what has been previously unquestioned, we learn. And such a process is not beyond the common man. In revolutions around the world, these past thirty years, he has demonstrated again and again this inner dynamic of all tragedy.

Insistence upon the rank of the tragic hero, or the so-called nobility of his character, is really but a clinging to the outward forms of tragedy. If rank or nobility of character was indispensable, then it would follow that the problems of those with rank were the particular problems of tragedy. But surely the right of one monarch to capture the domain from another no longer raises our passions, nor are our concepts of justice what they were to the mind of an Elizabethan king.

The quality in such plays that does shake us, however, derives from the underlying fear of being displaced, the disaster inherent in being torn away from our chosen image of what and who we are in this world. Among us today this fear is as strong, and perhaps stronger, than it ever was. In fact, it is the common man who knows this fear best.

Now, if it is true that tragedy is the consequence of a man's total compulsion to evaluate himself justly, his destruction in the attempt posits a wrong or an evil in his environment. And this is precisely the morality of tragedy and its lesson. The discovery of the moral law, which is what the enlightenment of tragedy consists of, is not the discovery of some abstract or metaphysical quantity.

The tragic right is a condition of life, a condition in which the human personality is able to flower and realize itself. The wrong is the condition which suppresses man, perverts the flowing out of his love and creative instinct. Tragedy enlightens—and it must, in that it points the heroic finger at the enemy of man's freedom. The thrust for freedom is the quality in tragedy which exalts. The revolutionary questioning of the stable environment is what terrifies. In no way is the common man debarred from such thoughts or such actions.

Seen in this light, our lack of tragedy may be partially accounted for by the turn which modern literature has taken toward the purely psychiatric view of life, or the purely sociological. If all our miseries, our indignities, are born and bred within our minds, then all action, let alone the heroic action, is obviously impossible.

And if society alone is responsible for the cramping of our lives, then the protagonist must needs be so pure and faultless as to force us to deny his validity as a character. From neither of these views can tragedy derive, simply because neither represents a balanced concept of life. Above all else, tragedy requires the finest appreciation by the writer of cause and effect.

No tragedy can therefore come about when its author fears to question absolutely everything, when he regards any institution, habit or custom as being either everlasting, immutable or inevitable. In the tragic view the need of man to wholly realize himself is the only fixed star, and whatever it is that hedges his nature and lowers it is ripe for attack and examination. Which is not to say that tragedy must preach revolution.

The Greeks could probe the very heavenly origin of their ways and return to confirm the rightness of laws. And Job could face God in anger, demanding his right, and end in submission. But for a moment everything is in suspension, nothing is accepted, and in this stretching and tearing apart of the cosmos, in the very action of so doing, the character gains "size," the tragic stature which is spuriously attached to the royal or the high born in our minds. The commonest of men may take on that stature to the extent of his willingness to throw all he has into the contest, the battle to secure his rightful place in his world.

There is a misconception of tragedy with which I have been struck in review after review, and in many conversations with writers and readers alike. It is the idea that tragedy is of necessity allied to pessimism. Even the dictionary says nothing more about the word than that it means a story with a sad or unhappy ending. This impression is so firmly fixed that I almost hesitate to claim that in truth tragedy implies more optimism in its author than does comedy, and that its final result ought to be the reinforcement of the onlooker's brightest opinions of the human animal.

For, if it is true to say that in essence the tragic hero is intent upon claiming his whole due as a personality, and if this struggle must be total and without reservation, then it automatically demonstrates the indestructible will of man to achieve his humanity.

The possibility of victory must be there in tragedy. Where pathos rules, where pathos is finally derived, a character has fought a battle he could not possibly have won. The pathetic is achieved when the protagonist is, by virtue of his witlessness, his insensitivity, or the very air he gives off, incapable of grappling with a much superior force.

Pathos truly is the mode for the pessimist. But tragedy requires a nicer balance between what is possible and what is impossible. And it is curious, although edifying, that the plays we revere, century after century, are the tragedies. In them, and in them alone, lies the belief—optimistic, if you will—in the perfectibility of man.

It is time, I think, that we who are without kings took up this bright thread of our history and followed it to the only place it can possibly lead in our time— the heart and spirit of the average man.

Maria Irene Fornes (b. 1930)

FINDING A WAY OUT   1988

I don't romanticize pain. In my work people are always trying to find a way out, rather than feeling a romantic attachment to their prison. Some people complain that my work doesn't offer the solution. But the reason for that is that I feel that characters don't have to get out, it's *you* who has to get out. Characters are not real people. If characters were real people, I would have opened the door for them at the top of it—there would be no play. The play is there as a lesson, because I feel that art ultimately is a teacher. You go to a museum to look at a painting and that painting teaches you something. You may not look at a Cézanne and say, "I know now what I have to do." But it gives you something, a charge of some understanding, some knowledge that you have in your heart. And if art doesn't do that, I am not interested in it.

—Interview with David Savran, *In Their Own Words*

August Wilson (b. 1945)

INTERVIEWER: Your plays are set in the past—*Joe Turner's Come and Gone* in 1911, *Ma Rainey's Black Bottom* in 1927, *Fences* in the 1950s. Do you ever consider writing about what's happening today?

WILSON: I suspect eventually I will get to that. Right now I enjoy the benefit of the historical perspective. You can look back to a character in 1936, for instance, and you can see him going down a particular path that you know did not work out for that character. Part of what I'm trying to do is to see some of the choices that we as blacks in America have made. Maybe we have made some incorrect choices. By writing about that, you can illuminate the choices.

INTERVIEWER: Give me an example of a choice that you think may have been the wrong one.

WILSON: I think we should have stayed in the South. We attempted to plant what in essence was an emerging culture, a culture that had grown out of our experience of 200 years as slaves in the South. The cities of the urban North have not been hospitable. If we had stayed in the South, we could have strengthened the culture. . . .

INTERVIEWER: One of your characters has said, "Everyone has to find his own song." How do these people find their song?

WILSON: They have it. They just have to realize that, and then they have to learn how to sing it. In that particular case, in *Joe Turner*, the song was the African identity. It was connecting yourself to that and understanding that this is who you are. Then you can go out in the world and sing your song as an African. . . .

INTERVIEWER: But if blacks keep looking for the African in them, if they keep returning spiritually or emotionally to their roots, can they ever come to terms with living in these two worlds? Aren't they always going to be held by the past in a way that is potentially destructive?

WILSON: It's not potentially destructive at all. To say that I am an African, and I can participate in this society as an African, is to say that I don't have to adopt European values, European aesthetics, and European ways of doing things in order to live in the world. We would not be here had we not learned to adapt to American culture. Blacks know more about whites in white culture and white life than whites know about blacks. We *have* to know because our survival depends on it. White people's survival does not depend on knowing blacks. . . .

INTERVIEWER: I was going to suggest that maybe the black middle class possesses [a] warrior spirit today in the sense that they're struggling in a white man's world to make it, to provide for their children, to keep that house, to pay that mortgage, to send those kids to school, to live responsibly. There's a struggle going on there in the black middle class.

WILSON: There probably is a struggle. But the real struggle, since an African first set foot on the continent, is the affirmation of the value of oneself. If in order to participate in American society and in order to accomplish some of the things which the black middle class has accomplished, you have had to give up that self, then you are not affirming the value of the African being. You're saying that in order to do that, I must become like someone else.

I was in the bus station in St. Paul, and I saw six Japanese-Americans sitting down having breakfast. I simply sat there and observed them. They chattered among themselves very politely, and they ate their breakfast, got up, paid the bill, and walked out. I sat there and considered, what would have been the difference if six black guys had come in there and sat down? What are the cultural differences? The first thing I discovered is that none of those Japanese guys played the jukebox. It never entered their minds to play the jukebox. The first thing when six black guys walk in there, somebody's going to go over to the jukebox. Somebody's going to come up and say, "Hey, Rodney, man, play this" and he's going to say, "No, man, play your own record. I ain't playin' what you want. I'm playin' my record, man. Put your own quarter in there." And he's going to make his selection.

The second thing I noticed, no one said anything to the waitress. Now six black guys are going to say, "Hey, mama, what's happenin'? What's your phone number? No, don't talk to him, he can't read. Give your phone number to me." The guy's going to get up to play another record, somebody's going to steal a piece of bacon off his plate, he's going to come back and say, "Man, who's been messin' with my food, I ain't playin' with you all, don't be messin' with my food." When the time comes to pay the bill, it's going to be, "Hey, Joe, loan me a dollar, man." Right?

So if you were a white person observing that, you would say, "They don't know how to act, they're too loud, they don't like one another, the guy wouldn't let him play the record, the guy stole food off his plate." But if you go to those six guys and say, "What's the situation here?" you'll find out they're the greatest of friends, and they're just having breakfast, the same way the Japanese guys had breakfast. But they do it a little differently. This is just who they are in the world.

INTERVIEWER: You've answered my question. I was going to ask you, don't you grow weary of thinking black, writing black, being asked questions about blacks?

WILSON: How could one grow weary of that? Whites don't get tired of thinking white or being who they are. I'm just who I am. You never transcend who you are. Black is not limiting. There's no idea in the world that is not contained by black life. I could write forever about the black experience in America.

—"August Wilson's America," interview with Bill Moyers in *American Theatre*

SUPPLEMENT: WRITING

Writing about Literature

All of us have some powers of reasoning and perception. And when we come to a story, a poem, or a play, we can do little other than to trust whatever powers we have, like one who enters a shadowy room, clutching a decent candle.

After all, in the study of literature, common sense (poet Gerard Manley Hopkins said) is never out of place. For most of a class hour, a renowned English professor rhapsodized about the arrangement of the contents of W.H. Auden's *Collected Poems*. Auden, he claimed, was a master of thematic continuity, who had brilliantly placed the poems in the best possible order, in which (to the ingenious mind) they complemented each other. Near the end of the hour, his theories were punctured—with a great inaudible pop—when a student, timidly raising a hand, pointed out that Auden had arranged the poems in the book not according to theme but in alphabetical order according to the first word of each poem. The professor's jaw dropped: "Why didn't you say that sooner?" The student was apologetic: "I—I was afraid I'd sound too *ordinary*."

Emerson makes a similar point in his essay, "The American Scholar": "Meek young men grow up in libraries, believing it their duty to accept the views which Cicero, which Locke, which Bacon have given; forgetful that Cicero, Locke, and Bacon were only young men in libraries when they wrote these books." Don't be afraid to state a conviction, though it seems obvious. Does it matter that you may be repeating something that, once upon a time or even just the other day, has been said before? There are excellent old ideas as well as new.

SOME APPROACHES TO LITERATURE

Most writers of critical essays follow a few familiar approaches to stories, poems, and plays. Underlying each of these four approaches is a specific way of regarding the nature of a work of literature.

1. *The Work by Itself.* This view assumes a story, poem, or play to be an individual text, existing on its page, which we can read and understand in its own right, without necessarily studying the life of its author, or the age in which it was written, or its possible effect on its readers. This is the approach in most papers written in reponse to college assignments; to study just the work (and not its backgrounds or its influence) does not require the student to spend prolonged time doing research in a library. The three common ways of writing a paper discussed in this book—explication, analysis, and comparison and contrast—deal mainly with the work of literature in itself.

2. *The Work as Imitation of Life.* Aristotle called the art of writing a tragedy *mimesis*: the imitation or re-creation of an action that is serious and complete in itself. From this classic theory in the *Poetics* comes the view that a work of literature in some ways imitates the world or the civilization in which it was produced. We can say that Ibsen's play *A Doll House* places before our eyes actors whose lifelike speeches and movements represent members of an upper middle-class society in provincial Norway in the late nineteenth century and that the play reflects their beliefs and attitudes. Not only the subject and theme of a work imitate life in this view: John Ciardi remarked that the heroic couplet, dominant stanza form in poetry read by educated people in eighteenth-century England, reflects, in its exact form and its use of antithesis, the rhythms of the minuet—another contemporary form, fashionable also among the well-to-do: "now on this hand, now on that." The writer considering literature as imitation usually studies the world that the literary work imitates. He or she goes into the ideas underlying the writer's society, showing how the themes, assumptions, and conventions of the writer's work arose out of that time and that place. Obviously, this analysis takes more research than one can do for a weekly paper; it is usually the approach taken for a book or a dissertation, or perhaps an honors thesis or a term paper. (The other two approaches we will mention also take research.) Reasonably short studies of the relation between the work and its world are, however, possible: "World War II as Seen in Henry Reed's 'Naming of Parts' "; "Faulkner's 'Barn Burning': A Mirror of Mississippi?"

3. *The Work as Expression.* In this view, a work of literature expresses the feelings of the person who wrote it; therefore, to study it, one studies the author's life. Typical paper topics: "*A Glass Menagerie* and the Early Life of Tennessee Williams"; "Sylvia Plath's Lost Father and Her View of Him in 'Daddy.' " To write any truly deep-reaching biographical criticism takes research, clearly, but one could write a term paper on topics such as these by reading a biography.

    Biographical criticism fell into temporary disrepute around 1920, when T.S. Eliot questioned the assumption that a poem must be a personal statement of the poet's thoughts and emotions.[1] Eliot and other

---

[1]See Eliot's essay "Tradition and the Individual Talent," in *Selected Essays* (New York: Harcourt, 1932).

critics did much to clear the air of speculation that "To Autumn" may have been shaped by what Keats had had for breakfast. Evidently, in any search for what went on in an author's mind, and for the influence of life upon work, absolute certainty is unattainable. Besides, such an approach can be grossly reductive—holding, for example, that Shakespeare was sad when he wrote his tragedies and especially happy when he wrote A *Midsummer Night's Dream*. Still, some works do gain in meaning from even a slight knowledge of the author's biography. In reading *Moby-Dick*, it helps to know that Herman Melville served aboard a whaling vessel.

4. *The Work as Influence.* From this perspective, a literary work is a force that affects people. It stirs responses in them, rouses their emotions, perhaps argues for ideas that change their minds. The artist, said Tolstoi in a famous pronouncement (*What Is Art?*), "hands on to others those feelings he himself has felt, that they too may be moved, and experience them." Part of the function of art, Tolstoi continued, is to enlighten and to lead its audience into an acceptance of better moral attitudes (religious faith, or a sense of social justice). The critic who takes this approach generally deals with the ideas that a literary work imparts and the reception of those ideas by a particular audience: "Did *Uncle Tom's Cabin* Cause the Civil War?"; "The Early Reception of Allen Ginsberg's *Howl*"; "Ed Bullin's Plays and Their Newly Proud Black Audience." As you can see, this whole approach is closely related to viewing a literary work as an imitation of life. Still another way of discussing a work's influence is to trace its effect upon other writers: "Robert Frost's Debt to Emily Dickinson"; "*Moby-Dick* and William Faulkner's *The Bear*: Two Threatened Wildernesses."

BEGINNING

Offered a choice of literary works to write about, you probably will do best if, instead of choosing what you think will impress your instructor, you choose what appeals to you. And how to find out what appeals? Whether you plan to write a short paper that requires no research beyond the story or poem or play itself, or a long term paper that will take you to the library, the first stage of your project is reading—and note taking. To concentrate your attention, one time-honored method is to read with a pencil, marking (if the book is yours) passages that stand out in importance, jotting brief notes in a margin ("*Key symbol—this foreshadows the ending*"; "*Dramatic irony*"; "*IDIOT!!!*"; or other possibly useful remarks). In a long story or poem or play, some students asterisk passages that cry for comparison; for instance, all the places in which they find the same theme or symbol. Later, at a glance, they can review the highlights of a work and, when writing a paper about it, quickly refer to evidence. This method shoots holes in a book's resale value, but many find the sacrifice worthwhile. Patient souls who dislike butchering a book prefer to take notes on looseleaf notebook paper, holding one sheet beside a page in the book and giving it the book's page number. Later, in writing a paper, they can place book page and companion note page together again. This method has the advantage of affording a lot of room for note taking; it is a good one for short poems closely packed with complexities.

But by far the most popular method of taking notes (besides writing on the pages of books) is to write on index cards—the 3 × 5 kind, for brief notes and titles; 5 × 8 cards for longer notes. Write on one side only; notes on the back of the card usually get overlooked later. Cards are easy to shuffle and, in organizing your material, to deal. To save work, instead of copying out on a card the title and author of a book you're taking a note from, just keep a numbered list of the books you're using. Then, when making a note, you need write only the book's identifying number on the card in order to identify your source. (Later, when writing footnotes, you can translate the number into title, author, and other information.)

Now that coin-operated photocopy machines are to be found in many libraries, you no longer need to spend hours copying by hand whole poems and longer passages. If accuracy is essential (surely it is) and if a poem or passage is long enough to be worth the investment of a few cents, you can lay photocopied material into place in your paper with transparent tape or rubber cement. The latest copyright law permits students and scholars to reproduce books and periodicals in this fashion; it does not, however, permit making a dozen or more copies for public sale.

Certain literary works, because they offer intriguing difficulties, have attracted professional critics by the score. On library shelves, great phalanxes of critical books now stand at the side of James Joyce's complex novels *Ulysses* and *Finnegans Wake*, and T.S. Eliot's allusive poem *The Waste Land*. The student who undertakes to study such works seriously is well advised to profit from the critics' labors. Chances are, too, that even in discussing a relatively uncomplicated work you will want to seek the aid of the finest critics. If you quote them, quote them exactly, in quotation marks, and give them credit. When employed in any but the most superlative student paper, a brilliant phrase (or even a not-so-brilliant sentence) from a renowned critic is likely to stand out like a golf ball in a garter snake's midriff, and most English instructors are likely to recognize it. If you rip off the critic's words, then go ahead and steal the whole essay, for good critics write in seamless unities. Then, when apprehended, you can exclaim—like the student whose term paper was found to be the work of a well-known scholar— "I've been robbed! That paper cost me twenty dollars!" But of course the worst rip-off is the one the student inflicted on himself, having got nothing for his money out of a college course but a little practice in touch typing.

Taking notes on your readings, you will want to jot down the title of every book you might refer to in your paper, and the page number of any passage you might wish to quote. Even if you summarize a critic's idea in your own words, rather than quote, you have to give credit to your source. Nothing is cheaper to give than proper credit. Certainly it's easier to take notes while you read than to have to run back to the library during the final typing.

Choose a topic appropriate to the assigned length of your paper. How do you know the probable length of your discussion until you write it? When in doubt, you are better off to define your topic narrowly. Your paper will be stronger if you go deeper into your subject than if you choose some gigantic subject and then find yourself able to touch on it only superficially. A thorough explication of a short story is hardly possible in a paper of 250 words. There are, in truth, four-line poems whose surface 250 words might only begin to scratch. A profound topic ("The Character of Shakespeare's Hamlet") might overflow a book; but a topic more narrowly defined ("Hamlet's Views of Acting"; "Hamlet's Puns") might result in a more nearly manageable term paper. You can narrow and focus a large topic while you work your way into it. A general interest in "Hemingway's Heroes" might lead you, in reading, taking notes, and thinking further, to the narrower topic, "Jake Barnes: Spokesman for Hemingway's Views of War."

Many student writers find it helpful, in defining a topic, to state an emerging idea for a paper in a provisional **thesis sentence:** a summing-up of the one main idea or argument that the paper will embody. (A thesis sentence is for your own use; you don't have to implant it in your paper unless your instructor asks for it.) A good statement of a thesis is not just a disembodied subject; it comes with both subject and verb. ("The Downfall of Oedipus Rex" is not yet a complete idea for a paper; "What Caused the Downfall of Oedipus Rex?" is.) A thesis sentence may help you see for yourself what the author is *saying about* a subject. Not a full thesis, and not a sentence, "The Isolation of Laura in *The Glass Menagerie*" might be a decent title for a paper. But it isn't a useful thesis because it doesn't indicate what one might say about that isolation (nor what Tennessee Williams is saying about it). It may be obvious that isolation isn't desirable, but a clearer and more workable thesis sentence might be, "In *The Glass Menagerie*, the playwright shows how Laura's isolation leads her to take refuge in a world of dreams."

DISCOVERING AND PLANNING

Writing is not likely to proceed in a straight line. Like thought, it often goes by fits and starts, by charges and retreats and mopping-up operations. All the while you take notes, you discover material to write about; all the while you tool over your topic in your mind, you plan. It is the nature of ideas, those headstrong things, to happen in any order they desire. While you continue to plan, while you write a draft, and while you revise, expect to keep discovering new thoughts—perhaps the best thoughts of all. If you do, be sure to let them in.

Topic in hand (which may get drastically changed as you continue), you begin to sort out your miscellaneous notes, thoughts, and impressions. If you can see that you haven't had enough ideas, you may wish to **brainstorm**—to set yourself, say, fifteen minutes in which to write down as fast as you can all the ideas on your topic that come into your head, without worrying whether they are going to be useful. (You can look over the results and decide that later.) Another method of discovery is to **freewrite:** to write rapidly and uncritically, letting your thoughts tumble onto paper as fast as your pen, typewriter, or word processor can capture them. Sometimes these methods will goad the unconscious into coming up with unexpectedly good ideas; at least, you will generate more potentially useful raw material.

To outline or not to outline? Unless your topic, by its nature, suggests some obvious way to organize your paper ("An Explication of a Wordsworth Sonnet" might mean simply working through the poem line by line), then some kind of outline will probably help. In high school or other prehistoric times, you perhaps learned how to construct a beautiful outline, laid out with Roman numerals, capital letters, arabic numerals, and lower-case letters. It was a thing of beauty and symmetry, and possibly even had something to do with paper writing. But if now you are skeptical of the value of outlining, reflect: not every outline needs to be detailed and elaborate. Some students, of course, find it helpful to outline in detail—particularly if they are planning a long term paper involving several literary works, comparing and contrasting several aspects of them. For a 500-word analysis of a short story's figures of speech, though, all you might need is a simple list of points to make, scribbled down in the order in which you will make them. This order is probably not, of course, the order in which the points first occurred to you. Thoughts, when they first come to mind, can be a confused rabble.

While granting the need for order in a piece of writing, the present writer confesses that he is a reluctant outliner. His tendency (or curse) is to want to keep whatever random thoughts occur to him; to polish his prose right then and there; and finally to try to juggle his disconnected paragraphs into something like logical order. The usual result is that he has large blocks of illogical thought left over. This process is wasteful, and if you can learn to live with an outline, then you belong to the legion of the blessed and will never know the pain of scrapping pages that cost you hours. On the other hand, you will never know the joy of meandering—of bursting into words and surprising yourself. As novelist E.M. Forster remarked, "How do I know what I think until I see what I say?"

An outline, if you use one, is not meant to stand as an achievement in itself. It should—as Ezra Pound said literary criticism ought to do—consume itself and disappear. Here is a once-valuable outline not worth keeping—a very informal one that enabled a student to organize the paper that appears on page 1474, "The Hearer of 'The Tell-Tale Heart.'" Before he wrote, the student jotted down the ideas that had occurred to him. Looking them over, he could see that certain ones predominated. Since the aim of his paper was to analyze Poe's story for its point of view, he began with some notes about the narrator of the story. His other leading ideas had emerged as questions: is the story supposed to be a ghost story or an account of a delusion? Can we read the whole thing as a nightmare, having no reality outside the narrator's mind? Having seen that his thoughts weren't a totally disconnected jumble, he drew connections. Going down his list, he numbered with the same numbers those ideas that belonged together.

Point of view

1 Killer is mad—can listen in on Hell.

2 He is obsessed with the Evil Eye.

1 He thinks he is sane, we know he's mad.

Old man rich—a miser?

4 { Is this a ghost story? NO! Natural explanations for the heartbeat:

His mind is playing tricks.

Hears his <u>own</u> heart (Hoffman's idea).

3 Maybe the whole story is only his dream?

Poe must have been crazy too.

The numbers now showed him the order in which he planned to take up each of his four chief ideas. Labeling with the number "1" his remarks about the narrator, he decided to open his paper with them and to declare at once that they indicated the story's point of view. As you can tell from his finished paper, he discarded two notions that didn't seem to relate to his purpose: the point about the old man's wealth and the speculation (which he realized he couldn't prove) that Poe himself was mad. Having completed this rough outline, he felt encouraged to return to Poe's story and on rereading it noticed a few additional points, which you will find in his paper. His outline didn't tell him exactly what to say at every moment, but it was clear and easy to follow.

DRAFTING AND REVISING

Seated at last, or striking some other businesslike stance,[2] you prepare to write, only to find yourself besieged with petty distractions. All of a sudden you remember a friend you had promised to call, some dry cleaning you were supposed to pick up, a neglected Coke (in another room) growing warmer and flatter by the minute. If your paper is to be written, you have one course of action: to collar these thoughts and for the moment banish them.

When first you draft your paper—that is, when you write it out in the rough—you will probably do best to write rapidly. At this early stage, you don't need to be fussy about spelling, grammar, and punctuation. To be sure, those picayune details matter, but you can worry about them later on, when you are **editing** (combing through your draft repairing grammar, cutting excess words, making small verbal improvements) and **proofreading** (going over your finished paper line by line, checking it for typographical or other mistakes). Right now, it is more important to get your thoughts down on paper in a steady flow than to keep taking time out to check spellings in the dictionary. Forge ahead, and don't be too nastily self-critical. Perhaps when you write your draft you won't even want to look at all those notes on your reading that you collected so industriously. When you

---

[2]R.H. Super of the University of Michigan wrote a definitive biography of Walter Savage Landor while standing up, typing on a machine atop a filing cabinet.

come to a place where a note will fit, you might just insert a reminder to yourself, such as SEE CARD 19, or SEE ARISTOTLE ON COMEDY.

Let us admit that writing about literature is a fussier kind of writing than turning out a narrative essay called "My Most Exciting Experience." You may need to draft some of your paper slowly and painstakingly. You'll find yourself coping with all sorts of small problems, many of them simple and mechanical. What, for instance, will you call the author whose work you are dealing with? Decide at the outset. Most critics favor the author's last name alone: "Dickinson implies . . . " ("Miss Dickinson" or "Ms. Dickinson" may sound fussily polite; "Emily," too chummy.) Will you include footnotes in your paper and, if so, do you know how they work? (Some pointers on handling the pesky things will come in a few pages.)

You will want to give credit to any critics who helped you out, and properly to do so is to be painstaking. To paraphrase a critic, you do more than just rearrange the critic's words and phrases; you translate them into language of your own. Say you wish to refer to an insight of Randall Jarrell, who comments on the images of spider, flower, and moth in Robert Frost's poem "Design":

> Notice how the *heal-all*, because of its name, is the one flower in all the world picked to be the altar for this Devil's Mass; notice how holding up the moth brings something ritual and hieratic, a ghostly, ghastly formality to this priest and its sacrificial victim. . . .

It would be incorrect to say, without quotation marks:

> Frost picks the heal-all as the one flower in all the world to be the altar for
> this Devil's Mass. There is a ghostly, ghastly formality to the spider holding
> up the moth, like a priest holding a sacrificial victim.

That rewording, although not exactly in Jarrell's language, manages to steal his memorable phrases without giving him credit. Nor is it sufficient just to list Jarrell's essay in a bibliography at the end of your paper. If you do, you are still a crook; you merely point to the scene of your crime. What is needed, clearly, is to think through Jarrell's words to the point he is making; and if you want to keep any of his striking phrases (and why not?), put them in quotation marks:

> As Randall Jarrell points out, Frost portrays the spider as a kind of priest in
> a Mass, or Black Mass, elevating the moth like an object for sacrifice, with "a
> ghostly, ghastly formality."

To be scrupulous in your acknowledgment, tell where you found your quotation from Jarrell, citing the book and the page. (See "Documenting Your Sources," page 1465) But unless your instructor expects you to write such a formal, documented paper, the passage as it now stands would make sufficiently clear your source, and your obligation.

One more word of Dutch-uncle warning. In this book you are offered a vocabulary with which to discuss literature: a flurry of terms such as *irony, symbol,* and *image*, printed in **boldface** when first introduced. In your writing you may decide to enlist a few of them. And yet, critical terminology—especially if unfamiliar—can tempt a beginning critic to sling it about. Nothing can be less sophisticated, or more misleading, than a technical term grandly misapplied: "The *myth-symbolism* of this *rime scheme* leaves one aghast." Far better to choose plain words you're already at ease with. Your instructor, no doubt, has met many a critical term and is not likely to be impressed by the mere sight of another one. Knowingly selected and placed, a critical term can help sharpen a thought and make it easier to handle. Clearly it is less cumbersome to refer to the *tone* of a story than to have to say, "the way the author feels about what she is talking about." But the paper-writer who declares, "The tone of this poem is full of ironic imagery," fries words to a hash—mixed up and indigestible.

When you write your first draft, by the way, leave plenty of space between lines and leave enormous margins. Then, when later thoughts come to you, you can easily squeeze them in.

Does any writer write perfectly on first try and drop ideas with a single shot? Some writers have claimed to do so—among them the English novelist Anthony Trollope, who thought it "unmanly" not to write a thought right the first time. Jack Kerouac, leading novelist of the beat generation of the 1950s, believed in spontaneous prose. He used to write entire novels on uncut ribbons of teletype paper, thus saving himself the interruption of stopping at the bottom of each page. His specialty, though, was fiction of ecstasy and hallucination, not essays in explication, or comparison and contrast. For most of us, however, good writing is largely a matter of revising—of going back over our first thoughts word by word. Painstaking revision is more than a matter of tidying grammar and spelling: in the process of reconsidering our words, we sometimes discover fresher and sharper ideas. "Writing and rewriting," says John Updike, "are a constant search for what one is saying."

To achieve effective writing, you have to have the courage to be wild. Aware that no reader need see your rough drafts, you can treat them mercilessly—scissor them apart, rearrange their pieces, reassemble them into a stronger order, using staples or tape or glue. The art of revising calls for a textbook in itself, but here are a few simple suggestions:

1. Insofar as your deadline allows, be willing to revise as many times as need be.
2. Don't think of revision as the simple chore of fixing up spelling mistakes. That's proofreading, and it comes last. When you revise, be willing to cut and slash, to discover new insights, to move blocks of words around so that they follow in a stronger order. Stand ready to question your whole approach to a work of literature, to entertain the notion of throwing everything you have written into the wastebasket and starting over again.
3. At this stage, you may find it helpful to enlist outside advice—from your instructor, from your roommate or your mate, from any friend who will read your rough draft and give you a reaction. If you can enlist such a willing reader ask: What isn't clear to you?

4. If you (or your willing reader) should find any places that aren't readily understandable, single them out for rewriting. After all, you don't need to revise a whole draft if only parts of it need work. Try rewriting any especially troublesome passage or paragraph.

5. Short, skimpy paragraphs of one or two sentences may indicate places that call for more thought, or more material. Can you supply them with more evidence, more explanation, more example and illustration?

6. A time-tested method of revising is to lay aside your manuscript for a while, forget about it, and then after a long interval (the Roman poet Horace recommended nine years, but obviously that won't do), go back to it for a fresh look. If you have time, take a nap or a walk, or at least a yawn and a stretch, before you take yet another look.

7. When your paper is in a *last* draft—that's the time to edit it. Once you have your ideas in firm shape, you can check those uncertain spellings, look up the agreement of verbs in a grammar book or handbook, make your pronouns and numbers agree, cut needless words, pull out a weak word and send in a stronger one. Back when you were drafting, to get prematurely fussy about such small things might have frozen you up. But once you feel satisfied that you have made yourself clear, you can be as fussy as you like.

If you type your papers, it is a great help to become a reasonably expert typist—one whose method is other than the Christopher Columbus method (to discover a key and land on it). Then you can revise while you retype. All to what end? "Each clear sentence," according to Robert Russell, "is that much ground stripped clean of the undergrowth of one's own confusion. Sometimes it's thrilling to feel you have written even a single paragraph that makes sense."[3]

THE FORM OF YOUR FINISHED PAPER

Now that you have smoothed your final draft as fleck-free as you can, your instructor may have specific advice for the form of your finished paper. If none is forthcoming, it is only reasonable

1. to choose standard letter-size (8½ × 11) paper;
2. to give your name at the top of your title page;
3. to leave an inch or more of margin on all four sides of each page, and a few inches of blank paper or an additional sheet after your conclusion, so that your instructor can offer comment;
4. to doublespace, or (if you handwrite) to use paper with widely spaced lines.

And what of titles of works discussed: when to put them in quotation marks, when to underline them? One rule of thumb is that titles of works shorter than

---

[3]*To Catch an Angel* (New York: Vanguard, 1962) 301.

book length rate quotation marks (poems, short stories, articles); but titles of books (including book-length poems: *The Odyssey*), plays, and periodicals take underlining. (In a manuscript to be set in type, an underline is a signal to the compositor to use *italics*.)

DOCUMENTING YOUR SOURCES

When you quote from other writers, when you lift their information, when you summarize or paraphrase their ideas, make sure you give them their due. Document everything you take. Identify the writer by name; cite the very book, magazine, newspaper, pamphlet, letter, or other source you are using, and the page or pages you are indebted to.

By so doing, you invite your readers to go to your original source and check up on you. Most readers won't bother, of course, but at least your invitation enlists their confidence. Besides, the duty to document keeps you carefully looking at your sources—and so helps keep your writing accurate and responsible.

The latest and most efficient way for writers to document their sources is that recommended in the *MLA Handbook for Writers of Research Papers*, 3rd ed. (New York: Modern Language Association of America, 1988). In the long run, whether you write an immense term paper citing a hundred sources or a short paper citing only three or four, the MLA's advice will save you and your reader time and trouble.

These pointers cannot take the place of the *MLA Handbook* itself; but the gist of the method is this. Begin by listing your sources: all the works from which you're going to quote, summarize, paraphrase, or take information. Later on, when you type up your paper in finished form, you're going to *end* it with a neat copy of this list (once called a *bibliography*, now entitled "Works Cited"). But right now, in writing your paper, every time you refer to one of these works, you need give only enough information to help a reader locate it in under "Works Cited." Usually, you can just give (in parentheses) an author's last name and a page citation. You incorporate this information right in the text of your paper, most often at the end of a sentence:

> One recent investigation has suggested that few people who submit poems to
> small literary magazines bother to read those magazines; or indeed, bother to
> read poems by anybody else (Horton 108-09).

Say you will want to cite *two* books or magazine articles by Horton—how to tell them apart? In your text, condense the title of each article into a word or two.

> One recent investigation has shown that few people who submit poems to small
> literary magazines bother to read those magazines (Horton, "Magazines"
> 108-09).

If you have mentioned the name of the author in the body of your paper, you need give only the page number:

> As a recent investigator, Louise Horton, has suggested, few people who submit poems to small literary magazines bother to read those magazines (108-09).

The beauty of this method is that you don't have to stop every two minutes to write a footnote identifying your source in full detail. At the end of your paper, in your list of works cited, your reader can find a fuller description of your source—in this case, a magazine article:

> Horton, Louise. "Who Reads Small Literary Magazines and What Good Do They Do?" Texas Review Spring/Summer 1984: 108-13.

It's imperative to keep citations in your text brief and snappy, lest they hinder the flow of your prose. You may wish to append a note supplying a passage of less important (yet possibly valuable) information or making careful qualifying statements ("On the other hand, not every expert agrees. John Binks finds that poets are often a little magazine's only cash customers; while Molly MacGuire maintains that . . . "). If you want to put in some such aside, and suspect that you couldn't give it in your text without interrupting your paper awkwardly, then cast it into a **footnote** (a note placed at the bottom of a page) or an **endnote** (a note placed at the end of a paper). Given a choice, most writers prefer endnotes. Far easier to collect all the notes at the end of a paper than to use footnotes—as any writer knows who has had to retype pages and pages again and again, to make the footnotes fit.[4]

How do you drop in such notes? The number of each consecutive note comes (following any punctuation) after the last word of a sentence. So that the number will stand out, you roll your typewriter carriage up a click (or order your word-processor to do a superscript), thus lifting the number slightly above the usual level of your prose.

> as other observers have claimed.[1]

When you come to type the footnote or endnote itself, skip five spaces, elevate the number again, and proceed.

> [1]John Binks, to name only one such observer, finds . . .

Although now useful mainly for such slightly longwinded asides, footnotes and endnotes are time-honored ways to document *all* sources in a research paper. Indeed, some instructors still prefer them to the new MLA guidelines, and urge students to use such notes to indicate every writer cited. Though such notes take more work, they have the advantage of hiding dull data away from your reader's

---

[4]Nowadays, some word-processing programs make life easier for footnotes by helping to format each footnote and by automatically dropping it in at the bottom of its page.

eyes, enabling you to end sentences with powerful bangs and inconspicuous note numbers instead of whimpering parentheses (Glutz-Finnegan, *Lesser Corollary* 1029–30). Besides, in a brief paper containing only one citation or two, to use footnotes or endnotes may be simpler and less showy than to compile a Works Cited list that has only two entries.

Large-mindedly, the *MLA Handbook* tolerates the continued use of footnotes and endnotes for documentation—indeed, offers advice for their preparation, which we will follow here. If you do use footnotes or endnotes to document all your sources, here is how to format them. A note identifying a magazine article looks like this:

[16]Louise Horton, "Who Reads Small Literary Magazines and What Good Do They Do?" Texas Review Spring/Summer 1984: 108-109.

Notice that, in notes, the author's first name comes first. (In a list of Works Cited, you work differently: you put last name first, so that you can readily arrange your list of authors in easy-to-consult alphabetical order.) A footnote or endnote for a reference to a book (and not a magazine article) looks like this:

[17]Elizabeth Frank, Louise Bogan: A Portrait (New York: Knopf, 1985) 59-60.

Should you return later to cite another place in Frank's book, you need not repeat all its information. Just write:

[18]Frank 192.

If in your paper you refer to *two* books by Elizabeth Frank, give the full title of each in the first note citing it. Then, if you cite it again, use a shortened form of its title:

[19]Frank, Bogan 192.

Your readers should not have to interrupt their reading of your essay to glance down at a note simply to find out whom you are quoting. It is poor form to write:

Dylan Thomas's poem "Fern Hill" is a memory of the poet's childhood: of his Aunt Ann Jones's farm, where he spent his holidays. "Time, which has an art to throw dust on all things, broods over the poem."[1] The farm, indeed, is a lost paradise—a personal garden of Eden.

[1]William York Tindall, A Reader's Guide to Dylan Thomas (New York: Noonday, 1962) 268.

That is annoying, because the reader has to stop reading and look at the footnote to find out who made that resonant statement about Time brooding over the poem. A better way:

"Time," as William York Tindall has observed, "which has an art to throw dust on all things, broods over the poem."[1]

Your footnote or endnote then cites Tindall's book:

[1]A Reader's Guide to Dylan Thomas (New York: Noonday, 1962) 268.

What to do now but hand in your paper? "And good riddance," you may feel, after all your work. But a good paper is not only worth submitting, it is worth keeping. If you return to it, after a while, you may find to your surprise that it will preserve and even renew what you have learned.

KEEPING A JOURNAL

The essay is not, of course, the only medium in which you can write your responses to literature. Many instructors ask students to keep a **journal:** a day-to-day account of what they read and how they react to it. A great advantage in keeping a journal is that you can express your thoughts and feelings immediately, before they grow cold. You can set down all your miscellaneous reactions to what you read, whether or not they fit into a paper topic. (If you have to write a paper later on, your journal just might suggest topics galore.) Depending on what your instructor thinks essential, your journal may take in all your reading for the course; or you may concentrate on the work of some writer or writers, or on one kind of story. As you read (or afterward), you can jot down anything you notice that you wish to remember. Does a theme in a story, or a line of dialogue, strike you forcefully? Make a note of it. Does something in the story not make sense? Record your bewilderment. Your journal is personal: a place for you to sound off, to express your feelings. Don't just copy your class notes into it; don't simply quote the stories. Mere length of your entries will not impress your instructor, either: try for insights. A paragraph or two will probably suffice to set down your main reactions to most stories. In keeping a journal (a kind of writing primarily for yourself), you don't rewrite; and so you need not feel obliged to polish your prose. Your aim is to store information without delay; to wrap words around your reactions and observations.

Keeping a journal will be satisfying only if you keep it up to date. Record your feelings and insights while you still have a story freshly in mind. Get weeks behind and have to grind out a journal from scratch, the night before it is due, and the whole project will decay into meaningless drudgery. But faithfully do a little reading and a little writing every day or so, and you will find yourself keeping track of the life of your mind. When your journal is closed, you will have a lively record not only of the literature you have read, but also of your involvement with it.

The Girl Writing Her English Paper

lies on one hip by the fire,
blond, in jeans.

The wreckage of her labor, elegant as Eden
or petals from a tree,
surrounds her—

a little farm, smoke rising from the ashtray,
book, notebooks, papers, fields;
a poem's furrows.

If the lights were to go out suddenly,
stars would be overhead,
the edge of the wood still and dark.

Writing about a Story

Like any coherent, forceful essay, a good discussion of fiction doesn't just toss forth a random lot of impressions. It makes some point about which the writer feels strongly. In order to write a meaningful paper, then, you need something you *want* to say—a meaningful topic. For suggestions on finding such a topic (also some pointers on organizing, writing, revising, and finishing your paper), please see "Writing about Literature," which begins on page 1455. The advice there may be applied to papers on fiction, poetry, and drama. Some methods especially useful for writing about stories are gathered in the present chapter.

Unlike a brief poem, or a painting you can take in with one long glance, a work of fiction—even a short story—may be too complicated to hold all at once in the mind's eye. Before you can write about it, you may need to give it two or more careful readings, and even then, as you begin to think further about it, you will probably have to thumb through it to reread passages. The first time through, perhaps it is best just to read attentively, open to whatever pleasure and wisdom the story may afford. On second look, you may find it useful to read with pencil in hand, either to mark your personal copy or to take notes to jog your memory. To see the design and meaning of a story need not be a boring chore—any more than it is to land a fighting fish and to study it with admiration.

In this chapter, all the discussions and examples refer to Edgar Allan Poe's short story "The Tell-Tale Heart" (page 41). If you haven't already read it, you can do so in only a few minutes, so that the rest of this chapter will make more sense to you.

EXPLICATING

Explication is the patient unfolding of meanings in a work of literature. An explication—that is, an essay that follows this method—proceeds carefully through a story, poem, or play, usually interpreting it line by line—perhaps even word by word. A good explication dwells on details, as well as on larger things. It brings them to the attention of a reader who might have missed them (the reader probably hasn't read so closely as the writer of the explication). Alert and willing to take pains, the writer of such an essay notices anything meaningful that isn't obvious, whether it is a colossal theme suggested by a symbol or a little hint contained in a single word.

To write an honest explication of a story takes time and space, probably too much time and space to devote to a long and complex story unless you are writing a huge term paper, an honors thesis, or a dissertation. A thorough explication of Nathaniel Hawthorne's "Young Goodman Brown" would be likely to run much longer than the rich and intriguing short story itself. Ordinarily, the method of explication is best suited to a paper that deals only with a short passage or section of a story: a key scene, a crucial conversation, a statement of theme, an opening or closing paragraph. Storytellers who are especially fond of language invite closer attention to their words than others do. Edgar Allan Poe, for one, is a poet sensitive to the rhythms of his sentences and a symbolist whose stories abound in suggestions. Here is an explication, by a student, of a short but essential passage in "The Tell-Tale Heart." The passage occurs in the third paragraph of the story, and (to help us follow the explication) the student quotes it in full at the beginning of her paper.

By Lantern Light: An Explication of a Passage in "The Tell-Tale Heart"

And every night, about midnight, I turned the latch of his door and opened it -- oh, so gently! And then, when I had made an opening sufficient for my head, I put in a dark lantern, all closed, closed, so that no light shone out, and then I thrust in my head. Oh, you would have laughed to see how cunningly I thrust it in! I moved it slowly -- very, very slowly, so that I might not disturb the old man's sleep. It took me an hour to place my whole head within the opening so far that I could see him as he lay upon his bed. Ha! -- would a madman have been so wise as this? And then, when my head was well in the room, I undid the lantern cautiously -- oh, so cautiously -- cautiously (for the hinges creaked) -- I undid it just so much that a single thin ray fell upon the vulture eye. And this I did for seven long nights -- every night just at midnight -- but I found the eye always closed; and so it was impossible to do the work; for it was not the old man who vexed me, but his Evil Eye.

Although Poe has indicated in the first lines of his story that the person who addresses us is insane, it is only when we come to the speaker's account of his preparations for murdering the old man that we imagine him in action, and

so find his madness fully revealed. Even more convincingly than his earlier
words (for we might think that someone who claims to hear things in heaven
[*possibly* inserted above "might think"]
and hell is a religious mystic), these preparations reveal him to be mad. What
strikes us is that they are so elaborate and meticulous. A significant detail is the
exactness of his schedule for spying: "every night just at midnight." The words
with which he describes his motions also convey the most extreme care (and I
will indicate them with italics): "how wisely I proceeded -- with what caution,"
"I turned the latch of his door and opened it -- oh, so gently!" "how cunningly I
thrust [my head] in! I moved it slowly, very slowly," "I undid the lantern
cautiously -- oh, so cautiously -- cautiously." Taking a whole hour to intrude his
head into the room, he asks, "Ha! would a madman be as wise as this?" But of
course the word wise is unconsciously ironic, for clearly it is not wisdom the
speaker displays, but an absurd degree of care, an almost fiendish ingenuity. Such
behavior, I understand, is typical of certain mental illnesses. All his careful preparations that he thinks prove him sane only convince us instead that he is mad.

Obviously his behavior is self-defeating. He wants to catch the "vulture eye"
open, and yet he takes all these pains not to disturb the old man's sleep. If he behaved logically, he might go barging into the bedroom with his lantern ablaze,
shouting at the top of his voice. And yet, if we can see things his way, there is a
strange logic to his reasoning. He regards the eye as a creature in itself, quite
apart from its possessor. "It was not," he says, "the old man who vexed me, but
his Evil Eye." Apparently, to be inspired to do his deed, the madman needs to
behold the eye -- at least, this is my understanding of his remark, "I found the
eye always closed; and so it was impossible to do the work." Poe's choice of the
word work, by the way, is also revealing. Murder is made to seem a duty or a
job; and anyone who so regards murder is either extremely cold-blooded, like a
hired killer for a gangland assassination, or else deranged. Besides, the word
suggests again the curious sense of detachment that the speaker feels toward the
owner of the eye.

In still another of his assumptions, the speaker shows that he is madly logical, or operating on the logic of a dream. There seems a dreamlike relationship
between his dark lantern "all closed, closed, so that no light shone out," and the
sleeping victim. When the madman opens his lantern so that it emits a single
ray, he is hoping that the eye in the old man's head will be open too, letting out

its corresponding gleam. The latch that he turns so gently, too, seems like the eye, whose lid needs to be opened in order for the murderer to go ahead. It is as though the speaker is <u>trying</u> to get the eyelid to lift. By taking such great pains and by going through all this nightly ritual, he is practicing some kind of magic, whose rules are laid down not by our logic, but by the logic of dreams.

An unusually well-written paper, "By Lantern Light" cost the student two or three careful revisions. Rather than attempting to say something about *everything* in the passage from Poe, she selects only the details that strike her as most meaningful. In her very first sentence, she briefly shows us how the passage functions in the context of Poe's story: how it clinches our suspicions that the narrator is mad. In writing her paper, the student went by the following rough, simple outline—nothing more than a list of the points she wanted to express:

1. Speaker's extreme care and exactness—typical of some mental illnesses.

2. Speaker doesn't act by usual logic but by a crazy logic.

3. Dreamlike connection between latch & lantern and old man's eye.

As she wrote, she followed her brief list, setting forth her ideas one at a time, one idea to a paragraph. There is a different (and still easier) way to organize an explication: just work through the original passage line by line or sentence by sentence. The danger of this procedure is that you may find yourself falling into a boring singsong: "In the first sentence I noticed . . . ," "In the next sentence . . . ," "Now in the third sentence . . . ," "Finally, in the last paragraph. . . . " (If you choose to organize an explication in such a way, then boldly vary your transitions.) Notice that the student who wrote "By Lantern Light" doesn't inch through the passage sentence by sentence but freely takes up its details in whatever order she likes. Less fussy than Poe's madman, she neatly writes in three corrections, saving herself retyping. And why, in her first paragraph, does she change Poe's word *it* to *my head?* Coming upon a piece of sentence quoted out of context, the reader might forget what *it* refers to—and so the writer places the alteration in brackets, to indicate that the charged words are her own.

In a long critical essay in which we don't adhere to one method all the way through, the method of explication may appear from time to time—as when the critic, in discussing a story, stops to unravel a particularly knotty passage. But useful as it may be to know how to write an explication of fiction, it is probably still more useful (in most literature courses) to know how to write an analysis.

ANALYZING

Assignment: "Write an **analysis** of a story or novel." What do you do? Following the method of analysis (from the Greek: "breaking up"), you separate a story or novel into its components, then (usually) select one part for close study. One likely topic for an analysis might be "The Character of James Thurber's Mr. Martin" (referring to "The Catbird Seat"), in which the writer would concentrate on showing us Martin's highly individual features and traits of personality. Other typical analyses might be written about, say, "Folk Humor in Mark Twain's *Huckleberry Finn*," or "Gothic Elements in a Story by Joyce Carol Oates" (referring to "Where Are You Going, Where Have You Been?"), or "The Unidentified Narrator in 'A Rose for Emily.' " To be sure, no element of a story dwells in isolation from the story's other elements. In "The Tell-Tale Heart," the madness of the leading character apparently makes it necessary to tell the story from a special point of view and probably helps determine the author's choice of theme, setting, symbolism, tone, style, and ironies. But it would be mind-boggling to try to study all those elements simultaneously. For this reason, when we write an analysis we generally study just one element, though we may suggest—probably at the start of the essay—its relation to the whole story. Indeed, analysis is the method used in this book, in which, chapter by chapter, we have separated fiction into its components of plot, point of view, character, tone and style, and so on. If you have read the discussion on the plot of "Godfather Death" (page 4), or the attempt to state the theme of Hemmingway's "A Clean, Well-Lighted Place" (page 112), then you have already read some brief essays in analysis. Here is a student-written analysis of "The Tell-Tale Heart," dealing with just one element—the story's point of view.

The Hearer of the Tell-Tale Heart

Although there are many things we do not know about the narrator of Edgar Allan Poe's story "The Tell-Tale Heart"—is he a son? a servant? a companion?—there is one thing we are sure of from the start. He is mad. In the opening paragraph, Poe makes the narrator's condition unmistakeable, not only from his excited and worked-up speech (full of dashes and exclamation points), but also from his wild claims. He says it is merely some disease which has sharpened his senses that has made people call him crazy. Who but a madman, however, would say, "I heard all things in the heaven and in the earth," and brag how his ear is a kind of CB radio, listening in on Hell? Such a statement leaves no doubt that the point of view in the story is an ironic one.

Because the participating narrator is telling his story in the first person, some details in the story stand out more than others. When the narrator goes on to tell how he watches the old man sleeping, he rivets his attention on the old man's "vulture eye." When a ray from his lantern finds the Evil Eye open, he says, "I could see nothing else of the old man's face or person." Actually, the reader can see almost nothing else about the old man anywhere in the rest of the story. All we are told is that the old man treated the younger man well, and we gather that the old man was rich, because his house is full of treasures. We do not have a clear idea of what the old man looks like, though, nor do we know how he talks, for we are not given any of his words. Our knowledge of him is mainly confined to his eye and its effect on the narrator. This confinement gives that symbolic eye a lot of importance in the story. The narrator tells us all we know and directs our attention to parts of it.

This point of view raises an interesting question. Since we are *on the narrator* dependent for all our information, how do we know the whole story isn't just a nightmare in his demented mind? We have really no way to be sure it isn't, as far as I can see. I assume, however, that there really is a dark shuttered house and an old man and real policemen who start snooping around when screams are heard in the neighborhood, because it is a more memorable story if it is a crazy man's view of reality than if it is all just a terrible dream. But we can't take stock in the madman's interpretation of what happens. Poe keeps putting distances between what the narrator says and what we are supposed to think, apparently. For instance: the narrator has boasted that he is calm and clear in the head, but as soon as he starts (in the second paragraph) trying to explain why he killed the old man, we gather that he is confused, to say the least. "I think it was his eye!" the narrator exclaims, as if not quite sure. As he goes on to explain how he conducted the murder, we realize that he is a man with a fixed idea working with a patience that is certainly mad, almost diabolical.

Some readers might wonder if "The Tell-Tale Heart" is a story of the supernatural. Is the heartbeat that the narrator hears a ghost come back to haunt him? Here, I think, the point of view is our best guide to what to believe. The simple explanation for the heartbeat is this: it is all in the madman's mind. Perhaps he feels such guilt that he starts hearing things. Another explanation is possible, one suggested by Daniel Hoffman, a critic who has discussed the story: the killer hears the sound of his own heart.[1] Hoffman's explanation (which I don't like as well as mine) also is a natural one, and it fits the story as a whole. Back when the narrator first entered the old man's bedroom to kill him, the heartbeat sounded so loud to him that he was afraid the neighbors would hear it too. Evidently they didn't, and so Hoffman may be right in thinking that the sound was only that of his own heart pounding in his ears. Whichever explanation you take, it is a more down-to-earth and reasonable explanation than that (as the narrator believes) the heart is still alive, even though its owner has been cut to pieces. Then, too, the police keep chatting. If they heard the heartbeat too, wouldn't they leap to their feet, draw their guns, and look all around the room? As the author has kept showing us in the rest of the story, the narrator's view of things is ~~always~~ untrustworthy. You don't kill someone just because you dislike the look in his eye. You don't think that such a murder is funny. For all its Gothic atmosphere of the old dark house with a secret hidden inside, "The Tell-Tale Heart" is not a ghost story. We have only to see its point of view to know it is a study in abnormal psychology.

_____

[1] *Poe Poe Poe Poe Poe Poe Poe* (New York: Anchor, 1973), 227.

A temptation in writing an analysis is to want to include all sorts of insights that the writer proudly wishes to display, even though they aren't related to the main idea. In the preceding essay, the student resists this temptation admirably. In fairly plump and ample paragraphs, he works out his ideas, and he supports his contentions with specific references to Poe's story. Although his paper is not brilliantly written and contains no insight so fresh as the suggestion (by the writer of the first paper) that the madman's lantern is like the old man's head, still, it is a good brief analysis. By sticking faithfully to his purpose and by confronting the problems he raises ("how do we know the whole story isn't just a nightmare?"), the writer persuades us that he understands not only the story's point of view, but the story in its entirety.

Our analysis so far deals with one element in Poe's story: point of view. In another familiar writting assignment, the **card report,** one is asked to analyze a story into its *several* elements. Usually confined to the front and back of one 5 × 8-inch index card, such a report is just as challenging to write as an essay, if not more so. To do the job well, you have to see the story in its elements, then specify them succinctly and accurately. Here (on the following pages) is a typical card report listing and detailing the essentials of "The Tell-Tale Heart." In this assignment, the student was asked to include:

1. The title of the story and the date of its original publication.
2. The author's name and dates.
3. The name (if any) of the main character, together with a description of that character's dominant traits or features.

4. Other characters in the story, dealt with in the same fashion.
5. A short description of the setting.
6. The narrator of the story. (To identify him or her is, of course, to define the point of view from which the story is told.)

(Student's name)   (Course and section)

Story: "The Tell-Tale Heart," 1850
Author: Edgar Allan Poe (1809-1849)

Central character: An unnamed younger man whom people call mad, who claims that a nervous disease has greatly sharpened his sense perceptions. He is proud of his own cleverness. Other characters: The old man, whose leading feature is one pale blue, filmed eye; said to be rich, kind, and lovable. Also three policemen, not individually described.

Setting: A shuttered house full of wind, mice, and treasures; pitch dark even in the afternoon.

Narrator: The madman himself.

Events in summary: (1) Dreading one vulturelike eye of the old man he shares a house with, a madman determines to kill its owner. (2) Each night he spies on the sleeping old man, but finding the eye shut, he stays his hand. (3) On the eighth night, finding the eye open, he suffocates its owner beneath the mattress and conceals the dismembered body under the floor of the bedchamber. (4) Entertaining some inquiring police officers in the very room where the body lies hidden, the killer again hears (or thinks he hears) the beat of his victim's heart. (5) Terrified, convinced that the police also hear the heartbeat growing louder, the killer confesses.

Tone: Horror at the events described, skepticism toward the narrator's claims to be sane, detachment from his gaiety and laughter.

Front of Card

7. A terse summary of the main events of the story, given in chronological order.
8. A description of the general tone of the story, as well as it can be sensed: the author's feelings toward the central character or the main events.
9. Some comments on the style in which the story is written. (Brief illustrative quotations are helpful, insofar as space permits.)
10. Whatever kinds of irony the story contains and what they contribute to the story.
11. In a sentence, the story's main theme.
12. Leading symbols (if the story has any), with an educated guess at whatever each symbol suggests.

13. Finally, an evaluation of the story as a whole, concisely setting forth the student's opinion of it. (Some instructors regard this as the most important part of the report, and most students find that, by the time they have so painstakingly separated the ingredients of the story, they have arrived at a definite opinion of it.)

Style: Written as if told aloud by a deranged man eager to be believed, the story is punctuated by laughter, interjections ("Hearken!"), nervous halts, and fresh beginnings -- indicated by dashes that grown more frequent as the story goes on and the narrator becomes more excited. Poe often relies on general adjectives ("mournful," "hideous," "hellish") to convey atmosphere; also on exact details: the lantern that emits "a single dim ray, like the thread of a spider."

Irony: The whole story is ironic in its point of view. Presumably the author is not mad, nor does he share the madman's self-admiration, nor join in his glee ("I then smiled gaily, to find the deed so far done"). Many of the narrator's statements therefore seem verbal ironies: his account of taking an hour to move his head through the bedroom door.

Theme: Possibly "Murder will out," but I really don't find any theme either stated or clearly implied.

Symbols: The vulture eye, called an Evil Eye (in superstition, one that can implant a curse), perhaps suggesting too the all-seeing eye of God the Father, from whom no guilt can be conceealed. The ghostly heartbeat, sound of the victim coming back to be avenged (or the God who cannot be slain?). Death watches: beetles said to be death omens, whose ticking sound foreshadows the sound of the tell-tale heart "as a watch makes when enveloped in cotton."

Evaluation: Despite the overwrought style (to me slightly comic-bookish), a powerful story, admirable for its concision and for its memorable portrait of a deranged killer. Poe knows how it is to be mad.

Back of Card

To fit so much on one card is, admittedly, somewhat like trying to engrave the Declaration of Independence on the head of a pin. The student who wrote this succinct report had to spoil a few trial cards before he was able to do it. Every word has to count, and making them count is a discipline worthwhile in almost any sort of expository writing. Some students enjoy the challenge. In doing such a report, though you may feel severely limited, you'll probably be surprised at how thoroughly you come to understand a story. Besides, if you care to keep the card for future reference, it won't take much storage room. A longer story, even a novel, may be analyzed in the same way; but insist on taking a second card if you are asked to analyze some especially hefty and complicated novel—say, Leo Tolstoi's panoramic, thousand-page *War and Peace*.

COMPARING AND CONTRASTING

If you were to write on "The Humor of Frank O'Connor's 'First Confession' and Alice Munro's 'The Found Boat,' " you would probably employ one or two other methods. You might use **comparison**, placing the two stories side by side and pointing out their similarities; or you might use **contrast**, pointing out their differences. Most of the time, in dealing with a pair of stories, you will find them similar in some ways and different in others; and so you will be using both methods in writing your paper. No law requires you to devote equal space to each method. You might have to do more contrasting than comparing, or the other way around. If the stories are obviously similar but subtly different, you will probably compare them briefly, listing the similarities and then, at greater length, contrast them by calling attention to their important differences. If, however, the stories at first glance seem as different as peas and polecats yet are in fact closely related, you'll probably spend most of your time comparing them rather than contrasting them. (You might not just compare and contrast but also analyze, in that you might select one element of the stories for your investigation.) Other topics for papers involving two stories might be "The Experience of Coming of Age in James Joyce's 'Araby' and William Faulkner's 'Barn Burning' "; and "Mother and Daughter Relationships in Jamaica Kincaid's 'Girl' and Tillie Olsen's 'I Stand Here Ironing.' "

Your paper, of course, will hang together better if you choose a pair of stories that apparently have much in common than if you choose two as unlike as cow and cantaloupe. Before you start writing, think: Do the two stories I've selected throw some light on each other? An essay that likened W. Somerset Maugham's terse, ironic fable "The Appointment in Samarra" with William Faulkner's rich, complex "Barn Burning" just might reveal unexpected similarities. More likely, it would seem strained and pointless.

You can also write an essay in comparison and contrast that deals with just one story. You might consider, say, the attitudes of the younger waiter and the older waiter in Hemingway's "A Clean, Well-Lighted Place." In Flannery O'Connor's "Revelation," you might contrast Mrs. Turpin's smug view of herself with young Mary Grace's merciless view of her.

If your topic calls for both comparison and contrast and you are dealing with two stories, don't write the first half of your paper all about one story, then pivot and write the second half about the other, never permitting the two to mingle. The result probably would not be a unified essay in contrast and comparison but two separate commentaries yoked together. One workable way to organize such a paper is to make (before you begin) a brief list of points to look for in each story, then, as you write, to consider each point—first in one story and then in the other.

Here is a simple outline for an essay bringing together William Faulkner's "A Rose for Emily" and Flannery O'Connor's "Revelation." The topic is "Two Would-be Aristocrats: The Characters of Emily Grierson and Mrs. Turpin."

1. Character's view of her own innate superiority

   a. Emily

   b. Mrs. Turpin

2. Author's evaluation of character's moral worth

   a Emily

   b. Mrs. Turpin

3. Character's ability to change

   a. Emily

   b. Mrs. Turpin

It is best, however, not to follow such an outline in plodding, mechanical fashion ("Well, now it's time to whip over to Mrs. Turpin again"), lest your readers feel they are watching a back-and-forth tennis match. Some points are bound to interest you more than others, and, when they do, you will want to give them greater emphasis.

SUGGESTIONS FOR WRITING

What kinds of topics are likely to result in papers that will reveal something about works of fiction? Here is a list of typical topics, suitable to papers of various lengths, offered in the hope of stimulating your own ideas. For other topics, see Suggestions for Writing at the end of every chapter. For specific advice on finding a topic of your own, see "Discovering and Planning," page 1459.

TOPICS FOR BRIEF PAPERS *(250–500 words)*

1. Consider a short story in which the central character has to make a decision or must take some decisive step that will alter the rest of his or her life. Faulkner's "Barn Burning" is one such story; another is Updike's "A & P." As concisely and as thoroughly as you can, explain the nature of the character's decision, the reasons for it, and its probable consequences (as suggested by what the author tells us).
2. Write an informal (rather than a complete) explication of the opening paragraph or first few lines of a story. Show us how it prepares us for what will happen. (An alternate topic: take instead a *closing* paragraph and sum up whatever insight it leaves us with.) Don't feel obliged to deal with everything in the passage, as you would do in writing a more nearly complete explication. Within this suggested word length, limit your discussion to whatever strikes you as most essential.

3. Make a card report (see page 1476) on a short story in the Stories for Further Reading or one suggested by your instructor. Include all the elements in the report illustrated in this chapter (unless your instructor wishes you to emphasize some element or offers other advice).
4. Show how reading a specific short story caused you to change or modify an attitude or opinion you once had.
5. Just for fun, try writing a different ending to one of the short stories in this anthology. What does this exercise suggest about the wisdom of the author in ending things as done in the original? (Try to keep a sense of the author's style.)
6. Another wild idea: Write a *sequel* to one of your favorite short stories—or at least the beginning of a sequel, enough to give your reader a sense of it.
7. Argue from your own experience that a character in any story behaves (or doesn't behave) as people behave in life.

TOPICS FOR MORE EXTENDED PAPERS *(600–1,000 words)*

1. Choose a short passage (one of, say, three or four sentences) in a story, a passage that interests you. Perhaps it will contain a decisive movement in a plot, a revealing comment on a character, or a statement of the story's major theme. Then write a reasonably thorough explication. Like the writer of the paper "By Lantern Light" (page 1471), go through the passage in some detail, noticing words that especially convey the author's meanings.
2. Write an analysis of a short story, singling out an element such as the author's voice (tone, style, irony), point of view, character, theme, symbolism, or Gothic elements (if the story has any). Try to show how this element functions in the story as a whole. For a typical paper in response to this assignment, see "The Hearer of 'The Tell-Tale Heart' " (page 1474).
3. Analyze a story in which a character experiences some realization or revelation. How does the writer prepare us for the moment of enlightenment? What is the nature of each realization or revelation? How does it affect the character? Stories to consider might include "Miss Brill," "Gimpel the Fool," "Greasy Lake," "Araby," "The Chrysanthemums," "The Death of Ivan Ilych," "Revelation," "The Lover of Horses," "The Man Who Did Not Smile," and "Roman Fever."
4. Explore how humor functions in a story. What is funny? How is humor implied by the story's style or tone? Does humor help set forth a theme or reveal character? Any of the following stories deserves exploration: "A & P," "Gimpel the Fool," "Greasy Lake," "Harrison Bergeron," "Where I'm Calling From," "Revelation," "The Spirit of Giving," "First Confession," "The Conversion of the Jews," and "The Catbird Seat."
5. For anyone interested in a career in teaching: Explain how you would teach a story, either to an imaginary class or to the class you belong to now. Perhaps you might arrange with your instructor to write about a story your class hasn't read yet; and then, after writing your paper, actually to teach the story in class.
6. See if you can discover a new Stephen Crane—another journalist who brings literary skill to reporting (as Crane does in "The Open Boat"). In an essay, examine some news story, interview, or feature that you think reads like excellent fiction. Point out whatever elements of good storytelling you find in it. (Is there a plot? Lively dialogue? Suspense? Vivid style? Thought-provoking theme? Rounded characters, or at least memorable ones? Shrewd choice of a point of view?) For such a story, consult your daily newspaper or a weekly news magazine. Supply a clipping or copy of your discovery along with your finished paper.
7. If your daily newspaper lacks literary quality but you'd like to try that last topic, see any of the following books. Each contains some reporting that will show you storytelling art:

Nora Ephron, *Crazy Salad: Some Things About Women* (New York: Knopf, 1975). Includes a portrait of the first woman umpire and a cutthroat national baking competition.

John Hersey, *Hiroshima* (New York: Knopf, 1946). The first atomic holocaust as seen by six survivors.

Garrison Keillor, *Lake Wobegon Days* (New York: Viking, 1985). Gentle comic reports of a practically vanished small-town way of life.

Tracy Kidder, *Among Schoolchildren* (Boston: Todd/Houghton Mifflin, 1989). Close observations of a year in the life of an elementary school teacher.

Lillian Ross, *Reporting* (New York: Dodd, 1981). Seven classic essays in journalism, among them a profile of Ernest Hemingway.

Hunter S. Thompson, *The Great Shark Hunt* (New York: Summit Books, 1979). Reports of politics, sports, and pleasure-seeking in the 1960s and 1970s.

Tom Wolfe, *The Right Stuff* (New York: Farrar, 1979). The story of America's first astronauts.

TOPICS FOR LONG PAPERS (1,500 WORDS OR MORE)

1. Selecting a short story from the anthology in this book, or taking one suggested by your instructor, write an informal essay setting forth (as thoroughly as you can) your understanding of it. Point out any difficulties you encountered in first reading the story, for the benefit of other students who might meet the same difficulties. If you find particularly complicated passages, briefly explicate them. An ample statement of the meaning of the story probably will not deal only with plot or only with theme but will also consider how the story is written and structured.
2. Dealing with a single element of fiction, write an analysis of Tolstoi's *The Death of Ivan Ilych* or of some other long story that your instructor suggests.
3. Take a short story in which most of the events take place in the physical world (rather than inside some character's mind), and translate it into a one-act play, complete with stage directions. After you have done so, you might present a reading of it with the aid of other members of the class and then perhaps discuss what you had to do to the story to make a play of it.
4. Taking an author in this book whose work appeals to you, read at least three or four of his or her other stories. Then write an analysis of them, concentrating on an element of fiction that you find present in all. (Note: In Chapter 10, three fine writers are represented by three stories apiece.)
5. Again going beyond this book if necessary, compare and contrast two writers' handling of a similar theme. Let your essay build to a conclusion in which you state your opinion: which author's expression of theme is deeper or more memorable?

Writing a Story

FINDING A STORY

Whether or not you aspire to be a new Katherine Mansfield or D.H. Lawrence, writing a story may reveal to you much firsthand knowledge. At the very least, you may learn some of the ways in which a good story is crafted, and you may acquire a keener sense of the art it requires. Then, when you read stories in the future, you will enjoy them as an insider does.

Not everyone, of course, is a born storyteller. If someone tells you of something that happened the other day and practically puts you to sleep, you realize that it takes both talent and skill to recognize a story worth telling and to narrate it effectively. Yet most people who can write expository prose clearly and vigorously can, with enough effort, write at least a brief story that will satisfy themselves, and perhaps others. Generally, the skilled writer of fiction is a skilled reader of fiction, too. Among famed storytellers, Erskine Caldwell, author of *Tobacco Road*, may be the only one to claim that reading never did him any good. Before you attempt a story of your own, you would do well to read the works of master storytellers—as many as possible. In this book, you'll find a fair sampling; but if you are serious about wanting to write stories, you will want to read whole collections by authors you admire. Read not only for entertainment, read critically. Notice how a story is woven together. For what possible purpose does the writer tell it from one point of view instead of from another? What do the actions of the characters show us about the kinds of people they are? Are events given in chronological order? If not, what does the writer achieve by so departing from chronology? Such questions may seem dry, but if you apply them to living stories, they may help give you a few insights into the storyteller's art.

Some beginning writers, remarked Flannery O'Connor, think they know what a story is until they try to write one—"Then they find themselves writing a sketch with an essay woven through it, or an editorial with a character in it, or a case history with a moral, or some other mongrel thing."[1] But what, exactly, is a story? According to O'Connor, it is a form of writing in which characters and events influence each other. "If you start with a real personality, a real character," she explained to an audience of aspiring writers, "then something is bound to happen."[2] This would seem another way of saying, "Character is action"—the words of a master storyteller, Henry James.[3]

For an event to be charged with meaning in fiction, it has to produce an effect on someone. E. M. Forster, has explained, "Consider the death of a queen. If it is in a story we say, 'and then?' "[4] In such a story a writer might tell how the queen's death in some way altered the life of an obscure commoner. Read outstanding short stories of the past century and, in most, you will find a character led to act—or left, as a result of some dramatic event, deeply illumined and fundamentally changed. Most stories in this book exhibit the tradition that James defined: stories in which characters think, feel, and react, causing things to happen. Recently, however, many fiction writers have experimented with radically different concepts of character (discussed briefly in Chapter Three). As a result, in many contemporary stories, character seems hardly to matter and events sometimes occur without apparent human control. If recent fiction intrigues you, then closely read the stories of Margaret Atwood, T. Coraghessan Boyle, Raymond Carver, Bobbie Ann Mason, Alice Munro, and Joyce Carol Oates (all represented in this book), as well as those of John Barth, Donald Barthelme, Samuel Beckett, and others. You will meet a few stories in which writers appear to devise new rules for storytelling. If you are a novice at writing fiction, however, you might do well, before trying to change the rules, to watch a fair number of games first.

Let us assume that you have a working sense of the nature of a short story. Where do you find a story to tell? Evidently, if you take Flannery O'Connor's advice and start with a "real character," to unfold a story you have only to imagine that character in some dramatic situation or confrontation. Then you imagine how he or she will respond to it. In O'Connor's own story "Revelation," we see her procedure. First she establishes the nature of Mrs. Turpin, a racist prig full of smug self-congratulation. Then, after a flung textbook strikes Mrs. Turpin in the brow, O'Connor shows us her main character going through anguished change. Of course, there is no one approved and infallible method of story-finding. Writers begin with anything that sparks them into motion. Henry James could find the germ for a story—even for a whole novel—in an anecdote told him at a dinner party. Another source of seedling stories, for novelist and short story writer J. F. Powers, is small human-interest items in a daily newspaper. Robert Ludlum, author of popular spy novels, says, "I start with an idea, with something that outrages, amuses, or interests me. Then I try to find the story line that will support

[1]"The Nature and Aim of Fiction" in *Mystery and Manners*, ed. Sally and Robert Fitzgerald (New York: Farrar, 1961), 66.
[2]"Writing Short Stories," *Mystery and Manners*, 106.
[3]"Anthony Trollope" (1883), reprinted in part in *Theory of Fiction: Henry James*, ed. James E. Miller, Jr. (Lincoln: U of Nebraska P, 1972), 200.
[4]*Apsects of the Novel*, quoted by Eric S. Rabkin in the epigraph for his study *Narrative Suspense* (Ann Arbor: U of Michigan P, 1973).

the basic idea."[5] (Ludlum, no Flannery O'Connor-like prober of souls, writes a kind of fiction in which ingenious plot, not character, counts most.)

Endless stories surround you, if only you can recognize them. Your daily life may prove your most fruitful source. You need not live a story in order to write it, though: you can overhear it or observe it in the lives of others. As an aid to memory, many distinguished fiction writers have kept notebooks. There, in rough form, they record whatever sticks in their minds as grist for stories. F. Scott Fitzgerald filled his notebook with "Things Overheard," "Nonsense and Stray Phrases," "Scenes," "Situations," and "Descriptions of Girls." Nathaniel Hawthorne jotted down hundreds of ideas for stories he meant to write. (One that didn't materialize: "A stove possessed by a Devil.") In his own profound notebooks, Henry James not only saved bits and scraps (such as names he thought up for possible characters), he analyzed his stories as he worked on them, listing problems and solutions. Some writers, whether or not they ever turn their notebooks into finished stories, find that notebook-keeping sharpens their powers of observation. Keep such a notebook, after your own fashion, and you may well find yourself opening your eyes wide to the stories that surround you, and also fine-tuning your ears.

THE PROCESS OF STORYTELLING

In the heyday of pulp magazines (so called for their cheap paper) many professional writers of fiction relied on a mechanical gadget called Plotto—a sort of writer's Ouija board. Constructing a story for *Dime Western* or *Spicy Detective*, a writer would spin a little tin arrow to a number, then look up the number in an accompanying book. A few spins would indicate all the necessary ingredients: type of hero, type of villain, setting, kind of conflict, complication ("an earthquake"), crisis, climax, and conclusion. When the writer cooked the ingredients into a story, the result brought a penny a word.

Some more highly literate storytellers, though they don't own a Plotto board, lay out the elements of a story before they write. One believer in thorough planning was P. G. Wodehouse, author of ingeniously plotted novels of screwball dwellers in posh mansions in rural England. Everything in a story, declared Wodehouse, should be carefully figured out ahead of time: "Once you go saying to yourself, 'This is a pretty weak plot as it stands, but I'm such a hell of a writer that my magic touch will make it OK,' you're sunk."[6] Other writers, less insistent on firm scaffolding, begin writing with only a character or a situation in mind, letting themselves be surprised (along with the reader) as the story unfolds. Flannery O'Connor, it would seem, was such a writer. In her short story "Good Country People," a Bible salesman steals a woman's artificial leg. O'Connor has recalled that she didn't know he was going to do so until ten or twelve lines before she

[5]Reply to a questioner, quoted by Robert Charm, "From Pen to Podium," Boston *Globe*, 11 May 1982: 15.
[6]Interview with Gerald Clarke, *Paris Review* 64 (1975): 155.

came to describe the theft. Yet, she later realized, the salesman's astonishing act followed from the kind of man he was and from the nature of his victim.[7]

Whether they lay plans carefully or casually, writers often will meet a surprise in the act of telling a story. At times a character will behave unpredictably, especially a lifelike character who grows larger under the pen. Tolstoi, who began writing *Anna Karenina* determined to condemn an unfaithful woman, found himself, as he wrote his immense novel, coming to view his adulterous main character with greater compassion. He had imagined Anna as physically unattractive and boorish in her manners, but his descriptions of her became kinder and more sympathetic as he wrote on.

Like runners who first limber up their muscles before hitting the track, some writers warm up before they write. George Fox, author of popular novels (*Amok, Without Music*) and filmscripts, starts out by writing "a lot of drivel about the hero's childhood, about the setting, about a certain car." Perhaps none of this "drivel" will appear in his finished story. As he writes a description of a character, things start to happen, and the story begins to move. Then Fox drops ten or twenty pages of warm-up exercise into his trashbasket. Hero and setting, he finds, have become vivid in his imagination.

Early in writing a story, you have to make crucial decisions. One is your choice of the person to narrate the story—the point of view. Tolstoi, in writing *The Death of Ivan Ilych*, at first cast his story into the form of a diary kept by Ivan during his last days. Later, as Tolstoi reviewed what he had written, he decided against this device. He then completely rewrote the story in the third person. No doubt he had realized that the story required a narrator able to see Ivan both from without and from within. Such a narrator, besides, could survive Ivan's death and portray his mourners. In effective storytelling, perhaps a writer's most important decision is to select the most appropriate point of view. How to decide which point of view is best? Try telling the story to yourself in different ways, as if through the eyes of different narrators.

Still another decision that greatly matters is how thoroughly each part of your story needs to be told. Which events will you set forth in brief summaries, which in full scenes? Drawing a scene, you visualize it in detail. You thus enable your readers to see it in their minds' eyes as if they beheld it on a stage or a screen. In John Updike's "A & P," most of the story takes place in one extended scene in a supermarket, including a few interior thoughts of Sammy, the narrator. That we may visualize the action, Updike includes plenty of physical details: the story takes place "under the fluorescent lights, against all those stacked packages," and the girls who trigger Sammy's big decision are described with loving care. For another vivid scene, see Faulkner's "Barn Burning," in which the boy's father marches into Major de Spain's mansion, streaking the rug with filth. In a well-told story, we usually find the most highly dramatic moments set forth in scenes. For as long as a scene transpires, the reader lives it.

In employing the method of **summary,** you tell what happens in fewer words. You boil down events to their essentials and set them forth in a more general

[7]"Writing Short Stories," *Mystern and Manners* 100.

way. In the Grimm brothers' "Godfather Death," we find summary in the statement, "It wasn't long before the young man had become the most famous doctor in the world." In this one sentence, the taleteller covers events that, if told in scenes, might have required many chapters. Summary is the method of narration most of us employ in conversation: "I was in a little car crash last night. A truck slammed me in the tailgate and stove in my rear end." In fiction, a story containing scenes may also employ summary—for the less dramatic events, perhaps, or for getting over a long expanse of time that doesn't need to be chronicled in detail. In Singer's "Gimpel the Fool" the narrator summarizes: "I wandered over the land and good people did not neglect me. After many years I became old and white. . . . " Here, Singer's apparent purpose isn't to give us a complete history of Gimpel's later life. Instead, it is to show that, during his years of wandering, the supposed fool becomes a wiser man. Summary may also be valuable to supply background information that the reader needs. With wonderful economy, D. H. Lawrence begins "The Rocking-Horse Winner" with a summary: "There was a woman who was beautiful, who started with all the advantages, yet she had no luck. She married for love, and the love turned to dust." In a few words, summary can convey all the information we need more effectively than many scenes.

To decide which events to summarize and which to depict in scenes is a challenge to many storytellers. Beginning writers sometimes tell too large a part of their story in sketchy summary form, neglecting to set forth the dramatic moments in detailed scenes—and therefore, failing to milk these moments for all they are worth. Still, good storytellers know that, although vivid scenes are what readers best remember, summary at times is indispensable. With a short passage of summary, the writer can move along quickly to a scene. Divide your story into scenes, P. G. Wodehouse advised, "and have as little stuff in between as possible."[8]

Some writers, when shifting scenes, don't even use summary. To waft a character from one place to another, they will end a scene, leave some white space, and open the next scene with the character already arrived at a destination. Perhaps they will use a **time-marker,** or a brief phrase of transition, to indicate that some while has gone by: *"An hour later"*—that's the time-marker—"Cassidy was shoving open the bleary glass door of the Tenth Precinct Station."

A word of warning: Don't pretend to feelings you don't feel, or attitudes you can't call your own. In later life, Eudora Welty recalled with amusement the opening line of a story she had written as a girl trying to maintain a sophistication she hadn't really had: "Monsieur Boule inserted a delicate dagger into Mademoiselle's left side and departed with a poised immediacy."[9]

Some storytellers work slowly, taking pains to find the right words on their first try. Others, like Frank O'Connor, dash off a rough draft of a story, saving the pains for later. O'Connor would start writing "any sort of rubbish which will cover the main outlines of the story," just to get it down in writing and be able to look at it. "When I draft a story I never think of writing nice sentences," he explained. "It's the design of the story which to me is most important, the thing

[8]Interview with Clarke, 152.
[9]*One Writer's Beginnings* (Cambridge: Harvard UP, 1984), 85–6

that tells you there's a bad gap in the narrative here and you really ought to fill that up in some way or another."[10] Satisfied with his design, O'Connor would then work on the story's texture, rewriting a story as many as fifty times. " 'First Confession,' " he said, "has appeared in three quite different forms from the first day when *Lovat Dickson's Magazine* printed it, so I may now hope its ghost has ceased to haunt me."[11]

Not every writer of fiction believes in profound revision. "You know," Ann Beattie told a writers' conference, "I'm not capable of major revision at all. That's why I throw things out a lot."[12] D. H. Lawrence was another believer in letting first thoughts stand. If dissatisfied with a story, he would write the whole thing over from scratch. This strenuous custom accounts for there being at least three complete and separate versions of his novel *Lady Chatterley's Lover*.

At the opposite extreme is the "bleeder," the writer who lets go of each word as reluctantly as though it were a drop of blood. Perhaps the most celebrated bleeder in literary history was Gustave Flaubert, who rewrote his work with masochistic devotion, seeking to reflect in his style the clarity and precision of classical music. "May I die like a dog," he wrote to a friend, "rather than hasten the ripening of a sentence by a single second!"[13] (See other remarks by Flaubert upon his labors, page 487.)

Most professional writers of fiction probably reside somewhere between perfectionism and "Oh, let it all hang out." If, in looking over what they have written they spy a passage they can improve, they improve it. Because it is usually easier to delete than to amplify, some write at great length, putting in everything they can think of, and then, in revising the story, shorten it. Georges Simenon, French writer of mystery novels, sometimes reduced his first versions by as much as half. James Thurber distrusted too-obvious delight in one's own words. In writing a humorous story, he observed, "you're likely to be very gleeful with what you've first put down." But careful rewriting can transfer the glee from writer to reader. "You go over and over it . . . to make the piece sound less as if you were having a lot of fun with it yourself."[14]

If we can generalize at all, it may be safe to say that most professional writers first write a much rougher version of a story than they finish with. Although in some of his working habits Truman Capote may have been unique (he wrote *second* drafts on a peculiar kind of yellow paper), he was like most writers in bringing a story to completion stage by stage. After writing a first draft in longhand, Capote would type another draft, which he then retired for a week or a month. "When I take it out again," he said, "I read it as coldly as possible, then read it aloud to a friend or two, and decide what changes I want to make and whether

[10]Interview with Anthony Whittier, *Writers at Work: The Paris Review Interviews* (New York: Viking, 1959) 167–8.
[11]Foreword to the *Stories of Frank O'Connor* (New York: Knopf, 1952).
[12]Quoted by Gelarch Asayesh, news story on the New England Writers' Conference, Boston *Globe*, 8 July 1982.
[13]Letter to Maxim du Camp, June 19, 1852, *Selected Letters*, tr. Francis Steegmuller (New York: Vintage, 1957) 132.
[14]Interview with George Plimpton and Max Steele, *Writers* 88.

or not I want to publish it." (Capote threw away hundreds of thousands of words that didn't seem publishable.) "But if all goes well, I type the final version on white paper."[15]

As you can see, professional writers of fiction tend to be patient and demanding self-critics. They cultivate an ability to step out of themselves and to inspect a story as though with a reader's eyes. To be sure, problems will appear, problems deeper than whether to delete an adjective. A major character may prove useless and a minor character may assume swaggering proportions. A plot that had rolled along smoothly may run into a pothole and fall apart. Mark Twain, in writing *Huckleberry Finn*, called his masterpiece "that damned book" as he struggled with it. For seven years he kept casting aside his manuscript and returning to it. Something in him seemed unwilling to finish the book, and in the midst of his labors on it he took time out to produce his autobiographical *Life on the Mississippi* and an inferior but more tractable novel, *The Prince and the Pauper*. In spinning forth a story, every veteran writer of fiction perhaps has encountered knots. Fortunately, in trying to undo them, the writer has a powerful ally: the unconscious. Joyce Carol Oates has suggested a remedy for writer's block caused by running into deep problems. When the mind halts before a problem it can't solve, the writer had best put aside the story for a while, and sleep on it, until the trustworthy unconscious comes up with a solution.[16]

To write a novel that will soar to the top of bestseller lists and set every reviewer to babbling praise—this is a cherished American dream. In actuality, your chances of achieving great rewards from fiction are somewhat like your chances of winning a million dollars by playing blackjack at Las Vegas. Although a few professional writers make a living by regularly churning out paperback novels in some popular genre such as romance, Gothic, or science fiction, few serious first novelists meet much favor these days with readers or publishers. If you write short stories, you will find it even harder to reach a wide audience. Little magazines, with circulations of a few hundred dedicated readers, are today the principal medium for short fiction. Lately, however, hope for the short story has blossomed. Collections of stories by distinguished old hands (Eudora Welty, John Cheever) have proved bestsellers; and more and more publishers, including some university presses, have been welcoming volumes of stories.

Like poets, most short-story writers nowadays practice their demanding art for reasons other than the prospects of money and renown. What satisfactions reside in writing short stories? May you discover them, by writing a story that pleases you, your instructor, and your friends.

SUGGESTIONS FOR WRITING

1. Reviewing the illustrations of fable and tale in Chapter 1 (those by W. Somerset Maugham and the brothers Grimm), write a brief supernatural or fantastic tale, or a fable with a point to it.

---

[15]Interview with Pati Hill, *Writers* 296–7.
[16]Cited by Rust Hills, *Writing in General and the Short Story in Particular* (Boston: Houghton, 1977) 191.

2. In three separate paragraphs, try beginning a story in three distinctly different ways. You might try, for instance, relating an incident from three points of view; or try beginning a story with a summary, the opening of a scene, and a descriptive passage introducing a person or a setting.

3. Recount a dream you vividly remember, in which something exciting or astonishing occurred. (This is an exercise; the result does not have to be a complete story. You may find, though, that a longer story will suggest itself.)

4. Here is a writing exercise suggested by novelist R. V. Cassill. Take the first three paragraphs of a story you admire, and with the text open beside you, write three parallel paragraphs of careful imitation. Keep the same number of sentences, of the same general length and complexity. Imitate any proper names, characteristic detail, "emotional state of the characters." Reproduce the point of view. "In a word," says Cassill, "you cannot do this sort of imitation without thinking pretty nimbly about what you are doing. You are performing one of the kinds of thought that is part of original composition." (From *Writing Fiction*, New York: Pocket Books, 1962.)

5. Following George Fox's method of warming up, write ten or more pages of carefree exercise material, portraying in detail some strong and colorful character or a weak and appealing one. If the character you envision interests you, try to imagine such a person confronted with some challenge. Then go on to write the story that ensues.

6. Recall some dramatic event in your life or some event that you know from vivid secondhand reports. Bring it alive in the form of a scene, including dialogue and description if they seem necessary.

7. Write a skeletal novel in summary form, taking three or four pages to encompass all the main events in it. Then select one dramatic moment from your summary and present it in the form of a scene of about 1,000 to 2,000 words.

8. Invent names for ten or twelve imaginary characters, wildly assorted in age, walk of life, and personality. Then describe in two or three sentences the person each name suggests to you. (Here are three memorable fictional names from the novels of Henry James, for instance: Lambert Strether, Fleda Vetch, and Mrs. Bread.)

9. Following the procedure of J. F. Powers, scan a newspaper for some two-inch-long comic or touching story of relatively small news value but of much human interest. Write the tale or short story it suggests to you.

10. Choose a place you know well and write a story that might have happened there twenty-five, fifty, or a hundred years ago. An alternative idea might be to set your story in the future. (For inspiration, see "Harison Bergeron," or a current science-fiction magazine.)

11. In a short story, show how a brief moment alters the course of a character's life. For illustrations of such stories, see "A&P," "Greasy Lake," "Revelation," and "The Jilting of Granny Weatherall."

Writing about a Poem

Assignment: a paper about a poem. You can approach it as a grim duty, of course: any activity can so be regarded. For Don Juan, in Spanish legend, even the act of love became a chore. But the act of writing, like the act of love, is much easier if your feelings take part in it. Write about anything you dislike and don't understand, and you not only set yourself the labors of Hercules, but you guarantee your reader discouragingly hard labor, too.

To write about a poem informatively, you need first to experience it. It helps to live with the poem for as long as possible: there is little point in trying to encompass the poem in a ten-minute tour of inspection on the night before the paper falls due. However challenging, writing about poetry has immediate rewards, and, to mention just one, the poem you spend time with and write about is going to mean much more to you than poems skimmed ever do.

Most of the problems you will meet in writing about a poem will be the same ones you meet in writing about a play or a story: finding a topic, organizing your thoughts, writing, revising. For general advice on writing papers about any kind of literature, see "Writing about Literature" on page 1455. In a few ways, however, a poem requires a different approach. In this chapter we will deal briefly with some of them and will offer a few illustrations of papers that students have written. These papers may not be works of inimitable genius, but they are pretty good papers, the likes of which most students can write with a modest investment of time and care.

Briefer than most stories and most plays, lyric poems *look* easier to write about. They call, however, for your keenest attention. You may find that, before you can discuss a short poem, you will have to read it slowly and painstakingly, with your mind (like your pencil) sharp and ready. Unlike a play or a short story, a lyric poem tends to have very little plot, and perhaps you will find little to say about what happens in it. In order to understand a poem, you'll need to notice elements other than narrative: the connotations or suggestions of its words, surely, and the rhythm of phrases and lines. The subtleties of language, almost apart from story, are so essential to a poem (and so elusive) that Robert Frost was moved to say, "Poetry is what gets lost in translation." Once in a while, of course, you'll read a story whose prose abounds in sounds, rhythms, figures of speech, imagery, and other elements you expect of poetry. Certain novels of Herman Melville and William Faulkner contain paragraphs that, if extracted, seem in themselves prose poems—so lively are they in their wordplay, so rich in metaphor. But such writing is exceptional, and the main business of most fiction is to get a story told. An extreme case of a fiction writer who didn't want his prose to sound poetic is Georges Simenon, best known for his mystery novels, who said that whenever he noticed in his manuscript any word or phrase that called attention to itself, he struck it out. That method of writing would never do for a poet, who revels in words and phrases that fix themselves in memory. It is safe to say that, in order to write well about a poem, you have to read it carefully enough to remember at least part of it word for word.

Let's consider three commonly useful approaches to writing about poetry.

EXPLICATING

In an **explication** (literally, "an unfolding") of a poem, a writer explains the entire poem in detail, unraveling any complexities to be found in it. This method is a valuable one in approaching a lyric poem, especially if the poem is rich in complexities (or in suggestions worth rendering explicit). Most poems that you'll ever be asked to explicate are short enough to discuss thoroughly within a limited time; fully to explicate a long and involved work, such as John Milton's epic *Paradise Lost*, might require a lifetime. (To explicate a short passage of Milton's long poem would be a more usual course assignment.)

All the details or suggestions in a poem that a sensitive and intelligent reader might consider, the writer of an explication considers and tries to unfold. These might include allusions, the denotations or connotations of words, the possible meanings of symbols, the effects of certain sounds and rhythms and formal elements (rime schemes, for instance), the sense of any statements that contain irony, and other particulars. Not intent on ripping a poem to pieces, the author of a useful explication instead tries to show how each part contributes to the whole.

An explication is easy to organize. You can start with the first line of the poem and keep working straight on through. An explication should not be confused with a paraphrase. A paraphrase simply puts the words of the poem into other words; it is a sort of translation, useful in getting at the plain prose sense and therefore especially helpful in clarifying a poem's main theme. Perhaps in writing an explication you will wish to do some paraphrasing; but an explication (unlike a paraphrase) does not simply restate: it explains a poem, in great detail.

Here, for example, is a famous poem by Robert Frost, followed by a student's concise explication. (The assignment was to explain whatever in "Design" seemed most essential, in not more than 750 words.)

Robert Frost (1874–1963)*

DESIGN

1936

I found a dimpled spider, fat and white,
On a white heal-all, holding up a moth
Like a white piece of rigid satin cloth—
Assorted characters of death and blight
Mixed ready to begin the morning right,   5
Like the ingredients of a witches' broth—
A snow-drop spider, a flower like a froth,
And dead wings carried like a paper kite.

What had that flower to do with being white,
The wayside blue and innocent heal-all?   10
What brought the kindred spider to that height,
Then steered the white moth thither in the night?
What but design of darkness to appall?—
If design govern in a thing so small.

An Unfolding of Robert Frost's "Design"

"I always wanted to be very observing," Robert Frost once said, after reading his poem "Design" to an audience. Then he added, "But I have always been afraid of my own observations" (Cook 126–27). What could he have observed that could scare him? Let's observe the poem close up.

Starting with the title, "Design," any reader of this poem will find it full of meaning. As Webster's New World Dictionary defines design, the word can denote among other things a plan, or "purpose; intention; aim." Some arguments for the existence of God (I remember from Sunday School) are based on the "argument from design": that because the world shows a systematic order, there must be a Designer who made it. But the word design can also mean "a secret or sinister scheme"—such as we attribute to a "designing person." As we shall see, Frost's poem incorporates all of these meanings. His poem raises the old philosophic question of whether there is a Designer, an evil Designer, or no Designer at all. Frost probably read William James on this question, as a critic has shown convincingly (Poirier 245–50).

Like many other sonnets, the poem is divided into two parts. The first eight lines draw a picture centering on the spider, who at first seems almost jolly. It is dimpled and fat like a baby, or Santa Claus. It stands on a wild flower whose name, heal-all, seems an irony: a heal-all is supposed to cure any disease, but it certainly has no power to restore life to the dead moth. (Later, in line ten, we learn that the heal-all used to be blue. Presumably it has died and become bleached-looking.) In this second line we discover, too, that the spider has hold of another creature. Right away we might feel sorry for the moth, were it not for the simile applied to it in line three: "Like a white piece of rigid satin cloth." Suddenly the moth becomes not a creature but a piece of fabric—lifeless and dead—and yet satin has connotations also beautiful. For me satin, used in rich ceremonial costumes such as coronations gowns and brides' dresses, has a formality and luxury about it. Besides, there is great accuracy in the word: the smooth and slightly plush surface of satin is like the powder-smooth surface of moths' wings. But this "cloth," rigid and white, could be the lining to Dracula's coffin.

In the fifth line an invisible hand enters. The characters are "mixed" like ingredients in an evil potion. Some force doing the mixing is behind the scene. The characters in themselves are innocent enough, but when brought together and concocted, their whiteness and look of rigor mortis are overwhelming. There is something diabolical in the spider's feast. The "morning right" echoes the word rite, a ritual—in this case apparently a Black Mass or a Witches' Sabbath. The simile in line seven ("a flower like a froth") is more ambiguous and harder to describe. A froth is white, foamy, and delicate—something found on a brook in the woods or on a beach after a wave recedes. However, in the natural world, froth also can be ugly: the foam on a dead dog's mouth. The dualism in nature—its beauty and its horror—is there in that one simile.

So far, the poem has portrayed a small, frozen scene, with the dimpled killer holding its victim as innocently as a boy holds a kite. Already, Frost has hinted that Nature may be, as Radcliffe Squires suggests, "nothing but an ash-white plain without love or faith or hope, where ignorant appetites cross by chance" (87). Now, in the last six lines of the sonnet, Frost comes out and directly states his theme. What else could bring these deathly pale, stiff things together "but design of darkness to appall?" The question is clearly rhetorical, meant to be answered, "Why, nothing but that, of course!" I take the next-to-last line to mean, What except a design so dark and sinister that we're appalled by it? "Appall," by the way, is the second pun in the poem: it sounds like a pall or shroud. Steered carries the suggestion of a steering-wheel or rudder that some pilot had to control. Like the word brought, it implies that some Captain charted the paths of spider, heal-all, and moth, so that they arrived together.

Having suggested that the universe is in the hands of that sinister Captain (Fate? the Devil?), Frost adds *final* a note of doubt. The Bible tells us that "His eye is on the sparrow," but at the moment the poet doesn't seem sure. Maybe, he hints, when things in the universe drop below a certain size, they pass completely out of the Designer's notice. When creatures are that little, maybe He doesn't bother to govern them, but lets them run wild. And possibly the same *mindless* idiotic chance is all that governs human lives. Maybe we're not even sinners in the hands of an angry God, but amazingly are nothing but little dice being slung. And that—because it is even more senseless—is the worst suspicion of all.

Works Cited

Cook, Reginald. Robert Frost: A Living Voice. Amherst: U of Massachusetts P, 1974.

Poirier, Richard. Robert Frost: The Work of Knowing. New York: Oxford UP, 1977.

Squires, Radcliffe. The Major Themes of Robert Frost. Ann Arbor: U of Michigan P, 1963.

This excellent paper, while finding something worth unfolding in every line in Frost's poem, does so without seeming mechanical. Notice that, although the student proceeds through the poem from the title to the last line, she takes up points when necessary, in any sequence. In paragraph two, the writer looks ahead to the end of the poem and briefly states its main theme. (She does so in order to relate this theme to the poem's title.) In the third paragraph, she deals with the poem's *later* image of the heal-all, relating it to the first image. Along the way, she comments on the form of the poem ("Like many other sonnets"), on its similes and puns, its denotations and connotations.

Incidentally, this paper demonstrates good use of manuscript form, following the *MLA Handbook*, 3rd ed. Brief references (in parentheses) tell us where the writer found Frost's remarks before an audience, name the critic (Poirier) who showed that Frost had read the philosopher William James, and give page numbers for these sources and for another, a book by Radcliffe Squires. At the end of the paper, a list of these works cited uses abbreviations for *University* and *Press* that the *MLA*

Handbook recommends (but doesn't insist upon). This paper demonstrates, too, how to make final corrections without retyping. In the last paragraph, notice how the student legibly added a word and neatly changed another word by crossing it out and writing a substitute above it. In her next-to-last sentence, the writer clearly strikes out a superfluous letter.

It might seem that to work through a poem line by line is a lockstep task; and yet there can be high excitement in it. Randall Jarrell once wrote an explication of "Design" in which he managed to convey such excitement. In the following passage taken from it, see if you can sense the writer's joy in his work. (Don't, incidentally, feel obliged to compare the quality of your own insights with Jarrell's, nor the quality of your own prose with his. Be fair to yourself: unlike most students, Jarrell had the advantage of being an excellent poet and a gifted critic; besides, he had read and pondered Frost for years before he wrote his essay, and as a teacher he probably had taught "Design" many times.)

> Frost's details are so diabolically good that it seems criminal to leave some unremarked; but notice how *dimpled, fat,* and *white* (all but one; all but one) come from our regular description of any baby; notice how the *heal-all,* because of its name, is the one flower in all the world picked to be the altar for this Devil's Mass; notice how *holding up* the moth brings something ritual and hieratic, a ghostly, ghastly formality, to this priest and its sacrificial victim; notice how terrible to the fingers, how full of the stilling rigor of death, that *white piece of rigid satin cloth* is. And *assorted characters of death and blight* is, like so many things in this poem, sharply ambiguous: *a mixed bunch of actors* or *diverse representative signs.* The tone of the phrase *assorted characters of death and blight* is beautifully developed in the ironic Breakfast-Club-calisthenics, Radio-Kitchen heartiness of *mixed ready to begin the morning right* (which assures us, so unreassuringly, that this isn't any sort of Strindberg *Spook Sonata,* but hard fact), and concludes in the *ingredients* of the witches' broth, giving the soup a sort of cuddly shimmer that the cauldron in *Macbeth* never had; the *broth,* even, is brought to life—we realize that witches' broth *is* broth, to be supped with a long spoon.[1]

Evidently, Jarrell's cultural interests are broad: ranging from August Strindberg's ground-breaking modern drama down to the Breakfast Club (a once-popular radio program that cheerfully exhorted its listeners to march around their tables). And yet breadth of knowledge, however much it deepens and enriches Jarrell's writing, isn't all that he brings to the reading of poetry. For him, an explication isn't a dull plod, but a voyage of discovery. His prose—full of figures of speech (*diabolically good, cuddly shimmer*)—conveys the apparent delight he takes in showing off his findings. Such a joy, of course, can't be acquired deliberately. But it can grow the more you read and study poetry.

[1]From *Poetry and the Age* (New York: Knopf, 1953).

ANALYZING

An **analysis** of a poem, like a news commentator's analysis of a crisis in the Middle East or a chemist's analysis of an unknown fluid, separates its subject into elements as a means to understanding that subject—to see what composes it. Usually, the writer of such an essay singles out one of those elements for attention: "Imagery of Light and Darkness in Frost's 'Design' "; "The Character of Satan in *Paradise Lost.*"

Like explication, analysis can be particularly useful in dealing with a short poem. Unlike explication (which inches through a poem line by line), analysis often suits a long poem too, because it allows the writer to discuss just one manageable element in the poem. A good analysis casts intense light upon a poem from one direction. If you care enough about a poem, and about some perspective on it—its theme, say, or its symbolism, or its singability—writing an analysis can enlighten and give pleasure.

In this book you probably have met a few brief analyses: the discussion of connotations in John Masefield's "Cargoes" (page 561), for instance, or the examination of symbols in T. S. Eliot's "The *Boston Evening Transcript*" (page 702). In fact, most of the discussions in this book are analytic. Temporarily, we have separated the whole art of poetry into elements such as tone, irony, literal meaning, suggestions, imagery, figures of speech, sound, rhythm, and so on. No element of a poem, of course, exists apart from all the other elements. Still, by taking a closer look at particular elements, one at a time, we see them more clearly and more easily study them.

Long analyses of metrical feet, rime schemes, and identations tend to make ponderous reading: such formal and technical elements are perhaps the hardest to discuss engagingly. And yet formal analysis (at least a little of it) can be interesting and illuminating: it can measure the very pulse beat of lines. If you do care about the technical side of poetry, then write about it, by all means. You will probably find it helpful to learn the terms for the various meters, stanzas, fixed forms, and other devices, so that you can summon them to your aid with confidence. Here is a short formal analysis of "Design" by a student who evidently cares for technicalities yet who manages not to be a bore in talking about them. Concentrating on the sonnet form of Frost's poem, the student actually casts light upon the poem in its entirety.

The Design of "Design"

For "Design," the sonnet form has at least two advantages. First, as in most strict *Italian* sonnets, the argument of the poem falls into two parts. In the octave Frost draws his pale still-life of spider, flower, and moth; then in the sestet he contemplates the meaning of it. The sestet deals with a more general idea: the possible existence of a vindictive deity who causes the spider to catch the moth, and no doubt also causes other suffering. Frost weaves his own little web. The unwary reader is led into the poem by its opening story, and pretty soon is struggling with more than he expected. Even the rime scheme, by the way, has something to do with the poem's meaning. The word white ends the first line of the sestet. The same sound is echoed in the rimes that follow. All in all, half the lines in the poem end in an "ite." It seems as if Frost places great weight on the whiteness of his little scene, for the riming words both introduce the term white and keep reminding us of it.

A sonnet has a familiar design, and that is its second big advantage to this particular poem. In a way, writing "Design" as a sonnet almost seems a foxy joke. (I can just imagine Frost chuckling to himself, wondering if anyone will get it.) A sonnet, being a classical form, is an orderly world with certain laws in it. There is ready-made irony in its containing a meditation on whether there is any order in the universe at large. Obviously there's design in back of the poem, but is there any design to insect life, or human life? Whether or not the poet can answer this question (and it seems he can't), at least he discovers an order *while* writing the poem. Actually, that is just what Frost said a poet achieves: "a momentary stay against confusion."[1]

Although design clearly governs in this poem—in "this thing so small"—the design isn't entirely predictable. The poem starts out as an Italian sonnet, with just two riming sounds; then (unlike an Italian sonnet) it keeps the "ite" rimes going. It ends in a couplet, like a Shakespearean sonnet. From these unexpected departures from the pattern of the Italian sonnet announced in the opening lines, I get the impression that Frost's poem is somewhat like the larger universe. It looks perfectly orderly, until you notice the small details in it.

[1]Robert Frost, "The Figure a Poem Makes," preface, Complete Poems of Robert Frost (New York: Holt, 1949) vi.

Unlike the student paper on pages 1493–1495, that documented its references (inside parentheses), "The Design of 'Design' " uses an endnote to cite its one outside source. (In so doing, it follows the form for such notes suggested in the *MLA Handbook, 3rd ed.*) To do so seems sensible here. This writer doesn't need a list of works cited, for such a list might have looked skimpy, like a one-car funeral. (In the endnote, by the way, *Holt* is a short, MLA-recommended contraction for the full name of the publisher: Holt, Rinehart, and Winston, Inc.)

COMPARING AND CONTRASTING

To write a **comparison** of two poems, you place them side by side and point out their likenesses; to write a **contrast,** you point out their differences. If you wish, you can combine the two methods in the same paper. For example, even though you may emphasize similarities you may also call attention to differences, or vice versa.

Such a paper makes most sense if you pair two poems that have much in common. It would be possible to compare William McGonagall's unintentionally comic poem "The Albion Battleship Calamity" with John Milton's profound "Lycidas," but comparison would be difficult, perhaps futile. Though both poems are in English, the two seem hopelessly remote from each other in diction, in tone, in complexity, and in worth.

Having found, however, a couple of poems that throw light on each other, you then go on in your paper to show further, unsuspected resemblances—not just the ones that are obvious (" 'Design' and 'Wing-Spread' are both about bugs"). The interesting resemblances are ones that take thinking to discover. Similarly, you may want to show noteworthy differences—besides those your reader will see without any help.

In comparing two poems, you may be tempted to discuss one of them and be done with it, then spend the latter half of your paper discussing the other. This simple way of organizing an essay can be dangerous if it leads you to keep the two poems in total isolation from each other. The whole idea of such an assignment, of course, is to get you to do some comparing. There is nothing wrong in discussing all of poem A first, then discussing poem B—*if* in discussing B you keep looking back at A. Another procedure is to keep comparing the two poems all the way through your paper—dealing first, let's say, with their themes; then with their metaphors; and finally with their respective merits.

More often than not, a comparison is an analysis: a study of a theme common to two poems, for instance; or of two poets' similar fondness for the myth of Eden. But you also can evaluate poems by comparing and contrasting them: placing them side by side in order to decide which poet deserves the brighter laurels. Here, for example, is a paper that considers "Design" and "Wing-Spread," a poem of Abbie Huston Evans (first printed in 1938, two years later than Frost's poem). By comparing and contrasting the two poems for (1) their language and (2) their themes, this student shows us reasons for his evaluation.

"Wing-Spread" Does a Dip

> The midge spins out to safety
>
> Through the spider's rope;
>
> But the moth, less lucky,
>
> Has to grope.

Mired in glue-like cable   5

See him foundered swing

By the gap he opened

With his wing,

Dusty web enlacing

All that blue and beryl.   10

In a netted universe

Wing-spread is peril.

—Abbie Huston Evans

"Wing-Spread," quoted above, is a good poem, but it is not in the same class
with "Design." Both poets show us a murderous spider and an unlucky moth,
but there are two reasons for Robert Frost's superiority. One is his more suggestive use of language, the other is his more memorable theme.

Let's start with language. "Design" is full of words and phrases rich in suggestions. "Wing-Spread," by comparison, contains few. To take just one example, Frost's "dimpled spider, fat and white" is certainly a more suggestive
description. Actually, Evans doesn't describe her spider; she just says, "the
spider's rope." (I have to hand Evans the palm for showing us the spider and
moth in action. In Frost's view, they are dead and petrified—but I guess that is
the impression he is after.) In "Design," the spider's dimples show that it is like
a chubby little kid, who further turns out to be a kite-flier. This seems an odd,
almost freaky way to look at a spider. I find it more refreshing than Evans's
view (although I like her word cable, suggesting that the spider's web is a kind
of suspension bridge). Frost's word-choice—his harping on white—paints a more
striking scene than Evans's slightly vague "All that blue and beryl." Except for
her personification of the moth in her second stanza, Evans doesn't go in for
any figures of speech, and even that one isn't a clear personification—she simply
gives the moth a sex by referring to it as "him." Frost's striking metaphors, similes, and puns (right, appall) show him, as usual, to be a master of figures of
speech. He calls the moth's wings "satin cloth" and "a paper kite"; Evans just
refers in line 8 to a moth's wing. As far as the language of the two poems goes,
you might as well compare a vase full with flowers and a single flower stuck

in a vase. (That is a poor metaphor, since Frost's poem contains only one flower, but I hope you will know what I mean.)

In fairness to Evans, I would say that she picks a pretty good solitary flower. And her poem has powerful sounds: short lines with the riming words coming at us again and again very frequently. In theme, however, "Wing-Spread" seems much more narrow than "Design." The first time I read Evans's poem all I felt was: Ho hum, the moth too was wide and got stuck. The second time I read it, I figured that she is saying something with a universal application. This comes out in line 11, in "a netted universe." That is the most interesting phrase in her poem, one that you can think about. Netted makes me imagine the universe as being full of nets rigged by someone who is fishing for us. Maybe, like Frost, Evans sees an evil plan operating. She does not, though, investigate it. She says that the midge escapes because it is tiny. On the other hand, things with wide wing-spreads get stuck. Her theme as I read it is, "Be small and inconspicuous if you want to survive," or maybe, "Isn't it too bad that in this world the big beautiful types crack up and die, while the miserable little puny punks keep sailing?" Now, that is a valuable idea. I have often thought that very same thing myself. But Frost's closing note ("If design govern in a thing so small") is really devastating, because it raises a huge uncertainty. "Wing-Spread" leaves us with not much besides a moth stuck in a web, and a moral. In both language and theme, "Design" climbs to a higher altitude.

HOW TO QUOTE A POEM

Preparing to discuss a short poem, it is a good idea to emulate the student who wrote on "Wing-Spread" and to quote the whole text of poem at the beginning of your paper, with its lines numbered. Then you can refer to it with ease, and your instructor, without having to juggle a book, can follow you.

Quoted to illustrate some point, memorable lines can add interest to your paper, and good commentators on poetry tend to be apt quoters, helping their readers to experience a word, a phrase, a line, or a passage that otherwise might be neglected. However, to quote from poetry is slightly more awkward than to quote from prose. There are lines to think about—important and meaningful units whose shape you will need to preserve. If you are quoting more than a couple of lines, it is good policy to arrange your quotation just as its lines occur in the poem, white space and all:

At the outset, the poet tells us of his discovery of

<blockquote>
a dimpled spider, fat and white,

On a white heal-all, holding up a moth

Like a white piece of rigid satin cloth—
</blockquote>

and implies that the small killer is both childlike and sinister.

But if you are quoting less than two lines of verse, it would seem wasteful of paper to write:

<blockquote>
The color white preoccupies Frost. The spider is

fat and white,

On a white heal-all

and even the victim moth is pale, too.
</blockquote>

In such a case, it saves space to transform Frost's line arrangement into prose:

<blockquote>
The color white preoccupies Frost. The spider is "fat and white,/On a white

heal-all"—and even the victim moth is pale, too.
</blockquote>

Here, a diagonal (/) indicates the writer's respect for where the poet's lines begin and end. Some writers prefer to note line-breaks without diagonals, just by keeping the initial capital letter of a line (if there is any): "fat and white, On a white heal-all . . . . " Incidentally, the ellipsis (. . .) in that last remark indicates that words are omitted from the end of Frost's sentence; the fourth dot is a period. Some writers—meticulous souls—also stick in an ellipsis at the *beginning* of a quotation, if they're leaving out words from the beginning of a sentence in the original:

<blockquote>
The color white preoccupies Frost in his description of the spider " . . . fat and

white,/On a white heal-all . . . . "
</blockquote>

Surely there's no need for an initial ellipsis, though, if you begin quoting at the beginning of a sentence. No need for a final ellipsis, either, if your quotation goes right to the end of a sentence in the original. If it is obvious that only a phrase is being quoted, no need for an ellipsis in any case:

<blockquote>
The speaker says he "found a dimpled spider" and he goes on to portray it as

a kite-flying boy.
</blockquote>

If you leave out whole lines, indicate the omission by an ellipsis all by itself on a line:

<blockquote>
The midge spins out to safety

Through the spider's rope;

. . .

In a netted universe

Wing-spread is peril.
</blockquote>

BEFORE YOU BEGIN

Ready at last to write, you will have spent considerable time in reading, thinking, and feeling. After having chosen your topic, you probably will have taken a further look at the poem or poems you have picked, letting further thoughts and feelings come to you. The quality of your paper will depend, above all, upon the quality of your readiness to write.

Exploring a poem, a sensitive writer handles it with care and affection as though it were a living animal, and, done with it, leaves it still alive. The unfeeling writer, on the other hand, disassembles the poem in a dull, mechanical way, like someone with a blunt ax filling an order for one horse-skeleton. Again, to write well is a matter of engaging your feelings. Writing to a deadline, on an assigned topic, you easily can sink into a drab, workaday style, especially if you regard the poet as some uninspired builder of chicken-coops who hammers themes and images into place, and then slaps the whole thing with a coat of words. Certain expressions, if you lean on them habitually, may tempt you to think of the poet in that way. Here, for instance, is a discussion—by a plodding writer—of Robert Frost's poem.

> The symbols Frost uses in "Design" are very successful. Frost makes the spider stand for Nature. He wants us to see Nature as blind and cruel. He also employs good sounds. He uses a lot of i's because he is trying to make you think of falling rain.

(Underscored words are worth questioning.) What's wrong with that comment? While understandable, the words *uses* and *employs* seem to lead the writer to see Frost only as a conscious tool-manipulator. To be sure, Frost in a sense "uses" symbols, but did he grab hold of them and lay them into his poem? For all we know, perhaps the symbols arrived quite unbidden and used the poet. To write a good poem, Frost maintained, a poet himself has to be surprised. (How, by the way, can we hope to know what a poet *wants* to do? And there isn't much point in saying that the poet is *trying to* do something. He has already done it if he has written a good poem.) At least, it is likely that Frost didn't plan to fulfill a certain quota of i-sounds. Writing his poem, not by following a blueprint but probably by bringing it slowly to the surface of his mind (like Elizabeth Bishop's hooked fish), Frost no doubt had enough to do without trying to engineer the reactions of his possible audience. Like all true symbols, Frost's spider doesn't *stand for* anything. The writer would be closer to the truth to say that the spider *suggests* or *reminds us* of Nature or of certain forces in the natural world. (Symbols just hint, they don't indicate.)

After the student discussed the paper in a conference, he rewrote the first two sentences like this:

> The symbols in Frost's "Design" are highly effective. The spider, for instance, suggests the blindness and cruelty of Nature. Frost's word-sounds, too, are part of the meaning of his poem, for the i's remind the reader of falling rain.

Not every reader of "Design" will hear rain falling, but the student's revision probably comes closer to describing the experience of the poem most of us know.

In writing about poetry, an occasional note of self-doubt can be useful: now and then a *perhaps* or a *possibly*, an *it seems* or a modest *I suppose*. Such expressions may seem timid shilly-shallying, but at least they keep the writer from thinking, "I know all there is to know about this poem."

Facing the showdown with your empty sheaf of paper, however, you can't worry forever about your critical vocabulary. To do so is to risk the fate of the centipede in a bit of comic verse, who was running along efficiently until someone asked, "Pray, which leg comes after which?," whereupon "He lay distracted in a ditch/Considering how to run." It is a safe bet that your instructor is human. Your main task as a writer is to communicate to another human being your sensitive reading of a poem.

SUGGESTIONS FOR WRITING

TOPICS FOR BRIEF PAPERS *(250–500 words)*

1. Write a concise *explication* of a short poem of your choice, or one suggested by your instructor. In a paper this brief, probably you won't have room to explain everything in the poem; explain what you think most needs explaining. (An illustration of one such explication appears on page 1493.)
2. Write an *analysis* of a short poem, first deciding which one of its elements to deal with. (An illustration of such an analysis appears on page 1497.) For examples, here are a few specific topics:

   "Kinds of Irony in Hardy's 'The Workbox'"

   "The Attitude of the Speaker in Marvell's 'To His Coy Mistress'"

   "The Theme of Pastan's 'Ethics'"

   "An Extended Metaphor in Yeats's 'Long-legged Fly.'" (Explain the one main comparison that the poem makes and show how the whole poem makes it. Other likely possibilities for a paper on extended metaphor: Baca's "Spliced Wire," Chappell's "Skin Flick," Dickinson's "Because I could not stop for Death," Dove's "Daystar," Frost's "The Silken Tent," Lowell's "Skunk Hour," Rich's "Aunt Jennifer's Tigers.")

   "The Rhythms of Plath's 'Daddy'"

   (To locate any of these poems, see the Index to Authors, Titles, and Quotations at the back of this book.)
3. Select a poem in which the main speaker is a character who for any reason interests you. You might consider, for instance, Betjeman's "In Westminster Abbey," Browning's "Soliloquy of the Spanish Cloister," Dove's "Daystar," or Eliot's "Love Song of J. Alfred Prufrock." Then write a brief profile of this character, drawing only on what the poem tells you (or reveals). What is the character's approximate age? Situation in life? Attitude toward self? Attitude toward others? General personality? Do you find this character admirable?
4. Although each of these poems tells a story, what happens in the poem isn't necessarily obvious: Cummings's "anyone lived in a pretty how town," Eliot's "Love Song of J. Alfred Prufrock," Digges's "For *The Daughters of Hannah* Bible Class . . . ," Stafford's "At the Klamath Berry Festival," Winters's "At the San Francisco Airport," James Wright's "A Blessing." Choose one of these poems and in a paragraph sum up what you think hap-

pens in it. Then in a second paragraph ask yourself: what, *besides* the element of story, did you consider in order to understand the poem?

5. Think of someone you know (or someone you can imagine) whose attitude toward poetry in general is dislike. Suggest a poem for that person to read—a poem that you like—and, addressing your skeptical reader, point out whatever you find to enjoy in it that you think the skeptic just might enjoy too.

6. Keeping in mind what Coleridge and Jarrell have to say about "obscurity" in poetry (see their statements in Criticism: On Poetry, pages 940 and 946), write a brief defense of some poem you like against the possible charge that it is obscure.

TOPICS FOR MORE EXTENSIVE PAPERS (600–1,000 *words*)

1. Write an explication of a poem short enough for you to work though line by line—for instance, Emily Dickinson's "My Life had stood—a loaded Gun" or MacLeish's "The End of the World." As if offering your reading experience to a friend who hadn't read the poem before, try to point out all the leading difficulties you encountered, and set forth in detail your understanding of any lines that contain such difficulties.

2. Write an explication of a longer poem—for instance, Eliot's "Love Song of J. Alfred Prufrock," Hardy's "Convergence of the Twain," Rich's "Trying to Talk with a Man," or Stevens's "Peter Quince at the Clavier." Although you will not be able to go through every line of the poem, explain what you think most needs explaining.

3. In this book, you will find from five to twelve poems by each of these poets: Blake, Dickinson, Donne, Eliot, Frost, Hardy, Hopkins, Housman, Langston Hughes, Keats, Roethke, Shakespeare, Stevens, Tennyson, Whitman, William Carlos Williams, Wordsworth, Wilbur, and Yeats; and multiple selections for many more. (See Index to Authors, Titles, and Quotations.) After you read a few poems by a poet who interests you, write an analysis of *more than one* of the poet's poems. To do this, you will need to select just one characteristic theme (or other element) to deal with—something typical of the poet's work, not found only in a single poem. Here are a few specific topics for such an analysis:

"What Angers William Blake? A Look at Three Poems of Protest"

"How Emily Dickinson's Lyrics Resemble Hymns"

"The Humor of Robert Frost"

"Folk Elements in the Poetry of Langston Hughes"

"John Keats's Sensuous Imagery"

"The Vocabulary of Music in Poems of Wallace Stevens"

"Non-free Verse: Patterns of Sound in Three Poems of William Carlos Williams"

4. Compare and contrast two poems in order to evaluate them: which is more satisfying and effective poetry? To make a meaningful comparison, be sure to choose two poems that genuinely have much in common: perhaps a similar theme or subject. (For an illustration of such a paper, see the one given in this chapter. For suggestions of poems to compare, see the Anthology.)

5. Evaluate by the method of comparison two versions of a poem: early and late drafts, perhaps, or two translations from another language. For parallel versions to work on, see Chapter Twenty-six, "Alternatives."

6. If the previous topic appeals to you, consider this. In 1912, twenty-four years before he printed "Design," Robert Frost sent a correspondent this early version:

IN WHITE

A dented spider like a snow drop white
On a white Heal-all, holding up a moth
Like a white piece of lifeless satin cloth—
Saw ever curious eye so strange a sight?—
Portent in little, assorted death and blight   5
Like ingredients of a witches' broth?—
The beady spider, the flower like a froth,
And the moth carried like a paper kite.

What had that flower to do with being white,
The blue prunella every child's delight.   10
What brought the kindred spider to that height?
(Make we no thesis of the miller's plight.)
What but design of darkness and of night?
Design, design! Do I use the word aright?

Compare "In White" with "Design." In what respects is the finished poem superior?

TOPICS FOR LONG PAPERS (1,500 words or more)

1. Write a line-by-line explication of a poem rich in matters to explain, or a longer poem that offers ample difficulty. While relatively short, Donne's "A Valediction: Forbidding Mourning" or Hopkins's "The Windhover" are poems that will take a good bit of time to explicate; but even a short, apparently simple poem such as Frost's "Stopping by Woods on a Snowy Evening" can provide more than enough to explicate thoughtfully in a longer paper.

2. Write an analysis of the work of one poet (as suggested above, in the third topic for more extensive papers) in which you go beyond this book to read an entire collection of that poet's work.

3. Write an analysis of a certain theme (or other element) that you find in the work of two or more poets. It is probable that in your conclusion you will want to set the poets' work side by side, comparing or contrasting it, and perhaps making some evaluation. Sample topics:

   "Langston Hughes, Gwendolyn Brooks, and Dudley Randall as Prophets of Social Change"

   "What It Is to Be a Woman: The Special Knowledge of Sylvia Plath, Anne Sexton, and Adrienne Rich"

   "Language of Science in Some Poems of Eberhart, Merrill, and Ammons"

4. Taking a passage from "Criticism: On Poetry," see what light it will cast on a poem that interests you. You might test Gray's "Elegy" by Poe's dictum that there is no such thing as a long poem. (Does the "Elegy" flag in intensity?) Or try reading several poems of Robert Frost, looking for the "sound of sense" (which Frost explains in his letter to John Bartlett on page 942.)

Writing a Poem

HOW DOES A POEM BEGIN?

After you have read much poetry and (as Keats said) "traveled in the realms of gold," it is natural to want to write a poem. And why shouldn't you? Whether or not you aspire ever to publish your work, the attempt itself offers profound satisfactions; and it offers, too, a way to become a finer reader of poetry. To learn how to carry a football may not equip you to play for the Oilers, but it may help you appreciate the timing and skill of an Earl Campbell. In a roughly similar way, you may find yourself better able to perceive the artistry of an excellent sonnet from having written a sonnet of your own—even a merely acceptable one.

Poems, like new comets, tend to arrive mysteriously. Sometimes they go burning right past a serious, hard-working poet only to dawn, as though by accident, upon a madman, an idler, or a child. This may be why no one has ever devised a formula for synthesizing memorable poems. "A good poet," said Randall Jarrell, "is someone who manages, in a lifetime of standing out in thunderstorms, to be struck by lightning five or six times." In this view, poetic inspiration, like grace, is something beyond human control. Still, most of the best lightning bolts tend to strike those poets who keep waiting patiently, writing and rewriting and discarding, keeping their lightning rods lifted as they work. As Louis Pasteur said—speaking of scientists—"Chance favors the prepared mind."

Teachers of creative writing do not promise to create poets. All they can try to create is an atmosphere in which good poems may be written, given a hearing, and perhaps rendered stronger and more concise. As a member of a class or writing workshop, you have certain advantages. At least, you have companions in your struggles and chagrins. You may even find a sympathetic audience.

Even though the writing of poetry cannot be taught with great efficiency, some knowledge useful to poets can be imparted. What does a poet need to know? Half-jokingly, W. H. Auden once proposed a College for Bards with this curriculum:

1. In addition to English, at least one ancient language, probably Greek or Hebrew, and two modern languages would be required.
2. Thousands of lines of poetry in these languages would be learned by heart.
3. The library would contain no books of literary criticism, and the only critical exercise required of students would be the writing of parodies.
4. Courses in prosody, rhetoric, and comparative philology would be required of all students, and every student would have to select three courses out of courses in mathematics, natural history, geology, meteorology, archeology, mythology, liturgics, and cooking.
5. Every student would be required to look after a domestic animal and cultivate a garden plot.[1]

Auden, though he pokes fun at the notion of systematically training poets, makes constructive suggestions. He would have the aspiring poet study languages and something besides literature, and store up some poetry in memory. William Butler Yeats, too, thought that poets learn mainly by reading the work of other poets. There can be no "singing school" except the study of great poems—monuments, Yeats calls them, of the human soul's magnificence. (See "Sailing to Byzantium," page 753.)

Begin by reading. Don't limit yourself to poems assigned for college credit. Until you explore poetry more widely and roam around in it, how will you know what kind you most care to write? Pick up current poetry magazines. Read an **anthology** of contemporary poets or a **collection** of poems by a contemporary. (An *anthology* represents the work of many poets; a *collection* gathers a single poet's poems.) Crack open a survey of older literature. Browse in bookshops. Lift some dust from library stacks. Read methodically or read by whim. Whatever poetry you come to love may nourish a poem you will write.

As you read, make your own personal, selective anthology. Don't let in a poem of Tennyson just because your instructor thinks it is great stuff, let it in only because you cherish it. Instead of just banging out Xerox copies of the poems you admire, you would do well to copy them by hand into a book with blank pages, or to type them on looseleaf notebook paper. By doing so, you'll pay close attention to them, and you'll grow accustomed to seeing excellent poetry (no matter whose) flow from your fingertips. If you would please the ghost of W. H. Auden, you'll say aloud the poems from your personal anthology until you know them by heart. The suggestion that you memorize poetry may strike you as boring, but its benefits may be surprising. You just might transfer some poetry from your head down to your viscera and into your bones. Then, the music of words, especially their rhythms, will become part of you. Your own work may well prove richer for knowing poetry on a deeper level than that of the mind and eye.

It would save time, of course, not to read anything, but simply to look into your heart and write. And yet, because poetry is (among other things) an art of

[1]"The Poet and the City" in *The Dyer's Hand* (New York: Random, 1962).

choosing words and arranging them, the usual result of just looking into one's heart and writing is a lot of words hastily chosen and stodgily arranged. "But," the novice might protest, "why should I read Keats and Yeats and the Beats? I don't want to be influenced by all those old birds—I want to be myself!" Excellent poets, though they may be bundles of influences, are still themselves. In truth, when you are starting out, you can learn a great deal by deliberately imitating the work of any excellent poets you deeply love. Spenser studied Chaucer; Keats studied Spenser; Tennyson and Stevens studied Keats. (Auden said he began by imitating Thomas Hardy, because Hardy's work looked imitable.) If you borrow any mannerisms from your models, they will probably disappear as soon as you gain in confidence. Although the novice poet is sometimes urged, "Discover your own voice!" such advice can lead to a painful self-consciousness. Your own voice is probably the last thing to concern yourself about. Certainly it would be a mistake to settle on any one particular voice or style before you have practiced singing in many registers. Imitate whomever you choose, and see what you can do best. Try a Levertovian lyric or a Miltonic meditation. Let out a Whitmanic yawp. Express what you feel in the strongest words you can find, and your voice will take care of itself. It will be your own, in the end, though Donne or Emily Dickinson went into the training of it.

From your reading, you will probably notice that long-lasting poems—those that remain in print after a century or more—tend to express powerful feelings. "In poetry," as Ezra Pound observed, "only emotion endures." Certainly, to name only one instance, the ballad of "Edward" remains vital after hundreds of years, still brimming with sorrow and hate. Asked by a student, "What shall I write about?" Karl Shapiro replied, "Praise something—anything!"—and that is good advice. Although it is possible to write a memorable poem out of piddling, nugatory feelings (or a poem about being unable to feel anything, like Eliot's "The *Boston Evening Transcript*"), a poem written out of love, or loathing, is more likely to radiate energy. (One of John Donne's most energetic poems begins with the impassioned outburst, "For God's sake hold your tongue, and let me love.")

Very often, beginning to write a poem is a process of discovering, and opening, some deep resource of feeling. You have to search within yourself; no map can lead you to such a discovery. Whatever quickens your imagination is your resource. It may be a dream or a nightmare. It may be the memory of some moving experience. At times, your resource may lie in some unexpected place. You might want to write—as Whitman, Keats, and Elizabeth Bishop did—a deeply felt poem about a spider, a piece of ancient pottery, or a filling station.

This is not to say that you can mechanically cram your past life into your poetry-mill and grind it into poems. Although poems may rise from your experience, sometimes in becoming a poem the experience will "suffer a sea change / Into something rich and strange" (like the drowned man's bones in the song in Shakespeare's *Tempest*). You have to leave room for your imagination freely to operate, to transform the raw matter of experience however it will. You will probably limit and constrict your poetry if you regard it as a diary to be kept—as a complete and faithful transcript of what happens to you. Your imagination may yearn to improve upon the literal truth for the sake of the truth of art. Inevitably, a successful poem (even one that sticks to the facts) will be more than journalism. It will be, as Robert Frost memorably described it, "a performance in words."

If it takes feelings to write a memorable poem, yet in poetry the hardest thing to do is to talk about those feelings directly. Readers grow weary of poets who bleat, "Woe is me! I'm so lonely! How miserably sterile I feel!" But probably no reader has ever failed to sympathize with the poet who begins, "Western wind, when wilt thou blow, / The small rain down can rain?" Such a poem does not *discuss* the poet's feelings. It utters them, and it points to objects in the world that invite the reader to feel similarly.

Drink or drugs, by the way, seem of little aid to poets in search of inspiration. The trouble with trying to write while stoned (according to one contemporary) is that poetry may seem too far below you to be worth noticing. Coleridge's visionary "Kubla Khan," though possibly inspired by an opium dream, was written by daylight, after the poet for years had stored his mind with descriptions of exotic landscapes in accounts of travel and exploration. In this regard, the poet Robert Wallace has made an excellent suggestion: "Get high on what you write." Some poets try to prod the unconscious by natural means. Donald Hall has testified to the advantages of rising before dawn and writing poetry when thoughts seem fruitful, being close to dream. (However, some writers who try Hall's method find themselves staring sleepily at blank paper.)

Novice poets sometimes begin a poem in a language clouded not with dream, but with gaseous abstraction:

> Indifferent cosmos!
> O ye cryptic force!
> Don't you notice our pitiful human
> Agonies and sufferings?
> Are we mere tools of careless, crushing Fate?

Far better for a poet to open his eyes and begin with whatever small object he sees:

> I found a dimpled spider, fat and white,
> On a white heal-all, holding up a moth . . .

Unlike the novice's complaint about the indifference of the universe, Robert Frost's lines on a similar theme are many times more inviting—more striking, more definite.

Poetry, then, tends to inhere not in abstract editorial stands, but in particulars. William Carlos Williams's brief poem about eating the plums in the ice box (page 535) may not be great, but it is human, and hard to forget. Sources of poems may lie before your eyes. Although poets can learn from reading other poets' work, they can also learn from the testimony of their own senses. In the best poems, as the following poem reminds us, there is always a quality that cannot be distilled from schools and libraries: a freshness that comes only from contact with the living world.

Frederick Morgan (b. 1922)

THE MASTER   1982

When Han Kan was summoned
to the imperial capital
it was suggested he sit at the feet of
the illustrious senior court painter
to learn from him the refinements of the art.   5

"No, thank you," he replied,
"I shall apprentice myself to the stables."

And he installed himself and his brushes amid the dung and the flies,
and studied the horses—their bodies' keen alertness—
eye-sparkle of one, another's sensitive stance,   10
the way a third moved graceful in his bulk—
and painted at last the emperor's favorite,
the charger named "Nightshining White,"

whose likeness after centuries still dazzles.

The advice of W. Somerset Maugham to aspiring novelists may be useful to poets,
too: Keep a notebook of memorable things you observe, of revealing bits of conversation you overhear. Jot them down for no purpose except to gain skill in recording them. Don't feel duty-bound to work this material into anything you write.
It will serve its purpose, even though none of it proves of any further use to you.

All right, then, how is your poem to begin? Some poets begin with something to say, then strive for the best way of saying it. Others start with nothing
much in mind. In the grip of strong but perhaps woolly and indefinite feelings,
they play around with words until they discover to their surprise that they have
said something. Evidently, a poem can arise from any adequate provocation.
T. S. Eliot, speaking of the habits of poets in general, but probably referring to his
own, said that at times a rhythm will begin to course through a poet's mind even
before there are words to embody it. Some poets begin from a memorable image;
Ezra Pound said he began writing "In a Station of the Metro" from being haunted
by a glimpse of a woman's face. Following still another procedure, Dylan Thomas
and many other poets have taken some promising line or phrase that swam to
mind, and without knowing where it might lead, have trustingly gone on with
it. Clearly, what matters isn't whether you begin with an idea or an emotion, a
rhythm or an image, a phrase or a line. What matters is that, somehow, you begin.

Plunge in and blunder about. Why be afraid of a blank sheet of paper? You're
writing only a first draft. No one is judging you. True poets, as they start to write
a poem, don't worry whether a reader will find it admirable. They are too busy
finding the words for an idea (or emotion, or rhythm) before it can get away. If
you begin to write in a state of high excitement, by all means keep going until
you simmer down. Let the words flow. Are some of them not the right ones? Have

you misspelled something? No matter, you can make repairs later. Go on with your task and, whatever you do, don't stop to congratulate yourself on your splendid workmanship, or to contemplate the poetic process. The point may be expressed in this "Ars Poetica," or poem about how poetry is written:

The goose that laid the golden egg
Died looking up its crotch
To find out how its sphincter worked.
Would you lay well? Don't watch.

Later on, of course, you will want to examine your first draft critically; but for now, write as though you were divinely inspired and sustained. When you revise and try to amend your faults, you can view yourself as the lowest sinner. When you write a first draft, you are (with any luck) bringing something out of obscure depths, raising it to the surface. It may mean more than you consciously know. If you are going ahead blindly—that is, if you have begun to write without any burning idea in mind—let the poem choose its own direction. See where it wants to go. Be reluctant to bark orders to it.

A quite different method of composition, which some poets find fruitful, is to compose a poem entirely in the mind, revolving it around and around, saying it over to oneself and trying to perfect it before setting it down on paper. The result tends to have a certain seamless consistency. This method, though, will probably work only for poets who write short poems in rime and meter—devices that help to hold a poem in the mind—or for those with excellent memories.

In a first draft, it is usually a good idea to write everything out in great detail, even at the risk of driveling. If, when you revise, you discover that changes are necessary, it is generally easier to delete than to amplify. A common reason for failure—for the poem that nobody knows what to make of, or feel any positive reaction toward—is mistakenly to assume that the reader is as thoroughly grounded in the facts behind the poem as the poet is. Sometimes, however, a reader will fail to grasp a poem because some vital bit of knowledge still lies within the poet's mind, folded like a green bud. In your first draft, spell out the background of the poem. Define its setting, flesh out any people in it. Show us how they relate to one another, and why they behave the way they do. Perhaps you will set down a lot of unnecessary explanation, but when you revise, you will then have all the matter arrayed before you, and you can easily see what to cut, or to retain.

Special challenges face anyone who writes a poem in meter and rime. Most students who attempt a traditionally formal poem, such as a ballad or a sonnet, quickly discover that to write skillfully in meter and rime is difficult. Thwarted by the requirements of strict form, they feel hindered from saying what they want to say. "This straitjacket isn't for me," they conclude hastily.

True, writing a poem in rime is at first an odd and unsettling experience. It is like walking blindfolded down a dark road with your hand in the hand of an inexorable guide. With the conscious, lighted portion of your mind, you may want to express some idea. But a line that ends in *year* must be followed by another ending in *atmosphere, beer, bier, bombardier, cashier, deer, friction-gear, frontier,* or some other word that probably would not have occurred if the rime scheme had not suggested it. As Rolfe Humphries once pointed out, rime sometimes "makes you think of better things than you would all by yourself." Far from being a coldly rational process of filling a form with wordage, to write a riming poem is to pit yourself against (or to enter into a playful relationship with) some of the wildest and most chaotic forces of the unconscious.

Learn to write a decent poem in rimed stanzas, and you will have at your fingertips certain skills useful in writing poems of any kind. You will know, for instance, how to condense a thought to its gist, from having wrestled with metrical lines that allow you only so many syllables. In revising and finishing your poem, you will become an old hand at replacing stumbling words and phrases with rhythmic ones, at choosing words for their sounds as well as their senses. This won't be easy. Although the iambic rhythm is native to English, learning to speak in it with ease and grace is almost like learning a foreign language. Alexander Pope's observation remains accurate:

> True ease in writing comes from art, not chance,
> As those move easiest who have learned to dance.

With practice, the day will come when a rime or a metrical line will spring to your lips almost thoughtlessly. And then, even if you decide to write poetry in *open* forms, you will do so from choice, not from inability to do otherwise. Proponents of closed form or open form sometimes assume that their favorite kind of form is intrinsically superior; but in truth the form of an excellent poem, whether open or closed, is whatever the poem requires. The poet's task is to discover it.

Whatever your formal preference, it is probably a mistake to try to plan out the direction of your poetic career and then grimly oblige yourself to go in it. Better to write a hundred poems and place them in a row, and see where they have taken you. Your life will shape what you write and the words you write in. Richard Hugo, speaking hyperbolically, has argued that the study of poetry writing fulfills a unique function: "Creative writing is the last class you can go to where your life as an individual is important."[2] Professors of mathematics, natural history, and geology might well argue that individual lives matter in their disciplines, too; but Hugo is surely right in at least one regard. Writing a poem calls for a kind of knowledge that only a poet can provide.

By the way, if a poem doesn't come to you all in one sitting, don't despair. Forget about it for a while. It may need time to gather its forces. Many poets carefully save their fragments: lines and passages that arrive easily, but which do not immediately want to go anywhere. In dry seasons, when inspiration is scarce, they can look back over their notebooks, and sometimes a fragment will spring to life at last and grow into an entire poem. Try this and see if you have any luck with it. For many, being a poet is like being a beggar: like standing with outstretched bowl by the side of a road, hoping for charity. Thankful poets keep whatever a passing Muse may throw, whether it is a Brasher doubloon or only a bent bottlecap.

---

[2]Quoted by Harriet Heyman, "Eleven American Poets," *Life* (Apr. 1981), 89.

ON BLOTTING OUT LINES

Your first draft is done, and the excitement of writing it has cooled. Your next step is to take a step back from it.

A hard but necessary part of being a poet is to try to see your work through a reader's eyes. How to reread it with detachment? The advice of the Roman poet Horace—to put aside a poem for nine years—may seem too discouraging. At least, you can put your poem aside for a week, or even overnight. You may then take a more nearly objective look at it. To help distance yourself from it, try reading it aloud—at least to yourself. Friends may be asked for their criticism, but it is a rare friend who is also a competent critic of poetry. Probably it is best to try to cultivate your own faculties for tough and demanding self-criticism.

Told that his friend Shakespeare in writing his plays never blotted out a line, Ben Jonson wished he had blotted a thousand. (Scholars, by the way, think that even Shakespeare blotted many lines.) Although there is a school of thought that holds for total spontaneity in writing and for leaving words just the way they land on a page, most poets probably feel that second thoughts, too, can be spontaneous, and often more memorable. If you regard your first draft as holy writ and refuse to make any changes in it, you may be preserving a work of genius, but more probably you will be passing up your chance to write a good poem. Poets usually don't mind revision; in fact, they find the task fascinating. "What happiness!" exclaimed Yeats, in a letter to a friend, on facing months of demanding rewriting. (It was Yeats, incidentally, who pointed out that, no less than the original act of writing a poem, the act of revision may be inspired.) A contemporary poet, James Dickey, says he writes a poem over and over in many ways. "After I've tried every possible way I can think of," he explains, "I finally get maybe not absolutely the right poem, but the poem that is less wrong than the others."[3]

Is there not a danger that much revision will drain the life out of a poem—or cause it to become ornate and needlessly complicated? Perhaps; but more often, the poem that seems beautifully simple, as if casually dropped from the lips, is the result of hard work; while the poem that the poet didn't retouch makes difficult reading. As you can tell from the two versions Yeats made of his "Old Pensioner," the one written a half-century later, far from lacking in life, seems the more youthful and spontaneous. (For this and other illustrations of poets' revisions, see pages 727–731.)

Working on your second draft, you have the leisure to look up spellings and to verify information. For the poet who is stuck for a rime, a riming dictionary will suggest some likely—and some outlandish—possibilities. When in such a fix, you will probably do better to proceed down the alphabet (*air, bear, bare, care, dare* . . .) and discover a rime among common words you know already. Rimes will strike your reader as reached-for and strange if you enlist them from far beyond your vocabulary.

---

[3]*Self-Interviews*, edited by Barbara and James Reiss (New York: Doubleday, 1970) 64.

Some poets make a typewritten first draft, then revise in longhand. When additions, deletions, and substitutions accumulate and the page becomes too cross-hatched to decipher, they type a fresh version (keeping the old version just in case they botch the revision and want to go back to the original and start over). Some poets—Richard Wilbur is one—prefer to keep working on a single poem till it is done; others simultaneously revise many poems, going around and making fresh moves like a chess master playing all comers.

In your first draft, when you were trying to include everything essential, you could allow yourself a multitude of words. But in revising and striving for concision, you have to select what is essential and decide what to leave out. Ask yourself whether every line—every word—deserves the room it occupies. Does it *do* anything? To decide, imagine your poem without the word or line. Begin your inspection with your opening lines. Are they valuable, or do they only delay the reader's entry into something more essential? What if, instead, the poem began with some line that now comes later? Opening lines, of course, don't have to be sensational, but there is much to be said for a beginning that stops the reader in his tracks and hangs on to him:

You do not do, you do not do
Any more, black shoe
In which I have lived like a foot . . .

(To quote Sylvia Plath's brilliant opening to "Daddy.") Samuel Johnson, that down-to-earth critic, insisted that a writer's first duty is to excite the reader of his work "to *read it through*," and to that purpose it helps to be interesting. Don't be afraid to be obvious. Go ahead and say, if necessary, "I started Early—Took my Dog—/And visited the Sea," or whatever will begin a story or clearly set forth a situation. Excellent poems may be clear and yet be profound—like bodies of water.

Here are some other questions to ask yourself while you revise:

1. Does this poem express what I feel? Does it claim to feel more than I do—that is, is it sentimental? Or does it hang back, afraid to declare itself? (If it does, see if you can persuade the feelings out into the open.) The advice of W. D. Snodgrass is worth remembering:

Our only hope as artists is to continually ask ourselves, "Am I writing what I *really* think? Not what is acceptable; not what my favorite intellectual would think in this situation; not what I wish I felt. Only what I cannot help thinking."[4]

2. Somewhere in its first half-dozen lines, does the poem offer the reader any temptation to go on reading? If so, something will have been begun: perhaps a story, dramatic situation, metaphor, or intriguing perplexity. To recognize it, you will need to put yourself into the reader's seat. One veteran teacher of poetry-writing, John Ciardi, placed great weight on engaging a reader early. Ciardi some-

---

[4]"Finding a Poem," In *Radical Pursuit* (New York: Harper, 1974) 32.

times penciled a line underneath the line in the poem at which, out of boredom or disgust, he quit reading.

3. Is there anything in my poem that doesn't make sense to me? (*Careful! Such a difficulty may not be a fault!*) Does the difficulty come in stating something I feel to be valuable, or is it just an unsuccessful attempt to say something unimportant or needlessly explanatory? If it is the latter, away with it.

Here is some further advice, from Ezra Pound:

> Use no superfluous word, no adjective which does not reveal something.
>
> Don't use such an expression as 'dim lands *of peace.*' It dulls the image. It mixes an abstraction with the concrete. It comes from the writer's not realizing that the natural object is always the *adequate* symbol.
>
> Go in fear of abstractions. Do not retell in mediocre verse what has already been done in good prose. Don't think any intelligent person is going to be deceived when you try to shirk all the difficulties of the unspeakably difficult art of good prose by chopping your composition into line lengths . . . .
>
> Don't be 'viewy'—leave that to the writers of pretty little philosophic essays. Don't be descriptive; remember that the painter can describe a landscape much better than you can, and that he has to know a deal more about it.
>
> When Shakespeare talks of the 'Dawn in russet mantle clad' he presents something which the painter does not present. There is in this line of his nothing that one can call description; he presents . . . .
>
> If you are using a symmetrical form, don't put in what you want to say and then fill up the remaining vacuums with slush.[5]

In Pound's view, a poet ought to pay attention to vivid detail, and usually that is good advice. But like all general advice to poets, it is not to be followed absolutely. Some details may point us nowhere. They distract us from what matters, and they will need to be cut. Thomas Hardy probably wouldn't have improved "Channel Firing" by naming the brand of beer Parson Thirdly preferred, nor by describing the picture on its label.

Evidently, the details to render vividly are the ones that mean the most. Unless you agree with Edgar Allan Poe that a short intense poem is the only true poem (see page 942), revision isn't a matter of polishing an entire poem to a level of high intensity. Long poems, said T. S. Eliot in "The Music of Poetry," naturally contain prosaic passages as well as intensely "poetic" ones. See the advice of Yeats on the need for putting in a bit of dullness now and again (page 729).

Of all the skills a poet has, one of the most valuable is to know where to end lines. If your poem happens to be written in meter and rime, where to end lines is clearly suggested for you: lines end on riming words, or they end when their metrical expectation has been fulfilled. (An iambic pentameter line stops

---

[5]Excerpts from "A Retrospect," *Literary Essays of Ezra Pound*, ed. T. S. Eliot (New York: New Directions, 1954) 4–6.

on its tenth syllable, give or take a syllable or two.) But in "free verse" or formally open poetry, you do not have any guidance other than your mind and eye and ear. To place your line breaks effectively calls for much care during revision, and at all times, a certain sensibility. Because the ending of a line compels your readers to make a slight pause—at least a moment for their eyes to relocate at the beginning of the next line—the placement of these pauses is a great resource to you. If most of your lines end on strong words (such as verbs and nouns), the effect is different from that of slicing your lines after weak words (such as articles—*a*, *the*—or prepositions). To see this truth for yourself, study the ways in which lines end in William Carlos Williams's "The Dance" (page 681).

Early in life, William Carlos Williams decided that it seemed pretentious to begin each line with a capital. Such avoidance of convention is neither right nor wrong, and your choice depends on the effect you are after. Any evident attempt to defy convention calls attention to itself. Say "i think, therefore i am," and you aren't necessarily being modest. The effect is as though you were to print the letter *I* in red. E. E. Cummings, who favored the small letter *i*, was, according to many who knew him, an egotist.

When should you declare your poem done? Never, according to the French poet Paul Valéry, who said that a poem is never finished, only abandoned in despair. Other poets feel a definite sense of completion—as did Yeats, to whom a poem came shut with a click. But if you hear no such click, just stop when you see no more verbiage to prune, no more weak words to tighten.

If by now a title for your poem hasn't occurred to you, you may want to consider one. Some poets, to be sure, dispense with any title—as was the usual practice of Cummings and Emily Dickinson. To a reader, however, a title may be a help. If a poem is difficult, its title can show the reader how to take hold of it. An explicit title can supply needed background, tell us who is speaking, or explain a dramatic situation. By calling his poem "Soliloquy of the Spanish Cloister," Robert Browning indicates that we listen in on the thoughts of a single character, a monk in a religious order. Even a flatly indicative title ("Stopping by a Market in Pismo Beach to Buy Wine for a Wedding Present") may be more helpful to a reader than a merely decorative title ("Subterfuge with Sea-green Raisins"). Some poems, however, seem to thrive under titles that intrigue or tantalize without telling everything: "The Portent," "Disillusionment of Ten O'Clock," "Daystar," "The Listeners."

REACHING AN AUDIENCE

Few contemporary poets seem to follow the custom of Emily Dickinson and store their poems in the family attic. Most poets want to share their work with the world, and some, as soon as they have written a first poem, rush to send it to a magazine. Hopes of instant acclaim, of course, often meet with disappointment. "Don't imagine," Ezra Pound warned, "that you can please the expert before you have spent at least as much effort on the art of verse as the average piano teacher spends on the art of music." Nevertheless, if you master your art, it is reasonable to expect that sooner or later people will listen to it.

In a writing class, you already have an audience: your fellow students, your instructor. Still, some beginning poets feel reluctant to display their work even to friendly eyes. They have an uncomfortable sense, at first, that they are being asked to parade their inmost emotions in public, while at the same time they risk being ridiculed for their weak artistry. That is why a writing class needs to agree that the poems its members share are to be regarded as works of the imagination, not as personal diaries. As for the risk of ridicule, nobody expects the beginner to be T. S. Eliot. Probably you will find your fellow students reading your poems as considerately and sympathetically as (they trust) you'll read theirs. As for your instructor, don't worry. He or she has seen worse poems.

If you *enjoy* reading your poems aloud, live audiences may be yours for the asking. Does your campus have a coffeehouse or other room in which to hold readings? Audience responses, while sometimes misleading, can encourage you. Be aware, however, that audiences like to laugh together and often prefer funny, outrageous, immediately understandable poems to more difficult, subtle ones that require more than one hearing. If any of your fellow student poets are interested, it may be even more valuable to form a small group for mutual criticism and support.

Some novice poets crave early publication, and some who hurry into print are later sorry. Should the day arrive, however, when, tired of staring at a tall stack of beautiful finished poems, you just have to break into print, why not begin near home? Submit poems to your campus literary magazine, if there is any. If there isn't, can you see about starting one? Another alternative is to bring out your own magazine of limited circulation, with the aid of a mimeograph or a copier. Eventually, you may decide that your work belongs in magazines of wider readership—but first make sure it is ready. Unlike your fellow students and your instructor, who know you personally and are likely to sympathize with your creative labors, the editor of a national magazine, to whom you are only a licked stamp, cares for nothing but what you can show on cold white paper. A writing class may deal patiently with a faulted poem, taking time to rummage it for meaning, but the glance of an overworked editor will be more cursory. A bungled opening, a cliché, a line of bombast or sentiment, and back goes the manuscript with a rejection slip. Not that this threat should discourage you. Just realize that, in trying to print your poems, you'll be venturing forth into a crowded marketplace.

At the moment, American poetry seems in the throes of an inflation: Karl Shapiro, somewhat grimly, has called it a "poetry glut." For a number of reasons (including, no doubt, the popularity of creative writing programs), thousands of people today are trying to throng into print. Perhaps, in a world of social-security numbers sorted out into zip-code areas, they feel nameless, and so hope to make a lasting name—however small—by writing poetry. Whatever the explanation, in the latest *Directory of American Poets and Fiction Writers*, 4,855 published poets are listed—an incomplete listing at that.[6] Although the ranks of poets are thick, recent years have been seen a dwindling in the number of paying markets for a

<hr>

[6] 1989–90 edition (New York: Poets & Writers, 1989).

poem. Few magazines currently sold on newsstands regularly print poetry: *The Atlantic, The New Yorker, Yankee*—the list expires.

Still, poets need not consign their work to their attics. Lately, in noncommercial publishing, there has been a tremendous explosion of energy. As the latest *International Directory of Little Magazines and Small Presses* will indicate,[7] literary publishers now number in the thousands. **Little magazines,** periodicals edited and published as labors of love, exist not to turn a profit but to turn up new writing. A few such magazines, thick and printed handsomely, appear on more or less regular schedules. The majority, less expensively produced, usually lag behind their declared frequencies. Most little magazines, if well established, reach an audience of perhaps 500 to 5,000.[8]

Read a magazine before sending it your work; if need be, write off (and pay) for a sample copy. There is no sense in offering, say, a pastoral elegy in heroic couplets to the radically experimental *Hanging Loose*, or a pornographic punk-rock song to *The American Scholar*. Decent respect for editors requires that along with your poems you enclose a stamped, self-addressed envelope; send original copies, not carbons or Xeroxes; and submit a poem to one magazine at a time.

Delmore Schwartz once made a brilliant observation: a poet is wise to write as much and to publish as little as possible. With so many noncommercial publishers, it is a safe bet that any halfway competent poet who persists in licking stamps will break into print sooner or later. Yet the difficulty for poets today is not merely to be printed, but to be read. Ours seems a time of more good voices than good listeners. It is, besides, an age of disagreement and diversity. Ask any published poets what they think of poetry, and they will probably tell you that most poetry now being printed, other than their own, is bad or mediocre. But ask any six poets (selected at random) which other poets among their contemporaries they admire, and you will receive six lists of names with little duplication. To add to the confusion about what is excellent (or, some might say, to add to the merriment), most literary critics, as if discouraged by the vastness of the task of keeping up with contemporary poetry, have folded their practices. (To be sure, a very few brave and overworked critics of contemporary poetry are still operating.) Some poets feel that, since criticism isn't a help to them anyhow, who needs it? Still, without critics, who used to be poets' most devoted readers, it is more difficult for excellence to be recognized. Two truths seem evident. It is hard for a new poet today to gain an audience and a reputation. And yet, in the last few years, despite all odds, several excellent new poets have succeeded in doing so.

---

[7]Edited by Len Fulton and Ellen Ferber, and published annually by Dustbooks, Box 100, Paradise, CA 95969. It may be in the reference department of your library.

[8]Among the heftier and more faithfully appearing little magazines are *Antaeus, Boulevard, Grand Street, Hudson Review, Paris Review, Ploughshares,* and *Threepenny Review;* also those reviews subsidized by universities (*Georgia Review, Massachusetts Review, TriQuarterly, Sewanee Review,* and others). *Poetry,* which printed the early poems of Eliot, Frost, Marianne Moore, and Stevens, still issues monthly from Chicago, as essential as ever. The influential *American Poetry Review,* a bimonthly in tabloid newspaper format, claims the largest circulation of any little magazine: according to one report, more than 20,000.

If you are a dedicated poet, and your work truly deserves your dedication, you'll keep faith that you will eventually find your audience. You'll listen to the voice of your Muse, not to the siren warblings of the marketplace. (In John Ciardi's view, it is hardly possible to prostitute your talent for poetry, anyway, there being so few paying customers.) You will become a severer critic of your own work than your fellow students or your instructor. Although when you send out your poems to the handsome magazines you'll have to elbow through a crowd, you can be sure that, among contenders for immortality, there can no more be any rivalry than there is among gold prospectors. That is, when poets strike paydirt and achieve renown, it is usually because they have stalwart backs, eyes for a gleam, and likely claims, not because they know someone at the assay office.

Apparently, poets are not paid in bullion. In fact, nowhere in the English-speaking world at the moment is the writing of poems a full-time paying occupation. Most poets survive by other honest trades (such as teaching), receiving nothing or almost nothing for their poems, making a spare dollar from an occasional reading. Still most derive ample compensation. No one has better summed up the payment of being a poet than John Keats, in a letter to a friend: "I should write for the mere yearning and fondness I have for the beautiful, even if my night's labors should be burnt every morning and no eye shine upon them." For any poet so intently dedicated, writing a poem is today—as it always has been—its own considerable, immediate reward.

SUGGESTIONS FOR WRITING

Doing finger exercises is generally less fruitful to a poet than trying to write poems. Here are a few suggestions that might result in poems, if they arouse any responses in you.

1. Try to recall, and recapture in a poem, some experience that deeply moved you. The experience does not have to be anything world-shaking or traumatic; it might be as small as a memory from early childhood, a chance meeting with someone, a visit to a beach, the realization that some ordinary object is beautiful.
2. Try writing a poem in a voice *remote* from your own—speaking, say, as a character in history or fiction or film; an ordinary citizen in a different place or time; a child; an octogenarian. (For one famous illustration of a poet's speaking through a mask or persona, see Robert Browning's "Soliloquy of the Spanish Cloister," page 792. Presumably Browning set himself a problem: What would a hate-filled, envious monk think and mutter about a devout brother? Then, having imagined such a character, the poet found the character some artful and appropriate words.)
3. Attempt a poem in which you convey the joy of performing some simple, familiar, routine act: running, driving a car, peeling an orange, stroking a cat, changing a baby—or whatever you like to do.
4. Here is an experiment suggested by Ezra Pound: Write words to a well-known tune "in such a way that the words will not be distorted when one sings them."
5. Here is a suggestion that Nancy Willard has given to her student poets: Write a poem that responds to another poem. (First, find a poem you feel strongly compelled to respond to.)
6. Find, in a current magazine, or anthology, a poem that strikes you as silly, pretentious, or simple-minded. Write a take-off on it.
7. The aim of the following experiment is to lead you to wrestle with arbitrary difficulties. Observe some limitation that may seem to you pointless, but which might set

up a certain tension within your poem—provide a bottle (to echo Richard Wilbur) for your genie to try to burst out of. For instance, write a poem entirely in simple declarative subject-plus-verb sentences. Write a poem that is all one metaphor (like, for example, Emily Dickinson's "Because I could not stop for Death" or Whitman's "A Noiseless Patient Spider." Write a poem in blank verse (the form of Tennyson's "Ulysses"). Or, as Theodore Roethke was fond of asking his students to do, write a poem without adjectives.

8. Write a poem in praise of someone you admire, allowing yourself no general terms (*beautiful, wonderful,* etc.); try to describe the person in language so specific that a reader, too, will find your subject admirable.

9. Write a curse in verse: a damnation of someone or something you can't abide.

10. From an opening line (or lines) supplied by your instructor, try to develop a poem. Then compare the result with poems developed by others from the same beginning.

11. In verse (whether rimed or open), write a letter to a friend. For neoclassical examples, see the works of Swift and Pope (the latter's "Epistle to Dr. Arbuthnot" and other epistles in particular); for less formal contemporary examples, see Richard Hugo's collection *31 Letters and 13 Dreams* (New York: Norton, 1977)—mostly verse-letters to fellow poets.

12. Write a poem in the form of a dialogue between two people. (Christina Rossetti's "Uphill," page 709, may help illustrate such an exchange of speeches.)

13. Intently observe something for twenty or thirty minutes, then write a poem full of images through which your reader, too, can apprehend it. An excellent object for scrutiny would be any small living thing that will stand still long enough: an animal, bird, tropical fish, insect, or plant.

14. In a bookstore or library, select a book of poems that appeals to you. Take it home and read it thoroughly. If you have chosen well, the book may quicken your feelings and encourage you, too, to devote yourself to words. See if you can write a poem suggested or inspired by it—not necessarily an imitation.

Writing about a Play

METHODS

How is writing about a play any different from writing about a short story or a poem? Differences will quickly appear if you are writing about a play you have actually seen performed. Although, like a story or a poem, a play in print is usually the work of one person (and it is relatively fixed and changeless), a play on stage may be the joint effort of seventy or eighty people—actors, director, costumers, set designers, and technicians—and in its many details it may change from season to season, or even from night to night. Later on in this chapter, you will find some advice on reviewing a performance of a play, as you might do for a class assignment or for publication in, say, a campus newspaper. But in a literature course, for the most part, you will probably write about the plays you quietly read, and behold only in the theater of your mind. At least one advantage in writing about a printed play is that you can always go back and reread it, unlike the reviewer who, unless provided with a script, has nothing but memory to rely on.

Before you begin to write, it makes sense to read the *whole* play—not just the dialogue, but also everything in italics: descriptions of scenes, instructions to the actors, and other stage directions. This point may seem obvious, but the meaning of a scene, or even of an entire play, may depend on the tone of voice in which an actor is supposed to deliver a line. At the end of *A Doll House*, we need to pay attention to what Ibsen tells the actor playing Helmer—"*A sudden hope leaps in him*"—if we are to understand that, when Nora departs, she ignores Helmer's last desperate hope for a reconciliation, and she slams the door emphatically. And of course there is a resounding meaning in the final stage direction, in "the sound of a door slamming shut."

Taking notes on passages you will want to quote or refer to in your paper, you can use a concise method for keeping track of them. Jot down the numbers of act, scene, and line—for instance: I, ii, 42. Later, when you write, this handy shorthand will save space, and you can use it both in footnotes and in the body of your essay. Even if you do without footnotes, you can still indicate the exact lines you are quoting, or referring to:

Iago's hypocrisy, apparent in his famous defense of his

good name (III, iii, 157–161), is aptly summed up by

Roderigo, who accuses him: "Your words and perfor-

mances are no kin together" (IV, ii, 180–181).

Any of the methods frequently applied in writing about fiction and poetry— explication, analysis, comparison and contrast—can serve in writing about a play. All three methods are discussed in "Writing about a Story," and again in "Writing about a Poem." (For student papers that illustrate explication, see pages 1471 and 1493; analysis, pages 1474 and 1497; comparison and contrast, page 1499.) For using these methods to write about plays in particular, here are a few suggestions.

A whole play is too much to cover in an ordinary **explication**—a detailed, line-by-line unfolding of meaning. An explication of *Othello* could take years; a more reasonable class assignment would be to explicate a single key speech or passage from a play: Iago's description of a "deserving woman" (*Othello*, II, i, 145–57); or the first song of the chorus in *Oedipus the King*.

If you decide to write an essay by the method of **comparison and contrast** (two methods, actually, but they usually work together), you might set two plays side by side and point out their similarities and differences. Again, watch out: do not bite off more than you can chew. A profound topic—"The Self-deceptions of Othello and Oedipus"—might do for a three-hundred-page dissertation, but an essay of a mere thousand words could treat it only sketchily. Probably the dual methods of comparison and contrast are most useful for a long term paper on a large but finite topic: "Attitudes Toward Marriage in *A Doll House* and *Trifles*," "Synge and Lady Gregory as Observers of Rural Life." In a shorter paper, you might confine your comparing and contrasting to the same play: "Willy's Illusions and Biff's in *Death of a Salesman*."

For writing about drama, **analysis** (a separation into elements) is an especially useful method. You can consider just one element in a play, and so your topic tends to be humanly manageable—"Animal Imagery in Some Speeches from *Othello*," or "The Theme of Fragility in *The Glass Menagerie*." Not all plays, however, contain every element you might find in fiction and poetry. Unlike a short story or a novel, a play does not ordinarily have a narrator. In most plays, the point of view is that of the audience, who see the events not through some narrator's eyes, but through their own.[1] And though it is usual for a short story to be written in an all-pervading style, some plays seem written in as many styles as there are speaking characters. (But you might well argue that in David Grene's translation of *Oedipus the King*, a consistently elevated style informs all the speeches, or that in Susan Glaspell's *Trifles* both main characters speak the same language.) Rime schemes and metrical patterns, elements familiar in traditional poetry, are seldom found in contemporary plays, which tend to sound like ordinary conversation. To be sure, some plays *are* written in poetic forms: the blank verse of the greater portion of *Othello*. (If, by the way, you wish any advice to heed in quoting passages from a play in blank verse or in rime, see "How To Quote a Poem," on page 1501.) Despite whatever some plays may lack, most plays have more than enough elements for analysis, including characters, themes, tone, irony, imagery, figures of speech, symbols, myths, and conventions.

Ready to begin writing an analysis of a play, you might think at first that one element—the plot—ought to be particularly easy to detach from the rest, and write about. But beware. In a good play (as in a good novel or short story), plot and character and theme are likely to be one, not perfectly simple to tell apart. Besides, if in your essay you were to summarize the events in the play, and then stop, you wouldn't tell your readers much that they couldn't observe for themselves just by reading the play, or by seeing it. In a meaningful, informative analysis, the writer does not merely isolate an element, but also shows how it functions within its play and why it is necessary to the whole.

WRITING A CARD REPORT

Instead of an essay, some instructors like to assign a **card report.** If asked to write a card report on a play, you will find yourself writing a kind of analysis. To do so, you first single out elements of a play, then you list them on 5 × 8-inch index cards as concisely as possible. Such an exercise is often assigned in a class studying fiction; and one student's card report on the Edgar Allan Poe story, "The Tell-Tale Heart," appears on page 1477. When you deal with a play, however, you will need to include some elements different from those in a short story. And because a full-length play may take more room to summarize than a short story, your instructor may suggest that, if necessary, you take two cards (four sides) for your report. Still, in order to write a good card report, you have to be both brief and specific. Before you start, sort out your impressions of the play, and try to decide which characters, scenes, and lines of dialogue are the most important and

---

[1]Point of view in drama is a study in itself; this mere mention grossly simplifies the matter. Some playwrights attempt to govern what the spectator sees, trying to make the stage become the mind of a character. An obvious example is the classic German film *The Cabinet of Dr. Caligari*, in which the scenery is distorted as though perceived by a lunatic. Some plays contain characters who act as narrators, directly addressing the audience in much the way that first-person narrators in fiction often address the reader. In Tennessee Williams's *The Glass Menagerie*, Tom Wingfield behaves like such a narrator, introducing scenes, commenting on the action. So does the psychiatrist Martin Dysart in Peter Shaffer's *Equus* (1974). But such a character in a play does not alter our angle of vision, our physical point of view.

memorable. Reducing your scattered impressions to essentials, you will have to reexamine what you have read; and when you get done, you will know the play much more thoroughly. It is not easy to write readable comments within so small a space; and you might find such a report taking as much thought and effort as any analysis you have ever written in essay form.

Here is an example: a card report on Susan Glaspell's one-act play, *Trifles*. (For the play itself, see page 956.) By including only the elements that seemed most important, the writer managed to analyze the brief play on the front and back of one card. Still, he managed to work in a few pertinent quotations to give a sense of the play's remarkable language, and to make a few observations of his own. Although the report does not say everything about Glaspell's little masterpiece, an adequate criticism of the play could hardly be much briefer. For this report, the writer was assigned to include:

1. The playwright's name, nationality, and dates.
2. The title of the play and the date of its first performance.

Front of Card

(Student's name)   (Course and section)
Susan Glaspell, American, 1882–1948   Trifles, 1916

    Central characters: Mrs. Peters, the sheriff's nervous wife, dutiful but independent, not "married to the law"—whose sorrows make her able to sympathize with a woman accused of murder. Mrs. Hale, who knows the accused; more decisive.

    Other characters: The County Attorney, self-important but shortsighted. The Sheriff, a man of only middling intelligence, another sexist pig. Hale, a farmer, a cautious man. Not seen on stage, two others are central: Minnie Foster (Wright), the accused, a music lover reduced to near despair by years of grim marriage and isolation; and John Wright, the victim, known for his cruelty.

    Scene: The kitchen of a gloomy farmhouse in Nebraska after the arrest of a wife on suspicion of murder; little things left in disarray.

    Major dramatic question: Why did Minnie Wright kill her husband? When this question is answered, a new major dramatic question is raised: Will Mrs. Peters and Mrs. Hale cover up incriminating evidence?

    Events: In the exposition, Sheriff and C.A., investigating the death of Wright, hear Hale tell how he found the body and a distracted Mrs. Wright. Then (1) C.A. starts looking for a motive. (2) His jeering at Mrs. Wright (and all women) for their concern with "trifles" cause Mrs. Peters and Mrs. Hale to rally to the woman's defense. [continued on back of card]

3. The central character of characters, with a brief description that includes leading traits.
4. Other characters, also described.
5. The scene or scenes and, if the play does not take place in the present, the time of its action.
6. The dramatic question. This question is whatever the play leads us to ask ourselves: some conflict whose outcome we wonder about, some uncertainty to whose resolution we look forward. (For a more detailed discussion of dramatic questions, see page 968.)
7. A brief summary of the play's principal events, in the order in which the playwright presents them. If you are reporting on a play longer than *Trifles*, you may find it simplest to take each act, perhaps each scene, and sum up what happens in it.

Back of Card

[Events, continued] (3) When the two women find evidence that Mrs. Wright had panicked (a patch of wild sewing in a quilt), Mrs. Hale destroys it. (4) Mrs. Peters finds more evidence: a wrecked birdcage. (5) The women find a canary with its neck wrung and realize that Minnie killed her husband in a similar way. (6) The women align themselves with Minnie when Mrs. Peters recalls her own sorrows, and Mrs. Hale decides her own failure to visit Minnie was "a crime." (7) The C.A. unwittingly provides Mrs. Peters with a means to smuggle out the canary. (8) The two women unite to seize the evidence.

Tone: Made clear in the women's dialogue: mingled horror and sadness at what has happened, compassion for a fellow woman, smoldering resentment toward men who crush women.

Language: The plain speech of farm people, with a dash of rural Midwestern slang (red-up for tidy; Hale's remark that the accused was "kind of done up"). Unschooled speech: Mrs. Hale says ain't—and yet her speech rises at moments to simple poetry: "She used to sing. He killed that too." Glaspell hints the self-importance of the County Attorney by his heavy reliance on the first person.

Central theme: Women, in their supposed concern for trifles, see more deeply than men do.

Symbols: The broken birdcage and the dead canary, both suggesting the music and the joy that John Wright stifled in Minnie.

Evaluation: A powerful, successful realistic play that conveys its theme with great economy—in its views, more than seventy years ahead of its time.

8. The tone of the play, as best you can detect it. Try to describe the playwright's apparent feelings toward the characters or what happens to them.
9. The language spoken in the play: try to describe it. Does any character speak with a choice of words or with figures of speech that strike you as unusual, distinctive, poetic—or maybe dull and drab? Does language indicate a character's background or place of birth? Brief quotations, in what space you have, will be valuable.
10. In a sentence, try to sum up the play's central theme. If you find none, say so. But plays often contain more themes than one—which of them seems most clearly borne out by the main events?
11. Any symbols you notice, and believe to matter. Try to state in a few words what each suggests.
12. A concise evaluation of the play: what did you think of it? (For more suggestions on being a drama critic, see Chapter Thirty-six, "Evaluating a Play.")

REVIEWING A PLAY

Writing a **play review,** a brief critical account of an actual performance, involves making an evaluation. To do so, you first have to decide what to evaluate: the work of the playwright; the work of the actors, director, and production staff; or the work of both. If the play is some classic of Shakespeare or Ibsen, evidently the more urgent task for a reviewer is not to evaluate the playwright's work, but to evaluate the success of the actors, director, and production staff in interpreting it. To be sure, a reviewer's personal feelings toward a play (even a towering classic) may deserve mention. Writing of an Ibsen masterpiece, the critic H. L. Mencken made the memorable comment that, next to being struck down by a taxicab and having his hat smashed, he could think of no worse punishment than going to another production of *Rosmersholm*. But a newer, less well-known play is probably more in need of evaluation.

To judge a live performance is, in many ways, more of a challenge than to judge a play read in a book. Obviously there is much to consider besides the playwright's script: acting, direction, costumes, sets, lighting, perhaps music, anything else that contributes to one's total experience in the theater. Still, many students find that to write a play review is more stimulating—and even more fun— than most writing assignments. And although the student with experience in acting or in stagecraft may be a more knowing reviewer than the student without such experience, the latter may prove just as capable in responding to a play and in judging it fairly and perceptively.

In the chapter "Evaluating a Play," we assumed that in order to judge a play one has to understand it, and be aware of its conventions. (For a list of things to consider in judging a play, whether staged or printed, see pages 1235–36.) Some plays will evoke a strong positive or negative response in the reviewer, either at once or by the time the final curtain tumbles; others will need to be pondered.

Incidentally, harsh evaluations sometimes tempt a reviewer to flashes of wit. One celebrated flash is Eugene Field's observation of an actor in a production of *Hamlet*, that "he played the king as though he were in constant fear that somebody else was going to play the ace." The comment isn't merely nasty; it implies that Field had closely watched the actor's performance and had discerned what was wrong with it. Readers, of course, have a right to expect that reviewers do not just sneer (or gush praise), but clearly set forth reasons for their feelings.

Reviewing plays seems an art with few fixed rules, but in general, an adequate play review usually gives us a small summary of the play—for the reader unacquainted with it—and perhaps also indicates what the play is about: its theme. If the play is familiar and often performed, some comment on the director's whole approach to it may be useful. Is the production exactly what you'd expect, or are there any fresh and apparently original innovations? And if the production is fresh, does it achieve its freshness by violating the play? (The director of one college production of *Othello*—a fresh, but not entirely successful, innovation—emphasized the play's being partly set in Venice by staging it in the campus swimming pool, with actors floating about on barges and a homemade gondola.) Does the play seem firmly directed, so that the actors neither lag nor hurry, and so that they speak and gesture not in an awkward, stylized manner, but naturally? Are they well cast? Usually, also, a reviewer pays attention to the performances of the leading actors, or principals; and to the costumes, sets, and lighting, if these are noteworthy. The theater itself may deserve mention. Is it distractingly uncomfortable? For this play, is it strikingly suitable or unsuitable? (*Othello* afloat might seem awkward and artificial. We may be so nervous about the gondola tipping over that we can't pay attention to the lines.) And if, all along, the reviewer has not been making clear an opinion of the play and its production, an opinion will probably come in the concluding paragraph.

For further pointers, read a few professional play reviews in magazines such as *The New Yorker, Time, Newsweek, The New Criterion, American Theatre,* and others; or on the entertainment pages of a metropolitan newspaper. Here is a good, concise review of an amateur production of *Trifles* as it might be written for a college newspaper, but similar to what your instructor might ask you to write for a course assignment.

<u>Trifles Scores Mixed Success</u>
in Monday Players' Production

Women have come a long way since 1916. At least, that impression was conveyed yesterday when the Monday Players presented Susan Glaspell's classic one-act play <u>Trifles</u> in Alpaugh Theater.

At first, in Glaspell's taut story of two subjugated farm women who figure out why a fellow farm woman strangled her husband, Lloyd Fox and Cal Federicci get to strut around. As a small-town sheriff and a county attorney, they lord it over the womenfolk, making sexist-pig remarks about women in general. Fox and Federicci obviously enjoy themselves as the pompous types that Glaspell means them to be.

But of course it is the women with their keen eyes for small details who prove the superior detectives. In the demanding roles of the two Nebraska Miss Marples, Kathy Betts and Ruth Fine cope as best they can with what is asked of them. Fine is especially convincing. As Mrs. Hale, a friend of the wife accused of the murder, she projects a growing sense of independence. Visibly smarting under the verbal lashes of the menfolk, she seems to straighten her spine inch by inch as the play goes on.

Unluckily for Betts, director Alvin Klein seems determined to view Mrs. Peters as a comedian. Though Glaspell's stage directions call the woman "nervous," I doubt she is supposed to be quite so fidgety as Betts makes her. Betts vibrates like a tuning fork every time a new clue turns up, and when obliged to smell a dead canary bird (another clue), you would think she was whiffing a dead hippopotamus. Mrs. Peters, whose sad past includes a lost baby and a kitten some maniac chopped up with a hatchet, is no figure of fun to my mind. Played for laughs, her character fails to grow visibly on stage, as Fine makes Mrs. Hale grow.

Klein, be it said in his favor, makes the quiet action proceed at a brisk pace. Feminists in the audience must have been a little embarrassed, though, by his having Betts and Fine deliver every speech defending women in an extra-loud voice. After all, Glaspell makes her points clear enough just by showing us what she shows. Not everything is overstated, however. As a farmer who found the murder victim, Cal Valdez acts his part with quiet authority.

Despite flaws in its direction, this powerful play still spellbinds an audience. Anna Winterbright's set, seen last week as a background for Dracula and just slightly touched up, provides appropriate gloom.

SUGGESTIONS FOR WRITING

Finding a topic you care to write about is, of course, your most important step toward writing a valuable paper. (For some general advice on topic-finding, see pages 1459–1460.) The following list of suggestions is not meant to replace your own ideas but to stimulate them.

TOPICS FOR BRIEF PAPERS (250–500 words)

1. When the curtain comes down on the conclusion of some plays, the audience is left to decide exactly what finally happened. In a short informal essay, state your interpretation

of the conclusion of one of these plays: *The Workhouse Ward, The Glass Menagerie, Joe Turner's Come and Gone.* Don't just give a plot summary; tell what you think the conclusion means.
2. Sum up the main suggestions you find in one of these meaningful objects (or actions): the handkerchief in *Othello*; the Christmas tree in *A Doll House* (or Nora's doing a wild tarantella); Willy Loman's planting a garden in *Death of a Salesman*, Laura's collection of figurines in *The Glass Menagerie.*
3. Here is an exercise in being terse. Write a card report on a short, one-scene play (other than *Trifles*) and confine your remarks to both sides of one 5 × 8-inch card. (For further instructions see page 1524.) Possible subjects: *Riders to the Sea, The Workhouse Ward, The Man in a Case.*
4. Review a play you have seen within recent memory and have felt strongly about (or against). Give your opinion of *either* the performance or the playwright's writing, with reasons for your evaluation.
5. Write an essay entitled "Why I Prefer Plays to Films" (or vice versa). Cite some plays and films to support your argument. (If you have never seen any professional plays, pick some other topic.)

TOPICS FOR MORE EXTENDED PAPERS (600–1,000 *words*)

1. From a play you have enjoyed, choose a passage that strikes you as difficult, worth reading closely. Try to pick a passage not longer than about 200 words, or twenty lines. Explicate it, working through it sentence by sentence or line by line. For instance, any of these passages might be considered memorable (and essential to their plays):

   Oedipus to Teiresias, speech beginning, "Wealth, sovereignty and skill outmatching skill" (*Oedipus the King*, 416–443).

   Iago's soliloquy, "Thus do I ever make my fool my purse" (*Othello*, I, iii, 356–377).

   Tom Wingfield's opening speech, "Yes, I have tricks in my pocket," through "I think the rest of the play will explain itself. . . ." (*The Glass Menagerie*, Scene I).
2. Take just a single line or sentence from a play—one that stands out for some reason as greatly important. Perhaps it states a theme, reveals a character, or serves as a crisis (or turning point). Write an essay demonstrating its importance: how it functions, why it is necessary. Some possible lines:

   Iago to Roderigo: "I am not what I am" (*Othello*, I, i, 62).

   Amanda to Tom: "You live in a dream; you manufacture illusions!" (*The Glass Menagerie*, VII).

   Charley to Biff: "A salesman is got to dream, boy. It comes with the territory" (*Death of a Salesman*, the closing Requiem).
3. Write an essay in analysis, in which you single out an element of a play for examination—character, plot, setting, theme, dramatic irony, tone, language, symbolism, conventions, or any other element. Try to relate this element to the play as a whole. Sample topics: "The Function of Teiresias in *Oedipus the King*," "Imagery of Poison in *Othello* (or *A Doll House*)," "Irony in *Antigone*," "Williams's Use of Magic-Lantern Slides in *The Glass Menagerie*," "The Theme of Success in *Death of a Salesman*," "Magic in *Joe Turner's Come and Gone.*"
4. Compare a character, situation, or theme in a play with a similar element in a short story. For instance: women's role in society as seen in *Trifles* and in Tillie Olsen's "I Stand Here Ironing"; pretending to be what one isn't in *The Real Inspector Hound* and in James Thurber's "The Catbird Seat"; "The Ocean as an Opponent in *Riders to the Sea* and Stephen Crane's 'The Open Boat.'"

5. Imagine a completely different ending for a play you have read, one that especially interests you. Briefly summarize the new resolution you have in mind. Then, looking back over the play's earlier scenes, tell what would happen to the rest of the play if it were to acquire this new ending. What else would need to be changed? What, if anything, does this exercise reveal?

6. In an essay, consider how you would go about staging a play of Shakespeare, Molière, or some other classic, in modern dress, with sets representing the world of today. What problems would you face? Can such an attempt ever succeed?

Topics for Long Papers *(1,500 words or more)*

1. Choosing any of the three works in Chapter Thirty-seven, "Plays for Further Reading," or taking some other modern or contemporary play your instructor suggests, report any difficulties you encountered in reading and responding to it. Explicate any troublesome passages for the benefit of other readers.

2. Compare and contrast two plays—a play in this book and another play by the same author—with attention to one element. For instance: "The Theme of Woman's Independence in Ibsen's *A Doll House* and *Hedda Gabler*"; "Antirealism in the Stagecraft of Tennessee Williams: *The Glass Menagerie* and *Camino Real*"; or "Christian Symbols and Allusions in Williams's *Menagerie* and *Night of the Iguana*."

3. Compare and contrast in *The Glass Menagerie* and *Death of a Salesman* the elements of dream-life and fantasy.

4. For at least a month, keep a journal of your experience in watching drama on stage, movie screen, or television. Make use of any skills you have learned from your reading and study of plays, and try to demonstrate how you have become a more critical and perceptive member of the viewing audience.

5. If you have ever acted or taken part in staging plays, consult with your instructor and see whether you both find that your experience could enable you to write a substantial paper. With the aid of specific recollections, perhaps, you might sum up what you have learned about the nature of drama or about what makes a play effective.

6. Watch a film version of a play, then read the original as produced on stage. What differences do you find, and how do you account for them? You might, for instance, compare the film *Driving Miss Daisy* with Alfred Uhry's stage play of the same name.

Writing a Play

"Playwriting," declares one novice playwright, "is a cinch. You have a bunch of actors standing or sitting around, and all you have to do is give them lines." Yet there is more to the writing of a play than that, if we are to believe some of our leading playwrights' testimony.

Unless a play is a closet drama, to be read but not performed, it is both a literary work and—when it comes alive in a theater—a team effort involving actors, director, producer, and many other specialists. For this reason, it is no accident that some of the finest playwrights have themselves been actors: Shakespeare, Molière, Harold Pinter. Writing a play calls for a sense of what will "go" on stage: what will keep an audience intently listening and watching. This sort of knowledge isn't acquired only from reading in a library. To write a good play, it may help to read masterpieces; but it is also essential to see plays performed, and if possible, to take part in them. Edward Albee, although not an actor himself, has remarked: "I've read and seen hundreds of plays, starting with Sophocles right up to the present day. As a playwright I imagine that in one fashion or another I've been influenced by every single play I've ever experienced."[1]

The effective playwright writes with a glowing stage in mind, not merely setting down words but visualizing their end result. What particular arrangement of people on stage, what physical objects or properties, what sets and costumes, what "stage business" (or visible activity that interests the spectator) will help make the play watchable? In *The Glass Menagerie*, an audience finds it fascinating to behold Laura arranging her collection of glass figurines with loving care, as the light glitters on them. Playwrights who make good use of the stage often lead us to focus upon something. The drama critic George Jean Nathan remarked, somewhat sarcastically, that he had never seen an American play fail if its set featured

---

[1]Interview with William Flanagan, *The Paris Review* 39 (Fall 1966) 106.

the headlight of a train that slowly moved across the rear of the stage, or if its set contained a large crystal chandelier. Why is it, he wondered, that "no actor, however incompetent, who has put a putty mole on his cheek and adorned himself with a seedy frock coat and stovepipe hat has failed completely in impressing the critics that he was a pretty good Lincoln?"[2] The answer may be that, at the very least, the audience is given something to watch—will Honest Abe's putty mole fall off?

Such matters may seem trivial, but a play, to be effective on the boards, has to engage not only our minds and our emotions, but also our senses. Of course, the mere entrance of an actor can interest an audience tremendously—as does, in *The Glass Menagerie*, the long-awaited arrival of Jim, the gentleman caller. In all dramatic literature, it would be hard to find a more entertaining departure from a stage than that of Shakespeare's Antigonus in *A Winter's Tale*: "Exit, pursued by a bear." To help playwrights become more aware of their bodies and their senses, Maria Irene Fornes, whenever she teaches a workshop in play writing, begins by having her students do some physical exercises, stretching and relaxing as dancers and runners do. After this warm-up, Fornes often asks students to visualize something unseen, perhaps draw a picture of it. The purpose of these exercises, Fornes asserts, is to overcome any tendency to think of playwriting as "how to phrase something, how to say something, rather than to let out what's underneath."[3]

How does a play begin? Evidently the playwright first needs a dramatic situation and some characters whom an audience will care for. To find these, William Alfred, author of *Hogan's Goat* and other plays, recommends first building up a "police file" on any likely characters, amassing a sheaf of imagined facts that include each character's childhood fears, hurts, and other earliest memories. One's own personal history may supply inspiration, as it seems to have done in *The Glass Menagerie*, a play apparently full of memories drawn from the playwright's early life. Although the painfully shy Laura is not an exact portrait of his sister Rose (Laura "was like Miss Rose only in her inescapable 'difference,' " Williams has written), the name of Rose suggests Laura's nickname "Blue Roses." A young woman with "lovely, heartbreaking eyes," Rose felt acute anxiety in male company. She was pressed by her mother to make a painful social début at the Knoxville Country Club. For a time she was courted by a junior executive, an ambitious young man who soon suspended his attentions. After the break-up, Rose suffered from mysterious illnesses, showed symptoms of withdrawal, and eventually was committed to the Missouri State Asylum. (Williams tells her story in his *Memoirs*.[4]) Like Tom Wingfield, apparently Williams as a young man was a restless dreamer and aspiring writer who left home to wander the country.

Not all plays, of course, begin in autobiography. As a playwright Shakespeare, a refurbisher of old plays and tales and a cribber from history, seems more

[2]"Marginalia," *The World of George Jean Nathan*, ed. Charles Angoff (New York: Knopf, 1952) 470.
[3]Quoted by Neena Beber, "Dramaticus Instructus," *American Theatre* (Jan. 1990) 24.
[4](New York: Doubleday, 1975) 116–28.

interested in others' lives than in his own. In fact, he seldom invented his own stories. Only two of his thirty-six plays (*The Tempest* and *Love's Labor's Lost*) are based on plots that, as far as we know, he originated. Edward Albee urges novice playwrights in search of inspiration to read plays by other people: "Know what everyone has written. But don't always read masterpieces, read some failures too. If anything, it's encouraging."[5]

Some playwrights carefully plan their plots before they write; others are more willing to let their characters hand them a surprise. Recalling a time when he and Elliott Nugent were collaborating on a comedy, *The Male Animal*, James Thurber recalled that Nugent was a believer in thorough plotting, who searched for the most effective possible moment at which to ring down the curtain on an act.

> Nugent would say, "Well, Thurber, we've got our problem, we've got all these people in the living room. Now what are we going to do with them?" I'd say that I didn't know and couldn't tell him until I'd sat down at the typewriter and found out.[6]

For Albee, writing a play is a matter of finishing it in the unconscious mind, then sitting down to write and finding out what it is. Spending from six months to a year and a half in reflecting on what to write, Albee begins setting words on paper only when he "more or less" knows what is going to happen (although not exactly how the characters will move from one situation to another).

> I write a first draft quite rapidly. Read it over. Make a few pencil corrections, where I think I've got the rhythms wrong in the speeches, for example, and then retype the whole thing. And in the retyping I discover that maybe one or two more speeches will come in. One or two more things will happen, but not much. Usually what I put down first is what we go into rehearsal with.[7]

Whether a believer in strict, thorough advance plotting or in letting a play take shape in the typewriter, a playwright cannot tell an actor *everything* to do on stage. Plays that stay alive for centuries provide roles that actors enjoy taking. A great character leaves an actor room for interpretation: how to play Hamlet or Othello is a challenge that fine actors welcome. An incompetent playwright, according to Frank O'Connor, will "pull an actor because he'll tell him what to do, but a really good playwright will give you a part that you can do what you like with."[8] A good playwright, too, has an ear for dialogue that sounds human. Harold Pinter, the English playwright whose characters usually speak the most ordinary, unpoetic sort of speech, says that as he writes each line he reads it aloud to himself. Silences, and their placement, are equally important. In French, a

[5]Talk to students at Johns Hopkins University quoted by Dick Carpenter, "Names and Faces," *Boston Globe* 13 Apr. 1983.
[6]Interview with George Plimpton and Max Steele, *Writers at Work: The Paris Review Interviews* (New York: Viking 1959) 87.
[7]Flanagan, 116.
[8]Interview with Anthony Whittier, *Writers at Work* 169.

famous play by Jean-Jacques Bernard, *Martine*, centers on a simple peasant girl who loses the great love of her life—and her one chance for happiness. Because she is inarticulate, she falls silent at moments when it is clear to the audience that her emotions are intense.

Once a play is finished, the playwright stands to learn from seeing it performed. Broadway plays, when they go into rehearsal, often involve the playwright who watches, prepared to change, add, or delete passages that do not seem to work when actually staged. Even if the performance of a play is just a reading of the script by a playwright's friends or by fellow students in a class, the novice playwright will find the experience valuable. Do certain lines give the actors unnecessary difficulty? Does the stage seem cluttered with people who have nothing to do but stand around? These are the sorts of discoveries that sometimes only a production will afford. Besides, the prime pleasure in writing a play may be to see it brought to life.

SUGGESTIONS FOR WRITING

1. In collaboration with another student (or others), write a one-act play from five to ten minutes in playing time, for two or three actors. Cast it, rehearse it, revise it if necessary, and then perform it in front of your class.
2. Write a scene (or perhaps just a page-long passage) that might be inserted without violence into one of the plays in this book. A play with a relatively free and episodic structure (such as *Joe Turner's Come and Gone*) might better admit such an addition than a more tightly constructed one (such as *A Doll House*). As best you can, imitate the playwright's language and stage directions. Keep the characters consistent with their natures in the rest of the play. Then read aloud to the class that portion containing your addition (together with some of the original text), and see if anyone can detect where the playwright's words stop and yours begin.
3. Transform a short story you admire into a script for a play in one act. Include a description of sets, lighting, and costumes; stage directions; and advice for the actors wherever necessary. Some likely stories to consider are "Godfather Death," "A & P," "Average Waves in Unprotected Waters," "Young Goodman Brown," "Cathedral," "First Confession," "The Catbird Seat," and "Roman Fever."

ACKNOWLEDGMENTS

Continued from page ii.

Maxine Chernoff. "The Spirit of Giving" first appeared in *Bop*, stories by Maxine Chernoff, Coffee House Press, 1986. Reprinted by permission of the publisher. Copyright © 1986 by Maxine Chernoff.

William Faulkner. "A Rose for Emily." Copyright 1930 and renewed 1958 by William Faulkner. "Barn Burning." Copyright 1939 and renewed 1967 by Estelle Faulkner and Jill Faulkner Summers. Both reprinted from *Collected Stories of William Faulkner* by permission of Random House, Inc.

Stanley Fish. Excerpt reprinted by permission of the publishers from *Is There a Text in This Class?* by Stanley Fish, Cambridge, Mass.: Harvard University Press. Copyright © 1980 by the President and Fellows of Harvard College.

Gustave Flaubert. Excerpt from *Madame Bovary* by Gustave Flaubert, translated by Francis Steegmuller. Copyright © 1957 by Francis Steegmuller. Reprinted by permission of Random House, Inc.

Tess Gallagher. "The Lover of Horses" from *The Lover of Horses* by Tess Gallagher. Copyright © 1982, 1986 by Tess Gallagher. Reprinted by permission of HarperCollins Publishers.

Jakob and Wilhelm Grimm. "Godfather Death" from *The Juniper Tree and Other Tales from the Brothers Grimm*, translated by Lore Segal and Randall Jarrell. Copyright © 1973 by Lore Segal. Reprinted by permission of Farrar, Straus and Giroux, Inc.

Ernest Hemingway. "A Clean, Well-Lighted Place." Reprinted with permission of Charles Scribner's Sons, an imprint of Macmillan Publishing Company, from *Winner Take Nothing* by Ernest Hemingway. Copyright 1933 by Charles Scribner's Sons; renewal copyright © 1961 by Mary Hemingway.

Langston Hughes. "On the Road" from *Laughing to Keep from Crying*. Reprinted by permission of Harold Ober Associates Incorporated. Copyright 1952 by Langston Hughes. Copyright renewed 1980 by George Houston Bass.

Shirley Jackson. "The Lottery" from *The Lottery* by Shirley Jackson. Copyright 1948, 1949 by Shirley Jackson. Renewal copyright © 1976, 1977 by Laurence Hyman, Barry Hyman, Mrs. Sarah Webster and Mrs. Joanne Schnurer. Reprinted by permission of Farrar, Straus and Giroux, Inc.

James Joyce. "Araby." From *Dubliners* by James Joyce. Copyright 1916 by B. W. Heubsch. Definitive text copyright © 1967 by the estate of James Joyce. Reprinted by permission of Viking Penguin, a division of Penguin Books USA Inc. Excerpt from *Stephen Hero* reprinted by permission of Jonathan Cape Ltd. and The Society of Authors as the literary representative of the Estate of James Joyce.

Franz Kafka. "The Bucket Rider." From *The Penal Colony: Stories and Short Pieces* by Franz Kafka, translated by Willa and Edwin Muir. Translation copyright 1948 and renewed 1976 by Schocken Books, Inc. Reprinted by permission of the publisher.

Yasunari Kawabata. "The Man Who Did Not Smile" excerpted from *Palm of the Hand Stories*, copyright © 1988 by Yasunari Kawabata, translated by Lane Dunlop and J. Martin Holman. Reprinted by permission of North Point Press.

Jamaica Kincaid. "Girl" from *At the Bottom of the River* by Jamaica Kincaid. Copyright © 1978, 1979, 1981, 1982, 1983 by Jamaica Kincaid. Reprinted by permission of Farrar, Straus and Giroux, Inc.

D. H. Lawrence. "The Rocking Horse Winner." From *The Complete Short Stories of D. H. Lawrence*, Volume III. Copyright 1933 by the Estate of D. H. Lawrence. Copyright renewed © 1961 by Angelo Ravagli and C. M. Weekley, Executors of the Estate of Frieda Lawrence Ravagli. Reprinted by permission of Viking Penguin, a division of Penguin Books USA Inc.

Katherine Mansfield. "Miss Brill." Copyright 1920 by Alfred A. Knopf, Inc. and renewed 1948 by John Middleton Murry. Reprinted from *The Short Stories of Katherine Mansfield* by permission of Alfred A. Knopf, Inc. Excerpt from January 17, 1921 letter to Richard Murry from *The Letters of Katherine Mansfield*, edited by John Middleton Murry, reprinted by permission of The Society of Authors as the literary representative of the Estate of Katherine Mansfield.

Bobbie Ann Mason. "Big Bertha Stories" from *Love Life*. Stories by Bobbie Ann Mason. Copyright © 1988 by Bobbie Ann Mason. Reprinted by permission of HarperCollins Publishers.

W. Somerset Maugham. "The Appointment in Samarra" from *Sheppey* by W. Somerset Maugham. Copyright 1933 by W. Somerset Maugham. Used by permission of Doubleday, a division of Bantam Doubleday, Dell Publishing Group, Inc., and A. P. Watt Limited on behalf of The Royal Literary Fund.

Alice Munro. "The Found Boat" from *Something I've Been Meaning to Tell You*. © 1974, Alice Munro. All rights reserved. Available in paperback through The New American Library. Reprinted by permission of Virginia Barber Literary Agency, Inc.

Joyce Carol Oates. "Where Are You Going, Where Have You Been?" from *The Wheel of Love and Other Stories*. Copyright © 1970 by Joyce Carol Oates. Reprinted by permission of John Hawkins & Associates, Inc.

Flannery O'Connor. "A Good Man Is Hard to Find" from *A Good Man Is Hard to Find and Other Stories*, copyright 1953 by Flannery O'Connor and renewed 1981 by Mrs. Regina O'Connor, reprinted by permission of Harcourt Brace Jovanovich, Inc. "Everything that Riss Must Converge" and "Revelation" from *Everything That Rises Must Converge* by Flannery O'Connor. Copyright © 1961, 1965 by the Estate of Mary Flannery O'Connor. Reprinted by permission by Farrar, Straus and Giroux, Inc. Excerpt from *Mystery and Manners* by Flannery O'Connor. Copyright © 1967, 1969 by the Estate of Mary Flannery O'Connor. Reprinted by permission of Farrar, Straus and Giroux, Inc.

Frank O'Connor. "First Confession." Copyright 1951 by Frank O'Connor. Reprinted from *Collected Stories* by Frank O'Connor, by permission of Alfred A. Knopf, Inc. and Joan Daves.

Tillie Olsen. "I Stand Here Ironing." from *Tell Me a Riddle* by Tillie Olsen. Copyright © 1956, 1957, 1960, 1961 by Tillie Olsen. Reprinted by permission of Delacorte Press/Seymour Lawrence, a division of Bantam, Doubleday, Dell Publishing Group, Inc.

Katherine Anne Porter. "The Jilting of Granny Weatherall" from *Flowering Judas and Other Stories*, copyright 1930 and renewed 1958 by Katherine Anne Porter, reprinted with permission of Harcourt Brace Jovanovich, Inc.

Philip Roth. "The Conversion of the Jews." From *Goodbye Columbus* by Philip Roth. Copyright © 1959 by Philip Roth. Reprinted by permission of Houghton Mifflin Company.

Isaac Bashevis Singer. "Gimpel the Fool," translated by Saul Bellow. From *A Treasury of*

Yiddish Stories, edited by Irving Howe and Eliezer Greenberg. Copyright 1953, 1954 by The Viking Press, Inc. Copyright renewed 1981 by Isaac Bashevis Singer. Reprinted by permission of Viking Penguin, a division of Penguin Books USA Inc.

John Steinbeck. "The Chrysanthemums." From The Long Valley by John Steinbeck. Copyright 1937, renewed © 1965 by John Steinbeck. Reprinted by permission of Viking Penguin, a division of Penguin Books USA Inc.

James Thurber. "The Unicorn in the Garden." Copyright 1940 James Thurber Copyright © 1968 Helen Thurber. From Fables for Our Time, published by Harper & Row. "The Catbird Seat." Copyright 1945 James Thurber. Copyright © 1973 Helen W. Thurber and Rosemary T. Sauers. From The Thurber Carnival, published by Harper & Row. Reprinted by permission.

Leo Tolstoi. "The Death of Ivan Ilych" from The Death of Ivan Ilych and Other Stories by Leo Tolstoi, translated by Louise and Aylmer Maude, published by Oxford University Press.

Anne Tyler. "Average Waves in Unprotected Waters." Reprinted by permission of Russell & Volkening as agents for the author. Copyright © 1977 by Anne Tyler. Appeared originally in The New Yorker.

Kurt Vonnegut, Jr. "Harrison Bergeron." From Welcome to the Monkey House by Kurt Vonnegut, Jr. Copyright © 1961 by Kurt Vonnegut, Jr. Originally published in Fantasy and Science Fiction Magazine. Reprinted by permission of Delacorte Press/Seymour Lawrence, a division of Bantam, Doubleday, Dell Publishing Group, Inc.

John Updike. "A & P." Copyright © 1962 by John Updike. Reprinted from Pigeon Feathers and Other Stories, by John Updike, by permission of Alfred A. Knopf, Inc.

Edith Wharton. "Roman Fever." Reprinted with permission of Charles Scribner's Sons, an imprint of Macmillan Publishing Company, from Roman Fever and Other Stories by Edith Wharton. Copyright 1934 by Liberty Magazine: renewal copyright © 1962 by William R. Tyler.

William Carlos Williams. "The Use of Force." From William Carlos Williams: The Doctor Stories. Copyright 1933 by William Carlos Williams. Reprinted by permission of New Directions Publishing Corporation.

POETRY

Dick Allen. "Night Driving" from Flight and Pursuit, Poems by Dick Allen. Copyright © 1987 by Dick Allen. Reprinted by permission of Louisiana State University Press.

A. R. Ammons. "Spring Coming" is reprinted from Collected Poems, 1951–1971, by A. R. Ammons, by permission of W.W. Norton & Company, Inc. Copyright © 1972 by A. R. Ammons.

John Ashbery. "At North Farm" from A Wave by John Ashbery. Copyright © 1984 by John Ashbery. All rights reserved. Reprinted by permission of Viking Penguin, a division of Penguin Books USA Inc. Originally appeared in The New Yorker. "The Cathedral Is" from As We Know by John Ashbery. Copyright © 1979 by John Ashbery. Reprinted by permission of Viking Penguin Inc.

Margaret Atwood. "All Bread" from Selected Poems II: Poems Selected and New 1976–1986 by Margaret Atwood. Copyright © 1987 by Margaret Atwood. Reprinted by permission of Houghton Mifflin Company and Oxford University Press Canada. Margaret Atwood, "you fit into me" from Power Politics (Toronto: House of Anansi Press, 1971). Reprinted by permission.

W. H. Auden. "James Watt" from Academic Graffiti, by W. H. Auden. Copyright © 1960 by W. H. Auden. Reprinted by permission of Random House, Inc. "As I Walked Out One Evening," "Musée des Beaux Arts" and "The Unknown Citizen" Copyright 1940 and renewed 1968 by W. H. Auden. Reprinted from W. H. Auden: Collected Poems, edited by Edward Mendelson, by permission of Random House, Inc. and Faber and Faber Ltd.

David B. Axelrod. "Once in a While a Protest Poem" from A Dream of Feet by David B. Axelrod. Reprinted by permission of the poet and Cross Cultural Communications.

Jimmy Santiago Baca. "Spliced Wire" from What's Happening by Jimmy Santiago Baca. Copyright © 1982 by Jimmy Santiago Baca. Reprinted by permission of Curbstone Press.

R. L. Barth. "The Insert" from Forced Marching to the Sea: Vietnam War Poems by R. L. Barth (1983). Reprinted by permission of Perivale Press. "Definition," Copyright © 1989 by R. L. Barth. Reprinted by permission of the author. "Readers and listeners praise my books" from Earthenware: XLIV Epigrams from Martial, translated by R. L. Barth. Copyright © 1988 by R. L. Barth. Reprinted by permission.

Max Beerbohm. "On the imprint of the first English edition of The Works of Max Beerbohm" from Max in Verse. Reprinted by permission of Sir Geoffrey Keynes.

Hilaire Belloc. "The Hippopotamus" from Cautionary Verses by Hilaire Belloc. Published 1940 by Gerald Duckworth & Co. Ltd., 1941 by Alfred A. Knopf, Inc. Reprinted by permission of the publishers.

Bruce Bennett "Leader," © 1984 by Bruce Bennett. Used by permission.

E. C. Bentley. "Sir Christopher Wren" from Clerihews Complete by E. C. Bentley. © E. C. Bentley. Reprinted by permission of Curtis Brown London.

John Betjeman. "In Westminster Abbey" from Collected Poems by John Betjeman (Houghton Mifflin Company, 1959). Reprinted by permission of John Murray Publishers Ltd.

Elizabeth Bishop. "The Fish," "Filling Station," "One Art," "Sestina," and lines from "Little Exercise" from The Complete Poems 1927–1979 by Elizabeth Bishop. Copyright 1940, 1946, 1949, 1952, 1953, © 1955, 1956, 1959, 1960, 1961, 1962, 1964, 1965, by Elizabeth Bishop. Copyright © 1979, 1983 by Alice Helen Methfessel. Reprinted by permission of Farrar, Straus & Giroux, Inc.

Robert Bly. "Driving to Town Late to Mail a Letter" from Silence in the Snowy Fields by Robert Bly (Wesleyan University Press, 1962) and "Inward Conversation." Reprinted by permission of the poet.

Louise Bogan. "The Dream" from The Blue Estuaries by Louise Bogan. Copyright 1938, © 1968 by Louise Bogan. Reprinted by permission of Farrar, Straus & Giroux, Inc.

Richard Brautigan. "Haiku Ambulance" from The Pill Versus the Springhill Mine Disaster by Richard Brautigan. Copyright © 1965 by Richard Brautigan. Reprinted by permission of Houghton Mifflin Company/Seymour Lawrence.

Van K. Brock. Quotation of three lines from "Driving at Dawn" from The Hard Essential Landscape by Van K. Brock (University Presses of Florida, 1979). Copyright © 1979 by Van K. Brock. Reprinted by permission.

Joseph Brodsky. "Belfast Tune" from To Urania by Joseph Brodsky. Copyright © 1981, 1982, 1983, 1984, 1985, 1987, 1988 by Joseph Brodsky. Reprinted by permission of Farrar, Straus & Giroux, Inc.

Gwendolyn Brooks. "A Black Wedding Song" from To Disembark by Gwendolyn Brooks. Copyright © 1981 by Gwendolyn Brooks. Reprinted by permission of Third World Press, Chicago. "The Bean Eaters" from *Selected Poems* by Gwendolyn Brooks. Copyright © 1944, 1945, 1949, 1959, 1960, 1963 by Gwendolyn Brooks Blakely. Reprinted by permission of the author. "We Real Cool" and "The Rites for Cousin Vit" from *Blacks* by Gwendolyn Brooks (Chicago: The David Company). Copyright © 1987 by Gwendolyn Brooks Blakely. Reprinted by permission of the author.

Kenneth Burke. "The Habit of Imperfect Rhyming" from *Collected Poems, 1915–1967* by Kenneth Burke. Copyright © 1968 Kenneth Burke. Reprinted by permission of The University of California Press.

Taniguchi Buson. "The Sudden Chilliness" from *An Introduction to Haiku* by Harold G. Henderson. Copyright © 1958 by Harold G. Henderson. Reprinted by permission of Doubleday & Company, Inc.

Fred Chappell. "Skin Flick" from *The World Between the Eyes* by Fred Chappell. Copyright © 1971 by Fred Chappell. Reprinted by permission of Louisiana State University Press.

Geoffrey Chaucer. Lines from Part I. "Merciles Beaute" from *The Works of Geoffrey Chaucer*. Second Edition, edited by F. N. Robinson (1957). Reprinted by permission of Houghton Mifflin Company.

G. K. Chesterton. "The Donkey" from *The Wild Knight and Other Poems* by G. K. Chesterton (London: J. M. Dent & Sons Ltd.)

John Ciardi. "In Place of a Curse" from *Selected Poems* by John Ciardi. Copyright © 1984 by John Ciardi. Reprinted by permission of The University of Arkansas Press.

Lucille Clifton. "winnie song" copyright © 1987 by Lucille Clifton. Reprinted from *Next: New Poems* by Lucille Clifton with the permission of BOA Editions, Ltd.

William Cole. From "Some River Rhymes" by William Cole from *Light Year '85* edited by Robert Wallace (Cleveland, Ohio: Bits Press, 1984). Reprinted by permission of the author.

Leo Connellan. "Scott Huff" from *New and Collected Poems* by Leo Connellan (New York: Paragon House). Copyright © 1989 by Leo Connellan. Reprinted by permission of the author.

Cid Corman. Translation of the haiku by Issa from *One Man's Moon, Fifth Haiku* used with permission of Gnomon Press and the author.

Frances Cornford. "The Watch" from *Collected Poems* by Frances Cornford (Cresset Press) Reprinted by permission of Barrie & Jenkins Ltd.

Robert Crawford. "My Iambic Pentameter Lines." Copyright © 1986 by Robert J. Crawford. Used by permission of the poet.

Robert Creeley. "Oh No" reprinted with permission of Charles Scribner's Sons, an imprint of Macmillan Publishing Company, from *For Love: Poems 1950–1960* by Robert Creeley. Copyright © 1962 by Robert Creeley.

Countee Cullen. "For a Lady I Know" from *On These I Stand* by Countee Cullen. Copyright 1925 by Harper & Row, Publishers, Inc.; renewed 1953 by Ida M. Cullen. Reprinted by permission of GRM Associates, Inc., as agents for the Estate of Ida M. Cullen.

E. E. Cummings. "anyone lived in a pretty how town" and "a politician is an arse upon" are reprinted from *Complete Poems, 1913–1962* by E. E. Cummings, by permission of Liveright Publishing Corporation. Copyright © 1923, 1925, 1931, 1935, 1938, 1939, 1940, 1944, 1945, 1946, 1947, 1948, 1949, 1950, 1951, 1952, 1953, 1954, 1955, 1956, 1957, 1958, 1959, 1960, 1961, 1962 by the Trustees for the E. E. Cummings Trust. Copyright © 1961, 1963, 1968 by Marion Morehouse Cummings. "Buffalo Bill's" and "in Just-" reprinted from *Tulips and Chimneys* by E. E. Cummings, edited by George James Firmage, by permission of Liveright Publishing Corporation. Copyright 1923, 1925 and renewed 1951, 1953 by E. E. Cummings. Copyright © 1973, 1976 by the Trustees of the E. E. Cummings Trust. Copyright © 1973, 1976 by George James Firmage.

J. V. Cunningham. "This Humanist whom no beliefs constrained," "Friend, on this scaffold Thomas More lies dead," "Motto for a Sundial" and "You serve the best wines always, my dear sir" from *The Exclusions of a Rhyme* by J. V. Cunningham. Copyright © 1971 by J. V. Cunningham. Reprinted with the permission of The University of Ohio Press, Athens.

D. J. Jazzy Jeff and the Fresh Prince. Lyrics from "Parents Just Don't Understand" by D. J. Jazzy Jeff and the Fresh Prince. Copyright © 1988 Zomba Recording Corporation. Reprinted by permission of Zomba Enterprises, Inc.

Peter Davison. "The Last Word" ("Four Love Poems," #IV), reprinted with permission of Atheneum Publishers, an imprint of Macmillan Publishing Company, from *Pretending To Be Asleep* by Peter Davison. Copyright © 1970 by Peter Davison.

Walter de la Mare. "The Listeners" by Walter de la Mare. Reprinted by permission of The Literary Trustees of Walter de la Mare and The Society of Authors as their representative.

Emily Dickinson. "Because I could not stop for Death," "I heard a Fly buzz — when I died," "I like to see it lap the Miles," "I started Early — Took my Dog," "The Lightning is a yellow Fork," "The Soul selects her own Society," "Victory comes late," "It dropped so low — in my regard." "A Dying Tiger — moaned for drink," "My life had stood — a Loaded Gun," and lines from "Hope is the thing with feathers" reprinted by permission of the publishers and Trustees of Amherst College from *The Poems of Emily Dickinson*, edited by Thomas H. Johnson, Cambridge, Mass., The Belknap Press of Harvard University Press, copyright 1951, © 1955, 1979, 1983 by the President and Fellows of Harvard College. Twenty-two lines from "My Life had stood — a Loaded Gun," from *The Complete Poems of Emily Dickinson*, edited by Thomas H. Johnson. Copyright 1929 by Martha Dickinson Bianchi; copyright © renewed 1957 by Mary L. Hampson. By permission of Little, Brown and Company in association with the Atlantic Monthly Press.

Emanuel di Pasquale. "Rain" reprinted by permission of the poet. "A Sensual, For Ezra Pound" copyright © 1989 by Emanuel di Pasquale. Reprinted from *Genesis* by Emanuel di Pasquale with the permission of BOA Editions, Ltd.

Deborah Digges. "For the Daughters of Hannah Bible Class of Tipton, Missouri's Women's Prison: Mother's Day, 1959" reprinted with permission of Atheneum Publishers, an imprint of Macmillan Publishing Company from *Vesper Sparrows* by Deborah Digges. Copyright © 1986 by Deborah Digges.

Hilda Doolittle. "Heat" and "Helen" from *Collected Poems* by Hilda Doolittle. Copyright © 1982 by the Estate of Hilda Doolittle. Reprinted by permission of New Directions Publishing Corporation.

Rita Dove. "Daystar" reprinted from *Thomas and Beulah* by Rita Dove, by permission of Carnegie-Mellon University Press. Copyright © 1986 by Rita Dove.

Richard Eberhart. "The Fury of Aerial Bombardment" from *Collected Poems 1930–1976* by Richard Eberhart. Copyright © 1960, 1976 by Richard Eberhart. Reprinted by permission of Oxford University Press, Inc.

T. S. Eliot. "Journey of the Magi," "Virginia," "The Love Song of J. Alfred Prufrock," "The Boston Evening Transcript," and "Preludes I" from *Collected Poems 1909–1962* by T. S. Eliot. Copyright 1936 by Harcourt Brace Jovanovich, Inc. and copyright © 1963, 1964 by T. S. Eliot, reprinted by permission of the publisher. Excerpt from "Tradition and the

Individual Talent" in *Selected Essays* by T. S. Eliot, copyright 1950 by Harcourt Brace Jovanovich, Inc. and renewed 1978 by Esme Valerie Eliot, reprinted by permission of the publisher.

Louise Erdrich. "Indian Boarding School: The Runaways" from *Jacklight* by Louise Erdrich. Copyright © 1984 by Louise Erdrich. Reprinted by permission of Henry Holt and Company, Inc.

Donald Finkel. "Gesture" reprinted with permission of Atheneum Publishers, an imprint of Macmillan Publishing Company from *The Garbage Wars* by Donald Finkel. Copyright © 1970 by Donald Finkel.

Robert Flanagan. "Reply to an Eviction Notice" from *Once You Learn You Never Forget* by Robert Flanagan (Fiddlehead Poetry Books, 1978). Reprinted by permission of the author.

Robert Francis. "Catch" from *The Orb Weaver* by Robert Francis. Copyright 1950 by Robert Francis. Reprinted by permission of Wesleyan University Press.

Robert Frost. "Birches," "The Road Not Taken," "Out, Out—". Copyright 1916 by Holt, Rinehart and Winston and renewed 1944 by Robert Frost. Reprinted from *The Poetry of Robert Frost* edited by Edward Connery Lathem, by permission of Henry Holt and Company, Inc. "Desert Places," "Design," "Stopping by Woods on a Snowy Evening," "The Secret Sits," "Never Again Would Birds' Song Be the Same," "Fire and Ice," "The Silken Tent," and "Away!" from *The Poetry of Robert Frost* edited by Edward Connery Lathem. Copyright © 1969 by Holt, Rinehart and Winston, Inc. Copyright © 1962 by Robert Frost. Copyright © 1975 by Lesley Frost Ballantine. Reprinted by permission of Henry Holt and Company, Inc. "In White" from *The Dimensions of Robert Frost* edited by Reginald L. Cook. Copyright © 1958 by Reginald L. Cook. Reprinted by permission of Henry Holt and Company, Inc. Letter to John Bartlett (no. 53) from *Selected Letters of Robert Frost* edited by Lawrance Thompson. Copyright © 1964 by Lawrance Thompson and Holt, Reinhart and Winston. Reprinted by permission of Henry Holt and Company, Inc.

Sandra M. Gilbert and Susan Gubar. From the Introduction to the poems of Emily Dickinson from *The Norton Anthology of Literature by Women, The Tradition in English,* edited by Sandra M. Gilbert and Susan Gubar, by permission of W. W. Norton & Company, Inc. Copyright © 1985 by Sandra M. Gilbert and Susan Gubar.

Gary Gildner. "First Practice" reprinted from *First Practice* by Gary Gildner. By permission of the University of Pittsburgh Press. © 1969 by Gary Gildner.

Allen Ginsberg. "A Supermarket in California" from *Collected Poems 1947–1980* by Allen Ginsberg. Poem Copyright © 1955 by Allen Ginsberg. Reprinted by permission of Harper & Row, Publishers, Inc.

Dana Gioia. "California Hills in August" by Dana Gioia from *The New Yorker*, August 9, 1982. Reprinted by permission.

Paul Goodman. Three lines from "Hokku" from *Collected Poems* by Paul Goodman. Copyright © 1973 by The Estate of Paul Goodman. Reprinted by permission of Sally Goodman.

Robert Graves. "Down Wanton Down" from *Collected Poems* by Robert Graves. Copyright © 1975 by Robert Graves. Reprinted by permission of Oxford University Press, Inc. and A P Watt Limited on behalf of The Executors of the Estate of Robert Graves.

Linda Gregg. "The Grub" from *Too Bright to See* by Linda Gregg. Copyright © 1981 by Linda Gregg. Reprinted by permission of Graywolf Press.

Ronald Gross. "Yield" from *Pop Poems* by Ronald Gross. Copyright © 1967 by Ronald Gross. Reprinted by permission of Simon & Schuster, Inc.

Bruce Guernsey. "Glove" from *The Invention of the Telephone* by Bruce Guernsey (Urbana, Illinois: Stormline Press, 1987). Reprinted by permission of the author.

Arthur Guiterman. "On the Vanity of Earthly Greatness" from *Gaily the Troubadour* by Arthur Guiterman. Copyright 1936 by E. P. Dutton; renewed 1954 by Mrs. Vita Lindo Guiterman. Reprinted by permission of Louise H. Sclove.

R. S. Gwynn. "Scenes from the Playroom" from *The Drive-In: Poems* by R. S. Gwynn. Copyright © 1986 by R. S. Gwynn. Reprinted by permission of the University of Missouri Press.

John Haines. "Winter News" from *News from the Glacier: Selected Poems 1960–1980* by John Haines. Copyright © 1964 by John Haines. Reprinted by permission of Wesleyan University Press.

Donald Hall. "Names of Horses" by Donald Hall from *The New Yorker*, September 14, 1977. Reprinted by permission.

Penny Harter. "broken bowl" from *In the Broken Curve* by Penny Harter. Copyright © 1984 by Penny Harter. Reprinted by permission of Burnt Lake Press.

Robert Hayden. "Those Winter Sundays" is reprinted from *Collected Poems* of Robert Hayden, edited by Frederick Glaysher, by permission of Liveright Publishing Corporation. Copyright © 1985 by Erma Hayden.

James Hayford. "Dry Noon," "Behind the Wall," and "Under the Holy Eye" from *Star in the Shed Window: Collected Poems* by James Hayford. Copyright © 1989 by James Hayford. Reprinted with the permission of The New England Press, Inc., Shelburne, VT.

Seamus Heaney. "Digging" and "Mother of the Groom" from *Poems 1965–1975* by Seamus Heaney. Copyright © 1966, 1969, 1972, 1975, 1980 by Seamus Heaney. Reprinted by permission of Farrar, Straus & Giroux, Inc. and Faber and Faber Ltd.

Anthony Hecht. "The Vow" from *The Hard Hours* by Anthony Hecht. Copyright © 1967 by Anthony Hecht. Reprinted by permission of the author.

Michael Heffernan. "Living Room" from *The Man at Home* by Michael Heffernan. Copyright © 1988 by Michael Heffernan. Reprinted by permission of The University of Arkansas Press.

Geoffrey Hill. "Merlin" from *Collected Poems* by Geoffrey Hill. Copyright © 1985 by Geoffrey Hill. Reprinted by permission of Oxford University Press, Inc.

John Hollander. "Swan and Shadow" reprinted with permission of Atheneum Publishers, an imprint of Macmillan Publishing Company from *Types of Shape* by John Hollander. Copyright © 1969 by John Hollander.

Garrett Hongo. "The Cadence of Silk" from *The River of Heaven* by Garrett Hongo. Copyright © 1988 by Garrett Hongo. Reprinted by permission of Alfred A. Knopf, Inc. "The Hongo Store" from *Yellow Light* by Garret Kaoru Hongo. Copyright © 1982 by Garret Kaoru Hongo. Reprinted by permission of Wesleyan University Press.

Richard Howard. "Meditation" from *Les Fleurs du Mal* by Charles Baudelaire, translated by Richard Howard. Translation copyright © 1982 by Richard Howard. Reprinted by permission of David R. Godine, Publisher, Boston.

A. E. Housman. "Eight O'Clock," "Loveliest of trees, the cherry now," "To an Athlete Dying Young," "When I was one-and-twenty," and "With rue my heart is laden," from *The Collected Poems of A. E. Housman.* Copyright © 1965 by Holt, Rinehart and Winston, Inc. Reprinted by permission of Henry Holt and Company, Inc.

Langston Hughes. "Dream Boogie" and "Green Memory" from *Selected Poems of Langston Hughes.* Copyright 1951 by Langston Hughes. Copyright renewed 1979 by George Houston Bass. Reprinted by permission of Harold Ober Associates Incorporated.

"Dream Deferred" from *The Panther and the Lash: Poems of Our Times*, by Langston Hughes. Copyright 1951 by Langston Hughes. Reprinted by permission of Alfred A. Knopf, Inc. "Homecoming" from *Selected Poems of Langston Hughes*. Copyright © 1959 by Langston Hughes. Reprinted by permission of Alfred A. Knopf, Inc. "Island" from *Selected Poems of Langston Hughes*. Copyright © 1959 by Langston Hughes. Copyright renewed 1987 by George Houston Bass. Reprinted by permission of Harold Ober Associates Incorporated.

T. E. Hulme. "Image" from *The Life and Opinions of T. E. Hulme* by Alun R. Jones. Copyright 1960 by Alun R. Jones. Reprinted by permission of Beacon Press.

Virgil Hutton. "Dusk over the lake" first appeared in *Modern Haiku*, 1984. By permission of the poet and the publisher.

Randall Jarrell. "The Death of the Ball Turret Gunner" (Copyright 1945, renewed © 1973 by Mary von Schrader Jarrell). Reprinted from *The Complete Poems* by Randall Jarrell by permission of Farrar, Straus & Giroux, Inc. Two excerpts from *Poetry and the Age* by Randall Jarrell. Copyright 1952, 1953 by Randall Jarrell. Reprinted by permission of Mary von Schrader Jarrell. "Well Water" reprinted with permission of Macmillan Publishing Company from *The Lost World* by Randall Jarrell. Copyright © 1965 by Randall Jarrell.

Robinson Jeffers. "The Stone-Cutters" from *The Selected Poetry of Robinson Jeffers*. Copyright 1924 and renewed 1952 by Robinson Jeffers. Reprinted by permission of Random House, Inc.

Elizabeth Jennings. "Delay" from *Collected Poems 1953–1985* by Elizabeth Jennings. Copyright © Elizabeth Jennings 1986 (Macmillan, London). Reprinted by permission of David Higham Associates Limited.

Donald Justice. "On the Death of Friends in Childhood" from *The Summer Anniversaries* by Donald Justice. Copyright © 1960 by Donald Justice. Reprinted by permission of Wesleyan University Press.

Greg Keeler. Lines from "There Ain't No Such Thing as a Montana Cowboy," *The Limberlost Review*, 1979. Reprinted by permission of the poet.

Jane Kenyon. "The Suitor" from *From Room to Room*, © 1978 by Jane Kenyon. Reprinted courtesy of Alice James Books, 138 Mt. Auburn St., Cambridge, MA 02138.

James C. Kilgore. "The White Man Pressed the Locks" from *Poets on the Platform*. Copyright © 1970 by James C. Kilgore. Reprinted by permission. All rights reserved.

Hugh Kingsmill. "What, still alive at twenty-two" from *The Best of Hugh Kingsmill*. Reprinted by permission of Victor Gollancz Ltd.

Bill Knott. "Poem" from *The Naomi Poems: Corpse and Beans* by Saint Geraud. Copyright © 1968 by William Knott. Reprinted by permission of Allyn & Bacon, Inc.

Kenneth Koch. "Mending Sump" by Kenneth Koch. Copyright © 1960 by Kenneth Koch. Reprinted by permission of the author.

Ted Kooser. "A Child's Grave Marker" reprinted from *One World At A Time* by Ted Kooser, by permission of the University of Pittsburgh Press. Copyright © 1985 by Ted Kooser.

Philip Larkin. "Home is so Sad" from *The Whitsun Weddings* by Philip Larkin. Reprinted by permission of Faber and Faber Ltd. "Wedding Wind" and "Poetry of Departures" from *The Less Deceived* by Philip Larkin. © the Estate of Philip Larkin 1988. Reprinted by permission of the Marvell Press, England.

D. H. Lawrence. "Piano" and "Bavarian Gentians." From *The Complete Poems of D. H. Lawrence*, ed. by Vivian de Sola Pinto and F. Warren Roberts. Copyright © 1964, 1971 by Angelo Ravagli and C. M. Weekleu, Executors of The Estate of Frieda Lawrence Ravagli. Reprinted by permission of Viking Penguin Inc.

Irving Layton. "The Bull Calf" from *A Red Carpet for the Sun*. Reprinted by permission of the poet.

Brad Leithauser. "Trauma" from *Hundreds of Fireflies* by Brad Leithauser. Copyright © 1981 by Brad Leithauser. Reprinted by permission of Alfred A. Knopf, Inc.

John Lennon and Paul McCartney. *"Eleanor Rigby"* by John Lennon and Paul McCartney. Copyright © 1966 NORTHERN SONGS LTD. All Rights for the U.S., Canada and Mexico Controlled and Administered by SBK BLACKWOOD MUSIC INC. Under License from ATV MUSIC (MACLEN). All Rights Reserved. International Copyright Secured. Used by permission.

Denise Levertov. "Leaving Forever" and "Six Variations, iii" from *Poems 1960–1967* by Denise Levertov. Copyright © 1958, 1963, 1964, 1969 by Denise Levertov Goodman. "Leaving Forever" was first published in *Poetry*. Reprinted by permission of New Directions Publishing Corporation. "Divorcing" from *The Freeing of the Dust* by Denise Levertov. Copyright © 1975 by Denise Levertov. Reprinted by permission of New Directions Publishing Corporation.

Philip Levine. "Animals Are Passing from Our Lives" from *Not This Pig* by Philip Levine. Copyright © 1968 by Philip Levine. Reprinted by permission of Wesleyan University Press.

Janet Lewis. "Girl Help" from *Poems 1924–1944* by Janet Lewis. Copyright 1950 by Janet Lewis. Reprinted with the permission of The Ohio University Press, Athens.

Stephen Shu Ning Liu. "My Father's Martial Art" by Stephen Shu Ning Liu. Copyright © 1981 by The Antioch Review, Vol. 39, No. 3, Summer 1981. Reprinted by permission of the Editors.

Federico Garcia Lorca. "La Guitarra" from *Obras Completas* by Federico Garcia Lorca. Copyright 1954 Aguilar S.A. de Ediciones. Reprinted by permission of New Directions Publishing Corporation.

Robert Lowell. "Meditation" from *Imitations* by Robert Lowell. Copyright © 1958, 1959, 1960, 1961 by Robert Lowell. "Skunk Hour" from *Life Studies* by Robert Lowell. Copyright © 1956, 1959 by Robert Lowell. Reprinted by permission of Farrar, Straus & Giroux, Inc.

Hugh MacDiarmid. "Wheesht, Wheesht" reprinted with permission of Macmillan Publishing Company from *Collected Poems* by Hugh MacDiarmid. © Christopher Murray Grieve 1948, 1962.

Archibald MacLeish. "The End of the World" from *New and Collected Poems 1917–1982* by Archibald MacLeish. Lines from "Ars Poetica." Copyright © 1985 by The Estate of Archibald MacLeish. Reprinted by permission of Houghton Mifflin Company.

Charles Martin. "Rough Draft" from *Steal the Bacon* by Charles Martin. Copyright © 1987 by The Johns Hopkins University Press. Reprinted by permission.

John Masefield. "Cargoes" reprinted with permission of Macmillan Publishing Company from *Poems* by John Masefield (New York: Macmillan, 1953).

Rod McKuen. "Thoughts on Capital Punishment" from *Stanyan Street and Other Sorrows* by Rod McKuen. Copyright 1954, © 1960, 1962, 1963, 1964, 1965, 1966 by Rod McKuen. Reprinted by permission of Random House, Inc.

James Merrill. "Laboratory Poem" reprinted with permission of Atheneum Publishers, an imprint of Macmillan Publishing Company from *The Country of A Thousand Years of Peace* by James Merrill. Copyright © 1958, 1970 by James Merrill. Originally appeared in *Poetry*.

W. S. Merwin. "Song of Man Chipping an

Arrowhead" reprinted with permission of Atheneum Publishers, an imprint of Macmillan Publishing Company from *Writings to an Unfinished Accompaniment* by W. S. Merwin. Copyright © 1972, 1973 by W. S. Merwin. Originally appeared in *Poetry*. "Elegy" reprinted with permission of Atheneum Publishers, an imprint of Macmillan Publishing Company from *The Carrier of Ladders* by W. S. Merwin. Copyright © 1970 by W. S. Merwin.

Charlotte Mew. "The Farmer's Bride" from *Collected Poems and Prose* by Charlotte Mew, edited by Val Warner. Copyright © 1981 The Estate of Charlotte Mew. Reprinted by permission of Carcanet Press Ltd.

Josephine Miles. "Reason" from *Poems 1930–1960* by Josephine Miles. Copyright © 1960 by Indiana University Press. Reprinted by permission.

Edna St. Vincent Millay. "Counting-out Rhyme" by Edna St. Vincent Millay. From *Collected Poems*, Harper & Row. Copyright © 1928, 1955 by Edna St. Vincent Millay and Norma Millay Ellis. Reprinted by permission. "Recuerdo" by Edna St. Vincent Millay. From *Collected Poems* (Harper & Row). Copyright 1922, 1950 by Edna St. Vincent Millay. Reprinted by permission.

Marianne Moore. "The Mind is an Enchanting Thing" and "The Wood-Weasel" reprinted with permission of Macmillan Publishing Company from *Collected Poems* by Marianne Moore. Copyright 1944 and renewed 1972, by Marianne Moore.

Edwin Morgan. "Siesta of a Hungarian Snake" from *The Second Life* by Edwin Morgan. Copyright © 1968 by Edwin Morgan and Edinburgh University Press. Reprinted by permission of Edinburgh University Press.

Frederick Morgan. "The Master" from *Northbrook* by Frederick Morgan. Copyright © 1982 by Frederick Morgan. Reprinted by permission of University of Illinois Press.

Howard Moss. "Shall I Compare Thee to a Summer's Day" (from "Modified Sonnets") reprinted with permission of Atheneum Publishers, an imprint of Macmillan Publishing Company from *A Swim Off the Rocks* by Howard Moss. Copyright © 1976 by Howard Moss.

Howard Nemerov. "The Snow Globe" from *The Collected Poems of Howard Nemerov*. Copyright © 1977 by Howard Nemerov. Reprinted by permission of the author.

Lorine Niedecker. From *From This Condensery: The Complete Writing of Lorine Niedecker*, edited by Robert J. Bertholf. Copyright © Cid Corman, Literary executor of Lorine Niedecker Estate. Reprinted by permission.

John Frederick Nims. "Love Poem" from *The Iron Pastoral*. Copyright, 1947, by John Frederick Nims. "Contemplation" from *Of Flesh and Bone*. Copyright © 1967 by Rutgers University. Reprinted by permission of the poet.

David Ogilvy. First four lines from "Carnation Milk" reprinted with permission of Atheneum Publishers, an imprint of Macmillan Publishing Company, from *Confessions of an Advertising Man* by David Ogilvy.

Sharon Olds. "The One Girl at the Boys Party" from *The Dead and the Living*, by Sharon Olds. Copyright © 1983 by Sharon Olds. Reprinted by permission of Alfred A. Knopf, Inc.

Mary Oliver. "Rain in Ohio" from *American Primitive* by Mary Oliver. Copyright © 1981 by Mary Oliver. First appeared in the *Atlantic Monthly*. Reprinted by permission of Little, Brown and Company.

Charles Olson. "La Chute" by Charles Olson. Reprinted by permission of Richard H. Schimmelpfeng for the Estate of Charles Olson.

Wilfred Owen. "Anthem for Doomed Youth" and "Dulce et Decorum Est" from *Collected Poems by*

Wilfred Owen. Copyright 1946, 1963 by Chatto & Windus Ltd. Reprinted by permission of New Directions Publishing Corporation, The Hogarth Press and the Estate of Wilfred Owen.

Dorothy Parker. "Résumé" from *The Portable Dorothy Parker*. Copyright © 1926, 1954 by Dorothy Parker. Reprinted by permission of Viking Penguin Inc.

Linda Pastan. "Ethics" is reprinted from *Waiting For My Life*, Poems by Linda Pastan, by permission of the author and W. W. Norton & Company, Inc. Copyright © 1981 by Linda Pastan. "Jump Cabling" from *Light Year '85* (Bits Press), Reprinted by permission of the poet.

Laurence Perrine. "Janus," *Poetry*, June 1984. Copyright © 1984 by Laurence Perrine. Reprinted by permission of the poet.

Robert Phillips. "Running on Empty" from *Running on Empty, New Poems* by Robert Phillips. Copyright 1984, Robert Phillips. Reprinted by permission of the poet.

Sylvia Plath "Daddy" (Copyright © 1963 by Ted Hughes) and "Morning Song" (Copyright © 1961 by Ted Hughes) from *Ariel* by Sylvia Plath. Published by Harper & Row, Publishers, Inc. and Faber and Faber, London Copyright Ted Hughes, 1965. "Metaphors" from *Crossing the Water* by Sylvia Plath. Copyright © 1960 by Ted Hughes. Published by Harper & Row, Publishers, Inc. and Faber and Faber, London. Copyright Ted Hughes, 1971. Reprinted by permission of Harper & Row, Publishers, Inc. and Olwyn Hughes, representing the estate of Sylvia Plath.

Ezra Pound. First six lines from "Ill Hiang Niao" reprinted by permission of the publishers from Ezra Pound, *Shih-Ching: The Classic Anthology Defined by Confucius*; Cambridge, Mass.: Harvard University Press. Copyright 1954 by the President and Fellows of Harvard College. From *ABC of Reading* by Ezra Pound. Copyright 1934 by Ezra Pound. Reprinted by permission of New Directions Publishing Corporation. "A Retrospect" from *Literary Essays* by Ezra Pound. Copyright 1935 by Ezra Pound. Reprinted by permission of New Directions Publishing Corporation. "In a Station of the Metro" and "The River-Merchant's Wife: A Letter" from *Personae* by Ezra Pound. Copyright 1926 by Ezra Pound. Reprinted by permission of New Directions Publishing Corporation.

Paul Ramsey. "A Poet Defended" from *Light Year '85* (Bits Press). Reprinted by permission of the poet.

Dudley Randall. "Ballad of Birmingham" and "Old Witherington" from *A Litany of Friends: New and Selected Poems* by Dudley Randall. Copyright © 1981 by Dudley Randall. Reprinted by permission of the author.

John Crowe Ransom. "Bells for John Whiteside's Daughter" from *Selected Poems, Third Edition, Revised and Enlarged*, by John Crowe Ransom. Copyright 1924 by Alfred A. Knopf, Inc. and renewed 1952 by John Crowe Ransom. Reprinted by permission of Alfred A. Knopf, Inc.

Adrienne Rich. "Aunt Jennifer's Tigers," "The Ninth Symphony of Beethoven Understood at Last as a Sexual Message," and "Trying to Talk with a Man" are reprinted from *The Fact of a Doorframe, Poems Selected and New, 1950–1984*, by Adrienne Rich, by permission of W. W. Norton & Company, Inc. Copyright © 1984 by Adrienne Rich. Copyright © 1975, 1978 by W. W. Norton & Company, Inc. Copyright © 1981 by Adrienne Rich.

Henry Reed. "Naming of Parts" from *A Map of Verona* by Henry Reed (1946). Reprinted by permission of John Tydeman.

Kenneth Rexroth. "A Dawn in a Tree of Birds" from *New Poems* by Kenneth Rexroth. Copyright © 1974 by Kenneth Rexroth. Reprinted by permission of New Directions Publishing Corporation.

John Ridland. "The Lazy Man's Haiku" by John

Ridland. Reprinted by permission of the author. From "Elegy for My Aunt" by John Ridland. Reprinted by permission of the author.

Theodore Roethke. "I Knew a Woman" (Copyright 1954 by Theodore Roethke). "My Papa's Waltz" (Copyright 1942 by Hearst Magazines, Inc.), "Root Cellar" (Copyright 1943 by Modern Poetry Association, Inc.), "Night Crow" (Copyright 1944 by Saturday Review Association, Inc.), and "Elegy for Jane" (Copyright 1950 by Theodore Roethke). Reprinted from *The Collected Poems of Theodore Roethke* by permission of Doubleday & Company, Inc.

Raymond Roseliep. "campfire extinguished" from *Listen to Light Haiku* by Raymond Roseliep. Copyright © 1980 by Raymond Roseliep (Alembic Press, Ithaca, N.Y.). Reprinted by permission.

Gibbons Ruark. "Waiting for You with the Swallows" from *Keeping Company* by Gibbons Ruark. Copyright © 1983 by The Johns Hopkins University Press. Reprinted by permission.

Paul Ruffin "Hotel Fire: New Orleans" from *Lighting the Furnace Pilot* (Spoon River Poetry Press, 1980). Reprinted by permission of the poet.

Carl Sandburg. "Fog" from *Chicago Poems* by Carl Sandburg, copyright 1916 by Holt, Rinehart and Winston, Inc. and renewed 1944 by Carl Sandburg, reprinted by permission of Harcourt Brace Jovanovich, Inc.

Aram Saroyan. From "crickets" from *Works* by Aram Saroyan. Copyright © 1966 by Aram Saroyan. Reprinted by permission of the author.

Gjertrud Schnackenberg. "Signs" from *The Lamplite Answer*. Copyright © 1982, 1985, by Gjertrud Schnackenberg. Reprinted by permission of Farrar, Straus & Giroux, Inc.

Robert Scholes. From *Semiotics and Interpretation* by Robert Scholes. Copyright © 1982 by Yale University. Reprinted by permission of Yale University Press.

Grace Schulman. "Hemispheres" from *Hemispheres* by Grace Schulman. Copyright © 1984 by Grace Schulman. Reprinted by permission of the author.

Herbert Scott. "The Grocer's Children" from *Groceries* by Herbert Scott (University of Pittsburg Press, 1976). Reprinted by permission of *Poetry Now*.

Bettie Sellers. "In the Counselor's Waiting Room" from *Morning of the Red-Tailed Hawk* by Bettie Sellers (University Center, MI: Green River Press, 1981). Reprinted by permission.

Anne Sexton. "The Kiss" and 2 lines from "Eighteen Days Without You" from *Love Poems* by Anne Sexton. Copyright © 1967, 1968, 1969 by Anne Sexton. Reprinted by permission of Houghton Mifflin Company.

Harvey Shapiro. "National Cold Storage Company" from *National Cold Storage Company* by Harvey Shapiro. Copyright © 1964 by Harvey Shapiro. Reprinted by permission of Wesleyan University Press.

Karl Shapiro. "The Dirty Word" from *Selected Poems* by Karl Shapiro. Copyright 1947 by Karl Shapiro. Reprinted by permission of Wieser & Wieser Inc.

Richard Shelton. "Mexico" by Richard Shelton from *The New Yorker*, April 5, 1976. Copyright © 1976 The New Yorker Magazine, Inc. Reprinted by permission.

Charles Simic. "The Butcher Shop" from *Dismantling the Silence* by Charles Simic. Copyright © 1971 by Charles Simic. Reprinted by permission of the publisher, George Braziller, Inc.

Paul Simon. Lyrics from "Richard Cory" by Paul Simon. Copyright © 1966 by Paul Simon. Reprinted by permission of Paul Simon Music.

L. E. Sissman. Lines from "In and Out: A Home Away from Home" from *Dying: An Introduction* by L. E. Sissman. Copyright © 1967 by L. E. Sissman. By

permission of Little, Brown and Company in association with the Atlantic Monthly Press.

Knute Skinner. "The Cold Irish Earth" from *A Close Sky Over Killas Puglanane* (The Dolman Press Ltd., 1968). Reprinted by permission of the poet and the publisher.

David R. Slavitt. "Titanic" from *Big Nose*, Poems by David R. Slavitt. Copyright © 1983 by David R. Slavitt. Copyright © 1983 by David R. Slavitt. Reprinted by permission of Louisiana State University Press.

Stevie Smith. "I Remember" from *Collected Poems* by Stevie Smith. Copyright © 1972 by Stevie Smith. Reprinted by permission of New Directions Publishing Corporation. "The Englishwoman" from *The Collected Poems of Stevie Smith*. Copyright © 1972 by Stevie Smith. Reprinted by permission of New Directions Publishing Corporation.

William Jay Smith. "American Primitive" from *The Traveler's Tree: New and Selected Poems* by William Jay Smith. Copyright © 1989 by William Jay Smith. Reprinted by permission of Persea Books, Inc.

W. D. Snodgrass. "Seeing You Have . . . " from *Selected Poems 1957–1987* by W. D. Snodgrass. Copyright © 1987 by W. D. Snodgrass. Reprinted by permission of Soho Press, Inc.

Gary Snyder. From "Hitch Haiku" from *The Back Country* by Gary Snyder. Copyright © 1968 by Gary Snyder. Reprinted by permission of New Directions Publishing Corporation. "Mid-August at Sourdough Mountain Lookout" from *Riprap* by Gary Snyder (Kyoto: Origin Press, 1959). Reprinted by permission of the poet.

Wole Soyinka. Excerpt: "The Lost Tribe," from "New York, U.S.A." in *Mandela's Earth and Other Poems*, by Wole Soyinka. Copyright © 1988 by Wole Soyinka. Reprinted by permission of Random House, Inc.

Bruce Springsteen. "Born to Run." Copyright © 1975 Bruce Springsteen. Reprinted by permission of Bruce Springsteen. All rights reserved.

William Stafford. "Traveling Through the Dark" copyright © 1960 by William Stafford and "At The Klamath Berry Festival" copyright © 1961 by William Stafford, from *Stories That Could Be True*, copyright © 1970 by William Stafford. Reprinted by permission of Harper & Row, Publishers, Inc.

Jon Stallworthy. "Sindhi Woman" is reprinted from *The Anzac Sonata*, New and Selected Poems, by Jon Stallworthy, by permission of W. W. Norton & Company, Inc. and Chatto & Windus. Copyright © 1986 by Jon Stallworthy.

George Starbuck. "Margaret Are You Drug" from "Translations from the English" in *White Paper: Poems* by George Starbuck. Copyright © 1965 by George Starbuck. First appeared in *The Atlantic*. By permission of Little, Brown and Company in association with the Atlantic Monthly Press.

Timothy Steele. "Here Lies Sir Tact." Reprinted by permission of Louisiana State University Press from *Uncertainties and Rest* by Timothy Steele, copyright © 1979. "Waiting For The Storm" from *Sapphics Against Anger and Other Poems*, by Timothy Steele. Copyright © 1986 by Timothy Steele. Reprinted by permission of Random House, Inc.

James Stephens. "A Glass of Beer" reprinted with permission of Macmillan Publishing Company and The Society of Authors from *Collected Poems* by James Stephens. Copyright 1918 by Macmillan Publishing Company, renewed 1946 by James Stephens. "The Wind" reprinted with permission of Macmillan Publishing Company and The Society of Authors from *Collected Poems* by James Stephens. Copyright 1915 by Macmillan Publishing Company, renewed 1943 by James Stephens.

Wallace Stevens. "The Emperor of Ice Cream," "Disillusionment of Ten O'Clock," "Thirteen Ways of

Looking at a Blackbird," "Anecdote of the Jar" and seven lines from "Sunday Morning" from *The Collected Poems of Wallace Stevens.* Copyright 1923 and renewed 1951 by Wallace Stevens. Reprinted by permission of Alfred A. Knopf, Inc. "Peter Quince at the Clavier" Copyright 1942 by Wallace Stevens. Reprinted from *The Collected Poems of Wallace Stevens,* by permission of Alfred A. Knopf, Inc. Nine proverbs from "Adagia" from *Opus Posthumous* by Wallace Stevens, edited by Samuel French Morse. Copyright © 1957 by Elsie Stevens and Holly Stevens. Reprinted by permission of Alfred A. Knopf, Inc. "Metamorphosis" copyright 1942 by Wallace Stevens. Reprinted from *The Collected Poems by Wallace Stevens,* by permission of Alfred A. Knopf, Inc.

Michael Stillman. "In Memoriam John Coltrane" from *Memories of Grace Street* by Michael Stillman, reprinted from *Occident* (Berkeley, Fall 1971). Reprinted by permission of the poet.

Ruth Stone. "Secondhand Coat" by Ruth Stone from *The Iowa Review,* Vol. 12:2/3, Spring/Summer 1981. Reprinted by permission of the author.

Dabney Stuart. "Crib Death" from *Don't Look Back, Poems* by Dabney Stuart. Copyright © 1987 by Dabney Stuart. Reprinted by permission of Louisiana State University Press.

John Tagliabue. "Maine vastly covered with much snow" from *The Great Day Poems: 1962–1983* by John Tagliabue (The Alembic Press, 1984). Reprinted by permission of the publisher.

Henry Taylor. "Riding a One-Eyed Horse" from *An Afternoon of Pocket Billiards* by Henry Taylor (Salt Lake City: University of Utah Press Poetry Series, 1975). Copyright © 1975 by Henry Taylor. Reprinted by permission of the University of Utah Press.

Dylan Thomas. "Fern Hill" and "Do not go gentle into that good night" from *The Poems of Dylan Thomas.* Copyright 1939, 1946 by New Directions Publishing Corporation, 1952 by Dylan Thomas. Reprinted by permission of New Directions Publishing Corporation and David Higham Associates, Ltd. One line from *Under Milk Wood* by Dylan Thomas. Copyright 1954 by New Directions Corporation. All Rights Reserved. Reprinted by permission of New Directions Publishing Corporation.

Jean Toomer. "Reapers" is reprinted from *Cane* by Jean Toomer, by permission of Liveright Publishing Corporation. Copyright 1923 by Boni & Liveright. Copyright renewed 1951 by Jean Toomer.

John Updike. "Ex-Basketball Player" from *The Carpentered Hen and Other Tame Creatures,* by John Updike. Copyright © 1957, 1982 by John Updike. Reprinted by permission of Alfred A. Knopf, Inc. "Winter Ocean" from *Telephone Poles and Other Poems,* by John Updike. Copyright © 1960 by John Updike. Reprinted by permission of Alfred A. Knopf, Inc.

Nicholas Virgilio. "On the cardboard box" from *Selected Haiku,* Second Edition, Augmented by Nicholas A. Virgilio. Copyright © 1988 by Nicholas A. Virgilio. Reprinted by permission of Burnt Lake Press.

Keith Waldrop. "Proposition II" from *The Garden of Effort* (Burning Deck Publishers, 1975). Translation of "Guitar" from Federico Garcia Lorca. Reprinted by permission.

Rosmarie Waldrop. "The Relaxed Abalone" from *The Relaxed Abalone: Or What-You-May-Find* by Rosmarie Waldrop (Burning Deck Publishers, 1970). Reprinted by permission.

Robert Wallace. "The Girl Writing Her English Paper" from *The Common Summer: New and Selected Poems* by Robert Wallace (Carnegie-Mellon University Press, 1989). Reprinted by permission of the publisher.

Emma Lee Warrior. "How I Came To Have A Man's Name" by Emma Lee Warrior from *Harper's Anthology of 20th Century Native American Poetry* edited by Duane Niatum. Copyright © 1988 by Duane Niatum. Reprinted by permission of Harper & Row, Publishers, Inc.

James Whitehead. "The Country Music Star Begins His Politics" from *Local Men and Domains: Two Books of Poetry* by James Whitehead. Copyright © 1966, 1979, 1987 by James Whitehead. Reprinted by permission of the University of Illinois Press.

Ruth Whitman. "Castoff Skin" from *The Passion of Lizzie Borden."* Copyright © 1973 by Ruth Whitman. Reprinted by permission of October House.

Richard Wilbur. "In the Elegy Season" and "A Simile for Her Smile" from *Ceremony and Other Poems,* copyright 1950 and renewed 1978 by Richard Wilbur, reprinted by permission of Harcourt Brace Jovanovich, Inc. "Transit" from *New and Collected Poems,* copyright © 1987 by Richard Wilbur, reprinted by permission of Harcourt Brace Jovanovich, Inc. "Sleepless at Crown Point," copyright © 1973 by Richard Wilbur, and "The Writer," copyright © 1971 by Richard Wilbur, from *The Mind Reader,* reprinted by permission of Harcourt Brace Jovanovich, Inc.

Nancy Willard. "Marriage Amulet" is reprinted from *Carpenter of the Sun,* poems by Nancy Willard, by permission of Liveright Publishing Corporation. Copyright © 1974 by Nancy Willard.

Miller Williams. "Mecanic on Duty at All Times" from *Imperfect Love* by Miller Williams. Copyright © 1986 by Miller Williams. Reprinted by permission of Louisiana State University Press.

Peter Williams. "When she was here, Li Bo, she was like cold summer lager." Copyright © 1978 by Peter Williams. First appeared in *Taxi,* a publication of the William Carlos Williams Poetry Center of the Paterson (NJ) Public Library. Reprinted by permission of the poet.

William Carlos Williams. "The Dance" from *Collected Poems Vol. II, 1939–1962* by William Carlos Williams. Copyright 1954 by William Carlos Williams. Reprinted by permission of New Directions Publishing Corporation. "The Great Figure," "Spring and All," "Poem," "This Is Just to Say," "The Red Wheelbarrow," "To Waken an Old Lady," "The Descent of Winter" and "The Waitress" from *The Collected Poems Vol. 1, 1909–1939,* by William Carlos Williams. Copyright 1938 by New Directions Publishing Corporation. Reprinted by permission of New Directions Publishing Corporation. From *Interviews With William Carlos Williams.* Copyright © 1976 by the Estate of William Carlos Williams. Reprinted by permission of New Directions Publishing Corporation.

Yvor Winters. "At the San Francisco Airport" from *Collected Poems* by Yvor Winters. Copyright 1952, © 1960 by Yvor Winters. Reprinted with the permission of The Ohio University Press, Athens.

James Wright. "A Blessing" and "Autumn Begins in Martins Ferry, Ohio" from *The Branch Will Not Break* by James Wright. Copyright © 1961, 1962 by James Wright. Reprinted by permission of Wesleyan University Press. "Saying Dante Aloud" from *Moments of an Italian Summer.* Copyright © 1976 by James Wright. Reprinted by permission of The Dryad Press.

Richard Wright. "Haiku" from *Richard Wright Reader.* Edited by Ellen Wright and Michael Fabre. Copyright © 1978 by Ellen Wright and Michael Fabre. Reprinted by permission of Harper & Row, Publishers, Inc.

Elinor Wylie. "The Eagle and the Mole" from *Collected Poems of Elinor Wylie.* Copyright 1932 by Alfred A. Knopf, Inc. and renewed 1960 by Edwina C. Rubenstein. Reprinted by permission of Alfred A. Knopf, Inc.

William Butler Yeats. "Crazy Jane Talks with the Bishop" reprinted with permission of Macmillan Publishing Company, A P Watt Limited on behalf of Michael B. Yeats, and Macmillan London Ltd. from *The Poems of W. B. Yeats: A New Edition,* edited by Richard J. Finneran. Copyright 1933 by Macmillan Publishing Company, renewed 1961 by Bertha Georgie Yeats. "The Magi" reprinted with permission of Macmillan Publishing Company, A P Watt Limited on behalf of Michael B. Yeats, and Macmillan London Ltd. from *The Poems of W. B. Yeats: A New Edition,* edited by Richard J. Finneran. Copyright 1916 by Macmillan Publishing Company, renewed 1944 by Bertha Georgie Yeats. "Sailing to Byzantium" reprinted with permission of Macmillan Publishing Company, A P Watt Limited on behalf of Michael B. Yeats, and Macmillan London Ltd. from *The Poems of W. B. Yeats: A New Edition,* edited by Richard J. Finneran. Copyright 1928 by Macmillan Publishing Company, renewed 1956 by Georgie Yeats. "The Second Coming" reprinted with permission of Macmillan Publishing Company, A P Watt Limited on behalf of Michael B. Yeats, and Macmillan London Ltd. from *The Poems of W. B. Yeats: A New Edition,* edited by Richard J. Finneran. Copyright 1924 by Macmillan Publishing Company, renewed 1952 by Bertha Georgie Yeats. "The Lake Isle of Innisfree" and "The Lamentation of the Old Pensioner" from *The Poems of W. B. Yeats: A New Edition* edited by Richard J. Finneran (New York: Macmillan, 1983). Reprinted by permission of A P Watt Limited on behalf of Michael B. Yeats and Macmillan London Ltd. "Long-legged Fly" reprinted with permission of Macmillan Publishing Company, A P Watt Limited on behalf of Michael B. Yeats, and Macmillan London Ltd. from *The Poems of W. B. Yeats: A New Edition,* edited by Richard J. Finneran. Copyright 1940 by Georgie Yeats, renewed 1968 by Bertha Georgie Yeats, Michael Butler Yeats and Anne Yeats. "Who Goes with Fergus?" from *The Poems of W. B. Yeats,* edited by Richard J. Finneran, reprinted by permission of Michael Yeats and Macmillan (London) Ltd. "Leda and the Swan." Copyright 1928 by Macmillan Publishing Company, renewed 1956 by Bertha Georgie Yeats. Reprinted with permission of Macmillan Publishing Company, Michael Yeats, and Macmillan (London) Ltd from *The Poems of W. B. Yeats,* edited by Richard J. Finneran.

Paul Zimmer. "The Day Zimmer Lost Religion" from *The Zimmer Poems* by Paul Zimmer. Copyright © 1976 by Paul Zimmer. Reprinted by permission of The Dryad Press.

DRAMA

Edward Albee. Excerpt from "Which Theatre Is the Absurd One" by Edward Albee *The New York Times* (Magazine), February 25, 1962, reprinted by permission of the William Morris Agency on behalf of the author. Copyright © 1962 by Edward Albee.

Aristotle. Excerpts from *Poetics* as translated by L. J. Potts in *Aristotle on the Art of Fiction,* 1959, Cambridge University Press. Reprinted by permission of Cambridge University Press.

E. R. Dodds. Excerpt from "On Misunderstanding the *Oedipus Rex*" by E. R. Dodds from *Greece & Rome,* vol. XIII (1966). Reprinted by permission of Oxford University Press.

W. C. Fields. *Stolen Bonds.* Copyright 1928 by W. C. Fields. All rights reserved. Reprinted by permission.

Maria Irene Fornes. *A Vietnamese Wedding.* Copyright 1971 by Maria Irene Fornes. Reprinted by permission. CAUTION NOTE: Professionals and amateurs are hereby warned that *A Vietnamese Wedding* is fully protected under the Copyright Laws of the United States of America, the British Commonwealth, including the Dominion of Canada, and all other countries of the International Copyright Union and Universal Copyright Convention, and are subject to royalty. All rights, including professional, amateur, motion picture, recitation, lecturing, public reading, radio and television broadcasting, and the rights of translation into foreign languages are strictly reserved. Particular emphasis is laid on the question of readings, permission for which must be secured from the author's agent in writing. All inquiries concerning the amateur and professional production rights to *A Vietnamese Wedding* by Maria Irene Fornes should be addressed to the author's agent, Helen Merrill, Ltd., 435 West 23rd Street, Suite 1A, New York, NY 10011, USA. No amateur performance of any of the plays may be given without obtaining, in advance, the written permission of Helen Merrill, Ltd. All inquiries concerning rights (other than production rights) should also be addressed to Helen Merrill, Ltd. Excerpt from an interview with Maria Irene Fornes, from *In Their Own Words: Contemporary American Playwrights* by David Savran, copyright © 1988 by David Savran, published by Theatre Communications Group, Inc. Used by permission.

Sigmund Freud. Excerpt from *The Interpretation of Dreams* by Sigmund Freud, translated and edited by James Strachey, published in the United States by Basic Books, Inc., New York, by arrangement with George Allen Unwin Ltd. and The Hogarth Press Ltd., London.

Susan Glaspell. *Trifles.* From *Plays* by Susan Glaspell. Copyright 1920 by Dodd, Mead & Company, Inc., copyright renewed 1948 by Susan Glaspell. Reprinted by permission of the Estate of Susan Glaspell. Inquiries concerning performance rights should be directed to Baker's Plays, 100 Chauncy Street, Boston, MA 02111.

Henrik Ibsen. *A Doll's House* from *Henrik Ibsen: The Complete Major Prose Plays* translated by Rolfe Fjelde. Copyright © 1965, 1970, 1978 by Rolfe Fjelde. Reprinted by permission of New American Library, a division of Penguin Books USA Inc. CAUTION: Professionals and amateurs are warned hereby that this translation is fully protected under the copyright laws of the United States, the British Empire, including the Dominion of Canada, and all other countries of the Copyright Union and are subject to royalty. All rights, including professional, amateur, motion picture, radio, television, audio and visual recording and reproduction are reserved. All inquiries should be addressed as follows: Eastern United States: Samuel French, Inc., 25 West 45th Street, New York, NY 10036. Western United States: Samuel French, Inc., 7623 Sunset Boulevard., Hollywood, CA 90046. Canada: Samuel French Canada Ltd. 80 Richmond Street East, Toronto, Ontario, Canada M5C 1P1. United Kingdom: Michael Imison, Dr. Jan Van Loewen Ltd., International Copyright Agency, 81/83 Shaftesbury Avenue, London W1V 85X, England.

Arthur Miller. *Death of a Salesman.* Copyright 1949, renewed © 1977 by Arthur Miller. Reprinted by permission of Viking Penguin, a division of Penguin Books USA Inc. CAUTION: This play in its printed form is designed for the reading public only. All dramatic rights in it are fully protected by copyright and no public or private performance— professional or amateur—may be given without the written permission of the author and the payment of royalty. As the courts have also ruled that the public reading of a play constitutes a public performance, no such reading may be given except under the conditions stated above. Communication should be addressed to the author's representative, International Creative Management, Inc., 40 West 57th Street, New York, NY 10019. "Tragedy and the Common Man" from *The Theater Essays of Arthur Miller* by Arthur Miller. Copyright 1949, renewed © 1977 by Arthur Miller. Reprinted by permission of Viking Penguin, a division of Penguin Books USA Inc.

Charles Paul Segal. Excerpt from "Sophocles' Praise of Man and the Conflicts of the *Antigone*" as published in *Sophocles: A Collection of Critical Essays* (Twentieth Century Views Series; Prentice-Hall, 1966). Reprinted by permission of the author.

William Shakespeare. *The Tragedy of Othello*, edited with notes by Alvin Kernan. Copyright © 1963 by Alvin Kernan. Reprinted by permission of New American Library, a division of Penguin Books USA Inc.

Bernard Shaw. Excerpt from *The Quintessence of Ibsenism* reprinted by permission of The Society of Authors on behalf of the Bernard Shaw Estate.

Sophocles, *Oedipus the King*, translated by David Grene (Copyright, 1942, by The University of Chicago), and *Antigone*, translated by Elizabeth Wyckoff (Copyright, 1954, by The University of Chicago) from David Grene and Richmond Lattimore, eds., *The Complete Greek Tragedies: Volume II: Sophocles*. Reprinted by permission of the publisher, the University of Chicago Press.

Tom Stoppard. *The Real Inspector Hound*. Reprinted by permission of Grove Weidenfeld, a division of Wheatland Corporation, and Faber and Faber Ltd. Copyright © 1968 by Tom Stoppard.

Wendy Wasserstein. *The Man in a Case*. Copyright © 1986 by Wendy Wasserstein. Reprinted from *Orchards: Seven Short Stories by Anton Chekhov and Seven Plays They Have Inspired*, by permission of Alfred A. Knopf, Inc.

Tennessee Williams. *The Glass Menagerie*. Copyright 1945 by Tennessee Williams and Edwina D. Williams and renewed 1973 by Tennessee Williams. Reprinted by permission of Random House, Inc.

August Wilson. *Joe Turner's Come and Gone*. Copyright © 1988 by August Wilson. Reprinted by arrangement with New American Library, a Division of Penguin Books USA Inc., New York, NY. Excerpts from the August Wilson interview in *Bill Moyers: A World of Ideas* by Bill Moyers, copyright © 1989 by Public Affairs Television, Inc. Used by permission of Doubleday, a division of Bantam, Doubleday, Dell Publishing Group, Inc.

Virginia Woolf. Excerpt from "A Room of One's Own" in *A Room of One's Own* by Virginia Woolf, copyright 1929 by Harcourt Brace Jovanovich, Inc. and renewed 1957 by Leonard Woolf, reprinted by permission of the Executors of the Estate of Virginia Woolf and the publishers, Harcourt Brace Jovanovich, Inc. and The Hogarth Press.

PICTURE ACKNOWLEDGMENTS

FICTION

4 Brown Brothers 9 UPI/Bettmann 15 AP/Wide World 24 Bern Keating/Black Star 31 Published by Alfred A. Knopf, Inc. 35 Random House, Photo: Carole Dufrechon 41 The Bettmann Archive 50 Rollie McKenna 58 Jerry Bauer 59 Reuters/UPI/Bettmann 68 Jerry Bauer 83 Library of Congress 87 The Bettmann Archive 99 Courtesy Viking Press, Photo: Pablo Campos 1988 112 UPI/Bettmann 131 Berenice Abbott/Commerce Graphics 136 Jerry Bauer 147 Newark Public Library Photo 165 The Essex Institute, Salem, Ma. 175 AP/Wide World 185 AP/Wide World 194 Erich Hartmann/Magnum Photos 201 Jerry Bauer 218 The Bettmann Archive 259 Jerry Bauer 297 The Bettmann Archive 319 AP/Wide World 357 The Bettmann Archive 364 UPI/Bettmann 369 Willa Cather Pioneer Memorial Collection, Nebraska State Historical Society 384 Vintage Press, Photo: Carole Harmel 388 Jerry Bauer 379 UPI/Bettmann 401 Courtesy Schoken Books 403 Burt Glinn/Magnum Photos 407 Photo: Muray/The Bettmann Archive 418 Jerry Bauer 429 Jerry Bauer 442 Elliott Erwitt/Magnum Photos 448 Photo: Bob McLeod, San Francisco Examiner/AP/Wide World 454 Elliott Erwitt/Magnum Photos 471 The Bettmann Archive 481 John D. Schiff Courtesy New Directions

POETRY

680 Kunsthistorisches Museum, Vienna 765 Gail H. Raub 767 Deniele Hayford 780 Jerry Bauer 781 The Bettmann Archive 783 Musees Royaux Des Beaux-Arts de Belgique 786 Thomas Victor, Courtesy Farrar, Straus and Giroux 788 The Bettmann Archive 791 AP/Wide World 797 The Bettmann Archive 801 The Bettmann Archive 805 AP/Wide World 815 AP/Wide World 818 The Bettmann Archive 824 The Bettmann Archive 827 Ellen Foscus Johnson 829 National Portrait Gallery, London 833 UPI/Bettmann 834 Ted Russell, Courtesy Farrar, Straus & Giroux 837 National Portrait Gallery, London 842 David Geier/Courtesy New Directions 851 AP/Wide World 855 George Murphy/Courtesy Norton 860 Reprinted by permission HarperCollins-Publishers, Inc. 861 Coris De Rachewiltz/Courtesy New Directions 862 Billy Williams 865 Colleen McKay/Courtesy W.W. Norton & Company 867 Courtesy University of Washington 869 UPI/Bettmann 871 National Portrait Gallery, London 878 Hulton Picture Library, The Bettmann Archive 882 The Bettmann Archive 884 The Bettmann Archive 890 The National Archives 891 AP/Wide World 894 John D. Schiff/Courtesy New Directions 896 The Bettmann Archive 897 AP/Wide World 900 Pirie MacDonald, The Royal Photographic Society

DRAMA

956 AP/Wide World 972 The Bettmann Archive 983 UPI/Bettmann 990 The Bettmann Archive 999 The Bettmann Archive 1046 National Portrait Gallery, London 1139 The Bettmann Archive 1191 Kim Zumwalt 1202 UPI/Bettmann 1238 Reuters/UPI/Bettmann 1336 AP/Wide World 1342 The Bettmann Archive 1388 AP/Wide World

INDEX TO FIRST LINES OF POETRY

The kingdom of heaven is likened unto a man which sowed good seed in his field, 706

The king sits in Dumferling toune, 504

The lanky hank of a she in the inn over there, 519

The license plate was another state and year, 893

The Lightning is a yellow Fork, 703

The master, the swabber, the boatswain, and I, 644

The midge spins out to safety, 1499

The Mind is an Enchanting Thing, 851

The National Cold Storage Company contains, 719

The only response, 751

The piercing chill I feel, 569

The radiance of that star that leans on me, 835

The readers of the Boston Evening Transcript, 702

There are no deadlier Americans, 636

There is a garden in her face, 757

There ought to be capital punishment for cars, 748

There was an old man of Khartoum, 674

There was such speed in her little body, 863

There were three ravens sat on a tree, 775

The robin cries: rain! 583

The sea is calm tonight, 778

The selfsame surface that billowed once with, 794

The silver swan, who living had no note, 618

The Soul, reaching, throwing out for love, 731

The splendor falls on castle walls, 629

The terra cotta girl, 529

The thing could barely stand. Yet taken, 840

The time you won your town the race, 832

The tusks that clashed in mighty brawls, 755

The war chief danced the old way—, 880

The whiskey on your breath, 510

The wind blew all my wedding-day, 516

The wind stood up and gave a shout, 593

The winter evening settles down, 571

The Wood-Weasel, 503

The world and I when young, 767

The world is charged with the grandeur of God, 635

The world is too much with us; late and soon, 717

They eat beans mostly, this old yellow pair, 565

They flee from me that sometime did me sekë, 898

They say that Richard Cory owns, 610

They say the wells, 575

They sing their dearest songs—, 818

Think tonight of sixteen, 751

This Englishwoman is so refined, 672

This Humanist whom no beliefs contrained, 672

This is the terminal: the light, 895

This living hand, now warm and capable, 662

This love is a rich cry over, 790

Thou are indeed just, Lord, if I contend, 830

Thou ill-formed offspring of my feeble brain, 511

Threading the palm, a web of little lines, 710

Three drunks, a leg on one quite gone, bereft, 672

Three Summers since I chose a maid, 849

Today we have naming of parts. Yesterday, 863

To freight cars in the air, 657

To see a world in a grain of sand, 590

Traveling through the dark I found a deer, 749

Treason doth never prosper; what's the reason? 671

True Ease in Writing comes from Art, not Chance, 621

Turning and turning in the widening gyre, 718

'Twas brillig, and the slithy toves, 554

'Twas in the year of 1898, and on the 21st of June, 743

Two boys uncoached are tossing a poem together, 769
Two roads diverged in a yellow wood, 708
Tyger! Tyger! burning bright, 788

Victory comes late, 680

Wave of sorrow, 834
We dance round in a ring and suppose, 601
We four lads from Liverpool are—, 736
We lie back to back. Curtains, 600
We never said farewell, nor even looked, 519
We real cool. We, 646
We shall not ever meet them bearded in heaven, 836
Western wind, when wilt thou blow, 778
We stood by a pond that winter day, 705
We were very tired, we were very merry—, 850
What happens to a dream deferred? 833
What of earls with whom you have supped, 527
What on earth deserves our trust? 856
What passing-bells for these who die as cattle? 854
What shall we find behind this wall, 766
What she remembers, 822
What, still alive at twenty-two, 737
What thoughts I have of you tonight, Walt Whitman, 813
Wheesht, wheesht, my foolish hert, 548
When daisies pied and violets blue, 872
Whenever Richard Cory went down town, 610
When fishes flew and forests walked, 795
When God at first made man, 597
When Han Kan was summoned, 1511
When he came home Mother said he looked, 843
When icicles hang by the wall, 873
When I consider how my light is spent, 850
When I have fears that I may cease to be, 838
When I lived in Seattle, I loved watching, 826
When, in disgrace with Fortune and men's eyes, 872

When I saw that clumsy crow, 611
When I saw your head bow, I knew I had beaten you, 539
When I see birches bend to left and right, 811
When I take my girl to the swimming party, 854
When I was one-and-twenty, 656
When maidens are young, and in their spring, 625
When my mother died I was very young, 532
When our cars touched, 691
When she was here, Li Bo, she was like cold summer lager, 591
While my hair was still cut straight across my forehead, 861
Who does not love the *Titanic?* 875
Who says you're like one of the dog days? 586
Whose woods these are I think I know, 812
Who will go drive with Fergus now, 623
Who would I show it to, 947
"Why dois your brand sae drap wi' bluid, 774
With rue my heart is laden, 639
With serving still, 648

Yet once more, O ye laurels, and once more, 720
Yield, 665
Yillow, yillow, yillow, 555
You are polishing me like old wood, 892
You can feel the muscles and veins rippling in widening and rising circles . . . 638
You claim his poems are garbage. Balderdash! 673
You do not do, you do not do, 857
You fit into me, 601
Your smiling, or the hope, the thought of it, 589
Your ÿen two wol slee me sodenly; 690
You that with allegory's curious frame, 710
You will carry this suture, 633
You would think the fury of aerial bombardment, 552

INDEX TO AUTHORS AND TITLES

Each page number immediately following a writer's name indicates a quotation from that writer. A number in *italics* refers you to the page on which you will find the writer's biography.

To the Student

Part of our job as publishers is to try to improve our textbooks. In revising them, we pay close attention to the experience of both instructors and students who have used the previous edition. At some time your instructor will be asked to comment on *Literature: An Introduction to Fiction, Poetry, and Drama*, 5th Edition, but right now we would like to hear from you. After all, though your instructor assigned this book, you are the one who paid for it.

Please help us by completing this questionnaire and returning it to the English Literature Acquisitions Editor, HarperCollins Publishers, College Division, 10 East 53rd Street, New York, NY 10022.

School: _____

Instructor's name: _____

Title of course: _____

1. How did you like *Literature?* _____

   _____

2. Did you find it too easy? _____ Too difficult? _____ About right? _____

3. Which statement comes closest to expressing your feelings about reading and studying literature? Please check one, or supply your own statement.

   _____ Love to read literature. It's my favorite subject.

   _____ Usually enjoy reading most literature.

   _____ Can take it or leave it.

   _____ Don't usually find much of interest in most literature.

   _____ Literature just is not for me.

4. In general, which form of literature do you most enjoy reading and find most rewarding? Please rate in 1, 2, 3 order:

   _____ Fiction _____ Poetry _____ Drama

5. Which chapters of the book did you find most interesting? _____

   _____

6. Which chapters did you like least? _____

   _____

7. Which stories were your favorites? _____

_____

Were there any you disliked? _____

_____

8. Which poems were your favorites? _____

_____

Were they any you disliked? _____

_____

9. Which plays were your favorites? _____

_____

Were there any you disliked? _____

_____

10. Are any writers not included whom you would have liked to study? _____

_____

11. Did you find the supplement on writing very helpful? _____ Somewhat

helpful? _____ Of no help? _____ How could we make it more useful to

you? _____

_____

12. Any other suggestions or reactions: _____

_____

May we quote you in our advertising efforts? Yes _____ No _____

Signature _____ Date _____

Mailing address _____

Thank you!

INDEX TO TERMS

INDEX TO TERMS